Peterson's
Two-Year
Colleges
2013

PETERSON'S
Publishing

About Peterson's Publishing

Peterson's Publishing provides the accurate, dependable, high-quality education content and guidance you need to succeed. No matter where you are on your academic or professional path, you can rely on Peterson's print and digital publications for the most up-to-date education exploration data, expert test-prep tools, and top-notch career success resources—everything you need to achieve your goals.

Visit us online at www.petersonspublishing.com and let Peterson's help you achieve your goals.

For more information, contact Peterson's Publishing, 2000 Lenox Drive, Lawrenceville, NJ 08648; 800-338-3282 Ext. 54229; or find us on the World Wide Web at www.petersonspublishing.com.

Bernadette Webster, Managing Editor; Jill C. Schwartz, Editor; John Wells, Research Project Manager; Cathleen Fee, Nicole Gallo, Research Associates; Phyllis Johnson, Software Engineer; Ray Golaszewski, Publishing Operations Manager; Linda M. Williams, Composition Manager; Carrie Hansen, Christine Lucht, Bailey Williams, Fulfillment Team

ISSN 0894-9328
ISBN-13: 978-0-7689-3610-0
ISBN-10: 0-7689-3610-1

Printed in the United States of America

10 9 8 7 6 5 4 3 2 1   14 13 12

Forty-third Edition

Contents

Certified Chain of Custody

60% Certified Fiber Sourcing and
40% Post-Consumer Recycled

www.sfiprogram.org

*This label applies to the text stock.

Sustainability—Its Importance to Peterson's Publishing

What does sustainability mean to Peterson's? As a leading publisher, we are aware that our business has a direct impact on vital resources—most especially the trees that are used to make our books. Peterson's Publishing is proud that its products are certified by the Sustainable Forestry Initiative (SFI) and that all of its books are printed on paper that is 40% post-consumer waste using vegetable-based ink.

Being a part of the Sustainable Forestry Initiative (SFI) means that all of our vendors—from paper suppliers to printers—have undergone rigorous audits to demonstrate that they are maintaining a sustainable environment.

Peterson's continuously strives to find new ways to incorporate sustainability throughout all aspects of its business.

A Note from the Peterson's Editors

For nearly 50 years, Peterson's has given students and parents the most comprehensive, up-to-date information on undergraduate institutions in the United States. Peterson's researches the data published in Peterson's Two-Year Colleges each year. The information is furnished by the colleges and is accurate at the time of publishing.

This guide also features advice and tips on the college search and selection process, such as how to decide if a two-year college is right for you, how to approach transferring between colleges, and what's in store for adults returning to college. If you seem to be getting more, not less, anxious about choosing and getting into the right college, Peterson's Two-Year Colleges provides just the right help, giving you the information you need to make important college decisions and ace the admission process.

Opportunities abound for students, and this guide can help you find what you want in a number of ways:

"What You Need to Know About Two-Year Colleges" outlines the basic features and advantages of two-year colleges. "Surviving Standardized Tests" gives an overview of the common examinations students take prior to attending college. "Who's Paying for This? Financial Aid Basics" provides guidelines for financing your college education. "Frequently Asked Questions About Transferring" takes a look at the two-year college scene from the perspective of a student who is looking toward the day when he or she may pursue additional education at a four-year institution. "Returning to School: Advice for Adult Students" is an analysis of the pros and cons (mostly pros) of returning to college after already having begun a professional career. "What International Students Need to Know About Admission to U.S. Colleges and Universities" is an article written particularly for students overseas who are considering a U.S. college education. "Community Colleges and the New Green Economy" offers information on some exciting "green" programs at community colleges throughout the United States, as well as two insightful essays by Mary F. T. Spilde, President, Lane Community College and James DeHaven, V.P. of Economic and Business Development, Kalamazoo Valley Community College. Finally, "How to Use This Guide" gives details on the data in this guide: what terms mean and why they're here.

- If you already have specifics in mind, such as a particular institution or major, turn to the easy-to-use **Two-Year Colleges At-a-Glance Chart** or **Indexes.** You can look up a particular feature—location and programs offered—or use the alphabetical index and immediately find the colleges that meet your criteria.

- For information about particular colleges, turn to the **Profiles of Two-Year Colleges** section. Here, our comprehensive college profiles are arranged alphabetically by state. They provide a complete picture of need-to-know information about every accredited two-year college—from admission to graduation, including expenses, financial aid, majors, and campus safety. All the information you need to apply is placed together at the conclusion of each college **Profile.** Display ads, which appear near some of the institutions' profiles, have been provided and paid for by those colleges or universities that wished to supplement their profile data with additional information about their institution.

- In addition, two-page narrative descriptions, which appear as **College Close-Ups,** are paid for and written by college officials and offer great detail about each college. They are edited to provide a consistent format across entries for your ease of comparison.

Peterson's publishes a full line of books—education exploration, test prep, financial aid, and career preparation. Peterson's publications can be found at high school guidance offices, college libraries and career centers, and your local bookstore and library. Peterson's books are now also available as eBooks.

We welcome any comments or suggestions you may have about this publication. Your feedback will help us make educational dreams possible for you—and others like you.

Colleges will be pleased to know that Peterson's helped you in your selection. Admissions staff members are more than happy to answer questions, address specific problems and help in any way they can. The editors at Peterson's wish you great success in your college search.

The College
Admissions Process:
An Overview

What You Need to Know About Two-Year Colleges

David R. Pierce

Two-year colleges—better known as community colleges—are often called "the people's colleges." With their open-door policies (admission is open to individuals with a high school diploma or its equivalent), community colleges provide access to higher education for millions of Americans who might otherwise be excluded from higher education. Community college students are diverse and of all ages, races, and economic backgrounds. While many community college students enroll full-time, an equally large number attend on a part-time basis so they can fulfill employment and family commitments as they advance their education.

Community colleges can also be referred to as either technical or junior colleges, and they may either be under public or independent control. What unites two-year colleges is that they are regionally accredited, postsecondary institutions, whose highest credential awarded is the associate degree. With few exceptions, community colleges offer a comprehensive curriculum, which includes transfer, technical, and continuing education programs.

IMPORTANT FACTORS IN A COMMUNITY COLLEGE EDUCATION

The student who attends a community college can count on receiving high-quality instruction in a supportive learning community. This setting frees the student to pursue his or her own goals, nurture special talents, explore new fields of learning, and develop the capacity for lifelong learning.

From the student's perspective, four characteristics capture the essence of community colleges:

1. They are community-based institutions that work in close partnership with high schools, community groups, and employers in extending high-quality programs at convenient times and places.

2. Community colleges are cost effective. Annual tuition and fees at public community colleges average approximately half those at public four-year colleges and less than 15 percent of private four-year institutions. In addition, since most community colleges are generally close to their students' homes, these students can also save a significant amount of money on the room, board, and transportation expenses traditionally associated with a college education.

3. Community colleges provide a caring environment, with faculty members who are expert instructors, known for excellent teaching and meeting students at the point of their individual needs, regardless of age, sex, race, current job status, or previous academic preparation. Community colleges join a strong curriculum with a broad range of counseling and career services that are intended to assist students in making the most of their educational opportunities.

4. Many offer comprehensive programs, including transfer curricula in such liberal arts programs as chemistry, psychology, and business management, that lead directly to a baccalaureate degree and career programs that prepare students for employment or assist those already employed in upgrading their skills. For those students who need to strengthen their academic skills, community colleges also offer a wide range of developmental programs in mathematics, languages, and learning skills, designed to prepare the student for success in college studies.

GETTING TO KNOW YOUR TWO-YEAR COLLEGE

The first step in determining the quality of a community college is to check the status of its accreditation. Once you have established that a community college is appropriately accredited, find out as much as you can about the programs and services it has to offer. Much of that information can be found in materials the college provides. However, the best way to learn about a college is to visit in person.

During a campus visit, be prepared to ask a lot of questions. Talk to students, faculty members, administrators, and counselors about the college and its programs, particularly those in which you have a special interest. Ask about available certificates and associate degrees. Don't be shy. Do what you can to dig below the surface. Ask college officials about the transfer rate to four-year colleges. If a college emphasizes student services, find out what particular assistance is offered, such as educational or career guidance. Colleges are eager to provide you with the information you need to make informed decisions.

3

COMMUNITY COLLEGES CAN SAVE YOU MONEY

If you are able to live at home while you attend college, you will certainly save money on room and board, but it does cost something to commute. Many two-year colleges offer you instruction in your own home through online learning programs or through home study courses that can save both time and money. Look into all the options, and be sure to add up all the costs of attending various colleges before deciding which is best for you.

FINANCIAL AID

Many students who attend community colleges are eligible for a range of federal financial aid programs, state aid, and on-campus jobs. Your high school counselor or the financial aid officer at a community college will also be able to help you. It is in your interest to apply for financial aid months in advance of the date you intend to start your college program, so find out early what assistance is available to you. While many community colleges are able to help students who make a last-minute decision to attend college, either through short-term loans or emergency grants, if you are considering entering college and think you might need financial aid, it is best to find out as much as you can as early as you can.

WORKING AND GOING TO SCHOOL

Many two-year college students maintain full-time or part-time employment while they earn their degrees. Over the years, a steadily growing number of students have chosen to attend community colleges while they fulfill family and employment responsibilities. To enable these students to balance the demands of home, work, and school, most community colleges offer classes at night and on weekends.

For the full-time student, the usual length of time it takes to obtain an associate degree is two years. However, your length of study will depend on the course load you take: the fewer credits you earn each term, the longer it will take you to earn a degree. To assist you in moving more quickly toward earning your degree, many community colleges now award credit through examination or for equivalent knowledge gained through relevant life experiences. Be certain to find out the credit options that are available to you at the college in which you are interested. You may discover that it will take less time to earn a degree than you first thought.

PREPARATION FOR TRANSFER

Studies have repeatedly shown that students who first attend a community college and then transfer to a four-year college or university do at least as well academically as the students who entered the four-year institutions as freshmen. Most community colleges have agreements with nearby four-year institutions to make transfer of credits easier. If you are thinking of transferring, be sure to meet with a counselor or faculty adviser before choosing your courses. You will want to map out a course of study with transfer in mind. Make sure you also find out the credit-transfer requirements of the four-year institution you might want to attend.

ATTENDING A TWO-YEAR COLLEGE IN ANOTHER REGION

Although many community colleges serve a specific county or district, they are committed (to the extent of their ability) to the goal of equal educational opportunity without regard to economic status, race, creed, color, sex, or national origin. Independent two-year colleges recruit from a much broader geographical area—throughout the United States and, increasingly, around the world.

Although some community colleges do provide on-campus housing for their students, most do not. However, even if on-campus housing is not available, most colleges do have housing referral services.

NEW CAREER OPPORTUNITIES

Community colleges realize that many entering students are not sure about the field in which they want to focus their studies or the career they would like to pursue. Often, students discover fields and careers they never knew existed. Community colleges have the resources to help students identify areas of career interest and to set challenging occupational goals.

Once a career goal is set, you can be confident that a community college will provide job-relevant, technical education. About half of the students who take courses for credit at community colleges do so to prepare for employment or to acquire or upgrade skills for their current job. Especially helpful in charting a career path is the assistance of a counselor or a faculty adviser, who can discuss job opportunities in your chosen field and help you map out your course of study.

In addition, since community colleges have close ties to their communities, they are in constant contact with leaders in business, industry, organized labor, and public life. Community colleges work with these individuals and their organizations to prepare students for direct entry into the world of work. For example, some community colleges have established partnerships with local businesses and industries to provide specialized training programs. Some also provide the academic portion of apprenticeship training, while others offer extensive job-shadowing and cooperative education opportunities. Be sure to examine all of the career-preparation opportunities offered by the community colleges in which you are interested.

David R. Pierce is the former President of the American Association of Community Colleges.

Surviving Standardized Tests

WHAT ARE STANDARDIZED TESTS?

Colleges and universities in the United States use tests to help evaluate applicants' readiness for admission or to place them in appropriate courses. The tests that are most frequently used by colleges are the ACT of American College Testing, Inc., and the College Board's SAT. In addition, the Educational Testing Service (ETS) offers the TOEFL test, which evaluates the English-language proficiency of nonnative speakers. The tests are offered at designated testing centers located at high schools and colleges throughout the United States and U.S. territories and at testing centers in various countries throughout the world.

Upon request, special accommodations for students with documented visual, hearing, physical, or learning disabilities are available. Examples of special accommodations include tests in Braille or large print and such aids as a reader, recorder, magnifying glass, or sign language interpreter. Additional testing time may be allowed in some instances. Contact the appropriate testing program or your guidance counselor for details on how to request special accommodations.

THE ACT

The ACT is a standardized college entrance examination that measures knowledge and skills in English, mathematics, reading, and science reasoning and the application of these skills to future academic tasks. The ACT consists of four multiple-choice tests.

Test 1: English
- 75 questions, 45 minutes
- Usage and mechanics
- Rhetorical skills

Test 2: Mathematics
- 60 questions, 60 minutes
- Pre-algebra
- Elementary algebra
- Intermediate algebra
- Coordinate geometry
- Plane geometry
- Trigonometry

Test 3: Reading
- 40 questions, 35 minutes
- Prose fiction
- Humanities
- Social studies
- Natural sciences

Test 4: Science
- 40 questions, 35 minutes
- Data representation
- Research summary
- Conflicting viewpoints

Each section is scored from 1 to 36 and is scaled for slight variations in difficulty. Students are not penalized for incorrect responses. The composite score is the average of the four scaled scores. The ACT Plus Writing includes the four multiple-choice tests and a writing test, which measures writing skills emphasized in high school English classes and in entry-level college composition courses.

To prepare for the ACT, ask your guidance counselor for a free guidebook called "Preparing for the ACT." Besides providing general test-preparation information and additional test-taking strategies, this guidebook describes the content and format of the four ACT subject area tests, summarizes test administration procedures followed at ACT test centers, and includes a practice test. Peterson's publishes *The Real ACT Prep Guide* that includes five official ACT tests.

THE SAT

The SAT measures developed critical reading and mathematical reasoning abilities as they relate to successful performance in college. It is intended to supplement the secondary school record and other information about the student in assessing readiness for college. There is one unscored, experimental section on the exam, which is used for equating and/or pretesting purposes and can cover either the mathematics or critical reading area.

Critical Reading
- 67 questions, 70 minutes
- Sentence completion
- Passage-based reading

DON'T FORGET TO . . .

- ☐ Take the SAT or ACT before application deadlines.
- ☐ Note that test registration deadlines precede test dates by about six weeks.
- ☐ Register to take the TOEFL test if English is not your native language and you are planning on studying at a North American college.
- ☐ Practice your test-taking skills with *Peterson's Master the SAT, The Real ACT Prep Guide* (published by Peterson's).
- ☐ Contact the College Board or American College Testing, Inc., in advance if you need special accommodations when taking tests.

Mathematics
- 54 questions, 70 minutes
- Multiple-choice
- Student-produced response (grid-ins)

Writing
- 49 questions plus essay, 60 minutes
- Identifying sentence errors
- Improving paragraphs
- Improving sentences
- Essay

Students receive one point for each correct response and lose a fraction of a point for each incorrect response (except for student-produced responses). These points are totaled to produce the raw scores, which are then scaled to equalize the scores for slight variations in difficulty for various editions of the test. The critical reading, writing, and mathematics scaled scores range from 200–800 per section. The total scaled score range is from 600–2400.

SAT SUBJECT TESTS

Subject Tests are required by some institutions for admission and/or placement in freshman-level courses. Each Subject Test measures one's knowledge of a specific subject and the ability to apply that knowledge. Students should check with each institution for its specific requirements. In general, students are required to take three Subject Tests (one English, one mathematics, and one of their choice).

Subject Tests are given in the following areas: biology, chemistry, Chinese, French, German, Italian, Japanese, Korean, Latin, literature, mathematics, modern Hebrew, physics, Spanish, U.S. history, and world history. These tests are 1 hour long and are primarily multiple-choice tests. Three Subject Tests may be taken on one test date.

Scored like the SAT, students gain a point for each correct answer and lose a fraction of a point for each incorrect answer. The raw scores are then converted to scaled scores that range from 200 to 800.

THE TOEFL INTERNET-BASED TEST (IBT)

The Test of English as a Foreign Language Internet-Based Test (TOEFL iBT) is designed to help assess a student's grasp of English if it is not the student's first language. Performance on the TOEFL test may help interpret scores on the critical reading sections of the SAT. The test consists of four integrated sections: speaking, listening, reading, and writing. The TOEFL iBT emphasizes integrated skills. The paper-based versions of the TOEFL will continue to be administered in certain countries where the Internet-based version has not yet been introduced. For further information, visit www.toefl.org.

WHAT OTHER TESTS SHOULD I KNOW ABOUT?

The AP Program

This program allows high school students to try college-level work and build valuable skills and study habits in the process. Subject matter is explored in more depth in AP courses than in other high school classes. A qualifying score on an AP test— which varies from school to school—can earn you college credit or advanced placement. Getting qualifying grades on enough exams can even earn you a full year's credit and sophomore standing at more than 1,500 higher-education institutions. There are more than thirty AP courses across multiple subject areas, including art history, biology, and computer science. Speak to your guidance counselor for information about your school's offerings.

College-Level Examination Program (CLEP)

The CLEP enables students to earn college credit for what they already know, whether it was learned in school, through independent study, or through other experiences outside of the classroom. More than 2,900 colleges and universities now award credit for qualifying scores on one or more of the 33 CLEP exams. The exams, which are 90 minutes in length and are primarily multiple choice, are administered at participating colleges and universities. For more information, check out the Web site at www.collegeboard.com/clep.

WHAT CAN I DO TO PREPARE FOR THESE TESTS?

Know what to expect. Get familiar with how the tests are structured, how much time is allowed, and the directions for each type of question. Get plenty of rest the night before the test and eat breakfast that morning.

There are a variety of products, from books to software to videos, available to help you prepare for most standardized tests. Find the learning style that suits you best. As for which products to buy, there are two major categories— those created by the test makers and those created by private companies. The best approach is to talk to someone who has been through the process and find out which product or products he or she recommends.

Some students report significant increases in scores after participating in coaching programs. Longer-term programs (40 hours) seem to raise scores more than short-term programs (20 hours), but beyond 40 hours, score gains are minor. Math scores appear to benefit more from coaching than critical reading scores.

Resources

There is a variety of ways to prepare for standardized tests— find a method that fits your schedule and your budget. But you should definitely prepare. Far too many students walk into these tests cold, either because they find standardized tests frightening or annoying or they just haven't found the time to study. The key is that these exams are standardized. That means these tests are largely the same from administration to administration; they always test the same concepts. They have to, or else you couldn't compare the scores of people who took the tests on different dates. The numbers or words may change, but the underlying content doesn't.

So how do you prepare? At the very least, you should review relevant material, such as math formulas and commonly used vocabulary words, and know the directions for each question type or test section. You should take at least one practice test and review your mistakes so you don't make them again on the test day. Beyond that, you know best how much preparation you need. You'll also find lots of material in libraries or bookstores to help you: books and software from the test makers and from other publishers (including Peterson's) or live courses that range from national test-preparation companies to teachers at your high school who offer classes.

Top 10 Ways Not to Take the Test

10. Cramming the night before the test.

9. Not becoming familiar with the directions before you take the test.

8. Not becoming familiar with the format of the test before you take it.

7. Not knowing how the test is graded.

6. Spending too much time on any one question.

5. Second-guessing yourself.

4. Not checking spelling, grammar, and sentence structure in essays.

3. Writing a one-paragraph essay.

2. Forgetting to take a deep breath to keep from—

1. Losing It!

Who's Paying for This?
Financial Aid Basics

A college education can be expensive—costing more than $150,000 for four years at some of the higher priced private colleges and universities. Even at the lower cost state colleges and universities, the cost of a four-year education can approach $60,000. Determining how you and your family will come up with the necessary funds to pay for your education requires planning, perseverance, and learning as much as you can about the options that are available to you. But before you get discouraged, College Board statistics show that 53 percent of full-time students attend four-year public and private colleges with tuition and fees less than $9000, while 20 percent attend colleges that have tuition and fees more than $36,000. College costs tend to be less in the western states and higher in New England.

Paying for college should not be looked at as a four-year financial commitment. For many families, paying the total cost of a student's college education out of current income and savings is usually not realistic. For families that have planned ahead and have financial savings established for higher education, the burden is a lot easier. But for most, meeting the cost of college requires the pooling of current income and assets and investing in longer-term loan options. These family resources, together with financial assistance from state, federal, and institutional sources, enable millions of students each year to attend the institution of their choice.

FINANCIAL AID PROGRAMS

There are three types of financial aid:

1. Gift-aid—Scholarships and grants are funds that do not have to be repaid.
2. Loans—Loans must be repaid, usually after graduation; the amount you have to pay back is the total you've borrowed plus any accrued interest. This is considered a source of self-help aid.
3. Student employment—Student employment is a job arranged for you by the financial aid office. This is another source of self-help aid.

The federal government has four major grant programs—the Federal Pell Grant, the Federal Supplemental Educational Opportunity Grant, Academic Competitiveness Grants (ACG), and SMART grants. ACG and SMART grants are limited to students who qualify for a Pell grant and are awarded to a select group of students. Overall, these grants are targeted to low-to-moderate income families with significant financial need. The federal government also sponsors a student employment program called the Federal Work-Study Program, which offers jobs both on and off campus, and several loan programs, including those for students and for parents of undergraduate students.

There are two types of student loan programs: subsidized and unsubsidized. The subsidized Federal Direct Loan and the Federal Perkins Loan are need-based, government-subsidized loans. Students who borrow through these programs do not have to pay interest on the loan until after they graduate or leave school. The unsubsidized Federal Direct Loan and the Federal Direct PLUS Loan Program are not based on need, and borrowers are responsible for the interest while the student is in school. These loans are administered by different methods. Once you choose your college, the financial aid office will guide you through this process.

After you've submitted your financial aid application and you've been accepted for admission, each college will send you a letter describing your financial aid award. Most award letters show estimated college costs, how much you and your family are expected to contribute, and the amount and types of aid you have been awarded. Most students are awarded aid from a combination of sources and programs. Hence, your award is often called a financial aid "package."

SOURCES OF FINANCIAL AID

Millions of students and families apply for financial aid each year. Financial aid from all sources exceeds $143 billion per year. The largest single source of aid is the federal government, which will award more than $100 billion this year.

The next largest source of financial aid is found in the college and university community. Most of this aid is awarded to students who have a demonstrated need based on the Federal Methodology. Some institutions use a different formula, the Institutional Methodology (IM), to award their own funds in conjunction with other forms of aid. Institutional aid may be either need-based or non-need based. Aid that is not based on need is usually awarded for a student's academic performance (merit awards), specific talents or abilities, or to attract the type of students a college seeks to enroll.

Another source of financial aid is from state government. All states offer grant and/or scholarship aid, most of which is need-based. However, more and more states are offering substantial merit-based aid programs. Most state programs award aid only to students attending college in their home state.

Other sources of financial aid include:

- Private agencies
- Foundations

- Corporations
- Clubs
- Fraternal and service organizations
- Civic associations
- Unions
- Religious groups that award grants, scholarships, and low-interest loans
- Employers that provide tuition reimbursement benefits for employees and their children

More information about these different sources of aid is available from high school guidance offices, public libraries, college financial aid offices, directly from the sponsoring organizations, and on the Web at www.petersons.com and www.finaid.org.

HOW NEED-BASED FINANCIAL AID IS AWARDED

When you apply for aid, your family's financial situation is analyzed using a government-approved formula called the Federal Methodology. This formula looks at five items:

1. Demographic information of the family
2. Income of the parents
3. Assets of the parents
4. Income of the student
5. Assets of the student

This analysis determines the amount you and your family are expected to contribute toward your college expenses, called your Expected Family Contribution or EFC. If the EFC is equal to or more than the cost of attendance at a particular college, then you do not demonstrate financial need. However, even if you don't have financial need, you may still qualify for aid, as there are grants, scholarships, and loan programs that are not need-based.

If the cost of your education is greater than your EFC, then you do demonstrate financial need and qualify for assistance. The amount of your financial need that can be met varies from school to school. Some are able to meet your full need, while others can only cover a certain percentage of need. Here's the formula:

> Cost of Attendance
> − Expected Family Contribution
> = Financial Need

The EFC remains constant, but your need will vary according to the costs of attendance at a particular college. In general, the higher the tuition and fees at a particular college, the higher the cost of attendance will be. Expenses for books and supplies, room and board, transportation, and other miscellaneous items are included in the overall cost of attendance. It is important to remember that you do not have to be "needy" to qualify for financial aid. Many middle and upper-middle income families qualify for need-based financial aid.

APPLYING FOR FINANCIAL AID

Every student must complete the Free Application for Federal Student Aid (FAFSA) to be considered for financial aid. The FAFSA is available from your high school guidance office, many public libraries, colleges in your area, or directly from the U.S. Department of Education.

Students are encouraged to apply for federal student aid on the Web. The electronic version of the FAFSA can be accessed at http://www.fafsa.ed.gov. Both the student and at least one parent must apply for a federal PIN at http:// www.pin.ed.gov. The PIN serves as your electronic signature when applying for aid on the Web.

To award their own funds, some colleges require an additional application, the CSS/Financial Aid PROFILE® form. The PROFILE asks supplemental questions that some colleges and awarding agencies feel provide a more accurate assessment of the family's ability to pay for college. It is up to the college to decide whether it will use only the FAFSA or both the FAFSA and the PROFILE. PROFILE applications are available from the high school guidance office and on the Web. Both the paper application and the Web site list those colleges and programs that require the PROFILE application.

If Every College You're Applying to for Fall 2013 Requires the FAFSA

. . . then it's pretty simple: Complete the FAFSA after January 1, 2013, being certain to send it in before any college-imposed deadlines. (You are not permitted to send in the 2013–14 FAFSA before January 1, 2013.) Most college FAFSA application deadlines are in February or early March. It is easier if you have all your financial records for the previous year available, but if that is not possible, you are strongly encouraged to use estimated figures.

After you send in your FAFSA, either with the paper application or electronically, you'll receive a Student Aid Report (SAR) that includes all of the information you reported and shows your EFC. If you provided an e-mail address, the SAR is sent to you electronically; otherwise, you will receive a paper copy in the mail. Be sure to review the SAR, checking to see if the information you reported is accurately represented. If you used estimated numbers to complete the FAFSA, you may have to resubmit the SAR with any corrections to the data. The college(s) you have designated on the FAFSA will receive the information you reported and will use that data to make their decision. In many instances, the colleges to which you've applied will ask you to send copies of your and your parents' federal income tax returns for 2011, plus any other documents needed to verify the information you reported.

If a College Requires the PROFILE

Step 1: Register for the CSS/Financial Aid PROFILE in the fall of your senior year in high school. You can apply for the PROFILE online at http://profileonline.collegeboard.com/ prf/ index.jsp. Registration information with a list of the colleges that require the PROFILE is available in most high school guidance offices. There is a fee for using the Financial Aid

PROFILE application ($25 for the first college, which includes the $9 application fee, and $16 for each additional college). You must pay for the service by credit card when you register. If you do not have a credit card, you will be billed. A limited number of fee waivers are automatically granted to first-time applicants based on the financial information provided on the PROFILE.

Step 2: Fill out your customized CSS/Financial Aid PROFILE. Once you register, your application will be immediately available online and will have questions that all students must complete, questions which must be completed by the student's parents (unless the student is independent and the colleges or programs selected do not require parental information), and *may* have supplemental questions needed by one or more of your schools or programs. If required, those will be found in Section Q of the application.

In addition to the PROFILE application you complete online, you may also be required to complete a Business/ Farm Supplement via traditional paper format. Completion of this form is not a part of the online process. If this form is required, instructions on how to download and print the supplemental form are provided. If your biological or adoptive parents are separated or divorced and your colleges and programs require it, your noncustodial parent may be asked to complete the Noncustodial PROFILE.

Once you complete and submit your PROFILE application, it will be processed and sent directly to your requested colleges and programs.

IF YOU DON'T QUALIFY FOR NEED-BASED AID

If you are not eligible for need-based aid, you can still find ways to lessen your burden.

Here are some suggestions:

- Search for merit scholarships. You can start at the initial stages of your application process. College merit awards are increasingly important as more and more colleges award these to students they especially want to attract. As a result, applying to a college at which your qualifications put you at the top of the entering class may give you a larger merit award. Another source of aid to look for is private scholarships that are given for special skills and talents. Additional information can be found at and at www.finaid.org.

- Seek employment during the summer and the academic year. The student employment office at your college can help you locate a school-year job. Many colleges and local businesses have vacancies remaining after they have hired students who are receiving Federal Work-Study Program financial aid.

- Borrow through the unsubsidized Federal Direct Loan program. This is generally available to all students. The terms and conditions are similar to the subsidized loans. The biggest difference is that the borrower is responsible for the interest while still in college, although the government permits students to delay paying the interest right away and add the accrued interest to the total amount owed. You must file the FAFSA to be considered.

- After you've secured what you can through scholarships, working, and borrowing, you and your parents will be expected to meet your share of the college bill (the Expected Family Contribution). Many colleges offer monthly payment plans that spread the cost over the academic year. If the monthly payments are too high, parents can borrow through the Federal Direct PLUS Loan Program, through one of the many private education loan programs available, or through home equity loans and lines of credit. Families seeking assistance in financing college expenses should inquire at the financial aid office about what programs are available at the college. Some families seek the advice of professional financial advisers and tax consultants.

Frequently Asked Questions About Transferring

Muriel M. Shishkoff

Among the students attending two-year colleges are a large number who began their higher education knowing they would eventually transfer to a four-year school to obtain their bachelor's degree. There are many reasons why students go this route. Upon graduating from high school, some simply do not have definite career goals. Although they don't want to put their education on hold, they prefer not to pay exorbitant amounts in tuition while trying to "find themselves." As the cost of a university education escalates—even in public institutions—the option of spending the freshman and sophomore years at a two-year college looks attractive to many students. Others attend a two-year college because they are unable to meet the initial entrance standards—a specified grade point average (GPA), standardized test scores, or knowledge of specific academic subjects—required by the four-year school of their choice. Many such students praise the community college system for giving them the chance to be, academically speaking, "born again." In addition, students from other countries often find that they can adapt more easily to language and cultural changes at a two-year school before transferring to a larger, more diverse four-year college.

If your plan is to attend a two-year college with the ultimate goal of transferring to a four-year school, you will be pleased to know that the increased importance of the community college route to a bachelor's degree is recognized by all segments of higher education. As a result, many two-year schools have revised their course outlines and established new courses in order to comply with the programs and curricular offerings of the universities. Institutional improvements to make transferring easier have also proliferated at both the two-and four-year levels. The generous transfer policies of the Pennsylvania, New York, and Florida state university systems, among others, reflect this attitude; these systems accept all credits from students who have graduated from accredited community colleges.

If you are interested in moving from a two-year college to a four-year school, the sooner you make up your mind that you are going to make the switch, the better position you will be in to transfer successfully (that is, without having wasted valuable time and credits). The ideal point at which to make such a decision is **before** you register for classes at your two-year school; a counselor can help you plan your course work with an eye toward fulfilling the requirements needed for your major course of study.

Naturally, it is not always possible to plan your transferring strategy that far in advance, but keep in mind that the key to a successful transfer is **preparation,** and preparation takes time—time to think through your objectives and time to plan the right classes to take.

As students face the prospect of transferring from a two-year to a four-year school, many thoughts and concerns about this complicated and often frustrating process race through their minds. Here are answers to the questions that are most frequently asked by transferring students.

Q Does every college and university accept transfer students?

A Most four-year institutions accept transfer students, but some do so more enthusiastically than others. Graduating from a community college is an advantage at, for example, Arizona State University and the University of Massachusetts Boston; both accept more community college transfer students than traditional freshmen. At the State University of New York at Albany, graduates of two-year transfer programs within the State University of New York System are given priority for upper-division (i.e., junior- and senior-level) vacancies.

Schools offering undergraduate work at the upper division only are especially receptive to transfer applications. On the other hand, some schools accept only a few transfer students; others refuse entrance to sophomores or those in their final year. Princeton University requires an "excellent academic record and particularly compelling reasons to transfer." Check the catalogs of several colleges for their transfer requirements before you make your final choice.

Q Do students who go directly from high school to a four-year college do better academically than transfer students from community colleges?

A On the contrary: some institutions report that transfers from two-year schools who persevere until graduation do *better* than those who started as freshmen in a four-year college.

Q Why is it so important that my two-year college be accredited?

A Four-year colleges and universities accept transfer credits only from schools formally recognized by a regional, national, or professional educational agency. This accreditation signifies that an institution or program of study meets or exceeds a minimum level of educational quality necessary for meeting stated educational objectives.

Q After enrolling at a four-year school, may I still make up necessary courses at a community college?

A Some institutions restrict credit after transfer to their own facilities. Others allow students to take a limited number of transfer courses after matriculation, depending on the subject matter. A few provide opportunities for cross-registration or dual enrollment, which means taking classes on more than one campus.

Q What do I need to do to transfer?

A First, send for your high school and college transcripts. Having chosen the school you wish to transfer to, check its admission requirements against your transcripts. If you find that you are admissible, file an application as early as possible before the deadline. Part of the process will be asking your former schools to send official transcripts to the admission office, i.e., not the copies you used in determining your admissibility.

Plan your transfer program with the head of your new department as soon as you have decided to transfer. Determine the recommended general education pattern and necessary preparation for your major. At your present school, take the courses you will need to meet transfer requirements for the new school.

Q What qualifies me for admission as a transfer student?

A Admission requirements for most four-year institutions vary. Depending on the reputation or popularity of the school and program you wish to enter, requirements may be quite selective and competitive. Usually, you will need to show satisfactory test scores, an academic record up to a certain standard, and completion of specific subject matter.

Transfer students can be eligible to enter a four-year school in a number of ways: by having been eligible for admission directly upon graduation from high school, by making up shortcomings in grades (or in subject matter not covered in high school) at a community college, or by satisfactory completion of necessary courses or credit hours at another postsecondary institution. Ordinarily, students coming from a community college or from another four-year institution must meet or exceed the receiving institution's standards for freshmen and show appropriate college-level course work taken since high school. Students who did not graduate from high school can present proof of proficiency through results on the General Educational Development (GED) test.

Q Are exceptions ever made for students who don't meet all the requirements for transfer?

A Extenuating circumstances, such as disability, low family income, refugee or veteran status, or athletic talent, may permit the special enrollment of students who would not otherwise be eligible but who demonstrate the potential for academic success. Consult the appropriate office—the Educational Opportunity Program, the disabled students' office, the athletic department, or the academic dean—to see whether an exception can be made in your case.

Q How far in advance do I need to apply for transfer?

A Some schools have a rolling admission policy, which means that they process transfer applications as they are received, all year long. With other schools, you must apply during the priority filing period, which can be up to a year before you wish to enter. Check the date with the admission office at your prospective campus.

Q Is it possible to transfer courses from several different institutions?

A Institutions ordinarily accept the courses that they consider transferable, regardless of the number of accredited schools involved. However, there is the danger of exceeding the maximum number of credit hours that can be transferred from all other schools or earned through credit by examination, extension courses, or correspondence courses. The limit placed on transfer credits varies from school to school, so read the catalog carefully to avoid taking courses you won't be able to use. To avoid duplicating courses, keep attendance at different campuses to a minimum.

Q What is involved in transferring from a semester system to a quarter or trimester system?

A In the semester system, the academic calendar is divided into two equal parts. The quarter system is more aptly named trimester, since the academic calendar is divided into three equal terms (not counting a summer session). To convert semester units into quarter units or credit hours, simply multiply the semester units by one and a half. Conversely, multiply quarter units by two thirds to come up with semester units. If you are used to a semester system of fifteen- to sixteen-week courses, the ten-week courses of the quarter system may seem to fly by.

Q Why might a course be approved for transfer credit by one four-year school but not by another?

A The beauty of postsecondary education in the United States lies in its variety. Entrance policies and graduation requirements are designed to reflect and serve each institution's mission. Because institutional policies vary so widely, schools may interpret the subject matter of a course from quite different points of view. Given that the granting of transfer credit indicates that a course is viewed as being, in effect, parallel to one offered by the receiving institution, it is easy to see how this might be the case at one university and not another.

Q Must I take a foreign language to transfer?

A Foreign language proficiency is often required for admission to a four-year institution; such proficiency also often figures in certain majors or in the general education pattern. Often, two or three years of a single language in high school will do the trick. Find out if scores received on Advanced Placement (AP) examinations, placement examinations given by the foreign language department, or SAT Subject Tests will be accepted in lieu of college course work.

Q Will the school to which I'm transferring accept pass/ no pass, pass/fail, or credit/no credit grades in lieu of letter grades?

A Usually, a limit is placed on the number of these courses you can transfer, and there may be other restrictions as well. If you want to use other-than-letter grades for the fulfillment of general education requirements or lower-division (freshman and sophomore) preparation for the major, check with the receiving institution.

Q Which is more important for transfer—my grade point average or my course completion pattern?

A Some schools believe that your past grades indicate academic potential and overshadow prior preparation for a specific degree program. Others require completion of certain introductory courses before transfer to prepare you for upper-division work in your major. In any case, appropriate course selection will cut down the time to graduation and increase your chances of making a successful transfer.

Q What happens to my credits if I change majors?

A If you change majors after admission, your transferable course credit should remain fairly intact. However, because you may need extra or different preparation for your new major, some of the courses you've taken may now be useful only as electives. The need for additional lower-level preparation may mean you're staying longer at your new school than you originally planned. On the other hand, you may already have taken courses that count toward your new major as part of the university's general education pattern.

Excerpted from *Transferring Made Easy: A Guide to Changing Colleges Successfully,* by Muriel M. Shishkoff, © 1991 by Muriel M. Shishkoff (published by Peterson's).

Returning to School: Advice for Adult Students

Sandra Cook, Ph.D.
Assistant Vice President for Academic Affairs, Enrollment Services, San Diego State University

Many adults think for a long time about returning to school without taking any action. One purpose of this article is to help the "thinkers" finally make some decisions by examining what is keeping them from action. Another purpose is to describe not only some of the difficulties and obstacles that adult students may face when returning to school but also tactics for coping with them.

If you have been thinking about going back to college, and believing that you are the only person your age contemplating college, you should know that approximately 7 million adult students are currently enrolled in higher education institutions. This number represents 50 percent of total higher education enrollments. The majority of adult students are enrolled at two-year colleges.

There are many reasons why adult students choose to attend a two-year college. Studies have shown that the three most important criteria that adult students consider when choosing a college are location, cost, and availability of the major or program desired. Most two-year colleges are public institutions that serve a geographic district, making them readily accessible to the community. Costs at most two-year colleges are far less than at other types of higher education institutions. For many students who plan to pursue a bachelor's degree, completing their first two years of college at a community college is an affordable means to that end. If you are interested in an academic program that will transfer to a four-year institution, most two-year colleges offer the "general education" courses that compose most freshman and sophomore years. If you are interested in a vocational or technical program, two-year colleges excel in providing this type of training.

SETTING THE STAGE

There are three different "stages" in the process of adults returning to school. The first stage is uncertainty. Do I really want to go back to school? What will my friends or family think? Can I compete with those 18-year-old whiz kids? Am I too old? The second stage is choice. Once the decision to return has been made, you must choose where you will attend. There are many criteria to use in making this decision. The third stage is support. You have just added another role to your already-too-busy life. There are, however, strategies that

will help you accomplish your goals—perhaps not without struggle, but with grace and humor nonetheless. Let's look at each of these stages.

UNCERTAINTY

Why are you thinking about returning to school? Is it to

- fulfill a dream that had to be delayed?
- become more educationally well-rounded?
- fill an intellectual void in your life?

These reasons focus on personal growth.

If you are returning to school to

- meet people and make friends
- attain and enjoy higher social status and prestige among friends, relatives, and associates
- understand/study a cultural heritage
- have a medium in which to exchange ideas

You are interested in social and cultural opportunities.

If you are like most adult students, you want to

- qualify for a new occupation
- enter or reenter the job market
- increase earnings potential
- qualify for a more challenging position in the same field of work

You are seeking career growth.

Understanding the reasons why you want to go back to school is an important step in setting your educational goals and will help you to establish some criteria for selecting a college. However, don't delay your decision because you have not been able to clearly define your motives. Many times, these aren't clear until you have already begun the process, and they may change as you move through your college experience.

Assuming you agree that additional education will benefit you, what is it that keeps you from returning to school? You may have a litany of excuses running through your mind:

- I don't have time.
- I can't afford it.
- I'm too old to learn.
- My friends will think I'm crazy.

- I'll be older than the teachers and other students.
- My family can't survive without me to take care of them every minute.
- I'll be X years old when I finish.
- I'm afraid.
- I don't know what to expect.

And that is just what these are—excuses. You can make school, like anything else in your life, a priority or not. If you really want to return, you can. The more you understand your motivation for returning to school and the more you understand what excuses are keeping you from taking action, the easier your task will be.

If you think you don't have time: The best way to decide how attending class and studying can fit into your schedule is to keep track of what you do with your time each day for several weeks. Completing a standard time-management grid (each day is plotted out by the half hour) is helpful for visualizing how your time is spent. For each 3-credit-hour class you take, you will need to find 3 hours for class plus 6 to 9 hours for reading-studying-library time. This study time should be spaced evenly throughout the week, not loaded up on one day. It is not possible to learn or retain the material that way. When you examine your grid, see where there are activities that could be replaced with school and study time. You may decide to give up your bowling league or some time in front of the TV. Try not to give up sleeping, and don't cut out every moment of free time. Here are some suggestions that have come from adults who have returned to school:

- Enroll in a time-management workshop. It helps you rethink how you use your time.
- Don't think you have to take more than one course at a time. You may eventually want to work up to taking more, but consider starting with one. (It is more than you are taking now!)
- If you have a family, start assigning to them those household chores that you usually do—and don't redo what they do.
- Use your lunch hour or commuting time for reading.

If you think you cannot afford it: As mentioned earlier, two-year colleges are extremely affordable. If you cannot afford the tuition, look into the various financial aid options. Most federal and state funds are available to full- and part-time students. Loans are also available. While many people prefer not to accumulate a debt for school, these same people will think nothing of taking out a loan to buy a car. After five or six years, which is the better investment? Adult students who work should look into whether their company has a tuition-reimbursement policy. There are also private scholarships, available through foundations, service organizations, and clubs, that are focused on adult learners. Your public library, the Web, and a college financial aid adviser are three excellent sources for reference materials regarding financial aid.

If you think you are too old to learn: This is pure myth. A number of studies have shown that adult learners perform as well as, or better than, traditional-age students.

If you are afraid your friends will think you're crazy: Who cares? Maybe they will, maybe they won't. Usually, they will admire your courage and be just a little jealous of your ambition (although they'll never tell you that). Follow your dreams, not theirs.

If you are concerned because the teachers or students will be younger than you: Don't be. The age differences that may be apparent in other settings evaporate in the classroom. If anything, an adult in the classroom strikes fear into the hearts of some 18-year-olds because adults have been known to be prepared, ask questions, be truly motivated, and be there to learn!

If you think your family will have a difficult time surviving while you are in school: If you have done everything for them up to now, they might struggle. Consider this an opportunity to help them become independent and self-sufficient. Your family can only make you feel guilty if you let them. You are not abandoning them; you are becoming an educational role model. When you are happy and working toward your goals, everyone benefits. Admittedly, it sometimes takes time for them to realize this. For single parents, there are schools that offer support groups, child care, and cooperative babysitting.

If you're appalled at the thought of being X years old when you graduate in Y years: How old will you be in Y years if you don't go back to school?

If you are afraid or don't know what to expect: Know that these are natural feelings when one encounters any new situation. Adult students find that their fears usually dissipate once they begin classes. Fear of trying is usually the biggest roadblock to the reentry process.

No doubt you have dreamed up a few more reasons for not making the decision to return to school. Keep in mind that what you are doing is making up excuses, and you are using these excuses to release you from the obligation to make a decision about your life. The thought of returning to college can be scary. Anytime anyone ventures into unknown territory, there is a risk, but taking risks is a necessary component of personal and professional growth. It is your life, and you alone are responsible for making the decisions that determine its course. Education is an investment in your future.

CHOICE

Once you have decided to go back to school, your next task is to decide where to go. If your educational goals are well defined (e.g., you want to pursue a degree in order to change careers), then your task is a bit easier. But even if your educational goals are still evolving, do not defer your return. Many students who enter higher education with a specific major in mind change that major at least once.

Most students who attend a public two-year college choose the community college in the district in which they live. This is generally the closest and least expensive option if the school offers the programs you want. If you are planning to begin your education at a two-year college and then transfer to a four-year school, there are distinct advantages to choosing your four-year school early. Many community and four-year colleges have "articulation" agreements that designate what credits from the two-year school will transfer to the four-year college and how. Some four-year institutions accept an associate degree as equivalent to the freshman and sophomore years, regardless of the courses you have taken. Some four-year schools accept two-year college work only on a course-by-course basis. If you can identify which school you will transfer to, you can know in advance exactly how your two-year credits will apply, preventing an unexpected loss of credit or time.

Each institution of higher education is distinctive. Your goal in choosing a college is to come up with the best student-institution fit—matching your needs with the offerings and characteristics of the school. The first step in choosing a college is to determine what criteria are most important to you in attaining your educational goals. Location, cost, and program availability are the three main factors that influence an adult student's college choice. In considering location, don't forget that some colleges have conveniently located branch campuses. In considering cost, remember to explore your financial aid options before ruling out an institution because of its tuition. Program availability should include not only the major in which you are interested, but also whether or not classes in that major are available when you can take them.

Some additional considerations beyond location, cost, and programs are:

- Does the school have a commitment to adult students and offer appropriate services, such as child care, tutoring, and advising?

- Are classes offered at times when you can take them?

- Are there academic options for adults, such as credit for life or work experience, credit by examination (including CLEP), credit for military service, or accelerated programs?

- Is the faculty sensitive to the needs of adult learners?

Once you determine which criteria are vital in your choice of an institution, you can begin to narrow your choices. There are myriad ways for you to locate the information you desire. Many newspapers publish a "School Guide" several times a year in which colleges and universities advertise to an adult student market. In addition, schools themselves publish catalogs, class schedules, and promotional materials that contain much of the information you need, and they are yours for the asking. Many colleges sponsor information sessions and open houses that allow you to visit the campus and ask questions. An appointment with an adviser is a good way to assess the fit between you and the institution. Be sure to bring your questions with you to your interview.

SUPPORT

Once you have made the decision to return to school and have chosen the institution that best meets your needs, take some additional steps to ensure your success during your crucial first semester. Take advantage of institutional support and build some social support systems of your own. Here are some ways of doing just that:

- Plan to participate in any orientation programs. These serve the threefold purpose of providing you with a great deal of important information, familiarizing you with the campus and its facilities, and giving you the opportunity to meet and begin networking with other students.

- Take steps to deal with any academic weaknesses. Take mathematics and writing placement tests if you have reason to believe you may need some extra help in these areas. It is not uncommon for adult students to need a math refresher course or a program to help alleviate math anxiety. Ignoring a weakness won't make it go away.

- Look into adult reentry programs. Many institutions offer adults workshops focusing on ways to improve study skills, textbook reading, test-taking, and time-management skills.

- Build new support networks by joining an adult student organization, making a point of meeting other adult students through workshops, or actively seeking out a "study buddy" in each class—that invaluable friend who shares and understands your experience.

- Incorporate your new status as "student" into your family life. Doing your homework with your children at a designated "homework time" is a valuable family activity and reinforces the importance of education.

- Make sure you take a reasonable course load in your first semester. It is far better to have some extra time on your hands and to succeed magnificently than to spend the entire semester on the brink of a breakdown. Also, whenever possible, try to focus your first courses not only on requirements, but also on areas of personal interest.

- Faculty members, advisers, and student affairs personnel are there to help you during difficult times—let them assist you as often as necessary.

After completing your first semester, you will probably look back in wonder at why you thought going back to school was so imposing. Certainly, it's not without its occasional exasperations. But, as with life, keeping things in perspective and maintaining your sense of humor make the difference between just coping and succeeding brilliantly.

What International Students Need to Know About Admission to U.S. Colleges and Universities

Kitty M. Villa

There are two principles to remember about admission to a university in the United States. First, applying is almost never a one-time request for admission but an ongoing process that may involve several exchanges of information between applicant and institution. "Admission process" or "application process" means that a "yes" or "no" is usually not immediate, and requests for additional information are to be expected. To successfully manage this process, you must be prepared to send additional information when requested and then wait for replies. You need a thoughtful balance of persistence to communicate regularly and effectively with your selected universities and patience to endure what can be a very long process.

The second principle involves a marketplace analogy. The most successful applicants are alert to opportunities to create a positive impression that sets them apart from other applicants. They are able to market themselves to their target institution. Institutions are also trying to attract the highest-quality student that they can. The admissions process presents you with the opportunity to analyze your strengths and weaknesses as a student and to look for ways to present yourself in the most marketable manner.

FIRST STEP—SELECTING INSTITUTIONS

With thousands of institutions of higher education in the United States, how do you begin to narrow your choices down to the institutions that are best for you? There are many factors to consider, and you must ultimately decide which factors are most important to you.

Location

You may spend several years studying in the United States. Do you prefer an urban or rural campus? Large or small metropolitan area? If you need to live on campus, will you be unhappy at a university where most students commute from off-campus housing? How do you feel about extremely hot summers or cold winters? Eliminating institutions that do not match your preferences in terms of location will narrow your choices.

Recommendations from Friends, Professors, or Others

There are valid academic reasons to consider the recommendations of people who know you well and have firsthand knowledge about particular institutions. Friends and contacts may be able to provide you with "inside information" about the campus or its academic programs to which published sources have no access. You should carefully balance anecdotal information with your own research and your own impressions. However, current and former students, professors, and others may provide excellent information during the application process.

Your Own Academic and Career Goals

Consideration of your academic goals is more complex than it may seem at first glance. All institutions do not offer the same academic programs. The application form usually provides a definitive listing of the academic programs offered by an institution. A course catalog describes the degree program and all the courses offered. In addition to printed sources, there is a tremendous amount of institutional information available on the Web. Program descriptions, even course descriptions and course syllabi, are often available to peruse online.

You may be interested in the rankings of either the university or of a program of study. Keep in mind, however, that rankings usually assume that quality is quantifiable. Rankings are usually based on presumptions about how data relate to quality and are likely to be unproven. It is important to carefully consider the source and the criteria of any ranking information before believing and acting upon it.

Your Own Educational Background

You may be concerned about the interpretation of your educational credentials, since your country's degree nomenclature and the grading scale may differ from those in the United States. Universities use reference books about the educational systems of other countries to help them understand specific educational credentials. Generally, these credentials are interpreted by each institution; there is not a single interpretation that applies to every institution. The lack of uniformity is good

17

news for most students, since it means that students from a wide variety of educational backgrounds can find a U.S. university that is appropriate to their needs.

To choose an appropriate institution, you can and should do an informal self-evaluation of your educational background. This self-analysis involves three important questions:

1. How Many Years of Study Have You Completed?
Completion of secondary school with at least twelve total years of education usually qualifies students to apply for undergraduate (bachelor's) degree programs. Completion of a university degree program that involves at least sixteen years of total education qualifies one to apply for admission to graduate (master's) degree programs in the United States.

2. Does the Education That You Have Completed in Your Country Provide Access to Further Study in the United States?
Consider the kind of institution where you completed your previous studies. If educational opportunities in your country are limited, it may be necessary to investigate many U.S. institutions and programs in order to find a match.

3. Are Your Previous Marks or Grades Excellent, Average, or Poor?
Your educational record influences your choice of U.S. institutions. If your grades are average or poor, it may be advisable to apply to several institutions with minimally difficult or noncompetitive entrance levels.

YOU are one of the best sources of information about the level and quality of your previous studies. Awareness of your educational assets and liabilities will serve you well throughout the application process.

SECOND STEP—PLANNING AND ASSEMBLING THE APPLICATION

Planning and assembling a university application can be compared to the construction of a building. First, you must start with a solid foundation, which is the application form itself. The application, often available online as well as in paper form, usually contains a wealth of useful information, such as deadlines, fees, and degree programs available at that institution. To build a solid application, it is best to begin well in advance of the application deadline.

How to Obtain the Application Form
Application forms and links to institutional Web sites may also be available at a U.S. educational advising center associated with the American Embassy or Consulate in your country. These centers are excellent resources for international students and provide information about standardized test administration, scholarships, and other matters to students who are interested in studying in the United States. Your local U.S. Embassy or Consulate can guide you to the nearest educational advising center.

What Are the Key Components of a Complete Application?
Institutional requirements vary, but the standard components of a complete application include the following:

- Transcript
- Required standardized examination scores
- Evidence of financial support
- Letters of recommendation
- Application fee

Transcript
A complete academic record or transcript includes all courses completed, grades earned, and degrees awarded. Most universities require an official transcript to be sent directly from the school or university. In many other countries, however, the practice is to issue official transcripts and degree certificates directly to the student. If you have only one official copy of your transcript, it may be a challenge to get additional certified copies that are acceptable to U.S. universities. Some institutions will issue additional official copies for application purposes.

If your institution does not provide this service, you may have to seek an alternate source of certification. As a last resort, you may send a photocopy of your official transcript, explain that you have only one original, and ask the university for advice on how to deal with this situation.

Required Standardized Examination Scores
Arranging to take standardized examinations and earning the required scores seem to cause the most anxiety for international students.

The university application form usually indicates which examinations are required. The standardized examination required most often for undergraduate admission is the Test of English as a Foreign Language (TOEFL). Institutions may also require the SAT of undergraduate applicants. These standardized examinations are administered by the Educational Testing Service (ETS).

These examinations are offered in almost every country of the world. It is advisable to begin planning for standardized examinations at least six months prior to the application deadline of your desired institutions. Test centers fill up quickly, so it is important to register as soon as possible. Information about the examinations is available at U.S. educational advising centers associated with embassies or consulates.

Most universities require that the original test scores, not a student copy, be sent directly by the testing service. When you register for the test, be sure to indicate that the testing service should send the test scores directly to the universities.

You should begin your application process before you receive your test scores. Delaying submission of your application until the test scores arrive may cause you to miss deadlines and negatively affect the outcome of your application. If you want to know your scores in order to assess your chances of admission to an institution with rigorous admission standards, you should take the tests early.

Many universities in the United States set minimum required scores on the TOEFL or other standardized examinations. Test scores are an important factor, but most institutions also look at a number of other factors in their consideration of a candidate for admission.

For More Information

Questions about test formats, locations, dates, and registration may be addressed to:

ETS Corporate Headquarters
Rosedale Road
Princeton, New Jersey 08541
Web sites: http://www.ets.org
                http://www.ets.org/toefl/
Phone: 609-921-9000
Fax: 609-734-5410

Evidence of Financial Support

Evidence of financial support is required to issue immigration documents to admitted students. This is part of a complete application package but usually plays no role in determining admission. Most institutions make admissions decisions without regard to the source and amount of financial support.

Letters of Recommendation

Most institutions require one or more letters of recommendation. The best letters are written by former professors, employers, or others who can comment on your academic achievements or professional potential.

Some universities provide a special form for the letters of recommendation. If possible, use the forms provided. If you are applying to a large number of universities, however, or if your recommenders are not available to complete several forms, it may be necessary for you to duplicate a general recommendation letter.

Application Fee

Most universities also require an application fee, ranging from $25 to $100, which must be paid to initiate consideration of the application.

Completing the Application Form

Whether sent by mail or electronically, the application form must be neat and thoroughly filled out. Although parts of the application may not seem to apply to you or your situation, do your best to answer all the questions.

Remember that this is a process. You provide information, and your proposed university then may request clarification and further information. If you have questions, it is better to initiate the entire process by submitting the application form rather than asking questions before you apply. The university will be better able to respond to you after it has your application. Always complete as much as you can. Do not permit uncertainty about the completion of the application form to cause unnecessary delays.

THIRD STEP—DISTINGUISH YOUR APPLICATION

To distinguish your application—to market yourself successfully—is ultimately the most important part of the application process. As you select your prospective universities, begin to analyze your strengths and weaknesses as a prospective student. As you complete your application, you should strive to create a positive impression and set yourself apart from other applicants, to highlight your assets and bring these qualities to the attention of the appropriate university administrators and professors. Applying early is a very easy way to distinguish your application.

Deadline or Guideline?

The application deadline is the last date that an application for a given semester will be accepted. Often, the application will specify that all required documents and information be submitted before the deadline date. To meet the deadlines, start the application process early. This also gives you more time to take—and perhaps retake and improve—the required standardized tests.

Admissions deliberations may take several weeks or months. In the meantime, most institutions accept additional information, including improved test scores, after the posted deadline.

Even if your application is initially rejected, you may be able to provide additional information to change the decision. You can request reconsideration based on additional information, such as improved test scores, strong letters of recommendation, or information about your class rank. Applying early allows more time to improve your application. Also, some students may decide not to accept their offers of admission, leaving room for offers to students on a waiting list. Reconsideration of the admission decisions can occur well beyond the application deadline.

Think of the deadline as a guideline rather than an impermeable barrier. Many factors—the strength of the application, your research interests, the number of spaces available at the proposed institution—can override the enforcement of an application deadline. So, if you lack a test score or transcript by the official deadline, you may still be able to apply and be accepted.

Statement of Purpose

The statement of purpose is your first and perhaps best opportunity to present yourself as an excellent candidate for admission. Whether or not a personal history essay or statement of purpose is required, always include a carefully written statement of purpose with your applications. A compelling statement of purpose does not have to be lengthy, but it should include some basic components:

- Part One—Introduce yourself and describe your educational background. This is your opportunity to describe any facet of your educational experience that you wish to emphasize. Perhaps you attended a highly ranked secondary school or university in your home country. Mention the name and any noteworthy characteristics of the secondary school or university from which you graduated. Explain the grading scale used at your university. Do not forget to mention your rank in your graduating class and any honors you may have received. This is not the time to be modest.

- Part Two—Describe your current academic and career interests and goals. Think about how these will fit into those of the institution to which you are applying, and mention the reasons why you have selected that institution.

- Part Three—Describe your long-term goals. When you finish your program of study, what do you plan to do next? If you already have a job offer or a career plan, describe it. Give some thought to how you'll demonstrate that studying in the United States. will ultimately benefit others.

Use Personal Contacts When Possible

Appropriate and judicious use of your own network of contacts can be very helpful. Friends, former professors, former students of your selected institutions, and others may be willing to advise you during the application process and provide you with introductions to key administrators or professors. If suggested, you may wish to contact certain professors or administrators by mail, phone, or *E-mail*. A personal visit to discuss your interest in the institution may be appropriate. Whatever your choice of communication, try to make the encounter pleasant and personal. Your goal is to make a positive impression, not to rush the admission decision.

There is no single right way to be admitted to U.S. universities. The same characteristics that make the educational choice in the United States so difficult—the number of institutions and the variety of programs of study—are the same attributes that allow so many international students to find the institution that's right for them.

Kitty M. Villa is the former Assistant Director, International Office, at the University of Texas at Austin.

Community Colleges and the New Green Economy

Community colleges are a focal point for state and national efforts to create a green economy and workforce. As the United States transforms its economy into a "green" one, community colleges are leading the way—filling the need for both educated technicians whose skills can cross industry lines as well as those technicians who are able to learn new skills as technologies evolve.

Community colleges have been at the heart of the Obama administration's economic recovery strategy, with $12 billion allocated over this decade. President Obama has extolled community colleges as "the unsung heroes of America's education system," essential to our country's success in the "global competition to lead in the growth of industries of the twenty-first century." With the support of state governments, and, more importantly, local and international business partners, America's community colleges are rising to meet the demands of the new green economy. Community colleges are training workers to work in fields such as renewable energy, energy efficiency, wind energy, green building, and sustainability. The programs are as diverse as the campuses housing them.

Here is a quick look at just some of the exciting "green" programs available at community colleges throughout the United States.

At Mesalands Community College in Tucumcari, New Mexico, the new North American Wind Research and Training Center provides state-of-the-art facilities for research and training qualified technicians in wind energy technology. The Center includes a facility for applied research in collaboration with Sandia National Laboratories—the first-ever such partnership between a national laboratory and a community college. It also provides associate degree training for wind energy technicians, meeting the fast-growing demand for "windsmiths" in the western part of the country—jobs that pay $45,000–$60,000 per year. For more information, visit http://www.mesalands.edu/wind/default.htm.

Cape Cod Community College (CCCC) in Massachusetts has become one of the nation's leading colleges in promoting and integrating sustainability and green practices throughout all campus operations and technical training programs. Ten years ago, Cape Wind Associates, Cape Cod's first wind farm, provided $50,000 to jumpstart CCCC's wind technician program—considered a state model for community-based clean energy workforce development and education. In addition, hundreds of CCCC students have earned degrees in coastal management, solar technology, wastewater, and other careers, including cleanup of Superfund sites at an abandoned military base. Visit http://www.capecod.edu/web/guest for more information.

At Oakland Community College in Michigan, more than 350 students are enrolled in the college's Renewable Energies and Sustainable Living program and its related courses. Students gain field experience refurbishing public buildings with renewable materials, performing energy audits for the government, and working with small businesses and hospitals to reduce waste and pollution. To learn more, visit http://www.oaklandcc.edu/est/.

In 2007, Columbia Gorge Community College in Oregon became the first community college in the Pacific Northwest to offer training programs for the windpower generation industry. The college offers a one-year certificate and a two-year Associate of Applied Science (A.A.S.) degree in renewable energy technology. The Renewable Energy Technology program was designed in collaboration with industry partners from the wind energy industry and the power generation industry. Students are prepared for employment in a broad range of industries, including hydro-generation, wind-generation, automated manufacturing, and engineering technology, and the College plans to add solar array technology to this list as well. For more information, visit http://www.cgcc.cc.or.us/Academics/WindTechnologyPage.cfm.

Central Carolina Community College (CCCC) in Pittsboro, North Carolina, has been leading the way in "green" programs for more than a decade. It offered a sustainable agriculture class at its Chatham campus in 1996 and soon became the first community college in the nation to offer an Associate in Applied Science degree in sustainable agriculture and the first in North Carolina to offer an associate degree in biofuels. In addition, it was the first North Carolina community college to offer a North American Board of Certified Energy Practitioners (NABCEP)–approved solar PV panel installation course as part of its green building/renewable energy program. In 2010, CCCC added an associate degree in sustainable technology and launched its new Natural Chef culinary arts program. The College also offers an ecotourism certificate as well as certificates in other green programs. For more information about Central Carolina Community College's green programs, visit http://www.cccc.edu/green.

The Green Jobs Academy at Bucks County Community College in Pennsylvania is an exciting new venture that includes a variety of academic and private industry partners that include Gamesa, Lockheed Martin, Dow, Veterans Green Jobs, and PECO, an Excelon Company. The Green Jobs Academy provides both long- and short-term training programs that are geared toward workers, who are looking for new skill sets in the green and sustainability industries. Courses include Hazardous Site Remediation & Preliminary Assessments, PV Solar Design, NABCEP (*North American*

Board of Certified Energy Practitioners) PV Solar Entry Level Program (40 hours), Electric Vehicle Conversion Workshop, Wind Energy Apprentice, Certified Green Supply Chain Professional, Certified Indoor Air Quality Manager, a Veterans' Weatherization Training Program, and many others. For details, visit http://www.bucks.edu/academics/cwd/green/.

At Cascadia Community College in Bothell, Washington, thanks to a grant from Puget Sound Energy (PSE), students in the Energy Informatics class designed a kiosk screen that shows the energy usage and solar generation at the local 21 Acres Center for Local Food and Sustainable Living. The PSE grant supports the classroom materials for renewable energy education and the Web-based monitoring software that allows students and interested community members to track how much energy is being generated as the weather changes. For more information, visit http://www.cascadia.edu/Default.aspx.

At Grand Rapids Community College, the federally funded Pathways to Prosperity program is successfully preparing low-income residents for jobs in fields such as renewable energy. Approximately 200 people have completed the program, which began in 2010 thanks to a $4-million grant from the Department of Labor, and found jobs in industries ranging from energy-efficient building construction to alternative energy and sustainable manufacturing. For additional information, check out http://cms.grcc.edu/workforce-training/pathways-prosperity or https://learning.grcc.edu/pathways/Overview.asp.

Linn-Benton Community College (LBCC) in Albany, Oregon, is now offering training for the Oregon Green Technology Certificate. Oregon Green Tech is a federally funded program that is designed to prepare entry-level workers with foundational skills for a variety of industries associated with or in support of green jobs. Students learn skills in green occupations that include green energy production; manufacturing, construction, installation, monitoring, and repair of equipment for solar, wind, wave, and bio-energy; building retro-fitting; process recycling; hazardous materials removal work; and more. LBCC is one of ten Oregon community colleges to provide training for the Green Technology Certificate, offered through the Oregon Consortium and Oregon Workforce Alliance. Visit http://www.linnbenton.edu for additional information.

The Santa Fe Community College Sustainable Technology Center in New Mexico offers several green jobs training programs along with various noncredit courses. It also provides credit programs from certificates in green building systems, environmental technology training, and solar energy training as well as an Associate in Applied Science (A.A.S.) degree in environmental technology. For more information, go online to http://www.sfcc.edu/sustainable_technologies_center.

In Colorado, Red Rocks Community College (RRCC) offers degree and certificate programs in renewable energy (solar photovoltaic, solar thermal, and wind energy technology), energy and industrial maintenance, energy operations and process technology, environmental technology, water quality management, and energy audit. RRCC has made a commitment to the national challenge of creating and sustaining a green workforce and instructs students about the issues of energy, environmental stewardship, and renewable resources across the college curriculum. For more information, visit http://www.rrcc.edu/green/.

Next you'll find two essays about other green community college programs. The first essay was written by the president of Lane Community College in Eugene, Oregon, about the role Lane and other community colleges are playing in creating a workforce for the green economy. Then, read a first-hand account of the new Wind Turbine Training Program at Kalamazoo Valley Community College in Kalamazoo, Michigan—a program that has more applicants than spaces and one whose students are being hired BEFORE they even graduate. It's clear that there are exciting "green" programs at community colleges throughout the United States.

The Role of Community Colleges in Creating a Workforce for the Green Economy

by Mary F.T. Spilde, President
Lane Community College

Community colleges are expected to play a leadership role in educating and training the workforce for the green economy. Due to close connections with local and regional labor markets, colleges assure a steady supply of skilled workers by developing and adapting programs to respond to the needs of business and industry. Further, instead of waiting for employers to create job openings, many colleges are actively engaged in local economic development to help educate potential employers to grow their green business opportunities and to participate in the creation of the green economy.

As the green movement emerges there has been confusion about what constitutes a green job. It is now clear that many of the green jobs span several economic sectors such as renewable energy, construction, manufacturing, transportation and agriculture. It is predicted that there will be many middle skill jobs requiring more than a high school diploma but less than a bachelor's degree. This is precisely the unique role that community colleges play. Community colleges develop training programs, including pre-apprenticeship, that ladder the curriculum to take lower skilled workers through a relevant and sequenced course of study that provides a clear pathway to career track jobs. As noted in Going Green: The Vital Role of Community Colleges in Building a Sustainable Future and Green Workforce, community colleges are strategically positioned to work with employers to redefine skills and competencies needed by the green workforce and to create the framework for new and expanded green career pathways.

While there will be new occupations such as solar and wind technologists, the majority of the jobs will be in the energy management sector—retrofitting the built environment. For example, President Obama called for retrofitting more than 75 percent of federal buildings and more than 2 million homes to make them more energy-efficient. The second major area for growth will be the "greening" of existing jobs as they evolve to incorporate green practices. Both will require new knowledge, skills and abilities. For community colleges, this means developing new programs that meet newly created industry standards and adapting existing programs and courses to integrate green skills. The key is to create a new talent pool of environmentally conscious, highly skilled workers.

These two areas show remarkable promise for education and training leading to high wage/high demand jobs:

- Efficiency and energy management: There is a need for auditors and energy efficiency experts to retrofit existing buildings. Consider how much built environment we have in this country, and it's not difficult to see that this is where the vast amount of jobs are now and will be in the future.
- Greening of existing jobs: There are few currently available jobs that environmental sustainability will not impact. Whether it is jobs in construction, such as plumbers, electricians, heating and cooling technicians, painters, and building supervisors, or chefs, farmers, custodians, architects, automotive technicians and interior designers, all will need to understand how to lessen their impact on the environment.

Lane Community College offers a variety of degree and certificate programs to prepare students to enter the energy efficiency fields. Lane has offered an Energy Management program since the late 1980s—before it was hip to be green! Students in this program learn to apply basic principles of physics and analysis techniques to the description and measurement of energy in today's building systems, with the goal of evaluating and recommending alternative energy solutions that will result in greater energy efficiency and energy cost savings. Students gain a working understanding of energy systems in today's built environment and the tools to analyze and quantify energy efficiency efforts. The program began with an emphasis in residential energy efficiency/solar energy systems and has evolved to include commercial energy efficiency and renewable energy system installation technology.

The Renewable Energy Technician program is offered as a second-year option within the Energy Management program. Course work prepares students for employment designing and installing solar electric and domestic hot water systems. Renewable Energy students, along with Energy Management students, take a first-year curriculum in commercial energy efficiency giving them a solid background that includes residential energy efficiency, HVAC systems, lighting, and physics and math. In the second year, Renewable Energy students diverge from the Energy Management curriculum and take course work that starts with two courses in electricity fundamentals and one course in energy economics. In the following terms, students learn to design, install, and develop a thorough understanding of photovoltaics and domestic hot water systems.

Recent additions to Lane's offerings are Sustainability Coordinator and Water Conservation Technician degrees. Both programs were added to meet workforce demand.

Lane graduates find employment in a wide variety of disciplines and may work as facility managers, energy auditors, energy program coordinators, or control system specialists, for such diverse employers as engineering firms, public and private utilities, energy equipment companies, and departments of energy and as sustainability leaders within public and private sector organizations.

Lane Community College also provides continuing education for working professionals. The Sustainable Building Advisor (SBA) Certificate Program is a nine-month, specialized training program for working professionals. Graduate are able to advise employers or clients on strategies and tools for implementing sustainable building practices. Benefits from participating in the SBA program often include saving long-term building operating costs; improving the environmental, social, and economic viability of the region; and reducing environmental impacts and owner liability—not to mention the chance to improve one's job skills in a rapidly growing field.

The Building Operators Certificate is a professional development program created by The Northwest Energy Efficiency Council. It is offered through the Northwest Energy Education Institute at Lane. The certificate is designed for operations and maintenance staff working in public or private commercial buildings. It certifies individuals in energy and resource-efficient operation of building systems at two levels: Level I–Building System Maintenance and Level II–Equipment Troubleshooting and Maintenance.

Lane Community College constantly scans the environment to assess workforce needs and develop programs that provide highly skilled employees. Lane, like most colleges, publishes information in its catalog on workforce demand and wages so that students can make informed decisions about program choice.

Green jobs will be a large part of a healthy economy. Opportunities will abound for those who take advantage of programs with a proven record of connecting with employers and successfully educating students to meet high skills standards.

Establishing a World-Class Wind Turbine Technician Academy

by James DeHaven, Vice President of Economic & Business Development
Kalamazoo Valley Community College

When Kalamazoo Valley Community College (KVCC) decided it wanted to become involved in the training of utility-grade technicians for wind-energy jobs, early on the choice was made to avoid another "me too" training course.

Our program here in Southwest Michigan, 30 miles from Lake Michigan, had to meet industry needs and industry standards.

It was also obvious from the start that the utility-grade or large wind industry had not yet adopted any uniform training standards in the United States.

Of course, these would come, but why should the college wait when European standards were solidly established and working well in Germany, France, Denmark and Great Britain?

As a result, in 2009, KVCC launched its Wind Turbine Technician Academy, the first of its kind in the United States. The noncredit academy runs 8 hours a day, five days a week, for twenty-six weeks of intense training in electricity, mechanics, wind dynamics, safety, and climbing. The college developed this program rather quickly—in eight months—to fast-track individuals into this emerging field.

KVCC based its program on the training standards forged by the Bildungszentrum fur Erneuerebare Energien (BZEE)—the Renewable Energy Education Center. Located in Husum, Germany, the BZEE was created and supported by major wind-turbine manufacturers, component makers, and enterprises that provide operation and maintenance services.

As wind-energy production increased throughout Europe, the need for high-quality, industry-driven, international standards emerged. The BZEE has become the leading trainer for wind-turbine technicians across Europe and now in Asia.

With the exception of one college in Canada, the standards are not yet available in North America. When Kalamazoo Valley realized it could be the first college or university in the United States to offer this training program—that was enough motivation to move forward.

For the College to become certified by the BZEE, it needed to hire and send an electrical instructor and a mechanical instructor to Germany for six weeks of "train the trainer." The instructors not only had to excel in their respective fields, they also needed to be able to climb the skyscraper towers supporting megawatt-class turbines—a unique combination of skills to possess. Truly, individuals who fit this job description don't walk through the door everyday—but we found them! Amazingly, we found a top mechanical instructor who was a part-time fireman and comfortable with tall ladder rescues and a skilled electrical instructor who used to teach rappelling off the Rockies to the Marine Corps.

In addition to employing new instructors, the College needed a working utility-grade nacelle that could fit in its training lab that would be located in the KVCC Michigan Technical Education Center. So one of the instructors traveled to Denmark and purchased a 300-kilowatt turbine.

Once their own training was behind them and the turbine was on its way from the North Sea, the instructors quickly turned to crafting the curriculum necessary for our graduates to earn both an academy certificate from KVCC and a certification from the BZEE.

Promoting the innovative program to qualified potential students across the country was the next step. News releases were published throughout Michigan, and they were also picked up on the Internet. Rather quickly, KVCC found itself with more than 500 requests for applications for a program built for 16 students.

Acceptance into the academy includes a medical release, a climbing test, reading and math tests, relevant work experience, and, finally, an interview. Students in the academy's pioneer class, which graduated in spring 2010, ranged in age from their late teens to early 50s. They hailed from throughout Michigan, Indiana, Ohio, and Illinois as well as from Puerto Rico and Great Britain.

The students brought with them degrees in marketing, law, business, science, and architecture, as well as entrepreneurial experiences in several businesses, knowledge of other languages, military service, extensive travel, and electrical, computer, artistic, and technical/mechanical skills.

Kalamazoo Valley's academy has provided some high-value work experiences for the students in the form of two collaborations with industry that has allowed them to maintain and/or repair actual utility-grade turbines, including those at the 2.5 megawatt size. This hands-on experience will add to the attractiveness of the graduates in the market place. Potential employers were recently invited to an open house where they could see the lab and meet members of this pioneer class.

The College's Turbine Technician Academy has also attracted a federal grant for $550,000 to expand its program through additional equipment purchases. The plan is to erect our own climbing tower. Climbing is a vital part of any valid program, and yet wind farms cannot afford to shut turbines down just for climb-training.

When the students are asked what best distinguishes the Kalamazoo Valley program, their answers point to the experienced instructors and the working lab, which is constantly changing to offer the best training experiences.

Industry continues to tell us that community colleges need to offer fast-track training programs of this caliber if the nation is to reach the U.S. Department of Energy's goal of 20 percent renewable energy by 2030. This would require more than 1,500 new technicians each year.

With that in mind, KVCC plans to host several BZEE orientation programs for other community colleges in order to encourage them to consider adopting the European training standards and start their own programs.

Meanwhile, applications are continuing to stream in from across the country for the next Wind Turbine Technician Academy program at Kalamazoo Valley Community College.

(A video about the program is available at www.mteckvcc.com/windtechacademy.html.)

How to Use This Guide

*P*eterson's *Two-Year Colleges 2013* contains a wealth of information for anyone interested in colleges offering associate degrees. This section details the criteria that institutions must meet to be included in this guide and provides information about research procedures used by Peterson's.

QUICK-REFERENCE CHART

The **Two-Year Colleges At-a-Glance Chart** is a geographically arranged table that lists colleges by name and city within the state, or country in which they are located. Areas listed include the United States, Canada, and other countries; the institutions are included because they are accredited by recognized U.S. accrediting bodies (see **Criteria for Inclusion** section).

The At-a-Glance chart contains basic information that enables you to compare institutions quickly according to broad characteristics such as degrees awarded, enrollment, application requirements, financial aid availability, and numbers of sports and majors offered. A dagger (†) after the institution's name indicates that an institution has an entry in the **College Close-Ups** section.

Column 1: Degrees Awarded

C= *college transfer associate degree:* the degree awarded after a "university-parallel" program, equivalent to the first two years of a bachelor's degree.

T= *terminal associate degree:* the degree resulting from a one-to three-year program providing training for a specific occupation.

B= *bachelor's degree (baccalaureate):* the degree resulting from a liberal arts, science, professional, or preprofessional program normally lasting four years, although in some cases an accelerated program can be completed in three years.

M= *master's degree:* the first graduate (postbaccalaureate) degree in the liberal arts and sciences and certain professional fields, usually requiring one to two years of full-time study.

D= *doctoral degree* (research/scholarship, professional practice, or other)

Column 2: Institutional Control

Private institutions are designated as one of the following:

Ind = *independent* (nonprofit)

I-R = *independent-religious:* nonprofit; sponsored by or affiliated with a particular religious group or having a nondenominational or interdenominational religious orientation.

Prop = *proprietary* (profit-making)

Public institutions are designated by the source of funding, as follows:

Fed = *federal*

St = *state*

Comm = *commonwealth* (Puerto Rico)

Terr = *territory* (U.S. territories)

Cou = *county*

Dist = *district:* an administrative unit of public education, often having boundaries different from units of local government.

City = *city*

St-L = *state and local:* local may refer to county, district, or city.

St-R = *state-related:* funded primarily by the state but administratively autonomous.

Column 3: Student Body

M= *men only* (100% of student body)

PM = *coed, primarily men*

W= *women only* (100% of student body)

PW = *coed, primarily women*

M/W = *coeducational*

Column 4: Undergraduate Enrollment

The figure shown represents the number of full-time and part-time students enrolled in undergraduate degree programs as of fall 2011.

Columns 5–7: Enrollment Percentages

Figures are shown for the percentages of the fall 2011 undergraduate enrollment made up of students attending part-time (column 5) and students 25 years of age or older (column 6). Also listed is the percentage of students in the last graduating class who completed a college-transfer associate program and went directly on to four-year colleges (column 7).

For columns 8 through 15, the following letter codes are used: Y = yes; N = no; R = recommended; S = for some.

Columns 8–10: Admission Policies

The information in these columns shows whether the college has an open admission policy (column 8) whereby virtually all applicants are accepted without regard to standardized test scores, grade average, or class rank; whether a high school equivalency certificate is accepted in place of a high school diploma for admission consideration (column 9); and whether a high school transcript (column 10) is required as part of the application process. In column 10, the combination of the codes R and S indicates that a high school transcript is recommended for all applicants (R) or required for some (S).

Columns 11–12: Financial Aid

These columns show which colleges offer the following types of financial aid: need-based aid (column 11) and part-time jobs (column 12), including those offered through the federal government's Federal Work-Study program.

Columns 13–15: Services and Facilities

These columns show which colleges offer the following: career counseling (column 13) on either an individual or group basis, job placement services (column 14) for individual students, and college-owned or -operated housing facilities (column 16) for noncommuting students.

Column 16: Sports

This figure indicates the number of sports that a college offers at the intramural and/or intercollegiate levels.

Column 17: Majors

This figure indicates the number of major fields of study in which a college offers degree programs.

PROFILES OF TWO-YEAR COLLEGES AND SPECIAL MESSAGES

The **Profiles of Two-Year Colleges** contain basic data in capsule form for quick review and comparison. The following outline of the **Profile** format shows the section headings and the items that each section covers. Any item that does not apply to a particular college or for which no information was supplied is omitted from that college's **Profile.** Display ads, which appear near some of the institution's profiles, have been provided and paid for by those colleges that chose to supplement their profile with additional information.

Bulleted Highlights

The bulleted highlights section features important information, for quick reference and comparison. The number of possible bulleted highlights that an ideal **Profile** would have if all questions were answered in a timely manner follow. However, not every institution provides all of the information necessary to fill out every bulleted line. In such instances, the line will not appear.

First Bullet

Institutional control: Private institutions are designated as independent (nonprofit), proprietary (profit-making), or independent, with a specific religious denomination or affiliation. Nondenominational or interdenominational religious orientation is possible and would be indicated.

Public institutions are designated by the source of funding. Designations include federal, state, province, commonwealth (Puerto Rico), territory (U.S. territories), county, district (an administrative unit of public education, often having boundaries different from units of local government), city, state and local (local may refer to county, district, or city), or state-related (funded primarily by the state but administratively autonomous).

Religious affiliation is also noted here.

Institutional type: Each institution is classified as one of the following:

Primarily two-year college: Awards baccalaureate degrees, but the vast majority of students are enrolled in two-year programs.

Four-year college: Awards baccalaureate degrees; may also award associate degrees; does not award graduate (postbaccalaureate) degrees.

Upper-level institution: Awards baccalaureate degrees, but entering students must have at least two years of previous college-level credit; may also offer graduate degrees.

Comprehensive institution: Awards baccalaureate degrees; may also award associate degrees; offers graduate degree programs, primarily at the master's, specialist's, or professional level, although one or two doctoral programs may be offered.

University: Offers four years of undergraduate work plus graduate degrees through the doctorate in more than two academic or professional fields.

Founding date: If the year an institution was chartered differs from the year when instruction actually began, the earlier date is given.

System or administrative affiliation: Any coordinate institutions or system affiliations are indicated. An institution that has separate colleges or campuses for men and women but shares facilities and courses is termed a coordinate institution. A formal administrative grouping of institutions, either private or public, of which the college is a part, or the name of a single institution with which the college is administratively affiliated, is a system.

Second Bullet

Setting: Schools are designated as urban (located within a major city), suburban (a residential area within commuting distance of a major city), small-town (a small but compactly settled area not within commuting distance of a major city), or rural (a remote and sparsely populated area). The phrase *easy access to...* indicates that the campus is within an hour's drive of the nearest major metropolitan area that has a population greater than 500,000.

Third Bullet

Endowment: The total dollar value of funds and/or property donated to the institution or the multicampus educational system of which the institution is a part.

Fourth Bullet

Student body: An institution is coed (coeducational—admits men and women), primarily (80 percent or more) women, primarily men, women only, or men only.

Undergraduate students: Represents the number of full-time and part-time students enrolled in undergraduate degree programs as of fall 2011. The percentage of full-time undergraduates and the percentages of men and women are given.

Category Overviews
Undergraduates

For fall 2011, the number of full- and part-time undergraduate students is listed. This list provides the number of states and U.S. territories, including the District of Columbia and Puerto Rico (or for Canadian institutions, provinces and territories), and other countries from which undergraduates come. Percentages of undergraduates who are part-time or full-time students; transfers in; live on campus; out-of-state; Black or African American, non-Hispanic/Latino; Hispanic/Latino; Asian, non-Hispanic/Latino; Native Hawaiian or other Pacific Islander, non-Hispanic/Latino; American Indian or Alaska Native, non-Hispanic/Latino are given.

Retention: The percentage of freshmen (or, for upper-level institutions, entering students) who returned the following year for the fall term.

Freshmen

Admission: Figures are given for the number of students who applied for fall 2011 admission, the number of those who were admitted, and the number who enrolled. Freshman statistics include the average high school GPA; the percentage of freshmen who took the SAT and received critical reading, writing, and math scores above 500, above 600, and above 700; as well as the percentage of freshmen taking the ACT who received a composite score of 18 or higher.

Faculty

Total: The total number of faculty members; the percentage of full-time faculty members as of fall 2011; and the percentage of full-time faculty members who hold doctoral/first professional/ terminal degrees.

Student-faculty ratio: The school's estimate of the ratio of matriculated undergraduate students to faculty members teaching undergraduate courses.

Majors

This section lists the major fields of study offered by the college.

Academics

Calendar: Most colleges indicate one of the following: 4-1-4, 4-4-1, or a similar arrangement (two terms of equal length plus an abbreviated winter or spring term, with the numbers referring to months); semesters; trimesters; quarters; 3-3 (three courses for each of three terms); modular (the academic year is divided into small blocks of time; courses of varying lengths

are assembled according to individual programs); or standard year (for most Canadian institutions).

Degrees: This names the full range of levels of certificates, diplomas, and degrees, including prebaccalaureate, graduate, and professional, that are offered by this institution:

Associate degree: Normally requires at least two but fewer than four years of full-time college work or its equivalent.

Bachelor's degree (baccalaureate): Requires at least four years but not more than five years of full-time college-level work or its equivalent. This includes all bachelor's degrees in which the normal four years of work are completed in three years and bachelor's degrees conferred in a five-year cooperative (work-study plan) program. A cooperative plan provides for alternate class attendance and employment in business, industry, or government. This allows students to combine actual work experience with their college studies.

Master's degree: Requires the successful completion of a program of study of at least the full-time equivalent of one but not more than two years of work beyond the bachelor's degree.

Doctoral degree (doctorate; research/scholarship, professional, or other): The highest degree in graduate study. The doctoral degree classification includes Doctor of Education, Doctor of Juridical Science, Doctor of Public Health, Doctor of Philosophy, Doctor of Podiatry, Doctor of Veterinary Medicine, and many more.

Post-master's certificate: Requires completion of an organized program of study of 24 credit hours beyond the master's degree but does not meet the requirements of academic degrees at the doctoral level.

Special study options: Details are next given here on study options available at each college:

Accelerated degree program: Students may earn a bachelor's degree in three academic years.

Academic remediation for entering students: Instructional courses designed for students deficient in the general competencies necessary for a regular postsecondary curriculum and educational setting.

Adult/continuing education programs: Courses offered for nontraditional students who are currently working or are returning to formal education.

Advanced placement: Credit toward a degree awarded for acceptable scores on College Board Advanced Placement (AP) tests.

Cooperative (co-op) education programs: Formal arrangements with off-campus employers allowing students to combine work and study in order to gain degree-related experience, usually extending the time required to complete a degree.

Distance learning: For-credit courses that can be accessed off-campus via cable television, the Internet, satellite, DVD, correspondence course, or other media.

Double major: A program of study in which a student concurrently completes the requirements of two majors.

English as a second language (ESL): A course of study designed specifically for students whose native language is not English.

External degree programs: A program of study in which students earn credits toward a degree through a combination of independent study, college courses, proficiency examinations, and personal experience. External degree programs require minimal or no classroom attendance.

Freshmen honors college: A separate academic program for talented freshmen.

Honors programs: Any special program for very able students offering the opportunity for educational enrichment, independent study, acceleration, or some combination of these.

Independent study: Academic work, usually undertaken outside the regular classroom structure, chosen or designed by the student with departmental approval and instructor supervision.

Internships: Any short-term, supervised work experience usually related to a student's major field, for which the student earns academic credit. The work can be full- or part-time, on or off-campus, paid or unpaid.

Off-campus study: A formal arrangement with one or more domestic institutions under which students may take courses at the other institution(s) for credit.

Part-time degree program: Students may earn a degree through part-time enrollment in regular session (daytime) classes or evening, weekend, or summer classes.

Self-designed major: Program of study based on individual interests, designed by the student with the assistance of an adviser.

Services for LD students: Special help for learning-disabled students with resolvable difficulties, such as dyslexia.

Study abroad: An arrangement by which a student completes part of the academic program studying in another country. A college may operate a campus abroad or it may have a cooperative agreement with other U.S. institutions or institutions in other countries.

Summer session for credit: Summer courses through which students may make up degree work or accelerate their program.

Tutorials: Undergraduates can arrange for special in-depth academic assignments (not for remediation)

working with faculty members one-on-one or in small groups.

ROTC: Army, Naval, or Air Force Reserve Officers' Training Corps programs offered either on campus, at a branch campus [designated by a (b)], or at a cooperating host institution [designated by (c)].

Unusual degree programs: Nontraditional programs such as a 3-2 degree program, in which three years of liberal arts study is followed by two years of study in a professional field at another institution (or in a professional division of the same institution), resulting in two bachelor's degrees or a bachelor's and a master's degree.

Student Life

Housing options: The institution's policy about whether students are permitted to live off-campus or are required to live on campus for a specified period; whether freshmen-only, coed, single-sex, cooperative, and disabled student housing options are available; whether campus housing is leased by the school and/or provided by a third party; whether freshman applicants are given priority for college housing. The phrase *college housing not available* indicates that no college-owned or -operated housing facilities are provided for undergraduates and that noncommuting students must arrange for their own accommodations.

Activities and organizations: Lists information on drama-theater groups, choral groups, marching bands, student-run campus newspapers, student-run radio stations, and social organizations (sororities, fraternities, eating clubs, etc.) and how many are represented on campus.

Campus security: Campus safety measures including 24-hour emergency response devices (telephones and alarms) and patrols by trained security personnel, student patrols, late-night transport-escort service, and controlled dormitory access (key, security card, etc.).

Student services: Information provided indicates services offered to students by the college, such as legal services, health clinics, personal-psychological counseling, and women's centers.

Athletics

Membership in one or more of the following athletic associations is indicated by initials.

NCAA: National Collegiate Athletic Association

NAIA: National Association of Intercollegiate Athletics

NCCAA: National Christian College Athletic Association

NJCAA: National Junior College Athletic Association

USCAA: United States Collegiate Athletic Association

CIS: Canadian Interuniversity Sports

The overall NCAA division in which all or most intercollegiate teams compete is designated by a roman numeral I, II, or

III. All teams that do not compete in this division are listed as exceptions.

Sports offered by the college are divided into two groups: intercollegiate (**M** or **W** following the name of each sport indicates that it is offered for men or women) and intramural. An **s** in parentheses following an **M** or **W** for an intercollegiate sport indicates that athletic scholarships (or grants-in-aid) are offered for men or women in that sport, and a c indicates a club team as opposed to a varsity team.

Standardized Tests

The most commonly required standardized tests are the ACT, SAT, and SAT Subject Tests. These and other standardized tests may be used for selective admission, as a basis for counseling or course placement, or for both purposes. This section notes if a test is used for admission or placement and whether it is required, required for some, or recommended.

In addition to the ACT and SAT, the following standardized entrance and placement examinations are referred to by their initials:

ABLE: Adult Basic Learning Examination

ACT ASSET: ACT Assessment of Skills for Successful Entry and Transfer

ACT PEP: ACT Proficiency Examination Program

CAT: California Achievement Tests

CELT: Comprehensive English Language Test

CPAt: Career Programs Assessment

CPT: Computerized Placement Test

DAT: Differential Aptitude Test

LSAT: Law School Admission Test

MAPS: Multiple Assessment Program Service

MCAT: Medical College Admission Test

MMPI: Minnesota Multiphasic Personality Inventory

OAT: Optometry Admission Test

PAA: Prueba de Aptitude Académica (Spanish-language version of the SAT)

PCAT: Pharmacy College Admission Test

PSAT/NMSQT: Preliminary SAT National Merit Scholarship Qualifying Test

SCAT: Scholastic College Aptitude Test

SRA: Scientific Research Association (administers verbal, arithmetical, and achievement tests)

TABE: Test of Adult Basic Education

TASP: Texas Academic Skills Program

TOEFL: Test of English as a Foreign Language (for international students whose native language is not English)

WPCT: Washington Pre-College Test

Costs

Costs are given for the 2012–13 academic year or for the 2011–12 academic year if 2012–13 figures were not yet available. Annual expenses may be expressed as a comprehensive fee (including full-time tuition, mandatory fees, and college room and board) or as separate figures for full-time tuition, fees, room and board, or room only. For public institutions where tuition differs according to residence, separate figures are given for area or state residents and for nonresidents. Part-time tuition is expressed in terms of a per-unit rate (per credit, per semester hour, etc.) as specified by the institution.

The tuition structure at some institutions is complex in that freshmen and sophomores may be charged a different rate from that for juniors and seniors, a professional or vocational division may have a different fee structure from the liberal arts division of the same institution, or part-time tuition may be prorated on a sliding scale according to the number of credit hours taken. Tuition and fees may vary according to academic program, campus/location, class time (day, evening, weekend), course/credit load, course level, degree level, reciprocity agreements, and student level. Room and board charges are reported as an average for one academic year and may vary according to the board plan selected, campus/location, type of housing facility, or student level. If no college-owned or -operated housing facilities are offered, the phrase *college housing not available* will appear in the Housing section of the Student Life paragraph.

Tuition payment plans that may be offered to undergraduates include tuition prepayment, installment payments, and deferred payment. A tuition prepayment plan gives a student the option of locking in the current tuition rate for the entire term of enrollment by paying the full amount in advance rather than year by year. Colleges that offer such a prepayment plan may also help the student to arrange financing.

The availability of full or partial undergraduate tuition waivers to minority students, children of alumni, employees or their children, adult students, and senior citizens may be listed.

Financial Aid

The number of Federal Work Study and/or part-time jobs and average earnings are listed. Financial aid deadlines are given as well.

Applying

Application and admission options include the following:

Early admission: Highly qualified students may matriculate before graduating from high school.

Early action plan: An admission plan that allows students to apply and be notified of an admission decision well in advance of the regular notification dates. If accepted, the candidate is not committed to enroll; students may reply to the offer under the college's regular reply policy.

Early decision plan: A plan that permits students to apply and be notified of an admission decision (and financial aid offer, if applicable) well in advance of the regular notification date. Applicants agree to accept an offer of admission and to withdraw their applications from other colleges. Candidates who are not accepted under early decision are automatically considered with the regular applicant pool, without prejudice.

Deferred entrance: The practice of permitting accepted students to postpone enrollment, usually for a period of one academic term or year.

Application fee: The fee required with an application is noted. This is typically nonrefundable, although under certain specified conditions it may be waived or returned.

Requirements: Other application requirements are grouped into three categories: required for all, required for some, and recommended. They may include an essay, standardized test scores, a high school transcript, a minimum high school grade point average (expressed as a number on a scale of 0 to 4.0, where 4.0 equals A, 3.0 equals B, etc.), letters of recommendation, an interview on campus or with local alumni, and, for certain types of schools or programs, special requirements such as a musical audition or an art portfolio.

Application deadlines and notification dates: Admission application deadlines and dates for notification of acceptance or rejection are given either as specific dates or as **rolling** and **continuous.** Rolling means that applications are processed as they are received, and qualified students are accepted as long as there are openings. Continuous means that applicants are notified of acceptance or rejection as applications are processed up until the date indicated or the actual beginning of classes. The application deadline and the notification date for transfers are given if they differ from the dates for freshmen. Early decision and early action application deadlines and notification dates are also indicated when relevant.

Admissions Contact

The name, title, and phone number of the person to contact for application information are given at the end of the Profile. The admission office address is listed in most cases. Toll-free phone numbers may also be included. The admission office fax number and *E-mail* address, if available, are listed, provided the school wanted them printed for use by prospective students. Finally, the URL of the institution's Web site is provided.

Additional Information

Each college that has a **College Close-Up** in the guide will have a cross-reference appended to the Profile, referring you directly to that **College Close-Up.**

COLLEGE CLOSE-UPS

These narrative descriptions provide an inside look at certain colleges, shifting the focus to a variety of other factors that should also be considered. The descriptions provide a wealth of statistics that are crucial components in the college decision-making equation—components such as tuition, financial aid, and major fields of study. Prepared exclusively by college officials, the descriptions are designed to help give students a better sense of the individuality of each institution, in terms that include campus environment, student activities, and lifestyle. Such quality-of-life intangibles can be the deciding factors in the college selection process. The absence of any college or university does not constitute an editorial decision on the part of Peterson's. In essence, these descriptions are an open forum for colleges, on a voluntary basis, to communicate their particular message to prospective college students. The colleges included have paid a fee to Peterson's to provide this information. The **College Close-Ups** are edited to provide a consistent format across entries for your ease of comparison.

INDEXES

2011–12 Changes in Institutions

Here you will find an alphabetical listing of institutions that have recently closed, merged with other institutions, or changed their name or status.

Associate Degree Programs at Two-and Four-Year Colleges

These indexes present hundreds of undergraduate fields of study that are currently offered most widely according to the colleges' responses on *Peterson's Annual Survey of Undergraduate Institutions*. The majors appear in alphabetical order, each followed by an alphabetical list of the schools that offer an associate-level program in that field. Liberal Arts and Studies indicates a general program with no specified major. The terms used for the majors are those of the U.S. Department of Education Classification of Instructional Programs (CIPs). Many institutions, however, use different terms. Readers should refer to the **College Close-Up** in this book for the school's exact terminology. In addition, although the term "major" is used in this guide, some colleges may use other terms, such as "concentration," "program of study," or "field."

DATA COLLECTION PROCEDURES

The data contained in the **Profiles** of Two-Year Colleges and **Indexes** were researched in winter and spring 2011 through *Peterson's Annual Survey of Undergraduate Institutions.* Questionnaires were sent to the more than 1,800 colleges that meet the outlined inclusion criteria. All data included in this edition have been submitted by officials (usually admission and financial aid officers, registrars, or institutional research personnel) at the colleges themselves. All usable information received in time for publication has been included. The omission of any particular item from the **Profiles** of Two-Year Colleges and **Indexes** listing signifies either that the item is not applicable to that institution or that data were not available. Because of the comprehensive editorial review that takes place in our offices and because all material comes directly from college officials, Peterson's has every reason to believe that the information presented in this guide is accurate at the time of printing. However, students should check with a specific college or university at the time of application to verify such figures as tuition and fees, which may have changed since the publication of this volume.

CRITERIA FOR INCLUSION IN THIS BOOK

Peterson's Two-Year Colleges 2013 covers accredited institutions in the United States, U.S. territories, and other countries that award the associate degree as their most popular undergraduate offering (a few also offer bachelor's, master's, or doctoral degrees). The term two-year college is the commonly used designation for institutions that grant the associate degree, since two years is the normal duration of the traditional associate degree program. However, some programs may be completed in one year, others require three years, and, of course, part-time programs may take a considerably longer period. Therefore, "two-year college" should be understood as a conventional term that accurately describes most of the institutions included in this guide but which should not be taken literally in all cases. Also included are some non-degree-granting institutions, usually branch campuses of a multicampus system, which offer the equivalent of the first two years of a bachelor's degree, transferable to a bachelor's degree–granting institution.

To be included in this guide, an institution must have full accreditation or be a candidate for accreditation (preaccreditation) status by an institutional or specialized accrediting body recognized by the U.S. Department of Education or the Council for Higher Education Accreditation (CHEA). Institutional accrediting bodies, which review each institution as a whole, include the six regional associations of schools and colleges (Middle States, New England, North Central, Northwest, Southern, and Western), each of which is responsible for a specified portion of the United States and its territories. Other institutional accrediting bodies are national in scope and accredit specific kinds of institutions (e.g., Bible colleges, independent colleges, and rabbinical and Talmudic schools). Program registration by the New York State Board of Regents is considered to be the equivalent of institutional accreditation, since the board requires that all programs offered by an institution meet its standards before recognition is granted. This guide also includes institutions outside the United States that are accredited by these U.S. accrediting bodies. There are recognized specialized or professional accrediting bodies in more than forty different fields, each of which is authorized to accredit institutions or specific programs in its particular field. For specialized institutions that offer programs in one field only, we designate this to be the equivalent of institutional accreditation. A full explanation of the accrediting process and complete information on recognized, institutional (regional and national), and specialized accrediting bodies can be found online at www.chea.org or at www.ed.gov//admins/finaid/accred/ index.html.

Quick-Reference Chart

Two-Year Colleges At-a-Glance

This chart includes the names and locations of accredited two-year colleges in the United States, Canada, and other countries and shows institutions' responses to the *Peterson's Annual Survey of Undergraduate Institutions*. If an institution submitted incomplete data, one or more columns opposite the institution's name is blank. A dagger after the school name indicates that the institution has one or more entries in the *College Close-Ups* section. If a school does not appear, it did not report any of the information.

Key: Y—Yes; N—No; R—Recommended; S—For Some

Column legend:
- Degrees Awarded: College Transfer Associate (C); Terminal Associate (T); Bachelor's (B); Master's (M); Doctoral (D)
- Institutional Control: County, District, City, Federal, State, Commonwealth, State and Local, State-Related (St, St-L, Cou); Independent, Independent-Religious, Proprietary (Ind, Prop)
- Student Body: Men, Primarily Men (M); Women, Primarily Women (PW); Coed (M/W)

Institution	Location	Degrees	Control	Body	Enroll.	% Part-Time	% 25 or Older	% Grads to 4-Yr	HS Equiv. Accepted	Open Adm.	HS Transcript Req.	Need-Based Aid	Part-Time Jobs	Career Counseling	Job Placement	College Housing	Sports	Majors
UNITED STATES																		
Alabama																		
Bevill State Community College	Sumiton	C,T	St	M/W	4,704	43	37		Y	Y	Y	Y	Y	Y	Y			13
Brown Mackie College–Birmingham†	Birmingham	C,T,B	Prop	M/W														
Chattahoochee Valley Community College	Phenix City	C,T	St	M/W	1,697	44	38		Y	Y	Y	Y	Y			N	3	13
Gadsden State Community College	Gadsden	C,T	St	M/W	6,733	42	36	18	Y	Y	Y	Y	Y	Y	Y	N	5	23
H. Councill Trenholm State Technical College	Montgomery	T	St	M/W	1,721		48		Y	Y	Y	Y	Y	Y	Y	N		20
ITT Technical Institute	Bessemer	T,B	Prop	M/W							Y	Y	Y	Y		N		17
ITT Technical Institute	Madison	T,B	Prop	M/W												N		13
ITT Technical Institute	Mobile	T,B	Prop	M/W												N		13
Jefferson State Community College	Birmingham	C,T	St	M/W	9,460	63	41		Y	Y	S	Y	Y	Y	Y	N		19
Lawson State Community College	Birmingham	C,T	St	M/W	4,205	39	33		Y	Y	Y	Y	Y	Y	Y	Y	4	14
Lurleen B. Wallace Community College	Andalusia	C	St	M/W	1,779	41	37		Y	Y	Y	Y	Y	Y	Y	N	3	12
Northeast Alabama Community College	Rainsville	C,T	St	M/W	3,294	45			Y	Y		Y	Y	Y	Y	N		11
Northwest-Shoals Community College	Muscle Shoals	C	St	M/W	3,939	47	30	12	Y	Y	Y	Y	Y	Y	Y	N	4	14
Prince Institute of Professional Studies	Montgomery	T	Prop	PW	63													
Reid State Technical College	Evergreen	T	St	M/W	699	30	13		Y		Y	Y	Y	Y	Y	N		3
Alaska																		
Ilisagvik College	Barrow	C	St		288	86												
University of Alaska Anchorage, Kenai Peninsula College	Soldotna	C,T,B	St	M/W	1,934													
University of Alaska Anchorage, Kodiak College	Kodiak	C,T	St	M/W	479				Y	Y	S	Y		Y		N		8
Arizona																		
Arizona Western College	Yuma	C,T	St-L	M/W	8,545	67												
Brown Mackie College–Phoenix†	Phoenix	T,B	Prop	M/W														
Brown Mackie College–Tucson†	Tucson	C,T,B	Prop	M/W														
Chandler-Gilbert Community College	Chandler	C,T	St-L	M/W	14,030	68	25		Y			Y	Y	Y	N	6		37
Cochise College	Sierra Vista	C,T	St-L	M/W	4,288	76	48	43	Y	R		Y	Y	Y	Y	Y	3	54
CollegeAmerica–Flagstaff	Flagstaff	T,B	Prop	M/W	300													
Eastern Arizona College	Thatcher	C,T	St-L	M/W	6,997	69	55		Y		R	Y	Y	Y	Y	Y	10	49
GateWay Community College	Phoenix	C,T	St-L	M/W	716	73			Y		S	Y	Y	Y		N	5	54
Glendale Community College	Glendale	C,T	St-L	M/W	20,154	65												
ITT Technical Institute	Phoenix	T,B	Prop	M/W								Y		Y	Y	N		12
ITT Technical Institute	Phoenix	T,B	Prop	M/W												N		10
ITT Technical Institute	Tucson	T,B	Prop	M/W							Y		Y	Y	Y	N		13
Kaplan College, Phoenix Campus	Phoenix	T	Prop	M/W								Y				N		3
Mesa Community College	Mesa	C,T	St-L	M/W	28,000													
Mohave Community College	Kingman	C,T	St	M/W	6,107	72	54		Y					Y				34
Phoenix College	Phoenix	C,T	Cou	M/W	13,000													
Pima Community College	Tucson	C,T	St-L	M/W	36,823	63												
Pima Medical Institute	Mesa		Prop	M/W														
Pima Medical Institute	Mesa	T,B	Prop	M/W	958													
Pima Medical Institute	Tucson	T,B	Prop	M/W	900													
Scottsdale Community College	Scottsdale	C,T	St-L	M/W	11,345	68	37		Y			Y	Y	Y		N	13	25
Yavapai College	Prescott	C,T	St-L	M/W	8,276	77												
Arkansas																		
Arkansas State University–Mountain Home	Mountain Home	T	St	M/W	1,472	38	41		Y	Y	Y	Y	Y	Y	Y	N		14
College of the Ouachitas	Malvern	C,T	St	M/W	1,407	58			Y	Y	Y	Y	Y	Y	Y	N		15
ITT Technical Institute	Little Rock	T,B	Prop	M/W							Y	Y	Y	Y		N		13
Ozarka College	Melbourne	C,T	St	M/W	1,600		43		Y	Y		Y	Y			N		8
University of Arkansas Community College at Morrilton	Morrilton	C,T	St	M/W	2,299	35	37		Y	Y	Y	Y	Y	Y	Y	N	5	16
California																		
American Academy of Dramatic Arts	Hollywood	C	Ind	M/W	188													
Antelope Valley College	Lancaster	C,T	St-L	M/W	15,108	68												
Berkeley City College	Berkeley	C,T	St-L	M/W	7,645		65	0	Y		R	Y	Y	Y		N		32
College of the Canyons	Santa Clarita	C,T	St-L	M/W	22,968		29		Y		R	Y	Y	Y	Y	N	11	51
De Anza College	Cupertino	C,T	St-L	M/W	25,191	56												
Deep Springs College	Deep Springs	C	Ind	M	26		0	75	N	Y	Y					Y	13	1
East Los Angeles College	Monterey Park	C,T	St-L	M/W	31,749	75												
Fashion Careers College	San Diego	C,T	Prop	PW	91													
FIDM/The Fashion Institute of Design & Merchandising, Los Angeles Campus†	Los Angeles	C,T,B	Prop	M/W	4,424	13												
FIDM/The Fashion Institute of Design & Merchandising, Orange County Campus	Irvine	C,T	Prop	PW	372	6												
FIDM/The Fashion Institute of Design & Merchandising, San Diego Campus	San Diego	C,T	Prop	PW	292	10												
FIDM/The Fashion Institute of Design & Merchandising, San Francisco Campus	San Francisco	C,T	Prop	M/W	960	15												

This chart includes the names and locations of accredited two-year colleges in the United States, Canada, and other countries and shows institutions' responses to the *Peterson's Annual Survey of Undergraduate Institutions.* If an institution submitted incomplete data, one or more columns opposite the institution's name is blank. A dagger after the school name indicates that the institution has one or more entries in the *College Close-Ups* section. If a school does not appear, it did not report any of the information.

Y—Yes; N—No; R—Recommended; S—For Some

Column legend: Degrees Awarded — College Transfer Associate (C), Terminal Associate (T), Bachelor's (B), Master's (M), Doctoral (D). Then Institutional Control, Student Body, Undergraduate Enrollment, Percent Attending Part-Time, Percent of Grads Going on to Four-Year Colleges, Percent 25 Years of Age or Older, Open Admissions, High School Equivalency Certificate Accepted, High School Transcript Required, Need-Based Aid Required, Part-Time Jobs Available, Career Counseling Available, Job Placement Services Available, College Housing Available, Number of Sports Offered, Number of Majors Offered.

College	Location	Degrees	Control	Student Body	Undergrad Enroll	% Part-Time	% Grads→4yr	% 25+	Open Adm	HS Equiv	HS Transcript	Need-Based Aid	Part-Time Jobs	Career Counseling	Job Placement	College Housing	Sports	Majors
Foothill College	Los Altos Hills	C,T	St-L	M/W	18,342	80	50		Y			R	Y	Y	Y	N	8	55
Gavilan College	Gilroy	C,T	St-L	M/W	8,382		56	12	Y	Y			Y	Y	Y	N	6	42
Golden West College	Huntington Beach	C,T	St-L	M/W	13,226													
ITT Technical Institute	Culver City	T,B	Prop	M/W														11
ITT Technical Institute	Lathrop	T,B	Prop	M/W						Y		Y	Y			N		14
ITT Technical Institute	Oakland	T,B	Prop	M/W														10
ITT Technical Institute	Orange	T,B	Prop	M/W						Y		Y	Y			N		16
ITT Technical Institute	Oxnard	C,T,B	Prop	M/W						Y		Y	Y	Y		N		13
ITT Technical Institute	Rancho Cordova	T,B	Prop	M/W						Y		Y				N		15
ITT Technical Institute	San Bernardino	T,B	Prop	M/W						Y		Y	Y			N		14
ITT Technical Institute	San Diego	T,B	Prop	M/W						Y		Y	Y			N		11
ITT Technical Institute	San Dimas	T,B	Prop	M/W						Y		Y	Y			N		13
ITT Technical Institute	Sylmar	T,B	Prop	M/W						Y		Y	Y			N		16
ITT Technical Institute	Torrance	T,B	Prop	M/W								Y	Y			N		12
ITT Technical Institute	West Covina	T,B	Prop	M/W														11
Kaplan College, Bakersfield Campus	Bakersfield	T	Prop	M/W							Y							1
Kaplan College, Chula Vista Campus	Chula Vista	T	Prop	M/W							Y							1
Kaplan College, Fresno Campus	Clovis	T	Prop	M/W							Y							1
Kaplan College, Modesto Campus	Salida	T	Prop	PW							Y							2
Kaplan College, Palm Springs Campus	Palm Springs	T	Prop	M/W							Y							1
Kaplan College, Riverside Campus	Riverside	T	Prop	M/W							Y							2
Kaplan College, Sacramento Campus	Sacramento	T	Prop	M/W							Y							1
Kaplan College, San Diego Campus	San Diego	T	Prop	M/W							Y				Y			2
Kaplan College, Stockton Campus	Stockton	T	Prop	M/W							Y							1
Kaplan College, Vista Campus	Vista	T	Prop	M/W							Y							1
Los Angeles Harbor College	Wilmington	C,T	St-L	M/W	10,181	72	35		Y				Y	Y	Y	Y	N	6	23
Mendocino College	Ukiah	C,T	St-L	M/W	3,753	68	40	25	Y		Y	Y	Y	Y	Y	N	7	34
Moreno Valley College	Moreno Valley	C,T	St-L	M/W	10,413				Y								N	8
MTI College	Sacramento	C,T	Prop	M/W	900		62			Y	Y	Y	Y	Y	Y		3	7
Norco College	Norco	C,T	St-L	M/W	9,674				Y								N	7
Orange Coast College	Costa Mesa	C,T	St-L	M/W	24,239	58	70		Y				Y	Y	Y	N	14	99
Pima Medical Institute	Chula Vista	T,B	Prop	M/W	813													
Reedley College	Reedley	C,T	St-L	M/W	14,573				Y		Y	Y	Y	Y	Y	Y	9	39
Riverside City College	Riverside	T	St-L	M/W	18,586		33		Y				Y	Y			N	18
San Diego City College	San Diego	C	St-L	M/W	18,626			61	Y		S	Y	Y	Y		N	16	66
San Joaquin Valley College	Bakersfield	T	Prop	M/W	541		41		N	Y							N	10
San Joaquin Valley College	Fresno	T	Prop	M/W	675		46			Y							N	11
San Joaquin Valley College	Hanford		Prop	M/W														
San Joaquin Valley College	Hesperia		Prop	M/W														
San Joaquin Valley College	Rancho Cordova	T	Prop	M/W	619		66		N	Y							N	8
San Joaquin Valley College	Salida	T	Prop	M/W	254		46		N	Y								6
San Joaquin Valley College	Temecula		Prop	M/W														
San Joaquin Valley College	Visalia	T	Ind	M/W	895		48		N	Y	S	Y		Y	Y	N		16
San Joaquin Valley College–Fresno Aviation Campus	Fresno	T	Prop	M/W	59		54		N	Y							N	1
San Joaquin Valley College–Online	Visalia	T	Prop	M/W	887		55		N	Y								6
Santa Barbara City College	Santa Barbara	T	St-L	M/W	18,092	56												
Santa Monica College	Santa Monica	C,T	St-L	M/W	31,138	64	23		Y	Y	Y	Y	Y	Y	Y	N	10	36
Santa Rosa Junior College	Santa Rosa	C,T	St-L	M/W	23,224		54		Y			Y	Y	Y			15	70
Solano Community College	Fairfield	C,T	St-L	M/W	10,927													
WyoTech Fremont	Fremont	T	Prop	M/W	1,596													

Colorado

College	Location	Degrees	Control	Student Body	Undergrad Enroll	% Part-Time	% Grads→4yr	% 25+	Open Adm	HS Equiv	HS Transcript	Need-Based Aid	Part-Time Jobs	Career Counseling	Job Placement	College Housing	Sports	Majors
Colorado Mountain College	Glenwood Springs	C,T,B	Dist	M/W	2,465		70		Y		Y	Y	Y	Y	Y	Y	6	24
Colorado Mountain College, Alpine Campus	Steamboat Springs	C,T,B	Dist	M/W	1,550		30		Y		Y	Y	Y	Y	Y	Y	6	21
Colorado Mountain College, Timberline Campus	Leadville	C,T,B	Dist	M/W	1,209		55		Y		Y	Y	Y	Y	Y	Y	6	12
Colorado School of Trades	Lakewood	T	Prop	M/W	134			4		Y	Y							1
Front Range Community College	Westminster	C,T	St	M/W	20,092	63	43		Y		Y	Y	Y	Y	N			27
Institute of Business & Medical Careers	Fort Collins	T	Priv	M/W	302		20		Y	Y	Y	Y	Y	Y	Y			9
ITT Technical Institute	Aurora	T,B	Prop	M/W														10
ITT Technical Institute	Thornton	T,B	Prop	M/W						Y		Y	Y			N		12
Lamar Community College	Lamar	C,T	St	M/W	1,084	55												
Northeastern Junior College	Sterling	C,T	St	M/W	2,113	48	34		Y			Y	Y	Y	Y		15	59
Otero Junior College	La Junta	C,T	St	M/W	1,660	48	25		Y	Y	R	Y	Y	Y	Y		6	24
Pima Medical Institute	Colorado Springs		Prop	M/W														
Pima Medical Institute	Denver	T,B	Prop	M/W	922													
Pueblo Community College	Pueblo	C,T	St	M/W	7,736													
Red Rocks Community College	Lakewood	C,T	St	M/W	9,541	66	53		Y			Y	Y	Y	N			52

Connecticut

College	Location	Degrees	Control	Student Body	Undergrad Enroll	% Part-Time	% Grads→4yr	% 25+	Open Adm	HS Equiv	HS Transcript	Need-Based Aid	Part-Time Jobs	Career Counseling	Job Placement	College Housing	Sports	Majors
Gateway Community College	New Haven	C,T	St	M/W	7,261	66	42		Y	Y	Y	Y	Y	Y		N	4	35
Goodwin College	East Hartford	C,T,B	Prop	M/W	3,116	84	65		Y	Y	Y	Y	Y	Y	Y	N	4	24
Housatonic Community College	Bridgeport	C,T	St	M/W	5,975				Y	Y	Y	Y	Y	Y		N		24
Manchester Community College	Manchester	C,T	St	M/W	7,499	62			Y	Y	Y	Y	Y	Y		N	4	31
Middlesex Community College	Middletown	C,T	St	M/W	2,952	60												
Northwestern Connecticut Community College	Winsted	C,T	St	M/W	1,701	70	40		Y	Y	Y	Y	Y	Y		N		35
Norwalk Community College	Norwalk	C,T	St	M/W	6,740	62												
Three Rivers Community College	Norwich	C,T	St	M/W	5,154	68			Y	Y	R	Y	Y	Y		N	2	39
Tunxis Community College	Farmington	C,T	St	M/W	4,740	61	38		Y	Y	Y	Y	Y	Y				23

This chart includes the names and locations of accredited two-year colleges in the United States, Canada, and other countries and shows institutions' responses to the *Peterson's Annual Survey of Undergraduate Institutions*. If an institution submitted incomplete data, one or more columns opposite the institution's name is blank. A dagger after the school name indicates that the institution has one or more entries in the *College Close-Ups* section. If a school does not appear, it did not report any of the information.

Y—Yes; N—No; R—Recommended; S—For Some

Column headers (diagonal labels):
- **Degrees Awarded:** College Transfer Associate (C), Terminal Associate (T), Bachelor's (B), Master's (M), Doctoral (D)
- **Institutional Control:** County, District, City, State and Local, State-Related, Federal, State, Commonwealth, Territory, Independent, Independent-Religious, Proprietary
- **Student Body:** Men, Primarily Men, Women, Primarily Women, Coed

Institution	Location	Degrees Awarded	Institutional Control	Student Body	Undergraduate Enrollment	Percent Attending Part-Time	Percent 25 Years of Age or Older	Percent of Grads Going on to Four-Year Colleges	High School Equivalency Certificate Accepted	Open Admissions	High School Transcript Required	Need-Based Aid Available	Part-Time Jobs Available	Career Counseling Available	Job Placement Services Available	College Housing Available	Number of Sports Offered	Number of Majors Offered
Delaware																		
Delaware Technical & Community College, Jack F. Owens Campus	Georgetown	C,T	St	M/W	4,741	56	40		Y	Y	S	Y	Y			N	4	52
Delaware Technical & Community College, Stanton/Wilmington Campus	Newark	C,T	St	M/W	6,978	61	37			Y	S	Y	Y			N	5	64
Delaware Technical & Community College, Terry Campus	Dover	C,T	St	M/W	3,323	57	45		Y	Y	S	Y	Y			N	3	44
Florida																		
Brown Mackie College–Miami†	Miami	T,B	Prop	M/W														
Chipola College	Marianna	C,T,B	St	M/W	2,341	57	37		Y	Y	Y	Y	Y	Y	Y	N	4	19
College of Business and Technology	Miami	C,B	Prop	M/W	1,098		70		Y	Y	Y			Y	Y			7
College of Central Florida	Ocala	C,T,B	St-L	M/W	8,766	58	32		Y	Y	Y	Y	Y	Y	Y	N	5	19
Daytona State College	Daytona Beach	C,T,B	St	M/W	18,838	54												
Florida State College at Jacksonville	Jacksonville	C,T,B	St	M/W	30,863	65	46		Y	Y	Y		Y	Y	Y		11	93
Gulf Coast State College	Panama City	C,T,B	St	M/W	6,436	62	44		Y	Y	Y	Y	Y	Y	Y	N	4	30
Hillsborough Community College	Tampa	C,T	St	M/W	28,329	58	38		Y	Y	Y	Y	Y	Y	Y	Y	5	40
Indian River State College	Fort Pierce	C,T,B	St	M/W	17,528	65	39	77	Y	Y	Y	Y	Y	Y	Y	N	7	92
ITT Technical Institute	Bradenton	T,B	Prop	M/W														12
ITT Technical Institute	Fort Lauderdale	T,B	Prop	M/W						Y		Y				N		13
ITT Technical Institute	Fort Myers	T,B	Prop	M/W														11
ITT Technical Institute	Jacksonville	T,B	Prop	M/W						Y		Y				N		12
ITT Technical Institute	Lake Mary	T,B	Prop	M/W						Y		Y	Y					15
ITT Technical Institute	Miami	T,B	Prop	M/W						Y		Y	Y			N		14
ITT Technical Institute	Orlando	T,B	Prop	M/W														12
ITT Technical Institute	Pinellas Park	T,B	Prop	M/W												N		11
ITT Technical Institute	Tallahassee	T,B	Prop	M/W														11
ITT Technical Institute	Tampa	T,B	Prop	M/W						Y		Y	Y			N		14
Kaplan College, Jacksonville Campus	Jacksonville	T	Prop	M/W													2	3
Kaplan College, Pembroke Pines Campus	Pembroke Pines	T	Prop	M/W							Y							3
Lake-Sumter Community College	Leesburg	C	St-L	M/W	4,929	67												
Miami Dade College	Miami	C,T,B	St-L	M/W	63,766	58	36		Y	Y	Y	Y	Y	Y	Y	N	4	142
Northwest Florida State College	Niceville	C,T,B	St-L	M/W	10,317		44		Y	Y	Y	Y	Y	Y	Y	N	3	57
Palm Beach State College	Lake Worth	C,T,B	St	M/W	29,534	63	33		Y	Y	Y	Y	Y	Y	Y	N	4	67
Pasco-Hernando Community College	New Port Richey	C,T	St	M/W	12,167		35		Y	Y	Y	Y	Y	Y	Y	N	6	19
Pensacola State College	Pensacola	C,T,B	St	M/W	11,531	58	41		Y	Y	Y	Y	Y	Y	Y	N	16	101
Polk State College	Winter Haven	C,T,B	St	M/W	11,529	66	37		Y	Y	Y	Y	Y	Y	Y	N	7	25
Rasmussen College Fort Myers	Fort Myers	C,T,B	Prop	M/W	723		65			Y	Y		Y	Y	Y			23
Rasmussen College New Port Richey	New Port Richey	C,T,B	Prop	M/W	896		71			Y	Y	Y	Y	Y	Y			23
Rasmussen College Ocala	Ocala	C,T,B	Prop	PW	1,256		71		Y	Y	Y	Y	Y	Y	Y			22
Seminole State College of Florida	Sanford	C,T,B	St-L	M/W	18,514	58	43		Y	Y	Y	Y	Y	Y	Y	N	3	50
State College of Florida Manatee-Sarasota	Bradenton	C,T,B	St	M/W	11,303	57	41		Y	Y	Y	Y	Y	Y	Y	N	5	96
Tallahassee Community College	Tallahassee	C,T	St-L	M/W	13,477	46			Y	Y	Y	Y	Y	Y	Y	N	6	30
Valencia College	Orlando	C,T	St	M/W	42,631	58	40		Y	Y	S	Y	Y	Y	Y	N		43
Georgia																		
Albany Technical College	Albany	T	St	M/W	4,918	42	65		Y	Y	Y					N		17
Altamaha Technical College	Jesup	T	St	M/W	1,499	73	51		Y	Y	Y					N		9
Athens Technical College	Athens	T	St	M/W	5,323	71	67		Y	Y	Y	Y				N		27
Atlanta Technical College	Atlanta	T	St	M/W	4,779	69	66		Y	Y	Y					N		11
Augusta Technical College	Augusta	T	St	M/W	4,631	66	57		Y	Y	Y	Y				N		24
Bainbridge College	Bainbridge	C,T	St	M/W	3,712		55			Y	S	Y	Y	Y	Y	N	2	33
Brown Mackie College–Atlanta†	Atlanta	T	Prop	M/W														
Central Georgia Technical College	Macon	T	St	M/W	6,187	57	61		Y	Y	Y	Y				N		27
Chattahoochee Technical College	Marietta	T	St	M/W	12,158	69	61		Y	Y	Y	Y				N		22
Columbus Technical College	Columbus	T	St	M/W	4,164	71	53		Y	Y	Y	Y				N		24
Darton College	Albany	C,T	St	M/W	5,854	51												
Emory University, Oxford College	Oxford	C,B	I-R	M/W	936	0		98	N	N	Y	Y	Y	Y		Y	9	1
Georgia Highlands College	Rome	C,T	St	M/W	5,522	46	27		N	Y	Y	Y	Y		Y	N	9	26
Georgia Military College	Milledgeville	C,T	St-L	M/W	6,081	31												
Georgia Northwestern Technical College	Rome	T	St	M/W	6,506	63	57		Y	Y	Y					N		13
Georgia Piedmont Technical College	Clarkston	T	St	M/W	4,544	75	54		Y	Y	Y	Y	Y			N		27
Gwinnett Technical College	Lawrenceville	T	St	M/W	6,787	63	59		Y	Y	Y	Y				N		27
ITT Technical Institute	Atlanta	T,B	Prop	M/W												N		9
ITT Technical Institute	Duluth	T,B	Prop	M/W						Y		Y				N		11
ITT Technical Institute	Kennesaw	T,B	Prop	M/W												N		12
Lanier Technical College	Oakwood	T	St	M/W	3,722	75	56		Y	Y	Y					N		21
Middle Georgia Technical College	Warner Robbins	T	St	M/W	4,045	68	56		Y	Y	Y	Y				N		11
Moultrie Technical College	Moultrie	T	St	M/W	2,308	59	51		Y	Y	Y					N		10
North Georgia Technical College	Clarkesville	T	St	M/W	2,670	57	47		Y	Y	Y							10
Oconee Fall Line Technical College–North Campus	Sandersville	T	St	M/W	1,934	68	50		Y	Y	Y					N		5
Oconee Fall Line Technical College–South Campus	Dublin	T	St	M/W	1,817	52												
Ogeechee Technical College	Statesboro	T	St	M/W	2,298	60	58		Y	Y	Y					N		24
Okefenokee Technical College	Waycross	T	St	M/W	1,432	70	50		Y	Y	Y					N		11
Savannah Technical College	Savannah	T	St	M/W	4,998	67	50		Y	Y	Y	Y				N		16
Southeastern Technical College	Vidalia	T	St	M/W	1,910	70	49		Y	Y	Y					N		13
Southern Crescent Technical College	Griffin	T	St	M/W	5,381	62	57		Y	Y	Y	Y						23
South Georgia Technical College	Americus	T	St	M/W	2,361	53	53		Y	Y	Y							15
Southwest Georgia Technical College	Thomasville	T	St	M/W	1,871	78	49		Y	Y	Y	Y	Y			N		11
Waycross College	Waycross	C,T	St	M/W	1,118													
West Georgia Technical College	Waco	T	St	M/W	7,845	73	51		Y	Y	Y	Y				N		17
Wiregrass Georgia Technical College	Valdosta	T	St	M/W	4,743	60	52		Y	Y	Y					N		15

This chart includes the names and locations of accredited two-year colleges in the United States, Canada, and other countries and shows institutions' responses to the *Peterson's Annual Survey of Undergraduate Institutions*. If an institution submitted incomplete data, one or more columns opposite the institution's name is blank. A dagger after the school name indicates that the institution has one or more entries in the *College Close-Ups* section. If a school does not appear, it did not report any of the information.

Y—Yes; N—No; R—Recommended; S—For Some

Degrees Awarded: College Transfer Associate (C); Terminal Associate (T); Bachelor's (B); Master's (M); Doctoral (D)

Institution	Location	Degrees Awarded	Institutional Control	Student Body	Undergraduate Enrollment	Percent Attending Part-Time	Percent 25 Years of Age or Older	Percent of Grads Going on to Four-Year Colleges	Open Admissions	High School Equivalency Certificate Accepted	High School Transcript Required	Need-Based Aid Required	Part-Time Jobs Available	Career Counseling Available	Job Placement Services Available	College Housing Available	Number of Sports Offered	Number of Majors Offered
Hawaii																		
Hawaii Tokai International College	Honolulu	C,T	Ind	M/W	57	2												
Honolulu Community College	Honolulu	C,T	St	M/W	4,567	64												
Leeward Community College	Pearl City	C,T	St	M/W	7,942	58												
Idaho																		
Brown Mackie College–Boise†	Boise	T,B	Prop	M/W														
Eastern Idaho Technical College	Idaho Falls	T	St	M/W	830		60	0	Y	Y	Y	Y	Y	Y	Y	N		17
ITT Technical Institute	Boise	T,B	Prop	M/W							Y			Y	Y	N		13
North Idaho College	Coeur d'Alene	C,T	St-L	M/W	5,723	40												
Illinois																		
City Colleges of Chicago, Harry S. Truman College	Chicago	C,T	St-L	M/W	13,174		65		Y	Y		Y	Y	Y	Y	N	1	12
College of DuPage	Glen Ellyn	C,T	St-L	M/W	26,209	64				Y		Y	Y	Y	Y	N	12	84
College of Lake County	Grayslake	C,T	Dist	M/W	17,388	70	39			Y		S	Y	Y	Y	N	9	40
Danville Area Community College	Danville	C,T	St-L	M/W	3,713	58												
Elgin Community College	Elgin	C,T	St-L	M/W	11,811	65	36			Y		S	Y	Y	Y	N	8	35
Fox College	Bedford Park	T	Priv	M/W	417											N		8
Harper College	Palatine	C,T	St-L	M/W	15,989	60	39		Y	Y	Y	Y	Y	Y		N	12	66
Highland Community College	Freeport	C,T	St-L	M/W	2,222	47	39		Y	Y	R,S	Y	Y	Y		N	5	17
Illinois Central College	East Peoria	C,T	St-L	M/W	12,286	62	40			Y		Y	Y	Y			6	53
Illinois Eastern Community Colleges, Frontier Community College	Fairfield	C,T	St-L	M/W	2,194	87	49		Y	Y	Y	Y	Y	Y	Y	N		14
Illinois Eastern Community Colleges, Lincoln Trail College	Robinson	C,T	St-L	M/W	1,066	56	40		Y	Y	Y	Y	Y	Y	Y		3	11
Illinois Eastern Community Colleges, Olney Central College	Olney	C,T	St-L	M/W	1,524	52	41		Y	Y	Y	Y	Y	Y	Y		3	15
Illinois Eastern Community Colleges, Wabash Valley College	Mount Carmel	C,T	St-L	M/W	5,456	88	58		Y	Y	Y	Y	Y	Y	Y	N	3	21
Illinois Valley Community College	Oglesby	C,T	Dist	M/W	4,355	57	33	64	Y		Y	Y	Y	Y	Y	N	6	42
ITT Technical Institute	Mount Prospect	T,B	Prop	M/W							Y			Y	Y	N		13
ITT Technical Institute	Oak Brook	T,B	Prop	M/W							Y			Y	Y	N		12
ITT Technical Institute	Orland Park	T,B	Prop	M/W							Y			Y	Y	N		14
John Wood Community College	Quincy	C,T	Dist	M/W	2,390	51	37	66	Y	Y	Y	Y	Y	Y	Y	N	4	28
Kankakee Community College	Kankakee	C,T	St-L	M/W	4,419	57	43	27	Y	Y	Y	Y	Y	Y	Y	N	5	40
Kaskaskia College	Centralia	C,T	St-L	M/W	5,286	60	40		Y	Y	Y	Y	Y	Y	Y	N	9	35
Lincoln Land Community College	Springfield	C,T	Dist	M/W	7,337	56	40			Y		R	Y	Y	Y		6	40
McHenry County College	Crystal Lake	C,T	St-L	M/W	6,494	64	32			Y		R	R	Y	Y		6	24
Moraine Valley Community College	Palos Hills	C,T	St-L	M/W	18,169	60	32	87	Y	Y	Y	Y	Y	Y	Y	N	12	36
Morton College	Cicero	C,T	St-L	M/W														
Rasmussen College Aurora	Aurora	C,T,B	Prop	M/W	443		61					Y	Y	Y	Y		N		14
Rasmussen College Rockford	Rockford	C,T,B	Prop	M/W	881		67					Y	Y	Y	Y		N		14
Sauk Valley Community College	Dixon	C,T	Dist	M/W	2,492	49												
Shawnee Community College	Ullin	C,T	St-L	M/W	3,190	70	54		Y	Y	Y	Y	Y	Y		N	4	23
South Suburban College	South Holland	C,T	St-L	M/W	7,579		52		Y	Y	Y	Y	Y	Y		N	5	23
Southwestern Illinois College	Belleville	C,T	Dist	M/W	12,779	59	41		Y	Y	Y	Y	Y	Y	Y	N	5	60
Vet Tech Institute at Fox College	Tinley Park	T	Priv	M/W	158						Y						N		1
Waubonsee Community College	Sugar Grove	C,T	Dist	M/W	10,428	62												
Indiana																		
Ancilla College	Donaldson	C,T	I-R	M/W	533	32	38		Y	Y	Y	Y	Y	Y		N	7	13
Brown Mackie College–Fort Wayne†	Fort Wayne	T,B	Prop	M/W														
Brown Mackie College–Indianapolis†	Indianapolis	T,B	Prop	M/W														
Brown Mackie College–Merrillville†	Merrillville	T,B	Prop	M/W														
Brown Mackie College–Michigan City†	Michigan City	C,T,B	Prop	M/W														
Brown Mackie College–South Bend†	South Bend	C,T,B	Prop	PW														
Harrison College	Anderson	T	Prop	M/W	280	78												
Harrison College	Columbus	T	Prop	M/W	254	20												
Harrison College	Indianapolis	T,B	Prop	M/W	2,668	35												
Harrison College	Indianapolis	T	Prop	M/W	321	25												
Harrison College	Lafayette	T,B	Prop	M/W	350	18												
Harrison College	Muncie	T,B	Prop	PW	229	18												
International Business College	Indianapolis	T	Priv	M/W	355						Y			Y		Y		11
ITT Technical Institute	Fort Wayne	T,B	Prop	M/W							Y			Y	Y	N		17
ITT Technical Institute	Merrillville	T,B	Prop	M/W							Y								11
ITT Technical Institute	Newburgh	T,B	Prop	M/W							Y			Y	Y	N		14
Ivy Tech Community College–Bloomington	Bloomington	C,T	St	M/W	6,218	54	45		Y		Y	Y	Y	Y	Y	N		27
Ivy Tech Community College–Central Indiana	Indianapolis	C,T	St	M/W	22,354	66	53		Y		Y	Y	Y	Y	Y	N	6	42
Ivy Tech Community College–Columbus	Columbus	C,T	St	M/W	5,553	67	53		Y		Y	Y	Y	Y	Y	N		32
Ivy Tech Community College–East Central	Muncie	C,T	St	M/W	8,902	51	52		Y		Y	Y	Y	Y	Y	N		38
Ivy Tech Community College–Kokomo	Kokomo	C,T	St	M/W	5,403	60	63		Y		Y	Y	Y	Y	Y	N		31
Ivy Tech Community College–Lafayette	Lafayette	C,T	St	M/W	7,339	51	45		Y		Y	Y	Y	Y	Y	N		42
Ivy Tech Community College–North Central	South Bend	C,T	St	M/W	8,662	68	62		Y		Y	Y	Y	Y	Y	N		42
Ivy Tech Community College–Northeast	Fort Wayne	C,T	St	M/W	11,538	60	55		Y		Y	Y	Y	Y	Y	N		39
Ivy Tech Community College–Northwest	Gary	C,T	St	M/W	11,429	54	56		Y		Y	Y	Y	Y	Y	N		42
Ivy Tech Community College–Richmond	Richmond	C,T	St	M/W	3,883	64	64		Y		Y	Y	Y	Y	Y	N	1	30
Ivy Tech Community College–Southeast	Madison	C,T	St	M/W	2,816	56	51		Y		Y	Y	Y	Y	Y	N		18
Ivy Tech Community College–Southern Indiana	Sellersburg	C,T	St	M/W	5,413	64	57		Y		Y	Y	Y	Y	Y	N		31
Ivy Tech Community College–Southwest	Evansville	C,T	St	M/W	6,287	61	56		Y		Y	Y	Y	Y	Y	N		42
Ivy Tech Community College–Wabash Valley	Terre Haute	C,T	St	M/W	6,137	56	53		Y		Y	Y	Y	Y	Y	N	2	44
Kaplan College, Hammond Campus	Hammond	T	Prop	M/W								Y					N		3
Kaplan College, Northwest Indianapolis Campus	Indianapolis	T	Prop	PW								Y							1

This chart includes the names and locations of accredited two-year colleges in the United States, Canada, and other countries and shows institutions' responses to the *Peterson's Annual Survey of Undergraduate Institutions*. If an institution submitted incomplete data, one or more columns opposite the institution's name is blank. A dagger after the school name indicates that the institution has one or more entries in the *College Close-Ups* section. If a school does not appear, it did not report any of the information.

Y—Yes; N—No; R—Recommended; S—For Some

Institution	City	Degrees Awarded	Institutional Control	Student Body	Undergrad Enrollment	% Women	% Attending Part-Time	% 25 or Older	% Grads to Four-Year Colleges	HS Equivalency Cert. Accepted	Open Admissions	HS Transcript Required	Need-Based Aid Required	Part-Time Jobs Available	Career Counseling Available	Job Placement Services Available	College Housing Available	No. of Sports Offered	No. of Majors Offered
Kaplan College, Southeast Indianapolis Campus	Indianapolis	T	Prop	M/W															1
Vet Tech Institute at International Business College	Fort Wayne	T	Priv	M/W	159												Y		1
Vet Tech Institute at International Business College	Indianapolis	T	Priv	M/W	116											Y	Y		1
Vincennes University	Vincennes	C,T,B	St	M/W	17,140	61				Y	Y	Y	Y	Y				Y	9	126
Vincennes University Jasper Campus	Jasper	C,T,B	St	M/W	915															
Iowa																			
Brown Mackie College–Quad Cities†	Bettendorf	T	Prop	M/W															
Hawkeye Community College	Waterloo	C,T	St-L	M/W	6,290	55	23		Y	Y	Y	Y	Y	Y	Y	Y	N	8	33
Iowa Lakes Community College	Estherville	C,T	St-L	M/W	3,102	46	26		Y	Y			Y	Y	Y	Y	Y	17	189
ITT Technical Institute	Cedar Rapids	T,B	Prop	M/W															10
ITT Technical Institute	Clive	T,B	Prop	M/W													N		11
Northeast Iowa Community College	Calmar	C,T	St-L	M/W	5,051	57	26	50	Y		R	Y	Y	Y	Y	N		7	29
North Iowa Area Community College	Mason City	C	St-L	M/W	3,744	47													
St. Luke's College	Sioux City	T	Ind	M/W	192	28													
Southeastern Community College	West Burlington	C	St-L	M/W	3,341	46	32		Y			Y	Y	Y		Y		6	29
Western Iowa Tech Community College	Sioux City	C,T	St	M/W	6,787	55			Y		Y	R	Y	Y	Y	Y		7	37
Kansas																			
Allen Community College	Iola	C,T	St-L	M/W	2,277														
Barton County Community College	Great Bend	C,T	St-L	M/W	4,723	78													
Brown Mackie College–Kansas City†	Lenexa	T	Prop	M/W															
Brown Mackie College–Salina†	Salina	C,T	Prop	M/W															
Colby Community College	Colby	C,T	St-L	M/W	1,462	51	12		Y	Y	Y	Y	Y	Y	Y	Y	10	24
Cowley County Community College and Area Vocational–Technical School	Arkansas City	C,T	St-L	M/W	4,328	46	13		Y	Y	Y	Y	Y	Y		Y	10	43
Dodge City Community College	Dodge City	C,T	St-L	M/W	1,807														
Hesston College	Hesston	C,T	I-R	M/W	448	12													
Hutchinson Community College and Area Vocational School	Hutchinson	C,T	St-L	M/W	5,560	53	41	72	Y	Y	R	Y	Y	Y	Y	Y	13	43
Kansas City Kansas Community College	Kansas City	C,T	St-L	M/W	7,555	62	59		Y	Y	Y	Y	Y	Y	Y	N	8	27
Pratt Community College	Pratt	C,T	St-L	M/W	1,664	55													
Kentucky																			
Bluegrass Community and Technical College	Lexington	C,T	St	M/W	11,596	52			Y	Y	R,S	Y	Y	Y	Y	N	2	31
Brown Mackie College–Hopkinsville†	Hopkinsville	C,T	Prop	M/W															
Brown Mackie College–Louisville†	Louisville	T,B	Prop	M/W															
Brown Mackie College–Northern Kentucky†	Fort Mitchell	C,T,B	Prop	M/W															
Gateway Community and Technical College	Covington	C	St	M/W	4,799														
ITT Technical Institute	Louisville	T,B	Prop	M/W					Y		Y	Y			N			15
Owensboro Community and Technical College	Owensboro	C,T	St	M/W	7,095	71	15		Y	Y	Y	Y	Y	Y	Y			20
Spencerian College	Louisville	T	Prop	PW	1,012	33			Y	Y	Y	Y		Y	Y	Y		13
Sullivan College of Technology and Design	Louisville	T,B	Prop	M/W	582	38	59	0	N	Y	Y	Y		Y	Y	Y		45
West Kentucky Community and Technical College	Paducah	C,T	St	M/W	5,709	56	55		Y	Y	S	Y	Y	Y	Y	N	4	14
Louisiana																			
Career Technical College	Monroe	T	Prop	M/W	756	27	57		N	Y	Y			Y	Y	N		12
Elaine P. Nunez Community College	Chalmette	C,T	St	M/W	2,413	64													
ITI Technical College	Baton Rouge	T	Prop	PM	393		46		Y	Y	Y			Y	Y			7
ITT Technical Institute	Baton Rouge	T,B	Prop	M/W												N		11
ITT Technical Institute	St. Rose	T,B	Prop	M/W						Y		Y	Y		N		13
Maine																			
Central Maine Community College	Auburn	C,T	St	M/W	2,905	51	41		N	Y	Y	Y	Y	Y	Y	Y	6	22
Central Maine Medical Center College of Nursing and Health Professions	Lewiston	T	Ind	M/W	200	93												
Southern Maine Community College	South Portland	C,T	St	M/W	7,482	56	37		Y	Y	Y	Y	Y	Y	Y	Y	10	33
York County Community College	Wells	C,T	St	M/W	1,631	60	51		Y	Y	Y	Y	Y	Y	Y	Y	8	13
Maryland																			
Anne Arundel Community College	Arnold	C,T	St-L	M/W	17,957	70	42		Y			Y	Y	Y	Y	N	8	49
Carroll Community College	Westminster	C,T	St-L	M/W	4,041	59	29		Y		Y	Y	Y	Y		N	2	27
Cecil College	North East	C	Cou	M/W	2,545	58	33		Y	Y	Y	Y	Y	Y		N	7	37
College of Southern Maryland	La Plata	C,T	St-L	M/W	9,153	62	35		Y		R	Y	Y	Y		N	7	33
The Community College of Baltimore County	Baltimore	C,T	Cou	M/W	26,271	66				Y	Y		Y			N	6	49
Frederick Community College	Frederick	C,T	St-L	M/W	6,233	62												
Garrett College	McHenry	C,T	St-L	M/W	902	22	20		Y		Y	Y	Y	Y	Y	Y	9	13
Hagerstown Community College	Hagerstown	C,T	St-L	M/W	4,714	69	42	77	Y		S	Y	Y	Y		N	12	26
Harford Community College	Bel Air	C,T	St-L	M/W	7,132	59	32	84	Y			Y	Y	Y			12	38
Howard Community College	Columbia	C,T	St-L	M/W	10,081				Y		S	Y	Y	Y		N	7	54
ITT Technical Institute	Owings Mills	T,B	Prop	M/W												N		11
Montgomery College	Rockville	C,T	St-L	M/W	26,996	64	31	89	Y		R	Y	Y	Y	Y		9	44
TESST College of Technology	Baltimore	T	Prop	M/W								Y						1
TESST College of Technology	Beltsville	T	Prop	M/W								Y	Y					3
TESST College of Technology	Towson	T	Prop	M/W								Y						2
Massachusetts																			
Berkshire Community College	Pittsfield	C,T	St	M/W	2,566	60	41	41	Y	Y		Y	Y	Y		N		19
Bristol Community College	Fall River	C,T	St	M/W	8,893													
Bunker Hill Community College	Boston	C,T	St	M/W	12,934	65	48		Y		Y	Y	Y	Y	Y	N	7	57
Holyoke Community College	Holyoke	C,T	St	M/W	7,119	50	13		Y		Y	Y	Y	Y	Y	N	7	22

This chart includes the names and locations of accredited two-year colleges in the United States, Canada, and other countries and shows institutions' responses to the *Peterson's Annual Survey of Undergraduate Institutions*. If an institution submitted incomplete data, one or more columns opposite the institution's name is blank. A dagger after the school name indicates that the institution has one or more entries in the *College Close-Ups* section. If a school does not appear, it did not report any of the information.

Column key: **Degrees Awarded** — College Transfer Associate (C); Terminal Associate (T); Bachelor's (B); Master's (M); Doctoral (D). **Institutional Control** — County, District, City; Federal; State and Local; State-Related; Independent; Independent-Religious; Proprietary; Territory. **Student Body** — Men, Primarily Men; Women, Primarily Women; Coed. Y—Yes; N—No; R—Recommended; S—For Some

Institution	Location	Degrees Awarded	Institutional Control	Student Body	Undergrad Enrollment	% Women	% Attending Part-Time	% Grads to 4-Yr Colleges	% 25 or Older	HS Equiv. Cert. Accepted	Open Admissions	HS Transcript Required	Need-Based Aid Available	Part-Time Jobs Available	Career Counseling Available	Job Placement Services Available	College Housing Available	No. of Sports Offered	No. of Majors Offered
ITT Technical Institute	Norwood	T,B	Prop	M/W									Y		Y	Y	N		8
ITT Technical Institute	Wilmington	T,B	Prop	M/W									Y		Y	Y	N		9
Massachusetts Bay Community College	Wellesley Hills	C,T	St	M/W	5,276	60	39			Y	Y		Y	Y	Y	Y	N	9	30
Mount Wachusett Community College	Gardner	C,T	St	M/W	4,755	58	46			Y	Y	Y	Y	Y	Y	Y	N	8	28
Northern Essex Community College	Haverhill	C,T	St	M/W	7,036	64	51			Y	Y	Y	Y	Y	Y	Y	N	10	58
North Shore Community College	Danvers	C,T	St	M/W	7,284		40	45		Y	Y	S	Y	Y	Y	Y	N		40
Quinsigamond Community College	Worcester	C,T	St	M/W	9,130	56	38			Y	Y	Y	Y	Y		Y	N	6	37
Springfield Technical Community College	Springfield	C,T	St	M/W	6,899	56	40			Y	Y	Y	Y	Y	Y	Y	N	8	61
Michigan																			
Grand Rapids Community College	Grand Rapids	C,T	Dist	M/W	17,575	62	36			Y	Y		Y	Y	Y	Y	N	11	37
ITT Technical Institute	Canton	T,B	Prop	M/W									Y		Y	Y	N		16
ITT Technical Institute	Dearborn	T,B	Prop	M/W															10
ITT Technical Institute	Swartz Creek	C,B	Prop	M/W															15
ITT Technical Institute	Troy	T,B	Prop	M/W									Y		Y	Y	N		15
ITT Technical Institute	Wyoming	T,B	Prop	M/W									Y		Y	Y	N		15
Jackson Community College	Jackson	C,T	Cou	M/W	6,988	55	45			Y	Y		Y			Y	Y	8	26
Kaplan Career Institute, Dearborn Campus	Detroit	T	Prop	M/W															1
Kirtland Community College	Roscommon	C,T	Dist	M/W	1,815	58	47			Y	Y		Y	Y	Y	Y	N	3	34
Lake Michigan College	Benton Harbor	C,T	Dist	M/W	4,654	66	49	50		Y		Y	Y	Y	Y		N	4	62
Lansing Community College	Lansing	C,T	St-L	M/W	20,640	72	47			Y		S	Y	Y	Y	Y	Y	6	88
Macomb Community College	Warren	C,T	Dist	M/W	23,969	65	36			Y			Y	Y	Y	Y	N	11	72
Mid Michigan Community College	Harrison	C,T	St-L	M/W	4,885	55	29			Y		R	Y	Y	Y	Y	N	3	37
Monroe County Community College	Monroe	C,T	Cou	M/W	4,440	61	45			Y	Y	Y	Y		Y	Y	N	2	42
Montcalm Community College	Sidney	C,T	St-L	M/W	2,062	66	41			Y		R	Y	Y			N	1	23
Mott Community College	Flint	C,T	Dist	M/W	11,760	65	50			Y		Y	Y	Y	Y	Y	N	7	45
Muskegon Community College	Muskegon	C,T	St-L	M/W	5,579	66				Y	Y	Y	Y	Y	Y	Y	N	8	43
Oakland Community College	Bloomfield Hills	C,T	St-L	M/W	29,158	67	55			Y		R	Y	Y	Y	Y	N	7	98
St. Clair County Community College	Port Huron	C,T	St-L	M/W	4,590	57	37			Y		Y	Y	Y	Y	Y	N	5	29
Southwestern Michigan College	Dowagiac	C,T	St-L	M/W	3,029	50	38			Y	Y	Y	Y				Y	9	34
Minnesota																			
Alexandria Technical and Community College	Alexandria	C,T	St	M/W	2,347														
Anoka-Ramsey Community College	Coon Rapids	C,T	St	M/W	7,475		29			Y	Y	S	Y	Y	Y	Y	N	10	23
Anoka-Ramsey Community College, Cambridge Campus	Cambridge	C,T	St	M/W	2,682		34			Y	Y	S	Y	Y	Y	Y	N	7	22
Central Lakes College	Brainerd	C,T	St	M/W	4,378														
Century College	White Bear Lake	C,T	St	M/W	10,707	57	43			Y	Y	Y	Y	Y	Y		N	8	36
Dakota County Technical College	Rosemount	C,T	St	M/W	3,672	54													
Duluth Business University	Duluth	T	Prop	PW	367														
The Institute of Production and Recording	Minneapolis	C,T	Prop	M/W	456	15					Y	Y	Y		Y	Y	N		2
Inver Hills Community College	Inver Grove Heights	C,T	St	M/W	6,342	61													
Itasca Community College	Grand Rapids	C,T	St	M/W	1,299		28			Y	Y	Y	Y	Y	Y	Y	Y	8	30
ITT Technical Institute	Brooklyn Center	T,B	Prop	M/W															8
ITT Technical Institute	Eden Prairie	T,B	Prop	M/W															12
Lake Superior College	Duluth	C,T	St	M/W	4,366	45													
Mesabi Range Community and Technical College	Virginia	C,T	St	M/W	1,467														
Minneapolis Business College	Roseville	T	Priv	PW	377						Y							Y		9
Minneapolis Community and Technical College	Minneapolis	C,T	St	M/W	9,991	62	53			Y	Y	Y	Y	Y	Y	Y	N		46
Minnesota School of Business–Brooklyn Center	Brooklyn Center	C,T,B	Prop	M/W	620	77	43				Y	Y	Y		Y	Y	N		10
Minnesota School of Business–Plymouth	Minneapolis	C,T,B	Prop	M/W	487	77	43				Y	Y	Y		Y	Y	N		13
Minnesota School of Business–Richfield	Richfield	T,B	Prop	M/W	1,738	70	46				Y	Y	Y			Y	N		17
Minnesota School of Business–St. Cloud	Waite Park	C,T,B	Prop	M/W	921	49	37				Y	Y			Y	Y	N		14
Minnesota School of Business–Shakopee	Shakopee	C,T,B	Prop	M/W	390	61	41				Y	Y			Y	Y	N		12
Minnesota State College–Southeast Technical	Winona	C,T	St	M/W	2,237	40	47			Y	Y	Y	Y	Y			Y		27
Minnesota State Community and Technical College	Fergus Falls	C,T	St	M/W	6,925														
Minnesota West Community and Technical College	Pipestone	C,T	St	M/W	3,464	52													
Normandale Community College	Bloomington	C,T	St	M/W	9,871	56				Y	Y	S	Y	Y	Y	Y	N	14	26
North Hennepin Community College	Brooklyn Park	C,T	St	M/W	7,456	63	44			Y	Y	R	Y	Y	Y	Y	N	14	28
Northland Community and Technical College–Thief River Falls & East Grand Forks	Thief River Falls	C,T	St	M/W	4,135	53													
Northwest Technical College	Bemidji	T	St	M/W	1,384	62	48			Y	Y		Y	Y			Y		16
Rainy River Community College	International Falls	C,T	St	M/W	344		54			Y	Y	R	Y	Y	Y	Y	Y	16	6
Rasmussen College Bloomington	Bloomington	C,T,B	Prop	M/W	611		69				Y	Y	Y	Y	Y	Y	N		21
Rasmussen College Brooklyn Park	Brooklyn Park	C,T,B	Prop	M/W	1,015		69				Y	Y	Y	Y	Y	Y	N		22
Rasmussen College Eagan	Eagan	C,T,B	Prop	PW	923		70				Y	Y	Y	Y	Y	Y	N		21
Rasmussen College Lake Elmo/Woodbury	Lake Elmo	C,T,B	Prop	M/W	735		69				Y	Y	Y	Y	Y	Y	N		22
Rasmussen College Mankato	Mankato	C,T,B	Prop	PW	797		64				Y	Y	Y	Y	Y	Y	N		22
Rasmussen College Moorhead	Moorhead	C,T,B	Prop	M/W	525		62				Y	Y	Y	Y	Y	Y	N		21
Rasmussen College St. Cloud	St. Cloud	C,T,B	Prop	PW	1,017		69				Y	Y	Y	Y	Y	Y	N		23
St. Cloud Technical & Community College	St. Cloud	C,T	St	M/W	4,883	44	15											N	4	37
Mississippi																			
Copiah-Lincoln Community College	Wesson	C,T	St-L	M/W	3,709	19	20			Y	Y	Y	Y	Y	Y	Y	Y	8	45
Southwest Mississippi Community College	Summit	C,T	St-L	M/W	2,053	13	29			Y	Y	Y	Y	Y	Y	Y	Y	5	50
Missouri																			
Anthem College–Maryland Heights	Maryland Heights	T	Prop	M/W	281	70	0			Y	Y	Y			Y	Y	N		7
Brown Mackie College–St. Louis†	Fenton	T,B	Prop	M/W															
Crowder College	Neosho	C,T	St-L	M/W	5,219	53	12			Y	Y	Y	Y	Y	Y	Y	Y	4	35
Culinary Institute of St. Louis at Hickey College	St. Louis	T	Priv	M/W	85											Y	Y		1
ITT Technical Institute	Arnold	T,B	Prop	M/W									Y		Y	Y	N		18

This chart includes the names and locations of accredited two-year colleges in the United States, Canada, and other countries and shows institutions' responses to the *Peterson's Annual Survey of Undergraduate Institutions*. If an institution submitted incomplete data, one or more columns opposite the institution's name is blank. A dagger after the school name indicates that the institution has one or more entries in the *College Close-Ups* section. If a school does not appear, it did not report any of the information.

Y—Yes; N—No; R—Recommended; S—For Some

Column headers (diagonal):
Degrees Awarded — College Transfer Associate (C), Terminal Associate (T), Bachelor's (B), Master's (M), Doctoral (D) · Institutional Control — County, District, City, State and Local, State-Related; Federal, State, Commonwealth, Territory; Independent, Independent-Religious, Proprietary · Student Body — Men, Primarily Men, Women, Primarily Women, Coed · Undergraduate Enrollment · Percent Attending Part-Time · Percent 25 Years of Age or Older · Percent of Grads Going on to Four-Year Colleges · High School Equivalency Certificate Accepted · Open Admissions · High School Transcript Required · Need-Based Aid Available · Part-Time Jobs Available · Career Counseling Services Available · Job Placement Services Available · College Housing Available · Number of Sports Offered · Number of Majors Offered

Institution	Location	Degrees	Control	Student Body	Undergrad Enroll	% Part-Time	% 25+	% to 4-Yr	HS Equiv	Open Adm	HS Transcript	Need Aid	PT Jobs	Career Couns	Job Place	Housing	# Sports	# Majors
ITT Technical Institute	Earth City	T,B	Prop	M/W								Y		Y	Y		N	18
ITT Technical Institute	Kansas City	T,B	Prop	M/W														13
Jefferson College	Hillsboro	C,T	St	M/W	6,192	45												
Linn State Technical College	Linn	T	St	PM	1,168	14	14											
Metropolitan Community College–Blue River	Independence	C,T	St-L	M/W	3,483	57	36	Y			Y		Y	Y	Y	N	9	23
Metropolitan Community College–Business & Technology Campus	Kansas City	C,T	St-L	M/W	852	70	68	Y				Y	Y	Y	N			43
Metropolitan Community College–Longview	Lee's Summit	C,T	St-L	M/W	6,209	58	30	Y		Y	Y		Y	Y	N		5	24
Metropolitan Community College–Maple Woods	Kansas City	C,T	St-L	M/W	5,332	60	30	Y	Y		Y	Y	Y	Y	Y	N	4	19
Metropolitan Community College–Penn Valley	Kansas City	C,T	St-L	M/W	5,409	70	39	Y	Y	Y	Y	Y	Y	Y	Y	N	1	31
Mineral Area College	Park Hills	C,T	Dist	M/W	3,958	40	34	Y		Y	Y	Y	Y	Y	Y	Y	5	33
Missouri State University–West Plains	West Plains	C,T	St	M/W	2,142	40	38	Y	Y	S	Y	Y	Y	Y	Y		2	21
Saint Charles Community College	Cottleville	C,T	St	M/W	8,202	47												
Southeast Missouri Hospital College of Nursing and Health Sciences	Cape Girardeau	C,T	Ind	M/W	196	87	66	N	Y	Y						N		2
Vet Tech Institute at Hickey College	St. Louis	T	Priv	M/W	134											Y		1
Wentworth Military Academy and College	Lexington	C,T	Ind	M/W	941	91												
Montana																		
Dawson Community College	Glendive	C,T	St-L	M/W	603	53	21	Y		Y	Y	Y	Y	Y		10	14
Montana State University–Great Falls College of Technology	Great Falls	C,T	St	M/W	1,874	48	58	55	Y	Y	Y	Y	Y	Y		N		24
The University of Montana–Helena College of Technology	Helena	C,T	St	M/W	1,679	52	55		Y	Y	S	Y	Y	Y	Y	N		16
Nebraska																		
Central Community College–Columbus Campus	Columbus	C,T	St-L	M/W	2,872	82	39	Y	Y	Y	Y	Y	Y	Y		6	17
Central Community College–Grand Island Campus	Grand Island	C,T	St-L	M/W	3,469	88	46	Y	Y	Y	Y	Y	Y	Y	Y	4	18
Central Community College–Hastings Campus	Hastings	C,T	St-L	M/W	2,966	66	36	Y	Y	Y	Y	Y	Y	Y		6	37
Creative Center	Omaha	T,B	Prop	M/W				N	Y	Y			Y	Y	N		3
ITT Technical Institute	Omaha	T,B	Prop	M/W					Y		Y				N		13
Mid-Plains Community College	North Platte	C,T	Dist	M/W	2,623	62	33	Y	Y	Y	Y	Y	Y	N		5	18
Northeast Community College	Norfolk	C,T	St-L	M/W	5,161	58	57	Y		R,S	Y	Y	Y	Y	Y	8	96
Nevada																		
Great Basin College	Elko	C,T,B	St	M/W	3,691	69												
ITT Technical Institute	Henderson	T,B	Prop	M/W							Y		Y	Y		N		16
ITT Technical Institute	North Las Vegas	T,B	Prop	M/W														13
Kaplan College, Las Vegas Campus	Las Vegas	T	Prop	M/W														4
Pima Medical Institute	Las Vegas	T,B	Prop	M/W	820													
Truckee Meadows Community College	Reno	C,T	St	M/W	12,587	72	43	39	Y			Y	Y	Y		N		51
New Hampshire																		
Hesser College, Concord	Concord	T,B	Prop	M/W														6
Hesser College, Manchester	Manchester	T,B	Prop	M/W									Y	Y	Y			11
Hesser College, Nashua	Nashua	T,B	Prop	M/W														6
Hesser College, Portsmouth	Portsmouth	T,B	Prop	M/W								Y						8
Hesser College, Salem	Salem	T,B	Prop	M/W								Y						6
Nashua Community College	Nashua	C,T	St	M/W	2,100													
White Mountains Community College	Berlin	C,T	St	M/W	922	62		Y	Y	Y	Y	Y	Y		N		18
New Jersey																		
Burlington County College	Pemberton	C,T	Cou	M/W	10,298	47	36	Y	Y	Y	Y	Y	Y	Y	N	6	58
ITT Technical Institute	Marlton	T	Prop	M/W														3
Ocean County College	Toms River	C,T	Cou	M/W	10,317	45	27	Y		S	Y	Y	Y		N	12	17
Raritan Valley Community College	Branchburg	C,T	Cou	M/W	8,370	53	28	Y	Y	Y	Y	Y	Y	N		5	57
Salem Community College	Carneys Point	C,T	Cou	M/W	1,321		33	Y	Y	Y	Y	Y	Y	N		5	13
Union County College	Cranford	C,T	St-L	M/W	12,416	53	41	Y	Y		Y	Y	Y	N		6	50
New Mexico																		
Brown Mackie College–Albuquerque†	Albuquerque	T,B	Prop	M/W														
Central New Mexico Community College	Albuquerque	C,T	St	M/W	29,948	67												
Clovis Community College	Clovis	C,T	St	M/W	4,175	76												
Do&nna Ana Community College	Las Cruces	C,T	St-L	M/W	8,891	55	38	Y	Y	Y	Y	Y	Y	Y	Y		22
ITT Technical Institute	Albuquerque	T,B	Prop	M/W					Y		Y		Y	Y	N		16
New Mexico State University–Alamogordo	Alamogordo	C,T	St	M/W	3,371	70	47	Y	Y	Y	Y	Y	Y	N			21
Pima Medical Institute	Albuquerque		Prop	M/W														
Pima Medical Institute	Albuquerque	T,B	Prop	M/W	716													
San Juan College	Farmington	C,T	St	M/W	9,470	66	58	Y		Y	Y	Y	Y	N		16	50
Santa Fe Community College	Santa Fe	C,T	St-L	M/W	4,856	66												
Southwestern Indian Polytechnic Institute	Albuquerque	C,T	Fed	M/W	480	15	38	N	Y	Y	Y	Y			Y	3	17
New York																		
The Art Institute of New York City†	New York	C,T	Prop	M/W														6
ASA The College For Excellence	Brooklyn	T	Prop	M/W	6,475													
Borough of Manhattan Community College of the City University of New York	New York	C,T	St-L	M/W	22,534	35												
Cayuga County Community College	Auburn	C,T	St-L	M/W	4,825	50	34	Y	Y	Y	Y	Y	Y	Y	Y	7	34
Clinton Community College	Plattsburgh	C,T	St-L	M/W	1,780		29	Y	Y	Y	Y	Y	Y	Y		5	16
Corning Community College	Corning	C,T	St-L	M/W	5,298	53	35	Y	Y	Y	Y	Y	Y	N		10	47
Dutchess Community College	Poughkeepsie	C,T	St-L	M/W	10,329	47	24	Y	Y	Y	Y	Y	Y	N		10	41
Ellis School of Nursing	Schenectady	C,T	Ind	PW	120	75	65				Y		Y					1

This chart includes the names and locations of accredited two-year colleges in the United States, Canada, and other countries and shows institutions' responses to the *Peterson's Annual Survey of Undergraduate Institutions*. If an institution submitted incomplete data, one or more columns opposite the institution's name is blank. A dagger after the school name indicates that the institution has one or more entries in the *College Close-Ups* section. If a school does not appear, it did not report any of the information.

Column legend for Degrees Awarded: College Transfer Associate (C), Terminal Associate (T), Bachelor's (B), Master's (M), Doctoral (D). Institutional Control abbreviations include County/District/City/State and Local, State-Related, Independent, Independent-Religious, Proprietary, Federal, State, Commonwealth, Territory. Student Body (Undergraduate Coed): Men, Primarily Men, Women, Primarily Women, Coed.

Y—Yes; N—No; R—Recommended; S—For Some

Institution	City	Degrees	Control	Body	Enroll.	% P-T	% 25+	% to 4-Yr	HS Equiv.	Open Adm.	HS Trans.	Need-Based Aid	P-T Jobs	Career Couns.	Job Place.	Housing	Sports	Majors
Elmira Business Institute	Elmira	C,T	Priv	PW	235	18	70		Y	Y	Y	Y	Y	Y	Y	N		4
Erie Community College	Buffalo	C,T	St-L	M/W	3,495	25	42		Y	Y	Y	Y	Y	Y	Y	N	14	16
Erie Community College, North Campus	Williamsville	C,T	St-L	M/W	6,410	35	35		Y	Y	Y	Y	Y	Y	Y	N	14	26
Erie Community College, South Campus	Orchard Park	C,T	St-L	M/W	4,271	40	26		Y	Y	Y	Y	Y	Y	Y	N	14	18
Fashion Institute of Technology†	New York	C,T,B,M	St-L	PW	10,023	29	23		N	Y	Y	Y	Y	Y	Y		9	20
Fiorello H. LaGuardia Community College of the City University of New York	Long Island City	C,T	St-L	M/W	17,563	41	29	54	Y	Y	Y	Y	Y	Y	Y	N	8	46
Fulton-Montgomery Community College	Johnstown	C,T	St-L	M/W	2,833	34			Y	Y	Y	Y	Y	Y		Y	13	38
Genesee Community College	Batavia	C,T	St-L	M/W	7,200	50	36		Y	Y	Y	R	Y	Y	Y	N		8
Island Drafting and Technical Institute	Amityville	C,T	Prop	M/W	116		45	0	Y	Y	R	Y	Y	Y		N		8
ITT Technical Institute	Albany	T	Prop	M/W						Y		Y	Y	Y		N		8
ITT Technical Institute	Getzville	T	Prop	M/W						Y		Y	Y	Y		N		7
ITT Technical Institute	Liverpool	T	Prop	M/W						Y		Y	Y	Y		N		6
Jamestown Business College	Jamestown	T,B	Prop	M/W	317	4	49		N	Y	Y	Y		Y	Y	N	8	3
Jamestown Community College	Jamestown	C,T	St-L	M/W	3,926	30	30	55	Y	Y	Y	Y	Y	Y	Y	Y	13	37
Jefferson Community College	Watertown	C,T	St-L	M/W	4,026	44			N	Y	Y	Y	Y	Y	Y	N	6	23
Kingsborough Community College of the City University of New York	Brooklyn	C,T	St-L	M/W	19,261	42	27		Y	Y	Y		Y	Y	Y	N	7	40
Long Island Business Institute	Flushing	C	Prop	PW	596	40	65	0	Y	Y			Y		Y	N		5
Mohawk Valley Community College	Utica	C,T	St-L	M/W	7,640	36	32		Y		S	Y	Y	Y	Y	Y	14	51
Monroe Community College	Rochester	C,T	St-L	M/W	17,699	38	40		Y	Y	Y	Y	Y	Y	Y	N	17	67
New York Career Institute	New York	T	Prop	PW	771				N	Y	Y	Y	Y	Y	Y	N		3
Niagara County Community College	Sanborn	C,T	St-L	M/W	7,177	39	27		Y	Y	Y	Y	Y	Y	Y	Y	12	40
Onondaga Community College	Syracuse	C,T	St-L	M/W	12,731	46	20		Y	Y	Y	Y	Y	Y	Y	Y	12	39
Phillips Beth Israel School of Nursing	New York		Ind	M/W	251	93											N		1
Rockland Community College	Suffern	C,T	St-L	M/W	7,986	40			Y		Y	Y	Y	Y	Y	N	11	41
St. Elizabeth College of Nursing	Utica	T	Ind	M/W	217	33	46			N	Y	Y		Y		N		1
St. Joseph's College of Nursing	Syracuse	T	I-R	M/W	273	39				Y	Y	Y		Y		Y		1
State University of New York College of Environmental Science & Forestry, Ranger School	Wanakena	C,T	St	PM	58		15	35	N	Y	Y	Y	Y	Y	Y	Y	7	3
State University of New York College of Technology at Alfred	Alfred	C,T,B	St	M/W	3,617	9	15		N	Y	Y	Y	Y	Y	Y	Y	17	79
Suffolk County Community College	Selden	C,T	St-L	M/W	28,294											Y	14	31
Sullivan County Community College	Loch Sheldrake	C,T	St-L	M/W	1,705	33	26	36	Y	Y	Y	Y	Y	Y	Y	Y	22	34
Tompkins Cortland Community College	Dryden	C,T	St-L	M/W	3,850	23	29		Y	Y	Y	Y	Y	Y	Y	N	11	47
Westchester Community College	Valhalla	C,T	St-L	M/W	13,969	47	29		Y	Y	Y	Y	Y	Y	Y	N		11
Wood Tobe–Coburn School	New York	T	Priv	PW	483				N	Y			Y					10
North Carolina																		
Alamance Community College	Graham	C,T	St	M/W	5,512	51										N		18
Beaufort County Community College	Washington	C,T	St	M/W	1,933				Y	Y	S	S	Y	Y	Y	N	7	34
Cape Fear Community College	Wilmington	C,T	St	M/W	9,247	56	40		Y	Y	S	S	Y	Y	Y	Y		3
Carolinas College of Health Sciences	Charlotte	T	Pub	M/W	424	86	61		N	Y	S	Y	Y	Y	Y	N	4	35
Catawba Valley Community College	Hickory	C,T	St-L	M/W	5,114	62	44		Y	Y	Y	Y	Y	Y	Y	N	5	29
Central Carolina Community College	Sanford	C,T	St-L	M/W	2,477		50		Y	Y	S	Y	Y	Y	Y	N	7	49
Fayetteville Technical Community College	Fayetteville	C,T	St	M/W	11,737	59	59	9	Y	Y	S	Y	Y	Y		N	4	54
Guilford Technical Community College	Jamestown	C,T	St-L	M/W	14,745	41	49		Y	Y	Y	Y	Y			N		11
ITT Technical Institute	Cary	T,B	Prop	M/W												N		11
ITT Technical Institute	Charlotte	T,B	Prop	M/W												N		12
ITT Technical Institute	High Point	T,B	Prop	M/W												N	2	17
James Sprunt Community College	Kenansville	C,T	St	M/W	1,587	50	41	1	Y	Y	Y	Y	Y	Y		N	2	23
Johnston Community College	Smithfield	C,T	St	M/W	4,410	48	40		Y	Y	Y	Y	Y	Y		N	4	2
Kaplan College, Charlotte Campus	Charlotte	T	Prop	M/W												Y		10
King's College	Charlotte	T	Priv	M/W	637													
Martin Community College	Williamston	C,T	St	M/W	755	37										N		10
Montgomery Community College	Troy	C,T	St	M/W	756	50	52		Y	Y		Y	Y	Y		N	5	32
Randolph Community College	Asheboro	C,T	St	M/W	2,967	49	39	53	Y	Y			Y	Y		N	7	19
Rockingham Community College	Wentworth	C,T	St	M/W	2,631	54	41		Y	Y			Y	Y	Y	N		
Sandhills Community College	Pinehurst	C,T	St	M/W	4,571											N		22
Wilson Community College	Wilson	C,T	St	M/W	1,899	51	51		Y	Y	Y	Y	Y	Y	Y	N		
North Dakota																		
Dakota College at Bottineau	Bottineau	C,T	St	M/W	812	49	37		Y	Y	Y	Y	Y	Y	Y	Y	9	71
Lake Region State College	Devils Lake	C,T	St	M/W	2,056	75	24	52	Y	Y	Y	Y	Y	Y	Y	Y	9	37
North Dakota State College of Science	Wahpeton	C,T	St	M/W	3,127	43	79		Y	Y		Y	Y		Y	N	8	47
Rasmussen College Bismarck	Bismarck	C,T,B	Prop	M/W	289		67			Y	Y	Y		Y	Y	N		20
Rasmussen College Fargo	Fargo	C,T,B	Prop	M/W	418		68			Y	Y			Y		N		18
Ohio																		
The Art Institute of Ohio–Cincinnati	Cincinnati	C,T,B	Prop	M/W														9
ATS Institute of Technology	Highland Heights	C	Prop	M/W	353													11
Bradford School	Columbus	T	Priv	PW	705				N	Y			Y			Y		
Brown Mackie College–Akron†	Akron	T	Prop	M/W														
Brown Mackie College–Cincinnati†	Cincinnati	T	Prop	M/W														
Brown Mackie College–Findlay†	Findlay	T	Prop	M/W														
Brown Mackie College–North Canton†	Canton	T	Prop	M/W														1
The Christ College of Nursing and Health Sciences	Cincinnati	T	Priv	M/W	346	42	38					Y	Y			N		
Cincinnati State Technical and Community College	Cincinnati	C,T	St	M/W	10,995	62												3
Cleveland Institute of Electronics	Cleveland	T	Prop	PM	1,826		85		Y	Y	Y			Y			Y	1
Columbus Culinary Institute at Bradford School	Columbus	T	Priv	M/W	293													
Eastern Gateway Community College	Steubenville	C,T	St-L	M/W	2,209	45												

This chart includes the names and locations of accredited two-year colleges in the United States, Canada, and other countries and shows institutions' responses to the *Peterson's Annual Survey of Undergraduate Institutions*. If an institution submitted incomplete data, one or more columns opposite the institution's name is blank. A dagger after the school name indicates that the institution has one or more entries in the *College Close-Ups* section. If a school does not appear, it did not report any of the information.

Y—Yes; N—No; R—Recommended; S—For Some

College	City	Degrees Awarded	Institutional Control	Student Body	Undergraduate Enrollment	Percent Attending Part-Time	Percent 25 Years of Age or Older	Percent of Grads Going on to Four-Year Colleges	Open Admissions	High School Equivalency Certificate Accepted	High School Transcript Required	Need-Based Aid Required	Part-Time Jobs Available	Job Placement Services Available	Career Counseling Available	College Housing Available	Number of Sports Offered	Number of Majors Offered
Edison Community College	Piqua	C,T	St	M/W	3,457	63	55	47	Y	Y	Y		Y	Y	Y	N	3	37
ETI Technical College of Niles	Niles	T	Prop	M/W	212	33	45	24		Y	Y	Y	Y		Y	Y	N		11
Good Samaritan College of Nursing and Health Science	Cincinnati	T	Prop	M/W	313	58	46			Y	Y	Y	Y		Y		N		1
Harrison College	Grove City	T	Prop	M/W	99	12											N		1
International College of Broadcasting	Dayton	C,T	Priv	M/W	84		35						Y		Y	Y	Y		2
ITT Technical Institute	Akron	T,B	Prop	M/W							Y		Y	Y	Y			13
ITT Technical Institute	Columbus	T,B	Prop	M/W														12
ITT Technical Institute	Dayton	T,B	Prop	M/W						Y		Y	Y		N			13
ITT Technical Institute	Hilliard	T,B	Prop	M/W														13
ITT Technical Institute	Maumee	T,B	Prop	M/W											N			11
ITT Technical Institute	Norwood	C,B	Prop	M/W						Y		Y	Y		N			16
ITT Technical Institute	Strongsville	T,B	Prop	M/W						Y		Y	Y		N			21
ITT Technical Institute	Warrensville Heights	T,B	Prop	M/W						Y		Y	Y		N			13
ITT Technical Institute	Youngstown	T,B	Prop	M/W						Y		Y	Y		N			14
Kaplan Career Institute, Cleveland Campus	Cleveland	T	Prop	M/W														1
Kaplan College, Cincinnati Campus	Cincinnati	T	Prop	M/W					Y									1
Kaplan College, Columbus Campus	Columbus	T	Prop	M/W					Y									2
Kaplan College, Dayton Campus	Dayton	T	Prop	M/W					Y		Y							3
Kent State University at Ashtabula	Ashtabula	C,T,B	St	M/W	2,451	50	55		Y	Y	Y	Y	Y	Y	Y	N		29
Kent State University at East Liverpool	East Liverpool	C,B	St	M/W	1,491	41	53		Y	Y	Y	Y	Y	Y	Y	N		14
Kent State University at Salem	Salem	C,T,B	St	M/W	2,018	32	47		Y	Y	Y	Y	Y	Y	Y	N		17
Kent State University at Trumbull	Warren	C,T,B	St	M/W	3,205	39	51		Y	Y	Y	Y	Y	Y	Y	N	5	19
Kent State University at Tuscarawas	New Philadelphia	C,B	St	M/W	2,659	43	48		Y	Y	Y	Y	Y	Y	Y	N	2	20
Lincoln College of Technology	Franklin	T	Prop	M/W														
Marion Technical College	Marion	C,T	St	M/W	2,765													
Owens Community College	Toledo	C,T	St	M/W	17,173	60	51		Y		R	Y	Y	Y	Y	N	11	55
School of Advertising Art	Kettering	T	Prop	M/W	116													
Southern State Community College	Hillsboro	C,T	St	M/W	3,350	41		25	Y	Y	R	Y	Y	Y	Y	N	5	31
Stark State College	North Canton	C,T	St-L	M/W	15,536	65	54		Y	Y	Y	Y	Y	Y	Y	N		49
Terra State Community College	Fremont	C,T	St	M/W	3,566	57	43		Y	Y	Y	S	Y	Y	Y	N	6	67
The University of Akron–Wayne College	Orrville	C,T,B	St	M/W	2,502	47	40		Y	Y	S	Y	Y	Y	Y	N	4	61
Vet Tech Institute at Bradford School	Columbus	T	Priv	M/W	194												Y		1

Oklahoma

College	City	Degrees Awarded	Institutional Control	Student Body	Undergraduate Enrollment	Percent Attending Part-Time	Percent 25 Years of Age or Older	Percent of Grads Going on to Four-Year Colleges	Open Admissions	High School Equivalency Certificate Accepted	High School Transcript Required	Need-Based Aid Required	Part-Time Jobs Available	Job Placement Services Available	Career Counseling Available	College Housing Available	Number of Sports Offered	Number of Majors Offered
Brown Mackie College–Oklahoma City†	Oklahoma City		Prop	M/W														
Brown Mackie College–Tulsa†	Tulsa	T,B	Prop	M/W														
Carl Albert State College	Poteau	C,T	St	M/W	2,460	44	35		Y		Y	Y	Y	Y	Y	Y	6	29
Clary Sage College	Tulsa	T	Prop	PW	322				Y	Y	Y			Y	Y	N		3
Community Care College	Tulsa	T	Prop	PW	942		51		Y	Y	Y			Y	Y	N		12
ITT Technical Institute	Tulsa	T,B	Prop	M/W												N		15
Murray State College	Tishomingo	C,T	St	M/W	2,674				Y	Y	Y		Y	Y	Y	Y	5	26
Oklahoma City Community College	Oklahoma City	C,T	St	M/W	14,941	62	44		Y		S	Y	Y	Y	N	7	59
Oklahoma State University, Oklahoma City	Oklahoma City	C,T,B	St	M/W	7,721		52		Y	Y		Y	Y	Y	Y	N		46
Oklahoma Technical College	Tulsa	T	Prop	PM					Y	Y			Y		N		4
Platt College	Oklahoma City	T	Prop	M/W	357													
Southwestern Oklahoma State University at Sayre	Sayre	C,T	St-L	M/W	643	60	49		Y	Y		Y	Y	Y	Y	N		10

Oregon

College	City	Degrees Awarded	Institutional Control	Student Body	Undergraduate Enrollment	Percent Attending Part-Time	Percent 25 Years of Age or Older	Percent of Grads Going on to Four-Year Colleges	Open Admissions	High School Equivalency Certificate Accepted	High School Transcript Required	Need-Based Aid Required	Part-Time Jobs Available	Job Placement Services Available	Career Counseling Available	College Housing Available	Number of Sports Offered	Number of Majors Offered
American College of Healthcare Sciences	Portland	T,M	Ind	M/W														
Central Oregon Community College	Bend	C,T	Dist	M/W	7,142	54	55		Y	Y		Y	Y	Y	Y	11	56
ITT Technical Institute	Portland	T,B	Prop	M/W						Y		Y	Y		N		18
Linn-Benton Community College	Albany	C,T	St-L	M/W	6,922	49												
Oregon Coast Community College	Newport	C,T	Pub	M/W	535	62												
Rogue Community College	Grants Pass	C,T	St-L	M/W	5,828	56	52		Y	Y		Y	Y	Y	Y	N	6	25
Umpqua Community College	Roseburg	C,T	St-L	M/W	3,233	46		31	Y		R	Y	Y	Y	Y	N	2	53

Pennsylvania

College	City	Degrees Awarded	Institutional Control	Student Body	Undergraduate Enrollment	Percent Attending Part-Time	Percent 25 Years of Age or Older	Percent of Grads Going on to Four-Year Colleges	Open Admissions	High School Equivalency Certificate Accepted	High School Transcript Required	Need-Based Aid Required	Part-Time Jobs Available	Job Placement Services Available	Career Counseling Available	College Housing Available	Number of Sports Offered	Number of Majors Offered
Antonelli Institute	Erdenheim	T	Prop	M/W	203				Y	Y		Y	Y		Y		2
The Art Institute of York–Pennsylvania	York	T,B	Prop	M/W														5
Bradford School	Pittsburgh	T	Priv	M/W	582				Y		Y		Y		Y		11
Bucks County Community College	Newtown	C,T	Cou	M/W	10,300	67	32	45	Y	Y	Y	Y	Y	Y	Y	N	10	59
Career Training Academy	Pittsburgh	T	Prop	M/W	84		54	0	N		Y		Y		Y	N		3
Community College of Allegheny County	Pittsburgh	C,T	Cou	M/W	20,372	60	46				R	Y	Y		N	15	115
Community College of Philadelphia	Philadelphia	C,T	St-L	M/W	39,270		53	71	Y	Y	R	S	Y	Y	N	N	8	39
Consolidated School of Business	York	T	Prop	PW	176		41		Y	Y	S	Y	Y	Y	Y	N	7	7
Delaware County Community College	Media	C,T	St-L	M/W	13,248		56	72	Y	Y	Y		Y		N	9	57
Douglas Education Center	Monessen	T	Prop	M/W	334													
Harrisburg Area Community College	Harrisburg	C,T	St-L	M/W	23,210	62												
ITT Technical Institute	Bensalem	T	Prop	M/W						Y		Y	Y		N		5
ITT Technical Institute	Dunmore	T	Prop	M/W													5
ITT Technical Institute	Harrisburg	T	Prop	M/W													6
ITT Technical Institute	King of Prussia	T	Prop	M/W													5
ITT Technical Institute	Pittsburgh	T	Prop	M/W											N		6
ITT Technical Institute	Tarentum	T	Prop	M/W						Y		Y	Y		N		7
JNA Institute of Culinary Arts	Philadelphia	T	Prop	M/W	92													
Kaplan Career Institute, Broomall Campus	Broomall	T	Prop	M/W							Y		Y	Y		1
Kaplan Career Institute, Franklin Mills Campus	Philadelphia	T	Prop	M/W						Y		Y	Y		3
Kaplan Career Institute, Harrisburg Campus	Harrisburg	T	Prop	M/W						Y		Y	Y		4
Kaplan Career Institute, ICM Campus	Pittsburgh	T	Prop	M/W						Y		Y	Y		6
Kaplan Career Institute, Philadelphia Campus	Philadelphia	T	Prop	M/W						Y		Y	Y		1
Lehigh Carbon Community College	Schnecksville	C,T	St-L	M/W	7,710	65	41	33	Y		S	Y	Y	Y	Y	N	8	58

This chart includes the names and locations of accredited two-year colleges in the United States, Canada, and other countries and shows institutions' responses to the *Peterson's Annual Survey of Undergraduate Institutions*. If an institution submitted incomplete data, one or more columns opposite the institution's name is blank. A dagger after the school name indicates that the institution has one or more entries in the *College Close-Ups* section. If a school does not appear, it did not report any of the information.

Y—Yes; N—No; R—Recommended; S—For Some

Column legend (diagonal headers):
- Degrees Awarded: College Transfer Associate (C), Terminal Associate (T), Bachelor's (B), Master's (M), Doctoral (D)
- Institutional Control: County District City, State and Local, State-Related, Federal, State Commonwealth, Territory, Independent-Religious, Independent, Proprietary
- Student Body: Men, Primarily Men, Women, Primarily Women, Coed
- Undergraduate Enrollment
- Percent Attending Part-Time
- Percent 25 Years of Age or Older
- Percent of Grads Going on to Four-Year Colleges
- Open Admissions
- High School Equivalency Certificate Accepted
- High School Transcript Required
- Need-Based Aid Required
- Part-Time Jobs Available
- Career Counseling Available
- Job Placement Services Available
- College Housing Available
- Number of Sports Offered
- Number of Majors Offered

Institution	City	Degrees	Control	Student Body	Undergrad Enroll.	% Part-Time	% 25+	% Grads to 4-yr	Open Adm.	HS Equiv.	HS Transcript	Need-Based Aid	Part-Time Jobs	Career Counseling	Job Placement	College Housing	# Sports	# Majors
Montgomery County Community College	Blue Bell	C,T	Cou	M/W	13,985	60	37	68	Y	Y	Y	Y	Y	Y	Y	N	13	59
Newport Business Institute	Williamsport	T	Prop	PW	108													
Northampton Community College	Bethlehem	C,T	St-L	M/W	11,350	56	36	68	Y	Y	R,S	Y	Y	Y	Y	N	10	60
Orleans Technical Institute	Philadelphia	C,T	Ind	M/W	533	25	61		N	Y	Y	Y		Y	Y	N		1
Pennco Tech	Bristol	T	Prop	M/W	400	39	40	1		Y	Y	Y		Y	Y	Y		2
Penn State Beaver	Monaca	C,T,B,M	St-R	M/W	870	20	11		N	Y	Y	Y	Y			Y	10	118
Penn State Brandywine	Media	C,T,B	St-R	M/W	1,628	15	11		N	Y	Y	Y	Y			N	10	120
Penn State DuBois	DuBois	C,T,B,M	St-R	M/W	795	24	28		N	Y	Y	Y	Y			N	7	127
Penn State Fayette, The Eberly Campus	Uniontown	C,T,B	St-R	M/W	956	18	29		N	Y	Y	Y	Y			Y	12	124
Penn State Greater Allegheny	McKeesport	C,T,B,M	St-R	M/W	701	12	12		N	Y	Y	Y	Y			Y	8	119
Penn State Hazleton	Hazleton	C,T,B	St-R	M/W	1,172	5	8		N	Y	Y	Y	Y			Y	8	125
Penn State Lehigh Valley	Fogelsville	C,T,B	St-R	M/W	915	19	15		N	Y	Y	Y	Y	Y	Y	N	13	119
Penn State Mont Alto	Mont Alto	C,T,B	St-R	M/W	1,217	21	21		N	Y	Y	Y	Y			Y	10	120
Penn State New Kensington	New Kensington	C,T,B,M	St-R	M/W	800	26	22		N	Y	Y	Y	Y				13	124
Penn State Schuylkill	Schuylkill Haven	C,T,B	St-R	M/W	1,012	16	15		N	Y	Y	Y	Y				8	124
Penn State Shenango	Sharon	C,T,B	St-R	M/W	651	40	55		N	Y	Y	Y	Y			N	7	124
Penn State Wilkes-Barre	Lehman	C,T,B	St-R	M/W	678	15	11		N	Y	Y	Y	Y			N	11	122
Penn State Worthington Scranton	Dunmore	C,T,B	St-R	M/W	1,270	20	21		N	Y	Y	Y	Y			N	10	119
Penn State York	York	C,T,B,M	St-R	M/W	1,259	32	27		N	Y	Y	Y	Y			N		126
Pennsylvania Highlands Community College	Johnstown	C,T	St-L	M/W	2,543													
Pittsburgh Technical Institute	Oakdale	T	Prop	M/W	1,939		21		Y	Y	Y			Y	Y	Y	N	5	13
The Restaurant School at Walnut Hill College	Philadelphia	T,B	Prop	M/W	402		12		Y	Y	Y	Y		Y	Y	Y			4
Triangle Tech, Inc.–DuBois School	DuBois	T	Prop	PM	329													
University of Pittsburgh at Titusville	Titusville	C,B	St-R	M/W	514	14										Y		1
Vet Tech Institute	Pittsburgh	T	Priv	M/W	363					Y			Y	Y	Y	Y	N	10	1
Westmoreland County Community College	Youngwood	C,T	Cou	M/W	6,943	53	40		Y			Y	Y	Y	Y	N		72
The Williamson Free School of Mechanical Trades	Media	T	Ind	M	270													7
YTI Career Institute–York	York	T	Priv	M/W	680		45		Y	Y	Y	Y	Y	Y	Y			7
Rhode Island																		
Community College of Rhode Island	Warwick	C,T	St	M/W	17,893	66	37		Y	Y		Y	Y	Y	Y	N	8	49
South Carolina																		
Aiken Technical College	Aiken	C,T	St-L	M/W	3,045	57	40		Y	Y	R	Y	Y			N	2	20
Brown Mackie College–Greenville†	Greenville	T,B	Prop	M/W														15
Central Carolina Technical College	Sumter	C,T	St	M/W	4,522	64	49		Y	Y	S	Y	Y	Y	Y	N		8
Denmark Technical College	Denmark	C,T	St	M/W	1,607	17	17		Y	Y	Y	Y	Y	Y	Y	Y		6	8
Forrest College	Anderson	C,T	Prop	M/W	94	19	60			Y	Y	Y	Y	Y		N		10
ITT Technical Institute	Columbia	T,B	Prop	M/W												N		10
ITT Technical Institute	Greenville	T,B	Prop	M/W						Y		Y	Y	Y		N		14
ITT Technical Institute	Myrtle Beach	T,B	Prop	M/W														9
ITT Technical Institute	North Charleston	T,B	Prop	M/W														8
Midlands Technical College	Columbia	C,T	St-L	M/W	12,078	53												
Spartanburg Community College	Spartanburg	C,T	St	M/W	5,871	47												39
Trident Technical College	Charleston	C,T	St-L	M/W	16,781	55	50		Y	Y	S	Y	Y	Y	Y	N		2
University of South Carolina Union	Union	C	St	M/W	500	50	33		N	Y	S	Y	Y			N	1	
South Dakota																		
Kilian Community College	Sioux Falls	C,T	Ind	M/W	335	88	61		Y	Y	Y	Y	Y	Y		N		16
Lake Area Technical Institute	Watertown	T	St	M/W	1,600				N	Y	Y	Y	Y	Y	Y	N	3	33
Mitchell Technical Institute	Mitchell	T	St	M/W	1,055	14	28		Y	Y	Y	Y	Y	Y	Y	Y	6	26
Southeast Technical Institute	Sioux Falls	T	St	M/W	2,507	24	27		N	Y	Y	Y	Y	Y	Y	Y	3	51
Western Dakota Technical Institute	Rapid City	T	St	M/W	1,045	18	51		Y	Y	Y	Y	Y	Y		N		11
Tennessee																		
Chattanooga State Community College	Chattanooga	C,T	St	M/W	10,438	54	41		Y	Y	R,S	Y	Y	Y	Y	N	3	26
Cleveland State Community College	Cleveland	C,T	St	M/W	3,814	44	39	39	Y	Y	Y	Y	Y	Y	Y	N	8	13
Dyersburg State Community College	Dyersburg	C,T	St	M/W	3,751	55	41	62	Y	Y	Y	Y	Y	Y	Y	N	4	13
Fountainhead College of Technology	Knoxville	C,T,B	Prop	M/W	219		64		Y	Y						N		10
ITT Technical Institute	Chattanooga	T,B	Prop	M/W												N		15
ITT Technical Institute	Cordova	T,B	Prop	M/W										Y	Y	N		10
ITT Technical Institute	Johnson City	T,B	Prop	M/W														16
ITT Technical Institute	Knoxville	T,B	Prop	M/W										Y		Y	N		18
ITT Technical Institute	Nashville	T,B	Prop	M/W										Y	Y		N		18
John A. Gupton College	Nashville	C,T	Ind	M/W	127	19												2
Kaplan Career Institute, Nashville Campus	Nashville	T	Prop	M/W										Y					7
Motlow State Community College	Tullahoma	C,T	St	M/W	4,910	57	28		Y	Y	Y	Y	Y	Y	Y	N	8	7
Nossi College of Art	Goodlettsville	C,B	Ind	M/W	660													
Volunteer State Community College	Gallatin	C,T	St	M/W	8,653	54	35		Y	Y	Y	Y	Y	Y	Y	N	3	17
Texas																		
Alvin Community College	Alvin	C,T	St-L	M/W	5,794	73	35		Y	Y	S	Y	Y	Y	Y	N	3	33
Amarillo College	Amarillo	C,T	St-L	M/W	11,456	67	36		Y		Y	Y	Y	Y	Y	N	5	83
Austin Community College	Austin	C,T	St-L	M/W	45,100		42		Y	Y	Y	Y	Y	Y	Y	N	5	90
Brookhaven College	Farmers Branch	C,T	Cou	M/W	13,705	79	50		Y	Y	Y			Y	Y	N	5	26
Brown Mackie College–San Antonio†	San Antonio	C,T,B	Prop	M/W														
Clarendon College	Clarendon	C,T	St-L	M/W	1,583													
Collin County Community College District	McKinney	C,T	St-L	M/W	27,069	62										N		1
Dallas Institute of Funeral Service	Dallas	C,T	Ind	M/W	141		52		Y	Y	Y		Y	Y				1
Eastfield College	Mesquite	C,T	St-L	M/W	12,403	76												
El Centro College	Dallas	C,T	Cou	M/W	10,581	77	49		Y	Y	S	Y	Y	Y	Y	N		37

This chart includes the names and locations of accredited two-year colleges in the United States, Canada, and other countries and shows institutions' responses to the *Peterson's Annual Survey of Undergraduate Institutions.* If an institution submitted incomplete data, one or more columns opposite the institution's name is blank. A dagger after the school name indicates that the institution has one or more entries in the *College Close-Ups* section. If a school does not appear, it did not report any of the information.

Y—Yes; N—No; R—Recommended; S—For Some

Degrees Awarded: College Transfer Associate (C); Terminal Associate (T); Bachelor's (B), Master's (M), Doctoral (D)
Institutional Control: County, District, City, State and Local State-Related; Independent, Independent-Religious, Proprietary, Territory; Federal, State, Commonwealth, Territory
Student Body: Men, Primarily Men, Women, Primarily Women, Coed

Name	City	Degrees	Control	Body	Enroll	%PT	%25+	%→4yr	HS Equiv	Open Adm	HS Transcript	Need Aid	PT Jobs	Career	Job Place	Housing	Sports	Majors
El Paso Community College	El Paso	C,T	Cou	M/W	30,723	61	30		Y	Y		Y	Y	Y	Y	N	10	65
Frank Phillips College	Borger	C,T	St-L	M/W	1,247	45												
Hallmark College of Technology	San Antonio	T,B	Prop	M/W	356													
Hallmark Institute of Aeronautics	San Antonio	T	Priv	M/W	227													
Houston Community College System	Houston	C,T	St-L	M/W	63,015	70	40		Y		S	Y	Y	Y	Y	N		61
ITT Technical Institute	Arlington	T,B	Prop	M/W							Y		Y	Y		N		11
ITT Technical Institute	Austin	T,B	Prop	M/W							Y	Y	Y	Y		N	N	11
ITT Technical Institute	DeSoto	T,B	Prop	M/W							Y		Y	Y		N		9
ITT Technical Institute	Houston	T,B	Prop	M/W							Y	Y	Y	Y		N		10
ITT Technical Institute	Houston	T,B	Prop	M/W							Y	Y	Y	Y		N	N	10
ITT Technical Institute	Richardson	T,B	Prop	M/W							Y	Y	Y	Y		N		13
ITT Technical Institute	San Antonio	T,B	Prop	M/W							Y	Y	Y	Y		N		11
ITT Technical Institute	Waco	T,B	Prop	M/W							Y		Y	Y		N		9
ITT Technical Institute	Webster	T,B	Prop	M/W							Y		Y	Y		N		10
Kaplan College, Arlington Campus	Arlington	T	Prop	M/W							Y					N		2
Kaplan College, Beaumont Campus	Beaumont	T	Prop	M/W														2
Kaplan College, Brownsville Campus	Brownsville	T	Prop	M/W														2
Kaplan College, Corpus Christi Campus	Corpus Christi	T	Prop	M/W														1
Kaplan College, Dallas Campus	Dallas	T	Prop	M/W							Y							2
Kaplan College, El Paso Campus	El Paso	T	Prop	M/W														2
Kaplan College, Fort Worth Campus	Fort Worth	T	Prop	M/W														1
Kaplan College, Laredo Campus	Laredo	T	Prop	M/W														1
Kaplan College, Lubbock Campus	Lubbock	T	Prop	M/W														1
Kaplan College, Midland Campus	Midland	T	Prop	M/W														1
Kaplan College, San Antonio Campus	San Antonio	T	Prop	M/W														2
Kaplan College, San Antonio–San Pedro Area Campus	San Antonio	T	Prop	M/W														2
KD Studio	Dallas	T	Prop	M/W	177		27		Y	Y	Y	Y		Y		N	Y	3
Kilgore College	Kilgore	C,T	St-L	M/W	6,391	53	34		Y	Y	Y	Y	Y	Y	N	Y	6	69
Lone Star College–CyFair	Cypress	C,T	St-L	M/W	18,107	73												
Lone Star College–Kingwood	Kingwood	C,T	St-L	M/W	10,879	77												
Lone Star College–Montgomery	Conroe	C,T	St-L	M/W	12,653	74												
Lone Star College–North Harris	Houston	C,T	St-L	M/W	16,356	80												
Lone Star College–Tomball	Tomball	C,T	St-L	M/W	11,344	80												
Mountain View College	Dallas	C,T	St-L	M/W	8,463													
Panola College	Carthage	C,T	St-L	M/W	2,562	56	34		Y	Y	R,S	Y	Y	Y	Y	Y	7	11
Pima Medical Institute	Houston		Prop	M/W														
St. Philip's College	San Antonio	C,T	Dist	M/W	10,710	79	51		Y	Y	Y	Y	Y	Y	Y	N	5	67
San Jacinto College District	Pasadena	C,T	St-L	M/W	29,392	68	30		Y	Y	Y		Y	Y	N	N	13	100
Tarrant County College District	Fort Worth	C,T	Cou	M/W	49,108	64	37		Y	Y			Y	Y	Y	N	6	42
Texarkana College	Texarkana	C,T	St-L	M/W	4,484		38		Y	Y	Y	Y	Y	Y	Y	Y	3	37
Texas School of Business, Friendswood Campus	Friendswood	T	Prop	M/W														1
Texas School of Business, Houston North Campus	Houston	T	Prop	M/W														1
Texas State Technical College Harlingen	Harlingen	C,T	St	M/W	5,807	61	31		Y	Y	Y	Y	Y	Y	Y	Y	11	39
Trinity Valley Community College	Athens	C,T	St-L	M/W	7,579	60												
Tyler Junior College	Tyler	C,T	St-L	M/W	11,540	50	29		Y	Y	Y	Y	Y	Y	Y	Y	9	58
Vet Tech Institute of Houston	Houston	T	Priv	M/W	348											N		1
Wade College	Dallas	C,T,B	Prop	PW	238													

Utah

Name	City	Degrees	Control	Body	Enroll	%PT	%25+	%→4yr	HS Equiv	Open Adm	HS Transcript	Need Aid	PT Jobs	Career	Job Place	Housing	Sports	Majors
ITT Technical Institute	Murray	T,B	Prop	M/W							Y		Y	Y		N		16
Salt Lake Community College	Salt Lake City	C,T	St	M/W	31,999	71	38		Y				Y	Y	Y	N	6	69
Snow College	Ephraim	C,T	St	M/W	4,465	34	12		Y				Y	Y	Y	Y	14	55

Vermont

Name	City	Degrees	Control	Body	Enroll	%PT	%25+	%→4yr	HS Equiv	Open Adm	HS Transcript	Need Aid	PT Jobs	Career	Job Place	Housing	Sports	Majors
Community College of Vermont	Montpelier	C,T	St	M/W	7,116		50	50	Y	Y		Y	Y	Y		N		25

Virginia

Name	City	Degrees	Control	Body	Enroll	%PT	%25+	%→4yr	HS Equiv	Open Adm	HS Transcript	Need Aid	PT Jobs	Career	Job Place	Housing	Sports	Majors
ACT College	Arlington	T	Prop	M/W	501		57		Y		R			Y	Y			5
Dabney S. Lancaster Community College	Clifton Forge	C,T	St	M/W	1,437	63												
ITT Technical Institute	Chantilly	T,B	Prop	M/W							Y		Y	Y		N		13
ITT Technical Institute	Norfolk	T,B	Prop	M/W							Y	Y	Y	Y		N	N	14
ITT Technical Institute	Richmond	T,B	Prop	M/W							Y		Y	Y		N		13
ITT Technical Institute	Salem	T,B	Prop	M/W							Y		Y	Y				13
ITT Technical Institute	Springfield	T,B	Prop	M/W							Y		Y	Y		N		14
John Tyler Community College	Chester	C,T	St	M/W	10,797	71	32		Y		R	Y	Y	Y	Y	N	N	28
J. Sargeant Reynolds Community College	Richmond	C,T	St	M/W	13,370	70			Y	Y	R	Y	Y	Y	Y	N		26
Kaplan College, Chesapeake Campus	Chesapeake	T	Prop	M/W														3
Mountain Empire Community College	Big Stone Gap	C,T	St	M/W	3,404													
Paul D. Camp Community College	Franklin	C,T	St	M/W	1,579													
Piedmont Virginia Community College	Charlottesville	C,T	St	M/W	5,683	79	29		Y		S	Y	Y	Y	Y	N	8	24
Southside Virginia Community College	Alberta	C,T	St	M/W	6,353	70												
Southwest Virginia Community College	Richlands	C,T	St	M/W	3,755	61	31		Y	Y		Y	Y	Y	Y	N	N	14
Virginia Western Community College	Roanoke	C,T	St	M/W	8,557	70	38		Y	Y		R,S	Y	Y	Y	N	4	25
Wytheville Community College	Wytheville	C,T	St	M/W	3,792		33		Y			R		Y	Y	N	N	21

Washington

Name	City	Degrees	Control	Body	Enroll	%PT	%25+	%→4yr	HS Equiv	Open Adm	HS Transcript	Need Aid	PT Jobs	Career	Job Place	Housing	Sports	Majors
The Art Institute of Seattle†	Seattle	T,B	Prop	M/W														14
Bellingham Technical College	Bellingham	C,T	St	M/W	2,864													
Big Bend Community College	Moses Lake	C,T	St	M/W	2,340	39			Y		S	Y	Y	Y	Y	N	4	14
Cascadia Community College	Bothell	C,T	St	M/W	2,697	54	0		Y							N	N	3
Clark College	Vancouver	C,T	St	M/W	12,744	50	38				S	Y				N	N	8	37

This chart includes the names and locations of accredited two-year colleges in the United States, Canada, and other countries and shows institutions' responses to the *Peterson's Annual Survey of Undergraduate Institutions*. If an institution submitted incomplete data, one or more columns opposite the institution's name is blank. A dagger after the school name indicates that the institution has one or more entries in the *College Close-Ups* section. If a school does not appear, it did not report any of the information.

Legend: Y—Yes; N—No; R—Recommended; S—For Some

Column headings (left to right): Degrees Awarded — College Transfer Associate (C), Terminal Associate (T), Bachelor's (B), Master's (M), Doctoral (D) | Institutional Control — County, District, City, State and Local, State-Related; Federal, State, Commonwealth, Territory; Independent, Independent-Religious, Proprietary | Student Body — Men, Primarily Men, Women, Primarily Women, Coed | Undergraduate Enrollment | Percent Attending Part-Time | Percent 25 Years of Age or Older | Percent of Grads Going on to Four-Year Colleges | High School Equivalency Certificate Accepted | High School Transcript Required | Open Admissions | Need-Based Aid Available | Part-Time Jobs Available | Career Counseling Available | Job Placement Services Available | College Housing Available | Number of Sports Offered | Number of Majors Offered

Institution	Location	Degrees	Control	Body	Enroll	% PT	% 25+	% Grad 4-yr	HS Equiv	HS Transcr	Open Adm	Need Aid	PT Jobs	Career	Job Place	Housing	Sports	Majors
Grays Harbor College	Aberdeen	C,T	St	M/W	2,526	37		51	Y			Y	Y	Y	Y	N	7	44
Highline Community College	Des Moines	C,T	St	M/W	6,743	42		51	Y									13
ITT Technical Institute	Everett	T,B	Prop	M/W						Y				Y	Y	N		17
ITT Technical Institute	Seattle	T,B	Prop	M/W					Y	Y				Y	Y	N		13
ITT Technical Institute	Spokane Valley	T,B	Prop	M/W					Y	Y				Y	Y	N		20
Lower Columbia College	Longview	C,T	St	M/W	4,252	39	55	55	Y	Y		R	Y	Y	Y	N	5	24
North Seattle Community College	Seattle	C,T	St	M/W	6,303	69	65		Y	Y		S	S	Y	Y	N	9	25
Olympic College	Bremerton	C,T,B	St	M/W	8,503		49		Y	Y		S	S	Y	Y	N	11	20
Peninsula College	Port Angeles	C,T,B	St	M/W	3,321													
Pima Medical Institute	Renton		Prop	M/W														
Pima Medical Institute	Seattle	T,B	Prop	M/W	357													
Wenatchee Valley College	Wenatchee	C,T	St-L	M/W	3,637													
Yakima Valley Community College	Yakima	C,T	St	M/W	4,479	38												
West Virginia																		
Blue Ridge Community and Technical College	Martinsburg	C,T	St	M/W	4,317	73	57		Y	Y	Y			Y	Y	N		15
ITT Technical Institute	Huntington	T	Prop	M/W										Y		N		10
Potomac State College of West Virginia University	Keyser	C,T,B	St	M/W	1,836	23			Y	Y		R	Y	Y	Y	N		8
West Virginia Junior College–Bridgeport	Bridgeport	C,T	Prop	M/W	514		30		Y	Y		R		S	Y	Y	N		22
West Virginia Northern Community College	Wheeling	C,T	St	M/W	2,994	52	51		Y	Y		S	Y	Y	Y	N	5	22
Wisconsin																		
Blackhawk Technical College	Janesville	C,T	Dist	M/W	3,278	57	59	0	Y	Y	Y	Y	Y		Y	N		24
Bryant & Stratton College - Milwaukee Campus	Milwaukee	T,B	Prop	M/W	828	44												28
Chippewa Valley Technical College	Eau Claire	C,T	Dist	M/W	6,058	52	43		Y	Y	S	Y	Y	Y	Y	N	6	44
Fox Valley Technical College	Appleton	C,T	St-L	M/W	10,873	73	50		Y	Y		Y	Y	Y	Y	N		51
Gateway Technical College	Kenosha	T	St-L	M/W	9,157	79	56		Y			Y		Y	Y	N		15
ITT Technical Institute	Green Bay	T,B	Prop	M/W						Y				Y		N		14
ITT Technical Institute	Greenfield	T,B	Prop	M/W						Y				Y		N		11
ITT Technical Institute	Madison	T	Prop	M/W										Y		N		1
Kaplan College, Milwaukee Campus	Milwaukee	T	Prop	M/W														
Moraine Park Technical College	Fond du Lac	C,T	Dist	M/W	6,734	82	69		Y	Y	Y	Y			Y	N		68
Rasmussen College Green Bay	Green Bay	C,T,B	Prop	M/W	649		77					Y			Y	N		22
University of Wisconsin–Fox Valley	Menasha	C,T	St	M/W	1,797	42						Y	Y	Y	Y	Y	9	2
University of Wisconsin–Richland	Richland Center	C	St	M/W	476	38	18					Y	Y	Y	Y			
University of Wisconsin–Sheboygan	Sheboygan	C	St	M/W													10	1
University of Wisconsin–Waukesha	Waukesha	C	St	M/W	2,234	49	28		N	Y		Y	Y	Y	Y	N		37
Waukesha County Technical College	Pewaukee	T	St-L	M/W	9,449	77	50		Y		Y					N		21
Wisconsin Indianhead Technical College	Shell Lake	T	Dist	M/W	3,718	58	60											
Wyoming																		
Casper College	Casper	C,T	St-L	M/W	4,306	51	40	40	Y	Y	Y	Y	Y	Y	Y	Y	10	99
Central Wyoming College	Riverton	C,T	St-L	M/W	2,242	59	42	54	Y	Y		R	Y	Y	Y	Y	15	62
Laramie County Community College	Cheyenne	C,T	Dist	M/W	4,527	51	40	64	Y	Y		R	S	Y	Y	Y	12	59
Northwest College	Powell	C,T	St-L	M/W	2,051	38	30		Y	Y		Y	Y	Y		Y	11	62
Sheridan College	Sheridan	C,T	St-L	M/W	3,940	63												
CANADA																		
Alberta																		
Southern Alberta Institute of Technology	Calgary	T,B	Prov	M/W	7,672	9												
OTHER COUNTRIES																		
Palau																		
Palau Community College	Koror	C,T	Terr	M/W	694	33			Y	Y		Y	Y	Y	Y	Y	7	14

Profiles
of Two-Year
Colleges

ALABAMA

Alabama Southern Community College
Monroeville, Alabama

Director of Admissions Ms. Jana S. Horton, Registrar, Alabama Southern Community College, PO Box 2000, Monroeville, AL 36461. *Phone:* 251-575-3156 Ext. 252. *E-mail:* jhorton@ascc.edu. *Web site:* http://www.ascc.edu/.

Bevill State Community College
Sumiton, Alabama

- **State-supported** 2-year, founded 1969, part of Alabama College System
- **Rural** 245-acre campus with easy access to Birmingham
- **Endowment** $142,934
- **Coed,** 4,704 undergraduate students, 57% full-time, 64% women, 36% men

Undergraduates 2,697 full-time, 2,007 part-time. 17% Black or African American, non-Hispanic/Latino; 1% Hispanic/Latino; 0.3% Asian, non-Hispanic/Latino; 0.3% American Indian or Alaska Native, non-Hispanic/Latino; 0.6% Two or more races, non-Hispanic/Latino; 2% Race/ethnicity unknown.
Freshmen *Admission:* 1,241 enrolled.
Faculty *Total:* 327, 35% full-time, 16% with terminal degrees.
Majors Administrative assistant and secretarial science; child-care and support services management; computer and information sciences; drafting and design technology; electrician; emergency medical technology (EMT paramedic); general studies; heating, ventilation, air conditioning and refrigeration engineering technology; industrial electronics technology; legal assistant/paralegal; liberal arts and sciences/liberal studies; registered nursing/registered nurse; tool and die technology.
Academics *Calendar:* semesters. *Degree:* certificates and associate. *Special study options:* academic remediation for entering students, adult/continuing education programs, advanced placement credit, cooperative education, honors programs, off-campus study, part-time degree program, services for LD students, summer session for credit.
Library 31,690 titles, 192 serial subscriptions, an OPAC, a Web page.
Student Life *Housing Options:* coed. Campus housing is university owned. *Activities and Organizations:* choral group, Student Government Association, Campus Ministries, Circle K, Outdoors men Club, Students Against Destructive Decisions. *Campus security:* 24-hour emergency response devices.
Financial Aid Of all full-time matriculated undergraduates who enrolled in 2010, 88 Federal Work-Study jobs (averaging $1807).
Applying *Options:* electronic application, early admission, deferred entrance. *Required:* high school transcript. *Application deadlines:* rolling (freshmen), rolling (transfers).
Freshman Application Contact Bevill State Community College, PO Box 800, Sumiton, AL 35148. *Phone:* 205-387-0511 Ext. 5813. *Toll-free phone:* 800-648-3271. *Web site:* http://www.bscc.edu/.

Bishop State Community College
Mobile, Alabama

Freshman Application Contact Bishop State Community College, 351 North Broad Street, Mobile, AL 36603-5898. *Phone:* 251-405-7000. *Toll-free phone:* 800-523-7235. *Web site:* http://bishop.edu/.

Brown Mackie College–Birmingham
Birmingham, Alabama

- **Proprietary** 4-year, part of Education Management Corporation
- **Coed**

Academics *Degrees:* diplomas, associate, and bachelor's.
Costs (2011–12) *Tuition:* Tuition varies by program. Students should contact Brown Mackie College for tuition information.
Freshman Application Contact Brown Mackie College–Birmingham, 105 Vulcan Road, Suite 400, Birmingham, AL 35209. *Phone:* 205-909-1500. *Toll-free phone:* 888-299-4699. *Web site:* http://www.brownmackie.edu/birmingham.

See page 344 for the College Close-Up.

Calhoun Community College
Decatur, Alabama

Freshman Application Contact Admissions Office, Calhoun Community College, PO Box 2216, Decatur, AL 35609-2216. *Phone:* 256-306-2593. *Toll-free phone:* 800-626-3628. *Fax:* 256-306-2941. *E-mail:* admissions@calhoun.edu. *Web site:* http://www.calhoun.edu/.

Central Alabama Community College
Alexander City, Alabama

Freshman Application Contact Ms. Donna Whaley, Central Alabama Community College, 1675 Cherokee Road, Alexander City, AL 35011-0699. *Phone:* 256-234-6346 Ext. 6232. *Toll-free phone:* 800-634-2657. *Web site:* http://www.cacc.edu/.

Chattahoochee Valley Community College
Phenix City, Alabama

- **State-supported** 2-year, founded 1974, part of Alabama College System
- **Small-town** 103-acre campus
- **Coed,** 1,697 undergraduate students, 56% full-time, 64% women, 36% men

Undergraduates 944 full-time, 753 part-time. 42% Black or African American, non-Hispanic/Latino; 4% Hispanic/Latino; 1% Asian, non-Hispanic/Latino; 0.2% Native Hawaiian or other Pacific Islander, non-Hispanic/Latino; 0.5% American Indian or Alaska Native, non-Hispanic/Latino; 0.6% Two or more races, non-Hispanic/Latino; 2% Race/ethnicity unknown; 16% transferred in. *Retention:* 54% of full-time freshmen returned.
Freshmen *Admission:* 405 applied, 405 admitted, 405 enrolled.
Faculty *Total:* 124, 28% full-time. *Student/faculty ratio:* 20:1.
Majors Accounting; administrative assistant and secretarial science; business administration and management; computer and information sciences; criminal justice/police science; design and visual communications; fire services administration; general studies; homeland security, law enforcement, firefighting and protective services related; liberal arts and sciences/liberal studies; medical/clinical assistant; music history, literature, and theory; registered nursing/registered nurse.
Academics *Calendar:* semesters. *Degree:* certificates and associate. *Special study options:* academic remediation for entering students, adult/continuing education programs, advanced placement credit, distance learning, honors programs, off-campus study, part-time degree program, services for LD students, student-designed majors, summer session for credit.
Library Estelle Bain Owens Learning Resource Center and Library with 56,307 titles, 88 serial subscriptions, a Web page.
Student Life *Housing:* college housing not available. *Activities and Organizations:* drama/theater group, choral group. *Campus security:* 24-hour emergency response devices and patrols. *Student services:* personal/psychological counseling.
Athletics Member NJCAA. *Intercollegiate sports:* baseball M, basketball M/W, softball W.
Financial Aid Of all full-time matriculated undergraduates who enrolled in 2010, 1,258 were judged to have need. 46 Federal Work-Study jobs (averaging $2233).
Applying *Options:* early admission. *Required:* high school transcript. *Application deadlines:* rolling (freshmen), rolling (transfers). *Notification:* continuous (freshmen), continuous (transfers).
Freshman Application Contact Chattahoochee Valley Community College, 2602 College Drive, Phenix City, AL 36869-7928. *Phone:* 334-291-4929. *Web site:* http://www.cv.edu/.

Community College of the Air Force
Maxwell Air Force Base, Alabama

Freshman Application Contact C.M. Sgt. Robert McAlexander, Director of Admissions/Registrar, Community College of the Air Force, 130 West Maxwell Boulevard, Building 836, Maxwell Air Force Base, Maxwell AFB, AL 36112-6613. *Phone:* 334-953-6436. *Fax:* 334-953-8211. *E-mail:* ronald.hall@maxwell.af.mil. *Web site:* http://www.au.af.mil/au/ccaf/.

Enterprise State Community College

Enterprise, Alabama

Director of Admissions Mr. Gary Deas, Associate Dean of Students/Registrar, Enterprise State Community College, PO Box 1300, Enterprise, AL 36331-1300. *Phone:* 334-347-2623 Ext. 2233. *E-mail:* gdeas@eocc.edu. *Web site:* http://www.escc.edu/.

Gadsden State Community College

Gadsden, Alabama

- **State-supported** 2-year, founded 1965, part of Alabama Community College System
- **Small-town** 275-acre campus with easy access to Birmingham
- **Coed,** 6,733 undergraduate students, 58% full-time, 62% women, 38% men

Undergraduates 3,926 full-time, 2,807 part-time. Students come from 17 states and territories; 60 other countries; 1% are from out of state; 22% Black or African American, non-Hispanic/Latino; 3% Hispanic/Latino; 0.9% Asian, non-Hispanic/Latino; 0.1% Native Hawaiian or other Pacific Islander, non-Hispanic/Latino; 0.4% American Indian or Alaska Native, non-Hispanic/Latino; 1% Two or more races, non-Hispanic/Latino; 0.8% Race/ethnicity unknown; 61% transferred in; 2% live on campus.

Freshmen *Admission:* 3,696 enrolled.

Faculty *Total:* 357, 43% full-time. *Student/faculty ratio:* 18:1.

Majors Accounting technology and bookkeeping; administrative assistant and secretarial science; child-care and support services management; civil engineering technology; clinical/medical laboratory technology; communication and journalism related; computer and information sciences; court reporting; criminal justice/police science; drafting and design technology; electrical, electronic and communications engineering technology; emergency medical technology (EMT paramedic); general studies; heating, ventilation, air conditioning and refrigeration engineering technology; industrial mechanics and maintenance technology; legal assistant/paralegal; liberal arts and sciences/liberal studies; manufacturing engineering technology; radiologic technology/science; registered nursing/registered nurse; sales, distribution, and marketing operations; substance abuse/addiction counseling; tool and die technology.

Academics *Calendar:* semesters. *Degree:* certificates and associate. *Special study options:* academic remediation for entering students, adult/continuing education programs, advanced placement credit, cooperative education, distance learning, English as a second language, external degree program, honors programs, internships, part-time degree program, services for LD students, study abroad, summer session for credit. *ROTC:* Army (b).

Library Meadows Library with 115,901 titles, 144 serial subscriptions, 7,080 audiovisual materials, an OPAC, a Web page.

Student Life *Housing Options:* coed. Campus housing is university owned. *Activities and Organizations:* drama/theater group, choral group, National Society of Leadership and Success, Student Government Association, Circle K, International Club, Cardinal Spirit Club. *Campus security:* 24-hour patrols. *Student services:* personal/psychological counseling.

Athletics Member NJCAA. *Intercollegiate sports:* baseball M(s), basketball M(s)/W(s), softball W(s), tennis M(s), volleyball W(s).

Costs (2011–12) *Tuition:* state resident $3852 full-time, $107 per credit hour part-time; nonresident $7704 full-time, $214 per credit hour part-time. Full-time tuition and fees vary according to reciprocity agreements. Part-time tuition and fees vary according to reciprocity agreements. *Required fees:* $684 full-time, $19 per credit hour part-time. *Room and board:* $3200. *Waivers:* minority students, adult students, senior citizens, and employees or children of employees.

Applying *Options:* early admission, deferred entrance. *Required:* high school transcript. *Application deadlines:* rolling (freshmen), rolling (transfers).

Freshman Application Contact Mrs. Jennie Dobson, Admissions and Records, Gadsden State Community College, Allen Hall, Gadsden, AL 35902-0227. *Phone:* 256-549-8210. *Toll-free phone:* 800-226-5563. *Fax:* 256-549-8205. *E-mail:* info@gadsdenstate.edu. *Web site:* http://www.gadsdenstate.edu/.

George Corley Wallace State Community College

Selma, Alabama

Director of Admissions Ms. Sunette Newman, Registrar, George Corley Wallace State Community College, PO Box 2530, Selma, AL 36702. *Phone:* 334-876-9305. *Web site:* http://www.wccs.edu/.

George C. Wallace Community College

Dothan, Alabama

Freshman Application Contact Mr. Keith Saulsberry, Director, Enrollment Services/Registrar, George C. Wallace Community College, 1141 Wallace Drive, Dothan, AL 36303. *Phone:* 334-983-3521 Ext. 2470. *Toll-free phone:* 800-543-2426. *Fax:* 334-983-3600. *E-mail:* ksaulsberry@wallace.edu. *Web site:* http://www.wallace.edu/.

H. Councill Trenholm State Technical College

Montgomery, Alabama

- **State-supported** 2-year, founded 1962, part of Alabama Department of Postsecondary Education
- **Urban** 81-acre campus
- **Coed,** 1,721 undergraduate students

Undergraduates Students come from 2 states and territories; 1% are from out of state; 62% Black or African American, non-Hispanic/Latino; 0.6% Hispanic/Latino; 0.8% Asian, non-Hispanic/Latino; 0.3% American Indian or Alaska Native, non-Hispanic/Latino; 0.1% Two or more races, non-Hispanic/Latino; 1% Race/ethnicity unknown. *Retention:* 50% of full-time freshmen returned.

Freshmen *Admission:* 1,133 applied, 545 admitted.

Faculty *Total:* 134, 51% full-time, 5% with terminal degrees. *Student/faculty ratio:* 10:1.

Majors Accounting technology and bookkeeping; administrative assistant and secretarial science; automotive engineering technology; child-care and support services management; computer and information sciences; culinary arts; dental assisting; diagnostic medical sonography and ultrasound technology; drafting and design technology; electrician; emergency medical technology (EMT paramedic); graphic and printing equipment operation/production; heating, ventilation, air conditioning and refrigeration engineering technology; industrial electronics technology; industrial mechanics and maintenance technology; machine tool technology; manufacturing engineering technology; medical/clinical assistant; physical therapy technology; radiologic technology/science.

Academics *Calendar:* semesters. *Degree:* certificates, diplomas, and associate. *Special study options:* academic remediation for entering students, adult/continuing education programs, advanced placement credit, cooperative education, distance learning, external degree program, independent study, internships, part-time degree program, services for LD students, summer session for credit.

Library Trenholm State Learning Resources plus 1 other with 61,245 titles, 9,135 serial subscriptions, 1,097 audiovisual materials, an OPAC, a Web page.

Student Life *Housing:* college housing not available. *Activities and Organizations:* student-run newspaper, Student Government Association, College Ambassadors, Photography Club, Skills USA - VICA, Student Leadership Academy. *Campus security:* 24-hour emergency response devices and patrols, late-night transport/escort service. *Student services:* personal/psychological counseling.

Standardized Tests *Required for some:* ACT (for admission).

Costs (2012–13) *Tuition:* state resident $2784 full-time, $116 per unit part-time; nonresident $5568 full-time, $232 per unit part-time. *Required fees:* $456 full-time, $19 per unit part-time. *Waivers:* senior citizens and employees or children of employees.

Applying *Options:* early admission. *Required:* high school transcript. *Application deadlines:* rolling (freshmen), rolling (out-of-state freshmen), rolling (transfers).

Freshman Application Contact Mrs. Tennie McBryde, Registrar, H. Councill Trenholm State Technical College, Montgomery, AL 36108. *Phone:* 334-420-4306. *Toll-free phone:* 866-753-4544. *Fax:* 334-420-4201. *E-mail:* tmcbryde@trenholmstate.edu. *Web site:* http://www.trenholmstate.edu/.

ITT Technical Institute

Bessemer, Alabama

- **Proprietary** primarily 2-year, founded 1994, part of ITT Educational Services, Inc.
- **Suburban** campus
- **Coed**

Majors Business administration and management; communications technology; computer and information systems security; computer software and media applications related; computer software engineering; computer software technology; construction management; criminal justice/law enforcement administration; drafting and design technology; electrical, electronic and communications engineering technology; forensic science and technology; game and interactive media design; graphic communications; legal assistant/

paralegal; network and system administration; project management; registered nursing/registered nurse.

Academics *Calendar:* quarters. *Degrees:* associate and bachelor's.

Student Life *Housing:* college housing not available. *Campus security:* 24-hour emergency response devices.

Freshman Application Contact Director of Recruitment, ITT Technical Institute, 6270 Park South Drive, Bessemer, AL 35022. *Phone:* 205-497-5700. *Toll-free phone:* 800-488-7033. *Web site:* http://www.itt-tech.edu/.

ITT Technical Institute
Madison, Alabama

- **Proprietary** primarily 2-year, part of ITT Educational Services, Inc.
- **Coed**

Majors Business administration and management; communications technology; computer and information systems security; computer software technology; criminal justice/law enforcement administration; drafting and design technology; electrical, electronic and communications engineering technology; forensic science and technology; graphic communications; legal assistant/paralegal; network and system administration; project management; registered nursing/registered nurse.

Academics *Degrees:* associate and bachelor's.

Student Life *Housing:* college housing not available.

Freshman Application Contact Director of Recruitment, ITT Technical Institute, 9238 Madison Boulevard, Suite 500, Madison, AL 35758. *Phone:* 256-542-2900. *Toll-free phone:* 877-628-5960. *Web site:* http://www.itt-tech.edu/.

ITT Technical Institute
Mobile, Alabama

- **Proprietary** primarily 2-year, part of ITT Educational Services, Inc.
- **Coed**

Majors Business administration and management; communications technology; computer and information systems security; construction management; criminal justice/law enforcement administration; drafting and design technology; electrical, electronic and communications engineering technology; forensic science and technology; graphic communications; legal assistant/paralegal; network and system administration; project management; registered nursing/registered nurse.

Academics *Degrees:* associate and bachelor's.

Student Life *Housing:* college housing not available.

Freshman Application Contact Director of Recruitment, ITT Technical Institute, Office Mall South, 3100 Cottage Hill Road, Building 3, Mobile, AL 36606. *Phone:* 251-472-4760. *Toll-free phone:* 877-327-1013. *Web site:* http://www.itt-tech.edu/.

James H. Faulkner State Community College
Bay Minette, Alabama

Freshman Application Contact Ms. Carmelita Mikkelsen, Director of Admissions and High School Relations, James H. Faulkner State Community College, 1900 Highway 31 South, Bay Minette, AL 36507. *Phone:* 251-580-2213. *Toll-free phone:* 800-231-3752. *Fax:* 251-580-2285. *E-mail:* cmikkelsen@faulknerstate.edu. *Web site:* http://www.faulknerstate.edu/.

Jefferson Davis Community College
Brewton, Alabama

Director of Admissions Ms. Robin Sessions, Registrar, Jefferson Davis Community College, PO Box 958, Brewton, AL 36427-0958. *Phone:* 251-867-4832. *Web site:* http://www.jdcc.edu/.

Jefferson State Community College
Birmingham, Alabama

- **State-supported** 2-year, founded 1965, part of Alabama Community College System
- **Suburban** 351-acre campus
- **Coed,** 9,460 undergraduate students, 37% full-time, 60% women, 40% men

Undergraduates 3,516 full-time, 5,944 part-time. Students come from 35 states and territories; 70 other countries; 2% are from out of state; 23% Black or African American, non-Hispanic/Latino; 3% Hispanic/Latino; 2% Asian, non-Hispanic/Latino; 0.1% Native Hawaiian or other Pacific Islander, non-Hispanic/Latino; 0.2% American Indian or Alaska Native, non-Hispanic/

Latino; 2% Two or more races, non-Hispanic/Latino; 0.8% international; 10% transferred in.

Freshmen *Admission:* 4,046 applied, 4,046 admitted, 1,860 enrolled. *Average high school GPA:* 2.79.

Faculty *Total:* 405, 32% full-time, 14% with terminal degrees. *Student/faculty ratio:* 26:1.

Majors Accounting technology and bookkeeping; administrative assistant and secretarial science; child-care and support services management; clinical/medical laboratory technology; computer and information sciences; construction engineering technology; criminal justice/police science; emergency medical technology (EMT paramedic); engineering technology; fire services administration; funeral service and mortuary science; general studies; hospitality administration; liberal arts and sciences/liberal studies; office management; physical therapy technology; radiologic technology/science; registered nursing/registered nurse; veterinary/animal health technology.

Academics *Calendar:* semesters. *Degree:* certificates and associate. *Special study options:* academic remediation for entering students, adult/continuing education programs, advanced placement credit, distance learning, English as a second language, honors programs, independent study, internships, part-time degree program, services for LD students, summer session for credit. *ROTC:* Army (c), Air Force (c).

Library Jefferson State Libraries plus 4 others with 135,893 titles, 290 serial subscriptions, 1,505 audiovisual materials, an OPAC, a Web page.

Student Life *Housing:* college housing not available. *Activities and Organizations:* drama/theater group, student-run newspaper, radio station, choral group, Student Government Association, Phi Theta Kappa, Sigma Kappa Delta, Jefferson State Ambassadors, Students in Free Enterprise (SIFE). *Campus security:* 24-hour patrols.

Costs (2011–12) *Tuition:* state resident $3690 full-time, $123 per semester hour part-time; nonresident $6450 full-time, $215 per semester hour part-time. Full-time tuition and fees vary according to course load. Part-time tuition and fees vary according to course load. *Waivers:* senior citizens and employees or children of employees.

Financial Aid Of all full-time matriculated undergraduates who enrolled in 2010, 189 Federal Work-Study jobs (averaging $1926).

Applying *Options:* electronic application, early admission, early action, deferred entrance. *Required for some:* high school transcript. *Application deadline:* rolling (freshmen). *Notification:* continuous (freshmen), continuous (transfers).

Freshman Application Contact Mrs. Lillian Owens, Director of Admissions and Retention, Jefferson State Community College, 2601 Carson Road, Birmingham, AL 35215-3098. *Phone:* 205-853-1200 Ext. 7990. *Toll-free phone:* 800-239-5900. *Fax:* 205-856-6070. *E-mail:* lowens@jeffstateonline.com. *Web site:* http://www.jeffstateonline.com/.

J. F. Drake State Technical College
Huntsville, Alabama

Freshman Application Contact Mrs. Monica Sudeall, Registrar, J. F. Drake State Technical College, Huntsville, AL 35811. *Phone:* 256-539-8161. *Toll-free phone:* 888-413-7253. *Fax:* 256-551-3142. *E-mail:* sudeall@drakestate.edu. *Web site:* http://www.drakestate.edu/.

Lawson State Community College
Birmingham, Alabama

- **State-supported** 2-year, founded 1949, part of Alabama Community College System
- **Urban** 30-acre campus
- **Coed,** 4,208 undergraduate students, 61% full-time, 61% women, 39% men

Undergraduates 2,579 full-time, 1,626 part-time. Students come from 11 states and territories; 1% are from out of state; 77% Black or African American, non-Hispanic/Latino; 1% Hispanic/Latino; 0.4% Asian, non-Hispanic/Latino; 0.1% Native Hawaiian or other Pacific Islander, non-Hispanic/Latino; 0.1% American Indian or Alaska Native, non-Hispanic/Latino; 0.5% Two or more races, non-Hispanic/Latino; 8% Race/ethnicity unknown; 0.2% international; 6% transferred in; 1% live on campus. *Retention:* 55% of full-time freshmen returned.

Freshmen *Admission:* 1,637 applied, 1,354 admitted, 1,079 enrolled.

Faculty *Total:* 252, 38% full-time. *Student/faculty ratio:* 19:1.

Majors Accounting technology and bookkeeping; administrative assistant and secretarial science; automotive engineering technology; building/construction finishing, management, and inspection related; business administration and management; child-care and support services management; computer and information sciences; criminal justice/police science; drafting and design technology; general studies; industrial electronics technology; liberal arts and sciences/liberal studies; registered nursing/registered nurse; social work.

Academics *Calendar:* semesters. *Degree:* certificates and associate. *Special study options:* academic remediation for entering students, adult/continuing education programs, advanced placement credit, cooperative education, distance learning, internships, part-time degree program, services for LD students, summer session for credit.

Library Lawson State Library with 50,859 titles, 253 serial subscriptions, an OPAC.

Student Life *Housing Options:* coed. Campus housing is university owned. *Activities and Organizations:* choral group, Student Government Association, Phi Theta Kappa, Kappa Beta Delta Honor Society, Phi Beta Lambda, Social Work Club. *Campus security:* 24-hour emergency response devices and patrols, controlled dormitory access. *Student services:* personal/psychological counseling.

Athletics Member NJCAA. *Intercollegiate sports:* baseball M, basketball M/W, volleyball W. *Intramural sports:* weight lifting M.

Costs (2012–13) *Tuition:* state resident $3240 full-time, $108 per credit hour part-time; nonresident $6480 full-time, $216 per credit hour part-time. *Required fees:* $850 full-time, $28 per credit hour part-time. *Room and board:* $4000; room only: $3000. *Payment plan:* installment. *Waivers:* senior citizens and employees or children of employees.

Financial Aid Of all full-time matriculated undergraduates who enrolled in 2010, 91 Federal Work-Study jobs (averaging $3000).

Applying *Options:* electronic application. *Required:* high school transcript. *Application deadlines:* rolling (freshmen), rolling (transfers). *Notification:* continuous (freshmen), continuous (transfers).

Freshman Application Contact Mr. Jeff Shelley, Director of Admissions and Records, Lawson State Community College, 3060 Wilson Road, SW, Birmingham, AL 35221-1798. *Phone:* 205-929-6361. *Fax:* 205-923-7106. *E-mail:* jshelley@lawsonstate.edu. *Web site:* http://www.lawsonstate.edu/.

Lurleen B. Wallace Community College

Andalusia, Alabama

- **State-supported** 2-year, founded 1969, part of Alabama College System
- **Small-town** 200-acre campus
- **Coed,** 1,779 undergraduate students, 59% full-time, 66% women, 34% men

Undergraduates 1,052 full-time, 727 part-time. 4% are from out of state; 23% Black or African American, non-Hispanic/Latino; 1% Hispanic/Latino; 0.7% Asian, non-Hispanic/Latino; 0.3% American Indian or Alaska Native, non-Hispanic/Latino; 0.8% Two or more races, non-Hispanic/Latino; 0.3% Race/ethnicity unknown. *Retention:* 52% of full-time freshmen returned.

Freshmen *Admission:* 437 enrolled.

Faculty *Total:* 120, 46% full-time, 5% with terminal degrees. *Student/faculty ratio:* 15:1.

Majors Accounting technology and bookkeeping; administrative assistant and secretarial science; child-care and support services management; computer and information sciences; drafting and design technology; electrician; emergency medical technology (EMT paramedic); forest technology; general studies; industrial electronics technology; liberal arts and sciences/liberal studies; registered nursing/registered nurse.

Academics *Calendar:* semesters. *Degree:* certificates, diplomas, and associate. *Special study options:* part-time degree program.

Library Lurleen B. Wallace Library plus 2 others with an OPAC, a Web page.

Student Life *Housing:* college housing not available. *Activities and Organizations:* drama/theater group, choral group. *Student services:* personal/psychological counseling.

Athletics Member NJCAA. *Intercollegiate sports:* baseball M(s), basketball M(s)/W(s), softball W(s).

Costs (2012–13) *Tuition:* state resident $3270 full-time, $109 per credit hour part-time; nonresident $6540 full-time, $218 per credit hour part-time. Full-time tuition and fees vary according to course load. Part-time tuition and fees vary according to course load. *Required fees:* $690 full-time. *Waivers:* senior citizens and employees or children of employees.

Financial Aid Of all full-time matriculated undergraduates who enrolled in 2010, 903 were judged to have need.

Applying *Required:* high school transcript. *Application deadlines:* rolling (freshmen), rolling (transfers).

Freshman Application Contact Lurleen B. Wallace Community College, PO Box 1418, Andalusia, AL 36420-1418. *Phone:* 334-881-2273. *Web site:* http://www.lbwcc.edu/.

Marion Military Institute

Marion, Alabama

Director of Admissions Director of Admissions, Marion Military Institute, 1101 Washington Street, Marion, AL 36756. *Phone:* 800-664-1842 Ext. 306. *Toll-free phone:* 800-664-1842. *Web site:* http://www.marionmilitary.edu/.

Northeast Alabama Community College

Rainsville, Alabama

- **State-supported** 2-year, founded 1963, part of Alabama Community College System
- **Rural** 117-acre campus
- **Coed,** 3,294 undergraduate students, 55% full-time, 61% women, 39% men

Undergraduates 1,805 full-time, 1,489 part-time. 2% Black or African American, non-Hispanic/Latino; 4% Hispanic/Latino; 0.4% Asian, non-Hispanic/Latino; 0.1% Native Hawaiian or other Pacific Islander, non-Hispanic/Latino; 3% American Indian or Alaska Native, non-Hispanic/Latino; 0.3% Two or more races, non-Hispanic/Latino; 0.4% international. *Retention:* 58% of full-time freshmen returned.

Freshmen *Admission:* 774 enrolled.

Faculty *Total:* 177, 33% full-time. *Student/faculty ratio:* 24:1.

Majors Administrative assistant and secretarial science; business administration and management; business/commerce; child-care and support services management; computer and information sciences; drafting and design technology; emergency medical technology (EMT paramedic); industrial electronics technology; industrial mechanics and maintenance technology; medical/clinical assistant; registered nursing/registered nurse.

Academics *Calendar:* quarters. *Degree:* certificates and associate. *Special study options:* academic remediation for entering students, accelerated degree program, adult/continuing education programs, advanced placement credit, distance learning, double majors, English as a second language, honors programs, part-time degree program, services for LD students, summer session for credit.

Library Cecil B. Word Learning Resources Center with 62,648 titles, 115 serial subscriptions, an OPAC.

Student Life *Housing:* college housing not available. *Activities and Organizations:* drama/theater group, choral group. *Campus security:* 24-hour emergency response devices and patrols, late-night transport/escort service. *Student services:* personal/psychological counseling.

Costs (2012–13) *Tuition:* state resident $3210 full-time, $107 per semester hour part-time; nonresident $6420 full-time, $214 per semester hour part-time. *Required fees:* $720 full-time, $24 per semester hour part-time. *Waivers:* senior citizens and employees or children of employees.

Financial Aid Of all full-time matriculated undergraduates who enrolled in 2010, 40 Federal Work-Study jobs (averaging $2500).

Applying *Application deadlines:* rolling (freshmen), rolling (transfers). *Notification:* continuous (freshmen), continuous (transfers).

Freshman Application Contact Northeast Alabama Community College, PO Box 159, Rainsville, AL 35986-0159. *Phone:* 256-228-6001 Ext. 2325. *Web site:* http://www.nacc.edu/.

Northwest-Shoals Community College

Muscle Shoals, Alabama

- **State-supported** 2-year, founded 1963, part of Alabama Department of Postsecondary Education
- **Small-town** 210-acre campus
- **Coed,** 3,939 undergraduate students, 53% full-time, 56% women, 44% men

Undergraduates 2,081 full-time, 1,858 part-time. Students come from 6 states and territories; 2 other countries; 3% are from out of state; 11% Black or African American, non-Hispanic/Latino; 3% Hispanic/Latino; 0.3% Asian, non-Hispanic/Latino; 0.5% American Indian or Alaska Native, non-Hispanic/Latino; 0.4% Two or more races, non-Hispanic/Latino; 0.2% Race/ethnicity unknown; 0.1% international; 7% transferred in.

Freshmen *Admission:* 1,674 applied, 1,674 admitted, 893 enrolled.

Faculty *Total:* 233, 36% full-time, 6% with terminal degrees. *Student/faculty ratio:* 20:1.

Majors Administrative assistant and secretarial science; child-care and support services management; child development; computer and information sciences; criminal justice/police science; drafting and design technology; emergency medical technology (EMT paramedic); environmental engineering technology; general studies; industrial electronics technology; industrial mechanics and maintenance technology; liberal arts and sciences/liberal studies; multi/interdisciplinary studies related; registered nursing/registered nurse.

Academics *Calendar:* semesters. *Degree:* certificates and associate. *Special study options:* academic remediation for entering students, accelerated degree program, adult/continuing education programs, advanced placement credit, cooperative education, distance learning, honors programs, independent study, part-time degree program, services for LD students, summer session for credit.

Library Larry W. McCoy Learning Resource Center and James Glasgow Library with 71,360 titles, 50 serial subscriptions, 1,499 audiovisual materials, an OPAC.

Student Life *Housing:* college housing not available. *Activities and Organizations:* choral group, Student Government Association, Science Club, Phi Theta Kappa, Baptist Campus Ministry, Northwest-Shoals Singers. *Campus security:* 24-hour emergency response devices and patrols. *Student services:* personal/psychological counseling.

Athletics *Intramural sports:* basketball M/W, softball M/W, table tennis M/W, tennis M/W.

Standardized Tests *Required:* COMPASS Placement Test for English and Math (for admission).

Costs (2012–13) *Tuition:* state resident $3270 full-time, $109 per credit hour part-time; nonresident $6540 full-time, $218 per credit hour part-time. Full-time tuition and fees vary according to program. Part-time tuition and fees vary according to program. *Required fees:* $810 full-time, $27 per credit hour part-time. *Waivers:* senior citizens and employees or children of employees.

Financial Aid Of all full-time matriculated undergraduates who enrolled in 2011, 46 Federal Work-Study jobs (averaging $1616). *Financial aid deadline:* 6/1.

Applying *Options:* electronic application. *Required:* high school transcript. *Application deadlines:* rolling (freshmen), rolling (transfers). *Notification:* continuous (transfers).

Freshman Application Contact Mr. Charles Taylor, Associate Dean of Student Development Services, Northwest-Shoals Community College, PO Box 2545, Muscle Shoals, AL 35662. *Phone:* 256-331-5462. *Toll-free phone:* 800-645-8967. *Fax:* 256-331-5366. *E-mail:* taylor@nwscc.edu. *Web site:* http://www.nwscc.edu/.

Prince Institute of Professional Studies

Montgomery, Alabama

- **Proprietary** 2-year, founded 1976
- **Suburban** campus
- **Coed, primarily women**

Undergraduates *Retention:* 100% of full-time freshmen returned.

Faculty *Student/faculty ratio:* 13:1.

Academics *Calendar:* quarters. *Degree:* certificates and associate.

Costs (2011–12) *Tuition:* $2800 full-time. *Required fees:* $295 full-time.

Financial Aid Of all full-time matriculated undergraduates who enrolled in 2009, 88 applied for aid, 88 were judged to have need. *Average percent of need met:* 72. *Average financial aid package:* $3101.

Applying *Options:* electronic application. *Application fee:* $125. *Required:* high school transcript, interview.

Freshman Application Contact Kellie Brescia, Director of Admissions, Prince Institute of Professional Studies, 7735 Atlanta Highway, Montgomery, AL 35117. *Phone:* 334-271-1670. *Toll-free phone:* 877-853-5569. *Fax:* 334-271-1671. *E-mail:* admissions@princeinstitute.edu. *Web site:* http://www.princeinstitute.edu/.

Reid State Technical College

Evergreen, Alabama

- **State-supported** 2-year, founded 1966, part of Alabama Community College System
- **Rural** 26-acre campus
- **Coed,** 699 undergraduate students, 70% full-time, 61% women, 39% men

Undergraduates 491 full-time, 208 part-time. Students come from 2 states and territories; 1% are from out of state; 59% Black or African American, non-Hispanic/Latino; 0.6% Hispanic/Latino; 0.3% Asian, non-Hispanic/Latino; 0.1% Native Hawaiian or other Pacific Islander, non-Hispanic/Latino; 0.9% American Indian or Alaska Native, non-Hispanic/Latino; 0.3% Race/ethnicity unknown.

Freshmen *Admission:* 122 applied, 122 admitted, 122 enrolled.

Faculty *Total:* 37, 73% full-time, 11% with terminal degrees. *Student/faculty ratio:* 12:1.

Majors Administrative assistant and secretarial science; child-care and support services management; electrical, electronic and communications engineering technology.

Academics *Calendar:* semesters. *Degree:* certificates, diplomas, and associate. *Special study options:* academic remediation for entering students, adult/continuing education programs, double majors, independent study, internships, part-time degree program, services for LD students, summer session for credit.

Library Edith A. Gray Library with 4,157 titles, 99 serial subscriptions, 298 audiovisual materials, a Web page.

Student Life *Housing:* college housing not available. *Activities and Organizations:* Student Government Association, Phi Beta Lambda, National Vocational-Technical Society, Ambassadors, Who's Who. *Campus security:* 24-hour emergency response devices, day and evening security guard. *Student services:* personal/psychological counseling.

Costs (2012–13) *Tuition:* state resident $3210 full-time, $112 per credit hour part-time; nonresident $6420 full-time, $224 per credit hour part-time. Full-time tuition and fees vary according to course load and program. Part-time tuition and fees vary according to course load and program. *Required fees:* $900 full-time, $30 per credit hour part-time. *Waivers:* senior citizens and employees or children of employees.

Financial Aid Of all full-time matriculated undergraduates who enrolled in 2010, 35 Federal Work-Study jobs (averaging $1500).

Applying *Options:* early admission. *Required:* high school transcript. *Application deadlines:* rolling (freshmen), rolling (transfers).

Freshman Application Contact Dr. Alesia Stuart, Public Relations/Marketing/Associate Dean of Workforce Development, Reid State Technical College, Evergreen, AL 36401-0588. *Phone:* 251-578-1313 Ext. 108. *E-mail:* akstuart@rstc.edu. *Web site:* http://www.rstc.edu/.

Remington College–Mobile Campus

Mobile, Alabama

Freshman Application Contact Remington College–Mobile Campus, 828 Downtowner Loop West, Mobile, AL 36609-5404. *Phone:* 251-343-8200. *Toll-free phone:* 800-560-6192. *Web site:* http://www.remingtoncollege.edu/.

Shelton State Community College

Tuscaloosa, Alabama

Freshman Application Contact Ms. Loretta Jones, Assistant to the Dean of Students, Shelton State Community College, 9500 Old Greensboro Road, Tuscaloosa, AL 35405. *Phone:* 205-391-2236. *Fax:* 205-391-3910. *Web site:* http://www.sheltonstate.edu/.

Snead State Community College

Boaz, Alabama

Freshman Application Contact Dr. Greg Chapman, Director of Instruction, Snead State Community College, PO Box 734, Boaz, AL 35957-0734. *Phone:* 256-840-4111. *Fax:* 256-593-7180. *E-mail:* gchapman@snead.edu. *Web site:* http://www.snead.edu/.

Southern Union State Community College

Wadley, Alabama

Freshman Application Contact Admissions Office, Southern Union State Community College, PO Box 1000, Roberts Street, Wadley, AL 36276. *Phone:* 256-395-5157. *E-mail:* info@suscc.edu. *Web site:* http://www.suscc.edu/.

Wallace State Community College

Hanceville, Alabama

Director of Admissions Ms. Linda Sperling, Director of Admissions, Wallace State Community College, PO Box 2000, 801 Main Street, Hanceville, AL 35077-2000. *Phone:* 256-352-8278. *Toll-free phone:* 866-350-9722. *Web site:* http://www.wallacestate.edu/.

ALASKA

Charter College

Anchorage, Alaska

Director of Admissions Ms. Lily Sirianni, Vice President, Charter College, 2221 East Northern Lights Boulevard, Suite 120, Anchorage, AK 99508. *Phone:* 907-277-1000. *Toll-free phone:* 888-200-9942. *Web site:* http://www.chartercollege.edu/.

Ilisagvik College

Barrow, Alaska

- **State-supported** 2-year, founded 1995
- **Rural** campus
- **Coed**

Undergraduates 39 full-time, 249 part-time. Students come from 3 states and territories; 3 other countries.

Faculty *Student/faculty ratio:* 6:1.

Academics *Calendar:* semesters. *Degree:* certificates, diplomas, and associate. *Special study options:* academic remediation for entering students, cooperative education, distance learning, double majors, English as a second language, independent study, internships, off-campus study, part-time degree program, services for LD students, summer session for credit.

Student Life *Campus security:* 24-hour emergency response devices and patrols, controlled dormitory access.

Standardized Tests *Required:* ACT ASSET (for admission).

Costs (2011–12) *Tuition:* state resident $2400 full-time, $100 per credit hour part-time; nonresident $3600 full-time, $150 per credit hour part-time. *Required fees:* $260 full-time. *Room and board:* $10,650; room only: $4050.

Applying *Required:* high school transcript, minimum 2.0 GPA. *Required for some:* copy of Alaska Native Shareholder/Native American Tribal Affiliation card if native.

Freshman Application Contact Janelle Everett, Recruiter, Ilisagvik College, UIC/Narl, Barrow, AK 99723. *Phone:* 907-852-1799. *Toll-free phone:* 800-478-7337. *E-mail:* janelle.everett@ilisagvik.edu. *Web site:* http://www.ilisagvik.edu/.

University of Alaska Anchorage, Kenai Peninsula College

Soldotna, Alaska

- **State-supported** primarily 2-year, founded 1964, part of University of Alaska System
- **Rural** 360-acre campus
- **Coed**

Academics *Calendar:* semesters. *Degrees:* certificates, associate, and bachelor's. *Special study options:* academic remediation for entering students, adult/continuing education programs, advanced placement credit, cooperative education, distance learning, English as a second language, part-time degree program, services for LD students.

Student Life *Campus security:* 24-hour emergency response devices.

Standardized Tests *Required:* ACT, SAT or ACCUPLACER scores (for admission).

Costs (2011–12) *Tuition:* state resident $4905 full-time, $154 per credit hour part-time; nonresident $4905 full-time, $154 per credit hour part-time. *Required fees:* $405 full-time.

Financial Aid Of all full-time matriculated undergraduates who enrolled in 2010, 50 Federal Work-Study jobs (averaging $3000). 50 state and other part-time jobs (averaging $3000).

Applying *Options:* electronic application. *Application fee:* $40. *Required:* high school transcript.

Freshman Application Contact Ms. Shelly Love Blatchford, Admission and Registration Coordinator, University of Alaska Anchorage, Kenai Peninsula College, 156 College Road, Soldotna, AK 99669-9798. *Phone:* 907-262-0311. *Toll-free phone:* 877-262-0330. *Web site:* http://www.kpc.alaska.edu/.

University of Alaska Anchorage, Kodiak College

Kodiak, Alaska

- **State-supported** 2-year, founded 1968, part of University of Alaska System
- **Rural** 68-acre campus
- **Coed,** 479 undergraduate students, 31% full-time, 90% women, 10% men

Undergraduates 148 full-time, 331 part-time. Students come from 18 states and territories; 3 other countries; 2% Black or African American, non-Hispanic/Latino; 8% Hispanic/Latino; 6% Asian, non-Hispanic/Latino; 0.8% Native Hawaiian or other Pacific Islander, non-Hispanic/Latino; 12% American Indian or Alaska Native, non-Hispanic/Latino; 6% Two or more races, non-Hispanic/Latino; 4% Race/ethnicity unknown; 2% international.

Freshmen *Admission:* 56 applied, 43 admitted.

Faculty *Total:* 41, 27% full-time, 10% with terminal degrees. *Student/faculty ratio:* 13:1.

Majors Accounting; accounting technology and bookkeeping; building construction technology; computer programming (specific applications); computer technology/computer systems technology; construction management; occupational safety and health technology; welding technology.

Academics *Calendar:* semesters. *Degree:* certificates and associate. *Special study options:* academic remediation for entering students, adult/continuing education programs, advanced placement credit, distance learning, double majors, part-time degree program, study abroad, summer session for credit.

Library Carolyn Floyd Library with 21,000 titles, 39 serial subscriptions, 2,400 audiovisual materials, an OPAC, a Web page.

Student Life *Housing:* college housing not available. *Activities and Organizations:* PHI THETA KAPPA, Student Government.

Standardized Tests *Required:* ACCUPLACER (for admission).

Costs (2012–13) *Tuition:* state resident $4320 full-time, $144 per credit part-time; nonresident $17,400 full-time, $580 per credit part-time. *Required fees:* $335 full-time, $8 per credit part-time, $5 per term part-time. *Payment plan:* installment. *Waivers:* senior citizens and employees or children of employees.

Applying *Options:* electronic application. *Application fee:* $40. *Required for some:* high school transcript. *Application deadlines:* rolling (freshmen), rolling (out-of-state freshmen), rolling (transfers).

Freshman Application Contact University of Alaska Anchorage, Kodiak College, 117 Benny Benson Drive, Kodiak, AK 99615-6643. *Phone:* 907-486-1235. *Toll-free phone:* 800-486-7660. *Web site:* http://www.koc.alaska.edu/.

University of Alaska Anchorage, Matanuska-Susitna College

Palmer, Alaska

Freshman Application Contact Ms. Sandra Gravley, Student Services Director, University of Alaska Anchorage, Matanuska-Susitna College, PO Box 2889, Palmer, AK 99645-2889. *Phone:* 907-745-9712. *Fax:* 907-745-9747. *E-mail:* info@matsu.alaska.edu. *Web site:* http://www.matsu.alaska.edu/.

University of Alaska, Prince William Sound Community College

Valdez, Alaska

Freshman Application Contact Mr. Nathan J. Platt, Director of Student Services, University of Alaska, Prince William Sound Community College, PO Box 97, Valdez, AK 99686-0097. *Phone:* 907-834-1631. *Toll-free phone:* 800-478-8800. *E-mail:* studentservices@pwscc.edu. *Web site:* http://www.pwscc.edu/.

University of Alaska Southeast, Ketchikan Campus

Ketchikan, Alaska

Freshman Application Contact Admissions Office, University of Alaska Southeast, Ketchikan Campus, 2600 7th Avenue, Ketchikan, AK 99901-5798. *Phone:* 907-225-6177. *Toll-free phone:* 888-550-6177. *Fax:* 907-225-3895. *E-mail:* ketch.info@uas.alaska.edu. *Web site:* http://www.ketch.alaska.edu/.

University of Alaska Southeast, Sitka Campus

Sitka, Alaska

Freshman Application Contact Cynthia Rogers, Coordinator of Admissions, University of Alaska Southeast, Sitka Campus, 1332 Seward Avenue, Sitka, AK 99835-9418. *Phone:* 907-747-7705. *Toll-free phone:* 800-478-6653. *Fax:* 907-747-7793. *E-mail:* cynthia.rogers@uas.alaska.edu. *Web site:* http://www.uas.alaska.edu/.

AMERICAN SAMOA

American Samoa Community College

Pago Pago, American Samoa

Director of Admissions Sifagatogo Tuitasi, Admissions, American Samoa Community College, PO Box 2609, Pago Pago, AS 96799-2609. *Phone:* 684-699-1141. *E-mail:* admissions@amsamoa.edu. *Web site:* http://www.amsamoa.edu/.

ARIZONA

Anthem College–Phoenix
Phoenix, Arizona

Freshman Application Contact Mr. Glen Husband, Vice President of Admissions, Anthem College–Phoenix, 1515 East Indian School Road, Phoenix, AZ 85014-4901. *Phone:* 602-279-9700. *Toll-free phone:* 855-331-7767. *Web site:* http://anthem.edu/phoenix-arizona/.

Arizona Automotive Institute
Glendale, Arizona

Director of Admissions Director of Admissions, Arizona Automotive Institute, 6829 North 46th Avenue, Glendale, AZ 85301-3597. *Phone:* 623-934-7273 Ext. 211. *Toll-free phone:* 800-321-5861 (in-state); 800-321-5961 (out-of-state). *Fax:* 623-937-5000. *E-mail:* info@azautoinst.com. *Web site:* http://www.aai.edu/.

Arizona College of Allied Health
Glendale, Arizona

Freshman Application Contact Admissions Department, Arizona College of Allied Health, 4425 West Olive Avenue, Suite 300, Glendale, AZ 85302-3843. *Phone:* 602-222-9300. *E-mail:* lhicks@arizonacollege.edu. *Web site:* http://www.arizonacollege.edu/.

Arizona Western College
Yuma, Arizona

- **State and locally supported** 2-year, founded 1962, part of Arizona State Community College System
- **Rural** 640-acre campus
- **Coed**

Undergraduates 2,834 full-time, 5,711 part-time. Students come from 37 states and territories; 31 other countries; 3% are from out of state; 3% Black or African American, non-Hispanic/Latino; 57% Hispanic/Latino; 1% Asian, non-Hispanic/Latino; 0.4% Native Hawaiian or other Pacific Islander, non-Hispanic/Latino; 2% American Indian or Alaska Native, non-Hispanic/Latino; 0.1% Two or more races, non-Hispanic/Latino; 3% Race/ethnicity unknown; 9% international; 3% live on campus.

Faculty *Student/faculty ratio:* 21:1.

Academics *Calendar:* semesters. *Degree:* certificates and associate. *Special study options:* academic remediation for entering students, adult/continuing education programs, advanced placement credit, cooperative education, distance learning, English as a second language, honors programs, independent study, part-time degree program, services for LD students, summer session for credit.

Student Life *Campus security:* 24-hour emergency response devices and patrols, student patrols, late-night transport/escort service.

Athletics Member NJCAA.

Standardized Tests *Required for some:* SAT or ACT (for admission).

Costs (2011–12) *Tuition:* state resident $1680 full-time, $70 per credit hour part-time; nonresident $6840 full-time, $80 per credit hour part-time. Full-time tuition and fees vary according to course load and program. Part-time tuition and fees vary according to course load and program. *Room and board:* $5610; room only: $2110. Room and board charges vary according to board plan.

Financial Aid Of all full-time matriculated undergraduates who enrolled in 2010, 350 Federal Work-Study jobs (averaging $1500). 100 state and other part-time jobs (averaging $1800).

Applying *Options:* electronic application, early admission, deferred entrance.

Freshman Application Contact Amy Pignatore, Director of Admissions/Registrar, Arizona Western College, PO Box 929, Yuma, AZ 85366. *Phone:* 928-317-7600. *Toll-free phone:* 888-293-0392. *Fax:* 928-344-7712. *E-mail:* amy.pignatore@azwestern.edu. *Web site:* http://www.azwestern.edu/.

Brown Mackie College–Phoenix
Phoenix, Arizona

- **Proprietary** primarily 2-year, part of Education Management Corporation
- **Coed**

Academics *Degrees:* diplomas, associate, and bachelor's.

Costs (2011–12) *Tuition:* Tuition varies by program. Students should contact Brown Mackie College for tuition information.

Freshman Application Contact Brown Mackie College–Phoenix, 13430 North Black Canyon Highway, Suite 190, Phoenix, AZ 85029. *Phone:* 602-337-3044. *Toll-free phone:* 866-824-4793. *Web site:* http://www.brownmackie.edu/phoenix/.

See page 378 for the College Close-Up.

Brown Mackie College–Tucson
Tucson, Arizona

- **Proprietary** primarily 2-year, founded 1972, part of Education Management Corporation
- **Suburban** campus
- **Coed**

Academics *Degrees:* diplomas, associate, and bachelor's.

Costs (2011–12) *Tuition:* Tuition varies by program. Students should contact Brown Mackie College for tuition information.

Freshman Application Contact Brown Mackie College–Tucson, 4585 East Speedway, Suite 204, Tucson, AZ 85712. *Phone:* 520-319-3300. *Web site:* http://www.brownmackie.edu/tucson/.

See page 390 for the College Close-Up.

The Bryman School of Arizona
Phoenix, Arizona

Freshman Application Contact Admissions Office, The Bryman School of Arizona, 2250 West Peoria Avenue, Phoenix, AZ 85029. *Phone:* 602-274-4300. *Toll-free phone:* 866-381-6383 (in-state); 866-391-6383 (out-of-state). *Fax:* 602-248-9087. *Web site:* http://www.brymanschool.edu/.

Carrington College - Mesa
Mesa, Arizona

Director of Admissions Valentina Colmone, Campus Director, Carrington College - Mesa, 630 West Southern Avenue, Mesa, AZ 85210. *Phone:* 480-212-1600. *E-mail:* vcolmone@apollocollege.edu. *Web site:* http://carrington.edu/.

Carrington College - Phoenix
Phoenix, Arizona

Director of Admissions Admissions Director, Carrington College - Phoenix, 8503 North 27th Avenue, Phoenix, AZ 85051. *Phone:* 602-324-5505. *Web site:* http://carrington.edu/.

Carrington College - Phoenix Westside
Phoenix, Arizona

Director of Admissions Cindy Nestor, Admissions, Carrington College - Phoenix Westside, 2701 West Bethany Home Road, Phoenix, AZ 85017. *Phone:* 602-433-1222. *Fax:* 602-433-1222. *E-mail:* cnestor@apollocollege.com. *Web site:* http://carrington.edu/.

Carrington College - Tucson
Tucson, Arizona

Director of Admissions Mr. Dennis C. Wilson, Executive Director, Carrington College - Tucson, 3550 North Oracle Road, Tucson, AZ 85705. *Phone:* 520-888-5885. *Fax:* 520-887-3005. *E-mail:* dwilson@apollo.edu. *Web site:* http://carrington.edu/.

Central Arizona College
Coolidge, Arizona

Freshman Application Contact Dr. James Moore, Dean of Records and Admissions, Central Arizona College, 8470 North Overfield Road, Coolidge, AZ 85128. *Phone:* 520-494-5261. *Toll-free phone:* 800-237-9814. *Fax:* 520-426-5083. *E-mail:* james.moore@centralaz.edu. *Web site:* http://www.centralaz.edu/.

Chandler-Gilbert Community College
Chandler, Arizona

- **State and locally supported** 2-year, founded 1985, part of Maricopa County Community College District System
- **Suburban** 80-acre campus with easy access to Phoenix
- **Coed**, 14,030 undergraduate students, 32% full-time, 53% women, 47% men

Undergraduates 4,424 full-time, 9,606 part-time. Students come from 38 states and territories; 37 other countries; 2% are from out of state; 4% Black or African American, non-Hispanic/Latino; 19% Hispanic/Latino; 5% Asian, non-Hispanic/Latino; 0.3% Native Hawaiian or other Pacific Islander, non-Hispanic/Latino; 1% American Indian or Alaska Native, non-Hispanic/Latino; 2% Two or more races, non-Hispanic/Latino; 11% Race/ethnicity unknown; 0.5% international; 4% transferred in. *Retention:* 61% of full-time freshmen returned.

Freshmen *Admission:* 2,932 enrolled.

Faculty *Total:* 645, 20% full-time. *Student/faculty ratio:* 25:1.

Majors Accounting; accounting technology and bookkeeping; airline pilot and flight crew; business administration and management; business administration, management and operations related; business/commerce; business, management, and marketing related; computer and information sciences; computer and information sciences and support services related; computer programming; computer programming (vendor/product certification); computer systems analysis; computer systems networking and telecommunications; criminal justice/safety; data entry/microcomputer applications; data modeling/warehousing and database administration; dietetic technology; dietitian assistant; dramatic/theater arts; electromechanical technology; elementary education; fine/studio arts; general studies; information technology; kinesiology and exercise science; liberal arts and sciences and humanities related; liberal arts and sciences/liberal studies; lineworker; massage therapy; mechanic and repair technologies related; music management; organizational behavior; physical sciences; psychology; registered nursing/registered nurse; social work; visual and performing arts.

Academics *Calendar:* semesters. *Degree:* certificates, diplomas, and associate. *Special study options:* academic remediation for entering students, advanced placement credit, English as a second language, freshman honors college, honors programs, independent study, part-time degree program, services for LD students, study abroad, summer session for credit.

Library Chandler-Gilbert Community College Library with an OPAC.

Student Life *Housing:* college housing not available. *Activities and Organizations:* student-run newspaper, radio station, choral group. *Campus security:* 24-hour emergency response devices and patrols, late-night transport/escort service. *Student services:* personal/psychological counseling.

Athletics Member NJCAA. *Intercollegiate sports:* baseball M, basketball M/W, golf M/W, soccer M/W, softball W, volleyball W.

Costs (2012–13) *Tuition:* area resident $1824 full-time, $76 per credit hour part-time; state resident $7200 full-time, $300 per credit hour part-time; nonresident $7608 full-time, $317 per credit hour part-time. Full-time tuition and fees vary according to reciprocity agreements. Part-time tuition and fees vary according to reciprocity agreements. *Required fees:* $30 full-time, $15 per term part-time. *Payment plans:* installment, deferred payment. *Waivers:* employees or children of employees.

Applying *Options:* electronic application.

Freshman Application Contact Ryan Cain, Coordinator of Enrollment Services, Chandler-Gilbert Community College, 2626 East Pecos Road, Chandler, AZ 85225-2479. *Phone:* 480-732-7044. *E-mail:* ryan.cain@cgcmail.maricopa.edu. *Web site:* http://www.cgc.maricopa.edu/.

Cochise College
Sierra Vista, Arizona

- **State and locally supported** 2-year, founded 1977
- **Small-town** 518-acre campus with easy access to Tucson
- **Coed**, 4,288 undergraduate students, 24% full-time, 54% women, 46% men

Undergraduates 1,024 full-time, 3,264 part-time. Students come from 21 states and territories; 8 other countries; 3% are from out of state; 5% Black or African American, non-Hispanic/Latino; 45% Hispanic/Latino; 2% Asian, non-Hispanic/Latino; 0.5% Native Hawaiian or other Pacific Islander, non-Hispanic/Latino; 0.8% American Indian or Alaska Native, non-Hispanic/Latino; 2% Two or more races, non-Hispanic/Latino; 3% Race/ethnicity unknown; 0.1% international; 2% transferred in. *Retention:* 48% of full-time freshmen returned.

Freshmen *Admission:* 1,257 applied, 1,257 admitted, 785 enrolled. *Average high school GPA:* 2.72.

Faculty *Total:* 405, 23% full-time. *Student/faculty ratio:* 11:1.

Majors Administrative assistant and secretarial science; aerospace ground equipment technology; agricultural business and management; airline pilot and

flight crew; anthropology; art; art teacher education; automobile/automotive mechanics technology; avionics maintenance technology; biology/biological sciences; building construction technology; business administration and management; chemistry teacher education; computer and information systems security; computer programming; computer science; computer systems networking and telecommunications; criminal justice/police science; culinary arts; data processing and data processing technology; dramatic/theater arts; early childhood education; economics; electrical, electronic and communications engineering technology; elementary education; emergency medical technology (EMT paramedic); engineering; English; English/language arts teacher education; fire science/firefighting; foreign languages and literatures; foreign language teacher education; game and interactive media design; general studies; health and physical education/fitness; history; history teacher education; humanities; information science/studies; intelligence; journalism; logistics, materials, and supply chain management; mathematics; mathematics teacher education; music; philosophy; physics; political science and government; psychology; registered nursing/registered nurse; social work; sociology; speech communication and rhetoric; welding technology.

Academics *Calendar:* semesters. *Degree:* certificates and associate. *Special study options:* academic remediation for entering students, adult/continuing education programs, cooperative education, distance learning, English as a second language, honors programs, independent study, internships, part-time degree program, services for LD students, summer session for credit.

Library Charles DiPeso Library/Andrea Cracchiolo Library with 98,962 titles, 6,364 serial subscriptions, 3,108 audiovisual materials, an OPAC, a Web page.

Student Life *Housing Options:* coed, disabled students. Campus housing is university owned. *Activities and Organizations:* drama/theater group, student-run newspaper, Student Nurses, Phi Theta Kappa, Circle K International. *Campus security:* 24-hour emergency response devices and patrols. *Student services:* personal/psychological counseling.

Athletics Member NJCAA. *Intercollegiate sports:* baseball M(s), basketball M(s)/W(s), soccer W(s).

Costs (2012–13) *Tuition:* state resident $2100 full-time, $70 per credit hour part-time; nonresident $8700 full-time, $290 per credit hour part-time. Full-time tuition and fees vary according to program. Part-time tuition and fees vary according to program. *Room and board:* $5600.

Financial Aid Of all full-time matriculated undergraduates who enrolled in 2011, 1,260 applied for aid, 1,105 were judged to have need. In 2011, 38 non-need-based awards were made. *Average financial aid package:* $6137. *Average need-based loan:* $3258. *Average need-based gift aid:* $3813. *Average non-need-based aid:* $816.

Applying *Options:* electronic application, deferred entrance. *Recommended:* high school transcript. *Application deadlines:* rolling (freshmen), rolling (out-of-state freshmen), rolling (transfers). *Notification:* continuous (freshmen), continuous (out-of-state freshmen), continuous (transfers).

Freshman Application Contact Ms. Debbie Quick, Director of Admissions and Records, Cochise College, 901 North Colombo Avenue, Sierra Vista, AZ 85635-2317. *Phone:* 520-515-3640. *Toll-free phone:* 800-593-9567. *Fax:* 520-515-5452. *E-mail:* quickd@cochise.edu. *Web site:* http://www.cochise.edu/.

Coconino Community College
Flagstaff, Arizona

Freshman Application Contact Miss Veronica Hipolito, Director of Student Services, Coconino Community College, 2800 South Lone Tree Road, Flagstaff, AZ 86001. *Phone:* 928-226-4334 Ext. 4334. *Toll-free phone:* 800-350-7122. *Fax:* 928-226-4114. *E-mail:* veronica.hipolito@coconino.edu. *Web site:* http://www.coconino.edu/.

CollegeAmerica–Flagstaff
Flagstaff, Arizona

- **Proprietary** primarily 2-year
- **Coed**

Undergraduates *Retention:* 60% of full-time freshmen returned.

Faculty *Student/faculty ratio:* 33:1.

Academics *Degrees:* associate and bachelor's.

Costs (2011–12) *Tuition:* Tuition cost varies by program. Prospective students should contact the school for current tuition costs.

Freshman Application Contact CollegeAmerica–Flagstaff, 3012 East Route 66, Flagstaff, AZ 86004. *Phone:* 928-213-6060. *Toll-free phone:* 800-622-2894. *Web site:* http://www.collegeamerica.edu/.

Diné College
Tsaile, Arizona

Freshman Application Contact Mrs. Louise Litzin, Registrar, Diné College, PO Box 67, Tsaile, AZ 86556. *Phone:* 928-724-6633. *Toll-free phone:* 877-

988-DINE. *Fax:* 928-724-3349. *E-mail:* louise@dinecollege.edu. *Web site:* http://www.dinecollege.edu/.

Eastern Arizona College

Thatcher, Arizona

- **State and locally supported** 2-year, founded 1888, part of Arizona State Community College System
- **Small-town** campus
- **Endowment** $3.6 million
- **Coed,** 6,997 undergraduate students, 31% full-time, 54% women, 46% men

Undergraduates 2,154 full-time, 4,843 part-time. Students come from 34 states and territories; 25 other countries; 5% are from out of state; 4% Black or African American, non-Hispanic/Latino; 19% Hispanic/Latino; 1% Asian, non-Hispanic/Latino; 0.1% Native Hawaiian or other Pacific Islander, non-Hispanic/Latino; 7% American Indian or Alaska Native, non-Hispanic/Latino; 0.6% Two or more races, non-Hispanic/Latino; 0.3% Race/ethnicity unknown; 0.6% international; 2% transferred in; 5% live on campus.

Freshmen *Admission:* 1,100 applied, 1,100 admitted, 1,786 enrolled.

Faculty *Total:* 276, 32% full-time, 10% with terminal degrees. *Student/faculty ratio:* 25:1.

Majors Anthropology; art; art teacher education; automobile/automotive mechanics technology; biology/biological sciences; business administration and management; business, management, and marketing related; business teacher education; chemistry; civil engineering technology; commercial and advertising art; cosmetology; criminal justice/law enforcement administration; criminal justice/police science; dramatic/theater arts; early childhood education; elementary education; emergency medical technology (EMT paramedic); English; entrepreneurship; environmental biology; fire science/firefighting; foreign languages and literatures; forestry; geology/earth science; health and physical education/fitness; health/medical preparatory programs related; history; industrial electronics technology; industrial mechanics and maintenance technology; information science/studies; liberal arts and sciences/liberal studies; machine shop technology; mathematics; mining technology; multi/interdisciplinary studies related; music; pharmacy technician; physics; political science and government; premedical studies; pre-pharmacy studies; psychology; registered nursing/registered nurse; secondary education; sociology; technology/industrial arts teacher education; welding technology; wildlife biology.

Academics *Calendar:* semesters. *Degree:* certificates and associate. *Special study options:* academic remediation for entering students, adult/continuing education programs, advanced placement credit, cooperative education, distance learning, double majors, independent study, internships, part-time degree program, services for LD students, study abroad, summer session for credit.

Library Alumni Library with an OPAC, a Web page.

Student Life *Housing Options:* men-only, women-only. Campus housing is university owned. *Activities and Organizations:* drama/theater group, choral group, marching band, Latter-Day Saints Student Association, Criminal Justice Student Association, Multicultural Council, Phi Theta Kappa, Mark Allen Dorm Club. *Campus security:* 24-hour emergency response devices, late-night transport/escort service, controlled dormitory access, 20-hour patrols by trained security personnel. *Student services:* personal/psychological counseling.

Athletics Member NJCAA. *Intercollegiate sports:* baseball M(s), basketball M(s)/W(s), football M(s), golf M/W, softball W(s), volleyball W(s). *Intramural sports:* basketball M/W, racquetball M/W, swimming and diving M/W, table tennis M/W, tennis M/W, volleyball M/W.

Costs (2012–13) *Tuition:* state resident $1760 full-time; nonresident $8360 full-time. *Room and board:* $5390. Room and board charges vary according to board plan. *Waivers:* senior citizens and employees or children of employees.

Financial Aid Of all full-time matriculated undergraduates who enrolled in 2010, 1,610 applied for aid, 1,468 were judged to have need, 72 had their need fully met. In 2010, 133 non-need-based awards were made. *Average percent of need met:* 56%. *Average financial aid package:* $5999. *Average need-based gift aid:* $5241. *Average non-need-based aid:* $3122.

Applying *Options:* electronic application, early admission, deferred entrance. *Recommended:* high school transcript. *Application deadlines:* rolling (freshmen), rolling (transfers). *Notification:* continuous (freshmen).

Freshman Application Contact Erline Norton, Records Assistant, Eastern Arizona College, 615 North Stadium Avenue, Thatcher, AZ 85552-0769. *Phone:* 928-428-8250. *Toll-free phone:* 800-678-3808. *Fax:* 928-428-2578. *E-mail:* admissions@eac.edu. *Web site:* http://www.eac.edu/.

Estrella Mountain Community College

Avondale, Arizona

Freshman Application Contact Estrella Mountain Community College, 3000 North Dysart Road, Avondale, AZ 85392. *Phone:* 623-935-8812. *Web site:* http://www.emc.maricopa.edu/.

Everest College

Phoenix, Arizona

Freshman Application Contact Mr. Jim Askins, Director of Admissions, Everest College, 10400 North 25th Avenue, Suite 190, Phoenix, AZ 85021. *Phone:* 602-942-4141. *Toll-free phone:* 888-741-4270. *Fax:* 602-943-0960. *E-mail:* jaskins@cci.edu. *Web site:* http://www.everest.edu/.

GateWay Community College

Phoenix, Arizona

- **State and locally supported** 2-year, founded 1968, part of Maricopa County Community College District System
- **Urban** 20-acre campus
- **Coed,** 6,801 undergraduate students, 3% full-time, 5% women, 6% men

Undergraduates 191 full-time, 525 part-time. 11% Black or African American, non-Hispanic/Latino; 26% Hispanic/Latino; 4% Asian, non-Hispanic/Latino; 0.2% Native Hawaiian or other Pacific Islander, non-Hispanic/Latino; 4% American Indian or Alaska Native, non-Hispanic/Latino; 9% Race/ethnicity unknown; 1% international.

Freshmen *Admission:* 716 applied, 716 admitted, 716 enrolled.

Faculty *Total:* 490, 20% full-time. *Student/faculty ratio:* 18:1.

Majors Accounting; accounting and computer science; accounting technology and bookkeeping; administrative assistant and secretarial science; aeronautical/aerospace engineering technology; automobile/automotive mechanics technology; biotechnology; business administration and management; business administration, management and operations related; business automation/technology/data entry; business/commerce; cabinetmaking and millwork; carpentry; clinical laboratory science/medical technology; computer and information sciences; computer systems networking and telecommunications; construction/heavy equipment/earthmoving equipment operation; court reporting; diagnostic medical sonography and ultrasound technology; electrician; electromechanical technology; elementary education; energy management and systems technology; general studies; health and medical administrative services related; health/health-care administration; heating, air conditioning, ventilation and refrigeration maintenance technology; heating, ventilation, air conditioning and refrigeration engineering technology; industrial and product design; ironworking; liberal arts and sciences/liberal studies; lineworker; management information systems; manufacturing engineering technology; marketing/marketing management; masonry; medical radiologic technology; medical transcription; nuclear medical technology; occupational safety and health technology; organizational behavior; painting and wall covering; personal and culinary services related; physical sciences; physical therapy technology; pipefitting and sprinkler fitting; plumbing technology; radiologic technology/science; registered nursing/registered nurse; respiratory care therapy; sheet metal technology; surgical technology; water quality and wastewater treatment management and recycling technology; web page, digital/multimedia and information resources design.

Academics *Calendar:* semesters. *Degree:* certificates, diplomas, and associate. *Special study options:* academic remediation for entering students, accelerated degree program, adult/continuing education programs, advanced placement credit, cooperative education, distance learning, double majors, English as a second language, freshman honors college, honors programs, independent study, internships, off-campus study, part-time degree program, services for LD students, study abroad, summer session for credit. *ROTC:* Army (c), Air Force (c).

Library GateWay Library with an OPAC.

Student Life *Housing:* college housing not available. *Campus security:* 24-hour emergency response devices and patrols, student patrols, late-night transport/escort service. *Student services:* personal/psychological counseling, women's center.

Athletics Member NJCAA. *Intercollegiate sports:* baseball M, cross-country running M/W, golf M/W, soccer M/W, softball W.

Applying *Options:* electronic application, early admission, deferred entrance. *Required for some:* high school transcript, interview. *Application deadlines:* rolling (freshmen), rolling (transfers). *Notification:* continuous (freshmen), continuous (transfers).

Freshman Application Contact Director of Admissions and Records, GateWay Community College, 108 North 40th Street, Phoenix, AZ 85034. *Phone:* 602-286-8200. *Fax:* 602-286-8200. *E-mail:* enroll@gatewaycc.edu. *Web site:* http://www.gatewaycc.edu/.

Glendale Community College
Glendale, Arizona

- **State and locally supported** 2-year, founded 1965, part of Maricopa County Community College District System
- **Suburban** 222-acre campus with easy access to Phoenix
- **Endowment** $1.2 million
- **Coed**

Undergraduates 7,126 full-time, 13,028 part-time. Students come from 51 states and territories; 92 other countries; 8% are from out of state; 7% transferred in. *Retention:* 64% of full-time freshmen returned.

Faculty *Student/faculty ratio:* 24:1.

Academics *Calendar:* semesters. *Degree:* certificates and associate. *Special study options:* academic remediation for entering students, adult/continuing education programs, advanced placement credit, cooperative education, distance learning, double majors, English as a second language, freshman honors college, honors programs, internships, off-campus study, part-time degree program, services for LD students, study abroad, summer session for credit. *ROTC:* Army (c), Air Force (c).

Student Life *Campus security:* 24-hour patrols, student patrols, late-night transport/escort service.

Athletics Member NJCAA.

Costs (2011–12) *Tuition:* state resident $1824 full-time, $76 per semester hour part-time; nonresident $7608 full-time, $317 per semester hour part-time. Full-time tuition and fees vary according to program and reciprocity agreements. Part-time tuition and fees vary according to course load, program, and reciprocity agreements. *Required fees:* $30 full-time, $15 per term part-time.

Financial Aid Of all full-time matriculated undergraduates who enrolled in 2010, 350 Federal Work-Study jobs (averaging $1700).

Applying *Options:* electronic application. *Required for some:* high school transcript.

Freshman Application Contact Ms. Mary Blackwell, Dean of Enrollment Services, Glendale Community College, 6000 West Olive Avenue, Glendale, AZ 85302. *Phone:* 623-435-3305. *Fax:* 623-845-3303. *E-mail:* info@gc.maricopa.edu. *Web site:* http://www.gc.maricopa.edu/.

ITT Technical Institute
Phoenix, Arizona

- **Proprietary** primarily 2-year, founded 1972, part of ITT Educational Services, Inc.
- **Urban** campus
- **Coed**

Majors Business administration and management; communications technology; computer and information systems security; criminal justice/law enforcement administration; drafting and design technology; electrical, electronic and communications engineering technology; forensic science and technology; graphic communications; legal assistant/paralegal; network and system administration; project management; registered nursing/registered nurse.

Academics *Calendar:* quarters. *Degrees:* associate and bachelor's.

Student Life *Housing:* college housing not available.

Financial Aid Of all full-time matriculated undergraduates who enrolled in 2010, 10 Federal Work-Study jobs (averaging $4000).

Freshman Application Contact Director of Recruitment, ITT Technical Institute, 10220 North 25th Avenue, Suite 100, Phoenix, AZ 85021. *Phone:* 602-749-7900. *Toll-free phone:* 877-221-1132. *Web site:* http://www.itt-tech.edu/.

ITT Technical Institute
Phoenix, Arizona

- **Proprietary** primarily 2-year, part of ITT Educational Services, Inc.
- **Coed**

Majors Business administration and management; communications technology; computer and information systems security; drafting and design technology; electrical, electronic and communications engineering technology; forensic science and technology; graphic communications; legal assistant/paralegal; network and system administration; project management.

Academics *Calendar:* quarters. *Degrees:* associate and bachelor's.

Freshman Application Contact Director of Recruitment, ITT Technical Institute, 1840 N. 95th Avenue, Suite 132, Phoenix, AZ 85037. *Phone:* 623-474-7900. *Toll-free phone:* 800-210-1178. *Web site:* http://www.itt-tech.edu/.

ITT Technical Institute
Tucson, Arizona

- **Proprietary** primarily 2-year, founded 1984, part of ITT Educational Services, Inc.
- **Urban** campus
- **Coed**

Majors Business administration and management; communications technology; computer and information systems security; construction management; criminal justice/law enforcement administration; drafting and design technology; electrical, electronic and communications engineering technology; forensic science and technology; game and interactive media design; graphic communications; legal assistant/paralegal; network and system administration; project management.

Academics *Calendar:* quarters. *Degrees:* associate and bachelor's.

Student Life *Housing:* college housing not available.

Freshman Application Contact Director of Recruitment, ITT Technical Institute, 1455 West River Road, Tucson, AZ 85704. *Phone:* 520-408-7488. *Toll-free phone:* 800-870-9730. *Web site:* http://www.itt-tech.edu/.

Kaplan College, Phoenix Campus
Phoenix, Arizona

- **Proprietary** 2-year, founded 1972
- **Coed**

Majors Criminal justice/law enforcement administration; respiratory care therapy; veterinary/animal health technology.

Academics *Calendar:* continuous. *Degree:* diplomas and associate.

Freshman Application Contact Kaplan College, Phoenix Campus, 13610 North Black Canyon Highway, Suite 104, Phoenix, AZ 85029. *Phone:* 602-548-1955. *Toll-free phone:* 800-935-1857. *Web site:* http://phoenix.kaplancollege.com/.

Lamson College
Tempe, Arizona

Freshman Application Contact Lamson College, 875 West Elliot Road, Suite 206, Tempe, AZ 85284. *Phone:* 480-898-7000. *Toll-free phone:* 800-915-2194. *Web site:* http://www.lamsoncollege.edu/.

Le Cordon Bleu College of Culinary Arts in Scottsdale
Scottsdale, Arizona

Director of Admissions Le Cordon Bleu College of Culinary Arts in Scottsdale, 8100 East Camelback Road, Suite 1001, Scottsdale, AZ 85251-3940. *Toll-free phone:* 888-557-4222. *Web site:* http://www.chefs.edu/SCOTTSDALE.

Mesa Community College
Mesa, Arizona

- **State and locally supported** 2-year, founded 1965, part of Maricopa County Community College District System
- **Urban** 160-acre campus with easy access to Phoenix
- **Coed**

Undergraduates Students come from 18 states and territories; 4% are from out of state.

Academics *Calendar:* semesters. *Degree:* certificates and associate. *Special study options:* academic remediation for entering students, adult/continuing education programs, advanced placement credit, cooperative education, distance learning, English as a second language, freshman honors college, honors programs, independent study, off-campus study, part-time degree program, services for LD students, student-designed majors, study abroad, summer session for credit. *ROTC:* Army (c), Air Force (c).

Student Life *Campus security:* 24-hour emergency response devices and patrols, student patrols.

Athletics Member NJCAA.

Costs (2011–12) *Tuition:* area resident $1824 full-time, $76 per credit hour part-time; state resident $7200 full-time, $317 per credit hour part-time; nonresident $7608 full-time, $317 per credit hour part-time. Full-time tuition and fees vary according to course load and reciprocity agreements. Part-time tuition and fees vary according to course load and reciprocity agreements.

Applying *Options:* electronic application, early admission, deferred entrance.

Freshman Application Contact Ms. Kathleen Perales, Manager, Recruitment, Mesa Community College, 1833 West Southern Avenue, Mesa, AZ 85202-4866. *Phone:* 480-461-7751. *Toll-free phone:* 866-532-4983. *Fax:*

480-654-7379. *E-mail:* admissions@mc.maricopa.edu. *Web site:* http://www.mesacc.edu/.

Mohave Community College
Kingman, Arizona

- **State-supported** 2-year, founded 1971
- **Small-town** 160-acre campus
- **Coed,** 6,107 undergraduate students, 28% full-time, 64% women, 36% men

Undergraduates 1,707 full-time, 4,400 part-time. Students come from 16 states and territories; 5% are from out of state; 1% Black or African American, non-Hispanic/Latino; 17% Hispanic/Latino; 2% Asian, non-Hispanic/Latino; 0.6% Native Hawaiian or other Pacific Islander, non-Hispanic/Latino; 1% American Indian or Alaska Native, non-Hispanic/Latino; 2% Two or more races, non-Hispanic/Latino; 1% Race/ethnicity unknown.
Freshmen *Admission:* 1,031 enrolled.
Faculty *Total:* 363, 21% full-time. *Student/faculty ratio:* 18:1.
Majors Accounting; art; automobile/automotive mechanics technology; building/construction finishing, management, and inspection related; business administration and management; computer and information sciences related; computer programming (specific applications); computer science; criminal justice/police science; culinary arts; dental assisting; dental hygiene; drafting and design technology; education; emergency medical technology (EMT paramedic); English; fire science/firefighting; heating, air conditioning, ventilation and refrigeration maintenance technology; history; information technology; legal assistant/paralegal; liberal arts and sciences/liberal studies; mathematics; medical/clinical assistant; personal and culinary services related; pharmacy technician; physical therapy technology; psychology; registered nursing/registered nurse; sociology; substance abuse/addiction counseling; surgical technology; truck and bus driver/commercial vehicle operation/instruction; welding technology.
Academics *Calendar:* semesters. *Degree:* certificates and associate. *Special study options:* academic remediation for entering students, adult/continuing education programs, cooperative education, distance learning, English as a second language, independent study, part-time degree program, summer session for credit.
Library Mohave Community College Library with 45,849 titles, 476 serial subscriptions, an OPAC, a Web page.
Student Life *Housing:* college housing not available. *Activities and Organizations:* Art Club, Phi Theta Kappa, Computer Club (MC4), Science Club, student government. *Campus security:* late-night transport/escort service.
Costs (2011–12) *Tuition:* state resident $2220 full-time, $74 per credit hour part-time; nonresident $8880 full-time, $296 per credit hour part-time. Full-time tuition and fees vary according to program. Part-time tuition and fees vary according to program. *Required fees:* $240 full-time, $8 per credit part-time. *Payment plans:* installment, deferred payment. *Waivers:* employees or children of employees.
Applying *Options:* electronic application, early admission, deferred entrance. *Application deadlines:* rolling (freshmen), rolling (transfers). *Notification:* continuous (freshmen), continuous (transfers).
Freshman Application Contact Ms. Jann Woods, Dean of Student Services, Mohave Community College, 1971 Jagerson Ave, Kingman, AZ 86409. *Phone:* 928-757-0803. *Toll-free phone:* 888-664-2832. *Fax:* 928-757-0808. *E-mail:* jwoods@mohave.edu. *Web site:* http://www.mohave.edu/.

Northland Pioneer College
Holbrook, Arizona

Freshman Application Contact Ms. Suzette Willis, Coordinator of Admissions, Northland Pioneer College, PO Box 610, Holbrook, AZ 86025. *Phone:* 928-536-6271. *Toll-free phone:* 800-266-7845. *Fax:* 928-536-6212. *Web site:* http://www.npc.edu/.

Paradise Valley Community College
Phoenix, Arizona

Freshman Application Contact Paradise Valley Community College, 18401 North 32nd Street, Phoenix, AZ 85032-1200. *Phone:* 602-787-7020. *Web site:* http://www.pvc.maricopa.edu/.

The Paralegal Institute, Inc.
Phoenix, Arizona

Freshman Application Contact Patricia Yancy, Director of Admissions, The Paralegal Institute, Inc., 2933 West Indian School Road, Drawer 11408, Phoenix, AZ 85061-1408. *Phone:* 602-212-0501. *Toll-free phone:* 800-354-

1254. *Fax:* 602-212-0502. *E-mail:* paralegalinst@mindspring.com. *Web site:* http://www.theparalegalinstitute.edu/.

Phoenix College
Phoenix, Arizona

- **County-supported** 2-year, founded 1920, part of Maricopa County Community College District System
- **Urban** 52-acre campus
- **Coed**

Undergraduates 3,375 full-time, 9,625 part-time. 12% Black or African American, non-Hispanic/Latino; 35% Hispanic/Latino; 3% Asian, non-Hispanic/Latino; 0.1% Native Hawaiian or other Pacific Islander, non-Hispanic/Latino; 4% American Indian or Alaska Native, non-Hispanic/Latino; 12% Race/ethnicity unknown; 0.5% international.
Faculty *Student/faculty ratio:* 20:1.
Academics *Calendar:* semesters. *Degree:* certificates, diplomas, and associate. *Special study options:* academic remediation for entering students, adult/continuing education programs, advanced placement credit, cooperative education, distance learning, English as a second language, freshman honors college, honors programs, independent study, internships, off-campus study, part-time degree program, services for LD students, study abroad, summer session for credit. *ROTC:* Army (c), Navy (c), Air Force (c).
Student Life *Campus security:* 24-hour emergency response devices, student patrols, late-night transport/escort service.
Athletics Member NCAA, NJCAA. All NCAA Division II.
Costs (2011–12) *Tuition:* area resident $1824 full-time, $76 per credit hour part-time; state resident $7200 full-time, $300 per credit hour part-time; nonresident $7608 full-time, $317 per credit hour part-time. Full-time tuition and fees vary according to reciprocity agreements. Part-time tuition and fees vary according to course load and reciprocity agreements. *Required fees:* $30 full-time, $15 per term part-time.
Financial Aid Of all full-time matriculated undergraduates who enrolled in 2010, 220 Federal Work-Study jobs (averaging $4800).
Applying *Options:* electronic application, early admission, deferred entrance.
Freshman Application Contact Ms. Kathleen French, Director of Admissions, Registration, and Records, Phoenix College, 1202 West Thomas Road, Phoenix, AZ 85013. *Phone:* 602-285-7503. *Fax:* 602-285-7813. *E-mail:* kathy.french@pcmail.maricopa.edu. *Web site:* http://www.pc.maricopa.edu/.

Pima Community College
Tucson, Arizona

- **State and locally supported** 2-year, founded 1966
- **Urban** 486-acre campus with easy access to Tucson
- **Endowment** $4.1 million
- **Coed**

Undergraduates 13,700 full-time, 23,123 part-time. Students come from 31 states and territories; 31 other countries; 4% are from out of state; 4% Black or African American, non-Hispanic/Latino; 34% Hispanic/Latino; 2% Asian, non-Hispanic/Latino; 0.2% Native Hawaiian or other Pacific Islander, non-Hispanic/Latino; 3% American Indian or Alaska Native, non-Hispanic/Latino; 2% Two or more races, non-Hispanic/Latino; 13% Race/ethnicity unknown; 2% international; 6% transferred in. *Retention:* 66% of full-time freshmen returned.
Faculty *Student/faculty ratio:* 29:1.
Academics *Calendar:* semesters. *Degrees:* certificates, diplomas, associate, and postbachelor's certificates. *Special study options:* academic remediation for entering students, accelerated degree program, adult/continuing education programs, advanced placement credit, cooperative education, distance learning, double majors, English as a second language, honors programs, independent study, internships, off-campus study, part-time degree program, services for LD students, student-designed majors, summer session for credit. *ROTC:* Army (c), Navy (c), Air Force (c).
Student Life *Campus security:* 24-hour emergency response devices and patrols, late-night transport/escort service.
Athletics Member NJCAA.
Costs (2011–12) *Tuition:* state resident $1404 full-time, $59 per credit hour part-time; nonresident $7056 full-time, $98 per credit hour part-time. Full-time tuition and fees vary according to course load and program. Part-time tuition and fees vary according to course load and program. *Required fees:* $128 full-time, $5 per credit hour part-time, $10 per term part-time. *Payment plans:* installment, deferred payment.
Applying *Options:* electronic application.
Freshman Application Contact Michael Tulino, Director of Admissions and Registrar, Pima Community College, 4905B East Broadway Boulevard, Tucson, AZ 85709-1120. *Phone:* 520-206-4640. *Fax:* 520-206-4790. *E-mail:* mtulino@pima.edu. *Web site:* http://www.pima.edu/.

Pima Medical Institute

Mesa, Arizona

- **Proprietary** 2-year
- **Urban** campus
- **Coed**

Academics *Special study options:* cooperative education, distance learning, internships.
Standardized Tests *Required:* Wonderlic Scholastic Level Exam (for admission).
Applying *Required:* high school transcript, interview.
Freshman Application Contact Pima Medical Institute, 2160 S. Power Road, Mesa, AZ 85209. *Phone:* 480-898-9898. *Web site:* http://www.pmi.edu/.

Pima Medical Institute

Mesa, Arizona

- **Proprietary** primarily 2-year, founded 1985, part of Vocational Training Institutes, Inc.
- **Urban** campus
- **Coed**

Academics *Calendar:* modular. *Degrees:* certificates, associate, and bachelor's. *Special study options:* distance learning.
Standardized Tests *Required:* Wonderlic aptitude test (for admission).
Applying *Required:* interview. *Required for some:* high school transcript.
Freshman Application Contact Admissions Office, Pima Medical Institute, 957 South Dobson Road, Mesa, AZ 85202. *Phone:* 480-644-0267 Ext. 225. *Toll-free phone:* 800-477-PIMA (in-state); 888-477-PIMA (out-of-state). *Web site:* http://www.pmi.edu/.

Pima Medical Institute

Tucson, Arizona

- **Proprietary** primarily 2-year, founded 1972, part of Vocational Training Institutes, Inc.
- **Urban** campus
- **Coed**

Academics *Calendar:* modular. *Degrees:* certificates, associate, and bachelor's. *Special study options:* academic remediation for entering students, accelerated degree program, adult/continuing education programs, cooperative education, distance learning, internships.
Standardized Tests *Required:* Wonderlic Scholastic Level Exam (for admission).
Applying *Options:* early admission. *Required:* interview. *Required for some:* high school transcript.
Freshman Application Contact Admissions Office, Pima Medical Institute, 3350 East Grant Road, Tucson, AZ 85716. *Phone:* 520-326-1600 Ext. 5112. *Toll-free phone:* 800-477-PIMA (in-state); 888-477-PIMA (out-of-state). *Web site:* http://www.pmi.edu/.

The Refrigeration School

Phoenix, Arizona

Freshman Application Contact Ms. Heather Haskell, The Refrigeration School, 4210 East Washington Street. *Phone:* 602-275-7133. *Toll-free phone:* 888-943-4822. *Fax:* 602-267-4811. *E-mail:* heather@rsiaz.edu. *Web site:* http://www.refrigerationschool.com/.

Rio Salado College

Tempe, Arizona

Freshman Application Contact Laurel Redman, Director, Instruction Support Services and Student Development, Rio Salado College, 2323 West 14th Street, Tempe 85281. *Phone:* 480-517-8563. *Toll-free phone:* 800-729-1197. *Fax:* 480-517-8199. *E-mail:* admission@riomail.maricopa.edu. *Web site:* http://www.rio.maricopa.edu/.

Scottsdale Community College

Scottsdale, Arizona

- **State and locally supported** 2-year, founded 1969, part of Maricopa County Community College District System
- **Urban** 160-acre campus with easy access to Phoenix
- **Coed,** 11,345 undergraduate students, 32% full-time, 52% women, 48% men

Undergraduates 3,628 full-time, 7,717 part-time. Students come from 33 states and territories; 33 other countries; 1% are from out of state; 5% Black or African American, non-Hispanic/Latino; 14% Hispanic/Latino; 2% Asian, non-Hispanic/Latino; 0.3% Native Hawaiian or other Pacific Islander, non-Hispanic/Latino; 4% American Indian or Alaska Native, non-Hispanic/Latino; 2% Two or more races, non-Hispanic/Latino; 8% Race/ethnicity unknown; 1% international; 75% transferred in.
Faculty *Total:* 776, 20% full-time, 12% with terminal degrees. *Student/faculty ratio:* 17:1.
Majors Accounting; administrative assistant and secretarial science; business administration and management; criminal justice/law enforcement administration; culinary arts; dramatic/theater arts; electrical, electronic and communications engineering technology; emergency medical technology (EMT paramedic); environmental design/architecture; equestrian studies; fashion merchandising; finance; fire science/firefighting; hospitality administration; hotel/motel administration; information science/studies; interior design; kindergarten/preschool education; mathematics; medical administrative assistant and medical secretary; photography; public administration; real estate; registered nursing/registered nurse; special products marketing.
Academics *Calendar:* semesters. *Degree:* certificates, diplomas, and associate. *Special study options:* academic remediation for entering students, adult/continuing education programs, advanced placement credit, cooperative education, English as a second language, honors programs, internships, off-campus study, part-time degree program, services for LD students, study abroad, summer session for credit.
Library Scottsdale Community College Library with an OPAC, a Web page.
Student Life *Housing:* college housing not available. *Activities and Organizations:* drama/theater group, student-run newspaper, radio station, choral group, Student Leadership Forum, International Community Club, Phi Theta Kappa, Music Industry Club, SCC ASID-Interior Design group. *Campus security:* 24-hour emergency response devices and patrols, student patrols, late-night transport/escort service, 24-hour automatic surveillance cameras. *Student services:* personal/psychological counseling.
Athletics Member NCAA, NJCAA. All NCAA Division II. *Intercollegiate sports:* baseball M, basketball M/W, cross-country running M/W, football M, golf M/W, soccer M/W, softball W, tennis M/W, track and field M/W, volleyball W. *Intramural sports:* archery M/W, badminton M/W, basketball M/W, racquetball M/W, track and field M/W, volleyball M/W.
Costs (2012–13) *Tuition:* area resident $2280 full-time, $76 per credit part-time; state resident $8550 full-time, $285 per credit part-time; nonresident $9510 full-time, $317 per credit part-time. Full-time tuition and fees vary according to program. Part-time tuition and fees vary according to program. *Required fees:* $30 full-time. *Payment plan:* deferred payment. *Waivers:* employees or children of employees.
Financial Aid Of all full-time matriculated undergraduates who enrolled in 2010, 75 Federal Work-Study jobs (averaging $2000). *Financial aid deadline:* 7/15.
Applying *Options:* electronic application, early admission. *Application deadline:* rolling (freshmen). *Notification:* continuous (freshmen).
Freshman Application Contact Ms. Fran Watkins, Director of Admissions and Records, Scottsdale Community College, 9000 East Chaparral Road, Scottsdale, AZ 85256. *Phone:* 480-423-6133. *Fax:* 480-423-6200. *E-mail:* fran.watkins@sccmail.maricopa.edu. *Web site:* http://www.scottsdalecc.edu/.

Sessions College for Professional Design

Tempe, Arizona

Freshman Application Contact Admissions, Sessions College for Professional Design, 398 South Mlll Avenue, Suite 300, Tempe, AZ 85281. *Phone:* 480-212-1704. *Toll-free phone:* 800-258-4115. *E-mail:* admissions@sessions.edu. *Web site:* http://www.sessions.edu/.

South Mountain Community College

Phoenix, Arizona

Director of Admissions Dean of Enrollment Services, South Mountain Community College, 7050 South Twenty-fourth Street, Phoenix, AZ 85040. *Phone:* 602-243-8120. *Web site:* http://www.southmountaincc.edu/.

Southwest Institute of Healing Arts

Tempe, Arizona

Director of Admissions Katie Yearous, Student Advisor, Southwest Institute of Healing Arts, 1100 East Apache Boulevard, Tempe, AZ 85281. *Phone:* 480-994-9244. *Toll-free phone:* 888-504-9106. *E-mail:* joannl@swiha.net. *Web site:* http://www.swiha.org/.

Tohono O'odham Community College

Sells, Arizona

Freshman Application Contact Admissions, Tohono O'odham Community College, PO Box 3129, Sells, AZ 85634. *Phone:* 520-383-8401. *E-mail:* info@tocc.cc.az.us. *Web site:* http://www.tocc.cc.az.us/.

Universal Technical Institute

Avondale, Arizona

Freshman Application Contact Director of Admission, Universal Technical Institute, 10695 West Pierce Street, Avondale, AZ 85323. *Phone:* 623-245-4600. *Toll-free phone:* 800-510-5072. *Fax:* 623-245-4601. *Web site:* http://www.uti.edu/.

Yavapai College

Prescott, Arizona

- **State and locally supported** 2-year, founded 1966, part of Arizona State Community College System
- **Small-town** 100-acre campus
- **Coed**

Undergraduates 1,917 full-time, 6,359 part-time. Students come from 30 states and territories; 18% are from out of state; 5% live on campus.

Faculty *Student/faculty ratio:* 15:1.

Academics *Calendar:* semesters. *Degree:* certificates and associate. *Special study options:* academic remediation for entering students, adult/continuing education programs, advanced placement credit, cooperative education, distance learning, English as a second language, honors programs, independent study, internships, off-campus study, part-time degree program, services for LD students, summer session for credit. *ROTC:* Army (c), Air Force (c).

Student Life *Campus security:* 24-hour emergency response devices and patrols, student patrols, late-night transport/escort service, controlled dormitory access.

Athletics Member NJCAA.

Costs (2011–12) *Tuition:* state resident $1608 full-time, $67 per credit hour part-time; nonresident $10,008 full-time, $175 per credit hour part-time. *Room and board:* $5892. Room and board charges vary according to board plan.

Financial Aid Of all full-time matriculated undergraduates who enrolled in 2010, 100 Federal Work-Study jobs (averaging $2000).

Applying *Options:* early admission, deferred entrance. *Required:* high school transcript. *Required for some:* essay or personal statement.

Freshman Application Contact Mrs. Sheila Jarrell, Admissions, Registration, and Records Manager, Yavapai College, 1100 East Sheldon Street, Prescott, AZ 86301-3297. *Phone:* 928-776-2107. *Toll-free phone:* 800-922-6787. *Fax:* 928-776-2151. *E-mail:* registration@yc.edu. *Web site:* http://www.yc.edu/.

ARKANSAS

Arkansas Northeastern College

Blytheville, Arkansas

Freshman Application Contact Mrs. Leslie Wells, Admissions Counselor, Arkansas Northeastern College, PO Box 1109, Blytheville, AR 72316. *Phone:* 870-762-1020 Ext. 1118. *Fax:* 870-763-1654. *E-mail:* lwells@anc.edu. *Web site:* http://www.anc.edu/.

Arkansas State University–Beebe

Beebe, Arkansas

Freshman Application Contact Mr. Ronald Hudson, Coordinator of Student Recruitment, Arkansas State University–Beebe, PO Box 1000, Beebe, AR 72012. *Phone:* 501-882-8860. *Toll-free phone:* 800-632-9985. *E-mail:* rdhudson@asub.edu. *Web site:* http://www.asub.edu/.

Arkansas State University–Mountain Home

Mountain Home, Arkansas

- **State-supported** 2-year, founded 2000, part of Arkansas State University System
- **Small-town** 136-acre campus
- **Coed,** 1,472 undergraduate students, 62% full-time, 64% women, 36% men

Undergraduates 917 full-time, 555 part-time. Students come from 18 states and territories; 1 other country; 2% are from out of state; 0.2% Black or African American, non-Hispanic/Latino; 1% Hispanic/Latino; 0.5% Asian, non-Hispanic/Latino; 0.2% Native Hawaiian or other Pacific Islander, non-Hispanic/Latino; 0.8% American Indian or Alaska Native, non-Hispanic/Latino; 3% Two or more races, non-Hispanic/Latino; 0.1% Race/ethnicity unknown; 7% transferred in. *Retention:* 49% of full-time freshmen returned.

Freshmen *Admission:* 715 applied, 336 admitted, 263 enrolled. *Average high school GPA:* 2.27.

Faculty *Total:* 79, 61% full-time, 16% with terminal degrees. *Student/faculty ratio:* 19:1.

Majors Administrative assistant and secretarial science; business/commerce; criminal justice/law enforcement administration; criminal justice/police science; early childhood education; education (multiple levels); emergency medical technology (EMT paramedic); forensic science and technology; funeral service and mortuary science; information science/studies; liberal arts and sciences/liberal studies; middle school education; respiratory care therapy; welding technology.

Academics *Calendar:* semesters. *Degree:* certificates and associate. *Special study options:* academic remediation for entering students, advanced placement credit, cooperative education, distance learning, English as a second language, honors programs, independent study, internships, part-time degree program, services for LD students, summer session for credit. *ROTC:* Army (b).

Library Norma Wood Library with 38,324 titles, 24,650 serial subscriptions, 9,205 audiovisual materials, an OPAC, a Web page.

Student Life *Housing:* college housing not available. *Activities and Organizations:* Phi Theta Kappa, Circle K, Criminal Justice Club, Mortuary Science Club, Student Ambassadors. *Campus security:* during operation hours security is present and available as needed.

Standardized Tests *Recommended:* SAT or ACT (for admission), COMPASS, ASSET.

Costs (2012–13) *Tuition:* state resident $2016 full-time; nonresident $3408 full-time. Full-time tuition and fees vary according to course load. Part-time tuition and fees vary according to course load. *Required fees:* $408 full-time. *Payment plan:* installment. *Waivers:* children of alumni, senior citizens, and employees or children of employees.

Financial Aid Of all full-time matriculated undergraduates who enrolled in 2011, 730 applied for aid, 689 were judged to have need, 34 had their need fully met. In 2011, 6 non-need-based awards were made. *Average percent of need met:* 45%. *Average financial aid package:* $8214. *Average need-based loan:* $1788. *Average need-based gift aid:* $1872. *Average non-need-based aid:* $2213.

Applying *Options:* electronic application. *Required:* high school transcript. *Recommended:* placement scores, GED scores accepted. *Notification:* continuous (freshmen).

Freshman Application Contact Ms. Delba Parrish, Admissions Coordinator, Arkansas State University–Mountain Home, 1600 South College Street, Mountain Home, AR 72653. *Phone:* 870-508-6180. *Fax:* 870-508-6287. *E-mail:* dparrish@asumh.edu. *Web site:* http://www.asumh.edu/.

Arkansas State University–Newport

Newport, Arkansas

Director of Admissions Robert Summers, Director of Admissions/Registrar, Arkansas State University–Newport, 7648 Victory Boulevard, Newport, AR 72112. *Phone:* 870-512-7800. *Toll-free phone:* 800-976-1676. *Fax:* 870-512-7825. *E-mail:* robert.summers@asun.edu. *Web site:* http://www.asun.edu/.

Black River Technical College

Pocahontas, Arkansas

Director of Admissions Director of Admissions, Black River Technical College, 1410 Highway 304 East, Pocahontas, AR 72455. *Phone:* 870-892-4565. *Web site:* http://www.blackrivertech.edu/.

College of the Ouachitas

Malvern, Arkansas

- **State-supported** 2-year, founded 1972
- **Small-town** 11-acre campus
- **Coed,** 1,407 undergraduate students, 42% full-time, 60% women, 40% men

Undergraduates 592 full-time, 815 part-time. 12% Black or African American, non-Hispanic/Latino; 3% Hispanic/Latino; 0.4% Asian, non-Hispanic/Latino; 0.1% Native Hawaiian or other Pacific Islander, non-Hispanic/Latino; 0.4% American Indian or Alaska Native, non-Hispanic/Latino; 3% Two or more races, non-Hispanic/Latino; 0.2% international.

Freshmen *Admission:* 153 enrolled. *Test scores:* ACT scores over 18: 62%; ACT scores over 24: 9%.

Faculty *Total:* 98, 40% full-time, 9% with terminal degrees.

Majors Accounting; administrative assistant and secretarial science; automobile/automotive mechanics technology; business administration and management; child-care and support services management; computer and information sciences; industrial technology; legal administrative assistant/secretary; legal assistant/paralegal; liberal arts and sciences/liberal studies; licensed practical/vocational nurse training; machine tool technology; management information systems; marketing/marketing management; medical administrative assistant and medical secretary.

Academics *Calendar:* semesters. *Degree:* certificates and associate. *Special study options:* academic remediation for entering students, accelerated degree program, advanced placement credit, cooperative education, distance learning, double majors, independent study, internships, part-time degree program, services for LD students, summer session for credit.

Library Ouachita Technical College Library/Learning Resource Center with 8,000 titles, 100 serial subscriptions, 1,200 audiovisual materials, an OPAC, a Web page.

Student Life *Housing:* college housing not available. *Campus security:* 24-hour patrols. *Student services:* personal/psychological counseling.

Standardized Tests *Recommended:* SAT or ACT (for admission), ACT COMPASS or ASSET.

Costs (2012–13) *Tuition:* state resident $1860 full-time; nonresident $3720 full-time. No tuition increase for student's term of enrollment. *Required fees:* $542 full-time, $17 per credit part-time, $16 per credit part-time. *Payment plan:* installment. *Waivers:* senior citizens and employees or children of employees.

Financial Aid Of all full-time matriculated undergraduates who enrolled in 2010, 18 Federal Work-Study jobs (averaging $2400).

Applying *Options:* electronic application, early admission, deferred entrance. *Required:* high school transcript. *Application deadlines:* rolling (freshmen), rolling (transfers).

Freshman Application Contact Kathy Lazenby, Counselor, College of the Ouachitas, One College Circle, Malvern, AR 72104. *Phone:* 501-337-5000 Ext. 1103. *Toll-free phone:* 800-337-0266. *Fax:* 501-337-9382. *E-mail:* klazenby@coto.edu. *Web site:* http://www.coto.edu/.

Cossatot Community College of the University of Arkansas

De Queen, Arkansas

Freshman Application Contact Cossatot Community College of the University of Arkansas, DeQueen, AR 71832. *Phone:* 870-584-4471. *Toll-free phone:* 800-844-4471. *Web site:* http://www.cccua.edu/.

Crowley's Ridge College

Paragould, Arkansas

Freshman Application Contact Amanda Drake, Director of Admissions, Crowley's Ridge College, 100 College Drive, Paragould, AR 72450-9731. *Phone:* 870-236-6901. *Toll-free phone:* 800-264-1096. *Fax:* 870-236-7748. *E-mail:* njoneshi@crc.pioneer.paragould.ar.us. *Web site:* http://www.crc.edu/.

East Arkansas Community College

Forrest City, Arkansas

Freshman Application Contact Ms. DeAnna Adams, Director of Enrollment Management/Institutional Research, East Arkansas Community College, 1700 Newcastle Road, Forrest City, AR 72335-2204. *Phone:* 870-633-4480. *Toll-free phone:* 877-797-3222. *Fax:* 870-633-3840. *E-mail:* dadams@eacc.edu. *Web site:* http://www.eacc.edu/.

ITT Technical Institute

Little Rock, Arkansas

- **Proprietary** primarily 2-year, founded 1993, part of ITT Educational Services, Inc.
- **Urban** campus
- **Coed**

Majors Business administration and management; communications technology; computer and information systems security; construction management; criminal justice/law enforcement administration; drafting and design technology; electrical, electronic and communications engineering technology; forensic science and technology; game and interactive media design; graphic communications; legal assistant/paralegal; network and system administration; project management.

Academics *Calendar:* quarters. *Degrees:* associate and bachelor's.

Student Life *Housing:* college housing not available.

Freshman Application Contact Director of Recruitment, ITT Technical Institute, 12200 Westhaven Drive, Little Rock, AR 72211. *Phone:* 501-565-5550. *Toll-free phone:* 800-359-4429. *Web site:* http://www.itt-tech.edu/.

Mid-South Community College

West Memphis, Arkansas

Freshman Application Contact Jeremy Reece, Director of Admissions, Mid-South Community College, 2000 West Broadway, West Memphis, AR 72301. *Phone:* 870-733-6786. *Toll-free phone:* 866-733-6722. *Fax:* 870-733-6719. *E-mail:* jreece@midsouthcc.edu. *Web site:* http://www.midsouthcc.edu/.

National Park Community College

Hot Springs, Arkansas

Director of Admissions Dr. Allen B. Moody, Director of Institutional Services/Registrar, National Park Community College, 101 College Drive, Hot Springs, AR 71913. *Phone:* 501-760-4222. *E-mail:* bmoody@npcc.edu. *Web site:* http://www.npcc.edu/.

North Arkansas College

Harrison, Arkansas

Freshman Application Contact Mrs. Charla Jennings, Director of Admissions, North Arkansas College, 1515 Pioneer Drive, Harrison, AR 72601. *Phone:* 870-391-3221. *Toll-free phone:* 800-679-6622. *Fax:* 870-391-3339. *E-mail:* charlam@northark.edu. *Web site:* http://www.northark.edu/.

NorthWest Arkansas Community College

Bentonville, Arkansas

Freshman Application Contact NorthWest Arkansas Community College, One College Drive, Bentonville, AR 72712. *Phone:* 479-636-9222. *Toll-free phone:* 800-995-6922. *Fax:* 479-619-4116. *E-mail:* admissions@nwacc.edu. *Web site:* http://www.nwacc.edu/.

Ozarka College

Melbourne, Arkansas

- **State-supported** 2-year, founded 1973
- **Rural** 40-acre campus
- **Coed,** 1,600 undergraduate students

Undergraduates 1% are from out of state.

Faculty *Total:* 71, 44% full-time, 4% with terminal degrees. *Student/faculty ratio:* 20:1.

Majors Automobile/automotive mechanics technology; business automation/technology/data entry; criminal justice/law enforcement administration; culinary arts; health information/medical records technology; information science/studies; liberal arts and sciences/liberal studies; middle school education.

Academics *Calendar:* semesters. *Degree:* certificates and associate. *Special study options:* academic remediation for entering students, advanced placement credit, distance learning, external degree program, internships, services for LD students, summer session for credit.

Library Ozarka College Library with 10,500 titles, 4,000 serial subscriptions, an OPAC.

Student Life *Housing:* college housing not available. *Activities and Organizations:* drama/theater group, VICA (Vocational Industrial Clubs of America), Phi Beta Lambda, Drama Club, HOSA, Phi Theta Kappa. *Campus security:* security patrols after business hours. *Student services:* personal/psychological counseling.

Applying *Options:* electronic application, deferred entrance. *Required:* high school transcript. *Required for some:* essay or personal statement, interview. *Recommended:* minimum 2.0 GPA. *Application deadlines:* 8/19 (freshmen), 8/15 (transfers).
Freshman Application Contact Ms. Amanda Dobbs, Director of Admissions, Ozarka College, PO Box 10, Melbourne, AR 72556. *Phone:* 870-368-7371 Ext. 2013. *Toll-free phone:* 800-821-4335. *E-mail:* amanda.dobbs@ozarka.edu. *Web site:* http://www.ozarka.edu/.

Phillips Community College of the University of Arkansas
Helena, Arkansas

Director of Admissions Mr. Lynn Boone, Registrar, Phillips Community College of the University of Arkansas, PO Box 785, Helena, AR 72342-0785. *Phone:* 870-338-6474. *Web site:* http://www.pccua.edu/.

Pulaski Technical College
North Little Rock, Arkansas

Freshman Application Contact Mr. Clark Atkins, Director of Admissions, Pulaski Technical College, 3000 West Scenic Drive, North Little Rock, AR 72118. *Phone:* 501-812-2734. *Fax:* 501-812-2316. *E-mail:* catkins@pulaskitech.edu. *Web site:* http://www.pulaskitech.edu/.

Remington College–Little Rock Campus
Little Rock, Arkansas

Director of Admissions Brian Maggio, Director of Recruitment, Remington College–Little Rock Campus, 19 Remington Drive, Little Rock, AR 72204. *Phone:* 501-312-0007. *Fax:* 501-225-3819. *E-mail:* brian.maggio@remingtoncollege.edu. *Web site:* http://www.remingtoncollege.edu/.

Rich Mountain Community College
Mena, Arkansas

Director of Admissions Dr. Steve Rook, Dean of Students, Rich Mountain Community College, 1100 College Drive, Mena, AR 71953. *Phone:* 479-394-7622 Ext. 1400. *Web site:* http://www.rmcc.edu/.

South Arkansas Community College
El Dorado, Arkansas

Freshman Application Contact Mr. Dean Inman, Director of Enrollment Services, South Arkansas Community College, PO Box 7010, El Dorado, AR 71731-7010. *Phone:* 870-864-7142. *Toll-free phone:* 800-955-2289. *Fax:* 870-864-7109. *E-mail:* dinman@southark.edu. *Web site:* http://www.southark.edu/.

Southeast Arkansas College
Pine Bluff, Arkansas

Freshman Application Contact Ms. Barbara Dunn, Coordinator of Admissions and Enrollment Management, Southeast Arkansas College, 1900 Hazel Street, Pine Bluff, AR 71603. *Phone:* 870-543-5957. *Toll-free phone:* 888-SEARK TC (in-state); 888-SEARC TC (out-of-state). *Fax:* 870-543-5956. *E-mail:* bdunn@seark.edu. *Web site:* http://www.seark.edu/.

Southern Arkansas University Tech
Camden, Arkansas

Freshman Application Contact Mrs. Beverly Ellis, Admissions Analyst, Southern Arkansas University Tech, PO Box 3499, Camden, AR 71711-1599. *Phone:* 870-574-4558. *Fax:* 870-574-4478. *E-mail:* bellis@sautech.edu. *Web site:* http://www.sautech.edu/.

University of Arkansas Community College at Batesville
Batesville, Arkansas

Freshman Application Contact Ms. Sharon Gage, Admissions Coordinator, University of Arkansas Community College at Batesville, PO Box 3350, Batesville, AR 72503. *Phone:* 870-612-2042. *Toll-free phone:* 800-508-7878.
Fax: 870-612-2129. *E-mail:* sgage@uaccb.edu. *Web site:* http://www.uaccb.edu/.

University of Arkansas Community College at Hope
Hope, Arkansas

Freshman Application Contact University of Arkansas Community College at Hope, PO Box 140, Hope, AR 71802. *Phone:* 870-772-8174. *Web site:* http://www.uacch.edu/.

University of Arkansas Community College at Morrilton
Morrilton, Arkansas

- **State-supported** 2-year, founded 1961, part of University of Arkansas System
- **Rural** 70-acre campus
- **Coed,** 2,299 undergraduate students, 65% full-time, 60% women, 40% men

Undergraduates 1,486 full-time, 813 part-time. Students come from 3 states and territories; 9% Black or African American, non-Hispanic/Latino; 4% Hispanic/Latino; 0.7% Asian, non-Hispanic/Latino; 0.1% Native Hawaiian or other Pacific Islander, non-Hispanic/Latino; 0.5% American Indian or Alaska Native, non-Hispanic/Latino; 4% Two or more races, non-Hispanic/Latino; 0.2% Race/ethnicity unknown; 0.7% international; 11% transferred in.
Freshmen *Admission:* 1,422 applied, 939 admitted, 587 enrolled. *Average high school GPA:* 2.77. *Test scores:* ACT scores over 18: 78%; ACT scores over 24: 25%; ACT scores over 30: 1%.
Faculty *Total:* 118, 58% full-time, 6% with terminal degrees. *Student/faculty ratio:* 23:1.
Majors Autobody/collision and repair technology; automobile/automotive mechanics technology; business/commerce; child development; commercial and advertising art; computer technology/computer systems technology; criminal justice/law enforcement administration; drafting and design technology; education (multiple levels); forensic science and technology; general studies; heating, air conditioning, ventilation and refrigeration maintenance technology; liberal arts and sciences/liberal studies; petroleum technology; registered nursing/registered nurse; surveying technology.
Academics *Calendar:* semesters. *Degree:* certificates and associate. *Special study options:* academic remediation for entering students, advanced placement credit, distance learning, double majors, internships, part-time degree program, services for LD students, summer session for credit.
Library E. Allen Gordon Library with 17,134 titles, 64 serial subscriptions, 1,681 audiovisual materials, an OPAC, a Web page.
Student Life *Housing:* college housing not available. *Activities and Organizations:* drama/theater group, choral group, Student Government Association, Phi Beta Lambda, Student Practical Nurses Organization, Computer Information Systems Club, Early Childhood Development Organization. *Campus security:* 24-hour emergency response devices, campus alert system. *Student services:* personal/psychological counseling.
Athletics *Intramural sports:* basketball M/W, football M/W, table tennis M/W, ultimate Frisbee M/W, volleyball M/W.
Standardized Tests *Recommended:* SAT or ACT (for admission), ACT Compass Exam.
Costs (2011–12) *Tuition:* area resident $2280 full-time, $76 per credit hour part-time; state resident $2490 full-time, $83 per credit hour part-time; nonresident $3600 full-time, $120 per credit hour part-time. Full-time tuition and fees vary according to course load and program. Part-time tuition and fees vary according to course load and program. *Required fees:* $655 full-time, $21 per credit hour part-time, $25 per term part-time. *Payment plan:* installment. *Waivers:* senior citizens and employees or children of employees.
Financial Aid Of all full-time matriculated undergraduates who enrolled in 2011, 1,279 applied for aid, 1,139 were judged to have need, 289 had their need fully met. 20 Federal Work-Study jobs (averaging $1269). In 2011, 84 non-need-based awards were made. *Average percent of need met:* 51%. *Average financial aid package:* $6740. *Average need-based loan:* $1767. *Average need-based gift aid:* $2225. *Average non-need-based aid:* $880. *Financial aid deadline:* 7/1.
Applying *Options:* electronic application, early admission, deferred entrance. *Required:* high school transcript. *Required for some:* immunization records and prior college transcript(s). *Application deadlines:* rolling (freshmen), rolling (transfers). *Notification:* continuous (freshmen), continuous (transfers).
Freshman Application Contact Ms. Rachel Mullins, Coordinator of Recruitment, University of Arkansas Community College at Morrilton, 1537 University Boulevard, Morrilton, AR 72110. *Phone:* 501-977-2174. *Toll-free phone:* 800-264-1094. *Fax:* 501-977-2123. *E-mail:* mullins@uaccm.edu. *Web site:* http://www.uaccm.edu/.

CALIFORNIA

Academy of Couture Art
West Hollywood, California

Admissions Office Contact Academy of Couture Art, Pacific Design Center, 8687 Melrose Avenue, Suite G520, West Hollywood, CA 90069. *Web site:* http://www.academyofcoutureart.com/.

Allan Hancock College
Santa Maria, California

Freshman Application Contact Ms. Adela Esquivel Swinson, Director of Admissions and Records, Allan Hancock College, 800 South College Drive, Santa Maria, CA 93454-6399. *Phone:* 805-922-6966 Ext. 3272. *Toll-free phone:* 866-342-5242. *Fax:* 805-922-3477. *Web site:* http://www.hancockcollege.edu/.

American Academy of Dramatic Arts
Hollywood, California

- **Independent** 2-year, founded 1974
- **Suburban** 4-acre campus with easy access to Los Angeles
- **Endowment** $1.7 million
- **Coed**

Undergraduates 188 full-time. Students come from 37 states and territories; 15 other countries; 59% are from out of state; 7% Black or African American, non-Hispanic/Latino; 11% Hispanic/Latino; 2% Asian, non-Hispanic/Latino; 0.5% American Indian or Alaska Native, non-Hispanic/Latino; 9% Two or more races, non-Hispanic/Latino; 5% Race/ethnicity unknown; 20% international.

Faculty *Student/faculty ratio:* 12:1.

Academics *Calendar:* continuous. *Degree:* certificates, diplomas, and associate. *Special study options:* internships.

Student Life *Campus security:* 24-hour emergency response devices, 8-hour patrols by trained security personnel.

Costs (2011–12) *Tuition:* $29,900 full-time. *Required fees:* $600 full-time.

Financial Aid Of all full-time matriculated undergraduates who enrolled in 2010, 15 Federal Work-Study jobs (averaging $2000).

Applying *Options:* deferred entrance. *Application fee:* $50. *Required:* essay or personal statement, high school transcript, 2 letters of recommendation, interview, audition. *Recommended:* minimum 2.0 GPA.

Freshman Application Contact American Academy of Dramatic Arts, 1336 North La Brea Avenue, Hollywood, CA 90028. *Phone:* 323-464-2777. *Toll-free phone:* 800-222-2867. *Web site:* http://www.aada.org/.

American Career College
Anaheim, California

Director of Admissions Susan Pailet, Senior Executive Director of Admission, American Career College, 1200 North Magnolia Avenue, Anaheim, CA 92801. *Phone:* 714-952-9066. *Toll-free phone:* 877-832-0790. *E-mail:* info@americancareer.com. *Web site:* http://americancareercollege.edu/.

American Career College
Los Angeles, California

Director of Admissions Tamra Adams, Director of Admissions, American Career College, 4021 Rosewood Avenue, Los Angeles, CA 90004-2932. *Phone:* 323-668-7555. *Toll-free phone:* 877-832-0790. *E-mail:* info@americancareer.com. *Web site:* http://americancareercollege.edu/.

American Career College
Ontario, California

Director of Admissions Juan Tellez, Director of Admissions, American Career College, 3130 East Sedona Court, Ontario, CA 91764. *Phone:* 951-739-0788. *Toll-free phone:* 877-832-0790. *E-mail:* info@americancareer.com. *Web site:* http://americancareercollege.edu/.

American River College
Sacramento, California

Freshman Application Contact American River College, 4700 College Oak Drive, Sacramento, CA 95841-4286. *Phone:* 916-484-8171. *Web site:* http://www.arc.losrios.edu/.

Antelope Valley College
Lancaster, California

- **State and locally supported** 2-year, founded 1929, part of California Community College System
- **Suburban** 135-acre campus with easy access to Los Angeles
- **Endowment** $299,569
- **Coed**

Undergraduates 4,802 full-time, 10,306 part-time. Students come from 7 states and territories; 1% are from out of state; 16% transferred in. *Retention:* 68% of full-time freshmen returned.

Faculty *Student/faculty ratio:* 45:1.

Academics *Calendar:* semesters. *Degree:* certificates and associate. *Special study options:* academic remediation for entering students, adult/continuing education programs, advanced placement credit, cooperative education, distance learning, English as a second language, honors programs, independent study, part-time degree program, services for LD students, student-designed majors, summer session for credit. *ROTC:* Air Force (c).

Student Life *Campus security:* 24-hour emergency response devices and patrols, late-night transport/escort service.

Costs (2011–12) *Tuition:* state resident $864 full-time, $36 per unit part-time; nonresident $5328 full-time, $222 per unit part-time. Full-time tuition and fees vary according to course load. Part-time tuition and fees vary according to course load. *Required fees:* $2 full-time, $1 per term part-time.

Applying *Options:* electronic application, early admission. *Required:* high school transcript. *Recommended:* assessment.

Freshman Application Contact Welcome Center, Antelope Valley College, 3041 West Avenue K, Lancaster, CA 93536-5426. *Phone:* 661-722-6331. *Web site:* http://www.avc.edu/.

Anthem College–Sacramento
Sacramento, California

Freshman Application Contact Admissions Office, Anthem College–Sacramento, 9738 Lincoln Village Drive, Suite 100, Sacramento, CA 95827. *Phone:* 916-929-9700. *Toll-free phone:* 855-331-7768. *Web site:* http://anthem.edu/sacramento-california/.

Applied Professional Training, Inc.
Carlsbad, California

Director of Admissions Monica Hoffman, Director of Admissions/Registrar, Applied Professional Training, Inc., 5751 Palmer Way, Suite D, PO Box 131717, Carlsbad, CA 92013. *Phone:* 800-431-8488. *Toll-free phone:* 800-431-8488. *Fax:* 888-431-8588. *E-mail:* aptc@aptc.com. *Web site:* http://www.aptc.edu/.

Aviation & Electronic Schools of America
Colfax, California

Freshman Application Contact Admissions Office, Aviation & Electronic Schools of America, 111 South Railroad Street, PO Box 1810, Colfax, CA 95713-1810. *Phone:* 530-346-6792. *Toll-free phone:* 800-345-2742. *Fax:* 530-346-8466. *E-mail:* aesa@aesa.com. *Web site:* http://www.aesa.com/.

Bakersfield College
Bakersfield, California

Freshman Application Contact Bakersfield College, 1801 Panorama Drive, Bakersfield, CA 93305-1299. *Phone:* 661-395-4301. *Web site:* http://www.bakersfieldcollege.edu/.

Barstow Community College
Barstow, California

Director of Admissions Heather Caldon, Manager of Admissions and Records, Barstow Community College, 2700 Barstow Road, Barstow, CA 92311-6699. *Phone:* 760-252-2411 Ext. 7236. *Fax:* 760-252-6754. *E-mail:* hcaldon@barstow.edu. *Web site:* http://www.barstow.edu/.

Berkeley City College
Berkeley, California

- **State and locally supported** 2-year, founded 1974, part of California Community College System
- **Urban** campus with easy access to San Francisco
- **Coed**, 7,645 undergraduate students

Undergraduates 1% are from out of state; 18% Black or African American, non-Hispanic/Latino; 12% Hispanic/Latino; 16% Asian, non-Hispanic/Latino; 0.5% Native Hawaiian or other Pacific Islander, non-Hispanic/Latino; 0.5% American Indian or Alaska Native, non-Hispanic/Latino; 3% Two or more races, non-Hispanic/Latino; 31% Race/ethnicity unknown.
Freshmen *Admission:* 7,090 applied, 7,090 admitted.
Faculty *Total:* 277, 19% full-time. *Student/faculty ratio:* 35:1.
Majors Accounting; accounting and business/management; American Sign Language (ASL); art; biology/biotechnology laboratory technician; business administration and management; business administration, management and operations related; business/commerce; business, management, and marketing related; computer and information sciences; computer and information sciences related; computer and information systems security; computer graphics; computer software and media applications related; creative writing; data entry/microcomputer applications related; English; fine/studio arts; general studies; liberal arts and sciences/liberal studies; medical administrative assistant and medical secretary; office management; psychology; public health education and promotion; public health related; sign language interpretation and translation; social sciences related; social work related; sociology; Spanish; web page, digital/multimedia and information resources design; writing.
Academics *Calendar:* semesters. *Degree:* certificates and associate. *Special study options:* academic remediation for entering students, adult/continuing education programs, cooperative education, distance learning, double majors, English as a second language, independent study, internships, off-campus study, part-time degree program, services for LD students, student-designed majors, study abroad, summer session for credit.
Library Susan A. Duncan Library plus 1 other with an OPAC, a Web page.
Student Life *Housing:* college housing not available. *Activities and Organizations:* choral group, Civic Engagement Club, Global Studies Club, Indigenous Student Alliance, The National Society of Leadership and Success, The Digital Arts Club (DAC). *Campus security:* 24-hour patrols. *Student services:* health clinic, personal/psychological counseling.
Costs (2012–13) *Tuition:* state resident $1380 full-time, $46 per unit part-time; nonresident $6390 full-time, $213 per unit part-time. Full-time tuition and fees vary according to class time, course load, and program. Part-time tuition and fees vary according to class time, course load, and program. *Required fees:* $170 full-time, $46 per unit part-time, $690 per term part-time. *Waivers:* minority students, children of alumni, adult students, senior citizens, and employees or children of employees.
Financial Aid Of all full-time matriculated undergraduates who enrolled in 2010, 43 Federal Work-Study jobs (averaging $3000).
Applying *Options:* electronic application, early admission, deferred entrance. *Recommended:* high school transcript. *Application deadlines:* rolling (freshmen), rolling (out-of-state freshmen), rolling (transfers). *Notification:* continuous (freshmen), continuous (out-of-state freshmen), continuous (transfers).
Freshman Application Contact Dr. May Kuang-chi Chen, Vice President of Student Services, Berkeley City College, 2050 Center Street, Berkeley, CA 94704. *Phone:* 510-981-2820. *Fax:* 510-841-7333. *E-mail:* mrivas@peralta.edu. *Web site:* http://www.berkeleycitycollege.edu/.

Bryan College
Gold River, California

Freshman Application Contact Bryan College, 2317 Gold Meadow Way, Gold River, CA 95670. *Phone:* 916-649-2400. *Toll-free phone:* 866-649-2400. *Web site:* http://www.bryancollege.edu/.

Butte College
Oroville, California

Freshman Application Contact Ms. Nancy Jenson, Registrar, Butte College, 3536 Butte Campus Drive, Oroville, CA 95965-8399. *Phone:* 530-895-2361. *Web site:* http://www.butte.edu/.

Cabrillo College
Aptos, California

Freshman Application Contact Tama Bolton, Director of Admissions and Records, Cabrillo College, 6500 Soquel Drive, Aptos, CA 95003-3194. *Phone:* 831-477-3548. *Fax:* 831-479-5782. *E-mail:* tabolton@cabrillo.edu. *Web site:* http://www.cabrillo.edu/.

California Culinary Academy
San Francisco, California

Director of Admissions Ms. Nancy Seyfert, Vice President of Admissions, California Culinary Academy, 625 Polk Street, San Francisco, CA 94102-3368. *Phone:* 800-229-2433 Ext. 275. *Toll-free phone:* 800-229-2433 (in-state); 800-BAYCHEF (out-of-state). *Web site:* http://www.baychef.com/.

Cambridge Junior College
Yuba City, California

Freshman Application Contact Admissions Office, Cambridge Junior College, 990-A Klamath Lane, Yuba City, CA 95993. *Phone:* 530-674-9199. *Fax:* 530-671-7319. *Web site:* http://cambridge.edu/.

Canada College
Redwood City, California

Freshman Application Contact Canada College, 4200 Farm Hill Boulevard, Redwood City, CA 94061-1099. *Phone:* 650-306-3125. *Web site:* http://www.canadacollege.edu/.

Carrington College California - Pleasant Hill
Pleasant Hill, California

Admissions Office Contact Carrington College California - Pleasant Hill, 380 Civic Drive, Suite 300, Pleasant Hill, CA 94523. *Web site:* http://carrington.edu/.

Carrington College California - San Jose
San Jose, California

Director of Admissions Admissions Director, Carrington College California - San Jose, 6201 San Ignacio Avenue, San Jose, CA 95119. *Phone:* 408-360-0840. *Web site:* http://carrington.edu/.

Carrington College California - San Leandro
San Leandro, California

Admissions Office Contact Carrington College California - San Leandro, 15555 East 14th Street, Suite 500, San Leandro, CA 94578. *Web site:* http://carrington.edu/.

Carrington College of California - Antioch
Antioch, California

Freshman Application Contact Admissions Director, Carrington College of California - Antioch, 2157 Country Hills Drive, Antioch, CA 94509. *Phone:* 925-522-7777. *Web site:* http://carrington.edu/.

Carrington College of California - Citrus Heights
Citrus Heights, California

Admissions Office Contact Carrington College of California - Citrus Heights, 7301 Greenback Lane, Suite A, Citrus Heights, CA 95621. *Web site:* http://carrington.edu/.

Carrington College of California - Emeryville
Emeryville, California

Freshman Application Contact Admissions Office, Carrington College of California - Emeryville, 6001 Shellmound Street, Suite 145, Emeryville, CA 94608. *Phone:* 510-601-0133. *Fax:* 510-623-9822. *Web site:* http://carrington.edu/.

Carrington College of California - Sacramento

Sacramento, California

Admissions Office Contact Carrington College of California - Sacramento, 8909 Folsom Boulevard, Sacramento, CA 95826. *Web site:* http://carrington.edu/.

Cerritos College

Norwalk, California

Director of Admissions Ms. Stephanie Murguia, Director of Admissions and Records, Cerritos College, 11110 Alondra Boulevard, Norwalk, CA 90650-6298. *Phone:* 562-860-2451. *E-mail:* smurguia@cerritos.edu. *Web site:* http://www.cerritos.edu/.

Cerro Coso Community College

Ridgecrest, California

Freshman Application Contact Mrs. Heather Ootash, Counseling/Matriculation Coordinator, Cerro Coso Community College, 3000 College Heights Boulevard, Ridgecrest, CA 93555. *Phone:* 760-384-6291. *Fax:* 760-375-4776. *E-mail:* hostash@cerrocoso.edu. *Web site:* http://www.cerrocoso.edu/.

Chabot College

Hayward, California

Director of Admissions Paulette Lino, Director of Admissions and Records, Chabot College, 25555 Hesperian Boulevard, Hayward, CA 94545-5001. *Phone:* 510-723-6700. *Web site:* http://www.chabotcollege.edu/.

Chaffey College

Rancho Cucamonga, California

Freshman Application Contact Erlinda Martinez, Coordinator of Admissions, Chaffey College, 5885 Haven Avenue, Rancho Cucamonga, CA 91737-3002. *Phone:* 909-652-6610. *E-mail:* erlinda.martinez@chaffey.edu. *Web site:* http://www.chaffey.edu/.

Citrus College

Glendora, California

Freshman Application Contact Admissions and Records, Citrus College, Glendora, CA 91741-1899. *Phone:* 626-914-8511. *Fax:* 626-914-8613. *E-mail:* admissions@citruscollege.edu. *Web site:* http://www.citruscollege.edu/.

City College of San Francisco

San Francisco, California

Freshman Application Contact Ms. Mary Lou Leyba-Frank, Dean of Admissions and Records, City College of San Francisco, 50 Phelan Avenue, San Francisco, CA 94112-1821. *Phone:* 415-239-3291. *Fax:* 415-239-3936. *E-mail:* mleyba@ccsf.edu. *Web site:* http://www.ccsf.edu/.

Coastline Community College

Fountain Valley, California

Freshman Application Contact Jennifer McDonald, Director of Admissions and Records, Coastline Community College, 11460 Warner Avenue, Fountain Valley, CA 92708-2597. *Phone:* 714-241-6163. *Web site:* http://www.coastline.edu/.

Coleman University

San Marcos, California

Director of Admissions Senior Admissions Officer, Coleman University, 1284 West San Marcos Boulevard, San Marcos, CA 92078. *Phone:* 760-747-3990. *Fax:* 760-752-9808. *Web site:* http://www.coleman.edu/.

College of Alameda

Alameda, California

Freshman Application Contact College of Alameda, 555 Ralph Appezzato Memorial Parkway, Alameda, CA 94501-2109. *Phone:* 510-748-2204. *Web site:* http://alameda.peralta.edu/.

College of Marin

Kentfield, California

Freshman Application Contact College of Marin, 835 College Avenue, Kentfield, CA 94904. *Phone:* 415-485-9414. *Web site:* http://www.marin.edu/

College of San Mateo

San Mateo, California

Director of Admissions Mr. Henry Villareal, Dean of Admissions and Records, College of San Mateo, 1700 West Hillsdale Boulevard, San Mateo, CA 94402-3784. *Phone:* 650-574-6590. *E-mail:* csmadmission@smccd.edu. *Web site:* http://www.collegeofsanmateo.edu/.

College of the Canyons

Santa Clarita, California

- **State and locally supported** 2-year, founded 1969, part of California Community College System
- **Suburban** 224-acre campus with easy access to Los Angeles
- **Coed,** 22,968 undergraduate students

Undergraduates 3% are from out of state; 6% Black or African American, non-Hispanic/Latino; 36% Hispanic/Latino; 8% Asian, non-Hispanic/Latino; 0.4% Native Hawaiian or other Pacific Islander, non-Hispanic/Latino; 0.5% American Indian or Alaska Native, non-Hispanic/Latino; 0.4% Two or more races, non-Hispanic/Latino; 2% Race/ethnicity unknown; 0.5% international.

Faculty *Total:* 630, 28% full-time. *Student/faculty ratio:* 38:1.

Majors Accounting technology and bookkeeping; administrative assistant and secretarial science; animation, interactive technology, video graphics and special effects; architectural drafting and CAD/CADD; art; athletic training; automobile/automotive mechanics technology; biological and physical sciences; building/construction site management; business administration and management; child-care provision; cinematography and film/video production; computer science; computer systems networking and telecommunications; criminal justice/police science; dramatic/theater arts; English; fire prevention and safety technology; French; graphic design; health and physical education/fitness; history; hospitality administration; hotel/motel administration; interior design; intermedia/multimedia; journalism; landscaping and groundskeeping; legal assistant/paralegal; liberal arts and sciences/liberal studies; library and archives assisting; manufacturing engineering technology; mathematics; music; parks, recreation and leisure; photography; pre-engineering; psychology; radio and television; real estate; registered nursing/registered nurse; restaurant, culinary, and catering management; sales, distribution, and marketing operations; sign language interpretation and translation; small business administration; social sciences; sociology; Spanish; surveying technology; water quality and wastewater treatment management and recycling technology; welding technology.

Academics *Calendar:* semesters. *Degree:* certificates and associate. *Special study options:* academic remediation for entering students, adult/continuing education programs, advanced placement credit, cooperative education, distance learning, double majors, English as a second language, honors programs, independent study, internships, off-campus study, part-time degree program, services for LD students, study abroad, summer session for credit.

Library College of the Canyons Library with 58,528 titles, 146 serial subscriptions, 7,760 audiovisual materials, an OPAC, a Web page.

Student Life *Housing:* college housing not available. *Activities and Organizations:* drama/theater group, choral group, Communication Studies Club, Gamma Beta Phi, Grad Club, American Medical Student Association, COC Honors Club. *Campus security:* 24-hour emergency response devices, late-night transport/escort service. *Student services:* health clinic, personal/psychological counseling, women's center.

Athletics *Intercollegiate sports:* baseball M, basketball M/W, cross-country running M/W, football M, golf M/W, ice hockey M(c), soccer M/W, softball W, swimming and diving M/W, track and field M/W, volleyball W.

Costs (2012–13) *Tuition:* state resident $1152 full-time, $46 per unit part-time; nonresident $5232 full-time, $201 per unit part-time. *Required fees:* $46 full-time.

Applying *Options:* electronic application, early admission. *Recommended:* high school transcript. *Application deadlines:* rolling (freshmen), rolling (transfers). *Notification:* continuous (freshmen), continuous (transfers).

Freshman Application Contact Ms. Jasmine Ruys, Director, Admissions and Records and Online Services, College of the Canyons, 26455 Rockwell Canyon Road, Santa Clarita, CA 91355. *Phone:* 661-362-3280. *Fax:* 661-254-7996. *E-mail:* jasmine.ruys@canyons.edu. *Web site:* http://www.canyons.edu/.

College of the Desert
Palm Desert, California

Freshman Application Contact College of the Desert, 43-500 Monterey Avenue, Palm Desert, CA 92260-9305. *Phone:* 760-346-8041 Ext. 7441. *Web site:* http://www.collegeofthedesert.edu/.

College of the Redwoods
Eureka, California

Freshman Application Contact Director of Enrollment Management, College of the Redwoods, 7351 Tompkins Hill Road, Eureka, CA 95501-9300. *Phone:* 707-476-4100. *Toll-free phone:* 800-641-0400. *Fax:* 707-476-4400. *Web site:* http://www.redwoods.edu/.

College of the Sequoias
Visalia, California

Freshman Application Contact Ms. Lisa Hott, Director for Admissions, College of the Sequoias, 915 South Mooney Boulevard, Visalia, CA 93277-2234. *Phone:* 559-737-4844. *Fax:* 559-737-4820. *Web site:* http://www.cos.edu/.

College of the Siskiyous
Weed, California

Freshman Application Contact Recruitment and Admissions, College of the Siskiyous, 800 College Avenue, Weed, CA 96094-2899. *Phone:* 530-938-5555. *Toll-free phone:* 888-397-4339. *E-mail:* admissions-weed@siskyous.edu. *Web site:* http://www.siskiyous.edu/.

Columbia College
Sonora, California

Freshman Application Contact Admissions Office, Columbia College, 11600 Columbia College Drive, Sonora, CA 95370. *Phone:* 209-588-5231. *Fax:* 209-588-5337. *E-mail:* ccadmissions@yosemite.edu. *Web site:* http://www.gocolumbia.edu/.

Community Christian College
Redlands, California

Freshman Application Contact Enrique D. Melendez, Assistant Director of Admissions, Community Christian College, 251 Tennessee Street, Redlands, CA 92373. *Phone:* 909-222-9556. *Fax:* 909-335-9101. *E-mail:* emelendez@cccollege.edu. *Web site:* http://www.cccollege.edu/.

Concorde Career College
Garden Grove, California

Freshman Application Contact Chris Becker, Director, Concorde Career College, 12951 Euclid Street, Suite 101, Garden Grove, CA 92840. *Phone:* 714-703-1900. *Fax:* 714-530-4737. *E-mail:* cbecker@concorde.edu. *Web site:* http://www.concorde.edu/.

Concorde Career College
North Hollywood, California

Freshman Application Contact Madeline Volker, Director, Concorde Career College, 12412 Victory Boulevard, North Hollywood, CA 91606. *Phone:* 818-766-8151. *Fax:* 818-766-1587. *E-mail:* mvolker@concorde.edu. *Web site:* http://www.concorde.edu/.

Contra Costa College
San Pablo, California

Freshman Application Contact Admissions and Records Office, Contra Costa College, San Pablo, CA 94806. *Phone:* 510-235-7800 Ext. 7500. *Fax:* 510-412-0769. *E-mail:* A&R@contracosta.edu. *Web site:* http://www.contracosta.edu/.

Copper Mountain College
Joshua Tree, California

Freshman Application Contact Dr. Laraine Turk, Associate Dean of Student Services, Copper Mountain College, 6162 Rotary Way, Joshua Tree, CA 92252. *Phone:* 760-366-5290. *Toll-free phone:* 866-366-3791. *Web site:* http://www.cmccd.edu/.

Cosumnes River College
Sacramento, California

Freshman Application Contact Admissions and Records, Cosumnes River College, 8401 Center Parkway, Sacramento, CA 95823-5799. *Phone:* 916-691-7411. *Web site:* http://www.crc.losrios.edu/.

Crafton Hills College
Yucaipa, California

Director of Admissions Larry Aycock, Admissions and Records Coordinator, Crafton Hills College, 11711 Sand Canyon Road, Yucaipa, CA 92399-1799. *Phone:* 909-389-3663. *E-mail:* laycock@craftonhills.edu. *Web site:* http://www.craftonhills.edu/.

Cuesta College
San Luis Obispo, California

Freshman Application Contact Cuesta College, PO Box 8106, San Luis Obispo, CA 93403-8106. *Phone:* 805-546-3130 Ext. 2262. *Web site:* http://www.cuesta.edu/.

Cuyamaca College
El Cajon, California

Freshman Application Contact Ms. Susan Topham, Dean of Admissions and Records, Cuyamaca College, 900 Rancho San Diego Parkway, El Cajon, CA 92019-4304. *Phone:* 619-660-4302. *Fax:* 619-660-4575. *E-mail:* susan.topham@gcccd.edu. *Web site:* http://www.cuyamaca.net/.

Cypress College
Cypress, California

Freshman Application Contact Admissions Office, Cypress College, 9200 Valley View, Cypress, CA 90630-5897. *Phone:* 714-484-7346. *Fax:* 714-484-7446. *E-mail:* admissions@cypresscollege.edu. *Web site:* http://www.cypresscollege.edu/.

De Anza College
Cupertino, California

- **State and locally supported** 2-year, founded 1967, part of California Community College System
- **Suburban** 112-acre campus with easy access to San Francisco, San Jose
- **Coed**

Undergraduates 11,139 full-time, 14,052 part-time. 3% Black or African American, non-Hispanic/Latino; 12% Hispanic/Latino; 33% Asian, non-Hispanic/Latino; 0.6% Native Hawaiian or other Pacific Islander, non-Hispanic/Latino; 0.5% American Indian or Alaska Native, non-Hispanic/Latino; 9% Two or more races, non-Hispanic/Latino; 13% Race/ethnicity unknown.

Faculty *Student/faculty ratio:* 36:1.

Academics *Calendar:* quarters. *Degree:* certificates, diplomas, and associate. *Special study options:* academic remediation for entering students, adult/continuing education programs, advanced placement credit, cooperative education, distance learning, English as a second language, external degree program, honors programs, independent study, internships, part-time degree program, services for LD students, student-designed majors, study abroad, summer session for credit. *ROTC:* Army (c), Air Force (c).

Student Life *Campus security:* 24-hour emergency response devices, student patrols, late-night transport/escort service.

Athletics Member NCAA. All Division II.

Costs (2011–12) *Tuition:* state resident $864 full-time; nonresident $5724 full-time. *Required fees:* $167 full-time.

Applying *Options:* early admission. *Application fee:* $22.

Freshman Application Contact De Anza College, 21250 Stevens Creek Boulevard, Cupertino, CA 95014-5793. *Phone:* 408-864-8292. *Web site:* http://www.deanza.fhda.edu/.

Deep Springs College
Deep Springs, California

- **Independent** 2-year, founded 1917
- **Rural** 3000-acre campus
- **Endowment** $13.6 million
- **Men only,** 26 undergraduate students, 100% full-time

Undergraduates 26 full-time. Students come from 16 states and territories; 2 other countries; 80% are from out of state; 62% transferred in; 100% live on campus. *Retention:* 92% of full-time freshmen returned.

Freshmen *Admission:* 140 applied, 12 admitted, 26 enrolled. *Average high school GPA:* 3.87. *Test scores:* SAT critical reading scores over 500: 100%; SAT math scores over 500: 100%; SAT writing scores over 500: 100%; SAT critical reading scores over 600: 100%; SAT math scores over 600: 95%; SAT writing scores over 600: 100%; SAT critical reading scores over 700: 95%; SAT math scores over 700: 80%; SAT writing scores over 700: 80%.

Faculty *Total:* 8, 38% full-time, 100% with terminal degrees. *Student/faculty ratio:* 5:1.

Majors Liberal arts and sciences/liberal studies.

Academics *Calendar:* 6 seven-week terms. *Degree:* associate. *Special study options:* accelerated degree program, cooperative education, distance learning, freshman honors college, honors programs, independent study, internships, student-designed majors, summer session for credit.

Library Mossner Library of Deep Springs with 20,000 titles, 60 serial subscriptions, an OPAC.

Student Life *Housing:* on-campus residence required through sophomore year. *Options:* men-only. Campus housing is university owned. Freshman campus housing is guaranteed. *Activities and Organizations:* drama/theater group, choral group, Student Self-Government, Labor Program, Applications Committee, Review Committee, Curriculum Committee. *Campus security:* late-night transport/escort service. *Student services:* personal/psychological counseling, legal services.

Athletics *Intramural sports:* archery M(c), basketball M, cross-country running M, equestrian sports M, football M, riflery M, rock climbing M, soccer M, swimming and diving M, table tennis M, ultimate Frisbee M, water polo M, weight lifting M.

Standardized Tests *Required:* SAT and SAT Subject Tests or ACT (for admission).

Costs (2011–12) *Tuition:* No tuition increase for student's term of enrollment. All students receive full scholarship covering tuition, room, and board.

Applying *Required:* essay or personal statement, high school transcript, interview. *Application deadlines:* 11/15 (freshmen), 11/15 (transfers). *Notification:* 4/15 (freshmen), 4/15 (transfers).

Freshman Application Contact David Neidorf, President, Deep Springs College, HC 72, Box 45001, Dyer, NV 89010-9803. *Phone:* 760-872-2000 Ext. 45. *Fax:* 760-874-0314. *E-mail:* apcom@deepsprings.edu. *Web site:* http://www.deepsprings.edu/.

Diablo Valley College
Pleasant Hill, California

Freshman Application Contact Ileana Dorn, Director of Admissions and Records, Diablo Valley College, Pleasant Hill, CA 94523-1529. *Phone:* 925-685-1230 Ext. 2330. *Fax:* 925-609-8085. *E-mail:* idorn@dvc.edu. *Web site:* http://www.dvc.edu/.

East Los Angeles College
Monterey Park, California

- **State and locally supported** 2-year, founded 1945, part of Los Angeles Community College District System
- **Urban** 84-acre campus with easy access to Los Angeles
- **Coed**

Undergraduates 8,063 full-time, 23,686 part-time. Students come from 17 states and territories; 0.1% are from out of state; 11% transferred in.

Academics *Calendar:* semesters. *Degree:* certificates and associate. *Special study options:* academic remediation for entering students, accelerated degree program, adult/continuing education programs, advanced placement credit, cooperative education, distance learning, double majors, English as a second language, freshman honors college, honors programs, independent study, internships, off-campus study, part-time degree program, services for LD students, student-designed majors, study abroad, summer session for credit.

Student Life *Campus security:* 24-hour emergency response devices and patrols, late-night transport/escort service, Los Angeles County Sheriff Substation.

Standardized Tests *Required:* mathematics and English placement tests, international students require TOEFL score of 450, CBT score 133, IBT score 45 or higher (for admission).

Costs (2011–12) *Tuition:* state resident $1080 full-time, $36 per unit part-time; nonresident $6780 full-time, $226 per unit part-time. No tuition increase for student's term of enrollment. *Required fees:* $22 full-time.

Financial Aid Of all full-time matriculated undergraduates who enrolled in 2010, 189 Federal Work-Study jobs (averaging $3000).

Applying *Options:* electronic application, early admission. *Recommended:* high school transcript, English and mathematics placement test.

Freshman Application Contact Mr. Jeremy Allred, Associate Dean of Admissions, East Los Angeles College, 1301 Avenida Cesar Chavez, Monterey Park, CA 91754. *Phone:* 323-265-8801. *Fax:* 323-265-8688. *E-mail:* allredjp@elac.edu. *Web site:* http://www.elac.edu/.

El Camino College
Torrance, California

Director of Admissions Mr. William Mulrooney, Director of Admissions, El Camino College, 16007 Crenshaw Boulevard, Torrance, CA 90506-0001. *Phone:* 310-660-3418. *Toll-free phone:* 866-ELCAMINO. *Fax:* 310-660-6779. *E-mail:* wmulrooney@elcamino.edu. *Web site:* http://www.elcamino.edu/.

Empire College
Santa Rosa, California

Freshman Application Contact Ms. Dahnja Barker, Admissions Officer, Empire College, 3035 Cleveland Avenue, Santa Rosa, CA 95403. *Phone:* 707-546-4000. *Toll-free phone:* 877-395-8535. *Web site:* http://www.empcol.edu/.

Everest College
City of Industry, California

Freshman Application Contact Admissions Office, Everest College, 12801 Crossroads Parkway South, City of Industry, CA 91746. *Phone:* 562-908-2500. *Toll-free phone:* 888-741-4270. *Fax:* 562-908-7656. *Web site:* http://www.everest.edu/.

Everest College
Ontario, California

Freshman Application Contact Admissions Office, Everest College, 1819 South Excise Avenue, Ontario, CA 91761. *Phone:* 909-484-4311. *Toll-free phone:* 888-741-4270. *Fax:* 909-484-1162. *Web site:* http://www.everest.edu/campus/ontario/.

Everest College
Rancho Cucamonga, California

Admissions Office Contact Everest College, 9616 Archibald Avenue, Suite 100, Rancho Cucamonga, CA 91730. *Toll-free phone:* 888-741-4270. *Web site:* http://www.everest-college.com/.

Evergreen Valley College
San Jose, California

Freshman Application Contact Evergreen Valley College, 3095 Yerba Buena Road, San Jose, CA 95135-1598. *Phone:* 408-270-6423. *Web site:* http://www.evc.edu/.

Fashion Careers College
San Diego, California

- **Proprietary** 2-year, founded 1979
- **Urban** campus with easy access to San Diego
- **Coed, primarily women**

Undergraduates 91 full-time. Students come from 18 states and territories; 2 other countries; 20% are from out of state.

Academics *Calendar:* quarters. *Degree:* certificates and associate. *Special study options:* adult/continuing education programs, cooperative education, distance learning, double majors, internships.

Student Life *Campus security:* 24-hour emergency response devices.

Standardized Tests *Required:* Wonderlic aptitude test (for admission).

Costs (2011–12) *Tuition:* $21,900 full-time. Full-time tuition and fees vary according to class time, course load, degree level, and program. *Required fees:* $525 full-time.

Financial Aid Of all full-time matriculated undergraduates who enrolled in 2010, 10 Federal Work-Study jobs (averaging $1760).

Applying *Options:* electronic application. *Application fee:* $25. *Required:* essay or personal statement, high school transcript, interview.

Freshman Application Contact Ms. Ronny Catarcio, Admissions Advisory, Fashion Careers College, 1923 Morena Boulevard, San Diego, CA 92110. *Phone:* 619-275-4700 Ext. 328. *Fax:* 619-275-0635. *E-mail:* ronny@fashioncareerscollege.com. *Web site:* http://www.fashioncareerscollege.com/.

Feather River College

Quincy, California

Freshman Application Contact Leslie Mikesell, Interim Director of Admissions and Records, Feather River College, 570 Golden Eagle Avenue, Quincy, CA 95971-9124. *Phone:* 530-283-0202 Ext. 600. *Toll-free phone:* 800-442-9799. *E-mail:* lmikesell@frc.edu. *Web site:* http://www.frc.edu/.

FIDM/The Fashion Institute of Design & Merchandising, Los Angeles Campus

Los Angeles, California

- **Proprietary** primarily 2-year, founded 1969, part of The Fashion Institute of Design and Merchandising/FIDM
- **Urban** campus
- **Coed**

Undergraduates 3,849 full-time, 575 part-time. Students come from 45 states and territories; 10 other countries; 37% are from out of state; 18% transferred in. *Retention:* 91% of full-time freshmen returned.

Faculty *Student/faculty ratio:* 16:1.

Academics *Calendar:* quarters. *Degrees:* associate and bachelor's (also includes Orange County Campus). *Special study options:* academic remediation for entering students, adult/continuing education programs, advanced placement credit, cooperative education, distance learning, English as a second language, independent study, internships, part-time degree program, services for LD students, study abroad, summer session for credit.

Student Life *Campus security:* 24-hour emergency response devices and patrols, late-night transport/escort service.

Standardized Tests *Recommended:* SAT or ACT (for admission).

Financial Aid Of all full-time matriculated undergraduates who enrolled in 2010, 88 Federal Work-Study jobs (averaging $2935).

Applying *Options:* electronic application, deferred entrance. *Application fee:* $225. *Required:* essay or personal statement, high school transcript, minimum 2.0 GPA, 3 letters of recommendation, interview, major-determined project.

Freshman Application Contact Ms. Susan Aronson, Director of Admissions, FIDM/The Fashion Institute of Design & Merchandising, Los Angeles Campus, Los Angeles, CA 90015. *Phone:* 213-624-1201. *Toll-free phone:* 800-624-1200. *Fax:* 213-624-4799. *E-mail:* saronson@fidm.com. *Web site:* http://www.fidm.edu/.

See Display ad below and page 398 for the College Close-Up.

FIDM/The Fashion Institute of Design & Merchandising, Orange County Campus

Irvine, California

- **Proprietary** 2-year, founded 1981, part of The Fashion Institute of Design and Merchandising/FIDM
- **Coed**, primarily women

Undergraduates 351 full-time, 21 part-time. Students come from 15 states and territories; 2 other countries; 13% are from out of state; 3% Black or African American, non-Hispanic/Latino; 31% Hispanic/Latino; 15% Asian, non-Hispanic/Latino; 3% Native Hawaiian or other Pacific Islander, non-Hispanic/Latino; 1% American Indian or Alaska Native, non-Hispanic/Latino; 1% Two or more races, non-Hispanic/Latino; 7% Race/ethnicity unknown; 3% international; 28% transferred in. *Retention:* 67% of full-time freshmen returned.

Faculty *Student/faculty ratio:* 17:1.

Academics *Calendar:* quarters. *Degree:* associate. *Special study options:* academic remediation for entering students, adult/continuing education programs, advanced placement credit, cooperative education, distance learning, English as a second language, independent study, internships, part-time degree program, services for LD students, study abroad, summer session for credit.

Student Life *Campus security:* 24-hour emergency response devices and patrols, late-night transport/escort service.

Applying *Options:* deferred entrance. *Application fee:* $225. *Required:* essay or personal statement, high school transcript, minimum 2.0 GPA, 3 letters of recommendation, interview, entrance requirement project.

Freshman Application Contact Admissions, FIDM/The Fashion Institute of Design & Merchandising, Orange County Campus, 17590 Gillette Avenue, Irvine, CA 92614-5610. *Phone:* 949-851-6200. *Toll-free phone:* 888-974-3436. *Fax:* 949-851-6808. *Web site:* http://www.fidm.com/.

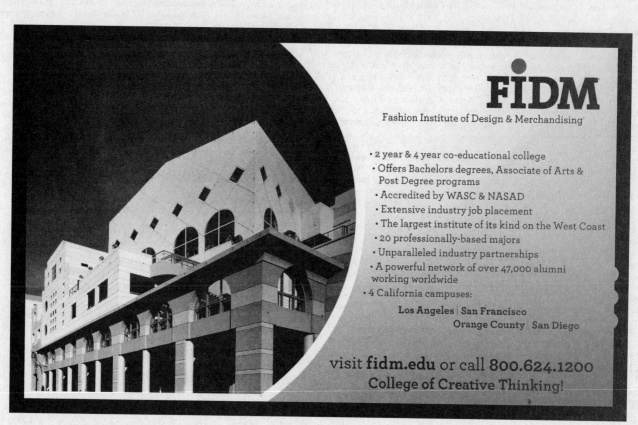

FIDM/The Fashion Institute of Design & Merchandising, San Diego Campus
San Diego, California

- **Proprietary** 2-year, founded 1985, part of The Fashion Institute of Design and Merchandising/FIDM
- **Urban** campus
- **Coed, primarily women**

Undergraduates 264 full-time, 28 part-time. Students come from 10 states and territories; 2 other countries; 4% are from out of state; 4% Black or African American, non-Hispanic/Latino; 30% Hispanic/Latino; 10% Asian, non-Hispanic/Latino; 2% Native Hawaiian or other Pacific Islander, non-Hispanic/Latino; 0.7% American Indian or Alaska Native, non-Hispanic/Latino; 3% Two or more races, non-Hispanic/Latino; 7% Race/ethnicity unknown; 2% international; 30% transferred in. *Retention:* 50% of full-time freshmen returned.
Faculty *Student/faculty ratio:* 21:1.
Academics *Calendar:* quarters. *Degree:* associate. *Special study options:* academic remediation for entering students, adult/continuing education programs, advanced placement credit, cooperative education, distance learning, English as a second language, independent study, internships, part-time degree program, services for LD students, study abroad, summer session for credit.
Student Life *Campus security:* 24-hour emergency response devices and patrols.
Standardized Tests *Recommended:* SAT or ACT (for admission).
Applying *Options:* electronic application, deferred entrance. *Application fee:* $225. *Required:* essay or personal statement, high school transcript, minimum 2.0 GPA, 3 letters of recommendation, interview, major-determined project.
Freshman Application Contact Ms. Susan Aronson, Director of Admissions, FIDM/The Fashion Institute of Design & Merchandising, San Diego Campus, San Diego, CA 92101. *Phone:* 213-624-1200 Ext. 5400. *Toll-free phone:* 800-243-3436. *Fax:* 619-232-4322. *E-mail:* info@fidm.com. *Web site:* http://www.fidm.com/.

FIDM/The Fashion Institute of Design & Merchandising, San Francisco Campus
San Francisco, California

- **Proprietary** 2-year, founded 1973, part of The Fashion Institute of Design and Merchandising/FIDM
- **Urban** campus
- **Coed**

Undergraduates 815 full-time, 145 part-time. Students come from 13 states and territories; 3 other countries; 8% are from out of state; 6% Black or African American, non-Hispanic/Latino; 20% Hispanic/Latino; 15% Asian, non-Hispanic/Latino; 2% Native Hawaiian or other Pacific Islander, non-Hispanic/Latino; 0.2% American Indian or Alaska Native, non-Hispanic/Latino; 5% Two or more races, non-Hispanic/Latino; 9% Race/ethnicity unknown; 5% international; 25% transferred in. *Retention:* 67% of full-time freshmen returned.
Faculty *Student/faculty ratio:* 20:1.
Academics *Calendar:* quarters. *Degree:* associate. *Special study options:* academic remediation for entering students, adult/continuing education programs, advanced placement credit, cooperative education, distance learning, English as a second language, honors programs, independent study, internships, off-campus study, part-time degree program, services for LD students, study abroad, summer session for credit.
Student Life *Campus security:* 24-hour emergency response devices and patrols.
Standardized Tests *Recommended:* SAT or ACT (for admission).
Applying *Options:* electronic application, deferred entrance. *Application fee:* $225. *Required:* essay or personal statement, high school transcript, 3 letters of recommendation, interview, major-determined project.
Freshman Application Contact Ms. Susan Aronson, Director of Admissions, FIDM/The Fashion Institute of Design & Merchandising, San Francisco Campus, San Francisco, CA 94108. *Phone:* 213-624-1201. *Toll-free phone:* 800-422-3436. *Fax:* 415-296-7299. *E-mail:* info@fidm.com. *Web site:* http://www.fidm.edu/.

Folsom Lake College
Folsom, California

Freshman Application Contact Admissions Office, Folsom Lake College, 10 College Parkway, Folsom, CA 95630. *Phone:* 916-608-6500. *Web site:* http://www.flc.losrios.edu/.

Foothill College
Los Altos Hills, California

- **State and locally supported** 2-year, founded 1958, part of Foothill-DeAnza Community College District
- **Suburban** 122-acre campus with easy access to San Jose
- **Endowment** $15.0 million
- **Coed,** 18,342 undergraduate students, 20% full-time, 51% women, 49% men

Undergraduates 3,728 full-time, 14,614 part-time. Students come from 16 states and territories; 75 other countries; 1% are from out of state; 37% transferred in.
Freshmen *Admission:* 5,697 applied, 5,697 admitted, 1,266 enrolled.
Faculty *Total:* 462, 41% full-time. *Student/faculty ratio:* 45:1.
Majors Accounting; American studies; anthropology; art; art history, criticism and conservation; athletic training; biology/biological sciences; business administration and management; chemistry; child development; classics and classical languages; communication; comparative literature; computer science; dental assisting; dental hygiene; diagnostic medical sonography and ultrasound technology; dramatic/theater arts; economics; electrical, electronic and communications engineering technology; emergency medical technology (EMT paramedic); English; fine/studio arts; geography; graphic design; history; international business/trade/commerce; Japanese; liberal arts and sciences/liberal studies; mathematics; medical radiologic technology; music; music technology; nanotechnology; natural sciences; ornamental horticulture; pharmacy technician; philosophy; photography; physical education teaching and coaching; physician assistant; physics; political science and government; pre-law studies; psychology; radiologic technology/science; real estate; respiratory care therapy; social sciences; sociology; Spanish; special education (administration); theater design and technology; veterinary/animal health technology; women's studies.
Academics *Calendar:* quarters. *Degree:* certificates and associate. *Special study options:* academic remediation for entering students, accelerated degree program, adult/continuing education programs, advanced placement credit, cooperative education, distance learning, English as a second language, honors programs, independent study, internships, off-campus study, part-time degree program, services for LD students, student-designed majors, study abroad, summer session for credit. *ROTC:* Army (c), Air Force (c).
Library Hubert H. Semans Library with 70,000 titles, 450 serial subscriptions, 5,150 audiovisual materials, an OPAC, a Web page.
Student Life *Housing:* college housing not available. *Activities and Organizations:* drama/theater group, student-run newspaper, radio station, choral group. *Campus security:* 24-hour emergency response devices and patrols, late-night transport/escort service. *Student services:* health clinic, personal/psychological counseling, legal services.
Athletics Member NJCAA. *Intercollegiate sports:* basketball M/W, football M, soccer M/W, softball W, swimming and diving M/W, tennis M, volleyball W, water polo W. *Intramural sports:* basketball M/W, football M/W, softball M/W, volleyball M/W.
Costs (2012–13) *Tuition:* state resident $1116 full-time, $31 per unit part-time; nonresident $6588 full-time, $183 per unit part-time. Full-time tuition and fees vary according to course load. Part-time tuition and fees vary according to course load. *Required fees:* $138 full-time. *Waivers:* employees or children of employees.
Financial Aid Of all full-time matriculated undergraduates who enrolled in 2010, 80 Federal Work-Study jobs (averaging $1300). 210 state and other part-time jobs.
Applying *Options:* electronic application. *Recommended:* high school transcript. *Application deadlines:* rolling (freshmen), rolling (out-of-state freshmen), rolling (transfers). *Notification:* continuous (freshmen), continuous (out-of-state freshmen), continuous (transfers).
Freshman Application Contact Ms. Shawna Aced, Registrar, Foothill College, Admissions and Records, 12345 El Monte Road, Los Altos Hills, CA 94022. *Phone:* 650-949-7771. *E-mail:* acedshawna@hda.edu. *Web site:* http://www.foothill.edu/.

Fresno City College
Fresno, California

Freshman Application Contact Office Assistant, Fresno City College, 1101 East University Avenue, Fresno, CA 93741-0002. *Phone:* 559-442-4600 Ext. 8604. *Fax:* 559-237-4232. *E-mail:* fcc.admissions@fresnocitycollege.edu. *Web site:* http://www.fresnocitycollege.edu/.

Fullerton College
Fullerton, California

Director of Admissions Mr. Albert Abutin, Dean of Admissions and Records, Fullerton College, 321 East Chapman Avenue, Fullerton, CA 92832-2095.

Phone: 714-992-7076. *Fax:* 714-992-9903. *E-mail:* aabutin@fullcoll.edu. *Web site:* http://www.fullcoll.edu/.

Gavilan College

Gilroy, California

- **State and locally supported** 2-year, founded 1919, part of California Community College System
- **Rural** 150-acre campus with easy access to San Jose
- **Coed,** 8,382 undergraduate students

Undergraduates 5% Black or African American, non-Hispanic/Latino; 43% Hispanic/Latino; 4% Asian, non-Hispanic/Latino; 2% Native Hawaiian or other Pacific Islander, non-Hispanic/Latino; 1% American Indian or Alaska Native, non-Hispanic/Latino; 10% Race/ethnicity unknown. *Retention:* 70% of full-time freshmen returned.

Faculty *Total:* 324, 23% full-time, 12% with terminal degrees. *Student/faculty ratio:* 30:1.

Majors Accounting technology and bookkeeping; administrative assistant and secretarial science; airframe mechanics and aircraft maintenance technology; art; biological and physical sciences; biology/biological sciences; business administration and management; business/commerce; carpentry; child-care provision; cinematography and film/video production; computer graphics; computer programming; computer science; computer systems networking and telecommunications; corrections; cosmetology; criminal justice/police science; data entry/microcomputer applications; desktop publishing and digital imaging design; drafting and design technology; dramatic/theater arts; engineering; English; family resource management; general studies; health and physical education/fitness; health/medical preparatory programs related; liberal arts and sciences/liberal studies; licensed practical/vocational nurse training; mathematics; medical administrative assistant and medical secretary; music; network and system administration; physical sciences; real estate; registered nursing/registered nurse; rhetoric and composition; social sciences; Spanish; theater design and technology; visual and performing arts.

Academics *Calendar:* semesters. *Degree:* certificates, diplomas, and associate. *Special study options:* academic remediation for entering students, adult/continuing education programs, advanced placement credit, cooperative education, distance learning, English as a second language, honors programs, independent study, internships, part-time degree program, services for LD students, study abroad, summer session for credit.

Library Gavilan Library with 60,587 titles, 2,541 serial subscriptions, an OPAC, a Web page.

Student Life *Housing:* college housing not available. *Activities and Organizations:* drama/theater group, student-run newspaper, choral group, EOPS, Rho Alpha Mu (Honor Society), Science Alliance, TADAA Drama Club, Vets Club. *Campus security:* 24-hour emergency response devices. *Student services:* health clinic, personal/psychological counseling.

Athletics *Intercollegiate sports:* baseball M, basketball M, football M, soccer M, softball W, volleyball W.

Costs (2012–13) *Tuition:* state resident $36 per unit part-time; nonresident $216 per unit part-time. Full-time tuition and fees vary according to course load. Part-time tuition and fees vary according to course load. *Required fees:* $36 per unit part-time. *Waivers:* employees or children of employees.

Financial Aid Of all full-time matriculated undergraduates who enrolled in 2010, 50 Federal Work-Study jobs (averaging $2000). *Financial aid deadline:* 6/30.

Applying *Application deadlines:* rolling (freshmen), rolling (out-of-state freshmen), rolling (transfers). *Notification:* continuous (freshmen), continuous (out-of-state freshmen), continuous (transfers).

Freshman Application Contact Gavilan College, 5055 Santa Teresa Boulevard, Gilroy, CA 95020-9599. *Phone:* 408-848-4754. *Web site:* http://www.gavilan.edu/.

Glendale Community College

Glendale, California

Freshman Application Contact Ms. Sharon Combs, Dean, Admissions, and Records, Glendale Community College, 1500 North Verdugo Road, Glendale, CA 91208. *Phone:* 818-240-1000 Ext. 5910. *E-mail:* scombs@glendale.edu. *Web site:* http://www.glendale.edu/.

Golden West College

Huntington Beach, California

- **State and locally supported** 2-year, founded 1966, part of Coast Community College District System
- **Suburban** 122-acre campus with easy access to Los Angeles
- **Endowment** $880,684
- **Coed**

Undergraduates 4,291 full-time, 8,935 part-time. Students come from 28 other countries.

Faculty *Student/faculty ratio:* 34:1.

Academics *Calendar:* semesters (summer session). *Degree:* certificates and associate. *Special study options:* academic remediation for entering students, adult/continuing education programs, advanced placement credit, cooperative education, distance learning, English as a second language, external degree program, honors programs, independent study, internships, part-time degree program, services for LD students, student-designed majors, study abroad, summer session for credit. *ROTC:* Air Force (c).

Student Life *Campus security:* 24-hour emergency response devices and patrols, late-night transport/escort service.

Athletics Member NJCAA.

Costs (2011–12) *Tuition:* state resident $1008 full-time, $36 per unit part-time; nonresident $6496 full-time, $232 per unit part-time. *Required fees:* $122 full-time, $31 per term part-time.

Applying *Options:* early admission. *Required for some:* essay or personal statement. *Recommended:* high school transcript.

Freshman Application Contact Golden West College, PO Box 2748, 15744 Golden West Street, Huntington Beach, CA 92647-2748. *Phone:* 714-892-7711 Ext. 58196. *Web site:* http://www.goldenwestcollege.edu/.

Golf Academy of America

Carlsbad, California

Director of Admissions Ms. Deborah Wells, Admissions Coordinator, Golf Academy of America, 1950 Camino Vida Roble, Suite 125, Carlsbad, CA 92008. *Phone:* 760-414-1501. *Toll-free phone:* 800-342-7342. *E-mail:* sdga@sdgagolf.com. *Web site:* http://www.golfacademy.edu/.

Grossmont College

El Cajon, California

Freshman Application Contact Admissions Office, Grossmont College, 8800 Grossmont College Drive, El Cajon, CA 92020-1799. *Phone:* 619-644-7186. *Web site:* http://www.grossmont.edu/.

Hartnell College

Salinas, California

Director of Admissions Director of Admissions, Hartnell College, 411 Central Avenue, Salinas, CA 93901. *Phone:* 831-755-6711. *Fax:* 831-759-6014. *Web site:* http://www.hartnell.edu/.

Heald College–Concord

Concord, California

Freshman Application Contact Director of Admissions, Heald College–Concord, 5130 Commercial Circle, Concord, CA 94520. *Phone:* 925-288-5800. *Toll-free phone:* 800-88-HEALD. *Fax:* 925-288-5896. *E-mail:* concordinfo@heald.edu. *Web site:* http://www.heald.edu/.

Heald College–Fresno

Fresno, California

Freshman Application Contact Director of Admissions, Heald College–Fresno, 255 West Bullard Avenue, Fresno, CA 93704-1706. *Phone:* 559-438-4222. *Toll-free phone:* 800-88-HEALD. *Fax:* 559-438-0948. *E-mail:* fresnoinfo@heald.edu. *Web site:* http://www.heald.edu/.

Heald College–Hayward

Hayward, California

Freshman Application Contact Director of Admissions, Heald College–Hayward, 25500 Industrial Boulevard, Hayward, CA 94545. *Phone:* 510-783-2100. *Toll-free phone:* 800-88-HEALD. *Fax:* 510-783-3287. *E-mail:* harwardinfo@heald.edu. *Web site:* http://www.heald.edu/.

Heald College–Rancho Cordova

Rancho Cordova, California

Freshman Application Contact Director of Admissions, Heald College–Rancho Cordova, 2910 Prospect Park Drive, Rancho Cordova, CA 95670-6005. *Phone:* 916-638-1616. *Toll-free phone:* 800-88-HEALD. *Fax:* 916-638-1580. *E-mail:* ranchocordovainfo@heald.edu. *Web site:* http://www.heald.edu/.

Heald College–Roseville

Roseville, California

Freshman Application Contact Director of Admissions, Heald College–Roseville, 7 Sierra Gate Plaza, Roseville, CA 95678. *Phone:* 916-789-8600. *Toll-free phone:* 800-88-HEALD. *Fax:* 916-789-8606. *E-mail:* rosevilleinfo@heald.edu. *Web site:* http://www.heald.edu/.

Heald College–Salinas

Salinas, California

Freshman Application Contact Director of Admissions, Heald College–Salinas, 1450 North Main Street, Salinas, CA 93906. *Phone:* 831-443-1700. *Toll-free phone:* 800-88-HEALD. *Fax:* 831-443-1050. *E-mail:* salinasinfo@heald.edu. *Web site:* http://www.heald.edu/.

Heald College–San Francisco

San Francisco, California

Freshman Application Contact Director of Admissions, Heald College–San Francisco, 350 Mission Street, San Francisco, CA 94105. *Phone:* 415-808-3000. *Toll-free phone:* 800-88-HEALD. *Fax:* 415-808-3005. *E-mail:* sanfranciscoinfo@heald.edu. *Web site:* http://www.heald.edu/.

Heald College–San Jose

Milpitas, California

Freshman Application Contact Director of Admissions, Heald College–San Jose, 341 Great Mall Parkway, Milpitas, CA 95035. *Phone:* 408-934-4900. *Toll-free phone:* 800-88-HEALD. *Fax:* 408-934-7777. *E-mail:* sanjoseinfo@heald.edu. *Web site:* http://www.heald.edu/.

Heald College–Stockton

Stockton, California

Freshman Application Contact Director of Admissions, Heald College–Stockton, 1605 East March Lane, Stockton, CA 95210. *Phone:* 209-473-5200. *Toll-free phone:* 800-88-HEALD. *Fax:* 209-477-2739. *E-mail:* stocktoninfo@heald.edu. *Web site:* http://www.heald.edu/.

Imperial Valley College

Imperial, California

Director of Admissions Dawn Chun, Associate Dean of Admissions and Records, Imperial Valley College, 380 East Aten Road, PO Box 158, Imperial, CA 92251-0158. *Phone:* 760-352-8320 Ext. 200. *Web site:* http://www.imperial.edu/.

Irvine Valley College

Irvine, California

Director of Admissions Mr. John Edwards, Director of Admissions, Records, and Enrollment Services, Irvine Valley College, 5500 Irvine Center Drive, Irvine, CA 92618. *Phone:* 949-451-5416. *Web site:* http://www.ivc.edu/.

ITT Technical Institute

Culver City, California

- **Proprietary** primarily 2-year, part of ITT Educational Services, Inc.
- **Coed**

Majors Business administration and management; communications technology; computer and information systems security; criminal justice/law enforcement administration; drafting and design technology; electrical, electronic and communications engineering technology; forensic science and technology; graphic communications; legal assistant/paralegal; network and system administration; project management.
Academics *Calendar:* quarters. *Degrees:* associate and bachelor's.
Freshman Application Contact Director of Recruitment, ITT Technical Institute, 6101 W. Centinela Avenue, Suite 180, Culver City, CA 90230. *Phone:* 310-417-5800. *Toll-free phone:* 800-215-6151. *Web site:* http://www.itt-tech.edu/.

ITT Technical Institute

Lathrop, California

- **Proprietary** primarily 2-year, founded 1997, part of ITT Educational Services, Inc.
- **Coed**

Majors Business administration and management; communications technology; computer and information systems security; computer systems networking and telecommunications; construction management; criminal justice/law enforcement administration; drafting and design technology; electrical, electronic and communications engineering technology; forensic science and technology; game and interactive media design; graphic communications; legal assistant/paralegal; network and system administration; project management.
Academics *Calendar:* quarters. *Degrees:* associate and bachelor's.
Student Life *Housing:* college housing not available.
Freshman Application Contact Director of Recruitment, ITT Technical Institute, 16916 South Harlan Road, Lathrop, CA 95330. *Phone:* 209-858-0077. *Toll-free phone:* 800-346-1786. *Web site:* http://www.itt-tech.edu/.

ITT Technical Institute

Oakland, California

- **Proprietary** primarily 2-year, part of ITT Educational Services, Inc.
- **Coed**

Majors Business administration and management; communications technology; computer and information systems security; drafting and design technology; electrical, electronic and communications engineering technology; forensic science and technology; graphic communications; legal assistant/paralegal; network and system administration; project management.
Academics *Calendar:* quarters. *Degrees:* associate and bachelor's.
Freshman Application Contact Director of Recruitment, ITT Technical Institute, 7901 Oakport Street, Suite 3000, Oakland, CA 94621. *Phone:* 510-553-2800. *Toll-free phone:* 877-442-5833. *Web site:* http://www.itt-tech.edu/.

ITT Technical Institute

Orange, California

- **Proprietary** primarily 2-year, founded 1982, part of ITT Educational Services, Inc.
- **Suburban** campus
- **Coed**

Majors Business administration and management; communications technology; computer and information systems security; computer systems networking and telecommunications; construction management; criminal justice/law enforcement administration; drafting and design technology; electrical, electronic and communications engineering technology; forensic science and technology; game and interactive media design; graphic communications; health information/medical records technology; legal assistant/paralegal; network and system administration; project management; system, networking, and LAN/WAN management.
Academics *Calendar:* quarters. *Degrees:* associate and bachelor's.
Student Life *Housing:* college housing not available.
Financial Aid Of all full-time matriculated undergraduates who enrolled in 2010, 20 Federal Work-Study jobs (averaging $5000).
Freshman Application Contact Director of Recruitment, ITT Technical Institute, 4000 West Metropolitan Drive, Suite 100, Orange, CA 92868. *Phone:* 714-941-2400. *Web site:* http://www.itt-tech.edu/.

ITT Technical Institute

Oxnard, California

- **Proprietary** primarily 2-year, founded 1993, part of ITT Educational Services, Inc.
- **Urban** campus
- **Coed**

Majors Business administration and management; communications technology; computer and information systems security; criminal justice/law enforcement administration; drafting and design technology; electrical, electronic and communications engineering technology; forensic science and technology; game and interactive media design; graphic communications; information technology project management; legal assistant/paralegal; network and system administration; project management.
Academics *Calendar:* quarters. *Degrees:* associate and bachelor's.

Student Life *Housing:* college housing not available.
Freshman Application Contact Director of Recruitment, ITT Technical Institute, 2051 Solar Drive, Suite 150, Oxnard, CA 93036. *Phone:* 805-988-0143. *Toll-free phone:* 800-530-1582. *Web site:* http://www.itt-tech.edu/.

ITT Technical Institute
Rancho Cordova, California

- **Proprietary** primarily 2-year, founded 1954, part of ITT Educational Services, Inc.
- **Urban** campus
- **Coed**

Majors Business administration and management; communications technology; computer and information systems security; computer systems networking and telecommunications; construction management; criminal justice/law enforcement administration; drafting and design technology; electrical, electronic and communications engineering technology; forensic science and technology; game and interactive media design; graphic communications; legal assistant/paralegal; network and system administration; project management; registered nursing/registered nurse.
Academics *Calendar:* quarters. *Degrees:* associate and bachelor's.
Student Life *Housing:* college housing not available.
Freshman Application Contact Director of Recruitment, ITT Technical Institute, 10863 Gold Center Drive, Rancho Cordova, CA 95670-6034. *Phone:* 916-851-3900. *Toll-free phone:* 800-488-8466. *Web site:* http://www.itt-tech.edu/.

ITT Technical Institute
San Bernardino, California

- **Proprietary** primarily 2-year, founded 1987, part of ITT Educational Services, Inc.
- **Urban** campus
- **Coed**

Majors Business administration and management; communications technology; computer and information systems security; construction management; criminal justice/law enforcement administration; drafting and design technology; electrical, electronic and communications engineering technology; forensic science and technology; game and interactive media design; graphic communications; health information/medical records technology; legal assistant/paralegal; network and system administration; project management.
Academics *Calendar:* quarters. *Degrees:* associate and bachelor's.
Student Life *Housing:* college housing not available.
Freshman Application Contact Director of Recruitment, ITT Technical Institute, 670 East Carnegie Drive, San Bernardino, CA 92408. *Phone:* 909-806-4600. *Toll-free phone:* 800-888-3801. *Web site:* http://www.itt-tech.edu/.

ITT Technical Institute
San Diego, California

- **Proprietary** primarily 2-year, founded 1981, part of ITT Educational Services, Inc.
- **Suburban** campus
- **Coed**

Majors Communications technology; computer and information systems security; construction management; criminal justice/law enforcement administration; drafting and design technology; electrical, electronic and communications engineering technology; forensic science and technology; graphic communications; legal assistant/paralegal; network and system administration; project management.
Academics *Calendar:* quarters. *Degrees:* associate and bachelor's.
Student Life *Housing:* college housing not available.
Freshman Application Contact Director of Recruitment, ITT Technical Institute, 9680 Granite Ridge Drive, San Diego, CA 92123. *Phone:* 858-571-8500. *Toll-free phone:* 800-883-0380. *Web site:* http://www.itt-tech.edu/.

ITT Technical Institute
San Dimas, California

- **Proprietary** primarily 2-year, founded 1982, part of ITT Educational Services, Inc.
- **Suburban** campus
- **Coed**

Majors Business administration and management; communications technology; computer and information systems security; construction management; criminal justice/law enforcement administration; drafting and design technology; electrical, electronic and communications engineering technology; forensic science and technology; graphic communications; health information/medical records technology; legal assistant/paralegal; network and system administration; project management.
Academics *Calendar:* quarters. *Degrees:* associate and bachelor's.
Student Life *Housing:* college housing not available.
Financial Aid Of all full-time matriculated undergraduates who enrolled in 2010, 20 Federal Work-Study jobs (averaging $4500).
Freshman Application Contact Director of Recruitment, ITT Technical Institute, 650 West Cienega Avenue, San Dimas, CA 91773. *Phone:* 909-971-2300. *Toll-free phone:* 800-414-6522. *Web site:* http://www.itt-tech.edu/.

ITT Technical Institute
Sylmar, California

- **Proprietary** primarily 2-year, founded 1982, part of ITT Educational Services, Inc.
- **Urban** campus
- **Coed**

Majors Business administration and management; communications technology; computer and information systems security; computer systems networking and telecommunications; construction management; criminal justice/law enforcement administration; drafting and design technology; electrical, electronic and communications engineering technology; forensic science and technology; game and interactive media design; graphic communications; health information/medical records technology; legal assistant/paralegal; network and system administration; project management; system, networking, and LAN/WAN management.
Academics *Calendar:* quarters. *Degrees:* associate and bachelor's.
Student Life *Housing:* college housing not available.
Freshman Application Contact Director of Recruitment, ITT Technical Institute, 12669 Encinitas Avenue, Sylmar, CA 91342-3664. *Phone:* 818-364-5151. *Toll-free phone:* 800-363-2086 (in-state); 800-636-2086 (out-of-state). *Web site:* http://www.itt-tech.edu/.

ITT Technical Institute
Torrance, California

- **Proprietary** primarily 2-year, founded 1987, part of ITT Educational Services, Inc.
- **Urban** campus
- **Coed**

Majors Business administration and management; communications technology; computer and information systems security; construction management; criminal justice/law enforcement administration; drafting and design technology; electrical, electronic and communications engineering technology; forensic science and technology; graphic communications; legal assistant/paralegal; network and system administration; project management.
Academics *Calendar:* quarters. *Degrees:* associate and bachelor's.
Student Life *Housing:* college housing not available.
Financial Aid Of all full-time matriculated undergraduates who enrolled in 2010, 6 Federal Work-Study jobs (averaging $4000).
Freshman Application Contact Director of Recruitment, ITT Technical Institute, 2555 West 190th Street, Suite 125, Torrance, CA 90504. *Phone:* 310-965-5900. *Web site:* http://www.itt-tech.edu/.

ITT Technical Institute
West Covina, California

- **Proprietary** primarily 2-year, part of ITT Educational Services, Inc.
- **Coed**

Majors Business administration and management; communications technology; computer and information systems security; criminal justice/law enforcement administration; drafting and design technology; electrical, electronic and communications engineering technology; forensic science and technology; graphic communications; legal assistant/paralegal; network and system administration; project management.
Academics *Calendar:* quarters. *Degrees:* associate and bachelor's.
Freshman Application Contact Director of Recruitment, ITT Technical Institute, 1530 W. Cameron Avenue, West Covina, CA 91790. *Phone:* 626-813-3681. *Toll-free phone:* 877-480-2766. *Web site:* http://www.itt-tech.edu/.

Kaplan College, Bakersfield Campus
Bakersfield, California

- **Proprietary** 2-year
- **Coed**

Majors Criminal justice/law enforcement administration.
Academics *Degree:* diplomas and associate.

Freshman Application Contact Kaplan College, Bakersfield Campus, 1914 Wible Road, Bakersfield, CA 93304. *Phone:* 661-836-6300. *Toll-free phone:* 800-935-1857. *Web site:* http://bakersfield.kaplancollege.com/.

Kaplan College, Chula Vista Campus

Chula Vista, California

- **Proprietary** 2-year
- **Coed**

Majors Criminal justice/law enforcement administration.
Academics *Degree:* diplomas and associate.
Freshman Application Contact Kaplan College, Chula Vista Campus, 555 Broadway, Chula Vista, CA 91910. *Phone:* 877-473-3052. *Toll-free phone:* 800-935-1857. *Web site:* http://chulavista.kaplancollege.com/.

Kaplan College, Fresno Campus

Clovis, California

- **Proprietary** 2-year
- **Coed**

Majors Criminal justice/law enforcement administration.
Academics *Degree:* diplomas and associate.
Freshman Application Contact Kaplan College, Fresno Campus, 44 Shaw Avenue, Clovis, CA 93612. *Phone:* 559-325-5100. *Toll-free phone:* 800-935-1857. *Web site:* http://fresno.kaplancollege.com/.

Kaplan College, Modesto Campus

Salida, California

- **Proprietary** 2-year
- **Coed, primarily women**

Majors Criminal justice/law enforcement administration; respiratory therapy technician.
Academics *Calendar:* semesters. *Degree:* diplomas and associate.
Freshman Application Contact Kaplan College, Modesto Campus, 5172 Kiernan Court, Salida, CA 95368. *Phone:* 209-543-7000. *Toll-free phone:* 800-935-1857. *Web site:* http://modesto.kaplancollege.com/.

Kaplan College, Palm Springs Campus

Palm Springs, California

- **Proprietary** 2-year
- **Coed**

Majors Criminal justice/law enforcement administration.
Academics *Degree:* diplomas and associate.
Freshman Application Contact Kaplan College, Palm Springs Campus, 2475 East Tahquitz Canyon Way, Palm Springs, CA 92262. *Phone:* 760-778-3540. *Toll-free* *phone:* 800-935-1857. *Web site:* http://palm-springs.kaplancollege.com/.

Kaplan College, Riverside Campus

Riverside, California

- **Proprietary** 2-year
- **Coed**

Majors Criminal justice/law enforcement administration; health information/medical records technology.
Academics *Degree:* diplomas and associate.
Freshman Application Contact Kaplan College, Riverside Campus, 4040 Vine Street, Riverside, CA 92507. *Phone:* 951-276-1704. *Toll-free phone:* 800-935-1857. *Web site:* http://riverside.kaplancollege.com/.

Kaplan College, Sacramento Campus

Sacramento, California

- **Proprietary** 2-year
- **Coed**

Majors Criminal justice/law enforcement administration.
Academics *Calendar:* semesters. *Degree:* diplomas and associate.
Freshman Application Contact Kaplan College, Sacramento Campus, 4330 Watt Avenue, Suite 400, Sacramento, CA 95821. *Phone:* 916-649-8168. *Toll-free phone:* 800-935-1857. *Web site:* http://sacramento.kaplancollege.com/.

Kaplan College, San Diego Campus

San Diego, California

- **Proprietary** 2-year, founded 1976
- **Urban** campus
- **Coed**

Majors Criminal justice/law enforcement administration; health information/medical records technology.
Academics *Calendar:* semesters. *Degrees:* diplomas and associate (also includes Vista campus).
Freshman Application Contact Kaplan College, San Diego Campus, 9055 Balboa Avenue, San Diego, CA 92123. *Phone:* 858-279-4500. *Toll-free phone:* 800-935-1857. *Web site:* http://san-diego.kaplancollege.com/.

Kaplan College, Stockton Campus

Stockton, California

- **Proprietary** 2-year
- **Coed**

Majors Criminal justice/law enforcement administration.
Academics *Degree:* diplomas and associate.
Freshman Application Contact Kaplan College, Stockton Campus, 722 West March Lane, Stockton, CA 95207. *Phone:* 209-954-4208. *Toll-free phone:* 800-935-1857. *Web site:* http://stockton.kaplancollege.com/.

Kaplan College, Vista Campus

Vista, California

- **Proprietary** 2-year
- **Coed**

Majors Criminal justice/law enforcement administration.
Academics *Degree:* diplomas and associate.
Freshman Application Contact Kaplan College, Vista Campus, 2022 University Drive, Vista, CA 92083. *Phone:* 760-630-1555. *Toll-free phone:* 800-935-1857. *Web site:* http://vista.kaplancollege.com/.

Lake Tahoe Community College

South Lake Tahoe, California

Freshman Application Contact Office of Admissions and Records, Lake Tahoe Community College, One College Drive, South Lake Tahoe, CA 96150. *Phone:* 530-541-4660 Ext. 211. *Fax:* 530-541-7852. *E-mail:* admissions@ltcc.edu. *Web site:* http://www.ltcc.edu/.

Laney College

Oakland, California

Freshman Application Contact Mrs. Barbara Simmons, District Admissions Officer, Laney College, 900 Fallon Street, Oakland, CA 94607-4893. *Phone:* 510-466-7369. *Web site:* http://www.laney.edu/.

Las Positas College

Livermore, California

Director of Admissions Mrs. Sylvia R. Rodriguez, Director of Admissions and Records, Las Positas College, 3000 Campus Hill Drive, Livermore, CA 94551. *Phone:* 925-373-4942. *Web site:* http://www.laspositascollege.edu/.

Lassen Community College District

Susanville, California

Freshman Application Contact Mr. Chris J. Alberico, Registrar, Lassen Community College District, Highway 139, PO Box 3000, Susanville, CA 96130. *Phone:* 530-257-6181. *Web site:* http://www.lassencollege.edu/.

Le Cordon Bleu College of Culinary Arts in Los Angeles

Pasadena, California

Director of Admissions Nora Sandoval, Registrar, Le Cordon Bleu College of Culinary Arts in Los Angeles, 521 East Green Street, Pasadena, CA 91101. *Phone:* 626-229-1300. *Fax:* 626-204-3905. *E-mail:* nsandoval@la.chefs.edu. *Web site:* http://www.chefs.edu/Los-Angeles.

Long Beach City College
Long Beach, California

Director of Admissions Mr. Ross Miyashiro, Dean of Admissions and Records, Long Beach City College, 4901 East Carson Street, Long Beach, CA 90808-1780. *Phone:* 562-938-4130. *Web site:* http://www.lbcc.edu/.

Los Angeles City College
Los Angeles, California

Freshman Application Contact Elaine Geismar, Director of Student Assistance Center, Los Angeles City College, 855 North Vermont Avenue, Los Angeles, CA 90029-3590. *Phone:* 323-953-4340. *Web site:* http://www.lacitycollege.edu/.

Los Angeles County College of Nursing and Allied Health
Los Angeles, California

Freshman Application Contact Admissions Office, Los Angeles County College of Nursing and Allied Health, 1237 North Mission Road, Los Angeles, CA 90033. *Phone:* 323-226-4911. *Web site:* http://www.dhs.co.la.ca.us/wps/portal/collegeofnursing/.

Los Angeles Harbor College
Wilmington, California

- **State and locally supported** 2-year, founded 1949, part of Los Angeles Community College District System
- **Suburban** 80-acre campus with easy access to Los Angeles
- **Coed,** 10,181 undergraduate students, 28% full-time, 61% women, 39% men

Undergraduates 2,812 full-time, 7,369 part-time. Students come from 14 states and territories; 15 other countries.
Freshmen *Admission:* 1,526 enrolled. *Average high school GPA:* 2.5.
Faculty *Total:* 422, 27% full-time. *Student/faculty ratio:* 47:1.
Majors Accounting; administrative assistant and secretarial science; architectural engineering technology; automobile/automotive mechanics technology; biology/biological sciences; business administration and management; computer engineering technology; criminal justice/police science; data processing and data processing technology; developmental and child psychology; drafting and design technology; electrical, electronic and communications engineering technology; electromechanical technology; engineering technology; fire science/firefighting; information science/studies; legal administrative assistant/secretary; liberal arts and sciences/liberal studies; medical administrative assistant and medical secretary; physics; pre-engineering; real estate; registered nursing/registered nurse.
Academics *Calendar:* semesters. *Degree:* certificates and associate. *Special study options:* academic remediation for entering students, accelerated degree program, adult/continuing education programs, advanced placement credit, cooperative education, distance learning, double majors, English as a second language, freshman honors college, honors programs, independent study, off-campus study, part-time degree program, services for LD students, study abroad, summer session for credit.
Library Harbor College Library with 89,768 titles, 21 serial subscriptions, 35 audiovisual materials, an OPAC, a Web page.
Student Life *Housing:* college housing not available. *Activities and Organizations:* drama/theater group, student-run newspaper, television station, choral group, Alpha Gamma Sigma, EOP&S, Creando Un Nuevo Futuro, Psychology Club, Honors Transfer Program. *Campus security:* 24-hour emergency response devices and patrols, late-night transport/escort service. *Student services:* health clinic, personal/psychological counseling, legal services.
Athletics *Intercollegiate sports:* baseball M, basketball M, football M, soccer M/W, softball W, volleyball W.
Costs (2012–13) *Tuition:* state resident $958 full-time; nonresident $5898 full-time. *Required fees:* $2 full-time.
Financial Aid Of all full-time matriculated undergraduates who enrolled in 2010, 100 Federal Work-Study jobs (averaging $1800).
Applying *Options:* electronic application, early admission, deferred entrance. *Application deadlines:* 9/3 (freshmen), 9/3 (out-of-state freshmen), 9/3 (transfers).
Freshman Application Contact Los Angeles Harbor College, 1111 Figueroa Place, Wilmington, CA 90744-2397. *Phone:* 310-233-4091. *Web site:* http://www.lahc.edu/.

Los Angeles Mission College
Sylmar, California

Freshman Application Contact Ms. Angela Merrill, Admissions Supervisor, Los Angeles Mission College, 13356 Eldridge Avenue, Sylmar, CA 91342-3245. *Phone:* 818-364-7658. *Web site:* http://www.lamission.edu/.

Los Angeles Pierce College
Woodland Hills, California

Director of Admissions Ms. Shelley L. Gerstl, Dean of Admissions and Records, Los Angeles Pierce College, 6201 Winnetka Avenue, Woodland Hills, CA 91371-0001. *Phone:* 818-719-6448. *Web site:* http://www.piercecollege.edu/.

Los Angeles Southwest College
Los Angeles, California

Director of Admissions Dan W. Walden, Dean of Academic Affairs, Los Angeles Southwest College, 1600 West Imperial Highway, Los Angeles, CA 90047-4810. *Phone:* 323-242-5511. *Web site:* http://www.lasc.edu/.

Los Angeles Trade-Technical College
Los Angeles, California

Director of Admissions Dr. Raul Cardoza, Los Angeles Trade-Technical College, 400 West Washington Boulevard, Los Angeles, CA 90015-4108. *Phone:* 213-763-5301. *E-mail:* CardozaRJ@lattc.edu. *Web site:* http://www.lattc.edu/.

Los Angeles Valley College
Van Nuys, California

Director of Admissions Mr. Florentino Manzano, Associate Dean, Los Angeles Valley College, 5800 Fulton Avenue, Van Nuys, CA 91401-4096. *Phone:* 818-947-2353. *E-mail:* manzanf@lavc.edu. *Web site:* http://www.lavc.cc.ca.us/.

Los Medanos College
Pittsburg, California

Freshman Application Contact Ms. Gail Newman, Director of Admissions and Records, Los Medanos College, 2700 East Leland Road, Pittsburg, CA 94565-5197. *Phone:* 925-439-2181 Ext. 7500. *Web site:* http://www.losmedanos.net/.

Mendocino College
Ukiah, California

- **State and locally supported** 2-year, founded 1973, part of California Community College System
- **Rural** 127-acre campus
- **Endowment** $6.3 million
- **Coed,** 3,753 undergraduate students, 32% full-time, 61% women, 39% men

Undergraduates 1,200 full-time, 2,553 part-time. Students come from 16 states and territories; 2 other countries; 4% Black or African American, non-Hispanic/Latino; 23% Hispanic/Latino; 2% Asian, non-Hispanic/Latino; 1% Native Hawaiian or other Pacific Islander, non-Hispanic/Latino; 6% American Indian or Alaska Native, non-Hispanic/Latino; 9% Race/ethnicity unknown; 0.6% international; 3% transferred in.
Freshmen *Admission:* 907 applied, 907 admitted, 355 enrolled.
Faculty *Total:* 271, 19% full-time, 3% with terminal degrees. *Student/faculty ratio:* 16:1.
Majors Accounting; administrative assistant and secretarial science; agriculture; art; automobile/automotive mechanics technology; biology/biological sciences; business administration and management; chemistry; child development; criminal justice/law enforcement administration; criminal justice/police science; data processing and data processing technology; developmental and child psychology; dramatic/theater arts; English; fiber, textile and weaving arts; finance; French; health professions related; human services; information science/studies; kindergarten/preschool education; liberal arts and sciences/liberal studies; mathematics; music; ornamental horticulture; physical education teaching and coaching; physical sciences; psychology; real estate; rhetoric and composition; social sciences; Spanish; substance abuse/addiction counseling.
Academics *Calendar:* semesters. *Degree:* certificates and associate. *Special study options:* academic remediation for entering students, adult/continuing education programs, advanced placement credit, cooperative education, dis-

tance learning, English as a second language, honors programs, independent study, internships, part-time degree program, services for LD students, summer session for credit.

Library Lowery Library with 27,441 titles, 275 serial subscriptions, a Web page.

Student Life *Housing:* college housing not available. *Activities and Organizations:* drama/theater group, student-run radio station, choral group. *Campus security:* late-night transport/escort service, security patrols 6 pm to 10 pm.

Athletics Member NJCAA. *Intercollegiate sports:* baseball M, basketball M/W, football M, soccer W, volleyball W. *Intramural sports:* table tennis M/W, tennis M/W.

Costs (2012–13) *Tuition:* state resident $1380 full-time; nonresident $7350 full-time. Full-time tuition and fees vary according to course load. Part-time tuition and fees vary according to course load. *Required fees:* $32 full-time.

Financial Aid *Financial aid deadline:* 5/20.

Applying *Options:* electronic application, early admission, deferred entrance. *Required:* high school transcript. *Application deadlines:* rolling (freshmen), rolling (transfers). *Notification:* continuous (freshmen), continuous (transfers).

Freshman Application Contact Mendocino College, 1000 Hensley Creek Road, Ukiah, CA 95482-0300. *Phone:* 707-468-3103. *Web site:* http://www.mendocino.edu/.

Merced College
Merced, California

Freshman Application Contact Ms. Cherie Davis, Associate Registrar, Merced College, 3600 M Street, Merced, CA 95348-2898. *Phone:* 209-384-6188. *Fax:* 209-384-6339. *Web site:* http://www.mccd.edu/.

Merritt College
Oakland, California

Freshman Application Contact Ms. Barbara Simmons, District Admissions Officer, Merritt College, 12500 Campus Drive, Oakland, CA 94619-3196. *Phone:* 510-466-7369. *E-mail:* hperdue@peralta.cc.ca.us. *Web site:* http://www.merritt.edu/.

MiraCosta College
Oceanside, California

Freshman Application Contact Director of Admissions, MiraCosta College, One Barnard Drive, Oceanside, CA 92056-3899. *Phone:* 760-795-6620. *Toll-free phone:* 888-201-8480. *E-mail:* admissions@miracosta.edu. *Web site:* http://www.miracosta.edu/.

Mission College
Santa Clara, California

Director of Admissions Daniel Sanidad, Dean of Student Services, Mission College, 3000 Mission College Boulevard, Santa Clara, CA 95054-1897. *Phone:* 408-855-5139. *Web site:* http://www.missioncollege.org/.

Modesto Junior College
Modesto, California

Freshman Application Contact Ms. Susie Agostini, Dean of Matriculation, Admissions, and Records, Modesto Junior College, 435 College Avenue, Modesto, CA 95350. *Phone:* 209-575-6470. *Fax:* 209-575-6859. *E-mail:* mjcadmissions@mail.yosemite.cc.ca.us. *Web site:* http://www.mjc.edu/.

Monterey Peninsula College
Monterey, California

Director of Admissions Ms. Vera Coleman, Registrar, Monterey Peninsula College, 980 Fremont Street, Monterey, CA 93940-4799. *Phone:* 831-646-4007. *E-mail:* vcoleman@mpc.edu. *Web site:* http://www.mpc.edu/.

Moorpark College
Moorpark, California

Freshman Application Contact Ms. Katherine Colborn, Registrar, Moorpark College, 7075 Campus Road, Moorpark, CA 93021-2899. *Phone:* 805-378-1415. *Web site:* http://www.moorparkcollege.edu/.

Moreno Valley College
Moreno Valley, California

- **State and locally supported** 2-year, founded 2010
- **Suburban** campus
- **Coed,** 10,413 undergraduate students

Faculty *Total:* 437, 17% full-time.

Majors Accounting; computer programming; dental hygiene; early childhood education; fire science/firefighting; health and physical education/fitness; medical/clinical assistant; physician assistant.

Academics *Degree:* associate. *Special study options:* academic remediation for entering students, distance learning, English as a second language, honors programs.

Student Life *Housing:* college housing not available. *Campus security:* late-night transport/escort service.

Costs (2012–13) *Tuition:* state resident $5280 full-time; nonresident $6360 full-time. Full-time tuition and fees vary according to course load. Part-time tuition and fees vary according to course load.

Applying *Options:* electronic application. *Application deadlines:* rolling (freshmen), rolling (transfers). *Notification:* continuous (freshmen), continuous (transfers).

Freshman Application Contact Jamie Clifton, Director, Enrollment Services, Moreno Valley College, 16130 Lasselle Street, Moreno Valley, CA 92551. *Phone:* 951-571-6293. *E-mail:* admissions@mvc.edu. *Web site:* http://www.rcc.edu/morenovalley/index.cfm.

Mt. San Antonio College
Walnut, California

Freshman Application Contact Dr. George Bradshaw, Dean of Enrollment Management, Mt. San Antonio College, Walnut, CA 91789. *Phone:* 909-594-5611 Ext. 4505. *Web site:* http://www.mtsac.edu/.

Mt. San Jacinto College
San Jacinto, California

Freshman Application Contact Mt. San Jacinto College, 1499 North State Street, San Jacinto, CA 92583-2399. *Phone:* 951-639-5212. *Web site:* http://www.msjc.edu/.

MTI College
Sacramento, California

- **Proprietary** 2-year, founded 1965
- **Suburban** 5-acre campus with easy access to Sacramento
- **Coed,** 900 undergraduate students
- 62% of applicants were admitted

Freshmen *Admission:* 629 applied, 390 admitted.

Faculty *Student/faculty ratio:* 15:1.

Majors Business administration and management; legal assistant/paralegal; system, networking, and LAN/WAN management.

Academics *Calendar:* continuous. *Degree:* diplomas and associate.

Standardized Tests *Required:* MTI Assessment (for admission).

Financial Aid Of all full-time matriculated undergraduates who enrolled in 2010, 35 Federal Work-Study jobs (averaging $1722).

Applying *Application fee:* $50. *Required:* essay or personal statement, high school transcript, interview.

Freshman Application Contact Director of Admissions, MTI College, 5221 Madison Avenue, Sacramento, CA 95841. *Phone:* 916-339-1500. *Fax:* 916-339-0305. *Web site:* http://www.mticollege.edu/.

Napa Valley College
Napa, California

Director of Admissions Mr. Oscar De Haro, Vice President of Student Services, Napa Valley College, 2277 Napa-Vallejo Highway, Napa, CA 94558-6236. *Phone:* 707-253-3000. *Toll-free phone:* 800-826-1077. *E-mail:* odeharo@napavalley.edu. *Web site:* http://www.napavalley.edu/.

Norco College
Norco, California

- **State and locally supported** 2-year, founded 2010
- **Urban** 141-acre campus with easy access to Los Angeles
- **Coed,** 9,674 undergraduate students

Faculty *Total:* 271, 25% full-time.

Majors Accounting; business/commerce; computer programming; early childhood education; engineering technology; marketing/marketing management; real estate.

Academics *Degree:* associate. *Special study options:* academic remediation for entering students, distance learning, English as a second language, honors programs.

Student Life *Housing:* college housing not available.

Costs (2012–13) *Tuition:* state resident $5280 full-time; nonresident $6360 full-time. Full-time tuition and fees vary according to course load. Part-time tuition and fees vary according to course load.

Applying *Options:* electronic application. *Application deadlines:* rolling (freshmen), rolling (transfers). *Notification:* continuous (freshmen), continuous (transfers).

Freshman Application Contact Mark DeAsis, Director, Enrollment Services, Norco College, 2001 Third Street, Norco, CA 92860. *E-mail:* admissionsnorco@norcocollege.edu. *Web site:* http://www.rcc.edu/norco/index.cfm.

Ohlone College
Fremont, California

Freshman Application Contact Christopher Williamson, Director of Admissions and Records, Ohlone College, 43600 Mission Boulevard, Fremont, CA 94539-5884. *Phone:* 510-659-6518. *Fax:* 510-659-7321. *E-mail:* cwilliamson@ohlone.edu. *Web site:* http://www.ohlone.edu/.

Orange Coast College
Costa Mesa, California

- **State and locally supported** 2-year, founded 1947, part of Coast Community College District System
- **Suburban** 164-acre campus with easy access to Los Angeles
- **Endowment** $10.0 million
- **Coed,** 24,239 undergraduate students, 42% full-time, 49% women, 51% men

Undergraduates 10,094 full-time, 14,145 part-time. Students come from 52 states and territories; 69 other countries; 2% are from out of state; 2% Black or African American, non-Hispanic/Latino; 25% Hispanic/Latino; 23% Asian, non-Hispanic/Latino; 0.5% Native Hawaiian or other Pacific Islander, non-Hispanic/Latino; 0.4% American Indian or Alaska Native, non-Hispanic/Latino; 3% Two or more races, non-Hispanic/Latino; 3% Race/ethnicity unknown; 3% international; 8% transferred in. *Retention:* 79% of full-time freshmen returned.

Freshmen *Admission:* 4,205 enrolled.

Faculty *Total:* 758, 28% full-time. *Student/faculty ratio:* 38:1.

Majors Accounting; administrative assistant and secretarial science; aeronautics/aviation/aerospace science and technology; airline pilot and flight crew; anthropology; architectural engineering technology; art; athletic training; avionics maintenance technology; behavioral sciences; biology/biological sciences; building/home/construction inspection; business administration and management; cardiovascular technology; chemistry; child-care and support services management; child-care provision; cinematography and film/video production; clinical laboratory science/medical technology; commercial and advertising art; communications technology; computer engineering technology; computer graphics; computer programming; computer programming (specific applications); computer typography and composition equipment operation; construction engineering technology; culinary arts; dance; data entry/microcomputer applications related; data processing and data processing technology; dental hygiene; dietetics; drafting and design technology; dramatic/theater arts; economics; electrical and power transmission installation; electrical, electronic and communications engineering technology; electrical/electronics equipment installation and repair; emergency medical technology (EMT paramedic); engineering; English; family and consumer economics related; family and consumer sciences/human sciences; fashion merchandising; film/cinema/video studies; food science; foods, nutrition, and wellness; food technology and processing; French; geography; geology/earth science; German; health professions related; heating, air conditioning, ventilation and refrigeration maintenance technology; history; horticultural science; hotel/motel administration; housing and human environments; human development and family studies; humanities; industrial and product design; industrial radiologic technology; information science/studies; interior design; journalism; kindergarten/preschool education; kinesiology and exercise science; liberal arts and sciences/liberal studies; machine shop technology; machine tool technology; marine maintenance and ship repair technology; marketing/marketing management; mass communication/media; mathematics; medical administrative assistant and medical secretary; medical/clinical assistant; music; musical instrument fabrication and repair; music management; natural sciences; nuclear medical technology; ornamental horticulture; philosophy; photography; physical education teaching and coaching; physics; political science and

government; religious studies; respiratory care therapy; restaurant, culinary, and catering management; retailing; selling skills and sales; social sciences; sociology; Spanish; special products marketing; welding technology; word processing.

Academics *Calendar:* semesters plus summer session. *Degree:* certificates and associate. *Special study options:* academic remediation for entering students, adult/continuing education programs, advanced placement credit, cooperative education, distance learning, double majors, English as a second language, external degree program, freshman honors college, honors programs, internships, off-campus study, part-time degree program, services for LD students, student-designed majors, study abroad, summer session for credit. *ROTC:* Army (c), Air Force (c).

Library Library with 100,314 titles, 208 serial subscriptions, 3,776 audiovisual materials, an OPAC, a Web page.

Student Life *Housing:* college housing not available. *Activities and Organizations:* drama/theater group, student-run newspaper, choral group, Architecture Club, Circle K, Doctors of Tomorrow, Speech, Theater, and Debate, Vietnamese Student Association. *Campus security:* 24-hour emergency response devices and patrols, student patrols, late-night transport/escort service. *Student services:* health clinic, personal/psychological counseling, legal services.

Athletics *Intercollegiate sports:* baseball M, basketball M/W, bowling M(c)/W(c), crew M/W, cross-country running M/W, football M, golf M/W, soccer M/W, softball W, swimming and diving M/W, tennis M/W, track and field M/W, volleyball W, water polo M/W.

Costs (2012–13) *Tuition:* state resident $1112 full-time, $36 per unit part-time; nonresident $6992 full-time. *Required fees:* $902 full-time, $61 per term part-time.

Financial Aid Of all full-time matriculated undergraduates who enrolled in 2010, 108 Federal Work-Study jobs (averaging $3000). *Financial aid deadline:* 5/28.

Applying *Options:* electronic application. *Application deadlines:* rolling (freshmen), rolling (transfers). *Notification:* continuous (freshmen), continuous (transfers).

Freshman Application Contact Dean of Enrollment Services, Orange Coast College, 2701 Fairview Road, Costa Mesa, CA 92926. *Phone:* 714-432-5788. *Fax:* 714-432-5072. *Web site:* http://www.orangecoastcollege.edu/.

Oxnard College
Oxnard, California

Freshman Application Contact Ms. Susan Cabral, Registrar, Oxnard College, 4000 South Rose Avenue, Oxnard, CA 93033-6699. *Phone:* 805-986-5843. *Fax:* 805-986-5943. *E-mail:* scabral@vcccd.edu. *Web site:* http://www.oxnardcollege.edu/.

Palomar College
San Marcos, California

Freshman Application Contact Mr. Herman Lee, Director of Enrollment Services, Palomar College, 1140 West Mission Road, San Marcos, CA 92069-1487. *Phone:* 760-744-1150 Ext. 2171. *Fax:* 760-744-2932. *E-mail:* admissions@palomar.edu. *Web site:* http://www.palomar.edu/.

Palo Verde College
Blythe, California

Freshman Application Contact Diana Rodriguez, Vice President of Student Services, Palo Verde College, 1 College Drive, Blythe, CA 92225. *Phone:* 760-921-5428. *Fax:* 760-921-3608. *E-mail:* diana.rodriguez@paloverde.edu. *Web site:* http://www.paloverde.edu/.

Pasadena City College
Pasadena, California

Freshman Application Contact Pasadena City College, 1570 East Colorado Boulevard, Pasadena, CA 91106-2041. *Phone:* 626-585-7805. *Fax:* 626-585-7915. *Web site:* http://www.pasadena.edu/.

Pima Medical Institute
Chula Vista, California

- **Proprietary** primarily 2-year, founded 1998
- **Urban** campus
- **Coed**

Academics *Calendar:* modular. *Degrees:* certificates, associate, and bachelor's. *Special study options:* cooperative education, distance learning, internships.

Standardized Tests *Required:* Wonderlic Scholastic Level Exam (for admission).

Applying *Required:* high school transcript, interview.

Freshman Application Contact Admissions Office, Pima Medical Institute, 780 Bay Boulevard, Suite 101, Chula Vista, CA 91910. *Phone:* 619-425-3200. *Toll-free phone:* 800-477-PIMA (in-state); 888-477-PIMA (out-of-state). *Web site:* http://www.pmi.edu/.

Platt College
Alhambra, California

Director of Admissions Mr. Detroit Whiteside, Director of Admissions, Platt College, 1000 South Fremont A9W, Alhambra, CA 91803. *Phone:* 323-258-8050. *Toll-free phone:* 888-866-6697 (in-state); 888-80-PLATT (out-of-state). *Web site:* http://www.plattcollege.edu/.

Platt College
Ontario, California

Director of Admissions Ms. Jennifer Abandonato, Director of Admissions, Platt College, 3700 Inland Empire Boulevard, Suite 400, Ontario, CA 91764. *Phone:* 909-941-9410. *Toll-free phone:* 888-80-PLATT. *Web site:* http://www.plattcollege.edu/.

Porterville College
Porterville, California

Director of Admissions Ms. Judy Pope, Director of Admissions and Records/ Registrar, Porterville College, 100 East College Avenue, Porterville, CA 93257-6058. *Phone:* 559-791-2222. *Web site:* http://www.pc.cc.ca.us/.

Professional Golfers Career College
Temecula, California

Freshman Application Contact Mr. Mark Bland, Director of Admissions, Professional Golfers Career College, 26109 Ynez Road, Temecula, CA 92591. *Phone:* 951-719-2994. *Toll-free phone:* 800-877-4380. *Fax:* 951-719-1643. *E-mail:* Mark@golfcollege.edu. *Web site:* http://www.golfcollege.edu/.

Reedley College
Reedley, California

- **State and locally supported** 2-year, founded 1926, part of State Center Community College District System
- **Rural** 350-acre campus
- **Coed,** 14,573 undergraduate students

Undergraduates Students come from 15 states and territories; 2% Black or African American, non-Hispanic/Latino; 41% Hispanic/Latino; 5% Asian, non-Hispanic/Latino; 0.1% American Indian or Alaska Native, non-Hispanic/ Latino; 21% Race/ethnicity unknown.

Faculty *Total:* 844, 23% full-time.

Majors Accounting; administrative assistant and secretarial science; agricultural business and management; agricultural mechanization related; agriculture; animal sciences; art; automobile/automotive mechanics technology; avionics maintenance technology; biology/biological sciences; business/commerce; child-care and support services management; commercial and advertising art; computer and information sciences; corrections and criminal justice related; criminal justice/police science; dental assisting; English; entrepreneurship; fine arts related; foreign languages and literatures; general studies; health and physical education/fitness; horticultural science; hospitality administration; information science/studies; liberal arts and sciences/liberal studies; machine tool technology; management science; mathematics; music performance; natural resources management and policy related; office occupations and clerical services; physical sciences; plant sciences; precision metal working related; social sciences; voice and opera; welding technology.

Academics *Calendar:* semesters. *Degree:* certificates, diplomas, and associate. *Special study options:* academic remediation for entering students, adult/ continuing education programs, advanced placement credit, cooperative education, distance learning, English as a second language, freshman honors college, honors programs, independent study, part-time degree program, services for LD students, study abroad, summer session for credit. *ROTC:* Air Force (c).

Library Reedley College Library with 36,000 titles, 217 serial subscriptions, an OPAC.

Student Life *Housing Options:* coed. Campus housing is university owned. *Activities and Organizations:* drama/theater group, student-run newspaper, choral group. *Campus security:* 24-hour emergency response devices, late-night transport/escort service, 24-hour on-campus police dispatcher. *Student services:* personal/psychological counseling.

Athletics *Intercollegiate sports:* baseball M, basketball M/W, football M, golf M, softball W, tennis M/W, track and field M/W, volleyball W. *Intramural sports:* basketball M/W, football M/W, swimming and diving M/W, tennis M/ W, track and field M/W, volleyball M/W.

Applying *Required:* high school transcript. *Application deadlines:* rolling (freshmen), rolling (transfers). *Notification:* continuous until 8/1 (freshmen), continuous until 8/1 (transfers).

Freshman Application Contact Admissions and Records Office, Reedley College, 995 North Reed Avenue, Reedley, CA 93654. *Phone:* 559-638-0323. *Fax:* 559-637-2523. *Web site:* http://www.reedleycollege.edu/.

Rio Hondo College
Whittier, California

Director of Admissions Ms. Judy G. Pearson, Director of Admissions and Records, Rio Hondo College, 3600 Workman Mill Road, Whittier, CA 90601-1699. *Phone:* 562-692-0921 Ext. 3153. *Web site:* http://www.riohondo.edu/.

Riverside City College
Riverside, California

- **State and locally supported** 2-year, founded 1916, part of California Community College System
- **Suburban** 108-acre campus with easy access to Los Angeles
- **Coed,** 18,586 undergraduate students

Faculty *Total:* 665, 33% full-time.

Majors Accounting; autobody/collision and repair technology; automobile/ automotive mechanics technology; business administration and management; computer programming; cosmetology; culinary arts; early childhood education; graphic and printing equipment operation/production; heating, air conditioning, ventilation and refrigeration maintenance technology; human services; licensed practical/vocational nurse training; marketing/marketing management; office management; real estate; registered nursing/registered nurse; sign language interpretation and translation; welding technology.

Academics *Calendar:* semesters. *Degree:* certificates and associate. *Special study options:* academic remediation for entering students, distance learning, English as a second language, honors programs, study abroad.

Student Life *Housing:* college housing not available. *Campus security:* late-night transport/escort service.

Costs (2012–13) *Tuition:* state resident $5280 full-time; nonresident $6360 full-time. Full-time tuition and fees vary according to course load. Part-time tuition and fees vary according to course load.

Applying *Options:* electronic application. *Application deadlines:* rolling (freshmen), rolling (transfers). *Notification:* continuous (freshmen), continuous (transfers).

Freshman Application Contact Joy Chambers, Dean of Enrollment Services, Riverside City College, Riverside, CA 92506. *Phone:* 951-222-8600. *Fax:* 951-222-8037. *E-mail:* admissionsriverside@rcc.edu. *Web site:* http:// www.rcc.edu/.

Sacramento City College
Sacramento, California

Director of Admissions Mr. Sam T. Sandusky, Dean, Student Services, Sacramento City College, 3835 Freeport Boulevard, Sacramento, CA 95822-1386. *Phone:* 916-558-2438. *Web site:* http://www.scc.losrios.edu/.

Saddleback College
Mission Viejo, California

Freshman Application Contact Admissions Office, Saddleback College, 28000 Marguerite Parkway, Mission Viejo, CA 92692. *Phone:* 949-582-4555. *Fax:* 949-347-8315. *E-mail:* earaiza@saddleback.edu. *Web site:* http:// www.saddleback.edu/.

Sage College
Moreno Valley, California

Admissions Office Contact Sage College, 12125 Day Street, Building L, Moreno Valley, CA 92557-6720. *Toll-free phone:* 888-755-SAGE. *Web site:* http://www.sagecollege.edu/.

The Salvation Army College for Officer Training at Crestmont

Rancho Palos Verdes, California

Freshman Application Contact Capt. Kevin Jackson, Director of Curriculum, The Salvation Army College for Officer Training at Crestmont, 30840 Hawthorne Boulevard, Rancho Palos Verdes, CA 90275. *Phone:* 310-544-6442. *Fax:* 310-265-6520. *Web site:* http://www.crestmont.edu/.

San Bernardino Valley College

San Bernardino, California

Director of Admissions Ms. Helena Johnson, Director of Admissions and Records, San Bernardino Valley College, 701 South Mount Vernon Avenue, San Bernardino, CA 92410-2748. *Phone:* 909-384-4401. *Web site:* http://www.valleycollege.edu/.

San Diego City College

San Diego, California

- **State and locally supported** 2-year, founded 1914, part of San Diego Community College District System
- **Urban** 60-acre campus with easy access to San Diego, Tijuana
- **Endowment** $166,270
- **Coed,** 18,626 undergraduate students

Undergraduates 13% Black or African American, non-Hispanic/Latino; 42% Hispanic/Latino; 9% Asian, non-Hispanic/Latino; 0.6% Native Hawaiian or other Pacific Islander, non-Hispanic/Latino; 0.6% American Indian or Alaska Native, non-Hispanic/Latino; 9% Race/ethnicity unknown.

Faculty *Total:* 803, 21% full-time, 16% with terminal degrees. *Student/faculty ratio:* 35:1.

Majors Accounting; administrative assistant and secretarial science; African American/Black studies; anthropology; art; artificial intelligence; automobile/automotive mechanics technology; behavioral sciences; biology/biological sciences; business administration and management; carpentry; commercial and advertising art; computer engineering technology; consumer services and advocacy; cosmetology; court reporting; data processing and data processing technology; developmental and child psychology; drafting and design technology; dramatic/theater arts; electrical, electronic and communications engineering technology; emergency medical technology (EMT paramedic); engineering technology; English; environmental engineering technology; fashion merchandising; finance; graphic and printing equipment operation/production; Hispanic-American, Puerto Rican, and Mexican-American/Chicano studies; hospitality administration; industrial technology; insurance; interior design; journalism; labor and industrial relations; Latin American studies; legal administrative assistant/secretary; legal assistant/paralegal; liberal arts and sciences/liberal studies; licensed practical/vocational nurse training; machine tool technology; marketing/marketing management; mathematics; modern languages; music; occupational safety and health technology; parks, recreation and leisure; photography; physical education teaching and coaching; physical sciences; political science and government; pre-engineering; psychology; radio and television; real estate; registered nursing/registered nurse; rhetoric and composition; social sciences; social work; sociology; special products marketing; teacher assistant/aide; telecommunications technology; tourism and travel services management; transportation and materials moving related; welding technology.

Academics *Calendar:* semesters. *Degree:* certificates and associate. *Special study options:* academic remediation for entering students, adult/continuing education programs, cooperative education, distance learning, English as a second language, external degree program, honors programs, independent study, off-campus study, part-time degree program, services for LD students, student-designed majors, summer session for credit. *ROTC:* Air Force (c).

Library San Diego City College Library with 88,000 titles, 191 serial subscriptions, 950 audiovisual materials, an OPAC.

Student Life *Housing:* college housing not available. *Activities and Organizations:* drama/theater group, student-run newspaper, radio station, choral group, Alpha Gamma Sigma, Association of United Latin American Students, MECHA, Afrikan Student Union, Student Nurses Association. *Campus security:* 24-hour emergency response devices and patrols, late-night transport/escort service. *Student services:* health clinic, personal/psychological counseling.

Athletics *Intercollegiate sports:* baseball M, basketball M/W, cross-country running M/W, football M, golf M/W, soccer M/W, softball W, tennis M/W, track and field M/W, volleyball M/W. *Intramural sports:* archery M/W, badminton M/W, baseball M, basketball M/W, bowling M/W, racquetball M/W, soccer M/W, softball W, swimming and diving M/W, tennis M/W, track and field M/W, volleyball M/W, weight lifting M/W.

Costs (2012–13) *Tuition:* state resident $1380 full-time; nonresident $6870 full-time. *Required fees:* $50 full-time.

Financial Aid Of all full-time matriculated undergraduates who enrolled in 2010, 90 Federal Work-Study jobs (averaging $3844). 19 state and other part-time jobs (averaging $2530).

Applying *Options:* electronic application. *Required for some:* high school transcript. *Application deadlines:* rolling (freshmen), rolling (transfers).

Freshman Application Contact Ms. Lou Humphries, Registrar/Supervisor of Admissions, Records, Evaluations and Veterans, San Diego City College, 1313 Park Boulevard, San Diego, CA 92101-4787. *Phone:* 619-388-3474. *Fax:* 619-388-3505. *E-mail:* lhumphri@sdccd.edu. *Web site:* http://www.sdcity.edu/.

San Diego Mesa College

San Diego, California

Freshman Application Contact Ms. Cheri Sawyer, Admissions Supervisor, San Diego Mesa College, 7250 Mesa College Drive, San Diego, CA 92111. *Phone:* 619-388-2686. *Fax:* 619-388-2960. *E-mail:* csawyer@sdccd.edu. *Web site:* http://www.sdmesa.edu/.

San Diego Miramar College

San Diego, California

Freshman Application Contact Ms. Dana Andras, Admissions Supervisor, San Diego Miramar College, 10440 Black Mountain Road, San Diego, CA 92126-2999. *Phone:* 619-536-7854. *E-mail:* dmaxwell@sdccd.cc.ca.us. *Web site:* http://www.sdmiramar.edu/.

San Joaquin Delta College

Stockton, California

Freshman Application Contact Ms. Catherine Mooney, Registrar, San Joaquin Delta College, 5151 Pacific Avenue, Stockton, CA 95207. *Phone:* 209-954-5635. *Fax:* 209-954-5769. *E-mail:* admissions@deltacollege.edu. *Web site:* http://www.deltacollege.edu/.

San Joaquin Valley College

Bakersfield, California

- **Proprietary** 2-year, founded 1977, part of San Joaquin Valley College
- **Coed,** 541 undergraduate students, 100% full-time, 65% women, 35% men

Undergraduates 541 full-time. Students come from 6 states and territories; 2 other countries; 1% are from out of state.

Faculty *Total:* 67, 54% full-time. *Student/faculty ratio:* 12:1.

Majors Business administration and management; corrections; dental assisting; heating, ventilation, air conditioning and refrigeration engineering technology; homeland security, law enforcement, firefighting and protective services related; medical/clinical assistant; medical insurance/medical billing; pharmacy technician; respiratory care therapy; surgical technology.

Academics *Degree:* associate.

Student Life *Activities and Organizations:* CAMA Club, RACT Club, Business Club, Student Council, National Technical Honor Society.

Costs (2012–13) *Tuition:* $29,750 full-time. No tuition increase for student's term of enrollment. *Payment plan:* installment.

Applying *Required for some:* essay or personal statement, interview. *Application deadlines:* rolling (freshmen), rolling (transfers). *Notification:* continuous (freshmen), continuous (transfers).

Freshman Application Contact Enrollment Services Director, San Joaquin Valley College, 201 New Stine Road, Bakersfield, CA 93309. *Phone:* 661-834-0126. *Toll-free phone:* 866-544-7898. *Fax:* 661-834-8124. *E-mail:* admissions@sjvc.edu. *Web site:* http://www.sjvc.edu/.

San Joaquin Valley College

Fresno, California

- **Proprietary** 2-year, part of San Joaquin Valley College
- **Coed,** 675 undergraduate students, 100% full-time, 68% women, 32% men

Undergraduates 675 full-time. Students come from 4 states and territories; 3% are from out of state.

Freshmen *Admission:* 185 enrolled.

Faculty *Total:* 71, 44% full-time. *Student/faculty ratio:* 10:1.

Majors Business administration and management; construction management; corrections; dental assisting; health and medical administrative services related; heating, ventilation, air conditioning and refrigeration engineering

technology; industrial technology; medical/clinical assistant; pharmacy technician; surgical technology; veterinary/animal health technology.
Academics *Degree:* certificates and associate.
Student Life *Housing:* college housing not available. *Activities and Organizations:* Associated Student Body, American Medical Technologists, State and County Dental Assistants Association, Arts and Entertainment.
Costs (2012–13) *Tuition:* $29,750 full-time.
Applying *Required for some:* essay or personal statement, 1 letter of recommendation, interview. *Application deadlines:* rolling (freshmen), rolling (transfers). *Notification:* continuous (freshmen), continuous (transfers).
Freshman Application Contact Enrollment Services Director, San Joaquin Valley College, 295 East Sierra Avenue, Fresno, CA 93710. *Phone:* 559-448-8282. *Fax:* 559-448-8250. *E-mail:* admissions@sjvc.edu. *Web site:* http://www.sjvc.edu/.

San Joaquin Valley College
Hanford, California

- **Proprietary** 2-year
- **Coed**

Academics *Degree:* certificates.
Costs (2012–13) *Tuition:* $29,750 full-time.
Freshman Application Contact San Joaquin Valley College, 215 West 7th Street, Hanford, CA 93230. *Web site:* http://www.sjvc.edu/.

San Joaquin Valley College
Hesperia, California

- **Proprietary** 2-year
- **Coed**

Costs (2012–13) *Tuition:* $31,950 full-time.
Freshman Application Contact San Joaquin Valley College, 9331 Mariposa Road, Hesperia, CA 92344. *Web site:* http://www.sjvc.edu/.

San Joaquin Valley College
Rancho Cordova, California

- **Proprietary** 2-year, part of San Joaquin Valley College
- **Coed,** 619 undergraduate students, 100% full-time, 65% women, 35% men

Undergraduates 619 full-time.
Freshmen *Admission:* 68 enrolled.
Faculty *Total:* 50, 38% full-time. *Student/faculty ratio:* 17:1.
Majors Business administration and management; corrections; dental assisting; heating, ventilation, air conditioning and refrigeration engineering technology; medical/clinical assistant; medical office management; pharmacy technician; respiratory therapy technician.
Academics *Degree:* certificates and associate.
Student Life *Housing:* college housing not available. *Activities and Organizations:* Associated Student Body, Diversity Committee.
Costs (2012–13) *Tuition:* $43,120 full-time.
Applying *Required for some:* essay or personal statement, 1 letter of recommendation, interview. *Application deadlines:* rolling (freshmen), rolling (transfers). *Notification:* continuous (freshmen), continuous (transfers).
Freshman Application Contact Enrollment Services Director, San Joaquin Valley College, 11050 Olson Drive, Suite 100, Rancho Cordova, CA 95670. *Phone:* 916-638-7582. *Fax:* 916-638-7553. *E-mail:* admissions@sjvc.edu. *Web site:* http://www.sjvc.edu/.

San Joaquin Valley College
Rancho Cucamonga, California

Freshman Application Contact Enrollment Services Director, San Joaquin Valley College, 10641 Church Street, Rancho Cucamonga, CA 91730. *Phone:* 909-948-7582. *Fax:* 909-948-3860. *E-mail:* admissions@sjvc.edu. *Web site:* http://www.sjvc.edu/.

San Joaquin Valley College
Salida, California

- **Proprietary** 2-year, part of San Joaquin Valley College
- **Coed,** 254 undergraduate students, 100% full-time, 86% women, 14% men

Undergraduates 254 full-time. Students come from 3 states and territories; 3% are from out of state.
Freshmen *Admission:* 104 enrolled.
Faculty *Total:* 17, 65% full-time. *Student/faculty ratio:* 18:1.

Majors Business administration and management; corrections and criminal justice related; industrial technology; medical/clinical assistant; medical office assistant; pharmacy technician.
Academics *Degree:* certificates and associate.
Student Life *Activities and Organizations:* Associated Student Body, Book Club.
Costs (2012–13) *Tuition:* $29,750 full-time.
Applying *Required for some:* essay or personal statement, 1 letter of recommendation, interview. *Application deadlines:* rolling (freshmen), rolling (transfers). *Notification:* continuous (freshmen), continuous (transfers).
Freshman Application Contact Enrollment Services Director, San Joaquin Valley College, 5380 Pirrone Road, Salida, CA 95368. *Phone:* 209-543-8800. *Fax:* 209-543-8320. *E-mail:* admissions@sjvc.edu. *Web site:* http://www.sjvc.edu/.

San Joaquin Valley College
Temecula, California

- **Proprietary** 2-year
- **Coed**

Costs (2012–13) *Tuition:* $31,950 full-time.
Freshman Application Contact San Joaquin Valley College, 27270 Madison Avenue, Suite 305, Temecula, CA 92590. *Web site:* http://www.sjvc.edu/.

San Joaquin Valley College
Visalia, California

- **Independent** 2-year, founded 1977, part of San Joaquin Valley College
- **Small-town** campus
- **Coed,** 895 undergraduate students, 100% full-time, 76% women, 24% men

Undergraduates 895 full-time. Students come from 17 states and territories; 2% are from out of state.
Freshmen *Admission:* 233 enrolled.
Faculty *Total:* 129, 53% full-time. *Student/faculty ratio:* 9:1.
Majors Business/commerce; computer and information sciences and support services related; corrections; dental assisting; dental hygiene; health and medical administrative services related; human resources management; industrial technology; licensed practical/vocational nurse training; medical administrative assistant and medical secretary; medical/clinical assistant; medical office assistant; pharmacy technician; physician assistant; registered nursing/registered nurse; respiratory care therapy.
Academics *Calendar:* semesters. *Degree:* certificates and associate. *Special study options:* academic remediation for entering students.
Library SJVC Visalia Campus Library with 4,720 titles, 53 serial subscriptions, 125 audiovisual materials.
Student Life *Housing:* college housing not available. *Activities and Organizations:* Associated Student Body, Students in Free Enterprise (SIFE), American Medical Technologists, National and Technical Honor Society. *Campus security:* late-night transport/escort service, full-time security personnel.
Costs (2012–13) *Tuition:* $29,750 full-time. No tuition increase for student's term of enrollment. *Payment plan:* installment.
Applying *Required for some:* essay or personal statement, high school transcript, interview. *Application deadlines:* rolling (freshmen), rolling (transfers). *Notification:* continuous (freshmen), continuous (transfers).
Freshman Application Contact Enrollment Services Director, San Joaquin Valley College, 8400 West Mineral King Boulevard, Visalia, CA 93291. *Phone:* 559-651-2500. *Fax:* 559-734-9048. *E-mail:* admissions@sjvc.edu. *Web site:* http://www.sjvc.edu/.

San Joaquin Valley College–Fresno Aviation Campus
Fresno, California

- **Proprietary** 2-year, part of San Joaquin Valley College
- **Coed,** 59 undergraduate students, 100% full-time, 3% women, 97% men

Undergraduates 59 full-time.
Freshmen *Admission:* 25 enrolled.
Faculty *Total:* 5, 100% full-time. *Student/faculty ratio:* 12:1.
Majors Airframe mechanics and aircraft maintenance technology.
Academics *Degree:* associate.
Student Life *Housing:* college housing not available. *Activities and Organizations:* RC Club (radio controlled airplane).
Costs (2012–13) *Tuition:* $27,265 full-time. No tuition increase for student's term of enrollment. *Payment plan:* installment.
Applying *Required for some:* essay or personal statement, interview. *Application deadlines:* rolling (freshmen), rolling (transfers). *Notification:* continuous (freshmen), continuous (transfers).

Freshman Application Contact Enrollment Services Coordinator, San Joaquin Valley College–Fresno Aviation Campus, 4985 East Anderson Avenue, Fresno, CA 93727. *Phone:* 559-453-0123. *Fax:* 599-453-0133. *E-mail:* admissions@sjvc.edu. *Web site:* http://www.sjvc.edu/.

San Joaquin Valley College–Online
Visalia, California

- **Proprietary** 2-year, part of San Joaquin Valley College
- **Suburban** campus with easy access to Fresno
- **Coed,** 887 undergraduate students, 100% full-time, 72% women, 28% men

Undergraduates 887 full-time. Students come from 14 states and territories; 31% are from out of state. *Retention:* 77% of full-time freshmen returned.
Freshmen *Admission:* 247 enrolled.
Faculty *Total:* 41, 2% full-time. *Student/faculty ratio:* 21:1.
Majors Business administration and management; construction management; criminal justice/law enforcement administration; human resources management and services related; medical/clinical assistant; medical office management.
Academics *Degree:* certificates and associate.
Costs (2012–13) *Tuition:* $30,800 full-time. No tuition increase for student's term of enrollment.
Applying *Options:* electronic application. *Required for some:* essay or personal statement, interview. *Application deadlines:* rolling (freshmen), rolling (transfers). *Notification:* continuous (freshmen), continuous (transfers).
Freshman Application Contact Enrollment Services Director, San Joaquin Valley College–Online, 801 S. Akers Street, Suite 150, Visalia, CA 93277. *E-mail:* admissions@sjvc.edu. *Web site:* http://www.sjvc.edu/campus/SJVC_Online/.

San Jose City College
San Jose, California

Freshman Application Contact Mr. Carlo Santos, Director of Admissions/Registrar, San Jose City College, 2100 Moorpark Avenue, San Jose, CA 95128-2799. *Phone:* 408-288-3707. *Fax:* 408-298-1935. *Web site:* http://www.sjcc.edu/.

Santa Ana College
Santa Ana, California

Freshman Application Contact Mrs. Christie Steward, Admissions Clerk, Santa Ana College, 1530 West 17th Street, Santa Ana, CA 92706-3398. *Phone:* 714-564-6053. *Web site:* http://www.sac.edu/.

Santa Barbara City College
Santa Barbara, California

- **State and locally supported** 2-year, founded 1908, part of California Community College System
- **Small-town** 65-acre campus
- **Endowment** $21.1 million
- **Coed**

Undergraduates 7,952 full-time, 10,140 part-time. Students come from 46 states and territories; 66 other countries; 6% are from out of state; 3% Black or African American, non-Hispanic/Latino; 29% Hispanic/Latino; 3% Asian, non-Hispanic/Latino; 1% Native Hawaiian or other Pacific Islander, non-Hispanic/Latino; 0.7% American Indian or Alaska Native, non-Hispanic/Latino; 4% Two or more races, non-Hispanic/Latino; 3% Race/ethnicity unknown; 10% international; 5% transferred in.
Faculty *Student/faculty ratio:* 27:1.
Academics *Calendar:* semesters. *Degree:* certificates and associate. *Special study options:* academic remediation for entering students, adult/continuing education programs, advanced placement credit, cooperative education, distance learning, double majors, English as a second language, honors programs, independent study, internships, part-time degree program, services for LD students, study abroad, summer session for credit. *ROTC:* Army (c).
Student Life *Campus security:* 24-hour emergency response devices and patrols, late-night transport/escort service.
Costs (2011–12) *Tuition:* nonresident $210 per unit part-time. Full-time tuition and fees vary according to course load. Part-time tuition and fees vary according to course load. *Required fees:* $36 per unit part-time, $43 per term part-time.
Applying *Options:* electronic application, early admission. *Recommended:* high school transcript.
Freshman Application Contact Ms. Allison Curtis, Director of Admissions and Records, Santa Barbara City College, Santa Barbara, CA 93109. *Phone:*

805-965-0581 Ext. 2352. *Fax:* 805-962-0497. *E-mail:* admissions@sbcc.edu. *Web site:* http://www.sbcc.edu/.

Santa Monica College
Santa Monica, California

- **State and locally supported** 2-year, founded 1929, part of California Community College System
- **Urban** 40-acre campus with easy access to Los Angeles
- **Coed,** 31,138 undergraduate students, 36% full-time, 55% women, 45% men

Undergraduates 11,160 full-time, 19,978 part-time. 10% Black or African American, non-Hispanic/Latino; 32% Hispanic/Latino; 12% Asian, non-Hispanic/Latino; 0.3% Native Hawaiian or other Pacific Islander, non-Hispanic/Latino; 0.3% American Indian or Alaska Native, non-Hispanic/Latino; 3% Two or more races, non-Hispanic/Latino; 4% Race/ethnicity unknown; 10% international.
Freshmen *Admission:* 4,560 enrolled.
Faculty *Total:* 1,303, 24% full-time.
Majors Accounting; administrative assistant and secretarial science; animation, interactive technology, video graphics and special effects; anthropology; apparel and textile marketing management; art; biological and physical sciences; business administration and management; child development; commercial photography; computer programming; computer science; cosmetology; dance; data entry/microcomputer applications; data modeling/warehousing and database administration; digital communication and media/multimedia; dramatic/theater arts; fashion/apparel design; film/cinema/video studies; graphic design; health and physical education/fitness; interior design; journalism; legal administrative assistant/secretary; liberal arts and sciences/liberal studies; music; office management; radio and television; registered nursing/registered nurse; respiratory care therapy; rhetoric and composition; sales, distribution, and marketing operations; selling skills and sales; special education–early childhood; women's studies.
Academics *Calendar:* semester plus optional winter and summer terms. *Degree:* certificates and associate. *Special study options:* academic remediation for entering students, adult/continuing education programs, advanced placement credit, cooperative education, distance learning, English as a second language, honors programs, independent study, internships, part-time degree program, services for LD students, study abroad, summer session for credit. *ROTC:* Army (c).
Library Santa Monica College Library with 101,317 titles, 389 serial subscriptions, an OPAC, a Web page.
Student Life *Housing:* college housing not available. *Activities and Organizations:* drama/theater group, student-run newspaper, choral group. *Campus security:* 24-hour emergency response devices and patrols, student patrols, late-night transport/escort service. *Student services:* health clinic, personal/psychological counseling, women's center, legal services.
Athletics *Intercollegiate sports:* basketball M/W, cross-country running M/W, football M, soccer W, softball W, swimming and diving M/W, tennis W, track and field M/W, volleyball M/W, water polo M/W.
Costs (2012–13) *Tuition:* state resident $1080 full-time, $36 per unit part-time; nonresident $8250 full-time, $275 per unit part-time. Full-time tuition and fees vary according to course load. Part-time tuition and fees vary according to course load. *Required fees:* $49 full-time. *Payment plan:* deferred payment.
Financial Aid Of all full-time matriculated undergraduates who enrolled in 2010, 450 Federal Work-Study jobs (averaging $3000).
Applying *Options:* early admission. *Required:* high school transcript. *Application deadlines:* 8/30 (freshmen), 8/30 (transfers). *Notification:* continuous until 8/30 (freshmen), continuous until 8/30 (transfers).
Freshman Application Contact Santa Monica College, 1900 Pico Boulevard, Santa Monica, CA 90405-1628. *Phone:* 310-434-4774. *Web site:* http://www.smc.edu/.

Santa Rosa Junior College
Santa Rosa, California

- **State and locally supported** 2-year, founded 1918, part of California Community College System
- **Urban** 100-acre campus with easy access to San Francisco
- **Endowment** $25.0 million
- **Coed,** 23,224 undergraduate students, 31% full-time, 55% women, 45% men

Undergraduates 7,239 full-time, 15,985 part-time. Students come from 40 other countries; 2% are from out of state.
Freshmen *Admission:* 5,804 applied, 5,804 admitted.
Faculty *Total:* 1,302, 22% full-time, 13% with terminal degrees. *Student/faculty ratio:* 22:1.
Majors Agricultural business and management; agricultural communication/journalism; agroecology and sustainable agriculture; American Sign Language

(ASL); animal sciences; anthropology; art; art history, criticism and conservation; automobile/automotive mechanics technology; behavioral sciences; biology/biological sciences; business administration and management; chemistry; child development; civil engineering technology; communication; computer science; criminal justice/law enforcement administration; culinary arts; dance; dental hygiene; diesel mechanics technology; dietetic technology; digital communication and media/multimedia; dramatic/theater arts; economics; electrical, electronic and communications engineering technology; emergency medical technology (EMT paramedic); engineering; English; environmental studies; fashion/apparel design; fashion merchandising; fire science/firefighting; floriculture/floristry management; graphic design; history; horse husbandry/equine science and management; humanities; human resources management; human services; interior design; landscaping and groundskeeping; Latin American studies; legal assistant/paralegal; liberal arts and sciences/liberal studies; mathematics; medical/clinical assistant; music related; natural resources/conservation; natural sciences; nursing practice; nutrition sciences; parks, recreation and leisure facilities management; pharmacy technician; philosophy; physical education teaching and coaching; physics; political science and government; psychology; radiologic technology/science; real estate; registered nursing/registered nurse; religious studies; restaurant/food services management; social sciences; sociology; Spanish; surveying technology; women's studies.

Academics *Calendar:* semesters. *Degree:* certificates and associate. *Special study options:* academic remediation for entering students, adult/continuing education programs, advanced placement credit, cooperative education, distance learning, English as a second language, independent study, internships, off-campus study, part-time degree program, services for LD students, study abroad, summer session for credit.

Library Doyle Library plus 1 other with 182,464 titles, 22,584 serial subscriptions, 13,951 audiovisual materials, an OPAC, a Web page.

Student Life *Activities and Organizations:* drama/theater group, student-run newspaper, choral group, AG Ambassadors, MECHA, Alpha Gamma Sigma, Phi Theta Kappa, Puente. *Campus security:* 24-hour emergency response devices and patrols, student patrols. *Student services:* health clinic, personal/psychological counseling.

Athletics Member NJCAA. *Intercollegiate sports:* baseball M, basketball M/W, cross-country running M/W, football M, golf M, ice hockey M(c), rugby M(c), soccer M/W, softball W, swimming and diving M/W, tennis M/W, track and field M/W, volleyball W, water polo M/W, wrestling M.

Costs (2012–13) *One-time required fee:* $36. *Tuition:* state resident $0 full-time; nonresident $5880 full-time, $199 per unit part-time. Full-time tuition and fees vary according to course load. Part-time tuition and fees vary according to course load. *Required fees:* $1104 full-time, $46 per unit part-time, $18 per term part-time. *Payment plans:* installment, deferred payment.

Financial Aid Of all full-time matriculated undergraduates who enrolled in 2009, 135 Federal Work-Study jobs (averaging $2210). 43 state and other part-time jobs (averaging $7396).

Applying *Options:* electronic application, early admission. *Application deadlines:* rolling (freshmen), rolling (out-of-state freshmen), rolling (transfers). *Notification:* continuous (freshmen), continuous (out-of-state freshmen), continuous (transfers).

Freshman Application Contact Ms. Diane Traversi, Director of Enrollment Services, Santa Rosa Junior College, 1501 Mendocino Avenue, Santa Rosa, CA 95401. *Phone:* 707-527-4510. *Fax:* 707-527-4798. *E-mail:* admininfo@santarosa.edu. *Web site:* http://www.santarosa.edu/.

Santiago Canyon College
Orange, California

Freshman Application Contact Denise Pennock, Admissions and Records, Santiago Canyon College, 8045 East Chapman Avenue, Orange, CA 92869. *Phone:* 714-564-4000. *Web site:* http://www.sccollege.edu/.

School of Urban Missions
Oakland, California

Freshman Application Contact Admissions, School of Urban Missions, 735 105th Avenue, Oakland, CA 94603. *Phone:* 510-567-6174. *Toll-free phone:* 888-567-6174. *Fax:* 510-568-1024. *Web site:* http://www.sum.edu/.

Shasta College
Redding, California

Director of Admissions Dr. Kevin O'Rorke, Dean of Enrollment Services, Shasta College, PO Box 496006, 11555 Old Oregon Trail, Redding, CA 96049-6006. *Phone:* 530-242-7669. *Web site:* http://www.shastacollege.edu/.

Sierra College
Rocklin, California

Freshman Application Contact Sierra College, 5000 Rocklin Road, Rocklin, CA 95677-3397. *Phone:* 916-660-7341. *Web site:* http://www.sierracollege.edu/.

Skyline College
San Bruno, California

Freshman Application Contact Terry Stats, Admissions Office, Skyline College, 3300 College Drive, San Bruno, CA 94066-1698. *Phone:* 650-738-4251. *E-mail:* stats@smccd.net. *Web site:* http://skylinecollege.net/.

Solano Community College
Fairfield, California

- **State and locally supported** 2-year, founded 1945, part of California Community College System
- **Suburban** 192-acre campus with easy access to Sacramento, San Francisco
- **Coed**

Undergraduates Students come from 43 states and territories; 6 other countries; 1% are from out of state.

Faculty *Student/faculty ratio:* 27:1.

Academics *Calendar:* semesters. *Degree:* certificates, diplomas, and associate. *Special study options:* academic remediation for entering students, adult/continuing education programs, advanced placement credit, cooperative education, distance learning, double majors, English as a second language, honors programs, independent study, off-campus study, part-time degree program, services for LD students, study abroad, summer session for credit.

Student Life *Campus security:* 24-hour patrols, student patrols, late-night transport/escort service.

Costs (2011–12) *Tuition:* state resident $1080 full-time, $36 per unit part-time; nonresident $6990 full-time, $233 per unit part-time. Full-time tuition and fees vary according to course load. Part-time tuition and fees vary according to course load. *Required fees:* $36 full-time, $1 per unit part-time, $13 per term part-time.

Financial Aid Of all full-time matriculated undergraduates who enrolled in 2010, 125 Federal Work-Study jobs (averaging $2000). 30 state and other part-time jobs (averaging $2000).

Applying *Options:* electronic application, early admission, deferred entrance.

Freshman Application Contact Solano Community College, 4000 Suisun Valley Road, Fairfield, CA 94534. *Phone:* 707-864-7000 Ext. 4313. *Web site:* http://www.solano.edu/.

South Coast College
Orange, California

Director of Admissions South Coast College, 2011 West Chapman Avenue, Orange, CA 92868. *Toll-free phone:* 877-568-6130. *Web site:* http://www.southcoastcollege.com/.

Southwestern College
Chula Vista, California

Freshman Application Contact Director of Admissions and Records, Southwestern College, 900 Otay Lakes Road, Chula Vista, CA 91910-7299. *Phone:* 619-421-6700 Ext. 5215. *Fax:* 619-482-6489. *Web site:* http://www.swc.edu/.

Stanbridge College
Irvine, California

Admissions Office Contact Stanbridge College, 2041 Business Center Drive, Irvine, CA 92612. *Web site:* http://www.stanbridge.edu/.

Taft College
Taft, California

Freshman Application Contact Harold Russell III, Director of Financial Aid and Admissions, Taft College, 29 Emmons Park Drive, Taft, CA 93268-2317. *Phone:* 661-763-7763. *Fax:* 661-763-7758. *E-mail:* hrussell@taft.org. *Web site:* http://www.taftcollege.edu/.

Unitek College
Fremont, California

Admissions Office Contact Unitek College, 4670 Auto Mall Parkway, Fremont, CA 94538. *Web site:* http://www.unitekcollege.edu/.

Ventura College
Ventura, California

Freshman Application Contact Ms. Susan Bricker, Registrar, Ventura College, 4667 Telegraph Road, Ventura, CA 93003-3899. *Phone:* 805-654-6456. *Fax:* 805-654-6357. *E-mail:* sbricker@vcccd.net. *Web site:* http://www.venturacollege.edu/.

Victor Valley College
Victorville, California

Freshman Application Contact Ms. Greta Moon, Director of Admissions and Records (Interim), Victor Valley College, 18422 Bear Valley Road, Victorville, CA 92395. *Phone:* 760-245-4271. *Fax:* 760-843-7707. *E-mail:* moong@vvc.edu. *Web site:* http://www.vvc.edu/.

West Hills Community College
Coalinga, California

Freshman Application Contact Sandra Dagnino, West Hills Community College, 300 Cherry Lane, Coalinga, CA 93210-1399. *Phone:* 559-934-3203. *Toll-free phone:* 800-266-1114. *Fax:* 559-934-2830. *E-mail:* sandradagnino@westhillscollege.com. *Web site:* http://www.westhillscollege.com/.

West Los Angeles College
Culver City, California

Director of Admissions Mr. Len Isaksen, Director of Admissions, West Los Angeles College, 9000 Overland Avenue, Culver City, CA 90230-3519. *Phone:* 310-287-4255. *Web site:* http://www.lacolleges.net/.

West Valley College
Saratoga, California

Freshman Application Contact Ms. Barbara Ogilive, Supervisor, Admissions and Records, West Valley College, 14000 Fruitvale Avenue, Saratoga, CA 95070-5698. *Phone:* 408-741-4630. *E-mail:* barbara_ogilvie@westvalley.edu. *Web site:* http://www.westvalley.edu/.

Woodland Community College
Woodland, California

Admissions Office Contact Woodland Community College, 2300 East Gibson Road, Woodland, CA 95776. *Web site:* http://www.yccd.edu/woodland/.

WyoTech Fremont
Fremont, California

- **Proprietary** 2-year, founded 1966
- **Urban** campus
- **Coed**
- 80% of applicants were admitted

Faculty *Student/faculty ratio:* 25:1.
Academics *Calendar:* continuous. *Degree:* certificates, diplomas, and associate. *Special study options:* academic remediation for entering students.
Student Life *Campus security:* security personnel.
Freshman Application Contact Admissions Department, WyoTech Fremont, 200 Whitney Place, Fremont, CA 94539-7663. *Phone:* 510-580-3507. *Toll-free phone:* 888-577-7559. *Fax:* 510-490-8599. *Web site:* http://www.wyotech.edu/.

WyoTech Long Beach
Long Beach, California

Freshman Application Contact Admissions Office, WyoTech Long Beach, 2161 Technology Place, Long Beach, CA 90810. *Phone:* 562-624-9530. *Toll-free phone:* 888-577-7559. *Fax:* 562-437-8111. *Web site:* http://www.wyotech.edu/campus/long_beach.

WyoTech Sacramento
West Sacramento, California

Freshman Application Contact Admissions Office, WyoTech Sacramento, 980 Riverside Parkway, West Sacramento, CA 95605-1507. *Phone:* 916-376-8888. *Toll-free phone:* 888-577-7559. *Fax:* 916-617-2059. *Web site:* http://www.wyotech.com/.

Yuba College
Marysville, California

Director of Admissions Dr. David Farrell, Dean of Student Development, Yuba College, 2088 North Beale Road, Marysville, CA 95901-7699. *Phone:* 530-741-6705. *Web site:* http://www.yccd.edu/.

COLORADO

Aims Community College
Greeley, Colorado

Freshman Application Contact Ms. Susie Gallardo, Admissions Technician, Aims Community College, Box 69, 5401 West 20th Street, Greeley, CO 80632-0069. *Phone:* 970-330-8008 Ext. 6624. *E-mail:* wgreen@chiron.aims.edu. *Web site:* http://www.aims.edu/.

Anthem College Aurora
Aurora, Colorado

Director of Admissions Amy Marshall, Director of Admissions, Anthem College Aurora, 350 Blackhawk Street, Aurora, CO 80011. *Phone:* 720-859-7900. *Toll-free phone:* 855-268-4363. *Web site:* http://www.anthem.edu/aurora-colorado/.

Arapahoe Community College
Littleton, Colorado

Freshman Application Contact Arapahoe Community College, 5900 South Santa Fe Drive, PO Box 9002, Littleton, CO 80160-9002. *Phone:* 303-797-5621. *Web site:* http://www.arapahoe.edu/.

Bel–Rea Institute of Animal Technology
Denver, Colorado

Director of Admissions Ms. Paulette Kaufman, Director, Bel–Rea Institute of Animal Technology, 1681 South Dayton Street, Denver, CO 80247. *Phone:* 303-751-8700. *Toll-free phone:* 800-950-8001. *E-mail:* admissions@bel-rea.com. *Web site:* http://www.bel-rea.com/.

Boulder College of Massage Therapy
Boulder, Colorado

Freshman Application Contact Admissions Office, Boulder College of Massage Therapy, 6255 Longbow Drive, Boulder, CO 80301. *Phone:* 303-530-2100. *Toll-free phone:* 800-442-5131. *Fax:* 303-530-2204. *E-mail:* admissions@bcmt.org. *Web site:* http://www.bcmt.org/.

CollegeAmerica–Colorado Springs
Colorado Springs, Colorado

Freshman Application Contact CollegeAmerica–Colorado Springs, 3645 Citadel Drive South, Colorado Springs, CO 80909. *Phone:* 719-637-0600. *Toll-free phone:* 800-622-2894. *Web site:* http://www.collegeamerica.edu/.

CollegeAmerica–Denver
Denver, Colorado

Freshman Application Contact Admissions Office, CollegeAmerica–Denver, 1385 South Colorado Boulevard, Denver, CO 80222. *Phone:* 303-300-8740. *Toll-free phone:* 800-622-2894. *Web site:* http://www.collegeamerica.edu/.

CollegeAmerica–Fort Collins
Fort Collins, Colorado

Director of Admissions Ms. Anna DiTorrice-Mull, Director of Admissions, CollegeAmerica–Fort Collins, 4601 South Mason Street, Fort Collins, CO 80525-3740. *Phone:* 970-223-6060 Ext. 8002. *Toll-free phone:* 800-622-2894. *Web site:* http://www.collegeamerica.edu/.

Colorado Mountain College
Glenwood Springs, Colorado

- **District-supported** primarily 2-year, founded 1965, part of Colorado Mountain College District System
- **Rural** 680-acre campus
- **Coed,** 2,465 undergraduate students

Undergraduates 44% live on campus.
Freshmen *Average high school GPA:* 2.4.
Faculty *Total:* 28. *Student/faculty ratio:* 12:1.
Majors Accounting; behavioral sciences; biological and physical sciences; biology/biological sciences; business administration and management; commercial and advertising art; computer and information sciences and support services related; computer engineering technology; computer systems networking and telecommunications; criminal justice/law enforcement administration; data entry/microcomputer applications related; dramatic/theater arts; English; humanities; liberal arts and sciences/liberal studies; licensed practical/vocational nurse training; mathematics; natural sciences; photography; psychology; registered nursing/registered nurse; social sciences; therapeutic recreation; veterinary/animal health technology.
Academics *Calendar:* semesters. *Degrees:* certificates, associate, and bachelor's. *Special study options:* academic remediation for entering students, adult/continuing education programs, advanced placement credit, cooperative education, distance learning, double majors, English as a second language, honors programs, independent study, internships, part-time degree program, services for LD students, study abroad, summer session for credit.
Library Quigley Library with 36,000 titles, 70 serial subscriptions, an OPAC, a Web page.
Student Life *Housing:* on-campus residence required for freshman year. *Options:* coed, disabled students. Campus housing is university owned. Freshman applicants given priority for college housing. *Activities and Organizations:* drama/theater group, student-run newspaper, student government, Outdoor activities, World Awareness Society, Peer Mentors, Student Activities Board. *Campus security:* 24-hour emergency response devices, student patrols, controlled dormitory access. *Student services:* health clinic, personal/psychological counseling.
Athletics Member NCAA, NJCAA. All NCAA Division I. *Intramural sports:* basketball M/W, rock climbing M/W, skiing (cross-country) M/W, skiing (downhill) M/W, ultimate Frisbee M/W, volleyball M/W.
Standardized Tests *Recommended:* SAT or ACT (for admission).
Costs (2012–13) *Tuition:* area resident $1590 full-time; state resident $2670 full-time; nonresident $8370 full-time. *Required fees:* $180 full-time. *Room and board:* $7928.
Applying *Options:* electronic application, early admission, deferred entrance. *Required:* high school transcript. *Application deadlines:* rolling (freshmen), rolling (out-of-state freshmen), rolling (transfers).
Freshman Application Contact Vicky Butler, Admissions Assistant, Colorado Mountain College, 3000 CR 114, Glenwood Springs, CO 81601. *Phone:* 970-947-8276. *Toll-free phone:* 800-621-8559. *E-mail:* Vvalentine@coloradomtn.edu. *Web site:* http://www.coloradomtn.edu/.

Colorado Mountain College, Alpine Campus
Steamboat Springs, Colorado

- **District-supported** primarily 2-year, founded 1965, part of Colorado Mountain College District System
- **Small-town** 10-acre campus
- **Coed,** 1,550 undergraduate students

Undergraduates 44% live on campus.
Freshmen *Average high school GPA:* 2.4.
Faculty *Total:* 25. *Student/faculty ratio:* 12:1.
Majors Accounting; behavioral sciences; biological and physical sciences; biology/biological sciences; business administration and management; computer engineering technology; consumer merchandising/retailing management; data entry/microcomputer applications related; English; fine/studio arts; geology/earth science; hospitality administration; hotel/motel administration; humanities; liberal arts and sciences/liberal studies; marketing/marketing management; mathematics; parks, recreation and leisure facilities management; physical sciences; pre-engineering; social sciences.

Academics *Calendar:* semesters. *Degrees:* certificates, associate, and bachelor's. *Special study options:* academic remediation for entering students, adult/continuing education programs, advanced placement credit, cooperative education, distance learning, double majors, English as a second language, honors programs, independent study, internships, off-campus study, part-time degree program, services for LD students, study abroad, summer session for credit.
Library Main Library plus 1 other with 25,000 titles, 50 serial subscriptions, an OPAC, a Web page.
Student Life *Housing:* on-campus residence required for freshman year. *Options:* coed, disabled students. Campus housing is university owned. *Activities and Organizations:* student-run newspaper, student government, Forensics Team, Ski Club, International Club, Phi Theta Kappa. *Campus security:* 24-hour emergency response devices, student patrols, controlled dormitory access. *Student services:* health clinic, personal/psychological counseling.
Athletics Member NCAA, NJCAA. All NCAA Division I. *Intercollegiate sports:* skiing (downhill) M/W. *Intramural sports:* basketball M/W, skiing (cross-country) M/W, skiing (downhill) M/W, soccer M/W, ultimate Frisbee M/W, volleyball M/W.
Standardized Tests *Recommended:* SAT or ACT (for admission).
Costs (2012–13) *Tuition:* area resident $1590 full-time; state resident $2670 full-time; nonresident $8370 full-time. *Required fees:* $180 full-time. *Room and board:* $7928; room only: $4160. Room and board charges vary according to board plan. *Payment plan:* installment. *Waivers:* senior citizens.
Financial Aid Of all full-time matriculated undergraduates who enrolled in 2010, 40 Federal Work-Study jobs (averaging $1173). 62 state and other part-time jobs (averaging $1060).
Applying *Options:* electronic application, early admission, deferred entrance. *Required:* high school transcript. *Application deadlines:* rolling (freshmen), rolling (out-of-state freshmen), rolling (transfers).
Freshman Application Contact Ms. Stephanie Fletcher, Admissions Assistant, Colorado Mountain College, Alpine Campus, 1330 Bob Adams Drive, Steamboat Springs, CO 80487. *Phone:* 970-870-4417 Ext. 4417. *Toll-free phone:* 800-621-8559. *E-mail:* stephaniefletcher@coloradomtn.edu. *Web site:* http://www.coloradomtn.edu/.

Colorado Mountain College, Timberline Campus
Leadville, Colorado

- **District-supported** primarily 2-year, founded 1965, part of Colorado Mountain College District System
- **Rural** 200-acre campus
- **Coed,** 1,209 undergraduate students

Undergraduates 30% live on campus.
Freshmen *Average high school GPA:* 2.4.
Faculty *Total:* 16. *Student/faculty ratio:* 12:1.
Majors Accounting; business/commerce; corrections; criminal justice/law enforcement administration; early childhood education; environmental studies; general studies; historic preservation and conservation; land use planning and management; liberal arts and sciences/liberal studies; parks, recreation and leisure; parks, recreation and leisure facilities management.
Academics *Calendar:* semesters. *Degrees:* certificates, associate, and bachelor's. *Special study options:* academic remediation for entering students, adult/continuing education programs, advanced placement credit, cooperative education, distance learning, double majors, English as a second language, honors programs, independent study, internships, off-campus study, part-time degree program, services for LD students, student-designed majors, study abroad, summer session for credit.
Library Leadville Campus Library plus 1 other with 25,000 titles, 50 serial subscriptions, an OPAC, a Web page.
Student Life *Housing:* on-campus residence required for freshman year. *Options:* coed, disabled students. Campus housing is university owned. Freshman applicants given priority for college housing. *Activities and Organizations:* Environmental Club, Outdoor Club, Student Activities Board. *Campus security:* 24-hour emergency response devices, student patrols, controlled dormitory access. *Student services:* health clinic, personal/psychological counseling.
Athletics Member NCAA, NJCAA. All NCAA Division I. *Intramural sports:* basketball M, rock climbing M/W, skiing (cross-country) M/W, skiing (downhill) M/W, soccer M/W, volleyball M/W.
Standardized Tests *Recommended:* SAT or ACT (for admission).
Costs (2012–13) *Tuition:* area resident $1590 full-time; state resident $2670 full-time; nonresident $8370 full-time. *Required fees:* $180 full-time. *Room and board:* $7928. Room and board charges vary according to board plan. *Payment plan:* installment. *Waivers:* senior citizens.
Applying *Options:* electronic application, early admission, deferred entrance. *Required:* high school transcript. *Application deadlines:* rolling (freshmen), rolling (out-of-state freshmen), rolling (transfers).

Freshman Application Contact Ms. Kate Kenoyer, Admissions Assistant, Colorado Mountain College, Timberline Campus, 901South Highway 24, Leadville, CO 80461. *Phone:* 719-486-4292. *Toll-free phone:* 800-621-8559. *E-mail:* joinus@coloradomtn.edu. *Web site:* http://www.coloradomtn.edu/.

Colorado Northwestern Community College
Rangely, Colorado

Director of Admissions Mr. Gene Bilodeau, Registrar, Colorado Northwestern Community College, 500 Kennedy Drive, Rangely, CO 81648-3598. *Phone:* 970-824-1103. *Toll-free phone:* 800-562-1105. *E-mail:* gene.bilodeau@cncc.edu. *Web site:* http://www.cncc.edu/.

Colorado School of Healing Arts
Lakewood, Colorado

Freshman Application Contact Colorado School of Healing Arts, 7655 West Mississippi Avenue, Suite 100, Lakewood, CO 80220. *Phone:* 303-986-2320. *Toll-free phone:* 800-233-7114. *Fax:* 303-980-6594. *Web site:* http://www.csha.net/.

Colorado School of Trades
Lakewood, Colorado

- **Proprietary** 2-year, founded 1947
- **Suburban** campus
- **Coed,** 134 undergraduate students, 100% full-time, 1% women, 99% men
- **87%** of applicants were admitted

Undergraduates 134 full-time. 88% are from out of state.
Freshmen *Admission:* 174 applied, 152 admitted, 30 enrolled.
Faculty *Total:* 10. *Student/faculty ratio:* 12:1.
Majors Gunsmithing.
Academics *Degree:* associate.
Costs (2012–13) *Tuition:* $18,900 full-time. No tuition increase for student's term of enrollment. *Payment plan:* installment.
Applying *Application fee:* $25. *Required:* essay or personal statement, high school transcript, interview.
Freshman Application Contact Colorado School of Trades, 1575 Hoyt Street, Lakewood, CO 80215-2996. *Phone:* 303-233-4697 Ext. 44. *Toll-free phone:* 800-234-4594. *Web site:* http://www.schooloftrades.com/.

Community College of Aurora
Aurora, Colorado

Freshman Application Contact Community College of Aurora, 16000 East Centre Tech Parkway, Aurora, CO 80011-9036. *Phone:* 303-360-4701. *Web site:* http://www.ccaurora.edu/.

Community College of Denver
Denver, Colorado

Freshman Application Contact Mr. Michael Rusk, Dean of Students, Community College of Denver, PO Box 173363, Campus Box 201, Denver, CO 80127-3363. *Phone:* 303-556-6325. *Fax:* 303-556-2431. *E-mail:* enrollment_services@ccd.edu. *Web site:* http://www.ccd.edu/.

Everest College
Aurora, Colorado

Freshman Application Contact Everest College, 14280 East Jewell Avenue, Suite 100, Aurora, CO 80014. *Phone:* 303-745-6244. *Toll-free phone:* 888-741-4270. *Web site:* http://www.everest.edu/.

Everest College
Colorado Springs, Colorado

Director of Admissions Director of Admissions, Everest College, 1815 Jet Wing Drive, Colorado Springs, CO 80916. *Phone:* 719-630-6580. *Toll-free phone:* 888-741-4270. *Fax:* 719-638-6818. *Web site:* http://www.everest.edu/.

Everest College
Denver, Colorado

Freshman Application Contact Admissions Office, Everest College, 9065 Grant Street, Denver, CO 80229-4339. *Phone:* 303-457-2757. *Toll-free phone:* 888-741-4270. *Fax:* 303-457-4030. *Web site:* http://www.everest.edu/.

Front Range Community College
Westminster, Colorado

- **State-supported** 2-year, founded 1968, part of Community Colleges of Colorado System
- **Suburban** 90-acre campus with easy access to Denver
- **Endowment** $294,302
- **Coed,** 20,092 undergraduate students, 37% full-time, 57% women, 43% men

Undergraduates 7,445 full-time, 12,647 part-time. Students come from 44 states and territories; 26 other countries; 2% are from out of state; 2% Black or African American, non-Hispanic/Latino; 13% Hispanic/Latino; 3% Asian, non-Hispanic/Latino; 0.4% Native Hawaiian or other Pacific Islander, non-Hispanic/Latino; 0.9% American Indian or Alaska Native, non-Hispanic/Latino; 1% Two or more races, non-Hispanic/Latino; 10% Race/ethnicity unknown; 1% international; 9% transferred in. *Retention:* 43% of full-time freshmen returned.
Freshmen *Admission:* 8,187 applied, 8,187 admitted, 3,634 enrolled.
Faculty *Total:* 1,118, 19% full-time. *Student/faculty ratio:* 23:1.
Majors Accounting technology and bookkeeping; animal health; animation, interactive technology, video graphics and special effects; applied horticulture/horticulture operations; architectural engineering technology; automobile/automotive mechanics technology; CAD/CADD drafting/design technology; dietitian assistant; early childhood education; electrical, electronic and communications engineering technology; emergency medical technology (EMT paramedic); general studies; health information/medical records technology; heating, ventilation, air conditioning and refrigeration engineering technology; hospitality administration; interior design; legal assistant/paralegal; liberal arts and sciences and humanities related; liberal arts and sciences/liberal studies; masonry; medical office assistant; registered nursing/registered nurse; science technologies related; sign language interpretation and translation; veterinary/animal health technology; welding technology; wildlife, fish and wildlands science and management.
Academics *Calendar:* semesters. *Degree:* certificates and associate. *Special study options:* academic remediation for entering students, advanced placement credit, cooperative education, distance learning, double majors, English as a second language, freshman honors college, honors programs, independent study, internships, off-campus study, part-time degree program, services for LD students, student-designed majors, study abroad, summer session for credit. *ROTC:* Army (c), Air Force (c).
Library College Hill Library with an OPAC, a Web page.
Student Life *Housing:* college housing not available. *Activities and Organizations:* drama/theater group, student-run newspaper, Student Government Association, Student Colorado Registry of Interpreters for the Deaf, Students in Free Enterprise (SIFE), Gay Straight Alliance, Recycling Club. *Campus security:* 24-hour patrols, late-night transport/escort service. *Student services:* personal/psychological counseling.
Costs (2011–12) *Tuition:* state resident $2540 full-time, $106 per credit hour part-time; nonresident $10,423 full-time, $434 per credit hour part-time. Full-time tuition and fees vary according to location and program. Part-time tuition and fees vary according to location and program. *Required fees:* $223 full-time, $223 per year part-time, $11 per term part-time. *Waivers:* employees or children of employees.
Financial Aid Of all full-time matriculated undergraduates who enrolled in 2010, 165 Federal Work-Study jobs (averaging $1316). 277 state and other part-time jobs (averaging $1635).
Applying *Options:* electronic application, early admission, deferred entrance. *Application deadlines:* rolling (freshmen), rolling (out-of-state freshmen), rolling (transfers). *Notification:* continuous (freshmen), continuous (out-of-state freshmen), continuous (transfers).
Freshman Application Contact Ms. Yolanda Espinoza, Registrar, Front Range Community College, Westminster, CO 80031. *Phone:* 303-404-5000. *Fax:* 303-439-2614. *E-mail:* yolanda.espinoza@frontrange.edu. *Web site:* http://www.frontrange.edu/.

Heritage College
Denver, Colorado

Freshman Application Contact Admissions Office, Heritage College, 12 Lakeside Lane, Denver, CO 80212-7413. *Web site:* http://www.heritage-education.com/.

Institute of Business & Medical Careers
Fort Collins, Colorado

- **Private** 2-year, founded 1987
- **Suburban** campus with easy access to Denver
- **Coed**, 302 undergraduate students, 100% full-time, 89% women, 11% men
- 100% of applicants were admitted

Undergraduates 302 full-time. Students come from 1 other state; 2% are from out of state. *Retention:* 69% of full-time freshmen returned.
Freshmen *Admission:* 366 applied, 366 admitted, 302 enrolled.
Faculty *Total:* 34, 32% full-time. *Student/faculty ratio:* 14:1.
Majors Accounting technology and bookkeeping; business administration and management; legal administrative assistant/secretary; legal assistant/paralegal; massage therapy; medical administrative assistant and medical secretary; medical/clinical assistant; office occupations and clerical services; pharmacy technician.
Academics *Calendar:* continuous. *Degree:* certificates, diplomas, and associate. *Special study options:* accelerated degree program, cooperative education, honors programs, internships.
Student Life *Housing:* college housing not available. *Activities and Organizations:* student-run newspaper, Alpha Beta Kappa, Circle of Hope, Relay for Life.
Costs (2012–13) *Tuition:* $11,340 full-time. Full-time tuition and fees vary according to course load and program. Part-time tuition and fees vary according to course load and program. No tuition increase for student's term of enrollment. *Payment plans:* tuition prepayment, installment. *Waivers:* employees or children of employees.
Financial Aid Of all full-time matriculated undergraduates who enrolled in 2010, 831 applied for aid, 788 were judged to have need, 663 had their need fully met. 37 Federal Work-Study jobs (averaging $2149). *Average percent of need met:* 73%. *Average financial aid package:* $7500. *Average need-based loan:* $3500. *Average need-based gift aid:* $3205.
Applying *Application fee:* $75. *Required:* high school transcript, interview. *Application deadline:* rolling (freshmen).
Freshman Application Contact Mr. Kevin McNeil, Regional Director of Admissions, Institute of Business & Medical Careers, 3842 South Mason Street, Fort Collins, CO 80525. *Phone:* 970-223-2669 Ext. 1105. *Toll-free phone:* 800-495-2669. *E-mail:* kmcneil@ibmc.edu. *Web site:* http://www.ibmc.edu/.

IntelliTec College
Colorado Springs, Colorado

Director of Admissions Director of Admissions, IntelliTec College, 2315 East Pikes Peak Avenue, Colorado Springs, CO 80909-6030. *Phone:* 719-632-7626. *Toll-free phone:* 800-748-2282. *Web site:* http://www.intelliteccollege.edu/.

IntelliTec College
Grand Junction, Colorado

Freshman Application Contact Admissions, IntelliTec College, 772 Horizon Drive, Grand Junction, CO 81506. *Phone:* 970-245-8101. *Toll-free phone:* 800-748-2282. *Fax:* 970-243-8074. *Web site:* http://www.intelliteccollege.edu/.

IntelliTec Medical Institute
Colorado Springs, Colorado

Director of Admissions Michelle Squibb, Admissions Representative, IntelliTec Medical Institute, 2345 North Academy Boulevard, Colorado Springs, CO 80909. *Phone:* 719-596-7400. *Toll-free phone:* 800-748-2282. *Web site:* http://www.intelliteccollege.edu/.

ITT Technical Institute
Aurora, Colorado

- **Proprietary** primarily 2-year
- **Coed**

Majors Business administration and management; communications technology; computer and information systems security; drafting and design technology; electrical, electronic and communications engineering technology; forensic science and technology; graphic communications; legal assistant/paralegal; network and system administration; project management.
Academics *Degrees:* associate and bachelor's.

Freshman Application Contact Director of Recruitment, ITT Technical Institute, 12500 East Iliff Avenue, Suite 100, Aurora, CO 80014. *Phone:* 303-695-6317. *Toll-free phone:* 877-832-8460. *Web site:* http://www.itt-tech.edu/.

ITT Technical Institute
Thornton, Colorado

- **Proprietary** primarily 2-year, founded 1984, part of ITT Educational Services, Inc.
- **Suburban** campus
- **Coed**

Majors Business administration and management; communications technology; computer and information systems security; construction management; criminal justice/law enforcement administration; drafting and design technology; electrical, electronic and communications engineering technology; forensic science and technology; graphic communications; legal assistant/paralegal; network and system administration; project management.
Academics *Calendar:* quarters. *Degrees:* associate and bachelor's.
Student Life *Housing:* college housing not available.
Freshman Application Contact Director of Recruitment, ITT Technical Institute, 500 East 84th Avenue, Suite B12, Thornton, CO 80229. *Phone:* 303-288-4488. *Toll-free phone:* 800-395-4488. *Web site:* http://www.itt-tech.edu/.

Lamar Community College
Lamar, Colorado

- **State-supported** 2-year, founded 1937, part of Colorado Community College and Occupational Education System
- **Small-town** 125-acre campus
- **Endowment** $136,000
- **Coed**

Undergraduates 485 full-time, 599 part-time. Students come from 28 states and territories; 4 other countries; 16% are from out of state; 4% transferred in; 20% live on campus.
Faculty *Student/faculty ratio:* 15:1.
Academics *Calendar:* semesters. *Degree:* certificates, diplomas, and associate. *Special study options:* academic remediation for entering students, adult/continuing education programs, advanced placement credit, cooperative education, distance learning, double majors, English as a second language, independent study, internships, part-time degree program, services for LD students, student-designed majors, summer session for credit.
Student Life *Campus security:* 24-hour emergency response devices and patrols, student patrols, late-night transport/escort service, controlled dormitory access.
Athletics Member NJCAA.
Applying *Options:* electronic application, early admission.
Freshman Application Contact Director of Admissions, Lamar Community College, 2401 South Main Street, Lamar, CO 81052-3999. *Phone:* 719-336-1592. *Toll-free phone:* 800-968-6920. *E-mail:* admissions@lamarcc.edu. *Web site:* http://www.lamarcc.edu/.

Lincoln College of Technology
Denver, Colorado

Director of Admissions Jennifer Hash, Assistant Director of Admissions, Lincoln College of Technology, 460 South Lipan Street, Denver, CO 80223-2025. *Phone:* 800-347-3232 Ext. 43032. *Web site:* http://www.lincolnedu.com/campus/denver-co/.

Morgan Community College
Fort Morgan, Colorado

Freshman Application Contact Ms. Kim Maxwell, Morgan Community College, 920 Barlow Road, Fort Morgan, CO 80701-4399. *Phone:* 970-542-3111. *Toll-free phone:* 800-622-0216. *Fax:* 970-867-6608. *E-mail:* kim.maxwell@morgancc.edu. *Web site:* http://www.morgancc.edu/.

Northeastern Junior College
Sterling, Colorado

- **State-supported** 2-year, founded 1941, part of Colorado Community College and Occupational Education System
- **Small-town** 65-acre campus
- **Endowment** $5.2 million
- **Coed**, 2,113 undergraduate students, 52% full-time, 59% women, 41% men

Undergraduates 1,108 full-time, 1,005 part-time. Students come from 20 states and territories; 6 other countries; 4% are from out of state; 7% Black or

African American, non-Hispanic/Latino; 10% Hispanic/Latino; 0.4% Asian, non-Hispanic/Latino; 0.3% Native Hawaiian or other Pacific Islander, non-Hispanic/Latino; 0.9% American Indian or Alaska Native, non-Hispanic/Latino; 2% Two or more races, non-Hispanic/Latino; 13% Race/ethnicity unknown; 0.6% international; 42% transferred in; 57% live on campus. *Retention:* 55% of full-time freshmen returned.

Freshmen *Admission:* 1,420 applied, 1,420 admitted, 564 enrolled. *Average high school GPA:* 2.68.

Faculty *Total:* 100, 49% full-time, 3% with terminal degrees. *Student/faculty ratio:* 22:1.

Majors Accounting; agricultural business and management; agricultural economics; agricultural mechanization; agricultural teacher education; agriculture; agronomy and crop science; anatomy; animal sciences; applied mathematics; art; art teacher education; automobile/automotive mechanics technology; biological and physical sciences; biology/biological sciences; business administration and management; business teacher education; child development; clinical laboratory science/medical technology; computer engineering technology; computer science; corrections; cosmetology; criminal justice/police science; dramatic/theater arts; drawing; economics; education; elementary education; emergency medical technology (EMT paramedic); English; equestrian studies; family and consumer sciences/human sciences; farm and ranch management; fashion merchandising; fine/studio arts; health professions related; history; humanities; journalism; kindergarten/preschool education; legal administrative assistant/secretary; liberal arts and sciences/liberal studies; licensed practical/vocational nurse training; marketing/marketing management; mathematics; medical administrative assistant and medical secretary; music; music teacher education; natural sciences; physical education teaching and coaching; physical sciences; pre-engineering; psychology; registered nursing/registered nurse; social sciences; social work; trade and industrial teacher education; zoology/animal biology.

Academics *Calendar:* semesters. *Degree:* certificates and associate. *Special study options:* academic remediation for entering students, accelerated degree program, adult/continuing education programs, advanced placement credit, cooperative education, distance learning, double majors, English as a second language, honors programs, independent study, internships, part-time degree program, services for LD students, summer session for credit.

Library Monahan Library with 30,042 titles, 112 serial subscriptions, an OPAC, a Web page.

Student Life *Housing:* on-campus residence required for freshman year. *Options:* coed, women-only. Campus housing is university owned. Freshman campus housing is guaranteed. *Activities and Organizations:* drama/theater group, choral group, Associated Student Government, Post Secondary Agriculture (PAS), Crossroads, Students in Free Enterprise (SIFE), NJC Ambassadors. *Campus security:* 24-hour emergency response devices, late-night transport/escort service, controlled dormitory access. *Student services:* health clinic, personal/psychological counseling.

Athletics Member NCAA, NJCAA. All NCAA Division I. *Intercollegiate sports:* baseball M(s), basketball M(s)/W(s), equestrian sports M(s)/W(s), golf M(s)/W(s), soccer M(s), softball W(s), volleyball W(s). *Intramural sports:* badminton M/W, baseball M/W, basketball M/W, bowling M/W, cheerleading M/W, football M, golf M/W, racquetball M/W, soccer M/W, softball M/W, tennis M/W, ultimate Frisbee M/W, volleyball M/W, weight lifting M/W.

Costs (2012–13) *Tuition:* state resident $3176 full-time, $106 per credit hour part-time; nonresident $10,421 full-time, $347 per credit hour part-time. Full-time tuition and fees vary according to course load. Part-time tuition and fees vary according to course load. *Required fees:* $596 full-time, $22 per credit hour part-time, $12 per term part-time. *Room and board:* $6010; room only: $2732. Room and board charges vary according to board plan and housing facility. *Payment plan:* installment. *Waivers:* senior citizens and employees or children of employees.

Applying *Options:* electronic application, early admission, deferred entrance. *Required:* high school transcript. *Application deadlines:* rolling (freshmen), rolling (out-of-state freshmen), rolling (transfers). *Notification:* continuous until 8/1 (freshmen), continuous (out-of-state freshmen), continuous until 8/1 (transfers).

Freshman Application Contact Andy Long, Director of Admissions, Northeastern Junior College, 100 College Avenue, Sterling, CO 80751-2399. *Phone:* 970-521-7000. *Toll-free phone:* 800-626-4637. *E-mail:* andy.long@njc.edu. *Web site:* http://www.njc.edu/.

Otero Junior College
La Junta, Colorado

- **State-supported** 2-year, founded 1941, part of Colorado Community College System
- **Rural** 40-acre campus
- **Coed,** 1,660 undergraduate students, 52% full-time, 61% women, 39% men

Undergraduates 870 full-time, 790 part-time. 17% live on campus.
Freshmen *Admission:* 318 enrolled.

Faculty *Total:* 75, 44% full-time.

Majors Administrative assistant and secretarial science; agricultural business and management; automobile/automotive mechanics technology; biological and physical sciences; biology/biological sciences; business administration and management; child development; comparative literature; data processing and data processing technology; dramatic/theater arts; elementary education; history; humanities; kindergarten/preschool education; legal administrative assistant/secretary; liberal arts and sciences/liberal studies; mathematics; medical administrative assistant and medical secretary; modern languages; political science and government; pre-engineering; psychology; registered nursing/registered nurse; social sciences.

Academics *Calendar:* semesters. *Degree:* certificates and associate. *Special study options:* academic remediation for entering students, adult/continuing education programs, advanced placement credit, distance learning, external degree program, internships, part-time degree program, summer session for credit.

Library Wheeler Library with 36,701 titles, 183 serial subscriptions, an OPAC.

Student Life *Housing:* on-campus residence required for freshman year. *Options:* men-only, women-only. Campus housing is university owned. *Activities and Organizations:* drama/theater group, student-run newspaper, choral group. *Campus security:* 24-hour patrols, late-night transport/escort service. *Student services:* personal/psychological counseling.

Athletics Member NJCAA. *Intercollegiate sports:* baseball M(s), basketball M(s)/W(s), golf M(s)/W(s), soccer M(s), softball W(s), volleyball W(s). *Intramural sports:* basketball M, volleyball M/W.

Costs (2011–12) *Tuition:* state resident $2540 full-time; nonresident $5034 full-time. *Required fees:* $254 full-time. *Room and board:* $5462. Room and board charges vary according to board plan and housing facility. *Payment plans:* installment, deferred payment.

Financial Aid Of all full-time matriculated undergraduates who enrolled in 2010, 30 Federal Work-Study jobs (averaging $2000). 100 state and other part-time jobs (averaging $2000).

Applying *Options:* electronic application, early admission. *Recommended:* high school transcript. *Application deadlines:* 8/30 (freshmen), 8/30 (transfers). *Notification:* continuous (freshmen), continuous (transfers).

Freshman Application Contact Mr. Jeff Paolucci, Vice President for Student Services, Otero Junior College, 1802 Colorado Avenue, La Junta, CO 81050-3415. *Phone:* 719-384-6833. *Fax:* 719-384-6933. *E-mail:* jan.schiro@ojc.edu. *Web site:* http://www.ojc.edu/.

Pikes Peak Community College
Colorado Springs, Colorado

Freshman Application Contact Pikes Peak Community College, 5675 South Academy Boulevard, Colorado Springs, CO 80906-5498. *Phone:* 719-540-7041. *Toll-free phone:* 866-411-7722. *Web site:* http://www.ppcc.edu/.

Pima Medical Institute
Colorado Springs, Colorado

- **Proprietary** 2-year
- **Urban** campus
- **Coed**

Academics *Special study options:* cooperative education, distance learning, internships.

Standardized Tests *Required:* Wonderlic Scholastic Level Exam (for admission).

Applying *Required:* high school transcript, interview.

Freshman Application Contact Pima Medical Institute, 3770 Citadel Drive North, Colorado Springs, CO 80909. *Phone:* 719-482-7462. *Web site:* http://www.pmi.edu/.

Pima Medical Institute
Denver, Colorado

- **Proprietary** primarily 2-year, founded 1988, part of Vocational Training Institutes, Inc.
- **Urban** campus
- **Coed**

Academics *Calendar:* modular. *Degrees:* certificates, associate, and bachelor's. *Special study options:* academic remediation for entering students, cooperative education, distance learning, internships.

Standardized Tests *Required:* Wonderlic Scholastic Level Exam (for admission).

Applying *Required:* interview. *Required for some:* high school transcript.

Freshman Application Contact Admissions Office, Pima Medical Institute, 1701 West 72nd Avenue, Suite 130, Denver, CO 80221. *Phone:* 303-426-

1800. *Toll-free phone:* 800-477-PIMA (in-state); 888-477-PIMA (out-of-state). *Web site:* http://www.pmi.edu/.

Platt College
Aurora, Colorado

Freshman Application Contact Admissions Office, Platt College, 3100 South Parker Road, Suite 200, Aurora, CO 80014-3141. *Phone:* 303-369-5151. *Web site:* http://www.plattcolorado.edu/.

Prince Institute–Rocky Mountains Campus
Westminster, Colorado

Director of Admissions Director of Admissions, Prince Institute–Rocky Mountains Campus, 9051 Harlan Street, Unit 20, Westminster, CO 80031. *Phone:* 303-427-5292. *Toll-free phone:* 866-712-2425. *Web site:* http://www.princeinstitute.edu/.

Pueblo Community College
Pueblo, Colorado

- **State-supported** 2-year, founded 1933, part of Colorado Community College System
- **Urban** 35-acre campus
- **Endowment** $1.1 million
- **Coed**

Undergraduates 3,054 full-time, 4,682 part-time. Students come from 24 states and territories; 6 other countries; 1% are from out of state; 3% Black or African American, non-Hispanic/Latino; 31% Hispanic/Latino; 1% Asian, non-Hispanic/Latino; 3% American Indian or Alaska Native, non-Hispanic/Latino; 7% Race/ethnicity unknown. *Retention:* 59% of full-time freshmen returned.
Faculty *Student/faculty ratio:* 19:1.
Academics *Calendar:* semesters. *Degree:* certificates and associate. *Special study options:* academic remediation for entering students, accelerated degree program, advanced placement credit, cooperative education, distance learning, double majors, English as a second language, honors programs, independent study, internships, part-time degree program, services for LD students, summer session for credit.
Student Life *Campus security:* 24-hour emergency response devices, late-night transport/escort service.
Costs (2011–12) *One-time required fee:* $10. *Tuition:* state resident $3176 full-time, $96 per credit part-time; nonresident $13,029 full-time, $414 per credit part-time. Full-time tuition and fees vary according to course load, location, and program. Part-time tuition and fees vary according to course load, location, and program. *Required fees:* $511 full-time, $19 per credit hour part-time, $51 per term part-time.
Financial Aid Of all full-time matriculated undergraduates who enrolled in 2010, 2,010 applied for aid, 1,508 were judged to have need, 450 had their need fully met. 60 Federal Work-Study jobs (averaging $3750). 170 state and other part-time jobs (averaging $3750). In 2010, 50. *Average percent of need met:* 50. *Average financial aid package:* $5500. *Average need-based loan:* $2000. *Average need-based gift aid:* $3500. *Average non-need-based aid:* $300. *Average indebtedness upon graduation:* $15,000.
Applying *Options:* electronic application, early admission, deferred entrance.
Freshman Application Contact Ms. Barbara Benedict, Assistant Director of Admissions and Records, Pueblo Community College, 900 West Orman Avenue, Pueblo, CO 81004. *Phone:* 719-549-3039. *Toll-free phone:* 888-642-6017. *Fax:* 719-549-3012. *Web site:* http://www.pueblocc.edu/.

Red Rocks Community College
Lakewood, Colorado

- **State-supported** 2-year, founded 1969, part of Colorado Community College and Occupational Education System
- **Urban** 141-acre campus with easy access to Denver
- **Coed,** 9,541 undergraduate students, 34% full-time, 50% women, 50% men

Undergraduates 3,211 full-time, 6,330 part-time. Students come from 38 states and territories; 11 other countries; 5% are from out of state; 2% Black or African American, non-Hispanic/Latino; 15% Hispanic/Latino; 2% Asian, non-Hispanic/Latino; 0.4% Native Hawaiian or other Pacific Islander, non-Hispanic/Latino; 2% American Indian or Alaska Native, non-Hispanic/Latino; 2% Two or more races, non-Hispanic/Latino; 9% Race/ethnicity unknown; 1% international; 9% transferred in.
Freshmen *Admission:* 4,052 applied, 4,052 admitted, 1,586 enrolled.
Faculty *Total:* 532, 17% full-time. *Student/faculty ratio:* 23:1.

Majors Accounting technology and bookkeeping; animation, interactive technology, video graphics and special effects; autobody/collision and repair technology; automobile/automotive mechanics technology; building construction technology; business administration and management; business administration, management and operations related; cinematography and film/video production; computer programming; computer systems networking and telecommunications; construction trades; cosmetology; criminal justice/police science; culinary arts; data modeling/warehousing and database administration; diagnostic medical sonography and ultrasound technology; digital communication and media/multimedia; drafting and design technology; early childhood education; educational/instructional technology; electrician; electromechanical and instrumentation and maintenance technologies related; emergency medical technology (EMT paramedic); energy management and systems technology; fire science/firefighting; game and interactive media design; general studies; holistic health; homeland security, law enforcement, firefighting and protective services related; industrial technology; interior design; liberal arts and sciences and humanities related; liberal arts and sciences/liberal studies; machine shop technology; management information systems; manufacturing engineering technology; medical office management; motorcycle maintenance and repair technology; parks, recreation and leisure; parts and warehousing operations and maintenance technology; photography; radiologic technology/science; real estate; registered nursing, nursing administration, nursing research and clinical nursing related; science technologies related; theater design and technology; vehicle maintenance and repair technologies; water quality and wastewater treatment management and recycling technology; web/multimedia management and webmaster; web page, digital/multimedia and information resources design; welding technology; woodworking.
Academics *Calendar:* semesters. *Degree:* certificates and associate. *Special study options:* academic remediation for entering students, adult/continuing education programs, cooperative education, distance learning, English as a second language, honors programs, off-campus study, part-time degree program, services for LD students, study abroad, summer session for credit. *ROTC:* Army (c), Air Force (c).
Library Marvin Buckels Library with 38,204 titles, 84 serial subscriptions, 4,098 audiovisual materials, an OPAC, a Web page.
Student Life *Housing:* college housing not available. *Activities and Organizations:* drama/theater group. *Campus security:* 24-hour emergency response devices and patrols. *Student services:* personal/psychological counseling.
Costs (2011–12) *Tuition:* state resident $3176 full-time, $106 per credit hour part-time; nonresident $13,029 full-time, $434 per credit hour part-time. Full-time tuition and fees vary according to program and reciprocity agreements. Part-time tuition and fees vary according to program and reciprocity agreements. *Required fees:* $9 per credit hour part-time, $12 per term part-time. *Payment plans:* installment, deferred payment. *Waivers:* employees or children of employees.
Financial Aid Of all full-time matriculated undergraduates who enrolled in 2010, 21 Federal Work-Study jobs (averaging $5000). 95 state and other part-time jobs (averaging $5000).
Applying *Options:* electronic application, early admission. *Application deadlines:* rolling (freshmen), rolling (out-of-state freshmen), rolling (transfers). *Notification:* continuous (freshmen), continuous (out-of-state freshmen), continuous (transfers).
Freshman Application Contact Admissions Office, Red Rocks Community College, 13300 West 6th Avenue, Lakewood, CO 80228-1255. *Phone:* 303-914-6360. *Fax:* 303-914-6919. *E-mail:* admissions@rrcc.edu. *Web site:* http://www.rrcc.edu/.

Redstone College–Denver
Broomfield, Colorado

Freshman Application Contact Redstone College–Denver, 10851 West 120th Avenue, Broomfield, CO 80021. *Phone:* 303-466-7383. *Toll-free phone:* 877-801-1025. *Web site:* http://www.redstone.edu/.

Remington College–Colorado Springs Campus
Colorado Springs, Colorado

Freshman Application Contact Remington College–Colorado Springs Campus, 6050 Erin Park Drive, #250, Colorado Springs, CO 80918. *Phone:* 719-532-1234 Ext. 202. *Web site:* http://www.remingtoncollege.edu/.

Trinidad State Junior College
Trinidad, Colorado

Freshman Application Contact Dr. Sandra Veltri, Vice President of Student/Academic Affairs, Trinidad State Junior College, 600 Prospect Street, Trinidad, CO 81082. *Phone:* 719-846-5559. *Toll-free phone:* 800-621-8752.

Fax: 719-846-5620. *E-mail:* sandy.veltri@trinidadstate.edu. *Web site:* http://www.trinidadstate.edu/.

CONNECTICUT

Asnuntuck Community College

Enfield, Connecticut

Freshman Application Contact Timothy St. James, Director of Admissions, Asnuntuck Community College, 170 Elm Street, Enfield, CT 06082-3800. *Phone:* 860-253-3087. *Fax:* 860-253-3014. *E-mail:* tstjames@acc.commnet.edu. *Web site:* http://www.acc.commnet.edu/.

Capital Community College

Hartford, Connecticut

Freshman Application Contact Ms. Jackie Phillips, Director of the Welcome and Advising Center, Capital Community College, 950 Main Street, Hartford, CT 06103. *Phone:* 860-906-5078. *Toll-free phone:* 800-894-6126. *E-mail:* jphillips@ccc.commnet.edu. *Web site:* http://www.ccc.commnet.edu/.

Gateway Community College

New Haven, Connecticut

- **State-supported** 2-year, founded 1992, part of Connecticut Community–Technical College System
- **Urban** 5-acre campus with easy access to New York City
- **Coed,** 7,261 undergraduate students, 34% full-time, 59% women, 41% men

Undergraduates 2,490 full-time, 4,771 part-time.
Freshmen *Admission:* 3,522 applied, 3,428 admitted, 1,377 enrolled.
Faculty *Total:* 443, 14% full-time, 3% with terminal degrees. *Student/faculty ratio:* 20:1.
Majors Accounting; automobile/automotive mechanics technology; avionics maintenance technology; biomedical technology; business administration and management; computer and information sciences related; computer engineering related; computer engineering technology; computer graphics; computer typography and composition equipment operation; consumer merchandising/retailing management; data entry/microcomputer applications; data processing and data processing technology; dietetics; electrical, electronic and communications engineering technology; engineering-related technologies; engineering technology; fashion merchandising; fire science/firefighting; gerontology; hotel/motel administration; human services; industrial radiologic technology; industrial technology; kindergarten/preschool education; legal administrative assistant/secretary; liberal arts and sciences/liberal studies; mechanical engineering/mechanical technology; medical administrative assistant and medical secretary; mental health counseling; nuclear medical technology; registered nursing/registered nurse; special products marketing; substance abuse/addiction counseling; word processing.
Academics *Calendar:* semesters. *Degree:* certificates and associate. *Special study options:* academic remediation for entering students, adult/continuing education programs, advanced placement credit, distance learning, English as a second language, external degree program, independent study, internships, off-campus study, part-time degree program, services for LD students, summer session for credit.
Library Gateway Community College Library plus 2 others with 46,090 titles, 275 serial subscriptions, 3,121 audiovisual materials, an OPAC, a Web page.
Student Life *Housing:* college housing not available. *Activities and Organizations:* drama/theater group, student-run newspaper. *Campus security:* late-night transport/escort service. *Student services:* personal/psychological counseling, women's center.
Athletics Member NJCAA. *Intercollegiate sports:* baseball M, basketball M/W, soccer M, softball W.
Costs (2012–13) *Tuition:* state resident $3168 full-time, $132 per credit part-time; nonresident $9504 full-time, $396 per credit part-time. *Required fees:* $402 full-time. *Payment plan:* installment. *Waivers:* senior citizens and employees or children of employees.
Financial Aid Of all full-time matriculated undergraduates who enrolled in 2010, 43 Federal Work-Study jobs, 105 state and other part-time jobs.
Applying *Options:* early admission, deferred entrance. *Application fee:* $20. *Required:* high school transcript. *Required for some:* essay or personal statement, interview. *Application deadlines:* 9/1 (freshmen), 9/1 (transfers). *Notification:* continuous until 9/1 (freshmen), continuous until 9/1 (transfers).
Freshman Application Contact Ms. Kim Shea, Director of Admissions, Gateway Community College, New Haven, CT 06511. *Phone:* 203-789-7043.

Toll-free phone: 800-390-7723. *Fax:* 203-285-2018. *E-mail:* gateway_ctc@commnet.edu. *Web site:* http://www.gwcc.commnet.edu/.

Goodwin College

East Hartford, Connecticut

- **Proprietary** primarily 2-year, founded 1999
- **Suburban** 660-acre campus with easy access to Hartford
- **Endowment** $3.4 million
- **Coed,** 3,116 undergraduate students, 16% full-time, 83% women, 17% men

Undergraduates 496 full-time, 2,620 part-time. 1% are from out of state; 24% Black or African American, non-Hispanic/Latino; 19% Hispanic/Latino; 2% Asian, non-Hispanic/Latino; 0.1% Native Hawaiian or other Pacific Islander, non-Hispanic/Latino; 0.3% American Indian or Alaska Native, non-Hispanic/Latino; 2% Two or more races, non-Hispanic/Latino; 0.4% Race/ethnicity unknown; 23% transferred in. *Retention:* 44% of full-time freshmen returned.
Freshmen *Admission:* 537 applied, 537 admitted, 381 enrolled.
Faculty *Total:* 261, 22% full-time. *Student/faculty ratio:* 11:1.
Majors Accounting technology and bookkeeping; business administration and management; business/commerce; child-care and support services management; child development; criminal justice/law enforcement administration; entrepreneurship; environmental studies; health services/allied health/health sciences; homeland security; homeland security, law enforcement, firefighting and protective services related; human resources management; human services; liberal arts and sciences/liberal studies; medical administrative assistant and medical secretary; medical/clinical assistant; medical insurance coding; medical insurance/medical billing; nonprofit management; occupational therapist assistant; office management; organizational behavior; registered nursing/registered nurse; respiratory care therapy.
Academics *Calendar:* semesters. *Degrees:* certificates, associate, and bachelor's. *Special study options:* academic remediation for entering students, adult/continuing education programs, advanced placement credit, distance learning, double majors, English as a second language, internships, off-campus study, part-time degree program, services for LD students, summer session for credit.
Library Hoffman Family Library with an OPAC.
Student Life *Housing:* college housing not available. *Activities and Organizations:* student-run newspaper, choral group. *Campus security:* 24-hour emergency response devices, evening security patrolman. *Student services:* personal/psychological counseling.
Athletics *Intramural sports:* basketball M, football M/W, soccer M/W, softball M/W.
Costs (2012–13) *Tuition:* $18,900 full-time, $590 per credit hour part-time. Full-time tuition and fees vary according to course load and program. Part-time tuition and fees vary according to course load and program. *Required fees:* $500 full-time. *Payment plan:* installment. *Waivers:* employees or children of employees.
Financial Aid Of all full-time matriculated undergraduates who enrolled in 2010, 662 applied for aid, 644 were judged to have need. 74 Federal Work-Study jobs (averaging $2745). In 2010, 11 non-need-based awards were made. *Average percent of need met:* 25%. *Average financial aid package:* $8029. *Average need-based loan:* $3231. *Average need-based gift aid:* $5404. *Average non-need-based aid:* $3333.
Applying *Options:* electronic application, early admission, early decision, early action, deferred entrance. *Application fee:* $50. *Required:* essay or personal statement, high school transcript, minimum 2.0 GPA, medical exam. *Recommended:* 2 letters of recommendation, interview. *Application deadlines:* rolling (freshmen), rolling (transfers), 6/1 (early action). *Early decision deadline:* 3/1. *Notification:* continuous (freshmen), continuous (transfers), 3/15 (early decision), 6/15 (early action).
Freshman Application Contact Mr. Nicholas Lentino, Director of Admissions, Goodwin College, One Riverside Drive, East Hartford, CT 06118. *Phone:* 860-727-6765. *Toll-free phone:* 800-889-3282. *Fax:* 860-291-9550. *E-mail:* nlantino@goodwin.edu. *Web site:* http://www.goodwin.edu/.

Housatonic Community College

Bridgeport, Connecticut

- **State-supported** 2-year, founded 1965, part of Connecticut Community–Technical College System
- **Urban** 4-acre campus with easy access to New York City
- **Coed,** 5,975 undergraduate students

Undergraduates 29% Black or African American, non-Hispanic/Latino; 25% Hispanic/Latino; 3% Asian, non-Hispanic/Latino; 0.1% Native Hawaiian or other Pacific Islander, non-Hispanic/Latino; 0.2% American Indian or Alaska Native, non-Hispanic/Latino; 2% Two or more races, non-Hispanic/Latino; 3% Race/ethnicity unknown.
Faculty *Total:* 391, 18% full-time. *Student/faculty ratio:* 14:1.

Majors Accounting; administrative assistant and secretarial science; art; avionics maintenance technology; business administration and management; child development; clinical/medical laboratory technology; commercial and advertising art; computer typography and composition equipment operation; criminal justice/law enforcement administration; data processing and data processing technology; environmental studies; humanities; human services; journalism; liberal arts and sciences/liberal studies; mathematics; mental health counseling; physical therapy; pre-engineering; public administration; registered nursing/registered nurse; social sciences; substance abuse/addiction counseling.

Academics *Calendar:* semesters. *Degree:* certificates and associate. *Special study options:* academic remediation for entering students, adult/continuing education programs, advanced placement credit, cooperative education, distance learning, double majors, English as a second language, honors programs; independent study, internships, part-time degree program, services for LD students, summer session for credit. *ROTC:* Army (c). *Unusual degree programs:* nursing with Bridgeport Hospital.

Library Housatonic Community College Library with 30,000 titles, 300 serial subscriptions, an OPAC, a Web page.

Student Life *Housing:* college housing not available. *Activities and Organizations:* drama/theater group, student-run newspaper, Student Senate, Association of Latin American Students, Community Action Network, Drama Club. *Campus security:* 24-hour emergency response devices, late-night transport/escort service. *Student services:* health clinic, personal/psychological counseling, women's center.

Financial Aid Of all full-time matriculated undergraduates who enrolled in 2010, 70 Federal Work-Study jobs (averaging $2850).

Applying *Options:* electronic application, deferred entrance. *Application fee:* $20. *Required:* high school transcript. *Required for some:* interview. *Application deadlines:* rolling (freshmen), rolling (transfers). *Notification:* continuous (freshmen), continuous (transfers).

Freshman Application Contact Ms. Delores Y. Curtis, Director of Admissions, Housatonic Community College, 900 Lafayette Boulevard, Bridgeport, CT 06604-4704. *Phone:* 203-332-5102. *Web site:* http://www.hctc.commnet.edu/.

Lincoln College of New England
Suffield, Connecticut

Freshman Application Contact Director of Admissions, Lincoln College of New England, 1760 Mapleton Avenue, Suffield, CT 06078. *Phone:* 860-628-4751. *Toll-free phone:* 800-825-0087. *E-mail:* admissions@lincolncollegene.edu. *Web site:* http://www.lincolncollegene.edu/.

Manchester Community College
Manchester, Connecticut

- **State-supported** 2-year, founded 1963, part of Connecticut Community–Technical College System
- **Small-town** campus
- **Coed,** 7,499 undergraduate students, 38% full-time, 53% women, 47% men

Undergraduates 2,819 full-time, 4,680 part-time. 15% Black or African American, non-Hispanic/Latino; 7% Hispanic/Latino; 4% Asian, non-Hispanic/Latino; 0.2% Native Hawaiian or other Pacific Islander, non-Hispanic/Latino; 0.1% American Indian or Alaska Native, non-Hispanic/Latino; 3% Two or more races, non-Hispanic/Latino; 8% Race/ethnicity unknown; 0.4% international; 12% transferred in.

Freshmen *Admission:* 1,507 enrolled.

Faculty *Total:* 503, 20% full-time. *Student/faculty ratio:* 19:1.

Majors Accounting; administrative assistant and secretarial science; business administration and management; clinical/medical laboratory technology; commercial and advertising art; criminal justice/law enforcement administration; dramatic/theater arts; engineering science; fine/studio arts; general studies; hotel/motel administration; human services; industrial engineering; industrial technology; information science/studies; journalism; kindergarten/preschool education; legal administrative assistant/secretary; legal assistant/paralegal; liberal arts and sciences/liberal studies; management information systems; marketing/marketing management; medical administrative assistant and medical secretary; music; occupational therapist assistant; physical therapy technology; respiratory care therapy; social work; speech communication and rhetoric; surgical technology; teacher assistant/aide.

Academics *Calendar:* semesters. *Degree:* certificates and associate. *Special study options:* adult/continuing education programs, part-time degree program.

Student Life *Housing:* college housing not available.

Athletics Member NJCAA. *Intercollegiate sports:* baseball M, basketball M/W, soccer M/W, softball W.

Costs (2011–12) *Tuition:* state resident $3096 full-time; nonresident $9288 full-time. *Required fees:* $394 full-time. *Payment plan:* installment. *Waivers:* senior citizens and employees or children of employees.

Financial Aid Of all full-time matriculated undergraduates who enrolled in 2010, 80 Federal Work-Study jobs (averaging $2000). 45 state and other part-time jobs (averaging $2000).

Applying *Options:* electronic application. *Application fee:* $20. *Required:* high school transcript. *Application deadlines:* rolling (freshmen), rolling (transfers). *Notification:* continuous (freshmen), continuous (transfers).

Freshman Application Contact Director of Admissions, Manchester Community College, PO Box 1046, Manchester, CT 06045-1046. *Phone:* 860-512-3210. *Fax:* 860-512-3221. *Web site:* http://www.mcc.commnet.edu/.

Middlesex Community College
Middletown, Connecticut

- **State-supported** 2-year, founded 1966, part of Connecticut Community–Technical College System
- **Suburban** 38-acre campus with easy access to Hartford
- **Endowment** $287,691
- **Coed**

Undergraduates 1,186 full-time, 1,766 part-time. Students come from 6 states and territories; 10 other countries; 1% are from out of state; 9% transferred in. *Retention:* 54% of full-time freshmen returned.

Faculty *Student/faculty ratio:* 22:1.

Academics *Calendar:* semesters. *Degree:* certificates and associate. *Special study options:* academic remediation for entering students, adult/continuing education programs, advanced placement credit, cooperative education, distance learning, double majors, English as a second language, honors programs, independent study, internships, off-campus study, part-time degree program, services for LD students, summer session for credit.

Student Life *Campus security:* 24-hour emergency response devices and patrols.

Standardized Tests *Required:* CPT (for admission).

Costs (2011–12) *Tuition:* state resident $3096 full-time, $129 per credit part-time; nonresident $9288 full-time, $387 per credit part-time. Full-time tuition and fees vary according to course load, degree level, and program. Part-time tuition and fees vary according to course load, degree level, and program. *Required fees:* $394 full-time, $79 per course part-time.

Financial Aid Of all full-time matriculated undergraduates who enrolled in 2010, 50 Federal Work-Study jobs (averaging $5000). 2 state and other part-time jobs (averaging $5000).

Applying *Options:* electronic application, early admission, deferred entrance. *Application fee:* $20. *Required:* high school transcript.

Freshman Application Contact Mensimah Shabazz, Director of Admissions, Middlesex Community College, Middletown, CT 06457-4889. *Phone:* 860-343-5742. *Fax:* 860-344-3055. *E-mail:* mshabazz@mxcc.commnet.edu. *Web site:* http://www.mxcc.commnet.edu/.

Naugatuck Valley Community College
Waterbury, Connecticut

Freshman Application Contact Ms. Lucretia Sveda, Director of Enrollment Services, Naugatuck Valley Community College, Waterbury, CT 06708. *Phone:* 203-575-8016. *Fax:* 203-596-8766. *E-mail:* lsveda@nvcc.commnet.edu. *Web site:* http://www.nvcc.commnet.edu/.

Northwestern Connecticut Community College
Winsted, Connecticut

- **State-supported** 2-year, founded 1965, part of Connecticut State Colleges and Universities
- **Small-town** 5-acre campus with easy access to Hartford
- **Coed,** 1,701 undergraduate students, 30% full-time, 67% women, 33% men

Undergraduates 511 full-time, 1,190 part-time. Students come from 3 states and territories; 0.5% are from out of state; 2% Black or African American, non-Hispanic/Latino; 7% Hispanic/Latino; 0.9% Asian, non-Hispanic/Latino; 0.1% Native Hawaiian or other Pacific Islander, non-Hispanic/Latino; 2% Two or more races, non-Hispanic/Latino; 4% Race/ethnicity unknown; 0.2% international; 10% transferred in. *Retention:* 60% of full-time freshmen returned.

Freshmen *Admission:* 242 enrolled.

Majors Accounting; administrative assistant and secretarial science; art; behavioral sciences; biology/biological sciences; business administration and management; child development; commercial and advertising art; communications technology; computer engineering technology; computer graphics; computer programming; computer science; criminal justice/law enforcement administration; criminal justice/police science; electrical, electronic and communications engineering technology; engineering; English; health professions related; human services; information science/studies; kindergarten/preschool education; legal assistant/paralegal; liberal arts and sciences/liberal studies; mathematics; medical/clinical assistant; parks, recreation and leisure; parks, recreation and leisure facilities management; physical sciences; pre-engineering; sign language interpretation and translation; social sciences; substance abuse/addiction counseling; therapeutic recreation; veterinary/animal health technology.

Academics *Calendar:* semesters. *Degree:* certificates and associate. *Special study options:* academic remediation for entering students, adult/continuing education programs, advanced placement credit, cooperative education, distance learning, double majors, English as a second language, independent study, internships, part-time degree program, services for LD students, summer session for credit.

Library Northwestern Connecticut Community–Technical College Learning Center with an OPAC.

Student Life *Housing:* college housing not available. *Activities and Organizations:* student-run newspaper. *Campus security:* evening security patrols.

Applying *Options:* deferred entrance. *Application fee:* $20. *Application deadlines:* rolling (freshmen), rolling (transfers). *Notification:* continuous (freshmen), continuous (transfers).

Freshman Application Contact Admissions Office, Northwestern Connecticut Community College, Park Place East, Winsted, CT 06098-1798. *Phone:* 860-738-6330. *Fax:* 860-738-6437. *E-mail:* admissions@nwcc.commnet.edu. *Web site:* http://www.nwcc.commnet.edu/.

Norwalk Community College

Norwalk, Connecticut

- **State-supported** 2-year, founded 1961, part of Connecticut Community–Technical College System
- **Suburban** 30-acre campus with easy access to New York City
- **Endowment** $16.7 million
- **Coed**

Undergraduates 2,531 full-time, 4,209 part-time. Students come from 9 states and territories; 44 other countries; 4% are from out of state; 6% transferred in.
Faculty *Student/faculty ratio:* 18:1.
Academics *Calendar:* semesters. *Degree:* certificates and associate. *Special study options:* academic remediation for entering students, adult/continuing education programs, advanced placement credit, cooperative education, distance learning, English as a second language, freshman honors college, honors programs, independent study, internships, part-time degree program, services for LD students, summer session for credit.
Student Life *Campus security:* late-night transport/escort service, all buildings are secured each evening; there are foot patrols and vehicle patrols by security from 8am to 11pm.
Costs (2011–12) *Tuition:* state resident $6980 full-time, $129 per credit part-time; nonresident $20,860 full-time, $387 per credit part-time. Full-time tuition and fees vary according to course load and program. Part-time tuition and fees vary according to course load and program. *Required fees:* $800 full-time, $70 per term part-time.
Financial Aid Of all full-time matriculated undergraduates who enrolled in 2010, 42 Federal Work-Study jobs (averaging $2581). 60 state and other part-time jobs (averaging $2046).
Applying *Options:* electronic application, deferred entrance. *Application fee:* $20. *Required:* high school transcript.
Freshman Application Contact Mr. Curtis Antrum, Admissions Counselor, Norwalk Community College, 188 Richards Avenue, Norwalk, CT 06854-1655. *Phone:* 203-857-7060. *Fax:* 203-857-3335. *E-mail:* admissions@ncc.commnet.edu. *Web site:* http://www.ncc.commnet.edu/.

Quinebaug Valley Community College

Danielson, Connecticut

Freshman Application Contact Dr. Toni Moumouris, Director of Admissions, Quinebaug Valley Community College, 742 Upper Maple Street, Danielson, CT 06239. *Phone:* 860-774-1130 Ext. 318. *Fax:* 860-774-7768. *E-mail:* qu_isd@commnet.edu. *Web site:* http://www.qvcc.commnet.edu/.

St. Vincent's College

Bridgeport, Connecticut

Freshman Application Contact Mr. Joseph Marrone, Director of Admissions and Recruitment Marketing, St. Vincent's College, 2800 Main Street, Bridgeport, CT 06606-4292. *Phone:* 203-576-5515. *Toll-free phone:* 800-873-1013. *Fax:* 203-576-5893. *E-mail:* jmarrone@stvincentscollege.edu. *Web site:* http://www.stvincentscollege.edu/.

Three Rivers Community College

Norwich, Connecticut

- **State-supported** 2-year, founded 1963, part of Connecticut Community–Technical College System
- **Suburban** 40-acre campus with easy access to Hartford
- **Coed,** 5,154 undergraduate students, 32% full-time, 58% women, 42% men

Undergraduates 1,650 full-time, 3,504 part-time. 1% are from out of state; 8% Black or African American, non-Hispanic/Latino; 13% Hispanic/Latino; 3% Asian, non-Hispanic/Latino; 0.2% Native Hawaiian or other Pacific Islander, non-Hispanic/Latino; 0.8% American Indian or Alaska Native, non-Hispanic/Latino; 3% Two or more races, non-Hispanic/Latino; 5% Race/ethnicity unknown; 0.1% international; 7% transferred in.
Freshmen *Admission:* 511 applied, 506 admitted, 1,025 enrolled.
Faculty *Total:* 315, 24% full-time, 3% with terminal degrees. *Student/faculty ratio:* 18:1.
Majors Accounting; administrative assistant and secretarial science; architectural engineering technology; avionics maintenance technology; business administration and management; civil engineering technology; computer engineering technology; computer programming; consumer merchandising/retailing management; corrections; criminal justice/law enforcement administration; data processing and data processing technology; drafting and design technology; dramatic/theater arts; electrical, electronic and communications engineering technology; engineering; engineering science; engineering technology; environmental engineering technology; fire science/firefighting; hospitality administration; hotel/motel administration; human services; hydrology and water resources science; industrial technology; kindergarten/preschool education; laser and optical technology; legal administrative assistant/secretary; liberal arts and sciences/liberal studies; marketing/marketing management; mechanical engineering/mechanical technology; nuclear/nuclear power technology; pre-engineering; professional, technical, business, and scientific writing; public administration; registered nursing/registered nurse; special products marketing; substance abuse/addiction counseling; tourism and travel services management.
Academics *Calendar:* semesters. *Degrees:* certificates and associate (engineering technology programs are offered on the Thames Valley Campus; liberal arts, transfer and career programs are offered on the Mohegan Campus). *Special study options:* adult/continuing education programs, part-time degree program.
Library Three Rivers Community College Learning Resource Center plus 1 other with an OPAC.
Student Life *Housing:* college housing not available. *Campus security:* 24-hour emergency response devices, late-night transport/escort service, 14-hour patrols by trained security personnel.
Athletics *Intramural sports:* baseball M(c)/W(c), golf M(c)/W(c).
Costs (2011–12) *Tuition:* state resident $3096 full-time, $129 per credit hour part-time; nonresident $10,036 full-time, $387 per credit hour part-time. Full-time tuition and fees vary according to course load and reciprocity agreements. Part-time tuition and fees vary according to course load and reciprocity agreements. *Required fees:* $394 full-time, $79 per course part-time. *Payment plan:* installment. *Waivers:* senior citizens and employees or children of employees.
Financial Aid Of all full-time matriculated undergraduates who enrolled in 2010, 1,135 applied for aid, 967 were judged to have need, 266 had their need fully met. *Average percent of need met:* 48%. *Average financial aid package:* $2631. *Average need-based loan:* $3308. *Average need-based gift aid:* $2409.
Applying *Options:* electronic application, early admission, deferred entrance. *Required for some:* minimum 3.0 GPA. *Recommended:* high school transcript. *Application deadlines:* rolling (freshmen), rolling (transfers). *Notification:* continuous (freshmen), continuous (transfers).
Freshman Application Contact Ms. Aida García, Admissions and Recruitment Counselor, Three Rivers Community College, 574 New London Turnpike, Norwich, CT 06360. *Phone:* 860-383-5268. *Fax:* 860-885-1684. *E-mail:* admissions@trcc.commnet.edu. *Web site:* http://www.trcc.commnet.edu/.

Tunxis Community College

Farmington, Connecticut

- **State-supported** 2-year, founded 1969, part of Connecticut Community–Technical College System
- **Suburban** 12-acre campus with easy access to Hartford
- **Coed,** 4,740 undergraduate students, 39% full-time, 57% women, 43% men

Undergraduates 1,857 full-time, 2,883 part-time. Students come from 6 states and territories; 2% are from out of state; 7% Black or African American, non-Hispanic/Latino; 13% Hispanic/Latino; 3% Asian, non-Hispanic/Latino; 0.1% Native Hawaiian or other Pacific Islander, non-Hispanic/Latino; 0.1% Ameri-

can Indian or Alaska Native, non-Hispanic/Latino; 8% Race/ethnicity unknown; 0.4% international. *Retention:* 59% of full-time freshmen returned.
Freshmen *Admission:* 805 enrolled.
Faculty *Total:* 239, 28% full-time, 12% with terminal degrees. *Student/faculty ratio:* 31:1.
Majors Accounting; administrative assistant and secretarial science; art; business administration and management; commercial and advertising art; corrections; criminal justice/law enforcement administration; data processing and data processing technology; dental hygiene; design and applied arts related; engineering; engineering technology; fashion merchandising; forensic science and technology; human services; information science/studies; kindergarten/preschool education; legal administrative assistant/secretary; liberal arts and sciences/liberal studies; marketing/marketing management; medical administrative assistant and medical secretary; physical therapy; substance abuse/addiction counseling.
Academics *Calendar:* semesters. *Degree:* certificates and associate. *Special study options:* academic remediation for entering students, adult/continuing education programs, cooperative education, distance learning, double majors, English as a second language, honors programs, independent study, internships, part-time degree program, services for LD students, summer session for credit.
Library Tunxis Community College Library with 33,866 titles, 285 serial subscriptions, an OPAC.
Student Life *Housing:* college housing not available. *Activities and Organizations:* drama/theater group, student-run newspaper, Phi Theta Kappa, Student American Dental Hygiene Association (SADHA), Human Services Club, student newspaper, Criminal Justice Club. *Campus security:* 24-hour emergency response devices.
Costs (2012–13) *Tuition:* state resident $3168 full-time, $132 per credit hour part-time; nonresident $9504 full-time, $396 per credit hour part-time. *Required fees:* $402 full-time, $114 per term part-time, $332 per term part-time. *Payment plan:* installment. *Waivers:* senior citizens and employees or children of employees.
Applying *Options:* deferred entrance. *Application fee:* $20. *Required:* high school transcript. *Application deadlines:* rolling (freshmen), rolling (transfers).
Freshman Application Contact Mr. Peter McCluskey, Director of Admissions, Tunxis Community College, 271 Scott Swamp Road, Farmington, CT 06032. *Phone:* 860-255-3550. *Fax:* 860-255-3559. *E-mail:* pmccluskey@txcc.commnet.edu. *Web site:* http://www.tunxis.commnet.edu/.

DELAWARE

Delaware College of Art and Design
Wilmington, Delaware

Freshman Application Contact Ms. Allison Gullo, Delaware College of Art and Design, 600 North Market Street, Wilmington, DE 19801. *Phone:* 302-622-8867 Ext. 111. *Fax:* 302-622-8870. *E-mail:* agullo@dcad.edu. *Web site:* http://www.dcad.edu/.

Delaware Technical & Community College, Jack F. Owens Campus
Georgetown, Delaware

- **State-supported** 2-year, founded 1967, part of Delaware Technical and Community College System
- **Small-town** campus
- **Coed,** 4,741 undergraduate students, 44% full-time, 64% women, 36% men

Undergraduates 2,096 full-time, 2,645 part-time. 19% Black or African American, non-Hispanic/Latino; 6% Hispanic/Latino; 2% Asian, non-Hispanic/Latino; 0.1% Native Hawaiian or other Pacific Islander, non-Hispanic/Latino; 0.4% American Indian or Alaska Native, non-Hispanic/Latino; 2% Two or more races, non-Hispanic/Latino; 0.3% Race/ethnicity unknown; 3% international; 3% transferred in. *Retention:* 56% of full-time freshmen returned.
Freshmen *Admission:* 1,701 applied, 1,701 admitted, 1,009 enrolled.
Majors Accounting; aeronautical/aerospace engineering technology; agricultural business and management; agricultural production; applied horticulture/horticulture operations; architectural engineering technology; automobile/automotive mechanics technology; biology/biological sciences; biology/biotechnology laboratory technician; business automation/technology/data entry; business/commerce; civil engineering technology; clinical/medical laboratory assistant; computer and information sciences; computer technology/computer systems technology; construction management; criminal justice/law enforce-

ment administration; criminal justice/police science; customer service support/call center/teleservice operation; diagnostic medical sonography and ultrasound technology; drafting and design technology; early childhood education; e-commerce; education (multiple levels); electrical, electronic and communications engineering technology; elementary education; emergency medical technology (EMT paramedic); energy management and systems technology; entrepreneurship; heating, air conditioning, ventilation and refrigeration maintenance technology; human services; kindergarten/preschool education; legal administrative assistant/secretary; licensed practical/vocational nurse training; management information systems; marketing/marketing management; mathematics teacher education; mechanical drafting and CAD/CADD; medical/clinical assistant; middle school education; nuclear engineering technology; occupational therapist assistant; office management; physical therapy technology; poultry science; radiologic technology/science; registered nursing/registered nurse; respiratory therapy technician; surveying technology; turf and turfgrass management; veterinary/animal health technology; water quality and wastewater treatment management and recycling technology.
Academics *Calendar:* semesters. *Degree:* certificates, diplomas, and associate. *Special study options:* part-time degree program.
Library Stephen J. Betze Library.
Student Life *Housing:* college housing not available. *Campus security:* 24-hour emergency response devices, late-night transport/escort service.
Athletics Member NJCAA. *Intercollegiate sports:* baseball M(s), golf M, softball W(s). *Intramural sports:* football M/W.
Costs (2011–12) *Tuition:* state resident $2742 full-time, $114 per credit hour part-time; nonresident $6856 full-time, $286 per credit hour part-time. *Required fees:* $238 full-time, $7 per credit hour part-time, $25 per term part-time. *Payment plan:* deferred payment. *Waivers:* senior citizens and employees or children of employees.
Financial Aid Of all full-time matriculated undergraduates who enrolled in 2010, 250 Federal Work-Study jobs (averaging $2000).
Applying *Options:* electronic application, early admission, deferred entrance. *Application fee:* $10. *Required for some:* high school transcript. *Application deadline:* rolling (freshmen). *Notification:* continuous (freshmen).
Freshman Application Contact Ms. Claire McDonald, Admissions Counselor, Delaware Technical & Community College, Jack F. Owens Campus, PO Box 610, Georgetown, DE 19947. *Phone:* 302-856-5400. *Fax:* 302-856-9461. *Web site:* http://www.dtcc.edu/.

Delaware Technical & Community College, Stanton/Wilmington Campus
Newark, Delaware

- **State-supported** 2-year, founded 1968, part of Delaware Technical and Community College System
- **Urban** campus
- **Coed,** 6,978 undergraduate students, 39% full-time, 59% women, 41% men

Undergraduates 2,706 full-time, 4,272 part-time. 26% Black or African American, non-Hispanic/Latino; 8% Hispanic/Latino; 4% Asian, non-Hispanic/Latino; 0.2% Native Hawaiian or other Pacific Islander, non-Hispanic/Latino; 0.3% American Indian or Alaska Native, non-Hispanic/Latino; 3% Two or more races, non-Hispanic/Latino; 1% Race/ethnicity unknown; 2% international; 4% transferred in. *Retention:* 55% of full-time freshmen returned.
Freshmen *Admission:* 3,154 applied, 3,154 admitted, 1,601 enrolled.
Majors Accounting; agricultural business and management; architectural engineering technology; automobile/automotive mechanics technology; biology/biological sciences; biology/biotechnology laboratory technician; business administration and management; business automation/technology/data entry; business/commerce; CAD/CADD drafting/design technology; cardiovascular technology; chemical technology; civil drafting and CAD/CADD; computer and information sciences; computer engineering technology; computer systems networking and telecommunications; construction management; criminal justice/law enforcement administration; criminal justice/police science; culinary arts; customer service management; customer service support/call center/teleservice operation; dental hygiene; diagnostic medical sonography and ultrasound technology; drafting and design technology; early childhood education; education (multiple levels); electrical, electronic and communications engineering technology; electrocardiograph technology; elementary education; emergency care attendant (EMT ambulance); emergency medical technology (EMT paramedic); energy management and systems technology; engineering/industrial management; fire prevention and safety technology; fire science/firefighting; fire services administration; heating, ventilation, air conditioning and refrigeration engineering technology; histologic technology/histotechnologist; hotel/motel administration; human services; kindergarten/preschool education; kinesiology and exercise science; management information systems; management science; manufacturing engineering technology; marketing/marketing management; mathematics teacher education; mechanical engineering/

mechanical technology; medical/clinical assistant; middle school education; nuclear engineering technology; nuclear medical technology; occupational therapist assistant; office management; operations research; physical therapy technology; radiologic technology/science; registered nursing/registered nurse; respiratory therapy technician; restaurant, culinary, and catering management; science technologies related; substance abuse/addiction counseling; surveying technology.

Academics *Calendar:* semesters. *Degree:* certificates, diplomas, and associate. *Special study options:* part-time degree program. *ROTC:* Air Force (c).

Library Stanton Campus Library and John Eugene Derrickson Memorial Library.

Student Life *Housing:* college housing not available. *Campus security:* 24-hour emergency response devices, late-night transport/escort service.

Athletics Member NJCAA. *Intercollegiate sports:* basketball M(s)/W(s), soccer M(s), softball W(s). *Intramural sports:* basketball M/W, football M/W, softball W, volleyball M/W.

Costs (2011–12) *Tuition:* state resident $2742 full-time, $114 per credit hour part-time; nonresident $6856 full-time, $286 per credit hour part-time. *Required fees:* $238 full-time, $7 per credit hour part-time, $25 per term part-time. *Payment plan:* deferred payment. *Waivers:* senior citizens and employees or children of employees.

Applying *Options:* electronic application, early admission, deferred entrance. *Application fee:* $10. *Required for some:* high school transcript. *Application deadlines:* rolling (freshmen), rolling (transfers). *Notification:* continuous (freshmen), continuous (transfers).

Freshman Application Contact Ms. Rebecca Bailey, Admissions Coordinator, Wilmington, Delaware Technical & Community College, Stanton/Wilmington Campus, 333 Shipley Street, Wilmington, DE 19713. *Phone:* 302-571-5343. *Fax:* 302-577-2548. *Web site:* http://www.dtcc.edu/.

Delaware Technical & Community College, Terry Campus

Dover, Delaware

- **State-supported** 2-year, founded 1972, part of Delaware Technical and Community College System
- **Small-town** campus
- **Coed,** 3,323 undergraduate students, 43% full-time, 65% women, 35% men

Undergraduates 1,425 full-time, 1,898 part-time. 28% Black or African American, non-Hispanic/Latino; 5% Hispanic/Latino; 2% Asian, non-Hispanic/Latino; 0.2% Native Hawaiian or other Pacific Islander, non-Hispanic/Latino; 0.5% American Indian or Alaska Native, non-Hispanic/Latino; 3% Two or more races, non-Hispanic/Latino; 2% Race/ethnicity unknown; 1% international; 4% transferred in. *Retention:* 52% of full-time freshmen returned.

Freshmen *Admission:* 1,266 applied, 1,266 admitted, 767 enrolled.

Majors Accounting; agricultural business and management; architectural engineering technology; bilingual and multilingual education; biomedical technology; business administration and management; business automation/technology/data entry; business/commerce; civil engineering technology; commercial and advertising art; computer and information sciences; computer engineering technology; computer systems networking and telecommunications; computer technology/computer systems technology; construction management; criminal justice/law enforcement administration; criminal justice/police science; culinary arts; digital communication and media/multimedia; drafting and design technology; early childhood education; e-commerce; education (multiple levels); electrical, electronic and communications engineering technology; electromechanical technology; elementary education; emergency medical technology (EMT paramedic); energy management and systems technology; entrepreneurship; hotel/motel administration; human resources management; human services; interior design; kindergarten/preschool education; legal administrative assistant/secretary; management information systems; marketing/marketing management; mathematics teacher education; medical/clinical assistant; middle school education; office management; photography; registered nursing/registered nurse; substance abuse/addiction counseling.

Academics *Calendar:* semesters. *Degree:* certificates, diplomas, and associate. *Special study options:* part-time degree program. *ROTC:* Air Force (c).

Student Life *Housing:* college housing not available. *Campus security:* 24-hour emergency response devices, late-night transport/escort service.

Athletics Member NJCAA. *Intercollegiate sports:* lacrosse M(s), soccer M(s)/W(s), softball W(s).

Costs (2011–12) *Tuition:* state resident $2980 full-time, $114 per credit hour part-time; nonresident $7095 full-time, $286 per credit hour part-time. *Required fees:* $238 full-time, $7 per credit hour part-time, $25 per term part-time. *Payment plan:* deferred payment. *Waivers:* senior citizens and employees or children of employees.

Financial Aid Of all full-time matriculated undergraduates who enrolled in 2010, 50 Federal Work-Study jobs (averaging $1500).

Applying *Options:* electronic application, early admission, deferred entrance. *Application fee:* $10. *Required for some:* high school transcript. *Application deadline:* rolling (freshmen). *Notification:* continuous (freshmen).

Freshman Application Contact Mrs. Maria Harris, Admissions Officer, Delaware Technical & Community College, Terry Campus, 100 Campus Drive, Dover, DE 19904. *Phone:* 302-857-1020. *Fax:* 302-857-1296. *E-mail:* terry-info@dtcc.edu. *Web site:* http://www.dtcc.edu/terry/.

FLORIDA

Anthem College–Orlando

Orlando, Florida

Freshman Application Contact Admissions Office, Anthem College–Orlando, 3710 Maguire Boulevard, Orlando, FL 32803. *Toll-free phone:* 855-824-0055. *Web site:* http://anthem.edu/orlando-florida/.

ATI Career Training Center

Fort Lauderdale, Florida

Director of Admissions Director of Admissions, ATI Career Training Center, 2880 NW 62nd Street, Fort Lauderdale, FL 33309-9731. *Phone:* 954-973-4760. *Toll-free phone:* 888-209-8264. *Web site:* http://www.aticareertraining.edu/.

ATI College of Health

Miami, Florida

Director of Admissions Admissions, ATI College of Health, 1395 NW 167th Street, Suite 200, Miami, FL 33169-5742. *Phone:* 305-628-1000. *Toll-free phone:* 888-209-8264. *Fax:* 305-628-1461. *E-mail:* admissions@atienterprises.edu. *Web site:* http://www.aticareertraining.edu/.

Brevard Community College

Cocoa, Florida

Freshman Application Contact Ms. Stephanie Burnette, Registrar, Brevard Community College, Cocoa, FL 32922-6597. *Phone:* 321-433-7271. *Fax:* 321-433-7172. *E-mail:* cocoaadmissions@brevardcc.edu. *Web site:* http://www.brevardcc.edu/.

Broward College

Fort Lauderdale, Florida

Freshman Application Contact Willie J. Alexander, Associate Vice President for Student Affairs/College Registrar, Broward College, 225 East Las Olas Boulevard, Fort Lauderdale, FL 33301. *Phone:* 954-201-7471. *Fax:* 954-201-7466. *E-mail:* walexand@broward.edu. *Web site:* http://www.broward.edu/.

Brown Mackie College–Miami

Miami, Florida

- **Proprietary** primarily 2-year, part of Education Management Corporation
- **Coed**

Academics *Degrees:* diplomas, associate, and bachelor's.

Costs (2011–12) *Tuition:* Tuition varies by program. Students should contact Brown Mackie College for tuition information.

Freshman Application Contact Brown Mackie College–Miami, One Herald Plaza, Miami, FL 33132. *Phone:* 305-341-6600. *Toll-free phone:* 866-505-0335. *Web site:* http://www.brownmackie.edu/miami/.

See page 368 for the College Close-Up.

Central Florida Institute

Palm Harbor, Florida

Director of Admissions Carol Bruno, Director of Admissions, Central Florida Institute, 30522 US Highway 19 North, Suite 300, Palm Harbor, FL 34684. *Phone:* 727-786-4707. *Toll-free phone:* 888-831-8303. *Web site:* http://www.cfinstitute.com/.

Centura Institute
Orlando, Florida

Director of Admissions John DiBenedetto, Director of Admissions, Centura Institute, 6359 Edgewater Drive, Orlando, FL 32810. *Phone:* 407-275-9696. *Toll-free phone:* 888-312-1320. *Fax:* 407-275-4499. *E-mail:* admcircorl@centura.edu. *Web site:* http://www.centurainstitute.edu/.

Chipola College
Marianna, Florida

- **State-supported** primarily 2-year, founded 1947
- **Rural** 105-acre campus
- **Coed,** 2,341 undergraduate students, 43% full-time, 61% women, 39% men

Undergraduates 1,016 full-time, 1,325 part-time. Students come from 7 states and territories; 6 other countries; 8% are from out of state; 16% Black or African American, non-Hispanic/Latino; 2% Hispanic/Latino; 0.9% Asian, non-Hispanic/Latino; 0.8% American Indian or Alaska Native, non-Hispanic/Latino; 2% Two or more races, non-Hispanic/Latino; 0.2% Race/ethnicity unknown; 6% transferred in.
Freshmen *Admission:* 249 enrolled. *Average high school GPA:* 2.5. *Test scores:* SAT critical reading scores over 500: 16%; SAT math scores over 500: 36%; ACT scores over 18: 81%; SAT critical reading scores over 600: 4%; SAT math scores over 600: 12%; ACT scores over 24: 25%; ACT scores over 30: 3%.
Faculty *Total:* 133, 30% full-time, 14% with terminal degrees. *Student/faculty ratio:* 24:1.
Majors Accounting; agriculture; agronomy and crop science; art; biological and physical sciences; business administration and management; clinical laboratory science/medical technology; computer and information sciences related; computer science; education; finance; liberal arts and sciences/liberal studies; mass communication/media; mathematics teacher education; pre-engineering; registered nursing/registered nurse; science teacher education; secondary education; social work.
Academics *Calendar:* semesters. *Degrees:* certificates, associate, and bachelor's. *Special study options:* academic remediation for entering students, adult/continuing education programs, advanced placement credit, distance learning, honors programs, independent study, part-time degree program, services for LD students, summer session for credit.
Library Chipola Library with 37,740 titles, 226 serial subscriptions.
Student Life *Housing:* college housing not available. *Activities and Organizations:* drama/theater group, student-run newspaper, choral group, Drama/Theater Group. *Campus security:* night security personnel.
Athletics Member NJCAA. *Intercollegiate sports:* baseball M(s), basketball M(s)/W(s), softball W(s).
Costs (2011–12) *Tuition:* state resident $3000 full-time, $100 per semester hour part-time; nonresident $8557 full-time, $285 per semester hour part-time. Full-time tuition and fees vary according to degree level. Part-time tuition and fees vary according to degree level. *Required fees:* $40 full-time.
Applying *Options:* early admission. *Required:* high school transcript. *Application deadlines:* rolling (freshmen), rolling (transfers). *Notification:* continuous (freshmen), continuous (transfers).
Freshman Application Contact Mrs. Kathy L. Rehberg, Registrar, Chipola College, 3094 Indian Circle, Marianna, FL 32446-3065. *Phone:* 850-718-2233. *Fax:* 850-718-2287. *E-mail:* rehbergk@chipola.edu. *Web site:* http://www.chipola.edu/.

City College
Casselberry, Florida

Director of Admissions Ms. Kimberly Bowden, Director of Admissions, City College, 853 Semoran Boulevard, Suite 200, Casselberry, FL 32707-5342. *Phone:* 352-335-4000. *Fax:* 352-335-4303. *E-mail:* kbowden@citycollege.edu. *Web site:* http://www.citycollegeorlando.edu/.

City College
Fort Lauderdale, Florida

Freshman Application Contact City College, 2000 West Commercial Boulevard, Suite 200, Fort Lauderdale, FL 33309. *Phone:* 954-492-5353. *Toll-free phone:* 866-314-5681. *Web site:* http://www.citycollege.edu/.

City College
Gainesville, Florida

Freshman Application Contact Admissions Office, City College, 7001 Northwest 4th Boulevard, Gainesville, FL 32607. *Phone:* 352-335-4000. *Web site:* http://www.citycollege.edu/.

City College
Miami, Florida

Freshman Application Contact Admissions Office, City College, 9300 South Dadeland Boulevard, Suite PH, Miami, FL 33156. *Phone:* 305-666-9242. *Fax:* 305-666-9243. *Web site:* http://www.citycollege.edu/.

College of Business and Technology
Miami, Florida

- **Proprietary** primarily 2-year, founded 1988
- **Coed,** 1,098 undergraduate students, 100% full-time, 37% women, 63% men

Undergraduates 1,098 full-time. Students come from 4 states and territories; 11% Black or African American, non-Hispanic/Latino; 85% Hispanic/Latino; 0.1% Asian, non-Hispanic/Latino; 0.1% Native Hawaiian or other Pacific Islander, non-Hispanic/Latino; 0.7% American Indian or Alaska Native, non-Hispanic/Latino; 0.2% Two or more races, non-Hispanic/Latino; 0.8% Race/ethnicity unknown; 3% transferred in.
Freshmen *Admission:* 1,463 applied, 1,098 admitted, 1,098 enrolled. *Average high school GPA:* 2.8.
Faculty *Total:* 28, 43% full-time, 100% with terminal degrees. *Student/faculty ratio:* 15:1.
Majors Accounting; business administration and management; computer graphics; computer systems networking and telecommunications; heating, air conditioning, ventilation and refrigeration maintenance technology; medical/clinical assistant; system, networking, and LAN/WAN management.
Academics *Calendar:* semesters. *Degrees:* certificates, diplomas, associate, and bachelor's. *Special study options:* academic remediation for entering students, accelerated degree program, adult/continuing education programs, advanced placement credit, cooperative education, distance learning, double majors, English as a second language, honors programs, independent study, internships, off-campus study, part-time degree program, services for LD students, summer session for credit.
Library The Bill Clinton Library plus 1 other with 700,000 titles, 200,000 serial subscriptions, 1,200 audiovisual materials, an OPAC, a Web page.
Student Life *Housing Options:* Campus housing is provided by a third party. *Activities and Organizations:* student-run newspaper.
Costs (2012–13) *Tuition:* $10,920 full-time. *Required fees:* $1400 full-time. *Payment plan:* installment.
Applying *Options:* electronic application. *Application fee:* $25. *Required:* essay or personal statement, high school transcript, minimum 2.6 GPA, 2 letters of recommendation, interview.
Freshman Application Contact Ms. Ivis Delgado, Admissions Representative, College of Business and Technology, 8230 West Flagler Street, Miami, FL 33144. *Phone:* 305-273-4499 Ext. 2204. *Toll-free phone:* 866-626-8842. *Fax:* 305-485-4411. *E-mail:* admissions@cbt.edu. *Web site:* http://www.cbt.edu/.

College of Central Florida
Ocala, Florida

- **State and locally supported** primarily 2-year, founded 1957, part of Florida Community College System
- **Small-town** 139-acre campus
- **Endowment** $40.1 million
- **Coed,** 8,766 undergraduate students, 42% full-time, 62% women, 38% men

Undergraduates 3,666 full-time, 5,100 part-time.
Freshmen *Admission:* 1,345 enrolled. *Test scores:* SAT critical reading scores over 500: 42%; SAT math scores over 500: 39%; SAT writing scores over 500: 42%; ACT scores over 18: 77%; SAT math scores over 600: 8%; ACT scores over 24: 29%; ACT scores over 30: 5%.
Faculty *Total:* 611, 21% full-time, 10% with terminal degrees. *Student/faculty ratio:* 18:1.
Majors Accounting technology and bookkeeping; automobile/automotive mechanics technology; business/commerce; drafting and design technology; early childhood education; emergency medical technology (EMT paramedic); fire science/firefighting; health information/medical records technology; human services; information technology; landscaping and groundskeeping; liberal arts and sciences/liberal studies; marketing/marketing management; office management; parks, recreation and leisure; physical therapy technology; registered nursing/registered nurse; restaurant, culinary, and catering management; veterinary/animal health technology.
Academics *Calendar:* semesters. *Degrees:* certificates, diplomas, associate, and bachelor's. *Special study options:* academic remediation for entering students, adult/continuing education programs, advanced placement credit, cooperative education, distance learning, English as a second language, freshman

honors college, honors programs, independent study, internships, part-time degree program, services for LD students, summer session for credit.

Library Learning Resources Center plus 1 other with 60,558 titles, 412 serial subscriptions, 6,244 audiovisual materials, an OPAC, a Web page.

Student Life *Housing:* college housing not available. *Activities and Organizations:* drama/theater group, student-run newspaper, choral group, Student Activities Board, African-American Student Union, ROC (Realizing Our Cause), Gay Straight Alliance, Musagettas. *Campus security:* 24-hour emergency response devices and patrols, student patrols, late-night transport/escort service. *Student services:* personal/psychological counseling.

Athletics Member NJCAA. *Intercollegiate sports:* baseball M(s), basketball M(s)/W(s), softball W(s), tennis W(s), volleyball W(s).

Standardized Tests *Recommended:* SAT (for admission), ACT (for admission), SAT or ACT (for admission), SAT and SAT Subject Tests or ACT (for admission), SAT Subject Tests (for admission).

Costs (2011–12) *Tuition:* state resident $2274 full-time, $99 per credit hour part-time; nonresident $9096 full-time, $371 per credit hour part-time. Full-time tuition and fees vary according to course level, degree level, and program. Part-time tuition and fees vary according to course level, degree level, and program. *Required fees:* $682 full-time, $23 per credit hour part-time. *Waivers:* employees or children of employees.

Financial Aid Of all full-time matriculated undergraduates who enrolled in 2010, 85 Federal Work-Study jobs (averaging $1505).

Applying *Options:* early admission. *Application fee:* $30. *Required:* high school transcript. *Application deadlines:* rolling (freshmen), rolling (transfers). *Notification:* continuous (freshmen), continuous (transfers).

Freshman Application Contact Ms. Devona Sewell, Registrar, Admission and Records, College of Central Florida, 3001 SW College Road, Ocala, FL 34474. *Phone:* 352-237-2111 Ext. 1398. *Fax:* 352-873-5882. *E-mail:* sewelld@cf.edu. *Web site:* http://www.cf.edu/.

Daytona State College
Daytona Beach, Florida

- **State-supported** primarily 2-year, founded 1958, part of Florida Community College System
- **Suburban** 100-acre campus with easy access to Orlando
- **Coed**

Undergraduates 8,605 full-time, 10,233 part-time. Students come from 51 states and territories; 52 other countries; 9% are from out of state; 16% Black or African American, non-Hispanic/Latino; 10% Hispanic/Latino; 2% Asian, non-Hispanic/Latino; 0.5% American Indian or Alaska Native, non-Hispanic/Latino; 0.4% Two or more races, non-Hispanic/Latino; 1% Race/ethnicity unknown; 0.4% international; 3% transferred in. *Retention:* 81% of full-time freshmen returned.

Faculty *Student/faculty ratio:* 22:1.

Academics *Calendar:* semesters. *Degrees:* certificates, diplomas, associate, bachelor's, and postbachelor's certificates. *Special study options:* academic remediation for entering students, adult/continuing education programs, advanced placement credit, cooperative education, distance learning, double majors, English as a second language, external degree program, freshman honors college, honors programs, independent study, internships, off-campus study, part-time degree program, services for LD students, study abroad, summer session for credit. *ROTC:* Army (c), Air Force (c).

Student Life *Campus security:* 24-hour emergency response devices and patrols, late-night transport/escort service.

Athletics Member NJCAA.

Costs (2011–12) *Tuition:* state resident $2847 full-time, $95 per credit hour part-time; nonresident $10,737 full-time, $358 per credit hour part-time. Full-time tuition and fees vary according to course level, course load, degree level, and program. Part-time tuition and fees vary according to course level, course load, degree level, and program. *Required fees:* $60 full-time, $30 per term part-time.

Financial Aid Of all full-time matriculated undergraduates who enrolled in 2010, 193 Federal Work-Study jobs (averaging $1542).

Applying *Options:* electronic application, early admission, deferred entrance. *Required:* high school transcript.

Freshman Application Contact Mrs. Karen Sanders, Director of Admissions and Recruitment, Daytona State College, 1200 International Speedway Boulevard, Daytona Beach, FL 32114. *Phone:* 386-506-3050. *E-mail:* sanderk@daytonastate.edu. *Web site:* http://www.daytonastate.edu/.

Edison State College
Fort Myers, Florida

Freshman Application Contact Lauren Willison, Admissions Specialist, Edison State College, 8099 College Parkway, Fort Myers, FL 33919. *Phone:* 239-489-9257. *Toll-free phone:* 800-749-2ECC. *E-mail:* Lauren.Willison@edison.edu. *Web site:* http://www.edison.edu/.

Everest Institute
Fort Lauderdale, Florida

Freshman Application Contact Admissions Office, Everest Institute, 1040 Bayview Drive, Fort Lauderdale, FL 33304. *Phone:* 954-630-0066. *Toll-free phone:* 888-741-4270. *Web site:* http://www.everest.edu/.

Everest Institute
Hialeah, Florida

Director of Admissions Director of Admissions, Everest Institute, 530 West 49th Street, Hialeah, FL 33012. *Phone:* 305-558-9500. *Toll-free phone:* 888-741-4270. *Fax:* 305-558-4419. *Web site:* http://www.everest.edu/.

Everest Institute
Miami, Florida

Director of Admissions Director of Admissions, Everest Institute, 111 Northwest 183rd Street, Second Floor, Miami, FL 33169. *Phone:* 305-949-9500. *Toll-free phone:* 888-741-4270. *Web site:* http://www.everest.edu/.

Everest Institute
Miami, Florida

Freshman Application Contact Director of Admissions, Everest Institute, 9020 Southwest 137th Avenue, Miami, FL 33186. *Phone:* 305-386-9900. *Toll-free phone:* 888-741-4270. *Fax:* 305-388-1740. *Web site:* http://www.everest.edu/.

Everest University
Orange Park, Florida

Freshman Application Contact Admissions Office, Everest University, 805 Wells Road, Orange Park, FL 32073. *Phone:* 904-264-9122. *Web site:* http://www.everest.edu/.

Florida Career College
Miami, Florida

Director of Admissions Mr. David Knobel, President, Florida Career College, 1321 Southwest 107 Avenue, Suite 201B, Miami, FL 33174. *Phone:* 305-553-6065. *Toll-free phone:* 888-852-7272. *Web site:* http://www.careercollege.edu/.

Florida College of Natural Health
Bradenton, Florida

Freshman Application Contact Admissions Office, Florida College of Natural Health, 616 67th Street Circle East, Bradenton, FL 34208. *Phone:* 941-744-1244. *Toll-free phone:* 800-966-7117. *Fax:* 941-744-1242. *Web site:* http://www.fcnh.com/.

Florida College of Natural Health
Maitland, Florida

Freshman Application Contact Admissions Office, Florida College of Natural Health, 2600 Lake Lucien Drive, Suite 140, Maitland, FL 32751. *Phone:* 407-261-0319. *Toll-free phone:* 800-393-7337. *Web site:* http://www.fcnh.com/.

Florida College of Natural Health
Miami, Florida

Director of Admissions Admissions Coordinator, Florida College of Natural Health, 7925 Northwest 12th Street, Suite 201, Miami, FL 33126. *Phone:* 305-597-9599. *Toll-free phone:* 800-599-9599. *Fax:* 305-597-9110. *Web site:* http://www.fcnh.com/.

Florida College of Natural Health
Pompano Beach, Florida

Freshman Application Contact Admissions Office, Florida College of Natural Health, 2001 West Sample Road, Suite 100, Pompano Beach, FL 33064. *Phone:* 954-975-6400. *Toll-free phone:* 800-541-9299. *Web site:* http://www.fcnh.com/.

Florida Gateway College

Lake City, Florida

Freshman Application Contact Florida Gateway College, Lake City, FL 32025-8703. *Fax:* 386-755-1521. *E-mail:* admissions@mail.lakecity.cc.fl.us. *Web site:* http://www.fgc.edu/.

Florida Keys Community College

Key West, Florida

Director of Admissions Ms. Cheryl A. Malsheimer, Director of Admissions and Records, Florida Keys Community College, 5901 College Road, Key West, FL 33040-4397. *Phone:* 305-296-9081 Ext. 201. *Web site:* http://www.fkcc.edu/.

The Florida School of Traditional Midwifery

Gainseville, Florida

Freshman Application Contact Admissions Office, The Florida School of Traditional Midwifery, 810 East University Avenue, 2nd Floor, Gainseville, FL 32601. *Phone:* 352-338-0766. *Fax:* 352-338-2013. *E-mail:* info@midwiferyschool.org. *Web site:* http://www.midwiferyschool.org/.

Florida State College at Jacksonville

Jacksonville, Florida

- **State-supported** primarily 2-year, founded 1963, part of Florida College System
- **Urban** 825-acre campus
- **Endowment** $28.8 million
- **Coed,** 30,863 undergraduate students, 35% full-time, 60% women, 40% men

Undergraduates 10,778 full-time, 20,085 part-time. 28% Black or African American, non-Hispanic/Latino; 4% Hispanic/Latino; 3% Asian, non-Hispanic/Latino; 0.6% Native Hawaiian or other Pacific Islander, non-Hispanic/Latino; 0.5% American Indian or Alaska Native, non-Hispanic/Latino; 1% Two or more races, non-Hispanic/Latino; 15% Race/ethnicity unknown; 0.8% international; 7% transferred in. *Retention:* 36% of full-time freshmen returned.

Freshmen *Admission:* 8,562 applied, 4,148 admitted, 4,864 enrolled.

Faculty *Total:* 1,205, 34% full-time, 18% with terminal degrees. *Student/faculty ratio:* 29:1.

Majors Accounting; administrative assistant and secretarial science; aircraft powerplant technology; airframe mechanics and aircraft maintenance technology; airline pilot and flight crew; architectural drafting and CAD/CADD; architectural engineering technology; autobody/collision and repair technology; automobile/automotive mechanics technology; aviation/airway management; banking and financial support services; biomedical technology; business administration and management; business administration, management and operations related; child-care and support services management; child-care provision; civil engineering technology; commercial and advertising art; computer and information sciences; computer and information sciences and support services related; computer and information sciences related; computer and information systems security; computer engineering technology; computer graphics; computer hardware engineering; computer/information technology services administration related; computer programming; computer programming related; computer programming (specific applications); computer programming (vendor/product certification); computer software and media applications related; computer software engineering; computer systems analysis; computer systems networking and telecommunications; construction engineering technology; criminal justice/law enforcement administration; criminal justice/police science; culinary arts; data entry/microcomputer applications; data entry/microcomputer applications related; data modeling/warehousing and database administration; dental hygiene; design and visual communications; diagnostic medical sonography and ultrasound technology; dietetics; dietitian assistant; drafting and design technology; early childhood education; electrical, electronic and communications engineering technology; emergency medical technology (EMT paramedic); engineering technology; fashion merchandising; fire prevention and safety technology; fire science/firefighting; fire services administration; food service systems administration; health information/medical records administration; homeland security, law enforcement, firefighting and protective services related; hospitality administration; hospitality and recreation marketing; hotel/motel administration; human services; information science/studies; information technology; instrumentation technology;

insurance; interior design; legal assistant/paralegal; liberal arts and sciences/liberal studies; machine shop technology; marketing/marketing management; masonry; medical office management; medical radiologic technology; network and system administration; nuclear/nuclear power technology; office management; office occupations and clerical services; physical therapy technology; printmaking; real estate; registered nursing/registered nurse; respiratory care therapy; retailing; sign language interpretation and translation; substance abuse/addiction counseling; theater design and technology; tourism and travel services marketing; visual and performing arts related; water quality and wastewater treatment management and recycling technology; web/multimedia management and webmaster; web page, digital/multimedia and information resources design; word processing.

Academics *Calendar:* semesters. *Degrees:* certificates, diplomas, associate, and bachelor's. *Special study options:* academic remediation for entering students, accelerated degree program, adult/continuing education programs, advanced placement credit, cooperative education, distance learning, double majors, English as a second language, honors programs, independent study, internships, off-campus study, part-time degree program, services for LD students, study abroad, summer session for credit. *ROTC:* Navy (c).

Library Florida State College at Jacksonville Library and Learning Commons plus 7 others with 211,361 titles, 3,299 serial subscriptions, 21,541 audiovisual materials, an OPAC, a Web page.

Student Life *Activities and Organizations:* drama/theater group, student-run newspaper, radio and television station, choral group, Phi Theta Kappa, Forensic Team, Brain Bowl Team, International Student Association, DramaWorks. *Campus security:* 24-hour emergency response devices and patrols, late-night transport/escort service. *Student services:* personal/psychological counseling, women's center.

Athletics Member NJCAA. *Intercollegiate sports:* baseball M(s), basketball M(s)/W(s), softball W(s), tennis W(s), volleyball W(s). *Intramural sports:* badminton M/W, basketball M/W, bowling M/W, football M/W, golf M/W, soccer M/W, softball M/W, table tennis M/W, tennis M/W, volleyball M/W.

Costs (2011–12) *Tuition:* state resident $2387 full-time, $99 per credit hour part-time; nonresident $9171 full-time, $382 per credit hour part-time. Full-time tuition and fees vary according to degree level and program. Part-time tuition and fees vary according to degree level and program. *Payment plan:* installment. *Waivers:* employees or children of employees.

Applying *Options:* electronic application, early admission, deferred entrance. *Application fee:* $25. *Required:* high school transcript. *Application deadlines:* rolling (freshmen), rolling (out-of-state freshmen), rolling (transfers).

Freshman Application Contact Dr. Peter Biegel, AVP, Enrollment Management, Florida State College at Jacksonville, 501 West State Street, Jacksonville, FL 32202. *Phone:* 904-632-3131. *Toll-free phone:* 888-873-1145. *Fax:* 904-632-5105. *E-mail:* pbiegel@fscj.edu. *Web site:* http://www.fscj.edu/.

Florida Technical College

DeLand, Florida

Freshman Application Contact Mr. Bill Atkinson, Director, Florida Technical College, 1450 South Woodland Boulevard, 3rd Floor, DeLand, FL 32720. *Phone:* 386-734-3303. *Fax:* 386-734-5150. *Web site:* http://www.flatech.edu/.

Florida Technical College

Orlando, Florida

Director of Admissions Ms. Jeanette E. Muschlitz, Director of Admissions, Florida Technical College, 12689 Challenger Parkway, Orlando, FL 32826. *Phone:* 407-678-5600. *Web site:* http://www.flatech.edu/.

Fortis College

Tampa, Florida

Freshman Application Contact Admissions Office, Fortis College, 3910 US Highway 301 North, Suite 200, Tampa, FL 33619-1259. *Phone:* 813-620-1446. *Toll-free phone:* 855-4-FORTIS. *Fax:* 813-620-1641. *Web site:* http://www.fortis.edu/.

Fortis College

Winter Park, Florida

Freshman Application Contact Admissions Office, Fortis College, 1573 West Fairbanks Avenue, Suite 100, Winter Park, FL 32789. *Phone:* 407-843-3984. *Toll-free phone:* 855-4-FORTIS. *Fax:* 407-843-9828. *Web site:* http://www.fortis.edu/.

Gulf Coast State College

Panama City, Florida

- **State-supported** primarily 2-year, founded 1957
- **Suburban** 80-acre campus
- **Endowment** $25.9 million
- **Coed,** 6,436 undergraduate students, 38% full-time, 63% women, 37% men

Undergraduates 2,414 full-time, 4,022 part-time. Students come from 21 states and territories; 6% are from out of state; 11% Black or African American, non-Hispanic/Latino; 8% Hispanic/Latino; 2% Asian, non-Hispanic/Latino; 0.2% Native Hawaiian or other Pacific Islander, non-Hispanic/Latino; 0.5% American Indian or Alaska Native, non-Hispanic/Latino; 3% Two or more races, non-Hispanic/Latino; 2% Race/ethnicity unknown; 0.6% international; 4% transferred in.
Freshmen *Admission:* 653 enrolled.
Faculty *Total:* 304, 38% full-time. *Student/faculty ratio:* 21:1.
Majors Accounting technology and bookkeeping; business administration and management; child-care provision; cinematography and film/video production; civil engineering technology; computer/information technology services administration related; computer programming (specific applications); computer technology/computer systems technology; construction engineering technology; criminal justice/law enforcement administration; dental hygiene; diagnostic medical sonography and ultrasound technology; drafting and design technology; electrical, electronic and communications engineering technology; electrician; electromechanical and instrumentation and maintenance technologies related; emergency medical technology (EMT paramedic); executive assistant/executive secretary; fire prevention and safety technology; hospitality administration; legal assistant/paralegal; liberal arts and sciences/liberal studies; management information systems and services related; medical radiologic technology; physical therapy technology; psychiatric/mental health services technology; radio and television; registered nursing/registered nurse; respiratory care therapy; restaurant, culinary, and catering management.
Academics *Calendar:* semesters. *Degrees:* certificates, associate, and bachelor's. *Special study options:* academic remediation for entering students, accelerated degree program, adult/continuing education programs, advanced placement credit, cooperative education, distance learning, double majors, English as a second language, external degree program, honors programs, independent study, off-campus study, part-time degree program, services for LD students, summer session for credit.
Library Gulf Coast State College Library with 117,901 titles, 124 serial subscriptions, 5,204 audiovisual materials, an OPAC, a Web page.
Student Life *Housing:* college housing not available. *Activities and Organizations:* drama/theater group, student-run newspaper, television station, choral group. *Campus security:* late-night transport/escort service, patrols by trained security personnel during campus hours. *Student services:* personal/psychological counseling.
Athletics Member NJCAA. *Intercollegiate sports:* baseball M(s), basketball M(s)/W(s), softball W(s), volleyball W(s).
Costs (2012–13) *One-time required fee:* $20. *Tuition:* state resident $2370 full-time, $99 per credit hour part-time; nonresident $8635 full-time, $360 per credit hour part-time. Full-time tuition and fees vary according to degree level. Part-time tuition and fees vary according to degree level.
Financial Aid Of all full-time matriculated undergraduates who enrolled in 2010, 145 Federal Work-Study jobs (averaging $3200). 60 state and other part-time jobs (averaging $2600).
Applying *Options:* electronic application, early admission, deferred entrance. *Application fee:* $20. *Required:* high school transcript. *Application deadlines:* rolling (freshmen), rolling (transfers). *Notification:* continuous (freshmen).
Freshman Application Contact Mrs. Jackie Kuczenski, Administrative Secretary of Admissions, Gulf Coast State College, 5230 West U.S. Highway 98, Panama City, FL 32401. *Phone:* 850-769-1551 Ext. 4892. *Fax:* 850-913-3308. *E-mail:* jkuczenski@gulfcoast.edu. *Web site:* http://www.gulfcoast.edu/

Hillsborough Community College

Tampa, Florida

- **State-supported** 2-year, founded 1968, part of Florida College System
- **Urban** campus with easy access to Tampa, Clearwater, St. Petersburg
- **Coed,** 28,329 undergraduate students, 42% full-time, 57% women, 43% men

Undergraduates 11,903 full-time, 16,426 part-time. Students come from 38 states and territories; 121 other countries; 0.7% are from out of state; 19% Black or African American, non-Hispanic/Latino; 24% Hispanic/Latino; 3% Asian, non-Hispanic/Latino; 0.2% Native Hawaiian or other Pacific Islander, non-Hispanic/Latino; 0.5% American Indian or Alaska Native, non-Hispanic/Latino; 1% Two or more races, non-Hispanic/Latino; 9% Race/ethnicity unknown; 2% international; 15% transferred in.

Freshmen *Admission:* 5,229 enrolled.
Faculty *Total:* 1,459, 20% full-time, 13% with terminal degrees. *Student/faculty ratio:* 25:1.
Majors Accounting technology and bookkeeping; aquaculture; architectural engineering technology; biology/biotechnology laboratory technician; building/construction site management; business administration and management; child-care and support services management; cinematography and film/video production; computer/information technology services administration related; computer programming (specific applications); computer systems analysis; computer technology/computer systems technology; criminal justice/law enforcement administration; dental hygiene; diagnostic medical sonography and ultrasound technology; dietitian assistant; electrical, electronic and communications engineering technology; emergency medical technology (EMT paramedic); engineering technology; environmental control technologies related; executive assistant/executive secretary; fire prevention and safety technology; hospitality administration; landscaping and groundskeeping; legal assistant/paralegal; liberal arts and sciences/liberal studies; management information systems; management information systems and services related; medical radiologic technology; nuclear medical technology; operations management; opticianry; optometric technician; psychiatric/mental health services technology; registered nursing/registered nurse; respiratory care therapy; restaurant, culinary, and catering management; restaurant/food services management; special education–individuals with hearing impairments; veterinary/animal health technology.
Academics *Calendar:* semesters. *Degree:* certificates and associate. *Special study options:* academic remediation for entering students, advanced placement credit, cooperative education, distance learning, English as a second language, honors programs, off-campus study, part-time degree program, services for LD students, summer session for credit. *ROTC:* Army (c), Air Force (c).
Library Main Library plus 5 others with 170,615 titles, 1,283 serial subscriptions, 50,000 audiovisual materials, an OPAC, a Web page.
Student Life *Housing Options:* Campus housing is provided by a third party. *Activities and Organizations:* drama/theater group, student-run newspaper, radio station, choral group, Student Government Association, Student Nursing Association, Phi Theta Kappa, International Students, Radiography Club. *Campus security:* 24-hour emergency response devices and patrols, late-night transport/escort service, emergency call box locations. *Student services:* personal/psychological counseling.
Athletics Member NJCAA. *Intercollegiate sports:* baseball M(s), basketball M(s)/W(s), softball W(s), tennis W(s), volleyball W(s).
Standardized Tests *Required:* Florida's Postsecondary Education Readiness Test (PERT) (for admission).
Costs (2011–12) *Tuition:* state resident $2422 full-time, $101 per credit hour part-time; nonresident $8850 full-time, $369 per credit hour part-time. *Payment plan:* installment.
Applying *Options:* electronic application, early admission. *Required:* high school transcript. *Application deadlines:* 8/8 (freshmen), 8/8 (out-of-state freshmen), 8/8 (transfers). *Notification:* continuous (freshmen), continuous (out-of-state freshmen), continuous (transfers).
Freshman Application Contact Ms. Katherine Durkee, College Registrar, Hillsborough Community College, PO Box 31127, Tampa, FL 33631-3127. *Phone:* 813-259-6565. *E-mail:* kdurkee@hccfl.edu. *Web site:* http://www.hccfl.edu/.

Indian River State College

Fort Pierce, Florida

- **State-supported** primarily 2-year, founded 1960, part of Florida Community College System
- **Small-town** 310-acre campus
- **Coed,** 17,528 undergraduate students, 35% full-time, 60% women, 40% men

Undergraduates 6,177 full-time, 11,351 part-time. Students come from 28 states and territories; 130 other countries; 13% are from out of state; 17% Black or African American, non-Hispanic/Latino; 14% Hispanic/Latino; 2% Asian, non-Hispanic/Latino; 0.2% Native Hawaiian or other Pacific Islander, non-Hispanic/Latino; 0.2% American Indian or Alaska Native, non-Hispanic/Latino; 0.8% Two or more races, non-Hispanic/Latino; 3% Race/ethnicity unknown; 1% international; 14% transferred in.
Freshmen *Admission:* 1,855 applied, 1,855 admitted, 2,123 enrolled. *Average high school GPA:* 2.83.
Faculty *Total:* 967, 22% full-time, 16% with terminal degrees. *Student/faculty ratio:* 22:1.
Majors Accounting; administrative assistant and secretarial science; agricultural business and management; airline pilot and flight crew; anthropology; apparel and textiles; architectural drafting and CAD/CADD; art teacher education; automobile/automotive mechanics technology; banking and financial support services; biology/biological sciences; biology teacher education; business administration and management; carpentry; chemistry; child development; civil engineering technology; clinical/medical laboratory technology;

computer engineering technology; computer programming; computer science; computer typography and composition equipment operation; consumer merchandising/retailing management; corrections; cosmetology; criminal justice/law enforcement administration; criminal justice/police science; criminal justice/safety; culinary arts; dental hygiene; drafting and design technology; dramatic/theater arts; economics; education; electrical, electronic and communications engineering technology; emergency medical technology (EMT paramedic); engineering; engineering technology; English; family and consumer sciences/human sciences; fashion merchandising; finance; fire science/firefighting; foods, nutrition, and wellness; forestry; French; health/health-care administration; health information/medical records administration; heating, air conditioning, ventilation and refrigeration maintenance technology; history; hotel/motel administration; humanities; human services; hydrology and water resources science; industrial radiologic technology; information science/studies; interior design; journalism; kindergarten/preschool education; language interpretation and translation; legal assistant/paralegal; liberal arts and sciences/liberal studies; library and information science; licensed practical/vocational nurse training; marine science/merchant marine officer; marketing/marketing management; mathematics; mathematics teacher education; medical administrative assistant and medical secretary; music; organizational behavior; pharmacy; philosophy; physical education teaching and coaching; physical therapy; physical therapy technology; physics; political science and government; pre-engineering; psychology; registered nursing/registered nurse; respiratory care therapy; rhetoric and composition; science teacher education; social sciences; social work; sociology; Spanish; special education; special products marketing; surveying technology; teacher assistant/aide.

Academics *Calendar:* semesters. *Degrees:* certificates, diplomas, associate, and bachelor's. *Special study options:* academic remediation for entering students, adult/continuing education programs, advanced placement credit, distance learning, English as a second language, independent study, part-time degree program, services for LD students, summer session for credit.

Library Charles S. Miley Learning Resource Center with 112,032 titles, 200 serial subscriptions, 3,577 audiovisual materials, an OPAC, a Web page.

Student Life *Housing:* college housing not available. *Activities and Organizations:* drama/theater group, choral group. *Campus security:* 24-hour emergency response devices and patrols. *Student services:* health clinic, personal/psychological counseling, women's center.

Athletics Member NJCAA. *Intercollegiate sports:* baseball M(s), basketball M(s)/W(s), softball W(s), swimming and diving M(s)/W(s), volleyball W(s). *Intramural sports:* basketball M/W, racquetball M/W, soccer M, volleyball M/W.

Applying *Options:* early admission, deferred entrance. *Required:* high school transcript. *Application deadlines:* rolling (freshmen), rolling (transfers). *Notification:* continuous (freshmen), continuous (transfers).

Freshman Application Contact Mr. Steven Payne, Dean of Educational Services, Indian River State College, 3209 Virginia Avenue, Fort Pierce, FL 34981-5596. *Phone:* 772-462-7805. *Toll-free phone:* 866-792-4772. *E-mail:* spayne@ircc.edu. *Web site:* http://www.irsc.edu/.

ITT Technical Institute
Bradenton, Florida

- **Proprietary** primarily 2-year, part of ITT Educational Services, Inc.
- **Coed**

Majors Business administration and management; communications technology; computer and information systems security; criminal justice/law enforcement administration; drafting and design technology; electrical, electronic and communications engineering technology; forensic science and technology; graphic communications; legal assistant/paralegal; network and system administration; project management; registered nursing/registered nurse.

Academics *Calendar:* quarters. *Degrees:* associate and bachelor's.

Freshman Application Contact Director of Recruitment, ITT Technical Institute, 8039 Cooper Creek Boulevard, Bradenton, FL 34201. *Phone:* 941-309-9200. *Toll-free phone:* 800-342-8684. *Web site:* http://www.itt-tech.edu/.

ITT Technical Institute
Fort Lauderdale, Florida

- **Proprietary** primarily 2-year, founded 1991, part of ITT Educational Services, Inc.
- **Suburban** campus
- **Coed**

Majors Business administration and management; communications technology; computer and information systems security; construction management; criminal justice/law enforcement administration; drafting and design technology; electrical, electronic and communications engineering technology; graphic communications; health information/medical records technology; legal assistant/paralegal; network and system administration; project management; registered nursing/registered nurse.

Academics *Calendar:* quarters. *Degrees:* associate and bachelor's.

Student Life *Housing:* college housing not available.

Freshman Application Contact Director of Recruitment, ITT Technical Institute, 3401 South University Drive, Fort Lauderdale, FL 33328-2021. *Phone:* 954-476-9300. *Toll-free phone:* 800-488-7797. *Web site:* http://www.itt-tech.edu/.

ITT Technical Institute
Fort Myers, Florida

- **Proprietary** primarily 2-year
- **Coed**

Majors Business administration and management; communications technology; computer and information systems security; drafting and design technology; electrical, electronic and communications engineering technology; forensic science and technology; graphic communications; legal assistant/paralegal; network and system administration; project management; registered nursing/registered nurse.

Academics *Degrees:* associate and bachelor's.

Freshman Application Contact Director of Recruitment, ITT Technical Institute, 13500 Powers Court, Suite 100, Fort Myers, FL 33912. *Phone:* 239-603-8700. *Toll-free phone:* 877-485-5313. *Web site:* http://www.itt-tech.edu/.

ITT Technical Institute
Jacksonville, Florida

- **Proprietary** primarily 2-year, founded 1991, part of ITT Educational Services, Inc.
- **Urban** campus
- **Coed**

Majors Business administration and management; communications technology; computer and information systems security; criminal justice/law enforcement administration; drafting and design technology; electrical, electronic and communications engineering technology; forensic science and technology; graphic communications; legal assistant/paralegal; network and system administration; project management; registered nursing/registered nurse.

Academics *Calendar:* quarters. *Degrees:* associate and bachelor's.

Student Life *Housing:* college housing not available.

Financial Aid Of all full-time matriculated undergraduates who enrolled in 2010, 5 Federal Work-Study jobs.

Freshman Application Contact Director of Recruitment, ITT Technical Institute, 7011 A.C. Skinner Parkway, Suite 140, Jacksonville, FL 32256. *Phone:* 904-573-9100. *Toll-free phone:* 800-318-1264. *Web site:* http://www.itt-tech.edu/.

ITT Technical Institute
Lake Mary, Florida

- **Proprietary** primarily 2-year, founded 1989, part of ITT Educational Services, Inc.
- **Suburban** campus
- **Coed**

Majors Business administration and management; communications technology; computer and information systems security; computer software technology; construction management; criminal justice/law enforcement administration; drafting and design technology; electrical, electronic and communications engineering technology; forensic science and technology; graphic communications; health information/medical records technology; legal assistant/paralegal; network and system administration; project management; registered nursing/registered nurse.

Academics *Calendar:* quarters. *Degrees:* associate and bachelor's.

Freshman Application Contact Director of Recruitment, ITT Technical Institute, 1400 South International Parkway, Lake Mary, FL 32746. *Phone:* 407-660-2900. *Toll-free phone:* 866-489-8441. *Fax:* 407-660-2566. *Web site:* http://www.itt-tech.edu/.

ITT Technical Institute
Miami, Florida

- **Proprietary** primarily 2-year, founded 1996, part of ITT Educational Services, Inc.
- **Coed**

Majors Business administration and management; communications technology; computer and information systems security; construction management; criminal justice/law enforcement administration; drafting and design technology; electrical, electronic and communications engineering technology; forensic science and technology; graphic communications; health information/

medical records technology; legal assistant/paralegal; network and system administration; project management; registered nursing/registered nurse.
Academics *Calendar:* quarters. *Degrees:* associate and bachelor's.
Student Life *Housing:* college housing not available.
Freshman Application Contact Director of Recruitment, ITT Technical Institute, 7955 NW 12th Street, Suite 119, Miami, FL 33126. *Phone:* 305-477-3080. *Web site:* http://www.itt-tech.edu/.

ITT Technical Institute
Orlando, Florida

- **Proprietary** primarily 2-year, part of ITT Educational Services, Inc.
- **Coed**

Majors Business administration and management; communications technology; computer and information systems security; criminal justice/law enforcement administration; drafting and design technology; electrical, electronic and communications engineering technology; forensic science and technology; graphic communications; legal assistant/paralegal; network and system administration; project management; registered nursing/registered nurse.
Academics *Calendar:* quarters. *Degrees:* associate and bachelor's.
Freshman Application Contact Director of Recruitment, ITT Technical Institute, 8301 Southpark Circle, Suite 100, Orlando, FL 32819. *Phone:* 407-371-6000. *Toll-free phone:* 877-201-4367. *Web site:* http://www.itt-tech.edu/.

ITT Technical Institute
Pinellas Park, Florida

- **Proprietary** primarily 2-year, part of ITT Educational Services, Inc.
- **Coed**

Majors Business administration and management; communications technology; computer and information systems security; drafting and design technology; electrical, electronic and communications engineering technology; forensic science and technology; graphic communications; legal assistant/paralegal; network and system administration; project management; registered nursing/registered nurse.
Academics *Degrees:* associate and bachelor's.
Student Life *Housing:* college housing not available.
Freshman Application Contact Director of Recruitment, ITT Technical Institute, 877 Executive Center Drive W, Suite 100, Pinellas Park, FL 33702. *Phone:* 727-209-4700. *Toll-free phone:* 866-488-5084. *Web site:* http://www.itt-tech.edu/.

ITT Technical Institute
Tallahassee, Florida

- **Proprietary** primarily 2-year
- **Coed**

Majors Business administration and management; communications technology; computer and information systems security; drafting and design technology; electrical, electronic and communications engineering technology; forensic science and technology; graphic communications; legal assistant/paralegal; network and system administration; project management; registered nursing/registered nurse.
Academics *Degrees:* associate and bachelor's.
Freshman Application Contact Director of Recruitment, ITT Technical Institute, 2639 North Monroe Street, Building A, Suite 100, Tallahassee, FL 32303. *Phone:* 850-422-6300. *Toll-free phone:* 877-230-3559. *Web site:* http://www.itt-tech.edu/.

ITT Technical Institute
Tampa, Florida

- **Proprietary** primarily 2-year, founded 1981, part of ITT Educational Services, Inc.
- **Suburban** campus
- **Coed**

Majors Business administration and management; communications technology; computer and information systems security; construction management; criminal justice/law enforcement administration; drafting and design technology; electrical, electronic and communications engineering technology; forensic science and technology; game and interactive media design; graphic communications; health information/medical records technology; network and system administration; project management; registered nursing/registered nurse.
Academics *Calendar:* quarters. *Degrees:* associate and bachelor's.
Student Life *Housing:* college housing not available.

Freshman Application Contact Director of Recruitment, ITT Technical Institute, 4809 Memorial Highway, Tampa, FL 33634-7151. *Phone:* 813-885-2244. *Toll-free phone:* 800-825-2831. *Web site:* http://www.itt-tech.edu/.

Kaplan College, Jacksonville Campus
Jacksonville, Florida

- **Proprietary** 2-year
- **Coed**

Majors Computer systems networking and telecommunications; criminal justice/law enforcement administration.
Academics *Degree:* diplomas and associate.
Freshman Application Contact Director of Admissions, Kaplan College, Jacksonville Campus, 7450 Beach Boulevard, Jacksonville, FL 32216. *Phone:* 904-855-2405. *Web site:* http://jacksonville.kaplancollege.com/.

Kaplan College, Pembroke Pines Campus
Pembroke Pines, Florida

- **Proprietary** 2-year
- **Coed**

Majors Computer systems networking and telecommunications; criminal justice/law enforcement administration; medical office management.
Academics *Degree:* diplomas and associate.
Freshman Application Contact Kaplan College, Pembroke Pines Campus, 10131 Pines Boulevard, Pembroke Pines, FL 33026. *Phone:* 954-885-3500. *Toll-free phone:* 800-935-1857. *Web site:* http://pembroke-pines.kaplancollege.com/.

Keiser Career College–Greenacres
Greenacres, Florida

Freshman Application Contact Admissions Office, Keiser Career College–Greenacres, 6812 Forest Hill Boulevard, Suite D-1, Greenacres, FL 33413. *Web site:* http://www.keisercareer.edu/kcc2009/ga_campus.htm.

Key College
Dania, Florida

Director of Admissions Mr. Ronald H. Dooley, President and Director of Admissions, Key College, 225 East Dania Beach Boulevard, Dania, FL 33004. *Phone:* 954-581-2223 Ext. 23. *Toll-free phone:* 800-581-8292. *Web site:* http://www.keycollege.edu/.

Lake-Sumter Community College
Leesburg, Florida

- **State and locally supported** 2-year, founded 1962, part of Florida College System
- **Suburban** 112-acre campus with easy access to Orlando
- **Endowment** $3.9 million
- **Coed**

Undergraduates 1,641 full-time, 3,288 part-time. 1% are from out of state; 5% transferred in.
Faculty *Student/faculty ratio:* 17:1.
Academics *Calendar:* semesters. *Degree:* certificates, diplomas, and associate. *Special study options:* academic remediation for entering students, adult/continuing education programs, advanced placement credit, cooperative education, distance learning, double majors, independent study, internships, off-campus study, part-time degree program, services for LD students, summer session for credit.
Student Life *Campus security:* 24-hour emergency response devices.
Athletics Member NJCAA.
Financial Aid Of all full-time matriculated undergraduates who enrolled in 2009, 420 applied for aid, 420 were judged to have need. 39 Federal Work-Study jobs (averaging $1701). In 2009, 95. *Average financial aid package:* $3166. *Average need-based gift aid:* $1912. *Average non-need-based aid:* $770.
Applying *Options:* electronic application. *Application fee:* $25. *Required:* high school transcript.
Freshman Application Contact Ms. Bonnie Yanick, Enrollment Specialist, Lake-Sumter Community College, 9501 U.S. Highway 441, Leesburg, FL 34788-8751. *Phone:* 352-365-3561. *Fax:* 352-365-3553. *E-mail:* admissinquiry@lscc.edu. *Web site:* http://www.lscc.edu/.

Le Cordon Bleu College of Culinary Arts in Orlando

Orlando, Florida

Admissions Office Contact Le Cordon Bleu College of Culinary Arts in Orlando, 8511 Commodity Circle, Suite 100, Orlando, FL 32819. *Toll-free phone:* 888-793-3222. *Web site:* http://www.chefs.edu/Orlando.

Le Cordon Bleu College of Culinary Arts, Miami

Miramar, Florida

Freshman Application Contact Admissions Office, Le Cordon Bleu College of Culinary Arts, Miami, 3221 Enterprise Way, Miramar, FL 33025. *Phone:* 954-628-4000. *Toll-free phone:* 888-569-3222. *Web site:* http://www.miamiculinary.com/.

Lincoln College of Technology

West Palm Beach, Florida

Director of Admissions Mr. Kevin Cassidy, Director of Admissions, Lincoln College of Technology, 2410 Metro Centre Boulevard, West Palm Beach, FL 33407. *Phone:* 561-842-8324 Ext. 117. *Fax:* 561-842-9503. *Web site:* http://www.lincolnedu.com/.

MedVance Institute

Palm Springs, Florida

Director of Admissions Campus Director, MedVance Institute, 1630 South Congress Avenue, Palm Springs, FL 33461. *Phone:* 561-304-3466. *Toll-free phone:* 877-606-3382. *Fax:* 561-304-3471. *Web site:* http://www.medvance.edu/.

Miami Dade College

Miami, Florida

- **State and locally supported** primarily 2-year, founded 1960, part of Florida College System
- **Urban** campus
- **Endowment** $176.1 million
- **Coed,** 63,766 undergraduate students, 42% full-time, 59% women, 41% men

Undergraduates 26,634 full-time, 37,132 part-time. Students come from 45 states and territories; 186 other countries; 1% are from out of state; 16% Black or African American, non-Hispanic/Latino; 70% Hispanic/Latino; 1% Asian, non-Hispanic/Latino; 0.1% Native Hawaiian or other Pacific Islander, non-Hispanic/Latino; 0.1% American Indian or Alaska Native, non-Hispanic/Latino; 0.2% Two or more races, non-Hispanic/Latino; 2% Race/ethnicity unknown; 2% international; 2% transferred in.

Freshmen *Admission:* 11,764 applied, 11,764 admitted, 13,498 enrolled.

Faculty *Total:* 2,462, 29% full-time, 19% with terminal degrees. *Student/faculty ratio:* 30:1.

Majors Accounting technology and bookkeeping; administrative assistant and secretarial science; aeronautics/aviation/aerospace science and technology; agriculture; airline pilot and flight crew; air traffic control; American studies; anthropology; architectural drafting and CAD/CADD; architectural engineering technology; art; Asian studies; audiology and speech-language pathology; aviation/airway management; behavioral sciences; biology/biological sciences; biology teacher education; biomedical technology; biotechnology; business administration and management; business administration, management and operations related; chemistry; chemistry teacher education; child development; cinematography and film/video production; civil engineering technology; clinical/medical laboratory technology; commercial and advertising art; comparative literature; computer engineering technology; computer graphics; computer programming; computer science; computer software technology; computer technology/computer systems technology; construction engineering technology; cooking and related culinary arts; court reporting; criminal justice/law enforcement administration; criminal justice/police science; culinary arts; dance; data processing and data processing technology; dental hygiene; diagnostic medical sonography and ultrasound technology; dietetics; dietetic technology; drafting and design technology; dramatic/theater arts; economics; education; education related; electrical and electronic engineering technologies related; electrical, electronic and communications engineering technology; elementary education; emergency medical technology (EMT paramedic); engi-

neering; engineering related; engineering technology; English; environmental engineering technology; finance; fire science/firefighting; food science; forestry; French; funeral service and mortuary science; general studies; geology/earth science; German; health information/medical records administration; health/medical preparatory programs related; health professions related; health services/allied health/health sciences; heating, air conditioning, ventilation and refrigeration maintenance technology; heating, ventilation, air conditioning and refrigeration engineering technology; histologic technician; history; homeland security, law enforcement, firefighting and protective services related; horticultural science; hospitality administration; humanities; human services; industrial technology; information science/studies; interior design; international relations and affairs; Italian; journalism; kindergarten/preschool education; landscaping and groundskeeping; Latin American studies; legal administrative assistant/secretary; legal assistant/paralegal; management information systems; marketing/marketing management; mass communication/media; mathematics; mathematics teacher education; medical/clinical assistant; middle school education; music; music performance; music teacher education; natural sciences; nonprofit management; nuclear medical technology; ophthalmic technology; ornamental horticulture; parks, recreation and leisure; philosophy; photographic and film/video technology; photography; physical education teaching and coaching; physical sciences; physical therapy technology; physics; physics teacher education; plant nursery management; political science and government; Portuguese; pre-engineering; psychology; public administration; radio and television; radio and television broadcasting technology; radiologic technology/science; recording arts technology; registered nursing/registered nurse; respiratory care therapy; respiratory therapy technician; science teacher education; sign language interpretation and translation; social sciences; social work; sociology; Spanish; special education; substance abuse/addiction counseling; teacher assistant/aide; telecommunications technology; tourism and travel services management.

Academics *Calendar:* 16-16-6-6. *Degrees:* certificates, associate, bachelor's, and postbachelor's certificates. *Special study options:* academic remediation for entering students, accelerated degree program, adult/continuing education programs, advanced placement credit, cooperative education, distance learning, English as a second language, freshman honors college, honors programs, independent study, internships, off-campus study, part-time degree program, services for LD students, study abroad, summer session for credit. *ROTC:* Army (b), Air Force (b).

Library Miami Dade College Learning Resources plus 8 others with 365,224 titles, 29,847 audiovisual materials, an OPAC, a Web page.

Student Life *Housing:* college housing not available. *Activities and Organizations:* drama/theater group, student-run newspaper, radio and television station, choral group, Student Government Association, Phi Theta Kappa, Phi Beta Lambda (Business), Future Educators of America Professional, Kappa Delta Pi Honor Society (Education), national fraternities. *Campus security:* 24-hour emergency response devices and patrols, mass communication emergency notification systems. *Student services:* personal/psychological counseling, legal services.

Athletics Member NCAA, NJCAA. All NCAA Division I. *Intercollegiate sports:* baseball M(s), basketball M(s)/W(s), softball W(s), volleyball W(s).

Costs (2011–12) *One-time required fee:* $30. *Tuition:* state resident $2365 full-time, $79 per credit hour part-time; nonresident $9466 full-time, $316 per credit hour part-time. Full-time tuition and fees vary according to course load, degree level, and program. Part-time tuition and fees vary according to course load, degree level, and program. *Required fees:* $780 full-time, $27 per credit hour part-time. *Waivers:* employees or children of employees.

Financial Aid Of all full-time matriculated undergraduates who enrolled in 2010, 800 Federal Work-Study jobs (averaging $5000). 125 state and other part-time jobs (averaging $5000).

Applying *Options:* electronic application, early admission. *Application fee:* $30. *Required:* high school transcript. *Required for some:* some programs such as Honors College have additional admissions requirements. *Application deadlines:* rolling (freshmen), rolling (out-of-state freshmen), rolling (transfers). *Notification:* continuous (freshmen), continuous (out-of-state freshmen), continuous (transfers).

Freshman Application Contact Mrs. Dulce Beltran, College Registrar, Miami Dade College, 11011 SW 104th Street, Miami, FL 33176. *Phone:* 305-237-2206. *Fax:* 305-237-2532. *E-mail:* dbeltran@mdc.edu. *Web site:* http://www.mdc.edu/.

North Florida Community College

Madison, Florida

Freshman Application Contact Mr. Bobby Scott, North Florida Community College, 325 Northwest Turner Davis Drive, Madison, FL 32340. *Phone:* 850-973-9450. *Toll-free phone:* 866-937-6322. *Fax:* 850-973-1697. *Web site:* http://www.nfcc.edu/.

Northwest Florida State College
Niceville, Florida

- **State and locally supported** primarily 2-year, founded 1963, part of Florida College System
- **Small-town** 264-acre campus
- **Endowment** $28.6 million
- **Coed**, 10,317 undergraduate students

Undergraduates Students come from 18 states and territories.

Faculty *Total:* 310, 31% full-time. *Student/faculty ratio:* 15:1.

Majors Accounting; administrative assistant and secretarial science; art; atmospheric sciences and meteorology; automobile/automotive mechanics technology; avionics maintenance technology; biological and physical sciences; biology/biological sciences; business administration and management; chemistry; child development; clinical laboratory science/medical technology; commercial and advertising art; computer engineering related; computer programming; computer programming (specific applications); computer science; computer systems networking and telecommunications; construction engineering technology; criminal justice/law enforcement administration; criminal justice/police science; data entry/microcomputer applications; dietetics; divinity/ministry; drafting and design technology; education; electrical, electronic and communications engineering technology; elementary education; engineering; family and consumer sciences/home economics teacher education; fashion merchandising; finance; foods, nutrition, and wellness; heating, air conditioning, ventilation and refrigeration maintenance technology; hotel/motel administration; humanities; human resources management; information technology; interior design; kindergarten/preschool education; legal assistant/paralegal; legal studies; liberal arts and sciences/liberal studies; mathematics; mathematics teacher education; modern languages; music; physical education teaching and coaching; physics; purchasing, procurement/acquisitions and contracts management; real estate; registered nursing/registered nurse; science teacher education; social sciences; social work; welding technology; word processing.

Academics *Calendar:* semesters plus summer sessions. *Degrees:* certificates, associate, and bachelor's. *Special study options:* academic remediation for entering students, accelerated degree program, adult/continuing education programs, advanced placement credit, distance learning, English as a second language, independent study, part-time degree program, services for LD students, summer session for credit. *ROTC:* Army (b).

Library Northwest Florida State College Learning Resources Center with 106,383 titles, 399 serial subscriptions, 10,219 audiovisual materials, an OPAC, a Web page.

Student Life *Housing:* college housing not available. *Activities and Organizations:* drama/theater group, choral group. *Student services:* women's center.

Athletics Member NJCAA. *Intercollegiate sports:* baseball M(s), basketball M(s)/W(s), softball W(s). *Intramural sports:* basketball M/W.

Standardized Tests *Required for some:* ACT, SAT I, ACT ASSET, MAPS, or Florida College Entry Placement Test are used for placement not admission.

Applying *Options:* electronic application. *Required:* high school transcript. *Application deadlines:* rolling (freshmen), rolling (transfers). *Notification:* continuous (freshmen), continuous (transfers).

Freshman Application Contact Ms. Christine Bishop, Dean Enrollment Services, Northwest Florida State College, 100 College Boulevard, Niceville, FL 32578. *Phone:* 850-729-5373. *Fax:* 850-729-5323. *E-mail:* registrar@nwfsc.edu. *Web site:* http://www.nwfsc.edu/.

Palm Beach State College
Lake Worth, Florida

- **State-supported** primarily 2-year, founded 1933, part of Florida College System
- **Urban** 150-acre campus with easy access to West Palm Beach
- **Endowment** $23.0 million
- **Coed**, 29,534 undergraduate students, 37% full-time, 58% women, 42% men

Undergraduates 10,913 full-time, 18,621 part-time. Students come from 49 states and territories; 146 other countries; 5% are from out of state; 5% transferred in.

Freshmen *Admission:* 5,127 applied, 5,127 admitted, 5,127 enrolled.

Faculty *Total:* 1,473, 19% full-time, 16% with terminal degrees. *Student/faculty ratio:* 43:1.

Majors Accounting; administrative assistant and secretarial science; airline pilot and flight crew; apparel and textiles; art; art history, criticism and conservation; biology/biological sciences; botany/plant biology; building/construction finishing, management, and inspection related; business administration and management; ceramic arts and ceramics; chemistry; commercial and advertising art; comparative literature; computer and information sciences and support services related; computer programming; computer programming (specific applications); computer science; criminal justice/law enforcement administration; criminal justice/police science; data processing and data processing technology; dental hygiene; drafting and design technology; dramatic/theater arts; economics; education; electrical, electronic and communications engineering technology; elementary education; English; family and consumer sciences/human sciences; fashion/apparel design; fashion merchandising; finance; fire science/firefighting; foods, nutrition, and wellness; health teacher education; history; hotel/motel administration; industrial radiologic technology; interior design; journalism; kindergarten/preschool education; legal administrative assistant/secretary; liberal arts and sciences/liberal studies; marketing/marketing management; mass communication/media; mathematics; music; network and system administration; occupational therapy; philosophy; photography; physical education teaching and coaching; physical sciences; physical therapy; political science and government; pre-engineering; psychology; registered nursing/registered nurse; religious studies; social sciences; social work; special products marketing; surveying technology; web page, digital/multimedia and information resources design; word processing; zoology/animal biology.

Academics *Calendar:* semesters. *Degrees:* certificates, diplomas, associate, and bachelor's. *Special study options:* academic remediation for entering students, adult/continuing education programs, advanced placement credit, cooperative education, distance learning, double majors, English as a second language, freshman honors college, honors programs, independent study, internships, off-campus study, part-time degree program, services for LD students, student-designed majors, study abroad, summer session for credit.

Library Harold C. Manor Library plus 3 others with 151,000 titles, 1,474 serial subscriptions, an OPAC, a Web page.

Student Life *Housing:* college housing not available. *Activities and Organizations:* drama/theater group, student-run newspaper, choral group, student government, Phi Theta Kappa, Students for International Understanding, Black Student Union, Drama Club, national fraternities. *Campus security:* 24-hour emergency response devices and patrols. *Student services:* health clinic, women's center.

Athletics Member NJCAA. *Intercollegiate sports:* baseball M(s), basketball M(s)/W(s), softball W(s), volleyball W(s).

Standardized Tests *Recommended:* SAT and SAT Subject Tests or ACT (for admission).

Costs (2011–12) *One-time required fee:* $20. *Tuition:* state resident $2304 full-time, $96 per credit hour part-time; nonresident $8376 full-time, $349 per credit hour part-time. *Required fees:* $10 full-time, $10 per term part-time. *Waivers:* employees or children of employees.

Applying *Options:* electronic application, early admission, deferred entrance. *Application fee:* $20. *Application deadlines:* 8/20 (freshmen), 8/20 (transfers). *Notification:* continuous until 8/20 (freshmen), continuous until 8/20 (transfers).

Freshman Application Contact Ms. Anne Guiler, Coordinator of Distance Learning, Palm Beach State College, Lake Worth, FL 33461. *Phone:* 561-868-3032. *Fax:* 561-868-3584. *E-mail:* enrollmt@palmbeachstate.edu. *Web site:* http://www.palmbeachstate.edu/.

Pasco-Hernando Community College
New Port Richey, Florida

- **State-supported** 2-year, founded 1972, part of Florida College System
- **Suburban** 142-acre campus with easy access to Tampa
- **Endowment** $34.7 million
- **Coed**, 12,167 undergraduate students

Undergraduates 1% are from out of state; 5% Black or African American, non-Hispanic/Latino; 8% Hispanic/Latino; 2% Asian, non-Hispanic/Latino; 0.5% American Indian or Alaska Native, non-Hispanic/Latino; 8% Race/ethnicity unknown.

Faculty *Total:* 390, 30% full-time. *Student/faculty ratio:* 26:1.

Majors Business administration and management; computer programming related; computer programming (specific applications); computer systems networking and telecommunications; computer technology/computer systems technology; criminal justice/law enforcement administration; dental hygiene; drafting and design technology; e-commerce; emergency medical technology (EMT paramedic); human services; information technology; legal assistant/paralegal; liberal arts and sciences/liberal studies; marketing/marketing management; physical therapy technology; radiologic technology/science; registered nursing/registered nurse; web page, digital/multimedia and information resources design.

Academics *Calendar:* semesters. *Degree:* certificates, diplomas, and associate. *Special study options:* academic remediation for entering students, accelerated degree program, adult/continuing education programs, advanced placement credit, cooperative education, distance learning, double majors, honors programs, independent study, internships, off-campus study, part-time degree program, services for LD students, study abroad, summer session for credit. *ROTC:* Army (c).

Library Alric Pottberg Library plus 3 others with 183,588 titles, an OPAC, a Web page.

Student Life *Housing:* college housing not available. *Activities and Organizations:* drama/theater group, choral group, Student Government Association, Phi Theta Kappa, Phi Beta Lambda, Human Services, PHCC Cares. *Campus security:* 24-hour patrols. *Student services:* personal/psychological counseling.

Athletics *Intercollegiate sports:* baseball M(s), basketball M(s), cross-country running W(s), softball W(s), volleyball W(s). *Intramural sports:* cheerleading M/W.

Standardized Tests *Recommended:* SAT and SAT Subject Tests or ACT (for admission), CPT.

Costs (2011–12) *Tuition:* state resident $95 per credit hour part-time; nonresident $361 per credit hour part-time. *Payment plans:* installment, deferred payment.

Financial Aid Of all full-time matriculated undergraduates who enrolled in 2010, 83 Federal Work-Study jobs (averaging $3201).

Applying *Options:* electronic application. *Application fee:* $25. *Required:* high school transcript. *Application deadlines:* rolling (freshmen), rolling (transfers). *Notification:* continuous (freshmen), continuous (transfers).

Freshman Application Contact Ms. Debra Bullard, Director of Admissions and Student Records, Pasco-Hernando Community College, New Port Richey, FL 34654-5199. *Phone:* 727-816-3261. *Toll-free phone:* 877-TRY-PHCC. *Fax:* 727-816-3389. *E-mail:* bullard@phcc.edu. *Web site:* http://www.phcc.edu/.

Pensacola State College
Pensacola, Florida

- **State-supported** primarily 2-year, founded 1948, part of Florida College System
- **Urban** 130-acre campus
- **Coed,** 11,531 undergraduate students, 42% full-time, 62% women, 38% men

Undergraduates 4,799 full-time, 6,732 part-time. Students come from 15 states and territories; 1% are from out of state; 16% Black or African American, non-Hispanic/Latino; 5% Hispanic/Latino; 3% Asian, non-Hispanic/Latino; 0.3% Native Hawaiian or other Pacific Islander, non-Hispanic/Latino; 1% American Indian or Alaska Native, non-Hispanic/Latino; 4% Two or more races, non-Hispanic/Latino; 1% Race/ethnicity unknown; 0.4% international; 6% transferred in.

Freshmen *Admission:* 1,359 enrolled.

Faculty *Total:* 203, 100% full-time, 20% with terminal degrees. *Student/faculty ratio:* 25:1.

Majors Accounting; accounting technology and bookkeeping; administrative assistant and secretarial science; agriculture; art; art teacher education; automobile/automotive mechanics technology; banking and financial support services; biochemistry; biology/biological sciences; botany/plant biology; building/property maintenance; business administration and management; business administration, management and operations related; business/commerce; chemical technology; chemistry; child-care and support services management; child-care provision; cinematography and film/video production; civil engineering; civil engineering technology; commercial and advertising art; communications technology; computer and information sciences; computer and information sciences related; computer engineering; computer programming; computer programming (specific applications); computer science; computer systems analysis; construction engineering technology; consumer services and advocacy; cooking and related culinary arts; criminal justice/law enforcement administration; dental hygiene; diagnostic medical sonography and ultrasound technology; dietetics; drafting and design technology; dramatic/theater arts; early childhood education; education; electrical and electronics engineering; electrical, electronic and communications engineering technology; elementary education; emergency medical technology (EMT paramedic); engineering; English; executive assistant/executive secretary; fire prevention and safety technology; fire science/firefighting; food service systems administration; foods, nutrition, and wellness; forest resources production and management; forestry; forest technology; geology/earth science; graphic design; hazardous materials management and waste technology; health information/medical records administration; history; hospitality administration; hospitality and recreation marketing; information science/studies; journalism; landscaping and groundskeeping; legal administrative assistant/secretary; legal assistant/paralegal; liberal arts and sciences/liberal studies; management information systems; management information systems and services related; management science; manufacturing engineering technology; mathematics; medical radiologic technology; music; music teacher education; natural resources management and policy; nursing science; office management; operations management; ornamental horticulture; philosophy; photographic and film/video technology; physical education teaching and coaching; physical therapy technology; physics; pre-dentistry studies; pre-law studies; premedical studies; prenursing studies; pre-pharmacy studies; pre-veterinary studies; psychology; registered nursing/registered nurse; religious studies; restaurant, culinary, and catering management; sociology; special education; speech communication and rhetoric; zoology/animal biology.

Academics *Calendar:* semesters. *Degrees:* certificates, diplomas, associate, and bachelor's. *Special study options:* academic remediation for entering students, adult/continuing education programs, advanced placement credit, cooperative education, distance learning, double majors, external degree program, honors programs, independent study, part-time degree program, services for LD students, summer session for credit. *ROTC:* Army (b).

Library Learning Resource Center plus 2 others.

Student Life *Housing:* college housing not available. *Activities and Organizations:* drama/theater group, student-run newspaper, choral group. *Campus security:* 24-hour emergency response devices and patrols, student patrols, late-night transport/escort service. *Student services:* health clinic, personal/psychological counseling.

Athletics Member NJCAA. *Intercollegiate sports:* baseball M(s), basketball M(s)/W(s), softball W(s), volleyball W. *Intramural sports:* archery M/W, badminton M/W, basketball M/W, bowling M/W, cross-country running M/W, gymnastics M/W, racquetball M/W, sailing M/W, swimming and diving M/W, tennis M/W, track and field M/W, volleyball M/W, weight lifting M/W, wrestling M.

Costs (2011–12) *One-time required fee:* $30. *Tuition:* state resident $2352 full-time, $98 per credit hour part-time; nonresident $8870 full-time, $370 per credit hour part-time. Full-time tuition and fees vary according to degree level. Part-time tuition and fees vary according to degree level. *Waivers:* senior citizens and employees or children of employees.

Financial Aid Of all full-time matriculated undergraduates who enrolled in 2010, 120 Federal Work-Study jobs (averaging $3000).

Applying *Options:* early admission. *Application fee:* $30. *Required:* high school transcript. *Application deadlines:* 8/30 (freshmen), 8/30 (transfers). *Notification:* continuous until 8/30 (freshmen), continuous until 8/30 (transfers).

Freshman Application Contact Ms. Martha Caughey, Registrar, Pensacola State College, 1000 College Boulevard, Pensacola, FL 32504-8998. *Phone:* 850-484-1600. *Fax:* 850-484-1829. *Web site:* http://www.pensacolastate.edu/.

Polk State College
Winter Haven, Florida

- **State-supported** primarily 2-year, founded 1964, part of Florida College System
- **Suburban** 98-acre campus with easy access to Orlando, Tampa
- **Endowment** $14.7 million
- **Coed,** 11,529 undergraduate students, 34% full-time, 63% women, 37% men

Undergraduates 3,914 full-time, 7,615 part-time. Students come from 9 states and territories; 60 other countries; 1% are from out of state; 19% Black or African American, non-Hispanic/Latino; 15% Hispanic/Latino; 2% Asian, non-Hispanic/Latino; 0.1% Native Hawaiian or other Pacific Islander, non-Hispanic/Latino; 0.3% American Indian or Alaska Native, non-Hispanic/Latino; 2% Two or more races, non-Hispanic/Latino; 3% Race/ethnicity unknown; 0.8% international; 2% transferred in. *Retention:* 62% of full-time freshmen returned.

Freshmen *Admission:* 2,055 enrolled. *Test scores:* SAT math scores over 500: 56%; SAT writing scores over 500: 45%; ACT scores over 18: 100%; SAT math scores over 600: 2%; SAT writing scores over 600: 5%; ACT scores over 24: 20%; SAT math scores over 700: 1%; ACT scores over 30: 2%.

Faculty *Total:* 707, 26% full-time, 13% with terminal degrees. *Student/faculty ratio:* 19:1.

Majors Accounting technology and bookkeeping; business administration and management; business administration, management and operations related; cardiovascular technology; child development; corrections; criminal justice/law enforcement administration; data processing and data processing technology; diagnostic medical sonography and ultrasound technology; electrical and power transmission installation; emergency medical technology (EMT paramedic); finance; fire science/firefighting; health information/medical records administration; information science/studies; liberal arts and sciences/liberal studies; marketing/marketing management; medical administrative assistant and medical secretary; occupational therapist assistant; physical therapy technology; pre-engineering; radiologic technology/science; registered nursing/registered nurse; respiratory care therapy; transportation/mobility management.

Academics *Calendar:* semesters 16-16-6-6. *Degrees:* certificates, associate, and bachelor's. *Special study options:* academic remediation for entering students, accelerated degree program, adult/continuing education programs, advanced placement credit, cooperative education, distance learning, double majors, English as a second language, honors programs, independent study, off-campus study, part-time degree program, services for LD students, study abroad, summer session for credit. *ROTC:* Army (c).

Library Polk State College Libraries plus 1 other with 162,767 titles, 217 serial subscriptions, 3,434 audiovisual materials, an OPAC, a Web page.

Student Life *Housing:* college housing not available. *Activities and Organizations:* drama/theater group, choral group, Florida Student Nursing Association, SLAM (Student's Living a Message), Eagleteers, Student Government Association, SALO (Student Activities and Leadership Office). *Campus security:* 24-hour emergency response devices and patrols. *Student services:* personal/psychological counseling.

Athletics Member NJCAA. *Intercollegiate sports:* baseball M(s), basketball M(s), soccer W(s), softball W(s), volleyball W(s). *Intramural sports:* basketball M/W, bowling M/W, football M/W, volleyball M/W.

Costs (2011–12) *Tuition:* state resident $3114 full-time, $104 per credit hour part-time; nonresident $11,677 full-time, $389 per credit hour part-time. Full-time tuition and fees vary according to course level, course load, and degree level. Part-time tuition and fees vary according to course level, course load, and degree level. *Waivers:* employees or children of employees.

Applying *Options:* electronic application, early admission, deferred entrance. *Required:* high school transcript. *Application deadlines:* rolling (freshmen), rolling (transfers). *Notification:* continuous (freshmen), continuous (transfers).

Freshman Application Contact Polk State College, 999 Avenue H, NE, Winter Haven, FL 33881-4299. *Phone:* 863-297-1010 Ext. 5016. *Web site:* http://www.polk.edu/.

Rasmussen College Fort Myers

Fort Myers, Florida

- **Proprietary** primarily 2-year, part of Rasmussen College System
- **Suburban** campus
- **Coed,** 723 undergraduate students

Faculty *Student/faculty ratio:* 22:1.

Majors Accounting; accounting and business/management; business administration and management; computer and information systems security; computer science; computer software engineering; corrections and criminal justice related; early childhood education; graphic communications related; health/health-care administration; health information/medical records administration; health information/medical records technology; human resources management; human services; information resources management; legal assistant/paralegal; management information systems and services related; marketing/marketing management; medical administrative assistant and medical secretary; medical/clinical assistant; pharmacy technician; registered nursing/registered nurse; web page, digital/multimedia and information resources design.

Academics *Degrees:* certificates, diplomas, associate, and bachelor's. *Special study options:* academic remediation for entering students, accelerated degree program, adult/continuing education programs, distance learning, double majors, internships, part-time degree program, summer session for credit.

Library Rasmussen College Library - Fort Myers with 1,846 titles, 47 serial subscriptions, 120 audiovisual materials, an OPAC, a Web page.

Student Life *Housing:* college housing not available.

Standardized Tests *Required:* Internal Exam (for admission).

Costs (2012–13) *Tuition:* $12,600 full-time. Full-time tuition and fees vary according to course level, course load, degree level, location, and program. Part-time tuition and fees vary according to course level, course load, degree level, location, and program. *Required fees:* $40 full-time. *Payment plans:* installment, deferred payment. *Waivers:* employees or children of employees.

Applying *Options:* electronic application, early admission, deferred entrance. *Application fee:* $20. *Required:* high school transcript, minimum 2.0 GPA, interview. *Application deadlines:* rolling (freshmen), rolling (transfers).

Freshman Application Contact Susan Hammerstrom, Director of Admissions, Rasmussen College Fort Myers, 9160 Forum Corporate Parkway, Suite 100, Fort Myers, FL 33905. *Phone:* 239-477-2100. *Toll-free phone:* 888-549-6755. *E-mail:* susan.hammerstrom@rasmussen.edu. *Web site:* http://www.rasmussen.edu/.

Rasmussen College New Port Richey

New Port Richey, Florida

- **Proprietary** primarily 2-year, part of Rasmussen College System
- **Suburban** campus
- **Coed,** 896 undergraduate students

Faculty *Student/faculty ratio:* 22:1.

Majors Accounting; accounting and business/management; business administration and management; computer and information systems security; computer science; computer software engineering; corrections and criminal justice related; early childhood education; graphic communications related; health/health-care administration; health information/medical records administration; health information/medical records technology; human resources management; human services; information resources management; legal assistant/paralegal; management information systems and services related; marketing/marketing management; medical administrative assistant and medical secre-

tary; medical/clinical assistant; pharmacy technician; registered nursing/registered nurse; web page, digital/multimedia and information resources design.

Academics *Degrees:* certificates, diplomas, associate, and bachelor's. *Special study options:* academic remediation for entering students, accelerated degree program, adult/continuing education programs, distance learning, double majors, internships, part-time degree program, summer session for credit.

Library Rasmussen College Library - New Port Richey with 1,893 titles, 12 serial subscriptions, 74 audiovisual materials, an OPAC, a Web page.

Student Life *Housing:* college housing not available.

Standardized Tests *Required:* Internal Exam (for admission).

Costs (2012–13) *Tuition:* $12,600 full-time. Full-time tuition and fees vary according to course level, course load, degree level, location, and program. Part-time tuition and fees vary according to course level, course load, degree level, location, and program. *Required fees:* $40 full-time. *Payment plans:* installment, deferred payment. *Waivers:* employees or children of employees.

Financial Aid Of all full-time matriculated undergraduates who enrolled in 2010, 6 Federal Work-Study jobs.

Applying *Options:* electronic application, early admission, deferred entrance. *Application fee:* $20. *Required:* high school transcript, minimum 2.0 GPA, interview. *Application deadlines:* rolling (freshmen), rolling (transfers).

Freshman Application Contact Susan Hammerstrom, Director of Admissions, Rasmussen College New Port Richey, 8661 Citizens Drive, New Port Richey, FL 34654. *Phone:* 727-942-0069. *Toll-free phone:* 888-549-6755. *E-mail:* susan.hammerstrom@rasmussen.edu. *Web site:* http://www.rasmussen.edu/.

Rasmussen College Ocala

Ocala, Florida

- **Proprietary** primarily 2-year, founded 1984, part of Rasmussen College System
- **Suburban** campus with easy access to Orlando
- **Coed, primarily women,** 1,256 undergraduate students

Faculty *Student/faculty ratio:* 22:1.

Majors Accounting; accounting and business/management; business administration and management; computer and information systems security; computer science; computer software engineering; corrections and criminal justice related; early childhood education; graphic communications related; health/health-care administration; health information/medical records administration; health information/medical records technology; human resources management; human services; information resources management; legal assistant/paralegal; management information systems and services related; marketing/marketing management; medical administrative assistant and medical secretary; medical/clinical assistant; pharmacy technician; web page, digital/multimedia and information resources design.

Academics *Calendar:* quarters. *Degrees:* certificates, diplomas, associate, and bachelor's. *Special study options:* academic remediation for entering students, accelerated degree program, adult/continuing education programs, distance learning, double majors, internships, part-time degree program, summer session for credit.

Library Rasmussen College Library - Ocala with 1,719 titles, 25 serial subscriptions, 151 audiovisual materials, an OPAC, a Web page.

Student Life *Housing:* college housing not available.

Standardized Tests *Required:* Internal Exam (for admission).

Costs (2012–13) *Tuition:* $12,600 full-time. Full-time tuition and fees vary according to course level, course load, degree level, location, and program. Part-time tuition and fees vary according to course level, course load, degree level, location, and program. *Required fees:* $40 full-time. *Payment plans:* installment, deferred payment. *Waivers:* employees or children of employees.

Applying *Options:* electronic application, early admission, deferred entrance. *Application fee:* $20. *Required:* high school transcript, minimum 2.0 GPA, interview. *Application deadlines:* rolling (freshmen), rolling (transfers).

Freshman Application Contact Susan Hammerstrom, Director of Admissions, Rasmussen College Ocala, 2221 Southwest 19th Avenue Road, Ocala, FL 34471. *Phone:* 352-629-1941. *Toll-free phone:* 888-549-6755. *E-mail:* susan.hammerstrom@rasmussen.edu. *Web site:* http://www.rasmussen.edu/.

Remington College–Largo Campus

Largo, Florida

Director of Admissions Kathy McCabe, Director of Recruitment, Remington College–Largo Campus, 8550 Ulmerton Road, Largo, FL 33771. *Phone:* 727-532-1999. *Toll-free phone:* 800-560-6192. *Fax:* 727-530-7710. *E-mail:* kathy.mccabe@remingtoncollege.edu. *Web site:* http://www.remingtoncollege.edu/.

Remington College–Tampa Campus
Tampa, Florida

Freshman Application Contact Remington College–Tampa Campus, 2410 East Busch Boulevard, Tampa, FL 33612-8410. *Phone:* 813-932-0701. *Toll-free phone:* 800-560-6192. *Web site:* http://www.remingtoncollege.edu/.

St. Johns River Community College
Palatka, Florida

Director of Admissions Dean of Admissions and Records, St. Johns River Community College, 5001 Saint Johns Avenue, Palatka, FL 32177-3897. *Phone:* 386-312-4032. *Fax:* 386-312-4289. *Web site:* http://www.sjrcc.edu/.

Sanford-Brown Institute
Fort Lauderdale, Florida

Director of Admissions Scott Nelowet, Sanford-Brown Institute, 1201 West Cypress Creek Road, Fort Lauderdale, FL 33309. *Phone:* 904-363-6221. *Toll-free phone:* 888-742-0333. *Fax:* 904-363-6824. *E-mail:* snelowet@sbjacksonville.com. *Web site:* http://www.sbftlauderdale.com/.

Sanford-Brown Institute
Jacksonville, Florida

Freshman Application Contact Denise Neal, Assistant Director of Admissions, Sanford-Brown Institute, 10255 Fortune Parkway, Suite 501. *Phone:* 904-380-2912. *Toll-free phone:* 888-577-5333. *Fax:* 904-363-6824. *E-mail:* dneal@sbjacksonville.com. *Web site:* http://www.sbjacksonville.com/

Sanford-Brown Institute
Tampa, Florida

Admissions Office Contact Sanford-Brown Institute, 5701 East Hillsborough Avenue, Tampa, FL 33610. *Toll-free phone:* 888-450-0333. *Web site:* http://www.sbtampa.com/.

Seminole State College of Florida
Sanford, Florida

- **State and locally supported** primarily 2-year, founded 1966
- **Small-town** 200-acre campus with easy access to Orlando
- **Endowment** $8.3 million
- **Coed,** 18,514 undergraduate students, 42% full-time, 59% women, 41% men

Undergraduates 7,692 full-time, 10,822 part-time. Students come from 88 other countries; 0.5% are from out of state; 18% Black or African American, non-Hispanic/Latino; 21% Hispanic/Latino; 2% Asian, non-Hispanic/Latino; 0.3% Native Hawaiian or other Pacific Islander, non-Hispanic/Latino; 0.3% American Indian or Alaska Native, non-Hispanic/Latino; 2% Two or more races, non-Hispanic/Latino; 2% Race/ethnicity unknown; 2% international; 4% transferred in.
Freshmen *Admission:* 8,978 applied, 8,978 admitted, 2,844 enrolled.
Faculty *Total:* 795, 30% full-time, 14% with terminal degrees. *Student/faculty ratio:* 27:1.
Majors Accounting; administrative assistant and secretarial science; architectural engineering technology; automobile/automotive mechanics technology; banking and financial support services; building/construction finishing, management, and inspection related; business administration and management; child development; civil engineering technology; computer and information sciences and support services related; computer and information sciences related; computer and information systems security; computer engineering related; computer engineering technology; computer graphics; computer hardware engineering; computer/information technology services administration related; computer programming; computer programming related; computer programming (specific applications); computer programming (vendor/product certification); computer software and media applications related; computer software engineering; computer systems networking and telecommunications; construction engineering technology; criminal justice/law enforcement administration; data entry/microcomputer applications; data entry/microcomputer applications related; data modeling/warehousing and database administration; data processing and data processing technology; drafting and design technology; electrical, electronic and communications engineering technology; emergency medical technology (EMT paramedic); finance; fire science/firefighting; industrial technology; information science/studies; information technology; interior design; legal assistant/paralegal; liberal arts and sciences/liberal studies; marketing/marketing management; network and system administration;

physical therapy; registered nursing/registered nurse; respiratory care therapy; telecommunications technology; web/multimedia management and webmaster; web page, digital/multimedia and information resources design; word processing.
Academics *Calendar:* semesters. *Degrees:* certificates, diplomas, associate, and bachelor's. *Special study options:* academic remediation for entering students, accelerated degree program, adult/continuing education programs, advanced placement credit, cooperative education, distance learning, double majors, English as a second language, external degree program, honors programs, independent study, internships, part-time degree program, services for LD students, study abroad, summer session for credit. *ROTC:* Army (b).
Library Seminole State College Library - SLM plus 7 others with 120,548 titles, 352 serial subscriptions, 7,211 audiovisual materials, an OPAC, a Web page.
Student Life *Housing:* college housing not available. *Activities and Organizations:* drama/theater group, student-run newspaper, choral group, Phi Beta Lambda, Phi Theta Kappa, Student Government Association, Sigma Phi Gamma, Hispanic Student Association. *Campus security:* 24-hour emergency response devices and patrols. *Student services:* personal/psychological counseling.
Athletics Member NJCAA. *Intercollegiate sports:* baseball M(s), golf W(s), softball W(s).
Standardized Tests *Required:* CPT (for admission). *Recommended:* ACT (for admission).
Costs (2012–13) *Tuition:* state resident $3131 full-time, $104 per credit hour part-time; nonresident $11,456 full-time, $382 per credit hour part-time. Full-time tuition and fees vary according to degree level and program. Part-time tuition and fees vary according to degree level and program. *Payment plan:* deferred payment. *Waivers:* senior citizens and employees or children of employees.
Applying *Options:* electronic application, early admission, deferred entrance. *Required:* high school transcript, minimum 2.0 GPA. *Application deadlines:* rolling (freshmen), rolling (transfers). *Notification:* continuous (freshmen), continuous (transfers).
Freshman Application Contact Ms. Pamela Mennechey, Associate Vice President - Student Recruitment and Enrollment, Seminole State College of Florida, Sanford, FL 32773-6199. *Phone:* 407-708-2050. *Fax:* 407-708-2395. *E-mail:* admissions@scc-fl.edu. *Web site:* http://www.seminolestate.edu/.

Southern Technical College
Auburndale, Florida

Director of Admissions Mr. Charles Owens, Admissions Office, Southern Technical College, 298 Havendale Boulevard, Auburndale, FL 33823. *Phone:* 863-967-8822. *Web site:* http://www.southerntech.edu/.

South Florida Community College
Avon Park, Florida

Director of Admissions Ms. Annie Alexander-Harvey, Dean of Student Services, South Florida Community College, 600 West College Drive, Avon Park, FL 33825-9356. *Phone:* 863-453-6661 Ext. 7107. *Web site:* http://www.sfcc.cc.fl.us/.

Southwest Florida College
Tampa, Florida

Director of Admissions Admissions, Southwest Florida College, 3910 Riga Boulevard, Tampa, FL 33619. *Phone:* 813-630-4401. *Toll-free phone:* 877-493-5147. *Web site:* http://www.swfc.edu/.

State College of Florida Manatee-Sarasota
Bradenton, Florida

- **State-supported** primarily 2-year, founded 1957, part of Florida Community College System
- **Suburban** 100-acre campus with easy access to Tampa-St. Petersburg
- **Coed,** 11,303 undergraduate students, 43% full-time, 60% women, 40% men

Undergraduates 4,881 full-time, 6,422 part-time. Students come from 29 states and territories; 47 other countries; 2% are from out of state; 10% Black or African American, non-Hispanic/Latino; 12% Hispanic/Latino; 2% Asian, non-Hispanic/Latino; 0.5% American Indian or Alaska Native, non-Hispanic/Latino; 0.7% Two or more races, non-Hispanic/Latino; 4% Race/ethnicity unknown; 1% international; 5% transferred in. *Retention:* 59% of full-time freshmen returned.

Freshmen *Admission:* 2,736 applied, 2,736 admitted, 1,541 enrolled. *Test scores:* SAT critical reading scores over 500: 32%; SAT math scores over 500: 31%; SAT writing scores over 500: 33%; ACT scores over 18: 56%; SAT critical reading scores over 600: 6%; SAT math scores over 600: 6%; SAT writing scores over 600: 6%; ACT scores over 24: 16%; ACT scores over 30: 3%.

Faculty *Total:* 407, 37% full-time.

Majors Accounting; administrative assistant and secretarial science; advertising; African American/Black studies; American government and politics; American studies; art; art history, criticism and conservation; Asian studies; astronomy; biology/biological sciences; biology teacher education; business administration and management; business/commerce; business/managerial economics; chemistry; chemistry teacher education; child development; civil engineering technology; commercial and advertising art; community health services counseling; computer and information sciences; computer and information sciences related; computer engineering technology; computer graphics; computer programming; computer programming related; construction engineering technology; criminal justice/safety; dietetics; drafting and design technology; dramatic/theater arts; economics; electrical, electronic and communications engineering technology; engineering; English; English/language arts teacher education; family and consumer sciences/home economics teacher education; finance; fine/studio arts; fire science/firefighting; foreign language teacher education; French; German; health/health-care administration; health teacher education; history; hospital and health-care facilities administration; humanities; information science/studies; jazz/jazz studies; Jewish/Judaic studies; journalism; kindergarten/preschool education; Latin American studies; legal assistant/paralegal; liberal arts and sciences/liberal studies; mass communication/media; mathematics teacher education; medical radiologic technology; music; music performance; music teacher education; music theory and composition; occupational therapist assistant; occupational therapy; philosophy; physical education teaching and coaching; physical therapy; physical therapy technology; physician assistant; physics; physics teacher education; pre-pharmacy studies; psychology; public administration; radio and television; radio and television broadcasting technology; radiologic technology/science; registered nursing/registered nurse; religious studies; respiratory care therapy; rhetoric and composition; Russian, Central European, East European and Eurasian studies; Russian studies; science teacher education; social psychology; social sciences; social studies teacher education; social work; Spanish; statistics; technology/industrial arts teacher education; trade and industrial teacher education; vocational rehabilitation counseling; women's studies.

Academics *Calendar:* semesters. *Degrees:* certificates, associate, and bachelor's. *Special study options:* academic remediation for entering students, advanced placement credit, cooperative education, distance learning, English as a second language, honors programs, independent study, part-time degree program, services for LD students, summer session for credit.

Library Sara Harlee Library plus 1 other with 65,386 titles, 378 serial subscriptions, an OPAC, a Web page.

Student Life *Housing:* college housing not available. *Activities and Organizations:* drama/theater group, student-run newspaper, choral group, Student Government Association, Phi Theta Kappa, American Chemical Society Student Affiliate, Campus Ministry, Medical Community Club. *Campus security:* 24-hour emergency response devices and patrols, late-night transport/escort service.

Athletics Member NJCAA. *Intercollegiate sports:* baseball M(s), basketball M(s), softball W(s), volleyball W(s). *Intramural sports:* basketball M/W, softball M/W, volleyball M/W, weight lifting M/W.

Costs (2012–13) *Tuition:* state resident $2460 full-time, $102 per credit part-time; nonresident $9276 full-time, $387 per credit part-time.

Financial Aid Of all full-time matriculated undergraduates who enrolled in 2010, 82 Federal Work-Study jobs (averaging $2800). *Financial aid deadline:* 8/15.

Applying *Options:* early admission. *Required:* high school transcript. *Application deadlines:* 8/20 (freshmen), 8/20 (transfers). *Notification:* continuous (freshmen), continuous (transfers).

Freshman Application Contact Ms. MariLynn Lewy, AVP, Student Services, State College of Florida Manatee-Sarasota, Bradenton, FL 34206. *Phone:* 941-752-5384. *Fax:* 941-727-6380. *E-mail:* lewym@scf.edu. *Web site:* http://www.scf.edu/.

Tallahassee Community College
Tallahassee, Florida

- **State and locally supported** 2-year, founded 1966, part of Florida Community College System
- **Suburban** 258-acre campus
- **Endowment** $6.9 million
- **Coed,** 13,477 undergraduate students, 54% full-time, 53% women, 47% men

Undergraduates 7,251 full-time, 6,226 part-time. 36% Black or African American, non-Hispanic/Latino; 8% Hispanic/Latino; 1% Asian, non-His-

panic/Latino; 0.1% Native Hawaiian or other Pacific Islander, non-Hispanic/Latino; 0.2% American Indian or Alaska Native, non-Hispanic/Latino; 3% Two or more races, non-Hispanic/Latino; 5% Race/ethnicity unknown; 0.9% international; 9% transferred in.

Freshmen *Admission:* 2,325 applied, 2,325 admitted, 2,642 enrolled.

Faculty *Total:* 868, 22% full-time, 18% with terminal degrees. *Student/faculty ratio:* 23:1.

Majors Accounting technology and bookkeeping; administrative assistant and secretarial science; business administration and management; civil engineering technology; computer and information sciences; computer graphics; computer programming; computer programming (specific applications); computer systems networking and telecommunications; construction engineering technology; criminal justice/law enforcement administration; data processing and data processing technology; dental hygiene; emergency medical technology (EMT paramedic); engineering; film/cinema/video studies; health information/medical records technology; kindergarten/preschool education; legal administrative assistant/secretary; legal assistant/paralegal; liberal arts and sciences/liberal studies; management information systems; marketing/marketing management; network and system administration; parks, recreation and leisure; public administration; registered nursing/registered nurse; respiratory care therapy; word processing.

Academics *Calendar:* semesters. *Degree:* certificates and associate. *Special study options:* academic remediation for entering students, accelerated degree program, adult/continuing education programs, advanced placement credit, distance learning, English as a second language, external degree program, honors programs, independent study, off-campus study, part-time degree program, services for LD students, study abroad, summer session for credit. *ROTC:* Army (c), Navy (c), Air Force (c).

Library Tallahassee Community College Library with 236,009 titles, 14,459 serial subscriptions, 4,576 audiovisual materials, an OPAC.

Student Life *Housing:* college housing not available. *Activities and Organizations:* drama/theater group, student-run newspaper, choral group, Student Government Association, International Student Organization, Phi Theta Kappa, Model United Nations, Honors Council. *Campus security:* 24-hour emergency response devices and patrols, late-night transport/escort service. *Student services:* personal/psychological counseling.

Athletics Member NJCAA. *Intercollegiate sports:* baseball M(s), basketball M(s)/W(s), softball W(s). *Intramural sports:* basketball M/W, football M/W, soccer M/W, softball M/W, volleyball M/W.

Costs (2012–13) *Tuition:* state resident $2518 full-time, $97 per credit hour part-time; nonresident $9724 full-time, $373 per credit hour part-time. Full-time tuition and fees vary according to course load. Part-time tuition and fees vary according to course load. No tuition increase for student's term of enrollment. *Payment plan:* installment. *Waivers:* employees or children of employees.

Financial Aid Of all full-time matriculated undergraduates who enrolled in 2009, 265 Federal Work-Study jobs (averaging $2395).

Applying *Options:* electronic application, early admission, deferred entrance. *Required:* high school transcript. *Application deadlines:* 8/1 (freshmen), 8/1 (transfers).

Freshman Application Contact Student Success Center, Tallahassee Community College, 444 Appleyard Drive, Tallahassee, FL 32304-2895. *Phone:* 850-201-8555. *E-mail:* admissions@tcc.fl.edu. *Web site:* http://www.tcc.fl.edu/.

Valencia College
Orlando, Florida

- **State-supported** 2-year, founded 1967, part of Florida Community College System
- **Urban** 629-acre campus with easy access to Orlando
- **Endowment** $47.9 million
- **Coed,** 42,631 undergraduate students, 42% full-time, 57% women, 43% men
- **90%** of applicants were admitted

Undergraduates 17,759 full-time, 24,872 part-time. Students come from 51 other countries; 3% are from out of state; 17% Black or African American, non-Hispanic/Latino; 30% Hispanic/Latino; 4% Asian, non-Hispanic/Latino; 0.3% Native Hawaiian or other Pacific Islander, non-Hispanic/Latino; 0.3% American Indian or Alaska Native, non-Hispanic/Latino; 1% Two or more races, non-Hispanic/Latino; 8% Race/ethnicity unknown; 1% international; 9% transferred in. *Retention:* 70% of full-time freshmen returned.

Freshmen *Admission:* 10,180 applied, 9,133 admitted, 8,210 enrolled.

Faculty *Total:* 1,465, 25% full-time, 6% with terminal degrees. *Student/faculty ratio:* 35:1.

Majors Accounting; administrative assistant and secretarial science; business administration and management; cardiovascular technology; cinematography and film/video production; civil engineering technology; commercial and advertising art; computer engineering technology; computer programming; computer programming related; computer programming (specific applica-

tions); construction engineering technology; criminal justice/law enforcement administration; culinary arts; data entry/microcomputer applications; dental hygiene; diagnostic medical sonography and ultrasound technology; drafting and design technology; dramatic/theater arts; electrical, electronic and communications engineering technology; emergency medical technology (EMT paramedic); environmental engineering technology; fire science/firefighting; hospitality administration; human resources management; industrial technology; information technology; legal administrative assistant/secretary; legal assistant/paralegal; liberal arts and sciences/liberal studies; marketing/marketing management; medical administrative assistant and medical secretary; medical radiologic technology; office management; ornamental horticulture; physical education teaching and coaching; pre-engineering; radiologic technology/science; registered nursing/registered nurse; respiratory care therapy; surveying technology; tourism and travel services management; word processing.
Academics *Calendar:* semesters. *Degree:* certificates, diplomas, and associate. *Special study options:* academic remediation for entering students, accelerated degree program, adult/continuing education programs, advanced placement credit, cooperative education, distance learning, double majors, English as a second language, freshman honors college, honors programs, independent study, internships, part-time degree program, services for LD students, study abroad, summer session for credit. *ROTC:* Army (c).
Library Learning Resources Center plus 4 others with 220,390 titles, 1,894 serial subscriptions, 19,978 audiovisual materials, an OPAC, a Web page.
Student Life *Housing:* college housing not available. *Activities and Organizations:* drama/theater group, student-run newspaper, choral group. *Campus security:* 24-hour emergency response devices and patrols, student patrols, late-night transport/escort service. *Student services:* personal/psychological counseling.
Costs (2011–12) *Tuition:* state resident $2377 full-time, $99 per credit hour part-time; nonresident $9005 full-time, $375 per credit hour part-time. Full-time tuition and fees vary according to course level, degree level, and program. Part-time tuition and fees vary according to course level, degree level, and program. *Payment plans:* tuition prepayment, installment. *Waivers:* senior citizens and employees or children of employees.
Financial Aid Of all full-time matriculated undergraduates who enrolled in 2010, 21,366 applied for aid, 17,532 were judged to have need, 485 had their need fully met. 242 Federal Work-Study jobs (averaging $2608). 27 state and other part-time jobs (averaging $2738). In 2010, 93 non-need-based awards were made. *Average percent of need met:* 46%. *Average financial aid package:* $7383. *Average need-based loan:* $3242. *Average need-based gift aid:* $3430. *Average non-need-based aid:* $642.
Applying *Options:* early admission, deferred entrance. *Application fee:* $35. *Required for some:* high school transcript. *Application deadlines:* 8/12 (freshmen), 8/12 (out-of-state freshmen), 8/12 (transfers).
Freshman Application Contact Sonja Boles, Director of Admissions and Records, Valencia College, Orlando, FL 32802-3028. *Phone:* 407-582-1552. *E-mail:* sboles1@valenciacollege.edu. *Web site:* http://valenciacollege.edu/.

GEORGIA

Albany Technical College
Albany, Georgia

- **State-supported** 2-year, founded 1961, part of Technical College System of Georgia
- **Coed,** 4,918 undergraduate students, 58% full-time, 64% women, 36% men

Undergraduates 2,863 full-time, 2,055 part-time. 0.3% are from out of state; 81% Black or African American, non-Hispanic/Latino; 0.8% Hispanic/Latino; 0.3% Asian, non-Hispanic/Latino; 0.1% American Indian or Alaska Native, non-Hispanic/Latino; 0.6% Two or more races, non-Hispanic/Latino; 0.3% Race/ethnicity unknown. *Retention:* 59% of full-time freshmen returned.
Freshmen *Admission:* 796 enrolled.
Majors Accounting; adult development and aging; child development; computer and information sciences; corrections and criminal justice related; culinary arts; drafting and design technology; electrical and electronic engineering technologies related; forest technology; hotel/motel administration; human development and family studies related; industrial technology; manufacturing engineering technology; marketing/marketing management; medical radiologic technology; pharmacy technician; tourism and travel services management.
Academics *Calendar:* quarters. *Degree:* certificates, diplomas, and associate. *Special study options:* distance learning.
Library Albany Technical College Library and Media Center.
Student Life *Housing:* college housing not available.
Applying *Options:* early admission. *Application fee:* $23. *Required:* high school transcript.

Freshman Application Contact Albany Technical College, 1704 South Slappey Boulevard, Albany, GA 31701. *Phone:* 229-430-3520. *Toll-free phone:* 877-261-3113. *Web site:* http://www.albanytech.edu/.

Altamaha Technical College
Jesup, Georgia

- **State-supported** 2-year, part of Technical College System of Georgia
- **Coed,** 1,499 undergraduate students, 27% full-time, 55% women, 45% men

Undergraduates 399 full-time, 1,100 part-time. 30% Black or African American, non-Hispanic/Latino; 2% Hispanic/Latino; 0.5% Asian, non-Hispanic/Latino; 0.5% American Indian or Alaska Native, non-Hispanic/Latino; 2% Race/ethnicity unknown. *Retention:* 66% of full-time freshmen returned.
Freshmen *Admission:* 262 enrolled.
Majors Administrative assistant and secretarial science; child development; computer programming; computer systems networking and telecommunications; criminal justice/safety; information science/studies; machine tool technology; manufacturing engineering technology; marketing/marketing management.
Academics *Calendar:* quarters. *Degree:* certificates, diplomas, and associate. *Special study options:* distance learning.
Student Life *Housing:* college housing not available.
Applying *Options:* early admission. *Application fee:* $24. *Required:* high school transcript.
Freshman Application Contact Altamaha Technical College, 1777 West Cherry Street, Jesup, GA 31545. *Phone:* 912-427-1958. *Toll-free phone:* 800-645-8284. *Web site:* http://www.altamahatech.edu/.

Andrew College
Cuthbert, Georgia

Freshman Application Contact Ms. Bridget Kurkowski, Director of Admission, Andrew College, 413 College Street, Cuthbert, GA 39840. *Phone:* 229-732-5986. *Toll-free phone:* 800-664-9250. *Fax:* 229-732-2176. *E-mail:* admissions@andrewcollege.edu. *Web site:* http://www.andrewcollege.edu/.

Anthem College–Atlanta
Atlanta, Georgia

Director of Admissions Frank Webster, Office Manager, Anthem College–Atlanta, 2450 Piedmont Road NE, Atlanta, GA 30324. *Phone:* 770-988-9877. *Toll-free phone:* 855-268-4360. *Fax:* 770-988-8824. *E-mail:* ckusema@hightechschools.com. *Web site:* http://anthem.edu/atlanta-georgia/.

Athens Technical College
Athens, Georgia

- **State-supported** 2-year, founded 1958, part of Technical College System of Georgia
- **Suburban** campus
- **Coed,** 5,323 undergraduate students, 29% full-time, 68% women, 32% men

Undergraduates 1,560 full-time, 3,763 part-time. 0.3% are from out of state; 23% Black or African American, non-Hispanic/Latino; 3% Hispanic/Latino; 4% Asian, non-Hispanic/Latino; 0.3% American Indian or Alaska Native, non-Hispanic/Latino; 0.2% Two or more races, non-Hispanic/Latino; 8% Race/ethnicity unknown. *Retention:* 56% of full-time freshmen returned.
Freshmen *Admission:* 634 enrolled.
Majors Accounting; administrative assistant and secretarial science; biology/biotechnology laboratory technician; child development; clinical laboratory science/medical technology; communications technology; computer programming; computer systems networking and telecommunications; criminal justice/law enforcement administration; dental assisting; dental hygiene; diagnostic medical sonography and ultrasound technology; electrical, electronic and communications engineering technology; emergency medical technology (EMT paramedic); hotel/motel administration; information science/studies; legal assistant/paralegal; licensed practical/vocational nurse training; logistics, materials, and supply chain management; marketing/marketing management; medical radiologic technology; physical therapy; registered nursing/registered nurse; respiratory care therapy; surgical technology; tourism and travel services management; veterinary/animal health technology.
Academics *Calendar:* quarters. *Degree:* certificates, diplomas, and associate. *Special study options:* distance learning.
Student Life *Housing:* college housing not available.
Financial Aid Of all full-time matriculated undergraduates who enrolled in 2010, 34 Federal Work-Study jobs (averaging $3090).
Applying *Options:* early admission. *Application fee:* $20. *Required:* high school transcript.

Freshman Application Contact Athens Technical College, 800 US Highway 29 North, Athens, GA 30601-1500. *Phone:* 706-355-5008. *Web site:* http://www.athenstech.edu/.

Atlanta Metropolitan College

Atlanta, Georgia

Freshman Application Contact Ms. Audrey Reid, Director, Office of Admissions, Atlanta Metropolitan College, 1630 Metropolitan Parkway, SW, Atlanta, GA 30310-4498. *Phone:* 404-756-4004. *Fax:* 404-756-4407. *E-mail:* admissions@atlm.edu. *Web site:* http://www.atlm.edu/.

Atlanta Technical College

Atlanta, Georgia

- **State-supported** 2-year, founded 1945, part of Technical College System of Georgia
- **Coed,** 4,779 undergraduate students, 31% full-time, 61% women, 39% men

Undergraduates 1,463 full-time, 3,316 part-time. 0.2% are from out of state; 94% Black or African American, non-Hispanic/Latino; 1% Hispanic/Latino; 0.8% Asian, non-Hispanic/Latino; 0.1% American Indian or Alaska Native, non-Hispanic/Latino; 0.7% Race/ethnicity unknown. *Retention:* 50% of full-time freshmen returned.

Freshmen *Admission:* 748 enrolled.

Majors Accounting; child development; computer programming; culinary arts; dental hygiene; health information/medical records technology; hotel/motel administration; information technology; legal assistant/paralegal; marketing/marketing management; tourism and travel services management.

Academics *Calendar:* quarters. *Degree:* certificates, diplomas, and associate. *Special study options:* distance learning, study abroad.

Student Life *Housing:* college housing not available.

Applying *Options:* early admission. *Application fee:* $20. *Required:* high school transcript.

Freshman Application Contact Atlanta Technical College, 1560 Metropolitan Parkway, SW, Atlanta, GA 30310. *Phone:* 404-225-4455. *Web site:* http://www.atlantatech.edu/.

Augusta Technical College

Augusta, Georgia

- **State-supported** 2-year, founded 1961, part of Technical College System of Georgia
- **Urban** campus
- **Coed,** 4,631 undergraduate students, 34% full-time, 62% women, 38% men

Undergraduates 1,596 full-time, 3,035 part-time. 2% are from out of state; 52% Black or African American, non-Hispanic/Latino; 2% Hispanic/Latino; 2% Asian, non-Hispanic/Latino; 0.3% American Indian or Alaska Native, non-Hispanic/Latino; 0.1% Two or more races, non-Hispanic/Latino; 2% Race/ethnicity unknown. *Retention:* 49% of full-time freshmen returned.

Freshmen *Admission:* 760 enrolled.

Majors Accounting; administrative assistant and secretarial science; biotechnology; business administration and management; cardiovascular technology; child development; computer programming; computer systems networking and telecommunications; criminal justice/safety; culinary arts; e-commerce; electrical, electronic and communications engineering technology; emergency medical technology (EMT paramedic); fire science/firefighting; information science/studies; marketing/marketing management; mechanical engineering/mechanical technology; medical radiologic technology; occupational therapist assistant; parks, recreation and leisure facilities management; pharmacy technician; respiratory care therapy; respiratory therapy technician; surgical technology.

Academics *Calendar:* quarters. *Degree:* certificates, diplomas, and associate. *Special study options:* distance learning.

Library Information Technology Center.

Student Life *Housing:* college housing not available.

Applying *Options:* early admission. *Application fee:* $20. *Required:* high school transcript.

Freshman Application Contact Augusta Technical College, 3200 Augusta Tech Drive, Augusta, GA 30906. *Phone:* 706-771-4150. *Web site:* http://www.augustatech.edu/.

Bainbridge College

Bainbridge, Georgia

- **State-supported** 2-year, founded 1972, part of University System of Georgia
- **Small-town** 160-acre campus
- **Coed,** 3,712 undergraduate students, 54% full-time, 70% women, 30% men

Undergraduates 1,999 full-time, 1,713 part-time. Students come from 4 states and territories; 2% are from out of state; 58% Black or African American, non-Hispanic/Latino; 1% Hispanic/Latino; 0.5% Asian, non-Hispanic/Latino; 0.2% American Indian or Alaska Native, non-Hispanic/Latino; 0.6% Two or more races, non-Hispanic/Latino; 3% Race/ethnicity unknown.

Freshmen *Admission:* 1,002 applied, 736 admitted.

Faculty *Total:* 205, 35% full-time, 18% with terminal degrees.

Majors Accounting; administrative assistant and secretarial science; agriculture; art; biology/biological sciences; business administration and management; business teacher education; chemistry; criminal justice/law enforcement administration; data processing and data processing technology; drafting and design technology; dramatic/theater arts; education; electrical, electronic and communications engineering technology; elementary education; English; family and consumer sciences/human sciences; forestry; health teacher education; history; information science/studies; journalism; kindergarten/preschool education; liberal arts and sciences/liberal studies; licensed practical/vocational nurse training; marketing/marketing management; mathematics; political science and government; psychology; registered nursing/registered nurse; rhetoric and composition; sociology; welding technology.

Academics *Calendar:* semesters. *Degree:* certificates and associate. *Special study options:* academic remediation for entering students, adult/continuing education programs, advanced placement credit, distance learning, double majors, independent study, part-time degree program, services for LD students, study abroad, summer session for credit.

Library Bainbridge College Library with 44,453 titles, 82 serial subscriptions, 3,712 audiovisual materials, an OPAC.

Student Life *Housing:* college housing not available. *Activities and Organizations:* drama/theater group, Canoe Club, Alpha Beta Gamma, Circle K, Sigma Kappa Delta, Student Government Association. *Campus security:* 24-hour patrols.

Athletics *Intramural sports:* table tennis M/W, volleyball M/W.

Standardized Tests *Required for some:* SAT or ACT (for admission), ACT COMPASS.

Costs (2011–12) *Tuition:* state resident $1976 full-time, $82 per credit hour part-time; nonresident $7478 full-time, $312 per credit hour part-time. Full-time tuition and fees vary according to course load. Part-time tuition and fees vary according to course load. *Required fees:* $888 full-time, $444 per term part-time. *Waivers:* senior citizens and employees or children of employees.

Applying *Options:* electronic application, early admission. *Required for some:* high school transcript, minimum 1.8 GPA, 3 letters of recommendation, interview, immunizations/waivers, medical records and criminal. *Application deadlines:* rolling (freshmen), rolling (transfers). *Notification:* continuous (freshmen), continuous (transfers).

Freshman Application Contact Mrs. Connie Snyder, Director of Admissions and Records, Bainbridge College, 2500 East Shotwell Street, Bainbridge, GA 39819. *Phone:* 229-248-2504. *Toll-free phone:* 866-825-1715 (in-state); 888-825-1715 (out-of-state). *Fax:* 229-248-2525. *E-mail:* csnyder@bainbridge.edu. *Web site:* http://www.bainbridge.edu/.

Brown Mackie College–Atlanta

Atlanta, Georgia

- **Proprietary** 2-year, part of Education Management Corporation
- **Urban** campus
- **Coed**

Academics *Degree:* diplomas and associate.

Costs (2011–12) *Tuition:* Tuition varies by program. Students should contact Brown Mackie College for tuition information.

Freshman Application Contact Brown Mackie College–Atlanta, 4370 Peachtree Road, NE, Atlanta, GA 30319. *Phone:* 404-799-4500. *Web site:* http://www.brownmackie.edu/atlanta/.

See page 342 for the College Close-Up.

Central Georgia Technical College

Macon, Georgia

- **State-supported** 2-year, founded 1966, part of Technical College System of Georgia
- **Suburban** campus
- **Coed,** 6,187 undergraduate students, 43% full-time, 66% women, 34% men

Undergraduates 2,685 full-time, 3,502 part-time. 64% Black or African American, non-Hispanic/Latino; 0.8% Hispanic/Latino; 0.7% Asian, non-Hispanic/Latino; 0.3% American Indian or Alaska Native, non-Hispanic/Latino; 0.4% Two or more races, non-Hispanic/Latino; 0.9% Race/ethnicity unknown. *Retention:* 43% of full-time freshmen returned.

Freshmen *Admission:* 737 enrolled.

Majors Accounting; administrative assistant and secretarial science; adult development and aging; banking and financial support services; business administration and management; cabinetmaking and millwork; cardiovascular technology; carpentry; child-care and support services management; child development; clinical/medical laboratory technology; computer programming; computer systems networking and telecommunications; criminal justice/safety; dental hygiene; drafting and design technology; e-commerce; electrical, electronic and communications engineering technology; hotel/motel administration; industrial technology; information science/studies; legal assistant/paralegal; marketing/marketing management; medical radiologic technology; tourism and travel services management; veterinary/animal health technology; web page, digital/multimedia and information resources design.

Academics *Calendar:* quarters. *Degree:* certificates, diplomas, and associate. *Special study options:* distance learning.

Student Life *Housing:* college housing not available.

Financial Aid Of all full-time matriculated undergraduates who enrolled in 2010, 175 Federal Work-Study jobs (averaging $2000). *Financial aid deadline:* 9/1.

Applying *Options:* early admission. *Application fee:* $15. *Required:* high school transcript.

Freshman Application Contact Central Georgia Technical College, 3300 Macon Tech Drive, Macon, GA 31206. *Phone:* 770-531-6332. *Toll-free phone:* 866-430-0135. *Web site:* http://www.centralgatech.edu/.

Chattahoochee Technical College

Marietta, Georgia

- **State-supported** 2-year, founded 1961, part of Technical College System of Georgia
- **Suburban** campus
- **Coed,** 12,158 undergraduate students, 31% full-time, 62% women, 38% men

Undergraduates 3,731 full-time, 8,427 part-time. 0.1% are from out of state; 33% Black or African American, non-Hispanic/Latino; 6% Hispanic/Latino; 2% Asian, non-Hispanic/Latino; 0.2% Native Hawaiian or other Pacific Islander, non-Hispanic/Latino; 0.4% American Indian or Alaska Native, non-Hispanic/Latino; 2% Two or more races, non-Hispanic/Latino; 1% Race/ethnicity unknown; 0.4% international. *Retention:* 49% of full-time freshmen returned.

Freshmen *Admission:* 2,056 enrolled.

Majors Accounting; administrative assistant and secretarial science; automobile/automotive mechanics technology; biomedical technology; business administration and management; child development; civil engineering technology; computer and information systems security; computer programming; computer systems networking and telecommunications; criminal justice/safety; culinary arts; drafting and design technology; electrical, electronic and communications engineering technology; fire science/firefighting; horticultural science; information science/studies; logistics, materials, and supply chain management; marketing/marketing management; medical radiologic technology; parks, recreation and leisure facilities management; web page, digital/multimedia and information resources design.

Academics *Calendar:* quarters. *Degree:* certificates, diplomas, and associate. *Special study options:* distance learning.

Student Life *Housing:* college housing not available.

Financial Aid Of all full-time matriculated undergraduates who enrolled in 2010, 40 Federal Work-Study jobs (averaging $2500).

Applying *Options:* early admission. *Application fee:* $15. *Required:* high school transcript.

Freshman Application Contact Chattahoochee Technical College, 980 South Cobb Drive, SE, Marietta, GA 30060. *Phone:* 770-757-3408. *Web site:* http://www.chattahoocheetech.edu/.

Columbus Technical College

Columbus, Georgia

- **State-supported** 2-year, founded 1961, part of Technical College System of Georgia
- **Urban** campus
- **Coed,** 4,164 undergraduate students, 29% full-time, 70% women, 30% men

Undergraduates 1,188 full-time, 2,976 part-time. 14% are from out of state; 45% Black or African American, non-Hispanic/Latino; 7% Hispanic/Latino; 2% Asian, non-Hispanic/Latino; 0.3% Native Hawaiian or other Pacific Islander, non-Hispanic/Latino; 0.4% American Indian or Alaska Native, non-Hispanic/Latino; 1% Two or more races, non-Hispanic/Latino; 2% Race/ethnicity unknown; 0.1% international. *Retention:* 45% of full-time freshmen returned.

Freshmen *Admission:* 620 enrolled.

Majors Accounting; administrative assistant and secretarial science; automobile/automotive mechanics technology; child development; computer engineering related; computer systems networking and telecommunications; dental hygiene; diagnostic medical sonography and ultrasound technology; drafting and design technology; electrical, electronic and communications engineering technology; emergency medical technology (EMT paramedic); health information/medical records technology; horticultural science; industrial technology; information science/studies; machine tool technology; mechanical engineering/mechanical technology; medical office management; medical radiologic technology; pharmacy technician; registered nursing/registered nurse; respiratory therapy technician; surgical technology; web page, digital/multimedia and information resources design.

Academics *Calendar:* quarters. *Degree:* certificates, diplomas, and associate. *Special study options:* distance learning.

Library Columbus Technical College Library.

Student Life *Housing:* college housing not available.

Financial Aid Of all full-time matriculated undergraduates who enrolled in 2010, 6 Federal Work-Study jobs (averaging $2000).

Applying *Options:* early admission. *Application fee:* $25. *Required:* high school transcript.

Freshman Application Contact Columbus Technical College, 928 Manchester Expressway, Columbus, GA 31904-6572. *Phone:* 706-649-1901. *Web site:* http://www.columbustech.edu/.

Darton College

Albany, Georgia

- **State-supported** 2-year, founded 1965, part of University System of Georgia
- **Urban** 185-acre campus
- **Endowment** $978,169
- **Coed**

Undergraduates 2,874 full-time, 2,980 part-time. Students come from 24 states and territories; 46 other countries; 7% are from out of state; 42% Black or African American, non-Hispanic/Latino; 1% Hispanic/Latino; 0.9% Asian, non-Hispanic/Latino; 0.2% American Indian or Alaska Native, non-Hispanic/Latino; 0.3% Two or more races, non-Hispanic/Latino; 0.8% Race/ethnicity unknown; 1% international; 10% transferred in. *Retention:* 45% of full-time freshmen returned.

Faculty *Student/faculty ratio:* 21:1.

Academics *Calendar:* semesters. *Degrees:* certificates, associate, and post-bachelor's certificates. *Special study options:* academic remediation for entering students, accelerated degree program, adult/continuing education programs, advanced placement credit, cooperative education, distance learning, double majors, English as a second language, honors programs, independent study, off-campus study, part-time degree program, services for LD students, student-designed majors, study abroad, summer session for credit. *ROTC:* Army (c).

Student Life *Campus security:* 24-hour emergency response devices and patrols, student patrols, late-night transport/escort service, controlled dormitory access.

Athletics Member NJCAA.

Standardized Tests *Required:* non-traditional students must take the COMPASS test (for admission). *Required for some:* SAT or ACT (for admission), SAT Subject Tests (for admission). *Recommended:* SAT or ACT (for admission), SAT Subject Tests (for admission).

Costs (2011–12) *Tuition:* state resident $1976 full-time, $82 per semester hour part-time; nonresident $7478 full-time, $312 per semester hour part-time. Part-time tuition and fees vary according to course load. $2470 for 15 credits/semester in-state; $9348 for 15 credits/semester out-of-state. *Required fees:* $1064 full-time, $455 per course part-time. *Room and board:* $7680. Room and board charges vary according to board plan and housing facility.

Financial Aid Of all full-time matriculated undergraduates who enrolled in 2010, 60 Federal Work-Study jobs.

Applying *Options:* electronic application, deferred entrance. *Application fee:* $20. *Required:* minimum 2.0 GPA, proof of immunization. *Required for some:* high school transcript.

Freshman Application Contact Darton College, 2400 Gillionville Road, Albany, GA 31707-3098. *Phone:* 229-430-6740. *Toll-free phone:* 866-775-1214. *Web site:* http://www.darton.edu/.

East Georgia College
Swainsboro, Georgia

Freshman Application Contact East Georgia College, 131 College Circle, Swainsboro, GA 30401-2699. *Phone:* 478-289-2017. *Web site:* http://www.ega.edu/.

Emory University, Oxford College
Oxford, Georgia

- **Independent Methodist** primarily 2-year, founded 1836
- **Small-town** 150-acre campus with easy access to Atlanta
- **Endowment** $39.0 million
- **Coed,** 936 undergraduate students, 100% full-time, 53% women, 47% men

Undergraduates 936 full-time. Students come from 45 states and territories; 29 other countries; 61% are from out of state; 14% Black or African American, non-Hispanic/Latino; 6% Hispanic/Latino; 29% Asian, non-Hispanic/Latino; 0.1% Native Hawaiian or other Pacific Islander, non-Hispanic/Latino; 0.3% American Indian or Alaska Native, non-Hispanic/Latino; 3% Two or more races, non-Hispanic/Latino; 4% Race/ethnicity unknown; 15% international; 99% live on campus. *Retention:* 90% of full-time freshmen returned.

Freshmen *Admission:* 3,683 applied, 2,013 admitted, 440 enrolled. *Average high school GPA:* 3.54. *Test scores:* SAT critical reading scores over 500: 95%; SAT math scores over 500: 97%; SAT writing scores over 500: 95%; ACT scores over 18: 100%; SAT critical reading scores over 600: 60%; SAT math scores over 600: 71%; SAT writing scores over 600: 65%; ACT scores over 24: 88%; SAT critical reading scores over 700: 19%; SAT math scores over 700: 26%; SAT writing scores over 700: 21%; ACT scores over 30: 29%.

Faculty *Total:* 85, 67% full-time, 74% with terminal degrees. *Student/faculty ratio:* 14:1.

Majors Liberal arts and sciences/liberal studies.

Academics *Calendar:* semesters. *Degrees:* associate and bachelor's. *Special study options:* advanced placement credit, double majors, independent study, internships, off-campus study, services for LD students, study abroad, summer session for credit. *ROTC:* Army (c), Navy (c), Air Force (c). *Unusual degree programs:* 3-2 engineering with Georgia Institute of Technology.

Library Hoke O'Kelly Library with 92,681 titles, 167 serial subscriptions, 1,352 audiovisual materials, an OPAC, a Web page.

Student Life *Housing:* on-campus residence required through sophomore year. *Options:* coed, women-only, disabled students. Campus housing is university owned. Freshman campus housing is guaranteed. *Activities and Organizations:* drama/theater group, student-run newspaper, choral group, Residence Hall Association, intramurals/junior varsity sports, Student Government Association, Student Admissions Association, Volunteer Oxford. *Campus security:* 24-hour emergency response devices and patrols, student patrols, late-night transport/escort service, controlled dormitory access. *Student services:* health clinic, personal/psychological counseling.

Athletics Member NJCAA. *Intercollegiate sports:* basketball M, soccer W, tennis M/W. *Intramural sports:* badminton M/W, baseball M(c), basketball M/W, football M, soccer M/W, swimming and diving M/W, tennis M/W, ultimate Frisbee M/W, volleyball M/W.

Standardized Tests *Required:* SAT or ACT (for admission). *Required for some:* SAT Subject Tests (for admission).

Costs (2012–13) *Comprehensive fee:* $47,054 includes full-time tuition ($36,100), mandatory fees ($478), and room and board ($10,476). Part-time tuition: $1504 per contact hour. *Room and board:* college room only: $7196. *Payment plan:* installment. *Waivers:* employees or children of employees.

Financial Aid Of all full-time matriculated undergraduates who enrolled in 2010, 225 Federal Work-Study jobs (averaging $1600).

Applying *Options:* electronic application, early admission, early action, deferred entrance. *Application fee:* $50. *Required:* essay or personal statement, high school transcript, 1 letter of recommendation. *Required for some:* interview. *Recommended:* minimum 3.0 GPA, 2 letters of recommendation. *Application deadlines:* 1/15 (freshmen), 11/1 (early action). *Notification:* continuous until 4/1 (freshmen), 12/15 (early action).

Freshman Application Contact Emory University, Oxford College, 100 Hamill Street, PO Box 1328, Oxford, GA 30054. *Phone:* 770-784-8328. *Toll-free phone:* 800-723-8328. *Web site:* http://oxford.emory.edu/.

Gainesville State College
Oakwood, Georgia

Freshman Application Contact Mr. Mack Palmour, Director of Admissions, Gainesville State College, PO Box 1358, Gainesville, GA 30503. *Phone:* 678-717-3641. *Fax:* 678-717-3751. *E-mail:* admissions@gsc.edu. *Web site:* http://www.gsc.edu/.

Georgia Highlands College
Rome, Georgia

- **State-supported** 2-year, founded 1970, part of University System of Georgia
- **Suburban** 226-acre campus with easy access to Atlanta
- **Endowment** $1.4 million
- **Coed,** 5,522 undergraduate students, 54% full-time, 63% women, 37% men

Undergraduates 2,976 full-time, 2,546 part-time. Students come from 35 states and territories; 30 other countries; 1% are from out of state; 17% Black or African American, non-Hispanic/Latino; 7% Hispanic/Latino; 2% Asian, non-Hispanic/Latino; 0.2% Native Hawaiian or other Pacific Islander, non-Hispanic/Latino; 0.3% American Indian or Alaska Native, non-Hispanic/Latino; 2% Two or more races, non-Hispanic/Latino; 0.5% Race/ethnicity unknown; 8% transferred in. *Retention:* 55% of full-time freshmen returned.

Freshmen *Admission:* 2,333 applied, 2,284 admitted, 1,130 enrolled. *Average high school GPA:* 2.7.

Faculty *Total:* 245, 54% full-time, 29% with terminal degrees. *Student/faculty ratio:* 27:1.

Majors Accounting; agriculture; art; biological and physical sciences; business administration and management; clinical laboratory science/medical technology; computer programming; criminal justice/police science; criminal justice/safety; dental hygiene; economics; English; foreign languages and literatures; geology/earth science; history; human services; journalism; liberal arts and sciences/liberal studies; marketing/marketing management; philosophy; political science and government; psychology; radiologic technology/science; registered nursing/registered nurse; secondary education; sociology.

Academics *Calendar:* semesters. *Degree:* associate. *Special study options:* academic remediation for entering students, advanced placement credit, cooperative education, distance learning, double majors, honors programs, independent study, part-time degree program, services for LD students, study abroad, summer session for credit.

Library Georgia Highlands College Library - Floyd Campus plus 1 other with 70,302 titles, 248 serial subscriptions, 7,185 audiovisual materials, an OPAC, a Web page.

Student Life *Housing:* college housing not available. *Activities and Organizations:* drama/theater group, student-run newspaper, Highlands Association of Nursing Students, Green Highlands, Black Awareness Society, Political Science Association, Phi Theta Kappa. *Campus security:* 24-hour emergency response devices and patrols, emergency phone/email alert system. *Student services:* personal/psychological counseling.

Athletics *Intramural sports:* basketball M/W, bowling M/W, football M/W, golf M/W, table tennis M/W, tennis M/W, ultimate Frisbee M/W, volleyball M/W, weight lifting M/W.

Costs (2011–12) *Tuition:* state resident $1979 full-time, $82 per credit hour part-time; nonresident $7478 full-time, $312 per credit hour part-time. Full-time tuition and fees vary according to course load. Part-time tuition and fees vary according to course load. *Required fees:* $934 full-time, $447 per term part-time. *Waivers:* senior citizens.

Financial Aid Of all full-time matriculated undergraduates who enrolled in 2010, 50 Federal Work-Study jobs (averaging $3500).

Applying *Options:* electronic application, deferred entrance. *Application fee:* $20. *Required:* high school transcript, minimum 2.0 GPA. *Required for some:* minimum 2.2 GPA. *Application deadlines:* rolling (freshmen), rolling (out-of-state freshmen), rolling (transfers). *Notification:* continuous (freshmen), continuous (out-of-state freshmen), continuous (transfers).

Freshman Application Contact Sandra Davis, Director of Admissions, Georgia Highlands College, 3175 Cedartown Highway, Rome, GA 30161. *Phone:* 706-295-6339. *Toll-free phone:* 800-332-2406. *Fax:* 706-295-6341. *E-mail:* sdavis@highlands.edu. *Web site:* http://www.highlands.edu/.

Georgia Military College
Milledgeville, Georgia

- **State and locally supported** 2-year, founded 1879
- **Small-town** 40-acre campus
- **Endowment** $9.4 million
- **Coed**

Undergraduates 4,198 full-time, 1,883 part-time. Students come from 33 states and territories; 5% are from out of state; 42% Black or African American, non-Hispanic/Latino; 3% Hispanic/Latino; 1% Asian, non-Hispanic/Latino; 0.4% American Indian or Alaska Native, non-Hispanic/Latino; 2% Two or more races, non-Hispanic/Latino; 2% Race/ethnicity unknown; 37% transferred in. *Retention:* 48% of full-time freshmen returned.

Faculty *Student/faculty ratio:* 14:1.

Academics *Calendar:* quarters. *Degree:* associate. *Special study options:* academic remediation for entering students, advanced placement credit, cooperative education, distance learning, double majors, external degree program, independent study, off-campus study, part-time degree program, services for LD students, study abroad, summer session for credit. *ROTC:* Army (b).

Student Life *Campus security:* 24-hour emergency response devices and patrols, controlled dormitory access.

Athletics Member NJCAA.

Standardized Tests *Required for some:* SAT or ACT (for admission). *Recommended:* SAT or ACT (for admission).

Financial Aid Of all full-time matriculated undergraduates who enrolled in 2011, 4,394 applied for aid, 4,394 were judged to have need, 4,292 had their need fully met. In 2011, 1414. *Average percent of need met:* 54. *Average financial aid package:* $6285. *Average need-based loan:* $3510. *Average need-based gift aid:* $6826. *Average non-need-based aid:* $15,237.

Applying *Options:* electronic application, early admission, deferred entrance. *Application fee:* $35. *Required:* high school transcript.

Freshman Application Contact Georgia Military College, 201 East Greene Street, Old Capitol Building, Milledgeville, GA 31061-3398. *Phone:* 478-387-4948. *Toll-free phone:* 800-342-0413. *Web site:* http://www.gmc.cc.ga.us/.

Georgia Northwestern Technical College
Rome, Georgia

- **State-supported** 2-year, founded 1962, part of Technical College System of Georgia
- **Coed**, 6,506 undergraduate students, 37% full-time, 67% women, 33% men

Undergraduates 2,411 full-time, 4,095 part-time. 0.9% are from out of state; 11% Black or African American, non-Hispanic/Latino; 4% Hispanic/Latino; 0.5% Asian, non-Hispanic/Latino; 0.1% Native Hawaiian or other Pacific Islander, non-Hispanic/Latino; 0.2% American Indian or Alaska Native, non-Hispanic/Latino; 1% Two or more races, non-Hispanic/Latino; 0.1% Race/ethnicity unknown. *Retention:* 49% of full-time freshmen returned.

Freshmen *Admission:* 997 enrolled.

Majors Accounting; child development; computer programming; criminal justice/safety; environmental engineering technology; fire science/firefighting; information science/studies; legal assistant/paralegal; marketing/marketing management; medical office management; respiratory therapy technician; surgical technology; web page, digital/multimedia and information resources design.

Academics *Calendar:* quarters. *Degree:* certificates, diplomas, and associate. *Special study options:* distance learning.

Student Life *Housing:* college housing not available.

Applying *Options:* early admission. *Application fee:* $15. *Required:* high school transcript.

Freshman Application Contact Georgia Northwestern Technical College, One Maurice Culberson Drive, Rome, GA 30161. *Phone:* 706-295-6933. *Toll-free phone:* 866-983-GNTC. *Web site:* http://www.gntc.edu/.

Georgia Perimeter College
Decatur, Georgia

Freshman Application Contact Georgia Perimeter College, 3251 Panthersville Road, Decatur, GA 30034-3897. *Phone:* 678-891-3250. *Toll-free phone:* 888-696-2780. *Web site:* http://www.gpc.edu/.

Georgia Piedmont Technical College
Clarkston, Georgia

- **State-supported** 2-year, founded 1961, part of Technical College System of Georgia
- **Suburban** campus
- **Coed**, 4,544 undergraduate students, 25% full-time, 62% women, 38% men

Undergraduates 1,140 full-time, 3,404 part-time. 1% are from out of state; 77% Black or African American, non-Hispanic/Latino; 2% Hispanic/Latino; 2% Asian, non-Hispanic/Latino; 0.1% Native Hawaiian or other Pacific Islander, non-Hispanic/Latino; 0.2% American Indian or Alaska Native, non-Hispanic/Latino; 0.9% Two or more races, non-Hispanic/Latino; 0.8% Race/

ethnicity unknown; 0.2% international. *Retention:* 46% of full-time freshmen returned.

Freshmen *Admission:* 601 enrolled.

Majors Accounting; administrative assistant and secretarial science; automobile/automotive mechanics technology; business/commerce; clinical/medical laboratory technology; computer engineering technology; computer programming; computer systems networking and telecommunications; criminal justice/safety; drafting and design technology; electrical, electronic and communications engineering technology; electromechanical technology; engineering technology; heating, ventilation, air conditioning and refrigeration engineering technology; industrial technology; information science/studies; instrumentation technology; legal administrative assistant/secretary; legal assistant/paralegal; machine tool technology; marketing/marketing management; medical/clinical assistant; operations management; ophthalmic laboratory technology; opticianry; surgical technology; telecommunications technology.

Academics *Calendar:* quarters. *Degree:* certificates, diplomas, and associate. *Special study options:* distance learning.

Student Life *Housing:* college housing not available.

Financial Aid Of all full-time matriculated undergraduates who enrolled in 2010, 7,200 applied for aid, 7,100 were judged to have need. 145 Federal Work-Study jobs (averaging $4000). *Average financial aid package:* $4500. *Average need-based gift aid:* $4500.

Applying *Options:* early admission. *Application fee:* $25. *Required:* high school transcript.

Freshman Application Contact Georgia Piedmont Technical College, 495 North Indian Creek Drive, Clarkston, GA 30021-2397. *Phone:* 404-297-9522 Ext. 1229. *Web site:* http://www.gptc.edu/.

Gordon College
Barnesville, Georgia

Freshman Application Contact Gordon College, 419 College Drive, Barnesville, GA 30204-1762. *Phone:* 678-359-5021. *Toll-free phone:* 800-282-6504. *Web site:* http://www.gdn.edu/.

Gupton-Jones College of Funeral Service
Decatur, Georgia

Freshman Application Contact Ms. Beverly Wheaton, Registrar, Gupton-Jones College of Funeral Service, 5141 Snapfinger Woods Drive, Decatur, GA 30035-4022. *Phone:* 770-593-2257. *Toll-free phone:* 800-848-5352. *Web site:* http://www.gupton-jones.edu/.

Gwinnett Technical College
Lawrenceville, Georgia

- **State-supported** 2-year, founded 1984, part of Technical College System of Georgia
- **Suburban** campus
- **Coed**, 6,787 undergraduate students, 37% full-time, 62% women, 38% men

Undergraduates 2,514 full-time, 4,273 part-time. 0.1% are from out of state; 34% Black or African American, non-Hispanic/Latino; 10% Hispanic/Latino; 6% Asian, non-Hispanic/Latino; 0.1% Native Hawaiian or other Pacific Islander, non-Hispanic/Latino; 0.3% American Indian or Alaska Native, non-Hispanic/Latino; 2% Two or more races, non-Hispanic/Latino; 3% Race/ethnicity unknown. *Retention:* 51% of full-time freshmen returned.

Freshmen *Admission:* 643 enrolled.

Majors Accounting; administrative assistant and secretarial science; automobile/automotive mechanics technology; building/construction finishing, management, and inspection related; business administration and management; computer programming; computer science; computer systems networking and telecommunications; drafting and design technology; electrical, electronic and communications engineering technology; emergency medical technology (EMT paramedic); horticultural science; hotel/motel administration; information science/studies; interior design; machine tool technology; management information systems; marketing/marketing management; medical/clinical assistant; medical radiologic technology; ornamental horticulture; photography; physical therapy; physical therapy technology; respiratory care therapy; tourism and travel services management; veterinary/animal health technology.

Academics *Calendar:* quarters. *Degree:* certificates, diplomas, and associate. *Special study options:* distance learning.

Library Gwinnett Technical Institute Media Center.

Student Life *Housing:* college housing not available.

Financial Aid Of all full-time matriculated undergraduates who enrolled in 2010, 20 Federal Work-Study jobs (averaging $2100).

Applying *Options:* early admission. *Application fee:* $20. *Required:* high school transcript.
Freshman Application Contact Gwinnett Technical College, 5150 Sugarloaf Parkway, Lawrenceville, GA 30043-5702. *Phone:* 678-762-7580 Ext. 434. *Web site:* http://www.gwinnetttech.edu/.

Interactive College of Technology
Chamblee, Georgia

Freshman Application Contact Director of Admissions, Interactive College of Technology, 5303 New Peachtree Road, Chamblee, GA 30341. *Phone:* 770-216-2960. *Toll-free phone:* 800-447-2011. *Fax:* 770-216-2988. *Web site:* http://www.ict-ils.edu/.

ITT Technical Institute
Atlanta, Georgia

- **Proprietary** primarily 2-year, part of ITT Educational Services, Inc.
- **Coed**

Majors CAD/CADD drafting/design technology; computer and information systems security; computer engineering technology; construction management; criminal justice/law enforcement administration; design and visual communications; electrical, electronic and communications engineering technology; legal assistant/paralegal; system, networking, and LAN/WAN management.
Academics *Degrees:* associate and bachelor's.
Student Life *Housing:* college housing not available.
Freshman Application Contact Director of Recruitment, ITT Technical Institute, 485 Oak Place, Suite 800, Atlanta, GA 30349. *Phone:* 404-765-4600. *Toll-free phone:* 877-488-6102 (in-state); 877-788-6102 (out-of-state). *Web site:* http://www.itt-tech.edu/.

ITT Technical Institute
Duluth, Georgia

- **Proprietary** primarily 2-year, founded 2003, part of ITT Educational Services, Inc.
- **Coed**

Majors CAD/CADD drafting/design technology; computer and information systems security; computer engineering technology; computer software technology; construction management; criminal justice/law enforcement administration; design and visual communications; electrical, electronic and communications engineering technology; legal assistant/paralegal; project management; system, networking, and LAN/WAN management.
Academics *Calendar:* quarters. *Degrees:* associate and bachelor's.
Student Life *Housing:* college housing not available.
Freshman Application Contact Director of Recruitment, ITT Technical Institute, 10700 Abbotts Bridge Road, Duluth, GA 30097. *Phone:* 678-957-8510. *Toll-free phone:* 866-489-8818. *Web site:* http://www.itt-tech.edu/.

ITT Technical Institute
Kennesaw, Georgia

- **Proprietary** primarily 2-year, founded 2004, part of ITT Educational Services, Inc.
- **Coed**

Majors CAD/CADD drafting/design technology; computer and information systems security; computer engineering technology; computer software technology; construction management; criminal justice/law enforcement administration; design and visual communications; electrical, electronic and communications engineering technology; game and interactive media design; legal assistant/paralegal; project management; system, networking, and LAN/WAN management.
Academics *Calendar:* quarters. *Degrees:* associate and bachelor's.
Freshman Application Contact Director of Recruitment, ITT Technical Institute, 2065 ITT Tech Way NW, Kennesaw, GA 30144. *Phone:* 770-426-2300. *Toll-free phone:* 877-231-6415 (in-state); 800-231-6415 (out-of-state). *Web site:* http://www.itt-tech.edu/.

Lanier Technical College
Oakwood, Georgia

- **State-supported** 2-year, founded 1964, part of Technical College System of Georgia
- **Coed,** 3,722 undergraduate students, 25% full-time, 65% women, 35% men

Undergraduates 932 full-time, 2,790 part-time. 2% are from out of state; 10% Black or African American, non-Hispanic/Latino; 7% Hispanic/Latino; 2%

Asian, non-Hispanic/Latino; 0.6% American Indian or Alaska Native, non-Hispanic/Latino; 0.7% Two or more races, non-Hispanic/Latino; 0.6% Race/ethnicity unknown; 0.1% international. *Retention:* 50% of full-time freshmen returned.
Freshmen *Admission:* 442 enrolled.
Majors Accounting; administrative assistant and secretarial science; banking and financial support services; child development; computer and information systems security; computer programming; computer science; computer systems networking and telecommunications; criminal justice/safety; drafting and design technology; electrical, electronic and communications engineering technology; fire science/firefighting; health professions related; industrial technology; information science/studies; interior design; marketing/marketing management; medical radiologic technology; occupational safety and health technology; surgical technology; web page, digital/multimedia and information resources design.
Academics *Calendar:* quarters. *Degree:* certificates, diplomas, and associate. *Special study options:* distance learning.
Student Life *Housing:* college housing not available.
Applying *Options:* early admission. *Application fee:* $15. *Required:* high school transcript.
Freshman Application Contact Lanier Technical College, 2990 Landrum Education Drive, PO Box 58, Oakwood, GA 30566. *Phone:* 770-531-6332. *Web site:* http://www.laniertech.edu/.

Le Cordon Bleu College of Culinary Arts, Atlanta
Tucker, Georgia

Freshman Application Contact Admissions Office, Le Cordon Bleu College of Culinary Arts, Atlanta, 1957 Lakeside Parkway, Tucker, GA 30084. *Toll-free phone:* 888-549-8222. *Web site:* http://www.atlantaculinary.com/.

Middle Georgia College
Cochran, Georgia

Freshman Application Contact Ms. Jennifer Brannon, Director of Admissions, Middle Georgia College, 1100 2nd Street, Southeast, Cochran, GA 31014. *Phone:* 478-934-3103. *Fax:* 478-934-3403. *E-mail:* admissions@mgc.edu. *Web site:* http://www.mgc.edu/.

Middle Georgia Technical College
Warner Robbins, Georgia

- **State-supported** 2-year, founded 1973, part of Technical College System of Georgia
- **Coed,** 4,045 undergraduate students, 32% full-time, 59% women, 41% men

Undergraduates 1,305 full-time, 2,740 part-time. 2% are from out of state; 42% Black or African American, non-Hispanic/Latino; 3% Hispanic/Latino; 1% Asian, non-Hispanic/Latino; 0.1% Native Hawaiian or other Pacific Islander, non-Hispanic/Latino; 0.3% American Indian or Alaska Native, non-Hispanic/Latino; 1% Two or more races, non-Hispanic/Latino; 2% Race/ethnicity unknown. *Retention:* 64% of full-time freshmen returned.
Freshmen *Admission:* 974 enrolled.
Majors Accounting; administrative assistant and secretarial science; airframe mechanics and aircraft maintenance technology; child development; computer systems networking and telecommunications; dental hygiene; drafting and design technology; information science/studies; marketing/marketing management; medical radiologic technology; web page, digital/multimedia and information resources design.
Academics *Calendar:* quarters. *Degree:* certificates, diplomas, and associate. *Special study options:* distance learning.
Student Life *Housing:* college housing not available.
Applying *Options:* early admission. *Application fee:* $15. *Required:* high school transcript.
Freshman Application Contact Middle Georgia Technical College, 80 Cohen Walker Drive, Warner Robbins, GA 31088. *Phone:* 478-988-6800. *Toll-free phone:* 800-474-1031. *Web site:* http://www.middlegatech.edu/.

Moultrie Technical College
Moultrie, Georgia

- **State-supported** 2-year, founded 1964, part of Technical College System of Georgia
- **Coed,** 2,308 undergraduate students, 41% full-time, 64% women, 36% men

Undergraduates 948 full-time, 1,360 part-time. 0.5% are from out of state; 37% Black or African American, non-Hispanic/Latino; 4% Hispanic/Latino;

0.3% Asian, non-Hispanic/Latino; 0.3% American Indian or Alaska Native, non-Hispanic/Latino; 0.3% Two or more races, non-Hispanic/Latino; 2% Race/ethnicity unknown. *Retention:* 52% of full-time freshmen returned.

Freshmen *Admission:* 335 enrolled.

Majors Accounting; administrative assistant and secretarial science; child development; civil engineering technology; computer systems networking and telecommunications; criminal justice/safety; electrical, electronic and communications engineering technology; information science/studies; marketing/marketing management; web page, digital/multimedia and information resources design.

Academics *Calendar:* quarters. *Degree:* certificates, diplomas, and associate. *Special study options:* distance learning.

Student Life *Housing:* college housing not available.

Applying *Options:* early admission. *Application fee:* $20. *Required:* high school transcript.

Freshman Application Contact Moultrie Technical College, 800 Veterans Parkway North, Moultrie, GA 31788. *Phone:* 229-528-4581. *Web site:* http://www.moultrietech.edu/.

North Georgia Technical College

Clarkesville, Georgia

- **State-supported** 2-year, founded 1943, part of Technical College System of Georgia
- **Coed,** 2,670 undergraduate students, 43% full-time, 60% women, 40% men

Undergraduates 1,138 full-time, 1,532 part-time. 7% Black or African American, non-Hispanic/Latino; 2% Hispanic/Latino; 0.9% Asian, non-Hispanic/Latino; 0.4% American Indian or Alaska Native, non-Hispanic/Latino; 1% Two or more races, non-Hispanic/Latino; 0.8% Race/ethnicity unknown. *Retention:* 53% of full-time freshmen returned.

Freshmen *Admission:* 606 enrolled.

Majors Administrative assistant and secretarial science; computer systems networking and telecommunications; criminal justice/safety; culinary arts; heating, ventilation, air conditioning and refrigeration engineering technology; horticultural science; industrial technology; parks, recreation and leisure facilities management; turf and turfgrass management; web page, digital/multimedia and information resources design.

Academics *Calendar:* quarters. *Degree:* certificates, diplomas, and associate. *Special study options:* distance learning.

Student Life *Housing Options:* coed.

Applying *Options:* early admission. *Application fee:* $15. *Required:* high school transcript.

Freshman Application Contact North Georgia Technical College, 1500 Georgia Highway 197, North, PO Box 65, Clarkesville, GA 30523. *Phone:* 706-754-7724. *Web site:* http://www.northgatech.edu/.

Oconee Fall Line Technical College– North Campus

Sandersville, Georgia

- **State-supported** 2-year, part of Technical College System of Georgia
- **Coed,** 1,934 undergraduate students, 32% full-time, 63% women, 37% men

Undergraduates 628 full-time, 1,306 part-time. 46% Black or African American, non-Hispanic/Latino; 1% Hispanic/Latino; 0.3% Asian, non-Hispanic/Latino; 0.2% American Indian or Alaska Native, non-Hispanic/Latino; 0.7% Two or more races, non-Hispanic/Latino; 0.6% Race/ethnicity unknown. *Retention:* 34% of full-time freshmen returned.

Freshmen *Admission:* 222 enrolled.

Majors Accounting; administrative assistant and secretarial science; child development; computer systems networking and telecommunications; information science/studies.

Academics *Calendar:* quarters. *Degree:* certificates, diplomas, and associate. *Special study options:* distance learning.

Student Life *Housing:* college housing not available.

Applying *Options:* early admission. *Application fee:* $20. *Required:* high school transcript.

Freshman Application Contact Oconee Fall Line Technical College–North Campus, 1189 Deepstep Road, Sandersville, GA 31082. *Phone:* 478-553-2050. *Toll-free phone:* 877-399-8324. *Web site:* http://www.oftc.edu/.

Oconee Fall Line Technical College– South Campus

Dublin, Georgia

- **State-supported** 2-year, founded 1984, part of Technical College System of Georgia
- **Small-town** campus with easy access to Atlanta
- **Coed**

Undergraduates 875 full-time, 942 part-time. 44% Black or African American, non-Hispanic/Latino; 0.3% Hispanic/Latino; 0.1% Asian, non-Hispanic/Latino; 0.3% Native Hawaiian or other Pacific Islander, non-Hispanic/Latino; 0.2% American Indian or Alaska Native, non-Hispanic/Latino; 0.3% Two or more races, non-Hispanic/Latino; 0.7% Race/ethnicity unknown. *Retention:* 54% of full-time freshmen returned.

Academics *Calendar:* quarters. *Degree:* certificates, diplomas, and associate. *Special study options:* distance learning.

Applying *Options:* early admission. *Application fee:* $15. *Required:* high school transcript.

Freshman Application Contact Oconee Fall Line Technical College–South Campus, 560 Pinehill Road, Dublin, GA 31021. *Phone:* 478-274-7837. *Toll-free phone:* 800-200-4484. *Web site:* http://www.oftc.edu/.

Ogeechee Technical College

Statesboro, Georgia

- **State-supported** 2-year, founded 1989, part of Technical College System of Georgia
- **Small-town** campus
- **Coed,** 2,298 undergraduate students, 40% full-time, 69% women, 31% men

Undergraduates 914 full-time, 1,384 part-time. 36% Black or African American, non-Hispanic/Latino; 2% Hispanic/Latino; 0.7% Asian, non-Hispanic/Latino; 0.2% American Indian or Alaska Native, non-Hispanic/Latino; 1% Two or more races, non-Hispanic/Latino; 0.3% Race/ethnicity unknown. *Retention:* 50% of full-time freshmen returned.

Freshmen *Admission:* 302 enrolled.

Majors Accounting; administrative assistant and secretarial science; agribusiness; automobile/automotive mechanics technology; banking and financial support services; child development; computer systems networking and telecommunications; construction trades; culinary arts; dental hygiene; forest technology; funeral service and mortuary science; health information/medical records technology; hotel/motel administration; information science/studies; interior design; legal assistant/paralegal; marketing/marketing management; opticianry; tourism and travel services management; veterinary/animal health technology; water quality and wastewater treatment management and recycling technology; wildlife, fish and wildlands science and management; wood science and wood products/pulp and paper technology.

Academics *Calendar:* quarters. *Degree:* certificates, diplomas, and associate. *Special study options:* distance learning.

Student Life *Housing:* college housing not available.

Applying *Options:* early admission. *Application fee:* $25. *Required:* high school transcript.

Freshman Application Contact Ogeechee Technical College, One Joe Kennedy Boulevard, Statesboro, GA 30458. *Phone:* 912-871-1600. *Toll-free phone:* 800-646-1316. *Web site:* http://www.ogeecheetech.edu/.

Okefenokee Technical College

Waycross, Georgia

- **State-supported** 2-year, part of Technical College System of Georgia
- **Small-town** campus
- **Coed,** 1,432 undergraduate students, 30% full-time, 67% women, 33% men

Undergraduates 429 full-time, 1,003 part-time. 0.1% are from out of state; 25% Black or African American, non-Hispanic/Latino; 3% Hispanic/Latino; 0.4% Asian, non-Hispanic/Latino; 0.6% American Indian or Alaska Native, non-Hispanic/Latino; 0.3% Two or more races, non-Hispanic/Latino; 0.4% Race/ethnicity unknown. *Retention:* 47% of full-time freshmen returned.

Freshmen *Admission:* 258 enrolled.

Majors Administrative assistant and secretarial science; child development; clinical/medical laboratory technology; computer systems networking and telecommunications; computer technology/computer systems technology; criminal justice/police science; forest technology; information science/studies; occupational safety and health technology; respiratory therapy technician; surgical technology.

Academics *Calendar:* quarters. *Degree:* certificates, diplomas, and associate. *Special study options:* distance learning.

Student Life *Housing:* college housing not available.

Applying *Options:* early admission. *Application fee:* $20. *Required:* high school transcript.

Freshman Application Contact Okefenokee Technical College, 1701 Carswell Avenue, Waycross, GA 31503. *Phone:* 912-338-5251. *Toll-free phone:* 877-ED-AT-OTC. *Web site:* http://www.okefenokeetech.edu/.

Savannah Technical College
Savannah, Georgia

- **State-supported** 2-year, founded 1929, part of Technical College System of Georgia
- **Urban** campus
- **Coed,** 4,998 undergraduate students, 33% full-time, 67% women, 33% men

Undergraduates 1,648 full-time, 3,350 part-time. 2% are from out of state; 46% Black or African American, non-Hispanic/Latino; 6% Hispanic/Latino; 2% Asian, non-Hispanic/Latino; 0.2% Native Hawaiian or other Pacific Islander, non-Hispanic/Latino; 0.5% American Indian or Alaska Native, non-Hispanic/Latino; 2% Two or more races, non-Hispanic/Latino; 0.4% Race/ethnicity unknown; 1% international. *Retention:* 42% of full-time freshmen returned.

Freshmen *Admission:* 872 enrolled.

Majors Accounting; administrative assistant and secretarial science; automobile/automotive mechanics technology; child development; computer systems networking and telecommunications; criminal justice/safety; culinary arts; electrical, electronic and communications engineering technology; fire science/firefighting; heating, ventilation, air conditioning and refrigeration engineering technology; hotel/motel administration; industrial technology; information technology; marketing/marketing management; surgical technology; tourism and travel services management.

Academics *Calendar:* quarters. *Degree:* certificates, diplomas, and associate. *Special study options:* distance learning.

Student Life *Housing:* college housing not available.

Applying *Options:* early admission. *Application fee:* $20. *Required:* high school transcript.

Freshman Application Contact Savannah Technical College, 5717 White Bluff Road, Savannah, GA 31405. *Phone:* 912-443-5711. *Toll-free phone:* 800-769-6362. *Web site:* http://www.savannahtech.edu/.

Southeastern Technical College
Vidalia, Georgia

- **State-supported** 2-year, founded 1989, part of Technical College System of Georgia
- **Coed,** 1,910 undergraduate students, 30% full-time, 72% women, 28% men

Undergraduates 576 full-time, 1,334 part-time. 1% are from out of state; 34% Black or African American, non-Hispanic/Latino; 3% Hispanic/Latino; 0.1% Asian, non-Hispanic/Latino; 0.4% American Indian or Alaska Native, non-Hispanic/Latino; 0.2% Two or more races, non-Hispanic/Latino; 0.1% Race/ethnicity unknown; 0.1% international. *Retention:* 55% of full-time freshmen returned.

Freshmen *Admission:* 223 enrolled.

Majors Accounting; administrative assistant and secretarial science; child development; computer systems networking and telecommunications; criminal justice/safety; dental hygiene; design and visual communications; electrical, electronic and communications engineering technology; information science/studies; marketing/marketing management; medical radiologic technology; respiratory therapy technician; web page, digital/multimedia and information resources design.

Academics *Calendar:* quarters. *Degree:* certificates, diplomas, and associate. *Special study options:* distance learning.

Student Life *Housing:* college housing not available.

Applying *Options:* early admission. *Application fee:* $20. *Required:* high school transcript.

Freshman Application Contact Southeastern Technical College, 3001 East First Street, Vidalia, GA 30474. *Phone:* 912-538-3121. *Web site:* http://www.southeasterntech.edu/.

Southern Crescent Technical College
Griffin, Georgia

- **State-supported** 2-year, founded 1965, part of Technical College System of Georgia
- **Small-town** campus
- **Coed,** 5,381 undergraduate students, 38% full-time, 68% women, 32% men

Undergraduates 2,058 full-time, 3,323 part-time. 0.1% are from out of state; 42% Black or African American, non-Hispanic/Latino; 3% Hispanic/Latino;

1% Asian, non-Hispanic/Latino; 0.1% Native Hawaiian or other Pacific Islander, non-Hispanic/Latino; 0.2% American Indian or Alaska Native, non-Hispanic/Latino; 2% Two or more races, non-Hispanic/Latino; 0.2% Race/ethnicity unknown. *Retention:* 53% of full-time freshmen returned.

Freshmen *Admission:* 756 enrolled.

Majors Accounting; administrative assistant and secretarial science; automobile/automotive mechanics technology; business administration and management; child development; computer and information systems security; computer programming; computer systems networking and telecommunications; criminal justice/safety; drafting and design technology; electrical, electronic and communications engineering technology; emergency medical technology (EMT paramedic); heating, ventilation, air conditioning and refrigeration engineering technology; horticultural science; industrial technology; legal assistant/paralegal; manufacturing engineering technology; marketing/marketing management; medical radiologic technology; pharmacy technician; respiratory therapy technician; surgical technology; web page, digital/multimedia and information resources design.

Academics *Calendar:* quarters. *Degree:* certificates, diplomas, and associate. *Special study options:* distance learning.

Library Griffin Technical College Library.

Applying *Options:* early admission. *Application fee:* $15. *Required:* high school transcript.

Freshman Application Contact Southern Crescent Technical College, 501 Varsity Road, Griffin, GA 30223. *Phone:* 770-646-6160. *Web site:* http://www.sctech.edu/.

South Georgia College
Douglas, Georgia

Freshman Application Contact South Georgia College, 100 West College Park Drive, Douglas, GA 31533-5098. *Phone:* 912-260-4419. *Toll-free phone:* 800-342-6364. *Web site:* http://www.sgc.edu/.

South Georgia Technical College
Americus, Georgia

- **State-supported** 2-year, founded 1948, part of Technical College System of Georgia
- **Coed,** 2,361 undergraduate students, 47% full-time, 54% women, 46% men

Undergraduates 1,102 full-time, 1,259 part-time. 1% are from out of state; 58% Black or African American, non-Hispanic/Latino; 1% Hispanic/Latino; 0.7% Asian, non-Hispanic/Latino; 0.2% American Indian or Alaska Native, non-Hispanic/Latino; 1% Race/ethnicity unknown. *Retention:* 47% of full-time freshmen returned.

Freshmen *Admission:* 476 enrolled.

Majors Accounting; administrative assistant and secretarial science; child development; computer systems networking and telecommunications; criminal justice/safety; culinary arts; drafting and design technology; electrical, electronic and communications engineering technology; heating, ventilation, air conditioning and refrigeration engineering technology; horticultural science; industrial technology; information science/studies; legal assistant/paralegal; manufacturing engineering technology; marketing/marketing management.

Academics *Calendar:* quarters. *Degree:* certificates, diplomas, and associate. *Special study options:* distance learning.

Applying *Options:* early admission. *Application fee:* $20. *Required:* high school transcript.

Freshman Application Contact South Georgia Technical College, 900 South Georgia Tech Parkway, Americus, GA 31709. *Phone:* 229-931-2299. *Web site:* http://www.southgatech.edu/.

Southwest Georgia Technical College
Thomasville, Georgia

- **State-supported** 2-year, founded 1963, part of Technical College System of Georgia
- **Coed,** 1,871 undergraduate students, 22% full-time, 70% women, 30% men

Undergraduates 405 full-time, 1,466 part-time. 2% are from out of state; 35% Black or African American, non-Hispanic/Latino; 2% Hispanic/Latino; 0.6% Asian, non-Hispanic/Latino; 0.1% Native Hawaiian or other Pacific Islander, non-Hispanic/Latino; 0.5% American Indian or Alaska Native, non-Hispanic/Latino; 0.4% Two or more races, non-Hispanic/Latino; 0.6% Race/ethnicity unknown. *Retention:* 56% of full-time freshmen returned.

Freshmen *Admission:* 251 enrolled.

Majors Accounting; administrative assistant and secretarial science; agricultural mechanization; child development; computer systems networking and telecommunications; criminal justice/safety; information science/studies; medical radiologic technology; registered nursing/registered nurse; respiratory care therapy; surgical technology.

Academics *Calendar:* quarters. *Degree:* certificates, diplomas, and associate. *Special study options:* distance learning.

Student Life *Housing:* college housing not available.

Applying *Options:* electronic application, early admission. *Application fee:* $20. *Required:* high school transcript.

Freshman Application Contact Southwest Georgia Technical College, 15689 US 19 North, Thomasville, GA 31792. *Phone:* 229-225-5089. *Web site:* http://www.southwestgatech.edu/.

Waycross College

Waycross, Georgia

- **State-supported** 2-year, founded 1976, part of University System of Georgia
- **Small-town** 150-acre campus
- **Coed**

Undergraduates 3% are from out of state. *Retention:* 58% of full-time freshmen returned.

Faculty *Student/faculty ratio:* 19:1.

Academics *Calendar:* semesters. *Degree:* certificates and associate. *Special study options:* academic remediation for entering students, adult/continuing education programs, advanced placement credit, distance learning, off-campus study, part-time degree program, study abroad, summer session for credit.

Student Life *Campus security:* late-night transport/escort service, security guards.

Athletics Member NJCAA.

Standardized Tests *Recommended:* SAT or ACT (for admission).

Costs (2011–12) *Tuition:* state resident $2470 full-time; nonresident $9348 full-time. Full-time tuition and fees vary according to course load. Part-time tuition and fees vary according to course load. *Required fees:* $704 full-time.

Financial Aid Of all full-time matriculated undergraduates who enrolled in 2010, 20 Federal Work-Study jobs (averaging $2000).

Applying *Options:* electronic application, early admission, deferred entrance. *Application fee:* $20. *Required:* high school transcript.

Freshman Application Contact Waycross College, 2001 South Georgia Parkway, Waycross, GA 31503-9248. *Phone:* 912-449-7600. *Web site:* http://www.waycross.edu/.

West Georgia Technical College

Waco, Georgia

- **State-supported** 2-year, founded 1966, part of Technical College System of Georgia
- **Coed,** 7,845 undergraduate students, 27% full-time, 71% women, 29% men

Undergraduates 2,082 full-time, 5,763 part-time. 3% are from out of state; 29% Black or African American, non-Hispanic/Latino; 3% Hispanic/Latino; 0.8% Asian, non-Hispanic/Latino; 0.1% Native Hawaiian or other Pacific Islander, non-Hispanic/Latino; 0.5% American Indian or Alaska Native, non-Hispanic/Latino; 2% Race/ethnicity unknown. *Retention:* 52% of full-time freshmen returned.

Freshmen *Admission:* 1,255 enrolled.

Majors Accounting; administrative assistant and secretarial science; automobile/automotive mechanics technology; child development; computer systems networking and telecommunications; criminal justice/safety; electrical, electronic and communications engineering technology; fire science/firefighting; health information/medical records technology; industrial technology; information science/studies; marketing/marketing management; medical radiologic technology; pharmacy technician; plastics and polymer engineering technology; social work; web page, digital/multimedia and information resources design.

Academics *Calendar:* quarters. *Degree:* certificates, diplomas, and associate. *Special study options:* distance learning.

Student Life *Housing:* college housing not available.

Financial Aid Of all full-time matriculated undergraduates who enrolled in 2010, 68 Federal Work-Study jobs (averaging $800).

Applying *Options:* early admission. *Application fee:* $25. *Required:* high school transcript.

Freshman Application Contact West Georgia Technical College, 176 Murphy Campus Boulevard, Waco, GA 30182. *Phone:* 770-537-5719. *Web site:* http://www.westgatech.edu/.

Wiregrass Georgia Technical College

Valdosta, Georgia

- **State-supported** 2-year, founded 1963, part of Technical College System of Georgia
- **Suburban** campus
- **Coed,** 4,743 undergraduate students, 40% full-time, 70% women, 30% men

Undergraduates 1,894 full-time, 2,849 part-time. 1% are from out of state; 37% Black or African American, non-Hispanic/Latino; 2% Hispanic/Latino; 0.6% Asian, non-Hispanic/Latino; 0.1% Native Hawaiian or other Pacific Islander, non-Hispanic/Latino; 0.4% American Indian or Alaska Native, non-Hispanic/Latino; 0.6% Two or more races, non-Hispanic/Latino; 1% Race/ethnicity unknown. *Retention:* 48% of full-time freshmen returned.

Freshmen *Admission:* 642 enrolled.

Majors Accounting; administrative assistant and secretarial science; banking and financial support services; child development; computer and information systems security; computer programming; computer systems networking and telecommunications; criminal justice/safety; drafting and design technology; e-commerce; fire science/firefighting; machine tool technology; marketing/marketing management; medical radiologic technology; web page, digital/multimedia and information resources design.

Academics *Calendar:* quarters. *Degree:* certificates, diplomas, and associate. *Special study options:* distance learning.

Student Life *Housing:* college housing not available.

Applying *Options:* early admission. *Application fee:* $15. *Required:* high school transcript.

Freshman Application Contact Wiregrass Georgia Technical College, 4089 Val Tech Road, Valdosta, GA 31602. *Phone:* 229-468-2278. *Web site:* http://www.wiregrass.edu/.

GUAM

Guam Community College

Barrigada, Guam

Freshman Application Contact Mr. Patrick L. Clymer, Registrar, Guam Community College, PO Box 23069, Sesame Street, Barrigada, GU 96921. *Phone:* 671-735-5561. *Fax:* 671-735-5531. *E-mail:* patrick.clymer@guamcc.edu. *Web site:* http://www.guamcc.net/.

HAWAII

Hawaii Community College

Hilo, Hawaii

Director of Admissions Mrs. Tammy M. Tanaka, Admissions Specialist, Hawaii Community College, 200 West Kawili Street, Hilo, HI 96720-4091. *Phone:* 808-974-7661. *Web site:* http://www.hawcc.hawaii.edu/.

Hawaii Tokai International College

Honolulu, Hawaii

- **Independent** 2-year, founded 1992, part of Tokai University Educational System (Japan)
- **Urban** campus
- **Coed**

Undergraduates 56 full-time, 1 part-time. Students come from 3 states and territories; 3 other countries; 26% Race/ethnicity unknown; 74% international; 60% live on campus. *Retention:* 88% of full-time freshmen returned.

Faculty *Student/faculty ratio:* 4:1.

Academics *Calendar:* quarters. *Degree:* certificates, diplomas, and associate. *Special study options:* English as a second language, part-time degree program, study abroad, summer session for credit.

Student Life *Campus security:* 24-hour patrols.

Standardized Tests *Required for some:* TOEFL score of 450 PBT for international students.

Costs (2011–12) *Comprehensive fee:* $17,730 includes full-time tuition ($10,050), mandatory fees ($420), and room and board ($7260). Full-time tuition and fees vary according to course load and program. Part-time tuition: $425 per credit hour. Part-time tuition and fees vary according to course load and program. *Required fees:* $140 per term part-time. *Room and board:* college room only: $5100. Room and board charges vary according to board plan and housing facility.

Applying *Options:* deferred entrance. *Application fee:* $50. *Required:* essay or personal statement, high school transcript, minimum 2.5 GPA. *Required for some:* interview. *Recommended:* 1 letter of recommendation.

Freshman Application Contact Ms. Morna Dexter, Director, Student Services, Hawaii Tokai International College, 2241 Kapiolani Boulevard, Honolulu, HI 96826. *Phone:* 808-983-4187. *Fax:* 808-983-4173. *E-mail:* studentservices@tokai.edu. *Web site:* http://www.hawaiitokai.edu/.

Heald College–Honolulu
Honolulu, Hawaii

Freshman Application Contact Director of Admissions, Heald College–Honolulu, 1500 Kapiolani Boulevard, Honolulu, HI 96814. *Phone:* 808-955-1500. *Toll-free phone:* 800-88-HEALD. *Fax:* 808-955-6964. *E-mail:* honoluluinfo@heald.edu. *Web site:* http://www.heald.edu/.

Honolulu Community College
Honolulu, Hawaii

- **State-supported** 2-year, founded 1920, part of University of Hawaii System
- **Urban** 20-acre campus
- **Coed**

Undergraduates 1,640 full-time, 2,927 part-time. Students come from 32 states and territories; 16 other countries; 2% are from out of state; 10% transferred in. *Retention:* 55% of full-time freshmen returned.

Academics *Calendar:* semesters. *Degree:* certificates and associate. *Special study options:* academic remediation for entering students, accelerated degree program, advanced placement credit, cooperative education, distance learning, English as a second language, internships, part-time degree program, services for LD students, student-designed majors, summer session for credit. *ROTC:* Army (c), Air Force (c).

Student Life *Campus security:* 24-hour emergency response devices.

Standardized Tests *Required for some:* TOEFL required for international applicants.

Financial Aid Of all full-time matriculated undergraduates who enrolled in 2010, 30 Federal Work-Study jobs (averaging $1600).

Applying *Options:* early admission.

Freshman Application Contact Ms. Grace Funai, Admissions Office, Honolulu Community College, 874 Dillingham Boulevard, Honolulu, HI 96817. *Phone:* 808-845-9129. *E-mail:* honcc@hawaii.edu. *Web site:* http://www.honolulu.hawaii.edu/.

Kapiolani Community College
Honolulu, Hawaii

Freshman Application Contact Kapiolani Community College, 4303 Diamond Head Road, Honolulu, HI 96816-4421. *Phone:* 808-734-9555. *Web site:* http://kapiolani.hawaii.edu/page/home.

Kauai Community College
Lihue, Hawaii

Freshman Application Contact Mr. Leighton Oride, Admissions Officer and Registrar, Kauai Community College, 3-1901 Kaumualii Highway, Lihue, HI 96766. *Phone:* 808-245-8225. *Fax:* 808-245-8297. *E-mail:* arkauai@hawaii.edu. *Web site:* http://kauai.hawaii.edu/.

Leeward Community College
Pearl City, Hawaii

- **State-supported** 2-year, founded 1968, part of University of Hawaii System
- **Suburban** 49-acre campus with easy access to Honolulu
- **Coed**

Undergraduates 3,296 full-time, 4,646 part-time. Students come from 31 states and territories; 13 other countries; 0.8% are from out of state; 2% Black or African American, non-Hispanic/Latino; 11% Hispanic/Latino; 37% Asian, non-Hispanic/Latino; 12% Native Hawaiian or other Pacific Islander, non-Hispanic/Latino; 0.3% American Indian or Alaska Native, non-Hispanic/Latino; 26% Two or more races, non-Hispanic/Latino; 1% Race/ethnicity unknown; 0.5% international; 7% transferred in. *Retention:* 65% of full-time freshmen returned.

Faculty *Student/faculty ratio:* 23:1.

Academics *Calendar:* semesters. *Degree:* certificates and associate. *Special study options:* academic remediation for entering students, advanced placement credit, cooperative education, distance learning, English as a second language, honors programs, independent study, internships, off-campus study, part-time degree program, services for LD students, study abroad, summer session for credit. *ROTC:* Air Force (c).

Student Life *Campus security:* 24-hour emergency response devices and patrols, late-night transport/escort service.

Costs (2011–12) *One-time required fee:* $25. *Tuition:* state resident $2328 full-time, $97 per credit part-time; nonresident $6960 full-time, $290 per credit part-time. Full-time tuition and fees vary according to course load. Part-time tuition and fees vary according to course load. *Required fees:* $45 full-time, $1 per credit part-time, $18 per term part-time.

Applying *Options:* electronic application, early admission. *Application fee:* $25. *Required for some:* high school transcript.

Freshman Application Contact Ms. Anna Donald, Office Assistant, Leeward Community College, 96-045 Ala Ike, Pearl City, HI 96782-3393. *Phone:* 808-455-0642. *Web site:* http://www.lcc.hawaii.edu/.

Remington College–Honolulu Campus
Honolulu, Hawaii

Director of Admissions Louis LaMair, Director of Recruitment, Remington College–Honolulu Campus, 1111 Bishop Street, Suite 400, Honolulu, HI 96813. *Phone:* 808-942-1000. *Fax:* 808-533-3064. *E-mail:* louis.lamair@remingtoncollege.edu. *Web site:* http://www.remingtoncollege.edu/.

University of Hawaii Maui College
Kahului, Hawaii

Freshman Application Contact Mr. Stephen Kameda, Director of Admissions and Records, University of Hawaii Maui College, 310 Kaahumanu Avenue, Kahului, HI 96732. *Phone:* 808-984-3267. *Toll-free phone:* 800-479-6692. *Fax:* 808-242-9618. *E-mail:* kameda@hawaii.edu. *Web site:* http://maui.hawaii.edu/.

Windward Community College
Kaneohe, Hawaii

Director of Admissions Geri Imai, Registrar, Windward Community College, 45-720 Keaahala Road, Kaneohe, HI 96744-3528. *Phone:* 808-235-7430. *E-mail:* gerii@hawaii.edu. *Web site:* http://www.wcc.hawaii.edu/.

IDAHO

Brown Mackie College–Boise
Boise, Idaho

- **Proprietary** primarily 2-year, part of Education Management Corporation
- **Coed**

Academics *Degrees:* diplomas, associate, and bachelor's.

Costs (2011–12) *Tuition:* Tuition varies by program. Students should contact Brown Mackie College for tuition information.

Freshman Application Contact Brown Mackie College–Boise, 9050 West Overland Road, Suite 100, Boise, ID 83709. *Phone:* 208-321-8800. *Web site:* http://www.brownmackie.edu/boise/.

See page 346 for the College Close-Up.

Carrington College - Boise
Boise, Idaho

Director of Admissions Director of Admissions, Carrington College - Boise, 1122 North Liberty Street, Boise, ID 83704. *Phone:* 208-377-8080 Ext. 35. *Web site:* http://carrington.edu/.

College of Southern Idaho
Twin Falls, Idaho

Freshman Application Contact Director of Admissions, Registration, and Records, College of Southern Idaho, PO Box 1238, Twin Falls, ID 83303-1238. *Phone:* 208-732-6232. *Toll-free phone:* 800-680-0274. *Fax:* 208-736-3014. *Web site:* http://www.csi.edu/.

Eastern Idaho Technical College

Idaho Falls, Idaho

- State-supported 2-year, founded 1970
- Small-town 40-acre campus
- Endowment $789,503
- Coed, 830 undergraduate students, 37% full-time, 64% women, 36% men

Undergraduates 307 full-time, 523 part-time. Students come from 5 states and territories; 2 other countries; 0.7% Black or African American, non-Hispanic/Latino; 11% Hispanic/Latino; 1% Asian, non-Hispanic/Latino; 0.1% Native Hawaiian or other Pacific Islander, non-Hispanic/Latino; 1% American Indian or Alaska Native, non-Hispanic/Latino; 0.6% Two or more races, non-Hispanic/Latino; 11% Race/ethnicity unknown; 0.2% international.
Freshmen *Admission:* 300 applied, 177 admitted.
Faculty *Total:* 87, 47% full-time. *Student/faculty ratio:* 11:1.
Majors Accounting; administrative assistant and secretarial science; automobile/automotive mechanics technology; computer systems networking and telecommunications; dental assisting; desktop publishing and digital imaging design; diesel mechanics technology; fire science/firefighting; legal assistant/paralegal; licensed practical/vocational nurse training; marketing/marketing management; medical/clinical assistant; nuclear and industrial radiologic technologies related; registered nursing/registered nurse; surgical technology; truck and bus driver/commercial vehicle operation/instruction; welding technology.
Academics *Calendar:* semesters. *Degree:* certificates and associate. *Special study options:* academic remediation for entering students, adult/continuing education programs, advanced placement credit, distance learning, English as a second language, part-time degree program, services for LD students, summer session for credit.
Library Richard and Lila Jordan Library plus 1 other with 18,000 titles, 125 serial subscriptions, 150 audiovisual materials, an OPAC, a Web page.
Student Life *Housing:* college housing not available. *Campus security:* 24-hour patrols. *Student services:* personal/psychological counseling.
Standardized Tests *Required:* COMPASS (for admission).
Financial Aid Of all full-time matriculated undergraduates who enrolled in 2010, 37 Federal Work-Study jobs (averaging $1176). 11 state and other part-time jobs (averaging $1619).
Applying *Options:* deferred entrance. *Application fee:* $10. *Required:* high school transcript, interview. *Required for some:* essay or personal statement. *Application deadline:* rolling (freshmen).
Freshman Application Contact Annalea Avery, Director of Admissions/Career Placement, Eastern Idaho Technical College, 1600 South 25th East, Idaho Falls, ID 83404. *Phone:* 208-524-3000 Ext. 3337. *Toll-free phone:* 800-662-0261. *Fax:* 208-524-0429. *E-mail:* Annalea.avery@my.eitc.edu. *Web site:* http://www.eitc.edu/.

ITT Technical Institute

Boise, Idaho

- Proprietary primarily 2-year, founded 1906, part of ITT Educational Services, Inc.
- Urban campus
- Coed

Majors Business administration and management; communications technology; computer and information systems security; construction management; criminal justice/law enforcement administration; drafting and design technology; electrical, electronic and communications engineering technology; forensic science and technology; graphic communications; legal assistant/paralegal; network and system administration; project management; registered nursing/registered nurse.
Academics *Calendar:* quarters. *Degrees:* associate and bachelor's.
Student Life *Housing:* college housing not available.
Financial Aid Of all full-time matriculated undergraduates who enrolled in 2010, 9 Federal Work-Study jobs (averaging $5500).
Freshman Application Contact Director of Recruitment, ITT Technical Institute, 12302 West Explorer Drive, Boise, ID 83713. *Phone:* 208-322-8844. *Toll-free phone:* 800-666-4888. *Fax:* 208-322-0173. *Web site:* http://www.itt-tech.edu/.

North Idaho College

Coeur d'Alene, Idaho

- State and locally supported 2-year, founded 1933
- Small-town 42-acre campus
- Coed

Undergraduates 3,437 full-time, 2,286 part-time. 0.9% Black or African American, non-Hispanic/Latino; 3% Hispanic/Latino; 1% Asian, non-Hispanic/Latino; 0.3% Native Hawaiian or other Pacific Islander, non-Hispanic/Latino; 2% American Indian or Alaska Native, non-Hispanic/Latino; 8% Two or more races, non-Hispanic/Latino.
Faculty *Student/faculty ratio:* 17:1.
Academics *Calendar:* semesters. *Degree:* certificates and associate. *Special study options:* academic remediation for entering students, adult/continuing education programs, advanced placement credit, cooperative education, distance learning, English as a second language, independent study, internships, off-campus study, part-time degree program, services for LD students, summer session for credit. *ROTC:* Army (c).
Student Life *Campus security:* 24-hour emergency response devices and patrols, late-night transport/escort service.
Athletics Member NJCAA.
Costs (2011–12) *Tuition:* area resident $1680 full-time, $70 per credit hour part-time; state resident $2680 full-time, $112 per credit hour part-time; nonresident $6232 full-time, $260 per credit hour part-time. *Required fees:* $1084 full-time. *Room and board:* $7000; room only: $4000.
Financial Aid Of all full-time matriculated undergraduates who enrolled in 2010, 142 Federal Work-Study jobs (averaging $1425). 106 state and other part-time jobs (averaging $1327).
Applying *Options:* electronic application, early admission, deferred entrance. *Application fee:* $25. *Required for some:* essay or personal statement, high school transcript, county residency certificate.
Freshman Application Contact North Idaho College, 1000 West Garden Avenue, Coeur d Alene, ID 83814-2199. *Phone:* 208-769-3303. *Toll-free phone:* 877-404-4536 Ext. 3311. *E-mail:* admit@nic.edu. *Web site:* http://www.nic.edu/.

ILLINOIS

Benedictine University at Springfield

Springfield, Illinois

Freshman Application Contact Kevin Hinkle, Associate Director of Admissions, Benedictine University at Springfield, 1500 North Fifth Street, Springfield, IL 62702. *Phone:* 217-525-1420 Ext. 321. *Toll-free phone:* 800-635-7289. *Fax:* 217-525-1497. *E-mail:* khinkle@sci.edu. *Web site:* http://www1.ben.edu/springfield/.

Black Hawk College

Moline, Illinois

Freshman Application Contact Ms. Vashti Berry, College Recruiter, Black Hawk College, 6600-34th Avenue, Moline, IL 61265. *Phone:* 309-796-5341. *Toll-free phone:* 800-334-1311. *E-mail:* berryv@bhc.edu. *Web site:* http://www.bhc.edu/.

Carl Sandburg College

Galesburg, Illinois

Director of Admissions Ms. Carol Kreider, Dean of Student Support Services, Carl Sandburg College, 2400 Tom L. Wilson Boulevard, Galesburg, IL 61401-9576. *Phone:* 309-341-5234. *Web site:* http://www.sandburg.edu/.

City Colleges of Chicago, Harold Washington College

Chicago, Illinois

Freshman Application Contact Admissions Office, City Colleges of Chicago, Harold Washington College, 30 East Lake Street, Chicago, IL 60601-2449. *Phone:* 312-553-6010. *Web site:* http://hwashington.ccc.edu/.

City Colleges of Chicago, Harry S. Truman College

Chicago, Illinois

- State and locally supported 2-year, founded 1956, part of City Colleges of Chicago
- Urban 5-acre campus
- Coed, 13,174 undergraduate students

Faculty *Student/faculty ratio:* 34:1.
Majors Accounting; automobile/automotive mechanics technology; biological and physical sciences; business administration and management; child-care provision; computer systems networking and telecommunications; criminal justice/safety; general studies; information technology; liberal arts and sci-

ences/liberal studies; mechanical drafting and CAD/CADD; registered nursing/registered nurse.

Academics *Calendar:* semesters. *Degree:* certificates, diplomas, and associate. *Special study options:* academic remediation for entering students, adult/continuing education programs, advanced placement credit, cooperative education, distance learning, English as a second language, honors programs, internships, part-time degree program, services for LD students, summer session for credit.

Student Life *Housing:* college housing not available. *Activities and Organizations:* drama/theater group. *Campus security:* 24-hour patrols, late-night transport/escort service. *Student services:* personal/psychological counseling.

Athletics Member NJCAA. *Intercollegiate sports:* basketball M.

Costs (2011–12) *Tuition:* $89 per credit hour part-time; state resident $174 per credit hour part-time; nonresident $230 per credit hour part-time. Full-time tuition and fees vary according to course level, course load, degree level, and program. Part-time tuition and fees vary according to course level, course load, degree level, and program. *Payment plans:* installment, deferred payment. *Waivers:* senior citizens and employees or children of employees.

Financial Aid Of all full-time matriculated undergraduates who enrolled in 2010, 150 Federal Work-Study jobs (averaging $3000).

Applying *Options:* early admission, deferred entrance. *Application deadlines:* rolling (freshmen), rolling (transfers). *Notification:* continuous until 9/8 (freshmen), continuous until 9/8 (transfers).

Freshman Application Contact City Colleges of Chicago, Harry S. Truman College, 1145 West Wilson Avenue, Chicago, IL 60640-5616. *Phone:* 773-907-4000 Ext. 1112. *Web site:* http://www.trumancollege.edu/.

City Colleges of Chicago, Kennedy-King College

Chicago, Illinois

Freshman Application Contact Admissions Office, City Colleges of Chicago, Kennedy-King College, 6301 South Halstead Street, Chicago, IL 60621. *Phone:* 773-602-5062. *Fax:* 773-602-5055. *Web site:* http://kennedyking.ccc.edu/.

City Colleges of Chicago, Malcolm X College

Chicago, Illinois

Freshman Application Contact Ms. Kimberly Hollingsworth, Dean of Student Services, City Colleges of Chicago, Malcolm X College, 1900 West Van Buren Street, Chicago, IL 60612-3145. *Phone:* 312-850-7120. *Fax:* 312-850-7119. *E-mail:* khollingsworth@ccc.edu. *Web site:* http://malcolmx.ccc.edu/.

City Colleges of Chicago, Olive-Harvey College

Chicago, Illinois

Freshman Application Contact City Colleges of Chicago, Olive-Harvey College, 10001 South Woodlawn Avenue, Chicago, IL 60628-1645. *Phone:* 773-291-6362. *Web site:* http://oliveharvey.ccc.edu/.

City Colleges of Chicago, Richard J. Daley College

Chicago, Illinois

Freshman Application Contact City Colleges of Chicago, Richard J. Daley College, 7500 South Pulaski Road, Chicago, IL 60652-1242. *Phone:* 773-838-7606. *Web site:* http://daley.ccc.edu/.

City Colleges of Chicago, Wilbur Wright College

Chicago, Illinois

Freshman Application Contact Ms. Amy Aiello, Assistant Dean of Student Services, City Colleges of Chicago, Wilbur Wright College, Chicago, IL 60634. *Phone:* 773-481-8207. *Fax:* 773-481-8185. *E-mail:* aaiello@ccc.edu. *Web site:* http://wright.ccc.edu/.

College of DuPage

Glen Ellyn, Illinois

- **State and locally supported** 2-year, founded 1967
- **Suburban** 297-acre campus with easy access to Chicago
- **Endowment** $7.4 million
- **Coed,** 26,209 undergraduate students, 36% full-time, 53% women, 47% men

Undergraduates 9,464 full-time, 16,745 part-time. Students come from 24 states and territories; 1% are from out of state; 7% Black or African American, non-Hispanic/Latino; 22% Hispanic/Latino; 9% Asian, non-Hispanic/Latino; 0.2% American Indian or Alaska Native, non-Hispanic/Latino; 2% Two or more races, non-Hispanic/Latino; 1% Race/ethnicity unknown; 0.4% international; 13% transferred in. *Retention:* 60% of full-time freshmen returned.

Freshmen *Admission:* 3,360 applied, 2,918 admitted, 3,411 enrolled.

Faculty *Total:* 1,134, 24% full-time, 25% with terminal degrees. *Student/faculty ratio:* 21:1.

Majors Accounting; administrative assistant and secretarial science; automobile/automotive mechanics technology; baking and pastry arts; biological and physical sciences; building/property maintenance; business administration and management; child-care and support services management; child-care provision; child development; cinematography and film/video production; commercial and advertising art; communications systems installation and repair technology; communications technology; computer installation and repair technology; computer programming (specific applications); computer typography and composition equipment operation; corrections; criminal justice/law enforcement administration; criminal justice/police science; culinary arts; data entry/microcomputer applications related; dental hygiene; design and visual communications; desktop publishing and digital imaging design; drafting and design technology; drafting/design engineering technologies related; electrical, electronic and communications engineering technology; electrical/electronics equipment installation and repair; electromechanical technology; emergency medical technology (EMT paramedic); engineering; fashion and fabric consulting; fashion/apparel design; fashion merchandising; fire science/firefighting; graphic and printing equipment operation/production; health/health-care administration; health information/medical records administration; health information/medical records technology; heating, air conditioning, ventilation and refrigeration maintenance technology; hospital and health-care facilities administration; hospitality administration; hotel/motel administration; human services; industrial electronics technology; industrial technology; interior design; landscaping and groundskeeping; legal administrative assistant/secretary; liberal arts and sciences/liberal studies; library and archives assisting; library and information science; machine tool technology; manufacturing engineering technology; marketing/marketing management; massage therapy; medical radiologic technology; merchandising; nuclear medical technology; occupational therapist assistant; occupational therapy; office management; ornamental horticulture; photography; physical therapy technology; plastics and polymer engineering technology; precision production trades; real estate; registered nursing/registered nurse; respiratory care therapy; restaurant, culinary, and catering management; retailing; robotics technology; sales, distribution, and marketing operations; selling skills and sales; speech-language pathology; substance abuse/addiction counseling; surgical technology; tourism and travel services management; tourism and travel services marketing; tourism promotion; transportation and materials moving related; welding technology.

Academics *Calendar:* semesters. *Degree:* certificates and associate. *Special study options:* academic remediation for entering students, accelerated degree program, adult/continuing education programs, advanced placement credit, cooperative education, distance learning, double majors, English as a second language, external degree program, honors programs, independent study, internships, off-campus study, part-time degree program, services for LD students, student-designed majors, study abroad, summer session for credit.

Library College of DuPage Library with 203,300 titles, 6,005 serial subscriptions, an OPAC, a Web page.

Student Life *Housing:* college housing not available. *Activities and Organizations:* drama/theater group, student-run newspaper, choral group, Latino Ethnic Awareness Association, The Christian Group, Phi Theta Kappa, International Students Organization, Muslim Student Association. *Campus security:* 24-hour emergency response devices and patrols, student patrols, late-night transport/escort service. *Student services:* health clinic, personal/psychological counseling.

Athletics Member NJCAA. *Intercollegiate sports:* baseball M, basketball M/W, golf M, soccer M/W, softball M/W. *Intramural sports:* basketball M/W, cross-country running M/W, football M, golf M, ice hockey M, racquetball M/W, soccer M/W, softball W, tennis M/W, track and field M/W, volleyball W.

Standardized Tests *Recommended:* ACT (for admission).

Costs (2011–12) *Tuition:* area resident $3960 full-time, $132 per credit hour part-time; state resident $9570 full-time, $319 per credit hour part-time; nonresident $11,670 full-time, $389 per credit hour part-time. Full-time tuition and fees vary according to program. Part-time tuition and fees vary according to program. *Payment plans:* installment, deferred payment. *Waivers:* senior citizens and employees or children of employees.

Financial Aid Of all full-time matriculated undergraduates who enrolled in 2010, 424 Federal Work-Study jobs (averaging $4135).

Applying *Options:* early admission, deferred entrance. *Application fee:* $20. *Application deadlines:* rolling (freshmen), rolling (out-of-state freshmen), rolling (transfers). *Notification:* continuous (freshmen), continuous (out-of-state freshmen), continuous (transfers).

Freshman Application Contact College of DuPage, IL. *E-mail:* admissions@cod.edu. *Web site:* http://www.cod.edu/.

College of Lake County

Grayslake, Illinois

- **District-supported** 2-year, founded 1967, part of Illinois Community College Board
- **Suburban** 226-acre campus with easy access to Chicago, Milwaukee
- **Coed,** 17,388 undergraduate students, 30% full-time, 56% women, 44% men

Undergraduates 5,212 full-time, 12,176 part-time. Students come from 31 other countries; 1% are from out of state; 9% Black or African American, non-Hispanic/Latino; 23% Hispanic/Latino; 6% Asian, non-Hispanic/Latino; 0.2% American Indian or Alaska Native, non-Hispanic/Latino; 10% Race/ethnicity unknown; 1% international.

Freshmen *Admission:* 1,791 enrolled.

Faculty *Total:* 1,027, 20% full-time, 15% with terminal degrees. *Student/faculty ratio:* 17:1.

Majors Accounting technology and bookkeeping; administrative assistant and secretarial science; architectural drafting and CAD/CADD; art; automobile/automotive mechanics technology; biological and physical sciences; business administration and management; business automation/technology/data entry; chemical technology; child-care provision; civil engineering technology; computer installation and repair technology; computer programming (specific applications); computer systems networking and telecommunications; construction engineering technology; criminal justice/police science; dental hygiene; electrical, electronic and communications engineering technology; electrician; engineering; fire prevention and safety technology; heating, air conditioning, ventilation and refrigeration maintenance technology; industrial mechanics and maintenance technology; landscaping and groundskeeping; liberal arts and sciences/liberal studies; machine shop technology; mechanical engineering/mechanical technology; medical office management; medical radiologic technology; music; music teacher education; natural resources management and policy; ornamental horticulture; professional, technical, business, and scientific writing; registered nursing/registered nurse; restaurant, culinary, and catering management; selling skills and sales; social work; substance abuse/addiction counseling; turf and turfgrass management.

Academics *Calendar:* semesters. *Degree:* certificates and associate. *Special study options:* academic remediation for entering students, adult/continuing education programs, advanced placement credit, cooperative education, distance learning, double majors, English as a second language, honors programs, independent study, internships, off-campus study, part-time degree program, services for LD students, student-designed majors, study abroad, summer session for credit.

Library College of Lake County Library plus 1 other with 106,842 titles, 766 serial subscriptions, an OPAC, a Web page.

Student Life *Housing:* college housing not available. *Activities and Organizations:* drama/theater group, student-run newspaper, radio station, choral group, Latino Alliance, Men of Vision, Asian Student Alliance, Student Government Association, Anime. *Campus security:* 24-hour emergency response devices and patrols, late-night transport/escort service. *Student services:* health clinic, personal/psychological counseling, women's center.

Athletics Member NJCAA. *Intercollegiate sports:* baseball M(s), basketball M(s)/W(s), cross-country running M(s)/W(s), golf M(s), soccer M(s)/W(s), softball W(s), tennis M(s)/W(s), volleyball W(s). *Intramural sports:* cheerleading W, golf M/W.

Costs (2012–13) *Tuition:* area resident $2790 full-time, $93 per credit hour part-time; state resident $6990 full-time, $233 per credit hour part-time; nonresident $9420 full-time, $314 per credit hour part-time. *Required fees:* $480 full-time, $16 per credit hour part-time. *Payment plan:* installment. *Waivers:* senior citizens and employees or children of employees.

Financial Aid Of all full-time matriculated undergraduates who enrolled in 2010, 98 Federal Work-Study jobs (averaging $1311).

Applying *Options:* electronic application, early admission, deferred entrance. *Required for some:* high school transcript, interview. *Application deadlines:* rolling (freshmen), rolling (transfers). *Notification:* continuous (freshmen), continuous (transfers).

Freshman Application Contact Director, Student Recruitment, College of Lake County, Grayslake, IL 60030-1198. *Phone:* 847-543-2383. *Fax:* 847-543-3061. *Web site:* http://www.clcillinois.edu/.

The College of Office Technology

Chicago, Illinois

Director of Admissions Mr. William Bolton, Director of Admissions, The College of Office Technology, 1520 West Division Street, Chicago, IL 60622. *Phone:* 773-278-0042. *Toll-free phone:* 800-953-6161. *E-mail:* bbolton@cot.edu. *Web site:* http://www.cot.edu/.

Danville Area Community College

Danville, Illinois

- **State and locally supported** 2-year, founded 1946, part of Illinois Community College Board
- **Small-town** 50-acre campus
- **Coed**

Undergraduates 1,564 full-time, 2,149 part-time. 7% are from out of state; 5% transferred in.

Faculty *Student/faculty ratio:* 26:1.

Academics *Calendar:* semesters. *Degree:* certificates and associate. *Special study options:* academic remediation for entering students, adult/continuing education programs, advanced placement credit, cooperative education, distance learning, double majors, English as a second language, independent study, internships, part-time degree program, services for LD students, summer session for credit.

Student Life *Campus security:* 24-hour patrols.

Athletics Member NJCAA.

Financial Aid Of all full-time matriculated undergraduates who enrolled in 2008, 60 Federal Work-Study jobs (averaging $2500). 113 state and other part-time jobs (averaging $4500).

Applying *Options:* early admission, deferred entrance. *Required:* high school transcript.

Freshman Application Contact Danville Area Community College, 2000 East Main Street, Danville, IL 61832-5199. *Phone:* 217-443-8803. *Web site:* http://www.dacc.edu/.

Elgin Community College

Elgin, Illinois

- **State and locally supported** 2-year, founded 1949, part of Illinois Community College Board
- **Suburban** 145-acre campus with easy access to Chicago
- **Coed,** 11,811 undergraduate students, 35% full-time, 55% women, 45% men

Undergraduates 4,086 full-time, 7,725 part-time. Students come from 10 states and territories; 12 other countries; 0.1% are from out of state; 6% Black or African American, non-Hispanic/Latino; 30% Hispanic/Latino; 6% Asian, non-Hispanic/Latino; 0.1% Native Hawaiian or other Pacific Islander, non-Hispanic/Latino; 0.3% American Indian or Alaska Native, non-Hispanic/Latino; 3% Race/ethnicity unknown; 0.9% international; 0.5% transferred in.

Freshmen *Admission:* 1,278 admitted, 1,278 enrolled.

Faculty *Student/faculty ratio:* 27:1.

Majors Accounting; administrative assistant and secretarial science; animation, interactive technology, video graphics and special effects; automobile/automotive mechanics technology; baking and pastry arts; biological and physical sciences; biology/biotechnology laboratory technician; business administration and management; CAD/CADD drafting/design technology; clinical/medical laboratory technology; computer and information systems security; criminal justice/police science; culinary arts; data entry/microcomputer applications; design and visual communications; engineering; entrepreneurship; executive assistant/executive secretary; fine/studio arts; fire science/firefighting; graphic design; health and physical education/fitness; heating, air conditioning, ventilation and refrigeration maintenance technology; industrial mechanics and maintenance technology; legal assistant/paralegal; liberal arts and sciences/liberal studies; machine tool technology; marketing/marketing management; music; physical therapy technology; radiologic technology/science; registered nursing/registered nurse; restaurant, culinary, and catering management; retailing; social work.

Academics *Calendar:* semesters. *Degree:* certificates, diplomas, and associate. *Special study options:* academic remediation for entering students, accelerated degree program, advanced placement credit, cooperative education, distance learning, double majors, English as a second language, honors programs, independent study, internships, off-campus study, part-time degree program, services for LD students, study abroad, summer session for credit.

Library Renner Learning Resource Center with an OPAC, a Web page.

Student Life *Housing:* college housing not available. *Activities and Organizations:* drama/theater group, student-run newspaper, choral group, Phi Theta Kappa Honor Society, Organization of Latin American Students, Asian Filipino Club, Amnesty International, Student Government. *Campus security:*

grounds are patrolled Sunday-Saturday 7am-11pm during the academic year. *Student services:* personal/psychological counseling, legal services.

Athletics Member NJCAA. *Intercollegiate sports:* baseball M(s), basketball M(s)/W(s), cross-country running M(s)/W(s), golf M(s), soccer M(s)/W(s), softball W(s), tennis M(s)/W(s), volleyball W(s).

Costs (2011–12) *Tuition:* area resident $2970 full-time, $99 per credit hour part-time; state resident $10,081 full-time, $336 per credit hour part-time; nonresident $13,358 full-time, $445 per credit hour part-time. *Required fees:* $10 full-time. *Payment plan:* installment. *Waivers:* senior citizens and employees or children of employees.

Applying *Options:* electronic application. *Required for some:* high school transcript, some academic programs have additional departmental admission requirements that students must meet. *Application deadlines:* rolling (freshmen), rolling (transfers). *Notification:* continuous (freshmen), continuous (transfers).

Freshman Application Contact Admissions, Recruitment, and Student Life, Elgin Community College, 1700 Spartan Drive, Elgin, IL 60123. *Phone:* 847-214-7414. *E-mail:* admissions@elgin.edu. *Web site:* http://www.elgin.edu/.

Fox College
Bedford Park, Illinois

- **Private** 2-year, founded 1932
- **Suburban** campus
- **Coed,** 417 undergraduate students
- 62% of applicants were admitted

Freshmen *Admission:* 1,071 applied, 667 admitted.

Majors Accounting technology and bookkeeping; administrative assistant and secretarial science; graphic design; hotel/motel administration; medical/clinical assistant; physical therapy technology; retailing; veterinary/animal health technology.

Academics *Degree:* diplomas and associate. *Special study options:* accelerated degree program, internships.

Student Life *Housing:* college housing not available.

Freshman Application Contact Admissions Office, Fox College, 6640 South Cicero, Bedford Park, IL 60638. *Phone:* 708-444-4500. *Web site:* http://www.foxcollege.edu/.

Gem City College
Quincy, Illinois

Director of Admissions Admissions Director, Gem City College, PO Box 179, Quincy, IL 62301. *Phone:* 217-222-0391. *Web site:* http://www.gemcitycollege.com/.

Harper College
Palatine, Illinois

- **State and locally supported** 2-year, founded 1965, part of Illinois Community College Board
- **Suburban** 200-acre campus with easy access to Chicago
- **Endowment** $2.6 million
- **Coed,** 15,989 undergraduate students, 40% full-time, 56% women, 44% men

Undergraduates 6,414 full-time, 9,575 part-time. Students come from 9 states and territories; 1% are from out of state; 6% Black or African American, non-Hispanic/Latino; 13% Hispanic/Latino; 11% Asian, non-Hispanic/Latino; 0.1% American Indian or Alaska Native, non-Hispanic/Latino; 8% Race/ethnicity unknown; 0.2% international; 4% transferred in. *Retention:* 61% of full-time freshmen returned.

Freshmen *Admission:* 4,303 applied, 4,303 admitted, 1,874 enrolled. *Test scores:* ACT scores over 18: 77%; ACT scores over 24: 26%; ACT scores over 30: 4%.

Faculty *Total:* 892, 23% full-time. *Student/faculty ratio:* 22:1.

Majors Accounting; administrative assistant and secretarial science; architectural drafting and CAD/CADD; architectural engineering technology; art; banking and financial support services; biology/biological sciences; business administration and management; cardiovascular technology; chemistry; childcare provision; computer and information sciences; computer programming; computer programming (specific applications); computer science; criminal justice/law enforcement administration; cyber/computer forensics and counterterrorism; dental hygiene; diagnostic medical sonography and ultrasound technology; dietetics; dietetic technology; early childhood education; electrical, electronic and communications engineering technology; elementary education; emergency medical technology (EMT paramedic); engineering; English; environmental studies; fashion and fabric consulting; fashion/apparel design; fashion merchandising; finance; fine/studio arts; fire science/firefighting; food service systems administration; health teacher education; heating, air conditioning, ventilation and refrigeration maintenance technology; history; home-

land security; hospitality administration; humanities; human services; interior design; international business/trade/commerce; legal administrative assistant/secretary; legal assistant/paralegal; liberal arts and sciences/liberal studies; marketing/marketing management; mathematics; medical administrative assistant and medical secretary; medical/clinical assistant; music; nanotechnology; philosophy; physical education teaching and coaching; physical sciences; psychology; public relations, advertising, and applied communication related; radiologic technology/science; registered nursing/registered nurse; sales, distribution, and marketing operations; small business administration; sociology and anthropology; speech communication and rhetoric; theater/theater arts management; web page, digital/multimedia and information resources design.

Academics *Calendar:* semesters. *Degree:* certificates and associate. *Special study options:* academic remediation for entering students, accelerated degree program, adult/continuing education programs, advanced placement credit, cooperative education, distance learning, English as a second language, honors programs, independent study, internships, part-time degree program, services for LD students, study abroad, summer session for credit.

Library Harper College Library with 121,982 titles, 155 serial subscriptions, 20,754 audiovisual materials, an OPAC, a Web page.

Student Life *Housing:* college housing not available. *Activities and Organizations:* drama/theater group, student-run newspaper, radio station, choral group, Student Radio Station, Program Board, Student Senate, Nursing Club, Phi Theta Kappa. *Campus security:* 24-hour emergency response devices and patrols, late-night transport/escort service. *Student services:* health clinic, personal/psychological counseling, women's center, legal services.

Athletics Member NJCAA. *Intercollegiate sports:* baseball M, basketball M/W, cross-country running M/W, football M, soccer M/W, softball W, track and field M/W, volleyball W, wrestling M. *Intramural sports:* baseball M, basketball M, football M, racquetball M/W, softball M/W, table tennis M/W, tennis M/W, volleyball M/W.

Costs (2012–13) *Tuition:* area resident $3075 full-time; state resident $10,785 full-time; nonresident $13,050 full-time. Full-time tuition and fees vary according to course load. Part-time tuition and fees vary according to course load. *Required fees:* $537 full-time. *Payment plan:* installment. *Waivers:* senior citizens and employees or children of employees.

Financial Aid Of all full-time matriculated undergraduates who enrolled in 2010, 85 Federal Work-Study jobs (averaging $1210).

Applying *Options:* electronic application, early admission, deferred entrance. *Application fee:* $25. *Required:* high school transcript. *Application deadlines:* rolling (freshmen), rolling (transfers). *Notification:* continuous (freshmen), continuous (transfers).

Freshman Application Contact Admissions Office, Harper College, 1200 West Algonquin Road, Palatine, IL 60067. *Phone:* 847-925-6700. *Fax:* 847-925-6044. *E-mail:* admissions@harpercollege.edu. *Web site:* http://goforward.harpercollege.edu/.

Heartland Community College
Normal, Illinois

Freshman Application Contact Ms. Candace Brownlee, Director of Student Recruitment, Heartland Community College, 1500 West Raab Road, Normal, IL 61761. *Phone:* 309-268-8041. *Fax:* 309-268-7992. *E-mail:* candace.brownlee@heartland.edu. *Web site:* http://www.heartland.edu/.

Highland Community College
Freeport, Illinois

- **State and locally supported** 2-year, founded 1962, part of Illinois Community College Board
- **Rural** 240-acre campus
- **Coed,** 2,222 undergraduate students, 53% full-time, 61% women, 39% men

Undergraduates 1,186 full-time, 1,036 part-time. 2% are from out of state; 11% Black or African American, non-Hispanic/Latino; 1% Hispanic/Latino; 1% Asian, non-Hispanic/Latino; 0.1% Native Hawaiian or other Pacific Islander, non-Hispanic/Latino; 2% American Indian or Alaska Native, non-Hispanic/Latino; 3% Two or more races, non-Hispanic/Latino; 2% Race/ethnicity unknown; 3% transferred in.

Freshmen *Admission:* 605 applied, 605 admitted, 450 enrolled. *Test scores:* ACT scores over 18: 69%; ACT scores over 24: 19%; ACT scores over 30: 1%.

Faculty *Total:* 142, 32% full-time, 6% with terminal degrees. *Student/faculty ratio:* 19:1.

Majors Accounting; administrative assistant and secretarial science; agricultural business and management; autobody/collision and repair technology; automobile/automotive mechanics technology; biological and physical sciences; engineering; general studies; graphic design; health information/medical records technology; heavy equipment maintenance technology; information technology; liberal arts and sciences/liberal studies; mathematics teacher education; medical/clinical assistant; registered nursing/registered nurse; teacher assistant/aide.

Academics *Calendar:* semesters. *Degree:* certificates and associate. *Special study options:* academic remediation for entering students, adult/continuing education programs, advanced placement credit, cooperative education, distance learning, English as a second language, external degree program, honors programs, independent study, internships, part-time degree program, services for LD students, student-designed majors, summer session for credit.

Library Clarence Mitchell Library with 71 serial subscriptions, 6,843 audiovisual materials, an OPAC, a Web page.

Student Life *Housing:* college housing not available. *Activities and Organizations:* drama/theater group, student-run newspaper, radio station, choral group, Phi Theta Kappa, Royal Scots, Prairie Wind, intramurals, Collegiate Choir. *Campus security:* 24-hour emergency response devices and patrols. *Student services:* personal/psychological counseling.

Athletics Member NJCAA. *Intercollegiate sports:* baseball M(s), basketball M(s)/W(s), golf M(s)/W(s), softball W(s), volleyball W(s). *Intramural sports:* basketball M/W, volleyball M/W.

Costs (2011–12) *Tuition:* area resident $2970 full-time, $99 per credit hour part-time; state resident $4470 full-time, $149 per credit hour part-time; nonresident $4950 full-time, $165 per credit hour part-time. Full-time tuition and fees vary according to program and reciprocity agreements. Part-time tuition and fees vary according to program and reciprocity agreements. *Required fees:* $270 full-time, $9 per credit hour part-time. *Payment plans:* installment, deferred payment. *Waivers:* minority students, senior citizens, and employees or children of employees.

Financial Aid Of all full-time matriculated undergraduates who enrolled in 2010, 1,030 applied for aid, 911 were judged to have need. 52 Federal Work-Study jobs (averaging $1604). In 2010, 76 non-need-based awards were made. *Average percent of need met:* 33%. *Average financial aid package:* $6319. *Average need-based loan:* $3060. *Average need-based gift aid:* $4695. *Average non-need-based aid:* $3044.

Applying *Options:* electronic application, early admission, deferred entrance. *Required for some:* high school transcript, 1 letter of recommendation. *Recommended:* high school transcript. *Application deadlines:* rolling (freshmen), rolling (transfers).

Freshman Application Contact Mr. Jeremy Bradt, Director, Enrollment and Records, Highland Community College, 2998 West Pearl City Road, Freeport, IL 61032. *Phone:* 815-235-6121 Ext. 3500. *Fax:* 815-235-6130. *E-mail:* jeremy.bradt@highland.edu. *Web site:* http://www.highland.edu/.

Illinois Central College

East Peoria, Illinois

- **State and locally supported** 2-year, founded 1967, part of Illinois Community College Board
- **Suburban** 430-acre campus
- **Coed,** 12,286 undergraduate students, 38% full-time, 57% women, 43% men

Undergraduates 4,718 full-time, 7,568 part-time. 1% are from out of state; 13% Black or African American, non-Hispanic/Latino; 3% Hispanic/Latino; 2% Asian, non-Hispanic/Latino; 0.2% Native Hawaiian or other Pacific Islander, non-Hispanic/Latino; 0.5% American Indian or Alaska Native, non-Hispanic/Latino; 1% Race/ethnicity unknown; 0.1% international.

Freshmen *Admission:* 1,480 enrolled.

Faculty *Total:* 658, 29% full-time. *Student/faculty ratio:* 19:1.

Majors Accounting; accounting technology and bookkeeping; administrative assistant and secretarial science; agricultural business and management; agricultural mechanics and equipment technology; agricultural production; applied horticulture/horticulture operations; automobile/automotive mechanics technology; banking and financial support services; business administration and management; child-care provision; clinical/medical laboratory technology; communications technology; community health services counseling; computer programming; construction engineering; corrections; criminal justice/police science; crop production; culinary arts; data entry/microcomputer applications; data processing and data processing technology; dental hygiene; diesel mechanics technology; electrical, electronic and communications engineering technology; engineering; fire science/firefighting; forensic science and technology; general studies; graphic design; heating, ventilation, air conditioning and refrigeration engineering technology; industrial technology; legal assistant/paralegal; liberal arts and sciences/liberal studies; library and archives assisting; manufacturing engineering technology; mechanical engineering/mechanical technology; mental health counseling; occupational therapist assistant; physical therapy technology; platemaking/imaging; psychiatric/mental

health services technology; radiologic technology/science; registered nursing/registered nurse; respiratory care therapy; retailing; robotics technology; sign language interpretation and translation; substance abuse/addiction counseling; surgical technology; teacher assistant/aide; web/multimedia management and webmaster; welding technology.

Academics *Calendar:* semesters. *Degree:* certificates and associate. *Special study options:* academic remediation for entering students, adult/continuing education programs, advanced placement credit, English as a second language, honors programs, internships, part-time degree program, services for LD students, summer session for credit.

Library Main Library plus 2 others.

Student Life *Activities and Organizations:* drama/theater group, student-run newspaper, radio station, choral group. *Campus security:* 24-hour emergency response devices, late-night transport/escort service. *Student services:* health clinic, personal/psychological counseling.

Athletics Member NJCAA. *Intercollegiate sports:* baseball M, basketball M/W, golf M, soccer M/W, softball W, volleyball W.

Costs (2012–13) *Tuition:* area resident $2448 full-time, $102 per credit hour part-time; state resident $5400 full-time, $225 per credit hour part-time; nonresident $5400 full-time, $225 per credit hour part-time. *Payment plan:* installment. *Waivers:* senior citizens and employees or children of employees.

Financial Aid Of all full-time matriculated undergraduates who enrolled in 2011, 6,521 applied for aid, 5,525 were judged to have need.

Applying *Options:* electronic application, early admission. *Required:* high school transcript. *Application deadlines:* rolling (freshmen), rolling (out-of-state freshmen), rolling (transfers). *Notification:* continuous (freshmen), continuous (out-of-state freshmen), continuous (transfers).

Freshman Application Contact Illinois Central College, One College Drive, East Peoria, IL 61635-0001. *Phone:* 309-694-5784. *Web site:* http://www.icc.edu/.

Illinois Eastern Community Colleges, Frontier Community College

Fairfield, Illinois

- **State and locally supported** 2-year, founded 1976, part of Illinois Eastern Community College System
- **Rural** 8-acre campus
- **Coed,** 2,194 undergraduate students, 13% full-time, 58% women, 42% men

Undergraduates 281 full-time, 1,913 part-time. 0.5% Black or African American, non-Hispanic/Latino; 0.8% Hispanic/Latino; 0.5% Asian, non-Hispanic/Latino; 0.2% American Indian or Alaska Native, non-Hispanic/Latino.

Freshmen *Admission:* 108 enrolled.

Faculty *Total:* 235, 2% full-time. *Student/faculty ratio:* 21:1.

Majors Administrative assistant and secretarial science; automobile/automotive mechanics technology; biological and physical sciences; business automation/technology/data entry; corrections; emergency care attendant (EMT ambulance); engineering; fire science/firefighting; general studies; health information/medical records technology; information technology; liberal arts and sciences/liberal studies; quality control technology; registered nursing/registered nurse.

Academics *Calendar:* semesters. *Degree:* certificates and associate. *Special study options:* academic remediation for entering students, adult/continuing education programs, advanced placement credit, cooperative education, distance learning, double majors, English as a second language, external degree program, independent study, part-time degree program, services for LD students, student-designed majors, summer session for credit.

Library 19,244 titles, 96 serial subscriptions, 2,659 audiovisual materials.

Student Life *Housing:* college housing not available.

Costs (2012–13) *Tuition:* area resident $2368 full-time, $74 per semester hour part-time; state resident $7252 full-time, $227 per semester hour part-time; nonresident $9561 full-time, $299 per semester hour part-time. *Required fees:* $490 full-time, $15 per credit hour part-time, $5 per term part-time. *Waivers:* senior citizens and employees or children of employees.

Applying *Options:* early admission, deferred entrance. *Required:* high school transcript. *Application deadlines:* rolling (freshmen), rolling (transfers). *Notification:* continuous (freshmen), continuous (transfers).

Freshman Application Contact Ms. Mary Atkins, Coordinator of Registration and Records, Illinois Eastern Community Colleges, Frontier Community College, Frontier Drive, Fairfield, IL 62837. *Phone:* 618-842-3711 Ext. 4111. *Fax:* 618-842-6340. *E-mail:* atkinsm@iecc.edu. *Web site:* http://www.iecc.edu/fcc/.

Illinois Eastern Community Colleges, Lincoln Trail College

Robinson, Illinois

- **State and locally supported** 2-year, founded 1969, part of Illinois Eastern Community College System
- **Rural** 120-acre campus
- **Coed,** 1,066 undergraduate students, 44% full-time, 60% women, 40% men

Undergraduates 472 full-time, 594 part-time. 1% are from out of state; 3% Black or African American, non-Hispanic/Latino; 0.8% Hispanic/Latino; 1% Asian, non-Hispanic/Latino; 0.1% Native Hawaiian or other Pacific Islander, non-Hispanic/Latino; 0.1% American Indian or Alaska Native, non-Hispanic/Latino.

Freshmen *Admission:* 176 enrolled.

Faculty *Total:* 86, 21% full-time. *Student/faculty ratio:* 20:1.

Majors Biological and physical sciences; business automation/technology/data entry; computer systems networking and telecommunications; corrections; general studies; health information/medical records administration; liberal arts and sciences/liberal studies; mechanical engineering/mechanical technology; quality control technology; teacher assistant/aide; telecommunications technology.

Academics *Calendar:* semesters. *Degree:* certificates and associate. *Special study options:* academic remediation for entering students, adult/continuing education programs, advanced placement credit, cooperative education, distance learning, double majors, English as a second language, external degree program, independent study, internships, part-time degree program, services for LD students, student-designed majors, summer session for credit.

Library Eagleton Learning Resource Center plus 1 other with 15,563 titles, 34 serial subscriptions, 652 audiovisual materials.

Student Life *Housing:* college housing not available. *Activities and Organizations:* drama/theater group, choral group, national fraternities.

Athletics Member NJCAA. *Intercollegiate sports:* baseball M(s), basketball M(s)/W(s), softball W(s). *Intramural sports:* baseball M, basketball M, softball W.

Costs (2012–13) *Tuition:* area resident $2368 full-time, $74 per semester hour part-time; state resident $7252 full-time, $227 per semester hour part-time; nonresident $9561 full-time, $299 per semester hour part-time. *Required fees:* $490 full-time, $15 per semester hour part-time, $5 per term part-time. *Waivers:* senior citizens and employees or children of employees.

Applying *Options:* early admission, deferred entrance. *Required:* high school transcript. *Application deadlines:* rolling (freshmen), rolling (transfers). *Notification:* continuous (freshmen), continuous (transfers).

Freshman Application Contact Ms. Becky Mikeworth, Director of Admissions, Illinois Eastern Community Colleges, Lincoln Trail College, 11220 State Highway 1, Robinson, IL 62454. *Phone:* 618-544-8657 Ext. 1137. *Fax:* 618-544-7423. *E-mail:* mikeworthb@iecc.edu. *Web site:* http://www.iecc.edu/ltc/.

Illinois Eastern Community Colleges, Olney Central College

Olney, Illinois

- **State and locally supported** 2-year, founded 1962, part of Illinois Eastern Community College System
- **Rural** 128-acre campus
- **Coed,** 1,524 undergraduate students, 48% full-time, 65% women, 35% men

Undergraduates 738 full-time, 786 part-time. 1% are from out of state; 2% Black or African American, non-Hispanic/Latino; 1% Hispanic/Latino; 0.9% Asian, non-Hispanic/Latino; 0.2% Native Hawaiian or other Pacific Islander, non-Hispanic/Latino; 0.3% American Indian or Alaska Native, non-Hispanic/Latino; 0.1% international.

Freshmen *Admission:* 270 enrolled.

Faculty *Total:* 117, 36% full-time. *Student/faculty ratio:* 17:1.

Majors Accounting; administrative assistant and secretarial science; autobody/collision and repair technology; automobile/automotive mechanics technology; biological and physical sciences; business automation/technology/data entry; corrections; criminal justice/police science; engineering; general studies; industrial mechanics and maintenance technology; liberal arts and sciences/liberal studies; medical administrative assistant and medical secretary; medical radiologic technology; registered nursing/registered nurse.

Academics *Calendar:* semesters. *Degree:* certificates and associate. *Special study options:* academic remediation for entering students, adult/continuing education programs, advanced placement credit, cooperative education, dis-

tance learning, double majors, English as a second language, external degree program, independent study, internships, part-time degree program, services for LD students, student-designed majors, summer session for credit.

Library Anderson Learning Resources Center plus 1 other with 21,020 titles, 22 serial subscriptions, 1,156 audiovisual materials.

Student Life *Housing:* college housing not available. *Activities and Organizations:* drama/theater group, student-run newspaper, choral group.

Athletics Member NJCAA. *Intercollegiate sports:* baseball M(s), basketball M(s)/W(s), softball W(s). *Intramural sports:* baseball M, basketball M/W, softball W.

Costs (2012–13) *Tuition:* area resident $2368 full-time, $74 per semester hour part-time; state resident $7252 full-time, $227 per semester hour part-time; nonresident $9561 full-time, $299 per semester hour part-time. *Required fees:* $490 full-time, $15 per semester hour part-time, $5 per term part-time. *Waivers:* senior citizens and employees or children of employees.

Applying *Options:* early admission, deferred entrance. *Required:* high school transcript. *Application deadlines:* rolling (freshmen), rolling (transfers). *Notification:* continuous (freshmen), continuous (transfers).

Freshman Application Contact Ms. Chris Webber, Assistant Dean for Student Services, Illinois Eastern Community Colleges, Olney Central College, 305 North West Street, Olney, IL 62450. *Phone:* 618-395-7777 Ext. 2005. *Fax:* 618-392-5212. *E-mail:* webberc@iecc.edu. *Web site:* http://www.iecc.edu/occ/.

Illinois Eastern Community Colleges, Wabash Valley College

Mount Carmel, Illinois

- **State and locally supported** 2-year, founded 1960, part of Illinois Eastern Community College System
- **Rural** 40-acre campus
- **Coed,** 5,456 undergraduate students, 12% full-time, 39% women, 61% men

Undergraduates 661 full-time, 4,795 part-time. 3% are from out of state; 2% Black or African American, non-Hispanic/Latino; 0.8% Hispanic/Latino; 1% Asian, non-Hispanic/Latino; 0.3% American Indian or Alaska Native, non-Hispanic/Latino.

Freshmen *Admission:* 251 enrolled.

Faculty *Total:* 126, 28% full-time. *Student/faculty ratio:* 46:1.

Majors Administrative assistant and secretarial science; agricultural business and management; agricultural production; biological and physical sciences; business administration and management; business automation/technology/data entry; child development; corrections; diesel mechanics technology; electrical, electronic and communications engineering technology; energy management and systems technology; engineering; general studies; industrial technology; legal assistant/paralegal; liberal arts and sciences/liberal studies; machine tool technology; manufacturing engineering technology; mining technology; radio and television; social work.

Academics *Calendar:* semesters. *Degree:* certificates and associate. *Special study options:* academic remediation for entering students, adult/continuing education programs, advanced placement credit, cooperative education, distance learning, double majors, English as a second language, external degree program, independent study, internships, part-time degree program, services for LD students, student-designed majors, summer session for credit.

Library Bauer Media Center plus 1 other with 32,811 titles, 21,649 serial subscriptions, 1,480 audiovisual materials.

Student Life *Housing:* college housing not available. *Activities and Organizations:* drama/theater group, student-run newspaper, radio and television station, choral group.

Athletics Member NJCAA. *Intercollegiate sports:* baseball M(s), basketball M(s)/W(s), softball W(s). *Intramural sports:* baseball M, basketball M/W, softball W.

Costs (2012–13) *Tuition:* area resident $2368 full-time, $74 per semester hour part-time; state resident $7252 full-time, $227 per semester hour part-time; nonresident $9561 full-time, $299 per semester hour part-time. *Required fees:* $490 full-time, $15 per semester hour part-time, $5 per term part-time. *Waivers:* senior citizens and employees or children of employees.

Applying *Options:* early admission, deferred entrance. *Required:* high school transcript. *Application deadlines:* rolling (freshmen), rolling (transfers). *Notification:* continuous (freshmen), continuous (transfers).

Freshman Application Contact Mrs. Diana Spear, Assistant Dean for Student Services, Illinois Eastern Community Colleges, Wabash Valley College, 2200 College Drive, Mt. Carmel, IL 62863. *Phone:* 618-262-8641 Ext. 3101. *Fax:* 618-262-8641. *E-mail:* speard@iecc.edu. *Web site:* http://www.iecc.edu/wvc/

Illinois Valley Community College

Oglesby, Illinois

- **District-supported** 2-year, founded 1924, part of Illinois Community College Board
- **Rural** 410-acre campus with easy access to Chicago
- **Endowment** $3.7 million
- **Coed**, 4,355 undergraduate students, 43% full-time, 60% women, 40% men

Undergraduates 1,881 full-time, 2,474 part-time. Students come from 1 other state; 1% are from out of state; 2% Black or African American, non-Hispanic/Latino; 9% Hispanic/Latino; 1% Asian, non-Hispanic/Latino; 0.3% American Indian or Alaska Native, non-Hispanic/Latino; 0.2% Two or more races, non-Hispanic/Latino; 53% Race/ethnicity unknown; 37% transferred in. *Retention:* 52% of full-time freshmen returned.

Freshmen *Admission:* 366 enrolled.

Faculty *Total:* 270, 34% full-time. *Student/faculty ratio:* 18:1.

Majors Accounting; automobile/automotive mechanics technology; biological and physical sciences; business administration and management; business automation/technology/data entry; CAD/CADD drafting/design technology; child-care provision; child development; computer programming; computer systems networking and telecommunications; corrections; criminal justice/law enforcement administration; criminal justice/police science; data processing and data processing technology; drafting and design technology; drafting/design engineering technologies related; early childhood education; education; electrical, electronic and communications engineering technology; electrician; elementary education; engineering; English; floriculture/floristry management; forensic science and technology; general studies; graphic design; industrial technology; information technology; journalism; juvenile corrections; landscaping and groundskeeping; liberal arts and sciences/liberal studies; marketing/marketing management; massage therapy; mechanical engineering/mechanical technology; network and system administration; pre-engineering; registered nursing/registered nurse; selling skills and sales; social work; teacher assistant/aide.

Academics *Calendar:* semesters. *Degree:* certificates and associate. *Special study options:* academic remediation for entering students, advanced placement credit, distance learning, English as a second language, honors programs, independent study, internships, off-campus study, part-time degree program, services for LD students, student-designed majors, study abroad, summer session for credit.

Library Jacobs Library with 55,473 titles, 14,981 serial subscriptions, 1,379 audiovisual materials, an OPAC, a Web page.

Student Life *Housing:* college housing not available. *Activities and Organizations:* drama/theater group, student-run newspaper, choral group, Chemistry Club, Student Embassadors, Phi Theta Kappa, Illinois Valley Leaders for Service, Student Veterans Association. *Campus security:* 24-hour emergency response devices and patrols, late-night transport/escort service. *Student services:* personal/psychological counseling.

Athletics Member NJCAA. *Intercollegiate sports:* baseball M, basketball M/W, golf M, softball W, tennis M/W. *Intramural sports:* basketball M, volleyball W.

Standardized Tests *Recommended:* ACT (for admission).

Costs (2012–13) *Tuition:* area resident $2720 full-time, $84 per credit part-time; state resident $7808 full-time, $244 per credit part-time; nonresident $8720 full-time, $273 per credit part-time. Full-time tuition and fees vary according to course load. Part-time tuition and fees vary according to course load. *Required fees:* $247 full-time, $7 per credit hour part-time, $5 part-time. *Payment plan:* deferred payment. *Waivers:* senior citizens and employees or children of employees.

Financial Aid Of all full-time matriculated undergraduates who enrolled in 2010, 81 Federal Work-Study jobs (averaging $955).

Applying *Options:* electronic application, early admission, deferred entrance. *Required:* high school transcript. *Application deadlines:* rolling (freshmen), rolling (transfers). *Notification:* continuous (freshmen), continuous (transfers).

Freshman Application Contact Mr. Mark Grzybowski, Director of Admissions and Records, Illinois Valley Community College, Oglesby, IL 61348. *Phone:* 815-224-0437. *Fax:* 815-224-3033. *E-mail:* mark_grzybowski@ivcc.edu. *Web site:* http://www.ivcc.edu/.

ITT Technical Institute

Mount Prospect, Illinois

- **Proprietary** primarily 2-year, founded 1986, part of ITT Educational Services, Inc.
- **Suburban** campus
- **Coed**

Majors CAD/CADD drafting/design technology; communications technology; computer and information systems security; computer engineering technology; construction management; criminal justice/law enforcement administration; design and visual communications; electrical, electronic and communications engineering technology; game and interactive media design; legal assistant/paralegal; network and system administration; project management; system, networking, and LAN/WAN management.

Academics *Calendar:* quarters. *Degrees:* associate and bachelor's.

Student Life *Housing:* college housing not available.

Freshman Application Contact Director of Recruitment, ITT Technical Institute, 1401 Feehanville Drive, Mount Prospect, IL 60056. *Phone:* 847-375-8800. *Web site:* http://www.itt-tech.edu/.

ITT Technical Institute

Oak Brook, Illinois

- **Proprietary** primarily 2-year, founded 1998, part of ITT Educational Services, Inc.
- **Coed**

Majors CAD/CADD drafting/design technology; computer and information systems security; computer engineering technology; computer software engineering; computer software technology; construction management; criminal justice/law enforcement administration; design and visual communications; electrical, electronic and communications engineering technology; legal assistant/paralegal; project management; system, networking, and LAN/WAN management.

Academics *Calendar:* quarters. *Degrees:* associate and bachelor's.

Student Life *Housing:* college housing not available.

Freshman Application Contact Director of Recruitment, ITT Technical Institute, 800 Jorie Boulevard, Suite 100, Oak Brook, IL 60523. *Phone:* 630-472-7000. *Toll-free phone:* 877-488-0001. *Web site:* http://www.itt-tech.edu/.

ITT Technical Institute

Orland Park, Illinois

- **Proprietary** primarily 2-year, founded 1993, part of ITT Educational Services, Inc.
- **Suburban** campus
- **Coed**

Majors CAD/CADD drafting/design technology; computer and information systems security; computer engineering technology; computer software engineering; computer software technology; construction management; criminal justice/law enforcement administration; design and visual communications; electrical, electronic and communications engineering technology; information technology project management; legal assistant/paralegal; project management; registered nursing/registered nurse; system, networking, and LAN/WAN management.

Academics *Calendar:* quarters. *Degrees:* associate and bachelor's.

Student Life *Housing:* college housing not available.

Financial Aid Of all full-time matriculated undergraduates who enrolled in 2010, 6 Federal Work-Study jobs (averaging $4000).

Freshman Application Contact Director of Recruitment, ITT Technical Institute, 11551 184th Place, Orland Park, IL 60467. *Phone:* 708-326-3200. *Web site:* http://www.itt-tech.edu/.

John A. Logan College

Carterville, Illinois

Director of Admissions Mr. Terry Crain, Dean of Student Services, John A. Logan College, 700 Logan College Road, Carterville, IL 62918-9900. *Phone:* 618-985-3741 Ext. 8382. *Fax:* 618-985-4433. *E-mail:* terrycrain@jalc.edu. *Web site:* http://www.jalc.edu/.

John Wood Community College

Quincy, Illinois

- **District-supported** 2-year, founded 1974, part of Illinois Community College Board
- **Small-town** campus
- **Coed**, 2,390 undergraduate students, 49% full-time, 59% women, 41% men

Undergraduates 1,178 full-time, 1,212 part-time. Students come from 18 states and territories; 7% are from out of state; 4% Black or African American, non-Hispanic/Latino; 0.8% Hispanic/Latino; 0.6% Asian, non-Hispanic/Latino; 0.1% Native Hawaiian or other Pacific Islander, non-Hispanic/Latino; 0.4% American Indian or Alaska Native, non-Hispanic/Latino; 1% Two or more races, non-Hispanic/Latino; 4% Race/ethnicity unknown; 9% transferred in.

Freshmen *Admission:* 530 enrolled. *Test scores:* ACT scores over 18: 67%; ACT scores over 24: 17%; ACT scores over 30: 1%.

Faculty *Total:* 258, 22% full-time, 7% with terminal degrees. *Student/faculty ratio:* 13:1.

Majors Accounting; administrative assistant and secretarial science; agricultural business and management; animal sciences; applied horticulture/horticulture operations; biological and physical sciences; business administration and management; CAD/CADD drafting/design technology; carpentry; child-care provision; clinical/medical laboratory technology; criminal justice/police science; electrician; emergency medical technology (EMT paramedic); executive assistant/executive secretary; fire science/firefighting; general studies; graphic design; legal administrative assistant/secretary; liberal arts and sciences/liberal studies; management information systems; manufacturing engineering technology; medical staff services technology; office management; radiologic technology/science; registered nursing, nursing administration, nursing research and clinical nursing related; restaurant, culinary, and catering management; selling skills and sales.

Academics *Calendar:* semesters. *Degree:* certificates and associate. *Special study options:* academic remediation for entering students, accelerated degree program, adult/continuing education programs, advanced placement credit, cooperative education, distance learning, English as a second language, external degree program, independent study, internships, off-campus study, part-time degree program, services for LD students, student-designed majors, study abroad, summer session for credit.

Library Academic Support Center with 18,000 titles, 160 serial subscriptions, 2,000 audiovisual materials, an OPAC, a Web page.

Student Life *Housing:* college housing not available. *Activities and Organizations:* choral group, Phi Theta Kappa, Agriculture Club, BACCHUS, Music Educators National Conference, Student Nurses Organization. *Campus security:* 24-hour emergency response devices, late-night transport/escort service, campus police department, 911-enhanced phone system.

Athletics Member NJCAA. *Intercollegiate sports:* baseball M(s), basketball M(s)/W(s), softball W(s). *Intramural sports:* basketball M/W, volleyball M/W.

Standardized Tests *Recommended:* ACT (for admission).

Costs (2012–13) *Tuition:* area resident $3600 full-time, $120 per credit hour part-time; state resident $6900 full-time, $230 per credit hour part-time; nonresident $6900 full-time, $230 per credit hour part-time. Full-time tuition and fees vary according to program and reciprocity agreements. Part-time tuition and fees vary according to program and reciprocity agreements. *Required fees:* $300 full-time, $10 per credit hour part-time. *Payment plan:* installment. *Waivers:* employees or children of employees.

Applying *Options:* electronic application, early admission. *Required:* high school transcript. *Application deadlines:* rolling (freshmen), rolling (out-of-state freshmen), rolling (transfers). *Notification:* continuous (freshmen), continuous (out-of-state freshmen), continuous (transfers).

Freshman Application Contact Mr. Lee Wibbell, Director of Admissions, John Wood Community College, Quincy, IL 62305-8736. *Phone:* 217-641-4339. *Fax:* 217-224-4208. *E-mail:* admissions@jwcc.edu. *Web site:* http://www.jwcc.edu/.

Joliet Junior College
Joliet, Illinois

Freshman Application Contact Ms. Jennifer Kloberdanz, Director of Admissions and Recruitment, Joliet Junior College, 1215 Houbolt Road, Joliet, IL 60431. *Phone:* 815-729-9020 Ext. 2414. *E-mail:* admission@jjc.edu. *Web site:* http://www.jjc.edu/.

Kankakee Community College
Kankakee, Illinois

- **State and locally supported** 2-year, founded 1966, part of Illinois Community College Board
- **Small-town** 178-acre campus with easy access to Chicago
- **Endowment** $4.5 million
- **Coed,** 4,419 undergraduate students, 43% full-time, 63% women, 37% men

Undergraduates 1,897 full-time, 2,522 part-time. Students come from 24 states and territories; 6 other countries; 0.8% are from out of state; 17% Black or African American, non-Hispanic/Latino; 7% Hispanic/Latino; 0.9% Asian, non-Hispanic/Latino; 0.1% Native Hawaiian or other Pacific Islander, non-Hispanic/Latino; 0.4% American Indian or Alaska Native, non-Hispanic/Latino; 0.7% Two or more races, non-Hispanic/Latino; 1% Race/ethnicity unknown; 0.1% international; 41% transferred in. *Retention:* 59% of full-time freshmen returned.

Freshmen *Admission:* 361 enrolled. *Average high school GPA:* 3. *Test scores:* ACT scores over 18: 67%; ACT scores over 24: 21%; ACT scores over 30: 2%.

Faculty *Total:* 196, 37% full-time.

Majors Accounting; administrative assistant and secretarial science; agriculture; applied horticulture/horticulture operations; automobile/automotive mechanics technology; avionics maintenance technology; biological and physical sciences; business/commerce; business, management, and marketing related; child development; clinical/medical laboratory technology; construction management; criminal justice/law enforcement administration; drafting and design technology; electrical, electronic and communications engineering technology; elementary education; emergency medical technology (EMT paramedic); engineering; fine/studio arts; general studies; graphic design; heating, air conditioning, ventilation and refrigeration maintenance technology; horticultural science; industrial radiologic technology; information science/studies; legal assistant/paralegal; machine tool technology; marketing/marketing management; mathematics teacher education; medical office assistant; physical therapy technology; psychology; radiologic technology/science; registered nursing/registered nurse; respiratory care therapy; secondary education; special education; teacher assistant/aide; visual and performing arts related; welding technology.

Academics *Calendar:* semesters. *Degrees:* certificates, diplomas, and associate (also offers continuing education program with significant enrollment not reflected in profile). *Special study options:* academic remediation for entering students, advanced placement credit, distance learning, English as a second language, honors programs, independent study, internships, off-campus study, part-time degree program, services for LD students, student-designed majors, study abroad, summer session for credit. *ROTC:* Army (c).

Library Kankakee Community College Learning Resource Center with 42,861 titles, 140 serial subscriptions, 4,475 audiovisual materials, an OPAC, a Web page.

Student Life *Housing:* college housing not available. *Activities and Organizations:* drama/theater group, Phi Theta Kappa, Hort, Student Nursing, Gay Straight Alliance, Student Advisory Council. *Campus security:* 24-hour patrols, late-night transport/escort service.

Athletics Member NJCAA. *Intercollegiate sports:* baseball M(s), basketball M(s)/W(s), soccer M, softball W(s), volleyball W(s). *Intramural sports:* basketball M.

Costs (2012–13) *Tuition:* area resident $3000 full-time; state resident $4660 full-time; nonresident $14,143 full-time. *Required fees:* $390 full-time. *Payment plan:* installment. *Waivers:* senior citizens and employees or children of employees.

Financial Aid Of all full-time matriculated undergraduates who enrolled in 2010, 70 Federal Work-Study jobs (averaging $1100). *Financial aid deadline:* 10/1.

Applying *Options:* electronic application, early admission. *Required:* high school transcript. *Application deadlines:* rolling (freshmen), rolling (transfers). *Notification:* continuous (freshmen), continuous (transfers).

Freshman Application Contact Ms. Michelle Driscoll, Kankakee Community College, 100 College Drive, Kankakee, IL 60901. *Phone:* 815-802-8520. *Fax:* 815-802-8521. *E-mail:* mdriscoll@kcc.edu. *Web site:* http://www.kcc.edu/.

Kaskaskia College
Centralia, Illinois

- **State and locally supported** 2-year, founded 1966, part of Illinois Community College Board
- **Rural** 195-acre campus with easy access to St. Louis
- **Endowment** $5.2 million
- **Coed,** 5,286 undergraduate students, 40% full-time, 61% women, 39% men

Undergraduates 2,097 full-time; 3,189 part-time. Students come from 8 states and territories; 5 other countries; 1% are from out of state; 6% Black or African American, non-Hispanic/Latino; 2% Hispanic/Latino; 0.5% Asian, non-Hispanic/Latino; 0.1% Native Hawaiian or other Pacific Islander, non-Hispanic/Latino; 0.3% American Indian or Alaska Native, non-Hispanic/Latino; 1% Two or more races, non-Hispanic/Latino; 0.4% Race/ethnicity unknown; 0.3% international; 32% transferred in.

Freshmen *Admission:* 984 applied, 984 admitted, 1,516 enrolled.

Faculty *Total:* 223, 33% full-time, 7% with terminal degrees. *Student/faculty ratio:* 26:1.

Majors Accounting; agriculture; applied horticulture/horticulture operations; architectural drafting and CAD/CADD; autobody/collision and repair technology; automobile/automotive mechanics technology; biological and physical sciences; business automation/technology/data entry; business/commerce; carpentry; child-care provision; clinical/medical laboratory technology; criminal justice/law enforcement administration; culinary arts; electrical, electronic and communications engineering technology; emergency medical technology (EMT paramedic); engineering; executive assistant/executive secretary; general studies; health information/medical records technology; industrial mechanics and maintenance technology; information science/studies; juvenile corrections; liberal arts and sciences/liberal studies; mathematics teacher education; network and system administration; occupational therapist assistant;

physical therapy technology; radiologic technology/science; registered nursing/registered nurse; respiratory care therapy; teacher assistant/aide; veterinary/animal health technology; web/multimedia management and webmaster; welding technology.

Academics *Calendar:* semesters. *Degree:* certificates and associate. *Special study options:* academic remediation for entering students, accelerated degree program, adult/continuing education programs, cooperative education, distance learning, double majors, English as a second language, honors programs, independent study, internships, off-campus study, part-time degree program, services for LD students, study abroad, summer session for credit.

Library Kaskaskia College Library with 18,293 titles, 84 serial subscriptions, 508 audiovisual materials, an OPAC, a Web page.

Student Life *Housing:* college housing not available. *Activities and Organizations:* drama/theater group, student-run newspaper, choral group, Phi Theta Kappa, Student Practical Nurses, Student Radiology Club, Intramural Sports, Criminal Justice. *Campus security:* 24-hour emergency response devices and patrols, late-night transport/escort service. *Student services:* personal/psychological counseling.

Athletics Member NJCAA. *Intercollegiate sports:* baseball M(s), basketball M(s)/W(s), cheerleading M(s)/W(s), cross-country running M(s)/W(s), golf M(s)/W(s), soccer M(s)/W(s), softball W(s), tennis M(s), volleyball W(s).

Standardized Tests *Recommended:* ACT (for admission).

Costs (2011–12) *Tuition:* area resident $2688 full-time, $84 per credit hour part-time; state resident $5280 full-time, $165 per credit hour part-time; nonresident $12,480 full-time, $390 per credit hour part-time. Full-time tuition and fees vary according to program. Part-time tuition and fees vary according to program. *Required fees:* $384 full-time, $12 per credit hour part-time. *Payment plan:* installment. *Waivers:* senior citizens and employees or children of employees.

Financial Aid Of all full-time matriculated undergraduates who enrolled in 2010, 1,502 applied for aid, 1,147 were judged to have need, 206 had their need fully met. 85 Federal Work-Study jobs (averaging $3131). 132 state and other part-time jobs (averaging $2992). In 2010, 90 non-need-based awards were made. *Average percent of need met:* 34%. *Average financial aid package:* $5420. *Average need-based loan:* $3245. *Average need-based gift aid:* $4125. *Average non-need-based aid:* $2221.

Applying *Options:* early admission, deferred entrance. *Required:* high school transcript. *Required for some:* interview. *Application deadlines:* rolling (freshmen), rolling (transfers). *Notification:* continuous (freshmen), continuous (transfers).

Freshman Application Contact Jan Ripperda, Manager of Records and Registration, Kaskaskia College, 27210 College Road, Centralia, IL 62801. *Phone:* 618-545-3041. *Toll-free phone:* 800-642-0859. *Fax:* 618-532-1990. *E-mail:* jripperda@kaskaskia.edu. *Web site:* http://www.kaskaskia.edu/.

Kishwaukee College
Malta, Illinois

Freshman Application Contact Ms. Sally Misciasci, Admission Analyst, Kishwaukee College, 21193 Malta Road, Malta, IL 60150. *Phone:* 815-825-2086 Ext. 400. *Web site:* http://www.kishwaukeecollege.edu/.

Lake Land College
Mattoon, Illinois

Freshman Application Contact Mr. Jon VanDyke, Dean of Admission Services, Lake Land College, Mattoon, IL 61938-9366. *Phone:* 217-234-5378. *E-mail:* admissions@lakeland.cc.il.us. *Web site:* http://www.lakelandcollege.edu/.

Le Cordon Bleu College of Culinary Arts in Chicago
Chicago, Illinois

Freshman Application Contact Mr. Matthew Verratti, Vice President of Admissions and Marketing, Le Cordon Bleu College of Culinary Arts in Chicago, 361 West Chestnut, Chicago, IL 60610. *Phone:* 312-873-2064. *Toll-free phone:* 888-295-7222. *Fax:* 312-798-2903. *E-mail:* mverratti@chicnet.org. *Web site:* http://www.chefs.edu/chicago/.

Lewis and Clark Community College
Godfrey, Illinois

Freshman Application Contact Lewis and Clark Community College, 5800 Godfrey Road, Godfrey, IL 62035-2466. *Phone:* 618-468-5100. *Toll-free phone:* 800-YES-LCCC. *Web site:* http://www.lc.edu/.

Lincoln College
Lincoln, Illinois

Director of Admissions Gretchen Bree, Director of Admissions, Lincoln College, 300 Keokuk Street, Lincoln, IL 62656-1699. *Phone:* 217-732-3155 Ext. 256. *Toll-free phone:* 800-569-0558. *E-mail:* gbree@lincolncollege.edu. *Web site:* http://www.lincolncollege.edu/.

Lincoln Land Community College
Springfield, Illinois

- **District-supported** 2-year, founded 1967, part of Illinois Community College Board
- **Suburban** 441-acre campus with easy access to St. Louis
- **Endowment** $2.2 million
- **Coed,** 7,337 undergraduate students, 44% full-time, 58% women, 42% men

Undergraduates 3,262 full-time, 4,075 part-time. Students come from 14 states and territories; 1% are from out of state; 10% Black or African American, non-Hispanic/Latino; 2% Hispanic/Latino; 1% Asian, non-Hispanic/Latino; 0.1% Native Hawaiian or other Pacific Islander, non-Hispanic/Latino; 0.4% American Indian or Alaska Native, non-Hispanic/Latino; 6% Race/ethnicity unknown; 0.1% international; 0.9% transferred in. *Retention:* 52% of full-time freshmen returned.

Freshmen *Admission:* 954 enrolled. *Test scores:* ACT scores over 18: 65%; ACT scores over 24: 13%; ACT scores over 30: 1%.

Faculty *Total:* 375, 35% full-time, 8% with terminal degrees. *Student/faculty ratio:* 22:1.

Majors Accounting; administrative assistant and secretarial science; agricultural production; airframe mechanics and aircraft maintenance technology; architectural drafting and CAD/CADD; autobody/collision and repair technology; automobile/automotive mechanics technology; aviation/airway management; biological and physical sciences; building/property maintenance; business automation/technology/data entry; business/commerce; child-care provision; computer programming; computer programming (specific applications); computer systems networking and telecommunications; construction engineering technology; criminal justice/police science; early childhood education; electrical, electronic and communications engineering technology; emergency medical technology (EMT paramedic); engineering; fine/studio arts; fire science/firefighting; general studies; graphic design; hospitality administration; industrial electronics technology; industrial technology; landscaping and groundskeeping; legal administrative assistant/secretary; liberal arts and sciences/liberal studies; medical office assistant; music; occupational therapist assistant; radiologic technology/science; registered nursing/registered nurse; special education; surgical technology; teacher assistant/aide.

Academics *Calendar:* semesters. *Degree:* certificates and associate. *Special study options:* academic remediation for entering students, accelerated degree program, adult/continuing education programs, advanced placement credit, distance learning, English as a second language, external degree program, honors programs, independent study, internships, off-campus study, part-time degree program, services for LD students, study abroad, summer session for credit.

Library Learning Resource Center with 65,000 titles, 10,000 serial subscriptions, an OPAC, a Web page.

Student Life *Housing:* college housing not available. *Activities and Organizations:* drama/theater group, student-run newspaper, choral group, Student Government Association, Phi Theta Kappa, Gay/Straight Alliance, Epicurean Club, Madrigals. *Campus security:* 24-hour emergency response devices and patrols, late-night transport/escort service. *Student services:* health clinic, personal/psychological counseling.

Athletics Member NJCAA. *Intercollegiate sports:* baseball M(s), basketball M(s)/W(s), soccer M(s), softball W(s), volleyball W(s). *Intramural sports:* basketball M/W, cheerleading W, volleyball W.

Applying *Options:* electronic application, early admission, deferred entrance. *Recommended:* high school transcript. *Application deadlines:* rolling (freshmen), rolling (transfers). *Notification:* continuous (freshmen), continuous (transfers).

Freshman Application Contact Mr. Ron Gregoire, Executive Director of Admissions and Records, Lincoln Land Community College, 5250 Shepherd Road, PO Box 19256, Springfield, IL 62794-9256. *Phone:* 217-786-2243. *Toll-free phone:* 800-727-4161. *Fax:* 217-786-2492. *E-mail:* ron.gregoire@llcc.edu. *Web site:* http://www.llcc.edu/.

MacCormac College
Chicago, Illinois

Director of Admissions Mr. David Grassi, Director of Admissions, MacCormac College, 506 South Wabash Avenue, Chicago, IL 60605-1667. *Phone:* 312-922-1884 Ext. 102. *Web site:* http://www.maccormac.edu/.

McHenry County College
Crystal Lake, Illinois

- **State and locally supported** 2-year, founded 1967, part of Illinois Community College Board
- **Suburban** 168-acre campus with easy access to Chicago
- **Coed,** 6,494 undergraduate students, 36% full-time, 56% women, 44% men

Undergraduates 2,346 full-time, 4,148 part-time. 0.1% are from out of state; 1% Black or African American, non-Hispanic/Latino; 10% Hispanic/Latino; 2% Asian, non-Hispanic/Latino; 0.4% American Indian or Alaska Native, non-Hispanic/Latino; 1% Race/ethnicity unknown; 0.7% international; 1% transferred in.
Freshmen *Admission:* 2,654 applied, 2,654 admitted, 1,267 enrolled. *Average high school GPA:* 2.25.
Faculty *Total:* 362, 26% full-time. *Student/faculty ratio:* 23:1.
Majors Accounting; administrative assistant and secretarial science; animation, interactive technology, video graphics and special effects; applied horticulture/horticulture operations; automobile/automotive mechanics technology; biological and physical sciences; building/home/construction inspection; business administration and management; child-care provision; computer and information systems security; criminal justice/police science; electrical, electronic and communications engineering technology; emergency medical technology (EMT paramedic); engineering; fine/studio arts; fire science/firefighting; general studies; health and physical education/fitness; information technology; liberal arts and sciences/liberal studies; music; operations management; registered nursing/registered nurse; selling skills and sales.
Academics *Calendar:* semesters. *Degree:* certificates and associate. *Special study options:* academic remediation for entering students, accelerated degree program, adult/continuing education programs, advanced placement credit, cooperative education, distance learning, English as a second language, honors programs, independent study, internships, part-time degree program, services for LD students, study abroad, summer session for credit.
Library McHenry County College Library with 40,000 titles, 330 serial subscriptions, 6,000 audiovisual materials, an OPAC, a Web page.
Student Life *Housing:* college housing not available. *Activities and Organizations:* drama/theater group, student-run newspaper, choral group, Phi Theta Kappa, Student Senate, Equality Club, Writer's Block, Latinos Unidos. *Campus security:* 24-hour emergency response devices and patrols, late-night transport/escort service. *Student services:* personal/psychological counseling.
Athletics Member NJCAA. *Intercollegiate sports:* baseball M(s), basketball M(s)/W(s), soccer M(s), softball W(s), tennis M(s)/W(s), volleyball W(s).
Costs (2011–12) *Tuition:* area resident $2700 full-time, $90 per credit part-time; state resident $7766 full-time, $259 per credit hour part-time; nonresident $9491 full-time, $316 per credit hour part-time. Full-time tuition and fees vary according to course load. Part-time tuition and fees vary according to course load. *Required fees:* $284 full-time, $9 per credit hour part-time, $7 per credit hour part-time. *Payment plan:* installment. *Waivers:* senior citizens and employees or children of employees.
Financial Aid Of all full-time matriculated undergraduates who enrolled in 2010, 200 Federal Work-Study jobs (averaging $3700). 130 state and other part-time jobs (averaging $2000).
Applying *Options:* electronic application, early admission, deferred entrance. *Application fee:* $15. *Recommended:* high school transcript. *Application deadlines:* rolling (freshmen), rolling (out-of-state freshmen), rolling (transfers). *Notification:* continuous (freshmen), continuous (out-of-state freshmen), continuous (transfers).
Freshman Application Contact Anne Weaver, New Student Enrollment Specialist, McHenry County College, 8900 US Highway 14, Crystal Lake, IL 60012-2761. *Phone:* 815-455-7782. *E-mail:* admissions@mchenry.edu. *Web site:* http://www.mchenry.edu/.

Moraine Valley Community College
Palos Hills, Illinois

- **State and locally supported** 2-year, founded 1967, part of Illinois Community College Board
- **Suburban** 294-acre campus with easy access to Chicago
- **Endowment** $13.6 million
- **Coed,** 18,169 undergraduate students, 40% full-time, 51% women, 49% men

Undergraduates 7,307 full-time, 10,862 part-time. Students come from 7 states and territories; 42 other countries; 11% Black or African American, non-Hispanic/Latino; 17% Hispanic/Latino; 2% Asian, non-Hispanic/Latino; 0.2% American Indian or Alaska Native, non-Hispanic/Latino; 1% Two or more races, non-Hispanic/Latino; 9% Race/ethnicity unknown; 1% international; 1% transferred in. *Retention:* 62% of full-time freshmen returned.
Freshmen *Admission:* 1,194 enrolled. *Test scores:* ACT scores over 18: 74%; ACT scores over 24: 16%; ACT scores over 30: 1%.

Faculty *Total:* 753, 24% full-time, 7% with terminal degrees. *Student/faculty ratio:* 30:1.
Majors Administrative assistant and secretarial science; automobile/automotive mechanics technology; biological and physical sciences; business administration and management; business/commerce; child-care provision; computer and information systems security; criminal justice/police science; emergency medical technology (EMT paramedic); fire prevention and safety technology; fire science/firefighting; graphic design; health information/medical records technology; heating, air conditioning, ventilation and refrigeration maintenance technology; human resources management; industrial electronics technology; instrumentation technology; liberal arts and sciences/liberal studies; management information systems; mathematics teacher education; mechanical engineering/mechanical technology; parks, recreation and leisure facilities management; radiologic technology/science; registered nursing/registered nurse; respiratory care therapy; restaurant, culinary, and catering management; retailing; science teacher education; small business administration; special education; substance abuse/addiction counseling; system, networking, and LAN/WAN management; teacher assistant/aide; tourism and travel services management; visual and performing arts; web/multimedia management and webmaster.
Academics *Calendar:* semesters. *Degree:* certificates and associate. *Special study options:* academic remediation for entering students, accelerated degree program, adult/continuing education programs, advanced placement credit, cooperative education, distance learning, double majors, English as a second language, honors programs, independent study, internships, off-campus study, part-time degree program, services for LD students, study abroad, summer session for credit.
Library Library with 71,328 titles, 411 serial subscriptions, 10,347 audiovisual materials, an OPAC, a Web page.
Student Life *Housing:* college housing not available. *Activities and Organizations:* drama/theater group, student-run newspaper, choral group, student newspaper, Speech Team, Alliance of Latin American Students, Phi Theta Kappa, Arab Student Union. *Campus security:* 24-hour emergency response devices and patrols, late-night transport/escort service, safety and security programs. *Student services:* personal/psychological counseling, women's center.
Athletics Member NJCAA. *Intercollegiate sports:* baseball M(s), basketball M(s)/W(s), cross-country running M(s)/W(s), golf M(s), soccer M(s)/W(s), softball W(s), tennis M(s)/W(s), volleyball W(s). *Intramural sports:* basketball M/W, football M/W, skiing (downhill) M/W, soccer M/W, table tennis M/W, ultimate Frisbee M/W, volleyball M/W.
Costs (2012–13) *Tuition:* area resident $3120 full-time, $104 per credit part-time; state resident $7740 full-time, $258 per hour part-time; nonresident $9060 full-time, $302 per hour part-time. *Required fees:* $276 full-time, $9 per credit hour part-time, $3 per term part-time. *Payment plan:* installment. *Waivers:* senior citizens and employees or children of employees.
Financial Aid Of all full-time matriculated undergraduates who enrolled in 2010, 84 Federal Work-Study jobs (averaging $2500). 260 state and other part-time jobs (averaging $2200).
Applying *Options:* electronic application, early admission, deferred entrance. *Required:* high school transcript. *Application deadlines:* rolling (freshmen), rolling (transfers). *Notification:* continuous (freshmen), continuous (transfers).
Freshman Application Contact Ms. Claudia Roselli, Director, Admissions and Recruitment, Moraine Valley Community College, 9000 West College Parkway, Palos Hills, IL 60465-0937. *Phone:* 708-974-5357. *Fax:* 708-974-0681. *E-mail:* roselli@morainevalley.edu. *Web site:* http://www.morainevalley.edu/.

Morrison Institute of Technology
Morrison, Illinois

Freshman Application Contact Mrs. Tammy Pruis, Admission Secretary, Morrison Institute of Technology, 701 Portland Avenue, Morrison, IL 61270. *Phone:* 815-772-7218. *Fax:* 815-772-7584. *E-mail:* admissions@morrison.tec.il.us. *Web site:* http://www.morrisontech.edu/.

Morton College
Cicero, Illinois

- **State and locally supported** 2-year, founded 1924, part of Illinois Community College Board
- **Suburban** 25-acre campus with easy access to Chicago
- **Coed**

Undergraduates Students come from 7 states and territories; 8 other countries; 0.6% are from out of state; 5% Black or African American, non-Hispanic/Latino; 74% Hispanic/Latino; 1% Asian, non-Hispanic/Latino; 0.1% Native Hawaiian or other Pacific Islander, non-Hispanic/Latino; 8% Race/ethnicity unknown; 0.1% international. *Retention:* 57% of full-time freshmen returned.
Faculty *Student/faculty ratio:* 23:1.

Academics *Calendar:* semesters. *Degree:* certificates and associate. *Special study options:* academic remediation for entering students, adult/continuing education programs, advanced placement credit, distance learning, English as a second language, internships, part-time degree program, services for LD students, student-designed majors, summer session for credit.

Student Life *Campus security:* 24-hour patrols, security cameras.

Athletics Member NJCAA.

Costs (2011–12) *Tuition:* area resident $2528 full-time, $79 per credit hour part-time; state resident $6624 full-time, $207 per credit hour part-time; non-resident $8672 full-time, $271 per credit hour part-time. *Required fees:* $468 full-time, $14 per credit hour part-time, $10 per term part-time.

Financial Aid Of all full-time matriculated undergraduates who enrolled in 2010, 15 Federal Work-Study jobs (averaging $2000).

Applying *Application fee:* $10.

Freshman Application Contact Morton College, 3801 South Central Avenue, Cicero, IL 60804-4398. *Phone:* 708-656-8000 Ext. 401. *Web site:* http://www.morton.edu/.

Northwestern College

Rosemont, Illinois

Freshman Application Contact Northwestern College, 9700 West Higgins Road, Suite 750, Rosemont, IL 60018. *Phone:* 773-481-3730. *Toll-free phone:* 888-205-2283. *Web site:* http://www.northwesterncollege.edu/.

Oakton Community College

Des Plaines, Illinois

Freshman Application Contact Mr. Dale Cohen, Admissions Specialist, Oakton Community College, 1600 East Golf Road, Des Plaines, IL 60016-1268. *Phone:* 847-635-1703. *Fax:* 847-635-1890. *E-mail:* dcohen@oakton.edu. *Web site:* http://www.oakton.edu/.

Parkland College

Champaign, Illinois

Freshman Application Contact Admissions Representative, Parkland College, Champaign, IL 61821-1899. *Phone:* 217-351-2482. *Toll-free phone:* 800-346-8089. *Fax:* 217-351-2640. *E-mail:* mhenry@parkland.edu. *Web site:* http://www.parkland.edu/.

Prairie State College

Chicago Heights, Illinois

Freshman Application Contact Jaime Miller, Director of Admissions, Prairie State College, 202 South Halsted Street, Chicago Heights, IL 60411. *Phone:* 708-709-3513. *E-mail:* jmmiller@prairiestate.edu. *Web site:* http://www.prairiestate.edu/.

Rasmussen College Aurora

Aurora, Illinois

- **Proprietary** primarily 2-year, part of Rasmussen College System
- **Suburban** campus
- **Coed,** 443 undergraduate students

Faculty *Student/faculty ratio:* 22:1.

Majors Accounting; business administration and management; corrections and criminal justice related; early childhood education; graphic communications related; health/health-care administration; health information/medical records administration; health information/medical records technology; legal assistant/paralegal; management information systems and services related; medical administrative assistant and medical secretary; medical/clinical assistant; pharmacy technician; web page, digital/multimedia and information resources design.

Academics *Degrees:* certificates, diplomas, associate, and bachelor's. *Special study options:* academic remediation for entering students, accelerated degree program, adult/continuing education programs, distance learning, double majors, internships, part-time degree program, summer session for credit.

Library Rasmussen College Library - Aurora with 1,875 titles, 34 serial subscriptions, 464 audiovisual materials, an OPAC, a Web page.

Student Life *Housing:* college housing not available.

Standardized Tests *Required:* Internal Exam (for admission).

Costs (2012–13) *Tuition:* $12,600 full-time. Full-time tuition and fees vary according to course level, course load, degree level, location, and program. Part-time tuition and fees vary according to course level, course load, degree level, location, and program. *Required fees:* $40 full-time. *Payment plans:* installment, deferred payment. *Waivers:* employees or children of employees.

Applying *Options:* electronic application, early admission, deferred entrance. *Application fee:* $40. *Required:* high school transcript, minimum 2.0 GPA, interview. *Application deadlines:* rolling (freshmen), rolling (transfers).

Freshman Application Contact Susan Hammerstrom, Director of Admissions, Rasmussen College Aurora, 2363 Sequoia Drive, Aurora, IL 60506. *Phone:* 630-888-3500. *Toll-free phone:* 888-549-6755. *E-mail:* susan.hammerstrom@rasmussen.edu. *Web site:* http://www.rasmussen.edu/.

Rasmussen College Rockford

Rockford, Illinois

- **Proprietary** primarily 2-year, part of Rasmussen College System
- **Suburban** campus
- **Coed,** 881 undergraduate students

Faculty *Student/faculty ratio:* 22:1.

Majors Accounting; business administration and management; corrections and criminal justice related; early childhood education; graphic communications related; health/health-care administration; health information/medical records administration; health information/medical records technology; legal assistant/paralegal; management information systems and services related; medical administrative assistant and medical secretary; medical/clinical assistant; pharmacy technician; web page, digital/multimedia and information resources design.

Academics *Degrees:* certificates, diplomas, associate, and bachelor's. *Special study options:* academic remediation for entering students, accelerated degree program, adult/continuing education programs, distance learning, double majors, internships, part-time degree program, summer session for credit.

Library Rasmussen College Library - Rockford with 1,912 titles, 18 serial subscriptions, 275 audiovisual materials, an OPAC, a Web page.

Student Life *Housing:* college housing not available.

Standardized Tests *Required:* Internal Exam (for admission).

Costs (2012–13) *Tuition:* $12,600 full-time. Full-time tuition and fees vary according to course level, course load, degree level, location, and program. Part-time tuition and fees vary according to course level, course load, degree level, location, and program. *Required fees:* $40 full-time. *Payment plans:* installment, deferred payment. *Waivers:* employees or children of employees.

Applying *Options:* electronic application, early admission, deferred entrance. *Application fee:* $40. *Required:* high school transcript, minimum 2.0 GPA, interview. *Application deadlines:* rolling (freshmen), rolling (transfers).

Freshman Application Contact Susan Hammerstrom, Director of Admissions, Rasmussen College Rockford, 6000 East State Street, Fourth Floor, Rockford, IL 61108-2513. *Phone:* 815-316-4800. *Toll-free phone:* 888-549-6755. *E-mail:* susan.hammerstrom@rasmussen.edu. *Web site:* http://www.rasmussen.edu/.

Rend Lake College

Ina, Illinois

Freshman Application Contact Mr. Jason Swann, Recruiter, Rend Lake College, 468 North Ken Gray Parkway, Ina, IL 62846-9801. *Phone:* 618-437-5321 Ext. 1265. *Toll-free phone:* 800-369-5321. *Fax:* 618-437-5677. *E-mail:* swannj@rlc.edu. *Web site:* http://www.rlc.edu/.

Richland Community College

Decatur, Illinois

Freshman Application Contact Ms. JoAnn Wirey, Director of Admissions and Records, Richland Community College, Decatur, IL 62521. *Phone:* 217-875-7200 Ext. 284. *Fax:* 217-875-7783. *E-mail:* jwirey@richland.edu. *Web site:* http://www.richland.edu/.

Rockford Career College

Rockford, Illinois

Director of Admissions Ms. Barbara Holliman, Director of Admissions, Rockford Career College, 1130 South Alpine Road, Suite 100, Rockford, IL 61108. *Phone:* 815-965-8616 Ext. 16. *Web site:* http://www.rockfordcareercollege.edu/.

Rock Valley College

Rockford, Illinois

Freshman Application Contact Rock Valley College, 3301 North Mulford Road, Rockford, IL 61114-5699. *Phone:* 815-921-4283. *Toll-free phone:* 800-973-7821. *Web site:* http://www.rockvalleycollege.edu/.

Sauk Valley Community College

Dixon, Illinois

- **District-supported** 2-year, founded 1965, part of Illinois Community College Board
- **Rural** 165-acre campus
- **Endowment** $1.1 million
- **Coed**

Undergraduates 1,269 full-time, 1,223 part-time.

Faculty *Student/faculty ratio:* 22:1.

Academics *Calendar:* semesters. *Degree:* certificates and associate. *Special study options:* academic remediation for entering students, accelerated degree program, adult/continuing education programs, cooperative education, distance learning, English as a second language, honors programs, independent study, internships, off-campus study, part-time degree program, services for LD students, student-designed majors, summer session for credit.

Student Life *Campus security:* 24-hour emergency response devices and patrols, late-night transport/escort service.

Athletics Member NJCAA.

Standardized Tests *Recommended:* ACT (for admission).

Costs (2011–12) *Tuition:* area resident $3168 full-time, $99 per credit hour part-time; state resident $8160 full-time, $255 per credit hour part-time; nonresident $9248 full-time, $289 per credit hour part-time. Full-time tuition and fees vary according to course load. Part-time tuition and fees vary according to course load. *Room and board:* $6228. Room and board charges vary according to housing facility.

Financial Aid Of all full-time matriculated undergraduates who enrolled in 2009, 961 applied for aid, 837 were judged to have need, 40 had their need fully met. In 2009, 19. *Average percent of need met:* 47. *Average financial aid package:* $4425. *Average need-based loan:* $2243. *Average need-based gift aid:* $4745. *Average non-need-based aid:* $2631.

Applying *Options:* electronic application, early admission, deferred entrance. *Recommended:* high school transcript.

Freshman Application Contact Sauk Valley Community College, 173 Illinois Route 2, Dixon, IL 61021. *Phone:* 815-288-5511 Ext. 378. *Web site:* http://www.svcc.edu/.

Shawnee Community College

Ullin, Illinois

- **State and locally supported** 2-year, founded 1967, part of Illinois Community College Board
- **Rural** 163-acre campus
- **Coed,** 3,190 undergraduate students, 30% full-time, 55% women, 45% men

Undergraduates 942 full-time, 2,248 part-time. Students come from 6 states and territories; 2 other countries; 4% are from out of state; 17% Black or African American, non-Hispanic/Latino; 3% Hispanic/Latino; 0.3% Asian, non-Hispanic/Latino; 0.3% American Indian or Alaska Native, non-Hispanic/Latino; 0.3% Race/ethnicity unknown.

Freshmen *Admission:* 731 applied, 731 admitted, 392 enrolled. *Test scores:* ACT scores over 18: 69%; ACT scores over 24: 17%.

Faculty *Total:* 212, 20% full-time, 4% with terminal degrees. *Student/faculty ratio:* 20:1.

Majors Accounting; administrative assistant and secretarial science; agricultural business and management; agriculture; agronomy and crop science; animal sciences; automobile/automotive mechanics technology; biological and physical sciences; business administration and management; child development; cosmetology; criminal justice/police science; electrical, electronic and communications engineering technology; horticultural science; human services; information science/studies; legal administrative assistant/secretary; liberal arts and sciences/liberal studies; medical administrative assistant and medical secretary; registered nursing/registered nurse; social work; welding technology; wildlife, fish and wildlands science and management.

Academics *Calendar:* semesters. *Degree:* certificates and associate. *Special study options:* academic remediation for entering students, accelerated degree program, adult/continuing education programs, advanced placement credit, distance learning, double majors, English as a second language, external degree program, independent study, internships, off-campus study, part-time degree program, services for LD students, summer session for credit.

Library Shawnee Community College Library with 46,313 titles, 148 serial subscriptions, 1,842 audiovisual materials, an OPAC, a Web page.

Student Life *Housing:* college housing not available. *Activities and Organizations:* drama/theater group, choral group, Phi Theta Kappa, Phi Beta Lambda, Music Club, Student Senate, Future Teachers Organization. *Campus security:* 24-hour patrols. *Student services:* personal/psychological counseling.

Athletics Member NJCAA. *Intercollegiate sports:* baseball M(s), basketball M(s)/W(s), softball W(s). *Intramural sports:* weight lifting M/W.

Standardized Tests *Required for some:* ACT (for admission). *Recommended:* ACT (for admission).

Costs (2012–13) *Tuition:* area resident $2208 full-time, $92 per credit hour part-time; state resident $3312 full-time, $138 per credit hour part-time; nonresident $3696 full-time, $154 per credit hour part-time. *Payment plans:* installment, deferred payment. *Waivers:* senior citizens and employees or children of employees.

Financial Aid Of all full-time matriculated undergraduates who enrolled in 2010, 60 Federal Work-Study jobs (averaging $2000). 50 state and other part-time jobs (averaging $2000).

Applying *Options:* electronic application, early admission, deferred entrance. *Required:* high school transcript. *Application deadlines:* rolling (freshmen), rolling (transfers). *Notification:* continuous (freshmen), continuous (transfers).

Freshman Application Contact Mrs. Erin King, Recruiter/Advisor, Shawnee Community College, 8364 Shawnee College Road, Ullin, IL 62992. *Phone:* 618-634-3200. *Toll-free phone:* 800-481-2242. *Fax:* 618-634-3300. *E-mail:* erink@shawneecc.edu. *Web site:* http://www.shawneecc.edu/.

Solex College

Wheeling, Illinois

Freshman Application Contact Solex College, 350 East Dundee Road, Wheeling, IL 60090. *Web site:* http://www.solex.edu/.

Southeastern Illinois College

Harrisburg, Illinois

Freshman Application Contact Dr. David Nudo, Director of Counseling, Southeastern Illinois College, 3575 College Road, Harrisburg, IL 62946-4925. *Phone:* 618-252-5400 Ext. 2430. *Toll-free phone:* 866-338-2742. *Web site:* http://www.sic.edu/.

South Suburban College

South Holland, Illinois

- **State and locally supported** 2-year, founded 1927, part of Illinois Community College Board
- **Suburban** campus with easy access to Chicago
- **Coed,** 7,579 undergraduate students, 37% full-time, 69% women, 31% men

Undergraduates 2,769 full-time, 4,810 part-time. 6% are from out of state; 68% Black or African American, non-Hispanic/Latino; 9% Hispanic/Latino; 0.9% Asian, non-Hispanic/Latino; 0.2% American Indian or Alaska Native, non-Hispanic/Latino; 0.4% Two or more races, non-Hispanic/Latino; 2% Race/ethnicity unknown. *Retention:* 58% of full-time freshmen returned.

Freshmen *Admission:* 873 applied, 873 admitted. *Average high school GPA:* 2.33.

Faculty *Total:* 700, 40% full-time. *Student/faculty ratio:* 22:1.

Majors Accounting; accounting technology and bookkeeping; architectural drafting and CAD/CADD; biological and physical sciences; building/home/construction inspection; CAD/CADD drafting/design technology; child-care provision; construction engineering technology; court reporting; criminal justice/safety; electrical, electronic and communications engineering technology; executive assistant/executive secretary; fine/studio arts; information technology; kinesiology and exercise science; legal assistant/paralegal; liberal arts and sciences/liberal studies; nursing administration; occupational therapist assistant; office management; radiologic technology/science; small business administration; social work.

Academics *Calendar:* semesters. *Degree:* certificates and associate. *Special study options:* academic remediation for entering students, adult/continuing education programs, advanced placement credit, cooperative education, distance learning, English as a second language, honors programs, internships, off-campus study, part-time degree program, services for LD students, study abroad, summer session for credit.

Library South Suburban College Library with 32,066 titles, 142 serial subscriptions, an OPAC, a Web page.

Student Life *Housing:* college housing not available. *Activities and Organizations:* drama/theater group, choral group. *Campus security:* 24-hour emergency response devices and patrols.

Athletics Member NJCAA. *Intercollegiate sports:* baseball M, basketball M/W, soccer M/W, softball W, volleyball W.

Costs (2012–13) *Tuition:* area resident $3300 full-time; state resident $8640 full-time; nonresident $10,290 full-time. Full-time tuition and fees vary according to course load and reciprocity agreements. Part-time tuition and fees vary according to course load and reciprocity agreements. *Required fees:* $473 full-time. *Payment plan:* installment. *Waivers:* senior citizens and employees or children of employees.

Financial Aid Of all full-time matriculated undergraduates who enrolled in 2010, 121 Federal Work-Study jobs (averaging $1750).

Applying *Options:* early admission, deferred entrance. *Required:* high school transcript. *Required for some:* essay or personal statement. *Recommended:* essay or personal statement, minimum 2.0 GPA. *Application deadlines:* rolling (freshmen), rolling (transfers). *Notification:* continuous (freshmen), continuous (transfers).

Freshman Application Contact Tiffane Jones, Admissions, South Suburban College, 15800 South State Street, South Holland, IL 60473-1270. *Phone:* 708-596-2000 Ext. 2158. *E-mail:* admissionsquestions@ssc.edu. *Web site:* http://www.ssc.edu/.

Southwestern Illinois College
Belleville, Illinois

- **District-supported** 2-year, founded 1946, part of Illinois Community College Board
- **Suburban** 341-acre campus with easy access to St. Louis
- **Endowment** $5.2 million
- **Coed,** 12,779 undergraduate students, 41% full-time, 56% women, 44% men

Undergraduates 5,276 full-time, 7,503 part-time. Students come from 12 states and territories; 1% are from out of state; 23% Black or African American, non-Hispanic/Latino; 2% Hispanic/Latino; 1% Asian, non-Hispanic/Latino; 0.4% Native Hawaiian or other Pacific Islander, non-Hispanic/Latino; 0.4% American Indian or Alaska Native, non-Hispanic/Latino; 5% Race/ethnicity unknown; 4% transferred in.

Freshmen *Admission:* 1,147 applied, 1,147 admitted, 1,147 enrolled.

Faculty *Total:* 728, 21% full-time, 30% with terminal degrees. *Student/faculty ratio:* 23:1.

Majors Accounting; administrative assistant and secretarial science; airframe mechanics and aircraft maintenance technology; airline pilot and flight crew; applied horticulture/horticulture operations; autobody/collision and repair technology; aviation/airway management; biological and physical sciences; carpentry; child-care provision; clinical/medical laboratory technology; computer and information sciences; computer/information technology services administration related; computer programming; concrete finishing; construction trades; criminal justice/law enforcement administration; data modeling/warehousing and database administration; desktop publishing and digital imaging design; electrical and power transmission installation; electrical, electronic and communications engineering technology; electrician; emergency medical technology (EMT paramedic); fine/studio arts; fire science/firefighting; general studies; health information/medical records technology; heating, air conditioning, ventilation and refrigeration maintenance technology; industrial mechanics and maintenance technology; information technology; ironworking; legal administrative assistant/secretary; legal assistant/paralegal; liberal arts and sciences/liberal studies; machine tool technology; manufacturing engineering technology; masonry; massage therapy; mathematics teacher education; mechanical drafting and CAD/CADD; medical/clinical assistant; medical office assistant; music; music teacher education; network and system administration; painting and wall covering; physical therapy technology; pipefitting and sprinkler fitting; radiologic technology/science; registered nursing/registered nurse; respiratory care therapy; restaurant, culinary, and catering management; selling skills and sales; sheet metal technology; sign language interpretation and translation; small business administration; social work; teacher assistant/aide; web/multimedia management and webmaster; welding technology.

Academics *Calendar:* semesters. *Degree:* certificates, diplomas, and associate. *Special study options:* academic remediation for entering students, accelerated degree program, adult/continuing education programs, advanced placement credit, cooperative education, distance learning, double majors, English as a second language, internships, off-campus study, part-time degree program, services for LD students, study abroad, summer session for credit. *ROTC:* Army (c), Air Force (c).

Library Southwestern Illinois College Library with 85,265 titles, 60 serial subscriptions, 6,902 audiovisual materials, an OPAC, a Web page.

Student Life *Housing:* college housing not available. *Activities and Organizations:* drama/theater group, student-run newspaper, choral group, College Activities Board, Phi Theta Kappa, Student Nurses Association, Horticulture Club, Data Processing Management Association. *Campus security:* 24-hour emergency response devices and patrols, late-night transport/escort service. *Student services:* personal/psychological counseling.

Athletics Member NJCAA. *Intercollegiate sports:* baseball M(s), basketball M(s)/W(s), soccer M(s)/W(s), softball W(s), volleyball W(s).

Standardized Tests *Required for some:* ACT (for admission), ACT ASSET or ACT COMPASS.

Costs (2012–13) *Tuition:* area resident $2850 full-time, $95 per credit hour part-time; state resident $7290 full-time, $243 per credit hour part-time; nonresident $10,950 full-time, $365 per credit hour part-time. Full-time tuition and fees vary according to course load. Part-time tuition and fees vary according to course load. *Required fees:* $120 full-time, $4 per credit hour part-time. *Pay-

ment plan:* installment. *Waivers:* senior citizens and employees or children of employees.

Financial Aid Of all full-time matriculated undergraduates who enrolled in 2010, 170 Federal Work-Study jobs (averaging $1537). 179 state and other part-time jobs (averaging $1004).

Applying *Options:* early admission, deferred entrance. *Required:* high school transcript. *Application deadlines:* rolling (freshmen), rolling (out-of-state freshmen), rolling (transfers).

Freshman Application Contact Michelle Birk, Dean of Enrollment Services, Southwestern Illinois College, 2500 Carlyle Road, Belleville, IL 62221. *Phone:* 618-235-2700 Ext. 5400. *Toll-free phone:* 866-942-SWIC. *Fax:* 618-222-9768. *E-mail:* michelle.birk@swic.edu. *Web site:* http://www.southwestern.cc.il.us/.

Spoon River College
Canton, Illinois

Freshman Application Contact Ms. Missy Wilkinson, Director of Admissions and Records, Spoon River College, 23235 North County 22, Canton, IL 61520-9801. *Phone:* 309-649-6305. *Toll-free phone:* 800-334-7337. *Fax:* 309-649-6235. *E-mail:* info@spoonrivercollege.edu. *Web site:* http://www.src.edu/.

Taylor Business Institute
Chicago, Illinois

Director of Admissions Mr. Rashed Jahangir, Taylor Business Institute, 318 West Adams, Chicago, IL 60606. *Web site:* http://www.tbiil.edu/.

Triton College
River Grove, Illinois

Freshman Application Contact Ms. Mary-Rita Moore, Dean of Admissions, Triton College, 2000 Fifth Avenue, River Grove, IL 60171. *Phone:* 708-456-0300 Ext. 3679. *Fax:* 708-583-3162. *E-mail:* mpatrice@triton.edu. *Web site:* http://www.triton.edu/.

Vet Tech Institute at Fox College
Tinley Park, Illinois

- **Private** 2-year, founded 2006
- **Suburban** campus
- **Coed,** 158 undergraduate students
- 56% of applicants were admitted

Freshmen *Admission:* 514 applied, 289 admitted.

Majors Veterinary/animal health technology.

Academics *Degree:* associate. *Special study options:* accelerated degree program, internships.

Student Life *Housing:* college housing not available.

Freshman Application Contact Admissions Office, Vet Tech Institute at Fox College, 18020 South Oak Park Avenue, Tinley Park, IL 60477. *Phone:* 888-884-3694. *Toll-free phone:* 888-884-3694. *Web site:* http://www.vettechinstitute.edu/chicago.

Waubonsee Community College
Sugar Grove, Illinois

- **District-supported** 2-year, founded 1966, part of Illinois Community College Board
- **Small-town** 243-acre campus with easy access to Chicago
- **Endowment** $1.1 million
- **Coed**

Undergraduates 3,927 full-time, 6,501 part-time. Students come from 12 states and territories; 8% Black or African American, non-Hispanic/Latino; 22% Hispanic/Latino; 2% Asian, non-Hispanic/Latino; 0.3% American Indian or Alaska Native, non-Hispanic/Latino; 3% transferred in. *Retention:* 65% of full-time freshmen returned.

Faculty *Student/faculty ratio:* 18:1.

Academics *Calendar:* semesters. *Degree:* certificates and associate. *Special study options:* academic remediation for entering students, accelerated degree program, advanced placement credit, distance learning, English as a second language, honors programs, independent study, internships, off-campus study, part-time degree program, services for LD students, study abroad, summer session for credit. *ROTC:* Army (c).

Student Life *Campus security:* 24-hour emergency response devices and patrols, late-night transport/escort service.

Athletics Member NJCAA.

Costs (2011–12) *Tuition:* area resident $2850 full-time, $95 per semester hour part-time; state resident $7933 full-time, $265 per semester hour part-time; nonresident $8698 full-time, $290 per semester hour part-time. Full-time tuition and fees vary according to reciprocity agreements. Part-time tuition and fees vary according to reciprocity agreements. *Required fees:* $150 full-time, $5 per semester hour part-time.

Financial Aid Of all full-time matriculated undergraduates who enrolled in 2010, 23 Federal Work-Study jobs (averaging $2000).

Freshman Application Contact Joy Sanders, Admissions Manager, Waubonsee Community College, Route 47 at Waubonsee Drive, Sugar Grove, IL 60554. *Phone:* 630-466-7900 Ext. 5756. *Fax:* 630-466-6663. *E-mail:* admissions@waubonsee.edu. *Web site:* http://www.waubonsee.edu/.

Worsham College of Mortuary Science
Wheeling, Illinois

Director of Admissions President, Worsham College of Mortuary Science, 495 Northgate Parkway, Wheeling, IL 60090-2646. *Phone:* 847-808-8444. *Web site:* http://www.worshamcollege.com/.

INDIANA

Ancilla College
Donaldson, Indiana

- **Independent Roman Catholic** 2-year, founded 1937
- **Rural** 63-acre campus with easy access to Chicago
- **Endowment** $3.7 million
- **Coed,** 533 undergraduate students, 68% full-time, 65% women, 35% men

Undergraduates 364 full-time, 169 part-time. Students come from 6 states and territories; 3 other countries; 6% are from out of state; 6% Black or African American, non-Hispanic/Latino; 5% Hispanic/Latino; 0.4% American Indian or Alaska Native, non-Hispanic/Latino; 2% Two or more races, non-Hispanic/Latino; 0.9% Race/ethnicity unknown; 0.8% international; 13% transferred in. *Retention:* 48% of full-time freshmen returned.

Freshmen *Admission:* 809 applied, 506 admitted, 135 enrolled. *Average high school GPA:* 2.52. *Test scores:* SAT critical reading scores over 500: 13%; SAT math scores over 500: 23%; ACT scores over 18: 41%; SAT critical reading scores over 600: 2%; ACT scores over 24: 1%.

Faculty *Total:* 45, 44% full-time, 16% with terminal degrees. *Student/faculty ratio:* 18:1.

Majors Behavioral sciences; biological and physical sciences; biology/biological sciences; business administration and management; criminal justice/safety; early childhood education; elementary education; general studies; health services/allied health/health sciences; history; mass communication/media; registered nursing/registered nurse; secondary education.

Academics *Calendar:* semesters. *Degree:* certificates and associate. *Special study options:* academic remediation for entering students, accelerated degree program, adult/continuing education programs, advanced placement credit, cooperative education, distance learning, double majors, independent study, internships, part-time degree program, services for LD students, student-designed majors, summer session for credit.

Library Ball Library with 27,859 titles, 152 serial subscriptions, 1,499 audiovisual materials, an OPAC, a Web page.

Student Life *Housing:* college housing not available. *Activities and Organizations:* student-run newspaper, Student Government Association, Student Nursing Organization, Ancilla Student Ambassadors, Phi Theta Kappa. *Campus security:* 24-hour patrols, late-night transport/escort service. *Student services:* personal/psychological counseling.

Athletics Member NJCAA. *Intercollegiate sports:* baseball M(s), basketball M(s)/W(s), cheerleading M(s)/W(s), golf M(s)/W(s), soccer M(s), softball W(s), volleyball W(s).

Standardized Tests *Required for some:* SAT or ACT (for admission). *Recommended:* SAT or ACT (for admission).

Costs (2012–13) *Tuition:* $13,650 full-time, $455 per credit part-time. Full-time tuition and fees vary according to course load and program. Part-time tuition and fees vary according to course load and program. *Required fees:* $230 full-time, $55 per term part-time. *Payment plan:* installment. *Waivers:* employees or children of employees.

Financial Aid Of all full-time matriculated undergraduates who enrolled in 2010, 28 Federal Work-Study jobs (averaging $1820). 16 state and other part-time jobs (averaging $1000). *Financial aid deadline:* 3/1.

Applying *Options:* electronic application. *Required:* high school transcript. *Application deadlines:* rolling (freshmen), rolling (transfers).

Freshman Application Contact Ms. Sarah lawrence, Director of Admissions, Ancilla College, 9601 Union Road, Donaldson, IN 46513. *Phone:* 574-936-8898 Ext. 396. *Toll-free phone:* 866-ANCILLA. *Fax:* 574-935-1773. *E-mail:* admissions@ancilla.edu. *Web site:* http://www.ancilla.edu/.

Aviation Institute of Maintenance–Indianapolis
Indianapolis, Indiana

Freshman Application Contact Admissions Office, Aviation Institute of Maintenance–Indianapolis, 7251 West McCarty Street, Indianapolis, IN 46241. *Toll-free phone:* 888-349-5387. *Web site:* http://www.aviationmaintenance.edu/.

Brown Mackie College–Fort Wayne
Fort Wayne, Indiana

- **Proprietary** primarily 2-year, part of Education Management Corporation
- **Coed**

Academics *Calendar:* quarters. *Degrees:* certificates, diplomas, associate, and bachelor's.

Costs (2011–12) *Tuition:* Tuition varies by program. Students should contact Brown Mackie College for tuition information.

Freshman Application Contact Brown Mackie College–Fort Wayne, 3000 East Coliseum Boulevard, Fort Wayne, IN 46805. *Phone:* 260-484-4400. *Toll-free phone:* 866-433-2289. *Web site:* http://www.brownmackie.edu/fortwayne/.

See page 354 for the College Close-Up.

Brown Mackie College–Indianapolis
Indianapolis, Indiana

- **Proprietary** primarily 2-year, part of Education Management Corporation
- **Coed**

Academics *Degrees:* certificates, diplomas, associate, and bachelor's.

Costs (2011–12) *Tuition:* Tuition varies by program. Students should contact Brown Mackie College for tuition information.

Freshman Application Contact Brown Mackie College–Indianapolis, 1200 North Meridian Street, Suite 100, Indianapolis, IN 46204. *Phone:* 317-554-8301. *Toll-free phone:* 866-255-0279. *Web site:* http://www.brownmackie.edu/indianapolis/.

See page 360 for the College Close-Up.

Brown Mackie College–Merrillville
Merrillville, Indiana

- **Proprietary** primarily 2-year, founded 1890, part of Education Management Corporation
- **Small-town** campus
- **Coed**

Academics *Calendar:* quarters. *Degrees:* certificates, diplomas, associate, and bachelor's.

Costs (2011–12) *Tuition:* Tuition varies by program. Students should contact Brown Mackie College for tuition information.

Freshman Application Contact Brown Mackie College–Merrillville, 1000 East 80th Place, Suite 205S, Merrillville, IN 46410. *Phone:* 219-769-3321. *Toll-free phone:* 800-258-3321. *Web site:* http://www.brownmackie.edu/merrillville/.

See page 366 for the College Close-Up.

Brown Mackie College–Michigan City
Michigan City, Indiana

- **Proprietary** primarily 2-year, part of Education Management Corporation
- **Rural** campus
- **Coed**

Academics *Calendar:* quarters. *Degrees:* certificates, diplomas, associate, and bachelor's.

Costs (2011–12) *Tuition:* Tuition varies by program. Students should contact Brown Mackie College for tuition information.

Freshman Application Contact Brown Mackie College–Michigan City, 325 East US Highway 20, Michigan City, IN 46360. *Phone:* 219-877-3100. *Toll-*

free phone: 800-519-2416. *Web site:* http://www.brownmackie.edu/michigancity/.

See page 370 for the College Close-Up.

Brown Mackie College–South Bend
South Bend, Indiana

- **Proprietary** primarily 2-year, founded 1882, part of Education Management Corporation
- **Urban** campus
- **Coed, primarily women**

Academics *Calendar:* quarters. *Degrees:* certificates, associate, and bachelor's.

Costs (2011–12) *Tuition:* Tuition varies by program. Students should contact Brown Mackie College for tuition information.

Freshman Application Contact Brown Mackie College–South Bend, 3454 Douglas Road, South Bend, IN 46635. *Phone:* 574-237-0774. *Toll-free phone:* 800-743-2447. *Web site:* http://www.brownmackie.edu/southbend/.

See page 388 for the College Close-Up.

College of Court Reporting
Hobart, Indiana

Freshman Application Contact Ms. Nicky Rodriquez, Director of Admissions, College of Court Reporting, 111 West Tenth Street, Suite 111, Hobart, IN 46342. *Phone:* 219-942-1459 Ext. 222. *Toll-free phone:* 866-294-3974. *Fax:* 219-942-1631. *E-mail:* nrodriquez@ccr.edu. *Web site:* http://www.ccr.edu/.

Harrison College
Anderson, Indiana

- **Proprietary** 2-year, founded 1902
- **Small-town** campus with easy access to Indianapolis
- **Coed**

Undergraduates 62 full-time, 218 part-time. 14% Black or African American, non-Hispanic/Latino; 0.4% American Indian or Alaska Native, non-Hispanic/Latino; 0.4% Two or more races, non-Hispanic/Latino; 22% transferred in. *Retention:* 50% of full-time freshmen returned.

Faculty *Student/faculty ratio:* 16:1.

Academics *Calendar:* quarters. *Degree:* certificates, diplomas, and associate. *Special study options:* adult/continuing education programs, cooperative education, distance learning, double majors, independent study, internships, part-time degree program.

Standardized Tests *Required:* Wonderlic Scholastic Level Exam (SLE) (for admission).

Costs (2011–12) *Tuition:* Full-time tuition and fees vary according to course load and program. Part-time tuition and fees vary according to course load and program. No tuition increase for student's term of enrollment. Tuition ranges from $300 to $400 a credit depending upon program of study. *Required fees:* $435 full-time, $145 per term part-time.

Applying *Options:* electronic application, early admission. *Application fee:* $50. *Required:* high school transcript, interview.

Freshman Application Contact Mr. Kynan Simison, Director of Admissions, Harrison College, 140 East 53rd Street, Anderson, IN 46013. *Phone:* 765-644-7514. *Toll-free phone:* 888-544-4422. *Fax:* 765-664-5724. *E-mail:* kynan.simison@harrison.edu. *Web site:* http://www.harrison.edu/.

Harrison College
Columbus, Indiana

- **Proprietary** 2-year
- **Rural** campus
- **Coed**
- **100% of applicants were admitted**

Undergraduates 203 full-time, 51 part-time. 1% Black or African American, non-Hispanic/Latino; 2% Hispanic/Latino; 0.4% Race/ethnicity unknown; 15% transferred in. *Retention:* 40% of full-time freshmen returned.

Faculty *Student/faculty ratio:* 15:1.

Academics *Calendar:* quarters. *Degree:* certificates, diplomas, and associate. *Special study options:* adult/continuing education programs, cooperative education, distance learning, double majors, independent study, internships, part-time degree program.

Standardized Tests *Required:* Wonderlic Scholastic Level Exam (SLE) (for admission).

Costs (2011–12) *Tuition:* Full-time tuition and fees vary according to course load and program. Part-time tuition and fees vary according to course load and program. No tuition increase for student's term of enrollment. Tuition ranges from $300 to $400 a credit depending upon program of study. *Required fees:* $435 full-time, $145 per term part-time.

Applying *Options:* electronic application. *Application fee:* $50. *Required:* high school transcript, interview.

Freshman Application Contact Ms. Gina Pate, Director of Admissions, Harrison College, 2222 Poshard Drive, Columbus, IN 47203. *Phone:* 812-379-9000. *Toll-free phone:* 888-544-4422. *Fax:* 812-375-0414. *E-mail:* gina.pate@harrison.edu. *Web site:* http://www.harrison.edu/.

Harrison College
Elkhart, Indiana

Freshman Application Contact Matt Brady, Director of Admissions, Harrison College, 56075 Parkway Avenue, Elkhart, IN 46516. *Phone:* 574-522-0397. *Toll-free phone:* 888-544-4422. *E-mail:* matt.brady@harrison.edu. *Web site:* http://www.harrison.edu/.

Harrison College
Evansville, Indiana

Freshman Application Contact Mr. Bryan Barber, Harrison College, 4601 Theater Drive, Evansville, IN 47715. *Phone:* 812-476-6000. *Toll-free phone:* 888-544-4422 (in-state); 888-554-4422 (out-of-state). *Fax:* 812-471-8576. *E-mail:* bryan.barber@harrison.edu. *Web site:* http://www.harrison.edu/.

Harrison College
Fort Wayne, Indiana

Freshman Application Contact Mr. Matt Wallace, Associate Director of Admissions, Harrison College, 6413 North Clinton Street, Fort Wayne, IN 46825. *Phone:* 260-471-7667. *Toll-free phone:* 888-544-4422. *Fax:* 260-471-6918. *E-mail:* matt.wallace@harrison.edu. *Web site:* http://www.harrison.edu/

Harrison College
Indianapolis, Indiana

- **Proprietary** primarily 2-year, founded 1902
- **Urban** 1-acre campus with easy access to Indianapolis
- **Coed**

Undergraduates 1,740 full-time, 928 part-time. Students come from 32 states and territories; 1 other country; 17% Black or African American, non-Hispanic/Latino; 2% Hispanic/Latino; 0.5% Asian, non-Hispanic/Latino; 0.3% American Indian or Alaska Native, non-Hispanic/Latino; 0.6% Two or more races, non-Hispanic/Latino; 36% Race/ethnicity unknown; 12% transferred in. *Retention:* 44% of full-time freshmen returned.

Faculty *Student/faculty ratio:* 16:1.

Academics *Calendar:* quarters. *Degrees:* certificates, diplomas, associate, and bachelor's. *Special study options:* adult/continuing education programs, cooperative education, distance learning, double majors, internships, part-time degree program, summer session for credit.

Student Life *Campus security:* 24-hour patrols.

Standardized Tests *Required:* Wonderlic Scholastic Level Exam (SLE) (for admission).

Costs (2011–12) *Tuition:* Full-time tuition and fees vary according to course load and program. Part-time tuition and fees vary according to course load and program. No tuition increase for student's term of enrollment. Tuition ranges from $300 to $400 a credit depending upon program of study. *Required fees:* $435 full-time, $145 per term part-time.

Applying *Options:* electronic application. *Application fee:* $50. *Required:* high school transcript, interview.

Freshman Application Contact Mr. Ted Lukomski, Director of Admissions, Harrison College, 550 East Washington Street, Indianapolis, IN 46204. *Phone:* 317-264-5656. *Toll-free phone:* 888-544-4422. *Fax:* 317-264-5650. *E-mail:* ted.lukomski@ibcschools.edu. *Web site:* http://www.harrison.edu/.

Harrison College
Indianapolis, Indiana

- **Proprietary** 2-year
- **Urban** campus
- **Coed**

Undergraduates 241 full-time, 80 part-time. 6% Black or African American, non-Hispanic/Latino; 1% Hispanic/Latino; 0.3% Native Hawaiian or other Pacific Islander, non-Hispanic/Latino; 2% Two or more races, non-Hispanic/Latino; 10% Race/ethnicity unknown; 10% transferred in. *Retention:* 58% of full-time freshmen returned.

Faculty *Student/faculty ratio:* 13:1.

Academics *Calendar:* quarters. *Degree:* certificates, diplomas, and associate. *Special study options:* adult/continuing education programs.
Standardized Tests *Required:* Wonderlic Scholastic Level Exam (for admission).
Costs (2011–12) *Tuition:* Full-time tuition and fees vary according to course load and program. Part-time tuition and fees vary according to course load and program. No tuition increase for student's term of enrollment. Tuition ranges from $300 to $400 a credit depending upon program of study. *Required fees:* $435 full-time, $145 per term part-time.
Applying *Application fee:* $50. *Required:* high school transcript, interview.
Freshman Application Contact Mr. Matt Stein, Director of Admissions, Harrison College, 6300 Technology Center Drive, Indianapolis, IN 46278. *Phone:* 317-873-6500. *Toll-free phone:* 888-544-4422. *Fax:* 317-733-6266. *E-mail:* matthew.stein@harrison.edu. *Web site:* http://www.harrison.edu/.

Harrison College
Indianapolis, Indiana

Freshman Application Contact Jan Carter, Director of Admissions, Harrison College, 8150 Brookville Road, Indianapolis, IN 46239. *Phone:* 317-375-8000. *Toll-free phone:* 888-544-4422. *Fax:* 317-351-1871. *E-mail:* jan.carter@harrison.edu. *Web site:* http://www.harrison.edu/.

Harrison College
Lafayette, Indiana

- **Proprietary** primarily 2-year
- **Small-town** campus
- **Coed**

Undergraduates 286 full-time, 64 part-time. 5% Black or African American, non-Hispanic/Latino; 6% Hispanic/Latino; 0.6% Asian, non-Hispanic/Latino; 0.3% Native Hawaiian or other Pacific Islander, non-Hispanic/Latino; 0.3% American Indian or Alaska Native, non-Hispanic/Latino; 1% Two or more races, non-Hispanic/Latino; 17% transferred in. *Retention:* 45% of full-time freshmen returned.
Faculty *Student/faculty ratio:* 15:1.
Academics *Calendar:* quarters. *Degrees:* certificates, diplomas, associate, and bachelor's. *Special study options:* adult/continuing education programs, cooperative education, distance learning, double majors, independent study, internships, part-time degree program.
Standardized Tests *Required:* Wonderlic Scholastic Level Exam (SLE) (for admission).
Costs (2011–12) *Tuition:* Full-time tuition and fees vary according to course load and program. Part-time tuition and fees vary according to course load and program. No tuition increase for student's term of enrollment. Tuition ranges from $300 to $400 a credit depending upon program of study. *Required fees:* $435 full-time, $145 per term part-time.
Applying *Options:* electronic application. *Application fee:* $50. *Required:* high school transcript, interview.
Freshman Application Contact Ms. Stacy Golleher, Associate Director of Admissions, Harrison College, 4705 Meijer Court, Lafayette, IN 47905. *Phone:* 765-447-9550. *Toll-free phone:* 888-544-4422. *Fax:* 765-447-0868. *E-mail:* stacy.golleher@harrison.edu. *Web site:* http://www.harrison.edu/.

Harrison College
Muncie, Indiana

- **Proprietary** primarily 2-year
- **Small-town** campus
- **Coed, primarily women**

Undergraduates 187 full-time, 42 part-time. 12% Black or African American, non-Hispanic/Latino; 2% Two or more races, non-Hispanic/Latino. *Retention:* 52% of full-time freshmen returned.
Faculty *Student/faculty ratio:* 16:1.
Academics *Calendar:* quarters. *Degrees:* certificates, diplomas, associate, and bachelor's. *Special study options:* adult/continuing education programs, cooperative education, distance learning, double majors, independent study, part-time degree program.
Standardized Tests *Required:* Wonderlic Scholastic Level Exam (SLE) (for admission).
Costs (2011–12) *Tuition:* Full-time tuition and fees vary according to course load and program. Part-time tuition and fees vary according to course load and program. No tuition increase for student's term of enrollment. Tuition ranges from $300 to $400 a credit depending upon program of study. *Required fees:* $435 full-time, $145 per term part-time.
Applying *Options:* electronic application. *Application fee:* $50. *Required:* high school transcript, interview.
Freshman Application Contact Mr. Jeremy Linder, Associate Director of Admissions, Harrison College, Muncie, IN 47303. *Phone:* 765-288-8681.

Toll-free phone: 888-544-4422. *Fax:* 765-288-8797. *E-mail:* Jeremy.linder@harrison.edu. *Web site:* http://www.harrison.edu/.

Harrison College
Terre Haute, Indiana

Freshman Application Contact Sarah Stultz, Associate Director of Admissions, Harrison College, 1378 South State Road 46, Terre Haute, IN 47803. *Phone:* 812-877-2100. *Toll-free phone:* 888-544-4422. *Fax:* 812-877-4440. *E-mail:* sarah.stultz@harrison.edu. *Web site:* http://www.harrison.edu/.

International Business College
Indianapolis, Indiana

- **Private** 2-year, founded 1889
- **Suburban** campus
- **Coed,** 355 undergraduate students
- **73% of applicants were admitted**

Freshmen *Admission:* 1,054 applied, 768 admitted.
Majors Accounting technology and bookkeeping; administrative assistant and secretarial science; computer programming; computer systems networking and telecommunications; dental assisting; graphic design; hotel/motel administration; legal administrative assistant/secretary; legal assistant/paralegal; medical/clinical assistant; veterinary/animal health technology.
Academics *Calendar:* semesters. *Degree:* diplomas and associate. *Special study options:* accelerated degree program, internships.
Freshman Application Contact Admissions Office, International Business College, 7205 Shadeland Station, Indianapolis, IN 46256. *Phone:* 317-813-2300. *Toll-free phone:* 800-589-6500. *Web site:* http://www.ibcindianapolis.edu/.

ITT Technical Institute
Fort Wayne, Indiana

- **Proprietary** primarily 2-year, founded 1967, part of ITT Educational Services, Inc.
- **Coed**

Majors Business administration and management; communications technology; computer and information systems security; computer software engineering; computer software technology; construction management; criminal justice/law enforcement administration; drafting and design technology; electrical, electronic and communications engineering technology; forensic science and technology; game and interactive media design; graphic communications; industrial technology; legal assistant/paralegal; network and system administration; project management; registered nursing/registered nurse.
Academics *Calendar:* quarters. *Degrees:* associate and bachelor's.
Student Life *Housing:* college housing not available.
Freshman Application Contact Director of Recruitment, ITT Technical Institute, 2810 Dupont Commerce Court, Fort Wayne, IN 46825. *Phone:* 260-497-6200. *Toll-free phone:* 800-866-4488. *Fax:* 260-497-6299. *Web site:* http://www.itt-tech.edu/.

ITT Technical Institute
Merrillville, Indiana

- **Proprietary** primarily 2-year
- **Coed**

Majors Business administration and management; communications technology; computer and information systems security; drafting and design technology; electrical, electronic and communications engineering technology; forensic science and technology; graphic communications; legal assistant/paralegal; network and system administration; project management; registered nursing/registered nurse.
Academics *Degrees:* associate and bachelor's.
Freshman Application Contact Director of Recruitment, ITT Technical Institute, 8488 Georgia Street, Merrillville, IN 46410. *Phone:* 219-738-6100. *Toll-free phone:* 877-418-8134. *Web site:* http://www.itt-tech.edu/.

ITT Technical Institute
Newburgh, Indiana

- **Proprietary** primarily 2-year, founded 1966, part of ITT Educational Services, Inc.
- **Coed**

Majors Business administration and management; communications technology; computer and information systems security; computer engineering technology; criminal justice/law enforcement administration; drafting and design technology; electrical, electronic and communications engineering technology;

forensic science and technology; graphic communications; industrial technology; legal assistant/paralegal; network and system administration; project management; registered nursing/registered nurse.

Academics *Calendar:* quarters. *Degrees:* associate and bachelor's.

Student Life *Housing:* college housing not available.

Freshman Application Contact Director of Recruitment, ITT Technical Institute, 10999 Stahl Road, Newburgh, IN 47630-7430. *Phone:* 812-858-1600. *Toll-free phone:* 800-832-4488. *Web site:* http://www.itt-tech.edu/.

Ivy Tech Community College–Bloomington

Bloomington, Indiana

- **State-supported** 2-year, founded 2001, part of Ivy Tech Community College System
- **Coed,** 6,218 undergraduate students, 46% full-time, 58% women, 42% men

Undergraduates 2,839 full-time, 3,379 part-time. 1% are from out of state; 5% Black or African American, non-Hispanic/Latino; 3% Hispanic/Latino; 1% Asian, non-Hispanic/Latino; 0.6% American Indian or Alaska Native, non-Hispanic/Latino; 1% Two or more races, non-Hispanic/Latino; 5% Race/ethnicity unknown; 5% transferred in. *Retention:* 46% of full-time freshmen returned.

Freshmen *Admission:* 2,141 applied, 2,141 admitted, 1,048 enrolled.

Faculty *Total:* 343, 21% full-time. *Student/faculty ratio:* 24:1.

Majors Accounting technology and bookkeeping; building/property maintenance; business administration and management; business automation/technology/data entry; cabinetmaking and millwork; child-care and support services management; computer and information sciences; criminal justice/safety; early childhood education; electrical, electronic and communications engineering technology; electrician; emergency medical technology (EMT paramedic); executive assistant/executive secretary; general studies; heating, air conditioning, ventilation and refrigeration maintenance technology; human services; industrial technology; legal assistant/paralegal; liberal arts and sciences/liberal studies; library and archives assisting; machine tool technology; mechanic and repair technologies related; mechanics and repair; pipefitting and sprinkler fitting; psychiatric/mental health services technology; registered nursing/registered nurse; tool and die technology.

Academics *Calendar:* semesters. *Degree:* certificates and associate. *Special study options:* academic remediation for entering students, adult/continuing education programs, advanced placement credit, distance learning, external degree program, internships, part-time degree program, services for LD students, summer session for credit.

Library 5,516 titles, 97 serial subscriptions, 1,281 audiovisual materials, an OPAC, a Web page.

Student Life *Activities and Organizations:* student government, Phi Theta Kappa. *Campus security:* late-night transport/escort service.

Costs (2012–13) *Tuition:* state resident $3335 full-time, $111 per credit hour part-time; nonresident $7182 full-time, $239 per credit hour part-time. *Required fees:* $120 full-time, $60 per term part-time. *Payment plans:* installment, deferred payment. *Waivers:* senior citizens and employees or children of employees.

Financial Aid Of all full-time matriculated undergraduates who enrolled in 2010, 51 Federal Work-Study jobs (averaging $3259).

Applying *Options:* electronic application, deferred entrance. *Required:* high school transcript. *Required for some:* interview. *Application deadlines:* rolling (freshmen), rolling (transfers). *Notification:* continuous (freshmen), continuous (transfers).

Freshman Application Contact Mr. Neil Frederick, Assistant Director of Admissions, Ivy Tech Community College–Bloomington, 200 Daniels Way, Bloomington, IN 47404. *Phone:* 812-330-6026. *Toll-free phone:* 888-IVYLINE. *Fax:* 812-332-8147. *E-mail:* nfrederi@ivytech.edu. *Web site:* http://www.ivytech.edu/.

Ivy Tech Community College–Central Indiana

Indianapolis, Indiana

- **State-supported** 2-year, founded 1963, part of Ivy Tech Community College System
- **Urban** 10-acre campus
- **Coed,** 22,354 undergraduate students, 34% full-time, 59% women, 41% men

Undergraduates 7,497 full-time, 14,857 part-time. 1% are from out of state; 29% Black or African American, non-Hispanic/Latino; 5% Hispanic/Latino; 2% Asian, non-Hispanic/Latino; 0.4% American Indian or Alaska Native, non-Hispanic/Latino; 2% Two or more races, non-Hispanic/Latino; 3% Race/eth-

nicity unknown; 5% transferred in. *Retention:* 52% of full-time freshmen returned.

Freshmen *Admission:* 3,002 enrolled.

Faculty *Total:* 826, 22% full-time. *Student/faculty ratio:* 32:1.

Majors Accounting technology and bookkeeping; automobile/automotive mechanics technology; biotechnology; building/property maintenance; business administration and management; business automation/technology/data entry; cabinetmaking and millwork; carpentry; child-care and support services management; child development; computer and information sciences; criminal justice/safety; design and visual communications; drafting and design technology; early childhood education; electrical, electronic and communications engineering technology; electrician; executive assistant/executive secretary; general studies; heating, air conditioning, ventilation and refrigeration maintenance technology; hospitality administration related; human services; industrial production technologies related; industrial technology; legal assistant/paralegal; liberal arts and sciences/liberal studies; machine shop technology; machine tool technology; masonry; mechanics and repair; medical/clinical assistant; medical radiologic technology; occupational safety and health technology; occupational therapist assistant; painting and wall covering; pipefitting and sprinkler fitting; psychiatric/mental health services technology; registered nursing/registered nurse; respiratory care therapy; sheet metal technology; surgical technology; tool and die technology.

Academics *Calendar:* semesters. *Degree:* certificates and associate. *Special study options:* academic remediation for entering students, adult/continuing education programs, advanced placement credit, cooperative education, distance learning, English as a second language, internships, off-campus study, part-time degree program, services for LD students, summer session for credit.

Library 20,247 titles, 138 serial subscriptions, 2,135 audiovisual materials, an OPAC, a Web page.

Student Life *Housing:* college housing not available. *Activities and Organizations:* student-run newspaper, student government, Phi Theta Kappa, Human Services Club, Administrative Office Assistants Club, Radiology Club. *Campus security:* 24-hour emergency response devices and patrols, late-night transport/escort service. *Student services:* personal/psychological counseling.

Athletics *Intramural sports:* baseball M, basketball M/W, cheerleading W, golf M/W, softball W, volleyball M/W.

Costs (2012–13) *Tuition:* state resident $3335 full-time, $111 per credit hour part-time; nonresident $7182 full-time, $239 per credit hour part-time. *Required fees:* $120 full-time, $60 per term part-time. *Payment plans:* installment, deferred payment. *Waivers:* senior citizens and employees or children of employees.

Financial Aid Of all full-time matriculated undergraduates who enrolled in 2010, 92 Federal Work-Study jobs (averaging $3766).

Applying *Options:* electronic application, early admission, deferred entrance. *Required:* high school transcript. *Required for some:* interview. *Application deadlines:* rolling (freshmen), rolling (transfers). *Notification:* continuous (freshmen), continuous (transfers).

Freshman Application Contact Ms. Tracy Funk, Director of Admissions, Ivy Tech Community College–Central Indiana, 50 West Fall Creek Parkway North Drive, Indianapolis, IN 46208-4777. *Phone:* 317-921-4371. *Toll-free phone:* 888-IVYLINE. *Fax:* 317-917-5919. *E-mail:* tfunk@ivytech.edu. *Web site:* http://www.ivytech.edu/.

Ivy Tech Community College–Columbus

Columbus, Indiana

- **State-supported** 2-year, founded 1963, part of Ivy Tech Community College System
- **Small-town** campus with easy access to Indianapolis
- **Coed,** 5,553 undergraduate students, 33% full-time, 66% women, 34% men

Undergraduates 1,825 full-time, 3,728 part-time. 1% are from out of state; 2% Black or African American, non-Hispanic/Latino; 2% Hispanic/Latino; 0.8% Asian, non-Hispanic/Latino; 0.3% American Indian or Alaska Native, non-Hispanic/Latino; 0.8% Two or more races, non-Hispanic/Latino; 6% Race/ethnicity unknown; 2% transferred in. *Retention:* 52% of full-time freshmen returned.

Freshmen *Admission:* 788 enrolled.

Faculty *Total:* 291, 19% full-time. *Student/faculty ratio:* 23:1.

Majors Accounting technology and bookkeeping; automobile/automotive mechanics technology; building/property maintenance; business administration and management; business automation/technology/data entry; cabinetmaking and millwork; child-care and support services management; computer and information sciences; design and visual communications; drafting and design technology; early childhood education; electrical and power transmission installation; electrical, electronic and communications engineering technology; executive assistant/executive secretary; general studies; heating, air conditioning, ventilation and refrigeration maintenance technology; human services; industrial technology; legal assistant/paralegal; liberal arts and sciences/liberal studies; library and archives assisting; machine tool technology; masonry; mechanic and repair technologies related; mechanics and repair; medical/clinical assistant; medical radiologic technology; pipefitting and sprinkler fitting; psychiatric/mental health services technology; robotics technology; surgical technology; tool and die technology.

Academics *Calendar:* semesters. *Degree:* certificates and associate. *Special study options:* academic remediation for entering students, adult/continuing education programs, advanced placement credit, distance learning, internships, part-time degree program, services for LD students, summer session for credit.

Library 7,855 titles, 13,382 serial subscriptions, 989 audiovisual materials, an OPAC, a Web page.

Student Life *Housing:* college housing not available. *Activities and Organizations:* student government, Phi Theta Kappa, LPN Club. *Campus security:* late-night transport/escort service, trained evening security personnel, escort service.

Costs (2012–13) *Tuition:* state resident $3335 full-time, $111 per credit hour part-time; nonresident $7182 full-time, $239 per credit hour part-time. *Required fees:* $120 full-time, $60 per term part-time. *Payment plans:* installment, deferred payment. *Waivers:* senior citizens and employees or children of employees.

Financial Aid Of all full-time matriculated undergraduates who enrolled in 2010, 26 Federal Work-Study jobs (averaging $1694).

Applying *Options:* electronic application, early admission, deferred entrance. *Required:* high school transcript. *Required for some:* interview. *Application deadlines:* rolling (freshmen), rolling (transfers). *Notification:* continuous (freshmen), continuous (transfers).

Freshman Application Contact Alisa Deck, Director of Admissions, Ivy Tech Community College–Columbus, 4475 Central Avenue, Columbus, IN 47203-1868. *Phone:* 812-374-5129. *Toll-free phone:* 888-IVY-LINE. *Fax:* 812-372-0331. *E-mail:* adeck@ivytech.edu. *Web site:* http://www.ivytech.edu/.

Ivy Tech Community College–East Central

Muncie, Indiana

- **State-supported** 2-year, founded 1968, part of Ivy Tech Community College System
- **Suburban** 15-acre campus with easy access to Indianapolis
- **Coed,** 8,902 undergraduate students, 49% full-time, 63% women, 37% men

Undergraduates 4,404 full-time, 4,498 part-time. 1% are from out of state; 9% Black or African American, non-Hispanic/Latino; 2% Hispanic/Latino; 0.6% Asian, non-Hispanic/Latino; 0.4% American Indian or Alaska Native, non-Hispanic/Latino; 2% Two or more races, non-Hispanic/Latino; 4% Race/ethnicity unknown; 3% transferred in. *Retention:* 48% of full-time freshmen returned.

Freshmen *Admission:* 1,690 enrolled.

Faculty *Total:* 548, 20% full-time. *Student/faculty ratio:* 23:1.

Majors Accounting technology and bookkeeping; automobile/automotive mechanics technology; building/property maintenance; business administration and management; business automation/technology/data entry; cabinetmaking and millwork; carpentry; child-care and support services management; computer and information sciences; construction trades; construction trades related; criminal justice/safety; early childhood education; electrical, electronic and communications engineering technology; electrician; executive assistant/executive secretary; general studies; heating, air conditioning, ventilation and refrigeration maintenance technology; hospitality administration; hospitality administration related; human services; industrial mechanics and maintenance technology; industrial production technologies related; industrial technology; legal assistant/paralegal; liberal arts and sciences/liberal studies; library and archives assisting; machine tool technology; masonry; medical/clinical assistant; medical radiologic technology; painting and wall covering; physical therapy technology; pipefitting and sprinkler fitting; psychiatric/mental health services technology; registered nursing/registered nurse; surgical technology; tool and die technology.

Academics *Calendar:* semesters. *Degree:* certificates and associate. *Special study options:* academic remediation for entering students, adult/continuing education programs, advanced placement credit, distance learning, internships, part-time degree program, services for LD students.

Library 5,779 titles, 145 serial subscriptions, 6,266 audiovisual materials, an OPAC, a Web page.

Student Life *Housing:* college housing not available. *Activities and Organizations:* Business Professionals of America, Skills USA - VICA, student government, Phi Theta Kappa, Human Services Club.

Costs (2012–13) *Tuition:* state resident $3335 full-time, $111 per credit hour part-time; nonresident $7182 full-time, $239 per credit hour part-time. *Required fees:* $120 full-time, $60 per term part-time. *Payment plans:* installment, deferred payment. *Waivers:* senior citizens and employees or children of employees.

Financial Aid Of all full-time matriculated undergraduates who enrolled in 2010, 65 Federal Work-Study jobs (averaging $2666).

Applying *Options:* electronic application, early admission, deferred entrance. *Required:* high school transcript. *Required for some:* interview. *Application deadlines:* rolling (freshmen), rolling (transfers). *Notification:* continuous (freshmen), continuous (transfers).

Freshman Application Contact Ms. Mary Lewellen, Ivy Tech Community College–East Central, 4301 South Cowan Road, Muncie, IN 47302-9448. *Phone:* 765-289-2291 Ext. 391. *Toll-free phone:* 888-IVY-LINE. *Fax:* 765-289-2292. *E-mail:* mlewelle@ivytech.edu. *Web site:* http://www.ivytech.edu/.

Ivy Tech Community College– Kokomo

Kokomo, Indiana

- **State-supported** 2-year, founded 1968, part of Ivy Tech Community College System
- **Small-town** 20-acre campus with easy access to Indianapolis
- **Coed,** 5,403 undergraduate students, 40% full-time, 64% women, 36% men

Undergraduates 2,178 full-time, 3,225 part-time. 7% Black or African American, non-Hispanic/Latino; 2% Hispanic/Latino; 0.6% Asian, non-Hispanic/Latino; 0.6% American Indian or Alaska Native, non-Hispanic/Latino; 1% Two or more races, non-Hispanic/Latino; 2% Race/ethnicity unknown; 3% transferred in. *Retention:* 53% of full-time freshmen returned.

Freshmen *Admission:* 816 enrolled.

Faculty *Total:* 338, 22% full-time. *Student/faculty ratio:* 20:1.

Majors Accounting technology and bookkeeping; automobile/automotive mechanics technology; building/property maintenance; business administration and management; business automation/technology/data entry; cabinetmaking and millwork; child-care and support services management; computer and information sciences; construction trades related; criminal justice/safety; drafting and design technology; early childhood education; electrical, electronic and communications engineering technology; electrician; emergency medical technology (EMT paramedic); executive assistant/executive secretary; general studies; heating, air conditioning, ventilation and refrigeration maintenance technology; human services; industrial technology; legal assistant/paralegal; liberal arts and sciences/liberal studies; library and archives assisting; machine tool technology; mechanic and repair technologies related; mechanics and repair; medical/clinical assistant; pipefitting and sprinkler fitting; psychiatric/mental health services technology; surgical technology; tool and die technology.

Academics *Calendar:* semesters. *Degree:* certificates and associate. *Special study options:* academic remediation for entering students, adult/continuing education programs, advanced placement credit, distance learning, internships, part-time degree program, services for LD students, summer session for credit.

Library 5,177 titles, 99 serial subscriptions, 772 audiovisual materials, an OPAC, a Web page.

Student Life *Housing:* college housing not available. *Activities and Organizations:* student-run newspaper, student government, Collegiate Secretaries International, Licensed Practical Nursing Club, Phi Theta Kappa. *Campus security:* 24-hour emergency response devices, late-night transport/escort service. *Student services:* personal/psychological counseling.

Costs (2012–13) *Tuition:* state resident $3335 full-time, $111 per credit hour part-time; nonresident $7182 full-time, $239 per credit hour part-time. *Required fees:* $120 full-time, $60 per term part-time. *Payment plans:* installment, deferred payment. *Waivers:* senior citizens and employees or children of employees.

Financial Aid Of all full-time matriculated undergraduates who enrolled in 2010, 45 Federal Work-Study jobs (averaging $1829).

Applying *Options:* electronic application, early admission. *Required:* high school transcript. *Required for some:* interview. *Application deadlines:* rolling (freshmen), rolling (transfers). *Notification:* continuous (freshmen), continuous (transfers).

Freshman Application Contact Mr. Mike Federspill, Director of Admissions, Ivy Tech Community College–Kokomo, 1815 East Morgan Street, Kokomo, IN 46903-1373. *Phone:* 765-459-0561 Ext. 233. *Toll-free phone:* 888-IVY-LINE. *Fax:* 765-454-5111. *E-mail:* mfedersp@ivytech.edu. *Web site:* http://www.ivytech.edu/.

Ivy Tech Community College–Lafayette

Lafayette, Indiana

- **State-supported** 2-year, founded 1968, part of Ivy Tech Community College System
- **Suburban** campus with easy access to Indianapolis
- **Coed,** 7,339 undergraduate students, 49% full-time, 56% women, 44% men

Undergraduates 3,609 full-time, 3,730 part-time. 5% Black or African American, non-Hispanic/Latino; 6% Hispanic/Latino; 1% Asian, non-Hispanic/Latino; 0.6% American Indian or Alaska Native, non-Hispanic/Latino; 1% Two or more races, non-Hispanic/Latino; 2% Race/ethnicity unknown; 4% transferred in. *Retention:* 52% of full-time freshmen returned.
Freshmen *Admission:* 1,231 enrolled.
Faculty *Total:* 431, 23% full-time. *Student/faculty ratio:* 23:1.
Majors Accounting; accounting technology and bookkeeping; automobile/automotive mechanics technology; biotechnology; building/property maintenance; business administration and management; business automation/technology/data entry; cabinetmaking and millwork; carpentry; child-care and support services management; computer and information sciences; drafting and design technology; early childhood education; electrical, electronic and communications engineering technology; electrician; executive assistant/executive secretary; general studies; heating, air conditioning, ventilation and refrigeration maintenance technology; human services; industrial production technologies related; industrial technology; ironworking; legal assistant/paralegal; liberal arts and sciences/liberal studies; library and archives assisting; lineworker; machine tool technology; masonry; mechanic and repair technologies related; mechanics and repair; medical/clinical assistant; painting and wall covering; pipefitting and sprinkler fitting; psychiatric/mental health services technology; quality control and safety technologies related; quality control technology; registered nursing/registered nurse; respiratory care therapy; robotics technology; sheet metal technology; surgical technology; tool and die technology.
Academics *Calendar:* semesters. *Degree:* certificates and associate. *Special study options:* academic remediation for entering students, advanced placement credit, distance learning, internships, part-time degree program, services for LD students, summer session for credit.
Library 8,043 titles, 200 serial subscriptions, 2,234 audiovisual materials, an OPAC, a Web page.
Student Life *Housing:* college housing not available. *Activities and Organizations:* student-run newspaper, student government, Phi Theta Kappa, LPN Club, Accounting Club, Student Computer Technology Association. *Student services:* personal/psychological counseling.
Costs (2012–13) *Tuition:* state resident $3335 full-time, $111 per credit hour part-time; nonresident $7182 full-time, $239 per credit hour part-time. *Required fees:* $120 full-time, $60 per term part-time. *Payment plans:* installment, deferred payment. *Waivers:* senior citizens and employees or children of employees.
Financial Aid Of all full-time matriculated undergraduates who enrolled in 2010, 65 Federal Work-Study jobs (averaging $2222). 1 state and other part-time job (averaging $2436).
Applying *Options:* electronic application. *Required:* high school transcript. *Required for some:* interview. *Application deadlines:* rolling (freshmen), rolling (transfers). *Notification:* continuous (freshmen), continuous (transfers).
Freshman Application Contact Mr. Ivan Hernanadez, Director of Admissions, Ivy Tech Community College–Lafayette, 3101 South Creasy Lane, PO Box 6299, Lafayette, IN 47903. *Phone:* 765-269-5116. *Toll-free phone:* 888-IVY-LINE. *Fax:* 765-772-9293. *E-mail:* ihernand@ivytech.edu. *Web site:* http://www.ivytech.edu/.

Ivy Tech Community College–North Central

South Bend, Indiana

- **State-supported** 2-year, founded 1968, part of Ivy Tech Community College System
- **Suburban** 4-acre campus
- **Coed,** 8,662 undergraduate students, 32% full-time, 63% women, 37% men

Undergraduates 2,761 full-time, 5,901 part-time. 2% are from out of state; 20% Black or African American, non-Hispanic/Latino; 8% Hispanic/Latino; 1% Asian, non-Hispanic/Latino; 0.6% American Indian or Alaska Native, non-Hispanic/Latino; 2% Two or more races, non-Hispanic/Latino; 3% Race/ethnicity unknown; 5% transferred in. *Retention:* 50% of full-time freshmen returned.
Freshmen *Admission:* 1,375 enrolled.
Faculty *Total:* 433, 24% full-time. *Student/faculty ratio:* 22:1.

Majors Accounting technology and bookkeeping; automobile/automotive mechanics technology; biotechnology; building/property maintenance; business administration and management; business automation/technology/data entry; cabinetmaking and millwork; carpentry; child-care and support services management; clinical/medical laboratory technology; computer and information sciences; criminal justice/safety; design and visual communications; early childhood education; educational/instructional technology; electrical, electronic and communications engineering technology; electrician; emergency medical technology (EMT paramedic); executive assistant/executive secretary; general studies; heating, air conditioning, ventilation and refrigeration maintenance technology; hospitality administration; human services; industrial production technologies related; industrial technology; interior design; ironworking; legal assistant/paralegal; liberal arts and sciences/liberal studies; library and archives assisting; machine tool technology; masonry; mechanic and repair technologies related; mechanics and repair; medical/clinical assistant; painting and wall covering; pipefitting and sprinkler fitting; registered nursing/registered nurse; robotics technology; sheet metal technology; telecommunications technology; tool and die technology.
Academics *Calendar:* semesters. *Degree:* certificates and associate. *Special study options:* academic remediation for entering students, adult/continuing education programs, advanced placement credit, distance learning, English as a second language, internships, off-campus study, part-time degree program, services for LD students, summer session for credit.
Library 6,246 titles, 90 serial subscriptions, 689 audiovisual materials, an OPAC, a Web page.
Student Life *Housing:* college housing not available. *Activities and Organizations:* Phi Theta Kappa, student government, LPN Club. *Campus security:* 24-hour emergency response devices and patrols, late-night transport/escort service, security during open hours. *Student services:* personal/psychological counseling, women's center.
Costs (2012–13) *Tuition:* state resident $3335 full-time, $111 per credit hour part-time; nonresident $7182 full-time, $239 per credit hour part-time. *Required fees:* $120 full-time, $60 per term part-time. *Payment plans:* installment, deferred payment. *Waivers:* senior citizens and employees or children of employees.
Financial Aid Of all full-time matriculated undergraduates who enrolled in 2010, 100 Federal Work-Study jobs (averaging $1538).
Applying *Options:* electronic application, early admission, deferred entrance. *Required:* high school transcript. *Required for some:* interview. *Application deadlines:* rolling (freshmen), rolling (transfers). *Notification:* continuous (freshmen), continuous (transfers).
Freshman Application Contact Ms. Pam Decker, Director of Admissions, Ivy Tech Community College–North Central, 220 Dean Johnson Boulevard, South Bend, IN 46601-3415. *Phone:* 574-289-7001. *Toll-free phone:* 888-IVY-LINE. *Fax:* 574-236-7177. *E-mail:* pdecker@ivytech.edu. *Web site:* http://www.ivytech.edu/.

Ivy Tech Community College–Northeast

Fort Wayne, Indiana

- **State-supported** 2-year, founded 1969, part of Ivy Tech Community College System
- **Urban** 22-acre campus
- **Coed,** 11,538 undergraduate students, 40% full-time, 59% women, 41% men

Undergraduates 4,669 full-time, 6,869 part-time. 3% are from out of state; 19% Black or African American, non-Hispanic/Latino; 5% Hispanic/Latino; 2% Asian, non-Hispanic/Latino; 0.6% American Indian or Alaska Native, non-Hispanic/Latino; 2% Two or more races, non-Hispanic/Latino; 3% Race/ethnicity unknown; 5% transferred in. *Retention:* 49% of full-time freshmen returned.
Freshmen *Admission:* 2,040 enrolled.
Faculty *Total:* 547, 24% full-time. *Student/faculty ratio:* 26:1.
Majors Accounting technology and bookkeeping; automobile/automotive mechanics technology; building/property maintenance; business administration and management; business automation/technology/data entry; cabinetmaking and millwork; child-care and support services management; computer and information sciences; construction trades; construction trades related; drafting and design technology; early childhood education; electrical, electronic and communications engineering technology; electrician; executive assistant/executive secretary; general studies; heating, air conditioning, ventilation and refrigeration maintenance technology; hospitality administration; hospitality administration related; human services; industrial production technologies related; industrial technology; ironworking; legal assistant/paralegal; liberal arts and sciences/liberal studies; library and archives assisting; machine tool technology; masonry; massage therapy; mechanics and repair; medical/clinical assistant; occupational safety and health technology; painting and wall covering; pipefitting and sprinkler fitting; psychiatric/mental health services

technology; respiratory care therapy; robotics technology; sheet metal technology; tool and die technology.

Academics *Calendar:* semesters. *Degree:* certificates and associate. *Special study options:* adult/continuing education programs, advanced placement credit, distance learning, English as a second language, internships, part-time degree program, services for LD students, summer session for credit.

Library 18,389 titles, 110 serial subscriptions, 3,397 audiovisual materials, an OPAC, a Web page.

Student Life *Housing:* college housing not available. *Activities and Organizations:* student-run newspaper, student government, LPN Club, Phi Theta Kappa. *Campus security:* 24-hour emergency response devices and patrols, late-night transport/escort service.

Costs (2012–13) *Tuition:* state resident $3335 full-time, $111 per credit hour part-time; nonresident $7182 full-time, $239 per credit hour part-time. *Required fees:* $120 full-time, $60 per term part-time. *Payment plans:* installment, deferred payment. *Waivers:* senior citizens and employees or children of employees.

Financial Aid Of all full-time matriculated undergraduates who enrolled in 2010, 40 Federal Work-Study jobs (averaging $4041).

Applying *Options:* early admission. *Required:* high school transcript. *Required for some:* interview. *Application deadlines:* rolling (freshmen), rolling (transfers). *Notification:* continuous (freshmen), continuous (transfers).

Freshman Application Contact Mr. Steve Scheer, Director of Admissions, Ivy Tech Community College–Northeast, 3800 North Anthony Boulevard, Ft. Wayne, IN 46805-1489. *Phone:* 260-480-4221. *Toll-free phone:* 888-IVY-LINE. *Fax:* 260-480-2053. *E-mail:* sscheer@ivytech.edu. *Web site:* http://www.ivytech.edu/.

Ivy Tech Community College–Northwest

Gary, Indiana

- **State-supported** 2-year, founded 1963, part of Ivy Tech Community College System
- **Urban** 13-acre campus with easy access to Chicago
- **Coed,** 11,429 undergraduate students, 46% full-time, 68% women, 32% men

Undergraduates 5,258 full-time, 6,171 part-time. 1% are from out of state; 27% Black or African American, non-Hispanic/Latino; 10% Hispanic/Latino; 0.7% Asian, non-Hispanic/Latino; 0.3% American Indian or Alaska Native, non-Hispanic/Latino; 1% Two or more races, non-Hispanic/Latino; 8% Race/ethnicity unknown; 4% transferred in. *Retention:* 49% of full-time freshmen returned.

Freshmen *Admission:* 1,766 enrolled.

Faculty *Total:* 447, 28% full-time. *Student/faculty ratio:* 25:1.

Majors Accounting technology and bookkeeping; automobile/automotive mechanics technology; building/construction finishing, management, and inspection related; building/property maintenance; business administration and management; business automation/technology/data entry; cabinetmaking and millwork; carpentry; child-care and support services management; computer and information sciences; construction trades; criminal justice/safety; drafting and design technology; early childhood education; electrical, electronic and communications engineering technology; electrician; executive assistant/executive secretary; funeral service and mortuary science; general studies; heating, air conditioning, ventilation and refrigeration maintenance technology; hospitality administration; human services; industrial technology; ironworking; legal assistant/paralegal; liberal arts and sciences/liberal studies; library and archives assisting; machine tool technology; masonry; mechanic and repair technologies related; mechanics and repair; medical/clinical assistant; occupational safety and health technology; painting and wall covering; pipefitting and sprinkler fitting; psychiatric/mental health services technology; registered nursing/registered nurse; respiratory care therapy; sheet metal technology; surgical technology; telecommunications technology; tool and die technology.

Academics *Calendar:* semesters. *Degree:* certificates and associate. *Special study options:* academic remediation for entering students, adult/continuing education programs, advanced placement credit, distance learning, internships, part-time degree program, services for LD students, summer session for credit.

Library 13,805 titles, 160 serial subscriptions, 4,295 audiovisual materials, an OPAC, a Web page.

Student Life *Housing:* college housing not available. *Activities and Organizations:* Phi Theta Kappa, LPN Club, Computer Club, student government, Business Club. *Campus security:* 24-hour emergency response devices, late-night transport/escort service.

Costs (2011–12) *Tuition:* state resident $3234 full-time, $108 per credit hour part-time; nonresident $6906 full-time, $230 per credit hour part-time. *Required fees:* $120 full-time, $60 per hour part-time.

Financial Aid Of all full-time matriculated undergraduates who enrolled in 2010, 74 Federal Work-Study jobs (averaging $2131).

Applying *Options:* electronic application, deferred entrance. *Required:* high school transcript. *Required for some:* interview. *Application deadlines:* rolling (freshmen), rolling (transfers). *Notification:* continuous (freshmen), continuous (transfers).

Freshman Application Contact Ms. Twilla Lewis, Associate Dean of Student Affairs, Ivy Tech Community College–Northwest, 1440 East 35th Avenue, Gary, IN 46409-499. *Phone:* 219-981-1111 Ext. 2273. *Toll-free phone:* 888-IVY-LINE. *Fax:* 219-981-4415. *E-mail:* tlewis@ivytech.edu. *Web site:* http://www.ivytech.edu/.

Ivy Tech Community College–Richmond

Richmond, Indiana

- **State-supported** 2-year, founded 1963, part of Ivy Tech Community College System
- **Small-town** 23-acre campus with easy access to Indianapolis
- **Coed,** 3,883 undergraduate students, 36% full-time, 66% women, 34% men

Undergraduates 1,382 full-time, 2,501 part-time. 6% are from out of state; 4% Black or African American, non-Hispanic/Latino; 1% Hispanic/Latino; 0.2% Asian, non-Hispanic/Latino; 0.6% American Indian or Alaska Native, non-Hispanic/Latino; 1% Two or more races, non-Hispanic/Latino; 2% Race/ethnicity unknown; 3% transferred in. *Retention:* 50% of full-time freshmen returned.

Freshmen *Admission:* 674 enrolled.

Faculty *Total:* 205, 20% full-time. *Student/faculty ratio:* 23:1.

Majors Accounting technology and bookkeeping; automobile/automotive mechanics technology; building/property maintenance; business administration and management; business automation/technology/data entry; cabinetmaking and millwork; child-care and support services management; computer and information sciences; construction trades; construction trades related; early childhood education; electrical, electronic and communications engineering technology; electrician; executive assistant/executive secretary; general studies; heating, air conditioning, ventilation and refrigeration maintenance technology; human services; industrial production technologies related; industrial technology; legal assistant/paralegal; liberal arts and sciences/liberal studies; library and archives assisting; machine tool technology; mechanics and repair; medical/clinical assistant; pipefitting and sprinkler fitting; psychiatric/mental health services technology; registered nursing/registered nurse; robotics technology; tool and die technology.

Academics *Calendar:* semesters. *Degree:* certificates and associate. *Special study options:* academic remediation for entering students, adult/continuing education programs, advanced placement credit, distance learning, independent study, internships, off-campus study, part-time degree program, services for LD students, summer session for credit.

Student Life *Housing:* college housing not available. *Activities and Organizations:* student-run newspaper, student government, Phi Theta Kappa, LPN Club, CATS 2000, Business Professionals of America. *Campus security:* 24-hour emergency response devices, late-night transport/escort service. *Student services:* personal/psychological counseling.

Athletics *Intramural sports:* softball M/W.

Costs (2012–13) *Tuition:* state resident $3335 full-time, $111 per credit hour part-time; nonresident $7182 full-time, $239 per credit hour part-time. *Required fees:* $120 full-time, $60 per term part-time. *Payment plans:* installment, deferred payment. *Waivers:* senior citizens and employees or children of employees.

Financial Aid Of all full-time matriculated undergraduates who enrolled in 2010, 14 Federal Work-Study jobs (averaging $3106). 1 state and other part-time job (averaging $3380).

Applying *Options:* electronic application, early admission. *Required:* high school transcript. *Required for some:* interview. *Application deadlines:* rolling (freshmen), rolling (transfers). *Notification:* continuous (freshmen), continuous (transfers).

Freshman Application Contact Christine Seger, Director of Admissions, Ivy Tech Community College–Richmond, 2325 Chester Boulevard, Richmond, IN 47374-1298. *Phone:* 765-966-2656 Ext. 1212. *Toll-free phone:* 888-IVY-LINE. *Fax:* 765-962-8741. *E-mail:* crethlake@ivytech.edu. *Web site:* http://www.ivytech.edu/richmond/.

Ivy Tech Community College–Southeast

Madison, Indiana

- **State-supported** 2-year, founded 1963, part of Ivy Tech Community College System
- **Small-town** 5-acre campus with easy access to Louisville
- **Coed,** 2,816 undergraduate students, 44% full-time, 69% women, 31% men

Undergraduates 1,246 full-time, 1,570 part-time. 5% are from out of state; 0.8% Black or African American, non-Hispanic/Latino; 1% Hispanic/Latino; 0.4% Asian, non-Hispanic/Latino; 0.5% American Indian or Alaska Native, non-Hispanic/Latino; 0.6% Two or more races, non-Hispanic/Latino; 10% Race/ethnicity unknown; 3% transferred in. *Retention:* 56% of full-time freshmen returned.

Freshmen *Admission:* 502 enrolled.

Faculty *Total:* 198, 24% full-time. *Student/faculty ratio:* 18:1.

Majors Accounting technology and bookkeeping; business administration and management; business automation/technology/data entry; child-care and support services management; computer and information sciences; early childhood education; electrical, electronic and communications engineering technology; executive assistant/executive secretary; general studies; human services; industrial technology; legal assistant/paralegal; liberal arts and sciences/liberal studies; library and archives assisting; licensed practical/vocational nurse training; medical/clinical assistant; psychiatric/mental health services technology; registered nursing/registered nurse.

Academics *Calendar:* semesters. *Degree:* certificates and associate. *Special study options:* academic remediation for entering students, advanced placement credit, distance learning, internships, part-time degree program, services for LD students, summer session for credit.

Library 9,027 titles, 14,299 serial subscriptions, 1,341 audiovisual materials, an OPAC, a Web page.

Student Life *Housing:* college housing not available. *Activities and Organizations:* student government, Phi Theta Kappa, LPN Club. *Campus security:* 24-hour emergency response devices.

Costs (2012–13) *Tuition:* state resident $3335 full-time, $111 per credit hour part-time; nonresident $7182 full-time, $239 per credit hour part-time. *Required fees:* $120 full-time, $60 per term part-time. *Payment plans:* installment, deferred payment. *Waivers:* senior citizens and employees or children of employees.

Financial Aid Of all full-time matriculated undergraduates who enrolled in 2010, 26 Federal Work-Study jobs (averaging $1696).

Applying *Options:* electronic application. *Required:* high school transcript. *Required for some:* interview. *Application deadlines:* rolling (freshmen), rolling (transfers). *Notification:* continuous (freshmen), continuous (transfers).

Freshman Application Contact Ms. Cindy Hutcherson, Assistant Director of Admission/Career Counselor, Ivy Tech Community College–Southeast, 590 Ivy Tech Drive, Madison, IN 47250-1881. *Phone:* 812-265-2580 Ext. 4142. *Toll-free phone:* 888-IVY-LINE. *Fax:* 812-265-4028. *E-mail:* chutcher@ivytech.edu. *Web site:* http://www.ivytech.edu/.

Ivy Tech Community College–Southern Indiana

Sellersburg, Indiana

- **State-supported** 2-year, founded 1968, part of Ivy Tech Community College System
- **Small-town** 63-acre campus with easy access to Louisville
- **Coed,** 5,413 undergraduate students, 36% full-time, 57% women, 43% men

Undergraduates 1,941 full-time, 3,472 part-time. 13% are from out of state; 8% Black or African American, non-Hispanic/Latino; 2% Hispanic/Latino; 0.6% Asian, non-Hispanic/Latino; 0.6% American Indian or Alaska Native, non-Hispanic/Latino; 1% Two or more races, non-Hispanic/Latino; 3% Race/ethnicity unknown; 6% transferred in. *Retention:* 52% of full-time freshmen returned.

Freshmen *Admission:* 1,043 enrolled.

Faculty *Total:* 243, 25% full-time. *Student/faculty ratio:* 26:1.

Majors Accounting technology and bookkeeping; automobile/automotive mechanics technology; building/property maintenance; business administration and management; business automation/technology/data entry; cabinetmaking and millwork; carpentry; child-care and support services management; computer and information sciences; design and visual communications; early childhood education; electrical, electronic and communications engineering technology; electrician; executive assistant/executive secretary; general studies; heating, air conditioning, ventilation and refrigeration maintenance technology; human services; industrial technology; legal assistant/paralegal; liberal arts and sciences/liberal studies; library and archives assisting; machine tool

technology; masonry; mechanics and repair; medical/clinical assistant; pipefitting and sprinkler fitting; psychiatric/mental health services technology; registered nursing/registered nurse; respiratory care therapy; sheet metal technology; tool and die technology.

Academics *Calendar:* semesters. *Degree:* certificates and associate. *Special study options:* academic remediation for entering students, adult/continuing education programs, advanced placement credit, cooperative education, distance learning, internships, part-time degree program, services for LD students, summer session for credit.

Library 7,634 titles, 66 serial subscriptions, 648 audiovisual materials, an OPAC, a Web page.

Student Life *Housing:* college housing not available. *Activities and Organizations:* Phi Theta Kappa, Practical Nursing Club, Medical Assistant Club, Accounting Club, student government. *Campus security:* late-night transport/escort service.

Costs (2012–13) *Tuition:* state resident $3335 full-time, $111 per credit hour part-time; nonresident $7182 full-time, $239 per credit hour part-time. *Required fees:* $60 per term part-time. *Payment plans:* installment, deferred payment. *Waivers:* senior citizens and employees or children of employees.

Financial Aid Of all full-time matriculated undergraduates who enrolled in 2010, 20 Federal Work-Study jobs (averaging $5007). 1 state and other part-time job (averaging $6080).

Applying *Options:* electronic application, early admission, deferred entrance. *Required:* high school transcript. *Required for some:* interview. *Application deadlines:* rolling (freshmen), rolling (transfers). *Notification:* continuous (freshmen), continuous (transfers).

Freshman Application Contact Ben Harris, Director of Admissions, Ivy Tech Community College–Southern Indiana, 8204 Highway 311, Sellersburg, IN 47172-1897. *Phone:* 812-246-3301 Ext. 4137. *Toll-free phone:* 888-IVY-LINE. *Fax:* 812-246-9905. *E-mail:* bharris88@ivytech.edu. *Web site:* http://www.ivytech.edu/.

Ivy Tech Community College–Southwest

Evansville, Indiana

- **State-supported** 2-year, founded 1963, part of Ivy Tech Community College System
- **Suburban** 15-acre campus
- **Coed,** 6,287 undergraduate students, 39% full-time, 55% women, 45% men

Undergraduates 2,467 full-time, 3,820 part-time. 3% are from out of state; 10% Black or African American, non-Hispanic/Latino; 2% Hispanic/Latino; 0.5% Asian, non-Hispanic/Latino; 0.4% American Indian or Alaska Native, non-Hispanic/Latino; 1% Two or more races, non-Hispanic/Latino; 3% Race/ethnicity unknown; 4% transferred in. *Retention:* 50% of full-time freshmen returned.

Freshmen *Admission:* 966 enrolled.

Faculty *Total:* 341, 25% full-time. *Student/faculty ratio:* 22:1.

Majors Accounting technology and bookkeeping; automobile/automotive mechanics technology; boilermaking; building/property maintenance; business administration and management; business automation/technology/data entry; cabinetmaking and millwork; carpentry; child-care and support services management; computer and information sciences; construction/heavy equipment/earthmoving equipment operation; criminal justice/safety; design and visual communications; early childhood education; electrical, electronic and communications engineering technology; electrician; emergency medical technology (EMT paramedic); executive assistant/executive secretary; general studies; graphic design; heating, air conditioning, ventilation and refrigeration maintenance technology; human services; industrial production technologies related; industrial technology; interior design; ironworking; legal assistant/paralegal; liberal arts and sciences/liberal studies; library and archives assisting; machine tool technology; masonry; mechanic and repair technologies related; mechanics and repair; medical/clinical assistant; painting and wall covering; pipefitting and sprinkler fitting; psychiatric/mental health services technology; registered nursing/registered nurse; robotics technology; sheet metal technology; surgical technology; tool and die technology.

Academics *Calendar:* semesters. *Degree:* certificates and associate. *Special study options:* academic remediation for entering students, advanced placement credit, cooperative education, distance learning, independent study, internships, part-time degree program, services for LD students, summer session for credit.

Library 7,082 titles, 107 serial subscriptions, 1,755 audiovisual materials, an OPAC, a Web page.

Student Life *Housing:* college housing not available. *Activities and Organizations:* student government, Phi Theta Kappa, LPN Club, National Association of Industrial Technology, Design Club. *Campus security:* late-night transport/escort service.

Costs (2012–13) *Tuition:* state resident $3335 full-time, $111 per credit hour part-time; nonresident $7182 full-time, $239 per credit hour part-time. *Required fees:* $120 full-time, $60 per term part-time. *Payment plans:* installment, deferred payment. *Waivers:* senior citizens and employees or children of employees.

Financial Aid Of all full-time matriculated undergraduates who enrolled in 2010, 65 Federal Work-Study jobs (averaging $2264).

Applying *Options:* electronic application, early admission, deferred entrance. *Required:* high school transcript. *Required for some:* interview. *Application deadlines:* rolling (freshmen), rolling (transfers). *Notification:* continuous (freshmen), continuous (transfers).

Freshman Application Contact Ms. Denise Johnson-Kincade, Director of Admissions, Ivy Tech Community College–Southwest, 3501 First Avenue, Evansville, IN 47710-3398. *Phone:* 812-429-1430. *Toll-free phone:* 888-IVY-LINE. *Fax:* 812-429-9878. *E-mail:* ajohnson@ivytech.edu. *Web site:* http://www.ivytech.edu/.

Ivy Tech Community College–Wabash Valley

Terre Haute, Indiana

- **State-supported** 2-year, founded 1966, part of Ivy Tech Community College System
- **Suburban** 55-acre campus with easy access to Indianapolis
- **Coed,** 6,137 undergraduate students, 44% full-time, 57% women, 43% men

Undergraduates 2,720 full-time, 3,417 part-time. 5% are from out of state; 4% Black or African American, non-Hispanic/Latino; 1% Hispanic/Latino; 0.5% Asian, non-Hispanic/Latino; 0.4% American Indian or Alaska Native, non-Hispanic/Latino; 0.9% Two or more races, non-Hispanic/Latino; 4% Race/ethnicity unknown; 5% transferred in. *Retention:* 50% of full-time freshmen returned.

Freshmen *Admission:* 842 enrolled.

Faculty *Total:* 280, 34% full-time. *Student/faculty ratio:* 25:1.

Majors Accounting technology and bookkeeping; airframe mechanics and aircraft maintenance technology; allied health diagnostic, intervention, and treatment professions related; automobile/automotive mechanics technology; building/property maintenance; business administration and management; cabinetmaking and millwork; carpentry; child-care and support services management; clinical/medical laboratory technology; computer and information sciences; construction/heavy equipment/earthmoving equipment operation; criminal justice/safety; design and visual communications; early childhood education; electrical, electronic and communications engineering technology; electrician; emergency medical technology (EMT paramedic); executive assistant/executive secretary; general studies; heating, air conditioning, ventilation and refrigeration maintenance technology; human services; industrial production technologies related; industrial technology; ironworking; legal assistant/paralegal; liberal arts and sciences/liberal studies; library and archives assisting; machine tool technology; masonry; mechanics and repair; medical/clinical assistant; medical radiologic technology; occupational safety and health technology; office management; painting and wall covering; pipefitting and sprinkler fitting; psychiatric/mental health services technology; quality control and safety technologies related; registered nursing/registered nurse; robotics technology; sheet metal technology; surgical technology; tool and die technology.

Academics *Calendar:* semesters. *Degree:* certificates and associate. *Special study options:* academic remediation for entering students, adult/continuing education programs, advanced placement credit, distance learning, internships, part-time degree program, services for LD students, summer session for credit.

Library 4,403 titles, 77 serial subscriptions, 406 audiovisual materials, an OPAC, a Web page.

Student Life *Housing:* college housing not available. *Activities and Organizations:* student government, Phi Theta Kappa, LPN Club, National Association of Industrial Technology. *Campus security:* 24-hour emergency response devices. *Student services:* personal/psychological counseling, women's center.

Athletics *Intramural sports:* basketball M/W, volleyball M/W.

Costs (2012–13) *Tuition:* state resident $3335 full-time, $111 per credit hour part-time; nonresident $7182 full-time, $239 per credit hour part-time. *Required fees:* $120 full-time, $60 per term part-time. *Payment plans:* installment, deferred payment. *Waivers:* senior citizens and employees or children of employees.

Financial Aid Of all full-time matriculated undergraduates who enrolled in 2010, 51 Federal Work-Study jobs (averaging $2110). 1 state and other part-time job (averaging $2963).

Applying *Options:* electronic application, early admission, deferred entrance. *Required:* high school transcript. *Required for some:* interview. *Application deadlines:* rolling (freshmen), rolling (transfers). *Notification:* continuous (freshmen), continuous (transfers).

Freshman Application Contact Mr. Michael Fisher, Director of Admissions, Ivy Tech Community College–Wabash Valley, 7999 U.S. Highway 41 South,

Terre Haute, IN 47802-4898. *Phone:* 812-298-2300. *Toll-free phone:* 888-IVY-LINE. *Fax:* 812-298-2291. *E-mail:* mfisher@ivytech.edu. *Web site:* http://www.ivytech.edu/.

Kaplan College, Hammond Campus

Hammond, Indiana

- **Proprietary** 2-year, founded 1962
- **Suburban** campus
- **Coed**

Majors Computer systems networking and telecommunications; massage therapy; medical/clinical assistant.

Academics *Calendar:* quarters. *Degree:* diplomas and associate.

Freshman Application Contact Kaplan College, Hammond Campus, 7833 Indianapolis Boulevard, Hammond, IN 46324. *Phone:* 219-844-0100. *Toll-free phone:* 800-935-1857. *Web site:* http://hammond.kaplancollege.com/.

Kaplan College, Northwest Indianapolis Campus

Indianapolis, Indiana

- **Proprietary** 2-year
- **Coed, primarily women**

Majors Medical office management.

Academics *Degree:* diplomas and associate.

Freshman Application Contact Kaplan College, Northwest Indianapolis Campus, 7302 Woodland Drive, Indianapolis, IN 46278. *Phone:* 317-299-6001. *Toll-free phone:* 800-935-1857. *Web site:* http://nwindianapolis.kaplancollege.com/.

Kaplan College, Southeast Indianapolis Campus

Indianapolis, Indiana

- **Proprietary** 2-year
- **Coed**

Majors Criminal justice/law enforcement administration.

Academics *Degree:* diplomas and associate.

Freshman Application Contact Director of Admissions, Kaplan College, Southeast Indianapolis Campus, 4200 South East Street, Suite 7, Indianapolis, IN 46227. *Phone:* 317-782-0315. *Web site:* http://www.seindianapolis.kaplancollege.com/.

Lincoln College of Technology

Indianapolis, Indiana

Director of Admissions Ms. Cindy Ryan, Director of Admissions, Lincoln College of Technology, 7225 Winton Drive, Building 128, Indianapolis, IN 46268. *Phone:* 317-632-5553. *Web site:* http://www.lincolnedu.com/.

Mid-America College of Funeral Service

Jeffersonville, Indiana

Freshman Application Contact Mr. Richard Nelson, Dean of Students, Mid-America College of Funeral Service, 3111 Hamburg Pike, Jeffersonville, IN 47130-9630. *Phone:* 812-288-8878. *Toll-free phone:* 800-221-6158. *Fax:* 812-288-5942. *E-mail:* macfs@mindspring.com. *Web site:* http://www.mid-america.edu/.

Vet Tech Institute at International Business College

Fort Wayne, Indiana

- **Private** 2-year, founded 2005
- **Suburban** campus
- **Coed,** 159 undergraduate students
- 42% of applicants were admitted

Freshmen *Admission:* 352 applied, 148 admitted.

Majors Veterinary/animal health technology.

Academics *Degree:* associate. *Special study options:* accelerated degree program, internships.

Freshman Application Contact Admissions Office, Vet Tech Institute at International Business College, 5699 Coventry Lane, Fort Wayne, IN 46804.

Phone: 800-589-6363. *Toll-free phone:* 800-589-6363. *Web site:* http://www.vettechinstitute.edu/.

Vet Tech Institute at International Business College

Indianapolis, Indiana

- **Private** 2-year, founded 2007
- **Suburban** campus
- **Coed,** 116 undergraduate students
- 46% of applicants were admitted

Freshmen *Admission:* 420 applied, 194 admitted.

Majors Veterinary/animal health technology.

Academics *Degree:* associate. *Special study options:* accelerated degree program, internships.

Freshman Application Contact Admissions Office, Vet Tech Institute at International Business College, 7205 Shadeland Station, Indianapolis, IN 46256. *Phone:* 800-589-6500. *Toll-free phone:* 877-835-7297. *Web site:* http://www.vettechinstitute.edu/indianapolis.

Vincennes University

Vincennes, Indiana

- **State-supported** primarily 2-year, founded 1801
- **Small-town** 100-acre campus
- **Coed,** 17,140 undergraduate students, 39% full-time, 46% women, 54% men

Undergraduates 6,701 full-time, 10,439 part-time. Students come from 36 states and territories; 32 other countries; 11% Black or African American, non-Hispanic/Latino; 2% Hispanic/Latino; 0.5% Asian, non-Hispanic/Latino; 0.2% Native Hawaiian or other Pacific Islander, non-Hispanic/Latino; 0.3% American Indian or Alaska Native, non-Hispanic/Latino; 1% Two or more races, non-Hispanic/Latino; 12% Race/ethnicity unknown; 0.7% international; 2% transferred in.

Freshmen *Admission:* 3,833 enrolled.

Faculty *Student/faculty ratio:* 17:1.

Majors Accounting technology and bookkeeping; administrative assistant and secretarial science; agricultural business and management; agricultural engineering; agriculture; aircraft powerplant technology; airline pilot and flight crew; American Sign Language (ASL); anthropology; applied horticulture/horticulture operations; architectural drafting and CAD/CADD; art; art teacher education; art therapy; autobody/collision and repair technology; automobile/automotive mechanics technology; behavioral sciences; biochemistry; biological and physical sciences; biology/biological sciences; biotechnology; building/home/construction inspection; business administration and management; business and personal/financial services marketing; business/commerce; chemistry; chemistry teacher education; child-care and support services management; child-care provision; civil engineering; civil engineering technology; commercial and advertising art; communications technology; computer and information sciences; computer/information technology services administration related; computer programming; computer science; computer systems networking and telecommunications; construction trades; corrections; corrections and criminal justice related; cosmetology; criminal justice/police science; culinary arts; design and applied arts related; diesel mechanics technology; dietetics; dramatic/theater arts; early childhood education; economics; education; electrical, electronic and communications engineering technology; elementary education; emergency medical technology (EMT paramedic); engineering technology; English; English/language arts teacher education; family and consumer sciences/home economics teacher education; family and consumer sciences/human sciences; fashion merchandising; finance; fire science/firefighting; food science; foreign languages and literatures; foreign languages related; funeral service and mortuary science; geology/earth science; graphic and printing equipment operation/production; health and physical education/fitness; health/health-care administration; health information/medical records technology; history; hospitality administration; hotel/motel administration; industrial technology; journalism; legal assistant/paralegal; liberal arts and sciences/liberal studies; manufacturing engineering technology; marketing/marketing management; massage therapy; mathematics; mathematics teacher education; mechanical drafting and CAD/CADD; mechanical engineering/mechanical technology; medical radiologic technology; music; music teacher education; natural resources/conservation; nuclear medical technology; ophthalmic and optometric support services and allied professions related; parks, recreation and leisure; pharmacy technician; philosophy; photojournalism; physical education teaching and coaching; physical sciences; physical therapy technology; political science and government; pre-dentistry studies; premedical studies; pre-pharmacy studies; pre-veterinary studies; psychology; public relations/image management; radio and television broadcasting technology; recording arts technology; registered nursing/registered nurse; restaurant, culi-

nary, and catering management; robotics technology; science teacher education; secondary education; securities services administration; security and loss prevention; sheet metal technology; social work; sociology; special education; sport and fitness administration/management; surgical technology; surveying technology; teacher assistant/aide; theater design and technology; tool and die technology; web/multimedia management and webmaster; woodworking.

Academics *Calendar:* semesters. *Degrees:* certificates, associate, and bachelor's. *Special study options:* academic remediation for entering students, adult/continuing education programs, advanced placement credit, distance learning, double majors, external degree program, off-campus study, part-time degree program, summer session for credit. *ROTC:* Army (c), Air Force (c).

Library Shake Learning Resource Center.

Student Life *Housing:* on-campus residence required for freshman year. *Options:* coed, men-only, women-only, disabled students. Campus housing is university owned. Freshman campus housing is guaranteed. *Activities and Organizations:* drama/theater group, student-run newspaper, radio and television station, choral group, national fraternities, national sororities. *Campus security:* 24-hour emergency response devices and patrols, student patrols, late-night transport/escort service, controlled dormitory access, surveillance cameras. *Student services:* health clinic, personal/psychological counseling.

Athletics Member NJCAA. *Intercollegiate sports:* baseball M, basketball M/W, bowling M, cross-country running M/W, golf M, swimming and diving M/W, tennis M, track and field M/W, volleyball W.

Financial Aid Of all full-time matriculated undergraduates who enrolled in 2010, 220 Federal Work-Study jobs (averaging $1072).

Applying *Options:* electronic application, early admission, deferred entrance. *Application fee:* $20. *Required:* high school transcript. *Required for some:* interview. *Application deadlines:* rolling (freshmen), rolling (transfers). *Notification:* continuous until 8/1 (freshmen), continuous (transfers).

Freshman Application Contact Vincennes University, 1002 North First Street, Vincennes, IN 47591-5202. *Phone:* 800-742-9198. *Toll-free phone:* 800-742-9198. *Web site:* http://www.vinu.edu/.

Vincennes University Jasper Campus

Jasper, Indiana

- **State-supported** primarily 2-year, founded 1970, part of Vincennes University
- **Small-town** 140-acre campus
- **Coed**

Undergraduates Students come from 1 other state; 1 other country.

Faculty *Student/faculty ratio:* 16:1.

Academics *Calendar:* semesters. *Degrees:* certificates, associate, and bachelor's. *Special study options:* academic remediation for entering students, adult/continuing education programs, advanced placement credit, distance learning, part-time degree program, summer session for credit.

Financial Aid Of all full-time matriculated undergraduates who enrolled in 2010, 3 Federal Work-Study jobs (averaging $3200).

Applying *Application fee:* $20. *Required:* high school transcript.

Freshman Application Contact Ms. Louann Gilbert, Admissions Director, Vincennes University Jasper Campus, 850 College Avenue, Jasper, IN 47546-9393. *Phone:* 812-482-3030. *Toll-free phone:* 800-809-VUJC. *Fax:* 812-481-5960. *E-mail:* lagilbert@vinu.edu. *Web site:* http://vujc.vinu.edu/.

IOWA

Brown Mackie College–Quad Cities

Bettendorf, Iowa

- **Proprietary** 2-year, part of Education Management Corporation
- **Coed**

Academics *Degree:* diplomas and associate.

Costs (2011–12) *Tuition:* Tuition varies by program. Students should contact Brown Mackie College for tuition information.

Freshman Application Contact Brown Mackie College–Quad Cities, 2119 East Kimberly Road, Bettendorf, IA 52722. *Phone:* 309-762-2100. *Toll-free phone:* 888-420-1652. *Web site:* http://www.brownmackie.edu/quad-cities/.

See page 380 for the College Close-Up.

Clinton Community College

Clinton, Iowa

Freshman Application Contact Mr. Gary Mohr, Executive Director of Enrollment Management and Marketing, Clinton Community College, 1000 Lincoln Boulevard, Clinton, IA 52732-6299. *Phone:* 563-336-3322. *Toll-free* *phone:* 800-462-3255. *Fax:* 563-336-3350. *E-mail:* gmohr@eicc.edu. *Web site:* http://www.eicc.edu/ccc/.

Des Moines Area Community College

Ankeny, Iowa

Freshman Application Contact Mr. Michael Lentsch, Director of Enrollment Management, Des Moines Area Community College, 2006 South Ankeny Boulevard, Ankeny, IA 50021-8995. *Phone:* 515-964-6216. *Toll-free phone:* 800-362-2127. *Fax:* 515-964-6391. *E-mail:* mjleutsch@dmacc.edu. *Web site:* http://www.dmacc.edu/.

Ellsworth Community College

Iowa Falls, Iowa

Director of Admissions Mrs. Nancy Walters, Registrar, Ellsworth Community College, 1100 College Avenue, Iowa Falls, IA 50126-1199. *Phone:* 641-648-4611. *Toll-free phone:* 800-ECC-9235. *Web site:* http://www.iavalley.cc.ia.us/ecc/.

Hawkeye Community College

Waterloo, Iowa

- **State and locally supported** 2-year, founded 1966
- **Rural** 320-acre campus
- **Endowment** $1.9 million
- **Coed,** 6,290 undergraduate students, 45% full-time, 56% women, 44% men

Undergraduates 2,848 full-time, 3,442 part-time. 1% are from out of state; 8% Black or African American, non-Hispanic/Latino; 3% Hispanic/Latino; 1% Asian, non-Hispanic/Latino; 0.1% Native Hawaiian or other Pacific Islander, non-Hispanic/Latino; 0.4% American Indian or Alaska Native, non-Hispanic/Latino; 1% Two or more races, non-Hispanic/Latino; 0.3% international; 33% transferred in.

Freshmen *Admission:* 5,858 applied, 4,328 admitted, 1,176 enrolled. *Test scores:* ACT scores over 18: 49%; ACT scores over 24: 13%; ACT scores over 30: 2%.

Faculty *Total:* 344, 35% full-time, 7% with terminal degrees. *Student/faculty ratio:* 22:1.

Majors Accounting; agricultural/farm supplies retailing and wholesaling; agricultural power machinery operation; animal/livestock husbandry and production; applied horticulture/horticulture operations; architectural drafting and CAD/CADD; autobody/collision and repair technology; automobile/automotive mechanics technology; child-care provision; civil engineering technology; clinical/medical laboratory technology; commercial photography; computer/information technology services administration related; computer systems networking and telecommunications; criminal justice/police science; dental hygiene; diesel mechanics technology; electrical, electronic and communications engineering technology; executive assistant/executive secretary; graphic communications; human resources management; interior design; liberal arts and sciences/liberal studies; machine tool technology; medical administrative assistant and medical secretary; multi/interdisciplinary studies related; natural resources management and policy; occupational therapist assistant; physical therapy technology; registered nursing/registered nurse; respiratory care therapy; sales, distribution, and marketing operations; web page, digital/multimedia and information resources design.

Academics *Calendar:* semesters. *Degree:* certificates, diplomas, and associate. *Special study options:* academic remediation for entering students, adult/continuing education programs, advanced placement credit, cooperative education, distance learning, English as a second language, external degree program, part-time degree program, services for LD students, study abroad, summer session for credit. *ROTC:* Army (c).

Library Hawkeye Community College Library with 152,216 titles, 249 serial subscriptions, 2,099 audiovisual materials, an OPAC, a Web page.

Student Life *Housing:* college housing not available. *Activities and Organizations:* Student Senate, Phi Theta Kappa, Student Ambassadors, All Ag/Horticulture, IAAP. *Campus security:* 24-hour patrols. *Student services:* health clinic, personal/psychological counseling, women's center.

Athletics *Intramural sports:* badminton M/W, basketball M/W, bowling M/W, cross-country running M/W, golf M/W, soccer M/W, table tennis M/W, volleyball M/W.

Standardized Tests *Required:* COMPASS or the equivalent from ACT or accredited college course(s) (for admission). *Required for some:* ACT (for admission).

Costs (2011–12) *Tuition:* state resident $3696 full-time, $132 per credit hour part-time; nonresident $4396 full-time, $157 per credit hour part-time. Full-time tuition and fees vary according to course load and program. Part-time tuition and fees vary according to course load and program. *Required fees:*

$168 full-time, $6 per credit hour part-time. *Payment plans:* installment, deferred payment. *Waivers:* employees or children of employees.

Applying *Options:* electronic application, deferred entrance. *Required:* high school transcript. *Application deadlines:* rolling (freshmen), rolling (out-of-state freshmen), rolling (transfers). *Notification:* continuous (freshmen), continuous (out-of-state freshmen), continuous (transfers).

Freshman Application Contact Ms. Holly Grimm-See, Associate Director, Admissions and Recruitment, Hawkeye Community College, PO Box 8015, Waterloo, IA 50704-8015. *Phone:* 319-296-4277. *Toll-free phone:* 800-670-4769. *Fax:* 319-296-2505. *E-mail:* holly.grimm-see@hawkeyecollege.edu. *Web site:* http://www.hawkeyecollege.edu/.

Indian Hills Community College

Ottumwa, Iowa

Freshman Application Contact Mrs. Jane Sapp, Admissions Officer, Indian Hills Community College, 525 Grandview Avenue, Building #1, Ottumwa, IA 52501-1398. *Phone:* 641-683-5155. *Toll-free phone:* 800-726-2585. *Web site:* http://www.ihcc.cc.ia.us/.

Iowa Central Community College

Fort Dodge, Iowa

Freshman Application Contact Mrs. Deb Bahls, Coordinator of Admissions, Iowa Central Community College, 330 Avenue M, Fort Dodge, IA 50501-5798. *Phone:* 515-576-0099 Ext. 2402. *Toll-free phone:* 800-362-2793. *Fax:* 515-576-7724. *E-mail:* bahls@iowacentral.com. *Web site:* http://www.iccc.cc.ia.us/.

Iowa Lakes Community College

Estherville, Iowa

- **State and locally supported** 2-year, founded 1967, part of Iowa Community College System
- **Small-town** 20-acre campus
- **Endowment** $6.5 million
- **Coed,** 3,102 undergraduate students, 54% full-time, 53% women, 47% men

Undergraduates 1,663 full-time, 1,439 part-time. Students come from 33 states and territories; 6 other countries; 3% Black or African American, non-Hispanic/Latino; 3% Hispanic/Latino; 1% Asian, non-Hispanic/Latino; 0.4% Native Hawaiian or other Pacific Islander, non-Hispanic/Latino; 0.4% American Indian or Alaska Native, non-Hispanic/Latino; 0.4% Two or more races, non-Hispanic/Latino; 4% Race/ethnicity unknown; 0.6% international; 37% live on campus. *Retention:* 59% of full-time freshmen returned.

Freshmen *Admission:* 1,425 applied, 1,318 admitted, 490 enrolled.

Faculty *Total:* 171, 53% full-time. *Student/faculty ratio:* 24:1.

Majors Accounting; accounting technology and bookkeeping; administrative assistant and secretarial science; agribusiness; agricultural business and management; agricultural business and management related; agricultural business technology; agricultural economics; agricultural/farm supplies retailing and wholesaling; agricultural mechanics and equipment technology; agricultural mechanization; agricultural power machinery operation; agricultural production; agricultural production related; agricultural teacher education; agriculture; agronomy and crop science; airline pilot and flight crew; animal/livestock husbandry and production; animal sciences; art; art history, criticism and conservation; art teacher education; astronomy; athletic training; autobody/collision and repair technology; automobile/automotive mechanics technology; aviation/airway management; behavioral sciences; biological and physical sciences; biology/biological sciences; botany/plant biology; broadcast journalism; business administration and management; business automation/technology/data entry; business machine repair; business teacher education; carpentry; ceramic arts and ceramics; chemistry; child-care provision; child development; chiropractic assistant; commercial and advertising art; communication and journalism related; comparative literature; computer and information sciences related; computer graphics; computer/information technology services administration related; computer programming; computer science; computer software technology; computer systems networking and telecommunications; construction engineering technology; construction management; construction trades; consumer merchandising/retailing management; cooking and related culinary arts; corrections; criminal justice/law enforcement administration; criminal justice/police science; crop production; culinary arts related; data entry/microcomputer applications; data processing and data processing technology; design and applied arts related; desktop publishing and digital imaging design; developmental and child psychology; drawing; early childhood education; ecology; economics; education; elementary education; emergency care attendant (EMT ambulance); energy management and systems technology; engineering; English; environmental design/architecture; environmental education; environmental engineering technology; environmental studies; family and consumer sciences/human sciences; farm and ranch management; fashion merchandising; finance; fine/studio arts; fishing and fisheries sciences and management; flight instruction; food preparation; foods and nutrition related; food service and dining room management; foreign languages and literatures; forestry; general studies; geology/earth science; graphic and printing equipment operation/production; graphic communications; graphic design; health and physical education/fitness; health/health-care administration; history; hospitality administration; hotel/motel administration; humanities; human resources management and services related; hydrology and water resources science; information technology; institutional food workers; jazz/jazz studies; journalism; keyboard instruments; kindergarten/preschool education; landscaping and groundskeeping; legal administrative assistant/secretary; legal assistant/paralegal; legal studies; liberal arts and sciences and humanities related; liberal arts and sciences/liberal studies; marine maintenance and ship repair technology; marketing/marketing management; massage therapy; mass communication/media; mathematics; medical administrative assistant and medical secretary; medical/clinical assistant; medical office assistant; medical office computer specialist; medical reception; medical transcription; merchandising, sales, and marketing operations related (general); motorcycle maintenance and repair technology; music; music teacher education; natural resources/conservation; natural sciences; network and system administration; office management; office occupations and clerical services; parks, recreation and leisure; percussion instruments; pharmacy; philosophy; photography; physical education teaching and coaching; physical sciences; political science and government; pre-dentistry studies; pre-engineering; pre-law studies; premedical studies; prenursing studies; pre-pharmacy studies; pre-veterinary studies; printing press operation; psychology; radio and television; radio and television broadcasting technology; real estate; receptionist; registered nursing/registered nurse; rehabilitation and therapeutic professions related; restaurant, culinary, and catering management; restaurant/food services management; retailing; rhetoric and composition; sales, distribution, and marketing operations; science teacher education; selling skills and sales; small business administration; small engine mechanics and repair technology; social sciences; social work; sociology; soil science and agronomy; Spanish; sport and fitness administration/management; surgical technology; system, networking, and LAN/WAN management; technology/industrial arts teacher education; trade and industrial teacher education; turf and turfgrass management; voice and opera; water, wetlands, and marine resources management; welding technology; wildlife biology; wildlife, fish and wildlands science and management; woodwind instruments; word processing.

Academics *Calendar:* semesters. *Degree:* certificates, diplomas, and associate. *Special study options:* academic remediation for entering students, accelerated degree program, adult/continuing education programs, advanced placement credit, cooperative education, distance learning, English as a second language, honors programs, independent study, internships, part-time degree program, services for LD students, summer session for credit.

Library Iowa Lakes Community College Library plus 2 others with 25,305 titles, 3,651 serial subscriptions, 1,175 audiovisual materials, an OPAC.

Student Life *Housing Options:* coed, disabled students. Campus housing is university owned. Freshman campus housing is guaranteed. *Activities and Organizations:* drama/theater group, student-run newspaper, radio and television station, choral group, music, Criminal Justice, nursing clubs, Environmental Studies, Business. *Campus security:* 24-hour emergency response devices, student patrols.

Athletics Member NJCAA. *Intercollegiate sports:* baseball M(s), basketball M(s)/W(s), cross-country running M(s)/W(s), golf M(s)/W(s), soccer M(s)/W(s), softball W(s), swimming and diving M(s)/W(s), volleyball W(s), wrestling M(s). *Intramural sports:* basketball M/W, football M/W, golf M/W, racquetball M/W, skiing (cross-country) M/W, skiing (downhill) M/W, soccer M/W, softball M/W, swimming and diving M/W, table tennis M/W, tennis M/W, ultimate Frisbee M/W, volleyball M/W, weight lifting M/W, wrestling M.

Applying *Options:* electronic application. *Required for some:* interview. *Application deadlines:* rolling (freshmen), rolling (out-of-state freshmen), rolling (transfers).

Freshman Application Contact Ms. Anne Stansbury Johnson, Director of Admission, Iowa Lakes Community College, 3200 College Drive, Emmetsburg, IA 50536. *Phone:* 712-852-3554 Ext. 5254. *Toll-free phone:* 800-521-5054. *Fax:* 712-852-2152. *E-mail:* info@iowalakes.edu. *Web site:* http://www.iowalakes.edu/.

Iowa Western Community College

Council Bluffs, Iowa

Freshman Application Contact Ms. Tori Christie, Director of Admissions, Iowa Western Community College, 2700 College Road, Box 4-C, Council Bluffs, IA 51502. *Phone:* 712-325-3288. *Toll-free phone:* 800-432-5852. *E-mail:* admissions@iwcc.edu. *Web site:* http://www.iwcc.edu/.

ITT Technical Institute

Cedar Rapids, Iowa

- **Proprietary** primarily 2-year
- **Coed**

Majors Business administration and management; communications technology; computer and information systems security; drafting and design technology; electrical, electronic and communications engineering technology; forensic science and technology; graphic communications; legal assistant/paralegal; network and system administration; project management.

Academics *Degrees:* associate and bachelor's.

Freshman Application Contact Director of Recruitment, ITT Technical Institute, 3735 Queen Court SW, Cedar Rapids, IA 52404. *Phone:* 319-297-3400. *Toll-free phone:* 877-320-4625. *Web site:* http://www.itt-tech.edu/.

ITT Technical Institute

Clive, Iowa

- **Proprietary** primarily 2-year, part of ITT Educational Services, Inc.
- **Coed**

Majors Business administration and management; communications technology; computer and information systems security; criminal justice/law enforcement administration; drafting and design technology; electrical, electronic and communications engineering technology; forensic science and technology; graphic communications; legal assistant/paralegal; network and system administration; project management.

Academics *Degrees:* associate and bachelor's.

Student Life *Housing:* college housing not available.

Freshman Application Contact Director of Recruitment, ITT Technical Institute, 1860 Northwest 118th Street, Suite 110, Clive, IA 50325. *Phone:* 515-327-5500. *Toll-free phone:* 877-526-7312. *Web site:* http://www.itt-tech.edu/.

Kaplan University, Cedar Falls

Cedar Falls, Iowa

Freshman Application Contact Kaplan University, Cedar Falls, 7009 Nordic Drive, Cedar Falls, IA 50613. *Phone:* 319-277-0220. *Toll-free phone:* 866-527-5268 (in-state); 800-527-5268 (out-of-state). *Web site:* http://www.cedarfalls.kaplanuniversity.edu/.

Kaplan University, Cedar Rapids

Cedar Rapids, Iowa

Freshman Application Contact Kaplan University, Cedar Rapids, 3165 Edgewood Parkway, SW, Cedar Rapids, IA 52404. *Phone:* 319-363-0481. *Toll-free phone:* 866-527-5268 (in-state); 800-527-5268 (out-of-state). *Web site:* http://www.cedarrapids.kaplanuniversity.edu/.

Kaplan University, Council Bluffs

Council Bluffs, Iowa

Freshman Application Contact Kaplan University, Council Bluffs, 1751 Madison Avenue, Council Bluffs, IA 51503. *Phone:* 712-328-4212. *Toll-free phone:* 866-527-5268 (in-state); 800-527-5268 (out-of-state). *Web site:* http://www.councilbluffs.kaplanuniversity.edu/.

Kaplan University, Des Moines

Urbandale, Iowa

Freshman Application Contact Kaplan University, Des Moines, 4655 121st Street, Urbandale, IA 50323. *Phone:* 515-727-2100. *Toll-free phone:* 866-527-5268 (in-state); 800-527-5268 (out-of-state). *Web site:* http://www.desmoines.kaplanuniversity.edu/.

Kirkwood Community College

Cedar Rapids, Iowa

Freshman Application Contact Kirkwood Community College, PO Box 2068, Cedar Rapids, IA 52406-2068. *Phone:* 319-398-5517. *Toll-free phone:* 800-332-2055. *Web site:* http://www.kirkwood.cc.ia.us/.

Marshalltown Community College

Marshalltown, Iowa

Freshman Application Contact Ms. Deana Inman, Director of Admissions, Marshalltown Community College, 3700 South Center Street, Marshalltown,

IA 50158-4760. *Phone:* 641-752-7106. *Toll-free phone:* 866-622-4748. *Fax:* 641-752-8149. *Web site:* http://www.marshalltowncommunitycollege.com/.

Muscatine Community College

Muscatine, Iowa

Freshman Application Contact Gary Mohr, Executive Director of Enrollment Management and Marketing, Muscatine Community College, 152 Colorado Street, Muscatine, IA 52761-5396. *Phone:* 563-336-3322. *Toll-free phone:* 800-351-4669. *Fax:* 563-336-3350. *E-mail:* gmohr@eicc.edu. *Web site:* http://www.eicc.edu/.

Northeast Iowa Community College

Calmar, Iowa

- **State and locally supported** 2-year, founded 1966, part of Iowa Area Community Colleges System
- **Rural** 210-acre campus
- **Endowment** $558,880
- **Coed,** 5,051 undergraduate students, 43% full-time, 61% women, 39% men

Undergraduates 2,192 full-time, 2,859 part-time. Students come from 23 states and territories; 4 other countries; 9% are from out of state; 3% Black or African American, non-Hispanic/Latino; 2% Hispanic/Latino; 0.4% Asian, non-Hispanic/Latino; 0.3% American Indian or Alaska Native, non-Hispanic/Latino; 0.8% Two or more races, non-Hispanic/Latino; 4% Race/ethnicity unknown; 0.1% international; 7% transferred in. *Retention:* 55% of full-time freshmen returned.

Freshmen *Admission:* 1,586 applied, 1,183 admitted, 778 enrolled.

Faculty *Total:* 347, 33% full-time, 6% with terminal degrees. *Student/faculty ratio:* 17:1.

Majors Accounting; administrative assistant and secretarial science; agribusiness; agricultural and food products processing; agricultural power machinery operation; agricultural production; automobile/automotive mechanics technology; business administration and management; business automation/technology/data entry; clinical/medical laboratory technology; computer programming (specific applications); construction trades; cosmetology; crop production; dairy husbandry and production; desktop publishing and digital imaging design; electrical, electronic and communications engineering technology; electrician; emergency medical technology (EMT paramedic); energy management and systems technology; fire science/firefighting; health information/medical records technology; liberal arts and sciences/liberal studies; plumbing technology; radiologic technology/science; registered nursing/registered nurse; respiratory care therapy; sales, distribution, and marketing operations; social work.

Academics *Calendar:* semesters. *Degree:* certificates, diplomas, and associate. *Special study options:* academic remediation for entering students, adult/continuing education programs, advanced placement credit, cooperative education, distance learning, double majors, external degree program, honors programs, internships, off-campus study, part-time degree program, services for LD students, summer session for credit.

Library Wilder Resource Center & Burton Payne Library plus 2 others with 44,835 titles, 341 serial subscriptions, 7,326 audiovisual materials, an OPAC, a Web page.

Student Life *Housing:* college housing not available. *Activities and Organizations:* student-run newspaper, choral group, national fraternities, national sororities. *Campus security:* security personnel on weeknights. *Student services:* personal/psychological counseling.

Athletics *Intramural sports:* basketball M/W, bowling M/W, football M, golf M/W, skiing (downhill) M/W, softball M/W, volleyball M/W.

Costs (2011–12) *Tuition:* state resident $4640 full-time, $145 per credit hour part-time; nonresident $4640 full-time, $145 per credit hour part-time. Full-time tuition and fees vary according to course load and program. Part-time tuition and fees vary according to course load and program. *Required fees:* $416 full-time, $13 per credit hour part-time. *Payment plan:* installment. *Waivers:* senior citizens and employees or children of employees.

Applying *Options:* electronic application. *Recommended:* high school transcript. *Application deadlines:* rolling (freshmen), rolling (out-of-state freshmen), rolling (transfers). *Notification:* continuous (freshmen), continuous (out-of-state freshmen), continuous (transfers).

Freshman Application Contact Ms. Brynn McConnell, Admissions Representative, Northeast Iowa Community College, Calmar, IA 52132. *Phone:* 563-562-3263 Ext. 307. *Toll-free phone:* 800-728-CALMAR. *Fax:* 563-562-4369. *E-mail:* mcconnellb@nicc.edu. *Web site:* http://www.nicc.edu/.

North Iowa Area Community College

Mason City, Iowa

- **State and locally supported** 2-year, founded 1918, part of Iowa Community College System
- **Rural** 320-acre campus
- **Coed**

Undergraduates 1,994 full-time, 1,750 part-time. 23% are from out of state; 3% Black or African American, non-Hispanic/Latino; 3% Hispanic/Latino; 1% Asian, non-Hispanic/Latino; 0.4% American Indian or Alaska Native, non-Hispanic/Latino; 0.6% Two or more races, non-Hispanic/Latino; 3% Race/ethnicity unknown; 0.8% international; 9% live on campus.

Faculty *Student/faculty ratio:* 17:1.

Academics *Calendar:* semesters. *Degree:* certificates, diplomas, and associate. *Special study options:* academic remediation for entering students, advanced placement credit, cooperative education, distance learning, English as a second language, external degree program, honors programs, internships, part-time degree program, services for LD students, student-designed majors, study abroad, summer session for credit.

Student Life *Campus security:* 24-hour emergency response devices.

Athletics Member NJCAA.

Costs (2011–12) *Tuition:* state resident $3666 full-time, $122 per semester hour part-time; nonresident $5499 full-time, $183 per semester hour part-time. Full-time tuition and fees vary according to course load. Part-time tuition and fees vary according to course load. *Required fees:* $738 full-time, $24 per semester hour part-time. *Room and board:* $5197. Room and board charges vary according to housing facility.

Financial Aid Of all full-time matriculated undergraduates who enrolled in 2010, 125 Federal Work-Study jobs (averaging $2000). 4 state and other part-time jobs (averaging $2000).

Applying *Options:* electronic application.

Freshman Application Contact Ms. Rachel McGuire, Director of Admissions, North Iowa Area Community College, 500 College Drive, Mason City, IA 50401. *Phone:* 641-422-4104. *Toll-free phone:* 888-GO NIACC Ext. 4245. *Fax:* 641-422-4385. *E-mail:* request@niacc.edu. *Web site:* http://www.niacc.edu/.

Northwest Iowa Community College

Sheldon, Iowa

Director of Admissions Ms. Lisa Story, Director of Enrollment Management, Northwest Iowa Community College, 603 West Park Street, Sheldon, IA 51201-1046. *Phone:* 712-324-5061 Ext. 115. *Toll-free phone:* 800-352-4907. *E-mail:* lstory@nwicc.edu. *Web site:* http://www.nwicc.edu/.

St. Luke's College

Sioux City, Iowa

- **Independent** 2-year, founded 1967, part of St. Luke's Regional Medical Center
- **Rural** 3-acre campus with easy access to Omaha
- **Endowment** $1.1 million
- **Coed**

Undergraduates 138 full-time, 54 part-time. Students come from 16 states and territories; 1 other country; 38% are from out of state; 1% Black or African American, non-Hispanic/Latino; 3% Hispanic/Latino; 3% Asian, non-Hispanic/Latino; 2% American Indian or Alaska Native, non-Hispanic/Latino; 20% transferred in. *Retention:* 100% of full-time freshmen returned.

Faculty *Student/faculty ratio:* 8:1.

Academics *Calendar:* semesters. *Degree:* certificates and associate. *Special study options:* advanced placement credit, cooperative education, summer session for credit.

Student Life *Campus security:* 24-hour emergency response devices and patrols, late-night transport/escort service.

Standardized Tests *Required:* SAT or ACT (for admission).

Costs (2011–12) *Tuition:* $15,300 full-time, $425 per quarter hour part-time. Full-time tuition and fees vary according to course load, degree level, and program. Part-time tuition and fees vary according to course load and degree level. *Required fees:* $1025 full-time, $1025 per year part-time. *Payment plans:* installment, deferred payment.

Financial Aid Of all full-time matriculated undergraduates who enrolled in 2011, 155 applied for aid, 155 were judged to have need, 25 had their need fully met. 3 Federal Work-Study jobs (averaging $1046). *Average percent of need met:* 75. *Average financial aid package:* $7257. *Average need-based loan:* $4089. *Average need-based gift aid:* $6444. *Average indebtedness upon graduation:* $23,831.

Applying *Options:* electronic application. *Application fee:* $50. *Required:* essay or personal statement, high school transcript, minimum 2.5 GPA, interview.

Freshman Application Contact Ms. Sherry McCarthy, Admissions Coordinator, St. Luke's College, 2720 Stone Park Boulevard, Sioux City, IA 51104. *Phone:* 712-279-3149. *Toll-free phone:* 800-352-4660 Ext. 3149. *Fax:* 712-233-8017. *E-mail:* mccartsj@stlukes.org. *Web site:* http://stlukescollege.edu/.

Scott Community College

Bettendorf, Iowa

Freshman Application Contact Mr. Gary Mohr, Executive Director of Enrollment Management and Marketing, Scott Community College, 500 Belmont Road, Bettendorf, IA 52722-6804. *Phone:* 563-336-3322. *Toll-free phone:* 800-895-0811. *Fax:* 563-336-3350. *E-mail:* gmohr@eicc.edu. *Web site:* http://www.eicc.edu/scc/.

Southeastern Community College

West Burlington, Iowa

- **State and locally supported** 2-year, founded 1968, part of Iowa Department of Education Division of Community Colleges
- **Small-town** 160-acre campus
- **Coed,** 3,341 undergraduate students, 54% full-time, 61% women, 39% men

Undergraduates 1,797 full-time, 1,544 part-time. 15% are from out of state; 5% Black or African American, non-Hispanic/Latino; 4% Hispanic/Latino; 1% Asian, non-Hispanic/Latino; 0.2% Native Hawaiian or other Pacific Islander, non-Hispanic/Latino; 0.7% American Indian or Alaska Native, non-Hispanic/Latino; 2% Two or more races, non-Hispanic/Latino; 2% Race/ethnicity unknown; 0.7% international; 3% transferred in.

Freshmen *Admission:* 848 applied, 480 admitted, 399 enrolled. *Average high school GPA:* 2.64. *Test scores:* ACT scores over 18: 57%; ACT scores over 24: 15%; ACT scores over 30: 2%.

Faculty *Total:* 158, 44% full-time, 6% with terminal degrees. *Student/faculty ratio:* 15:1.

Majors Accounting; administrative assistant and secretarial science; agricultural business and management; agronomy and crop science; artificial intelligence; automobile/automotive mechanics technology; biomedical technology; business administration and management; child development; computer programming; construction engineering technology; cosmetology; criminal justice/law enforcement administration; drafting and design technology; electrical, electronic and communications engineering technology; emergency medical technology (EMT paramedic); engineering related; industrial radiologic technology; information science/studies; liberal arts and sciences/liberal studies; licensed practical/vocational nurse training; machine tool technology; mechanical engineering/mechanical technology; medical/clinical assistant; registered nursing/registered nurse; respiratory care therapy; substance abuse/addiction counseling; trade and industrial teacher education; welding technology.

Academics *Calendar:* semesters. *Degree:* certificates, diplomas, and associate. *Special study options:* adult/continuing education programs, part-time degree program.

Library Yohe Memorial Library.

Student Life *Housing Options:* coed, men-only, disabled students. Campus housing is university owned. *Campus security:* controlled dormitory access, night patrols by trained security personnel.

Athletics Member NJCAA. *Intercollegiate sports:* baseball M(s), basketball M(s), softball W(s), volleyball W(s). *Intramural sports:* basketball M, bowling M/W, softball M/W, volleyball M/W, weight lifting M/W.

Financial Aid Of all full-time matriculated undergraduates who enrolled in 2010, 1,639 applied for aid, 1,494 were judged to have need. In 2010, 38 non-need-based awards were made. *Average financial aid package:* $6717. *Average need-based loan:* $3068. *Average need-based gift aid:* $4667. *Average non-need-based aid:* $1605.

Applying *Options:* early admission, deferred entrance. *Application deadlines:* rolling (freshmen), rolling (transfers). *Notification:* continuous (freshmen).

Freshman Application Contact Ms. Stacy White, Admissions, Southeastern Community College, 1500 West Agency Road, West Burlington, IA 52655-0180. *Phone:* 319-752-2731 Ext. 8137. *Toll-free phone:* 866-722-4692. *E-mail:* admoff@scciowa.edu. *Web site:* http://www.scciowa.edu/.

Southwestern Community College

Creston, Iowa

Freshman Application Contact Ms. Lisa Carstens, Admissions Coordinator, Southwestern Community College, 1501 West Townline Street, Creston, IA 50801. *Phone:* 641-782-7081 Ext. 453. *Toll-free phone:* 800-247-4023. *Fax:* 641-782-3312. *E-mail:* carstens@swcciowa.edu. *Web site:* http://www.swcciowa.edu/.

Vatterott College

Des Moines, Iowa

Freshman Application Contact Mr. Henry Franken, Co-Director, Vatterott College, 7000 Fleur Drive, Suite 290, Des Moines, IA 50321. *Phone:* 515-309-9000. *Toll-free phone:* 888-553-6627. *Fax:* 515-309-0366. *Web site:* http://www.vatterott-college.edu/.

Western Iowa Tech Community College

Sioux City, Iowa

- **State-supported** 2-year, founded 1966, part of Iowa Department of Education Division of Community Colleges
- **Suburban** campus
- **Coed,** 6,787 undergraduate students, 45% full-time, 58% women, 42% men

Undergraduates 3,083 full-time, 3,704 part-time. 6% Black or African American, non-Hispanic/Latino; 13% Hispanic/Latino; 1% Asian, non-Hispanic/Latino; 0.1% Native Hawaiian or other Pacific Islander, non-Hispanic/Latino; 5% American Indian or Alaska Native, non-Hispanic/Latino; 3% Two or more races, non-Hispanic/Latino; 7% Race/ethnicity unknown; 0.7% international.

Freshmen *Admission:* 801 enrolled. *Test scores:* ACT scores over 18: 63%; ACT scores over 24: 13%; ACT scores over 30: 1%.

Faculty *Total:* 366, 21% full-time, 8% with terminal degrees. *Student/faculty ratio:* 25:1.

Majors Accounting; administrative assistant and secretarial science; agricultural/farm supplies retailing and wholesaling; autobody/collision and repair technology; automobile/automotive mechanics technology; biomedical technology; business administration and management; business automation/technology/data entry; carpentry; child-care and support services management; child-care provision; clinical/medical laboratory technology; criminal justice/law enforcement administration; criminal justice/police science; dental hygiene; electrical, electronic and communications engineering technology; emergency medical technology (EMT paramedic); executive assistant/executive secretary; fire science/firefighting; human resources management; industrial mechanics and maintenance technology; interior design; legal administrative assistant/secretary; liberal arts and sciences/liberal studies; machine tool technology; medical administrative assistant and medical secretary; multi/interdisciplinary studies related; musical instrument fabrication and repair; nursing assistant/aide and patient care assistant/aide; occupational therapist assistant; physical therapy technology; registered nursing/registered nurse; sales, distribution, and marketing operations; securities services administration; surgical technology; tool and die technology; turf and turfgrass management.

Academics *Calendar:* semesters. *Degree:* certificates, diplomas, and associate. *Special study options:* adult/continuing education programs, part-time degree program.

Library Western Iowa Tech Community College Library Services.

Student Life *Housing Options:* coed. *Campus security:* 24-hour emergency response devices and patrols.

Athletics *Intramural sports:* basketball M/W, bowling M/W, football M/W, soccer M/W, softball W, volleyball M/W, wrestling M/W.

Standardized Tests *Required:* SAT or ACT (for admission). *Recommended:* ACT (for admission).

Financial Aid Of all full-time matriculated undergraduates who enrolled in 2010, 148 Federal Work-Study jobs (averaging $1000). 2 state and other part-time jobs (averaging $2500).

Applying *Options:* early admission, deferred entrance. *Recommended:* high school transcript. *Application deadlines:* rolling (freshmen), rolling (transfers). *Notification:* continuous (freshmen), continuous (transfers).

Freshman Application Contact Lora Vanderzwaag, Director of Admissions, Western Iowa Tech Community College, 4647 Stone Avenue, PO Box 5199, Sioux City, IA 51102-5199. *Phone:* 712-274-6400. *Toll-free phone:* 800-352-4649 Ext. 6403. *Fax:* 712-274-6441. *Web site:* http://www.witcc.edu/.

KANSAS

Allen Community College
Iola, Kansas

- **State and locally supported** 2-year, founded 1923, part of Kansas State Board of Regents
- **Small-town** 88-acre campus
- **Coed**

Undergraduates Students come from 20 states and territories; 8 other countries; 9% are from out of state; 4% Black or African American, non-Hispanic/Latino; 4% Hispanic/Latino; 0.8% Asian, non-Hispanic/Latino; 0.8% Native Hawaiian or other Pacific Islander, non-Hispanic/Latino; 2% American Indian or Alaska Native, non-Hispanic/Latino; 0.6% international. *Retention:* 56% of full-time freshmen returned.
Faculty *Student/faculty ratio:* 17:1.
Academics *Calendar:* semesters. *Degree:* certificates and associate. *Special study options:* academic remediation for entering students, adult/continuing education programs, cooperative education, distance learning, English as a second language, independent study, internships, part-time degree program, services for LD students, student-designed majors, summer session for credit.
Athletics Member NJCAA.
Standardized Tests *Required:* SAT or ACT (for admission).
Costs (2011–12) *Tuition:* state resident $1410 full-time, $47 per hour part-time; nonresident $1410 full-time, $47 per hour part-time. Full-time tuition and fees vary according to course load. Part-time tuition and fees vary according to course load. *Required fees:* $540 full-time, $18 per hour part-time. *Room and board:* $4300; room only: $3600. Room and board charges vary according to housing facility.
Financial Aid Of all full-time matriculated undergraduates who enrolled in 2008, 510 applied for aid, 411 were judged to have need, 384 had their need fully met. 40 Federal Work-Study jobs (averaging $2600). 112 state and other part-time jobs (averaging $2600). In 2008, 22. *Average percent of need met:* 80. *Average financial aid package:* $4738. *Average need-based loan:* $2482. *Average need-based gift aid:* $3257. *Average non-need-based aid:* $1241.
Applying *Options:* electronic application, early admission, deferred entrance. *Required:* high school transcript.
Freshman Application Contact Rebecca Bilderback, Director of Admissions, Allen Community College, 1801 North Cottonwood, Iola, KS 66749. *Phone:* 620-365-5116 Ext. 267. *Fax:* 620-365-7406. *E-mail:* bilderback@allencc.edu. *Web site:* http://www.allencc.edu/.

Barton County Community College
Great Bend, Kansas

- **State and locally supported** 2-year, founded 1969, part of Kansas Board of Regents
- **Rural** 140-acre campus
- **Endowment** $4.4 million
- **Coed**

Undergraduates 1,028 full-time, 3,695 part-time. Students come from 49 states and territories; 23 other countries; 7% are from out of state; 4% transferred in; 8% live on campus.
Faculty *Student/faculty ratio:* 23:1.
Academics *Calendar:* semesters. *Degree:* certificates and associate. *Special study options:* academic remediation for entering students, accelerated degree program, adult/continuing education programs, advanced placement credit, cooperative education, distance learning, double majors, English as a second language, external degree program, honors programs, independent study, internships, part-time degree program, services for LD students, summer session for credit.
Student Life *Campus security:* 24-hour emergency response devices and patrols.
Athletics Member NJCAA.
Costs (2011–12) *Tuition:* area resident $1620 full-time, $54 per credit hour part-time; state resident $1710 full-time, $57 per credit hour part-time; nonresident $2640 full-time, $88 per credit hour part-time. Full-time tuition and fees vary according to course load. Part-time tuition and fees vary according to course load. *Required fees:* $900 full-time, $30 per credit hour part-time. *Room and board:* $4784. Room and board charges vary according to board plan. *Payment plans:* installment, deferred payment.
Applying *Options:* electronic application, early admission. *Recommended:* high school transcript.
Freshman Application Contact Mr. Todd Moore, Director of Admissions and Promotions, Barton County Community College, 245 Northeast 30th Road, Great Bend, KS 67530. *Phone:* 620-792-9241. *Toll-free phone:* 800-722-6842. *Fax:* 620-786-1160. *E-mail:* admissions@bartonccc.edu. *Web site:* http://www.bartonccc.edu/.

Brown Mackie College–Kansas City
Lenexa, Kansas

- **Proprietary** 2-year, founded 1892, part of Education Management Corporation
- **Suburban** campus
- **Coed**

Academics *Calendar:* quarters. *Degree:* certificates, diplomas, and associate.
Costs (2011–12) *Tuition:* Tuition varies by program. Students should contact Brown Mackie College for tuition information.
Freshman Application Contact Brown Mackie College–Kansas City, 9705 Lenexa Drive, Lenexa, KS 66215. *Phone:* 913-768-1900. *Toll-free phone:* 800-635-9101. *Web site:* http://www.brownmackie.edu/kansascity/.

See page 362 for the College Close-Up.

Brown Mackie College–Salina
Salina, Kansas

- **Proprietary** 2-year, founded 1892, part of Education Management Corporation
- **Small-town** campus
- **Coed**

Academics *Calendar:* modular. *Degree:* certificates, diplomas, and associate.
Costs (2011–12) *Tuition:* Tuition varies by program. Students should contact Brown Mackie College for tuition information.
Freshman Application Contact Brown Mackie College–Salina, 2106 South 9th Street, Salina, KS 67401-2810. *Phone:* 785-825-5422. *Toll-free phone:* 800-365-0433. *Web site:* http://www.brownmackie.edu/salina/.

See page 384 for the College Close-Up.

Butler Community College
El Dorado, Kansas

Freshman Application Contact Mr. Glenn Lygrisse, Interim Director of Enrollment Management, Butler Community College, 901 South Haverhill Road, El Dorado, KS 67042. *Phone:* 316-321-2222. *Fax:* 316-322-3109. *E-mail:* admissions@butlercc.edu. *Web site:* http://www.butlercc.edu/.

Cloud County Community College
Concordia, Kansas

Director of Admissions Kim Reynolds, Director of Admissions, Cloud County Community College, 2221 Campus Drive, PO Box 1002, Concordia, KS 66901-1002. *Phone:* 785-243-1435 Ext. 214. *Toll-free phone:* 800-729-5101. *Web site:* http://www.cloud.edu/.

Coffeyville Community College
Coffeyville, Kansas

Freshman Application Contact Stacia Meek, Admissions Counselor/Marketing Event Coordinator, Coffeyville Community College, 400 West 11th Street, Coffeyville, KS 67337-5063. *Phone:* 620-252-7100. *Toll-free phone:* 877-51-RAVEN. *E-mail:* staciam@coffeyville.edu. *Web site:* http://www.coffeyville.edu/.

Colby Community College
Colby, Kansas

- **State and locally supported** 2-year, founded 1964, part of Kansas State Board of Education
- **Small-town** 80-acre campus
- **Endowment** $3.4 million
- **Coed**, 1,462 undergraduate students, 49% full-time, 63% women, 37% men

Undergraduates 722 full-time, 740 part-time. Students come from 15 states and territories; 5 other countries; 30% are from out of state; 6% Black or African American, non-Hispanic/Latino; 6% Hispanic/Latino; 2% Asian, non-Hispanic/Latino; 0.1% Native Hawaiian or other Pacific Islander, non-Hispanic/Latino; 0.7% American Indian or Alaska Native, non-Hispanic/Latino; 5% international; 6% transferred in; 30% live on campus.
Freshmen *Admission:* 622 applied, 622 admitted, 221 enrolled. *Average high school GPA:* 2.96. *Test scores:* ACT scores over 18: 67%; ACT scores over 24: 12%; ACT scores over 30: 2%.
Faculty *Total:* 153, 38% full-time, 11% with terminal degrees. *Student/faculty ratio:* 11:1.
Majors Administrative assistant and secretarial science; agribusiness; agricultural business and management; agricultural teacher education; agronomy and

crop science; broadcast journalism; business administration and management; child-care and support services management; child development; computer and information sciences; computer and information sciences related; criminal justice/law enforcement administration; criminal justice/police science; dental hygiene; engineering related; farm and ranch management; horse husbandry/equine science and management; liberal arts and sciences/liberal studies; licensed practical/vocational nurse training; physical therapy technology; radio and television; registered nursing/registered nurse; substance abuse/addiction counseling; veterinary/animal health technology.

Academics *Calendar:* semesters. *Degree:* certificates, diplomas, and associate. *Special study options:* academic remediation for entering students, adult/continuing education programs, advanced placement credit, cooperative education, distance learning, double majors, honors programs, internships, part-time degree program, services for LD students, student-designed majors, summer session for credit.

Library Davis Library with 34,000 titles, 463 serial subscriptions, 600 audiovisual materials, an OPAC.

Student Life *Housing:* on-campus residence required for freshman year. *Options:* coed, men-only, women-only. Campus housing is university owned. *Activities and Organizations:* drama/theater group, student-run newspaper, radio and television station, choral group, KSNEA, Physical Therapist Assistants Club, Block and Bridle, SVTA, COPNS. *Campus security:* 24-hour emergency response devices and patrols. *Student services:* health clinic, personal/psychological counseling.

Athletics Member NJCAA. *Intercollegiate sports:* baseball M(s), basketball M(s)/W(s), cheerleading M(s)/W(s), cross-country running M(s)/W(s), equestrian sports M/W, golf M(s)/W(s), softball W(s), track and field M(s)/W(s), volleyball W(s), wrestling M(s). *Intramural sports:* basketball M/W, softball M/W, volleyball M/W.

Standardized Tests *Recommended:* SAT or ACT (for admission).

Costs (2012–13) *Tuition:* state resident $1824 full-time, $57 per credit part-time; nonresident $3488 full-time, $109 per credit part-time. Full-time tuition and fees vary according to course load and program. Part-time tuition and fees vary according to course load and program. *Required fees:* $1120 full-time, $35 per credit part-time. *Room and board:* $4910. Room and board charges vary according to housing facility. *Payment plan:* installment. *Waivers:* senior citizens and employees or children of employees.

Financial Aid Of all full-time matriculated undergraduates who enrolled in 2010, 95 Federal Work-Study jobs (averaging $1500). 30 state and other part-time jobs (averaging $2000).

Applying *Options:* electronic application, early admission, deferred entrance. *Required:* high school transcript. *Required for some:* interview. *Application deadlines:* rolling (freshmen), rolling (out-of-state freshmen), rolling (transfers). *Notification:* continuous (freshmen), continuous (out-of-state freshmen), continuous (transfers).

Freshman Application Contact Ms. Nikol Nolan, Admissions Director, Colby Community College, Colby, KS 67701-4099. *Phone:* 785-462-3984 Ext. 5496. *Toll-free phone:* 888-634-9350. *Fax:* 785-460-4691. *E-mail:* admissions@colbycc.edu. *Web site:* http://www.colbycc.edu/.

Cowley County Community College and Area Vocational–Technical School

Arkansas City, Kansas

- **State and locally supported** 2-year, founded 1922, part of Kansas State Board of Education
- **Small-town** 19-acre campus
- **Endowment** $4.7 million
- **Coed,** 4,328 undergraduate students, 54% full-time, 62% women, 38% men

Undergraduates 2,328 full-time, 2,000 part-time. 10% are from out of state; 11% live on campus. *Retention:* 55% of full-time freshmen returned.

Freshmen *Admission:* 1,010 applied, 1,010 admitted, 1,010 enrolled. *Average high school GPA:* 2.94. *Test scores:* ACT scores over 18: 72%; ACT scores over 24: 20%; ACT scores over 30: 1%.

Faculty *Total:* 253, 19% full-time. *Student/faculty ratio:* 26:1.

Majors Accounting; administrative assistant and secretarial science; agriculture; art; automobile/automotive mechanics technology; biology/biological sciences; business administration and management; chemistry; child-care and support services management; child development; computer and information sciences; computer and information systems security; computer graphics; computer programming (specific applications); computer science; cosmetology; criminal justice/law enforcement administration; criminal justice/police science; dietetics and clinical nutrition services related; drafting and design technology; dramatic/theater arts; education; electromechanical and instrumentation and maintenance technologies related; elementary education; emergency medical technology (EMT paramedic); engineering technology;

entrepreneurship; hotel/motel administration; industrial radiologic technology; journalism; legal administrative assistant/secretary; liberal arts and sciences/liberal studies; machine tool technology; marketing/marketing management; medical insurance coding; medical transcription; music; physical and biological anthropology; pre-engineering; religious studies; social work; technology/industrial arts teacher education; welding technology.

Academics *Calendar:* semesters. *Degree:* certificates, diplomas, and associate. *Special study options:* academic remediation for entering students, accelerated degree program, adult/continuing education programs, advanced placement credit, cooperative education, distance learning, external degree program, independent study, off-campus study, part-time degree program, services for LD students, summer session for credit.

Library Renn Memorial Library with 27,000 titles, 12,000 serial subscriptions, 1,000 audiovisual materials, an OPAC, a Web page.

Student Life *Housing Options:* coed, men-only, women-only. Campus housing is university owned. *Activities and Organizations:* drama/theater group, student-run newspaper, choral group, Academic Civic Engagement through Services (ACES), Peers Advocating for Wellness (PAWS), Phi Theta Kappa, Student Government Association, Phi Beta Lambda. *Campus security:* 24-hour emergency response devices and patrols, student patrols, late-night transport/escort service, controlled dormitory access, residence hall entrances are locked at night. *Student services:* health clinic, personal/psychological counseling.

Athletics Member NJCAA. *Intercollegiate sports:* baseball M(s), basketball M(s)/W(s), cross-country running M(s)/W(s), soccer M(s)/W(s), softball W(s), tennis M(s)/W(s), track and field M(s)/W(s), volleyball W(s). *Intramural sports:* basketball M/W, bowling M/W, football M, softball M/W, tennis M/W, volleyball M/W.

Standardized Tests *Recommended:* ACT (for admission).

Costs (2011–12) *Tuition:* area resident $1536 full-time, $48 per credit hour part-time; state resident $1856 full-time, $58 per credit hour part-time; nonresident $3360 full-time, $105 per credit hour part-time. *Required fees:* $832 full-time, $26 per credit hour part-time. *Room and board:* $4450. Room and board charges vary according to board plan. *Payment plan:* installment. *Waivers:* employees or children of employees.

Financial Aid Of all full-time matriculated undergraduates who enrolled in 2011, 1,733 applied for aid, 1,331 were judged to have need, 481 had their need fully met. 91 Federal Work-Study jobs (averaging $1151). 74 state and other part-time jobs (averaging $1034). *Average financial aid package:* $6658. *Average need-based loan:* $2834. *Average need-based gift aid:* $4596. *Average indebtedness upon graduation:* $1668.

Applying *Options:* electronic application, early admission. *Required:* high school transcript. *Application deadlines:* rolling (freshmen), rolling (out-of-state freshmen), rolling (transfers). *Notification:* continuous (freshmen), continuous (out-of-state freshmen), continuous (transfers).

Freshman Application Contact Ms. Lory West, Director of Admissions, Cowley County Community College and Area Vocational–Technical School, PO Box 1147, Arkansas City, KS 67005. *Phone:* 620-441-5594. *Toll-free phone:* 800-593-CCCC. *Fax:* 620-441-5350. *E-mail:* admissions@cowley.edu. *Web site:* http://www.cowley.edu/.

Dodge City Community College

Dodge City, Kansas

- **State and locally supported** 2-year, founded 1935, part of Kansas State Board of Education
- **Small-town** 143-acre campus
- **Coed**

Undergraduates 1,807 full-time. Students come from 24 states and territories; 10% are from out of state; 20% live on campus.

Faculty *Student/faculty ratio:* 18:1.

Academics *Calendar:* semesters. *Degree:* certificates and associate. *Special study options:* academic remediation for entering students, adult/continuing education programs, advanced placement credit, cooperative education, English as a second language, external degree program, internships, part-time degree program, student-designed majors, summer session for credit.

Athletics Member NJCAA.

Applying *Options:* electronic application, early admission, deferred entrance. *Required:* high school transcript.

Freshman Application Contact Dodge City Community College, 2501 North 14th Avenue, Dodge City, KS 67801-2399. *Phone:* 620-225-1321. *Web site:* http://www.dc3.edu/.

Donnelly College

Kansas City, Kansas

Freshman Application Contact Mr. Edward Marquez, Director of Admissions, Donnelly College, 608 North 18th Street, Kansas City, KS 66102.

Phone: 913-621-8713. Fax: 913-621-8719. E-mail: admissions@ donnelly.edu. Web site: http://www.donnelly.edu/.

Flint Hills Technical College

Emporia, Kansas

Freshman Application Contact Admissions Office, Flint Hills Technical College, 3301 West 18th Avenue, Emporia, KS 66801. Phone: 620-341-1325. Toll-free phone: 800-711-6947. Web site: http://www.fhtc.edu/.

Fort Scott Community College

Fort Scott, Kansas

Director of Admissions Mrs. Mert Barrows, Director of Admissions, Fort Scott Community College, 2108 South Horton, Fort Scott, KS 66701. Phone: 620-223-2700 Ext. 353. Toll-free phone: 800-874-3722. Web site: http://www.fortscott.edu/.

Garden City Community College

Garden City, Kansas

Freshman Application Contact Office of Admissions, Garden City Community College, 801 Campus Drive, Garden City, KS 67846. Phone: 620-276-9531. Toll-free phone: 800-658-1696. Fax: 620-276-9650. E-mail: admissions@gcccks.edu. Web site: http://www.gcccks.edu/.

Hesston College

Hesston, Kansas

- **Independent Mennonite** 2-year, founded 1909
- **Small-town** 50-acre campus with easy access to Wichita
- **Coed**

Undergraduates 396 full-time, 52 part-time. Students come from 30 states and territories; 11 other countries; 45% are from out of state; 6% Black or African American, non-Hispanic/Latino; 5% Hispanic/Latino; 0.9% Asian, non-Hispanic/Latino; 0.2% Native Hawaiian or other Pacific Islander, non-Hispanic/Latino; 2% American Indian or Alaska Native, non-Hispanic/Latino; 2% Two or more races, non-Hispanic/Latino; 1% Race/ethnicity unknown; 8% international; 9% transferred in; 73% live on campus. Retention: 78% of full-time freshmen returned.

Faculty Student/faculty ratio: 12:1.

Academics Calendar: semesters. Degree: associate. Special study options: academic remediation for entering students, advanced placement credit, cooperative education, double majors, English as a second language, independent study, internships, part-time degree program, services for LD students, summer session for credit.

Student Life Campus security: 24-hour emergency response devices, controlled dormitory access.

Athletics Member NJCAA.

Standardized Tests Required: SAT or ACT (for admission).

Costs (2011–12) Comprehensive fee: $28,818 includes full-time tuition ($21,312), mandatory fees ($340), and room and board ($7166). Full-time tuition and fees vary according to program. Part-time tuition: $888 per hour. Part-time tuition and fees vary according to course load and program. Required fees: $85 per term part-time.

Financial Aid Of all full-time matriculated undergraduates who enrolled in 2010, 120 Federal Work-Study jobs (averaging $800).

Applying Options: electronic application, early admission, deferred entrance. Application fee: $15. Required: high school transcript, 2 letters of recommendation. Required for some: interview.

Freshman Application Contact Joel Kauffman, Vice President of Admissions, Hesston College, Hesston, KS 67062. Phone: 620-327-8222. Toll-free phone: 800-995-2757. Fax: 620-327-8300. E-mail: admissions@ hesston.edu. Web site: http://www.hesston.edu/.

Highland Community College

Highland, Kansas

Director of Admissions Ms. Cheryl Rasmussen, Vice President of Student Services, Highland Community College, 606 West Main Street, Highland, KS 66035. Phone: 785-442-6020. Fax: 785-442-6106. Web site: http://www.highlandcc.edu/.

Hutchinson Community College and Area Vocational School

Hutchinson, Kansas

- **State and locally supported** 2-year, founded 1928, part of Kansas Board of Regents
- **Small-town** 47-acre campus
- **Coed,** 5,560 undergraduate students, 47% full-time, 59% women, 41% men

Undergraduates 2,639 full-time, 2,921 part-time. Students come from 42 states and territories; 6 other countries; 8% are from out of state; 7% Black or African American, non-Hispanic/Latino; 7% Hispanic/Latino; 0.9% Asian, non-Hispanic/Latino; 1% American Indian or Alaska Native, non-Hispanic/Latino; 6% Race/ethnicity unknown; 0.5% international; 7% transferred in; 7% live on campus. Retention: 63% of full-time freshmen returned.

Freshmen Admission: 1,208 enrolled. Average high school GPA: 2.85. Test scores: ACT scores over 18: 74%; ACT scores over 24: 22%; ACT scores over 30: 2%.

Faculty Total: 359, 31% full-time, 6% with terminal degrees. Student/faculty ratio: 18:1.

Majors Administrative assistant and secretarial science; agricultural mechanization; agriculture; autobody/collision and repair technology; automobile/automotive mechanics technology; biology/biological sciences; biotechnology; business and personal/financial services marketing; business/commerce; carpentry; child-care and support services management; communications technology; computer and information sciences; computer systems analysis; criminal justice/police science; drafting and design technology; education; educational/instructional technology; electrical/electronics equipment installation and repair; emergency medical technology (EMT paramedic); engineering; English; family and consumer sciences/human sciences; farm and ranch management; fire science/firefighting; foreign languages and literatures; health information/medical records technology; legal assistant/paralegal; liberal arts and sciences/liberal studies; machine tool technology; manufacturing engineering technology; mathematics; medical radiologic technology; physical sciences; physical therapy technology; psychology; registered nursing/registered nurse; respiratory care therapy; retailing; social sciences; speech communication and rhetoric; visual and performing arts; welding technology.

Academics Calendar: semesters. Degree: certificates and associate. Special study options: academic remediation for entering students, adult/continuing education programs, advanced placement credit, cooperative education, distance learning, double majors, English as a second language, honors programs, independent study, internships, part-time degree program, services for LD students, student-designed majors, summer session for credit. ROTC: Army (c).

Library John F. Kennedy Library plus 1 other with 43,600 titles, 136 serial subscriptions, 2,962 audiovisual materials, an OPAC, a Web page.

Student Life Housing Options: men-only, women-only. Campus housing is university owned. Activities and Organizations: drama/theater group, student-run newspaper, choral group, Black Leadership League, Hispanic American Leadership Organization, Campus Crusade for Christ, Circle K, Block and Bridle Club. Campus security: 24-hour emergency response devices and patrols, student patrols, late-night transport/escort service, controlled dormitory access. Student services: health clinic, personal/psychological counseling.

Athletics Member NJCAA. Intercollegiate sports: baseball M(s), basketball M(s)/W(s), cheerleading M(s)/W(s), cross-country running M(s)/W(s), football M(s), golf M(s), soccer W(s), softball W(s), track and field M(s)/W(s), volleyball W(s). Intramural sports: badminton M/W, basketball M/W, football M/W, racquetball M/W, soccer M/W, tennis M/W, track and field M/W, volleyball M/W.

Costs (2012–13) Tuition: state resident $2144 full-time, $67 per hour part-time; nonresident $3136 full-time, $98 per hour part-time. Required fees: $544 full-time, $17 per hour part-time. Room and board: $5150. Room and board charges vary according to board plan. Payment plan: installment.

Applying Options: electronic application, early admission, deferred entrance. Required for some: interview. Recommended: high school transcript. Application deadlines: rolling (freshmen), rolling (transfers).

Freshman Application Contact Mr. Corbin Strobel, Director of Admissions, Hutchinson Community College and Area Vocational School, 1300 North Plum, Hutchinson, KS 67501. Phone: 620-665-3536. Toll-free phone: 888-GO-HUTCH. Fax: 620-665-3301. E-mail: strobelc@hutchcc.edu. Web site: http://www.hutchcc.edu/.

Independence Community College

Independence, Kansas

Freshman Application Contact Ms. Sally A. Ciufulescu, Director of Admissions, Independence Community College, Brookside Drive and College Avenue, PO Box 708, Independence, KS 67301-0708. Phone: 620-332-5400. Toll-free phone: 800-842-6063. Fax: 620-331-0946. E-mail: sciufulescu@ indycc.edu. Web site: http://www.indycc.edu/.

Johnson County Community College

Overland Park, Kansas

Director of Admissions Dr. Charles J. Carlsen, President, Johnson County Community College, 12345 College Boulevard, Overland Park, KS 66210-1299. *Phone:* 913-469-8500 Ext. 3806. *Web site:* http://www.johnco.cc.ks.us/

Kansas City Kansas Community College

Kansas City, Kansas

- **State and locally supported** 2-year, founded 1923
- **Urban** 148-acre campus
- **Endowment** $1.1 million
- **Coed,** 7,555 undergraduate students, 38% full-time, 64% women, 36% men

Undergraduates 2,903 full-time, 4,652 part-time. Students come from 27 states and territories; 13 other countries; 5% are from out of state; 29% Black or African American, non-Hispanic/Latino; 10% Hispanic/Latino; 2% Asian, non-Hispanic/Latino; 0.2% Native Hawaiian or other Pacific Islander, non-Hispanic/Latino; 0.6% American Indian or Alaska Native, non-Hispanic/Latino; 2% Two or more races, non-Hispanic/Latino; 5% Race/ethnicity unknown; 2% international; 4% transferred in.

Freshmen *Admission:* 970 admitted, 970 enrolled.

Faculty *Total:* 480, 31% full-time. *Student/faculty ratio:* 17:1.

Majors Accounting; accounting and business/management; administrative assistant and secretarial science; business administration and management; CAD/CADD drafting/design technology; child-care and support services management; computer engineering technology; computer software technology; computer systems networking and telecommunications; corrections; corrections and criminal justice related; criminal justice/police science; desktop publishing and digital imaging design; early childhood education; emergency medical technology (EMT paramedic); fire protection related; fire science/firefighting; funeral service and mortuary science; hazardous materials management and waste technology; legal assistant/paralegal; liberal arts and sciences/liberal studies; marketing/marketing management; recording arts technology; registered nursing/registered nurse; respiratory care therapy; respiratory therapy technician; substance abuse/addiction counseling.

Academics *Calendar:* semesters. *Degree:* certificates, diplomas, and associate. *Special study options:* academic remediation for entering students, adult/continuing education programs, advanced placement credit, cooperative education, distance learning, English as a second language, external degree program, freshman honors college, honors programs, independent study, internships, part-time degree program, services for LD students, summer session for credit.

Library Kansas City Kansas Community College Library plus 1 other with 75,000 titles, 200 serial subscriptions, 7,000 audiovisual materials, an OPAC, a Web page.

Student Life *Housing:* college housing not available. *Activities and Organizations:* drama/theater group, student-run newspaper, choral group, Student Senate, Phi Theta Kappa, Drama Club, The African American Student Union, Collegiate Educators Music Club. *Campus security:* 24-hour emergency response devices and patrols, student patrols, late-night transport/escort service. *Student services:* health clinic, personal/psychological counseling, women's center.

Athletics Member NJCAA. *Intercollegiate sports:* baseball M(s), basketball M(s)/W(s), cross-country running M(s)/W(s), golf M(s), soccer M(s), softball W(s), track and field M(s)/W(s), volleyball W(s).

Costs (2011–12) *Tuition:* state resident $1988 full-time, $71 per credit hour part-time; nonresident $4900 full-time, $175 per credit hour part-time. Full-time tuition and fees vary according to course load. Part-time tuition and fees vary according to course load. *Required fees:* $364 full-time, $13 per credit hour part-time. *Payment plan:* installment. *Waivers:* employees or children of employees.

Financial Aid Of all full-time matriculated undergraduates who enrolled in 2010, 125 Federal Work-Study jobs (averaging $3000).

Applying *Options:* electronic application. *Required:* high school transcript. *Application deadlines:* rolling (freshmen), rolling (transfers). *Notification:* continuous (freshmen), continuous (transfers).

Freshman Application Contact Dr. Denise McDowell, Dean of Enrollment Management/Registrar, Kansas City Kansas Community College, Admissions Office, 7250 State Avenue, Kansas City, KS 66112. *Phone:* 913-288-7694. *Fax:* 913-288-7648. *E-mail:* dmcdowell@kckcc.edu. *Web site:* http://www.kckcc.edu/.

Labette Community College

Parsons, Kansas

Freshman Application Contact Ms. Tammy Fuentez, Director of Admission, Labette Community College, 200 South 14th Street, Parsons, KS 67357-4299. *Phone:* 620-421-6700. *Toll-free phone:* 888-522-3883. *Fax:* 620-421-0180. *Web site:* http://www.labette.edu/.

Manhattan Area Technical College

Manhattan, Kansas

Freshman Application Contact Mr. Rick Smith, Coordinator of Admissions and Recruitment, Manhattan Area Technical College, 3136 Dickens Avenue, Manhattan, KS 66503. *Phone:* 785-587-2800 Ext. 104. *Toll-free phone:* 800-352-7575. *Fax:* 913-587-2804. *Web site:* http://www.matc.net/.

National American University

Overland Park, Kansas

Freshman Application Contact Admissions Office, National American University, 10310 Mastin, Overland Park, KS 66212. *Web site:* http://www.national.edu/.

Neosho County Community College

Chanute, Kansas

Freshman Application Contact Ms. Lisa Last, Dean of Student Development, Neosho County Community College, 800 West 14th Street, Chanute, KS 66720. *Phone:* 620-431-2820 Ext. 213. *Toll-free phone:* 800-729-6222. *Fax:* 620-431-0082. *E-mail:* llast@neosho.edu. *Web site:* http://www.neosho.edu/.

North Central Kansas Technical College

Beloit, Kansas

Freshman Application Contact Ms. Judy Heidrick, Director of Admissions, North Central Kansas Technical College, PO Box 507, 3033 US Highway 24, Beloit, KS 67420. *Toll-free phone:* 800-658-4655. *E-mail:* jheidrick@ncktc.tec.ks.us. *Web site:* http://www.ncktc.edu/.

Northwest Kansas Technical College

Goodland, Kansas

Admissions Office Contact Northwest Kansas Technical College, PO Box 668, 1209 Harrison Street, Goodland, KS 67735. *Toll-free phone:* 800-316-4127. *Web site:* http://www.nwktc.edu/.

Pratt Community College

Pratt, Kansas

- **State and locally supported** 2-year, founded 1938, part of Kansas State Board of Education
- **Rural** 80-acre campus with easy access to Wichita
- **Endowment** $3.0 million
- **Coed**

Undergraduates 751 full-time, 913 part-time. Students come from 32 states and territories; 14 other countries; 14% are from out of state; 8% transferred in; 35% live on campus. *Retention:* 60% of full-time freshmen returned.

Faculty *Student/faculty ratio:* 15:1.

Academics *Calendar:* semesters. *Degree:* certificates and associate. *Special study options:* academic remediation for entering students, adult/continuing education programs, advanced placement credit, cooperative education, distance learning, internships, part-time degree program, summer session for credit.

Student Life *Campus security:* 24-hour patrols, late-night transport/escort service, controlled dormitory access.

Athletics Member NJCAA.

Standardized Tests *Required for some:* ASSET.

Costs (2011–12) *Tuition:* state resident $1666 full-time, $51 per credit hour part-time; nonresident $1870 full-time, $57 per credit hour part-time. Full-time tuition and fees vary according to program. Part-time tuition and fees vary according to program. *Required fees:* $1088 full-time, $34 per credit hour part-time. *Room and board:* $4992. Room and board charges vary according to board plan and housing facility.

Financial Aid Of all full-time matriculated undergraduates who enrolled in 2010, 77 Federal Work-Study jobs (averaging $800). 25 state and other part-time jobs (averaging $800). *Financial aid deadline:* 8/1.

Applying *Options:* electronic application, early admission. *Required:* high school transcript.

Freshman Application Contact Ms. Theresa Ziehr, Office Assistant, Student Services, Pratt Community College, 348 Northeast State Road 61, Pratt, KS 67124. *Phone:* 620-450-2217. *Toll-free phone:* 800-794-3091. *Fax:* 620-672-5288. *E-mail:* theresaz@prattcc.edu. *Web site:* http://www.prattcc.edu/.

Seward County Community College
Liberal, Kansas

Director of Admissions Dr. Gerald Harris, Dean of Student Services, Seward County Community College, PO Box 1137, Liberal, KS 67905-1137. *Phone:* 620-624-1951 Ext. 617. *Toll-free phone:* 800-373-9951. *Web site:* http://www.sccc.edu/.

Wichita Area Technical College
Wichita, Kansas

Freshman Application Contact Ms. Jessica Ross, Dean, Enrollment Management, Wichita Area Technical College, Wichita, KS 67211-2099. *Phone:* 316-677-9400. *Fax:* 316-677-9555. *E-mail:* info@watc.edu. *Web site:* http://www.wichitatech.com/.

KENTUCKY

Ashland Community and Technical College
Ashland, Kentucky

Freshman Application Contact Ashland Community and Technical College, 1400 College Drive, Ashland, KY 41101-3683. *Phone:* 606-326-2008. *Toll-free phone:* 800-928-4256. *Web site:* http://www.ashland.kctcs.edu/.

ATA College
Louisville, Kentucky

Freshman Application Contact Admissions Office, ATA College, 10180 Linn Station Road, Suite A200, Louisville, KY 40223. *Phone:* 502-371-8330. *Fax:* 502-371-8598. *Web site:* http://www.ata.edu/.

Beckfield College
Florence, Kentucky

Freshman Application Contact Mrs. Leah Boerger, Director of Admissions, Beckfield College, 16 Spiral Drive, Florence, KY 41042. *Phone:* 859-371-9393. *E-mail:* lboerger@beckfield.edu. *Web site:* http://www.beckfield.edu/.

Big Sandy Community and Technical College
Prestonsburg, Kentucky

Director of Admissions Jimmy Wright, Director of Admissions, Big Sandy Community and Technical College, One Bert T. Combs Drive, Prestonsburg, KY 41653-1815. *Phone:* 606-886-3863. *Toll-free phone:* 888-641-4132. *E-mail:* jimmy.wright@kctcs.edu. *Web site:* http://www.bigsandy.kctcs.edu/.

Bluegrass Community and Technical College
Lexington, Kentucky

- **State-supported** 2-year, founded 1965, part of Kentucky Community and Technical College System
- **Urban** 10-acre campus
- **Endowment** $967,117
- **Coed,** 11,596 undergraduate students, 48% full-time, 56% women, 44% men

Undergraduates 5,539 full-time, 6,057 part-time. Students come from 16 states and territories; 26 other countries; 13% Black or African American, non-

Hispanic/Latino; 3% Hispanic/Latino; 1% Asian, non-Hispanic/Latino; 0.1% Native Hawaiian or other Pacific Islander, non-Hispanic/Latino; 0.3% American Indian or Alaska Native, non-Hispanic/Latino; 2% Two or more races, non-Hispanic/Latino; 2% Race/ethnicity unknown; 0.5% international; 4% transferred in; 3% live on campus.

Freshmen *Admission:* 1,889 enrolled.

Faculty *Total:* 846, 31% full-time. *Student/faculty ratio:* 18:1.

Majors Architectural drafting and CAD/CADD; automobile/automotive mechanics technology; business administration and management; carpentry; child-care provision; civil engineering technology; computer and information sciences; data processing and data processing technology; dental hygiene; dental laboratory technology; electrical, electronic and communications engineering technology; electrician; engineering technology; environmental engineering technology; executive assistant/executive secretary; fire science/firefighting; heating, air conditioning, ventilation and refrigeration maintenance technology; industrial electronics technology; industrial mechanics and maintenance technology; liberal arts and sciences/liberal studies; machine shop technology; medical administrative assistant and medical secretary; medical/clinical assistant; medical radiologic technology; multi/interdisciplinary studies related; nuclear medical technology; registered nursing/registered nurse; respiratory care therapy; surgical technology; teacher assistant/aide; welding technology.

Academics *Calendar:* semesters. *Degree:* certificates, diplomas, and associate. *Special study options:* academic remediation for entering students, accelerated degree program, adult/continuing education programs, advanced placement credit, cooperative education, distance learning, double majors, English as a second language, honors programs, part-time degree program, services for LD students, summer session for credit. *ROTC:* Army (c), Air Force (c).

Library Bluegrass Community and Technical College Library with 27,000 titles, 250 serial subscriptions, an OPAC, a Web page.

Student Life *Housing:* college housing not available. *Options:* coed. Campus housing is provided by a third party. Freshman applicants given priority for college housing. *Activities and Organizations:* drama/theater group, student-run newspaper, choral group, Student Nursing Association, intramural sports, Enlace (Latino Student Association), International Students' Association, Student American Dental Hygienists Association. *Campus security:* 24-hour emergency response devices and patrols, late-night transport/escort service. *Student services:* personal/psychological counseling.

Athletics *Intramural sports:* basketball M/W, soccer M/W.

Costs (2012–13) *Tuition:* state resident $3240 full-time, $135 per credit part-time; nonresident $11,160 full-time, $465 per credit part-time. *Required fees:* $50 full-time, $25 per term part-time. *Waivers:* senior citizens and employees or children of employees.

Applying *Options:* electronic application, early admission. *Application fee:* $20. *Required for some:* high school transcript. *Recommended:* high school transcript. *Application deadlines:* 8/2 (freshmen), 8/2 (transfers).

Freshman Application Contact Mrs. Shelbie Hugle, Director of Admission Services, Bluegrass Community and Technical College, 470 Cooper Drive, Lexington, KY 40506. *Phone:* 859-246-6216. *Toll-free phone:* 800-744-4872 (in-state); 866-744-4872 (out-of-state). *E-mail:* shelbie.hugle@kctcs.edu. *Web site:* http://www.bluegrass.kctcs.edu/.

Bowling Green Technical College
Bowling Green, Kentucky

Director of Admissions Mark Garrett, Chief Student Affairs Officer, Bowling Green Technical College, 1845 Loop Drive, Bowling Green, KY 42101. *Phone:* 270-901-1114. *Toll-free phone:* 800-790-0990. *Web site:* http://www.bowlinggreen.kctcs.edu/.

Brown Mackie College–Hopkinsville
Hopkinsville, Kentucky

- **Proprietary** 2-year, part of Education Management Corporation
- **Small-town** campus
- **Coed**

Academics *Calendar:* quarters. *Degree:* diplomas and associate.

Costs (2011–12) *Tuition:* Tuition varies by program. Students should contact Brown Mackie College for tuition information.

Freshman Application Contact Brown Mackie College–Hopkinsville, 4001 Fort Cambell Boulevard, Hopkinsville, KY 42240. *Phone:* 270-886-1302. *Toll-free phone:* 800-359-4753. *Web site:* http://www.brownmackie.edu/Hopkinsville/.

See page 358 for the College Close-Up.

Brown Mackie College–Louisville

Louisville, Kentucky

- **Proprietary** primarily 2-year, founded 1972, part of Education Management Corporation
- **Suburban** campus
- **Coed**

Academics *Calendar:* quarters. *Degrees:* certificates, diplomas, associate, and bachelor's.

Costs (2011–12) *Tuition:* Tuition varies by program. Students should contact Brown Mackie College for tuition information.

Freshman Application Contact Brown Mackie College–Louisville, 3605 Fern Valley Road, Louisville, KY 40219. *Phone:* 502-968-7191. *Toll-free phone:* 800-999-7387. *Web site:* http://www.brownmackie.edu/louisville/.

See page 364 for the College Close-Up.

Brown Mackie College–Northern Kentucky

Fort Mitchell, Kentucky

- **Proprietary** primarily 2-year, founded 1927, part of Education Management Corporation
- **Suburban** campus
- **Coed**

Academics *Calendar:* quarters. *Degrees:* certificates, diplomas, associate, and bachelor's.

Costs (2011–12) *Tuition:* Tuition varies by program. Students should contact Brown Mackie College for tuition information.

Freshman Application Contact Brown Mackie College–Northern Kentucky, 309 Buttermilk Pike, Fort Mitchell, KY 41017-2191. *Phone:* 859-341-5627. *Toll-free phone:* 800-888-1445. *Web site:* http://www.brownmackie.edu/northernkentucky/.

See page 374 for the College Close-Up.

Daymar College

Bellevue, Kentucky

Freshman Application Contact Cathy Baird, Director of Admissions, Daymar College, 119 Fairfield Avenue, Bellevue, KY 41073. *Phone:* 859-291-0800. *Toll-free phone:* 877-258-7796. *Fax:* 859-491-7500. *Web site:* http://www.daymarcollege.edu/.

Daymar College

Bowling Green, Kentucky

Freshman Application Contact Mrs. Traci Henderson, Admissions Director, Daymar College, 2421 Fitzgerald Industrial Drive, Bowling Green, KY 42101. *Phone:* 270-843-6750. *Toll-free phone:* 877-258-7796. *E-mail:* thenderson@daymarcollege.edu. *Web site:* http://www.daymarcollege.edu/.

Daymar College

Louisville, Kentucky

Director of Admissions Mr. Patrick Carney, Director of Admissions, Daymar College, 4400 Breckenridge Lane, Suite 415, Louisville, KY 40218. *Toll-free phone:* 877-258-7796. *Web site:* http://www.daymarcollege.edu/.

Daymar College

Owensboro, Kentucky

Freshman Application Contact Ms. Vickie McDougal, Director of Admissions, Daymar College, 3361 Buckland Square, Owensboro, KY 42301. *Phone:* 270-926-4040. *Toll-free phone:* 877-258-7796. *Fax:* 270-685-4090. *E-mail:* info@daymarcollege.edu. *Web site:* http://www.daymarcollege.edu/.

Daymar College

Paducah, Kentucky

Freshman Application Contact Daymar College, 509 South 30th Street, Paducah, KY 42001. *Phone:* 270-444-9950. *Toll-free phone:* 877-258-7796. *Web site:* http://www.daymarcollege.edu/.

Elizabethtown Community and Technical College

Elizabethtown, Kentucky

Freshman Application Contact Elizabethtown Community and Technical College, 620 College Street Road, Elizabethtown, KY 42701. *Phone:* 270-706-8800. *Toll-free phone:* 877-246-2322. *Web site:* http://www.elizabethtown.kctcs.edu/.

Gateway Community and Technical College

Covington, Kentucky

- **State-supported** 2-year, founded 1961, part of Kentucky Community and Technical College System
- **Suburban** campus with easy access to Cincinnati
- **Coed**

Undergraduates 10% Black or African American, non-Hispanic/Latino; 2% Hispanic/Latino; 0.4% Asian, non-Hispanic/Latino; 0.2% Native Hawaiian or other Pacific Islander, non-Hispanic/Latino; 0.3% American Indian or Alaska Native, non-Hispanic/Latino; 1% Two or more races, non-Hispanic/Latino; 1% Race/ethnicity unknown.

Faculty *Student/faculty ratio:* 19:1.

Academics *Calendar:* semesters. *Degree:* certificates, diplomas, and associate. *Special study options:* academic remediation for entering students, cooperative education, distance learning, internships, part-time degree program, services for LD students, summer session for credit.

Standardized Tests *Required:* ACT or ACT COMPASS (for admission).

Costs (2011–12) *Tuition:* state resident $3240 full-time, $135 per credit hour part-time; nonresident $11,160 full-time, $465 per credit hour part-time. Full-time tuition and fees vary according to course load. Part-time tuition and fees vary according to course load. No tuition increase for student's term of enrollment. *Required fees:* $40 per term part-time.

Applying *Options:* electronic application, early admission. *Required:* high school transcript.

Freshman Application Contact Gateway Community and Technical College, 1025 Amsterdam Road, Covington, KY 41011. *Phone:* 859-442-4176. *E-mail:* andre.washington@kctcs.edu. *Web site:* http://www.gateway.kctcs.edu/.

Hazard Community and Technical College

Hazard, Kentucky

Freshman Application Contact Director of Admissions, Hazard Community and Technical College, 1 Community College Drive, Hazard, KY 41701-2403. *Phone:* 606-487-3102. *Toll-free phone:* 800-246-7521. *Web site:* http://www.hazard.kctcs.edu/.

Henderson Community College

Henderson, Kentucky

Freshman Application Contact Ms. Teresa Hamiton, Admissions Counselor, Henderson Community College, 2660 South Green Street, Henderson, KY 42420-4623. *Phone:* 270-827-1867 Ext. 354. *Toll-free phone:* 800-696-9958. *Web site:* http://www.henderson.kctcs.edu/.

Hopkinsville Community College

Hopkinsville, Kentucky

Freshman Application Contact Ms. Janet Level, Student Records, Hopkinsville Community College, Room 135, English Education Center, 202 Bastogne Avenue, Fort Campbell, KY. *Phone:* 270-707-3918. *Toll-free phone:* 866-534-2224. *Fax:* 270-707-3973. *E-mail:* janet.level@kctcs.edu. *Web site:* http://hopkinsville.kctcs.edu/.

ITT Technical Institute

Louisville, Kentucky

- **Proprietary** primarily 2-year, founded 1993, part of ITT Educational Services, Inc.
- **Suburban** campus
- **Coed**

Majors Business administration and management; communications technology; computer and information systems security; computer software and media applications related; computer software technology; construction management;

criminal justice/law enforcement administration; drafting and design technology; electrical, electronic and communications engineering technology; game and interactive media design; graphic communications; legal assistant/paralegal; network and system administration; project management; registered nursing/registered nurse.

Academics *Calendar:* quarters. *Degrees:* associate and bachelor's.

Student Life *Housing:* college housing not available.

Freshman Application Contact Director of Recruitment, ITT Technical Institute, 9500 Ormsby Station Road, Suite 100, Louisville, KY 40223. *Phone:* 502-327-7424. *Toll-free phone:* 888-790-7427. *Web site:* http://www.itt-tech.edu/.

Jefferson Community and Technical College

Louisville, Kentucky

Freshman Application Contact Ms. Melanie Vaughan-Cooke, Admissions Coordinator, Jefferson Community and Technical College, Louisville, KY 40202. *Phone:* 502-213-4000. *Fax:* 502-213-2540. *Web site:* http://www.jefferson.kctcs.edu/.

Lincoln College of Technology

Florence, Kentucky

Freshman Application Contact Director of Admission, Lincoln College of Technology, 8095 Connector Drive, Florence, KY 41042. *Phone:* 859-282-9999. *Web site:* http://www.lincolnedu.com/.

Madisonville Community College

Madisonville, Kentucky

Director of Admissions Mr. Jay Parent, Registrar, Madisonville Community College, 2000 College Drive, Madisonville, KY 42431-9185. *Phone:* 270-821-2250. *Web site:* http://www.madcc.kctcs.edu/.

Maysville Community and Technical College

Maysville, Kentucky

Director of Admissions Ms. Patee Massie, Registrar, Maysville Community and Technical College, 1755 US 68, Maysville, KY 41056. *Phone:* 606-759-7141. *Fax:* 606-759-5818. *E-mail:* ccsmayrg@ukcc.uky.edu. *Web site:* http://www.maysville.kctcs.edu/.

Maysville Community and Technical College

Morehead, Kentucky

Director of Admissions Patee Massie, Registrar, Maysville Community and Technical College, 609 Viking Drive, Morehead, KY 40351. *Phone:* 606-759-7141 Ext. 66184. *Web site:* http://www.maysville.kctcs.edu/.

National College

Danville, Kentucky

Director of Admissions James McGuire, Campus Director, National College, 115 East Lexington Avenue, Danville, KY 40422. *Phone:* 859-236-6991. *Toll-free phone:* 888-9-JOBREADY. *Web site:* http://www.national-college.edu/.

National College

Florence, Kentucky

Director of Admissions Mr. Terry Kovacs, Campus Director, National College, 7627 Ewing Boulevard, Florence, KY 41042. *Phone:* 859-525-6510. *Toll-free phone:* 888-9-JOBREADY. *Web site:* http://www.national-college.edu/.

National College

Lexington, Kentucky

Director of Admissions Kim Thomasson, Campus Director, National College, 2376 Sir Barton Way, Lexington, KY 40509. *Phone:* 859-253-0621. *Toll-free phone:* 888-9-JOBREADY. *Web site:* http://www.national-college.edu/.

National College

Louisville, Kentucky

Director of Admissions Vincent C. Tinebra, Campus Director, National College, 3950 Dixie Highway, Louisville, KY 40216. *Phone:* 502-447-7634. *Toll-free phone:* 888-9-JOBREADY. *Web site:* http://www.national-college.edu/.

National College

Pikeville, Kentucky

Director of Admissions Tammy Riley, Campus Director, National College, 288 South Mayo Trail, Suite 2, Pikeville, KY 41501. *Phone:* 606-478-7200. *Toll-free phone:* 888-9-JOBREADY. *Web site:* http://www.national-college.edu/.

National College

Richmond, Kentucky

Director of Admissions Ms. Keeley Gadd, Campus Director, National College, 139 South Killarney Lane, Richmond, KY 40475. *Phone:* 859-623-8956. *Toll-free phone:* 888-9-JOBREADY. *Web site:* http://www.national-college.edu/.

Owensboro Community and Technical College

Owensboro, Kentucky

- **State-supported** 2-year, founded 1986, part of Kentucky Community and Technical College System
- **Suburban** 102-acre campus
- **Coed,** 7,095 undergraduate students, 29% full-time, 53% women, 47% men

Undergraduates 2,074 full-time, 5,021 part-time. Students come from 7 states and territories; 1 other country; 2% are from out of state; 5% Black or African American, non-Hispanic/Latino; 1% Hispanic/Latino; 0.3% Asian, non-Hispanic/Latino; 0.1% Native Hawaiian or other Pacific Islander, non-Hispanic/Latino; 0.2% American Indian or Alaska Native, non-Hispanic/Latino; 1% Two or more races, non-Hispanic/Latino; 0.4% Race/ethnicity unknown.

Freshmen *Admission:* 725 enrolled.

Faculty *Total:* 212, 46% full-time, 9% with terminal degrees. *Student/faculty ratio:* 28:1.

Majors Agriculture; business administration and management; computer and information sciences; computer/information technology services administration related; criminal justice/police science; data entry/microcomputer applications; diagnostic medical sonography and ultrasound technology; electrical, electronic and communications engineering technology; executive assistant/executive secretary; fire science/firefighting; human services; information technology; kindergarten/preschool education; liberal arts and sciences/liberal studies; medical radiologic technology; network and system administration; precision production trades; registered nursing/registered nurse; social work; word processing.

Academics *Calendar:* semesters. *Degree:* certificates, diplomas, and associate. *Special study options:* academic remediation for entering students, adult/continuing education programs, advanced placement credit, cooperative education, distance learning, double majors, English as a second language, external degree program, honors programs, independent study, off-campus study, part-time degree program, services for LD students, student-designed majors, study abroad, summer session for credit.

Library Learning Resource Center with 25,600 titles, 24,614 serial subscriptions, an OPAC, a Web page.

Student Life *Activities and Organizations:* drama/theater group, student-run newspaper, radio and television station, choral group, Student Government Association. *Campus security:* 24-hour emergency response devices, late-night transport/escort service.

Standardized Tests *Recommended:* SAT or ACT (for admission).

Costs (2012–13) *Tuition:* state resident $3240 full-time, $135 per credit part-time; nonresident $11,160 full-time, $465 per credit part-time. Full-time tuition and fees vary according to reciprocity agreements. Part-time tuition and fees vary according to reciprocity agreements. *Payment plan:* installment. *Waivers:* senior citizens and employees or children of employees.

Financial Aid Of all full-time matriculated undergraduates who enrolled in 2011, 46 Federal Work-Study jobs (averaging $5760). *Financial aid deadline:* 4/1.

Applying *Options:* electronic application. *Required:* high school transcript. *Application deadlines:* rolling (freshmen), rolling (transfers). *Notification:* continuous (freshmen), continuous (transfers).

Freshman Application Contact Ms. Barbara Tipmore, Admissions Counselor, Owensboro Community and Technical College, 4800 New Hartford Road, Owensboro, KY 42303. *Phone:* 270-686-4530. *Toll-free phone:* 866-755-6282. *E-mail:* barb.tipmore@kctcs.edu. *Web site:* http://www.octc.kctcs.edu/.

Somerset Community College

Somerset, Kentucky

Freshman Application Contact Director of Admission, Somerset Community College, 808 Monticello Street, Somerset, KY 42501-2973. *Phone:* 606-451-6630. *Toll-free phone:* 877-629-9722. *E-mail:* somerset-admissions@kctcs.edu. *Web site:* http://www.somerset.kctcs.edu/.

Southeast Kentucky Community and Technical College

Cumberland, Kentucky

Freshman Application Contact Southeast Kentucky Community and Technical College, 700 College Road, Cumberland, KY 40823-1099. *Phone:* 606-589-2145 Ext. 13018. *Toll-free phone:* 888-274-SECC. *Web site:* http://www.southeast.kctcs.edu/.

Spencerian College

Louisville, Kentucky

- **Proprietary** 2-year, founded 1892
- **Urban** 10-acre campus
- **Coed, primarily women,** 1,012 undergraduate students, 67% full-time, 86% women, 14% men

Undergraduates 675 full-time, 337 part-time. 21% Black or African American, non-Hispanic/Latino; 2% Hispanic/Latino; 0.4% Asian, non-Hispanic/Latino; 0.3% Native Hawaiian or other Pacific Islander, non-Hispanic/Latino; 14% Two or more races, non-Hispanic/Latino; 2% Race/ethnicity unknown; 1% live on campus.

Freshmen *Admission:* 266 admitted, 266 enrolled.

Faculty *Total:* 101, 47% full-time, 5% with terminal degrees. *Student/faculty ratio:* 14:1.

Majors Accounting; accounting and business/management; accounting technology and bookkeeping; business administration and management; cardiovascular technology; clinical/medical laboratory technology; massage therapy; medical insurance/medical billing; office management; radiologic technology/science; registered nursing/registered nurse; respiratory care therapy; surgical technology.

Academics *Calendar:* quarters. *Degree:* certificates, diplomas, and associate. *Special study options:* distance learning, internships, off-campus study, summer session for credit.

Library Spencerian College Learning Resource Center with 1,650 titles, 31,000 serial subscriptions, 277 audiovisual materials, an OPAC, a Web page.

Student Life *Housing Options:* coed. Campus housing is university owned.

Costs (2011–12) *Comprehensive fee:* $25,780 includes full-time tuition ($15,870), mandatory fees ($2170), and room and board ($7740). Full-time tuition and fees vary according to class time and program. Part-time tuition: $265 per credit hour. Part-time tuition and fees vary according to class time and program. *Required fees:* $50 per course part-time. *Room and board:* college room only: $5355. *Payment plan:* installment. *Waivers:* employees or children of employees.

Applying *Application fee:* $100. *Required:* high school transcript. *Required for some:* essay or personal statement, interview. *Notification:* continuous (freshmen), continuous (out-of-state freshmen), continuous (transfers).

Freshman Application Contact Spencerian College, 4627 Dixie Highway, Louisville, KY 40216. *Phone:* 502-447-1000 Ext. 7808. *Toll-free phone:* 800-264-1799. *Web site:* http://www.spencerian.edu/.

Spencerian College–Lexington

Lexington, Kentucky

Freshman Application Contact Spencerian College–Lexington, 1575 Winchester Road, Lexington, KY 40505. *Phone:* 859-223-9608 Ext. 5430. *Toll-free phone:* 800-456-3253. *Web site:* http://www.spencerian.edu/.

Sullivan College of Technology and Design

Louisville, Kentucky

- **Proprietary** primarily 2-year, founded 1961, part of The Sullivan University System, Inc.
- **Suburban** 10-acre campus with easy access to Louisville
- **Coed,** 582 undergraduate students, 62% full-time, 34% women, 66% men

Undergraduates 360 full-time, 222 part-time. Students come from 16 states and territories; 5 other countries; 15% are from out of state; 20% Black or African American, non-Hispanic/Latino; 4% Hispanic/Latino; 0.7% Asian, non-Hispanic/Latino; 0.2% Native Hawaiian or other Pacific Islander, non-Hispanic/Latino; 7% Two or more races, non-Hispanic/Latino; 4% transferred in; 6% live on campus. *Retention:* 72% of full-time freshmen returned.

Freshmen *Admission:* 323 applied, 151 admitted, 121 enrolled.

Faculty *Total:* 81, 42% full-time. *Student/faculty ratio:* 12:1.

Majors Animation, interactive technology, video graphics and special effects; architectural drafting and CAD/CADD; architectural engineering technology; architecture related; artificial intelligence; CAD/CADD drafting/design technology; civil drafting and CAD/CADD; computer and information sciences; computer and information sciences and support services related; computer and information systems security; computer engineering technology; computer graphics; computer hardware engineering; computer hardware technology; computer installation and repair technology; computer programming (vendor/product certification); computer systems networking and telecommunications; computer technology/computer systems technology; desktop publishing and digital imaging design; digital communication and media/multimedia; drafting and design technology; drafting/design engineering technologies related; electrical and electronic engineering technologies related; electrical, electronic and communications engineering technology; electrical/electronics equipment installation and repair; electrical/electronics maintenance and repair technology related; electromechanical and instrumentation and maintenance technologies related; engineering technologies and engineering related; engineering technology; graphic and printing equipment operation/production; graphic communications; graphic communications related; graphic design; heating, ventilation, air conditioning and refrigeration engineering technology; housing and human environments; industrial electronics technology; industrial mechanics and maintenance technology; information technology; interior design; manufacturing engineering technology; mechanical drafting and CAD/CADD; mechanical engineering/mechanical technology; network and system administration; robotics technology; web page, digital/multimedia and information resources design.

Academics *Calendar:* quarters. *Degrees:* certificates, diplomas, associate, and bachelor's. *Special study options:* academic remediation for entering students, accelerated degree program, adult/continuing education programs, advanced placement credit, double majors, independent study, internships, part-time degree program, services for LD students, summer session for credit.

Library Sullivan College of Technology and Design Library with 2,576 titles, 65 serial subscriptions, 199 audiovisual materials, an OPAC, a Web page.

Student Life *Housing Options:* coed. Campus housing is university owned and leased by the school. Freshman campus housing is guaranteed. *Activities and Organizations:* ASID, IIDA, ADDA, ADFED, Skills USA. *Campus security:* late-night transport/escort service, controlled dormitory access, telephone alarm device during hours school is open; patrols by trained security personnel while classes are in session.

Standardized Tests *Required:* Career Performance Assessment Test (CPAt) or ACT or SAT scores in place of CPAt results (for admission). *Recommended:* SAT or ACT (for admission).

Costs (2012–13) *Tuition:* $16,890 full-time. Full-time tuition and fees vary according to course load, degree level, and program. Part-time tuition and fees vary according to course load, degree level, and program. No tuition increase for student's term of enrollment. *Room only:* Room and board charges vary according to board plan. *Payment plan:* installment. *Waivers:* employees or children of employees.

Applying *Options:* electronic application, deferred entrance. *Application fee:* $100. *Required:* high school transcript, interview. *Application deadlines:* rolling (freshmen), rolling (out-of-state freshmen), rolling (transfers). *Notification:* continuous (freshmen), continuous (out-of-state freshmen), continuous (transfers).

Freshman Application Contact Mr. Aamer Z. Chauhdri, Director of Admissions, Sullivan College of Technology and Design, 3901 Atkinson Square Drive, Louisville, KY 40218. *Phone:* 502-456-6509 Ext. 8220. *Toll-free phone:* 800-884-6528. *Fax:* 502-456-2341. *E-mail:* achauhdri@sctd.edu. *Web site:* http://www.sctd.edu/.

West Kentucky Community and Technical College

Paducah, Kentucky

- **State-supported** 2-year, founded 1932, part of Kentucky Community and Technical College System
- **Small-town** 117-acre campus
- **Coed,** 5,709 undergraduate students, 44% full-time, 57% women, 43% men

Undergraduates 2,527 full-time, 3,182 part-time. Students come from 20 states and territories; 1 other country; 6% are from out of state; 7% Black or African American, non-Hispanic/Latino; 2% Hispanic/Latino; 0.6% Asian, non-Hispanic/Latino; 0.1% Native Hawaiian or other Pacific Islander, non-Hispanic/Latino; 0.4% American Indian or Alaska Native, non-Hispanic/Latino; 1% Two or more races, non-Hispanic/Latino; 6% Race/ethnicity unknown; 12% transferred in. *Retention:* 60% of full-time freshmen returned.
Freshmen *Admission:* 754 enrolled. *Test scores:* ACT scores over 18: 91%; ACT scores over 24: 37%; ACT scores over 30: 7%.
Majors Accounting; business administration and management; computer and information sciences; court reporting; criminal justice/law enforcement administration; culinary arts; diagnostic medical sonography and ultrasound technology; electrician; fire science/firefighting; machine shop technology; physical therapy technology; registered nursing/registered nurse; respiratory care therapy; surgical technology.
Academics *Calendar:* semesters. *Degree:* certificates, diplomas, and associate. *Special study options:* academic remediation for entering students, adult/continuing education programs, cooperative education, distance learning, English as a second language, honors programs, independent study, internships, part-time degree program, study abroad.
Library WKCTC Matheson Library with 74,676 titles, 155 serial subscriptions, 5,043 audiovisual materials, an OPAC, a Web page.
Student Life *Housing:* college housing not available. *Activities and Organizations:* drama/theater group, choral group. *Campus security:* late-night transport/escort service, 14-hour patrols by trained security personnel.
Athletics *Intramural sports:* basketball M/W, golf M/W, soccer M/W, volleyball M/W.
Standardized Tests *Required:* SAT or ACT (for admission). *Recommended:* ACT (for admission).
Costs (2011–12) *Tuition:* state resident $4050 full-time, $135 per credit hour part-time; nonresident $13,950 full-time, $465 per credit hour part-time. *Waivers:* senior citizens and employees or children of employees.
Financial Aid Of all full-time matriculated undergraduates who enrolled in 2010, 50 Federal Work-Study jobs (averaging $1650).
Applying *Options:* early admission. *Required for some:* high school transcript. *Application deadlines:* rolling (freshmen), rolling (transfers).
Freshman Application Contact Mr. Jerry Anderson, Admissions Counselor, West Kentucky Community and Technical College, 4810 Alben Barkley Drive, Paducah, KY 42002-7380. *Phone:* 270-554-3266. *E-mail:* jerry.anderson@kctcs.edu. *Web site:* http://www.westkentucky.kctcs.edu/.

LOUISIANA

Baton Rouge Community College

Baton Rouge, Louisiana

Director of Admissions Nancy Clay, Interim Executive Director for Enrollment Services, Baton Rouge Community College, 5310 Florida Boulevard, Baton Rouge, LA 70806. *Phone:* 225-216-8700. *Toll-free phone:* 800-601-4558. *Web site:* http://www.mybrcc.edu/.

Baton Rouge School of Computers

Baton Rouge, Louisiana

Freshman Application Contact Admissions Office, Baton Rouge School of Computers, 10425 Plaza Americana, Baton Rouge, LA 70816. *Phone:* 225-923-2524. *Toll-free phone:* 888-920-BRSC. *Fax:* 225-923-2979. *E-mail:* admissions@brsc.net. *Web site:* http://www.brsc.edu/.

Blue Cliff College–Lafayette

Lafayette, Louisiana

Freshman Application Contact Admissions Office, Blue Cliff College–Lafayette, 100 Asma Boulevard, Suite 350, Lafayette, LA 70508-3862. *Toll-free phone:* 800-514-2609. *Web site:* http://www.bluecliffcollege.com/.

Blue Cliff College–Shreveport

Shreveport, Louisiana

Freshman Application Contact Blue Cliff College–Shreveport, 8731 Park Plaza Drive, Shreveport, LA 71105. *Toll-free phone:* 800-516-6597. *Web site:* http://www.bluecliffcollege.com/.

Bossier Parish Community College

Bossier City, Louisiana

Freshman Application Contact Ms. Ann Jampole, Director of Admissions, Bossier Parish Community College, 2719 Airline Drive North, Bossier City, LA 71111-5801. *Phone:* 318-678-6166. *Fax:* 318-742-8664. *Web site:* http://www.bpcc.edu/.

Camelot College

Baton Rouge, Louisiana

Freshman Application Contact Camelot College, 2618 Wooddale Boulevard, Suite A, Baton Rouge, LA 70805. *Phone:* 225-928-3005. *Toll-free phone:* 800-470-3320. *Web site:* http://www.camelotcollege.com/.

Cameron College

New Orleans, Louisiana

Admissions Office Contact Cameron College, 2740 Canal Street, New Orleans, LA 70119. *Web site:* http://www.cameroncollege.com/.

Capital Area Technical College–Baton Rouge Campus

Baton Rouge, Louisiana

Freshman Application Contact Ms. Amber Aguillard, Admissions Officer, Capital Area Technical College–Baton Rouge Campus, 3250 North Acadian Thruway, East, Baton Rouge, LA 70805. *Phone:* 225-359-9263. *Fax:* 225-359-9354. *E-mail:* aaguillard@ltc.edu. *Web site:* http://region2.ltc.edu/.

Career Technical College

Monroe, Louisiana

- **Proprietary** 2-year, founded 1985, part of Delta Career Education Corporation
- **Small-town** campus with easy access to Shreveport
- **Coed,** 756 undergraduate students, 73% full-time, 73% women, 27% men

Undergraduates 550 full-time, 206 part-time. Students come from 3 states and territories; 1% are from out of state; 54% Black or African American, non-Hispanic/Latino; 0.7% Hispanic/Latino; 0.4% Asian, non-Hispanic/Latino; 0.3% Native Hawaiian or other Pacific Islander, non-Hispanic/Latino; 0.3% American Indian or Alaska Native, non-Hispanic/Latino; 0.5% Two or more races, non-Hispanic/Latino; 0.7% Race/ethnicity unknown; 9% transferred in. *Retention:* 90% of full-time freshmen returned.
Freshmen *Admission:* 756 enrolled. *Average high school GPA:* 2.5.
Faculty *Total:* 41, 66% full-time. *Student/faculty ratio:* 20:1.
Majors Administrative assistant and secretarial science; business administration and management; computer and information sciences and support services related; corrections and criminal justice related; legal administrative assistant/secretary; management science; massage therapy; medical/clinical assistant; medical office management; radiologic technology/science; respiratory therapy technician; surgical technology.
Academics *Calendar:* quarters. *Degree:* diplomas and associate. *Special study options:* academic remediation for entering students, adult/continuing education programs, advanced placement credit, cooperative education, double majors, independent study, internships.
Library Library & Information Resources Network.
Student Life *Housing:* college housing not available. *Activities and Organizations:* student-run newspaper, MAC Club, Scrub Club, Ambassadors, Rad Tech Club, Resp Therapy Club. *Campus security:* 24-hour emergency response devices, late-night transport/escort service, evening security guard.
Standardized Tests *Required:* SLE-Wonderlic Scholastic Level Exam; Math Proficiency Exam; English Proficiency Exam (for admission).
Costs (2012–13) *One-time required fee:* $120. *Tuition:* $8532 full-time, $237 per credit part-time. Full-time tuition and fees vary according to course load and program. Part-time tuition and fees vary according to course load and program. No tuition increase for student's term of enrollment. *Required fees:* $1275 full-time. *Payment plans:* tuition prepayment, installment. *Waivers:* employees or children of employees.

Applying *Options:* deferred entrance. *Application fee:* $40. *Required:* high school transcript, interview. *Application deadlines:* rolling (freshmen), rolling (out-of-state freshmen), rolling (transfers). *Notification:* continuous (freshmen), continuous (out-of-state freshmen), continuous (transfers).
Freshman Application Contact Mrs. Susan Boudreaux, Admissions Office, Career Technical College, 2319 Louisville Avenue, Monroe, LA 71201. *Phone:* 318-323-2889. *Toll-free phone:* 800-923-1947. *Fax:* 318-324-9883. *E-mail:* susan.boudreaux@careertc.edu. *Web site:* http://www.careertc.edu/.

Delgado Community College

New Orleans, Louisiana

Freshman Application Contact Ms. Gwen Boute, Director of Admissions, Delgado Community College, 501 City Park Avenue, New Orleans, LA 70119-4399. *Phone:* 504-671-5010. *Fax:* 504-483-1895. *E-mail:* enroll@dcc.edu. *Web site:* http://www.dcc.edu/.

Delta College of Arts and Technology

Baton Rouge, Louisiana

Freshman Application Contact Ms. Beulah Laverghe-Brown, Admissions Director, Delta College of Arts and Technology, 7380 Exchange Place, Baton Rouge, LA 70806-3851. *Phone:* 225-928-7770. *Fax:* 225-927-9096. *E-mail:* bbrown@deltacollege.com. *Web site:* http://www.deltacollege.com/.

Delta School of Business & Technology

Lake Charles, Louisiana

Freshman Application Contact Jeffery Tibodeaux, Director of Admissions, Delta School of Business & Technology, 517 Broad Street, Lake Charles, LA 70601. *Phone:* 337-439-5765. *Web site:* http://www.deltatech.edu/.

Elaine P. Nunez Community College

Chalmette, Louisiana

- **State-supported** 2-year, founded 1992, part of Louisiana Community and Technical College System
- **Suburban** 20-acre campus with easy access to New Orleans
- **Endowment** $1.2 million
- **Coed**

Undergraduates 879 full-time, 1,534 part-time. 14% transferred in. *Retention:* 59% of full-time freshmen returned.
Faculty *Student/faculty ratio:* 25:1.
Academics *Calendar:* semesters. *Degree:* certificates, diplomas, and associate. *Special study options:* academic remediation for entering students, adult/continuing education programs, advanced placement credit, cooperative education, distance learning, double majors, independent study, internships, off-campus study, part-time degree program, services for LD students, student-designed majors, summer session for credit.
Student Life *Campus security:* 24-hour emergency response devices, late-night transport/escort service, security cameras.
Standardized Tests *Recommended:* ACT (for admission).
Costs (2011–12) *Tuition:* state resident $2606 full-time; nonresident $5448 full-time. Part-time tuition and fees vary according to course load. *Required fees:* $494 full-time.
Financial Aid Of all full-time matriculated undergraduates who enrolled in 2010, 70 Federal Work-Study jobs (averaging $1452).
Applying *Options:* early admission, deferred entrance. *Application fee:* $10. *Required for some:* high school transcript.
Freshman Application Contact Mrs. Becky Maillet, Elaine P. Nunez Community College, 3710 Paris Road, Chalmette, LA 70043. *Phone:* 504-278-6477. *E-mail:* bmaillet@nunez.edu. *Web site:* http://www.nunez.edu/.

Fletcher Technical Community College

Houma, Louisiana

Director of Admissions Admissions Office, Fletcher Technical Community College, 310 St. Charles Street, Houma, LA 70360. *Phone:* 985-857-3659. *Web site:* http://www.ftcc.edu/.

Fortis College

Baton Rouge, Louisiana

Director of Admissions Ms. Sheri Kirley, Associate Director of Admissions, Fortis College, 9255 Interline Avenue, Baton Rouge, LA 70809. *Phone:* 225-248-1015. *Web site:* http://www.fortis.edu/.

Gretna Career College

Gretna, Louisiana

Freshman Application Contact Admissions Office, Gretna Career College, 1415 Whitney Avenue, Gretna, LA 70053-5835. *Phone:* 504-366-5409. *Fax:* 504-365-1004. *Web site:* http://gccla.edu/.

ITI Technical College

Baton Rouge, Louisiana

- **Proprietary** 2-year, founded 1973
- **Suburban** 10-acre campus
- **Coed, primarily men,** 393 undergraduate students, 100% full-time, 18% women, 82% men

Undergraduates 393 full-time. Students come from 3 states and territories; 1% are from out of state. *Retention:* 72% of full-time freshmen returned.
Freshmen *Admission:* 435 applied, 371 admitted, 75 enrolled.
Faculty *Total:* 51, 47% full-time, 49% with terminal degrees. *Student/faculty ratio:* 15:1.
Majors Chemical technology; computer technology/computer systems technology; drafting and design technology; electrical, electronic and communications engineering technology; information technology; instrumentation technology; office occupations and clerical services.
Academics *Calendar:* continuous. *Degree:* certificates and associate. *Special study options:* internships.
Library ITI Technical College Library with 1,260 titles.
Student Life *Campus security:* electronic alarm devices are activated during non-business hours and security cameras monitor campus 24 hours.
Applying *Required:* high school transcript, interview.
Freshman Application Contact Mrs. Marcia Stevens, Admissions Director, ITI Technical College, 13944 Airline Highway, Baton Rouge, LA 70817. *Phone:* 225-752-4230 Ext. 261. *Toll-free phone:* 888-211-7165. *Fax:* 225-756-0903. *E-mail:* mstevens@iticollege.edu. *Web site:* http://www.iticollege.edu/.

ITT Technical Institute

Baton Rouge, Louisiana

- **Proprietary** primarily 2-year
- **Coed**

Majors Business administration and management; communications technology; computer and information systems security; criminal justice/law enforcement administration; drafting and design technology; electrical, electronic and communications engineering technology; forensic science and technology; graphic communications; legal assistant/paralegal; network and system administration; project management.
Academics *Degrees:* associate and bachelor's.
Student Life *Housing:* college housing not available.
Freshman Application Contact Director of Recruitment, ITT Technical Institute, 14111 Airline Highway, Suite 101, Baton Rouge, LA 70817. *Phone:* 225-754-5800. *Toll-free phone:* 800-295-8485. *Web site:* http://www.itt-tech.edu/.

ITT Technical Institute

St. Rose, Louisiana

- **Proprietary** primarily 2-year, founded 1998, part of ITT Educational Services, Inc.
- **Coed**

Majors Business administration and management; communications technology; computer and information systems security; construction management; criminal justice/law enforcement administration; drafting and design technology; electrical, electronic and communications engineering technology; forensic science and technology; game and interactive media design; graphic communications; legal assistant/paralegal; network and system administration; project management.
Academics *Calendar:* quarters. *Degrees:* associate and bachelor's.
Student Life *Housing:* college housing not available.
Freshman Application Contact Director of Recruitment, ITT Technical Institute, 140 James Drive East, St. Rose, LA 70087. *Phone:* 504-463-0338. *Toll-free phone:* 866-463-0338. *Web site:* http://www.itt-tech.edu/.

Louisiana Delta Community College
Monroe, Louisiana

Admissions Office Contact Louisiana Delta Community College, 7500 Millhaven Road, Monroe, LA 71203. *Toll-free phone:* 866-500-LDCC. *Web site:* http://www.ladelta.edu/.

Louisiana State University at Eunice
Eunice, Louisiana

Freshman Application Contact Ms. Gracie Guillory, Director of Financial Aid, Louisiana State University at Eunice, PO Box 1129, Eunice, LA 70535-1129. *Phone:* 337-550-1282. *Toll-free phone:* 888-367-5783. *Web site:* http://www.lsue.edu/.

Northeast Louisiana Technical College–Northeast Campus
Winnsboro, Louisiana

Director of Admissions Admissions Office, Northeast Louisiana Technical College–Northeast Campus, 1710 Warren Street, Winnsboro, LA 71295. *Phone:* 318-435-2163. *Toll-free phone:* 877-842-6956. *Web site:* http://www.ltc.edu/.

Northshore Technical College–Florida Parishes Campus
Greensburg, Louisiana

Director of Admissions Mrs. Sharon G. Hornsby, Campus Dean, Northshore Technical College–Florida Parishes Campus, PO Box 1300, Greensburg, LA 70441. *Phone:* 225-222-4251. *Toll-free phone:* 800-827-9750. *Web site:* http://www.ltc.edu/.

Remington College–Baton Rouge Campus
Baton Rouge, Louisiana

Director of Admissions Monica Butler-Johnson, Director of Recruitment, Remington College–Baton Rouge Campus, 10551 Coursey Boulevard, Baton Rouge, LA 70816. *Phone:* 225-236-3200. *Fax:* 225-922-3250. *E-mail:* monica.johnson@remingtoncollege.edu. *Web site:* http://www.remingtoncollege.edu/.

Remington College–Lafayette Campus
Lafayette, Louisiana

Freshman Application Contact Remington College–Lafayette Campus, 303 Rue Louis XIV, Lafayette, LA 70508. *Phone:* 337-981-4010. *Toll-free phone:* 800-560-6192. *Web site:* http://www.remingtoncollege.edu/.

Remington College–Shreveport
Shreveport, Louisiana

Freshman Application Contact Marc Wright, Remington College–Shreveport, 2106 Bert Kouns Industrial Loop, Shreveport, LA 71118. *Phone:* 318-671-4000. *Web site:* http://www.remingtoncollege.edu/shreveport/.

River Parishes Community College
Sorrento, Louisiana

Director of Admissions Ms. Allison Dauzat, Dean of Students and Enrollment Management, River Parishes Community College, PO Box 310, Sorrento, LA 70778. *Phone:* 225-675-8270. *Fax:* 225-675-5478. *E-mail:* adauzat@rpcc.cc.la.us. *Web site:* http://www.rpcc.edu/.

South Central Louisiana Technical College–Young Memorial Campus
Morgan City, Louisiana

Director of Admissions Ms. Melanie Henry, Admissions Office, South Central Louisiana Technical College–Young Memorial Campus, 900 Youngs Road, Morgan City, LA 70381. *Phone:* 504-380-2436. *Fax:* 504-380-2440. *Web site:* http://www.ltc.edu/.

Southern University at Shreveport
Shreveport, Louisiana

Freshman Application Contact Ms. Juanita Johnson, Acting Admissions Records Technician, Southern University at Shreveport, 3050 Martin Luther King, Jr. Drive, Shreveport, LA 71107. *Phone:* 318-674-3342. *Toll-free phone:* 800-458-1472. *Web site:* http://www.susla.edu/.

South Louisiana Community College
Lafayette, Louisiana

Freshman Application Contact Metilda Wilson, Dean of Student Services, South Louisiana Community College, 320 Devalcourt, Lafayette, LA 70506. *Phone:* 337-521-8909. *Web site:* http://www.southlouisiana.edu/.

Sowela Technical Community College
Lake Charles, Louisiana

Director of Admissions Admissions Office, Sowela Technical Community College, 3820 J. Bennett Johnston Avenue, Lake Charles, LA 70616-6950. *Phone:* 337-491-2698. *Web site:* http://www.sowela.edu/.

MAINE

Beal College
Bangor, Maine

Freshman Application Contact Admissions Assistant, Beal College, 99 Farm Road, Bangor, ME 04401. *Phone:* 207-947-4591. *Toll-free phone:* 800-660-7351. *Fax:* 207-947-0208. *E-mail:* admissions@bealcollege.edu. *Web site:* http://www.bealcollege.edu/.

Central Maine Community College
Auburn, Maine

- **State-supported** 2-year, founded 1964, part of Maine Community College System
- **Small-town** 135-acre campus
- **Endowment** $280,384
- **Coed,** 2,905 undergraduate students, 49% full-time, 54% women, 46% men

Undergraduates 1,426 full-time, 1,479 part-time. Students come from 9 states and territories; 5 other countries; 8% are from out of state; 2% Black or African American, non-Hispanic/Latino; 1% Hispanic/Latino; 0.7% Asian, non-Hispanic/Latino; 0.5% American Indian or Alaska Native, non-Hispanic/Latino; 0.7% Two or more races, non-Hispanic/Latino; 18% Race/ethnicity unknown; 0.3% international; 2% transferred in; 8% live on campus.

Freshmen *Admission:* 2,070 applied, 714 admitted, 702 enrolled. *Test scores:* SAT critical reading scores over 500: 22%; SAT math scores over 500: 22%; SAT writing scores over 500: 18%; SAT critical reading scores over 600: 3%; SAT math scores over 600: 3%; SAT writing scores over 600: 3%; SAT writing scores over 700: 1%.

Faculty *Total:* 233, 21% full-time, 1% with terminal degrees. *Student/faculty ratio:* 13:1.

Majors Accounting technology and bookkeeping; administrative assistant and secretarial science; architectural engineering technology; automobile/automotive mechanics technology; business administration and management; child development; communications systems installation and repair technology; computer installation and repair technology; construction engineering technology; construction trades related; criminal justice/law enforcement administration; electromechanical technology; graphic and printing equipment operation/production; human services; liberal arts and sciences/liberal studies; licensed practical/vocational nurse training; machine tool technology; medical/clinical assistant; multi/interdisciplinary studies related; registered nursing/registered nurse; teacher assistant/aide; vehicle maintenance and repair technologies related.

Academics *Calendar:* semesters. *Degree:* certificates, diplomas, and associate. *Special study options:* academic remediation for entering students, accelerated degree program, adult/continuing education programs, advanced placement credit, cooperative education, distance learning, English as a second language, independent study, internships, part-time degree program, services for LD students, summer session for credit.

Library Central Maine Community College Library with 15,914 titles, 200 serial subscriptions, 2 audiovisual materials, an OPAC, a Web page.

Student Life *Housing Options:* coed, men-only, women-only. Campus housing is university owned. Freshman applicants given priority for college housing. *Activities and Organizations:* drama/theater group. *Campus security:* 24-hour emergency response devices, student patrols, controlled dormitory access, night patrols by police.

Athletics Member USCAA. *Intercollegiate sports:* baseball M, basketball M/W, golf M/W, soccer M/W, softball W, volleyball M/W.

Standardized Tests *Recommended:* SAT (for admission).

Costs (2011–12) *One-time required fee:* $185. *Tuition:* state resident $2580 full-time, $86 per credit hour part-time; nonresident $5220 full-time, $172 per credit hour part-time. Full-time tuition and fees vary according to course load and program. Part-time tuition and fees vary according to course load and program. *Required fees:* $744 full-time, $16 per credit hour part-time. *Room and board:* $8586; room only: $4150. Room and board charges vary according to housing facility. *Payment plan:* installment. *Waivers:* employees or children of employees.

Financial Aid Of all full-time matriculated undergraduates who enrolled in 2010, 89 Federal Work-Study jobs (averaging $1200). *Financial aid deadline:* 8/1.

Applying *Options:* electronic application, deferred entrance. *Application fee:* $20. *Required:* high school transcript. *Application deadlines:* rolling (freshmen), rolling (transfers). *Notification:* continuous (freshmen), continuous (transfers).

Freshman Application Contact Ms. Joan Nichols, Admissions Assistant, Central Maine Community College, 1250 Turner Street, Auburn, ME 04210. *Phone:* 207-755-5273. *Toll-free phone:* 800-891-2002. *Fax:* 207-755-5493. *E-mail:* enroll@cmcc.edu. *Web site:* http://www.cmcc.edu/.

Central Maine Medical Center College of Nursing and Health Professions
Lewiston, Maine

- **Independent** 2-year, founded 1891
- **Urban** campus
- **Coed**

Undergraduates 14 full-time, 186 part-time. Students come from 2 states and territories; 1% are from out of state; 5% live on campus.

Faculty *Student/faculty ratio:* 10:1.

Academics *Calendar:* semesters. *Degree:* associate. *Special study options:* advanced placement credit, off-campus study, services for LD students, summer session for credit.

Student Life *Campus security:* 24-hour emergency response devices and patrols, late-night transport/escort service, controlled dormitory access.

Standardized Tests *Required:* SAT or ACT (for admission), Kaplan Entrance Exam (for admission).

Costs (2011–12) *Tuition:* $7245 full-time, $210 per credit hour part-time. *Required fees:* $1630 full-time. *Room only:* $1900. Room and board charges vary according to housing facility.

Financial Aid Of all full-time matriculated undergraduates who enrolled in 2010, 5 applied for aid, 4 were judged to have need. *Average financial aid package:* $17,200. *Average need-based loan:* $4000. *Average need-based gift aid:* $7700.

Applying *Options:* electronic application. *Application fee:* $40. *Required:* essay or personal statement, high school transcript.

Freshman Application Contact Ms. Dagmar Jenison, Assistant Registrar, Central Maine Medical Center College of Nursing and Health Professions, 70 Middle Street, Lewiston, ME 04240. *Phone:* 207-795-2843. *Fax:* 207-795-2849. *E-mail:* jenisod@cmhc.org. *Web site:* http://www.cmmccollege.edu/.

Eastern Maine Community College
Bangor, Maine

Freshman Application Contact Mr. W. Gregory Swett, Director of Admissions, Eastern Maine Community College, 354 Hogan Road, Bangor, ME 04401. *Phone:* 207-974-4680. *Toll-free phone:* 800-286-9357. *Fax:* 207-974-4683. *E-mail:* admissions@emcc.edu. *Web site:* http://www.emcc.edu/.

Kaplan University
Lewiston, Maine

Freshman Application Contact Kaplan University, 475 Lisbon Street, Lewiston, ME 04240. *Phone:* 207-333-3300. *Toll-free phone:* 866-527-5268 (in-state); 800-527-5268 (out-of-state). *Web site:* http://www.kaplanuniversity.edu/.

Kaplan University
South Portland, Maine

Freshman Application Contact Kaplan University, 265 Western Avenue, South Portland, ME 04106. *Phone:* 207-774-6126. *Toll-free phone:* 866-527-

5268 (in-state); 800-527-5268 (out-of-state). *Web site:* http://www.kaplanuniversity.edu/.

Kennebec Valley Community College
Fairfield, Maine

Freshman Application Contact Mr. Jim Bourgoin, Director of Admissions, Kennebec Valley Community College, Fairfield, ME 04937-1367. *Phone:* 207-453-5035. *Toll-free phone:* 800-528-5882. *Fax:* 207-453-5011. *E-mail:* admissions@kvcc.me.edu. *Web site:* http://www.kvcc.me.edu/.

Northern Maine Community College
Presque Isle, Maine

Freshman Application Contact Ms. Nancy Gagnon, Admissions Secretary, Northern Maine Community College, 33 Edgemont Drive, Presque Isle, ME 04769-2016. *Phone:* 207-768-2785. *Toll-free phone:* 800-535-6682. *Fax:* 207-768-2848. *E-mail:* ngagnon@nmcc.edu. *Web site:* http://www.nmcc.edu/.

Southern Maine Community College
South Portland, Maine

- **State-supported** 2-year, founded 1946, part of Maine Community College System
- **Urban** 80-acre campus
- **Coed**, 7,482 undergraduate students, 44% full-time, 49% women, 51% men

Undergraduates 3,315 full-time, 4,167 part-time. Students come from 28 states and territories; 58 other countries; 4% are from out of state; 4% Black or African American, non-Hispanic/Latino; 2% Hispanic/Latino; 2% Asian, non-Hispanic/Latino; 0.1% Native Hawaiian or other Pacific Islander, non-Hispanic/Latino; 0.6% American Indian or Alaska Native, non-Hispanic/Latino; 1% Two or more races, non-Hispanic/Latino; 12% Race/ethnicity unknown; 0.4% international; 8% transferred in; 5% live on campus. *Retention:* 53% of full-time freshmen returned.

Freshmen *Admission:* 1,401 enrolled.

Faculty *Total:* 482, 23% full-time. *Student/faculty ratio:* 20:1.

Majors Applied horticulture/horticulture operations; architectural drafting and CAD/CADD; automobile/automotive mechanics technology; biotechnology; business administration and management; cardiovascular technology; computer engineering technology; construction trades; criminal justice/police science; culinary arts; dietetic technology; digital communication and media/multimedia; early childhood education; electrical, electronic and communications engineering technology; emergency medical technology (EMT paramedic); environmental engineering technology; fire science/firefighting; health information/medical records technology; heating, air conditioning, ventilation and refrigeration maintenance technology; hotel/motel administration; liberal arts and sciences and humanities related; machine tool technology; marine biology and biological oceanography; materials engineering; medical/clinical assistant; medical radiologic technology; mental and social health services and allied professions related; plumbing technology; pre-engineering; radiologic technology/science; registered nursing/registered nurse; respiratory care therapy; surgical technology.

Academics *Calendar:* semesters. *Degree:* certificates and associate. *Special study options:* academic remediation for entering students, advanced placement credit, distance learning, double majors, English as a second language, honors programs, independent study, internships, off-campus study, part-time degree program, services for LD students, study abroad, summer session for credit.

Library Southern Maine Community College Library with an OPAC, a Web page.

Student Life *Housing Options:* coed. Campus housing is university owned. *Activities and Organizations:* drama/theater group, student-run newspaper, choral group, Student Senate. *Campus security:* 24-hour emergency response devices and patrols, student patrols, late-night transport/escort service, controlled dormitory access. *Student services:* personal/psychological counseling.

Athletics Member USCAA. *Intercollegiate sports:* baseball M, basketball M/W, golf M/W, soccer M/W, softball W. *Intramural sports:* cheerleading M(c)/W, cross-country running M(c)/W(c), ice hockey M(c), rock climbing M(c)/W(c), soccer M/W, volleyball M/W.

Standardized Tests *Recommended:* SAT or ACT (for admission), ACCUPLACER.

Financial Aid Of all full-time matriculated undergraduates who enrolled in 2010, 130 Federal Work-Study jobs (averaging $1500).

Applying *Options:* electronic application. *Application fee:* $20. *Required:* high school transcript or proof of high school graduation. *Application deadlines:* rolling (freshmen), rolling (out-of-state freshmen), rolling (transfers).

Notification: continuous (freshmen), continuous (out-of-state freshmen), continuous (transfers).

Freshman Application Contact Amy Lee, Associate Dean for Enrollment Services, Southern Maine Community College, 2 Fort Road, South, Portland, ME 04106. *Phone:* 207-741-5800. *Toll-free phone:* 877-282-2182. *Fax:* 207-741-5760. *E-mail:* alee@smccme.edu. *Web site:* http://www.smccme.edu/.

Washington County Community College
Calais, Maine

Director of Admissions Mr. Kent Lyons, Admissions Counselor, Washington County Community College, One College Drive, Calais, ME 04619. *Phone:* 207-454-1000. *Toll-free phone:* 800-210-6932. *Web site:* http://www.wccc.me.edu/.

York County Community College
Wells, Maine

- **State-supported** 2-year, founded 1994, part of Maine Community College System
- **Small-town** 84-acre campus with easy access to Boston
- **Endowment** $804,057
- **Coed,** 1,631 undergraduate students, 40% full-time, 64% women, 36% men

Undergraduates 649 full-time, 982 part-time. Students come from 11 states and territories; 8 other countries; 3% are from out of state; 0.9% Black or African American, non-Hispanic/Latino; 2% Hispanic/Latino; 0.8% Asian, non-Hispanic/Latino; 0.8% American Indian or Alaska Native, non-Hispanic/Latino; 2% Two or more races, non-Hispanic/Latino; 11% Race/ethnicity unknown; 0.2% international; 10% transferred in. *Retention:* 54% of full-time freshmen returned.

Freshmen *Admission:* 282 enrolled.

Faculty *Total:* 77, 22% full-time. *Student/faculty ratio:* 18:1.

Majors Accounting; architectural drafting and CAD/CADD; business administration and management; child development; construction trades related; criminal justice/safety; culinary arts; design and visual communications; health services/allied health/health sciences; liberal arts and sciences and humanities related; management information systems; medical/clinical assistant; multi/interdisciplinary studies related.

Academics *Calendar:* semesters. *Degree:* certificates and associate. *Special study options:* academic remediation for entering students, accelerated degree program, adult/continuing education programs, advanced placement credit, cooperative education, distance learning, internships, part-time degree program, services for LD students, summer session for credit.

Library Library and Learning Resource Center plus 1 other with 14,000 titles, 93 serial subscriptions, 1,926 audiovisual materials, an OPAC, a Web page.

Student Life *Housing:* college housing not available. *Activities and Organizations:* student-run newspaper, Student Senate, The Voice Student Newspaper, Phi Theta Kappa, Photography Club, Culinary Arts Club. *Campus security:* 24-hour emergency response devices, late-night transport/escort service.

Athletics *Intramural sports:* basketball M/W, bowling M/W, cross-country running M/W, football M/W, ice hockey M/W, skiing (downhill) M/W, softball M/W, ultimate Frisbee M/W.

Financial Aid Of all full-time matriculated undergraduates who enrolled in 2010, 512 applied for aid, 441 were judged to have need, 23 had their need fully met. 26 Federal Work-Study jobs (averaging $1200). In 2010, 8 non-need-based awards were made. *Average percent of need met:* 52%. *Average financial aid package:* $6359. *Average need-based loan:* $2926. *Average need-based gift aid:* $5131. *Average non-need-based aid:* $687.

Applying *Options:* electronic application. *Application fee:* $20. *Required:* high school transcript, interview. *Application deadlines:* rolling (freshmen), rolling (transfers).

Freshman Application Contact York County Community College, 112 College Drive, Wells, ME 04090. *Phone:* 207-216-4406 Ext. 311. *Toll-free phone:* 800-580-3820. *Web site:* http://www.yccc.edu/.

MARSHALL ISLANDS

College of the Marshall Islands
Majuro, Marshall Islands, Marshall Islands

Freshman Application Contact Ms. Rosita Capelle, Director of Admissions and Records, College of the Marshall Islands, PO Box 1258, Majuro, MH 96960, Marshall Islands. *Phone:* 692-625-6823. *Fax:* 692-625-7203. *E-mail:* cmiadmissions@cmi.edu. *Web site:* http://www.cmi.edu/.

MARYLAND

Allegany College of Maryland
Cumberland, Maryland

Freshman Application Contact Ms. Cathy Nolan, Director of Admissions and Registration, Allegany College of Maryland, Cumberland, MD 21502. *Phone:* 301-784-5000 Ext. 5202. *Fax:* 301-784-5220. *E-mail:* cnolan@allegany.edu. *Web site:* http://www.allegany.edu/.

Anne Arundel Community College
Arnold, Maryland

- **State and locally supported** 2-year, founded 1961
- **Suburban** 230-acre campus with easy access to Baltimore and Washington, DC
- **Coed,** 17,957 undergraduate students, 30% full-time, 61% women, 39% men

Undergraduates 5,331 full-time, 12,626 part-time. Students come from 25 states and territories; 18% Black or African American, non-Hispanic/Latino; 4% Hispanic/Latino; 3% Asian, non-Hispanic/Latino; 0.2% Native Hawaiian or other Pacific Islander, non-Hispanic/Latino; 0.5% American Indian or Alaska Native, non-Hispanic/Latino; 1% Two or more races, non-Hispanic/Latino; 10% Race/ethnicity unknown; 1% international.

Freshmen *Admission:* 3,084 enrolled.

Faculty *Total:* 1,068, 25% full-time. *Student/faculty ratio:* 18:1.

Majors Accounting technology and bookkeeping; architectural drafting and CAD/CADD; biology/biological sciences; business administration and management; business administration, management and operations related; business/commerce; chemistry teacher education; child-care and support services management; clinical/medical laboratory technology; communications technologies and support services related; computer and information sciences; computer and information systems security; computer/information technology services administration related; computer software and media applications related; computer systems networking and telecommunications; criminal justice/law enforcement administration; criminal justice/police science; early childhood education; electrical and electronics engineering; electrical, electronic and communications engineering technology; elementary education; engineering; English/language arts teacher education; entrepreneurship; fire prevention and safety technology; graphic design; health and physical education/fitness; health information/medical records technology; hotel/motel administration; legal assistant/paralegal; liberal arts and sciences and humanities related; liberal arts and sciences/liberal studies; management information systems; management information systems and services related; mathematics; mathematics teacher education; medical administrative assistant and medical secretary; medical radiologic technology; occupational safety and health technology; parks, recreation, leisure, and fitness studies related; physical therapy technology; physics teacher education; pre-law studies; psychiatric/mental health services technology; public health; registered nursing/registered nurse; Spanish language teacher education; substance abuse/addiction counseling; surgical technology.

Academics *Calendar:* semesters. *Degree:* certificates and associate. *Special study options:* academic remediation for entering students, accelerated degree program, adult/continuing education programs, advanced placement credit, cooperative education, distance learning, English as a second language, freshman honors college, honors programs, independent study, internships, part-time degree program, services for LD students, summer session for credit. *ROTC:* Army (c), Air Force (c).

Library Andrew G. Truxal Library with 144,694 titles, 403 serial subscriptions, 8,060 audiovisual materials, an OPAC, a Web page.

Student Life *Housing:* college housing not available. *Activities and Organizations:* drama/theater group, student-run newspaper, choral group, Drama Club, Student Association, Black Student Union, International Student Association, Chemistry Club. *Campus security:* 24-hour emergency response devices and patrols, student patrols, late-night transport/escort service. *Student services:* health clinic, personal/psychological counseling.

Athletics Member NJCAA. *Intercollegiate sports:* baseball M(s), basketball M(s)/W(s), cross-country running M(s)/W(s), golf M, lacrosse M(s)/W(s), soccer M(s)/W(s), softball W(s), volleyball W.

Costs (2012–13) *Tuition:* area resident $2700 full-time; state resident $5190 full-time; nonresident $9180 full-time. Full-time tuition and fees vary according to course load. Part-time tuition and fees vary according to course load. *Required fees:* $500 full-time. *Payment plan:* installment. *Waivers:* senior citizens and employees or children of employees.

Financial Aid Of all full-time matriculated undergraduates who enrolled in 2010, 104 Federal Work-Study jobs (averaging $1900). 55 state and other part-time jobs (averaging $1740).

Applying *Options:* early admission, deferred entrance. *Application deadlines:* rolling (freshmen), rolling (transfers).

Freshman Application Contact Mr. Thomas McGinn, Director of Enrollment Development and Admissions, Anne Arundel Community College, 101 College Parkway, Arnold, MD 21012-1895. *Phone:* 410-777-2240. *Fax:* 410-777-2246. *E-mail:* 4info@aacc.edu. *Web site:* http://www.aacc.edu/.

Baltimore City Community College
Baltimore, Maryland

Freshman Application Contact Baltimore City Community College, 2901 Liberty Heights Avenue, Baltimore, MD 21215-7893. *Phone:* 410-462-8311. *Toll-free phone:* 888-203-1261. *Web site:* http://www.bccc.edu/.

Carroll Community College
Westminster, Maryland

- **State and locally supported** 2-year, founded 1993, part of Maryland Higher Education Commission
- **Suburban** 80-acre campus with easy access to Baltimore
- **Endowment** $4.1 million
- **Coed,** 4,041 undergraduate students, 41% full-time, 61% women, 39% men

Undergraduates 1,647 full-time, 2,394 part-time. Students come from 7 states and territories; 6 other countries; 1% are from out of state; 3% Black or African American, non-Hispanic/Latino; 2% Hispanic/Latino; 1% Asian, non-Hispanic/Latino; 0.1% Native Hawaiian or other Pacific Islander, non-Hispanic/Latino; 0.3% American Indian or Alaska Native, non-Hispanic/Latino; 0.8% Two or more races, non-Hispanic/Latino; 1% Race/ethnicity unknown; 0.3% international; 7% transferred in.
Freshmen *Admission:* 818 applied, 818 admitted, 818 enrolled.
Faculty *Total:* 275, 27% full-time, 3% with terminal degrees. *Student/faculty ratio:* 17:1.
Majors Accounting; architectural drafting and CAD/CADD; art; business administration and management; child-care and support services management; computer and information sciences; computer engineering; computer graphics; criminal justice/police science; education (multiple levels); electrical and electronics engineering; emergency care attendant (EMT ambulance); forensic science and technology; general studies; health information/medical records technology; health professions related; kindergarten/preschool education; kinesiology and exercise science; legal studies; liberal arts and sciences/liberal studies; management information systems; multi/interdisciplinary studies related; music; physical therapy technology; psychology; registered nursing/registered nurse; theater design and technology.
Academics *Calendar:* semesters plus winter session. *Degree:* certificates and associate. *Special study options:* academic remediation for entering students, advanced placement credit, distance learning, English as a second language, honors programs, independent study, internships, part-time degree program, services for LD students, summer session for credit.
Library Random House Learning Resources Center with 118,417 titles, 197 serial subscriptions, 3,478 audiovisual materials, an OPAC, a Web page.
Student Life *Housing:* college housing not available. *Activities and Organizations:* drama/theater group, choral group, Student Government Organization, Carroll Community Chorus, Campus Activities Board, Green Team, Academic Communities (Creativity, Education, Great Ideas, Health and Wellness). *Campus security:* 24-hour emergency response devices, late-night transport/escort service.
Athletics *Intramural sports:* basketball M/W, soccer M/W.
Financial Aid Of all full-time matriculated undergraduates who enrolled in 2010, 46 Federal Work-Study jobs (averaging $1331).
Applying *Required:* high school transcript. *Application deadlines:* rolling (freshmen), rolling (out-of-state freshmen), rolling (transfers). *Notification:* continuous (freshmen), continuous (out-of-state freshmen), continuous (transfers).
Freshman Application Contact Ms. Candace Edwards, Director of Admissions, Carroll Community College, 1601 Washington Road, Westminster, MD 21157. *Phone:* 410-386-8405. *Toll-free phone:* 888-221-9748. *Fax:* 410-386-8446. *E-mail:* cedwards@carrollcc.edu. *Web site:* http://www.carrollcc.edu/.

Cecil College
North East, Maryland

- **County-supported** 2-year, founded 1968
- **Small-town** 105-acre campus with easy access to Baltimore
- **Coed,** 2,545 undergraduate students, 42% full-time, 62% women, 38% men

Undergraduates 1,071 full-time, 1,474 part-time. Students come from 13 states and territories; 16 other countries; 9% are from out of state; 9% Black or African American, non-Hispanic/Latino; 3% Hispanic/Latino; 1% Asian, non-Hispanic/Latino; 0.1% Native Hawaiian or other Pacific Islander, non-Hispanic/Latino; 0.4% American Indian or Alaska Native, non-Hispanic/Latino; 2% Two or more races, non-Hispanic/Latino; 0.4% Race/ethnicity unknown; 0.5% international.
Freshmen *Admission:* 761 applied, 761 admitted, 761 enrolled.
Faculty *Total:* 267, 18% full-time, 5% with terminal degrees. *Student/faculty ratio:* 13:1.
Majors Accounting technology and bookkeeping; biology/biological sciences; business administration and management; business administration, management and operations related; business/commerce; business/corporate communications; child-care and support services management; commercial photography; computer and information sciences; computer programming; computer programming (specific applications); criminal justice/police science; data processing and data processing technology; education; elementary education; emergency medical technology (EMT paramedic); fire science/firefighting; general studies; graphic design; health services/allied health/health sciences; horse husbandry/equine science and management; information science/studies; information technology; kindergarten/preschool education; liberal arts and sciences/liberal studies; logistics, materials, and supply chain management; management information systems; marketing/marketing management; mathematics; photography; physical sciences; physics; public relations/image management; registered nursing/registered nurse; transportation and materials moving related; transportation/mobility management; web page, digital/multimedia and information resources design.
Academics *Calendar:* semesters. *Degree:* certificates and associate. *Special study options:* academic remediation for entering students, accelerated degree program, adult/continuing education programs, advanced placement credit, cooperative education, distance learning, double majors, English as a second language, independent study, internships, off-campus study, part-time degree program, services for LD students, summer session for credit.
Library Cecil County Veterans Memorial Library with 58,251 titles, 39 serial subscriptions, 793 audiovisual materials, an OPAC, a Web page.
Student Life *Housing:* college housing not available. *Activities and Organizations:* drama/theater group, Student Government, Non-traditional Student Organization, Student Nurses Association, national fraternities. *Campus security:* 24-hour emergency response devices, late-night transport/escort service. *Student services:* personal/psychological counseling, women's center.
Athletics Member NJCAA. *Intercollegiate sports:* baseball M(s), basketball M(s)/W(s), cheerleading W, soccer M(s)/W(s), softball W(s), tennis W(s), volleyball W(s).
Costs (2011–12) *Tuition:* area resident $2700 full-time, $90 per credit hour part-time; state resident $5400 full-time, $180 per credit hour part-time; nonresident $6750 full-time, $225 per credit hour part-time. *Required fees:* $362 full-time. *Payment plan:* deferred payment. *Waivers:* senior citizens and employees or children of employees.
Applying *Options:* electronic application, early admission, deferred entrance. *Required:* high school transcript. *Application deadlines:* rolling (freshmen), rolling (out-of-state freshmen), rolling (transfers). *Notification:* continuous (freshmen), continuous (out-of-state freshmen), continuous (transfers).
Freshman Application Contact Dr. Diane Lane, Cecil College, One Seahawk Drive, North East, MD 21901-1999. *Phone:* 410-287-1002. *Fax:* 410-287-1001. *E-mail:* dlane@cecil.edu. *Web site:* http://www.cecil.edu/.

Chesapeake College
Wye Mills, Maryland

Freshman Application Contact Randy Holliday, Director of Student Recruitment and Outreach, Chesapeake College, PO Box 8, Wye Mills, MD 21679-0008. *Phone:* 410-822-5400. *Fax:* 410-827-5875. *E-mail:* rholliday@chesapeake.edu. *Web site:* http://www.chesapeake.edu/.

College of Southern Maryland
La Plata, Maryland

- **State and locally supported** 2-year, founded 1958
- **Rural** 175-acre campus with easy access to Washington, DC
- **Coed,** 9,153 undergraduate students, 38% full-time, 62% women, 38% men

Undergraduates 3,484 full-time, 5,669 part-time. 24% Black or African American, non-Hispanic/Latino; 5% Hispanic/Latino; 2% Asian, non-Hispanic/Latino; 0.4% Native Hawaiian or other Pacific Islander, non-Hispanic/Latino; 0.6% American Indian or Alaska Native, non-Hispanic/Latino; 4% Two or more races, non-Hispanic/Latino; 1% Race/ethnicity unknown; 0.3% international; 4% transferred in.
Freshmen *Admission:* 2,084 applied, 2,084 admitted, 1,817 enrolled.
Faculty *Total:* 557, 22% full-time, 11% with terminal degrees.
Majors Accounting; accounting technology and bookkeeping; building/construction finishing, management, and inspection related; business administration and management; business/commerce; child-care and support services management; clinical/medical laboratory technology; computer and informa-

tion sciences; computer programming; criminal justice/law enforcement administration; early childhood education; education; electrician; elementary education; emergency medical technology (EMT paramedic); engineering; engineering technologies and engineering related; environmental engineering technology; fire prevention and safety technology; fire science/firefighting; health and physical education related; hospitality administration; information technology; legal assistant/paralegal; liberal arts and sciences and humanities related; liberal arts and sciences/liberal studies; licensed practical/vocational nurse training; lineworker; massage therapy; mental and social health services and allied professions related; multi/interdisciplinary studies related; physical therapy technology; registered nursing/registered nurse.

Academics *Calendar:* semesters. *Degree:* certificates and associate. *Special study options:* academic remediation for entering students, accelerated degree program, adult/continuing education programs, advanced placement credit, cooperative education, distance learning, honors programs, internships, part-time degree program, services for LD students, study abroad, summer session for credit.

Library College of Southern Maryland Library with 44,896 titles, 166 serial subscriptions, an OPAC, a Web page.

Student Life *Housing:* college housing not available. *Activities and Organizations:* drama/theater group, student-run newspaper, television station, choral group, Spanish Club, Nursing Student Association, Science Club, Black Student Union, BACCHUS. *Campus security:* 24-hour emergency response devices and patrols. *Student services:* personal/psychological counseling, women's center.

Athletics Member NJCAA. *Intercollegiate sports:* baseball M, basketball M/W, golf M, soccer M/W, softball W, tennis M, volleyball W.

Costs (2012–13) *Tuition:* area resident $3948 full-time, $107 per credit part-time; state resident $6826 full-time, $185 per credit part-time; nonresident $8819 full-time, $239 per credit hour part-time. Full-time tuition and fees vary according to course load. Part-time tuition and fees vary according to course load. *Payment plan:* deferred payment. *Waivers:* senior citizens and employees or children of employees.

Financial Aid Of all full-time matriculated undergraduates who enrolled in 2010, 25 Federal Work-Study jobs (averaging $1200).

Applying *Options:* electronic application, early admission, deferred entrance. *Recommended:* high school transcript. *Application deadlines:* rolling (freshmen), rolling (transfers). *Notification:* continuous (freshmen), continuous (transfers).

Freshman Application Contact Information Center Coordinator, College of Southern Maryland, PO Box 910, La Plata, MD 20646-0910. *Phone:* 301-934-7520 Ext. 7765. *Toll-free phone:* 800-933-9177. *Fax:* 301-934-7698. *E-mail:* info@csmd.edu. *Web site:* http://www.csmd.edu/.

The Community College of Baltimore County
Baltimore, Maryland

- **County-supported** 2-year, founded 1957
- **Suburban** 350-acre campus
- **Coed**, 26,271 undergraduate students, 34% full-time, 62% women, 38% men

Undergraduates 8,973 full-time, 17,298 part-time. 36% Black or African American, non-Hispanic/Latino; 3% Hispanic/Latino; 2% Asian, non-Hispanic/Latino; 0.2% Native Hawaiian or other Pacific Islander, non-Hispanic/Latino; 0.4% American Indian or Alaska Native, non-Hispanic/Latino; 2% Two or more races, non-Hispanic/Latino; 5% Race/ethnicity unknown; 8% international.

Freshmen *Admission:* 4,799 enrolled.

Faculty *Total:* 1,416, 30% full-time, 8% with terminal degrees.

Majors Administrative assistant and secretarial science; aeronautics/aviation/aerospace science and technology; architectural drafting and CAD/CADD; autobody/collision and repair technology; automobile/automotive mechanics technology; building/construction finishing, management, and inspection related; building/construction site management; business administration and management; business administration, management and operations related; business/commerce; chemistry teacher education; child-care and support services management; commercial and advertising art; computer and information sciences; computer systems networking and telecommunications; criminal justice/police science; dental hygiene; diesel mechanics technology; early childhood education; education; elementary education; emergency medical technology (EMT paramedic); engineering; engineering technologies and engineering related; funeral service and mortuary science; geography; hotel/motel administration; hydraulics and fluid power technology; labor and industrial relations; legal assistant/paralegal; liberal arts and sciences and humanities related; liberal arts and sciences/liberal studies; management information systems; mathematics teacher education; medical administrative assistant and medical secretary; medical informatics; medical radiologic technology; occupational safety and health technology; occupational therapy; parks, recreation

and leisure; physics teacher education; psychiatric/mental health services technology; respiratory care therapy; science technologies related; sign language interpretation and translation; Spanish language teacher education; substance abuse/addiction counseling; veterinary/animal health technology; visual and performing arts.

Academics *Calendar:* semesters. *Degree:* certificates and associate. *Special study options:* academic remediation for entering students, advanced placement credit, cooperative education, distance learning, English as a second language, honors programs, independent study, internships, off-campus study, services for LD students, study abroad, summer session for credit.

Student Life *Housing:* college housing not available. *Campus security:* 24-hour emergency response devices and patrols, late-night transport/escort service.

Athletics Member NJCAA. *Intercollegiate sports:* baseball M(s), basketball M(s)/W(s), lacrosse M(s)/W(s), soccer M(s)/W(s), softball W(s), volleyball W(s).

Standardized Tests *Recommended:* SAT or ACT (for admission).

Costs (2011–12) *Tuition:* area resident $3090 full-time; state resident $5880 full-time; nonresident $8820 full-time. *Required fees:* $682 full-time. *Payment plan:* installment. *Waivers:* employees or children of employees.

Applying *Required:* high school transcript. *Application deadlines:* rolling (freshmen), rolling (out-of-state freshmen), rolling (transfers).

Freshman Application Contact Ms. Diane Drake, Director of Admissions, The Community College of Baltimore County, 7201 Rossville Boulevard, Baltimore, MD 21228. *Phone:* 443-840-4392. *E-mail:* ddrake@ccbcmd.edu. *Web site:* http://www.ccbcmd.edu/.

Frederick Community College
Frederick, Maryland

- **State and locally supported** 2-year, founded 1957
- **Small-town** 100-acre campus with easy access to Baltimore and Washington, DC
- **Endowment** $4.0 million
- **Coed**

Undergraduates 2,359 full-time, 3,874 part-time. 1% are from out of state. *Retention:* 45% of full-time freshmen returned.

Faculty *Student/faculty ratio:* 12:1.

Academics *Calendar:* semesters. *Degree:* certificates and associate. *Special study options:* academic remediation for entering students, adult/continuing education programs, advanced placement credit, cooperative education, distance learning, English as a second language, freshman honors college, honors programs, independent study, internships, off-campus study, part-time degree program, services for LD students, study abroad, summer session for credit. *ROTC:* Army (c).

Student Life *Campus security:* 24-hour emergency response devices and patrols, late-night transport/escort service.

Athletics Member NJCAA.

Costs (2011–12) *Tuition:* area resident $3180 full-time, $106 per credit part-time; state resident $6900 full-time, $230 per credit part-time; nonresident $9360 full-time, $312 per credit part-time. *Required fees:* $627 full-time, $18 per credit part-time, $52 per term part-time.

Financial Aid Of all full-time matriculated undergraduates who enrolled in 2010, 25 Federal Work-Study jobs (averaging $1368). 14 state and other part-time jobs (averaging $2715).

Applying *Options:* electronic application. *Recommended:* high school transcript.

Freshman Application Contact Ms. Lisa A. Freel, Director of Admissions, Frederick Community College, 7932 Opossumtown Pike, Frederick, MD 21702. *Phone:* 301-846-2468. *Fax:* 301-624-2799. *E-mail:* admissions@frederick.edu. *Web site:* http://www.frederick.edu/.

Garrett College
McHenry, Maryland

- **State and locally supported** 2-year, founded 1966
- **Rural** 62-acre campus
- **Coed**, 902 undergraduate students, 78% full-time, 54% women, 46% men

Undergraduates 706 full-time, 196 part-time. 19% Black or African American, non-Hispanic/Latino; 2% Hispanic/Latino; 0.3% Asian, non-Hispanic/Latino; 0.2% American Indian or Alaska Native, non-Hispanic/Latino; 0.1% Race/ethnicity unknown; 0.1% international; 7% transferred in; 19% live on campus. *Retention:* 56% of full-time freshmen returned.

Freshmen *Admission:* 1,108 applied, 806 admitted, 269 enrolled. *Average high school GPA:* 3.31. *Test scores:* ACT scores over 18: 20%; ACT scores over 24: 7%.

Faculty *Total:* 77, 25% full-time, 13% with terminal degrees. *Student/faculty ratio:* 20:1.

Majors Business administration and management; business automation/technology/data entry; business/commerce; corrections; early childhood education; education; electrical and electronics engineering; elementary education; liberal arts and sciences and humanities related; liberal arts and sciences/liberal studies; management information systems; sport and fitness administration/management; wildlife, fish and wildlands science and management.
Academics *Calendar:* semesters. *Degree:* certificates and associate. *Special study options:* academic remediation for entering students, adult/continuing education programs, advanced placement credit, cooperative education, distance learning, double majors, external degree program, honors programs, independent study, internships, part-time degree program, services for LD students, summer session for credit.
Library Learning Resource Center with 48,127 titles, 73 serial subscriptions, 2,859 audiovisual materials, an OPAC, a Web page.
Student Life *Housing Options:* coed, disabled students. Campus housing is university owned and leased by the school. *Activities and Organizations:* drama/theater group, student-run newspaper, SGA, International Club. *Campus security:* 24-hour emergency response devices and patrols, controlled dormitory access. *Student services:* health clinic, personal/psychological counseling.
Athletics Member NJCAA. *Intercollegiate sports:* baseball M(s), basketball M(s)/W(s), cross-country running M/W, golf M, softball W, volleyball W. *Intramural sports:* basketball M/W, football M/W, rock climbing M/W, ultimate Frisbee M/W.
Standardized Tests *Recommended:* SAT or ACT (for admission).
Costs (2011–12) *One-time required fee:* $15. *Tuition:* area resident $2520 full-time, $90 per credit hour part-time; state resident $6048 full-time, $216 per credit hour part-time; nonresident $7140 full-time, $255 per credit hour part-time. Full-time tuition and fees vary according to location and reciprocity agreements. Part-time tuition and fees vary according to location and reciprocity agreements. *Required fees:* $702 full-time, $24 per credit hour part-time, $15 per term part-time. *Room and board:* $7782; room only: $5192. Room and board charges vary according to board plan and housing facility. *Payment plans:* installment, deferred payment. *Waivers:* senior citizens and employees or children of employees.
Financial Aid Of all full-time matriculated undergraduates who enrolled in 2011, 552 applied for aid, 496 were judged to have need, 30 had their need fully met. In 2011, 6 non-need-based awards were made. *Average percent of need met:* 34%. *Average financial aid package:* $4907. *Average need-based loan:* $1860. *Average need-based gift aid:* $3383. *Average non-need-based aid:* $179.
Applying *Options:* early admission, deferred entrance. *Required:* high school transcript. *Application deadlines:* rolling (freshmen), rolling (out-of-state freshmen), rolling (transfers). *Notification:* continuous (freshmen), continuous (out-of-state freshmen), continuous (transfers).
Freshman Application Contact Mrs. Rachelle Davis, Director of Admissions, Garrett College, 687 Mosser Road, McHenry, MD 21541. *Phone:* 301-387-3044. *Toll-free phone:* 866-55-GARRETT. *E-mail:* admissions@garrettcollege.edu. *Web site:* http://www.garrettcollege.edu/.

Hagerstown Community College

Hagerstown, Maryland

- **State and locally supported** 2-year, founded 1946
- **Suburban** 319-acre campus with easy access to Baltimore and Washington, DC
- **Coed,** 4,714 undergraduate students, 31% full-time, 61% women, 39% men

Undergraduates 1,467 full-time, 3,247 part-time. Students come from 12 states and territories; 21% are from out of state; 11% Black or African American, non-Hispanic/Latino; 5% Hispanic/Latino; 2% Asian, non-Hispanic/Latino; 0.6% American Indian or Alaska Native, non-Hispanic/Latino; 0.8% Two or more races, non-Hispanic/Latino; 4% Race/ethnicity unknown; 10% transferred in. *Retention:* 63% of full-time freshmen returned.
Freshmen *Admission:* 979 enrolled.
Faculty *Total:* 262, 29% full-time, 6% with terminal degrees. *Student/faculty ratio:* 18:1.
Majors Accounting technology and bookkeeping; animation, interactive technology, video graphics and special effects; biology/biotechnology laboratory technician; business administration and management; business/commerce; child-care and support services management; commercial and advertising art; computer and information sciences; criminal justice/police science; early childhood education; education; electromechanical technology; elementary education; emergency medical technology (EMT paramedic); engineering; health information/medical records administration; industrial technology; liberal arts and sciences and humanities related; liberal arts and sciences/liberal studies; management information systems; mechanical engineering/mechanical technology; medical radiologic technology; psychiatric/mental health services technology; registered nursing/registered nurse; transportation/mobility management; web page, digital/multimedia and information resources design.

Academics *Calendar:* semesters. *Degree:* certificates and associate. *Special study options:* academic remediation for entering students, accelerated degree program, adult/continuing education programs, advanced placement credit, cooperative education, distance learning, English as a second language, honors programs, independent study, internships, off-campus study, part-time degree program, services for LD students, student-designed majors, summer session for credit.
Library William Brish Library with 45,705 titles, 228 serial subscriptions, an OPAC, a Web page.
Student Life *Housing:* college housing not available. *Activities and Organizations:* drama/theater group, student-run newspaper, choral group, Phi Theta Kappa, Robinwood Players Theater Club, Association of Nursing Students, Radiography Club, Art and Design Club. *Campus security:* 24-hour patrols, student patrols. *Student services:* health clinic, personal/psychological counseling.
Athletics Member NJCAA. *Intercollegiate sports:* baseball M(s), basketball M(s)/W(s), cross-country running M(s)/W(s), golf M/W, soccer M(s)/W, softball W(s), track and field M(s)/W(s), volleyball W(s). *Intramural sports:* cheerleading M/W, golf M/W, lacrosse M/W, table tennis M/W, tennis M/W.
Costs (2011–12) *Tuition:* area resident $3090 full-time, $103 per credit hour part-time; state resident $4830 full-time, $161 per credit hour part-time; nonresident $6360 full-time, $212 per credit hour part-time. *Required fees:* $350 full-time, $10 per credit hour part-time, $25 per term part-time. *Payment plan:* installment. *Waivers:* senior citizens and employees or children of employees.
Financial Aid Of all full-time matriculated undergraduates who enrolled in 2010, 27 Federal Work-Study jobs (averaging $2955).
Applying *Options:* electronic application, early admission, deferred entrance. *Required for some:* high school transcript, selective admissions for RN, LPN, EMT, and radiography programs. *Application deadlines:* rolling (freshmen), rolling (out-of-state freshmen), rolling (transfers). *Notification:* continuous (freshmen), continuous (out-of-state freshmen), continuous (transfers).
Freshman Application Contact Assistant Director, Admissions, Records and Registration, Hagerstown Community College, 11400 Robinwood Drive, Hagerstown, MD 21742-6514. *Phone:* 240-500-2338. *Fax:* 301-791-9165. *E-mail:* admissions@hagerstowncc.edu. *Web site:* http://www.hagerstowncc.edu/.

Harford Community College

Bel Air, Maryland

- **State and locally supported** 2-year, founded 1957
- **Small-town** 331-acre campus with easy access to Baltimore
- **Coed,** 7,132 undergraduate students, 41% full-time, 60% women, 40% men

Undergraduates 2,917 full-time, 4,215 part-time. 14% Black or African American, non-Hispanic/Latino; 4% Hispanic/Latino; 2% Asian, non-Hispanic/Latino; 0.1% Native Hawaiian or other Pacific Islander, non-Hispanic/Latino; 0.4% American Indian or Alaska Native, non-Hispanic/Latino; 3% Two or more races, non-Hispanic/Latino; 0.7% Race/ethnicity unknown; 0.5% international.
Freshmen *Admission:* 1,527 enrolled. *Test scores:* SAT critical reading scores over 500: 100%; SAT math scores over 500: 100%; SAT critical reading scores over 600: 40%; SAT math scores over 600: 44%; SAT critical reading scores over 700: 3%; SAT math scores over 700: 2%.
Faculty *Total:* 387, 26% full-time, 12% with terminal degrees. *Student/faculty ratio:* 22:1.
Majors Accounting; accounting technology and bookkeeping; business administration and management; business/commerce; CAD/CADD drafting/design technology; chemistry teacher education; commercial photography; communications technologies and support services related; computer and information sciences; computer and information systems security; criminal justice/police science; design and visual communications; early childhood education; education; electroneurodiagnostic/electroencephalographic technology; elementary education; engineering; engineering technologies and engineering related; English/language arts teacher education; environmental studies; industrial production technologies related; interior design; legal assistant/paralegal; legal studies; liberal arts and sciences and humanities related; liberal arts and sciences/liberal studies; management information systems; mathematics teacher education; medical/clinical assistant; multi/interdisciplinary studies related; physics teacher education; psychiatric/mental health services technology; registered nursing/registered nurse; science technologies related; Spanish language teacher education; substance abuse/addiction counseling; theater design and technology; visual and performing arts.
Academics *Calendar:* semesters. *Degree:* certificates, diplomas, and associate. *Special study options:* academic remediation for entering students, adult/continuing education programs, advanced placement credit, cooperative education, distance learning, double majors, English as a second language, honors programs, independent study, internships, part-time degree program, services for LD students, student-designed majors, study abroad, summer session for credit.

Library Harford Community College Library with 55,972 titles, 129 serial subscriptions, 1,758 audiovisual materials, an OPAC, a Web page.

Student Life *Activities and Organizations:* drama/theater group, student-run newspaper, radio station, choral group, Student Association, Paralegal Club, Multi-National Students Association, Student Nurses Association, Gamers Guild. *Campus security:* 24-hour patrols, late-night transport/escort service. *Student services:* personal/psychological counseling.

Athletics Member NJCAA. *Intercollegiate sports:* baseball M(s), basketball M(s)/W(s), cheerleading M(c)/W(c), cross-country running M(s)/W(s), golf M(s), lacrosse M(s)/W(s), soccer M(s)/W(s), softball W(s), tennis M(s)/W(s), volleyball W(s). *Intramural sports:* badminton M/W, basketball M/W, football M/W, soccer M/W, softball M/W, tennis M/W, volleyball M/W.

Costs (2012–13) *Tuition:* area resident $2460 full-time; state resident $4920 full-time; nonresident $7380 full-time. *Required fees:* $295 full-time. *Waivers:* senior citizens and employees or children of employees.

Financial Aid Of all full-time matriculated undergraduates who enrolled in 2011, 1,774 applied for aid, 1,260 were judged to have need. 71 Federal Work-Study jobs (averaging $2020).

Applying *Options:* electronic application. *Application deadlines:* rolling (freshmen), rolling (transfers). *Notification:* continuous (transfers).

Freshman Application Contact Ms. Donna Strasavich, Enrollment Specialist, Harford Community College, 401 Thomas Run Road, Bel Air, MD 21015-1698. *Phone:* 443-412-2311. *Fax:* 443-412-2169. *E-mail:* sendinfo@harford.edu. *Web site:* http://www.harford.edu/.

Howard Community College
Columbia, Maryland

- **State and locally supported** 2-year, founded 1966
- **Suburban** 122-acre campus with easy access to Baltimore and Washington, DC
- **Coed,** 10,081 undergraduate students, 37% full-time, 57% women, 43% men

Undergraduates 3,712 full-time, 6,369 part-time. 27% Black or African American, non-Hispanic/Latino; 8% Hispanic/Latino; 13% Asian, non-Hispanic/Latino; 0.2% Native Hawaiian or other Pacific Islander, non-Hispanic/Latino; 0.3% American Indian or Alaska Native, non-Hispanic/Latino; 3% Two or more races, non-Hispanic/Latino; 2% Race/ethnicity unknown. *Retention:* 66% of full-time freshmen returned.

Faculty *Total:* 724, 24% full-time. *Student/faculty ratio:* 19:1.

Majors Accounting; administrative assistant and secretarial science; architecture; art; biological and physical sciences; biomedical technology; biotechnology; business administration and management; cardiovascular technology; child development; clinical laboratory science/medical technology; computer and information sciences related; computer graphics; computer/information technology services administration related; computer science; computer systems networking and telecommunications; consumer merchandising/retailing management; criminal justice/law enforcement administration; data entry/microcomputer applications; design and applied arts related; dramatic/theater arts; electrical, electronic and communications engineering technology; elementary education; emergency medical technology (EMT paramedic); engineering; environmental studies; fashion merchandising; financial planning and services; general studies; health teacher education; information science/studies; information technology; kindergarten/preschool education; legal administrative assistant/secretary; liberal arts and sciences/liberal studies; licensed practical/vocational nurse training; medical administrative assistant and medical secretary; music; nuclear medical technology; office management; photography; physical sciences; pre-dentistry studies; premedical studies; pre-pharmacy studies; pre-veterinary studies; psychology; registered nursing/registered nurse; secondary education; social sciences; sport and fitness administration/management; substance abuse/addiction counseling; telecommunications technology; theater design and technology.

Academics *Calendar:* semesters. *Degree:* certificates and associate. *Special study options:* academic remediation for entering students, adult/continuing education programs, advanced placement credit, cooperative education, distance learning, double majors, English as a second language, external degree program, freshman honors college, honors programs, off-campus study, part-time degree program, services for LD students, study abroad, summer session for credit.

Library Howard Community College Library with 45,707 titles, 39,910 serial subscriptions, 2,636 audiovisual materials, an OPAC, a Web page.

Student Life *Housing:* college housing not available. *Activities and Organizations:* drama/theater group, student-run newspaper, choral group, Phi Theta Kappa, Nursing Club, Black Leadership Organization, student newspaper, Student Government Association. *Campus security:* 24-hour emergency response devices and patrols, late-night transport/escort service. *Student services:* personal/psychological counseling.

Athletics Member NJCAA. *Intercollegiate sports:* basketball M/W, cross-country running M/W, lacrosse M/W, soccer M/W, track and field M/W, volleyball W. *Intramural sports:* basketball M/W, lacrosse M, softball W.

Standardized Tests *Required for some:* SAT or ACT (for admission).

Costs (2011–12) *Tuition:* area resident $3570 full-time, $119 per credit hour part-time; state resident $6060 full-time, $202 per credit hour part-time; nonresident $7410 full-time, $247 per credit hour part-time. *Required fees:* $598 full-time, $20 per credit hour part-time. *Payment plan:* installment. *Waivers:* senior citizens and employees or children of employees.

Applying *Options:* electronic application, early admission, deferred entrance. *Application fee:* $25. *Required for some:* essay or personal statement, high school transcript, 2 letters of recommendation. *Application deadlines:* rolling (freshmen), rolling (out-of-state freshmen), rolling (transfers). *Notification:* continuous (freshmen), continuous (out-of-state freshmen), continuous (transfers).

Freshman Application Contact Ms. Christy Thomson, Associate Director of Admissions, Howard Community College, Columbia, MD 21044-3197. *Phone:* 443-518-4599. *Fax:* 443-518-4589. *E-mail:* hsinfo@howardcc.edu. *Web site:* http://www.howardcc.edu/.

ITT Technical Institute
Owings Mills, Maryland

- **Proprietary** primarily 2-year, founded 2005
- **Coed**

Majors CAD/CADD drafting/design technology; computer and information systems security; computer engineering technology; computer software and media applications related; computer systems networking and telecommunications; construction management; design and visual communications; electrical, electronic and communications engineering technology; game and interactive media design; information technology project management; system, networking, and LAN/WAN management.

Academics *Calendar:* quarters. *Degrees:* associate and bachelor's.

Student Life *Housing:* college housing not available.

Freshman Application Contact Director of Recruitment, ITT Technical Institute, 11301 Red Run Boulevard, Owings Mills, MD 21117. *Phone:* 443-394-7115. *Toll-free phone:* 877-411-6782. *Web site:* http://www.itt-tech.edu/.

Kaplan University, Hagerstown Campus
Hagerstown, Maryland

Freshman Application Contact Kaplan University, Hagerstown Campus, 18618 Crestwood Drive, Hagerstown, MD 21742-2797. *Phone:* 301-739-2680 Ext. 217. *Toll-free phone:* 866-527-5268 (in-state); 800-527-5268 (out-of-state). *Web site:* http://www.ku-hagerstown.com/.

Montgomery College
Rockville, Maryland

- **State and locally supported** 2-year, founded 1946
- **Suburban** 333-acre campus with easy access to Washington, DC
- **Endowment** $18.5 million
- **Coed,** 26,996 undergraduate students, 36% full-time, 53% women, 47% men

Undergraduates 9,728 full-time, 17,268 part-time. Students come from 28 states and territories; 167 other countries; 4% are from out of state; 24% Black or African American, non-Hispanic/Latino; 19% Hispanic/Latino; 12% Asian, non-Hispanic/Latino; 0.3% Native Hawaiian or other Pacific Islander, non-Hispanic/Latino; 0.3% American Indian or Alaska Native, non-Hispanic/Latino; 2% Two or more races, non-Hispanic/Latino; 0.1% Race/ethnicity unknown; 11% international; 5% transferred in.

Freshmen *Admission:* 10,796 applied, 10,796 admitted, 4,042 enrolled.

Faculty *Total:* 1,309, 40% full-time, 29% with terminal degrees. *Student/faculty ratio:* 20:1.

Majors Accounting technology and bookkeeping; American Sign Language (ASL); animation, interactive technology, video graphics and special effects; applied horticulture/horticulture operations; architectural drafting and CAD/CADD; art; automobile/automotive mechanics technology; biology/biotechnology laboratory technician; building/construction finishing, management, and inspection related; business/commerce; chemistry teacher education; child-care provision; commercial and advertising art; commercial photography; communications technologies and support services related; computer and information sciences; computer and information systems security; criminal justice/police science; crisis/emergency/disaster management; data entry/microcomputer applications; diagnostic medical sonography and ultrasound technology; early childhood education; elementary education; engineering; English/language arts teacher education; fire prevention and safety technology; geography; health information/medical records technology; hotel/motel administration; interior design; legal assistant/paralegal; liberal arts and sciences and humanities related; liberal arts and sciences/liberal studies; manage-

ment information systems and services related; mathematics teacher education; medical radiologic technology; physical therapy technology; physics teacher education; psychiatric/mental health services technology; registered nursing/registered nurse; Spanish language teacher education; speech communication and rhetoric; surgical technology; web page, digital/multimedia and information resources design.
Academics *Calendar:* semesters. *Degree:* certificates and associate. *Special study options:* academic remediation for entering students, accelerated degree program, adult/continuing education programs, advanced placement credit, cooperative education, distance learning, double majors, English as a second language, external degree program, honors programs, independent study, internships, off-campus study, part-time degree program, services for LD students, study abroad, summer session for credit. *ROTC:* Air Force (c).
Library Montgomery College Library plus 1 other with 389,913 titles, 54,930 serial subscriptions, 28,346 audiovisual materials, an OPAC, a Web page.
Student Life *Activities and Organizations:* drama/theater group, student-run newspaper, choral group. *Campus security:* 24-hour emergency response devices and patrols, late-night transport/escort service. *Student services:* personal/psychological counseling, women's center.
Athletics Member NJCAA. *Intercollegiate sports:* baseball M, basketball M/W, soccer M/W, softball W, tennis M/W, track and field M/W, volleyball W. *Intramural sports:* baseball M, basketball M/W, cheerleading W, football M, soccer M/W, softball W, tennis M/W, track and field M/W, volleyball W.
Costs (2012–13) *One-time required fee:* $25. *Tuition:* area resident $2688 full-time, $110 per credit part-time; state resident $5496 full-time, $225 per credit part-time; nonresident $7560 full-time, $308 per credit part-time. Full-time tuition and fees vary according to course load. Part-time tuition and fees vary according to course load. *Required fees:* $874 full-time, $36 per credit part-time. *Payment plans:* installment, deferred payment. *Waivers:* senior citizens and employees or children of employees.
Applying *Options:* electronic application, early admission, deferred entrance. *Application fee:* $25. *Recommended:* high school transcript, interview. *Application deadlines:* rolling (freshmen), rolling (out-of-state freshmen), rolling (transfers). *Notification:* continuous (freshmen), continuous (out-of-state freshmen), continuous (transfers).
Freshman Application Contact Montgomery College, 51 Mannakee Street, Rockville, MD 20850. *Phone:* 240-567-5034. *Web site:* http://www.montgomerycollege.edu/.

Prince George's Community College

Largo, Maryland

Freshman Application Contact Ms. Vera Bagley, Director of Admissions and Records, Prince George's Community College, 301 Largo Road, Largo, MD 20774-2199. *Phone:* 301-322-0801. *Fax:* 301-322-0119. *E-mail:* enrollmentservices@pgcc.edu. *Web site:* http://www.pgcc.edu/.

TESST College of Technology

Baltimore, Maryland

- **Proprietary** 2-year, founded 1956
- **Coed**

Majors Computer systems networking and telecommunications.
Academics *Calendar:* quarters. *Degree:* certificates and associate.
Freshman Application Contact TESST College of Technology, 1520 South Caton Avenue, Baltimore, MD 21227. *Phone:* 410-644-6400. *Toll-free phone:* 800-935-1857. *Web site:* http://www.baltimore.tesst.com/.

TESST College of Technology

Beltsville, Maryland

- **Proprietary** 2-year, founded 1967
- **Coed**

Majors Computer systems networking and telecommunications; criminal justice/safety; health information/medical records technology.
Academics *Calendar:* quarters. *Degree:* certificates and associate.
Applying *Application fee:* $20.
Freshman Application Contact TESST College of Technology, 4600 Powder Mill Road, Beltsville, MD 20705. *Phone:* 301-937-8448. *Toll-free phone:* 800-935-1857. *Web site:* http://www.beltsville.tesst.com/.

TESST College of Technology

Towson, Maryland

- **Proprietary** 2-year, founded 1992
- **Coed**

Majors Computer systems networking and telecommunications; criminal justice/safety.
Academics *Calendar:* quarters. *Degree:* certificates and associate.

Freshman Application Contact TESST College of Technology, 803 Glen Eagles Court, Towson, MD 21286. *Phone:* 410-296-5350. *Toll-free phone:* 800-935-1857. *Web site:* http://www.towson.tesst.com/.

Wor-Wic Community College

Salisbury, Maryland

Freshman Application Contact Mr. Richard Webster, Director of Admissions, Wor-Wic Community College, 32000 Campus Drive, Salisbury, MD 21804. *Phone:* 410-334-2895. *Fax:* 410-334-2954. *E-mail:* admissions@worwic.edu. *Web site:* http://www.worwic.edu/.

MASSACHUSETTS

Bay State College

Boston, Massachusetts

Freshman Application Contact Kim Olds, Director of Admissions, Bay State College, 122 Commonwealth Avenue, Boston, MA 02116. *Phone:* 617-217-9115. *Toll-free phone:* 800-81-LEARN. *Fax:* 617-536-1735. *E-mail:* admissions@baystate.edu. *Web site:* http://www.baystate.edu/.

See next page for Display ad and page 336 for the College Close-Up.

Benjamin Franklin Institute of Technology

Boston, Massachusetts

Freshman Application Contact Ms. Brittainy Johnson, Associate Director of Admissions, Benjamin Franklin Institute of Technology, Boston, MA 02116. *Phone:* 617-423-4630 Ext. 122. *Toll-free phone:* 877-400-BFIT. *Fax:* 617-482-3706. *E-mail:* bjohnson@bfit.edu. *Web site:* http://www.bfit.edu/.

Berkshire Community College

Pittsfield, Massachusetts

- **State-supported** 2-year, founded 1960, part of Massachusetts Public Higher Education System
- **Rural** 180-acre campus
- **Endowment** $6.0 million
- **Coed,** 2,566 undergraduate students, 40% full-time, 60% women, 40% men

Undergraduates 1,034 full-time, 1,532 part-time. Students come from 5 states and territories; 11 other countries; 4% are from out of state; 5% Black or African American, non-Hispanic/Latino; 7% Hispanic/Latino; 2% Asian, non-Hispanic/Latino; 0.1% Native Hawaiian or other Pacific Islander, non-Hispanic/Latino; 0.4% American Indian or Alaska Native, non-Hispanic/Latino; 2% Two or more races, non-Hispanic/Latino; 3% Race/ethnicity unknown; 0.7% international; 5% transferred in.
Freshmen *Admission:* 796 applied, 527 admitted, 519 enrolled. *Average high school GPA:* 2.78.
Faculty *Total:* 229, 22% full-time, 73% with terminal degrees. *Student/faculty ratio:* 16:1.
Majors Business administration and management; business automation/technology/data entry; business/commerce; community organization and advocacy; computer and information sciences; criminal justice/safety; electrical, electronic and communications engineering technology; engineering; environmental studies; fire science/firefighting; health professions related; hospitality administration; human services; international/global studies; liberal arts and sciences/liberal studies; physical therapy technology; registered nursing/registered nurse; respiratory care therapy; visual and performing arts.
Academics *Calendar:* semesters. *Degree:* certificates and associate. *Special study options:* academic remediation for entering students, accelerated degree program, adult/continuing education programs, advanced placement credit, cooperative education, distance learning, double majors, English as a second language, honors programs, independent study, internships, off-campus study, part-time degree program, services for LD students, summer session for credit.
Library Jonathan Edwards Library plus 1 other with 77,497 titles, 263 serial subscriptions, 13,227 audiovisual materials, an OPAC, a Web page.
Student Life *Housing:* college housing not available. *Activities and Organizations:* drama/theater group, student-run newspaper, choral group, Mass PIRG, Student Nurse Organization, Student Senate, Diversity Club, LPN Organization. *Campus security:* 24-hour emergency response devices and patrols, late-night transport/escort service. *Student services:* personal/psychological counseling.

Costs (2012–13) *One-time required fee:* $10. *Tuition:* state resident $624 full-time, $26 per credit part-time; nonresident $6240 full-time, $260 per credit part-time. Full-time tuition and fees vary according to class time, course load, program, and reciprocity agreements. Part-time tuition and fees vary according to class time, course load, program, and reciprocity agreements. *Required fees:* $4440 full-time, $159 per credit part-time, $25 per term part-time. *Payment plan:* installment. *Waivers:* senior citizens and employees or children of employees.

Financial Aid Of all full-time matriculated undergraduates who enrolled in 2010, 80 Federal Work-Study jobs (averaging $1600).

Applying *Options:* deferred entrance. *Application fee:* $10. *Required:* high school transcript. *Recommended:* interview. *Application deadlines:* rolling (freshmen), rolling (out-of-state freshmen), rolling (transfers). *Notification:* continuous (freshmen), continuous (out-of-state freshmen), continuous (transfers).

Freshman Application Contact Ms. Tina Schettini, Enrollment Services, Berkshire Community College, 1350 West Street, Pittsfield, MA 01201-5786. *Phone:* 413-236-1635. *Toll-free phone:* 800-816-1233. *Fax:* 413-496-9511. *E-mail:* tschetti@berkshirecc.edu. *Web site:* http://www.berkshirecc.edu/.

Bristol Community College
Fall River, Massachusetts

- **State-supported** 2-year, founded 1965, part of Massachusetts Community College System
- **Urban** 105-acre campus with easy access to Boston
- **Endowment** $3.9 million
- **Coed**

Undergraduates Students come from 10 states and territories; 21 other countries; 9% are from out of state; 6% Black or African American, non-Hispanic/Latino; 5% Hispanic/Latino; 2% Asian, non-Hispanic/Latino; 0.6% American Indian or Alaska Native, non-Hispanic/Latino; 15% Race/ethnicity unknown; 0.3% international.

Academics *Calendar:* semesters. *Degree:* certificates and associate. *Special study options:* academic remediation for entering students, adult/continuing education programs, cooperative education, distance learning, English as a second language, honors programs, independent study, internships, off-campus study, part-time degree program, services for LD students, student-designed majors, summer session for credit.

Student Life *Campus security:* 24-hour emergency response devices and patrols, student patrols, late-night transport/escort service.

Athletics Member NJCAA.

Costs (2011–12) *Tuition:* state resident $576 full-time, $24 per credit part-time; nonresident $5520 full-time, $230 per credit part-time. Full-time tuition and fees vary according to course load. Part-time tuition and fees vary according to course load. *Required fees:* $3582 full-time, $146 per credit hour part-time.

Financial Aid Of all full-time matriculated undergraduates who enrolled in 2010, 205 Federal Work-Study jobs (averaging $1627). 65 state and other part-time jobs (averaging $1478).

Applying *Application fee:* $10. *Required:* high school transcript.

Freshman Application Contact Mr. Rodney S. Clark, Dean of Admissions, Bristol Community College, 777 Elsbree Street, Fall River, MA 02720. *Phone:* 508-678-2811 Ext. 2177. *Fax:* 508-730-3265. *E-mail:* rodney.clark@bristolcc.edu. *Web site:* http://www.bristolcc.edu/.

Bunker Hill Community College
Boston, Massachusetts

- **State-supported** 2-year, founded 1973
- **Urban** 21-acre campus
- **Endowment** $2.4 million
- **Coed,** 12,934 undergraduate students, 35% full-time, 56% women, 44% men

Undergraduates 4,486 full-time, 8,448 part-time. Students come from 78 other countries; 19% Black or African American, non-Hispanic/Latino; 24% Hispanic/Latino; 10% Asian, non-Hispanic/Latino; 0.5% American Indian or Alaska Native, non-Hispanic/Latino; 12% Two or more races, non-Hispanic/Latino; 9% Race/ethnicity unknown; 6% international; 7% transferred in.

Freshmen *Admission:* 4,179 applied, 4,090 admitted, 2,401 enrolled.

Faculty *Total:* 691, 21% full-time. *Student/faculty ratio:* 19:1.

Majors Accounting; art; bioengineering and biomedical engineering; biology/biological sciences; biotechnology; business administration and management; business administration, management and operations related; business operations support and secretarial services related; cardiovascular technology;

chemistry; clinical/medical laboratory technology; computer and information sciences and support services related; computer and information systems security; computer/information technology services administration related; computer programming; computer programming (specific applications); computer science; computer systems networking and telecommunications; criminal justice/law enforcement administration; criminal justice/police science; culinary arts; data entry/microcomputer applications; design and visual communications; diagnostic medical sonography and ultrasound technology; dramatic/theater arts; early childhood education; education; electrical/electronics maintenance and repair technology related; engineering; English; entrepreneurship; finance; fire prevention and safety technology; foreign languages and literatures; general studies; health information/medical records administration; history; hospitality administration; hospitality administration related; hotel/motel administration; human services; international business/trade/commerce; legal assistant/paralegal; mass communication/media; mathematics; medical administrative assistant and medical secretary; medical radiologic technology; music; operations management; physics; psychology; registered nursing/registered nurse; respiratory therapy technician; sociology; speech communication and rhetoric; tourism and travel services management; web page, digital/multimedia and information resources design.

Academics *Calendar:* semesters. *Degree:* certificates and associate. *Special study options:* academic remediation for entering students, advanced placement credit, cooperative education, distance learning, English as a second language, external degree program, honors programs, independent study, internships, part-time degree program, services for LD students, study abroad, summer session for credit.

Library Bunker Hill Community College Library with 62,872 titles, 211 serial subscriptions, 11,475 audiovisual materials, an OPAC, a Web page.

Student Life *Housing:* college housing not available. *Activities and Organizations:* drama/theater group, student-run radio station, choral group, Alpha Kappa Mu Honor Society, Asian-Pacific Students Association, African Students Club, Latinos Unidos Club, Haitian Students Club. *Campus security:* 24-hour emergency response devices and patrols, late-night transport/escort service. *Student services:* health clinic, personal/psychological counseling.

Athletics Member NJCAA. *Intercollegiate sports:* baseball M, basketball M/W, golf M/W, soccer M/W, softball W. *Intramural sports:* basketball M/W, table tennis M/W, tennis M/W.

Costs (2012–13) *Tuition:* state resident $576 full-time, $24 per credit hour part-time; nonresident $5520 full-time, $230 per credit hour part-time. Full-time tuition and fees vary according to course load. Part-time tuition and fees vary according to course load. *Required fees:* $117 per credit hour part-time. *Payment plan:* installment. *Waivers:* minority students, senior citizens, and employees or children of employees.

Financial Aid Of all full-time matriculated undergraduates who enrolled in 2010, 135 Federal Work-Study jobs (averaging $2376).

Applying *Options:* deferred entrance. *Application fee:* $10. *Required:* high school transcript. *Application deadlines:* rolling (freshmen), rolling (transfers). *Notification:* continuous (freshmen), continuous (transfers).

Freshman Application Contact Mr. William Sakamoto, Associate Vice President of Academic Affairs and Enrollment Services, Bunker Hill Community College, 250 New Rutherford Avenue, Boston, MA 02129. *Phone:* 617-228-2346. *Fax:* 617-228-2082. *Web site:* http://www.bhcc.mass.edu/.

Cape Cod Community College

West Barnstable, Massachusetts

Freshman Application Contact Director of Admissions, Cape Cod Community College, 2240 Iyannough Road, West Barnstable, MA 02668-1599. *Phone:* 508-362-2131 Ext. 4311. *Toll-free phone:* 877-846-3672. *Fax:* 508-375-4089. *E-mail:* admiss@capecod.edu. *Web site:* http://www.capecod.edu/.

Dean College

Franklin, Massachusetts

Freshman Application Contact Mr. James Fowler, Dean College, 99 Main Street, Franklin, MA 02038. *Phone:* 508-541-1547. *Toll-free phone:* 877-TRY-DEAN. *Fax:* 508-541-8726. *E-mail:* jfowler@dean.edu. *Web site:* http://www.dean.edu/.

FINE Mortuary College, LLC

Norwood, Massachusetts

Freshman Application Contact Dean Marsha Wise, Admissions Office, FINE Mortuary College, LLC, 150 Kerry Place, Norwood, MA 02062. *Phone:* 781-762-1211. *Fax:* 781-762-7177. *E-mail:* mwise@fine-ne.com. *Web site:* http://www.fine-ne.com/.

Greenfield Community College

Greenfield, Massachusetts

Freshman Application Contact Mr. Herbert Hentz, Assistant Director of Admission, Greenfield Community College, 1 College Drive, Greenfield, MA 01301-9739. *Phone:* 413-775-1000. *Fax:* 413-773-5129. *E-mail:* admission@gcc.mass.edu. *Web site:* http://www.gcc.mass.edu/.

Holyoke Community College

Holyoke, Massachusetts

- **State-supported** 2-year, founded 1946, part of Massachusetts Public Higher Education System
- **Small-town** 135-acre campus
- **Endowment** $8.7 million
- **Coed,** 7,119 undergraduate students, 50% full-time, 62% women, 38% men

Undergraduates 3,571 full-time, 3,548 part-time. Students come from 12 states and territories; 1% are from out of state; 7% Black or African American, non-Hispanic/Latino; 19% Hispanic/Latino; 2% Asian, non-Hispanic/Latino; 0.5% American Indian or Alaska Native, non-Hispanic/Latino; 2% Two or more races, non-Hispanic/Latino; 2% Race/ethnicity unknown; 0.3% international; 8% transferred in.

Freshmen *Admission:* 1,741 admitted, 1,730 enrolled.

Faculty *Total:* 518, 25% full-time, 20% with terminal degrees. *Student/faculty ratio:* 18:1.

Majors Accounting technology and bookkeeping; administrative assistant and secretarial science; art; business administration and management; child-care and support services management; computer programming (specific applications); criminal justice/safety; engineering; environmental control technologies related; geography; health and physical education/fitness; hospitality administration related; liberal arts and sciences and humanities related; liberal arts and sciences/liberal studies; medical radiologic technology; music; opticianry; registered nursing/registered nurse; retailing; social work; sport and fitness administration/management; veterinary/animal health technology.

Academics *Calendar:* semesters. *Degree:* certificates and associate. *Special study options:* academic remediation for entering students, adult/continuing education programs, advanced placement credit, cooperative education, distance learning, double majors, English as a second language, external degree program, honors programs, independent study, internships, off-campus study, part-time degree program, services for LD students, student-designed majors, study abroad, summer session for credit. *ROTC:* Army (c), Air Force (c).

Library Elaine Marieb Library plus 1 other with 88,149 titles, 29,599 serial subscriptions, 9,327 audiovisual materials, an OPAC, a Web page.

Student Life *Housing:* college housing not available. *Activities and Organizations:* drama/theater group, student-run newspaper, radio station, Drama Club, Japanese Anime Club, Student Senate, LISA Club, STRIVE. *Campus security:* 24-hour emergency response devices and patrols, late-night transport/escort service. *Student services:* health clinic, personal/psychological counseling, women's center.

Athletics Member NJCAA. *Intercollegiate sports:* baseball M, basketball M/W, cross-country running M/W, golf M/W, soccer M/W, softball W, volleyball W.

Costs (2011–12) *Tuition:* state resident $576 full-time, $129 per credit part-time; nonresident $5520 full-time, $335 per credit part-time. Full-time tuition and fees vary according to course load. Part-time tuition and fees vary according to course load. *Required fees:* $2700 full-time, $90 per term part-time. *Payment plan:* installment. *Waivers:* senior citizens and employees or children of employees.

Applying *Options:* electronic application, early admission, deferred entrance. *Required:* high school transcript. *Recommended:* interview. *Application deadlines:* rolling (freshmen), rolling (transfers). *Notification:* continuous (freshmen), continuous (transfers).

Freshman Application Contact Ms. Marcia Rosbury-Henne, Director of Admissions and Transfer Affairs, Holyoke Community College, Admission Office, Holyoke, MA 01040. *Phone:* 413-552-2321. *Fax:* 413-552-2045. *E-mail:* admissions@hcc.edu. *Web site:* http://www.hcc.edu/.

ITT Technical Institute

Norwood, Massachusetts

- **Proprietary** primarily 2-year, founded 1990, part of ITT Educational Services, Inc.
- **Suburban** campus
- **Coed**

Majors CAD/CADD drafting/design technology; computer and information systems security; computer engineering technology; computer software and media applications related; electrical, electronic and communications engineering technology; game and interactive media design; system, networking, and LAN/WAN management; web/multimedia management and webmaster.

Academics *Calendar:* quarters. *Degrees:* associate and bachelor's.

Student Life *Housing:* college housing not available.

Freshman Application Contact Director of Recruitment, ITT Technical Institute, 333 Providence Highway, Norwood, MA 02062. *Phone:* 781-278-7200. *Toll-free phone:* 800-879-8324. *Web site:* http://www.itt-tech.edu/.

ITT Technical Institute
Wilmington, Massachusetts

- **Proprietary** primarily 2-year, founded 2000, part of ITT Educational Services, Inc.
- **Coed**

Majors CAD/CADD drafting/design technology; computer and information systems security; computer engineering technology; computer software and media applications related; electrical, electronic and communications engineering technology; game and interactive media design; system, networking, and LAN/WAN management; web/multimedia management and webmaster; web page, digital/multimedia and information resources design.

Academics *Calendar:* quarters. *Degrees:* associate and bachelor's.

Student Life *Housing:* college housing not available.

Freshman Application Contact Director of Recruitment, ITT Technical Institute, 200 Ballardvale Street, Suite 200, Wilmington, MA 01887. *Phone:* 978-658-2636. *Toll-free phone:* 800-430-5097. *Web site:* http://www.itt-tech.edu/.

Labouré College
Boston, Massachusetts

Director of Admissions Ms. Gina M. Morrissette, Director of Admissions, Labouré College, 2120 Dorchester Avenue, Boston, MA 02124-5698. *Phone:* 617-296-8300. *Web site:* http://www.laboure.edu/.

Marian Court College
Swampscott, Massachusetts

Director of Admissions Bryan Boppert, Director of Admissions, Marian Court College, 35 Little's Point Road, Swampscott, MA 01907-2840. *Phone:* 781-309-5230. *Fax:* 781-309-5286. *Web site:* http://www.mariancourt.edu/.

Massachusetts Bay Community College
Wellesley Hills, Massachusetts

- **State-supported** 2-year, founded 1961
- **Suburban** 84-acre campus with easy access to Boston
- **Coed,** 5,276 undergraduate students, 40% full-time, 57% women, 43% men

Undergraduates 2,128 full-time, 3,148 part-time. Students come from 11 states and territories; 99 other countries; 2% are from out of state; 17% Black or African American, non-Hispanic/Latino; 13% Hispanic/Latino; 4% Asian, non-Hispanic/Latino; 0.1% Native Hawaiian or other Pacific Islander, non-Hispanic/Latino; 0.5% American Indian or Alaska Native, non-Hispanic/Latino; 8% Race/ethnicity unknown; 2% international; 5% transferred in. *Retention:* 53% of full-time freshmen returned.

Freshmen *Admission:* 1,890 applied, 1,887 admitted, 1,147 enrolled.

Faculty *Total:* 382, 23% full-time. *Student/faculty ratio:* 17:1.

Majors Accounting; automotive engineering technology; biological and physical sciences; biology/biotechnology laboratory technician; business administration and management; business/commerce; chemical technology; child-care and support services management; computer and information sciences; computer engineering technology; computer science; criminal justice/law enforcement administration; drafting and design technology; engineering technology; environmental engineering technology; forensic science and technology; general studies; hospitality administration; human services; information science/studies; international relations and affairs; legal assistant/paralegal; liberal arts and sciences/liberal studies; mechanical engineering/mechanical technology; medical radiologic technology; physical therapy technology; registered nursing/registered nurse; respiratory care therapy; social sciences; speech communication and rhetoric.

Academics *Calendar:* semesters. *Degree:* certificates and associate. *Special study options:* academic remediation for entering students, adult/continuing education programs, advanced placement credit, cooperative education, distance learning, honors programs, internships, part-time degree program, services for LD students, summer session for credit.

Library Perkins Library with 51,429 titles, 280 serial subscriptions, 4,780 audiovisual materials, an OPAC, a Web page.

Student Life *Housing:* college housing not available. *Activities and Organizations:* drama/theater group, student-run newspaper, Student Government Association, Latino Student Organization, New World Society Club, Mass Bay Players, Student Occupational Therapy Association. *Campus security:* 24-hour emergency response devices and patrols. *Student services:* health clinic, personal/psychological counseling.

Athletics Member NJCAA. *Intercollegiate sports:* baseball M, basketball M/W, cross-country running M/W, golf M/W, soccer M/W, softball W, tennis M/W, volleyball W. *Intramural sports:* ice hockey M, soccer M/W.

Costs (2012–13) *Tuition:* state resident $576 full-time, $24 per credit part-time; nonresident $5520 full-time, $230 per credit part-time. *Required fees:* $3600 full-time.

Financial Aid Of all full-time matriculated undergraduates who enrolled in 2010, 59 Federal Work-Study jobs (averaging $1840).

Applying *Options:* electronic application, deferred entrance. *Application fee:* $20. *Application deadlines:* rolling (freshmen), rolling (transfers). *Notification:* continuous (freshmen), continuous (transfers).

Freshman Application Contact Ms. Donna Raposa, Director of Admissions, Massachusetts Bay Community College, 50 Oakland Street, Wellesley Hills, MA 02481. *Phone:* 781-239-2500. *Fax:* 781-239-1047. *E-mail:* info@massbay.edu. *Web site:* http://www.massbay.edu/.

Massasoit Community College
Brockton, Massachusetts

Freshman Application Contact Michelle Hughes, Director of Admissions, Massasoit Community College, 1 Massasoit Boulevard, Brockton, MA 02302-3996. *Phone:* 508-588-9100. *Toll-free phone:* 800-CAREERS. *Web site:* http://www.massasoit.mass.edu/.

Middlesex Community College
Bedford, Massachusetts

Director of Admissions Ms. Laurie Dimitrov, Director, Admissions and Recruitment, Middlesex Community College, Springs Road, Bedford, MA 01730-1655. *Phone:* 978-656-3207. *Toll-free phone:* 800-818-3434. *E-mail:* orellanad@middlesex.cc.ma.us. *Web site:* http://www.middlesex.mass.edu/.

Mount Wachusett Community College
Gardner, Massachusetts

- **State-supported** 2-year, founded 1963, part of Massachusetts Public Higher Education System
- **Small-town** 270-acre campus with easy access to Boston
- **Endowment** $3.4 million
- **Coed,** 4,755 undergraduate students, 42% full-time, 65% women, 35% men

Undergraduates 2,016 full-time, 2,739 part-time. Students come from 10 states and territories; 4% are from out of state; 7% Black or African American, non-Hispanic/Latino; 13% Hispanic/Latino; 2% Asian, non-Hispanic/Latino; 0.1% Native Hawaiian or other Pacific Islander, non-Hispanic/Latino; 0.4% American Indian or Alaska Native, non-Hispanic/Latino; 2% Two or more races, non-Hispanic/Latino; 3% Race/ethnicity unknown; 0.9% international; 6% transferred in. *Retention:* 54% of full-time freshmen returned.

Freshmen *Admission:* 1,922 applied, 1,922 admitted, 1,010 enrolled.

Faculty *Total:* 237, 31% full-time. *Student/faculty ratio:* 23:1.

Majors Allied health and medical assisting services related; alternative and complementary medical support services related; art; automobile/automotive mechanics technology; biotechnology; child-care and support services management; child development; clinical/medical laboratory technology; computer and information sciences; computer graphics; computer technology/computer systems technology; corrections; criminal justice/law enforcement administration; criminal justice/safety; dental hygiene; environmental studies; fire prevention and safety technology; general studies; human services; legal assistant/paralegal; liberal arts and sciences/liberal studies; medical/clinical assistant; physical therapy technology; plastics and polymer engineering technology; psychiatric/mental health services technology; radio and television broadcasting technology; registered nursing/registered nurse; web page, digital/multimedia and information resources design.

Academics *Calendar:* semesters. *Degree:* certificates and associate. *Special study options:* academic remediation for entering students, accelerated degree program, adult/continuing education programs, advanced placement credit, cooperative education, distance learning, double majors, English as a second language, honors programs, independent study, internships, part-time degree program, services for LD students, study abroad, summer session for credit.

Library LaChance Library with 53,763 titles, 2,495 audiovisual materials, an OPAC, a Web page.

Student Life *Housing:* college housing not available. *Activities and Organizations:* drama/theater group, student-run newspaper, choral group, Art Club,

Dental Hygienist Club, International Club, Student Government Association, Student Nurses Association. *Campus security:* 24-hour emergency response devices and patrols. *Student services:* health clinic, personal/psychological counseling.

Athletics *Intramural sports:* badminton M/W, basketball M/W, football M/W, soccer M/W, softball M/W, table tennis M/W, volleyball M/W, water polo M/W.

Standardized Tests *Required for some:* SAT (for admission). *Recommended:* SAT (for admission), ACT (for admission), SAT or ACT (for admission), SAT and SAT Subject Tests or ACT (for admission), SAT Subject Tests (for admission).

Costs (2011–12) *Tuition:* state resident $750 full-time, $25 per credit hour part-time; nonresident $6900 full-time, $230 per credit hour part-time. Full-time tuition and fees vary according to program and reciprocity agreements. Part-time tuition and fees vary according to program and reciprocity agreements. *Required fees:* $4800 full-time, $160 per credit hour part-time, $125 per term part-time. *Payment plan:* installment. *Waivers:* senior citizens and employees or children of employees.

Financial Aid Of all full-time matriculated undergraduates who enrolled in 2010, 47 Federal Work-Study jobs (averaging $2228).

Applying *Options:* electronic application, early admission. *Application fee:* $10. *Required:* high school transcript. *Required for some:* 2 letters of recommendation. *Recommended:* interview. *Application deadlines:* rolling (freshmen), rolling (transfers). *Notification:* continuous (freshmen), continuous (transfers).

Freshman Application Contact Mr. Ryan Forsythe, Director of Admissions, Mount Wachusett Community College, 444 Green Street, Gardner, MA 01440-1000. *Phone:* 978-632-6600 Ext. 110. *Fax:* 978-630-9554. *E-mail:* admissions@mwcc.mass.edu. *Web site:* http://www.mwcc.mass.edu/.

Northern Essex Community College

Haverhill, Massachusetts

- **State-supported** 2-year, founded 1960
- **Suburban** 106-acre campus with easy access to Boston
- **Endowment** $4.5 million
- **Coed,** 7,036 undergraduate students, 36% full-time, 62% women, 38% men

Undergraduates 2,515 full-time, 4,521 part-time. Students come from 6 states and territories; 17% are from out of state; 3% Black or African American, non-Hispanic/Latino; 30% Hispanic/Latino; 1% Asian, non-Hispanic/Latino; 0.9% Native Hawaiian or other Pacific Islander, non-Hispanic/Latino; 0.2% American Indian or Alaska Native, non-Hispanic/Latino; 0.9% Two or more races, non-Hispanic/Latino; 4% Race/ethnicity unknown; 0.7% international; 5% transferred in. *Retention:* 59% of full-time freshmen returned.

Freshmen *Admission:* 2,960 applied, 2,817 admitted, 1,185 enrolled.

Faculty *Total:* 657, 16% full-time. *Student/faculty ratio:* 22:1.

Majors Accounting; administrative assistant and secretarial science; biological and physical sciences; business administration and management; business teacher education; civil engineering technology; commercial and advertising art; computer and information sciences; computer engineering technology; computer graphics; computer programming; computer programming related; computer programming (specific applications); computer science; computer systems networking and telecommunications; computer typography and composition equipment operation; criminal justice/law enforcement administration; dance; data processing and data processing technology; dental assisting; dramatic/theater arts; education; electrical, electronic and communications engineering technology; elementary education; engineering science; finance; general studies; health information/medical records administration; history; hotel/motel administration; human services; industrial radiologic technology; international relations and affairs; journalism; kindergarten/preschool education; legal assistant/paralegal; liberal arts and sciences/liberal studies; machine tool technology; marketing/marketing management; materials science; medical administrative assistant and medical secretary; medical transcription; mental health counseling; music; parks, recreation and leisure; physical education teaching and coaching; political science and government; radiologic technology/science; real estate; registered nursing/registered nurse; respiratory care therapy; respiratory therapy technician; sign language interpretation and translation; telecommunications technology; tourism and travel services management; web/multimedia management and webmaster; web page, digital/multimedia and information resources design; women's studies.

Academics *Calendar:* semesters. *Degree:* certificates and associate. *Special study options:* academic remediation for entering students, adult/continuing education programs, advanced placement credit, cooperative education, distance learning, double majors, English as a second language, freshman honors college, honors programs, independent study, internships, off-campus study, part-time degree program, services for LD students, study abroad, summer session for credit. *ROTC:* Air Force (c).

Library Bentley Library with 61,120 titles, 598 serial subscriptions, an OPAC.

Student Life *Housing:* college housing not available. *Activities and Organizations:* drama/theater group, student-run newspaper. *Campus security:* 24-hour emergency response devices and patrols. *Student services:* health clinic, personal/psychological counseling, women's center.

Athletics Member NJCAA. *Intercollegiate sports:* baseball M, basketball M/W, cross-country running M/W, volleyball M/W. *Intramural sports:* basketball M/W, cross-country running M/W, football M/W, golf M/W, racquetball M/W, skiing (cross-country) M/W, skiing (downhill) M/W, weight lifting M/W.

Standardized Tests *Required:* Psychological Corporation Aptitude Test for Practical Nursing (for admission).

Costs (2011–12) *Tuition:* state resident $600 full-time, $25 per credit hour part-time; nonresident $6384 full-time, $266 per credit hour part-time. *Required fees:* $2928 full-time, $122 per credit hour part-time. *Payment plan:* installment. *Waivers:* employees or children of employees.

Financial Aid Of all full-time matriculated undergraduates who enrolled in 2010, 74 Federal Work-Study jobs (averaging $1759).

Applying *Options:* early admission. *Application fee:* $25. *Required:* high school transcript. *Application deadlines:* rolling (freshmen), rolling (transfers). *Notification:* continuous (freshmen), continuous (transfers).

Freshman Application Contact Ms. Laurie Dimitrov, Director of Admissions, Northern Essex Community College, Haverhill, MA 01830. *Phone:* 978-556-3616. *Fax:* 978-556-3155. *Web site:* http://www.necc.mass.edu/.

North Shore Community College

Danvers, Massachusetts

- **State-supported** 2-year, founded 1965
- **Suburban** campus with easy access to Boston
- **Endowment** $5.2 million
- **Coed,** 7,284 undergraduate students

Undergraduates Students come from 9 states and territories; 8 other countries; 2% are from out of state; 9% Black or African American, non-Hispanic/Latino; 18% Hispanic/Latino; 4% Asian, non-Hispanic/Latino; 0.1% Native Hawaiian or other Pacific Islander, non-Hispanic/Latino; 0.4% American Indian or Alaska Native, non-Hispanic/Latino; 2% Two or more races, non-Hispanic/Latino; 3% Race/ethnicity unknown; 0.2% international.

Freshmen *Admission:* 4,696 applied, 3,879 admitted.

Faculty *Total:* 496, 27% full-time, 33% with terminal degrees. *Student/faculty ratio:* 17:1.

Majors Accounting; administrative assistant and secretarial science; airline pilot and flight crew; biology/biotechnology laboratory technician; business administration and management; child development; computer and information sciences related; computer engineering technology; computer graphics; computer programming; computer programming (specific applications); computer science; criminal justice/law enforcement administration; culinary arts; data entry/microcomputer applications; engineering science; fire science/firefighting; foods, nutrition, and wellness; gerontology; health professions related; hospitality administration; information science/studies; interdisciplinary studies; kindergarten/preschool education; legal administrative assistant/secretary; legal assistant/paralegal; liberal arts and sciences/liberal studies; marketing/marketing management; medical administrative assistant and medical secretary; medical radiologic technology; mental health counseling; occupational therapy; physical therapy technology; pre-engineering; registered nursing/registered nurse; respiratory care therapy; substance abuse/addiction counseling; tourism and travel services management; veterinary/animal health technology; web page, digital/multimedia and information resources design.

Academics *Calendar:* semesters. *Degree:* certificates and associate. *Special study options:* academic remediation for entering students, accelerated degree program, adult/continuing education programs, advanced placement credit, cooperative education, distance learning, English as a second language, honors programs, independent study, internships, part-time degree program, services for LD students, summer session for credit.

Library Learning Resource Center plus 2 others with 71,183 titles, 248 serial subscriptions, 6,016 audiovisual materials, an OPAC.

Student Life *Housing:* college housing not available. *Activities and Organizations:* drama/theater group, student-run newspaper, Program Council, student government, performing arts, student newspaper, Phi Theta Kappa. *Campus security:* 24-hour emergency response devices and patrols, late-night transport/escort service. *Student services:* health clinic, personal/psychological counseling, women's center.

Financial Aid Of all full-time matriculated undergraduates who enrolled in 2009, 1,658 applied for aid, 1,438 were judged to have need, 23 had their need fully met. 123 Federal Work-Study jobs (averaging $1359). In 2009, 11 non-need-based awards were made. *Average percent of need met:* 18%. *Average financial aid package:* $6856. *Average need-based loan:* $1639. *Average need-based gift aid:* $2522. *Average non-need-based aid:* $614.

Applying *Options:* electronic application, early admission. *Required for some:* high school transcript, interview. *Application deadlines:* rolling (freshmen), rolling (transfers). *Notification:* continuous (freshmen), continuous (transfers).

Freshman Application Contact Ms. Lisa Barrett, Academic Counselor, North Shore Community College, Danvers, MA 01923. *Phone:* 978-762-4000 Ext. 6225. *Fax:* 978-762-4015. *E-mail:* lbarrett@northshore.edu. *Web site:* http://www.northshore.edu/.

Quincy College
Quincy, Massachusetts

Freshman Application Contact Paula Smith, Dean, Enrollment Services, Quincy College, 34 Coddington Street, Quincy, MA 02169-4522. *Phone:* 617-984-1700. *Toll-free phone:* 800-698-1700. *Fax:* 617-984-1779. *E-mail:* psmith@quincycollege.edu. *Web site:* http://www.quincycollege.edu/.

Quinsigamond Community College
Worcester, Massachusetts

- **State-supported** 2-year, founded 1963, part of Massachusetts System of Higher Education
- **Urban** 57-acre campus with easy access to Boston
- **Endowment** $384,927
- **Coed,** 9,130 undergraduate students, 44% full-time, 57% women, 43% men

Undergraduates 4,001 full-time, 5,129 part-time. Students come from 26 states and territories; 31 other countries; 1% are from out of state; 11% Black or African American, non-Hispanic/Latino; 14% Hispanic/Latino; 4% Asian, non-Hispanic/Latino; 0.1% Native Hawaiian or other Pacific Islander, non-Hispanic/Latino; 0.4% American Indian or Alaska Native, non-Hispanic/Latino; 1% Two or more races, non-Hispanic/Latino; 5% Race/ethnicity unknown; 0.3% international. *Retention:* 59% of full-time freshmen returned.
Freshmen *Admission:* 4,311 applied, 2,455 admitted, 1,923 enrolled.
Faculty *Total:* 564, 23% full-time, 14% with terminal degrees. *Student/faculty ratio:* 21:1.
Majors Alternative and complementary medicine related; automobile/automotive mechanics technology; bioengineering and biomedical engineering; biotechnology; business administration and management; business/commerce; civil engineering technology; computer and information systems security; computer engineering technology; computer graphics; computer programming (specific applications); computer science; computer systems analysis; criminal justice/police science; data modeling/warehousing and database administration; dental hygiene; dental services and allied professions related; electrical, electronic and communications engineering technology; electromechanical technology; emergency medical technology (EMT paramedic); executive assistant/executive secretary; fire services administration; general studies; health services/allied health/health sciences; hospitality administration; human services; kindergarten/preschool education; liberal arts and sciences/liberal studies; manufacturing engineering technology; medical administrative assistant and medical secretary; occupational therapy; radiologic technology/science; registered nursing/registered nurse; respiratory care therapy; restaurant/food services management; telecommunications technology; web page, digital/multimedia and information resources design.
Academics *Calendar:* semesters. *Degree:* certificates and associate. *Special study options:* academic remediation for entering students, accelerated degree program, advanced placement credit, cooperative education, distance learning, double majors, English as a second language, honors programs, independent study, internships, off-campus study, part-time degree program, services for LD students, summer session for credit. *ROTC:* Army (c).
Library Alden Library with 60,280 titles, 220 serial subscriptions, 2,719 audiovisual materials, an OPAC, a Web page.
Student Life *Housing:* college housing not available. *Activities and Organizations:* drama/theater group, student-run newspaper, Phi Theta Kappa, academic-related clubs, Student Senate, Chess Club, Business Club. *Campus security:* 24-hour emergency response devices and patrols, late-night transport/escort service. *Student services:* personal/psychological counseling.
Athletics Member NJCAA. *Intercollegiate sports:* baseball M, basketball M/W, softball W. *Intramural sports:* basketball M/W, soccer M/W, ultimate Frisbee M/W, volleyball M/W.
Costs (2012–13) *Tuition:* state resident $576 full-time, $24 per credit hour part-time; nonresident $5520 full-time, $230 per credit hour part-time. Full-time tuition and fees vary according to course load and program. Part-time tuition and fees vary according to course load and program. *Required fees:* $4176 full-time, $154 per credit hour part-time, $245 per credit hour part-time. *Payment plan:* installment. *Waivers:* senior citizens and employees or children of employees.
Applying *Options:* electronic application. *Application fee:* $20. *Required:* high school transcript. *Required for some:* interview. *Application deadlines:* rolling (freshmen), rolling (out-of-state freshmen), rolling (transfers). *Notifi-*

cation: continuous (freshmen), continuous (out-of-state freshmen), continuous (transfers).
Freshman Application Contact Quinsigamond Community College, 670 West Boylston Street, Worcester, MA 01606-2092. *Phone:* 508-854-4260. *Web site:* http://www.qcc.edu/.

Roxbury Community College
Roxbury Crossing, Massachusetts

Director of Admissions Mr. Milton Samuels, Director, Admissions, Roxbury Community College, 1234 Columbus Avenue, Roxbury Crossing, MA 02120-3400. *Phone:* 617-541-5310. *Web site:* http://www.rcc.mass.edu/.

Springfield Technical Community College
Springfield, Massachusetts

- **State-supported** 2-year, founded 1967
- **Urban** 34-acre campus
- **Coed,** 6,899 undergraduate students, 44% full-time, 58% women, 42% men

Undergraduates 3,015 full-time, 3,884 part-time. 3% are from out of state; 14% Black or African American, non-Hispanic/Latino; 22% Hispanic/Latino; 2% Asian, non-Hispanic/Latino; 0.6% American Indian or Alaska Native, non-Hispanic/Latino; 1% Two or more races, non-Hispanic/Latino; 10% Race/ethnicity unknown; 0.6% international; 10% transferred in.
Freshmen *Admission:* 3,189 applied, 2,774 admitted, 1,275 enrolled.
Faculty *Total:* 368, 41% full-time. *Student/faculty ratio:* 17:1.
Majors Accounting; administrative assistant and secretarial science; animation, interactive technology, video graphics and special effects; automotive engineering technology; biology/biological sciences; biotechnology; building/construction finishing, management, and inspection related; business administration and management; business/commerce; chemistry; civil engineering technology; clinical/medical laboratory technology; commercial and advertising art; commercial photography; computer and information systems security; computer engineering technology; computer programming (specific applications); computer science; criminal justice/police science; data processing and data processing technology; dental hygiene; diagnostic medical sonography and ultrasound technology; early childhood education; electrical, electronic and communications engineering technology; electromechanical technology; elementary education; engineering; executive assistant/executive secretary; finance; fine/studio arts; fire prevention and safety technology; fire science/firefighting; general studies; heating, ventilation, air conditioning and refrigeration engineering technology; landscaping and groundskeeping; laser and optical technology; liberal arts and sciences/liberal studies; marketing/marketing management; massage therapy; mathematics; mechanical engineering/mechanical technology; medical administrative assistant and medical secretary; medical/clinical assistant; medical insurance coding; network and system administration; nuclear medical technology; occupational therapist assistant; physical therapy technology; physics; premedical studies; radio and television broadcasting technology; radiologic technology/science; recording arts technology; registered nursing/registered nurse; respiratory care therapy; secondary education; small business administration; sport and fitness administration/management; surgical technology; telecommunications technology; web page, digital/multimedia and information resources design.
Academics *Calendar:* semesters. *Degree:* certificates and associate. *Special study options:* academic remediation for entering students, adult/continuing education programs, advanced placement credit, cooperative education, distance learning, English as a second language, honors programs, independent study, internships, off-campus study, part-time degree program, services for LD students, summer session for credit.
Library Springfield Technical Community College Library with an OPAC, a Web page.
Student Life *Housing:* college housing not available. *Activities and Organizations:* Phi Theta Kappa, Landscape Design Club, Dental Hygiene Club, Clinical Lab Science Club, Physical Therapist Assistant Club. *Campus security:* 24-hour emergency response devices and patrols, late-night transport/escort service. *Student services:* health clinic, personal/psychological counseling.
Athletics Member NJCAA. *Intercollegiate sports:* basketball M/W, golf M, soccer M/W, wrestling M. *Intramural sports:* basketball M/W, cross-country running M/W, golf M/W, skiing (cross-country) M/W, volleyball M/W, weight lifting M/W.
Standardized Tests *Required for some:* SAT (for admission).
Costs (2011–12) *Tuition:* state resident $750 full-time, $25 per credit part-time; nonresident $7260 full-time, $242 per credit part-time. Full-time tuition and fees vary according to course load and reciprocity agreements. Part-time tuition and fees vary according to course load and reciprocity agreements. No tuition increase for student's term of enrollment. *Required fees:* $4026 full-

time, $152 per credit part-time, $108 per term part-time. *Payment plan:* installment. *Waivers:* senior citizens and employees or children of employees.

Financial Aid Of all full-time matriculated undergraduates who enrolled in 2010, 124 Federal Work-Study jobs (averaging $2400).

Applying *Options:* electronic application. *Application fee:* $10. *Required:* high school transcript. *Required for some:* interview. *Application deadlines:* rolling (freshmen), rolling (transfers).

Freshman Application Contact Mr. Ray Blair, Springfield Technical Community College, Springfield, MA 01105. *Phone:* 413-781-7822 Ext. 4868. *E-mail:* rblair@stcc.edu. *Web site:* http://www.stcc.edu/.

Urban College of Boston

Boston, Massachusetts

Director of Admissions Dr. Henry J. Johnson, Director of Enrollment Services/Registrar, Urban College of Boston, 178 Tremont Street, Boston, MA 02111. *Phone:* 617-348-6353. *Web site:* http://www.urbancollegeofboston.org/.

MICHIGAN

Alpena Community College

Alpena, Michigan

Freshman Application Contact Mr. Mike Kollien, Director of Admissions, Alpena Community College, 665 Johnson, Alpena, MI 49707. *Phone:* 989-358-7339. *Toll-free phone:* 888-468-6222. *Fax:* 989-358-7540. *E-mail:* kollienm@alpenacc.edu. *Web site:* http://www.alpenacc.edu/.

Bay de Noc Community College

Escanaba, Michigan

Freshman Application Contact Bay de Noc Community College, 2001 North Lincoln Road, Escanaba, MI 49829-2511. *Phone:* 906-786-5802 Ext. 1276. *Toll-free phone:* 800-221-2001. *Web site:* http://www.baycollege.edu/.

Bay Mills Community College

Brimley, Michigan

Freshman Application Contact Ms. Elaine Lehre, Admissions Officer, Bay Mills Community College, 12214 West Lakeshore Drive, Brimley, MI 49715. *Phone:* 906-248-3354. *Toll-free phone:* 800-844-BMCC. *Fax:* 906-248-3351. *Web site:* http://www.bmcc.edu/.

Delta College

University Center, Michigan

Freshman Application Contact Mr. Gary Brasseur, Associate Director of Admissions, Delta College, 1961 Delta Road, University Center, MI 48710. *Phone:* 989-686-9590. *Fax:* 989-667-2202. *E-mail:* admit@delta.edu. *Web site:* http://www.delta.edu/.

Glen Oaks Community College

Centreville, Michigan

Freshman Application Contact Ms. Beverly M. Andrews, Director of Admissions/Registrar, Glen Oaks Community College, 62249 Shimmel Road, Centreville, MI 49032-9719. *Phone:* 269-467-9945 Ext. 248. *Toll-free phone:* 888-994-7818. *Web site:* http://www.glenoaks.edu/.

Gogebic Community College

Ironwood, Michigan

Freshman Application Contact Ms. Jeanne Graham, Director of Admissions, Gogebic Community College, E4946 Jackson Road, Ironwood, MI 49938. *Phone:* 906-932-4231 Ext. 306. *Toll-free phone:* 800-682-5910. *Fax:* 906-932-2339. *E-mail:* jeanneg@gogebic.edu. *Web site:* http://www.gogebic.edu/.

Grand Rapids Community College

Grand Rapids, Michigan

- **District-supported** 2-year, founded 1914, part of Michigan Department of Education
- **Urban** 35-acre campus
- **Endowment** $31.2 million
- **Coed,** 17,575 undergraduate students, 38% full-time, 53% women, 47% men

Undergraduates 6,690 full-time, 10,885 part-time. Students come from 8 states and territories; 23 other countries; 1% are from out of state; 12% Black or African American, non-Hispanic/Latino; 7% Hispanic/Latino; 3% Asian, non-Hispanic/Latino; 0.8% American Indian or Alaska Native, non-Hispanic/Latino; 0.1% Two or more races, non-Hispanic/Latino; 12% Race/ethnicity unknown; 0.1% international; 7% transferred in.

Freshmen *Admission:* 11,861 applied, 3,919 enrolled. *Average high school GPA:* 3.2. *Test scores:* ACT scores over 18: 73%; ACT scores over 24: 26%; ACT scores over 30: 2%.

Faculty *Total:* 863, 28% full-time, 10% with terminal degrees. *Student/faculty ratio:* 23:1.

Majors Architectural engineering technology; architecture; art; automobile/automotive mechanics technology; business administration and management; chemistry; child-care and support services management; computer engineering technology; computer programming; computer science; corrections; criminal justice/law enforcement administration; criminal justice/police science; culinary arts; dental hygiene; drafting and design technology; electrical, electronic and communications engineering technology; elementary education; engineering; English; fashion merchandising; foreign languages and literatures; forestry; geology/earth science; heating, air conditioning, ventilation and refrigeration maintenance technology; industrial technology; landscaping and groundskeeping; liberal arts and sciences/liberal studies; library and information science; licensed practical/vocational nurse training; mass communication/media; medical administrative assistant and medical secretary; music; plastics and polymer engineering technology; quality control technology; registered nursing/registered nurse; welding technology.

Academics *Calendar:* semesters. *Degree:* certificates and associate. *Special study options:* academic remediation for entering students, adult/continuing education programs, advanced placement credit, cooperative education, distance learning, English as a second language, honors programs, independent study, internships, off-campus study, part-time degree program, services for LD students, study abroad, summer session for credit.

Library Arthur Andrews Memorial Library plus 1 other with 200,000 titles, 18,000 serial subscriptions, 3,500 audiovisual materials, an OPAC, a Web page.

Student Life *Housing:* college housing not available. *Activities and Organizations:* drama/theater group, student-run newspaper, choral group, Student Congress, Phi Theta Kappa, Hispanic Student Organization, Asian Student Organization, Service Learning Advisory Board. *Campus security:* 24-hour emergency response devices, late-night transport/escort service. *Student services:* personal/psychological counseling.

Athletics Member NJCAA. *Intercollegiate sports:* baseball M(s), basketball M(s)/W(s), golf M(s), softball W(s), tennis M(s)/W(s), volleyball W(s). *Intramural sports:* badminton M/W, basketball M/W, skiing (cross-country) M/W, skiing (downhill) M/W, soccer M/W, swimming and diving M/W, tennis M/W, volleyball M/W.

Standardized Tests *Required for some:* ACT ASSET. *Recommended:* SAT or ACT (for admission).

Costs (2011–12) *Tuition:* area resident $2865 full-time, $96 per contact hour part-time; state resident $6285 full-time, $210 per contact hour part-time; non-resident $9405 full-time, $314 per contact hour part-time. Full-time tuition and fees vary according to course load. Part-time tuition and fees vary according to course load. *Required fees:* $259 full-time, $6 per contact hour part-time, $47 per term part-time. *Payment plan:* installment. *Waivers:* employees or children of employees.

Financial Aid Of all full-time matriculated undergraduates who enrolled in 2008, 6,142 applied for aid, 4,896 were judged to have need, 1,012 had their need fully met. In 2008, 96 non-need-based awards were made. *Average financial aid package:* $4850. *Average need-based loan:* $2764. *Average need-based gift aid:* $3984. *Average non-need-based aid:* $1051.

Applying *Options:* electronic application, early admission, deferred entrance. *Required:* high school transcript. *Application deadline:* 8/30 (freshmen). *Notification:* continuous (freshmen), continuous (transfers).

Freshman Application Contact Ms. Diane Patrick, Director of Admissions, Grand Rapids Community College, Grand Rapids, MI 49503-3201. *Phone:* 616-234-4100. *Fax:* 616-234-4005. *E-mail:* dpatrick@grcc.edu. *Web site:* http://www.grcc.edu/.

Henry Ford Community College
Dearborn, Michigan

Freshman Application Contact Admissions Office, Henry Ford Community College, 5101 Evergreen Road, Dearborn, MI 48128-1495. *Phone:* 313-845-6403. *Toll-free phone:* 800-585-HFCC. *Fax:* 313-845-6464. *E-mail:* enroll@hfcc.edu. *Web site:* http://www.hfcc.edu/.

ITT Technical Institute
Canton, Michigan

- **Proprietary** primarily 2-year, founded 2002, part of ITT Educational Services, Inc.
- **Coed**

Majors Business administration and management; communications technology; computer and information systems security; computer software engineering; computer software technology; construction management; criminal justice/law enforcement administration; drafting and design technology; electrical, electronic and communications engineering technology; forensic science and technology; game and interactive media design; graphic communications; legal assistant/paralegal; network and system administration; project management; registered nursing/registered nurse.

Academics *Calendar:* quarters. *Degrees:* associate and bachelor's.

Student Life *Housing:* college housing not available.

Freshman Application Contact Director of Recruitment, ITT Technical Institute, 1905 South Haggerty Road, Canton, MI 48188-2025. *Phone:* 784-397-7800. *Toll-free phone:* 800-247-4477. *Web site:* http://www.itt-tech.edu/.

ITT Technical Institute
Dearborn, Michigan

- **Proprietary** primarily 2-year, part of ITT Educational Services, Inc.
- **Coed**

Majors Business administration and management; communications technology; computer and information systems security; drafting and design technology; electrical, electronic and communications engineering technology; forensic science and technology; graphic communications; legal assistant/paralegal; network and system administration; project management.

Academics *Calendar:* quarters. *Degrees:* associate and bachelor's.

Freshman Application Contact Director of Recruitment, ITT Technical Institute, 19855 W. Outer Drive, Suite L10W, Dearborn, MI 48124. *Phone:* 313-278-5208. *Toll-free phone:* 800-605-0801. *Web site:* http://www.itt-tech.edu/.

ITT Technical Institute
Swartz Creek, Michigan

- **Proprietary** primarily 2-year, founded 2005, part of ITT Educational Services, Inc.
- **Coed**

Majors Business administration and management; communications technology; computer and information systems security; computer software and media applications related; computer software technology; construction management; criminal justice/law enforcement administration; drafting and design technology; electrical, electronic and communications engineering technology; forensic science and technology; graphic communications; information technology project management; legal assistant/paralegal; network and system administration; project management.

Academics *Calendar:* quarters. *Degrees:* associate and bachelor's.

Freshman Application Contact Director of Recruitment, ITT Technical Institute, 6359 Miller Road, Swartz Creek, MI 48473. *Phone:* 810-628-2500. *Toll-free phone:* 800-514-6564. *Web site:* http://www.itt-tech.edu/.

ITT Technical Institute
Troy, Michigan

- **Proprietary** primarily 2-year, founded 1987, part of ITT Educational Services, Inc.
- **Coed**

Majors Business administration and management; communications technology; computer and information systems security; computer software and media applications related; construction management; criminal justice/law enforcement administration; drafting and design technology; electrical, electronic and communications engineering technology; forensic science and technology; game and interactive media design; graphic communications; legal assistant/paralegal; network and system administration; project management; web/multimedia management and webmaster.

Academics *Calendar:* quarters. *Degrees:* associate and bachelor's.

Student Life *Housing:* college housing not available.

Freshman Application Contact Director of Recruitment, ITT Technical Institute, 1522 East Big Beaver Road, Troy, MI 48083-1905. *Phone:* 248-524-1800. *Toll-free phone:* 800-832-6817. *Fax:* 248-524-1965. *Web site:* http://www.itt-tech.edu/.

ITT Technical Institute
Wyoming, Michigan

- **Proprietary** primarily 2-year, part of ITT Educational Services, Inc.
- **Coed**

Majors Business administration and management; communications technology; computer and information systems security; computer software engineering; computer software technology; construction management; criminal justice/law enforcement administration; drafting and design technology; electrical, electronic and communications engineering technology; forensic science and technology; graphic communications; information technology project management; legal assistant/paralegal; network and system administration; project management.

Academics *Calendar:* quarters. *Degrees:* associate and bachelor's.

Student Life *Housing:* college housing not available.

Freshman Application Contact Director of Recruitment, ITT Technical Institute, 1980 Metro Court SW, Wyoming, MI 49519. *Phone:* 616-406-1200. *Toll-free phone:* 800-632-4676. *Web site:* http://www.itt-tech.edu/.

Jackson Community College
Jackson, Michigan

- **County-supported** 2-year, founded 1928
- **Suburban** 580-acre campus with easy access to Detroit
- **Coed,** 6,988 undergraduate students, 45% full-time, 61% women, 39% men

Undergraduates 3,120 full-time, 3,868 part-time. 1% are from out of state; 9% Black or African American, non-Hispanic/Latino; 4% Hispanic/Latino; 0.5% Asian, non-Hispanic/Latino; 0.8% American Indian or Alaska Native, non-Hispanic/Latino; 1% Two or more races, non-Hispanic/Latino; 5% Race/ethnicity unknown; 0.2% international; 2% live on campus.

Freshmen *Admission:* 1,415 enrolled.

Faculty *Total:* 452, 21% full-time. *Student/faculty ratio:* 21:1.

Majors Accounting and finance; administrative assistant and secretarial science; airline pilot and flight crew; automobile/automotive mechanics technology; business administration and management; computer and information sciences and support services related; construction trades related; corrections; criminal justice/law enforcement administration; data processing and data processing technology; diagnostic medical sonography and ultrasound technology; early childhood education; electrical, electronic and communications engineering technology; emergency medical technology (EMT paramedic); executive assistant/executive secretary; general studies; graphic design; heating, ventilation, air conditioning and refrigeration engineering technology; liberal arts and sciences/liberal studies; licensed practical/vocational nurse training; marketing/marketing management; medical/clinical assistant; medical insurance/medical billing; medical radiologic technology; medical transcription; registered nursing/registered nurse.

Academics *Calendar:* semesters. *Degree:* certificates and associate. *Special study options:* adult/continuing education programs, part-time degree program.

Library Atkinson Learning Resources Center plus 1 other.

Student Life *Housing Options:* coed. Campus housing is university owned. *Campus security:* 24-hour emergency response devices and patrols, student patrols, late-night transport/escort service, controlled dormitory access.

Athletics Member NJCAA. *Intercollegiate sports:* baseball M(s), basketball M(s)/W(s), cross-country running M(s)/W(s), golf M(s)/W(s), ice hockey M(c), soccer M(s)/W(s), softball W(s), volleyball W(s).

Applying *Options:* electronic application, early admission. *Application deadlines:* rolling (freshmen), rolling (transfers). *Notification:* continuous (freshmen), continuous (transfers).

Freshman Application Contact Ms. Julie Hand, Assistant Dean of Enrollment Services, Jackson Community College, 2111 Emmons Road, Jackson, MI 49201. *Phone:* 517-796-8425. *Toll-free phone:* 888-522-7344. *Fax:* 517-796-8631. *E-mail:* admissions@jccmi.edu. *Web site:* http://www.jccmi.edu/.

Kalamazoo Valley Community College
Kalamazoo, Michigan

Freshman Application Contact Kalamazoo Valley Community College, PO Box 4070, Kalamazoo, MI 49003-4070. *Phone:* 269-488-4207. *Web site:* http://www.kvcc.edu/.

Kaplan Career Institute, Dearborn Campus

Detroit, Michigan

- **Proprietary** 2-year
- **Coed**

Majors Criminal justice/law enforcement administration.
Academics *Degree:* diplomas and associate.
Freshman Application Contact Director of Admissions, Kaplan Career Institute, Dearborn Campus, 18440 Ford Road, Detroit, MI 48228. *Phone:* 313-425-4314. *Web site:* http://dearborn.kaplancareerinstitute.com/.

Kellogg Community College

Battle Creek, Michigan

Freshman Application Contact Ms. Denise Newman, Director of Enrollment Services, Kellogg Community College, 450 North Avenue, Battle Creek, MI 49017. *Phone:* 269-965-3931 Ext. 2620. *Fax:* 269-965-4133. *E-mail:* harriss@kellogg.edu. *Web site:* http://www.kellogg.edu/.

Keweenaw Bay Ojibwa Community College

Baraga, Michigan

Freshman Application Contact Megan Shanahan, Admissions Officer, Keweenaw Bay Ojibwa Community College, 111 Beartown Road, Baraga, MI 49908. *Phone:* 909-353-4600. *E-mail:* megan@kbocc.org. *Web site:* http://www.kbocc.org/.

Kirtland Community College

Roscommon, Michigan

- **District-supported** 2-year, founded 1966
- **Rural** 180-acre campus
- **Coed,** 1,815 undergraduate students, 42% full-time, 63% women, 37% men

Undergraduates 762 full-time, 1,053 part-time. Students come from 5 states and territories; 1 other country; 0.7% Black or African American, non-Hispanic/Latino; 2% Hispanic/Latino; 0.4% Asian, non-Hispanic/Latino; 1% American Indian or Alaska Native, non-Hispanic/Latino; 0.7% Two or more races, non-Hispanic/Latino; 7% Race/ethnicity unknown; 0.3% international.
Freshmen *Admission:* 967 applied, 967 admitted, 298 enrolled. *Test scores:* ACT scores over 18: 66%; ACT scores over 24: 6%; ACT scores over 30: 1%.
Faculty *Total:* 139, 28% full-time. *Student/faculty ratio:* 19:1.
Majors Administrative assistant and secretarial science; art; automobile/automotive mechanics technology; biological and physical sciences; business administration and management; cardiovascular technology; computer systems analysis; corrections; cosmetology; creative writing; criminal justice/law enforcement administration; drafting and design technology; education (multiple levels); electrical, electronic and communications engineering technology; fire services administration; general studies; graphic design; heating, air conditioning, ventilation and refrigeration maintenance technology; industrial and product design; industrial technology; information science/studies; legal administrative assistant/secretary; liberal arts and sciences/liberal studies; licensed practical/vocational nurse training; management information systems; medical administrative assistant and medical secretary; nail technician and manicurist; pharmacy technician; registered nursing/registered nurse; small engine mechanics and repair technology; surgical technology; teacher assistant/aide; web/multimedia management and webmaster; welding technology.
Academics *Calendar:* semesters. *Degree:* certificates and associate. *Special study options:* academic remediation for entering students, adult/continuing education programs, advanced placement credit, cooperative education, distance learning, English as a second language, honors programs, independent study, internships, part-time degree program, summer session for credit.
Library Kirtland Community College Library with 33,000 titles, 331 serial subscriptions, an OPAC.
Student Life *Housing:* college housing not available. *Activities and Organizations:* drama/theater group, student-run newspaper. *Campus security:* 24-hour emergency response devices, student patrols, late-night transport/escort service, campus warning siren, uniformed armed police officers.
Athletics Member NJCAA. *Intercollegiate sports:* basketball M(s)/W(s), cross-country running M(s)/W(s), golf M(s)/W(s).
Standardized Tests *Recommended:* ACT (for admission).
Costs (2012–13) *Tuition:* area resident $2580 full-time; state resident $3570 full-time; nonresident $5940 full-time. *Required fees:* $270 full-time. *Payment plan:* installment. *Waivers:* minority students, senior citizens, and employees or children of employees.

Financial Aid Of all full-time matriculated undergraduates who enrolled in 2010, 50 Federal Work-Study jobs (averaging $1253). 28 state and other part-time jobs (averaging $1647).
Applying *Options:* electronic application. *Application deadlines:* rolling (freshmen), rolling (transfers). *Notification:* continuous until 8/22 (freshmen), continuous until 8/22 (transfers).
Freshman Application Contact Ms. Michelle Vyskocil, Dean of Student Services, Kirtland Community College, 10775 North Saint Helen Road, Roscommon, MI 48653. *Phone:* 989-275-5000 Ext. 248. *Fax:* 989-275-6789. *E-mail:* registrar@kirtland.edu. *Web site:* http://www.kirtland.edu/.

Lake Michigan College

Benton Harbor, Michigan

- **District-supported** 2-year, founded 1946, part of Michigan Department of Education
- **Small-town** 260-acre campus
- **Endowment** $9.8 million
- **Coed,** 4,654 undergraduate students, 34% full-time, 61% women, 39% men

Undergraduates 1,601 full-time, 3,053 part-time. Students come from 8 states and territories; 46 other countries; 2% are from out of state; 17% Black or African American, non-Hispanic/Latino; 6% Hispanic/Latino; 1% Asian, non-Hispanic/Latino; 0.1% Native Hawaiian or other Pacific Islander, non-Hispanic/Latino; 0.6% American Indian or Alaska Native, non-Hispanic/Latino; 1% Two or more races, non-Hispanic/Latino; 8% Race/ethnicity unknown; 6% transferred in. *Retention:* 55% of full-time freshmen returned.
Freshmen *Admission:* 1,878 applied, 1,869 admitted, 808 enrolled. *Average high school GPA:* 2.8.
Faculty *Total:* 329, 17% full-time, 10% with terminal degrees. *Student/faculty ratio:* 18:1.
Majors Accounting; administrative assistant and secretarial science; applied horticulture/horticulture operations; art; biology/biological sciences; business administration and management; casino management; chemistry; communication; computer and information sciences; corrections; criminal justice/law enforcement administration; dental assisting; diagnostic medical sonography and ultrasound technology; drafting and design technology; dramatic/theater arts; early childhood education; elementary education; emergency medical technology (EMT paramedic); energy management and systems technology; English; environmental science; foreign languages and literatures; general studies; geography; geology/earth science; graphic design; health and physical education/fitness; history; hospitality administration; humanities; industrial technology; landscaping and groundskeeping; legal administrative assistant/secretary; liberal arts and sciences/liberal studies; machine tool technology; magnetic resonance imaging (MRI) technology; manufacturing engineering; marketing/marketing management; mass communication/media; mathematics; medical administrative assistant and medical secretary; medical radiologic technology; music; philosophy; physical sciences; physics; political science and government; precision production related; pre-dentistry studies; pre-engineering; pre-law studies; premedical studies; pre-pharmacy studies; pre-veterinary studies; psychology; radiologic technology/science; registered nursing/registered nurse; secondary education; sociology; turf and turfgrass management; viticulture and enology.
Academics *Calendar:* semesters. *Degree:* certificates and associate. *Special study options:* academic remediation for entering students, adult/continuing education programs, cooperative education, distance learning, English as a second language, honors programs, independent study, off-campus study, part-time degree program, services for LD students, student-designed majors, summer session for credit.
Library William Hessel Library with 104,728 titles, 24,060 serial subscriptions, 4,925 audiovisual materials, an OPAC, a Web page.
Student Life *Housing:* college housing not available. *Activities and Organizations:* drama/theater group, choral group, International Club, Phi Theta Kappa, Student Senate, Movie Club, LMC Sky Kings (Sky Diving Club). *Campus security:* 24-hour emergency response devices, contracted campus security force.
Athletics Member NJCAA. *Intercollegiate sports:* baseball M(s), basketball M(s)/W(s), softball W(s), volleyball W(s).
Costs (2012–13) *Tuition:* area resident $2430 full-time, $81 per contact hour part-time; state resident $3660 full-time, $122 per contact hour part-time; nonresident $4770 full-time, $159 per contact hour part-time. *Required fees:* $1050 full-time, $35 per contact hour part-time. *Payment plans:* installment, deferred payment. *Waivers:* senior citizens and employees or children of employees.
Applying *Options:* electronic application. *Required:* high school transcript. *Required for some:* interview. *Application deadlines:* rolling (freshmen), rolling (transfers). *Notification:* continuous (freshmen), continuous (transfers).
Freshman Application Contact Mr. Louis Thomas, Lead Admissions Specialist, Lake Michigan College, 2755 East Napier Avenue, Benton Harbor, MI 49022-1899. *Phone:* 269-927-6584. *Toll-free phone:* 800-252-1LMC.

Fax: 269-927-6718. *E-mail:* thomas@lakemichigancollege.edu. *Web site:* http://www.lakemichigancollege.edu/.

Lansing Community College
Lansing, Michigan

- **State and locally supported** 2-year, founded 1957, part of Michigan Department of Education
- **Urban** 28-acre campus
- **Endowment** $6.8 million
- **Coed,** 20,640 undergraduate students, 28% full-time, 55% women, 45% men

Undergraduates 5,869 full-time, 14,771 part-time. Students come from 25 states and territories; 40 other countries; 12% Black or African American, non-Hispanic/Latino; 2% Hispanic/Latino; 2% Asian, non-Hispanic/Latino; 0.4% Native Hawaiian or other Pacific Islander, non-Hispanic/Latino; 0.9% American Indian or Alaska Native, non-Hispanic/Latino; 2% Two or more races, non-Hispanic/Latino; 12% Race/ethnicity unknown; 1% international; 0.8% transferred in.

Freshmen *Admission:* 5,121 enrolled.

Faculty *Total:* 2,144, 10% full-time. *Student/faculty ratio:* 12:1.

Majors Accounting related; accounting technology and bookkeeping; African American/Black studies; agricultural business and management; aircraft powerplant technology; airframe mechanics and aircraft maintenance technology; American studies; animation, interactive technology, video graphics and special effects; architectural engineering technology; architectural technology; art; art history, criticism and conservation; autobody/collision and repair technology; automobile/automotive mechanics technology; banking and financial support services; biology/biological sciences; biotechnology; business administration and management; business/commerce; chemical technology; chemistry; child-care provision; cinematography and film/video production; civil engineering technology; community organization and advocacy; computer and information sciences; computer programming (specific applications); computer systems networking and telecommunications; computer technology/computer systems technology; construction/heavy equipment/earthmoving equipment operation; corrections; criminal justice/police science; customer service support/call center/teleservice operation; diagnostic medical sonography and ultrasound technology; dramatic/theater arts; e-commerce; economics; electrical and power transmission installation; electrician; electromechanical technology; elementary education; emergency medical technology (EMT paramedic); energy management and systems technology; engineering; English; environmental engineering technology; fashion merchandising; fire science/firefighting; foreign languages and literatures; geography; graphic design; health and physical education/fitness; heating, air conditioning, ventilation and refrigeration maintenance technology; histologic technician; history; hotel/motel administration; humanities; human resources management; industrial production technologies related; international business/trade/commerce; international relations and affairs; juvenile corrections; legal assistant/paralegal; liberal arts and sciences/liberal studies; licensed practical/vocational nurse training; management information systems; mathematics; mechanical drafting and CAD/CADD; music; music performance; philosophy; photography; political science and government; premedical studies; psychology; real estate; religious studies; sales, distribution, and marketing operations; secondary education; selling skills and sales; sign language interpretation and translation; social sciences; sociology; surgical technology; surveying technology; teacher assistant/aide; veterinary/animal health technology; welding technology.

Academics *Calendar:* semesters. *Degrees:* certificates, associate, and post-bachelor's certificates. *Special study options:* academic remediation for entering students, adult/continuing education programs, advanced placement credit, cooperative education, distance learning, double majors, English as a second language, external degree program, honors programs, independent study, internships, part-time degree program, services for LD students, study abroad, summer session for credit. *ROTC:* Army (c), Air Force (c).

Library Abel Sykes Technology and Learning Center plus 1 other with 147,963 titles, 168 serial subscriptions, 6,127 audiovisual materials, an OPAC, a Web page.

Student Life *Activities and Organizations:* drama/theater group, student-run newspaper, radio station, choral group, American Marketing Association, Phi Theta Kappa, Future Teachers' Club, Health Career Related Clubs (Dental Hygiene, Nurses), Gay-Straight Alliance, national fraternities, national sororities. *Campus security:* 24-hour emergency response devices and patrols, student patrols, late-night transport/escort service. *Student services:* personal/psychological counseling, women's center.

Athletics Member NJCAA. *Intercollegiate sports:* baseball M(s), basketball M(s)/W(s), cross-country running M(s)/W(s), softball W(s), track and field M/W, volleyball W(s).

Costs (2012–13) *Tuition:* area resident $2370 full-time, $79 per credit hour part-time; state resident $4740 full-time, $158 per credit hour part-time; non-resident $7110 full-time, $237 per credit hour part-time. *Required fees:* $200 full-time, $5 per credit hour part-time, $25 per term part-time. *Room and* board: $7100. *Payment plan:* installment. *Waivers:* senior citizens and employees or children of employees.

Financial Aid Of all full-time matriculated undergraduates who enrolled in 2010, 125 Federal Work-Study jobs (averaging $2636). 122 state and other part-time jobs (averaging $2563).

Applying *Options:* electronic application, early admission, deferred entrance. *Required for some:* essay or personal statement, high school transcript, 2 letters of recommendation, interview. *Application deadlines:* rolling (freshmen), rolling (transfers).

Freshman Application Contact Ms. Tammy Grossbauer, Director of Admissions/Registrar, Lansing Community College, 1121 - Enrollment Services, PO BOX 40010, Lansing, MI 48901. *Phone:* 517-483-9886. *Toll-free phone:* 800-644-4LCC. *Fax:* 517-483-1170. *E-mail:* grossbt@lcc.edu. *Web site:* http://www.lcc.edu/.

Macomb Community College
Warren, Michigan

- **District-supported** 2-year, founded 1954, part of Michigan Public Community College System
- **Suburban** 384-acre campus with easy access to Detroit
- **Endowment** $12.3 million
- **Coed,** 23,969 undergraduate students, 35% full-time, 52% women, 48% men

Undergraduates 8,441 full-time, 15,528 part-time. Students come from 4 states and territories. *Retention:* 70% of full-time freshmen returned.

Freshmen *Admission:* 1,360 enrolled.

Faculty *Total:* 1,102, 20% full-time, 10% with terminal degrees. *Student/faculty ratio:* 27:1.

Majors Accounting; administrative assistant and secretarial science; agriculture; architectural drafting and CAD/CADD; automobile/automotive mechanics technology; automotive engineering technology; biology/biological sciences; business administration and management; business automation/technology/data entry; business/commerce; cabinetmaking and millwork; chemistry; child-care and support services management; civil engineering technology; commercial and advertising art; computer programming; computer programming (specific applications); construction engineering technology; criminal justice/law enforcement administration; criminal justice/police science; culinary arts; drafting and design technology; drafting/design engineering technologies related; electrical, electronic and communications engineering technology; electrical/electronics equipment installation and repair; electromechanical technology; emergency medical technology (EMT paramedic); energy management and systems technology; engineering related; finance; fire prevention and safety technology; forensic science and technology; general studies; graphic and printing equipment operation/production; heating, air conditioning, ventilation and refrigeration maintenance technology; heating, ventilation, air conditioning and refrigeration engineering technology; industrial mechanics and maintenance technology; industrial technology; international/global studies; legal assistant/paralegal; legal studies; liberal arts and sciences/liberal studies; machine tool technology; manufacturing engineering technology; marketing/marketing management; mathematics; mechanical drafting and CAD/CADD; mechanical engineering/mechanical technology; mechanic and repair technologies related; medical/clinical assistant; mental health counseling; metallurgical technology; music performance; occupational therapist assistant; operations management; physical therapy technology; plastics and polymer engineering technology; plumbing technology; pre-engineering; quality control and safety technologies related; quality control technology; registered nursing/registered nurse; respiratory care therapy; robotics technology; sheet metal technology; social psychology; speech communication and rhetoric; surgical technology; surveying technology; tool and die technology; veterinary/animal health technology; welding technology.

Academics *Calendar:* semesters. *Degree:* certificates and associate. *Special study options:* academic remediation for entering students, adult/continuing education programs, advanced placement credit, cooperative education, English as a second language, honors programs, internships, off-campus study, part-time degree program, services for LD students, student-designed majors, summer session for credit.

Library Library of South Campus, Library of Center Campus with 159,226 titles, 4,240 serial subscriptions, an OPAC.

Student Life *Housing:* college housing not available. *Activities and Organizations:* drama/theater group, Phi Beta Kappa, Adventure Unlimited, Alpha Rho Rho, SADD. *Campus security:* 24-hour emergency response devices and patrols, late-night transport/escort service, security phones in parking lots, surveillance cameras. *Student services:* health clinic, personal/psychological counseling.

Athletics Member NJCAA. *Intercollegiate sports:* baseball M(s), basketball M(s), cross-country running M(s)/W(s), soccer M(s), softball W(s), track and field M(s)/W(s), volleyball W(s). *Intramural sports:* baseball M, basketball M, bowling M/W, cross-country running M/W, football M/W, skiing (cross-country) M/W, skiing (downhill) M/W, volleyball M/W.

Costs (2011–12) *Tuition:* area resident $2604 full-time, $84 per credit hour part-time; state resident $3968 full-time, $128 per credit hour part-time; non-resident $5177 full-time, $159 per credit hour part-time. Full-time tuition and fees vary according to course load. Part-time tuition and fees vary according to course load. *Required fees:* $100 full-time, $50 per term part-time. *Waivers:* senior citizens and employees or children of employees.

Applying *Options:* early admission, deferred entrance. *Application deadlines:* rolling (freshmen), rolling (transfers).

Freshman Application Contact Mr. Brian Bouwman, Coordinator of Admissions and Transfer Credit, Macomb Community College, G312, 14500 East 12 Mile Road, Warren, MI 48088-3896. *Phone:* 586-445-7246. *Toll-free phone:* 866-MACOMB1. *Fax:* 586-445-7140. *E-mail:* stevensr@macomb.edu. *Web site:* http://www.macomb.edu/.

Mid Michigan Community College

Harrison, Michigan

- **State and locally supported** 2-year, founded 1965, part of Michigan Department of Education
- **Rural** 560-acre campus
- **Coed,** 4,885 undergraduate students, 45% full-time, 59% women, 41% men

Undergraduates 2,193 full-time, 2,692 part-time. 0.5% are from out of state; 3% Black or African American, non-Hispanic/Latino; 3% Hispanic/Latino; 0.2% Asian, non-Hispanic/Latino; 0.4% Native Hawaiian or other Pacific Islander, non-Hispanic/Latino; 2% American Indian or Alaska Native, non-Hispanic/Latino; 0.1% Two or more races, non-Hispanic/Latino; 7% Race/ethnicity unknown; 0.6% international; 4% transferred in. *Retention:* 43% of full-time freshmen returned.

Freshmen *Admission:* 785 applied, 785 admitted, 1,336 enrolled.

Faculty *Total:* 264, 17% full-time, 2% with terminal degrees. *Student/faculty ratio:* 26:1.

Majors Accounting; administrative assistant and secretarial science; art; auto-mobile/automotive mechanics technology; biological and physical sciences; biology/biological sciences; business administration and management; chemistry; child-care provision; child development; corrections; criminal justice/law enforcement administration; drafting and design technology; dramatic/theater arts; education (multiple levels); elementary education; fire science/firefighting; general studies; heating, air conditioning, ventilation and refrigeration maintenance technology; industrial radiologic technology; information science/studies; legal administrative assistant/secretary; liberal arts and sciences/liberal studies; licensed practical/vocational nurse training; machine tool technology; marketing/marketing management; mathematics; medical administrative assistant and medical secretary; medical/clinical assistant; medical transcription; pharmacy; physical therapy; pre-engineering; psychology; registered nursing/registered nurse; secondary education; sociology.

Academics *Calendar:* semesters. *Degree:* certificates and associate. *Special study options:* academic remediation for entering students, adult/continuing education programs, advanced placement credit, cooperative education, distance learning, honors programs, independent study, internships, part-time degree program, services for LD students, summer session for credit.

Library Charles A. Amble Library with 29,450 titles, 200 serial subscriptions.

Student Life *Housing:* college housing not available. *Activities and Organizations:* drama/theater group, MC2, Phi Theta Kappa, Art Club, ECHO, Japan Culture Club. *Campus security:* 24-hour emergency response devices. *Student services:* personal/psychological counseling.

Athletics *Intercollegiate sports:* basketball M(c)/W(c), ice hockey M(c), soccer M(c)/W(c).

Costs (2012–13) *Tuition:* area resident $2360 full-time, $93 per contact hour part-time; state resident $4550 full-time, $182 per contact hour part-time; non-resident $8396 full-time, $334 per contact hour part-time. Full-time tuition and fees vary according to course load. Part-time tuition and fees vary according to course load. *Required fees:* $20 per term part-time. *Payment plan:* installment. *Waivers:* employees or children of employees.

Financial Aid Of all full-time matriculated undergraduates who enrolled in 2010, 50 Federal Work-Study jobs (averaging $3600). 50 state and other part-time jobs (averaging $3600).

Applying *Options:* electronic application, early admission. *Recommended:* high school transcript. *Application deadlines:* rolling (freshmen), rolling (transfers). *Notification:* continuous (freshmen), continuous (transfers).

Freshman Application Contact Jennifer Casebeer, Admissions Specialist, Mid Michigan Community College, 1375 South Clare Avenue, Harrison, MI 48625-9447. *Phone:* 989-386-6661. *E-mail:* apply@midmich.edu. *Web site:* http://www.midmich.edu/.

Monroe County Community College

Monroe, Michigan

- **County-supported** 2-year, founded 1964, part of Michigan Department of Education
- **Small-town** 150-acre campus with easy access to Detroit, Toledo
- **Coed,** 4,440 undergraduate students, 39% full-time, 59% women, 41% men

Undergraduates 1,712 full-time, 2,728 part-time. Students come from 3 other countries; 4% are from out of state; 50% transferred in.

Freshmen *Admission:* 1,700 applied, 1,698 admitted, 776 enrolled. *Average high school GPA:* 2.5.

Faculty *Total:* 197, 27% full-time.

Majors Accounting; administrative assistant and secretarial science; architectural engineering technology; art; biology/biological sciences; business administration and management; child development; clinical laboratory science/medical technology; computer and information sciences related; computer engineering technology; computer graphics; computer programming (specific applications); criminal justice/police science; criminal justice/safety; culinary arts; data processing and data processing technology; drafting and design technology; electrical, electronic and communications engineering technology; elementary education; English; finance; funeral service and mortuary science; industrial technology; information technology; journalism; legal administrative assistant/secretary; liberal arts and sciences/liberal studies; marketing/marketing management; mass communication/media; mathematics; medical administrative assistant and medical secretary; physical therapy; pre-engineering; psychology; registered nursing/registered nurse; respiratory care therapy; rhetoric and composition; social work; web/multimedia management and webmaster; web page, digital/multimedia and information resources design; welding technology; word processing.

Academics *Calendar:* semesters. *Degree:* certificates and associate. *Special study options:* academic remediation for entering students, advanced placement credit, independent study, part-time degree program, services for LD students, summer session for credit.

Library Campbell Learning Resource Center with 47,352 titles, 321 serial subscriptions, an OPAC.

Student Life *Housing:* college housing not available. *Activities and Organizations:* drama/theater group, student-run newspaper, choral group, student government, Society of Auto Engineers, Oasis, Nursing Students Organization. *Campus security:* police patrols during open hours.

Athletics *Intramural sports:* soccer M/W, volleyball M/W.

Standardized Tests *Required:* ACT, ACT COMPASS (for admission). *Required for some:* ACT (for admission). *Recommended:* ACT (for admission).

Costs (2011–12) *Tuition:* area resident $1872 full-time, $78 per contact hour part-time; state resident $3120 full-time, $130 per contact hour part-time; non-resident $3456 full-time, $144 per contact hour part-time. *Required fees:* $204 full-time, $6 per contact hour part-time, $30 per term part-time. *Payment plan:* installment. *Waivers:* senior citizens and employees or children of employees.

Applying *Options:* early admission, deferred entrance. *Required:* high school transcript, Baseline cut scores on ACT or COMPASS. *Application deadline:* rolling (transfers). *Notification:* continuous (freshmen), continuous (transfers).

Freshman Application Contact Mr. Mark V. Hall, Director of Admissions and Guidance Services, Monroe County Community College, 1555 South Raisinville Road, Monroe, MI 48161. *Phone:* 734-384-4261. *Toll-free phone:* 877-YES-MCCC. *Fax:* 734-242-9711. *E-mail:* mhall@monroeccc.edu. *Web site:* http://www.monroeccc.edu/.

Montcalm Community College

Sidney, Michigan

- **State and locally supported** 2-year, founded 1965, part of Michigan Department of Education
- **Rural** 240-acre campus with easy access to Grand Rapids
- **Endowment** $4.7 million
- **Coed,** 2,062 undergraduate students, 34% full-time, 66% women, 34% men

Undergraduates 698 full-time, 1,364 part-time. 0.4% Black or African American, non-Hispanic/Latino; 0.4% Asian, non-Hispanic/Latino; 0.4% American Indian or Alaska Native, non-Hispanic/Latino; 2% Two or more races, non-Hispanic/Latino; 7% Race/ethnicity unknown; 0.2% international.

Freshmen *Admission:* 869 applied, 869 admitted, 235 enrolled. *Average high school GPA:* 2.72. *Test scores:* ACT scores over 18: 74%; ACT scores over 24: 15%.

Faculty *Total:* 138, 22% full-time, 67% with terminal degrees. *Student/faculty ratio:* 31:1.

Majors Accounting; administrative assistant and secretarial science; automobile/automotive mechanics technology; business administration and management; child-care and support services management; child-care provision;

computer installation and repair technology; corrections; cosmetology; criminal justice/law enforcement administration; data processing and data processing technology; drafting and design technology; electrical, electronic and communications engineering technology; emergency medical technology (EMT paramedic); entrepreneurship; general studies; industrial engineering; industrial technology; liberal arts and sciences/liberal studies; medical administrative assistant and medical secretary; registered nursing/registered nurse; teacher assistant/aide; welding technology.

Academics *Calendar:* semesters. *Degree:* certificates and associate. *Special study options:* academic remediation for entering students, adult/continuing education programs, advanced placement credit, cooperative education, distance learning, double majors, independent study, internships, off-campus study, part-time degree program, services for LD students, study abroad, summer session for credit.

Library Montcalm Community College Library with 29,848 titles, 3,670 serial subscriptions, an OPAC, a Web page.

Student Life *Housing:* college housing not available. *Activities and Organizations:* drama/theater group, choral group, Nursing Club, Native American Club, Phi Theta Kappa, Business Club, Judo Club. *Student services:* personal/psychological counseling.

Athletics *Intramural sports:* volleyball M/W.

Costs (2012–13) *Tuition:* area resident $2490 full-time, $83 per credit part-time; state resident $4590 full-time, $153 per credit part-time; nonresident $6840 full-time, $228 per credit part-time. *Required fees:* $270 full-time, $9 per credit part-time. *Waivers:* senior citizens and employees or children of employees.

Financial Aid Of all full-time matriculated undergraduates who enrolled in 2010, 57 Federal Work-Study jobs (averaging $2000).

Applying *Options:* electronic application, early admission, deferred entrance. *Recommended:* high school transcript. *Application deadlines:* rolling (freshmen), rolling (transfers). *Notification:* continuous (freshmen), continuous (transfers).

Freshman Application Contact Ms. Debra Alexander, Associate Dean of Student Services, Montcalm Community College, 2800 College Drive, SW, Sidney, MI 48885. *Phone:* 989-328-1276. *Toll-free phone:* 877-328-2111. *E-mail:* admissions@montcalm.edu. *Web site:* http://www.montcalm.edu/.

Mott Community College
Flint, Michigan

- **District-supported** 2-year, founded 1923, part of Michigan Workforce Programs/Postsecondary Services/Community College Services
- **Urban** 32-acre campus with easy access to Detroit
- **Endowment** $36.8 million
- **Coed,** 11,760 undergraduate students, 35% full-time, 60% women, 40% men

Undergraduates 4,066 full-time, 7,694 part-time. Students come from 2 states and territories; 21% Black or African American, non-Hispanic/Latino; 3% Hispanic/Latino; 0.5% Asian, non-Hispanic/Latino; 1% American Indian or Alaska Native, non-Hispanic/Latino; 1% Two or more races, non-Hispanic/Latino; 15% Race/ethnicity unknown; 0.2% international; 2% transferred in.

Freshmen *Admission:* 705 enrolled.

Faculty *Total:* 572, 24% full-time, 11% with terminal degrees. *Student/faculty ratio:* 22:1.

Majors Accounting technology and bookkeeping; administrative assistant and secretarial science; architectural engineering technology; automobile/automotive mechanics technology; baking and pastry arts; biology/biological sciences; business administration and management; business/commerce; cinematography and film/video production; communications technology; community health services counseling; computer programming; computer programming (specific applications); computer systems networking and telecommunications; criminal justice/police science; culinary arts; dental assisting; dental hygiene; drafting and design technology; early childhood education; electrical, electronic and communications engineering technology; emergency medical technology (EMT paramedic); engineering technologies and engineering related; entrepreneurship; fire prevention and safety technology; food service systems administration; general studies; graphic design; health information/medical records technology; heating, ventilation, air conditioning and refrigeration engineering technology; histologic technician; liberal arts and sciences/liberal studies; manufacturing engineering technology; marketing/marketing management; mechanical engineering/mechanical technology; medical radiologic technology; occupational therapist assistant; photography; physical therapy technology; precision production related; registered nursing/registered nurse; respiratory care therapy; salon/beauty salon management; sign language interpretation and translation; web page, digital/multimedia and information resources design.

Academics *Calendar:* semesters. *Degree:* certificates and associate. *Special study options:* academic remediation for entering students, accelerated degree program, adult/continuing education programs, advanced placement credit,

cooperative education, distance learning, double majors, English as a second language, honors programs, independent study, internships, part-time degree program, services for LD students, summer session for credit.

Library Charles Stewart Mott Library with 86,611 titles, 170 serial subscriptions, 89 audiovisual materials, an OPAC, a Web page.

Student Life *Housing:* college housing not available. *Activities and Organizations:* student-run newspaper, choral group, Phi Theta Kappa, Dental Hygiene, Student Physical Therapist Assistants, Respiratory Care Student Society, GSA (Gay Straight Alliance). *Campus security:* 24-hour emergency response devices and patrols, student patrols, late-night transport/escort service. *Student services:* health clinic, personal/psychological counseling.

Athletics Member NJCAA. *Intercollegiate sports:* baseball M(s), basketball M(s)/W(s), cross-country running M(s)/W(s), golf M(s), softball W(s), volleyball W(s). *Intramural sports:* cheerleading W(c).

Costs (2012–13) *Tuition:* area resident $2593 full-time, $108 per contact hour part-time; state resident $3882 full-time, $162 per contact hour part-time; nonresident $5181 full-time, $216 per contact hour part-time. Full-time tuition and fees vary according to course load. Part-time tuition and fees vary according to course load. *Required fees:* $257 full-time, $6 per contact hour part-time, $108 per term part-time. *Payment plan:* installment. *Waivers:* senior citizens and employees or children of employees.

Financial Aid Of all full-time matriculated undergraduates who enrolled in 2010, 15,695 applied for aid, 14,858 were judged to have need, 374 had their need fully met. 3,243 Federal Work-Study jobs (averaging $297). In 2010, 130 non-need-based awards were made. *Average percent of need met:* 71%. *Average financial aid package:* $7432. *Average need-based loan:* $167. *Average need-based gift aid:* $3885. *Average non-need-based aid:* $1526.

Applying *Options:* electronic application, early admission, deferred entrance. *Required:* high school transcript. *Application deadline:* 8/31 (freshmen). *Notification:* continuous (transfers).

Freshman Application Contact Mr. Troy Boquette, Interim Executive Dean of Student Services, Mott Community College, 1401 East Court Street, Flint, MI 48503. *Phone:* 810-762-0243. *Toll-free phone:* 800-852-8614. *Fax:* 810-232-9503. *E-mail:* troy.boquette@mcc.edu. *Web site:* http://www.mcc.edu/.

Muskegon Community College
Muskegon, Michigan

- **State and locally supported** 2-year, founded 1926, part of Michigan Department of Education
- **Small-town** 112-acre campus with easy access to Grand Rapids
- **Coed,** 5,579 undergraduate students, 34% full-time, 59% women, 41% men

Undergraduates 1,886 full-time, 3,693 part-time. 9% Black or African American, non-Hispanic/Latino; 4% Hispanic/Latino; 0.7% Asian, non-Hispanic/Latino; 0.1% Native Hawaiian or other Pacific Islander, non-Hispanic/Latino; 1% American Indian or Alaska Native, non-Hispanic/Latino; 2% Two or more races, non-Hispanic/Latino; 19% Race/ethnicity unknown; 0.1% international.

Freshmen *Admission:* 524 applied, 506 admitted, 716 enrolled.

Faculty *Total:* 318, 31% full-time. *Student/faculty ratio:* 20:1.

Majors Accounting; administrative assistant and secretarial science; advertising; anthropology; applied mathematics; art; art history, criticism and conservation; art teacher education; automobile/automotive mechanics technology; biology/biotechnology laboratory technician; biomedical technology; business administration and management; business machine repair; chemical engineering; child development; commercial and advertising art; criminal justice/law enforcement administration; data processing and data processing technology; design and applied arts related; developmental and child psychology; drafting and design technology; economics; education; electrical, electronic and communications engineering technology; electromechanical technology; elementary education; engineering technology; finance; hospitality administration; hospitality and recreation marketing; hotel/motel administration; industrial technology; information science/studies; legal administrative assistant/secretary; liberal arts and sciences/liberal studies; machine tool technology; marketing/marketing management; medical administrative assistant and medical secretary; parks, recreation and leisure; registered nursing/registered nurse; special products marketing; transportation and materials moving related; welding technology.

Academics *Calendar:* semesters. *Degree:* associate. *Special study options:* academic remediation for entering students, adult/continuing education programs, cooperative education, honors programs, part-time degree program, student-designed majors, summer session for credit.

Library Hendrik Meijer and Technology Center with 48,597 titles, 450 serial subscriptions.

Student Life *Housing:* college housing not available. *Activities and Organizations:* drama/theater group, student-run newspaper, choral group, Respiratory Therapy, Hispanic Student Organization, Black Student Alliance, International Club, Rotaract. *Campus security:* 24-hour emergency response devices, on-campus security officer. *Student services:* personal/psychological counseling.

Athletics Member NJCAA. *Intercollegiate sports:* baseball M, basketball M(s)/W(s), golf M/W, softball W, tennis M/W, volleyball W(s), wrestling M. *Intramural sports:* basketball M/W, skiing (downhill) M(c)/W(c).
Costs (2012–13) *Tuition:* area resident $1980 full-time; state resident $3432 full-time; nonresident $4704 full-time. *Payment plan:* deferred payment.
Financial Aid Of all full-time matriculated undergraduates who enrolled in 2010, 250 Federal Work-Study jobs (averaging $2500). 50 state and other part-time jobs (averaging $2500).
Applying *Options:* electronic application, early admission, deferred entrance. *Required:* high school transcript. *Application deadlines:* rolling (freshmen), rolling (transfers). *Notification:* continuous (freshmen), continuous (transfers).
Freshman Application Contact Ms. Darlene Peklar, Enrollment Generalist, Muskegon Community College, 221 South Quarterline Road, Muskegon, MI 49442-1493. *Phone:* 231-777-0366. *Toll-free phone:* 866-711-4622. *E-mail:* Dalene.Peklar@muskegoncc.edu. *Web site:* http://www.muskegoncc.edu/.

North Central Michigan College
Petoskey, Michigan

Director of Admissions Ms. Julieanne Tobin, Director of Enrollment Management, North Central Michigan College, 1515 Howard Street, Petoskey, MI 49770-8717. *Phone:* 231-439-6511. *Toll-free phone:* 888-298-6605. *E-mail:* jtobin@ncmich.edu. *Web site:* http://www.ncmich.edu/.

Northwestern Michigan College
Traverse City, Michigan

Freshman Application Contact Mr. James Bensley, Coordinator of Admissions, Northwestern Michigan College, 1701 East Front Street, Traverse City, MI 49686-3061. *Phone:* 231-995-1034. *Toll-free phone:* 800-748-0566. *Fax:* 616-955-1339. *E-mail:* welcome@nmc.edu. *Web site:* http://www.nmc.edu/.

Oakland Community College
Bloomfield Hills, Michigan

- **State and locally supported** 2-year, founded 1964
- **Suburban** 540-acre campus with easy access to Detroit
- **Endowment** $1.1 million
- **Coed**, 29,158 undergraduate students, 33% full-time, 58% women, 42% men

Undergraduates 9,628 full-time, 19,530 part-time. Students come from 12 states and territories; 49 other countries; 0.1% are from out of state; 28% Black or African American, non-Hispanic/Latino; 3% Hispanic/Latino; 2% Asian, non-Hispanic/Latino; 0.1% Native Hawaiian or other Pacific Islander, non-Hispanic/Latino; 0.6% American Indian or Alaska Native, non-Hispanic/Latino; 2% Two or more races, non-Hispanic/Latino; 7% Race/ethnicity unknown; 5% international. *Retention:* 41% of full-time freshmen returned.
Freshmen *Admission:* 9,854 applied, 9,854 admitted, 3,908 enrolled.
Faculty *Total:* 1,340, 18% full-time. *Student/faculty ratio:* 26:1.
Majors Accounting and business/management; accounting technology and bookkeeping; adult development and aging; architectural engineering technology; art; biotechnology; business administration and management; business automation/technology/data entry; carpentry; ceramic arts and ceramics; child-care and support services management; commercial and advertising art; community health services counseling; computer and information sciences and support services related; computer and information systems security; computer hardware technology; computer/information technology services administration related; computer programming; computer systems analysis; computer technology/computer systems technology; construction management; corrections; cosmetology; court reporting; criminalistics and criminal science; criminal justice/law enforcement administration; criminal justice/police science; culinary arts; data processing and data processing technology; dental hygiene; diagnostic medical sonography and ultrasound technology; drafting and design technology; dramatic/theater arts and stagecraft related; electrical, electronic and communications engineering technology; electrician; electromechanical technology; electroneurodiagnostic/electroencephalographic technology; emergency medical technology (EMT paramedic); engineering; entrepreneurship; fashion merchandising; film/cinema/video studies; fire science/firefighting; general studies; graphic design; health/health-care administration; health professions related; heating, ventilation, air conditioning and refrigeration engineering technology; histologic technician; histologic technology/histotechnologist; hotel/motel administration; illustration; industrial production technologies related; industrial technology; interior design; international business/trade/commerce; international/global studies; kinesiology and exercise science; landscaping and groundskeeping; legal assistant/paralegal; liberal arts and sciences and humanities related; liberal arts and sciences/liberal studies; library and archives assisting; machine tool technology; management information systems; manufacturing engineering technology; massage therapy;

mechanical drafting and CAD/CADD; mechanics and repair; medical/clinical assistant; medical radiologic technology; medical transcription; music performance; music theory and composition; nanotechnology; nuclear medical technology; occupational therapist assistant; office management; pharmacy technician; photographic and film/video technology; photography; physical therapy technology; pipefitting and sprinkler fitting; precision metal working related; radio and television broadcasting technology; registered nursing/registered nurse; respiratory care therapy; restaurant/food services management; retail management; robotics technology; salon/beauty salon management; science technologies related; sign language interpretation and translation; surgical technology; tool and die technology; veterinary/animal health technology; voice and opera; welding technology.
Academics *Calendar:* semesters. *Degree:* certificates and associate. *Special study options:* academic remediation for entering students, adult/continuing education programs, advanced placement credit, cooperative education, distance learning, English as a second language, internships, off-campus study, part-time degree program, services for LD students, study abroad, summer session for credit.
Library Main Library plus 5 others with 263,563 titles, 1,159 serial subscriptions, 8,835 audiovisual materials, an OPAC, a Web page.
Student Life *Housing:* college housing not available. *Activities and Organizations:* drama/theater group, choral group, Phi Theta Kappa, Gamers Guild, BELIEVERS, Criminal Justice Student Organization, Student Government. *Campus security:* 24-hour emergency response devices, late-night transport/escort service. *Student services:* personal/psychological counseling, women's center.
Athletics Member NJCAA. *Intercollegiate sports:* basketball M(s)/W(s), cross-country running M(s)/W(s), golf M(s), soccer M(c), softball W(s), track and field M(s)(c)/W(s)(c), volleyball W(s).
Costs (2011–12) *Tuition:* area resident $2001 full-time, $67 per credit hour part-time; state resident $3387 full-time, $113 per credit hour part-time; nonresident $4752 full-time, $158 per credit hour part-time. Full-time tuition and fees vary according to course load. Part-time tuition and fees vary according to course load. *Required fees:* $70 full-time, $35 per term part-time. *Waivers:* senior citizens and employees or children of employees.
Financial Aid Of all full-time matriculated undergraduates who enrolled in 2011, 4,119 applied for aid, 3,688 were judged to have need, 2 had their need fully met. 193 Federal Work-Study jobs (averaging $3921). In 2011, 42 non-need-based awards were made. *Average percent of need met:* 43%. *Average financial aid package:* $4549. *Average need-based loan:* $1004. *Average need-based gift aid:* $4787. *Average non-need-based aid:* $1550.
Applying *Options:* electronic application, deferred entrance. *Recommended:* high school transcript, interview. *Application deadlines:* rolling (freshmen), rolling (transfers). *Notification:* continuous (freshmen), continuous (transfers).
Freshman Application Contact Stephan M. Linden, Registrar, Oakland Community College, 2480 Opdyke Road, Bloomfield Hills, MI 48304-2266. *Phone:* 248-341-2192. *Fax:* 248-341-2099. *E-mail:* smlinden@oaklandcc.edu. *Web site:* http://www.oaklandcc.edu/.

Saginaw Chippewa Tribal College
Mount Pleasant, Michigan

Freshman Application Contact Ms. Tracy Reed, Admissions Officer/Registrar/Financial Aid, Saginaw Chippewa Tribal College, 2274 Enterprise Drive, Mount Pleasant, MI 48858. *Phone:* 989-775-4123. *Fax:* 989-775-4528. *E-mail:* treed@sagchip.org. *Web site:* http://www.sagchip.edu/.

St. Clair County Community College
Port Huron, Michigan

- **State and locally supported** 2-year, founded 1923, part of Michigan Department of Education
- **Small-town** 25-acre campus with easy access to Detroit
- **Coed**, 4,590 undergraduate students, 43% full-time, 59% women, 41% men

Undergraduates 1,959 full-time, 2,631 part-time. 4% Black or African American, non-Hispanic/Latino; 2% Hispanic/Latino; 0.4% Asian, non-Hispanic/Latino; 0.1% Native Hawaiian or other Pacific Islander, non-Hispanic/Latino; 1% American Indian or Alaska Native, non-Hispanic/Latino; 2% Two or more races, non-Hispanic/Latino; 3% Race/ethnicity unknown; 0.4% international; 30% transferred in. *Retention:* 61% of full-time freshmen returned.
Freshmen *Admission:* 877 enrolled.
Faculty *Total:* 294, 24% full-time. *Student/faculty ratio:* 20:1.
Majors Accounting technology and bookkeeping; architectural engineering technology; business/commerce; commercial and advertising art; computer programming; criminal justice/police science; data processing and data processing technology; electrical, electronic and communications engineering technology; energy management and systems technology; engineering; executive assistant/executive secretary; health information/medical records technol-

ogy; industrial production technologies related; journalism; kindergarten/preschool education; landscaping and groundskeeping; liberal arts and sciences/liberal studies; marketing/marketing management; massage therapy; mechanical drafting and CAD/CADD; medical administrative assistant and medical secretary; medical/clinical assistant; office management; radio and television broadcasting technology; robotics technology; teacher assistant/aide; transportation and materials moving related; web/multimedia management and webmaster; welding technology.

Academics *Calendar:* semesters. *Degree:* certificates and associate. *Special study options:* academic remediation for entering students, adult/continuing education programs, advanced placement credit, cooperative education, distance learning, honors programs, independent study, part-time degree program, summer session for credit.

Library Library plus 1 other with an OPAC, a Web page.

Student Life *Housing:* college housing not available. *Activities and Organizations:* drama/theater group, student-run newspaper, radio station, Phi Theta Kappa, Zombie Defense Council, Marketing and Management Club, Gay-Straight Alliance, Criminal Justice Club. *Campus security:* 24-hour emergency response devices, late-night transport/escort service, patrols by security until 10 pm. *Student services:* personal/psychological counseling.

Athletics Member NJCAA. *Intercollegiate sports:* baseball M(s), basketball M(s)/W(s), golf M, softball W(s), volleyball W(s).

Costs (2012–13) *Tuition:* area resident $2835 full-time, $95 per contact hour part-time; state resident $5520 full-time, $184 per contact hour part-time; non-resident $8040 full-time, $268 per contact hour part-time. Full-time tuition and fees vary according to course load and location. Part-time tuition and fees vary according to course load and location. *Required fees:* $418 full-time, $10 per contact hour part-time. *Payment plan:* deferred payment. *Waivers:* senior citizens and employees or children of employees.

Financial Aid Of all full-time matriculated undergraduates who enrolled in 2010, 40 Federal Work-Study jobs (averaging $2888). 40 state and other part-time jobs (averaging $1610).

Applying *Options:* electronic application, early admission. *Required:* high school transcript. *Application deadlines:* rolling (freshmen), rolling (transfers).

Freshman Application Contact St. Clair County Community College, 323 Erie Street, PO Box 5015, Port Huron, MI 48061-5015. *Phone:* 810-989-5501. *Toll-free phone:* 800-553-2427. *Web site:* http://www.sc4.edu/.

Schoolcraft College
Livonia, Michigan

Freshman Application Contact Ms. Cheryl Hagen, Dean of Student Services, Schoolcraft College, 18600 Haggerty Road, Livonia, MI 48152-2696. *Phone:* 734-462-4426. *Fax:* 734-462-4553. *E-mail:* admissions@schoolcraft.edu. *Web site:* http://www.schoolcraft.edu/.

Southwestern Michigan College
Dowagiac, Michigan

- **State and locally supported** 2-year, founded 1964
- **Rural** 240-acre campus
- **Coed,** 3,029 undergraduate students, 50% full-time, 62% women, 38% men

Undergraduates 1,501 full-time, 1,528 part-time. Students come from 7 states and territories; 12 other countries; 12% are from out of state; 9% Black or African American, non-Hispanic/Latino; 3% Hispanic/Latino; 0.7% Asian, non-Hispanic/Latino; 0.1% Native Hawaiian or other Pacific Islander, non-Hispanic/Latino; 1% American Indian or Alaska Native, non-Hispanic/Latino; 3% Two or more races, non-Hispanic/Latino; 5% Race/ethnicity unknown; 1% international; 38% transferred in; 9% live on campus. *Retention:* 59% of full-time freshmen returned.

Freshmen *Admission:* 1,958 applied, 1,936 admitted, 635 enrolled.

Faculty *Total:* 154, 38% full-time, 21% with terminal degrees. *Student/faculty ratio:* 22:1.

Majors Accounting technology and bookkeeping; administrative assistant and secretarial science; automobile/automotive mechanics technology; business administration and management; computer programming; computer support specialist; computer systems networking and telecommunications; construction management; drafting and design technology; early childhood education; electrical, electronic and communications engineering technology; emergency medical technology (EMT paramedic); engineering technology; executive assistant/executive secretary; fire science/firefighting; general studies; graphic design; health information/medical records technology; hotel/motel administration; industrial mechanics and maintenance technology; industrial production technologies related; liberal arts and sciences/liberal studies; machine tool technology; mechatronics, robotics, and automation engineering; medical/clinical assistant; meeting and event planning; prenursing studies; professional,

technical, business, and scientific writing; registered nursing/registered nurse; social work; teacher assistant/aide; theater design and technology; tool and die technology; welding technology.

Academics *Calendar:* semesters. *Degree:* certificates and associate. *Special study options:* academic remediation for entering students, accelerated degree program, adult/continuing education programs, advanced placement credit, cooperative education, distance learning, double majors, English as a second language, independent study, internships, part-time degree program, services for LD students, summer session for credit.

Library Fred L. Mathews Library with 31,203 titles, 30,634 serial subscriptions, 2,986 audiovisual materials, an OPAC, a Web page.

Student Life *Housing Options:* coed. Campus housing is university owned. *Activities and Organizations:* drama/theater group, choral group, Dionysus Drama Club, Synergy Dance Club, SMC Community of Veterans, Alpha Kappa Omega, SMC Green Club. *Campus security:* 24-hour emergency response devices and patrols, controlled dormitory access, day and evening police patrols.

Athletics *Intramural sports:* basketball M/W, football M/W, golf M/W, racquetball M/W, rock climbing M/W, soccer M/W, softball M/W, tennis M/W, volleyball M/W.

Costs (2011–12) *Tuition:* area resident $2581 full-time, $99 per contact hour part-time; state resident $3334 full-time, $128 per contact hour part-time; non-resident $3634 full-time, $140 per contact hour part-time. *Required fees:* $988 full-time, $38 per contact hour part-time. *Room and board:* $7543; room only: $5305. *Payment plan:* installment. *Waivers:* employees or children of employees.

Financial Aid Of all full-time matriculated undergraduates who enrolled in 2010, 125 Federal Work-Study jobs (averaging $1000). 75 state and other part-time jobs (averaging $1000).

Applying *Options:* electronic application, deferred entrance. *Required:* high school transcript. *Required for some:* interview. *Application deadlines:* rolling (freshmen), rolling (transfers). *Notification:* continuous (freshmen), continuous (transfers).

Freshman Application Contact Ms. Angela Palsak, Associate Dean of Students, Southwestern Michigan College, Dowagiac, MI 49047. *Phone:* 269-782-1000 Ext. 1310. *Toll-free phone:* 800-456-8675. *Fax:* 269-782-1331. *E-mail:* apalsak@swmich.edu. *Web site:* http://www.swmich.edu/.

Washtenaw Community College
Ann Arbor, Michigan

Freshman Application Contact Washtenaw Community College, 4800 East Huron River Drive, PO Box D-1, Ann Arbor, MI 48106. *Phone:* 734-973-3315. *Web site:* http://www.wccnet.edu/.

Wayne County Community College District
Detroit, Michigan

Freshman Application Contact Office of Enrollment Management and Student Services, Wayne County Community College District, 801 West Fort Street, Detroit, MI 48226-9975. *Phone:* 313-496-2634. *E-mail:* caafjh@wccc.edu. *Web site:* http://www.wcccd.edu/.

West Shore Community College
Scottville, Michigan

Freshman Application Contact Wendy Fought, Director of Admissions, West Shore Community College, PO Box 277, 3000 North Stiles Road, Scottville, MI 49454-0277. *Phone:* 231-843-5503. *Fax:* 231-845-3944. *E-mail:* admissions@westshore.edu. *Web site:* http://www.westshore.edu/.

MICRONESIA

College of Micronesia–FSM
Kolonia Pohnpei, Federated States of Micronesia, Micronesia

Freshman Application Contact Rita Hinga, Student Services Specialist, College of Micronesia–FSM, PO Box 159, Kolonia Pohnpei, FM 96941-0159, Micronesia. *Phone:* 691-320-3795 Ext. 15. *E-mail:* rhinga@comfsm.fm. *Web site:* http://www.comfsm.fm/.

MINNESOTA

Alexandria Technical and Community College

Alexandria, Minnesota

- **State-supported** 2-year, founded 1961, part of Minnesota State Colleges and Universities System
- **Small-town** 106-acre campus
- **Coed**

Undergraduates 1,580 full-time, 767 part-time. Students come from 18 states and territories; 4% are from out of state; 1% Black or African American, non-Hispanic/Latino; 1% Hispanic/Latino; 0.6% Asian, non-Hispanic/Latino; 0.2% Native Hawaiian or other Pacific Islander, non-Hispanic/Latino; 1% American Indian or Alaska Native, non-Hispanic/Latino.
Faculty *Student/faculty ratio:* 19:1.
Academics *Calendar:* semesters. *Degree:* certificates, diplomas, and associate. *Special study options:* academic remediation for entering students, advanced placement credit, distance learning, double majors, independent study, internships, part-time degree program, services for LD students, student-designed majors, summer session for credit.
Student Life *Campus security:* student patrols, late-night transport/escort service, security cameras inside and outside.
Costs (2011–12) *Tuition:* state resident $5261 full-time, $155 per credit part-time; nonresident $5261 full-time, $155 per credit part-time. Full-time tuition and fees vary according to program. Part-time tuition and fees vary according to program. *Required fees:* $588 full-time, $18 per credit part-time. *Room and board:* $5200.
Financial Aid Of all full-time matriculated undergraduates who enrolled in 2010, 94 Federal Work-Study jobs (averaging $1871).
Applying *Options:* electronic application, early admission, deferred entrance. *Application fee:* $20. *Required:* high school transcript, interview.
Freshman Application Contact Janet Dropik, Admissions Receptionist, Alexandria Technical and Community College, 1601 Jefferson Street, Alexandria, MN 56308. *Phone:* 320-762-4520. *Toll-free phone:* 888-234-1222. *Fax:* 320-762-4603. *E-mail:* admissionsrep@alextech.edu. *Web site:* http://www.alextech.edu/.

Anoka-Ramsey Community College

Coon Rapids, Minnesota

- **State-supported** 2-year, founded 1965, part of Minnesota State Colleges and Universities System
- **Suburban** 100-acre campus with easy access to Minneapolis-St. Paul
- **Coed,** 7,475 undergraduate students

Undergraduates 4% are from out of state; 7% Black or African American, non-Hispanic/Latino; 5% Hispanic/Latino; 4% Asian, non-Hispanic/Latino; 0.1% Native Hawaiian or other Pacific Islander, non-Hispanic/Latino; 0.5% American Indian or Alaska Native, non-Hispanic/Latino; 4% Two or more races, non-Hispanic/Latino; 1% Race/ethnicity unknown; 0.3% international. *Retention:* 43% of full-time freshmen returned.
Freshmen *Admission:* 2,913 applied, 1,524 admitted.
Faculty *Total:* 241, 39% full-time. *Student/faculty ratio:* 31:1.
Majors Accounting; accounting technology and bookkeeping; bioengineering and biomedical engineering; biology/biological sciences; biomedical technology; business administration and management; business/commerce; community health and preventive medicine; computer science; computer systems networking and telecommunications; dramatic/theater arts; environmental science; fine/studio arts; health services/allied health/health sciences; holistic health; human resources management; liberal arts and sciences/liberal studies; multi/interdisciplinary studies related; music; physical therapy technology; pre-engineering; registered nursing/registered nurse; sales, distribution, and marketing operations.
Academics *Calendar:* semesters. *Degree:* certificates and associate. *Special study options:* academic remediation for entering students, accelerated degree program, advanced placement credit, cooperative education, distance learning, double majors, honors programs, independent study, internships, off-campus study, part-time degree program, services for LD students, study abroad, summer session for credit. *ROTC:* Air Force (c).
Library Coon Rapids Campus Library with 42,349 titles, 158 serial subscriptions, 1,961 audiovisual materials, an OPAC, a Web page.
Student Life *Housing:* college housing not available. *Activities and Organizations:* drama/theater group, student-run newspaper, choral group, student government, Phi Theta Kappa, Multicultural Club, CRU (Campus Christian group), Salmagundi (student newspaper). *Campus security:* 24-hour emergency response devices, late-night transport/escort service. *Student services:* personal/psychological counseling.

Athletics Member NJCAA. *Intercollegiate sports:* baseball M, basketball M/W, soccer M/W, softball W, volleyball W. *Intramural sports:* basketball M/W, bowling M/W, football M/W, golf M/W, ice hockey M/W, soccer M/W, softball M/W, tennis M/W, volleyball M/W.
Costs (2011–12) *Tuition:* state resident $4181 full-time, $139 per credit part-time; nonresident $4181 full-time, $139 per credit part-time. Full-time tuition and fees vary according to course load and program. Part-time tuition and fees vary according to course load and program. *Required fees:* $568 full-time, $21 per credit part-time. *Payment plans:* installment, deferred payment. *Waivers:* senior citizens and employees or children of employees.
Financial Aid Of all full-time matriculated undergraduates who enrolled in 2010, 111 Federal Work-Study jobs (averaging $4000). 151 state and other part-time jobs (averaging $4000).
Applying *Options:* electronic application, early admission, deferred entrance. *Application fee:* $20. *Required for some:* high school transcript. *Application deadlines:* rolling (freshmen), rolling (out-of-state freshmen), rolling (transfers). *Notification:* continuous (freshmen), continuous (out-of-state freshmen), continuous (transfers).
Freshman Application Contact Admissions Department, Anoka-Ramsey Community College, 11200 Mississippi Boulevard, NW, Coon Rapids, MN 55433-3470. *Phone:* 763-433-1300. *Fax:* 763-433-1521. *E-mail:* admissions@anokaramsey.edu. *Web site:* http://www.anokaramsey.edu/.

Anoka-Ramsey Community College, Cambridge Campus

Cambridge, Minnesota

- **State-supported** 2-year, founded 1965, part of Minnesota State Colleges and Universities System
- **Small-town** campus
- **Coed,** 2,682 undergraduate students

Undergraduates 3% are from out of state; 1% Black or African American, non-Hispanic/Latino; 3% Hispanic/Latino; 1% Asian, non-Hispanic/Latino; 0.1% Native Hawaiian or other Pacific Islander, non-Hispanic/Latino; 0.4% American Indian or Alaska Native, non-Hispanic/Latino; 3% Two or more races, non-Hispanic/Latino; 2% Race/ethnicity unknown; 0.1% international. *Retention:* 52% of full-time freshmen returned.
Freshmen *Admission:* 668 applied, 342 admitted.
Faculty *Total:* 58, 45% full-time. *Student/faculty ratio:* 36:1.
Majors Accounting; accounting technology and bookkeeping; bioengineering and biomedical engineering; biology/biological sciences; biomedical technology; business administration and management; business/commerce; community health and preventive medicine; computer science; computer systems networking and telecommunications; dramatic/theater arts; environmental science; fine/studio arts; health services/allied health/health sciences; holistic health; human resources management; liberal arts and sciences/liberal studies; multi/interdisciplinary studies related; music; pre-engineering; registered nursing/registered nurse; sales, distribution, and marketing operations.
Academics *Calendar:* semesters. *Degree:* certificates and associate. *Special study options:* academic remediation for entering students, accelerated degree program, advanced placement credit, cooperative education, distance learning, double majors, honors programs, independent study, internships, off-campus study, part-time degree program, services for LD students, study abroad, summer session for credit. *ROTC:* Air Force (c).
Library Cambridge Campus Library with 26,829 titles, 134 serial subscriptions, 1,598 audiovisual materials, an OPAC, a Web page.
Student Life *Housing:* college housing not available. *Activities and Organizations:* drama/theater group, student-run newspaper, choral group. *Campus security:* 24-hour emergency response devices, late-night transport/escort service. *Student services:* personal/psychological counseling.
Athletics Member NJCAA. *Intercollegiate sports:* baseball M, basketball M/W, soccer M/W, softball W, volleyball W. *Intramural sports:* bowling M/W, golf M/W, volleyball M/W.
Costs (2011–12) *Tuition:* state resident $4181 full-time, $139 per credit part-time; nonresident $4181 full-time, $139 per credit part-time. Full-time tuition and fees vary according to course load and program. Part-time tuition and fees vary according to course load and program. *Required fees:* $568 full-time, $21 per credit part-time. *Payment plans:* installment, deferred payment. *Waivers:* senior citizens and employees or children of employees.
Applying *Options:* electronic application, early admission, deferred entrance. *Application fee:* $20. *Required for some:* high school transcript. *Application deadlines:* rolling (freshmen), rolling (out-of-state freshmen), rolling (transfers). *Notification:* continuous (freshmen), continuous (out-of-state freshmen), continuous (transfers).
Freshman Application Contact Admissions Department, Anoka-Ramsey Community College, Cambridge Campus, 300 Spirit River Drive South, Cambridge, MN 55008-5706. *Phone:* 763-433-1300. *Fax:* 763-433-1841. *E-mail:* admissions@anokaramsey.edu. *Web site:* http://www.anokaramsey.edu/.

Anoka Technical College

Anoka, Minnesota

Director of Admissions Mr. Robert Hoenie, Director of Admissions, Anoka Technical College, 1355 West Highway 10, Anoka, MN 55303. *Phone:* 763-576-4746. *E-mail:* info@anokatech.edu. *Web site:* http://www.anokatech.edu/

Anthem College–St. Louis Park

St. Louis Park, Minnesota

Freshman Application Contact Admissions Office, Anthem College–St. Louis Park, 5100 Gamble Drive, St. Louis Park, MN 55416. *Toll-free phone:* 855-331-7769. *Web site:* http://anthem.edu/minneapolis-minnesota/.

Brown College

Mendota Heights, Minnesota

Freshman Application Contact Mr. Mark Fredrichs, Registrar, Brown College, 1440 Northland Drive, Mendota Heights, MN 55120. *Phone:* 651-905-3400. *Toll-free phone:* 866-551-0049. *Fax:* 651-905-3550. *Web site:* http://www.browncollege.edu/.

Central Lakes College

Brainerd, Minnesota

- **State-supported** 2-year, founded 1938, part of Minnesota State Colleges and Universities System
- **Small-town** campus
- **Endowment** $3.4 million
- **Coed**

Undergraduates 2,517 full-time, 1,861 part-time. Students come from 12 states and territories; 0.3% are from out of state; 2% Black or African American, non-Hispanic/Latino; 0.8% Hispanic/Latino; 0.9% Asian, non-Hispanic/Latino; 0.1% Native Hawaiian or other Pacific Islander, non-Hispanic/Latino; 3% American Indian or Alaska Native, non-Hispanic/Latino; 0.2% Race/ethnicity unknown.

Faculty *Student/faculty ratio:* 20:1.

Academics *Calendar:* semesters. *Degree:* certificates, diplomas, and associate. *Special study options:* academic remediation for entering students, advanced placement credit, distance learning, English as a second language, external degree program, independent study, internships, off-campus study, part-time degree program, services for LD students, summer session for credit.

Student Life *Campus security:* 24-hour emergency response devices and patrols, student patrols, late-night transport/escort service.

Athletics Member NJCAA.

Applying *Options:* electronic application, deferred entrance. *Application fee:* $20. *Required:* high school transcript.

Freshman Application Contact Ms. Rose Tretter, Central Lakes College, 501 West College Drive, Brainerd, MN 56401-3904. *Phone:* 218-855-8036. *Toll-free phone:* 800-933-0346. *Fax:* 218-855-8220. *E-mail:* cdaniels@clcmn.edu. *Web site:* http://www.clcmn.edu/.

Century College

White Bear Lake, Minnesota

- **State-supported** 2-year, founded 1970, part of Minnesota State Colleges and Universities System
- **Suburban** 150-acre campus with easy access to Minneapolis-St. Paul
- **Coed**, 10,707 undergraduate students, 43% full-time, 55% women, 45% men

Undergraduates 4,637 full-time, 6,070 part-time. Students come from 43 states and territories; 43 other countries; 6% are from out of state; 11% Black or African American, non-Hispanic/Latino; 6% Hispanic/Latino; 15% Asian, non-Hispanic/Latino; 0.1% Native Hawaiian or other Pacific Islander, non-Hispanic/Latino; 0.5% American Indian or Alaska Native, non-Hispanic/Latino; 4% Two or more races, non-Hispanic/Latino; 0.5% Race/ethnicity unknown; 1% international; 41% transferred in.

Freshmen *Admission:* 3,444 applied, 3,444 admitted, 1,671 enrolled.

Faculty *Total:* 391, 52% full-time. *Student/faculty ratio:* 25:1.

Majors Accounting; administrative assistant and secretarial science; building/property maintenance; business administration and management; CAD/CADD drafting/design technology; computer and information systems security; computer science; computer systems networking and telecommunications; computer technology/computer systems technology; cosmetology; criminalistics and criminal science; criminal justice/police science; criminal justice/safety; dental assisting; dental hygiene; digital communication and media/multimedia;

emergency medical technology (EMT paramedic); energy management and systems technology; greenhouse management; heating, air conditioning, ventilation and refrigeration maintenance technology; homeland security, law enforcement, firefighting and protective services related; horticultural science; human services; interior design; landscaping and groundskeeping; language interpretation and translation; liberal arts and sciences/liberal studies; marketing/marketing management; medical administrative assistant and medical secretary; music; orthotics/prosthetics; radiologic technology/science; registered nursing/registered nurse; sport and fitness administration/management; substance abuse/addiction counseling; teacher assistant/aide.

Academics *Calendar:* semesters. *Degree:* certificates, diplomas, and associate. *Special study options:* academic remediation for entering students, advanced placement credit, distance learning, double majors, English as a second language, honors programs, internships, part-time degree program, services for LD students, study abroad, summer session for credit. *ROTC:* Air Force (c).

Library Century College Library with 93,913 titles, 220 serial subscriptions, 10,526 audiovisual materials, an OPAC.

Student Life *Housing:* college housing not available. *Activities and Organizations:* drama/theater group, student-run newspaper, choral group, Asian Student Association, Intercultural Club, Student Senate, Phi Theta Kappa, Planning Activities Committee. *Campus security:* late-night transport/escort service, day patrols. *Student services:* personal/psychological counseling.

Athletics Member NJCAA. *Intercollegiate sports:* baseball M, soccer M/W, softball W. *Intramural sports:* badminton M/W, basketball M/W, bowling M/W, soccer M/W, softball M/W, table tennis M/W, volleyball M/W.

Costs (2011–12) *Tuition:* state resident $4644 full-time, $155 per semester hour part-time; nonresident $4644 full-time, $155 per semester hour part-time. Full-time tuition and fees vary according to course load, program, and reciprocity agreements. Part-time tuition and fees vary according to course load, program, and reciprocity agreements. *Required fees:* $557 full-time, $19 per semester hour part-time. *Payment plan:* installment. *Waivers:* senior citizens and employees or children of employees.

Financial Aid Of all full-time matriculated undergraduates who enrolled in 2010, 81 Federal Work-Study jobs (averaging $2763). 85 state and other part-time jobs (averaging $2646).

Applying *Options:* electronic application, deferred entrance. *Application fee:* $20. *Required:* high school transcript. *Application deadlines:* rolling (freshmen), rolling (transfers).

Freshman Application Contact Ms. Christine Paulos, Admissions Director, Century College, 3300 Century Avenue North, White Bear Lake, MN 55110. *Phone:* 651-779-2619. *Toll-free phone:* 800-228-1978. *Fax:* 651-773-1796. *E-mail:* admissions@century.edu. *Web site:* http://www.century.edu/.

Dakota County Technical College

Rosemount, Minnesota

- **State-supported** 2-year, founded 1970, part of Minnesota State Colleges and Universities System
- **Suburban** 100-acre campus with easy access to Minneapolis-St. Paul
- **Endowment** $3.2 million
- **Coed**

Undergraduates 1,690 full-time, 1,982 part-time. Students come from 8 states and territories; 28 other countries; 3% are from out of state; 7% Black or African American, non-Hispanic/Latino; 3% Hispanic/Latino; 3% Asian, non-Hispanic/Latino; 0.8% American Indian or Alaska Native, non-Hispanic/Latino; 6% Race/ethnicity unknown; 0.8% international; 17% transferred in.

Faculty *Student/faculty ratio:* 30:1.

Academics *Calendar:* semesters. *Degree:* certificates, diplomas, and associate. *Special study options:* academic remediation for entering students, cooperative education, distance learning, double majors, English as a second language, independent study, internships, part-time degree program, services for LD students, student-designed majors, summer session for credit.

Student Life *Campus security:* 24-hour emergency response devices, late-night transport/escort service.

Athletics Member NJCAA.

Costs (2011–12) *Tuition:* state resident $4680 full-time; nonresident $4680 full-time. Full-time tuition and fees vary according to program. Part-time tuition and fees vary according to program. *Required fees:* $630 full-time. *Payment plans:* installment, deferred payment.

Applying *Options:* electronic application. *Application fee:* $20. *Required for some:* high school transcript.

Freshman Application Contact Mr. Patrick Lair, Admissions Director, Dakota County Technical College, 1300 East 145th Street, Rosemount, MN 55068. *Phone:* 651-423-8399. *Toll-free phone:* 877-YES-DCTC. *Fax:* 651-423-8775. *E-mail:* admissions@dctc.mnscu.edu. *Web site:* http://www.dctc.edu/.

Duluth Business University

Duluth, Minnesota

- Proprietary 2-year, founded 1891
- Urban 2-acre campus
- Coed, primarily women

Academics *Calendar:* quarters. *Degree:* diplomas and associate.
Applying *Application fee:* $35.
Freshman Application Contact Mr. Mark Traux, Director of Admissions, Duluth Business University, 4724 Mike Colalillo Drive, Duluth, MN 55807. *Phone:* 218-722-4000. *Toll-free phone:* 800-777-8406. *Fax:* 218-628-2127. *E-mail:* markt@dbumn.edu. *Web site:* http://www.dbumn.edu/.

Dunwoody College of Technology

Minneapolis, Minnesota

Freshman Application Contact Bonney Bielen, Director of Admissions and Student Services, Dunwoody College of Technology, 818 Dunwoody Boulevard, Minneapolis, MN 55403. *Phone:* 612-374-5800. *Toll-free phone:* 800-292-4625. *Web site:* http://www.dunwoody.edu/.

Fond du Lac Tribal and Community College

Cloquet, Minnesota

Freshman Application Contact Kathie Jubie, Admissions Representative, Fond du Lac Tribal and Community College, 2101 14th Street, Cloquet, MN 55720. *Phone:* 218-879-0808. *Toll-free phone:* 800-657-3712. *E-mail:* admissions@fdltcc.edu. *Web site:* http://www.fdltcc.edu/.

Hennepin Technical College

Brooklyn Park, Minnesota

Freshman Application Contact Hennepin Technical College, 9000 Brooklyn Boulevard, Brooklyn Park, MN 55445. *Phone:* 763-488-2415. *Toll-free phone:* 800-345-4655 (in-state); 800-645-4655 (out-of-state). *Web site:* http://www.hennepintech.edu/.

Herzing University

Minneapolis, Minnesota

Freshman Application Contact Ms. Shelly Larson, Director of Admissions, Herzing University, 5700 West Broadway, Minneapolis, MN 55428. *Phone:* 763-231-3155. *Toll-free phone:* 800-596-0724. *Fax:* 763-535-9205. *E-mail:* info@mpls.herzing.edu. *Web site:* http://www.herzing.edu/.

Hibbing Community College

Hibbing, Minnesota

Freshman Application Contact Admissions, Hibbing Community College, 1515 East 25th Street, Hibbing, MN 55746. *Phone:* 218-262-7200. *Toll-free phone:* 800-224-4HCC. *Fax:* 218-262-6717. *E-mail:* admissions@hibbing.edu. *Web site:* http://www.hcc.mnscu.edu/.

The Institute of Production and Recording

Minneapolis, Minnesota

- Proprietary 2-year, part of Globe Education Network (GEN) which is composed of Globe University, Minnesota School of Business, Broadview University, The Institute of Production and Recording and Minnesota School of Cosmetology
- Urban 4-acre campus with easy access to Minneapolis-St. Paul
- Coed, 456 undergraduate students, 85% full-time, 14% women, 86% men

Undergraduates 389 full-time, 67 part-time. Students come from 28 states and territories; 6% are from out of state; 8% Black or African American, non-Hispanic/Latino; 5% Hispanic/Latino; 2% Asian, non-Hispanic/Latino; 0.2% Native Hawaiian or other Pacific Islander, non-Hispanic/Latino; 0.9% American Indian or Alaska Native, non-Hispanic/Latino; 5% Two or more races, non-Hispanic/Latino; 9% Race/ethnicity unknown; 16% transferred in.
Freshmen *Admission:* 127 enrolled.
Faculty *Total:* 38, 5% with terminal degrees. *Student/faculty ratio:* 10:1.
Majors Music management; recording arts technology.
Academics *Degree:* associate. *Special study options:* academic remediation for entering students, accelerated degree program, adult/continuing education

programs, advanced placement credit, internships, part-time degree program, services for LD students, summer session for credit.
Library Institute of Production and Recording Campus Library with 1,640 titles, 53,111 serial subscriptions, 2,079 audiovisual materials, an OPAC, a Web page.
Student Life *Housing:* college housing not available. *Campus security:* 24-hour emergency response devices, late-night transport/escort service.
Standardized Tests *Required:* AccuPlacer is required of all applicants unless documentation of a minimum ACT composite score of 21 or documentation of a minimum composite score of 1485 on the SAT is presented (for admission).
Applying *Options:* electronic application. *Application fee:* $50. *Required:* high school transcript, interview. *Required for some:* essay or personal statement, 2 letters of recommendation. *Application deadlines:* rolling (freshmen), rolling (out-of-state freshmen), rolling (transfers). *Notification:* continuous (freshmen), continuous (out-of-state freshmen), continuous (transfers).
Freshman Application Contact The Institute of Production and Recording, 312 Washington Avenue North, Minneapolis, MN 55401. *Phone:* 612-375-1900. *Web site:* http://www.ipr.edu/.

Inver Hills Community College

Inver Grove Heights, Minnesota

- State-supported 2-year, founded 1969, part of Minnesota State Colleges and Universities System
- Suburban 100-acre campus with easy access to Minneapolis-St. Paul
- Coed

Undergraduates 2,502 full-time, 3,840 part-time. Students come from 19 states and territories; 2% are from out of state; 11% Black or African American, non-Hispanic/Latino; 5% Hispanic/Latino; 6% Asian, non-Hispanic/Latino; 0.3% Native Hawaiian or other Pacific Islander, non-Hispanic/Latino; 1% American Indian or Alaska Native, non-Hispanic/Latino; 2% Race/ethnicity unknown; 0.6% international; 5% transferred in.
Academics *Calendar:* semesters. *Degree:* certificates and associate. *Special study options:* academic remediation for entering students, accelerated degree program, advanced placement credit, cooperative education, distance learning, English as a second language, external degree program, honors programs, independent study, internships, off-campus study, part-time degree program, services for LD students, summer session for credit. *ROTC:* Army (c), Air Force (c).
Student Life *Campus security:* late-night transport/escort service, evening police patrol.
Costs (2011–12) *Tuition:* state resident $3720 full-time, $155 per credit hour part-time; nonresident $3720 full-time, $155 per credit hour part-time. Full-time tuition and fees vary according to course load, location, program, and reciprocity agreements. Part-time tuition and fees vary according to course load, location, program, and reciprocity agreements. *Required fees:* $402 full-time, $17 per credit hour part-time.
Financial Aid Of all full-time matriculated undergraduates who enrolled in 2009, 3,600 applied for aid, 3,250 were judged to have need. 175 Federal Work-Study jobs (averaging $2300). 153 state and other part-time jobs (averaging $2300). *Average percent of need met:* 48. *Average financial aid package:* $4300. *Average need-based loan:* $4200. *Average need-based gift aid:* $3800.
Applying *Options:* electronic application. *Application fee:* $20. *Required for some:* high school transcript. *Recommended:* high school transcript.
Freshman Application Contact Mr. Casey Carmody, Admissions Representative, Inver Hills Community College, 2500 East 80th Street, Inver Grove Heights, MN 55076-3224. *Phone:* 651-450-3589. *Fax:* 651-450-3677. *E-mail:* admissions@inverhills.edu. *Web site:* http://www.inverhills.edu/.

Itasca Community College

Grand Rapids, Minnesota

- State-supported 2-year, founded 1922, part of Minnesota State Colleges and Universities System,, Northeastern Higher Education District
- Rural 24-acre campus
- Endowment $4.0 million
- Coed, 1,299 undergraduate students, 76% full-time, 45% women, 55% men

Undergraduates 983 full-time, 316 part-time. Students come from 2 other countries; 4% are from out of state; 3% Black or African American, non-Hispanic/Latino; 0.4% Hispanic/Latino; 0.5% Asian, non-Hispanic/Latino; 0.2% Native Hawaiian or other Pacific Islander, non-Hispanic/Latino; 4% American Indian or Alaska Native, non-Hispanic/Latino; 3% Race/ethnicity unknown; 10% live on campus. *Retention:* 53% of full-time freshmen returned.
Freshmen *Admission:* 946 applied, 946 admitted.
Faculty *Total:* 77, 56% full-time, 3% with terminal degrees. *Student/faculty ratio:* 17:1.

Majors Accounting; American Indian/Native American studies; business administration and management; chemical engineering; civil engineering; computer engineering; computer engineering related; education; education (multiple levels); engineering; engineering related; engineering science; engineering technology; environmental studies; fishing and fisheries sciences and management; forestry; forest technology; general studies; geography; human services; liberal arts and sciences/liberal studies; licensed practical/vocational nurse training; mechanical engineering; natural resources/conservation; natural resources management and policy; nuclear engineering; pre-engineering; psychology; special education–early childhood; wildlife, fish and wildlands science and management.

Academics *Calendar:* semesters. *Degree:* certificates, diplomas, and associate. *Special study options:* academic remediation for entering students, adult/continuing education programs, advanced placement credit, cooperative education, double majors, independent study, internships, off-campus study, part-time degree program, services for LD students, study abroad, summer session for credit.

Library Itasca Community College Library with 28,790 titles, 280 serial subscriptions, an OPAC, a Web page.

Student Life *Housing Options:* coed. Campus housing is university owned. *Activities and Organizations:* Student Association, Circle K, Student Ambassadors, Minority Student Club, Psychology Club. *Campus security:* student patrols, late-night transport/escort service, controlled dormitory access, evening patrols by trained security personnel.

Athletics Member NJCAA. *Intercollegiate sports:* baseball M, basketball M/W, football M, softball W, volleyball W, wrestling M. *Intramural sports:* basketball M, bowling M/W, softball M/W, table tennis M/W, volleyball M/W.

Applying *Options:* electronic application. *Required:* high school transcript. *Application deadlines:* 8/20 (freshmen), 8/20 (transfers). *Notification:* continuous (freshmen), continuous (transfers).

Freshman Application Contact Ms. Candace Perry, Director of Enrollment Services, Itasca Community College, Grand Rapids, MN 55744. *Phone:* 218-322-2340. *Toll-free phone:* 800-996-6422. *Fax:* 218-327-4350. *E-mail:* iccinfo@itascacc.edu. *Web site:* http://www.itascacc.edu/.

ITT Technical Institute
Brooklyn Center, Minnesota

- **Proprietary** primarily 2-year, part of ITT Educational Services, Inc.
- **Coed**

Majors Business administration and management; communications technology; computer and information systems security; drafting and design technology; electrical, electronic and communications engineering technology; graphic communications; network and system administration; project management.

Academics *Calendar:* quarters. *Degrees:* associate and bachelor's.

Freshman Application Contact Director of Recruitment, ITT Technical Institute, 6120 Earle Brown Drive, Suite 100, Brooklyn Center, MN 55430. *Phone:* 763-549-5900. *Toll-free phone:* 800-216-8883. *Web site:* http://www.itt-tech.edu/.

ITT Technical Institute
Eden Prairie, Minnesota

- **Proprietary** primarily 2-year, founded 2003, part of ITT Educational Services, Inc.
- **Coed**

Majors Business administration and management; communications technology; computer and information systems security; computer software engineering; computer software technology; drafting and design technology; electrical, electronic and communications engineering technology; forensic science and technology; graphic communications; legal assistant/paralegal; network and system administration; project management.

Academics *Calendar:* quarters. *Degrees:* associate and bachelor's.

Freshman Application Contact Director of Recruitment, ITT Technical Institute, 8911 Columbine Road, Eden Prairie, MN 55347. *Phone:* 952-914-5300. *Toll-free phone:* 888-488-9646. *Web site:* http://www.itt-tech.edu/.

Lake Superior College
Duluth, Minnesota

- **State-supported** 2-year, founded 1995, part of Minnesota State Colleges and Universities System
- **Urban** 105-acre campus
- **Endowment** $476,618
- **Coed**

Undergraduates 2,380 full-time, 1,986 part-time. Students come from 29 states and territories; 3 other countries; 9% are from out of state; 39% transferred in. *Retention:* 56% of full-time freshmen returned.

Faculty *Student/faculty ratio:* 13:1.

Academics *Calendar:* semesters. *Degree:* certificates, diplomas, and associate. *Special study options:* academic remediation for entering students, advanced placement credit, distance learning, double majors, English as a second language, independent study, internships, part-time degree program, services for LD students, summer session for credit.

Student Life *Campus security:* late-night transport/escort service, 15-hour patrols by trained security personnel.

Costs (2011–12) *Tuition:* state resident $3984 full-time, $133 per credit part-time; nonresident $8169 full-time, $272 per credit part-time. Full-time tuition and fees vary according to course load and reciprocity agreements. Part-time tuition and fees vary according to course load and reciprocity agreements. *Required fees:* $624 full-time, $21 per credit part-time. *Payment plans:* installment, deferred payment.

Financial Aid Of all full-time matriculated undergraduates who enrolled in 2010, 72 Federal Work-Study jobs (averaging $2720). 103 state and other part-time jobs (averaging $2720).

Applying *Options:* early admission, deferred entrance. *Application fee:* $20. *Required for some:* high school transcript.

Freshman Application Contact Ms. Melissa Leno, Director of Admissions, Lake Superior College, 2101 Trinity Road, Duluth, MN 55811. *Phone:* 218-723-4895. *Toll-free phone:* 800-432-2884. *Fax:* 218-733-5945. *E-mail:* enroll@lsc.edu. *Web site:* http://www.lsc.edu/.

Le Cordon Bleu College of Culinary Arts
Saint Paul, Minnesota

Freshman Application Contact Admissions Office, Le Cordon Bleu College of Culinary Arts, 1315 Mendota Heights Road, Saint Paul, MN 55120. *Phone:* 651-675-4700. *Toll-free phone:* 888-348-5222. *Web site:* http://www.twincitiesculinary.com/.

Leech Lake Tribal College
Cass Lake, Minnesota

Freshman Application Contact Ms. Shelly Braford, Recruiter, Leech Lake Tribal College, PO Box 180, 6945 Littlewolf Road NW, Cass Lake, MN 56633. *Phone:* 218-335-4200 Ext. 4270. *Fax:* 218-335-4217. *E-mail:* shelly.braford@lltc.edu. *Web site:* http://www.lltc.edu/.

Mesabi Range Community and Technical College
Virginia, Minnesota

- **State-supported** 2-year, founded 1918, part of Minnesota State Colleges and Universities System
- **Small-town** 30-acre campus
- **Coed**

Undergraduates Students come from 6 states and territories; 2 other countries; 4% are from out of state; 10% live on campus.

Faculty *Student/faculty ratio:* 24:1.

Academics *Calendar:* semesters. *Degree:* certificates, diplomas, and associate. *Special study options:* academic remediation for entering students, adult/continuing education programs, advanced placement credit, cooperative education, independent study, internships, off-campus study, part-time degree program, services for LD students, student-designed majors, study abroad, summer session for credit.

Student Life *Campus security:* late-night transport/escort service.

Athletics Member NJCAA.

Costs (2011–12) *Tuition:* state resident $4546 full-time, $152 per credit hour part-time; nonresident $5670 full-time, $189 per credit hour part-time. Full-time tuition and fees vary according to reciprocity agreements. Part-time tuition and fees vary according to reciprocity agreements. *Required fees:* $564 full-time, $19 per credit hour part-time. *Room and board:* room only: $3972.

Financial Aid Of all full-time matriculated undergraduates who enrolled in 2011, 168 Federal Work-Study jobs (averaging $1227). 82 state and other part-time jobs (averaging $1380).

Applying *Options:* early admission, deferred entrance. *Application fee:* $20. *Required:* high school transcript.

Freshman Application Contact Ms. Brenda Kochevar, Enrollment Services Director, Mesabi Range Community and Technical College, Virginia, MN 55792. *Phone:* 218-749-0314. *Toll-free phone:* 800-657-3860. *Fax:* 218-749-0318. *E-mail:* b.kochevar@mr.mnscu.edu. *Web site:* http://www.mesabirange.edu/.

Minneapolis Business College

Roseville, Minnesota

- **Private** 2-year, founded 1874
- **Suburban** campus with easy access to Minneapolis-St. Paul
- **Coed, primarily women,** 377 undergraduate students
- 89% of applicants were admitted

Freshmen *Admission:* 574 applied, 513 admitted.

Majors Accounting technology and bookkeeping; administrative assistant and secretarial science; computer programming; computer systems networking and telecommunications; graphic design; hotel/motel administration; legal administrative assistant/secretary; legal assistant/paralegal; medical/clinical assistant.

Academics *Degree:* diplomas and associate. *Special study options:* accelerated degree program, internships.

Freshman Application Contact Admissions Office, Minneapolis Business College, 1711 West County Road B, Roseville, MN 55113. *Phone:* 651-636-7406. *Toll-free phone:* 800-279-5200. *Web site:* http://www.minneapolisbusinesscollege.edu/.

Minneapolis Community and Technical College

Minneapolis, Minnesota

- **State-supported** 2-year, founded 1965, part of Minnesota State Colleges and Universities System
- **Urban** 22-acre campus
- **Coed,** 9,991 undergraduate students, 38% full-time, 53% women, 47% men

Undergraduates 3,758 full-time, 6,233 part-time. Students come from 31 states and territories; 31% Black or African American, non-Hispanic/Latino; 8% Hispanic/Latino; 5% Asian, non-Hispanic/Latino; 0.1% Native Hawaiian or other Pacific Islander, non-Hispanic/Latino; 2% American Indian or Alaska Native, non-Hispanic/Latino; 8% Two or more races, non-Hispanic/Latino; 1% Race/ethnicity unknown; 2% international; 12% transferred in.

Freshmen *Admission:* 1,551 admitted, 1,548 enrolled.

Faculty *Total:* 477, 33% full-time. *Student/faculty ratio:* 27:1.

Majors Accounting; accounting technology and bookkeeping; administrative assistant and secretarial science; air traffic control; allied health diagnostic, intervention, and treatment professions related; animation, interactive technology, video graphics and special effects; biology/biological sciences; biotechnology; business administration and management; business automation/technology/data entry; chemistry; child-care and support services management; child development; cinematography and film/video production; commercial photography; community organization and advocacy; computer and information systems security; computer programming; computer systems networking and telecommunications; criminal justice/police science; criminal justice/safety; culinary arts; dental assisting; design and visual communications; digital communication and media/multimedia; dramatic/theater arts; education; education (multiple levels); electroneurodiagnostic/electroencephalographic technology; fine/studio arts; heating, air conditioning, ventilation and refrigeration maintenance technology; human services; liberal arts and sciences/liberal studies; library and archives assisting; mathematics; network and system administration; philosophy; photographic and film/video technology; playwriting and screenwriting; polysomnography; public administration; recording arts technology; registered nursing/registered nurse; restaurant/food services management; substance abuse/addiction counseling; web page, digital/multimedia and information resources design.

Academics *Calendar:* semesters. *Degree:* certificates, diplomas, and associate. *Special study options:* academic remediation for entering students, accelerated degree program, adult/continuing education programs, advanced placement credit, distance learning, English as a second language, honors programs, independent study, internships, off-campus study, part-time degree program, services for LD students, study abroad, summer session for credit.

Library Minneapolis Community and Technical College Library.

Student Life *Housing:* college housing not available. *Activities and Organizations:* drama/theater group, student-run newspaper, choral group, Student Senate, College Choirs, Student African American Brotherhood /B2B, Science Club, Phi Theta Kappa. *Campus security:* 24-hour emergency response devices and patrols, late-night transport/escort service. *Student services:* health clinic, personal/psychological counseling, women's center, legal services.

Costs (2012–13) *Tuition:* state resident $4523 full-time; nonresident $4523 full-time. *Required fees:* $669 full-time.

Applying *Options:* electronic application, early admission, deferred entrance. *Application fee:* $20. *Required:* high school transcript. *Application deadlines:* rolling (freshmen), rolling (transfers). *Notification:* continuous (freshmen), continuous (transfers).

Freshman Application Contact Minneapolis Community and Technical College, 1501 Hennepin Avenue, Minneapolis, MN 55403. *Phone:* 612-659-6200. *Toll-free phone:* 800-247-0911. *E-mail:* admissions.office@minneapolis.edu. *Web site:* http://www.mctc.mnscu.edu/.

Minneapolis Media Institute

Edina, Minnesota

Admissions Office Contact Minneapolis Media Institute, 4100 West 76th Street, Edina, MN 55435. *Toll-free phone:* 800-236-4997. *Web site:* http://www.mediainstitute.edu/minneapolis.

Minnesota School of Business–Brooklyn Center

Brooklyn Center, Minnesota

- **Proprietary** primarily 2-year, founded 1989, part of Globe Education Network (GEN) which is composed of Globe University, Minnesota School of Business, Broadview University, The Institute of Production and Recording and Minnesota School of Cosmetology
- **Suburban** 4-acre campus with easy access to Minneapolis-St. Paul
- **Coed,** 620 undergraduate students, 23% full-time, 68% women, 32% men
- 68% of applicants were admitted

Undergraduates 145 full-time, 475 part-time. Students come from 2 states and territories; 0.2% are from out of state; 22% Black or African American, non-Hispanic/Latino; 1% Hispanic/Latino; 7% Asian, non-Hispanic/Latino; 1% American Indian or Alaska Native, non-Hispanic/Latino; 2% Two or more races, non-Hispanic/Latino; 40% Race/ethnicity unknown; 14% transferred in. *Retention:* 38% of full-time freshmen returned.

Freshmen *Admission:* 675 applied, 457 admitted, 48 enrolled.

Faculty *Total:* 100, 15% full-time, 14% with terminal degrees. *Student/faculty ratio:* 10:1.

Majors Accounting; business administration and management; criminal justice/law enforcement administration; health/health-care administration; information technology; legal assistant/paralegal; marketing/marketing management; massage therapy; medical administrative assistant and medical secretary; medical/clinical assistant.

Academics *Calendar:* quarters. *Degrees:* diplomas, associate, and bachelor's. *Special study options:* academic remediation for entering students, accelerated degree program, adult/continuing education programs, advanced placement credit, internships, part-time degree program, services for LD students, summer session for credit.

Library Brooklyn Center Campus Library with 3,076 titles, 53,133 serial subscriptions, 132 audiovisual materials, an OPAC, a Web page.

Student Life *Housing:* college housing not available. *Campus security:* 24-hour emergency response devices, late-night transport/escort service.

Standardized Tests *Required:* AccuPlacer is required of all applicants unless documentation of a minimum ACT composite score of 21 or documentation of a minimum composite score of 1485 on the SAT is presented (for admission).

Applying *Options:* electronic application. *Application fee:* $50. *Required:* high school transcript, interview. *Required for some:* essay or personal statement, 2 letters of recommendation. *Application deadlines:* rolling (freshmen), rolling (out-of-state freshmen), rolling (transfers). *Notification:* continuous (freshmen), continuous (out-of-state freshmen), continuous (transfers).

Freshman Application Contact Minnesota School of Business–Brooklyn Center, 5910 Shingle Creek Parkway, Brooklyn Center, MN 55430. *Phone:* 763-566-7777. *Web site:* http://www.msbcollege.edu/.

Minnesota School of Business–Plymouth

Minneapolis, Minnesota

- **Proprietary** primarily 2-year, founded 2002, part of Globe Education Network (GEN) which is composed of Globe University, Minnesota School of Business, Broadview University, The Institute of Production and Recording and Minnesota School of Cosmetology
- **Suburban** 7-acre campus with easy access to Minneapolis-St. Paul
- **Coed,** 487 undergraduate students, 23% full-time, 74% women, 26% men

Undergraduates 114 full-time, 373 part-time. Students come from 1 other state; 6% Black or African American, non-Hispanic/Latino; 2% Hispanic/Latino; 0.8% Asian, non-Hispanic/Latino; 0.2% Native Hawaiian or other Pacific Islander, non-Hispanic/Latino; 0.8% American Indian or Alaska Native, non-Hispanic/Latino; 2% Two or more races, non-Hispanic/Latino; 11% Race/ethnicity unknown; 14% transferred in. *Retention:* 44% of full-time freshmen returned.

Freshmen *Admission:* 40 enrolled.

Faculty *Total:* 36, 22% full-time, 47% with terminal degrees. *Student/faculty ratio:* 21:1.

Majors Accounting; architectural drafting and CAD/CADD; business administration and management; computer systems networking and telecommunications; financial forensics and fraud investigation; information technology; marketing/marketing management; massage therapy; mechanical drafting and CAD/CADD; medical administrative assistant and medical secretary; medical/clinical assistant; physical fitness technician; veterinary/animal health technology.

Academics *Calendar:* quarters. *Degrees:* diplomas, associate, and bachelor's. *Special study options:* academic remediation for entering students, accelerated degree program, adult/continuing education programs, advanced placement credit, internships, part-time degree program, services for LD students, summer session for credit.

Library Plymouth Campus Library with 2,773 titles, 53,143 serial subscriptions, 52 audiovisual materials, an OPAC, a Web page.

Student Life *Housing:* college housing not available. *Campus security:* 24-hour emergency response devices, late-night transport/escort service.

Standardized Tests *Required:* AccuPlacer is required of all applicants unless documentation of a minimum ACT composite score of 21 or documentation of a minimum composite score of 1485 on the SAT is presented (for admission).

Applying *Options:* electronic application. *Application fee:* $50. *Required:* high school transcript, interview, High school transcript or GED required of all applicants. *Required for some:* essay or personal statement, 2 letters of recommendation. *Application deadlines:* rolling (freshmen), rolling (out-of-state freshmen), rolling (transfers). *Notification:* continuous (freshmen), continuous (out-of-state freshmen), continuous (transfers).

Freshman Application Contact Minnesota School of Business–Plymouth, Plymouth, MN 55447. *Phone:* 763-476-2000. *Fax:* 763-476-1000. *Web site:* http://www.msbcollege.edu/.

Minnesota School of Business– Richfield

Richfield, Minnesota

- **Proprietary** primarily 2-year, founded 1877, part of Globe Education Network (GEN) which is composed of Globe University, Minnesota School of Business, Broadview University, The Institute of Production and Recording and Minnesota School of Cosmetology
- **Urban** 3-acre campus with easy access to Minneapolis-St. Paul
- **Coed,** 1,738 undergraduate students, 30% full-time, 64% women, 36% men

Undergraduates 524 full-time, 1,214 part-time. Students come from 9 states and territories; 1% are from out of state; 9% Black or African American, non-Hispanic/Latino; 2% Hispanic/Latino; 3% Asian, non-Hispanic/Latino; 0.1% Native Hawaiian or other Pacific Islander, non-Hispanic/Latino; 1% American Indian or Alaska Native, non-Hispanic/Latino; 2% Two or more races, non-Hispanic/Latino; 12% Race/ethnicity unknown; 0.2% international; 18% transferred in. *Retention:* 28% of full-time freshmen returned.

Freshmen *Admission:* 144 enrolled.

Faculty *Total:* 177, 12% full-time, 15% with terminal degrees. *Student/faculty ratio:* 16:1.

Majors Accounting; animation, interactive technology, video graphics and special effects; business administration and management; computer programming; computer systems networking and telecommunications; criminal justice/law enforcement administration; financial forensics and fraud investigation; graphic design; health/health-care administration; information technology; legal assistant/paralegal; marketing/marketing management; medical administrative assistant and medical secretary; medical/clinical assistant; music related; physical fitness technician; registered nursing/registered nurse.

Academics *Calendar:* quarters. *Degrees:* diplomas, associate, and bachelor's. *Special study options:* academic remediation for entering students, accelerated degree program, adult/continuing education programs, advanced placement credit, internships, part-time degree program, services for LD students, summer session for credit.

Library Richfield Campus Library with 20,058 titles, 85,016 serial subscriptions, 4,265 audiovisual materials, an OPAC, a Web page.

Student Life *Housing:* college housing not available. *Campus security:* 24-hour emergency response devices, late-night transport/escort service.

Standardized Tests *Required:* AccuPlacer is required of all applicants unless documentation of a minimum ACT composite score of 21 or documentation of a minimum composite score of 1485 on the SAT is presented (for admission).

Applying *Options:* electronic application. *Application fee:* $50. *Required:* high school transcript, interview, High school transcript or GED required of all applicants. Application fee for Nursing Program is $100. *Required for some:* essay or personal statement, 2 letters of recommendation. *Application deadlines:* rolling (freshmen), rolling (out-of-state freshmen), rolling (transfers). *Notification:* continuous (freshmen), continuous (out-of-state freshmen), continuous (transfers).

Freshman Application Contact Minnesota School of Business–Richfield, 1401 West 76th Street, Suite 500, Richfield, MN 55423. *Phone:* 612-861-2000. *Toll-free phone:* 800-752-4223. *Web site:* http://www.msbcollege.edu/.

Minnesota School of Business– St. Cloud

Waite Park, Minnesota

- **Proprietary** primarily 2-year, founded 2004, part of Globe Education Network (GEN) which is composed of Globe University, Minnesota School of Business, Broadview University, The Institute of Production and Recording and Minnesota School of Cosmetology
- **Small-town** 2-acre campus
- **Coed,** 921 undergraduate students, 51% full-time, 72% women, 28% men

Undergraduates 468 full-time, 453 part-time. Students come from 1 other state; 2% Black or African American, non-Hispanic/Latino; 1% Hispanic/Latino; 1% Asian, non-Hispanic/Latino; 0.8% American Indian or Alaska Native, non-Hispanic/Latino; 0.8% Two or more races, non-Hispanic/Latino; 7% Race/ethnicity unknown; 0.1% international; 16% transferred in. *Retention:* 47% of full-time freshmen returned.

Freshmen *Admission:* 109 enrolled.

Faculty *Total:* 61, 30% full-time, 20% with terminal degrees. *Student/faculty ratio:* 22:1.

Majors Accounting; business administration and management; computer systems networking and telecommunications; criminal justice/law enforcement administration; graphic design; health/health-care administration; information technology; legal assistant/paralegal; marketing/marketing management; massage therapy; medical administrative assistant and medical secretary; medical/clinical assistant; physical fitness technician; veterinary/animal health technology.

Academics *Calendar:* quarters. *Degrees:* diplomas, associate, and bachelor's. *Special study options:* academic remediation for entering students, accelerated degree program, adult/continuing education programs, advanced placement credit, internships, part-time degree program, services for LD students, summer session for credit.

Library St. Cloud Campus Library with 3,549 titles, 53,154 serial subscriptions, 199 audiovisual materials, an OPAC, a Web page.

Student Life *Housing:* college housing not available. *Campus security:* 24-hour emergency response devices, late-night transport/escort service.

Standardized Tests *Required:* AccuPlacer is required of all applicants unless documentation of a minimum ACT composite score of 21 or documentation of a minimum composite score of 1485 on the SAT is presented (for admission).

Applying *Options:* electronic application. *Application fee:* $50. *Required:* high school transcript, interview, High school transcript or GED required of all applicants. *Required for some:* essay or personal statement, 2 letters of recommendation. *Application deadlines:* rolling (freshmen), rolling (out-of-state freshmen), rolling (transfers). *Notification:* continuous (freshmen), continuous (out-of-state freshmen), continuous (transfers).

Freshman Application Contact Minnesota School of Business–St. Cloud, 1201 2nd Street South, Waite Park, MN 56387. *Phone:* 320-257-2000. *Toll-free phone:* 866-403-3333. *Web site:* http://www.msbcollege.edu/.

Minnesota School of Business– Shakopee

Shakopee, Minnesota

- **Proprietary** primarily 2-year, founded 2004, part of Globe Education Network (GEN) which is composed of Globe University, Minnesota School of Business, Broadview University, The Institute of Production and Recording and Minnesota School of Cosmetology
- **Suburban** 1-acre campus
- **Coed,** 390 undergraduate students, 39% full-time, 81% women, 19% men

Undergraduates 154 full-time, 236 part-time. Students come from 1 other state; 2% Black or African American, non-Hispanic/Latino; 3% Hispanic/Latino; 4% Asian, non-Hispanic/Latino; 1% American Indian or Alaska Native, non-Hispanic/Latino; 1% Two or more races, non-Hispanic/Latino; 9% Race/ethnicity unknown; 0.8% international; 14% transferred in. *Retention:* 20% of full-time freshmen returned.

Freshmen *Admission:* 35 enrolled.

Faculty *Total:* 36, 36% full-time, 36% with terminal degrees. *Student/faculty ratio:* 15:1.

Majors Accounting; business administration and management; computer systems networking and telecommunications; criminal justice/law enforcement administration; financial forensics and fraud investigation; health/health-care administration; information technology; legal assistant/paralegal; marketing/

marketing management; medical administrative assistant and medical secretary; medical/clinical assistant; veterinary/animal health technology.

Academics *Calendar:* quarters. *Degrees:* diplomas, associate, and bachelor's. *Special study options:* academic remediation for entering students, accelerated degree program, adult/continuing education programs, advanced placement credit, internships, part-time degree program, services for LD students, summer session for credit.

Library Shakopee Campus Library with 2,987 titles, 53,132 serial subscriptions, 28 audiovisual materials, an OPAC, a Web page.

Student Life *Housing:* college housing not available. *Campus security:* 24-hour emergency response devices, late-night transport/escort service.

Standardized Tests *Required:* AccuPlacer is required of all applicants unless documentation of a minimum ACT composite score of 21 or documentation of a minimum composite score of 1485 on the SAT is presented (for admission).

Applying *Options:* electronic application. *Application fee:* $50. *Required:* high school transcript, interview, High school transcript or GED required of all applicants. *Required for some:* essay or personal statement, 2 letters of recommendation. *Application deadlines:* rolling (freshmen), rolling (out-of-state freshmen), rolling (transfers). *Notification:* continuous (freshmen), continuous (out-of-state freshmen), continuous (transfers).

Freshman Application Contact Minnesota School of Business–Shakopee, 1200 Shakopee Town Square, Shakopee, MN 55379. *Phone:* 952-345-1200. *Toll-free phone:* 866-766-1200. *Web site:* http://www.msbcollege.edu/.

Minnesota State College–Southeast Technical

Winona, Minnesota

- **State-supported** 2-year, founded 1992, part of Minnesota State Colleges and Universities System

- **Small-town** 132-acre campus with easy access to Minneapolis-St. Paul

- **Coed,** 2,237 undergraduate students, 60% full-time, 61% women, 39% men

Undergraduates 1,350 full-time, 887 part-time. 27% are from out of state; 4% Black or African American, non-Hispanic/Latino; 1% Hispanic/Latino; 2% Asian, non-Hispanic/Latino; 0.1% Native Hawaiian or other Pacific Islander, non-Hispanic/Latino; 0.8% American Indian or Alaska Native, non-Hispanic/Latino; 0.1% Race/ethnicity unknown; 0.4% international; 49% transferred in.

Freshmen *Admission:* 612 enrolled.

Faculty *Total:* 183, 37% full-time. *Student/faculty ratio:* 19:1.

Majors Accounting; accounting technology and bookkeeping; administrative assistant and secretarial science; autobody/collision and repair technology; biomedical technology; business administration and management; CAD/CADD drafting/design technology; carpentry; computer programming; computer systems networking and telecommunications; computer technology/computer systems technology; cosmetology; criminal justice/safety; early childhood education; electrical, electronic and communications engineering technology; heating, air conditioning, ventilation and refrigeration maintenance technology; industrial mechanics and maintenance technology; legal administrative assistant/secretary; massage therapy; medical administrative assistant and medical secretary; multi/interdisciplinary studies related; radiologic technology/science; registered nursing/registered nurse; retailing; sales, distribution, and marketing operations; selling skills and sales; web page, digital/multimedia and information resources design.

Academics *Calendar:* semesters. *Degree:* certificates, diplomas, and associate. *Special study options:* distance learning, double majors, internships.

Library Learning Resource Center.

Student Life *Campus security:* 24-hour emergency response devices, late-night transport/escort service.

Applying *Options:* electronic application. *Application fee:* $20. *Required:* high school transcript. *Recommended:* interview. *Application deadlines:* rolling (freshmen), rolling (out-of-state freshmen), rolling (transfers). *Notification:* continuous (freshmen), continuous (out-of-state freshmen), continuous (transfers).

Freshman Application Contact Admissions, SE Technical, Minnesota State College–Southeast Technical, 1250 Homer Road, PO Box 409, Winona, MN 55987. *Phone:* 877-853-8324. *Toll-free phone:* 800-372-8164. *Fax:* 507-453-2715. *E-mail:* enrollmentservices@southeastmn.edu. *Web site:* http://www.southeastmn.edu/.

Minnesota State Community and Technical College

Fergus Falls, Minnesota

- **State-supported** 2-year, founded 1960, part of Minnesota State Colleges and Universities System

- **Rural** campus

- **Coed**

Undergraduates 4% Black or African American, non-Hispanic/Latino; 1% Hispanic/Latino; 1% Asian, non-Hispanic/Latino; 0.2% Native Hawaiian or other Pacific Islander, non-Hispanic/Latino; 3% American Indian or Alaska Native, non-Hispanic/Latino; 4% Race/ethnicity unknown; 2% live on campus.

Faculty *Student/faculty ratio:* 18:1.

Academics *Calendar:* semesters. *Degree:* certificates, diplomas, and associate. *Special study options:* academic remediation for entering students, accelerated degree program, advanced placement credit, cooperative education, distance learning, double majors, English as a second language, freshman honors college, honors programs, independent study, internships, off-campus study, part-time degree program, services for LD students, study abroad, summer session for credit.

Student Life *Campus security:* 24-hour emergency response devices, late-night transport/escort service, security for special events.

Athletics Member NJCAA.

Costs (2011–12) *Tuition:* state resident $4622 full-time, $155 per credit hour part-time; nonresident $4622 full-time, $155 per credit hour part-time. Full-time tuition and fees vary according to location and program. Part-time tuition and fees vary according to location and program. *Required fees:* $500 full-time, $15 per credit part-time. *Room and board:* room only: $2850. Room and board charges vary according to board plan and housing facility.

Financial Aid *Financial aid deadline:* 7/1.

Applying *Options:* electronic application, early admission, deferred entrance. *Application fee:* $20. *Required:* high school transcript.

Freshman Application Contact Ms. Carrie Brimhall, Dean of Enrollment Management, Minnesota State Community and Technical College, Fergus Falls, MN 56537-1009. *Phone:* 218-736-1528. *Toll-free phone:* 877-450-3322. *E-mail:* carrie.brimhall@minnesota.edu. *Web site:* http://www.minnesota.edu/.

Minnesota State Community and Technical College–Detroit Lakes

Detroit Lakes, Minnesota

Director of Admissions Mr. Dale Westley, Enrollment Manager, Minnesota State Community and Technical College–Detroit Lakes, 900 Highway 34, E, Detroit Lakes, MN 56501. *Phone:* 218-846-3777. *Toll-free phone:* 800-492-4836. *Web site:* http://www.minnesota.edu/.

Minnesota State Community and Technical College–Moorhead

Moorhead, Minnesota

Director of Admissions Laurie McKeever, Enrollment Manager, Minnesota State Community and Technical College–Moorhead, 1900 28th Avenue, South, Moorhead, MN 56560. *Phone:* 218-299-6583. *Toll-free phone:* 800-426-5603. *Fax:* 218-299-6810. *Web site:* http://www.minnesota.edu/.

Minnesota State Community and Technical College–Wadena

Wadena, Minnesota

Director of Admissions Mr. Paul Drange, Enrollment Manager, Minnesota State Community and Technical College–Wadena, 405 Colfax Avenue, SW, PO Box 566, Wadena, MN 56482. *Phone:* 218-631-7818. *Toll-free phone:* 800-247-2007. *Web site:* http://www.minnesota.edu/.

Minnesota West Community and Technical College

Pipestone, Minnesota

- **State-supported** 2-year, founded 1967, part of Minnesota State Colleges and Universities System
- **Rural** campus
- **Coed**

Undergraduates 1,659 full-time, 1,805 part-time. Students come from 30 states and territories; 2 other countries; 10% are from out of state; 8% transferred in. *Retention:* 63% of full-time freshmen returned.

Faculty *Student/faculty ratio:* 13:1.

Academics *Calendar:* semesters. *Degrees:* certificates, diplomas, and associate (profile contains information from Canby, Granite Falls, Jackson, and Worthington campuses). *Special study options:* academic remediation for entering students, advanced placement credit, cooperative education, distance learning, double majors, external degree program, honors programs, independent study, internships, part-time degree program, services for LD students, summer session for credit.

Athletics Member NJCAA.

Applying *Options:* electronic application. *Application fee:* $20. *Required:* high school transcript.

Freshman Application Contact Ms. Crystal Strouth, College Registrar, Minnesota West Community and Technical College, 1450 Collegeway, Worthington, MN 56187. *Phone:* 507-372-3451. *Toll-free phone:* 800-658-2330. *Fax:* 507-372-5803. *E-mail:* crystal.strouth@mnwest.edu. *Web site:* http://www.mnwest.edu/.

National American University

Bloomington, Minnesota

Freshman Application Contact Ms. Jennifer Michaelson, Admissions Assistant, National American University, 321 Kansas City Street, Rapid City, SD 57201. *Phone:* 605-394-4827. *Toll-free phone:* 866-628-6387. *E-mail:* jmichaelson@national.edu. *Web site:* http://www.national.edu/.

National American University

Brooklyn Center, Minnesota

Freshman Application Contact Admissions Office, National American University, 6200 Shingle Creek Parkway, Suite 130, Brooklyn Center, MN 55430. *Web site:* http://www.national.edu/.

Normandale Community College

Bloomington, Minnesota

- **State-supported** 2-year, founded 1968, part of Minnesota State Colleges and Universities System
- **Suburban** 90-acre campus with easy access to Minneapolis-St. Paul
- **Coed,** 9,904 undergraduate students, 44% full-time, 55% women, 45% men

Undergraduates 4,382 full-time, 5,489 part-time. 16% Black or African American, non-Hispanic/Latino; 4% Hispanic/Latino; 9% Asian, non-Hispanic/Latino; 0.3% Native Hawaiian or other Pacific Islander, non-Hispanic/Latino; 0.8% American Indian or Alaska Native, non-Hispanic/Latino; 2% Race/ethnicity unknown. *Retention:* 49% of full-time freshmen returned.

Freshmen *Admission:* 1,520 applied, 1,520 admitted, 1,359 enrolled. *Average high school GPA:* 3.1.

Faculty *Total:* 358, 54% full-time.

Majors Art; business administration, management and operations related; computer and information sciences; computer programming (specific applications); computer science; computer technology/computer systems technology; creative writing; criminal justice/police science; criminal justice/safety; dental hygiene; dietetics; elementary education; engineering fields related; food science; health information/medical records administration; health information/medical records technology; hospitality administration; liberal arts and sciences and humanities related; liberal arts and sciences/liberal studies; mechanical engineering/mechanical technology; music; nanotechnology; registered nursing/registered nurse; special education; theater design and technology; visual and performing arts.

Academics *Calendar:* semesters. *Degree:* certificates and associate. *Special study options:* academic remediation for entering students, accelerated degree program, adult/continuing education programs, advanced placement credit, cooperative education, distance learning, English as a second language, external degree program, independent study, internships, off-campus study, part-time degree program, services for LD students, student-designed majors, study abroad, summer session for credit.

Library Library plus 1 other with 93,000 titles, 600 serial subscriptions, 40,000 audiovisual materials, an OPAC, a Web page.

Student Life *Housing:* college housing not available. *Activities and Organizations:* drama/theater group, student-run newspaper, choral group, Program Board (NPB), Student Senate, Phi Theta Kappa, Inter-Varsity Christian Fellowship, Spanish Club. *Campus security:* 24-hour emergency response devices, student patrols, late-night transport/escort service. *Student services:* personal/psychological counseling.

Athletics *Intramural sports:* archery M/W, badminton M/W, basketball M/W, bowling M/W, football M/W, ice hockey M/W, lacrosse M/W, racquetball M/W, soccer M/W, softball M/W, table tennis M/W, tennis M/W, volleyball M/W, weight lifting M/W.

Costs (2011–12) *Tuition:* state resident $4704 full-time, $157 per credit hour part-time; nonresident $4704 full-time, $157 per credit hour part-time. Full-time tuition and fees vary according to program and reciprocity agreements. Part-time tuition and fees vary according to program and reciprocity agreements. *Required fees:* $744 full-time, $25 per credit hour part-time. *Payment plan:* installment. *Waivers:* senior citizens and employees or children of employees.

Applying *Options:* electronic application, deferred entrance. *Application fee:* $20. *Required for some:* high school transcript. *Application deadlines:* rolling (freshmen), rolling (transfers). *Notification:* continuous (freshmen), continuous (transfers).

Freshman Application Contact Admissions Office, Normandale Community College, Normandy Community College, 9700 France Avenue South, Bloomington, MN 55431. *Phone:* 952-358-8201. *Toll-free phone:* 866-880-8740. *Fax:* 952-358-8230. *E-mail:* information@normandale.edu. *Web site:* http://www.normandale.edu/.

North Hennepin Community College

Brooklyn Park, Minnesota

- **State-supported** 2-year, founded 1966, part of Minnesota State Colleges and Universities System
- **Suburban** 80-acre campus
- **Endowment** $697,321
- **Coed,** 7,456 undergraduate students, 38% full-time, 57% women, 43% men

Undergraduates 2,796 full-time, 4,660 part-time. Students come from 11 states and territories; 58 other countries; 0.3% are from out of state; 20% Black or African American, non-Hispanic/Latino; 2% Hispanic/Latino; 12% Asian, non-Hispanic/Latino; 0.2% Native Hawaiian or other Pacific Islander, non-Hispanic/Latino; 1% American Indian or Alaska Native, non-Hispanic/Latino; 2% Race/ethnicity unknown; 1% international; 13% transferred in. *Retention:* 56% of full-time freshmen returned.

Freshmen *Admission:* 3,192 applied, 2,094 admitted, 1,314 enrolled.

Faculty *Total:* 248, 42% full-time, 6% with terminal degrees. *Student/faculty ratio:* 30:1.

Majors Accounting; biology/biological sciences; building/construction site management; building/home/construction inspection; business administration and management; chemistry; clinical/medical laboratory technology; computer science; construction management; criminal justice/law enforcement administration; criminal justice/police science; criminal justice/safety; engineering; finance; fine/studio arts; graphic design; histologic technology/histotechnologist; history; legal assistant/paralegal; liberal arts and sciences/liberal studies; management information systems; marketing/marketing management; mathematics; multi/interdisciplinary studies related; physical education teaching and coaching; pre-engineering; registered nursing/registered nurse; small business administration.

Academics *Calendar:* semesters. *Degree:* certificates and associate. *Special study options:* academic remediation for entering students, accelerated degree program, adult/continuing education programs, advanced placement credit, distance learning, double majors, English as a second language, external degree program, honors programs, independent study, internships, off-campus study, part-time degree program, services for LD students, student-designed majors, study abroad, summer session for credit. *ROTC:* Army (c), Navy (c), Air Force (c).

Library Learning Resource Center with 52,849 titles, 8,000 serial subscriptions, 3,244 audiovisual materials, an OPAC, a Web page.

Student Life *Housing:* college housing not available. *Activities and Organizations:* drama/theater group, choral group, Muslim Student Association, Phi Theta Kappa, Student Anime Game Club, Multicultural Club. *Campus security:* 24-hour emergency response devices, student patrols, late-night transport/escort service. *Student services:* personal/psychological counseling.

Athletics *Intramural sports:* badminton M/W, basketball M/W, bowling M/W, cross-country running M/W, football M/W, golf M/W, ice hockey M/W, rock climbing M/W, soccer M/W, softball M/W, table tennis M/W, tennis M/W, volleyball M/W, weight lifting M/W.

Costs (2011–12) *Tuition:* state resident $3828 full-time, $159 per credit hour part-time; nonresident $3828 full-time, $159 per credit hour part-time. Full-

time tuition and fees vary according to course load, location, and program. Part-time tuition and fees vary according to course load, location, and program. *Required fees:* $348 full-time, $15 per credit hour part-time. *Payment plan:* installment. *Waivers:* senior citizens and employees or children of employees.
Financial Aid Of all full-time matriculated undergraduates who enrolled in 2009, 100 Federal Work-Study jobs, 100 state and other part-time jobs.
Applying *Options:* electronic application, early admission, deferred entrance. *Application fee:* $20. *Recommended:* high school transcript. *Application deadlines:* rolling (freshmen), rolling (transfers). *Notification:* continuous (freshmen), continuous (transfers).
Freshman Application Contact Ms. Alison Leintz, Admissions Specialist, North Hennepin Community College, 7411 85th Ave N., Brooklyn Park, MN 55445. *Phone:* 763-424-0722. *Toll-free phone:* 800-818-0395. *Fax:* 763-424-0929. *E-mail:* aleintz@nhcc.edu. *Web site:* http://www.nhcc.edu/.

Northland Community and Technical College–Thief River Falls & East Grand Forks
Thief River Falls, Minnesota

- **State-supported** 2-year, founded 1965, part of Minnesota State Colleges and Universities System
- **Small-town** 239-acre campus
- **Coed**

Undergraduates 1,946 full-time, 2,189 part-time. Students come from 19 states and territories; 1 other country; 45% are from out of state; 10% transferred in.
Faculty *Student/faculty ratio:* 21:1.
Academics *Calendar:* semesters. *Degree:* certificates, diplomas, and associate. *Special study options:* academic remediation for entering students, adult/continuing education programs, advanced placement credit, distance learning, double majors, internships, off-campus study, part-time degree program, services for LD students, summer session for credit.
Student Life *Campus security:* student patrols, late-night transport/escort service.
Athletics Member NJCAA.
Costs (2011–12) *Tuition:* state resident $5291 full-time, $174 per credit hour part-time; nonresident $5291 full-time, $174 per credit hour part-time. Full-time tuition and fees vary according to course load. Part-time tuition and fees vary according to course load. *Required fees:* $531 full-time, $19 per credit hour part-time.
Financial Aid Of all full-time matriculated undergraduates who enrolled in 2010, 75 Federal Work-Study jobs (averaging $2500). 40 state and other part-time jobs (averaging $2500).
Applying *Options:* electronic application, early admission, deferred entrance. *Application fee:* $20. *Required:* high school transcript.
Freshman Application Contact Mr. Eugene Klinke, Director of Enrollment Management and Multicultural Services, Northland Community and Technical College–Thief River Falls & East Grand Forks, 1101 Highway One East, Thief River Falls, MN 56701. *Phone:* 218-683-8554. *Toll-free phone:* 800-959-6282. *Fax:* 218-683-8980. *E-mail:* eugene.klinke@northlandcollege.edu. *Web site:* http://www.northlandcollege.edu/.

Northwest Technical College
Bemidji, Minnesota

- **State-supported** 2-year, founded 1993, part of Minnesota State Colleges and Universities System
- **Small-town** campus
- **Coed,** 1,384 undergraduate students, 38% full-time, 70% women, 30% men

Undergraduates 522 full-time, 862 part-time. 8% are from out of state; 2% Black or African American, non-Hispanic/Latino; 3% Hispanic/Latino; 0.4% Asian, non-Hispanic/Latino; 0.2% Native Hawaiian or other Pacific Islander, non-Hispanic/Latino; 9% American Indian or Alaska Native, non-Hispanic/Latino; 5% Two or more races, non-Hispanic/Latino; 1% Race/ethnicity unknown; 0.1% international; 15% transferred in; 4% live on campus. *Retention:* 36% of full-time freshmen returned.
Freshmen *Admission:* 278 admitted, 142 enrolled.
Faculty *Total:* 66, 41% full-time. *Student/faculty ratio:* 21:1.
Majors Accounting; administrative assistant and secretarial science; automobile/automotive mechanics technology; business administration and management; child-care and support services management; computer systems networking and telecommunications; dental assisting; energy management and systems technology; engine machinist; industrial safety technology; industrial technology; licensed practical/vocational nurse training; manufacturing engineering technology; medical administrative assistant and medical secretary;

registered nursing/registered nurse; sales, distribution, and marketing operations.
Academics *Calendar:* semesters. *Degree:* certificates, diplomas, and associate. *Special study options:* part-time degree program.
Library Northwest Technical College Learning Enrichment Center.
Student Life *Housing Options:* coed, disabled students. Campus housing is provided by a third party.
Costs (2011–12) *Tuition:* state resident $5040 full-time, $168 per credit part-time; nonresident $5040 full-time, $168 per credit part-time. Full-time tuition and fees vary according to program. Part-time tuition and fees vary according to program. *Required fees:* $289 full-time, $10 per credit part-time. *Room and board:* $6690; room only: $4210. Room and board charges vary according to board plan. *Payment plan:* installment. *Waivers:* senior citizens and employees or children of employees.
Applying *Options:* electronic application. *Application fee:* $20. *Required:* high school transcript. *Application deadlines:* rolling (freshmen), rolling (transfers). *Notification:* continuous (freshmen), continuous (transfers).
Freshman Application Contact Ms. Kari Kantack-Miller, Diversity and Enrollment Representative, Northwest Technical College, 905 Grant Avenue, Southeast, Bemidji, MN 56601. *Phone:* 218-333-6645. *Toll-free phone:* 800-942-8324. *Fax:* 218-333-6694. *E-mail:* kari.kantack@ntcmn.edu. *Web site:* http://www.ntcmn.edu/.

Northwest Technical Institute
Eagan, Minnesota

Freshman Application Contact Northwest Technical Institute, 950 Blue Gentian Road, Suite 500, Eagan, MN 55121. *Phone:* 952-944-0080 Ext. 103. *Toll-free phone:* 800-443-4223. *Web site:* http://www.nti.edu/.

Pine Technical College
Pine City, Minnesota

Freshman Application Contact Pine Technical College, 900 4th Street SE, Pine City, MN 55063. *Phone:* 320-629-5100. *Toll-free phone:* 800-521-7463. *Web site:* http://www.pinetech.edu/.

Rainy River Community College
International Falls, Minnesota

- **State-supported** 2-year, founded 1967, part of Minnesota State Colleges and Universities System
- **Small-town** 80-acre campus
- **Coed,** 344 undergraduate students, 78% full-time, 62% women, 38% men

Undergraduates 268 full-time, 76 part-time. 13% Black or African American, non-Hispanic/Latino; 0.9% Hispanic/Latino; 1% Asian, non-Hispanic/Latino; 5% American Indian or Alaska Native, non-Hispanic/Latino; 8% international.
Faculty *Total:* 25, 40% full-time. *Student/faculty ratio:* 15:1.
Majors Administrative assistant and secretarial science; biological and physical sciences; business administration and management; liberal arts and sciences/liberal studies; pre-engineering; real estate.
Academics *Calendar:* semesters. *Degree:* certificates, diplomas, and associate. *Special study options:* academic remediation for entering students, adult/continuing education programs, advanced placement credit, cooperative education, honors programs, independent study, internships, part-time degree program, services for LD students, summer session for credit.
Library Rainy River Community College Library with 20,000 titles, an OPAC.
Student Life *Housing Options:* disabled students. Campus housing is university owned. *Activities and Organizations:* drama/theater group, Anishinaabe Student Coalition, Student Senate, Black Student Association. *Campus security:* 24-hour emergency response devices, late-night transport/escort service, controlled dormitory access. *Student services:* personal/psychological counseling.
Athletics Member NJCAA. *Intercollegiate sports:* basketball M/W, ice hockey W, softball W, volleyball W. *Intramural sports:* archery M/W, badminton M/W, baseball M, bowling M/W, cheerleading M/W, cross-country running M/W, ice hockey M, skiing (cross-country) M/W, skiing (downhill) M/W, swimming and diving M/W, table tennis M/W, tennis M/W, volleyball M/W, weight lifting M/W.
Costs (2011–12) *Tuition:* state resident $4280 full-time; nonresident $5465 full-time. Full-time tuition and fees vary according to program and reciprocity agreements. Part-time tuition and fees vary according to program and reciprocity agreements. *Required fees:* $594 full-time. *Room and board:* room only: $2900. Room and board charges vary according to housing facility. *Payment plan:* installment. *Waivers:* employees or children of employees.
Applying *Options:* electronic application, early admission, deferred entrance. *Application fee:* $20. *Recommended:* high school transcript. *Application*

deadlines: rolling (freshmen), rolling (out-of-state freshmen), rolling (transfers). *Notification:* continuous (freshmen), continuous (out-of-state freshmen), continuous (transfers).

Freshman Application Contact Ms. Berta Hagen, Registrar, Rainy River Community College, 1501 Highway 71, International Falls, MN 56649. *Phone:* 218-285-2207. *Toll-free phone:* 800-456-3996. *Fax:* 218-285-2314. *E-mail:* bhagen@rrcc.mnscu.edu. *Web site:* http://www.rrcc.mnscu.edu/.

Rasmussen College Bloomington

Bloomington, Minnesota

- **Proprietary** primarily 2-year, founded 1904, part of Rasmussen College System
- **Suburban** campus
- **Coed,** 611 undergraduate students

Faculty *Student/faculty ratio:* 22:1.

Majors Accounting; business administration and management; computer and information systems security; computer science; computer software engineering; corrections and criminal justice related; criminal justice/police science; early childhood education; graphic communications related; health/health-care administration; health information/medical records administration; health information/medical records technology; human resources management; human services; legal assistant/paralegal; management information systems and services related; marketing/marketing management; medical administrative assistant and medical secretary; medical/clinical assistant; pharmacy technician; web page, digital/multimedia and information resources design.

Academics *Calendar:* quarters. *Degrees:* certificates, diplomas, associate, and bachelor's. *Special study options:* academic remediation for entering students, accelerated degree program, adult/continuing education programs, distance learning, double majors, internships, part-time degree program, summer session for credit.

Library Rasmussen College Library - Bloomington with 2,443 titles, 29 serial subscriptions, 355 audiovisual materials, an OPAC, a Web page.

Student Life *Housing:* college housing not available.

Standardized Tests *Required:* Internal Exam (for admission).

Costs (2012–13) *Tuition:* $14,220 full-time. Full-time tuition and fees vary according to course level, course load, degree level, location, and program. Part-time tuition and fees vary according to course level, course load, degree level, location, and program. *Required fees:* $40 full-time. *Payment plans:* installment, deferred payment. *Waivers:* employees or children of employees.

Financial Aid Of all full-time matriculated undergraduates who enrolled in 2010, 3 state and other part-time jobs (averaging $4338).

Applying *Options:* electronic application, early admission, deferred entrance. *Application fee:* $40. *Required:* high school transcript, minimum 2.0 GPA, interview. *Application deadlines:* rolling (freshmen), rolling (transfers).

Freshman Application Contact Susan Hammerstrom, Director of Admissions, Rasmussen College Bloomington, 440 West 78th Street, Bloomington, MN 55345. *Phone:* 952-545-2000. *Toll-free phone:* 888-549-6755. *Web site:* http://www.rasmussen.edu/.

Rasmussen College Brooklyn Park

Brooklyn Park, Minnesota

- **Proprietary** primarily 2-year, part of Rasmussen College System
- **Suburban** campus
- **Coed,** 1,015 undergraduate students

Faculty *Student/faculty ratio:* 22:1.

Majors Accounting; business administration and management; computer and information systems security; computer science; computer software engineering; corrections and criminal justice related; criminal justice/police science; early childhood education; graphic communications related; health/health-care administration; health information/medical records administration; health information/medical records technology; human resources management; human services; legal assistant/paralegal; management information systems and services related; marketing/marketing management; medical administrative assistant and medical secretary; medical/clinical assistant; pharmacy technician; surgical technology; web page, digital/multimedia and information resources design.

Academics *Degrees:* certificates, diplomas, associate, and bachelor's. *Special study options:* academic remediation for entering students, accelerated degree program, adult/continuing education programs, distance learning, double majors, internships, part-time degree program, summer session for credit.

Library Rasmussen College Library - Brooklyn Park with 2,680 titles, 26 serial subscriptions, 223 audiovisual materials, an OPAC, a Web page.

Student Life *Housing:* college housing not available.

Standardized Tests *Required:* Internal Exam (for admission).

Costs (2012–13) *Tuition:* $14,220 full-time. Full-time tuition and fees vary according to course level, course load, degree level, location, and program. Part-time tuition and fees vary according to course level, course load, degree

level, location, and program. *Required fees:* $40 full-time. *Payment plans:* installment, deferred payment. *Waivers:* employees or children of employees.

Applying *Options:* electronic application, early admission, deferred entrance. *Application fee:* $40. *Required:* high school transcript, minimum 2.0 GPA, interview. *Application deadlines:* rolling (freshmen), rolling (transfers).

Freshman Application Contact Susan Hammerstrom, Director of Admissions, Rasmussen College Brooklyn Park, 8301 93rd Avenue North, Brooklyn Park, MN 55445-1512. *Phone:* 763-493-4500. *Toll-free phone:* 888-549-6755. *E-mail:* susan.hammerstrom@rasmussen.edu. *Web site:* http://www.rasmussen.edu/.

Rasmussen College Eagan

Eagan, Minnesota

- **Proprietary** primarily 2-year, founded 1904, part of Rasmussen College System
- **Suburban** campus
- **Coed, primarily women,** 923 undergraduate students

Faculty *Student/faculty ratio:* 22:1.

Majors Accounting; business administration and management; computer and information systems security; computer science; computer software engineering; corrections and criminal justice related; criminal justice/police science; early childhood education; graphic communications related; health/health-care administration; health information/medical records administration; health information/medical records technology; human resources management; human services; legal assistant/paralegal; management information systems and services related; marketing/marketing management; medical administrative assistant and medical secretary; medical/clinical assistant; pharmacy technician; web page, digital/multimedia and information resources design.

Academics *Calendar:* quarters. *Degrees:* certificates, diplomas, associate, and bachelor's. *Special study options:* academic remediation for entering students, accelerated degree program, adult/continuing education programs, distance learning, double majors, internships, part-time degree program, summer session for credit.

Library Rasmussen College Library - Eagan with 1,995 titles, 25 serial subscriptions, 216 audiovisual materials, an OPAC, a Web page.

Student Life *Housing:* college housing not available.

Standardized Tests *Required:* Internal Exam (for admission).

Costs (2012–13) *Tuition:* $14,220 full-time. Full-time tuition and fees vary according to course level, course load, degree level, location, and program. Part-time tuition and fees vary according to course level, course load, degree level, location, and program. *Required fees:* $40 full-time. *Payment plans:* installment, deferred payment. *Waivers:* employees or children of employees.

Applying *Options:* electronic application, early admission, deferred entrance. *Application fee:* $40. *Required:* high school transcript, minimum 2.0 GPA, interview. *Application deadlines:* rolling (freshmen), rolling (transfers).

Freshman Application Contact Susan Hammerstrom, Director of Admissions, Rasmussen College Eagan, 3500 Federal Drive, Eagan, MN 55122-1346. *Phone:* 651-687-9000. *Toll-free phone:* 888-549-6755. *E-mail:* susan.hammerstrom@rasmussen.edu. *Web site:* http://www.rasmussen.edu/.

Rasmussen College Lake Elmo/ Woodbury

Lake Elmo, Minnesota

- **Proprietary** primarily 2-year, part of Rasmussen College System
- **Suburban** campus
- **Coed,** 735 undergraduate students

Faculty *Student/faculty ratio:* 22:1.

Majors Accounting; business administration and management; clinical/medical laboratory technology; computer and information systems security; computer science; computer software engineering; corrections and criminal justice related; criminal justice/police science; early childhood education; graphic communications related; health/health-care administration; health information/medical records administration; health information/medical records technology; human resources management; human services; legal assistant/paralegal; management information systems and services related; marketing/marketing management; medical administrative assistant and medical secretary; medical/clinical assistant; pharmacy technician; web page, digital/multimedia and information resources design.

Academics *Degrees:* certificates, diplomas, associate, and bachelor's. *Special study options:* academic remediation for entering students, accelerated degree program, adult/continuing education programs, distance learning, double majors, internships, part-time degree program, summer session for credit.

Library Rasmussen College Library - Lake Elmo with 1,970 titles, 25 serial subscriptions, 83 audiovisual materials, an OPAC, a Web page.

Student Life *Housing:* college housing not available.

Standardized Tests *Required:* Internal Exam (for admission).

Costs (2012–13) *Tuition:* $14,220 full-time. Full-time tuition and fees vary according to course level, course load, degree level, location, and program. Part-time tuition and fees vary according to course level, course load, degree level, location, and program. *Required fees:* $40 full-time. *Payment plans:* installment, deferred payment. *Waivers:* employees or children of employees.
Applying *Options:* electronic application, early admission, deferred entrance. *Application fee:* $40. *Required:* high school transcript, minimum 2.0 GPA, interview. *Application deadlines:* rolling (freshmen), rolling (transfers).
Freshman Application Contact Susan Hammerstrom, Director of Admissions, Rasmussen College Lake Elmo/Woodbury, 8565 Eagle Point Circle, Lake Elmo, MN 55042. *Phone:* 651-259-6600. *Toll-free phone:* 888-549-6755. *E-mail:* susan.hammerstrom@rasmussen.edu. *Web site:* http://www.rasmussen.edu/.

Rasmussen College Mankato
Mankato, Minnesota

- **Proprietary** primarily 2-year, founded 1904, part of Rasmussen College System
- **Suburban** campus
- **Coed, primarily women,** 797 undergraduate students

Faculty *Student/faculty ratio:* 22:1.
Majors Accounting; business administration and management; clinical/medical laboratory technology; computer and information systems security; computer science; computer software engineering; corrections and criminal justice related; criminal justice/police science; early childhood education; graphic communications related; health/health-care administration; health information/medical records administration; health information/medical records technology; human resources management; human services; legal assistant/paralegal; management information systems and services related; marketing/marketing management; medical administrative assistant and medical secretary; medical/clinical assistant; pharmacy technician; web page, digital/multimedia and information resources design.
Academics *Calendar:* quarters. *Degrees:* certificates, diplomas, associate, and bachelor's. *Special study options:* academic remediation for entering students, accelerated degree program, adult/continuing education programs, distance learning, double majors, internships, part-time degree program, summer session for credit.
Library Rasmussen College Library - Mankato with 1,635 titles, 19 serial subscriptions, 199 audiovisual materials, an OPAC, a Web page.
Student Life *Housing:* college housing not available.
Standardized Tests *Required:* Internal Exam (for admission).
Costs (2012–13) *Tuition:* $14,220 full-time. Full-time tuition and fees vary according to course level, course load, degree level, location, and program. Part-time tuition and fees vary according to course level, course load, degree level, location, and program. *Required fees:* $40 full-time. *Payment plans:* installment, deferred payment. *Waivers:* employees or children of employees.
Financial Aid Of all full-time matriculated undergraduates who enrolled in 2010, 15 Federal Work-Study jobs (averaging $4000). 13 state and other part-time jobs (averaging $4000).
Applying *Options:* electronic application, early admission, deferred entrance. *Application fee:* $40. *Required:* high school transcript, minimum 2.0 GPA, interview. *Application deadlines:* rolling (freshmen), rolling (transfers).
Freshman Application Contact Susan Hammerstrom, Director of Admissions, Rasmussen College Mankato, 130 Saint Andrews Drive, Mankato, MN 56001. *Phone:* 507-625-6556. *Toll-free phone:* 888-549-6755. *E-mail:* susan.hammerstrom@rasmussen.edu. *Web site:* http://www.rasmussen.edu/.

Rasmussen College Moorhead
Moorhead, Minnesota

- **Proprietary** primarily 2-year, part of Rasmussen College System
- **Suburban** campus
- **Coed,** 525 undergraduate students

Faculty *Student/faculty ratio:* 22:1.
Majors Accounting; business administration and management; clinical/medical laboratory technology; computer and information systems security; computer science; computer software engineering; corrections and criminal justice related; early childhood education; graphic communications related; health/health-care administration; health information/medical records administration; health information/medical records technology; human services; legal assistant/paralegal; management information systems and services related; marketing/marketing management; medical administrative assistant and medical secretary; medical/clinical assistant; pharmacy technician; web page, digital/multimedia and information resources design.
Academics *Degrees:* certificates, diplomas, associate, and bachelor's. *Special study options:* academic remediation for entering students, accelerated degree

program, adult/continuing education programs, distance learning, double majors, internships, part-time degree program, summer session for credit.
Library Rasmussen College Library - Moorhead with 537 titles, 19 serial subscriptions, 70 audiovisual materials, an OPAC, a Web page.
Student Life *Housing:* college housing not available.
Standardized Tests *Required:* Internal Exam (for admission).
Costs (2012–13) *Tuition:* $14,220 full-time. Full-time tuition and fees vary according to course level, course load, degree level, location, and program. Part-time tuition and fees vary according to course level, course load, degree level, location, and program. *Required fees:* $40 full-time. *Payment plans:* installment, deferred payment. *Waivers:* employees or children of employees.
Applying *Options:* electronic application, early admission, deferred entrance. *Application fee:* $40. *Required:* high school transcript, minimum 2.0 GPA, interview. *Application deadlines:* rolling (freshmen), rolling (transfers).
Freshman Application Contact Susan Hammerstrom, Director of Admissions, Rasmussen College Moorhead, 1250 29th Avenue South, Moorhead, MN 56560. *Phone:* 218-304-6200. *Toll-free phone:* 888-549-6755. *E-mail:* susan.hammerstrom@rasmussen.edu. *Web site:* http://www.rasmussen.edu/.

Rasmussen College St. Cloud
St. Cloud, Minnesota

- **Proprietary** primarily 2-year, founded 1904, part of Rasmussen College System
- **Suburban** campus
- **Coed, primarily women,** 1,017 undergraduate students

Faculty *Student/faculty ratio:* 22:1.
Majors Accounting; blood bank technology; business administration and management; clinical/medical laboratory technology; computer and information systems security; computer science; computer software engineering; corrections and criminal justice related; criminal justice/police science; early childhood education; graphic communications related; health/health-care administration; health information/medical records administration; health information/medical records technology; human services; legal assistant/paralegal; management information systems and services related; marketing/marketing management; medical administrative assistant and medical secretary; medical/clinical assistant; pharmacy technician; surgical technology; web page, digital/multimedia and information resources design.
Academics *Calendar:* quarters. *Degrees:* certificates, diplomas, associate, and bachelor's. *Special study options:* academic remediation for entering students, accelerated degree program, adult/continuing education programs, distance learning, double majors, internships, part-time degree program, summer session for credit.
Library Rasmussen College Library - St. Cloud with 2,529 titles, 29 serial subscriptions, 516 audiovisual materials, an OPAC, a Web page.
Student Life *Housing:* college housing not available.
Standardized Tests *Required:* Internal Exam (for admission).
Costs (2012–13) *Tuition:* $14,220 full-time. Full-time tuition and fees vary according to course level, course load, degree level, location, and program. Part-time tuition and fees vary according to course level, course load, degree level, location, and program. *Required fees:* $40 full-time. *Payment plans:* installment, deferred payment. *Waivers:* employees or children of employees.
Financial Aid Of all full-time matriculated undergraduates who enrolled in 2010, 34 Federal Work-Study jobs (averaging $866). 51 state and other part-time jobs (averaging $700).
Applying *Options:* electronic application, early admission, deferred entrance. *Application fee:* $40. *Required:* high school transcript, minimum 2.0 GPA, interview. *Application deadlines:* rolling (freshmen), rolling (transfers).
Freshman Application Contact Susan Hammerstrom, Director of Admissions, Rasmussen College St. Cloud, 226 Park Avenue South, St. Cloud, MN 56301-3713. *Phone:* 320-251-5600. *Toll-free phone:* 888-549-6755. *E-mail:* susan.hammerstrom@rasmussen.edu. *Web site:* http://www.rasmussen.edu/.

Ridgewater College
Willmar, Minnesota

Freshman Application Contact Ms. Linda Barron, Admissions Assistant, Ridgewater College, PO Box 1097, Willmar, MN 56201-1097. *Phone:* 320-222-5976. *Toll-free phone:* 800-722-1151. *E-mail:* linda.barron@ridgewater.edu. *Web site:* http://www.ridgewater.edu/.

Riverland Community College
Austin, Minnesota

Freshman Application Contact Ms. Renee Njos, Admission Secretary, Riverland Community College, Austin, MN 55912. *Phone:* 507-433-0820.

Toll-free phone: 800-247-5039. *Fax:* 507-433-0515. *E-mail:* admissions@riverland.edu. *Web site:* http://www.riverland.edu/.

Rochester Community and Technical College
Rochester, Minnesota

Director of Admissions Mr. Troy Tynsky, Director of Admissions, Rochester Community and Technical College, 851 30th Avenue, SE, Rochester, MN 55904-4999. *Phone:* 507-280-3509. *Web site:* http://www.rctc.edu/.

St. Cloud Technical & Community College
St. Cloud, Minnesota

- **State-supported** 2-year, founded 1948, part of Minnesota State Colleges and Universities System
- **Urban** 35-acre campus with easy access to Minneapolis-St. Paul
- **Coed,** 4,883 undergraduate students, 56% full-time, 52% women, 48% men

Undergraduates 2,742 full-time, 2,141 part-time. Students come from 15 states and territories; 3 other countries; 1% are from out of state; 36% transferred in.

Freshmen *Admission:* 1,984 applied, 1,924 admitted, 1,092 enrolled. *Average high school GPA:* 3.16.

Faculty *Total:* 214, 49% full-time, 7% with terminal degrees. *Student/faculty ratio:* 23:1.

Majors Accounting; advertising; architectural drafting and CAD/CADD; autobody/collision and repair technology; automobile/automotive mechanics technology; banking and financial support services; business administration and management; cardiovascular technology; carpentry; child-care and support services management; civil engineering technology; computer programming; computer programming (specific applications); computer systems networking and telecommunications; dental assisting; dental hygiene; diagnostic medical sonography and ultrasound technology; electrical and power transmission installation; electrical, electronic and communications engineering technology; emergency medical technology (EMT paramedic); executive assistant/executive secretary; health information/medical records technology; heating, air conditioning, ventilation and refrigeration maintenance technology; instrumentation technology; legal administrative assistant/secretary; licensed practical/vocational nurse training; machine tool technology; mechanical drafting and CAD/CADD; medium/heavy vehicle and truck technology; plumbing technology; registered nursing/registered nurse; sales, distribution, and marketing operations; surgical technology; teacher assistant/aide; water quality and wastewater treatment management and recycling technology; web page, digital/multimedia and information resources design; welding technology.

Academics *Calendar:* semesters. *Degree:* certificates, diplomas, and associate. *Special study options:* academic remediation for entering students, adult/continuing education programs, advanced placement credit, cooperative education, distance learning, English as a second language, independent study, internships, part-time degree program, services for LD students, summer session for credit.

Library Learning Resource Center plus 1 other with 10,000 titles, 600 serial subscriptions, an OPAC, a Web page.

Student Life *Housing:* college housing not available. *Activities and Organizations:* drama/theater group, student-run newspaper, Student Senate, Distributive Education Club of America, Business Professionals of America, Child and Adult Care Education, Central Minnesota Builders Association. *Campus security:* late-night transport/escort service. *Student services:* personal/psychological counseling, women's center.

Athletics Member NJCAA. *Intercollegiate sports:* baseball M, basketball M/W, softball W, volleyball W. *Intramural sports:* volleyball M/W.

Costs (2011–12) *Tuition:* state resident $4628 full-time, $154 per semester hour part-time; nonresident $4628 full-time, $154 per semester hour part-time. Full-time tuition and fees vary according to course load and program. Part-time tuition and fees vary according to course load and program. *Required fees:* $521 full-time, $17 per semester hour part-time. *Payment plan:* installment. *Waivers:* senior citizens and employees or children of employees.

Financial Aid Of all full-time matriculated undergraduates who enrolled in 2010, 51 Federal Work-Study jobs (averaging $2010). 84 state and other part-time jobs (averaging $2060).

Applying *Options:* electronic application, early admission, deferred entrance. *Application fee:* $20. *Required:* high school transcript. *Required for some:* essay or personal statement, interview. *Application deadlines:* rolling (freshmen), rolling (transfers). *Notification:* continuous until 8/1 (freshmen), continuous until 8/1 (transfers).

Freshman Application Contact Ms. Jodi Elness, Admissions Office, St. Cloud Technical & Community College, 1540 Northway Drive, St. Cloud, MN

56303. *Phone:* 320-308-5089. *Toll-free phone:* 800-222-1009. *Fax:* 320-308-5981. *E-mail:* jelness@sctcc.edu. *Web site:* http://www.sctcc.edu/.

Saint Paul College–A Community & Technical College
St. Paul, Minnesota

Freshman Application Contact Ms. Sarah Carrico, Saint Paul College–A Community & Technical College, 235 Marshall Avenue, Saint Paul, MN 55102. *Phone:* 651-846-1424. *Toll-free phone:* 800-227-6029. *Fax:* 651-846-1703. *E-mail:* admissions@saintpaul.edu. *Web site:* http://www.saintpaul.edu/.

South Central College
North Mankato, Minnesota

Freshman Application Contact Ms. Beverly Herda, Director of Admissions, South Central College, 1920 Lee Boulevard, North Mankato, MN 56003. *Phone:* 507-389-7334. *Fax:* 507-388-9951. *Web site:* http://southcentral.edu/.

Vermilion Community College
Ely, Minnesota

Freshman Application Contact Mr. Todd Heiman, Director of Enrollment Services, Vermilion Community College, 1900 East Camp Street, Ely, MN 55731-1996. *Phone:* 218-365-7224. *Toll-free phone:* 800-657-3608. *Web site:* http://www.vcc.edu/.

MISSISSIPPI

Antonelli College
Hattiesburg, Mississippi

Freshman Application Contact Mrs. Karen Gautreau, Director, Antonelli College, 1500 North 31st Avenue, Hattiesburg, MS 39401. *Phone:* 601-583-4100. *Fax:* 601-583-0839. *E-mail:* admissionsh@antonellicollege.edu. *Web site:* http://www.antonellicollege.edu/.

Antonelli College
Jackson, Mississippi

Freshman Application Contact Antonelli College, 2323 Lakeland Drive, Jackson, MS 39232. *Phone:* 601-362-9991. *Web site:* http://www.antonellicollege.edu/.

Coahoma Community College
Clarksdale, Mississippi

Freshman Application Contact Mrs. Wanda Holmes, Director of Admissions and Records, Coahoma Community College, Clarksdale, MS 38614-9799. *Phone:* 662-621-4205. *Toll-free phone:* 866-470-1CCC. *Web site:* http://www.ccc.cc.ms.us/.

Copiah-Lincoln Community College
Wesson, Mississippi

- **State and locally supported** 2-year, founded 1928, part of Mississippi Community College Board
- **Rural** 525-acre campus with easy access to Jackson
- **Endowment** $2.5 million
- **Coed,** 3,709 undergraduate students, 81% full-time, 63% women, 37% men

Undergraduates 3,016 full-time, 693 part-time. Students come from 11 states and territories; 1 other country; 45% Black or African American, non-Hispanic/Latino; 0.7% Hispanic/Latino; 0.1% Asian, non-Hispanic/Latino; 0.2% American Indian or Alaska Native, non-Hispanic/Latino; 0.1% Two or more races, non-Hispanic/Latino; 0.8% Race/ethnicity unknown; 30% live on campus.

Freshmen *Admission:* 911 enrolled.

Faculty *Total:* 138.

Majors Accounting; agribusiness; agricultural business and management; agricultural business and management related; agricultural business technology; agricultural economics; agricultural/farm supplies retailing and wholesaling; agriculture; architecture; art teacher education; biological and physical sciences; biology/biological sciences; business administration and management; chemistry; child development; civil engineering technology; clinical/ medical laboratory technology; computer programming; cosmetology; criminal justice/police science; data processing and data processing technology; drafting and design technology; economics; education; electrical, electronic and communications engineering technology; elementary education; engineering; English; family and consumer sciences/home economics teacher education; farm and ranch management; food technology and processing; forestry; French; health teacher education; history; industrial radiologic technology; journalism; liberal arts and sciences/liberal studies; library and information science; music teacher education; physical education teaching and coaching; registered nursing/registered nurse; special products marketing; trade and industrial teacher education; wood science and wood products/pulp and paper technology.

Academics *Calendar:* semesters. *Degree:* certificates and associate. *Special study options:* academic remediation for entering students, adult/continuing education programs, advanced placement credit, honors programs, part-time degree program, student-designed majors, summer session for credit.

Library Oswalt Memorial Library with 34,357 titles, 166 serial subscriptions.

Student Life *Housing Options:* Campus housing is university owned. *Activities and Organizations:* drama/theater group, student-run newspaper, radio station, choral group, marching band. *Campus security:* 24-hour patrols. *Student services:* health clinic, personal/psychological counseling.

Athletics Member NJCAA. *Intercollegiate sports:* baseball M(s), basketball M(s)/W(s), football M(s), golf M/W, softball W, tennis M/W, track and field M. *Intramural sports:* basketball M/W, football M, golf M/W, tennis M/W, volleyball M/W.

Costs (2012–13) *Tuition:* state resident $2100 full-time; nonresident $3900 full-time. *Room and board:* Room and board charges vary according to board plan. *Waivers:* senior citizens and employees or children of employees.

Financial Aid Of all full-time matriculated undergraduates who enrolled in 2010, 125 Federal Work-Study jobs (averaging $1000).

Applying *Options:* early admission. *Required:* high school transcript. *Application deadlines:* rolling (freshmen), rolling (transfers).

Freshman Application Contact Vanessa Alexander, Director of Distance Learning, Copiah-Lincoln Community College, PO Box 649, Wesson, MS 39191-0457. *Phone:* 601-643-8619. *Fax:* 601-643-8222. *E-mail:* vanessa.alexander@colin.edu. *Web site:* http://www.colin.edu/.

Copiah-Lincoln Community College–Natchez Campus
Natchez, Mississippi

Freshman Application Contact Copiah-Lincoln Community College–Natchez Campus, 11 Co-Lin Circle, Natchez, MS 39120-8446. *Phone:* 601-442-9111 Ext. 224. *Web site:* http://www.colin.edu/.

East Central Community College
Decatur, Mississippi

Director of Admissions Ms. Donna Luke, Director of Admissions, Records, and Research, East Central Community College, PO Box 129, Decatur, MS 39327-0129. *Phone:* 601-635-2111 Ext. 206. *Toll-free phone:* 877-462-3222. *Web site:* http://www.eccc.cc.ms.us/.

East Mississippi Community College
Scooba, Mississippi

Director of Admissions Ms. Melinda Sciple, Admissions Officer, East Mississippi Community College, PO Box 158, Scooba, MS 39358-0158. *Phone:* 662-476-5041. *Web site:* http://www.eastms.edu/.

Hinds Community College
Raymond, Mississippi

Director of Admissions Ms. Ginger Turner, Director of Admissions and Records, Hinds Community College, PO Box 1100, Raymond, MS 39154-1100. *Phone:* 601-857-3280. *Toll-free phone:* 800-HINDSCC. *Fax:* 601-857-3539. *Web site:* http://www.hindscc.edu/.

Holmes Community College
Goodman, Mississippi

Director of Admissions Dr. Lynn Wright, Dean of Admissions and Records, Holmes Community College, PO Box 369, Goodman, MS 39079-0369.

Phone: 601-472-2312 Ext. 1023. *Toll-free phone:* 800-HOLMES-4. *Web site:* http://www.holmescc.edu/.

Itawamba Community College
Fulton, Mississippi

Freshman Application Contact Mr. Larry Boggs, Director of Student Recruitment and Scholarships, Itawamba Community College, 602 West Hill Street, Fulton, MS 38843. *Phone:* 601-862-8252. *E-mail:* laboggs@iccms.edu. *Web site:* http://www.iccms.edu/.

Jones County Junior College
Ellisville, Mississippi

Director of Admissions Mrs. Dianne Speed, Director of Admissions and Records, Jones County Junior College, 900 South Court Street, Ellisville, MS 39437-3901. *Phone:* 601-477-4025. *Web site:* http://www.jcjc.edu/.

Meridian Community College
Meridian, Mississippi

Freshman Application Contact Ms. Angela Payne, Director of Admissions, Meridian Community College, 910 Highway 19 North, Meridian, MS 39307. *Phone:* 601-484-8357. *Toll-free phone:* 800-MCC-THE-1. *E-mail:* apayne@meridiancc.edu. *Web site:* http://www.meridiancc.edu/.

Mississippi Delta Community College
Moorhead, Mississippi

Director of Admissions Mr. Joseph F. Ray Jr., Vice President of Admissions, Mississippi Delta Community College, PO Box 668, Highway 3 and Cherry Street, Moorhead, MS 38761-0668. *Phone:* 662-246-6308. *Web site:* http://www.msdelta.edu/.

Mississippi Gulf Coast Community College
Perkinston, Mississippi

Freshman Application Contact Mr. Ladd Taylor, Director of Admissions, Mississippi Gulf Coast Community College, Perkinston, MS 39573. *Phone:* 601-928-6264. *Fax:* 601-928-6299. *E-mail:* ladd.taylor@mgccc.edu. *Web site:* http://www.mgccc.edu/.

Northeast Mississippi Community College
Booneville, Mississippi

Freshman Application Contact Office of Enrollment Services, Northeast Mississippi Community College, 101 Cunningham Boulevard, Booneville, MS 38829. *Phone:* 662-720-7239. *Toll-free phone:* 800-555-2154. *E-mail:* admitme@nemcc.edu. *Web site:* http://www.nemcc.edu/.

Northwest Mississippi Community College
Senatobia, Mississippi

Director of Admissions Ms. Deanna Ferguson, Director of Admissions and Recruiting, Northwest Mississippi Community College, 4975 Highway 51 North, Senatobia, MS 38668-1701. *Phone:* 662-562-3222. *Web site:* http://www.northwestms.edu/.

Pearl River Community College
Poplarville, Mississippi

Freshman Application Contact Mr. J. Dow Ford, Director of Admissions, Pearl River Community College, 101 Highway 11 North, Poplarville, MS 39470. *Phone:* 601-403-1000. *E-mail:* dford@prcc.edu. *Web site:* http://www.prcc.edu/.

Southwest Mississippi Community College

Summit, Mississippi

- **State and locally supported** 2-year, founded 1918, part of Mississippi State Board for Community and Junior Colleges
- **Rural** 701-acre campus
- **Coed,** 2,053 undergraduate students, 87% full-time, 64% women, 36% men

Undergraduates 1,785 full-time, 268 part-time. Students come from 8 states and territories; 1 other country; 6% are from out of state; 43% Black or African American, non-Hispanic/Latino; 0.3% Hispanic/Latino; 0.5% Asian, non-Hispanic/Latino; 0.4% American Indian or Alaska Native, non-Hispanic/Latino; 0.2% Two or more races, non-Hispanic/Latino; 0.2% Race/ethnicity unknown; 45% transferred in; 35% live on campus. *Retention:* 50% of full-time freshmen returned.

Freshmen *Admission:* 567 enrolled.

Faculty *Total:* 90, 79% full-time. *Student/faculty ratio:* 24:1.

Majors Accounting; administrative assistant and secretarial science; advertising; automobile/automotive mechanics technology; biological and physical sciences; biology/biological sciences; business administration and management; business teacher education; carpentry; chemistry; computer programming related; computer science; computer systems networking and telecommunications; construction engineering technology; cosmetology; diesel mechanics technology; early childhood education; education; electrical, electronic and communications engineering technology; elementary education; emergency medical technology (EMT paramedic); engineering; English; fashion merchandising; finance; health information/medical records technology; health professions related; heating, air conditioning, ventilation and refrigeration maintenance technology; history; humanities; information technology; legal administrative assistant/secretary; liberal arts and sciences/liberal studies; licensed practical/vocational nurse training; marketing/marketing management; massage therapy; medical insurance/medical billing; music; music teacher education; network and system administration; nursing assistant/aide and patient care assistant/aide; occupational safety and health technology; petroleum technology; physical education teaching and coaching; physical sciences; registered nursing/registered nurse; social sciences; web/multimedia management and webmaster; welding technology; well drilling.

Academics *Calendar:* semesters. *Degree:* certificates and associate. *Special study options:* academic remediation for entering students, adult/continuing education programs, advanced placement credit, distance learning, part-time degree program, summer session for credit.

Library Library Learning Resources Center (LLRC) with 34,000 titles, 150 serial subscriptions, an OPAC.

Student Life *Housing Options:* men-only, women-only. Campus housing is university owned. *Activities and Organizations:* student-run newspaper, choral group, marching band. *Campus security:* 24-hour patrols.

Athletics Member NJCAA. *Intercollegiate sports:* baseball M(s), basketball M(s)/W(s), football M(s), soccer M(s)/W(s), softball W(s). *Intramural sports:* basketball M/W.

Costs (2011–12) *Tuition:* state resident $1950 full-time, $100 per credit hour part-time; nonresident $4650 full-time, $215 per credit hour part-time. Full-time tuition and fees vary according to class time. Part-time tuition and fees vary according to class time and course load. *Required fees:* $140 full-time, $70 per term part-time. *Room and board:* $2730. Room and board charges vary according to board plan. *Payment plan:* deferred payment. *Waivers:* senior citizens.

Financial Aid Of all full-time matriculated undergraduates who enrolled in 2010, 85 Federal Work-Study jobs (averaging $698). 6 state and other part-time jobs (averaging $550).

Applying *Required:* high school transcript. *Application deadlines:* 8/1 (freshmen), 8/1 (out-of-state freshmen), 8/1 (transfers).

Freshman Application Contact Mr. Matthew Calhoun, Vice President of Admissions and Records, Southwest Mississippi Community College, 1156 College Drive, Summit, MS 39666. *Phone:* 601-276-2001. *Fax:* 601-276-3888. *E-mail:* mattc@smcc.edu. *Web site:* http://www.smcc.cc.ms.us/.

Virginia College at Jackson

Jackson, Mississippi

Director of Admissions Director of Admissions, Virginia College at Jackson, 5360 I-55 North, Jackson, MS 39211. *Phone:* 601-977-0960. *Web site:* http://www.vc.edu/.

MISSOURI

American College of Technology

Saint Joseph, Missouri

Director of Admissions Richard Lingle, Lead Admission Coordinator, American College of Technology, 2300 Frederick Avenue, Saint Joseph, MO 64506. *Phone:* 800-908-9329 Ext. 13. *Toll-free phone:* 800-908-9329. *E-mail:* ricahrd@acot.edu. *Web site:* http://www.acot.edu/.

Anthem College–Kansas City

Kansas City, Missouri

Freshman Application Contact Admissions Office, Anthem College–Kansas City, 9001 State Line Road, Kansas City, MO 64114. *Phone:* 816-444-4300. *Toll-free phone:* 855-464-2684. *Fax:* 816-444-4494. *Web site:* http://anthem.edu/kansas-city-missouri/.

Anthem College–Maryland Heights

Maryland Heights, Missouri

- **Proprietary** 2-year
- **Urban** 1-acre campus with easy access to St. Louis
- **Coed,** 281 undergraduate students, 100% full-time, 85% women, 15% men

Undergraduates 281 full-time. Students come from 1 other state; 1 other country; 43% Black or African American, non-Hispanic/Latino; 2% Hispanic/Latino; 0.7% Asian, non-Hispanic/Latino; 4% Two or more races, non-Hispanic/Latino; 1% Race/ethnicity unknown; 0.4% international.

Freshmen *Admission:* 34 applied, 34 admitted, 34 enrolled.

Faculty *Total:* 24, 42% full-time, 92% with terminal degrees. *Student/faculty ratio:* 21:1.

Majors Dental assisting; health and medical administrative services related; massage therapy; medical/clinical assistant; medical insurance/medical billing; pharmacy technician; surgical technology.

Academics *Degree:* certificates and associate. *Special study options:* academic remediation for entering students, internships.

Library Anthem College Library - consists of Library Word and Ebrary with 69,000 titles, 25 serial subscriptions, 75 audiovisual materials, an OPAC.

Student Life *Housing:* college housing not available. *Campus security:* 24-hour emergency response devices and patrols.

Applying *Application fee:* $20. *Required:* high school transcript, interview, Entrance Assessment Tests. *Application deadlines:* rolling (freshmen), rolling (out-of-state freshmen), rolling (transfers).

Freshman Application Contact Mr. Brad Coleman, Admissions Office, Anthem College–Maryland Heights, 13723 Riverport Drive, Maryland Heights, MO 63043. *Phone:* 314-595-3400. *Toll-free phone:* 855-526-8436. *Fax:* 314-739-5133. *Web site:* http://anthem.edu/maryland-heights-missouri/.

Aviation Institute of Maintenance–Kansas City

Kansas City, Missouri

Freshman Application Contact Aviation Institute of Maintenance–Kansas City, 4100 Raytown Road, Kansas City, MO 64129. *Phone:* 816-753-9920. *Toll-free phone:* 888-349-5387. *Fax:* 816-753-9941. *Web site:* http://www.aviationmaintenance.edu/.

Brown Mackie College–St. Louis

Fenton, Missouri

- **Proprietary** primarily 2-year, part of Education Management Corporation
- **Coed**

Academics *Degrees:* diplomas, associate, and bachelor's.

Costs (2011–12) *Tuition:* Tuition varies by program. Students should contact Brown Mackie College for tuition information.

Freshman Application Contact Brown Mackie College–St. Louis, #2 Soccer Park Road, Fenton, MO 63026. *Phone:* 636-651-3290. *Web site:* http://www.brownmackie.edu/st-louis/.

See page 382 for the College Close-Up.

Concorde Career College

Kansas City, Missouri

Freshman Application Contact Deborah Crow, Director, Concorde Career College, 3239 Broadway, Kansas City, MO 64111-2407. *Phone:* 816-531-5223. *Fax:* 816-756-3231. *E-mail:* dcrow@concorde.edu. *Web site:* http://www.concorde.edu/.

Cottey College

Nevada, Missouri

Freshman Application Contact Ms. Judi Steege, Director of Admission, Cottey College, 1000 West Austin Boulevard, Nevada, MO 64772. *Phone:* 417-667-8181. *Toll-free phone:* 888-526-8839. *Fax:* 417-667-8103. *E-mail:* enrollmgt@cottey.edu. *Web site:* http://www.cottey.edu/.

Crowder College

Neosho, Missouri

- **State and locally supported** 2-year, founded 1963, part of Missouri Coordinating Board for Higher Education
- **Rural** 608-acre campus
- **Coed,** 5,219 undergraduate students, 47% full-time, 63% women, 37% men

Undergraduates 2,479 full-time, 2,740 part-time. Students come from 19 states and territories; 25 other countries; 4% are from out of state; 2% Black or African American, non-Hispanic/Latino; 6% Hispanic/Latino; 1% Asian, non-Hispanic/Latino; 0.4% Native Hawaiian or other Pacific Islander, non-Hispanic/Latino; 2% American Indian or Alaska Native, non-Hispanic/Latino; 0.2% Two or more races, non-Hispanic/Latino; 2% Race/ethnicity unknown; 0.5% international; 0.8% transferred in; 10% live on campus.

Freshmen *Admission:* 1,111 enrolled.

Faculty *Total:* 436, 19% full-time, 7% with terminal degrees. *Student/faculty ratio:* 12:1.

Majors Administrative assistant and secretarial science; agribusiness; agriculture; art; biology/biological sciences; business administration and management; business automation/technology/data entry; computer systems networking and telecommunications; construction engineering technology; drafting and design technology; dramatic/theater arts; education; electrical, electronic and communications engineering technology; elementary education; environmental engineering technology; environmental health; executive assistant/executive secretary; farm and ranch management; fire science/firefighting; general studies; industrial technology; legal administrative assistant/secretary; liberal arts and sciences/liberal studies; mass communication/media; mathematics; mathematics and computer science; medical administrative assistant and medical secretary; music; physical education teaching and coaching; physical sciences; poultry science; pre-engineering; psychology; public relations/image management; registered nursing/registered nurse.

Academics *Calendar:* semesters. *Degree:* certificates and associate. *Special study options:* academic remediation for entering students, adult/continuing education programs, advanced placement credit, cooperative education, English as a second language, freshman honors college, honors programs, independent study, part-time degree program, student-designed majors, study abroad, summer session for credit.

Library Bill & Margot Lee Library with 42,019 titles, 183 serial subscriptions, 6,330 audiovisual materials, an OPAC, a Web page.

Student Life *Housing Options:* men-only, women-only. Campus housing is university owned. *Activities and Organizations:* drama/theater group, student-run newspaper, choral group, Phi Theta Kappa, Students in Free Enterprise (SIFE), Baptist Student Union, Student Senate, Student Ambassadors. *Campus security:* 24-hour patrols. *Student services:* personal/psychological counseling.

Athletics Member NJCAA. *Intercollegiate sports:* baseball M(s), basketball W(s), soccer M(s).

Costs (2011–12) *Tuition:* area resident $2190 full-time, $73 per credit hour part-time; state resident $3000 full-time, $100 per credit hour part-time; nonresident $3840 full-time, $128 per credit hour part-time. *Required fees:* $340 full-time. *Room and board:* $3870. *Payment plan:* installment. *Waivers:* senior citizens and employees or children of employees.

Financial Aid Of all full-time matriculated undergraduates who enrolled in 2010, 150 Federal Work-Study jobs (averaging $1000).

Applying *Application fee:* $25. *Required:* high school transcript. *Application deadlines:* rolling (freshmen), rolling (transfers). *Notification:* continuous (freshmen).

Freshman Application Contact Mr. Jim Riggs, Admissions Coordinator, Crowder College, Neosho, MO 64850. *Phone:* 417-451-3223 Ext. 5466. *Toll-free phone:* 866-238-7788. *Fax:* 417-455-5731. *E-mail:* jimriggs@crowder.edu. *Web site:* http://www.crowder.edu/.

Culinary Institute of St. Louis at Hickey College

St. Louis, Missouri

- **Private** 2-year, founded 2009
- **Suburban** campus
- **Coed,** 85 undergraduate students

Majors Cooking and related culinary arts.

Academics *Degree:* associate.

Freshman Application Contact Admissions Office, Culinary Institute of St. Louis at Hickey College, 2700 North Lindbergh Boulevard, St. Louis, MO 63114. *Phone:* 314-434-2212. *Web site:* http://www.ci-stl.com/.

East Central College

Union, Missouri

Freshman Application Contact Miss Megen Poynter, Admissions Coordinator, East Central College, 1964 Prairie Dell Road, Union, MO 63084. *Phone:* 636-584-6564. *Fax:* 636-584-7347. *E-mail:* poynterm@eastcentral.edu. *Web site:* http://www.eastcentral.edu/.

Everest College

Springfield, Missouri

Freshman Application Contact Admissions Office, Everest College, 1010 West Sunshine, Springfield, MO 65807-2488. *Phone:* 417-864-7220. *Toll-free phone:* 888-741-4270. *Fax:* 417-864-5697. *Web site:* http://www.everest.edu/campus/springfield/.

Heritage College

Kansas City, Missouri

Freshman Application Contact Admissions Office, Heritage College, 1200 East 104th Street, Suite 300, Kansas City, MO 64131. *Phone:* 816-942-5474. *Toll-free phone:* 888-334-7339. *E-mail:* info@heritage-education.com. *Web site:* http://www.heritage-education.com/.

IHM Health Studies Center

St. Louis, Missouri

Freshman Application Contact Admissions Director, IHM Health Studies Center, 2500 Abbott Place, St. Louis, MO 63143. *Phone:* 314-768-1234. *Fax:* 314-768-1595. *E-mail:* info@ihmhealthstudies.edu. *Web site:* http://www.ihmhealthstudies.com/.

ITT Technical Institute

Arnold, Missouri

- **Proprietary** primarily 2-year, founded 1997, part of ITT Educational Services, Inc.
- **Coed**

Majors Business administration and management; communications technology; computer and information systems security; computer software and media applications related; computer software engineering; computer software technology; construction management; criminal justice/law enforcement administration; drafting and design technology; electrical, electronic and communications engineering technology; forensic science and technology; game and interactive media design; graphic communications; information technology project management; legal assistant/paralegal; network and system administration; project management; web/multimedia management and webmaster.

Academics *Calendar:* quarters. *Degrees:* associate and bachelor's.

Student Life *Housing:* college housing not available.

Freshman Application Contact Director of Recruitment, ITT Technical Institute, 1930 Meyer Drury Drive, Arnold, MO 63010. *Phone:* 636-464-6600. *Toll-free phone:* 888-488-1082. *Web site:* http://www.itt-tech.edu/.

ITT Technical Institute

Earth City, Missouri

- **Proprietary** primarily 2-year, founded 1936, part of ITT Educational Services, Inc.
- **Suburban** campus
- **Coed**

Majors Business administration and management; communications technology; computer and information systems security; computer software and media applications related; computer software engineering; computer software tech-

nology; construction management; criminal justice/law enforcement administration; drafting and design technology; electrical, electronic and communications engineering technology; forensic science and technology; game and interactive media design; graphic communications; legal assistant/paralegal; network and system administration; project management; registered nursing/registered nurse; system, networking, and LAN/WAN management.
Academics *Calendar:* quarters. *Degrees:* associate and bachelor's.
Student Life *Housing:* college housing not available.
Freshman Application Contact Director of Recruitment, ITT Technical Institute, 3640 Corporate Trail Drive, Earth City, MO 63045. *Phone:* 314-298-7800. *Toll-free phone:* 800-235-5488. *Web site:* http://www.itt-tech.edu/.

ITT Technical Institute
Kansas City, Missouri

- **Proprietary** primarily 2-year, founded 2004, part of ITT Educational Services, Inc.
- **Coed**

Majors Business administration and management; communications technology; computer and information systems security; computer software technology; construction management; criminal justice/law enforcement administration; drafting and design technology; electrical, electronic and communications engineering technology; forensic science and technology; graphic communications; information technology project management; legal assistant/paralegal; project management.
Academics *Calendar:* quarters. *Degrees:* associate and bachelor's.
Freshman Application Contact Director of Recruitment, ITT Technical Institute, 9150 East 41st Terrace, Kansas City, MO 64133. *Phone:* 816-276-1400. *Toll-free phone:* 877-488-1442. *Web site:* http://www.itt-tech.edu/.

Jefferson College
Hillsboro, Missouri

- **State-supported** 2-year, founded 1963
- **Rural** 480-acre campus with easy access to St. Louis
- **Coed**

Undergraduates 3,429 full-time, 2,763 part-time. 12% are from out of state; 2% Black or African American, non-Hispanic/Latino; 0.6% Hispanic/Latino; 0.5% Asian, non-Hispanic/Latino; 0.1% Native Hawaiian or other Pacific Islander, non-Hispanic/Latino; 0.5% American Indian or Alaska Native, non-Hispanic/Latino; 3% Race/ethnicity unknown; 0.3% international.
Academics *Calendar:* semesters. *Degree:* certificates, diplomas, and associate. *Special study options:* academic remediation for entering students, adult/continuing education programs, advanced placement credit, distance learning, English as a second language, freshman honors college, honors programs, internships, off-campus study, part-time degree program, services for LD students, summer session for credit.
Student Life *Campus security:* 24-hour patrols.
Athletics Member NJCAA.
Costs (2011–12) *One-time required fee:* $25. *Tuition:* area resident $2550 full-time, $85 per credit hour part-time; state resident $3840 full-time, $128 per credit hour part-time; nonresident $5100 full-time, $170 per credit hour part-time. Full-time tuition and fees vary according to program. Part-time tuition and fees vary according to program. *Room and board:* $5794. Room and board charges vary according to housing facility.
Financial Aid Of all full-time matriculated undergraduates who enrolled in 2010, 2,759 applied for aid, 2,100 were judged to have need, 111 had their need fully met. 106 Federal Work-Study jobs (averaging $1030). 157 state and other part-time jobs (averaging $1358). In 2010, 151. *Average percent of need met:* 57. *Average financial aid package:* $5167. *Average need-based loan:* $2985. *Average need-based gift aid:* $2364. *Average non-need-based aid:* $1775.
Applying *Options:* electronic application, early admission. *Application fee:* $25. *Required:* high school transcript.
Freshman Application Contact Ms. Julie Fraser, Director of Admissions and Financial Aid, Jefferson College, 1000 Viking Drive, Hillsboro, MO 63050-2441. *Phone:* 636-797-3000. *Fax:* 636-789-5103. *E-mail:* admissions@jeffco.edu. *Web site:* http://www.jeffco.edu/.

Linn State Technical College
Linn, Missouri

- **State-supported** 2-year, founded 1961
- **Rural** 249-acre campus
- **Coed, primarily men,** 1,168 undergraduate students, 86% full-time, 13% women, 87% men
- **63% of applicants were admitted**

Undergraduates 1,001 full-time, 167 part-time. Students come from 7 states and territories; 4% are from out of state; 2% Black or African American, non-

Hispanic/Latino; 0.3% Hispanic/Latino; 0.3% Asian, non-Hispanic/Latino; 0.5% American Indian or Alaska Native, non-Hispanic/Latino; 0.3% Two or more races, non-Hispanic/Latino; 2% Race/ethnicity unknown; 14% transferred in; 15% live on campus. *Retention:* 77% of full-time freshmen returned.
Freshmen *Admission:* 1,024 applied, 645 admitted, 498 enrolled. *Average high school GPA:* 2.87.
Faculty *Total:* 96, 88% full-time. *Student/faculty ratio:* 12:1.
Majors Aircraft powerplant technology; airframe mechanics and aircraft maintenance technology; autobody/collision and repair technology; automobile/automotive mechanics technology; civil engineering technology; computer programming; computer systems networking and telecommunications; drafting and design technology; electrical, electronic and communications engineering technology; electrical/electronics equipment installation and repair; electrician; heating, air conditioning, ventilation and refrigeration maintenance technology; heavy equipment maintenance technology; lineworker; machine tool technology; management information systems; manufacturing engineering technology; medium/heavy vehicle and truck technology; motorcycle maintenance and repair technology; nuclear/nuclear power technology; physical therapy technology; turf and turfgrass management; welding technology.
Academics *Calendar:* semesters. *Degree:* certificates and associate. *Special study options:* academic remediation for entering students, adult/continuing education programs, cooperative education, distance learning, double majors, independent study, internships, off-campus study, part-time degree program, services for LD students, summer session for credit. *ROTC:* Army (c).
Library Linn State Technical College Library with 18,725 titles, 130 serial subscriptions, 2,040 audiovisual materials, an OPAC, a Web page.
Student Life *Housing Options:* coed, men-only, women-only, disabled students. Campus housing is university owned. *Activities and Organizations:* Skills USA, Phi Theta Kappa, Student Government Association, Aviation Club, Electricity Club. *Campus security:* 24-hour emergency response devices, student patrols, controlled dormitory access, indoor and outdoor surveillance cameras. *Student services:* personal/psychological counseling.
Athletics *Intramural sports:* archery M/W, basketball M/W, bowling M/W, football M/W, golf M/W, riflery M/W, softball M/W, table tennis M/W, volleyball M/W.
Standardized Tests *Required:* COMPASS (for admission). *Required for some:* ACT (for admission).
Costs (2011–12) *One-time required fee:* $50. *Tuition:* state resident $4470 full-time, $149 per credit hour part-time; nonresident $8940 full-time, $298 per credit hour part-time. Full-time tuition and fees vary according to course load and program. Part-time tuition and fees vary according to course load and program. *Required fees:* $1080 full-time, $36 per credit hour part-time. *Room and board:* $4120; room only: $3120. Room and board charges vary according to board plan. *Payment plan:* installment. *Waivers:* employees or children of employees.
Financial Aid Of all full-time matriculated undergraduates who enrolled in 2010, 70 Federal Work-Study jobs (averaging $769).
Applying *Options:* electronic application. *Required:* high school transcript. *Required for some:* essay or personal statement, 1 letter of recommendation, interview, some require high school attendance, mechanical test. *Application deadlines:* rolling (freshmen), rolling (out-of-state freshmen), rolling (transfers). *Notification:* continuous (freshmen), continuous (out-of-state freshmen), continuous (transfers).
Freshman Application Contact Linn State Technical College, One Technology Drive, Linn, MO 65051-9606. *Phone:* 573-897-5196. *Toll-free phone:* 800-743-TECH. *Web site:* http://www.linnstate.edu/.

Metro Business College
Cape Girardeau, Missouri

Director of Admissions Ms. Kyla Evans, Admissions Director, Metro Business College, 1732 North Kingshighway, Cape Girardeau, MO 63701. *Phone:* 573-334-9181. *Toll-free phone:* 888-206-4545. *Fax:* 573-334-0617. *Web site:* http://www.metrobusinesscollege.edu/.

Metro Business College
Jefferson City, Missouri

Freshman Application Contact Ms. Cheri Chockley, Campus Director, Metro Business College, 1407 Southwest Boulevard, Jefferson City, MO 65109. *Phone:* 573-635-6600. *Toll-free phone:* 888-206-4545. *Fax:* 573-635-6999. *E-mail:* cheri@metrobusinesscollege.edu. *Web site:* http://www.metrobusinesscollege.edu/.

Metro Business College
Rolla, Missouri

Freshman Application Contact Admissions Office, Metro Business College, 1202 East Highway 72, Rolla, MO 65401. *Phone:* 573-364-8464. *Toll-free phone:* 888-206-4545. *Fax:* 573-364-8077. *E-mail:* inforolla@metrobusinesscollege.edu. *Web site:* http://www.metrobusinesscollege.edu/.

Metropolitan Community College–Blue River
Independence, Missouri

- **State and locally supported** 2-year, founded 1997, part of Metropolitan Community Colleges System
- **Suburban** campus with easy access to Kansas City
- **Endowment** $3.3 million
- **Coed,** 3,483 undergraduate students, 43% full-time, 60% women, 40% men

Undergraduates 1,482 full-time, 2,001 part-time. Students come from 2 states and territories; 6% Black or African American, non-Hispanic/Latino; 7% Hispanic/Latino; 1% Asian, non-Hispanic/Latino; 0.5% Native Hawaiian or other Pacific Islander, non-Hispanic/Latino; 0.3% American Indian or Alaska Native, non-Hispanic/Latino; 6% Two or more races, non-Hispanic/Latino; 2% Race/ethnicity unknown; 3% transferred in. *Retention:* 52% of full-time freshmen returned.
Freshmen *Admission:* 788 applied, 788 admitted, 788 enrolled.
Faculty *Total:* 236, 18% full-time, 9% with terminal degrees. *Student/faculty ratio:* 20:1.
Majors Accounting technology and bookkeeping; administrative assistant and secretarial science; business administration and management; computer and information sciences related; computer science; criminal justice/police science; fire science/firefighting; information science/studies; liberal arts and sciences/liberal studies.
Academics *Calendar:* semesters. *Degree:* certificates and associate. *Special study options:* academic remediation for entering students, accelerated degree program, adult/continuing education programs, advanced placement credit, cooperative education, distance learning, English as a second language, honors programs, independent study, internships, off-campus study, part-time degree program, study abroad.
Library Blue River Community College Library with 10,098 titles, 62 serial subscriptions, 567 audiovisual materials, an OPAC, a Web page.
Student Life *Housing:* college housing not available. *Activities and Organizations:* choral group. *Campus security:* 24-hour emergency response devices and patrols.
Athletics Member NJCAA. *Intercollegiate sports:* soccer M/W.
Costs (2011–12) *One-time required fee:* $30. *Tuition:* area resident $2460 full-time, $82 per credit hour part-time; state resident $4530 full-time, $151 per credit hour part-time; nonresident $6150 full-time, $205 per credit hour part-time. Full-time tuition and fees vary according to class time, course load, location, program, and reciprocity agreements. Part-time tuition and fees vary according to class time, course load, location, program, and reciprocity agreements. *Required fees:* $150 full-time. *Payment plan:* installment. *Waivers:* senior citizens and employees or children of employees.
Applying *Options:* early admission, deferred entrance. *Application deadlines:* rolling (freshmen), rolling (transfers).
Freshman Application Contact Dr. Jon Burke, Dean of Student Development, Metropolitan Community College–Blue River, Independence, MO 64057. *Phone:* 816-604-6118. *Fax:* 816-655-6014. *Web site:* http://www.mcckc.edu/.

Metropolitan Community College–Business & Technology Campus
Kansas City, Missouri

- **State and locally supported** 2-year, founded 1995, part of Metropolitan Community Colleges System
- **Urban** 23-acre campus
- **Endowment** $3.3 million
- **Coed,** 852 undergraduate students, 30% full-time, 12% women, 88% men
- 100% of applicants were admitted

Undergraduates 258 full-time, 594 part-time. Students come from 3 states and territories; 2% are from out of state; 14% Black or African American, non-Hispanic/Latino; 6% Hispanic/Latino; 2% Asian, non-Hispanic/Latino; 0.3% Native Hawaiian or other Pacific Islander, non-Hispanic/Latino; 0.6% American Indian or Alaska Native, non-Hispanic/Latino; 5% Two or more races,

non-Hispanic/Latino; 2% Race/ethnicity unknown; 3% transferred in. *Retention:* 37% of full-time freshmen returned.
Freshmen *Admission:* 160 applied, 160 admitted, 160 enrolled.
Faculty *Total:* 85, 21% full-time, 1% with terminal degrees. *Student/faculty ratio:* 11:1.
Majors Accounting; accounting technology and bookkeeping; artificial intelligence; building/construction site management; business administration and management; business/commerce; carpentry; computer and information sciences; computer and information sciences and support services related; computer and information sciences related; computer and information systems security; computer graphics; computer/information technology services administration related; computer programming; computer programming related; computer programming (specific applications); computer programming (vendor/product certification); computer science; computer software and media applications related; computer systems analysis; computer systems networking and telecommunications; data entry/microcomputer applications; data entry/microcomputer applications related; data modeling/warehousing and database administration; data processing and data processing technology; drafting and design technology; electrical, electronic and communications engineering technology; engineering; engineering-related technologies; environmental engineering technology; glazier; information science/studies; information technology; liberal arts and sciences/liberal studies; machine shop technology; management information systems and services related; masonry; network and system administration; quality control technology; system, networking, and LAN/WAN management; web/multimedia management and webmaster; web page, digital/multimedia and information resources design; word processing.
Academics *Calendar:* semesters. *Degree:* certificates and associate. *Special study options:* academic remediation for entering students, distance learning.
Library Learning Resource Center/Library with 10,098 titles, 14 serial subscriptions, 165 audiovisual materials, an OPAC.
Student Life *Housing:* college housing not available. *Campus security:* 24-hour patrols, late-night transport/escort service.
Costs (2011–12) *One-time required fee:* $30. *Tuition:* area resident $2460 full-time, $82 per credit hour part-time; state resident $4530 full-time, $151 per credit hour part-time; nonresident $6150 full-time, $205 per credit hour part-time. Full-time tuition and fees vary according to class time, course load, location, program, and reciprocity agreements. Part-time tuition and fees vary according to class time, course load, location, program, and reciprocity agreements. *Required fees:* $150 full-time. *Payment plan:* installment. *Waivers:* senior citizens and employees or children of employees.
Applying *Application deadlines:* rolling (freshmen), rolling (transfers).
Freshman Application Contact Mr. Tom Wheeler, Dean of Instruction, Metropolitan Community College–Business & Technology Campus, Kansas City, MO 64120. *Phone:* 816-604-5240. *Web site:* http://www.mcckc.edu/.

Metropolitan Community College–Longview
Lee's Summit, Missouri

- **State and locally supported** 2-year, founded 1969, part of Metropolitan Community Colleges System
- **Suburban** 147-acre campus with easy access to Kansas City
- **Endowment** $3.3 million
- **Coed,** 6,209 undergraduate students, 42% full-time, 57% women, 43% men

Undergraduates 2,631 full-time, 3,578 part-time. Students come from 7 states and territories; 18% Black or African American, non-Hispanic/Latino; 6% Hispanic/Latino; 1% Asian, non-Hispanic/Latino; 0.2% Native Hawaiian or other Pacific Islander, non-Hispanic/Latino; 0.3% American Indian or Alaska Native, non-Hispanic/Latino; 6% Two or more races, non-Hispanic/Latino; 3% Race/ethnicity unknown; 3% transferred in. *Retention:* 48% of full-time freshmen returned.
Freshmen *Admission:* 1,392 applied, 1,392 admitted, 1,392 enrolled.
Faculty *Total:* 271, 31% full-time, 36% with terminal degrees. *Student/faculty ratio:* 26:1.
Majors Accounting; administrative assistant and secretarial science; agricultural mechanization; automobile/automotive mechanics technology; biological and physical sciences; biology/biological sciences; business administration and management; chemistry; computer and information sciences related; computer programming; computer science; computer typography and composition equipment operation; corrections; criminal justice/law enforcement administration; criminal justice/police science; data processing and data processing technology; engineering; heavy equipment maintenance technology; human services; legal administrative assistant/secretary; liberal arts and sciences/liberal studies; marketing/marketing management; medical administrative assistant and medical secretary; pre-engineering.
Academics *Calendar:* semesters. *Degree:* certificates and associate. *Special study options:* academic remediation for entering students, accelerated degree

program, adult/continuing education programs, advanced placement credit, cooperative education, distance learning, English as a second language, honors programs, independent study, internships, off-campus study, part-time degree program, study abroad.

Library Longview Community College Library with 10,098 titles, 288 serial subscriptions, an OPAC, a Web page.

Student Life *Housing:* college housing not available. *Activities and Organizations:* drama/theater group, student-run newspaper, choral group, student newspaper, student government, Phi Theta Kappa, Longview Mighty Voices Choir, Longview Broadcasting Network, national fraternities. *Campus security:* 24-hour patrols. *Student services:* personal/psychological counseling.

Athletics Member NJCAA. *Intercollegiate sports:* baseball M(s), cross-country running W(s), volleyball W(s). *Intramural sports:* basketball M/W, swimming and diving M/W, volleyball M/W.

Costs (2011–12) *One-time required fee:* $30. *Tuition:* area resident $2460 full-time, $82 per credit hour part-time; state resident $4530 full-time, $151 per credit hour part-time; nonresident $6150 full-time, $205 per credit hour part-time. Full-time tuition and fees vary according to class time, course load, location, program, and reciprocity agreements. Part-time tuition and fees vary according to class time, course load, location, program, and reciprocity agreements. *Required fees:* $150 full-time. *Payment plan:* installment. *Waivers:* senior citizens and employees or children of employees.

Applying *Options:* early admission, deferred entrance. *Application deadlines:* rolling (freshmen), rolling (transfers).

Freshman Application Contact Ms. Janet Cline, Dean of Student Development, Metropolitan Community College–Longview, 500 Southwest Longview Road, Lee's Summit, MO 64081-2105. *Phone:* 816-604-2249. *Fax:* 816-672-2040. *E-mail:* janet.cline@mcckc.edu. *Web site:* http://www.mcckc.edu/.

Metropolitan Community College–Maple Woods

Kansas City, Missouri

- **State and locally supported** 2-year, founded 1969, part of Metropolitan Community Colleges System
- **Suburban** 205-acre campus
- **Endowment** $3.3 million
- **Coed,** 5,332 undergraduate students, 40% full-time, 60% women, 40% men

Undergraduates 2,121 full-time, 3,211 part-time. Students come from 2 states and territories; 1 other country; 7% Black or African American, non-Hispanic/Latino; 7% Hispanic/Latino; 3% Asian, non-Hispanic/Latino; 0.4% Native Hawaiian or other Pacific Islander, non-Hispanic/Latino; 0.5% American Indian or Alaska Native, non-Hispanic/Latino; 5% Two or more races, non-Hispanic/Latino; 2% Race/ethnicity unknown; 3% transferred in. *Retention:* 46% of full-time freshmen returned.

Freshmen *Admission:* 1,198 applied, 1,198 admitted, 1,198 enrolled.

Faculty *Total:* 233, 23% full-time, 9% with terminal degrees. *Student/faculty ratio:* 27:1.

Majors Accounting; administrative assistant and secretarial science; avionics maintenance technology; biological and physical sciences; biology/biological sciences; business administration and management; chemistry; computer and information sciences related; computer programming; computer science; criminal justice/law enforcement administration; criminal justice/police science; data processing and data processing technology; legal administrative assistant/secretary; liberal arts and sciences/liberal studies; marketing/marketing management; medical administrative assistant and medical secretary; pre-engineering; veterinary/animal health technology.

Academics *Calendar:* semesters. *Degree:* certificates and associate. *Special study options:* academic remediation for entering students, accelerated degree program, adult/continuing education programs, advanced placement credit, cooperative education, distance learning, English as a second language, honors programs, internships, off-campus study, part-time degree program, services for LD students, summer session for credit.

Library Maple Woods Community College Library with 10,098 titles, 151 serial subscriptions, 103 audiovisual materials, an OPAC.

Student Life *Housing:* college housing not available. *Activities and Organizations:* drama/theater group, student-run newspaper, choral group, Student Activities Council, Art Club, Friends of All Cultures, Phi Theta Kappa, Engineering Club, national fraternities. *Campus security:* 24-hour patrols, late-night transport/escort service. *Student services:* personal/psychological counseling.

Athletics Member NJCAA. *Intercollegiate sports:* baseball M(s), soccer M/W, softball W(s). *Intramural sports:* softball M/W, volleyball M/W.

Costs (2011–12) *One-time required fee:* $30. *Tuition:* area resident $2460 full-time, $82 per credit hour part-time; state resident $4530 full-time, $151 per credit hour part-time; nonresident $6150 full-time, $205 per credit hour part-time. Full-time tuition and fees vary according to class time, course load, location, program, and reciprocity agreements. Part-time tuition and fees vary according to class time, course load, location, program, and reciprocity agreements. *Required fees:* $150 full-time. *Payment plan:* installment. *Waivers:* senior citizens and employees or children of employees.

Applying *Options:* early admission, deferred entrance. *Application deadlines:* rolling (freshmen), rolling (transfers). *Notification:* continuous (freshmen), continuous (transfers).

Freshman Application Contact Ms. Shelli Allen, Dean of Student Development and Enrollment Management, Metropolitan Community College–Maple Woods, 2601 Northeast Barry Road, Kansas City, MO 64156-1299. *Phone:* 816-604-3175. *Fax:* 816-437-3351. *Web site:* http://www.mcckc.edu/.

Metropolitan Community College–Penn Valley

Kansas City, Missouri

- **State and locally supported** 2-year, founded 1969, part of Metropolitan Community Colleges System
- **Urban** 25-acre campus
- **Endowment** $3.3 million
- **Coed,** 5,409 undergraduate students, 30% full-time, 70% women, 30% men

Undergraduates 1,638 full-time, 3,771 part-time. Students come from 5 states and territories; 43 other countries; 5% are from out of state; 41% Black or African American, non-Hispanic/Latino; 9% Hispanic/Latino; 3% Asian, non-Hispanic/Latino; 0.2% Native Hawaiian or other Pacific Islander, non-Hispanic/Latino; 0.3% American Indian or Alaska Native, non-Hispanic/Latino; 5% Two or more races, non-Hispanic/Latino; 2% Race/ethnicity unknown; 2% international; 4% transferred in. *Retention:* 43% of full-time freshmen returned.

Freshmen *Admission:* 1,048 applied, 1,048 admitted, 1,048 enrolled.

Faculty *Total:* 283, 33% full-time, 30% with terminal degrees. *Student/faculty ratio:* 19:1.

Majors Accounting; administrative assistant and secretarial science; biological and physical sciences; biology/biological sciences; business administration and management; chemistry; child-care provision; commercial and advertising art; computer and information sciences related; computer science; corrections; criminal justice/law enforcement administration; criminal justice/police science; data processing and data processing technology; emergency medical technology (EMT paramedic); engineering; family and consumer sciences/human sciences; fashion/apparel design; fashion merchandising; health information/medical records administration; kindergarten/preschool education; legal administrative assistant/secretary; legal assistant/paralegal; liberal arts and sciences/liberal studies; marketing/marketing management; medical administrative assistant and medical secretary; occupational therapy; physical therapy; registered nursing/registered nurse; respiratory care therapy; special products marketing.

Academics *Calendar:* semesters. *Degree:* certificates and associate. *Special study options:* academic remediation for entering students, accelerated degree program, adult/continuing education programs, advanced placement credit, cooperative education, distance learning, English as a second language, honors programs, independent study, internships, off-campus study, part-time degree program, study abroad.

Library Penn Valley Community College Library with 10,098 titles, 89,242 serial subscriptions, an OPAC.

Student Life *Housing:* college housing not available. *Activities and Organizations:* drama/theater group, student-run newspaper, choral group, Black Student Association, Los Americanos, Phi Theta Kappa, Fashion Club, national fraternities. *Campus security:* 24-hour patrols. *Student services:* personal/psychological counseling.

Athletics Member NJCAA. *Intercollegiate sports:* basketball M(s)/W(s).

Costs (2011–12) *One-time required fee:* $30. *Tuition:* area resident $2460 full-time, $82 per credit hour part-time; state resident $4530 full-time, $151 per credit hour part-time; nonresident $6150 full-time, $205 per credit hour part-time. Full-time tuition and fees vary according to class time, course load, location, program, and reciprocity agreements. Part-time tuition and fees vary according to class time, course load, location, program, and reciprocity agreements. *Required fees:* $150 full-time. *Payment plan:* installment. *Waivers:* senior citizens and employees or children of employees.

Applying *Options:* early admission. *Required:* high school transcript. *Application deadlines:* rolling (freshmen), rolling (transfers).

Freshman Application Contact Dr. Lisa Minis, Dean of Student Services, Metropolitan Community College–Penn Valley, 3201 Southwest Trafficway, Kansas City, MO 64111. *Phone:* 816-604-4101. *Fax:* 816-759-4478. *Web site:* http://www.mcckc.edu/.

Midwest Institute

Kirkwood, Missouri

Freshman Application Contact Admissions Office, Midwest Institute, 10910 Manchester Road, Kirkwood, MO 63122. *Toll-free phone:* 800-695-5550. *Web site:* http://www.midwestinstitute.com/.

Midwest Institute

St. Louis, Missouri

Freshman Application Contact Admissions Office, Midwest Institute, 4260 Shoreline Drive, St. Louis, MO 63045. *Phone:* 314-344-4440. *Toll-free phone:* 800-695-5550. *Fax:* 314-344-0495. *Web site:* http://www.midwestinstitute.com/.

Mineral Area College

Park Hills, Missouri

- **District-supported** 2-year, founded 1922, part of Missouri Coordinating Board for Higher Education
- **Rural** 240-acre campus with easy access to St. Louis
- **Coed,** 3,958 undergraduate students, 60% full-time, 64% women, 36% men

Undergraduates 2,371 full-time, 1,587 part-time. Students come from 13 states and territories; 7 other countries; 1% are from out of state; 2% Black or African American, non-Hispanic/Latino; 0.8% Hispanic/Latino; 0.2% Asian, non-Hispanic/Latino; 1% American Indian or Alaska Native, non-Hispanic/Latino; 0.3% Two or more races, non-Hispanic/Latino; 5% Race/ethnicity unknown; 0.3% international; 4% transferred in. *Retention:* 68% of full-time freshmen returned.

Freshmen *Admission:* 1,004 enrolled.

Faculty *Total:* 262, 26% full-time. *Student/faculty ratio:* 15:1.

Majors Administrative assistant and secretarial science; agribusiness; applied horticulture/horticulture operations; autobody/collision and repair technology; automobile/automotive mechanics technology; business/commerce; carpentry; child-care provision; civil engineering technology; computer programming; criminal justice/police science; culinary arts; drafting and design technology; electrical, electronic and communications engineering technology; emergency medical technology (EMT paramedic); engineering technology; fire science/firefighting; general studies; graphic and printing equipment operation/production; health professions related; heating, ventilation, air conditioning and refrigeration engineering technology; heavy/industrial equipment maintenance technologies related; industrial technology; liberal arts and sciences/liberal studies; machine tool technology; operations management; precision production related; precision production trades; radio and television broadcasting technology; registered nursing/registered nurse; respiratory therapy technician; system, networking, and LAN/WAN management; technical teacher education.

Academics *Calendar:* semesters. *Degree:* certificates and associate. *Special study options:* academic remediation for entering students, advanced placement credit, distance learning, honors programs, internships, off-campus study, part-time degree program, services for LD students, summer session for credit.

Library C. H. Cozen Learning Resource Center with 32,228 titles, 214 serial subscriptions, 4,859 audiovisual materials, an OPAC, a Web page.

Student Life *Housing Options:* coed. Campus housing is university owned. *Activities and Organizations:* drama/theater group, choral group. *Campus security:* 24-hour patrols. *Student services:* personal/psychological counseling.

Athletics Member NJCAA. *Intercollegiate sports:* baseball M(s), basketball M(s)/W(s), golf M, softball W(s), volleyball W(s).

Costs (2012–13) *Tuition:* area resident $2490 full-time, $87 per hour part-time; state resident $3240 full-time, $115 per hour part-time; nonresident $3960 full-time, $143 per hour part-time. *Room and board:* room only: $3555. Room and board charges vary according to board plan and housing facility. *Payment plan:* installment. *Waivers:* senior citizens and employees or children of employees.

Financial Aid Of all full-time matriculated undergraduates who enrolled in 2010, 65 Federal Work-Study jobs (averaging $3708).

Applying *Options:* electronic application, early admission. *Application fee:* $15. *Required:* high school transcript. *Application deadlines:* rolling (freshmen), rolling (transfers). *Notification:* continuous (freshmen).

Freshman Application Contact Linda Huffman, Registrar, Mineral Area College, PO Box 1000, Park Hills, MO 63601-1000. *Phone:* 573-518-2130. *Fax:* 573-518-2166. *E-mail:* lhuffman@mineralarea.edu. *Web site:* http://www.mineralarea.edu/.

Missouri College

St. Louis, Missouri

Director of Admissions Mr. Doug Brinker, Admissions Director, Missouri College, 10121 Manchester Road, St. Louis, MO 63122-1583. *Phone:* 314-821-7700. *Toll-free phone:* 800-216-6732. *Fax:* 314-821-0891. *Web site:* http://www.mocollege.com/.

Missouri State University–West Plains

West Plains, Missouri

- **State-supported** 2-year, founded 1963, part of Missouri State University
- **Small-town** 20-acre campus
- **Endowment** $2.6 million
- **Coed,** 2,142 undergraduate students, 60% full-time, 60% women, 40% men

Undergraduates 1,284 full-time, 858 part-time. Students come from 26 states and territories; 7 other countries; 6% are from out of state; 2% Black or African American, non-Hispanic/Latino; 2% Hispanic/Latino; 1% Asian, non-Hispanic/Latino; 0.9% American Indian or Alaska Native, non-Hispanic/Latino; 6% Race/ethnicity unknown; 0.1% international; 4% transferred in; 4% live on campus. *Retention:* 46% of full-time freshmen returned.

Freshmen *Admission:* 970 applied, 709 admitted, 583 enrolled. *Average high school GPA:* 3.33. *Test scores:* ACT scores over 18: 71%; ACT scores over 24: 16%; ACT scores over 30: 1%.

Faculty *Total:* 114, 29% full-time, 14% with terminal degrees. *Student/faculty ratio:* 26:1.

Majors Accounting; agriculture; business administration and management; business/commerce; child-care and support services management; computer and information sciences related; computer graphics; computer programming (specific applications); criminal justice/law enforcement administration; criminal justice/police science; engineering; entrepreneurship; food science; general studies; horticultural science; industrial technology; information technology; legal assistant/paralegal; management information systems and services related; registered nursing/registered nurse; respiratory therapy technician.

Academics *Calendar:* semesters. *Degree:* certificates and associate. *Special study options:* academic remediation for entering students, advanced placement credit, cooperative education, distance learning, honors programs, internships, off-campus study, part-time degree program, services for LD students, study abroad, summer session for credit.

Library Garnett Library with 40,233 titles, 149 serial subscriptions, 1,280 audiovisual materials, an OPAC, a Web page.

Student Life *Housing Options:* men-only, women-only. Campus housing is university owned. *Activities and Organizations:* Student Government Association, Chi Alpha, Adult Students in Higher Education, Lambda Lambda Lambda, Programming Board. *Campus security:* access only with key. *Student services:* health clinic, personal/psychological counseling.

Athletics Member NJCAA. *Intercollegiate sports:* basketball M(s), volleyball W(s).

Costs (2011–12) *Tuition:* state resident $3210 full-time, $107 per credit part-time; nonresident $6714 full-time, $214 per credit part-time. Full-time tuition and fees vary according to course load, location, and program. Part-time tuition and fees vary according to course load and location. *Required fees:* $294 full-time, $5 per credit part-time, $72 per year part-time. *Room and board:* $5116. Room and board charges vary according to board plan. *Payment plan:* deferred payment. *Waivers:* senior citizens and employees or children of employees.

Financial Aid Of all full-time matriculated undergraduates who enrolled in 2010, 63 Federal Work-Study jobs (averaging $2000).

Applying *Options:* electronic application. *Application fee:* $15. *Required for some:* high school transcript. *Application deadlines:* 8/20 (freshmen), 8/20 (out-of-state freshmen), 8/20 (transfers). *Notification:* continuous (freshmen), continuous (out-of-state freshmen), continuous (transfers).

Freshman Application Contact Ms. Melissa Jett, Coordinator of Admissions, Missouri State University–West Plains, 128 Garfield, West Plains, MO 65775. *Phone:* 417-255-7955. *Toll-free phone:* 888-466-7897. *Fax:* 417-255-7959. *E-mail:* melissajett@missouristate.edu. *Web site:* http://wp.missouristate.edu/.

Moberly Area Community College

Moberly, Missouri

Freshman Application Contact Dr. James Grant, Dean of Student Services, Moberly Area Community College, Moberly, MO 65270-1304. *Phone:* 660-263-4110 Ext. 235. *Toll-free phone:* 800-622-2070. *Fax:* 660-263-2406. *E-mail:* info@macc.edu. *Web site:* http://www.macc.edu/.

North Central Missouri College

Trenton, Missouri

Freshman Application Contact Megan Goodin, Admissions Assistant, North Central Missouri College, Trenton, MO 64683. *Phone:* 660-359-3948 Ext. 1410. *E-mail:* megoodin@mail.ncmissouri.edu. *Web site:* http://www.ncmissouri.edu/.

Ozarks Technical Community College

Springfield, Missouri

Director of Admissions Mr. Jeff Jochems, Dean of Student Development, Ozarks Technical Community College, PO Box 5958, 1001 East Chestnut Expressway, Springfield, MO 65801. *Phone:* 417-895-7136. *Web site:* http://www.otc.edu/.

Pinnacle Career Institute

Kansas City, Missouri

Director of Admissions Ms. Ruth Matous, Director of Admissions, Pinnacle Career Institute, 1001 East 101st Terrace, Suite 325, Kansas City, MO 64131. *Phone:* 816-331-5700 Ext. 212. *Toll-free phone:* 877-241-3097. *Web site:* http://www.pcitraining.edu/.

Ranken Technical College

St. Louis, Missouri

Director of Admissions Ms. Elizabeth Keserauskis, Director of Admissions, Ranken Technical College, 4431 Finney Avenue, St. Louis, MO 63113. *Phone:* 314-371-0233 Ext. 4811. *Toll-free phone:* 866-4-RANKEN. *Web site:* http://www.ranken.edu/.

Saint Charles Community College

Cottleville, Missouri

- **State-supported** 2-year, founded 1986, part of Missouri Coordinating Board for Higher Education
- **Suburban** 234-acre campus with easy access to St. Louis
- **Coed**

Undergraduates 4,313 full-time, 3,889 part-time. Students come from 11 states and territories; 20 other countries; 5% transferred in. *Retention:* 64% of full-time freshmen returned.

Faculty *Student/faculty ratio:* 25:1.

Academics *Calendar:* semesters. *Degree:* certificates and associate. *Special study options:* academic remediation for entering students, adult/continuing education programs, advanced placement credit, cooperative education, distance learning, double majors, English as a second language, independent study, internships, part-time degree program, services for LD students, study abroad, summer session for credit.

Student Life *Campus security:* 24-hour emergency response devices and patrols, late-night transport/escort service, campus police officers on duty during normal operating hours.

Athletics Member NJCAA.

Costs (2011–12) *Tuition:* area resident $2040 full-time, $85 per credit hour part-time; state resident $3072 full-time, $128 per credit hour part-time; nonresident $4584 full-time, $191 per credit hour part-time.

Applying *Options:* electronic application, early admission, deferred entrance. *Required for some:* high school transcript, minimum 2.5 GPA. *Recommended:* high school transcript.

Freshman Application Contact Ms. Kathy Brockgreitens-Gober, Director of Admissions/Registrar/Financial Assistance, Saint Charles Community College, 4601 Mid Rivers Mall Drive, Cottleville, MO 63376-0975. *Phone:* 636-922-8229. *Fax:* 636-922-8236. *E-mail:* regist@stchas.edu. *Web site:* http://www.stchas.edu/.

St. Louis College of Health Careers

St. Louis, Missouri

Freshman Application Contact Admissions Office, St. Louis College of Health Careers, 909 South Taylor Avenue, St. Louis, MO 63110-1511. *Phone:* 314-652-0300. *Toll-free phone:* 888-789-4820. *Fax:* 314-652-4825. *Web site:* http://www.slchc.com/.

St. Louis Community College at Florissant Valley

St. Louis, Missouri

Freshman Application Contact Ms. Brenda Davenport, Manager of Admissions and Registration, St. Louis Community College at Florissant Valley, 3400 Pershall Road, St. Louis, MO 63135-1499. *Phone:* 314-513-4248. *Fax:* 314-513-4724. *Web site:* http://www.stlcc.edu/.

St. Louis Community College at Forest Park

St. Louis, Missouri

Freshman Application Contact Director of Admissions, St. Louis Community College at Forest Park, 5600 Oakland Avenue, St. Louis, MO 63110-1316. *Phone:* 314-644-9129. *Fax:* 314-644-9375. *E-mail:* fp_admissions@stlcc.edu. *Web site:* http://www.stlcc.edu/.

St. Louis Community College at Meramec

Kirkwood, Missouri

Freshman Application Contact Director of Admissions, St. Louis Community College at Meramec, 11333 Big Bend Boulevard, Kirkwood, MO 63122-5720. *Phone:* 314-984-7601. *Fax:* 314-984-7051. *E-mail:* mc-admissions@stlcc.edu. *Web site:* http://www.stlcc.edu/.

Sanford-Brown College

Fenton, Missouri

Director of Admissions Ms. Judy Wilga, Director of Admissions, Sanford-Brown College, 1203 Smizer Mill Road, Fenton, MO 63026. *Phone:* 636-349-4900 Ext. 102. *Toll-free phone:* 800-769-2433 (in-state); 888-769-2433 (out-of-state). *Fax:* 636-349-9170. *Web site:* http://www.sanford-brown.edu/.

Sanford-Brown College

St. Peters, Missouri

Director of Admissions Karl J. Petersen, Executive Director, Sanford-Brown College, 100 Richmond Center Boulevard, St. Peters, MO 63376. *Phone:* 636-949-2620. *Toll-free phone:* 888-793-2433. *Fax:* 636-949-5081. *E-mail:* karl.peterson@wix.net. *Web site:* http://www.sanford-brown.edu/.

Southeast Missouri Hospital College of Nursing and Health Sciences

Cape Girardeau, Missouri

- **Independent** 2-year, founded 1928
- **Rural** 1-acre campus
- **Coed**, 196 undergraduate students, 13% full-time, 80% women, 20% men

Undergraduates 25 full-time, 171 part-time. Students come from 3 states and territories; 5% are from out of state; 3% Black or African American, non-Hispanic/Latino; 0.5% Hispanic/Latino; 1% Asian, non-Hispanic/Latino; 0.5% Native Hawaiian or other Pacific Islander, non-Hispanic/Latino; 96% transferred in. *Retention:* 100% of full-time freshmen returned.

Freshmen *Admission:* 215 applied, 173 admitted, 7 enrolled. *Average high school GPA:* 2.5. *Test scores:* ACT scores over 18: 100%; ACT scores over 24: 27%; ACT scores over 30: 3%.

Faculty *Total:* 31, 71% full-time, 6% with terminal degrees. *Student/faculty ratio:* 5:1.

Majors Medical radiologic technology; registered nursing/registered nurse.

Academics *Calendar:* six 7-week terms per year. *Degrees:* certificates, associate, and postbachelor's certificates. *Special study options:* advanced placement credit.

Student Life *Housing:* college housing not available. *Campus security:* 24-hour emergency response devices and patrols, late-night transport/escort service, electronic campus access.

Standardized Tests *Required:* SAT or ACT (for admission), COMPASS and NLN also used for various programs and tracks (for admission).

Costs (2012–13) *Tuition:* $300 per credit part-time. Full-time tuition and fees vary according to course load and program. Part-time tuition and fees vary according to course load and program. *Required fees:* $21 per hour part-time. *Payment plan:* installment.

Applying *Application fee:* $50. *Required:* high school transcript, minimum 2.0 GPA, 1 letter of recommendation, Bridge Program requirement is a minimum score of 75 on NLN exam. COMPASS exam minimum scores are required for the associate degree programs of 75 in writing, 85 in reading, and 46 in Pre-Algebra. *Application deadlines:* rolling (freshmen), rolling (out-of-state freshmen), rolling (transfers). *Notification:* continuous (freshmen), continuous (out-of-state freshmen), continuous (transfers).

Freshman Application Contact Southeast Missouri Hospital College of Nursing and Health Sciences, 2001 William Street, Cape Girardeau, MO 63701. *Phone:* 573-334-6825 Ext. 12. *Web site:* http://www.southeastmissourihospitalcollege.edu/.

State Fair Community College

Sedalia, Missouri

Freshman Application Contact State Fair Community College, 3201 West 16th Street, Sedalia, MO 65301-2199. *Phone:* 660-596-7221. *Toll-free phone:* 877-311-7322. *Web site:* http://www.sfccmo.edu/.

Three Rivers Community College

Poplar Bluff, Missouri

Freshman Application Contact Ms. Marcia Fields, Director of Admissions and Recruiting, Three Rivers Community College, Poplar Bluff, MO 63901. *Phone:* 573-840-9675. *Toll-free phone:* 877-TRY-TRCC. *E-mail:* trytrcc@trcc.edu. *Web site:* http://www.trcc.edu/.

Vatterott College

Kansas City, Missouri

Admissions Office Contact Vatterott College, 8955 East 38th Terrace, Kansas City, MO 64129. *Toll-free phone:* 888-553-6627. *Web site:* http://www.vatterott-college.edu/.

Vatterott College

O'Fallon, Missouri

Director of Admissions Gertrude Bogan-Jones, Director of Admissions, Vatterott College, 927 East Terra Lane, O'Fallon, MO 63366. *Phone:* 636-978-7488. *Toll-free phone:* 888-553-6627. *Fax:* 636-978-5121. *E-mail:* ofallon@vatterott-college.edu. *Web site:* http://www.vatterott-college.edu/.

Vatterott College

St. Ann, Missouri

Director of Admissions Ann Farajallah, Director of Admissions, Vatterott College, 3925 Industrial Drive, St. Ann, MO 63074-1807. *Phone:* 314-264-1020. *Toll-free phone:* 888-553-6627. *Web site:* http://www.vatterott-college.edu/.

Vatterott College

St. Joseph, Missouri

Director of Admissions Director of Admissions, Vatterott College, 3131 Frederick Avenue, St. Joseph, MO 64506. *Phone:* 816-364-5399. *Toll-free phone:* 888-553-6627. *Fax:* 816-364-1593. *Web site:* http://www.vatterott-college.edu/.

Vatterott College

Sunset Hills, Missouri

Director of Admissions Director of Admission, Vatterott College, 12970 Maurer Industrial Drive, St. Louis, MO 63127. *Phone:* 314-843-4200. *Toll-free phone:* 888-553-6627. *Fax:* 314-843-1709. *Web site:* http://www.vatterott-college.edu/.

Vatterott College

Springfield, Missouri

Freshman Application Contact Mr. Scott Lester, Director of Admissions, Vatterott College, 1258 East Trafficway Street, Springfield, MO 65802. *Phone:* 417-831-8116. *Toll-free phone:* 888-553-6627. *Fax:* 417-831-5099.

E-mail: springfield@vatterott-college.edu. *Web site:* http://www.vatterott-college.edu/.

Vet Tech Institute at Hickey College

St. Louis, Missouri

- **Private** 2-year, founded 2007
- **Suburban** campus
- **Coed,** 134 undergraduate students
- 47% of applicants were admitted

Freshmen *Admission:* 574 applied, 268 admitted.

Majors Veterinary/animal health technology.

Academics *Degree:* associate. *Special study options:* accelerated degree program, internships.

Freshman Application Contact Admissions Office, Vet Tech Institute at Hickey College, 2780 North Lindbergh Boulevard, St. Louis, MO 63114. *Phone:* 888-884-1459. *Toll-free phone:* 888-884-1459. *Web site:* http://www.vettechinstitute.edu/.

Wentworth Military Academy and College

Lexington, Missouri

- **Independent** 2-year, founded 1880
- **Small-town** 130-acre campus with easy access to Kansas City
- **Coed**

Undergraduates 84 full-time, 857 part-time. Students come from 22 states and territories; 4 other countries; 43% are from out of state; 2% Black or African American, non-Hispanic/Latino; 2% Hispanic/Latino; 1% Asian, non-Hispanic/Latino; 1% Native Hawaiian or other Pacific Islander, non-Hispanic/Latino; 0.4% American Indian or Alaska Native, non-Hispanic/Latino; 1% Two or more races, non-Hispanic/Latino; 1% Race/ethnicity unknown; 2% international; 0.1% transferred in. *Retention:* 88% of full-time freshmen returned.

Faculty *Student/faculty ratio:* 10:1.

Academics *Calendar:* semesters. *Degree:* diplomas and associate. *Special study options:* academic remediation for entering students, adult/continuing education programs, advanced placement credit, distance learning, English as a second language, part-time degree program, student-designed majors, summer session for credit. *ROTC:* Army (b).

Student Life *Campus security:* 24-hour emergency response devices and patrols.

Athletics Member NJCAA.

Standardized Tests *Required for some:* SAT or ACT (for admission). *Recommended:* SAT or ACT (for admission).

Costs (2011–12) *Comprehensive fee:* $29,700. Full-time tuition and fees vary according to course load and program. Part-time tuition: $180 per credit. Part-time tuition and fees vary according to course load and program.

Applying *Application fee:* $100. *Required:* high school transcript.

Freshman Application Contact Capt. Mike Bellis, College Admissions Director, Wentworth Military Academy and College, 1880 Washington Avenue, Lexington, MO 64067. *Phone:* 660-259-2221 Ext. 1351. *Fax:* 660-259-2677. *E-mail:* admissions@wma.edu. *Web site:* http://www.wma.edu/.

MONTANA

Blackfeet Community College

Browning, Montana

Freshman Application Contact Ms. Deana M. McNabb, Registrar and Admissions Officer, Blackfeet Community College, PO Box 819, Browning, MT 59417-0819. *Phone:* 406-338-5421. *Toll-free phone:* 800-549-7457. *Fax:* 406-338-3272. *Web site:* http://www.bfcc.org/.

Chief Dull Knife College

Lame Deer, Montana

Freshman Application Contact Director of Admissions, Chief Dull Knife College, PO Box 98, 1 College Drive, Lame Deer, MT 59043-0098. *Phone:* 406-477-6215. *Web site:* http://www.cdkc.edu/.

Dawson Community College
Glendive, Montana

- **State and locally supported** 2-year, founded 1940, part of Montana University System
- **Rural** 300-acre campus
- **Endowment** $344,944
- **Coed,** 603 undergraduate students, 47% full-time, 58% women, 42% men

Undergraduates 284 full-time, 319 part-time.
Freshmen *Admission:* 98 enrolled.
Faculty *Total:* 26, 88% full-time. *Student/faculty ratio:* 26:1.
Majors Administrative assistant and secretarial science; agricultural business and management; agricultural power machinery operation; business/commerce; child-care provision; clinical/medical social work; community psychology; computer and information sciences; computer and information sciences related; criminal justice/police science; liberal arts and sciences/liberal studies; music; substance abuse/addiction counseling; welding technology.
Academics *Calendar:* semesters. *Degree:* certificates and associate. *Special study options:* academic remediation for entering students, adult/continuing education programs, distance learning, independent study, internships, part-time degree program, services for LD students, summer session for credit.
Library Jane Carey Memorial Library with 17,182 titles, 90 serial subscriptions, 1,127 audiovisual materials, an OPAC, a Web page.
Student Life *Housing Options:* coed. Campus housing is university owned. *Activities and Organizations:* drama/theater group, choral group, Phi Theta Kappa, Associated Student Body, Rodeo Club, Law Enforcement Club, Campus Corp. *Campus security:* 24-hour emergency response devices.
Athletics Member NJCAA. *Intercollegiate sports:* baseball M, basketball M(s)/W(s), equestrian sports M(s)/W(s), softball W. *Intramural sports:* basketball M/W, bowling M/W, golf M/W, racquetball M/W, softball M/W, table tennis M/W, tennis M/W, volleyball M/W.
Costs (2011–12) *Tuition:* area resident $1566 full-time, $52 per credit part-time; state resident $2673 full-time, $89 per credit part-time; nonresident $7329 full-time, $178 per credit part-time. *Required fees:* $1290 full-time, $43 per hour part-time. *Room and board:* $3300. *Waivers:* senior citizens and employees or children of employees.
Financial Aid Of all full-time matriculated undergraduates who enrolled in 2010, 45 Federal Work-Study jobs (averaging $1500). 17 state and other part-time jobs (averaging $1500).
Applying *Options:* deferred entrance. *Application fee:* $30. *Required:* high school transcript. *Application deadlines:* rolling (freshmen), rolling (transfers). *Notification:* continuous (freshmen), continuous (transfers).
Freshman Application Contact Dawson Community College, 300 College Drive, PO Box 421, Glendive, MT 59330-0421. *Phone:* 406-377-3396 Ext. 410. *Toll-free phone:* 800-821-8320. *Web site:* http://www.dawson.edu/.

Flathead Valley Community College
Kalispell, Montana

Freshman Application Contact Ms. Marlene C. Stoltz, Admissions/Graduation Coordinator, Flathead Valley Community College, 777 Grandview Drive, Kalispell, MT 59901-2622. *Phone:* 406-756-3846. *Toll-free phone:* 800-313-3822. *E-mail:* mstoltz@fvcc.cc.mt.us. *Web site:* http://www.fvcc.edu/.

Fort Belknap College
Harlem, Montana

Director of Admissions Ms. Dixie Brockie, Registrar and Admissions Officer, Fort Belknap College, PO Box 159, Harlem, MT 59526-0159. *Phone:* 406-353-2607 Ext. 233. *Fax:* 406-353-2898. *E-mail:* dbrockie@mail.fbcc.edu. *Web site:* http://www.fbcc.edu/.

Fort Peck Community College
Poplar, Montana

Director of Admissions Mr. Robert McAnally, Vice President for Student Services, Fort Peck Community College, PO Box 398, Poplar, MT 59255-0398. *Phone:* 406-768-6329. *Web site:* http://www.fpcc.edu/.

Little Big Horn College
Crow Agency, Montana

Freshman Application Contact Ms. Ann Bullis, Dean of Student Services, Little Big Horn College, Box 370, 1 Forest Lane, Crow Agency, MT 59022-0370. *Phone:* 406-638-2228 Ext. 50. *Web site:* http://www.lbhc.edu/.

Miles Community College
Miles City, Montana

Freshman Application Contact Mr. Jake Samuelson, Admissions Representative, Miles Community College, 2715 Dickinson Street, Miles City, MT 59301. *Phone:* 406-874-6178. *Toll-free phone:* 800-541-9281. *E-mail:* samuelsonj@milescc.edu. *Web site:* http://www.milescc.edu/.

Montana State University–Great Falls College of Technology
Great Falls, Montana

- **State-supported** 2-year, founded 1969, part of Montana University System
- **Small-town** 40-acre campus
- **Endowment** $11,300
- **Coed,** 1,874 undergraduate students, 52% full-time, 71% women, 29% men

Undergraduates 973 full-time, 901 part-time. Students come from 30 states and territories; 1 other country; 3% are from out of state; 1% Black or African American, non-Hispanic/Latino; 4% Hispanic/Latino; 1% Asian, non-Hispanic/Latino; 0.3% Native Hawaiian or other Pacific Islander, non-Hispanic/Latino; 6% American Indian or Alaska Native, non-Hispanic/Latino; 4% Two or more races, non-Hispanic/Latino; 1% Race/ethnicity unknown; 9% transferred in.
Freshmen *Admission:* 419 applied, 404 admitted, 338 enrolled. *Average high school GPA:* 2.71.
Faculty *Total:* 159, 27% full-time, 9% with terminal degrees. *Student/faculty ratio:* 16:1.
Majors Accounting technology and bookkeeping; business administration and management; computer systems networking and telecommunications; dental hygiene; dietetic technology; emergency medical technology (EMT paramedic); energy management and systems technology; entrepreneurship; fire science/firefighting; graphic design; health information/medical records technology; information technology; interior design; liberal arts and sciences and humanities related; licensed practical/vocational nurse training; medical/clinical assistant; medical insurance/medical billing; medical transcription; physical therapy technology; radiologic technology/science; respiratory care therapy; surgical technology; web page, digital/multimedia and information resources design; welding technology.
Academics *Calendar:* semesters. *Degree:* certificates and associate. *Special study options:* academic remediation for entering students, advanced placement credit, distance learning, double majors, English as a second language, independent study, internships, off-campus study, part-time degree program, services for LD students, summer session for credit.
Library Weaver Library with 8,813 titles, 43,202 serial subscriptions, 972 audiovisual materials, an OPAC, a Web page.
Student Life *Housing:* college housing not available. *Activities and Organizations:* The Associated Students of Montana State University - Great Falls (ASMSUGF), Native American Students, Veteran's Club - MSUGF, Anime Club, Lambda - MSUGF. *Campus security:* 24-hour emergency response devices.
Costs (2011–12) *Tuition:* state resident $2496 full-time, $104 per credit hour part-time; nonresident $8748 full-time, $364 per credit hour part-time. Full-time tuition and fees vary according to course load and program. Part-time tuition and fees vary according to course load and program. *Required fees:* $573 full-time, $20 per credit hour part-time, $50 per term part-time. *Payment plan:* deferred payment. *Waivers:* minority students, senior citizens, and employees or children of employees.
Financial Aid Of all full-time matriculated undergraduates who enrolled in 2010, 822 applied for aid, 751 were judged to have need, 16 had their need fully met. 49 Federal Work-Study jobs (averaging $2000). 26 state and other part-time jobs (averaging $2000). In 2010, 2 non-need-based awards were made. *Average percent of need met:* 68%. *Average financial aid package:* $9252. *Average need-based loan:* $3092. *Average need-based gift aid:* $5547. *Average non-need-based aid:* $375. *Average indebtedness upon graduation:* $15,052.
Applying *Options:* early admission. *Application fee:* $30. *Required:* high school transcript, proof of immunization. *Application deadlines:* rolling (freshmen), rolling (out-of-state freshmen), rolling (transfers). *Notification:* continuous (freshmen), continuous (out-of-state freshmen), continuous (transfers).
Freshman Application Contact Ms. Dana Freshly, Admissions, Montana State University–Great Falls College of Technology, 2100 16th Avenue South, Great Falls, MT 59405. *Phone:* 406-771-4300. *Toll-free phone:* 800-446-2698. *Fax:* 406-771-4329. *E-mail:* dfreshly@msugf.edu. *Web site:* http://www.msugf.edu/.

Salish Kootenai College

Pablo, Montana

Freshman Application Contact Ms. Jackie Moran, Admissions Officer, Salish Kootenai College, PO Box 70, Pablo, MT 59855-0117. *Phone:* 406-275-4866. *Fax:* 406-275-4810. *E-mail:* jackie_moran@skc.edu. *Web site:* http://www.skc.edu/.

Stone Child College

Box Elder, Montana

Director of Admissions Mr. Ted Whitford, Director of Admissions/Registrar, Stone Child College, RR1, Box 1082, Box Elder, MT 59521. *Phone:* 406-395-4313 Ext. 110. *E-mail:* uanet337@quest.ocsc.montana.edu. *Web site:* http://www.stonechild.edu/.

The University of Montana–Helena College of Technology

Helena, Montana

- **State-supported** 2-year, founded 1939, part of Montana University System
- **Small-town** campus
- **Coed,** 1,679 undergraduate students, 48% full-time, 57% women, 43% men

Undergraduates 813 full-time, 866 part-time. Students come from 10 states and territories; 2% are from out of state; 0.5% Black or African American, non-Hispanic/Latino; 3% Hispanic/Latino; 1% Asian, non-Hispanic/Latino; 5% American Indian or Alaska Native, non-Hispanic/Latino; 0.7% Two or more races, non-Hispanic/Latino; 6% Race/ethnicity unknown; 7% transferred in. *Retention:* 61% of full-time freshmen returned.

Freshmen *Admission:* 414 applied, 360 admitted, 276 enrolled.

Faculty *Total:* 140, 26% full-time. *Student/faculty ratio:* 15:1.

Majors Accounting technology and bookkeeping; airframe mechanics and aircraft maintenance technology; automobile/automotive mechanics technology; business automation/technology/data entry; carpentry; computer programming; diesel mechanics technology; executive assistant/executive secretary; fire science/firefighting; general studies; legal administrative assistant/secretary; licensed practical/vocational nurse training; machine tool technology; medical administrative assistant and medical secretary; office occupations and clerical services; welding technology.

Academics *Calendar:* semesters. *Degree:* certificates and associate. *Special study options:* academic remediation for entering students, adult/continuing education programs, distance learning, double majors, internships, part-time degree program, services for LD students, summer session for credit.

Library UM-Helena Library with 95,845 titles, 38,794 serial subscriptions, 6,219 audiovisual materials, an OPAC, a Web page.

Student Life *Housing:* college housing not available. *Activities and Organizations:* Student Senate, Circle K, College Christian Fellowship, Phi Theta Kappa. *Campus security:* late-night transport/escort service. *Student services:* personal/psychological counseling.

Costs (2012–13) *Tuition:* state resident $3030 full-time; nonresident $8326 full-time. Full-time tuition and fees vary according to course load and reciprocity agreements. Part-time tuition and fees vary according to course load and reciprocity agreements. *Required fees:* $672 full-time. *Payment plan:* installment. *Waivers:* minority students, senior citizens, and employees or children of employees.

Financial Aid Of all full-time matriculated undergraduates who enrolled in 2008, 445 applied for aid, 334 were judged to have need. 42 Federal Work-Study jobs (averaging $1549). 22 state and other part-time jobs (averaging $1476). In 2008, 37 non-need-based awards were made. *Average financial aid package:* $6368. *Average need-based loan:* $3428. *Average need-based gift aid:* $3111. *Average non-need-based aid:* $1769. *Average indebtedness upon graduation:* $14,068.

Applying *Options:* early admission, deferred entrance. *Application fee:* $30. *Required for some:* high school transcript. *Application deadlines:* rolling (freshmen), rolling (transfers).

Freshman Application Contact Mr. James Bisom, Admissions Representative/Recruiter, The University of Montana–Helena College of Technology, 1115 North Roberts Street, Helena, MT 59601. *Phone:* 406-444-5436. *Toll-free phone:* 800-241-4882. *Web site:* http://www.umhelena.edu/.

NEBRASKA

Central Community College–Columbus Campus

Columbus, Nebraska

- **State and locally supported** 2-year, founded 1968, part of Central Community College
- **Small-town** 90-acre campus
- **Coed,** 2,872 undergraduate students, 18% full-time, 59% women, 41% men

Undergraduates 523 full-time, 2,349 part-time. Students come from 38 states and territories; 24 other countries; 2% Black or African American, non-Hispanic/Latino; 13% Hispanic/Latino; 0.8% Asian, non-Hispanic/Latino; 0.2% Native Hawaiian or other Pacific Islander, non-Hispanic/Latino; 0.2% American Indian or Alaska Native, non-Hispanic/Latino; 0.9% Two or more races, non-Hispanic/Latino; 4% Race/ethnicity unknown; 4% transferred in; 17% live on campus.

Freshmen *Admission:* 347 enrolled.

Faculty *Total:* 99, 46% full-time.

Majors Administrative assistant and secretarial science; agricultural business and management; automobile/automotive mechanics technology; business administration and management; child-care and support services management; commercial and advertising art; computer and information sciences; criminal justice/safety; drafting and design technology; electrical, electronic and communications engineering technology; liberal arts and sciences/liberal studies; licensed practical/vocational nurse training; machine tool technology; marketing/marketing management; medical/clinical assistant; quality control technology; welding technology.

Academics *Calendar:* semesters plus six-week summer session. *Degree:* certificates, diplomas, and associate. *Special study options:* academic remediation for entering students, accelerated degree program, adult/continuing education programs, advanced placement credit, cooperative education, distance learning, English as a second language, external degree program, independent study, internships, off-campus study, part-time degree program, services for LD students, student-designed majors, summer session for credit.

Library Learning Resources Center with 14,047 titles, 66 serial subscriptions, 12 audiovisual materials, an OPAC.

Student Life *Housing Options:* coed. Campus housing is university owned. *Activities and Organizations:* drama/theater group, choral group, Phi Theta Kappa, Drama Club, Art Club, Cantari, Chorale. *Campus security:* 24-hour emergency response devices and patrols, controlled dormitory access, night security. *Student services:* personal/psychological counseling, women's center.

Athletics Member NJCAA. *Intercollegiate sports:* basketball M(s), golf M(s), softball W(s), volleyball W(s). *Intramural sports:* basketball M/W, football M, softball M/W, table tennis M/W, volleyball M/W.

Costs (2011–12) *Tuition:* state resident $1872 full-time, $78 per credit part-time; nonresident $2808 full-time, $117 per credit part-time. *Required fees:* $192 full-time, $8 per credit part-time. *Room and board:* $5734. Room and board charges vary according to board plan. *Payment plan:* deferred payment. *Waivers:* employees or children of employees.

Applying *Options:* electronic application, early admission. *Required:* high school transcript. *Required for some:* 3 letters of recommendation, interview. *Application deadlines:* rolling (freshmen), rolling (out-of-state freshmen), rolling (transfers). *Notification:* continuous (freshmen), continuous (out-of-state freshmen), continuous (transfers).

Freshman Application Contact Ms. Erica Leffler, Admissions/Recruiting Coordinator, Central Community College–Columbus Campus, PO Box 1027, Columbus, NE 68602-1027. *Phone:* 402-562-1296. *Toll-free phone:* 877-CCC-0780. *Fax:* 402-562-1201. *E-mail:* eleffler@cccneb.edu. *Web site:* http://www.cccneb.edu/.

Central Community College–Grand Island Campus

Grand Island, Nebraska

- **State and locally supported** 2-year, founded 1976, part of Central Community College
- **Small-town** 80-acre campus
- **Coed,** 3,469 undergraduate students, 12% full-time, 67% women, 33% men

Undergraduates 423 full-time, 3,046 part-time. Students come from 24 other countries; 2% Black or African American, non-Hispanic/Latino; 13% Hispanic/Latino; 1% Asian, non-Hispanic/Latino; 0.2% Native Hawaiian or other Pacific Islander, non-Hispanic/Latino; 0.5% American Indian or Alaska Native, non-Hispanic/Latino; 1% Two or more races, non-Hispanic/Latino; 4% Race/ethnicity unknown; 3% transferred in; 10% live on campus.

Freshmen *Admission:* 382 enrolled.
Faculty *Total:* 112. *Student/faculty ratio:* 15:1.
Majors Administrative assistant and secretarial science; automobile/automotive mechanics technology; business administration and management; child-care and support services management; child development; clinical/medical social work; computer and information sciences; criminal justice/safety; drafting and design technology; electrical, electronic and communications engineering technology; heating, air conditioning, ventilation and refrigeration maintenance technology; legal assistant/paralegal; liberal arts and sciences/liberal studies; licensed practical/vocational nurse training; medical/clinical assistant; network and system administration; registered nursing/registered nurse; welding technology.
Academics *Calendar:* semesters plus six-week summer session. *Degree:* certificates, diplomas, and associate. *Special study options:* academic remediation for entering students, accelerated degree program, adult/continuing education programs, advanced placement credit, cooperative education, distance learning, English as a second language, external degree program, independent study, internships, off-campus study, part-time degree program, services for LD students, student-designed majors, summer session for credit.
Library Central Community College–Grand Island Campus Library with 8,023 titles, 144 serial subscriptions, 142 audiovisual materials, an OPAC, a Web page.
Student Life *Housing Options:* coed. Campus housing is provided by a third party. Freshman applicants given priority for college housing. *Activities and Organizations:* Mid-Nebraska Users of Computers, Student Activities Organization, intramurals, TRIO, Phi Theta Kappa. *Student services:* personal/psychological counseling.
Athletics *Intramural sports:* bowling M/W, softball M/W, table tennis M/W, volleyball M/W.
Costs (2011–12) *Tuition:* state resident $1872 full-time, $78 per credit part-time; nonresident $2808 full-time, $117 per credit part-time. *Required fees:* $192 full-time, $8 per credit part-time. *Payment plan:* deferred payment. *Waivers:* employees or children of employees.
Applying *Options:* electronic application, early admission. *Required:* high school transcript. *Required for some:* 3 letters of recommendation, interview. *Application deadlines:* rolling (freshmen), rolling (out-of-state freshmen), rolling (transfers). *Notification:* continuous (freshmen), continuous (out-of-state freshmen), continuous (transfers).
Freshman Application Contact Michelle Lubken, Admissions Director, Central Community College–Grand Island Campus, PO Box 4903, Grand Island, NE 68802-4903. *Phone:* 308-398-7406 Ext. 406. *Toll-free phone:* 877-CCC-0780. *Fax:* 308-398-7398. *E-mail:* mlubken@cccneb.edu. *Web site:* http://www.cccneb.edu/.

Central Community College–Hastings Campus
Hastings, Nebraska

- **State and locally supported** 2-year, founded 1966, part of Central Community College
- **Small-town** 644-acre campus
- **Coed,** 2,966 undergraduate students, 34% full-time, 57% women, 43% men

Undergraduates 1,001 full-time, 1,965 part-time. Students come from 38 states and territories; 24 other countries; 0.7% Black or African American, non-Hispanic/Latino; 7% Hispanic/Latino; 0.9% Asian, non-Hispanic/Latino; 0.1% Native Hawaiian or other Pacific Islander, non-Hispanic/Latino; 0.4% American Indian or Alaska Native, non-Hispanic/Latino; 1% Two or more races, non-Hispanic/Latino; 5% Race/ethnicity unknown; 5% transferred in.
Freshmen *Admission:* 508 enrolled.
Faculty *Total:* 109, 45% full-time. *Student/faculty ratio:* 15:1.
Majors Administrative assistant and secretarial science; agricultural business and management; applied horticulture/horticulture operations; autobody/collision and repair technology; automobile/automotive mechanics technology; building/construction finishing, management, and inspection related; business administration and management; child-care and support services management; child development; clinical/medical laboratory technology; clinical/medical social work; commercial and advertising art; construction engineering technology; criminal justice/safety; dental assisting; dental hygiene; diesel mechanics technology; drafting and design technology; electrical, electronic and communications engineering technology; electrician; graphic and printing equipment operation/production; health information/medical records technology; heating, air conditioning, ventilation and refrigeration maintenance technology; hotel/motel administration; industrial mechanics and maintenance technology; industrial technology; liberal arts and sciences/liberal studies; library and archives assisting; logistics, materials, and supply chain management; machine tool technology; medical/clinical assistant; quality control technology; radio and television broadcasting technology; restaurant, culinary, and catering man-

agement; truck and bus driver/commercial vehicle operation/instruction; vehicle and vehicle parts and accessories marketing; welding technology.
Academics *Calendar:* semesters plus six-week summer session. *Degree:* certificates, diplomas, and associate. *Special study options:* academic remediation for entering students, accelerated degree program, adult/continuing education programs, advanced placement credit, cooperative education, distance learning, English as a second language, external degree program, independent study, internships, off-campus study, part-time degree program, services for LD students, student-designed majors, summer session for credit.
Library Nuckolls Library with 7,201 titles, 44 serial subscriptions, 11 audiovisual materials, an OPAC.
Student Life *Housing Options:* coed, men-only, women-only. Campus housing is university owned. *Activities and Organizations:* student-run radio station, Student Senate, Central Dormitory Council, Judicial Board, Seeds and Soils, Young Farmers and Ranchers. *Campus security:* 24-hour emergency response devices and patrols, controlled dormitory access. *Student services:* personal/psychological counseling, women's center.
Athletics *Intramural sports:* basketball M/W, bowling M/W, golf M/W, softball M/W, volleyball M/W, weight lifting M/W.
Costs (2011–12) *Tuition:* state resident $1872 full-time, $78 per credit part-time; nonresident $2808 full-time, $117 per credit part-time. *Required fees:* $192 full-time. *Room and board:* $5734. Room and board charges vary according to board plan. *Payment plan:* deferred payment. *Waivers:* employees or children of employees.
Financial Aid Of all full-time matriculated undergraduates who enrolled in 2010, 70 Federal Work-Study jobs (averaging $1200). 12 state and other part-time jobs (averaging $1250).
Applying *Options:* electronic application, early admission. *Required:* high school transcript. *Required for some:* 3 letters of recommendation, interview. *Application deadlines:* rolling (freshmen), rolling (out-of-state freshmen), rolling (transfers). *Notification:* continuous (freshmen), continuous (out-of-state freshmen), continuous (transfers).
Freshman Application Contact Mr. Robert Glenn, Admissions and Recruiting Director, Central Community College–Hastings Campus, PO Box 1024, East Highway 6, Hastings, NE 68902-1024. *Phone:* 402-461-2428. *Toll-free phone:* 877-CCC-0780. *E-mail:* rglenn@ccneb.edu. *Web site:* http://www.cccneb.edu/.

Creative Center
Omaha, Nebraska

- **Proprietary** primarily 2-year, founded 1993
- **Urban** 2-acre campus
- **Coed**

Faculty *Total:* 18, 22% full-time. *Student/faculty ratio:* 13:1.
Majors Computer graphics; design and visual communications; illustration.
Academics *Calendar:* semesters. *Degrees:* associate and bachelor's. *Special study options:* distance learning, part-time degree program, services for LD students.
Library Student Library plus 1 other.
Student Life *Housing:* college housing not available.
Costs (2011–12) *Tuition:* $23,600 full-time. Full-time tuition and fees vary according to course load, program, and student level. Part-time tuition and fees vary according to course load, program, and student level.
Applying *Application fee:* $100. *Required:* essay or personal statement, high school transcript, 1 letter of recommendation, interview, portfolio. *Application deadlines:* rolling (freshmen), rolling (out-of-state freshmen), rolling (transfers). *Notification:* continuous (freshmen), continuous (out-of-state freshmen), continuous (transfers).
Freshman Application Contact Mr. Richard Caldwell, Director of Admissions, Creative Center, 10850 Emmet Street, Omaha, NE 68164. *Phone:* 402-898-1000 Ext. 216. *Toll-free phone:* 888-898-1789. *Fax:* 402-898-1301. *E-mail:* rich_c@creativecenter.edu. *Web site:* http://www.creativecenter.edu/.

ITT Technical Institute
Omaha, Nebraska

- **Proprietary** primarily 2-year, founded 1991, part of ITT Educational Services, Inc.
- **Urban** campus
- **Coed**

Majors Business administration and management; communications technology; computer and information systems security; construction management; drafting and design technology; electrical, electronic and communications engineering technology; forensic science and technology; game and interactive media design; graphic communications; legal assistant/paralegal; network and system administration; project management; registered nursing/registered nurse.

Academics *Calendar:* quarters. *Degrees:* associate and bachelor's.
Student Life *Housing:* college housing not available.
Freshman Application Contact Director of Recruitment, ITT Technical Institute, 9814 M Street, Omaha, NE 68127-2056. *Phone:* 402-331-2900. *Toll-free phone:* 800-677-9260. *Web site:* http://www.itt-tech.edu/.

Kaplan University, Lincoln

Lincoln, Nebraska

Freshman Application Contact Kaplan University, Lincoln, 1821 K Street, Lincoln, NE 68501-2826. *Phone:* 402-474-5315. *Toll-free phone:* 866-527-5268 (in-state); 800-527-5268 (out-of-state). *Web site:* http://www.lincoln.kaplanuniversity.edu/.

Kaplan University, Omaha

Omaha, Nebraska

Freshman Application Contact Kaplan University, Omaha, 5425 North 103rd Street, Omaha, NE 68134. *Phone:* 402-572-8500. *Toll-free phone:* 866-527-5268 (in-state); 800-527-5268 (out-of-state). *Web site:* http://www.omaha.kaplanuniversity.edu/.

Little Priest Tribal College

Winnebago, Nebraska

Director of Admissions Ms. Karen Kemling, Director of Admissions and Records, Little Priest Tribal College, PO Box 270, Winnebago, NE 68071. *Phone:* 402-878-2380. *Web site:* http://www.littlepriest.edu/.

Metropolitan Community College

Omaha, Nebraska

Freshman Application Contact Ms. Maria Vazquez, Associate Vice President for Student Affairs, Metropolitan Community College, PO Box 3777, Omaha, NE 69103-0777. *Phone:* 402-457-2430. *Toll-free phone:* 800-228-9553. *Fax:* 402-457-2238. *E-mail:* mvazquez@mccneb.edu. *Web site:* http://www.mccneb.edu/.

Mid-Plains Community College

North Platte, Nebraska

- **District-supported** 2-year, founded 1973
- **Small-town** campus
- **Endowment** $8.1 million
- **Coed,** 2,623 undergraduate students, 38% full-time, 58% women, 42% men

Undergraduates 1,000 full-time, 1,623 part-time. Students come from 34 states and territories; 3 other countries; 8% are from out of state; 6% Black or African American, non-Hispanic/Latino; 8% Hispanic/Latino; 0.1% Asian, non-Hispanic/Latino; 0.1% Native Hawaiian or other Pacific Islander, non-Hispanic/Latino; 0.8% American Indian or Alaska Native, non-Hispanic/Latino; 1% Two or more races, non-Hispanic/Latino; 5% Race/ethnicity unknown; 1% international; 0.5% transferred in; 8% live on campus.
Freshmen *Admission:* 444 applied, 444 admitted, 444 enrolled.
Faculty *Total:* 285, 24% full-time, 2% with terminal degrees. *Student/faculty ratio:* 11:1.
Majors Administrative assistant and secretarial science; autobody/collision and repair technology; automobile/automotive mechanics technology; building/construction finishing, management, and inspection related; business administration and management; clinical/medical laboratory technology; commercial and advertising art; computer and information sciences; construction engineering technology; dental assisting; diesel mechanics technology; fire science/firefighting; heating, air conditioning, ventilation and refrigeration maintenance technology; liberal arts and sciences/liberal studies; licensed practical/vocational nurse training; registered nursing/registered nurse; transportation and materials moving related; welding technology.
Academics *Calendar:* semesters. *Degree:* certificates, diplomas, and associate. *Special study options:* academic remediation for entering students, accelerated degree program, adult/continuing education programs, advanced placement credit, cooperative education, distance learning, double majors, English as a second language, external degree program, independent study, internships, part-time degree program, services for LD students, summer session for credit.
Library McDonald-Belton L R C plus 1 other with 79,334 titles, 124 serial subscriptions, 1,803 audiovisual materials, an OPAC, a Web page.
Student Life *Housing Options:* coed, disabled students. Campus housing is university owned. *Activities and Organizations:* drama/theater group, student-run newspaper, choral group, Student Senate, Phi Theta Kappa, Phi Beta

Lambda, Intercollegiate Athletics, MPCC Student Nurses Association, national fraternities, national sororities. *Campus security:* controlled dormitory access, patrols by trained security personnel.
Athletics Member NJCAA. *Intercollegiate sports:* baseball M(s), basketball M(s)/W(s), golf M(s), softball W(s), volleyball W(s). *Intramural sports:* baseball M, basketball M/W, softball W, volleyball W.
Standardized Tests *Required for some:* COMPASS. *Recommended:* ACT (for admission).
Costs (2011–12) *Tuition:* state resident $2220 full-time, $74 per credit hour part-time; nonresident $2880 full-time, $96 per credit hour part-time. Full-time tuition and fees vary according to reciprocity agreements. Part-time tuition and fees vary according to reciprocity agreements. *Required fees:* $450 full-time, $15 per credit hour part-time. *Room and board:* $5300. Room and board charges vary according to board plan, housing facility, and location. *Payment plan:* installment. *Waivers:* senior citizens and employees or children of employees.
Financial Aid Of all full-time matriculated undergraduates who enrolled in 2010, 1,021 applied for aid, 896 were judged to have need, 114 had their need fully met. 60 Federal Work-Study jobs (averaging $779). In 2010, 82 non-need-based awards were made. *Average percent of need met:* 64%. *Average financial aid package:* $5525. *Average need-based loan:* $2477. *Average need-based gift aid:* $4497. *Average non-need-based aid:* $1274. *Average indebtedness upon graduation:* $8039.
Applying *Options:* electronic application, deferred entrance. *Required:* high school transcript. *Required for some:* 2 letters of recommendation, interview. *Application deadlines:* rolling (freshmen), rolling (transfers). *Notification:* continuous (freshmen), continuous (transfers).
Freshman Application Contact Mr. Michael Driskell, Area Recruiter, Mid-Plains Community College, 1101 Halligan Dr, North Platte, NE 69101. *Phone:* 308-535-3709. *Toll-free phone:* 800-658-4308 (in-state); 800-658-4348 (out-of-state). *Fax:* 308-534-5767. *E-mail:* driskellm@mpcc.edu. *Web site:* http://www.mpcc.edu/.

Myotherapy Institute

Lincoln, Nebraska

Freshman Application Contact Admissions Office, Myotherapy Institute, 6020 South 58th Street, Lincoln, NE 68516. *Phone:* 402-421-7410. *Web site:* http://www.myotherapy.edu/.

Nebraska College of Technical Agriculture

Curtis, Nebraska

Freshman Application Contact Kevin Martin, Assistant Admissions Coordinator, Nebraska College of Technical Agriculture, 404 East 7th Street, Curtis, NE 69025, NE 69025. *Phone:* 308-367-4124. *Toll-free phone:* 800-3CURTIS. *Web site:* http://www.ncta.unl.edu/.

Nebraska Indian Community College

Macy, Nebraska

Director of Admissions Ms. Theresa Henry, Admission Counselor, Nebraska Indian Community College, PO Box 428, Macy, NE 68039-0428. *Phone:* 402-837-5078. *Web site:* http://www.thenicc.edu/.

Northeast Community College

Norfolk, Nebraska

- **State and locally supported** 2-year, founded 1973, part of Nebraska Coordinating Commission for Postsecondary Education
- **Small-town** 205-acre campus
- **Coed,** 5,161 undergraduate students, 42% full-time, 46% women, 54% men

Undergraduates 2,169 full-time, 2,992 part-time. 6% are from out of state; 1% Black or African American, non-Hispanic/Latino; 6% Hispanic/Latino; 0.3% Asian, non-Hispanic/Latino; 0.9% American Indian or Alaska Native, non-Hispanic/Latino; 0.7% Two or more races, non-Hispanic/Latino; 3% Race/ethnicity unknown; 0.6% international; 5% transferred in; 6% live on campus. *Retention:* 65% of full-time freshmen returned.
Freshmen *Admission:* 1,644 applied, 1,644 admitted, 894 enrolled.
Faculty *Total:* 381, 30% full-time, 26% with terminal degrees. *Student/faculty ratio:* 16:1.
Majors Accounting; administrative assistant and secretarial science; agribusiness; agricultural mechanics and equipment technology; agricultural mechanization; agriculture; agriculture and agriculture operations related; agronomy and crop science; animal sciences; applied horticulture/horticultural business services related; applied horticulture/horticultural operations; architectural

drafting and CAD/CADD; art; autobody/collision and repair technology; auto-mobile/automotive mechanics technology; banking and financial support services; biological and biomedical sciences related; biology/biological sciences; building/construction finishing, management, and inspection related; business administration and management; business operations support and secretarial services related; chemistry; computer and information sciences; computer and information sciences and support services related; computer programming; computer programming (specific applications); computer science; corrections; criminal justice/police science; crop production; culinary arts; dairy science; diesel mechanics technology; dramatic/theater arts; early childhood education; education; electrician; electromechanical technology; elementary education; emergency medical technology (EMT paramedic); energy management and systems technology; engineering; English; entrepreneurship; farm and ranch management; finance and financial management services related; food service systems administration; general studies; graphic design; health aide; health and medical administrative services related; health and physical education/fitness; health/medical preparatory programs related; heating, air conditioning, ventilation and refrigeration maintenance technology; industrial mechanics and maintenance technology; international business/trade/commerce; journalism; legal administrative assistant/secretary; liberal arts and sciences/liberal studies; library and archives assisting; licensed practical/vocational nurse training; lineworker; livestock management; marketing/marketing management; mass communication/media; mathematics; medical administrative assistant and medical secretary; medical insurance coding; medical radiologic technology; medium/heavy vehicle and truck technology; merchandising; music management; music performance; music teacher education; office management; office occupations and clerical services; physical therapy technology; physics; pre-dentistry studies; pre-engineering; pre-law studies; premedical studies; prenursing studies; pre-pharmacy studies; pre-veterinary studies; psychology; radio and television broadcasting technology; real estate; recording arts technology; registered nursing/registered nurse; rhetoric and composition; secondary education; social sciences; surgical technology; veterinary/animal health technology; welding technology.

Academics *Calendar:* semesters. *Degree:* certificates, diplomas, and associate. *Special study options:* academic remediation for entering students, adult/continuing education programs, advanced placement credit, cooperative education, distance learning, double majors, English as a second language, internships, off-campus study, part-time degree program, services for LD students, summer session for credit.

Library Library Resource Center plus 1 other with an OPAC, a Web page.

Student Life *Housing Options:* disabled students. Campus housing is university owned. *Activities and Organizations:* drama/theater group, student-run newspaper, radio and television station, choral group. *Campus security:* 24-hour patrols, controlled dormitory access. *Student services:* personal/psychological counseling.

Athletics Member NJCAA. *Intercollegiate sports:* basketball M(s)/W(s), cheerleading W(s). *Intramural sports:* basketball M/W, bowling M/W, football M/W, soccer M/W, softball M/W, table tennis M/W, volleyball M/W.

Costs (2011–12) *Tuition:* state resident $2190 full-time, $73 per credit hour part-time; nonresident $2738 full-time, $91 per credit hour part-time. *Required fees:* $465 full-time. *Room and board:* $5936; room only: $3080. Room and board charges vary according to board plan and housing facility.

Financial Aid Of all full-time matriculated undergraduates who enrolled in 2010, 1,821 applied for aid, 1,512 were judged to have need, 240 had their need fully met. 81 Federal Work-Study jobs (averaging $1083). In 2010, 49 non-need-based awards were made. *Average percent of need met:* 56%. *Average financial aid package:* $6166. *Average need-based loan:* $2885. *Average need-based gift aid:* $3979. *Average non-need-based aid:* $1146. *Average indebtedness upon graduation:* $10,487.

Applying *Options:* electronic application, early admission. *Required for some:* high school transcript, minimum 2.0 GPA, 3 letters of recommendation, interview. *Recommended:* high school transcript. *Application deadlines:* rolling (freshmen), rolling (out-of-state freshmen), rolling (transfers). *Notification:* continuous (freshmen), continuous (out-of-state freshmen), continuous (transfers).

Freshman Application Contact Maureen Baker, Dean of Students, Northeast Community College, 801 East Benjamin Avenue, PO Box 469, Norfolk, NE 68702-0469. *Phone:* 402-844-7258. *Toll-free phone:* 800-348-9033 Ext. 7260. *Fax:* 402-844-7403. *E-mail:* admission@northeast.edu. *Web site:* http://www.northeast.edu/.

Omaha School of Massage Therapy and Healthcare of Herzing University
Omaha, Nebraska

Admissions Office Contact Omaha School of Massage Therapy and Healthcare of Herzing University, 9748 Park Drive, Omaha, NE 68127. *Web site:* http://www.osmhc.com/.

Southeast Community College, Beatrice Campus
Beatrice, Nebraska

Freshman Application Contact Admissions Office, Southeast Community College, Beatrice Campus, 4771 West Scott Road, Beatrice, NE 68310. *Phone:* 402-228-3468. *Toll-free phone:* 800-233-5027. *Fax:* 402-228-2218. *Web site:* http://www.southeast.edu/.

Southeast Community College, Lincoln Campus
Lincoln, Nebraska

Freshman Application Contact Admissions Office, Southeast Community College, Lincoln Campus, 8800 O Street, Lincoln, NE 68520-1299. *Phone:* 402-471-3333. *Toll-free phone:* 800-642-4075. *Fax:* 402-437-2404. *Web site:* http://www.southeast.edu/.

Southeast Community College, Milford Campus
Milford, Nebraska

Freshman Application Contact Admissions Office, Southeast Community College, Milford Campus, 600 State Street, Milford, NE 68405. *Phone:* 402-761-2131. *Toll-free phone:* 800-933-7223. *Fax:* 402-761-2324. *Web site:* http://www.southeast.edu/.

Vatterott College
Omaha, Nebraska

Freshman Application Contact Admissions Office, Vatterott College, 5318 South 136th Street, Omaha, NE 68137. *Phone:* 402-891-9411. *Toll-free phone:* 888-553-6627. *Fax:* 402-891-9413. *Web site:* http://www.vatterott-college.edu/.

Western Nebraska Community College
Sidney, Nebraska

Director of Admissions Mr. Troy Archuleta, Admissions and Recruitment Director, Western Nebraska Community College, 371 College Drive, Sidney, NE 69162. *Phone:* 308-635-6015. *Toll-free phone:* 800-222-9682. *E-mail:* rhovey@wncc.net. *Web site:* http://www.wncc.net/.

NEVADA

Anthem Institute–Las Vegas
Las Vegas, Nevada

Freshman Application Contact Admissions Office, Anthem Institute–Las Vegas, 2320 South Rancho Drive, Las Vegas, NV 89102. *Phone:* 702-385-6700. *Toll-free phone:* 855-331-7762. *Web site:* http://anthem.edu/las-vegas-nevada/.

Career College of Northern Nevada
Sparks, Nevada

Freshman Application Contact Ms. Laura Goldhammer, Director of Admissions, Career College of Northern Nevada, 1421 Pullman Drive, Sparks, NV 89434. *Phone:* 775-856-2266 Ext. 11. *Fax:* 775-856-0935. *E-mail:* lgoldhammer@ccnn4u.com. *Web site:* http://www.ccnn.edu/.

Carrington College - Las Vegas
Las Vegas, Nevada

Admissions Office Contact Carrington College - Las Vegas, 5740 South Eastern Avenue, Las Vegas, NV 89119. *Web site:* http://carrington.edu/.

Carrington College - Reno

Reno, Nevada

Admissions Office Contact Carrington College - Reno, 5580 Kietzke Lane, Reno, NV 89511. *Web site:* http://carrington.edu/.

College of Southern Nevada

North Las Vegas, Nevada

Freshman Application Contact Admissions and Records, College of Southern Nevada, 3200 East Cheyenne Avenue, North Las Vegas, NV 89030-4296. *Phone:* 702-651-4060. *Web site:* http://www.csn.edu/.

Everest College

Henderson, Nevada

Admissions Office Contact Everest College, 170 North Stephanie Street, 1st Floor, Henderson, NV 89074. *Toll-free phone:* 888-741-4270. *Web site:* http://www.everest.edu/campus/henderson/.

Great Basin College

Elko, Nevada

- **State-supported** primarily 2-year, founded 1967, part of University and Community College System of Nevada
- **Small-town** 45-acre campus
- **Endowment** $187,761
- **Coed**

Undergraduates 1,141 full-time, 2,550 part-time. Students come from 13 states and territories; 3% are from out of state; 5% live on campus. *Retention:* 77% of full-time freshmen returned.
Faculty *Student/faculty ratio:* 15:1.
Academics *Calendar:* semesters. *Degrees:* certificates, associate, bachelor's, and postbachelor's certificates. *Special study options:* academic remediation for entering students, accelerated degree program, adult/continuing education programs, cooperative education, distance learning, double majors, English as a second language, external degree program, independent study, off-campus study, part-time degree program, services for LD students, summer session for credit.
Student Life *Campus security:* late-night transport/escort service, evening patrols by trained security personnel.
Costs (2011–12) *Tuition:* state resident $2243 full-time, $69 per credit hour part-time; nonresident $8738 full-time, $146 per credit hour part-time. Full-time tuition and fees vary according to course level. Part-time tuition and fees vary according to course level. *Required fees:* $6 per credit hour part-time. *Room and board:* room only: $2299. Room and board charges vary according to housing facility.
Financial Aid Of all full-time matriculated undergraduates who enrolled in 2010, 35 Federal Work-Study jobs (averaging $1000). 50 state and other part-time jobs (averaging $1800).
Applying *Options:* electronic application, early admission, deferred entrance. *Application fee:* $10.
Freshman Application Contact Ms. Janice King, Director of Admissions and Registrar, Great Basin College, 1500 College Parkway, Elko, NV 89801-3348. *Phone:* 775-753-2361. *Fax:* 775-753-2311. *E-mail:* janicek@gwmail.gbcnv.edu. *Web site:* http://www.gbcnv.edu/.

ITT Technical Institute

Henderson, Nevada

- **Proprietary** primarily 2-year, founded 1997, part of ITT Educational Services, Inc.
- **Coed**

Majors Business administration and management; communications technology; computer and information systems security; computer software engineering; computer software technology; construction management; criminal justice/law enforcement administration; drafting and design technology; electrical, electronic and communications engineering technology; forensic science and technology; game and interactive media design; graphic communications; legal assistant/paralegal; network and system administration; project management; registered nursing/registered nurse.
Academics *Degrees:* associate and bachelor's.
Student Life *Housing:* college housing not available.
Financial Aid Of all full-time matriculated undergraduates who enrolled in 2010, 6 Federal Work-Study jobs (averaging $5000).
Freshman Application Contact Director of Recruitment, ITT Technical Institute, 168 North Gibson Road, Henderson, NV 89014. *Phone:* 702-558-5404. *Toll-free phone:* 800-488-8459. *Web site:* http://www.itt-tech.edu/.

ITT Technical Institute

North Las Vegas, Nevada

- **Proprietary** primarily 2-year, part of ITT Educational Services, Inc.
- **Coed**

Majors Business administration and management; communications technology; computer and information systems security; computer software technology; criminal justice/law enforcement administration; drafting and design technology; electrical, electronic and communications engineering technology; forensic science and technology; game and interactive media design; graphic communications; legal assistant/paralegal; network and system administration; project management.
Academics *Calendar:* quarters. *Degrees:* associate and bachelor's.
Freshman Application Contact Director of Recruitment, ITT Technical Institute, 3825 W. Cheyenne Avenue, Suite 600, North Las Vegas, NV 89032. *Phone:* 702-240-0967. *Toll-free phone:* 877-832-8442. *Web site:* http://www.itt-tech.edu/.

Kaplan College, Las Vegas Campus

Las Vegas, Nevada

- **Proprietary** 2-year, founded 1990
- **Coed**

Majors Criminal justice/law enforcement administration; health information/medical records technology; radiologic technology/science; registered nursing/registered nurse.
Academics *Degree:* diplomas and associate.
Freshman Application Contact Admissions Office, Kaplan College, Las Vegas Campus, 3535 West Sahara Avenue, Las Vegas, NV 89102. *Phone:* 702-368-2338. *Toll-free phone:* 800-935-1857. *Web site:* http://las-vegas.kaplancollege.com/.

Le Cordon Bleu College of Culinary Arts, Las Vegas

Las Vegas, Nevada

Freshman Application Contact Admissions Office, Le Cordon Bleu College of Culinary Arts, Las Vegas, 1451 Center Crossing Road, Las Vegas, NV 89144. *Toll-free phone:* 888-551-8222. *Web site:* http://www.vegasculinary.com/.

Pima Medical Institute

Las Vegas, Nevada

- **Proprietary** primarily 2-year, founded 2003, part of Vocational Training Institutes, Inc.
- **Urban** campus
- **Coed**

Academics *Calendar:* modular. *Degrees:* certificates, associate, and bachelor's. *Special study options:* advanced placement credit, distance learning, internships.
Standardized Tests *Required:* Wonderlic Scholastic Level Exam (for admission).
Applying *Required:* interview. *Required for some:* essay or personal statement, high school transcript.
Freshman Application Contact Admissions Office, Pima Medical Institute, 3333 East Flamingo Road, Las Vegas, NV 89121. *Phone:* 702-458-9650 Ext. 202. *Toll-free phone:* 800-477-PIMA. *Web site:* http://www.pmi.edu/.

Truckee Meadows Community College

Reno, Nevada

- **State-supported** 2-year, founded 1971, part of Nevada System of Higher Education
- **Suburban** 63-acre campus
- **Endowment** $9.0 million
- **Coed,** 12,587 undergraduate students, 28% full-time, 56% women, 44% men

Undergraduates 3,530 full-time, 9,057 part-time. Students come from 18 states and territories; 7% are from out of state; 3% Black or African American, non-Hispanic/Latino; 19% Hispanic/Latino; 5% Asian, non-Hispanic/Latino; 1% Native Hawaiian or other Pacific Islander, non-Hispanic/Latino; 2% American Indian or Alaska Native, non-Hispanic/Latino; 3% Two or more races, non-Hispanic/Latino; 1% Race/ethnicity unknown; 0.6% international; 5% transferred in. *Retention:* 62% of full-time freshmen returned.

Freshmen *Admission:* 3,666 applied, 3,666 admitted, 2,043 enrolled. *Test scores:* SAT critical reading scores over 500: 49%; SAT math scores over 500: 44%; SAT writing scores over 500: 34%; ACT scores over 18: 76%; SAT critical reading scores over 600: 11%; SAT math scores over 600: 9%; SAT writing scores over 600: 9%; ACT scores over 24: 12%; SAT critical reading scores over 700: 1%; SAT math scores over 700: 1%; SAT writing scores over 700: 1%; ACT scores over 30: 2%.

Faculty *Total:* 593, 30% full-time. *Student/faculty ratio:* 22:1.

Majors Administrative assistant and secretarial science; anthropology; architecture; automobile/automotive mechanics technology; biology/biological sciences; building construction technology; business administration and management; chemistry; civil engineering; computer programming; construction management; criminal justice/law enforcement administration; culinary arts; dance; dental hygiene; diesel mechanics technology; dietetics; dietetic technology; drafting and design technology; dramatic/theater arts; early childhood education; elementary education; engineering; English; entrepreneurship; environmental science; fine/studio arts; fire science/firefighting; general studies; geological and earth sciences/geosciences related; heating, ventilation, air conditioning and refrigeration engineering technology; history; landscape architecture; legal assistant/paralegal; logistics, materials, and supply chain management; manufacturing engineering technology; mathematics; mental health counseling; music; network and system administration; philosophy; physics; psychology; radiologic technology/science; registered nursing/registered nurse; special education; special education–elementary school; substance abuse/addiction counseling; veterinary/animal health technology; web/multimedia management and webmaster; welding technology.

Academics *Calendar:* semesters. *Degree:* certificates and associate. *Special study options:* academic remediation for entering students, accelerated degree program, adult/continuing education programs, advanced placement credit, distance learning, English as a second language, part-time degree program, services for LD students, summer session for credit. *ROTC:* Army (c).

Library Elizabeth Storm Library with an OPAC, a Web page.

Student Life *Housing:* college housing not available. *Activities and Organizations:* drama/theater group. *Campus security:* 24-hour emergency response devices and patrols, late-night transport/escort service. *Student services:* personal/psychological counseling.

Costs (2012–13) *Tuition:* state resident $2078 full-time, $69 per credit part-time; nonresident $5325 full-time, $146 per credit part-time. Full-time tuition and fees vary according to course load and program. Part-time tuition and fees vary according to course load and program. *Required fees:* $445 full-time, $15 per credit part-time. *Payment plans:* tuition prepayment, installment. *Waivers:* employees or children of employees.

Financial Aid Of all full-time matriculated undergraduates who enrolled in 2010, 126 Federal Work-Study jobs (averaging $5000). 368 state and other part-time jobs (averaging $5000).

Applying *Options:* early admission, deferred entrance. *Application fee:* $10. *Application deadlines:* 8/3 (freshmen), 8/3 (out-of-state freshmen), 8/3 (transfers). *Notification:* 3/1 (freshmen), 3/1 (out-of-state freshmen), 3/1 (transfers).

Freshman Application Contact Truckee Meadows Community College, 7000 Dandini Boulevard, Reno, NV 89512-3901. *Phone:* 775-3375616. *Web site:* http://www.tmcc.edu/.

Western Nevada College

Carson City, Nevada

Freshman Application Contact Admissions and Records, Western Nevada College, 2201 West College Parkway, Carson City, NV 89703. *Phone:* 775-445-2377. *Fax:* 775-445-3147. *E-mail:* wncc_aro@wncc.edu. *Web site:* http://www.wnc.edu/.

NEW HAMPSHIRE

Great Bay Community College

Portsmouth, New Hampshire

Freshman Application Contact Matt Thornton, Admissions Coordinator, Great Bay Community College, 320 Corporate Drive, Portsmouth, NH 03801. *Phone:* 603-427-7605. *Toll-free phone:* 800-522-1194. *E-mail:* askgreatbay@ccsnh.edu. *Web site:* http://www.greatbay.edu/.

Hesser College, Concord

Concord, New Hampshire

- **Proprietary** primarily 2-year
- **Coed**

Majors Accounting; business administration and management; criminal justice/law enforcement administration; liberal arts and sciences/liberal studies; physical therapy technology; psychology.

Academics *Degrees:* diplomas, associate, and bachelor's.

Freshman Application Contact Hesser College, Concord, 16 Foundry Street, Concord, NH 03301. *Phone:* 603-225-9200. *Toll-free phone:* 800-935-1824. *Web site:* http://www.hesser.edu/.

Hesser College, Manchester

Manchester, New Hampshire

- **Proprietary** primarily 2-year, founded 1900
- **Urban** campus
- **Coed**

Majors Accounting; business administration and management; communication; criminal justice/law enforcement administration; early childhood education; graphic design; legal assistant/paralegal; liberal arts and sciences/liberal studies; medical/clinical assistant; physical therapy technology; psychology.

Academics *Calendar:* semesters. *Degrees:* diplomas, associate, and bachelor's.

Financial Aid Of all full-time matriculated undergraduates who enrolled in 2010, 700 Federal Work-Study jobs (averaging $1000).

Freshman Application Contact Hesser College, Manchester, 3 Sundial Avenue, Manchester, NH 03103. *Phone:* 603-668-6660. *Toll-free phone:* 800-935-1824. *Web site:* http://www.hesser.edu/.

Hesser College, Nashua

Nashua, New Hampshire

- **Proprietary** primarily 2-year
- **Coed**

Majors Accounting; business administration and management; criminal justice/law enforcement administration; liberal arts and sciences/liberal studies; medical/clinical assistant; psychology.

Academics *Degrees:* diplomas, associate, and bachelor's.

Freshman Application Contact Hesser College, Nashua, 410 Amherst Street, Nashua, NH 03063. *Phone:* 603-883-0404. *Toll-free phone:* 800-935-1824. *Web site:* http://www.hesser.edu/.

Hesser College, Portsmouth

Portsmouth, New Hampshire

- **Proprietary** primarily 2-year
- **Coed**

Majors Accounting; business administration and management; criminal justice/law enforcement administration; early childhood education; legal assistant/paralegal; liberal arts and sciences/liberal studies; medical/clinical assistant; psychology.

Academics *Degrees:* diplomas, associate, and bachelor's.

Freshman Application Contact Hesser College, Portsmouth, 170 Commerce Way, Portsmouth, NH 03801. *Phone:* 603-436-5300. *Toll-free phone:* 800-935-1824. *Web site:* http://www.hesser.edu/.

Hesser College, Salem

Salem, New Hampshire

- **Proprietary** primarily 2-year
- **Coed**

Majors Accounting; business administration and management; criminal justice/law enforcement administration; liberal arts and sciences/liberal studies; medical/clinical assistant; psychology.

Academics *Degrees:* diplomas, associate, and bachelor's.

Freshman Application Contact Hesser College, Salem, 11 Manor Parkway, Salem, NH 03079. *Phone:* 603-898-3480. *Toll-free phone:* 800-935-1824. *Web site:* http://www.hesser.edu/.

Lakes Region Community College

Laconia, New Hampshire

Director of Admissions Wayne Fraser, Director of Admissions, Lakes Region Community College, 379 Belmont Road, Laconia, NH 03246. *Phone:* 603-524-3207 Ext. 766. *Toll-free phone:* 800-357-2992. *E-mail:* wfraser@ccsnh.edu. *Web site:* http://www.lrcc.edu/.

Manchester Community College

Manchester, New Hampshire

Freshman Application Contact Ms. Jacquie Poirier, Coordinator of Admissions, Manchester Community College, 1066 Front Street, Manchester, NH 03102-8518. *Phone:* 603-668-6706 Ext. 283. *Toll-free phone:* 800-924-3445. *E-mail:* jpoirier@nhctc.edu. *Web site:* http://www.manchestercommunitycollege.edu/.

Nashua Community College

Nashua, New Hampshire

- **State-supported** 2-year, founded 1967, part of Community College System of New Hampshire
- **Urban** 66-acre campus with easy access to Boston
- **Coed**

Undergraduates 950 full-time, 1,150 part-time.
Academics *Calendar:* semesters. *Degree:* certificates and associate. *Special study options:* academic remediation for entering students, adult/continuing education programs, cooperative education, distance learning, English as a second language, internships, part-time degree program, services for LD students, student-designed majors, summer session for credit.
Student Life *Campus security:* 24-hour emergency response devices, late-night transport/escort service.
Financial Aid Of all full-time matriculated undergraduates who enrolled in 2010, 35 Federal Work-Study jobs (averaging $1000).
Applying *Options:* deferred entrance. *Application fee:* $20. *Required:* high school transcript, interview. *Required for some:* TEAS testing for pre-nursing.
Freshman Application Contact Ms. Patricia Goodman, Vice President of Student Services, Nashua Community College, Nashua, NH 03063. *Phone:* 603-882-6923 Ext. 1529. *Fax:* 603-882-8690. *E-mail:* pgoodman@ccsnh.edu. *Web site:* http://www.nashuacc.edu/.

NHTI, Concord's Community College

Concord, New Hampshire

Freshman Application Contact Mr. Francis P. Meyer, Director of Admissions, NHTI, Concord's Community College, 31 College Drive, Concord, NH 03301-7412. *Phone:* 603-271-7131. *Toll-free phone:* 800-247-0179. *E-mail:* fmeyer@nhctc.edu. *Web site:* http://www.nhti.edu/.

River Valley Community College

Claremont, New Hampshire

Director of Admissions Charles Kusselow, Director of Admissions, River Valley Community College, 1 College Drive, Claremont, NH 03743. *Phone:* 603-542-7744 Ext. 5322. *Toll-free phone:* 800-837-0658. *Fax:* 603-543-1844. *E-mail:* ckusselow@ccsnh.edu. *Web site:* http://www.rivervalley.edu/.

White Mountains Community College

Berlin, New Hampshire

- **State-supported** 2-year, founded 1966, part of Community College System of New Hampshire
- **Rural** 325-acre campus
- **Coed,** 922 undergraduate students, 38% full-time, 66% women, 34% men

Undergraduates 348 full-time, 574 part-time.
Freshmen *Admission:* 189 enrolled.
Faculty *Total:* 253, 11% full-time, 0.4% with terminal degrees.
Majors Accounting; automobile/automotive mechanics technology; baking and pastry arts; business administration and management; computer and information sciences; computer engineering technology; criminal justice/safety; culinary arts; diesel mechanics technology; early childhood education; environmental studies; general studies; human services; liberal arts and sciences/liberal studies; medical office assistant; office management; registered nursing/registered nurse; surveying technology.
Academics *Calendar:* semesters. *Degree:* certificates, diplomas, and associate. *Special study options:* academic remediation for entering students, adult/continuing education programs, advanced placement credit, distance learning, double majors, external degree program, independent study, internships, part-time degree program, services for LD students, summer session for credit.
Library Fortier Library with 18,000 titles, 85 serial subscriptions, 350 audiovisual materials, an OPAC.
Student Life *Housing:* college housing not available. *Activities and Organizations:* Student Senate.
Standardized Tests *Required:* ACCUPLACER Placement Test, Pre National League of Nursing entrance exam (Nursing AS Degree) (for admission).

Costs (2012–13) *Tuition:* state resident $6300 full-time, $210 per credit part-time; nonresident $14,340 full-time, $478 per credit part-time. *Required fees:* $540 full-time, $18 per credit part-time. *Payment plan:* deferred payment. *Waivers:* senior citizens and employees or children of employees.
Applying *Options:* electronic application, deferred entrance. *Application fee:* $20. *Required:* high school transcript, placement test. *Required for some:* essay or personal statement. *Application deadlines:* rolling (freshmen), rolling (transfers). *Notification:* continuous (freshmen), continuous (transfers).
Freshman Application Contact Ms. Jamie Rivard, Program Assistant, White Mountains Community College, 2020 Riverside Drive, Berlin, NH 03570. *Phone:* 603-752-1113 Ext. 3000. *Toll-free phone:* 800-445-4525. *Fax:* 603-752-6335. *E-mail:* jrivard@ccsnh.edu. *Web site:* http://www.wmcc.edu/.

NEW JERSEY

Assumption College for Sisters

Mendham, New Jersey

Freshman Application Contact Sr. Gerardine Tantsits, Academic Dean/Registrar, Assumption College for Sisters, 350 Bernardsville Road, Mendham, NJ 07945-2923. *Phone:* 973-543-6528 Ext. 228. *Fax:* 973-543-1738. *E-mail:* deanregistrar@acs350.org. *Web site:* http://www.acs350.org/.

Atlantic Cape Community College

Mays Landing, New Jersey

Freshman Application Contact Mrs. Linda McLeod, Assistant Director, Admissions and College Recruitment, Atlantic Cape Community College, 5100 Black Horse Pike, Mays Landing, NJ 08330-2699. *Phone:* 609-343-5009. *Fax:* 609-343-4921. *E-mail:* accadmit@atlantic.edu. *Web site:* http://www.atlantic.edu/.

Bergen Community College

Paramus, New Jersey

Freshman Application Contact Admissions Office, Bergen Community College, 400 Paramus Road, Paramus, NJ 07652-1595. *Phone:* 201-447-7195. *E-mail:* admsoffice@bergen.edu. *Web site:* http://www.bergen.edu/.

Brookdale Community College

Lincroft, New Jersey

Director of Admissions Ms. Kim Toomey, Registrar, Brookdale Community College, 765 Newman Springs Road, Lincroft, NJ 07738-1597. *Phone:* 732-224-2268. *Web site:* http://www.brookdalecc.edu/.

Burlington County College

Pemberton, New Jersey

- **County-supported** 2-year, founded 1966
- **Suburban** 225-acre campus with easy access to Philadelphia
- **Coed,** 10,298 undergraduate students, 53% full-time, 58% women, 42% men

Undergraduates 5,483 full-time, 4,815 part-time. Students come from 17 states and territories; 1% are from out of state; 18% Black or African American, non-Hispanic/Latino; 8% Hispanic/Latino; 3% Asian, non-Hispanic/Latino; 0.2% Native Hawaiian or other Pacific Islander, non-Hispanic/Latino; 0.2% American Indian or Alaska Native, non-Hispanic/Latino; 2% Two or more races, non-Hispanic/Latino; 9% Race/ethnicity unknown; 2% international; 7% transferred in. *Retention:* 63% of full-time freshmen returned.
Freshmen *Admission:* 5,190 applied, 5,190 admitted, 2,303 enrolled.
Faculty *Total:* 682, 9% full-time, 1% with terminal degrees. *Student/faculty ratio:* 26:1.
Majors Accounting; agribusiness; American Sign Language (ASL); animation, interactive technology, video graphics and special effects; art; automotive engineering technology; biological and physical sciences; biology/biological sciences; biotechnology; business administration and management; chemical engineering; chemistry; commercial and advertising art; communication disorders sciences and services related; computer graphics; computer science; construction engineering technology; criminal justice/police science; dental hygiene; drafting and design technology; dramatic/theater arts; education; electrical, electronic and communications engineering technology; engineering; engineering technologies and engineering related; English; environmental science; fashion/apparel design; fire science/firefighting; food service systems administration; geological and earth sciences/geosciences related; graphic and printing equipment operation/production; graphic design; health information/

medical records technology; health services/allied health/health sciences; history; hospitality administration; human services; information technology; international/global studies; journalism; legal assistant/paralegal; liberal arts and sciences/liberal studies; management information systems; mathematics; medical radiologic technology; music; philosophy; physics; psychology; registered nursing/registered nurse; respiratory care therapy; restaurant/food services management; retailing; sales, distribution, and marketing operations; sign language interpretation and translation; social sciences; sociology.

Academics *Calendar:* semesters plus 2 summer terms. *Degree:* certificates and associate. *Special study options:* academic remediation for entering students, accelerated degree program, adult/continuing education programs, advanced placement credit, cooperative education, distance learning, double majors, English as a second language, honors programs, independent study, internships, part-time degree program, services for LD students, study abroad, summer session for credit.

Library Burlington County College Library plus 1 other with 92,400 titles, 1,750 serial subscriptions, an OPAC, a Web page.

Student Life *Housing:* college housing not available. *Activities and Organizations:* drama/theater group, student-run radio station, choral group, Student Government Association, Phi Theta Kappa, Creative Writing Guild. *Campus security:* 24-hour emergency response devices and patrols, late-night transport/escort service, electronic entrances to buildings and rooms, surveillance cameras. *Student services:* health clinic, personal/psychological counseling.

Athletics Member NJCAA. *Intercollegiate sports:* baseball M(s), basketball M(s)/W(s), golf M/W, soccer M/W, softball W. *Intramural sports:* archery M.

Costs (2011–12) *Tuition:* area resident $2760 full-time, $92 per credit part-time; state resident $3240 full-time, $108 per credit hour part-time; nonresident $5190 full-time, $173 per credit hour part-time. Full-time tuition and fees vary according to course load and program. Part-time tuition and fees vary according to course load and program. *Required fees:* $855 full-time, $29 per credit part-time. *Payment plans:* installment, deferred payment. *Waivers:* senior citizens and employees or children of employees.

Financial Aid Of all full-time matriculated undergraduates who enrolled in 2010, 100 Federal Work-Study jobs (averaging $1200). 100 state and other part-time jobs (averaging $2000).

Applying *Options:* electronic application, early admission, deferred entrance. *Application fee:* $20. *Required:* high school transcript. *Application deadlines:* rolling (freshmen), rolling (out-of-state freshmen), rolling (transfers). *Notification:* continuous (freshmen), continuous (out-of-state freshmen), continuous (transfers).

Freshman Application Contact Burlington County College, 601 Pemberton Browns Mills Road, Pemberton, NJ 08068. *Phone:* 609-894-9311 Ext. 1200. *Web site:* http://www.bcc.edu/.

Camden County College

Blackwood, New Jersey

Freshman Application Contact Donald Delaney, Outreach Coordinator, School and Community Academic Programs, Camden County College, PO Box 200, Blackwood, NJ 08012-0200. *Phone:* 856-227-7200 Ext. 4371. *Fax:* 856-374-4916. *E-mail:* ddelaney@camdencc.edu. *Web site:* http://www.camdencc.edu/.

See Display ad on this page and page 394 for the College Close-Up.

County College of Morris

Randolph, New Jersey

Freshman Application Contact County College of Morris, 214 Center Grove Road, Randolph, NJ 07869-2086. *Phone:* 973-328-5100. *Web site:* http://www.ccm.edu/.

Cumberland County College

Vineland, New Jersey

Freshman Application Contact Ms. Anne Daly-Eimer, Director of Admissions and Registration, Cumberland County College, PO Box 1500, College Drive, Vineland, NJ 08362. *Phone:* 856-691-8986. *Web site:* http://www.cccnj.edu/.

Essex County College

Newark, New Jersey

Freshman Application Contact Ms. Marva Mack, Director of Admissions, Essex County College, 303 University Avenue, Newark, NJ 07102. *Phone:* 973-877-3119. *Fax:* 973-623-6449. *Web site:* http://www.essex.edu/.

Gloucester County College

Sewell, New Jersey

Freshman Application Contact Ms. Judy Atkinson, Registrar/Admissions, Gloucester County College, 1400 Tanyard Road, Sewell, NJ 08080. *Phone:* 856-415-2209. *E-mail:* jatkinso@gccnj.edu. *Web site:* http://www.gccnj.edu/.

Hudson County Community College

Jersey City, New Jersey

Director of Admissions Mr. Robert Martin, Assistant Dean of Admissions, Hudson County Community College, 25 Journal Square, Jersey City, NJ 07306. *Phone:* 201-714-2115. *Fax:* 201-714-2136. *E-mail:* martin@hccc.edu. *Web site:* http://www.hccc.edu/.

ITT Technical Institute

Marlton, New Jersey

- **Proprietary** 2-year
- **Coed**

Majors CAD/CADD drafting/design technology; computer engineering technology; system, networking, and LAN/WAN management.

Academics *Degree:* associate.

Freshman Application Contact Director of Recruitment, ITT Technical Institute, 9000 Lincoln Drive East, Suite 100, Marlton, NJ 08053. *Phone:* 856-396-3500. *Toll-free phone:* 877-209-5410. *Web site:* http://www.itt-tech.edu/.

Mercer County Community College

Trenton, New Jersey

Freshman Application Contact Dr. L. Campbell, Dean for Student and Academic Services, Mercer County Community College, 1200 Old Trenton Road, PO Box B, Trenton, NJ 08690-1004. *Phone:* 609-586-4800 Ext. 3222. *Toll-free phone:* 800-392-MCCC. *Fax:* 609-586-6944. *E-mail:* admiss@mccc.edu. *Web site:* http://www.mccc.edu/.

Middlesex County College

Edison, New Jersey

Director of Admissions Mr. Peter W. Rice, Director of Admissions and Recruitment, Middlesex County College, 2600 Woodbridge Avenue, PO Box 3050, Edison, NJ 08818-3050. *Phone:* 732-906-4243. *Web site:* http://www.middlesexcc.edu/.

Ocean County College

Toms River, New Jersey

- **County-supported** 2-year, founded 1964, part of New Jersey Higher Education
- **Suburban** 275-acre campus with easy access to Philadelphia
- **Coed,** 10,317 undergraduate students, 55% full-time, 57% women, 43% men

Undergraduates 5,641 full-time, 4,676 part-time. Students come from 18 states and territories; 16 other countries; 2% are from out of state; 4% Black or African American, non-Hispanic/Latino; 6% Hispanic/Latino; 3% Asian, non-Hispanic/Latino; 0.3% American Indian or Alaska Native, non-Hispanic/Latino; 22% Race/ethnicity unknown; 4% transferred in. *Retention:* 70% of full-time freshmen returned.

Freshmen *Admission:* 3,981 applied, 3,981 admitted, 2,447 enrolled.

Faculty *Total:* 536, 20% full-time, 27% with terminal degrees. *Student/faculty ratio:* 29:1.

Majors Administrative assistant and secretarial science; broadcast journalism; business administration and management; business/commerce; communications technologies and support services related; computer and information sciences; criminal justice/police science; engineering; engineering technologies and engineering related; environmental science; fire prevention and safety technology; general studies; homeland security, law enforcement, firefighting and protective services related; human services; liberal arts and sciences/liberal studies; registered nursing/registered nurse; sign language interpretation and translation.

Academics *Calendar:* semesters. *Degree:* certificates, diplomas, and associate. *Special study options:* academic remediation for entering students, accelerated degree program, adult/continuing education programs, advanced placement credit, cooperative education, distance learning, English as a second language, honors programs, independent study, internships, part-time degree program, services for LD students, study abroad, summer session for credit.

Library Ocean County College Library with 87,773 titles, 300 serial subscriptions, 3,863 audiovisual materials, an OPAC, a Web page.

Student Life *Housing:* college housing not available. *Activities and Organizations:* drama/theater group, student-run newspaper, radio and television station, choral group, Student Activities Board, Veteran's Club, Student Government, OCC Vikings Cheerleaders, Speech and Theater Club. *Campus security:* 24-hour emergency response devices and patrols, late-night transport/escort service, security cameras in hallways and parking lots. *Student services:* personal/psychological counseling.

Athletics Member NJCAA. *Intercollegiate sports:* baseball M, basketball M/W, cross-country running M/W, golf M/W, soccer M/W, softball W, swimming and diving M/W, tennis M/W. *Intramural sports:* basketball M/W, cheerleading M(c)/W(c), ice hockey M, sailing M(c)/W(c), soccer M/W, softball W, volleyball M/W.

Standardized Tests *Required for some:* Accuplacer is required for degree seeking students. Waiver may be obtained by meeting institution's minimum ACT or SAT scores, or English and math transfer credits.

Costs (2012–13) *Tuition:* area resident $2940 full-time, $98 per credit part-time; state resident $3900 full-time, $130 per credit part-time; nonresident $6450 full-time, $215 per credit part-time. Full-time tuition and fees vary according to course load and program. Part-time tuition and fees vary according to program. *Required fees:* $30 per credit part-time, $20 per term part-time. *Payment plan:* installment. *Waivers:* senior citizens and employees or children of employees.

Financial Aid Of all full-time matriculated undergraduates who enrolled in 2010, 76 Federal Work-Study jobs (averaging $1300). 45 state and other part-time jobs (averaging $850).

Applying *Options:* electronic application. *Required for some:* high school transcript, Accuplacer testing required for degree seeking students not meeting minimum ACT or SAT institutional requirements. Selective admissions for nursing students. Please see our website for details. *Application deadlines:* rolling (freshmen), rolling (out-of-state freshmen), rolling (transfers). *Notification:* continuous (freshmen), continuous (out-of-state freshmen), continuous (transfers).

Freshman Application Contact Ocean County College, College Drive, PO Box 2001, Toms River, NJ 08754-2001. *Phone:* 732-255-0400 Ext. 2330. *Web site:* http://www.ocean.edu/.

Passaic County Community College

Paterson, New Jersey

Freshman Application Contact Mr. Patrick Noonan, Director of Admissions, Passaic County Community College, One College Boulevard, Paterson, NJ 07505-1179. *Phone:* 973-684-6304. *Web site:* http://www.pccc.cc.nj.us/.

Raritan Valley Community College

Branchburg, New Jersey

- **County-supported** 2-year, founded 1965
- **Small-town** 225-acre campus with easy access to New York City, Philadelphia
- **Endowment** $1.1 million
- **Coed,** 8,370 undergraduate students, 47% full-time, 53% women, 47% men

Undergraduates 3,893 full-time, 4,477 part-time. Students come from 11 states and territories; 1% are from out of state; 10% Black or African American, non-Hispanic/Latino; 15% Hispanic/Latino; 6% Asian, non-Hispanic/Latino; 0.3% Native Hawaiian or other Pacific Islander, non-Hispanic/Latino; 0.3% American Indian or Alaska Native, non-Hispanic/Latino; 1% Two or more races, non-Hispanic/Latino; 6% Race/ethnicity unknown; 2% international; 7% transferred in.

Freshmen *Admission:* 2,618 applied, 2,618 admitted, 1,588 enrolled.

Faculty *Total:* 521, 22% full-time. *Student/faculty ratio:* 22:1.

Majors Accounting related; accounting technology and bookkeeping; administrative assistant and secretarial science; animation, interactive technology, video graphics and special effects; automotive engineering technology; biotechnology; business administration and management; business/commerce; chemical technology; child-care provision; cinematography and film/video production; communication and media related; computer and information sciences and support services related; computer programming (vendor/product certification); computer systems networking and telecommunications; construction engineering technology; corrections; criminal justice/law enforcement administration; criminal justice/police science; critical incident response/special police operations; dance; dental assisting; dental hygiene; design and applied arts related; diesel mechanics technology; digital communication and media/multimedia; engineering science; engineering technologies and engineering related; English; financial planning and services; fine/studio arts; health and physical education/fitness; health information/medical records technology; health services/allied health/health sciences; heating, ventilation, air conditioning and refrigeration engineering technology; information technology; interior design; international business/trade/commerce; kindergarten/preschool education; kinesiology and exercise science; legal assistant/paralegal; liberal arts and sciences/liberal studies; lineworker; management information systems; manufacturing engineering technology; marketing/marketing management; medical/clinical assistant; meeting and event planning; multi-interdisciplinary studies related; music; opticianry; optometric technician; registered nursing/registered nurse; respiratory care therapy; restaurant, culinary, and catering management; small business administration; web page, digital/multimedia and information resources design.

Academics *Calendar:* semesters. *Degree:* certificates and associate. *Special study options:* academic remediation for entering students, adult/continuing education programs, advanced placement credit, cooperative education, distance learning, double majors, English as a second language, honors programs, independent study, internships, off-campus study, part-time degree program, services for LD students, summer session for credit. *ROTC:* Army (c), Air Force (c).

Library Evelyn S. Field Library with 143,559 titles, 26,810 serial subscriptions, 2,712 audiovisual materials, an OPAC, a Web page.

Student Life *Housing:* college housing not available. *Activities and Organizations:* drama/theater group, student-run radio station, choral group, Phi Theta Kappa, Orgullo Latino, Student Nurses Association, Business Club/SIFE, Environmental club. *Campus security:* 24-hour emergency response devices and patrols, late-night transport/escort service, 24-hour outdoor and indoor surveillance cameras; 24-hr mobile patrols; 24-hr communication center. *Student services:* personal/psychological counseling.

Athletics Member NJCAA. *Intercollegiate sports:* baseball M(s), basketball M(s)/W(s), golf M/W, soccer M/W, softball W(s).

Financial Aid Of all full-time matriculated undergraduates who enrolled in 2010, 12 Federal Work-Study jobs (averaging $2500).

Applying *Options:* electronic application, early admission. *Application fee:* $25. *Required:* high school transcript. *Application deadlines:* rolling (freshmen), rolling (transfers).

Freshman Application Contact Mr. Daniel Palubniak, Registrar, Enrollment Services, Raritan Valley Community College, PO Box 3300, Somerville, NJ 08876-1265. *Phone:* 908-526-1200 Ext. 8206. *Fax:* 908-704-3442. *E-mail:* dpalubni@raritanval.edu. *Web site:* http://www.raritanval.edu/.

Salem Community College
Carneys Point, New Jersey

- **County-supported** 2-year, founded 1972
- **Small-town** campus with easy access to Philadelphia
- **Coed,** 1,321 undergraduate students

Undergraduates 17% are from out of state; 22% Black or African American, non-Hispanic/Latino; 3% Hispanic/Latino; 0.8% Asian, non-Hispanic/Latino; 0.1% American Indian or Alaska Native, non-Hispanic/Latino; 3% Two or more races, non-Hispanic/Latino; 10% Race/ethnicity unknown.

Faculty *Total:* 112, 20% full-time. *Student/faculty ratio:* 20:1.

Majors Administrative assistant and secretarial science; biotechnology; business administration and management; computer graphics; energy management and systems technology; industrial and product design; liberal arts and sciences/liberal studies; licensed practical/vocational nurse training; medical insurance coding; nuclear/nuclear power technology; precision production related; registered nursing/registered nurse; sculpture.

Academics *Calendar:* semesters. *Degree:* certificates and associate. *Special study options:* academic remediation for entering students, adult/continuing education programs, advanced placement credit, cooperative education, distance learning, double majors, English as a second language, independent study, off-campus study, part-time degree program, services for LD students, summer session for credit.

Library Michael S. Cettei Memorial Library plus 1 other with an OPAC.

Student Life *Housing:* college housing not available. *Activities and Organizations:* choral group. *Campus security:* 24-hour emergency response devices and patrols, late-night transport/escort service. *Student services:* personal/psychological counseling, women's center.

Athletics Member NJCAA. *Intercollegiate sports:* baseball M, basketball M/W, golf M, soccer M/W, softball W.

Financial Aid Of all full-time matriculated undergraduates who enrolled in 2010, 756 applied for aid, 624 were judged to have need, 35 had their need fully met. 34 Federal Work-Study jobs (averaging $1137). In 2010, 39 non-need-based awards were made. *Average percent of need met:* 47%. *Average financial aid package:* $4663. *Average need-based loan:* $2304. *Average need-based gift aid:* $4284. *Average non-need-based aid:* $1652.

Applying *Options:* electronic application, early admission, deferred entrance. *Application fee:* $27. *Required:* high school transcript, Basic Skills test or minimum SAT scores. Students with a minimum score of 530 in math and 540 in English on the SAT are exempt from placement testing. *Required for some:* essay or personal statement. *Application deadlines:* rolling (freshmen), rolling (out-of-state freshmen), rolling (transfers). *Notification:* continuous (freshmen), continuous (transfers).

Freshman Application Contact Lynn Fishlock, Director of Enrollment and Transfer Services, Salem Community College, 460 Hollywood Avenue, Carneys Point, NJ 08069. *Phone:* 856-351-2701. *Fax:* 856-299-9193. *E-mail:* info@salemcc.edu. *Web site:* http://www.salemcc.edu/.

Sussex County Community College
Newton, New Jersey

Freshman Application Contact Mr. James Donohue, Director of Admissions and Registrar, Sussex County Community College, 1 College Hill Road, Newton, NJ 07860. *Phone:* 973-300-2219. *Fax:* 973-579-5226. *E-mail:* jdonohue@sussex.edu. *Web site:* http://www.sussex.edu/.

Union County College
Cranford, New Jersey

- **State and locally supported** 2-year, founded 1933, part of New Jersey Higher Education
- **Urban** 48-acre campus with easy access to New York City
- **Endowment** $8.8 million
- **Coed,** 12,416 undergraduate students, 47% full-time, 63% women, 37% men

Undergraduates 5,881 full-time, 6,535 part-time. Students come from 11 states and territories; 77 other countries; 2% are from out of state; 26% Black or African American, non-Hispanic/Latino; 25% Hispanic/Latino; 3% Asian, non-Hispanic/Latino; 0.4% Native Hawaiian or other Pacific Islander, non-Hispanic/Latino; 0.6% American Indian or Alaska Native, non-Hispanic/Latino; 20% Race/ethnicity unknown; 2% international; 4% transferred in. *Retention:* 53% of full-time freshmen returned.

Freshmen *Admission:* 4,239 applied, 2,430 admitted, 2,114 enrolled.

Faculty *Total:* 528, 35% full-time, 28% with terminal degrees. *Student/faculty ratio:* 26:1.

Majors Accounting technology and bookkeeping; allied health diagnostic, intervention, and treatment professions related; American Sign Language (ASL); American Sign Language related; animation, interactive technology, video graphics and special effects; automobile/automotive mechanics technology; biology/biological sciences; business administration and management; business/commerce; chemistry; civil engineering technology; computer and information sciences and support services related; computer science; criminal justice/law enforcement administration; criminal justice/police science; customer service support/call center/teleservice operation; dental assisting; dental hygiene; diagnostic medical sonography and ultrasound technology; electromechanical technology; emergency medical technology (EMT paramedic); engineering; fire prevention and safety technology; hospitality administration; hotel/motel administration; human services; information science/studies; information technology; language interpretation and translation; legal assistant/paralegal; liberal arts and sciences/liberal studies; licensed practical/vocational nurse training; management information systems; manufacturing engineering technology; marketing/marketing management; mass communication/media; mathematics; mechanical engineering/mechanical technology; medical radiologic technology; nuclear medical technology; physical therapy technology; radiologic technology/science; recording arts technology; registered nursing/registered nurse; rehabilitation and therapeutic professions related; respiratory care therapy; security and loss prevention; sign language interpretation and translation; sport and fitness administration/management; telecommunications technology.

Academics *Calendar:* semesters. *Degree:* certificates, diplomas, and associate. *Special study options:* academic remediation for entering students, accelerated degree program, adult/continuing education programs, advanced placement credit, distance learning, English as a second language, honors programs, independent study, internships, off-campus study, part-time degree program, services for LD students, student-designed majors, summer session for credit. *ROTC:* Air Force (c).

Library MacKay Library plus 2 others with 137,731 titles, 20,938 serial subscriptions, 3,610 audiovisual materials, an OPAC, a Web page.

Student Life *Housing:* college housing not available. *Activities and Organizations:* drama/theater group, student-run newspaper, radio and television station, SIGN, Business Management Club, Art Society, La Sociedad Hispanica de UCC, Architecture Club. *Campus security:* 24-hour emergency response devices and patrols, late-night transport/escort service. *Student services:* personal/psychological counseling.

Athletics Member NJCAA. *Intercollegiate sports:* baseball M, basketball M/W(s), golf M/W, soccer M, volleyball W. *Intramural sports:* cheerleading W.

Costs (2012–13) *Tuition:* area resident $2688 full-time, $112 per credit part-time; state resident $5376 full-time, $224 per credit part-time; nonresident $5376 full-time, $224 per credit part-time. Full-time tuition and fees vary according to course load. Part-time tuition and fees vary according to course load. *Required fees:* $918 full-time, $38 per credit part-time. *Payment plan:*

deferred payment. *Waivers:* senior citizens and employees or children of employees.

Financial Aid Of all full-time matriculated undergraduates who enrolled in 2010, 150 Federal Work-Study jobs (averaging $1700).

Applying *Options:* electronic application, early admission, deferred entrance. *Required:* high school transcript. *Required for some:* interview. *Application deadlines:* rolling (freshmen), rolling (transfers). *Notification:* continuous (freshmen), continuous (transfers).

Freshman Application Contact Ms. Nina Hernandez, Director of Admissions, Records, and Registration, Union County College, Cranford, NJ 07016. *Phone:* 908-709-7127. *Fax:* 908-709-7125. *E-mail:* hernandez@ucc.edu. *Web site:* http://www.ucc.edu/.

Warren County Community College

Washington, New Jersey

Freshman Application Contact Shannon Horwath, Associate Director of Admissions, Warren County Community College, 475 Route 57 West, Washington, NJ 07882-9605. *Phone:* 908-835-2300. *E-mail:* shorwath@warren.edu. *Web site:* http://www.warren.edu/.

NEW MEXICO

Brown Mackie College–Albuquerque

Albuquerque, New Mexico

- **Proprietary** primarily 2-year, part of Education Management Corporation
- **Coed**

Academics *Degrees:* associate and bachelor's.

Costs (2011–12) *Tuition:* Tuition varies by program. Students should contact Brown Mackie College for tuition information.

Freshman Application Contact Brown Mackie College–Albuquerque, 10500 Cooper Avenue NE, Albuquerque, NM 87123. *Phone:* 505-559-5200. *Toll-free phone:* 877-271-3488. *Web site:* http://www.brownmackie.edu/.

See page 340 for the College Close-Up.

Carrington College - Albuquerque

Albuquerque, New Mexico

Admissions Office Contact Carrington College - Albuquerque, 1001 Menaul Boulevard NE, Albuquerque, NM 87107. *Web site:* http://carrington.edu/.

Central New Mexico Community College

Albuquerque, New Mexico

- **State-supported** 2-year, founded 1965
- **Urban** 60-acre campus
- **Endowment** $892,730
- **Coed**

Undergraduates 9,818 full-time, 20,130 part-time. Students come from 31 states and territories; 5% transferred in. *Retention:* 58% of full-time freshmen returned.

Faculty *Student/faculty ratio:* 27:1.

Academics *Calendar:* trimesters. *Degree:* certificates and associate. *Special study options:* academic remediation for entering students, adult/continuing education programs, advanced placement credit, cooperative education, distance learning, double majors, English as a second language, internships, part-time degree program, services for LD students, summer session for credit. *ROTC:* Army (c), Navy (c), Air Force (c).

Student Life *Campus security:* 24-hour emergency response devices and patrols, late-night transport/escort service.

Costs (2011–12) *Tuition:* state resident $1737 full-time, $48 per credit hour part-time; nonresident $9025 full-time, $251 per credit hour part-time. Full-time tuition and fees vary according to course load. Part-time tuition and fees vary according to course load. *Required fees:* $120 full-time, $43 per term part-time.

Applying *Options:* electronic application.

Freshman Application Contact Ms. Jane Campbell, Director, Enrollment Services, Central New Mexico Community College, Albuquerque, NM 87106. *Phone:* 505-224-3160. *Fax:* 505-224-3237. *Web site:* http://www.cnm.edu/.

Clovis Community College

Clovis, New Mexico

- **State-supported** 2-year, founded 1990
- **Small-town** 25-acre campus
- **Endowment** $740,423
- **Coed**

Undergraduates 995 full-time, 3,180 part-time. Students come from 37 states and territories; 14% are from out of state; 8% transferred in. *Retention:* 43% of full-time freshmen returned.

Faculty *Student/faculty ratio:* 21:1.

Academics *Calendar:* semesters. *Degree:* certificates and associate. *Special study options:* academic remediation for entering students, adult/continuing education programs, advanced placement credit, cooperative education, distance learning, double majors, English as a second language, independent study, internships, part-time degree program, services for LD students, summer session for credit.

Student Life *Campus security:* student patrols, late-night transport/escort service.

Applying *Required:* high school transcript. *Required for some:* interview.

Freshman Application Contact Ms. Rosie Corrie, Director of Admissions and Records/Registrar, Clovis Community College, Clovis, NM 88101-8381. *Phone:* 575-769-4962. *Toll-free phone:* 800-769-1409. *Fax:* 575-769-4190. *E-mail:* admissions@clovis.edu. *Web site:* http://www.clovis.edu/.

Dona Ana Community College

Las Cruces, New Mexico

- **State and locally supported** 2-year, founded 1973, part of New Mexico State University System
- **Urban** 15-acre campus with easy access to El Paso
- **Endowment** $18,682
- **Coed,** 8,891 undergraduate students, 45% full-time, 57% women, 43% men

Undergraduates 4,037 full-time, 4,854 part-time. Students come from 14 states and territories; 1 other country; 12% are from out of state; 3% Black or African American, non-Hispanic/Latino; 65% Hispanic/Latino; 1% Asian, non-Hispanic/Latino; 2% American Indian or Alaska Native, non-Hispanic/Latino; 5% Race/ethnicity unknown; 2% international; 2% transferred in. *Retention:* 85% of full-time freshmen returned.

Freshmen *Admission:* 556 applied, 2,087 enrolled.

Faculty *Total:* 344. *Student/faculty ratio:* 21:1.

Majors Administrative assistant and secretarial science; architectural engineering technology; automobile/automotive mechanics technology; business administration and management; computer engineering technology; computer typography and composition equipment operation; consumer merchandising/retailing management; drafting and design technology; electrical, electronic and communications engineering technology; emergency medical technology (EMT paramedic); fashion merchandising; finance; fire science/firefighting; heating, air conditioning, ventilation and refrigeration maintenance technology; hospitality administration; hydrology and water resources science; industrial radiologic technology; legal assistant/paralegal; library and information science; registered nursing/registered nurse; respiratory care therapy; welding technology.

Academics *Calendar:* semesters. *Degree:* certificates and associate. *Special study options:* academic remediation for entering students, adult/continuing education programs, advanced placement credit, cooperative education, distance learning, English as a second language, freshman honors college, honors programs, internships, part-time degree program, services for LD students, summer session for credit. *ROTC:* Army (c), Air Force (c).

Library Library/Media Center with 17,140 titles, 213 serial subscriptions, an OPAC.

Student Life *Housing Options:* coed. Campus housing is university owned. *Activities and Organizations:* drama/theater group, student-run newspaper, radio and television station, choral group, marching band, national fraternities, national sororities. *Campus security:* 24-hour emergency response devices and patrols, late-night transport/escort service, controlled dormitory access. *Student services:* health clinic, personal/psychological counseling, women's center, legal services.

Standardized Tests *Recommended:* ACT, ACT ASSET, or ACT COMPASS.

Financial Aid Of all full-time matriculated undergraduates who enrolled in 2010, 15 Federal Work-Study jobs (averaging $2800). 106 state and other part-time jobs (averaging $2800). *Financial aid deadline:* 6/30.

Applying *Options:* electronic application, deferred entrance. *Application fee:* $20. *Required:* high school transcript. *Application deadline:* rolling (freshmen).

Freshman Application Contact Mrs. Ricci Montes, Admissions Advisor, Dona Ana Community College, MSC-3DA, Box 30001, 3400 South Espina

Street, Las Cruces, NM 88003-8001. *Phone:* 575-527-7683. *Toll-free phone:* 800-903-7503. *Fax:* 575-527-7515. *Web site:* http://dabcc-www.nmsu.edu/.

Eastern New Mexico University– Roswell

Roswell, New Mexico

Freshman Application Contact Eastern New Mexico University–Roswell, PO Box 6000, Roswell, NM 88202-6000. *Phone:* 505-624-7142. *Toll-free phone:* 800-243-6687 (in-state); 800-624-7000 (out-of-state). *Web site:* http://www.enmu.edu/.

ITT Technical Institute

Albuquerque, New Mexico

- **Proprietary** primarily 2-year, founded 1989, part of ITT Educational Services, Inc.
- **Coed**

Majors Business administration and management; communications technology; computer and information systems security; computer software engineering; computer software technology; construction management; criminal justice/law enforcement administration; drafting and design technology; electrical, electronic and communications engineering technology; forensic science and technology; graphic communications; health information/medical records technology; legal assistant/paralegal; network and system administration; project management; registered nursing/registered nurse.

Academics *Calendar:* quarters. *Degrees:* associate and bachelor's.

Student Life *Housing:* college housing not available.

Freshman Application Contact Director of Recruitment, ITT Technical Institute, 5100 Masthead Street, NE, Albuquerque, NM 87109. *Phone:* 505-828-1114. *Toll-free phone:* 800-636-1114. *Web site:* http://www.itt-tech.edu/.

Luna Community College

Las Vegas, New Mexico

Freshman Application Contact Ms. Henrietta Griego, Director of Admissions, Recruitment, and Retention, Luna Community College, PO Box 1510, Las Vegas, NM 87701. *Phone:* 505-454-2020. *Toll-free phone:* 800-588-7232 (in-state); 800-5888-7232 (out-of-state). *Fax:* 505-454-2588. *E-mail:* hgriego@luna.cc.nm.us. *Web site:* http://www.luna.edu/.

Mesalands Community College

Tucumcari, New Mexico

Director of Admissions Mr. Ken Brashear, Director of Enrollment Management, Mesalands Community College, 911 South Tenth Street, Tucumcari, NM 88401. *Phone:* 505-461-4413. *Web site:* http://www.mesalands.edu/.

National American University

Rio Rancho, New Mexico

Freshman Application Contact Admissions Office, National American University, 1601 Rio Rancho, Suite 200, Rio Rancho, NM 87124. *Web site:* http://www.national.edu/.

Navajo Technical College

Crownpoint, New Mexico

Director of Admissions Director of Admission, Navajo Technical College, PO Box 849, Crownpoint, NM 87313. *Phone:* 505-786-4100. *Web site:* http://www.navajotech.edu/.

New Mexico Junior College

Hobbs, New Mexico

Director of Admissions Mr. Robert Bensing, Dean of Enrollment Management, New Mexico Junior College, 5317 Lovington Highway, Hobbs, NM 88240-9123. *Phone:* 505-392-5092. *Toll-free phone:* 800-657-6260. *Web site:* http://www.nmjc.edu/.

New Mexico Military Institute

Roswell, New Mexico

Freshman Application Contact New Mexico Military Institute, Roswell, NM 88201-5173. *Phone:* 505-624-8050. *Toll-free phone:* 800-421-5376. *Fax:*

505-624-8058. *E-mail:* admissions@nmmi.edu. *Web site:* http://www.nmmi.edu/.

New Mexico State University– Alamogordo

Alamogordo, New Mexico

- **State-supported** 2-year, founded 1958, part of New Mexico State University System
- **Small-town** 540-acre campus
- **Endowment** $147,086
- **Coed,** 3,371 undergraduate students, 30% full-time, 64% women, 36% men

Undergraduates 1,005 full-time, 2,366 part-time. Students come from 26 states and territories; 15% are from out of state; 4% Black or African American, non-Hispanic/Latino; 38% Hispanic/Latino; 2% Asian, non-Hispanic/Latino; 0.1% Native Hawaiian or other Pacific Islander, non-Hispanic/Latino; 3% American Indian or Alaska Native, non-Hispanic/Latino; 1% Two or more races, non-Hispanic/Latino; 6% Race/ethnicity unknown; 2% international; 6% transferred in. *Retention:* 50% of full-time freshmen returned.

Freshmen *Admission:* 423 applied, 423 admitted, 331 enrolled. *Average high school GPA:* 2.73.

Faculty *Total:* 158, 34% full-time, 9% with terminal degrees. *Student/faculty ratio:* 20:1.

Majors Administrative assistant and secretarial science; animation, interactive technology, video graphics and special effects; biomedical technology; business/commerce; computer programming; criminal justice/safety; early childhood education; education; electrical, electronic and communications engineering technology; electrician; ethnic, cultural minority, gender, and group studies related; fine/studio arts; general studies; graphic design; human services; information technology; legal assistant/paralegal; liberal arts and sciences and humanities related; multi/interdisciplinary studies related; office occupations and clerical services; registered nursing/registered nurse.

Academics *Calendar:* semesters. *Degree:* certificates and associate. *Special study options:* academic remediation for entering students, adult/continuing education programs, advanced placement credit, distance learning, double majors, honors programs, independent study, internships, off-campus study, part-time degree program, services for LD students, study abroad, summer session for credit.

Library David H. Townsend Library with 50,000 titles, 350 serial subscriptions, an OPAC, a Web page.

Student Life *Housing:* college housing not available. *Activities and Organizations:* drama/theater group, choral group, Student Government, advocates for Children in Education, Phi Theta Kappa, Social Science Club, Student Veterans of America-Alamogordo. *Campus security:* 24-hour emergency response devices.

Costs (2012–13) *Tuition:* area resident $1824 full-time, $76 per credit hour part-time; state resident $2160 full-time, $90 per credit hour part-time; nonresident $4872 full-time, $203 per credit hour part-time. Full-time tuition and fees vary according to course load. *Required fees:* $96 full-time, $4 per credit hour part-time. *Payment plans:* installment, deferred payment. *Waivers:* senior citizens and employees or children of employees.

Financial Aid Of all full-time matriculated undergraduates who enrolled in 2010, 10 Federal Work-Study jobs (averaging $3300). 60 state and other part-time jobs (averaging $3300). *Financial aid deadline:* 5/1.

Applying *Options:* electronic application, early admission, deferred entrance. *Application fee:* $20. *Required:* high school transcript, minimum 2.0 GPA. *Application deadlines:* rolling (freshmen), rolling (out-of-state freshmen), rolling (transfers). *Notification:* continuous (freshmen), continuous (out-of-state freshmen), continuous (transfers).

Freshman Application Contact Ms. Bobi McDonald, Coordinator of Admissions and Records, New Mexico State University–Alamogordo, 2400 North Scenic Drive, Alamogordo, NM 88311-0477. *Phone:* 575-439-3700. *E-mail:* advisor@nmsua.nmsu.edu. *Web site:* http://nmsua.edu/.

New Mexico State University– Carlsbad

Carlsbad, New Mexico

Freshman Application Contact Ms. Everal Shannon, Records Specialist, New Mexico State University–Carlsbad, 1500 University Drive, Carlsbad, NM 88220. *Phone:* 575-234-9222. *Fax:* 575-885-4951. *E-mail:* eshannon@nmsu.edu. *Web site:* http://www.cavern.nmsu.edu/.

New Mexico State University–Grants
Grants, New Mexico

Director of Admissions Ms. Irene Lutz, Campus Student Services Officer, New Mexico State University–Grants, 1500 3rd Street, Grants, NM 87020-2025. *Phone:* 505-287-7981. *Web site:* http://grants.nmsu.edu/.

Northern New Mexico College
Espanola, New Mexico

Freshman Application Contact Mr. Mike L. Costello, Registrar, Northern New Mexico College, 921 Paseo de Onate, Espanola, NM 87532. *Phone:* 505-747-2193. *Fax:* 505-747-2191. *E-mail:* dms@nnmc.edu. *Web site:* http://www.nnmc.edu/.

Pima Medical Institute
Albuquerque, New Mexico

- **Proprietary** 2-year
- **Urban** campus
- **Coed**

Academics *Special study options:* cooperative education, distance learning, internships.
Standardized Tests *Required:* Wonderlic Scholastic Level Exam (for admission).
Applying *Required:* high school transcript, interview.
Freshman Application Contact Pima Medical Institute, 2305 San Pedro NE, Suite D, Albuquerque, NM 87110. *Phone:* 505-816-0556. *Web site:* http://www.pmi.edu/.

Pima Medical Institute
Albuquerque, New Mexico

- **Proprietary** primarily 2-year, founded 1985, part of Vocational Training Institutes, Inc.
- **Urban** campus
- **Coed**

Academics *Calendar:* modular. *Degrees:* certificates, associate, and bachelor's. *Special study options:* academic remediation for entering students, cooperative education, distance learning, internships, services for LD students.
Standardized Tests *Required:* Wonderlic Scholastic Level Exam (for admission).
Financial Aid Of all full-time matriculated undergraduates who enrolled in 2010, 6 Federal Work-Study jobs.
Applying *Options:* early admission. *Required:* interview. *Required for some:* high school transcript.
Freshman Application Contact Admissions Office, Pima Medical Institute, 4400 Cutler Avenue NE, Albuquerque, NM 87110. *Phone:* 505-881-1234. *Toll-free phone:* 800-477-PIMA (in-state); 888-477-PIMA (out-of-state). *Fax:* 505-881-5329. *Web site:* http://www.pmi.edu/.

San Juan College
Farmington, New Mexico

- **State-supported** 2-year, founded 1958, part of New Mexico Higher Education Department
- **Small-town** 698-acre campus
- **Endowment** $9.7 million
- **Coed,** 9,470 undergraduate students, 34% full-time, 47% women, 53% men

Undergraduates 3,230 full-time, 6,240 part-time. Students come from 49 states and territories; 27 other countries; 21% are from out of state; 1% Black or African American, non-Hispanic/Latino; 13% Hispanic/Latino; 0.5% Asian, non-Hispanic/Latino; 0.1% Native Hawaiian or other Pacific Islander, non-Hispanic/Latino; 36% American Indian or Alaska Native, non-Hispanic/Latino; 0.8% Two or more races, non-Hispanic/Latino; 4% Race/ethnicity unknown; 0.5% international; 4% transferred in.
Freshmen *Admission:* 1,033 applied, 1,033 admitted, 937 enrolled.
Faculty *Total:* 448, 34% full-time. *Student/faculty ratio:* 20:1.
Majors Accounting technology and bookkeeping; autobody/collision and repair technology; automobile/automotive mechanics technology; biology/biological sciences; business administration and management; carpentry; chemistry; child-care provision; clinical/medical laboratory technology; commercial and advertising art; cosmetology; data processing and data processing technology; dental hygiene; diesel mechanics technology; drafting and design technology; electrical, electronic and communications engineering technology;

elementary education; emergency medical technology (EMT paramedic); engineering; fire science/firefighting; general studies; geography; geology/earth science; health and physical education/fitness; health information/medical records technology; industrial mechanics and maintenance technology; industrial technology; instrumentation technology; landscaping and groundskeeping; legal assistant/paralegal; liberal arts and sciences/liberal studies; machine shop technology; mathematics; occupational safety and health technology; parks, recreation and leisure; physical sciences; physical therapy technology; physics; premedical studies; psychology; registered nursing/registered nurse; respiratory care therapy; secondary education; social work; solar energy technology; special education; surgical technology; theater design and technology; veterinary/animal health technology; welding technology.
Academics *Calendar:* semesters. *Degree:* certificates, diplomas, and associate. *Special study options:* academic remediation for entering students, adult/continuing education programs, advanced placement credit, cooperative education, distance learning, English as a second language, honors programs, independent study, internships, part-time degree program, services for LD students, summer session for credit.
Library San Juan College Library with 86,360 titles, 346 serial subscriptions, 4,775 audiovisual materials, an OPAC, a Web page.
Student Life *Housing:* college housing not available. *Activities and Organizations:* drama/theater group, student-run newspaper, radio station, choral group, national fraternities, national sororities. *Campus security:* 24-hour emergency response devices and patrols, late-night transport/escort service. *Student services:* personal/psychological counseling.
Athletics *Intramural sports:* archery M/W, badminton M/W, basketball M/W, bowling M/W, cross-country running M/W, football M/W, golf M/W, racquetball M/W, rock climbing M/W, skiing (cross-country) M/W, skiing (downhill) M/W, soccer M/W, softball M/W, table tennis M/W, tennis M/W, volleyball M/W.
Costs (2012–13) *Tuition:* state resident $1230 full-time, $41 per credit hour part-time; nonresident $3150 full-time, $105 per credit hour part-time. Full-time tuition and fees vary according to reciprocity agreements. *Required fees:* $180 full-time, $6 per credit part-time. *Payment plans:* tuition prepayment, installment. *Waivers:* senior citizens and employees or children of employees.
Financial Aid Of all full-time matriculated undergraduates who enrolled in 2010, 150 Federal Work-Study jobs (averaging $2500). 175 state and other part-time jobs (averaging $2500).
Applying *Options:* electronic application, early admission, deferred entrance. *Required:* high school transcript. *Application deadlines:* rolling (freshmen), rolling (transfers). *Notification:* continuous (freshmen), continuous (transfers).
Freshman Application Contact Ms. Skylar Maston, Enrollment Services Coordinator, San Juan College, 4601 College Blvd, Farmington, NM 87402. *Phone:* 505-566-3300. *Fax:* 505-566-3500. *E-mail:* mastons@sanjuancollege.edu. *Web site:* http://www.sanjuancollege.edu/.

Santa Fe Community College
Santa Fe, New Mexico

- **State and locally supported** 2-year, founded 1983
- **Suburban** 366-acre campus with easy access to Albuquerque
- **Coed**

Undergraduates 1,668 full-time, 3,188 part-time. Students come from 50 states and territories; 17 other countries; 11% are from out of state. *Retention:* 56% of full-time freshmen returned.
Faculty *Student/faculty ratio:* 17:1.
Academics *Calendar:* semesters. *Degree:* certificates and associate. *Special study options:* academic remediation for entering students, adult/continuing education programs, advanced placement credit, cooperative education, distance learning, double majors, English as a second language, external degree program, honors programs, independent study, internships, part-time degree program, services for LD students, summer session for credit.
Student Life *Campus security:* 24-hour emergency response devices and patrols, late-night transport/escort service.
Costs (2011–12) *Tuition:* area resident $1080 full-time, $36 per credit hour part-time; state resident $1410 full-time, $47 per credit hour part-time; nonresident $2550 full-time, $85 per credit hour part-time. Full-time tuition and fees vary according to reciprocity agreements. Part-time tuition and fees vary according to reciprocity agreements. *Required fees:* $144 full-time, $5 per credit hour part-time.
Applying *Options:* electronic application, early admission, deferred entrance. *Recommended:* high school transcript.
Freshman Application Contact Ms. Rebecca Estrada, Director of Recruitment, Santa Fe Community College, 6401 Richards Ave, Santa Fe, NM 87508. *Phone:* 505-428-1604. *Fax:* 505-428-1468. *E-mail:* rebecca.estrada@sfcc.edu. *Web site:* http://www.sfcc.edu/.

Southwestern Indian Polytechnic Institute

Albuquerque, New Mexico

- **Federally supported** 2-year, founded 1971
- **Suburban** 144-acre campus
- **Coed,** 480 undergraduate students, 85% full-time, 53% women, 47% men

Undergraduates 406 full-time, 74 part-time. Students come from 21 states and territories; 60% live on campus.

Freshmen *Admission:* 247 applied, 136 admitted, 158 enrolled. *Average high school GPA:* 2.11.

Faculty *Total:* 48, 29% full-time, 21% with terminal degrees. *Student/faculty ratio:* 15:1.

Majors Accounting technology and bookkeeping; business administration and management; business automation/technology/data entry; business/commerce; data processing and data processing technology; early childhood education; engineering; geographic information science and cartography; hospitality administration related; institutional food workers; instrumentation technology; liberal arts and sciences/liberal studies; management information systems and services related; manufacturing engineering technology; natural resources and conservation related; opticianry; system, networking, and LAN/WAN management.

Academics *Calendar:* trimesters. *Degree:* certificates and associate. *Special study options:* academic remediation for entering students, advanced placement credit, cooperative education, distance learning, double majors, internships, part-time degree program, services for LD students, summer session for credit.

Library Southwester Indian Polytechnic Institute Library with 27,000 titles, 715 serial subscriptions.

Student Life *Housing Options:* men-only, women-only. Campus housing is university owned. *Activities and Organizations:* Dance club, Student Senate, rodeo club, Natural Resources, Pow-wow club. *Campus security:* 24-hour emergency response devices and patrols, late-night transport/escort service. *Student services:* personal/psychological counseling.

Athletics *Intramural sports:* basketball M/W, softball M/W, volleyball M/W.

Costs (2012–13) *Tuition:* state resident $675 full-time, $150 per term part-time; nonresident $675 full-time, $150 per term part-time. *Room and board:* $165. *Payment plan:* deferred payment.

Financial Aid Of all full-time matriculated undergraduates who enrolled in 2010, 351 applied for aid, 351 were judged to have need, 23 had their need fully met. 14 Federal Work-Study jobs (averaging $661). 36 state and other part-time jobs (averaging $726). *Average percent of need met:* 27%. *Average financial aid package:* $2943. *Average need-based gift aid:* $2878.

Applying *Required:* high school transcript, Certificate of Indian Blood. *Application deadlines:* 7/30 (freshmen), 7/30 (transfers). *Notification:* continuous (freshmen).

Freshman Application Contact Southwestern Indian Polytechnic Institute, 9169 Coors, NW, Box 10146, Albuquerque, NM 87184-0146. *Phone:* 505-346-2324. *Toll-free phone:* 800-586-7474. *Web site:* http://www.sipi.edu/.

University of New Mexico–Gallup

Gallup, New Mexico

Director of Admissions Ms. Pearl A. Morris, Admissions Representative, University of New Mexico–Gallup, 200 College Road, Gallup, NM 87301-5603. *Phone:* 505-863-7576. *Web site:* http://www.gallup.unm.edu/.

University of New Mexico–Los Alamos Branch

Los Alamos, New Mexico

Freshman Application Contact Mrs. Irene K. Martinez, Enrollment Representative, University of New Mexico–Los Alamos Branch, 4000 University Drive, Los Alamos, NM 87544-2233. *Phone:* 505-662-0332. *E-mail:* L65130@unm.edu. *Web site:* http://www.la.unm.edu/.

University of New Mexico–Taos

Taos, New Mexico

Director of Admissions Vickie Alvarez, Student Enrollment Associate, University of New Mexico–Taos, 115 Civic Plaza Drive, Taos, NM 87571. *Phone:* 575-737-6425. *E-mail:* valvarez@unm.edu. *Web site:* http://taos.unm.edu/.

University of New Mexico–Valencia Campus

Los Lunas, New Mexico

Director of Admissions Richard M. Hulett, Director of Admissions and Recruitment, University of New Mexico–Valencia Campus, 280 La Entrada, Los Lunas, NM 87031-7633. *Phone:* 505-277-2446. *E-mail:* mhulett@unm.edu. *Web site:* http://www.unm.edu/~unmvc/.

NEW YORK

Adirondack Community College

Queensbury, New York

Freshman Application Contact Office of Admissions, Adirondack Community College, 640 Bay Road, Queensbury, NY 12804. *Phone:* 518-743-2264. *Toll-free phone:* 888-SUNY-ADK. *Fax:* 518-743-2200. *Web site:* http://www.sunyacc.edu/.

American Academy McAllister Institute of Funeral Service

New York, New York

Freshman Application Contact Mr. Norman Provost, Registrar, American Academy McAllister Institute of Funeral Service, 450 West 56th Street, New York, NY 10019-3602. *Phone:* 212-757-1190. *Toll-free phone:* 866-932-2264. *Web site:* http://www.funeraleducation.org/.

American Academy of Dramatic Arts

New York, New York

Freshman Application Contact Ms. Karen Higginbotham, Director of Admissions, American Academy of Dramatic Arts, 120 Madison Avenue, New York, NY 10016. *Phone:* 212-686-9244 Ext. 315. *Toll-free phone:* 800-463-8990. *Fax:* 212-696-1284. *E-mail:* admissions-ny@aada.org. *Web site:* http://www.aada.org/.

The Art Institute of New York City

New York, New York

- **Proprietary** 2-year, founded 1980, part of Education Management Corporation
- **Urban** campus
- **Coed**

Majors Cinematography and film/video production; fashion/apparel design; fashion merchandising; graphic design; interior design; web page, digital/multimedia and information resources design.

Academics *Calendar:* quarters. *Degree:* associate.

Costs (2011–12) *Tuition:* Tuition cost varies by program. Prospective students should contact the school for current tuition costs. Other charges include a starting kit for all first-quarter students. Kits vary in price, depending on the program of study.

Freshman Application Contact The Art Institute of New York City, 11 Beach Street, New York, NY 10013. *Phone:* 212-226-5500. *Toll-free phone:* 800-654-2433. *Web site:* http://www.artinstitutes.edu/newyork/.

See page 332 for the College Close-Up.

ASA The College For Excellence

Brooklyn, New York

- **Proprietary** 2-year, founded 1985
- **Urban** campus with easy access to New York City
- **Coed**

Academics *Calendar:* semesters. *Degree:* certificates and associate. *Special study options:* academic remediation for entering students, accelerated degree program, advanced placement credit, cooperative education, distance learning, English as a second language, internships, part-time degree program.

Athletics Member NJCAA.

Costs (2011–12) *Tuition:* $12,094 full-time.

Applying *Options:* electronic application. *Application fee:* $25. *Required:* high school transcript, interview.

Freshman Application Contact Admissions Office, ASA The College For Excellence, 81 Willoughby Street, Brooklyn, NY 11201. *Phone:* 718-522-9073. *Toll-free phone:* 877-679-8772. *Web site:* http://www.asa.edu/.

Berkeley College–Westchester Campus

White Plains, New York

Freshman Application Contact Director of Admissions, Berkeley College–Westchester Campus, White Plains, NY 10601. *Phone:* 914-694-1122. *Toll-free phone:* 800-446-5400. *Fax:* 914-328-9469. *E-mail:* info@berkeleycollege.edu. *Web site:* http://www.berkeleycollege.edu/.

Borough of Manhattan Community College of the City University of New York

New York, New York

- **State and locally supported** 2-year, founded 1963, part of City University of New York System
- **Urban** 5-acre campus
- **Coed**

Undergraduates 14,658 full-time, 7,876 part-time. 1% are from out of state; 31% Black or African American, non-Hispanic/Latino; 37% Hispanic/Latino; 11% Asian, non-Hispanic/Latino; 0.2% American Indian or Alaska Native, non-Hispanic/Latino; 7% international; 2% transferred in.

Faculty *Student/faculty ratio:* 24:1.

Academics *Calendar:* semesters. *Degree:* certificates and associate. *Special study options:* academic remediation for entering students, adult/continuing education programs, advanced placement credit, cooperative education, distance learning, English as a second language, honors programs, independent study, internships, off-campus study, part-time degree program, services for LD students, study abroad, summer session for credit.

Student Life *Campus security:* 24-hour patrols.

Athletics Member NJCAA.

Standardized Tests *Recommended:* SAT or ACT (for admission).

Costs (2011–12) *Tuition:* state resident $3600 full-time, $150 per credit part-time; nonresident $7200 full-time, $240 per credit part-time. Full-time tuition and fees vary according to course load. Part-time tuition and fees vary according to course load. *Required fees:* $318 full-time, $87 per term part-time.

Applying *Options:* electronic application, deferred entrance. *Application fee:* $65. *Required:* high school transcript.

Freshman Application Contact Dr. Eugenio Barrios, Director of Enrollment Management, Borough of Manhattan Community College of the City University of New York, 199 Chambers Street, Room S-300, New York, NY 10007. *Phone:* 212-220-1265. *Toll-free phone:* 866-583-5729 (in-state); 866-593-5729 (out-of-state). *Fax:* 212-220-2366. *E-mail:* admissions@bmcc.cuny.edu. *Web site:* http://www.bmcc.cuny.edu/.

Bramson ORT College

Forest Hills, New York

Freshman Application Contact Admissions Office, Bramson ORT College, 69-30 Austin Street, Forest Hills, NY 11375-4239. *Phone:* 718-261-5800. *Fax:* 718-575-5119. *E-mail:* admissions@bramsonort.edu. *Web site:* http://www.bramsonort.edu/.

Bronx Community College of the City University of New York

Bronx, New York

Freshman Application Contact Ms. Alba N. Cancetty, Admissions Officer, Bronx Community College of the City University of New York, 2155 University Avenue, Bronx, NY 10453. *Phone:* 718-289-5888. *E-mail:* admission@bcc.cuny.edu. *Web site:* http://www.bcc.cuny.edu/.

Broome Community College

Binghamton, New York

Freshman Application Contact Ms. Jenae Norris, Director of Admissions, Broome Community College, PO Box 1017, Upper Front Street, Binghamton, NY 13902. *Phone:* 607-778-5001. *Fax:* 607-778-5394. *E-mail:* admissions@sunybroome.edu. *Web site:* http://www.sunybroome.edu/.

Bryant & Stratton College - Albany Campus

Albany, New York

Freshman Application Contact Mr. Robert Ferrell, Director of Admissions, Bryant & Stratton College - Albany Campus, 1259 Central Avenue, Albany, NY 12205. *Phone:* 518-437-1802 Ext. 205. *Fax:* 518-437-1048. *Web site:* http://www.bryantstratton.edu/.

Bryant & Stratton College - Amherst Campus

Clarence, New York

Freshman Application Contact Mr. Brian K. Dioguardi, Director of Admissions, Bryant & Stratton College - Amherst Campus, Audubon Business Center, 40 Hazelwood Drive, Amherst, NY 14228. *Phone:* 716-691-0012. *Fax:* 716-691-0012. *E-mail:* bkdioguardi@bryantstratton.edu. *Web site:* http://www.bryantstratton.edu/.

Bryant & Stratton College - Buffalo Campus

Buffalo, New York

Freshman Application Contact Mr. Philip J. Struebel, Director of Admissions, Bryant & Stratton College - Buffalo Campus, 465 Main Street, Suite 400, Buffalo, NY 14203. *Phone:* 716-884-9120. *Fax:* 716-884-0091. *E-mail:* pjstruebel@bryantstratton.edu. *Web site:* http://www.bryantstratton.edu/.

Bryant & Stratton College - Greece Campus

Rochester, New York

Freshman Application Contact Bryant & Stratton College - Greece Campus, 150 Bellwood Drive, Rochester, NY 14606. *Phone:* 585-720-0660. *Web site:* http://www.bryantstratton.edu/.

Bryant & Stratton College - Henrietta Campus

Rochester, New York

Freshman Application Contact Bryant & Stratton College - Henrietta Campus, 1225 Jefferson Road, Rochester, NY 14623-3136. *Phone:* 585-292-5627 Ext. 101. *Web site:* http://www.bryantstratton.edu/.

Bryant & Stratton College - North Campus

Liverpool, New York

Freshman Application Contact Ms. Heather Macnik, Director of Admissions, Bryant & Stratton College - North Campus, 8687 Carling Road, Liverpool, NY 13090-1315. *Phone:* 315-652-6500. *Web site:* http://www.bryantstratton.edu/.

Bryant & Stratton College - Southtowns Campus

Orchard Park, New York

Freshman Application Contact Bryant & Stratton College - Southtowns Campus, 200 Redtail, Orchard Park, NY 14127. *Phone:* 716-677-9500. *Web site:* http://www.bryantstratton.edu/.

Bryant & Stratton College - Syracuse Campus

Syracuse, New York

Freshman Application Contact Ms. Dawn Rajkowski, Director of High School Enrollments, Bryant & Stratton College - Syracuse Campus, 953 James Street, Syracuse, NY 13203-2502. *Phone:* 315-472-6603 Ext. 248. *Fax:* 315-474-4383. *Web site:* http://www.bryantstratton.edu/.

Business Informatics Center, Inc.

Valley Stream, New York

Freshman Application Contact Admissions Office, Business Informatics Center, Inc., 134 South Central Avenue, Valley Stream, NY 11580-5431. *Phone:* 516-561-0050. *Fax:* 516-561-0074. *E-mail:* info@ thecollegeforbusiness.com. *Web site:* http://www.thecollegeforbusiness.com/.

Cayuga County Community College

Auburn, New York

- **State and locally supported** 2-year, founded 1953, part of State University of New York System
- **Small-town** 50-acre campus with easy access to Rochester, Syracuse
- **Endowment** $6.2 million
- **Coed,** 4,825 undergraduate students, 50% full-time, 61% women, 39% men

Undergraduates 2,394 full-time, 2,431 part-time. 4% Black or African American, non-Hispanic/Latino; 2% Hispanic/Latino; 0.6% Asian, non-Hispanic/Latino; 0.6% American Indian or Alaska Native, non-Hispanic/Latino; 21% Race/ethnicity unknown; 7% transferred in. *Retention:* 51% of full-time freshmen returned.

Freshmen *Admission:* 2,183 applied, 1,400 admitted, 734 enrolled.

Faculty *Total:* 277, 22% full-time. *Student/faculty ratio:* 24:1.

Majors Accounting technology and bookkeeping; art; business administration and management; child-care and support services management; communication and journalism related; communications systems installation and repair technology; computer and information sciences; computer and information sciences and support services related; corrections; criminal justice/police science; drafting and design technology; education (multiple levels); electrical, electronic and communications engineering technology; fine/studio arts; game and interactive media design; general studies; geography; graphic design; humanities; information science/studies; liberal arts and sciences/liberal studies; literature related; mathematics related; mechanical engineering; mechanical engineering/mechanical technology; music related; psychology related; radio, television, and digital communication related; registered nursing/registered nurse; science technologies related; sport and fitness administration/management; telecommunications technology; wine steward/sommelier; writing.

Academics *Calendar:* semesters. *Degree:* certificates and associate. *Special study options:* academic remediation for entering students, accelerated degree program, adult/continuing education programs, advanced placement credit, cooperative education, distance learning, double majors, honors programs, independent study, internships, off-campus study, part-time degree program, services for LD students, study abroad, summer session for credit. *ROTC:* Air Force (c).

Library Norman F. Bourke Memorial Library plus 2 others with 92,156 titles, 187 serial subscriptions, 5,240 audiovisual materials, an OPAC, a Web page.

Student Life *Housing Options:* coed. Campus housing is provided by a third party. *Activities and Organizations:* drama/theater group, student-run newspaper, radio and television station, choral group, Student Activity Board, Student Government, Criminal Justice Club, Tutor Club, Early Childhood Club. *Campus security:* security from 8 am to 9 pm. *Student services:* health clinic.

Athletics Member NJCAA. *Intercollegiate sports:* basketball M/W, bowling M/W, golf M/W, lacrosse M/W, soccer M/W, volleyball W. *Intramural sports:* basketball M/W, skiing (downhill) M/W, volleyball M/W.

Standardized Tests *Required for some:* SAT or ACT (for admission).

Costs (2012–13) *Tuition:* state resident $3820 full-time, $150 per credit hour part-time; nonresident $7640 full-time, $300 per credit hour part-time. Full-time tuition and fees vary according to class time, course load, location, and program. Part-time tuition and fees vary according to class time, course load, location, and program. *Required fees:* $700 full-time, $7 per credit part-time. *Payment plan:* installment. *Waivers:* senior citizens and employees or children of employees.

Financial Aid Of all full-time matriculated undergraduates who enrolled in 2010, 150 Federal Work-Study jobs (averaging $2000). 200 state and other part-time jobs (averaging $1000).

Applying *Options:* electronic application, deferred entrance. *Required:* high school transcript. *Required for some:* interview. *Application deadlines:* rolling (freshmen), rolling (transfers). *Notification:* continuous (freshmen), continuous (transfers).

Freshman Application Contact Cayuga County Community College, 197 Franklin Street, Auburn, NY 13021-3099. *Phone:* 315-255-1743 Ext. 2244. *Toll-free phone:* 866-598-8883. *Web site:* http://www.cayuga-cc.edu/.

Clinton Community College

Plattsburgh, New York

- **State and locally supported** 2-year, founded 1969, part of State University of New York System
- **Small-town** 100-acre campus
- **Coed,** 1,780 undergraduate students, 76% full-time, 55% women, 45% men

Undergraduates 1,351 full-time, 429 part-time. Students come from 5 states and territories; 2 other countries; 2% are from out of state; 10% live on campus.

Faculty *Total:* 165, 33% full-time. *Student/faculty ratio:* 14:1.

Majors Accounting; administrative assistant and secretarial science; biological and physical sciences; business administration and management; community organization and advocacy; computer/information technology services administration related; consumer merchandising/retailing management; criminal justice/law enforcement administration; criminal justice/police science; electrical, electronic and communications engineering technology; humanities; industrial technology; liberal arts and sciences/liberal studies; physical education teaching and coaching; registered nursing/registered nurse; social sciences.

Academics *Calendar:* semesters. *Degree:* certificates and associate. *Special study options:* academic remediation for entering students, adult/continuing education programs, advanced placement credit, cooperative education, distance learning, English as a second language, external degree program, independent study, internships, off-campus study, part-time degree program, services for LD students, student-designed majors, summer session for credit.

Library Clinton Community College Learning Resource Center plus 1 other with 43,000 titles, 113 serial subscriptions, 297 audiovisual materials, an OPAC, a Web page.

Student Life *Housing Options:* coed, disabled students. Campus housing is provided by a third party. Freshman campus housing is guaranteed. *Activities and Organizations:* drama/theater group, student-run newspaper, choral group, Athletics, Future Human Services Professionals, PTK (Honor Society), Drama Club, Criminal Justice Club. *Campus security:* 24-hour emergency response devices and patrols, late-night transport/escort service, controlled dormitory access. *Student services:* health clinic, personal/psychological counseling.

Athletics Member NJCAA. *Intercollegiate sports:* baseball M, basketball M/W, soccer M/W, softball W. *Intramural sports:* volleyball M/W.

Costs (2012–13) *Tuition:* state resident $3620 full-time, $151 per credit part-time; nonresident $8500 full-time, $350 per credit part-time. Full-time tuition and fees vary according to program. Part-time tuition and fees vary according to course load and program. *Required fees:* $464 full-time, $16 per credit part-time, $10 per credit part-time. *Room and board:* $8250; room only: $4300. Room and board charges vary according to board plan. *Payment plan:* tuition prepayment.

Financial Aid Of all full-time matriculated undergraduates who enrolled in 2010, 45 Federal Work-Study jobs (averaging $1260).

Applying *Options:* electronic application, deferred entrance. *Required:* high school transcript. *Required for some:* essay or personal statement, 3 letters of recommendation, interview. *Application deadlines:* 8/26 (freshmen), 9/3 (transfers). *Notification:* continuous (freshmen), continuous (transfers).

Freshman Application Contact Clinton Community College, 136 Clinton Point Drive, Plattsburgh, NY 12901-9573. *Phone:* 518-562-4100. *Toll-free phone:* 800-552-1160. *Web site:* http://clintoncc.suny.edu/.

Cochran School of Nursing

Yonkers, New York

Freshman Application Contact Cochran School of Nursing, 967 North Broadway, Yonkers, NY 10701. *Phone:* 914-964-4606. *Web site:* http://www.cochranschoolofnursing.us/.

The College of Westchester

White Plains, New York

Freshman Application Contact Mr. Dale T. Smith, Vice President, The College of Westchester, 325 Central Avenue, PO Box 710, White Plains, NY 10602. *Phone:* 914-948-4442 Ext. 311. *Toll-free phone:* 800-660-7093. *Fax:* 914-948-5441. *E-mail:* admissions@cw.edu. *Web site:* http://www.cw.edu/.

Columbia-Greene Community College

Hudson, New York

Freshman Application Contact Christine Pepitone, Director of Admissions, Columbia-Greene Community College, 4400 Route 23, Hudson, NY 12534-0327. *Phone:* 518-828-4181 Ext. 3388. *E-mail:* christine.pepitone@ sunycgcc.edu. *Web site:* http://www.sunycgcc.edu/.

Corning Community College

Corning, New York

- **State and locally supported** 2-year, founded 1956, part of State University of New York System
- **Rural** 500-acre campus
- **Endowment** $3.9 million
- **Coed,** 5,298 undergraduate students, 47% full-time, 57% women, 43% men

Undergraduates 2,471 full-time, 2,827 part-time. Students come from 12 states and territories; 18 other countries; 4% are from out of state; 4% Black or African American, non-Hispanic/Latino; 1% Hispanic/Latino; 0.8% Asian, non-Hispanic/Latino; 0.1% Native Hawaiian or other Pacific Islander, non-Hispanic/Latino; 0.4% American Indian or Alaska Native, non-Hispanic/Latino; 2% Two or more races, non-Hispanic/Latino; 13% Race/ethnicity unknown; 0.2% international; 4% transferred in. *Retention:* 58% of full-time freshmen returned.

Freshmen *Admission:* 2,328 applied, 2,269 admitted, 917 enrolled.

Faculty *Total:* 295, 34% full-time, 11% with terminal degrees. *Student/faculty ratio:* 24:1.

Majors Accounting; administrative assistant and secretarial science; auto-body/collision and repair technology; automobile/automotive mechanics technology; automotive engineering technology; biological and physical sciences; business administration and management; chemical technology; child-care provision; computer and information sciences; computer and information sciences related; computer graphics; computer/information technology services administration related; computer programming; computer programming related; computer science; computer systems networking and telecommunications; computer technology/computer systems technology; corrections and criminal justice related; criminal justice/law enforcement administration; drafting and design technology; education related; electrical, electronic and communications engineering technology; elementary education; emergency medical technology (EMT paramedic); environmental science; fine/studio arts; fire science/firefighting; general studies; health and physical education/fitness; hospitality administration related; humanities; human services; industrial technology; information technology; liberal arts and sciences/liberal studies; machine shop technology; machine tool technology; mathematics; mechanical engineering/mechanical technology; optical sciences; outdoor education; pre-engineering; registered nursing/registered nurse; social sciences; substance abuse/addiction counseling; word processing.

Academics *Calendar:* semesters. *Degree:* certificates and associate. *Special study options:* academic remediation for entering students, accelerated degree program, adult/continuing education programs, advanced placement credit, cooperative education, distance learning, double majors, English as a second language, honors programs, independent study, internships, off-campus study, part-time degree program, services for LD students, student-designed majors, study abroad, summer session for credit. *ROTC:* Army (c), Navy (c), Air Force (c).

Library Arthur A. Houghton, Jr. Library with 48,454 titles, 43,027 serial subscriptions, 860 audiovisual materials, an OPAC, a Web page.

Student Life *Housing:* college housing not available. *Activities and Organizations:* drama/theater group, student-run newspaper, radio station, choral group, Student Association, Nursing Society, Muse of Fire theatre group, WCEB radio station, International Foreign Language. *Campus security:* 24-hour emergency response devices and patrols, late-night transport/escort service. *Student services:* health clinic, personal/psychological counseling.

Athletics Member NJCAA. *Intercollegiate sports:* baseball M, basketball M/W, bowling M/W, golf M/W, soccer M/W, softball W, volleyball W. *Intramural sports:* basketball M/W, bowling M/W, cross-country running M/W, golf M/W, soccer M/W, softball M/W, table tennis M/W, volleyball M/W, weight lifting M/W.

Costs (2011–12) *Tuition:* state resident $3870 full-time, $161 per credit hour part-time; nonresident $7740 full-time, $322 per credit hour part-time. Part-time tuition and fees vary according to course load. *Required fees:* $435 full-time, $8 per credit hour part-time. *Payment plan:* installment. *Waivers:* senior citizens and employees or children of employees.

Financial Aid Of all full-time matriculated undergraduates who enrolled in 2010, 264 Federal Work-Study jobs (averaging $1128).

Applying *Options:* electronic application, early admission. *Application fee:* $25. *Required:* high school transcript. *Required for some:* interview. *Application deadlines:* rolling (freshmen), rolling (transfers). *Notification:* continuous (freshmen), continuous (transfers).

Freshman Application Contact Corning Community College, One Academic Drive, Corning, NY 14830-3297. *Phone:* 607-962-9427. *Toll-free phone:* 800-358-7171. *Web site:* http://www.corning-cc.edu/.

Crouse Hospital School of Nursing

Syracuse, New York

Freshman Application Contact Ms. Amy Graham, Enrollment Management Supervisor, Crouse Hospital School of Nursing, 736 Irving Avenue, Syracuse, NY 13210. *Phone:* 315-470-7481. *Fax:* 315-470-7925. *E-mail:* amygraham@crouse.org. *Web site:* http://www.crouse.org/nursing/.

Dorothea Hopfer School of Nursing at The Mount Vernon Hospital

Mount Vernon, New York

Director of Admissions Sandra Farrior, Coordinator of Student Services, Dorothea Hopfer School of Nursing at The Mount Vernon Hospital, 53 Valentine Street, Mount Vernon, NY 10550. *Phone:* 914-361-6472. *E-mail:* hopferadmissions@sshsw.org. *Web site:* http://www.ssmc.org/.

Dutchess Community College

Poughkeepsie, New York

- **State and locally supported** 2-year, founded 1957, part of State University of New York System
- **Suburban** 130-acre campus with easy access to New York City
- **Coed,** 10,329 undergraduate students, 53% full-time, 55% women, 45% men

Undergraduates 5,449 full-time, 4,880 part-time. 11% Black or African American, non-Hispanic/Latino; 12% Hispanic/Latino; 3% Asian, non-Hispanic/Latino; 0.1% Native Hawaiian or other Pacific Islander, non-Hispanic/Latino; 0.4% American Indian or Alaska Native, non-Hispanic/Latino; 1% Two or more races, non-Hispanic/Latino; 7% Race/ethnicity unknown; 0.5% international; 4% transferred in.

Freshmen *Admission:* 2,190 enrolled. *Average high school GPA:* 2.5.

Faculty *Total:* 491, 27% full-time, 7% with terminal degrees.

Majors Accounting; administrative assistant and secretarial science; architectural engineering technology; biological and physical sciences; business administration and management; child development; clinical/medical laboratory technology; commercial and advertising art; computer and information sciences; computer science; construction engineering technology; consumer merchandising/retailing management; criminal justice/law enforcement administration; criminal justice/safety; dietetics; electrical and electronics engineering; electrical, electronic and communications engineering technology; electromechanical technology; elementary education; emergency medical technology (EMT paramedic); engineering science; foods, nutrition, and wellness; humanities; information science/studies; kindergarten/preschool education; legal assistant/paralegal; liberal arts and sciences/liberal studies; mass communication/media; mathematics; medical/clinical assistant; mental health counseling; parks, recreation and leisure; physical therapy technology; psychiatric/mental health services technology; registered nursing/registered nurse; science teacher education; social sciences; special products marketing; speech communication and rhetoric; telecommunications technology; tourism and travel services management.

Academics *Calendar:* semesters. *Degree:* certificates and associate. *Special study options:* academic remediation for entering students, adult/continuing education programs, advanced placement credit, English as a second language, freshman honors college, honors programs, internships, off-campus study, part-time degree program, summer session for credit.

Library Dutchess Library with 158,166 titles, 293 serial subscriptions, an OPAC, a Web page.

Student Life *Housing:* college housing not available. *Activities and Organizations:* drama/theater group, student-run newspaper, radio station, choral group. *Campus security:* 24-hour emergency response devices and patrols, late-night transport/escort service. *Student services:* health clinic, personal/psychological counseling.

Athletics Member NJCAA. *Intercollegiate sports:* baseball M, basketball M/W, bowling M/W, golf M, soccer M/W, softball W, tennis M/W, volleyball W. *Intramural sports:* badminton M/W, basketball M/W, football M, soccer M/W, tennis M/W, volleyball M/W.

Costs (2012–13) *Tuition:* state resident $2900 full-time, $121 per credit hour part-time; nonresident $5800 full-time, $242 per credit hour part-time. *Required fees:* $420 full-time, $10 per credit hour part-time, $17 per term part-time. *Payment plan:* installment. *Waivers:* senior citizens and employees or children of employees.

Applying *Options:* early admission, deferred entrance. *Required:* high school transcript. *Application deadlines:* rolling (freshmen), rolling (transfers). *Notification:* continuous (freshmen), continuous (transfers).

Freshman Application Contact Dutchess Community College, 53 Pendell Road, Poughkeepsie, NY 12601-1595. *Phone:* 845-431-8010. *Web site:* http://www.sunydutchess.edu/.

Ellis School of Nursing

Schenectady, New York

- **Independent** 2-year, founded 1906
- **Urban** campus
- **Coed, primarily women,** 120 undergraduate students, 25% full-time, 79% women, 21% men

Undergraduates 30 full-time, 90 part-time. Students come from 3 states and territories; 3% Black or African American, non-Hispanic/Latino; 4% Hispanic/Latino; 2% Asian, non-Hispanic/Latino; 3% Native Hawaiian or other Pacific Islander, non-Hispanic/Latino; 2% Race/ethnicity unknown.

Freshmen *Admission:* 14 applied, 1 admitted, 1 enrolled.

Faculty *Student/faculty ratio:* 6:1.

Majors Registered nursing/registered nurse.

Academics *Degree:* associate.

Standardized Tests *Recommended:* SAT (for admission).

Costs (2011–12) *Tuition:* $7426 full-time, $4874 per year part-time. Full-time tuition and fees vary according to student level. Part-time tuition and fees vary according to student level. *Required fees:* $831 full-time, $429 per year part-time.

Applying *Options:* electronic application. *Application fee:* $40. *Required:* essay or personal statement, high school transcript, minimum 3.0 GPA, 2 letters of recommendation. *Application deadlines:* 1/15 (freshmen), rolling (transfers). *Notification:* 3/15 (freshmen).

Freshman Application Contact Carolyn Lansing, Student Services Coordinator, Ellis School of Nursing, 1101 Nott Street, Schenectady, NY 12308. *Phone:* 518-243-4471. *Fax:* 518-243-4470. *E-mail:* lansingc@ellismedicine.org. *Web site:* http://www.ellismedicine.org/AboutEllis/SchoolofNursing.aspx.

Elmira Business Institute

Elmira, New York

- **Private** 2-year, founded 1858
- **Urban** campus
- **Coed, primarily women,** 235 undergraduate students, 82% full-time, 88% women, 12% men

Undergraduates 192 full-time, 43 part-time. 10% are from out of state.

Freshmen *Admission:* 79 enrolled.

Faculty *Student/faculty ratio:* 9:1.

Majors Accounting; administrative assistant and secretarial science; medical/clinical assistant; medical insurance coding.

Academics *Calendar:* semesters. *Degree:* certificates and associate. *Special study options:* academic remediation for entering students, advanced placement credit, internships, part-time degree program.

Library Elmira Business Institute Library plus 1 other.

Student Life *Housing:* college housing not available. *Campus security:* 24-hour emergency response devices.

Costs (2012–13) *Tuition:* $11,700 full-time, $390 per credit hour part-time. Full-time tuition and fees vary according to program. Part-time tuition and fees vary according to program. No tuition increase for student's term of enrollment. *Required fees:* $100 full-time.

Financial Aid Of all full-time matriculated undergraduates who enrolled in 2011, 316 applied for aid, 306 were judged to have need. *Average percent of need met:* 85%. *Average financial aid package:* $30,450. *Average need-based loan:* $3500. *Average need-based gift aid:* $18,950. *Average indebtedness upon graduation:* $14,000.

Applying *Options:* electronic application. *Required:* high school transcript, interview. *Application deadline:* rolling (freshmen).

Freshman Application Contact Mrs. Lisa Roan, Admissions Director, Elmira Business Institute, Elmira, NY 14901. *Phone:* 607-733-7178. *Toll-free phone:* 800-843-1812. *E-mail:* info@ebi-college.com. *Web site:* http://www.ebi-college.com/.

Erie Community College

Buffalo, New York

- **State and locally supported** 2-year, founded 1971, part of State University of New York System
- **Urban** 1-acre campus
- **Coed,** 3,495 undergraduate students, 75% full-time, 61% women, 39% men

Undergraduates 2,631 full-time, 864 part-time. Students come from 18 states and territories; 4 other countries; 2% are from out of state; 33% Black or African American, non-Hispanic/Latino; 11% Hispanic/Latino; 2% Asian, non-Hispanic/Latino; 0.2% Native Hawaiian or other Pacific Islander, non-Hispanic/Latino; 0.6% American Indian or Alaska Native, non-Hispanic/Latino; 3% Two or more races, non-Hispanic/Latino; 4% Race/ethnicity unknown; 4% international; 7% transferred in.

Freshmen *Admission:* 756 enrolled.

Faculty *Total:* 225, 36% full-time. *Student/faculty ratio:* 17:1.

Majors Administrative assistant and secretarial science; building/property maintenance; business administration and management; child-care and support services management; community health services counseling; criminal justice/police science; culinary arts; humanities; legal assistant/paralegal; liberal arts and sciences/liberal studies; medical radiologic technology; middle school education; physical education teaching and coaching; public administration and social service professions related; registered nursing/registered nurse; substance abuse/addiction counseling.

Academics *Calendar:* semesters. *Degree:* certificates, diplomas, and associate. *Special study options:* academic remediation for entering students, adult/continuing education programs, advanced placement credit, cooperative education, distance learning, double majors, English as a second language, honors programs, independent study, internships, part-time degree program, services for LD students, student-designed majors, study abroad, summer session for credit. *ROTC:* Army (c).

Library Leon E. Butler Library with 26,269 titles, 152 serial subscriptions, 1,571 audiovisual materials, an OPAC, a Web page.

Student Life *Housing:* college housing not available. *Activities and Organizations:* drama/theater group, student-run newspaper, radio station, choral group. *Campus security:* 24-hour emergency response devices and patrols, late-night transport/escort service. *Student services:* health clinic, personal/psychological counseling, women's center.

Athletics Member NJCAA. *Intercollegiate sports:* baseball M, basketball M/W, bowling M/W, cheerleading W, cross-country running M/W, football M, golf M/W, ice hockey M, lacrosse W, soccer M/W, softball W, swimming and diving M/W, track and field M/W, volleyball W.

Costs (2011–12) *One-time required fee:* $50. *Tuition:* area resident $3600 full-time, $150 per credit hour part-time; state resident $7200 full-time, $300 per credit hour part-time; nonresident $7200 full-time, $300 per credit hour part-time. *Required fees:* $510 full-time, $5 per credit hour part-time; $60 per term part-time. *Payment plan:* installment. *Waivers:* senior citizens and employees or children of employees.

Applying *Options:* electronic application. *Required:* high school transcript. *Required for some:* interview. *Application deadlines:* rolling (freshmen), rolling (transfers). *Notification:* continuous (freshmen), continuous (transfers).

Freshman Application Contact Erie Community College, 121 Ellicott Street, Buffalo, NY 14203-2698. *Phone:* 716-851-1155. *Fax:* 716-270-2821. *Web site:* http://www.ecc.edu/.

Erie Community College, North Campus

Williamsville, New York

- **State and locally supported** 2-year, founded 1946, part of State University of New York System
- **Suburban** 120-acre campus with easy access to Buffalo
- **Coed,** 6,410 undergraduate students, 65% full-time, 50% women, 50% men

Undergraduates 4,183 full-time, 2,227 part-time. Students come from 23 states and territories; 22 other countries; 0.6% are from out of state; 13% Black or African American, non-Hispanic/Latino; 4% Hispanic/Latino; 2% Asian, non-Hispanic/Latino; 0.1% Native Hawaiian or other Pacific Islander, non-Hispanic/Latino; 0.5% American Indian or Alaska Native, non-Hispanic/Latino; 2% Two or more races, non-Hispanic/Latino; 4% Race/ethnicity unknown; 2% international; 10% transferred in.

Freshmen *Admission:* 1,315 enrolled. *Test scores:* SAT critical reading scores over 500: 70%; SAT math scores over 500: 76%; SAT critical reading scores over 600: 11%; SAT math scores over 600: 15%; SAT critical reading scores over 700: 1%.

Faculty *Total:* 384, 39% full-time. *Student/faculty ratio:* 17:1.

Majors Business administration and management; civil engineering technology; clinical/medical laboratory technology; computer and information sciences; construction management; criminal justice/police science; culinary arts; dental hygiene; dietitian assistant; electrical, electronic and communications engineering technology; engineering; geological and earth sciences/geosciences related; health information/medical records technology; humanities; industrial technology; information technology; liberal arts and sciences/liberal studies; mechanical engineering/mechanical technology; medical office management; occupational therapist assistant; office management; opticianry; physical education teaching and coaching; registered nursing/registered nurse; respiratory care therapy; restaurant, culinary, and catering management.

Academics *Calendar:* semesters plus summer sessions, winter intersession. *Degree:* certificates, diplomas, and associate. *Special study options:* academic remediation for entering students, adult/continuing education programs, advanced placement credit, cooperative education, distance learning, double majors, English as a second language, honors programs, independent study, internships, part-time degree program, services for LD students, student-designed majors, study abroad, summer session for credit. *ROTC:* Army (c).

Library Richard R. Dry Memorial Library with 53,554 titles, 211 serial subscriptions, 4,917 audiovisual materials, an OPAC, a Web page.

Student Life *Housing:* college housing not available. *Activities and Organizations:* drama/theater group, student-run newspaper, radio station, choral group. *Campus security:* 24-hour emergency response devices and patrols, late-night transport/escort service. *Student services:* health clinic, personal/psychological counseling, women's center.

Athletics Member NJCAA. *Intercollegiate sports:* baseball M, basketball M/W, bowling M/W, cheerleading W, cross-country running M/W, football M, golf M/W, ice hockey M, lacrosse W, soccer M/W, softball W, swimming and diving M/W, track and field M/W, volleyball W.

Costs (2011–12) *One-time required fee:* $50. *Tuition:* area resident $3600 full-time, $150 per credit hour part-time; state resident $7200 full-time, $300 per credit hour part-time; nonresident $7200 full-time, $300 per credit hour part-time. *Required fees:* $510 full-time, $5 per credit hour part-time, $60 per term part-time. *Payment plan:* installment. *Waivers:* senior citizens and employees or children of employees.

Applying *Options:* electronic application. *Required:* high school transcript. *Required for some:* interview. *Application deadlines:* rolling (freshmen), rolling (transfers). *Notification:* continuous (freshmen), continuous (transfers).

Freshman Application Contact Erie Community College, North Campus, 6205 Main Street, Williamsville, NY 14221-7095. *Phone:* 716-851-1455. *Fax:* 716-270-2961. *Web site:* http://www.ecc.edu/.

Erie Community College, South Campus
Orchard Park, New York

- **State and locally supported** 2-year, founded 1974, part of State University of New York System
- **Suburban** 110-acre campus with easy access to Buffalo
- **Coed,** 4,271 undergraduate students, 60% full-time, 45% women, 55% men

Undergraduates 2,542 full-time, 1,729 part-time. Students come from 16 states and territories; 3 other countries; 2% are from out of state; 5% Black or African American, non-Hispanic/Latino; 4% Hispanic/Latino; 0.5% Asian, non-Hispanic/Latino; 1% American Indian or Alaska Native, non-Hispanic/Latino; 2% Two or more races, non-Hispanic/Latino; 5% Race/ethnicity unknown; 0.6% international; 7% transferred in.

Freshmen *Admission:* 828 enrolled. *Test scores:* SAT critical reading scores over 500: 74%; SAT critical reading scores over 600: 13%; SAT critical reading scores over 700: 1%.

Faculty *Total:* 337, 28% full-time. *Student/faculty ratio:* 17:1.

Majors Architectural engineering technology; autobody/collision and repair technology; automobile/automotive mechanics technology; business administration and management; CAD/CADD drafting/design technology; communications systems installation and repair technology; computer technology/computer systems technology; criminal justice/police science; dental laboratory technology; emergency medical technology (EMT paramedic); fire services administration; graphic and printing equipment operation/production; humanities; information technology; liberal arts and sciences/liberal studies; office management; physical education teaching and coaching; speech communication and rhetoric.

Academics *Calendar:* semesters plus summer sessions, winter intersession. *Degree:* certificates, diplomas, and associate. *Special study options:* academic remediation for entering students, adult/continuing education programs, advanced placement credit, cooperative education, distance learning, double majors, English as a second language, honors programs, independent study, internships, part-time degree program, services for LD students, student-designed majors, study abroad, summer session for credit. *ROTC:* Army (c).

Library 47,892 titles, 188 serial subscriptions, 1,366 audiovisual materials, an OPAC, a Web page.

Student Life *Housing:* college housing not available. *Activities and Organizations:* drama/theater group, student-run newspaper, radio station, choral group. *Campus security:* 24-hour emergency response devices and patrols, late-night transport/escort service. *Student services:* health clinic, personal/psychological counseling, women's center.

Athletics Member NJCAA. *Intercollegiate sports:* baseball M, basketball M/W, bowling M/W, cheerleading W, cross-country running M/W, football M, golf M/W, ice hockey M, lacrosse W, soccer M/W, softball W, swimming and diving M/W, track and field M/W, volleyball W.

Costs (2011–12) *One-time required fee:* $50. *Tuition:* area resident $3600 full-time, $150 per credit hour part-time; state resident $7200 full-time, $300 per credit hour part-time; nonresident $7200 full-time, $300 per credit hour part-time. *Required fees:* $510 full-time, $5 per credit hour part-time, $60 per term part-time. *Payment plan:* installment. *Waivers:* senior citizens and employees or children of employees.

Applying *Options:* electronic application. *Required:* high school transcript. *Required for some:* interview. *Application deadlines:* rolling (freshmen), rolling (transfers). *Notification:* continuous (freshmen), continuous (transfers).

Freshman Application Contact Erie Community College, South Campus, 4041 Southwestern Boulevard, Orchard Park, NY 14127-2199. *Phone:* 716-851-1655. *Fax:* 716-851-1687. *Web site:* http://www.ecc.edu/.

Eugenio María de Hostos Community College of the City University of New York
Bronx, New York

Freshman Application Contact Mr. Roland Velez, Director of Admissions, Eugenio María de Hostos Community College of the City University of New York, 120 149th Street, Bronx, NY 10451. *Phone:* 718-319-7968. *Fax:* 718-319-7919. *E-mail:* admissions@hostos.cuny.edu. *Web site:* http://www.hostos.cuny.edu/.

Everest Institute
Rochester, New York

Freshman Application Contact Deanna Pfluke, Director of Admissions, Everest Institute, 1630 Portland Avenue, Rochester, NY 14621. *Phone:* 585-266-0430. *Toll-free phone:* 888-741-4270. *Fax:* 585-266-8243. *Web site:* http://www.everest.edu/campus/rochester/.

Fashion Institute of Technology
New York, New York

- **State and locally supported** comprehensive, founded 1944, part of State University of New York System
- **Urban** 5-acre campus with easy access to New York City
- **Endowment** $25.9 million
- **Coed, primarily women,** 10,023 undergraduate students, 71% full-time, 84% women, 16% men

Undergraduates 7,141 full-time, 2,882 part-time. 29% are from out of state; 7% transferred in; 24% live on campus. *Retention:* 87% of full-time freshmen returned.

Freshmen *Admission:* 4,417 applied, 1,916 admitted, 1,156 enrolled.

Faculty *Total:* 977, 24% full-time. *Student/faculty ratio:* 17:1.

Majors Advertising; animation, interactive technology, video graphics and special effects; apparel and textile manufacturing; commercial and advertising art; commercial photography; entrepreneurial and small business related; fashion/apparel design; fashion merchandising; fashion modeling; fine and studio arts management; fine/studio arts; graphic design; illustration; industrial and product design; interior design; international marketing; marketing research; merchandising, sales, and marketing operations related (specialized); metal and jewelry arts; special products marketing.

Academics *Calendar:* semesters. *Degrees:* certificates, associate, bachelor's, and master's. *Special study options:* academic remediation for entering students, adult/continuing education programs, advanced placement credit, distance learning, English as a second language, honors programs, internships, part-time degree program, services for LD students, study abroad, summer session for credit.

Library Gladys Marcus Library.

Student Life *Housing Options:* coed, women-only. Campus housing is university owned and is provided by a third party. Freshman applicants given priority for college housing. *Activities and Organizations:* drama/theater group, student-run newspaper, radio and television station, choral group, FITSA/Student Government, Merchandising Society/Style Shop, Delta Epilson Chi: Promoting Leadership in Marketing, Merchandising, and Advertising, PRSSA: Public Relations Student Society of America, Student Ambassadors. *Campus security:* 24-hour emergency response devices and patrols, late-night transport/escort service, controlled dormitory access. *Student services:* health clinic, personal/psychological counseling.

Athletics Member NJCAA. *Intercollegiate sports:* cheerleading M/W, cross-country running M/W, soccer W, swimming and diving M/W, table tennis M/W, tennis W, track and field M/W, volleyball W. *Intramural sports:* basketball M/W, table tennis M/W, tennis M/W, volleyball M/W.

Costs (2011–12) *Tuition:* state resident $5168 full-time, $215 per credit hour part-time; nonresident $13,550 full-time, $565 per credit hour part-time. Full-time tuition and fees vary according to degree level. Part-time tuition and fees vary according to degree level. *Required fees:* $435 full-time, $40 per credit hour part-time, $93 per term part-time. *Room and board:* $12,190. Room and board charges vary according to board plan and housing facility. *Payment plan:* installment. *Waivers:* employees or children of employees.

Financial Aid Of all full-time matriculated undergraduates who enrolled in 2009, 4,507 applied for aid, 3,512 were judged to have need, 459 had their need fully met. 553 Federal Work-Study jobs (averaging $1479). In 2009, 170 non-need-based awards were made. *Average percent of need met:* 63%. *Average financial aid package:* $11,305. *Average need-based loan:* $4298. *Average need-based gift aid:* $5355. *Average non-need-based aid:* $1676. *Average indebtedness upon graduation:* $24,143.

Applying *Options:* electronic application. *Application fee:* $50. *Required:* essay or personal statement, high school transcript. *Required for some:* portfolio for art and design programs. *Application deadlines:* 2/1 (freshmen), 2/1 (transfers). *Notification:* continuous until 4/1 (freshmen), continuous until 4/1 (transfers).

Freshman Application Contact Ms. Laura Arbrogast, Director of Admissions, Fashion Institute of Technology, Seventh Avenue at 27th Street, New York, NY 10001-5992. *Phone:* 212-217-3760. *Fax:* 212-217-3761. *E-mail:* fitinfo@fitnyc.edu. *Web site:* http://www.fitnyc.edu/.

See Display ad below and page 396 for the College Close-Up.

Finger Lakes Community College

Canandaigua, New York

Freshman Application Contact Ms. Bonnie B. Ritts, Director of Admissions, Finger Lakes Community College, 3325 Marvin Sands Drive, Canandaigua, NY 14424-8395. *Phone:* 585-394-3500 Ext. 7278. *Fax:* 585-394-5005. *E-mail:* admissions@flcc.edu. *Web site:* http://www.flcc.edu/.

Fiorello H. LaGuardia Community College of the City University of New York

Long Island City, New York

- **State and locally supported** 2-year, founded 1970, part of City University of New York System
- **Urban** 6-acre campus with easy access to New York City
- **Coed,** 17,563 undergraduate students, 59% full-time, 59% women, 41% men

Undergraduates 10,401 full-time, 7,162 part-time. Students come from 15 states and territories; 162 other countries; 2% are from out of state; 15% Black or African American, non-Hispanic/Latino; 36% Hispanic/Latino; 15% Asian, non-Hispanic/Latino; 0.9% American Indian or Alaska Native, non-Hispanic/Latino; 17% Race/ethnicity unknown; 6% international; 9% transferred in.

Freshmen *Admission:* 7,745 applied, 7,745 admitted, 3,190 enrolled.

Faculty *Total:* 1,128, 30% full-time, 24% with terminal degrees. *Student/faculty ratio:* 21:1.

Majors Accounting technology and bookkeeping; administrative assistant and secretarial science; adult development and aging; biology/biological sciences; business administration and management; civil engineering; commercial photography; computer and information sciences and support services related; computer installation and repair technology; computer programming; computer science; criminal justice/safety; data entry/microcomputer applications; dietetic technology; digital arts; dramatic/theater arts; electrical and electronics engineering; emergency medical technology (EMT paramedic); engineering science; English; environmental science; fine/studio arts; funeral service and mortuary science; gerontology; industrial and product design; information science/studies; legal assistant/paralegal; liberal arts and sciences/liberal studies; licensed practical/vocational nurse training; mechanical engineering; medical radiologic technology; occupational therapist assistant; philosophy; photographic and film/video technology; physical sciences; physical therapy technology; psychiatric/mental health services technology; recording arts technology; registered nursing/registered nurse; restaurant/food services management; Spanish; speech communication and rhetoric; teacher assistant/aide; tourism and travel services management; veterinary/animal health technology; visual and performing arts.

Academics *Calendar:* enhanced semester. *Degree:* certificates and associate. *Special study options:* academic remediation for entering students, accelerated degree program, adult/continuing education programs, advanced placement credit, cooperative education, distance learning, double majors, English as a second language, honors programs, independent study, internships, off-campus study, part-time degree program, services for LD students, student-designed majors, study abroad, summer session for credit.

Library Fiorello H. LaGuardia Community College Library Media Resources Center plus 1 other with 324,359 titles, 568 serial subscriptions, 3,505 audiovisual materials, an OPAC, a Web page.

Student Life *Housing:* college housing not available. *Activities and Organizations:* drama/theater group, student-run newspaper, radio station, Bangladesh Student Association, Christian Club, Chinese Club, Web Radio, Black Student Union. *Campus security:* 24-hour emergency response devices and patrols, late-night transport/escort service. *Student services:* health clinic, personal/psychological counseling, women's center, legal services.

Athletics *Intramural sports:* basketball M/W, bowling M/W, football M, soccer M/W, softball M/W, swimming and diving M/W, table tennis M/W, volleyball M/W.

Costs (2012–13) *Tuition:* state resident $3600 full-time, $150 per credit part-time; nonresident $7200 full-time, $240 per credit part-time. *Required fees:* $342 full-time, $86 per term part-time. *Payment plan:* installment. *Waivers:* senior citizens and employees or children of employees.

Financial Aid Of all full-time matriculated undergraduates who enrolled in 2010, 7,674 applied for aid, 7,208 were judged to have need, 118 had their need fully met. 343 Federal Work-Study jobs (averaging $650). *Average percent of need met:* 51%. *Average financial aid package:* $6079. *Average need-based loan:* $4319. *Average need-based gift aid:* $4743.

Applying *Options:* electronic application, early admission, deferred entrance. *Application fee:* $65. *Required:* high school transcript. *Application deadlines:* rolling (freshmen), rolling (transfers). *Notification:* continuous (freshmen), continuous (transfers).

Freshman Application Contact Ms. LaVora Desvigne, Director of Admissions, Fiorello H. LaGuardia Community College of the City University of New York, RM-147, 31-10 Thomson Avenue, Long Island City, NY 11101. *Phone:* 718-482-5114. *Fax:* 718-482-5112. *E-mail:* admissions@lagcc.cuny.edu. *Web site:* http://www.lagcc.cuny.edu/.

Fulton-Montgomery Community College
Johnstown, New York

- **State and locally supported** 2-year, founded 1964, part of State University of New York System
- **Rural** 195-acre campus
- **Endowment** $1.7 million
- **Coed**

Undergraduates 1,863 full-time, 970 part-time. Students come from 6 states and territories; 18 other countries; 1% are from out of state; 4% transferred in. *Retention:* 56% of full-time freshmen returned.
Faculty *Student/faculty ratio:* 24:1.
Academics *Calendar:* semesters plus winter session. *Degree:* certificates and associate. *Special study options:* academic remediation for entering students, accelerated degree program, adult/continuing education programs, advanced placement credit, cooperative education, distance learning, double majors, English as a second language, external degree program, honors programs, independent study, internships, off-campus study, part-time degree program, services for LD students, student-designed majors, study abroad, summer session for credit.
Student Life *Campus security:* weekend and night security.
Athletics Member NJCAA.
Costs (2011–12) *Tuition:* state resident $3194 full-time; nonresident $6388 full-time. Part-time tuition and fees vary according to course load. *Required fees:* $544 full-time. *Room and board:* $7320; room only: $5830. *Payment plans:* installment, deferred payment.
Financial Aid Of all full-time matriculated undergraduates who enrolled in 2010, 87 Federal Work-Study jobs (averaging $1500).
Applying *Options:* electronic application, early admission, deferred entrance. *Required:* high school transcript.
Freshman Application Contact Fulton-Montgomery Community College, 2805 State Highway 67, Johnstown, NY 12095-3790. *Phone:* 518-762-4651 Ext. 8301. *Web site:* http://www.fmcc.suny.edu/.

Genesee Community College
Batavia, New York

- **State and locally supported** 2-year, founded 1966, part of State University of New York System
- **Small-town** 256-acre campus with easy access to Buffalo, Rochester
- **Endowment** $2.9 million
- **Coed,** 7,200 undergraduate students, 50% full-time, 63% women, 37% men

Undergraduates 3,611 full-time, 3,589 part-time. Students come from 25 states and territories; 30 other countries; 1% are from out of state; 9% Black or African American, non-Hispanic/Latino; 2% Hispanic/Latino; 0.5% Asian, non-Hispanic/Latino; 0.1% Native Hawaiian or other Pacific Islander, non-Hispanic/Latino; 1% American Indian or Alaska Native, non-Hispanic/Latino; 0.5% Two or more races, non-Hispanic/Latino; 5% Race/ethnicity unknown; 3% international; 6% transferred in.
Freshmen *Admission:* 2,835 applied, 2,835 admitted, 1,291 enrolled.
Faculty *Total:* 375, 22% full-time. *Student/faculty ratio:* 18:1.
Majors Accounting; administrative assistant and secretarial science; business administration and management; clinical/medical laboratory technology; computer and information sciences related; computer engineering technology;

computer graphics; computer software and media applications related; criminal justice/law enforcement administration; criminology; drafting and design technology; dramatic/theater arts; education; electrical, electronic and communications engineering technology; elementary education; engineering science; fashion merchandising; gerontology; health professions related; hotel/motel administration; human services; information science/studies; kindergarten/preschool education; legal assistant/paralegal; liberal arts and sciences/liberal studies; marketing/marketing management; mass communication/media; mathematics; network and system administration; physical education teaching and coaching; physical therapy; polysomnography; psychology; registered nursing/registered nurse; respiratory care therapy; substance abuse/addiction counseling; tourism and travel services management; veterinary/animal health technology.
Academics *Calendar:* semesters. *Degree:* certificates and associate. *Special study options:* academic remediation for entering students, adult/continuing education programs, advanced placement credit, cooperative education, distance learning, double majors, English as a second language, honors programs, independent study, internships, part-time degree program, services for LD students, study abroad, summer session for credit.
Library Alfred C. O'Connell Library with 87,500 titles, 212 serial subscriptions, 5,922 audiovisual materials, an OPAC, a Web page.
Student Life *Housing Options:* disabled students. Campus housing is university owned. *Activities and Organizations:* drama/theater group, student-run newspaper, radio station, choral group, Student Government Association, Phi Theta Kappa, DECA, Student Activities Council, Forum Players. *Campus security:* 24-hour emergency response devices and patrols, student patrols, late-night transport/escort service, controlled dormitory access. *Student services:* health clinic, personal/psychological counseling.
Athletics Member NJCAA. *Intercollegiate sports:* baseball M(s), basketball M(s)/W(s), cheerleading M/W, golf M/W, lacrosse M(s)/W, soccer M/W, softball W, swimming and diving M/W, volleyball W(s). *Intramural sports:* badminton M/W, basketball M/W, soccer M/W, tennis M/W, track and field M/W, volleyball M/W, water polo M/W.
Standardized Tests *Recommended:* ACT (for admission).
Costs (2012–13) *Tuition:* state resident $140 per credit hour part-time; nonresident $160 per credit hour part-time. Full-time tuition and fees vary according to course load. Part-time tuition and fees vary according to course load. *Required fees:* $10 per credit hour part-time. *Room and board:* Room and board charges vary according to board plan and housing facility. *Payment plan:* installment. *Waivers:* senior citizens and employees or children of employees.
Financial Aid Of all full-time matriculated undergraduates who enrolled in 2009, 2,826 applied for aid, 2,520 were judged to have need, 980 had their need fully met. 145 Federal Work-Study jobs (averaging $1090). 68 state and other part-time jobs (averaging $1895). *Average percent of need met:* 68%. *Average financial aid package:* $4320. *Average need-based loan:* $3300. *Average need-based gift aid:* $2975. *Average indebtedness upon graduation:* $8750.
Applying *Options:* electronic application. *Required:* high school transcript. *Required for some:* 1 letter of recommendation. *Application deadlines:* rolling (freshmen), rolling (out-of-state freshmen), rolling (transfers). *Notification:* continuous (freshmen), continuous (out-of-state freshmen), continuous (transfers).
Freshman Application Contact Mrs. Tanya Lane-Martin, Director of Admissions, Genesee Community College, Batavia, NY 14020. *Phone:* 585-343-0055 Ext. 6413. *Toll-free phone:* 800-CALL GCC. *Fax:* 585-345-6892. *E-mail:* tmlanemartin@genesee.edu. *Web site:* http://www.genesee.edu/.

Helene Fuld College of Nursing of North General Hospital
New York, New York

Freshman Application Contact Helene Fuld College of Nursing of North General Hospital, 24 East 120th Street, New York, NY 10035. *Phone:* 212-616-7271. *Web site:* http://www.helenefuld.edu/.

Herkimer County Community College
Herkimer, New York

Director of Admissions Mr. Scott J. Hughes, Associate Dean for Enrollment Management, Herkimer County Community College, Reservoir Road, Herkimer, NY 13350. *Phone:* 315-866-0300 Ext. 278. *Toll-free phone:* 888-464-4222 Ext. 8278. *Web site:* http://www.herkimer.edu/.

Hudson Valley Community College
Troy, New York

Freshman Application Contact Ms. Marie Claire Bauer, Director of Admissions, Hudson Valley Community College, 80 Vandenburgh Avenue,

Troy, NY 12180-6096. *Phone:* 518-629-7309. *Toll-free phone:* 877-325-HVCC. *Web site:* http://www.hvcc.edu/.

Institute of Design and Construction
Brooklyn, New York

Director of Admissions Mr. Kevin Giannetti, Director of Admissions, Institute of Design and Construction, 141 Willoughby Street, Brooklyn, NY 11201-5317. *Phone:* 718-855-3661. *Web site:* http://www.idcbrooklyn.org/.

Island Drafting and Technical Institute
Amityville, New York

- **Proprietary** 2-year, founded 1957
- **Suburban** campus with easy access to New York City
- **Coed,** 116 undergraduate students, 100% full-time, 14% women, 86% men

Undergraduates 116 full-time. Students come from 1 other state; 18% Black or African American, non-Hispanic/Latino; 21% Hispanic/Latino; 0.9% Asian, non-Hispanic/Latino; 0.9% Two or more races, non-Hispanic/Latino. *Retention:* 80% of full-time freshmen returned.
Freshmen *Admission:* 67 applied, 54 admitted, 45 enrolled. *Average high school GPA:* 2.5.
Faculty *Total:* 11, 45% full-time. *Student/faculty ratio:* 15:1.
Majors Architectural drafting and CAD/CADD; computer and information sciences and support services related; computer and information systems security; computer systems networking and telecommunications; computer technology/computer systems technology; electrical, electronic and communications engineering technology; mechanical drafting and CAD/CADD; network and system administration.
Academics *Calendar:* semesters. *Degree:* certificates, diplomas, and associate. *Special study options:* accelerated degree program, adult/continuing education programs, summer session for credit.
Student Life *Housing:* college housing not available.
Costs (2011–12) *Tuition:* $14,850 full-time, $495 per credit hour part-time. No tuition increase for student's term of enrollment. *Required fees:* $150 full-time. *Payment plan:* installment.
Applying *Options:* early admission. *Application fee:* $25. *Required:* interview. *Recommended:* high school transcript. *Notification:* continuous (freshmen).
Freshman Application Contact John Olivio, Island Drafting and Technical Institute, Island Drafting and Technical Institute, 128 Broadway, Amityville, NY 11701. *Phone:* 631-691-8733 Ext. 14. *Fax:* 631-691-8738. *E-mail:* info@idti.edu. *Web site:* http://www.idti.edu/.

ITT Technical Institute
Albany, New York

- **Proprietary** 2-year, founded 1998, part of ITT Educational Services, Inc.
- **Coed**

Majors Communications technology; computer software and media applications related; design and visual communications; drafting and design technology; electrical, electronic and communications engineering technology; graphic communications; network and system administration; web/multimedia management and webmaster.
Academics *Calendar:* quarters. *Degree:* associate.
Student Life *Housing:* college housing not available.
Freshman Application Contact Director of Recruitment, ITT Technical Institute, 13 Airline Drive, Albany, NY 12205. *Phone:* 518-452-9300. *Toll-free phone:* 800-489-1191. *Web site:* http://www.itt-tech.edu/.

ITT Technical Institute
Getzville, New York

- **Proprietary** 2-year, part of ITT Educational Services, Inc.
- **Coed**

Majors Communications technology; computer software and media applications related; criminal justice/law enforcement administration; drafting and design technology; electrical, electronic and communications engineering technology; graphic communications; network and system administration.
Academics *Degree:* associate.
Student Life *Housing:* college housing not available.
Freshman Application Contact Director of Recruitment, ITT Technical Institute, 2295 Millersport Highway, PO Box 327, Getzville, NY 14068. *Phone:* 716-689-2200. *Toll-free phone:* 800-469-7593. *Web site:* http://www.itt-tech.edu/.

ITT Technical Institute
Liverpool, New York

- **Proprietary** 2-year, founded 1998, part of ITT Educational Services, Inc.
- **Coed**

Majors Communications technology; computer software and media applications related; drafting and design technology; electrical, electronic and communications engineering technology; graphic communications; network and system administration.
Academics *Calendar:* semesters. *Degree:* associate.
Student Life *Housing:* college housing not available.
Freshman Application Contact Director of Recruitment, ITT Technical Institute, 235 Greenfield Parkway, Liverpool, NY 13088. *Phone:* 315-461-8000. *Toll-free phone:* 877-488-0011. *Web site:* http://www.itt-tech.edu/.

Jamestown Business College
Jamestown, New York

- **Proprietary** primarily 2-year, founded 1886
- **Small-town** 1-acre campus
- **Coed,** 317 undergraduate students, 96% full-time, 70% women, 30% men

Undergraduates 304 full-time, 13 part-time. Students come from 2 states and territories; 11% are from out of state; 2% Black or African American, non-Hispanic/Latino; 4% Hispanic/Latino; 0.6% Asian, non-Hispanic/Latino; 0.3% Native Hawaiian or other Pacific Islander, non-Hispanic/Latino; 2% American Indian or Alaska Native, non-Hispanic/Latino; 0.6% Two or more races, non-Hispanic/Latino; 2% Race/ethnicity unknown; 13% transferred in.
Freshmen *Admission:* 101 applied, 99 admitted, 70 enrolled.
Faculty *Total:* 17, 41% full-time, 6% with terminal degrees. *Student/faculty ratio:* 32:1.
Majors Administrative assistant and secretarial science; business administration and management; medical/clinical assistant.
Academics *Calendar:* quarters. *Degrees:* certificates, associate, and bachelor's. *Special study options:* advanced placement credit, double majors, internships, part-time degree program, summer session for credit.
Library James Prendergast Library with 279,270 titles, 372 serial subscriptions, an OPAC, a Web page.
Student Life *Housing:* college housing not available. *Campus security:* 24-hour emergency response devices.
Athletics *Intramural sports:* basketball M(c)/W(c), racquetball M(c)/W(c), softball M(c)/W(c), swimming and diving M(c)/W(c), table tennis M(c)/W(c), tennis M(c)/W(c), volleyball M(c)/W(c), weight lifting M(c)/W(c).
Costs (2012–13) *One-time required fee:* $25. *Tuition:* $10,500 full-time, $292 per credit hour part-time. *Required fees:* $900 full-time, $150 per term part-time. *Waivers:* employees or children of employees.
Applying *Application fee:* $25. *Required:* essay or personal statement, high school transcript, interview. *Application deadlines:* rolling (freshmen), rolling (transfers).
Freshman Application Contact Mrs. Brenda Salemme, Director of Admissions and Placement, Jamestown Business College, 7 Fairmount Avenue, Box 429, Jamestown, NY 14702-0429. *Phone:* 716-664-5100. *Fax:* 716-664-3144. *E-mail:* brendasalemme@jamestownbusinesscollege.edu. *Web site:* http://www.jbcny.org/.

Jamestown Community College
Jamestown, New York

- **State and locally supported** 2-year, founded 1950, part of State University of New York System
- **Small-town** 107-acre campus
- **Endowment** $7.9 million
- **Coed,** 3,926 undergraduate students, 70% full-time, 58% women, 42% men

Undergraduates 2,746 full-time, 1,180 part-time. Students come from 14 states and territories; 9 other countries; 8% are from out of state; 3% Black or African American, non-Hispanic/Latino; 5% Hispanic/Latino; 0.6% Asian, non-Hispanic/Latino; 0.1% Native Hawaiian or other Pacific Islander, non-Hispanic/Latino; 1% American Indian or Alaska Native, non-Hispanic/Latino; 2% Two or more races, non-Hispanic/Latino; 0.5% Race/ethnicity unknown; 0.4% international; 6% transferred in; 6% live on campus.
Freshmen *Admission:* 2,161 applied, 2,077 admitted, 1,152 enrolled. *Average high school GPA:* 3.19.
Faculty *Total:* 378, 22% full-time. *Student/faculty ratio:* 16:1.
Majors Accounting; accounting technology and bookkeeping; administrative assistant and secretarial science; airline pilot and flight crew; biology/biological sciences; biology/biotechnology laboratory technician; business administration and management; commercial and advertising art; community organization and advocacy; computer programming; criminal justice/police

science; criminal justice/safety; data processing and data processing technology; early childhood education; electrical, electronic and communications engineering technology; elementary education; engineering; fine/studio arts; fire prevention and safety technology; fire science/firefighting; health information/medical records technology; humanities; human services; information technology; kindergarten/preschool education; liberal arts and sciences and humanities related; liberal arts and sciences/liberal studies; machine tool technology; mechanical engineering/mechanical technology; medical office assistant; music; occupational therapist assistant; office occupations and clerical services; physical education teaching and coaching; registered nursing/registered nurse; speech communication and rhetoric; welding technology.

Academics *Calendar:* semesters. *Degree:* certificates and associate. *Special study options:* academic remediation for entering students, adult/continuing education programs, advanced placement credit, distance learning, honors programs, independent study, internships, off-campus study, part-time degree program, services for LD students, study abroad, summer session for credit.

Library Hultquist Library with 86,539 titles, 329 serial subscriptions, 6,105 audiovisual materials, an OPAC, a Web page.

Student Life *Housing Options:* coed. Campus housing is university owned. *Activities and Organizations:* drama/theater group, student-run radio station, choral group, Nursing Club, Student Occupational Therapy Assistant (SOTA) Club, Earth Awareness, Deranged Nerd Alliance (DNA Club), Japanese Culture Club. *Student services:* health clinic, personal/psychological counseling.

Athletics Member NJCAA. *Intercollegiate sports:* baseball M, basketball M/W, cheerleading W, golf M/W, soccer M/W, softball W, swimming and diving M/W, volleyball W, wrestling M. *Intramural sports:* basketball M/W, bowling M/W, cross-country running M/W, softball M/W, table tennis M/W, tennis M/W, volleyball M/W.

Costs (2011–12) *Tuition:* state resident $3900 full-time, $163 per credit hour part-time; nonresident $7800 full-time, $294 per credit hour part-time. Full-time tuition and fees vary according to course load and program. Part-time tuition and fees vary according to course load and program. *Required fees:* $455 full-time, $15 per credit hour part-time. *Room and board:* $9100; room only: $6300. Room and board charges vary according to board plan. *Payment plan:* installment. *Waivers:* employees or children of employees.

Financial Aid Of all full-time matriculated undergraduates who enrolled in 2010, 85 Federal Work-Study jobs (averaging $1500). 85 state and other part-time jobs (averaging $1300).

Applying *Options:* electronic application, deferred entrance. *Required:* high school transcript. *Required for some:* standardized test scores used for placement, GEDs accepted. TOEFL (or equivalent) required for international students. *Application deadlines:* rolling (freshmen), rolling (out-of-state freshmen), rolling (transfers). *Notification:* continuous (freshmen), continuous (out-of-state freshmen), continuous (transfers).

Freshman Application Contact Ms. Wendy Present, Director of Admissions and Recruitment, Jamestown Community College, 525 Falconer Street, PO Box 20, Jamestown, NY 14702-0020. *Phone:* 716-338-1001. *Toll-free phone:* 800-388-8557. *Fax:* 716-338-1450. *E-mail:* admissions@mail.sunyjcc.edu. *Web site:* http://www.sunyjcc.edu/.

Jefferson Community College
Watertown, New York

- **State and locally supported** 2-year, founded 1961, part of State University of New York System
- **Small-town** 90-acre campus with easy access to Syracuse
- **Coed,** 4,026 undergraduate students, 56% full-time, 62% women, 38% men

Undergraduates 2,238 full-time, 1,788 part-time. Students come from 23 states and territories; 3 other countries; 6% Black or African American, non-Hispanic/Latino; 5% Hispanic/Latino; 1% Asian, non-Hispanic/Latino; 0.4% Native Hawaiian or other Pacific Islander, non-Hispanic/Latino; 0.9% American Indian or Alaska Native, non-Hispanic/Latino; 0.4% Two or more races, non-Hispanic/Latino; 7% Race/ethnicity unknown.

Freshmen *Admission:* 941 enrolled.

Faculty *Total:* 228, 36% full-time, 10% with terminal degrees. *Student/faculty ratio:* 18:1.

Majors Accounting; accounting technology and bookkeeping; animal/livestock husbandry and production; business administration and management; child-care and support services management; child development; computer and information sciences; computer and information sciences and support services related; computer/information technology services administration related; computer science; criminal justice/law enforcement administration; early childhood education; emergency medical technology (EMT paramedic); engineering science; fire prevention and safety technology; forest technology; hospitality administration; humanities; human services; legal assistant/paralegal; mathematics; office management; registered nursing/registered nurse.

Academics *Calendar:* semesters. *Degree:* certificates and associate. *Special study options:* academic remediation for entering students, advanced placement credit, cooperative education, distance learning, double majors, honors

programs, independent study, internships, part-time degree program, services for LD students, student-designed majors, summer session for credit.

Library Melvil Dewey Library with 152,238 titles, 146 serial subscriptions, 5,504 audiovisual materials, an OPAC, a Web page.

Student Life *Housing:* college housing not available. *Activities and Organizations:* student-run newspaper, Phi Theta Kappa, Dionysian Players, Military Loved One's Club, student-run newspaper, choral group. *Campus security:* 24-hour emergency response devices and patrols. *Student services:* health clinic, personal/psychological counseling.

Athletics Member NJCAA. *Intercollegiate sports:* baseball M, basketball M/W, lacrosse M/W, soccer M/W, softball W, volleyball W.

Standardized Tests *Recommended:* SAT or ACT (for admission).

Costs (2011–12) *Tuition:* state resident $3648 full-time, $152 per credit hour part-time; nonresident $5808 full-time, $242 per credit hour part-time. Full-time tuition and fees vary according to course load, location, program, and reciprocity agreements. Part-time tuition and fees vary according to course load, location, program, and reciprocity agreements. *Required fees:* $471 full-time, $15 per credit hour part-time. *Payment plan:* installment. *Waivers:* senior citizens and employees or children of employees.

Financial Aid Of all full-time matriculated undergraduates who enrolled in 2009, 1,748 applied for aid. 98 Federal Work-Study jobs (averaging $1093).

Applying *Options:* electronic application, early admission, deferred entrance. *Required:* high school transcript. *Required for some:* interview. *Application deadlines:* 9/6 (freshmen), rolling (transfers). *Notification:* continuous (freshmen), continuous (transfers).

Freshman Application Contact Ms. Rosanne N. Weir, Director of Admissions, Jefferson Community College, 1220 Coffeen Street, Watertown, NY 13601. *Phone:* 315-786-2277. *Toll-free phone:* 888-435-6522. *Fax:* 315-786-2459. *E-mail:* admissions@sunyjefferson.edu. *Web site:* http://www.sunyjefferson.edu/.

Kingsborough Community College of the City University of New York
Brooklyn, New York

- **State and locally supported** 2-year, founded 1963, part of City University of New York System
- **Urban** 72-acre campus with easy access to New York City
- **Coed,** 19,261 undergraduate students, 58% full-time, 56% women, 44% men

Undergraduates 11,205 full-time, 8,056 part-time. Students come from 10 states and territories; 136 other countries; 1% are from out of state; 33% Black or African American, non-Hispanic/Latino; 16% Hispanic/Latino; 13% Asian, non-Hispanic/Latino; 0.2% American Indian or Alaska Native, non-Hispanic/Latino; 3% international; 9% transferred in. *Retention:* 66% of full-time freshmen returned.

Freshmen *Admission:* 2,702 enrolled. *Average high school GPA:* 2.7.

Faculty *Total:* 944, 38% full-time, 28% with terminal degrees. *Student/faculty ratio:* 23:1.

Majors Accounting; administrative assistant and secretarial science; art; biology/biological sciences; broadcast journalism; business administration and management; chemistry; commercial and advertising art; community health services counseling; computer and information sciences; computer science; cooking and related culinary arts; criminal justice/law enforcement administration; data processing and data processing technology; design and applied arts related; dramatic/theater arts; early childhood education; education; elementary education; engineering science; fashion merchandising; health and physical education related; human services; journalism; labor and industrial relations; liberal arts and sciences/liberal studies; marine maintenance and ship repair technology; marketing/marketing management; mathematics; mental health counseling; music; parks, recreation and leisure; physical therapy; physical therapy technology; physics; psychiatric/mental health services technology; registered nursing/registered nurse; sport and fitness administration/management; teacher assistant/aide; tourism and travel services management.

Academics *Calendar:* semesters. *Degree:* associate. *Special study options:* academic remediation for entering students, adult/continuing education programs, advanced placement credit, distance learning, English as a second language, honors programs, independent study, internships, off-campus study, part-time degree program, services for LD students, summer session for credit.

Library Robert J. Kibbee Library with 198,343 titles, 335 serial subscriptions, 2,145 audiovisual materials, an OPAC.

Student Life *Housing:* college housing not available. *Activities and Organizations:* drama/theater group, student-run newspaper, radio station, choral group, Peer Advisors, Caribbean Club, DECA. *Campus security:* 24-hour emergency response devices and patrols. *Student services:* health clinic, personal/psychological counseling, women's center.

Athletics Member NJCAA. *Intercollegiate sports:* baseball M, basketball M/W, soccer M, softball W, tennis M/W, track and field M/W, volleyball W.

Intramural sports: baseball M, basketball M/W, soccer M, softball W, tennis M/W, track and field M/W, volleyball W.

Costs (2012–13) *Tuition:* state resident $3610 full-time, $150 per credit part-time; nonresident $7200 full-time, $240 per credit part-time. *Required fees:* $350 full-time, $92 per term part-time. *Payment plan:* installment. *Waivers:* senior citizens.

Applying *Application fee:* $65. *Required:* high school transcript. *Application deadlines:* 8/15 (freshmen), rolling (transfers).

Freshman Application Contact Mr. Robert Ingenito, Director of Admissions Information Center, Kingsborough Community College of the City University of New York, 2001 Oriental Boulevard, Brooklyn, NY 11235. *Phone:* 718-368-4600. *Fax:* 718-368-5356. *E-mail:* info@kbcc.cuny.edu. *Web site:* http://www.kbcc.cuny.edu/.

Long Island Business Institute

Flushing, New York

- **Proprietary** 2-year, founded 1968
- **Urban** campus with easy access to New York City
- **Coed, primarily women,** 596 undergraduate students, 60% full-time, 81% women, 19% men

Undergraduates 360 full-time, 236 part-time. Students come from 4 states and territories; 14 other countries; 1% are from out of state; 9% Black or African American, non-Hispanic/Latino; 18% Hispanic/Latino; 42% Asian, non-Hispanic/Latino; 0.2% Two or more races, non-Hispanic/Latino; 0.5% Race/ethnicity unknown; 4% international; 4% transferred in.

Freshmen *Admission:* 266 applied, 182 admitted, 150 enrolled.

Faculty *Total:* 90, 21% full-time, 1% with terminal degrees. *Student/faculty ratio:* 20:1.

Majors Accounting; business administration and management; court reporting; homeland security; medical office management.

Academics *Calendar:* semesters. *Degrees:* certificates, diplomas, and associate (information provided for Commack and Flushing campuses). *Special study options:* academic remediation for entering students, adult/continuing education programs, advanced placement credit, cooperative education, English as a second language, honors programs, independent study, part-time degree program, summer session for credit.

Library Flushing Main Campus Library, Commack Campus Library with 5,870 titles, 76 serial subscriptions, 909 audiovisual materials, an OPAC, a Web page.

Student Life *Housing:* college housing not available. *Activities and Organizations:* Small Business Club, Web Design Club, Investment Club, Court Reporting Alumni Association. *Campus security:* 24-hour emergency response devices.

Standardized Tests *Required:* COMPASS, CELSA (for admission).

Costs (2012–13) *Tuition:* $13,299 full-time, $375 per credit part-time. *Required fees:* $600 full-time, $200 per term part-time. *Payment plans:* installment, deferred payment.

Applying *Application fee:* $55. *Required:* essay or personal statement, high school transcript, interview. *Application deadlines:* rolling (freshmen), rolling (transfers).

Freshman Application Contact Mr. Ethan Yang, Director of Admissions, Long Island Business Institute, 136-18 39th Avenue, Flushing, NY 11354. *Phone:* 718-939-5100. *Fax:* 718-939-9235. *E-mail:* eyang@libi.edu. *Web site:* http://www.libi.edu/.

Long Island College Hospital School of Nursing

Brooklyn, New York

Freshman Application Contact Ms. Barbara Evans, Admissions Assistant, Long Island College Hospital School of Nursing, 350 Henry Street, 7th Floor, Brooklyn, NY 11201. *Phone:* 718-780-1071. *Fax:* 718-780-1936. *E-mail:* bevans@chpnet.org. *Web site:* http://www.futurenurselich.org/.

Memorial Hospital School of Nursing

Albany, New York

Freshman Application Contact Admissions Office, Memorial Hospital School of Nursing, 600 Northern Boulevard, Albany, NY 12204. *Web site:* http://www.nehealth.com/son/.

Mildred Elley School

Albany, New York

Director of Admissions Mr. Michael Cahalan, Enrollment Manager, Mildred Elley School, 855 Central Avenue, Albany, NY 12206. *Phone:* 518-786-3171

Ext. 227. *Toll-free phone:* 800-622-6327. *Web site:* http://www.mildred-elley.edu/.

Mohawk Valley Community College

Utica, New York

- **State and locally supported** 2-year, founded 1946, part of State University of New York System
- **Suburban** 80-acre campus
- **Endowment** $3.8 million
- **Coed,** 7,640 undergraduate students, 64% full-time, 55% women, 45% men

Undergraduates 4,904 full-time, 2,736 part-time. Students come from 12 states and territories; 13 other countries; 9% Black or African American, non-Hispanic/Latino; 6% Hispanic/Latino; 3% Asian, non-Hispanic/Latino; 0.1% Native Hawaiian or other Pacific Islander, non-Hispanic/Latino; 0.5% American Indian or Alaska Native, non-Hispanic/Latino; 2% Two or more races, non-Hispanic/Latino; 0.2% Race/ethnicity unknown; 1% international; 5% transferred in; 7% live on campus.

Freshmen *Admission:* 4,383 applied, 4,240 admitted, 1,757 enrolled. *Average high school GPA:* 2.7.

Faculty *Total:* 483, 30% full-time, 16% with terminal degrees. *Student/faculty ratio:* 23:1.

Majors Accounting technology and bookkeeping; administrative assistant and secretarial science; advertising; airframe mechanics and aircraft maintenance technology; art; banking and financial support services; building/property maintenance; business administration and management; chemical technology; civil engineering technology; commercial and advertising art; commercial photography; communications systems installation and repair technology; community organization and advocacy; computer and information sciences; computer and information sciences and support services related; computer programming; criminal justice/law enforcement administration; design and applied arts related; drafting and design technology; dramatic/theater arts; electrical and electronic engineering technologies related; electrical, electronic and communications engineering technology; electrical/electronics maintenance and repair technology related; elementary education; emergency medical technology (EMT paramedic); engineering; entrepreneurship; fire services administration; food service systems administration; heating, ventilation, air conditioning and refrigeration engineering technology; hotel/motel administration; humanities; industrial production technologies related; liberal arts and sciences and humanities related; liberal arts and sciences/liberal studies; management information systems and services related; mechanical engineering/mechanical technology; mechanical engineering technologies related; medical/clinical assistant; medical radiologic technology; nutrition sciences; parks, recreation and leisure facilities management; public administration; registered nursing/registered nurse; respiratory care therapy; restaurant, culinary, and catering management; secondary education; sign language interpretation and translation; substance abuse/addiction counseling; surveying technology.

Academics *Calendar:* semesters. *Degree:* certificates and associate. *Special study options:* academic remediation for entering students, advanced placement credit, distance learning, double majors, English as a second language, honors programs, independent study, internships, off-campus study, part-time degree program, services for LD students, student-designed majors, summer session for credit. *ROTC:* Army (c), Air Force (c).

Library Mohawk Valley Community College Library plus 1 other with an OPAC, a Web page.

Student Life *Housing Options:* coed, men-only, women-only, disabled students. Campus housing is provided by a third party. Freshman applicants given priority for college housing. *Activities and Organizations:* drama/theater group, student-run newspaper, choral group, Student Congress, Student Nurses Organization (SNO), Black Student Union, Ski Club, Returning Adult Student Association (RASA). *Campus security:* 24-hour emergency response devices and patrols, late-night transport/escort service, controlled dormitory access. *Student services:* health clinic, personal/psychological counseling.

Athletics Member NJCAA. *Intercollegiate sports:* baseball M, basketball M/W, bowling M/W, cross-country running M/W, golf M/W, ice hockey M, lacrosse M/W, soccer M/W, softball W, tennis M/W, track and field M/W, volleyball W. *Intramural sports:* basketball M/W, racquetball M/W, soccer M/W, tennis M/W, volleyball M/W, weight lifting M/W.

Costs (2011–12) *Tuition:* state resident $3480 full-time, $120 per credit hour part-time; nonresident $6960 full-time, $240 per credit hour part-time. *Required fees:* $530 full-time, $5 per credit hour part-time, $40 per term part-time. *Room and board:* $8660; room only: $5220. Room and board charges vary according to board plan. *Payment plan:* installment. *Waivers:* senior citizens and employees or children of employees.

Financial Aid Of all full-time matriculated undergraduates who enrolled in 2010, 229 Federal Work-Study jobs (averaging $1750).

Applying *Options:* electronic application, deferred entrance. *Required for some:* high school transcript. *Recommended:* interview. *Application deadlines:* rolling (freshmen), rolling (out-of-state freshmen), rolling (transfers).

Notification: continuous (freshmen), continuous (out-of-state freshmen), continuous (transfers).

Freshman Application Contact Mrs. Sandra Fiebiger, Data Processing Clerk, Admissions, Mohawk Valley Community College, Utica, NY 13501. *Phone:* 315-792-5640. *Toll-free phone:* 800-SEE-MVCC. *Fax:* 315-792-5527. *E-mail:* sandra.fiebiger@mvcc.edu. *Web site:* http://www.mvcc.edu/.

Monroe Community College
Rochester, New York

- **State and locally supported** 2-year, founded 1961, part of State University of New York System
- **Suburban** 314-acre campus with easy access to Buffalo
- **Coed,** 17,699 undergraduate students, 62% full-time, 53% women, 47% men

Undergraduates 10,992 full-time, 6,707 part-time. 18% Black or African American, non-Hispanic/Latino; 8% Hispanic/Latino; 3% Asian, non-Hispanic/Latino; 0.2% Native Hawaiian or other Pacific Islander, non-Hispanic/Latino; 0.4% American Indian or Alaska Native, non-Hispanic/Latino; 3% Two or more races, non-Hispanic/Latino; 0.6% Race/ethnicity unknown; 0.5% international. *Retention:* 63% of full-time freshmen returned.

Freshmen *Admission:* 4,206 enrolled. *Test scores:* SAT critical reading scores over 500: 34%; SAT math scores over 500: 41%; SAT writing scores over 500: 28%; ACT scores over 18: 71%; SAT critical reading scores over 600: 8%; SAT math scores over 600: 10%; SAT writing scores over 600: 5%; ACT scores over 24: 18%; SAT critical reading scores over 700: 1%; SAT math scores over 700: 1%; SAT writing scores over 700: 1%; ACT scores over 30: 2%.

Faculty *Total:* 959, 34% full-time, 10% with terminal degrees. *Student/faculty ratio:* 25:1.

Majors Accounting; administrative assistant and secretarial science; art; automobile/automotive mechanics technology; behavioral sciences; biological and physical sciences; biology/biological sciences; biology/biotechnology laboratory technician; business administration and management; chemical engineering; chemistry; civil engineering technology; commercial and advertising art; computer and information sciences and support services related; computer and information sciences related; computer engineering related; computer engineering technology; computer science; construction engineering technology; consumer merchandising/retailing management; corrections; criminal justice/law enforcement administration; criminal justice/police science; data processing and data processing technology; dental hygiene; electrical, electronic and communications engineering technology; engineering science; environmental studies; family and consumer sciences/human sciences; fashion/apparel design; fashion merchandising; fire science/firefighting; food technology and processing; forestry; graphic and printing equipment operation/production; health information/medical records administration; heating, air conditioning, ventilation and refrigeration maintenance technology; history; hotel/motel administration; human services; industrial radiologic technology; industrial technology; information science/studies; information technology; instrumentation technology; interior design; international business/trade/commerce; landscape architecture; laser and optical technology; legal administrative assistant/secretary; liberal arts and sciences/liberal studies; marketing/marketing management; mass communication/media; mathematics; mechanical engineering/mechanical technology; music; parks, recreation and leisure; physical education teaching and coaching; physics; political science and government; pre-pharmacy studies; quality control technology; registered nursing/registered nurse; social sciences; special products marketing; telecommunications technology; tourism and travel services management.

Academics *Calendar:* semesters. *Degree:* certificates and associate. *Special study options:* academic remediation for entering students, accelerated degree program, adult/continuing education programs, advanced placement credit, cooperative education, English as a second language, honors programs, internships, off-campus study, part-time degree program, services for LD students, summer session for credit. *ROTC:* Army (c), Air Force (c).

Library LeRoy V. Good Library plus 1 other with 110,748 titles, 745 serial subscriptions, 4,100 audiovisual materials, an OPAC.

Student Life *Housing Options:* Campus housing is university owned. *Activities and Organizations:* drama/theater group, student-run newspaper, radio station, choral group, student newspaper, Phi Theta Kappa, student government. *Campus security:* 24-hour emergency response devices, late-night transport/escort service. *Student services:* health clinic, personal/psychological counseling.

Athletics Member NJCAA. *Intercollegiate sports:* baseball M(s), basketball M(s)/W(s), golf M, ice hockey M(s), lacrosse M(s), soccer M(s)/W(s), softball W, swimming and diving M(s)/W(s), tennis M/W, volleyball W. *Intramural sports:* archery M/W, basketball M/W, bowling M/W, cheerleading W, cross-country running M/W, lacrosse W, racquetball M/W, rugby M, skiing (cross-country) M/W, soccer M/W, softball M/W, swimming and diving M/W, tennis M/W, volleyball M/W.

Applying *Options:* electronic application, early admission. *Application fee:* $20. *Required:* high school transcript. *Application deadlines:* rolling (freshmen), rolling (transfers). *Notification:* continuous (freshmen), continuous (transfers).

Freshman Application Contact Mr. Andrew Freeman, Director of Admissions, Monroe Community College, 1000 East Henrietta Road, Rochester, NY 14623-5780. *Phone:* 585-292-2231. *Fax:* 585-292-3860. *E-mail:* admissions@monroecc.edu. *Web site:* http://www.monroecc.edu/.

Nassau Community College
Garden City, New York

Freshman Application Contact Mr. Craig Wright, Vice President of Enrollment Management, Nassau Community College, Garden City, NY 11530. *Phone:* 516-572-7345. *E-mail:* admissions@sunynassau.edu. *Web site:* http://www.ncc.edu/.

New York Career Institute
New York, New York

- **Proprietary** 2-year, founded 1942
- **Urban** campus
- **Coed, primarily women,** 771 undergraduate students, 74% full-time, 92% women, 8% men

Undergraduates 567 full-time, 204 part-time. Students come from 4 states and territories; 8 other countries.

Faculty *Total:* 47, 19% full-time.

Majors Court reporting; legal assistant/paralegal; medical office assistant.

Academics *Calendar:* trimesters (semesters for evening division). *Degree:* certificates and associate. *Special study options:* academic remediation for entering students, advanced placement credit, cooperative education, internships, part-time degree program, summer session for credit.

Library 5,010 titles, 23 serial subscriptions.

Student Life *Housing:* college housing not available.

Costs (2011–12) *Tuition:* $12,450 full-time, $390 per credit hour part-time. Full-time tuition and fees vary according to class time. Part-time tuition and fees vary according to class time. *Required fees:* $150 full-time, $50 per term part-time. *Payment plan:* installment.

Applying *Application fee:* $50. *Required:* high school transcript, interview. *Application deadlines:* 9/21 (freshmen), 9/21 (transfers). *Notification:* continuous (freshmen), continuous (transfers).

Freshman Application Contact Mr. Larry Stieglitz, Director of Admissions, New York Career Institute, 11 Park Place, New York, NY 10007. *Phone:* 212-962-0002 Ext. 115. *Fax:* 212-385-7574. *E-mail:* lstieglitz@nyci.edu. *Web site:* http://www.nyci.com/.

Niagara County Community College
Sanborn, New York

- **State and locally supported** 2-year, founded 1962, part of State University of New York System
- **Rural** 287-acre campus with easy access to Buffalo
- **Endowment** $3.6 million
- **Coed,** 7,177 undergraduate students, 61% full-time, 57% women, 43% men

Undergraduates 4,389 full-time, 2,788 part-time. Students come from 11 states and territories; 5 other countries; 1% are from out of state; 9% Black or African American, non-Hispanic/Latino; 2% Hispanic/Latino; 1% Asian, non-Hispanic/Latino; 2% American Indian or Alaska Native, non-Hispanic/Latino; 5% Race/ethnicity unknown; 0.4% international; 4% transferred in; 4% live on campus.

Freshmen *Admission:* 1,775 applied, 1,775 admitted, 1,588 enrolled. *Average high school GPA:* 2.48.

Faculty *Total:* 386, 27% full-time, 11% with terminal degrees. *Student/faculty ratio:* 17:1.

Majors Accounting; administrative assistant and secretarial science; animal sciences; baking and pastry arts; biological and physical sciences; business administration and management; business, management, and marketing related; chemical technology; computer science; consumer merchandising/retailing management; criminal justice/law enforcement administration; culinary arts; design and applied arts related; drafting and design technology; drafting/design engineering technologies related; dramatic/theater arts; elementary education; fine/studio arts; general studies; hospitality administration; humanities; human services; information science/studies; liberal arts and sciences/liberal studies; mass communication/media; mathematics; medical/clinical assistant; medical radiologic technology; music; natural resources/conservation; occupational health and industrial hygiene; parks, recreation and leisure; physical education teaching and coaching; physical therapy technology; registered nursing/registered nurse; social sciences; sport and fitness

administration/management; surgical technology; tourism and travel services management; web page, digital/multimedia and information resources design.
Academics *Calendar:* semesters. *Degree:* certificates and associate. *Special study options:* academic remediation for entering students, adult/continuing education programs, advanced placement credit, cooperative education, double majors, honors programs, independent study, internships, off-campus study, part-time degree program, services for LD students, student-designed majors, study abroad, summer session for credit. *ROTC:* Army (c).
Library Henrietta G. Lewis Library with 98,214 titles, 334 serial subscriptions, 8,155 audiovisual materials, an OPAC, a Web page.
Student Life *Housing Options:* coed. Campus housing is provided by a third party. *Activities and Organizations:* drama/theater group, student-run newspaper, radio station, choral group, student radio station, Student Nurses Association, Phi Theta Kappa, Alpha Beta Gamma, Physical Education Club. *Campus security:* 24-hour emergency response devices and patrols, student patrols, late-night transport/escort service. *Student services:* health clinic, personal/psychological counseling.
Athletics Member NJCAA. *Intercollegiate sports:* baseball M, basketball M(s)/W(s), bowling M/W, golf M/W, lacrosse M/W, soccer M/W, softball W, volleyball W, wrestling M(s). *Intramural sports:* basketball M/W, racquetball M/W, soccer M/W, swimming and diving M/W, tennis M/W.
Costs (2011–12) *Tuition:* state resident $3624 full-time, $151 per credit hour part-time; nonresident $7248 full-time, $302 per credit hour part-time. Full-time tuition and fees vary according to course load and program. Part-time tuition and fees vary according to course load and program. *Required fees:* $334 full-time, $167 per term part-time. *Room and board:* room only: $6300. Room and board charges vary according to housing facility. *Payment plan:* installment. *Waivers:* senior citizens and employees or children of employees.
Financial Aid Of all full-time matriculated undergraduates who enrolled in 2010, 5,003 applied for aid, 5,003 were judged to have need. 117 Federal Work-Study jobs (averaging $2900). 95 state and other part-time jobs (averaging $145). *Average percent of need met:* 85%. *Average financial aid package:* $4222. *Average need-based loan:* $4302. *Average need-based gift aid:* $1369.
Applying *Options:* electronic application, early admission. *Required:* high school transcript. *Required for some:* minimum 2.0 GPA. *Notification:* continuous until 8/31 (freshmen), continuous until 8/31 (transfers).
Freshman Application Contact Ms. Kathy Saunders, Director of Enrollment Services, Niagara County Community College, 3111 Saunders Settlement Road, Sanborn, NY 14132. *Phone:* 716-614-6200. *Fax:* 716-614-6820. *E-mail:* admissions@niagaracc.suny.edu.
Web site: http://www.niagaracc.suny.edu/.

North Country Community College
Saranac Lake, New York

Freshman Application Contact Enrollment Management Assistant, North Country Community College, 23 Santanoni Avenue, PO Box 89, Saranac Lake, NY 12983-0089. *Phone:* 518-891-2915 Ext. 686. *Toll-free phone:* 800-TRY-NCCC (in-state); 888-TRY-NCCC (out-of-state). *Fax:* 518-891-0898. *E-mail:* info@nccc.edu. *Web site:* http://www.nccc.edu/.

Olean Business Institute
Olean, New York

Freshman Application Contact Olean Business Institute, 301 North Union Street, Olean, NY 14760-2691. *Phone:* 716-372-7978. *Web site:* http://www.obi.edu/.

Onondaga Community College
Syracuse, New York

- **State and locally supported** 2-year, founded 1962, part of State University of New York System
- **Suburban** 280-acre campus
- **Endowment** $6063
- **Coed,** 12,731 undergraduate students, 54% full-time, 52% women, 48% men

Undergraduates 6,816 full-time, 5,915 part-time. Students come from 15 states and territories; 22 other countries; 0.2% are from out of state; 10% Black or African American, non-Hispanic/Latino; 4% Hispanic/Latino; 2% Asian, non-Hispanic/Latino; 1% American Indian or Alaska Native, non-Hispanic/Latino; 1% Two or more races, non-Hispanic/Latino; 7% Race/ethnicity unknown; 0.5% international; 4% transferred in; 5% live on campus. *Retention:* 57% of full-time freshmen returned.
Freshmen *Admission:* 8,028 applied, 5,496 admitted, 2,497 enrolled.
Faculty *Total:* 684, 26% full-time. *Student/faculty ratio:* 25:1.
Majors Accounting; accounting technology and bookkeeping; architectural engineering technology; architectural technology; art; automobile/automotive mechanics technology; business administration and management; business/

commerce; computer engineering technology; computer science; computer systems networking and telecommunications; construction engineering technology; criminal justice/law enforcement administration; criminal justice/police science; design and applied arts related; education (multiple levels); electrical and electronic engineering technologies related; electrical, electronic and communications engineering technology; engineering science; environmental engineering technology; fire prevention and safety technology; general studies; health information/medical records technology; health professions related; homeland security, law enforcement, firefighting and protective services related; hospitality administration; humanities; interior design; liberal arts and sciences and humanities related; mechanical engineering/mechanical technology; music; parks, recreation and leisure; photography; physical therapy technology; public administration and social service professions related; radio and television; registered nursing/registered nurse; respiratory care therapy; speech communication and rhetoric.
Academics *Calendar:* semesters. *Degree:* certificates, diplomas, and associate. *Special study options:* academic remediation for entering students, accelerated degree program, adult/continuing education programs, advanced placement credit, cooperative education, distance learning, double majors, English as a second language, external degree program, honors programs, internships, part-time degree program, services for LD students, study abroad, summer session for credit. *ROTC:* Air Force (c).
Library Sidney B. Coulter Library with 106,670 titles, 245 serial subscriptions, 15,488 audiovisual materials, an OPAC, a Web page.
Student Life *Housing Options:* coed. Campus housing is provided by a third party. *Activities and Organizations:* drama/theater group, student-run newspaper, radio station, choral group. *Campus security:* 24-hour emergency response devices and patrols, controlled dormitory access. *Student services:* personal/psychological counseling.
Athletics Member NJCAA. *Intercollegiate sports:* badminton M/W, baseball M, basketball M/W, lacrosse M/W, soccer M/W, softball W, tennis M/W, volleyball W. *Intramural sports:* basketball M/W, golf M/W, skiing (downhill) M/W, swimming and diving M/W, table tennis M/W, tennis M/W, volleyball M/W.
Costs (2012–13) *Tuition:* area resident $4050 full-time, $161 per credit hour part-time; state resident $8100 full-time, $322 per credit hour part-time; nonresident $8100 full-time, $322 per credit hour part-time. Full-time tuition and fees vary according to program. Part-time tuition and fees vary according to course load and program. *Required fees:* $554 full-time, $115 per term part-time. *Room and board:* room only: $7082. Room and board charges vary according to board plan. *Payment plan:* installment. *Waivers:* senior citizens and employees or children of employees.
Financial Aid Of all full-time matriculated undergraduates who enrolled in 2010, 5,721 applied for aid, 5,086 were judged to have need, 267 had their need fully met. *Average percent of need met:* 68%. *Average financial aid package:* $6248. *Average need-based loan:* $2990. *Average need-based gift aid:* $4956.
Applying *Options:* electronic application. *Required:* high school transcript, some programs require specific prerequisite courses and/or tests to be admitted directly to the program; an alternate program is offered. *Required for some:* minimum 2.0 GPA, interview. *Application deadlines:* 8/12 (freshmen), 8/12 (transfers). *Notification:* continuous (freshmen), continuous (transfers).
Freshman Application Contact Mrs. Katherine Perry, Director of Admissions, Onondaga Community College, 4585 West Seneca Turnpike, Syracuse, NY 13215. *Phone:* 315-488-2602. *Fax:* 315-488-2107. *E-mail:* admissions@sunyocc.edu. *Web site:* http://www.sunyocc.edu/.

Orange County Community College
Middletown, New York

Freshman Application Contact Michael Roe, Director of Admissions and Recruitment, Orange County Community College, 115 South Street, Middletown, NY 10940. *Phone:* 845-341-4205. *Fax:* 845-343-1228. *E-mail:* apply@sunyorange.edu. *Web site:* http://www.sunyorange.edu/.

Phillips Beth Israel School of Nursing
New York, New York

- **Independent** 2-year, founded 1904
- **Urban** campus
- **Endowment** $1.2 million
- **Coed**

Undergraduates 17 full-time, 234 part-time. Students come from 9 states and territories; 6 other countries; 15% are from out of state; 23% Black or African American, non-Hispanic/Latino; 9% Hispanic/Latino; 14% Asian, non-Hispanic/Latino; 4% Native Hawaiian or other Pacific Islander, non-Hispanic/Latino; 40% transferred in. *Retention:* 84% of full-time freshmen returned.
Faculty *Student/faculty ratio:* 10:1.

Academics *Calendar:* semesters. *Degree:* associate. *Special study options:* academic remediation for entering students, advanced placement credit, cooperative education, distance learning, honors programs, off-campus study, part-time degree program, services for LD students, summer session for credit.
Student Life *Campus security:* 24-hour emergency response devices.
Standardized Tests *Required:* nursing exam (for admission). *Recommended:* SAT (for admission).
Costs (2011–12) *Tuition:* $16,400 full-time, $400 per credit part-time. Full-time tuition and fees vary according to course load. Part-time tuition and fees vary according to course load. *Required fees:* $2590 full-time.
Financial Aid *Financial aid deadline:* 6/1.
Applying *Options:* deferred entrance. *Application fee:* $50. *Required:* essay or personal statement, high school transcript, minimum 2.5 GPA, 2 letters of recommendation, interview.
Freshman Application Contact Mrs. Bernice Pass-Stern, Assistant Dean, Phillips Beth Israel School of Nursing, 776 Sixth Avenue, 4th Floor, New York, NY 10010-6354. *Phone:* 212-614-6176. *Fax:* 212-614-6109. *E-mail:* bstern@chpnet.org. *Web site:* http://www.futurenursebi.org/.

Plaza College
Jackson Heights, New York

Freshman Application Contact Dean Rose Ann Black, Dean of Administration, Plaza College, 74-09 37th Avenue, Jackson Heights, NY 11372. *Phone:* 718-779-1430. *E-mail:* info@plazacollege.edu. *Web site:* http://www.plazacollege.edu/.

Queensborough Community College of the City University of New York
Bayside, New York

Freshman Application Contact Ms. Ann Tullio, Director of Registration, Queensborough Community College of the City University of New York, 222-05 56th Avenue, Bayside, NY 11364. *Phone:* 718-631-6307. *Fax:* 718-281-5189. *Web site:* http://www.qcc.cuny.edu/.

Rockland Community College
Suffern, New York

- **State and locally supported** 2-year, founded 1959, part of State University of New York System
- **Suburban** 150-acre campus with easy access to New York City
- **Coed,** 7,986 undergraduate students, 60% full-time, 54% women, 46% men

Undergraduates 4,752 full-time, 3,234 part-time. 20% Black or African American, non-Hispanic/Latino; 19% Hispanic/Latino; 5% Asian, non-Hispanic/Latino; 0.4% American Indian or Alaska Native, non-Hispanic/Latino; 12% Race/ethnicity unknown; 2% international; 8% transferred in. *Retention:* 64% of full-time freshmen returned.
Freshmen *Admission:* 1,610 applied, 1,610 admitted, 1,581 enrolled.
Faculty *Total:* 707, 17% full-time. *Student/faculty ratio:* 20:1.
Majors Accounting; administrative assistant and secretarial science; advertising; art; automobile/automotive mechanics technology; biological and physical sciences; business administration and management; commercial and advertising art; computer and information sciences related; computer graphics; computer/information technology services administration related; computer programming; computer programming related; computer programming (specific applications); computer systems networking and telecommunications; criminal justice/law enforcement administration; culinary arts; data processing and data processing technology; design and applied arts related; developmental and child psychology; dietetics; drafting and design technology; dramatic/theater arts; electrical, electronic and communications engineering technology; emergency medical technology (EMT paramedic); finance; fine/studio arts; fire science/firefighting; health information/medical records administration; hospitality administration; human services; liberal arts and sciences/liberal studies; marketing/marketing management; mass communication/media; mathematics; network and system administration; occupational therapy; photography; registered nursing/registered nurse; respiratory care therapy; tourism and travel services management.
Academics *Calendar:* semesters. *Degree:* certificates and associate. *Special study options:* adult/continuing education programs, external degree program, part-time degree program.
Library Rockland Community College Library.
Student Life *Housing:* college housing not available. *Campus security:* 24-hour emergency response devices and patrols, student patrols, late-night transport/escort service.
Athletics Member NJCAA. *Intercollegiate sports:* baseball M(s), basketball M/W, bowling M/W, golf M(s), soccer M/W, softball W, tennis M/W, volley-

ball W. *Intramural sports:* basketball M/W, bowling M/W, field hockey M/W, football M/W, golf M, racquetball M/W, soccer M/W, softball M/W, tennis M/W, volleyball M/W.
Costs (2011–12) *Tuition:* state resident $3815 full-time, $158 per credit hour part-time; nonresident $7630 full-time, $316 per credit hour part-time. Full-time tuition and fees vary according to course load and program. Part-time tuition and fees vary according to course load and program. *Required fees:* $278 full-time, $4 per credit hour part-time. *Payment plans:* installment, deferred payment. *Waivers:* employees or children of employees.
Financial Aid Of all full-time matriculated undergraduates who enrolled in 2010, 49 Federal Work-Study jobs (averaging $2790). *Average need-based loan:* $4037. *Average need-based gift aid:* $3796.
Applying *Options:* early admission, deferred entrance. *Application fee:* $30. *Required:* high school transcript. *Application deadline:* rolling (freshmen).
Freshman Application Contact Rockland Community College, 145 College Road, Suffern, NY 10901-3699. *Phone:* 845-574-4237. *Toll-free phone:* 800-722-7666. *Web site:* http://www.sunyrockland.edu/.

St. Elizabeth College of Nursing
Utica, New York

- **Independent** 2-year, founded 1904
- **Small-town** 1-acre campus with easy access to Syracuse
- **Coed,** 217 undergraduate students, 67% full-time, 88% women, 12% men
- 60% of applicants were admitted

Undergraduates 145 full-time, 72 part-time. Students come from 4 states and territories; 1 other country; 1% are from out of state; 1% Black or African American, non-Hispanic/Latino; 1% Hispanic/Latino; 2% Asian, non-Hispanic/Latino; 0.9% American Indian or Alaska Native, non-Hispanic/Latino; 2% international; 42% transferred in. *Retention:* 75% of full-time freshmen returned.
Freshmen *Admission:* 42 applied, 25 admitted, 17 enrolled.
Faculty *Total:* 17. *Student/faculty ratio:* 10:1.
Majors Registered nursing/registered nurse.
Academics *Calendar:* semesters. *Degree:* associate. *Special study options:* academic remediation for entering students, advanced placement credit, off-campus study, part-time degree program, services for LD students.
Student Life *Housing:* college housing not available. *Campus security:* 24-hour emergency response devices and patrols. *Student services:* health clinic, personal/psychological counseling.
Standardized Tests *Required:* SAT or ACT (for admission). *Recommended:* SAT or ACT (for admission).
Costs (2012–13) *Tuition:* $12,750 full-time, $375 per credit hour part-time. Full-time tuition and fees vary according to course load, location, program, and student level. Part-time tuition and fees vary according to course load, location, program, and student level. *Required fees:* $1000 full-time, $500 per term part-time. *Payment plan:* installment.
Applying *Options:* electronic application. *Application fee:* $65. *Required:* high school transcript, 2 letters of recommendation. *Recommended:* minimum 3.0 GPA. *Application deadline:* rolling (freshmen). *Notification:* continuous (freshmen).
Freshman Application Contact Donna Ernst, Director of Recruitment, St. Elizabeth College of Nursing, 2215 Genesee Street, Utica, NY 13501. *Phone:* 315-798-8189. *E-mail:* dernst@secon.edu. *Web site:* http://www.secon.edu/.

St. Joseph's College of Nursing
Syracuse, New York

- **Independent Roman Catholic** 2-year, founded 1898
- **Urban** campus
- **Coed,** 273 undergraduate students, 61% full-time, 91% women, 9% men

Undergraduates 166 full-time, 107 part-time. Students come from 2 states and territories; 20% live on campus.
Freshmen *Admission:* 42 applied, 23 admitted, 10 enrolled. *Average high school GPA:* 3. *Test scores:* SAT critical reading scores over 500: 56%; SAT math scores over 500: 50%; ACT scores over 18: 100%; ACT scores over 24: 1%.
Faculty *Total:* 29, 55% full-time. *Student/faculty ratio:* 9:1.
Majors Registered nursing/registered nurse.
Academics *Calendar:* semesters. *Degree:* associate. *Special study options:* academic remediation for entering students, adult/continuing education programs, advanced placement credit, cooperative education, internships, part-time degree program, services for LD students.
Library St. Joseph's Hospital Health Center School of Nursing Library with 4,500 titles, 230 serial subscriptions, 500 audiovisual materials, an OPAC.
Student Life *Housing Options:* coed. Campus housing is university owned. Freshman applicants given priority for college housing. *Activities and Organizations:* New York State Student Nurse's Association, Syracuse Area Black

Nurses Association, Student Body Organization. *Campus security:* 24-hour patrols. *Student services:* health clinic, personal/psychological counseling, legal services.

Standardized Tests *Required:* SAT or ACT (for admission).

Costs (2012–13) *Tuition:* $16,592 full-time, $488 per credit hour part-time. Full-time tuition and fees vary according to course load. Part-time tuition and fees vary according to course load. *Required fees:* $200 full-time. *Room only:* $4400. *Payment plan:* installment. *Waivers:* employees or children of employees.

Applying *Options:* electronic application, deferred entrance. *Application fee:* $50. *Required:* essay or personal statement, high school transcript, minimum 3.0 GPA, 2 letters of recommendation, interview. *Application deadlines:* rolling (freshmen), rolling (out-of-state freshmen), rolling (transfers). *Notification:* continuous (freshmen), continuous (out-of-state freshmen), continuous (transfers).

Freshman Application Contact Ms. Felicia Corp, Recruiter, St. Joseph's College of Nursing, 206 Prospect Avenue, Syracuse, NY 13203. *Phone:* 315-448-5040. *Fax:* 315-448-5745. *E-mail:* collegeofnursing@sjhsyr.org. *Web site:* http://www.sjhsyr.org/nursing/.

St. Paul's School of Nursing
Flushing, New York

Director of Admissions Nancy Wolinski, Chairperson of Admissions, St. Paul's School of Nursing, 30-50 Whitestone Expressway, Suite 400, Flushing, NY 11354. *Phone:* 718-357-0500 Ext. 131. *E-mail:* nwolinski@svcmcny.org. *Web site:* http://www.stpaulsschoolofnursing.com/.

Samaritan Hospital School of Nursing
Troy, New York

Director of Admissions Ms. Jennifer Marrone, Student Services Coordinator, Samaritan Hospital School of Nursing, 2215 Burdett Avenue, Troy, NY 12180. *Phone:* 518-271-3734. *Fax:* 518-271-3303. *E-mail:* marronej@nehealth.com. *Web site:* http://www.nehealth.com/.

SBI Campus–an affiliate of Sanford-Brown
Melville, New York

Director of Admissions Ms. Cynthia Gamache, Director of Admissions, SBI Campus–an affiliate of Sanford-Brown, 320 South Service Road, Melville, NY 11747-3785. *Phone:* 631-370-3307. *Web site:* http://www.sbmelville.edu/.

Schenectady County Community College
Schenectady, New York

Freshman Application Contact Mr. David Sampson, Director of Admissions, Schenectady County Community College, 78 Washington Avenue, Schenectady, NY 12305-2294. *Phone:* 518-381-1370. *E-mail:* sampsodg@gw.sunysccc.edu. *Web site:* http://www.sunysccc.edu/.

Simmons Institute of Funeral Service
Syracuse, New York

Freshman Application Contact Ms. Vera Wightman, Director of Admissions, Simmons Institute of Funeral Service, 1828 South Avenue, Syracuse, NY 13207. *Phone:* 315-475-5142. *Toll-free phone:* 800-727-3536. *Fax:* 315-475-3817. *E-mail:* admissions@simmonsinstitute.com. *Web site:* http://www.simmonsinstitute.com/.

State University of New York College of Environmental Science & Forestry, Ranger School
Wanakena, New York

- **State-supported** 2-year, founded 1912, part of State University of New York
- **Rural** 2800-acre campus
- **Coed, primarily men,** 58 undergraduate students, 100% full-time, 17% women, 83% men

Undergraduates 58 full-time. Students come from 1 other state; 2% Hispanic/Latino; 2% Asian, non-Hispanic/Latino; 60% transferred in; 100% live on campus.

Faculty *Total:* 6, 100% full-time, 17% with terminal degrees. *Student/faculty ratio:* 9:1.

Majors Forest technology; natural resources/conservation; surveying technology.

Academics *Calendar:* semesters. *Degrees:* associate (The associate degrees offered at The Ranger School campus of SUNY-ESF are 1 + 1 programs enrolling students for the second year of study after they complete their first-year requirements at SUNY-ESF's Syracuse campus or the college of their choice). *Special study options:* advanced placement credit.

Library Ranger School Library with 1,500 titles, 60 serial subscriptions, an OPAC.

Student Life *Housing:* on-campus residence required through sophomore year. *Options:* coed. Campus housing is university owned. *Activities and Organizations:* Hockey Club, Outing Club. *Campus security:* 24-hour emergency response devices. *Student services:* health clinic, personal/psychological counseling, legal services.

Athletics *Intramural sports:* basketball M/W, ice hockey M/W, skiing (cross-country) M/W, skiing (downhill) M/W, softball M/W, volleyball M/W, weight lifting M/W.

Standardized Tests *Required:* SAT or ACT (for admission).

Costs (2012–13) *Tuition:* state resident $5570 full-time, $220 per credit hour part-time; nonresident $15,180 full-time, $597 per credit hour part-time. Full-time tuition and fees vary according to course load and location. Part-time tuition and fees vary according to course load and location. *Required fees:* $1260 full-time. *Room and board:* $10,020; room only: $2720. Room and board charges vary according to housing facility. *Payment plan:* installment.

Financial Aid Of all full-time matriculated undergraduates who enrolled in 2010, 43 applied for aid, 40 were judged to have need, 36 had their need fully met. 5 Federal Work-Study jobs (averaging $1801). In 2010, 2 non-need-based awards were made. *Average percent of need met:* 90%. *Average financial aid package:* $10,051. *Average need-based loan:* $4260. *Average need-based gift aid:* $7749. *Average non-need-based aid:* $2250.

Applying *Options:* electronic application, deferred entrance. *Application fee:* $50. *Required:* essay or personal statement, high school transcript, minimum 2.5 GPA. *Recommended:* essay or personal statement, high school transcript, minimum 2.5 GPA, interview. *Application deadline:* 3/1 (transfers).

Freshman Application Contact Ms. Susan Sanford, Director of Admissions, State University of New York College of Environmental Science & Forestry, Ranger School, 1 Forestry Drive, Syracuse, NY 13210-2779. *Phone:* 315-470-6600. *Fax:* 315-470-6933. *E-mail:* esfinfo@esf.edu. *Web site:* http://www.esf.edu/rangerschool/default.asp.

State University of New York College of Technology at Alfred
Alfred, New York

- **State-supported** primarily 2-year, founded 1908, part of The State University of New York System
- **Rural** 1084-acre campus
- **Endowment** $3.6 million
- **Coed,** 3,617 undergraduate students, 91% full-time, 38% women, 62% men

Undergraduates 3,279 full-time, 338 part-time. Students come from 35 states and territories; 19 other countries; 7% are from out of state; 9% Black or African American, non-Hispanic/Latino; 5% Hispanic/Latino; 2% Asian, non-Hispanic/Latino; 0.1% Native Hawaiian or other Pacific Islander, non-Hispanic/Latino; 0.3% American Indian or Alaska Native, non-Hispanic/Latino; 2% Two or more races, non-Hispanic/Latino; 4% Race/ethnicity unknown; 7% transferred in; 74% live on campus. *Retention:* 81% of full-time freshmen returned.

Freshmen *Admission:* 3,890 applied, 2,136 admitted, 1,082 enrolled. *Average high school GPA:* 3.3.

Faculty *Total:* 219, 83% full-time, 21% with terminal degrees. *Student/faculty ratio:* 18:1.

Majors Accounting technology and bookkeeping; agribusiness; agriculture; agroecology and sustainable agriculture; agronomy and crop science; animal sciences; architectural engineering technology; autobody/collision and repair technology; automotive engineering technology; baking and pastry arts; banking and financial support services; biology/biological sciences; business, management, and marketing related; CAD/CADD drafting/design technology; carpentry; community organization and advocacy; computer and information sciences; computer and information sciences and support services related; computer and information systems security; computer engineering technology; computer hardware technology; computer science; computer systems networking and telecommunications; construction engineering technology; construction trades related; cooking and related culinary arts; court reporting; culinary arts related; dairy science; data processing and data processing technology; design and applied arts related; diesel mechanics technology; digital arts; digital communication and media/multimedia; electrical, electronic and communications engineering technology; electrical/electronics equipment installation and repair; electrician; electromechanical technology; engineering; engineering technologies and engineering related; entrepreneurial and small business related; entrepreneurship; environmental science; finance; finance and financial management services related; financial planning and services; forensic science and technology; health information/medical records technology; heating, air conditioning, ventilation and refrigeration maintenance technology; heating, ventilation, air conditioning and refrigeration engineering technology; heavy equipment maintenance technology; humanities; human resources management; human services; industrial technology; information technology; interior architecture; interior design; liberal arts and sciences/liberal studies; machine tool technology; manufacturing engineering technology; marketing/marketing management; masonry; mechanical drafting and CAD/CADD; mechanical engineering/mechanical technology; merchandising, sales, and marketing operations related (general); network and system administration; plumbing technology; registered nursing/registered nurse; robotics technology; secondary education; sport and fitness administration/management; surveying technology; system, networking, and LAN/WAN management; urban forestry; vehicle maintenance and repair technologies related; veterinary/animal health technology; web/multimedia management and webmaster; welding technology.

Academics *Calendar:* semesters. *Degrees:* certificates, associate, and bachelor's. *Special study options:* academic remediation for entering students, adult/continuing education programs, advanced placement credit, cooperative education, distance learning, double majors, English as a second language, honors programs, independent study, internships, off-campus study, part-time degree program, services for LD students, student-designed majors, study abroad, summer session for credit. *ROTC:* Army (c).

Library Walter C. Hinkle Memorial Library plus 1 other with 61,639 titles, 68,689 serial subscriptions, 4,478 audiovisual materials, an OPAC, a Web page.

Student Life *Housing Options:* coed, men-only, women-only, disabled students. Campus housing is university owned. Freshman campus housing is guaranteed. *Activities and Organizations:* drama/theater group, student-run newspaper, radio station, choral group, Outdoor Recreation Club, International Club, intramural Sports, Pioneer Woodsmen Team, Black Student Union. *Campus security:* 24-hour emergency response devices and patrols, late-night transport/escort service, controlled dormitory access, residence hall entrance guards. *Student services:* health clinic, personal/psychological counseling.

Athletics Member NJCAA. *Intercollegiate sports:* baseball M, basketball M(s)/W(s), cross-country running M/W, equestrian sports M/W, football M(s), lacrosse M(s), soccer M/W, softball W, swimming and diving M/W, track and field M/W, volleyball W, wrestling M. *Intramural sports:* basketball M/W, football M(c), golf M/W, ice hockey M(c)/W(c), lacrosse M(c)/W(c), rock climbing M/W, soccer M/W, softball M/W, swimming and diving M(c)/W(c), tennis M/W, ultimate Frisbee M/W, volleyball M/W.

Standardized Tests *Required for some:* SAT or ACT (for admission). *Recommended:* SAT or ACT (for admission).

Costs (2012–13) *Tuition:* state resident $5570 full-time, $220 per credit hour part-time; nonresident $10,714 full-time, $406 per credit hour part-time. Full-time tuition and fees vary according to course load and degree level. Part-time tuition and fees vary according to course load and degree level. *Required fees:* $1272 full-time, $53 per credit hour part-time, $5 per credit hour part-time. *Room and board:* $10,450; room only: $6100. Room and board charges vary according to board plan and housing facility. *Payment plan:* installment. *Waivers:* employees or children of employees.

Financial Aid Of all full-time matriculated undergraduates who enrolled in 2010, 3,084 applied for aid, 2,722 were judged to have need, 256 had their need fully met. 228 Federal Work-Study jobs (averaging $861). In 2010, 99 non-need-based awards were made. *Average percent of need met:* 57%. *Average financial aid package:* $9568. *Average need-based loan:* $3760. *Average need-based gift aid:* $5759. *Average non-need-based aid:* $4307. *Average indebtedness upon graduation:* $29,772.

Applying *Options:* electronic application. *Application fee:* $50. *Required:* high school transcript, minimum 2.0 GPA. *Recommended:* essay or personal statement, interview. *Application deadlines:* rolling (freshmen), rolling (out-of-state freshmen), rolling (transfers). *Notification:* continuous (freshmen), continuous (out-of-state freshmen), continuous (transfers).

Freshman Application Contact Mrs. Deborah Goodrich, Associate Vice President for Enrollment Management, State University of New York College of Technology at Alfred, Huntington Administration Building, 10 Upper College Drive, Alfred, NY 14802. *Phone:* 607-587-4215. *Toll-free phone:* 800-4-ALFRED. *Fax:* 607-587-4299. *E-mail:* admissions@alfredstate.edu. *Web site:* http://www.alfredstate.edu/.

Suffolk County Community College
Selden, New York

- **State and locally supported** 2-year, founded 1959, part of State University of New York System
- **Small-town** 500-acre campus with easy access to New York City
- **Coed**

Undergraduates 13,853 full-time, 14,441 part-time. Students come from 14 states and territories; 1% are from out of state.
Faculty *Student/faculty ratio:* 18:1.
Academics *Calendar:* semesters. *Degree:* certificates, diplomas, and associate. *Special study options:* academic remediation for entering students, adult/continuing education programs, advanced placement credit, cooperative education, distance learning, English as a second language, freshman honors college, honors programs, independent study, internships, off-campus study, part-time degree program, services for LD students, study abroad, summer session for credit. *ROTC:* Army (c).
Student Life *Campus security:* 24-hour emergency response devices and patrols.
Athletics Member NJCAA.
Financial Aid Of all full-time matriculated undergraduates who enrolled in 2010, 109 Federal Work-Study jobs (averaging $1377).
Applying *Options:* electronic application, deferred entrance. *Application fee:* $35. *Required:* high school transcript. *Required for some:* interview.
Freshman Application Contact Suffolk County Community College, 533 College Road, Selden, NY 11784-2899. *Phone:* 631-451-4000. *Web site:* http://www.sunysuffolk.edu/.

Sullivan County Community College
Loch Sheldrake, New York

- **State and locally supported** 2-year, founded 1962, part of State University of New York System
- **Rural** 405-acre campus
- **Endowment** $934,330
- **Coed,** 1,705 undergraduate students, 67% full-time, 57% women, 43% men

Undergraduates 1,134 full-time, 571 part-time. Students come from 11 states and territories; 3 other countries; 2% are from out of state; 23% Black or African American, non-Hispanic/Latino; 14% Hispanic/Latino; 2% Asian, non-Hispanic/Latino; 0.5% American Indian or Alaska Native, non-Hispanic/Latino; 18% Race/ethnicity unknown; 0.2% international; 5% transferred in; 21% live on campus.
Freshmen *Admission:* 1,755 applied, 1,690 admitted, 448 enrolled.
Faculty *Total:* 113, 44% full-time, 13% with terminal degrees. *Student/faculty ratio:* 19:1.
Majors Accounting; administrative assistant and secretarial science; baking and pastry arts; business administration and management; commercial and advertising art; computer graphics; computer programming (specific applications); consumer merchandising/retailing management; corrections; culinary arts; data entry/microcomputer applications; electrical, electronic and communications engineering technology; elementary education; engineering science; environmental studies; hospitality administration; human services; information science/studies; kindergarten/preschool education; legal assistant/paralegal; liberal arts and sciences/liberal studies; marketing/marketing management; mathematics; photography; radio and television; registered nursing/registered nurse; sport and fitness administration/management; substance abuse/addiction counseling; surveying technology; tourism and travel services management; web/multimedia management and webmaster.
Academics *Calendar:* 4-1-4. *Degree:* certificates and associate. *Special study options:* academic remediation for entering students, adult/continuing education programs, advanced placement credit, distance learning, double majors, honors programs, independent study, internships, part-time degree program, services for LD students, summer session for credit.
Library Hermann Memorial Library plus 1 other with 65,699 titles, 400 serial subscriptions, an OPAC, a Web page.
Student Life *Housing Options:* coed. Campus housing is provided by a third party. Freshman applicants given priority for college housing. *Activities and Organizations:* student-run newspaper, radio station, Science Alliance, Black Student Union, Drama Club, Baking Club, Honor Society. *Campus security:* 24-hour emergency response devices and patrols. *Student services:* health clinic, personal/psychological counseling, legal services.
Athletics Member NJCAA. *Intercollegiate sports:* basketball M/W, cheerleading W, cross-country running M/W, golf M, softball W, volleyball W. *Intramural sports:* basketball M/W, bowling M/W, cross-country running M/W, football M, golf M/W, racquetball M/W, skiing (downhill) M/W, soccer M/W, softball M/W, table tennis M/W, tennis M/W, volleyball M/W, weight lifting M/W.

Costs (2012–13) *Tuition:* state resident $4180 full-time, $163 per credit hour part-time; nonresident $6720 full-time, $244 per credit hour part-time. Full-time tuition and fees vary according to program and student level. Part-time tuition and fees vary according to program and student level. *Required fees:* $562 full-time, $54 per credit hour part-time. *Room and board:* $8266; room only: $5338. Room and board charges vary according to board plan and housing facility. *Payment plans:* installment, deferred payment. *Waivers:* employees or children of employees.

Financial Aid Of all full-time matriculated undergraduates who enrolled in 2010, 1,214 applied for aid, 1,214 were judged to have need, 1,206 had their need fully met. 78 Federal Work-Study jobs (averaging $798). 61 state and other part-time jobs (averaging $1755). *Average percent of need met:* 100%. *Average financial aid package:* $5368. *Average need-based loan:* $4586. *Average need-based gift aid:* $5227.

Applying *Options:* electronic application, early admission, deferred entrance. *Application fee:* $20. *Required:* high school transcript. *Application deadlines:* rolling (freshmen), rolling (out-of-state freshmen), rolling (transfers). *Notification:* continuous (freshmen), continuous (out-of-state freshmen), continuous (transfers).

Freshman Application Contact Ms. Sari Rosenheck, Director of Admissions and Registration Services, Sullivan County Community College, 112 College Road, Loch Sheldrake, NY 12759. *Phone:* 845-434-5750 Ext. 4200. *Toll-free phone:* 800-577-5243. *Fax:* 845-434-4806. *E-mail:* sarir@sullivan.suny.edu. *Web site:* http://www.sullivan.suny.edu/.

TCI–The College of Technology
New York, New York

Freshman Application Contact Director of Admission, TCI–The College of Technology, 320 West 31st Street, New York, NY 10001-2705. *Phone:* 212-594-4000. *Toll-free phone:* 800-878-8246. *E-mail:* admissions@tcicollege.edu. *Web site:* http://www.tciedu.com/.

Tompkins Cortland Community College
Dryden, New York

- **State and locally supported** 2-year, founded 1968, part of State University of New York System
- **Rural** 250-acre campus with easy access to Syracuse
- **Endowment** $8.0 million
- **Coed,** 3,850 undergraduate students, 77% full-time, 55% women, 45% men

Undergraduates 2,968 full-time, 882 part-time. Students come from 19 states and territories; 26 other countries; 1% are from out of state; 8% Black or African American, non-Hispanic/Latino; 6% Hispanic/Latino; 1% Asian, non-Hispanic/Latino; 0.1% Native Hawaiian or other Pacific Islander, non-Hispanic/Latino; 0.5% American Indian or Alaska Native, non-Hispanic/Latino; 2% Two or more races, non-Hispanic/Latino; 0.1% Race/ethnicity unknown; 2% international; 10% transferred in; 21% live on campus.

Freshmen *Admission:* 1,122 enrolled.

Faculty *Total:* 324, 22% full-time, 15% with terminal degrees. *Student/faculty ratio:* 19:1.

Majors Accounting technology and bookkeeping; administrative assistant and secretarial science; biotechnology; business administration and management; business, management, and marketing related; child-care and support services management; commercial and advertising art; community organization and advocacy; computer and information sciences; computer and information sciences and support services related; construction trades related; creative writing; criminal justice/law enforcement administration; early childhood education; electrical, electronic and communications engineering technology; engineering; forensic science and technology; hotel/motel administration; humanities; information science/studies; international business/trade/commerce; kindergarten/preschool education; legal assistant/paralegal; liberal arts and sciences/liberal studies; natural resources/conservation; parks, recreation and leisure facilities management; parks, recreation, leisure, and fitness studies related; photography; radio and television broadcasting technology; registered nursing/registered nurse; speech communication and rhetoric; sport and fitness administration/management; substance abuse/addiction counseling; web/multimedia management and webmaster.

Academics *Calendar:* semesters. *Degree:* certificates and associate. *Special study options:* academic remediation for entering students, adult/continuing education programs, advanced placement credit, cooperative education, distance learning, double majors, English as a second language, honors programs, independent study, internships, off-campus study, part-time degree program, services for LD students, study abroad, summer session for credit.

Library Gerald A. Barry Memorial Library plus 1 other with 65,386 titles, 200 serial subscriptions, 3,445 audiovisual materials, an OPAC, a Web page.

Student Life *Housing Options:* coed. Campus housing is provided by a third party. *Activities and Organizations:* drama/theater group, College Entertainment Board, Sport Management Club, Nursing Club, Media Club, Writer's Guild. *Campus security:* 24-hour patrols, late-night transport/escort service, controlled dormitory access, armed peace officers. *Student services:* health clinic, personal/psychological counseling.

Athletics Member NJCAA. *Intercollegiate sports:* baseball M, basketball M/W, golf M/W, lacrosse M, soccer M/W, softball W, volleyball W. *Intramural sports:* archery M/W, badminton M/W, basketball M/W, bowling M/W, football M/W, golf M/W, lacrosse M/W, racquetball M/W, skiing (cross-country) M/W, skiing (downhill) M/W, soccer M/W, softball M/W, squash M/W, swimming and diving M/W, table tennis M/W, tennis M/W, ultimate Frisbee M/W, volleyball M/W, water polo M/W, weight lifting M/W, wrestling M/W.

Costs (2011–12) *Tuition:* state resident $3950 full-time, $143 per credit hour part-time; nonresident $8200 full-time, $296 per credit hour part-time. Part-time tuition and fees vary according to course load. *Required fees:* $655 full-time, $25 per credit hour part-time, $10 per term part-time. *Room and board:* $8680. Room and board charges vary according to board plan and housing facility. *Payment plans:* installment, deferred payment. *Waivers:* employees or children of employees.

Financial Aid Of all full-time matriculated undergraduates who enrolled in 2010, 150 Federal Work-Study jobs (averaging $1000). 150 state and other part-time jobs (averaging $1000).

Applying *Options:* electronic application, early admission, deferred entrance. *Application fee:* $15. *Required:* high school transcript. *Required for some:* essay or personal statement, interview. *Application deadlines:* rolling (freshmen), rolling (out-of-state freshmen), rolling (transfers). *Notification:* continuous (freshmen), continuous (out-of-state freshmen), continuous (transfers).

Freshman Application Contact Mr. Sandy Drumluk, Director of Admissions, Tompkins Cortland Community College, 170 North Street, PO Box 139, Dryden, NY 13053-0139. *Phone:* 607-844-6580. *Toll-free phone:* 888-567-8211. *Fax:* 607-844-6538. *E-mail:* admissions@tc3.edu. *Web site:* http://www.TC3.edu/.

Trocaire College
Buffalo, New York

Freshman Application Contact Mrs. Theresa Horner, Director of Records, Trocaire College, 360 Choate Avenue, Buffalo, NY 14220-2094. *Phone:* 716-827-2459. *Fax:* 716-828-6107. *E-mail:* info@trocaire.edu. *Web site:* http://www.trocaire.edu/.

Ulster County Community College
Stone Ridge, New York

Freshman Application Contact Admissions Office, Ulster County Community College, 491 Cottekill Road, Stone Ridge, NY 12484. *Phone:* 845-687-5022. *Toll-free phone:* 800-724-0833. *E-mail:* admissionsoffice@sunyulster.edu. *Web site:* http://www.sunyulster.edu/.

Utica School of Commerce
Utica, New York

Freshman Application Contact Senior Admissions Coordinator, Utica School of Commerce, 201 Bleecker Street, Utica, NY 13501-2280. *Phone:* 315-733-2300. *Toll-free phone:* 800-321-4USC. *Fax:* 315-733-9281. *Web site:* http://www.uscny.edu/.

Westchester Community College
Valhalla, New York

- **State and locally supported** 2-year, founded 1946, part of State University of New York System
- **Suburban** 218-acre campus with easy access to New York City
- **Coed,** 13,969 undergraduate students, 53% full-time, 53% women, 47% men

Undergraduates 7,410 full-time, 6,559 part-time. Students come from 9 states and territories; 0.5% are from out of state; 20% Black or African American, non-Hispanic/Latino; 27% Hispanic/Latino; 4% Asian, non-Hispanic/Latino; 0.2% Native Hawaiian or other Pacific Islander, non-Hispanic/Latino; 0.5% American Indian or Alaska Native, non-Hispanic/Latino; 0.7% Two or more races, non-Hispanic/Latino; 7% Race/ethnicity unknown; 7% transferred in.

Freshmen *Admission:* 2,726 enrolled.

Faculty *Total:* 1,102, 15% full-time. *Student/faculty ratio:* 18:1.

Majors Accounting; administrative assistant and secretarial science; apparel and textile manufacturing; business administration and management; child development; civil engineering technology; clinical laboratory science/medical technology; clinical/medical laboratory technology; community organization and advocacy; computer and information sciences; computer and information sciences and support services related; computer and information sciences related; computer and information systems security; computer science; computer systems networking and telecommunications; consumer merchandising/retailing management; corrections; culinary arts; dance; data processing and data processing technology; design and applied arts related; dietetics; education (multiple levels); electrical, electronic and communications engineering technology; emergency medical technology (EMT paramedic); energy management and systems technology; engineering science; engineering technology; environmental control technologies related; film/video and photographic arts related; finance; fine/studio arts; food technology and processing; humanities; information science/studies; international business/trade/commerce; legal assistant/paralegal; liberal arts and sciences/liberal studies; marketing/marketing management; mass communication/media; mechanical engineering/mechanical technology; public administration; registered nursing/registered nurse; respiratory care therapy; social sciences; substance abuse/addiction counseling; veterinary/animal health technology.

Academics *Calendar:* semesters. *Degree:* certificates and associate. *Special study options:* academic remediation for entering students, adult/continuing education programs, advanced placement credit, cooperative education, distance learning, double majors, English as a second language, honors programs, independent study, internships, off-campus study, part-time degree program, services for LD students, student-designed majors, study abroad, summer session for credit.

Library Harold L. Drimmer Library plus 1 other with 216,803 titles, 393 serial subscriptions, 7,573 audiovisual materials, an OPAC, a Web page.

Student Life *Housing:* college housing not available. *Activities and Organizations:* drama/theater group, student-run newspaper, radio station, choral group, Deca Fashion Retail, Future Educators, Respiratory Club, Black Student Union, Diversity Action. *Campus security:* 24-hour emergency response devices and patrols, late-night transport/escort service. *Student services:* health clinic, personal/psychological counseling, women's center.

Athletics Member NJCAA. *Intercollegiate sports:* baseball M, basketball M/W, bowling M/W, golf M, soccer M, softball W, volleyball W. *Intramural sports:* badminton M/W, basketball M/W, softball M/W, swimming and diving M/W, tennis M/W, volleyball M/W, weight lifting M/W.

Costs (2011–12) *Tuition:* state resident $4150 full-time, $173 per credit hour part-time; nonresident $12,450 full-time, $519 per credit hour part-time. *Required fees:* $363 full-time, $83 per term part-time. *Payment plan:* installment.

Financial Aid Of all full-time matriculated undergraduates who enrolled in 2010, 200 Federal Work-Study jobs (averaging $1000).

Applying *Options:* early admission. *Application fee:* $25. *Required:* high school transcript. *Recommended:* interview. *Application deadlines:* rolling (freshmen), rolling (transfers). *Notification:* continuous until 2/2 (freshmen), continuous (transfers).

Freshman Application Contact Ms. Gloria Leon, Director of Admissions, Westchester Community College, 75 Grasslands Road, Administration Building, Valhalla, NY 10595-1698. *Phone:* 914-606-6735. *Fax:* 914-606-6540. *E-mail:* admissions@sunywcc.edu. *Web site:* http://www.sunywcc.edu/

Wood Tobe–Coburn School

New York, New York

- **Private** 2-year, founded 1879, part of Bradford Schools, Inc.
- **Urban** campus
- **Coed, primarily women,** 483 undergraduate students
- 84% of applicants were admitted

Freshmen *Admission:* 1,269 applied, 1,072 admitted.

Majors Accounting technology and bookkeeping; administrative assistant and secretarial science; computer programming; computer systems networking and telecommunications; fashion/apparel design; graphic design; hotel/motel administration; medical/clinical assistant; retailing; tourism and travel services management.

Academics *Calendar:* semesters. *Degree:* diplomas and associate. *Special study options:* accelerated degree program, internships.

Student Life *Housing:* college housing not available.

Freshman Application Contact Admissions Office, Wood Tobe–Coburn School, 8 East 40th Street, New York, NY 10016. *Phone:* 212-686-9040. *Toll-free phone:* 800-394-9663. *Web site:* http://www.woodtobecoburn.edu/.

NORTH CAROLINA

Alamance Community College
Graham, North Carolina

- **State-supported** 2-year, founded 1959, part of North Carolina Community College System
- **Small-town** 48-acre campus
- **Endowment** $2.9 million
- **Coed**

Undergraduates 2,710 full-time, 2,802 part-time. Students come from 6 states and territories; 1% are from out of state; 20% transferred in.
Faculty *Student/faculty ratio:* 12:1.
Academics *Calendar:* semesters. *Degree:* certificates, diplomas, and associate. *Special study options:* academic remediation for entering students, adult/continuing education programs, cooperative education, distance learning, double majors, English as a second language, independent study, off-campus study, part-time degree program, services for LD students, summer session for credit.
Student Life *Campus security:* 24-hour emergency response devices and patrols, student patrols, late-night transport/escort service.
Costs (2011–12) *Tuition:* state resident $1995 full-time; nonresident $7754 full-time. Full-time tuition and fees vary according to course load. Part-time tuition and fees vary according to course load. *Required fees:* $30 full-time.
Financial Aid Of all full-time matriculated undergraduates who enrolled in 2010, 4,000 applied for aid, 3,000 were judged to have need. 200 Federal Work-Study jobs. *Average percent of need met:* 30. *Average financial aid package:* $4500. *Average need-based gift aid:* $4500. *Average indebtedness upon graduation:* $2500.
Applying *Options:* electronic application. *Required:* high school transcript.
Freshman Application Contact Ms. Elizabeth Brehler, Director for Enrollment Management, Alamance Community College, Graham, NC 27253-8000. *Phone:* 336-506-4120. *Fax:* 336-506-4264. *E-mail:* brehlere@alamancecc.edu. *Web site:* http://www.alamancecc.edu/.

Asheville-Buncombe Technical Community College
Asheville, North Carolina

Freshman Application Contact Asheville-Buncombe Technical Community College, 340 Victoria Road, Asheville, NC 28801-4897. *Phone:* 828-254-1921 Ext. 7520. *Web site:* http://www.abtech.edu/.

Beaufort County Community College
Washington, North Carolina

- **State-supported** 2-year, founded 1967, part of North Carolina Community College System
- **Rural** 67-acre campus
- **Coed,** 1,933 undergraduate students

Undergraduates 32% Black or African American, non-Hispanic/Latino; 2% Hispanic/Latino; 0.2% Asian, non-Hispanic/Latino; 0.6% American Indian or Alaska Native, non-Hispanic/Latino; 3% Race/ethnicity unknown.
Freshmen *Admission:* 856 applied, 856 admitted.
Majors Accounting; administrative assistant and secretarial science; automobile/automotive mechanics technology; business administration and management; clinical/medical laboratory technology; computer programming; criminal justice/law enforcement administration; criminal justice/police science; drafting and design technology; electrical, electronic and communications engineering technology; heavy equipment maintenance technology; information science/studies; kindergarten/preschool education; liberal arts and sciences/liberal studies; mechanical engineering/mechanical technology; medical office management; registered nursing/registered nurse; welding technology.
Academics *Calendar:* semesters. *Degree:* certificates, diplomas, and associate. *Special study options:* academic remediation for entering students, advanced placement credit, cooperative education, distance learning, English as a second language, part-time degree program, services for LD students, summer session for credit.
Library Beaufort Community College Library with 25,734 titles, 214 serial subscriptions, an OPAC, a Web page.
Student Life *Housing:* college housing not available. *Activities and Organizations:* Student Government Association, Gamma Beta Phi, BECANS-Nursing. *Campus security:* 24-hour emergency response devices and patrols, late-night transport/escort service. *Student services:* personal/psychological counseling.
Standardized Tests *Required:* ACCUPLACER, COMPASS, ASSET (for admission). *Recommended:* SAT or ACT (for admission).

Costs (2011–12) *Tuition:* state resident $2128 full-time, $67 per credit hour part-time; nonresident $8272 full-time, $259 per credit hour part-time. Part-time tuition and fees vary according to course load. *Required fees:* $64 full-time, $2 per credit hour part-time. *Waivers:* senior citizens.

Applying *Options:* electronic application. *Required for some:* high school transcript. *Application deadlines:* rolling (freshmen), rolling (out-of-state freshmen), rolling (transfers).

Freshman Application Contact Mr. Gary Burbage, Director of Admissions, Beaufort County Community College, PO Box 1069, 5337 US Highway 264 East, Washington, NC 27889-1069. *Phone:* 252-940-6233. *Fax:* 252-940-6393. *E-mail:* garyb@beaufortccc.edu. *Web site:* http://www.beaufortccc.edu/

Bladen Community College
Dublin, North Carolina

Freshman Application Contact Ms. Andrea Fisher, Enrollment Specialist, Bladen Community College, PO Box 266, Dublin, NC 28332. *Phone:* 910-879-5593. *Fax:* 910-879-5564. *E-mail:* acarterfisher@bladencc.edu. *Web site:* http://www.bladen.cc.nc.us/.

Blue Ridge Community College
Flat Rock, North Carolina

Freshman Application Contact Blue Ridge Community College, 180 West Campus Drive, Flat Rock, NC 28731. *Phone:* 828-694-1810. *Web site:* http://www.blueridge.edu/.

Brunswick Community College
Supply, North Carolina

Freshman Application Contact Admissions Counselor, Brunswick Community College, 50 College Road, PO Box 30, Supply, NC 28462-0030. *Phone:* 910-755-7300. *Toll-free phone:* 800-754-1050. *Fax:* 910-754-9609. *E-mail:* admissions@brunswickcc.edu. *Web site:* http://www.brunswickcc.edu/.

Caldwell Community College and Technical Institute
Hudson, North Carolina

Freshman Application Contact Carolyn Woodard, Director of Enrollment Management Services, Caldwell Community College and Technical Institute, 2855 Hickory Boulevard, Hudson, NC 28638. *Phone:* 828-726-2703. *Fax:* 828-726-2709. *E-mail:* cwoodard@cccti.edu. *Web site:* http://www.cccti.edu/.

Cape Fear Community College
Wilmington, North Carolina

- **State-supported** 2-year, founded 1959, part of North Carolina Community College System
- **Urban** 150-acre campus
- **Endowment** $4.3 million
- **Coed,** 9,247 undergraduate students, 44% full-time, 54% women, 46% men

Undergraduates 4,086 full-time, 5,161 part-time. Students come from 45 states and territories; 16 other countries; 7% are from out of state; 15% Black or African American, non-Hispanic/Latino; 4% Hispanic/Latino; 0.9% Asian, non-Hispanic/Latino; 0.8% American Indian or Alaska Native, non-Hispanic/Latino; 4% Race/ethnicity unknown; 10% transferred in.

Freshmen *Admission:* 4,825 applied, 2,515 admitted, 1,414 enrolled.

Faculty *Total:* 701, 41% full-time. *Student/faculty ratio:* 14:1.

Majors Accounting technology and bookkeeping; architectural engineering technology; automobile/automotive mechanics technology; building/property maintenance; business administration and management; chemical technology; cinematography and film/video production; computer systems networking and telecommunications; computer technology/computer systems technology; criminal justice/police science; culinary arts; dental hygiene; diagnostic medical sonography and ultrasound technology; early childhood education; electrical, electronic and communications engineering technology; electrical/electronics equipment installation and repair; electromechanical and instrumentation and maintenance technologies related; executive assistant/executive secretary; fire prevention and safety technology; hotel/motel administration; instrumentation technology; interior design; landscaping and groundskeeping; liberal arts and sciences/liberal studies; machine shop technology; marine maintenance and ship repair technology; mechanical engineering/mechanical technology; medical office management; medical radiologic technology; nuclear/nuclear power technology; occupational therapist assistant; oceanogra-

phy (chemical and physical); registered nursing/registered nurse; surgical technology.

Academics *Calendar:* semesters. *Degree:* certificates, diplomas, and associate. *Special study options:* academic remediation for entering students, adult/continuing education programs, advanced placement credit, cooperative education, distance learning, double majors, English as a second language, independent study, off-campus study, part-time degree program, services for LD students, summer session for credit.

Library Cape Fear Community College Library with 84,433 titles, 7,951 serial subscriptions, 15,311 audiovisual materials, an OPAC, a Web page.

Student Life *Housing:* college housing not available. *Activities and Organizations:* student-run newspaper, choral group, Nursing Club, Dental Hygiene Club, Pineapple Guild, Phi Theta Kappa, Occupational Therapy. *Campus security:* 24-hour emergency response devices and patrols, late-night transport/escort service, armed police officer. *Student services:* personal/psychological counseling.

Athletics Member NJCAA. *Intercollegiate sports:* basketball M, cheerleading M/W, golf M/W, soccer M/W, volleyball M/W. *Intramural sports:* softball M/W, tennis M/W.

Costs (2011–12) *Tuition:* state resident $2128 full-time, $67 per credit hour part-time; nonresident $8272 full-time, $259 per credit hour part-time. Full-time tuition and fees vary according to course load. Part-time tuition and fees vary according to course load. *Required fees:* $137 full-time. *Payment plans:* installment, deferred payment. *Waivers:* senior citizens and employees or children of employees.

Financial Aid Of all full-time matriculated undergraduates who enrolled in 2010, 107 Federal Work-Study jobs (averaging $1555).

Applying *Options:* electronic application, early admission. *Required for some:* high school transcript, interview, placement testing. *Application deadlines:* 8/15 (freshmen), rolling (transfers). *Notification:* continuous (freshmen), continuous (transfers).

Freshman Application Contact Ms. Linda Kasyan, Director of Enrollment Management, Cape Fear Community College, 411 North Front Street, Wilmington, NC 28401-3993. *Phone:* 910-362-7054. *Toll-free phone:* 877-799-2322. *Fax:* 910-362-7080. *E-mail:* admissions@cfcc.edu. *Web site:* http://www.cfcc.edu/.

Carolinas College of Health Sciences
Charlotte, North Carolina

- **Public** 2-year, founded 1990
- **Urban** 3-acre campus with easy access to Charlotte
- **Endowment** $1.8 million
- **Coed,** 424 undergraduate students, 14% full-time, 86% women, 14% men

Undergraduates 61 full-time, 363 part-time. Students come from 3 states and territories; 9% are from out of state; 12% Black or African American, non-Hispanic/Latino; 4% Hispanic/Latino; 3% Asian, non-Hispanic/Latino; 0.7% Native Hawaiian or other Pacific Islander, non-Hispanic/Latino; 0.5% American Indian or Alaska Native, non-Hispanic/Latino; 2% Two or more races, non-Hispanic/Latino; 4% Race/ethnicity unknown.

Freshmen *Admission:* 8 admitted, 8 enrolled. *Average high school GPA:* 3.45.

Faculty *Total:* 71, 37% full-time. *Student/faculty ratio:* 6:1.

Majors Medical radiologic technology; radiologic technology/science; registered nursing/registered nurse.

Academics *Calendar:* semesters. *Degree:* certificates, diplomas, and associate. *Special study options:* advanced placement credit, distance learning, independent study, services for LD students, summer session for credit.

Library AHEC Library with 9,810 titles, 503 serial subscriptions, an OPAC, a Web page.

Student Life *Housing Options:* Campus housing is provided by a third party. *Campus security:* 24-hour emergency response devices and patrols, late-night transport/escort service. *Student services:* health clinic, personal/psychological counseling.

Standardized Tests *Required for some:* SAT or ACT (for admission).

Costs (2012–13) *Tuition:* state resident $11,550 full-time, $297 per credit hour part-time; nonresident $11,550 full-time, $297 per credit hour part-time. Full-time tuition and fees vary according to course load and program. Part-time tuition and fees vary according to course load and program. *Required fees:* $585 full-time, $125 per term part-time. *Waivers:* employees or children of employees.

Financial Aid Of all full-time matriculated undergraduates who enrolled in 2008, 5 Federal Work-Study jobs (averaging $5500).

Applying *Options:* electronic application. *Application fee:* $50. *Required:* minimum 2.5 GPA. *Required for some:* high school transcript, 1 letter of recommendation, interview, SAT or ACT Test Scores.

Freshman Application Contact Ms. Nicki Sabourin, Admissions Representative, Carolinas College of Health Sciences, 1200 Blythe Boulevard, Charlotte, NC 28203. *Phone:* 704-355-5043. *Fax:* 704-355-9336.

E-mail: cchsinformation@carolinashealthcare.org.
Web site: http://www.carolinascollege.edu/.

Carteret Community College

Morehead City, North Carolina

Freshman Application Contact Ms. Margie Ward, Admissions Officer, Carteret Community College, 3505 Arendell Street, Morehead City, NC 28557-2989. *Phone:* 252-222-6155. *Fax:* 252-222-6265. *E-mail:* admissions@carteret.edu. *Web site:* http://www.carteret.edu/.

Catawba Valley Community College

Hickory, North Carolina

- **State and locally supported** 2-year, founded 1960, part of North Carolina Community College System
- **Small-town** 50-acre campus with easy access to Charlotte
- **Endowment** $1.3 million
- **Coed,** 5,114 undergraduate students, 38% full-time, 59% women, 41% men

Undergraduates 1,961 full-time, 3,153 part-time. Students come from 9 states and territories; 1 other country; 6% Black or African American, non-Hispanic/Latino; 0.2% Hispanic/Latino; 8% Asian, non-Hispanic/Latino; 0.1% Native Hawaiian or other Pacific Islander, non-Hispanic/Latino; 0.7% American Indian or Alaska Native, non-Hispanic/Latino; 0.4% Two or more races, non-Hispanic/Latino; 2% Race/ethnicity unknown; 25% transferred in.

Freshmen *Admission:* 2,587 applied, 2,148 admitted, 856 enrolled. *Average high school GPA:* 2.9.

Faculty *Total:* 548, 28% full-time. *Student/faculty ratio:* 7:1.

Majors Accounting technology and bookkeeping; applied horticulture/horticulture operations; architectural engineering technology; automobile/automotive mechanics technology; banking and financial support services; business administration and management; commercial and advertising art; computer engineering technology; computer programming; computer systems networking and telecommunications; criminal justice/safety; customer service management; cyber/computer forensics and counterterrorism; dental hygiene; early childhood education; e-commerce; electrical, electronic and communications engineering technology; electromechanical and instrumentation and maintenance technologies related; electroneurodiagnostic/electroencephalographic technology; emergency medical technology (EMT paramedic); fire prevention and safety technology; forensic science and technology; general studies; health information/medical records technology; industrial engineering; information technology; liberal arts and sciences/liberal studies; medical office management; medical radiologic technology; office management; photographic and film/video technology; polysomnography; registered nursing/registered nurse; respiratory care therapy; turf and turfgrass management.

Academics *Calendar:* semesters. *Degree:* certificates, diplomas, and associate. *Special study options:* academic remediation for entering students, adult/continuing education programs, advanced placement credit, cooperative education, distance learning, double majors, English as a second language, independent study, part-time degree program, services for LD students, student-designed majors, summer session for credit.

Library Learning Resource Center with 27,000 titles, 1,250 serial subscriptions, 700 audiovisual materials, an OPAC, a Web page.

Student Life *Housing:* college housing not available. *Activities and Organizations:* drama/theater group, choral group, Cosmetology Club- Cutting Edge, Phi Theta Kappa, Student Photographic Society, Theatre Arts Club. *Campus security:* 24-hour patrols. *Student services:* personal/psychological counseling.

Athletics Member NJCAA. *Intercollegiate sports:* baseball M, basketball M/W, cheerleading M/W, volleyball W.

Standardized Tests *Required:* COMPASS test series (for admission).

Costs (2012–13) *Tuition:* state resident $1683 full-time, $67 per credit hour part-time; nonresident $6291 full-time, $259 per credit part-time. Part-time tuition and fees vary according to course load. *Required fees:* $87 full-time, $5 per credit hour part-time, $11 per term part-time. *Payment plan:* installment. *Waivers:* senior citizens.

Applying *Options:* electronic application, early admission, deferred entrance. *Required:* high school transcript. *Required for some:* 1 letter of recommendation. *Application deadlines:* rolling (freshmen), rolling (out-of-state freshmen), rolling (transfers). *Notification:* continuous (freshmen), continuous (out-of-state freshmen), continuous (transfers).

Freshman Application Contact Catawba Valley Community College, 2550 Highway 70 SE, Hickory, NC 28602-9699. *Phone:* 828-327-7000 Ext. 4618. *Web site:* http://www.cvcc.edu/.

Central Carolina Community College

Sanford, North Carolina

- **State and locally supported** 2-year, founded 1962, part of North Carolina Community College System
- **Small-town** 41-acre campus
- **Endowment** $3.0 million
- **Coed,** 2,477 undergraduate students

Undergraduates Students come from 36 states and territories; 6% are from out of state.

Faculty *Total:* 627, 26% full-time. *Student/faculty ratio:* 10:1.

Majors Accounting; administrative assistant and secretarial science; automobile/automotive mechanics technology; business administration and management; computer/information technology services administration related; computer programming; computer programming (specific applications); computer systems networking and telecommunications; criminal justice/law enforcement administration; drafting and design technology; electrical, electronic and communications engineering technology; information science/studies; information technology; instrumentation technology; kindergarten/preschool education; laser and optical technology; legal administrative assistant/secretary; legal assistant/paralegal; liberal arts and sciences/liberal studies; marketing/marketing management; medical administrative assistant and medical secretary; medical/clinical assistant; operations management; quality control technology; radio and television; registered nursing/registered nurse; social work; telecommunications technology; veterinary/animal health technology.

Academics *Calendar:* semesters. *Degree:* certificates, diplomas, and associate. *Special study options:* academic remediation for entering students, adult/continuing education programs, advanced placement credit, distance learning, double majors, English as a second language, independent study, internships, part-time degree program, services for LD students, summer session for credit.

Library Library/Learning Resources Center plus 2 others with 50,479 titles, 240 serial subscriptions, 5,946 audiovisual materials, an OPAC, a Web page.

Student Life *Housing:* college housing not available. *Activities and Organizations:* student-run radio station. *Campus security:* 24-hour emergency response devices and patrols, student patrols, patrols by trained security personnel during operating hours. *Student services:* personal/psychological counseling.

Athletics Member NJCAA. *Intercollegiate sports:* basketball M/W, golf M/W, softball W, volleyball W. *Intramural sports:* bowling M/W, golf M/W, softball W, volleyball W.

Costs (2011–12) *Tuition:* state resident $2083 full-time; nonresident $7843 full-time. Full-time tuition and fees vary according to course load. Part-time tuition and fees vary according to course load. *Required fees:* $88 full-time. *Payment plan:* installment. *Waivers:* senior citizens.

Financial Aid Of all full-time matriculated undergraduates who enrolled in 2010, 70 Federal Work-Study jobs (averaging $1361). *Financial aid deadline:* 5/4.

Applying *Options:* electronic application, early admission, deferred entrance. *Required:* high school transcript. *Application deadlines:* rolling (freshmen), rolling (transfers). *Notification:* continuous (freshmen), continuous (transfers).

Freshman Application Contact Mrs. Jamie Tyson Childress, Registrar, Central Carolina Community College, 1105 Kelly Drive, Sanford, NC 27330-9000. *Phone:* 919-718-7239. *Toll-free phone:* 800-682-8353. *Fax:* 919-718-7380. *Web site:* http://www.cccc.edu/.

Central Piedmont Community College

Charlotte, North Carolina

Freshman Application Contact Ms. Linda McComb, Associate Dean, Central Piedmont Community College, PO Box 35009, Charlotte, NC 28235-5009. *Phone:* 704-330-6784. *Fax:* 704-330-6136. *Web site:* http://www.cpcc.edu/.

Cleveland Community College

Shelby, North Carolina

Freshman Application Contact Cleveland Community College, 137 South Post Road, Shelby, NC 28152. *Phone:* 704-484-6073. *Web site:* http://www.clevelandcc.edu/.

Coastal Carolina Community College

Jacksonville, North Carolina

Freshman Application Contact Ms. Heather Calihan, Counseling Coordinator, Coastal Carolina Community College, Jacksonville, NC 28546. *Phone:* 910-938-6241. *Fax:* 910-455-2767. *E-mail:* calihanh@coastal.cc.nc.us. *Web site:* http://www.coastalcarolina.edu/.

College of The Albemarle
Elizabeth City, North Carolina

Freshman Application Contact Mr. Kenny Krentz, Director of Admissions and International Students, College of The Albemarle, PO Box 2327, Elizabeth City, NC 27906-2327. *Phone:* 252-335-0821. *Fax:* 252-335-2011. *E-mail:* kkrentz@albemarle.edu. *Web site:* http://www.albemarle.edu/.

Craven Community College
New Bern, North Carolina

Freshman Application Contact Ms. Millicent Fulford, Recruiter, Craven Community College, 800 College Court, New Bern, NC 28562-4984. *Phone:* 252-638-7232. *Web site:* http://www.craven.cc.nc.us/.

Davidson County Community College
Lexington, North Carolina

Freshman Application Contact Davidson County Community College, PO Box 1287, Lexington, NC 27293-1287. *Phone:* 336-249-8186 Ext. 6715. *Fax:* 336-224-0240. *E-mail:* admissions@davidsonccc.edu. *Web site:* http://www.davidsonccc.edu/.

Durham Technical Community College
Durham, North Carolina

Director of Admissions Ms. Penny Augustine, Director of Admissions and Testing, Durham Technical Community College, 1637 Lawson Street, Durham, NC 27703-5023. *Phone:* 919-686-3619. *Web site:* http://www.durhamtech.edu/.

ECPI College of Technology
Charlotte, North Carolina

Admissions Office Contact ECPI College of Technology, 4800 Airport Center Parkway, Charlotte, NC 28208. *Toll-free phone:* 866-708-6167. *Web site:* http://www.ecpi.edu/.

ECPI College of Technology
Greensboro, North Carolina

Admissions Office Contact ECPI College of Technology, 7802 Airport Center Drive, Greensboro, NC 27409. *Toll-free phone:* 866-708-6170. *Web site:* http://www.ecpi.edu/.

Edgecombe Community College
Tarboro, North Carolina

Freshman Application Contact Ms. Jackie Heath, Admissions Officer, Edgecombe Community College, 2009 West Wilson Street, Tarboro, NC 27886-9399. *Phone:* 252-823-5166 Ext. 254. *Web site:* http://www.edgecombe.edu/.

Fayetteville Technical Community College
Fayetteville, North Carolina

- **State-supported** 2-year, founded 1961, part of North Carolina Community College System
- **Suburban** 209-acre campus with easy access to Raleigh
- **Endowment** $39,050
- **Coed,** 11,737 undergraduate students, 41% full-time, 64% women, 36% men

Undergraduates 4,760 full-time, 6,977 part-time. Students come from 38 states and territories; 83 other countries; 11% are from out of state; 46% Black or African American, non-Hispanic/Latino; 9% Hispanic/Latino; 1% Asian, non-Hispanic/Latino; 0.3% Native Hawaiian or other Pacific Islander, non-Hispanic/Latino; 3% American Indian or Alaska Native, non-Hispanic/Latino; 2% Two or more races, non-Hispanic/Latino; 3% Race/ethnicity unknown; 0.7% international; 20% transferred in.

Freshmen *Admission:* 4,794 applied, 4,794 admitted, 1,812 enrolled. *Average high school GPA:* 2.34.

Faculty *Total:* 814, 39% full-time. *Student/faculty ratio:* 15:1.

Majors Accounting; applied horticulture/horticulture operations; architectural engineering technology; automobile/automotive mechanics technology; banking and financial support services; building/construction finishing, management, and inspection related; business administration and management; civil engineering technology; commercial and advertising art; computer and information systems security; computer programming; computer systems networking and telecommunications; corrections and criminal justice related; criminal justice/safety; crisis/emergency/disaster management; culinary arts; dental hygiene; early childhood education; electrical, electronic and communications engineering technology; electrician; elementary education; emergency medical technology (EMT paramedic); fire prevention and safety technology; forensic science and technology; funeral service and mortuary science; game and interactive media design; heating, air conditioning, ventilation and refrigeration maintenance technology; hotel, motel, and restaurant management; human resources management; information science/studies; information technology; legal assistant/paralegal; liberal arts and sciences and humanities related; liberal arts and sciences/liberal studies; machine shop technology; marketing/marketing management; medical office management; nuclear medical technology; office management; operations management; pharmacy technician; physical therapy technology; public administration; radiologic technology/science; registered nursing/registered nurse; respiratory care therapy; speech-language pathology assistant; surgical technology; surveying technology.

Academics *Calendar:* semesters. *Degree:* certificates, diplomas, and associate. *Special study options:* academic remediation for entering students, adult/continuing education programs, advanced placement credit, cooperative education, distance learning, double majors, English as a second language, independent study, internships, off-campus study, part-time degree program, services for LD students, summer session for credit.

Library Paul H. Thompson Library plus 1 other with 70,819 titles, 308 serial subscriptions, 582 audiovisual materials, an OPAC, a Web page.

Student Life *Housing:* college housing not available. *Activities and Organizations:* Parents for Higher Education, Early Childhood Club, Phi Beta Lambda, Association of Nursing Students, African/American Heritage Club. *Campus security:* 24-hour emergency response devices and patrols, late-night transport/escort service, campus-wide emergency notification system. *Student services:* personal/psychological counseling.

Athletics *Intramural sports:* basketball M/W, bowling M/W, football M/W, golf M/W, softball M/W, tennis M/W, volleyball M/W.

Standardized Tests *Required:* ACCUPLACER is required or ACT and SAT scores in lieu of ACCUPLACER if the scores are no more than 5 years old or ASSET and COMPASS scores are also accepted if they are no more than 3 years old (for admission).

Costs (2011–12) *One-time required fee:* $25. *Tuition:* state resident $2128 full-time, $67 per credit hour part-time; nonresident $8272 full-time, $259 per credit hour part-time. Full-time tuition and fees vary according to course load. Part-time tuition and fees vary according to course load. *Required fees:* $90 full-time, $90 per term part-time. *Payment plan:* installment. *Waivers:* senior citizens and employees or children of employees.

Financial Aid Of all full-time matriculated undergraduates who enrolled in 2010, 75 Federal Work-Study jobs (averaging $2000). *Financial aid deadline:* 6/1.

Applying *Options:* electronic application. *Required for some:* essay or personal statement, high school transcript, interview. *Application deadlines:* rolling (freshmen), rolling (out-of-state freshmen), rolling (transfers). *Notification:* continuous (freshmen), continuous (out-of-state freshmen), continuous (transfers).

Freshman Application Contact Ms. Melissa Ann Jones, Registrar/Curriculum, Fayetteville Technical Community College, 2201 Hull Road, Fayetteville, NC 28303. *Phone:* 910-678-8474. *Fax:* 910-678-0085. *E-mail:* jonesma@faytechcc.edu. *Web site:* http://www.faytechcc.edu/.

Forsyth Technical Community College
Winston-Salem, North Carolina

Freshman Application Contact Admissions Office, Forsyth Technical Community College, 2100 Silas Creek Parkway, Winston-Salem, NC 27103-5197. *Phone:* 336-734-7556. *E-mail:* admissions@forsythtech.edu. *Web site:* http://www.forsythtech.edu/.

Gaston College
Dallas, North Carolina

Freshman Application Contact Terry Basier, Director of Enrollment Management and Admissions, Gaston College, 201 Highway 321 South, Dallas, NC 28034. *Phone:* 704-922-6214. *Fax:* 704-922-6443. *Web site:* http://www.gaston.edu/.

Guilford Technical Community College

Jamestown, North Carolina

- **State and locally supported** 2-year, founded 1958, part of North Carolina Community College System
- **Urban** 158-acre campus with easy access to Raleigh, Charlotte
- **Endowment** $8.9 million
- **Coed,** 14,745 undergraduate students, 59% full-time, 57% women, 43% men

Undergraduates 8,738 full-time, 6,007 part-time. Students come from 22 states and territories; 102 other countries; 0.3% are from out of state; 45% Black or African American, non-Hispanic/Latino; 4% Hispanic/Latino; 0.1% Asian, non-Hispanic/Latino; 1% Native Hawaiian or other Pacific Islander, non-Hispanic/Latino; 0.9% American Indian or Alaska Native, non-Hispanic/Latino; 3% Two or more races, non-Hispanic/Latino; 3% Race/ethnicity unknown; 0.8% international; 26% transferred in. *Retention:* 59% of full-time freshmen returned.

Freshmen *Admission:* 9,914 applied, 9,914 admitted, 1,849 enrolled. *Average high school GPA:* 2.28.

Faculty *Total:* 1,152, 32% full-time, 5% with terminal degrees. *Student/faculty ratio:* 23:1.

Majors Accounting technology and bookkeeping; agricultural power machinery operation; airline pilot and flight crew; architectural engineering technology; automobile/automotive mechanics technology; avionics maintenance technology; biology/biotechnology laboratory technician; building/property maintenance; business administration and management; chemical technology; civil engineering technology; commercial and advertising art; computer programming; computer systems analysis; computer systems networking and telecommunications; cosmetology; criminal justice/safety; culinary arts; dental hygiene; early childhood education; education related; electrical, electronic and communications engineering technology; electrician; electromechanical technology; emergency medical technology (EMT paramedic); fire prevention and safety technology; general studies; heating, air conditioning, ventilation and refrigeration maintenance technology; hotel/motel administration; human resources management; industrial production technologies related; information science/studies; information technology; legal assistant/paralegal; liberal arts and sciences and humanities related; liberal arts and sciences/liberal studies; logistics, materials, and supply chain management; machine shop technology; mechanical engineering/mechanical technology; medical/clinical assistant; medical office management; office management; pharmacy technician; physical therapy technology; psychiatric/mental health services technology; recording arts technology; registered nursing/registered nurse; substance abuse/addiction counseling; surgical technology; surveying technology; system, networking, and LAN/WAN management; telecommunications technology; turf and turfgrass management; vehicle maintenance and repair technologies related.

Academics *Calendar:* semesters. *Degree:* certificates, diplomas, and associate. *Special study options:* academic remediation for entering students, adult/continuing education programs, advanced placement credit, cooperative education, distance learning, double majors, English as a second language, external degree program, independent study, internships, off-campus study, part-time degree program, services for LD students, student-designed majors, summer session for credit. *ROTC:* Army (c), Air Force (c).

Library M. W. Bell Library plus 2 others with 115,666 titles, 13,821 serial subscriptions, 4,652 audiovisual materials, an OPAC, a Web page.

Student Life *Housing:* college housing not available. *Activities and Organizations:* drama/theater group, International Students Association, Steppin' N Style, Surgical Technology, Rotaract, Fellowship of Christian Athletes. *Campus security:* 24-hour emergency response devices and patrols, late-night transport/escort service. *Student services:* personal/psychological counseling.

Athletics Member NJCAA. *Intercollegiate sports:* baseball M(s), basketball M(s)/W(s), cheerleading W, volleyball W(s).

Applying *Options:* electronic application, early admission, deferred entrance. *Required:* high school transcript. *Required for some:* interview. *Application deadlines:* rolling (freshmen), rolling (transfers). *Notification:* continuous (freshmen), continuous (transfers).

Freshman Application Contact Guilford Technical Community College, PO Box 309, Jamestown, NC 27282-0309. *Phone:* 336-334-4822 Ext. 50125. *Web site:* http://www.gtcc.edu/.

Halifax Community College

Weldon, North Carolina

Director of Admissions Mrs. Scottie Dickens, Director of Admissions, Halifax Community College, PO Drawer 809, Weldon, NC 27890-0809. *Phone:* 252-536-7220. *Web site:* http://www.hcc.cc.nc.us/.

Haywood Community College

Clyde, North Carolina

Director of Admissions Ms. Debbie Rowland, Coordinator of Admissions, Haywood Community College, 185 Freedlander Drive, Clyde, NC 28721-9453. *Phone:* 828-627-4505. *Toll-free phone:* 866-GOTOHCC. *Web site:* http://www.haywood.edu/.

Isothermal Community College

Spindale, North Carolina

Freshman Application Contact Ms. Vickie Searcy, Enrollment Management Office, Isothermal Community College, PO Box 804, Spindale, NC 28160-0804. *Phone:* 828-286-3636 Ext. 251. *Fax:* 828-286-8109. *E-mail:* vsearcy@isothermal.edu. *Web site:* http://www.isothermal.edu/.

ITT Technical Institute

Cary, North Carolina

- **Proprietary** primarily 2-year, part of ITT Educational Services, Inc.
- **Coed**

Majors CAD/CADD drafting/design technology; computer and information systems security; computer engineering technology; computer software engineering; computer software technology; construction management; criminal justice/law enforcement administration; design and visual communications; electrical, electronic and communications engineering technology; project management; system, networking, and LAN/WAN management.

Academics *Degrees:* associate and bachelor's.

Student Life *Housing:* college housing not available.

Freshman Application Contact Director of Recruitment, ITT Technical Institute, 5520 Dillard Drive, Suite 100, Cary, NC 27518. *Phone:* 919-233-2520. *Toll-free phone:* 877-203-5533. *Web site:* http://www.itt-tech.edu/.

ITT Technical Institute

Charlotte, North Carolina

- **Proprietary** primarily 2-year
- **Coed**

Majors CAD/CADD drafting/design technology; computer and information systems security; computer engineering technology; computer software engineering; computer software technology; construction management; criminal justice/law enforcement administration; design and visual communications; electrical, electronic and communications engineering technology; project management; system, networking, and LAN/WAN management.

Academics *Degrees:* associate and bachelor's.

Student Life *Housing:* college housing not available.

Freshman Application Contact Director of Recruitment, ITT Technical Institute, 4135 Southstream Boulevard, Suite 200, Charlotte, NC 28217. *Phone:* 704-423-3100. *Toll-free phone:* 800-488-0173. *Web site:* http://www.itt-tech.edu/.

ITT Technical Institute

High Point, North Carolina

- **Proprietary** primarily 2-year, founded 2007, part of ITT Educational Services, Inc.
- **Coed**

Majors CAD/CADD drafting/design technology; computer and information systems security; computer engineering technology; computer software engineering; computer software technology; construction management; criminal justice/law enforcement administration; design and visual communications; electrical, electronic and communications engineering technology; project management; registered nursing/registered nurse; system, networking, and LAN/WAN management.

Academics *Calendar:* quarters. *Degrees:* associate and bachelor's.

Student Life *Housing:* college housing not available.

Freshman Application Contact Director of Recruitment, ITT Technical Institute, 4050 Piedmont Parkway, Suite 110, High Point, NC 27265. *Phone:* 336-819-5900. *Toll-free phone:* 877-536-5231. *Web site:* http://www.itt-tech.edu/.

James Sprunt Community College
Kenansville, North Carolina

- **State-supported** 2-year, founded 1964, part of North Carolina Community College System
- **Rural** 51-acre campus
- **Endowment** $1.0 million
- **Coed**, 1,587 undergraduate students, 50% full-time, 73% women, 27% men

Undergraduates 790 full-time, 797 part-time. Students come from 3 states and territories; 1% are from out of state; 43% Black or African American, non-Hispanic/Latino; 9% Hispanic/Latino; 0.4% Asian, non-Hispanic/Latino; 0.1% Native Hawaiian or other Pacific Islander, non-Hispanic/Latino; 0.6% American Indian or Alaska Native, non-Hispanic/Latino; 0.5% Two or more races, non-Hispanic/Latino; 0.4% Race/ethnicity unknown; 18% transferred in.
Freshmen *Admission:* 587 applied, 292 admitted, 212 enrolled.
Faculty *Total:* 135, 43% full-time, 4% with terminal degrees. *Student/faculty ratio:* 22:1.
Majors Accounting; agribusiness; animal sciences; business administration and management; child development; commercial and advertising art; criminal justice/safety; early childhood education; elementary education; general studies; information technology; institutional food workers; liberal arts and sciences and humanities related; liberal arts and sciences/liberal studies; medical/clinical assistant; registered nursing/registered nurse; viticulture and enology.
Academics *Calendar:* semesters. *Degree:* certificates, diplomas, and associate. *Special study options:* academic remediation for entering students, accelerated degree program, advanced placement credit, cooperative education, distance learning, double majors, English as a second language, independent study, internships, part-time degree program, services for LD students, summer session for credit.
Library James Sprunt Community College Library with 24,536 titles, 63 serial subscriptions, 1,073 audiovisual materials, an OPAC, a Web page.
Student Life *Housing:* college housing not available. *Activities and Organizations:* student-run newspaper, Student Nurses Association, Art Club, Alumni Association, National Technical-Vocational Honor Society, Phi Theta Kappa, national sororities. *Campus security:* day, evening and Saturday trained security personnel. *Student services:* personal/psychological counseling.
Athletics *Intercollegiate sports:* softball M/W, volleyball M/W.
Costs (2011–12) *Tuition:* state resident $2128 full-time, $67 per semester hour part-time; nonresident $8272 full-time, $259 per semester hour part-time. Full-time tuition and fees vary according to course load. Part-time tuition and fees vary according to course load. *Required fees:* $70 full-time, $35 per term part-time. *Waivers:* senior citizens.
Financial Aid Of all full-time matriculated undergraduates who enrolled in 2010, 35 Federal Work-Study jobs (averaging $1057).
Applying *Options:* electronic application. *Required:* high school transcript. *Application deadlines:* rolling (freshmen), rolling (transfers). *Notification:* continuous (freshmen), continuous (transfers).
Freshman Application Contact Ms. Lea Matthews, Admissions Specialist, James Sprunt Community College, Highway 11 South, 133 James Sprunt Drive, Kenansville, NC 28349. *Phone:* 910-296-6078. *Fax:* 910-296-1222. *E-mail:* lmatthews@jamessprunt.edu. *Web site:* http://www.jamessprunt.edu/.

Johnston Community College
Smithfield, North Carolina

- **State-supported** 2-year, founded 1969, part of North Carolina Community College System
- **Rural** 100-acre campus
- **Coed**, 4,410 undergraduate students, 52% full-time, 63% women, 37% men

Undergraduates 2,283 full-time, 2,127 part-time.
Freshmen *Admission:* 1,028 enrolled.
Faculty *Total:* 385, 37% full-time. *Student/faculty ratio:* 14:1.
Majors Accounting; accounting technology and bookkeeping; administrative assistant and secretarial science; business administration and management; commercial and advertising art; computer programming; criminal justice/police science; diesel mechanics technology; early childhood education; electrical, electronic and communications engineering technology; heating, air conditioning, ventilation and refrigeration maintenance technology; kindergarten/preschool education; landscaping and groundskeeping; legal assistant/paralegal; liberal arts and sciences/liberal studies; machine shop technology; machine tool technology; medical administrative assistant and medical secretary; medical/clinical assistant; medical office management; medical radiologic technology; office management; registered nursing/registered nurse.
Academics *Calendar:* semesters. *Degree:* certificates, diplomas, and associate. *Special study options:* academic remediation for entering students, adult/continuing education programs, advanced placement credit, cooperative education, distance learning, double majors, honors programs, independent study, part-time degree program, services for LD students, summer session for credit.
Library Johnston Community College Library plus 1 other with 33,094 titles, 197 serial subscriptions, an OPAC, a Web page.
Student Life *Housing:* college housing not available. *Activities and Organizations:* choral group. *Campus security:* 24-hour patrols. *Student services:* personal/psychological counseling.
Athletics Member NJCAA. *Intercollegiate sports:* golf M/W, softball M/W, volleyball M/W. *Intramural sports:* basketball M/W.
Standardized Tests *Required:* ACCUPLACER (for admission). *Recommended:* SAT or ACT (for admission).
Costs (2011–12) *Tuition:* state resident $2128 full-time, $67 per credit hour part-time; nonresident $8272 full-time, $285 per credit hour part-time. Full-time tuition and fees vary according to course load. Part-time tuition and fees vary according to course load. *Required fees:* $97 full-time. *Waivers:* senior citizens.
Financial Aid Of all full-time matriculated undergraduates who enrolled in 2010, 35 Federal Work-Study jobs (averaging $1853).
Applying *Options:* electronic application. *Required:* high school transcript, interview. *Application deadlines:* rolling (freshmen), rolling (transfers). *Notification:* continuous (freshmen), continuous (transfers).
Freshman Application Contact Dr. Pamela J. Harrell, Vice President of Student Services, Johnston Community College, Smithfield, NC 27577-2350. *Phone:* 919-209-2048. *Fax:* 919-989-7862. *E-mail:* pjharrell@johnstoncc.edu. *Web site:* http://www.johnstoncc.edu/.

Kaplan College, Charlotte Campus
Charlotte, North Carolina

- **Proprietary** 2-year
- **Coed**

Majors Computer systems networking and telecommunications; criminal justice/law enforcement administration.
Academics *Degree:* diplomas and associate.
Freshman Application Contact Director of Admissions, Kaplan College, Charlotte Campus, 6070 East Independence Boulevard, Charlotte, NC 28212. *Phone:* 704-567-3700. *Web site:* http://charlotte.kaplancollege.com/.

King's College
Charlotte, North Carolina

- **Private** 2-year, founded 1901
- **Suburban** campus
- **Coed**, 637 undergraduate students
- 77% of applicants were admitted

Freshmen *Admission:* 1,157 applied, 886 admitted.
Majors Accounting and business/management; accounting technology and bookkeeping; administrative assistant and secretarial science; computer programming; computer systems networking and telecommunications; graphic design; hotel/motel administration; legal administrative assistant/secretary; legal assistant/paralegal; medical/clinical assistant.
Academics *Calendar:* quarters. *Degree:* diplomas and associate. *Special study options:* accelerated degree program, internships.
Freshman Application Contact Admissions Office, King's College, 322 Lamar Avenue, Charlotte, NC 28204-2436. *Phone:* 704-372-0266. *Toll-free phone:* 800-768-2255. *Web site:* http://www.kingscollegecharlotte.edu/.

Lenoir Community College
Kinston, North Carolina

Freshman Application Contact Ms. Tammy Buck, Director of Enrollment Management, Lenoir Community College, PO Box 188, Kinston, NC 28502-0188. *Phone:* 252-527-6223 Ext. 309. *Fax:* 252-526-5112. *E-mail:* tbuck@lenoircc.edu. *Web site:* http://www.lenoircc.edu/.

Living Arts College
Raleigh, North Carolina

Freshman Application Contact Wayne Moseley, Admissions, Living Arts College, 3000 Wakefield Crossing Drive, Raleigh, NC 27614. *Phone:* 919-488-5912. *Toll-free phone:* 800-288-7442. *Fax:* 919-488-8490. *E-mail:* wmoseley@hdigi.com. *Web site:* http://www.higherdigital.com/.

Louisburg College
Louisburg, North Carolina

Freshman Application Contact Mr. Jim Schlimmer, Vice President for Enrollment Management, Louisburg College, 501 North Main Street,

Louisburg, NC 27549-2399. *Phone:* 919-497-3233. *Toll-free phone:* 800-775-0208. *Fax:* 919-496-1788. *E-mail:* admissions@louisburg.edu. *Web site:* http://www.louisburg.edu/.

Martin Community College
Williamston, North Carolina

- **State-supported** 2-year, founded 1968, part of North Carolina Community College System
- **Rural** 65-acre campus
- **Endowment** $32,015
- **Coed**

Undergraduates 475 full-time, 280 part-time. Students come from 1 other state; 0.8% are from out of state; 47% Black or African American, non-Hispanic/Latino; 0.3% Hispanic/Latino; 0.3% Asian, non-Hispanic/Latino; 0.3% American Indian or Alaska Native, non-Hispanic/Latino; 13% Race/ethnicity unknown; 27% transferred in.
Faculty *Student/faculty ratio:* 10:1.
Academics *Calendar:* semesters. *Degree:* certificates, diplomas, and associate. *Special study options:* academic remediation for entering students, advanced placement credit, distance learning, English as a second language, independent study, internships, off-campus study, part-time degree program, services for LD students, summer session for credit.
Student Life *Campus security:* 24-hour emergency response devices, part-time patrols by trained security personnel.
Financial Aid Of all full-time matriculated undergraduates who enrolled in 2010, 30 Federal Work-Study jobs (averaging $1200).
Applying *Options:* electronic application. *Required:* high school transcript. *Required for some:* interview.
Freshman Application Contact Martin Community College, 1161 Kehukee Park Road, Williamston, NC 27892. *Phone:* 252-792-1521 Ext. 243. *Web site:* http://www.martin.cc.nc.us/.

Mayland Community College
Spruce Pine, North Carolina

Director of Admissions Ms. Cathy Morrison, Director of Admissions, Mayland Community College, PO Box 547, Spruce Pine, NC 28777-0547. *Phone:* 828-765-7351 Ext. 224. *Toll-free phone:* 800-462-9526. *Web site:* http://www.mayland.edu/.

McDowell Technical Community College
Marion, North Carolina

Freshman Application Contact Mr. Rick L. Wilson, Director of Admissions, McDowell Technical Community College, 54 College Drive, Marion, NC 28752. *Phone:* 828-652-0632. *Fax:* 828-652-1014. *E-mail:* rickw@mcdowelltech.edu. *Web site:* http://www.mcdowelltech.edu/.

Mitchell Community College
Statesville, North Carolina

Freshman Application Contact Mr. Doug Rhoney, Counselor, Mitchell Community College, 500 West Broad, Statesville, NC 28677-5293. *Phone:* 704-878-3280. *Web site:* http://www.mitchellcc.edu/.

Montgomery Community College
Troy, North Carolina

- **State-supported** 2-year, founded 1967, part of North Carolina Community College System
- **Rural** 159-acre campus
- **Coed,** 756 undergraduate students, 50% full-time, 64% women, 36% men

Undergraduates 375 full-time, 381 part-time. Students come from 4 states and territories; 1% are from out of state; 22% Black or African American, non-Hispanic/Latino; 3% Hispanic/Latino; 2% Asian, non-Hispanic/Latino; 0.8% American Indian or Alaska Native, non-Hispanic/Latino; 0.3% Two or more races, non-Hispanic/Latino; 0.1% international.
Freshmen *Admission:* 90 enrolled.
Faculty *Total:* 76, 47% full-time.
Majors Accounting; administrative assistant and secretarial science; business administration and management; ceramic arts and ceramics; child-care and support services management; criminal justice/police science; forest technology; liberal arts and sciences/liberal studies; management information systems; medical/clinical assistant.

Academics *Calendar:* semesters. *Degree:* certificates, diplomas, and associate. *Special study options:* academic remediation for entering students, advanced placement credit, cooperative education, distance learning, English as a second language, part-time degree program, services for LD students, summer session for credit.
Library 23,000 titles, 100 serial subscriptions, 1,430 audiovisual materials, an OPAC.
Student Life *Housing:* college housing not available. *Activities and Organizations:* Student Government Association, Nursing Club, Gunsmithing Society, Medical Assisting Club, Forestry Club. *Student services:* personal/psychological counseling.
Costs (2011–12) *Tuition:* state resident $2128 full-time, $67 per credit hour part-time; nonresident $8272 full-time, $259 per credit hour part-time. Full-time tuition and fees vary according to course load. Part-time tuition and fees vary according to course load. *Required fees:* $75 full-time, $38 per term part-time. *Payment plan:* deferred payment. *Waivers:* senior citizens.
Financial Aid Of all full-time matriculated undergraduates who enrolled in 2010, 24 Federal Work-Study jobs (averaging $500).
Applying *Options:* electronic application, early admission, deferred entrance. *Required:* high school transcript. *Application deadlines:* rolling (freshmen), rolling (transfers). *Notification:* continuous (freshmen), continuous (transfers).
Freshman Application Contact Montgomery Community College, 1011 Page Street, Troy, NC 27371. *Phone:* 910-576-6222 Ext. 240. *Web site:* http://www.montgomery.edu/.

Nash Community College
Rocky Mount, North Carolina

Freshman Application Contact Ms. Dorothy Gardner, Admissions Officer, Nash Community College, PO Box 7488, Rocky Mount, NC 27804. *Phone:* 252-451-8300. *E-mail:* dgardner@nashcc.edu. *Web site:* http://www.nash.cc.nc.us/.

Pamlico Community College
Grantsboro, North Carolina

Director of Admissions Mr. Floyd H. Hardison, Admissions Counselor, Pamlico Community College, PO Box 185, Grantsboro, NC 28529-0185. *Phone:* 252-249-1851 Ext. 28. *Web site:* http://www.pamlico.cc.nc.us/.

Piedmont Community College
Roxboro, North Carolina

Freshman Application Contact Piedmont Community College, PO Box 1197, Roxboro, NC 27573-1197. *Phone:* 336-599-1181 Ext. 219. *Web site:* http://www.piedmont.cc.nc.us/.

Pitt Community College
Greenville, North Carolina

Freshman Application Contact Ms. Bev Webster, Interim Coordinator of Counseling, Pitt Community College, PO Drawer 7007, Greenville, NC 27835-7007. *Phone:* 252-493-7217. *Fax:* 252-321-4612. *E-mail:* pittadm@pcc.pitt.cc.nc.us. *Web site:* http://www.pittcc.edu/.

Randolph Community College
Asheboro, North Carolina

- **State-supported** 2-year, founded 1962, part of North Carolina Community College System
- **Small-town** 40-acre campus with easy access to Greensboro, Winston-Salem, High Point
- **Endowment** $8.9 million
- **Coed,** 2,967 undergraduate students, 51% full-time, 65% women, 35% men

Undergraduates 1,528 full-time, 1,439 part-time. Students come from 4 states and territories; 12 other countries; 1% are from out of state; 9% Black or African American, non-Hispanic/Latino; 7% Hispanic/Latino; 1% Asian, non-Hispanic/Latino; 0.1% Native Hawaiian or other Pacific Islander, non-Hispanic/Latino; 0.7% American Indian or Alaska Native, non-Hispanic/Latino; 10% Race/ethnicity unknown; 18% transferred in. *Retention:* 57% of full-time freshmen returned.
Freshmen *Admission:* 2,517 applied, 2,517 admitted, 646 enrolled. *Average high school GPA:* 2.8.
Faculty *Total:* 356, 26% full-time. *Student/faculty ratio:* 11:1.
Majors Accounting; autobody/collision and repair technology; automobile/automotive mechanics technology; biology/biotechnology laboratory technician; business administration and management; commercial and advertising

art; commercial photography; computer systems networking and telecommunications; cosmetology; criminal justice/safety; early childhood education; electrician; electromechanical and instrumentation and maintenance technologies related; entrepreneurship; funeral service and mortuary science; industrial electronics technology; information technology; interior design; liberal arts and sciences and humanities related; liberal arts and sciences/liberal studies; logistics, materials, and supply chain management; machine shop technology; medical/clinical assistant; medical office management; office management; photographic and film/video technology; photojournalism; physical therapy technology; pre-engineering; prenursing studies; radiologic technology/science; registered nursing/registered nurse.

Academics *Calendar:* semesters. *Degree:* certificates, diplomas, and associate. *Special study options:* academic remediation for entering students, adult/continuing education programs, advanced placement credit, cooperative education, distance learning, double majors, English as a second language, independent study, internships, off-campus study, part-time degree program, services for LD students, summer session for credit.

Library R. Alton Cox Learning Resources Center with 33,200 titles, 5,000 audiovisual materials, an OPAC, a Web page.

Student Life *Housing:* college housing not available. *Activities and Organizations:* Student Government Association, Phi Theta Kappa, Student Nurse Association, Phi Beta Lambda, Campus Crusaders. *Campus security:* 24-hour emergency response devices, security officer during open hours. *Student services:* personal/psychological counseling.

Athletics *Intramural sports:* basketball M/W, cheerleading M/W, football M/W, golf M/W, volleyball M/W.

Costs (2012–13) *Tuition:* state resident $2128 full-time, $67 per credit part-time; nonresident $8272 full-time, $259 per credit part-time. *Required fees:* $88 full-time, $3 per credit part-time. *Payment plan:* installment. *Waivers:* senior citizens.

Applying *Options:* electronic application, deferred entrance. *Application deadlines:* rolling (freshmen), rolling (transfers). *Notification:* continuous (freshmen), continuous (transfers).

Freshman Application Contact Ms. Brandi F. Hagerman, Director of Enrollment Management/Registrar, Randolph Community College, 629 Industrial Park Avenue, Asheboro, NC 27205. *Phone:* 336-633-0213. *Fax:* 336-629-9547. *E-mail:* bhagerman@randolph.edu. *Web site:* http://www.randolph.edu/.

Richmond Community College
Hamlet, North Carolina

Freshman Application Contact Daphne Stancil, Director of Admissions/Registrar, Richmond Community College, PO Box 1189, Hamlet, NC 28345-1189. *Phone:* 910-410-1732. *Fax:* 910-582-7102. *E-mail:* daphnes@richmondcc.edu. *Web site:* http://www.richmondcc.edu/.

Roanoke-Chowan Community College
Ahoskie, North Carolina

Director of Admissions Miss Sandra Copeland, Director, Counseling Services, Roanoke-Chowan Community College, 109 Community College Road, Ahoskie, NC 27910. *Phone:* 252-862-1225. *Web site:* http://www.roanokechowan.edu/.

Robeson Community College
Lumberton, North Carolina

Freshman Application Contact Ms. Judy Revels, Director of Admissions, Robeson Community College, PO Box 1420, 5160 Fayetteville Road, Lumberton, NC 28359-1420. *Phone:* 910-618-5680 Ext. 251. *Web site:* http://www.robeson.cc.nc.us/.

Rockingham Community College
Wentworth, North Carolina

- **State-supported** 2-year, founded 1964, part of North Carolina Community College System
- **Rural** 257-acre campus
- **Coed,** 2,631 undergraduate students, 46% full-time, 63% women, 37% men

Undergraduates 1,216 full-time, 1,415 part-time. Students come from 10 states and territories; 8 other countries; 1% are from out of state; 25% Black or African American, non-Hispanic/Latino; 2% Hispanic/Latino; 0.5% Asian, non-Hispanic/Latino; 0.1% Native Hawaiian or other Pacific Islander, non-Hispanic/Latino; 0.6% American Indian or Alaska Native, non-Hispanic/

Latino; 0.7% Two or more races, non-Hispanic/Latino; 1% Race/ethnicity unknown; 0.1% international; 18% transferred in.

Freshmen *Admission:* 485 enrolled.

Faculty *Total:* 111, 59% full-time, 9% with terminal degrees. *Student/faculty ratio:* 18:1.

Majors Accounting; banking and financial support services; biology/biotechnology laboratory technician; business administration and management; corrections and criminal justice related; criminal justice/police science; early childhood education; electrical, electronic and communications engineering technology; electrician; general studies; health/health-care administration; information technology; liberal arts and sciences/liberal studies; logistics, materials, and supply chain management; machine shop technology; medical office management; office management; registered nursing/registered nurse; respiratory care therapy.

Academics *Calendar:* semesters. *Degree:* certificates, diplomas, and associate. *Special study options:* academic remediation for entering students, adult/continuing education programs, advanced placement credit, cooperative education, part-time degree program, student-designed majors, summer session for credit.

Library Gerald B. James Library with 2,124 titles, 433 audiovisual materials, an OPAC, a Web page.

Student Life *Housing:* college housing not available. *Activities and Organizations:* student-run newspaper. *Campus security:* 24-hour emergency response devices and patrols. *Student services:* personal/psychological counseling.

Athletics Member NJCAA. *Intercollegiate sports:* baseball M, basketball M, golf M, volleyball W. *Intramural sports:* basketball W, cheerleading W, golf W, table tennis M/W, tennis M/W, volleyball M/W.

Costs (2012–13) *Tuition:* state resident $2128 full-time, $67 per credit part-time; nonresident $8272 full-time, $259 per credit part-time. Full-time tuition and fees vary according to course load. Part-time tuition and fees vary according to course load. *Required fees:* $116 full-time. *Payment plan:* installment.

Financial Aid Of all full-time matriculated undergraduates who enrolled in 2010, 37 Federal Work-Study jobs (averaging $2300).

Applying *Options:* electronic application, early admission, deferred entrance. *Application deadlines:* rolling (freshmen), rolling (transfers). *Notification:* continuous (freshmen), continuous (transfers).

Freshman Application Contact Mr. Derrick Satterfield, Director of Enrollment Services, Rockingham Community College, PO Box 38, Wentworth, NC 27375-0038. *Phone:* 336-342-4261 Ext. 2114. *Fax:* 336-342-1809. *E-mail:* admissions@rockinghamcc.edu. *Web site:* http://www.rockinghamcc.edu/.

Rowan-Cabarrus Community College
Salisbury, North Carolina

Freshman Application Contact Mrs. Gail Cummins, Director of Admissions and Recruitment, Rowan-Cabarrus Community College, PO Box 1595, Salisbury, NC 28145-1595. *Phone:* 704-637-0760. *Fax:* 704-633-6804. *Web site:* http://www.rccc.edu/.

Sampson Community College
Clinton, North Carolina

Director of Admissions Mr. William R. Jordan, Director of Admissions, Sampson Community College, PO Box 318, 1801 Sunset Avenue, Highway 24 West, Clinton, NC 28329-0318. *Phone:* 910-592-8084 Ext. 2022. *Web site:* http://www.sampsoncc.edu/.

Sandhills Community College
Pinehurst, North Carolina

- **State-supported** 2-year, founded 1963, part of North Carolina Community College System
- **Small-town** 240-acre campus
- **Endowment** $10.7 million
- **Coed**

Faculty *Student/faculty ratio:* 13:1.

Academics *Calendar:* semesters. *Degree:* certificates, diplomas, and associate. *Special study options:* academic remediation for entering students, advanced placement credit, cooperative education, distance learning, double majors, English as a second language, independent study, internships, off-campus study, part-time degree program, services for LD students, summer session for credit.

Student Life *Campus security:* 24-hour emergency response devices, security on duty until 12 am.

Athletics Member NJCAA.

Applying *Options:* electronic application, deferred entrance. *Required:* high school transcript.

Freshman Application Contact Mr. Isai Robledo, Recruiter, Sandhills Community College, 3395 Airport Road, Pinehurst, NC 28374-8299. *Phone:* 910-246-5365. *Toll-free phone:* 800-338-3944. *Fax:* 910-695-3981. *E-mail:* robledoi@sandhills.edu. *Web site:* http://www.sandhills.edu/.

South College–Asheville
Asheville, North Carolina

Freshman Application Contact Director of Admissions, South College–Asheville, 1567 Patton Avenue, Asheville, NC 28806. *Phone:* 828-277-5521. *Fax:* 828-277-6151. *Web site:* http://www.southcollegenc.edu/.

Southeastern Community College
Whiteville, North Carolina

Freshman Application Contact Ms. Sylvia Tart, Registrar, Southeastern Community College, PO Box 151, Whiteville, NC 28472. *Phone:* 910-642-7141 Ext. 249. *Fax:* 910-642-5658. *E-mail:* start@sccnc.edu. *Web site:* http://www.sccnc.edu/.

South Piedmont Community College
Polkton, North Carolina

Freshman Application Contact Ms. Jeania Martin, Admissions Coordinator, South Piedmont Community College, PO Box 126, Polkton, NC 28135-0126. *Phone:* 704-272-7635. *Toll-free phone:* 800-766-0319. *E-mail:* abaucom@vnet.net. *Web site:* http://www.spcc.edu/.

Southwestern Community College
Sylva, North Carolina

Freshman Application Contact Mr. Delos Monteith, Institutional Research and Planning Officer, Southwestern Community College, 447 College Drive, Sylva, NC 28779. *Phone:* 828-586-4091 Ext. 236. *Toll-free phone:* 800-447-4091 (in-state); 800-447-7091 (out-of-state). *Fax:* 828-586-3129. *E-mail:* delos@southwesterncc.edu. *Web site:* http://www.southwesterncc.edu/.

Stanly Community College
Albemarle, North Carolina

Freshman Application Contact Mrs. Denise B. Ross, Associate Dean, Admissions, Stanly Community College, 141 College Drive, Albemarle, NC 28001. *Phone:* 704-982-0121 Ext. 264. *Fax:* 704-982-0255. *E-mail:* dross7926@stanly.edu. *Web site:* http://www.stanly.edu/.

Surry Community College
Dobson, North Carolina

Freshman Application Contact Renita Hazelwood, Director of Admissions, Surry Community College, 630 South Main Street, Dobson, NC 27017. *Phone:* 336-386-3392. *Fax:* 336-386-3690. *E-mail:* hazelwoodr@surry.edu. *Web site:* http://www.surry.edu/.

Tri-County Community College
Murphy, North Carolina

Freshman Application Contact Dr. Jason Chambers, Director of Student Services and Admissions, Tri-County Community College, 21 Campus Circle, Murphy, NC 28906-7919. *Phone:* 828-837-6810. *Fax:* 828-837-3266. *E-mail:* jchambers@tricountycc.edu. *Web site:* http://www.tricountycc.edu/.

Vance-Granville Community College
Henderson, North Carolina

Freshman Application Contact Ms. Kathy Kutl, Admissions Officer, Vance-Granville Community College, PO Box 917, State Road 1126, Henderson, NC 27536. *Phone:* 252-492-2061 Ext. 3265. *Fax:* 252-430-0460. *Web site:* http://www.vgcc.edu/.

Wake Technical Community College
Raleigh, North Carolina

Director of Admissions Ms. Susan Bloomfield, Director of Admissions, Wake Technical Community College, 9101 Fayetteville Road, Raleigh, NC 27603-5696. *Phone:* 919-866-5452. *E-mail:* srbloomfield@waketech.edu. *Web site:* http://www.waketech.edu/.

Wayne Community College
Goldsboro, North Carolina

Freshman Application Contact Ms. Jennifer Parker, Associate/Director of Admissions and Records, Wayne Community College, PO Box 8002, Goldsboro, NC 27533. *Phone:* 919-735-5151 Ext. 6721. *Fax:* 919-736-9425. *E-mail:* jbparker@waynecc.edu. *Web site:* http://www.waynecc.edu/.

Western Piedmont Community College
Morganton, North Carolina

Freshman Application Contact Susan Williams, Director of Admissions, Western Piedmont Community College, 1001 Burkemont Avenue, Morganton, NC 28655-4511. *Phone:* 828-438-6051. *Fax:* 828-438-6065. *E-mail:* swilliams@wpcc.edu. *Web site:* http://www.wpcc.edu/.

Wilkes Community College
Wilkesboro, North Carolina

Freshman Application Contact Mr. Mac Warren, Director of Admissions, Wilkes Community College, PO Box 120, Wilkesboro, NC 28697. *Phone:* 336-838-6141. *Fax:* 336-838-6547. *E-mail:* mac.warren@wilkescc.edu. *Web site:* http://www.wilkescc.edu/.

Wilson Community College
Wilson, North Carolina

- **State-supported** 2-year, founded 1958, part of North Carolina Community College System
- **Small-town** 35-acre campus
- **Coed,** 1,899 undergraduate students, 49% full-time, 69% women, 31% men

Undergraduates 923 full-time, 976 part-time. Students come from 2 states and territories; 45% Black or African American, non-Hispanic/Latino; 5% Hispanic/Latino; 0.8% Asian, non-Hispanic/Latino; 0.1% Native Hawaiian or other Pacific Islander, non-Hispanic/Latino; 0.6% American Indian or Alaska Native, non-Hispanic/Latino; 0.1% Two or more races, non-Hispanic/Latino; 2% Race/ethnicity unknown; 0.1% international; 17% transferred in.

Freshmen *Admission:* 427 applied, 423 admitted, 262 enrolled.

Faculty *Total:* 227, 22% full-time, 1% with terminal degrees. *Student/faculty ratio:* 17:1.

Majors Accounting; biology/biotechnology laboratory technician; business administration and management; computer and information systems security; computer systems networking and telecommunications; criminal justice/safety; early childhood education; electrician; elementary education; fire prevention and safety technology; general studies; heating, air conditioning, ventilation and refrigeration maintenance technology; information technology; legal assistant/paralegal; liberal arts and sciences and humanities related; liberal arts and sciences/liberal studies; mechanical engineering/mechanical technology; medical office management; office management; registered nursing/registered nurse; sign language interpretation and translation; surgical technology.

Academics *Calendar:* semesters. *Degree:* certificates, diplomas, and associate. *Special study options:* academic remediation for entering students, advanced placement credit, cooperative education, distance learning, double majors, English as a second language, independent study, internships, part-time degree program, services for LD students, summer session for credit.

Library 38,466 titles, an OPAC.

Student Life *Housing:* college housing not available. *Campus security:* 11-hour patrols by trained security personnel.

Costs (2011–12) *Tuition:* state resident $2128 full-time, $67 per credit hour part-time; nonresident $8272 full-time, $259 per credit hour part-time. *Required fees:* $105 full-time, $1 per credit hour part-time, $31 per term part-time.

Financial Aid Of all full-time matriculated undergraduates who enrolled in 2010, 65 Federal Work-Study jobs (averaging $1500).

Applying *Options:* electronic application, deferred entrance. *Required:* high school transcript. *Application deadlines:* rolling (freshmen), rolling (transfers). *Notification:* continuous (freshmen), continuous (transfers).

Freshman Application Contact Mrs. Maegan Williams, Admissions Technician, Wilson Community College, Wilson, NC 27893-0305. *Phone:* 252-246-1275. *Fax:* 252-243-7148. *E-mail:* mwilliams@wilsoncc.edu. *Web site:* http://www.wilsoncc.edu/.

NORTH DAKOTA

Bismarck State College
Bismarck, North Dakota

Freshman Application Contact Greg Sturm, Dean of Admissions and Enrollment Services, Bismarck State College, PO Box 5587, Bismarck, ND 58506-5587. *Phone:* 701-224-5426. *Toll-free phone:* 800-445-5073. *Fax:* 701-224-5643. *E-mail:* gregory.sturm@bsc.nodak.edu. *Web site:* http://www.bismarckstate.edu/.

Cankdeska Cikana Community College
Fort Totten, North Dakota

Director of Admissions Mr. Ermen Brown Jr., Registrar, Cankdeska Cikana Community College, PO Box 269, Fort Totten, ND 58335-0269. *Phone:* 701-766-1342. *Toll-free phone:* 888-783-1463. *Web site:* http://www.littlehoop.edu/.

Dakota College at Bottineau
Bottineau, North Dakota

- **State-supported** 2-year, founded 1906, part of North Dakota University System
- **Rural** 35-acre campus
- **Coed,** 812 undergraduate students, 51% full-time, 48% women, 52% men

Undergraduates 414 full-time, 398 part-time. Students come from 37 states and territories; 5 other countries; 19% are from out of state; 5% Black or African American, non-Hispanic/Latino; 3% Hispanic/Latino; 0.4% Asian, non-Hispanic/Latino; 3% American Indian or Alaska Native, non-Hispanic/Latino; 0.9% Two or more races, non-Hispanic/Latino; 27% Race/ethnicity unknown; 4% international.

Freshmen *Admission:* 593 enrolled.

Faculty *Total:* 84, 33% full-time, 12% with terminal degrees. *Student/faculty ratio:* 18:1.

Majors Accounting; accounting related; accounting technology and bookkeeping; administrative assistant and secretarial science; adult development and aging; advertising; agriculture; applied horticulture/horticultural business services related; applied horticulture/horticulture operations; biology/biological sciences; business administration and management; business automation/technology/data entry; chemistry; child-care and support services management; child-care provision; computer and information sciences; computer and information sciences and support services related; computer software and media applications related; computer technology/computer systems technology; crop production; education; entrepreneurial and small business related; environmental engineering technology; executive assistant/executive secretary; fishing and fisheries sciences and management; floriculture/floristry management; general studies; greenhouse management; health and physical education/fitness; health services/allied health/health sciences; history; horticultural science; hospitality and recreation marketing; humanities; information science/studies; information technology; landscaping and groundskeeping; liberal arts and sciences and humanities related; liberal arts and sciences/liberal studies; licensed practical/vocational nurse training; marketing/marketing management; marketing related; mathematics; medical administrative assistant and medical secretary; medical/clinical assistant; medical insurance coding; medical office assistant; medical transcription; natural resources/conservation; network and system administration; office management; office occupations and clerical services; ornamental horticulture; parks, recreation and leisure; parks, recreation and leisure facilities management; parks, recreation, leisure, and fitness studies related; physical sciences; physical sciences related; premedical studies; prenursing studies; pre-veterinary studies; psychology; receptionist; registered nursing/registered nurse; science technologies related; small business administration; social sciences; teacher assistant/aide; urban forestry; wildlife, fish and wildlands science and management; zoology/animal biology.

Academics *Calendar:* semesters. *Degree:* certificates, diplomas, and associate. *Special study options:* academic remediation for entering students, advanced placement credit, cooperative education, distance learning, double majors, off-campus study, part-time degree program, services for LD students, summer session for credit.

Library Dakota College at Bottineau Library plus 1 other with 41,411 titles, 5,544 serial subscriptions, 1,339 audiovisual materials, an OPAC, a Web page.

Student Life *Housing:* on-campus residence required through sophomore year. *Options:* men-only, women-only. Campus housing is university owned. Freshman campus housing is guaranteed. *Activities and Organizations:* drama/theater group, student-run newspaper, Student Senate, Wildlife Club/Horticulture Club, Snowboarding Club, Phi Theta Kappa, Delta Epsilon Chi. *Campus security:* controlled dormitory access, security cameras. *Student services:* health clinic, personal/psychological counseling.

Athletics Member NJCAA. *Intercollegiate sports:* baseball M(s), basketball M(s)/W(s), football M(s), ice hockey M(s), softball W(s), volleyball W(s). *Intramural sports:* archery M/W, badminton M/W, basketball M/W, skiing (downhill) M/W, volleyball M/W.

Standardized Tests *Required:* ACT (for admission).

Financial Aid Of all full-time matriculated undergraduates who enrolled in 2010, 50 Federal Work-Study jobs (averaging $1100).

Applying *Options:* electronic application, early admission, deferred entrance. *Application fee:* $35. *Required:* high school transcript, immunization records. *Application deadlines:* rolling (freshmen), rolling (out-of-state freshmen), rolling (transfers).

Freshman Application Contact Mrs. Luann Soland, Admissions Counselor, Dakota College at Bottineau, 105 Simrall Boulevard, Bottineau, ND 58318. *Phone:* 701-228-5487. *Toll-free phone:* 800-542-6866. *Fax:* 701-228-5499. *E-mail:* jancy.brisson@dakotacollege.edu. *Web site:* http://www.dakotacollege.edu/.

Fort Berthold Community College
New Town, North Dakota

Freshman Application Contact Office of Admissions, Fort Berthold Community College, PO Box 490, 220 8th Avenue North, New Town, ND 58763-0490. *Phone:* 701-627-4738 Ext. 295. *Web site:* http://www.fortberthholdcc.edu/.

Lake Region State College
Devils Lake, North Dakota

- **State-supported** 2-year, founded 1941, part of North Dakota University System
- **Small-town** 120-acre campus
- **Coed,** 2,056 undergraduate students, 25% full-time, 56% women, 44% men

Undergraduates 518 full-time, 1,538 part-time. Students come from 35 states and territories; 8 other countries; 17% are from out of state; 4% Black or African American, non-Hispanic/Latino; 3% Hispanic/Latino; 0.4% Asian, non-Hispanic/Latino; 0.2% Native Hawaiian or other Pacific Islander, non-Hispanic/Latino; 6% American Indian or Alaska Native, non-Hispanic/Latino; 3% Two or more races, non-Hispanic/Latino; 0.2% Race/ethnicity unknown; 4% international; 9% transferred in; 20% live on campus. *Retention:* 45% of full-time freshmen returned.

Freshmen *Admission:* 293 applied, 266 admitted, 211 enrolled.

Faculty *Total:* 173, 20% full-time, 10% with terminal degrees. *Student/faculty ratio:* 12:1.

Majors Accounting; accounting technology and bookkeeping; administrative assistant and secretarial science; agricultural business and management; automobile/automotive mechanics technology; avionics maintenance technology; business administration and management; child-care and support services management; child-care provision; computer and information sciences; computer programming (specific applications); computer programming (vendor/product certification); computer science; computer systems networking and telecommunications; criminal justice/police science; electrical and electronic engineering technologies related; electrical and electronics engineering; electrical/electronics equipment installation and repair; executive assistant/executive secretary; fashion merchandising; information technology; legal administrative assistant/secretary; legal assistant/paralegal; liberal arts and sciences/liberal studies; licensed practical/vocational nurse training; management information systems; marketing research; medical administrative assistant and medical secretary; multi/interdisciplinary studies related; nursing assistant/aide and patient care assistant/aide; office management; office occupations and clerical services; pathologist assistant; physical fitness technician; sales, distribution, and marketing operations; sign language interpretation and translation; small business administration.

Academics *Calendar:* semesters. *Degree:* certificates, diplomas, and associate. *Special study options:* academic remediation for entering students, adult/continuing education programs, cooperative education, distance learning, double majors, English as a second language, freshman honors college, honors programs, internships, part-time degree program, summer session for credit.

Library Paul Hoghaug Library with 60,000 titles, 200 serial subscriptions, 2,000 audiovisual materials, an OPAC.

Student Life *Housing Options:* men-only, women-only. Campus housing is university owned. *Activities and Organizations:* drama/theater group, DECA, drama, SOTA (Students Other than Average), Student Senate, Computer Club. *Campus security:* 24-hour emergency response devices, controlled dormitory access. *Student services:* personal/psychological counseling.

Athletics Member NJCAA. *Intercollegiate sports:* basketball M(s)/W(s). *Intramural sports:* basketball M/W, football M/W, golf M/W, ice hockey M/W, softball M/W, table tennis M/W, volleyball M/W.

Standardized Tests *Required:* SAT or ACT (for admission), COMPASS (for admission).

Costs (2012–13) *Tuition:* state resident $3065 full-time, $128 per credit hour part-time; nonresident $3065 full-time, $128 per credit hour part-time. Full-time tuition and fees vary according to course load, location, and program. Part-time tuition and fees vary according to location and program. *Required fees:* $843 full-time, $28 per credit hour part-time. *Room and board:* $5046; room only: $1916. Room and board charges vary according to board plan and housing facility. *Payment plan:* installment. *Waivers:* minority students.

Financial Aid Of all full-time matriculated undergraduates who enrolled in 2011, 416 applied for aid, 340 were judged to have need, 335 had their need fully met. 33 Federal Work-Study jobs (averaging $1500). In 2011, 165 non-need-based awards were made. *Average percent of need met:* 58%. *Average financial aid package:* $8194. *Average need-based loan:* $3509. *Average need-based gift aid:* $5223. *Average non-need-based aid:* $823. *Average indebtedness upon graduation:* $15,063.

Applying *Options:* electronic application. *Application fee:* $35. *Required:* high school transcript, immunizations, transcripts. *Required for some:* interview. *Application deadlines:* rolling (freshmen), rolling (transfers). *Notification:* continuous (freshmen), continuous (transfers).

Freshman Application Contact Ms. Samantha Cordrey, Administrative Assistant, Admissions Office, Lake Region State College, 1801 College Drive North, Devils Lake, ND 58301. *Phone:* 701-662-1514. *Toll-free phone:* 800-443-1313. *Fax:* 701-662-1581. *E-mail:* kelsey.walters@lrsc.edu. *Web site:* http://www.lrsc.edu/.

North Dakota State College of Science

Wahpeton, North Dakota

- **State-supported** 2-year, founded 1903, part of North Dakota University System
- **Rural** 125-acre campus
- **Endowment** $9.3 million
- **Coed,** 3,127 undergraduate students, 57% full-time, 43% women, 57% men

Undergraduates 1,791 full-time, 1,336 part-time. Students come from 38 states and territories; 11 other countries; 41% are from out of state; 5% Black or African American, non-Hispanic/Latino; 1% Hispanic/Latino; 0.9% Asian, non-Hispanic/Latino; 1% American Indian or Alaska Native, non-Hispanic/Latino; 1% Two or more races, non-Hispanic/Latino; 0.9% Race/ethnicity unknown; 1% international; 6% transferred in; 52% live on campus.

Freshmen *Admission:* 1,125 applied, 849 admitted, 758 enrolled.

Faculty *Total:* 282, 41% full-time, 5% with terminal degrees. *Student/faculty ratio:* 13:1.

Majors Administrative assistant and secretarial science; agricultural business and management; agricultural mechanics and equipment technology; architectural engineering technology; autobody/collision and repair technology; automobile/automotive mechanics technology; biology/biotechnology laboratory technician; building construction technology; business administration and management; civil engineering technology; computer and information sciences; computer and information systems security; computer programming; computer support specialist; computer systems networking and telecommunications; construction engineering technology; culinary arts; data entry/microcomputer applications; dental assisting; dental hygiene; diesel mechanics technology; e-commerce; electrical and electronic engineering technologies related; emergency medical technology (EMT paramedic); energy management and systems technology; engineering technologies and engineering related; health information/medical records technology; heating, air conditioning, ventilation and refrigeration maintenance technology; heating, ventilation, air conditioning and refrigeration engineering technology; liberal arts and sciences/liberal studies; licensed practical/vocational nurse training; machine tool technology; manufacturing engineering technology; medical insurance coding; medical transcription; multi/interdisciplinary studies related; nanotechnology; occupational therapist assistant; pharmacy technician; plumbing technology; psychiatric/mental health services technology; registered nursing/registered nurse; science technologies related; small engine mechanics and repair technology; vehicle maintenance and repair technologies related; web page, digital/multimedia and information resources design; welding technology.

Academics *Calendar:* semesters. *Degree:* certificates, diplomas, and associate. *Special study options:* academic remediation for entering students, adult/continuing education programs, cooperative education, distance learning, dou-

ble majors, English as a second language, independent study, internships, part-time degree program, services for LD students, student-designed majors, summer session for credit.

Library Mildred Johnson Library with 66,770 titles, 146 serial subscriptions, 4,342 audiovisual materials, an OPAC, a Web page.

Student Life *Housing:* on-campus residence required for freshman year. *Options:* coed, men-only, women-only. Campus housing is university owned. Freshman campus housing is guaranteed. *Activities and Organizations:* drama/theater group, choral group, marching band, music, Drama Club, Inter-Varsity Christian Fellowship, Cultural Diversity, Habitat for Humanity. *Campus security:* 24-hour emergency response devices and patrols, student patrols, late-night transport/escort service, controlled dormitory access. *Student services:* health clinic, personal/psychological counseling, legal services.

Athletics Member NJCAA. *Intercollegiate sports:* basketball M(s)/W(s), football M(s), softball W, volleyball W(s). *Intramural sports:* baseball M, basketball M/W, cheerleading W, field hockey M/W, football M, racquetball M/W, softball M/W, volleyball M/W.

Standardized Tests *Required:* ACT (for admission).

Costs (2011–12) *Tuition:* state resident $4181 full-time, $137 per credit hour part-time; nonresident $10,179 full-time. Full-time tuition and fees vary according to program. Part-time tuition and fees vary according to program. *Room and board:* $5926. Room and board charges vary according to board plan. *Payment plan:* installment. *Waivers:* minority students, children of alumni, and employees or children of employees.

Financial Aid Of all full-time matriculated undergraduates who enrolled in 2009, 1,245 applied for aid, 925 were judged to have need, 904 had their need fully met. *Average percent of need met:* 62%. *Average financial aid package:* $7164. *Average need-based loan:* $3791. *Average need-based gift aid:* $3121.

Applying *Options:* electronic application, early admission. *Application fee:* $35. *Required:* high school transcript. *Application deadlines:* rolling (freshmen), rolling (out-of-state freshmen), rolling (transfers). *Notification:* continuous (freshmen), continuous (out-of-state freshmen), continuous (transfers).

Freshman Application Contact Ms. Karen Reilly, Director of Enrollment Services, North Dakota State College of Science, 800 North 6th Street, Wahpeton, ND 58076. *Phone:* 701-671-2189. *Toll-free phone:* 800-342-4325. *Fax:* 701-671-2332. *E-mail:* Karen.Reilly@ndscs.edu. *Web site:* http://www.ndscs.nodak.edu/.

Rasmussen College Bismarck

Bismarck, North Dakota

- **Proprietary** primarily 2-year, part of Rasmussen College System
- **Suburban** campus
- **Coed,** 289 undergraduate students

Faculty *Student/faculty ratio:* 22:1.

Majors Accounting; business administration and management; clinical/medical laboratory technology; computer and information systems security; computer science; computer software engineering; corrections and criminal justice related; early childhood education; graphic communications related; health/health-care administration; health information/medical records administration; health information/medical records technology; human resources management; human services; legal assistant/paralegal; management information systems and services related; marketing/marketing management; medical administrative assistant and medical secretary; medical/clinical assistant; web page, digital/multimedia and information resources design.

Academics *Degrees:* certificates, diplomas, associate, and bachelor's. *Special study options:* academic remediation for entering students, accelerated degree program, adult/continuing education programs, distance learning, double majors, internships, part-time degree program, summer session for credit.

Library Rasmussen College Library - Bismarck with 2,053 titles, 25 serial subscriptions, 235 audiovisual materials, an OPAC, a Web page.

Student Life *Housing:* college housing not available.

Standardized Tests *Required:* Internal Exam (for admission).

Costs (2012–13) *Tuition:* $12,600 full-time. Full-time tuition and fees vary according to course level, course load, degree level, location, and program. Part-time tuition and fees vary according to course level, course load, degree level, location, and program. *Required fees:* $40 full-time. *Payment plans:* installment, deferred payment. *Waivers:* employees or children of employees.

Applying *Options:* electronic application, early admission, deferred entrance. *Application fee:* $40. *Required:* high school transcript, minimum 2.0 GPA, interview. *Application deadlines:* rolling (freshmen), rolling (transfers).

Freshman Application Contact Susan Hammerstrom, Director of Admissions, Rasmussen College Bismarck, 1701 East Century Avenue, Bismarck, ND 58503. *Phone:* 701-530-9600. *Toll-free phone:* 888-549-6755. *E-mail:* susan.hammerstrom@rasmussen.edu. *Web site:* http://www.rasmussen.edu/.

Rasmussen College Fargo

Fargo, North Dakota

- **Proprietary** primarily 2-year, founded 1902, part of Rasmussen College System
- **Suburban** campus
- **Coed,** 418 undergraduate students

Faculty *Student/faculty ratio:* 22:1.

Majors Accounting; business administration and management; computer and information systems security; computer programming; computer science; computer software engineering; corrections and criminal justice related; early childhood education; graphic communications related; health/health-care administration; health information/medical records administration; human resources management; human services; legal assistant/paralegal; management information systems and services related; marketing/marketing management; medical administrative assistant and medical secretary; web page, digital/multimedia and information resources design.

Academics *Calendar:* quarters. *Degrees:* certificates, diplomas, associate, and bachelor's. *Special study options:* academic remediation for entering students, accelerated degree program, adult/continuing education programs, distance learning, double majors, internships, part-time degree program, summer session for credit.

Library Rasmussen College Library - Fargo with 1,717 titles, 19 serial subscriptions, 140 audiovisual materials, an OPAC, a Web page.

Student Life *Housing:* college housing not available.

Standardized Tests *Required:* Internal Exam (for admission).

Costs (2012–13) *Tuition:* $12,600 full-time. Full-time tuition and fees vary according to course level, course load, degree level, location, and program. Part-time tuition and fees vary according to course level, course load, degree level, location, and program. *Required fees:* $40 full-time. *Payment plans:* installment, deferred payment. *Waivers:* employees or children of employees.

Applying *Options:* electronic application, early admission, deferred entrance. *Application fee:* $40. *Required:* high school transcript, minimum 2.0 GPA, interview. *Application deadlines:* rolling (freshmen), rolling (transfers).

Freshman Application Contact Susan Hammerstrom, Director of Admissions, Rasmussen College Fargo, 4012 19th Avenue, SW, Fargo, ND 58103. *Phone:* 701-277-3889. *Toll-free phone:* 888-549-6755. *E-mail:* susan.hammerstrom@rasmussen.edu. *Web site:* http://www.rasmussen.edu/.

Sitting Bull College

Fort Yates, North Dakota

Director of Admissions Ms. Melody Silk, Director of Registration and Admissions, Sitting Bull College, 1341 92nd Street, Fort Yates, ND 58538-9701. *Phone:* 701-854-3864. *Fax:* 701-854-3403. *E-mail:* melodys@sbcl.edu. *Web site:* http://www.sittingbull.edu/.

Turtle Mountain Community College

Belcourt, North Dakota

Director of Admissions Ms. Joni LaFontaine, Admissions/Records Officer, Turtle Mountain Community College, Box 340, Belcourt, ND 58316-0340. *Phone:* 701-477-5605 Ext. 217. *E-mail:* jlafontaine@tm.edu. *Web site:* http://www.turtle-mountain.cc.nd.us/.

United Tribes Technical College

Bismarck, North Dakota

Freshman Application Contact Ms. Vivian Gillette, Director of Admissions, United Tribes Technical College, Bismarck, ND 58504. *Phone:* 701-255-3285 Ext. 1334. *Fax:* 701-530-0640. *E-mail:* vgillette@uttc.edu. *Web site:* http://www.uttc.edu/.

Williston State College

Williston, North Dakota

Freshman Application Contact Ms. Jan Solem, Director for Admission and Records, Williston State College, PO Box 1326, Williston, ND 58802-1326. *Phone:* 701-774-4554. *Toll-free phone:* 888-863-9455. *Fax:* 701-774-4211. *E-mail:* wsc.admission@wsc.nodak.edu. *Web site:* http://www.willistonstate.edu/.

NORTHERN MARIANA ISLANDS

Northern Marianas College

Saipan, Northern Mariana Islands

Freshman Application Contact Ms. Leilani M. Basa-Alam, Admission Specialist, Northern Marianas College, PO Box 501250, Saipan, MP 96950-1250. *Phone:* 670-234-3690 Ext. 1539. *Fax:* 670-235-4967. *E-mail:* leilanib@nmcnet.edu. *Web site:* http://www.nmcnet.edu/.

OHIO

Academy of Court Reporting

Cleveland, Ohio

Freshman Application Contact Director of Admissions, Academy of Court Reporting, 2044 Euclid Avenue, Cleveland, OH 44115. *Phone:* 216-861-3222. *Toll-free phone:* 888-314-7780. *Fax:* 216-861-4517. *Web site:* http://www.acr.edu/.

Akron Institute of Herzing University

Akron, Ohio

Admissions Office Contact Akron Institute of Herzing University, 1600 South Arlington Street, Suite 100, Akron, OH 44306. *Toll-free phone:* 800-311-0512. *Web site:* http://www.akroninstitute.com/.

Antonelli College

Cincinnati, Ohio

Freshman Application Contact Antonelli College, 124 East Seventh Street, Cincinnati, OH 45202. *Phone:* 513-241-4338. *Toll-free phone:* 877-500-4304. *Web site:* http://www.antonellicollege.edu/.

The Art Institute of Cincinnati

Cincinnati, Ohio

Director of Admissions Director of Admissions, The Art Institute of Cincinnati, 1171 East Kemper Road, Cincinnati, OH 45246. *Phone:* 513-751-1206. *Fax:* 513-751-1209. *Web site:* http://www.aic-arts.edu/.

The Art Institute of Ohio–Cincinnati

Cincinnati, Ohio

- **Proprietary** primarily 2-year, part of Education Management Corporation
- **Urban** campus
- **Coed**

Majors Advertising; animation, interactive technology, video graphics and special effects; cinematography and film/video production; culinary arts; fashion merchandising; graphic design; interior design; restaurant, culinary, and catering management; web page, digital/multimedia and information resources design.

Academics *Calendar:* continuous. *Degrees:* diplomas, associate, and bachelor's.

Costs (2011–12) *Tuition:* Tuition cost varies by program. Prospective students should contact the school for current tuition costs. Other charges include a starting kit for all first-quarter students. Kits vary in price, depending on the program of study.

Freshman Application Contact The Art Institute of Ohio–Cincinnati, 8845 Governors Hill Drive, Cincinnati, OH 45249-3317. *Phone:* 513-833-2400. *Toll-free phone:* 866-613-5184. *Web site:* http://www.artinstitutes.edu/cincinnati/.

ATS Institute of Technology

Highland Heights, Ohio

- **Proprietary** 2-year
- **Suburban** campus with easy access to Cleveland
- **Coed**

Academics *Degree:* diplomas and associate. *Special study options:* academic remediation for entering students, accelerated degree program, advanced placement credit, English as a second language, external degree program, part-time degree program. *Unusual degree programs:* nursing.

Student Life *Campus security:* security guard.
Standardized Tests *Required:* PSB (Psychological Service Bureau) exam is required except for those applying for Bridge program (for admission).
Costs (2011–12) *Tuition:* $40,000 full-time. Full-time tuition and fees vary according to course load, degree level, and program. Part-time tuition and fees vary according to course load and program.
Applying *Application fee:* $30. *Required:* high school transcript, minimum 2.5 GPA, interview, complete background check and physical evaluation. *Required for some:* essay or personal statement, 1 letter of recommendation.
Freshman Application Contact Admissions Office, ATS Institute of Technology, 325 Alpha Park, Highland Heights, OH 44143. *Phone:* 440-449-1700 Ext. 103. *E-mail:* info@atsinstitute.edu. *Web site:* http://www.atsinstitute.edu/.

Belmont Technical College

St. Clairsville, Ohio

Director of Admissions Michael Sterling, Director of Recruitment, Belmont Technical College, 120 Fox Shannon Place, St. Clairsville, OH 43950-9735. *Phone:* 740-695-9500 Ext. 1563. *Toll-free phone:* 800-423-1188. *E-mail:* msterling@btc.edu. *Web site:* http://www.btc.edu/.

Bowling Green State University-Firelands College

Huron, Ohio

Freshman Application Contact Debralee Divers, Director of Admissions and Financial Aid, Bowling Green State University-Firelands College, One University Drive, Huron, OH 44839-9791. *Phone:* 419-433-5560. *Toll-free phone:* 800-322-4787. *Fax:* 419-372-0604. *E-mail:* divers@bgsu.edu. *Web site:* http://www.firelands.bgsu.edu/.

Bradford School

Columbus, Ohio

- **Private** 2-year, founded 1911
- **Suburban** campus
- **Coed, primarily women,** 705 undergraduate students
- 50% of applicants were admitted

Freshmen *Admission:* 2,021 applied, 1,005 admitted.
Majors Accounting and business/management; business administration and management; computer programming; culinary arts; graphic design; legal administrative assistant/secretary; legal assistant/paralegal; medical/clinical assistant; system, networking, and LAN/WAN management; tourism and travel services management; veterinary/animal health technology.
Academics *Calendar:* semesters. *Degree:* diplomas and associate. *Special study options:* accelerated degree program, internships.
Freshman Application Contact Admissions Office, Bradford School, 2469 Stelzer Road, Columbus, OH 43219. *Phone:* 614-416-6200. *Toll-free phone:* 800-678-7981. *Web site:* http://www.bradfordschoolcolumbus.edu/.

Brown Mackie College–Akron

Akron, Ohio

- **Proprietary** 2-year, founded 1968, part of Education Management Corporation
- **Suburban** campus
- **Coed**

Academics *Calendar:* quarters. *Degree:* certificates, diplomas, and associate.
Costs (2011–12) *Tuition:* Tuition varies by program. Students should contact Brown Mackie College for tuition information.
Freshman Application Contact Brown Mackie College–Akron, 755 White Pond Drive, Suite 101, Akron, OH 44320. *Phone:* 330-869-3600. *Web site:* http://www.brownmackie.edu/akron/.

See page 338 for the College Close-Up.

Brown Mackie College–Cincinnati

Cincinnati, Ohio

- **Proprietary** 2-year, founded 1927, part of Education Management Corporation
- **Suburban** campus
- **Coed**

Academics *Calendar:* quarters. *Degree:* certificates, diplomas, and associate.

Costs (2011–12) *Tuition:* Tuition varies by program. Students should contact Brown Mackie College for tuition information.
Freshman Application Contact Brown Mackie College–Cincinnati, 1011 Glendale-Milford Road, Cincinnati, OH 45215. *Phone:* 513-771-2424. *Toll-free phone:* 800-888-1445. *Web site:* http://www.brownmackie.edu/cincinnati/

See page 348 for the College Close-Up.

Brown Mackie College–Findlay

Findlay, Ohio

- **Proprietary** 2-year, founded 1929, part of Education Management Corporation
- **Rural** campus
- **Coed**

Academics *Calendar:* continuous. *Degree:* diplomas and associate.
Costs (2011–12) *Tuition:* Tuition varies by program. Students should contact Brown Mackie College for tuition information.
Freshman Application Contact Brown Mackie College–Findlay, 1700 Fostoria Avenue, Suite 100, Findlay, OH 45840. *Phone:* 419-423-2211. *Toll-free phone:* 800-842-3687. *Web site:* http://www.brownmackie.edu/findlay/.

See page 352 for the College Close-Up.

Brown Mackie College–North Canton

Canton, Ohio

- **Proprietary** 2-year, founded 1929, part of Education Management Corporation
- **Suburban** campus
- **Coed**

Academics *Calendar:* quarters. *Degree:* diplomas and associate.
Costs (2011–12) *Tuition:* Tuition varies by program. Students should contact Brown Mackie College for tuition information.
Freshman Application Contact Brown Mackie College–North Canton, 4300 Munson Street NW, Canton, OH 44718-3674. *Phone:* 330-494-1214. *Web site:* http://www.brownmackie.edu/northcanton/.

See page 372 for the College Close-Up.

Bryant & Stratton College - Eastlake Campus

Eastlake, Ohio

Freshman Application Contact Ms. Melanie Pettit, Director of Admissions, Bryant & Stratton College - Eastlake Campus, 35350 Curtis Boulevard, Eastlake, OH 44095. *Phone:* 440-510-1112. *Web site:* http://www.bryantstratton.edu/.

Bryant & Stratton College - Parma Campus

Parma, Ohio

Freshman Application Contact Bryant & Stratton College - Parma Campus, 12955 Snow Road, Parma, OH 44130-1013. *Phone:* 216-265-3151. *Toll-free phone:* 866-948-0571. *Web site:* http://www.bryantstratton.edu/.

Central Ohio Technical College

Newark, Ohio

Freshman Application Contact Jacqueline Stewart, Admissions Representative, Central Ohio Technical College, 1179 University Drive, Newark, OH 43055-1767. *Phone:* 740-366-9222. *Toll-free phone:* 800-9NEWARK. *Fax:* 740-366-5047. *Web site:* http://www.cotc.edu/.

Chatfield College

St. Martin, Ohio

Freshman Application Contact Chatfield College, 20918 State Route 251, St. Martin, OH 45118-9705. *Phone:* 513-875-3344 Ext. 137. *Web site:* http://www.chatfield.edu/.

The Christ College of Nursing and Health Sciences
Cincinnati, Ohio

- **Private** 2-year
- **Urban** campus with easy access to Cincinnati
- **Coed,** 346 undergraduate students, 58% full-time, 92% women, 8% men
- 64% of applicants were admitted

Undergraduates 202 full-time, 144 part-time. 10% Black or African American, non-Hispanic/Latino; 1% Hispanic/Latino; 0.9% Asian, non-Hispanic/Latino; 0.9% Two or more races, non-Hispanic/Latino; 0.9% Race/ethnicity unknown; 22% transferred in.
Freshmen *Admission:* 70 applied, 45 admitted, 35 enrolled.
Faculty *Total:* 41, 61% full-time, 10% with terminal degrees. *Student/faculty ratio:* 7:1.
Majors Registered nursing/registered nurse.
Academics *Degree:* associate. *Special study options:* academic remediation for entering students, advanced placement credit, services for LD students, summer session for credit.
Library James N. Gamble Library.
Student Life *Housing:* college housing not available. *Campus security:* 24-hour emergency response devices and patrols, late-night transport/escort service. *Student services:* personal/psychological counseling.
Standardized Tests *Required:* SAT or ACT (for admission).
Costs (2012–13) *Tuition:* $12,600 full-time. Full-time tuition and fees vary according to course load. Part-time tuition and fees vary according to course load. *Payment plan:* installment.
Applying *Application fee:* $45. *Required:* high school transcript, minimum 2.8 GPA.
Freshman Application Contact Mr. Bradley Jackson, Admissions, The Christ College of Nursing and Health Sciences, 2139 Auburn Avenue, Cincinnati, OH 45219. *Phone:* 513-585-0016. *E-mail:* bradley.jackson@thechristcollege.edu. *Web site:* http://www.thechristcollege.edu/.

Cincinnati State Technical and Community College
Cincinnati, Ohio

- **State-supported** 2-year, founded 1966, part of Ohio Board of Regents
- **Urban** 46-acre campus
- **Coed**

Undergraduates 4,206 full-time, 6,789 part-time. Students come from 8 states and territories; 76 other countries; 10% are from out of state; 27% Black or African American, non-Hispanic/Latino; 1% Hispanic/Latino; 1% Asian, non-Hispanic/Latino; 0.9% American Indian or Alaska Native, non-Hispanic/Latino; 1% Two or more races, non-Hispanic/Latino; 6% Race/ethnicity unknown; 1% international. *Retention:* 51% of full-time freshmen returned.
Faculty *Student/faculty ratio:* 18:1.
Academics *Calendar:* 5 ten-week terms. *Degree:* certificates and associate. *Special study options:* academic remediation for entering students, advanced placement credit, cooperative education, distance learning, double majors, English as a second language, honors programs, independent study, internships, off-campus study, part-time degree program, services for LD students, student-designed majors, summer session for credit.
Student Life *Campus security:* 24-hour emergency response devices and patrols, late-night transport/escort service.
Athletics Member NJCAA.
Costs (2011–12) *One-time required fee:* $10. *Tuition:* state resident $4890 full-time, $89 per credit hour part-time; nonresident $9779 full-time, $178 per credit hour part-time. *Required fees:* $258 full-time, $6 per credit hour part-time, $31 per term part-time.
Financial Aid Of all full-time matriculated undergraduates who enrolled in 2010, 100 Federal Work-Study jobs (averaging $3500).
Applying *Options:* electronic application. *Required:* high school transcript.
Freshman Application Contact Ms. Gabriele Boeckermann, Director of Admission, Cincinnati State Technical and Community College, Cincinnati, OH 45223-2690. *Phone:* 513-569-1550. *Toll-free phone:* 877-569-0115. *Fax:* 513-569-1562. *E-mail:* adm@cincinnatistate.edu. *Web site:* http://www.cincinnatistate.edu/.

Clark State Community College
Springfield, Ohio

Freshman Application Contact Admissions Office, Clark State Community College, PO Box 570, Springfield, OH 45501-0570. *Phone:* 937-328-3858. *Fax:* 937-328-6133. *E-mail:* admissions@clarkstate.edu. *Web site:* http://www.clarkstate.edu/.

Cleveland Institute of Electronics
Cleveland, Ohio

- **Proprietary** 2-year, founded 1934
- **Coed, primarily men,** 1,826 undergraduate students

Undergraduates Students come from 52 states and territories; 70 other countries; 97% are from out of state.
Faculty *Total:* 8, 50% full-time, 13% with terminal degrees.
Majors Computer/information technology services administration related; computer software engineering; electrical, electronic and communications engineering technology.
Academics *Calendar:* continuous. *Degrees:* diplomas and associate (offers only external degree programs conducted through home study). *Special study options:* accelerated degree program, adult/continuing education programs, distance learning, external degree program, independent study, part-time degree program.
Library 5,000 titles, 38 serial subscriptions.
Costs (2011–12) *Tuition:* $1885 per term part-time. No tuition increase for student's term of enrollment. *Payment plans:* tuition prepayment, installment.
Applying *Options:* electronic application, early admission. *Required:* high school transcript. *Application deadlines:* rolling (freshmen), rolling (out-of-state freshmen), rolling (transfers). *Notification:* continuous (freshmen), continuous (out-of-state freshmen), continuous (transfers).
Freshman Application Contact Mr. Scott Katzenmeyer, Registrar, Cleveland Institute of Electronics, Cleveland, OH 44114. *Phone:* 216-781-9400. *Toll-free phone:* 800-243-6446. *Fax:* 216-781-0331. *E-mail:* instruct@cie-wc.edu. *Web site:* http://www.cie-wc.edu/.

Columbus Culinary Institute at Bradford School
Columbus, Ohio

- **Private** 2-year, founded 2006
- **Suburban** campus
- **Coed,** 293 undergraduate students
- 52% of applicants were admitted

Freshmen *Admission:* 916 applied, 476 admitted.
Majors Cooking and related culinary arts.
Academics *Calendar:* semesters. *Degree:* associate.
Freshman Application Contact Admissions Office, Columbus Culinary Institute at Bradford School, 2435 Stelzer Road, Columbus, OH 43219. *Phone:* 614-944-4200. *Toll-free phone:* 877-506-5006. *Web site:* http://www.columbusculinary.com/.

Columbus State Community College
Columbus, Ohio

Freshman Application Contact Ms. Tari Blaney, Director of Admissions, Columbus State Community College, Box 1609, Columbus, OH 43216-1609. *Phone:* 614-287-2669. *Toll-free phone:* 800-621-6407 Ext. 2669. *Fax:* 614-287-6019. *E-mail:* tblaney@cscc.edu. *Web site:* http://www.cscc.edu/.

Cuyahoga Community College
Cleveland, Ohio

Freshman Application Contact Mr. Kevin McDaniel, Director of Admissions and Records, Cuyahoga Community College, Cleveland, OH 44115. *Phone:* 216-987-4030. *Toll-free phone:* 800-954-8742. *Fax:* 216-696-2567. *Web site:* http://www.tri-c.edu/.

Davis College
Toledo, Ohio

Freshman Application Contact Ms. Dana Stern, Davis College, 4747 Monroe Street, Toledo, OH 43623-4307. *Phone:* 419-473-2700. *Toll-free phone:* 800-477-7021. *Fax:* 419-473-2472. *E-mail:* dstern@daviscollege.edu. *Web site:* http://daviscollege.edu/.

Daymar College
Chillicothe, Ohio

Freshman Application Contact Admissions Office, Daymar College, 1410 Industrial Drive, Chillicothe, OH 45601. *Phone:* 740-774-6300. *Toll-free phone:* 877-258-7796. *Fax:* 740-774-6317. *Web site:* http://www.daymarcollege.edu/.

Daymar College
Jackson, Ohio

Freshman Application Contact Admissions Office, Daymar College, 504 McCarty Lane, Jackson, OH 45640. *Phone:* 740-286-1554. *Toll-free phone:* 877-258-7796. *Fax:* 740-774-6317. *Web site:* http://www.daymarcollege.edu/

Daymar College
Lancaster, Ohio

Freshman Application Contact Holly Hankinson, Admissions Office, Daymar College, 1579 Victor Road, NW, Lancaster, OH 43130. *Phone:* 740-687-6126. *Toll-free phone:* 877-258-7796. *E-mail:* hhankinson@daymarcollege.edu. *Web site:* http://www.daymarcollege.edu/.

Daymar College
New Boston, Ohio

Freshman Application Contact Mike Bell, Admissions Representative, Daymar College, 3879 Rhodes Avenue, New Boston, OH 45662. *Phone:* 740-456-4124. *Toll-free phone:* 877-258-7796. *Web site:* http://www.daymarcollege.edu/.

Eastern Gateway Community College
Steubenville, Ohio

- **State and locally supported** 2-year, founded 1966, part of Ohio Board of Regents
- **Small-town** 83-acre campus with easy access to Pittsburgh
- **Coed**

Undergraduates 1,219 full-time, 990 part-time. 10% are from out of state.
Faculty *Student/faculty ratio:* 16:1.
Academics *Calendar:* semesters. *Degree:* certificates and associate. *Special study options:* academic remediation for entering students, accelerated degree program, adult/continuing education programs, cooperative education, distance learning, double majors, off-campus study, part-time degree program, services for LD students, summer session for credit.
Student Life *Campus security:* 24-hour emergency response devices, day and evening security.
Standardized Tests *Required for some:* SAT or ACT (for admission).
Financial Aid Of all full-time matriculated undergraduates who enrolled in 2010, 30 Federal Work-Study jobs (averaging $1500).
Applying *Options:* electronic application, early admission, deferred entrance. *Application fee:* $20. *Required for some:* high school transcript.
Freshman Application Contact Mrs. Kristen Taylor, Director of Admissions, Eastern Gateway Community College, 4000 Sunset Boulevard, Steubenville, OH 43952. *Phone:* 740-264-5591 Ext. 142. *Toll-free phone:* 800-68-COLLEGE. *Fax:* 740-266-2944. *E-mail:* kltaylor@egcc.edu. *Web site:* http://www.egcc.edu/.

Edison Community College
Piqua, Ohio

- **State-supported** 2-year, founded 1973, part of Ohio Board of Regents' University System of Ohio
- **Small-town** 130-acre campus with easy access to Cincinnati, Dayton
- **Endowment** $1.5 million
- **Coed,** 3,457 undergraduate students, 37% full-time, 65% women, 35% men

Undergraduates 1,279 full-time, 2,178 part-time. Students come from 2 states and territories; 4 other countries; 1% are from out of state; 2% Black or African American, non-Hispanic/Latino; 0.7% Hispanic/Latino; 0.6% Asian, non-Hispanic/Latino; 0.5% American Indian or Alaska Native, non-Hispanic/Latino; 0.9% Two or more races, non-Hispanic/Latino; 3% Race/ethnicity unknown; 0.1% international; 3% transferred in. *Retention:* 54% of full-time freshmen returned.
Freshmen *Admission:* 945 applied, 811 admitted, 639 enrolled. *Average high school GPA:* 2.95. *Test scores:* ACT scores over 18: 78%; ACT scores over 24: 20%; ACT scores over 30: 1%.
Faculty *Total:* 243, 23% full-time, 11% with terminal degrees. *Student/faculty ratio:* 17:1.
Majors Accounting; art; business administration and management; child development; clinical/medical laboratory technology; commercial and advertising art; computer and information sciences; computer and information systems security; computer programming; computer systems networking and telecommunications; criminal justice/police science; dramatic/theater arts; education; electrical, electronic and communications engineering technology;

electromechanical technology; executive assistant/executive secretary; health/medical preparatory programs related; human resources management; industrial technology; legal administrative assistant/secretary; legal assistant/paralegal; liberal arts and sciences/liberal studies; logistics, materials, and supply chain management; marketing/marketing management; mechanical drafting and CAD/CADD; mechanical engineering/mechanical technology; medical administrative assistant and medical secretary; medical/clinical assistant; medium/heavy vehicle and truck technology; physical therapy technology; prenursing studies; real estate; registered nursing/registered nurse; sales, distribution, and marketing operations; social work; speech communication and rhetoric; web page, digital/multimedia and information resources design.
Academics *Calendar:* semesters. *Degrees:* certificates, associate, and post-bachelor's certificates. *Special study options:* academic remediation for entering students, accelerated degree program, adult/continuing education programs, advanced placement credit, distance learning, double majors, English as a second language, honors programs, independent study, internships, off-campus study, part-time degree program, services for LD students, student-designed majors, summer session for credit,
Library Edison Community College Library with 29,851 titles, 542 serial subscriptions; 2,424 audiovisual materials, an OPAC, a Web page.
Student Life *Housing:* college housing not available. *Activities and Organizations:* drama/theater group, Campus Crusade for Christ, Student Ambassadors, Edison Stagelight Players, Writers Club, Edison Photo Society. *Campus security:* late-night transport/escort service, 18-hour patrols by trained security personnel. *Student services:* health clinic, personal/psychological counseling.
Athletics Member NJCAA. *Intercollegiate sports:* basketball M(s)/W(s), volleyball W(s). *Intramural sports:* baseball M(c).
Standardized Tests *Required:* ACT COMPASS (for admission).
Costs (2012–13) *Tuition:* state resident $3934 full-time, $131 per credit hour part-time; nonresident $7240 full-time, $241 per credit hour part-time. Full-time tuition and fees vary according to course load, program, and reciprocity agreements. Part-time tuition and fees vary according to course load, program, and reciprocity agreements. *Required fees:* $15 full-time. *Payment plans:* installment, deferred payment. *Waivers:* senior citizens and employees or children of employees.
Financial Aid Of all full-time matriculated undergraduates who enrolled in 2010, 42 Federal Work-Study jobs (averaging $3000).
Applying *Options:* electronic application. *Application fee:* $20. *Required:* high school transcript. *Application deadlines:* rolling (freshmen), rolling (out-of-state freshmen), rolling (transfers).
Freshman Application Contact Ms. Velina Bogart, Coordinator of Recruiting, Edison Community College, 1973 Edison Drive, Piqua, OH 45356. *Phone:* 937-778-7854. *Toll-free phone:* 800-922-3722. *Fax:* 937-778-4692. *E-mail:* vbogart@edisonohio.edu. *Web site:* http://www.edisonohio.edu/.

ETI Technical College of Niles
Niles, Ohio

- **Proprietary** 2-year, founded 1989
- **Small-town** 1-acre campus with easy access to Cleveland, Pittsburgh
- **Coed,** 212 undergraduate students, 67% full-time, 67% women, 33% men

Undergraduates 143 full-time, 69 part-time. Students come from 2 states and territories; 10% are from out of state; 8% transferred in.
Freshmen *Admission:* 40 applied, 34 admitted, 34 enrolled. *Average high school GPA:* 2.6.
Faculty *Total:* 23, 35% full-time. *Student/faculty ratio:* 7:1.
Majors Computer/information technology services administration related; computer programming (specific applications); computer programming (vendor/product certification); computer software and media applications related; computer software engineering; data entry/microcomputer applications; data entry/microcomputer applications related; electrical, electronic and communications engineering technology; legal assistant/paralegal; medical/clinical assistant; word processing.
Academics *Calendar:* semesters. *Degree:* diplomas and associate. *Special study options:* academic remediation for entering students, adult/continuing education programs, double majors, internships, part-time degree program, services for LD students.
Library Main Library plus 3 others with 3,000 titles, 20 serial subscriptions, a Web page.
Student Life *Housing:* college housing not available. *Activities and Organizations:* student-run newspaper, student government. *Campus security:* 24-hour emergency response devices.
Standardized Tests *Recommended:* SAT (for admission), ACT (for admission).
Costs (2012–13) *Tuition:* $7854 full-time, $281 per credit part-time. Full-time tuition and fees vary according to course load and program. Part-time tuition and fees vary according to course load and program. *Required fees:* $300 full-time, $400 per year part-time. *Payment plan:* installment. *Waivers:* employees or children of employees.

Financial Aid Of all full-time matriculated undergraduates who enrolled in 2009, 475 applied for aid, 370 were judged to have need, 450 had their need fully met. *Average percent of need met:* 100%. *Average financial aid package:* $15,250. *Average need-based loan:* $3500. *Average need-based gift aid:* $5750.

Applying *Options:* early admission, deferred entrance. *Application fee:* $50. *Required:* high school transcript, interview. *Application deadlines:* rolling (freshmen), rolling (transfers). *Notification:* continuous (freshmen), continuous (transfers).

Freshman Application Contact Ms. Diane Marsteller, Director of Admissions, ETI Technical College of Niles, 2076 Youngstown-Warren Road, Niles, OH 44446-4398. *Phone:* 330-652-9919 Ext. 16. *Fax:* 330-652-4399. *E-mail:* dianemarsteller@eticollege.edu. *Web site:* http://eticollege.edu/.

Fortis College
Centerville, Ohio

Freshman Application Contact Fortis College, 555 East Alex Bell Road, Centerville, OH 45459. *Phone:* 937-433-3410. *Toll-free phone:* 855-4-FORTIS. *Web site:* http://www.fortis.edu/.

Fortis College
Cuyahoga Falls, Ohio

Freshman Application Contact Admissions Office, Fortis College, 2545 Bailey Road, Cuyahoga Falls, OH 44221. *Phone:* 330-923-9959. *Fax:* 330-923-0886. *Web site:* http://www.fortis.edu/.

Fortis College
Ravenna, Ohio

Freshman Application Contact Admissions Office, Fortis College, 653 Enterprise Parkway, Ravenna, OH 44266. *Toll-free phone:* 855-4-FORTIS. *Web site:* http://www.fortis.edu/.

Gallipolis Career College
Gallipolis, Ohio

Freshman Application Contact Mr. Jack Henson, Director of Admissions, Gallipolis Career College, 1176 Jackson Pike, Suite 312, Gallipolis, OH 45631. *Phone:* 740-446-4367. *Toll-free phone:* 800-214-0452. *Fax:* 740-446-4124. *E-mail:* admissions@gallipoliscareercollege.com. *Web site:* http://www.gallipoliscareercollege.com/.

Good Samaritan College of Nursing and Health Science
Cincinnati, Ohio

- **Proprietary** 2-year
- **Urban** campus with easy access to Cincinnati
- **Coed,** 313 undergraduate students, 42% full-time, 88% women, 12% men

Undergraduates 131 full-time, 182 part-time. 7% are from out of state; 20% transferred in.

Freshmen *Admission:* 31 applied, 22 admitted, 7 enrolled. *Average high school GPA:* 3.1.

Faculty *Student/faculty ratio:* 7:1.

Majors Registered nursing/registered nurse.

Academics *Degree:* associate.

Student Life *Housing:* college housing not available.

Standardized Tests *Required:* SAT or ACT (for admission).

Costs (2011–12) *Tuition:* $15,660 full-time, $450 per credit hour part-time. *Required fees:* $1455 full-time, $215 per term part-time.

Financial Aid Of all full-time matriculated undergraduates who enrolled in 2010, 155 applied for aid, 149 were judged to have need. 8 state and other part-time jobs (averaging $750). In 2010, 8 non-need-based awards were made. *Average percent of need met:* 68%. *Average financial aid package:* $7488. *Average need-based loan:* $3477. *Average need-based gift aid:* $4260. *Average non-need-based aid:* $1100.

Applying *Options:* electronic application. *Application fee:* $40. *Required:* high school transcript, minimum 2.5 GPA, Required average GPA 2.25 in these high school courses: English, Math (Algebra required), Science (Chemistry required), and Social Studies.

Freshman Application Contact Admissions Office, Good Samaritan College of Nursing and Health Science, 375 Dixmyth Avenue, Cincinnati, OH 45220. *Phone:* 513-862-2743. *Fax:* 513-862-3572. *Web site:* http://www.gscollege.edu/.

Harrison College
Grove City, Ohio

- **Proprietary** 2-year
- **Coed**

Undergraduates 87 full-time, 12 part-time. 6% Black or African American, non-Hispanic/Latino; 3% Hispanic/Latino; 1% Asian, non-Hispanic/Latino; 1% Two or more races, non-Hispanic/Latino; 4% Race/ethnicity unknown; 15% transferred in. *Retention:* 69% of full-time freshmen returned.

Academics *Calendar:* quarters. *Degree:* associate.

Standardized Tests *Required:* Wonderlic Scholastic Level Exam (SLE) (for admission).

Costs (2011–12) *Tuition:* Full-time tuition and fees vary according to course load and program. Part-time tuition and fees vary according to course load and program. No tuition increase for student's term of enrollment. Tuition ranges from $300 to $400 a credit depending upon program of study. *Required fees:* $435 full-time, $145 per term part-time.

Applying *Options:* electronic application. *Application fee:* $50. *Required:* high school transcript, interview.

Freshman Application Contact Mark Jones, Harrison College, 3880 Jackpot Road, Grove City, OH 43123. *Phone:* 614-539-8800. *Toll-free phone:* 888-544-4422. *E-mail:* mark.jones@harrison.edu. *Web site:* http://www.harrison.edu/.

Herzing University
Toledo, Ohio

Admissions Office Contact Herzing University, 5212 Hill Avenue, Toledo, OH 43615. *Toll-free phone:* 800-596-0724. *Web site:* http://www.herzing.edu/toledo.

Hocking College
Nelsonville, Ohio

Director of Admissions Ms. Lyn Hull, Director of Admissions, Hocking College, 3301 Hocking Parkway, Nelsonville, OH 45764-9588. *Phone:* 740-753-3591 Ext. 2803. *Toll-free phone:* 877-462-5464. *E-mail:* hull_lyn@hocking.edu. *Web site:* http://www.hocking.edu/.

Hondros College
Westerville, Ohio

Director of Admissions Ms. Carol Thomas, Operations Manager, Hondros College, 4140 Executive Parkway, Westerville, OH 43081-3855. *Phone:* 614-508-7244. *Toll-free phone:* 888-HONDROS. *Web site:* http://www.hondros.edu/.

International College of Broadcasting
Dayton, Ohio

- **Private** 2-year, founded 1968
- **Urban** 1-acre campus
- **Coed,** 84 undergraduate students

Majors Radio and television; recording arts technology.

Academics *Calendar:* semesters. *Degree:* diplomas and associate.

Student Life *Housing Options:* Campus housing is provided by a third party.

Standardized Tests *Required:* Wonderlic aptitude test (for admission).

Costs (2012–13) *Tuition:* $29,120 full-time. No tuition increase for student's term of enrollment. *Payment plan:* tuition prepayment.

Applying *Application fee:* $100.

Freshman Application Contact International College of Broadcasting, 6 South Smithville Road, Dayton, OH 45431-1833. *Phone:* 937-258-8251. *Toll-free phone:* 800-517-7284. *Web site:* http://www.icbcollege.com/.

ITT Technical Institute
Akron, Ohio

- **Proprietary** primarily 2-year
- **Coed**

Majors Business administration and management; communications technology; computer and information systems security; computer software technology; construction management; criminal justice/law enforcement administration; drafting and design technology; electrical, electronic and communications engineering technology; forensic science and technology; graphic communications; legal assistant/paralegal; network and system administration; registered nursing/registered nurse.

Academics *Degrees:* associate and bachelor's.

Freshman Application Contact Director of Recruitment, ITT Technical Institute, 3428 West Market Street, Akron, OH 44333. *Phone:* 330-865-8600. *Toll-free phone:* 877-818-0154. *Web site:* http://www.itt-tech.edu/.

ITT Technical Institute
Columbus, Ohio

- **Proprietary** primarily 2-year, part of ITT Educational Services, Inc.
- **Coed**

Majors Business administration and management; communications technology; computer and information systems security; computer software technology; construction management; criminal justice/law enforcement administration; drafting and design technology; electrical, electronic and communications engineering technology; forensic science and technology; graphic communications; legal assistant/paralegal; network and system administration.
Academics *Calendar:* quarters. *Degrees:* associate and bachelor's.

Freshman Application Contact Director of Recruitment, ITT Technical Institute, 4717 Hilton Corporate Drive, Columbus, OH 43232. *Phone:* 614-868-2000. *Toll-free phone:* 877-233-8864. *Web site:* http://www.itt-tech.edu/.

ITT Technical Institute
Dayton, Ohio

- **Proprietary** primarily 2-year, founded 1935, part of ITT Educational Services, Inc.
- **Suburban** campus
- **Coed**

Majors Architectural drafting and CAD/CADD; business administration and management; communications technology; computer and information systems security; computer software technology; construction management; criminal justice/law enforcement administration; drafting and design technology; forensic science and technology; graphic communications; legal assistant/paralegal; network and system administration; registered nursing/registered nurse.
Academics *Calendar:* quarters. *Degrees:* associate and bachelor's.
Student Life *Housing:* college housing not available.
Freshman Application Contact Director of Recruitment, ITT Technical Institute, 3325 Stop 8 Road, Dayton, OH 45414. *Phone:* 937-264-7700. *Toll-free phone:* 800-568-3241. *Web site:* http://www.itt-tech.edu/.

ITT Technical Institute
Hilliard, Ohio

- **Proprietary** primarily 2-year, founded 2003, part of ITT Educational Services, Inc.
- **Coed**

Majors Business administration and management; communications technology; computer and information systems security; computer software technology; construction management; criminal justice/law enforcement administration; drafting and design technology; electrical, electronic and communications engineering technology; forensic science and technology; graphic communications; legal assistant/paralegal; network and system administration; registered nursing/registered nurse.
Academics *Calendar:* quarters. *Degrees:* associate and bachelor's.
Freshman Application Contact Director of Recruitment, ITT Technical Institute, 3781 Park Mill Run Drive, Hilliard, OH 43026. *Phone:* 614-771-4888. *Toll-free phone:* 888-483-4888. *Web site:* http://www.itt-tech.edu/.

ITT Technical Institute
Maumee, Ohio

- **Proprietary** primarily 2-year
- **Coed**

Majors Business administration and management; communications technology; computer and information systems security; computer software technology; construction management; criminal justice/law enforcement administration; drafting and design technology; electrical, electronic and communications engineering technology; graphic communications; legal assistant/paralegal; network and system administration.
Academics *Degrees:* associate and bachelor's.
Student Life *Housing:* college housing not available.
Freshman Application Contact Director of Recruitment, ITT Technical Institute, 1656 Henthorne Drive, Suite B, Maumee, OH 43537. *Phone:* 419-861-6500. *Toll-free phone:* 877-205-4639. *Web site:* http://www.itt-tech.edu/.

ITT Technical Institute
Norwood, Ohio

- **Proprietary** primarily 2-year, founded 1995, part of ITT Educational Services, Inc.
- **Coed**

Majors Accounting technology and bookkeeping; business administration and management; communications technology; computer and information systems security; computer software and media applications related; computer software technology; construction management; criminal justice/law enforcement administration; drafting and design technology; electrical, electronic and communications engineering technology; forensic science and technology; graphic communications; legal assistant/paralegal; network and system administration; registered nursing/registered nurse; web/multimedia management and webmaster.
Academics *Calendar:* quarters. *Degrees:* associate and bachelor's.
Student Life *Housing:* college housing not available.
Freshman Application Contact Director of Recruitment, ITT Technical Institute, 4750 Wesley Avenue, Norwood, OH 45212. *Phone:* 513-531-8300. *Toll-free phone:* 800-314-8324. *Web site:* http://www.itt-tech.edu/.

ITT Technical Institute
Strongsville, Ohio

- **Proprietary** primarily 2-year, founded 1994, part of ITT Educational Services, Inc.
- **Coed**

Majors Accounting technology and bookkeeping; business administration and management; CAD/CADD drafting/design technology; communications technology; computer and information systems security; computer engineering technology; computer software and media applications related; computer software technology; construction management; criminal justice/law enforcement administration; design and visual communications; drafting and design technology; electrical, electronic and communications engineering technology; forensic science and technology; graphic communications; legal assistant/paralegal; network and system administration; registered nursing/registered nurse; system, networking, and LAN/WAN management; web/multimedia management and webmaster; web page, digital/multimedia and information resources design.
Academics *Calendar:* quarters. *Degrees:* associate and bachelor's.
Student Life *Housing:* college housing not available.
Freshman Application Contact Director of Recruitment, ITT Technical Institute, 14955 Sprague Road, Strongsville, OH 44136. *Phone:* 440-234-9091. *Toll-free phone:* 800-331-1488. *Web site:* http://www.itt-tech.edu/.

ITT Technical Institute
Warrensville Heights, Ohio

- **Proprietary** primarily 2-year, founded 2005
- **Coed**

Majors Business administration and management; communications technology; computer and information systems security; computer software technology; construction management; criminal justice/law enforcement administration; drafting and design technology; electrical, electronic and communications engineering technology; forensic science and technology; graphic communications; legal assistant/paralegal; network and system administration; registered nursing/registered nurse.
Academics *Calendar:* quarters. *Degrees:* associate and bachelor's.
Student Life *Housing:* college housing not available.
Freshman Application Contact Director of Recruitment, ITT Technical Institute, 4700 Richmond Road, Warrensville Heights, OH 44128. *Phone:* 216-896-6500. *Toll-free phone:* 800-741-3494. *Web site:* http://www.itt-tech.edu/.

ITT Technical Institute
Youngstown, Ohio

- **Proprietary** primarily 2-year, founded 1967, part of ITT Educational Services, Inc.
- **Suburban** campus
- **Coed**

Majors Business administration and management; communications technology; computer and information systems security; computer software and media applications related; computer software engineering; construction management; criminal justice/law enforcement administration; drafting and design technology; electrical, electronic and communications engineering technology; forensic science and technology; graphic communications; legal assistant/paralegal; network and system administration; registered nursing/registered nurse.

Academics *Calendar:* quarters. *Degrees:* associate and bachelor's.
Student Life *Housing:* college housing not available.
Financial Aid Of all full-time matriculated undergraduates who enrolled in 2010, 5 Federal Work-Study jobs (averaging $3979).
Freshman Application Contact Director of Recruitment, ITT Technical Institute, 1030 North Meridian Road, Youngstown, OH 44509-4098. *Phone:* 330-270-1600. *Toll-free phone:* 800-832-5001. *Web site:* http://www.itt-tech.edu/.

James A. Rhodes State College
Lima, Ohio

Freshman Application Contact Mr. Scot Lingrell, Director, Student Advising and Development, James A. Rhodes State College, 4240 Campus Drive, Lima, OH 45804-3597. *Phone:* 419-995-8050. *E-mail:* peterl@ltc.tec.oh.us. *Web site:* http://www.rhodesstate.edu/.

Kaplan Career Institute, Cleveland Campus
Cleveland, Ohio

- **Proprietary** 2-year
- **Coed**

Majors Criminal justice/law enforcement administration.
Academics *Degree:* diplomas and associate.
Freshman Application Contact Admissions Office, Kaplan Career Institute, Cleveland Campus, 8720 Brookpark Road, Cleveland, OH 44129. *Toll-free phone:* 800-935-1857. *Web site:* http://cleveland.kaplancareerinstitute.com/.

Kaplan College, Cincinnati Campus
Cincinnati, Ohio

- **Proprietary** 2-year
- **Coed**

Majors Criminal justice/law enforcement administration.
Academics *Degree:* diplomas and associate.
Freshman Application Contact Kaplan College, Cincinnati Campus, 801 Linn Street, Cincinnati, OH 45203. *Phone:* 513-421-9900. *Toll-free phone:* 800-935-1857. *Web site:* http://cincinnati.kaplancollege.com/.

Kaplan College, Columbus Campus
Columbus, Ohio

- **Proprietary** 2-year
- **Coed**

Majors Criminal justice/law enforcement administration; medical office management.
Academics *Degree:* diplomas and associate.
Freshman Application Contact Kaplan College, Columbus Campus, 2745 Winchester Pike, Columbus, OH 43232. *Phone:* 614-456-4600. *Toll-free phone:* 800-935-1857. *Web site:* http://columbus.kaplancollege.com/.

Kaplan College, Dayton Campus
Dayton, Ohio

- **Proprietary** 2-year, founded 1971
- **Urban** campus
- **Coed**

Majors Computer systems networking and telecommunications; photographic and film/video technology; registered nursing/registered nurse.
Academics *Calendar:* quarters. *Degree:* diplomas and associate.
Freshman Application Contact Kaplan College, Dayton Campus, 2800 East River Road, Dayton, OH 45439. *Phone:* 937-294-6155. *Toll-free phone:* 800-935-1857. *Web site:* http://dayton.kaplancollege.com/.

Kent State University at Ashtabula
Ashtabula, Ohio

- **State-supported** primarily 2-year, founded 1958, part of Kent State University System
- **Small-town** 120-acre campus with easy access to Cleveland
- **Coed,** 2,451 undergraduate students, 50% full-time, 66% women, 34% men

Undergraduates 1,227 full-time, 1,224 part-time. Students come from 12 states and territories; 1 other country; 2% are from out of state; 6% Black or African American, non-Hispanic/Latino; 3% Hispanic/Latino; 0.7% Asian, non-Hispanic/Latino; 0.5% American Indian or Alaska Native, non-Hispanic/

Latino; 1% Two or more races, non-Hispanic/Latino; 3% Race/ethnicity unknown; 10% transferred in. *Retention:* 49% of full-time freshmen returned.
Freshmen *Admission:* 607 applied, 603 admitted, 419 enrolled. *Average high school GPA:* 2.68. *Test scores:* ACT scores over 18: 69%; ACT scores over 24: 10%; ACT scores over 30: 2%.
Faculty *Total:* 126, 41% full-time. *Student/faculty ratio:* 18:1.
Majors Accounting; administrative assistant and secretarial science; aerospace, aeronautical and astronautical/space engineering; business administration and management; computer engineering technology; criminal justice/police science; criminal justice/safety; electrical, electronic and communications engineering technology; engineering technology; English; environmental studies; finance; health/medical preparatory programs related; hospitality administration; human services; industrial technology; kindergarten/preschool education; legal administrative assistant/secretary; liberal arts and sciences/liberal studies; marketing/marketing management; materials science; mechanical engineering/mechanical technology; medical radiologic technology; physical therapy; real estate; registered nursing/registered nurse; respiratory care therapy; speech communication and rhetoric; viticulture and enology.
Academics *Calendar:* semesters. *Degrees:* certificates, associate, and bachelor's (also offers some upper-level and graduate courses). *Special study options:* academic remediation for entering students, advanced placement credit, distance learning, double majors, independent study, part-time degree program, services for LD students, student-designed majors, study abroad, summer session for credit.
Library Kent State at Ashtabula Library with 51,884 titles, 225 serial subscriptions, 640 audiovisual materials, an OPAC, a Web page.
Student Life *Housing:* college housing not available. *Activities and Organizations:* student government, student veterans association, student Nurses Association, Student Occupational Therapy Association (SOTA), Media Club. *Campus security:* 24-hour emergency response devices.
Standardized Tests *Required for some:* SAT or ACT (for admission). *Recommended:* SAT or ACT (for admission).
Costs (2011–12) *Tuition:* state resident $5288 full-time, $241 per credit hour part-time; nonresident $13,248 full-time, $603 per credit hour part-time. Full-time tuition and fees vary according to course level and course load. Part-time tuition and fees vary according to course level and course load. *Payment plans:* installment, deferred payment. *Waivers:* senior citizens and employees or children of employees.
Financial Aid Of all full-time matriculated undergraduates who enrolled in 2011, 880 applied for aid, 852 were judged to have need, 182 had their need fully met. In 2011, 7 non-need-based awards were made. *Average percent of need met:* 44%. *Average financial aid package:* $7753. *Average need-based loan:* $3568. *Average need-based gift aid:* $4829. *Average non-need-based aid:* $1426.
Applying *Options:* electronic application, early admission, deferred entrance. *Application fee:* $30. *Required:* high school transcript. *Application deadlines:* rolling (freshmen), rolling (transfers). *Notification:* continuous (freshmen), continuous (transfers).
Freshman Application Contact Kent State University at Ashtabula, 3300 Lake Road West, Ashtabula, OH 44004-2299. *Phone:* 440-964-4217. *Web site:* http://www.ashtabula.kent.edu/.

Kent State University at East Liverpool
East Liverpool, Ohio

- **State-supported** primarily 2-year, founded 1967, part of Kent State University System
- **Small-town** 4-acre campus with easy access to Pittsburgh
- **Coed,** 1,491 undergraduate students, 59% full-time, 68% women, 32% men

Undergraduates 883 full-time, 608 part-time. Students come from 8 states and territories; 2 other countries; 5% are from out of state; 4% Black or African American, non-Hispanic/Latino; 1% Hispanic/Latino; 0.3% Asian, non-Hispanic/Latino; 0.1% Native Hawaiian or other Pacific Islander, non-Hispanic/Latino; 0.3% American Indian or Alaska Native, non-Hispanic/Latino; 0.8% Two or more races, non-Hispanic/Latino; 3% Race/ethnicity unknown; 0.1% international; 6% transferred in. *Retention:* 54% of full-time freshmen returned.
Freshmen *Admission:* 211 applied, 203 admitted, 146 enrolled. *Average high school GPA:* 2.86. *Test scores:* SAT critical reading scores over 500: 67%; SAT math scores over 500: 67%; SAT writing scores over 500: 100%; ACT scores over 18: 52%; SAT critical reading scores over 600: 67%; SAT math scores over 600: 33%; SAT writing scores over 600: 67%; ACT scores over 24: 7%; SAT critical reading scores over 700: 33%.
Faculty *Total:* 77, 34% full-time. *Student/faculty ratio:* 18:1.
Majors Accounting; business administration and management; computer and information sciences related; computer engineering technology; criminal justice/law enforcement administration; English; legal administrative assistant/

secretary; legal assistant/paralegal; liberal arts and sciences/liberal studies; occupational therapy; physical therapy; psychology; registered nursing/registered nurse; speech communication and rhetoric.

Academics *Calendar:* semesters. *Degrees:* certificates, associate, and bachelor's (also offers some upper-level and graduate courses). *Special study options:* academic remediation for entering students, accelerated degree program, adult/continuing education programs, advanced placement credit, distance learning, double majors, freshman honors college, honors programs, independent study, internships, part-time degree program, services for LD students, student-designed majors, study abroad, summer session for credit.

Library Blair Memorial Library with 31,320 titles, 135 serial subscriptions, an OPAC, a Web page.

Student Life *Housing:* college housing not available. *Activities and Organizations:* student-run newspaper, Student Government, Student Nurses Association, Environmental Club, Occupational Therapist Assistant Club, Physical Therapist Assistant Club. *Campus security:* student patrols, late-night transport/escort service.

Standardized Tests *Required for some:* SAT or ACT (for admission). *Recommended:* SAT or ACT (for admission).

Costs (2011–12) *Tuition:* state resident $5288 full-time, $241 per credit hour part-time; nonresident $13,248 full-time, $603 per credit hour part-time. Full-time tuition and fees vary according to course level and course load. Part-time tuition and fees vary according to course level and course load. *Payment plans:* installment, deferred payment. *Waivers:* senior citizens and employees or children of employees.

Financial Aid Of all full-time matriculated undergraduates who enrolled in 2011, 473 applied for aid, 451 were judged to have need, 94 had their need fully met. In 2011, 1 non-need-based awards were made. *Average percent of need met:* 45%. *Average financial aid package:* $7873. *Average need-based loan:* $3481. *Average need-based gift aid:* $4787. *Average non-need-based aid:* $500.

Applying *Options:* electronic application, early admission, deferred entrance. *Application fee:* $30. *Required:* high school transcript. *Application deadlines:* rolling (freshmen), rolling (transfers). *Notification:* continuous (freshmen), continuous (transfers).

Freshman Application Contact Kent State University at East Liverpool, 400 East 4th Street, East Liverpool, OH 43920-3497. *Phone:* 330-382-7415. *Web site:* http://www.eliv.kent.edu/.

Kent State University at Salem
Salem, Ohio

- **State-supported** primarily 2-year, founded 1966, part of Kent State University System
- **Rural** 98-acre campus
- **Coed**, 2,018 undergraduate students, 68% full-time, 71% women, 29% men

Undergraduates 1,373 full-time, 645 part-time. Students come from 11 states and territories; 4 other countries; 2% are from out of state; 3% Black or African American, non-Hispanic/Latino; 2% Hispanic/Latino; 0.5% Asian, non-Hispanic/Latino; 0.6% American Indian or Alaska Native, non-Hispanic/Latino; 0.7% Two or more races, non-Hispanic/Latino; 3% Race/ethnicity unknown; 0.2% international; 8% transferred in. *Retention:* 54% of full-time freshmen returned.

Freshmen *Admission:* 418 applied, 405 admitted, 267 enrolled. *Average high school GPA:* 2.84. *Test scores:* SAT critical reading scores over 500: 67%; SAT math scores over 500: 33%; SAT writing scores over 500: 33%; ACT scores over 18: 71%; ACT scores over 24: 12%.

Faculty *Total:* 133, 34% full-time. *Student/faculty ratio:* 17:1.

Majors Administrative assistant and secretarial science; allied health diagnostic, intervention, and treatment professions related; applied horticulture/horticulture operations; business administration and management; business/commerce; computer programming (specific applications); criminal justice/safety; early childhood education; education; English; health and medical administrative services related; industrial technology; liberal arts and sciences/liberal studies; medical radiologic technology; psychology; registered nursing/registered nurse; speech communication and rhetoric.

Academics *Calendar:* semesters. *Degrees:* certificates, associate, and bachelor's (also offers some upper-level and graduate courses). *Special study options:* academic remediation for entering students, accelerated degree program, adult/continuing education programs, advanced placement credit, cooperative education, distance learning, double majors, freshman honors college, honors programs, independent study, internships, part-time degree program, services for LD students, student-designed majors, summer session for credit.

Library Kent State Salem Library with 19,000 titles, 163 serial subscriptions, 158 audiovisual materials, an OPAC, a Web page.

Student Life *Housing:* college housing not available. *Activities and Organizations:* choral group, Honors Club, Human Services Technology Club, Radiologic Technology Club, Student Government Organization, Students for Professional Nursing. *Campus security:* 24-hour emergency response devices,

late-night transport/escort service. *Student services:* personal/psychological counseling.

Athletics *Intramural sports:* basketball M/W, skiing (downhill) M/W, table tennis M/W, tennis M/W, volleyball M/W.

Standardized Tests *Required for some:* SAT or ACT (for admission). *Recommended:* SAT or ACT (for admission).

Costs (2011–12) *Tuition:* state resident $5288 full-time, $241 per credit hour part-time; nonresident $13,248 full-time, $603 per credit hour part-time. Full-time tuition and fees vary according to course level and course load. Part-time tuition and fees vary according to course level and course load. *Payment plans:* installment, deferred payment. *Waivers:* senior citizens and employees or children of employees.

Financial Aid Of all full-time matriculated undergraduates who enrolled in 2011, 894 applied for aid, 844 were judged to have need, 228 had their need fully met. In 2011, 9 non-need-based awards were made. *Average percent of need met:* 45%. *Average financial aid package:* $7217. *Average need-based loan:* $3496. *Average need-based gift aid:* $4489. *Average non-need-based aid:* $979.

Applying *Options:* electronic application, early admission, deferred entrance. *Application fee:* $30. *Required:* high school transcript. *Required for some:* essay or personal statement. *Application deadlines:* rolling (freshmen), rolling (transfers). *Notification:* continuous (freshmen), continuous (transfers).

Freshman Application Contact Kristin Toothman, Kent State University at Salem, 2491 State Route 45 South, Salem, OH 44460-9412. *Phone:* 330-337-4226. *E-mail:* ktoothm@kent.edu. *Web site:* http://www.salem.kent.edu/.

Kent State University at Trumbull
Warren, Ohio

- **State-supported** primarily 2-year, founded 1954, part of Kent State University System
- **Suburban** 200-acre campus with easy access to Cleveland
- **Coed**, 3,205 undergraduate students, 61% full-time, 64% women, 36% men

Undergraduates 1,971 full-time, 1,234 part-time. Students come from 16 states and territories; 3 other countries; 1% are from out of state; 12% Black or African American, non-Hispanic/Latino; 2% Hispanic/Latino; 0.7% Asian, non-Hispanic/Latino; 0.2% American Indian or Alaska Native, non-Hispanic/Latino; 1% Two or more races, non-Hispanic/Latino; 3% Race/ethnicity unknown; 0.4% international; 7% transferred in. *Retention:* 49% of full-time freshmen returned.

Freshmen *Admission:* 513 applied, 507 admitted, 392 enrolled. *Average high school GPA:* 2.65. *Test scores:* SAT critical reading scores over 500: 33%; SAT math scores over 500: 50%; SAT writing scores over 500: 17%; ACT scores over 18: 70%; SAT math scores over 600: 17%; ACT scores over 24: 12%; ACT scores over 30: 1%.

Faculty *Total:* 128, 45% full-time. *Student/faculty ratio:* 22:1.

Majors Accounting technology and bookkeeping; automobile/automotive mechanics technology; business administration and management; computer engineering technology; computer/information technology services administration related; computer technology/computer systems technology; criminal justice/safety; electrical, electronic and communications engineering technology; English; environmental engineering technology; general studies; industrial technology; legal assistant/paralegal; liberal arts and sciences/liberal studies; manufacturing engineering; mechanical engineering/mechanical technology; nursing science; speech communication and rhetoric; systems engineering.

Academics *Calendar:* semesters. *Degrees:* certificates, associate, and bachelor's (also offers some upper-level and graduate courses). *Special study options:* academic remediation for entering students, adult/continuing education programs, advanced placement credit, distance learning, double majors, freshman honors college, honors programs, independent study, internships, part-time degree program, services for LD students, student-designed majors, study abroad, summer session for credit.

Library Trumbull Campus Library with 65,951 titles, 759 serial subscriptions, an OPAC, a Web page.

Student Life *Housing:* college housing not available. *Activities and Organizations:* drama/theater group, National Student Nurses Association, Spot On Improv Group, Amnesty International, Campus Crusade for Christ, Student Veteran Organization. *Campus security:* 24-hour emergency response devices, late-night transport/escort service, patrols by trained security personnel during open hours. *Student services:* personal/psychological counseling.

Standardized Tests *Required for some:* SAT or ACT (for admission). *Recommended:* SAT or ACT (for admission).

Costs (2011–12) *Tuition:* state resident $5288 full-time, $241 per credit hour part-time; nonresident $13,248 full-time, $603 per credit hour part-time. Full-time tuition and fees vary according to course level and course load. Part-time tuition and fees vary according to course level and course load. *Payment plans:* installment, deferred payment. *Waivers:* senior citizens and employees or children of employees.

Financial Aid Of all full-time matriculated undergraduates who enrolled in 2011, 1,253 applied for aid, 1,198 were judged to have need, 292 had their need fully met. In 2011, 6 non-need-based awards were made. *Average percent of need met:* 45%. *Average financial aid package:* $7686. *Average need-based loan:* $3615. *Average need-based gift aid:* $4803. *Average non-need-based aid:* $1167.

Applying *Options:* electronic application, deferred entrance. *Application fee:* $30. *Required:* high school transcript. *Application deadlines:* rolling (freshmen), rolling (transfers). *Notification:* continuous (freshmen), continuous (transfers).

Freshman Application Contact Kent State University at Trumbull, Warren, OH 44483. *Phone:* 330-675-8935. *Web site:* http://www.trumbull.kent.edu/.

Kent State University at Tuscarawas
New Philadelphia, Ohio

- **State-supported** primarily 2-year, founded 1962, part of Kent State University System
- **Small-town** 172-acre campus with easy access to Cleveland
- **Coed,** 2,659 undergraduate students, 57% full-time, 60% women, 40% men

Undergraduates 1,510 full-time, 1,149 part-time. Students come from 7 states and territories; 4 other countries; 1% are from out of state; 2% Black or African American, non-Hispanic/Latino; 0.9% Hispanic/Latino; 0.4% Asian, non-Hispanic/Latino; 0.1% Native Hawaiian or other Pacific Islander, non-Hispanic/Latino; 0.3% American Indian or Alaska Native, non-Hispanic/Latino; 0.8% Two or more races, non-Hispanic/Latino; 3% Race/ethnicity unknown; 0.2% international; 7% transferred in. *Retention:* 62% of full-time freshmen returned.

Freshmen *Admission:* 542 applied, 519 admitted, 401 enrolled. *Average high school GPA:* 2.81. *Test scores:* ACT scores over 18: 80%; ACT scores over 24: 21%; ACT scores over 30: 1%.

Faculty *Total:* 139, 39% full-time. *Student/faculty ratio:* 20:1.

Majors Accounting; administrative assistant and secretarial science; animation, interactive technology, video graphics and special effects; business administration and management; communications technology; computer engineering technology; criminal justice/police science; early childhood education; electrical, electronic and communications engineering technology; engineering technologies and engineering related; engineering technology; environmental studies; industrial technology; liberal arts and sciences and humanities related; liberal arts and sciences/liberal studies; mechanical engineering/mechanical technology; plastics and polymer engineering technology; registered nursing/registered nurse; speech communication and rhetoric; veterinary/animal health technology.

Academics *Calendar:* semesters. *Degrees:* certificates, associate, and bachelor's (also offers some upper-level and graduate courses). *Special study options:* academic remediation for entering students, accelerated degree program, adult/continuing education programs, advanced placement credit, distance learning, double majors, freshman honors college, honors programs, independent study, internships, part-time degree program, services for LD students, student-designed majors, study abroad, summer session for credit.

Library Tuscarawas Campus Library with 63,880 titles, 208 serial subscriptions, 1,179 audiovisual materials, an OPAC, a Web page.

Student Life *Housing:* college housing not available. *Activities and Organizations:* drama/theater group, choral group, Society of Manufacturing Engineers, IEEE, Animation Imagineers, Justice Studies Club, Student Activities Council. **Athletics** *Intramural sports:* basketball M/W, volleyball M/W.

Standardized Tests *Required for some:* SAT or ACT (for admission). *Recommended:* SAT or ACT (for admission).

Costs (2011–12) *Tuition:* state resident $5288 full-time, $241 per credit hour part-time; nonresident $13,248 full-time, $603 per credit hour part-time. Full-time tuition and fees vary according to course level and course load. Part-time tuition and fees vary according to course level and course load. *Payment plans:* installment, deferred payment. *Waivers:* senior citizens and employees or children of employees.

Financial Aid Of all full-time matriculated undergraduates who enrolled in 2011, 1,137 applied for aid, 1,075 were judged to have need, 244 had their need fully met. In 2011, 7 non-need-based awards were made. *Average percent of need met:* 47%. *Average financial aid package:* $7391. *Average need-based loan:* $3423. *Average need-based gift aid:* $4577. *Average non-need-based aid:* $1111.

Applying *Options:* electronic application, early admission, deferred entrance. *Application fee:* $30. *Required:* high school transcript. *Application deadlines:* rolling (freshmen), rolling (transfers). *Notification:* continuous (freshmen), continuous (transfers).

Freshman Application Contact Mrs. Laurie R. Donley, Director of Enrollment Management and Student Services, Kent State University at Tuscarawas, 330 University Drive Northeast, New Philadelphia, OH 44663-9403. *Phone:* 330-339-3391 Ext. 47425. *Fax:* 330-339-3321. *E-mail:* ldonley@kent.edu. *Web site:* http://www.tusc.kent.edu/.

Lakeland Community College
Kirtland, Ohio

Freshman Application Contact Lakeland Community College, 7700 Clocktower Drive, Kirtland, OH 44094-5198. *Phone:* 440-525-7230. *Toll-free phone:* 800-589-8520. *Web site:* http://www.lakeland.cc.oh.us/.

Lincoln College of Technology
Cincinnati, Ohio

Freshman Application Contact Director of Admission, Lincoln College of Technology, 149 Northland Boulevard, Cincinnati, OH 45246-1122. *Phone:* 513-874-0432. *Fax:* 513-874-1330. *Web site:* http://www.lincolnedu.com/.

Lincoln College of Technology
Cincinnati, Ohio

Freshman Application Contact Admissions Director, Lincoln College of Technology, 632 Vine Street, Suite 200, Cincinnati, OH 45202-4304. *Phone:* 513-421-3212. *Fax:* 513-421-8325. *Web site:* http://www.lincolnedu.com/.

Lincoln College of Technology
Dayton, Ohio

Director of Admissions William Furlong, Director of Admissions, Lincoln College of Technology, 111 West First Street, Dayton, OH 45402-3003. *Phone:* 937-224-0061. *Web site:* http://www.lincolnedu.com/.

Lincoln College of Technology
Franklin, Ohio

- **Proprietary** 2-year, founded 1981
- **Suburban** campus with easy access to Cincinnati, Dayton
- **Coed**

Undergraduates Students come from 1 other state. *Retention:* 57% of full-time freshmen returned.

Academics *Calendar:* quarters. *Degree:* certificates, diplomas, and associate. *Special study options:* cooperative education, independent study.

Applying *Required:* high school transcript, interview.

Freshman Application Contact Admissions Director, Lincoln College of Technology, 201 East Second Street, Franklin, OH 45005. *Phone:* 937-746-6633. *Fax:* 937-746-6754. *Web site:* http://www.lincolnedu.com/.

Lorain County Community College
Elyria, Ohio

Director of Admissions Ms. Thalia Fountain, Interim Director of Enrollment Services, Lorain County Community College, 1005 Abbe Road, North, Elyria, OH 44035. *Phone:* 440-366-7683. *Toll-free phone:* 800-995-5222 Ext. 4032. *Fax:* 440-366-4150. *Web site:* http://www.lorainccc.edu/.

Marion Technical College
Marion, Ohio

- **State-supported** 2-year, founded 1971, part of University System of Ohio
- **Small-town** 180-acre campus with easy access to Columbus
- **Coed**

Undergraduates 5% Black or African American, non-Hispanic/Latino; 1% Hispanic/Latino; 0.5% Asian, non-Hispanic/Latino; 0.2% American Indian or Alaska Native, non-Hispanic/Latino; 2% Race/ethnicity unknown. *Retention:* 57% of full-time freshmen returned.

Faculty *Student/faculty ratio:* 18:1.

Academics *Calendar:* quarters. *Degree:* certificates and associate. *Special study options:* academic remediation for entering students, accelerated degree program, adult/continuing education programs, advanced placement credit, cooperative education, distance learning, double majors, independent study, internships, off-campus study, part-time degree program, services for LD students, student-designed majors, summer session for credit.

Standardized Tests *Required:* COMPASS or ACT (for admission). *Required for some:* ACT (for admission).

Costs (2011–12) *Tuition:* state resident $3852 full-time, $107 per credit hour part-time; nonresident $5760 full-time, $160 per credit hour part-time. Full-time tuition and fees vary according to course load and program. Part-time tuition and fees vary according to course load and program. *Required fees:* $300 full-time.

Financial Aid Of all full-time matriculated undergraduates who enrolled in 2010, 28 Federal Work-Study jobs (averaging $1200). 45 state and other part-time jobs (averaging $1000).

Applying *Options:* electronic application, early admission, deferred entrance. *Application fee:* $20. *Required:* high school transcript. *Required for some:* minimum 2.5 GPA, some programs are Limited Enrollment Programs with specific admission criteria. *Recommended:* interview.

Freshman Application Contact Mr. Joel Liles, Dean of Enrollment Services, Marion Technical College, 1467 Mount Vernon Avenue, Marion, OH 43302. *Phone:* 740-389-4636 Ext. 249. *Fax:* 740-389-6136. *E-mail:* enroll@ mtc.edu. *Web site:* http://www.mtc.edu/.

Miami-Jacobs Career College
Dayton, Ohio

Director of Admissions Mary Percell, Vice President of Information Services, Miami-Jacobs Career College, 110 N. Patterson Boulevard, Dayton, OH 45402. *Phone:* 937-461-5174 Ext. 118. *Web site:* http:// www.miamijacobs.edu/.

Miami University–Middletown Campus
Middletown, Ohio

Freshman Application Contact Diane Cantonwine, Assistant Director of Admission and Financial Aid, Miami University–Middletown Campus, 4200 East University Boulevard, Middletown, OH 45042-3497. *Phone:* 513-727-3346. *Toll-free phone:* 866-426-4643. *Fax:* 513-727-3223. *E-mail:* cantondm@muohio.edu. *Web site:* http://www.mid.muohio.edu/.

North Central State College
Mansfield, Ohio

Freshman Application Contact Ms. Nikia L. Fletcher, Director of Admissions, North Central State College, 2441 Kenwood Circle, PO Box 698, Mansfield, OH 44901-0698. *Phone:* 419-755-4813. *Toll-free phone:* 888-755-4899. *E-mail:* nfletcher@ncstatecollege.edu. *Web site:* http:// www.ncstatecollege.edu/.

Northwest State Community College
Archbold, Ohio

Director of Admissions Mr. Jeffrey Ferezan, Dean of Student Success and Advocacy Center, Northwest State Community College, 22-600 State Route 34, Archbold, OH 43502-9542. *Phone:* 419-267-1213. *Web site:* http:// www.northweststate.edu/.

Ohio Business College
Sandusky, Ohio

Freshman Application Contact Ohio Business College, 5202 Timber Commons Drive, Sandusky, OH 44870. *Phone:* 419-627-8345. *Toll-free phone:* 888-627-8345. *Web site:* http://www.ohiobusinesscollege.com/.

Ohio Business College
Sheffield Village, Ohio

Director of Admissions Mr. Jim Unger, Admissions Director, Ohio Business College, 5095 Waterford Drive, Sheffield Village, OH 44035. *Toll-free phone:* 888-514-3126. *Web site:* http://www.ohiobusinesscollege.com/.

Ohio College of Massotherapy
Akron, Ohio

Director of Admissions Mr. John Atkins, Director of Admissions and Marketing, Ohio College of Massotherapy, 225 Heritage Woods Drive, Akron, OH 44321. *Phone:* 330-665-1084 Ext. 11. *Toll-free phone:* 888-888-4325. *E-mail:* johna@ocm.edu. *Web site:* http://www.ocm.edu/.

The Ohio State University Agricultural Technical Institute
Wooster, Ohio

Freshman Application Contact Ms. Sarah Elvey, Admissions Counselor, The Ohio State University Agricultural Technical Institute, 1328 Dover Road, Wooster, OH 44691. *Phone:* 330-287-1228. *Toll-free phone:* 800-647-8283

Ext. 1327. *Fax:* 330-287-1333. *E-mail:* elvey.3@osu.edu. *Web site:* http:// www.ati.osu.edu/.

Ohio Technical College
Cleveland, Ohio

Director of Admissions Mr. Marc Brenner, President, Ohio Technical College, 1374 East 51st Street, Cleveland, OH 44103. *Phone:* 216-881-1700. *Toll-free phone:* 800-322-7000. *Fax:* 216-881-9145. *E-mail:* ohioauto@ aol.com. *Web site:* http://www.ohiotechnicalcollege.com/.

Ohio Valley College of Technology
East Liverpool, Ohio

Freshman Application Contact Mr. Scott S. Rogers, Director, Ohio Valley College of Technology, 16808 St. Clair Avenue, PO Box 7000, East Liverpool, OH 43920. *Phone:* 330-385-1070. *Web site:* http://www.ovct.edu/.

Owens Community College
Toledo, Ohio

- **State-supported** 2-year, founded 1966
- **Suburban** 420-acre campus with easy access to Detroit
- **Endowment** $1.3 million
- **Coed,** 17,173 undergraduate students, 40% full-time, 52% women, 48% men

Undergraduates 6,937 full-time, 10,236 part-time. Students come from 21 states and territories; 28 other countries; 3% are from out of state; 14% Black or African American, non-Hispanic/Latino; 6% Hispanic/Latino; 0.7% Asian, non-Hispanic/Latino; 0.1% Native Hawaiian or other Pacific Islander, non-Hispanic/Latino; 0.4% American Indian or Alaska Native, non-Hispanic/Latino; 2% Two or more races, non-Hispanic/Latino; 2% Race/ethnicity unknown; 0.6% international; 0.6% transferred in.

Freshmen *Admission:* 11,378 applied, 11,378 admitted, 2,610 enrolled. *Average high school GPA:* 2.48. *Test scores:* SAT critical reading scores over 500: 24%; SAT math scores over 500: 32%; SAT writing scores over 500: 20%; ACT scores over 18: 57%; SAT critical reading scores over 600: 8%; SAT math scores over 600: 8%; SAT writing scores over 600: 8%; ACT scores over 24: 8%.

Faculty *Total:* 1,582, 12% full-time, 8% with terminal degrees. *Student/faculty ratio:* 16:1.

Majors Accounting technology and bookkeeping; agricultural mechanization; architectural drafting and CAD/CADD; architectural engineering technology; automotive engineering technology; biomedical technology; business/commerce; commercial and advertising art; commercial photography; communications technology; computer and information systems security; computer engineering technology; computer programming (specific applications); construction engineering technology; corrections; criminal justice/law enforcement administration; criminal justice/police science; dental hygiene; diagnostic medical sonography and ultrasound technology; dietetics; early childhood education; education; electrical, electronic and communications engineering technology; energy management and systems technology; environmental engineering technology; executive assistant/executive secretary; fire prevention and safety technology; general studies; golf course operation and grounds management; health/health-care administration; health information/ medical records technology; industrial and product design; industrial technology; information technology; international business/trade/commerce; landscaping and groundskeeping; manufacturing engineering technology; massage therapy; medical administrative assistant and medical secretary; medical/ health management and clinical assistant; medical radiologic technology; music technology; nuclear medical technology; occupational therapist assistant; office management; operations management; physical therapy technology; public administration; quality control technology; registered nursing/ registered nurse; restaurant/food services management; sales, distribution, and marketing operations; surgical technology; tool and die technology; welding technology.

Academics *Calendar:* semesters. *Degree:* certificates and associate. *Special study options:* academic remediation for entering students, accelerated degree program, adult/continuing education programs, advanced placement credit, cooperative education, distance learning, double majors, English as a second language, honors programs, independent study, internships, part-time degree program, services for LD students, study abroad, summer session for credit. *ROTC:* Army (c), Air Force (c).

Library Owens Community College Library plus 1 other with 36,770 titles, 9,612 serial subscriptions, 13,470 audiovisual materials, an OPAC, a Web page.

Student Life *Housing:* college housing not available. *Activities and Organizations:* drama/theater group, student-run newspaper, choral group, Student Government, Raising Awareness Club, Environmental Club, First Year Experience,

Gamers. *Campus security:* 24-hour emergency response devices and patrols, student patrols, classroom doors that lock from the inside; campus alert system.

Athletics Member NJCAA. *Intercollegiate sports:* baseball M(s), basketball M(s)/W(s), golf M(s)/W, soccer M(s)/W(s), softball W(s), volleyball W(s). *Intramural sports:* basketball M/W, bowling M/W, football M, golf M/W, softball M/W, table tennis M/W, tennis M/W, volleyball M/W, weight lifting M.

Costs (2012–13) *Tuition:* state resident $3455 full-time, $123 per credit part-time; nonresident $6910 full-time, $247 per credit part-time. Full-time tuition and fees vary according to course load and reciprocity agreements. Part-time tuition and fees vary according to course load and reciprocity agreements. *Required fees:* $454 full-time, $16 per credit part-time, $16 per credit part-time. *Payment plans:* installment, deferred payment. *Waivers:* senior citizens and employees or children of employees.

Applying *Options:* electronic application, early admission. *Required for some:* minimum 2.0 GPA, interview. *Recommended:* high school transcript. *Application deadlines:* rolling (freshmen), rolling (out-of-state freshmen), rolling (transfers). *Notification:* continuous (freshmen), continuous (out-of-state freshmen), continuous (transfers).

Freshman Application Contact Mr. Cory Stine, Director, Admissions, Owens Community College, P.O. Box 10000, Toledo, OH 43699. *Phone:* 567-661-7515. *Toll-free phone:* 800-GO-OWENS. *Fax:* 567-661-7734. *E-mail:* cory_stine@owens.edu. *Web site:* http://www.owens.edu/.

Professional Skills Institute

Toledo, Ohio

Director of Admissions Ms. Hope Finch, Director of Marketing, Professional Skills Institute, 20 Arco Drive, Toledo, OH 43607. *Phone:* 419-531-9610. *Web site:* http://www.proskills.com/.

Remington College–Cleveland Campus

Cleveland, Ohio

Director of Admissions Director of Recruitment, Remington College–Cleveland Campus, 14445 Broadway Avenue, Cleveland, OH 44125. *Phone:* 216-475-7520. *Fax:* 216-475-6055. *Web site:* http://www.remingtoncollege.edu/.

Remington College–Cleveland West Campus

North Olmstead, Ohio

Freshman Application Contact Remington College–Cleveland West Campus, 26350 Brookpark Road, North Olmstead, OH 44070. *Phone:* 440-777-2560. *Web site:* http://www.remingtoncollege.edu/.

Rosedale Bible College

Irwin, Ohio

Director of Admissions Mr. John Showalter, Director of Enrollment Services, Rosedale Bible College, 2270 Rosedale Road, Irwin, OH 43029-9501. *Phone:* 740-857-1311. *Fax:* 740-857-1577. *E-mail:* pweber@rosedale.edu. *Web site:* http://www.rosedalebible.org/.

School of Advertising Art

Kettering, Ohio

- **Proprietary** 2-year, founded 1983
- **Suburban** 5-acre campus with easy access to Columbus
- **Coed**

Undergraduates 116 full-time. Students come from 3 states and territories; 2% are from out of state; 2% Black or African American, non-Hispanic/Latino; 2% Hispanic/Latino; 0.9% Native Hawaiian or other Pacific Islander, non-Hispanic/Latino; 4% Race/ethnicity unknown. *Retention:* 86% of full-time freshmen returned.

Faculty *Student/faculty ratio:* 14:1.

Academics *Calendar:* trimesters. *Degree:* diplomas and associate.

Costs (2011–12) *One-time required fee:* $100. *Tuition:* $21,960 full-time. *Required fees:* $1145 full-time.

Applying *Options:* electronic application. *Required:* high school transcript, minimum 2.0 GPA, interview. *Required for some:* essay or personal statement, 2 letters of recommendation.

Freshman Application Contact Ms. Abigail Heaney, Admissions, School of Advertising Art, 1725 East David Road, Kettering, OH 45440. *Phone:* 937-294-0592. *Toll-free phone:* 877-300-9866. *Fax:* 937-294-5869. *E-mail:* Abbie@saa.edu. *Web site:* http://www.saa.edu/.

Sinclair Community College

Dayton, Ohio

Freshman Application Contact Ms. Sara Smith, Director and Systems Manager, Outreach Services, Sinclair Community College, 444 West Third Street, Dayton, OH 45402-1460. *Phone:* 937-512-3060. *Toll-free phone:* 800-315-3000. *Fax:* 937-512-2393. *E-mail:* ssmith@sinclair.edu. *Web site:* http://www.sinclair.edu/.

Southern State Community College

Hillsboro, Ohio

- **State-supported** 2-year, founded 1975
- **Rural** 60-acre campus
- **Endowment** $1.9 million
- **Coed**, 3,350 undergraduate students, 59% full-time, 68% women, 32% men

Undergraduates 1,970 full-time, 1,380 part-time. 2% Black or African American, non-Hispanic/Latino; 0.5% Hispanic/Latino; 0.7% Asian, non-Hispanic/Latino; 0.1% Native Hawaiian or other Pacific Islander, non-Hispanic/Latino; 0.2% American Indian or Alaska Native, non-Hispanic/Latino; 1% Two or more races, non-Hispanic/Latino; 2% Race/ethnicity unknown.

Freshmen *Admission:* 443 applied, 443 admitted, 443 enrolled.

Faculty *Total:* 204, 29% full-time, 9% with terminal degrees. *Student/faculty ratio:* 17:1.

Majors Accounting technology and bookkeeping; administrative assistant and secretarial science; agricultural production; agriculture; business administration and management; business/commerce; CAD/CADD drafting/design technology; computer programming; computer programming (specific applications); computer systems analysis; computer technology/computer systems technology; corrections; criminal justice/law enforcement administration; criminal justice/police science; drafting and design technology; early childhood education; electrical, electronic and communications engineering technology; electromechanical technology; emergency medical technology (EMT paramedic); entrepreneurship; executive assistant/executive secretary; food technology and processing; human services; kindergarten/preschool education; liberal arts and sciences/liberal studies; medical/clinical assistant; real estate; registered nursing/registered nurse; respiratory care therapy; substance abuse/addiction counseling; teacher assistant/aide.

Academics *Calendar:* quarters. *Degree:* certificates and associate. *Special study options:* academic remediation for entering students, advanced placement credit, cooperative education, distance learning, double majors, independent study, internships, off-campus study, part-time degree program, services for LD students, student-designed majors, summer session for credit.

Library Learning Resources Center plus 3 others with 61,110 titles, 229 serial subscriptions, 3,365 audiovisual materials, an OPAC, a Web page.

Student Life *Housing:* college housing not available. *Activities and Organizations:* drama/theater group, choral group, Student Government Association, Drama Club. *Student services:* personal/psychological counseling.

Athletics Member USCAA. *Intercollegiate sports:* baseball M(c), basketball M(s)/W(s), soccer M(s), softball W(s), volleyball W(s).

Costs (2011–12) *Tuition:* state resident $3633 full-time, $93 per quarter hour part-time; nonresident $6933 full-time, $180 per quarter hour part-time. Full-time tuition and fees vary according to course load and reciprocity agreements. Part-time tuition and fees vary according to course load and reciprocity agreements. *Payment plan:* deferred payment. *Waivers:* senior citizens and employees or children of employees.

Financial Aid Of all full-time matriculated undergraduates who enrolled in 2011, 4,248 applied for aid, 3,547 were judged to have need, 3,452 had their need fully met. 56 Federal Work-Study jobs (averaging $1884). In 2011, 1457 non-need-based awards were made. *Average percent of need met:* 97%. *Average financial aid package:* $4570. *Average need-based loan:* $2247. *Average need-based gift aid:* $3560. *Average non-need-based aid:* $1549.

Applying *Options:* electronic application, early admission, deferred entrance. *Recommended:* high school transcript. *Application deadlines:* rolling (freshmen), rolling (transfers). *Notification:* continuous (freshmen), continuous (transfers).

Freshman Application Contact Ms. Wendy Johnson, Director of Admissions, Southern State Community College, Hillsboro, OH 45133. *Phone:* 937-393-3431 Ext. 2720. *Toll-free phone:* 800-628-7722. *Fax:* 937-393-6682. *E-mail:* wjohnson@sscc.edu. *Web site:* http://www.sscc.edu/.

Stark State College
North Canton, Ohio

- **State and locally supported** 2-year, founded 1970, part of Ohio Board of Regents
- **Suburban** 34-acre campus with easy access to Cleveland
- **Endowment** $2.1 million
- **Coed,** 15,536 undergraduate students, 35% full-time, 60% women, 40% men

Undergraduates 5,441 full-time, 10,095 part-time. Students come from 15 states and territories; 6 other countries; 0.8% are from out of state; 19% Black or African American, non-Hispanic/Latino; 0.8% Hispanic/Latino; 0.7% Asian, non-Hispanic/Latino; 0.1% Native Hawaiian or other Pacific Islander, non-Hispanic/Latino; 0.5% American Indian or Alaska Native, non-Hispanic/Latino; 2% Two or more races, non-Hispanic/Latino; 5% Race/ethnicity unknown; 5% transferred in. *Retention:* 45% of full-time freshmen returned.
Freshmen *Admission:* 3,067 enrolled. *Test scores:* ACT scores over 18: 48%; ACT scores over 24: 6%; ACT scores over 30: 1%.
Faculty *Total:* 730, 27% full-time. *Student/faculty ratio:* 23:1.
Majors Accounting; administrative assistant and secretarial science; architectural engineering technology; automobile/automotive mechanics technology; biomedical technology; business administration and management; child development; civil engineering technology; clinical/medical laboratory technology; computer and information sciences and support services related; computer and information sciences related; computer engineering related; computer hardware engineering; computer/information technology services administration related; computer programming; computer programming related; computer programming (specific applications); computer programming (vendor/product certification); computer software and media applications related; computer software engineering; computer systems networking and telecommunications; consumer merchandising/retailing management; court reporting; data entry/microcomputer applications; data entry/microcomputer applications related; dental hygiene; drafting and design technology; environmental studies; finance; fire science/firefighting; food technology and processing; health information/medical records administration; human services; industrial technology; information technology; international business/trade/commerce; legal administrative assistant/secretary; marketing/marketing management; mechanical engineering/mechanical technology; medical/clinical assistant; occupational therapy; operations management; physical therapy; registered nursing/registered nurse; respiratory care therapy; surveying technology; web/multimedia management and webmaster; web page, digital/multimedia and information resources design; word processing.
Academics *Calendar:* semesters. *Degree:* certificates and associate. *Special study options:* academic remediation for entering students, adult/continuing education programs, distance learning, external degree program, independent study, off-campus study, part-time degree program, services for LD students, student-designed majors, summer session for credit.
Library Learning Resource Center plus 1 other with 82,728 titles, 23,331 serial subscriptions, an OPAC.
Student Life *Housing:* college housing not available. *Activities and Organizations:* student-run newspaper, Phi Theta Kappa, Business Student Club, Institute of Management Accountants, Stark State College Association of Medical Assistants, Student Health Information Management Association. *Campus security:* 24-hour emergency response devices, late-night transport/escort service. *Student services:* personal/psychological counseling.
Standardized Tests *Recommended:* SAT or ACT (for admission).
Costs (2011–12) *Tuition:* state resident $4215 full-time, $141 per credit hour part-time; nonresident $6465 full-time, $216 per credit hour part-time. Full-time tuition and fees vary according to course load and program. Part-time tuition and fees vary according to program. *Payment plan:* installment. *Waivers:* senior citizens and employees or children of employees.
Financial Aid Of all full-time matriculated undergraduates who enrolled in 2010, 194 Federal Work-Study jobs (averaging $2383).
Applying *Options:* electronic application, early admission, deferred entrance. *Application fee:* $65. *Required:* high school transcript. *Application deadlines:* rolling (freshmen), rolling (transfers).
Freshman Application Contact Mr. Wallace Hoffer, Dean of Student Services, Stark State College, 6200 Frank Road, NW, Canton, OH 44720. *Phone:* 330-966-5450. *Toll-free phone:* 800-797-8275. *Fax:* 330-497-6313. *E-mail:* info@starkstate.edu. *Web site:* http://www.starkstate.edu/.

Stautzenberger College
Maumee, Ohio

Director of Admissions Ms. Karen Fitzgerald, Director of Admissions and Marketing, Stautzenberger College, 1796 Indian Wood Circle, Maumee, OH 43537. *Phone:* 419-866-0261. *Toll-free phone:* 800-552-5099. *Fax:* 419-867-9821. *E-mail:* klfitzgerald@stautzenberger.com. *Web site:* http://www.stautzen.edu/.

Terra State Community College
Fremont, Ohio

- **State-supported** 2-year, founded 1968, part of Ohio Board of Regents
- **Small-town** 100-acre campus with easy access to Toledo
- **Coed,** 3,566 undergraduate students, 43% full-time, 58% women, 42% men

Undergraduates 1,530 full-time, 2,036 part-time. Students come from 7 states and territories; 4 other countries; 0.2% are from out of state; 6% Black or African American, non-Hispanic/Latino; 8% Hispanic/Latino; 0.3% Asian, non-Hispanic/Latino; 0.4% American Indian or Alaska Native, non-Hispanic/Latino; 0.9% Two or more races, non-Hispanic/Latino; 3% Race/ethnicity unknown; 0.4% international; 2% transferred in. *Retention:* 40% of full-time freshmen returned.
Freshmen *Admission:* 653 applied, 653 admitted, 653 enrolled.
Faculty *Total:* 217, 21% full-time, 5% with terminal degrees. *Student/faculty ratio:* 20:1.
Majors Accounting; agricultural business and management; animation, interactive technology, video graphics and special effects; architectural engineering technology; art history, criticism and conservation; automotive engineering technology; banking and financial support services; biological and physical sciences; biology/biological sciences; business administration and management; business/commerce; chemistry; commercial and advertising art; computer and information sciences; computer programming; computer systems networking and telecommunications; criminal justice/police science; data processing and data processing technology; desktop publishing and digital imaging design; economics; education; electrical and electronic engineering technologies related; electrical, electronic and communications engineering technology; engineering; English; executive assistant/executive secretary; fine/studio arts; general studies; health/health-care administration; health information/medical records administration; health information/medical records technology; health professions related; heating, ventilation, air conditioning and refrigeration engineering technology; history; hospitality administration; humanities; kindergarten/preschool education; language interpretation and translation; liberal arts and sciences/liberal studies; manufacturing engineering technology; marketing/marketing management; mathematics; mechanical engineering/mechanical technology; mechanical engineering technologies related; medical administrative assistant and medical secretary; medical/clinical assistant; medical/health management and clinical assistant; medical insurance coding; medical office assistant; music; music management; music performance; music related; nuclear/nuclear power technology; operations management; physics; plastics and polymer engineering technology; psychology; real estate; registered nursing/registered nurse; robotics technology; sheet metal technology; social sciences; social work; teaching assistants/aides related; web page, digital/multimedia and information resources design; welding technology.
Academics *Calendar:* semesters. *Degree:* certificates, diplomas, and associate. *Special study options:* academic remediation for entering students, adult/continuing education programs, advanced placement credit, cooperative education, distance learning, double majors, independent study, internships, off-campus study, part-time degree program, services for LD students, student-designed majors, summer session for credit.
Library Learning Resource Center with 22,675 titles, 383 serial subscriptions, an OPAC, a Web page.
Student Life *Housing:* college housing not available. *Activities and Organizations:* choral group, Phi Theta Kappa, Student Activities Club, Society of Plastic Engineers, Koinonia, Student Senate. *Campus security:* 24-hour emergency response devices. *Student services:* personal/psychological counseling, legal services.
Athletics *Intramural sports:* basketball M/W, bowling M/W, football M, golf M/W, table tennis M/W, volleyball M/W.
Financial Aid Of all full-time matriculated undergraduates who enrolled in 2010, 57 Federal Work-Study jobs (averaging $1450).
Applying *Options:* electronic application, early admission, deferred entrance. *Required:* high school transcript. *Application deadlines:* rolling (freshmen), rolling (transfers).
Freshman Application Contact Ms. Kristen Taylor, Director of Admissions and Enrollment Services, Terra State Community College, 2830 Napoleon Road, Fremont, OH 43420. *Phone:* 419-559-2154. *Toll-free phone:* 866-AT-TERRA. *Fax:* 419-559-2352. *E-mail:* ktaylor01@terra.edu. *Web site:* http://www.terra.edu/.

Trumbull Business College
Warren, Ohio

Director of Admissions Admissions Office, Trumbull Business College, 3200 Ridge Road, Warren, OH 44484. *Phone:* 330-369-6792. *Toll-free phone:* 888-766-1598. *E-mail:* admissions@tbc-trumbullbusiness.com. *Web site:* http://www.tbc-trumbullbusiness.com/.

The University of Akron–Wayne College

Orrville, Ohio

- **State-supported** primarily 2-year, founded 1972, part of The University of Akron
- **Rural** 157-acre campus
- **Coed,** 2,502 undergraduate students, 53% full-time, 61% women, 39% men

Undergraduates 1,327 full-time, 1,175 part-time. Students come from 5 states and territories; 2 other countries; 8% Black or African American, non-Hispanic/Latino; 1% Hispanic/Latino; 0.6% Asian, non-Hispanic/Latino; 0.4% American Indian or Alaska Native, non-Hispanic/Latino; 1% Two or more races, non-Hispanic/Latino; 3% Race/ethnicity unknown; 3% transferred in. *Retention:* 48% of full-time freshmen returned.

Freshmen *Admission:* 859 applied, 780 admitted, 389 enrolled. *Average high school GPA:* 3.16. *Test scores:* ACT scores over 18: 69%; ACT scores over 24: 15%; ACT scores over 30: 1%.

Faculty *Total:* 174, 16% full-time, 22% with terminal degrees. *Student/faculty ratio:* 23:1.

Majors Administrative assistant and secretarial science; business administration and management; general studies; liberal arts and sciences/liberal studies; medical office management; social work.

Academics *Calendar:* semesters. *Degrees:* certificates, associate, and bachelor's. *Special study options:* academic remediation for entering students, adult/continuing education programs, advanced placement credit, cooperative education, distance learning, double majors, English as a second language, honors programs, independent study, internships, off-campus study, part-time degree program, services for LD students, summer session for credit. *ROTC:* Army (c), Air Force (c).

Library Wayne College Library with 19,541 titles, 124 serial subscriptions, 1,641 audiovisual materials, an OPAC, a Web page.

Student Life *Housing:* college housing not available. *Campus security:* 24-hour emergency response devices, late-night transport/escort service. *Student services:* personal/psychological counseling.

Athletics *Intercollegiate sports:* basketball M/W, cheerleading W, golf M, volleyball W. *Intramural sports:* basketball M/W, golf M, volleyball M/W.

Standardized Tests *Required for some:* SAT or ACT (for admission), ACT COMPASS. *Recommended:* SAT or ACT (for admission), ACT COMPASS.

Costs (2011–12) *Tuition:* state resident $5740 full-time; nonresident $13,526 full-time. Full-time tuition and fees vary according to course load and location. Part-time tuition and fees vary according to course load and location. *Required fees:* $170 full-time. *Payment plan:* installment. *Waivers:* employees or children of employees.

Financial Aid Of all full-time matriculated undergraduates who enrolled in 2010, 8 Federal Work-Study jobs (averaging $2200).

Applying *Options:* electronic application, early admission, deferred entrance. *Application fee:* $40. *Required for some:* high school transcript. *Application deadlines:* 8/30 (freshmen), 8/30 (transfers). *Notification:* continuous until 8/30 (freshmen), continuous until 8/30 (transfers).

Freshman Application Contact Ms. Alicia Broadus, Student Services Counselor, The University of Akron–Wayne College, Orrville, OH 44667. *Phone:* 800-221-8308 Ext. 8901. *Toll-free phone:* 800-221-8308. *Fax:* 330-684-8989. *E-mail:* wayneadmissions@uakron.edu. *Web site:* http://www.wayne.uakron.edu/.

University of Cincinnati Blue Ash

Cincinnati, Ohio

Freshman Application Contact Leigh Schlegal, Admission Counselor, University of Cincinnati Blue Ash, 9555 Plainfield Road, Cincinnati, OH 45236-1007. *Phone:* 513-745-5783. *Fax:* 513-745-5768. *Web site:* http://www.ucblueash.edu/.

University of Cincinnati Clermont College

Batavia, Ohio

Freshman Application Contact Mrs. Jamie Adkins, Records Management Officer, University of Cincinnati Clermont College, 4200 Clermont College Drive, Batavia, OH 45103. *Phone:* 513-732-5294. *Fax:* 513-732-5303. *E-mail:* jamie.adkins@uc.edu. *Web site:* http://www.ucclermont.edu/.

Vatterott College

Broadview Heights, Ohio

Director of Admissions Mr. Jack Chalk, Director of Admissions, Vatterott College, 5025 East Royalton Road, Broadview Heights, OH 44147. *Phone:* 440-526-1660. *Toll-free phone:* 888-553-6627. *Web site:* http://www.vatterott-college.edu/.

Vet Tech Institute at Bradford School

Columbus, Ohio

- **Private** 2-year, founded 2005
- **Suburban** campus
- **Coed,** 194 undergraduate students
- 31% of applicants were admitted

Freshmen *Admission:* 674 applied, 209 admitted.

Majors Veterinary/animal health technology.

Academics *Degree:* associate. *Special study options:* accelerated degree program, internships.

Freshman Application Contact Admissions Office, Vet Tech Institute at Bradford School, 2469 Stelzer Road, Columbus, OH 43219. *Phone:* 800-678-7981. *Toll-free phone:* 800-678-7981. *Web site:* http://www.vettechinstitute.edu/.

Virginia Marti College of Art and Design

Lakewood, Ohio

Freshman Application Contact Virginia Marti College of Art and Design, 11724 Detroit Avenue, PO Box 580, Lakewood, OH 44107-3002. *Phone:* 216-221-8584 Ext. 106. *Web site:* http://www.vmcad.edu/.

Washington State Community College

Marietta, Ohio

Freshman Application Contact Ms. Rebecca Peroni, Director of Admissions, Washington State Community College, 110 Coligate Drive, Marietta, OH 45750. *Phone:* 740-374-8716. *Fax:* 740-376-0257. *E-mail:* rperoni@wscc.edu. *Web site:* http://www.wscc.edu/.

Wright State University, Lake Campus

Celina, Ohio

Freshman Application Contact Sandra Gilbert, Student Services Officer, Wright State University, Lake Campus, 7600 State Route 703, Celina, OH 45822-2921. *Phone:* 419-586-0324. *Toll-free phone:* 800-237-1477. *Fax:* 419-586-0358. *Web site:* http://www.wright.edu/lake/.

Zane State College

Zanesville, Ohio

Director of Admissions Mr. Paul Young, Director of Admissions, Zane State College, 1555 Newark Road, Zanesville, OH 43701-2626. *Phone:* 740-454-2501 Ext. 1225. *Toll-free phone:* 800-686-8324. *E-mail:* pyoung@zanestate.edu. *Web site:* http://www.zanestate.edu/.

OKLAHOMA

Brown Mackie College–Oklahoma City

Oklahoma City, Oklahoma

- **Proprietary** 2-year, part of Education Management Corporation
- **Coed**

Costs (2011–12) *Tuition:* Tuition varies by program. Students should contact Brown Mackie College for tuition information.

Admissions Office Contact Brown Mackie College–Oklahoma City, 7101 Northwest Expressway, Suite 800, Oklahoma City, OK 73132. *Toll-free phone:* 888-229-3280. *Web site:* http://www.brownmackie.edu/oklahoma-city/

See page 376 for the College Close-Up.

Brown Mackie College–Tulsa

Tulsa, Oklahoma

- **Proprietary** primarily 2-year, part of Education Management Corporation
- **Coed**

Academics *Degrees:* diplomas, associate, and bachelor's.

Costs (2011–12) *Tuition:* Tuition varies by program. Students should contact Brown Mackie College for tuition information.

Freshman Application Contact Brown Mackie College–Tulsa, 4608 South Garnett, Suite 110, Tulsa, OK 74146. *Phone:* 918-628-3700. *Toll-free phone:* 888-794-8411. *Web site:* http://www.brownmackie.edu/tulsa/.

See page 392 for the College Close-Up.

Carl Albert State College

Poteau, Oklahoma

- **State-supported** 2-year, founded 1934, part of Oklahoma State Regents for Higher Education
- **Small-town** 78-acre campus
- **Endowment** $5.7 million
- **Coed,** 2,460 undergraduate students, 56% full-time, 66% women, 34% men

Undergraduates 1,373 full-time, 1,087 part-time. Students come from 16 states and territories; 9 other countries.

Freshmen *Admission:* 605 enrolled.

Faculty *Total:* 154, 33% full-time, 2% with terminal degrees. *Student/faculty ratio:* 16:1.

Majors Biology/biological sciences; business administration and management; business/commerce; child development; computer and information sciences; elementary education; engineering; engineering technologies and engineering related; English; film/cinema/video studies; fine arts related; foods, nutrition, and wellness; health professions related; health services/allied health/health sciences; hotel/motel administration; journalism; management information systems; mathematics; music related; physical education teaching and coaching; physical sciences; physical therapy technology; pre-law studies; radiologic technology/science; registered nursing/registered nurse; rhetoric and composition; secondary education; social sciences; telecommunications technology.

Academics *Calendar:* semesters. *Degree:* certificates and associate. *Special study options:* academic remediation for entering students, adult/continuing education programs, cooperative education, part-time degree program.

Library Joe E. White Library with 27,200 titles, 1,350 serial subscriptions, an OPAC.

Student Life *Housing Options:* Campus housing is university owned. *Activities and Organizations:* drama/theater group, student-run newspaper, radio station, choral group, Student Government Association, Phi Theta Kappa, Baptist Student Union, BACCHUS, Student Physical Therapist Assistant Association. *Campus security:* security guards. *Student services:* health clinic, personal/psychological counseling.

Athletics Member NJCAA. *Intercollegiate sports:* baseball M, basketball M(s)/W(s), softball M. *Intramural sports:* tennis M/W, volleyball M/W, weight lifting M.

Financial Aid Of all full-time matriculated undergraduates who enrolled in 2010, 136 Federal Work-Study jobs (averaging $1761).

Applying *Required:* high school transcript. *Application deadlines:* 8/13 (freshmen), 8/15 (transfers). *Notification:* continuous (freshmen), continuous (transfers).

Freshman Application Contact Dawn Webster, Admission Clerk, Carl Albert State College, 1507 South McKenna, Poteau, OK 74953-5208. *Phone:* 918-647-1300. *Fax:* 918-647-1306. *E-mail:* dwebster@carlalbert.edu. *Web site:* http://www.carlalbert.edu/.

Clary Sage College

Tulsa, Oklahoma

- **Proprietary** 2-year, part of Dental Directions, Inc.
- **Urban** 6-acre campus
- **Coed, primarily women,** 322 undergraduate students, 100% full-time, 98% women, 2% men

Undergraduates 322 full-time. Students come from 2 states and territories; 10% Black or African American, non-Hispanic/Latino; 3% Hispanic/Latino; 0.6% Asian, non-Hispanic/Latino; 3% American Indian or Alaska Native, non-Hispanic/Latino; 46% Race/ethnicity unknown.

Freshmen *Admission:* 95 enrolled.

Faculty *Total:* 26, 96% full-time. *Student/faculty ratio:* 13:1.

Majors Cosmetology; fashion/apparel design; interior design.

Academics *Degree:* diplomas and associate. *Special study options:* adult/continuing education programs, distance learning, internships, part-time degree program.

Student Life *Housing:* college housing not available. *Activities and Organizations:* Student Ambassadors. *Campus security:* security guard during hours of operation.. *Student services:* personal/psychological counseling.

Costs (2012–13) *Tuition:* $17,808 full-time. Full-time tuition and fees vary according to class time, course level, course load, degree level, location, program, and reciprocity agreements. Part-time tuition and fees vary according to class time, course level, location, and reciprocity agreements. *Required fees:* $2478 full-time. *Payment plans:* tuition prepayment, installment. *Waivers:* employees or children of employees.

Applying *Options:* electronic application. *Application fee:* $100. *Required:* essay or personal statement, high school transcript, interview. *Application deadlines:* rolling (freshmen), rolling (out-of-state freshmen), rolling (transfers). *Notification:* continuous (freshmen), continuous (out-of-state freshmen), continuous (transfers).

Freshman Application Contact Ms. Rebecca Banuelos, Director of Marketing, Clary Sage College, 3131 South Sheridan, Tulsa, OK 74145. *Phone:* 918-610-0027 Ext. 2002. *E-mail:* rbanuelos@communitycarecollege.edu. *Web site:* http://www.clarysagecollege.com/.

Community Care College

Tulsa, Oklahoma

- **Proprietary** 2-year, founded 1995, part of Dental Directions, Inc.
- **Urban** 6-acre campus
- **Coed, primarily women,** 942 undergraduate students, 100% full-time, 91% women, 9% men

Undergraduates 942 full-time. Students come from 14 states and territories; 11% are from out of state; 17% Black or African American, non-Hispanic/Latino; 4% Hispanic/Latino; 2% Asian, non-Hispanic/Latino; 10% American Indian or Alaska Native, non-Hispanic/Latino; 0.1% Two or more races, non-Hispanic/Latino; 7% Race/ethnicity unknown.

Freshmen *Admission:* 227 enrolled.

Faculty *Total:* 35, 100% full-time. *Student/faculty ratio:* 27:1.

Majors Business administration, management and operations related; dental assisting; early childhood education; health and physical education/fitness; health/health-care administration; legal assistant/paralegal; massage therapy; medical/clinical assistant; medical insurance coding; pharmacy technician; surgical technology; veterinary/animal health technology.

Academics *Calendar:* continuous. *Degree:* diplomas and associate. *Special study options:* adult/continuing education programs, distance learning, independent study, internships, services for LD students.

Student Life *Housing:* college housing not available. *Activities and Organizations:* Student Ambassadors. *Campus security:* campus security personnel are available during school hours. *Student services:* personal/psychological counseling.

Costs (2012–13) *Tuition:* $21,121 full-time. Full-time tuition and fees vary according to class time, course level, course load, degree level, location, program, and reciprocity agreements. Part-time tuition and fees vary according to class time, course level, location, and reciprocity agreements. *Required fees:* $2546 full-time. *Payment plans:* tuition prepayment, installment. *Waivers:* employees or children of employees.

Applying *Options:* electronic application. *Application fee:* $100. *Required:* essay or personal statement, high school transcript, interview. *Required for some:* 1 letter of recommendation. *Application deadlines:* rolling (freshmen), rolling (out-of-state freshmen). *Notification:* continuous (freshmen), continuous (out-of-state freshmen).

Freshman Application Contact Ms. Teresa L. Knox, Chief Executive Officer, Community Care College, 4242 South Sheridan, Tulsa, OK 74145. *Phone:* 918-610-0027 Ext. 2005. *Fax:* 918-610-0029. *E-mail:* tknox@communitycarecollege.edu. *Web site:* http://www.communitycarecollege.edu/.

Connors State College

Warner, Oklahoma

Freshman Application Contact Ms. Sonya Baker, Registrar, Connors State College, Route 1 Box 1000, Warner, OK 74469-9700. *Phone:* 918-463-6233. *Web site:* http://www.connorsstate.edu/.

Eastern Oklahoma State College

Wilburton, Oklahoma

Freshman Application Contact Ms. Leah McLaughlin, Director of Admissions, Eastern Oklahoma State College, 1301 West Main, Wilburton, OK 74578-4999. *Phone:* 918-465-1811. *Toll-free phone:* 855-534-3672. *Fax:* 918-465-2431. *E-mail:* lmiller@eosc.edu. *Web site:* http://www.eosc.edu/.

Heritage College
Oklahoma City, Oklahoma

Freshman Application Contact Admissions Office, Heritage College, 7100 I-35 Services Road, Suite 7118, Oklahoma City, OK 73149. *Phone:* 405-631-3399. *Toll-free phone:* 888-334-7339. *E-mail:* info@heritage-education.com. *Web site:* http://www.heritage-education.com/campus_oklahoma.htm.

ITT Technical Institute
Tulsa, Oklahoma

- **Proprietary** primarily 2-year, founded 2005
- **Coed**

Majors Business administration and management; communications technology; computer and information systems security; computer software engineering; computer software technology; construction management; criminal justice/law enforcement administration; drafting and design technology; electrical, electronic and communications engineering technology; forensic science and technology; graphic communications; legal assistant/paralegal; network and system administration; project management; registered nursing/registered nurse.

Academics *Calendar:* quarters. *Degrees:* associate and bachelor's.

Student Life *Housing:* college housing not available.

Freshman Application Contact Director of Recruitment, ITT Technical Institute, 4500 South 129th East Avenue, Suite 152, Tulsa, OK 74134. *Phone:* 918-615-3900. *Toll-free phone:* 800-514-6535. *Web site:* http://www.itt-tech.edu/.

Murray State College
Tishomingo, Oklahoma

- **State-supported** 2-year, founded 1908, part of Oklahoma State Regents for Higher Education
- **Rural** 120-acre campus
- **Coed,** 2,674 undergraduate students, 49% full-time, 70% women, 30% men

Undergraduates 1,317 full-time, 1,357 part-time. Students come from 19 states and territories; 9 other countries; 4% are from out of state; 5% Black or African American, non-Hispanic/Latino; 6% Hispanic/Latino; 0.3% Asian, non-Hispanic/Latino; 0.1% Native Hawaiian or other Pacific Islander, non-Hispanic/Latino; 13% American Indian or Alaska Native, non-Hispanic/Latino; 9% Two or more races, non-Hispanic/Latino; 2% Race/ethnicity unknown; 0.1% international; 11% live on campus. *Retention:* 49% of full-time freshmen returned.

Faculty *Total:* 152, 38% full-time. *Student/faculty ratio:* 20:1.

Majors Agricultural teacher education; agriculture; biological and biomedical sciences related; biology/biological sciences; chemistry; child-care provision; child development; computer and information sciences; corrections and criminal justice related; elementary education; fine arts related; general studies; gunsmithing; history; humanities; industrial production technologies related; information science/studies; management science; mathematics; natural resources and conservation related; occupational therapist assistant; physical education teaching and coaching; physical therapy technology; psychology related; registered nursing/registered nurse; veterinary/animal health technology.

Academics *Calendar:* semesters. *Degree:* associate. *Special study options:* academic remediation for entering students, advanced placement credit, distance learning, honors programs, internships, part-time degree program, services for LD students, summer session for credit.

Library Murray State College Library plus 1 other with 19,698 titles, 47 serial subscriptions, 1,316 audiovisual materials, an OPAC, a Web page.

Student Life *Housing:* on-campus residence required for freshman year. *Options:* coed, men-only, disabled students. Campus housing is university owned. Freshman campus housing is guaranteed. *Activities and Organizations:* drama/theater group, choral group. *Campus security:* 24-hour patrols. *Student services:* personal/psychological counseling.

Athletics Member NJCAA. *Intercollegiate sports:* baseball M(s), basketball M(s)/W(s), cheerleading M/W, golf M(s)/W(s), softball W(s). *Intramural sports:* basketball M/W.

Standardized Tests *Required:* SAT or ACT (for admission).

Financial Aid Of all full-time matriculated undergraduates who enrolled in 2010, 68 Federal Work-Study jobs (averaging $3354). 20 state and other part-time jobs (averaging $2516).

Applying *Options:* electronic application, early admission. *Required:* high school transcript. *Application deadlines:* rolling (freshmen), rolling (transfers). *Notification:* continuous (freshmen), continuous (transfers).

Freshman Application Contact Murray State College, One Murray Campus, Tishomingo, OK 73460-3130. *Phone:* 580-371-2371 Ext. 171. *Web site:* http://www.mscok.edu/.

Northeastern Oklahoma Agricultural and Mechanical College
Miami, Oklahoma

Freshman Application Contact Amy Ishmael, Vice President for Enrollment Management, Northeastern Oklahoma Agricultural and Mechanical College, 200 I Street, NE, Miami, OK 74354-6434. *Phone:* 918-540-6212. *Toll-free phone:* 800-464-6636. *Fax:* 918-540-6946. *E-mail:* neoadmission@neo.edu. *Web site:* http://www.neo.edu/.

Northern Oklahoma College
Tonkawa, Oklahoma

Freshman Application Contact Ms. Sheri Snyder, Director of College Relations, Northern Oklahoma College, 1220 East Grand Avenue, PO Box 310, Tonkawa, OK 74653-0310. *Phone:* 580-628-6290. *Web site:* http://www.north-ok.edu/.

Oklahoma City Community College
Oklahoma City, Oklahoma

- **State-supported** 2-year, founded 1969, part of Oklahoma State Regents for Higher Education
- **Urban** 143-acre campus
- **Endowment** $292,271
- **Coed,** 14,941 undergraduate students, 38% full-time, 58% women, 42% men

Undergraduates 5,647 full-time, 9,294 part-time. Students come from 23 states and territories; 41 other countries; 4% are from out of state; 11% Black or African American, non-Hispanic/Latino; 5% Hispanic/Latino; 4% Asian, non-Hispanic/Latino; 0.3% Native Hawaiian or other Pacific Islander, non-Hispanic/Latino; 7% American Indian or Alaska Native, non-Hispanic/Latino; 8% Race/ethnicity unknown; 4% international.

Freshmen *Admission:* 5,472 applied, 5,472 admitted, 2,805 enrolled. *Test scores:* ACT scores over 18: 70%; ACT scores over 24: 16%.

Faculty *Total:* 629, 24% full-time, 9% with terminal degrees. *Student/faculty ratio:* 28:1.

Majors Accounting; airframe mechanics and aircraft maintenance technology; American government and politics; architectural drafting and CAD/CADD; art; automobile/automotive mechanics technology; avionics maintenance technology; biology/biological sciences; biotechnology; broadcast journalism; business administration and management; chemistry; child development; cinematography and film/video production; commercial and advertising art; comparative literature; computer engineering technology; computer science; computer systems analysis; data entry/microcomputer applications; design and applied arts related; design and visual communications; diagnostic medical sonography and ultrasound technology; diesel mechanics technology; drafting and design technology; dramatic/theater arts; electrical, electronic and communications engineering technology; elementary education; emergency medical technology (EMT paramedic); engineering technologies and engineering related; finance; fine/studio arts; foreign languages and literatures; health information/medical records administration; history; humanities; liberal arts and sciences/liberal studies; manufacturing engineering technology; mass communication/media; mathematics; medical/clinical assistant; modern Greek; modern languages; multi/interdisciplinary studies related; music; occupational therapy; orthotics/prosthetics; parks, recreation and leisure facilities management; philosophy; physical therapy; physics; political science and government; pre-engineering; psychology; registered nursing/registered nurse; respiratory care therapy; sociology; surgical technology; system, networking, and LAN/WAN management.

Academics *Calendar:* semesters. *Degree:* certificates and associate. *Special study options:* academic remediation for entering students, accelerated degree program, advanced placement credit, cooperative education, distance learning, double majors, English as a second language, honors programs, independent study, internships, part-time degree program, services for LD students, student-designed majors, summer session for credit.

Library Keith Leftwich Memorial Library with 94,367 titles, 14,960 serial subscriptions, 14,250 audiovisual materials, an OPAC, a Web page.

Student Life *Housing:* college housing not available. *Activities and Organizations:* drama/theater group, student-run newspaper, choral group, Health Professions Association, Black Student Association, Nursing Student Association, Hispanic Organization Promoting Education (H.O.P.E), Phi Theta Kappa (Honorary). *Campus security:* 24-hour emergency response devices and patrols, late-night transport/escort service. *Student services:* personal/psychological counseling.

Athletics *Intramural sports:* basketball M/W, bowling M/W, football M/W, rock climbing M/W, soccer M(c)/W(c), volleyball M/W, weight lifting M/W.

Standardized Tests *Required for some:* ACT (for admission). *Recommended:* SAT or ACT (for admission).

Costs (2012–13) *One-time required fee:* $25. *Tuition:* state resident $2147 full-time, $72 per credit hour part-time; nonresident $6767 full-time, $226 per credit hour part-time. Full-time tuition and fees vary according to class time, course load, and program. Part-time tuition and fees vary according to class time, course load, and program. *Required fees:* $704 full-time, $23 per credit hour part-time. *Payment plan:* installment. *Waivers:* senior citizens and employees or children of employees.

Financial Aid Of all full-time matriculated undergraduates who enrolled in 2010, 4,062 applied for aid, 3,608 were judged to have need, 1,576 had their need fully met. 315 Federal Work-Study jobs (averaging $4800). 240 state and other part-time jobs (averaging $2502). In 2010, 321 non-need-based awards were made. *Average percent of need met:* 70%. *Average financial aid package:* $7351. *Average need-based loan:* $2801. *Average need-based gift aid:* $4769. *Average non-need-based aid:* $589.

Applying *Options:* electronic application. *Application fee:* $25. *Required for some:* high school transcript. *Application deadlines:* rolling (freshmen), rolling (out-of-state freshmen), rolling (transfers). *Notification:* continuous (freshmen), continuous (out-of-state freshmen), continuous (transfers).

Freshman Application Contact Mr. Jon Horinek, Director of Recruitment and Admissions, Oklahoma City Community College, 7777 South May Avenue, Oklahoma City, OK 73159. *Phone:* 405-682-7743. *Fax:* 405-682-7817. *E-mail:* jhorinek@occc.edu. *Web site:* http://www.occc.edu/.

Oklahoma State University Institute of Technology

Okmulgee, Oklahoma

Freshman Application Contact Mary Graves, Director, Admissions, Oklahoma State University Institute of Technology, 1801 East Fourth Street, Okmulgee, OK 74447-3901. *Phone:* 918-293-5298. *Toll-free phone:* 800-722-4471. *Fax:* 918-293-4643. *E-mail:* mary.r.graves@okstate.edu. *Web site:* http://www.osuit.edu/.

Oklahoma State University, Oklahoma City

Oklahoma City, Oklahoma

- **State-supported** primarily 2-year, founded 1961, part of Oklahoma State University
- **Urban** 110-acre campus
- **Coed,** 7,721 undergraduate students

Undergraduates Students come from 9 states and territories; 8 other countries; 1% are from out of state. *Retention:* 34% of full-time freshmen returned.

Freshmen *Admission:* 1,087 applied, 1,087 admitted.

Faculty *Total:* 381, 22% full-time. *Student/faculty ratio:* 20:1.

Majors Accounting; American Sign Language (ASL); architectural engineering technology; art; building/home/construction inspection; business administration and management; civil engineering technology; construction engineering technology; construction management; construction trades; criminal justice/police science; drafting and design technology; early childhood education; economics; electrical and power transmission installation; electrical, electronic and communications engineering technology; electrocardiograph technology; emergency medical technology (EMT paramedic); engineering technology; fire prevention and safety technology; fire science/firefighting; general studies; health/health-care administration; history; horticultural science; humanities; human services; illustration; information science/studies; information technology; language interpretation and translation; occupational safety and health technology; physics; pre-engineering; prenursing studies; professional, technical, business, and scientific writing; psychology; public administration and social service professions related; radiologic technology/science; registered nursing/registered nurse; sign language interpretation and translation; substance abuse/addiction counseling; surveying technology; turf and turfgrass management; veterinary/animal health technology; web page, digital/multimedia and information resources design.

Academics *Calendar:* semesters. *Degrees:* certificates, associate, and bachelor's. *Special study options:* academic remediation for entering students, advanced placement credit, cooperative education, distance learning, double majors, honors programs, independent study, part-time degree program, services for LD students, study abroad, summer session for credit.

Library Oklahoma State University-Oklahoma City Campus Library with 12,278 titles, 265 serial subscriptions, an OPAC, a Web page.

Student Life *Housing:* college housing not available. *Activities and Organizations:* Phi Theta Kappa, Deaf/Hearing Social Club, American Criminal Justice Association, Horticulture Club, Vet-Tech Club. *Campus security:* 24-hour patrols, late-night transport/escort service.

Costs (2011–12) *Tuition:* state resident $2534 full-time, $106 per credit hour part-time; nonresident $6836 full-time, $285 per credit hour part-time. Full-time tuition and fees vary according to course level, degree level, and program. Part-time tuition and fees vary according to course level, degree level, and program. No tuition increase for student's term of enrollment. *Required fees:* $30 full-time. *Payment plan:* installment. *Waivers:* senior citizens and employees or children of employees.

Applying *Options:* electronic application, early admission. *Required:* high school transcript. *Application deadlines:* rolling (freshmen), rolling (transfers). *Notification:* continuous (freshmen), continuous (transfers).

Freshman Application Contact Mr. Kyle Williams, Director, Enrollment Management, Oklahoma State University, Oklahoma City, 900 North Portland, AD202, Oklahoma City, OK 73107. *Phone:* 405-945-9152. *Toll-free phone:* 800-560-4099. *E-mail:* wilkylw@osuokc.edu. *Web site:* http://www.osuokc.edu/.

Oklahoma Technical College

Tulsa, Oklahoma

- **Proprietary** 2-year, part of Dental Directions, Inc.
- **Urban** 9-acre campus
- **Coed, primarily men**

Undergraduates Students come from 2 states and territories.

Faculty *Total:* 13, 100% full-time. *Student/faculty ratio:* 9:1.

Majors Automobile/automotive mechanics technology; barbering; diesel mechanics technology; welding technology.

Academics *Degree:* diplomas and associate. *Special study options:* adult/continuing education programs, distance learning, internships, services for LD students.

Student Life *Housing:* college housing not available. *Activities and Organizations:* Student Ambassadors. *Campus security:* Campus security is available during school hours. *Student services:* personal/psychological counseling.

Costs (2012–13) *Tuition:* $27,678 full-time. Full-time tuition and fees vary according to degree level, location, and program. Part-time tuition and fees vary according to degree level, location, and program. *Required fees:* $1884 full-time. *Payment plans:* tuition prepayment, installment. *Waivers:* employees or children of employees.

Applying *Options:* electronic application. *Application fee:* $100. *Required:* essay or personal statement, high school transcript, interview. *Required for some:* valid Oklahoma driver's license. *Application deadlines:* rolling (freshmen), rolling (out-of-state freshmen), rolling (transfers). *Notification:* continuous (freshmen), continuous (out-of-state freshmen), continuous (transfers).

Freshman Application Contact Ms. Rebecca Banuelos, Director of Marketing, Oklahoma Technical College, 4242 South Sheridan, Tulsa, OK 74145. *Phone:* 918-610-0027 Ext. 2002. *Fax:* 918-610-0029. *E-mail:* rbanuelos@communitycarecollege.edu. *Web site:* http://www.oklahomatechnicalcollege.com/.

Platt College

Moore, Oklahoma

Admissions Office Contact Platt College, 201 North Eastern Avenue, Moore, OK 73160. *Web site:* http://www.plattcolleges.edu/.

Platt College

Oklahoma City, Oklahoma

- **Proprietary** 2-year, founded 1979
- **Urban** campus with easy access to Oklahoma City
- **Coed**

Undergraduates 357 full-time. 30% Black or African American, non-Hispanic/Latino; 13% Hispanic/Latino; 2% Asian, non-Hispanic/Latino; 5% American Indian or Alaska Native, non-Hispanic/Latino.

Faculty *Student/faculty ratio:* 60:1.

Academics *Calendar:* continuous. *Degree:* diplomas and associate. *Special study options:* academic remediation for entering students, internships, part-time degree program.

Student Life *Campus security:* 24-hour emergency response devices, security officer for evening and Saturday classes.

Applying *Application fee:* $100.

Freshman Application Contact Ms. Kim Lamb, Director of Admissions, Platt College, 309 South Ann Arbor, Oklahoma City, OK 73128. *Phone:* 405-946-7799. *Fax:* 405-943-2150. *E-mail:* klamb@plattcollege.org. *Web site:* http://www.plattcolleges.edu/.

Platt College

Tulsa, Oklahoma

Director of Admissions Mrs. Susan Rone, Director, Platt College, 3801 South Sheridan Road, Tulsa, OK 74145-111. *Phone:* 918-663-9000. *Fax:* 918-622-1240. *E-mail:* susanr@plattcollege.org. *Web site:* http://www.plattcolleges.edu/.

Redlands Community College

El Reno, Oklahoma

Director of Admissions Ms. Tricia Hobson, Director, Enrollment Management, Redlands Community College, 1300 South Country Club Road, El Reno, OK 73036-5304. *Phone:* 405-262-2552 Ext. 1263. *Toll-free phone:* 866-415-6367. *Fax:* 405-422-1239. *E-mail:* hobsont@redlandscc.edu. *Web site:* http://www.redlandscc.edu/.

Rose State College

Midwest City, Oklahoma

Freshman Application Contact Ms. Mechelle Aitson-Roessler, Registrar and Director of Admissions, Rose State College, 6420 Southeast 15th Street, Midwest City, OK 73110-2799. *Phone:* 405-733-7308. *Toll-free phone:* 866-621-0987. *Fax:* 405-736-0203. *E-mail:* maitson@ms.rose.cc.ok.us. *Web site:* http://www.rose.edu/.

Seminole State College

Seminole, Oklahoma

Freshman Application Contact Mr. Chris Lindley, Director of Enrollment Management, Seminole State College, PO Box 351, 2701 Boren Boulevard, Seminole, OK 74818-0351. *Phone:* 405-382-9272. *Fax:* 405-382-9524. *E-mail:* lindley_c@ssc.cc.ok.us. *Web site:* http://www.ssc.cc.ok.us/.

Southwestern Oklahoma State University at Sayre

Sayre, Oklahoma

- **State and locally supported** 2-year, founded 1938, part of Southwestern Oklahoma State University
- **Rural** 6-acre campus
- **Coed,** 643 undergraduate students, 40% full-time, 74% women, 26% men

Undergraduates 258 full-time, 385 part-time. 2% Black or African American, non-Hispanic/Latino; 6% Hispanic/Latino; 0.6% Asian, non-Hispanic/Latino; 0.5% Native Hawaiian or other Pacific Islander, non-Hispanic/Latino; 5% American Indian or Alaska Native, non-Hispanic/Latino; 3% Two or more races, non-Hispanic/Latino.

Freshmen *Admission:* 85 admitted, 85 enrolled.

Faculty *Total:* 14, 100% full-time. *Student/faculty ratio:* 18:1.

Majors Business administration and management; clinical/medical laboratory technology; computer science; corrections; criminal justice/safety; general studies; medical radiologic technology; occupational therapist assistant; physical therapy technology; registered nursing/registered nurse.

Academics *Calendar:* semesters. *Degree:* diplomas and associate. *Special study options:* academic remediation for entering students, adult/continuing education programs, advanced placement credit, cooperative education, distance learning, independent study, part-time degree program, services for LD students, summer session for credit.

Library Oscar McMahan Library with 9,975 titles, 45 serial subscriptions, an OPAC, a Web page.

Student Life *Housing:* college housing not available.

Standardized Tests *Required for some:* ACT (for admission).

Costs (2011–12) *Tuition:* state resident $3660 full-time, $122 per credit hour part-time; nonresident $9720 full-time, $324 per credit hour part-time. *Required fees:* $930 full-time, $31 per credit hour part-time.

Applying *Application fee:* $15. *Required:* high school transcript. *Application deadlines:* rolling (freshmen), rolling (transfers).

Freshman Application Contact Ms. Kim Seymour, Registrar, Southwestern Oklahoma State University at Sayre, 409 East Mississippi Avenue, Sayre, OK 73662. *Phone:* 580-928-5533 Ext. 101. *Fax:* 580-928-1140. *E-mail:* kim.seymour@swosu.edu. *Web site:* http://www.swosu.edu/sayre/.

Spartan College of Aeronautics and Technology

Tulsa, Oklahoma

Freshman Application Contact Mr. Mark Fowler, Vice President of Student Records and Finance, Spartan College of Aeronautics and Technology, 8820 East Pine Street, PO Box 582833, Tulsa, OK 74158-2833. *Phone:* 918-836-6886. *Toll-free phone:* 800-331-1204 (in-state); 800-331-124 (out-of-state). *Web site:* http://www.spartan.edu/.

Tulsa Community College

Tulsa, Oklahoma

Freshman Application Contact Ms. Leanne Brewer, Director of Admissions and Records, Tulsa Community College, 6111 East Skelly Drive, Tulsa, OK 74135. *Phone:* 918-595-7811. *Fax:* 918-595-7910. *E-mail:* lbrewer@tulsacc.edu. *Web site:* http://www.tulsacc.edu/.

Tulsa Welding School

Tulsa, Oklahoma

Freshman Application Contact Mrs. Debbie Renee Burke, Vice President/Executive Director, Tulsa Welding School, 2545 East 11th Street, Tulsa, OK 74104. *Phone:* 918-587-6789 Ext. 2258. *Toll-free phone:* 888-765-5555. *Fax:* 918-295-6812. *E-mail:* dburke@twsweld.com. *Web site:* http://www.weldingschool.com/.

Vatterott College

Oklahoma City, Oklahoma

Freshman Application Contact Mr. Mark Hybers, Director of Admissions, Vatterott College, Oklahoma City, OK 73127. *Phone:* 405-945-0088 Ext. 4416. *Toll-free phone:* 888-553-6627. *Fax:* 405-945-0788. *E-mail:* mark.hybers@vatterott-college.edu. *Web site:* http://www.vatterott-college.edu/.

Vatterott College

Tulsa, Oklahoma

Freshman Application Contact Mr. Terry Queeno, Campus Director, Vatterott College, 4343 South 118th East Avenue, Suite A, Tulsa, OK 74146. *Phone:* 918-836-6656. *Toll-free phone:* 888-553-6627. *Fax:* 918-836-9698. *E-mail:* tulsa@vatterott-college.edu. *Web site:* http://www.vatterott-college.edu/.

Western Oklahoma State College

Altus, Oklahoma

Freshman Application Contact Dr. Larry W. Paxton, Director of Academic Services, Western Oklahoma State College, 2801 North Main, Altus, OK 73521. *Phone:* 580-477-7720. *Fax:* 580-477-7723. *E-mail:* larry.paxton@wosc.edu. *Web site:* http://www.wosc.edu/.

OREGON

American College of Healthcare Sciences

Portland, Oregon

- **Urban** campus
- **Coed**

Undergraduates Students come from 50 s[...]tries. *Retention:* 92% of full-time freshme[...]

Academics *Degrees:* certificates, diploma[...]elor's certificates.

Applying *Application fee:* $35. *Required[...]school transcript, standardized test scores[...]Committee. *Required for some:* interview[...]

Freshman Application Contact ACHS[...]Healthcare Sciences, 5940 SW Hood Av[...]503-244-0726. *Toll-free phone:* 800-487-[...]achs@achs.edu. *Web site:* http://www.ach[...]

Costs [...]
M[...]
time; sta[...]
$9270 full-[...]
Room and bo[...]
children of emplo[...]

Blue Mountain Community College
Pendleton, Oregon

Director of Admissions Ms. Theresa Bosworth, Director of Admissions, Blue Mountain Community College, 2411 Northwest Carden Avenue, PO Box 100, Pendleton, OR 97801-1000. *Phone:* 541-278-5774. *E-mail:* tbosworth@bluecc.edu. *Web site:* http://www.bluecc.edu/.

Carrington College - Portland
Portland, Oregon

Freshman Application Contact Admissions Office, Carrington College - Portland, 2004 Lloyd Center, 3rd Floor, Portland, OR 97232. *Phone:* 503-761-6100. *Web site:* http://carrington.edu/.

Central Oregon Community College
Bend, Oregon

- **District-supported** 2-year, founded 1949, part of Oregon Community College Association
- **Small-town** 193-acre campus
- **Endowment** $10.0 million
- **Coed,** 7,142 undergraduate students, 46% full-time, 54% women, 46% men

Undergraduates 3,319 full-time, 3,823 part-time. Students come from 10 states and territories; 5% are from out of state; 0.8% Black or African American, non-Hispanic/Latino; 7% Hispanic/Latino; 1% Asian, non-Hispanic/Latino; 0.3% Native Hawaiian or other Pacific Islander, non-Hispanic/Latino; 2% American Indian or Alaska Native, non-Hispanic/Latino; 0.5% Two or more races, non-Hispanic/Latino; 8% Race/ethnicity unknown; 6% transferred in; 1% live on campus. *Retention:* 55% of full-time freshmen returned.
Freshmen *Admission:* 1,481 applied, 1,481 admitted, 917 enrolled.
Faculty *Total:* 289, 38% full-time. *Student/faculty ratio:* 27:1.
Majors Accounting; administrative assistant and secretarial science; airline pilot and flight crew; art; automobile/automotive mechanics technology; biological and physical sciences; biology/biological sciences; business administration and management; CAD/CADD drafting/design technology; child-care and support services management; computer and information sciences related; computer science; computer systems networking and telecommunications; cooking and related culinary arts; customer service management; dental assisting; dietetics; drafting and design technology; early childhood education; education; electrical, electronic and communications engineering technology; emergency medical technology (EMT paramedic); engineering; fire science/firefighting; fishing and fisheries sciences and management; foreign languages and literatures; forestry; forest technology; health and physical education/fitness; health information/medical records technology; hotel/motel administration; humanities; industrial technology; kinesiology and exercise science; liberal arts and sciences/liberal studies; licensed practical/vocational nurse training; management information systems; manufacturing engineering technology; marketing/marketing management; massage therapy; mathematics; medical/clinical assistant; natural resources/conservation; physical sciences; physical therapy; polymer/plastics engineering; pre-law studies; premedical studies; pre-pharmacy studies; radiologic technology/science; registered nursing/registered nurse; retailing; social sciences; speech communication and rhetoric; sport and fitness administration/management; substance abuse/addiction counseling.
Academics *Calendar:* quarters. *Degree:* certificates and associate. *Special study options:* academic remediation for entering students, cooperative education, distance learning, double majors, English as a second language, independent study, internships, part-time degree program, student-designed majors, study abroad, summer session for credit. *ROTC:* Army (c).
Library COCC Library plus 1 other with 76,421 titles, 329 serial subscriptions, 3,570 audiovisual materials, an OPAC, a Web page.
Student Life *Housing Options:* coed. Campus housing is university owned. *Activities and Organizations:* drama/theater group, student-run newspaper, choral group, club sports, student newspaper, Criminal Justice Club, Aviation Club. *Campus security:* 24-hour emergency response devices and patrols, late-night transport/escort service. *Student services:* personal/psychological counseling.
Athletics *Intercollegiate sports:* golf M/W. *Intramural sports:* baseball M, basketball M/W, cross-country running M/W, football M, skiing (cross-country) M/W, skiing (downhill) M/W, soccer M/W, track and field M/W, volleyball W, weight lifting M/W.
(2011–12) *Tuition:* area resident $3420 full-time, $76 per credit part-time; resident $4545 full-time, $101 per credit part-time; nonresident time, $206 per credit part-time. *Required fees:* $171 full-time. $8196. *Payment plan:* installment. *Waivers:* employees or

Financial Aid Of all full-time matriculated undergraduates who enrolled in 2010, 725 Federal Work-Study jobs (averaging $2130).
Applying *Options:* electronic application. *Application fee:* $25. *Application deadlines:* rolling (freshmen), rolling (transfers). *Notification:* continuous (freshmen), continuous (transfers).
Freshman Application Contact Central Oregon Community College, 2600 Northwest College Way, Bend, OR 97701-5998. *Phone:* 541-383-7500. *Web site:* http://www.cocc.edu/.

Chemeketa Community College
Salem, Oregon

Freshman Application Contact Chemeketa Community College, 4000 Lancaster Drive NE, P.O. Box 14007, Salem, OR 97309. *Phone:* 503-399-5001. *Web site:* http://www.chemeketa.edu/.

Clackamas Community College
Oregon City, Oregon

Freshman Application Contact Ms. Tara Sprehe, Registrar, Clackamas Community College, 19600 South Molalla Avenue, Oregon City, OR 97045. *Phone:* 503-657-6958 Ext. 2742. *Fax:* 503-650-6654. *E-mail:* pattyw@clackamas.edu. *Web site:* http://www.clackamas.edu/.

Clatsop Community College
Astoria, Oregon

Freshman Application Contact Ms. Kristen Lee, Director, Enrollment Services, Clatsop Community College, 1653 Jerome Avenue, Astoria, OR 97103. *Phone:* 503-338-2326. *Toll-free phone:* 855-252-8767. *Fax:* 503-325-5738. *E-mail:* admissions@clatsopcc.edu. *Web site:* http://www.clatsopcc.edu/.

Columbia Gorge Community College
The Dalles, Oregon

Director of Admissions Ms. Karen Carter, Chief Student Services Officer, Columbia Gorge Community College, 400 East Scenic Drive, The Dalles, OR 97058. *Phone:* 541-506-6011. *E-mail:* kcarter@cgcc.cc.or.us. *Web site:* http://www.cgcc.cc.or.us/.

Everest College
Portland, Oregon

Freshman Application Contact Admissions Office, Everest College, 425 Southwest Washington Street, Portland, OR 97204. *Phone:* 503-222-3225. *Toll-free phone:* 888-741-4270. *Fax:* 503-228-6926. *Web site:* http://www.everest.edu/.

Heald College–Portland
Portland, Oregon

Freshman Application Contact Director of Admissions, Heald College–Portland, 6035 NE 78th Court, Portland, OR 97218. *Phone:* 503-229-0492. *Toll-free phone:* 800-88-HEALD. *Fax:* 503-229-0498. *E-mail:* portlandinfo@heald.edu. *Web site:* http://www.heald.edu/.

ITT Technical Institute
Portland, Oregon

- **Proprietary** primarily 2-year, founded 1971, part of ITT Educational Services, Inc.
- **Urban** campus
- **Coed**

Majors Business administration and management; communications technology; computer and information systems security; computer software engineering; computer software technology; computer systems networking and telecommunications; construction management; criminal justice/law enforcement administration; drafting and design technology; electrical, electronic and communications engineering technology; game and interactive media design; graphic communications; industrial technology; legal assistant/paralegal; network and system administration; project management; registered nursing/registered nurse; web/multimedia management and webmaster.
Academics *Calendar:* quarters. *Degrees:* associate and bachelor's.
Student Life *Housing:* college housing not available.
Financial Aid Of all full-time matriculated undergraduates who enrolled in 2010, 15 Federal Work-Study jobs (averaging $5000).

Freshman Application Contact Director of Recruitment, ITT Technical Institute, 9500 Northeast Cascades Parkway, Portland, OR 97220. *Phone:* 503-255-6500. *Toll-free phone:* 800-234-5488. *Web site:* http://www.itt-tech.edu/.

Klamath Community College

Klamath Falls, Oregon

Freshman Application Contact Admissions Office, Klamath Community College, 7390 South 6th Street, Klamath Falls, OR 97603. *Phone:* 541-882-3521. *Web site:* http://www.klamathcc.edu/.

Lane Community College

Eugene, Oregon

Director of Admissions Ms. Helen Garrett, Director of Admissions/Registrar, Lane Community College, 4000 East 30th Avenue, Eugene, OR 97405-0640. *Phone:* 541-747-4501 Ext. 2686. *Web site:* http://www.lanecc.edu/.

Le Cordon Bleu College of Culinary Arts in Portland

Portland, Oregon

Admissions Office Contact Le Cordon Bleu College of Culinary Arts in Portland, 921 Southwest Morrison Street, Suite 400, Portland, OR 97205. *Toll-free phone:* 888-891-6222. *Web site:* http://www.wci.edu/.

Linn-Benton Community College

Albany, Oregon

- **State and locally supported** 2-year, founded 1966
- **Small-town** 104-acre campus
- **Coed**

Undergraduates 3,556 full-time, 3,366 part-time. 2% Black or African American, non-Hispanic/Latino; 6% Hispanic/Latino; 1% Asian, non-Hispanic/Latino; 1% American Indian or Alaska Native, non-Hispanic/Latino; 6% Two or more races, non-Hispanic/Latino; 0.1% Race/ethnicity unknown; 0.3% international.

Faculty *Student/faculty ratio:* 20:1.

Academics *Calendar:* quarters. *Degree:* certificates and associate. *Special study options:* academic remediation for entering students, adult/continuing education programs, advanced placement credit, cooperative education, distance learning, English as a second language, independent study, internships, part-time degree program, services for LD students, student-designed majors, study abroad, summer session for credit. *ROTC:* Army (c), Air Force (c).

Student Life *Campus security:* 24-hour emergency response devices and patrols, student patrols, late-night transport/escort service.

Costs (2011–12) *Tuition:* state resident $3360 full-time, $84 per credit part-time; nonresident $7120 full-time, $178 per credit part-time.

Financial Aid Of all full-time matriculated undergraduates who enrolled in 2010, 290 Federal Work-Study jobs (averaging $1800).

Applying *Options:* electronic application, deferred entrance. *Application fee:* $30. *Required for some:* high school transcript.

Freshman Application Contact Ms. Christine Baker, Outreach Coordinator, Linn-Benton Community College, 6500 Pacific Boulevard, SW, Albany, OR 97321. *Phone:* 541-917-4813. *Fax:* 541-917-4838. *E-mail:* admissions@linnbenton.edu. *Web site:* http://www.linnbenton.edu/.

Mt. Hood Community College

Gresham, Oregon

Director of Admissions Dr. Craig Kolins, Associate Vice President of Enrollment Services, Mt. Hood Community College, 26000 Southeast Stark Street, Gresham, OR 97030-3300. *Phone:* 503-491-7265. *Web site:* http://www.mhcc.edu/.

Oregon Coast Community College

Newport, Oregon

- **Public** 2-year, founded 1987
- **Small-town** 24-acre campus
- **Coed**

Undergraduates 204 full-time, 331 part-time. Students come from 4 states and territories; 1% are from out of state; 0.9% Black or African American, non-Hispanic/Latino; 7% Hispanic/Latino; 2% Asian, non-Hispanic/Latino; 0.9% Native Hawaiian or other Pacific Islander, non-Hispanic/Latino; 2% American Indian or Alaska Native, non-Hispanic/Latino; 4% Two or more races, non-Hispanic/Latino; 2% Race/ethnicity unknown. *Retention:* 29% of full-time freshmen returned.

Faculty *Student/faculty ratio:* 14:1.

Academics *Calendar:* quarters. *Degree:* certificates and associate. *Special study options:* academic remediation for entering students, cooperative education, distance learning, English as a second language, honors programs, internships, part-time degree program, services for LD students, summer session for credit.

Standardized Tests *Required for some:* nursing entrance exam.

Freshman Application Contact Student Services, Oregon Coast Community College, 400 SE College Way, Newport, OR 97366. *Phone:* 541-265-2283. *Fax:* 541-265-3820. *E-mail:* webinfo@occc.cc.or.us. *Web site:* http://www.oregoncoastcc.org.

Portland Community College

Portland, Oregon

Freshman Application Contact PCC Admissions and Registration Office, Portland Community College, PO Box 19000, Portland, OR 97280. *Phone:* 503-977-8888. *Web site:* http://www.pcc.edu/.

Rogue Community College

Grants Pass, Oregon

- **State and locally supported** 2-year, founded 1970
- **Rural** 84-acre campus
- **Endowment** $6.6 million
- **Coed,** 5,828 undergraduate students, 44% full-time, 58% women, 42% men

Undergraduates 2,559 full-time, 3,269 part-time. Students come from 27 states and territories; 1 other country; 2% are from out of state; 0.8% Black or African American, non-Hispanic/Latino; 11% Hispanic/Latino; 2% Asian, non-Hispanic/Latino; 0.5% Native Hawaiian or other Pacific Islander, non-Hispanic/Latino; 2% American Indian or Alaska Native, non-Hispanic/Latino; 2% Two or more races, non-Hispanic/Latino; 4% Race/ethnicity unknown; 68% transferred in.

Freshmen *Admission:* 880 enrolled.

Faculty *Total:* 419, 20% full-time. *Student/faculty ratio:* 19:1.

Majors Accounting technology and bookkeeping; automobile/automotive mechanics technology; business administration and management; business/commerce; child-care and support services management; computer and information sciences; computer software technology; construction engineering technology; construction trades; criminal justice/police science; diesel mechanics technology; electrical and power transmission installation; electrical, electronic and communications engineering technology; emergency medical technology (EMT paramedic); fire prevention and safety technology; general studies; liberal arts and sciences/liberal studies; manufacturing engineering technology; marketing/marketing management; mechanics and repair; medical office computer specialist; registered nursing/registered nurse; social work; visual and performing arts; welding technology.

Academics *Calendar:* quarters. *Degree:* certificates and associate. *Special study options:* academic remediation for entering students, adult/continuing education programs, advanced placement credit, cooperative education, distance learning, double majors, English as a second language, independent study, internships, part-time degree program, services for LD students, study abroad, summer session for credit.

Library Rogue Community College Library with 33,000 titles, 275 serial subscriptions, an OPAC.

Student Life *Housing:* college housing not available. *Activities and Organizations:* drama/theater group, student-run newspaper, choral group. *Campus security:* 24-hour emergency response devices and patrols, late-night transport/escort service. *Student services:* personal/psychological counseling.

Athletics *Intramural sports:* badminton M/W, basketball M/W, soccer M/W, softball M/W, tennis M/W, volleyball M/W.

Costs (2011–12) *Tuition:* state resident $3060 full-time, $85 per credit hour part-time; nonresident $3744 full-time, $104 per credit hour part-time. Full-time tuition and fees vary according to course load. Part-time tuition and fees vary according to course load. *Required fees:* $549 full-time, $4 per credit hour part-time, $135 per term part-time. *Payment plan:* installment. *Waivers:* employees or children of employees.

Financial Aid Of all full-time matriculated undergraduates who enrolled in 2010, 2,053 applied for aid, 1,824 were judged to have need, 87 had their need fully met. 81 Federal Work-Study jobs (averaging $2416). In 2010, 48 non-need-based awards were made. *Average percent of need met:* 74%. *Average financial aid package:* $8800. *Average need-based loan:* $3417. *Average need-based gift aid:* $5146. *Average non-need-based aid:* $1307.

Applying *Options:* electronic application, early admission. *Application deadlines:* rolling (freshmen), rolling (out-of-state freshmen), rolling (transfers).

Freshman Application Contact Ms. Claudia Sullivan, Director of Enrollment Services, Rogue Community College, 3345 Redwood Highway, Grants Pass, OR 97527-9291. *Phone:* 541-956-7176. *Fax:* 541-471-3585. *E-mail:* csullivan@roguecc.edu. *Web site:* http://www.roguecc.edu/.

Southwestern Oregon Community College

Coos Bay, Oregon

Freshman Application Contact Miss Lela Wells, Southwestern Oregon Community College, Student First Stop, 1988 Newmark Avenue, Coos Bay, OR 97420. *Phone:* 541-888-7611. *Toll-free phone:* 800-962-2838. *E-mail:* lwells@socc.edu. *Web site:* http://www.socc.edu/.

Tillamook Bay Community College

Tillamook, Oregon

Freshman Application Contact Lori Gates, Tillamook Bay Community College, 4301 Third Street, Tillamook, OR 97141. *Phone:* 503-842-8222. *Fax:* 503-842-2214. *E-mail:* gates@tillamookbay.cc. *Web site:* http://www.tbcc.cc.or.us/.

Treasure Valley Community College

Ontario, Oregon

Freshman Application Contact Ms. Candace Bell, Office of Admissions and Student Services, Treasure Valley Community College, 650 College Boulevard, Ontario, OR 97914. *Phone:* 541-881-8822 Ext. 239. *Fax:* 541-881-2721. *E-mail:* clbell@tvcc.cc. *Web site:* http://www.tvcc.cc.or.us/.

Umpqua Community College

Roseburg, Oregon

- **State and locally supported** 2-year, founded 1964
- **Rural** 100-acre campus
- **Endowment** $6.1 million
- **Coed,** 3,233 undergraduate students, 54% full-time, 58% women, 42% men

Undergraduates 1,735 full-time, 1,498 part-time. Students come from 5 states and territories; 2 other countries; 12% transferred in.

Freshmen *Admission:* 250 applied, 250 admitted, 347 enrolled.

Faculty *Total:* 205, 31% full-time. *Student/faculty ratio:* 30:1.

Majors Accounting; administrative assistant and secretarial science; agriculture; anthropology; art; art history, criticism and conservation; art teacher education; automobile/automotive mechanics technology; behavioral sciences; biological and physical sciences; biology/biological sciences; business administration and management; chemistry; child development; civil engineering technology; computer engineering technology; computer science; cosmetology; criminal justice/law enforcement administration; desktop publishing and digital imaging design; dramatic/theater arts; economics; education; electrical, electronic and communications engineering technology; elementary education; emergency medical technology (EMT paramedic); engineering; English; fire science/firefighting; forestry; health teacher education; history; humanities; human resources management; journalism; kindergarten/preschool education; legal administrative assistant/secretary; liberal arts and sciences/liberal studies; marketing/marketing management; mathematics; medical administrative assistant and medical secretary; music; music teacher education; natural sciences; physical education teaching and coaching; physical sciences; political science and government; pre-engineering; psychology; registered nursing/registered nurse; social sciences; social work; sociology.

Academics *Calendar:* quarters. *Degree:* certificates and associate. *Special study options:* academic remediation for entering students, accelerated degree program, adult/continuing education programs, advanced placement credit, cooperative education, distance learning, English as a second language, honors programs, independent study, internships, part-time degree program, services for LD students, study abroad, summer session for credit.

Library Umpqua Community College Library with 41,000 titles, 350 serial subscriptions, an OPAC, a Web page.

Student Life *Housing:* college housing not available. *Activities and Organizations:* drama/theater group, student-run newspaper, choral group, Phi Theta Kappa, Computer Club, Phi Beta Lambda, Nursing Club, Umpqua Accounting Associates. *Campus security:* 24-hour emergency response devices and patrols. *Student services:* personal/psychological counseling.

Athletics *Intercollegiate sports:* basketball M(s)/W(s), volleyball W(s). *Intramural sports:* basketball M/W.

Costs (2011–12) *Tuition:* state resident $3876 full-time, $72 per credit hour part-time; nonresident $9248 full-time, $198 per credit hour part-time. *Required fees:* $300 full-time, $8 per credit hour part-time, $100 per term part-time. *Waivers:* employees or children of employees.

Financial Aid Of all full-time matriculated undergraduates who enrolled in 2010, 120 Federal Work-Study jobs (averaging $3000).

Applying *Options:* electronic application, early admission, deferred entrance. *Application fee:* $25. *Recommended:* high school transcript. *Application deadlines:* rolling (freshmen), rolling (transfers).

Freshman Application Contact Mr. Rich Robles, Recruiter, Umpqua Community College, PO Box 967, Roseburg, OR 97470-0226. *Phone:* 541-440-4600 Ext. 7661. *Fax:* 541-440-4612. *E-mail:* Richard.Robles@umpqua.edu. *Web site:* http://www.umpqua.edu/.

PENNSYLVANIA

Antonelli Institute

Erdenheim, Pennsylvania

- **Proprietary** 2-year, founded 1938
- **Suburban** 15-acre campus with easy access to Philadelphia
- **Coed,** 203 undergraduate students
- **85% of applicants were admitted**

Freshmen *Admission:* 270 applied, 229 admitted.

Majors Graphic design; photography.

Academics *Calendar:* semesters. *Degree:* associate. *Special study options:* adult/continuing education programs.

Costs (2011–12) *Tuition:* Photography AST Degree program: $20,780 per year. Graphic Design AST program: $18,680 per year.

Financial Aid Of all full-time matriculated undergraduates who enrolled in 2010, 5 Federal Work-Study jobs (averaging $2000).

Applying *Application deadline:* 9/6 (transfers).

Freshman Application Contact Admissions Office, Antonelli Institute, 300 Montgomery Avenue, Erdenheim, PA 19038. *Phone:* 800-722-7871. *Toll-free phone:* 800-722-7871. *Web site:* http://www.antonelli.edu/.

The Art Institute of York–Pennsylvania

York, Pennsylvania

- **Proprietary** primarily 2-year, founded 1952, part of Education Management Corporation
- **Suburban** campus
- **Coed**

Majors Apparel and accessories marketing; digital communication and media/multimedia; graphic design; interior design; web page, digital/multimedia and information resources design.

Academics *Calendar:* quarters. *Degrees:* associate and bachelor's.

Costs (2011–12) *Tuition:* Tuition cost varies by program. Prospective students should contact the school for current tuition costs. Other charges include a starting kit for all first-quarter students. Kits vary in price, depending on the program of study.

Freshman Application Contact The Art Institute of York–Pennsylvania, 1409 Williams Road, York, PA 17402-9012. *Phone:* 717-755-2300. *Toll-free phone:* 800-864-7725. *Web site:* http://www.artinstitutes.edu/york/.

Berks Technical Institute

Wyomissing, Pennsylvania

Freshman Application Contact Mr. Allan Brussolo, Academic Dean, Berks Technical Institute, 2205 Ridgewood Road, Wyomissing, PA 19610-1168. *Phone:* 610-372-1722. *Toll-free phone:* 866-591-8384. *Fax:* 610-376-4684. *E-mail:* abrussolo@berks.edu. *Web site:* http://www.berks.edu/.

Bidwell Training Center

Pittsburgh, Pennsylvania

Freshman Application Contact Admissions Office, Bidwell Training Center, 1815 Metropolitan Street, Pittsburgh, PA 15233. *Phone:* 412-322-1773. *Toll-free phone:* 800-516-1800. *E-mail:* admissions@mcg-btc.org. *Web site:* http://www.bidwell-training.org/.

Bradford School

Pittsburgh, Pennsylvania

- **Private** 2-year, founded 1968
- **Urban** campus
- **Coed**, 582 undergraduate students
- 87% of applicants were admitted

Freshmen *Admission:* 915 applied, 794 admitted.

Majors Accounting technology and bookkeeping; administrative assistant and secretarial science; computer programming; computer systems networking and telecommunications; dental assisting; graphic design; hotel/motel administration; legal administrative assistant/secretary; legal assistant/paralegal; medical/clinical assistant; retailing.

Academics *Degree:* diplomas and associate. *Special study options:* accelerated degree program, internships.

Freshman Application Contact Admissions Office, Bradford School, 125 West Station Square Drive, Pittsburgh, PA 15219. *Phone:* 412-391-6710. *Toll-free phone:* 800-391-6810. *Web site:* http://www.bradfordpittsburgh.edu/.

Bucks County Community College

Newtown, Pennsylvania

- **County-supported** 2-year, founded 1964
- **Suburban** 200-acre campus with easy access to Philadelphia
- **Endowment** $4.7 million
- **Coed**, 10,300 undergraduate students, 33% full-time, 56% women, 44% men

Undergraduates 3,434 full-time, 6,866 part-time. Students come from 11 states and territories; 31 other countries; 1% are from out of state; 5% Black or African American, non-Hispanic/Latino; 4% Hispanic/Latino; 2% Asian, non-Hispanic/Latino; 0.1% Native Hawaiian or other Pacific Islander, non-Hispanic/Latino; 1% American Indian or Alaska Native, non-Hispanic/Latino; 1% Two or more races, non-Hispanic/Latino; 18% Race/ethnicity unknown; 0.6% international; 74% transferred in. *Retention:* 62% of full-time freshmen returned.

Freshmen *Admission:* 5,002 applied, 4,906 admitted, 2,382 enrolled.

Faculty *Total:* 615, 28% full-time. *Student/faculty ratio:* 17:1.

Majors Accounting technology and bookkeeping; American studies; biology/biotechnology laboratory technician; biology teacher education; biotechnology; building/home/construction inspection; business administration and management; business/commerce; business, management, and marketing related; cabinetmaking and millwork; chemical technology; chemistry teacher education; child-care and support services management; child-care provision; cinematography and film/video production; commercial and advertising art; commercial photography; computer and information sciences; computer engineering technology; computer programming (specific applications); computer systems networking and telecommunications; criminal justice/safety; dramatic/theater arts; early childhood education; education; environmental science; food service systems administration; health and medical administrative services related; health professions related; historic preservation and conservation; history teacher education; human development and family studies; humanities; industrial technology; information science/studies; institutional food workers; journalism; legal assistant/paralegal; legal professions and studies related; liberal arts and sciences and humanities related; liberal arts and sciences/liberal studies; mathematics; medical insurance coding; medical office assistant; multi/interdisciplinary studies related; music; network and system administration; parks, recreation and leisure facilities management; physical education teaching and coaching; precision production trades; psychology; radio and television; registered nursing/registered nurse; retailing; speech communication and rhetoric; sport and fitness administration/management; tourism and travel services management; visual and performing arts; web page, digital/multimedia and information resources design.

Academics *Calendar:* semesters. *Degree:* certificates and associate. *Special study options:* academic remediation for entering students, adult/continuing education programs, advanced placement credit, cooperative education, distance learning, English as a second language, external degree program, independent study, internships, part-time degree program, services for LD students, student-designed majors, summer session for credit.

Library Bucks County Community College Library with 146,215 titles, 290 serial subscriptions, 2,738 audiovisual materials, an OPAC, a Web page.

Student Life *Housing:* college housing not available. *Activities and Organizations:* drama/theater group, student-run newspaper, television station, choral group, Phi Theta Kappa, Inter-Varsity Christian Fellowship, Drama Club, Habitat for Humanity, Future Teachers Organization. *Campus security:* 24-hour emergency response devices and patrols, late-night transport/escort service. *Student services:* personal/psychological counseling, women's center.

Athletics Member NJCAA. *Intercollegiate sports:* baseball M, basketball M/W, equestrian sports M/W, golf M/W, soccer M/W, tennis M/W, volleyball W.

Intramural sports: basketball M/W, soccer M/W, softball M/W, table tennis M/W, tennis M/W, ultimate Frisbee M/W, volleyball W.

Costs (2011–12) *Tuition:* area resident $3330 full-time, $111 per credit hour part-time; state resident $6660 full-time, $222 per credit hour part-time; non-resident $9990 full-time, $333 per credit hour part-time. Full-time tuition and fees vary according to course load and reciprocity agreements. Part-time tuition and fees vary according to course load and reciprocity agreements. *Required fees:* $974 full-time, $58 per credit hour part-time. *Payment plans:* installment, deferred payment. *Waivers:* senior citizens and employees or children of employees.

Financial Aid Of all full-time matriculated undergraduates who enrolled in 2009, 175 Federal Work-Study jobs (averaging $2023).

Applying *Options:* electronic application, early admission. *Required:* high school transcript. *Required for some:* essay or personal statement, interview.

Freshman Application Contact Ms. Marlene Barlow, Director of Admissions, Bucks County Community College, Newtown, PA 18940. *Phone:* 215-968-8137. *Fax:* 215-968-8110. *E-mail:* barlowm@bucks.edu. *Web site:* http://www.bucks.edu/.

Butler County Community College

Butler, Pennsylvania

Freshman Application Contact Ms. Patricia Bajuszik, Director of Admissions, Butler County Community College, College Drive, PO Box 1205, Butler, PA 16003-1203. *Phone:* 724-287-8711 Ext. 344. *Toll-free phone:* 888-826-2829. *Fax:* 724-287-4961. *E-mail:* pattie.bajoszik@bc3.edu. *Web site:* http://www.bc3.edu/.

Cambria-Rowe Business College

Indiana, Pennsylvania

Freshman Application Contact Mrs. Stacey Bell-Leger, Representative at Indiana Campus, Cambria-Rowe Business College, 422 South 13th Street, Indiana, PA 15701. *Phone:* 724-483-0222. *Toll-free phone:* 800-NEW-CAREER. *Fax:* 724-463-7246. *E-mail:* sbell-leger@crbc.net. *Web site:* http://www.crbc.net/.

Cambria-Rowe Business College

Johnstown, Pennsylvania

Freshman Application Contact Mrs. Amanda Artim, Director of Admissions, Cambria-Rowe Business College, 221 Central Avenue, Johnstown, PA 15902-2494. *Phone:* 814-536-5168. *Toll-free phone:* 800-NEWCAREER. *Fax:* 814-536-5160. *E-mail:* admissions@crbc.net. *Web site:* http://www.crbc.net/.

Career Training Academy

Monroeville, Pennsylvania

Freshman Application Contact Career Training Academy, 4314 Old William Penn Highway, Suite 103, Monroeville, PA 15146. *Phone:* 412-372-3900. *Toll-free phone:* 866-673-7773. *Web site:* http://www.careerta.edu/.

Career Training Academy

New Kensington, Pennsylvania

Freshman Application Contact Career Training Academy, 950 Fifth Avenue, New Kensington, PA 15068-6301. *Phone:* 724-337-1000. *Toll-free phone:* 866-673-7773. *Web site:* http://www.careerta.edu/.

Career Training Academy

Pittsburgh, Pennsylvania

- **Proprietary** 2-year
- **Suburban** campus with easy access to Pittsburgh
- **Coed**, 84 undergraduate students, 100% full-time, 92% women, 8% men

Undergraduates 84 full-time. Students come from 1 other state; 10% Black or African American, non-Hispanic/Latino.

Freshmen *Admission:* 10 enrolled. *Average high school GPA:* 2.

Faculty *Total:* 10, 70% full-time, 10% with terminal degrees. *Student/faculty ratio:* 9:1.

Majors Massage therapy; medical/clinical assistant; medical insurance coding.

Academics *Calendar:* continuous. *Degree:* diplomas and associate. *Special study options:* academic remediation for entering students, advanced placement credit, cooperative education, internships.

Student Life *Housing:* college housing not available. *Campus security:* 24-hour emergency response devices, late-night transport/escort service.

Costs (2011–12) *Tuition:* $11,280 full-time.

Applying *Application fee:* $30. *Required:* essay or personal statement, high school transcript, interview. *Application deadlines:* rolling (freshmen), rolling (out-of-state freshmen).

Freshman Application Contact Marcus Zimmerman, Career Training Academy, 1500 Northway Mall, Suite 200, Pittsburgh, PA 15237. *Phone:* 412-367-4000. *Toll-free phone:* 866-673-7773. *Fax:* 412-369-7223. *E-mail:* admission3@careerta.edu. *Web site:* http://www.careerta.edu/.

Commonwealth Technical Institute

Johnstown, Pennsylvania

Freshman Application Contact Ms. Rebecca Halza, Admissions Supervisor, Commonwealth Technical Institute, Hiram G. Andrews Center, 727 Goucher Street, Johnstown, PA 15905. *Phone:* 814-255-8200. *Toll-free phone:* 800-762-4211. *Fax:* 814-255-8283. *E-mail:* rhalza@state.pa.us. *Web site:* http://www.portal.state.pa.us/portal/server.pt/community/commonwealth_technical_institute/10361.

Community College of Allegheny County

Pittsburgh, Pennsylvania

- **County-supported** 2-year, founded 1966
- **Urban** 242-acre campus
- **Coed,** 20,372 undergraduate students, 40% full-time, 58% women, 42% men

Undergraduates 8,061 full-time, 12,311 part-time. 2% are from out of state.
Freshmen *Admission:* 4,538 enrolled.

Majors Accounting technology and bookkeeping; administrative assistant and secretarial science; airline pilot and flight crew; applied horticulture/horticulture operations; architectural drafting and CAD/CADD; art; athletic training; automotive engineering technology; aviation/airway management; banking and financial support services; biology/biological sciences; building/property maintenance; business administration and management; business automation/technology/data entry; business machine repair; carpentry; chemical technology; chemistry; child-care provision; child development; civil drafting and CAD/CADD; civil engineering technology; clinical/medical laboratory technology; commercial and advertising art; communications technologies and support services related; community health services counseling; computer engineering technology; computer systems networking and telecommunications; computer technology/computer systems technology; construction engineering technology; construction trades related; corrections; cosmetology and personal grooming arts related; court reporting; criminal justice/police science; culinary arts; diagnostic medical sonography and ultrasound technology; dietitian assistant; drafting and design technology; drafting/design engineering technologies related; dramatic/theater arts; education (specific levels and methods) related; education (specific subject areas) related; electrical, electronic and communications engineering technology; electroneurodiagnostic/electroencephalographic technology; energy management and systems technology; engineering technologies and engineering related; English; entrepreneurship; environmental engineering technology; fire prevention and safety technology; food service systems administration; foreign languages and literatures; general studies; greenhouse management; health and physical education/fitness; health information/medical records technology; health professions related; health unit coordinator/ward clerk; heating, air conditioning, ventilation and refrigeration maintenance technology; hotel/motel administration; housing and human environments related; human development and family studies related; humanities; human resources management; industrial technology; insurance; journalism; landscaping and groundskeeping; legal administrative assistant/secretary; legal assistant/paralegal; liberal arts and sciences/liberal studies; licensed practical/vocational nurse training; machine shop technology; management information systems; marketing/marketing management; mathematics; mechanical drafting and CAD/CADD; medical administrative assistant and medical secretary; medical/clinical assistant; medical radiologic technology; music; nuclear medical technology; nursing assistant/aide and patient care assistant/aide; occupational therapist assistant; office management; ornamental horticulture; perioperative/operating room and surgical nursing; pharmacy technician; physical therapy technology; physics; plant nursery management; psychiatric/mental health services technology; psychology; quality control technology; real estate; registered nursing/registered nurse; respiratory care therapy; restaurant, culinary, and catering management; retailing; robotics technology; science technologies related; sheet metal technology; sign language interpretation and translation; social sciences; social work; sociology; solar energy technology; substance abuse/addiction counseling; surgical technology; therapeutic recreation; tourism promotion; turf and turfgrass management; visual and performing arts related; welding technology.

Academics *Calendar:* semesters. *Degree:* certificates, diplomas, and associate. *Special study options:* part-time degree program.

Library Community College of Allegheny County Library.

Student Life *Housing:* college housing not available. *Campus security:* 24-hour emergency response devices and patrols, late-night transport/escort service.

Athletics Member NJCAA. *Intercollegiate sports:* baseball M, basketball M/W, bowling M/W, golf M/W, ice hockey M, softball W, table tennis M/W, tennis M/W, volleyball W. *Intramural sports:* badminton M/W, basketball M/W, bowling M/W, cross-country running M/W, football M, golf M/W, lacrosse M, racquetball M/W, softball M/W, table tennis M/W, tennis M/W, volleyball M/W, weight lifting M/W.

Applying *Recommended:* high school transcript. *Application deadlines:* rolling (freshmen), rolling (transfers). *Notification:* continuous (freshmen), continuous (transfers).

Freshman Application Contact Admissions Office, Community College of Allegheny County, 808 Ridge Avenue, Pittsburgh, PA 15212. *Phone:* 412-237-2511. *Web site:* http://www.ccac.edu/.

Community College of Beaver County

Monaca, Pennsylvania

Freshman Application Contact Enrollment Management, Community College of Beaver County, One Campus Drive, Monaca, PA 15061-2588. *Phone:* 724-480-3500. *Toll-free phone:* 800-335-0222. *E-mail:* admissions@ccbc.edu. *Web site:* http://www.ccbc.edu/.

Community College of Philadelphia

Philadelphia, Pennsylvania

- **State and locally supported** 2-year, founded 1964
- **Urban** 14-acre campus
- **Coed,** 39,270 undergraduate students

Undergraduates Students come from 50 other countries.
Faculty *Total:* 1,132, 35% full-time.

Majors Accounting; architectural engineering technology; art; automobile/automotive mechanics technology; business administration and management; chemical technology; clinical/medical laboratory technology; computer science; construction engineering technology; criminal justice/law enforcement administration; culinary arts; dental hygiene; drafting and design technology; education; engineering; engineering technology; facilities planning and management; finance; fire science/firefighting; forensic science and technology; health information/medical records administration; health professions related; hotel/motel administration; human services; kindergarten/preschool education; liberal arts and sciences/liberal studies; medical administrative assistant and medical secretary; medical/clinical assistant; medical radiologic technology; mental health counseling; music; occupational therapist assistant; photography; pre-engineering; psychology; recording arts technology; registered nursing/registered nurse; respiratory care therapy; sign language interpretation and translation.

Academics *Calendar:* semesters. *Degree:* certificates, diplomas, and associate. *Special study options:* academic remediation for entering students, accelerated degree program, adult/continuing education programs, advanced placement credit, cooperative education, distance learning, English as a second language, external degree program, honors programs, independent study, internships, off-campus study, part-time degree program, services for LD students, student-designed majors, study abroad, summer session for credit. *ROTC:* Army (c).

Library Main Campus Library plus 2 others with 110,000 titles, 420 serial subscriptions, an OPAC, a Web page.

Student Life *Housing:* college housing not available. *Activities and Organizations:* drama/theater group, student-run newspaper, choral group, Philadelphia L.E.A.D.S, Phi Theta Kappa, Student Government Association, Vanguard Student Newspaper, Fundraising Club. *Campus security:* 24-hour emergency response devices and patrols, phone/alert systems in classrooms/buildings. *Student services:* personal/psychological counseling, women's center.

Athletics *Intercollegiate sports:* baseball M, basketball M/W, cheerleading M/W, cross-country running M/W, soccer M, tennis M/W, track and field M/W, volleyball M/W. *Intramural sports:* basketball M/W, soccer M/W, tennis M/W, track and field M/W, volleyball M/W.

Costs (2011–12) *Tuition:* area resident $3312 full-time, $138 per credit hour part-time; state resident $6864 full-time, $286 per credit hour part-time; nonresident $10,416 full-time, $434 per credit hour part-time. Full-time tuition and fees vary according to program. Part-time tuition and fees vary according to program. *Payment plan:* installment. *Waivers:* senior citizens and employees or children of employees.

Applying *Options:* electronic application, early admission, deferred entrance. *Application fee:* $20. *Required for some:* high school transcript, allied health and nursing programs have specific entry requirements. *Application deadlines:* rolling (freshmen), rolling (transfers). *Notification:* continuous (freshmen), continuous (transfers).

Freshman Application Contact Community College of Philadelphia, 1700 Spring Garden Street, Philadelphia, PA 19130-3991. *Phone:* 215-751-8010. *Web site:* http://www.ccp.edu/.

Consolidated School of Business
Lancaster, Pennsylvania

Freshman Application Contact Ms. Libby Paul, Admissions Representative, Consolidated School of Business, 2124 Ambassador Circle, Lancaster, PA 17603. *Phone:* 717-394-6211. *Toll-free phone:* 800-541-8298. *Fax:* 717-394-6213. *E-mail:* lpaul@csb.edu. *Web site:* http://www.csb.edu/.

Consolidated School of Business
York, Pennsylvania

- **Proprietary** 2-year, founded 1981
- **Suburban** 6-acre campus with easy access to Baltimore
- **Coed, primarily women,** 176 undergraduate students, 100% full-time, 82% women, 18% men

Undergraduates 176 full-time.

Freshmen *Average high school GPA:* 2.8.

Faculty *Total:* 21, 86% full-time. *Student/faculty ratio:* 15:1.

Majors Accounting; business administration and management; health/healthcare administration; legal administrative assistant/secretary; medical administrative assistant and medical secretary; office management; tourism and travel services management.

Academics *Calendar:* continuous. *Degree:* diplomas and associate. *Special study options:* accelerated degree program, double majors, honors programs, independent study, internships, part-time degree program, services for LD students.

Student Life *Housing:* college housing not available. *Activities and Organizations:* student-run newspaper.

Applying *Options:* electronic application. *Required:* high school transcript, interview. *Application deadlines:* rolling (freshmen), rolling (transfers).

Freshman Application Contact Ms. Sandra Swanger, Admissions Representative, Consolidated School of Business, 1605 Clugston Road, York, PA 17404. *Phone:* 717-764-9550. *Toll-free phone:* 800-520-0691. *Fax:* 717-764-9469. *E-mail:* sswanger@csb.edu. *Web site:* http://www.csb.edu/.

Dean Institute of Technology
Pittsburgh, Pennsylvania

Director of Admissions Mr. Richard D. Ali, Admissions Director, Dean Institute of Technology, 1501 West Liberty Avenue, Pittsburgh, PA 15226-1103. *Phone:* 412-531-4433. *Web site:* http://www.deantech.edu/.

Delaware County Community College
Media, Pennsylvania

- **State and locally supported** 2-year, founded 1967
- **Suburban** 123-acre campus with easy access to Philadelphia
- **Endowment** $3.8 million
- **Coed,** 13,248 undergraduate students, 40% full-time, 56% women, 44% men

Undergraduates 5,360 full-time, 7,888 part-time. Students come from 9 states and territories; 53 other countries; 1% are from out of state; 25% Black or African American, non-Hispanic/Latino; 2% Hispanic/Latino; 4% Asian, non-Hispanic/Latino; 0.1% Native Hawaiian or other Pacific Islander, non-Hispanic/Latino; 0.2% American Indian or Alaska Native, non-Hispanic/Latino; 2% Two or more races, non-Hispanic/Latino; 5% Race/ethnicity unknown. *Retention:* 61% of full-time freshmen returned.

Freshmen *Admission:* 4,818 applied, 4,818 admitted.

Faculty *Total:* 802, 18% full-time. *Student/faculty ratio:* 24:1.

Majors Accounting technology and bookkeeping; animation, interactive technology, video graphics and special effects; anthropology; architectural engineering technology; automobile/automotive mechanics technology; biological and physical sciences; biomedical technology; building/property maintenance; business administration and management; CAD/CADD drafting/design technology; commercial and advertising art; communication and journalism related; computer and information sciences; computer programming (specific applications); computer systems networking and telecommunications; computer technology/computer systems technology; construction management; criminal justice/police science; data entry/microcomputer applications; early childhood education; e-commerce; education (multiple levels); electrical and power transmission installation; electrical, electronic and communications engineering technology; emergency medical technology (EMT paramedic); engineering; entrepreneurship; fine/studio arts; fire prevention and safety technology; general studies; health services/allied health/health sciences; health unit management/ward supervision; heating, air conditioning, ventilation and refrigeration maintenance technology; heating, ventilation, air conditioning and refrigeration engineering technology; hotel/motel administration; human services; industrial mechanics and maintenance technology; journalism; legal assistant/paralegal; liberal arts and sciences/liberal studies; machine tool technology; management information systems; mechanical engineering/mechanical technology; medical/clinical assistant; office management; psychology; registered nursing/registered nurse; respiratory care therapy; retailing; robotics technology; science technologies related; sociology; speech communication and rhetoric; surgical technology; telecommunications technology; web/multimedia management and webmaster; web page, digital/multimedia and information resources design.

Academics *Calendar:* semesters. *Degree:* certificates and associate. *Special study options:* academic remediation for entering students, adult/continuing education programs, advanced placement credit, cooperative education, distance learning, double majors, English as a second language, independent study, internships, part-time degree program, services for LD students, student-designed majors, summer session for credit.

Library Delaware County Community College Library with 55,779 titles, 249 serial subscriptions, 2,863 audiovisual materials, an OPAC, a Web page.

Student Life *Housing:* college housing not available. *Activities and Organizations:* drama/theater group, student-run newspaper, radio station, Business Society, Phi Theta Kappa, Student Government Association, Campus Bible Fellowship, Engineering Club. *Campus security:* 24-hour emergency response devices and patrols, late-night transport/escort service. *Student services:* health clinic, personal/psychological counseling.

Athletics Member NJCAA. *Intercollegiate sports:* baseball M, basketball M/W, golf M/W, soccer M, softball W, tennis M/W, volleyball W. *Intramural sports:* basketball M/W, lacrosse M(c), rugby W, volleyball W.

Financial Aid Of all full-time matriculated undergraduates who enrolled in 2010, 95 Federal Work-Study jobs (averaging $900).

Applying *Options:* early admission. *Application fee:* $25. *Required:* high school transcript. *Application deadlines:* rolling (freshmen), rolling (out-of-state freshmen), rolling (transfers). *Notification:* continuous (freshmen), continuous (out-of-state freshmen), continuous (transfers).

Freshman Application Contact Ms. Hope Diehl, Director of Admissions and Enrollment Services, Delaware County Community College, 901 South Media Line Road, Media, PA 19063-1094. *Phone:* 610-359-5050. *Fax:* 610-723-1530. *E-mail:* admiss@dccc.edu. *Web site:* http://www.dccc.edu/.

Douglas Education Center
Monessen, Pennsylvania

- **Proprietary** 2-year, founded 1904
- **Small-town** campus with easy access to Pittsburgh
- **Coed**

Undergraduates 334 full-time. Students come from 49 states and territories; 4 other countries; 32% are from out of state; 4% Black or African American, non-Hispanic/Latino; 4% Hispanic/Latino; 0.6% Asian, non-Hispanic/Latino; 0.6% Native Hawaiian or other Pacific Islander, non-Hispanic/Latino; 0.6% American Indian or Alaska Native, non-Hispanic/Latino; 1% Two or more races, non-Hispanic/Latino; 1% Race/ethnicity unknown; 1% international. *Retention:* 87% of full-time freshmen returned.

Faculty *Student/faculty ratio:* 16:1.

Academics *Degree:* diplomas and associate. *Special study options:* advanced placement credit.

Student Life *Campus security:* 24-hour emergency response devices.

Standardized Tests *Required:* Wonderlic aptitude test (for admission).

Financial Aid Of all full-time matriculated undergraduates who enrolled in 2010, 5 Federal Work-Study jobs (averaging $2500).

Applying *Application fee:* $50. *Required:* high school transcript, interview.

Freshman Application Contact Ms. Sherry Lee Walters, Director of Enrollment Services, Douglas Education Center, 130 Seventh Street, Monessen, PA 15062. *Phone:* 724-684-3684 Ext. 2181. *Toll-free phone:* 800-413-6013. *Web site:* http://www.dec.edu/.

DuBois Business College
DuBois, Pennsylvania

Director of Admissions Mrs. Lisa Doty, Director of Admissions, DuBois Business College, 1 Beaver Drive, DuBois, PA 15801-2401. *Phone:* 814-371-6920. *Toll-free phone:* 800-692-6213. *Fax:* 814-371-3947. *E-mail:* dotylj@dbcollege.com. *Web site:* http://www.dbcollege.com/.

Erie Business Center, Main

Erie, Pennsylvania

Freshman Application Contact Erie Business Center, Main, 246 West Ninth Street, Erie, PA 16501-1392. *Phone:* 814-456-7504. *Toll-free phone:* 800-352-3743. *Web site:* http://www.eriebc.edu/.

Erie Business Center, South

New Castle, Pennsylvania

Freshman Application Contact Erie Business Center, South, 170 Cascade Galleria, New Castle, PA 16101-3950. *Phone:* 724-658-9066. *Toll-free phone:* 800-722-6227. *E-mail:* admissions@eriebcs.com. *Web site:* http://www.eriebc.edu/.

Erie Institute of Technology

Erie, Pennsylvania

Freshman Application Contact Erie Institute of Technology, 940 Millcreek Mall, Erie, PA 16565. *Phone:* 814-868-9900. *Toll-free phone:* 866-868-3743. *Web site:* http://www.erieit.edu/.

Everest Institute

Pittsburgh, Pennsylvania

Director of Admissions Director of Admissions, Everest Institute, 100 Forbes Avenue, Suite 1200, Pittsburgh, PA 15222. *Phone:* 412-261-4520. *Toll-free phone:* 888-741-4270. *Fax:* 412-261-4546. *Web site:* http://www.everest.edu/.

Fortis Institute

Erie, Pennsylvania

Director of Admissions Guy M. Euliano, President, Fortis Institute, 5757 West 26th Street, Erie, PA 16506. *Phone:* 814-838-7673. *Fax:* 814-838-8642. *E-mail:* geuliano@tsbi.org. *Web site:* http://www.fortis.edu/.

Fortis Institute

Forty Fort, Pennsylvania

Freshman Application Contact Admissions Office, Fortis Institute, 166 Slocum Street, Forty Fort, PA 18704. *Phone:* 570-288-8400. *Web site:* http://www.fortis.edu/.

Harcum College

Bryn Mawr, Pennsylvania

Freshman Application Contact Office of Enrollment Management, Harcum College, 750 Montgomery Avenue, Bryn Mawr, PA 19010-3476. *Phone:* 610-526-6050. *E-mail:* enroll@harcum.edu. *Web site:* http://www.harcum.edu/.

Harrisburg Area Community College

Harrisburg, Pennsylvania

- **State and locally supported** 2-year, founded 1964
- **Urban** 212-acre campus
- **Endowment** $25.9 million
- **Coed**

Undergraduates 8,783 full-time, 14,427 part-time. Students come from 10 states and territories; 58 other countries; 1% are from out of state; 7% transferred in.

Faculty *Student/faculty ratio:* 22:1.

Academics *Calendar:* semesters. *Degree:* certificates, diplomas, and associate. *Special study options:* academic remediation for entering students, adult/continuing education programs, advanced placement credit, distance learning, double majors, English as a second language, honors programs, independent study, internships, part-time degree program, services for LD students, student-designed majors, study abroad, summer session for credit. *ROTC:* Army (b).

Student Life *Campus security:* 24-hour emergency response devices and patrols, late-night transport/escort service.

Costs (2011–12) *One-time required fee:* $35. *Tuition:* area resident $4095 full-time, $137 per credit hour part-time; state resident $5670 full-time, $189 per credit hour part-time; nonresident $8505 full-time, $284 per credit hour part-time. Full-time tuition and fees vary according to location and program. Part-time tuition and fees vary according to location and program. *Required fees:* $855 full-time, $29 per credit hour part-time.

Financial Aid Of all full-time matriculated undergraduates who enrolled in 2011, 4,396 applied for aid, 3,366 were judged to have need, 93 had their need fully met. In 2011, 13. *Average percent of need met:* 51. *Average financial aid package:* $6381. *Average need-based loan:* $3265. *Average need-based gift aid:* $2407. *Average non-need-based aid:* $981.

Applying *Options:* electronic application, early admission, deferred entrance. *Application fee:* $35. *Required for some:* high school transcript, 1 letter of recommendation, interview.

Freshman Application Contact Mrs. Vanita L. Cowan, Administrative Clerk, Admissions, Harrisburg Area Community College, Harrisburg, PA 17110. *Phone:* 717-780-2694. *Toll-free phone:* 800-ABC-HACC. *Fax:* 717-231-7674. *E-mail:* admit@hacc.edu. *Web site:* http://www.hacc.edu/.

Hussian School of Art

Philadelphia, Pennsylvania

Freshman Application Contact Director of Admissions, Hussian School of Art, The Bourse, Suite 300, 111 South Independence Mall East, Philadelphia, PA 19106. *Phone:* 215-574-9600. *Fax:* 215-574-9800. *E-mail:* info@hussianart.edu. *Web site:* http://www.hussianart.edu/.

ITT Technical Institute

Bensalem, Pennsylvania

- **Proprietary** 2-year, founded 2000, part of ITT Educational Services, Inc.
- **Coed**

Majors CAD/CADD drafting/design technology; computer engineering technology; criminal justice/law enforcement administration; design and visual communications; system, networking, and LAN/WAN management.

Academics *Calendar:* quarters. *Degree:* diplomas and associate.

Student Life *Housing:* college housing not available.

Freshman Application Contact Director of Recruitment, ITT Technical Institute, 3330 Tillman Drive, Bensalem, PA 19020. *Phone:* 215-702-6300. *Toll-free phone:* 866-488-8324. *Web site:* http://www.itt-tech.edu/.

ITT Technical Institute

Dunmore, Pennsylvania

- **Proprietary** 2-year, part of ITT Educational Services, Inc.
- **Coed**

Majors CAD/CADD drafting/design technology; computer engineering technology; criminal justice/law enforcement administration; design and visual communications; system, networking, and LAN/WAN management.

Academics *Calendar:* quarters. *Degree:* diplomas and associate.

Freshman Application Contact Director of Recruitment, ITT Technical Institute, 1000 Meade Street, Dunmore, PA 18512. *Phone:* 570-330-0600. *Toll-free phone:* 800-774-9791. *Web site:* http://www.itt-tech.edu/.

ITT Technical Institute

Harrisburg, Pennsylvania

- **Proprietary** 2-year, part of ITT Educational Services, Inc.
- **Coed**

Majors CAD/CADD drafting/design technology; computer engineering technology; computer software and media applications related; criminal justice/law enforcement administration; design and visual communications; system, networking, and LAN/WAN management.

Academics *Degree:* diplomas and associate.

Freshman Application Contact Director of Recruitment, ITT Technical Institute, 449 Eisenhower Boulevard, Suite 100, Harrisburg, PA 17111. *Phone:* 717-565-1700. *Toll-free phone:* 800-847-4756. *Web site:* http://www.itt-tech.edu/.

ITT Technical Institute

King of Prussia, Pennsylvania

- **Proprietary** 2-year, founded 2002, part of ITT Educational Services, Inc.
- **Coed**

Majors CAD/CADD drafting/design technology; computer engineering technology; criminal justice/law enforcement administration; design and visual communications; system, networking, and LAN/WAN management.

Academics *Calendar:* quarters. *Degree:* diplomas and associate.

Freshman Application Contact Director of Recruitment, ITT Technical Institute, 760 Moore Road, King of Prussia, PA 19406-1212. *Phone:* 610-491-8004. *Toll-free phone:* 866-902-8324. *Web site:* http://www.itt-tech.edu/.

ITT Technical Institute

Pittsburgh, Pennsylvania

- **Proprietary** 2-year, part of ITT Educational Services, Inc.
- **Coed**

Majors CAD/CADD drafting/design technology; computer engineering technology; computer software and media applications related; criminal justice/law enforcement administration; design and visual communications; system, networking, and LAN/WAN management.

Academics *Calendar:* quarters. *Degree:* diplomas and associate.

Student Life *Housing:* college housing not available.

Freshman Application Contact Director of Recruitment, ITT Technical Institute, 10 Parkway Center, Pittsburgh, PA 15220-3801. *Phone:* 412-937-9150. *Toll-free phone:* 800-353-8324. *Web site:* http://www.itt-tech.edu/.

ITT Technical Institute

Tarentum, Pennsylvania

- **Proprietary** 2-year, part of ITT Educational Services, Inc.
- **Coed**

Majors CAD/CADD drafting/design technology; computer engineering technology; computer software and media applications related; criminal justice/law enforcement administration; design and visual communications; system, networking, and LAN/WAN management; web/multimedia management and webmaster.

Academics *Calendar:* quarters. *Degree:* diplomas and associate.

Student Life *Housing:* college housing not available.

Freshman Application Contact Director of Recruitment, ITT Technical Institute, 100 Pittsburgh Mills Circle, Suite 100, Tarentum, PA 15084. *Phone:* 724-274-1400. *Toll-free phone:* 800-488-0121. *Web site:* http://www.itt-tech.edu/.

JNA Institute of Culinary Arts

Philadelphia, Pennsylvania

- **Proprietary** 2-year, founded 1988
- **Urban** campus with easy access to Philadelphia
- **Coed**

Undergraduates 92 full-time. 65% Black or African American, non-Hispanic/Latino; 4% Hispanic/Latino; 2% Asian, non-Hispanic/Latino. *Retention:* 52% of full-time freshmen returned.

Academics *Calendar:* continuous. *Degree:* associate.

Freshman Application Contact Admissions Office, JNA Institute of Culinary Arts, 1212 South Broad Street, Philadelphia, PA 19146. *Web site:* http://www.culinaryarts.com/.

Johnson College

Scranton, Pennsylvania

Freshman Application Contact Ms. Melissa Ide, Director of Enrollment Management, Johnson College, 3427 North Main Avenue, Scranton, PA 18508. *Phone:* 570-702-8910. *Toll-free phone:* 800-2WE-WORK. *Fax:* 570-348-2181. *E-mail:* admit@johnson.edu. *Web site:* http://www.johnson.edu/.

Kaplan Career Institute, Broomall Campus

Broomall, Pennsylvania

- **Proprietary** 2-year, founded 1958
- **Small-town** campus
- **Coed**

Majors Medical/clinical assistant.

Academics *Calendar:* quarters. *Degree:* diplomas and associate.

Freshman Application Contact Kaplan Career Institute, Broomall Campus, 1991 Sproul Road, Suite 42, Broomall, PA 19008. *Phone:* 610-353-3300. *Toll-free phone:* 800-935-1857. *Web site:* http://broomall.kaplancareerinstitute.com/.

Kaplan Career Institute, Franklin Mills Campus

Philadelphia, Pennsylvania

- **Proprietary** 2-year, founded 1981
- **Suburban** campus
- **Coed**

Majors Computer engineering technology; criminal justice/law enforcement administration; respiratory care therapy.

Academics *Calendar:* quarters. *Degree:* diplomas and associate.

Financial Aid Of all full-time matriculated undergraduates who enrolled in 2010, 30 Federal Work-Study jobs (averaging $2050).

Freshman Application Contact Kaplan Career Institute, Franklin Mills Campus, 125 Franklin Mills Boulevard, Philadelphia, PA 19154. *Phone:* 215-612-6600. *Toll-free phone:* 800-935-1857. *Web site:* http://franklin-mills.kaplancareerinstitute.com/.

Kaplan Career Institute, Harrisburg Campus

Harrisburg, Pennsylvania

- **Proprietary** 2-year, founded 1918
- **Suburban** campus
- **Coed**

Majors Business administration and management; computer systems networking and telecommunications; criminal justice/law enforcement administration; medical/clinical assistant.

Academics *Calendar:* quarters. *Degree:* diplomas and associate.

Freshman Application Contact Kaplan Career Institute, Harrisburg Campus, 5650 Derry Street, Harrisburg, PA 17111-3518. *Phone:* 717-558-1300. *Toll-free phone:* 800-935-1857. *Web site:* http://harrisburg.kaplancareerinstitute.com/.

Kaplan Career Institute, ICM Campus

Pittsburgh, Pennsylvania

- **Proprietary** 2-year, founded 1963
- **Urban** campus
- **Coed**

Majors Accounting and business/management; business administration and management; computer systems networking and telecommunications; criminal justice/law enforcement administration; medical/clinical assistant; occupational therapy.

Academics *Calendar:* continuous. *Degree:* diplomas and associate.

Freshman Application Contact Kaplan Career Institute, ICM Campus, 10 Wood Street, Pittsburgh, PA 15222-1977. *Phone:* 412-261-2647. *Toll-free phone:* 800-935-1857. *Web site:* http://pittsburgh.kaplancareerinstitute.com/.

Kaplan Career Institute, Philadelphia Campus

Philadelphia, Pennsylvania

- **Proprietary** 2-year
- **Coed**

Majors Criminal justice/law enforcement administration.

Academics *Degree:* diplomas and associate.

Freshman Application Contact Admissions Director, Kaplan Career Institute, Philadelphia Campus, 3010 Market Street, Philadelphia, PA 19104. *Toll-free phone:* 800-935-1857. *Web site:* http://philadelphia.kaplancareerinstitute.com/.

Keystone Technical Institute

Harrisburg, Pennsylvania

Freshman Application Contact Tom Bogush, Director of Admissions, Keystone Technical Institute, 2301 Academy Drive, Harrisburg, PA 17112. *Phone:* 717-545-4747. *Toll-free phone:* 800-400-3322. *Fax:* 717-901-9090. *E-mail:* info@acadcampus.com. *Web site:* http://www.kti.edu/.

Lackawanna College

Scranton, Pennsylvania

Freshman Application Contact Ms. Stacey Muchal, Associate Director of Admissions, Lackawanna College, 501 Vine Street, Scranton, PA 18509. *Phone:* 570-961-7868. *Toll-free phone:* 877-346-3552. *Fax:* 570-961-7843. *E-mail:* muchals@lackawanna.edu. *Web site:* http://www.lackawanna.edu/.

Lancaster General College of Nursing & Health Sciences

Lancaster, Pennsylvania

Freshman Application Contact Admissions Office, Lancaster General College of Nursing & Health Sciences, 410 North Lime Street, Lancaster, PA 17602. *Toll-free phone:* 800-622-5443. *Web site:* http://www.lancastergeneralcollege.edu/content/.

Lansdale School of Business

North Wales, Pennsylvania

Director of Admissions Ms. Marianne H. Johnson, Director of Admissions, Lansdale School of Business, 201 Church Road, North Wales, PA 19454-4148. *Phone:* 215-699-5700 Ext. 112. *Toll-free phone:* 800-219-0486. *Fax:* 215-699-8770. *E-mail:* mjohnson@lsb.edu. *Web site:* http://www.lsb.edu/.

Laurel Business Institute

Uniontown, Pennsylvania

Freshman Application Contact Mrs. Lisa Dolan, Laurel Business Institute, 11 East Penn Street, PO Box 877, Uniontown, PA 15401. *Phone:* 724-439-4900 Ext. 158. *Fax:* 724-439-3607. *E-mail:* ldolan@laurel.edu. *Web site:* http://www.laurel.edu/.

Laurel Technical Institute

Meadville, Pennsylvania

Freshman Application Contact Admissions Officer, Laurel Technical Institute, 628 Arch Street, Suite B105, Meadville, PA 16335. *Phone:* 814-724-0700. *Fax:* 814-724-2777. *E-mail:* lti.admission@laurel.edu. *Web site:* http://www.laurel.edu/lti/.

Laurel Technical Institute

Sharon, Pennsylvania

Freshman Application Contact Irene Lewis, Laurel Technical Institute, 335 Boyd Drive, Sharon, PA 16146. *Phone:* 724-983-0700. *Fax:* 724-983-8355. *E-mail:* info@biop.edu. *Web site:* http://www.laurel.edu/lti/.

Le Cordon Bleu Institute of Culinary Arts in Pittsburgh

Pittsburgh, Pennsylvania

Freshman Application Contact Ms. Juliette Mariani, Dean of Students, Le Cordon Bleu Institute of Culinary Arts in Pittsburgh, 717 Liberty Avenue, 19th Floor, Pittsburgh, PA 15222. *Phone:* 412-566-2433. *Toll-free phone:* 888-314-8222. *Fax:* 412-566-2434. *Web site:* http://www.chefs.edu/Pittsburgh.

Lehigh Carbon Community College

Schnecksville, Pennsylvania

- **State and locally supported** 2-year, founded 1967
- **Suburban** 254-acre campus with easy access to Philadelphia
- **Endowment** $2.1 million
- **Coed,** 7,710 undergraduate students, 35% full-time, 61% women, 39% men

Undergraduates 2,726 full-time, 4,984 part-time. Students come from 10 states and territories; 13 other countries; 0.4% are from out of state; 5% Black or African American, non-Hispanic/Latino; 15% Hispanic/Latino; 2% Asian, non-Hispanic/Latino; 0.2% American Indian or Alaska Native, non-Hispanic/Latino; 3% Two or more races, non-Hispanic/Latino; 7% Race/ethnicity unknown; 0.3% international; 53% transferred in. *Retention:* 54% of full-time freshmen returned.

Freshmen *Admission:* 4,352 applied, 4,352 admitted, 1,294 enrolled.

Faculty *Total:* 443, 20% full-time, 4% with terminal degrees. *Student/faculty ratio:* 35:1.

Majors Accounting technology and bookkeeping; aeronautics/aviation/aerospace science and technology; airline pilot and flight crew; animation, interactive technology, video graphics and special effects; art; biology/biological sciences; biotechnology; building/construction site management; business administration and management; business/commerce; chemical technology; computer and information sciences; computer and information systems security; computer programming; computer programming (specific applications);

computer systems networking and telecommunications; construction trades; criminal justice/law enforcement administration; criminal justice/safety; drafting and design technology; early childhood education; education; electrical, electronic and communications engineering technology; engineering; fashion/apparel design; game and interactive media design; general studies; geographic information science and cartography; graphic design; health information/medical records technology; heating, air conditioning, ventilation and refrigeration maintenance technology; horticultural science; humanities; human resources management; human services; industrial electronics technology; interior design; legal assistant/paralegal; liberal arts and sciences/liberal studies; manufacturing engineering technology; mathematics; mechanical engineering/mechanical technology; medical/clinical assistant; nanotechnology; occupational therapist assistant; physical sciences; physical therapy technology; psychology; radio and television broadcasting technology; recording arts technology; registered nursing/registered nurse; resort management; special education; speech communication and rhetoric; sport and fitness administration/management; teacher assistant/aide; veterinary/animal health technology; web page, digital/multimedia and information resources design.

Academics *Calendar:* semesters. *Degree:* certificates, diplomas, and associate. *Special study options:* academic remediation for entering students, advanced placement credit, cooperative education, distance learning, English as a second language, external degree program, honors programs, independent study, internships, part-time degree program, services for LD students, summer session for credit. *ROTC:* Army (c).

Library Rothrock Library with 96,508 titles, 336 serial subscriptions, 7,563 audiovisual materials, an OPAC, a Web page.

Student Life *Housing:* college housing not available. *Activities and Organizations:* drama/theater group, student-run radio station, choral group, Phi Theta Kappa, Justice Society, Students in Free Enterprise (SIFE), Student Government Association, WXLV 90.3FM college radio station. *Campus security:* 24-hour emergency response devices. *Student services:* personal/psychological counseling.

Athletics Member NJCAA. *Intercollegiate sports:* baseball M, basketball M/W, golf M/W, soccer M, softball W, volleyball W. *Intramural sports:* basketball M/W, soccer M/W, softball M/W, table tennis M/W, tennis M/W, volleyball M/W.

Standardized Tests *Required for some:* TEAS (for those applying to Nursing Program).

Costs (2012–13) *Tuition:* area resident $2820 full-time, $94 per credit part-time; state resident $5910 full-time, $197 per credit part-time; nonresident $9000 full-time; $300 per credit part-time. *Required fees:* $510 full-time, $17 per credit part-time. *Payment plan:* installment. *Waivers:* senior citizens and employees or children of employees.

Applying *Options:* electronic application. *Required for some:* essay or personal statement, high school transcript, interview. *Application deadlines:* rolling (freshmen), rolling (out-of-state freshmen), rolling (transfers). *Notification:* continuous (freshmen), continuous (out-of-state freshmen), continuous (transfers).

Freshman Application Contact Mr. Louis Hegyes, Director of Recruitment/Admissions, Lehigh Carbon Community College, 4525 Education Park Drive, Schnecksville, PA 18078. *Phone:* 610-799-1575. *Fax:* 610-799-1527. *E-mail:* admissions@lccc.edu. *Web site:* http://www.lccc.edu/.

Lincoln Technical Institute

Allentown, Pennsylvania

Freshman Application Contact Admissions Office, Lincoln Technical Institute, 5151 Tilghman Street, Allentown, PA 18104-3298. *Phone:* 610-398-5301. *Web site:* http://www.lincolnedu.com/.

Lincoln Technical Institute

Philadelphia, Pennsylvania

Director of Admissions Mr. James Kuntz, Executive Director, Lincoln Technical Institute, 9191 Torresdale Avenue, Philadelphia, PA 19136-1595. *Phone:* 215-335-0800. *Fax:* 215-335-1443. *E-mail:* jkuntz@lincolntech.com. *Web site:* http://www.lincolnedu.com/.

Luzerne County Community College

Nanticoke, Pennsylvania

Freshman Application Contact Mr. Francis Curry, Director of Admissions, Luzerne County Community College, 1333 South Prospect Street, Nanticoke, PA 18634-9804. *Phone:* 570-740-0337. *Toll-free phone:* 800-377-5222 Ext. 7337. *Fax:* 570-740-0238. *E-mail:* admissions@luzerne.edu. *Web site:* http://www.luzerne.edu/.

Manor College

Jenkintown, Pennsylvania

Director of Admissions I. Jerry Czenstuch, Vice President of Enrollment Management, Manor College, 700 Fox Chase Road, Jenkintown, PA 19046. *Phone:* 215-884-2216. *E-mail:* ftadmiss@manor.edu. *Web site:* http://www.manor.edu/.

McCann School of Business & Technology

Pottsville, Pennsylvania

Freshman Application Contact Ms. Linda Walinsky, Director, Pottsville Campus, McCann School of Business & Technology, 2650 Woodglen Road, Pottsville, PA 17901. *Phone:* 570-622-7622. *Fax:* 570-622-7770. *Web site:* http://www.mccannschool.com/.

Mercyhurst North East

North East, Pennsylvania

Director of Admissions Travis Lindahl, Director of Admissions, Mercyhurst North East, 16 West Division Street, North East, PA 16428. *Phone:* 814-725-6217. *Toll-free phone:* 866-846-6042. *Fax:* 814-725-6251. *E-mail:* neadmiss@mercyhurst.edu. *Web site:* http://northeast.mercyhurst.edu/.

Metropolitan Career Center

Philadelphia, Pennsylvania

Freshman Application Contact Admissions Office, Metropolitan Career Center, 100 South Broad Street, Suite 830, Philadelphia, PA 19110. *Phone:* 215-568-7861. *Web site:* http://www.careersinit.org/.

Montgomery County Community College

Blue Bell, Pennsylvania

- **County-supported** 2-year, founded 1964
- **Suburban** 186-acre campus with easy access to Philadelphia
- **Coed,** 13,985 undergraduate students, 40% full-time, 57% women, 43% men

Undergraduates 5,532 full-time, 8,453 part-time. Students come from 12 states and territories; 95 other countries; 1% are from out of state; 14% Black or African American, non-Hispanic/Latino; 5% Hispanic/Latino; 5% Asian, non-Hispanic/Latino; 0.2% Native Hawaiian or other Pacific Islander, non-Hispanic/Latino; 0.3% American Indian or Alaska Native, non-Hispanic/Latino; 1% Two or more races, non-Hispanic/Latino; 9% Race/ethnicity unknown; 2% international; 3% transferred in. *Retention:* 60% of full-time freshmen returned.

Freshmen *Admission:* 7,477 applied, 7,477 admitted, 4,370 enrolled.

Faculty *Total:* 754, 25% full-time. *Student/faculty ratio:* 22:1.

Majors Accounting; accounting technology and bookkeeping; administrative assistant and secretarial science; architectural drafting and CAD/CADD; art; automobile/automotive mechanics technology; baking and pastry arts; biology/biological sciences; biotechnology; business administration and management; business/commerce; business/corporate communications; CAD/CADD drafting/design technology; child-care and support services management; clinical/medical laboratory technology; commercial and advertising art; communications technologies and support services related; computer and information sciences; computer programming; computer systems networking and telecommunications; criminal justice/police science; culinary arts; dental hygiene; electrical, electronic and communications engineering technology; electromechanical technology; elementary education; engineering science; engineering technologies and engineering related; environmental science; fire prevention and safety technology; health and physical education/fitness; hospitality and recreation marketing; humanities; information science/studies; liberal arts and sciences/liberal studies; management information systems and services related; mathematics; mechanical drafting and CAD/CADD; mechanical engineering/mechanical technology; medical/clinical assistant; medical radiologic technology; network and system administration; physical education teaching and coaching; physical sciences; psychiatric/mental health services technology; psychology; radiologic technology/science; radio, television, and digital communication related; real estate; recording arts technology; registered nursing/registered nurse; sales, distribution, and marketing operations; secondary education; social sciences; speech communication and rhetoric; sur-

gical technology; teacher assistant/aide; tourism and travel services marketing; web/multimedia management and webmaster.

Academics *Calendar:* semesters. *Degree:* certificates and associate. *Special study options:* academic remediation for entering students, accelerated degree program, adult/continuing education programs, advanced placement credit, cooperative education, distance learning, English as a second language, honors programs, independent study, internships, part-time degree program, services for LD students, student-designed majors, study abroad, summer session for credit.

Library The Brendlinger Library/Branch Library Pottstown Campus plus 1 other with 87,895 titles, 366 serial subscriptions, 21,804 audiovisual materials, an OPAC, a Web page.

Student Life *Housing:* college housing not available. *Activities and Organizations:* drama/theater group, student-run newspaper, radio and television station, choral group, student government, Thrive (Christian Fellowship), radio station, Drama Club, African - American Student League. *Campus security:* 24-hour emergency response devices and patrols, late-night transport/escort service, bicycle patrol. *Student services:* health clinic, personal/psychological counseling.

Athletics Member NJCAA. *Intercollegiate sports:* baseball M, basketball M/W, soccer M/W, softball W, volleyball W. *Intramural sports:* badminton M/W, basketball M/W, bowling M/W, cross-country running M/W, football M, racquetball M/W, soccer M/W, table tennis M/W, tennis M/W, volleyball M/W, weight lifting M/W.

Costs (2011–12) *Tuition:* area resident $3090 full-time, $103 per credit hour part-time; state resident $6480 full-time, $206 per credit hour part-time; non-resident $9870 full-time, $309 per credit hour part-time. *Required fees:* $660 full-time, $22 per credit hour part-time. *Payment plan:* deferred payment. *Waivers:* senior citizens and employees or children of employees.

Financial Aid Of all full-time matriculated undergraduates who enrolled in 2010, 60 Federal Work-Study jobs (averaging $2500).

Applying *Options:* electronic application, early admission, deferred entrance. *Application fee:* $25. *Required:* high school transcript. *Required for some:* interview. *Application deadline:* rolling (transfers). *Notification:* continuous (freshmen), continuous (transfers).

Freshman Application Contact Ms. Penny Sawyer, Director of Admissions and Recruitment, Montgomery County Community College, Blue Bell, PA 19422. *Phone:* 215-641-6551. *Fax:* 215-619-7188. *E-mail:* admrec@admin.mc3.edu. *Web site:* http://www.mc3.edu/.

New Castle School of Trades

Pulaski, Pennsylvania

Freshman Application Contact Mr. James Catheline, Admissions Director, New Castle School of Trades, New Castle Youngstown Road, Route 422 RD1, Pulaski, PA 16143-9721. *Phone:* 724-964-8811. *Toll-free phone:* 800-837-8299. *Web site:* http://www.ncstrades.com/.

Newport Business Institute

Lower Burrell, Pennsylvania

Freshman Application Contact Admissions Coordinator, Newport Business Institute, Lower Burrell, PA 15068. *Phone:* 724-339-7542. *Toll-free phone:* 800-752-7695. *Fax:* 724-339-2950. *E-mail:* admissions@newportbusiness.com. *Web site:* http://www.nbi.edu/.

Newport Business Institute

Williamsport, Pennsylvania

- **Proprietary** 2-year, founded 1955
- **Small-town** campus
- **Coed, primarily women**

Undergraduates 108 full-time. 18% Black or African American, non-Hispanic/Latino; 0.9% Hispanic/Latino; 16% transferred in.

Faculty *Student/faculty ratio:* 9:1.

Academics *Calendar:* quarters. *Degree:* associate. *Special study options:* distance learning, internships, part-time degree program, summer session for credit.

Financial Aid *Financial aid deadline:* 8/1.

Applying *Options:* electronic application, deferred entrance. *Application fee:* $25. *Required:* high school transcript, interview.

Freshman Application Contact Ms. Ashley Wall, Admissions Representative, Newport Business Institute, 941 West Third Street, Williamsport, PA 17701. *Phone:* 570-326-2869. *Toll-free phone:* 800-962-6971. *Fax:* 570-326-2136. *E-mail:* admissions2_NBI@Comcast.net. *Web site:* http://www.nbi.edu/.

Northampton Community College

Bethlehem, Pennsylvania

- **State and locally supported** 2-year, founded 1967
- **Suburban** 165-acre campus with easy access to Philadelphia
- **Endowment** $29.9 million
- **Coed,** 11,350 undergraduate students, 44% full-time, 60% women, 40% men

Undergraduates 5,004 full-time, 6,346 part-time. Students come from 27 states and territories; 43 other countries; 2% are from out of state; 11% Black or African American, non-Hispanic/Latino; 18% Hispanic/Latino; 2% Asian, non-Hispanic/Latino; 0.2% Native Hawaiian or other Pacific Islander, non-Hispanic/Latino; 0.3% American Indian or Alaska Native, non-Hispanic/Latino; 1% Two or more races, non-Hispanic/Latino; 2% Race/ethnicity unknown; 0.8% international; 10% transferred in; 2% live on campus.

Freshmen *Admission:* 4,845 applied, 4,845 admitted, 2,436 enrolled.

Faculty *Total:* 721, 16% full-time, 20% with terminal degrees. *Student/faculty ratio:* 22:1.

Majors Accounting technology and bookkeeping; acting; administrative assistant and secretarial science; architectural engineering technology; athletic training; automobile/automotive mechanics technology; biology/biological sciences; biotechnology; business administration and management; business/commerce; CAD/CADD drafting/design technology; chemistry; computer and information systems security; computer installation and repair technology; computer programming; computer science; computer systems networking and telecommunications; construction management; criminal justice/safety; culinary arts; dental hygiene; diagnostic medical sonography and ultrasound technology; early childhood education; electrical, electronic and communications engineering technology; electrician; electromechanical technology; engineering; fine/studio arts; fire science/firefighting; fire services administration; funeral service and mortuary science; general studies; graphic design; heating, air conditioning, ventilation and refrigeration maintenance technology; hotel/motel administration; industrial electronics technology; interior design; journalism; legal administrative assistant/secretary; legal assistant/paralegal; liberal arts and sciences and humanities related; liberal arts and sciences/liberal studies; marketing/marketing management; mathematics; medical administrative assistant and medical secretary; middle school education; physics; quality control technology; radio and television broadcasting technology; radiologic technology/science; registered nursing/registered nurse; restaurant/food services management; secondary education; social work; speech communication and rhetoric; sport and fitness administration/management; surgical technology; teacher assistant/aide; veterinary/animal health technology; web page, digital/multimedia and information resources design.

Academics *Calendar:* semesters. *Degree:* certificates, diplomas, and associate. *Special study options:* academic remediation for entering students, adult/continuing education programs, advanced placement credit, distance learning, English as a second language, honors programs, independent study, internships, off-campus study, part-time degree program, services for LD students, student-designed majors, study abroad, summer session for credit.

Library Paul & Harriett Mack Library with 72,578 titles, 198 serial subscriptions, 10,802 audiovisual materials, an OPAC, a Web page.

Student Life *Housing Options:* coed. Campus housing is university owned. *Activities and Organizations:* drama/theater group, student-run newspaper, radio station, choral group, Phi Theta Kappa, Student Senate, College and Hospital Association of Radiologic Technologies Students (CHARTS), American Dental Hygiene Association (ADHA), International Student Organization. *Campus security:* 24-hour emergency response devices and patrols, controlled dormitory access. *Student services:* health clinic, personal/psychological counseling.

Athletics Member NJCAA. *Intercollegiate sports:* baseball M, basketball M/W, bowling M/W, golf M/W, soccer M, softball W, tennis M/W, volleyball M/W. *Intramural sports:* basketball M/W, cheerleading M(c)/W(c), soccer M/W, volleyball M/W, wrestling M(c).

Costs (2011–12) *Tuition:* area resident $2460 full-time, $82 per credit hour part-time; state resident $4920 full-time, $164 per credit hour part-time; nonresident $7380 full-time, $246 per credit hour part-time. Full-time tuition and fees vary according to course load. Part-time tuition and fees vary according to course load. *Required fees:* $960 full-time, $32 per credit hour part-time. *Room and board:* $7404; room only: $4216. Room and board charges vary according to board plan and housing facility. *Payment plan:* installment. *Waivers:* senior citizens and employees or children of employees.

Financial Aid Of all full-time matriculated undergraduates who enrolled in 2010, 2,443 applied for aid, 1,832 were judged to have need, 696 had their need fully met. 230 Federal Work-Study jobs (averaging $1175). 100 state and other part-time jobs (averaging $1933). *Average percent of need met:* 80%.

Applying *Options:* electronic application, deferred entrance. *Application fee:* $25. *Required for some:* high school transcript, minimum 2.5 GPA, interview,

interview required: rad, veterinary, and surgical technologies. *Recommended:* high school transcript. *Application deadlines:* rolling (freshmen), rolling (out-of-state freshmen), rolling (transfers). *Notification:* continuous (freshmen), continuous (out-of-state freshmen), continuous (transfers).

Freshman Application Contact Mr. James McCarthy, Director of Admissions, Northampton Community College, 3835 Green Pond Road, Bethlehem, PA 18020-7599. *Phone:* 610-861-5506. *Fax:* 610-861-5551. *E-mail:* jrmccarthy@northampton.edu. *Web site:* http://www.northampton.edu/.

Oakbridge Academy of Arts

Lower Burrell, Pennsylvania

Freshman Application Contact Matthew Belferman, Admissions Coordinator, Oakbridge Academy of Arts, 1250 Greensburg Road, Lower Burrell, PA 15068. *Phone:* 724-335-5336. *Toll-free phone:* 800-734-5601. *E-mail:* mbelferman@oaa.edu. *Web site:* http://oaa.edu/.

Orleans Technical Institute

Philadelphia, Pennsylvania

- **Independent** 2-year
- **Urban** 9-acre campus with easy access to Philadelphia
- **Coed,** 533 undergraduate students, 75% full-time, 30% women, 70% men

Undergraduates 400 full-time, 133 part-time. Students come from 3 states and territories; 5% are from out of state; 49% Black or African American, non-Hispanic/Latino; 11% Hispanic/Latino; 2% Asian, non-Hispanic/Latino; 0.6% Native Hawaiian or other Pacific Islander, non-Hispanic/Latino; 0.2% American Indian or Alaska Native, non-Hispanic/Latino; 0.2% Two or more races, non-Hispanic/Latino; 0.8% transferred in.

Freshmen *Admission:* 480 enrolled.

Faculty *Total:* 48, 56% full-time. *Student/faculty ratio:* 13:1.

Majors Court reporting.

Academics *Calendar:* trimesters. *Degree:* diplomas and associate. *Special study options:* academic remediation for entering students, cooperative education, internships, part-time degree program, summer session for credit.

Library Orleans Technical Institute Library and Learning Resource Center plus 1 other with 804 titles, 27 serial subscriptions, 7 audiovisual materials, an OPAC, a Web page.

Student Life *Housing:* college housing not available. *Campus security:* 24-hour emergency response devices.

Standardized Tests *Required:* Wonderlic (for admission).

Costs (2011–12) *Tuition:* $9320 full-time. Full-time tuition and fees vary according to class time, course load, degree level, and program. Part-time tuition and fees vary according to class time, course load, degree level, and program. No tuition increase for student's term of enrollment. *Required fees:* $860 full-time. *Payment plans:* tuition prepayment, installment.

Financial Aid Of all full-time matriculated undergraduates who enrolled in 2010, 5 Federal Work-Study jobs (averaging $4800). *Financial aid deadline:* 8/1.

Applying *Options:* electronic application. *Application fee:* $125. *Required:* high school transcript, interview. *Application deadlines:* rolling (freshmen), rolling (transfers).

Freshman Application Contact Mrs. Dorothy Stinson, Admissions Secretary, Orleans Technical Institute, 2770 Red Lion Road, Philadelphia, PA 19114. *Phone:* 215-728-4700. *Fax:* 215-745-1689. *E-mail:* stinsd@jevs.org. *Web site:* http://www.orleanstech.edu/.

Pace Institute

Reading, Pennsylvania

Director of Admissions Mr. Ed Levandowski, Director of Enrollment Management, Pace Institute, 606 Court Street, Reading, PA 19601. *Phone:* 610-375-1212. *Fax:* 610-375-1924. *Web site:* http://www.paceinstitute.com/.

Penn Commercial Business and Technical School

Washington, Pennsylvania

Director of Admissions Mr. Michael John Joyce, Director of Admissions, Penn Commercial Business and Technical School, 242 Oak Spring Road, Washington, PA 15301. *Phone:* 724-222-5330 Ext. 1. *Toll-free phone:* 888-309-7484. *E-mail:* mjoyce@penn-commercial.com. *Web site:* http://www.penncommercial.net/.

Pennco Tech
Bristol, Pennsylvania

- **Proprietary** 2-year, founded 1961, part of Pennco Institutes, Inc.
- **Suburban** 7-acre campus with easy access to Philadelphia
- **Coed,** 400 undergraduate students, 61% full-time, 20% women, 80% men

Undergraduates 245 full-time, 155 part-time. Students come from 6 states and territories; 3% are from out of state; 1% transferred in; 3% live on campus. *Retention:* 78% of full-time freshmen returned.
Freshmen *Admission:* 229 applied, 79 enrolled.
Faculty *Total:* 40, 75% full-time. *Student/faculty ratio:* 18:1.
Majors Autobody/collision and repair technology; vehicle maintenance and repair technologies related.
Academics *Calendar:* modular. *Degree:* certificates, diplomas, and associate. *Special study options:* academic remediation for entering students, adult/continuing education programs, advanced placement credit, double majors.
Library Resource Center with 6,000 titles, 30 serial subscriptions, a Web page.
Student Life *Housing Options:* men-only. Campus housing is university owned. *Campus security:* 24-hour emergency response devices, controlled dormitory access.
Costs (2012–13) *Tuition:* $21,500 full-time. Full-time tuition and fees vary according to class time, course load, and program. Part-time tuition and fees vary according to class time, course load, and program. *Room only:* $4000. *Payment plan:* installment. *Waivers:* employees or children of employees.
Applying *Application fee:* $100. *Required:* high school transcript, minimum 2.0 GPA, interview. *Required for some:* essay or personal statement. *Application deadlines:* rolling (freshmen), rolling (transfers).
Freshman Application Contact Pennco Tech, 3815 Otter Street, Bristol, PA 19007-3696. *Phone:* 215-785-0111. *Toll-free phone:* 800-575-9399. *Web site:* http://www.penncotech.com/.

Penn State Beaver
Monaca, Pennsylvania

- **State-related** primarily 2-year, founded 1964, part of Pennsylvania State University
- **Small-town** campus
- **Coed,** 870 undergraduate students, 80% full-time, 46% women, 54% men

Undergraduates 700 full-time, 170 part-time. 8% are from out of state; 11% Black or African American, non-Hispanic/Latino; 4% Hispanic/Latino; 2% Asian, non-Hispanic/Latino; 0.3% Native Hawaiian or other Pacific Islander, non-Hispanic/Latino; 0.1% American Indian or Alaska Native, non-Hispanic/Latino; 3% Two or more races, non-Hispanic/Latino; 2% Race/ethnicity unknown; 0.8% international; 6% transferred in; 23% live on campus. *Retention:* 71% of full-time freshmen returned.
Freshmen *Admission:* 737 applied, 637 admitted, 251 enrolled. *Average high school GPA:* 2.9. *Test scores:* SAT critical reading scores over 500: 38%; SAT math scores over 500: 45%; SAT writing scores over 500: 32%; SAT critical reading scores over 600: 9%; SAT math scores over 600: 15%; SAT writing scores over 600: 7%; SAT critical reading scores over 700: 3%; SAT math scores over 700: 2%; SAT writing scores over 700: 1%.
Faculty *Total:* 61, 56% full-time, 46% with terminal degrees. *Student/faculty ratio:* 18:1.
Majors Accounting; acting; actuarial science; adult and continuing education administration; advertising; aerospace, aeronautical and astronautical/space engineering; African American/Black studies; agribusiness; agricultural and extension education; agricultural business and management related; agricultural engineering; agricultural mechanization; agriculture; agronomy and crop science; animal sciences; animal sciences related; anthropology; applied economics; archeology; architectural engineering; art; art history, criticism and conservation; art teacher education; Asian studies (East); astronomy; atmospheric sciences and meteorology; biochemistry; bioengineering and biomedical engineering; biological and biomedical sciences related; biological and physical sciences; biology/biological sciences; biology/biotechnology laboratory technician; business administration and management; business/commerce; business/managerial economics; chemical engineering; chemistry; civil engineering; classics and classical languages; communication and journalism related; communication sciences and disorders; comparative literature; computer and information sciences; computer engineering; criminal justice/law enforcement administration; economics; electrical and electronics engineering; elementary education; engineering science; English; environmental/environmental health engineering; film/cinema/video studies; finance; food science; foreign language teacher education; forest sciences and biology; forest technology; French; geography; geological and earth sciences/geosciences related; geology/earth science; German; graphic design; health/health-care administration; history; horticultural science; hospitality administration related; human

development and family studies; human nutrition; industrial engineering; information science/studies; international relations and affairs; Italian; Japanese; Jewish/Judaic studies; journalism; kinesiology and exercise science; labor and industrial relations; landscaping and groundskeeping; Latin American studies; liberal arts and sciences/liberal studies; logistics, materials, and supply chain management; management information systems; marketing/marketing management; materials science; mathematics; mechanical engineering; medical microbiology and bacteriology; medieval and Renaissance studies; mining and mineral engineering; music; natural resources and conservation related; natural resources/conservation; nuclear engineering; organizational behavior; parks, recreation and leisure facilities management; petroleum engineering; philosophy; physics; political science and government; premedical studies; psychology; registered nursing/registered nurse; rehabilitation and therapeutic professions related; religious studies; Russian; secondary education; sociology; soil science and agronomy; Spanish; special education; speech communication and rhetoric; statistics; theater design and technology; toxicology; turf and turfgrass management; visual and performing arts; women's studies.
Academics *Calendar:* semesters. *Degrees:* certificates, associate, bachelor's, and master's. *Special study options:* adult/continuing education programs.
Student Life *Housing Options:* coed, disabled students. Campus housing is university owned. Freshman campus housing is guaranteed.
Athletics Member NJCAA. *Intercollegiate sports:* baseball M, basketball M, softball M/W, volleyball W. *Intramural sports:* basketball M/W, cheerleading M(c)/W(c), cross-country running M/W, football M, golf M/W, soccer M/W, softball M/W, table tennis M/W.
Standardized Tests *Required:* SAT or ACT (for admission).
Costs (2011–12) *Tuition:* state resident $12,242 full-time, $495 per credit part-time; nonresident $18,682 full-time, $778 per credit part-time. Full-time tuition and fees vary according to course level, degree level, location, program, and student level. Part-time tuition and fees vary according to course level, course load, degree level, location, program, and student level. *Required fees:* $860 full-time. *Room and board:* $8940; room only: $4770. Room and board charges vary according to board plan, housing facility, and location. *Payment plans:* installment, deferred payment. *Waivers:* employees or children of employees.
Financial Aid Of all full-time matriculated undergraduates who enrolled in 2010, 616 applied for aid, 532 were judged to have need, 27 had their need fully met. In 2010, 34 non-need-based awards were made. *Average percent of need met:* 65%. *Average financial aid package:* $10,048. *Average need-based loan:* $3914. *Average need-based gift aid:* $6366. *Average non-need-based aid:* $2157. *Average indebtedness upon graduation:* $33,530.
Applying *Options:* electronic application, early admission, deferred entrance. *Application fee:* $50. *Required:* high school transcript. *Required for some:* interview. *Recommended:* essay or personal statement. *Application deadlines:* rolling (freshmen), rolling (transfers). *Notification:* continuous (freshmen), continuous (transfers).
Freshman Application Contact Admissions Office, Penn State Beaver, 100 University Drive, Monaca, PA 15061. *Phone:* 724-773-3800. *Fax:* 724-773-3658. *E-mail:* br-admissions@psu.edu. *Web site:* http://www.br.psu.edu/.

Penn State Brandywine
Media, Pennsylvania

- **State-related** primarily 2-year, founded 1966, part of Pennsylvania State University
- **Small-town** campus
- **Coed,** 1,628 undergraduate students, 85% full-time, 42% women, 58% men

Undergraduates 1,390 full-time, 238 part-time. 5% are from out of state; 11% Black or African American, non-Hispanic/Latino; 4% Hispanic/Latino; 8% Asian, non-Hispanic/Latino; 0.1% Native Hawaiian or other Pacific Islander, non-Hispanic/Latino; 2% Two or more races, non-Hispanic/Latino; 3% Race/ethnicity unknown; 0.8% international; 5% transferred in. *Retention:* 72% of full-time freshmen returned.
Freshmen *Admission:* 1,260 applied, 1,050 admitted, 402 enrolled. *Average high school GPA:* 2.89. *Test scores:* SAT critical reading scores over 500: 37%; SAT math scores over 500: 46%; SAT writing scores over 500: 31%; SAT critical reading scores over 600: 6%; SAT math scores over 600: 14%; SAT writing scores over 600: 4%; SAT critical reading scores over 700: 1%; SAT math scores over 700: 2%; SAT writing scores over 700: 1%.
Faculty *Total:* 128, 44% full-time, 45% with terminal degrees. *Student/faculty ratio:* 18:1.
Majors Accounting; acting; actuarial science; adult and continuing education administration; advertising; aerospace, aeronautical and astronautical/space engineering; African American/Black studies; agribusiness; agricultural and extension education; agricultural business and management related; agricultural engineering; agricultural mechanization; agriculture; agronomy and crop science; American studies; animal sciences; animal sciences related; anthropology; applied economics; archeology; architectural engineering; art; art his-

tory, criticism and conservation; art teacher education; Asian studies (East); astronomy; atmospheric sciences and meteorology; biochemistry; bioengineering and biomedical engineering; biological and biomedical sciences related; biological and physical sciences; biology/biological sciences; biology/biotechnology laboratory technician; business administration and management; business/commerce; business/managerial economics; chemical engineering; chemistry; civil engineering; classics and classical languages; communication and journalism related; communication sciences and disorders; comparative literature; computer and information sciences; computer engineering; criminal justice/law enforcement administration; economics; electrical and electronics engineering; electrical, electronic and communications engineering technology; elementary education; engineering science; English; environmental/environmental health engineering; film/cinema/video studies; finance; food science; foreign language teacher education; forest sciences and biology; forest technology; French; geography; geological and earth sciences/geosciences related; geology/earth science; German; graphic design; health/health-care administration; history; horticultural science; hospitality administration related; human development and family studies; human nutrition; industrial engineering; information science/studies; international relations and affairs; Italian; Japanese; Jewish/Judaic studies; journalism; kinesiology and exercise science; labor and industrial relations; landscape architecture; landscaping and groundskeeping; Latin American studies; liberal arts and sciences/liberal studies; logistics, materials, and supply chain management; management information systems; marketing/marketing management; materials science; mathematics; mechanical engineering; medical microbiology and bacteriology; medieval and Renaissance studies; mining and mineral engineering; music; natural resources and conservation related; natural resources/conservation; nuclear engineering; organizational behavior; parks, recreation and leisure facilities management; petroleum engineering; philosophy; physics; political science and government; premedical studies; psychology; registered nursing/registered nurse; rehabilitation and therapeutic professions related; religious studies; Russian; secondary education; sociology; soil science and agronomy; Spanish; special education; speech communication and rhetoric; statistics; theater design and technology; turf and turfgrass management; visual and performing arts; women's studies.

Academics *Calendar:* semesters. *Degrees:* certificates, associate, and bachelor's. *Special study options:* adult/continuing education programs. *ROTC:* Army (c), Air Force (c).

Student Life *Housing:* college housing not available. *Campus security:* late-night transport/escort service, part-time trained security personnel.

Athletics Member NJCAA. *Intercollegiate sports:* baseball M, basketball M/W, soccer M/W, tennis M/W, volleyball W. *Intramural sports:* basketball M/W, cheerleading M(c)/W(c), golf M/W, ice hockey M(c)/W(c), lacrosse M/W, soccer M/W, softball W(c), tennis M/W, volleyball M(c)/W.

Standardized Tests *Required:* SAT or ACT (for admission).

Costs (2011–12) *Tuition:* state resident $12,242 full-time, $495 per credit part-time; nonresident $18,682 full-time, $778 per credit part-time. Full-time tuition and fees vary according to course level, degree level, location, program, and student level. Part-time tuition and fees vary according to course level, course load, degree level, location, program, and student level. *Required fees:* $860 full-time. *Payment plans:* installment, deferred payment. *Waivers:* employees or children of employees.

Financial Aid Of all full-time matriculated undergraduates who enrolled in 2010, 1,011 applied for aid, 776 were judged to have need, 35 had their need fully met. In 2010, 101 non-need-based awards were made. *Average percent of need met:* 61%. *Average financial aid package:* $9055. *Average need-based loan:* $3930. *Average need-based gift aid:* $6189. *Average non-need-based aid:* $2349. *Average indebtedness upon graduation:* $33,530.

Applying *Options:* electronic application, early admission, deferred entrance. *Application fee:* $50. *Required:* high school transcript. *Required for some:* interview. *Recommended:* essay or personal statement. *Application deadlines:* rolling (freshmen), rolling (transfers). *Notification:* continuous (freshmen), continuous (transfers).

Freshman Application Contact Admissions Office, Penn State Brandywine, 25 Yearsley Mill Road, Media, PA 19063-5596. *Phone:* 610-892-1200. *Fax:* 610-892-1320. *E-mail:* bwadmissions@psu.edu. *Web site:* http://www.brandywine.psu.edu/.

Penn State DuBois
DuBois, Pennsylvania

- **State-related** primarily 2-year, founded 1935, part of Pennsylvania State University
- **Small-town** campus
- **Coed,** 795 undergraduate students, 76% full-time, 49% women, 51% men

Undergraduates 602 full-time, 193 part-time. 3% are from out of state; 2% Black or African American, non-Hispanic/Latino; 2% Hispanic/Latino; 0.9% Asian, non-Hispanic/Latino; 0.2% Native Hawaiian or other Pacific Islander, non-Hispanic/Latino; 0.6% Two or more races, non-Hispanic/Latino; 1%

Race/ethnicity unknown; 3% transferred in. *Retention:* 74% of full-time freshmen returned.

Freshmen *Admission:* 433 applied, 379 admitted, 165 enrolled. *Average high school GPA:* 2.88. *Test scores:* SAT critical reading scores over 500: 31%; SAT math scores over 500: 45%; SAT writing scores over 500: 21%; SAT critical reading scores over 600: 6%; SAT math scores over 600: 9%; SAT writing scores over 600: 1%; SAT math scores over 700: 1%.

Faculty *Total:* 76, 61% full-time, 46% with terminal degrees. *Student/faculty ratio:* 12:1.

Majors Accounting; acting; actuarial science; adult and continuing education administration; advertising; aerospace, aeronautical and astronautical/space engineering; African American/Black studies; agribusiness; agricultural and extension education; agricultural business and management related; agricultural engineering; agricultural mechanization; agriculture; agronomy and crop science; animal sciences; animal sciences related; anthropology; applied economics; archeology; architectural engineering; art; art history, criticism and conservation; art teacher education; Asian studies (East); astronomy; atmospheric sciences and meteorology; biochemistry; bioengineering and biomedical engineering; biological and biomedical sciences related; biological and physical sciences; biology/biological sciences; biology/biotechnology laboratory technician; biomedical technology; business administration and management; business/commerce; business/managerial economics; chemical engineering; chemistry; civil engineering; classics and classical languages; clinical/medical laboratory technology; communication and journalism related; communication sciences and disorders; comparative literature; computer and information sciences; computer engineering; criminal justice/law enforcement administration; economics; electrical and electronics engineering; electrical, electronic and communications engineering technology; elementary education; engineering science; English; environmental/environmental health engineering; film/cinema/video studies; finance; food science; foreign language teacher education; forest sciences and biology; forest technology; French; geography; geological and earth sciences/geosciences related; geology/earth science; German; graphic design; health/health-care administration; history; horticultural science; hospitality administration related; human development and family studies; human nutrition; industrial engineering; information science/studies; international business/trade/commerce; international relations and affairs; Italian; Japanese; Jewish/Judaic studies; journalism; kinesiology and exercise science; labor and industrial relations; landscaping and groundskeeping; Latin American studies; liberal arts and sciences/liberal studies; management information systems; marketing/marketing management; materials science; mathematics; mechanical engineering; mechanical engineering/mechanical technology; medical microbiology and bacteriology; medieval and Renaissance studies; metallurgical technology; mining and mineral engineering; music; natural resources and conservation related; natural resources/conservation; nuclear engineering; occupational therapist assistant; organizational behavior; parks, recreation and leisure facilities management; petroleum engineering; philosophy; physical therapy technology; physics; political science and government; premedical studies; psychology; registered nursing/registered nurse; rehabilitation and therapeutic professions related; religious studies; Russian; secondary education; sociology; soil science and agronomy; Spanish; special education; speech communication and rhetoric; statistics; telecommunications technology; theater design and technology; toxicology; turf and turfgrass management; visual and performing arts; wildlife, fish and wildlands science and management; women's studies.

Academics *Calendar:* semesters. *Degrees:* certificates, associate, bachelor's, and master's. *Special study options:* adult/continuing education programs.

Student Life *Housing:* college housing not available.

Athletics Member NJCAA. *Intercollegiate sports:* basketball M, cross-country running M/W, golf M/W, volleyball W. *Intramural sports:* basketball M/W, football M, soccer M/W, table tennis M/W, volleyball M/W.

Standardized Tests *Required:* SAT or ACT (for admission).

Costs (2011–12) *Tuition:* state resident $12,242 full-time, $495 per credit part-time; nonresident $18,682 full-time, $778 per credit part-time. Full-time tuition and fees vary according to course level, degree level, location, program, and student level. Part-time tuition and fees vary according to course level, course load, degree level, location, program, and student level. *Required fees:* $752 full-time. *Payment plans:* installment, deferred payment. *Waivers:* employees or children of employees.

Financial Aid Of all full-time matriculated undergraduates who enrolled in 2010, 629 applied for aid, 579 were judged to have need, 22 had their need fully met. In 2010, 9 non-need-based awards were made. *Average percent of need met:* 63%. *Average financial aid package:* $10,915. *Average need-based loan:* $3824. *Average need-based gift aid:* $6242. *Average non-need-based aid:* $1022. *Average indebtedness upon graduation:* $33,530.

Applying *Options:* electronic application, early admission, deferred entrance. *Application fee:* $50. *Required:* high school transcript. *Required for some:* interview. *Recommended:* essay or personal statement. *Application deadlines:* rolling (freshmen), rolling (transfers). *Notification:* continuous (freshmen), continuous (transfers).

Freshman Application Contact Admissions Office, Penn State DuBois, College Place, DuBois, PA 15801-3199. *Phone:* 814-375-4720. *Toll-free phone:* 800-346-7627. *Fax:* 814-375-4784. *E-mail:* duboisinfo@psi.edu. *Web site:* http://www.ds.psu.edu/.

Penn State Fayette, The Eberly Campus

Uniontown, Pennsylvania

- **State-related** primarily 2-year, founded 1934, part of Pennsylvania State University
- **Small-town** campus
- **Coed,** 956 undergraduate students, 82% full-time, 57% women, 43% men

Undergraduates 781 full-time, 175 part-time. 3% are from out of state; 5% Black or African American, non-Hispanic/Latino; 1% Hispanic/Latino; 0.6% Asian, non-Hispanic/Latino; 0.1% American Indian or Alaska Native, non-Hispanic/Latino; 2% Two or more races, non-Hispanic/Latino; 2% Race/ethnicity unknown; 0.9% international; 6% transferred in. *Retention:* 74% of full-time freshmen returned.

Freshmen *Admission:* 555 applied, 497 admitted, 232 enrolled. *Average high school GPA:* 2.99. *Test scores:* SAT critical reading scores over 500: 26%; SAT math scores over 500: 39%; SAT writing scores over 500: 22%; SAT critical reading scores over 600: 4%; SAT math scores over 600: 11%; SAT writing scores over 600: 3%; SAT critical reading scores over 700: 1%; SAT math scores over 700: 1%.

Faculty *Total:* 90, 61% full-time, 39% with terminal degrees. *Student/faculty ratio:* 13:1.

Majors Accounting; acting; actuarial science; adult and continuing education administration; advertising; aerospace, aeronautical and astronautical/space engineering; African American/Black studies; agribusiness; agricultural and extension education; agricultural business and management related; agricultural engineering; agricultural mechanization; agriculture; agronomy and crop science; animal sciences; animal sciences related; anthropology; applied economics; archeology; architectural engineering; architectural engineering technology; art; art history, criticism and conservation; art teacher education; Asian studies (East); astronomy; atmospheric sciences and meteorology; biochemistry; bioengineering and biomedical engineering; biological and biomedical sciences related; biological and physical sciences; biology/biological sciences; biology/biotechnology laboratory technician; biomedical technology; business administration and management; business/commerce; business/managerial economics; chemical engineering; chemistry; civil engineering; classics and classical languages; communication and journalism related; communication sciences and disorders; comparative literature; computer and information sciences; computer engineering; criminal justice/law enforcement administration; criminal justice/safety; economics; electrical and electronics engineering; electrical, electronic and communications engineering technology; elementary education; engineering science; English; environmental/environmental health engineering; film/cinema/video studies; finance; food science; foreign language teacher education; forest sciences and biology; forest technology; French; geography; geological and earth sciences/geosciences related; geology/earth science; German; graphic design; health/health-care administration; history; horticultural science; hospitality administration related; human development and family studies; human nutrition; industrial engineering; information science/studies; international relations and affairs; Italian; Japanese; Jewish/Judaic studies; journalism; kinesiology and exercise science; labor and industrial relations; landscaping and groundskeeping; Latin American studies; liberal arts and sciences/liberal studies; logistics, materials, and supply chain management; management information systems; manufacturing engineering; marketing/marketing management; materials science; mathematics; mechanical engineering; medical microbiology and bacteriology; medieval and Renaissance studies; metallurgical technology; mining and mineral engineering; natural resources and conservation related; natural resources/conservation; nuclear engineering; organizational behavior; parks, recreation and leisure facilities management; petroleum engineering; philosophy; physics; political science and government; premedical studies; psychology; registered nursing/registered nurse; rehabilitation and therapeutic professions related; religious studies; Russian; secondary education; sociology; soil science and agronomy; Spanish; special education; speech communication and rhetoric; statistics; telecommunications technology; theater design and technology; toxicology; turf and turfgrass management; visual and performing arts; women's studies.

Academics *Calendar:* semesters. *Degrees:* certificates, associate, and bachelor's. *Special study options:* adult/continuing education programs. *ROTC:* Army (b).

Student Life *Housing:* college housing not available. *Campus security:* student patrols, 8-hour patrols by trained security personnel.

Athletics Member NJCAA. *Intercollegiate sports:* baseball M, basketball M, softball W, volleyball W. *Intramural sports:* badminton M/W, basketball M/

W, cheerleading M(c)/W(c), equestrian sports M(c)/W(c), football M/W, golf M(c)/W(c), softball M/W, tennis M/W, volleyball M/W, weight lifting M/W.

Standardized Tests *Required:* SAT or ACT (for admission).

Costs (2011–12) *Tuition:* state resident $12,242 full-time, $495 per credit part-time; nonresident $18,682 full-time, $778 per credit part-time. Full-time tuition and fees vary according to course level, degree level, location, program, and student level. Part-time tuition and fees vary according to course level, course load, degree level, location, program, and student level. *Required fees:* $798 full-time. *Payment plans:* installment, deferred payment. *Waivers:* employees or children of employees.

Financial Aid Of all full-time matriculated undergraduates who enrolled in 2010, 700 applied for aid, 625 were judged to have need, 36 had their need fully met. In 2010, 37 non-need-based awards were made. *Average percent of need met:* 65%. *Average financial aid package:* $10,432. *Average need-based loan:* $4029. *Average need-based gift aid:* $6414. *Average non-need-based aid:* $2399. *Average indebtedness upon graduation:* $33,530.

Applying *Options:* electronic application, early admission, deferred entrance. *Application fee:* $50. *Required:* high school transcript. *Required for some:* interview. *Recommended:* essay or personal statement. *Application deadlines:* rolling (freshmen), rolling (transfers). *Notification:* continuous (freshmen), continuous (transfers).

Freshman Application Contact Admissions Office, Penn State Fayette, The Eberly Campus, 1 University Drive, PO Box 519, Uniontown, PA 15401-0519. *Phone:* 724-430-4130. *Toll-free phone:* 877-568-4130. *Fax:* 724-430-4175. *E-mail:* feadm@psu.edu. *Web site:* http://www.fe.psu.edu/.

Penn State Greater Allegheny

McKeesport, Pennsylvania

- **State-related** primarily 2-year, founded 1947, part of Pennsylvania State University
- **Small-town** campus
- **Coed,** 701 undergraduate students, 88% full-time, 47% women, 53% men

Undergraduates 620 full-time, 81 part-time. 9% are from out of state; 29% Black or African American, non-Hispanic/Latino; 3% Hispanic/Latino; 2% Asian, non-Hispanic/Latino; 0.3% Native Hawaiian or other Pacific Islander, non-Hispanic/Latino; 0.2% American Indian or Alaska Native, non-Hispanic/Latino; 3% Two or more races, non-Hispanic/Latino; 2% Race/ethnicity unknown; 3% international; 4% transferred in; 29% live on campus. *Retention:* 70% of full-time freshmen returned.

Freshmen *Admission:* 719 applied, 583 admitted, 234 enrolled. *Average high school GPA:* 2.82. *Test scores:* SAT critical reading scores over 500: 29%; SAT math scores over 500: 34%; SAT writing scores over 500: 19%; SAT critical reading scores over 600: 9%; SAT math scores over 600: 11%; SAT writing scores over 600: 4%; SAT critical reading scores over 700: 1%; SAT math scores over 700: 2%; SAT writing scores over 700: 1%.

Faculty *Total:* 69, 52% full-time, 46% with terminal degrees. *Student/faculty ratio:* 14:1.

Majors Accounting; acting; actuarial science; adult and continuing education administration; advertising; aerospace, aeronautical and astronautical/space engineering; African American/Black studies; agribusiness; agricultural and extension education; agricultural business and management related; agricultural engineering; agricultural mechanization; agriculture; agronomy and crop science; animal sciences; animal sciences related; anthropology; applied economics; archeology; architectural engineering; art; art history, criticism and conservation; art teacher education; Asian studies (East); astronomy; atmospheric sciences and meteorology; biochemistry; bioengineering and biomedical engineering; biological and biomedical sciences related; biological and physical sciences; biology/biological sciences; biology/biotechnology laboratory technician; business administration and management; business/commerce; business/managerial economics; chemical engineering; chemistry; civil engineering; classics and classical languages; communication and journalism related; communication sciences and disorders; comparative literature; computer and information sciences; computer engineering; criminal justice/law enforcement administration; economics; electrical and electronics engineering; elementary education; engineering science; English; environmental/environmental health engineering; film/cinema/video studies; finance; food science; foreign language teacher education; forest sciences and biology; forest technology; French; geography; geological and earth sciences/geosciences related; geology/earth science; German; graphic design; health/health-care administration; history; horticultural science; hospitality administration related; human development and family studies; human nutrition; industrial engineering; information science/studies; international relations and affairs; Italian; Japanese; Jewish/Judaic studies; journalism; kinesiology and exercise science; labor and industrial relations; landscaping and groundskeeping; Latin American studies; liberal arts and sciences/liberal studies; logistics, materials, and supply chain management; management information systems; manufacturing engineering; marketing/marketing management; materials science; mathematics; mechanical engineering; medical microbiology and bacteriology; medieval and Renaissance studies; mining and mineral engineering; music; natural resources and conservation related; natural resources/conservation; nuclear engineering; organizational behavior; parks, recreation and leisure facilities management; petroleum engineering; philosophy; physics; political science and government; premedical studies; psychology; registered nursing/registered nurse; rehabilitation and therapeutic professions related; religious studies; Russian; secondary education; sociology; soil science and agronomy; Spanish; special education; speech communication and rhetoric; statistics; theater design and technology; toxicology; turf and turfgrass management; visual and performing arts; women's studies.

Academics *Calendar:* semesters. *Degrees:* certificates, associate, bachelor's, and master's. *Special study options:* adult/continuing education programs.

Student Life *Housing Options:* coed, disabled students. Campus housing is university owned. Freshman campus housing is guaranteed. *Campus security:* 24-hour patrols, controlled dormitory access.

Athletics Member NJCAA. *Intercollegiate sports:* baseball M, basketball M, softball W, volleyball W. *Intramural sports:* basketball M/W, cheerleading M(c)/W(c), football M/W, ice hockey M(c), racquetball M/W, skiing (cross-country) M(c)/W(c), skiing (downhill) M(c)/W(c), soccer M(c)/W(c), softball M/W, tennis M/W, volleyball M/W.

Standardized Tests *Required:* SAT or ACT (for admission).

Costs (2011–12) *Tuition:* state resident $12,242 full-time, $495 per credit part-time; nonresident $18,682 full-time, $778 per credit part-time. Full-time tuition and fees vary according to course level, degree level, location, program, and student level. Part-time tuition and fees vary according to course level, course load, degree level, location, program, and student level. *Required fees:* $860 full-time. *Room and board:* $8940; room only: $4770. Room and board charges vary according to board plan, housing facility, and location. *Payment plans:* installment, deferred payment. *Waivers:* employees or children of employees.

Financial Aid Of all full-time matriculated undergraduates who enrolled in 2010, 574 applied for aid, 522 were judged to have need, 29 had their need fully met. In 2010, 20 non-need-based awards were made. *Average percent of need met:* 67%. *Average financial aid package:* $11,373. *Average need-based loan:* $3743. *Average need-based gift aid:* $7339. *Average non-need-based aid:* $3212. *Average indebtedness upon graduation:* $33,530.

Applying *Options:* electronic application, early admission, deferred entrance. *Application fee:* $50. *Required:* high school transcript. *Required for some:* interview. *Recommended:* essay or personal statement. *Application deadlines:* rolling (freshmen), rolling (transfers). *Notification:* continuous (freshmen), continuous (transfers).

Freshman Application Contact Admissions Office, Penn State Greater Allegheny, 4000 University Drive, McKeesport, PA 15132-7698. *Phone:* 412-675-9010. *Fax:* 412-675-9046. *E-mail:* psuga@psu.edu. *Web site:* http://www.ga.psu.edu/.

Penn State Hazleton
Hazleton, Pennsylvania

- **State-related** primarily 2-year, founded 1934, part of Pennsylvania State University
- **Small-town** campus
- **Coed,** 1,172 undergraduate students, 95% full-time, 46% women, 54% men

Undergraduates 1,108 full-time, 64 part-time. 27% are from out of state; 13% Black or African American, non-Hispanic/Latino; 15% Hispanic/Latino; 4% Asian, non-Hispanic/Latino; 0.4% American Indian or Alaska Native, non-Hispanic/Latino; 2% Two or more races, non-Hispanic/Latino; 2% Race/ethnicity unknown; 1% international; 5% transferred in; 41% live on campus. *Retention:* 76% of full-time freshmen returned.

Freshmen *Admission:* 1,268 applied, 1,100 admitted, 458 enrolled. *Average high school GPA:* 2.83. *Test scores:* SAT critical reading scores over 500: 32%; SAT math scores over 500: 39%; SAT writing scores over 500: 27%; SAT critical reading scores over 600: 5%; SAT math scores over 600: 10%; SAT writing scores over 600: 2%; SAT math scores over 700: 1%.

Faculty *Total:* 83, 66% full-time, 48% with terminal degrees. *Student/faculty ratio:* 18:1.

Majors Accounting; acting; actuarial science; adult and continuing education administration; advertising; aerospace, aeronautical and astronautical/space engineering; African American/Black studies; agribusiness; agricultural and extension education; agricultural business and management related; agricultural engineering; agricultural mechanization; agriculture; agronomy and crop science; animal sciences; animal sciences related; anthropology; applied economics; archeology; architectural engineering; art; art history, criticism and conservation; art teacher education; Asian studies (East); astronomy; atmospheric sciences and meteorology; biochemistry; bioengineering and biomedical engineering; biological and biomedical sciences related; biological and physical sciences; biology/biological sciences; biology/biotechnology laboratory technician; biomedical technology; business administration and management; business/commerce; business/managerial economics; chemical

engineering; chemistry; civil engineering; classics and classical languages; clinical/medical laboratory technology; communication and journalism related; communication sciences and disorders; comparative literature; computer and information sciences; computer engineering; criminal justice/law enforcement administration; economics; electrical and electronics engineering; electrical, electronic and communications engineering technology; elementary education; engineering science; English; environmental/environmental health engineering; film/cinema/video studies; finance; food science; forest sciences and biology; forest technology; French; geography; geological and earth sciences/geosciences related; geology/earth science; German; graphic design; health/health-care administration; history; horticultural science; hospitality administration related; human development and family studies; human nutrition; industrial engineering; information science/studies; international relations and affairs; Italian; Japanese; Jewish/Judaic studies; journalism; kinesiology and exercise science; labor and industrial relations; landscaping and groundskeeping; Latin American studies; liberal arts and sciences/liberal studies; logistics, materials, and supply chain management; management information systems; manufacturing engineering; marketing/marketing management; materials science; mathematics; mechanical engineering; mechanical engineering/mechanical technology; medical microbiology and bacteriology; medieval and Renaissance studies; metallurgical technology; mining and mineral engineering; music; natural resources and conservation related; natural resources/conservation; nuclear engineering; organizational behavior; parks, recreation and leisure facilities management; petroleum engineering; philosophy; physical therapy technology; physics; political science and government; premedical studies; psychology; registered nursing/registered nurse; rehabilitation and therapeutic professions related; religious studies; Russian; secondary education; sociology; soil science and agronomy; Spanish; special education; speech communication and rhetoric; statistics; telecommunications technology; theater design and technology; toxicology; turf and turfgrass management; visual and performing arts; women's studies.

Academics *Calendar:* semesters. *Degrees:* certificates, associate, and bachelor's. *Special study options:* adult/continuing education programs. *ROTC:* Army (b), Air Force (c).

Student Life *Housing Options:* coed. Campus housing is university owned. Freshman campus housing is guaranteed. *Campus security:* 24-hour patrols, late-night transport/escort service, controlled dormitory access.

Athletics Member NJCAA. *Intercollegiate sports:* baseball M, basketball M/W, cheerleading M/W, soccer M, softball W(s), tennis M/W, volleyball M/W. *Intramural sports:* basketball M/W, skiing (downhill) M(c)/W(c), soccer M/W, volleyball M/W.

Standardized Tests *Required:* SAT or ACT (for admission).

Costs (2011–12) *Tuition:* state resident $12,242 full-time, $495 per credit part-time; nonresident $18,682 full-time, $778 per credit part-time. Full-time tuition and fees vary according to course level, degree level, location, program, and student level. Part-time tuition and fees vary according to course level, course load, degree level, location, program, and student level. *Required fees:* $806 full-time. *Room and board:* $8940; room only: $4770. Room and board charges vary according to board plan, housing facility, and location. *Payment plans:* installment, deferred payment. *Waivers:* employees or children of employees.

Financial Aid Of all full-time matriculated undergraduates who enrolled in 2010, 1,069 applied for aid, 949 were judged to have need, 26 had their need fully met. In 2010, 65 non-need-based awards were made. *Average percent of need met:* 61%. *Average financial aid package:* $9809. *Average need-based loan:* $3793. *Average need-based gift aid:* $6663. *Average non-need-based aid:* $2458. *Average indebtedness upon graduation:* $33,530.

Applying *Options:* electronic application, early admission, deferred entrance. *Application fee:* $50. *Required:* high school transcript. *Required for some:* interview. *Recommended:* essay or personal statement. *Application deadlines:* rolling (freshmen), rolling (transfers). *Notification:* continuous (freshmen), continuous (transfers).

Freshman Application Contact Admissions Office, Penn State Hazleton, Hazleton, PA 18202-1291. *Phone:* 570-450-3142. *Toll-free phone:* 800-279-8495. *Fax:* 570-450-3182. *E-mail:* admissions-hn@psu.edu. *Web site:* http://www.hn.psu.edu/.

Penn State Lehigh Valley
Fogelsville, Pennsylvania

- **State-related** primarily 2-year, founded 1912, part of Pennsylvania State University
- **Rural** campus
- **Coed,** 915 undergraduate students, 81% full-time, 43% women, 57% men

Undergraduates 738 full-time, 177 part-time. 4% are from out of state; 4% Black or African American, non-Hispanic/Latino; 14% Hispanic/Latino; 9% Asian, non-Hispanic/Latino; 0.1% Native Hawaiian or other Pacific Islander, non-Hispanic/Latino; 2% Two or more races, non-Hispanic/Latino; 2% Race/

ethnicity unknown; 0.5% international; 6% transferred in. *Retention:* 76% of full-time freshmen returned.

Freshmen *Admission:* 951 applied, 831 admitted, 260 enrolled. *Average high school GPA:* 2.87. *Test scores:* SAT critical reading scores over 500: 47%; SAT math scores over 500: 51%; SAT writing scores over 500: 37%; SAT critical reading scores over 600: 12%; SAT math scores over 600: 14%; SAT writing scores over 600: 8%; SAT critical reading scores over 700: 3%; SAT math scores over 700: 2%.

Faculty *Total:* 89, 37% full-time, 42% with terminal degrees. *Student/faculty ratio:* 16:1.

Majors Accounting; acting; actuarial science; adult and continuing education administration; advertising; aerospace, aeronautical and astronautical/space engineering; African American/Black studies; agribusiness; agricultural and extension education; agricultural business and management related; agricultural engineering; agricultural mechanization; agriculture; American studies; animal sciences; animal sciences related; anthropology; applied economics; archeology; architectural engineering; art; art history, criticism and conservation; art teacher education; Asian studies (East); astronomy; atmospheric sciences and meteorology; biochemistry; bioengineering and biomedical engineering; biological and biomedical sciences related; biological and physical sciences; biology/biological sciences; biology/biotechnology laboratory technician; business/commerce; business/managerial economics; chemical engineering; chemistry; civil engineering; classics and classical languages; communication and journalism related; communication sciences and disorders; comparative literature; computer and information sciences; computer engineering; criminal justice/law enforcement administration; economics; electrical and electronics engineering; elementary education; engineering science; English; environmental/environmental health engineering; film/cinema/video studies; finance; food science; foreign languages and literatures; forest sciences and biology; forest technology; French; geography; geological and earth sciences/geosciences related; geology/earth science; German; graphic design; health/health-care administration; history; horticultural science; hospitality administration related; human development and family studies; human nutrition; industrial engineering; information science/studies; international business/trade/commerce; international relations and affairs; Italian; Japanese; Jewish/Judaic studies; journalism; kinesiology and exercise science; labor and industrial relations; landscape architecture; landscaping and groundskeeping; Latin American studies; liberal arts and sciences/liberal studies; logistics, materials, and supply chain management; management information systems; management sciences and quantitative methods related; marketing/marketing management; materials science; mathematics; mechanical engineering; medical microbiology and bacteriology; medieval and Renaissance studies; mining and mineral engineering; natural resources and conservation related; natural resources/conservation; nuclear engineering; organizational behavior; parks, recreation and leisure facilities management; petroleum engineering; philosophy; physics; political science and government; premedical studies; professional, technical, business, and scientific writing; psychology; registered nursing/registered nurse; rehabilitation and therapeutic professions related; religious studies; Russian; secondary education; sociology; soil science and agronomy; Spanish; special education; speech communication and rhetoric; statistics; theater design and technology; turf and turfgrass management; visual and performing arts; women's studies.

Academics *Calendar:* semesters. *Degrees:* certificates, associate, and bachelor's (enrollment figures include students enrolled at The Graduate School at Penn State who are taking courses at this location). *Special study options:* adult/continuing education programs. *ROTC:* Army (c).

Student Life *Housing:* college housing not available.

Athletics Member NJCAA. *Intercollegiate sports:* baseball M, basketball M/W, bowling M(c)/W(c), cheerleading M/W, cross-country running M/W, football M(c), golf M(c)/W(c), ice hockey M(c)/W(c), skiing (downhill) M(c)/W(c), soccer M(c)/W, tennis M/W, volleyball M(c)/W. *Intramural sports:* badminton M/W, basketball M/W, football M/W, golf M/W, soccer M/W, volleyball M/W.

Standardized Tests *Required:* SAT or ACT (for admission).

Costs (2011–12) *Tuition:* state resident $12,242 full-time, $495 per credit part-time; nonresident $18,682 full-time, $778 per credit part-time. Full-time tuition and fees vary according to course level, degree level, location, program, and student level. Part-time tuition and fees vary according to course level, course load, degree level, location, program, and student level. *Required fees:* $852 full-time. *Payment plans:* installment, deferred payment. *Waivers:* employees or children of employees.

Financial Aid Of all full-time matriculated undergraduates who enrolled in 2010, 563 applied for aid, 451 were judged to have need, 14 had their need fully met. In 2010, 47 non-need-based awards were made. *Average percent of need met:* 63%. *Average financial aid package:* $9538. *Average need-based loan:* $3994. *Average need-based gift aid:* $6678. *Average non-need-based aid:* $1926. *Average indebtedness upon graduation:* $33,530.

Applying *Options:* electronic application, early admission, deferred entrance. *Application fee:* $50. *Required:* high school transcript. *Application deadlines:*

rolling (freshmen), rolling (transfers). *Notification:* continuous (freshmen), continuous (transfers).

Freshman Application Contact Admissions Office, Penn State Lehigh Valley, 2809 Saucon Valley Road, Fogelsville, PA 18051-9999. *Phone:* 610-285-5000. *Fax:* 610-285-5220. *E-mail:* admissions-lv@psu.edu. *Web site:* http://www.lv.psu.edu/.

Penn State Mont Alto
Mont Alto, Pennsylvania

- **State-related** primarily 2-year, founded 1929, part of Pennsylvania State University
- **Small-town** campus
- **Coed,** 1,217 undergraduate students, 79% full-time, 58% women, 42% men

Undergraduates 956 full-time, 261 part-time. 18% are from out of state; 12% Black or African American, non-Hispanic/Latino; 5% Hispanic/Latino; 2% Asian, non-Hispanic/Latino; 0.1% Native Hawaiian or other Pacific Islander, non-Hispanic/Latino; 0.1% American Indian or Alaska Native, non-Hispanic/Latino; 3% Two or more races, non-Hispanic/Latino; 1% Race/ethnicity unknown; 0.4% international; 5% transferred in; 35% live on campus. *Retention:* 76% of full-time freshmen returned.

Freshmen *Admission:* 947 applied, 803 admitted, 394 enrolled. *Average high school GPA:* 2.92. *Test scores:* SAT critical reading scores over 500: 35%; SAT math scores over 500: 38%; SAT writing scores over 500: 28%; SAT critical reading scores over 600: 6%; SAT math scores over 600: 10%; SAT writing scores over 600: 4%; SAT critical reading scores over 700: 1%.

Faculty *Total:* 114, 49% full-time, 32% with terminal degrees. *Student/faculty ratio:* 14:1.

Majors Accounting; acting; actuarial science; adult and continuing education administration; advertising; aerospace, aeronautical and astronautical/space engineering; African American/Black studies; agribusiness; agricultural and extension education; agricultural business and management related; agricultural engineering; agricultural mechanization; agriculture; agronomy and crop science; animal sciences; animal sciences related; anthropology; applied economics; archeology; architectural engineering; art; art history, criticism and conservation; art teacher education; Asian studies (East); astronomy; atmospheric sciences and meteorology; biochemistry; bioengineering and biomedical engineering; biological and biomedical sciences related; biological and physical sciences; biology/biological sciences; biology/biotechnology laboratory technician; business administration and management; business/commerce; business/managerial economics; chemical engineering; chemistry; civil engineering; classics and classical languages; communication and journalism related; communication sciences and disorders; comparative literature; computer and information sciences; computer engineering; criminal justice/law enforcement administration; economics; electrical and electronics engineering; elementary education; engineering science; English; environmental/environmental health engineering; film/cinema/video studies; finance; food science; foreign language teacher education; forest sciences and biology; forest technology; French; geography; geological and earth sciences/geosciences related; geology/earth science; German; graphic design; health/health-care administration; history; horticultural science; hospitality administration related; human development and family studies; human nutrition; industrial engineering; information science/studies; international relations and affairs; Italian; Japanese; Jewish/Judaic studies; journalism; kinesiology and exercise science; labor and industrial relations; landscaping and groundskeeping; Latin American studies; liberal arts and sciences/liberal studies; management information systems; marketing/marketing management; materials science; mathematics; mechanical engineering; medical microbiology and bacteriology; medieval and Renaissance studies; mining and mineral engineering; music; natural resources and conservation related; natural resources/conservation; nuclear engineering; occupational therapist assistant; occupational therapy; organizational behavior; parks, recreation and leisure facilities management; petroleum engineering; philosophy; physical therapy technology; physics; political science and government; premedical studies; psychology; registered nursing/registered nurse; rehabilitation and therapeutic professions related; religious studies; Russian; secondary education; sociology; soil science and agronomy; Spanish; special education; speech communication and rhetoric; statistics; theater design and technology; toxicology; turf and turfgrass management; visual and performing arts; women's studies.

Academics *Calendar:* semesters. *Degrees:* certificates, associate, and bachelor's. *Special study options:* adult/continuing education programs. *ROTC:* Army (c).

Student Life *Housing Options:* coed, disabled students. Campus housing is university owned. Freshman campus housing is guaranteed. *Campus security:* 24-hour patrols, controlled dormitory access.

Athletics Member NJCAA. *Intercollegiate sports:* basketball M/W, cheerleading M/W, cross-country running M/W, golf M/W, soccer M/W, softball W, tennis M/W, volleyball W. *Intramural sports:* badminton M/W, basketball M/

W, cheerleading M(c)/W(c), racquetball M/W, soccer M/W, softball W, volleyball M/W.

Standardized Tests *Required:* SAT or ACT (for admission).

Costs (2011–12) *Tuition:* state resident $12,242 full-time, $495 per credit part-time; nonresident $18,682 full-time, $778 per credit part-time. Full-time tuition and fees vary according to course level, degree level, location, program, and student level. Part-time tuition and fees vary according to course level, course load, degree level, location, program, and student level. *Required fees:* $860 full-time. *Room and board:* $8940; room only: $4770. Room and board charges vary according to board plan, housing facility, and location. *Payment plans:* installment, deferred payment. *Waivers:* employees or children of employees.

Financial Aid Of all full-time matriculated undergraduates who enrolled in 2010, 824 applied for aid, 710 were judged to have need, 31 had their need fully met. In 2010, 51 non-need-based awards were made. *Average percent of need met:* 64%. *Average financial aid package:* $10,515. *Average need-based loan:* $3797. *Average need-based gift aid:* $6448. *Average non-need-based aid:* $2460. *Average indebtedness upon graduation:* $33,530.

Applying *Options:* electronic application, early admission, deferred entrance. *Application fee:* $50. *Required:* high school transcript. *Required for some:* interview. *Recommended:* essay or personal statement. *Application deadlines:* rolling (freshmen), rolling (transfers). *Notification:* continuous (freshmen), continuous (transfers).

Freshman Application Contact Admissions Office, Penn State Mont Alto, 1 Campus Drive, Mont Alto, PA 17237-9703. *Phone:* 717-749-6130. *Toll-free phone:* 800-392-6173. *Fax:* 717-749-6132. *E-mail:* psuma@psu.edu. *Web site:* http://www.ma.psu.edu/.

Penn State New Kensington

New Kensington, Pennsylvania

- **State-related** primarily 2-year, founded 1958, part of Pennsylvania State University
- **Small-town** campus
- **Coed,** 800 undergraduate students, 74% full-time, 42% women, 59% men

Undergraduates 595 full-time, 205 part-time. 3% are from out of state; 5% Black or African American, non-Hispanic/Latino; 2% Hispanic/Latino; 0.7% Asian, non-Hispanic/Latino; 0.1% American Indian or Alaska Native, non-Hispanic/Latino; 0.7% Two or more races, non-Hispanic/Latino; 2% Race/ethnicity unknown; 5% transferred in. *Retention:* 74% of full-time freshmen returned.

Freshmen *Admission:* 528 applied, 422 admitted, 195 enrolled. *Average high school GPA:* 2.95. *Test scores:* SAT critical reading scores over 500: 34%; SAT math scores over 500: 45%; SAT writing scores over 500: 25%; SAT critical reading scores over 600: 7%; SAT math scores over 600: 9%; SAT writing scores over 600: 2%; SAT math scores over 700: 1%.

Faculty *Total:* 79, 47% full-time, 44% with terminal degrees. *Student/faculty ratio:* 13:1.

Majors Accounting; acting; actuarial science; adult and continuing education administration; advertising; aerospace, aeronautical and astronautical/space engineering; African American/Black studies; agribusiness; agricultural and extension education; agricultural business and management related; agricultural engineering; agricultural mechanization; agriculture; agronomy and crop science; animal sciences; animal sciences related; anthropology; applied economics; archeology; architectural engineering; art; art history, criticism and conservation; art teacher education; Asian studies (East); astronomy; atmospheric sciences and meteorology; biochemistry; bioengineering and biomedical engineering; biological and biomedical sciences related; biological and physical sciences; biology/biological sciences; biology/biotechnology laboratory technician; biomedical technology; business administration and management; business/commerce; business/managerial economics; chemical engineering; chemistry; civil engineering; classics and classical languages; communication and journalism related; communication sciences and disorders; comparative literature; computer and information sciences; computer engineering; computer engineering technology; criminal justice/law enforcement administration; economics; electrical and electronics engineering; electrical, electronic and communications engineering technology; elementary education; engineering science; English; environmental/environmental health engineering; film/cinema/video studies; finance; food science; forest sciences and biology; forest technology; French; geography; geological and earth sciences/geosciences related; geology/earth science; German; graphic design; health/health-care administration; history; horticultural science; hospitality administration related; human development and family studies; human nutrition; industrial engineering; information science/studies; international relations and affairs; Italian; Japanese; Jewish/Judaic studies; journalism; kinesiology and exercise science; labor and industrial relations; landscaping and groundskeeping; Latin American studies; liberal arts and sciences/liberal studies; logistics, materials, and supply chain management; management information systems; marketing/marketing management; materials science; mathematics; mechani-

cal engineering; mechanical engineering/mechanical technology; medical microbiology and bacteriology; medical radiologic technology; medieval and Renaissance studies; metallurgical technology; mining and mineral engineering; music; natural resources and conservation related; natural resources/conservation; nuclear engineering; organizational behavior; parks, recreation and leisure facilities management; petroleum engineering; philosophy; physics; political science and government; premedical studies; psychology; registered nursing/registered nurse; rehabilitation and therapeutic professions related; religious studies; Russian; secondary education; sociology; soil science and agronomy; Spanish; special education; speech communication and rhetoric; statistics; telecommunications technology; theater design and technology; toxicology; turf and turfgrass management; visual and performing arts; women's studies.

Academics *Calendar:* semesters. *Degrees:* certificates, associate, bachelor's, and master's. *Special study options:* adult/continuing education programs, external degree program. *ROTC:* Air Force (c).

Student Life *Campus security:* part-time trained security personnel.

Athletics Member NJCAA. *Intercollegiate sports:* baseball M, basketball M/W, cheerleading M/W, golf M/W, softball W, volleyball W. *Intramural sports:* badminton M/W, basketball M/W, bowling M/W, cheerleading M(c)/W(c), football M/W, ice hockey M(c)/W(c), racquetball M/W, skiing (downhill) M(c)/W(c), soccer M/W, softball W, volleyball M/W.

Standardized Tests *Required:* SAT or ACT (for admission).

Costs (2011–12) *Tuition:* state resident $12,242 full-time, $495 per credit part-time; nonresident $18,682 full-time, $778 per credit part-time. Full-time tuition and fees vary according to course level, degree level, location, program, and student level. Part-time tuition and fees vary according to course level, course load, degree level, location, program, and student level. *Required fees:* $806 full-time. *Payment plans:* installment, deferred payment. *Waivers:* employees or children of employees.

Financial Aid Of all full-time matriculated undergraduates who enrolled in 2010, 568 applied for aid, 498 were judged to have need, 20 had their need fully met. In 2010, 31 non-need-based awards were made. *Average percent of need met:* 64%. *Average financial aid package:* $9188. *Average need-based loan:* $3990. *Average need-based gift aid:* $5948. *Average non-need-based aid:* $1986. *Average indebtedness upon graduation:* $33,530.

Applying *Options:* electronic application, early admission, deferred entrance. *Application fee:* $50. *Required:* high school transcript. *Required for some:* interview. *Recommended:* essay or personal statement. *Application deadlines:* rolling (freshmen), rolling (transfers). *Notification:* continuous (freshmen), continuous (transfers).

Freshman Application Contact Admissions Office, Penn State New Kensington, 3550 Seventh Street Road, New Kensington, PA 15068. *Phone:* 724-334-5466. *Toll-free phone:* 888-968-7297. *Fax:* 724-334-6111. *E-mail:* nkadmissions@psu.edu. *Web site:* http://www.nk.psu.edu/.

Penn State Schuylkill

Schuylkill Haven, Pennsylvania

- **State-related** primarily 2-year, founded 1934, part of Pennsylvania State University
- **Small-town** campus
- **Coed,** 1,012 undergraduate students, 84% full-time, 53% women, 47% men

Undergraduates 851 full-time, 161 part-time. 20% are from out of state; 30% Black or African American, non-Hispanic/Latino; 7% Hispanic/Latino; 2% Asian, non-Hispanic/Latino; 0.1% Native Hawaiian or other Pacific Islander, non-Hispanic/Latino; 0.1% American Indian or Alaska Native, non-Hispanic/Latino; 2% Two or more races, non-Hispanic/Latino; 2% Race/ethnicity unknown; 0.9% international; 3% transferred in; 30% live on campus. *Retention:* 71% of full-time freshmen returned.

Freshmen *Admission:* 834 applied, 663 admitted, 332 enrolled. *Average high school GPA:* 2.66. *Test scores:* SAT critical reading scores over 500: 26%; SAT math scores over 500: 22%; SAT writing scores over 500: 19%; SAT critical reading scores over 600: 2%; SAT math scores over 600: 4%; SAT writing scores over 600: 3%.

Faculty *Total:* 74, 61% full-time, 50% with terminal degrees. *Student/faculty ratio:* 17:1.

Majors Accounting; acting; actuarial science; adult and continuing education administration; advertising; aerospace, aeronautical and astronautical/space engineering; African American/Black studies; agribusiness; agricultural and extension education; agricultural business and management related; agricultural engineering; agricultural mechanization; agriculture; American studies; animal sciences; animal sciences related; anthropology; applied economics; archeology; architectural engineering; art; art history, criticism and conservation; art teacher education; Asian studies (East); astronomy; atmospheric sciences and meteorology; biochemistry; bioengineering and biomedical engineering; biological and biomedical sciences related; biological and physical sciences; biology/biological sciences; biology/biotechnology laboratory technician; biomedical technology; business/commerce; business/managerial economics; chemical engineering; chemistry; civil engineering; classics and classical languages; clinical/medical laboratory technology; communication and journalism related; communication sciences and disorders; comparative literature; computer and information sciences; computer engineering; criminal justice/law enforcement administration; criminal justice/safety; economics; electrical and electronics engineering; electrical, electronic and communications engineering technology; elementary education; engineering science; English; environmental/environmental health engineering; film/cinema/video studies; finance; food science; forest sciences and biology; forest technology; French; geography; geological and earth sciences/geosciences related; geology/earth science; German; graphic design; health/health-care administration; history; horticultural science; hospitality administration related; human development and family studies; human nutrition; industrial engineering; information science/studies; international business/trade/commerce; international relations and affairs; Italian; Japanese; Jewish/Judaic studies; journalism; kinesiology and exercise science; labor and industrial relations; landscape architecture; landscaping and groundskeeping; Latin American studies; liberal arts and sciences/liberal studies; logistics, materials, and supply chain management; management information systems; management sciences and quantitative methods related; marketing/marketing management; materials science; mathematics; mechanical engineering; medical microbiology and bacteriology; medical radiologic technology; medieval and Renaissance studies; metallurgical technology; mining and mineral engineering; natural resources and conservation related; natural resources/conservation; nuclear engineering; organizational behavior; parks, recreation and leisure facilities management; petroleum engineering; philosophy; physics; political science and government; premedical studies; psychology; registered nursing/registered nurse; rehabilitation and therapeutic professions related; religious studies; Russian; secondary education; sociology; soil science and agronomy; Spanish; special education; speech communication and rhetoric; statistics; telecommunications technology; theater design and technology; turf and turfgrass management; visual and performing arts; women's studies.

Academics *Calendar:* semesters. *Degrees:* certificates, associate, and bachelor's (bachelor's degree programs completed at the Harrisburg campus). *Special study options:* adult/continuing education programs.

Student Life *Housing Options:* disabled students. *Campus security:* 24-hour patrols, controlled dormitory access.

Athletics Member NJCAA. *Intercollegiate sports:* basketball M, cross-country running M/W, golf M, soccer M, softball W, volleyball W. *Intramural sports:* basketball M/W, football M, soccer M/W, softball M/W, table tennis M/W, volleyball M/W.

Standardized Tests *Required:* SAT or ACT (for admission).

Costs (2011–12) *Tuition:* state resident $12,242 full-time, $495 per credit part-time; nonresident $18,682 full-time, $778 per credit part-time. Full-time tuition and fees vary according to course level, degree level, location, program, and student level. Part-time tuition and fees vary according to course level, course load, degree level, location, program, and student level. *Required fees:* $752 full-time. *Payment plans:* installment, deferred payment. *Waivers:* employees or children of employees.

Financial Aid Of all full-time matriculated undergraduates who enrolled in 2010, 791 applied for aid, 738 were judged to have need, 21 had their need fully met. In 2010, 16 non-need-based awards were made. *Average percent of need met:* 63%. *Average financial aid package:* $11,086. *Average need-based loan:* $3899. *Average need-based gift aid:* $7089. *Average non-need-based aid:* $1636. *Average indebtedness upon graduation:* $33,530.

Applying *Options:* electronic application, early admission, deferred entrance. *Application fee:* $50. *Required:* high school transcript. *Application deadlines:* rolling (freshmen), rolling (transfers). *Notification:* continuous (freshmen), continuous (transfers).

Freshman Application Contact Admissions Office, Penn State Schuylkill, 200 University Drive, Schuylkill Haven, PA 17972-2208. *Phone:* 570-385-6252. *Fax:* 570-385-6272. *E-mail:* sl-admissions@psu.edu. *Web site:* http://www.sl.psu.edu/.

Penn State Shenango

Sharon, Pennsylvania

- **State-related** primarily 2-year, founded 1965, part of Pennsylvania State University
- **Small-town** campus
- **Coed,** 651 undergraduate students, 60% full-time, 63% women, 37% men

Undergraduates 393 full-time, 258 part-time. 20% are from out of state; 7% Black or African American, non-Hispanic/Latino; 2% Hispanic/Latino; 0.4% Native Hawaiian or other Pacific Islander, non-Hispanic/Latino; 1% Two or more races, non-Hispanic/Latino; 3% Race/ethnicity unknown; 8% transferred in. *Retention:* 63% of full-time freshmen returned.

Freshmen *Admission:* 254 applied, 189 admitted, 101 enrolled. *Average high school GPA:* 2.83. *Test scores:* SAT critical reading scores over 500: 19%; SAT math scores over 500: 29%; SAT writing scores over 500: 13%; SAT critical reading scores over 600: 6%; SAT writing scores over 600: 3%.

Faculty *Total:* 68, 41% full-time, 40% with terminal degrees. *Student/faculty ratio:* 12:1.

Majors Accounting; acting; actuarial science; adult and continuing education administration; advertising; aerospace, aeronautical and astronautical/space engineering; African American/Black studies; agribusiness; agricultural and extension education; agricultural business and management related; agricultural engineering; agricultural mechanization; agriculture; agronomy and crop science; animal sciences; animal sciences related; anthropology; applied economics; archeology; architectural engineering; art; art history, criticism and conservation; art teacher education; Asian studies (East); astronomy; atmospheric sciences and meteorology; biochemistry; bioengineering and biomedical engineering; biological and biomedical sciences related; biological and physical sciences; biology/biological sciences; biology/biotechnology laboratory technician; biomedical technology; business administration and management; business/commerce; business/managerial economics; chemical engineering; chemistry; civil engineering; classics and classical languages; communication and journalism related; communication sciences and disorders; comparative literature; computer and information sciences; computer engineering; criminal justice/law enforcement administration; economics; electrical and electronics engineering; electrical, electronic and communications engineering technology; elementary education; engineering science; English; environmental/environmental health engineering; film/cinema/video studies; finance; food science; foreign language teacher education; forest sciences and biology; forest technology; French; geography; geological and earth sciences/geosciences related; geology/earth science; German; graphic design; health/health-care administration; history; horticultural science; hospitality administration related; human development and family studies; human nutrition; industrial engineering; information science/studies; international relations and affairs; Italian; Japanese; Jewish/Judaic studies; journalism; kinesiology and exercise science; labor and industrial relations; landscaping and groundskeeping; Latin American studies; liberal arts and sciences/liberal studies; logistics, materials, and supply chain management; management information systems; marketing/marketing management; materials science; mathematics; mechanical engineering/mechanical technology; medical microbiology and bacteriology; medieval and Renaissance studies; metallurgical technology; mining and mineral engineering; music; natural resources and conservation related; natural resources/conservation; nuclear engineering; organizational behavior; parks, recreation and leisure facilities management; petroleum engineering; philosophy; physical therapy technology; physics; political science and government; premedical studies; psychology; registered nursing/registered nurse; rehabilitation and therapeutic professions related; religious studies; Russian; secondary education; sociology; soil science and agronomy; Spanish; special education; speech communication and rhetoric; statistics; telecommunications technology; theater design and technology; toxicology; turf and turfgrass management; visual and performing arts; women's studies.

Academics *Calendar:* semesters. *Degrees:* certificates, associate, and bachelor's. *Special study options:* adult/continuing education programs.

Student Life *Housing:* college housing not available.

Athletics *Intramural sports:* basketball M(c)/W, bowling M/W, football M(c), golf M/W, softball M/W, tennis M/W, volleyball M/W.

Standardized Tests *Required:* SAT or ACT (for admission).

Costs (2011–12) *Tuition:* state resident $12,242 full-time, $495 per credit part-time; nonresident $18,682 full-time, $778 per credit part-time. Full-time tuition and fees vary according to course level, degree level, location, program, and student level. Part-time tuition and fees vary according to course level, course load, degree level, location, program, and student level. *Required fees:* $752 full-time. *Payment plans:* installment, deferred payment. *Waivers:* employees or children of employees.

Financial Aid Of all full-time matriculated undergraduates who enrolled in 2010, 393 applied for aid, 379 were judged to have need, 19 had their need fully met. In 2010, 12 non-need-based awards were made. *Average percent of need met:* 63%. *Average financial aid package:* $11,994. *Average need-based loan:* $4022. *Average need-based gift aid:* $6724. *Average non-need-based aid:* $3003. *Average indebtedness upon graduation:* $33,530.

Applying *Options:* electronic application, early admission, deferred entrance. *Application fee:* $50. *Required:* high school transcript. *Required for some:* interview. *Recommended:* essay or personal statement. *Application deadlines:* rolling (freshmen), rolling (transfers). *Notification:* continuous (freshmen), continuous (transfers).

Freshman Application Contact Admissions Office, Penn State Shenango, 147 Shenango Avenue, Sharon, PA 16146-1537. *Phone:* 724-983-2803. *Fax:* 724-983-2820. *E-mail:* psushenango@psu.edu. *Web site:* http://www.shenango.psu.edu/.

Penn State Wilkes-Barre

Lehman, Pennsylvania

- **State-related** primarily 2-year, founded 1916, part of Pennsylvania State University
- **Rural** campus
- **Coed,** 678 undergraduate students, 85% full-time, 35% women, 65% men

Undergraduates 579 full-time, 99 part-time. 6% are from out of state; 5% Black or African American, non-Hispanic/Latino; 3% Hispanic/Latino; 2% Asian, non-Hispanic/Latino; 0.3% American Indian or Alaska Native, non-Hispanic/Latino; 2% Two or more races, non-Hispanic/Latino; 0.8% Race/ethnicity unknown; 0.5% international; 6% transferred in. *Retention:* 73% of full-time freshmen returned.

Freshmen *Admission:* 549 applied, 482 admitted, 191 enrolled. *Average high school GPA:* 3.01. *Test scores:* SAT critical reading scores over 500: 46%; SAT math scores over 500: 53%; SAT writing scores over 500: 36%; SAT critical reading scores over 600: 10%; SAT math scores over 600: 15%; SAT writing scores over 600: 5%; SAT critical reading scores over 700: 1%; SAT math scores over 700: 2%.

Faculty *Total:* 57, 60% full-time, 49% with terminal degrees. *Student/faculty ratio:* 15:1.

Majors Accounting; acting; actuarial science; adult and continuing education administration; advertising; aerospace, aeronautical and astronautical/space engineering; African American/Black studies; agribusiness; agricultural and extension education; agricultural business and management related; agricultural engineering; agricultural mechanization; agriculture; agronomy and crop science; animal sciences; animal sciences related; anthropology; applied economics; archeology; architectural engineering; art; art history, criticism and conservation; art teacher education; astronomy; atmospheric sciences and meteorology; biochemistry; bioengineering and biomedical engineering; biological and biomedical sciences related; biological and physical sciences; biology/biological sciences; biology/biotechnology laboratory technician; business administration and management; business/commerce; business/managerial economics; chemical engineering; chemistry; civil engineering; classics and classical languages; communication and journalism related; communication sciences and disorders; comparative literature; computer and information sciences; computer engineering; criminal justice/law enforcement administration; criminal justice/safety; economics; electrical and electronics engineering; electrical, electronic and communications engineering technology; elementary education; engineering science; English; environmental/environmental health engineering; film/cinema/video studies; finance; food science; forest sciences and biology; forest technology; French; geography; geological and earth sciences/geosciences related; geology/earth science; German; graphic design; health/health-care administration; history; horticultural science; hospitality administration related; human development and family studies; human nutrition; industrial engineering; information science/studies; international relations and affairs; Italian; Japanese; Jewish/Judaic studies; journalism; kinesiology and exercise science; labor and industrial relations; landscape architecture; landscaping and groundskeeping; Latin American studies; liberal arts and sciences/liberal studies; management information systems; manufacturing engineering; marketing/marketing management; materials science; mathematics; mechanical engineering; medical microbiology and bacteriology; medieval and Renaissance studies; metallurgical technology; mining and mineral engineering; music; natural resources and conservation related; natural resources/conservation; nuclear engineering; organizational behavior; parks, recreation and leisure facilities management; petroleum engineering; philosophy; physics; political science and government; premedical studies; psychology; registered nursing/registered nurse; rehabilitation and therapeutic professions related; religious studies; Russian; secondary education; sociology; soil science and agronomy; Spanish; special education; speech communication and rhetoric; statistics; surveying technology; telecommunications technology; theater design and technology; toxicology; turf and turfgrass management; visual and performing arts; women's studies.

Academics *Calendar:* semesters. *Degrees:* certificates, associate, and bachelor's (enrollment figures include students enrolled at The Graduate School at Penn State who are taking courses at this location). *Special study options:* adult/continuing education programs. *ROTC:* Army (c), Air Force (c).

Student Life *Housing:* college housing not available.

Athletics Member NJCAA. *Intercollegiate sports:* baseball M, basketball M, cross-country running M/W, golf M/W, soccer M/W, volleyball W. *Intramural sports:* basketball M/W, bowling M(c)/W(c), cheerleading M(c)/W(c), football M, racquetball M/W, softball W, volleyball M(c)/W.

Standardized Tests *Required:* SAT or ACT (for admission).

Costs (2011–12) *Tuition:* state resident $12,242 full-time, $495 per credit part-time; nonresident $18,682 full-time, $778 per credit part-time. Full-time tuition and fees vary according to course level, degree level, location, program, and student level. Part-time tuition and fees vary according to course level, course load, degree level, location, program, and student level. *Required fees:*

$752 full-time. *Payment plans:* installment, deferred payment. *Waivers:* employees or children of employees.

Financial Aid Of all full-time matriculated undergraduates who enrolled in 2010, 519 applied for aid, 442 were judged to have need, 20 had their need fully met. In 2010, 32 non-need-based awards were made. *Average percent of need met:* 65%. *Average financial aid package:* $9669. *Average need-based loan:* $3988. *Average need-based gift aid:* $5934. *Average non-need-based aid:* $2388. *Average indebtedness upon graduation:* $33,530.

Applying *Options:* electronic application, early admission, deferred entrance. *Application fee:* $50. *Required:* high school transcript. *Required for some:* interview. *Recommended:* essay or personal statement. *Application deadlines:* rolling (freshmen), rolling (transfers). *Notification:* continuous (freshmen), continuous (transfers).

Freshman Application Contact Admissions Office, Penn State Wilkes-Barre, PO PSU, Lehman, PA 18627-0217. *Phone:* 570-675-9238. *Fax:* 570-675-9113. *E-mail:* wbadmissions@psu.edu. *Web site:* http://www.wb.psu.edu/.

Penn State Worthington Scranton

Dunmore, Pennsylvania

- **State-related** primarily 2-year, founded 1923, part of Pennsylvania State University
- **Small-town** campus
- **Coed,** 1,270 undergraduate students, 80% full-time, 51% women, 49% men

Undergraduates 1,011 full-time, 259 part-time. 2% are from out of state; 1% Black or African American, non-Hispanic/Latino; 4% Hispanic/Latino; 4% Asian, non-Hispanic/Latino; 0.2% American Indian or Alaska Native, non-Hispanic/Latino; 1% Two or more races, non-Hispanic/Latino; 2% Race/ethnicity unknown; 0.2% international; 3% transferred in. *Retention:* 71% of full-time freshmen returned.

Freshmen *Admission:* 799 applied, 653 admitted, 318 enrolled. *Average high school GPA:* 2.83. *Test scores:* SAT critical reading scores over 500: 38%; SAT math scores over 500: 41%; SAT writing scores over 500: 29%; SAT critical reading scores over 600: 7%; SAT math scores over 600: 6%; SAT writing scores over 600: 3%; SAT critical reading scores over 700: 1%.

Faculty *Total:* 100, 52% full-time, 40% with terminal degrees. *Student/faculty ratio:* 16:1.

Majors Accounting; acting; actuarial science; adult and continuing education administration; advertising; aerospace, aeronautical and astronautical/space engineering; African American/Black studies; agribusiness; agricultural and extension education; agricultural business and management related; agricultural engineering; agricultural mechanization; agriculture; agronomy and crop science; American studies; animal sciences; animal sciences related; anthropology; applied economics; archeology; architectural engineering; architectural engineering technology; art; art history, criticism and conservation; art teacher education; Asian studies (East); astronomy; atmospheric sciences and meteorology; biochemistry; bioengineering and biomedical engineering; biological and biomedical sciences related; biological and physical sciences; biology/biological sciences; biology/biotechnology laboratory technician; business administration and management; business/commerce; business/managerial economics; chemical engineering; chemistry; civil engineering; classics and classical languages; communication and journalism related; communication sciences and disorders; comparative literature; computer and information sciences; computer engineering; criminal justice/law enforcement administration; economics; electrical and electronics engineering; electrical, electronic and communications engineering technology; elementary education; engineering science; English; environmental/environmental health engineering; film/cinema/video studies; finance; food science; foreign language teacher education; forest sciences and biology; forest technology; French; geography; geological and earth sciences/geosciences related; geology/earth science; German; graphic design; health/health-care administration; history; horticultural science; hospitality administration related; human development and family studies; human nutrition; industrial engineering; information science/studies; international relations and affairs; Italian; Japanese; Jewish/Judaic studies; journalism; kinesiology and exercise science; labor and industrial relations; landscaping and groundskeeping; Latin American studies; liberal arts and sciences/liberal studies; management information systems; marketing/marketing management; materials science; mathematics; mechanical engineering; medical microbiology and bacteriology; medieval and Renaissance studies; mining and mineral engineering; music; natural resources and conservation related; natural resources/conservation; nuclear engineering; organizational behavior; parks, recreation and leisure facilities management; petroleum engineering; philosophy; physics; political science and government; premedical studies; psychology; registered nursing/registered nurse; rehabilitation and therapeutic professions related; religious studies; Russian; secondary education; sociology; soil science and agronomy; Spanish; special education; speech communication and rhetoric; statistics; theater design and technology; turf and turfgrass management; visual and performing arts; women's studies.

Academics *Calendar:* semesters. *Degrees:* certificates, associate, and bachelor's. *Special study options:* adult/continuing education programs. *ROTC:* Army (c), Air Force (c).
Student Life *Housing:* college housing not available.
Athletics Member NJCAA. *Intercollegiate sports:* baseball M, basketball M/W, cheerleading M/W, cross-country running M/W, soccer M, softball W, volleyball W. *Intramural sports:* basketball M/W, bowling M(c)/W(c), skiing (downhill) M(c)/W(c), soccer M/W, softball M/W, volleyball M/W(c), weight lifting M(c)/W(c).
Standardized Tests *Required:* SAT or ACT (for admission).
Costs (2011–12) *Tuition:* state resident $12,242 full-time, $495 per credit part-time; nonresident $18,682 full-time, $778 per credit part-time. Full-time tuition and fees vary according to course level, degree level, location, program, and student level. Part-time tuition and fees vary according to course level, course load, degree level, location, program, and student level. *Required fees:* $724 full-time. *Payment plans:* installment, deferred payment. *Waivers:* employees or children of employees.
Financial Aid Of all full-time matriculated undergraduates who enrolled in 2010, 940 applied for aid, 829 were judged to have need, 27 had their need fully met. In 2010, 38 non-need-based awards were made. *Average percent of need met:* 63%. *Average financial aid package:* $9201. *Average need-based loan:* $3899. *Average need-based gift aid:* $5986. *Average non-need-based aid:* $2452. *Average indebtedness upon graduation:* $33,530.
Applying *Options:* electronic application, early admission, deferred entrance. *Application fee:* $50. *Required:* high school transcript. *Required for some:* interview. *Recommended:* essay or personal statement. *Application deadlines:* rolling (freshmen), rolling (transfers). *Notification:* continuous (freshmen), continuous (transfers).
Freshman Application Contact Admissions Office, Penn State Worthington Scranton, 120 Ridge View Drive, Dunmore, PA 18512-1699. *Phone:* 570-963-2500. *Fax:* 570-963-2524. *E-mail:* wsadmissions@psu.edu. *Web site:* http://www.sn.psu.edu/.

Penn State York

York, Pennsylvania

- **State-related** primarily 2-year, founded 1926, part of Pennsylvania State University
- **Suburban** campus
- **Coed,** 1,259 undergraduate students, 68% full-time, 44% women, 56% men

Undergraduates 862 full-time, 397 part-time. 9% are from out of state; 8% Black or African American, non-Hispanic/Latino; 6% Hispanic/Latino; 5% Asian, non-Hispanic/Latino; 0.2% American Indian or Alaska Native, non-Hispanic/Latino; 3% Two or more races, non-Hispanic/Latino; 2% Race/ethnicity unknown; 4% international; 4% transferred in. *Retention:* 77% of full-time freshmen returned.
Freshmen *Admission:* 1,200 applied, 947 admitted, 282 enrolled. *Average high school GPA:* 2.92. *Test scores:* SAT critical reading scores over 500: 41%; SAT math scores over 500: 50%; SAT writing scores over 500: 34%; SAT critical reading scores over 600: 9%; SAT math scores over 600: 13%; SAT writing scores over 600: 8%; SAT critical reading scores over 700: 2%; SAT math scores over 700: 2%.
Faculty *Total:* 110, 51% full-time, 45% with terminal degrees. *Student/faculty ratio:* 14:1.
Majors Accounting; acting; actuarial science; adult and continuing education administration; advertising; aerospace, aeronautical and astronautical/space engineering; African American/Black studies; agribusiness; agricultural and extension education; agricultural business and management related; agricultural engineering; agricultural mechanization; agriculture; agronomy and crop science; American studies; animal sciences; animal sciences related; anthropology; applied economics; archeology; architectural engineering; art; art history, criticism and conservation; art teacher education; Asian studies (East); astronomy; atmospheric sciences and meteorology; biochemistry; bioengineering and biomedical engineering; biological and biomedical sciences related; biological and physical sciences; biology/biological sciences; biology/biotechnology laboratory technician; biomedical technology; business administration and management; business/commerce; business/managerial economics; chemical engineering; chemistry; civil engineering; classics and classical languages; communication and journalism related; communication sciences and disorders; comparative literature; computer and information sciences; computer engineering; criminal justice/law enforcement administration; economics; electrical and electronics engineering; electrical, electronic and communications engineering technology; elementary education; engineering science; English; environmental/environmental health engineering; film/cinema/video studies; finance; food science; foreign language teacher education; forest sciences and biology; forest technology; French; geography; geological and earth sciences/geosciences related; geology/earth science; German; graphic design; health/health-care administration; history; horticultural science; hospitality administration related; human development and family studies; human nutrition;

industrial engineering; industrial technology; information science/studies; international relations and affairs; Italian; Japanese; Jewish/Judaic studies; journalism; kinesiology and exercise science; labor and industrial relations; landscaping and groundskeeping; Latin American studies; liberal arts and sciences/liberal studies; logistics, materials, and supply chain management; management information systems; manufacturing engineering; marketing/marketing management; materials science; mathematics; mechanical engineering; mechanical engineering/mechanical technology; medical microbiology and bacteriology; medieval and Renaissance studies; metallurgical technology; mining and mineral engineering; music; natural resources and conservation related; natural resources/conservation; nuclear engineering; organizational behavior; parks, recreation and leisure facilities management; petroleum engineering; philosophy; physics; political science and government; premedical studies; psychology; registered nursing/registered nurse; rehabilitation and therapeutic professions related; religious studies; Russian; secondary education; sociology; soil science and agronomy; Spanish; special education; speech communication and rhetoric; statistics; telecommunications technology; theater design and technology; toxicology; turf and turfgrass management; visual and performing arts; women's studies.
Academics *Calendar:* semesters. *Degrees:* certificates, associate, bachelor's, and master's (also offers up to 2 years of most bachelor's degree programs offered at University Park campus). *Special study options:* adult/continuing education programs.
Student Life *Housing:* college housing not available.
Athletics Member NJCAA.
Standardized Tests *Required:* SAT or ACT (for admission).
Costs (2011–12) *Tuition:* state resident $12,242 full-time, $495 per credit part-time; nonresident $18,682 full-time, $778 per credit part-time. Full-time tuition and fees vary according to course level, degree level, location, program, and student level. Part-time tuition and fees vary according to course level, course load, degree level, location, program, and student level. *Required fees:* $724 full-time. *Payment plans:* installment, deferred payment. *Waivers:* employees or children of employees.
Financial Aid Of all full-time matriculated undergraduates who enrolled in 2010, 730 applied for aid, 586 were judged to have need, 31 had their need fully met. In 2010, 60 non-need-based awards were made. *Average percent of need met:* 60%. *Average financial aid package:* $8964. *Average need-based loan:* $3848. *Average need-based gift aid:* $5964. *Average non-need-based aid:* $2640. *Average indebtedness upon graduation:* $33,530.
Applying *Options:* electronic application, early admission, deferred entrance. *Application fee:* $50. *Required:* high school transcript. *Required for some:* interview. *Recommended:* essay or personal statement. *Application deadlines:* rolling (freshmen), rolling (transfers). *Notification:* continuous (freshmen), continuous (transfers).
Freshman Application Contact Admissions Office, Penn State York, 1031 Edgecomb Avenue, York, PA 17403-3398. *Phone:* 717-771-4040. *Toll-free phone:* 800-778-6227. *Fax:* 717-771-4005. *E-mail:* ykadmission@psu.edu. *Web site:* http://www.yk.psu.edu/.

Pennsylvania Highlands Community College

Johnstown, Pennsylvania

- **State and locally supported** 2-year, founded 1994
- **Small-town** campus
- **Coed**

Undergraduates 955 full-time, 1,588 part-time. Students come from 4 states and territories; 2% are from out of state. *Retention:* 34% of full-time freshmen returned.
Faculty *Student/faculty ratio:* 13:1.
Academics *Calendar:* semesters. *Degree:* certificates, diplomas, and associate. *Special study options:* academic remediation for entering students, adult/continuing education programs, advanced placement credit, cooperative education, distance learning, honors programs, independent study, internships, part-time degree program, services for LD students.
Athletics Member NJCAA.
Costs (2011–12) *Tuition:* area resident $2900 full-time, $96 per credit part-time; state resident $5800 full-time, $192 per credit part-time; nonresident $8700 full-time, $288 per credit part-time. Full-time tuition and fees vary according to course load and reciprocity agreements. Part-time tuition and fees vary according to course load and reciprocity agreements. *Required fees:* $1260 full-time, $35 per credit part-time.
Financial Aid Of all full-time matriculated undergraduates who enrolled in 2010, 25 Federal Work-Study jobs (averaging $2500).
Applying *Application fee:* $20.
Freshman Application Contact Mr. Jeff Maul, Admissions Officer, Pennsylvania Highlands Community College, 101 Community College Way, Johnstown, PA 15904. *Phone:* 814-262-6431. *E-mail:* jmaul@pennhighlands.edu. *Web site:* http://www.pennhighlands.edu/.

Pennsylvania Institute of Technology
Media, Pennsylvania

Freshman Application Contact Ms. Angela Cassetta, Dean of Enrollment Management, Pennsylvania Institute of Technology, 800 Manchester Avenue, Media, PA 19063-4036. *Phone:* 610-892-1550 Ext. 1553. *Toll-free phone:* 800-422-0025. *Fax:* 610-892-1510. *E-mail:* info@pit.edu. *Web site:* http://www.pit.edu/.

Pennsylvania School of Business
Allentown, Pennsylvania

Freshman Application Contact Mr. Bill Barber, Director, Pennsylvania School of Business, 406 West Hamilton Street, Allentown, PA 18101. *Phone:* 610-841-3333. *Fax:* 610-841-3334. *E-mail:* wbarber@pennschoolofbusiness.edu. *Web site:* http://www.psb.edu/.

Pittsburgh Institute of Aeronautics
Pittsburgh, Pennsylvania

Freshman Application Contact Mr. Vincent J. Mezza, Director of Admissions, Pittsburgh Institute of Aeronautics, PO Box 10897, Pittsburgh, PA 15236-0897. *Phone:* 412-346-2100. *Toll-free phone:* 800-444-1440. *Fax:* 412-466-5013. *E-mail:* admissions@pia.edu. *Web site:* http://www.pia.edu/.

Pittsburgh Institute of Mortuary Science, Incorporated
Pittsburgh, Pennsylvania

Freshman Application Contact Ms. Karen Rocco, Registrar, Pittsburgh Institute of Mortuary Science, Incorporated, 5808 Baum Boulevard, Pittsburgh, PA 15206-3706. *Phone:* 412-362-8500 Ext. 105. *Fax:* 412-362-1684. *E-mail:* pims5808@aol.com. *Web site:* http://www.pims.edu/.

Pittsburgh Technical Institute
Oakdale, Pennsylvania

- **Proprietary** 2-year, founded 1946
- **Suburban** 180-acre campus with easy access to Pittsburgh
- **Coed,** 1,939 undergraduate students, 100% full-time, 39% women, 61% men
- 84% of applicants were admitted

Undergraduates 1,939 full-time. Students come from 20 states and territories; 1 other country; 18% are from out of state; 6% Black or African American, non-Hispanic/Latino; 0.9% Hispanic/Latino; 0.4% Asian, non-Hispanic/Latino; 0.1% Native Hawaiian or other Pacific Islander, non-Hispanic/Latino; 0.2% American Indian or Alaska Native, non-Hispanic/Latino; 2% Two or more races, non-Hispanic/Latino; 35% Race/ethnicity unknown; 12% transferred in; 40% live on campus. *Retention:* 67% of full-time freshmen returned.
Freshmen *Admission:* 2,011 applied, 1,693 admitted, 747 enrolled. *Average high school GPA:* 2.62.
Faculty *Total:* 127, 60% full-time. *Student/faculty ratio:* 25:1.
Majors Architectural drafting and CAD/CADD; business administration and management; computer graphics; computer programming; computer technology/computer systems technology; electrical, electronic and communications engineering technology; electrical/electronics equipment installation and repair; homeland security, law enforcement, firefighting and protective services related; hotel/motel administration; medical/health management and clinical assistant; medical office assistant; surgical technology; web page, digital/multimedia and information resources design.
Academics *Calendar:* quarters. *Degree:* certificates and associate. *Special study options:* academic remediation for entering students, advanced placement credit, cooperative education, distance learning, double majors, internships, services for LD students.
Library Library Resource Center with 10,159 titles, 163 serial subscriptions, 1,662 audiovisual materials, an OPAC.
Student Life *Housing Options:* coed. Campus housing is university owned and leased by the school. Freshman campus housing is guaranteed. *Activities and Organizations:* drama/theater group, choral group, American Society of Travel Agents (ASTA), MEDICS Club, Alpha Beta Gamma (ABG), Drama Club, Direct Connect. *Campus security:* 24-hour emergency response devices and patrols, controlled dormitory access. *Student services:* personal/psychological counseling.
Athletics *Intramural sports:* basketball M/W, soccer M/W, softball M/W, ultimate Frisbee M/W, volleyball M/W.
Costs (2012–13) *Comprehensive fee:* $23,710 includes full-time tuition ($15,250) and room and board ($8460). Full-time tuition and fees vary according to course load and program. No tuition increase for student's term of enrollment. *Room and board:* Room and board charges vary according to housing facility. *Payment plans:* installment, deferred payment. *Waivers:* children of alumni and employees or children of employees.
Applying *Options:* electronic application, deferred entrance. *Required:* high school transcript, interview. *Required for some:* essay or personal statement, certain programs require a criminal background check; some programs require applicants to be in top 50-80% of class; Practical Nursing requires entrance exam. *Recommended:* interview. *Application deadlines:* rolling (freshmen), rolling (out-of-state freshmen), rolling (transfers). *Notification:* continuous (freshmen), continuous (out-of-state freshmen), continuous (transfers).
Freshman Application Contact Ms. Nancy Goodlin, Admissions Office Assistant, Pittsburgh Technical Institute, 1111 McKee Road, Oakdale, PA 15071. *Phone:* 412-809-5100. *Toll-free phone:* 800-784-9675. *Fax:* 412-809-5351. *E-mail:* goodlin.nancy@pti.edu. *Web site:* http://www.pti.edu/.

Prism Career Institute
Upper Darby, Pennsylvania

Director of Admissions Ms. Dina Gentile, Director, Prism Career Institute, 6800 Market Street, Upper Darby, PA 19082. *Phone:* 610-789-6700. *Toll-free phone:* 800-571-2213. *Fax:* 610-789-5208. *E-mail:* dgentile@pjaschool.com. *Web site:* http://www.prismcareerinstitute.edu/.

Reading Area Community College
Reading, Pennsylvania

Director of Admissions Ms. Maria Mitchell, Associate Vice President of Enrollment Management and Student Services, Reading Area Community College, PO Box 1706, Reading, PA 19603-1706. *Phone:* 610-607-6224. *E-mail:* mmitchell@racc.edu. *Web site:* http://www.racc.edu/.

The Restaurant School at Walnut Hill College
Philadelphia, Pennsylvania

- **Proprietary** primarily 2-year, founded 1974
- **Urban** 2-acre campus
- **Coed,** 402 undergraduate students, 100% full-time, 56% women, 44% men
- 97% of applicants were admitted

Undergraduates 402 full-time. Students come from 4 other countries; 29% are from out of state; 14% Black or African American, non-Hispanic/Latino; 4% Hispanic/Latino; 2% Asian, non-Hispanic/Latino; 1% Two or more races, non-Hispanic/Latino; 32% Race/ethnicity unknown; 10% transferred in.
Freshmen *Admission:* 174 applied, 168 admitted, 278 enrolled.
Faculty *Total:* 19, 95% full-time. *Student/faculty ratio:* 22:1.
Majors Baking and pastry arts; culinary arts; hotel/motel administration; restaurant/food services management.
Academics *Calendar:* quarters. *Degrees:* associate and bachelor's. *Special study options:* internships, part-time degree program.
Library Alumni Resource Center with a Web page.
Student Life *Housing Options:* coed. Campus housing is leased by the school. *Activities and Organizations:* Wine Club, Book Club, Coffee & Tea Club, Craft Club, Flair Bartending. *Campus security:* 24-hour emergency response devices and patrols, student patrols, controlled dormitory access.
Standardized Tests *Recommended:* SAT or ACT (for admission).
Costs (2012–13) *One-time required fee:* $200. *Tuition:* $17,850 full-time. *Required fees:* $3750 full-time. *Room only:* $4600. Room and board charges vary according to housing facility. *Payment plans:* installment, deferred payment.
Applying *Options:* electronic application, early admission, early decision, deferred entrance. *Application fee:* $50. *Required:* essay or personal statement, high school transcript, 2 letters of recommendation, interview. *Required for some:* entrance exam. *Recommended:* minimum 2.0 GPA. *Application deadline:* rolling (freshmen).
Freshman Application Contact Miss Toni Morelli, Director of Admissions, The Restaurant School at Walnut Hill College, 4207 Walnut Street, Philadelphia, PA 19104-3518. *Phone:* 267-295-2353. *Fax:* 215-222-4219. *E-mail:* tmorelli@walnuthillcollege.edu. *Web site:* http://www.walnuthillcollege.edu/.

Rosedale Technical Institute
Pittsburgh, Pennsylvania

Freshman Application Contact Ms. Debbie Bier, Director of Admissions, Rosedale Technical Institute, 215 Beecham Drive, Suite 2, Pittsburgh, PA 15205-9791. *Phone:* 412-521-6200. *Toll-free phone:* 800-521-6262. *Fax:*

412-521-2520. *E-mail:* admissions@rosedaletech.org. *Web site:* http://www.rosedaletech.org/.

Sanford-Brown Institute–Pittsburgh

Pittsburgh, Pennsylvania

Director of Admissions Mr. Bruce E. Jones, Director of Admission, Sanford-Brown Institute–Pittsburgh, 421 Seventh Avenue, Pittsburgh, PA 15219-1907. *Phone:* 412-281-7083 Ext. 114. *Toll-free phone:* 888-270-6333. *Web site:* http://www.sanfordbrown.edu/.

Sanford-Brown Institute–Wilkins Township

Pittsburgh, Pennsylvania

Director of Admissions Timothy Babyok, Director of Admission, Sanford-Brown Institute–Wilkins Township, Penn Center East, 777 Penn Center Boulevard, Building 7, Pittsburgh, PA 15235. *Phone:* 412-373-6400. *Toll-free phone:* 888-381-2433. *Fax:* 412-374-0863. *Web site:* http://www.sanfordbrown.edu/Wilkins-Township/.

South Hills School of Business & Technology

Altoona, Pennsylvania

Freshman Application Contact Ms. Holly J. Emerick, Director of Admissions, South Hills School of Business & Technology, 508 58th Street, Altoona, PA 16602. *Phone:* 814-944-6134. *Fax:* 814-944-4684. *E-mail:* hemerick@southhills.edu. *Web site:* http://www.southhills.edu/.

South Hills School of Business & Technology

State College, Pennsylvania

Freshman Application Contact Ms. Diane M. Brown, Director of Admissions, South Hills School of Business & Technology, 480 Waupelani Drive, State College, PA 16801-4516. *Phone:* 814-234-7755 Ext. 2020. *Toll-free phone:* 888-282-7427. *Fax:* 814-234-0926. *E-mail:* admissions@southhills.edu. *Web site:* http://www.southhills.edu/.

Thaddeus Stevens College of Technology

Lancaster, Pennsylvania

Director of Admissions Ms. Erin Kate Nelsen, Director of Enrollment, Thaddeus Stevens College of Technology, 750 East King Street, Lancaster, PA 17602-3198. *Phone:* 717-299-7772. *Toll-free phone:* 800-842-3832. *Web site:* http://www.stevenscollege.edu/.

Triangle Tech–Greensburg School

Greensburg, Pennsylvania

Freshman Application Contact Mr. John Mazzarese, Vice President of Admissions, Triangle Tech–Greensburg School, 222 East Pittsburgh Street, Greensburg, PA 15601. *Phone:* 412-359-1000. *Toll-free phone:* 800-874-8324. *Web site:* http://www.triangle-tech.com/.

Triangle Tech Inc–Bethlehem

Bethlehem, Pennsylvania

Freshman Application Contact Triangle Tech Inc–Bethlehem, Lehigh Valley Industrial Park IV, 31 South Commerce Way, Bethlehem, PA 18017. *Web site:* http://www.triangle-tech.edu/.

Triangle Tech, Inc.–DuBois School

DuBois, Pennsylvania

- **Proprietary** 2-year, founded 1944, part of Triangle Tech Group, Inc.
- **Small-town** 5-acre campus
- **Coed, primarily men**

Undergraduates 329 full-time. Students come from 2 states and territories; 1 other country.

Faculty *Student/faculty ratio:* 15:1.

Academics *Calendar:* semesters. *Degree:* diplomas and associate. *Special study options:* academic remediation for entering students, advanced placement credit, off-campus study.

Applying *Options:* deferred entrance. *Required:* high school transcript, minimum 2.0 GPA, interview.

Freshman Application Contact Terry Kucic, Director of Admissions, Triangle Tech, Inc.–DuBois School, PO Box 551, DuBois, PA 15801. *Phone:* 814-371-2090. *Toll-free phone:* 800-874-8324. *Fax:* 814-371-9227. *E-mail:* tkucic@triangle-tech.com. *Web site:* http://www.triangle-tech.edu/.

Triangle Tech, Inc.–Erie School

Erie, Pennsylvania

Freshman Application Contact Admissions Representative, Triangle Tech, Inc.–Erie School, 2000 Liberty Street, Erie, PA 16502-2594. *Phone:* 814-453-6016. *Toll-free phone:* 800-874-8324 (in-state); 800-TRI-TECH (out-of-state). *Web site:* http://www.triangle-tech.com/.

Triangle Tech, Inc.–Pittsburgh School

Pittsburgh, Pennsylvania

Freshman Application Contact Director of Admissions, Triangle Tech, Inc.–Pittsburgh School, 1940 Perrysville Avenue, Pittsburgh, PA 15214-3897. *Phone:* 412-359-1000. *Toll-free phone:* 800-874-8324. *Fax:* 412-359-1012. *E-mail:* info@triangle-tech.edu. *Web site:* http://www.triangle-tech.edu/.

Triangle Tech, Inc.–Sunbury School

Sunbury, Pennsylvania

Freshman Application Contact Triangle Tech, Inc.–Sunbury School, 191 Performance Road, Sunbury, PA 17801. *Phone:* 412-359-1000. *Web site:* http://www.triangle-tech.edu/.

University of Pittsburgh at Titusville

Titusville, Pennsylvania

- **State-related** primarily 2-year, founded 1963, part of University of Pittsburgh System
- **Small-town** 10-acre campus
- **Endowment** $850,000
- **Coed**

Undergraduates 442 full-time, 72 part-time. Students come from 15 states and territories; 8% are from out of state; 19% Black or African American, non-Hispanic/Latino; 2% Hispanic/Latino; 2% Asian, non-Hispanic/Latino; 0.2% American Indian or Alaska Native, non-Hispanic/Latino; 3% Two or more races, non-Hispanic/Latino; 3% Race/ethnicity unknown; 8% transferred in; 55% live on campus.

Academics *Calendar:* semesters. *Degrees:* certificates, associate, and bachelor's. *Special study options:* academic remediation for entering students, advanced placement credit, distance learning, internships, part-time degree program, study abroad, summer session for credit.

Student Life *Campus security:* 24-hour emergency response devices and patrols, controlled dormitory access.

Athletics Member NJCAA.

Standardized Tests *Required:* SAT or ACT (for admission). *Recommended:* SAT (for admission).

Financial Aid Of all full-time matriculated undergraduates who enrolled in 2009, 429 applied for aid, 408 were judged to have need, 23 had their need fully met. In 2009, 10. *Average percent of need met:* 80. *Average financial aid package:* $15,305. *Average need-based loan:* $9451. *Average need-based gift aid:* $1992. *Average non-need-based aid:* $39,059.

Applying *Options:* electronic application, early admission, deferred entrance. *Application fee:* $45. *Required:* high school transcript, minimum 2.0 GPA. *Required for some:* essay or personal statement, 1 letter of recommendation. *Recommended:* interview.

Freshman Application Contact Mr. John R. Mumford, Executive Director of Enrollment Management, University of Pittsburgh at Titusville, PO Box 287, Titusville, PA 16354. *Phone:* 814-827-4409. *Toll-free phone:* 888-878-0462. *Fax:* 814-827-4519. *E-mail:* uptadm@pitt.edu. *Web site:* http://www.upt.pitt.edu/.

Valley Forge Military College

Wayne, Pennsylvania

Freshman Application Contact Maj. Greg Potts, Dean of Enrollment Management, Valley Forge Military College, 1001 Eagle Road, Wayne, PA 19087-3695. *Phone:* 610-989-1300. *Toll-free phone:* 800-234-8362. *Fax:*

610-688-1545. *E-mail:* admissions@vfmac.edu. *Web site:* http://www.vfmac.edu/.

See Display ad below and page 400 for the College Close-Up.

Vet Tech Institute

Pittsburgh, Pennsylvania

- **Private** 2-year, founded 1958
- **Urban** campus
- **Coed,** 363 undergraduate students
- 60% of applicants were admitted

Freshmen *Admission:* 540 applied, 325 admitted.

Majors Veterinary/animal health technology.

Academics *Calendar:* quarters. *Degree:* associate. *Special study options:* accelerated degree program, internships, summer session for credit.

Freshman Application Contact Admissions Office, Vet Tech Institute, 125 7th Street, Pittsburgh, PA 15222-3400. *Phone:* 412-391-7021. *Toll-free phone:* 800-570-0693. *Web site:* http://www.vettechinstitute.edu/.

Westmoreland County Community College

Youngwood, Pennsylvania

- **County-supported** 2-year, founded 1970
- **Rural** 85-acre campus with easy access to Pittsburgh
- **Endowment** $476,362
- **Coed,** 6,943 undergraduate students, 47% full-time, 64% women, 36% men

Undergraduates 3,268 full-time, 3,675 part-time. Students come from 5 states and territories; 0.2% are from out of state; 4% Black or African American, non-Hispanic/Latino; 1% Hispanic/Latino; 0.6% Asian, non-Hispanic/Latino; 0.2% Native Hawaiian or other Pacific Islander, non-Hispanic/Latino; 0.2% American Indian or Alaska Native, non-Hispanic/Latino; 0.8% Two or more races, non-Hispanic/Latino; 0.8% Race/ethnicity unknown; 2% transferred in. *Retention:* 48% of full-time freshmen returned.

Freshmen *Admission:* 2,988 applied, 2,988 admitted, 1,746 enrolled.

Faculty *Total:* 525, 18% full-time. *Student/faculty ratio:* 18:1.

Majors Accounting technology and bookkeeping; administrative assistant and secretarial science; applied horticulture/horticulture operations; architectural drafting and CAD/CADD; baking and pastry arts; banking and financial support services; biology/biotechnology laboratory technician; business administration and management; business/commerce; casino management; chemical technology; child-care provision; clinical/medical laboratory assistant; communications systems installation and repair technology; computer and information systems security; computer numerically controlled (CNC) machinist technology; computer programming; computer programming (specific applications); computer support specialist; computer systems networking and telecommunications; corrections; criminal justice/police science; criminal justice/safety; culinary arts; data entry/microcomputer applications; data processing and data processing technology; dental assisting; dental hygiene; diagnostic medical sonography and ultrasound technology; dietetic technology; early childhood education; electrical, electronic and communications engineering technology; family and community services; fire prevention and safety technology; floriculture/floristry management; food service and dining room management; graphic design; health and medical administrative services related; health information/medical records technology; heating, air conditioning, ventilation and refrigeration maintenance technology; homeland security, law enforcement, firefighting and protective services related; hotel/motel administration; human resources management; industrial mechanics and maintenance technology; legal assistant/paralegal; liberal arts and sciences/liberal studies; library and information science; licensed practical/vocational nurse training; machine tool technology; manufacturing engineering technology; mechanical drafting and CAD/CADD; mechanical engineering/mechanical technology; mechatronics, robotics, and automation engineering; medical/clinical assistant; medical insurance coding; medical office assistant; medical transcription; network and system administration; phlebotomy technology; physical science technologies related; pre-engineering; radio and television broadcasting technology; radiologic technology/science; real estate; registered nursing/registered nurse; restaurant, culinary, and catering management; sales, distribution, and marketing operations; special education–elementary school; tourism and travel services management; turf and turfgrass management; web page, digital/multimedia and information resources design; welding technology.

Academics *Calendar:* semesters. *Degree:* certificates, diplomas, and associate. *Special study options:* academic remediation for entering students, adult/

continuing education programs, advanced placement credit, cooperative education, distance learning, double majors, English as a second language, honors programs, independent study, internships, off-campus study, part-time degree program, services for LD students, summer session for credit.

Library Westmoreland County Community College Learning Resources Center with 64,000 titles, 250 serial subscriptions, 3,500 audiovisual materials, an OPAC, a Web page.

Student Life *Housing:* college housing not available. *Activities and Organizations:* drama/theater group, choral group, Phi Theta Kappa, Sigma Alpha Pi Leadership Society, Criminal Justice Fraternity, Gay Straight Alliance, SADAA/SADHA. *Campus security:* 24-hour emergency response devices and patrols, late-night transport/escort service. *Student services:* personal/psychological counseling.

Athletics Member NJCAA. *Intercollegiate sports:* baseball M, basketball M/W, bowling M/W, cross-country running M/W, golf M/W, soccer M/W, softball W, volleyball W. *Intramural sports:* basketball M/W, bowling M/W, golf M/W, skiing (downhill) M/W, volleyball M/W, weight lifting M/W.

Costs (2011–12) *Tuition:* area resident $2400 full-time, $80 per credit part-time; state resident $4800 full-time, $160 per credit part-time; nonresident $7200 full-time, $240 per credit part-time. Full-time tuition and fees vary according to course load. Part-time tuition and fees vary according to course load. *Required fees:* $510 full-time, $17 per credit part-time. *Payment plans:* installment, deferred payment. *Waivers:* senior citizens and employees or children of employees.

Applying *Options:* electronic application, early admission. *Application fee:* $15. *Application deadlines:* rolling (freshmen), rolling (transfers). *Notification:* continuous (freshmen), continuous (transfers).

Freshman Application Contact Mr. Andrew Colosimo, Admissions Coordinator, Westmoreland County Community College, 145 Pavillon Lane, Youngwood, PA 15697. *Phone:* 724-925-4064. *Toll-free phone:* 800-262-2103. *Fax:* 724-925-4292. *E-mail:* admission@wccc.edu. *Web site:* http://www.wccc.edu/.

The Williamson Free School of Mechanical Trades

Media, Pennsylvania

- **Independent** 2-year, founded 1888
- **Small-town** 222-acre campus with easy access to Philadelphia
- **Men only**

Undergraduates 270 full-time. Students come from 7 states and territories; 15% are from out of state; 100% live on campus.

Faculty *Student/faculty ratio:* 12:1.

Academics *Calendar:* semesters. *Degree:* diplomas and associate. *Special study options:* academic remediation for entering students, independent study, off-campus study.

Student Life *Campus security:* evening patrols, gate security.

Athletics Member NJCAA.

Standardized Tests *Required:* Armed Services Vocational Aptitude Battery (for admission).

Applying *Required:* essay or personal statement, high school transcript, minimum 2.0 GPA, interview, average performance or better on the Armed Services Vocational Aptitude Battery (ASVAB). *Required for some:* 3 letters of recommendation.

Freshman Application Contact Mr. Jay Merillat, Dean of Enrollments, The Williamson Free School of Mechanical Trades, 106 South New Middletown Road, Media, PA 19063. *Phone:* 610-566-1776 Ext. 235. *E-mail:* jmerillat@williamson.edu. *Web site:* http://www.williamson.edu/.

WyoTech Blairsville

Blairsville, Pennsylvania

Freshman Application Contact Mr. Tim Smyers, WyoTech Blairsville, 500 Innovation Drive, Blairsville, PA 15717. *Phone:* 724-459-2311. *Toll-free phone:* 888-577-7559. *Fax:* 724-459-6499. *E-mail:* tsmyers@wyotech.edu. *Web site:* http://www.wyotech.com/.

Yorktowne Business Institute

York, Pennsylvania

Director of Admissions Director of Admissions, Yorktowne Business Institute, West Seventh Avenue, York, PA 17404. *Phone:* 717-846-5000. *Toll-free phone:* 800-840-1004. *Web site:* http://www.ybi.edu/.

YTI Career Institute–York

York, Pennsylvania

- **Private** 2-year, founded 1967, part of York Technical Institute, LLC
- **Suburban** campus with easy access to Harrisburg
- **Coed,** 680 undergraduate students, 100% full-time, 44% women, 56% men

Undergraduates 680 full-time. Students come from 9 states and territories; 2% are from out of state; 9% Black or African American, non-Hispanic/Latino; 9% Hispanic/Latino; 1% Asian, non-Hispanic/Latino; 0.3% Native Hawaiian or other Pacific Islander, non-Hispanic/Latino; 0.1% American Indian or Alaska Native, non-Hispanic/Latino; 3% Two or more races, non-Hispanic/Latino.

Freshmen *Admission:* 500 enrolled.

Faculty *Total:* 69, 70% full-time. *Student/faculty ratio:* 15:1.

Majors Accounting; business administration and management; CAD/CADD drafting/design technology; computer and information sciences and support services related; electrical, electronic and communications engineering technology; medical/clinical assistant; parks, recreation and leisure facilities management.

Academics *Calendar:* continuous. *Degree:* diplomas and associate. *Special study options:* academic remediation for entering students, advanced placement credit, cooperative education, internships.

Student Life *Student services:* personal/psychological counseling.

Standardized Tests *Required:* ACT COMPASS (for admission).

Costs (2012–13) *One-time required fee:* $50. *Tuition:* $15,000 full-time. Full-time tuition and fees vary according to location and program. *Payment plan:* installment. *Waivers:* employees or children of employees.

Applying *Application fee:* $50. *Required:* high school transcript, minimum 2.0 GPA, interview. *Recommended:* admissions test.

Freshman Application Contact YTI Career Institute–York, 1405 Williams Road, York, PA 17402-9017. *Phone:* 717-757-1100 Ext. 318. *Toll-free phone:* 800-557-6335. *Web site:* http://www.yti.edu/.

PUERTO RICO

Centro de Estudios Multidisciplinarios

Rio Piedras, Puerto Rico

Director of Admissions Admissions Department, Centro de Estudios Multidisciplinarios, Calle 13 #1206, Ext. San Agustin, Rio Piedras, PR 00926. *Phone:* 787-765-4210 Ext. 115. *Toll-free phone:* 877-779-CDEM. *Web site:* http://www.cempr.edu/.

Huertas Junior College

Caguas, Puerto Rico

Director of Admissions Mrs. Barbara Hassim López, Director of Admissions, Huertas Junior College, PO Box 8429, Caguas, PR 00726. *Phone:* 787-743-1242. *Fax:* 787-743-0203. *E-mail:* huertas@huertas.org. *Web site:* http://www.huertas.edu/.

Humacao Community College

Humacao, Puerto Rico

Director of Admissions Ms. Xiomara Sanchez, Director of Admissions, Humacao Community College, PO Box 9139, Humacao, PR 00792. *Phone:* 787-852-2525. *Web site:* http://www.hccpr.edu/.

Instituto Comercial de Puerto Rico Junior College

San Juan, Puerto Rico

Freshman Application Contact Admissions Office, Instituto Comercial de Puerto Rico Junior College, 558 Munoz Rivera Avenue, PO Box 190304, San Juan, PR 00919-0304. *Phone:* 787-753-6335. *Web site:* http://www.icprjc.edu/.

Puerto Rico Technical Junior College

San Juan, Puerto Rico

Director of Admissions Admissions Department, Puerto Rico Technical Junior College, 703 Ponce De Leon Avenue, Hato Rey, San Juan, PR 00917. *Phone:* 787-751-0628 Ext. 28.

Ramírez College of Business and Technology

San Juan, Puerto Rico

Director of Admissions Mr. Arnaldo Castro, Director of Admissions, Ramírez College of Business and Technology, Avenue Ponce de Leon #70, San Juan, PR 00918. *Phone:* 787-763-3120. *E-mail:* ramirezcollege@prtc.net. *Web site:* http://www.galeon.com/ramirezcollege/.

RHODE ISLAND

Community College of Rhode Island

Warwick, Rhode Island

- **State-supported** 2-year, founded 1964
- **Urban** 205-acre campus with easy access to Boston
- **Coed,** 17,893 undergraduate students, 34% full-time, 61% women, 39% men

Undergraduates 6,094 full-time, 11,799 part-time. Students come from 19 states and territories; 4% are from out of state; 9% Black or African American, non-Hispanic/Latino; 15% Hispanic/Latino; 3% Asian, non-Hispanic/Latino; 0.6% American Indian or Alaska Native, non-Hispanic/Latino; 0.8% Two or more races, non-Hispanic/Latino; 7% Race/ethnicity unknown; 0.1% international.

Freshmen *Admission:* 6,891 applied, 6,868 admitted, 3,757 enrolled.

Faculty *Total:* 821, 39% full-time. *Student/faculty ratio:* 21:1.

Majors Accounting; administrative assistant and secretarial science; adult development and aging; art; banking and financial support services; biological and physical sciences; business administration and management; business/commerce; chemical technology; clinical/medical laboratory technology; computer and information sciences; computer engineering technology; computer programming (specific applications); computer systems networking and telecommunications; criminal justice/police science; crisis/emergency/disaster management; customer service management; dental hygiene; diagnostic medical sonography and ultrasound technology; dramatic/theater arts; early childhood education; electrical, electronic and communications engineering technology; electromechanical technology; engineering; fire science/firefighting; general studies; histologic technician; jazz/jazz studies; kindergarten/preschool education; legal administrative assistant/secretary; legal assistant/paralegal; liberal arts and sciences/liberal studies; licensed practical/vocational nurse training; marketing/marketing management; massage therapy; medical administrative assistant and medical secretary; mental health counseling; music; occupational therapist assistant; optician; physical therapy technology; radiologic technology/science; registered nursing/registered nurse; respiratory care therapy; social work; special education; substance abuse/addiction counseling; surveying engineering; web/multimedia management and webmaster.

Academics *Calendar:* semesters. *Degree:* certificates, diplomas, and associate. *Special study options:* academic remediation for entering students, adult/continuing education programs, advanced placement credit, cooperative education, distance learning, double majors, English as a second language, external degree program, honors programs, independent study, internships, off-campus study, part-time degree program, services for LD students, study abroad, summer session for credit. *ROTC:* Army (c).

Library Community College of Rhode Island Learning Resources Center plus 3 others with an OPAC, a Web page.

Student Life *Housing:* college housing not available. *Activities and Organizations:* drama/theater group, student-run newspaper, choral group, Distributive Education Clubs of America, Theater group - Players, Skills USA, Phi Theta Kappa, student government. *Campus security:* 24-hour emergency response devices and patrols. *Student services:* health clinic, personal/psychological counseling.

Athletics Member NJCAA. *Intercollegiate sports:* baseball M(s), basketball M(s)/W(s), golf M/W, soccer M(s)/W(s), softball W(s), tennis M/W, track and field M/W, volleyball W(s). *Intramural sports:* basketball M/W, volleyball M/W.

Costs (2011–12) *Tuition:* state resident $3356 full-time, $153 per credit hour part-time; nonresident $9496 full-time, $454 per credit hour part-time. Full-time tuition and fees vary according to program. Part-time tuition and fees vary according to course load and program. *Required fees:* $320 full-time, $12 per credit hour part-time, $27 per term part-time. *Payment plans:* installment, deferred payment. *Waivers:* senior citizens and employees or children of employees.

Financial Aid Of all full-time matriculated undergraduates who enrolled in 2010, 500 Federal Work-Study jobs (averaging $2500).

Applying *Options:* deferred entrance. *Application fee:* $20. *Application deadlines:* rolling (freshmen), rolling (transfers). *Notification:* continuous (freshmen).

Freshman Application Contact Community College of Rhode Island, Flanagan Campus, 1762 Louisquisset Pike, Lincoln, RI 02865-4585. *Phone:* 401-333-7490. *Fax:* 401-333-7122. *E-mail:* webadmission@ccri.edu. *Web site:* http://www.ccri.edu/.

SOUTH CAROLINA

Aiken Technical College

Aiken, South Carolina

- **State and locally supported** 2-year, founded 1972, part of South Carolina State Board for Technical and Comprehensive Education
- **Rural** 88-acre campus
- **Endowment** $4.1 million
- **Coed,** 3,045 undergraduate students, 43% full-time, 64% women, 36% men

Undergraduates 1,315 full-time, 1,730 part-time. 10% are from out of state; 33% Black or African American, non-Hispanic/Latino; 2% Hispanic/Latino; 0.6% Asian, non-Hispanic/Latino; 0.3% Native Hawaiian or other Pacific Islander, non-Hispanic/Latino; 0.7% American Indian or Alaska Native, non-Hispanic/Latino; 0.7% Two or more races, non-Hispanic/Latino; 1% Race/ethnicity unknown; 11% transferred in. *Retention:* 23% of full-time freshmen returned.

Freshmen *Admission:* 2,001 applied, 829 admitted, 587 enrolled.

Faculty *Total:* 184, 32% full-time. *Student/faculty ratio:* 31:1.

Majors Accounting; administrative assistant and secretarial science; automobile/automotive mechanics technology; child-care and support services management; computer engineering technology; computer programming; computer systems networking and telecommunications; criminal justice/law enforcement administration; data processing and data processing technology; early childhood education; electrical, electronic and communications engineering technology; industrial mechanics and maintenance technology; liberal arts and sciences/liberal studies; management science; marketing related; medical radiologic technology; multi/interdisciplinary studies related; radiation protection/health physics technology; registered nursing/registered nurse; sales, distribution, and marketing operations.

Academics *Calendar:* semesters. *Degree:* certificates, diplomas, and associate. *Special study options:* academic remediation for entering students, advanced placement credit, cooperative education, internships, off-campus study, part-time degree program, services for LD students, summer session for credit.

Library Aiken Technical College Library with 62,235 titles, 165 serial subscriptions, an OPAC, a Web page.

Student Life *Housing:* college housing not available. *Campus security:* 24-hour emergency response devices and patrols, late-night transport/escort service. *Student services:* personal/psychological counseling.

Athletics Member NJCAA. *Intercollegiate sports:* basketball M, softball W.

Costs (2012–13) *Tuition:* area resident $3432 full-time, $143 per credit hour part-time; state resident $3792 full-time, $158 per credit hour part-time; nonresident $9600 full-time, $400 per credit hour part-time. Full-time tuition and fees vary according to course load and reciprocity agreements. Part-time tuition and fees vary according to course load and reciprocity agreements. *Required fees:* $290 full-time, $5 per credit hour part-time, $85 per term part-time. *Payment plans:* installment, deferred payment.

Financial Aid Of all full-time matriculated undergraduates who enrolled in 2010, 48 Federal Work-Study jobs (averaging $3000).

Applying *Options:* electronic application, deferred entrance. *Recommended:* high school transcript. *Application deadlines:* rolling (freshmen), rolling (out-of-state freshmen), rolling (transfers). *Notification:* continuous (freshmen), continuous (out-of-state freshmen), continuous (transfers).

Freshman Application Contact Ms. Lisa Sommers, Aiken Technical College, PO Drawer 696, Aiken, SC 29802. *Phone:* 803-593-9231 Ext. 1584. *Fax:* 803-593-6526. *E-mail:* sommersl@atc.edu. *Web site:* http://www.atc.edu/.

Brown Mackie College–Greenville

Greenville, South Carolina

- **Proprietary** primarily 2-year, part of Education Management Corporation
- **Coed**

Academics *Degrees:* certificates, associate, and bachelor's.

Costs (2011–12) *Tuition:* Tuition varies by program. Students should contact Brown Mackie College for tuition information.

Freshman Application Contact Brown Mackie College–Greenville, Two Liberty Square, 75 Beattie Place, Suite 100, Greenville, SC 29601. *Phone:* 864-239-5300. *Toll-free phone:* 877-479-8465. *Web site:* http://www.brownmackie.edu/greenville/.

See page 356 for the College Close-Up.

Central Carolina Technical College

Sumter, South Carolina

- **State-supported** 2-year, founded 1963, part of South Carolina State Board for Technical and Comprehensive Education
- **Small-town** 70-acre campus with easy access to Columbia, SC
- **Endowment** $1.4 million
- **Coed,** 4,522 undergraduate students, 36% full-time, 70% women, 30% men

Undergraduates 1,607 full-time, 2,915 part-time. 1% are from out of state; 48% Black or African American, non-Hispanic/Latino; 2% Hispanic/Latino; 0.8% Asian, non-Hispanic/Latino; 0.1% American Indian or Alaska Native, non-Hispanic/Latino; 0.6% Two or more races, non-Hispanic/Latino; 5% Race/ethnicity unknown; 7% transferred in.

Freshmen *Admission:* 901 enrolled.

Faculty *Total:* 258, 38% full-time. *Student/faculty ratio:* 17:1.

Majors Accounting; administrative assistant and secretarial science; business administration and management; child-care and support services management; criminal justice/safety; data processing and data processing technology; environmental control technologies related; human services; industrial electronics technology; legal assistant/paralegal; liberal arts and sciences/liberal studies; natural resources management and policy; registered nursing/registered nurse; sales, distribution, and marketing operations; surgical technology.

Academics *Calendar:* semesters. *Degree:* certificates, diplomas, and associate. *Special study options:* academic remediation for entering students, accelerated degree program, adult/continuing education programs, advanced placement credit, cooperative education, distance learning, external degree program, independent study, internships, part-time degree program, services for LD students, summer session for credit.

Library Central Carolina Technical College Library with 27,878 titles, 135 serial subscriptions, 2,778 audiovisual materials, an OPAC, a Web page.

Student Life *Housing:* college housing not available. *Activities and Organizations:* Creative Arts Society, Phi Theta Kappa, Computer Club, National Student Nurses Association (local chapter), Natural Resources Management Club. *Campus security:* 24-hour emergency response devices, student patrols, security patrols parking lots and halls during working hours and off-duty police officers are deployed on main campus during peak hours. *Student services:* personal/psychological counseling.

Standardized Tests *Required:* COMPASS/ASSET (for admission). *Required for some:* SAT (for admission), ACT (for admission), SAT or ACT (for admission).

Costs (2011–12) *Tuition:* area resident $3476 full-time, $145 per credit hour part-time; state resident $4052 full-time, $169 per credit hour part-time; nonresident $6042 full-time, $252 per credit hour part-time. *Required fees:* $70 full-time. *Payment plan:* deferred payment. *Waivers:* senior citizens and employees or children of employees.

Applying *Options:* electronic application. *Required for some:* high school transcript. *Application deadlines:* rolling (freshmen), rolling (transfers).

Freshman Application Contact Ms. Barbara Wright, Director of Admissions and Counseling, Central Carolina Technical College, 506 North Guignard Drive, Sumter, SC 29150. *Phone:* 803-778-6695. *Toll-free phone:* 800-221-8711. *Fax:* 803-778-6696. *E-mail:* wrightb@cctech.edu. *Web site:* http://www.cctech.edu/.

Clinton Junior College

Rock Hill, South Carolina

Director of Admissions Robert M. Copeland, Vice President for Student Affairs, Clinton Junior College, PO Box 968, 1029 Crawford Road, Rock Hill, SC 29730. *Phone:* 803-327-7402. *Toll-free phone:* 877-837-9645. *Fax:* 803-327-3261. *E-mail:* rcopeland@clintonjrcollege.org. *Web site:* http://www.clintonjuniorcollege.edu/.

Denmark Technical College

Denmark, South Carolina

- **State-supported** 2-year, founded 1948, part of South Carolina State Board for Technical and Comprehensive Education
- **Rural** 53-acre campus
- **Coed,** 1,607 undergraduate students, 83% full-time, 58% women, 42% men

Undergraduates 1,329 full-time, 278 part-time. 5% are from out of state; 95% Black or African American, non-Hispanic/Latino; 0.3% Hispanic/Latino; 0.1% Asian, non-Hispanic/Latino; 0.2% American Indian or Alaska Native, non-Hispanic/Latino; 0.7% Race/ethnicity unknown; 3% transferred in. *Retention:* 50% of full-time freshmen returned.

Freshmen *Admission:* 660 enrolled.

Faculty *Total:* 46, 76% full-time. *Student/faculty ratio:* 21:1.

Majors Administrative assistant and secretarial science; automobile/automotive mechanics technology; business administration and management; computer and information sciences; criminal justice/law enforcement administration; engineering technology; human services; kindergarten/preschool education.

Academics *Calendar:* semesters. *Degree:* certificates, diplomas, and associate. *Special study options:* academic remediation for entering students, adult/continuing education programs, advanced placement credit, cooperative education, distance learning, independent study, internships, off-campus study, part-time degree program, summer session for credit.

Library Denmark Technical College Learning Resources Center with 18,735 titles, 195 serial subscriptions, 802 audiovisual materials, an OPAC.

Student Life *Housing Options:* men-only, women-only. Campus housing is university owned. Freshman applicants given priority for college housing. *Activities and Organizations:* choral group, Student Government Association, DTC Choir, athletics, Phi Theta Kappa Internal Honor Society, Esquire Club (men and women). *Campus security:* 24-hour patrols, late-night transport/escort service, 24-hour emergency contact line/alarm devices. *Student services:* health clinic, personal/psychological counseling.

Athletics Member NJCAA. *Intercollegiate sports:* basketball M/W, cheerleading W. *Intramural sports:* baseball M, basketball M/W, softball W, tennis M/W, volleyball M/W.

Standardized Tests *Required:* ACT, ASSET, COMPASS, and TEAS (Nursing) (for admission). *Recommended:* SAT or ACT (for admission).

Costs (2012–13) *Tuition:* state resident $2590 full-time; nonresident $4870 full-time. *Room and board:* $3566; room only: $1762.

Financial Aid Of all full-time matriculated undergraduates who enrolled in 2010, 250 Federal Work-Study jobs (averaging $2000).

Applying *Options:* electronic application, early admission, deferred entrance. *Application fee:* $10. *Required:* high school transcript. *Required for some:* essay or personal statement. *Application deadlines:* rolling (freshmen), rolling (out-of-state freshmen), rolling (transfers).

Freshman Application Contact Mrs. Faith Spells-Harrison, Administrative Specialist, Denmark Technical College, PO Box 327, 1126 Solomon Blatt Boulevard, Denmark, SC 29042. *Phone:* 803-793-5289. *Fax:* 803-793-5942. *E-mail:* spellsf@denmarktech.edu. *Web site:* http://www.denmarktech.edu/.

ECPI College of Technology

Charleston, South Carolina

Admissions Office Contact ECPI College of Technology, 7410 Northside Drive, Suite 100, Charleston, SC 29420. *Toll-free phone:* 866-708-6166. *Web site:* http://www.ecpi.edu/.

ECPI College of Technology

Columbia, South Carolina

Admissions Office Contact ECPI College of Technology, 250 Berryhill Road, #300, Columbia, SC 29210. *Toll-free phone:* 866-708-6168. *Web site:* http://www.ecpi.edu/.

ECPI College of Technology

Greenville, South Carolina

Admissions Office Contact ECPI College of Technology, 1001 Keys Drive, #100, Greenville, SC 29615. *Toll-free phone:* 866-708-6171. *Web site:* http://www.ecpi.edu/.

Florence-Darlington Technical College

Florence, South Carolina

Director of Admissions Shelley Fortin, Vice President for Enrollment Management and Student Services, Florence-Darlington Technical College, 2715 West Lucas Street, PO Box 100548, Florence, SC 29501-0548. *Phone:* 843-661-8111 Ext. 117. *Toll-free phone:* 800-228-5745. *E-mail:* shelley.fortin@fdtc.edu. *Web site:* http://www.fdtc.edu/.

Forrest College

Anderson, South Carolina

- **Proprietary** 2-year, founded 1946
- **Rural** 3-acre campus
- **Coed,** 94 undergraduate students, 81% full-time, 88% women, 12% men

Undergraduates 76 full-time, 18 part-time. Students come from 2 states and territories; 1% are from out of state; 10% transferred in.

Freshmen *Admission:* 41 applied, 34 admitted, 21 enrolled.

Faculty *Total:* 20, 10% full-time, 20% with terminal degrees. *Student/faculty ratio:* 5:1.

Majors Accounting; business administration and management; child-care and support services management; computer installation and repair technology; computer technology/computer systems technology; legal administrative assistant/secretary; legal assistant/paralegal; medical/clinical assistant; medical office management; office management.

Academics *Calendar:* quarters. *Degree:* certificates, diplomas, and associate. *Special study options:* advanced placement credit, cooperative education, distance learning, double majors, independent study, internships, part-time degree program, summer session for credit.

Library Forrest Junior College Library with 40,000 titles, 225 serial subscriptions, 2,200 audiovisual materials, an OPAC.

Student Life *Housing:* college housing not available. *Campus security:* 24-hour emergency response devices, late-night transport/escort service.

Standardized Tests *Required:* Gates-McGinnity (for admission).

Costs (2011–12) *Tuition:* $8820 full-time, $245 per credit hour part-time. *Required fees:* $375 full-time, $245 per credit hour part-time. *Payment plan:* deferred payment.

Financial Aid Of all full-time matriculated undergraduates who enrolled in 2011, 104 applied for aid, 102 were judged to have need.

Applying *Options:* electronic application, deferred entrance. *Application fee:* $50. *Required:* essay or personal statement, high school transcript, minimum 2.0 GPA, interview. *Recommended:* minimum 2.5 GPA. *Application deadlines:* rolling (freshmen), rolling (out-of-state freshmen), rolling (transfers). *Notification:* continuous (freshmen), continuous (out-of-state freshmen), continuous (transfers).

Freshman Application Contact Ms. Janie Turmon, Admissions and Placement Coordinator/Representative, Forrest College, 601 East River Street, Anderson, SC 29624. *Phone:* 864-225-7653 Ext. 210. *Fax:* 864-261-7471. *E-mail:* janieturmon@forrestcollege.com. *Web site:* http://www.forrestcollege.edu/.

Greenville Technical College

Greenville, South Carolina

Director of Admissions Carolyn Watkins, Dean of Admissions, Greenville Technical College, PO Box 5616, Greenville, SC 29606-5616. *Phone:* 864-250-8287. *Toll-free phone:* 800-992-1183 (in-state); 800-723-0673 (out-of-state). *E-mail:* carolyn.watkins@gvltec.edu. *Web site:* http://www.gvltec.edu/

Horry-Georgetown Technical College

Conway, South Carolina

Freshman Application Contact Mr. George Swindoll, Vice President for Enrollment, Development, and Registration, Horry-Georgetown Technical College, 2050 Highway 502 East, PO Box 261966, Conway, SC 29528-6066. *Phone:* 843-349-5277. *Fax:* 843-349-7501. *E-mail:* george.swindoll@hgtc.edu. *Web site:* http://www.hgtc.edu/.

ITT Technical Institute

Columbia, South Carolina

- **Proprietary** primarily 2-year, part of ITT Educational Services, Inc.
- **Coed**

Majors Communications technology; computer and information systems security; criminal justice/law enforcement administration; drafting and design technology; electrical, electronic and communications engineering technology; forensic science and technology; graphic communications; legal assistant/paralegal; network and system administration; project management.

Academics *Degrees:* associate and bachelor's.

Student Life *Housing:* college housing not available.

Freshman Application Contact Director of Recruitment, ITT Technical Institute, 1628 Browning Road, Suite 180, Columbia, SC 29210. *Phone:* 803-216-6000. *Toll-free phone:* 800-242-5158. *Web site:* http://www.itt-tech.edu/.

ITT Technical Institute

Greenville, South Carolina

- **Proprietary** primarily 2-year, founded 1992, part of ITT Educational Services, Inc.
- **Coed**

Majors CAD/CADD drafting/design technology; computer and information systems security; computer engineering technology; computer software and media applications related; computer software technology; construction management; criminal justice/law enforcement administration; design and visual communications; electrical, electronic and communications engineering technology; game and interactive media design; legal assistant/paralegal; project management; system, networking, and LAN/WAN management; web/multimedia management and webmaster.

Academics *Calendar:* quarters. *Degrees:* associate and bachelor's.

Student Life *Housing:* college housing not available.

Financial Aid Of all full-time matriculated undergraduates who enrolled in 2010, 3 Federal Work-Study jobs.

Freshman Application Contact Director of Recruitment, ITT Technical Institute, Independence Corporate Park, 6 Independence Pointe, Greenville, SC 29615. *Phone:* 864-288-0777. *Toll-free phone:* 800-932-4488. *Web site:* http://www.itt-tech.edu/.

ITT Technical Institute

Myrtle Beach, South Carolina

- **Proprietary** primarily 2-year, part of ITT Educational Services, Inc.
- **Coed**

Majors Communications technology; computer and information systems security; drafting and design technology; electrical, electronic and communications engineering technology; forensic science and technology; graphic communications; legal assistant/paralegal; network and system administration; project management.

Academics *Calendar:* quarters. *Degrees:* associate and bachelor's.

Freshman Application Contact Director of Recruitment, ITT Technical Institute, 9654 N. Kings Highway, Suite 101, Myrtle Beach, SC 29572. *Phone:* 843-497-7820. *Toll-free phone:* 877-316-7054. *Web site:* http://www.itt-tech.edu/.

ITT Technical Institute

North Charleston, South Carolina

- **Proprietary** primarily 2-year, part of ITT Educational Services, Inc.
- **Coed**

Majors CAD/CADD drafting/design technology; communications technology; computer and information systems security; drafting and design technology; electrical, electronic and communications engineering technology; graphic communications; network and system administration; project management.

Academics *Calendar:* quarters. *Degrees:* associate and bachelor's.

Freshman Application Contact Director of Recruitment, ITT Technical Institute, 2431 W. Aviation Avenue, North Charleston, SC 29406. *Phone:* 843-745-5700. *Toll-free phone:* 877-291-0900. *Web site:* http://www.itt-tech.edu/.

Midlands Technical College

Columbia, South Carolina

- **State and locally supported** 2-year, founded 1974, part of South Carolina State Board for Technical and Comprehensive Education
- **Suburban** 113-acre campus
- **Endowment** $5.1 million
- **Coed**

Undergraduates 5,697 full-time, 6,381 part-time. Students come from 30 states and territories; 3% are from out of state; 35% Black or African American, non-Hispanic/Latino; 2% Hispanic/Latino; 2% Asian, non-Hispanic/Latino; 0.5% American Indian or Alaska Native, non-Hispanic/Latino; 0.2% Two or more races, non-Hispanic/Latino; 4% Race/ethnicity unknown; 0.0% international; 10% transferred in.

Faculty *Student/faculty ratio:* 20:1.

Academics *Calendar:* semesters. *Degree:* certificates, diplomas, and associate. *Special study options:* academic remediation for entering students, adult/continuing education programs, advanced placement credit, cooperative education, distance learning, double majors, English as a second language, internships, part-time degree program, services for LD students, student-designed majors, summer session for credit.

Student Life *Campus security:* 24-hour emergency response devices and patrols, late-night transport/escort service.

Standardized Tests *Required for some:* ACT ASSET. *Recommended:* SAT or ACT (for admission).

Financial Aid Of all full-time matriculated undergraduates who enrolled in 2010, 138 Federal Work-Study jobs (averaging $2496).

Applying *Options:* electronic application, early admission, deferred entrance. *Application fee:* $35. *Required for some:* interview. *Recommended:* high school transcript.

Freshman Application Contact Ms. Sylvia Littlejohn, Director of Admissions, Midlands Technical College, PO Box 2408, Columbia, SC 29202. *Phone:* 803-738-8324. *Toll-free phone:* 800-922-8038. *Fax:* 803-790-7524. *E-mail:* admissions@midlandstech.edu. *Web site:* http://www.midlandstech.edu/.

Miller-Motte Technical College

Charleston, South Carolina

Freshman Application Contact Ms. Elaine Cue, Campus President, Miller-Motte Technical College, 8085 Rivers Avenue, Suite E, Charleston, SC 29406. *Phone:* 843-574-0101. *Toll-free phone:* 800-923-4162. *Fax:* 843-266-3424. *E-mail:* juliasc@miller-mott.net. *Web site:* http://www.miller-motte.edu/.

Northeastern Technical College

Cheraw, South Carolina

Freshman Application Contact Mrs. Mary K. Newton, Dean of Students, Northeastern Technical College, PO Drawer 1007, Cheraw, SC 29520-1007. *Phone:* 843-921-6935. *Toll-free phone:* 800-921-7399. *Fax:* 843-921-1476. *E-mail:* mpace@netc.edu. *Web site:* http://www.netc.edu/.

Orangeburg-Calhoun Technical College

Orangeburg, South Carolina

Freshman Application Contact Mr. Dana Rickards, Director of Recruitment, Orangeburg-Calhoun Technical College, 3250 St Matthews Road, NE, Orangeburg, SC 29118-8299. *Phone:* 803-535-1219. *Toll-free phone:* 800-813-6519. *Web site:* http://www.octech.edu/.

Piedmont Technical College

Greenwood, South Carolina

Director of Admissions Mr. Steve Coleman, Director of Admissions, Piedmont Technical College, 620 North Emerald Road, PO Box 1467, Greenwood, SC 29648-1467. *Phone:* 864-941-8603. *Toll-free phone:* 800-868-5528. *Web site:* http://www.ptc.edu/.

Spartanburg Community College

Spartanburg, South Carolina

- **State-supported** 2-year, founded 1961, part of South Carolina State Board for Technical and Comprehensive Education
- **Suburban** 104-acre campus with easy access to Charlotte
- **Coed**

Undergraduates 3,133 full-time, 2,738 part-time. Students come from 14 states and territories; 5 other countries; 2% are from out of state; 20% Black or African American, non-Hispanic/Latino; 2% Hispanic/Latino; 2% Asian, non-Hispanic/Latino; 0.2% American Indian or Alaska Native, non-Hispanic/Latino; 0.9% Two or more races, non-Hispanic/Latino; 29% Race/ethnicity unknown; 28% transferred in. *Retention:* 57% of full-time freshmen returned.

Faculty *Student/faculty ratio:* 16:1.

Academics *Calendar:* semesters condensed semesters plus summer sessions. *Degree:* certificates, diplomas, and associate. *Special study options:* academic remediation for entering students, adult/continuing education programs, advanced placement credit, cooperative education, distance learning, English as a second language, part-time degree program, services for LD students, summer session for credit.

Student Life *Campus security:* 24-hour emergency response devices and patrols.

Standardized Tests *Required for some:* SAT or ACT (for admission).

Costs (2011–12) *Tuition:* area resident $3536 full-time, $148 per credit hour part-time; state resident $4384 full-time, $183 per credit hour part-time; non-resident $7298 full-time, $305 per credit hour part-time. Full-time tuition and fees vary according to course load. *Required fees:* $40 full-time, $20 per term part-time.

Financial Aid Of all full-time matriculated undergraduates who enrolled in 2010, 53 Federal Work-Study jobs (averaging $2933).

Applying *Options:* electronic application, early admission. *Application fee:* $25. *Required:* high school transcript, interview, high school diploma, GED or equivalent.

Freshman Application Contact Kathy Jo Lancaster, Admissions Counselor, Spartanburg Community College, PO Box 4386, Spartanburg, SC 29305. *Phone:* 864-592-4815. *Toll-free phone:* 866-591-3700. *Fax:* 864-592-4564. *E-mail:* admissions@stcsc.edu. *Web site:* http://www.sccsc.edu/.

Spartanburg Methodist College

Spartanburg, South Carolina

Freshman Application Contact Daniel L. Philbeck, Vice President for Enrollment Management, Spartanburg Methodist College, 1000 Powell Mill Road, Spartanburg, SC 29301-5899. *Phone:* 864-587-4223. *Toll-free phone:* 800-772-7286. *Fax:* 864-587-4355. *E-mail:* admiss@smcsc.edu. *Web site:* http://www.smcsc.edu/.

Technical College of the Lowcountry

Beaufort, South Carolina

Freshman Application Contact Rhonda Cole, Admissions Services Manager, Technical College of the Lowcountry, 921 Ribaut Road, PO Box 1288, Beaufort, SC 29901-1288. *Phone:* 843-525-8229. *Fax:* 843-525-8285. *E-mail:* rcole@tcl.edu. *Web site:* http://www.tclonline.org/.

Tri-County Technical College

Pendleton, South Carolina

Director of Admissions Renae Frazier, Director, Recruitment and Admissions, Tri-County Technical College, PO Box 587, 7900 Highway 76, Pendleton, SC 29670-0587. *Phone:* 864-646-1550. *Fax:* 864-646-1890. *E-mail:* infocent@tctc.edu. *Web site:* http://www.tctc.edu/.

Trident Technical College

Charleston, South Carolina

- **State and locally supported** 2-year, founded 1964, part of South Carolina State Board for Technical and Comprehensive Education
- **Urban** campus
- **Coed,** 16,781 undergraduate students, 45% full-time, 62% women, 38% men

Undergraduates 7,553 full-time, 9,228 part-time. Students come from 71 other countries; 3% are from out of state; 31% Black or African American, non-Hispanic/Latino; 4% Hispanic/Latino; 1% Asian, non-Hispanic/Latino; 0.2% Native Hawaiian or other Pacific Islander, non-Hispanic/Latino; 0.8% American Indian or Alaska Native, non-Hispanic/Latino; 2% Two or more races, non-Hispanic/Latino; 2% Race/ethnicity unknown.

Freshmen *Admission:* 3,233 admitted, 3,133 enrolled.

Faculty *Total:* 820, 38% full-time. *Student/faculty ratio:* 22:1.

Majors Accounting; administrative assistant and secretarial science; airframe mechanics and aircraft maintenance technology; automobile/automotive mechanics technology; biological and physical sciences; business administration and management; child-care provision; civil engineering technology; clinical/medical laboratory technology; commercial and advertising art; computer engineering technology; computer graphics; computer/information technology services administration related; computer programming (specific applications); computer systems networking and telecommunications; criminal justice/law enforcement administration; culinary arts; dental hygiene; electrical, electronic and communications engineering technology; engineering technology; horticultural science; hotel/motel administration; human services; industrial technology; legal assistant/paralegal; legal studies; liberal arts and sciences/liberal studies; machine tool technology; marketing/marketing management; mechanical engineering/mechanical technology; medical administrative assistant and medical secretary; occupational therapy; physical therapy; registered nursing/registered nurse; respiratory care therapy; telecommunications technology; veterinary/animal health technology; web/multimedia management and webmaster; web page, digital/multimedia and information resources design.

Academics *Calendar:* semesters. *Degree:* certificates, diplomas, and associate. *Special study options:* academic remediation for entering students, accelerated degree program, advanced placement credit, cooperative education, distance learning, double majors, English as a second language, off-campus study, part-time degree program, services for LD students, summer session for credit.

Library Learning Resource Center plus 3 others with 139,773 titles, 785 serial subscriptions, 12,486 audiovisual materials, an OPAC, a Web page.

Student Life *Housing:* college housing not available. *Activities and Organizations:* drama/theater group, student-run newspaper, radio station, Phi Theta Kappa, Lex Artis Paralegal Society, Hospitality and Culinary Student Association, Partnership for Change in Communities and Families, Society of Student Leaders. *Campus security:* 24-hour emergency response devices and patrols, late-night transport/escort service. *Student services:* personal/psychological counseling.

Costs (2011–12) *Tuition:* area resident $3530 full-time, $146 per credit hour part-time; state resident $3916 full-time, $162 per credit hour part-time; non-resident $6682 full-time, $280 per credit hour part-time. Full-time tuition and fees vary according to course load. Part-time tuition and fees vary according to course load. *Required fees:* $50 full-time, $4 per credit hour part-time. *Payment plans:* installment, deferred payment. *Waivers:* senior citizens.

Applying *Options:* electronic application, early admission. *Application fee:* $30. *Required for some:* high school transcript. *Application deadlines:* 8/6 (freshmen), 8/6 (transfers). *Notification:* continuous (freshmen), continuous (transfers).

Freshman Application Contact Ms. Clara Martin, Admissions Director, Trident Technical College, Charleston, SC 29423-8067. *Phone:* 843-574-6326. *Fax:* 843-574-6109. *E-mail:* Clara.Martin@tridenttech.edu. *Web site:* http://www.tridenttech.edu/.

University of South Carolina Lancaster

Lancaster, South Carolina

Freshman Application Contact Susan Vinson, Admissions Counselor, University of South Carolina Lancaster, PO Box 889, Lancaster, SC 29721. *Phone:* 803-313-7000. *Fax:* 803-313-7116. *E-mail:* vinsons@mailbox.sc.edu. *Web site:* http://usclancaster.sc.edu/.

University of South Carolina Salkehatchie

Allendale, South Carolina

Freshman Application Contact Ms. Carmen Brown, Admissions Coordinator, University of South Carolina Salkehatchie, PO Box 617, Allendale, SC 29810. *Phone:* 803-584-3446. *Toll-free phone:* 800-922-5500. *Fax:* 803-584-3884. *E-mail:* cdbrown@mailbox.sc.edu. *Web site:* http://uscsalkehatchie.sc.edu/.

University of South Carolina Sumter

Sumter, South Carolina

Freshman Application Contact Mr. Keith Britton, Director of Admissions, University of South Carolina Sumter, 200 Miller Road, Sumter, SC 29150-2498. *Phone:* 803-938-3882. *Fax:* 803-938-3901. *E-mail:* kbritton@usc.sumter.edu. *Web site:* http://www.uscsumter.edu/.

University of South Carolina Union

Union, South Carolina

- **State-supported** 2-year, founded 1965, part of University of South Carolina System
- **Small-town** campus with easy access to Charlotte
- **Coed,** 500 undergraduate students, 50% full-time, 60% women, 40% men

Undergraduates 250 full-time, 250 part-time.

Freshmen *Admission:* 400 enrolled. *Average high school GPA:* 3.

Faculty *Total:* 38, 26% full-time. *Student/faculty ratio:* 14:1.

Majors Biological and physical sciences; liberal arts and sciences/liberal studies.

Academics *Calendar:* semesters. *Degree:* associate. *Special study options:* part-time degree program.

Library USC UNION CAMPUS LIBRARY plus 1 other.

Student Life *Housing:* college housing not available. *Activities and Organizations:* drama/theater group, student-run newspaper, choral group.

Athletics *Intramural sports:* baseball M(c).

Standardized Tests *Required:* SAT or ACT (for admission).

Costs (2011–12) *Tuition:* state resident $2850 full-time; nonresident $7152 full-time. *Required fees:* $246 full-time.

Financial Aid Of all full-time matriculated undergraduates who enrolled in 2010, 16 Federal Work-Study jobs (averaging $3400).

Applying *Application fee:* $40. *Required:* high school transcript. *Application deadline:* rolling (freshmen).

Freshman Application Contact Mr. Michael B. Greer, Director of Enrollment Services, University of South Carolina Union, PO Drawer 729, Union, SC 29379-0729. *Phone:* 864-429-8728. *E-mail:* tyoung@gwm.sc.edu. *Web site:* http://uscunion.sc.edu/.

Williamsburg Technical College

Kingstree, South Carolina

Freshman Application Contact Williamsburg Technical College, 601 Martin Luther King, Jr Avenue, Kingstree, SC 29556-4197. *Phone:* 843-355-4162. *Toll-free phone:* 800-768-2021. *Web site:* http://www.wiltech.edu/.

York Technical College

Rock Hill, South Carolina

Freshman Application Contact Mr. Kenny Aldridge, Admissions Department Manager, York Technical College, Rock Hill, SC 29730. *Phone:* 803-327-8008, *Toll-free phone:* 800-922-8324. *Fax:* 803-981-7237. *E-mail:* kaldridge@yorktech.com. *Web site:* http://www.yorktech.com/.

SOUTH DAKOTA

Kilian Community College

Sioux Falls, South Dakota

- **Independent** 2-year, founded 1977
- **Urban** 2-acre campus
- **Coed,** 335 undergraduate students, 12% full-time, 70% women, 30% men

Undergraduates 39 full-time, 296 part-time. Students come from 3 states and territories; 1% are from out of state; 13% Black or African American, non-Hispanic/Latino; 2% Hispanic/Latino; 1% Asian, non-Hispanic/Latino; 11% American Indian or Alaska Native, non-Hispanic/Latino; 12% Race/ethnicity unknown; 11% transferred in.

Freshmen *Admission:* 52 enrolled.

Faculty *Total:* 38, 13% full-time, 16% with terminal degrees. *Student/faculty ratio:* 9:1.

Majors Accounting; American Indian/Native American studies; business administration and management; counseling psychology; criminal justice/law enforcement administration; education; environmental studies; financial planning and services; history; information technology; liberal arts and sciences/liberal studies; medical office management; psychology; social work; sociology; substance abuse/addiction counseling.

Academics *Calendar:* trimesters. *Degree:* certificates and associate. *Special study options:* academic remediation for entering students, distance learning, double majors, English as a second language, independent study, off-campus study, part-time degree program, services for LD students, summer session for credit.

Library Sioux Falls Public Library with 78,000 titles, 395 serial subscriptions, an OPAC, a Web page.

Student Life *Housing:* college housing not available. *Activities and Organizations:* Phi Theta Kappa, Students in Free Enterprise (SIFE), Student Leadership. *Campus security:* late-night transport/escort service. *Student services:* personal/psychological counseling.

Costs (2011–12) *Tuition:* $9252 full-time, $257 per credit hour part-time. *Required fees:* $450 full-time, $150 per term part-time. *Payment plan:* installment. *Waivers:* senior citizens and employees or children of employees.

Financial Aid Of all full-time matriculated undergraduates who enrolled in 2010, 40 applied for aid, 40 were judged to have need. 15 Federal Work-Study jobs (averaging $3000). *Average percent of need met:* 36%. *Average financial aid package:* $9000. *Average need-based loan:* $4500. *Average need-based gift aid:* $4500.

Applying *Options:* electronic application, deferred entrance. *Application fee:* $25. *Required:* high school transcript. *Application deadlines:* rolling (freshmen), rolling (out-of-state freshmen), rolling (transfers).

Freshman Application Contact Ms. Mary Klockman, Director of Admissions, Kilian Community College, 300 East 6th Street, Sioux Falls, SD 57103. *Phone:* 605-221-3100. *Toll-free phone:* 800-888-1147. *Fax:* 605-336-2606. *E-mail:* info@killian.edu. *Web site:* http://www.kilian.edu/.

Lake Area Technical Institute

Watertown, South Dakota

- **State-supported** 2-year, founded 1964
- **Small-town** 40-acre campus
- **Coed,** 1,600 undergraduate students

Freshmen *Admission:* 800 applied.

Faculty *Student/faculty ratio:* 16:1.

Majors Agricultural business and management; agricultural production; aircraft powerplant technology; autobody/collision and repair technology; automobile/automotive mechanics technology; banking and financial support services; biology/biotechnology laboratory technician; carpentry; clinical/medical laboratory technology; computer programming; computer science; construction engineering technology; dental assisting; diesel mechanics technology; drafting and design technology; electrical, electronic and communications engineering technology; electrical/electronics equipment installation and repair; electromechanical technology; emergency medical technology (EMT paramedic); engineering technology; environmental science; human services; licensed practical/vocational nurse training; machine tool technology; manufacturing engineering technology; marketing/marketing management; medical/clinical assistant; occupational therapist assistant; physical therapy technology; robotics technology; sales, distribution, and marketing operations; small business administration; welding technology.

Academics *Calendar:* semesters. *Degree:* diplomas and associate. *Special study options:* academic remediation for entering students, internships, services for LD students.

Library Leonard H. Timmerman Library plus 1 other with 5,000 titles, 128 serial subscriptions.

Student Life *Housing:* college housing not available.

Athletics *Intramural sports:* basketball M/W, softball M/W, volleyball M/W.

Standardized Tests *Required:* ACT (for admission).

Applying *Options:* electronic application. *Application fee:* $20. *Required:* high school transcript. *Required for some:* essay or personal statement, 3 letters of recommendation, interview.

Freshman Application Contact Lake Area Technical Institute, 230 11th Street, NE, Watertown, SD 57201. *Phone:* 605-882-5284. *Toll-free phone:* 800-657-4344. *Web site:* http://www.lakeareatech.edu/.

Mitchell Technical Institute

Mitchell, South Dakota

- **State-supported** 2-year, founded 1968, part of South Dakota Board of Education
- **Rural** 90-acre campus
- **Endowment** $1.4 million
- **Coed,** 1,055 undergraduate students, 86% full-time, 33% women, 67% men

Undergraduates 903 full-time, 152 part-time. Students come from 14 states and territories; 7% are from out of state; 0.4% Black or African American, non-Hispanic/Latino; 1% Hispanic/Latino; 0.4% Asian, non-Hispanic/Latino; 5% American Indian or Alaska Native, non-Hispanic/Latino; 0.3% Two or more races, non-Hispanic/Latino; 1% Race/ethnicity unknown; 10% transferred in; 8% live on campus. *Retention:* 75% of full-time freshmen returned.

Freshmen *Admission:* 945 applied, 464 admitted, 358 enrolled. *Test scores:* ACT scores over 18: 75%; ACT scores over 24: 15%.

Faculty *Total:* 61, 93% full-time. *Student/faculty ratio:* 18:1.

Majors Accounting and business/management; agricultural mechanics and equipment technology; agricultural production; automation engineer technology; building construction technology; building/property maintenance; business automation/technology/data entry; clinical/medical laboratory technology; computer support specialist; construction trades related; culinary arts; electrician; energy management and systems technology; geographic information science and cartography; heating, air conditioning, ventilation and refrigeration maintenance technology; lineworker; medical/clinical assistant; medical office assistant; medical radiologic technology; network and system administration; radiologic technology/science; radio, television, and digital communication related; small engine mechanics and repair technology; speech-language pathology assistant; telecommunications technology; welding engineering technology.

Academics *Calendar:* semesters. *Degree:* certificates, diplomas, and associate. *Special study options:* academic remediation for entering students, advanced placement credit, cooperative education, distance learning, internships, part-time degree program, services for LD students, summer session for credit.

Library Instructional Services Center with 3,000 titles, 100 serial subscriptions, 300 audiovisual materials, an OPAC.

Student Life *Housing Options:* coed. Campus housing is provided by a third party. *Activities and Organizations:* Student Representative Board, Skills USA, Post-Secondary Agricultural Students, Rodeo Club, Student Veterans Organization. *Student services:* personal/psychological counseling.

Athletics *Intercollegiate sports:* equestrian sports M/W. *Intramural sports:* basketball M/W, bowling M/W, riflery M/W, softball M/W, volleyball M/W.

Standardized Tests *Required for some:* COMPASS. *Recommended:* ACT (for admission).

Costs (2011–12) *Tuition:* state resident $3420 full-time, $95 per credit hour part-time; nonresident $3420 full-time, $95 per credit hour part-time. Full-time tuition and fees vary according to course load and program. Part-time tuition and fees vary according to course load and program. *Required fees:* $2964 full-time, $69 per credit hour part-time. *Payment plan:* installment. *Waivers:* employees or children of employees.

Financial Aid Of all full-time matriculated undergraduates who enrolled in 2010, 52 Federal Work-Study jobs (averaging $1375).

Applying *Options:* electronic application. *Application fee:* $60. *Required:* high school transcript. *Required for some:* essay or personal statement, interview. *Recommended:* minimum 2.0 GPA. *Application deadlines:* rolling (freshmen), rolling (out-of-state freshmen), rolling (transfers). *Notification:* continuous (freshmen), continuous (out-of-state freshmen), continuous (transfers).

Freshman Application Contact Mr. Clayton Deuter, Director of Admissions, Mitchell Technical Institute, 1800 East Spruce Street, Mitchell, SD 57301. *Phone:* 605-995-3025. *Toll-free phone:* 800-684-1969. *Fax:* 605-995-3067. *E-mail:* clayton.deuter@mitchelltech.edu. *Web site:* http://www.mitchelltech.edu/.

National American University

Ellsworth AFB, South Dakota

Freshman Application Contact Admissions Office, National American University, 1000 Ellsworth Street, Suite 2400B, Ellsworth AFB, SD 57706. *Web site:* http://www.national.edu/.

Sisseton-Wahpeton College

Sisseton, South Dakota

Freshman Application Contact Sisseton-Wahpeton College, Old Agency Box 689, Sisseton, SD 57262. *Phone:* 605-698-3966 Ext. 1180. *Web site:* http://www.swc.tc/.

Southeast Technical Institute

Sioux Falls, South Dakota

- **State-supported** 2-year, founded 1968
- **Urban** 168-acre campus
- **Endowment** $768,716
- **Coed,** 2,507 undergraduate students, 76% full-time, 51% women, 49% men

Undergraduates 1,907 full-time, 600 part-time. Students come from 7 states and territories; 9% are from out of state; 2% Black or African American, non-Hispanic/Latino; 2% Hispanic/Latino; 0.8% Asian, non-Hispanic/Latino; 0.1% Native Hawaiian or other Pacific Islander, non-Hispanic/Latino; 2% American Indian or Alaska Native, non-Hispanic/Latino; 1% Two or more races, non-Hispanic/Latino; 3% Race/ethnicity unknown; 14% transferred in; 8% live on campus. *Retention:* 69% of full-time freshmen returned.

Freshmen *Admission:* 3,119 applied, 1,324 admitted, 596 enrolled. *Average high school GPA:* 2.73.

Faculty *Total:* 180, 46% full-time, 3% with terminal degrees. *Student/faculty ratio:* 18:1.

Majors Accounting; animation, interactive technology, video graphics and special effects; applied horticulture/horticulture operations; architectural engineering technology; autobody/collision and repair technology; automobile/automotive mechanics technology; banking and financial support services; biomedical technology; building/construction finishing, management, and inspection related; business administration and management; cardiovascular technology; child-care and support services management; child-care provision; civil engineering technology; clinical/medical laboratory science and allied professions related; clinical/medical laboratory technology; commercial and advertising art; computer and information sciences and support services related; computer and information systems security; computer/information technology services administration related; computer installation and repair technology; computer programming; computer programming related; computer software engineering; computer systems networking and telecommunications; computer technology/computer systems technology; construction engineering technology; criminal justice/police science; desktop publishing and digital imaging design; diagnostic medical sonography and ultrasound technology; diesel mechanics technology; electrical, electronic and communications engineering technology; electrical/electronics equipment installation and repair; electromechanical technology; electroneurodiagnostic/electroencephalographic technology; finance; health unit coordinator/ward clerk; heating, air conditioning, ventilation and refrigeration maintenance technology; horticultural science; industrial technology; licensed practical/vocational nurse training; marketing/marketing management; mechanical engineering/mechanical technology; merchandising, sales, and marketing operations related (general); nuclear medical technology; office occupations and clerical services; registered nursing/registered nurse; surgical technology; surveying technology; turf and turfgrass management; welding technology.

Academics *Calendar:* semesters. *Degree:* certificates, diplomas, and associate. *Special study options:* academic remediation for entering students, advanced placement credit, distance learning, double majors, independent study, internships, part-time degree program, services for LD students, summer session for credit.

Library Southeast Library with 10,643 titles, 158 serial subscriptions, an OPAC, a Web page.

Student Life *Housing Options:* coed. Campus housing is provided by a third party. *Activities and Organizations:* VICA (Vocational Industrial Clubs of America), American Landscape Contractors Association. *Campus security:* 24-hour patrols, late-night transport/escort service, controlled dormitory access. *Student services:* personal/psychological counseling.

Athletics *Intramural sports:* basketball M/W, bowling M/W, volleyball M/W.

Standardized Tests *Recommended:* ACT (for admission).

Costs (2011–12) *Tuition:* state resident $2850 full-time, $95 per credit hour part-time; nonresident $2850 full-time, $95 per credit hour part-time. Full-time tuition and fees vary according to program. Part-time tuition and fees vary according to program. *Required fees:* $1980 full-time, $66 per credit hour part-time. *Room and board:* room only: $4600. *Payment plan:* installment.

Financial Aid Of all full-time matriculated undergraduates who enrolled in 2010, 35 Federal Work-Study jobs (averaging $2550).

Applying *Options:* electronic application. *Required:* high school transcript, minimum 2.2 GPA. *Required for some:* interview, background check and drug testing. *Application deadlines:* rolling (freshmen), rolling (out-of-state freshmen), rolling (transfers). *Notification:* continuous (freshmen), continuous (out-of-state freshmen), continuous (transfers).

Freshman Application Contact Mr. Scott Dorman, Recruiter, Southeast Technical Institute, Sioux Falls, SD 57107. *Phone:* 605-367-4458. *Toll-free phone:* 800-247-0789. *Fax:* 605-367-8305. *E-mail:* scott.dorman@southeasttech.edu. *Web site:* http://www.southeasttech.edu/.

Western Dakota Technical Institute
Rapid City, South Dakota

- **State-supported** 2-year, founded 1968
- **Small-town** 5-acre campus
- **Coed,** 1,045 undergraduate students, 82% full-time, 45% women, 55% men

Undergraduates 862 full-time, 183 part-time. Students come from 12 states and territories; 3% are from out of state; 2% Black or African American, non-Hispanic/Latino; 2% Hispanic/Latino; 0.5% Asian, non-Hispanic/Latino; 0.2% Native Hawaiian or other Pacific Islander, non-Hispanic/Latino; 13% American Indian or Alaska Native, non-Hispanic/Latino; 0.9% Race/ethnicity unknown; 0.6% transferred in. *Retention:* 48% of full-time freshmen returned.

Freshmen *Admission:* 965 applied, 854 admitted, 305 enrolled. *Average high school GPA:* 3.25.

Faculty *Total:* 123, 37% full-time. *Student/faculty ratio:* 13:1.

Majors Accounting; architectural drafting and CAD/CADD; automobile/automotive mechanics technology; computer systems networking and telecommunications; criminal justice/police science; electrical/electronics equipment installation and repair; electromechanical technology; fire science/firefighting; legal assistant/paralegal; marketing/marketing management; medical transcription.

Academics *Calendar:* semesters. *Degree:* certificates, diplomas, and associate. *Special study options:* academic remediation for entering students, advanced placement credit, distance learning, independent study, internships, part-time degree program, services for LD students, summer session for credit.

Library Western Dakota Technical Institute Library with 7,903 titles, 185 serial subscriptions, 269 audiovisual materials, an OPAC, a Web page.

Student Life *Housing:* college housing not available. *Campus security:* 24-hour video surveillance.

Standardized Tests *Recommended:* SAT or ACT (for admission).

Costs (2012–13) *One-time required fee:* $200. *Tuition:* state resident $3528 full-time, $98 per credit hour part-time; nonresident $3528 full-time, $98 per credit hour part-time. Full-time tuition and fees vary according to course load and program. Part-time tuition and fees vary according to course load. *Required fees:* $2880 full-time, $80 per credit hour part-time. *Payment plans:* installment, deferred payment. *Waivers:* employees or children of employees.

Financial Aid Of all full-time matriculated undergraduates who enrolled in 2010, 85 Federal Work-Study jobs (averaging $1400).

Applying *Options:* electronic application. *Application fee:* $20. *Required:* high school transcript, Placement test. *Required for some:* essay or personal

statement, 3 letters of recommendation, interview. *Recommended:* minimum 2.0 GPA. *Application deadlines:* 8/1 (freshmen), 8/1 (transfers). *Notification:* continuous until 8/15 (freshmen), continuous until 8/15 (transfers).

Freshman Application Contact Jill Elder, Admissions Coordinator, Western Dakota Technical Institute, 800 Mickelson Drive, Rapid City, SD 57703. *Phone:* 605-718-2411. *Toll-free phone:* 800-544-8765. *Fax:* 605-394-2204. *E-mail:* jill.elder@wdt.edu. *Web site:* http://www.wdt.edu/.

TENNESSEE

Anthem Career College
Memphis, Tennessee

Freshman Application Contact Admissions Office, Anthem Career College, 5865 Shelby Oaks Circle, Suite 100, Memphis, TN 38134. *Toll-free phone:* 866-381-5623. *Web site:* http://www.anthem.edu/memphis-tennessee/.

Anthem Career College–Nashville
Nashville, Tennessee

Freshman Application Contact Admissions Office, Anthem Career College–Nashville, 560 Royal Parkway, Nashville, TN 37214. *Phone:* 615-902-9705. *Toll-free phone:* 866-381-5791. *Web site:* http://anthem.edu/nashville-tennessee/.

Chattanooga College–Medical, Dental and Technical Careers
Chattanooga, Tennessee

Director of Admissions Toney McFadden, Admission Director, Chattanooga College–Medical, Dental and Technical Careers, 3805 Brainerd Road, Chattanooga, TN 37411-3798. *Phone:* 423-624-0077. *Toll-free phone:* 877-313-2373. *Fax:* 423-624-1575. *Web site:* http://www.chattanoogacollege.edu/

Chattanooga State Community College
Chattanooga, Tennessee

- **State-supported** 2-year, founded 1965, part of Tennessee Board of Regents
- **Urban** 100-acre campus
- **Endowment** $6.8 million
- **Coed,** 10,438 undergraduate students, 46% full-time, 62% women, 38% men

Undergraduates 4,775 full-time, 5,663 part-time. Students come from 23 states and territories; 9 other countries; 11% are from out of state; 18% Black or African American, non-Hispanic/Latino; 2% Hispanic/Latino; 1% Asian, non-Hispanic/Latino; 0.2% American Indian or Alaska Native, non-Hispanic/Latino; 0.4% Race/ethnicity unknown; 210% transferred in.

Freshmen *Admission:* 1,758 applied, 1,758 admitted, 1,586 enrolled. *Average high school GPA:* 2.73.

Faculty *Total:* 699, 32% full-time. *Student/faculty ratio:* 19:1.

Majors Accounting technology and bookkeeping; business administration and management; child development; commercial and advertising art; community organization and advocacy; dental assisting; dental hygiene; education; electrical, electronic and communications engineering technology; engineering; engineering technology; fire science/firefighting; foods, nutrition, and wellness; general studies; health information/medical records technology; industrial technology; legal assistant/paralegal; liberal arts and sciences/liberal studies; management information systems; medical radiologic technology; operations management; physical therapy technology; registered nursing/registered nurse; respiratory care therapy; veterinary/animal health technology; web page, digital/multimedia and information resources design.

Academics *Calendar:* semesters. *Degree:* certificates, diplomas, and associate. *Special study options:* academic remediation for entering students, accelerated degree program, adult/continuing education programs, advanced placement credit, cooperative education, distance learning, double majors, external degree program, honors programs, independent study, internships, part-time degree program, services for LD students, summer session for credit.

Library Augusta R. Kolwyck Library with 161,086 titles, 256 serial subscriptions, 3,680 audiovisual materials, an OPAC, a Web page.

Student Life *Housing:* college housing not available. *Activities and Organizations:* drama/theater group, student-run newspaper, choral group, Black Stu-

dent Association, Adult Connections, Human Services Specialists, Student Government Association, Student Nurses Association. *Campus security:* 24-hour emergency response devices and patrols, late-night transport/escort service. *Student services:* personal/psychological counseling, women's center.
Athletics Member NJCAA. *Intercollegiate sports:* baseball M(s), basketball M(s)/W(s), softball W(s). *Intramural sports:* softball W.
Costs (2011–12) *Tuition:* state resident $3411 full-time, $129 per credit hour part-time; nonresident $13,035 full-time, $401 per credit hour part-time. *Required fees:* $315 full-time. *Payment plan:* deferred payment. *Waivers:* senior citizens and employees or children of employees.
Applying *Options:* electronic application, early admission, deferred entrance. *Application fee:* $15. *Required for some:* high school transcript, interview. *Recommended:* high school transcript. *Application deadlines:* rolling (freshmen), rolling (out-of-state freshmen), rolling (transfers). *Notification:* continuous (freshmen), continuous (out-of-state freshmen), continuous (transfers).
Freshman Application Contact Brad McCormick, Director Admissions and Records, Chattanooga State Community College, 4501 Amnicola Highway, Chattanooga, TN 37406. *Phone:* 423-697-4401 Ext. 3264. *Toll-free phone:* 866-547-3733. *Fax:* 423-697-4709. *E-mail:* brad.mccormick@chattanoogastate.edu. *Web site:* http://www.chattanoogastate.edu/.

Cleveland State Community College
Cleveland, Tennessee

- **State-supported** 2-year, founded 1967, part of Tennessee Board of Regents
- **Suburban** 83-acre campus
- **Endowment** $6.3 million
- **Coed,** 3,814 undergraduate students, 56% full-time, 62% women, 38% men

Undergraduates 2,117 full-time, 1,697 part-time. Students come from 12 states and territories; 4 other countries; 1% are from out of state; 6% Black or African American, non-Hispanic/Latino; 0.7% Hispanic/Latino; 1% Asian, non-Hispanic/Latino; 0.3% American Indian or Alaska Native, non-Hispanic/Latino; 0.3% Two or more races, non-Hispanic/Latino; 5% Race/ethnicity unknown; 0.1% international; 5% transferred in.
Freshmen *Admission:* 1,131 applied, 817 admitted, 817 enrolled. *Average high school GPA:* 2.94. *Test scores:* ACT scores over 18: 62%; ACT scores over 24: 7%.
Faculty *Total:* 188, 38% full-time, 13% with terminal degrees. *Student/faculty ratio:* 24:1.
Majors Administrative assistant and secretarial science; business administration and management; child development; community organization and advocacy; criminal justice/police science; general studies; industrial technology; kindergarten/preschool education; liberal arts and sciences and humanities related; liberal arts and sciences/liberal studies; public administration and social service professions related; registered nursing/registered nurse; science technologies related.
Academics *Calendar:* semesters. *Degree:* certificates and associate. *Special study options:* academic remediation for entering students, adult/continuing education programs, advanced placement credit, cooperative education, distance learning, double majors, external degree program, honors programs, independent study, internships, off-campus study, part-time degree program, services for LD students, summer session for credit.
Library Cleveland State Community College Library with 153,201 titles, 835 serial subscriptions, 9,639 audiovisual materials, an OPAC, a Web page.
Student Life *Housing:* college housing not available. *Activities and Organizations:* student-run newspaper, choral group, Human Services/Social Work, Computer Aided Design, Phi Theta Kappa, Student Nursing Association, Early Childhood Education. *Campus security:* 24-hour emergency response devices and patrols. *Student services:* personal/psychological counseling.
Athletics Member NJCAA. *Intercollegiate sports:* baseball M(s), basketball M(s)/W(s), softball W(s). *Intramural sports:* archery M/W, basketball M/W, bowling M/W, cheerleading M(c)/W(c), softball W, table tennis M/W, volleyball M/W.
Costs (2011–12) *Tuition:* state resident $3252 full-time, $129 per credit hour part-time; nonresident $13,356 full-time, $530 per credit hour part-time. Full-time tuition and fees vary according to course load. *Required fees:* $269 full-time, $14 per credit hour part-time. *Payment plan:* deferred payment. *Waivers:* senior citizens and employees or children of employees.
Financial Aid Of all full-time matriculated undergraduates who enrolled in 2010, 52 Federal Work-Study jobs (averaging $1025).
Applying *Options:* electronic application, early admission, deferred entrance. *Application fee:* $10. *Required:* high school transcript. *Application deadlines:* rolling (freshmen), rolling (transfers). *Notification:* continuous (freshmen), continuous (transfers).
Freshman Application Contact Ms. Midge Burnette, Director of Admissions and Records, Cleveland State Community College, Cleveland, TN 37320-3570. *Phone:* 423-472-7141 Ext. 212. *Toll-free phone:* 800-604-2722. *Fax:*

423-478-6255. *E-mail:* mburnette@clevelandstatecc.edu. *Web site:* http://www.clevelandstatecc.edu/.

Columbia State Community College
Columbia, Tennessee

Freshman Application Contact Mr. Joey Scruggs, Coordinator of Recruitment, Columbia State Community College, PO Box 1315, Columbia, TN 38402-1315. *Phone:* 931-540-2540. *E-mail:* scruggs@coscc.cc.tn.us. *Web site:* http://www.columbiastate.edu/.

Concorde Career College
Memphis, Tennessee

Freshman Application Contact Dee Vickers, Director, Concorde Career College, 5100 Poplar Avenue, Suite 132, Memphis, TN 38137. *Phone:* 901-761-9494. *Fax:* 901-761-3293. *E-mail:* dvickers@concorde.edu. *Web site:* http://www.concorde.edu/.

Daymar Institute
Nashville, Tennessee

Director of Admissions Admissions Office, Daymar Institute, 340 Plus Park Boulevard, Nashville, TN 37217. *Phone:* 615-361-7555. *Fax:* 615-367-2736. *Web site:* http://www.daymarinstitute.edu/.

Dyersburg State Community College
Dyersburg, Tennessee

- **State-supported** 2-year, founded 1969, part of Tennessee Board of Regents
- **Small-town** 100-acre campus with easy access to Memphis
- **Endowment** $5.2 million
- **Coed,** 3,751 undergraduate students, 45% full-time, 69% women, 31% men

Undergraduates 1,706 full-time, 2,045 part-time. Students come from 4 states and territories; 4 other countries; 22% Black or African American, non-Hispanic/Latino; 2% Hispanic/Latino; 0.4% Asian, non-Hispanic/Latino; 0.1% Native Hawaiian or other Pacific Islander, non-Hispanic/Latino; 0.4% American Indian or Alaska Native, non-Hispanic/Latino; 1% Two or more races, non-Hispanic/Latino; 1% Race/ethnicity unknown; 3% transferred in. *Retention:* 59% of full-time freshmen returned.
Freshmen *Admission:* 1,627 applied, 1,627 admitted, 864 enrolled. *Average high school GPA:* 2.66.
Faculty *Total:* 191, 28% full-time, 14% with terminal degrees. *Student/faculty ratio:* 19:1.
Majors Agriculture; business administration and management; child development; computer and information systems security; criminal justice/police science; education; emergency medical technology (EMT paramedic); health information/medical records technology; health services/allied health/health sciences; information science/studies; liberal arts and sciences/liberal studies; registered nursing/registered nurse; web page, digital/multimedia and information resources design.
Academics *Calendar:* semesters. *Degree:* certificates and associate. *Special study options:* academic remediation for entering students, adult/continuing education programs, advanced placement credit, distance learning, double majors, honors programs, independent study, part-time degree program, services for LD students, summer session for credit.
Library Learning Resource Center with 75,619 titles, 87 serial subscriptions, 1,137 audiovisual materials, an OPAC, a Web page.
Student Life *Housing:* college housing not available. *Activities and Organizations:* drama/theater group, choral group, student government, Phi Theta Kappa, Minority Association for Successful Students, Video Club, Psychology Club. *Campus security:* 24-hour patrols. *Student services:* personal/psychological counseling.
Athletics Member NJCAA. *Intercollegiate sports:* baseball M(s), basketball M(s)/W(s), cheerleading W(s), softball W(s).
Standardized Tests *Required:* SAT or ACT (for admission).
Costs (2012–13) *Tuition:* state resident $3377 full-time, $140 per credit hour part-time; nonresident $13,002 full-time, $542 per credit hour part-time. Part-time tuition and fees vary according to course load. *Required fees:* $281 full-time, $141 per term part-time. *Payment plan:* deferred payment. *Waivers:* senior citizens and employees or children of employees.
Financial Aid Of all full-time matriculated undergraduates who enrolled in 2010, 42 Federal Work-Study jobs (averaging $1728). 97 state and other part-time jobs (averaging $1323).
Applying *Options:* electronic application, early admission. *Application fee:* $10. *Required:* high school transcript. *Application deadlines:* rolling (fresh-

men), rolling (transfers). *Notification:* continuous (freshmen), continuous (transfers).

Freshman Application Contact Ms. Jordan Willis, Admissions Counselor, Dyersburg State Community College, Dyersburg, TN 38024. *Phone:* 731-286-3324. *Fax:* 731-286-3325. *E-mail:* willis@dscc.edu. *Web site:* http://www.dscc.edu/.

Fortis Institute
Cookeville, Tennessee

Director of Admissions Ms. Sharon Mellott, Director of Admissions, Fortis Institute, 1025 Highway 111, Cookeville, TN 38501. *Phone:* 931-526-3660. *Toll-free phone:* 855-4-FORTIS. *Web site:* http://www.fortis.edu/.

Fountainhead College of Technology
Knoxville, Tennessee

- **Proprietary** primarily 2-year, founded 1947
- **Suburban** 6-acre campus
- **Coed,** 219 undergraduate students

Undergraduates *Retention:* 82% of full-time freshmen returned.
Faculty *Student/faculty ratio:* 9:1.
Majors Communications technology; computer and information systems security; computer engineering technology; computer programming; electrical, electronic and communications engineering technology; health information/medical records technology; information technology; medical insurance coding.
Academics *Calendar:* semesters. *Degrees:* associate and bachelor's. *Special study options:* accelerated degree program, distance learning, summer session for credit.
Library an OPAC.
Student Life *Housing:* college housing not available. *Campus security:* 24-hour emergency response devices.
Standardized Tests *Required for some:* SAT or ACT (for admission).
Costs (2012–13) *Tuition:* $485 per credit hour part-time. No tuition increase for student's term of enrollment.
Applying *Required:* high school transcript, interview. *Application deadlines:* rolling (freshmen), rolling (transfers). *Notification:* continuous (freshmen), continuous (transfers).
Freshman Application Contact Mr. Todd Hill, Director of Admissions, Fountainhead College of Technology, 3203 Tazewell Pike, Knoxville, TN 37918-2530. *Phone:* 865-688-9422. *Toll-free phone:* 888-218-7335. *Fax:* 865-688-2419. *E-mail:* todd.hill@fountainheadcollege.edu. *Web site:* http://www.fountainheadcollege.edu/.

ITT Technical Institute
Chattanooga, Tennessee

- **Proprietary** primarily 2-year, part of ITT Educational Services, Inc.
- **Coed**

Majors Business administration and management; communications technology; computer and information systems security; drafting and design technology; electrical, electronic and communications engineering technology; forensic science and technology; graphic communications; legal assistant/paralegal; network and system administration; project management.
Academics *Degrees:* associate and bachelor's.
Student Life *Housing:* college housing not available.
Freshman Application Contact Director of Recruitment, ITT Technical Institute, 5600 Brainerd Road, Suite G-1, Chattanooga, TN 37411. *Phone:* 423-510-6800. *Toll-free phone:* 877-474-8312. *Web site:* http://www.itt-tech.edu/.

ITT Technical Institute
Cordova, Tennessee

- **Proprietary** primarily 2-year, founded 1994, part of ITT Educational Services, Inc.
- **Suburban** campus
- **Coed**

Majors Business administration and management; communications technology; computer and information systems security; computer software and media applications related; computer software technology; computer systems networking and telecommunications; construction management; criminal justice/law enforcement administration; drafting and design technology; electrical, electronic and communications engineering technology; forensic science and technology; graphic communications; legal assistant/paralegal; network and system administration; project management.
Academics *Calendar:* quarters. *Degrees:* associate and bachelor's.
Student Life *Housing:* college housing not available.
Freshman Application Contact Director of Recruitment, ITT Technical Institute, 7260 Goodlett Farms Parkway, Cordova, TN 38016. *Phone:* 901-381-0200. *Toll-free phone:* 866-444-5141. *Web site:* http://www.itt-tech.edu/.

ITT Technical Institute
Johnson City, Tennessee

- **Proprietary** primarily 2-year
- **Coed**

Majors Business administration and management; communications technology; computer and information systems security; drafting and design technology; electrical, electronic and communications engineering technology; forensic science and technology; graphic communications; legal assistant/paralegal; network and system administration; project management.
Academics *Degrees:* associate and bachelor's.
Freshman Application Contact Director of Recruitment, ITT Technical Institute, 4721 Lake Park Drive, Suite 100, Johnson City, TN 37615. *Phone:* 423-952-4400. *Toll-free phone:* 877-301-9691. *Web site:* http://www.itt-tech.edu/.

ITT Technical Institute
Knoxville, Tennessee

- **Proprietary** primarily 2-year, founded 1988, part of ITT Educational Services, Inc.
- **Suburban** campus
- **Coed**

Majors Business administration and management; communications technology; computer and information systems security; computer software engineering; computer software technology; computer systems networking and telecommunications; construction management; criminal justice/law enforcement administration; drafting and design technology; electrical, electronic and communications engineering technology; forensic science and technology; game and interactive media design; graphic communications; legal assistant/paralegal; network and system administration; project management.
Academics *Calendar:* quarters. *Degrees:* associate and bachelor's.
Student Life *Housing:* college housing not available.
Freshman Application Contact Director of Recruitment, ITT Technical Institute, 10208 Technology Drive, Knoxville, TN 37932. *Phone:* 865-671-2800. *Toll-free phone:* 800-671-2801. *Web site:* http://www.itt-tech.edu/.

ITT Technical Institute
Nashville, Tennessee

- **Proprietary** primarily 2-year, founded 1984, part of ITT Educational Services, Inc.
- **Urban** campus
- **Coed**

Majors Business administration and management; communications technology; computer and information systems security; computer software and media applications related; computer software engineering; computer software technology; computer systems networking and telecommunications; construction management; criminal justice/law enforcement administration; drafting and design technology; electrical, electronic and communications engineering technology; forensic science and technology; game and interactive media design; graphic communications; legal assistant/paralegal; network and system administration; project management; registered nursing/registered nurse.
Academics *Calendar:* quarters. *Degrees:* associate and bachelor's.
Student Life *Housing:* college housing not available.
Freshman Application Contact Director of Recruitment, ITT Technical Institute, 2845 Elm Hill Pike, Nashville, TN 37214. *Phone:* 615-889-8700. *Toll-free phone:* 800-331-8386. *Web site:* http://www.itt-tech.edu/.

Jackson State Community College
Jackson, Tennessee

Freshman Application Contact Ms. Andrea Winchester, Director of Admissions, Jackson State Community College, 2046 North Parkway, Jackson, TN 38301-3797. *Phone:* 731-425-8844 Ext. 484. *Toll-free phone:* 800-355-5722. *Fax:* 731-425-9559. *E-mail:* awinchester@jscc.edu. *Web site:* http://www.jscc.edu/.

John A. Gupton College

Nashville, Tennessee

- **Independent** 2-year, founded 1946
- **Urban** 1-acre campus with easy access to Nashville
- **Endowment** $60,000
- **Coed**

Undergraduates 103 full-time, 24 part-time. Students come from 11 states and territories; 15% are from out of state; 24% Black or African American, non-Hispanic/Latino; 0.8% Hispanic/Latino; 0.8% Native Hawaiian or other Pacific Islander, non-Hispanic/Latino; 47% transferred in; 11% live on campus.

Faculty *Student/faculty ratio:* 8:1.

Academics *Calendar:* semesters. *Degree:* diplomas and associate. *Special study options:* part-time degree program.

Student Life *Campus security:* controlled dormitory access, day patrols.

Standardized Tests *Required:* ACT (for admission).

Costs (2011–12) *Tuition:* $9056 full-time, $283 per semester hour part-time. Full-time tuition and fees vary according to course load. Part-time tuition and fees vary according to course load. *Required fees:* $70 full-time, $283 per semester hour part-time. *Room only:* $3600.

Financial Aid *Financial aid deadline:* 6/1.

Applying *Options:* deferred entrance. *Application fee:* $20. *Required:* essay or personal statement, high school transcript, 2 letters of recommendation.

Freshman Application Contact John A. Gupton College, 1616 Church Street, Nashville, TN 37203-2920. *Phone:* 615-327-3927. *Web site:* http://www.guptoncollege.edu/.

Kaplan Career Institute, Nashville Campus

Nashville, Tennessee

- **Proprietary** 2-year, founded 1981
- **Coed**

Majors Criminal justice/law enforcement administration; legal assistant/paralegal.

Academics *Degree:* certificates, diplomas, and associate.

Freshman Application Contact Kaplan Career Institute, Nashville Campus, 750 Envious Lane, Nashville, TN 37217. *Phone:* 615-269-9900. *Toll-free phone:* 800-935-1857. *Web site:* http://nashville.kaplancareerinstitute.com/.

Miller-Motte Technical College

Clarksville, Tennessee

Director of Admissions Ms. Lisa Teague, Director of Admissions, Miller-Motte Technical College, 1820 Business Park Drive, Clarksville, TN 37040. *Phone:* 800-558-0071. *E-mail:* lisateague@hotmail.com. *Web site:* http://www.miller-motte.edu/.

Motlow State Community College

Tullahoma, Tennessee

- **State-supported** 2-year, founded 1969, part of Tennessee Board of Regents
- **Rural** 187-acre campus with easy access to Nashville
- **Endowment** $4.6 million
- **Coed,** 4,910 undergraduate students, 43% full-time, 62% women, 38% men

Undergraduates 2,088 full-time, 2,822 part-time. Students come from 10 states and territories; 25 other countries; 1% are from out of state; 10% Black or African American, non-Hispanic/Latino; 4% Hispanic/Latino; 2% Asian, non-Hispanic/Latino; 0.2% Native Hawaiian or other Pacific Islander, non-Hispanic/Latino; 0.9% American Indian or Alaska Native, non-Hispanic/Latino; 2% Race/ethnicity unknown; 7% transferred in.

Freshmen *Admission:* 5,383 applied, 1,239 admitted, 1,239 enrolled.

Faculty *Total:* 244, 33% full-time, 14% with terminal degrees.

Majors Business administration and management; education; general studies; liberal arts and sciences/liberal studies; registered nursing/registered nurse; special education–early childhood; web page, digital/multimedia and information resources design.

Academics *Calendar:* semesters. *Degree:* certificates and associate. *Special study options:* academic remediation for entering students, accelerated degree program, adult/continuing education programs, advanced placement credit, cooperative education, distance learning, double majors, honors programs, independent study, part-time degree program, services for LD students, study abroad, summer session for credit.

Library Clayton-Glass Library with 141,263 titles, 9,411 serial subscriptions, 16,729 audiovisual materials, an OPAC, a Web page.

Student Life *Housing:* college housing not available. *Activities and Organizations:* drama/theater group, choral group, PTK Club, Communication Club, Student Government Association, Art Club, Baptist Student Union. *Campus security:* 24-hour patrols, late-night transport/escort service. *Student services:* personal/psychological counseling.

Athletics Member NJCAA. *Intercollegiate sports:* baseball M(s), basketball M(s)/W(s), softball W(s). *Intramural sports:* badminton M/W, basketball M/W, bowling M/W, golf M/W, tennis M/W, volleyball M/W.

Costs (2012–13) *Tuition:* state resident $3372 full-time; nonresident $13,272 full-time.

Financial Aid Of all full-time matriculated undergraduates who enrolled in 2011, 42 Federal Work-Study jobs (averaging $1678).

Applying *Options:* electronic application, early admission, deferred entrance. *Application fee:* $10. *Required:* high school transcript. *Application deadlines:* 8/13 (freshmen), 8/13 (transfers). *Notification:* continuous (freshmen), continuous (transfers).

Freshman Application Contact Ms. Sheri Mason, Assistant Director of Student Services, Motlow State Community College, Lynchburg, TN 37352-8500. *Phone:* 931-393-1764. *Toll-free phone:* 800-654-4877. *Fax:* 931-393-1681. *E-mail:* smason@mscc.edu. *Web site:* http://www.mscc.edu/.

Nashville Auto Diesel College

Nashville, Tennessee

Freshman Application Contact Ms. Peggie Werrbach, Director of Admissions, Nashville Auto Diesel College, 1524 Gallatin Road, Nashville, TN 37206. *Phone:* 615-226-3990 Ext. 8465. *Toll-free phone:* 800-228-NADC. *Fax:* 615-262-8466. *E-mail:* wpruitt@nadcedu.com. *Web site:* http://www.nadcedu.com/.

Nashville State Technical Community College

Nashville, Tennessee

Freshman Application Contact Mr. Beth Mahan, Coordinator of Recruitment, Nashville State Technical Community College, 120 White Bridge Road, Nashville, TN 37209-4515. *Phone:* 615-353-3214. *Toll-free phone:* 800-272-7363. *E-mail:* beth.mahan@nscc.edu. *Web site:* http://www.nscc.edu/.

National College

Bristol, Tennessee

Freshman Application Contact National College, 1328 Highway 11 West, Bristol, TN 37620. *Phone:* 423-878-4440. *Toll-free phone:* 888-9-JOBREADY. *Web site:* http://www.national-college.edu/.

National College

Knoxville, Tennessee

Director of Admissions Frank Alvey, Campus Director, National College, 8415 Kingston Pike, Knoxville, TN 37919. *Phone:* 865-539-2011. *Toll-free phone:* 888-9-JOBREADY. *Fax:* 865-539-2049. *Web site:* http://www.national-college.edu/.

National College

Nashville, Tennessee

Director of Admissions Jerry Lafferty, Campus Director, National College, 5042 Linbar Drive, Suite 200, Nashville, TN 37211. *Phone:* 615-333-3344. *Toll-free phone:* 888-9-JOBREADY. *Web site:* http://www.national-college.edu/.

North Central Institute

Clarksville, Tennessee

Freshman Application Contact Dale Wood, Director of Admissions, North Central Institute, 168 Jack Miller Boulevard, Clarksville, TN 37042. *Phone:* 931-431-9700. *Toll-free phone:* 800-603-4116. *Fax:* 931-431-9771. *E-mail:* admissions@nci.edu. *Web site:* http://www.nci.edu/.

Northeast State Technical Community College

Blountville, Tennessee

Freshman Application Contact Dr. Jon P. Harr, Vice President for Student Affairs, Northeast State Technical Community College, PO Box 246, Blountville, TN 37617. *Phone:* 423-323-0231. *Toll-free phone:* 800-836-7822. *Fax:* 423-323-0240. *E-mail:* jpharr@northeaststate.edu. *Web site:* http://www.northeaststate.edu/.

Nossi College of Art

Goodlettsville, Tennessee

- **Independent** primarily 2-year
- **Urban** 10-acre campus with easy access to Nashville
- **Coed**
- 63% of applicants were admitted

Undergraduates 660 full-time. Students come from 10 states and territories; 1 other country; 10% are from out of state; 16% Black or African American, non-Hispanic/Latino; 2% Hispanic/Latino; 0.8% Asian, non-Hispanic/Latino; 1% Race/ethnicity unknown. *Retention:* 75% of full-time freshmen returned.
Faculty *Student/faculty ratio:* 10:1.
Academics *Calendar:* semesters. *Degrees:* associate and bachelor's. *Special study options:* independent study, internships, services for LD students, summer session for credit.
Student Life *Campus security:* campus has a gated entrance, all doors are kept locked.
Costs (2011–12) *Tuition:* $14,100 full-time, $4700 per term part-time. Full-time tuition and fees vary according to course load, degree level, and program. Part-time tuition and fees vary according to course load, degree level, and program. No tuition increase for student's term of enrollment.
Applying *Options:* electronic application, early admission. *Application fee:* $100. *Required:* essay or personal statement, high school transcript, interview, portfolio of work is required for Associate or Bachelor of Graphic Art and Design program and the Bachelor of Illustration program.
Freshman Application Contact Ms. Mary Alexander, Admissions Director, Nossi College of Art, 590 Cheron Road, Madison, TN 37115. *Phone:* 615-514-2787 (ARTS). *Toll-free phone:* 888-986-ARTS. *Fax:* 615-514-2788. *E-mail:* admissions@nossi.edu. *Web site:* http://www.nossi.edu/.

Pellissippi State Technical Community College

Knoxville, Tennessee

Freshman Application Contact Director of Admissions and Records, Pellissippi State Technical Community College, PO Box 22990, Knoxville, TN 37933-0990. *Phone:* 865-694-6400. *Fax:* 865-539-7217. *Web site:* http://www.pstcc.edu/.

Remington College–Memphis Campus

Memphis, Tennessee

Director of Admissions Randal Hayes, Director of Recruitment, Remington College–Memphis Campus, 2731 Nonconnah Boulevard, Memphis, TN 38132-2131. *Phone:* 901-345-1000. *Fax:* 901-396-8310. *E-mail:* randal.hayes@remingtoncollege.edu. *Web site:* http://www.remingtoncollege.edu/.

Remington College–Nashville Campus

Nashville, Tennessee

Director of Admissions Mr. Frank Vivelo, Campus President, Remington College–Nashville Campus, 441 Donelson Pike, Suite 150, Nashville, TN 37214. *Phone:* 615-889-5520. *Fax:* 615-889-5528. *E-mail:* frank.vivelo@remingtoncollege.edu. *Web site:* http://www.remingtoncollege.edu/.

Roane State Community College

Harriman, Tennessee

Freshman Application Contact Admissions Office, Roane State Community College, 276 Patton Lane, Harriman, TN 37748. *Phone:* 865-882-4523. *Toll-free phone:* 866-462-7722 Ext. 4554. *E-mail:* admissions@roanestate.edu. *Web site:* http://www.roanestate.edu/.

Southwest Tennessee Community College

Memphis, Tennessee

Freshman Application Contact Ms. Cindy Meziere, Assistant Director of Recruiting, Southwest Tennessee Community College, PO Box 780, Memphis, TN 38103-0780. *Phone:* 901-333-4195. *Toll-free phone:* 877-717-STCC. *Fax:* 901-333-4473. *E-mail:* cmeziere@southwest.tn.edu. *Web site:* http://www.southwest.tn.edu/.

Vatterott College

Memphis, Tennessee

Admissions Office Contact Vatterott College, 2655 Dividend Drive, Memphis, TN 38132. *Toll-free phone:* 888-553-6627. *Web site:* http://www.vatterott-college.edu/.

Volunteer State Community College

Gallatin, Tennessee

- **State-supported** 2-year, founded 1970, part of Tennessee Board of Regents
- **Suburban** 100-acre campus with easy access to Nashville
- **Endowment** $121,219
- **Coed**, 8,653 undergraduate students, 46% full-time, 62% women, 38% men

Undergraduates 4,008 full-time, 4,645 part-time. Students come from 14 states and territories; 11 other countries; 0.3% are from out of state; 9% Black or African American, non-Hispanic/Latino; 3% Hispanic/Latino; 1% Asian, non-Hispanic/Latino; 0.1% Native Hawaiian or other Pacific Islander, non-Hispanic/Latino; 0.4% American Indian or Alaska Native, non-Hispanic/Latino; 1% Two or more races, non-Hispanic/Latino; 2% Race/ethnicity unknown; 0.4% international; 8% transferred in.
Freshmen *Admission:* 2,327 applied, 2,327 admitted, 1,621 enrolled. *Average high school GPA:* 2.98. *Test scores:* ACT scores over 18: 63%; ACT scores over 24: 8%.
Faculty *Total:* 387, 40% full-time, 11% with terminal degrees. *Student/faculty ratio:* 23:1.
Majors Business administration and management; child development; clinical/medical laboratory technology; criminal justice/police science; education; fire science/firefighting; general studies; health information/medical records technology; health professions related; legal assistant/paralegal; liberal arts and sciences/liberal studies; medical radiologic technology; ophthalmic technology; physical therapy technology; respiratory care therapy; veterinary/animal health technology; web page, digital/multimedia and information resources design.
Academics *Calendar:* semesters. *Degree:* certificates and associate. *Special study options:* academic remediation for entering students, accelerated degree program, adult/continuing education programs, advanced placement credit, distance learning, double majors, English as a second language, honors programs, independent study, internships, part-time degree program, services for LD students, study abroad, summer session for credit.
Library Thigpen Learning Resource Center with 123,245 titles, 177 serial subscriptions, 3,775 audiovisual materials, an OPAC, a Web page.
Student Life *Housing:* college housing not available. *Activities and Organizations:* drama/theater group, student-run newspaper, radio station, choral group, Gamma Beta Phi, Returning Woman's Organization, Phi Theta Kappa, Student Government Association, The Settler. *Campus security:* 24-hour emergency response devices and patrols, late-night transport/escort service. *Student services:* personal/psychological counseling.
Athletics Member NJCAA. *Intercollegiate sports:* baseball M(s), basketball M(s)/W(s), softball W(s).
Standardized Tests *Required for some:* SAT or ACT (for admission).
Costs (2011–12) *Tuition:* state resident $3096 full-time, $129 per credit hour part-time; nonresident $12,720 full-time, $630 per credit hour part-time. Full-time tuition and fees vary according to course load. Part-time tuition and fees vary according to course load. *Required fees:* $271 full-time, $9 per credit hour part-time, $23 per term part-time. *Payment plan:* deferred payment. *Waivers:* senior citizens and employees or children of employees.
Financial Aid Of all full-time matriculated undergraduates who enrolled in 2010, 3,686 applied for aid, 2,962 were judged to have need, 174 had their need fully met. 23 Federal Work-Study jobs (averaging $1749). In 2010, 68 non-need-based awards were made. *Average percent of need met:* 48%. *Average financial aid package:* $6043. *Average need-based loan:* $2828. *Average need-based gift aid:* $4817. *Average non-need-based aid:* $1728.
Applying *Options:* electronic application, early admission, deferred entrance. *Application fee:* $20. *Required:* high school transcript. *Required for some:*

minimum 2.0 GPA, interview. *Application deadlines:* 8/28 (freshmen), 8/28 (transfers). *Notification:* continuous (freshmen), continuous (transfers).

Freshman Application Contact Mr. Tim Amyx, Director of Admissions, Volunteer State Community College, 1480 Nashville Pike, Gallatin, TN 37066-3188. *Phone:* 615-452-8600 Ext. 3614. *Toll-free phone:* 888-335-8722. *Fax:* 615-230-4875. *E-mail:* admissions@volstate.edu. *Web site:* http://www.volstate.edu/.

Walters State Community College
Morristown, Tennessee

Freshman Application Contact Mr. Michael Campbell, Assistant Vice President for Student Affairs, Walters State Community College, 500 South Davy Crockett Parkway, Morristown, TN 37813-6899. *Phone:* 423-585-2682. *Toll-free phone:* 800-225-4770. *Fax:* 423-585-6876. *E-mail:* mike.campbell@ws.edu. *Web site:* http://www.ws.edu/.

TEXAS

Alvin Community College
Alvin, Texas

- **State and locally supported** 2-year, founded 1949
- **Suburban** 114-acre campus with easy access to Houston
- **Coed,** 5,794 undergraduate students, 27% full-time, 54% women, 46% men

Undergraduates 1,560 full-time, 4,234 part-time.

Freshmen *Admission:* 1,097 enrolled.

Faculty *Total:* 262, 37% full-time. *Student/faculty ratio:* 17:1.

Majors Accounting; administrative assistant and secretarial science; aeronautics/aviation/aerospace science and technology; art; biology/biological sciences; business administration and management; chemical technology; child development; computer engineering technology; computer programming; corrections; court reporting; criminal justice/police science; drafting and design technology; dramatic/theater arts; electrical, electronic and communications engineering technology; emergency medical technology (EMT paramedic); legal administrative assistant/secretary; legal assistant/paralegal; legal studies; liberal arts and sciences/liberal studies; marketing/marketing management; mathematics; medical administrative assistant and medical secretary; mental health counseling; music; physical education teaching and coaching; physical sciences; radio and television; registered nursing/registered nurse; respiratory care therapy; substance abuse/addiction counseling; voice and opera.

Academics *Calendar:* semesters. *Degree:* certificates, diplomas, and associate. *Special study options:* academic remediation for entering students, accelerated degree program, adult/continuing education programs, advanced placement credit, distance learning, double majors, English as a second language, honors programs, independent study, internships, part-time degree program, services for LD students, student-designed majors, study abroad, summer session for credit.

Library Alvin Community College Library with an OPAC, a Web page.

Student Life *Campus security:* 24-hour patrols, late-night transport/escort service. *Student services:* personal/psychological counseling.

Athletics Member NJCAA. *Intercollegiate sports:* baseball M(s), softball W(s). *Intramural sports:* soccer M(c)/W(c).

Financial Aid Of all full-time matriculated undergraduates who enrolled in 2010, 65 Federal Work-Study jobs (averaging $3300). 3 state and other part-time jobs (averaging $3000).

Applying *Options:* electronic application. *Required for some:* high school transcript. *Application deadlines:* rolling (freshmen), rolling (transfers).

Freshman Application Contact Alvin Community College, 3110 Mustang Road, Alvin, TX 77511-4898. *Phone:* 281-756-3531. *Web site:* http://www.alvincollege.edu/.

Amarillo College
Amarillo, Texas

- **State and locally supported** 2-year, founded 1929
- **Urban** 1542-acre campus
- **Endowment** $30.4 million
- **Coed,** 11,456 undergraduate students, 33% full-time, 61% women, 39% men

Undergraduates 3,835 full-time, 7,621 part-time. 5% Black or African American, non-Hispanic/Latino; 32% Hispanic/Latino; 3% Asian, non-Hispanic/Latino; 1% American Indian or Alaska Native, non-Hispanic/Latino; 2% Race/ethnicity unknown. *Retention:* 52% of full-time freshmen returned.

Freshmen *Admission:* 1,754 enrolled.

Faculty *Total:* 471, 47% full-time.

Majors Accounting; administrative assistant and secretarial science; airframe mechanics and aircraft maintenance technology; architectural engineering technology; art; automobile/automotive mechanics technology; behavioral sciences; biblical studies; biology/biological sciences; broadcast journalism; business administration and management; business teacher education; chemical technology; chemistry; child development; clinical laboratory science/medical technology; commercial and advertising art; computer engineering technology; computer programming; computer science; computer systems analysis; corrections; criminal justice/law enforcement administration; criminal justice/police science; dental hygiene; drafting and design technology; dramatic/theater arts; electrical, electronic and communications engineering technology; elementary education; emergency medical technology (EMT paramedic); engineering; English; environmental health; fine/studio arts; fire science/firefighting; funeral service and mortuary science; general studies; geology/earth science; health information/medical records administration; heating, air conditioning, ventilation and refrigeration maintenance technology; heavy equipment maintenance technology; history; industrial radiologic technology; information science/studies; instrumentation technology; interior design; journalism; laser and optical technology; legal administrative assistant/secretary; liberal arts and sciences/liberal studies; licensed practical/vocational nurse training; machine tool technology; mass communication/media; mathematics; medical administrative assistant and medical secretary; modern languages; music; music teacher education; natural sciences; nuclear medical technology; occupational therapy; photography; physical education teaching and coaching; physical sciences; physical therapy; physics; pre-engineering; pre-pharmacy studies; psychology; public relations/image management; radio and television; radiologic technology/science; real estate; registered nursing/registered nurse; religious studies; respiratory care therapy; rhetoric and composition; social sciences; social work; substance abuse/addiction counseling; telecommunications technology; tourism and travel services management; visual and performing arts.

Academics *Calendar:* semesters. *Degree:* certificates and associate. *Special study options:* academic remediation for entering students, adult/continuing education programs, advanced placement credit, cooperative education, distance learning, English as a second language, freshman honors college, honors programs, part-time degree program, services for LD students, summer session for credit.

Library Lynn Library Learning Center plus 2 others with 61,774 titles, 22,000 serial subscriptions, an OPAC, a Web page.

Student Life *Housing:* college housing not available. *Activities and Organizations:* drama/theater group, student-run newspaper, radio station, choral group, Student Government Association, College Republicans. *Campus security:* 24-hour emergency response devices, late-night transport/escort service, Campus police patrol Monday through Saturday, 0700 to 2300.

Athletics *Intramural sports:* basketball M/W, soccer M/W, softball M/W, tennis M/W, volleyball M/W.

Costs (2012–13) *Tuition:* area resident $1506 full-time, $63 per semester hour part-time; state resident $2034 full-time, $85 per semester hour part-time; nonresident $2994 full-time, $125 per semester hour part-time. Full-time tuition and fees vary according to course load. Part-time tuition and fees vary according to course load. *Payment plan:* installment. *Waivers:* senior citizens and employees or children of employees.

Financial Aid Of all full-time matriculated undergraduates who enrolled in 2010, 100 Federal Work-Study jobs (averaging $3000).

Applying *Options:* early admission, deferred entrance. *Required:* high school transcript. *Notification:* continuous (freshmen), continuous (transfers).

Freshman Application Contact Amarillo College, PO Box 447, Amarillo, TX 79178-0001. *Phone:* 806-371-5000. *Toll-free phone:* 800-227-8784. *Fax:* 806-371-5497. *E-mail:* askac@actx.edu. *Web site:* http://www.actx.edu/.

Angelina College
Lufkin, Texas

Freshman Application Contact Angelina College, PO Box 1768, Lufkin, TX 75902-1768. *Phone:* 936-633-5213. *Web site:* http://www.angelina.cc.tx.us/.

ATI Technical Training Center
Dallas, Texas

Freshman Application Contact Admissions Office, ATI Technical Training Center, 6627 Maple Avenue, Dallas, TX 75235. *Phone:* 214-352-2222. *Toll-free phone:* 888-209-8264. *Web site:* http://www.aticareertraining.edu/.

Austin Community College
Austin, Texas

- **State and locally supported** 2-year, founded 1972
- **Urban** campus with easy access to Austin
- **Endowment** $4.0 million
- **Coed,** 45,100 undergraduate students, 23% full-time, 56% women, 44% men

Undergraduates 10,596 full-time, 34,504 part-time. 8% Black or African American, non-Hispanic/Latino; 27% Hispanic/Latino; 5% Asian, non-Hispanic/Latino; 0.1% Native Hawaiian or other Pacific Islander, non-Hispanic/Latino; 0.9% American Indian or Alaska Native, non-Hispanic/Latino; 1% Two or more races, non-Hispanic/Latino; 6% Race/ethnicity unknown; 2% international.

Faculty *Total:* 2,107, 29% full-time, 21% with terminal degrees. *Student/faculty ratio:* 19:1.

Majors Accounting technology and bookkeeping; administrative assistant and secretarial science; animation, interactive technology, video graphics and special effects; anthropology; art; automobile/automotive mechanics technology; banking and financial support services; biology/biological sciences; biology/biotechnology laboratory technician; business administration and management; business/commerce; carpentry; chemistry; child development; clinical/medical laboratory technology; commercial and advertising art; commercial photography; computer and information sciences; computer programming; computer systems networking and telecommunications; corrections; creative writing; criminal justice/police science; culinary arts; dance; dental hygiene; diagnostic medical sonography and ultrasound technology; drafting and design technology; dramatic/theater arts; early childhood education; economics; electrical, electronic and communications engineering technology; emergency medical technology (EMT paramedic); engineering; environmental engineering technology; fire prevention and safety technology; foreign languages and literatures; French; general studies; geographic information science and cartography; geography; geology/earth science; German; health and physical education/fitness; health information/medical records technology; health teacher education; heating, ventilation, air conditioning and refrigeration engineering technology; history; hospitality administration; human services; international business/trade/commerce; Japanese; journalism; Latin; legal assistant/paralegal; marketing/marketing management; mathematics; middle school education; music; music management; occupational therapist assistant; philosophy; physical sciences; physical therapy technology; physics; political science and government; pre-dentistry studies; premedical studies; pre-pharmacy studies; pre-veterinary studies; professional, technical, business, and scientific writing; psychology; radio and television; radiologic technology/science; real estate; registered nursing/registered nurse; rhetoric and composition; Russian; secondary education; sign language interpretation and translation; social work; sociology; Spanish; substance abuse/addiction counseling; surgical technology; surveying technology; therapeutic recreation; watchmaking and jewelrymaking; welding technology; writing.

Academics *Calendar:* semesters. *Degree:* certificates and associate. *Special study options:* academic remediation for entering students, accelerated degree program, adult/continuing education programs, advanced placement credit, cooperative education, distance learning, English as a second language, honors programs, independent study, internships, part-time degree program, services for LD students, summer session for credit. *ROTC:* Army (c), Air Force (c).

Library Main Library plus 8 others with 181,409 titles, 47,619 serial subscriptions, 18,271 audiovisual materials, an OPAC, a Web page.

Student Life *Housing:* college housing not available. *Activities and Organizations:* student-run newspaper, Student Government Association (SGA), Phi Theta Kappa (PTK), Sigma Alpha Pi - National Honor Leadership Society (SAP), Center for Student Political Studies (CSPS), Circle K International (CKI). *Campus security:* 24-hour emergency response devices and patrols, late-night transport/escort service. *Student services:* personal/psychological counseling.

Athletics *Intramural sports:* basketball M/W, bowling M/W, golf M/W, soccer M/W, volleyball W.

Costs (2011–12) *Tuition:* area resident $2040 full-time, $68 per credit hour part-time; state resident $6300 full-time, $210 per credit hour part-time; nonresident $9420 full-time, $314 per credit hour part-time. Full-time tuition and fees vary according to course load. Part-time tuition and fees vary according to course load. *Payment plan:* installment. *Waivers:* senior citizens and employees or children of employees.

Financial Aid Of all full-time matriculated undergraduates who enrolled in 2010, 6,265 applied for aid, 5,288 were judged to have need. 427 Federal Work-Study jobs (averaging $1562). 72 state and other part-time jobs (averaging $1414). *Average need-based loan:* $1787. *Average need-based gift aid:* $2851.

Applying *Options:* electronic application. *Required:* high school transcript. *Application deadlines:* rolling (freshmen), rolling (transfers).

Freshman Application Contact Ms. Linda Kluck, Director, Admissions and Records, Austin Community College, 5930 Middle Fiskville Road, Austin, TX 78752. *Phone:* 512-223-7503. *Fax:* 512-223-7665. *E-mail:* admission@austincc.edu. *Web site:* http://www.austincc.edu/.

Blinn College
Brenham, Texas

Freshman Application Contact Mrs. Stephanie Wehring, Coordinator, Recruitment and Admissions, Blinn College, 902 College Avenue, Brenham, TX 77833-4049. *Phone:* 979-830-4152. *Fax:* 979-830-4110. *E-mail:* recruit@blinn.edu. *Web site:* http://www.blinn.edu/.

Brazosport College
Lake Jackson, Texas

Freshman Application Contact Brazosport College, 500 College Drive, Lake Jackson, TX 77566-3199. *Phone:* 979-230-3020. *Web site:* http://www.brazosport.edu/.

Brookhaven College
Farmers Branch, Texas

- **County-supported** 2-year, founded 1978, part of Dallas County Community College District System
- **Suburban** 200-acre campus with easy access to Dallas-Fort Worth
- **Coed,** 13,705 undergraduate students, 21% full-time, 59% women, 41% men

Undergraduates 2,889 full-time, 10,816 part-time. Students come from 28 states and territories; 10 other countries; 0.4% are from out of state; 19% Black or African American, non-Hispanic/Latino; 30% Hispanic/Latino; 11% Asian, non-Hispanic/Latino; 0.4% American Indian or Alaska Native, non-Hispanic/Latino; 0.7% Two or more races, non-Hispanic/Latino; 3% Race/ethnicity unknown; 0.5% international; 7% transferred in.

Freshmen *Admission:* 1,648 enrolled.

Faculty *Total:* 549, 24% full-time. *Student/faculty ratio:* 24:1.

Majors Accounting; automobile/automotive mechanics technology; business administration and management; business/commerce; child development; computer engineering technology; computer programming; computer technology/computer systems technology; design and visual communications; e-commerce; education (multiple levels); emergency medical technology (EMT paramedic); executive assistant/executive secretary; general studies; geographic information science and cartography; graphic design; humanities; information science/studies; liberal arts and sciences/liberal studies; marketing/marketing management; music; office management; radiologic technology/science; registered nursing/registered nurse; secondary education; speech communication and rhetoric.

Academics *Calendar:* semesters. *Degree:* certificates and associate. *Special study options:* academic remediation for entering students, adult/continuing education programs, advanced placement credit, cooperative education, distance learning, English as a second language, honors programs, independent study, internships, off-campus study, part-time degree program, services for LD students, student-designed majors, study abroad, summer session for credit.

Library Brookhaven College Learning Resources Center plus 1 other with an OPAC, a Web page.

Student Life *Housing:* college housing not available. *Activities and Organizations:* drama/theater group, student-run newspaper, choral group. *Campus security:* 24-hour emergency response devices and patrols, late-night transport/escort service. *Student services:* health clinic, personal/psychological counseling.

Athletics Member NJCAA. *Intercollegiate sports:* baseball M, basketball M, soccer W, volleyball W. *Intramural sports:* weight lifting M/W.

Standardized Tests *Required for some:* THEA.

Costs (2011–12) *Tuition:* area resident $1350 full-time, $45 per hour part-time; state resident $2490 full-time, $83 per hour part-time; nonresident $3960 full-time, $132 per hour part-time. Full-time tuition and fees vary according to course load. Part-time tuition and fees vary according to course load. *Payment plan:* installment. *Waivers:* senior citizens and employees or children of employees.

Applying *Options:* electronic application, early admission, deferred entrance. *Required:* high school transcript. *Application deadlines:* rolling (freshmen), rolling (transfers).

Freshman Application Contact Admissions Office, Brookhaven College, 3939 Valley View Lane, Farmers Branch, TX 75244-4997. *Phone:* 972-860-4883. *Fax:* 972-860-4886. *E-mail:* bhcAdmissions@dcccd.edu. *Web site:* http://www.brookhavencollege.edu/.

Brown Mackie College–Dallas

Bedford, Texas

Admissions Office Contact Brown Mackie College–Dallas, 2200 North Highway 121, Suite 270, Bedford, TX 76021. *Web site:* http://www.brownmackie.edu/dallas/.

See page 350 for the College Close-Up.

Brown Mackie College–San Antonio

San Antonio, Texas

- **Proprietary** 4-year, part of Education Management Corporation
- **Coed**

Academics *Degrees:* associate and bachelor's.
Costs (2011–12) *Tuition:* Tuition varies by program. Students should contact Brown Mackie College for tuition information.
Director of Admissions Director of Admissions, Brown Mackie College–San Antonio, 4715 Fredericksburg Road, Suite 100, San Antonio, TX 78229. *Phone:* 210-428-2210. *Toll-free phone:* 877-460-1714. *Web site:* http://www.brownmackie.edu/san-antonio.

See page 386 for the College Close-Up.

Cedar Valley College

Lancaster, Texas

Freshman Application Contact Admissions Office, Cedar Valley College, Lancaster, TX 75134-3799. *Phone:* 972-860-8206. *Fax:* 972-860-8207. *Web site:* http://www.cedarvalleycollege.edu/.

Center for Advanced Legal Studies

Houston, Texas

Freshman Application Contact Mr. James Scheffer, Center for Advanced Legal Studies, 3910 Kirby, Suite 200, Houston, TX 77098. *Phone:* 713-529-2778. *Toll-free phone:* 800-446-6931. *Fax:* 713-523-2715. *E-mail:* james.scheffer@paralegal.edu. *Web site:* http://www.paralegal.edu/.

Central Texas College

Killeen, Texas

Freshman Application Contact Admissions Office, Central Texas College, PO Box 1800, Killeen, TX 76540-1800. *Phone:* 254-526-1696. *Toll-free phone:* 800-223-4760 (in-state); 800-792-3348 (out-of-state). *Fax:* 254-526-1545. *E-mail:* admrec@ctcd.edu. *Web site:* http://www.ctcd.edu/.

Cisco College

Cisco, Texas

Freshman Application Contact Mr. Olin O. Odom III, Dean of Admission/Registrar, Cisco College, 101 College Heights, Cisco, TX 76437-9321. *Phone:* 254-442-2567 Ext. 5130. *E-mail:* oodom@cjc.edu. *Web site:* http://www.cisco.edu/.

Clarendon College

Clarendon, Texas

- **State and locally supported** 2-year, founded 1898
- **Rural** 109-acre campus
- **Endowment** $2.1 million
- **Coed**

Undergraduates Students come from 14 states and territories; 2 other countries; 4% are from out of state; 6% Black or African American, non-Hispanic/Latino; 19% Hispanic/Latino; 1% Asian, non-Hispanic/Latino; 0.6% American Indian or Alaska Native, non-Hispanic/Latino; 12% Race/ethnicity unknown; 0.3% international; 21% live on campus.
Faculty *Student/faculty ratio:* 19:1.
Academics *Calendar:* semesters. *Degree:* certificates and associate. *Special study options:* academic remediation for entering students, adult/continuing education programs, advanced placement credit, distance learning, double majors, English as a second language, independent study, part-time degree program, services for LD students, summer session for credit.
Student Life *Campus security:* 8-hour patrols by trained security personnel, Emergency notification system through text messaging.
Athletics Member NJCAA.
Financial Aid Of all full-time matriculated undergraduates who enrolled in 2010, 47 Federal Work-Study jobs (averaging $575). 12 state and other part-time jobs (averaging $485).

Applying *Options:* electronic application, early admission. *Required:* high school transcript. *Required for some:* interview.
Freshman Application Contact Ms. Martha Smith, Admissions Director, Clarendon College, PO Box 968, Clarendon, TX 79226. *Phone:* 806-874-3571 Ext. 106. *Toll-free phone:* 800-687-9737. *Fax:* 806-874-3201. *E-mail:* martha.smith@clarendoncollege.edu. *Web site:* http://www.clarendoncollege.edu/.

Coastal Bend College

Beeville, Texas

Freshman Application Contact Ms. Alicia Ulloa, Director of Admissions/Registrar, Coastal Bend College, Beeville, TX 78102-2197. *Phone:* 361-354-2245. *Toll-free phone:* 866-722-2838 (in-state); 866-262-2838 (out-of-state). *Fax:* 361-354-2254. *E-mail:* register@coastalbend.edu. *Web site:* http://www.coastalbend.edu/.

College of Health Care Professions

Houston, Texas

Freshman Application Contact Admissions Office, College of Health Care Professions, 240 Northwest Mall Boulevard, Houston, TX 77092. *Phone:* 713-425-3100. *Toll-free phone:* 800-487-6728. *Fax:* 713-425-3193. *Web site:* http://www.ahcp.edu/.

College of the Mainland

Texas City, Texas

Freshman Application Contact Ms. Kelly Musick, Registrar/Director of Admissions, College of the Mainland, 1200 Amburn Road, Texas City, TX 77591. *Phone:* 409-938-1211 Ext. 469. *Toll-free phone:* 888-258-8859 Ext. 8264. *Fax:* 409-938-3126. *E-mail:* sem@com.edu. *Web site:* http://www.com.edu/.

Collin County Community College District

McKinney, Texas

- **State and locally supported** 2-year, founded 1985
- **Suburban** 333-acre campus with easy access to Dallas-Fort Worth
- **Endowment** $4.2 million
- **Coed**

Undergraduates 10,216 full-time, 16,853 part-time. Students come from 48 states and territories; 109 other countries; 6% are from out of state; 11% Black or African American, non-Hispanic/Latino; 14% Hispanic/Latino; 8% Asian, non-Hispanic/Latino; 0.1% Native Hawaiian or other Pacific Islander, non-Hispanic/Latino; 0.6% American Indian or Alaska Native, non-Hispanic/Latino; 1% Two or more races, non-Hispanic/Latino; 3% Race/ethnicity unknown; 4% international; 12% transferred in. *Retention:* 62% of full-time freshmen returned.
Faculty *Student/faculty ratio:* 26:1.
Academics *Calendar:* semesters. *Degree:* certificates and associate. *Special study options:* academic remediation for entering students, adult/continuing education programs, advanced placement credit, cooperative education, distance learning, English as a second language, honors programs, internships, part-time degree program, services for LD students, summer session for credit. *ROTC:* Air Force (c).
Student Life *Campus security:* 24-hour emergency response devices and patrols, late-night transport/escort service.
Athletics Member NJCAA.
Standardized Tests *Required:* COMPASS (for admission).
Costs (2011–12) *Tuition:* area resident $810 full-time, $27 per semester hour part-time; state resident $1830 full-time, $61 per semester hour part-time; non-resident $3330 full-time, $111 per semester hour part-time. *Required fees:* $214 full-time, $7 per semester hour part-time.
Financial Aid Of all full-time matriculated undergraduates who enrolled in 2009, 3,737 applied for aid, 2,818 were judged to have need, 21 had their need fully met. In 2009, 169. *Average percent of need met:* 51. *Average financial aid package:* $5170. *Average need-based loan:* $3082. *Average need-based gift aid:* $4663. *Average non-need-based aid:* $618. *Average indebtedness upon graduation:* $4547.
Applying *Options:* electronic application. *Required:* high school transcript.
Freshman Application Contact Mr. Todd Fields, Registrar, Collin County Community College District, 2800 East Spring Creek Parkway, Plano, TX 75074. *Phone:* 972-881-5174. *Fax:* 972-881-5175. *E-mail:* tfields@collin.edu. *Web site:* http://www.collin.edu/.

Commonwealth Institute of Funeral Service

Houston, Texas

Freshman Application Contact Ms. Patricia Moreno, Registrar, Commonwealth Institute of Funeral Service, 415 Barren Springs Drive, Houston, TX 77090. *Phone:* 281-873-0262. *Toll-free phone:* 800-628-1580. *Fax:* 281-873-5232. *E-mail:* p.moreno@commonwealth.edu. *Web site:* http://www.commonwealth.edu/.

Computer Career Center

El Paso, Texas

Director of Admissions Ms. Sarah Hernandez, Registrar, Computer Career Center, 6101 Montana Avenue, El Paso, TX 79925. *Phone:* 915-779-8031. *Toll-free phone:* 866-442-4197. *Web site:* http://www.vistacollege.edu/.

Court Reporting Institute of Dallas

Dallas, Texas

Director of Admissions Ms. Debra Smith-Armstrong, Director of Admissions, Court Reporting Institute of Dallas, 8585 North Stemmons Freeway, Suite 200 North, Dallas, TX 75247. *Phone:* 214-350-9722 Ext. 227. *Toll-free phone:* 877-841-3557 (in-state); 888-841-3557 (out-of-state). *Web site:* http://www.crid.com/.

Court Reporting Institute of Houston

Houston, Texas

Freshman Application Contact Admissions Office, Court Reporting Institute of Houston, 13101 Northwest Freeway, Suite 100, Houston, TX 77040. *Phone:* 713-996-8300. *Toll-free phone:* 888-841-3557. *Web site:* http://www.crid.com/.

Culinary Institute LeNotre

Houston, Texas

Freshman Application Contact Admissions Office, Culinary Institute LeNotre, 7070 Allensby, Houston, TX 77022-4322. *Phone:* 713-358-5070. *Toll-free phone:* 888-LENOTRE. *Web site:* http://www.culinaryinstitute.edu/.

Dallas Institute of Funeral Service

Dallas, Texas

- **Independent** 2-year, founded 1945
- **Urban** 4-acre campus with easy access to Dallas-Fort Worth
- **Coed,** 141 undergraduate students, 100% full-time, 47% women, 53% men

Undergraduates 141 full-time. Students come from 7 states and territories; 11% are from out of state.
Freshmen *Admission:* 56 enrolled.
Faculty *Student/faculty ratio:* 17:1.
Majors Funeral service and mortuary science.
Academics *Calendar:* quarters. *Degree:* certificates and associate. *Special study options:* distance learning, services for LD students.
Student Life *Housing:* college housing not available. *Campus security:* 24-hour emergency response devices.
Costs (2011–12) *One-time required fee:* $50. *Tuition:* $12,000 full-time, $200 per quarter hour part-time. No tuition increase for student's term of enrollment. *Payment plan:* installment.
Applying *Application fee:* $50. *Required:* high school transcript.
Freshman Application Contact Director of Admissions, Dallas Institute of Funeral Service, 3909 South Buckner Boulevard, Dallas, TX 75227. *Phone:* 214-388-5466. *Toll-free phone:* 800-235-5444. *Fax:* 214-388-0316. *E-mail:* difs@dallasinstitute.edu. *Web site:* http://www.dallasinstitute.edu/.

Del Mar College

Corpus Christi, Texas

Freshman Application Contact Ms. Frances P. Jordan, Director of Admissions and Registrar, Del Mar College, 101 Baldwin, Corpus Christi, TX 78404. *Phone:* 361-698-1255. *Toll-free phone:* 800-652-3357. *Fax:* 361-698-1595. *E-mail:* fjordan@delmar.edu. *Web site:* http://www.delmar.edu/.

Eastfield College

Mesquite, Texas

- **State and locally supported** 2-year, founded 1970, part of Dallas County Community College District System
- **Suburban** 244-acre campus with easy access to Dallas-Fort Worth
- **Coed**

Undergraduates 3,026 full-time, 9,377 part-time. Students come from 7 states and territories; 26 other countries; 0.6% are from out of state; 2% transferred in.
Faculty *Student/faculty ratio:* 24:1.
Academics *Calendar:* semesters. *Degree:* certificates and associate. *Special study options:* academic remediation for entering students, adult/continuing education programs, advanced placement credit, cooperative education, distance learning, English as a second language, honors programs, part-time degree program, services for LD students, summer session for credit.
Student Life *Campus security:* 24-hour emergency response devices and patrols.
Athletics Member NJCAA.
Applying *Options:* early admission, deferred entrance. *Recommended:* high school transcript.
Freshman Application Contact Ms. Glynis Miller, Director of Admissions/Registrar, Eastfield College, 3737 Motley Drive, Mesquite, TX 75150-2099. *Phone:* 972-860-7010. *Fax:* 972-860-8306. *E-mail:* efc@dcccd.edu. *Web site:* http://www.efc.dcccd.edu/.

El Centro College

Dallas, Texas

- **County-supported** 2-year, founded 1966, part of Dallas County Community College District System
- **Urban** 2-acre campus
- **Coed,** 10,581 undergraduate students, 23% full-time, 67% women, 33% men

Undergraduates 2,427 full-time, 8,154 part-time. Students come from 20 states and territories; 40 other countries; 2% are from out of state; 36% Black or African American, non-Hispanic/Latino; 37% Hispanic/Latino; 3% Asian, non-Hispanic/Latino; 0.5% American Indian or Alaska Native, non-Hispanic/Latino; 0.2% Two or more races, non-Hispanic/Latino; 1% Race/ethnicity unknown; 1% international; 100% transferred in. *Retention:* 40% of full-time freshmen returned.
Freshmen *Admission:* 2,736 applied, 2,736 admitted, 1,599 enrolled.
Faculty *Total:* 503, 27% full-time, 9% with terminal degrees. *Student/faculty ratio:* 20:1.
Majors Accounting; apparel and accessories marketing; baking and pastry arts; biotechnology; business administration and management; business automation/technology/data entry; business/commerce; cardiovascular technology; clinical/medical laboratory technology; computer and information systems security; computer/information technology services administration related; computer programming; computer science; culinary arts; data processing and data processing technology; diagnostic medical sonography and ultrasound technology; emergency medical technology (EMT paramedic); executive assistant/executive secretary; fashion/apparel design; health information/medical records administration; information science/studies; interior design; legal administrative assistant/secretary; legal assistant/paralegal; licensed practical/vocational nurse training; medical/clinical assistant; medical radiologic technology; medical transcription; office occupations and clerical services; peace studies and conflict resolution; radiologic technology/science; registered nursing/registered nurse; respiratory care therapy; special products marketing; surgical technology; teacher assistant/aide; web page, digital/multimedia and information resources design.
Academics *Calendar:* semesters. *Degree:* certificates and associate. *Special study options:* academic remediation for entering students, adult/continuing education programs, advanced placement credit, cooperative education, distance learning, double majors, English as a second language, freshman honors college, honors programs, internships, part-time degree program, services for LD students, summer session for credit. *ROTC:* Army (c).
Library El Centro College Library with 77,902 titles, 224 serial subscriptions, 585 audiovisual materials, an OPAC, a Web page.
Student Life *Housing:* college housing not available. *Activities and Organizations:* choral group, Phi Theta Kappa, Student Government, Paralegal Student Association, El Centro Computer Society, Conflict Resolution Society. *Campus security:* 24-hour emergency response devices and patrols, late-night transport/escort service, *E-mail* and text message alerts. *Student services:* health clinic, personal/psychological counseling.
Costs (2011–12) *Tuition:* area resident $1080 full-time, $45 per credit hour part-time; state resident $1992 full-time, $83 per credit hour part-time; nonresident $3168 full-time, $132 per credit hour part-time. Full-time tuition and fees vary according to program. Part-time tuition and fees vary according to pro-

gram. *Payment plans:* installment, deferred payment. *Waivers:* senior citizens and employees or children of employees.

Applying *Options:* electronic application, early admission. *Required for some:* high school transcript, 1 letter of recommendation. *Application deadlines:* rolling (freshmen), rolling (transfers).

Freshman Application Contact Ms. Rebecca Garza, Director of Admissions and Registrar, El Centro College, Dallas, TX 75202. *Phone:* 214-860-2618. *Fax:* 214-860-2233. *E-mail:* rgarza@dcccd.edu. *Web site:* http://www.elcentrocollege.edu/.

El Paso Community College
El Paso, Texas

- **County-supported** 2-year, founded 1969
- **Urban** campus
- **Coed,** 30,723 undergraduate students, 39% full-time, 57% women, 43% men

Undergraduates 11,886 full-time, 18,837 part-time. 2% Black or African American, non-Hispanic/Latino; 85% Hispanic/Latino; 0.8% Asian, non-Hispanic/Latino; 0.1% Native Hawaiian or other Pacific Islander, non-Hispanic/Latino; 0.4% American Indian or Alaska Native, non-Hispanic/Latino; 0.7% Race/ethnicity unknown; 2% international.

Freshmen *Admission:* 5,451 enrolled.

Faculty *Total:* 1,452; 29% full-time, 9% with terminal degrees.

Majors Accounting; administrative assistant and secretarial science; adult development and aging; automobile/automotive mechanics technology; business administration and management; business automation/technology/data entry; business/commerce; child-care and support services management; child development; cinematography and film/video production; clinical/medical laboratory technology; commercial and advertising art; computer and information sciences; computer programming; corrections; corrections and criminal justice related; court reporting; criminal justice/police science; criminal justice/safety; culinary arts; dental assisting; dental hygiene; diagnostic medical sonography and ultrasound technology; dietetics; drafting and design technology; electrical, electronic and communications engineering technology; emergency medical technology (EMT paramedic); engineering; environmental engineering technology; fashion/apparel design; fire prevention and safety technology; general studies; health information/medical records administration; heating, air conditioning, ventilation and refrigeration maintenance technology; homeland security, law enforcement, firefighting and protective services related; hotel/motel administration; institutional food workers; interior design; international business/trade/commerce; kindergarten/preschool education; legal assistant/paralegal; liberal arts and sciences/liberal studies; machine tool technology; medical/clinical assistant; medical radiologic technology; middle school education; multi/interdisciplinary studies related; music; opticianry; optometric technician; pharmacy technician; physical therapy technology; plastics and polymer engineering technology; psychiatric/mental health services technology; radiologic technology/science; real estate; registered nursing/registered nurse; respiratory care therapy; sign language interpretation and translation; social work; speech communication and rhetoric; substance abuse/addiction counseling; surgical technology; system, networking, and LAN/WAN management; tourism and travel services management.

Academics *Calendar:* semesters. *Degree:* certificates and associate. *Special study options:* academic remediation for entering students, adult/continuing education programs, advanced placement credit, cooperative education, distance learning, English as a second language, external degree program, honors programs, internships, off-campus study, part-time degree program, services for LD students, summer session for credit. *ROTC:* Army (c).

Library El Paso Community College Learning Resource Center plus 4 others with 220,150 titles, 807 serial subscriptions, 14,734 audiovisual materials, an OPAC, a Web page.

Student Life *Housing:* college housing not available. *Activities and Organizations:* drama/theater group, student-run newspaper, radio and television station, choral group. *Campus security:* 24-hour patrols, late-night transport/escort service. *Student services:* personal/psychological counseling.

Athletics Member NJCAA. *Intercollegiate sports:* baseball M(s), softball W(s), track and field M/W. *Intramural sports:* basketball M/W, bowling M/W, cross-country running M/W, softball M/W, table tennis M/W, tennis M/W, volleyball M/W, weight lifting M/W.

Costs (2012–13) *Tuition:* state resident $1848 full-time, $67 per hour part-time; nonresident $2496 full-time, $94 per hour part-time. *Required fees:* $240 full-time, $10 per hour part-time.

Financial Aid Of all full-time matriculated undergraduates who enrolled in 2010, 750 Federal Work-Study jobs (averaging $1800). 50 state and other part-time jobs (averaging $1800).

Applying *Options:* early admission, deferred entrance. *Application fee:* $10. *Application deadlines:* 8/3 (freshmen), 8/3 (transfers).

Freshman Application Contact Daryle Hendry, Director of Admissions, El Paso Community College, PO Box 20500, El Paso, TX 79998-0500. *Phone:* 915-831-2580. *E-mail:* daryleh@epcc.edu. *Web site:* http://www.epcc.edu/.

Everest College
Arlington, Texas

Freshman Application Contact Admissions Office, Everest College, 300 Six Flags Drive, Suite 200, Arlington, TX 76011. *Phone:* 817-652-7790. *Toll-free phone:* 888-741-4270. *Fax:* 817-649-6033. *Web site:* http://www.everest.edu/.

Everest College
Dallas, Texas

Freshman Application Contact Admissions Office, Everest College, 6060 North Central Expressway, Suite 101, Dallas, TX 75206-5209. *Phone:* 214-234-4850. *Toll-free phone:* 888-741-4270. *Fax:* 214-696-6208. *Web site:* http://www.everest.edu/.

Everest College
Fort Worth, Texas

Freshman Application Contact Admissions Office, Everest College, 5237 North Riverside Drive, Suite 100, Fort Worth, TX 76137. *Phone:* 817-838-3000. *Toll-free phone:* 888-741-4270. *Fax:* 817-838-2040. *Web site:* http://www.everest.edu/.

Frank Phillips College
Borger, Texas

- **State and locally supported** 2-year, founded 1948
- **Small-town** 60-acre campus
- **Endowment** $919,464
- **Coed**

Undergraduates 686 full-time, 561 part-time. Students come from 15 states and territories; 6 other countries; 10% are from out of state; 6% transferred in; 20% live on campus. *Retention:* 52% of full-time freshmen returned.

Faculty *Student/faculty ratio:* 18:1.

Academics *Calendar:* semesters. *Degree:* certificates and associate. *Special study options:* academic remediation for entering students, accelerated degree program, adult/continuing education programs, advanced placement credit, cooperative education, distance learning, honors programs, internships, part-time degree program, services for LD students, summer session for credit.

Student Life *Campus security:* 24-hour emergency response devices and patrols, controlled dormitory access.

Athletics Member NJCAA.

Costs (2011–12) *Tuition:* area resident $864 full-time, $36 per hour part-time; state resident $1416 full-time, $59 per hour part-time; nonresident $1562 full-time, $66 per hour part-time. Full-time tuition and fees vary according to program. Part-time tuition and fees vary according to course load and program. *Required fees:* $1216 full-time, $44 per hour part-time, $80 per hour part-time. *Room and board:* $4220. Room and board charges vary according to housing facility.

Financial Aid Of all full-time matriculated undergraduates who enrolled in 2010, 24 Federal Work-Study jobs (averaging $5200). 6 state and other part-time jobs (averaging $4800). *Financial aid deadline:* 8/31.

Applying *Options:* electronic application, early admission, deferred entrance. *Required:* high school transcript.

Freshman Application Contact Ms. Michele Stevens, Director of Enrollment Management, Frank Phillips College, PO Box 5118, Borger, TX 79008-5118. *Phone:* 806-457-4200 Ext. 707. *Fax:* 806-457-4225. *E-mail:* mstevens@fpctx.edu. *Web site:* http://www.fpctx.edu/.

Galveston College
Galveston, Texas

Freshman Application Contact Galveston College, 4015 Avenue Q, Galveston, TX 77550-7496. *Phone:* 409-944-1234. *Web site:* http://www.gc.edu/.

Grayson County College
Denison, Texas

Freshman Application Contact Tana Adams, Lead Enrollment Advisor, Grayson County College, 6101 Grayson Drive, Denison, TX 75020-8299. *Phone:* 903-463-8627. *E-mail:* hallt@grayson.edu. *Web site:* http://www.grayson.edu/.

Hallmark College of Technology
San Antonio, Texas

- **Proprietary** primarily 2-year, founded 1969
- **Suburban** 3-acre campus
- **Coed**

Undergraduates 356 full-time. Students come from 1 other state; 15% Black or African American, non-Hispanic/Latino; 55% Hispanic/Latino; 0.6% Asian, non-Hispanic/Latino; 0.3% Native Hawaiian or other Pacific Islander, non-Hispanic/Latino; 4% Two or more races, non-Hispanic/Latino; 1% Race/ethnicity unknown.
Faculty *Student/faculty ratio:* 8:1.
Academics *Calendar:* continuous. *Degrees:* certificates, associate, and bachelor's. *Special study options:* accelerated degree program, internships.
Student Life *Campus security:* 24-hour emergency response devices.
Standardized Tests *Required:* Wonderlic aptitude test (for admission).
Costs (2011–12) *Tuition:* Full-time tuition and fees vary according to degree level and program. Tuition varies by program: AAS degree in Computer Network Systems Technology tuition is $30,800. Bachelor of Science tuition is $55,000. AAS in Medical Assistant tuition is $19,850. AAS in Medical Assistant tuition is $19,850. Each program has a $110 registration fee except for nursing, the registration fee is $25. Books, supplies and equipment is included in the tuition for each program. *Payment plans:* tuition prepayment, installment, deferred payment.
Applying *Application fee:* $110. *Required:* high school transcript, interview, tour. *Required for some:* essay or personal statement.
Freshman Application Contact Hallmark College of Technology, 10401 IH 10 West, San Antonio, TX 78230. *Phone:* 210-690-9000 Ext. 212. *Web site:* http://www.hallmarkcollege.edu/.

Hallmark Institute of Aeronautics
San Antonio, Texas

- **Private** 2-year
- **Urban** 2-acre campus
- **Coed**

Undergraduates 227 full-time. Students come from 1 other state; 10% Black or African American, non-Hispanic/Latino; 49% Hispanic/Latino; 1% Asian, non-Hispanic/Latino; 0.4% Native Hawaiian or other Pacific Islander, non-Hispanic/Latino; 3% Two or more races, non-Hispanic/Latino; 0.4% Race/ethnicity unknown; 2% transferred in.
Faculty *Student/faculty ratio:* 17:1.
Academics *Calendar:* continuous. *Degree:* diplomas and associate. *Special study options:* academic remediation for entering students.
Student Life *Campus security:* 24-hour emergency response devices and patrols.
Applying *Application fee:* $110. *Required:* high school transcript, interview, assessment, tour, background check.
Freshman Application Contact Hallmark Institute of Aeronautics, 8901 Wetmore Road, San Antonio, TX 78216. *Phone:* 210-826-1000 Ext. 106. *Web site:* http://www.hallmarkcollege.edu/programs-school-of-aeronautics.aspx/.

Hill College of the Hill Junior College District
Hillsboro, Texas

Freshman Application Contact Ms. Diane Harvey, Director of Admissions/Registrar, Hill College of the Hill Junior College District, 112 Lamar Drive, Hillsboro, TX 76645. *Phone:* 254-582-2555. *Fax:* 254-582-7591. *E-mail:* diharvey@hill-college.cc.tx.us. *Web site:* http://www.hillcollege.edu/.

Houston Community College System
Houston, Texas

- **State and locally supported** 2-year, founded 1971
- **Urban** campus
- **Coed**, 63,015 undergraduate students, 30% full-time, 59% women, 41% men

Undergraduates 19,039 full-time, 43,976 part-time. 10% are from out of state; 33% Black or African American, non-Hispanic/Latino; 29% Hispanic/Latino; 10% Asian, non-Hispanic/Latino; 0.3% Native Hawaiian or other Pacific Islander, non-Hispanic/Latino; 0.2% American Indian or Alaska Native, non-Hispanic/Latino; 1% Two or more races, non-Hispanic/Latino; 1% Race/ethnicity unknown; 9% international; 7% transferred in. *Retention:* 55% of full-time freshmen returned.
Freshmen *Admission:* 10,450 enrolled.
Faculty *Total:* 2,552, 30% full-time, 19% with terminal degrees. *Student/faculty ratio:* 25:1.

Majors Accounting; animation, interactive technology, video graphics and special effects; applied horticulture/horticulture operations; automobile/automotive mechanics technology; banking and financial support services; biology/biotechnology laboratory technician; business administration and management; business automation/technology/data entry; business/corporate communications; cardiovascular technology; chemical technology; child development; cinematography and film/video production; clinical/medical laboratory science and allied professions related; clinical/medical laboratory technology; commercial photography; computer engineering technology; computer programming; computer programming (specific applications); computer systems networking and telecommunications; construction engineering technology; cosmetology; court reporting; criminal justice/police science; culinary arts; desktop publishing and digital imaging design; drafting and design technology; emergency medical technology (EMT paramedic); fashion/apparel design; fashion merchandising; fire prevention and safety technology; geographic information science and cartography; graphic and printing equipment operation/production; health and physical education/fitness; health information/medical records technology; histologic technician; hotel/motel administration; instrumentation technology; interior design; international business/trade/commerce; legal assistant/paralegal; logistics, materials, and supply chain management; manufacturing engineering technology; marketing/marketing management; music management; music performance; music theory and composition; network and system administration; nuclear medical technology; occupational therapist assistant; physical therapy technology; psychiatric/mental health services technology; public administration; radio and television broadcasting technology; radiologic technology/science; real estate; registered nursing/registered nurse; respiratory care therapy; sign language interpretation and translation; tourism and travel services management; turf and turfgrass management.
Academics *Calendar:* semesters. *Degree:* certificates and associate. *Special study options:* adult/continuing education programs, part-time degree program. *ROTC:* Army (c), Air Force (c).
Student Life *Housing:* college housing not available. *Activities and Organizations:* drama/theater group, student-run newspaper, television station. *Campus security:* 24-hour emergency response devices and patrols, late-night transport/escort service. *Student services:* personal/psychological counseling.
Costs (2011–12) *Tuition:* area resident $930 full-time, $31 per credit hour part-time; state resident $2940 full-time, $98 per credit hour part-time; nonresident $3435 full-time, $115 per credit hour part-time. Full-time tuition and fees vary according to course load. Part-time tuition and fees vary according to course load. *Required fees:* $1092 full-time, $36 per credit hour part-time, $6 per term part-time. *Payment plan:* installment.
Applying *Required for some:* high school transcript, interview. *Application deadlines:* rolling (freshmen), rolling (transfers). *Notification:* continuous (transfers).
Freshman Application Contact Ms. Mary Lemburg, Registrar, Houston Community College System, 3100 Main Street, PO Box 667517, Houston, TX 77266-7517. *Phone:* 713-718-8500. *Toll-free phone:* 877-422-6111. *Fax:* 713-718-2111. *Web site:* http://www.hccs.edu/.

Howard College
Big Spring, Texas

Freshman Application Contact Ms. TaNeal Richardson, Assistant Registrar, Howard College, 1001 Birdwell Lane, Big Spring, TX 79720-3702. *Phone:* 432-264-5105. *Toll-free phone:* 866-HC-HAWKS. *Fax:* 432-264-5604. *E-mail:* trichardson@howardcollege.edu. *Web site:* http://www.howardcollege.edu/.

ITT Technical Institute
Arlington, Texas

- **Proprietary** primarily 2-year, founded 1982, part of ITT Educational Services, Inc.
- **Suburban** campus
- **Coed**

Majors Business administration and management; communications technology; computer and information systems security; computer software technology; construction management; drafting and design technology; electrical, electronic and communications engineering technology; graphic communications; legal assistant/paralegal; network and system administration; project management.
Academics *Calendar:* quarters. *Degrees:* associate and bachelor's.
Student Life *Housing:* college housing not available.
Freshman Application Contact Director of Recruitment, ITT Technical Institute, 551 Ryan Plaza Drive, Arlington, TX 76011. *Phone:* 817-794-5100. *Toll-free phone:* 888-288-4950. *Fax:* 817-275-8446. *Web site:* http://www.itt-tech.edu/.

ITT Technical Institute
Austin, Texas

- **Proprietary** primarily 2-year, founded 1985, part of ITT Educational Services, Inc.
- **Urban** campus
- **Coed**

Majors Accounting technology and bookkeeping; business administration and management; communications technology; computer and information systems security; computer software technology; drafting and design technology; electrical, electronic and communications engineering technology; graphic communications; legal assistant/paralegal; network and system administration; project management.

Academics *Calendar:* quarters. *Degrees:* associate and bachelor's.

Student Life *Housing:* college housing not available.

Financial Aid Of all full-time matriculated undergraduates who enrolled in 2010, 1 Federal Work-Study job.

Freshman Application Contact Director of Recruitment, ITT Technical Institute, 6330 Highway 290 East, Austin, TX 78723. *Phone:* 512-467-6800. *Toll-free phone:* 800-431-0677. *Fax:* 512-467-6677. *Web site:* http://www.itt-tech.edu/.

ITT Technical Institute
DeSoto, Texas

- **Proprietary** primarily 2-year
- **Coed**

Majors Business administration and management; communications technology; computer and information systems security; drafting and design technology; electrical, electronic and communications engineering technology; graphic communications; legal assistant/paralegal; network and system administration; project management.

Academics *Degrees:* associate and bachelor's.

Freshman Application Contact Director of Recruitment, ITT Technical Institute, 921 West Belt Line Road, Suite 181, DeSoto, TX 75115. *Phone:* 972-274-8600. *Toll-free phone:* 877-854-5728. *Web site:* http://www.itt-tech.edu/.

ITT Technical Institute
Houston, Texas

- **Proprietary** primarily 2-year, founded 1985, part of ITT Educational Services, Inc.
- **Suburban** campus
- **Coed**

Majors Business administration and management; communications technology; computer and information systems security; construction management; drafting and design technology; electrical, electronic and communications engineering technology; graphic communications; legal assistant/paralegal; network and system administration; project management.

Academics *Calendar:* quarters. *Degrees:* associate and bachelor's.

Student Life *Housing:* college housing not available.

Freshman Application Contact Director of Recruitment, ITT Technical Institute, 15651 North Freeway, Houston, TX 77090. *Phone:* 281-873-0512. *Toll-free phone:* 800-879-6486. *Web site:* http://www.itt-tech.edu/.

ITT Technical Institute
Houston, Texas

- **Proprietary** primarily 2-year, founded 1983, part of ITT Educational Services, Inc.
- **Urban** campus
- **Coed**

Majors Business administration and management; communications technology; computer and information systems security; construction management; drafting and design technology; electrical, electronic and communications engineering technology; graphic communications; legal assistant/paralegal; network and system administration; project management.

Academics *Calendar:* quarters. *Degrees:* associate and bachelor's.

Student Life *Housing:* college housing not available.

Freshman Application Contact Director of Recruitment, ITT Technical Institute, 2950 South Gessner, Houston, TX 77063-3751. *Phone:* 713-952-2294. *Toll-free phone:* 800-235-4787. *Web site:* http://www.itt-tech.edu/.

ITT Technical Institute
Richardson, Texas

- **Proprietary** primarily 2-year, founded 1989, part of ITT Educational Services, Inc.
- **Suburban** campus
- **Coed**

Majors Accounting technology and bookkeeping; business administration and management; communications technology; computer and information systems security; computer software technology; construction management; drafting and design technology; electrical, electronic and communications engineering technology; graphic communications; legal assistant/paralegal; network and system administration; project management; registered nursing/registered nurse.

Academics *Calendar:* quarters. *Degrees:* associate and bachelor's.

Student Life *Housing:* college housing not available.

Financial Aid Of all full-time matriculated undergraduates who enrolled in 2010, 5 Federal Work-Study jobs (averaging $5000).

Freshman Application Contact Director of Recruitment, ITT Technical Institute, 2101 Waterview Parkway, Richardson, TX 75080. *Phone:* 972-690-9100. *Toll-free phone:* 888-488-5761. *Web site:* http://www.itt-tech.edu/.

ITT Technical Institute
San Antonio, Texas

- **Proprietary** primarily 2-year, founded 1988, part of ITT Educational Services, Inc.
- **Urban** campus
- **Coed**

Majors Business administration and management; communications technology; computer and information systems security; computer software technology; construction management; drafting and design technology; electrical, electronic and communications engineering technology; graphic communications; legal assistant/paralegal; network and system administration; project management.

Academics *Calendar:* quarters. *Degrees:* associate and bachelor's.

Student Life *Housing:* college housing not available.

Freshman Application Contact Director of Recruitment, ITT Technical Institute, 5700 Northwest Parkway, San Antonio, TX 78249-3303. *Phone:* 210-694-4612. *Toll-free phone:* 800-880-0570. *Web site:* http://www.itt-tech.edu/.

ITT Technical Institute
Waco, Texas

- **Proprietary** primarily 2-year, part of ITT Educational Services, Inc.
- **Coed**

Majors Business administration and management; communications technology; computer and information systems security; drafting and design technology; electrical, electronic and communications engineering technology; graphic communications; legal assistant/paralegal; network and system administration; project management.

Academics *Calendar:* quarters. *Degrees:* associate and bachelor's.

Freshman Application Contact Director of Recruitment, ITT Technical Institute, 3700 S. Jack Kultgen Expressway, Suite 100, Waco, TX 76706. *Phone:* 254-881-2200. *Toll-free phone:* 877-201-7143. *Web site:* http://www.itt-tech.edu/.

ITT Technical Institute
Webster, Texas

- **Proprietary** primarily 2-year, founded 1995, part of ITT Educational Services, Inc.
- **Coed**

Majors Business administration and management; communications technology; computer and information systems security; computer software technology; drafting and design technology; electrical, electronic and communications engineering technology; graphic communications; legal assistant/paralegal; network and system administration; project management.

Academics *Calendar:* quarters. *Degrees:* associate and bachelor's.

Student Life *Housing:* college housing not available.

Freshman Application Contact Director of Recruitment, ITT Technical Institute, 1001 Magnolia Avenue, Webster, TX 77598. *Phone:* 281-316-4700. *Toll-free phone:* 888-488-9347. *Web site:* http://www.itt-tech.edu/.

Jacksonville College

Jacksonville, Texas

Freshman Application Contact Danny Morris, Director of Admissions, Jacksonville College, 105 B.J. Albritton Drive, Jacksonville, TX 75766. *Phone:* 903-589-7110. *Toll-free phone:* 800-256-8522. *E-mail:* admissions@jacksonville-college.org. *Web site:* http://www.jacksonville-college.edu/.

Kaplan College, Arlington Campus

Arlington, Texas

- **Proprietary** 2-year
- **Coed**

Majors Computer systems networking and telecommunications; criminal justice/law enforcement administration.

Academics *Degree:* diplomas and associate.

Freshman Application Contact Kaplan College, Arlington Campus, 2241 South Watson Road, Arlington, TX 76010. *Phone:* 866-249-2074. *Toll-free phone:* 800-935-1857. *Web site:* http://arlington.kaplancollege.com/.

Kaplan College, Beaumont Campus

Beaumont, Texas

- **Proprietary** 2-year
- **Coed**

Majors Computer systems networking and telecommunications; criminal justice/law enforcement administration.

Academics *Calendar:* continuous. *Degree:* diplomas and associate.

Freshman Application Contact Admissions Office, Kaplan College, Beaumont Campus, 6115 Eastex Freeway, Beaumont, TX 77706. *Phone:* 409-833-2722. *Toll-free phone:* 800-935-1857. *Web site:* http://beaumont.kaplancollege.com/.

Kaplan College, Brownsville Campus

Brownsville, Texas

- **Proprietary** 2-year
- **Coed**

Majors Medical office management.

Academics *Degree:* diplomas and associate.

Freshman Application Contact Director of Admissions, Kaplan College, Brownsville Campus, 1900 North Expressway, Suite O, Brownsville, TX 78521. *Phone:* 956-547-8200. *Web site:* http://brownsville.kaplancollege.com/.

Kaplan College, Corpus Christi Campus

Corpus Christi, Texas

- **Proprietary** 2-year
- **Coed**

Majors Criminal justice/law enforcement administration; medical office management.

Academics *Calendar:* other. *Degree:* diplomas and associate.

Freshman Application Contact Admissions Director, Kaplan College, Corpus Christi Campus, 1620 South Padre Island Drive, Suite 600, Corpus Christi, TX 78416. *Phone:* 361-852-2900. *Web site:* http://corpus-christi.kaplancollege.com/.

Kaplan College, Dallas Campus

Dallas, Texas

- **Proprietary** 2-year, founded 1987
- **Coed**

Majors Criminal justice/law enforcement administration; legal assistant/paralegal.

Academics *Degree:* diplomas and associate.

Freshman Application Contact Kaplan College, Dallas Campus, 12005 Ford Road, Suite 100, Dallas, TX 75234. *Phone:* 972-385-1446. *Toll-free phone:* 800-935-1857. *Web site:* http://dallas.kaplancollege.com/.

Kaplan College, El Paso Campus

El Paso, Texas

- **Proprietary** 2-year
- **Coed**

Majors Computer systems networking and telecommunications; criminal justice/law enforcement administration.

Academics *Degree:* diplomas and associate.

Freshman Application Contact Director of Admissions, Kaplan College, El Paso Campus, 8360 Burnham Road, Suite 100, El Paso, TX 79907. *Web site:* http://el-paso.kaplancollege.com/.

Kaplan College, Fort Worth Campus

Fort Worth, Texas

- **Proprietary** 2-year
- **Coed**

Majors Criminal justice/law enforcement administration.

Academics *Degree:* diplomas and associate.

Freshman Application Contact Director of Admissions, Kaplan College, Fort Worth Campus, 2001 Beach Street, Suite 201, Fort Worth, TX 76103. *Phone:* 817-413-2000. *Web site:* http://fort-worth.kaplancollege.com/.

Kaplan College, Laredo Campus

Laredo, Texas

- **Proprietary** 2-year
- **Coed**

Majors Criminal justice/law enforcement administration.

Academics *Degree:* diplomas and associate.

Freshman Application Contact Admissions Office, Kaplan College, Laredo Campus, 6410 McPherson Road, Laredo, TX 78041. *Phone:* 956-717-5909. *Toll-free phone:* 800-935-1857. *Web site:* http://laredo.kaplancollege.com/.

Kaplan College, Lubbock Campus

Lubbock, Texas

- **Proprietary** 2-year
- **Coed**

Majors Criminal justice/law enforcement administration.

Academics *Degree:* diplomas and associate.

Freshman Application Contact Admissions Office, Kaplan College, Lubbock Campus, 1421 Ninth Street, Lubbock, TX 79401. *Phone:* 806-765-7051. *Toll-free phone:* 800-935-1857. *Web site:* http://lubbock.kaplancollege.com/.

Kaplan College, Midland Campus

Midland, Texas

- **Proprietary** 2-year
- **Coed**

Majors Criminal justice/law enforcement administration.

Academics *Degree:* diplomas and associate.

Freshman Application Contact Director of Admissions, Kaplan College, Midland Campus, 4320 West Illinois Avenue, Suite A, Midland, TX 79703. *Phone:* 432-681-3390. *Toll-free phone:* 800-935-1857. *Web site:* http://midland.kaplancollege.com/.

Kaplan College, San Antonio Campus

San Antonio, Texas

- **Proprietary** 2-year
- **Coed**

Majors Health information/medical records technology; legal assistant/paralegal.

Academics *Degree:* certificates, diplomas, and associate.

Freshman Application Contact Admissions Office, Kaplan College, San Antonio Campus, 6441 NW Loop 410, San Antonio, TX 78238. *Phone:* 210-308-8584. *Toll-free phone:* 800-935-1857. *Web site:* http://wsan-antonio.kaplancollege.com/.

Kaplan College, San Antonio–San Pedro Area Campus

San Antonio, Texas

- **Proprietary** 2-year
- **Coed**

Majors Criminal justice/law enforcement administration; medical office management.

Academics *Degree:* diplomas and associate.

Freshman Application Contact Director of Admissions, Kaplan College, San Antonio–San Pedro Area Campus, 7142 San Pedro Avenue, Suite 100, San Antonio, TX 78216. *Toll-free phone:* 800-935-1857. *Web site:* http://nsan-antonio.kaplancollege.com/.

KD Studio

Dallas, Texas

- **Proprietary** 2-year, founded 1979
- **Urban** campus
- **Coed,** 177 undergraduate students

Undergraduates 9% are from out of state; 46% Black or African American, non-Hispanic/Latino; 18% Hispanic/Latino; 2% Asian, non-Hispanic/Latino. *Retention:* 69% of full-time freshmen returned.

Freshmen *Admission:* 21 applied, 21 admitted.

Faculty *Total:* 28, 100% full-time, 4% with terminal degrees. *Student/faculty ratio:* 6:1.

Majors Acting; film/cinema/video studies; musical theater.

Academics *Calendar:* semesters. *Degree:* associate. *Special study options:* cooperative education.

Library KD Studio Library with 800 titles, 15 serial subscriptions.

Student Life *Housing:* college housing not available. *Activities and Organizations:* drama/theater group, Student Council. *Campus security:* 24-hour emergency response devices and patrols.

Costs (2011–12) *Tuition:* $12,860 full-time, $348 per credit part-time. Full-time tuition and fees vary according to program. No tuition increase for student's term of enrollment. *Required fees:* $200 full-time, $200 per year part-time. *Payment plan:* installment.

Applying *Options:* deferred entrance. *Application fee:* $100. *Required:* essay or personal statement, high school transcript, interview, audition. *Application deadlines:* rolling (freshmen), rolling (transfers).

Freshman Application Contact Mr. T. A. Taylor, Director of Education, KD Studio, 2600 Stemmons Freeway, Suite 117, Dallas, TX 75207. *Phone:* 214-638-0484. *Toll-free phone:* 877-278-2283. *Fax:* 214-630-5140. *E-mail:* tataylor@kdstudio.com. *Web site:* http://www.kdstudio.com/.

Kilgore College

Kilgore, Texas

- **State and locally supported** 2-year, founded 1935
- **Small-town** 35-acre campus with easy access to Dallas-Fort Worth
- **Coed,** 6,391 undergraduate students, 47% full-time, 63% women, 37% men

Undergraduates 2,981 full-time, 3,410 part-time. Students come from 23 states and territories; 33 other countries; 1% are from out of state; 20% Black or African American, non-Hispanic/Latino; 11% Hispanic/Latino; 0.8% Asian, non-Hispanic/Latino; 0.5% American Indian or Alaska Native, non-Hispanic/Latino; 3% Two or more races, non-Hispanic/Latino; 0.5% Race/ethnicity unknown; 1% international; 7% transferred in; 7% live on campus. *Retention:* 48% of full-time freshmen returned.

Freshmen *Admission:* 1,279 enrolled.

Faculty *Total:* 398, 39% full-time. *Student/faculty ratio:* 17:1.

Majors Accounting technology and bookkeeping; aerospace, aeronautical and astronautical/space engineering; agriculture; architecture; art; autobody/collision and repair technology; automobile/automotive mechanics technology; biological and physical sciences; business administration and management; business/commerce; chemical engineering; chemistry; child-care and support services management; child-care provision; civil engineering; clinical/medical laboratory technology; commercial and advertising art; commercial photography; computer and information sciences; computer installation and repair technology; computer programming; computer systems networking and telecommunications; corrections; criminal justice/law enforcement administration; dance; diesel mechanics technology; drafting and design technology; dramatic/theater arts; electrical, electronic and communications engineering technology; elementary education; emergency medical technology (EMT paramedic); English; executive assistant/executive secretary; fashion merchandising; forestry; general studies; geology/earth science; health teacher education; heating, air conditioning, ventilation and refrigeration maintenance technology; journalism; legal assistant/paralegal; management information systems; mathematics; mechanical engineering; medical radiologic technology; metallurgical technology; multi/interdisciplinary studies related; music; occupational safety and health technology; occupational therapist assistant; operations management; petroleum engineering; physical education teaching and coaching; physical therapy; physical therapy technology; physics; pre-dentistry studies; pre-law studies; premedical studies; pre-pharmacy studies; pre-veterinary studies; psychology; radiologic technology/science; registered nursing/registered nurse; religious studies; social sciences; surgical technology; web/multimedia management and webmaster; welding technology.

Academics *Calendar:* semesters. *Degree:* certificates and associate. *Special study options:* academic remediation for entering students, adult/continuing education programs, advanced placement credit, cooperative education, distance learning, English as a second language, internships, part-time degree program, services for LD students, student-designed majors, summer session for credit.

Library Randolph C. Watson Library plus 1 other with 65,000 titles, 6,679 serial subscriptions, 13,351 audiovisual materials, an OPAC, a Web page.

Student Life *Housing Options:* coed, men-only, women-only. Campus housing is university owned. *Activities and Organizations:* drama/theater group, student-run newspaper, choral group, marching band. *Campus security:* 24-hour emergency response devices and patrols. *Student services:* personal/psychological counseling.

Athletics Member NJCAA. *Intercollegiate sports:* basketball M(s)/W(s), cheerleading M(s)/W(s), football M(s). *Intramural sports:* basketball M/W, football M/W, racquetball M/W, tennis M/W, volleyball M/W.

Costs (2011–12) *Tuition:* area resident $636 full-time, $27 per semester hour part-time; state resident $2112 full-time, $88 per semester hour part-time; non-resident $3168 full-time, $132 per semester hour part-time. *Required fees:* $624 full-time, $26 per semester hour part-time. *Room and board:* $4270. Room and board charges vary according to board plan and housing facility. *Payment plan:* installment. *Waivers:* senior citizens and employees or children of employees.

Financial Aid Of all full-time matriculated undergraduates who enrolled in 2010, 80 Federal Work-Study jobs (averaging $2500). *Financial aid deadline:* 6/1.

Applying *Options:* electronic application, early admission. *Required:* high school transcript. *Required for some:* interview. *Application deadlines:* rolling (freshmen), rolling (out-of-state freshmen), rolling (transfers).

Freshman Application Contact Kilgore College, 1100 Broadway Boulevard, Kilgore, TX 75662-3299. *Phone:* 903-983-8200. *E-mail:* register@kilgore.cc.tx.us. *Web site:* http://www.kilgore.edu/.

Lamar Institute of Technology

Beaumont, Texas

Freshman Application Contact Admissions Office, Lamar Institute of Technology, 855 East Lavaca, Beaumont, TX 77705. *Phone:* 409-880-8354. *Toll-free phone:* 800-950-6989. *Web site:* http://www.lit.edu/.

Lamar State College–Orange

Orange, Texas

Freshman Application Contact Kerry Olson, Director of Admissions and Financial Aid, Lamar State College–Orange, 410 Front Street, Orange, TX 77632. *Phone:* 409-882-3362. *Fax:* 409-882-3374. *Web site:* http://www.lsco.edu/.

Lamar State College–Port Arthur

Port Arthur, Texas

Freshman Application Contact Ms. Connie Nicholas, Registrar, Lamar State College–Port Arthur, PO Box 310, Port Arthur, TX 77641-0310. *Phone:* 409-984-6165. *Toll-free phone:* 800-477-5872. *Fax:* 409-984-6025. *E-mail:* nichoca@lamarpa.edu. *Web site:* http://www.lamarpa.edu/.

Laredo Community College

Laredo, Texas

Freshman Application Contact Ms. Josie Soliz, Admissions Records Supervisor, Laredo Community College, Laredo, TX 78040-4395. *Phone:* 956-721-5177. *Fax:* 956-721-5493. *Web site:* http://www.laredo.edu/.

Le Cordon Bleu College of Culinary Arts in Austin

Austin, Texas

Director of Admissions Paula Paulette, Vice President of Marketing and Admissions, Le Cordon Bleu College of Culinary Arts in Austin, 3110

Esperanza Crossing, Suite 100, Austin, TX 78758. *Phone:* 512-837-2665. *Toll-free phone:* 888-559-7222. *E-mail:* ppaulette@txca.com. *Web site:* http://www.chefs.edu/Austin.

Lee College

Baytown, Texas

Director of Admissions Ms. Becki Griffith, Registrar, Lee College, PO Box 818, Baytown, TX 77522-0818. *Phone:* 281-425-6399. *E-mail:* bgriffit@lee.edu. *Web site:* http://www.lee.edu/.

Lone Star College–CyFair

Cypress, Texas

- **State and locally supported** 2-year, founded 2002, part of Lone Star College System
- **Suburban** campus with easy access to Houston
- **Coed**

Undergraduates 4,855 full-time, 13,252 part-time. Students come from 19 states and territories; 68 other countries; 1% are from out of state; 0.4% Black or African American, non-Hispanic/Latino; 13% Hispanic/Latino; 10% Asian, non-Hispanic/Latino; 0.4% American Indian or Alaska Native, non-Hispanic/Latino; 9% Race/ethnicity unknown; 0.6% international.

Faculty *Student/faculty ratio:* 8:1.

Academics *Calendar:* semesters. *Degree:* certificates, diplomas, and associate. *Special study options:* academic remediation for entering students, accelerated degree program, adult/continuing education programs, advanced placement credit, cooperative education, distance learning, double majors, English as a second language, honors programs, independent study, internships, part-time degree program, services for LD students, study abroad, summer session for credit.

Student Life *Campus security:* 24-hour emergency response devices and patrols, late-night transport/escort service.

Costs (2011–12) *Tuition:* area resident $960 full-time, $40 per credit hour part-time; state resident $2640 full-time, $110 per credit hour part-time; nonresident $3000 full-time, $125 per credit hour part-time. Full-time tuition and fees vary according to program. Part-time tuition and fees vary according to program. *Required fees:* $416 full-time, $16 per credit hour part-time, $32 per term part-time.

Applying *Options:* electronic application, early admission.

Freshman Application Contact Admissions Office, Lone Star College–CyFair, 9191 Barker Cypress Road, Cypress, TX 77433-1383. *Phone:* 281-290-3200. *E-mail:* cfc.info@lonestar.edu. *Web site:* http://www.lonestar.edu/cyfair.

Lone Star College–Kingwood

Kingwood, Texas

- **State and locally supported** 2-year, founded 1984, part of Lone Star College System
- **Suburban** 264-acre campus with easy access to Houston
- **Coed**

Undergraduates 2,459 full-time, 8,420 part-time. Students come from 14 states and territories; 37 other countries; 1% are from out of state; 14% Black or African American, non-Hispanic/Latino; 20% Hispanic/Latino; 4% Asian, non-Hispanic/Latino; 0.5% American Indian or Alaska Native, non-Hispanic/Latino; 8% Race/ethnicity unknown; 0.7% international.

Faculty *Student/faculty ratio:* 7:1.

Academics *Calendar:* semesters. *Degree:* certificates and associate. *Special study options:* academic remediation for entering students, accelerated degree program, adult/continuing education programs, advanced placement credit, cooperative education, distance learning, double majors, English as a second language, honors programs, independent study, internships, part-time degree program, services for LD students, study abroad, summer session for credit.

Student Life *Campus security:* 24-hour emergency response devices and patrols, late-night transport/escort service.

Costs (2011–12) *Tuition:* area resident $960 full-time, $40 per credit hour part-time; state resident $2640 full-time, $110 per credit hour part-time; nonresident $3000 full-time, $125 per credit hour part-time. Full-time tuition and fees vary according to program. Part-time tuition and fees vary according to program. *Required fees:* $416 full-time, $16 per credit hour part-time, $32 per term part-time.

Financial Aid Of all full-time matriculated undergraduates who enrolled in 2009, 28 Federal Work-Study jobs, 6 state and other part-time jobs. *Financial aid deadline:* 4/1.

Applying *Options:* electronic application, early admission.

Freshman Application Contact Admissions Office, Lone Star College–Kingwood, 20000 Kingwood Drive, Kingwood, TX 77339. *Phone:* 281-312-1525. *Fax:* 281-312-1477. *E-mail:* kingwoodadvising@lonestar.edu. *Web site:* http://www.lonestar.edu/kingwood.htm.

Lone Star College–Montgomery

Conroe, Texas

- **State and locally supported** 2-year, founded 1995, part of Lone Star College System
- **Suburban** campus with easy access to Houston
- **Coed**

Undergraduates 3,331 full-time, 9,322 part-time. Students come from 25 states and territories; 48 other countries; 2% are from out of state; 9% Black or African American, non-Hispanic/Latino; 20% Hispanic/Latino; 4% Asian, non-Hispanic/Latino; 0.6% American Indian or Alaska Native, non-Hispanic/Latino; 4% Race/ethnicity unknown; 0.6% international.

Faculty *Student/faculty ratio:* 8:1.

Academics *Calendar:* semesters. *Degree:* certificates and associate. *Special study options:* academic remediation for entering students, adult/continuing education programs, advanced placement credit, cooperative education, distance learning, double majors, English as a second language, honors programs, independent study, internships, part-time degree program, services for LD students, study abroad, summer session for credit.

Student Life *Campus security:* 24-hour emergency response devices and patrols, late-night transport/escort service.

Costs (2011–12) *Tuition:* area resident $960 full-time, $40 per credit hour part-time; state resident $2640 full-time, $110 per credit hour part-time; nonresident $3000 full-time, $125 per credit hour part-time. Full-time tuition and fees vary according to program. Part-time tuition and fees vary according to program. *Required fees:* $416 full-time, $16 per credit hour part-time, $32 per term part-time.

Financial Aid Of all full-time matriculated undergraduates who enrolled in 2010, 25 Federal Work-Study jobs (averaging $2500). 4 state and other part-time jobs.

Applying *Options:* electronic application, early admission.

Freshman Application Contact Lone Star College–Montgomery, 3200 College Park Drive, Conroe, TX 77384. *Phone:* 936-273-7236. *Web site:* http://www.lonestar.edu/montgomery.

Lone Star College–North Harris

Houston, Texas

- **State and locally supported** 2-year, founded 1972, part of Lone Star College System
- **Suburban** campus with easy access to Houston
- **Coed**

Undergraduates 3,232 full-time, 13,124 part-time. Students come from 16 states and territories; 59 other countries; 0.9% are from out of state; 27% Black or African American, non-Hispanic/Latino; 34% Hispanic/Latino; 7% Asian, non-Hispanic/Latino; 0.3% American Indian or Alaska Native, non-Hispanic/Latino; 7% Race/ethnicity unknown; 1% international.

Faculty *Student/faculty ratio:* 7:1.

Academics *Calendar:* semesters. *Degree:* certificates and associate. *Special study options:* academic remediation for entering students, adult/continuing education programs, advanced placement credit, cooperative education, distance learning, double majors, English as a second language, honors programs, independent study, internships, part-time degree program, services for LD students, study abroad, summer session for credit.

Student Life *Campus security:* 24-hour emergency response devices and patrols, late-night transport/escort service.

Costs (2011–12) *Tuition:* area resident $960 full-time, $40 per credit hour part-time; state resident $2640 full-time, $110 per credit hour part-time; nonresident $3000 full-time, $125 per credit hour part-time. Full-time tuition and fees vary according to program. Part-time tuition and fees vary according to program. *Required fees:* $416 full-time, $16 per credit hour part-time, $32 per term part-time.

Applying *Options:* electronic application, early admission.

Freshman Application Contact Admissions Office, Lone Star College–North Harris, 2700 W. W. Thorne Drive, Houston, TX 77073-3499. *Phone:* 281-618-5410. *E-mail:* nhcounselor@lonestar.edu. *Web site:* http://www.lonestar.edu/northharris.

Lone Star College–Tomball
Tomball, Texas

- **State and locally supported** 2-year, founded 1988, part of Lone Star College System
- **Suburban** campus with easy access to Houston
- **Coed**

Undergraduates 2,267 full-time, 9,077 part-time. Students come from 12 states and territories; 51 other countries; 1% are from out of state; 11% Black or African American, non-Hispanic/Latino; 21% Hispanic/Latino; 7% Asian, non-Hispanic/Latino; 0.6% American Indian or Alaska Native, non-Hispanic/Latino; 4% Race/ethnicity unknown; 0.8% international.

Faculty *Student/faculty ratio:* 8:1.

Academics *Calendar:* semesters. *Degree:* certificates and associate. *Special study options:* academic remediation for entering students, adult/continuing education programs, advanced placement credit, cooperative education, distance learning, double majors, English as a second language, honors programs, independent study, internships, part-time degree program, services for LD students, study abroad, summer session for credit.

Student Life *Campus security:* 24-hour emergency response devices and patrols, late-night transport/escort service, trained security personnel during open hours.

Costs (2011–12) *Tuition:* area resident $960 full-time, $40 per credit hour part-time; state resident $2640 full-time, $110 per credit hour part-time; nonresident $3000 full-time, $125 per credit hour part-time. Full-time tuition and fees vary according to program. Part-time tuition and fees vary according to program. *Required fees:* $416 full-time, $16 per credit hour part-time, $32 per term part-time.

Financial Aid Of all full-time matriculated undergraduates who enrolled in 2010, 34 Federal Work-Study jobs (averaging $3000).

Applying *Options:* electronic application, early admission.

Freshman Application Contact Admissions Office, Lone Star College–Tomball, 30555 Tomball Parkway, Tomball, TX 77375-4036. *Phone:* 281-351-3310. *E-mail:* tcinfo@lonestar.edu. *Web site:* http://www.lonestar.edu/tomball.

Lon Morris College
Jacksonville, Texas

Freshman Application Contact Mr. Rafael Gonzalez, Director of Enrollment Management, Lon Morris College, 800 College Avenue, Jacksonville, TX 75766. *Phone:* 903-589-4059. *Toll-free phone:* 800-259-5753. *Web site:* http://www.lonmorris.edu/.

McLennan Community College
Waco, Texas

Freshman Application Contact Dr. Vivian G. Jefferson, Director, Admissions and Recruitment, McLennan Community College, 1400 College Drive, Waco, TX 76708. *Phone:* 254-299-8689. *Fax:* 254-299-8694. *E-mail:* vjefferson@mclennan.edu. *Web site:* http://www.mclennan.edu/.

Mountain View College
Dallas, Texas

- **State and locally supported** 2-year, founded 1970, part of Dallas County Community College District System
- **Urban** 200-acre campus
- **Coed**

Undergraduates 27% Black or African American, non-Hispanic/Latino; 50% Hispanic/Latino; 5% Asian, non-Hispanic/Latino; 0.4% American Indian or Alaska Native, non-Hispanic/Latino; 2% Race/ethnicity unknown; 0.3% international. *Retention:* 45% of full-time freshmen returned.

Faculty *Student/faculty ratio:* 27:1.

Academics *Calendar:* semesters. *Degree:* certificates and associate. *Special study options:* academic remediation for entering students, adult/continuing education programs, advanced placement credit, cooperative education, distance learning, double majors, English as a second language, external degree program, freshman honors college, honors programs, independent study, internships, part-time degree program, services for LD students, summer session for credit.

Student Life *Campus security:* 24-hour patrols, late-night transport/escort service.

Athletics Member NJCAA.

Financial Aid Of all full-time matriculated undergraduates who enrolled in 2010, 145 Federal Work-Study jobs (averaging $2700).

Applying *Options:* electronic application, early admission, deferred entrance. *Required:* high school transcript.

Freshman Application Contact Ms. Glenda Hall, Director of Admissions, Mountain View College, 4849 West Illinois Avenue, Dallas, TX 75211-6599. *Phone:* 214-860-8666. *Fax:* 214-860-8570. *E-mail:* ghall@dcccd.edu. *Web site:* http://www.mountainviewcollege.edu/.

Navarro College
Corsicana, Texas

Freshman Application Contact David Edwards, Registrar, Navarro College, 3200 West 7th Avenue, Corsicana, TX 75110-4899. *Phone:* 903-875-7348. *Toll-free phone:* 800-NAVARRO (in-state); 800-628-2776 (out-of-state). *Fax:* 903-875-7353. *E-mail:* david.edwards@navarrocollege.edu. *Web site:* http://www.navarrocollege.edu/.

North Central Texas College
Gainesville, Texas

Freshman Application Contact Melinda Carroll, Director of Admissions/Registrar, North Central Texas College, 1525 West California, Gainesville, TX 76240-4699. *Phone:* 940-668-7731. *Fax:* 940-668-7075. *E-mail:* mcarroll@nctc.edu. *Web site:* http://www.nctc.edu/.

Northeast Texas Community College
Mount Pleasant, Texas

Freshman Application Contact Ms. Sherry Keys, Director of Admissions, Northeast Texas Community College, PO Box 1307, Mount Pleasant, TX 75456-1307. *Phone:* 903-572-1911 Ext. 263. *Toll-free phone:* 800-870-0142. *Web site:* http://www.ntcc.edu/.

North Lake College
Irving, Texas

Freshman Application Contact Admissions/Registration Office (A405), North Lake College, 5001 North MacArthur Boulevard, Irving, TX 75038. *Phone:* 972-273-3183. *Web site:* http://www.northlakecollege.edu/.

Northwest Vista College
San Antonio, Texas

Freshman Application Contact Dr. Elaine Lang, Interim Director of Enrollment Management, Northwest Vista College, 3535 North Ellison Drive, San Antonio, TX 78251. *Phone:* 210-348-2016. *E-mail:* elang@accd.edu. *Web site:* http://www.alamo.edu/nvc/.

Odessa College
Odessa, Texas

Freshman Application Contact Ms. Tracy Hilliard, Associate Director, Admissions, Odessa College, 201 West University Avenue, Odessa, TX 79764. *Phone:* 432-335-6816. *Fax:* 432-335-6303. *E-mail:* thilliard@odessa.edu. *Web site:* http://www.odessa.edu/.

Palo Alto College
San Antonio, Texas

Freshman Application Contact Ms. Rachel Montejano, Director of Enrollment Management, Palo Alto College, 1400 West Villaret Boulevard, San Antonio, TX 78224. *Phone:* 210-921-5279. *Fax:* 210-921-5310. *E-mail:* pacar@accd.edu. *Web site:* http://www.alamo.edu/pac/.

Panola College
Carthage, Texas

- **State and locally supported** 2-year, founded 1947
- **Small-town** 35-acre campus
- **Endowment** $2.4 million
- **Coed**, 2,562 undergraduate students, 44% full-time, 70% women, 30% men

Undergraduates 1,134 full-time, 1,428 part-time. Students come from 23 states and territories; 11 other countries; 8% are from out of state; 22% Black or African American, non-Hispanic/Latino; 7% Hispanic/Latino; 0.7% Asian, non-Hispanic/Latino; 1% American Indian or Alaska Native, non-Hispanic/Latino; 0.4% Two or more races, non-Hispanic/Latino; 1% international; 12% transferred in; 8% live on campus. *Retention:* 39% of full-time freshmen returned.

Freshmen *Admission:* 474 admitted, 474 enrolled.

Faculty *Total:* 132, 46% full-time, 5% with terminal degrees. *Student/faculty ratio:* 19:1.

Majors Administrative assistant and secretarial science; business automation/technology/data entry; general studies; health information/medical records technology; industrial technology; information science/studies; middle school education; multi/interdisciplinary studies related; occupational therapist assistant; registered nursing/registered nurse; secondary education.

Academics *Calendar:* semesters. *Degree:* certificates and associate. *Special study options:* academic remediation for entering students, advanced placement credit, cooperative education, distance learning, English as a second language, part-time degree program, services for LD students, summer session for credit.

Library M. P. Baker Library with 103,639 titles, 31,932 serial subscriptions, 4,870 audiovisual materials, an OPAC, a Web page.

Student Life *Housing Options:* coed. Campus housing is university owned. *Activities and Organizations:* drama/theater group, student-run newspaper, choral group, Student Government Organization, Student Occupational Therapy Assistant Club, Baptist Student Ministries, Texas Nursing Student Association, Phi Theta Kappa. *Campus security:* controlled dormitory access.

Athletics Member NCAA, NJCAA. *Intercollegiate sports:* baseball M(s), basketball M(s)/W(s), volleyball W(s). *Intramural sports:* basketball M/W, football M/W, racquetball M/W, table tennis M/W, volleyball M/W, weight lifting M/W.

Applying *Options:* electronic application, early admission. *Required for some:* high school transcript. *Recommended:* high school transcript. *Application deadlines:* rolling (freshmen), rolling (out-of-state freshmen), rolling (transfers). *Notification:* continuous (freshmen), continuous (out-of-state freshmen), continuous (transfers).

Freshman Application Contact Mr. Jeremty Dorman, Registrar/Director of Admissions, Panola College, 1109 West Panola Street, Carthage, TX 75633-2397. *Phone:* 903-693-2009. *Fax:* 903-693-2031. *E-mail:* bsimpson@panola.edu. *Web site:* http://www.panola.edu/.

Paris Junior College
Paris, Texas

Freshman Application Contact Paris Junior College, 2400 Clarksville Street, Paris, TX 75460-6298. *Phone:* 903-782-0425. *Toll-free phone:* 800-232-5804. *Web site:* http://www.parisjc.edu/.

Pima Medical Institute
Houston, Texas

- **Proprietary** 2-year
- **Urban** campus
- **Coed**

Academics *Special study options:* cooperative education, distance learning, internships.

Standardized Tests *Required:* Wonderlic Scholastic Level Exam (for admission).

Applying *Required:* high school transcript, interview.

Freshman Application Contact Christopher Luebke, Corporate Director of Admissions, Pima Medical Institute, 2160 South Power Road, Mesa, AZ 85209. *Phone:* 480-610-6063. *E-mail:* cluebke@pmi.edu. *Web site:* http://www.pmi.edu/.

Ranger College
Ranger, Texas

Freshman Application Contact Dr. Jim Davis, Dean of Students, Ranger College, 1100 College Circle, Ranger, TX 76470. *Phone:* 254-647-3234 Ext. 110. *Web site:* http://www.ranger.cc.tx.us/.

Remington College–Dallas Campus
Garland, Texas

Director of Admissions Ms. Shonda Wisenhunt, Remington College–Dallas Campus, 1800 Eastgate Drive, Garland, TX 75041. *Phone:* 972-686-7878. *Fax:* 972-686-5116. *E-mail:* shonda.wisenhunt@remingtoncollege.edu. *Web site:* http://www.remingtoncollege.edu/.

Remington College–Fort Worth Campus
Fort Worth, Texas

Director of Admissions Marcia Kline, Director of Recruitment, Remington College–Fort Worth Campus, 300 East Loop 820, Fort Worth, TX 76112. *Phone:* 817-451-0017. *Toll-free phone:* 800-560-6192. *Fax:* 817-496-1257.

E-mail: marcia.kline@remingtoncollege.edu. *Web site:* http://www.remingtoncollege.edu/.

Remington College–Houston Campus
Houston, Texas

Director of Admissions Kevin Wilkinson, Director of Recruitment, Remington College–Houston Campus, 3110 Hayes Road, Suite 380, Houston, TX 77082. *Phone:* 281-899-1240. *Fax:* 281-597-8466. *E-mail:* kevin.wilkinson@remingtoncollege.edu. *Web site:* http://www.remingtoncollege.edu/houston/.

Remington College–Houston Southeast
Webster, Texas

Director of Admissions Lori Minor, Director of Recruitment, Remington College–Houston Southeast, 20985 Interstate 45 South, Webster, TX 77598. *Phone:* 281-554-1700. *Fax:* 281-554-1765. *E-mail:* lori.minor@remingtoncollege.edu. *Web site:* http://www.remingtoncollege.edu/houstonsoutheast/.

Remington College–North Houston Campus
Houston, Texas

Director of Admissions Edmund Flores, Director of Recruitment, Remington College–North Houston Campus, 11310 Greens Crossing Boulevard, Suite 300, Houston, TX 77067. *Phone:* 281-885-4450. *Fax:* 281-875-9964. *E-mail:* edmund.flores@remingtoncollege.edu. *Web site:* http://www.remingtoncollege.edu/.

Richland College
Dallas, Texas

Freshman Application Contact Ms. Carol McKinney, Department Assistant, Richland College, 12800 Abrams Road, Dallas, TX 75243-2199. *Phone:* 972-238-6100. *Web site:* http://www.rlc.dcccd.edu/.

St. Philip's College
San Antonio, Texas

- **District-supported** 2-year, founded 1898, part of Alamo Community College District System
- **Urban** 68-acre campus with easy access to San Antonio
- **Coed,** 10,710 undergraduate students, 21% full-time, 57% women, 43% men

Undergraduates 2,232 full-time, 8,478 part-time. Students come from 45 states and territories; 11 other countries; 1% are from out of state; 13% Black or African American, non-Hispanic/Latino; 50% Hispanic/Latino; 2% Asian, non-Hispanic/Latino; 0.4% American Indian or Alaska Native, non-Hispanic/Latino; 2% Two or more races, non-Hispanic/Latino; 0.3% international; 10% transferred in.

Freshmen *Admission:* 1,690 enrolled.

Faculty *Total:* 437, 43% full-time, 9% with terminal degrees. *Student/faculty ratio:* 15:1.

Majors Accounting; administrative assistant and secretarial science; aircraft powerplant technology; airframe mechanics and aircraft maintenance technology; art; autobody/collision and repair technology; automobile/automotive mechanics technology; biology/biological sciences; biomedical technology; building/construction finishing, management, and inspection related; business administration and management; CAD/CADD drafting/design technology; chemistry; clinical/medical laboratory technology; computer and information systems security; computer systems networking and telecommunications; computer technology/computer systems technology; construction engineering technology; criminal justice/law enforcement administration; culinary arts; data entry/microcomputer applications; diesel mechanics technology; dramatic/theater arts; dramatic/theater arts and stagecraft related; early childhood education; e-commerce; economics; education; electrical/electronics equipment installation and repair; electromechanical technology; energy management and systems technology; English; environmental science; geology/earth science; health information/medical records technology; heating, air conditioning, ventilation and refrigeration maintenance technology; history; hotel/motel administration; kinesiology and exercise science; legal administrative assistant/secretary; liberal arts and sciences/liberal studies; mathematics; medical administrative assistant and medical secretary; medical radiologic technology; music; natural resources/conservation; occupational safety and health technology; occupational therapist assistant; philosophy; physical therapy technology; political science and government; pre-dentistry studies; pre-engineering; pre-law studies; premedical studies; prenursing studies; pre-pharmacy studies; psychology; respiratory care therapy; restaurant/food services management; rhetoric and composition; social work; sociology; Spanish; system, networking, and LAN/WAN management; teacher assistant/aide; welding technology.

Academics *Calendar:* semesters. *Degree:* certificates, diplomas, and associate. *Special study options:* academic remediation for entering students, adult/continuing education programs, advanced placement credit, cooperative education, distance learning, double majors, English as a second language, honors programs, independent study, internships, off-campus study, part-time degree program, services for LD students, study abroad, summer session for credit. *ROTC:* Army (c).

Library Learning Resource Center plus 1 other with 77,979 titles, 212 serial subscriptions, 11,787 audiovisual materials, an OPAC, a Web page.

Student Life *Housing:* college housing not available. *Activities and Organizations:* drama/theater group, choral group, Student Government, Future United Latino Leaders of Change, Anime. *Campus security:* 24-hour emergency response devices and patrols, late-night transport/escort service. *Student services:* health clinic, women's center.

Athletics *Intramural sports:* basketball M/W, cheerleading M/W, table tennis M/W, volleyball M/W, weight lifting M/W.

Costs (2011–12) *Tuition:* area resident $1680 full-time, $56 per credit hour part-time; state resident $3360 full-time, $112 per credit hour part-time; nonresident $6720 full-time, $224 per credit hour part-time. *Required fees:* $300 full-time, $150 per term part-time. *Payment plan:* installment. *Waivers:* senior citizens and employees or children of employees.

Applying *Options:* electronic application, early admission. *Required:* high school transcript. *Application deadlines:* rolling (freshmen), rolling (transfers). *Notification:* continuous (freshmen), continuous (transfers).

Freshman Application Contact Ms. Penelope Velasco, Associate Director, Residency and Reports, St. Philip's College, 1801 Martin Luther King Drive, San Antonio, TX 78203-2098. *Phone:* 210-486-2283. *Fax:* 210-486-2103. *E-mail:* pvelasco@alamo.edu. *Web site:* http://www.alamo.edu/spc/.

San Antonio College
San Antonio, Texas

Director of Admissions Mr. J. Martin Ortega, Director of Admissions and Records, San Antonio College, 1300 San Pedro Avenue, San Antonio, TX 78212-4299. *Phone:* 210-733-2582. *Web site:* http://www.alamo.edu/sac/.

San Jacinto College District
Pasadena, Texas

- **State and locally supported** 2-year, founded 1961
- **Suburban** 445-acre campus with easy access to Houston
- **Endowment** $2.6 million
- **Coed,** 29,392 undergraduate students, 32% full-time, 57% women, 43% men

Undergraduates 9,266 full-time, 20,126 part-time. Students come from 45 states and territories; 74 other countries; 1% are from out of state; 10% Black or African American, non-Hispanic/Latino; 40% Hispanic/Latino; 5% Asian, non-Hispanic/Latino; 0.2% Native Hawaiian or other Pacific Islander, non-Hispanic/Latino; 0.3% American Indian or Alaska Native, non-Hispanic/Latino; 2% Two or more races, non-Hispanic/Latino; 9% Race/ethnicity unknown; 2% international; 25% transferred in.

Freshmen *Admission:* 12,473 applied, 12,473 admitted, 5,716 enrolled.

Faculty *Total:* 1,224, 40% full-time, 13% with terminal degrees. *Student/faculty ratio:* 22:1.

Majors Accounting; administrative assistant and secretarial science; agribusiness; agriculture; airline pilot and flight crew; art; autobody/collision and repair technology; automobile/automotive mechanics technology; aviation/airway management; baking and pastry arts; behavioral sciences; biology/biological sciences; biotechnology; business administration and management; business automation/technology/data entry; business/commerce; chemical process technology; chemical technology; chemistry; child development; clinical laboratory science/medical technology; clinical/medical laboratory technology; commercial and advertising art; computer and information sciences; computer and information systems security; computer programming; computer science; construction engineering technology; cosmetology; cosmetology, barber/styling, and nail instruction; criminal justice/police science; culinary arts; dance; design and visual communications; diagnostic medical sonography and ultrasound technology; diesel mechanics technology; digital communication and media/multimedia; drafting and design technology; dramatic/theater arts; education (multiple levels); electrical and power transmission installation; electrical, electronic and communications engineering technology; elementary education; emergency medical technology (EMT paramedic); engineering;

engineering mechanics; English; environmental science; film/cinema/video studies; fire prevention and safety technology; fire science/firefighting; food preparation; food service systems administration; foreign languages and literatures; general studies; geology/earth science; health and physical education/fitness; health information/medical records technology; heating, air conditioning, ventilation and refrigeration maintenance technology; Hispanic-American, Puerto Rican, and Mexican-American/Chicano studies; history; institutional food workers; instrumentation technology; interior design; international business/trade/commerce; journalism; kindergarten/preschool education; legal assistant/paralegal; licensed practical/vocational nurse training; management information systems; mathematics; medical administrative assistant and medical secretary; mental health counseling; middle school education; multi/interdisciplinary studies related; music; occupational safety and health technology; optometric technician; philosophy; physical sciences; physical therapy technology; physics; political science and government; psychology; radio and television broadcasting technology; radiologic technology/science; real estate; registered nursing/registered nurse; respiratory care therapy; restaurant, culinary, and catering management; rhetoric and composition; science teacher education; secondary education; social sciences; sociology; speech communication and rhetoric; surgical technology; system, networking, and LAN/WAN management; web/multimedia management and webmaster; welding technology.

Academics *Calendar:* semesters. *Degree:* certificates and associate. *Special study options:* academic remediation for entering students, accelerated degree program, adult/continuing education programs, advanced placement credit, cooperative education, distance learning, double majors, English as a second language, honors programs, part-time degree program, services for LD students, student-designed majors, study abroad, summer session for credit. *ROTC:* Army (c), Air Force (c).

Library Lee Davis Library (C), Edwin E. Lehr (N), and Parker Williams (S) with 271,976 titles, 539 serial subscriptions, 2,494 audiovisual materials, an OPAC, a Web page.

Student Life *Housing:* college housing not available. *Activities and Organizations:* drama/theater group, student-run newspaper, choral group, Phi Theta Kappa, Nurses Association, Student Government Association, ABG Radiography, Texas Student Education Association. *Campus security:* 24-hour emergency response devices and patrols, late-night transport/escort service.

Athletics Member NJCAA. *Intercollegiate sports:* baseball M, basketball M(s), cheerleading M(s), golf M, soccer M/W, softball W, tennis M/W, volleyball W(s). *Intramural sports:* basketball M/W, bowling M/W, football M/W, racquetball M/W, table tennis M/W, volleyball M/W, weight lifting M/W.

Costs (2011–12) *Tuition:* area resident $1486 full-time, $38 per credit hour part-time; state resident $2286 full-time, $63 per credit hour part-time; nonresident $3886 full-time, $113 per credit hour part-time. Full-time tuition and fees vary according to course load. Part-time tuition and fees vary according to course load. *Required fees:* $270 full-time, $135 per term part-time. *Payment plan:* installment. *Waivers:* senior citizens.

Applying *Options:* electronic application, early admission. *Required:* high school transcript. *Required for some:* interview.

Freshman Application Contact San Jacinto College District, 4624 Fairmont Parkway, Pasadena, TX 77504-3323. *Phone:* 281-998-6150. *Web site:* http://www.sanjac.edu/.

South Plains College
Levelland, Texas

Freshman Application Contact Mrs. Andrea Rangel, Dean of Admissions and Records, South Plains College, 1401 College Avenue, Levelland, TX 78336. *Phone:* 806-894-9611 Ext. 2370. *Fax:* 806-897-3167. *E-mail:* arangel@southplainscollege.edu. *Web site:* http://www.southplainscollege.edu/.

South Texas College
McAllen, Texas

Freshman Application Contact Mr. Matthew Hebbard, Director of Enrollment Services and Registrar, South Texas College, 3201 West Pecan, McAllen, TX 78501. *Phone:* 956-872-2147. *Toll-free phone:* 800-742-7822. *E-mail:* mshebbar@southtexascollege.edu. *Web site:* http://www.southtexascollege.edu/.

Southwest Institute of Technology
Austin, Texas

Freshman Application Contact Director of Admissions, Southwest Institute of Technology, 5424 Highway 290 West, Suite 200, Austin, TX 78735-8800. *Phone:* 512-892-2640. *Fax:* 512-892-1045. *Web site:* http://www.swse.net/.

Southwest Texas Junior College

Uvalde, Texas

Director of Admissions Mr. Joe C. Barker, Dean of Admissions and Student Services, Southwest Texas Junior College, 2401 Garner Field Road, Uvalde, TX 78801-6297. *Phone:* 830-278-4401 Ext. 7284. *Web site:* http://www.swtjc.edu/.

Tarrant County College District

Fort Worth, Texas

- **County-supported** 2-year, founded 1967
- **Urban** 667-acre campus
- **Endowment** $5.8 million
- **Coed,** 49,108 undergraduate students, 36% full-time, 58% women, 42% men

Undergraduates 17,591 full-time, 31,517 part-time. Students come from 39 states and territories; 17% Black or African American, non-Hispanic/Latino; 22% Hispanic/Latino; 6% Asian, non-Hispanic/Latino; 0.1% Native Hawaiian or other Pacific Islander, non-Hispanic/Latino; 0.5% American Indian or Alaska Native, non-Hispanic/Latino; 0.2% Two or more races, non-Hispanic/Latino; 0.7% Race/ethnicity unknown; 0.9% international.

Freshmen *Admission:* 9,212 applied, 9,212 admitted, 9,212 enrolled.

Faculty *Total:* 1,861, 35% full-time. *Student/faculty ratio:* 26:1.

Majors Accounting; administrative assistant and secretarial science; architectural engineering technology; automobile/automotive mechanics technology; avionics maintenance technology; business administration and management; clinical laboratory science/medical technology; clinical/medical laboratory technology; computer programming; computer science; construction engineering technology; consumer merchandising/retailing management; criminal justice/law enforcement administration; dental hygiene; developmental and child psychology; dietetics; drafting and design technology; educational/instructional technology; electrical, electronic and communications engineering technology; electromechanical technology; emergency medical technology (EMT paramedic); fashion merchandising; fire science/firefighting; food technology and processing; graphic and printing equipment operation/production; health information/medical records administration; heating, air conditioning, ventilation and refrigeration maintenance technology; horticultural science; industrial radiologic technology; legal assistant/paralegal; liberal arts and sciences/liberal studies; machine tool technology; marketing/marketing management; mechanical engineering/mechanical technology; mental health counseling; physical therapy; quality control technology; registered nursing/registered nurse; respiratory care therapy; sign language interpretation and translation; surgical technology; welding technology.

Academics *Calendar:* semesters. *Degree:* certificates and associate. *Special study options:* academic remediation for entering students, adult/continuing education programs, advanced placement credit, distance learning, English as a second language, honors programs, part-time degree program, services for LD students, summer session for credit. *ROTC:* Army (c), Air Force (c).

Library 197,352 titles, 1,649 serial subscriptions, 18,833 audiovisual materials, an OPAC, a Web page.

Student Life *Housing:* college housing not available. *Activities and Organizations:* drama/theater group, student-run newspaper, choral group. *Campus security:* 24-hour emergency response devices and patrols, late-night transport/escort service. *Student services:* health clinic, personal/psychological counseling.

Athletics *Intramural sports:* football M, golf M, sailing M/W, table tennis M, tennis M/W, volleyball M/W.

Costs (2012–13) *Tuition:* area resident $1248 full-time, $52 per credit hour part-time; state resident $1824 full-time, $76 per credit hour part-time; nonresident $4104 full-time, $171 per credit hour part-time. Full-time tuition and fees vary according to program. Part-time tuition and fees vary according to program. *Payment plan:* installment.

Financial Aid Of all full-time matriculated undergraduates who enrolled in 2010, 11,519 applied for aid, 10,184 were judged to have need. 754 Federal Work-Study jobs (averaging $2463). 85 state and other part-time jobs (averaging $2990). In 2010, 25 non-need-based awards were made. *Average need-based loan:* $2530. *Average need-based gift aid:* $2839. *Average non-need-based aid:* $619.

Applying *Options:* electronic application, early admission. *Application deadlines:* rolling (freshmen), rolling (transfers).

Freshman Application Contact Mr. Vikas Rajpurohit, Assistant Director of Admissions Services, Tarrant County College District, 1500 Houston Street, Fort Worth, TX 76102-6599. *Phone:* 817-515-5656. *E-mail:* vikas.rajpurohit@tccd.edu. *Web site:* http://www.tccd.edu/.

Temple College

Temple, Texas

Freshman Application Contact Ms. Carey Rose, Director of Admissions and Records, Temple College, 2600 South First Street, Temple, TX 76504. *Phone:* 254-298-8303. *Toll-free phone:* 800-460-4636. *E-mail:* carey.rose@templejc.edu. *Web site:* http://www.templejc.edu/.

Texarkana College

Texarkana, Texas

- **State and locally supported** 2-year, founded 1927
- **Urban** 90-acre campus
- **Coed,** 4,484 undergraduate students, 41% full-time, 63% women, 37% men

Undergraduates 1,819 full-time, 2,665 part-time. Students come from 7 states and territories; 8 other countries; 30% are from out of state; 22% Black or African American, non-Hispanic/Latino; 3% Hispanic/Latino; 1% Asian, non-Hispanic/Latino; 0.1% Native Hawaiian or other Pacific Islander, non-Hispanic/Latino; 0.6% American Indian or Alaska Native, non-Hispanic/Latino; 2% Two or more races, non-Hispanic/Latino; 3% Race/ethnicity unknown; 0.1% international; 2% live on campus.

Faculty *Total:* 227, 42% full-time. *Student/faculty ratio:* 20:1.

Majors Administrative assistant and secretarial science; agriculture; art; automobile/automotive mechanics technology; biology/biological sciences; business administration and management; business/commerce; chemistry; childcare and support services management; child development; computer and information sciences; cosmetology; criminal justice/law enforcement administration; criminal justice/safety; culinary arts; drafting and design technology; dramatic/theater arts; electrical, electronic and communications engineering technology; emergency medical technology (EMT paramedic); engineering; foreign languages and literatures; heating, air conditioning, ventilation and refrigeration maintenance technology; history; humanities; journalism; liberal arts and sciences/liberal studies; licensed practical/vocational nurse training; marketing/marketing management; mathematics; music; physics; political science and government; real estate; registered nursing/registered nurse; social sciences; substance abuse/addiction counseling; welding technology.

Academics *Calendar:* semesters. *Degree:* certificates and associate. *Special study options:* academic remediation for entering students, adult/continuing education programs, advanced placement credit, cooperative education, part-time degree program, services for LD students, summer session for credit.

Library Palmer Memorial Library with 46,700 titles, 646 serial subscriptions.

Student Life *Housing Options:* Campus housing is university owned. *Activities and Organizations:* drama/theater group, student-run newspaper, radio station, choral group, Black Student Association, Earth Club, Baptist Student Union, 21st Century Democrats, Young Republicans. *Campus security:* 24-hour patrols. *Student services:* personal/psychological counseling.

Athletics Member NJCAA. *Intercollegiate sports:* baseball M(s), golf M/W, softball W(s).

Costs (2012–13) *Tuition:* area resident $1170 full-time, $39 per semester hour part-time; state resident $2430 full-time, $81 per semester hour part-time; nonresident $3600 full-time, $120 per semester hour part-time. Full-time tuition and fees vary according to course load. Part-time tuition and fees vary according to course load. *Required fees:* $660 full-time. *Room and board:* room only: $2000. *Payment plan:* installment. *Waivers:* employees or children of employees.

Financial Aid Of all full-time matriculated undergraduates who enrolled in 2010, 30 Federal Work-Study jobs (averaging $3090).

Applying *Options:* early admission. *Required:* high school transcript. *Application deadlines:* rolling (freshmen), rolling (transfers).

Freshman Application Contact Mrs. Linda Bennett, Director of Admissions, Texarkana College, 2500 North Robison Road, Texarkana, TX 75599-0001. *Phone:* 903-838-4541 Ext. 3011. *Fax:* 903-832-5030. *E-mail:* linda.bennett@texarkanacollege.edu. *Web site:* http://www.texarkanacollege.edu/.

Texas School of Business, Friendswood Campus

Friendswood, Texas

- **Proprietary** 2-year
- **Coed**

Majors Criminal justice/safety.

Academics *Degree:* diplomas and associate.

Freshman Application Contact Admissions Office, Texas School of Business, Friendswood Campus, 3208 West Parkwood Avenue, Friendswood, TX 77546. *Web site:* http://www.friendswood.tsb.edu/.

Texas School of Business, Houston North Campus

Houston, Texas

- **Proprietary** 2-year
- **Coed**

Majors Criminal justice/safety.
Academics *Degree:* diplomas and associate.
Freshman Application Contact Admissions Office, Texas School of Business, Houston North Campus, 711 East Airtex Drive, Houston, TX 77073. *Phone:* 281-443-8900. *Web site:* http://www.north.tsb.edu/.

Texas Southmost College

Brownsville, Texas

Freshman Application Contact New Student Relations, Texas Southmost College, 80 Fort Brown, Brownsville, TX 78520-4991. *Phone:* 956-882-8860. *Toll-free phone:* 877-882-8721. *Fax:* 956-882-8959. *Web site:* http://www.utb.edu/.

Texas State Technical College Harlingen

Harlingen, Texas

- **State-supported** 2-year, founded 1967, part of Texas State Technical College System
- **Small-town** 125-acre campus
- **Coed,** 5,807 undergraduate students, 39% full-time, 53% women, 47% men

Undergraduates 2,285 full-time, 3,522 part-time. Students come from 20 states and territories; 2 other countries; 1% are from out of state; 0.7% Black or African American, non-Hispanic/Latino; 87% Hispanic/Latino; 0.6% Asian, non-Hispanic/Latino; 0.1% Native Hawaiian or other Pacific Islander, non-Hispanic/Latino; 0.1% American Indian or Alaska Native, non-Hispanic/Latino; 1% Two or more races, non-Hispanic/Latino; 2% Race/ethnicity unknown; 0.1% international; 39% transferred in; 5% live on campus.
Freshmen *Admission:* 4,987 applied, 4,987 admitted, 563 enrolled.
Faculty *Total:* 231, 64% full-time, 3% with terminal degrees. *Student/faculty ratio:* 16:1.
Majors Administrative assistant and secretarial science; agricultural business technology; aircraft powerplant technology; airframe mechanics and aircraft maintenance technology; autobody/collision and repair technology; automobile/automotive mechanics technology; biology/biological sciences; biomedical technology; business/commerce; chemical technology; commercial and advertising art; computer programming; computer systems networking and telecommunications; computer technology/computer systems technology; construction engineering technology; dental assisting; dental hygiene; dental laboratory technology; drafting and design technology; electromechanical technology; emergency medical technology (EMT paramedic); engineering; executive assistant/executive secretary; health information/medical records technology; health services/allied health/health sciences; heating, air conditioning, ventilation and refrigeration maintenance technology; information technology; institutional food workers; licensed practical/vocational nurse training; machine tool technology; mathematics; medical/clinical assistant; medical transcription; prenursing studies; surgical technology; teacher assistant/aide; telecommunications technology; tool and die technology; welding technology.
Academics *Calendar:* semesters. *Degree:* certificates and associate. *Special study options:* academic remediation for entering students, adult/continuing education programs, cooperative education, distance learning, double majors, English as a second language, internships, part-time degree program, services for LD students, summer session for credit.
Library Dr. J. Gilbert Leal Learning Resource Center with 51,289 titles, 80 serial subscriptions, 410 audiovisual materials, an OPAC, a Web page.
Student Life *Housing Options:* men-only, women-only, disabled students. Campus housing is university owned. *Activities and Organizations:* student-run newspaper, Student Government Association, VICA (Vocational Industrial Clubs of America), Business Professionals of America. *Campus security:* 24-hour emergency response devices and patrols, late-night transport/escort service, night watchman for housing area. *Student services:* health clinic, personal/psychological counseling, women's center.
Athletics *Intramural sports:* badminton M/W, basketball M/W, football M/W, racquetball M/W, soccer M/W, softball M/W, table tennis M/W, tennis M/W, track and field M/W, volleyball M/W, weight lifting M/W.
Costs (2012–13) *Tuition:* state resident $6098 full-time, $136 per credit hour part-time; nonresident $13,500 full-time, $300 per credit hour part-time. Full-time tuition and fees vary according to course load and program. Part-time tuition and fees vary according to course load and program. *Room and board:*

$7340. Room and board charges vary according to board plan and housing facility. *Payment plans:* installment, deferred payment.
Financial Aid Of all full-time matriculated undergraduates who enrolled in 2010, 120 Federal Work-Study jobs (averaging $2400). 15 state and other part-time jobs (averaging $2400).
Applying *Options:* electronic application, early admission, deferred entrance. *Required:* high school transcript. *Application deadlines:* rolling (freshmen), rolling (transfers). *Notification:* continuous (freshmen), continuous (transfers).
Freshman Application Contact Texas State Technical College Harlingen, 1902 North Loop 499, Harlingen, TX 78550-3697. *Phone:* 956-364-4100. *Toll-free phone:* 800-852-8784. *Web site:* http://www.harlingen.tstc.edu/.

Texas State Technical College– Marshall

Marshall, Texas

Director of Admissions Pat Robbins, Registrar, Texas State Technical College–Marshall, 2650 East End Boulevard South, Marshall, TX 75671. *Phone:* 903-935-1010. *Toll-free phone:* 888-382-8782. *Fax:* 903-923-3282. *E-mail:* Pat.Robbins@marshall.tstc.edu. *Web site:* http://www.marshall.tstc.edu/.

Texas State Technical College Waco

Waco, Texas

Freshman Application Contact Mr. Marcus Balch, Director, Recruiting Services, Texas State Technical College Waco, 3801 Campus Drive, Waco, TX 76705. *Phone:* 254-867-2026. *Toll-free phone:* 800-792-8784 Ext. 2362. *Fax:* 254-867-3827. *E-mail:* marcus.balch@tstc.edu. *Web site:* http://waco.tstc.edu/.

Texas State Technical College West Texas

Sweetwater, Texas

Freshman Application Contact Ms. Maria Aguirre-Acuna, Texas State Technical College West Texas, 300 Homer K Taylor Drive, Sweetwater, TX 79556-4108. *Phone:* 325-235-7349. *Toll-free phone:* 800-592-8784. *Fax:* 325-235-7443. *E-mail:* maria.aquirre@sweetwater.tstc.edu. *Web site:* http://www.westtexas.tstc.edu/.

Trinity Valley Community College

Athens, Texas

- **State and locally supported** 2-year, founded 1946
- **Rural** 65-acre campus with easy access to Dallas-Fort Worth
- **Endowment** $2.9 million
- **Coed**

Undergraduates 3,035 full-time, 4,544 part-time. Students come from 27 states and territories; 11 other countries; 1% are from out of state; 12% live on campus.
Faculty *Student/faculty ratio:* 26:1.
Academics *Calendar:* semesters. *Degree:* certificates, diplomas, and associate. *Special study options:* academic remediation for entering students, adult/continuing education programs, advanced placement credit, cooperative education, distance learning, double majors, English as a second language, honors programs, independent study, internships, part-time degree program, services for LD students, summer session for credit.
Student Life *Campus security:* 24-hour emergency response devices and patrols, controlled dormitory access.
Athletics Member NJCAA.
Costs (2011–12) *Tuition:* area resident $1920 full-time, $30 per semester hour part-time; state resident $3360 full-time, $78 per semester hour part-time; nonresident $4200 full-time, $106 per semester hour part-time. Full-time tuition and fees vary according to course load. Part-time tuition and fees vary according to course load. *Required fees:* $34 per semester hour part-time. *Room and board:* $4000. Room and board charges vary according to board plan.
Financial Aid Of all full-time matriculated undergraduates who enrolled in 2010, 80 Federal Work-Study jobs (averaging $1544). 40 state and other part-time jobs (averaging $1544).
Applying *Options:* electronic application, early admission. *Required:* high school transcript.
Freshman Application Contact Dr. Colette Hilliard, Dean of Enrollment Management and Registrar, Trinity Valley Community College, 100 Cardinal Drive, Athens, TX 75751. *Phone:* 903-675-6209 Ext. 209. *Web site:* http://www.tvcc.edu/.

Tyler Junior College

Tyler, Texas

- **State and locally supported** 2-year, founded 1926
- **Suburban** 85-acre campus
- **Coed,** 11,540 undergraduate students, 50% full-time, 59% women, 41% men

Undergraduates 5,722 full-time, 5,818 part-time. Students come from 40 states and territories; 53 other countries; 3% are from out of state; 23% Black or African American, non-Hispanic/Latino; 12% Hispanic/Latino; 1% Asian, non-Hispanic/Latino; 0.1% Native Hawaiian or other Pacific Islander, non-Hispanic/Latino; 0.7% American Indian or Alaska Native, non-Hispanic/Latino; 2% Race/ethnicity unknown; 1% international; 7% transferred in; 9% live on campus. *Retention:* 48% of full-time freshmen returned.
Freshmen *Admission:* 7,189 applied, 7,189 admitted, 2,571 enrolled.
Faculty *Total:* 547, 51% full-time. *Student/faculty ratio:* 21:1.
Majors Accounting; administrative assistant and secretarial science; agriculture; art; automobile/automotive mechanics technology; behavioral sciences; biology/biological sciences; business administration and management; chemistry; child development; clinical/medical laboratory technology; commercial and advertising art; computer and information sciences; computer and information sciences related; computer engineering technology; computer graphics; computer programming related; computer science; computer systems networking and telecommunications; criminal justice/law enforcement administration; criminal justice/police science; dance; data entry/microcomputer applications; dental hygiene; dramatic/theater arts; economics; emergency medical technology (EMT paramedic); engineering; environmental science; family and consumer sciences/human sciences; fire science/firefighting; geology/earth science; health/health-care administration; health information/medical records technology; horticultural science; industrial radiologic technology; information technology; legal administrative assistant/secretary; liberal arts and sciences/liberal studies; licensed practical/vocational nurse training; mathematics; medical administrative assistant and medical secretary; modern languages; optometric technician; photography; physical education teaching and coaching; physics; political science and government; psychology; registered nursing/registered nurse; respiratory care therapy; sign language interpretation and translation; social sciences; speech communication and rhetoric; substance abuse/addiction counseling; surgical technology; surveying technology; welding technology.
Academics *Calendar:* semesters. *Degree:* certificates and associate. *Special study options:* academic remediation for entering students, accelerated degree program, adult/continuing education programs, advanced placement credit, distance learning, English as a second language, freshman honors college, honors programs, part-time degree program, services for LD students, summer session for credit.
Library Vaughn Library and Learning Resource Center with 104,000 titles, 10,000 serial subscriptions, an OPAC.
Student Life *Housing Options:* men-only, women-only. Campus housing is university owned. *Activities and Organizations:* drama/theater group, student-run newspaper, choral group, marching band, student government, religious affiliation clubs, Phi Theta Kappa, national fraternities, national sororities. *Campus security:* 24-hour patrols, controlled dormitory access. *Student services:* health clinic, personal/psychological counseling.
Athletics Member NJCAA. *Intercollegiate sports:* baseball M, basketball M(s)/W(s), football M(s), golf M/W, soccer M(s)/W(s), tennis M(s)/W(s), volleyball W(s). *Intramural sports:* basketball M/W, racquetball M/W, volleyball M/W, weight lifting M/W.
Costs (2011–12) *Tuition:* area resident $720 full-time, $30 per credit hour part-time; state resident $1824 full-time, $76 per credit hour part-time; nonresident $2304 full-time, $96 per credit hour part-time. *Required fees:* $1140 full-time, $39 per credit hour part-time, $100 per term part-time. *Room and board:* $2700. Room and board charges vary according to housing facility. *Payment plan:* installment. *Waivers:* senior citizens.
Financial Aid Of all full-time matriculated undergraduates who enrolled in 2010, 8,866 applied for aid. 26 Federal Work-Study jobs, 22 state and other part-time jobs.
Applying *Options:* early admission. *Required:* high school transcript. *Application deadlines:* rolling (freshmen), rolling (transfers).
Freshman Application Contact Ms. Janna Chancey, Director of Enrollment Management, Tyler Junior College, PO Box 9020, Tyler, TX 75711-9020. *Phone:* 903-510-3325. *Toll-free phone:* 800-687-5680. *E-mail:* jcha@tjc.edu. *Web site:* http://www.tjc.edu/.

Universal Technical Institute

Houston, Texas

Director of Admissions Director of Admissions, Universal Technical Institute, 721 Lockhaven Drive, Houston, TX 77073-5598. *Phone:* 281-443-6262. *Toll-free phone:* 800-510-5072. *Fax:* 281-443-0610. *Web site:* http://www.uti.edu/.

Vernon College

Vernon, Texas

Director of Admissions Mr. Joe Hite, Dean of Admissions/Registrar, Vernon College, 4400 College Drive, Vernon, TX 76384-4092. *Phone:* 940-552-6291 Ext. 2204. *Web site:* http://www.vernoncollege.edu/.

Vet Tech Institute of Houston

Houston, Texas

- **Private** 2-year, founded 1958
- **Suburban** campus
- **Coed,** 348 undergraduate students
- 61% of applicants were admitted

Freshmen *Admission:* 572 applied, 350 admitted.
Majors Veterinary/animal health technology.
Academics *Degree:* associate. *Special study options:* accelerated degree program, internships.
Student Life *Housing:* college housing not available.
Freshman Application Contact Admissions Office, Vet Tech Institute of Houston, 4669 Southwest Freeway, Suite 100, Houston, TX 77027. *Phone:* 888-884-1468. *Toll-free phone:* 800-275-2736. *Web site:* http://www.vettechinstitute.edu/.

Victoria College

Victoria, Texas

Freshman Application Contact Ms. Lavern Dentler, Registrar, Victoria College, 2200 East Red River, Victoria, TX 77901-4494. *Phone:* 361-573-3291. *Toll-free phone:* 877-843-4369. *Fax:* 361-582-2525. *E-mail:* registrar@victoriacollege.edu. *Web site:* http://www.victoriacollege.edu/.

Virginia College at Austin

Austin, Texas

Admissions Office Contact Virginia College at Austin, 6301 East Highway 290, Austin, TX 78723. *Web site:* http://www.vc.edu/.

Wade College

Dallas, Texas

- **Proprietary** primarily 2-year, founded 1965
- **Urban** 175-acre campus
- **Coed, primarily women**

Undergraduates 5% are from out of state. *Retention:* 49% of full-time freshmen returned.
Faculty *Student/faculty ratio:* 15:1.
Academics *Calendar:* trimesters. *Degrees:* associate and bachelor's. *Special study options:* academic remediation for entering students, advanced placement credit, double majors, part-time degree program, summer session for credit.
Student Life *Campus security:* 24-hour emergency response devices and patrols, late-night transport/escort service, controlled dormitory access.
Applying *Options:* electronic application. *Required:* high school transcript, interview.
Freshman Application Contact Wade College, INFOMart, 1950 Stemmons Freeway, Suite 4080, LB 562, Dallas, TX 75207. *Phone:* 214-637-3530. *Toll-free phone:* 800-624-4850. *Web site:* http://www.wadecollege.edu/.

Weatherford College

Weatherford, Texas

Freshman Application Contact Mr. Ralph Willingham, Director of Admissions, Weatherford College, 225 College Park Drive, Weatherford, TX 76086-5699. *Phone:* 817-598-6248. *Toll-free phone:* 800-287-5471. *Fax:* 817-598-6205. *E-mail:* willingham@wc.edu. *Web site:* http://www.wc.edu/.

Western Technical College

El Paso, Texas

Freshman Application Contact Laura Pena, Director of Admissions, Western Technical College, 9451 Diana, El Paso, TX 79930-2610. *Phone:* 915-566-9621. *Toll-free phone:* 800-201-9232. *E-mail:* lpena@westerntech.edu. *Web site:* http://www.westerntech.edu/.

Western Technical College

El Paso, Texas

Freshman Application Contact Mr. Bill Terrell, Chief Admissions Officer, Western Technical College, 9624 Plaza Circle, El Paso, TX 79927. *Phone:* 915-532-3737 Ext. 117. *Fax:* 915-532-6946. *E-mail:* bterrell@wtc-ep.edu. *Web site:* http://www.westerntech.edu/.

Western Texas College

Snyder, Texas

Director of Admissions Dr. Jim Clifton, Dean of Student Services, Western Texas College, 6200 College Avenue, Snyder, TX 79549. *Phone:* 325-573-8511 Ext. 204. *Toll-free phone:* 888-GO-TO-WTC. *E-mail:* jclifton@wtc.cc.tx.us. *Web site:* http://www.wtc.edu/.

Westwood College–Houston South Campus

Houston, Texas

Freshman Application Contact Westwood College–Houston South Campus, 7322 Southwest Freeway #110, Houston, TX 77074. *Phone:* 713-777-4779. *Toll-free phone:* 866-340-3677. *Web site:* http://www.westwood.edu/.

Wharton County Junior College

Wharton, Texas

Freshman Application Contact Mr. Albert Barnes, Dean of Admissions and Registration, Wharton County Junior College, 911 Boling Highway, Wharton, TX 77488-3298. *Phone:* 979-532-6381. *E-mail:* albertb@wcjc.edu. *Web site:* http://www.wcjc.edu/.

UTAH

Everest College

West Valley City, Utah

Director of Admissions Director of Admissions, Everest College, 3280 West 3500 South, West Valley City, UT 84119. *Phone:* 801-840-4800. *Toll-free phone:* 888-741-4270. *Fax:* 801-969-0828. *Web site:* http://www.everest.edu/.

ITT Technical Institute

Murray, Utah

- **Proprietary** primarily 2-year, founded 1984, part of ITT Educational Services, Inc.
- **Suburban** campus
- **Coed**

Majors Business administration and management; communications technology; computer and information systems security; computer software engineering; computer software technology; construction management; criminal justice/law enforcement administration; drafting and design technology; electrical, electronic and communications engineering technology; forensic science and technology; game and interactive media design; graphic communications; graphic design; legal assistant/paralegal; network and system administration; project management.

Academics *Calendar:* quarters. *Degrees:* associate and bachelor's.

Student Life *Housing:* college housing not available.

Freshman Application Contact Director of Recruitment, ITT Technical Institute, 920 West Levoy Drive, Murray, UT 84123-2500. *Phone:* 801-263-3313. *Toll-free phone:* 800-365-2136. *Web site:* http://www.itt-tech.edu/.

LDS Business College

Salt Lake City, Utah

Freshman Application Contact Miss Dawn Fellows, Assistant Director of Admissions, LDS Business College, 95 North 300 West, Salt Lake City, UT 84101-3500. *Phone:* 801-524-8146. *Toll-free phone:* 800-999-5767. *Fax:* 801-524-1900. *E-mail:* DFellows@ldsbc.edu. *Web site:* http://www.ldsbc.edu/.

Provo College

Provo, Utah

Director of Admissions Mr. Gordon Peters, College Director, Provo College, 1450 West 820 North, Provo, UT 84601. *Phone:* 801-375-1861. *Toll-free phone:* 877-777-5886. *Fax:* 801-375-9728. *E-mail:* gordonp@provocollege.org. *Web site:* http://www.provocollege.edu/.

Salt Lake Community College

Salt Lake City, Utah

- **State-supported** 2-year, founded 1948, part of Utah System of Higher Education
- **Urban** 114-acre campus with easy access to Salt Lake City
- **Endowment** $818,597
- **Coed,** 31,999 undergraduate students, 29% full-time, 52% women, 48% men

Undergraduates 9,337 full-time, 22,662 part-time. 2% Black or African American, non-Hispanic/Latino; 11% Hispanic/Latino; 3% Asian, non-Hispanic/Latino; 1% Native Hawaiian or other Pacific Islander, non-Hispanic/Latino; 0.9% American Indian or Alaska Native, non-Hispanic/Latino; 0.8% Two or more races, non-Hispanic/Latino; 13% Race/ethnicity unknown; 1% international; 2% transferred in.

Freshmen *Admission:* 3,387 applied, 3,387 admitted, 3,387 enrolled.

Faculty *Total:* 1,254, 28% full-time. *Student/faculty ratio:* 23:1.

Majors Accounting technology and bookkeeping; airline pilot and flight crew; architectural engineering technology; autobody/collision and repair technology; avionics maintenance technology; biology/biological sciences; biology/biotechnology laboratory technician; building/construction finishing, management, and inspection related; business administration and management; chemistry; clinical/medical laboratory technology; computer and information sciences; computer science; cosmetology; criminal justice/law enforcement administration; culinary arts; dental hygiene; design and visual communications; diesel mechanics technology; drafting and design technology; economics; electrical, electronic and communications engineering technology; engineering; engineering technology; English; entrepreneurship; environmental engineering technology; finance; general studies; geology/earth science; graphic design; health professions related; heating, air conditioning, ventilation and refrigeration maintenance technology; history; human development and family studies; humanities; industrial radiologic technology; information science/studies; information technology; instrumentation technology; international/global studies; international relations and affairs; kinesiology and exercise science; legal assistant/paralegal; marketing/marketing management; mass communication/media; medical/clinical assistant; medical radiologic technology; music; occupational therapist assistant; photographic and film/video technology; physical sciences; physical therapy technology; physics; political science and government; psychology; public health related; quality control technology; radio and television broadcasting technology; registered nursing/registered nurse; sign language interpretation and translation; social work; sociology; speech communication and rhetoric; sport and fitness administration/management; surveying technology; teacher assistant/aide; telecommunications technology; welding technology.

Academics *Calendar:* semesters. *Degree:* certificates, diplomas, and associate. *Special study options:* academic remediation for entering students, advanced placement credit, cooperative education, distance learning, double majors, English as a second language, internships, part-time degree program, services for LD students, student-designed majors, study abroad, summer session for credit. *ROTC:* Army (c), Air Force (c).

Library Markosian Library plus 2 others with 152,537 titles, 21,736 serial subscriptions, 20,645 audiovisual materials, an OPAC, a Web page.

Student Life *Housing:* college housing not available. *Activities and Organizations:* drama/theater group, student-run newspaper, radio and television station, choral group, marching band. *Campus security:* 24-hour emergency response devices and patrols, late-night transport/escort service. *Student services:* health clinic, personal/psychological counseling.

Athletics Member NJCAA. *Intercollegiate sports:* baseball M(s), basketball M(s)/W(s), cheerleading M(s)/W(s), soccer M(c)/W(c), softball W(s), volleyball W(s).

Costs (2011–12) *Tuition:* state resident $2640 full-time, $110 per credit hour part-time; nonresident $9192 full-time, $383 per credit hour part-time. *Required fees:* $412 full-time, $23 per credit hour part-time. *Payment plan:* installment. *Waivers:* senior citizens and employees or children of employees.

Financial Aid Of all full-time matriculated undergraduates who enrolled in 2010, 132 Federal Work-Study jobs (averaging $2567).

Applying *Options:* electronic application, early admission. *Application fee:* $40. *Application deadlines:* rolling (freshmen), rolling (transfers).

Freshman Application Contact Ms. Kathy Thompson, Salt Lake Community College, Salt Lake City, UT 84130. *Phone:* 801-957-4485. *E-mail:* kathy.thompson@slcc.edu. *Web site:* http://www.slcc.edu/.

Snow College
Ephraim, Utah

- **State-supported** 2-year, founded 1888, part of Utah System of Higher Education
- **Rural** 50-acre campus
- **Endowment** $6.2 million
- **Coed,** 4,465 undergraduate students, 66% full-time, 52% women, 48% men

Undergraduates 2,943 full-time, 1,522 part-time. Students come from 34 states and territories; 12 other countries; 6% are from out of state; 1% Black or African American, non-Hispanic/Latino; 3% Hispanic/Latino; 0.5% Asian, non-Hispanic/Latino; 2% Native Hawaiian or other Pacific Islander, non-Hispanic/Latino; 1% American Indian or Alaska Native, non-Hispanic/Latino; 1% Two or more races, non-Hispanic/Latino; 3% Race/ethnicity unknown; 2% international; 2% transferred in. *Retention:* 47% of full-time freshmen returned.

Freshmen *Admission:* 2,764 applied, 2,764 admitted, 1,467 enrolled. *Average high school GPA:* 3.3.

Faculty *Total:* 319, 36% full-time, 5% with terminal degrees. *Student/faculty ratio:* 19:1.

Majors Accounting; administrative assistant and secretarial science; agricultural business and management; agriculture; animal sciences; art; automobile/automotive mechanics technology; biology/biological sciences; botany/plant biology; building/construction finishing, management, and inspection related; business administration and management; business teacher education; chemistry; child development; computer science; construction engineering technology; criminal justice/law enforcement administration; dance; dramatic/theater arts; economics; education; elementary education; family and community services; family and consumer sciences/human sciences; farm and ranch management; foods, nutrition, and wellness; forestry; French; geography; geology/earth science; history; humanities; information science/studies; Japanese; kindergarten/preschool education; liberal arts and sciences/liberal studies; mass communication/media; mathematics; music; music history, literature, and theory; music teacher education; philosophy; physical education teaching and coaching; physical sciences; physics; political science and government; pre-engineering; range science and management; science teacher education; sociology; soil science and agronomy; Spanish; trade and industrial teacher education; voice and opera; zoology/animal biology.

Academics *Calendar:* semesters. *Degree:* certificates, diplomas, and associate. *Special study options:* academic remediation for entering students, adult/continuing education programs, advanced placement credit, cooperative education, English as a second language, external degree program, honors programs, independent study, part-time degree program, services for LD students, summer session for credit.

Library Eccles Library with 51,352 titles, 201 serial subscriptions, 6,676 audiovisual materials, an OPAC, a Web page.

Student Life *Housing Options:* coed. Campus housing is university owned. *Activities and Organizations:* drama/theater group, student-run newspaper, radio station, choral group, Phi Beta Lambda, Latter-Day Saints Singers, International Student Society, BAAD Club (Alcohol and Drug Prevention), Dead Cats Society (Life Science Club). *Campus security:* 24-hour emergency response devices and patrols, student patrols, late-night transport/escort service. *Student services:* health clinic, personal/psychological counseling.

Athletics Member NJCAA. *Intercollegiate sports:* basketball M(s)/W(s), football M(s), softball W(s), volleyball W(s). *Intramural sports:* badminton M/W, basketball M/W, bowling M/W, football M/W, golf M/W, lacrosse M/W, racquetball M/W, soccer M/W, softball M/W, tennis M/W, ultimate Frisbee M/W, volleyball M/W, water polo M/W, wrestling M.

Standardized Tests *Recommended:* SAT or ACT (for admission).

Costs (2011–12) *Tuition:* state resident $2520 full-time, $150 per credit part-time; nonresident $9196 full-time, $600 per credit part-time. Full-time tuition and fees vary according to course load. Part-time tuition and fees vary according to course load. *Required fees:* $390 full-time, $30 per credit hour part-time. *Room and board:* $5000. Room and board charges vary according to board plan, housing facility, and location. *Payment plan:* installment. *Waivers:* employees or children of employees.

Financial Aid Of all full-time matriculated undergraduates who enrolled in 2010, 302 Federal Work-Study jobs (averaging $1017).

Applying *Options:* electronic application, early admission. *Application fee:* $30. *Required:* high school transcript. *Application deadlines:* 6/15 (freshmen), 6/1 (transfers). *Notification:* continuous (freshmen), continuous (transfers).

Freshman Application Contact Ms. Lorie Parry, Admissions Advisor, Snow College, 150 East College Avenue, Ephraim, UT 84627. *Phone:* 435-283-7144. *Fax:* 435-283-7157. *E-mail:* snowcollege@snow.edu. *Web site:* http://www.snow.edu/.

VERMONT

Community College of Vermont
Montpelier, Vermont

- **State-supported** 2-year, founded 1970, part of Vermont State Colleges System
- **Rural** campus
- **Coed,** 7,116 undergraduate students, 17% full-time, 69% women, 31% men

Undergraduates 1,187 full-time, 5,929 part-time. Students come from 18 states and territories; 3% are from out of state; 3% Black or African American, non-Hispanic/Latino; 2% Hispanic/Latino; 2% Asian, non-Hispanic/Latino; 0.1% Native Hawaiian or other Pacific Islander, non-Hispanic/Latino; 3% American Indian or Alaska Native, non-Hispanic/Latino; 2% Two or more races, non-Hispanic/Latino; 7% Race/ethnicity unknown.

Freshmen *Admission:* 798 applied, 798 admitted.

Faculty *Total:* 737, 12% with terminal degrees. *Student/faculty ratio:* 13:1.

Majors Accounting; administrative assistant and secretarial science; art; business administration and management; CAD/CADD drafting/design technology; child development; community organization and advocacy; computer and information sciences; computer science; computer systems networking and telecommunications; criminal justice/law enforcement administration; data entry/microcomputer applications; developmental and child psychology; digital communication and media/multimedia; early childhood education; education; environmental science; graphic design; hospitality administration; human services; industrial technology; information technology; liberal arts and sciences/liberal studies; social sciences; teacher assistant/aide.

Academics *Calendar:* semesters. *Degree:* certificates and associate. *Special study options:* academic remediation for entering students, accelerated degree program, adult/continuing education programs, advanced placement credit, cooperative education, distance learning, double majors, English as a second language, external degree program, independent study, internships, part-time degree program, services for LD students, student-designed majors, study abroad, summer session for credit.

Library Hartness Library plus 1 other with 59,000 titles, 36,500 serial subscriptions, 6,200 audiovisual materials, an OPAC, a Web page.

Student Life *Housing:* college housing not available.

Costs (2012–13) *Tuition:* state resident $6600 full-time, $220 per credit hour part-time; nonresident $13,350 full-time, $445 per credit hour part-time. *Required fees:* $100 full-time, $50 per term part-time. *Payment plan:* installment. *Waivers:* senior citizens and employees or children of employees.

Financial Aid Of all full-time matriculated undergraduates who enrolled in 2010, 84 Federal Work-Study jobs (averaging $2000).

Applying *Options:* electronic application. *Application deadlines:* rolling (freshmen), rolling (out-of-state freshmen), rolling (transfers). *Notification:* continuous (freshmen), continuous (out-of-state freshmen), continuous (transfers).

Freshman Application Contact Community College of Vermont, PO Box 489, Montpelier, VT 05601. *Phone:* 802-654-0505. *Toll-free phone:* 800-CCV-6686. *Web site:* http://www.ccv.edu/.

Landmark College
Putney, Vermont

Freshman Application Contact Admissions Main Desk, Landmark College, Putney, VT 05346. *Phone:* 802-387-6718. *Fax:* 802-387-6868. *E-mail:* admissions@landmark.edu. *Web site:* http://www.landmark.edu/.

New England Culinary Institute
Montpelier, Vermont

Freshman Application Contact Jan Knutsen, Vice President of Enrollment, New England Culinary Institute, 56 College Street, Montpelier, VT 05602-3115. *Toll-free phone:* 877-223-6324. *Fax:* 802-225-3280. *E-mail:* janknutsen@neci.edu. *Web site:* http://www.neci.edu/.

VIRGINIA

ACT College
Arlington, Virginia

- **Proprietary** 2-year, founded 1983
- **Coed,** 501 undergraduate students

Undergraduates 31% are from out of state.

Faculty *Total:* 29, 52% full-time. *Student/faculty ratio:* 21:1.

Majors Dental assisting; medical/clinical assistant; medical office assistant; pharmacy, pharmaceutical sciences, and administration related; radiologic technology/science.

Academics *Degree:* diplomas and associate. *Special study options:* academic remediation for entering students, cooperative education, honors programs, internships, part-time degree program, services for LD students.

Applying *Application fee:* $50. *Required:* interview. *Recommended:* high school transcript, 3 letters of recommendation.

Freshman Application Contact Admissions Office, ACT College, 1100 Wilson Boulevard, Arlington, VA 22209. *Phone:* 703-527-6660. *Toll-free phone:* 866-950-7979. *E-mail:* info@actcollege.edu. *Web site:* http://www.healthtraining.com/.

Advanced Technology Institute

Virginia Beach, Virginia

Freshman Application Contact Admissions Office, Advanced Technology Institute, 5700 Southern Boulevard, Suite 100, Virginia Beach, VA 23462. *Phone:* 757-490-1241. *Toll-free phone:* 888-468-1093. *Web site:* http://www.auto.edu/.

Aviation Institute of Maintenance–Chesapeake

Chesapeake, Virginia

Freshman Application Contact Aviation Institute of Maintenance–Chesapeake, 2211 South Military Highway, Chesapeake, VA 23320. *Phone:* 757-363-2121. *Toll-free phone:* 888-349-5387. *Fax:* 757-363-2044. *Web site:* http://www.aviationmaintenance.edu/.

Aviation Institute of Maintenance–Manassas

Manassas, Virginia

Freshman Application Contact Aviation Institute of Maintenance–Manassas, 9821 Godwin Drive, Manassas, VA 20110. *Phone:* 703-257-5515. *Toll-free phone:* 888-349-5387- (in-state); 888-349-5387 (out-of-state). *Fax:* 703-257-5523. *Web site:* http://www.aviationmaintenance.edu/.

Blue Ridge Community College

Weyers Cave, Virginia

Freshman Application Contact Blue Ridge Community College, PO Box 80, Weyers Cave, VA 24486-0080. *Phone:* 540-453-2217. *Toll-free phone:* 888-750-2722. *Web site:* http://www.brcc.edu/.

Bryant & Stratton College - Richmond Campus

Richmond, Virginia

Freshman Application Contact Mr. David K. Mayle, Director of Admissions, Bryant & Stratton College - Richmond Campus, 8141 Hull Street Road, Richmond, VA 23235-6411. *Phone:* 804-745-2444. *Fax:* 804-745-6884. *E-mail:* tlawson@bryanstratton.edu. *Web site:* http://www.bryantstratton.edu/.

Bryant & Stratton College - Virginia Beach

Virginia Beach, Virginia

Freshman Application Contact Bryant & Stratton College - Virginia Beach, 301 Centre Pointe Drive, Virginia Beach, VA 23462-4417. *Phone:* 757-499-7900 Ext. 173. *Web site:* http://www.bryantstratton.edu/.

Central Virginia Community College

Lynchburg, Virginia

Freshman Application Contact Admissions Office, Central Virginia Community College, 3506 Wards Road, Lynchburg, VA 24502-2498. *Phone:* 434-832-7633. *Toll-free phone:* 800-562-3060. *Fax:* 434-832-7793. *Web site:* http://www.cvcc.vccs.edu/.

Centura College

Chesapeake, Virginia

Director of Admissions Director of Admissions, Centura College, 932 Ventures Way, Chesapeake, VA 23320. *Phone:* 757-549-2121. *Toll-free phone:* 877-575-5627. *Fax:* 575-549-1196. *Web site:* http://www.centuracollege.edu/.

Centura College

Newport News, Virginia

Director of Admissions Victoria Whitehead, Director of Admissions, Centura College, 616 Denbigh Boulevard, Newport News, VA 23608. *Phone:* 757-874-2121. *Toll-free phone:* 877-575-5627. *Fax:* 757-874-3857. *E-mail:* admdircpen@centura.edu. *Web site:* http://www.centuracollege.edu/.

Centura College

Norfolk, Virginia

Director of Admissions Director of Admissions, Centura College, 7020 North Military Highway, Norfolk, VA 23518. *Phone:* 757-853-2121. *Toll-free phone:* 877-575-5627. *Fax:* 757-852-9017. *Web site:* http://www.centuracollege.edu/.

Centura College

Richmond, Virginia

Director of Admissions Terry Gates, Director of Admissions, Centura College, 7001 West Broad Street, Richmond, VA 23294. *Phone:* 804-672-2300. *Toll-free phone:* 877-575-5627. *Fax:* 804-672-3338. *Web site:* http://www.centuracollege.edu/.

Centura College

Richmond, Virginia

Freshman Application Contact Admissions Office, Centura College, 7914 Midlothian Turnpike, Richmond, VA 23235-5230. *Phone:* 804-330-0111. *Toll-free phone:* 877-575-5627. *Fax:* 804-330-3809. *Web site:* http://www.centuracollege.edu/.

Centura College

Virginia Beach, Virginia

Freshman Application Contact Admissions Office, Centura College, 2697 Dean Drive, Suite 100, Virginia Beach, VA 23452. *Phone:* 757-340-2121. *Toll-free phone:* 877-575-5627. *Fax:* 757-340-9704. *Web site:* http://www.centuracollege.edu/.

Dabney S. Lancaster Community College

Clifton Forge, Virginia

- **State-supported** 2-year, founded 1964, part of Virginia Community College System
- **Rural** 117-acre campus
- **Endowment** $3.3 million
- **Coed**

Undergraduates 527 full-time, 910 part-time. Students come from 5 states and territories; 6% are from out of state; 24% transferred in.

Faculty *Student/faculty ratio:* 15:1.

Academics *Calendar:* semesters. *Degree:* certificates, diplomas, and associate. *Special study options:* academic remediation for entering students, adult/continuing education programs, advanced placement credit, cooperative education, distance learning, honors programs, independent study, internships, part-time degree program, services for LD students, study abroad, summer session for credit.

Student Life *Campus security:* 24-hour emergency response devices.

Costs (2011–12) *Tuition:* state resident $2916 full-time, $122 per credit hour part-time; nonresident $7514 full-time, $313 per credit hour part-time. Full-time tuition and fees vary according to program and reciprocity agreements. Part-time tuition and fees vary according to program and reciprocity agreements. *Required fees:* $240 full-time, $10 per credit hour part-time.

Applying *Options:* electronic application, early admission, deferred entrance. *Recommended:* high school transcript, interview.

Freshman Application Contact Ms. Kathy Nicely, Registration Specialist, Dabney S. Lancaster Community College, Scott Hall, Clifton Forge, VA

24422. *Phone:* 540-863-2841. *Toll-free phone:* 877-73-DSLCC. *Fax:* 540-863-2915. *E-mail:* knicely@dslcc.edu. *Web site:* http://www.dslcc.edu/.

Danville Community College
Danville, Virginia

Freshman Application Contact Cathy Pulliam, Coordinator of Student Recruitment and Enrollment, Danville Community College, 1008 South Main Street, Danville, VA 24541-4088. *Phone:* 434-797-8538. *Toll-free phone:* 800-560-4291. *E-mail:* cpulliam@dcc.vccs.edu. *Web site:* http://www.dcc.vccs.edu/.

Eastern Shore Community College
Melfa, Virginia

Freshman Application Contact P. Bryan Smith, Dean of Student Services, Eastern Shore Community College, 29300 Lankford Highway, Melfa, VA 23410. *Phone:* 757-789-1732. *Toll-free phone:* 877-871-8455. *Fax:* 757-789-1737. *E-mail:* bsmith@es.vccs.edu. *Web site:* http://www.es.vccs.edu/.

ECPI College of Technology
Richmond, Virginia

Freshman Application Contact Director, ECPI College of Technology, 800 Moorefield Park Drive, Richmond, VA 23236. *Phone:* 804-330-5533. *Toll-free phone:* 800-986-1200. *Fax:* 804-330-5577. *E-mail:* agerard@ecpi.edu. *Web site:* http://www.ecpi.edu/.

Everest College
Arlington, Virginia

Freshman Application Contact Director of Admissions, Everest College, 801 North Quincy Street, Suite 500, Arlington, VA 22203. *Phone:* 703-248-8887. *Toll-free phone:* 888-741-4270. *Fax:* 703-351-2202. *Web site:* http://www.everest.edu/.

Germanna Community College
Locust Grove, Virginia

Freshman Application Contact Ms. Rita Dunston, Registrar, Germanna Community College, 10000 Germanna Point Drive, Fredericksburg, VA 22408. *Phone:* 540-891-3020. *Fax:* 540-891-3092. *Web site:* http://www.gcc.vccs.edu/.

ITT Technical Institute
Chantilly, Virginia

- **Proprietary** primarily 2-year, founded 2002, part of ITT Educational Services, Inc.
- **Coed**

Majors Business administration and management; communications technology; computer and information systems security; computer software and media applications related; construction management; criminal justice/law enforcement administration; drafting and design technology; electrical, electronic and communications engineering technology; forensic science and technology; graphic communications; legal assistant/paralegal; network and system administration; project management.
Academics *Calendar:* quarters. *Degrees:* associate and bachelor's.
Student Life *Housing:* college housing not available.
Freshman Application Contact Director of Recruitment, ITT Technical Institute, 14420 Abermarle Point Place, Suite 100, Chantilly, VA 20151. *Phone:* 703-263-2541. *Toll-free phone:* 888-895-8324. *Web site:* http://www.itt-tech.edu/.

ITT Technical Institute
Norfolk, Virginia

- **Proprietary** primarily 2-year, founded 1988, part of ITT Educational Services, Inc.
- **Suburban** campus
- **Coed**

Majors Business administration and management; communications technology; computer and information systems security; construction management; criminal justice/law enforcement administration; drafting and design technology; electrical, electronic and communications engineering technology; forensic science and technology; game and interactive media design; graphic communications; legal assistant/paralegal; project management; registered nursing/registered nurse; web/multimedia management and webmaster.

Academics *Calendar:* quarters. *Degrees:* associate and bachelor's.
Student Life *Housing:* college housing not available.
Financial Aid Of all full-time matriculated undergraduates who enrolled in 2010, 3 Federal Work-Study jobs (averaging $5000).
Freshman Application Contact Director of Recruitment, ITT Technical Institute, 863 Glenrock Road, Suite 100, Norfolk, VA 23502-3701. *Phone:* 757-466-1260. *Toll-free phone:* 888-253-8324. *Web site:* http://www.itt-tech.edu/.

ITT Technical Institute
Richmond, Virginia

- **Proprietary** primarily 2-year, founded 1999, part of ITT Educational Services, Inc.
- **Coed**

Majors Business administration and management; communications technology; computer and information systems security; construction management; criminal justice/law enforcement administration; drafting and design technology; electrical, electronic and communications engineering technology; forensic science and technology; game and interactive media design; graphic communications; legal assistant/paralegal; network and system administration; project management.
Academics *Calendar:* quarters. *Degrees:* associate and bachelor's.
Student Life *Housing:* college housing not available.
Freshman Application Contact Director of Recruitment, ITT Technical Institute, 300 Gateway Centre Parkway, Richmond, VA 23235. *Phone:* 804-330-4992. *Toll-free phone:* 888-330-4888. *Web site:* http://www.itt-tech.edu/.

ITT Technical Institute
Salem, Virginia

- **Proprietary** primarily 2-year
- **Coed**

Majors Business administration and management; communications technology; computer and information systems security; drafting and design technology; electrical, electronic and communications engineering technology; forensic science and technology; graphic communications; legal assistant/paralegal; network and system administration; project management; registered nursing/registered nurse.
Academics *Degrees:* associate and bachelor's.
Freshman Application Contact Director of Recruitment, ITT Technical Institute, 2159 Apperson Drive, Salem, VA 24153. *Phone:* 540-989-2500. *Toll-free phone:* 877-208-6132. *Web site:* http://www.itt-tech.edu/.

ITT Technical Institute
Springfield, Virginia

- **Proprietary** primarily 2-year, founded 2002, part of ITT Educational Services, Inc.
- **Coed**

Majors Business administration and management; communications technology; computer and information systems security; computer software technology; construction management; criminal justice/law enforcement administration; drafting and design technology; electrical, electronic and communications engineering technology; forensic science and technology; game and interactive media design; graphic communications; legal assistant/paralegal; network and system administration; project management.
Academics *Calendar:* quarters. *Degrees:* associate and bachelor's.
Student Life *Housing:* college housing not available.
Freshman Application Contact Director of Recruitment, ITT Technical Institute, 7300 Boston Boulevard, Springfield, VA 22153. *Phone:* 703-440-9535. *Toll-free phone:* 866-817-8324. *Web site:* http://www.itt-tech.edu/.

John Tyler Community College
Chester, Virginia

- **State-supported** 2-year, founded 1967, part of Virginia Community College System
- **Suburban** 160-acre campus with easy access to Richmond
- **Endowment** $2.1 million
- **Coed,** 10,797 undergraduate students, 29% full-time, 58% women, 42% men

Undergraduates 3,181 full-time, 7,616 part-time. Students come from 7 states and territories; 3 other countries; 26% Black or African American, non-Hispanic/Latino; 5% Hispanic/Latino; 3% Asian, non-Hispanic/Latino; 0.2% Native Hawaiian or other Pacific Islander, non-Hispanic/Latino; 0.5% American Indian or Alaska Native, non-Hispanic/Latino; 2% Two or more races, non-Hispanic/Latino; 2% Race/ethnicity unknown; 0.1% international; 5% transferred in. *Retention:* 60% of full-time freshmen returned.

Freshmen *Admission:* 1,387 enrolled.

Faculty *Total:* 548, 19% full-time. *Student/faculty ratio:* 23:1.

Majors Accounting related; administrative assistant and secretarial science; architectural engineering technology; architectural technology; business administration and management; business administration, management and operations related; business/commerce; child-care provision; computer and information sciences; criminal justice/law enforcement administration; electrical and electronics engineering; engineering; engineering technology; funeral service and mortuary science; general studies; humanities; human services; industrial electronics technology; industrial technology; information technology; liberal arts and sciences/liberal studies; management information systems; mechanical engineering/mechanical technology; mechanical engineering technologies related; mental and social health services and allied professions related; quality control and safety technologies related; registered nursing/registered nurse; visual and performing arts related.

Academics *Calendar:* semesters. *Degree:* certificates and associate. *Special study options:* academic remediation for entering students, adult/continuing education programs, advanced placement credit, distance learning, external degree program, honors programs, off-campus study, part-time degree program, services for LD students, study abroad, summer session for credit. *ROTC:* Army (c).

Library John Tyler Community College Learning Resource and Technology Center with 52,000 titles, 10,150 serial subscriptions, 1,335 audiovisual materials, an OPAC, a Web page.

Student Life *Housing:* college housing not available. *Activities and Organizations:* drama/theater group, choral group, Phi Theta Kappa -TauRho, Phi Theta Kappa - BOO, Art Club, Elements of Life Club, Funeral Services Club. *Campus security:* 24-hour emergency response devices and patrols.

Costs (2011–12) *Tuition:* state resident $2856 full-time, $119 per credit hour part-time; nonresident $7454 full-time, $311 per credit hour part-time. Full-time tuition and fees vary according to course load. Part-time tuition and fees vary according to course load. *Required fees:* $50 full-time, $25 per term part-time. *Payment plan:* installment. *Waivers:* senior citizens.

Applying *Options:* early admission, deferred entrance. *Recommended:* high school transcript. *Application deadline:* rolling (freshmen). *Notification:* continuous (freshmen).

Freshman Application Contact Ms. Joy James, Director of Admission, John Tyler Community College, 13101 Jefferson Davis Highway, Chester, VA 23831. *Phone:* 804-706-5214. *Toll-free phone:* 800-552-3490. *Fax:* 804-796-4362. *Web site:* http://www.jtcc.edu/.

J. Sargeant Reynolds Community College
Richmond, Virginia

- **State-supported** 2-year, founded 1972, part of Virginia Community College System
- **Suburban** 207-acre campus
- **Coed,** 13,370 undergraduate students, 30% full-time, 61% women, 39% men

Undergraduates 4,075 full-time, 9,295 part-time. 37% Black or African American, non-Hispanic/Latino; 3% Hispanic/Latino; 4% Asian, non-Hispanic/Latino; 1% American Indian or Alaska Native, non-Hispanic/Latino; 2% Race/ethnicity unknown.

Freshmen *Admission:* 2,180 enrolled.

Majors Administrative assistant and secretarial science; agricultural business and management; biological and physical sciences; business administration and management; business/commerce; clinical/medical laboratory technology; computer and information sciences; dental laboratory technology; electrical and electronic engineering technologies related; emergency medical technology (EMT paramedic); engineering; engineering technologies and engineering related; homeland security, law enforcement, firefighting and protective services related; industrial technology; liberal arts and sciences/liberal studies; management information systems; mental and social health services and allied professions related; occupational therapist assistant; optometric technician; public administration and social service professions related; registered nursing/registered nurse; respiratory care therapy; social sciences; special education; vehicle maintenance and repair technologies related; visual and performing arts related.

Academics *Calendar:* semesters. *Degree:* certificates and associate. *Special study options:* academic remediation for entering students, adult/continuing education programs, advanced placement credit, distance learning, English as a second language, independent study, internships, off-campus study, part-time degree program, services for LD students, summer session for credit.

Library J. Sargeant Reynolds Community College Library plus 3 others with 101,858 titles, 45,875 serial subscriptions, 2,483 audiovisual materials, an OPAC, a Web page.

Student Life *Housing:* college housing not available. *Activities and Organizations:* drama/theater group. *Campus security:* 24-hour emergency response devices and patrols, late-night transport/escort service, security during open hours. *Student services:* personal/psychological counseling.

Costs (2011–12) *Tuition:* state resident $3873 full-time, $129 per credit hour part-time; nonresident $9621 full-time, $321 per credit hour part-time. Full-time tuition and fees vary according to course load. Part-time tuition and fees vary according to course load. *Payment plan:* installment. *Waivers:* senior citizens.

Financial Aid Of all full-time matriculated undergraduates who enrolled in 2009, 14,628 applied for aid, 11,184 were judged to have need. 64 Federal Work-Study jobs (averaging $2600). In 2009, 121 non-need-based awards were made. *Average percent of need met:* 49%. *Average financial aid package:* $6950. *Average need-based loan:* $2792. *Average need-based gift aid:* $3400. *Average non-need-based aid:* $891. *Average indebtedness upon graduation:* $3891.

Applying *Options:* electronic application. *Required:* high school transcript. *Required for some:* interview. *Application deadlines:* rolling (freshmen), rolling (transfers). *Notification:* continuous (freshmen), continuous (transfers).

Freshman Application Contact Ms. Karen Pettis-Walden, Director of Admissions and Records, J. Sargeant Reynolds Community College, PO Box 85622, Richmond, VA 23285-5622. *Phone:* 804-523-5029. *Fax:* 804-371-3650. *E-mail:* kpettis-walden@reynolds.edu. *Web site:* http://www.reynolds.edu/.

Kaplan College, Chesapeake Campus
Chesapeake, Virginia

- **Proprietary** 2-year
- **Coed**

Majors Computer systems networking and telecommunications; criminal justice/law enforcement administration; medical office management.

Academics *Degree:* diplomas and associate.

Freshman Application Contact Admissions Director, Kaplan College, Chesapeake Campus, 1987 South Military Highway, Chesapeake, VA 23320. *Phone:* 757-494-6800. *Toll-free phone:* 800-935-1857. *Web site:* http://chesapeake.kaplancollege.com/.

Lord Fairfax Community College
Middletown, Virginia

Freshman Application Contact Karen Bucher, Director of Enrollment Management, Lord Fairfax Community College, 173 Skirmisher Lane, Middletown, VA 22645. *Phone:* 540-868-7132. *Toll-free phone:* 800-906-LFCC. *Fax:* 540-868-7005. *E-mail:* kbucher@lfcc.edu. *Web site:* http://www.lfcc.edu/.

Mountain Empire Community College
Big Stone Gap, Virginia

- **State-supported** 2-year, founded 1972, part of Virginia Community College System
- **Rural** campus
- **Coed**

Undergraduates 1,606 full-time, 1,798 part-time. Students come from 10 states and territories; 3% are from out of state; 2% Black or African American, non-Hispanic/Latino; 0.3% Hispanic/Latino; 0.3% Asian, non-Hispanic/Latino; 0.2% American Indian or Alaska Native, non-Hispanic/Latino; 0.2% Race/ethnicity unknown. *Retention:* 48% of full-time freshmen returned.

Academics *Calendar:* semesters. *Degree:* certificates and associate. *Special study options:* academic remediation for entering students, adult/continuing education programs, advanced placement credit, cooperative education, distance learning, double majors, external degree program, independent study, internships, part-time degree program, student-designed majors, summer session for credit.

Student Life *Campus security:* 24-hour emergency response devices and patrols.

Financial Aid Of all full-time matriculated undergraduates who enrolled in 2010, 150 Federal Work-Study jobs (averaging $1200). 30 state and other part-time jobs (averaging $650).

Applying *Options:* electronic application, early admission, deferred entrance. *Required:* high school transcript. *Required for some:* minimum 2.0 GPA.

Freshman Application Contact Mountain Empire Community College, 3441 Mountain Empire Road, Big Stone Gap, VA 24219. *Phone:* 276-523-2400 Ext. 219. *Web site:* http://www.mecc.edu/.

National College
Bluefield, Virginia

Freshman Application Contact National College, 100 Logan Street, PO Box 629, Bluefield, VA 24605-1405. *Phone:* 276-326-3621. *Toll-free phone:* 888-9-JOBREADY. *Web site:* http://www.national-college.edu/.

National College
Charlottesville, Virginia

Director of Admissions Kimberly Moore, Campus Director, National College, 1819 Emmet Street, Charlottesville, VA 22901. *Phone:* 434-295-0136. *Toll-free phone:* 888-9-JOBREADY. *Fax:* 434-979-8061. *Web site:* http://www.national-college.edu/.

National College
Danville, Virginia

Freshman Application Contact Admissions Office, National College, 734 Main Street, Danville, VA 24541-1819. *Phone:* 434-793-6822. *Toll-free phone:* 888-9-JOBREADY. *Web site:* http://www.national-college.edu/.

National College
Harrisonburg, Virginia

Director of Admissions Jack Evey, Campus Director, National College, 51 B Burgess Road, Harrisonburg, VA 22801-9709. *Phone:* 540-432-0943. *Toll-free phone:* 888-9-JOBREADY. *Web site:* http://www.national-college.edu/.

National College
Lynchburg, Virginia

Freshman Application Contact Admissions Representative, National College, 104 Candlewood Court, Lynchburg, VA 24502-2653. *Phone:* 804-239-3500. *Toll-free phone:* 888-9-JOBREADY. *Web site:* http://www.national-college.edu/.

National College
Martinsville, Virginia

Director of Admissions Mr. John Scott, Campus Director, National College, 10 Church Street, PO Box 232, Martinsville, VA 24114. *Phone:* 276-632-5621. *Toll-free phone:* 888-9-JOBREADY. *Web site:* http://www.national-college.edu/.

National College
Salem, Virginia

Freshman Application Contact Director of Admissions, National College, 1813 East Main Street, Salem, VA 24153. *Phone:* 540-986-1800. *Toll-free phone:* 888-9-JOBREADY. *Fax:* 540-444-4198. *Web site:* http://www.national-college.edu/.

New River Community College
Dublin, Virginia

Freshman Application Contact Ms. Margaret G. Taylor, Director of Student Services, New River Community College, PO Box 1127, Dublin, VA 24084-1127. *Phone:* 540-674-3600. *Toll-free phone:* 866-462-6722. *Fax:* 540-674-3644. *E-mail:* nrtaylm@nr.edu. *Web site:* http://www.nr.edu/.

Northern Virginia Community College
Annandale, Virginia

Director of Admissions Dr. Max L. Bassett, Dean of Academic and Student Services, Northern Virginia Community College, 4001 Wakefield Chapel Road, Annandale, VA 22003-3796. *Phone:* 703-323-3195. *Web site:* http://www.nvcc.edu/.

Patrick Henry Community College
Martinsville, Virginia

Freshman Application Contact Mr. Travis Tisdale, Coordinator, Admissions and Records, Patrick Henry Community College, Martinsville, VA 24115. *Phone:* 276-656-0311. *Toll-free phone:* 800-232-7997. *Fax:* 276-656-0352. *Web site:* http://www.ph.vccs.edu/.

Paul D. Camp Community College
Franklin, Virginia

- **State-supported** 2-year, founded 1971, part of Virginia Community College System
- **Small-town** 99-acre campus
- **Endowment** $500,000
- **Coed**

Undergraduates 426 full-time, 1,153 part-time. Students come from 2 states and territories; 2 other countries; 0.5% are from out of state; 38% Black or African American, non-Hispanic/Latino; 4% Race/ethnicity unknown. *Retention:* 66% of full-time freshmen returned.
Faculty *Student/faculty ratio:* 17:1.
Academics *Calendar:* semesters. *Degree:* certificates and associate. *Special study options:* academic remediation for entering students, adult/continuing education programs, advanced placement credit, cooperative education, distance learning, honors programs, independent study, internships, off-campus study, part-time degree program, summer session for credit.
Student Life *Campus security:* late-night transport/escort service.
Costs (2011–12) *Tuition:* state resident $2624 full-time, $109 per credit part-time; nonresident $7772 full-time, $302 per credit part-time. Full-time tuition and fees vary according to course load. Part-time tuition and fees vary according to course load.
Financial Aid Of all full-time matriculated undergraduates who enrolled in 2010, 30 Federal Work-Study jobs (averaging $2000).
Applying *Options:* electronic application, deferred entrance. *Required:* high school transcript.
Freshman Application Contact Dr. Joe Edenfield, Director of Admissions and Records, Paul D. Camp Community College, PO Box 737, 100 North College Drive, Franklin, VA 23851-0737. *Phone:* 757-569-6744. *E-mail:* jedenfield@pdc.edu. *Web site:* http://www.pdc.edu/.

Piedmont Virginia Community College
Charlottesville, Virginia

- **State-supported** 2-year, founded 1972, part of Virginia Community College System
- **Suburban** 114-acre campus with easy access to Richmond
- **Coed,** 5,683 undergraduate students, 21% full-time, 60% women, 40% men

Undergraduates 1,191 full-time, 4,492 part-time. Students come from 32 states and territories; 9 other countries; 14% Black or African American, non-Hispanic/Latino; 2% Hispanic/Latino; 4% Asian, non-Hispanic/Latino; 0.3% American Indian or Alaska Native, non-Hispanic/Latino; 2% Race/ethnicity unknown; 10% transferred in.
Freshmen *Admission:* 835 enrolled.
Faculty *Total:* 300, 24% full-time. *Student/faculty ratio:* 18:1.
Majors Accounting; biological and physical sciences; biotechnology; business administration and management; clinical/medical laboratory technology; computer and information sciences and support services related; computer engineering technology; computer programming; computer programming (specific applications); computer science; computer systems networking and telecommunications; criminal justice/police science; data processing and data processing technology; diagnostic medical sonography and ultrasound technology; education; emergency medical technology (EMT paramedic); engineering; general studies; liberal arts and sciences/liberal studies; marketing/marketing management; radiologic technology/science; registered nursing/registered nurse; visual and performing arts; web/multimedia management and webmaster.
Academics *Calendar:* semesters. *Degree:* certificates and associate. *Special study options:* academic remediation for entering students, adult/continuing education programs, advanced placement credit, cooperative education, distance learning, English as a second language, honors programs, independent study, internships, part-time degree program, services for LD students, summer session for credit. *ROTC:* Army (c).
Library Jessup Library with 37,261 titles, 139 serial subscriptions, 1,058 audiovisual materials, an OPAC, a Web page.
Student Life *Housing:* college housing not available. *Activities and Organizations:* drama/theater group, student-run newspaper, choral group, Phi Theta Kappa, Black Student Alliance, Science Club, Masquers, Christian Fellowship Club. *Campus security:* 24-hour emergency response devices and patrols, late-night transport/escort service.
Athletics *Intramural sports:* basketball M/W, golf M/W, soccer M/W, table tennis M/W, tennis M/W, ultimate Frisbee M/W, volleyball M/W, weight lifting M/W.
Costs (2011–12) *Tuition:* state resident $3345 full-time, $112 per credit hour part-time; nonresident $8643 full-time, $288 per credit hour part-time. Full-time tuition and fees vary according to course load. Part-time tuition and fees

vary according to course load. *Required fees:* $319 full-time, $11 per credit hour part-time. *Payment plan:* installment. *Waivers:* senior citizens.

Financial Aid Of all full-time matriculated undergraduates who enrolled in 2010, 50 Federal Work-Study jobs.

Applying *Options:* electronic application, early admission, deferred entrance. *Required for some:* high school transcript, for nursing program: completion of any developmental studies; grade C or better in high school or college developmental chemistry course; high school diploma/GED; and completion of nursing program application. *Application deadlines:* rolling (freshmen), rolling (transfers). *Notification:* continuous (freshmen), continuous (transfers).

Freshman Application Contact Ms. Mary Lee Walsh, Dean of Student Services, Piedmont Virginia Community College, 501 College Drive, Charlottesville, VA 22902-7589. *Phone:* 434-961-6540. *Fax:* 434-961-5425. *E-mail:* mwalsh@pvcc.edu. *Web site:* http://www.pvcc.edu/.

Rappahannock Community College
Glenns, Virginia

Freshman Application Contact Ms. Wilnet Willis, Admissions and Records Officer, Rappahannock Community College, Glenns Campus, PO Box 287, Glenns, VA 23149-0287. *Phone:* 804-758-6742. *Toll-free phone:* 800-836-9381. *Web site:* http://www.rappahannock.edu/.

Richard Bland College of The College of William and Mary
Petersburg, Virginia

Freshman Application Contact Office of Admissions, Richard Bland College of The College of William and Mary, 11301 Johnson Road, Petersburg, VA 23805-7100. *Phone:* 804-862-6249. *Web site:* http://www.rbc.edu/.

Southside Virginia Community College
Alberta, Virginia

- **State-supported** 2-year, founded 1970, part of Virginia Community College System
- **Rural** 207-acre campus
- **Endowment** $1.3 million
- **Coed**

Undergraduates 1,924 full-time, 4,429 part-time. Students come from 5 states and territories; 0.1% are from out of state.

Faculty *Student/faculty ratio:* 17:1.

Academics *Calendar:* semesters. *Degree:* certificates, diplomas, and associate. *Special study options:* academic remediation for entering students, advanced placement credit, distance learning, honors programs, off-campus study, part-time degree program, services for LD students, study abroad, summer session for credit. *ROTC:* Army (c).

Costs (2011–12) *Tuition:* state resident $3345 full-time, $112 per credit hour part-time; nonresident $8643 full-time, $288 per credit hour part-time. Full-time tuition and fees vary according to course load. Part-time tuition and fees vary according to course load. *Required fees:* $300 full-time, $10 per credit hour part-time.

Applying *Options:* electronic application, deferred entrance. *Required:* high school transcript, interview.

Freshman Application Contact Mr. Brent Richey, Dean of Enrollment Management, Southside Virginia Community College, 109 Campus Drive, Alberta, VA 23821. *Phone:* 434-949-1012. *Fax:* 434-949-7863. *E-mail:* rhina.jones@sv.vccs.edu. *Web site:* http://www.southside.edu/.

Southwest Virginia Community College
Richlands, Virginia

- **State-supported** 2-year, founded 1968, part of Virginia Community College System
- **Rural** 100-acre campus
- **Endowment** $8.5 million
- **Coed,** 3,755 undergraduate students, 39% full-time, 54% women, 46% men

Undergraduates 1,475 full-time, 2,280 part-time. Students come from 7 states and territories; 2% are from out of state; 3% Black or African American, non-Hispanic/Latino; 0.8% Hispanic/Latino; 0.4% Asian, non-Hispanic/Latino; 0.1% Native Hawaiian or other Pacific Islander, non-Hispanic/Latino; 0.4% American Indian or Alaska Native, non-Hispanic/Latino; 0.3% Two or more races, non-Hispanic/Latino; 0.3% Race/ethnicity unknown; 25% transferred in. *Retention:* 50% of full-time freshmen returned.

Freshmen *Admission:* 551 enrolled.

Faculty *Total:* 246, 19% full-time. *Student/faculty ratio:* 17:1.

Majors Accounting related; business administration, management and operations related; business operations support and secretarial services related; child-care provision; computer and information sciences; criminal justice/law enforcement administration; criminal justice/police science; electrical, electronic and communications engineering technology; emergency medical technology (EMT paramedic); liberal arts and sciences/liberal studies; mental and social health services and allied professions related; radiologic technology/science; registered nursing/registered nurse; respiratory care therapy.

Academics *Calendar:* semesters. *Degree:* certificates, diplomas, and associate. *Special study options:* academic remediation for entering students, adult/continuing education programs, advanced placement credit, distance learning, double majors, honors programs, internships, part-time degree program, summer session for credit.

Library Southwest Virginia Community College Library with 110,000 titles, 950 serial subscriptions, 900 audiovisual materials, an OPAC, a Web page.

Student Life *Housing:* college housing not available. *Activities and Organizations:* choral group, Phi Theta Kappa, Phi Beta Lambda, Intervoice, Helping Minds Club, Project ACHEIVE. *Campus security:* 24-hour emergency response devices and patrols, student patrols, heavily saturated camera system. *Student services:* personal/psychological counseling.

Standardized Tests *Required:* ASSET or COMPASS or VCCS Math (for admission).

Costs (2011–12) *Tuition:* state resident $2676 full-time, $112 per credit hour part-time; nonresident $6914 full-time, $288 per credit hour part-time. No tuition increase for student's term of enrollment. *Required fees:* $216 full-time, $9 per credit hour part-time. *Payment plans:* tuition prepayment, installment. *Waivers:* senior citizens.

Financial Aid Of all full-time matriculated undergraduates who enrolled in 2010, 150 Federal Work-Study jobs (averaging $1140).

Applying *Options:* electronic application, early admission, deferred entrance. *Required:* high school transcript, interview. *Application deadlines:* rolling (freshmen), rolling (transfers).

Freshman Application Contact Mr. Jim Farris, Director of Admissions, Records, and Counseling, Southwest Virginia Community College, Box SVCC, Richlands, VA 24641. *Phone:* 276-964-7300. *Toll-free phone:* 800-822-7822. *Fax:* 276-964-7716. *Web site:* http://www.sw.edu/.

Thomas Nelson Community College
Hampton, Virginia

Freshman Application Contact Ms. Jerri Newson, Admissions Office Manager, Thomas Nelson Community College, PO Box 9407, Hampton, VA 23670-0407. *Phone:* 757-825-2800. *Fax:* 757-825-2763. *E-mail:* admissions@tncc.edu. *Web site:* http://www.tncc.edu/.

Tidewater Community College
Norfolk, Virginia

Freshman Application Contact Kellie Sorey PhD, Registrar, Tidewater Community College, Norfolk, VA 23510. *Phone:* 757-822-1900. *E-mail:* CentralRecords@tcc.edu. *Web site:* http://www.tcc.edu/.

Virginia Highlands Community College
Abingdon, Virginia

Freshman Application Contact Karen Cheers, Acting · Director of Admissions, Records, and Financial Aid, Virginia Highlands Community College, PO Box 828, 100 VHCC Drive Abingdon, Abingdon, VA 24212. *Phone:* 276-739-2490. *Toll-free phone:* 877-207-6115. *E-mail:* kcheers@vhcc.edu. *Web site:* http://www.vhcc.edu/.

Virginia Western Community College
Roanoke, Virginia

- **State-supported** 2-year, founded 1966, part of Virginia Community College System
- **Suburban** 70-acre campus
- **Coed,** 8,557 undergraduate students, 30% full-time, 56% women, 44% men

Undergraduates 2,552 full-time, 6,005 part-time. Students come from 16 states and territories; 2 other countries; 1% are from out of state; 15% Black or African American, non-Hispanic/Latino; 2% Hispanic/Latino; 3% Asian, non-Hispanic/Latino; 0.3% Native Hawaiian or other Pacific Islander, non-Hispanic/Latino; 0.8% American Indian or Alaska Native, non-Hispanic/Latino; 0.8% Two or more races, non-Hispanic/Latino; 0.2% Race/ethnicity unknown; 0.3% international; 4% transferred in. *Retention:* 59% of full-time freshmen returned.

Freshmen *Admission:* 1,421 enrolled.

Faculty *Student/faculty ratio:* 23:1.

Majors Accounting; administrative assistant and secretarial science; art; automobile/automotive mechanics technology; biological and physical sciences; business administration and management; child development; civil engineering technology; commercial and advertising art; computer science; criminal justice/law enforcement administration; data processing and data processing technology; dental hygiene; education; electrical, electronic and communications engineering technology; engineering; industrial radiologic technology; kindergarten/preschool education; liberal arts and sciences/liberal studies; mechanical engineering/mechanical technology; mental health counseling; pre-engineering; radio and television; radiologic technology/science; registered nursing/registered nurse.

Academics *Calendar:* semesters. *Degree:* certificates and associate. *Special study options:* academic remediation for entering students, advanced placement credit, cooperative education, distance learning, double majors, English as a second language, honors programs, independent study, internships, part-time degree program, services for LD students, summer session for credit.

Library Brown Library with an OPAC, a Web page.

Student Life *Housing:* college housing not available. *Activities and Organizations:* drama/theater group, student-run newspaper. *Campus security:* 24-hour emergency response devices and patrols, late-night transport/escort service. *Student services:* personal/psychological counseling.

Athletics *Intramural sports:* baseball M, basketball M/W.

Applying *Options:* electronic application, early admission, deferred entrance. *Required for some:* high school transcript. *Recommended:* high school transcript. *Application deadlines:* rolling (freshmen), rolling (transfers). *Notification:* continuous (freshmen), continuous (transfers).

Freshman Application Contact Admissions Office, Virginia Western Community College, PO Box 14007, Roanoke, VA 24038. *Phone:* 540-857-7231. *Web site:* http://www.virginiawestern.edu/.

Wytheville Community College
Wytheville, Virginia

- **State-supported** 2-year, founded 1967, part of Virginia Community College System
- **Rural** 141-acre campus
- **Coed,** 3,792 undergraduate students, 36% full-time, 64% women, 36% men

Undergraduates 1,370 full-time, 2,422 part-time. 7% Black or African American, non-Hispanic/Latino; 1% Hispanic/Latino; 0.8% Asian, non-Hispanic/Latino; 0.1% Native Hawaiian or other Pacific Islander, non-Hispanic/Latino; 0.3% American Indian or Alaska Native, non-Hispanic/Latino; 2% Two or more races, non-Hispanic/Latino; 0.4% Race/ethnicity unknown. *Retention:* 59% of full-time freshmen returned.

Faculty *Student/faculty ratio:* 25:1.

Majors Accounting; administrative assistant and secretarial science; biological and physical sciences; business administration and management; civil engineering technology; clinical/medical laboratory technology; corrections; criminal justice/law enforcement administration; criminal justice/police science; dental hygiene; drafting and design technology; education; electrical, electronic and communications engineering technology; information science/studies; liberal arts and sciences/liberal studies; machine tool technology; mass communication/media; mechanical engineering/mechanical technology; medical administrative assistant and medical secretary; physical therapy; registered nursing/registered nurse.

Academics *Calendar:* semesters. *Degree:* certificates, diplomas, and associate. *Special study options:* academic remediation for entering students, adult/continuing education programs, advanced placement credit, distance learning, external degree program, part-time degree program, services for LD students, summer session for credit.

Library Wytheville Community College Library.

Student Life *Housing:* college housing not available. *Activities and Organizations:* drama/theater group, student-run newspaper. *Campus security:* 24-hour emergency response devices and patrols.

Athletics *Intercollegiate sports:* basketball M, volleyball W. *Intramural sports:* baseball M, golf M/W.

Financial Aid Of all full-time matriculated undergraduates who enrolled in 2010, 125 Federal Work-Study jobs (averaging $2592).

Applying *Options:* early admission. *Required:* high school transcript. *Required for some:* interview. *Application deadlines:* rolling (freshmen), rolling (transfers). *Notification:* continuous (freshmen), continuous (transfers).

Freshman Application Contact Wytheville Community College, 1000 East Main Street, Wytheville, VA 24382-3308. *Phone:* 276-223-4755. *Toll-free phone:* 800-468-1195. *Web site:* http://www.wcc.vccs.edu/.

WASHINGTON

The Art Institute of Seattle
Seattle, Washington

- **Proprietary** primarily 2-year, founded 1982, part of Education Management Corporation
- **Urban** campus
- **Coed**

Majors Animation, interactive technology, video graphics and special effects; baking and pastry arts; cinematography and film/video production; culinary arts; digital communication and media/multimedia; fashion/apparel design; fashion merchandising; graphic design; industrial and product design; interior design; photography; recording arts technology; restaurant, culinary, and catering management; web page, digital/multimedia and information resources design.

Academics *Calendar:* quarters. *Degrees:* diplomas, associate, and bachelor's.

Costs (2011–12) *Tuition:* Tuition cost varies by program. Prospective students should contact the school for current tuition costs. Other charges include a starting kit for all first-quarter students. Kits vary in price, depending on the program of study.

Freshman Application Contact The Art Institute of Seattle, 2323 Elliott Avenue, Seattle, WA 98121-1642. *Phone:* 206-448-6600. *Toll-free phone:* 800-275-2471. *Web site:* http://www.artinstitutes.edu/seattle/.

See page 334 for the College Close-Up.

Bates Technical College
Tacoma, Washington

Director of Admissions Director of Admissions, Bates Technical College, 1101 South Yakima Avenue, Tacoma, WA 98405-4895. *Phone:* 253-680-7000. *E-mail:* registration@bates.ctc.edu. *Web site:* http://www.bates.ctc.edu/

Bellevue College
Bellevue, Washington

Freshman Application Contact Morenika Jacobs, Associate Dean of Enrollment Services, Bellevue College, 3000 Landerholm Circle, SE, Bellevue, WA 98007-6484. *Phone:* 425-564-2205. *Fax:* 425-564-4065. *Web site:* http://www.bcc.ctc.edu/.

Bellingham Technical College
Bellingham, Washington

- **State-supported** 2-year, founded 1957, part of Washington State Board for Community and Technical Colleges (SBCTC)
- **Suburban** 21-acre campus with easy access to Vancouver
- **Coed**

Faculty *Student/faculty ratio:* 24:1.

Academics *Degree:* certificates and associate. *Special study options:* academic remediation for entering students, distance learning, English as a second language, internships, part-time degree program, services for LD students, summer session for credit.

Standardized Tests *Required:* ACCUPLACER entrance exam or waiver (for admission).

Costs (2011–12) *Tuition:* state resident $4050 full-time, $82 per credit part-time; nonresident $5468 full-time, $110 per credit part-time. Full-time tuition and fees vary according to course load and program. Part-time tuition and fees vary according to course load and program. *Required fees:* $600 full-time, $50 per course part-time.

Financial Aid Of all full-time matriculated undergraduates who enrolled in 2011, 30 Federal Work-Study jobs (averaging $1300).

Applying *Options:* early admission, deferred entrance. *Required for some:* high school transcript, some programs have prerequisites.

Freshman Application Contact Bellingham Technical College, 3028 Lindbergh Avenue, Bellingham, WA 98225. *Phone:* 360-752-8324. *Web site:* http://www.btc.ctc.edu/.

Big Bend Community College
Moses Lake, Washington

- **State-supported** 2-year, founded 1962
- **Small-town** 159-acre campus
- **Coed,** 2,340 undergraduate students, 63% full-time, 58% women, 42% men

Undergraduates 1,480 full-time, 860 part-time. 2% Black or African American, non-Hispanic/Latino; 39% Hispanic/Latino; 1% Asian, non-Hispanic/Latino; 0.3% Native Hawaiian or other Pacific Islander, non-Hispanic/Latino; 1% American Indian or Alaska Native, non-Hispanic/Latino; 5% Race/ethnicity unknown; 5% live on campus.

Faculty *Student/faculty ratio:* 21:1.

Majors Accounting technology and bookkeeping; agricultural production; airline pilot and flight crew; automobile/automotive mechanics technology; avionics maintenance technology; early childhood education; industrial electronics technology; industrial mechanics and maintenance technology; liberal arts and sciences/liberal studies; licensed practical/vocational nurse training; medical/clinical assistant; medical office management; registered nursing/registered nurse; welding technology.

Academics *Calendar:* quarters. *Degree:* certificates and associate. *Special study options:* academic remediation for entering students, advanced placement credit, cooperative education, distance learning, English as a second language, part-time degree program, services for LD students, summer session for credit.

Library Big Bend Community College Library with 42,378 titles, 113 serial subscriptions, 3,993 audiovisual materials, an OPAC, a Web page.

Student Life *Housing Options:* coed. Campus housing is university owned. *Activities and Organizations:* choral group. *Campus security:* 24-hour emergency response devices, late-night transport/escort service, controlled dormitory access. *Student services:* personal/psychological counseling.

Athletics *Intercollegiate sports:* baseball M, basketball M/W, softball W, volleyball W.

Costs (2012–13) *One-time required fee:* $30. *Tuition:* state resident $3585 full-time, $100 per credit hour part-time; nonresident $4005 full-time, $114 per credit hour part-time. Full-time tuition and fees vary according to course load and program. Part-time tuition and fees vary according to course load and program. *Required fees:* $5 per credit hour part-time. *Room and board:* $6138; room only: $2520. *Payment plan:* installment. *Waivers:* senior citizens.

Applying *Options:* electronic application, early admission, deferred entrance. *Application fee:* $30. *Required for some:* high school transcript. *Application deadlines:* rolling (freshmen), rolling (transfers). *Notification:* continuous (freshmen), continuous (transfers).

Freshman Application Contact Candis Lacher, Associate Vice President of Student Services, Big Bend Community College, 7662 Chanute Street, Moses Lake, WA 98837. *Phone:* 509-793-2061. *Toll-free phone:* 877-745-1212. *Fax:* 509-793-6243. *E-mail:* admissions@bigbend.edu. *Web site:* http://www.bigbend.edu/.

Carrington College - Spokane
Spokane, Washington

Director of Admissions Deanna Baker, Campus Director, Carrington College - Spokane, 10102 East Knox Avenue, Suite 200, Spokane, WA 99206. *Phone:* 509-532-8888. *Fax:* 509-533-5983. *Web site:* http://carrington.edu/.

Cascadia Community College
Bothell, Washington

- **State-supported** 2-year, founded 1999
- **Suburban** 128-acre campus
- **Coed,** 2,697 undergraduate students, 46% full-time, 49% women, 51% men

Undergraduates 1,240 full-time, 1,457 part-time. 2% Black or African American, non-Hispanic/Latino; 11% Hispanic/Latino; 10% Asian, non-Hispanic/Latino; 1% American Indian or Alaska Native, non-Hispanic/Latino; 2% Race/ethnicity unknown.

Freshmen *Admission:* 336 enrolled.

Faculty *Total:* 143, 26% full-time. *Student/faculty ratio:* 21:1.

Majors Liberal arts and sciences and humanities related; liberal arts and sciences/liberal studies; science technologies related.

Academics *Calendar:* quarters. *Degree:* certificates and associate. *Special study options:* academic remediation for entering students, accelerated degree program, adult/continuing education programs, advanced placement credit, cooperative education, distance learning, double majors, English as a second language, independent study, internships, off-campus study, part-time degree program, services for LD students, study abroad, summer session for credit.

Library UWB/CCC Campus Library with 73,749 titles, 850 serial subscriptions, 6,100 audiovisual materials, an OPAC, a Web page.

Student Life *Housing:* college housing not available. *Activities and Organizations:* drama/theater group, student-run newspaper. *Campus security:* 24-hour emergency response devices, late-night transport/escort service.

Costs (2012–13) *Tuition:* state resident $96 per credit hour part-time; nonresident $268 per credit hour part-time. *Waivers:* senior citizens and employees or children of employees.

Applying *Options:* electronic application. *Application deadlines:* rolling (freshmen), rolling (out-of-state freshmen), rolling (transfers). *Notification:* continuous (freshmen), continuous (out-of-state freshmen), continuous (transfers).

Freshman Application Contact Ms. Erin Blakeney, Dean for Student Success, Cascadia Community College, 18345 Campus Way, NE, Bothell, WA 98011. *Phone:* 425-352-8000. *Fax:* 425-352-8137. *E-mail:* admissions@cascadia.ctc.edu. *Web site:* http://www.cascadia.edu/.

Centralia College
Centralia, Washington

Freshman Application Contact Admissions Office, Centralia College, Centralia, WA 98531. *Phone:* 360-736-9391 Ext. 221. *Fax:* 360-330-7503. *E-mail:* admissions@centralia.edu. *Web site:* http://www.centralia.edu/.

Clark College
Vancouver, Washington

- **State-supported** 2-year, founded 1933, part of Washington State Board for Community and Technical Colleges
- **Urban** 101-acre campus with easy access to Portland
- **Coed,** 12,744 undergraduate students, 50% full-time, 58% women, 42% men

Undergraduates 6,414 full-time, 6,330 part-time. 3% are from out of state; 3% Black or African American, non-Hispanic/Latino; 7% Hispanic/Latino; 4% Asian, non-Hispanic/Latino; 0.5% Native Hawaiian or other Pacific Islander, non-Hispanic/Latino; 1% American Indian or Alaska Native, non-Hispanic/Latino; 6% Two or more races, non-Hispanic/Latino; 5% Race/ethnicity unknown; 3% transferred in.

Freshmen *Admission:* 1,406 applied, 1,406 admitted, 1,764 enrolled.

Faculty *Total:* 711, 29% full-time, 12% with terminal degrees. *Student/faculty ratio:* 23:1.

Majors Accounting technology and bookkeeping; applied horticulture/horticulture operations; automobile/automotive mechanics technology; baking and pastry arts; business administration and management; business automation/technology/data entry; computer programming; computer systems networking and telecommunications; construction engineering technology; culinary arts; data entry/microcomputer applications; dental hygiene; diesel mechanics technology; early childhood education; electrical, electronic and communications engineering technology; emergency medical technology (EMT paramedic); executive assistant/executive secretary; graphic communications; human resources management; landscaping and groundskeeping; legal administrative assistant/secretary; legal assistant/paralegal; liberal arts and sciences/liberal studies; machine tool technology; manufacturing engineering technology; medical administrative assistant and medical secretary; medical/clinical assistant; radiologic technology/science; registered nursing/registered nurse; retailing; selling skills and sales; sport and fitness administration/management; substance abuse/addiction counseling; surveying technology; telecommunications technology; web/multimedia management and webmaster; welding technology.

Academics *Calendar:* quarters. *Degree:* certificates, diplomas, and associate. *Special study options:* adult/continuing education programs, part-time degree program. *ROTC:* Army (c), Air Force (c).

Library Lewis D. Cannell Library.

Student Life *Housing:* college housing not available. *Campus security:* 24-hour patrols, late-night transport/escort service, security staff during hours of operation.

Athletics *Intercollegiate sports:* baseball M, basketball M(s)/W(s), cross-country running M(s)/W(s), fencing M(c)/W(c), soccer M(s)/W(s), softball W, track and field M(s)/W(s), volleyball W(s). *Intramural sports:* basketball M/W, fencing M/W, soccer M/W, softball M/W, volleyball M/W.

Costs (2011–12) *Tuition:* area resident $3743 full-time, $101 per credit hour part-time; state resident $4133 full-time, $114 per credit hour part-time; nonresident $8978 full-time, $273 per credit hour part-time. Full-time tuition and fees vary according to course load and reciprocity agreements. Part-time tuition and fees vary according to course load and reciprocity agreements. *Payment plan:* installment. *Waivers:* senior citizens and employees or children of employees.

Applying *Options:* electronic application, early admission, deferred entrance. *Application fee:* $20. *Required for some:* high school transcript, interview. *Application deadlines:* 7/30 (freshmen), rolling (transfers). *Notification:* continuous (freshmen), continuous (transfers).

Freshman Application Contact Ms. Sheryl Anderson, Director of Admissions, Clark College, Vancover, WA 98663. *Phone:* 360-992-2308. *Fax:* 360-992-2867. *E-mail:* admissions@clark.edu. *Web site:* http://www.clark.edu/.

Clover Park Technical College
Lakewood, Washington
Director of Admissions Ms. Judy Richardson, Registrar, Clover Park Technical College, 4500 Steilacoom Boulevard, SW, Lakewood, WA 98499. *Phone:* 253-589-5570. *Web site:* http://www.cptc.edu/.

Columbia Basin College
Pasco, Washington
Freshman Application Contact Admissions Department, Columbia Basin College, 2600 North 20th Avenue, Pasco, WA 99301-3397. *Phone:* 509-542-4524. *Fax:* 509-544-2023. *E-mail:* admissions@columbiabasin.edu. *Web site:* http://www.columbiabasin.edu/.

Edmonds Community College
Lynnwood, Washington
Freshman Application Contact Ms. Nancy Froemming, Enrollment Services Office Manager, Edmonds Community College, 20000 68th Avenue West, Lynwood, WA 98036-5999. *Phone:* 425-640-1853. *Fax:* 425-640-1159. *E-mail:* nanci.froemming@edcc.edu. *Web site:* http://www.edcc.edu/.

Everest College
Vancouver, Washington
Director of Admissions Ms. Renee Schiffhauer, Director of Admissions, Everest College, 120 Northeast 136th Avenue, Suite 130, Vancouver, WA 98684. *Phone:* 360-254-3282. *Toll-free phone:* 888-741-4270. *Fax:* 360-254-3035. *E-mail:* rschiffhauer@cci.edu. *Web site:* http://www.everest.edu/.

Everett Community College
Everett, Washington
Freshman Application Contact Ms. Linda Baca, Entry Services Manager, Everett Community College, 2000 Tower Street, Everett, WA 98201-1327. *Phone:* 425-388-9219. *Fax:* 425-388-9173. *E-mail:* admissions@everettcc.edu. *Web site:* http://www.everettcc.edu/.

Grays Harbor College
Aberdeen, Washington
- **State-supported** 2-year, founded 1930, part of Washington State Board for Community and Technical Colleges
- **Small-town** 125-acre campus
- **Endowment** $8.3 million
- **Coed**

Undergraduates 1,589 full-time, 937 part-time. Students come from 11 states and territories; 1 other country; 0.8% are from out of state; 3% Black or African American, non-Hispanic/Latino; 4% Hispanic/Latino; 2% Asian, non-Hispanic/Latino; 0.1% Native Hawaiian or other Pacific Islander, non-Hispanic/Latino; 4% American Indian or Alaska Native, non-Hispanic/Latino; 6% Two or more races, non-Hispanic/Latino; 2% Race/ethnicity unknown; 0.1% international; 17% transferred in. *Retention:* 57% of full-time freshmen returned.
Faculty *Student/faculty ratio:* 19:1.
Academics *Calendar:* quarters. *Degree:* certificates, diplomas, and associate. *Special study options:* academic remediation for entering students, accelerated degree program, adult/continuing education programs, advanced placement credit, cooperative education, distance learning, double majors, English as a second language, external degree program, honors programs, independent study, internships, part-time degree program, services for LD students, study abroad, summer session for credit.
Student Life *Campus security:* 24-hour emergency response devices, late-night transport/escort service.
Costs (2011–12) *Tuition:* state resident $3514 full-time, $96 per credit hour part-time; nonresident $8749 full-time, $268 per credit hour part-time. Full-time tuition and fees vary according to course load and program. Part-time tuition and fees vary according to program. *Required fees:* $275 full-time, $9 per contact hour part-time.
Financial Aid Of all full-time matriculated undergraduates who enrolled in 2010, 40 Federal Work-Study jobs (averaging $810). *Average financial aid package:* $5686.

Applying *Options:* electronic application, early admission. *Recommended:* high school transcript.
Freshman Application Contact Ms. Brenda Dell, Admissions Officer, Grays Harbor College, 1620 Edward P Smith Drive, Aberdeen, WA 98520-7599. *Phone:* 360-532-9020 Ext. 4026. *Toll-free phone:* 800-562-4830. *Web site:* http://www.ghc.edu/.

Green River Community College
Auburn, Washington
Freshman Application Contact Ms. Peggy Morgan, Program Support Supervisor, Green River Community College, 12401 Southeast 320th Street, Auburn, WA 98092-3699. *Phone:* 253-833-9111. *Fax:* 253-288-3454. *Web site:* http://www.greenriver.edu/.

Highline Community College
Des Moines, Washington
- **State-supported** 2-year, founded 1961, part of Washington State Board for Community and Technical Colleges
- **Suburban** 81-acre campus with easy access to Seattle
- **Endowment** $1.4 million
- **Coed**, 6,743 undergraduate students, 58% full-time, 58% women, 42% men

Undergraduates 3,932 full-time, 2,811 part-time. Students come from 6 states and territories; 50 other countries; 1% are from out of state; 11% Black or African American, non-Hispanic/Latino; 7% Hispanic/Latino; 15% Asian, non-Hispanic/Latino; 1% Native Hawaiian or other Pacific Islander, non-Hispanic/Latino; 0.7% American Indian or Alaska Native, non-Hispanic/Latino; 6% Two or more races, non-Hispanic/Latino; 11% Race/ethnicity unknown; 7% international; 71% transferred in. *Retention:* 57% of full-time freshmen returned.
Freshmen *Admission:* 4,445 applied, 4,445 admitted, 631 enrolled.
Faculty *Total:* 360, 40% full-time, 23% with terminal degrees. *Student/faculty ratio:* 19:1.
Majors Accounting; administrative assistant and secretarial science; art; behavioral sciences; biological and physical sciences; business administration and management; clinical/medical laboratory science and allied professions related; computer engineering technology; computer programming; computer systems networking and telecommunications; computer typography and composition equipment operation; criminal justice/law enforcement administration; criminal justice/police science; data entry/microcomputer applications related; dental hygiene; drafting and design technology; education; engineering; engineering technology; English; hotel/motel administration; humanities; human services; industrial technology; interior design; international business/trade/commerce; journalism; kindergarten/preschool education; legal administrative assistant/secretary; legal assistant/paralegal; library and information science; mathematics; medical/clinical assistant; music; natural sciences; pre-engineering; psychology; registered nursing/registered nurse; respiratory care therapy; Romance languages; social sciences; tourism and travel services management; transportation and materials moving related; web page, digital/multimedia and information resources design.
Academics *Calendar:* quarters. *Degree:* certificates, diplomas, and associate. *Special study options:* academic remediation for entering students, advanced placement credit, cooperative education, distance learning, English as a second language, freshman honors college, honors programs, independent study, internships, off-campus study, part-time degree program, services for LD students, student-designed majors, study abroad, summer session for credit. *ROTC:* Army (c), Air Force (c).
Library Highline Community College Library with 57,678 titles, 585 serial subscriptions, an OPAC, a Web page.
Student Life *Housing:* college housing not available. *Activities and Organizations:* drama/theater group, student-run newspaper, choral group, Black Student Union, Pacific Islander Club, Friends of Bosnia, United Latino Association, Muslim Student Association. *Campus security:* 24-hour emergency response devices and patrols, late-night transport/escort service. *Student services:* personal/psychological counseling, women's center.
Athletics Member NJCAA. *Intercollegiate sports:* basketball M(s)/W(s), cross-country running M(s)/W(s), soccer M(s)/W(s), softball W(s), track and field M(s)/W(s), volleyball W(s), wrestling M(s).
Costs (2012–13) *Tuition:* $108 per credit part-time; state resident $3968 full-time, $122 per credit part-time; nonresident $4416 full-time, $300 per credit part-time. Full-time tuition and fees vary according to course load and program. Part-time tuition and fees vary according to course load and program. *Required fees:* $75 full-time, $108 per credit part-time, $75 per term part-time. *Payment plan:* installment. *Waivers:* employees or children of employees.
Applying *Options:* electronic application. *Application fee:* $26. *Application deadlines:* rolling (freshmen), rolling (transfers).

Freshman Application Contact Ms. Michelle Kuwasaki, Director of Admissions, Highline Community College, 2400 South 240th Street, Des Moines, WA 98198-9800. *Phone:* 206-878-3710 Ext. 9800. *Web site:* http://www.highline.edu/.

ITT Technical Institute
Everett, Washington

- **Proprietary** primarily 2-year, part of ITT Educational Services, Inc.
- **Coed**

Majors Business administration and management; communications technology; computer and information systems security; construction management; criminal justice/law enforcement administration; drafting and design technology; electrical, electronic and communications engineering technology; forensic science and technology; game and interactive media design; graphic communications; legal assistant/paralegal; network and system administration; project management.

Academics *Degrees:* associate and bachelor's.

Freshman Application Contact Director of Recruitment, ITT Technical Institute, 1615 75th Street SW, Everett, WA 98203. *Phone:* 425-583-0200. *Toll-free phone:* 800-272-3791. *Web site:* http://www.itt-tech.edu/.

ITT Technical Institute
Seattle, Washington

- **Proprietary** primarily 2-year, founded 1932, part of ITT Educational Services, Inc.
- **Urban** campus
- **Coed**

Majors Business administration and management; communications technology; computer and information systems security; computer engineering technology; computer software and media applications related; computer software engineering; computer software technology; construction management; criminal justice/law enforcement administration; drafting and design technology; electrical, electronic and communications engineering technology; forensic science and technology; game and interactive media design; graphic communications; legal assistant/paralegal; network and system administration; project management.

Academics *Calendar:* quarters. *Degrees:* associate and bachelor's.

Student Life *Housing:* college housing not available.

Freshman Application Contact Director of Recruitment, ITT Technical Institute, 12720 Gateway Drive, Suite 100, Seattle, WA 98168-3333. *Phone:* 206-244-3300. *Toll-free phone:* 800-422-2029. *Web site:* http://www.itt-tech.edu/.

ITT Technical Institute
Spokane Valley, Washington

- **Proprietary** primarily 2-year, founded 1985, part of ITT Educational Services, Inc.
- **Suburban** campus
- **Coed**

Majors Business administration and management; communications technology; computer and information systems security; construction management; criminal justice/law enforcement administration; drafting and design technology; electrical, electronic and communications engineering technology; forensic science and technology; game and interactive media design; graphic communications; legal assistant/paralegal; network and system administration; project management.

Academics *Calendar:* quarters. *Degrees:* associate and bachelor's.

Student Life *Housing:* college housing not available.

Freshman Application Contact Director of Recruitment, ITT Technical Institute, 13518 East Indiana Avenue, Spokane Valley, WA 99216. *Phone:* 509-926-2900. *Toll-free phone:* 800-777-8324. *Web site:* http://www.itt-tech.edu/.

Lake Washington Technical College
Kirkland, Washington

Freshman Application Contact Shawn Miller, Registrar Enrollment Services, Lake Washington Technical College, 11605 132nd Avenue NE, Kirkland, WA 98034-8506. *Phone:* 425-739-8104. *E-mail:* jnfo@lwtc.edu. *Web site:* http://www.lwtc.edu/.

Lower Columbia College
Longview, Washington

- **State-supported** 2-year, founded 1934, part of Washington State Board for Community and Technical Colleges
- **Rural** 39-acre campus with easy access to Portland
- **Endowment** $12.0 million
- **Coed,** 4,252 undergraduate students, 61% full-time, 63% women, 37% men

Undergraduates 2,579 full-time, 1,673 part-time. Students come from 7 states and territories; 2 other countries; 2% are from out of state; 2% Black or African American, non-Hispanic/Latino; 6% Hispanic/Latino; 2% Asian, non-Hispanic/Latino; 0.1% Native Hawaiian or other Pacific Islander, non-Hispanic/Latino; 2% American Indian or Alaska Native, non-Hispanic/Latino; 2% Two or more races, non-Hispanic/Latino; 9% Race/ethnicity unknown; 11% transferred in. *Retention:* 53% of full-time freshmen returned.

Freshmen *Admission:* 388 enrolled.

Faculty *Total:* 222, 31% full-time. *Student/faculty ratio:* 24:1.

Majors Accounting; accounting technology and bookkeeping; administrative assistant and secretarial science; automobile/automotive mechanics technology; business administration and management; criminal justice/law enforcement administration; data entry/microcomputer applications; diesel mechanics technology; early childhood education; fire science/firefighting; industrial mechanics and maintenance technology; instrumentation technology; legal administrative assistant/secretary; liberal arts and sciences/liberal studies; machine tool technology; medical administrative assistant and medical secretary; medical/clinical assistant; registered nursing/registered nurse; substance abuse/addiction counseling; welding technology.

Academics *Calendar:* quarters. *Degree:* certificates, diplomas, and associate. *Special study options:* academic remediation for entering students, adult/continuing education programs, advanced placement credit, cooperative education, distance learning, English as a second language, external degree program, independent study, internships, part-time degree program, services for LD students, student-designed majors, summer session for credit.

Library Alan Thompson Library plus 1 other with 38,841 titles, 130 serial subscriptions, 4,573 audiovisual materials, an OPAC, a Web page.

Student Life *Housing:* college housing not available. *Activities and Organizations:* drama/theater group, choral group, Phi Theta Kappa, Biological Society, Electric Vehicle Club, American Sign Language Club, Global Medical Brigade. *Campus security:* 24-hour emergency response devices and patrols. *Student services:* personal/psychological counseling.

Athletics *Intercollegiate sports:* baseball M(s), basketball M(s)/W(s), soccer W(s), softball W(s), volleyball W(s).

Costs (2011–12) *One-time required fee:* $30. *Tuition:* state resident $3815 full-time, $104 per credit part-time; nonresident $4629 full-time, $128 per credit part-time. Full-time tuition and fees vary according to course load and reciprocity agreements. Part-time tuition and fees vary according to course load and reciprocity agreements. *Required fees:* $845 full-time. *Payment plan:* deferred payment. *Waivers:* senior citizens and employees or children of employees.

Financial Aid Of all full-time matriculated undergraduates who enrolled in 2010, 440 Federal Work-Study jobs (averaging $708). 447 state and other part-time jobs (averaging $2415).

Applying *Options:* electronic application. *Application fee:* $14. *Recommended:* high school transcript. *Application deadlines:* rolling (freshmen), rolling (transfers). *Notification:* continuous (freshmen).

Freshman Application Contact Ms. Lynn Lawrence, Director of Registration, Lower Columbia College, 1600 Maple Street, Longview, WA 98632. *Phone:* 360-442-2371. *Toll-free phone:* 866-900-2311. *Fax:* 360-442-2379. *E-mail:* registration@lowercolumbia.edu. *Web site:* http://www.lowercolumbia.edu/.

North Seattle Community College
Seattle, Washington

- **State-supported** 2-year, founded 1970, part of Seattle Community College District
- **Urban** 65-acre campus
- **Endowment** $4.4 million
- **Coed,** 6,303 undergraduate students, 31% full-time, 60% women, 40% men

Undergraduates 1,953 full-time, 4,350 part-time. Students come from 50 states and territories; 39 other countries; 5% are from out of state; 7% Black or African American, non-Hispanic/Latino; 7% Hispanic/Latino; 12% Asian, non-Hispanic/Latino; 1% Native Hawaiian or other Pacific Islander, non-Hispanic/Latino; 0.8% American Indian or Alaska Native, non-Hispanic/Latino; 8% Two or more races, non-Hispanic/Latino; 12% Race/ethnicity unknown; 23% transferred in.

Freshmen *Admission:* 5,726 applied, 5,726 admitted, 707 enrolled.

Faculty *Total:* 304, 29% full-time, 3% with terminal degrees. *Student/faculty ratio:* 20:1.

Majors Accounting technology and bookkeeping; administrative assistant and secretarial science; allied health and medical assisting services related; architectural drafting and CAD/CADD; art; biomedical technology; business/corporate communications; civil drafting and CAD/CADD; communications systems installation and repair technology; computer and information systems security; computer systems networking and telecommunications; early childhood education; electrical, electronic and communications engineering technology; heating, air conditioning, ventilation and refrigeration maintenance technology; liberal arts and sciences/liberal studies; licensed practical/vocational nurse training; mechanical drafting and CAD/CADD; medical/clinical assistant; music; pharmacy technician; real estate; registered nursing/registered nurse; telecommunications technology; watchmaking and jewelrymaking.

Academics *Calendar:* quarters. *Degree:* certificates, diplomas, and associate. *Special study options:* academic remediation for entering students, adult/continuing education programs, advanced placement credit, cooperative education, distance learning, English as a second language, external degree program, independent study, internships, part-time degree program, services for LD students, study abroad, summer session for credit. *ROTC:* Army (c).

Library North Seattle Community College Library with 52,496 titles, 594 serial subscriptions, an OPAC, a Web page.

Student Life *Housing:* college housing not available. *Activities and Organizations:* drama/theater group, choral group, Muslim Students Association, Indonesian Community Club, Literary Guild, Phi Theta Kappa, Vietnamese Student Association. *Campus security:* 24-hour emergency response devices, late-night transport/escort service, patrols by security. *Student services:* personal/psychological counseling, women's center.

Athletics *Intercollegiate sports:* basketball M/W. *Intramural sports:* basketball M/W.

Applying *Options:* electronic application, early admission, deferred entrance. *Required:* high school transcript. *Required for some:* essay or personal statement, English/Math Placement Test. *Application deadlines:* rolling (freshmen), rolling (transfers). *Notification:* continuous until 9/24 (freshmen), continuous until 9/24 (transfers).

Freshman Application Contact Ms. Betsy Abts, Registrar, North Seattle Community College, Seattle, WA 98103-3599. *Phone:* 206-934-3663. *Fax:* 206-934-3671. *E-mail:* arrc@seattlecolleges.edu. *Web site:* http://www.northseattle.edu/.

Northwest Indian College

Bellingham, Washington

Freshman Application Contact Office of Admissions, Northwest Indian College, 2522 Kwina Road, Bellingham, WA 98226. *Phone:* 360-676-2772. *Toll-free phone:* 866-676-2772. *Fax:* 360-392-4333. *E-mail:* admissions@nwic.edu. *Web site:* http://www.nwic.edu/.

Northwest School of Wooden Boatbuilding

Port Hadlock, Washington

Director of Admissions Student Services Coordinator, Northwest School of Wooden Boatbuilding, 42 North Water Street, Port Hadlock, WA 98339. *Phone:* 360-385-4948. *Fax:* 360-385-5089. *E-mail:* info@nwboatschool.org. *Web site:* http://www.nwboatschool.org/.

Olympic College

Bremerton, Washington

- **State-supported** primarily 2-year, founded 1946, part of Washington State Board for Community and Technical Colleges
- **Suburban** 33-acre campus with easy access to Seattle (30 miles by ferry)
- **Coed,** 8,503 undergraduate students

Undergraduates 4% Black or African American, non-Hispanic/Latino; 6% Hispanic/Latino; 8% Asian, non-Hispanic/Latino; 2% American Indian or Alaska Native, non-Hispanic/Latino; 0.8% international.

Freshmen *Admission:* 3,145 applied, 3,145 admitted.

Faculty *Total:* 509, 24% full-time.

Majors Accounting technology and bookkeeping; administrative assistant and secretarial science; airline pilot and flight crew; animation, interactive technology, video graphics and special effects; building/construction finishing, management, and inspection related; business administration and management; computer programming; computer systems networking and telecommunications; criminal justice/police science; culinary arts; drafting and design technology; early childhood education; electrical, electronic and communications engineering technology; electrician; hospitality administration; industrial technology; medical/clinical assistant; natural resources/conservation; organiza-

tional leadership; physical therapy technology; plumbing technology; registered nursing/registered nurse; substance abuse/addiction counseling; teacher assistant/aide; welding technology.

Academics *Calendar:* quarters. *Degrees:* certificates, diplomas, associate, and bachelor's. *Special study options:* academic remediation for entering students, adult/continuing education programs, advanced placement credit, cooperative education, distance learning, English as a second language, honors programs, independent study, internships, off-campus study, part-time degree program, services for LD students, summer session for credit.

Library Haselwood Library with 70,000 titles, 6,500 audiovisual materials, an OPAC, a Web page.

Student Life *Housing:* college housing not available. *Activities and Organizations:* drama/theater group, student-run newspaper, choral group, Phi Theta Kappa, International Student Club, Oceans (Nursing), ASOC, ADN. *Campus security:* 24-hour emergency response devices and patrols, student patrols, late-night transport/escort service. *Student services:* personal/psychological counseling.

Athletics *Intercollegiate sports:* baseball M(s), basketball M(s)/W(s), cross-country running M/W, golf M/W, soccer M(s)/W(s), softball W(s), volleyball W(s). *Intramural sports:* basketball M/W, table tennis M/W, volleyball M/W, weight lifting M/W.

Costs (2011–12) *Tuition:* state resident $3542 full-time, $96 per quarter hour part-time; nonresident $4007 full-time, $109 per quarter hour part-time. *Required fees:* $215 full-time, $4 per credit hour part-time, $48 per term part-time.

Financial Aid Of all full-time matriculated undergraduates who enrolled in 2010, 105 Federal Work-Study jobs (averaging $2380). 31 state and other part-time jobs (averaging $2880).

Applying *Options:* electronic application. *Required for some:* high school transcript. *Application deadlines:* rolling (freshmen), rolling (out-of-state freshmen), rolling (transfers).

Freshman Application Contact Ms. Jennifer Fyllingness, Director of Admissions and Outreach, Olympic College, 1600 Chester Avenue, Bremerton, WA 98337-1699. *Phone:* 360-475-7128. *Toll-free phone:* 800-259-6718. *Fax:* 360-475-7202. *E-mail:* jfyllingness@olympic.edu. *Web site:* http://www.olympic.edu/.

Peninsula College

Port Angeles, Washington

- **State-supported** primarily 2-year, founded 1961, part of Washington State Community and Technical Colleges
- **Small-town** 75-acre campus
- **Coed,** 3,321 undergraduate students, 51% full-time, 55% women, 45% men

Undergraduates 1,705 full-time, 1,616 part-time.

Faculty *Total:* 156, 37% full-time. *Student/faculty ratio:* 21:1.

Majors Accounting; automobile/automotive mechanics technology; biological and physical sciences; business administration and management; child-care and support services management; child development; civil engineering technology; commercial fishing; computer programming (vendor/product certification); criminal justice/law enforcement administration; data entry/microcomputer applications related; diesel mechanics technology; electrical, electronic and communications engineering technology; engineering technology; fishing and fisheries sciences and management; management science; office management; registered nursing/registered nurse; substance abuse/addiction counseling; web page, digital/multimedia and information resources design.

Academics *Calendar:* quarters. *Degrees:* certificates, associate, and bachelor's. *Special study options:* academic remediation for entering students, adult/continuing education programs, advanced placement credit, distance learning, English as a second language, honors programs, internships, part-time degree program, services for LD students, summer session for credit.

Library John D Glann Library with 33,736 titles, 383 serial subscriptions.

Student Life *Housing:* college housing not available. *Activities and Organizations:* student-run newspaper. *Campus security:* 8-hour patrols by trained security personnel. *Student services:* women's center.

Athletics *Intercollegiate sports:* basketball M/W, soccer M/W. *Intramural sports:* badminton M/W, basketball M/W, bowling M/W, football M, golf M, skiing (cross-country) M/W, soccer M/W, softball M/W, table tennis M/W, tennis M/W, volleyball M/W.

Financial Aid Of all full-time matriculated undergraduates who enrolled in 2010, 30 Federal Work-Study jobs (averaging $3600). 25 state and other part-time jobs (averaging $3600).

Applying *Required for some:* high school transcript. *Application deadlines:* rolling (freshmen), rolling (transfers). *Notification:* continuous (freshmen), continuous (transfers).

Freshman Application Contact Ms. Pauline Marvin, Peninsula College, 1502 East Lauridsen Boulevard, Port Angeles, WA 98362. *Phone:* 360-417-6596.

Toll-free phone: 877-452-9277. *Fax:* 360-457-8100. *E-mail:* admissions@pencol.edu. *Web site:* http://www.pc.ctc.edu/.

Pierce College at Puyallup
Puyallup, Washington

Director of Admissions Ms. Cindy Burbank, Director of Admissions, Pierce College at Puyallup, 1601 39th Avenue Southeast, Puyallup, WA 98374-2222. *Phone:* 253-964-6686. *Web site:* http://www.pierce.ctc.edu/.

Pima Medical Institute
Renton, Washington

- **Proprietary** 2-year
- **Urban** campus
- **Coed**

Academics *Special study options:* cooperative education, distance learning, internships.

Standardized Tests *Required:* Wonderlic Scholastic Level Exam (for admission).

Applying *Required:* high school transcript, interview.

Freshman Application Contact Pima Medical Institute, 555 South Renton Village Place, Renton, WA 98057. *Phone:* 425-228-9600. *Web site:* http://www.pmi.edu/.

Pima Medical Institute
Seattle, Washington

- **Proprietary** primarily 2-year, founded 1989, part of Vocational Training Institutes, Inc.
- **Urban** campus
- **Coed**

Academics *Calendar:* modular. *Degrees:* certificates, associate, and bachelor's. *Special study options:* distance learning.

Standardized Tests *Required:* Wonderlic aptitude test (for admission).

Applying *Required:* interview. *Required for some:* high school transcript.

Freshman Application Contact Admissions Office, Pima Medical Institute, 9709 Third Avenue NE, Suite 400, Seattle, WA 98115. *Phone:* 206-322-6100. *Toll-free phone:* 800-477-PIMA (in-state); 888-477-PIMA (out-of-state). *Web site:* http://www.pmi.edu/.

Renton Technical College
Renton, Washington

Director of Admissions Becky Riverman, Vice President for Student Services, Renton Technical College, 3000 NE Fourth Street, Renton, WA 98056. *Phone:* 425-235-2463. *Web site:* http://www.rtc.edu/.

Seattle Central Community College
Seattle, Washington

Freshman Application Contact Admissions Office, Seattle Central Community College, 1701 Broadway, Seattle, WA 98122-2400. *Phone:* 206-587-5450. *Web site:* http://www.seattlecentral.edu/.

Shoreline Community College
Shoreline, Washington

Director of Admissions Mr. Chris Linebarger, Director, Recruiting and Enrollment Services, Shoreline Community College, 16101 Greenwood Avenue North, Shoreline, WA 98133-5696. *Phone:* 206-546-4581. *Web site:* http://www.shore.ctc.edu/.

Skagit Valley College
Mount Vernon, Washington

Freshman Application Contact Ms. Karen Marie Bade, Admissions and Recruitment Coordinator, Skagit Valley College, 2405 College Way, Mount Vernon, WA 98273-5899. *Phone:* 360-416-7620. *E-mail:* karenmarie.bade@skagit.edu. *Web site:* http://www.skagit.edu/.

South Puget Sound Community College
Olympia, Washington

Freshman Application Contact Ms. Lyn Sharp, South Puget Sound Community College, 2011 Mottman Road, SW, Olympia, WA 98512-6292. *Phone:* 360-754-7711 Ext. 5237. *E-mail:* lsharp@spcc.ctc.edu. *Web site:* http://www.spscc.ctc.edu/.

South Seattle Community College
Seattle, Washington

Director of Admissions Ms. Kim Manderbach, Dean of Student Services/Registration, South Seattle Community College, 6000 16th Avenue, SW, Seattle, WA 98106-1499. *Phone:* 206-764-5378. *Fax:* 206-764-7947. *E-mail:* kimmanderb@sccd.ctc.edu. *Web site:* http://southseattle.edu/.

Spokane Community College
Spokane, Washington

Freshman Application Contact Ms. Brenda Burns, Researcher, District Institutional Research, Spokane Community College, Spokane, WA 99217-5399. *Phone:* 509-434-5242. *Toll-free phone:* 800-248-5644. *Fax:* 509-434-5249. *E-mail:* mlee@ccs.spokane.edu. *Web site:* http://www.scc.spokane.edu/.

Spokane Falls Community College
Spokane, Washington

Freshman Application Contact Admissions Office, Spokane Falls Community College, Admissions MS 3011, 3410 West Fort George Wright Drive, Spokane, WA 99224. *Phone:* 509-533-3401. *Toll-free phone:* 888-509-7944. *Fax:* 509-533-3852. *Web site:* http://www.spokanefalls.edu/.

Tacoma Community College
Tacoma, Washington

Freshman Application Contact Enrollment Services, Tacoma Community College, 6501 South 19th Street, Tacoma, WA 98466. *Phone:* 253-566-5325. *Fax:* 253-566-6034. *Web site:* http://www.tacomacc.edu/.

Walla Walla Community College
Walla Walla, Washington

Freshman Application Contact Walla Walla Community College, 500 Tausick Way, Walla Walla, WA 99362-9267. *Phone:* 509-522-2500. *Toll-free phone:* 877-992-9922. *Web site:* http://www.wwcc.edu/.

Wenatchee Valley College
Wenatchee, Washington

- **State and locally supported** 2-year, founded 1939, part of Washington State Board for Community and Technical Colleges
- **Rural** 56-acre campus
- **Coed**

Academics *Calendar:* quarters. *Degree:* certificates, diplomas, and associate. *Special study options:* academic remediation for entering students, adult/continuing education programs, advanced placement credit, cooperative education, distance learning, English as a second language, external degree program, independent study, part-time degree program, services for LD students, summer session for credit.

Student Life *Campus security:* 24-hour patrols, evening and late night security patrols.

Applying *Options:* electronic application, early admission, deferred entrance. *Required for some:* high school transcript.

Freshman Application Contact Ms. Cecilia Escobedo, Registrar/Admissions Coordinator, Wenatchee Valley College, 1300 Fifth Street, Wenatchee, WA 98801-1799. *Phone:* 509-682-6836. *E-mail:* cescobedo@wvc.edu. *Web site:* http://www.wvc.edu/.

Whatcom Community College
Bellingham, Washington

Freshman Application Contact Entry and Advising Center, Whatcom Community College, 237 West Kellogg Road, Bellingham, WA 98226-8003. *Phone:* 360-676-2170. *Fax:* 360-676-2171. *E-mail:* admit@whatcom.ctc.edu. *Web site:* http://www.whatcom.ctc.edu/.

Yakima Valley Community College

Yakima, Washington

- **State-supported** 2-year, founded 1928, part of Washington State Board for Community and Technical Colleges
- **Small-town** 20-acre campus
- **Coed**

Undergraduates 2,786 full-time, 1,693 part-time. 1% live on campus.
Faculty *Student/faculty ratio:* 20:1.
Academics *Calendar:* quarters. *Degree:* certificates and associate. *Special study options:* academic remediation for entering students, adult/continuing education programs, advanced placement credit, cooperative education, distance learning, English as a second language, internships, part-time degree program, services for LD students, summer session for credit.
Student Life *Campus security:* 24-hour emergency response devices, student patrols, late-night transport/escort service, controlled dormitory access.
Athletics Member NJCAA.
Standardized Tests *Required:* ACT COMPASS (for admission).
Costs (2011–12) *Tuition:* state resident $3850 full-time, $104 per credit hour part-time; nonresident $4250 full-time, $117 per credit hour part-time. Full-time tuition and fees vary according to course load. Part-time tuition and fees vary according to course load. *Required fees:* $308 full-time. *Room and board:* room only: $3240. Room and board charges vary according to housing facility. *Payment plans:* installment, deferred payment.
Financial Aid Of all full-time matriculated undergraduates who enrolled in 2010, 133 Federal Work-Study jobs (averaging $1164). 156 state and other part-time jobs (averaging $2083).
Applying *Application fee:* $20. *Required:* placement testing. *Required for some:* high school transcript, interview. *Recommended:* high school transcript.
Freshman Application Contact Denise Anderson, Registrar and Director for Enrollment Services, Yakima Valley Community College, PO Box 1647, Yakima, WA 98907-1647. *Phone:* 509-574-4702. *Fax:* 509-574-6879. *E-mail:* admis@yvcc.edu. *Web site:* http://www.yvcc.edu/.

WEST VIRGINIA

Blue Ridge Community and Technical College

Martinsburg, West Virginia

- **State-supported** 2-year, founded 1974
- **Small-town** campus
- **Coed,** 4,317 undergraduate students, 27% full-time, 67% women, 33% men

Undergraduates 1,161 full-time, 3,156 part-time. 5% are from out of state; 15% Black or African American, non-Hispanic/Latino; 3% Hispanic/Latino; 0.8% Asian, non-Hispanic/Latino; 0.2% Native Hawaiian or other Pacific Islander, non-Hispanic/Latino; 0.4% American Indian or Alaska Native, non-Hispanic/Latino; 3% Two or more races, non-Hispanic/Latino; 0.3% Race/ethnicity unknown; 4% transferred in. *Retention:* 54% of full-time freshmen returned.
Freshmen *Admission:* 403 enrolled. *Test scores:* SAT critical reading scores over 500: 45%; ACT scores over 18: 34%; SAT critical reading scores over 600: 10%; ACT scores over 24: 1%.
Faculty *Total:* 169, 35% full-time. *Student/faculty ratio:* 23:1.
Majors Automobile/automotive mechanics technology; business, management, and marketing related; criminal justice/safety; culinary arts; design and visual communications; electromechanical technology; emergency medical technology (EMT paramedic); fashion merchandising; fire science/firefighting; general studies; heating, air conditioning, ventilation and refrigeration maintenance technology; information technology; legal assistant/paralegal; office occupations and clerical services; quality control and safety technologies related.
Academics *Degree:* certificates and associate. *Special study options:* academic remediation for entering students, accelerated degree program, adult/continuing education programs, advanced placement credit, double majors, English as a second language, independent study, internships, part-time degree program, services for LD students.
Library Martinsburg Public Library.
Student Life *Housing:* college housing not available. *Activities and Organizations:* drama/theater group, national fraternities. *Campus security:* late-night transport/escort service. *Student services:* personal/psychological counseling.
Standardized Tests *Recommended:* SAT and SAT Subject Tests or ACT (for admission).
Costs (2012–13) *Tuition:* state resident $130 per credit hour part-time; nonresident $234 per credit hour part-time. Full-time tuition and fees vary according to course load. Part-time tuition and fees vary according to course load. *Waivers:* adult students, senior citizens, and employees or children of employees.
Applying *Options:* deferred entrance. *Application fee:* $25. *Required:* high school transcript. *Required for some:* interview.
Freshman Application Contact Brenda K. Neal, Director of Access, Blue Ridge Community and Technical College, 400 West Stephen Street, Martinsburg, WV 25401. *Phone:* 304-260-4380 Ext. 2109. *Fax:* 304-260-4376. *E-mail:* bneal@blueridgectc.edu. *Web site:* http://www.blueridgectc.edu/.

Bridgemont Community & Technical College

Montgomery, West Virginia

Director of Admissions Ms. Lisa Graham, Director of Admissions, Bridgemont Community & Technical College, 405 Fayette Pike, Montgomery, WV 25136. *Phone:* 304-442-3167. *Web site:* http://www.bridgemont.edu/.

Eastern West Virginia Community and Technical College

Moorefield, West Virginia

Freshman Application Contact Learner Support Services, Eastern West Virginia Community and Technical College, HC 65 Box 402, Moorefield, WV 26836. *Phone:* 304-434-8000. *Toll-free phone:* 877-982-2322. *Fax:* 304-434-7000. *E-mail:* askeast@eastern.wvnet.edu. *Web site:* http://www.eastern.wvnet.edu/.

Everest Institute

Cross Lanes, West Virginia

Freshman Application Contact Director of Admissions, Everest Institute, 5514 Big Tyler Road, Cross Lanes, WV 25313-1390. *Phone:* 304-776-6290. *Toll-free phone:* 888-741-4270. *Fax:* 304-776-6262. *Web site:* http://www.everest.edu/.

Huntington Junior College

Huntington, West Virginia

Director of Admissions Mr. James Garrett, Educational Services Director, Huntington Junior College, 900 Fifth Avenue, Huntington, WV 25701-2004. *Phone:* 304-697-7550. *Toll-free phone:* 800-344-4522. *Web site:* http://www.huntingtonjuniorcollege.com/.

ITT Technical Institute

Huntington, West Virginia

- **Proprietary** 2-year, part of ITT Educational Services, Inc.
- **Coed**

Majors Business administration and management; communications technology; computer software technology; drafting and design technology; electrical, electronic and communications engineering technology; forensic science and technology; graphic communications; legal assistant/paralegal; network and system administration; registered nursing/registered nurse.
Academics *Calendar:* quarters. *Degree:* associate.
Freshman Application Contact Director of Recruitment, ITT Technical Institute, 5183 US Route 60, Building 1, Suite 40, Huntington, WV 25705. *Phone:* 304-733-8700. *Toll-free phone:* 800-224-4695. *Web site:* http://www.itt-tech.edu/.

Kanawha Valley Community and Technical College

Institute, West Virginia

Freshman Application Contact Mr. Bryce Casto, Vice President, Student Affairs, Kanawha Valley Community and Technical College, 333 Sullivan Hall. *Phone:* 304-766-3140. *Fax:* 304-766-4158. *E-mail:* castosb@wvstateu.edu. *Web site:* http://www.kvctc.edu/.

Mountain State College

Parkersburg, West Virginia

Freshman Application Contact Ms. Judith Sutton, President, Mountain State College, 1508 Spring Street, Parkersburg, WV 26101-3993. *Phone:* 304-485-5487. *Toll-free phone:* 800-841-0201. *Fax:* 304-485-3524. *E-mail:* jsutton@msc.edu. *Web site:* http://www.msc.edu/.

Mountwest Community & Technical College

Huntington, West Virginia

Freshman Application Contact Dr. Tammy Johnson, Admissions Director, Mountwest Community & Technical College, 1 John Marshall Drive, Huntington, WV 25755. *Phone:* 304-696-3160. *Toll-free phone:* 866-676-5533. *Fax:* 304-696-3135. *E-mail:* admissions@marshall.edu. *Web site:* http://www.mctc.edu/.

New River Community and Technical College

Beckley, West Virginia

Director of Admissions Dr. Allen B. Withers, Vice President, Student Services, New River Community and Technical College, 167 Dye Drive, Beckley, WV 25801. *Phone:* 304-929-5011. *E-mail:* awithers@newriver.edu. *Web site:* http://www.newriver.edu/.

Pierpont Community & Technical College

Fairmont, West Virginia

Freshman Application Contact Mr. Steve Leadman, Director of Admissions and Recruiting, Pierpont Community & Technical College, 1201 Locust Avenue, Fairmont, WV 26554. *Phone:* 304-367-4892. *Toll-free phone:* 800-641-5678. *Fax:* 304-367-4789. *Web site:* http://www.pierpont.edu/.

Potomac State College of West Virginia University

Keyser, West Virginia

- **State-supported** primarily 2-year, founded 1901, part of West Virginia Higher Education Policy Commission
- **Small-town** 18-acre campus
- **Coed**

Undergraduates 1,415 full-time, 421 part-time. Students come from 18 states and territories; 3 other countries; 29% are from out of state; 14% Black or African American, non-Hispanic/Latino; 3% Hispanic/Latino; 0.7% Asian, non-Hispanic/Latino; 0.2% Native Hawaiian or other Pacific Islander, non-Hispanic/Latino; 1% American Indian or Alaska Native, non-Hispanic/Latino; 0.3% Two or more races, non-Hispanic/Latino; 2% Race/ethnicity unknown; 0.3% international; 4% transferred in. *Retention:* 50% of full-time freshmen returned.

Faculty *Student/faculty ratio:* 25:1.

Academics *Calendar:* semesters. *Degrees:* certificates, associate, and bachelor's. *Special study options:* academic remediation for entering students, adult/continuing education programs, advanced placement credit, distance learning, double majors, honors programs, independent study, internships, part-time degree program, services for LD students, study abroad, summer session for credit.

Student Life *Campus security:* 24-hour patrols, late-night transport/escort service, controlled dormitory access.

Athletics Member NJCAA.

Standardized Tests *Required for some:* SAT or ACT (for admission).

Costs (2011–12) *Tuition:* state resident $3058 full-time, $129 per credit hour part-time; nonresident $8990 full-time, $376 per credit hour part-time. Full-time tuition and fees vary according to degree level. Part-time tuition and fees vary according to course load and degree level. *Room and board:* $7290; room only: $3860. Room and board charges vary according to board plan and housing facility.

Financial Aid Of all full-time matriculated undergraduates who enrolled in 2010, 70 Federal Work-Study jobs (averaging $1300).

Applying *Options:* electronic application, early admission. *Required:* high school transcript.

Freshman Application Contact Ms. Beth Little, Director of Enrollment Services, Potomac State College of West Virginia University, 75 Arnold Street, Keyser, WV 26726. *Phone:* 304-788-6820. *Toll-free phone:* 800-262-7332 Ext. 6820. *Fax:* 304-788-6939. *E-mail:* go2psc@mail.wvu.edu. *Web site:* http://www.potomacstatecollege.edu/.

Southern West Virginia Community and Technical College

Mount Gay, West Virginia

Freshman Application Contact Mr. Roy Simmons, Registrar, Southern West Virginia Community and Technical College, PO Box 2900, Mt. Gay, WV 25637. *Phone:* 304-792-7160 Ext. 120. *Fax:* 304-792-7096. *E-mail:* admissions@southern.wvnet.edu. *Web site:* http://southernwv.edu/.

Valley College of Technology

Martinsburg, West Virginia

Freshman Application Contact Ms. Gail Kennedy, Admissions Director, Valley College of Technology, 287 Aikens Center, Martinsburg, WV 25404. *Phone:* 304-263-0878. *Fax:* 304-263-2413. *E-mail:* gkennedy@vct.edu. *Web site:* http://www.vct.edu/.

West Virginia Business College

Nutter Fort, West Virginia

Director of Admissions Robert Wright, Campus Director, West Virginia Business College, 116 Pennsylvania Avenue, Nutter Fort, WV 26301. *Phone:* 304-624-7695. *E-mail:* info@wvbc.edu. *Web site:* http://www.wvbc.edu/.

West Virginia Business College

Wheeling, West Virginia

Freshman Application Contact Ms. Karen D. Shaw, Director, West Virginia Business College, 1052 Main Street, Wheeling, WV 26003. *Phone:* 304-232-0361. *Fax:* 304-232-0363. *E-mail:* wvbcwheeling@stratuswave.net. *Web site:* http://www.wvbc.edu/.

West Virginia Junior College

Charleston, West Virginia

Freshman Application Contact West Virginia Junior College, 1000 Virginia Street East, Charleston, WV 25301-2817. *Phone:* 304-345-2820. *Toll-free phone:* 800-924-5208. *Web site:* http://www.wvjc.edu/.

West Virginia Junior College

Morgantown, West Virginia

Freshman Application Contact Admissions Office, West Virginia Junior College, 148 Willey Street, Morgantown, WV 26505-5521. *Phone:* 304-296-8282. *Web site:* http://www.wvjcmorgantown.edu/.

West Virginia Junior College–Bridgeport

Bridgeport, West Virginia

- **Proprietary** 2-year, founded 1922
- **Small-town** 3-acre campus with easy access to Pittsburgh
- **Coed,** 514 undergraduate students, 100% full-time, 80% women, 20% men

Undergraduates 514 full-time. Students come from 6 states and territories; 0.6% Black or African American, non-Hispanic/Latino; 10% transferred in. *Retention:* 77% of full-time freshmen returned.

Freshmen *Admission:* 514 enrolled. *Average high school GPA:* 2.5.

Faculty *Total:* 18, 44% full-time, 100% with terminal degrees. *Student/faculty ratio:* 18:1.

Majors Business administration and management; computer technology/computer systems technology; dental assisting; medical administrative assistant and medical secretary; medical/clinical assistant; medical insurance coding; pharmacy technician; web/multimedia management and webmaster.

Academics *Calendar:* quarters. *Degree:* associate. *Special study options:* cooperative education, distance learning, independent study, internships, services for LD students, summer session for credit.

Library WVJC Resource Center plus 1 other with an OPAC.

Student Life *Housing:* college housing not available. *Activities and Organizations:* Medical Club, FBLA (Business students), Computer Club, Dental Assisting Club, Pharmacy Tech Club. *Campus security:* 24-hour emergency response devices.

Standardized Tests *Recommended:* SAT or ACT (for admission).

Financial Aid Of all full-time matriculated undergraduates who enrolled in 2010, 10 Federal Work-Study jobs.

Applying *Options:* electronic application. *Required:* essay or personal statement, minimum 2.0 GPA, interview. *Required for some:* 1 letter of recommendation. *Recommended:* high school transcript. *Application deadline:* rolling (freshmen). *Notification:* continuous (freshmen).

Freshman Application Contact Mr. Adam Pratt, High School Admissions Coordinator, West Virginia Junior College–Bridgeport, 176 Thompson Drive, Bridgeport, WV 26330. *Phone:* 304-842-4007 Ext. 112. *Toll-free phone:* 800-470-5627. *Fax:* 304-842-8191. *E-mail:* admissions@wvjcinfo.net. *Web site:* http://www.wvjcinfo.net/.

West Virginia Northern Community College
Wheeling, West Virginia

- **State-supported** 2-year, founded 1972
- **Small-town** campus with easy access to Pittsburgh
- **Endowment** $587,145
- **Coed,** 2,994 undergraduate students, 48% full-time, 69% women, 31% men

Undergraduates 1,439 full-time, 1,555 part-time. Students come from 10 states and territories; 23% are from out of state; 5% Black or African American, non-Hispanic/Latino; 0.4% Hispanic/Latino; 0.4% Asian, non-Hispanic/Latino; 0.3% American Indian or Alaska Native, non-Hispanic/Latino; 0.6% Two or more races, non-Hispanic/Latino; 2% Race/ethnicity unknown; 11% transferred in.

Freshmen *Admission:* 501 applied, 501 admitted, 502 enrolled. *Average high school GPA:* 2.8.

Faculty *Total:* 201, 31% full-time, 3% with terminal degrees. *Student/faculty ratio:* 18:1.

Majors Administrative assistant and secretarial science; business/commerce; computer programming; criminal justice/police science; culinary arts; executive assistant/executive secretary; general studies; health information/medical records technology; heating, air conditioning, ventilation and refrigeration maintenance technology; hospitality administration; information technology; legal assistant/paralegal; liberal arts and sciences and humanities related; liberal arts and sciences/liberal studies; medical/clinical assistant; medical radiologic technology; multi/interdisciplinary studies related; registered nursing/registered nurse; respiratory care therapy; science technologies related; social work; surgical technology.

Academics *Calendar:* semesters. *Degree:* certificates and associate. *Special study options:* academic remediation for entering students, accelerated degree program, adult/continuing education programs, advanced placement credit, distance learning, double majors, honors programs, internships, part-time degree program, services for LD students, student-designed majors, summer session for credit.

Library Wheeling B&O Campus Library plus 2 others with 36,650 titles, 188 serial subscriptions, 3,495 audiovisual materials, an OPAC, a Web page.

Student Life *Housing:* college housing not available. *Activities and Organizations:* student-run newspaper, Community Outreach Opportunity Program (COOP). *Campus security:* police officer on staff during the day at Main Campus, security personnel during evening and during night classes.

Athletics *Intramural sports:* basketball M/W, bowling M/W, golf M/W, softball M/W, volleyball M/W.

Standardized Tests *Required for some:* Compass. *Recommended:* Compass.

Costs (2012–13) *Tuition:* state resident $87 per credit hour part-time; nonresident $286 per credit hour part-time. Full-time tuition and fees vary according to course load, program, reciprocity agreements, and student level. Part-time tuition and fees vary according to course load, program, reciprocity agreements, and student level. *Payment plan:* installment. *Waivers:* adult students, senior citizens, and employees or children of employees.

Applying *Options:* electronic application, early admission, deferred entrance. *Required for some:* high school transcript. *Application deadlines:* rolling (freshmen), rolling (transfers).

Freshman Application Contact Mr. Richard McCray, Assistant Director of Admissions, West Virginia Northern Community College, 1704 Market Street, Wheeling, WV 26003. *Phone:* 304-214-8838. *E-mail:* rmccray@northern.wvnet.edu. *Web site:* http://www.wvncc.edu/.

West Virginia University at Parkersburg
Parkersburg, West Virginia

Freshman Application Contact Christine Post, Associate Dean of Enrollment Management, West Virginia University at Parkersburg, 300 Campus Drive, Parkersburg, WV 26104. *Phone:* 304-424-8223 Ext. 223. *Toll-free phone:* 800-WVA-WVUP. *Fax:* 304-424-8332. *E-mail:* christine.post@mail.wvu.edu. *Web site:* http://www.wvup.edu/.

WISCONSIN

Blackhawk Technical College
Janesville, Wisconsin

- **District-supported** 2-year, founded 1968, part of Wisconsin Technical College System
- **Rural** 84-acre campus
- **Coed,** 3,278 undergraduate students, 43% full-time, 61% women, 39% men

Undergraduates 1,416 full-time, 1,862 part-time. Students come from 3 states and territories; 1% are from out of state; 7% Black or African American, non-Hispanic/Latino; 6% Hispanic/Latino; 0.6% Asian, non-Hispanic/Latino; 0.1% Native Hawaiian or other Pacific Islander, non-Hispanic/Latino; 0.4% American Indian or Alaska Native, non-Hispanic/Latino; 2% Two or more races, non-Hispanic/Latino; 12% Race/ethnicity unknown. *Retention:* 83% of full-time freshmen returned.

Freshmen *Admission:* 634 enrolled.

Faculty *Total:* 388, 28% full-time, 0.8% with terminal degrees. *Student/faculty ratio:* 17:1.

Majors Accounting; administrative assistant and secretarial science; business administration and management; clinical/medical laboratory technology; computer and information systems security; computer systems networking and telecommunications; criminal justice/police science; culinary arts; drafting/design engineering technologies related; early childhood education; electromechanical technology; fire science/firefighting; heating, air conditioning, ventilation and refrigeration maintenance technology; industrial engineering; industrial technology; legal administrative assistant/secretary; management science; marketing/marketing management; medical administrative assistant and medical secretary; physical therapy; radiologic technology/science; registered nursing/registered nurse; web/multimedia management and webmaster; web page, digital/multimedia and information resources design.

Academics *Calendar:* semesters. *Degree:* associate. *Special study options:* academic remediation for entering students, accelerated degree program, adult/continuing education programs, advanced placement credit, cooperative education, distance learning, English as a second language, external degree program, independent study, internships, part-time degree program, services for LD students, student-designed majors, summer session for credit.

Library Blackhawk Technical College Library with 101,024 titles, 300 serial subscriptions, 5,889 audiovisual materials, an OPAC.

Student Life *Housing:* college housing not available. *Activities and Organizations:* student-run newspaper, Student Government, Association of Information Technology Professionals, Criminal Justice, Epicurean Club, Phi Theta Kappa Honor Society. *Campus security:* student patrols. *Student services:* personal/psychological counseling, women's center.

Costs (2011–12) *Tuition:* state resident $3356 full-time, $118 per credit part-time; nonresident $5033 full-time, $174 per credit part-time. Full-time tuition and fees vary according to course load. Part-time tuition and fees vary according to course load. *Required fees:* $438 full-time, $6 per credit part-time. *Payment plan:* deferred payment. *Waivers:* senior citizens.

Financial Aid Of all full-time matriculated undergraduates who enrolled in 2010, 33 Federal Work-Study jobs (averaging $1150).

Applying *Options:* electronic application. *Application fee:* $30. *Required:* high school transcript. *Application deadlines:* rolling (freshmen), rolling (transfers). *Notification:* continuous (freshmen), continuous (transfers).

Freshman Application Contact Blackhawk Technical College, PO Box 5009, Janesville, WI 53547-5009. *Phone:* 608-757-7713. *Web site:* http://www.blackhawk.edu/.

Bryant & Stratton College - Milwaukee Campus
Milwaukee, Wisconsin

- **Proprietary** primarily 2-year, founded 1863, part of Bryant and Stratton College, Inc.
- **Urban** campus
- **Coed**

Undergraduates 460 full-time, 368 part-time. Students come from 1 other state; 33% transferred in. *Retention:* 70% of full-time freshmen returned.

Faculty *Student/faculty ratio:* 13:1.

Academics *Calendar:* semesters. *Degrees:* associate and bachelor's. *Special study options:* academic remediation for entering students, adult/continuing education programs, advanced placement credit, cooperative education, distance learning, double majors, independent study, internships, part-time degree program, summer session for credit.

Student Life *Campus security:* 24-hour emergency response devices and patrols.

Standardized Tests *Required:* CPAt; ACCUPLACER (for admission). *Recommended:* SAT or ACT (for admission).

Costs (2011–12) *Tuition:* $15,570 full-time, $519 per credit hour part-time. Full-time tuition and fees vary according to class time and course load. Part-time tuition and fees vary according to course load. *Required fees:* $125 full-time.

Applying *Options:* electronic application. *Required:* high school transcript, interview, entrance and placement evaluations.

Freshman Application Contact Mr. Dan Basile, Director of Admissions, Bryant & Stratton College - Milwaukee Campus, 310 West Wisconsin Avenue, Suite 500 East, Milwaukee, WI 53203-2214. *Phone:* 414-276-5200. *Web site:* http://www.bryantstratton.edu/.

Chippewa Valley Technical College

Eau Claire, Wisconsin

- **District-supported** 2-year, founded 1912, part of Wisconsin Technical College System
- **Urban** 255-acre campus
- **Coed,** 6,058 undergraduate students, 48% full-time, 56% women, 44% men

Undergraduates 2,902 full-time, 3,156 part-time. 2% are from out of state; 1% Black or African American, non-Hispanic/Latino; 2% Hispanic/Latino; 4% Asian, non-Hispanic/Latino; 0.2% Native Hawaiian or other Pacific Islander, non-Hispanic/Latino; 0.6% American Indian or Alaska Native, non-Hispanic/Latino; 1% Two or more races, non-Hispanic/Latino; 4% Race/ethnicity unknown.

Freshmen *Admission:* 1,977 enrolled.

Faculty *Total:* 491, 46% full-time, 7% with terminal degrees. *Student/faculty ratio:* 14:1.

Majors Accounting; administrative assistant and secretarial science; agricultural business and management related; applied horticulture/horticultural business services related; business administration and management; civil engineering technology; clinical/medical laboratory technology; computer programming; computer systems networking and telecommunications; criminal justice/police science; dental hygiene; diagnostic medical sonography and ultrasound technology; early childhood education; electromechanical technology; emergency medical technology (EMT paramedic); health information/medical records technology; heating, ventilation, air conditioning and refrigeration engineering technology; human resources management; legal assistant/paralegal; liberal arts and sciences/liberal studies; marketing/marketing management; medical radiologic technology; multi/interdisciplinary studies related; nanotechnology; physical therapy technology; registered nursing/registered nurse; respiratory care therapy; substance abuse/addiction counseling.

Academics *Calendar:* semesters. *Degree:* certificates, diplomas, and associate. *Special study options:* academic remediation for entering students, accelerated degree program, adult/continuing education programs, advanced placement credit, cooperative education, distance learning, double majors, English as a second language, honors programs, independent study, internships, part-time degree program, services for LD students, student-designed majors, summer session for credit.

Library The Learning Center with an OPAC, a Web page.

Student Life *Housing:* college housing not available. *Activities and Organizations:* Collegiate DECA. *Campus security:* 24-hour emergency response devices, late-night transport/escort service, security cameras. *Student services:* health clinic, personal/psychological counseling.

Standardized Tests *Required:* Compass, Accuplacer (for admission). *Recommended:* ACT (for admission).

Financial Aid Of all full-time matriculated undergraduates who enrolled in 2010, 218 Federal Work-Study jobs (averaging $875).

Applying *Options:* electronic application, early admission, deferred entrance. *Application fee:* $30. *Required for some:* high school transcript. *Application deadlines:* rolling (freshmen), rolling (transfers). *Notification:* continuous (freshmen), continuous (transfers).

Freshman Application Contact Admissions Office, Chippewa Valley Technical College, 620 W. Clairemont Avenue, Eau Claire, WI 54701. *Phone:* 715-833-6200. *Toll-free phone:* 800-547-2882. *Fax:* 715-833-6470. *E-mail:* infocenter@cvtc.edu. *Web site:* http://www.cvtc.edu/.

College of Menominee Nation

Keshena, Wisconsin

Director of Admissions Tessa James, Admissions Coordinator, College of Menominee Nation, PO Box 1179, Keshena, WI 54135. *Phone:* 715-799-5600 Ext. 3053. *Toll-free phone:* 800-567-2344. *E-mail:* tjames@menominee.edu. *Web site:* http://www.menominee.edu/.

Fox Valley Technical College

Appleton, Wisconsin

- **State and locally supported** 2-year, founded 1967, part of Wisconsin Technical College System
- **Suburban** 100-acre campus
- **Endowment** $1.9 million
- **Coed,** 10,873 undergraduate students, 27% full-time, 50% women, 50% men

Undergraduates 2,930 full-time, 7,943 part-time. Students come from 6 states and territories; 6 other countries; 0.8% are from out of state; 2% Black or African American, non-Hispanic/Latino; 3% Hispanic/Latino; 3% Asian, non-Hispanic/Latino; 0.1% Native Hawaiian or other Pacific Islander, non-Hispanic/Latino; 1% American Indian or Alaska Native, non-Hispanic/Latino; 0.4% Two or more races, non-Hispanic/Latino; 5% Race/ethnicity unknown.

Freshmen *Admission:* 1,184 applied, 941 admitted, 831 enrolled.

Faculty *Total:* 926, 35% full-time. *Student/faculty ratio:* 11:1.

Majors Accounting; administrative assistant and secretarial science; agricultural/farm supplies retailing and wholesaling; agricultural mechanization; airline pilot and flight crew; autobody/collision and repair technology; automobile/automotive mechanics technology; avionics maintenance technology; banking and financial support services; business administration and management; computer engineering technology; computer programming; computer systems analysis; computer systems networking and telecommunications; criminal justice/police science; dental hygiene; early childhood education; electrical, electronic and communications engineering technology; electromechanical technology; emergency medical technology (EMT paramedic); environmental control technologies related; fire prevention and safety technology; fire protection related; forensic science and technology; graphic and printing equipment operation/production; graphic communications; heavy equipment maintenance technology; hospitality administration; human resources management; instrumentation technology; interior design; manufacturing engineering technology; marketing/marketing management; mechanical drafting and CAD/CADD; medical office management; multi/interdisciplinary studies related; natural resources/conservation; occupational therapist assistant; operations management; registered nursing/registered nurse; restaurant, culinary, and catering management; substance abuse/addiction counseling; web/multimedia management and webmaster; welding technology.

Academics *Calendar:* semesters. *Degree:* certificates, diplomas, and associate. *Special study options:* academic remediation for entering students, accelerated degree program, advanced placement credit, cooperative education, distance learning, double majors, English as a second language, independent study, internships, off-campus study, part-time degree program, services for LD students, student-designed majors, study abroad, summer session for credit.

Library William M. Sirek Educational Resource Center plus 1 other with 48,000 titles, 103 serial subscriptions, 4,000 audiovisual materials, an OPAC, a Web page.

Student Life *Housing:* college housing not available. *Activities and Organizations:* student-run newspaper, Student Government Association, Phi Theta Kappa, Culinary Arts, Student Nurses, Post Secondary Agribusiness. *Campus security:* 24-hour emergency response devices, late-night transport/escort service, 16-hour patrols by trained security personnel. *Student services:* health clinic, personal/psychological counseling.

Athletics *Intercollegiate sports:* basketball M/W, volleyball W. *Intramural sports:* basketball M/W, football M/W, soccer M/W, softball M/W, table tennis M/W, volleyball M/W.

Costs (2011–12) *Tuition:* state resident $3356 full-time, $112 per credit part-time; nonresident $5034 full-time, $168 per credit part-time. *Required fees:* $488 full-time, $16 per credit part-time. *Payment plan:* installment.

Applying *Options:* electronic application, early admission, deferred entrance. *Application fee:* $30. *Required:* high school transcript. *Application deadlines:* rolling (freshmen), rolling (transfers).

Freshman Application Contact Admissions Center, Fox Valley Technical College, 1825 North Bluemound Drive, PO Box 2277, Appleton, WI 54912-2277. *Phone:* 920-735-5643. *Toll-free phone:* 800-735-3882. *Fax:* 920-735-2582. *Web site:* http://www.fvtc.edu/.

Gateway Technical College

Kenosha, Wisconsin

- **State and locally supported** 2-year, founded 1911, part of Wisconsin Technical College System
- **Urban** 10-acre campus with easy access to Chicago, Milwaukee
- **Coed,** 9,157 undergraduate students, 21% full-time, 61% women, 39% men

Undergraduates 1,882 full-time, 7,275 part-time. Students come from 12 states and territories; 15 other countries; 1% are from out of state; 15% Black or African American, non-Hispanic/Latino; 12% Hispanic/Latino; 1% Asian, non-Hispanic/Latino; 0.1% Native Hawaiian or other Pacific Islander, non-Hispanic/Latino; 0.6% American Indian or Alaska Native, non-Hispanic/Latino; 2% Two or more races, non-Hispanic/Latino; 0.9% Race/ethnicity unknown; 1% transferred in.

Freshmen *Admission:* 4,384 enrolled.

Faculty *Total:* 275, 100% full-time. *Student/faculty ratio:* 16:1.

Majors Accounting; administrative assistant and secretarial science; airline pilot and flight crew; applied horticulture/horticultural business services related; applied horticulture/horticulture operations; architectural engineering technology; automobile/automotive mechanics technology; biology/biotechnology laboratory technician; business administration and management; business operations support and secretarial services related; civil engineering technology; computer and information sciences and support services related; computer programming; computer programming (specific applications); computer support specialist; computer systems analysis; computer systems networking and telecommunications; criminal justice/police science; early childhood education; electrical, electronic and communications engineering technology; electromechanical technology; emergency medical technology (EMT paramedic); fire prevention and safety technology; fire science/firefighting; graphic design; health information/medical records administration; health information/medical records technology; heating, air conditioning, ventilation and refrigeration maintenance technology; heating, ventilation, air conditioning and refrigeration engineering technology; hotel/motel administration; hotel, motel, and restaurant management; industrial mechanics and maintenance technology; interior design; marketing/marketing management; mechanical drafting and CAD/CADD; medical radiologic technology; mental and social health services and allied professions related; multi/interdisciplinary studies related; operations management; physical therapy technology; professional, technical, business, and scientific writing; quality control technology; radio and television broadcasting technology; registered nursing/registered nurse; restaurant, culinary, and catering management; sign language interpretation and translation; surgical technology; surveying technology; teacher assistant/aide; transportation and highway engineering; web/multimedia management and webmaster.

Academics *Calendar:* semesters. *Degree:* certificates, diplomas, and associate. *Special study options:* academic remediation for entering students, advanced placement credit, cooperative education, distance learning, double majors, English as a second language, independent study, internships, part-time degree program, services for LD students, student-designed majors, summer session for credit.

Library Library/Learning Resources Center plus 3 others with an OPAC.

Student Life *Housing:* college housing not available. *Activities and Organizations:* student-run newspaper, radio station. *Campus security:* 24-hour emergency response devices and patrols, late-night transport/escort service. *Student services:* personal/psychological counseling.

Applying *Options:* electronic application, early admission, deferred entrance. *Application fee:* $30. *Required:* high school transcript. *Application deadlines:* rolling (freshmen), rolling (transfers). *Notification:* continuous (freshmen), continuous (transfers).

Freshman Application Contact Admissions, Gateway Technical College, 3520 30th Avenue, Kenosha, WI 53144-1690. *Phone:* 262-564-2300. *Fax:* 262-564-2301. *E-mail:* admissions@gtc.edu. *Web site:* http://www.gtc.edu/.

ITT Technical Institute

Green Bay, Wisconsin

- **Proprietary** primarily 2-year, founded 2000, part of ITT Educational Services, Inc.
- **Coed**

Majors Business administration and management; computer and information systems security; computer software engineering; computer software technology; construction management; criminal justice/law enforcement administration; drafting and design technology; electrical, electronic and communications engineering technology; forensic science and technology; game and interactive media design; graphic communications; information technology project management; legal assistant/paralegal; network and system administration; project management.

Academics *Calendar:* quarters. *Degrees:* associate and bachelor's.

Student Life *Housing:* college housing not available.

Freshman Application Contact Director of Recruitment, ITT Technical Institute, 470 Security Boulevard, Green Bay, WI 54313. *Phone:* 920-662-9000. *Toll-free phone:* 888-884-3626. *Fax:* 920-662-9384. *Web site:* http://www.itt-tech.edu/.

ITT Technical Institute

Greenfield, Wisconsin

- **Proprietary** primarily 2-year, founded 1968, part of ITT Educational Services, Inc.
- **Suburban** campus
- **Coed**

Majors Business administration and management; computer and information systems security; computer software and media applications related; computer software engineering; computer software technology; construction management; criminal justice/law enforcement administration; drafting and design technology; electrical, electronic and communications engineering technology; game and interactive media design; graphic communications; legal assistant/paralegal; network and system administration; project management.

Academics *Calendar:* quarters. *Degrees:* associate and bachelor's.

Student Life *Housing:* college housing not available.

Freshman Application Contact Director of Recruitment, ITT Technical Institute, 6300 West Layton Avenue, Greenfield, WI 53220-4612. *Phone:* 414-282-9494. *Web site:* http://www.itt-tech.edu/.

ITT Technical Institute

Madison, Wisconsin

- **Proprietary** primarily 2-year, part of ITT Educational Services, Inc.
- **Coed**

Majors Business administration and management; computer and information systems security; computer software engineering; computer software technology; criminal justice/law enforcement administration; drafting and design technology; electrical, electronic and communications engineering technology; graphic communications; legal assistant/paralegal; network and system administration; project management.

Academics *Degrees:* associate and bachelor's.

Freshman Application Contact Director of Recruitment, ITT Technical Institute, 2450 Rimrock Road, Suite 100, Madison, WI 53713. *Phone:* 608-288-6301. *Toll-free phone:* 877-628-5960. *Web site:* http://www.itt-tech.edu/.

Kaplan College, Milwaukee Campus

Milwaukee, Wisconsin

- **Proprietary** 2-year
- **Coed**

Majors Criminal justice/law enforcement administration.

Academics *Degree:* diplomas and associate.

Freshman Application Contact Director of Admissions, Kaplan College, Milwaukee Campus, 111 West Pleasant Street, Suite 101, Milwaukee, WI 53212. *Phone:* 414-225-4600. *Toll-free phone:* 800-935-1857. *Web site:* http://milwaukee.kaplancollege.com/.

Lac Courte Oreilles Ojibwa Community College

Hayward, Wisconsin

Freshman Application Contact Ms. Annette Wiggins, Registrar, Lac Courte Oreilles Ojibwa Community College, 13466 West Trepania Road, Hayward, WI 54843-2181. *Phone:* 715-634-4790 Ext. 104. *Toll-free phone:* 888-526-6221. *Web site:* http://www.lco.edu/.

Lakeshore Technical College

Cleveland, Wisconsin

Freshman Application Contact Lakeshore Technical College, 1290 North Avenue, Cleveland, WI 53015. *Phone:* 920-693-1339. *Toll-free phone:* 888-GO TO LTC. *Fax:* 920-693-3561. *Web site:* http://www.gotoltc.com/.

Madison Area Technical College

Madison, Wisconsin

Director of Admissions Ms. Maureen Menendez, Interim Admissions Administrator, Madison Area Technical College, 3550 Anderson Street, Madison, WI 53704-2599. *Phone:* 608-246-6212. *Toll-free phone:* 800-322-6282. *Web site:* http://www.matcmadison.edu/matc/.

Madison Media Institute

Madison, Wisconsin

Freshman Application Contact Mr. Chris K. Hutchings, President/Director, Madison Media Institute, 2702 Agriculture Drive, Madison, WI 53718.

Phone: 608-237-8301. *Toll-free phone:* 800-236-4997. *Web site:* http://www.madisonmedia.edu/.

Mid-State Technical College
Wisconsin Rapids, Wisconsin

Freshman Application Contact Ms. Carole Prochnow, Admissions Assistant, Mid-State Technical College, 500 32nd Street North, Wisconsin Rapids, WI 54494-5599. *Phone:* 715-422-5444. *Web site:* http://www.mstc.edu/.

Milwaukee Area Technical College
Milwaukee, Wisconsin

Freshman Application Contact Sarah Adams, Director, Enrollment Services, Milwaukee Area Technical College, 700 West State Street, Milwaukee, WI 53233-1443. *Phone:* 414-297-6595. *Fax:* 414-297-7800. *E-mail:* adamss4@matc.edu. *Web site:* http://www.matc.edu/.

Moraine Park Technical College
Fond du Lac, Wisconsin

- **District-supported** 2-year, founded 1967, part of Wisconsin Technical College System
- **Small-town** 40-acre campus with easy access to Milwaukee
- **Coed,** 6,734 undergraduate students, 18% full-time, 60% women, 40% men

Undergraduates 1,205 full-time, 5,529 part-time. 2% Black or African American, non-Hispanic/Latino; 3% Hispanic/Latino; 0.9% Asian, non-Hispanic/Latino; 0.6% American Indian or Alaska Native, non-Hispanic/Latino; 0.8% Two or more races, non-Hispanic/Latino; 3% Race/ethnicity unknown.
Freshmen *Admission:* 395 enrolled.
Faculty *Total:* 356, 40% full-time. *Student/faculty ratio:* 14:1.
Majors Accounting; administrative assistant and secretarial science; automotive engineering technology; blasting; business administration and management; carpentry; chiropractic assistant; civil engineering technology; clinical/medical laboratory technology; computer and information sciences and support services related; computer numerically controlled (CNC) machinist technology; computer programming related; computer systems networking and telecommunications; corrections; court reporting; early childhood education; electrician; electromechanical technology; emergency medical technology (EMT paramedic); food preparation; graphic communications; graphic design; hair styling and hair design; health information/medical records technology; heating, air conditioning, ventilation and refrigeration maintenance technology; heating, ventilation, air conditioning and refrigeration engineering technology; hotel/motel administration; human resources management; industrial electronics technology; industrial mechanics and maintenance technology; industrial production technologies related; industrial technology; legal administrative assistant/secretary; legal assistant/paralegal; licensed practical/vocational nurse training; lineworker; machine shop technology; marketing/marketing management; mechanical drafting and CAD/CADD; mechanical engineering technologies related; mechatronics, robotics, and automation engineering; medical/clinical assistant; medical insurance coding; medical office assistant; medical radiologic technology; medical transcription; merchandising, sales, and marketing operations related (general); metal fabricator; multi/interdisciplinary studies related; nursing assistant/aide and patient care assistant/aide; office occupations and clerical services; operations management; pharmacy technician; pipefitting and sprinkler fitting; plumbing technology; printing management; registered nursing/registered nurse; respiratory care therapy; restaurant, culinary, and catering management; structural engineering; substance abuse/addiction counseling; surgical technology; teacher assistant/aide; tool and die technology; veterinary/animal health technology; water quality and wastewater treatment management and recycling technology; web page, digital/multimedia and information resources design; welding technology.
Academics *Calendar:* semesters. *Degree:* certificates, diplomas, and associate. *Special study options:* academic remediation for entering students, accelerated degree program, adult/continuing education programs, advanced placement credit, distance learning, English as a second language, external degree program, independent study, internships, part-time degree program, services for LD students, summer session for credit.
Library Moraine Park Technical College Library/Learning Resource Center with 41,737 titles, 280 serial subscriptions, 11,438 audiovisual materials, an OPAC, a Web page.
Student Life *Housing:* college housing not available. *Campus security:* 24-hour emergency response devices. *Student services:* personal/psychological counseling.
Standardized Tests *Required:* ACT, ACCUPLACER OR COMPASS (for admission). *Required for some:* ACT (for admission).

Costs (2011–12) *Tuition:* state resident $3356 full-time, $112 per credit hour part-time; nonresident $5034 full-time, $168 per credit hour part-time. Full-time tuition and fees vary according to program. Part-time tuition and fees vary according to program. *Required fees:* $271 full-time, $9 per credit hour part-time. *Payment plans:* installment, deferred payment. *Waivers:* senior citizens.
Applying *Options:* electronic application, deferred entrance. *Application fee:* $30. *Required:* high school transcript, placement test. *Required for some:* interview. *Application deadlines:* rolling (freshmen), rolling (out-of-state freshmen), rolling (transfers). *Notification:* continuous (freshmen), continuous (out-of-state freshmen), continuous (transfers).
Freshman Application Contact Ms. Karen Jarvis, Student Services, Moraine Park Technical College, 235 North National Avenue, Fond du Lac, WI 54935. *Phone:* 920-924-3200. *Toll-free phone:* 800-472-4554. *Fax:* 920-924-3421. *E-mail:* kjarvis@morainepark.edu. *Web site:* http://www.morainepark.edu/.

Nicolet Area Technical College
Rhinelander, Wisconsin

Freshman Application Contact Ms. Susan Kordula, Director of Admissions, Nicolet Area Technical College, PO Box 518, Rhinelander, WI 54501. *Phone:* 715-365-4451. *Toll-free phone:* 800-544-3039. *E-mail:* inquire@nicoletcollege.edu. *Web site:* http://www.nicoletcollege.edu/.

Northcentral Technical College
Wausau, Wisconsin

Director of Admissions Ms. Carolyn Michalski, Team Leader, Student Services, Northcentral Technical College, 1000 West Campus Drive, Wausau, WI 54401-1899. *Phone:* 715-675-3331 Ext. 4285. *Web site:* http://www.ntc.edu/.

Northeast Wisconsin Technical College
Green Bay, Wisconsin

Freshman Application Contact Christine Lemerande, Program Enrollment Supervisor, Northeast Wisconsin Technical College, 2740 W Mason Street, PO Box 19042, Green Bay, WI 54307-9042. *Phone:* 920-498-5444. *Toll-free phone:* 888-385-6982. *Fax:* 920-498-6882. *Web site:* http://www.nwtc.edu/.

Rasmussen College Green Bay
Green Bay, Wisconsin

- **Proprietary** primarily 2-year, part of Rasmussen College System
- **Suburban** campus
- **Coed,** 649 undergraduate students

Faculty *Student/faculty ratio:* 22:1.
Majors Accounting; accounting and business/management; business administration and management; clinical/medical laboratory technology; computer and information systems security; computer science; computer software engineering; corrections and criminal justice related; early childhood education; graphic communications related; health/health-care administration; health information/medical records administration; health information/medical records technology; human resources management; human services; legal assistant/paralegal; management information systems and services related; marketing/marketing management; medical administrative assistant and medical secretary; medical/clinical assistant; pharmacy technician; web page, digital/multimedia and information resources design.
Academics *Degrees:* certificates, diplomas, associate, and bachelor's. *Special study options:* academic remediation for entering students, accelerated degree program, adult/continuing education programs, distance learning, double majors, internships, part-time degree program, summer session for credit.
Library Rasmussen College Library - Green Bay with 2,087 titles, 30 serial subscriptions, 147 audiovisual materials, an OPAC, a Web page.
Student Life *Housing:* college housing not available.
Standardized Tests *Required:* Internal Exam (for admission).
Costs (2012–13) *Tuition:* $12,600 full-time. Full-time tuition and fees vary according to course level, course load, degree level, location, and program. Part-time tuition and fees vary according to course level, course load, degree level, location, and program. *Required fees:* $40 full-time. *Payment plans:* installment, deferred payment. *Waivers:* employees or children of employees.
Applying *Options:* electronic application, early admission, deferred entrance. *Application fee:* $40. *Required:* high school transcript, minimum 2.0 GPA, interview. *Application deadlines:* rolling (freshmen), rolling (transfers).
Freshman Application Contact Susan Hammerstrom, Director of Admissions, Rasmussen College Green Bay, 940 South Taylor Street, Suite 100, Green Bay, WI 54303. *Phone:* 920-593-8400. *Toll-free phone:* 888-549-

6755. *E-mail:* susan.hammerstrom@rasmussen.edu. *Web site:* http://www.rasmussen.edu/.

Southwest Wisconsin Technical College

Fennimore, Wisconsin

Freshman Application Contact Student Services, Southwest Wisconsin Technical College, 1800 Bronson Boulevard, Fennimore, WI 53809-9778. *Phone:* 608-822-2354. *Toll-free phone:* 800-362-3322. *Fax:* 608-822-6019. *E-mail:* student-services@swtc.edu. *Web site:* http://www.swtc.edu/.

University of Wisconsin–Baraboo/Sauk County

Baraboo, Wisconsin

Freshman Application Contact Ms. Jan Gerlach, Assistant Director of Student Services, University of Wisconsin–Baraboo/Sauk County, Baraboo, WI 53913-1015. *Phone:* 608-355-5270. *E-mail:* booinfo@uwc.edu. *Web site:* http://www.baraboo.uwc.edu/.

University of Wisconsin–Barron County

Rice Lake, Wisconsin

Freshman Application Contact Assistant Dean for Student Services, University of Wisconsin–Barron County, 1800 College Drive, Rice Lake, WI 54868-2497. *Phone:* 715-234-8024. *Fax:* 715-234-8024. *Web site:* http://www.barron.uwc.edu/.

University of Wisconsin–Fond du Lac

Fond du Lac, Wisconsin

Freshman Application Contact University of Wisconsin–Fond du Lac, 400 University Drive, Fond du Lac, WI 54935. *Phone:* 920-929-1122. *Web site:* http://www.fdl.uwc.edu/.

University of Wisconsin–Fox Valley

Menasha, Wisconsin

- **State-supported** 2-year, founded 1933, part of University of Wisconsin System
- **Urban** 33-acre campus
- **Coed**

Undergraduates 1,037 full-time, 760 part-time. Students come from 3 states and territories; 4 other countries; 1% are from out of state.

Faculty *Student/faculty ratio:* 20:1.

Academics *Calendar:* semesters. *Degree:* certificates and associate. *Special study options:* academic remediation for entering students, accelerated degree program, adult/continuing education programs, advanced placement credit, cooperative education, distance learning, honors programs, independent study, off-campus study, part-time degree program, services for LD students, study abroad, summer session for credit.

Student Life *Campus security:* 24-hour emergency response devices, late-night transport/escort service.

Athletics Member NJCAA.

Standardized Tests *Required:* ACT (for admission).

Costs (2011–12) *Tuition:* state resident $4775 full-time; nonresident $11,758 full-time. Full-time tuition and fees vary according to course load and reciprocity agreements. Part-time tuition and fees vary according to course load and reciprocity agreements. *Payment plans:* installment, deferred payment.

Applying *Options:* electronic application, early admission. *Application fee:* $44. *Required:* essay or personal statement, high school transcript.

Freshman Application Contact University of Wisconsin–Fox Valley, 1478 Midway Road, Menasha, WI 54952. *Phone:* 920-832-2620. *Web site:* http://www.uwfox.uwc.edu/.

University of Wisconsin–Manitowoc

Manitowoc, Wisconsin

Freshman Application Contact Dr. Christopher Lewis, Assistant Campus Dean for Student Services, University of Wisconsin–Manitowoc, 705 Viebahn Street, Manitowoc, WI 54220-6699. *Phone:* 920-683-4707. *Fax:* 920-683-

4776. *E-mail:* christopher.lewis@uwc.edu. *Web site:* http://www.manitowoc.uwc.edu/.

University of Wisconsin–Marathon County

Wausau, Wisconsin

Freshman Application Contact Dr. Nolan Beck, Director of Student Services, University of Wisconsin–Marathon County, 518 South Seventh Avenue, Wausau, WI 54401-5396. *Phone:* 715-261-6238. *Toll-free phone:* 888-367-8962. *Fax:* 715-848-3568. *Web site:* http://www.uwmc.uwc.edu/.

University of Wisconsin–Marinette

Marinette, Wisconsin

Freshman Application Contact Ms. Cynthia M. Bailey, Assistant Campus Dean for Student Services, University of Wisconsin–Marinette, 750 West Bay Shore, Marinette, WI 54143-4299. *Phone:* 715-735-4301. *E-mail:* cynthia.bailey@uwc.edu. *Web site:* http://www.uwc.edu/.

University of Wisconsin–Marshfield/Wood County

Marshfield, Wisconsin

Freshman Application Contact Mr. Jeff Meece, Director of Student Services, University of Wisconsin–Marshfield/Wood County, 2000 West 5th Street, Marshfield, WI 54449. *Phone:* 715-389-6500. *Fax:* 715-384-1718. *Web site:* http://marshfield.uwc.edu/.

University of Wisconsin–Richland

Richland Center, Wisconsin

- **State-supported** 2-year, founded 1967, part of University of Wisconsin System
- **Rural** 135-acre campus
- **Coed,** 476 undergraduate students, 62% full-time, 54% women, 46% men

Undergraduates 294 full-time, 182 part-time. 4% Black or African American, non-Hispanic/Latino; 1% Hispanic/Latino; 1% Asian, non-Hispanic/Latino; 0.6% American Indian or Alaska Native, non-Hispanic/Latino; 2% Race/ethnicity unknown. *Retention:* 55% of full-time freshmen returned.

Freshmen *Admission:* 476 enrolled.

Faculty *Total:* 33, 45% full-time. *Student/faculty ratio:* 18:1.

Majors Biological and physical sciences; liberal arts and sciences/liberal studies.

Academics *Calendar:* semesters. *Degree:* associate. *Special study options:* academic remediation for entering students, adult/continuing education programs, advanced placement credit, distance learning, external degree program, independent study, off-campus study, part-time degree program, services for LD students, study abroad, summer session for credit.

Library Miller Memorial Library with 40,000 titles, 200 serial subscriptions, an OPAC, a Web page.

Student Life *Housing Options:* coed. Campus housing is provided by a third party. *Activities and Organizations:* drama/theater group, Student Senate, International Club, Campus Ambassadors, Educators of the Future, Natural Resources Club. *Student services:* personal/psychological counseling.

Athletics *Intercollegiate sports:* basketball M/W, volleyball W. *Intramural sports:* badminton M/W, basketball M/W, football M/W, golf M/W, racquetball M/W, swimming and diving M/W, table tennis M/W, tennis M/W, volleyball M/W.

Standardized Tests *Required:* SAT or ACT (for admission). *Recommended:* ACT (for admission).

Costs (2011–12) *Tuition:* state resident $5014 full-time, $188 per credit part-time; nonresident $11,998 full-time, $477 per credit part-time. Full-time tuition and fees vary according to reciprocity agreements. Part-time tuition and fees vary according to reciprocity agreements. *Required fees:* $479 full-time. *Room and board:* room only: $3400. Room and board charges vary according to board plan. *Payment plan:* installment. *Waivers:* senior citizens.

Applying *Options:* electronic application. *Application fee:* $44. *Required:* high school transcript. *Required for some:* interview. *Application deadlines:* rolling (freshmen), 9/1 (transfers). *Notification:* continuous until 9/1 (freshmen), continuous until 9/1 (transfers).

Freshman Application Contact Mr. John D. Poole, Assistant Campus Dean, University of Wisconsin–Richland, 1200 Highway 14 West, Richland Center, WI 53581. *Phone:* 608-647-8422. *Fax:* 608-647-2275. *E-mail:* john.poole@uwc.edu. *Web site:* http://richland.uwc.edu/.

University of Wisconsin–Rock County
Janesville, Wisconsin

Freshman Application Contact University of Wisconsin–Rock County, 2909 Kellogg Avenue, Janesville, WI 53546-5699. *Phone:* 608-758-6523. *Toll-free phone:* 888-INFO-UWC. *Web site:* http://rock.uwc.edu/.

University of Wisconsin–Sheboygan
Sheboygan, Wisconsin

- **State-supported** 2-year, founded 1933, part of University of Wisconsin System
- **Small-town** 75-acre campus with easy access to Milwaukee
- **Coed**

Academics *Calendar:* semesters. *Degree:* associate. *Special study options:* academic remediation for entering students, adult/continuing education programs, advanced placement credit, distance learning, English as a second language, independent study, off-campus study, part-time degree program, services for LD students, summer session for credit.
Student Life *Campus security:* 24-hour patrols by city police.
Applying *Options:* electronic application. *Application fee:* $44. *Required:* high school transcript. *Required for some:* interview.
Freshman Application Contact University of Wisconsin–Sheboygan, One University Drive, Sheboygan, WI 53081-4789. *Phone:* 920-459-6633. *Web site:* http://www.sheboygan.uwc.edu/.

University of Wisconsin–Washington County
West Bend, Wisconsin

Freshman Application Contact Mr. Dan Cebrario, Associate Director of Student Services, University of Wisconsin–Washington County, Student Services Office, 400 University Drive, West Bend, WI 53095. *Phone:* 262-335-5201. *Fax:* 262-335-5220. *E-mail:* dan.cibrario@uwc.edu. *Web site:* http://www.washington.uwc.edu/.

University of Wisconsin–Waukesha
Waukesha, Wisconsin

- **State-supported** 2-year, founded 1966, part of University of Wisconsin System
- **Suburban** 86-acre campus with easy access to Milwaukee
- **Coed,** 2,234 undergraduate students, 51% full-time, 47% women, 53% men

Undergraduates 1,145 full-time, 1,089 part-time. Students come from 2 other countries; 1% are from out of state; 3% Black or African American, non-Hispanic/Latino; 3% Hispanic/Latino; 2% Asian, non-Hispanic/Latino; 0.3% American Indian or Alaska Native, non-Hispanic/Latino; 0.4% Race/ethnicity unknown; 8% transferred in.
Freshmen *Admission:* 1,364 enrolled.
Faculty *Total:* 93, 66% full-time, 88% with terminal degrees. *Student/faculty ratio:* 24:1.
Majors Liberal arts and sciences/liberal studies.
Academics *Calendar:* semesters. *Degree:* associate. *Special study options:* academic remediation for entering students, advanced placement credit, distance learning, honors programs, internships, off-campus study, part-time degree program, services for LD students, study abroad, summer session for credit.
Library University of Wisconsin-Waukesha Library plus 1 other with 61,000 titles, 300 serial subscriptions.
Student Life *Housing:* college housing not available. *Activities and Organizations:* drama/theater group, student-run newspaper, choral group, Student Government, Student Activities Committee, Campus Crusade, Phi Theta Kappa, Circle K. *Campus security:* part-time patrols by trained security personnel. *Student services:* personal/psychological counseling.
Athletics Member NJCAA. *Intercollegiate sports:* basketball M/W, golf M/W, soccer M/W, tennis M/W, volleyball W. *Intramural sports:* basketball M, bowling M/W, cheerleading W, football M/W, skiing (downhill) M/W, table tennis M/W, volleyball M(c).
Standardized Tests *Required:* SAT or ACT (for admission).
Costs (2012–13) *Tuition:* state resident $4826 full-time, $204 per hour part-time; nonresident $11,810 full-time, $495 per hour part-time. Full-time tuition and fees vary according to course load and reciprocity agreements. Part-time tuition and fees vary according to course load and reciprocity agreements.

Required fees: $387 full-time. *Payment plan:* installment. *Waivers:* senior citizens.
Applying *Options:* electronic application, early admission, deferred entrance. *Application fee:* $44. *Required:* high school transcript. *Required for some:* interview. *Recommended:* essay or personal statement, admission interview may be recommended. *Application deadline:* rolling (freshmen). *Notification:* continuous (freshmen).
Freshman Application Contact Ms. Deb Kusick, Admissions Specialist, University of Wisconsin–Waukesha, 1500 North University Drive, Waukesha, WI 53188-2799. *Phone:* 262-521-5200. *Fax:* 262-521-5530. *E-mail:* deborah.kusick@uwc.edu. *Web site:* http://www.waukesha.uwc.edu/.

Waukesha County Technical College
Pewaukee, Wisconsin

- **State and locally supported** 2-year, founded 1923, part of Wisconsin Technical College System
- **Suburban** 137-acre campus with easy access to Milwaukee
- **Coed,** 9,449 undergraduate students, 23% full-time, 48% women, 52% men

Undergraduates 2,151 full-time, 7,298 part-time. 6% Black or African American, non-Hispanic/Latino; 5% Hispanic/Latino; 3% Asian, non-Hispanic/Latino; 0.9% American Indian or Alaska Native, non-Hispanic/Latino; 5% Race/ethnicity unknown.
Freshmen *Admission:* 517 enrolled.
Faculty *Total:* 910, 21% full-time.
Majors Accounting; administrative assistant and secretarial science; architectural drafting and CAD/CADD; autobody/collision and repair technology; automobile/automotive mechanics technology; business administration and management; business administration, management and operations related; computer and information sciences and support services related; computer programming; computer support specialist; computer systems networking and telecommunications; criminal justice/police science; dental hygiene; digital arts; early childhood education; electrical, electronic and communications engineering technology; electromechanical and instrumentation and maintenance technologies related; emergency medical technology (EMT paramedic); fire prevention and safety technology; graphic communications; graphic design; health information/medical records technology; hotel, motel, and restaurant management; interior design; international marketing; marketing/marketing management; mechanical drafting and CAD/CADD; medical radiologic technology; mental and social health services and allied professions related; multi/interdisciplinary studies related; operations management; physical therapy technology; real estate; registered nursing/registered nurse; restaurant, culinary, and catering management; surgical technology; teacher assistant/aide.
Academics *Calendar:* semesters. *Degree:* certificates, diplomas, and associate. *Special study options:* academic remediation for entering students, adult/continuing education programs, advanced placement credit, cooperative education, distance learning, English as a second language, part-time degree program, services for LD students, student-designed majors, summer session for credit.
Student Life *Housing:* college housing not available. *Campus security:* patrols by police officers 8 am to 10 pm.
Costs (2011–12) *Tuition:* state resident $3356 full-time, $112 per credit hour part-time; nonresident $5034 full-time, $168 per credit hour part-time. Full-time tuition and fees vary according to program. Part-time tuition and fees vary according to program. *Required fees:* $201 full-time, $7 per credit hour part-time. *Payment plans:* installment, deferred payment. *Waivers:* senior citizens.
Financial Aid Of all full-time matriculated undergraduates who enrolled in 2010, 40 Federal Work-Study jobs (averaging $2500). 100 state and other part-time jobs (averaging $2000).
Applying *Application fee:* $30. *Required:* high school transcript. *Required for some:* interview. *Application deadlines:* rolling (freshmen), rolling (transfers).
Freshman Application Contact Waukesha County Technical College, 800 Main Street, Pewaukee, WI 53072-4601. *Phone:* 262-691-5464. *Web site:* http://www.wctc.edu/.

Western Technical College
La Crosse, Wisconsin

Freshman Application Contact Ms. Jane Wells, Manager of Admissions, Registration, and Records, Western Technical College, PO Box 908, La Crosse, WI 54602-0908. *Phone:* 608-785-9158. *Toll-free phone:* 800-322-9982. *Fax:* 608-785-9094. *E-mail:* mildes@wwtc.edu. *Web site:* http://www.westerntc.edu/.

Wisconsin Indianhead Technical College

Shell Lake, Wisconsin

- **District-supported** 2-year, founded 1912, part of Wisconsin Technical College System
- **Urban** 113-acre campus
- **Endowment** $2.8 million
- **Coed,** 3,718 undergraduate students, 42% full-time, 62% women, 38% men

Undergraduates 1,545 full-time, 2,173 part-time. Students come from 4 states and territories; 1% are from out of state; 0.6% Black or African American, non-Hispanic/Latino; 0.5% Hispanic/Latino; 0.5% Asian, non-Hispanic/Latino; 0.1% Native Hawaiian or other Pacific Islander, non-Hispanic/Latino; 2% American Indian or Alaska Native, non-Hispanic/Latino; 1% Two or more races, non-Hispanic/Latino; 1% Race/ethnicity unknown; 3% international. *Retention:* 71% of full-time freshmen returned.
Freshmen *Admission:* 799 enrolled.
Faculty *Total:* 581, 26% full-time. *Student/faculty ratio:* 10:1.
Majors Accounting; administrative assistant and secretarial science; architectural engineering technology; business administration and management; computer installation and repair technology; computer systems networking and telecommunications; corrections; court reporting; criminal justice/police science; early childhood education; emergency medical technology (EMT paramedic); energy management and systems technology; finance; marketing/marketing management; mechanical drafting and CAD/CADD; medical administrative assistant and medical secretary; mental and social health services and allied professions related; multi/interdisciplinary studies related; occupational therapist assistant; operations management; web page, digital/multimedia and information resources design.
Academics *Calendar:* semesters. *Degree:* certificates, diplomas, and associate.
Student Life *Housing:* college housing not available. *Student services:* health clinic.
Applying *Options:* electronic application. *Application fee:* $30. *Application deadline:* rolling (freshmen).
Freshman Application Contact Mr. Steve Bitzer, Vice President, Student Affairs and Campus Administrator, Wisconsin Indianhead Technical College, 2100 Beaser Avenue, Ashland, WI 54806. *Phone:* 715-468-2815 Ext. 3149. *Toll-free phone:* 800-243-9482. *Fax:* 715-468-2819. *E-mail:* Steve.Bitzer@witc.edu. *Web site:* http://www.witc.edu/.

WYOMING

Casper College

Casper, Wyoming

- **State and locally supported** 2-year, founded 1945
- **Small-town** 200-acre campus
- **Coed,** 4,306 undergraduate students, 49% full-time, 59% women, 41% men

Undergraduates 2,090 full-time, 2,216 part-time. Students come from 38 states and territories; 20 other countries; 7% are from out of state; 2% Black or African American, non-Hispanic/Latino; 4% Hispanic/Latino; 0.5% Asian, non-Hispanic/Latino; 0.3% Native Hawaiian or other Pacific Islander, non-Hispanic/Latino; 1% American Indian or Alaska Native, non-Hispanic/Latino; 0.3% Two or more races, non-Hispanic/Latino; 1% Race/ethnicity unknown; 1% international; 6% transferred in; 10% live on campus. *Retention:* 57% of full-time freshmen returned.
Freshmen *Admission:* 1,053 applied, 1,053 admitted, 674 enrolled. *Average high school GPA:* 2.9. *Test scores:* ACT scores over 18: 71%; ACT scores over 24: 21%; ACT scores over 30: 1%.
Faculty *Total:* 264, 57% full-time, 19% with terminal degrees. *Student/faculty ratio:* 15:1.
Majors Accounting; accounting technology and bookkeeping; acting; administrative assistant and secretarial science; agricultural business and management; agriculture; airline pilot and flight crew; animal sciences; anthropology; art; art teacher education; athletic training; autobody/collision and repair technology; automobile/automotive mechanics technology; biology/biological sciences; business administration and management; business automation/technology/data entry; chemistry; clinical laboratory science/medical technology; computer programming; construction management; construction trades; criminal justice/law enforcement administration; crisis/emergency/disaster management; dance; diesel mechanics technology; drafting and design technology; economics; electrical, electronic and communications engineering technology; elementary education; emergency medical technology (EMT para-

medic); energy management and systems technology; engineering; English; entrepreneurship; environmental science; fine/studio arts; fire science/firefighting; foreign languages and literatures; forensic science and technology; general studies; geographic information science and cartography; geology/earth science; graphic design; history; hospitality administration; industrial mechanics and maintenance technology; international relations and affairs; kindergarten/preschool education; legal assistant/paralegal; liberal arts and sciences/liberal studies; machine tool technology; manufacturing engineering technology; marketing/marketing management; mathematics; mining technology; museum studies; music; musical theater; music performance; music teacher education; nutrition sciences; occupational therapist assistant; pharmacy technician; phlebotomy technology; photography; physical education teaching and coaching; physics; political science and government; pre-dentistry studies; pre-law studies; premedical studies; pre-occupational therapy; pre-optometry; pre-pharmacy studies; pre-physical therapy; pre-veterinary studies; psychology; radiologic technology/science; range science and management; registered nursing/registered nurse; respiratory care therapy; retailing; robotics technology; social studies teacher education; social work; sociology; speech communication and rhetoric; statistics related; substance abuse/addiction counseling; teacher assistant/aide; technology/industrial arts teacher education; theater design and technology; water quality and wastewater treatment management and recycling technology; web/multimedia management and webmaster; web page, digital/multimedia and information resources design; welding technology; wildlife, fish and wildlands science and management; women's studies.
Academics *Calendar:* semesters. *Degree:* certificates and associate. *Special study options:* academic remediation for entering students, accelerated degree program, advanced placement credit, cooperative education, distance learning, English as a second language, honors programs, independent study, internships, off-campus study, part-time degree program, services for LD students, summer session for credit.
Library Goodstein Foundation Library with 128,000 titles, 385 serial subscriptions, an OPAC, a Web page.
Student Life *Housing Options:* coed. Campus housing is university owned. *Activities and Organizations:* drama/theater group, student-run newspaper, choral group, Student Senate, Student Activities Board, Agriculture Club, Theater Club, Phi Theta Kappa. *Campus security:* 24-hour patrols, late-night transport/escort service. *Student services:* health clinic, personal/psychological counseling.
Athletics Member NJCAA. *Intercollegiate sports:* basketball M(s)/W(s), equestrian sports M/W, volleyball W(s). *Intramural sports:* basketball M/W, bowling M/W, football M/W, golf M/W, racquetball M/W, soccer M/W, softball M/W, tennis M/W.
Costs (2012–13) *Tuition:* state resident $1704 full-time, $71 per credit hour part-time; nonresident $5112 full-time, $216 per credit hour part-time. *Required fees:* $432 full-time, $18 per credit hour part-time. *Room and board:* $5300. Room and board charges vary according to board plan and housing facility. *Payment plan:* deferred payment. *Waivers:* senior citizens and employees or children of employees.
Financial Aid Of all full-time matriculated undergraduates who enrolled in 2010, 80 Federal Work-Study jobs (averaging $2000).
Applying *Options:* electronic application, early admission. *Required:* high school transcript. *Application deadlines:* 8/15 (freshmen), 8/15 (transfers). *Notification:* continuous until 8/15 (freshmen), continuous until 8/15 (transfers).
Freshman Application Contact Mrs. Kyla Foltz, Director of Admissions Services, Casper College, 125 College Drive, Casper, WY 82601. *Phone:* 307-268-2111. *Toll-free phone:* 800-442-2963. *Fax:* 307-268-2611. *E-mail:* kfoltz@caspercollege.edu. *Web site:* http://www.caspercollege.edu/.

Central Wyoming College

Riverton, Wyoming

- **State and locally supported** 2-year, founded 1966, part of Wyoming Community College Commission
- **Small-town** 200-acre campus
- **Endowment** $13.2 million
- **Coed,** 2,242 undergraduate students, 41% full-time, 58% women, 42% men

Undergraduates 911 full-time, 1,331 part-time. Students come from 45 states and territories; 9 other countries; 15% are from out of state; 0.7% Black or African American, non-Hispanic/Latino; 7% Hispanic/Latino; 1% Asian, non-Hispanic/Latino; 0.4% Native Hawaiian or other Pacific Islander, non-Hispanic/Latino; 12% American Indian or Alaska Native, non-Hispanic/Latino; 2% Two or more races, non-Hispanic/Latino; 2% Race/ethnicity unknown; 0.6% international; 7% transferred in; 11% live on campus. *Retention:* 54% of full-time freshmen returned.
Freshmen *Admission:* 642 applied, 642 admitted, 376 enrolled. *Average high school GPA:* 2.94. *Test scores:* SAT critical reading scores over 500: 39%; SAT math scores over 500: 31%; ACT scores over 18: 70%; SAT critical read-

ing scores over 600: 8%; SAT math scores over 600: 8%; ACT scores over 24: 17%.

Faculty *Total:* 152, 32% full-time, 46% with terminal degrees. *Student/faculty ratio:* 16:1.

Majors Accounting; accounting technology and bookkeeping; acting; administrative assistant and secretarial science; agricultural and domestic animal services related; agricultural business and management; American Indian/Native American studies; area studies related; art; athletic training; automobile/automotive mechanics technology; biology/biological sciences; business administration and management; business automation/technology/data entry; business/commerce; carpentry; child-care and support services management; commercial photography; computer science; computer technology/computer systems technology; criminal justice/law enforcement administration; culinary arts; customer service support/call center/teleservice operation; dental assisting; dramatic/theater arts; early childhood education; elementary education; emergency medical technology (EMT paramedic); engineering; English; environmental/environmental health engineering; environmental science; equestrian studies; fire science/firefighting; general studies; geology/earth science; graphic design; health services/allied health/health sciences; homeland security, law enforcement, firefighting and protective services related; hotel/motel administration; international/global studies; manufacturing engineering; mathematics; medical office assistant; music; occupational safety and health technology; office occupations and clerical services; parks, recreation and leisure; parks, recreation and leisure facilities management; physical sciences; pre-law studies; psychology; radio and television; range science and management; registered nursing/registered nurse; rehabilitation and therapeutic professions related; secondary education; selling skills and sales; social sciences; teacher assistant/aide; theater design and technology; welding technology.

Academics *Calendar:* semesters. *Degree:* certificates, diplomas, and associate. *Special study options:* academic remediation for entering students, adult/continuing education programs, advanced placement credit, cooperative education, distance learning, double majors, English as a second language, honors programs, independent study, off-campus study, part-time degree program, services for LD students, summer session for credit.

Library Central Wyoming College Library with 54,974 titles, 2,940 serial subscriptions, 1,450 audiovisual materials, an OPAC, a Web page.

Student Life *Housing Options:* coed. Campus housing is university owned. *Activities and Organizations:* drama/theater group, student-run radio and television station, choral group, Multi-Cultural Club, La Vida Nueva Club, Fellowship of College Christians, Quality Leaders, Science Club. *Campus security:* 24-hour emergency response devices, late-night transport/escort service, controlled dormitory access. *Student services:* personal/psychological counseling.

Athletics Member NJCAA. *Intercollegiate sports:* basketball M(s)/W(s), equestrian sports M(s)/W(s), volleyball W(s). *Intramural sports:* badminton M/W, basketball M/W, football M/W, rock climbing M/W, skiing (cross-country) M/W, skiing (downhill) M/W, soccer M/W, softball M/W, swimming and diving M/W, table tennis M/W, tennis M/W, ultimate Frisbee M/W, volleyball M/W, weight lifting M/W.

Costs (2012–13) *Tuition:* state resident $1800 full-time, $75 per credit part-time; nonresident $5400 full-time, $225 per credit part-time. Full-time tuition and fees vary according to course load, program, and reciprocity agreements. Part-time tuition and fees vary according to course load, program, and reciprocity agreements. *Required fees:* $672 full-time, $28 per credit part-time. *Room and board:* $4477; room only: $2167. Room and board charges vary according to board plan and housing facility. *Payment plans:* installment, deferred payment. *Waivers:* senior citizens and employees or children of employees.

Financial Aid Of all full-time matriculated undergraduates who enrolled in 2010, 620 applied for aid, 519 were judged to have need. 44 Federal Work-Study jobs (averaging $2527). *Financial aid deadline:* 6/30.

Applying *Options:* electronic application, early admission, deferred entrance. *Recommended:* high school transcript. *Application deadlines:* rolling (freshmen), rolling (out-of-state freshmen), rolling (transfers).

Freshman Application Contact Mrs. Mikal Dalley, Admissions Assistant, Central Wyoming College, 2660 Peck Avenue, Riverton, WY 82501-2273. *Phone:* 307-855-2119. *Toll-free phone:* 800-735-8418. *Fax:* 307-855-2065. *E-mail:* admit@cwc.edu. *Web site:* http://www.cwc.edu/.

Eastern Wyoming College

Torrington, Wyoming

Freshman Application Contact Dr. Rex Cogdill, Vice President for Students Services, Eastern Wyoming College, 3200 West C Street, Torrington, WY 82240. *Phone:* 307-532-8257. *Toll-free phone:* 866-327-8996. *Fax:* 307-532-8222. *E-mail:* rex.cogdill@ewc.wy.edu. *Web site:* http://www.ewc.wy.edu/.

Laramie County Community College

Cheyenne, Wyoming

- **District-supported** 2-year, founded 1968, part of Wyoming Community College Commission
- **Small-town** 271-acre campus
- **Endowment** $15.6 million
- **Coed,** 4,527 undergraduate students, 49% full-time, 59% women, 41% men

Undergraduates 2,228 full-time, 2,299 part-time. Students come from 26 states and territories; 9 other countries; 14% are from out of state; 2% Black or African American, non-Hispanic/Latino; 8% Hispanic/Latino; 1% Asian, non-Hispanic/Latino; 0.4% Native Hawaiian or other Pacific Islander, non-Hispanic/Latino; 0.7% American Indian or Alaska Native, non-Hispanic/Latino; 0.2% Two or more races, non-Hispanic/Latino; 3% Race/ethnicity unknown; 1% international; 7% transferred in; 5% live on campus. *Retention:* 77% of full-time freshmen returned.

Freshmen *Admission:* 1,582 applied, 1,582 admitted, 476 enrolled. *Average high school GPA:* 3.08. *Test scores:* ACT scores over 18: 68%; ACT scores over 24: 16%; ACT scores over 30: 1%.

Faculty *Total:* 381, 27% full-time, 3% with terminal degrees. *Student/faculty ratio:* 12:1.

Majors Accounting; agribusiness; agricultural business technology; agricultural production; agriculture; anthropology; art; autobody/collision and repair technology; automobile/automotive mechanics technology; biological and physical sciences; biology/biological sciences; business administration and management; business/commerce; chemistry; computer programming; computer science; corrections; criminal justice/law enforcement administration; dental hygiene; diagnostic medical sonography and ultrasound technology; diesel mechanics technology; digital communication and media/multimedia; drafting and design technology; early childhood education; economics; education; emergency medical technology (EMT paramedic); energy management and systems technology; engineering; English; entrepreneurship; equestrian studies; fire science/firefighting; heating, air conditioning, ventilation and refrigeration maintenance technology; history; homeland security, law enforcement, firefighting and protective services related; humanities; human services; legal assistant/paralegal; mass communication/media; mathematics; multi/interdisciplinary studies related; music; physical education teaching and coaching; physical therapy technology; political science and government; pre-law studies; pre-pharmacy studies; psychology; public administration; radiologic technology/science; registered nursing/registered nurse; religious studies; social sciences; sociology; Spanish; speech communication and rhetoric; surgical technology; wildlife, fish and wildlands science and management.

Academics *Calendar:* semesters. *Degree:* certificates and associate. *Special study options:* academic remediation for entering students, adult/continuing education programs, advanced placement credit, cooperative education, distance learning, double majors, English as a second language, honors programs, independent study, internships, off-campus study, part-time degree program, services for LD students, summer session for credit. *ROTC:* Army (c), Air Force (c).

Library Ludden Library plus 1 other with 56,351 titles, 188 serial subscriptions, 5,594 audiovisual materials, an OPAC, a Web page.

Student Life *Housing Options:* coed. Campus housing is university owned. *Activities and Organizations:* drama/theater group, student-run newspaper, choral group. *Campus security:* 24-hour emergency response devices and patrols, late-night transport/escort service, controlled dormitory access. *Student services:* personal/psychological counseling.

Athletics Member NJCAA. *Intercollegiate sports:* basketball M(s), cheerleading M(s)/W(s), equestrian sports M(s)/W(s), soccer M(s)/W(s), volleyball W(s). *Intramural sports:* basketball M/W, equestrian sports M/W, golf M/W, racquetball M/W, rock climbing M/W, skiing (cross-country) M/W, soccer M/W, softball M/W, table tennis M/W, ultimate Frisbee M/W, volleyball M/W.

Costs (2012–13) *One-time required fee:* $20. *Tuition:* state resident $1704 full-time, $71 per credit hour part-time; nonresident $5112 full-time, $213 per credit hour part-time. *Required fees:* $840 full-time, $35 per credit hour part-time. *Room and board:* $7086; room only: $4506.

Applying *Options:* electronic application, deferred entrance. *Application fee:* $20. *Required for some:* high school transcript, interview. *Application deadlines:* rolling (freshmen), rolling (out-of-state freshmen), rolling (transfers). *Notification:* continuous (freshmen), continuous (out-of-state freshmen), continuous (transfers).

Freshman Application Contact Ms. Holly Allison, Director of Admissions, Laramie County Community College, 1400 East College Drive, Cheyenne, WY 82007. *Phone:* 307-778-1117. *Toll-free phone:* 800-522-2993 Ext. 1357. *Fax:* 307-778-1360. *E-mail:* learnmore@lccc.wy.edu. *Web site:* http://www.lccc.wy.edu/.

Northwest College

Powell, Wyoming

- **State and locally supported** 2-year, founded 1946, part of Wyoming Community College Commission

- **Rural** 124-acre campus

- **Endowment** $6.5 million

- **Coed,** 2,051 undergraduate students, 62% full-time, 60% women, 40% men

Undergraduates 1,267 full-time, 784 part-time. Students come from 38 states and territories; 22 other countries; 24% are from out of state; 0.3% Black or African American, non-Hispanic/Latino; 7% Hispanic/Latino; 0.7% Asian, non-Hispanic/Latino; 2% American Indian or Alaska Native, non-Hispanic/Latino; 2% Two or more races, non-Hispanic/Latino; 0.2% Race/ethnicity unknown; 3% international; 5% transferred in. *Retention:* 50% of full-time freshmen returned.

Freshmen *Admission:* 418 enrolled.

Faculty *Total:* 164, 49% full-time. *Student/faculty ratio:* 14:1.

Majors Accounting; administrative assistant and secretarial science; aeronautics/aviation/aerospace science and technology; agribusiness; agricultural communication/journalism; agricultural production; agricultural teacher education; animal sciences; anthropology; archeology; art; athletic training; biology/biological sciences; broadcast journalism; business administration and management; business/commerce; CAD/CADD drafting/design technology; chemistry; cinematography and film/video production; commercial and advertising art; commercial photography; criminal justice/law enforcement administration; crop production; desktop publishing and digital imaging design; electrician; elementary education; engineering; English; equestrian studies; farm and ranch management; French; general studies; graphic and printing equipment operation/production; health and physical education/fitness; health/medical preparatory programs related; health services/allied health/health sciences; history; international relations and affairs; journalism; kindergarten/pre-school education; liberal arts and sciences/liberal studies; mathematics; music; natural resources management and policy; parks, recreation and leisure; physics; playwriting and screenwriting; political science and government; pre-pharmacy studies; psychology; radio and television; radio, television, and digital communication related; range science and management; registered nursing/registered nurse; secondary education; social sciences; sociology; Spanish; speech communication and rhetoric; veterinary/animal health technology; visual and performing arts related; welding technology.

Academics *Calendar:* semesters. *Degree:* certificates and associate. *Special study options:* academic remediation for entering students, adult/continuing education programs, advanced placement credit, cooperative education, distance learning, double majors, English as a second language, external degree program, independent study, internships, off-campus study, part-time degree program, services for LD students, study abroad, summer session for credit.

Library John Taggart Hinckley Library with 47,375 titles, 59,654 serial subscriptions, 28,531 audiovisual materials, an OPAC, a Web page.

Student Life *Housing:* on-campus residence required for freshman year. *Options:* coed, women-only, disabled students. Campus housing is university owned. Freshman campus housing is guaranteed. *Activities and Organizations:* drama/theater group, student-run newspaper, radio and television station, choral group. *Campus security:* 24-hour emergency response devices and patrols, late-night transport/escort service, controlled dormitory access. *Student services:* health clinic, personal/psychological counseling.

Athletics Member NJCAA. *Intercollegiate sports:* basketball M(s)/W(s), equestrian sports M(s)/W(s), soccer M(s)/W(s), volleyball W(s), wrestling M(s). *Intramural sports:* basketball M/W, football M/W, golf M/W, skiing (downhill) M/W, softball M/W, tennis M/W, ultimate Frisbee M/W, volleyball M/W.

Standardized Tests *Recommended:* SAT or ACT (for admission), ACT COMPASS.

Costs (2011–12) *Tuition:* state resident $1704 full-time, $71 per credit hour part-time; nonresident $5112 full-time, $213 per credit hour part-time. Full-time tuition and fees vary according to course load, location, and program. Part-time tuition and fees vary according to course load, location, and program. *Required fees:* $626 full-time, $21 per credit hour part-time. *Room and board:* $4460; room only: $1990. Room and board charges vary according to board plan and housing facility. *Payment plan:* installment. *Waivers:* children of alumni, senior citizens, and employees or children of employees.

Financial Aid Of all full-time matriculated undergraduates who enrolled in 2010, 115 Federal Work-Study jobs (averaging $2700). 215 state and other part-time jobs (averaging $2700).

Applying *Options:* electronic application. *Required:* high school transcript. *Required for some:* minimum 2.0 GPA. *Recommended:* minimum 2.0 GPA. *Application deadlines:* rolling (freshmen), rolling (out-of-state freshmen), rolling (transfers). *Notification:* continuous (freshmen), continuous (out-of-state freshmen), continuous (transfers).

Freshman Application Contact Mr. West Hernandez, Admissions Manager, Northwest College, 231 West 6th Street, Orendorff Building 1, Powell, WY 82435-1898. *Phone:* 307-754-6103. *Toll-free phone:* 800-560-4692. *Fax:* 307-754-6249. *E-mail:* west.hernandez@northwestcollege.edu. *Web site:* http://www.northwestcollege.edu/.

Sheridan College

Sheridan, Wyoming

- **State and locally supported** 2-year, founded 1948, part of Wyoming Community College Commission

- **Small-town** 124-acre campus

- **Endowment** $17.5 million

- **Coed**

Undergraduates 1,447 full-time, 2,493 part-time. Students come from 29 states and territories; 12 other countries; 18% are from out of state; 4% transferred in; 12% live on campus.

Faculty *Student/faculty ratio:* 21:1.

Academics *Calendar:* semesters. *Degree:* certificates and associate. *Special study options:* academic remediation for entering students, advanced placement credit, cooperative education, distance learning, double majors, English as a second language, independent study, internships, off-campus study, part-time degree program, services for LD students, summer session for credit.

Student Life *Campus security:* 24-hour emergency response devices, student patrols, controlled dormitory access, night patrols by certified officers.

Athletics Member NJCAA.

Costs (2011–12) *Tuition:* state resident $1704 full-time, $71 per credit hour part-time; nonresident $5112 full-time, $213 per credit hour part-time. Full-time tuition and fees vary according to course load, location, program, and reciprocity agreements. Part-time tuition and fees vary according to course load, location, program, and reciprocity agreements. *Required fees:* $690 full-time, $23 per credit hour part-time. *Room and board:* $4900. Room and board charges vary according to board plan, housing facility, and location.

Financial Aid Of all full-time matriculated undergraduates who enrolled in 2010, 92 Federal Work-Study jobs (averaging $1798).

Applying *Options:* electronic application, early admission, deferred entrance. *Required for some:* high school transcript. *Recommended:* high school transcript.

Freshman Application Contact Mr. Zane Garstad, Director of Enrollment Services, Sheridan College, PO Box 1500, Sheridan, WY 82801-1500. *Phone:* 307-674-6446 Ext. 2002. *Toll-free phone:* 800-913-9139 Ext. 2002. *Fax:* 307-674-7205. *E-mail:* admissions@sheridan.edu. *Web site:* http://www.sheridan.edu/.

Western Wyoming Community College

Rock Springs, Wyoming

Freshman Application Contact Director of Admissions, Western Wyoming Community College, PO Box 428, Rock Springs, WY 82902-0428. *Phone:* 307-382-1647. *Toll-free phone:* 800-226-1181. *Fax:* 307-382-1636. *E-mail:* admissions@wwcc.wy.edu. *Web site:* http://www.wwcc.wy.edu/.

WyoTech Laramie

Laramie, Wyoming

Director of Admissions Director of Admissions, WyoTech Laramie, 4373 North Third Street, Laramie, WY 82072-9519. *Phone:* 307-742-3776. *Toll-free phone:* 888-577-7559. *Fax:* 307-721-4854. *Web site:* http://www.wyotech.com/.

CANADA

ALBERTA

Southern Alberta Institute of Technology
Calgary, Alberta, Canada

- **Province-supported** primarily 2-year, founded 1916
- **Urban** 96-acre campus
- **Coed**

Undergraduates 6,954 full-time, 718 part-time.
Academics *Calendar:* trimesters. *Degrees:* certificates, diplomas, associate, and bachelor's. *Special study options:* cooperative education, distance learn-ing, independent study, internships, off-campus study, services for LD students.
Student Life *Campus security:* 24-hour emergency response devices and patrols, late-night transport/escort service.
Costs (2011–12) *Tuition:* Full-time tuition and fees vary according to class time, course load, and program. Part-time tuition and fees vary according to class time, course load, and program. Tuition varies according to program and course load. *Room and board:* Room and board charges vary according to housing facility.
Applying *Options:* electronic application, early admission, early decision. *Application fee:* $50 Canadian dollars. *Required:* high school transcript. *Required for some:* essay or personal statement, interview.
Freshman Application Contact Southern Alberta Institute of Technology, 1301 16th Avenue NW, Calgary, AB T2M 0L4, Canada. *Phone:* 403-284-8857. *Toll-free phone:* 877-284-SAIT. *Web site:* http://www.sait.ca/.

INTERNATIONAL

MEXICO

Westhill University
Sante Fe, Mexico

Freshman Application Contact Admissions, Westhill University, 56 Domingo Garcia Ramos, Zona Escolar, Prados de la Montana I, 05610 Sante Fe, Cuajimalpa, Mexico. *Phone:* 52-55 5292-1121. *Toll-free phone:* 877-403-4535. *E-mail:* admissions@westhill.edu.mx. *Web site:* http://www.westhill.edu.mx/.

PALAU

Palau Community College
Koror, Palau

- **Territory-supported** 2-year, founded 1969
- **Small-town** 30-acre campus
- **Endowment** $1.3 million
- **Coed,** 694 undergraduate students, 67% full-time, 58% women, 42% men

Undergraduates 463 full-time, 231 part-time. 2% transferred in; 20% live on campus.
Freshmen *Admission:* 283 applied, 165 admitted, 114 enrolled. *Average high school GPA:* 2.82.
Faculty *Total:* 65, 54% full-time. *Student/faculty ratio:* 16:1.
Majors Accounting; administrative assistant and secretarial science; agriculture; automobile/automotive mechanics technology; business teacher education; carpentry; construction engineering technology; criminal justice/police science; education; electrical, electronic and communications engineering technology; hotel/motel administration; liberal arts and sciences/liberal studies; natural resources and conservation related; registered nursing/registered nurse.
Academics *Calendar:* semesters. *Degree:* certificates and associate. *Special study options:* academic remediation for entering students, adult/continuing education programs, cooperative education, distance learning, double majors, English as a second language, internships, part-time degree program, summer session for credit.
Library Palau Community College Library with 28,458 titles, 1,888 serial subscriptions, 855 audiovisual materials, an OPAC.
Student Life *Housing Options:* coed, men-only. Campus housing is university owned. *Activities and Organizations:* Yapese Student Organization, Chuukes Student Organization, Palauans Student Organization, Environmental Club, Writing Club. *Campus security:* 24-hour emergency response devices and patrols, late-night transport/escort service, evening patrols by trained security personnel. *Student services:* health clinic, personal/psychological counseling, legal services.
Athletics *Intramural sports:* baseball M, basketball M, softball M/W, table tennis M/W, volleyball M/W, weight lifting M, wrestling M.
Costs (2011–12) *Tuition:* state resident $2640 full-time, $110 per credit hour part-time; nonresident $3000 full-time, $125 per credit hour part-time. Full-time tuition and fees vary according to course load. Part-time tuition and fees vary according to course load. *Required fees:* $610 full-time, $610 per term part-time. *Room and board:* $3381; room only: $1176. Room and board charges vary according to board plan, housing facility, and location. *Payment plan:* installment. *Waivers:* employees or children of employees.
Financial Aid *Financial aid deadline:* 6/30.
Applying *Options:* early admission, deferred entrance. *Application fee:* $10. *Required:* high school transcript, minimum 2.0 GPA. *Application deadlines:* 8/15 (freshmen), 8/15 (transfers). *Notification:* continuous (freshmen), continuous (transfers).
Freshman Application Contact Ms. Dahlia Katosang, Director of Admissions and Financial Aid, Palau Community College, PO Box 9, Koror, PW 96940-0009. *Phone:* 680-488-2471 Ext. 233. *Fax:* 680-488-4468. *E-mail:* dahliapcc@palaunet.com. *Web site:* http://www.palau.edu/.

College
Close-Ups

THE ART INSTITUTE OF NEW YORK CITY
NEW YORK, NEW YORK

The Art Institute
of New York City®

CREATE TOMORROW

A focused education from The Art Institute of New York City can help students turn their creative energy into a powerful tool that can make a difference in the world. Students are part of a collaborative and supportive community, where experienced instructors provide the guidance and skills needed to pursue a career in the creative economy.

The school's programs in the areas of design, media arts, and fashion give students the opportunity to learn by using professional-grade technology and to build a portfolio of work to show potential employers after graduation.

The Art Institute of New York City is accredited by the Accrediting Council for Independent Colleges and Schools to award associate degrees. The Accrediting Council for Independent Colleges and Schools is listed as a nationally recognized accrediting agency by the United States Department of Education and is recognized by the Council for Higher Education Accreditation. ACICS can be contacted at 750 First Street NE, Suite 980, Washington, D.C. 20002; phone: 202-336-6780.

The Art Institute of New York City has received permission to operate from the State of New York Board of Regents State Education Department, 89 Washington Avenue, 5 North Mezzanine, Albany, New York 12234; phone: 518-474-2593.

Academic Programs

No matter which course of study a student may choose, the professionals at The Art Institute of New York City will guide, support, and help each student as their talents evolve on their journey of personal and professional transformation. Students studying design learn to fine-tune their visual thinking and problem-solving skills, as they create everything from logos to TV ads. Programs in the area of media arts focus on utilizing technology to deliver information and entertainment, while studentsstudying fashion learn to design clothes for the runway or run a retail shop.

Associate degree programs are offered in the areas of digital filmmaking, fashion design, fashion merchandising and marketing, graphic design, interior design, and Web design and interactive media.

Costs

Tuition costs vary by program. Prospective students should contact the school for current tuition costs. Other charges include a starting kit for all first-quarter students. Kits vary in price, depending on the program of study.

Financial Aid

Financial aid is available for those who qualify. Students who require financial assistance should first complete and submit a Free Application for Federal Student Aid (FAFSA) and meet with a financial aid officer.

Faculty

Faculty members are experienced professionals who create a learning environment that is similar to the professional world students will face after graduation. Instructors are focused on helping students develop the skills they need to transform their creative potential into marketable skills.

Student Body Profile

Students come to The Art Institute of New York City from throughout the United States and abroad. The student population includes recent high school graduates, transfer students, and those who have left a previous employment situation to study and train for a new career. Students are creative, competitive, and open to new ideas. They place great value on an education that prepares them for an exciting entry-level position in the arts.

Student Activities

There are several events for students throughout the year that celebrate culture, health, and holidays. The Student Activities Office also provides shape-up and wellness programs for students, along with The Art Institute of New York City Celebrates Women program. Students are offered many opportunities to volunteer throughout the year. Culinary students work at various events throughout the city as well as open-house programs at the school.

Facilities and Resources

The Art Institute of New York City provides a learning environment with professional-grade technology applicable to each student's course of study. Students have the opportunity to build a portfolio of work that shows potential employers that they are trained to use the software, hardware, or equipment utilized within the industry. Depending upon the course of study, students are immersed in a creative environment—from classrooms to computer labs to studios—focused on relevant, hands-on education designed to prepare students for the real world. The school contains computer labs, drawing studios, a student bookstore, and an art gallery.

Location

The Art Institute of New York City is located in the SoHo/Tribeca district of New York City. Manhattan is a hub of contemporary style, and New York City provides a wealth of opportunities for students to explore their creative side. Broadway plays, art museums, music halls, and professional sports teams are just some of the many entertainment options available to students who make the Big Apple their home.

Admission Requirements

Applicants must complete an application form and write a 150-word essay to apply for admission to The Art Institute of New York City. A personal interview with an admissions representative is required. Applicants must provide official high school transcripts, proof of successful completion of the General Educational Development (GED) test, or transcripts from any college previously attended. There is a $50 application fee.

For the most recent information regarding admission requirements, prospective students should refer to the current academic catalog.

Application and Information

To obtain an application or make arrangements for an interview or tour of the school, prospective students should contact:

The Art Institute of New York City
11 Beach Street
New York, New York 10013
United States
Phone: 212-226-5500
       800-654-2433 (toll-free)
Fax: 212-966-0706
Web site: http://www.artinstitutes.edu/newyork

Over 50 schools: The Art Institute of Atlanta; The Art Institute of Atlanta—Decatur, A branch of The Art Institute of Atlanta; The Art Institute of Austin, A branch of The Art Institute of Houston; The Art Institute of California, a college of Argosy University, with locations in Hollywood, Inland Empire, Los Angeles, Orange County, Sacramento, San Diego, San Francisco, and Sunnyvale; The Art Institute of Charleston, A branch of The Art Institute of Atlanta; The Art Institute of Charlotte; The Art Institute of Colorado; The Art Institute of Dallas, A campus of South University; The Art Institute of Fort Lauderdale; The Art Institute of Fort Worth, A campus of South University; The Art Institute of Houston; The Art Institute of Houston—North, A branch of The Art Institute of Houston; The Art Institute of Indianapolis; The Art Institute of Jacksonville, A branch of Miami International University of Art & Design; The Art Institute of Las Vegas; The Art Institute of Michigan; The Art Institute of Michigan—Troy; The Art Institute of New York City; The Art Institute of Ohio—Cincinnati; The Art Institute of Philadelphia; The Art Institute of Phoenix; The Art Institute of Pittsburgh; The Art Institute of Portland; The Art Institute of Raleigh–Durham; The Art Institute of Salt Lake City; The Art Institute of San Antonio, A branch of The Art Institute of Houston; The Art Institute of Seattle; The Art Institute of Tampa, A branch of Miami International University of Art & Design; The Art Institute of Tennessee—Nashville, A branch of The Art Institute of Atlanta; The Art Institute of Tucson; The Art Institute of Vancouver; The Art Institute of Virginia Beach[1], A branch of The Art Institute of Atlanta; The Art Institute of Washington[1], A branch of The Art Institute of Atlanta; The Art Institute of Washington—Dulles[1], A branch of The Art Institute of Atlanta; The Art Institute of Wisconsin; The Art Institute of York—Pennsylvania; The Art Institutes International—Kansas City; The Art Institutes International Minnesota; The Illinois Institute of Art—Chicago; The Illinois Institute of Art—Schaumburg; The Illinois Institute of Art—Tinley Park; Miami International University of Art & Design; The New England Institute of Art

[1] Certified by SCHEV to operate in Virginia

See **aiprograms.info** for program duration, tuition, fees, and other costs, median debt, federal salary data, alumni success, and other important info. The Art Institutes is a system of over 50 schools throughout North America. Programs, credential levels, technology, and scheduling options vary by school, and employment opportunities are not guaranteed. Financial aid is available to those who qualify. Several institutions included in The Art Institutes system are campuses of South University or Argosy University. OH Registration # 04-01-1698B, AC0165, AC0080, Licensed by the Florida Commission for Independent Education, License No. 1287, 3427, 3110, 2581. Administrative office: 210 Sixth Avenue, 33rd Floor, Pittsburgh, PA 15222. ©2012 The Art Institutes International LLC.

THE ART INSTITUTE OF SEATTLE
SEATTLE, WASHINGTON

CREATE TOMORROW

A focused education from The Art Institute of Seattle can help students turn their creative energy into a powerful tool that can make a difference in the world. Students are part of a collaborative and supportive community, where experienced instructors provide the guidance and skills needed to pursue a career in the creative economy.

The school's programs in the areas of design, media arts, fashion, and culinary give students the opportunity to learn by using professional-grade technology and to build a portfolio of work to show potential employers after graduation.

The Art Institute of Seattle is accredited by the Northwest Commission on Colleges and Universities (NWCCU), an institutional accrediting body recognized by the United States Department of Education.

The Art Institute of Seattle is licensed under Chapter 28c.10RCW; inquiries or complaints regarding this or any other private vocational school may be made to the Workforce Training and Education Coordinating Board, 128 10th Avenue SW, P.O. Box 43105, Olympia, Washington 98504-3105; phone: 360-753-5662.

The Associate of Applied Arts in culinary arts degree program is accredited by the Accrediting Commission of the American Culinary Federation Education Foundation.

The interior design program leading to the Bachelor of Fine Arts degree is accredited by the Council for Interior Design Accreditation, 206 Grandville Avenue, Suite 350, Grand Rapids, Michigan 49503; www.accredit-id.org.

Academic Programs

No matter which course of study a student may choose, the professionals at The Art Institute of Seattle will guide, support, and help each student as their talents evolve on their journey of personal and professional transformation. Students studying design learn to fine-tune their visual thinking and problem-solving skills, as they create everything from logos to TV ads. Programs in the area of media arts focus on utilizing technology to deliver information and entertainment, while students studying fashion learn to design clothes for the runway or run a retail shop. Culinary programs focus on the fundamental techniques while exposing students to a full menu of international cuisines and management techniques.

Associate degrees are available in the areas of audio production, baking and pastry, culinary arts, fashion design, fashion marketing, graphic design, industrial design technology, interior design, photography, video production, and Web design and interactive media.

Bachelor's degree programs are available in the areas of audio design technology, culinary arts management, digital filmmaking and video production, fashion design, fashion marketing, game art and design, graphic design, industrial

design, interior design, media arts and animation, photography, and Web design and interactive media.

Diploma programs are offered in the areas of art of cooking, baking and pastry, digital design, digital image management, fashion retailing, residential design, Web design and development, and Web design and interactive communications.

The Art Institute of Seattle operates on a year-round, quarterly basis. Each quarter totals eleven weeks. Bachelor's degree programs are twelve quarters in length.

Costs

Tuition cost varies by program. Prospective students should contact the school for current tuition costs. Other charges include a starting kit for all first-quarter students. Kits vary in price, depending on the program of study.

Financial Aid

Financial aid is available for those who qualify. Students who require financial assistance should first complete and submit a Free Application for Federal Student Aid (FAFSA) and meet with a financial aid officer.

Faculty

Faculty members are experienced professionals who create a learning environment that is similar to the professional world students will face after graduation. Instructors are focused on helping students develop the skills they need to transform their creative potential into marketable skills.

Student Body Profile

Students come to The Art Institute of Seattle from throughout the United States and abroad. The student population includes recent high school graduates, transfer students, and those who have left a previous employment situation to study and train for a new career. Students are creative, competitive, and open to new ideas. They place great value on an education that prepares them for an exciting entry-level position in the arts.

Student Activities

The Art Institute of Seattle places high importance on student life, both inside and outside the classroom. The school provides an environment that encourages involvement in a wide variety of activities, including clubs and organizations, community service opportunities, and various committees designed to enhance the quality of student life. Numerous all-school programs and events are planned throughout the year to meet students' needs.

Facilities and Resources

The Art Institute of Seattle provides a learning environment with professional-grade technology applicable to each student's course of study. Students have the opportunity to build a portfolio of work that shows potential employers that they are trained to use the software, hardware, or equipment utilized within the industry. Depending upon the course of study, students are immersed in a creative environment—from classrooms to computer labs to studios—focused on relevant, hands-on education designed to prepare students for the real world.

The urban campus comprises three facilities. The school houses classrooms, audio and video studios, a student store, student lounges, copy centers, a gallery, a woodshop, a sculpture room, fashion display windows, a resource center, a technology center, and culinary facilities. The Art Institute of Seattle is also home to a public student-run restaurant.

Location

The Art Institute of Seattle is located in the city's Belltown district. Founded by Native Americans and traders, the city has retained respect for its different cultures and customs. People from all over the world come to study, work, and live in this city that is known for its friendly people and beautiful natural surroundings.

World-class companies, such as Microsoft, Boeing, Starbucks, Amazon.com, and Nordstrom, make their global headquarters in Seattle. As a gateway to the Pacific Rim, Seattle is a crossroads where creativity, technology, and business meet.

Admission Requirements

A student seeking admission to The Art Institute of Seattle is required to interview with an admissions representative (in person or over the phone). Applicants are required to have a high school diploma or a General Educational Development (GED) certificate and to submit an admissions application and an essay describing how an education at The Art Institute of Seattle may help the student to achieve career goals. For advanced placement, additional information, including college transcripts, letters of recommendation, or portfolio work, may be required. Students may apply for admission online.

The Art Institute of Seattle follows a rolling admissions schedule. Students are encouraged to apply for their chosen quarter early so that they may take advantage of orientation activities. Students may also apply until the actual start date for any given quarter, depending on space availability. There is a $50 application fee.

For the most recent information regarding admission requirements, please refer to the current academic catalog.

Application and Information

To obtain an application, make arrangements for an interview, or tour the school, prospective students should contact:

The Art Institute of Seattle
2323 Elliott Avenue
Seattle, Washington 98121-1642
Phone: 206-448-6600
       800-275-2471 (toll-free)
Fax: 206-269-0275
Web site: http://www.artinstitutes.edu/seattle

BAY STATE COLLEGE
BOSTON, MASSACHUSETTS

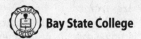

The College and Its Mission

Founded in 1946, Bay State College is a private, independent, coeducational institution located in Boston's historic Back Bay. Since its founding, Bay State College has been preparing graduates for outstanding careers and continued education.

Bay State College is a small, private college focused on passionate students who want to turn their interests into a rewarding career. The College offers associate and bachelor's degrees in a number of rewarding fields. Everyone at Bay State—from admissions counselors and professors to the career services team—helps to assist, guide, and advise students, from the moment they apply and throughout their careers. Located in Boston's Back Bay, the College offers the city of Boston as a campus, small classes, and one-on-one attention. For students seeking a career in one of the professions offered by Bay State, a degree program at the College could be a strong first step on their career path.

The College offers associate degrees and bachelor's degrees. The educational experience offered through the variety of programs prepares students to excel in the careers of their choice. Personalized attention is the cornerstone of a Bay State College education. Through the transformative power of its core values of quality, respect, and support, Bay State College has been able to assist students with setting and achieving goals that prepare them for careers and continued education.

Recognizing that one of the most important aspects of college is life outside the classroom, the Office of Student Affairs seeks to provide services from orientation through graduation and beyond. Special events throughout the year include a fashion show and a host of events produced by the Entertainment Management Association. Students also enjoy professional sports teams such as the Boston Celtics and Boston Red Sox.

Bay State College's campus experience can be whatever the student chooses it to be. It's not the typical college campus—its residence halls are actually brownstones along Boston's trendy Commonwealth Avenue and Bay State's quad could be Boston Common, the banks of the Charles River by the Esplanade, or Copley Square. That's the advantage of being located in Boston's Back Bay, which is also the safest neighborhood in the city. Students can relax at a favorite coffee shop, bike along the Charles River, ice skate on the Frog Pond, check out the city's nightlife, or take in a ball game at Fenway Park.

Bay State College is accredited by the New England Association of Schools and Colleges and is authorized to award the Associate in Science, Associate in Applied Science, and three Bachelor of Science degrees by the Commonwealth of Massachusetts. Bay State is a member of several professional educational associations. Its medical assisting program is accredited by the Accrediting Bureau of Health Education Schools (ABHES). The physical therapist assistant program is accredited by the Commission on Accreditation in Physical Therapy Education (CAPTE) of the American Physical Therapy Association (APTA).

Academic Programs

Bay State College operates on a semester calendar. The fall semester runs from early September to late December. The spring semester runs from late January until mid-May. A satellite campus is located in Middleborough, Massachusetts.

Bachelor's degrees are offered in criminal justice, entertainment management, fashion merchandising, and management.

Associate degrees are offered in business administration, criminal justice, early childhood education, entertainment management (with a concentration in audio production), fashion design, fashion merchandising, health studies, marketing, medical assisting, nursing, physical therapist assistant studies, retail business management, and hospitality management.

Bay State College also offers courses on-ground and online to working adults in its Evening and Online Division. The courses are offered in eight-week sessions and allow more flexibility for students who must balance work and family commitments while pursuing their education.

Bay State College reviews, enhances, and adds new programs to help graduates remain industry-current in their respective fields.

Off-Campus Programs

Many students cite Bay State's internship program as a turning point for them. Bay State internships allow students to gain hands-on experience and spend time working in their chosen fields. These valuable opportunities can give students an advantage when they apply for positions after they have completed school.

Bay State's Boston location allows the College to offer internships at many well-known companies and organizations. Students are able to apply what they've learned in the classroom and do meaningful work in their field of study. In addition, they build working relationships with people in their chosen profession. For more information on internships, prospective students may contact Tom Corrigan, Director of Career Services, at 617-217-9000.

Costs

Tuition charges are assessed on a per-credit-hour basis and vary depending upon program of study. This provides students with maximum flexibility based on individual financial and academic needs, making a Bay State College education more accommodating and affordable. Rates quoted below by program are for the 2012–13 academic year. Charges are not prorated unless noted. Program flow sheets may require more or less than 30 credits per academic year. Early childhood education, medical assisting, and health studies: $749 per credit, $22,470 (30 credits). Business, criminal justice, fashion merchandising, fashion design, entertainment management, and hospitality management: $768 per credit, $23,040 (30 credits). Nursing and physical therapy assistant: $781 per credit, $23,430 (30 credits).

Evening students pay $300 per credit. Room and board are $11,800 per year, the application fee is $40, the student services fee is $400 (for day students only), and the student activity fee is $50. The cost of books and additional fees vary by major. A residence hall security deposit of $300 and a technology fee of $250 are required of all resident students.

The fall tuition payment due date is July 1; the spring tuition payment is due December 1.

Financial Aid

Each student works with a personal advocate to thoroughly explain financial options and guide them through the financial aid application process. Many options are available: aid, grants and scholarships, federal programs, and private loans. Bay State College's Financial Aid Department and tuition planners can help students determine what aid may apply. Approximately 85 percent of students receive some form of financial assistance. Bay State College requires a completed Free Application for Federal Student Aid (FAFSA) form and signed federal tax forms. The College's institutional financial aid priority deadline is March 15. Financial aid is granted on a rolling basis.

Faculty

There are 72 faculty members, many holding advanced degrees and several holding doctoral degrees. The student-faculty ratio is 20:1.

Student Body Profile

There are approximately 1,200 students in degree programs in both the day and evening divisions.

Student Activities

Bay State College students participate in a multitude of activities offered by the College through existing student organizations.

Students also have the opportunity to create clubs and organizations that meet their interests. Existing organizations include the Student Government Association, Entertainment Management Association, Justice Society, the Criminal Justice Society, DEX, and the Early Childhood Education Club. Students produce an annual talent show as well as an annual fashion show that showcases student work from the College's fashion design program. An annual literary magazine also features the work of students throughout the College.

Facilities and Resources

Advisement/Counseling: Trained staff members assist students in selecting courses and programs of study. A counseling center is available to provide mental and physical health referrals to all students in need of such services. Referral networks are extensive, within a wide range of geographic areas, and provide access to a variety of public and private health agencies.

Specialized Services: The Office of Academic Development at Bay State College is designed to meet and support the various academic needs of the student body and serve as a resource for supplemental instruction, academic plans, learning accommodations, and other types of support. The Office of Academic Development operates on the belief that all students can achieve success in their courses by accessing support services and creating individual academic plans.

The Center for Learning and Academic Success (CLAS) at Bay State College is a key component available to help students achieve academic success. Students come to CLAS to get support in specific subject areas as well as study skills such as note-taking, reading comprehension, writing research papers, time management, and coping with exam anxiety. They utilize CLAS to develop study plans and strategies that positively impact their grades in all subjects. Students can also take advantage of the tutoring and seminars CLAS offers. CLAS's goal is to ensure that students are provided with exceptional academic support in all areas of study.

Career Planning/Placement: For many college students, the transition from student life to professional life is filled with questions and uncharted realities. Bay State College's Career Services Department offers students their own personal career advancement team. The department can help students learn to write a resume and cover letter, use social networks, practice interviewing skills, find the right job opportunity, and learn other career-related functions. Students even receive a Professionalism Grade, which lets future employers know they have what it takes to start contributing on day one. The Career Services Department at is determined to see each student succeed and offers valuable instruction that will serve students throughout their professional careers.

Library and Audiovisual Services: The library is staffed with trained librarians who are available to guide students in their research process. The library's resources include 7,500 books, eighty-five periodical subscriptions, and a dramatically increased reach through its online library resource databases that include ProQuest, InfoTrac, and LexisNexis. In addition, the library provides computer access and study space for students. The library catalog and databases are accessible from any Internet-ready terminal.

First-Year Experience: The First-Year Experience (FYE) is a 1-credit course that is required of all first-year students and takes place during the first three days that students are on campus. FYE combines social activities with an academic syllabus that is designed to ease the transition into the college experience. Through FYE, students have the opportunity to connect with their academic advisers as well as with other students in their academic programs. At the conclusion of FYE, students are on the road to mapping out their personal action plan for success. The plan, designed by students, guided by academic advisers, and revisited each semester, helps students set, monitor, and achieve academic and life goals. It also builds the preparation for lifelong accomplishment.

Location

Located in the historic city of Boston, Massachusetts, and surrounded by dozens of colleges and universities, Bay State College is an ideal setting in which to pursue a college degree. Tree-lined streets around the school are mirrored in the skyscrapers of the Back Bay. The College is located within walking distance of several major league sport franchises, concert halls, museums, the Freedom Trail, Boston Symphony Hall, the Boston Public Library, and the Boston Public Garden. World-class shopping and major cultural and sporting events help make college life a memorable experience.

The College is accessible by the MBTA and commuter rail and bus, and it is near Boston Logan International Airport.

Admission Requirements

Applicants must be a high school graduate, a current high school student working toward graduation, or a recipient of a GED certificate. The Office of Admissions requires that applicants to the associate degree programs have a minimum of a 2.0 GPA (on a 4.0 scale); if available, applicants may submit SAT and/or ACT scores. Applicants to bachelor's degree programs must have a minimum 2.3 GPA (on a 4.0 scale) and must also submit SAT or ACT scores. International applicants must also submit high school transcripts translated to English with an explanation of the grading system, financial documentation, and a minimum TOEFL score of 500 on the paper-based exam or 173 on the computer-based exam if English is not their native language.

The physical therapist assistant studies and nursing programs require a minimum 2.7 GPA (on a 4.0 scale) and the Evening Division has different or additional admission requirements. For more information about these programs, interested students should visit the Web site at http://www.baystate.edu.

A personal interview is required for all prospective students—parents are encouraged to attend. Applicants must receive the recommendation of a Bay State College Admissions Officer.

Application and Information

Applications are accepted on a rolling basis. A $40 fee is required at the time of application. Students are responsible for arranging for their official high school transcripts, test scores, and letters of recommendation to be submitted to Bay State College.

The Bay State College Admissions Office notifies applicants of a decision within one week of receipt of the transcript and other required documents. There is a $100 nonrefundable tuition deposit required upon acceptance to ensure a place in the class; the deposit is credited toward the tuition fee. Deposits are due within thirty days of acceptance. Once a student is accepted, a Bay State College representative creates a personalized financial plan that provides payment options for a Bay State College education.

Applications should be submitted to:

Admissions Office
Bay State College
122 Commonwealth Avenue
Boston, Massachusetts 02116
Phone: 800-81-LEARN (53276)
Fax: 617-249-0400 (eFax)
E-mail: admissions@baystate.edu
Web site: http://www.baystate.edu
        http://www.facebook.com/baystatecollege
        http://twitter.com/baystatecollege

Bay State College's main admissions and administrative building at 122 Commonwealth Avenue in the Back Bay.

BROWN MACKIE COLLEGE — AKRON
AKRON, OHIO

BROWN
MACKIE
COLLEGE
AKRON℠

The College and Its Mission

Brown Mackie College — Akron (Brown Mackie College) is one of over twenty-five locations in the Brown Mackie College family of schools (www.brownmackie.edu), which is dedicated to providing educational programs that prepare students to pursue entry-level positions in a competitive, rapidly changing workplace. Brown Mackie College's family of schools offers bachelor degree, associate degree, diploma, and certificate programs in health sciences, business, information technology, legal studies, and design to more than 20,000 students in the Midwest, Southeast, Southwest, and Western United States.

Brown Mackie College was founded in Cincinnati, Ohio, in February 1927, as a traditional business college. In March 1980, the college added a branch campus in Akron, Ohio. The college outgrew this space and relocated to its current address in January 2007.

Brown Mackie College — Akron is accredited by the Accrediting Council for Independent Colleges and Schools to award associate degrees and diplomas. The Accrediting Council for Independent Colleges and Schools (ACICS) is listed as a nationally recognized accrediting agency by the United States Department of Education and is recognized by the Council for Higher Education Accreditation. ACICS can be contacted at 750 First Street NE, Suite 980, Washington, D.C. 20002; phone: 202-336-6780.

Brown Mackie College — Akron is licensed by the Ohio State Board of Career Colleges and Schools, 30 East Broad Street, 24th Floor, Suite 2481, Columbus, Ohio 43215-3138; phone: 614-466-2752. Ohio registration #03-09-1685T.

The associate of applied science in medical assisting program is accredited by the Commission of Accreditation of Allied Health Education Programs upon the recommendation of the Curriculum Review Board of the Medical Assisting Education Review Board (MAERB). The Commission on Accreditation of Allied Health Education Programs can be contacted at 1361 Park Street Clearwater, Florida 33756; phone: 727-210-2350; www.caahep.org.

The associate of applied science in surgical technology program is accredited by the Commission on Accreditation of Allied Health Education Programs (www.caahep.org) upon the recommendation of the Accreditation Review Council on Education in Surgical Technology and Surgical Assisting (ARC/STSA). The Commission on Accreditation of Allied Health Education Programs is located at 1361 Park Street Clearwater, Florida 33756; phone: 727-210-2350; www.caahep.org.

The Associate of Applied Science in occupational therapy assistant program is accredited by the Accreditation Council for Occupational Therapy Education (ACOTE) of the American Occupational Therapy Association (AOTA), located at 4720 Montgomery Lane, P.O. Box 31220, Bethesda, Maryland 20824-1220; phone: 301-652-AOTA.

The Associate of Applied Science in veterinary technology program has provisional programmatic accreditation granted by the American Veterinary Medical Association (AVMA) through the Committee on Veterinary Technician Education and Activities (CVTEA).

The College is a nonresidential, smoke-free institution.

Academic Programs

Brown Mackie College — Akron provides higher education to traditional and nontraditional students through associate degree and diploma programs that can assist them in enhancing their career opportunities, broadening their perspectives through appropriate general education courses, thinking independently and critically, and improving problem-solving abilities.

Each college quarter comprises twelve weeks. Associate degree programs require a minimum of eight quarters to complete. Programs are offered on a year-round basis, providing students with the ability to work uninterrupted toward their degree. Brown Mackie College offers all programs in a unique One Course a Month format. This schedule allows students to focus studies on only one course for four weeks and has proven convenient for students with multiple obligations such as jobs and family.

Associate Degree Programs: The Associate of Applied Business degree is awarded in accounting technology, business management, criminal justice, and paralegal. The Associate of Applied Science degree is awarded in computer networking and applications, health care administration, information technology, medical assisting, occupational therapy assistant, pharmacy technology, surgical technology, and veterinary technology.

Diploma Programs: Brown Mackie College offers diploma programs in accounting, business, computer software applications, criminal justice, medical assistant, medical coding and billing, paralegal assistant, and practical nursing.

The American Medical Technologists (AMT), which offers the certification for Registered Medical Assistant (RMA), accepts the accreditation of Brown Mackie College — Akron. Students will qualify to take the RMA certification examination upon graduating the Brown Mackie College — Akron medical assisting and medical assistant programs. Graduates of the 48 credit-hour medical assistant program are not qualified to take the AMT/RMA exam.

Brown Mackie College — Akron does not guarantee third-party certification. Outside agencies control the requirements for certifications and are subject to change without notice to Brown Mackie College.

Costs

Tuition for the 2011–12 academic year was $294 per credit hour and $15 per credit hour for general fees. Tuition for the practical nursing program was $361 per credit hour and $25 per credit hour for general fees. Tuition for the surgical technology program was $340 per credit hour and $15 per credit hour for general fees. Tuition for the occupational therapy assistant program was $361 per credit hour and $15 per credit hour for general fees. The cost of textbooks and other instructional materials varies by program.

Financial Aid

Financial aid is available to those who qualify. The college maintains a full-time staff of Student Financial Services Advisors to assist qualified students in obtaining financial assistance. The college participates in several student aid programs. Forms of financial aid available through federal resources include the Federal Pell Grant Program, Federal Supplemental Educational Opportunity Grant (FSEOG) Program, Federal Work-Study Program, Federal Stafford Student Loan Program (subsidized and unsubsidized), and the Federal PLUS Loan Program. Eligible students may also apply for veterans' educational benefits. Students with physical or mental disabilities that are a handicap to employment may be eligible for training services through the state Agency for Vocational Rehabilitation. For further information, students should contact the Student Financial Services Office.

Each year, the college makes available President's Scholarships of $1000 each to qualifying seniors from area high schools. Up to three (3) scholarships may be awarded per high school. In order to qualify, a senior must be graduating from a participating high school, have maintained a cumulative grade point average of at least 2.0, and submitted a brief essay. The student's extracurricular activities and community service are also considered. These scholarships are available only to students enrolling in one of the college's degree programs. Students awarded the scholarship must enroll at Brown Mackie College between June and September immediately following their high school graduation. Applications for these scholarships can be obtained from the guidance departments of participating high schools. These applications must be completed and returned to Brown Mackie College by March 31.

Faculty

There are 20 full-time and 39 part-time faculty members. The student-faculty ratio is 17:1.

Facilities and Resources

Brown Mackie College provides media presentation rooms for special instructional needs, a library that provides instructional resources and academic support for both faculty members and students, and qualified and experienced faculty members who are committed to the academic and technical preparation of their students. Brown Mackie College is nonresidential; students who are unable to commute daily from their homes may request assistance from the Office of Admissions in locating off-campus housing. The college is accessible by public transportation and provides ample parking, available at no charge.

Location

Brown Mackie College — Akron is located at 755 White Pond Drive in Akron, Ohio.

Admission Requirements

Each applicant for admission is assigned to an Assistant Director of Admissions who directs the applicant through the steps of the admissions process, providing information on curriculum, policies, procedures, and services and assisting the applicant in setting necessary appointments and interviews.

To qualify for admission, each applicant must provide documentation of graduation from an accredited high school or from a state-approved secondary education curriculum or provide official documentation of high school graduation equivalency. All transcripts become the property of Brown Mackie College. Admission to Brown Mackie College is based upon the applicant meeting the stated requirements, a review of the applicant's previous education records, and a review of the applicant's career interests. If previous academic records indicate that the Brown Mackie College education and training programs would not benefit the applicant, the Brown Mackie College reserves the right to advise the applicant not to enroll. Special requirements for enrollment into certain programs are discussed in the descriptions of those programs.

For the most recent information regarding admission requirements, applicants should refer to the current academic catalog.

Application and Information

Applicants must complete and submit an application form along with documentation of graduation from an accredited high school or state-approved secondary education curriculum, or applicants must provide official documentation of high school graduation equivalency. Prospective students can go online to BMCprograms.info for program duration, tuition, fees and other costs, median debt, federal salary data, alumni success, programmatic accreditation, and other important details.

For additional information, prospective students should contact:

Senior Director of Admissions
Brown Mackie College — Akron
755 White Pond Drive
Akron, Ohio 44320
Phone: 330-869-3600
Fax: 330-869-3650
E-mail: bmcakadm@brownmackie.edu
Web site: http://www.brownmackie.edu/Akron

BROWN MACKIE COLLEGE — ALBUQUERQUE
ALBUQUERQUE, NEW MEXICO

The College and Its Mission

Brown Mackie College — Albuquerque (Brown Mackie College) is one of over twenty-five locations in the Brown Mackie College family of schools (www.brownmackie.edu), which is dedicated to providing educational programs that prepare students to pursue entry-level positions in a competitive, rapidly changing workplace. Brown Mackie College schools offer bachelor degree, associate degree, diploma, and certificate programs in health sciences, business, information technology, legal studies, and design to over 20,000 students in the Midwest, Southeast, Southwest, and Western United States.

Brown Mackie College was originally founded and approved by the Board of Trustees of Kansas Wesleyan College in Salina, Kansas on July 30, 1892. In 1938, the college was incorporated as the Brown Mackie School of Business under the ownership of Perry E. Brown and A.B. Mackie, former instructors at Kansas Wesleyan University in Salina, Kansas. Their last names formed the name of Brown Mackie. By January 1975, with improvements in curricula and higher degree-granting status, the Brown Mackie School of Business became Brown Mackie College.

Brown Mackie College — Albuquerque is accredited by the Accrediting Council for Independent Colleges and Schools to award associate degrees and diplomas. The Accrediting Council for Independent Colleges and Schools is listed as a nationally recognized accrediting agency by the United States Department of Education and is recognized by the Council for Higher Education Accreditation. ACICS can be contacted at 750 First Street NE, Suite 980, Washington, D.C. 20002; phone: 202-336-6780.

The Associate of Applied Science in occupational therapy assistant program is accredited by the Accreditation Council for Occupational Therapy Education (ACOTE) of the American Occupational Therapy Association (AOTA), located at 4720 Montgomery Lane, P.O. Box 31220, Bethesda, Maryland 20824; phone: 301-652-AOTA.

Academic Programs

Brown Mackie College — Albuquerque provides higher education to traditional and nontraditional students through associate degree and diploma programs that assist in enhancing their career opportunities, broadening their perspectives through appropriate general education courses, thinking independently and critically, and improving problem-solving abilities. The college strives to develop within its students the desire for lifelong and continued education.

Each college quarter comprises twelve weeks. Associate degree programs require a minimum of eight quarters to complete. Programs are offered on a year-round basis, providing students with the ability to work uninterrupted toward completion of their programs. The college offers all programs in a unique One Course a Month format. This allows students to focus studies on only one course for four weeks. This schedule has proven convenient for students with multiple obligations such as jobs and family.

Associate Degree Programs: The Associate of Applied Science degree is awarded in accounting technology, architectural design and drafting technology, business management, criminal justice, health care administration, information technology, medical assisting, occupational therapy assistant, paralegal, pharmacy technology, surgical technology, and veterinary technology.

Diploma Programs: Brown Mackie College — Albuquerque offers diploma programs in accounting, business, criminal justice, medical assistant, and paralegal assistant.

The American Medical Technologists (AMT), which offers the certification for Registered Medical Assistant (RMA), accepts the accreditation of Brown Mackie College — Albuquerque. Students will qualify to take the RMA certification examination upon graduating the Brown Mackie College — Albuquerque medical assisting and medical assistant programs. Graduates of the 48 credit-hour medical assistant program are not qualified to take the AMT/RMA exam.

Brown Mackie College — Albuquerque does not guarantee third-party certification. Outside agencies control the requirements for certifications and are subject to change without notice to Brown Mackie College.

Costs

Tuition in the 2011–12 academic year for all associate degrees and certificates was $324 per credit hour; fees were $20 per credit hour. Tuition for the occupational therapy assistant program was $355 per credit hour; fees were $20 per credit hour. Tuition for the surgical technology program was $339 per credit hour; fees were $20 per credit hour. The cost of textbooks and other instructional materials varies by program.

Financial Aid

Financial aid is available for those who qualify. Brown Mackie College maintains a full-time staff of Student Financial Services Advisors to assist qualified students in obtaining the financial assistance they require to meet their educational expenses. Available resources include federal and state aid, student loans from private lenders, and Federal Work-Study opportunities, both on and off college premises.

Each year, the college makes available President's Scholarships of $1000 each to qualifying seniors from area high schools. Up to three (3) scholarships may be awarded per high school. In order to qualify, a senior must have graduated from a participating high school, must have maintained a cumulative grade point average of at least 2.0, and submitted a brief essay. The student's extracurricular activities and community service are also considered. These scholarships are available only to students enrolling in one of the college's degree programs. Students awarded the scholarship must enroll at Brown Mackie College — Albuquerque between June and September immediately following their high school graduation. Applications for these scholarships can be obtained from the guidance departments of participating high schools. These applications must be completed and returned to the college by March 31.

Faculty

Experienced faculty members provide academic support and are committed to the academic and technical preparation of their students. The college has both full-time and part-time instructors, with a student-faculty ratio of 15:1.

Facilities and Resources

A modern facility, Brown Mackie College — Albuquerque offers more than 35,000 square feet. The college is equipped with multiple computer labs, housing over 100 computers. High-speed access to the Internet and other online resources are available to students and faculty. Multimedia classrooms are outfitted with overhead projectors, VCR/DVD players, and computers.

In 2012, Brown Mackie College — Albuquerque began its transition to using eTextbooks and computer tablets in the classroom. Utilizing these tablets to access expanded course material, students will be able to increase their acumen for using this technology and further enhance their educational experience. Students have the ability to directly download their eTextbooks to their tablet, eliminating the need to carry heavy, physical textbooks and reducing the overall cost of supplies.

Brown Mackie College is nonresidential; public transportation and ample parking at no cost are available. The campus is a smoke-free facility.

Location

Brown Mackie College — Albuquerque is conveniently located at 10500 Copper Avenue NE, in Albuquerque, New Mexico. The college has a generous parking area and is easily accessible by public transportation.

Admission Requirements

Each applicant for admission is assigned to an Assistant Director of Admissions who directs the applicant through the steps of the admissions process. They provide information on curriculum, policies, procedures, and services and assist the applicant in setting necessary appointments and interviews. To qualify for admission, each applicant must provide documentation of graduation from an accredited high school or from a state-approved secondary education curriculum or provide official documentation of high school graduation equivalency. All transcripts become the property of the college. Admission to the college is based on the applicant meeting the stated requirements, a review of the applicant's previous educational records, and a review of the applicant's career interests. If previous academic records indicate the college's education and training programs would not benefit the applicant, the college reserves the right to advise the applicant not to enroll. Special requirements for enrollment into certain programs are discussed in the descriptions of those programs.

For the most recent information regarding admission requirements, prospective students should refer to the current academic catalog.

Application and Information

Applicants must complete and submit an application form, along with documentation of graduation from an accredited high school or state-approved secondary education curriculum or official documentation of high school graduation equivalency.

Applicants can go online to BMCprograms.info for program duration, tuition, fees and other costs, median debt, federal salary data, alumni success, programmatic accreditation and other important information.

For additional information, prospective students should contact:

Director of Admissions
Brown Mackie College — Albuquerque
10500 Copper Avenue
Albuquerque, New Mexico 87123
Phone: 505-559-5200
      877-271-3488 (toll-free)
Fax: 505-559-5222
E-mail: bmcalbadm@brownmackie.edu
Web site: http://www.brownmackie.edu/Albuquerque

BROWN MACKIE COLLEGE — ATLANTA
ATLANTA, GEORGIA

The College and Its Mission

Brown Mackie College — Atlanta (Brown Mackie College) is one of over twenty-five locations in the Brown Mackie College family of schools (http://www.brownmackie.edu), which is dedicated to providing educational programs that prepare students to pursue entry-level positions in a competitive, rapidly changing workplace. Brown Mackie College schools offer bachelor degree, associate degree, certificate, and diploma programs in health sciences, business, information technology, legal studies, and design to over 20,000 students in the Midwest, Southeast, Southwest, and Western United States.

Brown Mackie College — Atlanta is accredited by the Accrediting Council for Independent Colleges and Schools (ACICS) to award associate degrees and diplomas. The Accrediting Council for Independent Colleges and Schools is listed as a nationally recognized accrediting agency by the United States Department of Education and is recognized by the Council for Higher Education Accreditation. ACICS can be contacted at 750 First Street NE, Suite 980, Washington, D.C. 20002; phone: 202-336-6780.

The Associate of Applied Science in occupational therapy assistant program is accredited by the Accreditation Council for Occupational Therapy Education (ACOTE) of the American Occupational Therapy Association (AOTA), located at 4720 Montgomery Lane, P.O. Box 31220, Bethesda, Maryland 20824; phone: 301-652-AOTA.

The Associate of Applied Science in surgical technology program is accredited by the Accrediting Bureau of Health Education Schools (http://www.abhes.org).

Brown Mackie College is a nonresidential, smoke-free institution.

Academic Programs

Brown Mackie College — Atlanta provides higher education to traditional and nontraditional students through associate degree and diploma programs that can assist students in enhancing their career opportunities, broadening their perspectives through appropriate general education courses, thinking independently and critically, and improving problem-solving abilities. Brown Mackie College strives to develop within its students the desire for lifelong and continued education.

Each college quarter comprises twelve weeks. Associate degree programs require a minimum of eight quarters to complete. Programs are offered on a year-round basis, providing students with the ability to work uninterrupted toward their degrees. Brown Mackie College offers all programs in a unique One Course a Month format. This schedule allows students to focus studies on only one course for four weeks and has proven convenient for students with multiple obligations such as jobs and family.

Associate Degree Programs: The Associate of Applied Business degree is awarded in accounting technology, business management, criminal justice, and paralegal. The Associate of Applied Science degree is awarded in early childhood education, health care administration, medical assisting, occupational therapy assistant, pharmacy technology, and surgical technology.

Diploma Programs: Brown Mackie College — Atlanta also offers diploma programs in accounting, business, criminal justice, medical assistant, and paralegal assistant.

The American Medical Technologists (AMT), which offers the certification for Registered Medical Assistant (RMA), accepts the accreditation of Brown Mackie College — Atlanta. Students will qualify to take the RMA certification examination upon graduating the Brown Mackie College — Atlanta medical assisting and medical assistant programs. Graduates of the 48 credit-hour medical assistant program are not qualified to take the AMT/RMA exam.

Costs

Tuition for the 2011–12 academic year was $346 per credit hour and $15 per credit hour for general fees. Tuition for the occupational therapy assistant program was $361 per credit hour and $15 per credit hour for general fees. Tuition for the surgical technology program was $340 per credit hour and $15 per credit hour for general fees. The cost of textbooks and other instructional materials varies by program.

Financial Aid

Financial aid is available to those who qualify. Brown Mackie College — Atlanta maintains a full-time staff of financial aid professionals to assist qualified students in obtaining financial assistance. The college participates in several student aid programs. Forms of financial aid available through federal resources include the Federal Pell Grant Program, Federal Supplemental Educational Opportunity Grant (FSEOG) Program, Federal Work-Study Program, Federal Perkins Loan Program, Federal Stafford Student Loan Program (subsidized and unsubsidized), and the Federal PLUS Loan Program. Eligible students may also apply for state awards and veterans' educational benefits. Students with physical or mental disabilities that are a handicap to employment may be eligible for training services through the state Agency for Vocational Rehabilitation. For further information, students should contact the Brown Mackie College — Atlanta Student Financial Services Office.

Each year, the college makes available President's Scholarships of $1000 each to qualifying seniors from area high schools. Up to three (3) scholarships may be awarded per high school. In order to qualify, a senior must be graduating from a participating high school, have maintained a cumulative grade point average of at least 2.0, and submitted a brief essay. The student's extracurricular activities and community service are also considered. The President's Scholarship is available only to students enrolling in one of the college's degree programs. Students awarded the scholarship must enroll at Brown Mackie College — Atlanta between June and September immediately following their high school graduation. Applications for these scholarships can be obtained from the guidance departments of participating high schools. These applications must be completed and returned to the college by March 31.

Faculty

There are 4 full-time and 5 part-time faculty members. The average student-faculty ratio is 19:1. Each student has a faculty and student adviser.

Facilities and Resources

Brown Mackie College — Atlanta comprises administrative offices, faculty and student lounges, a reception area, and spacious classrooms and laboratories. Instructional equipment includes personal computers, LANs, printers, and transcribers. The library provides support for the academic programs through volumes covering a broad range of subjects, as well as through Internet access. Vehicle parking is provided for both students and staff members.

Location

Brown Mackie College — Atlanta is located at 4370 Peachtree Road NE in Atlanta, Georgia, which is easily accessible from I-285 and the MARTA Brookhaven rail station.

Admission Requirements

Each applicant for admission is assigned to an Assistant Director of Admissions who directs the applicant through the steps of the admissions process, providing information on curriculum, policies, procedures, and services and assisting the applicant in setting necessary appointments and interviews.

To qualify for admission, each applicant must provide documentation of graduation from an accredited high school or from a state-approved secondary education curriculum or provide official documentation of high school graduation equivalency. All transcripts become the property of Brown Mackie College. Admission is based upon the applicant meeting the stated requirements, a review of the applicant's previous education records, and a review of the applicant's career interests. If previous academic records indicate that the Brown Mackie College education and training programs would not benefit the applicant, the college reserves the right to advise the applicant not to enroll. Special requirements for enrollment into certain programs are discussed in the descriptions of those programs.

For the most recent information regarding admission requirements, applicants should refer to the current academic catalog.

Application and Information

Applicants must complete and submit an application form along with documentation of graduation from an accredited high school or state-approved secondary education curriculum, or applicants must provide official documentation of high school graduation equivalency.

Applicants can go online to BMCprograms.info for program duration, tuition, fees and other costs, median debt, federal salary data, alumni success, programmatic accreditation and other important information.

For additional information, prospective students should contact:

Director of Admissions
Brown Mackie College — Atlanta
4370 Peachtree Road NE
Atlanta, Georgia 30319
Phone: 404-799-4500
      877-479-8419 (toll-free)
Fax: 404-799-4522
E-mail: bmcatadm@brownmackie.edu
Web site: http://www.brownmackie.edu/Atlanta

BROWN MACKIE COLLEGE — BIRMINGHAM
BIRMINGHAM, ALABAMA

The College and Its Mission

Brown Mackie College — Birmingham (Brown Mackie College) is one of over twenty-five locations in the Brown Mackie College family of schools (www.brownmackie.edu), which is dedicated to providing educational programs that prepare students to pursue entry-level positions in a competitive, rapidly changing workplace. Brown Mackie College schools offer bachelor degree, associate degree, diploma, and certificate programs in health sciences, business, information technology, legal studies, and design to over 20,000 students in the Midwest, Southeast, Southwest, and Western United States.

Brown Mackie College was originally founded and approved by the Board of Trustees of Kansas Wesleyan College in Salina, Kansas on July 30, 1892. In 1938, the college was incorporated as the Brown Mackie School of Business under the ownership of Perry E. Brown and A.B. Mackie, former instructors at Kansas Wesleyan University in Salina, Kansas. Their last names formed the name of Brown Mackie. By January 1975, with improvements in curricula and higher degree-granting status, the Brown Mackie School of Business became Brown Mackie College.

Brown Mackie College — Birmingham is accredited by the Accrediting Council for Independent Colleges and Schools to award associate degrees and diplomas. The Accrediting Council for Independent Colleges and Schools is listed as a nationally recognized accrediting agency by the United States Department of Education and is recognized by the Council for Higher Education Accreditation. ACICS can be contacted at 750 First Street NE, Suite 980, Washington, D.C. 20002; phone: 202-336-6780.

The Associate of Applied Science in occupational therapy assistant program has applied for accreditation by the Accreditation Council for Occupational Therapy Education (ACOTE) of the American Occupational Therapy Association (AOTA), 4720 Montgomery Lane, P.O. Box 31220, Bethesda, Maryland 20824-1220; phone: 301-652-AOTA.

Academic Programs

Brown Mackie College — Birmingham provides higher education to traditional and nontraditional students through associate degree and diploma programs that assist in enhancing their career opportunities, broadening their perspectives through appropriate general education courses, thinking independently and critically, and improving problem-solving abilities. The college strives to develop within its students the desire for lifelong and continued education.

Each college quarter comprises twelve weeks. Associate degree programs require a minimum of eight quarters to complete. Programs are offered on a year-round basis, providing students with the ability to work uninterrupted toward completion of their programs. The college offers all programs in a unique One Course a Month format. This allows students to focus studies on only one course for four weeks. This schedule has proven convenient for students with multiple obligations such as jobs and family.

Associate Degree Programs: The Associate of Science degree is awarded in accounting technology, architectural design and drafting technology, biomedical equipment technology, business management, graphic design, health care administration, information technology, medical assisting, paralegal, and surgical technology.

The Associate of Applied Science degree is awarded in occupational therapy assistant.

Diploma Programs: The college offers diploma programs in accounting, business, dental assistant, healthcare administrative specialist, medical assistant, and paralegal assistant.

The American Medical Technologists (AMT), which offers the certification for Registered Medical Assistant (RMA), accepts the accreditation of Brown Mackie College — Birmingham. Students will qualify to take the RMA certification examination upon graduating the Brown Mackie College — Birmingham medical assisting and medical assistant programs. Graduates of the 48 credit-hour medical assistant program are not qualified to take the AMT/RMA exam.

Brown Mackie College — Birmingham does not guarantee third-party certification. Outside agencies control the requirements for certifications and are subject to change without notice to Brown Mackie College.

Costs

Tuition in the 2011–12 academic year for all associate degrees and certificates was $315 per credit hour; fees were $15 per credit hour. Tuition for the surgical technology program was $350 per credit hour; fees were $15 per credit hour. Tuition for the occupational therapy assistant program was $381 per credit hour; fees were $15 per credit hour. The cost of textbooks and other instructional materials varies by program.

Financial Aid

Financial aid is available for those who qualify. Brown Mackie College maintains a full-time staff of Student Financial Services Advisors to assist qualified students in obtaining the financial assistance they require to meet their educational expenses. Available resources include federal and state aid, student loans from private lenders, and Federal Work-Study opportunities, both on and off college premises.

Each year, the college makes available President's Scholarships of $1000 each to qualifying seniors from area high schools. Up to three (3) scholarships may be awarded per high school. In order to qualify, a senior must have graduated from a participating high school, must be maintained a cumulative grade point average of at least 2.0, and submitted a brief essay. The student's extracurricular activities and community service are also considered. These scholarships are available only to students enrolling in one of the college's degree programs. Students awarded the scholarship must enroll at Brown Mackie College — Birmingham between June and September immediately following their high school graduation. Applications for these scholarships can be obtained from the guidance departments of participating high schools. These applications must be completed and returned to the college by March 31.

Faculty

Experienced faculty members provide academic support and are committed to the academic and technical preparation of their students. The college has both full-time and part-time instructors, with a student-faculty ratio of 15:1.

Facilities and Resources

A modern facility, Brown Mackie College offers approximately 35,000 square feet of classroom, computer and allied health labs, library, and office space. The college is equipped with multiple computer labs, housing over 100 computers. High-speed access to the Internet and other online resources are available to students and faculty. Multimedia classrooms are outfitted with overhead projectors, VCR/DVD players, and computers.

In 2012, Brown Mackie College began its transition to using eTextbooks and computer tablets in the classroom. Utilizing these tablets to access expanded course material, students will be able to increase their acumen for using this technology and further enhance their educational experience. Students have the ability to directly download their eTextbooks to their tablet, eliminating the need to carry heavy, physical textbooks and reducing the overall cost of supplies.

Brown Mackie College is nonresidential; public transportation and ample parking at no cost are available. The campus is a smoke-free facility.

Location

Brown Mackie College — Birmingham is conveniently located at 105 Vulcan Road, in Birmingham, Alabama. The college has a generous parking area and is easily accessible by public transportation.

Admission Requirements

Each applicant for admission is assigned to an Assistant Director of Admissions who directs the applicant through the steps of the admissions process. They provide information on curriculum, policies, procedures, and services and assist the applicant in setting necessary appointments and interviews. To qualify for admission, each applicant must provide documentation of graduation from an accredited high school or from a state-approved secondary education curriculum or provide official documentation of high school graduation equivalency. All transcripts become the property of the college. Admission to the college is based on the applicant meeting the stated requirements, a review of the applicant's previous educational records, and a review of the applicant's career interests. If previous academic records indicate the college's education and training programs would not benefit the applicant, the college reserves the right to advise the applicant not to enroll. Special requirements for enrollment into certain programs are discussed in the descriptions of those programs.

For the most recent information regarding admission requirements, prospective students should refer to the current academic catalog.

Application and Information

Applicants must complete and submit an application form, along with documentation of graduation from an accredited high school or state-approved secondary education curriculum or official documentation of high school graduation equivalency.

Prospective students should go online to BMCprograms.info for program duration, tuition, fees and other costs, median debt, federal salary data, alumni success, programmatic accreditation and other important information.

For additional information, prospective students should contact:

Director of Admissions
Brown Mackie College — Birmingham
105 Vulcan Road, Suite 100
Birmingham, Alabama 35209
Phone: 205-909-1500
        888-299-4699 (toll-free)
Fax: 205-909-1588
E-mail: bmbirmadm@brownmackie.edu
Web site: http://www.brownmackie.edu/Birmingham

BROWN MACKIE COLLEGE — BOISE

BOISE, IDAHO

BROWN
MACKIE
COLLEGE
BOISE℠

The College and Its Mission

Brown Mackie College — Boise (Brown Mackie College) is one of over twenty-five locations in the Brown Mackie College family of schools (www.brownmackie.edu), which is dedicated to providing educational programs that prepare students to pursue entry-level positions in a competitive, rapidly changing workplace. Brown Mackie College schools offer bachelor degree, associate degree, diploma, and certificate programs in health sciences, business, information technology, legal studies, and design to over 20,000 students in the Midwest, Southeast, Southwest, and Western United States.

Brown Mackie College — Boise is accredited by the Accrediting Council for Independent Colleges and Schools to award associate degrees and diplomas. The Accrediting Council for Independent Colleges and Schools is listed as a nationally recognized accrediting agency by the United States Department of Education and is recognized by the Council for Higher Education Accreditation. ACICS can be contacted at 750 First Street NE, Suite 980, Washington, D.C. 20002; phone: 202-336-6780.

The Associate of Applied Science in occupational therapy assistant program is accredited by the Accreditation Council for Occupational Therapy Education (ACOTE) of the American Occupational Therapy Association (AOTA), 4720 Montgomery Lane, P.O. Box 31220, Bethesda, Maryland 20824-1220; phone: 301-652-AOTA.

The Associate of Applied Science in veterinary technology program at Brown Mackie College — Boise is accredited by the American Veterinary Medical Association (AVMA) as a program for educating veterinary technicians. The American Veterinary Medical Association can be contacted at 1931 North Meacham Road, Suite 100, Schaumburg, Illinois 60173-4360; phone: 800-248-2862 (toll-free).

Academic Programs

Brown Mackie College — Boise provides higher education to traditional and nontraditional students through associate degree, and diploma programs that assist in enhancing their career opportunities, broadening their perspectives through appropriate general education courses, thinking independently and critically, and improving problem-solving abilities.

Each college quarter comprises twelve weeks. Associate degree programs require a minimum of eight quarters to complete. Programs are offered on a year-round basis, providing students with the opportunity to work uninterrupted toward completion of their programs. The college offers all programs in a unique One Course a Month format. This allows students to focus studies on only one course for four weeks. This schedule has proven convenient for students with multiple obligations such as jobs and family.

Associate Degree Programs: The Associate of Science degree is awarded in accounting technology, architectural design and drafting technology, bioscience laboratory technology, business management, criminal justice, health care administration, information technology, medical assisting, paralegal, and veterinary technology.

The Associate of Applied Science degree is awarded in occupational therapy assistant.

Diploma Programs: Diploma programs are offered in accounting, business, criminal justice, medical assistant, and paralegal assistant.

The American Medical Technologists (AMT), which offers the certification for Registered Medical Assistant (RMA), accepts the accreditation of Brown Mackie College — Boise. Students will qualify to take the RMA certification examination upon graduating the Brown Mackie College — Boise medical assisting and medical assistant programs. Graduates of the 48 credit-hour medical assistant program are not qualified to take the AMT/RMA exam.

Costs

Tuition for programs in the 2011–12 academic year was $324 per credit hour, with a $15 per credit hour general fee applied to instructional costs for activities and services. Textbooks and other instructional materials vary by program. Tuition for the occupational therapy assistant courses was $381 per credit hour with a $15 per credit fee applied to instructional costs for activities and services.

Financial Aid

Financial aid is available for those who qualify. The college maintains a full-time staff of Student Financial Services Advisors to assist qualified students in obtaining financial assistance. The college participates in several student aid programs. Forms of financial aid available through federal resources include the Federal Pell Grant Program, Federal Supplemental Educational Opportunity Grant (FSEOG) Program, Federal Work-Study Program, Federal Perkins Loan Program, Federal Stafford Student Loan Program (subsidized and unsubsidized), and the Federal PLUS Loan Program.

Each year, the college makes available President's Scholarships of $1000 each to qualifying seniors from area high schools. Up to three (3) scholarships may be awarded per high school. In order to qualify, a senior must be graduating from a participating high school, must be maintaining a cumulative grade point average of at least 2.0, and must submit a brief essay. The student's extracurricular activities and community service are also considered. The President's Scholarship is available only to students enrolling in one of the college's degree programs. Students awarded the scholarship must enroll at Brown Mackie College — Boise between June and September immediately following their high school graduation. Applications for these scholarships can be obtained from the guidance departments of participating high schools. These applications must be completed and returned to the college by March 31.

Faculty

There are 14 full-time and 34 part-time faculty members at the college. The average student-faculty ratio is 15:1. Each student is assigned to a program department chair as an advisor.

Facilities and Resources

Opened in 2008, this modern facility offers more than 40,000 square feet of tastefully decorated classrooms, laboratories, and office space designed to specifications of the college for its business, medical, and technical programs. Instructional equipment is comparable to current technology used in business and industry today. Modern classrooms for special instructional needs offer multimedia capabilities with surround sound and overhead projectors accessible through computer, or DVD. Internet access and instructional resources are available at the college's library. Experienced faculty members provide academic support and are committed to the academic and technical preparation of their students.

In 2012, Brown Mackie College — Boise began its transition to using eTextbooks and computer tablets in the classroom. Utilizing these tablets to access expanded course material, students will be able to increase their acumen for using this technology and further enhance their educational experience. Students have the ability to directly download their eTextbooks to their tablet, eliminating the need to carry heavy, physical textbooks and reducing the overall cost of supplies.

The campus is nonresidential; public transportation and ample parking at no cost are available.

Location

Brown Mackie College — Boise is conveniently located at 9050 West Overland Road in Boise, Idaho. The college has a generous parking area and is easily accessible by public transportation.

Admission Requirements

Each applicant for admission is assigned to an Assistant Director of Admissions who directs the applicant through the steps of the admissions process. They provide information on curriculum, policies, procedures, and services, and assist the applicant in setting necessary appointments and interviews. To qualify for admission, each applicant must provide documentation of graduation from an accredited high school or from a state-approved secondary education curriculum or provide official documentation of high school graduation equivalency. All transcripts become the property of the college.

As part of the admission process, students are given an assessment of academic skills. Although the results of this assessment do not determine eligibility for admission, they provide the college with a means of determining the need for academic support as well as a means by which the college can evaluate the effectiveness of its educational programs. All new students are required to complete this assessment, which is readministered at the end of the student's program so results may be compared with those of the initial administration.

In addition to the college's general admission requirements, applicants enrolling in the occupational therapy assistant program must document one of the following: a high school cumulative grade point average of at least 2.5, a score on the GED examination of at least 57 (557 if taken on or after January 15, 2002), or completion of 12 quarter-credit hours or 8 semester-credit hours of collegiate course work with a grade point average of at least 2.5. Credit hours may not include Professional Development (CF 1100), the Brown Mackie College — Boise course. Students entering the program must also have completed a biology course with a grade of at least a C (or an average of at least 2.0 on a 4.0 scale).

For the most recent information regarding admission requirements, prospective students should refer to the current academic catalog.

Application and Information

Applicants must complete and submit an application form, along with documentation of graduation from an accredited high school or state-approved secondary education curriculum or official documentation of high school graduation equivalency.

Applicants can go online to BMCprograms.info for program duration, tuition, fees and other costs, median debt, federal salary data, alumni success, programmatic accreditation and other important information.

For additional information, prospective students should contact:

Director of Admissions
Brown Mackie College — Boise
9050 West Overland Road
Suite 100
Boise, Idaho 83709
Phone: 208-321-8800
          888-810-9286 (toll-free)
Fax: 208-375-3249
E-mail: bmcboiadm@brownmackie.edu
Web site: http://www.brownmackie.edu/Boise

BROWN MACKIE COLLEGE — CINCINNATI

CINCINNATI, OHIO

The College and Its Mission

Brown Mackie College — Cincinnati (Brown Mackie College) is one of over twenty-five locations in the Brown Mackie College family of schools (www.brownmackie.edu), which is dedicated to providing educational programs that prepare students to pursue entry-level positions in a competitive, rapidly changing workplace. The Brown Mackie College family of schools offers bachelor degree, associate degree, diploma, and certificate programs in health sciences, business, information technology, legal studies, and design to more than 20,000 students in the Midwest, Southeast, Southwest, and Western United States.

Brown Mackie College—Cincinnati was founded in February 1927 as Southern Ohio Business College. In 1978, the college's main location was relocated from downtown Cincinnati to the Bond Hill–Roselawn area and in 1995 to its current location at 1011 Glendale-Milford Road in the community of Woodlawn.

Brown Mackie College — Cincinnati is accredited by the Accrediting Council for Independent Colleges and Schools to award associate degrees, diplomas, and certificates. The Accrediting Council for Independent Colleges and Schools is listed as a nationally recognized accrediting agency by the U.S. Department of Education and is recognized by the Council for Higher Education Accreditation. ACICS can be contacted at 750 First Street NE, Suite 980, Washington, D.C. 20002; phone: 202-336-6780.

The Brown Mackie College — Cincinnati Associate of Applied Science degree in surgical technology is accredited by the Commission on Accreditation of Allied Health Education Programs (www.caahep.org), upon the recommendation of the Accreditation Review Committee on Education in Surgical Technology. The Commission on Accreditation of Allied Health Education Programs is located at 1361 Park Street Clearwater, Florida 33756; phone: 727-210-2350.

The Brown Mackie College — Cincinnati veterinary technology program has provisional programmatic accreditation granted by the American Veterinary Medical Association (AVMA) through the Committee on Veterinary Technician Education and Activities (CVTEA).

The Associate of Applied Science in medical assisting program is accredited by the Commission on Accreditation of Allied Health Education Programs (www.caahep.org) upon the recommendation of the Curriculum Review Board of the Medical Assisting Education Review Board (MAERB). The Commission on Accreditation of Allied Health Education Programs can be contacted at 1361 Park Street Clearwater, Florida 33756; phone: 727-210-2350.

The practical nursing diploma program complies with the Ohio Board of Nursing guidelines as set forth in the Ohio Administrative Code, Chapter 4723-5. The program is administered at the following locations: Brown Mackie College — Cincinnati, Brown Mackie College — Findlay, Brown Mackie College — Akron, and Brown Mackie College — North Canton and all operate under the same approval. The Ohio Board of Nursing is located at 17 South High Street, Suite 400, Columbus, Ohio 43215-3413; phone: 614-466-3947.

Brown Mackie College — Cincinnati is licensed by the Ohio State Board of Career Colleges and Schools, 30 East Broad Street, 24th Floor, Suite 2481, Columbus, Ohio 43215-3138; phone: 614-466-2752. Ohio registration #03-09-1686T.

Brown Mackie College — Cincinnati is regulated by the Indiana Commission on Proprietary Education, 302 West Washington Street, Room E201, Indianapolis, Indiana 46204; phone: 800-227-5695 (toll-free) or 317-232-1320. Indiana advertising code: AC0150.

Academic Programs

Brown Mackie — Cincinnati provides higher education to traditional and nontraditional students through associate degrees, diploma, and certificate programs that can assist them in enhancing their career opportunities, broadening their perspectives through appropriate general education courses, thinking independently and critically, and improving problem-solving abilities. The college strives to develop within its students the desire for lifelong and continued education.

Each college quarter comprises twelve weeks. Associate degree programs require a minimum of eight quarters to complete. Programs are offered on a year-round basis, providing students with the ability to work uninterrupted toward their degrees. The college offers all programs in a unique One Course a Month format. This schedule allows students to focus studies on only one course for four weeks and has proven convenient for students with multiple obligations such as jobs and family.

Associate Degree Programs: The Associate of Applied Business degree is awarded in accounting technology, business management, computer networking and applications, criminal justice, information technology, office management, and paralegal. The Associate of Applied Science degree is awarded in architectural design and drafting technology, audio/video production, biomedical equipment technology, early childhood education, health care administration, medical assisting, pharmacy technology, surgical technology, and veterinary technology.

Diploma Programs: Diploma programs are offered in accounting, audio/video technician, business, criminal justice, medical assistant, paralegal assistant, and practical nursing.

Certificate Program: The college offers a certificate program in computer networking.

The American Medical Technologists (AMT), which offers the certification for Registered Medical Assistant (RMA), accepts the accreditation of Brown Mackie College — Cincinnati. Students will qualify to take the RMA certification examination upon graduating the Brown Mackie College — Cincinnati medical assisting and medical assistant programs. Graduates of the 48 credit-hour medical assistant program are not qualified to take the AMT/RMA exam.

Brown Mackie College — Cincinnati does not guarantee third-party certification. Outside agencies control the requirements for certifications and are subject to change without notice to Brown Mackie College.

Costs

Tuition for the 2011–12 academic year was $294 per credit hour and $15 per credit hour for general fees. Tuition for the practical nursing program was $361 per credit hour and $25 per credit hour for general fees. Tuition for the surgical technology program was $340 per credit hour and $15 per credit hour for general fees. The cost of textbooks and other instructional materials varies by program.

Financial Aid

Financial aid is available to those who qualify. Brown Mackie College maintains a full-time staff of Student Financial Services Advisers to assist qualified students in obtaining financial assistance. The college participates in several student aid programs. Forms of financial aid available to qualified students through federal resources include the Federal Pell Grant Program, Federal Supplemental Educational Opportunity Grant (FSEOG) Program, Federal Work-Study Program, Federal Perkins Loan Program, Federal Stafford Student Loan Program (subsidized and unsubsidized), and the Federal PLUS Loan Program. Eligible students may apply for state awards, such as veterans' educational benefits. Students with physical or mental disabilities that are a handicap to employment may be eligible for training services through the state Agency for Vocational Rehabilitation. For further information, students should contact the Student Financial Services Office.

Each year, the college makes available President's Scholarships of $1000 each to qualifying seniors from area high schools. Up to three (3) scholarships may be awarded per high school. In order to qualify, a senior must be graduating from a participating high school, have maintained a cumulative grade point average of at least 2.0, and submitted a brief essay. The student's extracurricular activities and community service are also considered. The President's Scholarship is available only to students enrolling in one of the college's degree programs. Students awarded the scholarship must enroll at Brown Mackie College — Cincinnati between June and September immediately following their high school graduation. Applications for these scholarships can be obtained from the guidance departments of participating high schools. These applications must be completed and returned to the college by March 31.

The Education Foundation was established in 2000 to offer scholarship support to students interested in continuing their education at one of the postsecondary, career-focused schools in the EDMC system. The number and amount of the awards can vary depending on the funds available. Scholarship applications are considered every quarter. At Brown Mackie College — Cincinnati, applicants must be currently enrolled in an associate degree program and in their fourth quarter or higher (but no further than their second-to-last quarter) at the time of application. Awards are made based on academic performance and potential, as well as financial need.

Faculty

There are 33 full-time and 90 part-time faculty members. The average student-faculty ratio is 20:1. Each student has a faculty and student adviser.

Academic Facilities

Brown Mackie College — Cincinnati consists of more than 57,000 square feet of classroom, laboratory, and office space at the main campus and more than 28,000 square feet at the learning site. Both sites are designed to specifications of the college for its business, computer, medical, and creative programs.

Location

Brown Mackie College — Cincinnati is located in the Woodlawn section of Cincinnati, Ohio. The college is accessible by public transportation and provides parking at no cost. For added convenience, the college also holds classes at the Norwood Learning Site at 4805 Montgomery Road in Norwood, Ohio.

Admission Requirements

Each applicant for admission is assigned to an Assistant Director of Admissions, who directs the applicant through the steps of the admissions process, providing information on curriculum, policies, procedures, and services and assisting the applicant in setting necessary appointments and interviews.

To qualify for admission, each applicant must provide documentation of graduation from an accredited high school or from a state-approved secondary education curriculum or provide official documentation of high school graduation equivalency. All transcripts become the property of the college. Admission to the college is based on the applicant meeting the stated requirements, a review of the applicant's previous educational records, and a review of the applicant's career interests. If previous academic records indicate that the college's education and training programs would not benefit the applicant, the college reserves the right to advise the applicant not to enroll. Special requirements for enrollment into certain programs are discussed in the descriptions of those programs.

For the most recent information regarding admission requirements, please refer to the current academic catalog.

Application and Information

Applicants must complete and submit an application form, along with documentation of graduation from an accredited high school or state-approved secondary education curriculum or official documentation of high school graduation equivalency.

Prospective students can go online to BMCprograms.info for program duration, tuition, fees and other costs, median debt, federal salary data, alumni success, programmatic accreditation, and other important details.

For additional information, prospective students should contact:

Senior Director of Admissions
Brown Mackie College — Cincinnati
1011 Glendale-Milford Road
Cincinnati, Ohio 45215
Phone: 512-771-2424
        800-888-1445 (toll-free)
Fax: 513-771-3413
E-mail: bmcciadm@brownmackie.edu
Web site: http://www.brownmackie.edu/Cincinnati

BROWN MACKIE COLLEGE — DALLAS/FORT WORTH

DALLAS, TEXAS

The College and Its Mission

Brown Mackie College — Dallas/Fort Worth (Brown Mackie College) is one of over twenty-five locations in the Brown Mackie College family of schools (www.brownmackie.edu), which is dedicated to providing educational programs that prepare students to pursue entry-level positions in a competitive, rapidly changing workplace. The Brown Mackie College family of schools offers bachelor degree, associate degree, diploma, and certificate programs in health sciences, business, information technology, legal studies, and design to more than 20,000 students in the Midwest, Southeast, Southwest, and Western United States.

Brown Mackie College — Dallas/Fort Worth is accredited by the Accrediting Council for Independent Colleges and Schools to award associate degrees and diplomas. The Accrediting Council for Independent Colleges and Schools is listed as a nationally recognized accrediting agency by the United States Department of Education and is recognized by the Council for Higher Education Accreditation. ACICS can be contacted at 750 First Street NE, Suite 980, Washington, D.C. 20002; phone: 202-336-6780.

Brown Mackie College — Dallas/Fort Worth is approved and regulated by the Texas Workforce Commission, Career Schools and Colleges, Austin, Texas.

Brown Mackie College — Dallas/Fort Worth holds a Certificate of Authorization acknowledging exemption from the Texas Higher Education Coordinating Board Regulations.

Academic Programs

Brown Mackie College — Dallas/Fort Worth provides higher education to traditional and nontraditional students through associate degree and diploma programs that assist them in enhancing their career opportunities, broadening their perspectives through appropriate general education courses, thinking independently and critically, and improving problem-solving abilities. The college strives to develop within its students the desire for lifelong and continued education.

Each college quarter comprises ten to twelve weeks. Associate degree programs require a minimum of eight quarters to complete. Programs are offered on a year-round basis, providing students with the ability to work uninterrupted toward their degrees. The college offers all programs in a unique One Course a Month format. This allows students to focus studies on only one course for four weeks. This schedule has proven convenient for students with multiple obligations such as jobs and family.

Associate Degree Programs: The Associate of Science degree is awarded in accounting technology, architectural design and drafting technology, business management, biomedical equipment technology, computer networking, graphic design, health care administration, information technology, and surgical technology.

Diploma Programs: Brown Mackie College offers a medical assistant diploma program.

The American Medical Technologists (AMT), which offers the certification for Registered Medical Assistant (RMA), accepts the accreditation of Brown Mackie College — Dallas/Fort Worth. Students will qualify to take the RMA certification examination upon graduating the Brown Mackie College — Dallas/Fort Worth medical assistant program. Graduates of the 48 credit-hour medical assistant program are not qualified to take the AMT/RMA exam.

Brown Mackie College — Dallas/Fort Worth does not guarantee third-party certification. Outside agencies control the requirements for certifications and are subject to change without notice to Brown Mackie College.

Costs

Tuition for the 2012 academic year was $324 per credit hour and general fees were $15 per credit hour, with some exceptions. The surgical technology tuition was $371 per credit hour and general fees were $15 per credit hour. The cost of textbooks and other instructional materials varies by program.

Financial Aid

Financial aid is available to those who qualify. The college maintains a full-time staff of Student Financial Services Advisers to assist qualified students in obtaining financial assistance. The college participates in several student aid programs. Forms of financial aid available through federal resources include Federal Pell Grants, Federal Supplemental Educational Opportunity Grants (FSEOG), Federal Work-Study Program awards, Federal Perkins Loans, Federal Stafford Student Loans (subsidized and unsubsidized), and Federal PLUS loans. Eligible students may apply for veterans' educational benefits. Students with physical or mental disabilities that are a handicap to employment may be eligible for training services through the state Vocational Rehabilitation Agency. For further information, students should contact the college Student Financial Services Office.

Each year, the college makes available President's Scholarships of $1000 each to qualifying seniors from area high schools. Up to three (3) scholarships may be awarded per high school. In order to qualify, a senior must have graduated from a participating high school, maintained a cumulative grade point average of at least 2.0, and submitted a brief essay. The student's extracurricular activities and community service are also considered. The President's Scholarship is available only to students enrolling in one of the college's degree programs. Students who receive the scholarship must enroll at Brown Mackie College — Dallas/Fort Worth between June and September immediately following their high school graduation. Applications for these scholarships can be obtained from the guidance departments of participating high schools. These applications must be completed and returned to the college by March 31.

Faculty

Classes at Brown Mackie College — Dallas/Fort Worth were scheduled to begin July 2, 2012. Faculty and student statistics were not available at time of publication.

Academic Facilities

Brown Mackie College — Dallas/Fort Worth offers media presentation rooms for special instructional needs and a library that provides instructional resources and academic support for both faculty members and students.

In 2012, Brown Mackie College — Dallas/Fort Worth began its transition to using eTextbooks and computer tablets in the classroom. Utilizing these tablets to access expanded course material, students will be able to increase their acumen for using this technology and further enhance their educational experience. Students have the ability to directly download their eTextbooks to their tablet, eliminating the need to carry heavy, physical textbooks and reducing the overall cost of supplies.

Brown Mackie College — Dallas/Fort Worth is nonresidential; public transportation and ample parking at no cost are available. The campus is a smoke-free facility.

Location

Brown Mackie College — Dallas/Fort Worth is conveniently located at 2200 North Highway 121, Suite 250, in Bedford, Texas. A spacious parking lot provides ample parking at no additional charge.

Admission Requirements

Each applicant for admission is assigned to an Assistant Director of Admissions, who directs the applicant through the steps of the admissions process, providing information on curriculum, policies, procedures, and services and assisting the applicant in setting necessary appointments and interviews. To qualify for admission, each applicant must provide documentation of graduation from an accredited high school or from a state-approved secondary education curriculum or provide official documentation of high school graduation equivalency. All transcripts become the property of the college. Admission to the college is based upon the applicant meeting the stated requirements, a review of the applicant's previous education records, and a review of the applicant's career interests. If previous academic records indicate the college's education and training programs would not benefit the applicant, the college reserves the right to advise the applicant not to enroll. Special requirements for enrollment into certain programs are discussed in the descriptions of those programs.

For the most recent information regarding admission requirements, prospective students should refer to the current academic catalog.

Application and Information

Applicants must complete and submit an application form, along with documentation of graduation from an accredited high school or state-approved secondary education curriculum or official documentation of high school graduation equivalency.

Prospective students can go online to BMCprograms.info for program duration, tuition, fees and other costs, median debt, federal salary data, alumni success, programmatic accreditation, and other important details.

For additional information, prospective students should contact:

Director of Admissions
Brown Mackie College — Dallas/Fort Worth
2200 North highway 121, Suite 250
Bedford, Texas 76021
Phone: 817-799-0500
      888-299-4799 (toll-free)
Fax: Not available at time of publication
E-mail: bmcdaladm@brownmackie.edu
Web site: http://www.brownmackie.edu/Dallas

BROWN MACKIE COLLEGE — FINDLAY
FINDLAY, OHIO

BROWN
MACKIE
COLLEGE
FINDLAY℠

The College and Its Mission

Brown Mackie — Findlay (Brown Mackie College) is one of over twenty-five locations in the Brown Mackie College family of schools (www.brownmackie.edu), which is dedicated to providing educational programs that prepare students to pursue entry-level positions in a competitive, rapidly changing workplace. The Brown Mackie College family of schools offers bachelor degree, associate degree, diploma, and certificate programs in health sciences, business, information technology, legal studies, and design to more than 20,000 students in the Midwest, Southeast, Southwest, and Western United States.

Brown Mackie College — Findlay was founded in 1926 by William H. Stautzenberger to provide solid business education at a reasonable cost. In 1960, the College was acquired by George R. Hawes, who served as its president until 1969. The college changed its name from Southern Ohio College–Findlay in 2001 to AEC Southern Ohio College; it was changed again to Brown Mackie College — Findlay in November 2004.

Brown Mackie College — Findlay is accredited by the Accrediting Council for Independent Colleges and Schools to award bachelor degrees, associate degrees, and diplomas. The Accrediting Council for Independent Colleges and Schools is listed as a nationally recognized accrediting agency by the United States Department of Education and is recognized by the Council for Higher Education Accreditation. ACICS can be contacted at 750 First Street NE, Suite 980, Washington, D.C. 20002; phone: 202-336-6780.

The Associate of Applied Science in occupational therapy assistant program is accredited by the Accreditation Council for Occupational Therapy Education (ACOTE) of the American Occupational Therapy Association (AOTA), located at 4720 Montgomery Lane, P.O. Box 31220, Bethesda, Maryland 20824-1220; phone: 301-652-AOTA.

The Associate of Science in surgical technology program is accredited by the Commission on Accreditation of Allied Health Education Programs (www.caahep.org) upon the recommendation of the Accreditation Review Committee on Education in Surgical Technology.

The Associate of Applied Science in veterinary technology program has provisional programmatic accreditation granted by the American Veterinary Medical Association (AVMA) through the Committee on Veterinary Technician Education and Activities (CVTEA).

Brown Mackie College — Findlay is licensed by the Ohio State Board of Career Colleges and Schools, 30 East Broad Street, 24th Floor, Suite 2481, Columbus, Ohio 43215-3138; phone: 614-466-2752. Ohio registration #03-09-1687T.

Academic Programs

Brown Mackie College — Findlay provides higher education to traditional and nontraditional students through associate degree and diploma programs that can assist them in enhancing their career opportunities, broadening their perspectives through appropriate general education courses, thinking independently and critically, and improving problem-solving abilities. The college strives to develop within its students the desire for lifelong and continued education.

Each college quarter comprises twelve weeks. Associate degree programs require a minimum of eight quarters to complete. Programs are offered on a year-round basis, providing students with the ability to work uninterrupted toward completion of their programs. The college offers all programs in a unique One Course a Month format. This schedule allows students to focus studies on only one course for four weeks and has proven convenient for students with multiple obligations such as jobs and family.

Associate Degree Programs: The Associate of Applied Business degree is awarded in accounting technology, business management, criminal justice, and paralegal. The Associate of Applied Science degree is awarded in architectural design and drafting technology, health care administration, medical assisting, occupational therapy assistant, pharmacy technology, surgical technology, and veterinary technology.

Diploma Programs: In addition to the associate degree programs, the college offers diploma programs in business, computer software applications, criminal justice, dental assisting, medical assistant, paralegal assistant, and practical nursing.

The American Medical Technologists (AMT), which offers the certification for Registered Medical Assistant (RMA), accepts the accreditation of Brown Mackie College — Findlay. Students will qualify to take the RMA certification examination upon graduating the Brown Mackie College — Findlay medical assisting and medical assistant programs. Graduates of the 48 credit-hour medical assistant program are not qualified to take the AMT/RMA exam.

Brown Mackie College — Findlay does not guarantee third-party certification. Outside agencies control the requirements for certifications and are subject to change without notice to Brown Mackie College.

Costs

Tuition for programs in the 2011–12 academic year was $294 per credit hour, with a $15 per credit hour general fee. Tuition for the practical nursing diploma program was $361 per credit hour, with a $25 per credit hour general fee. Tuition for the occupational therapy assistant program was $361 per credit hour, with a $15 per credit hour general fee. Tuition for the surgical technology program was $340 per credit hour, with a $15 per credit hour general fee. The length of the program determines total cost. The cost of textbooks and other instructional materials varies by program.

Financial Aid

Financial aid is available to those who qualify. The college maintains a full-time staff of Student Financial Services Advisers to assist qualified students in obtaining financial assistance. The college participates in several student aid programs. Forms of financial aid available through federal resources include the Federal DIRECT Pell Grant Program, Federal Supplemental Educational Opportunity Grant (FSEOG) Program, Federal Work-Study Program, Federal DIRECT Stafford Student Loan Program (subsidized and unsubsidized), the Federal DIRECT PLUS Loan Program, the Ohio College Opportunity Grant (OHCOG), and the Smart Grant. Eligible students may apply for state awards, such as the veterans' educational benefits. Students with physical or mental disabilities that are a handicap to employment may be eligible for training services through the state Agency for Vocational Rehabilitation. For further information, students should contact the college's Student Financial Services Office.

Each year, the college makes available President's Scholarships of $1000 each to qualifying seniors from area high schools. Up to three (3) scholarships may be awarded per high school. In order to qualify, a senior must be graduating from a participating high school, have maintained a cumulative grade point average of at least 2.0, and submitted a brief essay. The student's extracurricular activities and community service are also considered. The President's Scholarship is available only to students enrolling in one of the college's degree programs. Students awarded the scholarship must enroll at Brown Mackie College — Findlay between June and September immediately following their high school graduation. Applications for these scholarships can be obtained from the guidance departments of participating high schools. These applications must be completed and returned to the college by March 31.

Faculty

There are 27 full-time and 90 part-time adjunct instructors at the college. The average student-faculty ratio is 14:1. Each student is assigned a faculty adviser.

Academic Facilities

Brown Mackie College — Findlay is a nonresidential, smoke-free institution. Although the college does not offer residential housing, students who are unable to commute daily from their homes may request assistance from the Admissions Office in locating housing. Ample parking is available at no additional cost.

Location

Located at 1700 Fostoria Avenue, Suite 100, in Findlay, Ohio, the college is easily accessible from Interstate 75.

Admission Requirements

Each applicant for admission is assigned to an Assistant Director of Admissions, who directs the applicant through the steps of the admissions process, providing information on curriculum, policies, procedures, and services and assisting the applicant in setting necessary appointments and interviews.

To qualify for admission, each applicant must provide documentation of graduation from an accredited high school or from a state-approved secondary education curriculum or provide official documentation of high school graduation equivalency. All transcripts become the property of the college. Admission to the college is based upon the applicant meeting the stated requirements, a review of the applicant's previous educational records, and a review of the applicant's career interests. If previous academic records indicate that the college's education and training programs would not benefit the applicant, the college reserves the right to advise the applicant not to enroll. Special requirements for enrollment into certain programs are discussed in the descriptions of those programs.

For the most recent information regarding admission requirements, please refer to the current academic catalog.

Application and Information

Applicants must complete and submit an application form, along with documentation of graduation from an accredited high school or state-approved secondary education curriculum or official documentation of high school graduation equivalency.

Prospective students can go online to BMCprograms.info for program duration, tuition, fees and other costs, median debt, federal salary data, alumni success, programmatic accreditation, and other important details.

For additional information, prospective students should contact:

Director of Admissions
Brown Mackie College — Findlay
1700 Fostoria Avenue, Suite 100
Findlay, Ohio 45840
Phone: 419-423-2211
      800-842-3687 (toll-free)
Fax: 419-423-0725
E-mail: bmcfiadm@brownmackie.edu
Web site: http://www.brownmackie.edu/Findlay

BROWN MACKIE COLLEGE — FORT WAYNE

FORT WAYNE, INDIANA

The College and Its Mission

Brown Mackie College — Fort Wayne (Brown Mackie College) is one of over twenty-five locations in the Brown Mackie College family of schools (www.brownmackie.edu), which is dedicated to providing educational programs that prepare students to pursue entry-level positions in a competitive, rapidly changing workplace. Brown Mackie College schools offer bachelor degree, associate degree, diploma, and certificate programs in health sciences, business, information technology, legal studies, and design to over 20,000 students in the Midwest, Southeast, Southwest, and Western United States.

Brown Mackie College — Fort Wayne is one of the oldest institutions of its kind in the country and the oldest in the state of Indiana. Established in 1882 as the South Bend Commercial College, the school later changed its name to Michiana College. In 1930, the college was incorporated under the laws of the state of Indiana and was authorized to confer associate degrees and certificates in business. In 1992, the College in South Bend added a branch location in Fort Wayne, Indiana. In 2004, Michiana College changed its name to Brown Mackie College — Fort Wayne.

Brown Mackie College — Fort Wayne is accredited by the Accrediting Council for Independent Colleges and Schools to award associate degrees, diplomas, and certificates. The Accrediting Council for Independent Colleges and Schools is listed as a nationally recognized accrediting agency by the United States Department of Education and is recognized by the Council for Higher Education Accreditation. ACICS can be contacted at 750 First Street NE, Suite 980, Washington, D.C. 20002; phone: 202-336-6780.

The Associate of Science in surgical technology program is accredited by the Accrediting Bureau of Health Education Schools and by the Commission on Accreditation of Allied Health Education Programs (www.caahep.org) upon the recommendation of the Accreditation Review Council on Education in Surgical Technology and Surgical Assisting (ARC/STSA). The Commission on Accreditation of Allied Health Education Programs can be contacted at 1361 Park Street, Clearwater, Florida 33756; phone: 727-210-2350; www.caahep.org.

The Associate of Applied Science in occupational therapy assistant program is accredited by the Accreditation Council for Occupational Therapy Education (ACOTE) of the American Occupational Therapy Association (AOTA), located at 4720 Montgomery Lane, P.O. Box 31220, Bethesda, Maryland 20824-1220; phone: 301-652-AOTA.

The Associate of Applied Science in physical therapist assistant program at Brown Mackie College — Fort Wayne is accredited by the Commission on Accreditation in Physical Therapy Education (CAPTE), 1111 North Fairfax Street, Alexandria, Virginia 22314; phone: 703-706-3245; e-mail: accreditation@apta.org; www.capteonline.org.

The Associate of Science in medical assisting program is accredited by the Commission of Accreditation of Allied Health Education Programs (www.caahep.org) upon the recommendation of the Curriculum Review Board of the Medical Assisting Education Review Board (MAERB). The Commission on Accreditation of Allied Health Education Programs can be contacted at 1361 Park Street, Clearwater, Florida 33756; phone: 727-210-2350.

The Associate of Applied Science in veterinary technology program has provisional programmatic accreditation granted by the American Veterinary Medical Association (AVMA) through the Committee on Veterinary Technician Education and Activities (CVTEA).

Brown Mackie College — Fort Wayne does not guarantee third-party certification. Outside agencies control the requirements for certifications and are subject to change without notice to Brown Mackie College.

Brown Mackie College — Fort Wayne is regulated by the Indiana Commission on Proprietary Education, 302 West Washington Street, Room E201, Indianapolis, Indiana 46204; phone: 800-227-5695 (toll-free) or 317-232-1320. Indiana advertising code: AC-0109.

Academic Programs

Brown Mackie College — Fort Wayne provides higher education to traditional and nontraditional students through associate degree, diploma, and certificate programs that assist them in enhancing their career opportunities, broadening their perspectives through appropriate general education courses, thinking independently and critically, and improving problem-solving abilities. The college strives to develop within its students the desire for lifelong and continued education.

Each college quarter comprises twelve weeks. Associate degree programs require a minimum of eight quarters to complete. Programs are offered on a year-round basis, providing students with the ability to work uninterrupted toward their degrees. The college offers all programs in a unique One Course a Month format. This allows students to focus studies on only one course for four weeks. This schedule has proven convenient for students with multiple obligations such as jobs and family.

Associate Degree Programs: The Associate of Science degree is awarded in accounting technology, business management, criminal justice, health care administration, medical assisting, office management, paralegal, and surgical technology.

The Associate of Applied Science degree is awarded in biomedical equipment technology, health and fitness training, nursing, occupational therapy assistant, physical therapist assistant, and veterinary technology.

Diploma Program: A diploma is awarded in practical nursing.

Certificate Programs: The college offers certificate programs in accounting, business, criminal justice, fitness trainer, medical assistant, and paralegal assistant.

The American Medical Technologists (AMT), which offers the certification for Registered Medical Assistant (RMA), accepts the accreditation of Brown Mackie College — Fort Wayne. Students will qualify to take the RMA certification examination upon graduating the Brown Mackie College — Fort Wayne medical assisting and medical assistant programs. Graduates of the 48 credit-hour medical assistant program are not qualified to take the AMT/RMA exam.

Costs

Tuition in the 2011–12 academic year was $314 per credit hour with fees of $15 per credit hour for all programs except nursing, practical nursing, surgical technology, personal fitness training, occupational therapy assistant studies, and physical therapist assistant studies. Textbooks and other instructional materials vary by program. For the nursing program, tuition was $410 per credit hour; fees were $25 per credit hour. For the practical nursing program, tuition was $381 per credit hour; fees were $25 per credit hour. For the surgical technology program, tuition was $360 per credit hour; fees were $15. Tuition for the personal fitness training programs was $324 per credit hour;

fees were $25 per credit hour. Textbook expenses are estimated at $400 for the first term; $600 for the second term; and $100 for the third, fourth, and fifth terms. For certain courses in the occupational therapy assistant studies and physical therapist assistant studies programs, tuition was $381 per credit hour; fees were $15 per credit hour. Textbook expenses are estimated at $370 per quarter for the first six terms and $460 for the seventh term.

Financial Aid

The college maintains a full-time staff of Student Financial Services Advisers to assist qualified students in obtaining financial assistance. The college participates in several student aid programs. Forms of financial aid available through federal resources include the Federal Pell Grant Program, Federal Supplemental Educational Opportunity Grant (FSEOG) Program, Federal Work-Study Program, Federal Perkins Loan Program, Federal Stafford Student Loan Program (subsidized and unsubsidized), and the Federal PLUS Loan Program. Eligible students may apply for Indiana state awards, such as the Frank O'Bannon Grant Program (formerly the Indiana State Grant Program), the Higher Education Award, and Twenty-First Century Scholarships for high school students; for the Core 40 awards; and for veterans' educational benefits. For further information, students should contact the Student Financial Services Office.

Each year, the college makes available President's Scholarships of $1000 each to qualifying seniors from area high schools. Up to three (3) scholarships may be awarded per high school. In order to qualify, a senior must have graduated from a participating high school, maintained a cumulative grade point average of at least 2.0, and submitted a brief essay. The student's extracurricular activities and community service are also considered. The President's Scholarship is available only to students enrolling in one of the college's degree programs. Students awarded the scholarship must enroll at Brown Mackie College — Fort Wayne between June and September immediately following their high school graduation. Applications for these scholarships can be obtained from the guidance departments of participating high schools. These applications must be completed and returned to the college by March 31.

Faculty

The college has 45 full-time and 80 part-time instructors, with a student-faculty ratio of 15:1. Each student is assigned a faculty adviser.

Facilities and Resources

In 2005, the campus located in a 75,000-square-foot facility at 3000 East Coliseum Boulevard. Record enrollment allowed the institution to triple in size in less than one year. The three-story building offers a modern, professional environment for study. Ten classrooms are outfitted as "classrooms of the future," with an instructor workstation, full multimedia capabilities, a surround sound system, and projection screen that can be accessed by computer, DVD, or VHS equipment. The Brown Mackie College — Fort Wayne facility includes a criminal justice lab, surgical technology labs, medical labs, computer labs, and occupational and physical therapy labs, as well as a library and bookstore. The labs provide students with hands-on opportunities to apply knowledge and skills learned in the classroom. Students are welcome to use the labs when those facilities are not in use for scheduled classes.

In 2012, Brown Mackie College — Fort Wayne began its transition to using eTextbooks and computer tablets in the classroom. Utilizing these tablets to access expanded course material, students will be able to increase their acumen for using this technology and further enhance their educational experience. Students have the ability to directly download their eTextbooks to their tablet, eliminating the need to carry heavy, physical textbooks and reducing the overall cost of supplies.

The college is nonresidential; public transportation and ample parking at no cost are available. The campus is a smoke-free facility.

Location

Brown Mackie College — Fort Wayne is located at 3000 East Coliseum Boulevard in Fort Wayne, Indiana. The college facility is accessible by public transportation. Ample parking is provided at no additional charge. For added convenience, the college also operates a learning site at 2135 South Hannah Drive in Fort Wayne.

Admission Requirements

Each applicant for admission is assigned to an Assistant Director of Admissions, who directs the applicant through the steps of the admissions process, providing information on curriculum, policies, procedures, and services and assisting the applicant in setting necessary appointments and interviews. To qualify for admission, each applicant must provide documentation of graduation from an accredited high school or from a state-approved secondary education curriculum or provide official documentation of high school graduation equivalency. All transcripts become the property of the college. Admission to the college is based on the applicant meeting the stated requirements, a review of the applicant's previous educational records, and a review of the applicant's career interests. If previous academic records indicate the college's education and training programs would not benefit the applicant, the college reserves the right to advise the applicant not to enroll. Special requirements for enrollment into certain programs are discussed in the descriptions of those programs.

In addition to the college's general admission requirements, applicants enrolling in the practical nursing program must document the following, which must be completed and a record of proof must appear in the student's file prior to the start of the nursing fundamentals course. No student will be admitted to a clinical agency unless all paperwork is completed. This paperwork is a requirement of all contracted agencies. This paperwork includes records of (1) a complete physical, current to within six months of admission; (2) a two-step Mantoux test that is kept current throughout schooling; (3) a hepatitis B vaccination or signed refusal; (4) up-to-date immunizations, including tetanus and rubella; (5) a record of current CPR certification that is maintained throughout the student's clinical experience; and (6) hospitalization insurance or a signed waiver.

Application and Information

Applicants must complete and submit an application form, along with documentation of graduation from an accredited high school or state-approved secondary education curriculum or official documentation of high school graduation equivalency.

Prospective students can go online to BMCprograms.info for program duration, tuition, fees and other costs, median debt, federal salary data, alumni success, programmatic accreditation, and other important details.

For additional information, prospective students should contact:

Director of Admissions
Brown Mackie College — Fort Wayne
3000 East Coliseum Boulevard
Fort Wayne, Indiana 46805
Phone: 260-484-4400
        866-433-2289 (toll-free)
Fax: 260-484-2678
E-mail: bmcfwaadm@brownmackie.edu
Web site: http://www.brownmackie.edu/FortWayne

BROWN MACKIE COLLEGE — GREENVILLE
GREENVILLE, SOUTH CAROLINA

The College and Its Mission

Brown Mackie College — Greenville (Brown Mackie College) is one of over twenty-five locations in the Brown Mackie College family of schools (www.brownmackie.edu), which is dedicated to providing educational programs that prepare students to pursue entry-level positions in a competitive, rapidly changing workplace. Brown Mackie College schools offer bachelor degree, associate degree, diploma, and certificate programs in health sciences, business, information technology, and legal studies to over 20,000 students in the Midwest, Southeast, Southwest, and Western United States.

Brown Mackie College was originally founded and approved by the Board of Trustees of Kansas Wesleyan College in Salina, Kansas on July 30, 1892. In 1938, the college was incorporated as The Brown Mackie School of Business under the ownership of Perry E. Brown and A.B. Mackie, former instructors at Kansas Wesleyan University in Salina, Kansas. Their last names formed the name of Brown Mackie. By January 1975, with improvements in curricula and higher degree-granting status, The Brown Mackie School of Business became Brown Mackie College.

Brown Mackie College — Greenville is accredited by the Accrediting Council for Independent Colleges and Schools to award associate degrees and certificates. The Accrediting Council for Independent Colleges and Schools is listed as a nationally recognized accrediting agency by the United States Department of Education and is recognized by the Council for Higher Education Accreditation. ACICS can be contacted at 750 First Street NE, Suite 980, Washington, D.C. 20002; phone: 202-336-6780.

Brown Mackie College — Greenville is licensed by the South Carolina Commission on Higher Education, 1122 Lady Street, Suite 300, Columbia, South Carolina 29201; phone: 803-737-2260. Licensure indicates only that minimum standards have been met; it is not equal to or synonymous with accreditation by an accrediting agency recognized by the U.S. Department of Education.

The occupational therapy assistant program has applied for accreditation by the Accreditation Council for Occupational Therapy Education (ACOTE) of the American Occupational Therapy Association (AOTA), located at 4720 Montgomery Lane, P.O. Box 31220, Bethesda, Maryland 20824; phone: 301-652-AOTA.

The Brown Mackie College — Greenville Associate of Science in surgical technology program is accredited by the Accrediting Bureau of Health Education Schools.

Academic Programs

Brown Mackie College — Greenville provides higher education to traditional and nontraditional students through associate degree and certificate programs that assist in enhancing their career opportunities, broadening their perspectives through appropriate general education courses, thinking independently and critically, and improving problem-solving abilities. The college strives to develop within its students the desire for lifelong and continued education.

Each college quarter comprises twelve weeks. Associate degree programs require a minimum of eight quarters to complete. Programs are offered on a year-round basis, providing students with the ability to work uninterrupted toward completion of their degrees. The college offers all programs in a unique One Course a Month format. This allows students to focus studies on only one course for four weeks. This schedule has proven convenient for students with multiple obligations such as jobs and family.

Associate Degree Programs: The Associate of Applied Science degree is awarded in accounting technology, business management, criminal justice, health care administration, information technology, medical assisting, occupational therapy assistant, office management, paralegal, and surgical technology.

Certificate Programs: The certificate is awarded in accounting, business, criminal justice, medical assistant, and paralegal assistant.

The American Medical Technologists (AMT), which offers the certification for Registered Medical Assistant (RMA), accepts the accreditation of Brown Mackie College — Greenville. Students will qualify to take the RMA certification examination upon graduating the Brown Mackie College — Greenville medical assisting and medical assistant programs. Graduates of the 48 credit-hour medical assistant program are not qualified to take the AMT/RMA exam.

Brown Mackie College — Greenville does not guarantee third party certification. Outside agencies control the requirements for certifications and are subject to change without notice to Brown Mackie College.

Costs

Tuition in the 2011–12 academic year for most associate degrees and certificates was $294 per credit hour; fees were $15 per credit hour. Tuition for the occupational therapy assistant program was $361 per credit hour; fees were $15 per credit hour. Tuition for the surgical technology program was $340 per credit hour; fees were $15 per credit hour. The cost of textbooks and other instructional expenses vary by program.

Financial Aid

Financial aid is available for those who qualify. The college maintains a full-time staff of Student Financial Services Advisers to assist qualified students in obtaining the financial assistance they require to meet their educational expenses. Available resources include federal and state aid, student loans from private lenders, and Federal Work-Study opportunities, both on and off college premises.

Each year, the college makes available President's Scholarships of $1000 each to qualifying seniors from area high schools. Up to three (3) scholarships may be awarded per high school. In order to qualify, a senior must have graduated from a participating high school, maintained a cumulative grade point average of at least 2.0, and submitted a brief essay. The student's extracurricular activities and community service are also considered. The President's Scholarship is available only to students enrolling in one of the college's degree programs. Students awarded the scholarship must enroll at Brown Mackie College — Greenville between June and September immediately following their high school graduation. Applications for these scholarships can be obtained from the guidance departments of participating high schools. These applications must be completed and returned to the college by March 31.

Faculty

Experienced faculty members provide academic support and are committed to the academic and technical preparation of their students. The college has 9 full-time and 30 part-time instructors, with a student-faculty ratio of 24:1. Each student is assigned a faculty adviser.

Facilities and Resources

A modern facility, Brown Mackie College — Greenville offers nearly 50,000 square feet. The college is equipped with multiple computer labs housing over 100 computers. High-speed access to the Internet and other online resources are available for students and faculty. Multimedia classrooms are outfitted with overhead projectors, VCR/DVD players, and computers.

Brown Mackie College is nonresidential; public transportation and ample parking at no cost are available. The college is a smoke-free facility.

Location

Brown Mackie College — Greenville is conveniently located at Two Liberty Square, 75 Beattie Place, Suite 100, in Greenville, South Carolina. The college has a generous parking area and is easily accessible by public transportation.

Admission Requirements

Each applicant for admission is assigned to an Assistant Director of Admissions who directs the applicant through the steps of the admissions process. They provide information on curriculum, policies, procedures, and services and assist the applicant in setting necessary appointments and interviews. To qualify for admission, each applicant must provide documentation of graduation from an accredited high school or from a state-approved secondary education curriculum or provide official documentation of high school graduation equivalency. All transcripts become the property of the college. Admission to the college is based on the applicant meeting the stated requirements, a review of the applicant's previous educational records, and a review of the applicant's career interests. If previous academic records indicate the college's education and training programs would not benefit the applicant, the college reserves the right to advise the applicant not to enroll. Special requirements for enrollment into certain programs are discussed in the descriptions of those programs.

For the most recent information regarding admission requirements, prospective students should refer to the current academic catalog.

Application and Information

Applicants must complete and submit an application form along with documentation of graduation from an accredited high school or state-approved secondary education curriculum or official documentation of high school graduation equivalency.

Prospective students should go online to BMCprograms.info for program duration, tuition, fees and other costs, median debt, federal salary data, alumni success, programmatic accreditation, and other important details.

For additional information, prospective students should contact:

Director of Admissions
Brown Mackie College — Greenville
Two Liberty Square
75 Beattie Place, Suite 100
Greenville, South Carolina 29601
Phone: 864-239-5300
　　　　877-479-8465 (toll-free)
Fax: 864-232-4094
E-mail: bmcgrweb@brownmackie.edu
Web site: http://www.brownmackie.edu/greenville

BROWN MACKIE COLLEGE — HOPKINSVILLE
HOPKINSVILLE, KENTUCKY

The College and Its Mission

Brown Mackie College — Hopkinsville (Brown Mackie College) is one of over twenty-five locations in the Brown Mackie College family of schools (www.brownmackie.edu), which is dedicated to providing educational programs that prepare students to pursue entry-level positions in a competitive, rapidly changing workplace. Brown Mackie College schools offer bachelor degree, associate degree, certificate, and diploma programs in health sciences, business, information technology, legal studies, and design to over 20,000 students in the Midwest, Southeast, Southwest, and Western United States.

Brown Mackie College — Hopkinsville is accredited by the Accrediting Council for Independent Colleges and Schools (ACICS) to award associate degrees and diplomas. ACICS is listed as a nationally recognized accrediting agency by the United States Department of Education and is recognized by the Council for Higher Education Accreditation. ACICS can be contacted at 750 First Street NE, Suite 980, Washington, D.C. 20002; phone: 202-336-6780.

The Associate of Applied Science in occupational therapy assistant program is accredited by the Accreditation Council for Occupational Therapy Education (ACOTE) of the American Occupational Therapy Association (AOTA), located at 4720 Montgomery Lane, P.O. Box 31220, Bethesda, Maryland 20824-1220; phone: 301-652-AOTA.

Brown Mackie College — Hopkinsville is licensed by the Kentucky State Board for Proprietary Education and is authorized for operation as a postsecondary educational institution by the Tennessee Higher Education Commission (www.state.tn.us/thec).

Brown Mackie College is a nonresidential, smoke-free institution.

Academic Programs

Brown Mackie College — Hopkinsville provides higher education to traditional and nontraditional students through associate degree and diploma programs that can assist them in enhancing their career opportunities, broadening their perspectives through appropriate general education courses, thinking independently and critically, and improving problem-solving abilities.

Each college quarter comprises ten to twelve weeks. Programs are offered on a year-round basis, providing students with the ability to work uninterrupted toward their degrees. Brown Mackie College offers all programs in a unique One Course a Month format. This schedule allows students to focus studies on only one course for four weeks and has proven convenient for students with multiple obligations such as jobs and family.

Associate Degree Programs: Associate degree programs require a minimum of eight quarters to complete. The Associate of Applied Business degree is awarded in accounting technology, business management, criminal justice, and paralegal. The Associate of Applied Science degree is awarded in medical assisting, medical office management, and occupational therapy assistant.

Diploma Programs: Brown Mackie College also offers diploma programs in criminal justice, medical assistant, and medical coding and billing for healthcare.

The American Medical Technologists (AMT), which offers the certification for Registered Medical Assistant (RMA), accepts the accreditation of Brown Mackie College — Hopkinsville. Students will qualify to take the RMA certification examination upon graduating the Brown Mackie College — Hopkinsville medical assisting and medical assistant programs. Graduates of the 48 credit-hour medical assistant program are not qualified to take the AMT/RMA exam.

Costs

Tuition for the 2011–12 academic year was $294 per credit hour with a general fee of $15 per credit hour. Tuition for the occupational therapy assistant program was $361 per credit hour, with a general fee of $15 per credit hour. The cost of textbooks and other instructional materials varied by program.

Financial Aid

Financial aid is available to those who qualify. Brown Mackie College — Hopkinsville maintains a full-time staff of financial aid professionals to assist qualified students in obtaining the financial assistance they require to meet their educational expenses. The college participates in several student aid programs. Forms of financial aid available through federal resources include Federal Pell

Grants, Federal Supplemental Educational Opportunity Grants (FSEOG), the Federal Work-Study Program, Federal Stafford Student Loans (subsidized and unsubsidized), and the Federal PLUS Program. Students may apply for the College Access Program (CAP) grant. Eligible students may also apply for veterans' educational benefits. Students with physical or mental disabilities that are a handicap to employment may be eligible for training services through the State Vocational Rehabilitation Agency. For further information, students should contact the Brown Mackie College — Hopkinsville Student Financial Services Office.

Faculty

There are 3 full-time and approximately 15 adjunct instructors. The student-faculty ratio is 12:1.

Facilities and Resources

Brown Mackie College — Hopkinsville occupies a spacious building that has been specifically designed to provide a comfortable and effective environment for learning. The facility comprises approximately 17,100 square feet, including sixteen classrooms, two medical laboratories, an academic resource center, administrative and faculty offices, a bookstore, and a student lounge. Computer equipment for hands-on learning includes six networked laboratories. Medical equipment includes monocular and binocular microscopes, electrocardiograph, autoclave, centrifuge, and other equipment appropriate to hands-on laboratory and clinical instruction. Convenient parking is available to all students.

Location

Brown Mackie College — Hopkinsville is conveniently located at 4001 Fort Campbell Boulevard in Hopkinsville, Kentucky.

Admission Requirements

Each applicant for admission is assigned to an Assistant Director of Admissions who directs the applicant through the steps of the admissions process, providing information on curriculum, policies, procedures, and services and assisting the applicant in setting necessary appointments and interviews.

To qualify for admission, each applicant must provide documentation of graduation from an accredited high school or from a state-approved secondary education curriculum or provide official documentation of high school graduation equivalency. All transcripts become the property of Brown Mackie College. Admission to the college is based upon the applicant meeting the stated requirements, a review of the applicant's previous education records, and a review of the applicant's career interests. If previous academic records indicate that the Brown Mackie College education and training programs would not benefit the applicant, the college reserves the right to advise the applicant not to enroll. Special requirements for enrollment into certain programs are discussed in the descriptions of those programs.

For the most recent information regarding admission requirements, please refer to the current academic catalog.

Application and Information

Applicants must complete and submit an application form, along with documentation of graduation from an accredited high school or state-approved secondary education curriculum or provide official documentation of high school graduation equivalency.

Prospective students should go online to BMCprograms.info for program duration, tuition, fees and other costs, median debt, federal salary data, alumni success, programmatic accreditation, and other important details.

For additional information, prospective students should contact:

Senior Director of Admissions
Brown Mackie College — Hopkinsville
4001 Fort Campbell Boulevard
Hopkinsville, Kentucky 42240
Phone: 270-886-1302
        800-359-4753 (toll-free)
Fax: 270-886-3544
E-mail: bmchoadm@brownmackie.edu
Web site: http://www.brownmackie.edu/Hopkinsville

BROWN MACKIE COLLEGE — INDIANAPOLIS
INDIANAPOLIS, INDIANA

The College and Its Mission

Brown Mackie College — Indianapolis (Brown Mackie College) is one of over twenty-five locations in the Brown Mackie College family of schools (http://www.brownmackie.edu), which is dedicated to providing educational programs that prepare students to pursue entry-level positions in a competitive, rapidly changing workplace. The Brown Mackie College family of schools offers bachelor degree, associate degree, diploma, and certificate programs in health sciences, business, information technology, legal studies, and design to more than 20,000 students in the Midwest, Southeast, Southwest, and Western United States.

Brown Mackie College — Indianapolis was founded in 2007 as a branch of Brown Mackie College — Findlay, Ohio.

Brown Mackie College — Indianapolis is accredited by the Accrediting Council for Independent Colleges and Schools to award associate degrees, diplomas, and certificates. The Accrediting Council for Independent Colleges and Schools is listed as a nationally recognized accrediting agency by the United States Department of Education and is recognized by the Council for Higher Education Accreditation. ACICS can be contacted at 750 First Street NE, Suite 980, Washington, D.C. 20002; phone: 202-336-6780.

The occupational therapy assistant program is accredited by the Accreditation Council for Occupational Therapy Education (ACOTE) of the American Occupational Therapy Association (AOTA), 4720 Montgomery Lane, P.O. Box 31220, Bethesda, Maryland 20824-1220; phone: 301-652-2682.

Brown Mackie College — Indianapolis is regulated by the Indiana Commission on Proprietary Education, 302 West Washington Street, Indianapolis, Indiana 46204; phone: 317-232-1320 or 800-227-5695 (toll-free). Indiana advertising code: AC0078.

The Brown Mackie College — Indianapolis practical nursing diploma program is approved by the Indiana State Board of Nursing, 402 West Washington Street, Room W066, Indianapolis, Indiana 46204; phone: 317-234-2043.

Academic Programs

Brown Mackie College — Indianapolis provides higher education to traditional and nontraditional students through associate degree, diploma, and certificate programs that assist them in enhancing their career opportunities, broadening their perspectives through appropriate general education courses, thinking independently and critically, and improving problem-solving abilities. The college strives to develop within its students the desire for lifelong and continued education.

Each college quarter comprises twelve weeks. Associate degree programs require a minimum of eight quarters to complete. Programs are offered on a year-round basis, providing students with the ability to work uninterrupted toward their degrees. The college offers all programs in a unique One Course a Month format. This allows students to focus studies on only one course for four weeks. This schedule has proven convenient for students with multiple obligations such as jobs and family.

Associate Degree Programs: The Associate of Science degree is awarded in business management, criminal justice, health care administration, medical assisting, and paralegal. The Associate of Applied Science degree is awarded in occupational therapy assistant.

Diploma Program: The college offers a diploma program in practical nursing.

Certificate Programs: The college offers certificate programs in business and medical assistant.

The American Medical Technologists (AMT), which offers the certification for Registered Medical Assistant (RMA), accepts the accreditation of Brown Mackie College — Indianapolis. Students will qualify to take the RMA certification examination upon graduating the Brown Mackie College — Indianapolis medical assisting and medical assistant programs. Graduates of the 48 credit-hour medical assistant program are not qualified to take the AMT/RMA exam.

Brown Mackie College — Indianapolis does not guarantee third-party certification. Outside agencies control the requirements for certifications and are subject to change without notice to Brown Mackie College.

Costs

Tuition for most programs in the 2011–12 academic year was $312 per credit hour with a $15 per credit hour general fee. Tuition for the practical nursing diploma program was $361 per credit hour with a $25 per credit hour general fee applied to instructional costs for activities and services. For the occupational therapy assistant program, the tuition was $361 per credit hour with a $15 per credit hour general fee.

Financial Aid

Financial aid is available to those who qualify. The college maintains a full-time staff of Student Financial Services Advisers to assist qualified students in obtaining the financial assistance they require to meet their educational expenses. Available resources include federal and state aid, student loans from private lenders, and federal work-study opportunities, both on and off college premises.

Each year, the college makes available President's Scholarships of $1000 each to qualifying seniors from area high schools. Up to three (3) scholarships may be awarded per high school. In order to qualify, a senior must be graduating from a participating high school, must be maintaining a cumulative grade point average of at least 2.0, and must submit a brief essay. The student's extracurricular activities and community service are also considered. These scholarships are available only to students enrolling in one of the college's degree programs. Students awarded the scholarship must enroll at Brown Mackie College — Indianapolis between June and September immediately following their high school graduation. Applications for these scholarships can be obtained from the guidance departments of participating high schools. These applications must be completed and returned to the college by March 31.

Faculty

The college has 24 full-time instructors, 77 adjunct instructors, and 16 lab assistants, with a student-faculty ratio of 12:1. Faculty members provide tutoring and additional academic services to students as needed.

Facilities and Resources

Opened in January 2008, this modern facility offers more than 22,000 square feet of tastefully decorated classrooms, laboratories, and office space designed to the specifications of the college for its business, health-care, and technical programs. The Circle Centre Mall branch learning site boasts 25,000 square feet with 20 lecture rooms, computer labs, 2 medical labs, college store, and more. Instructional equipment is comparable to current technology used in business and industry today. Modern classrooms for special instructional needs offer multimedia capabilities with surround sound and overhead projectors accessible through computer, DVD, or VHS. Internet access and instructional resources are available at the college's library. Experienced faculty members provide academic support and are committed to the academic and technical preparation of their students.

Brown Mackie College — Indianapolis is nonresidential; public transportation and ample parking are available at no additional cost.

Location

Brown Mackie College — Indianapolis is conveniently located at 1200 North Meridian Street in Indianapolis, Indiana. The college has a generous parking area and is easily accessible by public transportation.

In November 2011 the college opened an innovative branch learning site on Level 4 of Circle Centre Mall located at 49 West Maryland Street in the heart of downtown Indianapolis. Daily shuttle service is provided to and from the main college.

Admission Requirements

Each applicant for admission is assigned to an Assistant Director of Admissions, who directs the applicant through the steps of the admissions process, providing information on curriculum, policies, procedures, and services and assisting the applicant in setting necessary appointments and interviews. To qualify for admission, each applicant must provide documentation of graduation from an accredited high school or from a state-approved secondary education curriculum or provide official documentation of high school graduation equivalency. All transcripts become the property of the college. Admission to the college is based on the applicant meeting the stated requirements, a review of the applicant's previous educational records, and a review of the applicant's career interests. If previous academic records indicate the college's education and training programs would not benefit the applicant, the college reserves the right to advise the applicant not to enroll. Special requirements for enrollment into certain programs are discussed in the descriptions of those programs.

In addition to the college's general admission requirements, applicants enrolling in the practical nursing program must document the following: fulfillment of Brown Mackie College — Indianapolis general requirements; complete physical (must be current to within six months of admission); two-step Mantoux TB skin test (must be current throughout schooling); hepatitis B vaccination or signed refusal; up-to-date immunizations, including tetanus and rubella; record of current CPR certification (certification must be current throughout the clinical experience through health care provider certification or the American Heart Association); and hospitalization insurance or a signed waiver.

For the most recent information regarding admission requirements, please refer to the current academic catalog.

Application and Information

Applicants must complete and submit an application form, along with documentation of graduation from an accredited high school or state-approved secondary education curriculum or official documentation of high school graduation equivalency.

Prospective students should go online to BMCprograms.info for program duration, tuition, fees and other costs, median debt, federal salary data, alumni success, programmatic accreditation, and other important details.

For additional information, prospective students should contact:

Director of Admissions
Brown Mackie College — Indianapolis
1200 North Meridian Street, Suite 100
Indianapolis, Indiana 46204
Phone: 317-554-8301
        866-255-0279 (toll-free)
Fax: 317-632-4557
E-mail: bmcindadm@brownmackie.edu
Web site: http://www.brownmackie.edu/Indianapolis

BROWN MACKIE COLLEGE — KANSAS CITY
LENEXA, KANSAS

The College and Its Mission

Brown Mackie College — Kansas City (Brown Mackie College) is one of over twenty-five locations in the Brown Mackie College family of schools (www.brownmackie.edu), which is dedicated to providing educational programs that prepare students to pursue entry-level positions in a competitive, rapidly changing workplace. Brown Mackie College schools offer bachelor degree, associate degree, certificate, and diploma programs in health sciences, business, information technology, legal studies, and design to over 20,000 students in the Midwest, Southeast, Southwest, and Western United States.

The college was originally founded in Salina, Kansas, in July 1892 as the Kansas Wesleyan School of Business. In 1938, the college was incorporated as the Brown Mackie School of Business under the ownership of former Kansas Wesleyan instructors Perry E. Brown and A. B. Mackie. It became Brown Mackie College in January 1975.

Brown Mackie College in Lenexa, Kansas is a branch of Brown Mackie College in Salina, Kansas which accredited by the Higher Learning Commission and is a member of the North Central Association (NCA), 230 South LaSalle Street, Suite 7-500, Chicago, Illinois 60604-1413; phone: 800-621-7440 (toll free); www.ncahlc.org.

Brown Mackie College in Lenexa, Kansas is approved and authorized to grant the Associate of Applied Science (AAS) degree by the Kansas Board of Regents, 1000 Southwest Jackson Street, Suite 520, Topeka, Kansas 66612-1368.

The Associate of Applied Science in occupational therapy assistant program is accredited by the Accreditation Council for Occupational Therapy Education (ACOTE) of the American Occupational Therapy Association (AOTA), located at 4720 Montgomery Lane, P.O. Box 31220, Bethesda, Maryland 20824; phone: 301-652-AOTA.

Brown Mackie College — Kansas City is nonresidential, smoke free, and provides ample parking at no additional cost.

Academic Programs

Brown Mackie College — Kansas City provides higher education to traditional and nontraditional students through associate degree, diploma, and certificate programs that can assist them in enhancing their career opportunities, broadening their perspectives through appropriate general education courses, thinking independently and critically, and improving problem-solving abilities. Brown Mackie College strives to develop within its students the desire for lifelong and continued education.

In most programs, students can participate in day or evening classes, which begin every month. Programs are offered on a year-round basis, providing students with the ability to work uninterrupted toward completion of their programs. Brown Mackie College offers all programs in a unique One Course a Month format. This schedule allows students to focus studies on only one course for four weeks and has proven convenient for students with multiple obligations such as jobs and family.

Associate Degree Programs: The Associate of Applied Science degree is awarded in accounting technology, architectural design and drafting technology, bioscience laboratory technology, business management, computer aided design and drafting technology, criminal justice, health and fitness training, health care administration, medical assisting, nursing, occupational therapy assistant, office management, paralegal, and veterinary technology.

Diploma Programs: Brown Mackie College — Kansas City also offers diploma programs in accounting, business, computer aided design and drafting technician, computer software applications, criminal justice, fitness trainer, medical assistant, medical insurance specialist, and paralegal assistant.

Certificate Program: A certificate program is offered in practical nursing.

The American Medical Technologists (AMT), which offers the certification for Registered Medical Assistant (RMA), accepts the accreditation of Brown Mackie College — Kansas City. Students will qualify to take the RMA certification examination upon graduating the Brown Mackie College — Kansas City medical assisting and medical assistant programs. Graduates of the 48 credit-hour medical assistant program are not qualified to take the AMT/RMA exam.

Costs

Tuition for programs in the 2011–12 academic year was $294 per credit hour and $15 per credit hour for general fees. Tuition for nursing programs was $361 per credit hour with general fees of $25 per credit hour. Tuition for the health and fitness training program was $304 per credit hour with general fees of $25 per credit hour. Tuition for the occupational therapy assistant program was $361 per credit hour with fees of $15 per credit hour. The cost of textbooks and other instructional materials varies by program.

Financial Aid

Financial aid is available to those who qualify. Brown Mackie College — Kansas City maintains a full-time staff of financial aid professionals to assist qualified students in obtaining financial assistance. The college participates in several student aid programs. Forms of financial aid available to qualified students through federal resources include Federal Pell Grants, Federal Supplemental Educational Opportunity Grants (FSEOG), Academic Competitiveness Grant, Federal Work-Study Program, Federal Perkins Loans, Federal Stafford Student Loans (subsidized and unsubsidized), Federal Direct Loans (subsidized and unsubsidized), and the Federal PLUS Program. Eligible students may apply for veterans' educational benefits. Students with physical or mental disabilities that are a handicap to employment may be eligible for training services through the state Vocational Rehabilitation Agency. For further information, students should contact the Brown Mackie College — Kansas City Student Financial Services Office.

Each year, the college makes available President's Scholarships of $1000 each to qualifying seniors from area high schools. Up to three (3) scholarships may be awarded per high school. In order to qualify, a senior must be graduating from a participating high school, have maintained a cumulative grade point average of at least 2.0, and submitted a brief essay. The student's extracurricular activities and community service are also considered. The President's Scholarship is available only to students enrolling in one of the college's degree programs. Students awarded the scholarship must enroll at Brown Mackie College — Kansas City between June and September immediately following their high school graduation. Applications for these scholarships can be obtained from the guidance departments of participating high schools. These applications must be completed and returned to the college by March 31.

Faculty

There are 23 full-time faculty members and 25 adjunct faculty members. The average class student-instructor ratio is 14:1.

Facilities and Resources

In addition to classrooms and computer labs, Brown Mackie College — Kansas City maintains a library of curriculum-related resources, technical and general education materials, academic and professional periodicals, and audiovisual resources. Internet access also is available for research. The college has a bookstore that stocks texts, courseware, and other educational supplies required for courses and a variety of personal, recreational, and gift items, including apparel, supplies, and general merchandise incorporating the Brown Mackie College logo. Hours are posted at the bookstore entrance.

Location

Brown Mackie College — Kansas City is located at 9705 Lenexa Drive in Lenexa, Kansas, just off Interstate 35

at 95th Street in Johnson County. The Olathe course site is located at 450 North Rogers Road, Suite 175, in Olathe, Kansas, just off Interstate 35 and Santa Fe Street in Johnson County.

Admission Requirements

Each applicant for admission is assigned to an Assistant Director of Admissions, who directs the applicant through the steps of the admissions process, providing information on curriculum, policies, procedures, and services and assisting the applicant in setting necessary appointments and interviews.

To qualify for admission, each applicant must provide documentation of graduation from an accredited high school or from a state-approved secondary education curriculum or provide official documentation of high school graduation equivalency. All transcripts become the property of Brown Mackie College — Kansas City. Admission to the college is based upon the applicant meeting the stated requirements, a review of the applicant's previous education records, and a review of the applicant's career interests. If previous academic records indicate that the Brown Mackie College education and training programs would not benefit the applicant, the college reserves the right to advise the applicant not to enroll. Special requirements for enrollment into certain programs are discussed in the descriptions of those programs.

For the most recent information regarding admission requirements, please refer to the current academic catalog.

Application and Information

Applicants must complete and submit an application form, along with documentation of graduation from an accredited high school or state-approved secondary education curriculum or official documentation of high school graduation equivalency.

Prospective students can go online to BMCprograms.info for program duration, tuition, fees and other costs, median debt, federal salary data, alumni success, programmatic accreditation, and other important details.

For additional information, prospective students should contact:

Director of Admissions
Brown Mackie College — Kansas City
9705 Lenexa Drive
Lenexa, Kansas 66215
Phone: 913-768-1900
        800-635-9101 (toll-free)
Fax: 913-495-9555
E-mail: bmckcadm@brownmackie.edu
Web site: http://www.brownmackie.edu/KansasCity

BROWN MACKIE COLLEGE — LOUISVILLE
LOUISVILLE, KENTUCKY

BROWN
MACKIE
COLLEGE
LOUISVILLE℠

The College and Its Mission

Brown Mackie College — Louisville (Brown Mackie College) is one of over twenty-five locations in the Brown Mackie College family of schools (www.brownmackie.edu), which is dedicated to providing educational programs that prepare students to pursue entry-level positions in a competitive, rapidly changing workplace. Brown Mackie College schools offer bachelor degree, associate degree, diploma, and certificate programs in health sciences, business, information technology, legal studies, and design to over 20,000 students in the Midwest, Southeast, Southwest, and Western United States.

Brown Mackie College — Louisville opened in 1972 as RETS Institute of Technology. The first RETS school was founded in 1935 in Detroit in response to the rapid growth of radio broadcasting and the need for qualified radio technicians. The RETS Institute changed its name to Brown Mackie College — Louisville in 2004.

Brown Mackie College — Louisville is accredited by the Accrediting Council for Independent Colleges and Schools to award associate degrees, diplomas, and certificates. The Accrediting Council for Independent Colleges and Schools is listed as a nationally recognized accrediting agency by the United States Department of Education. Its accreditation of degree-granting institutions is recognized by the Council for Higher Education Accreditation. ACICS can be contacted at 750 First Street NE, Suite 980, Washington, D.C. 20002; phone: 202-336-6780.

Brown Mackie College — Louisville is licensed by the Kentucky Council on Postsecondary Education, 1024 Capital Center Drive, Suite 320 Frankfort, Kentucky 40601.

Brown Mackie College — Louisville is regulated by the Indiana Commission on Proprietary Education, 302 West Washington Street, Indianapolis, Indiana 46204; phone: 317-232-1320 or 800-227-5695 (toll-free). Indiana advertising code: AC-0045.

The Associate of Applied Science in veterinary technology program has provisional programmatic accreditation granted by the American Veterinary Medical Association (AVMA) through the Committee on Veterinary Technician Education and Activities (CVTEA).

The Associate of Applied Science in surgical technology program is accredited by the Accrediting Bureau of Health Education Schools.

The Associate of Applied Science in occupational therapy assistant program is accredited by the Accreditation Council for Occupational Therapy Education (ACOTE) of the American Occupational Therapy Association (AOTA), located at 4720 Montgomery Lane, P.O. Box 31220, Bethesda, Maryland 20824-1220. ACOTE's telephone number is 301-652-AOTA.

The Associate of Applied Science in surgical technology program is accredited by the Commission on Accreditation of Allied Health Education Programs (www.caahep.org) upon the recommendation of the Accreditation Review Council on Education in Surgical Technology and Surgical Assisting (ARC/STSA). The Commission on Accreditation of Allied Health Education Programs can be contacted at 1361 Park Street, Clearwater, Florida 33756; phone: 727-210-2350

Academic Programs

Brown Mackie College — Louisville provides higher education to traditional and nontraditional students through associate degree, and diploma programs that assist in enhancing their career opportunities, broadening their perspectives through appropriate general education courses, thinking independently and critically, and improving problem-solving abilities.

Each college quarter comprises twelve weeks. Associate degree programs require a minimum of eight quarters to complete. Programs are offered on a year-round basis, providing students with the ability to work uninterrupted toward completion of their programs. The college offers all programs in a unique One Course a Month format. This allows students to focus studies on only one course for four weeks. This schedule has proven convenient for students with multiple obligations such as jobs and family.

Associate Degree Programs: The Associate of Applied Business degree is awarded in accounting technology, business management, computer networking and applications, criminal justice, and paralegal.

The Associate of Applied Science degree is awarded in biomedical equipment technology, electronics, graphic design, health care administration, medical assisting, occupational therapy assistant, pharmacy technology, surgical technology, and veterinary technology.

Diploma Program: The college offers a diploma program in practical nursing.

Certificate Program: The college offers a certificate program in computer networking.

The American Medical Technologists (AMT), which offers the certification for Registered Medical Assistant (RMA), accepts the accreditation of Brown Mackie College — Louisville. Students will qualify to take the RMA certification examination upon graduating the Brown Mackie College — Louisville medical assisting program.

Brown Mackie College — Louisville does not guarantee third-party certification. Outside agencies control the requirements for certifications and are subject to change without notice to Brown Mackie College.

Costs

Tuition for most programs in the 2011–12 academic year was $294 per credit hour, and the general fees were $15 per credit hour. The practical nursing diploma program was $361 per credit hour, and the general fees were $25 per credit hour. The surgical technology program was $340 per credit hour, and the general fees were $15 per credit hour. The occupational therapy program was $361 per credit hour, and the general fees were $15 per credit hour. The computer networking certificate program was $300 per credit hour, and the general fees were $25 per credit hour. The length of the program determines total cost. The cost of textbooks and other instructional materials varies by program.

Financial Aid

Financial aid is available for those who qualify. The college maintains a full-time staff of Student Financial Services Advisers to assist qualified students in obtaining financial assistance. The college participates in several student aid programs. Forms of financial aid available through federal resources include the Federal Pell Grant Program, Federal Supplemental Educational Opportunity Grant (FSEOG) Program, Federal Work-Study Program, Federal Perkins Loan Program, Federal Stafford Student Loan Program (subsidized and unsubsidized), and the Federal PLUS Loan Program.

Each year, the college makes available President's Scholarships of $1000 each to qualifying seniors from area high schools. Up to three (3) scholarships may be awarded per high school. In order to qualify, a senior must have graduated from a participating high school, maintained a cumulative grade point average of at least 2.0, and submitted a brief essay. The student's extracurricular activities and community service are also considered. The President's Scholarship is available only to students enrolling in one of the college's degree programs. Students awarded the scholarship must enroll at Brown Mackie College — Louisville between June and September immediately following their high school graduation. Applications for these scholarships can be obtained from the guidance departments of participating high schools. These applications must be completed and returned to the college by March 31.

Faculty

There are 32 full-time and over 100 part-time faculty members at the college. The average student-faculty ratio is 20:1.

Facilities and Resources

Brown Mackie College — Louisville has more than 69,000 square feet of multipurpose classrooms, including networked computer laboratories, electronics laboratories, veterinary technology labs, medical labs, nursing labs, a resource center, and offices for administrative personnel as well as for student services such as admissions, student financial services, and career-services assistance. In 2009, 6,000 square feet was opened at the Louisville location. Included in this build-out are an occupational therapy lab, a criminal justice lab, additional classrooms, and faculty space. In 2010, 25,000 square feet opened at this location. This build-out included a biomedical equipment lab, additional classrooms, a career services center, and additional faculty/administration space.

Brown Mackie College — Louisville is nonresidential; ample parking at no cost is available. Brown Mackie College is a smoke-free facility.

Location

Brown Mackie College — Louisville is conveniently located at 3605 Fern Valley Road in Louisville, Kentucky. The college has a generous parking area and is easily accessible by public transportation.

Admission Requirements

Each applicant for admission is assigned to an Assistant Director of Admissions, who directs the applicant through the steps of the admissions process, providing information on curriculum, policies, procedures, and services and assisting the applicant in setting necessary appointments and interviews.

To qualify for admission, each applicant must provide documentation of graduation from an accredited high school or from a state-approved secondary education curriculum or provide official documentation of high school graduation equivalency. All transcripts become the property of the college. Admission to the college is based on the applicant meeting the stated requirements, a review of the applicant's previous educational records, and a review of the applicant's career interests. If previous academic records indicate the college's education and training programs would not benefit the applicant, the college reserves the right to advise the applicant not to enroll. Special requirements for enrollment into certain programs are discussed in the descriptions of those programs.

In addition to the college's general admission requirements, applicants enrolling in either the occupational therapy assistant program or the surgical technology program must document one of the following: a high school cumulative grade point average of at least 2.5, a score on the GED examination of at least 57 (557 if taken on or after January 15, 2002), or completion of 12 quarter-credit hours or 8 semester-credit hours of collegiate course work with a grade point average of at least 2.5. Credit hours may not include Professional Development (CF 1100), the Brown Mackie College — Louisville course. Students entering the program must also have completed a biology course with a grade of at least a C (or an average of at least 2.0 on a 4.0 scale).

In addition to the college's general admission requirements, applicants enrolling in the practical nursing program must document the following, which must be completed and a record of proof must appear in the student's file prior to the start of the nursing fundamentals course. No student will be admitted to a clinical agency unless all paperwork is completed. The paperwork is a requirement of all contracted agencies. This paperwork includes records of (1) a complete physical, current to within six months of admission; (2) a two-step Mantoux test that is kept current throughout schooling; (3) a hepatitis B vaccination or signed refusal; (4) up-to-date immunizations, including tetanus and rubella; (5) a record of current CPR certification that is maintained throughout the student's clinical experience; and (6) hospitalization insurance or a signed waiver.

For the most recent information regarding admission requirements, prospective students should refer to the current academic catalog.

Application and Information

Applicants must complete and submit an application form along with documentation of graduation from an accredited high school or completion of state-approved secondary education curriculum or provide official documentation of high school graduation equivalency.

Prospective students may go online to BMCprograms.info for program duration, tuition, fees and other costs, median debt, federal salary data, alumni success, programmatic accreditation, and other important details.

For additional information, prospective students should contact:

Director of Admissions
Brown Mackie College — Louisville
3605 Fern Valley Road
Louisville, Kentucky 40219
Phone: 502-968-7191
    800-999-7387 (toll-free)
Fax: 502-357-9956
E-mail: bmcloadm@brownmackie.edu
Web site: http://www.brownmackie.edu/Louisville

BROWN MACKIE COLLEGE — MERRILLVILLE

MERRILLVILLE, INDIANA

The College and Its Mission

Brown Mackie College — Merrillville (Brown Mackie College) is one of over twenty-five locations in the Brown Mackie College family of schools (www.brownmackie.edu), which is dedicated to providing educational programs that prepare students to pursue entry-level positions in a competitive, rapidly changing workplace. Brown Mackie College schools offer bachelor degree, associate degree, diploma, and certificate programs in health sciences, business, information technology, legal studies, and design to over 20,000 students in the Midwest, Southeast, Southwest, and Western United States.

Founded in 1890 by A. N. Hirons as LaPorte Business College in LaPorte, Indiana, the institution later became known as Commonwealth Business College. In 1919, ownership was transferred to Grace and J. J. Moore, who successfully operated the college under the name of Reese School of Business for several decades. In 1975, the college came under the ownership of Steven C. Smith as Commonwealth Business College. A second location, now known as Brown Mackie College — Merrillville, was opened in 1984 in Merrillville, Indiana.

Brown Mackie College — Merrillville is accredited by the Accrediting Council for Independent Colleges and Schools to award associate degrees, diplomas, and certificates. The Accrediting Council for Independent Colleges and Schools is listed as a nationally recognized accrediting agency by the United States Department of Education and is recognized by the Council for Higher Education Accreditation. ACICS can be contacted at 750 First Street NE, Suite 980, Washington, D.C. 20002; phone: 202-336-6780.

The college is regulated by the Indiana Commission on Proprietary Education, 302 West Washington Street, Indianapolis, Indiana 46204; phone: 800-227-5695 (toll-free) or 317-232-1320. Indiana advertising code: AC0138.

The Associate of Science in surgical technology program is accredited by the Commission on Accreditation of Allied Health Education Programs (www.caahep.org) upon the recommendation of the Accreditation Review Committee on Education in Surgical Technology. The Commission on Accreditation of Allied Health Education Programs can be contacted at 1361 Park Street, Clearwater, Florida 33756; phone: 727-210-2350.

The Associate of Applied Science in occupational therapy assistant program is accredited by the Accreditation Council for Occupational Therapy Education (ACOTE) of the American Occupational Therapy Association (AOTA), located at 4720 Montgomery Lane, P.O. Box 31220, Bethesda, Maryland 20824-1220; phone: 301-652-AOTA.

The Associate of Science in medical assisting program is accredited by the Accrediting Bureau of Health Education Schools.

The college is a nonresidential, smoke-free institution.

Academic Programs

Brown Mackie College — Merrillville provides higher education to traditional and nontraditional students through associate degree, diploma, and certificate programs that assist in enhancing their career opportunities, broadening their perspectives through appropriate general education courses, thinking independently and critically, and improving problem-solving abilities. The college strives to develop within its students the desire for lifelong and continued education.

Each college quarter comprises ten to twelve weeks. Associate degree programs require a minimum of eight quarters to complete. Programs are offered on a year-round basis, providing students with the ability to work uninterrupted toward completion of their programs. The college offers all programs in a unique One Course a Month format. This allows students to focus on only one course for four weeks. This schedule has proven convenient for students with multiple obligations such as jobs and family.

Associate Degree Programs: The Associate of Science degree is awarded in accounting technology, business management, criminal justice, medical assisting, medical office management, paralegal, and surgical technology.

The Associate of Applied Science degree is awarded in occupational therapy assistant.

Certificate Programs: The college offers certificate programs in accounting, business, criminal justice, medical assistant, and paralegal assistant.

The American Medical Technologists (AMT), which offers the certification for Registered Medical Assistant (RMA), accepts the accreditation of Brown Mackie College — Merrillville. Students will qualify to take the RMA certification examination upon graduating the Brown Mackie College — Merrillville medical assisting and medical assistant programs. Graduates of the 48 credit-hour medical assistant program are not qualified to take the AMT/RMA exam.

Brown Mackie College — Merrillville does not guarantee third-party certification. Outside agencies control the requirements for certifications and are subject to change without notice to Brown Mackie College.

Costs

Tuition for most programs in the 2011–12 academic year was $294 per credit hour and fees were $15 per credit hour, with some exceptions. For the surgical technology program, tuition was $340 per credit hour and fees were $15 per credit hour. For the occupational therapy assistant program, tuition was $361 per credit hour and fees were $15 per credit hour. The length of the program determines total cost. Textbook fees vary according to program.

Financial Aid

Financial aid is available to those who qualify. The college maintains a full-time staff of Student Financial Services Advisers to assist qualified students in obtaining financial assistance. The college participates in several student aid programs. Forms of financial aid available through federal resources include the Federal Pell Grant Program, Federal Supplemental Educational Opportunity Grant (FSEOG) Program, Federal Work-Study Program, Federal Perkins Loan

Program, Federal Stafford Student Loan Program (subsidized and unsubsidized), and the Federal PLUS Loan Program. Eligible students may apply for Indiana state awards, such as the Higher Education Award and Twenty-First Century Scholarships for high school students, the Core 40 awards, and veterans' educational benefits. Students with physical or mental disabilities that are a handicap to employment may be eligible for training services through the state's Bureau of Vocational Rehabilitation. For further information, students should contact the college's Student Financial Services Office.

Each year, the college makes available President's Scholarships of $1000 each to qualifying seniors from area high schools. Up to three (3) scholarships may be awarded per high school. In order to qualify, a senior must be graduating from a participating high school, must be maintaining a cumulative grade point average of at least 2.0, and must submit a brief essay. The student's extracurricular activities and community service are also considered. These scholarships are available only to students enrolling in one of the college's degree programs. Students awarded the scholarship must enroll at Brown Mackie College — Merrillville between June and September immediately following their high school graduation. Applications for these scholarships can be obtained from the guidance departments of participating high schools. These applications must be completed and returned to the college by March 31.

Faculty

There are approximately 60 full-time and 25 part-time faculty members at the college, practitioners in their fields of expertise. The average student-faculty ratio is 17:1.

Facilities and Resources

Occupying 26,000 square feet, Brown Mackie College — Merrillville was opened to students in October 1998 in the Twin Towers complex of Merrillville and comprises several instructional rooms, including five computer labs with networked computers and four medical laboratories. The administrative offices, college library, and student lounge are all easily accessible to students. The college bookstore stocks texts, courseware, and other educational supplies required for courses at the college. Students also find a variety of personal, recreational, and gift items, including apparel, supplies, and general merchandise incorporating the college logo. Hours are posted at the bookstore entrance.

Location

Brown Mackie College — Merrillville is conveniently located in northwest Indiana at 1000 East 80th Place, Merrillville, in the Twin Towers business complex just west of the intersection of U.S. Route 30 and Interstate 65. A spacious parking lot provides ample parking at no additional charge.

Admission Requirements

Each applicant for admission is assigned to an Assistant Director of Admissions who directs the applicant through the steps of the admissions process, providing information on curriculum, policies, procedures, and services and assisting the applicant in setting necessary appointments and interviews. To qualify for admission, each applicant must provide documentation of graduation from an accredited high school or completion of a state-approved secondary education curriculum or provide official documentation of high school graduation equivalency. All transcripts become the property of the college.

As part of the admission process, students are given an assessment of academic skills. Although the results of this assessment do not determine eligibility for admission, they provide the college with a means of determining the need for academic support as well as a means by which the college can evaluate the effectiveness of its educational programs. All new students are required to complete this assessment, which is readministered at the end of the student's program so results may be compared with those of the initial administration.

In addition to the college's general admission requirements, applicants enrolling in the practical nursing program must document the following, which must be completed, and a record of proof must appear in the student's file prior to the start of the nursing fundamentals course. No student will be admitted to a clinical agency unless all paperwork is completed. The paperwork is a requirement of all contracted agencies. This paperwork includes records of (1) a complete physical, current to within six months of admission, (2) a two-step Mantoux test that is kept current throughout schooling, (3) a hepatitis B vaccination or signed refusal, (4) up-to-date immunizations, including tetanus and rubella, (5) a record of current CPR certification that is maintained throughout the student's clinical experience, and (6) hospitalization insurance or a signed waiver.

For the most recent information regarding admission requirements, please refer to the current academic catalog.

Application and Information

Applicants must complete and submit an application form along with documentation of graduation from an accredited high school or completion of state-approved secondary education curriculum or provide official documentation of high school graduation equivalency.

Prospective students can go online to BMCprograms.info for program duration, tuition, fees and other costs, median debt, federal salary data, alumni success, programmatic accreditation, and other important details.

For additional information, prospective students should contact:

Brown Mackie College — Merrillville
1000 East 80th Place, Suite 205M
Merrillville, Indiana 46410
Phone: 219-769-3321
        800-258-3321 (toll-free)
Fax: 219-738-1076
E-mail: bmcmeadm@brownmackie.edu
Web site: http://www.brownmackie.edu/Merrillville

BROWN MACKIE COLLEGE — MIAMI

MIAMI, FLORIDA

BROWN
MACKIE
COLLEGE
MIAMI℠

The College and Its Mission

Brown Mackie College — Miami (Brown Mackie College) is one of over twenty-five locations in the Brown Mackie College family of schools (www.brownmackie.edu), which is dedicated to providing educational programs that prepare students to pursue entry-level positions in a competitive, rapidly changing workplace. Brown Mackie College schools offer bachelor degree, associate degree, diploma, and certificate programs in health sciences, business, information technology, legal studies, criminal justice, early childhood education, and design to over 20,000 students in the Midwest, Southeast, Southwest, and Western United States.

Brown Mackie College — Miami, Florida is accredited by the Accrediting Council for Independent Colleges and Schools to award associate degrees and diplomas. The Accrediting Council for Independent Colleges and Schools is listed as a nationally recognized accrediting agency by the United States Department of Education and is recognized by the Council for Higher Education Accreditation. ACICS can be contacted at 750 First Street NE, Suite 980, Washington, D.C. 20002; phone: 202-336-6780.

Brown Mackie College — Miami is licensed by the Commission for Independent Education, Florida Department of Education. Additional information regarding this institution may be obtained by contacting the Commission at 325 West Gaines Street, Suite 1414, Tallahassee, Florida 32399-0400; phone: 888-224-6684 (toll-free).

The college is a nonresidential, smoke-free institution.

Academic Programs

Brown Mackie College — Miami provides higher education to traditional and nontraditional students through associate degree and diploma programs that assist them in enhancing their career opportunities, broadening their perspectives through appropriate general education courses, thinking independently and critically, and improving problem-solving abilities. The college strives to develop within its students the desire for lifelong and continued education.

Each college quarter comprises twelve weeks. Associate degree programs require a minimum of eight quarters to complete. Programs are offered on a year-round basis, providing students with the ability to work uninterrupted toward their degrees. The college offers all programs in a unique One Course a Month format. This allows students to focus studies on only one course for four weeks. This schedule has proven convenient for students with multiple obligations such as jobs and family.

Associate Degree Programs: The Associate of Science degree is awarded in accounting technology, architectural design and drafting technology, biomedical equipment technology, business management, computer networking, criminal justice, early childhood education, graphic design, health care administration, information technology, medical assisting, nursing, and paralegal.

Diploma Program: The college offers a medical assistant diploma program.

The American Medical Technologists (AMT), which offers the certification for Registered Medical Assistant (RMA), accepts the accreditation of Brown Mackie College — Miami. Students will qualify to take the RMA certification examination upon graduating the Brown Mackie College — Miami medical assisting program.

Brown Mackie College — Miami does not guarantee third-party certification. Outside agencies control the requirements for certifications and are subject to change without notice to Brown Mackie College.

Costs

Tuition in the 2011–12 academic year for all programs was $391 per credit hour; fees were $15 per credit hour. For the nursing program, tuition was $410 per credit hour; fees were $25 per credit hour. Textbooks and other instructional materials vary by program.

Financial Aid

Financial aid is available for those who qualify. The college maintains a full-time staff of Student Financial Services Advisers to assist qualified students in obtaining financial assistance. The college participates in several student aid programs. Forms of financial aid available to qualified students through federal resources include the Federal Pell Grant Program, Federal Supplemental Educational Opportunity Grant (FSEOG) Program, Federal Work-Study Program, Federal Perkins Loan Program, Federal Stafford Student Loan Program (subsidized and unsubsidized), Federal PLUS loan program, and Florida State grant program. Eligible students may apply for veterans' educational benefits. Students with physical or mental disabilities that are a handicap to employment may be eligible for training services through the state Agency for Vocational Rehabilitation. For further information, students should contact the Student Financial Services Office.

Each year, the college makes available President's Scholarships of $1000 each to qualifying seniors from area high schools. Up to three (3) scholarships may be awarded per high school. In order to qualify, a senior must be graduating from a participating high school, must be maintaining a cumulative grade point average of at least 2.0, and must submit a brief essay. The student's extracurricular activities and community service are also considered. The President's Scholarship is available only to students enrolling in one of the college's degree programs. Students awarded the scholarship must enroll at Brown Mackie College — Miami between June and September immediately following their high school graduation. Applications for these scholarships can be obtained from the guidance departments of participating high schools. These applications must be completed and returned to the college by March 31. Those awarded scholarships will be notified by April 30. A list of participating high schools may be obtained from the campus Admissions Office.

Faculty

There are 15 full-time and more than 50 adjunct faculty members at the college. The average student-faculty ratio is 17:1.

Facilities and Resources

Brown Mackie College — Miami is conveniently located at One Herald Plaza, Miami, Florida. The college occupies 50,000 square feet on the top floor of the Miami Herald building, which sits on beautiful Biscayne Bay and offers a clear view of Miami and the Miami Beach skylines.

The computer networking lab as well as multiple computer classrooms offers students a modern and professional environment for study. Four medical labs are used to instruct clinical medical skills as well as biomedical equipment use and repair. Each student has access to the technology, tools, and facilities needed to complete projects in each subject area. Students are welcome to use the labs when the labs are not in use for scheduled classes.

The college features a comfortable student lounge as well as an on-site eatery available during all class shifts. The college bookstore offers retail items including textbooks, kits specific to programs of study, and college apparel. The on-site library offers multimedia resources including books, periodicals, and electronic resources specific to all academic programs offered. Course delivery at Brown Mackie College — Miami includes on-ground as well as blended courses.

In 2012, Brown Mackie College — Miami began its transition to using eTextbooks and computer tablets in the classroom. Utilizing these tablets to access expanded course material, students will be able to increase their acumen for using this technology and further enhance their educational experience. Students have the ability to directly download their eTextbooks to their tablet, eliminating the need to carry heavy, physical textbooks and reducing the overall cost of supplies.

Location

Brown Mackie College — Miami occupies space within the newly renovated One Herald Plaza in Miami, Florida. It is conveniently located adjacent to the OMNI Metro Mover and bus stop, with access to Metro Rail and Florida's regional Tri-Rail system. Ample parking is also available.

Admission Requirements

Each applicant for admission is assigned to an assistant director of admissions who directs the applicant through the steps of the admissions process, providing information on curriculum, policies, procedures, and services, and assisting the applicant in setting necessary appointments and interviews. To qualify for admission, applicants must be a graduate of a public or private high school or a correspondence school or education center that is accredited by an agency that is recognized by the U.S. Department of Education or the State of Florida's Department of Education or any of its approved agents, or provides official documentation of high school graduation equivalency. As part of the admissions process applicants must sign a document attesting to graduation or completion and containing the information to obtain verification of such. Official high school transcripts or official documentation of high school graduation equivalency must be obtained within the first term (90 days) or the student will be withdrawn from the institution following established guidelines for withdrawn students noted in the catalog. Title IV aid will not be dispersed until verification of graduation or completion has been received by the college.

Students seeking entry into the college with a high school diploma completed in a foreign country must provide an original U.S. – equivalency evaluation from an evaluating agency which is a member of the National Association of Credential Evaluation Services (NACES) (http://www.naces.org/) or the Association of International Credential Evaluators, Inc. (AICES) (http://www.aice-eval.org/). The cost of evaluating the foreign transcript is borne by the applicant.

Brown Mackie College — Miami is authorized under Federal law to enroll nonimmigrant students. Applicants seeking entry into the college with a high school diploma completed in a foreign country must provide an original U. S. equivalency evaluation from a recognized evaluating agency. The cost of evaluating the foreign transcript is borne by the applicant.

For the most recent information regarding admission requirements, please refer to the current academic catalog.

Application and Information

Applicants must complete and submit an application form, along with documentation of graduation from an accredited high school or state-approved secondary education curriculum or official documentation of high school graduation equivalency.

Prospective students can go online to BMCprograms.info for program duration, tuition, fees and other costs, median debt, federal salary data, alumni success, programmatic accreditation, and other important details.

For additional information, prospective students should contact:

Director of Admissions
Brown Mackie College — Miami
One Herald Plaza
Miami, Florida 33132-1418
Phone: 305-341-6600
    866-505-0335 (toll-free)
Fax: 305-373-8814
E-mail: bmmiaadm@brownmackie.edu
Web site: http://www.brownmackie.edu/Miami

BROWN MACKIE COLLEGE — MICHIGAN CITY
MICHIGAN CITY, INDIANA

The College and Its Mission

Brown Mackie College — Michigan City (Brown Mackie College) is one of over twenty-five locations in the Brown Mackie College family of schools (www.brownmackie.edu), which is dedicated to providing educational programs that prepare students to pursue entry-level positions in a competitive, rapidly changing workplace. Brown Mackie College schools offer bachelor degree, associate degree, diploma, and certificate programs in health sciences, business, information technology, legal studies, and design to over 20,000 students in the Midwest, Southeast, Southwest, and Western United States.

Founded in 1890 by A. N. Hirons as LaPorte Business College in LaPorte, Indiana, the institution later became known as Commonwealth Business College. In 1919, ownership was transferred to Grace and J. J. Moore, who successfully operated the college under the name of Reese School of Business for several decades. In 1975, the college came under the ownership of Steven C. Smith as Commonwealth Business College. In 1997, the college relocated to its present site in Michigan City, Indiana. The college was acquired by Education Management Corporation (EDMC) on September 2, 2003, and changed its name to Brown Mackie College — Michigan City in November 2004.

Brown Mackie College — Michigan City is accredited by the Accrediting Council for Independent Colleges and Schools to award associate degrees and certificates. The Accrediting Council for Independent Colleges and Schools is listed as a nationally recognized accrediting agency by the United States Department of Education and is recognized by the Council for Higher Education Accreditation. ACICS can be contacted at 750 First Street NE, Suite 980, Washington, D.C. 20002; phone: 202-336-6780.

Brown Mackie College — Michigan City is regulated by the Indiana Commission on Proprietary Education, 302 West Washington Street, Indianapolis, Indiana 46204; phone: 317-232-1320 or 800-227-5695 (toll-free). IN Advertising Code: AC0138.

The Associate of Science in medical assisting program is accredited by the Accrediting Bureau of Health Education Schools.

The Associate of Science in surgical technology is accredited by the Commission on Accreditation of Allied Health Education Programs (www.caahep.org) upon the recommendation of the Accreditation Review Committee on Education in Surgical Technology. The Commission on Accreditation of Allied Health Education Programs can be contacted at 1361 Park Street, Clearwater, Florida 33756; phone: 727-210-2350.

The Associate of Science in veterinary technology program has provisional programmatic accreditation granted by the American Veterinary Medical Association (AVMA) through the Committee on Veterinary Technician Education and Activities (CVTEA).

The college is a nonresidential, smoke-free institution.

Academic Programs

Brown Mackie College — Michigan City provides higher education to traditional and nontraditional students through associate degree and certificate programs that assist in enhancing their career opportunities, broadening their perspectives through appropriate general education courses, thinking independently and critically, and improving problem-solving abilities. Brown Mackie College strives to develop within its students the desire for lifelong and continued education.

Each college quarter comprises twelve weeks. Associate degree programs require a minimum of eight quarters to complete. Programs are offered on a year-round basis, providing students with the ability to work uninterrupted toward their degrees. The college offers all programs in a unique One Course a Month format. This allows students to focus studies on only one course for four weeks. This schedule has proven convenient for students with multiple obligations such as jobs and family.

Associate Degree Programs: The Associate of Science degree is awarded in accounting technology, business management, criminal justice, health care administration, medical assisting, medical office management, paralegal, surgical technology, and veterinary technology.

Certificate Programs: The college offers certificate programs in accounting, business, criminal justice, medical assistant, medical coding and billing, and paralegal assistant.

The American Medical Technologists (AMT), which offers the certification for Registered Medical Assistant (RMA), accepts the accreditation of Brown Mackie College — Michigan City. Students will qualify to take the RMA certification examination upon graduating the Brown Mackie College — Michigan City medical assisting and medical assistant programs. Graduates of the 48 credit-hour medical assistant program are not qualified to take the AMT/RMA exam.

Brown Mackie College — Michigan City does not guarantee third-party certification. Outside agencies control the requirements for certifications and are subject to change without notice to Brown Mackie College.

Costs

Tuition in the 2011–12 academic year was $294 per credit hour and fees were $15 per credit hour. For the surgical technology program, the tuition was $340 per credit hour and fees were $15 per credit hour. Textbook fees vary according to the program.

Financial Aid

The college maintains a full-time staff of Student Financial Services Advisers to assist qualified students in obtaining financial assistance. The college participates in several student aid programs. Forms of financial aid available to qualified students through federal resources include the Federal Pell Grant Program, Federal Supplemental Educational Opportunity Grant (FSEOG) Program, Federal Work-Study Program, Federal Stafford Student Loan Program (subsidized and unsubsidized), and Federal PLUS loan program.

Eligible students may apply for Indiana state awards, such as the Higher Education Award and Twenty-First Century Scholarships for high school students, the Core 40 awards, and veterans' educational benefits. Students with physical or mental disabilities that are a handicap to employment may be eligible for training services through the state's Bureau of Vocational Rehabilitation. For further information, students should contact the Brown Mackie College — Michigan City Student Financial Services Office.

Each year, the college makes available President's Scholarships of $1000 each to qualifying seniors from area high schools. Up to three (3) scholarships may be awarded per high school. In order to qualify, a senior must be graduating from a participating high school, must be maintaining a cumulative grade point average of at least 2.0, and must submit a brief essay. The student's extracurricular activities and community service are also considered. These scholarships are available only to students enrolling in one of the college's degree programs. Students awarded the scholarship must enroll at Brown Mackie College — Michigan City between June and September immediately following their high school graduation. Applications for these scholarships can be obtained from the guidance departments of participating high schools. These applications must be completed and returned to the college by March 31.

Faculty

There are 9 full-time and 31 part-time faculty members at the college. The average student-faculty ratio is 13:1. Each student is assigned a department chair.

Facilities and Resources

In 2002, the college underwent a major renovation and added 3,360 square feet, for a total of 10,338 square feet of occupancy. An additional medical laboratory, a larger library, new classrooms, and a bookstore were added. All classrooms and the library are equipped with new technology, including multimedia projectors, surround-sound audio systems, VCRs, and DVD players. Five of the ten new classrooms are equipped with networked computer systems. The two medical laboratories contain newly acquired medical equipment and instructional tools and supplies. Administrative offices are easily accessible to students. In 2008, a learning site was opened at 1623 South Woodland Avenue, Michigan City, Indiana. Of approximately 6,500 square feet, this site is conveniently located within a mile of the main campus.

Location

Brown Mackie College — Michigan City is conveniently located in northwest Indiana, at 1001 East U.S. Highway 20, Michigan City, 1 mile north of Interstate 94, 1 mile east of the intersection of routes 20 and 421.

Admission Requirements

Each applicant for admission is assigned to an Assistant Director of Admissions, who directs the applicant through the steps of the admissions process, providing information on curriculum, policies, procedures, and services and assisting the applicant in setting necessary appointments and interviews. To qualify for admission, each applicant must provide documentation of graduation from an accredited high school or completion of a state-approved secondary education curriculum or provide official documentation of high school graduation equivalency. All transcripts become the property of the Brown Mackie College.

As part of the admission process, students are given an assessment of academic skills. Although the results of this assessment do not determine eligibility for admission, they provide the college with a means of determining the need for academic support, as well as a means by which the college can evaluate the effectiveness of its educational programs. All new students are required to complete this assessment.

For the most recent information regarding admission requirements, please refer to the current academic catalog.

Application and Information

Applicants must complete and submit an application form along with documentation of graduation from an accredited high school or completion of a state-approved secondary education curriculum or provide official documentation of high school graduation equivalency.

Prospective students can go online to BMCprograms.info for program duration, tuition, fees and other costs, median debt, federal salary data, alumni success, programmatic accreditation, and other important details.

For additional information, prospective students should contact:

Director of Admissions
Brown Mackie College — Michigan City
1001 East U.S. Highway 20
Michigan City, Indiana 46360
Phone: 219-877-3100
        800-519-2416 (toll-free)
Fax: 219-877-3110
E-mail: bmcmcadm@brownmackie.edu
Web site: http://www.brownmackie.edu/MichiganCity)

BROWN MACKIE COLLEGE — NORTH CANTON

NORTH CANTON, OHIO

The College and Its Mission

Brown Mackie College — North Canton (Brown Mackie College) one of over twenty-five locations in the Brown Mackie College family of schools (www.brownmackie.edu), which is dedicated to providing educational programs that prepare students to pursue entry-level positions in a competitive, rapidly changing workplace. The Brown Mackie College family of schools offers bachelor degree, associate degree, diploma, and certificate programs in health sciences, business, information technology, legal studies, and design to more than 20,000 students in the Midwest, Southeast, Southwest, and Western United States.

The college opened in the 1980s as the National Electronics Institute. In 2002, the Southern Ohio College took ownership. The following year it became part of the Brown Mackie College family of schools.

Brown Mackie College — North Canton is accredited by the Accrediting Council for Independent Colleges and Schools to award associate degrees and diplomas. The Accrediting Council for Independent Colleges and Schools is listed as a nationally recognized accrediting agency by the United States Department of Education and is recognized by the Council for Higher Education Accreditation. ACICS can be contacted at 750 First Street NE, Suite 980, Washington, D.C. 20002; phone: 202-336-6780.

Brown Mackie College — North Canton is licensed by the Ohio State Board of Career Colleges and Schools, 30 East Broad Street, 24th Floor, Suite 2481, Columbus, Ohio 43215-3138; phone: 614-466-2752. Ohio registration #03-09-1688T.

The Associate of Science in medical assisting program is accredited by the Accrediting Bureau of Health Education Schools.

The Associate of Science in surgical technology is accredited by the Commission on Accreditation of Allied Health Education Programs (www.caahep.org) upon the recommendation of the Accreditation Review Committee on Education in Surgical Technology. The Commission on Accreditation of Allied Health Education Programs can be contacted at 1361 Park Street, Clearwater, Florida 33756; phone: 727-210-2350.

The Associate of Science in veterinary technology program has provisional programmatic accreditation granted by the American Veterinary Medical Association (AVMA) through the Committee on Veterinary Technician Education and Activities (CVTEA).

Academic Programs

Brown Mackie College — North Canton provides higher education to traditional and nontraditional students through associate degree and diploma programs that can assist students in enhancing their career opportunities, broadening their perspectives through appropriate general education courses, thinking independently and critically, and improving problem-solving abilities. The college strives to develop within its students the desire for lifelong and continued education.

Each college quarter comprises twelve weeks. Associate degree programs require a minimum of eight quarters to complete. Programs are offered on a year-round basis, providing students with the ability to work uninterrupted toward their degrees. The college offers all programs in a unique One Course a Month format. This schedule allows students to focus studies on only one course for four weeks and has proven convenient for students with multiple obligations such as jobs and family.

Associate Degree Programs: The Associate of Applied Business degree is awarded in accounting technology, business management, computer networking and applications, criminal justice, and paralegal. The Associate of Applied Science degree is awarded in computer-aided design and drafting technology, health care administration, medical assisting, pharmacy technology, surgical technology, and veterinary technology.

Diploma Programs: The college also offers diploma programs in accounting, business, computer aided design and drafting technician, criminal justice, medical assistant, paralegal assistant, and practical nursing.

The American Medical Technologists (AMT), which offers the certification for Registered Medical Assistant (RMA), accepts the accreditation of Brown Mackie College — North Canton. Students will qualify to take the RMA certification examination upon graduating the Brown Mackie College — North Canton medical assisting and medical assistant programs. Graduates of the 48 credit-hour medical assistant program are not qualified to take the AMT/RMA exam.

Brown Mackie College — North Canton does not guarantee third-party certification. Outside agencies control the requirements for certifications and are subject to change without notice to Brown Mackie College.

Costs

Tuition for the 2011–12 academic year was $294 per credit hour and $15 per credit hour for general fees. The tuition for the surgical technology program was $340 per credit hour and $15 per credit hour for general fees. The tuition for the practical nursing program is $361 per credit hour and $25 per credit hour for general fees. The cost of textbooks and other instructional materials varies by program.

Financial Aid

Financial aid is available to those who qualify. The college maintains a full-time staff of Student Financial Services Advisers to assist qualified students in obtaining financial assistance.

The college participates in several student aid programs. Forms of financial aid available through federal resources include the Federal Pell Grant Program, Federal Supplemental Educational Opportunity Grant (FSEOG) Program, Federal Work-Study Program, Federal Perkins Loan Program, Federal Stafford Student Loan Program (subsidized and unsubsidized), and the Federal PLUS Loan Program. Eligible students may also apply for state awards and veterans' educational benefits. Students with physical or mental disabilities that are a handicap to employment may be eligible for training services through the state Agency for Vocational Rehabilitation. For further information, students should contact the Brown Mackie College — North Canton Student Financial Services Office.

Each year, the college makes available President's Scholarships of $1000 each to qualifying seniors from area high schools. Up to three (3) scholarships may be awarded per high school. In order to qualify, a senior must be graduating from a participating high school, must be maintaining a cumulative grade point average of at least 2.0, and must submit a brief essay. The student's extracurricular activities and community service are also considered. The President's Scholarship is available only to students enrolling in one of the college's degree programs. Students awarded the scholarship must enroll at Brown Mackie College — North Canton between June and September immediately following their high school graduation. Applications for these scholarships can be obtained from the guidance departments of participating high schools. These applications must be completed and returned to the college by March 31.

Faculty

There are approximately 20 full-time and approximately 35 part-time faculty members. The average student-faculty ratio is approximately 19:1. Each student has a faculty and student adviser.

Facilities and Resources

The college comprises administrative offices, faculty and student lounges, a reception area, and spacious classrooms and laboratories. Instructional equipment includes personal computers, LANs, printers, and LCD projectors. The library provides support for the academic programs through volumes covering a broad range of subjects, as well as through Internet access. Vehicle parking is provided for both students and staff members.

Location

Brown Mackie College — North Canton is located at 4300 Munson Street, NW in Canton, Ohio. The school is easily accessible from I-77 and Route 687 and by the SARTA bus line.

Admission Requirements

Each applicant for admission is assigned to an Assistant Director of Admissions, who directs the applicant through the steps of the admissions process, providing information on curriculum, policies, procedures, and services and assisting the applicant in setting necessary appointments and interviews. To qualify for admission, each applicant must provide documentation of graduation from an accredited high school or from a state-approved secondary education curriculum or provide official documentation of high school graduation equivalency. All transcripts become the property of the college. Admission to the college is based upon the applicant meeting the stated requirements, a review of the applicant's previous education records, and a review of the applicant's career interests. If previous academic records indicate that the college's education and training programs would not benefit the applicant, the college reserves the right to advise the applicant not to enroll. Special requirements for enrollment into certain programs are discussed in the descriptions of those programs.

For the most recent information regarding admission requirements, please refer to the current academic catalog.

Application and Information

Applicants must complete and submit an application form, along with documentation of graduation from an accredited high school or state-approved secondary education curriculum or official documentation of high school graduation equivalency.

Prospective students can go online to BMCprograms.info for program duration, tuition, fees and other costs, median debt, federal salary data, alumni success, programmatic accreditation, and other important details.

For additional information, prospective students should contact:

Director of Admissions
Brown Mackie College — North Canton
4300 Munson Street NW
Canton, Ohio 44718-3674
Phone: 330-494-1214
Fax: 330-494-8112
E-mail: bmcncweb@brownmackie.edu
Web site: http://www.brownmackie.edu/North-Canton)

BROWN MACKIE COLLEGE — NORTHERN KENTUCKY

FORT MITCHELL, KENTUCKY

The College and Its Mission

Brown Mackie College — Northern Kentucky (Brown Mackie College) is one of over twenty-five locations in the Brown Mackie College family of schools (www.brownmackie.edu), which is dedicated to providing educational programs that prepare students to pursue entry-level positions in a competitive, rapidly changing workplace. The Brown Mackie College family of schools offers bachelor degree, associate degree, diploma, and certificate programs in health sciences, business, information technology, legal studies, and design to more than 20,000 students in the Midwest, Southeast, Southwest, and Western United States.

The college was founded in Cincinnati, Ohio, in February 1927 as a traditional business college. In May 1981, the college opened a branch location in northern Kentucky, which moved in 1986 to its current location in Fort Mitchell.

Brown Mackie College — Northern Kentucky is accredited by the Accrediting Council for Independent Colleges and Schools to award associate degrees and diplomas. The Accrediting Council for Independent Colleges and Schools is listed as a nationally recognized accrediting agency by the United States Department of Education and is recognized by the Council for Higher Education Accreditation. ACICS can be contacted at 750 First Street NE, Suite 980, Washington, D.C. 20002; phone: 202-336-6780.

Brown Mackie College — Northern Kentucky is regulated by the Indiana Commission on Proprietary Education; 302 West Washington Street, Room E201, Indianapolis, Indiana 46204; phone: 317-232-1320 or 800-227-5695 (toll-free). Indiana Advertising Code: AC-0150.

Brown Mackie College — Northern Kentucky is licensed by the Ohio State Board of Career Colleges and Schools, 30 East Broad Street, 24th Floor, Suite 2481, Columbus, Ohio 43215-3138; phone: 614-466-2752. Ohio registration #06-03-1781T.

Brown Mackie College — Northern Kentucky is licensed by the Kentucky Council on Postsecondary Education, 1024 Capital Center Drive, Suite 320; Frankfort, Kentucky 40601

The Associate of Applied Science in occupational therapy assistant program is accredited by the Accreditation Council for Occupational Therapy Education (ACOTE) of the American Occupational Therapy Association (AOTA), located at 4720 Montgomery Lane, P.O. Box 31220, Bethesda, Maryland 20824; phone: 301-652-AOTA.

The Associate of Applied Science in surgical technology program is accredited by the Commission on Accreditation of Allied Health Education Programs (http://www.caahep.org) upon the recommendation of the Accreditation Review Council on Education in Surgical Technology and Surgical Assisting (ARC/STSA).

Academic Programs

Brown Mackie College — Northern Kentucky provides higher education to traditional and nontraditional students through bachelor's degree, associate degree, and diploma programs that assist them in enhancing their career opportunities, broadening their perspectives through appropriate general education courses, thinking independently and critically, and improving problem-solving abilities. The college strives to develop within its students the desire for lifelong and continued education.

Each college quarter comprises ten to twelve weeks. Associate degree programs require a minimum of eight quarters to complete. Programs are offered on a year-round basis, providing students with the ability to work uninterrupted toward their degrees. The college offers all programs in a unique One Course a Month format. This allows students to focus studies on only one course for four weeks. This schedule has proven convenient for students with multiple obligations such as jobs and family.

Associate Degree Programs: The Associate of Applied Business degree is awarded in accounting technology, business management, criminal justice, health care administration, information technology, and paralegal.

The Associate of Applied Science degree is awarded in computer-aided design and drafting technology, medical assisting, occupational therapy assistant, and surgical technology.

Diploma Programs: The college offers a diploma program in medical assistant and practical nursing.

The American Medical Technologists (AMT), which offers the certification for Registered Medical Assistant (RMA), accepts the accreditation of Brown Mackie College — Northern Kentucky. Students will qualify to take the RMA certification examination upon graduating the Brown Mackie College — Northern Kentucky medical assisting and medical assistant programs. Graduates of the 48 credit-hour medical assistant program are not qualified to take the AMT/RMA exam.

Brown Mackie College — Northern Kentucky does not guarantee third-party certification. Outside agencies control the requirements for certifications and are subject to change without notice to Brown Mackie College.

Costs

Tuition for the 2011–12 academic year was $294 per credit hour and general fees were $15 per credit hour, with some exceptions. The practical nursing program tuition was $361 per credit hour and general fees were $25 per credit hour. The surgical technology tuition was $340 per credit hour. Tuition for the occupational therapy assistant program was

$361 per credit hour and general fees were $15 per credit hour. The cost of textbooks and other instructional materials varies by program.

Financial Aid

Financial aid is available to those who qualify. The college maintains a full-time staff of Student Financial Services Advisers to assist qualified students in obtaining financial assistance. The college participates in several student aid programs. Forms of financial aid available through federal resources include Federal Pell Grants, Federal Supplemental Educational Opportunity Grants (FSEOG), Federal Work-Study Program awards, Federal Perkins Loans, Federal Stafford Student Loans (subsidized and unsubsidized), and Federal PLUS loans. Eligible students may apply for veterans' educational benefits. Students with physical or mental disabilities that are a handicap to employment may be eligible for training services through the state Vocational Rehabilitation Agency. For further information, students should contact the Student Financial Services Office.

Each year, the college makes available President's Scholarships of $1000 each to qualifying seniors from area high schools. Up to three (3) scholarships may be awarded per high school. In order to qualify, a senior have graduated from a participating high school, maintained a cumulative grade point average of at least 2.0, and submitted a brief essay. The student's extracurricular activities and community service are also considered. The President's Scholarship is available only to students enrolling in one of the college's degree programs. Students who receive the scholarship must enroll at Brown Mackie College — Northern Kentucky between June and September immediately following their high school graduation. Applications for these scholarships can be obtained from the guidance departments of participating high schools. These applications must be completed and returned to the college by March 31.

Faculty

There are 11 full-time and 30 adjunct faculty members. The student-faculty ratio is 15:1.

Facilities and Resources

Brown Mackie College offers media presentation rooms for special instructional needs and a library that provides instructional resources and academic support for both faculty members and students.

The college is nonresidential; public transportation and ample parking at no cost are available. The campus is a smoke-free facility.

Location

Brown Mackie College — Northern Kentucky is conveniently located at 309 Buttermilk Pike in Fort Mitchell, Kentucky. A spacious parking lot provides ample parking at no additional charge.

Admission Requirements

Each applicant for admission is assigned to an Assistant Director of Admissions, who directs the applicant through the steps of the admissions process, providing information on curriculum, policies, procedures, and services and assisting the applicant in setting necessary appointments and interviews. To qualify for admission, each applicant must provide documentation of graduation from an accredited high school or from a state-approved secondary education curriculum or provide official documentation of high school graduation equivalency. All transcripts become the property of the college. Admission to the college is based upon the applicant meeting the stated requirements, a review of the applicant's previous education records, and a review of the applicant's career interests. If previous academic records indicate the college's education and training programs would not benefit the applicant, the college reserves the right to advise the applicant not to enroll. Special requirements for enrollment into certain programs are discussed in the descriptions of those programs.

In addition to the college's general admission requirements, applicants enrolling in the practical nursing program must document the following, which must be completed, and a record of proof must appear in the student's file prior to the start of the nursing fundamentals course. No student will be admitted to a clinical agency unless all paperwork is completed. The paperwork is a requirement of all contracted agencies. This paperwork includes records of (1) a complete physical, current to within six months of admission; (2) a two-step Mantoux test that is kept current throughout schooling; (3) a hepatitis B vaccination or signed refusal; (4) up-to-date immunizations, including tetanus and rubella; (5) a record of current CPR certification that is maintained throughout the student's clinical experience; and (6) hospitalization insurance or a signed waiver.

For the most recent information regarding admission requirements, prospective students should refer to the current academic catalog.

Application and Information

Applicants must complete and submit an application form, along with documentation of graduation from an accredited high school or state-approved secondary education curriculum or official documentation of high school graduation equivalency.

Prospective students can go online to BMCprograms.info for program duration, tuition, fees and other costs, median debt, federal salary data, alumni success, programmatic accreditation, and other important details.

For additional information, prospective students should contact:

Director of Admissions
Brown Mackie College — Northern Kentucky
309 Buttermilk Pike
Fort Mitchell, Kentucky 41017
Phone: 859-341-5627
Fax: 859-341-6483
E-mail: bmcnkadm@brownmackie.edu
Web site: http://www.brownmackie.edu/NorthernKentucky

BROWN MACKIE COLLEGE — OKLAHOMA CITY
OKLAHOMA CITY, OKLAHOMA

The College and Its Mission

Brown Mackie College—Oklahoma City (Brown Mackie College) is one of over twenty-five locations in the Brown Mackie College family of schools (www.brownmackie.edu), which is dedicated to providing educational programs that prepare students to pursue entry-level positions in a competitive, rapidly changing workplace. Brown Mackie College schools offer bachelor degree, associate degree, certificate, and diploma programs in health sciences, business, information technology, legal studies, and design to over 20,000 students in the Midwest, Southeast, Southwest, and Western United States.

Brown Mackie College — Oklahoma City is a branch campus of Brown Mackie College — Salina which is accredited by the Higher Learning Commission and a member of the North Central Association, 230 South LaSalle Street, Suite 7-500, Chicago, Illinois 60604-1413; phone: 800-621-7440 (toll-free); www.ncahlc.org.

This institution has been granted authority to operate in Oklahoma by the Oklahoma State Regents for Higher Education (OSRHE), 655 Research Parkway, Suite 200, Oklahoma City, Oklahoma 73101; phone: 405-225-9100.

Brown Mackie College — Oklahoma City is a nonresidential, smoke-free institution.

Academic Programs

Brown Mackie College — Oklahoma City provides higher education to traditional and nontraditional students through associate degree programs that can assist students in enhancing their career opportunities, broadening their perspectives through appropriate general education courses, thinking independently and critically, and improving problem-solving abilities. Brown Mackie College strives to develop within its students the desire for lifelong and continued education.

Each college quarter comprises twelve weeks. Associate degree programs require a minimum of eight quarters to complete. Programs are offered on a year-round basis, providing students with the ability to work uninterrupted toward their degrees. Brown Mackie College offers all programs in a unique One Course a Month format. This schedule allows students to focus studies on only one course for four weeks and has proven convenient for students with multiple obligations such as jobs and family.

Associate Degree Programs: The Associate of Applied Science degree is awarded in accounting technology, business management, health care administration, medical assisting, occupational therapy assistant, office management, and paralegal.

The American Medical Technologists (AMT), which offers the certification for Registered Medical Assistant (RMA), accepts the accreditation of Brown Mackie College — Oklahoma City. Students will qualify to take the RMA certification examination upon graduating the Brown Mackie College — Oklahoma City medical assisting program.

Costs

Tuition for the 2011–12 academic year was $294 per credit hour, and $15 per credit hour for general fees. Tuition for the occupational therapy assistant program was $361 per credit hour, and $15 per credit hour for general fees. The cost of textbooks and other instructional materials varies by program.

Financial Aid

Financial aid is available to those who qualify. Brown Mackie College — Oklahoma City maintains a full-time staff of financial aid professionals to assist qualified students in obtaining financial assistance. The college participates in several student aid programs. Forms of financial aid available through federal resources include the Federal Pell Grant Program, Federal Supplemental Educational Opportunity Grant (FSEOG) Program, Federal Work-Study Program, Federal Perkins Loan Program, Federal Stafford Student Loan Program (subsidized and unsubsidized), and the Federal PLUS Loan Program. Eligible students may also apply for state awards and veterans' educational benefits. Students with physical or mental disabilities that are a handicap to employment may be eligible for training services through the state Agency for Vocational Rehabilitation. For further information, students should contact the Brown Mackie College — Oklahoma City Student Financial Services Office.

Each year, the college makes available President's Scholarships of $1000 each to qualifying seniors from area high schools. Up to three (3) scholarships may be awarded per high school. In order to qualify, a senior must be graduating from a participating high school, have maintained a cumulative grade point average of at least 2.0, and submitted a brief essay. The student's extracurricular activities and community service are also considered. The President's Scholarship is available only to students enrolling in one of the college's degree programs. Students awarded the scholarship must enroll at Brown Mackie College — Oklahoma City between June and September immediately following their high school graduation. Applications for these scholarships can be obtained from the guidance departments of participating high schools. These applications must be completed and returned to the college by March 31.

Faculty

Brown Mackie College — Oklahoma City has 5 full-time and 11 regular adjunct faculty members, with an average student-faculty ratio of 14:1.

Facilities and Resources

Brown Mackie College — Oklahoma City comprises administrative offices, faculty and student lounges, a reception area, and spacious classrooms and laboratories. Instructional equipment includes personal computers, LANs, printers, and transcribers. The library provides support for the academic programs through volumes covering a broad range of subjects, as well as through Internet access. Vehicle parking is provided for both students and staff members.

Location

Brown Mackie College — Oklahoma City is located at 7101 Northwest Expressway, Suite 800, in Oklahoma City, Oklahoma.

Admission Requirements

Each applicant for admission is assigned an Assistant Director of Admissions who directs the applicant through the steps of the admissions process, providing information on curriculum, policies, procedures, and services and assisting the applicant in setting necessary appointments and interviews.

To qualify for admission, each applicant must provide documentation of graduation from an accredited high school or from a state-approved secondary education curriculum or provide official documentation of high school graduation equivalency. All transcripts become the property of Brown Mackie College — Oklahoma City. Admission to the college is based upon the applicant meeting the stated requirements, a review of the applicant's previous education records, and a review of the applicant's career interests. If previous academic records indicate that the Brown Mackie College education and training programs would not benefit the applicant, the college reserves the right to advise the applicant not to enroll. Special requirements for enrollment into certain programs are discussed in the descriptions of those programs.

For the most recent information regarding admission requirements, please refer to the current academic catalog.

Application and Information

Applicants must complete and submit an application form along with documentation of graduation from an accredited high school or state-approved secondary education curriculum, or applicants must provide official documentation of high school graduation equivalency.

Prospective students can go online to BMCprograms.info for program duration, tuition, fees and other costs, median debt, federal salary data, alumni success, programmatic accreditation, and other important details.

For additional information, prospective students should contact:

Director of Admissions
Brown Mackie College — Oklahoma City
7101 Northwest Expressway, Suite 800
Oklahoma City, Oklahoma 73132
Phone: 405-621-8000
        888-229-3280 (toll-free)
Fax: 405-621-8055
E-mail: bmcokcadm@brownmackie.edu
Web site: http://www.brownmackie.edu/Oklahoma-City

BROWN MACKIE COLLEGE — PHOENIX

PHOENIX, ARIZONA

The College and Its Mission

Brown Mackie College — Phoenix (Brown Mackie College) is one of over twenty-five locations in the Brown Mackie College family of schools (www.brownmackie.edu), which is dedicated to providing educational programs that prepare students to pursue entry-level positions in a competitive, rapidly changing workplace. The Brown Mackie College family of schools offers bachelor degree, associate degree, diploma, and certificate programs in health sciences, business, information technology, legal studies, and design to over 20,000 students in the Midwest, Southeast, Southwest, and Western United States.

Brown Mackie College — Phoenix was founded in 2009 as a branch of Brown Mackie College — Tucson, Arizona.

Brown Mackie College — Phoenix is accredited by the Accrediting Council for Independent Colleges and Schools to award associate degrees and diplomas. The Accrediting Council for Independent Colleges and Schools is listed as a nationally recognized accrediting agency by the United States Department of Education and is recognized by the Council for Higher Education Accreditation. ACICS can be contacted at 750 First Street NE, Suite 980, Washington, D.C. 20002; phone: 202-336-6780.

The Associate of Applied Science in occupational therapy assistant program is accredited by the Accreditation Council for Occupational Therapy Education (ACOTE) of the American Occupational Therapy Association (AOTA), located at 4720 Montgomery Lane, P.O. Box 31220, Bethesda, Maryland 20824-1220; phone: 301-652-2682.

The Associate of Science in surgical technology program is accredited by the Accrediting Bureau of Health Education Schools.

Brown Mackie College — Phoenix is authorized by the Arizona State Board for Private Postsecondary Education, 1400 West Washington Street, Room 2560, Phoenix, Arizona 85007; phone: 602-542-5709; http://azppse.state.az.us.

The college is a nonresidential, smoke-free institution.

Academic Programs

Brown Mackie College provides higher education to traditional and nontraditional students through associate degree and diploma programs that assist in enhancing their career opportunities, broadening their perspectives through appropriate general education courses, thinking independently and critically, and improving problem-solving abilities. The college strives to develop within its students the desire for lifelong and continued education.

Each college quarter comprises twelve weeks. Associate degree programs require a minimum of eight quarters to complete. Programs are offered on a year-round basis, providing students with the ability to work uninterrupted toward completion of their programs. The college offers all programs in a unique One Course a Month format. This allows students to focus studies on only one course for four weeks. This schedule has proven convenient for students with multiple obligations such as jobs and family.

Associate Degree Programs: The Associate of Science degree is awarded in accounting technology, biomedical equipment technology, business management, criminal justice, health care administration, information technology, medical assisting, paralegal, and surgical technology.

The Associate of Applied Science degree is awarded in nursing and occupational therapy assistant.

Diploma Program: Brown Mackie College — Phoenix offers a medical assistant diploma program.

The American Medical Technologists (AMT), which offers the certification for Registered Medical Assistant (RMA), accepts the accreditation of Brown Mackie College — Phoenix. Students will qualify to take the RMA certification examination upon graduating the Brown Mackie College — Phoenix medical assisting and medical assistant programs. Graduates of the 48 credit-hour medical assistant program are not qualified to take the AMT/RMA exam.

Brown Mackie College — Phoenix does not guarantee third-party certification. Outside agencies control the requirements for certifications and are subject to change without notice to Brown Mackie College.

Costs

Tuition for programs in the 2011–12 academic year was $294 per credit hour, with a $15 per credit hour general fee applied to instructional costs for activities and services. For the surgical technology program, the tuition was $340 per credit hour with a $15 per credit hour general fee applied to instructional costs for activities. For the occupational therapy assistant program, the tuition was $361 per credit hour with a $15 per credit hour general fee applied to instructional costs for activities. For the nursing program, the tuition was $390 per credit hour with a $25 per credit hour general fee applied to instructional costs for activities. Textbooks and other instructional materials vary by program.

Financial Aid

Financial aid is available for those who qualify. The college maintains a full-time staff of Student Financial Services Advisers to assist qualified students in obtaining financial assistance. The college participates in several student aid programs. Forms of financial aid available to those who qualify through federal resources include the Federal Pell Grant Program, Federal Supplemental Educational Opportunity Grant (FSEOG) Program, Federal Work-Study Program, Federal Perkins Loan Program, Federal Stafford Student Loan Program (subsidized and unsubsidized), and the Federal PLUS Loan Program.

Each year, the college makes available President's Scholarships of $1000 each to qualifying seniors from area high schools. Up to three (3) scholarships may be awarded per high school. In order to qualify, a senior must be graduating from a participating high school, must be maintaining a cumulative grade point average of at least 2.0, and must submit a brief essay. The student's extracurricular activities and community service are also considered. The President's Scholarship is available only to students enrolling in one of the college's degree programs. Students awarded the scholarship must enroll at Brown Mackie College — Phoenix between June and September immediately following their high school graduation. Applications for these scholarships can be obtained from the guidance departments of participating high schools. These applications must be completed and returned to the college by March 31.

Faculty

Experienced faculty members provide academic support and are committed to the academic and technical preparation of their students. The college has both full- and part-time faculty members. The average student-faculty ratio is 14:1. Each student is assigned a program director as an adviser.

Facilities and Resources

Brown Mackie College — Phoenix has a variety of classrooms including computer labs housing the latest technology in the industry. High-speed access to the Internet and other online resources are available for students and faculty. Multimedia classrooms provide a learning environment equipped with overhead projectors, TVs, DVD/VCR players, computers, and sound systems.

Location

Brown Mackie College — Phoenix is conveniently located at 13430 North Black Canyon Highway, Suite 190, in Phoenix, Arizona. The college has a generous parking area and is easily accessible by public transportation.

Admission Requirements

Each applicant for admission is assigned to an Assistant Director of Admissions, who directs the applicant through the steps of the admissions process, providing information on curriculum, policies, procedures, and services and assisting the applicant in setting necessary appointments and interviews. To qualify for admission, each applicant must provide documentation of graduation from an accredited high school or from a state-approved secondary education curriculum or provide official documentation of high school graduation equivalency. All transcripts become the property of the college.

For the most recent information regarding admission requirements, please refer to the current academic catalog.

Application and Information

Applicants must complete and submit an application form, along with documentation of graduation from an accredited high school or state-approved secondary education curriculum or official documentation of high school graduation equivalency.

Prospective students can go online to BMCprograms.info for program duration, tuition, fees and other costs, median debt, federal salary data, alumni success, programmatic accreditation, and other important details.

For additional information, prospective students should contact:

Director of Admissions
Brown Mackie College — Phoenix
13430 North Black Canyon Highway, Suite 190
Phoenix, Arizona 85029
Phone: 602-337-3044
    866-824-4793 (toll-free)
Fax: 480-375-2450
E-mail: bmcpxadmn@brownmackie.edu
Web site: http://www.brownmackie.edu/Phoenix

BROWN MACKIE COLLEGE — QUAD CITIES

BETTENDORF, IOWA

BROWN
MACKIE
COLLEGE
QUAD CITIES℠

The College and Its Mission

Brown Mackie College — Quad Cities (Brown Mackie College) is one of over twenty-five locations in the Brown Mackie College family of schools (www.brownmackie.edu), which is dedicated to providing educational programs that prepare students to pursue entry-level positions in a competitive, rapidly changing workplace. Brown Mackie College schools offer bachelor degree, associate degree, certificate, and diploma programs in health sciences, business, information technology, legal studies, and design to over 20,000 students in the Midwest, Southeast, Southwest, and Western United States.

Founded in 1890 by A. N. Hirons as LaPorte Business College in LaPorte, Indiana, the institution later became known as Commonwealth Business College. In 1919, ownership was transferred to Grace and J. J. Moore, who successfully operated the college for almost thirty years. Following World War II, Harley and Stephanie Reese operated the college under the name of Reese School of Business for several decades.

In 1975, the college came under the ownership of Steven C. Smith as Commonwealth Business College. A second location, now known as Brown Mackie College — Merrillville, was opened in 1984 in Merrillville, Indiana, and a third location was opened a year later in Davenport, Iowa. In 1987, the Davenport site relocated to Moline, Illinois. In September 2003, the college changed ownership again and the name was changed to Brown Mackie College — Moline in November 2004. In 2010, the college moved to its current location in Bettendorf, Iowa, and changed its name to Brown Mackie College — Quad Cities.

Brown Mackie College — Quad Cities is accredited by the Accrediting Council for Independent Colleges and Schools (ACICS) to award associate degrees and diplomas. ACICS is listed as a nationally recognized accrediting agency by the United States Department of Education and is recognized by the Council for Higher Education Accreditation. ACICS can be contacted at 750 First Street NE, Suite 980, Washington, D.C. 20002; phone: 202-336-6780.

The Associate of Applied Science in occupational therapy assistant program has applied for accreditation by the Accreditation Council for Occupational Therapy Education (ACOTE) of the American Occupational Therapy Association (AOTA), located at 4720 Montgomery Lane, P.O. Box 31220, Bethesda, Maryland 20824; phone: 301-652-AOTA.

Brown Mackie College — Quad Cities is approved and registered by the Iowa College Student Aid Commission (ICSAC) under the authority of Chapters 261 and 261B of the Iowa Code. ICSCA can be contacted at 200 10th Street, fourth floor, Des Moines, Iowa 50309-3609; phone: 877-272-4456 (toll-free); www.iowacollegeaid.gov.

Academic Programs

Brown Mackie College — Quad Cities provides higher education to traditional and nontraditional students through associate degree and diploma programs that can assist them in enhancing their career opportunities, broadening their perspectives through appropriate general education courses, thinking independently and critically, and improving problem-solving abilities. The college strives to develop within its students the desire for lifelong and continued education.

Each college quarter comprises twelve weeks. Programs are offered on a year-round basis, providing students with the ability to work uninterrupted toward the completion of their programs. Brown Mackie College offers all programs in a unique One Course a Month format. This schedule allows students to focus studies on only one course for four weeks and has proven convenient for students with multiple obligations such as jobs and family.

Associate Degree Programs: The Associate of Applied Science degree is awarded in accounting technology, business management, criminal justice, health care administration, information technology, medical assisting, occupational therapy assistant, and paralegal.

Diploma Programs: Brown Mackie College — Quad Cities offers diploma programs in accounting, business, medical assistant, and medical coding and billing.

The American Medical Technologists (AMT), which offers the certification for Registered Medical Assistant (RMA), accepts the accreditation of Brown Mackie College — Quad Cities. Students will qualify to take the RMA certification examination upon graduating the Brown Mackie College — Quad Cities medical assisting and medical assistant programs. Graduates of the 48 credit-hour medical assistant program are not qualified to take the AMT/RMA exam.

Costs

Tuition for the 2011–12 academic year was $294 per credit hour and $15 per credit hour for general fees. Tuition for the occupational therapy assistant program was $361 per credit hour and $15 per credit hour for general fees. Textbook costs vary by program.

Financial Aid

Financial aid is available to those who qualify. Brown Mackie College — Quad Cities maintains a full-time staff of financial aid professionals to assist qualified students in obtaining the financial assistance they require to meet their educational expenses. The college participates in several student aid programs. Forms of financial aid available through federal resources include the Federal Pell Grant Program, Federal Supplemental Educational Opportunity Grant (FSEOG) Program, Federal Work-Study Program, Federal Perkins Loan Program, Federal Stafford Student Loan Program (subsidized and unsubsidized), and Federal PLUS loan program. Eligible students may apply for veterans' educational benefits. Students with physical or mental disabilities that are a handicap to employment may be eligible for training services through the state Agency for Vocational Rehabilitation. For further information, students should contact the Brown Mackie College — Quad Cities Student Financial Services Office.

Each year, the college makes available President's Scholarships of $1000 each to qualifying seniors from area high schools. Up to three (3) scholarships may be awarded per high school. In order to qualify, a senior must be graduating from a participating high school, have maintained a cumulative grade point average of at least 2.0, and submitted a brief essay. The student's extracurricular activities and community service are also considered. The President's Scholarship is available only to students enrolling in one of the college's degree programs. Students awarded the scholarship must enroll at Brown Mackie College — Quad Cities between June and September immediately following their high school graduation. Applications for these scholarships can be obtained from the guidance departments of participating high schools. These applications must be completed and returned to the college by March 31.

Faculty

Brown Mackie College — Quad Cities has 4 full-time and 43 regular adjunct faculty members, with an average student-faculty ratio of 12:1.

Facilities and Resources

Brown Mackie College — Quad Cities maintains a library of curriculum-related resources. Technical and general education materials, academic and professional periodicals, and audiovisual resources are available to both students and faculty members. Students have borrowing privileges at several local libraries. Internet access is available for research.

The college is a nonresidential, smoke-free institution.

Location

Brown Mackie College — Quad Cities is located at 2119 East Kimberly Road in Bettendorf, Iowa. The college is easily accessible by public transportation, and ample parking is available at no cost.

Admission Requirements

Each applicant for admission is assigned to an Assistant Director of Admissions, who directs the applicant through the steps of the admissions process, providing information on curriculum, policies, procedures, and services and assisting the applicant in setting necessary appointments and interviews.

To qualify for admission, each applicant must provide documentation of graduation from an accredited high school or from a state-approved secondary education curriculum or provide official documentation of high school graduation equivalency. All transcripts become the property of Brown Mackie College — Quad Cities. Admission to the college is based on the applicant meeting the above requirements, a review of the applicant's previous education records, and a review of the applicant's career interests. If previous academic records indicate that the Brown Mackie College education and training programs would not benefit the applicant, the college reserves the right to advise the applicant not to enroll. Special requirements for enrollment into certain programs are discussed in the descriptions of those programs.

Application and Information

Applicants must complete and submit an application form along with documentation of graduation from an accredited high school or state-approved secondary education curriculum, or applicants must provide official documentation of high school graduation equivalency.

Prospective students can go online to BMCprograms.info for program duration, tuition, fees and other costs, median debt, federal salary data, alumni success, programmatic accreditation, and other important details.

For further information, prospective students should contact:

Director of Admissions
Brown Mackie College — Quad Cities
2119 East Kimberly Road
Bettendorf, Iowa 52722
Phone: 563-344-1500
        888-420-1652 (toll-free)
Fax: 563-344-1501
E-mail: bmcmoadm@brownmackie.edu
Web site: http://www.brownmackie.edu/Quad-Cities

BROWN MACKIE COLLEGE — ST. LOUIS
FENTON, MISSOURI

The College and Its Mission

Brown Mackie College — St. Louis (Brown Mackie College) is one of over twenty-five locations in the Brown Mackie College family of schools (www.brownmackie.edu), which is dedicated to providing educational programs that prepare students to pursue entry-level positions in a competitive, rapidly changing workplace. The Brown Mackie College family of schools offers bachelor degree, associate degree, diploma, and certificate programs in health sciences, business, information technology, legal studies, and design to over 20,000 students in the Midwest, Southeast, Southwest, and Western United States.

Brown Mackie College was originally founded and approved by the Board of Trustees of Kansas Wesleyan College in Salina, Kansas on July 30, 1892. In 1938, the college was incorporated as The Brown Mackie School of Business under the ownership of Perry E. Brown and A. B. Mackie, former instructors at Kansas Wesleyan University in Salina, Kansas. Their last names formed the name of Brown Mackie. By January 1975, with improvements in curricula and higher degree-granting status, The Brown Mackie School of Business became Brown Mackie College.

Brown Mackie College — St. Louis is accredited by the Accrediting Council for Independent Colleges and Schools to award associate degrees and certificates. The Accrediting Council for Independent Colleges and Schools is listed as a nationally recognized accrediting agency by the United States Department of Education and is recognized by the Council for Higher Education Accreditation. ACICS can be contacted at 750 First Street NE, Suite 980, Washington, D.C. 20002; phone: 202-336-6780.

The Associate of Applied Science in occupational therapy assistant program is accredited by the Accreditation Council for Occupational Therapy Education (ACOTE) of the American Occupational Therapy Association (AOTA), located at 4720 Montgomery Lane, P.O. Box 31220, Bethesda, Maryland 20824-1220; phone: 301-652-AOTA.

Academic Programs

Brown Mackie College — St. Louis provides higher education to traditional and nontraditional students through associate degree programs that assist in enhancing their career opportunities, broadening their perspectives through appropriate general education courses, thinking independently and critically, and improving problem-solving abilities. The college strives to develop within its students the desire for lifelong and continued education.

Each college quarter comprises twelve weeks. Associate degree programs require a minimum of eight quarters to complete. Programs are offered on a year-round basis, providing students with the ability to work uninterrupted toward completion of their programs. The college offers all programs in a unique One Course a Month format. This allows students to focus studies on only one course for four weeks. This schedule has proven convenient for students with multiple obligations such as jobs and family.

Associate Degree Programs: The Associate of Applied Science degree is awarded in accounting technology, architectural design and drafting technology, business management, criminal justice, health care administration, information technology, medical assisting, nursing, occupational therapy assistant, office management, paralegal, pharmacy technology, surgical technology, and veterinary technology.

Certificate Programs: The college offers certificate programs in accounting, business, criminal justice, medical assistant, and paralegal assistant.

The American Medical Technologists (AMT), which offers the certification for Registered Medical Assistant (RMA), accepts the accreditation of Brown Mackie College — St. Louis. Students will qualify to take the RMA certification examination upon graduating the Brown Mackie College — St. Louis medical assisting and medical assistant programs. Graduates of the 48 credit-hour medical assistant program are not qualified to take the AMT/RMA exam.

Brown Mackie College — St. Louis does not guarantee third party certification. Outside agencies control the requirements for certifications and are subject to change without notice to Brown Mackie College.

Costs

Tuition in the 2011–12 academic year for all bachelor and associate degrees and diploma programs was $268 per credit hour; fees were $15 per credit hour. Tuition for the surgical technology program was $319 per credit hour; fees were $15 per credit hour. Tuition for the nursing program was $390 per credit hour; fees were $25 per credit hour. Tuition for the occupational therapy assistant program was $335 per credit hour; fees were $15 per credit hour. The cost of textbooks and other instructional materials varies by program.

Financial Aid

Financial aid is available for those who qualify. The college maintains a full-time staff of Student Financial Services Advisers to assist qualified students in obtaining the financial assistance they require to meet their educational expenses. Available resources include federal and state aid, student loans from private lenders, and Federal Work-Study opportunities, both on and off college premises.

Each year, the college makes available President's Scholarships of $1000 each to qualifying seniors from area high schools. Up to three (3) scholarships may be awarded per high school. In order to qualify, a senior must have graduated from a participating high school, maintained a cumulative grade point average of at least 2.0, and submitted a brief essay. The student's extracurricular activities and community service are also considered. These scholarships are available only to students enrolling in one of the college's degree programs. Students awarded the scholarship must enroll at Brown Mackie College — St. Louis between June and September immediately following their high school graduation. Applications for these scholarships can be obtained from the guidance departments of participating high schools. These applications must be completed and returned to the college by March 31.

Faculty

Experienced faculty members provide academic support and are committed to the academic and technical preparation of their students. The college has 12 full-time and 23 part-time instructors, with a student-faculty ratio of 20:1.

Facilities and Resources

A modern facility, Brown Mackie College — St. Louis offers more than 30,000 square feet of educational and administrative space. The college is equipped with multiple computer labs, housing over 200 computers. High-speed access to the Internet and other online resources are available for students and faculty. Multimedia classrooms are outfitted with overhead projectors, VCR/DVD players, and computers.

The campus is nonresidential. The college has a generous parking area and is easily accessible by public transportation. The campus is a smoke-free facility.

Location

Brown Mackie College — St. Louis is conveniently located at #2 Soccer Park Road in Fenton, Missouri. The college has a generous parking area and is easily accessible by public transportation.

Admission Requirements

Each applicant for admission is assigned to an Assistant Director of Admissions who directs the applicant through the steps of the admissions process. They provide information on curriculum, policies, procedures, and services and assist the applicant in setting necessary appointments and interviews. To qualify for admission, each applicant must provide documentation of graduation from an accredited high school or from a state-approved secondary education curriculum or provide official documentation of high school graduation equivalency. All transcripts become the property of the college. Admission to the college is based on the applicant meeting the stated requirements, a review of the applicant's previous educational records, and a review of the applicant's career interests. If previous academic records indicate the college's education and training programs would not benefit the applicant, the college reserves the right to advise the applicant not to enroll. Special requirements for enrollment into certain programs are discussed in the descriptions of those programs.

For the most recent information regarding admission requirements, prospective students should refer to the current academic catalog.

Application and Information

Applicants must complete and submit an application form, along with documentation of graduation from an accredited high school or state-approved secondary education curriculum or official documentation of high school graduation equivalency.

Prospective students can go online to BMCprograms.info for program duration, tuition, fees and other costs, median debt, federal salary data, alumni success, programmatic accreditation, and other important details.

For additional information, prospective students should contact:

Director of Admissions
Brown Mackie College — St. Louis
#2 Soccer Park Road
Fenton, Missouri 63026
Phone: 636-651-3290
　　　　888-874-4375 (toll-free)
Fax: 636-651-3349
E-mail: bmcstladm@brownmackie.edu
Web site: http://www.brownmackie.edu/StLouis

BROWN MACKIE COLLEGE — SALINA

SALINA, KANSAS

The College and Its Mission

Brown Mackie College — Salina (Brown Mackie College) is one of over twenty-five locations in the Brown Mackie College family of schools (www.brownmackie.edu), which is dedicated to providing educational programs that prepare students to pursue entry-level positions in a competitive, rapidly changing workplace. Brown Mackie College schools offer bachelor degree, associate degree, certificate, and diploma programs in health sciences, business, information technology, legal studies, and design to over 20,000 students in the Midwest, Southeast, Southwest, and Western United States.

The college was originally founded in July 1892 as the Kansas Wesleyan School of Business. In 1938, the college was incorporated as the Brown Mackie School of Business under the ownership of former Kansas Wesleyan instructors Perry E. Brown and A. B. Mackie; it became Brown Mackie College in January 1975.

Brown Mackie College — Salina is accredited by the Higher Learning Commission and is a member of the North Central Association (NCA), 230 South LaSalle Street, Suite 7-500, Chicago, Illinois 60604-1413; phone 800-621-7440 (toll-free); www.ncahlc.org.

The Associate of Applied Science in occupational therapy assistant program is accredited by the Accreditation Council for Occupational Therapy Education (ACOTE) of the American Occupational Therapy Association (AOTA), located at 4720 Montgomery Lane, P.O. Box 31220, Bethesda, Maryland 20824-1220; phone: 301-652-AOTA.

The Associate of Applied Science in veterinary technology program has provisional programmatic accreditation granted by the American Veterinary Medical Association (AVMA) through the Committee on Veterinary Technician Education and Activities (CVTEA).

Brown Mackie College — Salina is approved and authorized to grant the Associate of Applied Science (A.A.S.) and Associate of General Studies (A.G.D.) degrees by the Kansas Board of Regents, 1000 Southwest Jackson Street, Suite 520, Topeka, Kansas 66612-1368.

Academic Programs

Brown Mackie College — Salina provides higher education to traditional and nontraditional students through associate degree, diploma, and certificate programs that can assist them in enhancing their career opportunities, broadening their perspectives through appropriate general education courses, thinking independently and critically, and improving problem-solving abilities. The college strives to develop within its students the desire for lifelong and continued education.

In most programs, students can participate in day or evening classes, which begin every month. Programs are offered on a year-round basis, providing students with the ability to work uninterrupted toward completion of their programs. Brown Mackie College offers all programs in a unique One Course a Month format. This schedule allows students to focus studies on only one course for four weeks and has proven convenient for students with multiple obligations such as jobs and family.

Associate Degree Programs: The Associate of Applied Science degree is awarded in accounting technology, business management, computer aided design and drafting technology, computer networking and applications, criminal justice, general studies, health and fitness training, health care administration, medical assisting, nursing, occupational therapy assistant, and veterinary technology. An associate degree in general studies is also offered to create a greater level of flexibility for students who may be unsure of their career choice, who want a more generalized education, or who want to transfer to a baccalaureate program.

Diploma Programs: Brown Mackie College — Salina also offers diploma programs in bookkeeping specialist, general business, computer aided designer/drafter, criminal justice specialist, fitness trainer, medical assistant, medical insurance specialist, and networking specialist.

Certificate Programs: Certificate programs are offered in network engineer specialist, nurse aid, IV therapy for practical nurses, and practical nursing.

The American Medical Technologists (AMT), which offers the certification for Registered Medical Assistant (RMA), accepts the accreditation of Brown Mackie College — Salina. Students will qualify to take the RMA certification examination upon graduating the Brown Mackie College — Salina medical assisting and medical assistant programs. Graduates of the 48 credit-hour medical assistant program are not qualified to take the AMT/RMA exam.

Costs

Tuition for the 2011–12 academic year was $294 per credit hour and general fees were $15 per credit hour. Tuition for computer networking was $300 per credit hour and general fees were $25 per credit hour. Tuition for the nursing programs was $361 per credit hour and general fees were $25 per credit hour. Tuition for the occupational therapy assistant program was $361 per credit hour and general fees were $15 per credit hour. The cost of textbooks and other instructional materials varies by program.

Financial Aid

Financial aid is available to those who qualify. Brown Mackie College — Salina maintains a full-time staff of financial aid professionals to assist qualified students in obtaining financial assistance. The college participates in several student aid programs. Forms of financial aid that are available through federal resources include Federal Pell Grants, Federal Supplemental Educational Opportunity Grants (FSEOG), Academic Competitiveness Grant, Federal Work-Study Program awards, Federal Perkins Loans, Federal Stafford Student Loans (subsidized and unsubsidized), and Federal PLUS loans. Eligible students may apply for veterans' educational benefits. Students with physical or mental disabilities that are a handicap to employment may be eligible for training services through the state Vocational Rehabilitation Agency. For further information, students should contact the Brown Mackie College — Salina Student Financial Services Office.

Each year, the college makes available President's Scholarships of $1000 each to qualifying seniors from area high schools. Up to three (3) scholarships may be awarded per high school. In order to qualify, a senior must be graduating from a participating high school, have maintained a cumulative grade point average of at least 2.0, and submitted a brief essay. The student's extracurricular activities and community service are also considered. The President's Scholarship is available only to students enrolling in one of the college's degree programs. Students awarded the scholarship must enroll at Brown Mackie College — Salina between June and September immediately following their high school graduation. Applications for these scholarships can be obtained from the guidance departments of participating high schools. These applications must be completed and returned to the college by March 31.

The Merit Scholarship is a college-sponsored scholarship that may be awarded to students who demonstrate exceptional academic ability. To qualify for a Merit Scholarship, an applicant or student must have scored 21 or higher on the ACT or 900 or higher on the SAT. The maximum amount awarded by this scholarship to any student is $500.

Athletic scholarships may be awarded to students who participate in athletic programs that are sponsored by Brown Mackie College — Salina. Current sports are men's baseball, men's and women's basketball, and women's fast-pitch softball. Maximum awards for any applicant or student are determined by the college president. Further information is available from the Athletic Office. Recipients of athletic scholarships must achieve a cumulative grade point average of at least 2.0 by their graduation. Recipients who fail to maintain full-time status or the required grade point average forfeit their awards.

Faculty

There are 21 full-time and 19 adjunct faculty members. The average student-instructor ratio is 15:1.

Facilities and Resources

In addition to classrooms and computer labs, Brown Mackie College — Salina maintains a library of curriculum-related resources, technical and general education materials, academic and professional periodicals, and audiovisual resources. Internet access is also available for research. The college has a bookstore that stocks texts, courseware, and other educational supplies that are required for courses and a variety of personal, recreational, and gift items, including apparel, supplies, and general merchandise incorporating the Brown Mackie College logo. Hours are posted at the bookstore entrance.

Location

Brown Mackie College — Salina is located at 2106 South Ninth Street in Salina, Kansas.

Admission Requirements

Each applicant for admission is assigned to an Assistant Director of Admissions, who directs the applicant through the steps of the admissions process, providing information on curriculum, policies, procedures, and services and assisting the applicant in setting necessary appointments and interviews.

To qualify for admission, each applicant must provide documentation of graduation from an accredited high school or from a state-approved secondary education curriculum or provide official documentation of high school graduation equivalency. All transcripts become the property of Brown Mackie College. Admission to the college is based upon the applicant meeting the above requirements, a review of the applicant's previous education records, and a review of the applicant's career interests. If previous academic records indicate that the Brown Mackie College education and training programs would not benefit the applicant, the college reserves the right to advise the applicant not to enroll. Special requirements for enrollment into certain programs are discussed in the descriptions of those programs.

For the most recent information regarding admissions requirements, please refer to the most current academic catalog.

Application and Information

Applicants must complete and submit an application form, along with documentation of graduation from an accredited high school or state-approved secondary education curriculum or official documentation of high school graduation equivalency.

Prospective students can go online to BMCprograms.info for program duration, tuition, fees and other costs, median debt, federal salary data, alumni success, programmatic accreditation, and other important details.

For additional information, prospective students should contact:

Director of Admissions
Brown Mackie College — Salina
2106 South Ninth Street
Salina, Kansas 67401
Phone: 785-825-5422
        800-365-0433 (toll-free)
Fax: 785-827-7623
E-mail: bmcsaadm@brownmackie.edu
Web site: http://www.brownmackie.edu/Salina)

BROWN MACKIE COLLEGE —
SAN ANTONIO
SAN ANTONIO, TEXAS

The College and Its Mission

Brown Mackie College — San Antonio (Brown Mackie College) is one of over twenty-five locations in the Brown Mackie College family of schools (www.brownmackie.edu), which is dedicated to providing educational programs that prepare students to pursue entry-level positions in a competitive, rapidly changing workplace. The Brown Mackie College family of schools offers bachelor degree, associate degree, diploma, and certificate programs in health sciences, business, information technology, legal studies, and design to over 20,000 students in the Midwest, Southeast, Southwest, and Western United States.

Brown Mackie College was originally founded and approved by the Board of Trustees of Kansas Wesleyan College in Salina, Kansas on July 30, 1892. In 1938, the college was incorporated as the Brown Mackie School of Business under the ownership of Perry E. Brown and A. B. Mackie, former instructors at Kansas Wesleyan University in Salina, Kansas. Their last names formed the name of Brown Mackie. By January 1975, with improvements in curricula and higher degree-granting status, the Brown Mackie School of Business became Brown Mackie College.

Brown Mackie College — San Antonio is accredited by the Accrediting Council for Independent Colleges and Schools to award associate degrees. The Accrediting Council for Independent Colleges and Schools is listed as a nationally recognized accrediting agency by the United States Department of Education and is recognized by the Council for Higher Education Accreditation. ACICS can be contacted at 750 First Street NE, Suite 980, Washington, D.C. 20002; phone: 202-336-6780.

Brown Mackie College — San Antonio is approved and regulated by the Texas Workforce Commission, Career School and Colleges, Austin, Texas.

Brown Mackie College — San Antonio holds a Certificate of Authorization acknowledging exemption from Texas Higher Education Coordinating Board regulations.

Academic Programs

Brown Mackie College — San Antonio provides higher education to traditional and nontraditional students through associate degree programs that assist in enhancing their career opportunities, broadening their perspectives through appropriate general education courses, thinking independently and critically, and improving problem-solving abilities. The college strives to develop within its students the desire for lifelong and continued education.

Each college quarter comprises twelve weeks. Associate degree programs require a minimum of eight quarters to complete.

Programs are offered on a year-round basis, providing students with the ability to work uninterrupted toward completion of their programs. The college offers all programs in a unique One Course a Month format. This allows students to focus studies on only one course for four weeks. This schedule has proven convenient for students with multiple obligations such as jobs and family.

Associate Degree Programs: The Associate of Science degree is awarded in accounting technology, architectural design and drafting technology, business management, criminal justice, health care administration, information technology, medical assisting, paralegal, pharmacy technology, and surgical technology.

The American Medical Technologists (AMT), which offers the certification for Registered Medical Assistant (RMA), accepts the accreditation of Brown Mackie College — San Antonio. Students will qualify to take the RMA certification examination upon graduating the Brown Mackie College — San Antonio medical assisting program.

Brown Mackie College — San Antonio does not guarantee third-party certification. Outside agencies control the requirements for certifications and are subject to change without notice to Brown Mackie College.

Costs

Tuition in the 2011–12 academic year for all associate degrees was $324 per credit hour; fees were $15 per credit hour. Tuition for the surgical technology program was $360 per credit hour; fees were $15 per credit hour. The cost of textbooks and other instructional materials varies by program.

Financial Aid

Financial aid is available for those who qualify. The college maintains a full-time staff of Student Financial Services Advisers to assist qualified students in obtaining the financial assistance they require to meet their educational expenses. Available resources include federal and state aid, student loans from private lenders, and Federal Work-Study opportunities, both on and off college premises.

Each year, the college makes available President's Scholarships of $1000 each to qualifying seniors from area high schools. Up to three (3) scholarships may be awarded per high school. In order to qualify, a senior must have graduated from a participating high school, must be maintained a cumulative grade point average of at least 2.0, and submitted a brief essay. The student's extracurricular activities and community service are also considered. These scholarships are available only to students enrolling in one of the college's degree programs. Students awarded the scholarship must enroll at Brown Mackie College — San Antonio between June and September immediately following their high school graduation. Applications for these scholarships can be obtained from the guidance departments of participating high schools. These applications must be completed and returned to the college by March 31.

Faculty

Experienced faculty members provide academic support and are committed to the academic and technical preparation of their students. Brown Mackie College — San Antonio has both full-time and part-time instructors, with a student-faculty ratio of 15:1.

Facilities and Resources

A modern facility, Brown Mackie College — San Antonio offers more than 35,000 square feet. The College is equipped with multiple computer labs, housing over 100 computers. High-speed access to the Internet and other online resources are available to students and faculty. Multimedia classrooms are outfitted with overhead projectors, VCR/DVD players, and computers.

In 2012, Brown Mackie College — San Antonio began its transition to using eTextbooks and computer tablets in the classroom. Utilizing these tablets to access expanded course material, students will be able to increase their acumen for using this technology and further enhance their educational experience. Students have the ability to directly download their eTextbooks to their tablet, eliminating the need to carry heavy, physical textbooks and reducing the overall cost of supplies.

The college is nonresidential; public transportation and ample parking at no cost are available. The campus is a smoke-free facility.

Location

Brown Mackie College — San Antonio is conveniently located at 4715 Fredericksburg Road in San Antonio, Texas. The college has a generous parking area and is easily accessible by public transportation.

Admission Requirements

Each applicant for admission is assigned to an Assistant Director of Admissions who directs the applicant through the steps of the admissions process. They provide information on curriculum, policies, procedures, and services and assist the applicant in setting necessary appointments and interviews. To qualify for admission, each applicant must provide documentation of graduation from an accredited high school or from a state-approved secondary education curriculum or provide official documentation of high school graduation equivalency. All transcripts become the property of the college. Admission to the college is based on the applicant meeting the stated requirements, a review of the applicant's previous educational records, and a review of the applicant's career interests. If previous academic records indicate the college's education and training programs would not benefit the applicant, the college reserves the right to advise the applicant not to enroll. Special requirements for enrollment into certain programs are discussed in the descriptions of those programs.

For the most recent information regarding admission requirements, prospective students should refer to the current academic catalog.

Application and Information

Applicants must complete and submit an application form, along with documentation of graduation from an accredited high school or state-approved secondary education curriculum or official documentation of high school graduation equivalency.

Prospective students can go online to BMCprograms.info for program duration, tuition, fees and other costs, median debt, federal salary data, alumni success, programmatic accreditation, and other important details.

For additional information, prospective students should contact:

Director of Admissions
Brown Mackie College — San Antonio
4715 Fredericksburg Road, Suite 100
San Antonio, Texas 78229
Phone: 210-428-2210
      877-460-1714 (toll-free)
Fax: 210-428-2265
E-mail: bmsanadm@brownmackie.edu
Web site: http://www.brownmackie.edu/SanAntonio

BROWN MACKIE COLLEGE — SOUTH BEND

SOUTH BEND, INDIANA

BROWN
MACKIE
COLLEGE
SOUTH BEND℠

The College and Its Mission

Brown Mackie College — South Bend (Brown Mackie College) is one of over twenty-five locations in the Brown Mackie College family of schools (www.brownmackie.edu), which is dedicated to providing educational programs that prepare students to pursue entry-level positions in a competitive, rapidly changing workplace. The Brown Mackie College family of schools offers bachelor degree, associate degree, diploma, and certificate programs in health sciences, business, information technology, legal studies, and design to over 20,000 students in the Midwest, Southeast, Southwest, and Western United States.

Brown Mackie College — South Bend is one of the oldest institutions of its kind in the country and the oldest in the state of Indiana. Established in 1882 as the South Bend Commercial College, the school later changed its name to Michiana College. In 1930, the school was incorporated under the laws of the state of Indiana and was authorized to confer associate degrees and certificates in business. The college relocated to East Jefferson Boulevard in 1987. In September 2009, Brown Mackie College — South Bend officially opened a new 46,000-square-foot facility at 3454 Douglas Road in South Bend, Indiana.

Brown Mackie College — South Bend is accredited by the Accrediting Council for Independent Colleges and Schools to award associate degrees, diplomas, and certificates. The Accrediting Council for Independent Colleges and Schools is listed as a nationally recognized accrediting agency by the United States Department of Education and is recognized by the Council for Higher Education Accreditation. ACICS can be contacted at 750 First Street NE, Suite 980, Washington, D.C. 20002; phone: 202-336-6780.

Brown Mackie College — South Bend is regulated by the Indiana Commission on Proprietary Education, 302 West Washington Street, Indianapolis, Indiana 46204; phone: 317-232-1320 or 800-227-5695 (toll-free). Indiana advertising code AC-0110.

The practical nursing diploma program is accredited by the Indiana State Board of Nursing, 402 West Washington Street, Room W066, Indianapolis, Indiana 46204; phone: 317-234-2043.

The Associate of Science in medical assisting is accredited by the Commission on Accreditation of Allied Health Education Program (www.caahep.org) upon the recommendation of the Curriculum Review Board of the American Association of Medical Assistants Endowment (AAMAE). Commission on Accreditation of Allied Health Education Programs is located at 1361 Park Street, Clearwater, Florida 33756; phone: 727-210-2350.

The Associate of Applied Science in occupational therapy assistant program is accredited by the Accreditation Council for Occupational Therapy Education (ACOTE) of the American Occupational Therapy Association (AOTA), located at 4720 Montgomery Lane, P.O. Box 31220, Bethesda, Maryland 20824-1220; phone: 301-652-AOTA.

The Associate of Applied Science in physical therapist assistant program is accredited by the Commission on Accreditation in Physical Therapy Education (CAPTE) of the American Physical Therapy Association (APTA), 1111 North Fairfax Street, Alexandria, Virginia 22314; phone: 703-706-3241.

The Associate of Science in veterinary technology program has provisional programmatic accreditation granted by the American Veterinary Medical Association (AVMA) through the Committee on Veterinary Technician Education and Activities (CVTEA).

The college is a nonresidential, smoke-free institution.

Academic Programs

Brown Mackie College — South Bend provides higher education to traditional and nontraditional students through associate degrees, diploma, and certificate programs that assist in enhancing their career opportunities, broadening their perspectives through appropriate general education courses, thinking independently and critically, and improving problem-solving abilities.

Each college quarter comprises twelve weeks. Associate degree programs require a minimum of eight quarters to complete. Programs are offered on a year-round basis, providing students with the ability to work uninterrupted toward completion of their programs. The college offers all programs in a unique One Course a Month format. This allows students to focus studies on only one course for four weeks. This schedule has proven convenient for students with multiple obligations such as jobs and family.

Associate Degree Programs: The Associate of Science degree is awarded in accounting technology, business management, computer software technology, criminal justice, health care administration, information technology, medical assisting, paralegal, and veterinary technology.

The Associate of Applied Science degree is awarded in occupational therapy assistant and physical therapist assistant.

Diploma Program: The college offers a diploma program in practical nursing.

Certificate Programs: The college offers certificate programs in accounting, business, computer software applications, criminal justice, medical assistant, and paralegal assistant.

The American Medical Technologists (AMT), which offers the certification for Registered Medical Assistant (RMA), accepts the accreditation of Brown Mackie College — South Bend. Students will qualify to take the RMA certification examination upon graduating the Brown Mackie College — South Bend medical assisting and medical assistant programs. Graduates of the 48 credit-hour medical assistant program are not qualified to take the AMT/RMA exam.

Brown Mackie College — South Bend does not guarantee third-party certification. Outside agencies control the requirements for certifications and are subject to change without notice to Brown Mackie College.

Costs

Tuition for programs in the 2011–12 academic year was $294 per credit hour, with a $15 per credit hour general fee applied to instructional costs for activities and services. Textbooks and other instructional materials vary by program. Tuition for the practical nursing program was $361 per credit hour, with a $25 per credit hour general fee applied to instructional costs for activities and services. Tuition for the physical therapist assistant program was $361 per credit hour with a $15 per credit hour general fee. Tuition for the occupational therapy assistant program was $361 per credit hour with a $15 per credit hour general fee.

Financial Aid

Financial aid is available for those who qualify. The college maintains a full-time staff of Student Financial Services Advisers to assist qualified students in obtaining financial assistance. The college participates in several student aid programs. Forms of financial aid available through federal resources include the Federal Pell Grant Program, Federal Supplemental Educational Opportunity Grant (FSEOG) Program, Federal Work-Study Program, Federal Perkins Loan Program, Federal Stafford

Student Loan Program (subsidized and unsubsidized), and the Federal PLUS Loan Program.

Eligible students may apply for Indiana state awards, such as the Frank O'Bannon Grant Program (formerly the Indiana Higher Education Grant) and Twenty-First Century Scholars Program for high school students, the Core 40 awards, and veterans' educational benefits. Students with physical or mental disabilities that are a handicap may be eligible for training services through the state's Bureau of Vocational Rehabilitation. For further information, students should contact the Student Financial Services Office.

Each year, the college makes available President's Scholarships of $1000 each to qualifying seniors from area high schools. Up to three (3) scholarships may be awarded per high school. In order to qualify, a senior must be graduating from a participating high school, must be maintaining a cumulative grade point average of at least 2.0, and must submit a brief essay. The student's extracurricular activities and community service are also considered. The President's Scholarship is available only to students enrolling in one of the college's degree programs. Students awarded the scholarship must enroll at Brown Mackie College — South Bend between June and September immediately following their high school graduation. Applications for these scholarships can be obtained from the guidance departments of participating high schools. These applications must be completed and returned to the college by March 31.

Faculty

There are 29 full-time and 46 part-time faculty members at the college. The average student-faculty ratio is 12:1. Each student is assigned a program director as an adviser.

Facilities and Resources

Brown Mackie College — South Bend's new location has a generous parking area and is easily accessible by public transportation. The college's smoke-free, three-story 46,000 square foot building offers a modern, professional environment for study. The facility offers "classrooms of the future," with instructor workstations and full multimedia capabilities that include surround sound and projection screens that can be accessed by computer, DVD, and VHS machines. The new facility includes medical, computer, and occupational and physical therapy labs, as well as a library and bookstore. The labs provide students with hands-on opportunities to apply knowledge and skills learned in the classroom. The veterinary technology lab is 2,600 square feet and includes surgery areas, treatment areas, and kennels.

Location

Brown Mackie College — South Bend is conveniently located at 3454 Douglas Road in South Bend, Indiana. The college has a generous parking area and is also easily accessible by public transportation.

Admission Requirements

Each applicant for admission is assigned to an Assistant Director of Admissions, who directs the applicant through the steps of the admissions process, providing information on curriculum, policies, procedures, and services; and assisting the applicant in setting necessary appointments and interviews. To qualify for admission, each applicant must provide documentation of graduation from an accredited high school or from a state-approved secondary education curriculum or provide official documentation of high school graduation equivalency. All transcripts become the property of the college.

Admission to the college is based on the applicant meeting the stated requirements, a review of the applicant's previous educational records, and a review of the applicant's career interests. If previous academic records indicate the college's education and training programs would not benefit the applicant, the college reserves the right to advise the applicant not to enroll. Special requirements for enrollment into certain programs are discussed in the descriptions of those programs.

In addition to the college's general admission requirements, applicants enrolling in the occupational therapy assistant (OTA) program must also meet some additional requirements. They must complete COMPASS assessment before the first course is scheduled to determine if transitional courses are needed (minimal scores: reading 75, writing 60, math 51). If minimum scores or better are attained on all three sections the student is scheduled in CF1000–Professional Development. If the student's scores are below the minimum on any of the sections, the student is advised that they will be placed in transitional course(s). After successful completion of all the required transitional courses, the student will have one opportunity to retake the COMPASS assessment and achieve the minimum score(s). If the student does not successfully obtain the minimum scores in all three sections on the second attempt, the student will not be allowed to continue in the OTA program, but can be considered for another program at Brown Mackie College.

In addition to the college's general admission requirements, applicants enrolling in the physical therapist assistant program must document the following: a minimum high school cumulative grade point average of 3.0 on a 4.0 scale or minimum score of 600 on the GED examination (if taken on or after January 15, 2002) or 60 (if taken before January 15, 2002); a minimum of 12 quarter-credit hours or 9 semester-credit hours of consecutive collegiate coursework with a minimum GPA of 3.0 on a 4.0 scale (may be completed at Brown Mackie College); a biology course in high school or college with a minimum grade of a B (3.0 on a 4.0 scale); and 20 hours (total) of documented observation, volunteer, or employment hours in at least two different physical therapy settings with no less than 8 hours in one setting completed within the past three years.

In addition to the college's general admission requirements, applicants enrolling in the practical nursing program must document the following: fulfillment of Brown Mackie College — South Bend general requirements; complete physical (must be current to within six months of admission); two-step Mantoux TB skin test (must be current throughout schooling); hepatitis B vaccination or signed refusal; up-to-date immunizations, including tetanus and rubella; record of current CPR certification (certification must be current throughout the clinical experience through health-care provider certification or the American Heart Association); and hospitalization insurance or a signed waiver.

For the most recent administration regarding admission requirements, please refer to the current academic catalog.

Application and Information

Applicants must complete and submit an application form, along with documentation of graduation from an accredited high school or state-approved secondary education curriculum or official documentation of high school graduation equivalency.

Prospective students can go online to BMCprograms.info for program duration, tuition, fees and other costs, median debt, federal salary data, alumni success, programmatic accreditation, and other important details.

For additional information, prospective students should contact:

Director of Admissions
Brown Mackie College — South Bend
3454 Douglas Road
South Bend, Indiana 46635
Phone: 574-237-0774
        800-743-2447 (toll-free)
Fax: 574-237-3585
E-mail: bmcsbadm@brownmackie.edu
Web site: http://www.brownmackie.edu/SouthBend)

BROWN MACKIE COLLEGE — TUCSON
TUCSON, ARIZONA

The College and Its Mission

Brown Mackie College — Tucson (Brown Mackie College) is one of over twenty-five locations in the Brown Mackie College family of schools (www.brownmackie.edu), which is dedicated to providing educational programs that prepare students to pursue entry-level positions in a competitive, rapidly changing workplace. Brown Mackie College schools offer bachelor degree, associate degree, diploma, and certificate programs in health sciences, business, information technology, legal studies, and design to over 20,000 students in the Midwest, Southeast, Southwest, and Western United States.

Brown Mackie College was originally founded and approved by the Board of Trustees of Kansas Wesleyan College in Salina, Kansas on July 30, 1892. In 1938, the college was incorporated as The Brown Mackie School of Business under the ownership of Perry E. Brown and A. B. Mackie, former instructors at Kansas Wesleyan University in Salina, Kansas. Their last names formed the name of Brown Mackie. By January 1975, with improvements in curricula and higher degree-granting status, The Brown Mackie School of Business became Brown Mackie College.

Brown Mackie College entered the Arizona market in 2007 when it purchased a school that had been previously established in the Tucson area. That school had an established history in the community and was converted into what is now known as Brown Mackie College — Tucson. The historical timeline of Brown Mackie College — Tucson started in 1972 when Rockland West Corporation first formed a partnership with Lamson Business College. At that time the school was a career college that offered only short-term programs focusing on computer training and secretarial skills. In 1994 the college became accredited as a junior college and began offering associate degrees in academic subjects. The mission was then modified to include the goal of instilling in graduates an appreciation for lifelong learning through the general education courses that became a part of every program.

In 1996 the college applied for and received status as a senior college by the Accrediting Commission of Independent Colleges and Schools. This gave the school the ability to offer course work leading to a Bachelor of Science degree in business administration. Since then the program offerings for bachelor and associate degrees have expanded.

In 1986, the college moved from 5001 East Speedway to the 4585 East Speedway location where it remains today. In 2008, two of the college's three buildings were remodeled which resulted in updated classrooms; networked computer laboratories; new medical, surgical technology, and forensics laboratories; a larger library and offices for student services such as academics, admissions, and student financial services; and a full-service college store. In 2009, the third building was remodeled and provides newer classrooms and a new career services department.

Brown Mackie College — Tucson is accredited by the Accrediting Council for Independent Colleges and Schools to award associate degrees and certificates. The Accrediting Council for Independent Colleges and Schools is listed as a nationally recognized accrediting agency by the United States Department of Education and is recognized by the Council for Higher Education Accreditation. ACICS can be contacted at 750 First Street NE, Suite 980, Washington, D.C. 20002; phone: 202-336-6780.

Brown Mackie College — Tucson is authorized by the Arizona State Board for Private Post-secondary Education, 1400 West Washington Street, Room 2560, Phoenix, Arizona 85007; phone: 602-542-5709; http://azppse.state.az.us.

The Associate of Science in surgical technology program is accredited by the Accrediting Bureau of Health Education Schools.

The Associate of Applied Science in occupational therapy assistant program is accredited by the Accreditation Council for Occupational Therapy Education (ACOTE) of the American Occupational Therapy Association (AOTA), located at 4720 Montgomery Lane, P.O. Box 31220, Bethesda, Maryland 20824-1220; phone: 301-652-AOTA.

Academic Programs

Brown Mackie College — Tucson provides higher education to traditional and nontraditional students through associate degree and diploma programs that assist in enhancing their career opportunities, broadening their perspectives through appropriate general education courses, thinking independently and critically, and improving problem-solving abilities. The college strives to develop within its students the desire for lifelong and continued education.

Each college quarter comprises twelve weeks. Associate degree programs require a minimum of eight quarters to complete. Programs are offered on a year-round basis, providing students with the ability to work uninterrupted toward their degrees. The college offers all programs in a unique One Course a Month format. This allows students to focus studies on only one course for four weeks. This schedule has proven convenient for students with multiple obligations such as jobs and family.

Associate Degree Programs: The Associate of Science degree is awarded in accounting technology, business management, computer networking and security, criminal justice, graphic design, health care administration, information technology, medical assisting, paralegal, and surgical technology.

The Associate of Applied Science degree is awarded in biomedical equipment technology, health and fitness training, and occupational therapy assistant.

Diploma Program: A diploma is awarded in fitness trainer, medical assistant, and practical nursing.

The American Medical Technologists (AMT), which offers the certification for Registered Medical Assistant (RMA), accepts the accreditation of Brown Mackie College — Tucson. Students will qualify to take the RMA certification examination upon graduating the Brown Mackie College — Tucson medical assisting and medical assistant programs. Graduates of the 48 credit-hour medical assistant program are not qualified to take the AMT/RMA exam.

Brown Mackie College — Tucson does not guarantee third-party certification. Outside agencies control the requirements for certifications and are subject to change without notice to Brown Mackie College.

Costs

Tuition in the 2011–12 academic year for most associate and diploma programs was $324 per credit hour; fees were $15 per credit hour. Tuition for the health and fitness training program was $324 per credit hour; fees were $25 per credit hour. Tuition for the surgical technology program was $340 per credit hour; fees were $15 per credit hour. Tuition for the occupational therapy assistant program was $361 per credit hour; fees were $15 per credit hour. Tuition for the practical nursing program was $361 per credit hour; fees were $25 per credit hour. Textbook and other instructional expenses vary by program.

Financial Aid

Financial aid is available for those who qualify. The college maintains a full-time staff of Student Financial Services Advisers to assist qualified students in obtaining the financial assistance they require to meet their educational expenses. Available resources include federal and state aid, student loans from private lenders, and Federal Work-Study opportunities, both on and off college premises.

Each year, the college makes available President's Scholarships of $1000 each to qualifying seniors from area high schools. Up to three (3) scholarships may be awarded per high school. In order to qualify, a senior must be graduating from a participating high school, must be maintaining a cumulative grade point average of at least 2.0, and must submit a brief essay. The student's extracurricular activities and community service are also considered. These scholarships are available only to students enrolling in one of the college's degree programs. Students awarded the scholarship must enroll at Brown Mackie College — Tucson between June and September immediately following their high school graduation. Applications for these scholarships can be obtained from the guidance departments of participating high schools. These applications must be completed and returned to the college by March 31.

Faculty

Experienced faculty members provide academic support and are committed to the academic and technical preparation of their students. The college has 15 full-time and 35 part-time instructors, with a student-faculty ratio of 12:1. Each student is assigned a faculty adviser.

Facilities and Resources

A modern facility, Brown Mackie College — Tucson offers more than 31,000 square feet. The college is equipped with multiple computer labs housing over 200 computers. High-speed access to the Internet and other online resources are available for students and faculty. Multimedia classrooms are outfitted with overhead projectors, VCR/DVD players, and computers. The college is nonresidential; public transportation and parking at no cost are available.

Location

Brown Mackie College — Tucson is conveniently located at 4585 East Speedway Boulevard in Tucson, Arizona. The college has a generous parking area and is also easily accessible by public transportation.

Admission Requirements

Each applicant for admission is assigned to an Assistant Director of Admissions who directs the applicant through the steps of the admissions process. They provide information on curriculum, policies, procedures, and services and assist the applicant in setting necessary appointments and interviews. To qualify for admission, each applicant must provide documentation of graduation from an accredited high school or from a state-approved secondary education curriculum or provide official documentation of high school graduation equivalency. All transcripts become the property of the college. Admission to the college is based on the applicant meeting the stated requirements, a review of the applicant's previous educational records, and a review of the applicant's career interests. If previous academic records indicate the college's education and training programs would not benefit the applicant, the college reserves the right to advise the applicant not to enroll. Special requirements for enrollment into certain programs are discussed in the descriptions of those programs.

For the most recent information regarding admission requirements, please refer to the current academic catalog.

Application and Information

Applicants must complete and submit an application form, along with documentation of graduation from an accredited high school or state-approved secondary education curriculum or official documentation of high school graduation equivalency.

Prospective students can go online to BMCprograms.info for program duration, tuition, fees and other costs, median debt, federal salary data, alumni success, programmatic accreditation, and other important details.

For additional information, prospective students should contact:

Senior Director of Admissions
Brown Mackie College — Tucson
4585 East Speedway Boulevard, Suite 204
Tucson, Arizona 85712
Phone: 520-319-3300
Fax: 520-325-0108
E-mail: bmctuadm@brownmackie.edu
Web site: http://www.brownmackie.edu/Tucson

BROWN MACKIE COLLEGE — TULSA
TULSA, OKLAHOMA

The College and Its Mission

Brown Mackie College — Tulsa (Brown Mackie College) is one of over twenty-five locations in the Brown Mackie College family of schools (www.brownmackie.edu), which is dedicated to providing educational programs that prepare students to pursue entry-level positions in a competitive, rapidly changing workplace. Brown Mackie College schools offer bachelor degree, associate degree, diploma, and certificate programs in health sciences, business, information technology, legal studies, and design to over 20,000 students in the Midwest, Southeast, Southwest, and Western United States.

Brown Mackie College — Tulsa was founded in 2008 as a branch of Brown Mackie College — South Bend, Indiana.

Brown Mackie College — Tulsa is accredited by the Accrediting Council for Independent Colleges and Schools to award associate degrees and diplomas. The Accrediting Council for Independent Colleges and Schools is listed as a nationally recognized accrediting agency by the United States Department of Education and is recognized by the Council for Higher Education Accreditation. ACICS can be contacted at 750 First Street NE, Suite 980, Washington, D.C. 20002; phone: 202-336-6780.

This institution is licensed by the Oklahoma Board of Private Vocational Schools (OBPVS), 3700 North Classen Boulevard, Suite 250, Oklahoma City, Oklahoma 73118; phone: 405-528-3370.

This institution has been granted authority to operate in Oklahoma by the Oklahoma State Regents for Higher Education (OSRHE), 655 Research Parkway, Suite 200, Oklahoma City, Oklahoma 73101; phone: 405-225-9100; www.okhighered.org.

The occupational therapy assistant program is accredited by the Accreditation Council for Occupational Therapy Education (ACOTE) of the American Occupational Therapy Association (AOTA), located at 4720 Montgomery Lane, P.O. Box 31220, Bethesda, Maryland 20824; phone: 301-652-AOTA.

Academic Programs

Brown Mackie College — Tulsa provides higher education to traditional and nontraditional students through bachelor's degree, associate degree, and diploma programs that assist in enhancing their career opportunities, broadening their perspectives through appropriate general education courses, thinking independently and critically, and improving problem-solving abilities. The college strives to develop within its students the desire for lifelong and continued education.

Each college quarter comprises twelve weeks. Associate degree programs require a minimum of eight quarters to complete.

Programs are offered on a year-round basis, providing students with the ability to work uninterrupted toward completion of their programs. The college offers all programs in a unique One Course a Month format. This allows students to focus on only one course for four weeks. This schedule has proven convenient for students with multiple obligations such as jobs and family.

Associate Degree Programs: The Associate of Applied Science degree is awarded in accounting technology, business management, criminal justice, health care administration, information technology, medical assisting, nursing, occupational therapy assistant, paralegal, and surgical technology.

Diploma Programs: Diploma programs are offered in accounting, business, criminal justice, medical assistant, and paralegal assistant.

The American Medical Technologists (AMT), which offers the certification for Registered Medical Assistant (RMA), accepts the accreditation of Brown Mackie College — Tulsa. Students will qualify to take the RMA certification examination upon graduating the Brown Mackie College — Tulsa medical assisting and medical assistant programs. Graduates of the 48 credit-hour medical assistant program are not qualified to take the AMT/RMA exam.

Brown Mackie College — Tulsa does not guarantee third-party certification. Outside agencies control the requirements for certifications and are subject to change without notice to Brown Mackie College.

Costs

Tuition for programs in the 2011–12 academic year was $294 per credit hour, with a $15 per credit hour general fee applied to instructional costs for activities and services. Tuition for the occupational therapy program was $361 per credit hour with a $15 per credit hour general fee applied to instructional costs for activities. Tuition for the surgical technology program was $340 per credit hour with a $15 per credit hour general fee applied to instructional costs for activities. Tuition for the nursing program was $390 per credit hour with a $25 per credit hour general fee applied to instructional costs for activities. Textbooks and other instructional materials vary by program.

Financial Aid

Financial aid is available for those who qualify. The college maintains a full-time staff of Student Financial Services Advisers to assist qualified students in obtaining financial assistance. The college participates in several student aid programs. Forms of financial aid available through federal resources include the Federal Pell Grant Program, Federal

Supplemental Educational Opportunity Grant (FSEOG) Program, Federal Work-Study Program, Federal Perkins Loan Program, Federal Stafford Student Loan Program (subsidized and unsubsidized), and the Federal PLUS Loan Program.

Faculty

There are 10 full-time and several adjunct faculty members. The average class size is 14 students. Each student has a faculty and student adviser.

Facilities and Resources

Opened in 2008, this modern facility offers more than 25,000 square feet of tastefully decorated classrooms, laboratories, and office space designed to specifications of the college for its business, medical, and technical programs. Instructional equipment is comparable to current technology used in business and industry today. Modern classrooms for special instructional needs offer multimedia capabilities with surround sound and overhead projectors accessible through computer, DVD, or VHS. Internet access and instructional resources are available at the college's library. Experienced faculty members provide academic support and are committed to the academic and technical preparation of their students.

The college is nonresidential; public transportation and ample parking at no cost are available.

Location

Brown Mackie College — Tulsa is conveniently located at 4608 South Garnett Road, Suite 110 in Tulsa, Oklahoma. The college has a generous parking area and is easily accessible by public transportation.

Admission Requirements

Each applicant for admission is assigned to an Assistant Director of Admissions, who directs the applicant through the steps of the admissions process, providing information on curriculum, policies, procedures, and services and assisting the applicant in setting necessary appointments and interviews. To qualify for admission, applicants must be a graduate of a public or private high school or a correspondence school or education center that is accredited by an agency that is recognized by the U.S. or State of Oklahoma Department of Education or any of its approved agents. As part of the admissions process applicants must sign a document attesting to graduation or completion and containing the information to obtain verification of such. Verification must be obtained within the first term (90 days) or the student will be withdrawn from the institution following established guidelines for withdrawn students noted in the catalog. Title IV aid will not be dispersed until verification of graduation or completion has been received by the college. All transcripts become the property of the college.

Students are given an assessment of academic skills. Although the results of this assessment do not determine eligibility for admission, they provide the college with a means of determining the need for academic support.

For the most recent information regarding admission requirements, please refer to the current academic catalog.

Application and Information

Applicants must complete and submit an application form, along with documentation of graduation from an accredited high school or state-approved secondary education curriculum or official documentation of high school graduation equivalency.

Prospective students can go online to BMCprograms.info for program duration, tuition, fees and other costs, median debt, federal salary data, alumni success, programmatic accreditation, and other important details.

For additional information, prospective students should contact:

Senior Director of Admissions
Brown Mackie College — Tulsa
4608 South Garnett Road, Suite 110
Suite 110
Tulsa, Oklahoma 74146
Phone: 918-628-3700
          888-794-8411 (toll-free)
Fax: 918-828-9083
E-mail: bmctuladm@brownmackie.edu
Web site: http://www.brownmackie.edu/Tulsa

CAMDEN COUNTY COLLEGE
BLACKWOOD, NEW JERSEY

The College and Its Mission

Camden County College (CCC) is a fully-accredited comprehensive public community college in New Jersey. CCC provides accessible and affordable education. Since its inception in 1967, the College has grown to offer 100-plus associate degree and occupational certificate programs along with noncredit development courses and customized job training. The College also provides support services students need to transfer for further studies or begin a career. The College has three locations: the main campus in Blackwood, the Camden City Campus in the University District in Camden, and the William G. Rohrer Center in Cherry Hill, New Jersey. Satellite locations include the Regional Emergency Training Center (RETC) in Blackwood and the Technical Institute (TI) in Sicklerville.

The College is one of the largest community colleges in New Jersey and one of the most sophisticated in the nation. Recognized nationally as a leader in technology programs, the College is also regionally acknowledged as a vital resource for transfer education, customized training, and cultural events.

The main campus is situated on 320 sylvan acres near Philadelphia and New York, allowing students to take advantage of the cities for recreation, education, and work opportunities.

A capital initiative is transforming many of the facilities and structural amenities on the main campus. A new science building is under construction; roads, athletic fields, and parking are being upgraded. The College is easily accessible from Route 42 via Exit 7B, which leads directly into the College's main entrance.

College housing is not available. If not commuting, students may reside at local apartment complexes that are within walking distance of the main campus.

Over 20 student clubs and service organizations, national honor societies, and other activities are available. The College also has a student newspaper, the *Campus Press*, and a radio station.

A variety of athletic activities are offered for both experienced competitors and casual participants. Varsity teams for both men and women compete against other two-year college teams in the New Jersey Garden State Athletic Conference and Region XIX of the National Junior College Athletic Association. Men compete in soccer, golf, cross-country, basketball, and baseball. Women compete in soccer, golf, cross-country, basketball, and softball. Students can use College athletic facilities, including an all-weather quarter-mile track; an athletic center with a weight and fitness room; basketball/volleyball courts, and various outdoor playing fields.

Academic Programs

Camden County College offers the following associate degrees: A.A., A.S., A.F.A., and A.A.S., as well as C.T. and C.A. certificates.

The College operates on a fifteen- or thirteen-week semester and offers courses in arts, humanities, social sciences, business, computers, mathematics, health care, and science. Online and hybrid courses are offered. Summer sessions are five, seven, and eight weeks long; and online and weekend courses are offered as well. The College's academic calendar is accessible at www.camdencc.edu.

In general, approximately 60 credits are required to earn an associate degree and about 30 credits for a certificate. The total number of credits required varies by program.

Career programs (A.A.S.) include: accounting; addictions counseling; automotive technology (apprentice); automotive technology: GM/ASEP; biotechnology; biotechnology: cell and tissue culture option; biotechnology: forensic science option; CADD: computer-aided drafting and design; computer graphics; computer graphics: game design and development; computer information systems; computer information systems: personal computer option; computer integrated manufacturing/engineering technology; computer systems technology; dental assisting; dental hygiene; dietetic technology; engineering technology; electrical electronic engineering; engineering technology: electromechanical engineering; engineering technology: mechanical engineering; film and television production; finance; fire science technology; fire science technology: administration option; health information technology; health science; health science: certified medical assistant option; health science: surgical technology option; hospitality technology; management; management: business paraprofessional management option; management: small business management option; marketing; massage therapy; medical laboratory technology; office systems technology administrative assistant; office systems technology administrative assistant: information processing option; ophthalmic science technology; paralegal studies; paramedic sciences; paramedic sciences: paramedic educational management option; photonics: laser/electro-optic technology; photonics: laser/electro-optic technology fiber-optic option; respiratory therapy; sign language interpreter education; technical studies; veterinary technology; and video imaging.

Transfer programs (A.A./A.F.A./A.S.) include applied and fine arts option/liberal arts and science (A.A.); biology option/liberal arts and science (A.S.); business administration option/liberal arts and science (A.S.); business administration option: information systems track/liberal arts and science (A.S.); chemistry option/liberal arts and science (A.S.); communications option/liberal arts and science (A.A.); communications option: photojournalism track/liberal arts and science (A.A.); communications option: public relations/advertising track/liberal arts and science (A.A.); computer graphics option/liberal arts and science (A.A.); computer graphics option: electronic publishing track/liberal arts and science (A.A.); computer science (A.A.); computer science (A.S.); criminal justice (A.S.); dance option/liberal arts and science (A.A.); deaf studies option/liberal arts and science (A.A.); early childhood education option/liberal arts and science (A.A.); elementary/secondary education (A.S.); engineering science (A.S.); English option/liberal arts and science (A.A.); environmental science option/liberal arts and science (A.S.); food science option/liberal arts and science (A.S.); health and exercise science option/liberal arts and science (A.S.); history option/liberal arts and science (A.A.); human services (A.S.); human services: developmental disabilities option (A.S.); human services: early childhood education option (A.S.); international studies option/liberal arts and science (A.A.); language and culture option/liberal arts and science (A.A.); law, government, and politics option/liberal arts and science (A.A.); liberal arts and science (A.A.); liberal arts and science (A.S.); mathematics option/liberal arts and science (A.S.); music option/liberal arts and science (A.A.); nursing: Our Lady of Lourdes School of Nursing (A.S.); nursing: pre-nursing option/liberal arts and science (A.S.); photography option/liberal arts and science (A.A.); physics option/liberal arts and science (A.S.); pre-pharmacy option/liberal arts and science (A.S.); psychology option/liberal arts and science (A.A.); psychosocial rehabilitation and treatment (A.S.); secondary education in biology option/liberal arts and science (A.S.); secondary education in chemistry option/liberal arts and science (A.S.); secondary education in mathematics option/liberal arts and science (A.S.); speech option/liberal arts and science (A.A.); sport management (A.S.); studio art (A.F.A.); and theater option/liberal arts and science (A.A.).

Academic Certificate Programs (C.T.) offered are computer applications programming; computer graphics; computer integrated manufacturing technology; computer programming; computer systems technology; dental assisting; developmental disabilities; film and television production assistant; medical coding; nutrition care manager; office assistant; personal computer specialist; photonics: fiber-optic technical specialist; practical nursing; social services; Web design development

Certificate of Achievement Programs (C.A.) include addictions counseling; alternate energy engineering technology; automotive general technician; behavioral health care; CADD: computer-aided drafting and design; computer-aided manufacturing technician; computer science; computerized accounting specialist; crime and intelligence analysis; culinary; educational interpreter training;

electronic health records: implementation support specialist; electronic health records: practice workflow and information management redesign specialist; electronic health records: trainer; emergency and disaster management; fine art techniques; food services management; fundamentals of policing; hotel and resort management; industrial controls: programmable logic controller; instructional aide paraprofessional core; Linux/UNIX administration; massage therapy; meeting and event planning; Microsoft Office specialist; multi-skilled technician; music recording; ophthalmic medical technician; ophthalmic science apprentice; paramedic sciences; personal trainer; relational database management system using ORACLE; and surgical technology.

Off-Campus Programs

Camden County College has articulation agreements with regional four-year colleges and universities to offer bachelor's degree completion programs on the CCC campus. More information is available online at www.camdencc.edu.

Credit for Nontraditional Learning Experiences

CCC offers a number of opportunities including evaluating educational experiences approved by the American Council on Education and the Program on Non-Collegiate Sponsored Instruction and validating armed services training among others. More details can be found in the College *Catalog* at www.camdencc.edu.

Costs

For students who enter in September 2012, tuition costs are $101 per credit for in-county residents, $105 per credit for out-of-county residents, and $180 per credit for international students. The general service fee per credit is $26, the facility fee per credit is $4, and the insurance fee is $3 per semester. Course fees vary depending on courses taken, and hourly instruction fees vary depending on courses taken.

The cost of books and supplies is estimated to be $1450 for one year for a full-time student. Students who choose e-textbooks instead of new books can reduce the cost by up to 50 percent. Students can also save by participating in book rentals and buybacks. Actual costs depend on the specific courses chosen.

Financial Aid

Financial aid comes in the form of scholarships, grants, loans and work-study. Students are required to file a Free Application for Federal Student Aid (FAFSA) as soon as possible after January 1 of each year (the College's school code is 006865), as well as the College's authorization and certification form. Financial aid applications filed by May 1 and completed by June 1 of each year are given priority. Students must be admitted before an offer of financial aid can be made. Additional application information is available at www.camdencc.edu.

Faculty

The student-faculty ratio is 29:1. Faculty members are dedicated to teaching and supporting students throughout the academic year. In addition to the College's advisory staff, some faculty members may assist in providing academic advisement for their field of specialization. Full-time faculty members hold advanced degrees as do adjuncts.

Student Body Profile

Of the College's 23,052 credit students served in the financial year 2011, 75 percent are Camden County residents and 96 percent are New Jersey residents. Approximately 53 percent of the students are Caucasian, 22.1 percent African American, 5.3 percent Asian, 7.6 percent Hispanic, 0.08 percent American Indian/Alaskan native, 0.03 percent Native Hawaiian/Pacific Islander, 2.0 percent are two or more, and 8.9 unknown/not reported. The mean student age is 27.

Academic Facilities

The library is located on the Blackwood Campus, and an e-library is located at the Cherry Hill location. Students on the Camden City Campus have access to the Rutgers University library and gym located near CCC in the city's University District. CCC offers open-access computer labs, laser labs, automotive facility, vision care facility, dental facility, and numerous other laboratories. The Otto R. Mauke Community Center houses a cyber café, student activities offices, cafeteria, and student lounge areas. The facility

also contains student support offices including advising, a Barnes and Noble bookstore, student employment, student transfer, and international student offices. The Papiano Gymnasium hosts a fitness center and variety of indoor and outdoor sports.

Location

The 320-acre main campus is located in Blackwood, New Jersey. The College is easily reached from the interstate highway system, is located a short distance from the PATCO high-speed train line service to and from Philadelphia, and is available via NJ Transit buses. Lincoln Hall's Marlin Art Gallery and the Dennis Flyer Memorial Theatre, Little Theatre, and the Madison Connector Building's Civic Hall, home to the Center for Civic Leadership and Responsibility are venues for College, county, and regional communities. The facilities host musical concerts, dance performances, theatrical presentations, lectures, workshops, community events, and a regional arts center. The conference center on the Camden City Campus is used by businesses, community and government organizations. The Regional Emergency Training Center is used by continuing education, police, and fire service students. The Technical Institute provides training in a variety of trades.

Admission Requirements

The College has open enrollment. Students must be 18 years of age. A few selected programs have additional admission criteria. Prospective students should apply online at www.camdencc.edu. The Web site provides details about the enrollment process. There is no cost to apply to CCC.

Application and Information

Processing of applications for admission each year begins no later than February 15 for the fall semester and no later than October 1 for the spring semester. Rolling admission for a semester occurs through the last day of the semester.

Office of Admissions and Registration Services
Camden County College
P.O. Box 200
College Drive
Blackwood, New Jersey 08012
Phone: 856-227-7200
Website: http://www.camdencc.edu

The Connector Building contains light-filled atrium space for students to relax or purchase a beverage or snack at the Connector Café. In addition to lounge areas, it houses the Center for Civic Leadership and Responsibility, two auditoriums, and classrooms.

FASHION INSTITUTE OF TECHNOLOGY
State University of New York
NEW YORK, NEW YORK

The College and Its Mission

The Fashion Institute of Technology (FIT) is New York's celebrated urban college for creative and business talent. A State University of New York (SUNY) college of art, design, business, and technology, FIT is a dynamic mix of innovative achievers, original thinkers, and industry pioneers. FIT balances a real-world-based curriculum and hands-on instruction with a rigorous liberal arts foundation. The college marries design and business and supports individual creativity in a collaborative environment. It offers a complete college experience with a vibrant student and residential life.

With an extraordinary location at the center of New York City—world capital of the arts, business, and media—FIT maintains close ties with the design, fashion, advertising, communications, and international commerce industries. Academic departments consult with advisory boards of noted experts to ensure that the curriculum and classroom technology reflect current industry practices. The college's faculty of successful professionals brings experience to the classroom, while field trips, guest lectures, and sponsored competitions introduce students to the opportunities and challenges of their disciplines.

FIT's mission is to produce well-rounded graduates—doers and thinkers who raise the professional bar to become the next generation of business pacesetters and creative icons.

FIT's four residence halls house 2,300 students in fully furnished single-, double-, triple-, and quad-occupancy rooms and suites. All students taking 12 or more credits are eligible for FIT housing, and students may apply for housing no matter where they live. Students can choose either traditional or apartment-style accommodations. Various dining options and meal plans are available. Counselors and student staff members live in the residence halls, helping students adjust to college life and New York City.

FIT is accredited by the Middle States Association of Colleges and Schools, the National Association of Schools of Art and Design, and the Council for Interior Design Accreditation.

Academic Programs

FIT serves approximately 10,000 full-time, part-time, and evening/weekend students from the metropolitan area, New York State, across the country, and around the world, offering more than forty programs leading to the A.A.S., B.F.A., B.S., M.A., M.F.A., and M.P.S. degrees. Each undergraduate program includes a core of traditional liberal arts courses, providing students with a global perspective, critical-thinking skills, and the ability to communicate effectively. All degree programs are designed to prepare students for creative and business careers and to provide them with the prerequisite studies to go on to baccalaureate, master's, or doctoral degrees, if they wish.

All students complete a two-year A.A.S. program in their major area and the liberal arts. They may then choose to go on to a related, two-year B.F.A. or B.S. program or begin their careers with their A.A.S. degree, which qualifies them for entry-level positions.

Associate Degree Programs: For the A.A.S. degree, FIT offers eleven majors through its School of Art and Design and four through its Jay and Patty Baker School of Business and Technology. The A.A.S. programs are accessories design*, advertising and marketing communications*, communication design foundation*, fashion design*, fashion merchandising management* (with an online option), fine arts, illustration, interior design, jewelry design*, menswear, photography, production management: fashion and related industries, textile development and marketing*, textile/surface design*, and visual presentation and exhibition design. Programs with an asterisk (*) are also available in a one-year format for students with sufficient transferable credits.

Bachelor's Degree Programs: Many A.A.S. graduates choose to pursue a related, two-year baccalaureate program at the college. FIT offers twenty-four baccalaureate programs—thirteen B.F.A. programs through the School of Art and Design, ten B.S. programs

through the Baker School of Business and Technology, and one B.S. program through the School of Liberal Arts. The B.F.A. programs are accessories design, advertising design, computer animation and interactive media, fabric styling, fashion design (with specializations in children's wear, intimate apparel, knitwear, special occasion, and sportswear), fine arts, graphic design, illustration, interior design, packaging design, photography and the digital image, textile/surface design, and toy design. The B.S. programs are advertising and marketing communications, art history and museum professions, cosmetics and fragrance marketing, direct and interactive marketing, entrepreneurship for the fashion and design industries, fashion merchandising management, home products development, international trade and marketing for the fashion industries, production management: fashion and related industries, technical design, and textile development and marketing.

Liberal Arts Minors: The School of Liberal Arts offers FIT students the opportunity to minor in a variety of liberal arts areas in two forms: traditional subject-based minors and interdisciplinary minors unique to the FIT liberal arts curriculum. Selected minors include film and media, economics, Asian studies, and psychology.

Evening/Weekend Programs: FIT's School of Continuing Education and Professional Studies provides evening and weekend credit and noncredit classes to students and working professionals interested in pursuing a degree or certificate or furthering their knowledge of a particular industry, while balancing the demands of career or family. There are nine degree programs available through evening/weekend study: advertising and marketing communications (A.A.S. and B.S.), communication design foundation (A.A.S.), fashion design (A.A.S.), fashion merchandising management (A.A.S. and B.S.), graphic design (B.F.A.), illustration (B.F.A.), and international trade and marketing for the fashion industries (B.S.).

Honors Program: The Presidential Scholars honors program, available to academically exceptional students in all majors, offers special courses, projects, colloquia, and off-campus activities that broaden horizons and stimulate discourse. Presidential Scholars receive priority course registration and an annual merit stipend.

Internships: Internships are a required element of most programs and are available to all matriculated students. Nearly one third of FIT student interns are offered employment on completion of their internships; past sponsors include American Eagle Outfitters, Bloomingdale's, Calvin Klein, Estée Lauder, Fairchild Publications, MTV, and Saatchi & Saatchi.

Precollege Programs: Precollege programs (Saturday Live, Sunday Live, and Summer Live) are available to middle and high school students during the fall, spring, and summer. More than sixty courses provide the chance to learn in an innovative environment, develop art and design portfolios, explore the business and technological sides of many creative careers, and discover natural talents and abilities.

Off-Campus Programs

The study-abroad experience lets students immerse themselves in diverse cultures and prepares them to live and work in a global community. FIT has two programs in Italy—one in Milan, one in Florence—where students study fashion design or fashion merchandising management and gain firsthand experience in the dynamics of European fashion. FIT also offers study-abroad options in countries like Australia, China, England, France, and Mexico. Students can study abroad during the winter or summer sessions, for a semester, or for a full academic year.

Costs

As a SUNY college, FIT offers affordable tuition for both New York State residents and nonresidents. The 2011–12 associate-level tuition per semester for in-state residents was $1987; for nonresidents, $5961. Baccalaureate-level tuition per semester was $2734 for in-state residents and $7245 for nonresidents.

Per-semester housing costs were $6119–$6299 for traditional residence hall accommodations with mandatory meal plan and $5241–$9521 for apartment-style accommodations. Meal plans ranged from $1595 to $2045 per semester. Textbook costs and other nominal fees, such as locker rental or laboratory use, vary per program. All costs are subject to change.

Financial Aid

FIT offers scholarships, grants, loans, and work-study employment for students with financial need. Nearly all full-time, matriculated undergraduate students who complete the financial aid application process receive some type of assistance. The college directly administers its own institutional grants and scholarships, which are provided by the FIT Foundation.

College-administered funding includes Federal Pell Grants, Federal Perkins Loans, Federal Supplemental Educational Opportunity Grants, Federal Work-Study Program awards, and the Federal Family Educational Loan Program, which includes student and parent loans. New York State residents who meet eligibility guidelines may also receive Tuition Assistance Program (TAP) and/or Educational Opportunity Program (EOP) grants. Financial aid applicants must file the Free Application for Federal Student Aid (FAFSA) and should also apply to all available outside sources of aid. Additional documentation may be requested by the Financial Aid Office. Applications for financial aid should be completed prior to February 15 for fall admission or November 1 for spring admission.

Faculty

FIT's faculty is drawn from top professionals in academia, art, design, communications, and business, providing a curriculum rich in real-world experience and traditional educational values. Student-instructor interaction is encouraged, with a maximum class size of 25, and courses are structured to foster participation, independent thinking, and self-expression.

Student Body Profile

Fall 2011 enrollment was 10,223 with 8,179 students enrolled in degree programs. Thirty-seven percent of degree-seeking students are enrolled in the School of Art and Design; 41 percent are in the Baker School of Business and Technology. The average age of full-time degree seekers is 23. Forty-four percent of FIT's students are New York City residents, 23 percent are New York State (non–New York City) residents, and 24 percent are out-of-state residents or international students. The ethnic/racial makeup of the student body is approximately 0.15 percent American Indian or Alaskan, 11.68 percent Asian, 9.86 percent black, 16.93 percent Hispanic, 3.37 percent multiracial, 0.67 percent Native Hawaiian or Pacific Islander, and 57.33 percent white. There are 773 international students.

Student Activities

Participation in campus life is encouraged, and the college is home to more than seventy student organizations, societies, athletic teams, major-related groups, and clubs based on areas of interest. Each organization is open to all students who have paid their activity fee.

Student Government: The Student Council, the governing body of the Student Association, grants all students the privileges and responsibilities of citizens in a self-governing college community. Faculty committees often include student representatives, and the president of the student government sits on FIT's Board of Trustees.

Athletics: FIT has intercollegiate teams in cross-country, half marathon, outdoor track, dance, table tennis, tennis, soccer, swimming and diving, and volleyball. Athletics and Recreation offers group fitness classes at no extra cost to students. Open gym activities allow students to participate in team and individual sports.

Events: Concerts, dances, field trips, films, flea markets, and other events are planned by the Student Association and Programming Board and various clubs. Student-run publications include a campus newspaper, a literary and art magazine, and the FIT yearbook.

Facilities and Resources

FIT's campus provides its students with classrooms, laboratories, and studios that reflect the most advanced educational and industry practices. The Fred P. Pomerantz Art and Design Center houses drawing, painting, photography, printmaking, and sculpture studios; display and exhibit design rooms; a model-making work-shop; and a graphics printing service bureau. The Peter G. Scotese Computer-Aided Design and Communications Center provides the latest technology in computer graphics, design, photography, and animation. Other cutting-edge facilities include a professionally equipped fragrance-development laboratory—the only one of its kind on a U.S. college campus—cutting and sewing labs, a design/research lighting laboratory, knitting lab, broadcasting studio, multimedia foreign languages laboratory, and twenty-three computer labs containing Mac and PC workstations.

The Museum at FIT, New York City's only museum dedicated to fashion, contains one of the most important collections of fashion and textiles in the world. The museum operates year-round, and its exhibitions are free and open to the public. The Gladys Marcus Library provides more than 300,000 volumes of print, nonprint, and electronic materials. The periodicals collection includes over 500 current subscriptions, with a specialization in international design and trade publications; online resources include more than 90 searchable databases.

The David Dubinsky Student Center offers lounges, a game room, a student radio station, the Style Shop (a student-run boutique), a dining hall and full-service Starbucks, student government and club offices, comprehensive health services and a counseling center, two gyms, a state-of-the-art fitness center, and a dance studio.

Location

Occupying an entire block in Manhattan's Chelsea neighborhood, FIT makes extensive use of the city's creative, commercial, and cultural resources, providing students with unrivaled internship opportunities and professional connections. A wide range of cultural and entertainment options are available within a short walk of the campus, as is convenient access to several subway and bus lines and the city's major rail and bus transportation hubs.

Admission Requirements

Applicants for admission must be either candidates for or recipients of a high school diploma or a General Educational Development (GED) certificate. Admission is based on class rank, strength and performance in college-preparatory course work, and the student essay. A portfolio evaluation is required for art and design majors. Specific portfolio requirements are explained on FIT's Web site. SAT and ACT scores are required for placement in math and English classes and they are required for students applying to the Presidential Scholars honors program. Letters of recommendation are not required.

Transfer students must submit official transcripts for credit evaluation. Students may qualify for the one-year A.A.S. option if they hold a bachelor's degree or if they have a minimum of 30 transferable college credits, including 24 credits equivalent to FIT's liberal arts requirements.

Students seeking admission to a B.F.A. or B.S. program must hold an A.A.S. degree from FIT or an equivalent college degree and must meet the prerequisites for the specific major. Further requirements may include an interview with a departmental committee, review of academic standing, and portfolio review for applicants to B.F.A. programs. Any student who applies for baccalaureate-level transfer to FIT from a four-year program must have completed a minimum of 60 credits, including the requisite art or technical courses and the liberal arts requirements.

Application and Information

Students wishing to visit FIT are encouraged to attend a group information session and take a tour of FIT's campus. The visit schedule is available online at http://www.fitnyc.edu/visitfit. A virtual tour of the campus can be found at http://www.fitnyc.edu/virtualtour. Candidates may apply online at http://www.fitnyc.edu/admissions. More information is available by contacting:

Admissions

Fashion Institute of Technology

227 West 27 Street, Room C139

New York, New York 10001-5992

Phone: 212-217-3760

    800-GO-TO-FIT (toll-free)

Email: fitinfo@fitnyc.edu

Web site: http://www.fitnyc.edu

    http://www.facebook.com/FashionInstituteofTechnology

FIDM/FASHION INSTITUTE OF DESIGN & MERCHANDISING
LOS ANGELES, CALIFORNIA

The Institute and Its Mission

FIDM/Fashion Institute of Design & Merchandising provides a dynamic and exciting community of learning in the fashion, graphics, interior design, digital media, and entertainment industries. Students can launch into one of thousands of exciting careers in as little as two years. FIDM offers two-year and four-year degree programs—Associate of Arts (A.A.), A.A. professional designation, A.A. advanced study, and Bachelor of Science (B.S.).

FIDM offers a highly focused education that prepares students for the professional world. Students can choose from twenty specialized creative business and design majors.

Established in 1969, FIDM is a private college that enrolls more than 7,500 students a year and has graduated over 47,000 students. Graduates receive membership in the Alumni Association, which keeps them well connected while providing up-to-the-minute alumni news and information. FIDM alumni chapters can be found in thirty-five locations around the United States, Europe, and Asia.

Career planning and job placement are among the most important services offered by the college. Career assistance includes job search techniques, preparation for employment interviews, resume preparation, virtual portfolios, and job adjustment assistance. FIDM's full-time Career Center department and advisers partner one-on-one with current students and graduates to help them move forward on their career path, within their chosen major. Employers post over 19,000 jobs a year on FIDM's alumni job search site, which is available 24/7 exclusively to FIDM students and graduates. FIDM career advisers connect students to internships and directly to professionals in the industry. FIDM also offers job fairs, open portfolio days, and networking days to allow students to meet alumni and industry leaders face-to-face. Because of the college's long-standing industry relationships, many firms come to FIDM first to recruit its students. Over 90 percent of FIDM graduates in all majors are successfully employed in their field of study within six months of graduation. Some of FIDM's successful graduates include celebrity designers Nick Verreos, Monique Lhuillier, and the co-founder of Juicy Couture, as well as Hollywood costume designer Marlene Stewart.

FIDM's ethnically and culturally diverse student body is one of the factors that attracts students. The current population includes students from more than thirty different countries. The Student Activities Department plans and coordinates social activities, cultural events, and community projects. Student organizations include the ASID student chapter, Cross-Cultural Student Alliance, American Association of Textile Chemists and Colorists, Phi Theta Kappa honor society, and the Alumni Association. The students also produce *MODE*, the student magazine that promotes awareness about the design industry, current events, and FIDM student life.

FIDM is accredited by the Accrediting Commission for Community and Junior and Senior Colleges of the Western Association of Schools and Colleges (WASC) and the National Association of Schools of Art and Design (NASAD).

Academic Programs

FIDM offers two-year Associate of Arts (A.A.) degree programs, bachelor's degree programs, advanced study programs, and professional designation programs. There are 20 specialized creative business and design majors to choose from.

Students can choose from the following Associate of Arts degrees: Apparel Industry Management, Beauty Industry Merchandising and Marketing, Digital Media, Fashion Design, Fashion Knitwear Design, Graphic Design, Interior Design, Jewelry Design, Merchandise Marketing, Merchandising Product Development, Textile Design, and Visual Communications. All of these programs offer the highly specialized curriculum of a specific major combined with a core general education/liberal arts foundation.

Many FIDM A.A. graduates take their skills to the next level through FIDM's B.S. in Business Management program as well. Only FIDM graduates from A.A. majors are eligible to apply to the bachelor's program, which is offered at the Los Angeles and San Francisco campuses and available online. Students from all FIDM majors study and collaborate on business projects and take courses in accounting, human resource management, international finance, ethics, leadership, and more, giving them extensive knowledge of managing a business and the creative edge that is a growing necessity in the corporate world. FIDM's unique industry partnerships offer exciting opportunities for students through internships, events, and guest speakers, with companies such as Forever 21, JCPenney, Mattel, NBC Universal, Oakley, Smashbox, and Stila.

Students from other regionally accredited college programs have the opportunity to complement their previous college education by enrolling in FIDM's professional designation programs. Students can determine which credits will transfer and receive a personalized schedule toward completion of their professional designation program by consulting with FIDM admissions advisers. FIDM offers professional designation programs in Apparel Industry Management, Beauty Industry Management, Digital Media, Fashion Design, Fashion Knitwear Design, Graphic Design, Interior Design, International Manufacturing and Product Development, Jewelry Design, Textile Design, and Visual Communications. For more information about FIDM transfer programs, students can visit http://fidm.edu/go/admissionstransfer.

FIDM operates on a four-quarter academic calendar. New students may begin their studies at the start of any quarter throughout the year. Detailed information about FIDM majors and curriculum is also available online at http://fidm.edu/en/Majors/.

Department chairs and other trained staff members assist students in selecting the correct sequence of courses to complete degree requirements. The counseling department provides personal guidance and referral to outside counseling services and matches peer tutors to specific students' needs. Individual Development and Education Assistance (IDEA) Centers at each campus provide students with additional educational assistance in the areas of writing, mathematics, computer competency, study skills, research skills, and reading comprehension.

FIDM's eLearning program, which includes the B.S. in business management and some classes in other majors, ensures that a student's educational experience can take place anywhere. The online courses are designed to replicate the experience of classes on campus. Students in the eLearning program are granted the same high-quality education as students on campus and have immediate access to valuable campus resources, including the FIDM Library, career advisers, and instructors.

Off-Campus Programs

Internships are available within each major. Paid and volunteer positions provide work experience for students to gain practical application of classroom skills.

FIDM provides the opportunity for students to participate in academic study tours in Europe, Asia, and New York. These tours are specifically designed to broaden and enhance the specialized education offered at FIDM. Participants may earn academic credit under faculty-supervised directed studies. Exchange programs are also available with Esmod, Paris; Instituto Artictico dell' Abbigliamento Marangoni, Milan; Accademia Internazionale d'Alta Mode e d'Arte del Costume Koefia, Rome; St. Martins School of Art, London; College of Distributive Trades, London; and Janette Klein Design School, Mexico City.

Costs

For the 2011–12 academic year, tuition and fees started at $26,000, depending on the selected major. Textbooks and supplies started at $2100 per year, depending on the major. First-year application fees range from $225 for California residents to $525 for international students.

Financial Aid

There are several sources of financial funding available to the student, including federal financial aid and education loan programs, California state aid programs, institutional loan programs, and FIDM awards and scholarships. The FIDM Student Financial Services office and FIDM admissions advisers work one-on-one with students and parents to help them find funding for their FIDM education. More information on FIDM scholarships and financial aid can be found at http://fidm.edu/go/fidmscholarships.

Faculty

FIDM faculty members are selected as specialists in their fields, working professionals with impressive resumes and invaluable industry connections. They bring daily exposure from their industry into the classroom for the benefit of the students. In pursuit of the best faculty members, consideration is given to both academic excellence and practical experience.

Facilities and Resources

FIDM's award-winning campuses feature design studios with computer labs and innovative study spaces, spacious classrooms, imaginative common areas, and state-of-the-industry technology. Computer labs support and enhance the educational programs of the Institute. Specialized labs offer computerized cutting and marking; graphic, interior, and textile design; word processing; and database management.

The FIDM Library goes beyond traditional sources of information. It houses a print and electronic collection of over 2.5 million titles that encompass all subject areas, with an emphasis on fashion, interior design, retailing, and costume. The library subscribes to over 160 international and national periodicals, offering the latest information on art, design, graphics, fashion, beauty, business, and current trends. The FIDM Library also features an international video library, subscriptions to major predictive services, interior design workrooms, textile samples, a trimmings/findings collection, and access to the Internet.

The FIDM Museum & Galleries' permanent and study collections contain more than 12,000 garments from the eighteenth century to present day, including film and theater costumes. One of the largest collections in the United States, it features top designer holdings including Chanel, Yves Saint Laurent, Dior, and Lacroix. The collection also includes items from the California Historical Society (First Families), the Hollywood Collection, and the Rudi Gernreich Collection.

Location

FIDM's main campus is in the heart of downtown Los Angeles near the famed California Mart and Fashion District. There are additional California campuses in San Francisco, San Diego, and Orange County. A virtual tour of the campuses and their locations is available at http://fidm.edu/en/Visit+FIDM/Launch+Virtual+Tour.

FIDM Los Angeles is nestled at the center of an incredibly vibrant apparel and entertainment hub, surrounded by the fashion, entertainment, jewelry, and financial districts. It is situated next to beautiful Grand Hope Park, a tree-filled oasis amid the hustle and bustle of downtown Los Angeles. Newly renovated by acclaimed architect Clive Wilkinson, FIDM San Francisco stands in the heart of historic Union Square. The country's third-largest shopping area and stimulating atmosphere combined with the industry-based staff and faculty make this campus as incredible as the city in which it is located.

The FIDM Orange County campus is a dynamic visual experience with ultramodern lofts, an indoor/outdoor student lounge, eye-popping colors, and a one-of-a-kind audiovisual igloo. Also designed by world-renowned architect Clive Wilkinson, this campus has received several prestigious architectural awards and has been featured in numerous national magazines.

FIDM San Diego's gorgeous campus overlooks PETCO Park and is near the historic Gaslamp district and the San Diego harbor. FIDM's newest campus is sophisticated, stylish, and tech savvy, reflecting the importance of California's fastest-growing city and its appeal to the global industry.

Admission Requirements

Students are accepted into one of FIDM's specialized Associate of Arts degree programs which offer 16–25 challenging courses per major. Associate of Arts programs are designed for high school graduates or applicants with strong GED scores. These programs offer the highly specialized curriculum of a specific major, as well as a traditional liberal arts/ general studies foundation. Official transcripts from high school/secondary schools and all colleges/universities attended are needed to apply. International students must send transcripts accompanied by official English translations. Three recommendations from teachers, counselors, or employers are also required for admission. FIDM provides a reference request form on its Web site in the Admissions section under "How To Apply." All references must be sealed and mailed to the school when applying. An admissions essay portion and portfolio entrance project requirement, which is specific to the student's selected major, are also available on the Web site's Admissions section under "How To Apply."

For more information on the application process, prospective students can go to www.fidm.edu.

Application and Information

FIDM/Fashion Institute of Design & Merchandising
919 South Grand Avenue
Los Angeles, California 90015
United States
Phone: 800-624-1200 (toll-free)
Fax: 213-624-4799
Web site: http://www.fidm.edu
    http://www.facebook.com/home.php#!/FIDMCollege
    http://twitter.com/#!/FIDM

FIDM Los Angeles (exterior campus)

VALLEY FORGE MILITARY COLLEGE
WAYNE, PENNSYLVANIA

The College and Its Mission

Valley Forge Military College—The Military College of Pennsylvania™ (VFMC) is a private, coeducational residential college that offers the freshman and sophomore years of college. The primary mission of the College is to prepare students for transfer to competitive four-year colleges and universities. Established in 1935, the College has a long tradition of fostering personal growth through a comprehensive system built on the five cornerstones that make Valley Forge unique: academic excellence, character development, leadership, personal motivation, and physical development for all students regardless of race, creed, or national origin. The diverse student body represents more than nineteen states and four countries. The College has an excellent transfer record, with 95 percent of cadets accepted to their first- or second-choice schools. More than 63 percent were admitted to the top-tier schools in the country.

Valley Forge Military College is the only college in the northeastern United States that offers qualified freshmen the opportunity to participate in an Early Commissioning Program, leading to a commission as a second lieutenant in the U.S. Army Reserves or Army National Guard at the end of their sophomore year. The U.S. Air Force Academy, the U.S. Coast Guard Academy, the U.S. Military Academy, and the U.S. Naval Academy have all sponsored cadets through their Foundation Scholarship Programs and other programs to attend Valley Forge Military College.

In October 2007, the Pennsylvania House of Representatives adopted a resolution introduced by then state Representative Bryan Lentz, designating Valley Forge Military College as the official military college of the commonwealth of Pennsylvania. For the next two years, Valley Forge Military College used the trademarked tagline "The Military College of Pennsylvania™," and now the designation is official. This in no way will change the name of the school; it will remain Valley Forge Military College. This resolution sets in stone what many local citizens, family members, and alumni already know—Valley Forge provides elite military education and training for future leaders in every aspect of society and is in a class of its own.

The College is accredited by the Middle States Association of Colleges and Schools and is approved by the Pennsylvania State Council of Education and the Commission on Higher Education of the Pennsylvania State Department of Education. The College is a member of the National Association of Independent Colleges and Universities, the Association of Independent Colleges/Universities of Pennsylvania, the Pennsylvania Association of Two-Year Colleges, and the Association of Military Colleges and Schools in the United States.

Academic Programs

All students are required to complete an academic program of 60 credits, including a core program of approximately 45 credits designed to establish the essential competencies that are necessary for continued intellectual development and to facilitate the transfer process. Included in the core program are one semester of computer science, two semesters of English, one semester of literature, two semesters of mathematics, one semester of science, and one semester of Western civilization. Qualified cadets must also complete a minimum of two semesters of military science. To satisfy the requirement for the associate degree, cadets must complete at least 15 additional credits in courses related to their selected area of concentration. Associate degrees are awarded upon satisfactory completion of the degree requirements with a quality point average of 2.0 or higher.

Associate Degree Programs: Valley Forge Military College offers concentrations in business, criminal justice, general studies, leadership, and liberal arts, leading to an Associate of Arts degree, as well as concentrations in general studies, life sciences, physical sciences, and pre-engineering, leading to an Associate of Science degree.

Transfer Arrangements: Transfer of academic credits and completion of the baccalaureate degree are facilitated by established relationships with a number of outstanding colleges and universities, including agreements with the neighboring institutions of Cabrini College, Eastern University, and Rosemont College.

Credit for Nontraditional Learning Experiences

Valley Forge Military College may give credit for demonstrated proficiency in areas related to college-level courses. Sources used to determine such proficiency are the College-Level Examination Program (CLEP), Advanced Placement (AP) examinations, Defense Activity for Nontraditional Education Support (DANTES), and the Office of Education Credit and Credentials of the American Council on Education (ACE). All such requests must be approved by the Office of the Dean.

Costs

The annual charge for 2011–12 was $40,265. This charge included haircuts, maintenance, room and board, tuition, uniforms, and other fees. Optional expenses may include fee-based courses, such as aviation, driver's education, membership in the cavalry troop or artillery battery, or scuba. A fee is charged for Health Center confinement over 24 hours' duration. For information on the payment plan, students should contact the Business Office.

Financial Aid

The College offers a combination of merit- and need-based scholarships and grants as well as endowed scholarships based on donor specifications to help VFMC cadets finance their education. The academic scholarships reward incoming and returning cadets for demonstrated academic excellence. Performance scholarships are awarded to eligible cadets who participate in the athletic teams, band, or choir. To qualify for federal, state, and VFMC grants, students must file the Free Application for Federal Student Aid (FAFSA) by the published priority deadlines. In addition, qualified cadets in the advanced ROTC commissioning program are eligible for two-year, full-tuition scholarships. These scholarships are supplemented by assistance for room and board provided by the College. The FAFSA is also required for ROTC scholarship applications.

Valley Forge Military College offers federal student aid to eligible cadets in the form of Federal Pell Grants, Federal Supplemental Educational Opportunity Grants (FSEOG), Federal Work-Study (FWS) Program positions, Federal Stafford Student Loans, and Parent Loans for Undergraduate Students (PLUS) through the Federal Family Education Loan Program. Applicants must file the FAFSA and the VFMC financial aid application for consideration for all student aid.

Faculty

There are 12 full-time and 11 part-time faculty members holding the academic rank of assistant professor, associate professor, instructor, or professor. These faculty members are selected for their professional ability and strong personal leadership qualities; 50 percent of the full-time staff members hold doctorates in their field. Faculty members perform additional duties as advisers and athletic coaches of extracurricular activities. The

Military Science Department has 5 active-duty Army officers and 4 noncommissioned officers assigned as full-time faculty members for the ROTC program. The faculty-student ratio is approximately 1:12. Classes are small, and the classroom atmosphere contributes to a harmonious relationship between faculty members and the students.

Student Body Profile

The military structure of Valley Forge provides extraordinary opportunities for cadets to develop and exercise leadership abilities. The Corps of Cadets is a self-administering body organized in nine company units along military lines, with a cadet officer and noncommissioned officer organization for cadet control and administration. The College's cadets are appointed to major command positions in the Corps. The First Captain is generally a sophomore in the College. Cadet leadership and positive peer pressure within this structured setting result in a unique camaraderie among cadets. Cadets, through their student representatives, cooperate with the administration in enforcing regulations regarding student conduct. The Student Advisory Council represents the cadets in the school administration. The Dean's Council meets regularly to discuss aspects of academic life.

Student Activities

The proximity to many colleges and universities ensures a full schedule of local college-oriented events in addition to Valley Forge's own activities. Cadets are encouraged to become involved in community-service activities. The scholarship-supported Regimental Band has performed for U.S. presidents, royalty, and countless military and social events. The Regimental Chorus has performed at the Capitol Building in Washington, D.C.; New York's Carnegie Hall; and the Philadelphia Academy of Music. In addition, eligible students can participate in VFMC honor societies: Alpha Beta Gamma, Lambda Alpha Epsilon, or Phi Theta Kappa. Other available activities include Black Student Union, business and political clubs, flight training, French Club, participation in the local Radnor Fire Company, and Rotoract.

Sports: Athletics and physical well-being are important elements in a Valley Forge education. The aim of the program is to develop alertness, all-around fitness, character, competitive spirit, courage, esprit de corps, leadership, and genuine desire for physical and mental achievement. For students aspiring to compete at the Division I-A or Division I-AA level, Valley Forge's residential college football and basketball programs offer a distinctive opportunity that combines a strong academic transfer program with a highly successful athletic program that has habitually placed players at the national level. Continuing a legacy that began with its high school program, in only eight years, the College has placed 40 players on national-level teams in basketball and football. In the last seven years, the Valley Forge wrestling program has also produced 3 National Champions and 7 All-Americans in the National Collegiate Wrestling Association. Students may also compete at the collegiate level in men's and women's cross-country, men's and women's track and field, lacrosse, co-ed soccer, women's basketball, women's softball, women's volleyball, and tennis. Club and interscholastic teams are available in golf, and riflery.

Facilities and Resources

Campus buildings are equipped to meet student needs. A fiber-optic, Internet-capable computer network connects all campus classrooms, dormitory rooms, laboratories, and the library. All rooms are computer accessible and provide access to CadetNET, the institutional local area network. This network provides access to the library and the Internet. College classrooms are located in two buildings and contain biology, chemistry, and physics laboratories. A computer laboratory supports the computer science curriculum and student requirements through a local area network.

Library and Audiovisual Services: The May H. Baker Memorial Library is a learning resource center for independent study and research. The library has more than 100,000 volumes and audiovisual materials, microfilm, and periodicals and houses the Cadet Achievement Center. It provides online database access, membership in the Tri-State Library Consortium, and computer links to ACCESS Pennsylvania and other databases to support the College requirements.

Location

Valley Forge Military College is situated on a beautifully landscaped 100-acre campus in the Main Line community of Wayne, 15 miles west of Philadelphia and close to Valley Forge National Historic Park. Ample opportunities exist for cadets to enjoy cultural and entertainment resources and activities in the Philadelphia area.

Admission Requirements

Admission to the College is based upon review of an applicant's SAT or ACT scores, high school transcript, recommendations from a guidance counselor, and personal interview. Students may be accepted for midyear admission. Minimum requirements for admission on a nonprobation status are a high school diploma or equivalency diploma with a minimum 2.0 average, rank in the upper half of the class, and minimum combined SAT score of 850 or ACT score of 17. The College reviews the new SAT standards and scores on a case-by-case basis. An international student for whom English is a second language must have a minimum score of 550 on the paper-based version of the Test of English as a Foreign Language (TOEFL). Up to 20 percent of an entering class may be admitted on a conditional or probationary status, and individual entrance requirements may be waived by the Dean of the College for students who display a sincere commitment to pursuing a college degree.

Application and Information

Valley Forge Military College follows a program of rolling admissions. Applicants are notified of the admission decision as soon as their files are complete. A nonrefundable registration fee of $25 is required of all applicants.

For application forms and further information, students should contact:

College Admissions Officer
Valley Forge Military College
1001 Eagle Road
Wayne, Pennsylvania 19087
Phone: 800-234-VFMC (toll-free)
E-mail: admissions@vfmac.edu
Web site: http://college.vfmac.edu

On the campus of Valley Forge Military College.

Indexes

2011–12 Changes in Institutions

Following is an alphabetical listing of institutions that have recently closed, merged with other institutions, or changed their name or status. In the case of a name change, the former name appears first, followed by the new name.

Academy of Court Reporting (Akron, OH): *closed.*

The Academy of Health Care Professions (Houston, TX): *name changed to College of Health Care Professions.*

Allied College (Maryland Heights, MO): *name changed to Anthem College–Maryland Heights.*

Angley College (Deland, FL): *closed.*

Barstow College (Barstow, CA): *name changed to Barstow Community College.*

Berkeley College (Woodland Park, NJ): *now classified as 4-year college.*

Berkeley College–New York City Campus (New York, NY): *now classified as 4-year college.*

Bryant & Stratton College (Eastlake, OH): *name changed to Bryant & Stratton College - Eastlake Campus.*

Bryant & Stratton College (Parma, OH): *name changed to Bryant & Stratton College - Parma Campus.*

Bryant & Stratton College (Milwaukee, WI): *name changed to Bryant & Stratton College - Milwaukee Campus.*

Cambridge Career College (Yuba City, CA): *name changed to Cambridge Junior College.*

CHI Institute, Broomall Campus (Broomall, PA): *name changed to Kaplan Career Institute, Broomall Campus.*

CHI Institute, Franklin Mills Campus (Philadelphia, PA): *name changed to Kaplan Career Institute, Franklin Mills Campus.*

Colegio Universitario de San Juan (San Juan, PR): *now classified as 4-year college.*

Community & Technical College at West Virginia University Institute of Technology (Montgomery, WV): *name changed to Bridgemont Community & Technical College.*

Culinary Institute Alain & Marie LeNotre (Houston, TX): *name changed to Culinary Institute LeNotre.*

DeKalb Technical College (Clarkston, GA): *name changed to Georgia Piedmont Technical College.*

Denver Academy of Court Reporting (Westminster, CO): *name changed to Prince Institute–Rocky Mountains Campus.*

Edison State Community College (Piqua, OH): *name changed to Edison Community College.*

Ellis Hospital School of Nursing (Schenectady, NY): *name changed to Ellis School of Nursing.*

Everest Institute (Atlanta, GA): *no longer degree granting.*

The Florida School of Midwifery (Gainseville, FL): *name changed to The Florida School of Traditional Midwifery.*

Florida Technical College (Auburndale, FL): *name changed to Southern Technical College.*

Forrest Junior College (Anderson, SC): *name changed to Forrest College.*

Fortis College Cuyahoga Falls (Cuyahoga Falls, OH): *name changed to Fortis College.*

Fortis College–Ravenna (Ravenna, OH): *name changed to Fortis College.*

Gulf Coast Community College (Panama City, FL): *name changed to Gulf Coast State College.*

Heart of Georgia Technical College (Dublin, GA): *name changed to Oconee Fall Line Technical College–South Campus.*

High-Tech Institute (Phoenix, AZ): *name changed to Anthem College–Phoenix.*

High-Tech Institute (Sacramento, CA): *name changed to Anthem College–Sacramento.*

High-Tech Institute (Orlando, FL): *name changed to Anthem College–Orlando.*

High-Tech Institute (Marietta, GA): *name changed to Anthem College–Atlanta.*

High-Tech Institute (St. Louis Park, MN): *name changed to Anthem College–St. Louis Park.*

High-Tech Institute (Kansas City, MO): *name changed to Anthem College–Kansas City.*

High-Tech Institute (Las Vegas, NV): *name changed to Anthem Institute–Las Vegas.*

High-Tech Institute (Memphis, TN): *name changed to Anthem Career College.*

High-Tech Institute (Nashville, TN): *name changed to Anthem Career College–Nashville.*

Institute of American Indian Arts (Santa Fe, NM): *now classified as 4-year college.*

ITT Technical Institute (Indianapolis, IN): *now classified as 4-year college.*

Kaplan Career Institute, Harrisburg (Harrisburg, PA): *name changed to Kaplan Career Institute, Harrisburg Campus.*

Kaplan College, Arlington (Arlington, TX): *name changed to Kaplan College, Arlington Campus.*

Kaplan College, Dallas (Dallas, TX): *name changed to Kaplan College, Dallas Campus.*

Kaplan College, Denver Campus (Thornton, CO): *closed.*

Kaplan College–Las Vegas Campus (Las Vegas, NV): *name changed to Kaplan College, Las Vegas Campus.*

Kaplan College, Merrillville Campus (Merrillville, IN): *closed.*

Kaplan College, Panorama City Campus (Panorama City, CA): *closed.*

Kaplan College, Pembroke Pines (Pembroke Pines, FL): *name changed to Kaplan College, Pembroke Pines Campus.*

Kent State University at Geauga (Burton, OH): *now classified as 4-year college.*

Lincoln Technical Institute (Denver, CO): *name changed to Lincoln College of Technology.*

Lincoln Technical Institute (Indianapolis, IN): *name changed to Lincoln College of Technology.*

Lincoln Technical Institute (Plymouth Meeting, PA): *closed.*

Lonestar College–Cy-Fair (Cypress, TX): *name changed to Lone Star College–CyFair.*

Lonestar College–Kingwood (Kingwood, TX): *name changed to Lone Star College–Kingwood.*

Lonestar College–Montgomery (Conroe, TX): *name changed to Lone Star College–Montgomery.*

Lonestar College–North Harris (Houston, TX): *name changed to Lone Star College–North Harris.*

Lonestar College–Tomball (Tomball, TX): *name changed to Lone Star College–Tomball.*

Louisiana State University at Alexandria (Alexandria, LA): *now classified as 4-year college.*

Louisiana Technical College (Baton Rouge, LA): *name changed to Capital Area Technical College–Baton Rouge Campus.*

Louisiana Technical College–Florida Parishes Campus (Greensburg, LA): *name changed to Northshore Technical College–Florida Parishes Campus.*

Louisiana Technical College–Northeast Louisiana Campus (Winnsboro, LA): *name changed to Northeast Louisiana Technical College–Northeast Campus.*

Louisiana Technical College–Young Memorial Campus (Morgan City, LA): *name changed to South Central Louisiana Technical College–Young Memorial Campus.*

Maui Community College (Kahului, HI): *name changed to University of Hawaii Maui College.*

MedVance Institute (Baton Rouge, LA): *name changed to Fortis College.*

MedVance Institute (Cookeville, TN): *name changed to Fortis Institute.*

Miami–Jacobs College (Dayton, OH): *name changed to Miami-Jacobs Career College..*

Mid-America Baptist Theological Seminary (Cordova, TN): *now classified as 4-year college.*

New England Institute of Technology (Warwick, RI): *now classified as 4-year college.*

New York College of Health Professions (Syosset, NY): *now classified as 4-year college.*

New York Film Academy (Los Angeles, CA): *now classified as 4-year college.*

North Central Industrial Technical Education Center (Ridgway, PA): *closed.*

Northeast Kansas Technical Center of Highland Community College (Atchison, KS): *merged into a single entry for Highland Community College (Highland, KS).*

Northwest Aviation College (Auburn, WA): *closed.*

Orlando Culinary Academy (Orlando, FL): *name changed to Le Cordon Bleu College of Culinary Arts in Orlando.*

Ouachita Technical College (Malvern, AR): *name changed to College of the Ouachitas.*

Platt College (Cerritos, CA): *closed.*

Platt College (Huntington Beach, CA): *closed.*

Platt College–Los Angeles (Alhambra, CA): *name changed to Platt College.*

Rasmussen College Eden Prairie (Eden Prairie, MN): *name changed to Rasmussen College Bloomington.*

Rasmussen College Pasco County (Holiday, FL): *name changed to Rasmussen College New Port Richey.*

Rasmussen College Rockford, Illinois (Rockford, IL): *name changed to Rasmussen College Rockford.*

Riverside Community College District (Riverside, CA): *name changed to Riverside City College.*

St. Catharine College (St. Catharine, KY): *now classified as 4-year college.*

Sandersville Technical College (Sandersville, GA): *name changed to Oconee Fall Line Technical College–North Campus.*

Sanford-Brown College (Hazelwood, MO): *closed.*

Sanford-Brown Institute–Monroeville (Pittsburgh, PA): *name changed to Sanford-Brown Institute–Wilkins Township.*

Savannah River College (Augusta, GA): *closed.*

Scottsdale Culinary Institute (Scottsdale, AZ): *name changed to Le Cordon Bleu College of Culinary Arts in Scottsdale.*

Sisseton-Wahpeton Community College (Sisseton, SD): *name changed to Sisseton-Wahpeton College.*

Southwestern College of Business (Florence, KY): *name changed to Lincoln College of Technology.*

Southwestern College of Business (Cincinnati, OH): *name changed to Lincoln College of Technology.*

Southwestern College of Business (Cincinnati, OH): *name changed to Lincoln College of Technology.*

Southwestern College of Business (Dayton, OH): *name changed to Lincoln College of Technology.*

Southwestern College of Business (Franklin, OH): *name changed to Lincoln College of Technology.*

Stark State College of Technology (North Canton, OH): *name changed to Stark State College.*

TESST College of Technology (Alexandria, VA): *closed.*

Texas Culinary Academy (Austin, TX): *name changed to Le Cordon Bleu College of Culinary Arts in Austin.*

Tri-State Business Institute (Erie, PA): *name changed to Fortis Institute.*

Universidad Central del Caribe (Bayamón, PR): *now classified as 4-year college.*

University of Cincinnati Raymond Walters College (Cincinnati, OH): *name changed to University of Cincinnati Blue Ash.*

University of Northwestern Ohio (Lima, OH): *now classified as 4-year college.*

University of Puerto Rico at Carolina (Carolina, PR): *now classified as 4-year college.*

Utah State University–College of Eastern Utah (Price, UT): *merged into a single entry for Utah State University (Logan, UT) by request from the institution.*

Valencia Community College (Orlando, FL): *name changed to Valencia College.*

WyoTech (Fremont, CA): *name changed to WyoTech Fremont.*

WyoTech (West Sacramento, CA): *name changed to WyoTech Sacramento.*

WyoTech (Blairsville, PA): *name changed to WyoTech Blairsville.*

WyoTech (Laramie, WY): *name changed to WyoTech Laramie.*

Associate Degree Programs at Two-Year Colleges

ACCOUNTING

Aiken Tech Coll (SC)
Albany Tech Coll (GA)
Alvin Comm Coll (TX)
Amarillo Coll (TX)
Anoka-Ramsey Comm Coll (MN)
Anoka-Ramsey Comm Coll, Cambridge Campus (MN)
Athens Coll (GA)
Atlanta Tech Coll (GA)
Augusta Tech Coll (GA)
Bainbridge Coll (GA)
Beaufort County Comm Coll (NC)
Berkeley City Coll (CA)
Blackhawk Tech Coll (WI)
Brookhaven Coll (TX)
Bunker Hill Comm Coll (MA)
Burlington County Coll (NJ)
Carroll Comm Coll (MD)
Casper Coll (WY)
Central Carolina Comm Coll (NC)
Central Carolina Tech Coll (SC)
Central Georgia Tech Coll (GA)
Central Oregon Comm Coll (OR)
Central Wyoming Coll (WY)
Century Coll (MN)
Chandler-Gilbert Comm Coll (AZ)
Chattahoochee Tech Coll (GA)
Chattahoochee Valley Comm Coll (AL)
Chipola Coll (FL)
Chippewa Valley Tech Coll (WI)
City Colls of Chicago, Harry S. Truman College (IL)
Clinton Comm Coll (NY)
Coll of Business and Technology (FL)
Coll of DuPage (IL)
Coll of Southern Maryland (MD)
Coll of the Ouachitas (AR)
Colorado Mountain Coll (CO)
Colorado Mountain Coll, Alpine Campus (CO)
Colorado Mountain Coll, Timberline Campus (CO)
Columbus Tech Coll (GA)
Comm Coll of Philadelphia (PA)
Comm Coll of Rhode Island (RI)
Comm Coll of Vermont (VT)
Consolidated School of Business, York (PA)
Copiah-Lincoln Comm Coll (MS)
Corning Comm Coll (NY)
Cowley County Comm Coll and Area Vocational–Tech School (KS)
Dakota Coll at Bottineau (ND)
Delaware Tech & Comm Coll, Jack F. Owens Campus (DE)
Delaware Tech & Comm Coll, Stanton/Wilmington Campus (DE)
Delaware Tech & Comm Coll, Terry Campus (DE)
Dutchess Comm Coll (NY)
Eastern Idaho Tech Coll (ID)
Edison Comm Coll (OH)
El Centro Coll (TX)
Elgin Comm Coll (IL)
Elmira Business Inst (NY)
El Paso Comm Coll (TX)
Fayetteville Tech Comm Coll (NC)
Florida State Coll at Jacksonville (FL)
Foothill Coll (CA)
Forrest Coll (SC)
Fox Valley Tech Coll (WI)

GateWay Comm Coll (AZ)
Gateway Comm Coll (CT)
Gateway Tech Coll (WI)
Genesee Comm Coll (NY)
Georgia Highlands Coll (GA)
Georgia Northwestern Tech Coll (GA)
Georgia Piedmont Tech Coll (GA)
Gwinnett Tech Coll (GA)
Harford Comm Coll (MD)
Harper Coll (IL)
Hawkeye Comm Coll (IA)
Hesser Coll, Concord (NH)
Hesser Coll, Manchester (NH)
Hesser Coll, Nashua (NH)
Hesser Coll, Portsmouth (NH)
Hesser Coll, Salem (NH)
Highland Comm Coll (IL)
Highline Comm Coll (WA)
Housatonic Comm Coll (CT)
Houston Comm Coll System (TX)
Howard Comm Coll (MD)
Illinois Central Coll (IL)
Illinois Eastern Comm Colls, Olney Central College (IL)
Illinois Valley Comm Coll (IL)
Indian River State Coll (FL)
Iowa Lakes Comm Coll (IA)
Itasca Comm Coll (MN)
Ivy Tech Comm Coll–Lafayette (IN)
James Sprunt Comm Coll (NC)
Jamestown Comm Coll (NY)
Jefferson Comm Coll (NY)
Johnston Comm Coll (NC)
John Wood Comm Coll (IL)
Kankakee Comm Coll (IL)
Kansas City Kansas Comm Coll (KS)
Kaskaskia Coll (IL)
Kent State U at Ashtabula (OH)
Kent State U at East Liverpool (OH)
Kent State U at Tuscarawas (OH)
Kilian Comm Coll (SD)
Kingsborough Comm Coll of the City U of New York (NY)
Lake Michigan Coll (MI)
Lake Region State Coll (ND)
Lanier Tech Coll (GA)
Laramie County Comm Coll (WY)
Lincoln Land Comm Coll (IL)
Long Island Business Inst (NY)
Los Angeles Harbor Coll (CA)
Lower Columbia Coll (WA)
Macomb Comm Coll (MI)
Manchester Comm Coll (CT)
Massachusetts Bay Comm Coll (MA)
McHenry County Coll (IL)
Mendocino Coll (CA)
Metropolitan Comm Coll–Business & Technology Campus (MO)
Metropolitan Comm Coll–Longview (MO)
Metropolitan Comm Coll–Maple Woods (MO)
Metropolitan Comm Coll–Penn Valley (MO)
Middle Georgia Tech Coll (GA)
Mid Michigan Comm Coll (MI)
Minneapolis Comm and Tech Coll (MN)
Minnesota School of Business– Brooklyn Center (MN)
Minnesota School of Business– Plymouth (MN)
Minnesota School of Business– Richfield (MN)

Minnesota School of Business–St. Cloud (MN)
Minnesota School of Business– Shakopee (MN)
Minnesota State Coll–Southeast Tech (MN)
Missouri State U–West Plains (MO)
Mohave Comm Coll (AZ)
Monroe Comm Coll (NY)
Monroe County Comm Coll (MI)
Montcalm Comm Coll (MI)
Montgomery Comm Coll (NC)
Montgomery County Comm Coll (PA)
Moraine Park Tech Coll (WI)
Moreno Valley Coll (CA)
Moultrie Tech Coll (GA)
Muskegon Comm Coll (MI)
Niagara County Comm Coll (NY)
Norco Coll (CA)
Northeast Comm Coll (NE)
Northeastern Jr Coll (CO)
Northeast Iowa Comm Coll (IA)
Northern Essex Comm Coll (MA)
North Hennepin Comm Coll (MN)
North Shore Comm Coll (MA)
Northwest Coll (WY)
Northwestern Connecticut Comm Coll (CT)
Northwest Florida State Coll (FL)
Northwest Tech Coll (MN)
Oconee Fall Line Tech Coll–North Campus (GA)
Ogeechee Tech Coll (GA)
Oklahoma City Comm Coll (OK)
Oklahoma State U, Oklahoma City (OK)
Onondaga Comm Coll (NY)
Orange Coast Coll (CA)
Palau Comm Coll (Palau)
Palm Beach State Coll (FL)
Peninsula Coll (WA)
Pensacola State Coll (FL)
Piedmont Virginia Comm Coll (VA)
Randolph Comm Coll (NC)
Rasmussen Coll Aurora (IL)
Rasmussen Coll Bismarck (ND)
Rasmussen Coll Bloomington (MN)
Rasmussen Coll Brooklyn Park (MN)
Rasmussen Coll Eagan (MN)
Rasmussen Coll Fort Myers (FL)
Rasmussen Coll Green Bay (WI)
Rasmussen Coll Lake Elmo/Woodbury (MN)
Rasmussen Coll Mankato (MN)
Rasmussen Coll Moorhead (MN)
Rasmussen Coll New Port Richey (FL)
Rasmussen Coll Ocala (FL)
Rasmussen Coll St. Cloud (MN)
Reedley Coll (CA)
Riverside City Coll (CA)
Rockingham Comm Coll (NC)
Rockland Comm Coll (NY)
St. Cloud Tech & Comm Coll (MN)
St. Philip's Coll (TX)
San Diego City Coll (CA)
San Jacinto Coll District (TX)
Santa Monica Coll (CA)
Savannah Tech Coll (GA)
Scottsdale Comm Coll (AZ)
Seminole State Coll of Florida (FL)
Shawnee Comm Coll (IL)
Snow Coll (UT)
Southeastern Comm Coll (IA)
Southeastern Tech Coll (GA)

Southeast Tech Inst (SD)
Southern Crescent Tech Coll (GA)
South Georgia Tech Coll (GA)
South Suburban Coll (IL)
Southwestern Illinois Coll (IL)
Southwest Georgia Tech Coll (GA)
Southwest Mississippi Comm Coll (MS)
Spencerian Coll (KY)
Springfield Tech Comm Coll (MA)
Stark State Coll (OH)
State Coll of Florida Manatee-Sarasota (FL)
Sullivan County Comm Coll (NY)
Tarrant County Coll District (TX)
Terra State Comm Coll (OH)
Three Rivers Comm Coll (CT)
Trident Tech Coll (SC)
Tunxis Comm Coll (CT)
Tyler Jr Coll (TX)
Umpqua Comm Coll (OR)
U of Alaska Anchorage, Kodiak Coll (AK)
Valencia Coll (FL)
Virginia Western Comm Coll (VA)
Waukesha County Tech Coll (WI)
Westchester Comm Coll (NY)
Western Dakota Tech Inst (SD)
Western Iowa Tech Comm Coll (IA)
West Georgia Tech Coll (GA)
West Kentucky Comm and Tech Coll (KY)
White Mountains Comm Coll (NH)
Wilson Comm Coll (NC)
Wiregrass Georgia Tech Coll (GA)
Wisconsin Indianhead Tech Coll (WI)
Wytheville Comm Coll (VA)
York County Comm Coll (ME)
YTI Career Inst–York (PA)

ACCOUNTING AND BUSINESS/MANAGEMENT

Berkeley City Coll (CA)
Bradford School (OH)
Kansas City Kansas Comm Coll (KS)
Kaplan Career Inst, ICM Campus (PA)
King's Coll (NC)
Mitchell Tech Inst (SD)
Oakland Comm Coll (MI)
Spencerian Coll (KY)

ACCOUNTING AND COMPUTER SCIENCE

GateWay Comm Coll (AZ)

ACCOUNTING AND FINANCE

Jackson Comm Coll (MI)

ACCOUNTING RELATED

Dakota Coll at Bottineau (ND)
John Tyler Comm Coll (VA)
Lansing Comm Coll (MI)
Raritan Valley Comm Coll (NJ)
Southwest Virginia Comm Coll (VA)

ACCOUNTING TECHNOLOGY AND BOOKKEEPING

Anne Arundel Comm Coll (MD)
Anoka-Ramsey Comm Coll (MN)
Anoka-Ramsey Comm Coll, Cambridge Campus (MN)
Austin Comm Coll (TX)

Big Bend Comm Coll (WA)
Bradford School (PA)
Bucks County Comm Coll (PA)
Cape Fear Comm Coll (NC)
Casper Coll (WY)
Catawba Valley Comm Coll (NC)
Cayuga County Comm Coll (NY)
Cecil Coll (MD)
Central Maine Comm Coll (ME)
Central Wyoming Coll (WY)
Chandler-Gilbert Comm Coll (AZ)
Chattanooga State Comm Coll (TN)
Clark Coll (WA)
Coll of Central Florida (FL)
Coll of Lake County (IL)
Coll of Southern Maryland (MD)
Coll of the Canyons (CA)
Comm Coll of Allegheny County (PA)
Dakota Coll at Bottineau (ND)
Delaware County Comm Coll (PA)
Fiorello H. LaGuardia Comm Coll of the City U of New York (NY)
Fox Coll (IL)
Front Range Comm Coll (CO)
Gadsden State Comm Coll (AL)
GateWay Comm Coll (AZ)
Gavilan Coll (CA)
Goodwin Coll (CT)
Guilford Tech Comm Coll (NC)
Gulf Coast State Coll (FL)
Hagerstown Comm Coll (MD)
Harford Comm Coll (MD)
H. Councill Trenholm State Tech Coll (AL)
Hillsborough Comm Coll (FL)
Holyoke Comm Coll (MA)
Illinois Central Coll (IL)
Inst of Business & Medical Careers (CO)
International Business Coll, Indianapolis (IN)
Iowa Lakes Comm Coll (IA)
ITT Tech Inst, Norwood (OH)
ITT Tech Inst, Strongsville (OH)
ITT Tech Inst, Austin (TX)
ITT Tech Inst, Richardson (TX)
Ivy Tech Comm Coll–Bloomington (IN)
Ivy Tech Comm Coll–Central Indiana (IN)
Ivy Tech Comm Coll–Columbus (IN)
Ivy Tech Comm Coll–East Central (IN)
Ivy Tech Comm Coll–Kokomo (IN)
Ivy Tech Comm Coll–Lafayette (IN)
Ivy Tech Comm Coll–North Central (IN)
Ivy Tech Comm Coll–Northeast (IN)
Ivy Tech Comm Coll–Northwest (IN)
Ivy Tech Comm Coll–Richmond (IN)
Ivy Tech Comm Coll–Southeast (IN)
Ivy Tech Comm Coll–Southern Indiana (IN)
Ivy Tech Comm Coll–Southwest (IN)
Ivy Tech Comm Coll–Wabash Valley (IN)
Jamestown Comm Coll (NY)
Jefferson Comm Coll (NY)
Jefferson State Comm Coll (AL)
Johnston Comm Coll (NC)

Kent State U at Trumbull (OH)
Kilgore Coll (TX)
King's Coll (NC)
Lake Region State Coll (ND)
Lansing Comm Coll (MI)
Lawson State Comm Coll (AL)
Lehigh Carbon Comm Coll (PA)
Lower Columbia Coll (WA)
Lurleen B. Wallace Comm Coll (AL)
Metropolitan Comm Coll–Blue River (MO)
Metropolitan Comm Coll–Business & Technology Campus (MO)
Miami Dade Coll (FL)
Minneapolis Business Coll (MN)
Minneapolis Comm and Tech Coll (MN)
Minnesota State Coll–Southeast Tech (MN)
Mohawk Valley Comm Coll (NY)
Montana State U–Great Falls Coll of Technology (MT)
Montgomery Coll (MD)
Montgomery County Comm Coll (PA)
Mott Comm Coll (MI)
Northampton Comm Coll (PA)
North Seattle Comm Coll (WA)
Oakland Comm Coll (MI)
Olympic Coll (WA)
Onondaga Comm Coll (NY)
Owens Comm Coll, Toledo (OH)
Pensacola State Coll (FL)
Polk State Coll (FL)
Raritan Valley Comm Coll (NJ)
Red Rocks Comm Coll (CO)
Rogue Comm Coll (OR)
St. Clair County Comm Coll (MI)
Salt Lake Comm Coll (UT)
San Juan Coll (NM)
Southern State Comm Coll (OH)
South Suburban Coll (IL)
Southwestern Indian Polytechnic Inst (NM)
Southwestern Michigan Coll (MI)
Spencerian Coll (KY)
State U of New York Coll of Technology at Alfred (NY)
Tallahassee Comm Coll (FL)
Tompkins Cortland Comm Coll (NY)
Union County Coll (NJ)
U of Alaska Anchorage, Kodiak Coll (AK)
The U of Montana–Helena Coll of Technology (MT)
Vincennes U (IN)
Westmoreland County Comm Coll (PA)
Wood Tobe–Coburn School (NY)

ACTING

Casper Coll (WY)
Central Wyoming Coll (WY)
KD Studio (TX)
Northampton Comm Coll (PA)

ADMINISTRATIVE ASSISTANT AND SECRETARIAL SCIENCE

Aiken Tech Coll (SC)
Altamaha Tech Coll (GA)
Alvin Comm Coll (TX)
Amarillo Coll (TX)
Arkansas State U–Mountain Home (AR)
Athens Tech Coll (GA)
Augusta Tech Coll (GA)
Austin Comm Coll (TX)
Bainbridge Coll (GA)
Beaufort County Comm Coll (NC)
Bevill State Comm Coll (AL)
Blackhawk Tech Coll (WI)
Bradford School (PA)
Career Tech Coll (LA)
Casper Coll (WY)
Central Carolina Comm Coll (NC)
Central Carolina Tech Coll (SC)
Central Comm Coll–Columbus Campus (NE)
Central Comm Coll–Grand Island Campus (NE)
Central Comm Coll–Hastings Campus (NE)
Central Georgia Tech Coll (GA)
Central Maine Comm Coll (ME)
Central Oregon Comm Coll (OR)

Central Wyoming Coll (WY)
Century Coll (MN)
Chattahoochee Tech Coll (GA)
Chattahoochee Valley Comm Coll (AL)
Chippewa Valley Tech Coll (WI)
Cleveland State Comm Coll (TN)
Clinton Comm Coll (NY)
Cochise Coll, Sierra Vista (AZ)
Colby Comm Coll (KS)
Coll of DuPage (IL)
Coll of Lake County (IL)
Coll of the Canyons (CA)
Coll of the Ouachitas (AR)
Columbus Tech Coll (GA)
Comm Coll of Allegheny County (PA)
The Comm Coll of Baltimore County (MD)
Comm Coll of Rhode Island (RI)
Comm Coll of Vermont (VT)
Corning Comm Coll (NY)
Cowley County Comm Coll and Area Vocational–Tech School (KS)
Crowder Coll (MO)
Dakota Coll at Bottineau (ND)
Dawson Comm Coll (MT)
Denmark Tech Coll (SC)
Do&nna Ana Comm Coll (NM)
Dutchess Comm Coll (NY)
Eastern Idaho Tech Coll (ID)
Elgin Comm Coll (IL)
Elmira Business Inst (NY)
El Paso Comm Coll (TX)
Erie Comm Coll (NY)
Fiorello H. LaGuardia Comm Coll of the City U of New York (NY)
Florida State Coll at Jacksonville (FL)
Fox Coll (IL)
Fox Valley Tech Coll (WI)
Gadsden State Comm Coll (AL)
GateWay Comm Coll (AZ)
Gateway Tech Coll (WI)
Gavilan Coll (CA)
Genesee Comm Coll (NY)
Georgia Piedmont Tech Coll (GA)
Gwinnett Tech Coll (GA)
Harper Coll (IL)
H. Councill Trenholm State Tech Coll (AL)
Highland Comm Coll (IL)
Highline Comm Coll (WA)
Holyoke Comm Coll (MA)
Housatonic Comm Coll (CT)
Howard Comm Coll (MD)
Hutchinson Comm Coll and Area Vocational School (KS)
Illinois Central Coll (IL)
Illinois Eastern Comm Colls, Frontier Community College (IL)
Illinois Eastern Comm Colls, Olney Central College (IL)
Illinois Eastern Comm Colls, Wabash Valley College (IL)
Indian River State Coll (FL)
International Business Coll, Indianapolis (IN)
Iowa Lakes Comm Coll (IA)
Jackson Comm Coll (MI)
Jamestown Business Coll (NY)
Jamestown Comm Coll (NY)
Jefferson State Comm Coll (AL)
Johnston Comm Coll (NC)
John Tyler Comm Coll (VA)
John Wood Comm Coll (IL)
J. Sargeant Reynolds Comm Coll (VA)
Kankakee Comm Coll (IL)
Kansas City Kansas Comm Coll (KS)
Kent State U at Ashtabula (OH)
Kent State U at Salem (OH)
Kent State U at Tuscarawas (OH)
Kingsborough Comm Coll of the City U of New York (NY)
King's Coll (NC)
Kirtland Comm Coll (MI)
Lake Michigan Coll (MI)
Lake Region State Coll (ND)
Lanier Tech Coll (GA)
Lawson State Comm Coll (AL)
Lincoln Land Comm Coll (IL)
Los Angeles Harbor Coll (CA)
Lower Columbia Coll (WA)
Lurleen B. Wallace Comm Coll (AL)

Macomb Comm Coll (MI)
Manchester Comm Coll (CT)
McHenry County Coll (IL)
Mendocino Coll (CA)
Metropolitan Comm Coll–Blue River (MO)
Metropolitan Comm Coll–Longview (MO)
Metropolitan Comm Coll–Maple Woods (MO)
Metropolitan Comm Coll–Penn Valley (MO)
Miami Dade Coll (FL)
Middle Georgia Tech Coll (GA)
Mid Michigan Comm Coll (MI)
Mid-Plains Comm Coll, North Platte (NE)
Mineral Area Coll (MO)
Minneapolis Business Coll (MN)
Minneapolis Comm and Tech Coll (MN)
Minnesota State Coll–Southeast Tech (MN)
Mohawk Valley Comm Coll (NY)
Monroe Comm Coll (NY)
Monroe County Comm Coll (MI)
Montcalm Comm Coll (MI)
Montgomery Comm Coll (NC)
Montgomery County Comm Coll (PA)
Moraine Park Tech Coll (WI)
Moraine Valley Comm Coll (IL)
Mott Comm Coll (MI)
Moultrie Tech Coll (GA)
Muskegon Comm Coll (MI)
New Mexico State U–Alamogordo (NM)
Niagara County Comm Coll (NY)
Northampton Comm Coll (PA)
North Dakota State Coll of Science (ND)
Northeast Alabama Comm Coll (AL)
Northeast Comm Coll (NE)
Northeast Iowa Comm Coll (IA)
Northern Essex Comm Coll (MA)
North Georgia Tech Coll (GA)
North Seattle Comm Coll (WA)
North Shore Comm Coll (MA)
Northwest Coll (WY)
Northwestern Connecticut Comm Coll (CT)
Northwest Florida State Coll (FL)
Northwest-Shoals Comm Coll (AL)
Northwest Tech Coll (MN)
Ocean County Coll (NJ)
Oconee Fall Line Tech Coll–North Campus (GA)
Ogeechee Tech Coll (GA)
Okefenokee Tech Coll (GA)
Olympic Coll (WA)
Orange Coast Coll (CA)
Otero Jr Coll (CO)
Palau Comm Coll (Palau)
Palm Beach State Coll (FL)
Panola Coll (TX)
Pensacola State Coll (FL)
Rainy River Comm Coll (MN)
Raritan Valley Comm Coll (NJ)
Reedley Coll (CA)
Reid State Tech Coll (AL)
Rockland Comm Coll (NY)
St. Philip's Coll (TX)
Salem Comm Coll (NJ)
San Diego City Coll (CA)
San Jacinto Coll District (TX)
Santa Monica Coll (CA)
Savannah Tech Coll (GA)
Scottsdale Comm Coll (AZ)
Seminole State Coll of Florida (FL)
Shawnee Comm Coll (IL)
Snow Coll (UT)
Southeastern Comm Coll (IA)
Southeastern Tech Coll (GA)
Southern Crescent Tech Coll (GA)
Southern State Comm Coll (OH)
South Georgia Tech Coll (GA)
Southwestern Illinois Coll (IL)
Southwestern Michigan Coll (MI)
Southwest Georgia Tech Coll (GA)
Southwest Mississippi Comm Coll (MS)
Springfield Tech Comm Coll (MA)
Stark State Coll (OH)
State Coll of Florida Manatee-Sarasota (FL)
Sullivan County Comm Coll (NY)

Tallahassee Comm Coll (FL)
Tarrant County Coll District (TX)
Texarkana Coll (TX)
Texas State Tech Coll Harlingen (TX)
Three Rivers Comm Coll (CT)
Tompkins Cortland Comm Coll (NY)
Trident Tech Coll (SC)
Truckee Meadows Comm Coll (NV)
Tunxis Comm Coll (CT)
Tyler Jr Coll (TX)
Umpqua Comm Coll (OR)
The U of Akron–Wayne Coll (OH)
Valencia Coll (FL)
Vincennes U (IN)
Virginia Western Comm Coll (VA)
Waukesha County Tech Coll (WI)
Westchester Comm Coll (NY)
Western Iowa Tech Comm Coll (IA)
West Georgia Tech Coll (GA)
Westmoreland County Comm Coll (PA)
West Virginia Northern Comm Coll (WV)
Wiregrass Georgia Tech Coll (GA)
Wisconsin Indianhead Tech Coll (WI)
Wood Tobe–Coburn School (NY)
Wytheville Comm Coll (VA)

ADULT DEVELOPMENT AND AGING

Albany Tech Coll (GA)
Central Georgia Tech Coll (GA)
Comm Coll of Rhode Island (RI)
Dakota Coll at Bottineau (ND)
El Paso Comm Coll (TX)
Fiorello H. LaGuardia Comm Coll of the City U of New York (NY)
Oakland Comm Coll (MI)

ADVERTISING

Dakota Coll at Bottineau (ND)
Fashion Inst of Technology (NY)
Mohawk Valley Comm Coll (NY)
Muskegon Comm Coll (MI)
Rockland Comm Coll (NY)
St. Cloud Tech & Comm Coll (MN)
Southwest Mississippi Comm Coll (MS)
State Coll of Florida Manatee-Sarasota (FL)

AERONAUTICAL/AEROSPACE ENGINEERING TECHNOLOGY

Delaware Tech & Comm Coll, Jack F. Owens Campus (DE)
GateWay Comm Coll (AZ)

AERONAUTICS/AVIATION/ AEROSPACE SCIENCE AND TECHNOLOGY

Alvin Comm Coll (TX)
The Comm Coll of Baltimore County (MD)
Lehigh Carbon Comm Coll (PA)
Miami Dade Coll (FL)
Northwest Coll (WY)
Orange Coast Coll (CA)

AEROSPACE, AERONAUTICAL AND ASTRONAUTICAL/SPACE ENGINEERING

Kent State U at Ashtabula (OH)
Kilgore Coll (TX)

AEROSPACE GROUND EQUIPMENT TECHNOLOGY

Cochise Coll, Sierra Vista (AZ)

AFRICAN AMERICAN/BLACK STUDIES

Lansing Comm Coll (MI)
San Diego City Coll (CA)
State Coll of Florida Manatee-Sarasota (FL)

AGRIBUSINESS

Burlington County Coll (NJ)
Colby Comm Coll (KS)
Copiah-Lincoln Comm Coll (MS)
Crowder Coll (MO)

Iowa Lakes Comm Coll (IA)
James Sprunt Comm Coll (NC)
Laramie County Comm Coll (WY)
Mineral Area Coll (MO)
Northeast Comm Coll (NE)
Northeast Iowa Comm Coll (IA)
Northwest Coll (WY)
Ogeechee Tech Coll (GA)
San Jacinto Coll District (TX)
State U of New York Coll of Technology at Alfred (NY)

AGRICULTURAL AND DOMESTIC ANIMAL SERVICES RELATED

Central Wyoming Coll (WY)

AGRICULTURAL AND FOOD PRODUCTS PROCESSING

Northeast Iowa Comm Coll (IA)

AGRICULTURAL BUSINESS AND MANAGEMENT

Casper Coll (WY)
Central Comm Coll–Columbus Campus (NE)
Central Comm Coll–Hastings Campus (NE)
Central Wyoming Coll (WY)
Cochise Coll, Sierra Vista (AZ)
Colby Comm Coll (KS)
Copiah-Lincoln Comm Coll (MS)
Dawson Comm Coll (MT)
Delaware Tech & Comm Coll, Jack F. Owens Campus (DE)
Delaware Tech & Comm Coll, Stanton/Wilmington Campus (DE)
Delaware Tech & Comm Coll, Terry Campus (DE)
Highland Comm Coll (IL)
Illinois Central Coll (IL)
Illinois Eastern Comm Colls, Wabash Valley College (IL)
Indian River State Coll (FL)
Iowa Lakes Comm Coll (IA)
John Wood Comm Coll (IL)
J. Sargeant Reynolds Comm Coll (VA)
Lake Area Tech Inst (SD)
Lake Region State Coll (ND)
Lansing Comm Coll (MI)
North Dakota State Coll of Science (ND)
Northeastern Jr Coll (CO)
Otero Jr Coll (CO)
Reedley Coll (CA)
Santa Rosa Jr Coll (CA)
Shawnee Comm Coll (IL)
Snow Coll (UT)
Southeastern Comm Coll (IA)
Terra State Comm Coll (OH)
Vincennes U (IN)

AGRICULTURAL BUSINESS AND MANAGEMENT RELATED

Chippewa Valley Tech Coll (WI)
Copiah-Lincoln Comm Coll (MS)
Iowa Lakes Comm Coll (IA)
Penn State Beaver (PA)
Penn State Brandywine (PA)
Penn State DuBois (PA)
Penn State Fayette, The Eberly Campus (PA)
Penn State Greater Allegheny (PA)
Penn State Hazleton (PA)
Penn State Lehigh Valley (PA)
Penn State Mont Alto (PA)
Penn State New Kensington (PA)
Penn State Schuylkill (PA)
Penn State Shenango (PA)
Penn State Wilkes-Barre (PA)
Penn State Worthington Scranton (PA)
Penn State York (PA)

AGRICULTURAL BUSINESS TECHNOLOGY

Copiah-Lincoln Comm Coll (MS)
Iowa Lakes Comm Coll (IA)
Laramie County Comm Coll (WY)
Texas State Tech Coll Harlingen (TX)

AGRICULTURAL COMMUNICATION/ JOURNALISM
Northwest Coll (WY)
Santa Rosa Jr Coll (CA)

AGRICULTURAL ECONOMICS
Copiah-Lincoln Comm Coll (MS)
Iowa Lakes Comm Coll (IA)
Northeastern Jr Coll (CO)

AGRICULTURAL ENGINEERING
Vincennes U (IN)

AGRICULTURAL/FARM SUPPLIES RETAILING AND WHOLESALING
Copiah-Lincoln Comm Coll (MS)
Fox Valley Tech Coll (WI)
Hawkeye Comm Coll (IA)
Iowa Lakes Comm Coll (IA)
Western Iowa Tech Comm Coll (IA)

AGRICULTURAL MECHANICS AND EQUIPMENT TECHNOLOGY
Illinois Central Coll (IL)
Iowa Lakes Comm Coll (IA)
Mitchell Tech Inst (SD)
North Dakota State Coll of Science (ND)
Northeast Comm Coll (NE)

AGRICULTURAL MECHANIZATION
Fox Valley Tech Coll (WI)
Hutchinson Comm Coll and Area Vocational School (KS)
Iowa Lakes Comm Coll (IA)
Metropolitan Comm Coll–Longview (MO)
Northeast Comm Coll (NE)
Northeastern Jr Coll (CO)
Owens Comm Coll, Toledo (OH)
Southwest Georgia Tech Coll (GA)

AGRICULTURAL MECHANIZATION RELATED
Reedley Coll (CA)

AGRICULTURAL POWER MACHINERY OPERATION
Dawson Comm Coll (MT)
Guilford Tech Comm Coll (NC)
Hawkeye Comm Coll (IA)
Iowa Lakes Comm Coll (IA)
Northeast Iowa Comm Coll (IA)

AGRICULTURAL PRODUCTION
Big Bend Comm Coll (WA)
Delaware Tech & Comm Coll, Jack F. Owens Campus (DE)
Illinois Central Coll (IL)
Illinois Eastern Comm Colls, Wabash Valley College (IL)
Iowa Lakes Comm Coll (IA)
Lake Area Tech Inst (SD)
Laramie County Comm Coll (WY)
Lincoln Land Comm Coll (IL)
Mitchell Tech Inst (SD)
Northeast Iowa Comm Coll (IA)
Northwest Coll (WY)
Southern State Comm Coll (OH)

AGRICULTURAL PRODUCTION RELATED
Iowa Lakes Comm Coll (IA)

AGRICULTURAL TEACHER EDUCATION
Colby Comm Coll (KS)
Iowa Lakes Comm Coll (IA)
Murray State Coll (OK)
Northeastern Jr Coll (CO)
Northwest Coll (WY)

AGRICULTURE
Bainbridge Coll (GA)
Casper Coll (WY)
Chipola Coll (FL)
Copiah-Lincoln Comm Coll (MS)

Cowley County Comm Coll and Area Vocational–Tech School (KS)
Crowder Coll (MO)
Dakota Coll at Bottineau (ND)
Dyersburg State Comm Coll (TN)
Georgia Highlands Coll (GA)
Hutchinson Comm Coll and Area Vocational School (KS)
Iowa Lakes Comm Coll (IA)
Kankakee Comm Coll (IL)
Kaskaskia Coll (IL)
Kilgore Coll (TX)
Laramie County Comm Coll (WY)
Macomb Comm Coll (MI)
Mendocino Coll (CA)
Miami Dade Coll (FL)
Missouri State U–West Plains (MO)
Murray State Coll (OK)
Northeast Comm Coll (NE)
Northeastern Jr Coll (CO)
Owensboro Comm and Tech Coll (KY)
Palau Comm Coll (Palau)
Pensacola State Coll (FL)
Reedley Coll (CA)
San Jacinto Coll District (TX)
Shawnee Comm Coll (IL)
Snow Coll (UT)
Southern State Comm Coll (OH)
State U of New York Coll of Technology at Alfred (NY)
Texarkana Coll (TX)
Tyler Jr Coll (TX)
Umpqua Comm Coll (OR)
Vincennes U (IN)

AGRICULTURE AND AGRICULTURE OPERATIONS RELATED
Northeast Comm Coll (NE)

AGROECOLOGY AND SUSTAINABLE AGRICULTURE
Santa Rosa Jr Coll (CA)
State U of New York Coll of Technology at Alfred (NY)

AGRONOMY AND CROP SCIENCE
Chipola Coll (FL)
Colby Comm Coll (KS)
Iowa Lakes Comm Coll (IA)
Northeast Comm Coll (NE)
Northeastern Jr Coll (CO)
Shawnee Comm Coll (IL)
Southeastern Comm Coll (IA)
State U of New York Coll of Technology at Alfred (NY)

AIRCRAFT POWERPLANT TECHNOLOGY
Florida State Coll at Jacksonville (FL)
Lake Area Tech Inst (SD)
Lansing Comm Coll (MI)
Linn State Tech Coll (MO)
St. Philip's Coll (TX)
Texas State Tech Coll Harlingen (TX)
Vincennes U (IN)

AIRFRAME MECHANICS AND AIRCRAFT MAINTENANCE TECHNOLOGY
Amarillo Coll (TX)
Florida State Coll at Jacksonville (FL)
Gavilan Coll (CA)
Ivy Tech Comm Coll–Wabash Valley (IN)
Lansing Comm Coll (MI)
Lincoln Land Comm Coll (IL)
Linn State Tech Coll (MO)
Middle Georgia Tech Coll (GA)
Mohawk Valley Comm Coll (NY)
Oklahoma City Comm Coll (OK)
St. Philip's Coll (TX)
San Joaquin Valley Coll–Fresno Aviation Campus (CA)
Southwestern Illinois Coll (IL)
Texas State Tech Coll Harlingen (TX)
Trident Tech Coll (SC)
The U of Montana–Helena Coll of Technology (MT)

AIRLINE PILOT AND FLIGHT CREW
Big Bend Comm Coll (WA)
Casper Coll (WY)
Central Oregon Comm Coll (OR)
Chandler-Gilbert Comm Coll (AZ)
Cochise Coll, Sierra Vista (AZ)
Comm Coll of Allegheny County (PA)
Florida State Coll at Jacksonville (FL)
Fox Valley Tech Coll (WI)
Gateway Tech Coll (WI)
Guilford Tech Comm Coll (NC)
Indian River State Coll (FL)
Iowa Lakes Comm Coll (IA)
Jackson Comm Coll (MI)
Jamestown Comm Coll (NY)
Lehigh Carbon Comm Coll (PA)
Miami Dade Coll (FL)
North Shore Comm Coll (MA)
Olympic Coll (WA)
Orange Coast Coll (CA)
Palm Beach State Coll (FL)
Salt Lake Comm Coll (UT)
San Jacinto Coll District (TX)
Southwestern Illinois Coll (IL)
Vincennes U (IN)

AIR TRAFFIC CONTROL
Miami Dade Coll (FL)
Minneapolis Comm and Tech Coll (MN)

ALLIED HEALTH AND MEDICAL ASSISTING SERVICES RELATED
Mount Wachusett Comm Coll (MA)
North Seattle Comm Coll (WA)

ALLIED HEALTH DIAGNOSTIC, INTERVENTION, AND TREATMENT PROFESSIONS RELATED
Ivy Tech Comm Coll–Wabash Valley (IN)
Kent State U at Salem (OH)
Minneapolis Comm and Tech Coll (MN)
Union County Coll (NJ)

ALTERNATIVE AND COMPLEMENTARY MEDICAL SUPPORT SERVICES RELATED
Mount Wachusett Comm Coll (MA)

ALTERNATIVE AND COMPLEMENTARY MEDICINE RELATED
Quinsigamond Comm Coll (MA)

AMERICAN GOVERNMENT AND POLITICS
Oklahoma City Comm Coll (OK)
State Coll of Florida Manatee-Sarasota (FL)

AMERICAN INDIAN/NATIVE AMERICAN STUDIES
Central Wyoming Coll (WY)
Itasca Comm Coll (MN)
Kilian Comm Coll (SD)

AMERICAN SIGN LANGUAGE (ASL)
Berkeley City Coll (CA)
Burlington County Coll (NJ)
Montgomery Coll (MD)
Oklahoma State U, Oklahoma City (OK)
Santa Rosa Jr Coll (CA)
Union County Coll (NJ)
Vincennes U (IN)

AMERICAN SIGN LANGUAGE RELATED
Union County Coll (NJ)

AMERICAN STUDIES
Bucks County Comm Coll (PA)
Foothill Coll (CA)
Lansing Comm Coll (MI)
Miami Dade Coll (FL)

State Coll of Florida Manatee-Sarasota (FL)

ANATOMY
Northeastern Jr Coll (CO)

ANIMAL HEALTH
Front Range Comm Coll (CO)

ANIMAL/LIVESTOCK HUSBANDRY AND PRODUCTION
Hawkeye Comm Coll (IA)
Iowa Lakes Comm Coll (IA)
Jefferson Comm Coll (NY)

ANIMAL SCIENCES
Casper Coll (WY)
Iowa Lakes Comm Coll (IA)
James Sprunt Comm Coll (NC)
John Wood Comm Coll (IL)
Niagara County Comm Coll (NY)
Northeast Comm Coll (NE)
Northeastern Jr Coll (CO)
Northwest Coll (WY)
Reedley Coll (CA)
Santa Rosa Jr Coll (CA)
Shawnee Comm Coll (IL)
Snow Coll (UT)
State U of New York Coll of Technology at Alfred (NY)

ANIMATION, INTERACTIVE TECHNOLOGY, VIDEO GRAPHICS AND SPECIAL EFFECTS
The Art Inst of Seattle (WA)
Austin Comm Coll (TX)
Burlington County Coll (NJ)
Coll of the Canyons (CA)
Delaware County Comm Coll (PA)
Elgin Comm Coll (IL)
Front Range Comm Coll (CO)
Hagerstown Comm Coll (MD)
Houston Comm Coll System (TX)
Kent State U at Tuscarawas (OH)
Lansing Comm Coll (MI)
Lehigh Carbon Comm Coll (PA)
McHenry County Coll (IL)
Minneapolis Comm and Tech Coll (MN)
Minnesota School of Business–Richfield (MN)
Montgomery Coll (MD)
New Mexico State U–Alamogordo (NM)
Olympic Coll (WA)
Raritan Valley Comm Coll (NJ)
Red Rocks Comm Coll (CO)
Santa Monica Coll (CA)
Southeast Tech Inst (SD)
Springfield Tech Comm Coll (MA)
Sullivan Coll of Technology and Design (KY)
Terra State Comm Coll (OH)
Union County Coll (NJ)

ANTHROPOLOGY
Austin Comm Coll (TX)
Casper Coll (WY)
Cochise Coll, Sierra Vista (AZ)
Delaware County Comm Coll (PA)
Eastern Arizona Coll (AZ)
Foothill Coll (CA)
Indian River State Coll (FL)
Laramie County Comm Coll (WY)
Miami Dade Coll (FL)
Muskegon Comm Coll (MI)
Northwest Coll (WY)
Orange Coast Coll (CA)
San Diego City Coll (CA)
Santa Monica Coll (CA)
Santa Rosa Jr Coll (CA)
Truckee Meadows Comm Coll (NV)
Umpqua Comm Coll (OR)
Vincennes U (IN)

APPAREL AND ACCESSORIES MARKETING
El Centro Coll (TX)

APPAREL AND TEXTILE MANUFACTURING
Fashion Inst of Technology (NY)
Westchester Comm Coll (NY)

APPAREL AND TEXTILE MARKETING MANAGEMENT
Santa Monica Coll (CA)

APPAREL AND TEXTILES
Indian River State Coll (FL)
Palm Beach State Coll (FL)

APPLIED HORTICULTURE/ HORTICULTURAL BUSINESS SERVICES RELATED
Chippewa Valley Tech Coll (WI)
Dakota Coll at Bottineau (ND)
Gateway Tech Coll (WI)
Northeast Comm Coll (NE)

APPLIED HORTICULTURE/ HORTICULTURE OPERATIONS
Catawba Valley Comm Coll (NC)
Central Comm Coll–Hastings Campus (NE)
Clark Coll (WA)
Comm Coll of Allegheny County (PA)
Dakota Coll at Bottineau (ND)
Delaware Tech & Comm Coll, Jack F. Owens Campus (DE)
Fayetteville Tech Comm Coll (NC)
Front Range Comm Coll (CO)
Gateway Tech Coll (WI)
Hawkeye Comm Coll (IA)
Houston Comm Coll System (TX)
Illinois Central Coll (IL)
John Wood Comm Coll (IL)
Kankakee Comm Coll (IL)
Kaskaskia Coll (IL)
Kent State U at Salem (OH)
Lake Michigan Coll (MI)
McHenry County Coll (IL)
Mineral Area Coll (MO)
Montgomery Coll (MD)
Northeast Comm Coll (NE)
Southeast Tech Inst (SD)
Southern Maine Comm Coll (ME)
Southwestern Illinois Coll (IL)
Vincennes U (IN)
Westmoreland County Comm Coll (PA)

APPLIED MATHEMATICS
Muskegon Comm Coll (MI)
Northeastern Jr Coll (CO)

AQUACULTURE
Hillsborough Comm Coll (FL)

ARCHEOLOGY
Northwest Coll (WY)

ARCHITECTURAL DRAFTING AND CAD/CADD
Anne Arundel Comm Coll (MD)
Bluegrass Comm and Tech Coll (KY)
Carroll Comm Coll (MD)
Coll of Lake County (IL)
Coll of the Canyons (CA)
Comm Coll of Allegheny County (PA)
The Comm Coll of Baltimore County (MD)
Florida State Coll at Jacksonville (FL)
Harper Coll (IL)
Hawkeye Comm Coll (IA)
Indian River State Coll (FL)
Island Drafting and Tech Inst (NY)
ITT Tech Inst, Dayton (OH)
Kaskaskia Coll (IL)
Lincoln Land Comm Coll (IL)
Macomb Comm Coll (MI)
Miami Dade Coll (FL)
Minnesota School of Business–Plymouth (MN)
Montgomery Coll (MD)
Montgomery County Comm Coll (PA)
Northeast Comm Coll (NE)
North Seattle Comm Coll (WA)
Oklahoma City Comm Coll (OK)
Owens Comm Coll, Toledo (OH)
Pittsburgh Tech Inst, Oakdale (PA)
St. Cloud Tech & Comm Coll (MN)
Southern Maine Comm Coll (ME)
South Suburban Coll (IL)

Sullivan Coll of Technology and Design (KY)
Vincennes U (IN)
Waukesha County Tech Coll (WI)
Western Dakota Tech Inst (SD)
Westmoreland County Comm Coll (PA)
York County Comm Coll (ME)

ARCHITECTURAL ENGINEERING TECHNOLOGY
Amarillo Coll (TX)
Cape Fear Comm Coll (NC)
Catawba Valley Comm Coll (NC)
Central Maine Comm Coll (ME)
Comm Coll of Philadelphia (PA)
Delaware County Comm Coll (PA)
Delaware Tech & Comm Coll, Jack F. Owens Campus (DE)
Delaware Tech & Comm Coll, Stanton/Wilmington Campus (DE)
Delaware Tech & Comm Coll, Terry Campus (DE)
Do&nna Ana Comm Coll (NM)
Dutchess Comm Coll (NY)
Erie Comm Coll, South Campus (NY)
Fayetteville Tech Comm Coll (NC)
Florida State Coll at Jacksonville (FL)
Front Range Comm Coll (CO)
Gateway Tech Coll (WI)
Grand Rapids Comm Coll (MI)
Guilford Tech Comm Coll (NC)
Harper Coll (IL)
Hillsborough Comm Coll (FL)
John Tyler Comm Coll (VA)
Lansing Comm Coll (MI)
Los Angeles Harbor Coll (CA)
Miami Dade Coll (FL)
Monroe County Comm Coll (MI)
Mott Comm Coll (MI)
Northampton Comm Coll (PA)
North Dakota State Coll of Science (ND)
Oakland Comm Coll (MI)
Oklahoma State U, Oklahoma City (OK)
Onondaga Comm Coll (NY)
Orange Coast Coll (CA)
Owens Comm Coll, Toledo (OH)
Penn State Fayette, The Eberly Campus (PA)
Penn State Worthington Scranton (PA)
St. Clair County Comm Coll (MI)
Salt Lake Comm Coll (UT)
Seminole State Coll of Florida (FL)
Southeast Tech Inst (SD)
Stark State Coll (OH)
State U of New York Coll of Technology at Alfred (NY)
Sullivan Coll of Technology and Design (KY)
Tarrant County Coll District (TX)
Terra State Comm Coll (OH)
Three Rivers Comm Coll (CT)
Wisconsin Indianhead Tech Coll (WI)

ARCHITECTURAL TECHNOLOGY
John Tyler Comm Coll (VA)
Lansing Comm Coll (MI)
Onondaga Comm Coll (NY)

ARCHITECTURE
Copiah-Lincoln Comm Coll (MS)
Grand Rapids Comm Coll (MI)
Howard Comm Coll (MD)
Kilgore Coll (TX)
Truckee Meadows Comm Coll (NV)

ARCHITECTURE RELATED
Sullivan Coll of Technology and Design (KY)

AREA STUDIES RELATED
Central Wyoming Coll (WY)

ART
Alvin Comm Coll (TX)
Amarillo Coll (TX)
Austin Comm Coll (TX)

Bainbridge Coll (GA)
Berkeley City Coll (CA)
Bunker Hill Comm Coll (MA)
Burlington County Coll (NJ)
Carroll Comm Coll (MD)
Casper Coll (WY)
Cayuga County Comm Coll (NY)
Central Oregon Comm Coll (OR)
Central Wyoming Coll (WY)
Chipola Coll (FL)
Cochise Coll, Sierra Vista (AZ)
Coll of Lake County (IL)
Coll of the Canyons (CA)
Comm Coll of Allegheny County (PA)
Comm Coll of Philadelphia (PA)
Comm Coll of Rhode Island (RI)
Comm Coll of Vermont (VT)
Cowley County Comm Coll and Area Vocational–Tech School (KS)
Crowder Coll (MO)
Eastern Arizona Coll (AZ)
Edison Comm Coll (OH)
Foothill Coll (CA)
Gavilan Coll (CA)
Georgia Highlands Coll (GA)
Grand Rapids Comm Coll (MI)
Harper Coll (IL)
Highline Comm Coll (WA)
Holyoke Comm Coll (MA)
Housatonic Comm Coll (CT)
Howard Comm Coll (MD)
Iowa Lakes Comm Coll (IA)
Kilgore Coll (TX)
Kingsborough Comm Coll of the City U of New York (NY)
Kirtland Comm Coll (MI)
Lake Michigan Coll (MI)
Lansing Comm Coll (MI)
Laramie County Comm Coll (WY)
Lehigh Carbon Comm Coll (PA)
Mendocino Coll (CA)
Miami Dade Coll (FL)
Mid Michigan Comm Coll (MI)
Mohave Comm Coll (AZ)
Mohawk Valley Comm Coll (NY)
Monroe Comm Coll (NY)
Monroe County Comm Coll (MI)
Montgomery Coll (MD)
Montgomery County Comm Coll (PA)
Mount Wachusett Comm Coll (MA)
Muskegon Comm Coll (MI)
Normandale Comm Coll (MN)
Northeast Comm Coll (NE)
Northeastern Jr Coll (CO)
North Seattle Comm Coll (WA)
Northwest Coll (WY)
Northwestern Connecticut Comm Coll (CT)
Northwest Florida State Coll (FL)
Oakland Comm Coll (MI)
Oklahoma City Comm Coll (OK)
Oklahoma State U, Oklahoma City (OK)
Onondaga Comm Coll (NY)
Orange Coast Coll (CA)
Palm Beach State Coll (FL)
Pensacola State Coll (FL)
Reedley Coll (CA)
Rockland Comm Coll (NY)
St. Philip's Coll (TX)
San Diego City Coll (CA)
San Jacinto Coll District (TX)
Santa Monica Coll (CA)
Santa Rosa Jr Coll (CA)
Snow Coll (UT)
State Coll of Florida Manatee-Sarasota (FL)
Texarkana Coll (TX)
Tunxis Comm Coll (CT)
Tyler Jr Coll (TX)
Umpqua Comm Coll (OR)
Vincennes U (IN)
Virginia Western Comm Coll (VA)

ART HISTORY, CRITICISM AND CONSERVATION
Foothill Coll (CA)
Iowa Lakes Comm Coll (IA)
Lansing Comm Coll (MI)
Muskegon Comm Coll (MI)
Palm Beach State Coll (FL)
Santa Rosa Jr Coll (CA)

State Coll of Florida Manatee-Sarasota (FL)
Terra State Comm Coll (OH)
Umpqua Comm Coll (OR)

ARTIFICIAL INTELLIGENCE
Metropolitan Comm Coll–Business & Technology Campus (MO)
San Diego City Coll (CA)
Southeastern Comm Coll (IA)
Sullivan Coll of Technology and Design (KY)

ART TEACHER EDUCATION
Casper Coll (WY)
Cochise Coll, Sierra Vista (AZ)
Copiah-Lincoln Comm Coll (MS)
Eastern Arizona Coll (AZ)
Indian River State Coll (FL)
Iowa Lakes Comm Coll (IA)
Muskegon Comm Coll (MI)
Northeastern Jr Coll (CO)
Pensacola State Coll (FL)
Umpqua Comm Coll (OR)
Vincennes U (IN)

ART THERAPY
Vincennes U (IN)

ASIAN STUDIES
Miami Dade Coll (FL)
State Coll of Florida Manatee-Sarasota (FL)

ASTRONOMY
Iowa Lakes Comm Coll (IA)
State Coll of Florida Manatee-Sarasota (FL)

ATHLETIC TRAINING
Casper Coll (WY)
Central Wyoming Coll (WY)
Coll of the Canyons (CA)
Comm Coll of Allegheny County (PA)
Foothill Coll (CA)
Iowa Lakes Comm Coll (IA)
Northampton Comm Coll (PA)
Northwest Coll (WY)
Orange Coast Coll (CA)

ATMOSPHERIC SCIENCES AND METEOROLOGY
Northwest Florida State Coll (FL)

AUDIOLOGY AND SPEECH-LANGUAGE PATHOLOGY
Miami Dade Coll (FL)

AUTOBODY/COLLISION AND REPAIR TECHNOLOGY
Casper Coll (WY)
Central Comm Coll–Hastings Campus (NE)
The Comm Coll of Baltimore County (MD)
Corning Comm Coll (NY)
Erie Comm Coll, South Campus (NY)
Florida State Coll at Jacksonville (FL)
Fox Valley Tech Coll (WI)
Hawkeye Comm Coll (IA)
Highland Comm Coll (IL)
Hutchinson Comm Coll and Area Vocational School (KS)
Illinois Eastern Comm Colls, Olney Central College (IL)
Iowa Lakes Comm Coll (IA)
Kaskaskia Coll (IL)
Kilgore Coll (TX)
Lake Area Tech Inst (SD)
Lansing Comm Coll (MI)
Laramie County Comm Coll (WY)
Lincoln Land Comm Coll (IL)
Linn State Tech Coll (MO)
Mid-Plains Comm Coll, North Platte (NE)
Mineral Area Coll (MO)
Minnesota State Coll–Southeast Tech (MN)
North Dakota State Coll of Science (ND)
Northeast Comm Coll (NE)

Pennco Tech (PA)
Randolph Comm Coll (NC)
Red Rocks Comm Coll (CO)
Riverside City Coll (CA)
St. Cloud Tech & Comm Coll (MN)
St. Philip's Coll (TX)
Salt Lake Comm Coll (UT)
San Jacinto Coll District (TX)
San Juan Coll (NM)
Southeast Tech Inst (SD)
Southwestern Illinois Coll (IL)
State U of New York Coll of Technology at Alfred (NY)
Texas State Tech Coll Harlingen (TX)
U of Arkansas Comm Coll at Morrilton (AR)
Vincennes U (IN)
Waukesha County Tech Coll (WI)
Western Iowa Tech Comm Coll (IA)

AUTOMATION ENGINEER TECHNOLOGY
Mitchell Tech Inst (SD)

AUTOMOBILE/AUTOMOTIVE MECHANICS TECHNOLOGY
Aiken Tech Coll (SC)
Amarillo Coll (TX)
Austin Comm Coll (TX)
Beaufort County Comm Coll (NC)
Big Bend Comm Coll (WA)
Bluegrass Comm and Tech Coll (KY)
Blue Ridge Comm and Tech Coll (WV)
Brookhaven Coll (TX)
Cape Fear Comm Coll (NC)
Casper Coll (WY)
Catawba Valley Comm Coll (NC)
Central Carolina Comm Coll (NC)
Central Comm Coll–Columbus Campus (NE)
Central Comm Coll–Grand Island Campus (NE)
Central Comm Coll–Hastings Campus (NE)
Central Maine Comm Coll (ME)
Central Oregon Comm Coll (OR)
Central Wyoming Coll (WY)
Chattahoochee Tech Coll (GA)
City Colls of Chicago, Harry S. Truman College (IL)
Clark Coll (WA)
Cochise Coll, Sierra Vista (AZ)
Coll of Central Florida (FL)
Coll of DuPage (IL)
Coll of Lake County (IL)
Coll of the Canyons (CA)
Coll of the Ouachitas (AR)
Columbus Tech Coll (GA)
The Comm Coll of Baltimore County (MD)
Comm Coll of Philadelphia (PA)
Corning Comm Coll (NY)
Cowley County Comm Coll and Area Vocational–Tech School (KS)
Delaware County Comm Coll (PA)
Delaware Tech & Comm Coll, Jack F. Owens Campus (DE)
Delaware Tech & Comm Coll, Stanton/Wilmington Campus (DE)
Denmark Tech Coll (SC)
Do&nna Ana Comm Coll (NM)
Eastern Arizona Coll (AZ)
Eastern Idaho Tech Coll (ID)
Elgin Comm Coll (IL)
El Paso Comm Coll (TX)
Erie Comm Coll, South Campus (NY)
Fayetteville Tech Comm Coll (NC)
Florida State Coll at Jacksonville (FL)
Fox Valley Tech Coll (WI)
Front Range Comm Coll (CO)
GateWay Comm Coll (AZ)
Gateway Comm Coll (CT)
Gateway Tech Coll (WI)
Georgia Piedmont Tech Coll (GA)
Grand Rapids Comm Coll (MI)
Guilford Tech Comm Coll (NC)
Gwinnett Tech Coll (GA)
Hawkeye Comm Coll (IA)
Highland Comm Coll (IL)

Houston Comm Coll System (TX)
Hutchinson Comm Coll and Area Vocational School (KS)
Illinois Central Coll (IL)
Illinois Eastern Comm Colls, Frontier Community College (IL)
Illinois Eastern Comm Colls, Olney Central College (IL)
Illinois Valley Comm Coll (IL)
Indian River State Coll (FL)
Iowa Lakes Comm Coll (IA)
Ivy Tech Comm Coll–Central Indiana (IN)
Ivy Tech Comm Coll–Columbus (IN)
Ivy Tech Comm Coll–East Central (IN)
Ivy Tech Comm Coll–Kokomo (IN)
Ivy Tech Comm Coll–Lafayette (IN)
Ivy Tech Comm Coll–North Central (IN)
Ivy Tech Comm Coll–Northeast (IN)
Ivy Tech Comm Coll–Northwest (IN)
Ivy Tech Comm Coll–Richmond (IN)
Ivy Tech Comm Coll–Southern Indiana (IN)
Ivy Tech Comm Coll–Southwest (IN)
Ivy Tech Comm Coll–Wabash Valley (IN)
Jackson Comm Coll (MI)
Kankakee Comm Coll (IL)
Kaskaskia Coll (IL)
Kent State U at Trumbull (OH)
Kilgore Coll (TX)
Kirtland Comm Coll (MI)
Lake Area Tech Inst (SD)
Lake Region State Coll (ND)
Lansing Comm Coll (MI)
Laramie County Comm Coll (WY)
Lincoln Land Comm Coll (IL)
Linn State Tech Coll (MO)
Los Angeles Harbor Coll (CA)
Lower Columbia Coll (WA)
Macomb Comm Coll (MI)
McHenry County Coll (IL)
Mendocino Coll (CA)
Metropolitan Comm Coll–Longview (MO)
Mid Michigan Comm Coll (MI)
Mid-Plains Comm Coll, North Platte (NE)
Mineral Area Coll (MO)
Mohave Comm Coll (AZ)
Monroe Comm Coll (NY)
Montcalm Comm Coll (MI)
Montgomery Coll (MD)
Montgomery County Comm Coll (PA)
Moraine Valley Comm Coll (IL)
Mott Comm Coll (MI)
Mount Wachusett Comm Coll (MA)
Muskegon Comm Coll (MI)
Northampton Comm Coll (PA)
North Dakota State Coll of Science (ND)
Northeast Comm Coll (NE)
Northeastern Jr Coll (CO)
Northeast Iowa Comm Coll (IA)
Northwest Florida State Coll (FL)
Northwest Tech Coll (MN)
Ogeechee Tech Coll (GA)
Oklahoma City Comm Coll (OK)
Oklahoma Tech Coll (OK)
Onondaga Comm Coll (NY)
Otero Jr Coll (CO)
Ozarka Coll (AR)
Palau Comm Coll (Palau)
Peninsula Coll (WA)
Pensacola State Coll (FL)
Quinsigamond Comm Coll (MA)
Randolph Comm Coll (NC)
Red Rocks Comm Coll (CO)
Reedley Coll (CA)
Riverside City Coll (CA)
Rockland Comm Coll (NY)
Rogue Comm Coll (OR)
St. Cloud Tech & Comm Coll (MN)
St. Philip's Coll (TX)
San Diego City Coll (CA)
San Jacinto Coll District (TX)
San Juan Coll (NM)
Santa Rosa Jr Coll (CA)
Savannah Tech Coll (GA)
Seminole State Coll of Florida (FL)

Shawnee Comm Coll (IL)
Snow Coll (UT)
Southeastern Comm Coll (IA)
Southeast Tech Inst (SD)
Southern Crescent Tech Coll (GA)
Southern Maine Comm Coll (ME)
Southwestern Michigan Coll (MI)
Southwest Mississippi Comm Coll (MS)
Stark State Coll (OH)
Tarrant County Coll District (TX)
Texarkana Coll (TX)
Texas State Tech Coll Harlingen (TX)
Trident Tech Coll (SC)
Truckee Meadows Comm Coll (NV)
Tyler Jr Coll (TX)
Umpqua Comm Coll (OR)
Union County Coll (NJ)
U of Arkansas Comm Coll at Morrilton (AR)
The U of Montana–Helena Coll of Technology (MT)
Vincennes U (IN)
Virginia Western Comm Coll (VA)
Waukesha County Tech Coll (WI)
Western Dakota Tech Inst (SD)
Western Iowa Tech Comm Coll (IA)
West Georgia Tech Coll (GA)
White Mountains Comm Coll (NH)

AUTOMOTIVE ENGINEERING TECHNOLOGY
Burlington County Coll (NJ)
Comm Coll of Allegheny County (PA)
Corning Comm Coll (NY)
H. Councill Trenholm State Tech Coll (AL)
Lawson State Comm Coll (AL)
Macomb Comm Coll (MI)
Massachusetts Bay Comm Coll (MA)
Moraine Park Tech Coll (WI)
Owens Comm Coll, Toledo (OH)
Raritan Valley Comm Coll (NJ)
Springfield Tech Comm Coll (MA)
State U of New York Coll of Technology at Alfred (NY)
Terra State Comm Coll (OH)

AVIATION/AIRWAY MANAGEMENT
Comm Coll of Allegheny County (PA)
Florida State Coll at Jacksonville (FL)
Iowa Lakes Comm Coll (IA)
Lincoln Land Comm Coll (IL)
Miami Dade Coll (FL)
San Jacinto Coll District (TX)
Southwestern Illinois Coll (IL)

AVIONICS MAINTENANCE TECHNOLOGY
Big Bend Comm Coll (WA)
Cochise Coll, Sierra Vista (AZ)
Fox Valley Tech Coll (WI)
Gateway Comm Coll (CT)
Guilford Tech Comm Coll (NC)
Housatonic Comm Coll (CT)
Kankakee Comm Coll (IL)
Lake Region State Coll (ND)
Metropolitan Comm Coll–Maple Woods (MO)
Northwest Florida State Coll (FL)
Oklahoma City Comm Coll (OK)
Orange Coast Coll (CA)
Reedley Coll (CA)
Salt Lake Comm Coll (UT)
Tarrant County Coll District (TX)
Three Rivers Comm Coll (CT)

BAKING AND PASTRY ARTS
The Art Inst of Seattle (WA)
Clark Coll (WA)
Coll of DuPage (IL)
El Centro Coll (TX)
Elgin Comm Coll (IL)
Montgomery County Comm Coll (PA)
Mott Comm Coll (MI)
Niagara County Comm Coll (NY)
The Restaurant School at Walnut Hill Coll (PA)
San Jacinto Coll District (TX)

State U of New York Coll of Technology at Alfred (NY)
Sullivan County Comm Coll (NY)
Westmoreland County Comm Coll (PA)
White Mountains Comm Coll (NH)

BANKING AND FINANCIAL SUPPORT SERVICES
Austin Comm Coll (TX)
Catawba Valley Comm Coll (NC)
Central Georgia Tech Coll (GA)
Comm Coll of Allegheny County (PA)
Comm Coll of Rhode Island (RI)
Fayetteville Tech Comm Coll (NC)
Florida State Coll at Jacksonville (FL)
Fox Valley Tech Coll (WI)
Harper Coll (IL)
Houston Comm Coll System (TX)
Illinois Central Coll (IL)
Indian River State Coll (FL)
Lake Area Tech Inst (SD)
Lanier Tech Coll (GA)
Lansing Comm Coll (MI)
Mohawk Valley Comm Coll (NY)
Northeast Comm Coll (NE)
Ogeechee Tech Coll (GA)
Pensacola State Coll (FL)
Rockingham Comm Coll (NC)
St. Cloud Tech & Comm Coll (MN)
Seminole State Coll of Florida (FL)
Southeast Tech Inst (SD)
State U of New York Coll of Technology at Alfred (NY)
Terra State Comm Coll (OH)
Westmoreland County Comm Coll (PA)
Wiregrass Georgia Tech Coll (GA)

BARBERING
Oklahoma Tech Coll (OK)

BEHAVIORAL SCIENCES
Amarillo Coll (TX)
Ancilla Coll (IN)
Colorado Mountain Coll (CO)
Colorado Mountain Coll, Alpine Campus (CO)
Highline Comm Coll (WA)
Iowa Lakes Comm Coll (IA)
Miami Dade Coll (FL)
Monroe Comm Coll (NY)
Northwestern Connecticut Comm Coll (CT)
Orange Coast Coll (CA)
San Diego City Coll (CA)
San Jacinto Coll District (TX)
Santa Rosa Jr Coll (CA)
Tyler Jr Coll (TX)
Umpqua Comm Coll (OR)
Vincennes U (IN)

BIBLICAL STUDIES
Amarillo Coll (TX)

BILINGUAL AND MULTILINGUAL EDUCATION
Delaware Tech & Comm Coll, Terry Campus (DE)

BIOCHEMISTRY
Pensacola State Coll (FL)
Vincennes U (IN)

BIOENGINEERING AND BIOMEDICAL ENGINEERING
Anoka-Ramsey Comm Coll (MN)
Anoka-Ramsey Comm Coll, Cambridge Campus (MN)
Bunker Hill Comm Coll (MA)
Quinsigamond Comm Coll (MA)

BIOLOGICAL AND BIOMEDICAL SCIENCES RELATED
Murray State Coll (OK)
Northeast Comm Coll (NE)

BIOLOGICAL AND PHYSICAL SCIENCES
Ancilla Coll (IN)
Burlington County Coll (NJ)
Central Oregon Comm Coll (OR)

Chipola Coll (FL)
City Colls of Chicago, Harry S. Truman College (IL)
Clinton Comm Coll (NY)
Coll of DuPage (IL)
Coll of Lake County (IL)
Coll of the Canyons (CA)
Colorado Mountain Coll (CO)
Colorado Mountain Coll, Alpine Campus (CO)
Comm Coll of Rhode Island (RI)
Copiah-Lincoln Comm Coll (MS)
Corning Comm Coll (NY)
Delaware County Comm Coll (PA)
Dutchess Comm Coll (NY)
Elgin Comm Coll (IL)
Gavilan Coll (CA)
Georgia Highlands Coll (GA)
Highland Comm Coll (IL)
Highline Comm Coll (WA)
Howard Comm Coll (MD)
Illinois Eastern Comm Colls, Frontier Community College (IL)
Illinois Eastern Comm Colls, Lincoln Trail College (IL)
Illinois Eastern Comm Colls, Olney Central College (IL)
Illinois Eastern Comm Colls, Wabash Valley College (IL)
Illinois Valley Comm Coll (IL)
Iowa Lakes Comm Coll (IA)
John Wood Comm Coll (IL)
J. Sargeant Reynolds Comm Coll (VA)
Kankakee Comm Coll (IL)
Kaskaskia Coll (IL)
Kilgore Coll (TX)
Kirtland Comm Coll (MI)
Laramie County Comm Coll (WY)
Lincoln Land Comm Coll (IL)
Massachusetts Bay Comm Coll (MA)
McHenry County Coll (IL)
Metropolitan Comm Coll–Longview (MO)
Metropolitan Comm Coll–Maple Woods (MO)
Metropolitan Comm Coll–Penn Valley (MO)
Mid Michigan Comm Coll (MI)
Monroe Comm Coll (NY)
Moraine Valley Comm Coll (IL)
Niagara County Comm Coll (NY)
Northeastern Jr Coll (CO)
Northern Essex Comm Coll (MA)
Northwest Florida State Coll (FL)
Otero Jr Coll (CO)
Peninsula Coll (WA)
Penn State Beaver (PA)
Penn State DuBois (PA)
Penn State Fayette, The Eberly Campus (PA)
Penn State Greater Allegheny (PA)
Penn State New Kensington (PA)
Penn State Schuylkill (PA)
Penn State Shenango (PA)
Piedmont Virginia Comm Coll (VA)
Rainy River Comm Coll (MN)
Rockland Comm Coll (NY)
Santa Monica Coll (CA)
Shawnee Comm Coll (IL)
South Suburban Coll (IL)
Southwestern Illinois Coll (IL)
Southwest Mississippi Comm Coll (MS)
Terra State Comm Coll (OH)
Trident Tech Coll (SC)
Umpqua Comm Coll (OR)
U of South Carolina Union (SC)
U of Wisconsin–Richland (WI)
Vincennes U (IN)
Virginia Western Comm Coll (VA)
Wytheville Comm Coll (VA)

BIOLOGY/BIOLOGICAL SCIENCES
Alvin Comm Coll (TX)
Amarillo Coll (TX)
Ancilla Coll (IN)
Anne Arundel Comm Coll (MD)
Anoka-Ramsey Comm Coll (MN)
Anoka-Ramsey Comm Coll, Cambridge Campus (MN)
Austin Comm Coll (TX)
Bainbridge Coll (GA)
Bunker Hill Comm Coll (MA)
Burlington County Coll (NJ)
Carl Albert State Coll (OK)

Casper Coll (WY)
Cecil Coll (MD)
Central Oregon Comm Coll (OR)
Central Wyoming Coll (WY)
Cochise Coll, Sierra Vista (AZ)
Colorado Mountain Coll (CO)
Colorado Mountain Coll, Alpine Campus (CO)
Comm Coll of Allegheny County (PA)
Copiah-Lincoln Comm Coll (MS)
Cowley County Comm Coll and Area Vocational–Tech School (KS)
Crowder Coll (MO)
Dakota Coll at Bottineau (ND)
Delaware Tech & Comm Coll, Jack F. Owens Campus (DE)
Delaware Tech & Comm Coll, Stanton/Wilmington Campus (DE)
Eastern Arizona Coll (AZ)
Fiorello H. LaGuardia Comm Coll of the City U of New York (NY)
Foothill Coll (CA)
Gavilan Coll (CA)
Harper Coll (IL)
Hutchinson Comm Coll and Area Vocational School (KS)
Indian River State Coll (FL)
Iowa Lakes Comm Coll (IA)
Jamestown Comm Coll (NY)
Kingsborough Comm Coll of the City U of New York (NY)
Lake Michigan Coll (MI)
Lansing Comm Coll (MI)
Laramie County Comm Coll (WY)
Lehigh Carbon Comm Coll (PA)
Los Angeles Harbor Coll (CA)
Macomb Comm Coll (MI)
Mendocino Coll (CA)
Metropolitan Comm Coll–Longview (MO)
Metropolitan Comm Coll–Maple Woods (MO)
Metropolitan Comm Coll–Penn Valley (MO)
Miami Dade Coll (FL)
Mid Michigan Comm Coll (MI)
Minneapolis Comm and Tech Coll (MN)
Monroe Comm Coll (NY)
Monroe County Comm Coll (MI)
Montgomery County Comm Coll (PA)
Mott Comm Coll (MI)
Murray State Coll (OK)
Northampton Comm Coll (PA)
Northeast Comm Coll (NE)
Northeastern Jr Coll (CO)
North Hennepin Comm Coll (MN)
Northwest Coll (WY)
Northwestern Connecticut Comm Coll (CT)
Northwest Florida State Coll (FL)
Oklahoma City Comm Coll (OK)
Orange Coast Coll (CA)
Otero Jr Coll (CO)
Palm Beach State Coll (FL)
Pensacola State Coll (FL)
Reedley Coll (CA)
St. Philip's Coll (TX)
Salt Lake Comm Coll (UT)
San Diego City Coll (CA)
San Jacinto Coll District (TX)
San Juan Coll (NM)
Santa Rosa Jr Coll (CA)
Snow Coll (UT)
Southwest Mississippi Comm Coll (MS)
Springfield Tech Comm Coll (MA)
State Coll of Florida Manatee-Sarasota (FL)
State U of New York Coll of Technology at Alfred (NY)
Terra State Comm Coll (OH)
Texarkana Coll (TX)
Texas State Tech Coll Harlingen (TX)
Truckee Meadows Comm Coll (NV)
Tyler Jr Coll (TX)
Umpqua Comm Coll (OR)
Union County Coll (NJ)
Vincennes U (IN)

BIOLOGY/BIOTECHNOLOGY LABORATORY TECHNICIAN
Athens Tech Coll (GA)

Austin Comm Coll (TX)
Berkeley City Coll (CA)
Bucks County Comm Coll (PA)
Delaware Tech & Comm Coll, Jack F. Owens Campus (DE)
Delaware Tech & Comm Coll, Stanton/Wilmington Campus (DE)
Elgin Comm Coll (IL)
Gateway Tech Coll (WI)
Guilford Tech Comm Coll (NC)
Hagerstown Comm Coll (MD)
Hillsborough Comm Coll (FL)
Houston Comm Coll System (TX)
Jamestown Comm Coll (NY)
Lake Area Tech Inst (SD)
Massachusetts Bay Comm Coll (MA)
Monroe Comm Coll (NY)
Montgomery Coll (MD)
Muskegon Comm Coll (MI)
North Dakota State Coll of Science (ND)
North Shore Comm Coll (MA)
Randolph Comm Coll (NC)
Rockingham Comm Coll (NC)
Salt Lake Comm Coll (UT)
Westmoreland County Comm Coll (PA)
Wilson Comm Coll (NC)

BIOLOGY TEACHER EDUCATION
Bucks County Comm Coll (PA)
State Coll of Florida Manatee-Sarasota (FL)

BIOMEDICAL TECHNOLOGY
Anoka-Ramsey Comm Coll (MN)
Anoka-Ramsey Comm Coll, Cambridge Campus (MN)
Chattahoochee Tech Coll (GA)
Delaware County Comm Coll (PA)
Delaware Tech & Comm Coll, Terry Campus (DE)
Florida State Coll at Jacksonville (FL)
Gateway Comm Coll (CT)
Howard Comm Coll (MD)
Miami Dade Coll (FL)
Minnesota State Coll–Southeast Tech (MN)
Muskegon Comm Coll (MI)
New Mexico State U–Alamogordo (NM)
North Seattle Comm Coll (WA)
Owens Comm Coll, Toledo (OH)
Penn State DuBois (PA)
Penn State Fayette, The Eberly Campus (PA)
Penn State Hazleton (PA)
Penn State New Kensington (PA)
Penn State Schuylkill (PA)
Penn State Shenango (PA)
Penn State York (PA)
St. Philip's Coll (TX)
Southeastern Comm Coll (IA)
Southeast Tech Inst (SD)
Stark State Coll (OH)
Texas State Tech Coll Harlingen (TX)
Western Iowa Tech Comm Coll (IA)

BIOTECHNOLOGY
Augusta Tech Coll (GA)
Bucks County Comm Coll (PA)
Bunker Hill Comm Coll (MA)
Burlington County Coll (NJ)
El Centro Coll (TX)
GateWay Comm Coll (AZ)
Howard Comm Coll (MD)
Hutchinson Comm Coll and Area Vocational School (KS)
Ivy Tech Comm Coll–Central Indiana (IN)
Ivy Tech Comm Coll–Lafayette (IN)
Ivy Tech Comm Coll–North Central (IN)
Lansing Comm Coll (MI)
Lehigh Carbon Comm Coll (PA)
Miami Dade Coll (FL)
Minneapolis Comm and Tech Coll (MN)
Montgomery County Comm Coll (PA)
Mount Wachusett Comm Coll (MA)
Northampton Comm Coll (PA)

Oakland Comm Coll (MI)
Oklahoma City Comm Coll (OK)
Piedmont Virginia Comm Coll (VA)
Quinsigamond Comm Coll (MA)
Raritan Valley Comm Coll (NJ)
Salem Comm Coll (NJ)
San Jacinto Coll District (TX)
Southern Maine Comm Coll (ME)
Springfield Tech Comm Coll (MA)
Tompkins Cortland Comm Coll (NY)
Vincennes U (IN)

BLASTING
Moraine Park Tech Coll (WI)

BLOOD BANK TECHNOLOGY
Rasmussen Coll St. Cloud (MN)

BOILERMAKING
Ivy Tech Comm Coll–Southwest (IN)

BOTANY/PLANT BIOLOGY
Iowa Lakes Comm Coll (IA)
Palm Beach State Coll (FL)
Pensacola State Coll (FL)
Snow Coll (UT)

BROADCAST JOURNALISM
Amarillo Coll (TX)
Colby Comm Coll (KS)
Iowa Lakes Comm Coll (IA)
Kingsborough Comm Coll of the City U of New York (NY)
Northwest Coll (WY)
Ocean County Coll (NJ)
Oklahoma City Comm Coll (OK)

BUILDING/CONSTRUCTION FINISHING, MANAGEMENT, AND INSPECTION RELATED
Central Comm Coll–Hastings Campus (NE)
Coll of Southern Maryland (MD)
The Comm Coll of Baltimore County (MD)
Fayetteville Tech Comm Coll (NC)
Gwinnett Tech Coll (GA)
Ivy Tech Comm Coll–Northwest (IN)
Lawson State Comm Coll (AL)
Mid-Plains Comm Coll, North Platte (NE)
Mohave Comm Coll (AZ)
Montgomery Coll (MD)
Northeast Comm Coll (NE)
Olympic Coll (WA)
Palm Beach State Coll (FL)
St. Philip's Coll (TX)
Salt Lake Comm Coll (UT)
Seminole State Coll of Florida (FL)
Snow Coll (UT)
Southeast Tech Inst (SD)
Springfield Tech Comm Coll (MA)

BUILDING/CONSTRUCTION SITE MANAGEMENT
Coll of the Canyons (CA)
The Comm Coll of Baltimore County (MD)
Hillsborough Comm Coll (FL)
Lehigh Carbon Comm Coll (PA)
Metropolitan Comm Coll–Business & Technology Campus (MO)
North Hennepin Comm Coll (MN)

BUILDING CONSTRUCTION TECHNOLOGY
Cochise Coll, Sierra Vista (AZ)
Mitchell Tech Inst (SD)
North Dakota State Coll of Science (ND)
Red Rocks Comm Coll (CO)
Truckee Meadows Comm Coll (NV)
U of Alaska Anchorage, Kodiak Coll (AK)

BUILDING/HOME/ CONSTRUCTION INSPECTION
Bucks County Comm Coll (PA)
McHenry County Coll (IL)
North Hennepin Comm Coll (MN)

Oklahoma State U, Oklahoma City (OK)
Orange Coast Coll (CA)
South Suburban Coll (IL)
Vincennes U (IN)

BUILDING/PROPERTY MAINTENANCE
Cape Fear Comm Coll (NC)
Century Coll (MN)
Coll of DuPage (IL)
Comm Coll of Allegheny County (PA)
Delaware County Comm Coll (PA)
Erie Comm Coll (NY)
Guilford Tech Comm Coll (NC)
Ivy Tech Comm Coll–Bloomington (IN)
Ivy Tech Comm Coll–Central Indiana (IN)
Ivy Tech Comm Coll–Columbus (IN)
Ivy Tech Comm Coll–East Central (IN)
Ivy Tech Comm Coll–Kokomo (IN)
Ivy Tech Comm Coll–Lafayette (IN)
Ivy Tech Comm Coll–North Central (IN)
Ivy Tech Comm Coll–Northeast (IN)
Ivy Tech Comm Coll–Northwest (IN)
Ivy Tech Comm Coll–Richmond (IN)
Ivy Tech Comm Coll–Southern Indiana (IN)
Ivy Tech Comm Coll–Southwest (IN)
Ivy Tech Comm Coll–Wabash Valley (IN)
Lincoln Land Comm Coll (IL)
Mitchell Tech Inst (SD)
Mohawk Valley Comm Coll (NY)
Pensacola State Coll (FL)

BUSINESS ADMINISTRATION AND MANAGEMENT
Alvin Comm Coll (TX)
Amarillo Coll (TX)
Ancilla Coll (IN)
Anne Arundel Comm Coll (MD)
Anoka-Ramsey Comm Coll (MN)
Anoka-Ramsey Comm Coll, Cambridge Campus (MN)
Augusta Tech Coll (GA)
Austin Comm Coll (TX)
Bainbridge Coll (GA)
Beaufort County Comm Coll (NC)
Berkeley City Coll (CA)
Berkshire Comm Coll (MA)
Blackhawk Tech Coll (WI)
Bluegrass Comm and Tech Coll (KY)
Bradford School (OH)
Brookhaven Coll (TX)
Bucks County Comm Coll (PA)
Bunker Hill Comm Coll (MA)
Burlington County Coll (NJ)
Cape Fear Comm Coll (NC)
Career Tech Coll (LA)
Carl Albert State Coll (OK)
Carroll Comm Coll (MD)
Casper Coll (WY)
Catawba Valley Comm Coll (NC)
Cayuga County Comm Coll (NY)
Cecil Coll (MD)
Central Carolina Comm Coll (NC)
Central Carolina Tech Coll (SC)
Central Comm Coll–Columbus Campus (NE)
Central Comm Coll–Grand Island Campus (NE)
Central Comm Coll–Hastings Campus (NE)
Central Georgia Tech Coll (GA)
Central Maine Comm Coll (ME)
Central Oregon Comm Coll (OR)
Central Wyoming Coll (WY)
Century Coll (MN)
Chandler-Gilbert Comm Coll (AZ)
Chattahoochee Tech Coll (GA)
Chattahoochee Valley Comm Coll (AL)
Chattanooga State Comm Coll (TN)
Chipola Coll (FL)
Chippewa Valley Tech Coll (WI)

City Colls of Chicago, Harry S. Truman College (IL)
Clark Coll (WA)
Cleveland State Comm Coll (TN)
Clinton Comm Coll (NY)
Cochise Coll, Sierra Vista (AZ)
Colby Comm Coll (KS)
Coll of Business and Technology (FL)
Coll of DuPage (IL)
Coll of Lake County (IL)
Coll of Southern Maryland (MD)
Coll of the Canyons (CA)
Coll of the Ouachitas (AR)
Colorado Mountain Coll (CO)
Colorado Mountain Coll, Alpine Campus (CO)
Comm Coll of Allegheny County (PA)
The Comm Coll of Baltimore County (MD)
Comm Coll of Philadelphia (PA)
Comm Coll of Rhode Island (RI)
Comm Coll of Vermont (VT)
Consolidated School of Business, York (PA)
Copiah-Lincoln Comm Coll (MS)
Corning Comm Coll (NY)
Cowley County Comm Coll and Area Vocational–Tech School (KS)
Crowder Coll (MO)
Dakota Coll at Bottineau (ND)
Delaware County Comm Coll (PA)
Delaware Tech & Comm Coll, Stanton/Wilmington Campus (DE)
Delaware Tech & Comm Coll, Terry Campus (DE)
Denmark Tech Coll (SC)
Do&nna Ana Comm Coll (NM)
Dutchess Comm Coll (NY)
Dyersburg State Comm Coll (TN)
Eastern Arizona Coll (AZ)
Edison Comm Coll (OH)
El Centro Coll (TX)
Elgin Comm Coll (IL)
El Paso Comm Coll (TX)
Erie Comm Coll (NY)
Erie Comm Coll, North Campus (NY)
Erie Comm Coll, South Campus (NY)
Fayetteville Tech Comm Coll (NC)
Fiorello H. LaGuardia Comm Coll of the City U of New York (NY)
Florida State Coll at Jacksonville (FL)
Foothill Coll (CA)
Forrest Coll (SC)
Fox Valley Tech Coll (WI)
Garrett Coll (MD)
GateWay Comm Coll (AZ)
Gateway Comm Coll (CT)
Gateway Tech Coll (WI)
Gavilan Coll (CA)
Genesee Comm Coll (NY)
Georgia Highlands Coll (GA)
Goodwin Coll (CT)
Grand Rapids Comm Coll (MI)
Guilford Tech Comm Coll (NC)
Gulf Coast State Coll (FL)
Gwinnett Tech Coll (GA)
Hagerstown Comm Coll (MD)
Harford Comm Coll (MD)
Harper Coll (IL)
Hesser Coll, Concord (NH)
Hesser Coll, Manchester (NH)
Hesser Coll, Nashua (NH)
Hesser Coll, Portsmouth (NH)
Hesser Coll, Salem (NH)
Highline Comm Coll (WA)
Hillsborough Comm Coll (FL)
Holyoke Comm Coll (MA)
Housatonic Comm Coll (CT)
Houston Comm Coll System (TX)
Howard Comm Coll (MD)
Illinois Central Coll (IL)
Illinois Eastern Comm Colls, Wabash Valley College (IL)
Illinois Valley Comm Coll (IL)
Indian River State Coll (FL)
Inst of Business & Medical Careers (CO)
Iowa Lakes Comm Coll (IA)
Itasca Comm Coll (MN)
ITT Tech Inst, Bessemer (AL)

ITT Tech Inst, Madison (AL)
ITT Tech Inst, Mobile (AL)
ITT Tech Inst, Phoenix (AZ)
ITT Tech Inst, Tucson (AZ)
ITT Tech Inst (AR)
ITT Tech Inst, Lathrop (CA)
ITT Tech Inst, Orange (CA)
ITT Tech Inst, Oxnard (CA)
ITT Tech Inst, Rancho Cordova (CA)
ITT Tech Inst, San Bernardino (CA)
ITT Tech Inst, San Dimas (CA)
ITT Tech Inst, Sylmar (CA)
ITT Tech Inst, Torrance (CA)
ITT Tech Inst, Aurora (CO)
ITT Tech Inst, Thornton (CO)
ITT Tech Inst, Fort Lauderdale (FL)
ITT Tech Inst, Fort Myers (FL)
ITT Tech Inst, Jacksonville (FL)
ITT Tech Inst, Lake Mary (FL)
ITT Tech Inst, Miami (FL)
ITT Tech Inst, Pinellas Park (FL)
ITT Tech Inst, Tallahassee (FL)
ITT Tech Inst, Tampa (FL)
ITT Tech Inst (ID)
ITT Tech Inst, Fort Wayne (IN)
ITT Tech Inst, Merrillville (IN)
ITT Tech Inst, Newburgh (IN)
ITT Tech Inst, Cedar Rapids (IA)
ITT Tech Inst, Clive (IA)
ITT Tech Inst, Louisville (KY)
ITT Tech Inst, Baton Rouge (LA)
ITT Tech Inst, St. Rose (LA)
ITT Tech Inst, Canton (MI)
ITT Tech Inst, Swartz Creek (MI)
ITT Tech Inst, Troy (MI)
ITT Tech Inst, Wyoming (MI)
ITT Tech Inst, Eden Prairie (MN)
ITT Tech Inst, Earth City (MO)
ITT Tech Inst, Kansas City (MO)
ITT Tech Inst (NE)
ITT Tech Inst, Henderson (NV)
ITT Tech Inst (NM)
ITT Tech Inst, Akron (OH)
ITT Tech Inst, Columbus (OH)
ITT Tech Inst, Dayton (OH)
ITT Tech Inst, Hilliard (OH)
ITT Tech Inst, Maumee (OH)
ITT Tech Inst, Norwood (OH)
ITT Tech Inst, Strongsville (OH)
ITT Tech Inst, Warrensville Heights (OH)
ITT Tech Inst, Youngstown (OH)
ITT Tech Inst, Tulsa (OK)
ITT Tech Inst, Portland (OR)
ITT Tech Inst, Chattanooga (TN)
ITT Tech Inst, Cordova (TN)
ITT Tech Inst, Johnson City (TN)
ITT Tech Inst, Knoxville (TN)
ITT Tech Inst, Nashville (TN)
ITT Tech Inst, Arlington (TX)
ITT Tech Inst, Austin (TX)
ITT Tech Inst, DeSoto (TX)
ITT Tech Inst, Houston (TX)
ITT Tech Inst, Houston (TX)
ITT Tech Inst, Richardson (TX)
ITT Tech Inst, San Antonio (TX)
ITT Tech Inst, Webster (TX)
ITT Tech Inst (UT)
ITT Tech Inst, Chantilly (VA)
ITT Tech Inst, Norfolk (VA)
ITT Tech Inst, Richmond (VA)
ITT Tech Inst, Salem (VA)
ITT Tech Inst, Springfield (VA)
ITT Tech Inst, Everett (WA)
ITT Tech Inst, Seattle (WA)
ITT Tech Inst, Spokane Valley (WA)
ITT Tech Inst (WV)
ITT Tech Inst, Green Bay (WI)
ITT Tech Inst, Greenfield (WI)
ITT Tech Inst, Madison (WI)
Ivy Tech Comm Coll–Bloomington (IN)
Ivy Tech Comm Coll–Central Indiana (IN)
Ivy Tech Comm Coll–Columbus (IN)
Ivy Tech Comm Coll–East Central (IN)
Ivy Tech Comm Coll–Kokomo (IN)
Ivy Tech Comm Coll–Lafayette (IN)
Ivy Tech Comm Coll–North Central (IN)
Ivy Tech Comm Coll–Northeast (IN)
Ivy Tech Comm Coll–Northwest (IN)

Ivy Tech Comm Coll–Richmond (IN)
Ivy Tech Comm Coll–Southeast (IN)
Ivy Tech Comm Coll–Southern Indiana (IN)
Ivy Tech Comm Coll–Southwest (IN)
Ivy Tech Comm Coll–Wabash Valley (IN)
Jackson Comm Coll (MI)
James Sprunt Comm Coll (NC)
Jamestown Business Coll (NY)
Jamestown Comm Coll (NY)
Jefferson Comm Coll (NY)
Johnston Comm Coll (NC)
John Tyler Comm Coll (VA)
John Wood Comm Coll (IL)
J. Sargeant Reynolds Comm Coll (VA)
Kansas City Kansas Comm Coll (KS)
Kaplan Career Inst, Harrisburg Campus (PA)
Kaplan Career Inst, ICM Campus (PA)
Kent State U at Ashtabula (OH)
Kent State U at East Liverpool (OH)
Kent State U at Salem (OH)
Kent State U at Trumbull (OH)
Kent State U at Tuscarawas (OH)
Kilgore Coll (TX)
Kilian Comm Coll (SD)
Kingsborough Comm Coll of the City U of New York (NY)
Kirtland Comm Coll (MI)
Lake Michigan Coll (MI)
Lake Region State Coll (ND)
Lansing Comm Coll (MI)
Laramie County Comm Coll (WY)
Lawson State Comm Coll (AL)
Lehigh Carbon Comm Coll (PA)
Long Island Business Inst (NY)
Los Angeles Harbor Coll (CA)
Lower Columbia Coll (WA)
Macomb Comm Coll (MI)
Manchester Comm Coll (CT)
Massachusetts Bay Comm Coll (MA)
McHenry County Coll (IL)
Mendocino Coll (CA)
Metropolitan Comm Coll–Blue River (MO)
Metropolitan Comm Coll–Business & Technology Campus (MO)
Metropolitan Comm Coll–Longview (MO)
Metropolitan Comm Coll–Maple Woods (MO)
Metropolitan Comm Coll–Penn Valley (MO)
Miami Dade Coll (FL)
Mid Michigan Comm Coll (MI)
Mid-Plains Comm Coll, North Platte (NE)
Minneapolis Comm and Tech Coll (MN)
Minnesota School of Business– Brooklyn Center (MN)
Minnesota School of Business– Plymouth (MN)
Minnesota School of Business– Richfield (MN)
Minnesota School of Business–St. Cloud (MN)
Minnesota School of Business– Shakopee (MN)
Minnesota State Coll–Southeast Tech (MN)
Missouri State U–West Plains (MO)
Mohave Comm Coll (AZ)
Mohawk Valley Comm Coll (NY)
Monroe Comm Coll (NY)
Monroe County Comm Coll (MI)
Montana State U–Great Falls Coll of Technology (MT)
Montcalm Comm Coll (MI)
Montgomery Comm Coll (NC)
Montgomery County Comm Coll (PA)
Moraine Park Tech Coll (WI)
Moraine Valley Comm Coll (IL)
Motlow State Comm Coll (TN)
Mott Comm Coll (MI)
MTI Coll, Sacramento (CA)
Muskegon Comm Coll (MI)
Niagara County Comm Coll (NY)

Northampton Comm Coll (PA)
North Dakota State Coll of Science (ND)
Northeast Alabama Comm Coll (AL)
Northeast Comm Coll (NE)
Northeastern Jr Coll (CO)
Northeast Iowa Comm Coll (IA)
Northern Essex Comm Coll (MA)
North Hennepin Comm Coll (MN)
North Shore Comm Coll (MA)
Northwest Coll (WY)
Northwestern Connecticut Comm Coll (CT)
Northwest Florida State Coll (FL)
Northwest Tech Coll (MN)
Oakland Comm Coll (MI)
Ocean County Coll (NJ)
Oklahoma City Comm Coll (OK)
Oklahoma State U, Oklahoma City (OK)
Olympic Coll (WA)
Onondaga Comm Coll (NY)
Orange Coast Coll (CA)
Otero Jr Coll (CO)
Owensboro Comm and Tech Coll (KY)
Pasco-Hernando Comm Coll (FL)
Peninsula Coll (WA)
Pensacola State Coll (FL)
Piedmont Virginia Comm Coll (VA)
Pittsburgh Tech Inst, Oakdale (PA)
Polk State Coll (FL)
Quinsigamond Comm Coll (MA)
Rainy River Comm Coll (MN)
Randolph Comm Coll (NC)
Raritan Valley Comm Coll (NJ)
Rasmussen Coll Aurora (IL)
Rasmussen Coll Bloomington (MN)
Rasmussen Coll Brooklyn Park (MN)
Rasmussen Coll Eagan (MN)
Rasmussen Coll Fort Myers (FL)
Rasmussen Coll Green Bay (WI)
Rasmussen Coll Lake Elmo/Woodbury (MN)
Rasmussen Coll Mankato (MN)
Rasmussen Coll Moorhead (MN)
Rasmussen Coll New Port Richey (FL)
Rasmussen Coll Ocala (FL)
Rasmussen Coll St. Cloud (MN)
Red Rocks Comm Coll (CO)
Riverside City Coll (CA)
Rockingham Comm Coll (NC)
Rockland Comm Coll (NY)
Rogue Comm Coll (OR)
St. Cloud Tech & Comm Coll (MN)
St. Philip's Coll (TX)
Salem Comm Coll (NJ)
Salt Lake Comm Coll (UT)
San Diego City Coll (CA)
San Jacinto Coll District (TX)
San Joaquin Valley Coll, Bakersfield (CA)
San Joaquin Valley Coll, Fresno (CA)
San Joaquin Valley Coll, Rancho Cordova (CA)
San Joaquin Valley Coll, Salida (CA)
San Joaquin Valley Coll–Online (CA)
San Juan Coll (NM)
Santa Monica Coll (CA)
Santa Rosa Jr Coll (CA)
Scottsdale Comm Coll (AZ)
Seminole State Coll of Florida (FL)
Shawnee Comm Coll (IL)
Snow Coll (UT)
Southeastern Comm Coll (IA)
Southeast Tech Inst (SD)
Southern Crescent Tech Coll (GA)
Southern Maine Comm Coll (ME)
Southern State Comm Coll (OH)
Southwestern Indian Polytechnic Inst (NM)
Southwestern Michigan Coll (MI)
Southwestern Oklahoma State U at Sayre (OK)
Southwest Mississippi Comm Coll (MS)
Spencerian Coll (KY)
Springfield Tech Comm Coll (MA)
Stark State Coll (OH)
State Coll of Florida Manatee-Sarasota (FL)
Sullivan County Comm Coll (NY)
Tallahassee Comm Coll (FL)

Tarrant County Coll District (TX)
Terra State Comm Coll (OH)
Texarkana Coll (TX)
Three Rivers Comm Coll (CT)
Tompkins Cortland Comm Coll (NY)
Trident Tech Coll (SC)
Truckee Meadows Comm Coll (NV)
Tunxis Comm Coll (CT)
Tyler Jr Coll (TX)
Umpqua Comm Coll (OR)
Union County Coll (NJ)
The U of Akron–Wayne Coll (OH)
Valencia Coll (FL)
Vincennes U (IN)
Virginia Western Comm Coll (VA)
Volunteer State Comm Coll (TN)
Waukesha County Tech Coll (WI)
Westchester Comm Coll (NY)
Western Iowa Tech Comm Coll (IA)
West Kentucky Comm and Tech Coll (KY)
Westmoreland County Comm Coll (PA)
West Virginia Jr Coll–Bridgeport (WV)
White Mountains Comm Coll (NH)
Wilson Comm Coll (NC)
Wisconsin Indianhead Tech Coll (WI)
Wytheville Comm Coll (VA)
York County Comm Coll (ME)
YTI Career Inst–York (PA)

BUSINESS ADMINISTRATION, MANAGEMENT AND OPERATIONS RELATED
Anne Arundel Comm Coll (MD)
Berkeley City Coll (CA)
Bunker Hill Comm Coll (MA)
Cecil Coll (MD)
Chandler-Gilbert Comm Coll (AZ)
Comm Care Coll (OK)
The Comm Coll of Baltimore County (MD)
GateWay Comm Coll (AZ)
John Tyler Comm Coll (VA)
Normandale Comm Coll (MN)
Red Rocks Comm Coll (CO)
Southwest Virginia Comm Coll (VA)
Waukesha County Tech Coll (WI)

BUSINESS AND PERSONAL/FINANCIAL SERVICES MARKETING
Hutchinson Comm Coll and Area Vocational School (KS)
Vincennes U (IN)

BUSINESS AUTOMATION/TECHNOLOGY/DATA ENTRY
Berkshire Comm Coll (MA)
Casper Coll (WY)
Central Wyoming Coll (WY)
Clark Coll (WA)
Coll of Lake County (IL)
Comm Coll of Allegheny County (PA)
Crowder Coll (MO)
Dakota Coll at Bottineau (ND)
Delaware Tech & Comm Coll, Jack F. Owens Campus (DE)
Delaware Tech & Comm Coll, Stanton/Wilmington Campus (DE)
Delaware Tech & Comm Coll, Terry Campus (DE)
El Centro Coll (TX)
El Paso Comm Coll (TX)
Garrett Coll (MD)
GateWay Comm Coll (AZ)
Houston Comm Coll System (TX)
Illinois Eastern Comm Colls, Frontier Community College (IL)
Illinois Eastern Comm Colls, Lincoln Trail College (IL)
Illinois Eastern Comm Colls, Olney Central College (IL)
Illinois Eastern Comm Colls, Wabash Valley College (IL)
Illinois Valley Comm Coll (IL)
Iowa Lakes Comm Coll (IA)
Ivy Tech Comm Coll–Bloomington (IN)
Ivy Tech Comm Coll–Central Indiana (IN)
Ivy Tech Comm Coll–Columbus (IN)

Ivy Tech Comm Coll–East Central (IN)
Ivy Tech Comm Coll–Kokomo (IN)
Ivy Tech Comm Coll–Lafayette (IN)
Ivy Tech Comm Coll–North Central (IN)
Ivy Tech Comm Coll–Northeast (IN)
Ivy Tech Comm Coll–Northwest (IN)
Ivy Tech Comm Coll–Richmond (IN)
Ivy Tech Comm Coll–Southeast (IN)
Ivy Tech Comm Coll–Southern Indiana (IN)
Ivy Tech Comm Coll–Southwest (IN)
Kaskaskia Coll (IL)
Lincoln Land Comm Coll (IL)
Macomb Comm Coll (MI)
Minneapolis Comm and Tech Coll (MN)
Mitchell Tech Inst (SD)
Northeast Iowa Comm Coll (IA)
Oakland Comm Coll (MI)
Ozarka Coll (AR)
Panola Coll (TX)
San Jacinto Coll District (TX)
Southwestern Indian Polytechnic Inst (NM)
The U of Montana–Helena Coll of Technology (MT)
Western Iowa Tech Comm Coll (IA)

BUSINESS/COMMERCE
Anne Arundel Comm Coll (MD)
Anoka-Ramsey Comm Coll (MN)
Anoka-Ramsey Comm Coll, Cambridge Campus (MN)
Arkansas State U–Mountain Home (AR)
Austin Comm Coll (TX)
Berkeley City Coll (CA)
Berkshire Comm Coll (MA)
Brookhaven Coll (TX)
Bucks County Comm Coll (PA)
Carl Albert State Coll (OK)
Cecil Coll (MD)
Central Wyoming Coll (WY)
Chandler-Gilbert Comm Coll (AZ)
Coll of Central Florida (FL)
Coll of Southern Maryland (MD)
Colorado Mountain Coll, Timberline Campus (CO)
The Comm Coll of Baltimore County (MD)
Comm Coll of Rhode Island (RI)
Dawson Comm Coll (MT)
Delaware Tech & Comm Coll, Jack F. Owens Campus (DE)
Delaware Tech & Comm Coll, Stanton/Wilmington Campus (DE)
Delaware Tech & Comm Coll, Terry Campus (DE)
El Centro Coll (TX)
El Paso Comm Coll (TX)
Garrett Coll (MD)
GateWay Comm Coll (AZ)
Gavilan Coll (CA)
Georgia Piedmont Tech Coll (GA)
Goodwin Coll (CT)
Hagerstown Comm Coll (MD)
Harford Comm Coll (MD)
Hutchinson Comm Coll and Area Vocational School (KS)
John Tyler Comm Coll (VA)
J. Sargeant Reynolds Comm Coll (VA)
Kankakee Comm Coll (IL)
Kaskaskia Coll (IL)
Kent State U at Salem (OH)
Kilgore Coll (TX)
Lansing Comm Coll (MI)
Laramie County Comm Coll (WY)
Lehigh Carbon Comm Coll (PA)
Lincoln Land Comm Coll (IL)
Macomb Comm Coll (MI)
Massachusetts Bay Comm Coll (MA)
Metropolitan Comm Coll–Business & Technology Campus (MO)
Mineral Area Coll (MO)
Missouri State U–West Plains (MO)
Montgomery Coll (MD)
Montgomery County Comm Coll (PA)
Moraine Valley Comm Coll (IL)
Mott Comm Coll (MI)
New Mexico State U–Alamogordo (NM)

Norco Coll (CA)
Northampton Comm Coll (PA)
Northeast Alabama Comm Coll (AL)
Northwest Coll (WY)
Ocean County Coll (NJ)
Onondaga Comm Coll (NY)
Owens Comm Coll, Toledo (OH)
Penn State Beaver (PA)
Penn State Brandywine (PA)
Penn State DuBois (PA)
Penn State Fayette, The Eberly Campus (PA)
Penn State Greater Allegheny (PA)
Penn State Hazleton (PA)
Penn State Lehigh Valley (PA)
Penn State Mont Alto (PA)
Penn State New Kensington (PA)
Penn State Schuylkill (PA)
Penn State Shenango (PA)
Penn State Wilkes-Barre (PA)
Penn State Worthington Scranton (PA)
Penn State York (PA)
Pensacola State Coll (FL)
Quinsigamond Comm Coll (MA)
Raritan Valley Comm Coll (NJ)
Reedley Coll (CA)
Rogue Comm Coll (OR)
St. Clair County Comm Coll (MI)
San Jacinto Coll District (TX)
San Joaquin Valley Coll, Visalia (CA)
Southern State Comm Coll (OH)
Southwestern Indian Polytechnic Inst (NM)
Springfield Tech Comm Coll (MA)
State Coll of Florida Manatee-Sarasota (FL)
Terra State Comm Coll (OH)
Texarkana Coll (TX)
Texas State Tech Coll Harlingen (TX)
Union County Coll (NJ)
U of Arkansas Comm Coll at Morrilton (AR)
Vincennes U (IN)
Westmoreland County Comm Coll (PA)
West Virginia Northern Comm Coll (WV)

BUSINESS/CORPORATE COMMUNICATIONS
Cecil Coll (MD)
Houston Comm Coll System (TX)
Montgomery County Comm Coll (PA)
North Seattle Comm Coll (WA)

BUSINESS MACHINE REPAIR
Comm Coll of Allegheny County (PA)
Iowa Lakes Comm Coll (IA)
Muskegon Comm Coll (MI)

BUSINESS, MANAGEMENT, AND MARKETING RELATED
Berkeley City Coll (CA)
Blue Ridge Comm and Tech Coll (WV)
Bucks County Comm Coll (PA)
Chandler-Gilbert Comm Coll (AZ)
Eastern Arizona Coll (AZ)
Kankakee Comm Coll (IL)
Niagara County Comm Coll (NY)
Tompkins Cortland Comm Coll (NY)

BUSINESS/MANAGERIAL ECONOMICS
State Coll of Florida Manatee-Sarasota (FL)

BUSINESS OPERATIONS SUPPORT AND SECRETARIAL SERVICES RELATED
Bunker Hill Comm Coll (MA)
Gateway Tech Coll (WI)
Northeast Comm Coll (NE)
Southwest Virginia Comm Coll (VA)

BUSINESS TEACHER EDUCATION
Amarillo Coll (TX)
Bainbridge Coll (GA)
Eastern Arizona Coll (AZ)
Iowa Lakes Comm Coll (IA)

Northeastern Jr Coll (CO)
Northern Essex Comm Coll (MA)
Palau Comm Coll (Palau)
Snow Coll (UT)
Southwest Mississippi Comm Coll (MS)

CABINETMAKING AND MILLWORK
Bucks County Comm Coll (PA)
Central Georgia Tech Coll (GA)
GateWay Comm Coll (AZ)
Ivy Tech Comm Coll–Bloomington (IN)
Ivy Tech Comm Coll–Central Indiana (IN)
Ivy Tech Comm Coll–Columbus (IN)
Ivy Tech Comm Coll–East Central (IN)
Ivy Tech Comm Coll–Kokomo (IN)
Ivy Tech Comm Coll–Lafayette (IN)
Ivy Tech Comm Coll–North Central (IN)
Ivy Tech Comm Coll–Northeast (IN)
Ivy Tech Comm Coll–Northwest (IN)
Ivy Tech Comm Coll–Richmond (IN)
Ivy Tech Comm Coll–Southern Indiana (IN)
Ivy Tech Comm Coll–Southwest (IN)
Ivy Tech Comm Coll–Wabash Valley (IN)
Macomb Comm Coll (MI)

CAD/CADD DRAFTING/DESIGN TECHNOLOGY
Central Oregon Comm Coll (OR)
Century Coll (MN)
Comm Coll of Vermont (VT)
Delaware County Comm Coll (PA)
Delaware Tech & Comm Coll, Stanton/Wilmington Campus (DE)
Elgin Comm Coll (IL)
Erie Comm Coll, South Campus (NY)
Front Range Comm Coll (CO)
Harford Comm Coll (MD)
Illinois Valley Comm Coll (IL)
ITT Tech Inst, Atlanta (GA)
ITT Tech Inst, Duluth (GA)
ITT Tech Inst, Kennesaw (GA)
ITT Tech Inst, Mount Prospect (IL)
ITT Tech Inst, Oak Brook (IL)
ITT Tech Inst, Orland Park (IL)
ITT Tech Inst, Owings Mills (MD)
ITT Tech Inst, Norwood (MA)
ITT Tech Inst, Wilmington (MA)
ITT Tech Inst (NJ)
ITT Tech Inst, Cary (NC)
ITT Tech Inst, Charlotte (NC)
ITT Tech Inst, High Point (NC)
ITT Tech Inst, Strongsville (OH)
ITT Tech Inst, Bensalem (PA)
ITT Tech Inst, Dunmore (PA)
ITT Tech Inst, Harrisburg (PA)
ITT Tech Inst, King of Prussia (PA)
ITT Tech Inst, Pittsburgh (PA)
ITT Tech Inst, Tarentum (PA)
ITT Tech Inst, Greenville (SC)
John Wood Comm Coll (IL)
Kansas City Kansas Comm Coll (KS)
Minnesota State Coll–Southeast Tech (MN)
Montgomery County Comm Coll (PA)
Northampton Comm Coll (PA)
Northwest Coll (WY)
St. Philip's Coll (TX)
Southern State Comm Coll (OH)
South Suburban Coll (IL)
State U of New York Coll of Technology at Alfred (NY)
Sullivan Coll of Technology and Design (KY)
YTI Career Inst–York (PA)

CARDIOVASCULAR TECHNOLOGY
Augusta Tech Coll (GA)
Bunker Hill Comm Coll (MA)
Central Georgia Tech Coll (GA)
Delaware Tech & Comm Coll, Stanton/Wilmington Campus (DE)
El Centro Coll (TX)

Harper Coll (IL)
Houston Comm Coll System (TX)
Howard Comm Coll (MD)
Kirtland Comm Coll (MI)
Orange Coast Coll (CA)
Polk State Coll (FL)
St. Cloud Tech & Comm Coll (MN)
Southeast Tech Inst (SD)
Southern Maine Comm Coll (ME)
Spencerian Coll (KY)
Valencia Coll (FL)

CARPENTRY

Austin Comm Coll (TX)
Bluegrass Comm and Tech Coll (KY)
Central Georgia Tech Coll (GA)
Central Wyoming Coll (WY)
Comm Coll of Allegheny County (PA)
GateWay Comm Coll (AZ)
Gavilan Coll (CA)
Hutchinson Comm Coll and Area Vocational School (KS)
Indian River State Coll (FL)
Iowa Lakes Comm Coll (IA)
Ivy Tech Comm Coll–Central Indiana (IN)
Ivy Tech Comm Coll–East Central (IN)
Ivy Tech Comm Coll–Lafayette (IN)
Ivy Tech Comm Coll–North Central (IN)
Ivy Tech Comm Coll–Northwest (IN)
Ivy Tech Comm Coll–Southern Indiana (IN)
Ivy Tech Comm Coll–Southwest (IN)
Ivy Tech Comm Coll–Wabash Valley (IN)
John Wood Comm Coll (IL)
Kaskaskia Coll (IL)
Lake Area Tech Inst (SD)
Metropolitan Comm Coll–Business & Technology Campus (MO)
Mineral Area Coll (MO)
Minnesota State Coll–Southeast Tech (MN)
Moraine Park Tech Coll (WI)
Oakland Comm Coll (MI)
Palau Comm Coll (Palau)
St. Cloud Tech & Comm Coll (MN)
San Diego City Coll (CA)
San Juan Coll (NM)
Southwestern Illinois Coll (IL)
Southwest Mississippi Comm Coll (MS)
State U of New York Coll of Technology at Alfred (NY)
The U of Montana–Helena Coll of Technology (MT)
Western Iowa Tech Comm Coll (IA)

CASINO MANAGEMENT

Lake Michigan Coll (MI)
Westmoreland County Comm Coll (PA)

CERAMIC ARTS AND CERAMICS

Iowa Lakes Comm Coll (IA)
Montgomery Comm Coll (NC)
Oakland Comm Coll (MI)
Palm Beach State Coll (FL)

CHEMICAL ENGINEERING

Burlington County Coll (NJ)
Itasca Comm Coll (MN)
Kilgore Coll (TX)
Monroe Comm Coll (NY)
Muskegon Comm Coll (MI)

CHEMICAL PROCESS TECHNOLOGY

San Jacinto Coll District (TX)

CHEMICAL TECHNOLOGY

Alvin Comm Coll (TX)
Amarillo Coll (TX)
Bucks County Comm Coll (PA)
Cape Fear Comm Coll (NC)
Coll of Lake County (IL)
Comm Coll of Allegheny County (PA)

Comm Coll of Philadelphia (PA)
Comm Coll of Rhode Island (RI)
Corning Comm Coll (NY)
Delaware Tech & Comm Coll, Stanton/Wilmington Campus (DE)
Guilford Tech Comm Coll (NC)
Houston Comm Coll System (TX)
ITI Tech Coll (LA)
Lansing Comm Coll (MI)
Lehigh Carbon Comm Coll (PA)
Massachusetts Bay Comm Coll (MA)
Mohawk Valley Comm Coll (NY)
Niagara County Comm Coll (NY)
Pensacola State Coll (FL)
Raritan Valley Comm Coll (NJ)
San Jacinto Coll District (TX)
Texas State Tech Coll Harlingen (TX)
Westmoreland County Comm Coll (PA)

CHEMISTRY

Amarillo Coll (TX)
Austin Comm Coll (TX)
Bainbridge Coll (GA)
Bunker Hill Comm Coll (MA)
Burlington County Coll (NJ)
Casper Coll (WY)
Comm Coll of Allegheny County (PA)
Copiah-Lincoln Comm Coll (MS)
Cowley County Comm Coll and Area Vocational–Tech School (KS)
Dakota Coll at Bottineau (ND)
Eastern Arizona Coll (AZ)
Foothill Coll (CA)
Grand Rapids Comm Coll (MI)
Harper Coll (IL)
Indian River State Coll (FL)
Iowa Lakes Comm Coll (IA)
Kilgore Coll (TX)
Kingsborough Comm Coll of the City U of New York (NY)
Lake Michigan Coll (MI)
Lansing Comm Coll (MI)
Laramie County Comm Coll (WY)
Macomb Comm Coll (MI)
Mendocino Coll (CA)
Metropolitan Comm Coll–Longview (MO)
Metropolitan Comm Coll–Maple Woods (MO)
Metropolitan Comm Coll–Penn Valley (MO)
Miami Dade Coll (FL)
Mid Michigan Comm Coll (MI)
Minneapolis Comm and Tech Coll (MN)
Monroe Comm Coll (NY)
Murray State Coll (OK)
Northampton Comm Coll (PA)
Northeast Comm Coll (NE)
North Hennepin Comm Coll (MN)
Northwest Coll (WY)
Northwest Florida State Coll (FL)
Oklahoma City Comm Coll (OK)
Orange Coast Coll (CA)
Palm Beach State Coll (FL)
Pensacola State Coll (FL)
St. Philip's Coll (TX)
Salt Lake Comm Coll (UT)
San Jacinto Coll District (TX)
San Juan Coll (NM)
Santa Rosa Jr Coll (CA)
Snow Coll (UT)
Southwest Mississippi Comm Coll (MS)
Springfield Tech Comm Coll (MA)
State Coll of Florida Manatee-Sarasota (FL)
Terra State Comm Coll (OH)
Texarkana Coll (TX)
Truckee Meadows Comm Coll (NV)
Tyler Jr Coll (TX)
Umpqua Comm Coll (OR)
Union County Coll (NJ)
Vincennes U (IN)

CHEMISTRY TEACHER EDUCATION

Anne Arundel Comm Coll (MD)
Bucks County Comm Coll (PA)
Cochise Coll, Sierra Vista (AZ)

The Comm Coll of Baltimore County (MD)
Harford Comm Coll (MD)
Montgomery Coll (MD)
State Coll of Florida Manatee-Sarasota (FL)
Vincennes U (IN)

CHILD-CARE AND SUPPORT SERVICES MANAGEMENT

Aiken Tech Coll (SC)
Anne Arundel Comm Coll (MD)
Bevill State Comm Coll (AL)
Bucks County Comm Coll (PA)
Carroll Comm Coll (MD)
Cayuga County Comm Coll (NY)
Cecil Coll (MD)
Central Carolina Tech Coll (SC)
Central Comm Coll–Columbus Campus (NE)
Central Comm Coll–Grand Island Campus (NE)
Central Comm Coll–Hastings Campus (NE)
Central Georgia Tech Coll (GA)
Central Oregon Comm Coll (OR)
Central Wyoming Coll (WY)
Colby Comm Coll (KS)
Coll of DuPage (IL)
Coll of Southern Maryland (MD)
Coll of the Ouachitas (AR)
The Comm Coll of Baltimore County (MD)
Cowley County Comm Coll and Area Vocational–Tech School (KS)
Dakota Coll at Bottineau (ND)
El Paso Comm Coll (TX)
Erie Comm Coll (NY)
Florida State Coll at Jacksonville (FL)
Forrest Coll (SC)
Gadsden State Comm Coll (AL)
Goodwin Coll (CT)
Grand Rapids Comm Coll (MI)
Hagerstown Comm Coll (MD)
H. Councill Trenholm State Tech Coll (AL)
Hillsborough Comm Coll (FL)
Holyoke Comm Coll (MA)
Hutchinson Comm Coll and Area Vocational School (KS)
Ivy Tech Comm Coll–Bloomington (IN)
Ivy Tech Comm Coll–Central Indiana (IN)
Ivy Tech Comm Coll–Columbus (IN)
Ivy Tech Comm Coll–East Central (IN)
Ivy Tech Comm Coll–Kokomo (IN)
Ivy Tech Comm Coll–Lafayette (IN)
Ivy Tech Comm Coll–North Central (IN)
Ivy Tech Comm Coll–Northeast (IN)
Ivy Tech Comm Coll–Northwest (IN)
Ivy Tech Comm Coll–Richmond (IN)
Ivy Tech Comm Coll–Southeast (IN)
Ivy Tech Comm Coll–Southern Indiana (IN)
Ivy Tech Comm Coll–Southwest (IN)
Ivy Tech Comm Coll–Wabash Valley (IN)
Jefferson Comm Coll (NY)
Jefferson State Comm Coll (AL)
Kansas City Kansas Comm Coll (KS)
Kilgore Coll (TX)
Lake Region State Coll (ND)
Lawson State Comm Coll (AL)
Lurleen B. Wallace Comm Coll (AL)
Macomb Comm Coll (MI)
Massachusetts Bay Comm Coll (MA)
Minneapolis Comm and Tech Coll (MN)
Missouri State U–West Plains (MO)
Montcalm Comm Coll (MI)
Montgomery Comm Coll (NC)
Montgomery County Comm Coll (PA)
Mount Wachusett Comm Coll (MA)

Northeast Alabama Comm Coll (AL)
Northwest-Shoals Comm Coll (AL)
Northwest Tech Coll (MN)
Oakland Comm Coll (MI)
Orange Coast Coll (CA)
Peninsula Coll (WA)
Pensacola State Coll (FL)
Reedley Coll (CA)
Reid State Tech Coll (AL)
Rogue Comm Coll (OR)
St. Cloud Tech & Comm Coll (MN)
Southeast Tech Inst (SD)
Texarkana Coll (TX)
Tompkins Cortland Comm Coll (NY)
Vincennes U (IN)
Western Iowa Tech Comm Coll (IA)

CHILD-CARE PROVISION

Bluegrass Comm and Tech Coll (KY)
Bucks County Comm Coll (PA)
City Colls of Chicago, Harry S. Truman College (IL)
Coll of DuPage (IL)
Coll of Lake County (IL)
Coll of the Canyons (CA)
Comm Coll of Allegheny County (PA)
Corning Comm Coll (NY)
Dakota Coll at Bottineau (ND)
Dawson Comm Coll (MT)
Florida State Coll at Jacksonville (FL)
Gavilan Coll (CA)
Gulf Coast State Coll (FL)
Harper Coll (IL)
Hawkeye Comm Coll (IA)
Illinois Central Coll (IL)
Illinois Valley Comm Coll (IL)
Iowa Lakes Comm Coll (IA)
John Tyler Comm Coll (VA)
John Wood Comm Coll (IL)
Kaskaskia Coll (IL)
Kilgore Coll (TX)
Lake Region State Coll (ND)
Lansing Comm Coll (MI)
Lincoln Land Comm Coll (IL)
McHenry County Coll (IL)
Metropolitan Comm Coll–Penn Valley (MO)
Mid Michigan Comm Coll (MI)
Mineral Area Coll (MO)
Montcalm Comm Coll (MI)
Montgomery Coll (MD)
Moraine Valley Comm Coll (IL)
Murray State Coll (OK)
Orange Coast Coll (CA)
Pensacola State Coll (FL)
Raritan Valley Comm Coll (NJ)
San Juan Coll (NM)
Southeast Tech Inst (SD)
South Suburban Coll (IL)
Southwestern Illinois Coll (IL)
Southwest Virginia Comm Coll (VA)
Trident Tech Coll (SC)
Vincennes U (IN)
Western Iowa Tech Comm Coll (IA)
Westmoreland County Comm Coll (PA)

CHILD DEVELOPMENT

Albany Tech Coll (GA)
Altamaha Tech Coll (GA)
Alvin Comm Coll (TX)
Amarillo Coll (TX)
Athens Tech Coll (GA)
Atlanta Tech Coll (GA)
Augusta Tech Coll (GA)
Austin Comm Coll (TX)
Brookhaven Coll (TX)
Carl Albert State Coll (OK)
Central Comm Coll–Grand Island Campus (NE)
Central Comm Coll–Hastings Campus (NE)
Central Georgia Tech Coll (GA)
Central Maine Comm Coll (ME)
Chattahoochee Tech Coll (GA)
Chattanooga State Comm Coll (TN)
Cleveland State Comm Coll (TN)
Colby Comm Coll (KS)
Coll of DuPage (IL)
Columbus Tech Coll (GA)

Comm Coll of Allegheny County (PA)
Comm Coll of Vermont (VT)
Copiah-Lincoln Comm Coll (MS)
Cowley County Comm Coll and Area Vocational–Tech School (KS)
Dutchess Comm Coll (NY)
Dyersburg State Comm Coll (TN)
Edison Comm Coll (OH)
El Paso Comm Coll (TX)
Foothill Coll (CA)
Georgia Northwestern Tech Coll (GA)
Goodwin Coll (CT)
Housatonic Comm Coll (CT)
Houston Comm Coll System (TX)
Howard Comm Coll (MD)
Illinois Eastern Comm Colls, Wabash Valley College (IL)
Illinois Valley Comm Coll (IL)
Indian River State Coll (FL)
Iowa Lakes Comm Coll (IA)
Ivy Tech Comm Coll–Central Indiana (IN)
James Sprunt Comm Coll (NC)
Jefferson Comm Coll (NY)
Kankakee Comm Coll (IL)
Lanier Tech Coll (GA)
Mendocino Coll (CA)
Miami Dade Coll (FL)
Middle Georgia Tech Coll (GA)
Mid Michigan Comm Coll (MI)
Minneapolis Comm and Tech Coll (MN)
Monroe County Comm Coll (MI)
Moultrie Tech Coll (GA)
Mount Wachusett Comm Coll (MA)
Murray State Coll (OK)
Muskegon Comm Coll (MI)
Northeastern Jr Coll (CO)
North Shore Comm Coll (MA)
Northwestern Connecticut Comm Coll (CT)
Northwest Florida State Coll (FL)
Northwest-Shoals Comm Coll (AL)
Oconee Fall Line Tech Coll–North Campus (GA)
Ogeechee Tech Coll (GA)
Okefenokee Tech Coll (GA)
Oklahoma City Comm Coll (OK)
Otero Jr Coll (CO)
Peninsula Coll (WA)
Polk State Coll (FL)
San Jacinto Coll District (TX)
Santa Monica Coll (CA)
Santa Rosa Jr Coll (CA)
Savannah Tech Coll (GA)
Seminole State Coll of Florida (FL)
Shawnee Comm Coll (IL)
Snow Coll (UT)
Southeastern Comm Coll (IA)
Southeastern Tech Coll (GA)
Southern Crescent Tech Coll (GA)
South Georgia Tech Coll (GA)
Southwest Georgia Tech Coll (GA)
Stark State Coll (OH)
State Coll of Florida Manatee-Sarasota (FL)
Texarkana Coll (TX)
Tyler Jr Coll (TX)
Umpqua Comm Coll (OR)
U of Arkansas Comm Coll at Morrilton (AR)
Virginia Western Comm Coll (VA)
Volunteer State Comm Coll (TN)
Westchester Comm Coll (NY)
West Georgia Tech Coll (GA)
Wiregrass Georgia Tech Coll (GA)
York County Comm Coll (ME)

CHIROPRACTIC ASSISTANT

Iowa Lakes Comm Coll (IA)
Moraine Park Tech Coll (WI)

CINEMATOGRAPHY AND FILM/VIDEO PRODUCTION

The Art Inst of New York City (NY)
The Art Inst of Ohio–Cincinnati (OH)
The Art Inst of Seattle (WA)
Bucks County Comm Coll (PA)
Cape Fear Comm Coll (NC)
Coll of DuPage (IL)
Coll of the Canyons (CA)
El Paso Comm Coll (TX)

Gavilan Coll (CA)
Gulf Coast State Coll (FL)
Hillsborough Comm Coll (FL)
Houston Comm Coll System (TX)
Lansing Comm Coll (MI)
Minneapolis Comm and Tech Coll (MN)
Mott Comm Coll (MI)
Northwest Coll (WY)
Oklahoma City Comm Coll (OK)
Orange Coast Coll (CA)
Pensacola State Coll (FL)
Raritan Valley Comm Coll (NJ)
Red Rocks Comm Coll (CO)
Valencia Coll (FL)

CIVIL DRAFTING AND CAD/CADD

Comm Coll of Allegheny County (PA)
Delaware Tech & Comm Coll, Stanton/Wilmington Campus (DE)
North Seattle Comm Coll (WA)
Sullivan Coll of Technology and Design (KY)

CIVIL ENGINEERING

Fiorello H. LaGuardia Comm Coll of the City U of New York (NY)
Itasca Comm Coll (MN)
Kilgore Coll (TX)
Pensacola State Coll (FL)
Truckee Meadows Comm Coll (NV)
Vincennes U (IN)

CIVIL ENGINEERING TECHNOLOGY

Bluegrass Comm and Tech Coll (KY)
Chattahoochee Tech Coll (GA)
Chippewa Valley Tech Coll (WI)
Coll of Lake County (IL)
Comm Coll of Allegheny County (PA)
Copiah-Lincoln Comm Coll (MS)
Delaware Tech & Comm Coll, Jack F. Owens Campus (DE)
Delaware Tech & Comm Coll, Terry Campus (DE)
Eastern Arizona Coll (AZ)
Erie Comm Coll, North Campus (NY)
Fayetteville Tech Comm Coll (NC)
Florida State Coll at Jacksonville (FL)
Gadsden State Comm Coll (AL)
Gateway Tech Coll (WI)
Guilford Tech Comm Coll (NC)
Gulf Coast State Coll (FL)
Hawkeye Comm Coll (IA)
Indian River State Coll (FL)
Lansing Comm Coll (MI)
Linn State Tech Coll (MO)
Macomb Comm Coll (MI)
Miami Dade Coll (FL)
Mineral Area Coll (MO)
Mohawk Valley Comm Coll (NY)
Monroe Comm Coll (NY)
Moraine Park Tech Coll (WI)
Moultrie Tech Coll (GA)
North Dakota State Coll of Science (ND)
Northern Essex Comm Coll (MA)
Oklahoma State U, Oklahoma City (OK)
Peninsula Coll (WA)
Pensacola State Coll (FL)
Quinsigamond Comm Coll (MA)
St. Cloud Tech & Comm Coll (MN)
Santa Rosa Jr Coll (CA)
Seminole State Coll of Florida (FL)
Southeast Tech Inst (SD)
Springfield Tech Comm Coll (MA)
Stark State Coll (OH)
State Coll of Florida Manatee-Sarasota (FL)
Tallahassee Comm Coll (FL)
Three Rivers Comm Coll (CT)
Trident Tech Coll (SC)
Umpqua Comm Coll (OR)
Union County Coll (NJ)
Valencia Coll (FL)
Vincennes U (IN)
Virginia Western Comm Coll (VA)
Westchester Comm Coll (NY)
Wytheville Comm Coll (VA)

CLASSICS AND CLASSICAL LANGUAGES

Foothill Coll (CA)

CLINICAL LABORATORY SCIENCE/MEDICAL TECHNOLOGY

Amarillo Coll (TX)
Athens Tech Coll (GA)
Casper Coll (WY)
Chipola Coll (FL)
GateWay Comm Coll (AZ)
Georgia Highlands Coll (GA)
Howard Comm Coll (MD)
Monroe County Comm Coll (MI)
Northeastern Jr Coll (CO)
Northwest Florida State Coll (FL)
Orange Coast Coll (CA)
San Jacinto Coll District (TX)
Tarrant County Coll District (TX)
Westchester Comm Coll (NY)

CLINICAL/MEDICAL LABORATORY ASSISTANT

Delaware Tech & Comm Coll, Jack F. Owens Campus (DE)
Westmoreland County Comm Coll (PA)

CLINICAL/MEDICAL LABORATORY SCIENCE AND ALLIED PROFESSIONS RELATED

Highline Comm Coll (WA)
Houston Comm Coll System (TX)
Southeast Tech Inst (SD)

CLINICAL/MEDICAL LABORATORY TECHNOLOGY

Anne Arundel Comm Coll (MD)
Austin Comm Coll (TX)
Beaufort County Comm Coll (NC)
Blackhawk Tech Coll (WI)
Bunker Hill Comm Coll (MA)
Central Comm Coll—Hastings Campus (NE)
Central Georgia Tech Coll (GA)
Chippewa Valley Tech Coll (WI)
Coll of Southern Maryland (MD)
Comm Coll of Allegheny County (PA)
Comm Coll of Philadelphia (PA)
Comm Coll of Rhode Island (RI)
Copiah-Lincoln Comm Coll (MS)
Dutchess Comm Coll (NY)
Edison Comm Coll (OH)
El Centro Coll (TX)
Elgin Comm Coll (IL)
El Paso Comm Coll (TX)
Erie Comm Coll, North Campus (NY)
Gadsden State Comm Coll (AL)
Genesee Comm Coll (NY)
Georgia Piedmont Tech Coll (GA)
Hawkeye Comm Coll (IA)
Housatonic Comm Coll (CT)
Houston Comm Coll System (TX)
Illinois Central Coll (IL)
Indian River State Coll (FL)
Ivy Tech Comm Coll–North Central (IN)
Ivy Tech Comm Coll–Wabash Valley (IN)
Jefferson State Comm Coll (AL)
John Wood Comm Coll (IL)
J. Sargeant Reynolds Comm Coll (VA)
Kankakee Comm Coll (IL)
Kaskaskia Coll (IL)
Kilgore Coll (TX)
Lake Area Tech Inst (SD)
Manchester Comm Coll (CT)
Miami Dade Coll (FL)
Mid-Plains Comm Coll, North Platte (NE)
Mitchell Tech Inst (SD)
Montgomery County Comm Coll (PA)
Moraine Park Tech Coll (WI)
Mount Wachusett Comm Coll (MA)
Northeast Iowa Comm Coll (IA)
North Hennepin Comm Coll (MN)
Okefenokee Tech Coll (GA)
Penn State Hazleton (PA)
Penn State Schuylkill (PA)
Piedmont Virginia Comm Coll (VA)

Rasmussen Coll Bismarck (ND)
Rasmussen Coll Green Bay (WI)
Rasmussen Coll Lake Elmo/Woodbury (MN)
Rasmussen Coll Mankato (MN)
Rasmussen Coll Moorhead (MN)
Rasmussen Coll St. Cloud (MN)
St. Philip's Coll (TX)
Salt Lake Comm Coll (UT)
San Jacinto Coll District (TX)
San Juan Coll (NM)
Southeast Tech Inst (SD)
Southwestern Illinois Coll (IL)
Southwestern Oklahoma State U at Sayre (OK)
Spencerian Coll (KY)
Springfield Tech Comm Coll (MA)
Stark State Coll (OH)
Tarrant County Coll District (TX)
Trident Tech Coll (SC)
Tyler Jr Coll (TX)
Volunteer State Comm Coll (TN)
Westchester Comm Coll (NY)
Western Iowa Tech Comm Coll (IA)
Wytheville Comm Coll (VA)

CLINICAL/MEDICAL SOCIAL WORK

Central Comm Coll–Grand Island Campus (NE)
Central Comm Coll–Hastings Campus (NE)
Dawson Comm Coll (MT)

COMMERCIAL AND ADVERTISING ART

Amarillo Coll (TX)
Austin Comm Coll (TX)
Bucks County Comm Coll (PA)
Burlington County Coll (NJ)
Catawba Valley Comm Coll (NC)
Central Comm Coll—Columbus Campus (NE)
Central Comm Coll–Hastings Campus (NE)
Chattanooga State Comm Coll (TN)
Coll of DuPage (IL)
Colorado Mountain Coll (CO)
Comm Coll of Allegheny County (PA)
The Comm Coll of Baltimore County (MD)
Delaware County Comm Coll (PA)
Delaware Tech & Comm Coll, Terry Campus (DE)
Dutchess Comm Coll (NY)
Eastern Arizona Coll (AZ)
Edison Comm Coll (OH)
El Paso Comm Coll (TX)
Fashion Inst of Technology (NY)
Fayetteville Tech Comm Coll (NC)
Florida State Coll at Jacksonville (FL)
Guilford Tech Comm Coll (NC)
Hagerstown Comm Coll (MD)
Housatonic Comm Coll (CT)
Iowa Lakes Comm Coll (IA)
James Sprunt Comm Coll (NC)
Jamestown Comm Coll (NY)
Johnston Comm Coll (NC)
Kilgore Coll (TX)
Kingsborough Comm Coll of the City U of New York (NY)
Macomb Comm Coll (MI)
Manchester Comm Coll (CT)
Metropolitan Comm Coll—Penn Valley (MO)
Miami Dade Coll (FL)
Mid-Plains Comm Coll, North Platte (NE)
Mohawk Valley Comm Coll (NY)
Monroe Comm Coll (NY)
Montgomery Coll (MD)
Montgomery County Comm Coll (PA)
Muskegon Comm Coll (MI)
Northern Essex Comm Coll (MA)
Northwest Coll (WY)
Northwestern Connecticut Comm Coll (CT)
Northwest Florida State Coll (FL)
Oakland Comm Coll (MI)
Oklahoma City Comm Coll (OK)
Orange Coast Coll (CA)
Owens Comm Coll, Toledo (OH)
Palm Beach State Coll (FL)
Pensacola State Coll (FL)
Randolph Comm Coll (NC)

Reedley Coll (CA)
Rockland Comm Coll (NY)
St. Clair County Comm Coll (MI)
San Diego City Coll (CA)
San Jacinto Coll District (TX)
San Juan Coll (NM)
Southeast Tech Inst (SD)
Springfield Tech Comm Coll (MA)
State Coll of Florida Manatee-Sarasota (FL)
Sullivan County Comm Coll (NY)
Terra State Comm Coll (OH)
Texas State Tech Coll Harlingen (TX)
Tompkins Cortland Comm Coll (NY)
Trident Tech Coll (SC)
Tunxis Comm Coll (CT)
Tyler Jr Coll (TX)
U of Arkansas Comm Coll at Morrilton (AR)
Valencia Coll (FL)
Vincennes U (IN)
Virginia Western Comm Coll (VA)

COMMERCIAL FISHING

Peninsula Coll (WA)

COMMERCIAL PHOTOGRAPHY

Austin Comm Coll (TX)
Bucks County Comm Coll (PA)
Cecil Coll (MD)
Central Wyoming Coll (WY)
Fashion Inst of Technology (NY)
Fiorello H. LaGuardia Comm Coll of the City U of New York (NY)
Harford Comm Coll (MD)
Hawkeye Comm Coll (IA)
Houston Comm Coll System (TX)
Kilgore Coll (TX)
Minneapolis Comm and Tech Coll (MN)
Mohawk Valley Comm Coll (NY)
Montgomery Coll (MD)
Northwest Coll (WY)
Owens Comm Coll, Toledo (OH)
Randolph Comm Coll (NC)
Santa Monica Coll (CA)
Springfield Tech Comm Coll (MA)

COMMUNICATION

Foothill Coll (CA)
Hesser Coll, Manchester (NH)
Lake Michigan Coll (MI)
Santa Rosa Jr Coll (CA)

COMMUNICATION AND JOURNALISM RELATED

Cayuga County Comm Coll (NY)
Delaware County Comm Coll (PA)
Gadsden State Comm Coll (AL)
Iowa Lakes Comm Coll (IA)

COMMUNICATION AND MEDIA RELATED

Raritan Valley Comm Coll (NJ)

COMMUNICATION DISORDERS SCIENCES AND SERVICES RELATED

Burlington County Coll (NJ)

COMMUNICATIONS SYSTEMS INSTALLATION AND REPAIR TECHNOLOGY

Cayuga County Comm Coll (NY)
Central Maine Comm Coll (ME)
Coll of DuPage (IL)
Erie Comm Coll, South Campus (NY)
Mohawk Valley Comm Coll (NY)
North Seattle Comm Coll (WA)
Westmoreland County Comm Coll (PA)

COMMUNICATIONS TECHNOLOGIES AND SUPPORT SERVICES RELATED

Anne Arundel Comm Coll (MD)
Comm Coll of Allegheny County (PA)
Harford Comm Coll (MD)
Montgomery Coll (MD)
Montgomery County Comm Coll (PA)
Ocean County Coll (NJ)

COMMUNICATIONS TECHNOLOGY

Athens Tech Coll (GA)
Coll of DuPage (IL)
Fountainhead Coll of Technology (TN)
Hutchinson Comm Coll and Area Vocational School (KS)
Illinois Central Coll (IL)
ITT Tech Inst, Bessemer (AL)
ITT Tech Inst, Madison (AL)
ITT Tech Inst, Mobile (AL)
ITT Tech Inst, Phoenix (AZ)
ITT Tech Inst, Tucson (AZ)
ITT Tech Inst (AR)
ITT Tech Inst, Lathrop (CA)
ITT Tech Inst, Orange (CA)
ITT Tech Inst, Oxnard (CA)
ITT Tech Inst, Rancho Cordova (CA)
ITT Tech Inst, San Bernardino (CA)
ITT Tech Inst, San Diego (CA)
ITT Tech Inst, San Dimas (CA)
ITT Tech Inst, Sylmar (CA)
ITT Tech Inst, Torrance (CA)
ITT Tech Inst, Aurora (CO)
ITT Tech Inst, Thornton (CO)
ITT Tech Inst, Fort Lauderdale (FL)
ITT Tech Inst, Fort Myers (FL)
ITT Tech Inst, Jacksonville (FL)
ITT Tech Inst, Lake Mary (FL)
ITT Tech Inst, Miami (FL)
ITT Tech Inst, Pinellas Park (FL)
ITT Tech Inst, Tallahassee (FL)
ITT Tech Inst, Tampa (FL)
ITT Tech Inst (ID)
ITT Tech Inst, Mount Prospect (IL)
ITT Tech Inst, Fort Wayne (IN)
ITT Tech Inst, Merrillville (IN)
ITT Tech Inst, Newburgh (IN)
ITT Tech Inst, Cedar Rapids (IA)
ITT Tech Inst, Clive (IA)
ITT Tech Inst, Louisville (KY)
ITT Tech Inst, Baton Rouge (LA)
ITT Tech Inst, St. Rose (LA)
ITT Tech Inst, Canton (MI)
ITT Tech Inst, Swartz Creek (MI)
ITT Tech Inst, Troy (MI)
ITT Tech Inst, Wyoming (MI)
ITT Tech Inst, Eden Prairie (MN)
ITT Tech Inst, Arnold (MO)
ITT Tech Inst, Earth City (MO)
ITT Tech Inst, Kansas City (MO)
ITT Tech Inst (NE)
ITT Tech Inst, Henderson (NV)
ITT Tech Inst (NM)
ITT Tech Inst, Albany (NY)
ITT Tech Inst, Getzville (NY)
ITT Tech Inst, Liverpool (NY)
ITT Tech Inst, Akron (OH)
ITT Tech Inst, Columbus (OH)
ITT Tech Inst, Dayton (OH)
ITT Tech Inst, Hilliard (OH)
ITT Tech Inst, Maumee (OH)
ITT Tech Inst, Norwood (OH)
ITT Tech Inst, Strongsville (OH)
ITT Tech Inst, Warrensville Heights (OH)
ITT Tech Inst, Youngstown (OH)
ITT Tech Inst, Tulsa (OK)
ITT Tech Inst, Portland (OR)
ITT Tech Inst, Columbia (SC)
ITT Tech Inst, Chattanooga (TN)
ITT Tech Inst, Cordova (TN)
ITT Tech Inst, Johnson City (TN)
ITT Tech Inst, Knoxville (TN)
ITT Tech Inst, Nashville (TN)
ITT Tech Inst, Arlington (TX)
ITT Tech Inst, Austin (TX)
ITT Tech Inst, DeSoto (TX)
ITT Tech Inst, Houston (TX)
ITT Tech Inst, Houston (TX)
ITT Tech Inst, Richardson (TX)
ITT Tech Inst, San Antonio (TX)
ITT Tech Inst, Webster (TX)
ITT Tech Inst (UT)
ITT Tech Inst, Chantilly (VA)
ITT Tech Inst, Norfolk (VA)
ITT Tech Inst, Richmond (VA)
ITT Tech Inst, Salem (VA)
ITT Tech Inst, Springfield (VA)
ITT Tech Inst, Everett (WA)
ITT Tech Inst, Seattle (WA)
ITT Tech Inst, Spokane Valley (WA)
ITT Tech Inst (WV)
Kent State U at Tuscarawas (OH)
Mott Comm Coll (MI)

Northwestern Connecticut Comm Coll (CT)
Orange Coast Coll (CA)
Owens Comm Coll, Toledo (OH)
Pensacola State Coll (FL)
Vincennes U (IN)

COMMUNITY HEALTH AND PREVENTIVE MEDICINE
Anoka-Ramsey Comm Coll (MN)
Anoka-Ramsey Comm Coll, Cambridge Campus (MN)

COMMUNITY HEALTH SERVICES COUNSELING
Comm Coll of Allegheny County (PA)
Erie Comm Coll (NY)
Illinois Central Coll (IL)
Kingsborough Comm Coll of the City U of New York (NY)
Mott Comm Coll (MI)
Oakland Comm Coll (MI)
State Coll of Florida Manatee-Sarasota (FL)

COMMUNITY ORGANIZATION AND ADVOCACY
Berkshire Comm Coll (MA)
Chattanooga State Comm Coll (TN)
Cleveland State Comm Coll (TN)
Clinton Comm Coll (NY)
Comm Coll of Vermont (VT)
Jamestown Comm Coll (NY)
Lansing Comm Coll (MI)
Minneapolis Comm and Tech Coll (MN)
Mohawk Valley Comm Coll (NY)
State U of New York Coll of Technology at Alfred (NY)
Tompkins Cortland Comm Coll (NY)
Westchester Comm Coll (NY)

COMMUNITY PSYCHOLOGY
Dawson Comm Coll (MT)

COMPARATIVE LITERATURE
Foothill Coll (CA)
Iowa Lakes Comm Coll (IA)
Miami Dade Coll (FL)
Oklahoma City Comm Coll (OK)
Otero Jr Coll (CO)
Palm Beach State Coll (FL)

COMPUTER AND INFORMATION SCIENCES
Albany Tech Coll (GA)
Anne Arundel Comm Coll (MD)
Austin Comm Coll (TX)
Berkeley City Coll (CA)
Berkshire Comm Coll (MA)
Bevill State Comm Coll (AL)
Bluegrass Comm and Tech Coll (KY)
Bucks County Comm Coll (PA)
Carl Albert State Coll (OK)
Carroll Comm Coll (MD)
Cayuga County Comm Coll (NY)
Cecil Coll (MD)
Central Comm Coll–Columbus Campus (NE)
Central Comm Coll–Grand Island Campus (NE)
Chandler-Gilbert Comm Coll (AZ)
Chattahoochee Valley Comm Coll (AL)
Colby Comm Coll (KS)
Coll of Southern Maryland (MD)
Coll of the Ouachitas (AR)
The Comm Coll of Baltimore County (MD)
Comm Coll of Rhode Island (RI)
Comm Coll of Vermont (VT)
Corning Comm Coll (NY)
Cowley County Comm Coll and Area Vocational–Tech School (KS)
Dakota Coll at Bottineau (ND)
Dawson Comm Coll (MT)
Delaware County Comm Coll (PA)
Delaware Tech & Comm Coll, Jack F. Owens Campus (DE)

Delaware Tech & Comm Coll, Stanton/Wilmington Campus (DE)
Delaware Tech & Comm Coll, Terry Campus (DE)
Denmark Tech Coll (SC)
Dutchess Comm Coll (NY)
Edison Comm Coll (OH)
El Paso Comm Coll (TX)
Erie Comm Coll, North Campus (NY)
Florida State Coll at Jacksonville (FL)
Gadsden State Comm Coll (AL)
GateWay Comm Coll (AZ)
Hagerstown Comm Coll (MD)
Harford Comm Coll (MD)
Harper Coll (IL)
H. Councill Trenholm State Tech Coll (AL)
Hutchinson Comm Coll and Area Vocational School (KS)
Ivy Tech Comm Coll–Bloomington (IN)
Ivy Tech Comm Coll–Central Indiana (IN)
Ivy Tech Comm Coll–Columbus (IN)
Ivy Tech Comm Coll–East Central (IN)
Ivy Tech Comm Coll–Kokomo (IN)
Ivy Tech Comm Coll–Lafayette (IN)
Ivy Tech Comm Coll–North Central (IN)
Ivy Tech Comm Coll–Northeast (IN)
Ivy Tech Comm Coll–Northwest (IN)
Ivy Tech Comm Coll–Richmond (IN)
Ivy Tech Comm Coll–Southeast (IN)
Ivy Tech Comm Coll–Southern Indiana (IN)
Ivy Tech Comm Coll–Southwest (IN)
Ivy Tech Comm Coll–Wabash Valley (IN)
Jefferson Comm Coll (NY)
Jefferson State Comm Coll (AL)
John Tyler Comm Coll (VA)
J. Sargeant Reynolds Comm Coll (VA)
Kilgore Coll (TX)
Kingsborough Comm Coll of the City U of New York (NY)
Lake Michigan Coll (MI)
Lake Region State Coll (ND)
Lansing Comm Coll (MI)
Lawson State Comm Coll (AL)
Lehigh Carbon Comm Coll (PA)
Lurleen B. Wallace Comm Coll (AL)
Massachusetts Bay Comm Coll (MA)
Metropolitan Comm Coll–Business & Technology Campus (MO)
Mid-Plains Comm Coll, North Platte (NE)
Mohawk Valley Comm Coll (NY)
Montgomery Coll (MD)
Montgomery County Comm Coll (PA)
Mount Wachusett Comm Coll (MA)
Murray State Coll (OK)
Normandale Comm Coll (MN)
North Dakota State Coll of Science (ND)
Northeast Alabama Comm Coll (AL)
Northeast Comm Coll (NE)
Northern Essex Comm Coll (MA)
Northwest-Shoals Comm Coll (AL)
Ocean County Coll (NJ)
Owensboro Comm and Tech Coll (KY)
Penn State Schuylkill (PA)
Pensacola State Coll (FL)
Reedley Coll (CA)
Rogue Comm Coll (OR)
Salt Lake Comm Coll (UT)
San Jacinto Coll District (TX)
Southwestern Illinois Coll (IL)
Southwest Virginia Comm Coll (VA)
State Coll of Florida Manatee-Sarasota (FL)
State U of New York Coll of Technology at Alfred (NY)

Sullivan Coll of Technology and Design (KY)
Tallahassee Comm Coll (FL)
Terra State Comm Coll (OH)
Texarkana Coll (TX)
Tompkins Cortland Comm Coll (NY)
Tyler Jr Coll (TX)
Vincennes U (IN)
Westchester Comm Coll (NY)
West Kentucky Comm and Tech Coll (KY)
White Mountains Comm Coll (NH)

COMPUTER AND INFORMATION SCIENCES AND SUPPORT SERVICES RELATED
Bunker Hill Comm Coll (MA)
Career Tech Coll (LA)
Cayuga County Comm Coll (NY)
Chandler-Gilbert Comm Coll (AZ)
Colorado Mountain Coll (CO)
Dakota Coll at Bottineau (ND)
Fiorello H. LaGuardia Comm Coll of the City U of New York (NY)
Florida State Coll at Jacksonville (FL)
Gateway Tech Coll (WI)
Island Drafting and Tech Inst (NY)
Jackson Comm Coll (MI)
Jefferson Comm Coll (NY)
Metropolitan Comm Coll–Business & Technology Campus (MO)
Mohawk Valley Comm Coll (NY)
Monroe Comm Coll (NY)
Moraine Park Tech Coll (WI)
Northeast Comm Coll (NE)
Oakland Comm Coll (MI)
Palm Beach State Coll (FL)
Piedmont Virginia Comm Coll (VA)
Raritan Valley Comm Coll (NJ)
San Joaquin Valley Coll, Visalia (CA)
Seminole State Coll of Florida (FL)
Southeast Tech Inst (SD)
Stark State Coll (OH)
Sullivan Coll of Technology and Design (KY)
Tompkins Cortland Comm Coll (NY)
Union County Coll (NJ)
Waukesha County Tech Coll (WI)
Westchester Comm Coll (NY)
YTI Career Inst–York (PA)

COMPUTER AND INFORMATION SCIENCES RELATED
Berkeley City Coll (CA)
Central Oregon Comm Coll (OR)
Chipola Coll (FL)
Colby Comm Coll (KS)
Corning Comm Coll (NY)
Dawson Comm Coll (MT)
Florida State Coll at Jacksonville (FL)
Gateway Comm Coll (CT)
Genesee Comm Coll (NY)
Howard Comm Coll (MD)
Iowa Lakes Comm Coll (IA)
Kent State U at East Liverpool (OH)
Metropolitan Comm Coll–Blue River (MO)
Metropolitan Comm Coll–Business & Technology Campus (MO)
Metropolitan Comm Coll–Longview (MO)
Metropolitan Comm Coll–Maple Woods (MO)
Metropolitan Comm Coll–Penn Valley (MO)
Missouri State U–West Plains (MO)
Mohave Comm Coll (AZ)
Monroe Comm Coll (NY)
Monroe County Comm Coll (MI)
North Shore Comm Coll (MA)
Pensacola State Coll (FL)
Rockland Comm Coll (NY)
Seminole State Coll of Florida (FL)
Stark State Coll (OH)
State Coll of Florida Manatee-Sarasota (FL)
Tyler Jr Coll (TX)
Westchester Comm Coll (NY)

COMPUTER AND INFORMATION SYSTEMS SECURITY
Anne Arundel Comm Coll (MD)
Berkeley City Coll (CA)
Blackhawk Tech Coll (WI)
Bunker Hill Comm Coll (MA)
Century Coll (MN)
Chattahoochee Tech Coll (GA)
Cochise Coll, Sierra Vista (AZ)
Cowley County Comm Coll and Area Vocational–Tech School (KS)
Dyersburg State Comm Coll (TN)
Edison Comm Coll (OH)
El Centro Coll (TX)
Elgin Comm Coll (IL)
Fayetteville Tech Comm Coll (NC)
Florida State Coll at Jacksonville (FL)
Harford Comm Coll (MD)
Island Drafting and Tech Inst (NY)
Lanier Tech Coll (GA)
Lehigh Carbon Comm Coll (PA)
McHenry County Coll (IL)
Metropolitan Comm Coll–Business & Technology Campus (MO)
Minneapolis Comm and Tech Coll (MN)
Montgomery Coll (MD)
Moraine Valley Comm Coll (IL)
Northampton Comm Coll (PA)
North Dakota State Coll of Science (ND)
North Seattle Comm Coll (WA)
Oakland Comm Coll (MI)
Owens Comm Coll, Toledo (OH)
Quinsigamond Comm Coll (MA)
St. Philip's Coll (TX)
San Jacinto Coll District (TX)
Seminole State Coll of Florida (FL)
Southeast Tech Inst (SD)
Southern Crescent Tech Coll (GA)
Springfield Tech Comm Coll (MA)
Sullivan Coll of Technology and Design (KY)
Westchester Comm Coll (NY)
Westmoreland County Comm Coll (PA)
Wilson Comm Coll (NC)
Wiregrass Georgia Tech Coll (GA)

COMPUTER ENGINEERING
Carroll Comm Coll (MD)
Itasca Comm Coll (MN)
Pensacola State Coll (FL)

COMPUTER ENGINEERING RELATED
Columbus Tech Coll (GA)
Gateway Comm Coll (CT)
Itasca Comm Coll (MN)
Monroe Comm Coll (NY)
Northwest Florida State Coll (FL)
Seminole State Coll of Florida (FL)
Stark State Coll (OH)

COMPUTER ENGINEERING TECHNOLOGY
Aiken Tech Coll (SC)
Alvin Comm Coll (TX)
Amarillo Coll (TX)
Brookhaven Coll (TX)
Bucks County Comm Coll (PA)
Catawba Valley Comm Coll (NC)
Colorado Mountain Coll (CO)
Colorado Mountain Coll, Alpine Campus (CO)
Comm Coll of Allegheny County (PA)
Comm Coll of Rhode Island (RI)
Delaware Tech & Comm Coll, Stanton/Wilmington Campus (DE)
Delaware Tech & Comm Coll, Terry Campus (DE)
Do&nna Ana Comm Coll (NM)
Florida State Coll at Jacksonville (FL)
Fountainhead Coll of Technology (TN)
Fox Valley Tech Coll (WI)
Gateway Comm Coll (CT)
Genesee Comm Coll (NY)
Georgia Piedmont Tech Coll (GA)

Grand Rapids Comm Coll (MI)
Highline Comm Coll (WA)
Houston Comm Coll System (TX)
Indian River State Coll (FL)
ITT Tech Inst, Atlanta (GA)
ITT Tech Inst, Duluth (GA)
ITT Tech Inst, Kennesaw (GA)
ITT Tech Inst, Mount Prospect (IL)
ITT Tech Inst, Oak Brook (IL)
ITT Tech Inst, Orland Park (IL)
ITT Tech Inst, Newburgh (IN)
ITT Tech Inst, Owings Mills (MD)
ITT Tech Inst, Norwood (MA)
ITT Tech Inst, Wilmington (MA)
ITT Tech Inst (NJ)
ITT Tech Inst, Cary (NC)
ITT Tech Inst, Charlotte (NC)
ITT Tech Inst, High Point (NC)
ITT Tech Inst, Strongsville (OH)
ITT Tech Inst, Bensalem (PA)
ITT Tech Inst, Dunmore (PA)
ITT Tech Inst, Harrisburg (PA)
ITT Tech Inst, King of Prussia (PA)
ITT Tech Inst, Pittsburgh (PA)
ITT Tech Inst, Tarentum (PA)
ITT Tech Inst, Greenville (SC)
ITT Tech Inst, Seattle (WA)
Kansas City Kansas Comm Coll (KS)
Kaplan Career Inst, Franklin Mills Campus (PA)
Kent State U at Ashtabula (OH)
Kent State U at East Liverpool (OH)
Kent State U at Trumbull (OH)
Kent State U at Tuscarawas (OH)
Los Angeles Harbor Coll (CA)
Massachusetts Bay Comm Coll (MA)
Miami Dade Coll (FL)
Monroe Comm Coll (NY)
Monroe County Comm Coll (MI)
Northeastern Jr Coll (CO)
Northern Essex Comm Coll (MA)
North Shore Comm Coll (MA)
Northwestern Connecticut Comm Coll (CT)
Oklahoma City Comm Coll (OK)
Onondaga Comm Coll (NY)
Orange Coast Coll (CA)
Owens Comm Coll, Toledo (OH)
Penn State New Kensington (PA)
Piedmont Virginia Comm Coll (VA)
Quinsigamond Comm Coll (MA)
San Diego City Coll (CA)
Seminole State Coll of Florida (FL)
Southern Maine Comm Coll (ME)
Springfield Tech Comm Coll (MA)
State Coll of Florida Manatee-Sarasota (FL)
State U of New York Coll of Technology at Alfred (NY)
Sullivan Coll of Technology and Design (KY)
Three Rivers Comm Coll (CT)
Trident Tech Coll (SC)
Tyler Jr Coll (TX)
Umpqua Comm Coll (OR)
White Mountains Comm Coll (NH)

COMPUTER GRAPHICS
Berkeley City Coll (CA)
Burlington County Coll (NJ)
Carroll Comm Coll (MD)
Coll of Business and Technology (FL)
Corning Comm Coll (NY)
Cowley County Comm Coll and Area Vocational–Tech School (KS)
Creative Center (NE)
Florida State Coll at Jacksonville (FL)
Gateway Comm Coll (CT)
Gavilan Coll (CA)
Genesee Comm Coll (NY)
Howard Comm Coll (MD)
Iowa Lakes Comm Coll (IA)
Metropolitan Comm Coll–Business & Technology Campus (MO)
Miami Dade Coll (FL)
Missouri State U–West Plains (MO)
Monroe County Comm Coll (MI)
Mount Wachusett Comm Coll (MA)
Northern Essex Comm Coll (MA)
North Shore Comm Coll (MA)
Northwestern Connecticut Comm Coll (CT)

Orange Coast Coll (CA)
Pittsburgh Tech Inst, Oakdale (PA)
Quinsigamond Comm Coll (MA)
Rockland Comm Coll (NY)
Salem Comm Coll (NJ)
Seminole State Coll of Florida (FL)
State Coll of Florida Manatee-
Sarasota (FL)
Sullivan Coll of Technology and
Design (KY)
Sullivan County Comm Coll (NY)
Tallahassee Comm Coll (FL)
Trident Tech Coll (SC)
Tyler Jr Coll (TX)

**COMPUTER HARDWARE
ENGINEERING**

Florida State Coll at Jacksonville
(FL)
Seminole State Coll of Florida (FL)
Stark State Coll (OH)
Sullivan Coll of Technology and
Design (KY)

**COMPUTER HARDWARE
TECHNOLOGY**

Oakland Comm Coll (MI)
State U of New York Coll of
Technology at Alfred (NY)
Sullivan Coll of Technology and
Design (KY)

**COMPUTER/INFORMATION
TECHNOLOGY SERVICES
ADMINISTRATION RELATED**

Anne Arundel Comm Coll (MD)
Bunker Hill Comm Coll (MA)
Central Carolina Comm Coll (NC)
Cleveland Inst of Electronics (OH)
Clinton Comm Coll (NY)
Corning Comm Coll (NY)
El Centro Coll (TX)
ETI Tech Coll of Niles (OH)
Florida State Coll at Jacksonville
(FL)
Hawkeye Comm Coll (IA)
Hillsborough Comm Coll (FL)
Howard Comm Coll (MD)
Iowa Lakes Comm Coll (IA)
Jefferson Comm Coll (NY)
Kent State U at Trumbull (OH)
Metropolitan Comm Coll–Business
& Technology Campus (MO)
Oakland Comm Coll (MI)
Owensboro Comm and Tech Coll
(KY)
Rockland Comm Coll (NY)
Seminole State Coll of Florida (FL)
Southeast Tech Inst (SD)
Southwestern Illinois Coll (IL)
Stark State Coll (OH)
Trident Tech Coll (SC)
Vincennes U (IN)

**COMPUTER INSTALLATION
AND REPAIR TECHNOLOGY**

Central Maine Comm Coll (ME)
Coll of DuPage (IL)
Coll of Lake County (IL)
Fiorello H. LaGuardia Comm Coll of
the City U of New York (NY)
Forrest (SC)
Kilgore Coll (TX)
Montcalm Comm Coll (MI)
Northampton Comm Coll (PA)
Southeast Tech Inst (SD)
Sullivan Coll of Technology and
Design (KY)
Wisconsin Indianhead Tech Coll
(WI)

**COMPUTER NUMERICALLY
CONTROLLED (CNC)
MACHINIST TECHNOLOGY**

Moraine Park Tech Coll (WI)
Westmoreland County Comm Coll
(PA)

COMPUTER PROGRAMMING

Aiken Tech Coll (SC)
Altamaha Tech Coll (GA)
Alvin Comm Coll (TX)
Amarillo Coll (TX)
Athens Tech Coll (GA)
Atlanta Tech Coll (GA)
Augusta Tech Coll (GA)

Austin Comm Coll (TX)
Beaufort County Comm Coll (NC)
Bradford School (OH)
Bradford School (PA)
Brookhaven Coll (TX)
Bunker Hill Comm Coll (MA)
Casper Coll (WY)
Catawba Valley Comm Coll (NC)
Cecil Coll (MD)
Central Carolina Comm Coll (NC)
Central Georgia Tech Coll (GA)
Chandler-Gilbert Comm Coll (AZ)
Chattahoochee Tech Coll (GA)
Chippewa Valley Tech Coll (WI)
Clark Coll (WA)
Cochise Coll, Sierra Vista (AZ)
Coll of Southern Maryland (MD)
Copiah-Lincoln Comm Coll (MS)
Corning Comm Coll (NY)
Edison Comm Coll (OH)
El Centro Coll (TX)
El Paso Comm Coll (TX)
Fayetteville Tech Comm Coll (NC)
Fiorello H. LaGuardia Comm Coll of
the City U of New York (NY)
Florida State Coll at Jacksonville
(FL)
Fountainhead Coll of Technology
(TN)
Fox Valley Tech Coll (WI)
Gateway Tech Coll (WI)
Gavilan Coll (CA)
Georgia Highlands Coll (GA)
Georgia Northwestern Tech Coll
(GA)
Georgia Piedmont Tech Coll (GA)
Grand Rapids Comm Coll (MI)
Guilford Tech Comm Coll (NC)
Gwinnett Tech Coll (GA)
Harper Coll (IL)
Highline Comm Coll (WA)
Houston Comm Coll System (TX)
Illinois Central Coll (IL)
Illinois Valley Comm Coll (IL)
Indian River State Coll (FL)
International Business Coll,
Indianapolis (IN)
Iowa Lakes Comm Coll (IA)
Jamestown Comm Coll (NY)
Johnston Comm Coll (NC)
Kilgore Coll (TX)
King's Coll (NC)
Lake Area Tech Inst (SD)
Lanier Tech Coll (GA)
Laramie County Comm Coll (WY)
Lehigh Carbon Comm Coll (PA)
Lincoln Land Comm Coll (IL)
Linn State Tech Coll (MO)
Macomb Comm Coll (MI)
Metropolitan Comm Coll–Business
& Technology Campus (MO)
Metropolitan Comm Coll–Longview
(MO)
Metropolitan Comm Coll–Maple
Woods (MO)
Miami Dade Coll (FL)
Mineral Area Coll (MO)
Minneapolis Business Coll (MN)
Minneapolis Comm and Tech Coll
(MN)
Minnesota School of Business–
Richfield (MN)
Minnesota State Coll–Southeast
Tech (MN)
Mohawk Valley Comm Coll (NY)
Montgomery County Comm Coll
(PA)
Moreno Valley Coll (CA)
Mott Comm Coll (MI)
New Mexico State U–Alamogordo
(NM)
Norco Coll (CA)
Northampton Comm Coll (PA)
North Dakota State Coll of Science
(ND)
Northeast Comm Coll (NE)
Northern Essex Comm Coll (MA)
North Shore Comm Coll (MA)
Northwestern Connecticut Comm
Coll (CT)
Northwest Florida State Coll (FL)
Oakland Comm Coll (MI)
Olympic Coll (WA)
Orange Coast Coll (CA)
Palm Beach State Coll (FL)
Pensacola State Coll (FL)
Piedmont Virginia Comm Coll (VA)
Pittsburgh Tech Inst, Oakdale (PA)

Rasmussen Coll Fargo (ND)
Red Rocks Comm Coll (CO)
Riverside City Coll (CA)
Rockland Comm Coll (NY)
St. Clair County Comm Coll (MI)
St. Cloud Tech & Comm Coll (MN)
San Jacinto Coll District (TX)
Santa Monica Coll (CA)
Seminole State Coll of Florida (FL)
Southeastern Comm Coll (IA)
Southeast Tech Inst (SD)
Southern Crescent Tech Coll (GA)
Southern State Comm Coll (OH)
Southwestern Illinois Coll (IL)
Southwestern Michigan Coll (MI)
Stark State Coll (OH)
State Coll of Florida Manatee-
Sarasota (FL)
Tallahassee Comm Coll (FL)
Tarrant County Coll District (TX)
Terra State Comm Coll (OH)
Texas State Tech Coll Harlingen
(TX)
Three Rivers Comm Coll (CT)
Truckee Meadows Comm Coll (NV)
The U of Montana–Helena Coll of
Technology (MT)
Valencia Coll (FL)
Vincennes U (IN)
Waukesha County Tech Coll (WI)
Westmoreland County Comm Coll
(PA)
West Virginia Northern Comm Coll
(WV)
Wiregrass Georgia Tech Coll (GA)
Wood Tobe–Coburn School (NY)

**COMPUTER PROGRAMMING
RELATED**

Corning Comm Coll (NY)
Florida State Coll at Jacksonville
(FL)
Metropolitan Comm Coll–Business
& Technology Campus (MO)
Moraine Park Tech Coll (WI)
Northern Essex Comm Coll (MA)
Pasco-Hernando Comm Coll (FL)
Rockland Comm Coll (NY)
Seminole State Coll of Florida (FL)
Southeast Tech Inst (SD)
Southwest Mississippi Comm Coll
(MS)
Stark State Coll (OH)
State Coll of Florida Manatee-
Sarasota (FL)
Tyler Jr Coll (TX)
Valencia Coll (FL)

**COMPUTER PROGRAMMING
(SPECIFIC APPLICATIONS)**

Bucks County Comm Coll (PA)
Bunker Hill Comm Coll (MA)
Cecil Coll (MD)
Central Carolina Comm Coll (NC)
Coll of DuPage (IL)
Coll of Lake County (IL)
Comm Coll of Rhode Island (RI)
Cowley County Comm Coll and
Area Vocational–Tech School
(KS)
Delaware County Comm Coll (PA)
ETI Tech Coll of Niles (OH)
Florida State Coll at Jacksonville
(FL)
Gateway Tech Coll (WI)
Gulf Coast State Coll (FL)
Harper Coll (IL)
Hillsborough Comm Coll (FL)
Holyoke Comm Coll (MA)
Houston Comm Coll System (TX)
Kent State U at Salem (OH)
Lake Region State Coll (ND)
Lansing Comm Coll (MI)
Lehigh Carbon Comm Coll (PA)
Lincoln Land Comm Coll (IL)
Macomb Comm Coll (MI)
Metropolitan Comm Coll–Business
& Technology Campus (MO)
Missouri State U–West Plains (MO)
Mohave Comm Coll (AZ)
Monroe County Comm Coll (MI)
Mott Comm Coll (MI)
Normandale Comm Coll (MN)
Northeast Comm Coll (NE)
Northeast Iowa Comm Coll (IA)
Northern Essex Comm Coll (MA)
North Shore Comm Coll (MA)
Northwest Florida State Coll (FL)

Orange Coast Coll (CA)
Owens Comm Coll, Toledo (OH)
Palm Beach State Coll (FL)
Pasco-Hernando Comm Coll (FL)
Pensacola State Coll (FL)
Piedmont Virginia Comm Coll (VA)
Quinsigamond Comm Coll (MA)
Rockland Comm Coll (NY)
St. Cloud Tech & Comm Coll (MN)
Seminole State Coll of Florida (FL)
Southern State Comm Coll (OH)
Springfield Tech Comm Coll (MA)
Stark State Coll (OH)
Sullivan County Comm Coll (NY)
Tallahassee Comm Coll (FL)
Trident Tech Coll (SC)
U of Alaska Anchorage, Kodiak Coll
(AK)
Valencia Coll (FL)
Westmoreland County Comm Coll
(PA)

**COMPUTER PROGRAMMING
(VENDOR/PRODUCT
CERTIFICATION)**

Chandler-Gilbert Comm Coll (AZ)
ETI Tech Coll of Niles (OH)
Florida State Coll at Jacksonville
(FL)
Lake Region State Coll (ND)
Metropolitan Comm Coll–Business
& Technology Campus (MO)
Peninsula Coll (WA)
Raritan Valley Comm Coll (NJ)
Seminole State Coll of Florida (FL)
Stark State Coll (OH)
Sullivan Coll of Technology and
Design (KY)

COMPUTER SCIENCE

Amarillo Coll (TX)
Anoka-Ramsey Comm Coll (MN)
Anoka-Ramsey Comm Coll,
Cambridge Campus (MN)
Bunker Hill Comm Coll (MA)
Burlington County Coll (NJ)
Central Oregon Comm Coll (OR)
Central Wyoming Coll (WY)
Century Coll (MN)
Chipola Coll (FL)
Cochise Coll, Sierra Vista (AZ)
Coll of the Canyons (CA)
Comm Coll of Philadelphia (PA)
Comm Coll of Vermont (VT)
Corning Comm Coll (NY)
Cowley County Comm Coll and
Area Vocational–Tech School
(KS)
Dutchess Comm Coll (NY)
El Centro Coll (TX)
Fiorello H. LaGuardia Comm Coll of
the City U of New York (NY)
Foothill Coll (CA)
Gavilan Coll (CA)
Grand Rapids Comm Coll (MI)
Gwinnett Tech Coll (GA)
Harper Coll (IL)
Howard Comm Coll (MD)
Indian River State Coll (FL)
Iowa Lakes Comm Coll (IA)
Jefferson Comm Coll (NY)
Kingsborough Comm Coll of the
City U of New York (NY)
Lake Area Tech Inst (SD)
Lake Region State Coll (ND)
Lanier Tech Coll (GA)
Laramie County Comm Coll (WY)
Massachusetts Bay Comm Coll
(MA)
Metropolitan Comm Coll–Blue River
(MO)
Metropolitan Comm Coll–Business
& Technology Campus (MO)
Metropolitan Comm Coll–Longview
(MO)
Metropolitan Comm Coll–Maple
Woods (MO)
Metropolitan Comm Coll–Penn
Valley (MO)
Miami Dade Coll (FL)
Mohave Comm Coll (AZ)
Monroe Comm Coll (NY)
Niagara County Comm Coll (NY)
Normandale Comm Coll (MN)
Northampton Comm Coll (PA)
Northeast Comm Coll (NE)
Northeastern Jr Coll (CO)
Northern Essex Comm Coll (MA)

North Hennepin Comm Coll (MN)
North Shore Comm Coll (MA)
Northwestern Connecticut Comm
Coll (CT)
Northwest Florida State Coll (FL)
Oklahoma City Comm Coll (OK)
Onondaga Comm Coll (NY)
Palm Beach State Coll (FL)
Pensacola State Coll (FL)
Piedmont Virginia Comm Coll (VA)
Quinsigamond Comm Coll (MA)
Salt Lake Comm Coll (UT)
San Jacinto Coll District (TX)
Santa Monica Coll (CA)
Santa Rosa Jr Coll (CA)
Snow Coll (UT)
Southwestern Oklahoma State U at
Sayre (OK)
Southwest Mississippi Comm Coll
(MS)
Springfield Tech Comm Coll (MA)
State U of New York Coll of
Technology at Alfred (NY)
Tarrant County Coll District (TX)
Tyler Jr Coll (TX)
Umpqua Comm Coll (OR)
Union County Coll (NJ)
Vincennes U (IN)
Virginia Western Comm Coll (VA)
Westchester Comm Coll (NY)

**COMPUTER SOFTWARE AND
MEDIA APPLICATIONS
RELATED**

Anne Arundel Comm Coll (MD)
Berkeley City Coll (CA)
Dakota Coll at Bottineau (ND)
ETI Tech Coll of Niles (OH)
Florida State Coll at Jacksonville
(FL)
Genesee Comm Coll (NY)
ITT Tech Inst, Bessemer (AL)
ITT Tech Inst, Louisville (KY)
ITT Tech Inst, Owings Mills (MD)
ITT Tech Inst, Norwood (MA)
ITT Tech Inst, Wilmington (MA)
ITT Tech Inst, Swartz Creek (MI)
ITT Tech Inst, Troy (MI)
ITT Tech Inst, Arnold (MO)
ITT Tech Inst, Earth City (MO)
ITT Tech Inst, Albany (NY)
ITT Tech Inst, Getzville (NY)
ITT Tech Inst, Liverpool (NY)
ITT Tech Inst, Norwood (OH)
ITT Tech Inst, Strongsville (OH)
ITT Tech Inst, Youngstown (OH)
ITT Tech Inst, Harrisburg (PA)
ITT Tech Inst, Pittsburgh (PA)
ITT Tech Inst, Tarentum (PA)
ITT Tech Inst, Greenville (SC)
ITT Tech Inst, Cordova (TN)
ITT Tech Inst, Nashville (TN)
ITT Tech Inst, Chantilly (VA)
ITT Tech Inst, Seattle (WA)
ITT Tech Inst, Greenfield (WI)
Metropolitan Comm Coll–Business
& Technology Campus (MO)
Seminole State Coll of Florida (FL)
Stark State Coll (OH)

**COMPUTER SOFTWARE
ENGINEERING**

Cleveland Inst of Electronics (OH)
ETI Tech Coll of Niles (OH)
Florida State Coll at Jacksonville
(FL)
ITT Tech Inst, Youngstown (OH)
Rasmussen Coll Bismarck (ND)
Rasmussen Coll Bloomington (MN)
Rasmussen Coll Brooklyn Park
(MN)
Rasmussen Coll Eagan (MN)
Rasmussen Coll Fargo (ND)
Rasmussen Coll Fort Myers (FL)
Rasmussen Coll Green Bay (WI)
Rasmussen Coll Lake Elmo/
Woodbury (MN)
Rasmussen Coll Mankato (MN)
Rasmussen Coll Moorhead (MN)
Rasmussen Coll New Port Richey
(FL)
Rasmussen Coll Ocala (FL)
Rasmussen Coll St. Cloud (MN)
Seminole State Coll of Florida (FL)
Southeast Tech Inst (SD)
Stark State Coll (OH)

COMPUTER SOFTWARE TECHNOLOGY

Iowa Lakes Comm Coll (IA)
ITT Tech Inst, Bessemer (AL)
ITT Tech Inst, Madison (AL)
ITT Tech Inst, Lake Mary (FL)
ITT Tech Inst, Duluth (GA)
ITT Tech Inst, Kennesaw (GA)
ITT Tech Inst, Oak Brook (IL)
ITT Tech Inst, Orland Park (IL)
ITT Tech Inst, Fort Wayne (IN)
ITT Tech Inst, Louisville (KY)
ITT Tech Inst, Canton (MI)
ITT Tech Inst, Swartz Creek (MI)
ITT Tech Inst, Wyoming (MI)
ITT Tech Inst, Eden Prairie (MN)
ITT Tech Inst, Arnold (MO)
ITT Tech Inst, Earth City (MO)
ITT Tech Inst, Kansas City (MO)
ITT Tech Inst, Henderson (NV)
ITT Tech Inst (NM)
ITT Tech Inst, Cary (NC)
ITT Tech Inst, Charlotte (NC)
ITT Tech Inst, High Point (NC)
ITT Tech Inst, Akron (OH)
ITT Tech Inst, Columbus (OH)
ITT Tech Inst, Dayton (OH)
ITT Tech Inst, Hilliard (OH)
ITT Tech Inst, Maumee (OH)
ITT Tech Inst, Norwood (OH)
ITT Tech Inst, Strongsville (OH)
ITT Tech Inst, Warrensville Heights (OH)
ITT Tech Inst, Tulsa (OK)
ITT Tech Inst, Portland (OR)
ITT Tech Inst, Greenville (SC)
ITT Tech Inst, Cordova (TN)
ITT Tech Inst, Knoxville (TN)
ITT Tech Inst, Nashville (TN)
ITT Tech Inst, Arlington (TX)
ITT Tech Inst, Austin (TX)
ITT Tech Inst, Richardson (TX)
ITT Tech Inst, San Antonio (TX)
ITT Tech Inst, Webster (TX)
ITT Tech Inst (UT)
ITT Tech Inst, Springfield (VA)
ITT Tech Inst, Seattle (WA)
ITT Tech Inst (WV)
ITT Tech Inst, Green Bay (WI)
ITT Tech Inst, Greenfield (WI)
ITT Tech Inst, Madison (WI)
Kansas City Kansas Comm Coll (KS)
Miami Dade Coll (FL)
Rogue Comm Coll (OR)

COMPUTER SUPPORT SPECIALIST

Gateway Tech Coll (WI)
Mitchell Tech Inst (SD)
North Dakota State Coll of Science (ND)
Southwestern Michigan Coll (MI)
Waukesha County Tech Coll (WI)
Westmoreland County Comm Coll (PA)

COMPUTER SYSTEMS ANALYSIS

Amarillo Coll (TX)
Chandler-Gilbert Comm Coll (AZ)
Florida State Coll at Jacksonville (FL)
Fox Valley Tech Coll (WI)
Gateway Tech Coll (WI)
Guilford Tech Comm Coll (NC)
Hillsborough Comm Coll (FL)
Hutchinson Comm Coll and Area Vocational School (KS)
Kirtland Comm Coll (MI)
Metropolitan Comm Coll–Business & Technology Campus (MO)
Oakland Comm Coll (MI)
Oklahoma City Comm Coll (OK)
Pensacola State Coll (FL)
Quinsigamond Comm Coll (MA)
Southern State Comm Coll (OH)

COMPUTER SYSTEMS NETWORKING AND TELECOMMUNICATIONS

Aiken Tech Coll (SC)
Altamaha Tech Coll (GA)
Anne Arundel Comm Coll (MD)
Anoka-Ramsey Comm Coll (MN)

Anoka-Ramsey Comm Coll, Cambridge Campus (MN)
Athens Tech Coll (GA)
Augusta Tech Coll (GA)
Austin Comm Coll (TX)
Blackhawk Tech Coll (WI)
Bradford School (PA)
Bucks County Comm Coll (PA)
Bunker Hill Comm Coll (MA)
Cape Fear Comm Coll (NC)
Catawba Valley Comm Coll (NC)
Central Carolina Comm Coll (NC)
Central Georgia Tech Coll (GA)
Central Oregon Comm Coll (OR)
Century Coll (MN)
Chandler-Gilbert Comm Coll (AZ)
Chattahoochee Tech Coll (GA)
Chippewa Valley Tech Coll (WI)
City Colls of Chicago, Harry S. Truman College (IL)
Clark Coll (WA)
Cochise Coll, Sierra Vista (AZ)
Coll of Business and Technology (FL)
Coll of Lake County (IL)
Coll of the Canyons (CA)
Colorado Mountain Coll (CO)
Columbus Tech Coll (GA)
Comm Coll of Allegheny County (PA)
The Comm Coll of Baltimore County (MD)
Comm Coll of Rhode Island (RI)
Comm Coll of Vermont (VT)
Corning Comm Coll (NY)
Crowder Coll (MO)
Delaware County Comm Coll (PA)
Delaware Tech & Comm Coll, Stanton/Wilmington Campus (DE)
Delaware Tech & Comm Coll, Terry Campus (DE)
Eastern Idaho Tech Coll (ID)
Edison Comm Coll (OH)
Fayetteville Tech Comm Coll (NC)
Florida State Coll at Jacksonville (FL)
Fox Valley Tech Coll (WI)
GateWay Comm Coll (AZ)
Gateway Tech Coll (WI)
Gavilan Coll (CA)
Georgia Piedmont Tech Coll (GA)
Guilford Tech Comm Coll (NC)
Gwinnett Tech Coll (GA)
Hawkeye Comm Coll (IA)
Highline Comm Coll (WA)
Houston Comm Coll System (TX)
Howard Comm Coll (MD)
Illinois Eastern Comm Colls, Lincoln Trail College (IL)
Illinois Valley Comm Coll (IL)
International Business Coll, Indianapolis (IN)
Iowa Lakes Comm Coll (IA)
Island Drafting and Tech Inst (NY)
Kansas City Kansas Comm Coll (KS)
Kaplan Career Inst, Harrisburg Campus (PA)
Kaplan Career Inst, ICM Campus (PA)
Kaplan Coll, Arlington Campus (TX)
Kaplan Coll, Beaumont Campus (TX)
Kaplan Coll, Charlotte Campus (NC)
Kaplan Coll, Chesapeake Campus (VA)
Kaplan Coll, Dayton Campus (OH)
Kaplan Coll, El Paso Campus (TX)
Kaplan Coll, Hammond Campus (IN)
Kaplan Coll, Jacksonville Campus (FL)
Kaplan Coll, Pembroke Pines Campus (FL)
Kilgore Coll (TX)
King's Coll (NC)
Lake Region State Coll (ND)
Lanier Tech Coll (GA)
Lansing Comm Coll (MI)
Lehigh Carbon Comm Coll (PA)
Lincoln Land Comm Coll (IL)
Linn State Tech Coll (MO)
Metropolitan Comm Coll–Business & Technology Campus (MO)

Middle Georgia Tech Coll (GA)
Minneapolis Business Coll (MN)
Minneapolis Comm and Tech Coll (MN)
Minnesota School of Business–Plymouth (MN)
Minnesota School of Business–Richfield (MN)
Minnesota School of Business–St. Cloud (MN)
Minnesota School of Business–Shakopee (MN)
Minnesota State Coll–Southeast Tech (MN)
Montana State U–Great Falls Coll of Technology (MT)
Montgomery County Comm Coll (PA)
Moraine Park Tech Coll (WI)
Mott Comm Coll (MI)
Moultrie Tech Coll (GA)
Northampton Comm Coll (PA)
North Dakota State Coll of Science (ND)
Northern Essex Comm Coll (MA)
North Georgia Tech Coll (GA)
North Seattle Comm Coll (WA)
Northwest Florida State Coll (FL)
Northwest Tech Coll (MN)
Oconee Fall Line Tech Coll–North Campus (GA)
Ogeechee Tech Coll (GA)
Okefenokee Tech Coll (GA)
Olympic Coll (WA)
Onondaga Comm Coll (NY)
Pasco-Hernando Comm Coll (FL)
Piedmont Virginia Comm Coll (VA)
Randolph Comm Coll (NC)
Raritan Valley Comm Coll (NJ)
Red Rocks Comm Coll (CO)
Rockland Comm Coll (NY)
St. Cloud Tech & Comm Coll (MN)
St. Philip's Coll (TX)
Savannah Tech Coll (GA)
Seminole State Coll of Florida (FL)
Southeastern Tech Coll (GA)
Southeast Tech Inst (SD)
Southern Crescent Tech Coll (GA)
South Georgia Tech Coll (GA)
Southwestern Michigan Coll (MI)
Southwest Georgia Tech Coll (GA)
Southwest Mississippi Comm Coll (MS)
Stark State Coll (OH)
Sullivan Coll of Technology and Design (KY)
Tallahassee Comm Coll (FL)
Terra State Comm Coll (OH)
TESST Coll of Technology, Baltimore (MD)
TESST Coll of Technology, Beltsville (MD)
TESST Coll of Technology, Towson (MD)
Texas State Tech Coll Harlingen (TX)
Trident Tech Coll (SC)
Tyler Jr Coll (TX)
Vincennes U (IN)
Waukesha County Tech Coll (WI)
Westchester Comm Coll (NY)
Western Dakota Tech Inst (SD)
West Georgia Tech Coll (GA)
Westmoreland County Comm Coll (PA)
Wilson Comm Coll (NC)
Wiregrass Georgia Tech Coll (GA)
Wisconsin Indianhead Tech Coll (WI)
Wood Tobe–Coburn School (NY)

COMPUTER TECHNOLOGY/ COMPUTER SYSTEMS TECHNOLOGY

Brookhaven Coll (TX)
Cape Fear Comm Coll (NC)
Central Wyoming Coll (WY)
Century Coll (MN)
Comm Coll of Allegheny County (PA)
Corning Comm Coll (NY)
Dakota Coll at Bottineau (ND)
Delaware County Comm Coll (PA)
Delaware Tech & Comm Coll, Jack F. Owens Campus (DE)

Delaware Tech & Comm Coll, Terry Campus (DE)
Erie Comm Coll, South Campus (NY)
Forrest Coll (SC)
Gulf Coast State Coll (FL)
Hillsborough Comm Coll (FL)
Island Drafting and Tech Inst (NY)
ITI Tech Coll (LA)
Kent State U at Trumbull (OH)
Lansing Comm Coll (MI)
Miami Dade Coll (FL)
Minnesota State Coll–Southeast Tech (MN)
Mount Wachusett Comm Coll (MA)
Normandale Comm Coll (MN)
Oakland Comm Coll (MI)
Okefenokee Tech Coll (GA)
Pasco-Hernando Comm Coll (FL)
Pittsburgh Tech Inst, Oakdale (PA)
St. Philip's Coll (TX)
Southeast Tech Inst (SD)
Southern State Comm Coll (OH)
Sullivan Coll of Technology and Design (KY)
Texas State Tech Coll Harlingen (TX)
U of Alaska Anchorage, Kodiak Coll (AK)
U of Arkansas Comm Coll at Morrilton (AR)
West Virginia Jr Coll–Bridgeport (WV)

COMPUTER TYPOGRAPHY AND COMPOSITION EQUIPMENT OPERATION

Coll of DuPage (IL)
Do&nna Ana Comm Coll (NM)
Gateway Comm Coll (CT)
Highline Comm Coll (WA)
Housatonic Comm Coll (CT)
Indian River State Coll (FL)
Metropolitan Comm Coll–Longview (MO)
Northern Essex Comm Coll (MA)
Orange Coast Coll (CA)

CONCRETE FINISHING

Southwestern Illinois Coll (IL)

CONSTRUCTION ENGINEERING

Illinois Central Coll (IL)

CONSTRUCTION ENGINEERING TECHNOLOGY

Burlington County Coll (NJ)
Central Comm Coll–Hastings Campus (NE)
Central Maine Comm Coll (ME)
Clark Coll (WA)
Coll of Lake County (IL)
Comm Coll of Allegheny County (PA)
Comm Coll of Philadelphia (PA)
Crowder Coll (MO)
Dutchess Comm Coll (NY)
Florida State Coll at Jacksonville (FL)
Gulf Coast State Coll (FL)
Houston Comm Coll System (TX)
Iowa Lakes Comm Coll (IA)
Jefferson State Comm Coll (AL)
Lake Area Tech Inst (SD)
Lincoln Land Comm Coll (IL)
Macomb Comm Coll (MI)
Miami Dade Coll (FL)
Mid-Plains Comm Coll, North Platte (NE)
Monroe Comm Coll (NY)
North Dakota State Coll of Science (ND)
Northwest Florida State Coll (FL)
Oklahoma State U, Oklahoma City (OK)
Onondaga Comm Coll (NY)
Orange Coast Coll (CA)
Owens Comm Coll, Toledo (OH)
Palau Comm Coll (Palau)
Pensacola State Coll (FL)
Raritan Valley Comm Coll (NJ)
Rogue Comm Coll (OR)
St. Philip's Coll (TX)
San Jacinto Coll District (TX)

Seminole State Coll of Florida (FL)
Snow Coll (UT)
Southeastern Comm Coll (IA)
Southeast Tech Inst (SD)
South Suburban Coll (IL)
Southwest Mississippi Comm Coll (MS)
State Coll of Florida Manatee-Sarasota (FL)
State U of New York Coll of Technology at Alfred (NY)
Tallahassee Comm Coll (FL)
Tarrant County Coll District (TX)
Texas State Tech Coll Harlingen (TX)
Valencia Coll (FL)

CONSTRUCTION/HEAVY EQUIPMENT/EARTHMOVING EQUIPMENT OPERATION

GateWay Comm Coll (AZ)
Ivy Tech Comm Coll–Southwest (IN)
Ivy Tech Comm Coll–Wabash Valley (IN)
Lansing Comm Coll (MI)

CONSTRUCTION MANAGEMENT

Casper Coll (WY)
Delaware County Comm Coll (PA)
Delaware Tech & Comm Coll, Jack F. Owens Campus (DE)
Delaware Tech & Comm Coll, Stanton/Wilmington Campus (DE)
Delaware Tech & Comm Coll, Terry Campus (DE)
Erie Comm Coll, North Campus (NY)
Iowa Lakes Comm Coll (IA)
Kankakee Comm Coll (IL)
Northampton Comm Coll (PA)
North Hennepin Comm Coll (MN)
Oakland Comm Coll (MI)
Oklahoma State U, Oklahoma City (OK)
San Joaquin Valley Coll, Fresno (CA)
San Joaquin Valley Coll–Online (CA)
Southwestern Michigan Coll (MI)
Truckee Meadows Comm Coll (NV)
U of Alaska Anchorage, Kodiak Coll (AK)

CONSTRUCTION TRADES

Casper Coll (WY)
Iowa Lakes Comm Coll (IA)
Ivy Tech Comm Coll–East Central (IN)
Ivy Tech Comm Coll–Northeast (IN)
Ivy Tech Comm Coll–Northwest (IN)
Ivy Tech Comm Coll–Richmond (IN)
Lehigh Carbon Comm Coll (PA)
Northeast Iowa Comm Coll (IA)
Ogeechee Tech Coll (GA)
Oklahoma State U, Oklahoma City (OK)
Red Rocks Comm Coll (CO)
Rogue Comm Coll (OR)
Southern Maine Comm Coll (ME)
Southwestern Illinois Coll (IL)
Vincennes U (IN)

CONSTRUCTION TRADES RELATED

Central Maine Comm Coll (ME)
Comm Coll of Allegheny County (PA)
Ivy Tech Comm Coll–East Central (IN)
Ivy Tech Comm Coll–Kokomo (IN)
Ivy Tech Comm Coll–Northeast (IN)
Ivy Tech Comm Coll–Richmond (IN)
Jackson Comm Coll (MI)
Mitchell Tech Inst (SD)
State U of New York Coll of Technology at Alfred (NY)
Tompkins Cortland Comm Coll (NY)
York County Comm Coll (ME)

CONSUMER MERCHANDISING/RETAILING MANAGEMENT
Clinton Comm Coll (NY)
Colorado Mountain Coll, Alpine Campus (CO)
Do&nna Ana Comm Coll (NM)
Dutchess Comm Coll (NY)
Gateway Comm Coll (CT)
Howard Comm Coll (MD)
Indian River State Coll (FL)
Iowa Lakes Comm Coll (IA)
Monroe Comm Coll (NY)
Niagara County Comm Coll (NY)
Stark State Coll (OH)
Sullivan County Comm Coll (NY)
Tarrant County Coll District (TX)
Three Rivers Comm Coll (CT)
Westchester Comm Coll (NY)

CONSUMER SERVICES AND ADVOCACY
Pensacola State Coll (FL)
San Diego City Coll (CA)

COOKING AND RELATED CULINARY ARTS
Central Oregon Comm Coll (OR)
Columbus Culinary Inst at Bradford School (OH)
Culinary Inst of St. Louis at Hickey Coll (MO)
Iowa Lakes Comm Coll (IA)
Kingsborough Comm Coll of the City U of New York (NY)
Miami Dade Coll (FL)
Pensacola State Coll (FL)
State U of New York Coll of Technology at Alfred (NY)

CORRECTIONS
Alvin Comm Coll (TX)
Amarillo Coll (TX)
Austin Comm Coll (TX)
Cayuga County Comm Coll (NY)
Coll of DuPage (IL)
Colorado Mountain Coll, Timberline Campus (CO)
Comm Coll of Allegheny County (PA)
El Paso Comm Coll (TX)
Garrett Coll (MD)
Gavilan Coll (CA)
Grand Rapids Comm Coll (MI)
Illinois Central Coll (IL)
Illinois Eastern Comm Colls, Frontier Community College (IL)
Illinois Eastern Comm Colls, Lincoln Trail College (IL)
Illinois Eastern Comm Colls, Olney Central College (IL)
Illinois Eastern Comm Colls, Wabash Valley College (IL)
Illinois Valley Comm Coll (IL)
Indian River State Coll (FL)
Iowa Lakes Comm Coll (IA)
Jackson Comm Coll (MI)
Kansas City Kansas Comm Coll (KS)
Kilgore Coll (TX)
Kirtland Comm Coll (MI)
Lake Michigan Coll (MI)
Lansing Comm Coll (MI)
Laramie County Comm Coll (WY)
Metropolitan Comm Coll–Longview (MO)
Metropolitan Comm Coll–Penn Valley (MO)
Mid Michigan Comm Coll (MI)
Monroe Comm Coll (NY)
Montcalm Comm Coll (MI)
Moraine Park Tech Coll (WI)
Mount Wachusett Comm Coll (MA)
Northeast Comm Coll (NE)
Northeastern Jr Coll (CO)
Oakland Comm Coll (MI)
Owens Comm Coll, Toledo (OH)
Polk State Coll (FL)
Raritan Valley Comm Coll (NJ)
San Joaquin Valley Coll, Bakersfield (CA)
San Joaquin Valley Coll, Fresno (CA)
San Joaquin Valley Coll, Rancho Cordova (CA)
San Joaquin Valley Coll, Visalia (CA)
Southern State Comm Coll (OH)
Southwestern Oklahoma State U at Sayre (OK)
Sullivan County Comm Coll (NY)
Three Rivers Comm Coll (CT)
Tunxis Comm Coll (CT)
Vincennes U (IN)
Westchester Comm Coll (NY)
Westmoreland County Comm Coll (PA)
Wisconsin Indianhead Tech Coll (WI)
Wytheville Comm Coll (VA)

CORRECTIONS AND CRIMINAL JUSTICE RELATED
Albany Tech Coll (GA)
Career Tech Coll (LA)
Corning Comm Coll (NY)
El Paso Comm Coll (TX)
Fayetteville Tech Comm Coll (NC)
Kansas City Kansas Comm Coll (KS)
Murray State Coll (OK)
Rasmussen Coll Aurora (IL)
Rasmussen Coll Bismarck (ND)
Rasmussen Coll Bloomington (MN)
Rasmussen Coll Brooklyn Park (MN)
Rasmussen Coll Eagan (MN)
Rasmussen Coll Fort Myers (FL)
Rasmussen Coll Green Bay (WI)
Rasmussen Coll Lake Elmo/Woodbury (MN)
Rasmussen Coll Mankato (MN)
Rasmussen Coll Moorhead (MN)
Rasmussen Coll New Port Richey (FL)
Rasmussen Coll Ocala (FL)
Rasmussen Coll Rockford (IL)
Rasmussen Coll St. Cloud (MN)
Reedley Coll (CA)
Rockingham Comm Coll (NC)
San Joaquin Valley Coll, Salida (CA)

COSMETOLOGY
Century Coll (MN)
Clary Sage Coll (OK)
Copiah-Lincoln Comm Coll (MS)
Cowley County Comm Coll and Area Vocational–Tech School (KS)
Eastern Arizona Coll (AZ)
Gavilan Coll (CA)
Guilford Tech Comm Coll (NC)
Houston Comm Coll System (TX)
Indian River State Coll (FL)
Kirtland Comm Coll (MI)
Minnesota State Coll–Southeast Tech (MN)
Montcalm Comm Coll (MI)
Northeastern Jr Coll (CO)
Northeast Iowa Comm Coll (IA)
Oakland Comm Coll (MI)
Randolph Comm Coll (NC)
Red Rocks Comm Coll (CO)
Riverside City Coll (CA)
Salt Lake Comm Coll (UT)
San Diego City Coll (CA)
San Jacinto Coll District (TX)
San Juan Coll (NM)
Santa Monica Coll (CA)
Shawnee Comm Coll (IL)
Southeastern Comm Coll (IA)
Southwest Mississippi Comm Coll (MS)
Texarkana Coll (TX)
Umpqua Comm Coll (OR)
Vincennes U (IN)

COSMETOLOGY AND PERSONAL GROOMING ARTS RELATED
Comm Coll of Allegheny County (PA)

COSMETOLOGY, BARBER/STYLING, AND NAIL INSTRUCTION
San Jacinto Coll District (TX)

COUNSELING PSYCHOLOGY
Kilian Comm Coll (SD)

COURT REPORTING
Alvin Comm Coll (TX)

CORRECTIONS (continued)
Comm Coll of Allegheny County (PA)
El Paso Comm Coll (TX)
Gadsden State Comm Coll (AL)
GateWay Comm Coll (AZ)
Houston Comm Coll System (TX)
Long Island Business Inst (NY)
Miami Dade Coll (FL)
Moraine Park Tech Coll (WI)
New York Career Inst (NY)
Oakland Comm Coll (MI)
Orleans Tech Inst (PA)
San Diego City Coll (CA)
South Suburban Coll (IL)
Stark State Coll (OH)
State U of New York Coll of Technology at Alfred (NY)
West Kentucky Comm and Tech Coll (KY)
Wisconsin Indianhead Tech Coll (WI)

CREATIVE WRITING
Austin Comm Coll (TX)
Berkeley City Coll (CA)
Kirtland Comm Coll (MI)
Normandale Comm Coll (MN)
Tompkins Cortland Comm Coll (NY)

CRIMINALISTICS AND CRIMINAL SCIENCE
Century Coll (MN)
Oakland Comm Coll (MI)

CRIMINAL JUSTICE/LAW ENFORCEMENT ADMINISTRATION
Aiken Tech Coll (SC)
Amarillo Coll (TX)
Anne Arundel Comm Coll (MD)
Arkansas State U–Mountain Home (AR)
Athens Tech Coll (GA)
Bainbridge Coll (GA)
Beaufort County Comm Coll (NC)
Bunker Hill Comm Coll (MA)
Casper Coll (WY)
Central Carolina Comm Coll (NC)
Central Maine Comm Coll (ME)
Central Wyoming Coll (WY)
Clinton Comm Coll (NY)
Colby Comm Coll (KS)
Coll of DuPage (IL)
Coll of Southern Maryland (MD)
Colorado Mountain Coll (CO)
Colorado Mountain Coll, Timberline Campus (CO)
Comm Coll of Philadelphia (PA)
Comm Coll of Vermont (VT)
Corning Comm Coll (NY)
Cowley County Comm Coll and Area Vocational–Tech School (KS)
Delaware Tech & Comm Coll, Jack F. Owens Campus (DE)
Delaware Tech & Comm Coll, Stanton/Wilmington Campus (DE)
Delaware Tech & Comm Coll, Terry Campus (DE)
Denmark Tech Coll (SC)
Dutchess Comm Coll (NY)
Eastern Arizona Coll (AZ)
Florida State Coll at Jacksonville (FL)
Genesee Comm Coll (NY)
Goodwin Coll (CT)
Grand Rapids Comm Coll (MI)
Gulf Coast State Coll (FL)
Harper Coll (IL)
Hesser Coll, Concord (NH)
Hesser Coll, Manchester (NH)
Hesser Coll, Nashua (NH)
Hesser Coll, Portsmouth (NH)
Hesser Coll, Salem (NH)
Highline Comm Coll (WA)
Hillsborough Comm Coll (FL)
Housatonic Comm Coll (CT)
Howard Comm Coll (MD)
Illinois Valley Comm Coll (IL)
Indian River State Coll (FL)
Iowa Lakes Comm Coll (IA)
ITT Tech Inst, Tampa (FL)
ITT Tech Inst, Atlanta (GA)
ITT Tech Inst, Duluth (GA)
ITT Tech Inst, Kennesaw (GA)
ITT Tech Inst, Mount Prospect (IL)
ITT Tech Inst, Oak Brook (IL)
ITT Tech Inst, Orland Park (IL)
ITT Tech Inst, Louisville (KY)
ITT Tech Inst, Getzville (NY)
ITT Tech Inst, Cary (NC)
ITT Tech Inst, Charlotte (NC)
ITT Tech Inst, High Point (NC)
ITT Tech Inst, Portland (OR)
ITT Tech Inst, Bensalem (PA)
ITT Tech Inst, Dunmore (PA)
ITT Tech Inst, Harrisburg (PA)
ITT Tech Inst, King of Prussia (PA)
ITT Tech Inst, Pittsburgh (PA)
ITT Tech Inst, Tarentum (PA)
ITT Tech Inst, Greenville (SC)
ITT Tech Inst, Greenfield (WI)
ITT Tech Inst, Madison (WI)
Jackson Comm Coll (MI)
Jefferson Comm Coll (NY)
John Tyler Comm Coll (VA)
Kankakee Comm Coll (IL)
Kaplan Career Inst, Cleveland Campus (OH)
Kaplan Career Inst, Dearborn Campus (MI)
Kaplan Career Inst, Franklin Mills Campus (PA)
Kaplan Career Inst, Harrisburg Campus (PA)
Kaplan Career Inst, ICM Campus (PA)
Kaplan Career Inst, Nashville Campus (TN)
Kaplan Career Inst, Philadelphia Campus (PA)
Kaplan Coll, Arlington Campus (TX)
Kaplan Coll, Bakersfield Campus (CA)
Kaplan Coll, Beaumont Campus (TX)
Kaplan Coll, Charlotte Campus (NC)
Kaplan Coll, Chesapeake Campus (VA)
Kaplan Coll, Chula Vista Campus (CA)
Kaplan Coll, Cincinnati Campus (OH)
Kaplan Coll, Columbus Campus (OH)
Kaplan Coll, Corpus Christi Campus (TX)
Kaplan Coll, Dallas Campus (TX)
Kaplan Coll, El Paso Campus (TX)
Kaplan Coll, Fort Worth Campus (TX)
Kaplan Coll, Fresno Campus (CA)
Kaplan Coll, Jacksonville Campus (FL)
Kaplan Coll, Laredo Campus (TX)
Kaplan Coll, Las Vegas Campus, Las Vegas (NV)
Kaplan Coll, Lubbock Campus (TX)
Kaplan Coll, Midland Campus (TX)
Kaplan Coll, Milwaukee Campus (WI)
Kaplan Coll, Modesto Campus (CA)
Kaplan Coll, Palm Springs Campus (CA)
Kaplan Coll, Pembroke Pines Campus (FL)
Kaplan Coll, Phoenix Campus (AZ)
Kaplan Coll, Riverside Campus (CA)
Kaplan Coll, Sacramento Campus (CA)
Kaplan Coll, San Antonio–San Pedro Area Campus (TX)
Kaplan Coll, San Diego Campus (CA)
Kaplan Coll, Southeast Indianapolis Campus (IN)
Kaplan Coll, Stockton Campus (CA)
Kaplan Coll, Vista Campus (CA)
Kaskaskia Coll (IL)
Kent State U at East Liverpool (OH)
Kilgore Coll (TX)
Kilian Comm Coll (SD)
Kingsborough Comm Coll of the City U of New York (NY)
Kirtland Comm Coll (MI)
Lake Michigan Coll (MI)
Laramie County Comm Coll (WY)
Lehigh Carbon Comm Coll (PA)
Lower Columbia Coll (WA)
Macomb Comm Coll (MI)
Manchester Comm Coll (CT)
Massachusetts Bay Comm Coll (MA)
Mendocino Coll (CA)
Metropolitan Comm Coll–Longview (MO)
Metropolitan Comm Coll–Maple Woods (MO)
Metropolitan Comm Coll–Penn Valley (MO)
Miami Dade Coll (FL)
Mid Michigan Comm Coll (MI)
Minnesota School of Business–Brooklyn Center (MN)
Minnesota School of Business–Richfield (MN)
Minnesota School of Business–St. Cloud (MN)
Minnesota School of Business–Shakopee (MN)
Missouri State U–West Plains (MO)
Mohawk Valley Comm Coll (NY)
Monroe Comm Coll (NY)
Montcalm Comm Coll (MI)
Mount Wachusett Comm Coll (MA)
Muskegon Comm Coll (MI)
Niagara County Comm Coll (NY)
Northern Essex Comm Coll (MA)
North Hennepin Comm Coll (MN)
North Shore Comm Coll (MA)
Northwest Coll (WY)
Northwestern Connecticut Comm Coll (CT)
Northwest Florida State Coll (FL)
Oakland Comm Coll (MI)
Onondaga Comm Coll (NY)
Owens Comm Coll, Toledo (OH)
Ozarka Coll (AR)
Palm Beach State Coll (FL)
Pasco-Hernando Comm Coll (FL)
Peninsula Coll (WA)
Pensacola State Coll (FL)
Polk State Coll (FL)
Raritan Valley Comm Coll (NJ)
Rockland Comm Coll (NY)
St. Philip's Coll (TX)
Salt Lake Comm Coll (UT)
San Joaquin Valley Coll–Online (CA)
Santa Rosa Jr Coll (CA)
Scottsdale Comm Coll (AZ)
Seminole State Coll of Florida (FL)
Snow Coll (UT)
Southeastern Comm Coll (IA)
Southern State Comm Coll (OH)
Southwestern Illinois Coll (IL)
Southwest Virginia Comm Coll (VA)
Tallahassee Comm Coll (FL)
Tarrant County Coll District (TX)
Texarkana Coll (TX)
Three Rivers Comm Coll (CT)
Tompkins Cortland Comm Coll (NY)
Trident Tech Coll (SC)
Truckee Meadows Comm Coll (NV)
Tunxis Comm Coll (CT)
Tyler Jr Coll (TX)
Umpqua Comm Coll (OR)
Union County Coll (NJ)
U of Arkansas Comm Coll at Morrilton (AR)
Valencia Coll (FL)
Virginia Western Comm Coll (VA)
Western Iowa Tech Comm Coll (IA)
West Kentucky Comm and Tech Coll (KY)
Wytheville Comm Coll (VA)

CRIMINAL JUSTICE/POLICE SCIENCE
Alvin Comm Coll (TX)
Amarillo Coll (TX)
Anne Arundel Comm Coll (MD)
Arkansas State U–Mountain Home (AR)
Austin Comm Coll (TX)
Beaufort County Comm Coll (NC)
Blackhawk Tech Coll (WI)
Bunker Hill Comm Coll (MA)
Burlington County Coll (NJ)
Cape Fear Comm Coll (NC)
Carroll Comm Coll (MD)
Cayuga County Comm Coll (NY)
Cecil Coll (MD)
Century Coll (MN)
Chattahoochee Valley Comm Coll (AL)
Chippewa Valley Tech Coll (WI)
Cleveland State Comm Coll (TN)
Clinton Comm Coll (NY)

Cochise Coll, Sierra Vista (AZ)
Colby Comm Coll (KS)
Coll of DuPage (IL)
Coll of Lake County (IL)
Coll of the Canyons (CA)
Comm Coll of Allegheny County (PA)
The Comm Coll of Baltimore County (MD)
Comm Coll of Rhode Island (RI)
Copiah-Lincoln Comm Coll (MS)
Cowley County Comm Coll and Area Vocational–Tech School (KS)
Dawson Comm Coll (MT)
Delaware County Comm Coll (PA)
Delaware Tech & Comm Coll, Jack F. Owens Campus (DE)
Delaware Tech & Comm Coll, Stanton/Wilmington Campus (DE)
Delaware Tech & Comm Coll, Terry Campus (DE)
Dyersburg State Comm Coll (TN)
Eastern Arizona Coll (AZ)
Edison Comm Coll (OH)
Elgin Comm Coll (IL)
El Paso Comm Coll (TX)
Erie Comm Coll (NY)
Erie Comm Coll, North Campus (NY)
Erie Comm Coll, South Campus (NY)
Florida State Coll at Jacksonville (FL)
Fox Valley Tech Coll (WI)
Gadsden State Comm Coll (AL)
Gateway Tech Coll (WI)
Gavilan Coll (CA)
Georgia Highlands Coll (GA)
Grand Rapids Comm Coll (MI)
Hagerstown Comm Coll (MD)
Harford Comm Coll (MD)
Hawkeye Comm Coll (IA)
Highline Comm Coll (WA)
Houston Comm Coll System (TX)
Hutchinson Comm Coll and Area Vocational School (KS)
Illinois Central Coll (IL)
Illinois Eastern Comm Colls, Olney Central College (IL)
Illinois Valley Comm Coll (IL)
Indian River State Coll (FL)
Iowa Lakes Comm Coll (IA)
Jamestown Comm Coll (NY)
Jefferson State Comm Coll (AL)
Johnston Comm Coll (NC)
John Wood Comm Coll (IL)
Kansas City Kansas Comm Coll (KS)
Kent State U at Ashtabula (OH)
Kent State U at Tuscarawas (OH)
Lake Region State Coll (ND)
Lansing Comm Coll (MI)
Lawson State Comm Coll (AL)
Lincoln Land Comm Coll (IL)
Los Angeles Harbor Coll (CA)
Macomb Comm Coll (MI)
McHenry County Coll (IL)
Mendocino Coll (CA)
Metropolitan Comm Coll–Blue River (MO)
Metropolitan Comm Coll–Longview (MO)
Metropolitan Comm Coll–Maple Woods (MO)
Metropolitan Comm Coll–Penn Valley (MO)
Miami Dade Coll (FL)
Mineral Area Coll (MO)
Minneapolis Comm and Tech Coll (MN)
Missouri State U–West Plains (MO)
Mohave Comm Coll (AZ)
Monroe Comm Coll (NY)
Monroe County Comm Coll (MI)
Montgomery Coll (MD)
Montgomery Comm Coll (NC)
Montgomery County Comm Coll (PA)
Moraine Valley Comm Coll (IL)
Mott Comm Coll (MI)
Normandale Comm Coll (MN)
Northeast Comm Coll (NE)
Northeastern Jr Coll (CO)
North Hennepin Comm Coll (MN)

Northwestern Connecticut Comm Coll (CT)
Northwest Florida State Coll (FL)
Northwest-Shoals Comm Coll (AL)
Oakland Comm Coll (MI)
Ocean County Coll (NJ)
Okefenokee Tech Coll (GA)
Oklahoma State U, Oklahoma City (OK)
Olympic Coll (WA)
Onondaga Comm Coll (NY)
Owensboro Comm and Tech Coll (KY)
Owens Comm Coll, Toledo (OH)
Palau Comm Coll (Palau)
Palm Beach State Coll (FL)
Piedmont Virginia Comm Coll (VA)
Quinsigamond Comm Coll (MA)
Raritan Valley Comm Coll (NJ)
Rasmussen Coll Bloomington (MN)
Rasmussen Coll Brooklyn Park (MN)
Rasmussen Coll Eagan (MN)
Rasmussen Coll Lake Elmo/Woodbury (MN)
Rasmussen Coll Mankato (MN)
Rasmussen Coll St. Cloud (MN)
Red Rocks Comm Coll (CO)
Reedley Coll (CA)
Rockingham Comm Coll (NC)
Rogue Comm Coll (OR)
St. Clair County Comm Coll (MI)
San Jacinto Coll District (TX)
Shawnee Comm Coll (IL)
Southeast Tech Inst (SD)
Southern Maine Comm Coll (ME)
Southern State Comm Coll (OH)
Southwest Virginia Comm Coll (VA)
Springfield Tech Comm Coll (MA)
Terra State Comm Coll (OH)
Tyler Jr Coll (TX)
Union County Coll (NJ)
Vincennes U (IN)
Volunteer State Comm Coll (TN)
Waukesha County Tech Coll (WI)
Western Dakota Tech Inst (SD)
Western Iowa Tech Comm Coll (IA)
Westmoreland County Comm Coll (PA)
West Virginia Northern Comm Coll (WV)
Wisconsin Indianhead Tech Coll (WI)
Wytheville Comm Coll (VA)

CRIMINAL JUSTICE/SAFETY
Altamaha Tech Coll (GA)
Ancilla Coll (IN)
Augusta Tech Coll (GA)
Berkshire Comm Coll (MA)
Blue Ridge Comm and Tech Coll (WV)
Bucks County Comm Coll (PA)
Catawba Valley Comm Coll (NC)
Central Carolina Tech Coll (SC)
Central Comm Coll–Columbus Campus (NE)
Central Comm Coll–Grand Island Campus (NE)
Central Comm Coll–Hastings Campus (NE)
Central Georgia Tech Coll (GA)
Century Coll (MN)
Chandler-Gilbert Comm Coll (AZ)
Chattahoochee Tech Coll (GA)
City Colls of Chicago, Harry S. Truman College (IL)
Dutchess Comm Coll (NY)
El Paso Comm Coll (TX)
Fayetteville Tech Comm Coll (NC)
Fiorello H. LaGuardia Comm Coll of the City U of New York (NY)
Georgia Highlands Coll (GA)
Georgia Northwestern Tech Coll (GA)
Georgia Piedmont Tech Coll (GA)
Guilford Tech Comm Coll (NC)
Holyoke Comm Coll (MA)
Ivy Tech Comm Coll–Bloomington (IN)
Ivy Tech Comm Coll–Central Indiana (IN)
Ivy Tech Comm Coll–East Central (IN)
Ivy Tech Comm Coll–Kokomo (IN)
Ivy Tech Comm Coll–North Central (IN)

Ivy Tech Comm Coll–Northwest (IN)
Ivy Tech Comm Coll–Southwest (IN)
Ivy Tech Comm Coll–Wabash Valley (IN)
James Sprunt Comm Coll (NC)
Jamestown Comm Coll (NY)
Kent State U at Ashtabula (OH)
Kent State U at Salem (OH)
Kent State U at Trumbull (OH)
Lanier Tech Coll (GA)
Lehigh Carbon Comm Coll (PA)
Minneapolis Comm and Tech Coll (MN)
Minnesota State Coll–Southeast Tech (MN)
Monroe County Comm Coll (MI)
Moultrie Tech Coll (GA)
Mount Wachusett Comm Coll (MA)
New Mexico State U–Alamogordo (NM)
Normandale Comm Coll (MN)
Northampton Comm Coll (PA)
North Georgia Tech Coll (GA)
North Hennepin Comm Coll (MN)
Randolph Comm Coll (NC)
Savannah Tech Coll (GA)
Southeastern Tech Coll (GA)
Southern Crescent Tech Coll (GA)
South Georgia Tech Coll (GA)
South Suburban Coll (IL)
Southwestern Oklahoma State U at Sayre (OK)
Southwest Georgia Tech Coll (GA)
State Coll of Florida Manatee-Sarasota (FL)
TESST Coll of Technology, Beltsville (MD)
TESST Coll of Technology, Towson (MD)
Texarkana Coll (TX)
Texas School of Business, Friendswood Campus (TX)
Texas School of Business, Houston North Campus (TX)
West Georgia Tech Coll (GA)
Westmoreland County Comm Coll (PA)
White Mountains Comm Coll (NH)
Wilson Comm Coll (NC)
Wiregrass Georgia Tech Coll (GA)
York County Comm Coll (ME)

CRIMINOLOGY
Genesee Comm Coll (NY)

CRISIS/EMERGENCY/DISASTER MANAGEMENT
Casper Coll (WY)
Comm Coll of Rhode Island (RI)
Fayetteville Tech Comm Coll (NC)
Montgomery Coll (MD)

CRITICAL INCIDENT RESPONSE/SPECIAL POLICE OPERATIONS
Raritan Valley Comm Coll (NJ)

CROP PRODUCTION
Dakota Coll at Bottineau (ND)
Illinois Central Coll (IL)
Iowa Lakes Comm Coll (IA)
Northeast Comm Coll (NE)
Northeast Iowa Comm Coll (IA)
Northwest Coll (WY)

CULINARY ARTS
Albany Tech Coll (GA)
The Art Inst of Ohio–Cincinnati (OH)
The Art Inst of Seattle (WA)
Atlanta Tech Coll (GA)
Augusta Tech Coll (GA)
Austin Comm Coll (TX)
Blackhawk Tech Coll (WI)
Blue Ridge Comm and Tech Coll (WV)
Bradford School (OH)
Bunker Hill Comm Coll (MA)
Cape Fear Comm Coll (NC)
Central Wyoming Coll (WY)
Chattahoochee Tech Coll (GA)
Clark Coll (WA)
Cochise Coll, Sierra Vista (AZ)

Coll of DuPage (IL)
Comm Coll of Allegheny County (PA)
Comm Coll of Philadelphia (PA)
Delaware Tech & Comm Coll, Stanton/Wilmington Campus (DE)
Delaware Tech & Comm Coll, Terry Campus (DE)
El Centro Coll (TX)
Elgin Comm Coll (IL)
El Paso Comm Coll (TX)
Erie Comm Coll (NY)
Erie Comm Coll, North Campus (NY)
Fayetteville Tech Comm Coll (NC)
Florida State Coll at Jacksonville (FL)
Grand Rapids Comm Coll (MI)
Guilford Tech Comm Coll (NC)
H. Councill Trenholm State Tech Coll (AL)
Houston Comm Coll System (TX)
Illinois Central Coll (IL)
Indian River State Coll (FL)
Kaskaskia Coll (IL)
Macomb Comm Coll (MI)
Miami Dade Coll (FL)
Mineral Area Coll (MO)
Minneapolis Comm and Tech Coll (MN)
Mitchell Tech Inst (SD)
Mohave Comm Coll (AZ)
Monroe County Comm Coll (MI)
Montgomery County Comm Coll (PA)
Mott Comm Coll (MI)
Niagara County Comm Coll (NY)
Northampton Comm Coll (PA)
North Dakota State Coll of Science (ND)
Northeast Comm Coll (NE)
North Georgia Tech Coll (GA)
North Shore Comm Coll (MA)
Oakland Comm Coll (MI)
Ogeechee Tech Coll (GA)
Olympic Coll (WA)
Orange Coast Coll (CA)
Ozarka Coll (AR)
Red Rocks Comm Coll (CO)
The Restaurant School at Walnut Hill Coll (PA)
Riverside City Coll (CA)
Rockland Comm Coll (NY)
St. Philip's Coll (TX)
Salt Lake Comm Coll (UT)
San Jacinto Coll District (TX)
Santa Rosa Jr Coll (CA)
Savannah Tech Coll (GA)
Scottsdale Comm Coll (AZ)
Southern Maine Comm Coll (ME)
South Georgia Tech Coll (GA)
Sullivan County Comm Coll (NY)
Texarkana Coll (TX)
Trident Tech Coll (SC)
Truckee Meadows Comm Coll (NV)
Valencia Coll (FL)
Vincennes U (IN)
Westchester Comm Coll (NY)
West Kentucky Comm and Tech Coll (KY)
Westmoreland County Comm Coll (PA)
West Virginia Northern Comm Coll (WV)
White Mountains Comm Coll (NH)
York County Comm Coll (ME)

CULINARY ARTS RELATED
Iowa Lakes Comm Coll (IA)
State U of New York Coll of Technology at Alfred (NY)

CUSTOMER SERVICE MANAGEMENT
Catawba Valley Comm Coll (NC)
Central Oregon Comm Coll (OR)
Comm Coll of Rhode Island (RI)
Delaware Tech & Comm Coll, Stanton/Wilmington Campus (DE)

CUSTOMER SERVICE SUPPORT/CALL CENTER/TELESERVICE OPERATION
Central Wyoming Coll (WY)

Coll of DuPage (IL)
Comm Coll of Allegheny County (PA)
Comm Coll of Philadelphia (PA)
Delaware Tech & Comm Coll, Stanton/Wilmington Campus (DE)
Delaware Tech & Comm Coll, Jack F. Owens Campus (DE)
Delaware Tech & Comm Coll, Stanton/Wilmington Campus (DE)
Lansing Comm Coll (MI)
Union County Coll (NJ)

CYBER/COMPUTER FORENSICS AND COUNTERTERRORISM
Catawba Valley Comm Coll (NC)
Harper Coll (IL)

DAIRY HUSBANDRY AND PRODUCTION
Northeast Iowa Comm Coll (IA)

DAIRY SCIENCE
Northeast Comm Coll (NE)
State U of New York Coll of Technology at Alfred (NY)

DANCE
Austin Comm Coll (TX)
Casper Coll (WY)
Kilgore Coll (TX)
Miami Dade Coll (FL)
Northern Essex Comm Coll (MA)
Orange Coast Coll (CA)
Raritan Valley Comm Coll (NJ)
San Jacinto Coll District (TX)
Santa Monica Coll (CA)
Santa Rosa Jr Coll (CA)
Snow Coll (UT)
Truckee Meadows Comm Coll (NV)
Tyler Jr Coll (TX)
Westchester Comm Coll (NY)

DATA ENTRY/MICROCOMPUTER APPLICATIONS
Bunker Hill Comm Coll (MA)
Chandler-Gilbert Comm Coll (AZ)
Clark Coll (WA)
Comm Coll of Vermont (VT)
Delaware County Comm Coll (PA)
Elgin Comm Coll (IL)
ETI Tech Coll of Niles (OH)
Fiorello H. LaGuardia Comm Coll of the City U of New York (NY)
Florida State Coll at Jacksonville (FL)
Gateway Comm Coll (CT)
Gavilan Coll (CA)
Howard Comm Coll (MD)
Illinois Central Coll (IL)
Iowa Lakes Comm Coll (IA)
Lower Columbia Coll (WA)
Metropolitan Comm Coll–Business & Technology Campus (MO)
Montgomery Coll (MD)
North Dakota State Coll of Science (ND)
North Shore Comm Coll (MA)
Northwest Florida State Coll (FL)
Oklahoma City Comm Coll (OK)
Owensboro Comm and Tech Coll (KY)
St. Philip's Coll (TX)
Santa Monica Coll (CA)
Seminole State Coll of Florida (FL)
Stark State Coll (OH)
Sullivan County Comm Coll (NY)
Tyler Jr Coll (TX)
Valencia Coll (FL)
Westmoreland County Comm Coll (PA)

DATA ENTRY/MICROCOMPUTER APPLICATIONS RELATED
Berkeley City Coll (CA)
Coll of DuPage (IL)
Colorado Mountain Coll (CO)
Colorado Mountain Coll, Alpine Campus (CO)
ETI Tech Coll of Niles (OH)
Florida State Coll at Jacksonville (FL)
Highline Comm Coll (WA)
Metropolitan Comm Coll–Business & Technology Campus (MO)
Orange Coast Coll (CA)

Peninsula Coll (WA)
Seminole State Coll of Florida (FL)
Stark State Coll (OH)

DATA MODELING/ WAREHOUSING AND DATABASE ADMINISTRATION

Chandler-Gilbert Comm Coll (AZ)
Florida State Coll at Jacksonville (FL)
Metropolitan Comm Coll–Business & Technology Campus (MO)
Quinsigamond Comm Coll (MA)
Red Rocks Comm Coll (CO)
Santa Monica Coll (CA)
Seminole State Coll of Florida (FL)
Southwestern Illinois Coll (IL)

DATA PROCESSING AND DATA PROCESSING TECHNOLOGY

Aiken Tech Coll (SC)
Bainbridge Coll (GA)
Bluegrass Comm and Tech Coll (KY)
Cecil Coll (MD)
Central Carolina Tech Coll (SC)
Cochise Coll, Sierra Vista (AZ)
Copiah-Lincoln Comm Coll (MS)
El Centro Coll (TX)
Gateway Comm Coll (CT)
Housatonic Comm Coll (CT)
Illinois Central Coll (IL)
Illinois Valley Comm Coll (IL)
Iowa Lakes Comm Coll (IA)
Jackson Comm Coll (MI)
Jamestown Comm Coll (NY)
Kingsborough Comm Coll of the City U of New York (NY)
Los Angeles Harbor Coll (CA)
Mendocino Coll (CA)
Metropolitan Comm Coll–Business & Technology Campus (MO)
Metropolitan Comm Coll–Longview (MO)
Metropolitan Comm Coll–Maple Woods (MO)
Metropolitan Comm Coll–Penn Valley (MO)
Miami Dade Coll (FL)
Monroe Comm Coll (NY)
Monroe County Comm Coll (MI)
Montcalm Comm Coll (MI)
Muskegon Comm Coll (MI)
Northern Essex Comm Coll (MA)
Oakland Comm Coll (MI)
Orange Coast Coll (CA)
Otero Jr Coll (CO)
Palm Beach State Coll (FL)
Piedmont Virginia Comm Coll (VA)
Polk State Coll (FL)
Rockland Comm Coll (NY)
St. Clair County Comm Coll (MI)
San Diego City Coll (CA)
San Juan Coll (NM)
Seminole State Coll of Florida (FL)
Southwestern Indian Polytechnic Inst (NM)
Springfield Tech Comm Coll (MA)
State U of New York Coll of Technology at Alfred (NY)
Tallahassee Comm Coll (FL)
Terra State Comm Coll (OH)
Three Rivers Comm Coll (CT)
Tunxis Comm Coll (CT)
Virginia Western Comm Coll (VA)
Westchester Comm Coll (NY)
Westmoreland County Comm Coll (PA)

DENTAL ASSISTING

ACT Coll, Arlington (VA)
Anthem Coll–Maryland Heights (MO)
Athens Tech Coll (GA)
Bradford School (PA)
Central Comm Coll–Hastings Campus (NE)
Central Oregon Comm Coll (OR)
Central Wyoming Coll (WY)
Century Coll (MN)
Chattanooga State Comm Coll (TN)
Comm Care Coll (OK)
Eastern Idaho Tech Coll (ID)
El Paso Comm Coll (TX)
Foothill Coll (CA)

H. Councill Trenholm State Tech Coll (AL)
International Business Coll, Indianapolis (IN)
Lake Area Tech Inst (SD)
Lake Michigan Coll (MI)
Mid-Plains Comm Coll, North Platte (NE)
Minneapolis Comm and Tech Coll (MN)
Mohave Comm Coll (AZ)
Mott Comm Coll (MI)
North Dakota State Coll of Science (ND)
Northern Essex Comm Coll (MA)
Northwest Tech Coll (MN)
Raritan Valley Comm Coll (NJ)
Reedley Coll (CA)
St. Cloud Tech & Comm Coll (MN)
San Joaquin Valley Coll, Bakersfield (CA)
San Joaquin Valley Coll, Fresno (CA)
San Joaquin Valley Coll, Rancho Cordova (CA)
San Joaquin Valley Coll, Visalia (CA)
Texas State Tech Coll Harlingen (TX)
Union County Coll (NJ)
Westmoreland County Comm Coll (PA)
West Virginia Jr Coll–Bridgeport (WV)

DENTAL HYGIENE

Amarillo Coll (TX)
Athens Tech Coll (GA)
Atlanta Tech Coll (GA)
Austin Comm Coll (TX)
Bluegrass Comm and Tech Coll (KY)
Burlington County Coll (NJ)
Cape Fear Comm Coll (NC)
Catawba Valley Comm Coll (NC)
Central Comm Coll–Hastings Campus (NE)
Central Georgia Tech Coll (GA)
Century Coll (MN)
Chattanooga State Comm Coll (TN)
Chippewa Valley Tech Coll (WI)
Clark Coll (WA)
Colby Comm Coll (KS)
Coll of DuPage (IL)
Coll of Lake County (IL)
Columbus Tech Coll (GA)
The Comm Coll of Baltimore County (MD)
Comm Coll of Philadelphia (PA)
Comm Coll of Rhode Island (RI)
Delaware Tech & Comm Coll, Stanton/Wilmington Campus (DE)
El Paso Comm Coll (TX)
Erie Comm Coll, North Campus (NY)
Fayetteville Tech Comm Coll (NC)
Florida State Coll at Jacksonville (FL)
Foothill Coll (CA)
Fox Valley Tech Coll (WI)
Georgia Highlands Coll (GA)
Grand Rapids Comm Coll (MI)
Guilford Tech Comm Coll (NC)
Gulf Coast State Coll (FL)
Harper Coll (IL)
Hawkeye Comm Coll (IA)
Highline Comm Coll (WA)
Hillsborough Comm Coll (FL)
Illinois Central Coll (IL)
Indian River State Coll (FL)
Laramie County Comm Coll (WY)
Miami Dade Coll (FL)
Middle Georgia Tech Coll (GA)
Mohave Comm Coll (AZ)
Monroe Comm Coll (NY)
Montana State U–Great Falls Coll of Technology (MT)
Montgomery County Comm Coll (PA)
Moreno Valley Coll (CA)
Mott Comm Coll (MI)
Mount Wachusett Comm Coll (MA)
Normandale Comm Coll (MN)
Northampton Comm Coll (PA)
North Dakota State Coll of Science (ND)
Oakland Comm Coll (MI)

Ogeechee Tech Coll (GA)
Orange Coast Coll (CA)
Owens Comm Coll, Toledo (OH)
Palm Beach State Coll (FL)
Pasco-Hernando Comm Coll (FL)
Pensacola State Coll (FL)
Quinsigamond Comm Coll (MA)
Raritan Valley Comm Coll (NJ)
St. Cloud Tech & Comm Coll (MN)
Salt Lake Comm Coll (UT)
San Joaquin Valley Coll, Visalia (CA)
San Juan Coll (NM)
Santa Rosa Jr Coll (CA)
Southeastern Tech Coll (GA)
Springfield Tech Comm Coll (MA)
Stark State Coll (OH)
Tallahassee Comm Coll (FL)
Tarrant County Coll District (TX)
Texas State Tech Coll Harlingen (TX)
Trident Tech Coll (SC)
Truckee Meadows Comm Coll (NV)
Tunxis Comm Coll (CT)
Tyler Jr Coll (TX)
Union County Coll (NJ)
Valencia Coll (FL)
Virginia Western Comm Coll (VA)
Waukesha County Tech Coll (WI)
Western Iowa Tech Comm Coll (IA)
Westmoreland County Comm Coll (PA)
Wytheville Comm Coll (VA)

DENTAL LABORATORY TECHNOLOGY

Bluegrass Comm and Tech Coll (KY)
Erie Comm Coll, South Campus (NY)
J. Sargeant Reynolds Comm Coll (VA)
Texas State Tech Coll Harlingen (TX)

DENTAL SERVICES AND ALLIED PROFESSIONS RELATED

Quinsigamond Comm Coll (MA)

DESIGN AND APPLIED ARTS RELATED

Howard Comm Coll (MD)
Iowa Lakes Comm Coll (IA)
Kingsborough Comm Coll of the City U of New York (NY)
Mohawk Valley Comm Coll (NY)
Muskegon Comm Coll (MI)
Niagara County Comm Coll (NY)
Oklahoma City Comm Coll (OK)
Onondaga Comm Coll (NY)
Raritan Valley Comm Coll (NJ)
Rockland Comm Coll (NY)
State U of New York Coll of Technology at Alfred (NY)
Tunxis Comm Coll (CT)
Vincennes U (IN)
Westchester Comm Coll (NY)

DESIGN AND VISUAL COMMUNICATIONS

Blue Ridge Comm and Tech Coll (WV)
Brookhaven Coll (TX)
Bunker Hill Comm Coll (MA)
Chattahoochee Valley Comm Coll (AL)
Coll of DuPage (IL)
Creative Center (NE)
Elgin Comm Coll (IL)
Florida State Coll at Jacksonville (FL)
Harford Comm Coll (MD)
ITT Tech Inst, Atlanta (GA)
ITT Tech Inst, Duluth (GA)
ITT Tech Inst, Kennesaw (GA)
ITT Tech Inst, Mount Prospect (IL)
ITT Tech Inst, Oak Brook (IL)
ITT Tech Inst, Orland Park (IL)
ITT Tech Inst, Owings Mills (MD)
ITT Tech Inst, Albany (NY)
ITT Tech Inst, Cary (NC)
ITT Tech Inst, Charlotte (NC)
ITT Tech Inst, High Point (NC)
ITT Tech Inst, Strongsville (OH)
ITT Tech Inst, Bensalem (PA)
ITT Tech Inst, Dunmore (PA)

ITT Tech Inst, Harrisburg (PA)
ITT Tech Inst, King of Prussia (PA)
ITT Tech Inst, Pittsburgh (PA)
ITT Tech Inst, Tarentum (PA)
ITT Tech Inst, Greenville (SC)
Ivy Tech Comm Coll–Central Indiana (IN)
Ivy Tech Comm Coll–Columbus (IN)
Ivy Tech Comm Coll–North Central (IN)
Ivy Tech Comm Coll–Southern Indiana (IN)
Ivy Tech Comm Coll–Southwest (IN)
Ivy Tech Comm Coll–Wabash Valley (IN)
Minneapolis Comm and Tech Coll (MN)
Oklahoma City Comm Coll (OK)
Salt Lake Comm Coll (UT)
San Jacinto Coll District (TX)
Southeastern Tech Coll (GA)
York County Comm Coll (ME)

DESKTOP PUBLISHING AND DIGITAL IMAGING DESIGN

Coll of DuPage (IL)
Eastern Idaho Tech Coll (ID)
Gavilan Coll (CA)
Houston Comm Coll System (TX)
Iowa Lakes Comm Coll (IA)
Kansas City Kansas Comm Coll (KS)
Northeast Iowa Comm Coll (IA)
Northwest Coll (WY)
Southeast Tech Inst (SD)
Southwestern Illinois Coll (IL)
Sullivan Coll of Technology and Design (KY)
Terra State Comm Coll (OH)
Umpqua Comm Coll (OR)

DEVELOPMENTAL AND CHILD PSYCHOLOGY

Comm Coll of Vermont (VT)
Iowa Lakes Comm Coll (IA)
Los Angeles Harbor Coll (CA)
Mendocino Coll (CA)
Muskegon Comm Coll (MI)
Rockland Comm Coll (NY)
San Diego City Coll (CA)
Tarrant County Coll District (TX)

DIAGNOSTIC MEDICAL SONOGRAPHY AND ULTRASOUND TECHNOLOGY

Athens Tech Coll (GA)
Austin Comm Coll (TX)
Bunker Hill Comm Coll (MA)
Cape Fear Comm Coll (NC)
Chippewa Valley Tech Coll (WI)
Columbus Tech Coll (GA)
Comm Coll of Allegheny County (PA)
Comm Coll of Rhode Island (RI)
Delaware Tech & Comm Coll, Jack F. Owens Campus (DE)
Delaware Tech & Comm Coll, Stanton/Wilmington Campus (DE)
El Centro Coll (TX)
El Paso Comm Coll (TX)
Florida State Coll at Jacksonville (FL)
Foothill Coll (CA)
GateWay Comm Coll (AZ)
Gulf Coast State Coll (FL)
Harper Coll (IL)
H. Councill Trenholm State Tech Coll (AL)
Hillsborough Comm Coll (FL)
Jackson Comm Coll (MI)
Lake Michigan Coll (MI)
Lansing Comm Coll (MI)
Laramie County Comm Coll (WY)
Miami Dade Coll (FL)
Montgomery Coll (MD)
Northampton Comm Coll (PA)
Oakland Comm Coll (MI)
Oklahoma City Comm Coll (OK)
Owensboro Comm and Tech Coll (KY)
Owens Comm Coll, Toledo (OH)
Pensacola State Coll (FL)
Piedmont Virginia Comm Coll (VA)
Polk State Coll (FL)
Red Rocks Comm Coll (CO)

St. Cloud Tech & Comm Coll (MN)
San Jacinto Coll District (TX)
Southeast Tech Inst (SD)
Springfield Tech Comm Coll (MA)
Union County Coll (NJ)
Valencia Coll (FL)
West Kentucky Comm and Tech Coll (KY)
Westmoreland County Comm Coll (PA)

DIESEL MECHANICS TECHNOLOGY

Casper Coll (WY)
Central Comm Coll–Hastings Campus (NE)
Clark Coll (WA)
The Comm Coll of Baltimore County (MD)
Eastern Idaho Tech Coll (ID)
Hawkeye Comm Coll (IA)
Illinois Central Coll (IL)
Illinois Eastern Comm Colls, Wabash Valley College (IL)
Johnston Comm Coll (NC)
Kilgore Coll (TX)
Lake Area Tech Inst (SD)
Laramie County Comm Coll (WY)
Lower Columbia Coll (WA)
Mid-Plains Comm Coll, North Platte (NE)
North Dakota State Coll of Science (ND)
Northeast Comm Coll (NE)
Oklahoma City Comm Coll (OK)
Oklahoma Tech Coll (OK)
Peninsula Coll (WA)
Raritan Valley Comm Coll (NJ)
Rogue Comm Coll (OR)
St. Philip's Coll (TX)
Salt Lake Comm Coll (UT)
San Jacinto Coll District (TX)
San Juan Coll (NM)
Santa Rosa Jr Coll (CA)
Southeast Tech Inst (SD)
Southwest Mississippi Comm Coll (MS)
State U of New York Coll of Technology at Alfred (NY)
Truckee Meadows Comm Coll (NV)
The U of Montana–Helena Coll of Technology (MT)
Vincennes U (IN)
White Mountains Comm Coll (NH)

DIETETICS

Central Oregon Comm Coll (OR)
Dutchess Comm Coll (NY)
El Paso Comm Coll (TX)
Florida State Coll at Jacksonville (FL)
Gateway Comm Coll (CT)
Harper Coll (IL)
Miami Dade Coll (FL)
Normandale Comm Coll (MN)
Northwest Florida State Coll (FL)
Orange Coast Coll (CA)
Owens Comm Coll, Toledo (OH)
Pensacola State Coll (FL)
Rockland Comm Coll (NY)
State Coll of Florida Manatee-Sarasota (FL)
Tarrant County Coll District (TX)
Truckee Meadows Comm Coll (NV)
Vincennes U (IN)
Westchester Comm Coll (NY)

DIETETICS AND CLINICAL NUTRITION SERVICES RELATED

Cowley County Comm Coll and Area Vocational–Tech School (KS)

DIETETIC TECHNOLOGY

Chandler-Gilbert Comm Coll (AZ)
Fiorello H. LaGuardia Comm Coll of the City U of New York (NY)
Harper Coll (IL)
Miami Dade Coll (FL)
Montana State U–Great Falls Coll of Technology (MT)
Santa Rosa Jr Coll (CA)
Southern Maine Comm Coll (ME)
Truckee Meadows Comm Coll (NV)
Westmoreland County Comm Coll (PA)

DIETITIAN ASSISTANT
Chandler-Gilbert Comm Coll (AZ)
Comm Coll of Allegheny County (PA)
Erie Comm Coll, North Campus (NY)
Florida State Coll at Jacksonville (FL)
Front Range Comm Coll (CO)
Hillsborough Comm Coll (FL)

DIGITAL ARTS
Fiorello H. LaGuardia Comm Coll of the City U of New York (NY)
State U of New York Coll of Technology at Alfred (NY)
Waukesha County Tech Coll (WI)

DIGITAL COMMUNICATION AND MEDIA/MULTIMEDIA
Century Coll (MN)
Comm Coll of Vermont (VT)
Delaware Tech & Comm Coll, Terry Campus (DE)
Laramie County Comm Coll (WY)
Minneapolis Comm and Tech Coll (MN)
Raritan Valley Comm Coll (NJ)
Red Rocks Comm Coll (CO)
San Jacinto Coll District (TX)
Santa Monica Coll (CA)
Santa Rosa Jr Coll (CA)
Southern Maine Comm Coll (ME)
State U of New York Coll of Technology at Alfred (NY)
Sullivan Coll of Technology and Design (KY)

DIVINITY/MINISTRY
Northwest Florida State Coll (FL)

DRAFTING AND DESIGN TECHNOLOGY
Albany Tech Coll (GA)
Alvin Comm Coll (TX)
Amarillo Coll (TX)
Austin Comm Coll (TX)
Bainbridge Coll (GA)
Beaufort County Comm Coll (NC)
Bevill State Comm Coll (AL)
Burlington County Coll (NJ)
Casper Coll (WY)
Cayuga County Comm Coll (NY)
Central Carolina Comm Coll (NC)
Central Comm Coll–Columbus Campus (NE)
Central Comm Coll–Grand Island Campus (NE)
Central Comm Coll–Hastings Campus (NE)
Central Georgia Tech Coll (GA)
Central Oregon Comm Coll (OR)
Chattahoochee Tech Coll (GA)
Coll of Central Florida (FL)
Coll of DuPage (IL)
Columbus Tech Coll (GA)
Comm Coll of Allegheny County (PA)
Comm Coll of Philadelphia (PA)
Copiah-Lincoln Comm Coll (MS)
Corning Comm Coll (NY)
Cowley County Comm Coll and Area Vocational–Tech School (KS)
Crowder Coll (MO)
Delaware Tech & Comm Coll, Jack F. Owens Campus (DE)
Delaware Tech & Comm Coll, Stanton/Wilmington Campus (DE)
Delaware Tech & Comm Coll, Terry Campus (DE)
Do&nna Ana Comm Coll (NM)
El Paso Comm Coll (TX)
Florida State Coll at Jacksonville (FL)
Gadsden State Comm Coll (AL)
Gavilan Coll (CA)
Genesee Comm Coll (NY)
Georgia Piedmont Tech Coll (GA)
Grand Rapids Comm Coll (MI)
Gulf Coast State Coll (FL)
Gwinnett Tech Coll (GA)
H. Councill Trenholm State Tech Coll (AL)

Highline Comm Coll (WA)
Houston Comm Coll System (TX)
Hutchinson Comm Coll and Area Vocational School (KS)
Illinois Valley Comm Coll (IL)
Indian River State Coll (FL)
ITI Tech Coll (LA)
ITT Tech Inst, Bessemer (AL)
ITT Tech Inst, Madison (AL)
ITT Tech Inst, Mobile (AL)
ITT Tech Inst, Phoenix (AZ)
ITT Tech Inst, Tucson (AZ)
ITT Tech Inst (AR)
ITT Tech Inst, Lathrop (CA)
ITT Tech Inst, Orange (CA)
ITT Tech Inst, Oxnard (CA)
ITT Tech Inst, Rancho Cordova (CA)
ITT Tech Inst, San Bernardino (CA)
ITT Tech Inst, San Diego (CA)
ITT Tech Inst, San Dimas (CA)
ITT Tech Inst, Sylmar (CA)
ITT Tech Inst, Torrance (CA)
ITT Tech Inst, Aurora (CO)
ITT Tech Inst, Thornton (CO)
ITT Tech Inst, Fort Lauderdale (FL)
ITT Tech Inst, Fort Myers (FL)
ITT Tech Inst, Jacksonville (FL)
ITT Tech Inst, Lake Mary (FL)
ITT Tech Inst, Miami (FL)
ITT Tech Inst, Pinellas Park (FL)
ITT Tech Inst, Tallahassee (FL)
ITT Tech Inst, Tampa (FL)
ITT Tech Inst (ID)
ITT Tech Inst, Fort Wayne (IN)
ITT Tech Inst, Merrillville (IN)
ITT Tech Inst, Newburgh (IN)
ITT Tech Inst, Cedar Rapids (IA)
ITT Tech Inst, Clive (IA)
ITT Tech Inst, Louisville (KY)
ITT Tech Inst, Baton Rouge (LA)
ITT Tech Inst, St. Rose (LA)
ITT Tech Inst, Canton (MI)
ITT Tech Inst, Swartz Creek (MI)
ITT Tech Inst, Troy (MI)
ITT Tech Inst, Wyoming (MI)
ITT Tech Inst, Eden Prairie (MN)
ITT Tech Inst, Arnold (MO)
ITT Tech Inst, Earth City (MO)
ITT Tech Inst, Kansas City (MO)
ITT Tech Inst (NE)
ITT Tech Inst, Henderson (NV)
ITT Tech Inst (NM)
ITT Tech Inst, Albany (NY)
ITT Tech Inst, Getzville (NY)
ITT Tech Inst, Liverpool (NY)
ITT Tech Inst, Akron (OH)
ITT Tech Inst, Columbus (OH)
ITT Tech Inst, Dayton (OH)
ITT Tech Inst, Hilliard (OH)
ITT Tech Inst, Maumee (OH)
ITT Tech Inst, Norwood (OH)
ITT Tech Inst, Strongsville (OH)
ITT Tech Inst, Warrensville Heights (OH)
ITT Tech Inst, Youngstown (OH)
ITT Tech Inst, Tulsa (OK)
ITT Tech Inst, Portland (OR)
ITT Tech Inst, Columbia (SC)
ITT Tech Inst, Chattanooga (TN)
ITT Tech Inst, Cordova (TN)
ITT Tech Inst, Johnson City (TN)
ITT Tech Inst, Knoxville (TN)
ITT Tech Inst, Nashville (TN)
ITT Tech Inst, Arlington (TX)
ITT Tech Inst, Austin (TX)
ITT Tech Inst, DeSoto (TX)
ITT Tech Inst, Houston (TX)
ITT Tech Inst, Houston (TX)
ITT Tech Inst, Richardson (TX)
ITT Tech Inst, San Antonio (TX)
ITT Tech Inst, Webster (TX)
ITT Tech Inst (UT)
ITT Tech Inst, Chantilly (VA)
ITT Tech Inst, Norfolk (VA)
ITT Tech Inst, Richmond (VA)
ITT Tech Inst, Salem (VA)
ITT Tech Inst, Springfield (VA)
ITT Tech Inst, Everett (WA)
ITT Tech Inst, Seattle (WA)
ITT Tech Inst, Spokane Valley (WA)
ITT Tech Inst (WV)
ITT Tech Inst, Green Bay (WI)
ITT Tech Inst, Greenfield (WI)
ITT Tech Inst, Madison (WI)
Ivy Tech Comm Coll–Central Indiana (IN)

Ivy Tech Comm Coll–Columbus (IN)
Ivy Tech Comm Coll–Kokomo (IN)
Ivy Tech Comm Coll–Lafayette (IN)
Ivy Tech Comm Coll–Northeast (IN)
Ivy Tech Comm Coll–Northwest (IN)
Kankakee Comm Coll (IL)
Kilgore Coll (TX)
Kirtland Comm Coll (MI)
Lake Area Tech Inst (SD)
Lake Michigan Coll (MI)
Lanier Tech Coll (GA)
Laramie County Comm Coll (WY)
Lawson State Comm Coll (AL)
Lehigh Carbon Comm Coll (PA)
Linn State Tech Coll (MO)
Los Angeles Harbor Coll (CA)
Lurleen B. Wallace Comm Coll (AL)
Macomb Comm Coll (MI)
Massachusetts Bay Comm Coll (MA)
Metropolitan Comm Coll–Business & Technology Campus (MO)
Miami Dade Coll (FL)
Middle Georgia Tech Coll (GA)
Mid Michigan Comm Coll (MI)
Mineral Area Coll (MO)
Mohave Comm Coll (AZ)
Mohawk Valley Comm Coll (NY)
Monroe County Comm Coll (MI)
Montcalm Comm Coll (MI)
Mott Comm Coll (MI)
Muskegon Comm Coll (MI)
Niagara County Comm Coll (NY)
Northeast Alabama Comm Coll (AL)
Northwest Florida State Coll (FL)
Northwest-Shoals Comm Coll (AL)
Oakland Comm Coll (MI)
Oklahoma City Comm Coll (OK)
Oklahoma State U, Oklahoma City (OK)
Olympic Coll (WA)
Orange Coast Coll (CA)
Palm Beach State Coll (FL)
Pasco-Hernando Comm Coll (FL)
Pensacola State Coll (FL)
Red Rocks Comm Coll (CO)
Rockland Comm Coll (NY)
Salt Lake Comm Coll (UT)
San Diego City Coll (CA)
San Jacinto Coll District (TX)
San Juan Coll (NM)
Seminole State Coll of Florida (FL)
Southeastern Comm Coll (IA)
Southern Crescent Tech Coll (GA)
Southern State Comm Coll (OH)
South Georgia Tech Coll (GA)
Southwestern Michigan Coll (MI)
Stark State Coll (OH)
State Coll of Florida Manatee-Sarasota (FL)
Sullivan Coll of Technology and Design (KY)
Tarrant County Coll District (TX)
Texarkana Coll (TX)
Texas State Tech Coll Harlingen (TX)
Three Rivers Comm Coll (CT)
Truckee Meadows Comm Coll (NV)
U of Arkansas Comm Coll at Morrilton (AR)
Valencia Coll (FL)
Wiregrass Georgia Tech Coll (GA)
Wytheville Comm Coll (VA)

DRAFTING/DESIGN ENGINEERING TECHNOLOGIES RELATED
Blackhawk Tech Coll (WI)
Coll of DuPage (IL)
Comm Coll of Allegheny County (PA)
Illinois Valley Comm Coll (IL)
Macomb Comm Coll (MI)
Niagara County Comm Coll (NY)
Sullivan Coll of Technology and Design (KY)

DRAMATIC/THEATER ARTS
Alvin Comm Coll (TX)
Amarillo Coll (TX)
Anoka-Ramsey Comm Coll (MN)
Anoka-Ramsey Comm Coll, Cambridge Campus (MN)

Austin Comm Coll (TX)
Bainbridge Coll (GA)
Bucks County Comm Coll (PA)
Bunker Hill Comm Coll (MA)
Burlington County Coll (NJ)
Central Wyoming Coll (WY)
Chandler-Gilbert Comm Coll (AZ)
Cochise Coll, Sierra Vista (AZ)
Coll of the Canyons (CA)
Colorado Mountain Coll (CO)
Comm Coll of Allegheny County (PA)
Comm Coll of Rhode Island (RI)
Cowley County Comm Coll and Area Vocational–Tech School (KS)
Crowder Coll (MO)
Eastern Arizona Coll (AZ)
Edison Comm Coll (OH)
Fiorello H. LaGuardia Comm Coll of the City U of New York (NY)
Foothill Coll (CA)
Gavilan Coll (CA)
Genesee Comm Coll (NY)
Howard Comm Coll (MD)
Indian River State Coll (FL)
Kilgore Coll (TX)
Kingsborough Comm Coll of the City U of New York (NY)
Lake Michigan Coll (MI)
Lansing Comm Coll (MI)
Manchester Comm Coll (CT)
Mendocino Coll (CA)
Miami Dade Coll (FL)
Mid Michigan Comm Coll (MI)
Minneapolis Comm and Tech Coll (MN)
Mohawk Valley Comm Coll (NY)
Niagara County Comm Coll (NY)
Northeast Comm Coll (NE)
Northeastern Jr Coll (CO)
Northern Essex Comm Coll (MA)
Oklahoma City Comm Coll (OK)
Orange Coast Coll (CA)
Otero Jr Coll (CO)
Palm Beach State Coll (FL)
Pensacola State Coll (FL)
Rockland Comm Coll (NY)
St. Philip's Coll (TX)
San Diego City Coll (CA)
San Jacinto Coll District (TX)
Santa Monica Coll (CA)
Santa Rosa Jr Coll (CA)
Scottsdale Comm Coll (AZ)
Snow Coll (UT)
State Coll of Florida Manatee-Sarasota (FL)
Texarkana Coll (TX)
Three Rivers Comm Coll (CT)
Truckee Meadows Comm Coll (NV)
Tyler Jr Coll (TX)
Umpqua Comm Coll (OR)
Valencia Coll (FL)
Vincennes U (IN)

DRAMATIC/THEATER ARTS AND STAGECRAFT RELATED
Oakland Comm Coll (MI)
St. Philip's Coll (TX)

DRAWING
Iowa Lakes Comm Coll (IA)
Northeastern Jr Coll (CO)

EARLY CHILDHOOD EDUCATION
Aiken Tech Coll (SC)
Ancilla Coll (IN)
Anne Arundel Comm Coll (MD)
Arkansas State U–Mountain Home (AR)
Austin Comm Coll (TX)
Big Bend Comm Coll (WA)
Blackhawk Tech Coll (WI)
Bucks County Comm Coll (PA)
Bunker Hill Comm Coll (MA)
Cape Fear Comm Coll (NC)
Catawba Valley Comm Coll (NC)
Central Oregon Comm Coll (OR)
Central Wyoming Coll (WY)
Chippewa Valley Tech Coll (WI)
Clark Coll (WA)
Cochise Coll, Sierra Vista (AZ)
Coll of Central Florida (FL)
Coll of Southern Maryland (MD)

Colorado Mountain Coll, Timberline Campus (CO)
Comm Care Coll (OK)
The Comm Coll of Baltimore County (MD)
Comm Coll of Rhode Island (RI)
Comm Coll of Vermont (VT)
Delaware County Comm Coll (PA)
Delaware Tech & Comm Coll, Jack F. Owens Campus (DE)
Delaware Tech & Comm Coll, Stanton/Wilmington Campus (DE)
Delaware Tech & Comm Coll, Terry Campus (DE)
Eastern Arizona Coll (AZ)
Fayetteville Tech Comm Coll (NC)
Fox Valley Tech Coll (WI)
Front Range Comm Coll (CO)
Garrett Coll (MD)
Gateway Tech Coll (WI)
Guilford Tech Comm Coll (NC)
Hagerstown Comm Coll (MD)
Harford Comm Coll (MD)
Harper Coll (IL)
Hesser Coll, Manchester (NH)
Hesser Coll, Portsmouth (NH)
Illinois Valley Comm Coll (IL)
Iowa Lakes Comm Coll (IA)
Ivy Tech Comm Coll–Bloomington (IN)
Ivy Tech Comm Coll–Central Indiana (IN)
Ivy Tech Comm Coll–Columbus (IN)
Ivy Tech Comm Coll–East Central (IN)
Ivy Tech Comm Coll–Kokomo (IN)
Ivy Tech Comm Coll–Lafayette (IN)
Ivy Tech Comm Coll–North Central (IN)
Ivy Tech Comm Coll–Northeast (IN)
Ivy Tech Comm Coll–Northwest (IN)
Ivy Tech Comm Coll–Richmond (IN)
Ivy Tech Comm Coll–Southeast (IN)
Ivy Tech Comm Coll–Southern Indiana (IN)
Ivy Tech Comm Coll–Southwest (IN)
Ivy Tech Comm Coll–Wabash Valley (IN)
Jackson Comm Coll (MI)
James Sprunt Comm Coll (NC)
Jamestown Comm Coll (NY)
Jefferson Comm Coll (NY)
Johnston Comm Coll (NC)
Kansas City Kansas Comm Coll (KS)
Kent State U at Tuscarawas (OH)
Kingsborough Comm Coll of the City U of New York (NY)
Lake Michigan Coll (MI)
Laramie County Comm Coll (WY)
Lehigh Carbon Comm Coll (PA)
Lincoln Land Comm Coll (IL)
Lower Columbia Coll (WA)
Minnesota State Coll–Southeast Tech (MN)
Montgomery Coll (MD)
Moraine Park Tech Coll (WI)
Moreno Valley Coll (CA)
Mott Comm Coll (MI)
New Mexico State U–Alamogordo (NM)
Norco Coll (CA)
Northampton Comm Coll (PA)
Northeast Comm Coll (NE)
North Seattle Comm Coll (WA)
Oklahoma State U, Oklahoma City (OK)
Olympic Coll (WA)
Owens Comm Coll, Toledo (OH)
Pensacola State Coll (FL)
Randolph Comm Coll (NC)
Rasmussen Coll Aurora (IL)
Rasmussen Coll Bismarck (ND)
Rasmussen Coll Bloomington (MN)
Rasmussen Coll Brooklyn Park (MN)
Rasmussen Coll Eagan (MN)
Rasmussen Coll Fargo (ND)
Rasmussen Coll Fort Myers (FL)
Rasmussen Coll Green Bay (WI)

Rasmussen Coll Lake Elmo/ Woodbury (MN)
Rasmussen Coll Mankato (MN)
Rasmussen Coll Moorhead (MN)
Rasmussen Coll New Port Richey (FL)
Rasmussen Coll Ocala (FL)
Rasmussen Coll Rockford (IL)
Rasmussen Coll St. Cloud (MN)
Red Rocks Comm Coll (CO)
Riverside City Coll (CA)
Rockingham Comm Coll (NC)
St. Philip's Coll (TX)
Southern Maine Comm Coll (ME)
Southern State Comm Coll (OH)
Southwestern Indian Polytechnic Inst (NM)
Southwestern Michigan Coll (MI)
Southwest Mississippi Comm Coll (MS)
Springfield Tech Comm Coll (MA)
Tompkins Cortland Comm Coll (NY)
Truckee Meadows Comm Coll (NV)
Vincennes U (IN)
Waukesha County Tech Coll (WI)
Westmoreland County Comm Coll (PA)
White Mountains Comm Coll (NH)
Wilson Comm Coll (NC)
Wisconsin Indianhead Tech Coll (WI)

ECOLOGY
Iowa Lakes Comm Coll (IA)

E-COMMERCE
Augusta Tech Coll (GA)
Brookhaven Coll (TX)
Catawba Valley Comm Coll (NC)
Central Georgia Tech Coll (GA)
Delaware County Comm Coll (PA)
Delaware Tech & Comm Coll, Jack F. Owens Campus (DE)
Delaware Tech & Comm Coll, Terry Campus (DE)
Lansing Comm Coll (MI)
North Dakota State Coll of Science (ND)
Pasco-Hernando Comm Coll (FL)
St. Philip's Coll (TX)
Wiregrass Georgia Tech Coll (GA)

ECONOMICS
Austin Comm Coll (TX)
Casper Coll (WY)
Cochise Coll, Sierra Vista (AZ)
Copiah-Lincoln Comm Coll (MS)
Foothill Coll (CA)
Georgia Highlands Coll (GA)
Indian River State Coll (FL)
Iowa Lakes Comm Coll (IA)
Lansing Comm Coll (MI)
Laramie County Comm Coll (WY)
Miami Dade Coll (FL)
Muskegon Comm Coll (MI)
Northeastern Jr Coll (CO)
Oklahoma State U, Oklahoma City (OK)
Orange Coast Coll (CA)
Palm Beach State Coll (FL)
St. Philip's Coll (TX)
Salt Lake Comm Coll (UT)
Santa Rosa Jr Coll (CA)
Snow Coll (UT)
State Coll of Florida Manatee-Sarasota (FL)
Terra State Comm Coll (OH)
Tyler Jr Coll (TX)
Umpqua Comm Coll (OR)
Vincennes U (IN)

EDUCATION
Bainbridge Coll (GA)
Bucks County Comm Coll (PA)
Bunker Hill Comm Coll (MA)
Burlington County Coll (NJ)
Cecil Coll (MD)
Central Oregon Comm Coll (OR)
Chattanooga State Comm Coll (TN)
Chipola Coll (FL)
Coll of Southern Maryland (MD)
The Comm Coll of Baltimore County (MD)
Comm Coll of Philadelphia (PA)
Comm Coll of Vermont (VT)
Copiah-Lincoln Comm Coll (MS)

Cowley County Comm Coll and Area Vocational–Tech School (KS)
Crowder Coll (MO)
Dakota Coll at Bottineau (ND)
Dyersburg State Comm Coll (TN)
Edison Comm Coll (OH)
Garrett Coll (MD)
Genesee Comm Coll (NY)
Hagerstown Comm Coll (MD)
Harford Comm Coll (MD)
Highline Comm Coll (WA)
Hutchinson Comm Coll and Area Vocational School (KS)
Illinois Valley Comm Coll (IL)
Indian River State Coll (FL)
Iowa Lakes Comm Coll (IA)
Itasca Comm Coll (MN)
Kent State U at Salem (OH)
Kilian Comm Coll (SD)
Kingsborough Comm Coll of the City U of New York (NY)
Laramie County Comm Coll (WY)
Lehigh Carbon Comm Coll (PA)
Miami Dade Coll (FL)
Minneapolis Comm and Tech Coll (MN)
Mohave Comm Coll (AZ)
Motlow State Comm Coll (TN)
Muskegon Comm Coll (MI)
New Mexico State U–Alamogordo (NM)
Northeast Comm Coll (NE)
Northeastern Jr Coll (CO)
Northern Essex Comm Coll (MA)
Northwest Florida State Coll (FL)
Owens Comm Coll, Toledo (OH)
Palau Comm Coll (Palau)
Palm Beach State Coll (FL)
Pensacola State Coll (FL)
Piedmont Virginia Comm Coll (VA)
St. Philip's Coll (TX)
Snow Coll (UT)
Southwest Mississippi Comm Coll (MS)
Terra State Comm Coll (OH)
Umpqua Comm Coll (OR)
Vincennes U (IN)
Virginia Western Comm Coll (VA)
Volunteer State Comm Coll (TN)
Wytheville Comm Coll (VA)

EDUCATIONAL/ INSTRUCTIONAL TECHNOLOGY
Hutchinson Comm Coll and Area Vocational School (KS)
Ivy Tech Comm Coll–North Central (IN)
Red Rocks Comm Coll (CO)
Tarrant County Coll District (TX)

EDUCATION (MULTIPLE LEVELS)
Arkansas State U–Mountain Home (AR)
Brookhaven Coll (TX)
Carroll Comm Coll (MD)
Cayuga County Comm Coll (NY)
Delaware County Comm Coll (PA)
Delaware Tech & Comm Coll, Jack F. Owens Campus (DE)
Delaware Tech & Comm Coll, Stanton/Wilmington Campus (DE)
Delaware Tech & Comm Coll, Terry Campus (DE)
Itasca Comm Coll (MN)
Kirtland Comm Coll (MI)
Mid Michigan Comm Coll (MI)
Minneapolis Comm and Tech Coll (MN)
Onondaga Comm Coll (NY)
San Jacinto Coll District (TX)
U of Arkansas Comm Coll at Morrilton (AR)
Westchester Comm Coll (NY)

EDUCATION RELATED
Corning Comm Coll (NY)
Guilford Tech Comm Coll (NC)
Miami Dade Coll (FL)

EDUCATION (SPECIFIC LEVELS AND METHODS) RELATED
Comm Coll of Allegheny County (PA)

EDUCATION (SPECIFIC SUBJECT AREAS) RELATED
Comm Coll of Allegheny County (PA)

ELECTRICAL AND ELECTRONIC ENGINEERING TECHNOLOGIES RELATED
Albany Tech Coll (GA)
J. Sargeant Reynolds Comm Coll (VA)
Lake Region State Coll (ND)
Miami Dade Coll (FL)
Mohawk Valley Comm Coll (NY)
North Dakota State Coll of Science (ND)
Onondaga Comm Coll (NY)
Sullivan Coll of Technology and Design (KY)
Terra State Comm Coll (OH)

ELECTRICAL AND ELECTRONICS ENGINEERING
Anne Arundel Comm Coll (MD)
Carroll Comm Coll (MD)
Dutchess Comm Coll (NY)
Fiorello H. LaGuardia Comm Coll of the City U of New York (NY)
Garrett Coll (MD)
John Tyler Comm Coll (VA)
Lake Region State Coll (ND)
Pensacola State Coll (FL)

ELECTRICAL AND POWER TRANSMISSION INSTALLATION
Delaware County Comm Coll (PA)
Ivy Tech Comm Coll–Columbus (IN)
Lansing Comm Coll (MI)
Oklahoma State U, Oklahoma City (OK)
Orange Coast Coll (CA)
Polk State Coll (FL)
Rogue Comm Coll (OR)
St. Cloud Tech & Comm Coll (MN)
San Jacinto Coll District (TX)
Southwestern Illinois Coll (IL)

ELECTRICAL, ELECTRONIC AND COMMUNICATIONS ENGINEERING TECHNOLOGY
Aiken Tech Coll (SC)
Alvin Comm Coll (TX)
Amarillo Coll (TX)
Anne Arundel Comm Coll (MD)
Athens Tech Coll (GA)
Augusta Tech Coll (GA)
Austin Comm Coll (TX)
Bainbridge Coll (GA)
Beaufort County Comm Coll (NC)
Berkshire Comm Coll (MA)
Bluegrass Comm and Tech Coll (KY)
Burlington County Coll (NJ)
Cape Fear Comm Coll (NC)
Casper Coll (WY)
Catawba Valley Comm Coll (NC)
Cayuga County Comm Coll (NY)
Central Carolina Comm Coll (NC)
Central Comm Coll–Columbus Campus (NE)
Central Comm Coll–Grand Island Campus (NE)
Central Comm Coll–Hastings Campus (NE)
Central Georgia Tech Coll (GA)
Central Oregon Comm Coll (OR)
Chattahoochee Tech Coll (GA)
Chattanooga State Comm Coll (TN)
Clark Coll (WA)
Cleveland Inst of Electronics (OH)
Clinton Comm Coll (NY)
Cochise Coll, Sierra Vista (AZ)
Coll of DuPage (IL)
Coll of Lake County (IL)
Columbus Tech Coll (GA)
Comm Coll of Allegheny County (PA)
Comm Coll of Rhode Island (RI)

Copiah-Lincoln Comm Coll (MS)
Corning Comm Coll (NY)
Crowder Coll (MO)
Delaware County Comm Coll (PA)
Delaware Tech & Comm Coll, Jack F. Owens Campus (DE)
Delaware Tech & Comm Coll, Stanton/Wilmington Campus (DE)
Delaware Tech & Comm Coll, Terry Campus (DE)
Do&nna Ana Comm Coll (NM)
Dutchess Comm Coll (NY)
Edison Comm Coll (OH)
El Paso Comm Coll (TX)
Erie Comm Coll, North Campus (NY)
ETI Tech Coll of Niles (OH)
Fayetteville Tech Comm Coll (NC)
Florida State Coll at Jacksonville (FL)
Foothill Coll (CA)
Fountainhead Coll of Technology (TN)
Fox Valley Tech Coll (WI)
Front Range Comm Coll (CO)
Gadsden State Comm Coll (AL)
Gateway Comm Coll (CT)
Gateway Tech Coll (WI)
Genesee Comm Coll (NY)
Georgia Piedmont Tech Coll (GA)
Grand Rapids Comm Coll (MI)
Guilford Tech Comm Coll (NC)
Gulf Coast State Coll (FL)
Gwinnett Tech Coll (GA)
Harper Coll (IL)
Hawkeye Comm Coll (IA)
Hillsborough Comm Coll (FL)
Howard Comm Coll (MD)
Illinois Central Coll (IL)
Illinois Eastern Comm Colls, Wabash Valley College (IL)
Illinois Valley Comm Coll (IL)
Indian River State Coll (FL)
Island Drafting and Tech Inst (NY)
ITI Tech Coll (LA)
ITT Tech Inst, Bessemer (AL)
ITT Tech Inst, Madison (AL)
ITT Tech Inst, Mobile (AL)
ITT Tech Inst, Phoenix (AZ)
ITT Tech Inst, Tucson (AZ)
ITT Tech Inst (AR)
ITT Tech Inst, Lathrop (CA)
ITT Tech Inst, Orange (CA)
ITT Tech Inst, Oxnard (CA)
ITT Tech Inst, Rancho Cordova (CA)
ITT Tech Inst, San Bernardino (CA)
ITT Tech Inst, San Diego (CA)
ITT Tech Inst, San Dimas (CA)
ITT Tech Inst, Sylmar (CA)
ITT Tech Inst, Torrance (CA)
ITT Tech Inst, Aurora (CO)
ITT Tech Inst, Thornton (CO)
ITT Tech Inst, Fort Lauderdale (FL)
ITT Tech Inst, Fort Myers (FL)
ITT Tech Inst, Jacksonville (FL)
ITT Tech Inst, Lake Mary (FL)
ITT Tech Inst, Miami (FL)
ITT Tech Inst, Pinellas Park (FL)
ITT Tech Inst, Tallahassee (FL)
ITT Tech Inst, Tampa (FL)
ITT Tech Inst (ID)
ITT Tech Inst, Fort Wayne (IN)
ITT Tech Inst, Merrillville (IN)
ITT Tech Inst, Newburgh (IN)
ITT Tech Inst, Cedar Rapids (IA)
ITT Tech Inst, Clive (IA)
ITT Tech Inst, Louisville (KY)
ITT Tech Inst, Baton Rouge (LA)
ITT Tech Inst, St. Rose (LA)
ITT Tech Inst, Canton (MI)
ITT Tech Inst, Swartz Creek (MI)
ITT Tech Inst, Troy (MI)
ITT Tech Inst, Wyoming (MI)
ITT Tech Inst, Eden Prairie (MN)
ITT Tech Inst, Arnold (MO)
ITT Tech Inst, Earth City (MO)
ITT Tech Inst, Kansas City (MO)
ITT Tech Inst (NE)
ITT Tech Inst, Henderson (NV)
ITT Tech Inst, Albany (NY)
ITT Tech Inst, Getzville (NY)
ITT Tech Inst, Liverpool (NY)
ITT Tech Inst, Akron (OH)
ITT Tech Inst, Columbus (OH)
ITT Tech Inst, Hilliard (OH)
ITT Tech Inst, Maumee (OH)

ITT Tech Inst, Norwood (OH)
ITT Tech Inst, Strongsville (OH)
ITT Tech Inst, Warrensville Heights (OH)
ITT Tech Inst, Youngstown (OH)
ITT Tech Inst, Tulsa (OK)
ITT Tech Inst, Portland (OR)
ITT Tech Inst, Columbia (SC)
ITT Tech Inst, Chattanooga (TN)
ITT Tech Inst, Cordova (TN)
ITT Tech Inst, Johnson City (TN)
ITT Tech Inst, Knoxville (TN)
ITT Tech Inst, Nashville (TN)
ITT Tech Inst, Arlington (TX)
ITT Tech Inst, Austin (TX)
ITT Tech Inst, DeSoto (TX)
ITT Tech Inst, Houston (TX)
ITT Tech Inst, Houston (TX)
ITT Tech Inst, Richardson (TX)
ITT Tech Inst, San Antonio (TX)
ITT Tech Inst, Webster (TX)
ITT Tech Inst (UT)
ITT Tech Inst, Chantilly (VA)
ITT Tech Inst, Norfolk (VA)
ITT Tech Inst, Richmond (VA)
ITT Tech Inst, Salem (VA)
ITT Tech Inst, Springfield (VA)
ITT Tech Inst, Everett (WA)
ITT Tech Inst, Spokane Valley (WA)
ITT Tech Inst (WV)
ITT Tech Inst, Green Bay (WI)
ITT Tech Inst, Greenfield (WI)
ITT Tech Inst, Madison (WI)
Ivy Tech Comm Coll–Bloomington (IN)
Ivy Tech Comm Coll–Central Indiana (IN)
Ivy Tech Comm Coll–Columbus (IN)
Ivy Tech Comm Coll–East Central (IN)
Ivy Tech Comm Coll–Kokomo (IN)
Ivy Tech Comm Coll–Lafayette (IN)
Ivy Tech Comm Coll–North Central (IN)
Ivy Tech Comm Coll–Northeast (IN)
Ivy Tech Comm Coll–Northwest (IN)
Ivy Tech Comm Coll–Richmond (IN)
Ivy Tech Comm Coll–Southeast (IN)
Ivy Tech Comm Coll–Southern Indiana (IN)
Ivy Tech Comm Coll–Southwest (IN)
Ivy Tech Comm Coll–Wabash Valley (IN)
Jackson Comm Coll (MI)
Jamestown Comm Coll (NY)
Johnston Comm Coll (NC)
Kankakee Comm Coll (IL)
Kaskaskia Coll (IL)
Kent State U at Ashtabula (OH)
Kent State U at Trumbull (OH)
Kent State U at Tuscarawas (OH)
Kilgore Coll (TX)
Kirtland Comm Coll (MI)
Lake Area Tech Inst (SD)
Lanier Tech Coll (GA)
Lehigh Carbon Comm Coll (PA)
Lincoln Land Comm Coll (IL)
Linn State Tech Coll (MO)
Los Angeles Harbor Coll (CA)
Macomb Comm Coll (MI)
McHenry County Coll (IL)
Metropolitan Comm Coll–Business & Technology Campus (MO)
Miami Dade Coll (FL)
Mineral Area Coll (MO)
Minnesota State Coll–Southeast Tech (MN)
Mohawk Valley Comm Coll (NY)
Monroe Comm Coll (NY)
Monroe County Comm Coll (MI)
Montcalm Comm Coll (MI)
Montgomery County Comm Coll (PA)
Mott Comm Coll (MI)
Moultrie Tech Coll (GA)
Muskegon Comm Coll (MI)
New Mexico State U–Alamogordo (NM)
Northampton Comm Coll (PA)
Northeast Iowa Comm Coll (IA)
Northern Essex Comm Coll (MA)
North Seattle Comm Coll (WA)
Northwestern Connecticut Comm Coll (CT)
Northwest Florida State Coll (FL)
Oakland Comm Coll (MI)
Oklahoma City Comm Coll (OK)

Oklahoma State U, Oklahoma City (OK)
Olympic Coll (WA)
Onondaga Comm Coll (NY)
Orange Coast Coll (CA)
Owensboro Comm and Tech Coll (KY)
Owens Comm Coll, Toledo (OH)
Palau Comm Coll (Palau)
Palm Beach State Coll (FL)
Peninsula Coll (WA)
Penn State Brandywine (PA)
Penn State DuBois (PA)
Penn State Fayette, The Eberly Campus (PA)
Penn State Hazleton (PA)
Penn State New Kensington (PA)
Penn State Schuylkill (PA)
Penn State Shenango (PA)
Penn State Wilkes-Barre (PA)
Penn State Worthington Scranton (PA)
Penn State York (PA)
Pensacola State Coll (FL)
Pittsburgh Tech Inst, Oakdale (PA)
Quinsigamond Comm Coll (MA)
Reid State Tech Coll (AL)
Rockingham Comm Coll (NC)
Rockland Comm Coll (NY)
Rogue Comm Coll (OR)
St. Clair County Comm Coll (MI)
St. Cloud Tech & Comm Coll (MN)
Salt Lake Comm Coll (UT)
San Diego City Coll (CA)
San Jacinto Coll District (TX)
San Juan Coll (NM)
Santa Rosa Jr Coll (CA)
Savannah Tech Coll (GA)
Scottsdale Comm Coll (AZ)
Seminole State Coll of Florida (FL)
Shawnee Comm Coll (IL)
Southeastern Comm Coll (IA)
Southeastern Tech Coll (GA)
Southeast Tech Inst (SD)
Southern Crescent Tech Coll (GA)
Southern Maine Comm Coll (ME)
Southern State Comm Coll (OH)
South Georgia Tech Coll (GA)
South Suburban Coll (IL)
Southwestern Illinois Coll (IL)
Southwestern Michigan Coll (MI)
Southwest Mississippi Comm Coll (MS)
Southwest Virginia Comm Coll (VA)
Springfield Tech Comm Coll (MA)
State Coll of Florida Manatee-Sarasota (FL)
State U of New York Coll of Technology at Alfred (NY)
Sullivan Coll of Technology and Design (KY)
Sullivan County Comm Coll (NY)
Tarrant County Coll District (TX)
Terra State Comm Coll (OH)
Texarkana Coll (TX)
Three Rivers Comm Coll (CT)
Tompkins Cortland Comm Coll (NY)
Trident Tech Coll (SC)
Umpqua Comm Coll (OR)
Valencia Coll (FL)
Vincennes U (IN)
Virginia Western Comm Coll (VA)
Waukesha County Tech Coll (WI)
Westchester Comm Coll (NY)
Western Iowa Tech Comm Coll (IA)
West Georgia Tech Coll (GA)
Westmoreland County Comm Coll (PA)
Wytheville Comm Coll (VA)
YTI Career Inst–York (PA)

ELECTRICAL/ELECTRONICS EQUIPMENT INSTALLATION AND REPAIR
Cape Fear Comm Coll (NC)
Coll of DuPage (IL)
Hutchinson Comm Coll and Area Vocational School (KS)
Lake Area Tech Inst (SD)
Lake Region State Coll (ND)
Linn State Tech Coll (MO)
Macomb Comm Coll (MI)
Orange Coast Coll (CA)
Pittsburgh Tech Inst, Oakdale (PA)
St. Philip's Coll (TX)

Southeast Tech Inst (SD)
State U of New York Coll of Technology at Alfred (NY)
Sullivan Coll of Technology and Design (KY)
Western Dakota Tech Inst (SD)

ELECTRICAL/ELECTRONICS MAINTENANCE AND REPAIR TECHNOLOGY RELATED
Bunker Hill Comm Coll (MA)
Mohawk Valley Comm Coll (NY)
Sullivan Coll of Technology and Design (KY)

ELECTRICIAN
Bevill State Comm Coll (AL)
Bluegrass Comm and Tech Coll (KY)
Central Comm Coll–Hastings Campus (NE)
Coll of Lake County (IL)
Coll of Southern Maryland (MD)
Fayetteville Tech Comm Coll (NC)
GateWay Comm Coll (AZ)
Guilford Tech Comm Coll (NC)
Gulf Coast State Coll (FL)
H. Councill Trenholm State Tech Coll (AL)
Illinois Valley Comm Coll (IL)
Ivy Tech Comm Coll–Bloomington (IN)
Ivy Tech Comm Coll–Central Indiana (IN)
Ivy Tech Comm Coll–East Central (IN)
Ivy Tech Comm Coll–Kokomo (IN)
Ivy Tech Comm Coll–Lafayette (IN)
Ivy Tech Comm Coll–North Central (IN)
Ivy Tech Comm Coll–Northeast (IN)
Ivy Tech Comm Coll–Northwest (IN)
Ivy Tech Comm Coll–Richmond (IN)
Ivy Tech Comm Coll–Southern Indiana (IN)
Ivy Tech Comm Coll–Southwest (IN)
Ivy Tech Comm Coll–Wabash Valley (IN)
John Wood Comm Coll (IL)
Lansing Comm Coll (MI)
Linn State Tech Coll (MO)
Lurleen B. Wallace Comm Coll (AL)
Mitchell Tech Inst (SD)
Moraine Park Tech Coll (WI)
New Mexico State U–Alamogordo (NM)
Northampton Comm Coll (PA)
Northeast Comm Coll (NE)
Northeast Iowa Comm Coll (IA)
Northwest Coll (WY)
Oakland Comm Coll (MI)
Olympic Coll (WA)
Randolph Comm Coll (NC)
Red Rocks Comm Coll (CO)
Rockingham Comm Coll (NC)
Southwestern Illinois Coll (IL)
State U of New York Coll of Technology at Alfred (NY)
West Kentucky Comm and Tech Coll (KY)
Wilson Comm Coll (NC)

ELECTROCARDIOGRAPH TECHNOLOGY
Delaware Tech & Comm Coll, Stanton/Wilmington Campus (DE)
Oklahoma State U, Oklahoma City (OK)

ELECTROMECHANICAL AND INSTRUMENTATION AND MAINTENANCE TECHNOLOGIES RELATED
Cape Fear Comm Coll (NC)
Catawba Valley Comm Coll (NC)
Cowley County Comm Coll and Area Vocational–Tech School (KS)
Gulf Coast State Coll (FL)
Randolph Comm Coll (NC)
Red Rocks Comm Coll (CO)

Sullivan Coll of Technology and Design (KY)
Waukesha County Tech Coll (WI)

ELECTROMECHANICAL TECHNOLOGY
Blackhawk Tech Coll (WI)
Blue Ridge Comm and Tech Coll (WV)
Central Maine Comm Coll (ME)
Chandler-Gilbert Comm Coll (AZ)
Chippewa Valley Tech Coll (WI)
Coll of DuPage (IL)
Comm Coll of Rhode Island (RI)
Delaware Tech & Comm Coll, Terry Campus (DE)
Dutchess Comm Coll (NY)
Edison Comm Coll (OH)
Fox Valley Tech Coll (WI)
GateWay Comm Coll (AZ)
Gateway Tech Coll (WI)
Georgia Piedmont Tech Coll (GA)
Guilford Tech Comm Coll (NC)
Hagerstown Comm Coll (MD)
Lake Area Tech Inst (SD)
Lansing Comm Coll (MI)
Los Angeles Harbor Coll (CA)
Macomb Comm Coll (MI)
Montgomery County Comm Coll (PA)
Moraine Park Tech Coll (WI)
Muskegon Comm Coll (MI)
Northampton Comm Coll (PA)
Northeast Comm Coll (NE)
Oakland Comm Coll (MI)
Quinsigamond Comm Coll (MA)
St. Philip's Coll (TX)
Southeast Tech Inst (SD)
Southern State Comm Coll (OH)
Springfield Tech Comm Coll (MA)
State U of New York Coll of Technology at Alfred (NY)
Tarrant County Coll District (TX)
Texas State Tech Coll Harlingen (TX)
Union County Coll (NJ)
Western Dakota Tech Inst (SD)

ELECTRONEURODIAGNOSTIC / ELECTROENCEPHALOGRAPHIC TECHNOLOGY
Catawba Valley Comm Coll (NC)
Comm Coll of Allegheny County (PA)
Harford Comm Coll (MD)
Minneapolis Comm and Tech Coll (MN)
Oakland Comm Coll (MI)
Southeast Tech Inst (SD)

ELEMENTARY EDUCATION
Amarillo Coll (TX)
Ancilla Coll (IN)
Anne Arundel Comm Coll (MD)
Bainbridge Coll (GA)
Carl Albert State Coll (OK)
Casper Coll (WY)
Cecil Coll (MD)
Central Wyoming Coll (WY)
Chandler-Gilbert Comm Coll (AZ)
Cochise Coll, Sierra Vista (AZ)
Coll of Southern Maryland (MD)
The Comm Coll of Baltimore County (MD)
Copiah-Lincoln Comm Coll (MS)
Corning Comm Coll (NY)
Cowley County Comm Coll and Area Vocational–Tech School (KS)
Crowder Coll (MO)
Delaware Tech & Comm Coll, Jack F. Owens Campus (DE)
Delaware Tech & Comm Coll, Stanton/Wilmington Campus (DE)
Delaware Tech & Comm Coll, Terry Campus (DE)
Dutchess Comm Coll (NY)
Eastern Arizona Coll (AZ)
Fayetteville Tech Comm Coll (NC)
Garrett Coll (MD)
GateWay Comm Coll (AZ)
Genesee Comm Coll (NY)
Grand Rapids Comm Coll (MI)

Hagerstown Comm Coll (MD)
Harford Comm Coll (MD)
Harper Coll (IL)
Howard Comm Coll (MD)
Illinois Valley Comm Coll (IL)
Iowa Lakes Comm Coll (IA)
James Sprunt Comm Coll (NC)
Jamestown Comm Coll (NY)
Kankakee Comm Coll (IL)
Kilgore Coll (TX)
Kingsborough Comm Coll of the City U of New York (NY)
Lake Michigan Coll (MI)
Lansing Comm Coll (MI)
Miami Dade Coll (FL)
Mid Michigan Comm Coll (MI)
Mohawk Valley Comm Coll (NY)
Monroe County Comm Coll (MI)
Montgomery Coll (MD)
Montgomery County Comm Coll (PA)
Murray State Coll (OK)
Muskegon Comm Coll (MI)
Niagara County Comm Coll (NY)
Normandale Comm Coll (MN)
Northeast Comm Coll (NE)
Northeastern Jr Coll (CO)
Northern Essex Comm Coll (MA)
Northwest Coll (WY)
Oklahoma City Comm Coll (OK)
Otero Jr Coll (CO)
Palm Beach State Coll (FL)
Pensacola State Coll (FL)
San Jacinto Coll District (TX)
San Juan Coll (NM)
Snow Coll (UT)
Southwest Mississippi Comm Coll (MS)
Springfield Tech Comm Coll (MA)
Sullivan County Comm Coll (NY)
Truckee Meadows Comm Coll (NV)
Umpqua Comm Coll (OR)
Vincennes U (IN)
Wilson Comm Coll (NC)

EMERGENCY CARE ATTENDANT (EMT AMBULANCE)
Carroll Comm Coll (MD)
Delaware Tech & Comm Coll, Stanton/Wilmington Campus (DE)
Illinois Eastern Comm Colls, Frontier Community College (IL)
Iowa Lakes Comm Coll (IA)

EMERGENCY MEDICAL TECHNOLOGY (EMT PARAMEDIC)
Alvin Comm Coll (TX)
Amarillo Coll (TX)
Arkansas State U–Mountain Home (AR)
Athens Tech Coll (GA)
Augusta Tech Coll (GA)
Austin Comm Coll (TX)
Bevill State Comm Coll (AL)
Blue Ridge Comm and Tech Coll (WV)
Brookhaven Coll (TX)
Casper Coll (WY)
Catawba Valley Comm Coll (NC)
Cecil Coll (MD)
Central Oregon Comm Coll (OR)
Central Wyoming Coll (WY)
Century Coll (MN)
Chippewa Valley Tech Coll (WI)
Clark Coll (WA)
Cochise Coll, Sierra Vista (AZ)
Coll of Central Florida (FL)
Coll of DuPage (IL)
Coll of Southern Maryland (MD)
Columbus Tech Coll (GA)
The Comm Coll of Baltimore County (MD)
Corning Comm Coll (NY)
Cowley County Comm Coll and Area Vocational–Tech School (KS)
Delaware County Comm Coll (PA)
Delaware Tech & Comm Coll, Jack F. Owens Campus (DE)
Delaware Tech & Comm Coll, Stanton/Wilmington Campus (DE)

Delaware Tech & Comm Coll, Terry Campus (DE)
Do&nna Ana Comm Coll (NM)
Dutchess Comm Coll (NY)
Dyersburg State Comm Coll (TN)
Eastern Arizona Coll (AZ)
El Centro Coll (TX)
El Paso Comm Coll (TX)
Erie Comm Coll, South Campus (NY)
Fayetteville Tech Comm Coll (NC)
Fiorello H. LaGuardia Comm Coll of the City U of New York (NY)
Florida State Coll at Jacksonville (FL)
Foothill Coll (CA)
Fox Valley Tech Coll (WI)
Front Range Comm Coll (CO)
Gadsden State Comm Coll (AL)
Gateway Tech Coll (WI)
Guilford Tech Comm Coll (NC)
Gulf Coast State Coll (FL)
Gwinnett Tech Coll (GA)
Hagerstown Comm Coll (MD)
Harper Coll (IL)
H. Councill Trenholm State Tech Coll (AL)
Hillsborough Comm Coll (FL)
Houston Comm Coll System (TX)
Howard Comm Coll (MD)
Hutchinson Comm Coll and Area Vocational School (KS)
Indian River State Coll (FL)
Ivy Tech Comm Coll–Bloomington (IN)
Ivy Tech Comm Coll–Kokomo (IN)
Ivy Tech Comm Coll–North Central (IN)
Ivy Tech Comm Coll–Southwest (IN)
Ivy Tech Comm Coll–Wabash Valley (IN)
Jackson Comm Coll (MI)
Jefferson Comm Coll (NY)
Jefferson State Comm Coll (AL)
John Wood Comm Coll (IL)
J. Sargeant Reynolds Comm Coll (VA)
Kankakee Comm Coll (IL)
Kansas City Kansas Comm Coll (KS)
Kaskaskia Coll (IL)
Kilgore Coll (TX)
Lake Area Tech Inst (SD)
Lake Michigan Coll (MI)
Lansing Comm Coll (MI)
Laramie County Comm Coll (WY)
Lincoln Land Comm Coll (IL)
Lurleen B. Wallace Comm Coll (AL)
Macomb Comm Coll (MI)
McHenry County Coll (IL)
Metropolitan Comm Coll–Penn Valley (MO)
Miami Dade Coll (FL)
Mineral Area Coll (MO)
Mohave Comm Coll (AZ)
Mohawk Valley Comm Coll (NY)
Montana State U–Great Falls Coll of Technology (MT)
Montcalm Comm Coll (MI)
Moraine Park Tech Coll (WI)
Moraine Valley Comm Coll (IL)
Mott Comm Coll (MI)
North Dakota State Coll of Science (ND)
Northeast Alabama Comm Coll (AL)
Northeast Comm Coll (NE)
Northeastern Jr Coll (CO)
Northeast Iowa Comm Coll (IA)
Northwest-Shoals Comm Coll (AL)
Oakland Comm Coll (MI)
Oklahoma City Comm Coll (OK)
Oklahoma State U, Oklahoma City (OK)
Orange Coast Coll (CA)
Pasco-Hernando Comm Coll (FL)
Pensacola State Coll (FL)
Piedmont Virginia Comm Coll (VA)
Polk State Coll (FL)
Quinsigamond Comm Coll (MA)
Red Rocks Comm Coll (CO)
Rockland Comm Coll (NY)
Rogue Comm Coll (OR)
St. Cloud Tech & Comm Coll (MN)
San Diego City Coll (CA)
San Jacinto Coll District (TX)

San Juan Coll (NM)
Santa Rosa Jr Coll (CA)
Scottsdale Comm Coll (AZ)
Seminole State Coll of Florida (FL)
Southeastern Comm Coll (IA)
Southern Crescent Tech Coll (GA)
Southern Maine Comm Coll (ME)
Southern State Comm Coll (OH)
Southwestern Illinois Coll (IL)
Southwestern Michigan Coll (MI)
Southwest Mississippi Comm Coll (MS)
Southwest Virginia Comm Coll (VA)
Tallahassee Comm Coll (FL)
Tarrant County Coll District (TX)
Texarkana Coll (TX)
Texas State Tech Coll Harlingen (TX)
Tyler Jr Coll (TX)
Umpqua Comm Coll (OR)
Union County Coll (NJ)
Valencia Coll (FL)
Vincennes U (IN)
Waukesha County Tech Coll (WI)
Westchester Comm Coll (NY)
Western Iowa Tech Comm Coll (IA)
Wisconsin Indianhead Tech Coll (WI)

ENERGY MANAGEMENT AND SYSTEMS TECHNOLOGY
Casper Coll (WY)
Century Coll (MN)
Comm Coll of Allegheny County (PA)
Delaware Tech & Comm Coll, Jack F. Owens Campus (DE)
Delaware Tech & Comm Coll, Stanton/Wilmington Campus (DE)
Delaware Tech & Comm Coll, Terry Campus (DE)
GateWay Comm Coll (AZ)
Illinois Eastern Comm Colls, Wabash Valley College (IL)
Iowa Lakes Comm Coll (IA)
Lake Michigan Coll (MI)
Lansing Comm Coll (MI)
Laramie County Comm Coll (WY)
Macomb Comm Coll (MI)
Mitchell Tech Inst (SD)
Montana State U–Great Falls Coll of Technology (MT)
North Dakota State Coll of Science (ND)
Northeast Comm Coll (NE)
Northeast Iowa Comm Coll (IA)
Northwest Tech Coll (MN)
Owens Comm Coll, Toledo (OH)
Red Rocks Comm Coll (CO)
St. Clair County Comm Coll (MI)
St. Philip's Coll (TX)
Salem Comm Coll (NJ)
Westchester Comm Coll (NY)
Wisconsin Indianhead Tech Coll (WI)

ENGINEERING
Amarillo Coll (TX)
Anne Arundel Comm Coll (MD)
Austin Comm Coll (TX)
Berkshire Comm Coll (MA)
Bunker Hill Comm Coll (MA)
Burlington County Coll (NJ)
Carl Albert State Coll (OK)
Casper Coll (WY)
Central Oregon Comm Coll (OR)
Central Wyoming Coll (WY)
Chattanooga State Comm Coll (TN)
Cochise Coll, Sierra Vista (AZ)
Coll of DuPage (IL)
Coll of Lake County (IL)
Coll of Southern Maryland (MD)
The Comm Coll of Baltimore County (MD)
Comm Coll of Philadelphia (PA)
Comm Coll of Rhode Island (RI)
Copiah-Lincoln Comm Coll (MS)
Delaware County Comm Coll (PA)
Elgin Comm Coll (IL)
El Paso Comm Coll (TX)
Erie Comm Coll, North Campus (NY)
Gavilan Coll (CA)
Grand Rapids Comm Coll (MI)
Hagerstown Comm Coll (MD)
Harford Comm Coll (MD)
Harper Coll (IL)

Highland Comm Coll (IL)
Highline Comm Coll (WA)
Holyoke Comm Coll (MA)
Howard Comm Coll (MD)
Hutchinson Comm Coll and Area Vocational School (KS)
Illinois Central Coll (IL)
Illinois Eastern Comm Colls, Frontier Community College (IL)
Illinois Eastern Comm Colls, Olney Central College (IL)
Illinois Eastern Comm Colls, Wabash Valley College (IL)
Illinois Valley Comm Coll (IL)
Indian River State Coll (FL)
Iowa Lakes Comm Coll (IA)
Itasca Comm Coll (MN)
Jamestown Comm Coll (NY)
John Tyler Comm Coll (VA)
J. Sargeant Reynolds Comm Coll (VA)
Kankakee Comm Coll (IL)
Kaskaskia Coll (IL)
Lansing Comm Coll (MI)
Laramie County Comm Coll (WY)
Lehigh Carbon Comm Coll (PA)
Lincoln Land Comm Coll (IL)
McHenry County Coll (IL)
Metropolitan Comm Coll–Business & Technology Campus (MO)
Metropolitan Comm Coll–Longview (MO)
Metropolitan Comm Coll–Penn Valley (MO)
Miami Dade Coll (FL)
Missouri State U–West Plains (MO)
Mohawk Valley Comm Coll (NY)
Montgomery Coll (MD)
Northampton Comm Coll (PA)
Northeast Comm Coll (NE)
North Hennepin Comm Coll (MN)
Northwest Coll (WY)
Northwestern Connecticut Comm Coll (CT)
Northwest Florida State Coll (FL)
Oakland Comm Coll (MI)
Ocean County Coll (NJ)
Orange Coast Coll (CA)
Pensacola State Coll (FL)
Piedmont Virginia Comm Coll (VA)
St. Clair County Comm Coll (MI)
Salt Lake Comm Coll (UT)
San Jacinto Coll District (TX)
San Juan Coll (NM)
Santa Rosa Jr Coll (CA)
Southwestern Indian Polytechnic Inst (NM)
Southwest Mississippi Comm Coll (MS)
Springfield Tech Comm Coll (MA)
State Coll of Florida Manatee-Sarasota (FL)
State U of New York Coll of Technology at Alfred (NY)
Tallahassee Comm Coll (FL)
Terra State Comm Coll (OH)
Texarkana Coll (TX)
Texas State Tech Coll Harlingen (TX)
Three Rivers Comm Coll (CT)
Tompkins Cortland Comm Coll (NY)
Truckee Meadows Comm Coll (NV)
Tunxis Comm Coll (CT)
Tyler Jr Coll (TX)
Umpqua Comm Coll (OR)
Union County Coll (NJ)
Virginia Western Comm Coll (VA)

ENGINEERING FIELDS RELATED
Normandale Comm Coll (MN)

ENGINEERING/INDUSTRIAL MANAGEMENT
Delaware Tech & Comm Coll, Stanton/Wilmington Campus (DE)

ENGINEERING MECHANICS
San Jacinto Coll District (TX)

ENGINEERING RELATED
Colby Comm Coll (KS)
Itasca Comm Coll (MN)
Macomb Comm Coll (MI)
Miami Dade Coll (FL)
Southeastern Comm Coll (IA)

ENGINEERING-RELATED TECHNOLOGIES
Gateway Comm Coll (CT)
Metropolitan Comm Coll–Business & Technology Campus (MO)

ENGINEERING SCIENCE
Dutchess Comm Coll (NY)
Fiorello H. LaGuardia Comm Coll of the City U of New York (NY)
Genesee Comm Coll (NY)
Itasca Comm Coll (MN)
Jefferson Comm Coll (NY)
Kingsborough Comm Coll of the City U of New York (NY)
Manchester Comm Coll (CT)
Monroe Comm Coll (NY)
Montgomery County Comm Coll (PA)
Northern Essex Comm Coll (MA)
North Shore Comm Coll (MA)
Onondaga Comm Coll (NY)
Raritan Valley Comm Coll (NJ)
Sullivan County Comm Coll (NY)
Three Rivers Comm Coll (CT)
Westchester Comm Coll (NY)

ENGINEERING TECHNOLOGIES AND ENGINEERING RELATED
Burlington County Coll (NJ)
Carl Albert State Coll (OK)
Coll of Southern Maryland (MD)
Comm Coll of Allegheny County (PA)
The Comm Coll of Baltimore County (MD)
Harford Comm Coll (MD)
J. Sargeant Reynolds Comm Coll (VA)
Kent State U at Tuscarawas (OH)
Montgomery County Comm Coll (PA)
Mott Comm Coll (MI)
North Dakota State Coll of Science (ND)
Ocean County Coll (NJ)
Oklahoma City Comm Coll (OK)
Raritan Valley Comm Coll (NJ)
State U of New York Coll of Technology at Alfred (NY)
Sullivan Coll of Technology and Design (KY)

ENGINEERING TECHNOLOGY
Bluegrass Comm and Tech Coll (KY)
Chattanooga State Comm Coll (TN)
Comm Coll of Philadelphia (PA)
Cowley County Comm Coll and Area Vocational–Tech School (KS)
Denmark Tech Coll (SC)
Florida State Coll at Jacksonville (FL)
Gateway Comm Coll (CT)
Georgia Piedmont Tech Coll (GA)
Highline Comm Coll (WA)
Hillsborough Comm Coll (FL)
Indian River State Coll (FL)
Itasca Comm Coll (MN)
Jefferson State Comm Coll (AL)
John Tyler Comm Coll (VA)
Kent State U at Ashtabula (OH)
Kent State U at Tuscarawas (OH)
Lake Area Tech Inst (SD)
Los Angeles Harbor Coll (CA)
Massachusetts Bay Comm Coll (MA)
Miami Dade Coll (FL)
Mineral Area Coll (MO)
Muskegon Comm Coll (MI)
Norco Coll (CA)
Oklahoma State U, Oklahoma City (OK)
Peninsula Coll (WA)
Salt Lake Comm Coll (UT)
San Diego City Coll (CA)
Southwestern Michigan Coll (MI)
Sullivan Coll of Technology and Design (KY)
Three Rivers Comm Coll (CT)
Trident Tech Coll (SC)
Tunxis Comm Coll (CT)
Vincennes U (IN)
Westchester Comm Coll (NY)

ENGINE MACHINIST
Northwest Tech Coll (MN)

ENGLISH
Amarillo Coll (TX)
Bainbridge Coll (GA)
Berkeley City Coll (CA)
Bunker Hill Comm Coll (MA)
Burlington County Coll (NJ)
Carl Albert State Coll (OK)
Casper Coll (WY)
Central Wyoming Coll (WY)
Cochise Coll, Sierra Vista (AZ)
Coll of the Canyons (CA)
Colorado Mountain Coll (CO)
Colorado Mountain Coll, Alpine Campus (CO)
Comm Coll of Allegheny County (PA)
Copiah-Lincoln Comm Coll (MS)
Eastern Arizona Coll (AZ)
Fiorello H. LaGuardia Comm Coll of the City U of New York (NY)
Foothill Coll (CA)
Gavilan Coll (CA)
Georgia Highlands Coll (GA)
Grand Rapids Comm Coll (MI)
Harper Coll (IL)
Highline Comm Coll (WA)
Hutchinson Comm Coll and Area Vocational School (KS)
Illinois Valley Comm Coll (IL)
Indian River State Coll (FL)
Iowa Lakes Comm Coll (IA)
Kilgore Coll (TX)
Lake Michigan Coll (MI)
Lansing Comm Coll (MI)
Laramie County Comm Coll (WY)
Mendocino Coll (CA)
Miami Dade Coll (FL)
Mohave Comm Coll (AZ)
Monroe County Comm Coll (MI)
Northeast Comm Coll (NE)
Northeastern Jr Coll (CO)
Northwest Coll (WY)
Northwestern Connecticut Comm Coll (CT)
Orange Coast Coll (CA)
Palm Beach State Coll (FL)
Pensacola State Coll (FL)
Raritan Valley Comm Coll (NJ)
Reedley Coll (CA)
St. Philip's Coll (TX)
Salt Lake Comm Coll (UT)
San Diego City Coll (CA)
San Jacinto Coll District (TX)
Santa Rosa Jr Coll (CA)
Southwest Mississippi Comm Coll (MS)
State Coll of Florida Manatee-Sarasota (FL)
Terra State Comm Coll (OH)
Truckee Meadows Comm Coll (NV)
Umpqua Comm Coll (OR)
Vincennes U (IN)

ENGLISH/LANGUAGE ARTS TEACHER EDUCATION
Anne Arundel Comm Coll (MD)
Cochise Coll, Sierra Vista (AZ)
Harford Comm Coll (MD)
Montgomery Coll (MD)
State Coll of Florida Manatee-Sarasota (FL)
Vincennes U (IN)

ENTREPRENEURIAL AND SMALL BUSINESS RELATED
Dakota Coll at Bottineau (ND)
State U of New York Coll of Technology at Alfred (NY)

ENTREPRENEURSHIP
Anne Arundel Comm Coll (MD)
Bunker Hill Comm Coll (MA)
Casper Coll (WY)
Comm Coll of Allegheny County (PA)
Cowley County Comm Coll and Area Vocational–Tech School (KS)
Delaware County Comm Coll (PA)
Delaware Tech & Comm Coll, Jack F. Owens Campus (DE)
Delaware Tech & Comm Coll, Terry Campus (DE)
Eastern Arizona Coll (AZ)

Elgin Comm Coll (IL)
Goodwin Coll (CT)
Laramie County Comm Coll (WY)
Missouri State U–West Plains (MO)
Mohawk Valley Comm Coll (NY)
Montana State U–Great Falls Coll of Technology (MT)
Montcalm Comm Coll (MI)
Mott Comm Coll (MI)
Northeast Comm Coll (NE)
Oakland Comm Coll (MI)
Randolph Comm Coll (NC)
Reedley Coll (CA)
Salt Lake Comm Coll (UT)
Southern State Comm Coll (OH)
State U of New York Coll of Technology at Alfred (NY)
Truckee Meadows Comm Coll (NV)

ENVIRONMENTAL BIOLOGY
Eastern Arizona Coll (AZ)

ENVIRONMENTAL CONTROL TECHNOLOGIES RELATED
Central Carolina Tech Coll (SC)
Fox Valley Tech Coll (WI)
Hillsborough Comm Coll (FL)
Holyoke Comm Coll (MA)
Westchester Comm Coll (NY)

ENVIRONMENTAL DESIGN/ARCHITECTURE
Iowa Lakes Comm Coll (IA)
Scottsdale Comm Coll (AZ)

ENVIRONMENTAL EDUCATION
Iowa Lakes Comm Coll (IA)

ENVIRONMENTAL ENGINEERING TECHNOLOGY
Austin Comm Coll (TX)
Bluegrass Comm and Tech Coll (KY)
Coll of Southern Maryland (MD)
Comm Coll of Allegheny County (PA)
Crowder Coll (MO)
Dakota Coll at Bottineau (ND)
El Paso Comm Coll (TX)
Georgia Northwestern Tech Coll (GA)
Iowa Lakes Comm Coll (IA)
Kent State U at Trumbull (OH)
Lansing Comm Coll (MI)
Massachusetts Bay Comm Coll (MA)
Metropolitan Comm Coll–Business & Technology Campus (MO)
Miami Dade Coll (FL)
Northwest-Shoals Comm Coll (AL)
Onondaga Comm Coll (NY)
Owens Comm Coll, Toledo (OH)
Salt Lake Comm Coll (UT)
San Diego City Coll (CA)
Southern Maine Comm Coll (ME)
Three Rivers Comm Coll (CT)
Valencia Coll (FL)

ENVIRONMENTAL/ENVIRONMENTAL HEALTH ENGINEERING
Central Wyoming Coll (WY)

ENVIRONMENTAL HEALTH
Amarillo Coll (TX)
Crowder Coll (MO)

ENVIRONMENTAL SCIENCE
Anoka-Ramsey Comm Coll (MN)
Anoka-Ramsey Comm Coll, Cambridge Campus (MN)
Bucks County Comm Coll (PA)
Burlington County Coll (NJ)
Casper Coll (WY)
Central Wyoming Coll (WY)
Comm Coll of Vermont (VT)
Corning Comm Coll (NY)
Fiorello H. LaGuardia Comm Coll of the City U of New York (NY)
Lake Area Tech Inst (SD)
Lake Michigan Coll (MI)
Montgomery County Comm Coll (PA)
Ocean County Coll (NJ)

St. Philip's Coll (TX)
San Jacinto Coll District (TX)
State U of New York Coll of Technology at Alfred (NY)
Truckee Meadows Comm Coll (NV)
Tyler Jr Coll (TX)

ENVIRONMENTAL STUDIES
Berkshire Comm Coll (MA)
Colorado Mountain Coll, Timberline Campus (CO)
Goodwin Coll (CT)
Harford Comm Coll (MD)
Harper Coll (IL)
Housatonic Comm Coll (CT)
Howard Comm Coll (MD)
Iowa Lakes Comm Coll (IA)
Itasca Comm Coll (MN)
Kent State U at Ashtabula (OH)
Kent State U at Tuscarawas (OH)
Kilian Comm Coll (SD)
Monroe Comm Coll (NY)
Mount Wachusett Comm Coll (MA)
Santa Rosa Jr Coll (CA)
Stark State Coll (OH)
Sullivan County Comm Coll (NY)
White Mountains Comm Coll (NH)

EQUESTRIAN STUDIES
Central Wyoming Coll (WY)
Laramie County Comm Coll (WY)
Northeastern Jr Coll (CO)
Northwest Coll (WY)
Scottsdale Comm Coll (AZ)

ETHNIC, CULTURAL MINORITY, GENDER, AND GROUP STUDIES RELATED
New Mexico State U–Alamogordo (NM)

EXECUTIVE ASSISTANT/ EXECUTIVE SECRETARY
Bluegrass Comm and Tech Coll (KY)
Brookhaven Coll (TX)
Cape Fear Comm Coll (NC)
Clark Coll (WA)
Crowder Coll (MO)
Dakota Coll at Bottineau (ND)
Edison Comm Coll (OH)
El Centro Coll (TX)
Elgin Comm Coll (IL)
Gulf Coast State Coll (FL)
Hawkeye Comm Coll (IA)
Hillsborough Comm Coll (FL)
Ivy Tech Comm Coll–Bloomington (IN)
Ivy Tech Comm Coll–Central Indiana (IN)
Ivy Tech Comm Coll–Columbus (IN)
Ivy Tech Comm Coll–East Central (IN)
Ivy Tech Comm Coll–Kokomo (IN)
Ivy Tech Comm Coll–Lafayette (IN)
Ivy Tech Comm Coll–North Central (IN)
Ivy Tech Comm Coll–Northeast (IN)
Ivy Tech Comm Coll–Northwest (IN)
Ivy Tech Comm Coll–Richmond (IN)
Ivy Tech Comm Coll–Southeast (IN)
Ivy Tech Comm Coll–Southern Indiana (IN)
Ivy Tech Comm Coll–Southwest (IN)
Ivy Tech Comm Coll–Wabash Valley (IN)
Jackson Comm Coll (MI)
John Wood Comm Coll (IL)
Kaskaskia Coll (IL)
Kilgore Coll (TX)
Lake Region State Coll (ND)
Owensboro Comm and Tech Coll (KY)
Owens Comm Coll, Toledo (OH)
Pensacola State Coll (FL)
Quinsigamond Comm Coll (MA)
St. Clair County Comm Coll (MI)
St. Cloud Tech & Comm Coll (MN)
Southern State Comm Coll (OH)
South Suburban Coll (IL)

Southwestern Michigan Coll (MI)
Springfield Tech Comm Coll (MA)
Terra State Comm Coll (OH)
Texas State Tech Coll Harlingen (TX)
The U of Montana–Helena Coll of Technology (MT)
Western Iowa Tech Comm Coll (IA)
West Virginia Northern Comm Coll (WV)

FACILITIES PLANNING AND MANAGEMENT
Comm Coll of Philadelphia (PA)

FAMILY AND COMMUNITY SERVICES
Snow Coll (UT)
Westmoreland County Comm Coll (PA)

FAMILY AND CONSUMER ECONOMICS RELATED
Orange Coast Coll (CA)

FAMILY AND CONSUMER SCIENCES/HOME ECONOMICS TEACHER EDUCATION
Copiah-Lincoln Comm Coll (MS)
Northwest Florida State Coll (FL)
State Coll of Florida Manatee-Sarasota (FL)
Vincennes U (IN)

FAMILY AND CONSUMER SCIENCES/HUMAN SCIENCES
Bainbridge Coll (GA)
Hutchinson Comm Coll and Area Vocational School (KS)
Indian River State Coll (FL)
Iowa Lakes Comm Coll (IA)
Metropolitan Comm Coll–Penn Valley (MO)
Monroe Comm Coll (NY)
Northeastern Jr Coll (CO)
Orange Coast Coll (CA)
Palm Beach State Coll (FL)
Snow Coll (UT)
Tyler Jr Coll (TX)
Vincennes U (IN)

FAMILY RESOURCE MANAGEMENT
Gavilan Coll (CA)

FARM AND RANCH MANAGEMENT
Colby Comm Coll (KS)
Copiah-Lincoln Comm Coll (MS)
Crowder Coll (MO)
Hutchinson Comm Coll and Area Vocational School (KS)
Iowa Lakes Comm Coll (IA)
Northeast Comm Coll (NE)
Northeastern Jr Coll (CO)
Northwest Coll (WY)
Snow Coll (UT)

FASHION AND FABRIC CONSULTING
Coll of DuPage (IL)
Harper Coll (IL)

FASHION/APPAREL DESIGN
The Art Inst of New York City (NY)
The Art Inst of Seattle (WA)
Burlington County Coll (NJ)
Clary Sage Coll (OK)
Coll of DuPage (IL)
El Centro Coll (TX)
El Paso Comm Coll (TX)
Fashion Inst of Technology (NY)
Harper Coll (IL)
Houston Comm Coll System (TX)
Lehigh Carbon Comm Coll (PA)
Metropolitan Comm Coll–Penn Valley (MO)
Monroe Comm Coll (NY)
Palm Beach State Coll (FL)
Santa Monica Coll (CA)
Santa Rosa Jr Coll (CA)
Wood Tobe–Coburn School (NY)

FASHION MERCHANDISING
The Art Inst of New York City (NY)
The Art Inst of Ohio–Cincinnati (OH)
The Art Inst of Seattle (WA)
Blue Ridge Comm and Tech Coll (WV)
Coll of DuPage (IL)
Do&nna Ana Comm Coll (NM)
Fashion Inst of Technology (NY)
Florida State Coll at Jacksonville (FL)
Gateway Comm Coll (CT)
Genesee Comm Coll (NY)
Grand Rapids Comm Coll (MI)
Harper Coll (IL)
Houston Comm Coll System (TX)
Howard Comm Coll (MD)
Indian River State Coll (FL)
Iowa Lakes Comm Coll (IA)
Kilgore Coll (TX)
Kingsborough Comm Coll of the City U of New York (NY)
Lake Region State Coll (ND)
Lansing Comm Coll (MI)
Metropolitan Comm Coll–Penn Valley (MO)
Monroe Comm Coll (NY)
Northeastern Jr Coll (CO)
Northwest Florida State Coll (FL)
Oakland Comm Coll (MI)
Orange Coast Coll (CA)
Palm Beach State Coll (FL)
San Diego City Coll (CA)
Santa Rosa Jr Coll (CA)
Scottsdale Comm Coll (AZ)
Southwest Mississippi Comm Coll (MS)
Tarrant County Coll District (TX)
Tunxis Comm Coll (CT)
Vincennes U (IN)

FASHION MODELING
Fashion Inst of Technology (NY)

FIBER, TEXTILE AND WEAVING ARTS
Mendocino Coll (CA)

FILM/CINEMA/VIDEO STUDIES
Carl Albert State Coll (OK)
KD Studio (TX)
Oakland Comm Coll (MI)
Orange Coast Coll (CA)
San Jacinto Coll District (TX)
Santa Monica Coll (CA)
Tallahassee Comm Coll (FL)

FILM/VIDEO AND PHOTOGRAPHIC ARTS RELATED
Westchester Comm Coll (NY)

FINANCE
Bunker Hill Comm Coll (MA)
Chipola Coll (FL)
Comm Coll of Philadelphia (PA)
Do&nna Ana Comm Coll (NM)
Harper Coll (IL)
Indian River State Coll (FL)
Iowa Lakes Comm Coll (IA)
Kent State U at Ashtabula (OH)
Macomb Comm Coll (MI)
Mendocino Coll (CA)
Miami Dade Coll (FL)
Monroe County Comm Coll (MI)
Muskegon Comm Coll (MI)
Northern Essex Comm Coll (MA)
North Hennepin Comm Coll (MN)
Northwest Florida State Coll (FL)
Oklahoma City Comm Coll (OK)
Palm Beach State Coll (FL)
Polk State Coll (FL)
Rockland Comm Coll (NY)
Salt Lake Comm Coll (UT)
San Diego City Coll (CA)
Scottsdale Comm Coll (AZ)
Seminole State Coll of Florida (FL)
Southeast Tech Inst (SD)
Southwest Mississippi Comm Coll (MS)
Springfield Tech Comm Coll (MA)
Stark State Coll (OH)
State Coll of Florida Manatee-Sarasota (FL)

State U of New York Coll of Technology at Alfred (NY)
Tallahassee Comm Coll (FL)
Vincennes U (IN)
Westchester Comm Coll (NY)
Wisconsin Indianhead Tech Coll (WI)

FINANCE AND FINANCIAL MANAGEMENT SERVICES RELATED
Northeast Comm Coll (NE)

FINANCIAL PLANNING AND SERVICES
Howard Comm Coll (MD)
Kilian Comm Coll (SD)
Raritan Valley Comm Coll (NJ)

FINE ARTS RELATED
Carl Albert State Coll (OK)
Murray State Coll (OK)
Reedley Coll (CA)

FINE/STUDIO ARTS
Amarillo Coll (TX)
Anoka-Ramsey Comm Coll (MN)
Anoka-Ramsey Comm Coll, Cambridge Campus (MN)
Berkeley City Coll (CA)
Casper Coll (WY)
Cayuga County Comm Coll (NY)
Chandler-Gilbert Comm Coll (AZ)
Colorado Mountain Coll, Alpine Campus (CO)
Corning Comm Coll (NY)
Delaware County Comm Coll (PA)
Elgin Comm Coll (IL)
Fashion Inst of Technology (NY)
Fiorello H. LaGuardia Comm Coll of the City U of New York (NY)
Foothill Coll (CA)
Harper Coll (IL)
Iowa Lakes Comm Coll (IA)
Jamestown Comm Coll (NY)
Kankakee Comm Coll (IL)
Lincoln Land Comm Coll (IL)
Manchester Comm Coll (CT)
McHenry County Coll (IL)
Minneapolis Comm and Tech Coll (MN)
New Mexico State U–Alamogordo (NM)
Niagara County Comm Coll (NY)
Northampton Comm Coll (PA)
Northeastern Jr Coll (CO)
North Hennepin Comm Coll (MN)
Oklahoma City Comm Coll (OK)
Raritan Valley Comm Coll (NJ)
Rockland Comm Coll (NY)
South Suburban Coll (IL)
Southwestern Illinois Coll (IL)
Springfield Tech Comm Coll (MA)
State Coll of Florida Manatee-Sarasota (FL)
Terra State Comm Coll (OH)
Truckee Meadows Comm Coll (NV)
Westchester Comm Coll (NY)

FIRE PREVENTION AND SAFETY TECHNOLOGY
Anne Arundel Comm Coll (MD)
Austin Comm Coll (TX)
Bunker Hill Comm Coll (MA)
Cape Fear Comm Coll (NC)
Catawba Valley Comm Coll (NC)
Coll of Lake County (IL)
Coll of Southern Maryland (MD)
Coll of the Canyons (CA)
Comm Coll of Allegheny County (PA)
Delaware County Comm Coll (PA)
Delaware Tech & Comm Coll, Stanton/Wilmington Campus (DE)
El Paso Comm Coll (TX)
Fayetteville Tech Comm Coll (NC)
Florida State Coll at Jacksonville (FL)
Fox Valley Tech Coll (WI)
Gateway Tech Coll (WI)
Guilford Tech Comm Coll (NC)
Gulf Coast State Coll (FL)
Hillsborough Comm Coll (FL)
Houston Comm Coll System (TX)

Jamestown Comm Coll (NY)
Jefferson Comm Coll (NY)
Macomb Comm Coll (MI)
Montgomery Coll (MD)
Montgomery County Comm Coll (PA)
Moraine Valley Comm Coll (IL)
Mott Comm Coll (MI)
Mount Wachusett Comm Coll (MA)
Ocean County Coll (NJ)
Oklahoma State U, Oklahoma City (OK)
Onondaga Comm Coll (NY)
Owens Comm Coll, Toledo (OH)
Pensacola State Coll (FL)
Rogue Comm Coll (OR)
San Jacinto Coll District (TX)
Springfield Tech Comm Coll (MA)
Union County Coll (NJ)
Waukesha County Tech Coll (WI)
Westmoreland County Comm Coll (PA)
Wilson Comm Coll (NC)

FIRE PROTECTION RELATED
Fox Valley Tech Coll (WI)
Kansas City Kansas Comm Coll (KS)

FIRE SCIENCE/FIREFIGHTING
Amarillo Coll (TX)
Augusta Tech Coll (GA)
Berkshire Comm Coll (MA)
Blackhawk Tech Coll (WI)
Bluegrass Comm and Tech Coll (KY)
Blue Ridge Comm and Tech Coll (WV)
Burlington County Coll (NJ)
Casper Coll (WY)
Cecil Coll (MD)
Central Oregon Comm Coll (OR)
Central Wyoming Coll (WY)
Chattahoochee Tech Coll (GA)
Chattanooga State Comm Coll (TN)
Cochise Coll, Sierra Vista (AZ)
Coll of Central Florida (FL)
Coll of DuPage (IL)
Coll of Southern Maryland (MD)
Comm Coll of Philadelphia (PA)
Comm Coll of Rhode Island (RI)
Corning Comm Coll (NY)
Crowder Coll (MO)
Delaware Tech & Comm Coll, Stanton/Wilmington Campus (DE)
Do&nna Ana Comm Coll (NM)
Eastern Arizona Coll (AZ)
Eastern Idaho Tech Coll (ID)
Elgin Comm Coll (IL)
Florida State Coll at Jacksonville (FL)
Gateway Comm Coll (CT)
Gateway Tech Coll (WI)
Georgia Northwestern Tech Coll (GA)
Harper Coll (IL)
Hutchinson Comm Coll and Area Vocational School (KS)
Illinois Central Coll (IL)
Illinois Eastern Comm Colls, Frontier Community College (IL)
Indian River State Coll (FL)
Jamestown Comm Coll (NY)
John Wood Comm Coll (IL)
Kansas City Kansas Comm Coll (KS)
Lanier Tech Coll (GA)
Lansing Comm Coll (MI)
Laramie County Comm Coll (WY)
Lincoln Land Comm Coll (IL)
Los Angeles Harbor Coll (CA)
Lower Columbia Coll (WA)
McHenry County Coll (IL)
Metropolitan Comm Coll–Blue River (MO)
Miami Dade Coll (FL)
Mid Michigan Comm Coll (MI)
Mid-Plains Comm Coll, North Platte (NE)
Mineral Area Coll (MO)
Mohave Comm Coll (AZ)
Monroe Comm Coll (NY)
Montana State U–Great Falls Coll of Technology (MT)

Moraine Valley Comm Coll (IL)
Moreno Valley Coll (CA)
Northampton Comm Coll (PA)
Northeast Iowa Comm Coll (IA)
North Shore Comm Coll (MA)
Oakland Comm Coll (MI)
Oklahoma State U, Oklahoma City (OK)
Owensboro Comm and Tech Coll (KY)
Palm Beach State Coll (FL)
Pensacola State Coll (FL)
Polk State Coll (FL)
Red Rocks Comm Coll (CO)
Rockland Comm Coll (NY)
San Jacinto Coll District (TX)
San Juan Coll (NM)
Santa Rosa Jr Coll (CA)
Savannah Tech Coll (GA)
Scottsdale Comm Coll (AZ)
Seminole State Coll of Florida (FL)
Southern Maine Comm Coll (ME)
Southwestern Illinois Coll (IL)
Southwestern Michigan Coll (MI)
Springfield Tech Comm Coll (MA)
Stark State Coll (OH)
State Coll of Florida Manatee-Sarasota (FL)
Tarrant County Coll District (TX)
Three Rivers Comm Coll (CT)
Truckee Meadows Comm Coll (NV)
Tyler Jr Coll (TX)
Umpqua Comm Coll (OR)
The U of Montana–Helena Coll of Technology (MT)
Valencia Coll (FL)
Vincennes U (IN)
Volunteer State Comm Coll (TN)
Western Dakota Tech Inst (SD)
Western Iowa Tech Comm Coll (IA)
West Georgia Tech Coll (GA)
West Kentucky Comm and Tech Coll (KY)
Wiregrass Georgia Tech Coll (GA)

FIRE SERVICES ADMINISTRATION
Chattahoochee Valley Comm Coll (AL)
Delaware Tech & Comm Coll, Stanton/Wilmington Campus (DE)
Erie Comm Coll, South Campus (NY)
Jefferson State Comm Coll (AL)
Kirtland Comm Coll (MI)
Mohawk Valley Comm Coll (NY)
Northampton Comm Coll (PA)
Quinsigamond Comm Coll (MA)

FISHING AND FISHERIES SCIENCES AND MANAGEMENT
Central Oregon Comm Coll (OR)
Dakota Coll at Bottineau (ND)
Iowa Lakes Comm Coll (IA)
Itasca Comm Coll (MN)
Peninsula Coll (WA)

FLIGHT INSTRUCTION
Iowa Lakes Comm Coll (IA)

FLORICULTURE/FLORISTRY MANAGEMENT
Dakota Coll at Bottineau (ND)
Illinois Valley Comm Coll (IL)
Santa Rosa Jr Coll (CA)
Westmoreland County Comm Coll (PA)

FOOD PREPARATION
Iowa Lakes Comm Coll (IA)
Moraine Park Tech Coll (WI)
San Jacinto Coll District (TX)

FOODS AND NUTRITION RELATED
Iowa Lakes Comm Coll (IA)

FOOD SCIENCE
Miami Dade Coll (FL)
Missouri State U–West Plains (MO)
Normandale Comm Coll (MN)
Orange Coast Coll (CA)
Vincennes U (IN)

FOOD SERVICE AND DINING ROOM MANAGEMENT
Iowa Lakes Comm Coll (IA)
Westmoreland County Comm Coll (PA)

FOOD SERVICE SYSTEMS ADMINISTRATION
Bucks County Comm Coll (PA)
Burlington County Coll (NJ)
Comm Coll of Allegheny County (PA)
Florida State Coll at Jacksonville (FL)
Harper Coll (IL)
Mohawk Valley Comm Coll (NY)
Mott Comm Coll (MI)
Northeast Comm Coll (NE)
Pensacola State Coll (FL)
San Jacinto Coll District (TX)

FOODS, NUTRITION, AND WELLNESS
Carl Albert State Coll (OK)
Chattanooga State Comm Coll (TN)
Dutchess Comm Coll (NY)
Indian River State Coll (FL)
North Shore Comm Coll (MA)
Northwest Florida State Coll (FL)
Orange Coast Coll (CA)
Palm Beach State Coll (FL)
Pensacola State Coll (FL)
Snow Coll (UT)

FOOD TECHNOLOGY AND PROCESSING
Copiah-Lincoln Comm Coll (MS)
Monroe Comm Coll (NY)
Orange Coast Coll (CA)
Southern State Comm Coll (OH)
Stark State Coll (OH)
Tarrant County Coll District (TX)
Westchester Comm Coll (NY)

FOREIGN LANGUAGES AND LITERATURES
Austin Comm Coll (TX)
Bunker Hill Comm Coll (MA)
Casper Coll (WY)
Central Oregon Comm Coll (OR)
Cochise Coll, Sierra Vista (AZ)
Comm Coll of Allegheny County (PA)
Eastern Arizona Coll (AZ)
Georgia Highlands Coll (GA)
Grand Rapids Comm Coll (MI)
Hutchinson Comm Coll and Area Vocational School (KS)
Iowa Lakes Comm Coll (IA)
Lake Michigan Coll (MI)
Lansing Comm Coll (MI)
Oklahoma City Comm Coll (OK)
Reedley Coll (CA)
San Jacinto Coll District (TX)
Texarkana Coll (TX)
Vincennes U (IN)

FOREIGN LANGUAGES RELATED
Vincennes U (IN)

FOREIGN LANGUAGE TEACHER EDUCATION
Cochise Coll, Sierra Vista (AZ)
State Coll of Florida Manatee-Sarasota (FL)

FORENSIC SCIENCE AND TECHNOLOGY
Arkansas State U–Mountain Home (AR)
Carroll Comm Coll (MD)
Casper Coll (WY)
Catawba Valley Comm Coll (NC)
Comm Coll of Philadelphia (PA)
Fayetteville Tech Comm Coll (NC)
Fox Valley Tech Coll (WI)
Illinois Central Coll (IL)
Illinois Valley Comm Coll (IL)
ITT Tech Inst, Bessemer (AL)
ITT Tech Inst, Madison (AL)
ITT Tech Inst, Mobile (AL)
ITT Tech Inst, Phoenix (AZ)
ITT Tech Inst, Tucson (AZ)
ITT Tech Inst (AR)

ITT Tech Inst, Lathrop (CA)
ITT Tech Inst, Orange (CA)
ITT Tech Inst, Oxnard (CA)
ITT Tech Inst, Rancho Cordova (CA)
ITT Tech Inst, San Bernardino (CA)
ITT Tech Inst, San Diego (CA)
ITT Tech Inst, San Dimas (CA)
ITT Tech Inst, Sylmar (CA)
ITT Tech Inst, Torrance (CA)
ITT Tech Inst, Aurora (CO)
ITT Tech Inst, Thornton (CO)
ITT Tech Inst, Fort Myers (FL)
ITT Tech Inst, Jacksonville (FL)
ITT Tech Inst, Lake Mary (FL)
ITT Tech Inst, Miami (FL)
ITT Tech Inst, Pinellas Park (FL)
ITT Tech Inst, Tallahassee (FL)
ITT Tech Inst, Tampa (FL)
ITT Tech Inst (ID)
ITT Tech Inst, Fort Wayne (IN)
ITT Tech Inst, Merrillville (IN)
ITT Tech Inst, Newburgh (IN)
ITT Tech Inst, Cedar Rapids (IA)
ITT Tech Inst, Clive (IA)
ITT Tech Inst, Baton Rouge (LA)
ITT Tech Inst, St. Rose (LA)
ITT Tech Inst, Canton (MI)
ITT Tech Inst, Swartz Creek (MI)
ITT Tech Inst, Troy (MI)
ITT Tech Inst, Wyoming (MI)
ITT Tech Inst, Eden Prairie (MN)
ITT Tech Inst, Arnold (MO)
ITT Tech Inst, Earth City (MO)
ITT Tech Inst, Kansas City (MO)
ITT Tech Inst (NE)
ITT Tech Inst, Henderson (NV)
ITT Tech Inst (NM)
ITT Tech Inst, Akron (OH)
ITT Tech Inst, Columbus (OH)
ITT Tech Inst, Dayton (OH)
ITT Tech Inst, Hilliard (OH)
ITT Tech Inst, Norwood (OH)
ITT Tech Inst, Strongsville (OH)
ITT Tech Inst, Warrensville Heights (OH)
ITT Tech Inst, Youngstown (OH)
ITT Tech Inst, Tulsa (OK)
ITT Tech Inst, Columbia (SC)
ITT Tech Inst, Chattanooga (TN)
ITT Tech Inst, Cordova (TN)
ITT Tech Inst, Johnson City (TN)
ITT Tech Inst, Knoxville (TN)
ITT Tech Inst, Nashville (TN)
ITT Tech Inst (UT)
ITT Tech Inst, Chantilly (VA)
ITT Tech Inst, Norfolk (VA)
ITT Tech Inst, Richmond (VA)
ITT Tech Inst, Salem (VA)
ITT Tech Inst, Springfield (VA)
ITT Tech Inst, Everett (WA)
ITT Tech Inst, Seattle (WA)
ITT Tech Inst, Spokane Valley (WA)
ITT Tech Inst (WV)
ITT Tech Inst, Green Bay (WI)
Macomb Comm Coll (MI)
Massachusetts Bay Comm Coll (MA)
Tompkins Cortland Comm Coll (NY)
Tunxis Comm Coll (CT)
U of Arkansas Comm Coll at Morrilton (AR)

FOREST RESOURCES PRODUCTION AND MANAGEMENT
Pensacola State Coll (FL)

FORESTRY
Bainbridge Coll (GA)
Central Oregon Comm Coll (OR)
Copiah-Lincoln Comm Coll (MS)
Eastern Arizona Coll (AZ)
Grand Rapids Comm Coll (MI)
Indian River State Coll (FL)
Iowa Lakes Comm Coll (IA)
Itasca Comm Coll (MN)
Kilgore Coll (TX)
Miami Dade Coll (FL)
Monroe Comm Coll (NY)
Pensacola State Coll (FL)
Snow Coll (UT)
Umpqua Comm Coll (OR)

FOREST TECHNOLOGY
Albany Tech Coll (GA)
Central Oregon Comm Coll (OR)

Itasca Comm Coll (MN)
Jefferson Comm Coll (NY)
Lurleen B. Wallace Comm Coll (AL)
Montgomery Comm Coll (NC)
Ogeechee Tech Coll (GA)
Okefenokee Tech Coll (GA)
Penn State Mont Alto (PA)
Pensacola State Coll (FL)
State U of New York Coll of Environmental Science & Forestry, Ranger School (NY)

FRENCH
Austin Comm Coll (TX)
Coll of the Canyons (CA)
Copiah-Lincoln Comm Coll (MS)
Indian River State Coll (FL)
Mendocino Coll (CA)
Miami Dade Coll (FL)
Northwest Coll (WY)
Orange Coast Coll (CA)
Snow Coll (UT)
State Coll of Florida Manatee-Sarasota (FL)

FUNERAL SERVICE AND MORTUARY SCIENCE
Amarillo Coll (TX)
Arkansas State U–Mountain Home (AR)
The Comm Coll of Baltimore County (MD)
Dallas Inst of Funeral Service (TX)
Fayetteville Tech Comm Coll (NC)
Fiorello H. LaGuardia Comm Coll of the City U of New York (NY)
Ivy Tech Comm Coll–Northwest (IN)
Jefferson State Comm Coll (AL)
John Tyler Comm Coll (VA)
Kansas City Kansas Comm Coll (KS)
Miami Dade Coll (FL)
Monroe County Comm Coll (MI)
Northampton Comm Coll (PA)
Ogeechee Tech Coll (GA)
Randolph Comm Coll (NC)
Vincennes U (IN)

GAME AND INTERACTIVE MEDIA DESIGN
Cayuga County Comm Coll (NY)
Cochise Coll, Sierra Vista (AZ)
Fayetteville Tech Comm Coll (NC)
Lehigh Carbon Comm Coll (PA)
Red Rocks Comm Coll (CO)

GENERAL STUDIES
Amarillo Coll (TX)
Ancilla Coll (IN)
Austin Comm Coll (TX)
Berkeley City Coll (CA)
Bevill State Comm Coll (AL)
Blue Ridge Comm and Tech Coll (WV)
Brookhaven Coll (TX)
Bunker Hill Comm Coll (MA)
Carroll Comm Coll (MD)
Casper Coll (WY)
Catawba Valley Comm Coll (NC)
Cayuga County Comm Coll (NY)
Cecil Coll (MD)
Central Wyoming Coll (WY)
Chandler-Gilbert Comm Coll (AZ)
Chattahoochee Valley Comm Coll (AL)
Chattanooga State Comm Coll (TN)
City Colls of Chicago, Harry S. Truman College (IL)
Cleveland State Comm Coll (TN)
Cochise Coll, Sierra Vista (AZ)
Colorado Mountain Coll, Timberline Campus (CO)
Comm Coll of Allegheny County (PA)
Comm Coll of Rhode Island (RI)
Corning Comm Coll (NY)
Crowder Coll (MO)
Dakota Coll at Bottineau (ND)
Delaware County Comm Coll (PA)
El Paso Comm Coll (TX)
Front Range Comm Coll (CO)
Gadsden State Comm Coll (AL)
GateWay Comm Coll (AZ)
Gavilan Coll (CA)
Guilford Tech Comm Coll (NC)
Highland Comm Coll (IL)
Howard Comm Coll (MD)

Illinois Central Coll (IL)
Illinois Eastern Comm Colls, Frontier Community College (IL)
Illinois Eastern Comm Colls, Lincoln Trail College (IL)
Illinois Eastern Comm Colls, Olney Central College (IL)
Illinois Eastern Comm Colls, Wabash Valley College (IL)
Illinois Valley Comm Coll (IL)
Iowa Lakes Comm Coll (IA)
Itasca Comm Coll (MN)
Ivy Tech Comm Coll–Bloomington (IN)
Ivy Tech Comm Coll–Central Indiana (IN)
Ivy Tech Comm Coll–Columbus (IN)
Ivy Tech Comm Coll–East Central (IN)
Ivy Tech Comm Coll–Kokomo (IN)
Ivy Tech Comm Coll–Lafayette (IN)
Ivy Tech Comm Coll–North Central (IN)
Ivy Tech Comm Coll–Northeast (IN)
Ivy Tech Comm Coll–Northwest (IN)
Ivy Tech Comm Coll–Richmond (IN)
Ivy Tech Comm Coll–Southeast (IN)
Ivy Tech Comm Coll–Southern Indiana (IN)
Ivy Tech Comm Coll–Southwest (IN)
Ivy Tech Comm Coll–Wabash Valley (IN)
Jackson Comm Coll (MI)
James Sprunt Comm Coll (NC)
Jefferson State Comm Coll (AL)
John Tyler Comm Coll (VA)
John Wood Comm Coll (IL)
Kankakee Comm Coll (IL)
Kaskaskia Coll (IL)
Kilgore Coll (TX)
Kirtland Comm Coll (MI)
Lake Michigan Coll (MI)
Lawson State Comm Coll (AL)
Lehigh Carbon Comm Coll (PA)
Lincoln Land Comm Coll (IL)
Lurleen B. Wallace Comm Coll (AL)
Macomb Comm Coll (MI)
Manchester Comm Coll (CT)
Massachusetts Bay Comm Coll (MA)
McHenry County Coll (IL)
Miami Dade Coll (FL)
Mid Michigan Comm Coll (MI)
Mineral Area Coll (MO)
Missouri State U–West Plains (MO)
Montcalm Comm Coll (MI)
Motlow State Comm Coll (TN)
Mott Comm Coll (MI)
Mount Wachusett Comm Coll (MA)
Murray State Coll (OK)
New Mexico State U–Alamogordo (NM)
Niagara County Comm Coll (NY)
Northampton Comm Coll (PA)
Northeast Comm Coll (NE)
Northern Essex Comm Coll (MA)
Northwest Coll (WY)
Northwest-Shoals Comm Coll (AL)
Oakland Comm Coll (MI)
Ocean County Coll (NJ)
Oklahoma State U, Oklahoma City (OK)
Onondaga Comm Coll (NY)
Owens Comm Coll, Toledo (OH)
Panola Coll (TX)
Piedmont Virginia Comm Coll (VA)
Quinsigamond Comm Coll (MA)
Red Rocks Comm Coll (CO)
Reedley Coll (CA)
Rockingham Comm Coll (NC)
Rogue Comm Coll (OR)
Salt Lake Comm Coll (UT)
San Jacinto Coll District (TX)
San Juan Coll (NM)
Southwestern Illinois Coll (IL)
Southwestern Michigan Coll (MI)
Southwestern Oklahoma State U at Sayre (OK)
Springfield Tech Comm Coll (MA)
Terra State Comm Coll (OH)
Truckee Meadows Comm Coll (NV)
The U of Akron–Wayne Coll (OH)
U of Arkansas Comm Coll at Morrilton (AR)
The U of Montana–Helena Coll of Technology (MT)
Volunteer State Comm Coll (TN)

West Virginia Northern Comm Coll (WV)
White Mountains Comm Coll (NH)
Wilson Comm Coll (NC)

GEOGRAPHIC INFORMATION SCIENCE AND CARTOGRAPHY
Austin Comm Coll (TX)
Brookhaven Coll (TX)
Casper Coll (WY)
Houston Comm Coll System (TX)
Lehigh Carbon Comm Coll (PA)
Mitchell Tech Inst (SD)
Southwestern Indian Polytechnic Inst (NM)

GEOGRAPHY
Austin Comm Coll (TX)
Cayuga County Comm Coll (NY)
The Comm Coll of Baltimore County (MD)
Foothill Coll (CA)
Holyoke Comm Coll (MA)
Itasca Comm Coll (MN)
Lake Michigan Coll (MI)
Lansing Comm Coll (MI)
Montgomery Coll (MD)
Orange Coast Coll (CA)
San Juan Coll (NM)
Snow Coll (UT)

GEOLOGICAL AND EARTH SCIENCES/GEOSCIENCES RELATED
Burlington County Coll (NJ)
Erie Comm Coll, North Campus (NY)
Truckee Meadows Comm Coll (NV)

GEOLOGY/EARTH SCIENCE
Amarillo Coll (TX)
Austin Comm Coll (TX)
Casper Coll (WY)
Central Wyoming Coll (WY)
Colorado Mountain Coll, Alpine Campus (CO)
Eastern Arizona Coll (AZ)
Georgia Highlands Coll (GA)
Grand Rapids Comm Coll (MI)
Iowa Lakes Comm Coll (IA)
Kilgore Coll (TX)
Lake Michigan Coll (MI)
Miami Dade Coll (FL)
Orange Coast Coll (CA)
Pensacola State Coll (FL)
St. Philip's Coll (TX)
Salt Lake Comm Coll (UT)
San Jacinto Coll District (TX)
San Juan Coll (NM)
Snow Coll (UT)
Tyler Jr Coll (TX)
Vincennes U (IN)

GERMAN
Austin Comm Coll (TX)
Miami Dade Coll (FL)
Orange Coast Coll (CA)
State Coll of Florida Manatee-Sarasota (FL)

GERONTOLOGY
Fiorello H. LaGuardia Comm Coll of the City U of New York (NY)
Gateway Comm Coll (CT)
Genesee Comm Coll (NY)
North Shore Comm Coll (MA)

GLAZIER
Metropolitan Comm Coll–Business & Technology Campus (MO)

GOLF COURSE OPERATION AND GROUNDS MANAGEMENT
Owens Comm Coll, Toledo (OH)

GRAPHIC AND PRINTING EQUIPMENT OPERATION/PRODUCTION
Burlington County Coll (NJ)
Central Comm Coll–Hastings Campus (NE)
Central Maine Comm Coll (ME)

Coll of DuPage (IL)
Erie Comm Coll, South Campus (NY)
Fox Valley Tech Coll (WI)
H. Councill Trenholm State Tech Coll (AL)
Houston Comm Coll System (TX)
Iowa Lakes Comm Coll (IA)
Macomb Comm Coll (MI)
Mineral Area Coll (MO)
Monroe Comm Coll (NY)
Northwest Coll (WY)
Riverside City Coll (CA)
San Diego City Coll (CA)
Sullivan Coll of Technology and Design (KY)
Tarrant County Coll District (TX)
Vincennes U (IN)

GRAPHIC COMMUNICATIONS
Clark Coll (WA)
Fox Valley Tech Coll (WI)
Hawkeye Comm Coll (IA)
Iowa Lakes Comm Coll (IA)
ITT Tech Inst, Bessemer (AL)
ITT Tech Inst, Madison (AL)
ITT Tech Inst, Mobile (AL)
ITT Tech Inst, Phoenix (AZ)
ITT Tech Inst, Tucson (AZ)
ITT Tech Inst (AR)
ITT Tech Inst, Lathrop (CA)
ITT Tech Inst, Orange (CA)
ITT Tech Inst, Oxnard (CA)
ITT Tech Inst, Rancho Cordova (CA)
ITT Tech Inst, San Bernardino (CA)
ITT Tech Inst, San Diego (CA)
ITT Tech Inst, San Dimas (CA)
ITT Tech Inst, Sylmar (CA)
ITT Tech Inst, Torrance (CA)
ITT Tech Inst, Aurora (CO)
ITT Tech Inst, Thornton (CO)
ITT Tech Inst, Fort Lauderdale (FL)
ITT Tech Inst, Fort Myers (FL)
ITT Tech Inst, Jacksonville (FL)
ITT Tech Inst, Lake Mary (FL)
ITT Tech Inst, Miami (FL)
ITT Tech Inst, Pinellas Park (FL)
ITT Tech Inst, Tallahassee (FL)
ITT Tech Inst, Tampa (FL)
ITT Tech Inst (ID)
ITT Tech Inst, Fort Wayne (IN)
ITT Tech Inst, Merrillville (IN)
ITT Tech Inst, Newburgh (IN)
ITT Tech Inst, Cedar Rapids (IA)
ITT Tech Inst, Clive (IA)
ITT Tech Inst, Louisville (KY)
ITT Tech Inst, Baton Rouge (LA)
ITT Tech Inst, St. Rose (LA)
ITT Tech Inst, Canton (MI)
ITT Tech Inst, Swartz Creek (MI)
ITT Tech Inst, Troy (MI)
ITT Tech Inst, Wyoming (MI)
ITT Tech Inst, Eden Prairie (MN)
ITT Tech Inst, Arnold (MO)
ITT Tech Inst, Earth City (MO)
ITT Tech Inst, Kansas City (MO)
ITT Tech Inst (NE)
ITT Tech Inst, Henderson (NV)
ITT Tech Inst (NM)
ITT Tech Inst, Albany (NY)
ITT Tech Inst, Getzville (NY)
ITT Tech Inst, Liverpool (NY)
ITT Tech Inst, Akron (OH)
ITT Tech Inst, Columbus (OH)
ITT Tech Inst, Dayton (OH)
ITT Tech Inst, Hilliard (OH)
ITT Tech Inst, Maumee (OH)
ITT Tech Inst, Norwood (OH)
ITT Tech Inst, Strongsville (OH)
ITT Tech Inst, Warrensville Heights (OH)
ITT Tech Inst, Youngstown (OH)
ITT Tech Inst, Tulsa (OK)
ITT Tech Inst, Portland (OR)
ITT Tech Inst, Columbia (SC)
ITT Tech Inst, Chattanooga (TN)
ITT Tech Inst, Cordova (TN)
ITT Tech Inst, Johnson City (TN)
ITT Tech Inst, Knoxville (TN)
ITT Tech Inst, Nashville (TN)
ITT Tech Inst, Arlington (TX)
ITT Tech Inst, Austin (TX)
ITT Tech Inst, DeSoto (TX)
ITT Tech Inst, Houston (TX)
ITT Tech Inst, Houston (TX)
ITT Tech Inst, Richardson (TX)

ITT Tech Inst, San Antonio (TX)
ITT Tech Inst, Webster (TX)
ITT Tech Inst (UT)
ITT Tech Inst, Chantilly (VA)
ITT Tech Inst, Norfolk (VA)
ITT Tech Inst, Richmond (VA)
ITT Tech Inst, Salem (VA)
ITT Tech Inst, Springfield (VA)
ITT Tech Inst, Everett (WA)
ITT Tech Inst, Seattle (WA)
ITT Tech Inst, Spokane Valley (WA)
ITT Tech Inst (WV)
ITT Tech Inst, Green Bay (WI)
ITT Tech Inst, Greenfield (WI)
ITT Tech Inst, Madison (WI)
Moraine Park Tech Coll (WI)
Sullivan Coll of Technology and Design (KY)
Waukesha County Tech Coll (WI)

GRAPHIC COMMUNICATIONS RELATED
Rasmussen Coll Moorhead (MN)
Sullivan Coll of Technology and Design (KY)

GRAPHIC DESIGN
Anne Arundel Comm Coll (MD)
Antonelli Inst (PA)
The Art Inst of New York City (NY)
The Art Inst of Ohio–Cincinnati (OH)
The Art Inst of Seattle (WA)
The Art Inst of York–Pennsylvania (PA)
Bradford School (OH)
Bradford School (PA)
Brookhaven Coll (TX)
Burlington County Coll (NJ)
Casper Coll (WY)
Cayuga County Comm Coll (NY)
Cecil Coll (MD)
Central Wyoming Coll (WY)
Coll of the Canyons (CA)
Comm Coll of Vermont (VT)
Elgin Comm Coll (IL)
Foothill Coll (CA)
Fox Coll (IL)
Gateway Tech Coll (WI)
Hesser Coll, Manchester (NH)
Highland Comm Coll (IL)
Illinois Central Coll (IL)
Illinois Valley Comm Coll (IL)
International Business Coll, Indianapolis (IN)
Iowa Lakes Comm Coll (IA)
Ivy Tech Comm Coll–Southwest (IN)
Jackson Comm Coll (MI)
John Wood Comm Coll (IL)
Kankakee Comm Coll (IL)
King's Coll (NC)
Kirtland Comm Coll (MI)
Lake Michigan Coll (MI)
Lansing Comm Coll (MI)
Lehigh Carbon Comm Coll (PA)
Lincoln Land Comm Coll (IL)
Minneapolis Business Coll (MN)
Minnesota School of Business–Richfield (MN)
Minnesota School of Business–St. Cloud (MN)
Montana State U–Great Falls Coll of Technology (MT)
Moraine Park Tech Coll (WI)
Moraine Valley Comm Coll (IL)
Mott Comm Coll (MI)
New Mexico State U–Alamogordo (NM)
Northampton Comm Coll (PA)
Northeast Comm Coll (NE)
North Hennepin Comm Coll (MN)
Oakland Comm Coll (MI)
Salt Lake Comm Coll (UT)
Santa Monica Coll (CA)
Santa Rosa Jr Coll (CA)
Southwestern Michigan Coll (MI)
Sullivan Coll of Technology and Design (KY)
Waukesha County Tech Coll (WI)
Westmoreland County Comm Coll (PA)
Wood Tobe–Coburn School (NY)

GREENHOUSE MANAGEMENT
Century Coll (MN)

Comm Coll of Allegheny County (PA)
Dakota Coll at Bottineau (ND)

GUNSMITHING
Colorado School of Trades (CO)
Murray State Coll (OK)

HAIR STYLING AND HAIR DESIGN
Moraine Park Tech Coll (WI)

HAZARDOUS MATERIALS MANAGEMENT AND WASTE TECHNOLOGY
Kansas City Kansas Comm Coll (KS)
Pensacola State Coll (FL)

HEALTH AIDE
Northeast Comm Coll (NE)

HEALTH AND MEDICAL ADMINISTRATIVE SERVICES RELATED
Anthem Coll–Maryland Heights (MO)
Bucks County Comm Coll (PA)
GateWay Comm Coll (AZ)
Kent State U at Salem (OH)
Northeast Comm Coll (NE)
San Joaquin Valley Coll, Fresno (CA)
San Joaquin Valley Coll, Visalia (CA)
Westmoreland County Comm Coll (PA)

HEALTH AND PHYSICAL EDUCATION/FITNESS
Anne Arundel Comm Coll (MD)
Austin Comm Coll (TX)
Central Oregon Comm Coll (OR)
Cochise Coll, Sierra Vista (AZ)
Coll of the Canyons (CA)
Comm Care Coll (OK)
Comm Coll of Allegheny County (PA)
Corning Comm Coll (NY)
Dakota Coll at Bottineau (ND)
Eastern Arizona Coll (AZ)
Elgin Comm Coll (IL)
Gavilan Coll (CA)
Holyoke Comm Coll (MA)
Houston Comm Coll System (TX)
Iowa Lakes Comm Coll (IA)
Lake Michigan Coll (MI)
Lansing Comm Coll (MI)
McHenry County Coll (IL)
Montgomery County Comm Coll (PA)
Moreno Valley Coll (CA)
Northeast Comm Coll (NE)
Northwest Coll (WY)
Raritan Valley Comm Coll (NJ)
Reedley Coll (CA)
San Jacinto Coll District (TX)
San Juan Coll (NM)
Santa Monica Coll (CA)
Vincennes U (IN)

HEALTH AND PHYSICAL EDUCATION RELATED
Coll of Southern Maryland (MD)
Kingsborough Comm Coll of the City U of New York (NY)

HEALTH/HEALTH-CARE ADMINISTRATION
Coll of DuPage (IL)
Comm Care Coll (OK)
Consolidated School of Business, York (PA)
GateWay Comm Coll (AZ)
Iowa Lakes Comm Coll (IA)
Oakland Comm Coll (MI)
Oklahoma State U, Oklahoma City (OK)
Owens Comm Coll, Toledo (OH)
Rockingham Comm Coll (NC)
State Coll of Florida Manatee-Sarasota (FL)
Terra State Comm Coll (OH)

Tyler Jr Coll (TX)

HEALTH INFORMATION/MEDICAL RECORDS ADMINISTRATION
Amarillo Coll (TX)
Bunker Hill Comm Coll (MA)
Coll of DuPage (IL)
Comm Coll of Philadelphia (PA)
El Centro Coll (TX)
El Paso Comm Coll (TX)
Florida State Coll at Jacksonville (FL)
Gateway Tech Coll (WI)
Hagerstown Comm Coll (MD)
Illinois Eastern Comm Colls, Lincoln Trail College (IL)
Indian River State Coll (FL)
Metropolitan Comm Coll–Penn Valley (MO)
Miami Dade Coll (FL)
Monroe Comm Coll (NY)
Normandale Comm Coll (MN)
Northern Essex Comm Coll (MA)
Oklahoma City Comm Coll (OK)
Pensacola State Coll (FL)
Polk State Coll (FL)
Rockland Comm Coll (NY)
Stark State Coll (OH)
Tarrant County Coll District (TX)
Terra State Comm Coll (OH)

HEALTH INFORMATION/MEDICAL RECORDS TECHNOLOGY
Anne Arundel Comm Coll (MD)
Atlanta Tech Coll (GA)
Austin Comm Coll (TX)
Burlington County Coll (NJ)
Carroll Comm Coll (MD)
Catawba Valley Comm Coll (NC)
Central Comm Coll–Hastings Campus (NE)
Central Oregon Comm Coll (OR)
Chattanooga State Comm Coll (TN)
Chippewa Valley Tech Coll (WI)
Coll of Central Florida (FL)
Coll of DuPage (IL)
Columbus Tech Coll (GA)
Comm Coll of Allegheny County (PA)
Dyersburg State Comm Coll (TN)
Erie Comm Coll, North Campus (NY)
Fountainhead Coll of Technology (TN)
Front Range Comm Coll (CO)
Gateway Tech Coll (WI)
Highland Comm Coll (IL)
Houston Comm Coll System (TX)
Hutchinson Comm Coll and Area Vocational School (KS)
Illinois Eastern Comm Colls, Frontier Community College (IL)
ITT Tech Inst, Orange (CA)
ITT Tech Inst, San Bernardino (CA)
ITT Tech Inst, San Dimas (CA)
ITT Tech Inst, Sylmar (CA)
ITT Tech Inst, Fort Lauderdale (FL)
ITT Tech Inst, Lake Mary (FL)
ITT Tech Inst, Miami (FL)
ITT Tech Inst, Tampa (FL)
ITT Tech Inst (NM)
Jamestown Comm Coll (NY)
Kaplan Coll, Las Vegas Campus, Las Vegas (NV)
Kaplan Coll, Riverside Campus (CA)
Kaplan Coll, San Antonio Campus (TX)
Kaplan Coll, San Diego Campus (CA)
Kaskaskia Coll (IL)
Lehigh Carbon Comm Coll (PA)
Montana State U–Great Falls Coll of Technology (MT)
Montgomery Coll (MD)
Moraine Park Tech Coll (WI)
Moraine Valley Comm Coll (IL)
Mott Comm Coll (MI)
Normandale Comm Coll (MN)
North Dakota State Coll of Science (ND)
Northeast Iowa Comm Coll (IA)
Ogeechee Tech Coll (GA)

Onondaga Comm Coll (NY)
Owens Comm Coll, Toledo (OH)
Ozarka Coll (AR)
Panola Coll (TX)
Raritan Valley Comm Coll (NJ)
Rasmussen Coll Aurora (IL)
Rasmussen Coll Bismarck (ND)
Rasmussen Coll Bloomington (MN)
Rasmussen Coll Brooklyn Park (MN)
Rasmussen Coll Eagan (MN)
Rasmussen Coll Fort Myers (FL)
Rasmussen Coll Green Bay (WI)
Rasmussen Coll Lake Elmo/Woodbury (MN)
Rasmussen Coll Mankato (MN)
Rasmussen Coll Moorhead (MN)
Rasmussen Coll New Port Richey (FL)
Rasmussen Coll Ocala (FL)
Rasmussen Coll Rockford (IL)
Rasmussen Coll St. Cloud (MN)
St. Clair County Comm Coll (MI)
St. Cloud Tech & Comm Coll (MN)
St. Philip's Coll (TX)
San Jacinto Coll District (TX)
San Juan Coll (NM)
Southern Maine Comm Coll (ME)
Southwestern Illinois Coll (IL)
Southwestern Michigan Coll (MI)
Southwest Mississippi Comm Coll (MS)
State U of New York Coll of Technology at Alfred (NY)
Tallahassee Comm Coll (FL)
Terra State Comm Coll (OH)
TESST Coll of Technology, Beltsville (MD)
Texas State Tech Coll Harlingen (TX)
Tyler Jr Coll (TX)
Vincennes U (IN)
Volunteer State Comm Coll (TN)
Waukesha County Tech Coll (WI)
West Georgia Tech Coll (GA)
Westmoreland County Comm Coll (PA)
West Virginia Northern Comm Coll (WV)

HEALTH/MEDICAL PREPARATORY PROGRAMS RELATED

Eastern Arizona Coll (AZ)
Edison Comm Coll (OH)
Gavilan Coll (CA)
Miami Dade Coll (FL)
Northeast Comm Coll (NE)
Northwest Coll (WY)

HEALTH PROFESSIONS RELATED

Berkshire Comm Coll (MA)
Bucks County Comm Coll (PA)
Carl Albert State Coll (OK)
Carroll Comm Coll (MD)
Comm Coll of Allegheny County (PA)
Comm Coll of Philadelphia (PA)
Genesee Comm Coll (NY)
Lanier Tech Coll (GA)
Mendocino Coll (CA)
Miami Dade Coll (FL)
Mineral Area Coll (MO)
Northeastern Jr Coll (CO)
North Shore Comm Coll (MA)
Northwestern Connecticut Comm Coll (CT)
Oakland Comm Coll (MI)
Onondaga Comm Coll (NY)
Orange Coast Coll (CA)
Salt Lake Comm Coll (UT)
Southwest Mississippi Comm Coll (MS)
Terra State Comm Coll (OH)
Volunteer State Comm Coll (TN)

HEALTH SERVICES/ALLIED HEALTH/HEALTH SCIENCES

Ancilla Coll (IN)
Anoka-Ramsey Comm Coll (MN)
Anoka-Ramsey Comm Coll, Cambridge Campus (MN)
Burlington County Coll (NJ)
Carl Albert State Coll (OK)
Cecil Coll (MD)
Central Wyoming Coll (WY)

Dakota Coll at Bottineau (ND)
Delaware County Comm Coll (PA)
Dyersburg State Comm Coll (TN)
Goodwin Coll (CT)
Northwest Coll (WY)
Quinsigamond Comm Coll (MA)
Raritan Valley Comm Coll (NJ)
Texas State Tech Coll Harlingen (TX)
York County Comm Coll (ME)

HEALTH TEACHER EDUCATION

Austin Comm Coll (TX)
Bainbridge Coll (GA)
Copiah-Lincoln Comm Coll (MS)
Harper Coll (IL)
Howard Comm Coll (MD)
Kilgore Coll (TX)
Palm Beach State Coll (FL)
State Coll of Florida Manatee-Sarasota (FL)
Umpqua Comm Coll (OR)

HEALTH UNIT COORDINATOR/WARD CLERK

Comm Coll of Allegheny County (PA)
Southeast Tech Inst (SD)

HEALTH UNIT MANAGEMENT/WARD SUPERVISION

Delaware County Comm Coll (PA)

HEATING, AIR CONDITIONING, VENTILATION AND REFRIGERATION MAINTENANCE TECHNOLOGY

Amarillo Coll (TX)
Blackhawk Tech Coll (WI)
Bluegrass Comm and Tech Coll (KY)
Blue Ridge Comm and Tech Coll (WV)
Central Comm Coll–Grand Island Campus (NE)
Central Comm Coll–Hastings Campus (NE)
Century Coll (MN)
Coll of Business and Technology (FL)
Coll of DuPage (IL)
Coll of Lake County (IL)
Comm Coll of Allegheny County (PA)
Delaware County Comm Coll (PA)
Delaware Tech & Comm Coll, Jack F. Owens Campus (DE)
Do&nna Ana Comm Coll (NM)
Elgin Comm Coll (IL)
El Paso Comm Coll (TX)
Fayetteville Tech Comm Coll (NC)
GateWay Comm Coll (AZ)
Gateway Tech Coll (WI)
Grand Rapids Comm Coll (MI)
Guilford Tech Comm Coll (NC)
Harper Coll (IL)
Indian River State Coll (FL)
Ivy Tech Comm Coll–Bloomington (IN)
Ivy Tech Comm Coll–Central Indiana (IN)
Ivy Tech Comm Coll–Columbus (IN)
Ivy Tech Comm Coll–East Central (IN)
Ivy Tech Comm Coll–Kokomo (IN)
Ivy Tech Comm Coll–Lafayette (IN)
Ivy Tech Comm Coll–North Central (IN)
Ivy Tech Comm Coll–Northeast (IN)
Ivy Tech Comm Coll–Northwest (IN)
Ivy Tech Comm Coll–Richmond (IN)
Ivy Tech Comm Coll–Southern Indiana (IN)
Ivy Tech Comm Coll–Southwest (IN)
Ivy Tech Comm Coll–Wabash Valley (IN)
Johnston Comm Coll (NC)
Kankakee Comm Coll (IL)
Kilgore Coll (TX)
Kirtland Comm Coll (MI)
Lansing Comm Coll (MI)
Laramie County Comm Coll (WY)
Lehigh Carbon Comm Coll (PA)

Linn State Tech Coll (MO)
Macomb Comm Coll (MI)
Miami Dade Coll (FL)
Mid Michigan Comm Coll (MI)
Mid-Plains Comm Coll, North Platte (NE)
Minneapolis Comm and Tech Coll (MN)
Minnesota State Coll–Southeast Tech (MN)
Mitchell Tech Inst (SD)
Mohave Comm Coll (AZ)
Monroe Comm Coll (NY)
Moraine Park Tech Coll (WI)
Moraine Valley Comm Coll (IL)
Northampton Comm Coll (PA)
North Dakota State Coll of Science (ND)
Northeast Comm Coll (NE)
North Seattle Comm Coll (WA)
Northwest Florida State Coll (FL)
Orange Coast Coll (CA)
Riverside City Coll (CA)
St. Cloud Tech & Comm Coll (MN)
St. Philip's Coll (TX)
Salt Lake Comm Coll (UT)
San Jacinto Coll District (TX)
Southeast Tech Inst (SD)
Southern Maine Comm Coll (ME)
Southwestern Illinois Coll (IL)
Southwest Mississippi Comm Coll (MS)
State U of New York Coll of Technology at Alfred (NY)
Tarrant County Coll District (TX)
Texarkana Coll (TX)
Texas State Tech Coll Harlingen (TX)
U of Arkansas Comm Coll at Morrilton (AR)
Westmoreland County Comm Coll (PA)
West Virginia Northern Comm Coll (WV)
Wilson Comm Coll (NC)

HEATING, VENTILATION, AIR CONDITIONING AND REFRIGERATION ENGINEERING TECHNOLOGY

Austin Comm Coll (TX)
Bevill State Comm Coll (AL)
Chippewa Valley Tech Coll (WI)
Delaware County Comm Coll (PA)
Delaware Tech & Comm Coll, Stanton/Wilmington Campus (DE)
Front Range Comm Coll (CO)
Gadsden State Comm Coll (AL)
GateWay Comm Coll (AZ)
Gateway Tech Coll (WI)
Georgia Piedmont Tech Coll (GA)
H. Councill Trenholm State Tech Coll (AL)
Illinois Central Coll (IL)
Jackson Comm Coll (MI)
Macomb Comm Coll (MI)
Miami Dade Coll (FL)
Mineral Area Coll (MO)
Mohawk Valley Comm Coll (NY)
Moraine Park Tech Coll (WI)
Mott Comm Coll (MI)
North Dakota State Coll of Science (ND)
North Georgia Tech Coll (GA)
Oakland Comm Coll (MI)
Raritan Valley Comm Coll (NJ)
San Joaquin Valley Coll, Bakersfield (CA)
San Joaquin Valley Coll, Fresno (CA)
San Joaquin Valley Coll, Rancho Cordova (CA)
Savannah Tech Coll (GA)
Southern Crescent Tech Coll (GA)
South Georgia Tech Coll (GA)
Springfield Tech Comm Coll (MA)
State U of New York Coll of Technology at Alfred (NY)
Sullivan Coll of Technology and Design (KY)
Terra State Comm Coll (OH)
Truckee Meadows Comm Coll (NV)

HEAVY EQUIPMENT MAINTENANCE TECHNOLOGY

Amarillo Coll (TX)

Beaufort County Comm Coll (NC)
Fox Valley Tech Coll (WI)
Highland Comm Coll (IL)
Linn State Tech Coll (MO)
Metropolitan Comm Coll–Longview (MO)
State U of New York Coll of Technology at Alfred (NY)

HEAVY/INDUSTRIAL EQUIPMENT MAINTENANCE TECHNOLOGIES RELATED

Mineral Area Coll (MO)

HISPANIC-AMERICAN, PUERTO RICAN, AND MEXICAN-AMERICAN/CHICANO STUDIES

San Diego City Coll (CA)
San Jacinto Coll District (TX)

HISTOLOGIC TECHNICIAN

Comm Coll of Rhode Island (RI)
Houston Comm Coll System (TX)
Lansing Comm Coll (MI)
Miami Dade Coll (FL)
Mott Comm Coll (MI)
Oakland Comm Coll (MI)

HISTOLOGIC TECHNOLOGY/HISTOTECHNOLOGIST

Delaware Tech & Comm Coll, Stanton/Wilmington Campus (DE)
North Hennepin Comm Coll (MN)
Oakland Comm Coll (MI)

HISTORIC PRESERVATION AND CONSERVATION

Bucks County Comm Coll (PA)
Colorado Mountain Coll, Timberline Campus (CO)

HISTORY

Amarillo Coll (TX)
Ancilla Coll (IN)
Austin Comm Coll (TX)
Bainbridge Coll (GA)
Bunker Hill Comm Coll (MA)
Burlington County Coll (NJ)
Casper Coll (WY)
Cochise Coll, Sierra Vista (AZ)
Coll of the Canyons (CA)
Copiah-Lincoln Comm Coll (MS)
Dakota Coll at Bottineau (ND)
Eastern Arizona Coll (AZ)
Foothill Coll (CA)
Georgia Highlands Coll (GA)
Harper Coll (IL)
Indian River State Coll (FL)
Iowa Lakes Comm Coll (IA)
Kilian Comm Coll (SD)
Lake Michigan Coll (MI)
Lansing Comm Coll (MI)
Laramie County Comm Coll (WY)
Miami Dade Coll (FL)
Mohave Comm Coll (AZ)
Monroe Comm Coll (NY)
Murray State Coll (OK)
Northeastern Jr Coll (CO)
Northern Essex Comm Coll (MA)
North Hennepin Comm Coll (MN)
Northwest Coll (WY)
Oklahoma City Comm Coll (OK)
Oklahoma State U, Oklahoma City (OK)
Orange Coast Coll (CA)
Otero Jr Coll (CO)
Palm Beach State Coll (FL)
Pensacola State Coll (FL)
St. Philip's Coll (TX)
Salt Lake Comm Coll (UT)
San Jacinto Coll District (TX)
Santa Rosa Jr Coll (CA)
Snow Coll (UT)
Southwest Mississippi Comm Coll (MS)
State Coll of Florida Manatee-Sarasota (FL)
Terra State Comm Coll (OH)
Texarkana Coll (TX)
Truckee Meadows Comm Coll (NV)
Umpqua Comm Coll (OR)
Vincennes U (IN)

HISTORY TEACHER EDUCATION

Bucks County Comm Coll (PA)
Cochise Coll, Sierra Vista (AZ)

HOLISTIC HEALTH

Anoka-Ramsey Comm Coll (MN)
Anoka-Ramsey Comm Coll, Cambridge Campus (MN)
Red Rocks Comm Coll (CO)

HOMELAND SECURITY

Goodwin Coll (CT)
Harper Coll (IL)
Long Island Business Inst (NY)

HOMELAND SECURITY, LAW ENFORCEMENT, FIREFIGHTING AND PROTECTIVE SERVICES RELATED

Central Wyoming Coll (WY)
Century Coll (MN)
Chattahoochee Valley Comm Coll (AL)
El Paso Comm Coll (TX)
Goodwin Coll (CT)
J. Sargeant Reynolds Comm Coll (VA)
Laramie County Comm Coll (WY)
Miami Dade Coll (FL)
Ocean County Coll (NJ)
Onondaga Comm Coll (NY)
Pittsburgh Tech Inst, Oakdale (PA)
Red Rocks Comm Coll (CO)
San Joaquin Valley Coll, Bakersfield (CA)
Westmoreland County Comm Coll (PA)

HORSE HUSBANDRY/EQUINE SCIENCE AND MANAGEMENT

Cecil Coll (MD)
Colby Comm Coll (KS)
Santa Rosa Jr Coll (CA)

HORTICULTURAL SCIENCE

Century Coll (MN)
Chattahoochee Tech Coll (GA)
Columbus Tech Coll (GA)
Dakota Coll at Bottineau (ND)
Gwinnett Tech Coll (GA)
Kankakee Comm Coll (IL)
Lehigh Carbon Comm Coll (PA)
Miami Dade Coll (FL)
Missouri State U–West Plains (MO)
North Georgia Tech Coll (GA)
Oklahoma State U, Oklahoma City (OK)
Orange Coast Coll (CA)
Reedley Coll (CA)
Shawnee Comm Coll (IL)
Southeast Tech Inst (SD)
Southern Crescent Tech Coll (GA)
South Georgia Tech Coll (GA)
Tarrant County Coll District (TX)
Trident Tech Coll (SC)
Tyler Jr Coll (TX)

HOSPITAL AND HEALTH-CARE FACILITIES ADMINISTRATION

Coll of DuPage (IL)
State Coll of Florida Manatee-Sarasota (FL)

HOSPITALITY ADMINISTRATION

Austin Comm Coll (TX)
Berkshire Comm Coll (MA)
Bunker Hill Comm Coll (MA)
Burlington County Coll (NJ)
Casper Coll (WY)
Coll of DuPage (IL)
Coll of Southern Maryland (MD)
Coll of the Canyons (CA)
Colorado Mountain Coll, Alpine Campus (CO)
Comm Coll of Vermont (VT)
Do&nna Ana Comm Coll (NM)
Florida State Coll at Jacksonville (FL)
Fox Valley Tech Coll (WI)
Front Range Comm Coll (CO)
Gulf Coast State Coll (FL)
Harper Coll (IL)

Hillsborough Comm Coll (FL)
Iowa Lakes Comm Coll (IA)
Ivy Tech Comm Coll–East Central (IN)
Ivy Tech Comm Coll–North Central (IN)
Ivy Tech Comm Coll–Northeast (IN)
Ivy Tech Comm Coll–Northwest (IN)
Jefferson Comm Coll (NY)
Jefferson State Comm Coll (AL)
Lake Michigan Coll (MI)
Lincoln Land Comm Coll (IL)
Massachusetts Bay Comm Coll (MA)
Miami Dade Coll (FL)
Muskegon Comm Coll (MI)
Niagara County Comm Coll (NY)
Normandale Comm Coll (MN)
North Shore Comm Coll (MA)
Olympic Coll (WA)
Onondaga Comm Coll (NY)
Pensacola State Coll (FL)
Quinsigamond Comm Coll (MA)
Reedley Coll (CA)
Rockland Comm Coll (NY)
San Diego City Coll (CA)
Scottsdale Comm Coll (AZ)
Sullivan County Comm Coll (NY)
Terra State Comm Coll (OH)
Three Rivers Comm Coll (CT)
Union County Coll (NJ)
Valencia Coll (FL)
Vincennes U (IN)
West Virginia Northern Comm Coll (WV)

HOSPITALITY ADMINISTRATION RELATED

Bunker Hill Comm Coll (MA)
Corning Comm Coll (NY)
Holyoke Comm Coll (MA)
Ivy Tech Comm Coll–Central Indiana (IN)
Ivy Tech Comm Coll–East Central (IN)
Ivy Tech Comm Coll–Northeast (IN)
Penn State Beaver (PA)
Southwestern Indian Polytechnic Inst (NM)

HOSPITALITY AND RECREATION MARKETING

Dakota Coll at Bottineau (ND)
Florida State Coll at Jacksonville (FL)
Montgomery County Comm Coll (PA)
Muskegon Comm Coll (MI)
Pensacola State Coll (FL)

HOTEL/MOTEL ADMINISTRATION

Albany Tech Coll (GA)
Anne Arundel Comm Coll (MD)
Athens Tech Coll (GA)
Atlanta Tech Coll (GA)
Bradford School (PA)
Bunker Hill Comm Coll (MA)
Cape Fear Comm Coll (NC)
Carl Albert State Coll (OK)
Central Comm Coll–Hastings Campus (NE)
Central Georgia Tech Coll (GA)
Central Oregon Comm Coll (OR)
Central Wyoming Coll (WY)
Coll of DuPage (IL)
Coll of the Canyons (CA)
Colorado Mountain Coll, Alpine Campus (CO)
Comm Coll of Allegheny County (PA)
The Comm Coll of Baltimore County (MD)
Comm Coll of Philadelphia (PA)
Cowley County Comm Coll and Area Vocational–Tech School (KS)
Delaware County Comm Coll (PA)
Delaware Tech & Comm Coll, Stanton/Wilmington Campus (DE)
Delaware Tech & Comm Coll, Terry Campus (DE)
El Paso Comm Coll (TX)

Florida State Coll at Jacksonville (FL)
Fox Coll (IL)
Gateway Comm Coll (CT)
Gateway Tech Coll (WI)
Genesee Comm Coll (NY)
Guilford Tech Comm Coll (NC)
Gwinnett Tech Coll (GA)
Highline Comm Coll (WA)
Houston Comm Coll System (TX)
Indian River State Coll (FL)
International Business Coll, Indianapolis (IN)
Iowa Lakes Comm Coll (IA)
King's Coll (NC)
Lansing Comm Coll (MI)
Manchester Comm Coll (CT)
Minneapolis Business Coll (MN)
Mohawk Valley Comm Coll (NY)
Monroe Comm Coll (NY)
Montgomery Coll (MD)
Moraine Park Tech Coll (WI)
Muskegon Comm Coll (MI)
Northampton Comm Coll (PA)
Northern Essex Comm Coll (MA)
Northwest Florida State Coll (FL)
Oakland Comm Coll (MI)
Ogeechee Tech Coll (GA)
Orange Coast Coll (CA)
Palau Comm Coll (Palau)
Palm Beach State Coll (FL)
Pittsburgh Tech Inst, Oakdale (PA)
The Restaurant School at Walnut Hill Coll (PA)
St. Philip's Coll (TX)
Savannah Tech Coll (GA)
Scottsdale Comm Coll (AZ)
Southern Maine Comm Coll (ME)
Southwestern Michigan Coll (MI)
Three Rivers Comm Coll (CT)
Tompkins Cortland Comm Coll (NY)
Trident Tech Coll (SC)
Union County Coll (NJ)
Vincennes U (IN)
Westmoreland County Comm Coll (PA)
Wood Tobe–Coburn School (NY)

HOTEL, MOTEL, AND RESTAURANT MANAGEMENT

Fayetteville Tech Comm Coll (NC)
Gateway Tech Coll (WI)
Waukesha County Tech Coll (WI)

HOUSING AND HUMAN ENVIRONMENTS

Orange Coast Coll (CA)
Sullivan Coll of Technology and Design (KY)

HOUSING AND HUMAN ENVIRONMENTS RELATED

Comm Coll of Allegheny County (PA)

HUMAN DEVELOPMENT AND FAMILY STUDIES

Bucks County Comm Coll (PA)
Orange Coast Coll (CA)
Penn State Brandywine (PA)
Penn State DuBois (PA)
Penn State Fayette, The Eberly Campus (PA)
Penn State Mont Alto (PA)
Penn State New Kensington (PA)
Penn State Schuylkill (PA)
Penn State Shenango (PA)
Penn State Worthington Scranton (PA)
Penn State York (PA)
Salt Lake Comm Coll (UT)

HUMAN DEVELOPMENT AND FAMILY STUDIES RELATED

Albany Tech Coll (GA)
Comm Coll of Allegheny County (PA)

HUMANITIES

Brookhaven Coll (TX)
Bucks County Comm Coll (PA)
Cayuga County Comm Coll (NY)
Central Oregon Comm Coll (OR)

Clinton Comm Coll (NY)
Cochise Coll, Sierra Vista (AZ)
Colorado Mountain Coll (CO)
Colorado Mountain Coll, Alpine Campus (CO)
Comm Coll of Allegheny County (PA)
Corning Comm Coll (NY)
Dakota Coll at Bottineau (ND)
Dutchess Comm Coll (NY)
Erie Comm Coll (NY)
Erie Comm Coll, North Campus (NY)
Erie Comm Coll, South Campus (NY)
Harper Coll (IL)
Highline Comm Coll (WA)
Housatonic Comm Coll (CT)
Indian River State Coll (FL)
Iowa Lakes Comm Coll (IA)
Jamestown Comm Coll (NY)
Jefferson Comm Coll (NY)
John Tyler Comm Coll (VA)
Lake Michigan Coll (MI)
Lansing Comm Coll (MI)
Laramie County Comm Coll (WY)
Lehigh Carbon Comm Coll (PA)
Miami Dade Coll (FL)
Mohawk Valley Comm Coll (NY)
Montgomery County Comm Coll (PA)
Murray State Coll (OK)
Niagara County Comm Coll (NY)
Northeastern Jr Coll (CO)
Northwest Florida State Coll (FL)
Oklahoma City Comm Coll (OK)
Oklahoma State U, Oklahoma City (OK)
Onondaga Comm Coll (NY)
Orange Coast Coll (CA)
Otero Jr Coll (CO)
Salt Lake Comm Coll (UT)
Santa Rosa Jr Coll (CA)
Snow Coll (UT)
Southwest Mississippi Comm Coll (MS)
State Coll of Florida Manatee-Sarasota (FL)
State U of New York Coll of Technology at Alfred (NY)
Terra State Comm Coll (OH)
Texarkana Coll (TX)
Tompkins Cortland Comm Coll (NY)
Umpqua Comm Coll (OR)
Westchester Comm Coll (NY)

HUMAN RESOURCES MANAGEMENT

Anoka-Ramsey Comm Coll (MN)
Anoka-Ramsey Comm Coll, Cambridge Campus (MN)
Chippewa Valley Tech Coll (WI)
Clark Coll (WA)
Comm Coll of Allegheny County (PA)
Delaware Tech & Comm Coll, Terry Campus (DE)
Edison Comm Coll (OH)
Fayetteville Tech Comm Coll (NC)
Fox Valley Tech Coll (WI)
Goodwin Coll (CT)
Guilford Tech Comm Coll (NC)
Hawkeye Comm Coll (IA)
Lansing Comm Coll (MI)
Lehigh Carbon Comm Coll (PA)
Moraine Park Tech Coll (WI)
Moraine Valley Comm Coll (IL)
Northwest Florida State Coll (FL)
Rasmussen Coll Bloomington (MN)
Rasmussen Coll Brooklyn Park (MN)
Rasmussen Coll Eagan (MN)
Rasmussen Coll Fargo (ND)
Rasmussen Coll Fort Myers (FL)
Rasmussen Coll Green Bay (WI)
Rasmussen Coll Lake Elmo/Woodbury (MN)
Rasmussen Coll Mankato (MN)
Rasmussen Coll Moorhead (MN)
Rasmussen Coll New Port Richey (FL)
Rasmussen Coll Ocala (FL)
San Joaquin Valley Coll, Visalia (CA)
Santa Rosa Jr Coll (CA)

Umpqua Comm Coll (OR)
Valencia Coll (FL)
Western Iowa Tech Comm Coll (IA)
Westmoreland County Comm Coll (PA)

HUMAN RESOURCES MANAGEMENT AND SERVICES RELATED

Iowa Lakes Comm Coll (IA)
San Joaquin Valley Coll–Online (CA)

HUMAN SERVICES

Austin Comm Coll (TX)
Berkshire Comm Coll (MA)
Bunker Hill Comm Coll (MA)
Burlington County Coll (NJ)
Central Carolina Tech Coll (SC)
Central Maine Comm Coll (ME)
Century Coll (MN)
Coll of Central Florida (FL)
Coll of DuPage (IL)
Comm Coll of Philadelphia (PA)
Comm Coll of Vermont (VT)
Corning Comm Coll (NY)
Delaware County Comm Coll (PA)
Delaware Tech & Comm Coll, Jack F. Owens Campus (DE)
Delaware Tech & Comm Coll, Stanton/Wilmington Campus (DE)
Delaware Tech & Comm Coll, Terry Campus (DE)
Denmark Tech Coll (SC)
Florida State Coll at Jacksonville (FL)
Gateway Comm Coll (CT)
Genesee Comm Coll (NY)
Georgia Highlands Coll (GA)
Goodwin Coll (CT)
Harper Coll (IL)
Highline Comm Coll (WA)
Housatonic Comm Coll (CT)
Indian River State Coll (FL)
Itasca Comm Coll (MN)
Ivy Tech Comm Coll–Bloomington (IN)
Ivy Tech Comm Coll–Central Indiana (IN)
Ivy Tech Comm Coll–Columbus (IN)
Ivy Tech Comm Coll–East Central (IN)
Ivy Tech Comm Coll–Kokomo (IN)
Ivy Tech Comm Coll–Lafayette (IN)
Ivy Tech Comm Coll–North Central (IN)
Ivy Tech Comm Coll–Northeast (IN)
Ivy Tech Comm Coll–Northwest (IN)
Ivy Tech Comm Coll–Richmond (IN)
Ivy Tech Comm Coll–Southeast (IN)
Ivy Tech Comm Coll–Southern Indiana (IN)
Ivy Tech Comm Coll–Southwest (IN)
Ivy Tech Comm Coll–Wabash Valley (IN)
Jamestown Comm Coll (NY)
Jefferson Comm Coll (NY)
John Tyler Comm Coll (VA)
Kent State U at Ashtabula (OH)
Kingsborough Comm Coll of the City U of New York (NY)
Lake Area Tech Inst (SD)
Laramie County Comm Coll (WY)
Lehigh Carbon Comm Coll (PA)
Manchester Comm Coll (CT)
Massachusetts Bay Comm Coll (MA)
Mendocino Coll (CA)
Metropolitan Comm Coll–Longview (MO)
Miami Dade Coll (FL)
Minneapolis Comm and Tech Coll (MN)
Monroe Comm Coll (NY)
Mount Wachusett Comm Coll (MA)
New Mexico State U–Alamogordo (NM)
Niagara County Comm Coll (NY)
Northern Essex Comm Coll (MA)

Northwestern Connecticut Comm Coll (CT)
Ocean County Coll (NJ)
Oklahoma State U, Oklahoma City (OK)
Owensboro Comm and Tech Coll (KY)
Pasco-Hernando Comm Coll (FL)
Quinsigamond Comm Coll (MA)
Rasmussen Coll Bismarck (ND)
Rasmussen Coll Bloomington (MN)
Rasmussen Coll Brooklyn Park (MN)
Rasmussen Coll Eagan (MN)
Rasmussen Coll Fargo (ND)
Rasmussen Coll Fort Myers (FL)
Rasmussen Coll Green Bay (WI)
Rasmussen Coll Lake Elmo/Woodbury (MN)
Rasmussen Coll Mankato (MN)
Rasmussen Coll Moorhead (MN)
Rasmussen Coll New Port Richey (FL)
Rasmussen Coll Ocala (FL)
Rasmussen Coll St. Cloud (MN)
Riverside City Coll (CA)
Rockland Comm Coll (NY)
Santa Rosa Jr Coll (CA)
Shawnee Comm Coll (IL)
Southern State Comm Coll (OH)
Stark State Coll (OH)
State U of New York Coll of Technology at Alfred (NY)
Sullivan County Comm Coll (NY)
Three Rivers Comm Coll (CT)
Trident Tech Coll (SC)
Tunxis Comm Coll (CT)
Union County Coll (NJ)
White Mountains Comm Coll (NH)

HYDRAULICS AND FLUID POWER TECHNOLOGY

The Comm Coll of Baltimore County (MD)

HYDROLOGY AND WATER RESOURCES SCIENCE

Do&nna Ana Comm Coll (NM)
Indian River State Coll (FL)
Iowa Lakes Comm Coll (IA)
Three Rivers Comm Coll (CT)

ILLUSTRATION

Creative Center (NE)
Fashion Inst of Technology (NY)
Oakland Comm Coll (MI)
Oklahoma State U, Oklahoma City (OK)

INDUSTRIAL AND PRODUCT DESIGN

The Art Inst of Seattle (WA)
Fiorello H. LaGuardia Comm Coll of the City U of New York (NY)
GateWay Comm Coll (AZ)
Kirtland Comm Coll (MI)
Orange Coast Coll (CA)
Owens Comm Coll, Toledo (OH)
Salem Comm Coll (NJ)

INDUSTRIAL ELECTRONICS TECHNOLOGY

Bevill State Comm Coll (AL)
Big Bend Comm Coll (WA)
Bluegrass Comm and Tech Coll (KY)
Central Carolina Tech Coll (SC)
Coll of DuPage (IL)
Eastern Arizona Coll (AZ)
H. Councill Trenholm State Tech Coll (AL)
John Tyler Comm Coll (VA)
Lawson State Comm Coll (AL)
Lehigh Carbon Comm Coll (PA)
Lincoln Land Comm Coll (IL)
Lurleen B. Wallace Comm Coll (AL)
Moraine Park Tech Coll (WI)
Moraine Valley Comm Coll (IL)
Northampton Comm Coll (PA)
Northeast Alabama Comm Coll (AL)
Northwest-Shoals Comm Coll (AL)
Randolph Comm Coll (NC)
Sullivan Coll of Technology and Design (KY)

INDUSTRIAL ENGINEERING
Blackhawk Tech Coll (WI)
Catawba Valley Comm Coll (NC)
Manchester Comm Coll (CT)
Montcalm Comm Coll (MI)

INDUSTRIAL MECHANICS AND MAINTENANCE TECHNOLOGY
Aiken Tech Coll (SC)
Big Bend Comm Coll (WA)
Bluegrass Comm and Tech Coll (KY)
Casper Coll (WY)
Central Comm Coll–Hastings Campus (NE)
Coll of Lake County (IL)
Delaware County Comm Coll (PA)
Eastern Arizona Coll (AZ)
Elgin Comm Coll (IL)
Gadsden State Comm Coll (AL)
Gateway Tech Coll (WI)
H. Councill Trenholm State Tech Coll (AL)
Illinois Eastern Comm Colls, Olney Central College (IL)
Ivy Tech Comm Coll–East Central (IN)
Kaskaskia Coll (IL)
Lower Columbia Coll (WA)
Macomb Comm Coll (MI)
Minnesota State Coll–Southeast Tech (MN)
Moraine Park Tech Coll (WI)
Northeast Alabama Comm Coll (AL)
Northeast Comm Coll (NE)
Northwest-Shoals Comm Coll (AL)
San Juan Coll (NM)
Southwestern Illinois Coll (IL)
Southwestern Michigan Coll (MI)
Sullivan Coll of Technology and Design (KY)
Western Iowa Tech Comm Coll (IA)
Westmoreland County Comm Coll (PA)

INDUSTRIAL PRODUCTION TECHNOLOGIES RELATED
Guilford Tech Comm Coll (NC)
Harford Comm Coll (MD)
Ivy Tech Comm Coll–Central Indiana (IN)
Ivy Tech Comm Coll–East Central (IN)
Ivy Tech Comm Coll–Lafayette (IN)
Ivy Tech Comm Coll–North Central (IN)
Ivy Tech Comm Coll–Northeast (IN)
Ivy Tech Comm Coll–Richmond (IN)
Ivy Tech Comm Coll–Southwest (IN)
Ivy Tech Comm Coll–Wabash Valley (IN)
Lansing Comm Coll (MI)
Mohawk Valley Comm Coll (NY)
Moraine Park Tech Coll (WI)
Murray State Coll (OK)
Oakland Comm Coll (MI)
St. Clair County Comm Coll (MI)
Southwestern Michigan Coll (MI)

INDUSTRIAL RADIOLOGIC TECHNOLOGY
Amarillo Coll (TX)
Copiah-Lincoln Comm Coll (MS)
Cowley County Comm Coll and Area Vocational–Tech School (KS)
Do&nna Ana Comm Coll (NM)
Gateway Comm Coll (CT)
Indian River State Coll (FL)
Kankakee Comm Coll (IL)
Mid Michigan Comm Coll (MI)
Monroe Comm Coll (NY)
Northern Essex Comm Coll (MA)
Orange Coast Coll (CA)
Palm Beach State Coll (FL)
Salt Lake Comm Coll (UT)
Southeastern Comm Coll (IA)
Tarrant County Coll District (TX)
Tyler Jr Coll (TX)
Virginia Western Comm Coll (VA)

INDUSTRIAL SAFETY TECHNOLOGY
Northwest Tech Coll (MN)

INDUSTRIAL TECHNOLOGY
Albany Tech Coll (GA)
Blackhawk Tech Coll (WI)
Bucks County Comm Coll (PA)
Central Comm Coll–Hastings Campus (NE)
Central Georgia Tech Coll (GA)
Central Oregon Comm Coll (OR)
Chattanooga State Comm Coll (TN)
Cleveland State Comm Coll (TN)
Clinton Comm Coll (NY)
Coll of DuPage (IL)
Coll of the Ouachitas (AR)
Columbus Tech Coll (GA)
Comm Coll of Allegheny County (PA)
Comm Coll of Vermont (VT)
Corning Comm Coll (NY)
Crowder Coll (MO)
Edison Comm Coll (OH)
Erie Comm Coll, North Campus (NY)
Gateway Comm Coll (CT)
Georgia Piedmont Tech Coll (GA)
Grand Rapids Comm Coll (MI)
Hagerstown Comm Coll (MD)
Highline Comm Coll (WA)
Illinois Central Coll (IL)
Illinois Eastern Comm Colls, Wabash Valley College (IL)
Illinois Valley Comm Coll (IL)
Ivy Tech Comm Coll–Bloomington (IN)
Ivy Tech Comm Coll–Central Indiana (IN)
Ivy Tech Comm Coll–Columbus (IN)
Ivy Tech Comm Coll–East Central (IN)
Ivy Tech Comm Coll–Kokomo (IN)
Ivy Tech Comm Coll–Lafayette (IN)
Ivy Tech Comm Coll–North Central (IN)
Ivy Tech Comm Coll–Northeast (IN)
Ivy Tech Comm Coll–Northwest (IN)
Ivy Tech Comm Coll–Richmond (IN)
Ivy Tech Comm Coll–Southeast (IN)
Ivy Tech Comm Coll–Southern Indiana (IN)
Ivy Tech Comm Coll–Southwest (IN)
Ivy Tech Comm Coll–Wabash Valley (IN)
John Tyler Comm Coll (VA)
J. Sargeant Reynolds Comm Coll (VA)
Kent State U at Ashtabula (OH)
Kent State U at Salem (OH)
Kent State U at Trumbull (OH)
Kent State U at Tuscarawas (OH)
Kirtland Comm Coll (MI)
Lake Michigan Coll (MI)
Lanier Tech Coll (GA)
Lincoln Land Comm Coll (IL)
Macomb Comm Coll (MI)
Manchester Comm Coll (CT)
Miami Dade Coll (FL)
Mineral Area Coll (MO)
Missouri State U–West Plains (MO)
Monroe Comm Coll (NY)
Monroe County Comm Coll (MI)
Montcalm Comm Coll (MI)
Moraine Park Tech Coll (WI)
Muskegon Comm Coll (MI)
North Georgia Tech Coll (GA)
Northwest Tech Coll (MN)
Oakland Comm Coll (MI)
Olympic Coll (WA)
Owens Comm Coll, Toledo (OH)
Panola Coll (TX)
Penn State York (PA)
Red Rocks Comm Coll (CO)
San Diego City Coll (CA)
San Joaquin Valley Coll, Fresno (CA)
San Joaquin Valley Coll, Salida (CA)
San Joaquin Valley Coll, Visalia (CA)
San Juan Coll (NM)
Savannah Tech Coll (GA)
Seminole State Coll of Florida (FL)
Southeast Tech Inst (SD)
Southern Crescent Tech Coll (GA)
South Georgia Tech Coll (GA)
Stark State Coll (OH)
Three Rivers Comm Coll (CT)
Trident Tech Coll (SC)
Valencia Coll (FL)
West Georgia Tech Coll (GA)

INFORMATION RESOURCES MANAGEMENT
Rasmussen Coll Fort Myers (FL)
Rasmussen Coll New Port Richey (FL)
Rasmussen Coll Ocala (FL)

INFORMATION SCIENCE/ STUDIES
Altamaha Tech Coll (GA)
Amarillo Coll (TX)
Arkansas State U–Mountain Home (AR)
Athens Tech Coll (GA)
Augusta Tech Coll (GA)
Bainbridge Coll (GA)
Beaufort County Comm Coll (NC)
Brookhaven Coll (TX)
Bucks County Comm Coll (PA)
Cayuga County Comm Coll (NY)
Cecil Coll (MD)
Central Carolina Comm Coll (NC)
Central Georgia Tech Coll (GA)
Chattahoochee Tech Coll (GA)
Cochise Coll, Sierra Vista (AZ)
Columbus Tech Coll (GA)
Dakota Coll at Bottineau (ND)
Dutchess Comm Coll (NY)
Dyersburg State Comm Coll (TN)
Eastern Arizona Coll (AZ)
El Centro Coll (TX)
Fayetteville Tech Comm Coll (NC)
Fiorello H. LaGuardia Comm Coll of the City U of New York (NY)
Florida State Coll at Jacksonville (FL)
Genesee Comm Coll (NY)
Georgia Northwestern Tech Coll (GA)
Georgia Piedmont Tech Coll (GA)
Guilford Tech Comm Coll (NC)
Gwinnett Tech Coll (GA)
Howard Comm Coll (MD)
Indian River State Coll (FL)
Kankakee Comm Coll (IL)
Kaskaskia Coll (IL)
Kirtland Comm Coll (MI)
Lanier Tech Coll (GA)
Los Angeles Harbor Coll (CA)
Manchester Comm Coll (CT)
Massachusetts Bay Comm Coll (MA)
Mendocino Coll (CA)
Metropolitan Comm Coll–Blue River (MO)
Metropolitan Comm Coll–Business & Technology Campus (MO)
Miami Dade Coll (FL)
Middle Georgia Tech Coll (GA)
Mid Michigan Comm Coll (MI)
Monroe Comm Coll (NY)
Montgomery County Comm Coll (PA)
Moultrie Tech Coll (GA)
Murray State Coll (OK)
Muskegon Comm Coll (MI)
Niagara County Comm Coll (NY)
North Shore Comm Coll (MA)
Northwestern Connecticut Comm Coll (CT)
Oconee Fall Line Tech Coll–North Campus (GA)
Ogeechee Tech Coll (GA)
Okefenokee Tech Coll (GA)
Oklahoma State U, Oklahoma City (OK)
Orange Coast Coll (CA)
Ozarka Coll (AR)
Panola Coll (TX)
Penn State DuBois (PA)
Penn State Hazleton (PA)
Penn State Lehigh Valley (PA)
Penn State New Kensington (PA)
Penn State Schuylkill (PA)
Pensacola State Coll (FL)
Polk State Coll (FL)
Reedley Coll (CA)
Salt Lake Comm Coll (UT)
Scottsdale Comm Coll (AZ)
Seminole State Coll of Florida (FL)
Shawnee Comm Coll (IL)
Snow Coll (UT)
Southeastern Comm Coll (IA)
Southeastern Tech Coll (GA)
South Georgia Tech Coll (GA)

INFORMATION TECHNOLOGY
Atlanta Tech Coll (GA)
Blue Ridge Comm and Tech Coll (WV)
Burlington County Coll (NJ)
Catawba Valley Comm Coll (NC)
Cecil Coll (MD)
Central Carolina Comm Coll (NC)
Chandler-Gilbert Comm Coll (AZ)
City Colls of Chicago, Harry S. Truman College (IL)
Coll of Central Florida (FL)
Coll of Southern Maryland (MD)
Comm Coll of Vermont (VT)
Corning Comm Coll (NY)
Dakota Coll at Bottineau (ND)
Erie Comm Coll, North Campus (NY)
Erie Comm Coll, South Campus (NY)
Fayetteville Tech Comm Coll (NC)
Florida State Coll at Jacksonville (FL)
Fountainhead Coll of Technology (TN)
Guilford Tech Comm Coll (NC)
Highland Comm Coll (IL)
Howard Comm Coll (MD)
Illinois Eastern Comm Colls, Frontier Community College (IL)
Illinois Valley Comm Coll (IL)
Iowa Lakes Comm Coll (IA)
ITI Tech Coll (LA)
James Sprunt Comm Coll (NC)
Jamestown Comm Coll (NY)
John Tyler Comm Coll (VA)
Kilian Comm Coll (SD)
Lake Region State Coll (ND)
McHenry County Coll (IL)
Metropolitan Comm Coll–Business & Technology Campus (MO)
Missouri State U–West Plains (MO)
Mohave Comm Coll (AZ)
Monroe Comm Coll (NY)
Monroe County Comm Coll (MI)
Montana State U–Great Falls Coll of Technology (MT)
New Mexico State U–Alamogordo (NM)
Northwest Florida State Coll (FL)
Oklahoma State U, Oklahoma City (OK)
Owensboro Comm and Tech Coll (KY)
Owens Comm Coll, Toledo (OH)
Pasco-Hernando Comm Coll (FL)
Randolph Comm Coll (NC)
Raritan Valley Comm Coll (NJ)
Rockingham Comm Coll (NC)
Salt Lake Comm Coll (UT)
Savannah Tech Coll (GA)
Seminole State Coll of Florida (FL)
South Suburban Coll (IL)
Southwestern Illinois Coll (IL)
Southwest Mississippi Comm Coll (MS)
Stark State Coll (OH)
Sullivan Coll of Technology and Design (KY)
Texas State Tech Coll Harlingen (TX)
Tyler Jr Coll (TX)
Union County Coll (NJ)
Valencia Coll (FL)
West Virginia Northern Comm Coll (WV)
Wilson Comm Coll (NC)

INFORMATION TECHNOLOGY PROJECT MANAGEMENT
ITT Tech Inst, Kansas City (MO)

INSTITUTIONAL FOOD WORKERS
Bucks County Comm Coll (PA)
El Paso Comm Coll (TX)

Southwest Georgia Tech Coll (GA)
State Coll of Florida Manatee-Sarasota (FL)
Sullivan County Comm Coll (NY)
Tompkins Cortland Comm Coll (NY)
Tunxis Comm Coll (CT)
Union County Coll (NJ)
Westchester Comm Coll (NY)
West Georgia Tech Coll (GA)
Wytheville Comm Coll (VA)

Iowa Lakes Comm Coll (IA)
James Sprunt Comm Coll (NC)
San Jacinto Coll District (TX)
Southwestern Indian Polytechnic - Inst (NM)
Texas State Tech Coll Harlingen (TX)

INSTRUMENTATION TECHNOLOGY
Amarillo Coll (TX)
Cape Fear Comm Coll (NC)
Central Carolina Comm Coll (NC)
Florida State Coll at Jacksonville (FL)
Fox Valley Tech Coll (WI)
Georgia Piedmont Tech Coll (GA)
Houston Comm Coll System (TX)
ITI Tech Coll (LA)
Lower Columbia Coll (WA)
Monroe Comm Coll (NY)
Moraine Valley Comm Coll (IL)
St. Cloud Tech & Comm Coll (MN)
Salt Lake Comm Coll (UT)
San Jacinto Coll District (TX)
San Juan Coll (NM)
Southwestern Indian Polytechnic Inst (NM)

INSURANCE
Comm Coll of Allegheny County (PA)
Florida State Coll at Jacksonville (FL)
San Diego City Coll (CA)

INTELLIGENCE
Cochise Coll, Sierra Vista (AZ)

INTERDISCIPLINARY STUDIES
North Shore Comm Coll (MA)

INTERIOR ARCHITECTURE
State U of New York Coll of Technology at Alfred (NY)

INTERIOR DESIGN
Amarillo Coll (TX)
The Art Inst of New York City (NY)
The Art Inst of Ohio–Cincinnati (OH)
The Art Inst of Seattle (WA)
The Art Inst of York–Pennsylvania (PA)
Cape Fear Comm Coll (NC)
Century Coll (MN)
Clary Sage Coll (OK)
Coll of DuPage (IL)
Coll of the Canyons (CA)
Delaware Tech & Comm Coll, Terry Campus (DE)
El Centro Coll (TX)
El Paso Comm Coll (TX)
Fashion Inst of Technology (NY)
Florida State Coll at Jacksonville (FL)
Fox Valley Tech Coll (WI)
Front Range Comm Coll (CO)
Gateway Tech Coll (WI)
Gwinnett Tech Coll (GA)
Harford Comm Coll (MD)
Harper Coll (IL)
Hawkeye Comm Coll (IA)
Highline Comm Coll (WA)
Houston Comm Coll System (TX)
Indian River State Coll (FL)
Ivy Tech Comm Coll–North Central (IN)
Ivy Tech Comm Coll–Southwest (IN)
Lanier Tech Coll (GA)
Lehigh Carbon Comm Coll (PA)
Miami Dade Coll (FL)
Monroe Comm Coll (NY)
Montana State U–Great Falls Coll of Technology (MT)
Montgomery Coll (MD)
Northampton Comm Coll (PA)
Northwest Florida State Coll (FL)
Oakland Comm Coll (MI)
Ogeechee Tech Coll (GA)
Onondaga Comm Coll (NY)
Orange Coast Coll (CA)
Palm Beach State Coll (FL)
Randolph Comm Coll (NC)
Raritan Valley Comm Coll (NJ)
Red Rocks Comm Coll (CO)

San Diego City Coll (CA)
San Jacinto Coll District (TX)
Santa Monica Coll (CA)
Santa Rosa Jr Coll (CA)
Scottsdale Comm Coll (AZ)
Seminole State Coll of Florida (FL)
State U of New York Coll of
  Technology at Alfred (NY)
Sullivan Coll of Technology and
  Design (KY)
Waukesha County Tech Coll (WI)
Western Iowa Tech Comm Coll (IA)

INTERMEDIA/MULTIMEDIA
Coll of the Canyons (CA)

INTERNATIONAL BUSINESS/ TRADE/COMMERCE
Austin Comm Coll (TX)
Bunker Hill Comm Coll (MA)
El Paso Comm Coll (TX)
Foothill Coll (CA)
Harper Coll (IL)
Highline Comm Coll (WA)
Houston Comm Coll System (TX)
Lansing Comm Coll (MI)
Monroe Comm Coll (NY)
Northeast Comm Coll (NE)
Oakland Comm Coll (MI)
Owens Comm Coll, Toledo (OH)
Raritan Valley Comm Coll (NJ)
San Jacinto Coll District (TX)
Stark State Coll (OH)
Tompkins Cortland Comm Coll
  (NY)
Westchester Comm Coll (NY)

INTERNATIONAL/GLOBAL STUDIES
Berkshire Comm Coll (MA)
Burlington County Coll (NJ)
Central Wyoming Coll (WY)
Macomb Comm Coll (MI)
Oakland Comm Coll (MI)
Salt Lake Comm Coll (UT)

INTERNATIONAL MARKETING
Waukesha County Tech Coll (WI)

INTERNATIONAL RELATIONS AND AFFAIRS
Casper Coll (WY)
Lansing Comm Coll (MI)
Massachusetts Bay Comm Coll
  (MA)
Miami Dade Coll (FL)
Northern Essex Comm Coll (MA)
Northwest Coll (WY)
Salt Lake Comm Coll (UT)

IRONWORKING
GateWay Comm Coll (AZ)
Ivy Tech Comm Coll–Lafayette (IN)
Ivy Tech Comm Coll–North Central
  (IN)
Ivy Tech Comm Coll–Northeast (IN)
Ivy Tech Comm Coll–Northwest
  (IN)
Ivy Tech Comm Coll–Southwest
  (IN)
Ivy Tech Comm Coll–Wabash
  Valley (IN)
Southwestern Illinois Coll (IL)

ITALIAN
Miami Dade Coll (FL)

JAPANESE
Austin Comm Coll (TX)
Foothill Coll (CA)
Snow Coll (UT)

JAZZ/JAZZ STUDIES
Comm Coll of Rhode Island (RI)
Iowa Lakes Comm Coll (IA)
State Coll of Florida Manatee-
  Sarasota (FL)

JEWISH/JUDAIC STUDIES
State Coll of Florida Manatee-
  Sarasota (FL)

JOURNALISM
Amarillo Coll (TX)
Austin Comm Coll (TX)
Bainbridge Coll (GA)
Bucks County Comm Coll (PA)
Burlington County Coll (NJ)
Carl Albert State Coll (OK)
Cochise Coll, Sierra Vista (AZ)
Coll of the Canyons (CA)
Comm Coll of Allegheny County
  (PA)
Copiah-Lincoln Comm Coll (MS)
Cowley County Comm Coll and
  Area Vocational–Tech School
  (KS)
Delaware County Comm Coll (PA)
Georgia Highlands Coll (GA)
Highline Comm Coll (WA)
Housatonic Comm Coll (CT)
Illinois Valley Comm Coll (IL)
Indian River State Coll (FL)
Iowa Lakes Comm Coll (IA)
Kilgore Coll (TX)
Kingsborough Comm Coll of the
  City U of New York (NY)
Manchester Comm Coll (CT)
Miami Dade Coll (FL)
Monroe County Comm Coll (MI)
Northampton Comm Coll (PA)
Northeast Comm Coll (NE)
Northeastern Jr Coll (CO)
Northern Essex Comm Coll (MA)
Northwest Coll (WY)
Orange Coast Coll (CA)
Palm Beach State Coll (FL)
Pensacola State Coll (FL)
St. Clair County Comm Coll (MI)
San Diego City Coll (CA)
San Jacinto Coll District (TX)
Santa Monica Coll (CA)
State Coll of Florida Manatee-
  Sarasota (FL)
Texarkana Coll (TX)
Umpqua Comm Coll (OR)
Vincennes U (IN)

JUVENILE CORRECTIONS
Illinois Valley Comm Coll (IL)
Kaskaskia Coll (IL)
Lansing Comm Coll (MI)

KEYBOARD INSTRUMENTS
Iowa Lakes Comm Coll (IA)

KINDERGARTEN/PRESCHOOL EDUCATION
Bainbridge Coll (GA)
Beaufort County Comm Coll (NC)
Carroll Comm Coll (MD)
Casper Coll (WY)
Cecil Coll (MD)
Central Carolina Comm Coll (NC)
Cleveland State Comm Coll (TN)
Comm Coll of Philadelphia (PA)
Comm Coll of Rhode Island (RI)
Delaware Tech & Comm Coll, Jack
  F. Owens Campus (DE)
Delaware Tech & Comm Coll,
  Stanton/Wilmington Campus
  (DE)
Delaware Tech & Comm Coll, Terry
  Campus (DE)
Denmark Tech Coll (SC)
Dutchess Comm Coll (NY)
El Paso Comm Coll (TX)
Gateway Comm Coll (CT)
Genesee Comm Coll (NY)
Highline Comm Coll (WA)
Howard Comm Coll (MD)
Indian River State Coll (FL)
Iowa Lakes Comm Coll (IA)
Jamestown Comm Coll (NY)
Johnston Comm Coll (NC)
Kent State U at Ashtabula (OH)
Manchester Comm Coll (CT)
Mendocino Coll (CA)
Metropolitan Comm Coll–Penn
  Valley (MO)
Miami Dade Coll (FL)
Northeastern Jr Coll (CO)
Northern Essex Comm Coll (MA)
North Shore Comm Coll (MA)
Northwest Coll (WY)
Northwestern Connecticut Comm
  Coll (CT)
Northwest Florida State Coll (FL)

Orange Coast Coll (CA)
Otero Jr Coll (CO)
Owensboro Comm and Tech Coll
  (KY)
Palm Beach State Coll (FL)
Quinsigamond Comm Coll (MA)
Raritan Valley Comm Coll (NJ)
St. Clair County Comm Coll (MI)
San Jacinto Coll District (TX)
Scottsdale Comm Coll (AZ)
Snow Coll (UT)
Southern State Comm Coll (OH)
State Coll of Florida Manatee-
  Sarasota (FL)
Sullivan County Comm Coll (NY)
Tallahassee Comm Coll (FL)
Terra State Comm Coll (OH)
Three Rivers Comm Coll (CT)
Tompkins Cortland Comm Coll
  (NY)
Tunxis Comm Coll (CT)
Umpqua Comm Coll (OR)
Virginia Western Comm Coll (VA)

KINESIOLOGY AND EXERCISE SCIENCE
Carroll Comm Coll (MD)
Central Oregon Comm Coll (OR)
Chandler-Gilbert Comm Coll (AZ)
Delaware Tech & Comm Coll,
  Stanton/Wilmington Campus
  (DE)
Oakland Comm Coll (MI)
Orange Coast Coll (CA)
Raritan Valley Comm Coll (NJ)
St. Philip's Coll (TX)
Salt Lake Comm Coll (UT)
South Suburban Coll (IL)

LABOR AND INDUSTRIAL RELATIONS
The Comm Coll of Baltimore
  County (MD)
Kingsborough Comm Coll of the
  City U of New York (NY)
San Diego City Coll (CA)

LANDSCAPE ARCHITECTURE
Monroe Comm Coll (NY)
Truckee Meadows Comm Coll (NV)

LANDSCAPING AND GROUNDSKEEPING
Cape Fear Comm Coll (NC)
Century Coll (MN)
Clark Coll (WA)
Coll of Central Florida (FL)
Coll of DuPage (IL)
Coll of Lake County (IL)
Coll of the Canyons (CA)
Comm Coll of Allegheny County
  (PA)
Dakota Coll at Bottineau (ND)
Grand Rapids Comm Coll (MI)
Hillsborough Comm Coll (FL)
Illinois Valley Comm Coll (IL)
Iowa Lakes Comm Coll (IA)
Johnston Comm Coll (NC)
Lake Michigan Coll (MI)
Lincoln Land Comm Coll (IL)
Miami Dade Coll (FL)
Oakland Comm Coll (MI)
Owens Comm Coll, Toledo (OH)
Pensacola State Coll (FL)
St. Clair County Comm Coll (MI)
San Juan Coll (NM)
Santa Rosa Jr Coll (CA)
Springfield Tech Comm Coll (MA)

LAND USE PLANNING AND MANAGEMENT
Colorado Mountain Coll, Timberline
  Campus (CO)

LANGUAGE INTERPRETATION AND TRANSLATION
Century Coll (MN)
Indian River State Coll (FL)
Oklahoma State U, Oklahoma City
  (OK)
Terra State Comm Coll (OH)
Union County Coll (NJ)

LASER AND OPTICAL TECHNOLOGY
Amarillo Coll (TX)
Central Carolina Comm Coll (NC)
Monroe Comm Coll (NY)
Springfield Tech Comm Coll (MA)
Three Rivers Comm Coll (CT)

LATIN
Austin Comm Coll (TX)

LATIN AMERICAN STUDIES
Miami Dade Coll (FL)
San Diego City Coll (CA)
Santa Rosa Jr Coll (CA)
State Coll of Florida Manatee-
  Sarasota (FL)

LEGAL ADMINISTRATIVE ASSISTANT/SECRETARY
Alvin Comm Coll (TX)
Amarillo Coll (TX)
Blackhawk Tech Coll (WI)
Bradford School (OH)
Bradford School (PA)
Career Tech Coll (LA)
Central Carolina Comm Coll (NC)
Clark Coll (WA)
Coll of DuPage (IL)
Coll of the Ouachitas (AR)
Comm Coll of Allegheny County
  (PA)
Comm Coll of Rhode Island (RI)
Consolidated School of Business,
  York (PA)
Cowley County Comm Coll and
  Area Vocational–Tech School
  (KS)
Crowder Coll (MO)
Delaware Tech & Comm Coll, Jack
  F. Owens Campus (DE)
Delaware Tech & Comm Coll, Terry
  Campus (DE)
Edison Comm Coll (OH)
El Centro Coll (TX)
Forrest Coll (SC)
Gateway Comm Coll (CT)
Georgia Piedmont Tech Coll (GA)
Harper Coll (IL)
Highline Comm Coll (WA)
Howard Comm Coll (MD)
Inst of Business & Medical Careers
  (CO)
International Business Coll,
  Indianapolis (IN)
Iowa Lakes Comm Coll (IA)
John Wood Comm Coll (IL)
Kent State U at Ashtabula (OH)
Kent State U at East Liverpool (OH)
King's Coll (NC)
Kirtland Comm Coll (MI)
Lake Michigan Coll (MI)
Lake Region State Coll (ND)
Lincoln Land Comm Coll (IL)
Los Angeles Harbor Coll (CA)
Lower Columbia Coll (WA)
Manchester Comm Coll (CT)
Metropolitan Comm Coll–Longview
  (MO)
Metropolitan Comm Coll–Maple
  Woods (MO)
Metropolitan Comm Coll–Penn
  Valley (MO)
Miami Dade Coll (FL)
Mid Michigan Comm Coll (MI)
Minneapolis Business Coll (MN)
Minnesota State Coll–Southeast
  Tech (MN)
Monroe Comm Coll (NY)
Monroe County Comm Coll (MI)
Moraine Park Tech Coll (WI)
Muskegon Comm Coll (MI)
Northampton Comm Coll (PA)
Northeast Comm Coll (NE)
Northeastern Jr Coll (CO)
North Shore Comm Coll (MA)
Otero Jr Coll (CO)
Palm Beach State Coll (FL)
Pensacola State Coll (FL)
St. Cloud Tech & Comm Coll (MN)
St. Philip's Coll (TX)
San Diego City Coll (CA)
Santa Monica Coll (CA)
Shawnee Comm Coll (IL)
Southwestern Illinois Coll (IL)

Southwest Mississippi Comm Coll
  (MS)
Stark State Coll (OH)
Tallahassee Comm Coll (FL)
Three Rivers Comm Coll (CT)
Tunxis Comm Coll (CT)
Tyler Jr Coll (TX)
Umpqua Comm Coll (OR)
The U of Montana–Helena Coll of
  Technology (MT)
Valencia Coll (FL)
Western Iowa Tech Comm Coll (IA)

LEGAL ASSISTANT/ PARALEGAL
Alvin Comm Coll (TX)
Anne Arundel Comm Coll (MD)
Athens Tech Coll (GA)
Atlanta Tech Coll (GA)
Austin Comm Coll (TX)
Bevill State Comm Coll (AL)
Blue Ridge Comm and Tech Coll
  (WV)
Bradford School (OH)
Bradford School (PA)
Bucks County Comm Coll (PA)
Bunker Hill Comm Coll (MA)
Burlington County Coll (NJ)
Casper Coll (WY)
Central Carolina Comm Coll (NC)
Central Carolina Tech Coll (SC)
Central Comm Coll–Grand Island
  Campus (NE)
Central Georgia Tech Coll (GA)
Chattanooga State Comm Coll
  (TN)
Chippewa Valley Tech Coll (WI)
Clark Coll (WA)
Coll of Southern Maryland (MD)
Coll of the Canyons (CA)
Coll of the Ouachitas (AR)
Comm Care Coll (OK)
Comm Coll of Allegheny County
  (PA)
The Comm Coll of Baltimore
  County (MD)
Comm Coll of Rhode Island (RI)
Delaware County Comm Coll (PA)
Do&nna Ana Comm Coll (NM)
Dutchess Comm Coll (NY)
Eastern Idaho Tech Coll (ID)
Edison Comm Coll (OH)
El Centro Coll (TX)
Elgin Comm Coll (IL)
El Paso Comm Coll (TX)
Erie Comm Coll (NY)
ETI Tech Coll of Niles (OH)
Fayetteville Tech Comm Coll (NC)
Fiorello H. LaGuardia Comm Coll
  of the City U of New York (NY)
Florida State Coll at Jacksonville
  (FL)
Forrest Coll (SC)
Front Range Comm Coll (CO)
Gadsden State Comm Coll (AL)
Genesee Comm Coll (NY)
Georgia Northwestern Tech Coll
  (GA)
Georgia Piedmont Tech Coll (GA)
Guilford Tech Comm Coll (NC)
Gulf Coast State Coll (FL)
Harford Comm Coll (MD)
Harper Coll (IL)
Hesser Coll, Manchester (NH)
Hesser Coll, Portsmouth (NH)
Highline Comm Coll (WA)
Hillsborough Comm Coll (FL)
Houston Comm Coll System (TX)
Hutchinson Comm Coll and Area
  Vocational School (KS)
Illinois Central Coll (IL)
Illinois Eastern Comm Colls,
  Wabash Valley College (IL)
Indian River State Coll (FL)
Inst of Business & Medical Careers
  (CO)
International Business Coll,
  Indianapolis (IN)
Iowa Lakes Comm Coll (IA)
ITT Tech Inst, Bessemer (AL)
ITT Tech Inst, Madison (AL)
ITT Tech Inst, Mobile (AL)
ITT Tech Inst, Phoenix (AZ)
ITT Tech Inst, Tucson (AZ)
ITT Tech Inst (AR)
ITT Tech Inst, Lathrop (CA)

ITT Tech Inst, Orange (CA)
ITT Tech Inst, Oxnard (CA)
ITT Tech Inst, Rancho Cordova (CA)
ITT Tech Inst, San Bernardino (CA)
ITT Tech Inst, San Diego (CA)
ITT Tech Inst, San Dimas (CA)
ITT Tech Inst, Sylmar (CA)
ITT Tech Inst, Torrance (CA)
ITT Tech Inst, Aurora (CO)
ITT Tech Inst, Thornton (CO)
ITT Tech Inst, Fort Lauderdale (FL)
ITT Tech Inst, Fort Myers (FL)
ITT Tech Inst, Jacksonville (FL)
ITT Tech Inst, Lake Mary (FL)
ITT Tech Inst, Miami (FL)
ITT Tech Inst, Pinellas Park (FL)
ITT Tech Inst, Tallahassee (FL)
ITT Tech Inst, Atlanta (GA)
ITT Tech Inst, Duluth (GA)
ITT Tech Inst, Kennesaw (GA)
ITT Tech Inst (ID)
ITT Tech Inst, Mount Prospect (IL)
ITT Tech Inst, Oak Brook (IL)
ITT Tech Inst, Orland Park (IL)
ITT Tech Inst, Fort Wayne (IN)
ITT Tech Inst, Merrillville (IN)
ITT Tech Inst, Newburgh (IN)
ITT Tech Inst, Cedar Rapids (IA)
ITT Tech Inst, Clive (IA)
ITT Tech Inst, Louisville (KY)
ITT Tech Inst, Baton Rouge (LA)
ITT Tech Inst, St. Rose (LA)
ITT Tech Inst, Canton (MI)
ITT Tech Inst, Swartz Creek (MI)
ITT Tech Inst, Troy (MI)
ITT Tech Inst, Wyoming (MI)
ITT Tech Inst, Eden Prairie (MN)
ITT Tech Inst, Arnold (MO)
ITT Tech Inst, Earth City (MO)
ITT Tech Inst, Kansas City (MO)
ITT Tech Inst (NE)
ITT Tech Inst, Henderson (NV)
ITT Tech Inst (NM)
ITT Tech Inst, Akron (OH)
ITT Tech Inst, Columbus (OH)
ITT Tech Inst, Dayton (OH)
ITT Tech Inst, Hilliard (OH)
ITT Tech Inst, Maumee (OH)
ITT Tech Inst, Norwood (OH)
ITT Tech Inst, Strongsville (OH)
ITT Tech Inst, Warrensville Heights (OH)
ITT Tech Inst, Youngstown (OH)
ITT Tech Inst, Tulsa (OK)
ITT Tech Inst, Portland (OR)
ITT Tech Inst, Columbia (SC)
ITT Tech Inst, Greenville (SC)
ITT Tech Inst, Chattanooga (TN)
ITT Tech Inst, Cordova (TN)
ITT Tech Inst, Johnson City (TN)
ITT Tech Inst, Knoxville (TN)
ITT Tech Inst, Nashville (TN)
ITT Tech Inst, Arlington (TX)
ITT Tech Inst, Austin (TX)
ITT Tech Inst, DeSoto (TX)
ITT Tech Inst, Houston (TX)
ITT Tech Inst, Houston (TX)
ITT Tech Inst, Richardson (TX)
ITT Tech Inst, San Antonio (TX)
ITT Tech Inst, Webster (TX)
ITT Tech Inst (UT)
ITT Tech Inst, Chantilly (VA)
ITT Tech Inst, Norfolk (VA)
ITT Tech Inst, Richmond (VA)
ITT Tech Inst, Salem (VA)
ITT Tech Inst, Springfield (VA)
ITT Tech Inst, Everett (WA)
ITT Tech Inst, Seattle (WA)
ITT Tech Inst, Spokane Valley (WA)
ITT Tech Inst (WV)
ITT Tech Inst, Green Bay (WI)
ITT Tech Inst, Greenfield (WI)
ITT Tech Inst, Madison (WI)
Ivy Tech Comm Coll–Bloomington (IN)
Ivy Tech Comm Coll–Central Indiana (IN)
Ivy Tech Comm Coll–Columbus (IN)
Ivy Tech Comm Coll–East Central (IN)
Ivy Tech Comm Coll–Kokomo (IN)
Ivy Tech Comm Coll–Lafayette (IN)
Ivy Tech Comm Coll–North Central (IN)
Ivy Tech Comm Coll–Northeast (IN)
Ivy Tech Comm Coll–Northwest (IN)
Ivy Tech Comm Coll–Richmond (IN)

Ivy Tech Comm Coll–Southeast (IN)
Ivy Tech Comm Coll–Southern Indiana (IN)
Ivy Tech Comm Coll–Southwest (IN)
Ivy Tech Comm Coll–Wabash Valley (IN)
Jefferson Comm Coll (NY)
Johnston Comm Coll (NC)
Kankakee Comm Coll (IL)
Kansas City Kansas Comm Coll (KS)
Kaplan Career Inst, Nashville Campus (TN)
Kaplan Coll, Dallas Campus (TX)
Kaplan Coll, San Antonio Campus (TX)
Kent State U at East Liverpool (OH)
Kent State U at Trumbull (OH)
Kilgore Coll (TX)
King's Coll (NC)
Lake Region State Coll (ND)
Lansing Comm Coll (MI)
Laramie County Comm Coll (WY)
Lehigh Carbon Comm Coll (PA)
Macomb Comm Coll (MI)
Manchester Comm Coll (CT)
Massachusetts Bay Comm Coll (MA)
Metropolitan Comm Coll–Penn Valley (MO)
Miami Dade Coll (FL)
Minneapolis Business Coll (MN)
Minnesota School of Business– Brooklyn Center (MN)
Minnesota School of Business– Richfield (MN)
Minnesota School of Business–St. Cloud (MN)
Minnesota School of Business– Shakopee (MN)
Missouri State U–West Plains (MO)
Mohave Comm Coll (AZ)
Montgomery Coll (MD)
Moraine Park Tech Coll (WI)
Mount Wachusett Comm Coll (MA)
MTI Coll, Sacramento (CA)
New Mexico State U–Alamogordo (NM)
New York Career Inst (NY)
Northampton Comm Coll (PA)
Northern Essex Comm Coll (MA)
North Hennepin Comm Coll (MN)
North Shore Comm Coll (MA)
Northwestern Connecticut Comm Coll (CT)
Northwest Florida State Coll (FL)
Oakland Comm Coll (MI)
Ogeechee Tech Coll (GA)
Pasco-Hernando Comm Coll (FL)
Pensacola State Coll (FL)
Raritan Valley Comm Coll (NJ)
Rasmussen Coll Aurora (IL)
Rasmussen Coll Bismarck (ND)
Rasmussen Coll Bloomington (MN)
Rasmussen Coll Brooklyn Park (MN)
Rasmussen Coll Eagan (MN)
Rasmussen Coll Fargo (ND)
Rasmussen Coll Fort Myers (FL)
Rasmussen Coll Green Bay (WI)
Rasmussen Coll Lake Elmo/ Woodbury (MN)
Rasmussen Coll Mankato (MN)
Rasmussen Coll Moorhead (MN)
Rasmussen Coll New Port Richey (FL)
Rasmussen Coll Ocala (FL)
Rasmussen Coll Rockford (IL)
Rasmussen Coll St. Cloud (MN)
Salt Lake Comm Coll (UT)
San Diego City Coll (CA)
San Jacinto Coll District (TX)
San Juan Coll (NM)
Santa Rosa Jr Coll (CA)
Seminole State Coll of Florida (FL)
Southern Crescent Tech Coll (GA)
South Georgia Tech Coll (GA)
South Suburban Coll (IL)
Southwestern Illinois Coll (IL)
State Coll of Florida Manatee- Sarasota (FL)
Sullivan County Comm Coll (NY)
Tallahassee Comm Coll (FL)
Tarrant County Coll District (TX)
Tompkins Cortland Comm Coll (NY)
Trident Tech Coll (SC)
Truckee Meadows Comm Coll (NV)

Union County Coll (NJ)
Valencia Coll (FL)
Vincennes U (IN)
Volunteer State Comm Coll (TN)
Westchester Comm Coll (NY)
Western Dakota Tech Inst (SD)
Westmoreland County Comm Coll (PA)
West Virginia Northern Comm Coll (WV)
Wilson Comm Coll (NC)

LEGAL PROFESSIONS AND STUDIES RELATED
Bucks County Comm Coll (PA)

LEGAL STUDIES
Alvin Comm Coll (TX)
Carroll Comm Coll (MD)
Harford Comm Coll (MD)
Iowa Lakes Comm Coll (IA)
Macomb Comm Coll (MI)
Northwest Florida State Coll (FL)
Trident Tech Coll (SC)

LIBERAL ARTS AND SCIENCES AND HUMANITIES RELATED
Anne Arundel Comm Coll (MD)
Bucks County Comm Coll (PA)
Cascadia Comm Coll (WA)
Chandler-Gilbert Comm Coll (AZ)
Cleveland State Comm Coll (TN)
Coll of Southern Maryland (MD)
The Comm Coll of Baltimore County (MD)
Dakota Coll at Bottineau (ND)
Fayetteville Tech Comm Coll (NC)
Front Range Comm Coll (CO)
Garrett Coll (MD)
Guilford Tech Comm Coll (NC)
Hagerstown Comm Coll (MD)
Harford Comm Coll (MD)
Holyoke Comm Coll (MA)
Iowa Lakes Comm Coll (IA)
James Sprunt Comm Coll (NC)
Jamestown Comm Coll (NY)
Mohawk Valley Comm Coll (NY)
Montana State U–Great Falls Coll of Technology (MT)
Montgomery Coll (MD)
New Mexico State U–Alamogordo (NM)
Normandale Comm Coll (MN)
Northampton Comm Coll (PA)
Oakland Comm Coll (MI)
Onondaga Comm Coll (NY)
Randolph Comm Coll (NC)
Red Rocks Comm Coll (CO)
Southern Maine Comm Coll (ME)
West Virginia Northern Comm Coll (WV)
Wilson Comm Coll (NC)
York County Comm Coll (ME)

LIBERAL ARTS AND SCIENCES/ LIBERAL STUDIES
Aiken Tech Coll (SC)
Alvin Comm Coll (TX)
Amarillo Coll (TX)
Anne Arundel Comm Coll (MD)
Anoka-Ramsey Comm Coll (MN)
Anoka-Ramsey Comm Coll, Cambridge Campus (MN)
Arkansas State U–Mountain Home (AR)
Bainbridge Coll (GA)
Beaufort County Comm Coll (NC)
Berkeley City Coll (CA)
Berkshire Comm Coll (MA)
Bevill State Comm Coll (AL)
Big Bend Comm Coll (WA)
Bluegrass Comm and Tech Coll (KY)
Brookhaven Coll (TX)
Bucks County Comm Coll (PA)
Burlington County Coll (NJ)
Cape Fear Comm Coll (NC)
Carroll Comm Coll (MD)
Cascadia Comm Coll (WA)
Casper Coll (WY)
Catawba Valley Comm Coll (NC)
Cayuga County Comm Coll (NY)
Cecil Coll (MD)
Central Carolina Comm Coll (NC)
Central Carolina Tech Coll (SC)
Central Comm Coll–Columbus Campus (NE)

Central Comm Coll–Grand Island Campus (NE)
Central Comm Coll–Hastings Campus (NE)
Central Maine Comm Coll (ME)
Central Oregon Comm Coll (OR)
Century Coll (MN)
Chandler-Gilbert Comm Coll (AZ)
Chattahoochee Valley Comm Coll (AL)
Chattanooga State Comm Coll (TN)
Chipola Coll (FL)
Chippewa Valley Tech Coll (WI)
City Colls of Chicago, Harry S. Truman College (IL)
Clark Coll (WA)
Cleveland State Comm Coll (TN)
Clinton Comm Coll (NY)
Colby Comm Coll (KS)
Coll of Central Florida (FL)
Coll of DuPage (IL)
Coll of Lake County (IL)
Coll of Southern Maryland (MD)
Coll of the Canyons (CA)
Coll of the Ouachitas (AR)
Colorado Mountain Coll (CO)
Colorado Mountain Coll, Alpine Campus (CO)
Colorado Mountain Coll, Timberline Campus (CO)
Comm Coll of Allegheny County (PA)
The Comm Coll of Baltimore County (MD)
Comm Coll of Philadelphia (PA)
Comm Coll of Rhode Island (RI)
Comm Coll of Vermont (VT)
Copiah-Lincoln Comm Coll (MS)
Corning Comm Coll (NY)
Cowley County Comm Coll and Area Vocational-Tech School (KS)
Crowder Coll (MO)
Dakota Coll at Bottineau (ND)
Dawson Comm Coll (MT)
Deep Springs Coll (CA)
Delaware County Comm Coll (PA)
Dutchess Comm Coll (NY)
Dyersburg State Comm Coll (TN)
Eastern Arizona Coll (AZ)
Edison Comm Coll (OH)
Elgin Comm Coll (IL)
El Paso Comm Coll (TX)
Emory U, Oxford Coll (GA)
Erie Comm Coll (NY)
Erie Comm Coll, North Campus (NY)
Erie Comm Coll, South Campus (NY)
Fayetteville Tech Comm Coll (NC)
Fiorello H. LaGuardia Comm Coll of the City U of New York (NY)
Florida State Coll at Jacksonville (FL)
Foothill Coll (CA)
Front Range Comm Coll (CO)
Gadsden State Comm Coll (AL)
Garrett Coll (MD)
GateWay Comm Coll (AZ)
Gateway Comm Coll (CT)
Gavilan Coll (CA)
Genesee Comm Coll (NY)
Georgia Highlands Coll (GA)
Goodwin Coll (CT)
Grand Rapids Comm Coll (MI)
Guilford Tech Comm Coll (NC)
Gulf Coast State Coll (FL)
Hagerstown Comm Coll (MD)
Harford Comm Coll (MD)
Harper Coll (IL)
Hawkeye Comm Coll (IA)
Hesser Coll, Concord (NH)
Hesser Coll, Manchester (NH)
Hesser Coll, Nashua (NH)
Hesser Coll, Portsmouth (NH)
Hesser Coll, Salem (NH)
Highland Comm Coll (IL)
Hillsborough Comm Coll (FL)
Holyoke Comm Coll (MA)
Housatonic Comm Coll (CT)
Howard Comm Coll (MD)
Hutchinson Comm Coll and Area Vocational School (KS)
Illinois Central Coll (IL)
Illinois Eastern Comm Colls, Frontier Community College (IL)
Illinois Eastern Comm Colls, Lincoln Trail College (IL)

Illinois Eastern Comm Colls, Olney Central College (IL)
Illinois Eastern Comm Colls, Wabash Valley College (IL)
Illinois Valley Comm Coll (IL)
Indian River State Coll (FL)
Iowa Lakes Comm Coll (IA)
Itasca Comm Coll (MN)
Ivy Tech Comm Coll–Bloomington (IN)
Ivy Tech Comm Coll–Central Indiana (IN)
Ivy Tech Comm Coll–Columbus (IN)
Ivy Tech Comm Coll–East Central (IN)
Ivy Tech Comm Coll–Kokomo (IN)
Ivy Tech Comm Coll–Lafayette (IN)
Ivy Tech Comm Coll–North Central (IN)
Ivy Tech Comm Coll–Northeast (IN)
Ivy Tech Comm Coll–Northwest (IN)
Ivy Tech Comm Coll–Richmond (IN)
Ivy Tech Comm Coll–Southeast (IN)
Ivy Tech Comm Coll–Southern Indiana (IN)
Ivy Tech Comm Coll–Southwest (IN)
Ivy Tech Comm Coll–Wabash Valley (IN)
Jackson Comm Coll (MI)
James Sprunt Comm Coll (NC)
Jamestown Comm Coll (NY)
Jefferson State Comm Coll (AL)
Johnston Comm Coll (NC)
John Tyler Comm Coll (VA)
John Wood Comm Coll (IL)
J. Sargeant Reynolds Comm Coll (VA)
Kansas City Kansas Comm Coll (KS)
Kaskaskia Coll (IL)
Kent State U at Ashtabula (OH)
Kent State U at East Liverpool (OH)
Kent State U at Salem (OH)
Kent State U at Trumbull (OH)
Kent State U at Tuscarawas (OH)
Kilian Comm Coll (SD)
Kingsborough Comm Coll of the City U of New York (NY)
Kirtland Comm Coll (MI)
Lake Michigan Coll (MI)
Lake Region State Coll (ND)
Lansing Comm Coll (MI)
Lawson State Comm Coll (AL)
Lehigh Carbon Comm Coll (PA)
Lincoln Land Comm Coll (IL)
Los Angeles Harbor Coll (CA)
Lower Columbia Coll (WA)
Lurleen B. Wallace Comm Coll (AL)
Macomb Comm Coll (MI)
Manchester Comm Coll (CT)
Massachusetts Bay Comm Coll (MA)
McHenry County Coll (IL)
Mendocino Coll (CA)
Metropolitan Comm Coll–Blue River (MO)
Metropolitan Comm Coll–Business & Technology Campus (MO)
Metropolitan Comm Coll–Longview (MO)
Metropolitan Comm Coll–Maple Woods (MO)
Metropolitan Comm Coll–Penn Valley (MO)
Mid Michigan Comm Coll (MI)
Mid-Plains Comm Coll, North Platte (NE)
Mineral Area Coll (MO)
Minneapolis Comm and Tech Coll (MN)
Mohave Comm Coll (AZ)
Mohawk Valley Comm Coll (NY)
Monroe Comm Coll (NY)
Monroe County Comm Coll (MI)
Montcalm Comm Coll (MI)
Montgomery Coll (MD)
Montgomery Comm Coll (NC)
Montgomery County Comm Coll (PA)
Moraine Valley Comm Coll (IL)
Motlow State Comm Coll (TN)
Mott Comm Coll (MI)
Mount Wachusett Comm Coll (MA)
Muskegon Comm Coll (MI)
Niagara County Comm Coll (NY)
Normandale Comm Coll (MN)
Northampton Comm Coll (PA)

North Dakota State Coll of Science (ND)
Northeast Comm Coll (NE)
Northeastern Jr Coll (CO)
Northeast Iowa Comm Coll (IA)
Northern Essex Comm Coll (MA)
North Hennepin Comm Coll (MN)
North Seattle Comm Coll (WA)
North Shore Comm Coll (MA)
Northwest Coll (WY)
Northwestern Connecticut Comm Coll (CT)
Northwest Florida State Coll (FL)
Northwest-Shoals Comm Coll (AL)
Oakland Comm Coll (MI)
Ocean County Coll (NJ)
Oklahoma City Comm Coll (OK)
Orange Coast Coll (CA)
Otero Jr Coll (CO)
Owensboro Comm and Tech Coll (KY)
Ozarka Coll (AR)
Palau Comm Coll (Palau)
Palm Beach State Coll (FL)
Pasco-Hernando Comm Coll (FL)
Penn State Beaver (PA)
Penn State Brandywine (PA)
Penn State DuBois (PA)
Penn State Fayette, The Eberly Campus (PA)
Penn State Greater Allegheny (PA)
Penn State Hazleton (PA)
Penn State Lehigh Valley (PA)
Penn State Mont Alto (PA)
Penn State New Kensington (PA)
Penn State Schuylkill (PA)
Penn State Shenango (PA)
Penn State Wilkes-Barre (PA)
Penn State Worthington Scranton (PA)
Penn State York (PA)
Pensacola State Coll (FL)
Piedmont Virginia Comm Coll (VA)
Polk State Coll (FL)
Quinsigamond Comm Coll (MA)
Rainy River Comm Coll (MN)
Randolph Comm Coll (NC)
Raritan Valley Comm Coll (NJ)
Red Rocks Comm Coll (CO)
Reedley Coll (CA)
Rockingham Comm Coll (NC)
Rockland Comm Coll (NY)
Rogue Comm Coll (OR)
St. Clair County Comm Coll (MI)
St. Philip's Coll (TX)
Salem Comm Coll (NJ)
San Diego City Coll (CA)
San Juan Coll (NM)
Santa Monica Coll (CA)
Santa Rosa Jr Coll (CA)
Seminole State Coll of Florida (FL)
Shawnee Comm Coll (IL)
Snow Coll (UT)
Southeastern Comm Coll (IA)
Southern State Comm Coll (OH)
South Suburban Coll (IL)
Southwestern Illinois Coll (IL)
Southwestern Indian Polytechnic Inst (NM)
Southwestern Michigan Coll (MI)
Southwest Mississippi Comm Coll (MS)
Southwest Virginia Comm Coll (VA)
Springfield Tech Comm Coll (MA)
State Coll of Florida Manatee-Sarasota (FL)
State U of New York Coll of Technology at Alfred (NY)
Sullivan County Comm Coll (NY)
Tallahassee Comm Coll (FL)
Tarrant County Coll District (TX)
Terra State Comm Coll (OH)
Texarkana Coll (TX)
Three Rivers Comm Coll (CT)
Tompkins Cortland Comm Coll (NY)
Trident Tech Coll (SC)
Tunxis Comm Coll (CT)
Tyler Jr Coll (TX)
Umpqua Comm Coll (OR)
Union County Coll (NJ)
The U of Akron–Wayne Coll (OH)
U of Arkansas Comm Coll at Morrilton (AR)
U of South Carolina Union (SC)
U of Wisconsin–Richland (WI)
U of Wisconsin–Waukesha (WI)

Valencia Coll (FL)
Vincennes U (IN)
Virginia Western Comm Coll (VA)
Volunteer State Comm Coll (TN)
Westchester Comm Coll (NY)
Western Iowa Tech Comm Coll (IA)
Westmoreland County Comm Coll (PA)
West Virginia Northern Comm Coll (WV)
White Mountains Comm Coll (NH)
Wilson Comm Coll (NC)
Wytheville Comm Coll (VA)

LIBRARY AND ARCHIVES ASSISTING
Central Comm Coll–Hastings Campus (NE)
Coll of DuPage (IL)
Coll of the Canyons (CA)
Illinois Central Coll (IL)
Ivy Tech Comm Coll–Bloomington (IN)
Ivy Tech Comm Coll–Columbus (IN)
Ivy Tech Comm Coll–East Central (IN)
Ivy Tech Comm Coll–Kokomo (IN)
Ivy Tech Comm Coll–Lafayette (IN)
Ivy Tech Comm Coll–North Central (IN)
Ivy Tech Comm Coll–Northeast (IN)
Ivy Tech Comm Coll–Northwest (IN)
Ivy Tech Comm Coll–Richmond (IN)
Ivy Tech Comm Coll–Southeast (IN)
Ivy Tech Comm Coll–Southern Indiana (IN)
Ivy Tech Comm Coll–Southwest (IN)
Ivy Tech Comm Coll–Wabash Valley (IN)
Minneapolis Comm and Tech Coll (MN)
Northeast Comm Coll (NE)
Oakland Comm Coll (MI)

LIBRARY AND INFORMATION SCIENCE
Coll of DuPage (IL)
Copiah-Lincoln Comm Coll (MS)
Do&nna Ana Comm Coll (NM)
Grand Rapids Comm Coll (MI)
Highline Comm Coll (WA)
Indian River State Coll (FL)
Westmoreland County Comm Coll (PA)

LICENSED PRACTICAL/ VOCATIONAL NURSE TRAINING
Amarillo Coll (TX)
Athens Tech Coll (GA)
Bainbridge Coll (GA)
Big Bend Comm Coll (WA)
Central Comm Coll–Columbus Campus (NE)
Central Comm Coll–Grand Island Campus (NE)
Central Maine Comm Coll (ME)
Central Oregon Comm Coll (OR)
Colby Comm Coll (KS)
Coll of Southern Maryland (MD)
Coll of the Ouachitas (AR)
Colorado Mountain Coll (CO)
Comm Coll of Allegheny County (PA)
Comm Coll of Rhode Island (RI)
Dakota Coll at Bottineau (ND)
Delaware Tech & Comm Coll, Jack F. Owens Campus (DE)
Eastern Idaho Tech Coll (ID)
El Centro Coll (TX)
Fiorello H. LaGuardia Comm Coll of the City U of New York (NY)
Gavilan Coll (CA)
Grand Rapids Comm Coll (MI)
Howard Comm Coll (MD)
Indian River State Coll (FL)
Itasca Comm Coll (MN)
Ivy Tech Comm Coll–Southeast (IN)
Jackson Comm Coll (MI)

Kirtland Comm Coll (MI)
Lake Area Tech Inst (SD)
Lake Region State Coll (ND)
Lansing Comm Coll (MI)
Mid Michigan Comm Coll (MI)
Mid-Plains Comm Coll, North Platte (NE)
Montana State U–Great Falls Coll of Technology (MT)
Moraine Park Tech Coll (WI)
North Dakota State Coll of Science (ND)
Northeast Comm Coll (NE)
Northeastern Jr Coll (CO)
North Seattle Comm Coll (WA)
Northwest Tech Coll (MN)
Riverside City Coll (CA)
St. Cloud Tech & Comm Coll (MN)
Salem Comm Coll (NJ)
San Diego City Coll (CA)
San Jacinto Coll District (TX)
San Joaquin Valley Coll, Visalia (CA)
Southeastern Comm Coll (IA)
Southeast Tech Inst (SD)
Southwest Mississippi Comm Coll (MS)
Texarkana Coll (TX)
Texas State Tech Coll Harlingen (TX)
Tyler Jr Coll (TX)
Union County Coll (NJ)
The U of Montana–Helena Coll of Technology (MT)
Westmoreland County Comm Coll (PA)

LINEWORKER
Chandler-Gilbert Comm Coll (AZ)
Coll of Southern Maryland (MD)
GateWay Comm Coll (AZ)
Ivy Tech Comm Coll–Lafayette (IN)
Linn State Tech Coll (MO)
Mitchell Tech Inst (SD)
Moraine Park Tech Coll (WI)
Northeast Comm Coll (NE)
Raritan Valley Comm Coll (NJ)

LITERATURE RELATED
Cayuga County Comm Coll (NY)

LIVESTOCK MANAGEMENT
Northeast Comm Coll (NE)

LOGISTICS, MATERIALS, AND SUPPLY CHAIN MANAGEMENT
Athens Tech Coll (GA)
Cecil Coll (MD)
Central Comm Coll–Hastings Campus (NE)
Chattahoochee Tech Coll (GA)
Cochise Coll, Sierra Vista (AZ)
Edison Comm Coll (OH)
Guilford Tech Comm Coll (NC)
Houston Comm Coll System (TX)
Randolph Comm Coll (NC)
Rockingham Comm Coll (NC)
Truckee Meadows Comm Coll (NV)

MACHINE SHOP TECHNOLOGY
Bluegrass Comm and Tech Coll (KY)
Cape Fear Comm Coll (NC)
Coll of Lake County (IL)
Comm Coll of Allegheny County (PA)
Corning Comm Coll (NY)
Eastern Arizona Coll (AZ)
Fayetteville Tech Comm Coll (NC)
Florida State Coll at Jacksonville (FL)
Guilford Tech Comm Coll (NC)
Ivy Tech Comm Coll–Central Indiana (IN)
Johnston Comm Coll (NC)
Metropolitan Comm Coll–Business & Technology Campus (MO)
Moraine Park Tech Coll (WI)
Orange Coast Coll (CA)
Randolph Comm Coll (NC)
Red Rocks Comm Coll (CO)
Rockingham Comm Coll (NC)
San Juan Coll (NM)

West Kentucky Comm and Tech Coll (KY)

MACHINE TOOL TECHNOLOGY
Altamaha Tech Coll (GA)
Amarillo Coll (TX)
Casper Coll (WY)
Central Comm Coll–Columbus Campus (NE)
Central Comm Coll–Hastings Campus (NE)
Central Maine Comm Coll (ME)
Clark Coll (WA)
Coll of DuPage (IL)
Coll of the Ouachitas (AR)
Columbus Tech Coll (GA)
Corning Comm Coll (NY)
Cowley County Comm Coll and Area Vocational–Tech School (KS)
Delaware County Comm Coll (PA)
Elgin Comm Coll (IL)
El Paso Comm Coll (TX)
Georgia Piedmont Tech Coll (GA)
Gwinnett Tech Coll (GA)
Hawkeye Comm Coll (IA)
H. Councill Trenholm State Tech Coll (AL)
Hutchinson Comm Coll and Area Vocational School (KS)
Illinois Eastern Comm Colls, Wabash Valley College (IL)
Ivy Tech Comm Coll–Bloomington (IN)
Ivy Tech Comm Coll–Central Indiana (IN)
Ivy Tech Comm Coll–Columbus (IN)
Ivy Tech Comm Coll–East Central (IN)
Ivy Tech Comm Coll–Kokomo (IN)
Ivy Tech Comm Coll–Lafayette (IN)
Ivy Tech Comm Coll–North Central (IN)
Ivy Tech Comm Coll–Northeast (IN)
Ivy Tech Comm Coll–Northwest (IN)
Ivy Tech Comm Coll–Richmond (IN)
Ivy Tech Comm Coll–Southern Indiana (IN)
Ivy Tech Comm Coll–Southwest (IN)
Ivy Tech Comm Coll–Wabash Valley (IN)
Jamestown Comm Coll (NY)
Johnston Comm Coll (NC)
Kankakee Comm Coll (IL)
Lake Area Tech Inst (SD)
Lake Michigan Coll (MI)
Linn State Tech Coll (MO)
Lower Columbia Coll (WA)
Macomb Comm Coll (MI)
Mid Michigan Comm Coll (MI)
Mineral Area Coll (MO)
Muskegon Comm Coll (MI)
North Dakota State Coll of Science (ND)
Northern Essex Comm Coll (MA)
Oakland Comm Coll (MI)
Orange Coast Coll (CA)
Reedley Coll (CA)
St. Cloud Tech & Comm Coll (MN)
San Diego City Coll (CA)
Southeastern Comm Coll (IA)
Southern Maine Comm Coll (ME)
Southwestern Illinois Coll (IL)
Southwestern Michigan Coll (MI)
State U of New York Coll of Technology at Alfred (NY)
Tarrant County Coll District (TX)
Texas State Tech Coll Harlingen (TX)
Trident Tech Coll (SC)
The U of Montana–Helena Coll of Technology (MT)
Western Iowa Tech Comm Coll (IA)
Westmoreland County Comm Coll (PA)
Wiregrass Georgia Tech Coll (GA)
Wytheville Comm Coll (VA)

MAGNETIC RESONANCE IMAGING (MRI) TECHNOLOGY
Lake Michigan Coll (MI)

MANAGEMENT INFORMATION SYSTEMS
Anne Arundel Comm Coll (MD)
Burlington County Coll (NJ)
Carl Albert State Coll (OK)
Carroll Comm Coll (MD)
Cecil Coll (MD)
Central Oregon Comm Coll (OR)
Chattanooga State Comm Coll (TN)
Coll of the Ouachitas (AR)
Comm Coll of Allegheny County (PA)
The Comm Coll of Baltimore County (MD)
Delaware County Comm Coll (PA)
Delaware Tech & Comm Coll, Jack F. Owens Campus (DE)
Delaware Tech & Comm Coll, Stanton/Wilmington Campus (DE)
Delaware Tech & Comm Coll, Terry Campus (DE)
Garrett Coll (MD)
GateWay Comm Coll (AZ)
Gwinnett Tech Coll (GA)
Hagerstown Comm Coll (MD)
Harford Comm Coll (MD)
Hillsborough Comm Coll (FL)
John Tyler Comm Coll (VA)
John Wood Comm Coll (IL)
J. Sargeant Reynolds Comm Coll (VA)
Kilgore Coll (TX)
Kirtland Comm Coll (MI)
Lake Region State Coll (ND)
Lansing Comm Coll (MI)
Linn State Tech Coll (MO)
Manchester Comm Coll (CT)
Miami Dade Coll (FL)
Montgomery Comm Coll (NC)
Moraine Valley Comm Coll (IL)
North Hennepin Comm Coll (MN)
Oakland Comm Coll (MI)
Pensacola State Coll (FL)
Raritan Valley Comm Coll (NJ)
Red Rocks Comm Coll (CO)
San Jacinto Coll District (TX)
Tallahassee Comm Coll (FL)
Union County Coll (NJ)
York County Comm Coll (ME)

MANAGEMENT INFORMATION SYSTEMS AND SERVICES RELATED
Anne Arundel Comm Coll (MD)
Gulf Coast State Coll (FL)
Hillsborough Comm Coll (FL)
Metropolitan Comm Coll–Business & Technology Campus (MO)
Missouri State U–West Plains (MO)
Mohawk Valley Comm Coll (NY)
Montgomery Coll (MD)
Montgomery County Comm Coll (PA)
Pensacola State Coll (FL)
Rasmussen Coll Aurora (IL)
Rasmussen Coll Bismarck (ND)
Rasmussen Coll Bloomington (MN)
Rasmussen Coll Brooklyn Park (MN)
Rasmussen Coll Eagan (MN)
Rasmussen Coll Fargo (ND)
Rasmussen Coll Fort Myers (FL)
Rasmussen Coll Green Bay (WI)
Rasmussen Coll Lake Elmo/ Woodbury (MN)
Rasmussen Coll Mankato (MN)
Rasmussen Coll Moorhead (MN)
Rasmussen Coll New Port Richey (FL)
Rasmussen Coll Ocala (FL)
Rasmussen Coll Rockford (IL)
Rasmussen Coll St. Cloud (MN)
Southwestern Indian Polytechnic Inst (NM)

MANAGEMENT SCIENCE
Aiken Tech Coll (SC)
Blackhawk Tech Coll (WI)
Career Tech Coll (LA)
Delaware Tech & Comm Coll, Stanton/Wilmington Campus (DE)
Murray State Coll (OK)

Pensacola State Coll (FL)
Reedley Coll (CA)

MANUFACTURING ENGINEERING

Central Wyoming Coll (WY)
Kent State U at Trumbull (OH)
Lake Michigan Coll (MI)
Penn State Fayette, The Eberly Campus (PA)
Penn State Greater Allegheny (PA)
Penn State Hazleton (PA)
Penn State Wilkes-Barre (PA)
Penn State York (PA)

MANUFACTURING ENGINEERING TECHNOLOGY

Albany Tech Coll (GA)
Altamaha Tech Coll (GA)
Casper Coll (WY)
Central Oregon Comm Coll (OR)
Clark Coll (WA)
Coll of DuPage (IL)
Coll of the Canyons (CA)
Delaware Tech & Comm Coll, Stanton/Wilmington Campus (DE)
Fox Valley Tech Coll (WI)
Gadsden State Comm Coll (AL)
GateWay Comm Coll (AZ)
H. Councill Trenholm State Tech Coll (AL)
Houston Comm Coll System (TX)
Hutchinson Comm Coll and Area Vocational School (KS)
Illinois Central Coll (IL)
Illinois Eastern Comm Colls, Wabash Valley College (IL)
John Wood Comm Coll (IL)
Lake Area Tech Inst (SD)
Lehigh Carbon Comm Coll (PA)
Linn State Tech Coll (MO)
Macomb Comm Coll (MI)
Mott Comm Coll (MI)
North Dakota State Coll of Science (ND)
Northwest Tech Coll (MN)
Oakland Comm Coll (MI)
Oklahoma City Comm Coll (OK)
Owens Comm Coll, Toledo (OH)
Pensacola State Coll (FL)
Quinsigamond Comm Coll (MA)
Raritan Valley Comm Coll (NJ)
Red Rocks Comm Coll (CO)
Rogue Comm Coll (OR)
Southern Crescent Tech Coll (GA)
South Georgia Tech Coll (GA)
Southwestern Illinois Coll (IL)
Southwestern Indian Polytechnic Inst (NM)
Sullivan Coll of Technology and Design (KY)
Terra State Comm Coll (OH)
Truckee Meadows Comm Coll (NV)
Union County Coll (NJ)
Vincennes U (IN)
Westmoreland County Comm Coll (PA)

MARINE BIOLOGY AND BIOLOGICAL OCEANOGRAPHY

Southern Maine Comm Coll (ME)

MARINE MAINTENANCE AND SHIP REPAIR TECHNOLOGY

Cape Fear Comm Coll (NC)
Iowa Lakes Comm Coll (IA)
Kingsborough Comm Coll of the City U of New York (NY)
Orange Coast Coll (CA)

MARINE SCIENCE/MERCHANT MARINE OFFICER

Indian River State Coll (FL)

MARKETING/MARKETING MANAGEMENT

Albany Tech Coll (GA)
Altamaha Tech Coll (GA)
Alvin Comm Coll (TX)
Athens Tech Coll (GA)
Atlanta Tech Coll (GA)
Augusta Tech Coll (GA)
Austin Comm Coll (TX)

Bainbridge Coll (GA)
Blackhawk Tech Coll (WI)
Brookhaven Coll (TX)
Casper Coll (WY)
Cecil Coll (MD)
Central Carolina Comm Coll (NC)
Central Comm Coll–Columbus Campus (NE)
Central Georgia Tech Coll (GA)
Central Oregon Comm Coll (OR)
Century Coll (MN)
Chattahoochee Tech Coll (GA)
Chippewa Valley Tech Coll (WI)
Coll of Central Florida (FL)
Coll of DuPage (IL)
Coll of the Ouachitas (AR)
Colorado Mountain Coll, Alpine Campus (CO)
Comm Coll of Allegheny County (PA)
Comm Coll of Rhode Island (RI)
Cowley County Comm Coll and Area Vocational–Tech School (KS)
Dakota Coll at Bottineau (ND)
Delaware Tech & Comm Coll, Jack F. Owens Campus (DE)
Delaware Tech & Comm Coll, Stanton/Wilmington Campus (DE)
Delaware Tech & Comm Coll, Terry Campus (DE)
Eastern Idaho Tech Coll (ID)
Edison Comm Coll (OH)
Elgin Comm Coll (IL)
Fayetteville Tech Comm Coll (NC)
Florida State Coll at Jacksonville (FL)
Fox Valley Tech Coll (WI)
GateWay Comm Coll (AZ)
Gateway Tech Coll (WI)
Genesee Comm Coll (NY)
Georgia Highlands Coll (GA)
Georgia Northwestern Tech Coll (GA)
Georgia Piedmont Tech Coll (GA)
Gwinnett Tech Coll (GA)
Harper Coll (IL)
Houston Comm Coll System (TX)
Illinois Valley Comm Coll (IL)
Indian River State Coll (FL)
Iowa Lakes Comm Coll (IA)
Jackson Comm Coll (MI)
Kankakee Comm Coll (IL)
Kansas City Kansas Comm Coll (KS)
Kent State U at Ashtabula (OH)
Kingsborough Comm Coll of the City U of New York (NY)
Lake Area Tech Inst (SD)
Lake Michigan Coll (MI)
Lanier Tech Coll (GA)
Macomb Comm Coll (MI)
Manchester Comm Coll (CT)
Metropolitan Comm Coll–Longview (MO)
Metropolitan Comm Coll–Maple Woods (MO)
Metropolitan Comm Coll–Penn Valley (MO)
Miami Dade Coll (FL)
Middle Georgia Tech Coll (GA)
Mid Michigan Comm Coll (MI)
Minnesota School of Business–Brooklyn Center (MN)
Minnesota School of Business–Plymouth (MN)
Minnesota School of Business–Richfield (MN)
Minnesota School of Business–St. Cloud (MN)
Minnesota School of Business–Shakopee,(MN)
Monroe Comm Coll (NY)
Monroe County Comm Coll (MI)
Moraine Park Tech Coll (WI)
Mott Comm Coll (MI)
Moultrie Tech Coll (GA)
Muskegon Comm Coll (MI)
Norco Coll (CA)
Northampton Comm Coll (PA)
Northeast Comm Coll (NE)
Northeastern Jr Coll (CO)
Northern Essex Comm Coll (MA)
North Hennepin Comm Coll (MN)
North Shore Comm Coll (MA)
Ogeechee Tech Coll (GA)
Orange Coast Coll (CA)

Palm Beach State Coll (FL)
Pasco-Hernando Comm Coll (FL)
Piedmont Virginia Comm Coll (VA)
Polk State Coll (FL)
Raritan Valley Comm Coll (NJ)
Rasmussen Coll Bismarck (ND)
Rasmussen Coll Bloomington (MN)
Rasmussen Coll Brooklyn Park (MN)
Rasmussen Coll Eagan (MN)
Rasmussen Coll Fargo (ND)
Rasmussen Coll Fort Myers (FL)
Rasmussen Coll Green Bay (WI)
Rasmussen Coll Lake Elmo/Woodbury (MN)
Rasmussen Coll Mankato (MN)
Rasmussen Coll Moorhead (MN)
Rasmussen Coll New Port Richey (FL)
Rasmussen Coll Ocala (FL)
Rasmussen Coll St. Cloud (MN)
Riverside City Coll (CA)
Rockland Comm Coll (NY)
Rogue Comm Coll (OR)
St. Clair County Comm Coll (MI)
Salt Lake Comm Coll (UT)
San Diego City Coll (CA)
Savannah Tech Coll (GA)
Seminole State Coll of Florida (FL)
Southeastern Tech Coll (GA)
Southeast Tech Inst (SD)
Southern Crescent Tech Coll (GA)
South Georgia Tech Coll (GA)
Southwest Mississippi Comm Coll (MS)
Springfield Tech Comm Coll (MA)
Stark State Coll (OH)
State U of New York Coll of Technology at Alfred (NY)
Sullivan County Comm Coll (NY)
Tallahassee Comm Coll (FL)
Tarrant County Coll District (TX)
Terra State Comm Coll (OH)
Texarkana Coll (TX)
Three Rivers Comm Coll (CT)
Trident Tech Coll (SC)
Tunxis Comm Coll (CT)
Umpqua Comm Coll (OR)
Union County Coll (NJ)
Valencia Coll (FL)
Vincennes U (IN)
Waukesha County Tech Coll (WI)
Westchester Comm Coll (NY)
Western Dakota Tech Inst (SD)
West Georgia Tech Coll (GA)
Wiregrass Georgia Tech Coll (GA)
Wisconsin Indianhead Tech Coll (WI)

MARKETING RELATED

Aiken Tech Coll (SC)
Dakota Coll at Bottineau (ND)

MARKETING RESEARCH

Lake Region State Coll (ND)

MASONRY

Florida State Coll at Jacksonville (FL)
Front Range Comm Coll (CO)
GateWay Comm Coll (AZ)
Ivy Tech Comm Coll–Central Indiana (IN)
Ivy Tech Comm Coll–Columbus (IN)
Ivy Tech Comm Coll–East Central (IN)
Ivy Tech Comm Coll–Lafayette (IN)
Ivy Tech Comm Coll–North Central (IN)
Ivy Tech Comm Coll–Northeast (IN)
Ivy Tech Comm Coll–Northwest (IN)
Ivy Tech Comm Coll–Southern Indiana (IN)
Ivy Tech Comm Coll–Southwest (IN)
Ivy Tech Comm Coll–Wabash Valley (IN)
Metropolitan Comm Coll–Business & Technology Campus (MO)
Southwestern Illinois Coll (IL)
State U of New York Coll of Technology at Alfred (NY)

MASSAGE THERAPY

Anthem Coll–Maryland Heights (MO)
Career Tech Coll (LA)

Career Training Academy, Pittsburgh (PA)
Central Oregon Comm Coll (OR)
Chandler-Gilbert Comm Coll (AZ)
Coll of DuPage (IL)
Coll of Southern Maryland (MD)
Comm Care Coll (OK)
Comm Coll of Rhode Island (RI)
Illinois Valley Comm Coll (IL)
Inst of Business & Medical Careers (CO)
Iowa Lakes Comm Coll (IA)
Ivy Tech Comm Coll–Northeast (IN)
Kaplan Coll, Hammond Campus (IN)
Minnesota School of Business–Brooklyn Center (MN)
Minnesota School of Business–Plymouth (MN)
Minnesota School of Business–St. Cloud (MN)
Minnesota State Coll–Southeast Tech (MN)
Oakland Comm Coll (MI)
Owens Comm Coll, Toledo (OH)
St. Clair County Comm Coll (MI)
Southwestern Illinois Coll (IL)
Southwest Mississippi Comm Coll (MS)
Spencerian Coll (KY)
Springfield Tech Comm Coll (MA)
Vincennes U (IN)

MASS COMMUNICATION/MEDIA

Amarillo Coll (TX)
Ancilla Coll (IN)
Bunker Hill Comm Coll (MA)
Chipola Coll (FL)
Crowder Coll (MO)
Dutchess Comm Coll (NY)
Genesee Comm Coll (NY)
Grand Rapids Comm Coll (MI)
Iowa Lakes Comm Coll (IA)
Lake Michigan Coll (MI)
Laramie County Comm Coll (WY)
Miami Dade Coll (FL)
Monroe Comm Coll (NY)
Monroe County Comm Coll (MI)
Niagara County Comm Coll (NY)
Northeast Comm Coll (NE)
Oklahoma City Comm Coll (OK)
Orange Coast Coll (CA)
Palm Beach State Coll (FL)
Rockland Comm Coll (NY)
Salt Lake Comm Coll (UT)
Snow Coll (UT)
State Coll of Florida Manatee-Sarasota (FL)
Union County Coll (NJ)
Westchester Comm Coll (NY)
Wytheville Comm Coll (VA)

MATERIALS ENGINEERING

Southern Maine Comm Coll (ME)

MATERIALS SCIENCE

Kent State U at Ashtabula (OH)
Northern Essex Comm Coll (MA)

MATHEMATICS

Alvin Comm Coll (TX)
Amarillo Coll (TX)
Anne Arundel Comm Coll (MD)
Austin Comm Coll (TX)
Bainbridge Coll (GA)
Bucks County Comm Coll (PA)
Bunker Hill Comm Coll (MA)
Burlington County Coll (NJ)
Carl Albert State Coll (OK)
Casper Coll (WY)
Cecil Coll (MD)
Central Oregon Comm Coll (OR)
Central Wyoming Coll (WY)
Cochise Coll, Sierra Vista (AZ)
Coll of the Canyons (CA)
Colorado Mountain Coll (CO)
Colorado Mountain Coll, Alpine Campus (CO)
Comm Coll of Allegheny County (PA)
Corning Comm Coll (NY)
Crowder Coll (MO)
Dakota Coll at Bottineau (ND)
Dutchess Comm Coll (NY)
Eastern Arizona Coll (AZ)
Foothill Coll (CA)

Gavilan Coll (CA)
Genesee Comm Coll (NY)
Harper Coll (IL)
Highline Comm Coll (WA)
Housatonic Comm Coll (CT)
Hutchinson Comm Coll and Area Vocational School (KS)
Indian River State Coll (FL)
Iowa Lakes Comm Coll (IA)
Jefferson Comm Coll (NY)
Kilgore Coll (TX)
Kingsborough Comm Coll of the City U of New York (NY)
Lake Michigan Coll (MI)
Lansing Comm Coll (MI)
Laramie County Comm Coll (WY)
Lehigh Carbon Comm Coll (PA)
Macomb Comm Coll (MI)
Mendocino Coll (CA)
Miami Dade Coll (FL)
Mid Michigan Comm Coll (MI)
Minneapolis Comm and Tech Coll (MN)
Mohave Comm Coll (AZ)
Monroe Comm Coll (NY)
Monroe County Comm Coll (MI)
Montgomery County Comm Coll (PA)
Murray State Coll (OK)
Niagara County Comm Coll (NY)
Northampton Comm Coll (PA)
Northeast Comm Coll (NE)
Northeastern Jr Coll (CO)
North Hennepin Comm Coll (MN)
Northwest Coll (WY)
Northwestern Connecticut Comm Coll (CT)
Northwest Florida State Coll (FL)
Oklahoma City Comm Coll (OK)
Orange Coast Coll (CA)
Otero Jr Coll (CO)
Palm Beach State Coll (FL)
Pensacola State Coll (FL)
Reedley Coll (CA)
Rockland Comm Coll (NY)
St. Philip's Coll (TX)
San Diego City Coll (CA)
San Jacinto Coll District (TX)
San Juan Coll (NM)
Santa Rosa Jr Coll (CA)
Scottsdale Comm Coll (AZ)
Snow Coll (UT)
Springfield Tech Comm Coll (MA)
Sullivan County Comm Coll (NY)
Terra State Comm Coll (OH)
Texarkana Coll (TX)
Texas State Tech Coll Harlingen (TX)
Truckee Meadows Comm Coll (NV)
Tyler Jr Coll (TX)
Umpqua Comm Coll (OR)
Union County Coll (NJ)
Vincennes U (IN)

MATHEMATICS AND COMPUTER SCIENCE

Crowder Coll (MO)

MATHEMATICS RELATED

Cayuga County Comm Coll (NY)

MATHEMATICS TEACHER EDUCATION

Anne Arundel Comm Coll (MD)
Cochise Coll, Sierra Vista (AZ)
The Comm Coll of Baltimore County (MD)
Delaware Tech & Comm Coll, Jack F. Owens Campus (DE)
Delaware Tech & Comm Coll, Stanton/Wilmington Campus (DE)
Delaware Tech & Comm Coll, Terry Campus (DE)
Harford Comm Coll (MD)
Highland Comm Coll (IL)
Kankakee Comm Coll (IL)
Kaskaskia Coll (IL)
Montgomery Coll (MD)
Moraine Valley Comm Coll (IL)
Southwestern Illinois Coll (IL)
State Coll of Florida Manatee-Sarasota (FL)
Vincennes U (IN)

MECHANICAL DRAFTING AND CAD/CADD

City Colls of Chicago, Harry S. Truman College (IL)
Comm Coll of Allegheny County (PA)
Delaware Tech & Comm Coll, Jack F. Owens Campus (DE)
Edison Comm Coll (OH)
Fox Valley Tech Coll (WI)
Gateway Tech Coll (WI)
Island Drafting and Tech Inst (NY)
Lansing Comm Coll (MI)
Macomb Comm Coll (MI)
Minnesota School of Business–Plymouth (MN)
Montgomery County Comm Coll (PA)
Moraine Park Tech Coll (WI)
North Seattle Comm Coll (WA)
Oakland Comm Coll (MI)
St. Clair County Comm Coll (MI)
St. Cloud Tech & Comm Coll (MN)
Southwestern Illinois Coll (IL)
State U of New York Coll of Technology at Alfred (NY)
Sullivan Coll of Technology and Design (KY)
Vincennes U (IN)
Waukesha County Tech Coll (WI)
Westmoreland County Comm Coll (PA)
Wisconsin Indianhead Tech Coll (WI)

MECHANICAL ENGINEERING

Cayuga County Comm Coll (NY)
Fiorello H. LaGuardia Comm Coll of the City U of New York (NY)
Itasca Comm Coll (MN)
Kilgore Coll (TX)

MECHANICAL ENGINEERING/MECHANICAL TECHNOLOGY

Augusta Tech Coll (GA)
Beaufort County Comm Coll (NC)
Cape Fear Comm Coll (NC)
Cayuga County Comm Coll (NY)
Coll of Lake County (IL)
Columbus Tech Coll (GA)
Corning Comm Coll (NY)
Delaware County Comm Coll (PA)
Delaware Tech & Comm Coll, Stanton/Wilmington Campus (DE)
Edison Comm Coll (OH)
Erie Comm Coll, North Campus (NY)
Gateway Comm Coll (CT)
Guilford Tech Comm Coll (NC)
Hagerstown Comm Coll (MD)
Illinois Central Coll (IL)
Illinois Eastern Comm Colls, Lincoln Trail College (IL)
Illinois Valley Comm Coll (IL)
Jamestown Comm Coll (NY)
John Tyler Comm Coll (VA)
Kent State U at Ashtabula (OH)
Kent State U at Trumbull (OH)
Kent State U at Tuscarawas (OH)
Lehigh Carbon Comm Coll (PA)
Macomb Comm Coll (MI)
Massachusetts Bay Comm Coll (MA)
Mohawk Valley Comm Coll (NY)
Monroe Comm Coll (NY)
Montgomery County Comm Coll (PA)
Moraine Valley Comm Coll (IL)
Mott Comm Coll (MI)
Normandale Comm Coll (MN)
Onondaga Comm Coll (NY)
Penn State DuBois (PA)
Penn State Hazleton (PA)
Penn State New Kensington (PA)
Penn State Shenango (PA)
Penn State York (PA)
Southeastern Comm Coll (IA)
Southeast Tech Inst (SD)
Springfield Tech Comm Coll (MA)
Stark State Coll (OH)
State U of New York Coll of Technology at Alfred (NY)
Sullivan Coll of Technology and Design (KY)
Tarrant County Coll District (TX)

Terra State Comm Coll (OH)
Three Rivers Comm Coll (CT)
Trident Tech Coll (SC)
Union County Coll (NJ)
Vincennes U (IN)
Virginia Western Comm Coll (VA)
Westchester Comm Coll (NY)
Westmoreland County Comm Coll (PA)
Wilson Comm Coll (NC)
Wytheville Comm Coll (VA)

MECHANICAL ENGINEERING TECHNOLOGIES RELATED

John Tyler Comm Coll (VA)
Mohawk Valley Comm Coll (NY)
Moraine Park Tech Coll (WI)
Terra State Comm Coll (OH)

MECHANIC AND REPAIR TECHNOLOGIES RELATED

Chandler-Gilbert Comm Coll (AZ)
Ivy Tech Comm Coll–Bloomington (IN)
Ivy Tech Comm Coll–Columbus (IN)
Ivy Tech Comm Coll–Kokomo (IN)
Ivy Tech Comm Coll–Lafayette (IN)
Ivy Tech Comm Coll–North Central (IN)
Ivy Tech Comm Coll–Northwest (IN)
Ivy Tech Comm Coll–Southwest (IN)
Macomb Comm Coll (MI)

MECHANICS AND REPAIR

Ivy Tech Comm Coll–Bloomington (IN)
Ivy Tech Comm Coll–Central Indiana (IN)
Ivy Tech Comm Coll–Columbus (IN)
Ivy Tech Comm Coll–Kokomo (IN)
Ivy Tech Comm Coll–Lafayette (IN)
Ivy Tech Comm Coll–North Central (IN)
Ivy Tech Comm Coll–Northeast (IN)
Ivy Tech Comm Coll–Northwest (IN)
Ivy Tech Comm Coll–Richmond (IN)
Ivy Tech Comm Coll–Southern Indiana (IN)
Ivy Tech Comm Coll–Southwest (IN)
Ivy Tech Comm Coll–Wabash Valley (IN)
Oakland Comm Coll (MI)
Rogue Comm Coll (OR)

MECHATRONICS, ROBOTICS, AND AUTOMATION ENGINEERING

Moraine Park Tech Coll (WI)
Southwestern Michigan Coll (MI)
Westmoreland County Comm Coll (PA)

MEDICAL ADMINISTRATIVE ASSISTANT AND MEDICAL SECRETARY

Alvin Comm Coll (TX)
Amarillo Coll (TX)
Anne Arundel Comm Coll (MD)
Berkeley City Coll (CA)
Blackhawk Tech Coll (WI)
Bluegrass Comm and Tech Coll (KY)
Bunker Hill Comm Coll (MA)
Central Carolina Comm Coll (NC)
Century Coll (MN)
Clark Coll (WA)
Coll of the Ouachitas (AR)
Comm Coll of Allegheny County (PA)
The Comm Coll of Baltimore County (MD)
Comm Coll of Philadelphia (PA)
Comm Coll of Rhode Island (RI)
Consolidated School of Business, York (PA)
Crowder Coll (MO)
Dakota Coll at Bottineau (ND)
Edison Comm Coll (OH)

Gateway Comm Coll (CT)
Gavilan Coll (CA)
Goodwin Coll (CT)
Grand Rapids Comm Coll (MI)
Harper Coll (IL)
Hawkeye Comm Coll (IA)
Howard Comm Coll (MD)
Illinois Eastern Comm Colls, Olney Central College (IL)
Indian River State Coll (FL)
Inst of Business & Medical Careers (CO)
Iowa Lakes Comm Coll (IA)
Johnston Comm Coll (NC)
Kirtland Comm Coll (MI)
Lake Michigan Comm Coll (MI)
Lake Region State Coll (ND)
Los Angeles Harbor Coll (CA)
Lower Columbia Coll (WA)
Manchester Comm Coll (CT)
Metropolitan Comm Coll–Longview (MO)
Metropolitan Comm Coll–Maple Woods (MO)
Metropolitan Comm Coll–Penn Valley (MO)
Mid Michigan Comm Coll (MI)
Minnesota School of Business–Brooklyn Center (MN)
Minnesota School of Business–Plymouth (MN)
Minnesota School of Business–Richfield (MN)
Minnesota School of Business–St. Cloud (MN)
Minnesota School of Business–Shakopee (MN)
Minnesota State Coll–Southeast Tech (MN)
Monroe County Comm Coll (MI)
Montcalm Comm Coll (MI)
Muskegon Comm Coll (MI)
Northampton Comm Coll (PA)
Northeast Comm Coll (NE)
Northeastern Jr Coll (CO)
Northern Essex Comm Coll (MA)
North Shore Comm Coll (MA)
Northwest Tech Coll (MN)
Orange Coast Coll (CA)
Otero Jr Coll (CO)
Owens Comm Coll, Toledo (OH)
Polk State Coll (FL)
Quinsigamond Comm Coll (MA)
Rasmussen Coll Aurora (IL)
Rasmussen Coll Bismarck (ND)
Rasmussen Coll Bloomington (MN)
Rasmussen Coll Brooklyn Park (MN)
Rasmussen Coll Eagan (MN)
Rasmussen Coll Fargo (ND)
Rasmussen Coll Fort Myers (FL)
Rasmussen Coll Green Bay (WI)
Rasmussen Coll Lake Elmo/Woodbury (MN)
Rasmussen Coll Mankato (MN)
Rasmussen Coll Moorhead (MN)
Rasmussen Coll New Port Richey (FL)
Rasmussen Coll Ocala (FL)
Rasmussen Coll Rockford (IL)
Rasmussen Coll St. Cloud (MN)
St. Clair County Comm Coll (MI)
St. Philip's Coll (TX)
San Jacinto Coll District (TX)
San Joaquin Valley Coll, Visalia (CA)
Scottsdale Comm Coll (AZ)
Shawnee Comm Coll (IL)
Springfield Tech Comm Coll (MA)
Terra State Comm Coll (OH)
Trident Tech Coll (SC)
Tunxis Comm Coll (CT)
Tyler Jr Coll (TX)
Umpqua Comm Coll (OR)
The U of Montana–Helena Coll of Technology (MT)
Valencia Coll (FL)
Western Iowa Tech Comm Coll (IA)
West Virginia Jr Coll–Bridgeport (WV)
Wisconsin Indianhead Tech Coll (WI)
Wytheville Comm Coll (VA)

MEDICAL/CLINICAL ASSISTANT

ACT Coll, Arlington (VA)
Anthem Coll–Maryland Heights (MO)
Big Bend Comm Coll (WA)
Bluegrass Comm and Tech Coll (KY)
Bradford School (OH)
Bradford School (PA)
Career Tech Coll (LA)
Career Training Academy, Pittsburgh (PA)
Central Carolina Comm Coll (NC)
Central Comm Coll–Columbus Campus (NE)
Central Comm Coll–Grand Island Campus (NE)
Central Comm Coll–Hastings Campus (NE)
Central Maine Comm Coll (ME)
Central Oregon Comm Coll (OR)
Chattahoochee Valley Comm Coll (AL)
Clark Coll (WA)
Coll of Business and Technology (FL)
Comm Care Coll (OK)
Comm Coll of Allegheny County (PA)
Comm Coll of Philadelphia (PA)
Dakota Coll at Bottineau (ND)
Delaware County Comm Coll (PA)
Delaware Tech & Comm Coll, Jack F. Owens Campus (DE)
Delaware Tech & Comm Coll, Stanton/Wilmington Campus (DE)
Delaware Tech & Comm Coll, Terry Campus (DE)
Dutchess Comm Coll (NY)
Eastern Idaho Tech Coll (ID)
Edison Comm Coll (OH)
El Centro Coll (TX)
Elmira Business Inst (NY)
El Paso Comm Coll (TX)
ETI Tech Coll of Niles (OH)
Forrest Coll (SC)
Fox Coll (IL)
Georgia Piedmont Tech Coll (GA)
Goodwin Coll (CT)
Guilford Tech Comm Coll (NC)
Gwinnett Tech Coll (GA)
Harford Comm Coll (MD)
Harper Coll (IL)
H. Councill Trenholm State Tech Coll (AL)
Hesser Coll, Manchester (NH)
Hesser Coll, Nashua (NH)
Hesser Coll, Portsmouth (NH)
Hesser Coll, Salem (NH)
Highland Comm Coll (WA)
Highline Comm Coll (WA)
Inst of Business & Medical Careers (CO)
International Business Coll, Indianapolis (IN)
Iowa Lakes Comm Coll (IA)
Ivy Tech Comm Coll–Central Indiana (IN)
Ivy Tech Comm Coll–Columbus (IN)
Ivy Tech Comm Coll–East Central (IN)
Ivy Tech Comm Coll–Kokomo (IN)
Ivy Tech Comm Coll–Lafayette (IN)
Ivy Tech Comm Coll–North Central (IN)
Ivy Tech Comm Coll–Northeast (IN)
Ivy Tech Comm Coll–Northwest (IN)
Ivy Tech Comm Coll–Richmond (IN)
Ivy Tech Comm Coll–Southeast (IN)
Ivy Tech Comm Coll–Southern Indiana (IN)
Ivy Tech Comm Coll–Southwest (IN)
Ivy Tech Comm Coll–Wabash Valley (IN)
Jackson Comm Coll (MI)
James Sprunt Comm Coll (NC)
Jamestown Business Coll (NY)
Johnston Comm Coll (NC)
Kaplan Career Inst, Broomall Campus (PA)

Kaplan Career Inst, Harrisburg Campus (PA)
Kaplan Career Inst, ICM Campus (PA)
Kaplan Coll, Hammond Campus (IN)
King's Coll (NC)
Lake Area Tech Inst (SD)
Lehigh Carbon Comm Coll (PA)
Lower Columbia Coll (WA)
Macomb Comm Coll (MI)
Miami Dade Coll (FL)
Mid Michigan Comm Coll (MI)
Minneapolis Business Coll (MN)
Minnesota School of Business–Brooklyn Center (MN)
Minnesota School of Business–Plymouth (MN)
Minnesota School of Business–Richfield (MN)
Minnesota School of Business–St. Cloud (MN)
Minnesota School of Business–Shakopee (MN)
Mitchell Tech Inst (SD)
Mohave Comm Coll (AZ)
Mohawk Valley Comm Coll (NY)
Montana State U–Great Falls Coll of Technology (MT)
Montgomery Comm Coll (NC)
Montgomery County Comm Coll (PA)
Moraine Park Tech Coll (WI)
Moreno Valley Coll (CA)
Mount Wachusett Comm Coll (MA)
Niagara County Comm Coll (NY)
Northeast Alabama Comm Coll (AL)
North Seattle Comm Coll (WA)
Northwestern Connecticut Comm Coll (CT)
Oakland Comm Coll (MI)
Oklahoma City Comm Coll (OK)
Olympic Coll (WA)
Orange Coast Coll (CA)
Randolph Comm Coll (NC)
Raritan Valley Comm Coll (NJ)
Rasmussen Coll Aurora (IL)
Rasmussen Coll Bismarck (ND)
Rasmussen Coll Bloomington (MN)
Rasmussen Coll Brooklyn Park (MN)
Rasmussen Coll Eagan (MN)
Rasmussen Coll Fort Myers (FL)
Rasmussen Coll Green Bay (WI)
Rasmussen Coll Lake Elmo/Woodbury (MN)
Rasmussen Coll Mankato (MN)
Rasmussen Coll Moorhead (MN)
Rasmussen Coll New Port Richey (FL)
Rasmussen Coll Ocala (FL)
Rasmussen Coll Rockford (IL)
Rasmussen Coll St. Cloud (MN)
St. Clair County Comm Coll (MI)
Salt Lake Comm Coll (UT)
San Joaquin Valley Coll, Bakersfield (CA)
San Joaquin Valley Coll, Fresno (CA)
San Joaquin Valley Coll, Rancho Cordova (CA)
San Joaquin Valley Coll, Salida (CA)
San Joaquin Valley Coll, Visalia (CA)
San Joaquin Valley Coll–Online (CA)
Santa Rosa Jr Coll (CA)
Southeastern Comm Coll (IA)
Southern Maine Comm Coll (ME)
Southern State Comm Coll (OH)
Southwestern Illinois Coll (IL)
Southwestern Michigan Coll (MI)
Springfield Tech Comm Coll (MA)
Stark State Coll (OH)
Terra State Comm Coll (OH)
Texas State Tech Coll Harlingen (TX)
Westmoreland County Comm Coll (PA)
West Virginia Jr Coll–Bridgeport (WV)
West Virginia Northern Comm Coll (WV)
Wood Tobe–Coburn School (NY)

York County Comm Coll (ME)
YTI Career Inst–York (PA)

MEDICAL/HEALTH MANAGEMENT AND CLINICAL ASSISTANT

Owens Comm Coll, Toledo (OH)
Pittsburgh Tech Inst, Oakdale (PA)
Terra State Comm Coll (OH)

MEDICAL INFORMATICS

The Comm Coll of Baltimore County (MD)

MEDICAL INSURANCE CODING

Bucks County Comm Coll (PA)
Career Training Academy, Pittsburgh (PA)
Comm Care Coll (OK)
Cowley County Comm Coll and Area Vocational–Tech School (KS)
Dakota Coll at Bottineau (ND)
Elmira Business Inst (NY)
Fountainhead Coll of Technology (TN)
Goodwin Coll (CT)
Moraine Park Tech Coll (WI)
North Dakota State Coll of Science (ND)
Northeast Comm Coll (NE)
Salem Comm Coll (NJ)
Springfield Tech Comm Coll (MA)
Terra State Comm Coll (OH)
Westmoreland County Comm Coll (PA)
West Virginia Jr Coll–Bridgeport (WV)

MEDICAL INSURANCE/ MEDICAL BILLING

Anthem Coll–Maryland Heights (MO)
Goodwin Coll (CT)
Jackson Comm Coll (MI)
Montana State U–Great Falls Coll of Technology (MT)
San Joaquin Valley Coll, Bakersfield (CA)
Southwest Mississippi Comm Coll (MS)
Spencerian Coll (KY)

MEDICAL OFFICE ASSISTANT

ACT Coll, Arlington (VA)
Bucks County Comm Coll (PA)
Central Wyoming Coll (WY)
Dakota Coll at Bottineau (ND)
Front Range Comm Coll (CO)
Iowa Lakes Comm Coll (IA)
Jamestown Comm Coll (NY)
Kankakee Comm Coll (IL)
Lincoln Land Comm Coll (IL)
Mitchell Tech Inst (SD)
Moraine Park Tech Coll (WI)
New York Career Inst (NY)
Pittsburgh Tech Inst, Oakdale (PA)
San Joaquin Valley Coll, Salida (CA)
San Joaquin Valley Coll, Visalia (CA)
Southwestern Illinois Coll (IL)
Terra State Comm Coll (OH)
Westmoreland County Comm Coll (PA)
White Mountains Comm Coll (NH)

MEDICAL OFFICE COMPUTER SPECIALIST

Iowa Lakes Comm Coll (IA)
Rogue Comm Coll (OR)

MEDICAL OFFICE MANAGEMENT

Beaufort County Comm Coll (NC)
Big Bend Comm Coll (WA)
Cape Fear Comm Coll (NC)
Career Tech Coll (LA)
Catawba Valley Comm Coll (NC)
Coll of Lake County (IL)
Columbus Tech Coll (GA)
Erie Comm Coll, North Campus (NY)
Fayetteville Tech Comm Coll (NC)

Florida State Coll at Jacksonville (FL)
Forrest Coll (SC)
Fox Valley Tech Coll (WI)
Georgia Northwestern Tech Coll (GA)
Guilford Tech Comm Coll (NC)
Johnston Comm Coll (NC)
Kaplan Coll, Brownsville Campus (TX)
Kaplan Coll, Chesapeake Campus (VA)
Kaplan Coll, Columbus Campus (OH)
Kaplan Coll, Corpus Christi Campus (TX)
Kaplan Coll, Northwest Indianapolis Campus (IN)
Kaplan Coll, Pembroke Pines Campus (FL)
Kaplan Coll, San Antonio–San Pedro Area Campus (TX)
Kilian Comm Coll (SD)
Long Island Business Inst (NY)
Randolph Comm Coll (NC)
Red Rocks Comm Coll (CO)
Rockingham Comm Coll (NC)
San Joaquin Valley Coll, Rancho Cordova (CA)
San Joaquin Valley Coll–Online (CA)
The U of Akron–Wayne Coll (OH)
Wilson Comm Coll (NC)

MEDICAL RADIOLOGIC TECHNOLOGY

Aiken Tech Coll (SC)
Albany Tech Coll (GA)
Anne Arundel Comm Coll (MD)
Athens Tech Coll (GA)
Augusta Tech Coll (GA)
Bluegrass Comm and Tech Coll (KY)
Bunker Hill Comm Coll (MA)
Burlington County Coll (NJ)
Cape Fear Comm Coll (NC)
Carolinas Coll of Health Sciences (NC)
Catawba Valley Comm Coll (NC)
Central Georgia Tech Coll (GA)
Chattahoochee Tech Coll (GA)
Chattanooga State Comm Coll (TN)
Chippewa Valley Tech Coll (WI)
Coll of DuPage (IL)
Coll of Lake County (IL)
Columbus Tech Coll (GA)
Comm Coll of Allegheny County (PA)
The Comm Coll of Baltimore County (MD)
Comm Coll of Philadelphia (PA)
El Centro Coll (TX)
El Paso Comm Coll (TX)
Erie Comm Coll (NY)
Fiorello H. LaGuardia Comm Coll of the City U of New York (NY)
Florida State Coll at Jacksonville (FL)
Foothill Coll (CA)
GateWay Comm Coll (AZ)
Gateway Tech Coll (WI)
Gulf Coast State Coll (FL)
Gwinnett Tech Coll (GA)
Hagerstown Comm Coll (MD)
Hillsborough Comm Coll (FL)
Holyoke Comm Coll (MA)
Hutchinson Comm Coll and Area Vocational School (KS)
Illinois Eastern Comm Colls, Olney Central College (IL)
Ivy Tech Comm Coll–Central Indiana (IN)
Ivy Tech Comm Coll–Columbus (IN)
Ivy Tech Comm Coll–East Central (IN)
Ivy Tech Comm Coll–Wabash Valley (IN)
Jackson Comm Coll (MI)
Johnston Comm Coll (NC)
Kent State U at Ashtabula (OH)
Kent State U at Salem (OH)
Kilgore Coll (TX)
Lake Michigan Coll (MI)
Lanier Tech Coll (GA)
Massachusetts Bay Comm Coll (MA)
Middle Georgia Tech Coll (GA)
Mitchell Tech Inst (SD)

Mohawk Valley Comm Coll (NY)
Montgomery Coll (MD)
Montgomery County Comm Coll (PA)
Moraine Park Tech Coll (WI)
Mott Comm Coll (MI)
Niagara County Comm Coll (NY)
Northeast Comm Coll (NE)
North Shore Comm Coll (MA)
Oakland Comm Coll (MI)
Owensboro Comm and Tech Coll (KY)
Owens Comm Coll, Toledo (OH)
Penn State New Kensington (PA)
Penn State Schuylkill (PA)
Pensacola State Coll (FL)
St. Philip's Coll (TX)
Salt Lake Comm Coll (UT)
Southeastern Tech Coll (GA)
Southeast Missouri Hospital Coll of Nursing and Health Sciences (MO)
Southern Crescent Tech Coll (GA)
Southern Maine Comm Coll (ME)
Southwestern Oklahoma State U at Sayre (OK)
Southwest Georgia Tech Coll (GA)
State Coll of Florida Manatee-Sarasota (FL)
Union County Coll (NJ)
Valencia Coll (FL)
Vincennes U (IN)
Volunteer State Comm Coll (TN)
Waukesha County Tech Coll (WI)
West Georgia Tech Coll (GA)
West Virginia Northern Comm Coll (WV)
Wiregrass Georgia Tech Coll (GA)

MEDICAL RECEPTION

Iowa Lakes Comm Coll (IA)

MEDICAL STAFF SERVICES TECHNOLOGY

John Wood Comm Coll (IL)

MEDICAL TRANSCRIPTION

Cowley County Comm Coll and Area Vocational–Tech School (KS)
Dakota Coll at Bottineau (ND)
El Centro Coll (TX)
GateWay Comm Coll (AZ)
Iowa Lakes Comm Coll (IA)
Jackson Comm Coll (MI)
Mid Michigan Comm Coll (MI)
Montana State U–Great Falls Coll of Technology (MT)
Moraine Park Tech Coll (WI)
North Dakota State Coll of Science (ND)
Northern Essex Comm Coll (MA)
Oakland Comm Coll (MI)
Texas State Tech Coll Harlingen (TX)
Western Dakota Tech Inst (SD)
Westmoreland County Comm Coll (PA)

MEDIUM/HEAVY VEHICLE AND TRUCK TECHNOLOGY

Edison Comm Coll (OH)
Linn State Tech Coll (MO)
Northeast Comm Coll (NE)
St. Cloud Tech & Comm Coll (MN)

MEETING AND EVENT PLANNING

Raritan Valley Comm Coll (NJ)
Southwestern Michigan Coll (MI)

MENTAL AND SOCIAL HEALTH SERVICES AND ALLIED PROFESSIONS RELATED

Coll of Southern Maryland (MD)
Gateway Tech Coll (WI)
John Tyler Comm Coll (VA)
J. Sargeant Reynolds Comm Coll (VA)
Southern Maine Comm Coll (ME)
Southwest Virginia Comm Coll (VA)
Waukesha County Tech Coll (WI)
Wisconsin Indianhead Tech Coll (WI)

MENTAL HEALTH COUNSELING

Alvin Comm Coll (TX)
Comm Coll of Philadelphia (PA)
Comm Coll of Rhode Island (RI)
Dutchess Comm Coll (NY)
Gateway Comm Coll (CT)
Housatonic Comm Coll (CT)
Illinois Central Coll (IL)
Kingsborough Comm Coll of the City U of New York (NY)
Macomb Comm Coll (MI)
Northern Essex Comm Coll (MA)
North Shore Comm Coll (MA)
San Jacinto Coll District (TX)
Tarrant County Coll District (TX)
Truckee Meadows Comm Coll (NV)
Virginia Western Comm Coll (VA)

MERCHANDISING

Coll of DuPage (IL)
Northeast Comm Coll (NE)

MERCHANDISING, SALES, AND MARKETING OPERATIONS RELATED (GENERAL)

Iowa Lakes Comm Coll (IA)
Moraine Park Tech Coll (WI)
Southeast Tech Inst (SD)
State U of New York Coll of Technology at Alfred (NY)

METAL AND JEWELRY ARTS

Fashion Inst of Technology (NY)

METAL FABRICATOR

Moraine Park Tech Coll (WI)

METALLURGICAL TECHNOLOGY

Kilgore Coll (TX)
Macomb Comm Coll (MI)
Penn State DuBois (PA)
Penn State Fayette, The Eberly Campus (PA)
Penn State Hazleton (PA)
Penn State New Kensington (PA)
Penn State Schuylkill (PA)
Penn State Shenango (PA)
Penn State Wilkes-Barre (PA)
Penn State York (PA)

MIDDLE SCHOOL EDUCATION

Arkansas State U–Mountain Home (AR)
Austin Comm Coll (TX)
Delaware Tech & Comm Coll, Jack F. Owens Campus (DE)
Delaware Tech & Comm Coll, Stanton/Wilmington Campus (DE)
Delaware Tech & Comm Coll, Terry Campus (DE)
El Paso Comm Coll (TX)
Erie Comm Coll (NY)
Miami Dade Coll (FL)
Northampton Comm Coll (PA)
Ozarka Coll (AR)
Panola Coll (TX)
San Jacinto Coll District (TX)

MINING TECHNOLOGY

Casper Coll (WY)
Eastern Arizona Coll (AZ)
Illinois Eastern Comm Colls, Wabash Valley College (IL)

MODERN GREEK

Oklahoma City Comm Coll (OK)

MODERN LANGUAGES

Amarillo Coll (TX)
Northwest Florida State Coll (FL)
Oklahoma City Comm Coll (OK)
Otero Jr Coll (CO)
San Diego City Coll (CA)
Tyler Jr Coll (TX)

MOTORCYCLE MAINTENANCE AND REPAIR TECHNOLOGY

Iowa Lakes Comm Coll (IA)
Linn State Tech Coll (MO)
Red Rocks Comm Coll (CO)

MULTI/INTERDISCIPLINARY STUDIES RELATED

Aiken Tech Coll (SC)
Anoka-Ramsey Comm Coll (MN)
Anoka-Ramsey Comm Coll, Cambridge Campus (MN)
Bluegrass Comm and Tech Coll (KY)
Bucks County Comm Coll (PA)
Carroll Comm Coll (MD)
Central Maine Comm Coll (ME)
Chippewa Valley Tech Coll (WI)
Coll of Southern Maryland (MD)
Eastern Arizona Coll (AZ)
El Paso Comm Coll (TX)
Fox Valley Tech Coll (WI)
Gateway Tech Coll (WI)
Harford Comm Coll (MD)
Hawkeye Comm Coll (IA)
Kilgore Coll (TX)
Lake Region State Coll (ND)
Laramie County Comm Coll (WY)
Minnesota State Coll–Southeast Tech (MN)
Moraine Park Tech Coll (WI)
New Mexico State U–Alamogordo (NM)
North Dakota State Coll of Science (ND)
North Hennepin Comm Coll (MN)
Northwest-Shoals Comm Coll (AL)
Oklahoma City Comm Coll (OK)
Panola Coll (TX)
Raritan Valley Comm Coll (NJ)
San Jacinto Coll District (TX)
Waukesha County Tech Coll (WI)
Western Iowa Tech Comm Coll (IA)
West Virginia Northern Comm Coll (WV)
Wisconsin Indianhead Tech Coll (WI)
York County Comm Coll (ME)

MUSEUM STUDIES

Casper Coll (WY)

MUSIC

Alvin Comm Coll (TX)
Amarillo Coll (TX)
Anoka-Ramsey Comm Coll (MN)
Anoka-Ramsey Comm Coll, Cambridge Campus (MN)
Austin Comm Coll (TX)
Brookhaven Coll (TX)
Bucks County Comm Coll (PA)
Bunker Hill Comm Coll (MA)
Burlington County Coll (NJ)
Carroll Comm Coll (MD)
Casper Coll (WY)
Central Wyoming Coll (WY)
Century Coll (MN)
Cochise Coll, Sierra Vista (AZ)
Coll of Lake County (IL)
Coll of the Canyons (CA)
Comm Coll of Allegheny County (PA)
Comm Coll of Philadelphia (PA)
Comm Coll of Rhode Island (RI)
Cowley County Comm Coll and Area Vocational–Tech School (KS)
Crowder Coll (MO)
Dawson Comm Coll (MT)
Eastern Arizona Coll (AZ)
Elgin Comm Coll (IL)
El Paso Comm Coll (TX)
Foothill Coll (CA)
Gavilan Coll (CA)
Grand Rapids Comm Coll (MI)
Harper Coll (IL)
Highline Comm Coll (WA)
Holyoke Comm Coll (MA)
Howard Comm Coll (MD)
Indian River State Coll (FL)
Iowa Lakes Comm Coll (IA)
Jamestown Comm Coll (NY)
Kilgore Coll (TX)
Kingsborough Comm Coll of the City U of New York (NY)
Lake Michigan Coll (MI)
Lansing Comm Coll (MI)
Laramie County Comm Coll (WY)
Lincoln Land Comm Coll (IL)
Manchester Comm Coll (CT)
McHenry County Coll (IL)
Mendocino Coll (CA)
Miami Dade Coll (FL)
Monroe Comm Coll (NY)

Niagara County Comm Coll (NY)
Normandale Comm Coll (MN)
Northeastern Jr Coll (CO)
Northern Essex Comm Coll (MA)
North Seattle Comm Coll (WA)
Northwest Coll (WY)
Northwest Florida State Coll (FL)
Oklahoma City Comm Coll (OK)
Onondaga Comm Coll (NY)
Orange Coast Coll (CA)
Palm Beach State Coll (FL)
Pensacola State Coll (FL)
Raritan Valley Comm Coll (NJ)
St. Philip's Coll (TX)
Salt Lake Comm Coll (UT)
San Diego City Coll (CA)
San Jacinto Coll District (TX)
Santa Monica Coll (CA)
Snow Coll (UT)
Southwestern Illinois Coll (IL)
Southwest Mississippi Comm Coll (MS)
State Coll of Florida Manatee-Sarasota (FL)
Terra State Comm Coll (OH)
Texarkana Coll (TX)
Truckee Meadows Comm Coll (NV)
Umpqua Comm Coll (OR)
Vincennes U (IN)

MUSICAL INSTRUMENT FABRICATION AND REPAIR
Orange Coast Coll (CA)
Western Iowa Tech Comm Coll (IA)

MUSICAL THEATER
Casper Coll (WY)
KD Studio (TX)

MUSIC HISTORY, LITERATURE, AND THEORY
Chattahoochee Valley Comm Coll (AL)
Snow Coll (UT)

MUSIC MANAGEMENT
Austin Comm Coll (TX)
Chandler-Gilbert Comm Coll (AZ)
Houston Comm Coll System (TX)
The Inst of Production and Recording (MN)
Northeast Comm Coll (NE)
Orange Coast Coll (CA)
Terra State Comm Coll (OH)

MUSIC PERFORMANCE
Casper Coll (WY)
Houston Comm Coll System (TX)
Lansing Comm Coll (MI)
Macomb Comm Coll (MI)
Miami Dade Coll (FL)
Northeast Comm Coll (NE)
Oakland Comm Coll (MI)
Reedley Coll (CA)
State Coll of Florida Manatee-Sarasota (FL)
Terra State Comm Coll (OH)

MUSIC RELATED
Carl Albert State Coll (OK)
Cayuga County Comm Coll (NY)
Minnesota School of Business-Richfield (MN)
Santa Rosa Jr Coll (CA)
Terra State Comm Coll (OH)

MUSIC TEACHER EDUCATION
Amarillo Coll (TX)
Casper Coll (WY)
Coll of Lake County (IL)
Copiah-Lincoln Comm Coll (MS)
Iowa Lakes Comm Coll (IA)
Miami Dade Coll (FL)
Northeast Comm Coll (NE)
Northeastern Jr Coll (CO)
Pensacola State Coll (FL)
Snow Coll (UT)
Southwestern Illinois Coll (IL)
Southwest Mississippi Comm Coll (MS)
State Coll of Florida Manatee-Sarasota (FL)
Umpqua Comm Coll (OR)
Vincennes U (IN)

MUSIC TECHNOLOGY
Foothill Coll (CA)
Owens Comm Coll, Toledo (OH)

MUSIC THEORY AND COMPOSITION
Houston Comm Coll System (TX)
Oakland Comm Coll (MI)
State Coll of Florida Manatee-Sarasota (FL)

NAIL TECHNICIAN AND MANICURIST
Kirtland Comm Coll (MI)

NANOTECHNOLOGY
Chippewa Valley Tech Coll (WI)
Foothill Coll (CA)
Harper Coll (IL)
Lehigh Carbon Comm Coll (PA)
Normandale Comm Coll (MN)
North Dakota State Coll of Science (ND)
Oakland Comm Coll (MI)

NATURAL RESOURCES AND CONSERVATION RELATED
Murray State Coll (OK)
Palau Comm Coll (Palau)
Southwestern Indian Polytechnic Inst (NM)

NATURAL RESOURCES/CONSERVATION
Central Oregon Comm Coll (OR)
Dakota Coll at Bottineau (ND)
Fox Valley Tech Coll (WI)
Iowa Lakes Comm Coll (IA)
Itasca Comm Coll (MN)
Niagara County Comm Coll (NY)
Olympic Coll (WA)
St. Philip's Coll (TX)
Santa Rosa Jr Coll (CA)
State U of New York Coll of Environmental Science & Forestry, Ranger School (NY)
Tompkins Cortland Comm Coll (NY)
Vincennes U (IN)

NATURAL RESOURCES MANAGEMENT AND POLICY
Central Carolina Tech Coll (SC)
Coll of Lake County (IL)
Hawkeye Comm Coll (IA)
Itasca Comm Coll (MN)
Northwest Coll (WY)
Pensacola State Coll (FL)

NATURAL RESOURCES MANAGEMENT AND POLICY RELATED
Reedley Coll (CA)

NATURAL SCIENCES
Amarillo Coll (TX)
Colorado Mountain Coll (CO)
Foothill Coll (CA)
Highline Comm Coll (WA)
Iowa Lakes Comm Coll (IA)
Miami Dade Coll (FL)
Northeastern Jr Coll (CO)
Orange Coast Coll (CA)
Santa Rosa Jr Coll (CA)
Umpqua Comm Coll (OR)

NETWORK AND SYSTEM ADMINISTRATION
Bucks County Comm Coll (PA)
Central Comm Coll–Grand Island Campus (NE)
Dakota Coll at Bottineau (ND)
Florida State Coll at Jacksonville (FL)
Gavilan Coll (CA)
Genesee Comm Coll (NY)
Houston Comm Coll System (TX)
Illinois Valley Comm Coll (IL)
Iowa Lakes Comm Coll (IA)
Island Drafting and Tech Inst (NY)
ITT Tech Inst, Bessemer (AL)
ITT Tech Inst, Madison (AL)
ITT Tech Inst, Mobile (AL)

ITT Tech Inst, Phoenix (AZ)
ITT Tech Inst, Tucson (AZ)
ITT Tech Inst (AR)
ITT Tech Inst, Lathrop (CA)
ITT Tech Inst, Orange (CA)
ITT Tech Inst, Oxnard (CA)
ITT Tech Inst, Rancho Cordova (CA)
ITT Tech Inst, San Bernardino (CA)
ITT Tech Inst, San Diego (CA)
ITT Tech Inst, San Dimas (CA)
ITT Tech Inst, Sylmar (CA)
ITT Tech Inst, Torrance (CA)
ITT Tech Inst, Aurora (CO)
ITT Tech Inst, Thornton (CO)
ITT Tech Inst, Fort Lauderdale (FL)
ITT Tech Inst, Fort Myers (FL)
ITT Tech Inst, Jacksonville (FL)
ITT Tech Inst, Lake Mary (FL)
ITT Tech Inst, Miami (FL)
ITT Tech Inst, Pinellas Park (FL)
ITT Tech Inst, Tallahassee (FL)
ITT Tech Inst, Tampa (FL)
ITT Tech Inst (ID)
ITT Tech Inst, Mount Prospect (IL)
ITT Tech Inst, Fort Wayne (IN)
ITT Tech Inst, Merrillville (IN)
ITT Tech Inst, Newburgh (IN)
ITT Tech Inst, Cedar Rapids (IA)
ITT Tech Inst, Clive (IA)
ITT Tech Inst, Louisville (KY)
ITT Tech Inst, Baton Rouge (LA)
ITT Tech Inst, St. Rose (LA)
ITT Tech Inst, Canton (MI)
ITT Tech Inst, Swartz Creek (MI)
ITT Tech Inst, Troy (MI)
ITT Tech Inst, Wyoming (MI)
ITT Tech Inst, Eden Prairie (MN)
ITT Tech Inst, Arnold (MO)
ITT Tech Inst, Earth City (MO)
ITT Tech Inst (NE)
ITT Tech Inst, Henderson (NV)
ITT Tech Inst (NM)
ITT Tech Inst, Albany (NY)
ITT Tech Inst, Getzville (NY)
ITT Tech Inst, Liverpool (NY)
ITT Tech Inst, Akron (OH)
ITT Tech Inst, Columbus (OH)
ITT Tech Inst, Dayton (OH)
ITT Tech Inst, Hilliard (OH)
ITT Tech Inst, Maumee (OH)
ITT Tech Inst, Norwood (OH)
ITT Tech Inst, Strongsville (OH)
ITT Tech Inst, Warrensville Heights (OH)
ITT Tech Inst, Youngstown (OH)
ITT Tech Inst, Tulsa (OK)
ITT Tech Inst, Portland (OR)
ITT Tech Inst, Columbia (SC)
ITT Tech Inst, Chattanooga (TN)
ITT Tech Inst, Cordova (TN)
ITT Tech Inst, Johnson City (TN)
ITT Tech Inst, Knoxville (TN)
ITT Tech Inst, Nashville (TN)
ITT Tech Inst, Arlington (TX)
ITT Tech Inst, Austin (TX)
ITT Tech Inst, DeSoto (TX)
ITT Tech Inst, Houston (TX)
ITT Tech Inst, Houston (TX)
ITT Tech Inst, Richardson (TX)
ITT Tech Inst, San Antonio (TX)
ITT Tech Inst, Webster (TX)
ITT Tech Inst (UT)
ITT Tech Inst, Chantilly (VA)
ITT Tech Inst, Richmond (VA)
ITT Tech Inst, Salem (VA)
ITT Tech Inst, Springfield (VA)
ITT Tech Inst, Everett (WA)
ITT Tech Inst, Seattle (WA)
ITT Tech Inst, Spokane Valley (WA)
ITT Tech Inst (WV)
ITT Tech Inst, Green Bay (WI)
ITT Tech Inst, Greenfield (WI)
ITT Tech Inst, Madison (WI)
Kaskaskia Coll (IL)
Metropolitan Comm Coll–Business & Technology Campus (MO)
Minneapolis Comm and Tech Coll (MN)
Mitchell Tech Inst (SD)
Montgomery County Comm Coll (PA)
Owensboro Comm and Tech Coll (KY)
Palm Beach State Coll (FL)
Rockland Comm Coll (NY)
Seminole State Coll of Florida (FL)

Southwestern Illinois Coll (IL)
Southwest Mississippi Comm Coll (MS)
Springfield Tech Comm Coll (MA)
Sullivan Coll of Technology and Design (KY)
Tallahassee Comm Coll (FL)
Truckee Meadows Comm Coll (NV)
Westmoreland County Comm Coll (PA)

NONPROFIT MANAGEMENT
Goodwin Coll (CT)
Miami Dade Coll (FL)

NUCLEAR AND INDUSTRIAL RADIOLOGIC TECHNOLOGIES RELATED
Eastern Idaho Tech Coll (ID)

NUCLEAR ENGINEERING
Itasca Comm Coll (MN)

NUCLEAR ENGINEERING TECHNOLOGY
Delaware Tech & Comm Coll, Jack F. Owens Campus (DE)
Delaware Tech & Comm Coll, Stanton/Wilmington Campus (DE)

NUCLEAR MEDICAL TECHNOLOGY
Amarillo Coll (TX)
Bluegrass Comm and Tech Coll (KY)
Coll of DuPage (IL)
Comm Coll of Allegheny County (PA)
Delaware Tech & Comm Coll, Stanton/Wilmington Campus (DE)
Fayetteville Tech Comm Coll (NC)
GateWay Comm Coll (AZ)
Gateway Comm Coll (CT)
Hillsborough Comm Coll (FL)
Houston Comm Coll System (TX)
Howard Comm Coll (MD)
Miami Dade Coll (FL)
Oakland Comm Coll (MI)
Orange Coast Coll (CA)
Owens Comm Coll, Toledo (OH)
Southeast Tech Inst (SD)
Springfield Tech Comm Coll (MA)
Union County Coll (NJ)
Vincennes U (IN)

NUCLEAR/NUCLEAR POWER TECHNOLOGY
Cape Fear Comm Coll (NC)
Florida State Coll at Jacksonville (FL)
Linn State Tech Coll (MO)
Salem Comm Coll (NJ)
Terra State Comm Coll (OH)
Three Rivers Comm Coll (CT)

NURSING ADMINISTRATION
South Suburban Coll (IL)

NURSING ASSISTANT/AIDE AND PATIENT CARE ASSISTANT/AIDE
Comm Coll of Allegheny County (PA)
Lake Region State Coll (ND)
Moraine Park Tech Coll (WI)
Southwest Mississippi Comm Coll (MS)
Western Iowa Tech Comm Coll (IA)

NURSING PRACTICE
Santa Rosa Jr Coll (CA)

NUTRITION SCIENCES
Casper Coll (WY)
Mohawk Valley Comm Coll (NY)
Santa Rosa Jr Coll (CA)

OCCUPATIONAL HEALTH AND INDUSTRIAL HYGIENE
Niagara County Comm Coll (NY)

OCCUPATIONAL SAFETY AND HEALTH TECHNOLOGY
Anne Arundel Comm Coll (MD)
Central Wyoming Coll (WY)
The Comm Coll of Baltimore County (MD)
GateWay Comm Coll (AZ)
Ivy Tech Comm Coll–Central Indiana (IN)
Ivy Tech Comm Coll–Northeast (IN)
Ivy Tech Comm Coll–Northwest (IN)
Ivy Tech Comm Coll–Wabash Valley (IN)
Kilgore Coll (TX)
Lanier Tech Coll (GA)
Okefenokee Tech Coll (GA)
Oklahoma State U, Oklahoma City (OK)
St. Philip's Coll (TX)
San Diego City Coll (CA)
San Jacinto Coll District (TX)
San Juan Coll (NM)
Southwest Mississippi Comm Coll (MS)
U of Alaska Anchorage, Kodiak Coll (AK)

OCCUPATIONAL THERAPIST ASSISTANT
Augusta Tech Coll (GA)
Austin Comm Coll (TX)
Cape Fear Comm Coll (NC)
Casper Coll (WY)
Coll of DuPage (IL)
Comm Coll of Allegheny County (PA)
Comm Coll of Philadelphia (PA)
Comm Coll of Rhode Island (RI)
Delaware Tech & Comm Coll, Jack F. Owens Campus (DE)
Delaware Tech & Comm Coll, Stanton/Wilmington Campus (DE)
Erie Comm Coll, North Campus (NY)
Fiorello H. LaGuardia Comm Coll of the City U of New York (NY)
Fox Valley Tech Coll (WI)
Goodwin Coll (CT)
Hawkeye Comm Coll (IA)
Houston Comm Coll System (TX)
Illinois Central Coll (IL)
Ivy Tech Comm Coll–Central Indiana (IN)
Jamestown Comm Coll (NY)
J. Sargeant Reynolds Comm Coll (VA)
Kaskaskia Coll (IL)
Kilgore Coll (TX)
Lake Area Tech Inst (SD)
Lehigh Carbon Comm Coll (PA)
Lincoln Land Comm Coll (IL)
Macomb Comm Coll (MI)
Manchester Comm Coll (CT)
Mott Comm Coll (MI)
Murray State Coll (OK)
North Dakota State Coll of Science (ND)
Oakland Comm Coll (MI)
Owens Comm Coll, Toledo (OH)
Panola Coll (TX)
Penn State DuBois (PA)
Penn State Mont Alto (PA)
Polk State Coll (FL)
St. Philip's Coll (TX)
Salt Lake Comm Coll (UT)
South Suburban Coll (IL)
Southwestern Oklahoma State U at Sayre (OK)
Springfield Tech Comm Coll (MA)
State Coll of Florida Manatee-Sarasota (FL)
Western Iowa Tech Comm Coll (IA)
Wisconsin Indianhead Tech Coll (WI)

OCCUPATIONAL THERAPY
Amarillo Coll (TX)
Coll of DuPage (IL)
The Comm Coll of Baltimore County (MD)
Kaplan Career Inst, ICM Campus (PA)
Kent State U at East Liverpool (OH)

Metropolitan Comm Coll–Penn Valley (MO)
North Shore Comm Coll (MA)
Oklahoma City Comm Coll (OK)
Palm Beach State Coll (FL)
Quinsigamond Comm Coll (MA)
Rockland Comm Coll (NY)
Stark State Coll (OH)
State Coll of Florida Manatee-Sarasota (FL)
Trident Tech Coll (SC)

OCEANOGRAPHY (CHEMICAL AND PHYSICAL)

Cape Fear Comm Coll (NC)

OFFICE MANAGEMENT

Berkeley City Coll (CA)
Brookhaven Coll (TX)
Catawba Valley Comm Coll (NC)
Coll of Central Florida (FL)
Coll of DuPage (IL)
Comm Coll of Allegheny County (PA)
Consolidated School of Business, York (PA)
Dakota Coll at Bottineau (ND)
Delaware County Comm Coll (PA)
Delaware Tech & Comm Coll, Jack F. Owens Campus (DE)
Delaware Tech & Comm Coll, Stanton/Wilmington Campus (DE)
Delaware Tech & Comm Coll, Terry Campus (DE)
Erie Comm Coll, North Campus (NY)
Erie Comm Coll, South Campus (NY)
Fayetteville Tech Comm Coll (NC)
Florida State Coll at Jacksonville (FL)
Forrest Coll (SC)
Goodwin Coll (CT)
Guilford Tech Comm Coll (NC)
Howard Comm Coll (MD)
Iowa Lakes Comm Coll (IA)
Ivy Tech Comm Coll–Wabash Valley (IN)
Jefferson Comm Coll (NY)
Jefferson State Comm Coll (AL)
Johnston Comm Coll (NC)
John Wood Comm Coll (IL)
Lake Region State Coll (ND)
Northeast Comm Coll (NE)
Oakland Comm Coll (MI)
Owens Comm Coll, Toledo (OH)
Peninsula Coll (WA)
Pensacola State Coll (FL)
Randolph Comm Coll (NC)
Riverside City Coll (CA)
Rockingham Comm Coll (NC)
St. Clair County Comm Coll (MI)
Santa Monica Coll (CA)
South Suburban Coll (IL)
Spencerian Coll (KY)
Valencia Coll (FL)
White Mountains Comm Coll (NH)
Wilson Comm Coll (NC)

OFFICE OCCUPATIONS AND CLERICAL SERVICES

Blue Ridge Comm and Tech Coll (WV)
Central Wyoming Coll (WY)
Dakota Coll at Bottineau (ND)
El Centro Coll (TX)
Florida State Coll at Jacksonville (FL)
Inst of Business & Medical Careers (CO)
Iowa Lakes Comm Coll (IA)
ITI Tech Coll (LA)
Jamestown Comm Coll (NY)
Lake Region State Coll (ND)
Moraine Park Tech Coll (WI)
New Mexico State U–Alamogordo (NM)
Northeast Comm Coll (NE)
Reedley Coll (CA)
Southeast Tech Inst (SD)
The U of Montana–Helena Coll of Technology (MT)

OPERATIONS MANAGEMENT

Bunker Hill Comm Coll (MA)

Central Carolina Comm Coll (NC)
Chattanooga State Comm Coll (TN)
Fayetteville Tech Comm Coll (NC)
Fox Valley Tech Coll (WI)
Gateway Tech Coll (WI)
Georgia Piedmont Tech Coll (GA)
Hillsborough Comm Coll (FL)
Kilgore Coll (TX)
Macomb Comm Coll (MI)
McHenry County Coll (IL)
Mineral Area Coll (MO)
Moraine Park Tech Coll (WI)
Owens Comm Coll, Toledo (OH)
Pensacola State Coll (FL)
Stark State Coll (OH)
Terra State Comm Coll (OH)
Waukesha County Tech Coll (WI)
Wisconsin Indianhead Tech Coll (WI)

OPERATIONS RESEARCH

Delaware Tech & Comm Coll, Stanton/Wilmington Campus (DE)

OPHTHALMIC AND OPTOMETRIC SUPPORT SERVICES AND ALLIED PROFESSIONS RELATED

Vincennes U (IN)

OPHTHALMIC LABORATORY TECHNOLOGY

Georgia Piedmont Tech Coll (GA)

OPHTHALMIC TECHNOLOGY

Miami Dade Coll (FL)
Volunteer State Comm Coll (TN)

OPTICAL SCIENCES

Corning Comm Coll (NY)

OPTICIANRY

Comm Coll of Rhode Island (RI)
El Paso Comm Coll (TX)
Erie Comm Coll, North Campus (NY)
Georgia Piedmont Tech Coll (GA)
Hillsborough Comm Coll (FL)
Holyoke Comm Coll (MA)
Ogeechee Tech Coll (GA)
Raritan Valley Comm Coll (NJ)
Southwestern Indian Polytechnic Inst (NM)

OPTOMETRIC TECHNICIAN

El Paso Comm Coll (TX)
Hillsborough Comm Coll (FL)
J. Sargeant Reynolds Comm Coll (VA)
Raritan Valley Comm Coll (NJ)
San Jacinto Coll District (TX)
Tyler Jr Coll (TX)

ORGANIZATIONAL BEHAVIOR

Chandler-Gilbert Comm Coll (AZ)
GateWay Comm Coll (AZ)

ORGANIZATIONAL LEADERSHIP

Olympic Coll (WA)

ORNAMENTAL HORTICULTURE

Coll of DuPage (IL)
Coll of Lake County (IL)
Comm Coll of Allegheny County (PA)
Dakota Coll at Bottineau (ND)
Foothill Coll (CA)
Gwinnett Tech Coll (GA)
Mendocino Coll (CA)
Miami Dade Coll (FL)
Orange Coast Coll (CA)
Pensacola State Coll (FL)
Valencia Coll (FL)

ORTHOTICS/PROSTHETICS

Century Coll (MN)
Oklahoma City Comm Coll (OK)

OUTDOOR EDUCATION

Corning Comm Coll (NY)

PAINTING AND WALL COVERING

GateWay Comm Coll (AZ)
Ivy Tech Comm Coll–Central Indiana (IN)
Ivy Tech Comm Coll–East Central (IN)
Ivy Tech Comm Coll–Lafayette (IN)
Ivy Tech Comm Coll–North Central (IN)
Ivy Tech Comm Coll–Northeast (IN)
Ivy Tech Comm Coll–Northwest (IN)
Ivy Tech Comm Coll–Southwest (IN)
Ivy Tech Comm Coll–Wabash Valley (IN)
Southwestern Illinois Coll (IL)

PARKS, RECREATION AND LEISURE

Central Wyoming Coll (WY)
Coll of Central Florida (FL)
Coll of the Canyons (CA)
Colorado Mountain Coll, Timberline Campus (CO)
The Comm Coll of Baltimore County (MD)
Dakota Coll at Bottineau (ND)
Dutchess Comm Coll (NY)
Iowa Lakes Comm Coll (IA)
Kingsborough Comm Coll of the City U of New York (NY)
Miami Dade Coll (FL)
Monroe Comm Coll (NY)
Muskegon Comm Coll (MI)
Niagara County Comm Coll (NY)
Northern Essex Comm Coll (MA)
Northwest Coll (WY)
Northwestern Connecticut Comm Coll (CT)
Onondaga Comm Coll (NY)
Red Rocks Comm Coll (CO)
San Diego City Coll (CA)
San Juan Coll (NM)
Tallahassee Comm Coll (FL)
Vincennes U (IN)

PARKS, RECREATION AND LEISURE FACILITIES MANAGEMENT

Augusta Tech Coll (GA)
Bucks County Comm Coll (PA)
Central Wyoming Coll (WY)
Chattahoochee Tech Coll (GA)
Colorado Mountain Coll, Alpine Campus (CO)
Colorado Mountain Coll, Timberline Campus (CO)
Dakota Coll at Bottineau (ND)
Mohawk Valley Comm Coll (NY)
Moraine Valley Comm Coll (IL)
North Georgia Tech Coll (GA)
Northwestern Connecticut Comm Coll (CT)
Oklahoma City Comm Coll (OK)
Santa Rosa Jr Coll (CA)
Tompkins Cortland Comm Coll (NY)
YTI Career Inst–York (PA)

PARKS, RECREATION, LEISURE, AND FITNESS STUDIES RELATED

Anne Arundel Comm Coll (MD)
Dakota Coll at Bottineau (ND)
Tompkins Cortland Comm Coll (NY)

PARTS AND WAREHOUSING OPERATIONS AND MAINTENANCE TECHNOLOGY

Red Rocks Comm Coll (CO)

PATHOLOGIST ASSISTANT

Lake Region State Coll (ND)

PEACE STUDIES AND CONFLICT RESOLUTION

El Centro Coll (TX)

PERCUSSION INSTRUMENTS

Iowa Lakes Comm Coll (IA)

PERIOPERATIVE/OPERATING ROOM AND SURGICAL NURSING

Comm Coll of Allegheny County (PA)

PERSONAL AND CULINARY SERVICES RELATED

GateWay Comm Coll (AZ)
Mohave Comm Coll (AZ)

PETROLEUM ENGINEERING

Kilgore Coll (TX)

PETROLEUM TECHNOLOGY

Southwest Mississippi Comm Coll (MS)
U of Arkansas Comm Coll at Morrilton (AR)

PHARMACY

Indian River State Coll (FL)
Iowa Lakes Comm Coll (IA)
Mid Michigan Comm Coll (MI)

PHARMACY, PHARMACEUTICAL SCIENCES, AND ADMINISTRATION RELATED

ACT Coll, Arlington (VA)

PHARMACY TECHNICIAN

Albany Tech Coll (GA)
Anthem Coll–Maryland Heights (MO)
Augusta Tech Coll (GA)
Casper Coll (WY)
Columbus Tech Coll (GA)
Comm Care Coll (OK)
Comm Coll of Allegheny County (PA)
Eastern Arizona Coll (AZ)
El Paso Comm Coll (TX)
Fayetteville Tech Comm Coll (NC)
Foothill Coll (CA)
Guilford Tech Comm Coll (NC)
Inst of Business & Medical Careers (CO)
Kirtland Comm Coll (MI)
Mohave Comm Coll (AZ)
Moraine Park Tech Coll (WI)
North Dakota State Coll of Science (ND)
North Seattle Comm Coll (WA)
Oakland Comm Coll (MI)
Rasmussen Coll Aurora (IL)
Rasmussen Coll Bloomington (MN)
Rasmussen Coll Brooklyn Park (MN)
Rasmussen Coll Eagan (MN)
Rasmussen Coll Fort Myers (FL)
Rasmussen Coll Green Bay (WI)
Rasmussen Coll Lake Elmo/Woodbury (MN)
Rasmussen Coll Mankato (MN)
Rasmussen Coll Moorhead (MN)
Rasmussen Coll New Port Richey (FL)
Rasmussen Coll Ocala (FL)
Rasmussen Coll Rockford (IL)
Rasmussen Coll St. Cloud (MN)
San Joaquin Valley Coll, Bakersfield (CA)
San Joaquin Valley Coll, Fresno (CA)
San Joaquin Valley Coll, Rancho Cordova (CA)
San Joaquin Valley Coll, Salida (CA)
San Joaquin Valley Coll, Visalia (CA)
Santa Rosa Jr Coll (CA)
Southern Crescent Tech Coll (GA)
Vincennes U (IN)
West Georgia Tech Coll (GA)
West Virginia Jr Coll–Bridgeport (WV)

PHILOSOPHY

Austin Comm Coll (TX)
Burlington County Coll (NJ)
Cochise Coll, Sierra Vista (AZ)
Fiorello H. LaGuardia Comm Coll of the City U of New York (NY)
Foothill Coll (CA)

Georgia Highlands Coll (GA)
Harper Coll (IL)
Indian River State Coll (FL)
Iowa Lakes Comm Coll (IA)
Lake Michigan Coll (MI)
Lansing Comm Coll (MI)
Miami Dade Coll (FL)
Minneapolis Comm and Tech Coll (MN)
Oklahoma City Comm Coll (OK)
Orange Coast Coll (CA)
Palm Beach State Coll (FL)
Pensacola State Coll (FL)
St. Philip's Coll (TX)
San Jacinto Coll District (TX)
Santa Rosa Jr Coll (CA)
Snow Coll (UT)
State Coll of Florida Manatee-Sarasota (FL)
Truckee Meadows Comm Coll (NV)
Vincennes U (IN)

PHLEBOTOMY TECHNOLOGY

Casper Coll (WY)
Westmoreland County Comm Coll (PA)

PHOTOGRAPHIC AND FILM/VIDEO TECHNOLOGY

Catawba Valley Comm Coll (NC)
Fiorello H. LaGuardia Comm Coll of the City U of New York (NY)
Kaplan Coll, Dayton Campus (OH)
Miami Dade Coll (FL)
Minneapolis Comm and Tech Coll (MN)
Oakland Comm Coll (MI)
Pensacola State Coll (FL)
Randolph Comm Coll (NC)
Salt Lake Comm Coll (UT)

PHOTOGRAPHY

Amarillo Coll (TX)
Antonelli Inst (PA)
The Art Inst of Seattle (WA)
Casper Coll (WY)
Cecil Coll (MD)
Coll of DuPage (IL)
Coll of the Canyons (CA)
Colorado Mountain Coll (CO)
Comm Coll of Philadelphia (PA)
Delaware Tech & Comm Coll, Terry Campus (DE)
Foothill Coll (CA)
Gwinnett Tech Coll (GA)
Howard Comm Coll (MD)
Iowa Lakes Comm Coll (IA)
Lansing Comm Coll (MI)
Miami Dade Coll (FL)
Mott Comm Coll (MI)
Oakland Comm Coll (MI)
Onondaga Comm Coll (NY)
Orange Coast Coll (CA)
Palm Beach State Coll (FL)
Red Rocks Comm Coll (CO)
Rockland Comm Coll (NY)
San Diego City Coll (CA)
Scottsdale Comm Coll (AZ)
Sullivan County Comm Coll (NY)
Tompkins Cortland Comm Coll (NY)
Tyler Jr Coll (TX)

PHOTOJOURNALISM

Randolph Comm Coll (NC)
Vincennes U (IN)

PHYSICAL AND BIOLOGICAL ANTHROPOLOGY

Cowley County Comm Coll and Area Vocational–Tech School (KS)

PHYSICAL EDUCATION TEACHING AND COACHING

Alvin Comm Coll (TX)
Amarillo Coll (TX)
Bucks County Comm Coll (PA)
Carl Albert State Coll (OK)
Casper Coll (WY)
Clinton Comm Coll (NY)
Copiah-Lincoln Comm Coll (MS)
Crowder Coll (MO)
Erie Comm Coll (NY)
Erie Comm Coll, North Campus (NY)

Erie Comm Coll, South Campus (NY)
Foothill Coll (CA)
Genesee Comm Coll (NY)
Harper Coll (IL)
Indian River State Coll (FL)
Iowa Lakes Comm Coll (IA)
Jamestown Comm Coll (NY)
Kilgore Coll (TX)
Laramie County Comm Coll (WY)
Mendocino Coll (CA)
Miami Dade Coll (FL)
Monroe Comm Coll (NY)
Montgomery County Comm Coll (PA)
Murray State Coll (OK)
Niagara County Comm Coll (NY)
Northeastern Jr Coll (CO)
Northern Essex Comm Coll (MA)
North Hennepin Comm Coll (MN)
Northwest Florida State Coll (FL)
Orange Coast Coll (CA)
Palm Beach State Coll (FL)
Pensacola State Coll (FL)
San Diego City Coll (CA)
Santa Rosa Jr Coll (CA)
Snow Coll (UT)
Southwest Mississippi Comm Coll (MS)
State Coll of Florida Manatee-Sarasota (FL)
Tyler Jr Coll (TX)
Umpqua Comm Coll (OR)
Valencia Coll (FL)
Vincennes U (IN)

PHYSICAL FITNESS TECHNICIAN

Lake Region State Coll (ND)
Minnesota School of Business–Plymouth (MN)
Minnesota School of Business–Richfield (MN)
Minnesota School of Business–St. Cloud (MN)

PHYSICAL SCIENCES

Alvin Comm Coll (TX)
Amarillo Coll (TX)
Austin Comm Coll (TX)
Carl Albert State Coll (OK)
Cecil Coll (MD)
Central Oregon Comm Coll (OR)
Central Wyoming Coll (WY)
Chandler-Gilbert Comm Coll (AZ)
Colorado Mountain Coll, Alpine Campus (CO)
Crowder Coll (MO)
Dakota Coll at Bottineau (ND)
Fiorello H. LaGuardia Comm Coll of the City U of New York (NY)
GateWay Comm Coll (AZ)
Gavilan Coll (CA)
Harper Coll (IL)
Howard Comm Coll (MD)
Hutchinson Comm Coll and Area Vocational School (KS)
Iowa Lakes Comm Coll (IA)
Lake Michigan Coll (MI)
Lehigh Carbon Comm Coll (PA)
Mendocino Coll (CA)
Miami Dade Coll (FL)
Montgomery County Comm Coll (PA)
Northeastern Jr Coll (CO)
Northwestern Connecticut Comm Coll (CT)
Palm Beach State Coll (FL)
Reedley Coll (CA)
Salt Lake Comm Coll (UT)
San Diego City Coll (CA)
San Jacinto Coll District (TX)
San Juan Coll (NM)
Snow Coll (UT)
Southwest Mississippi Comm Coll (MS)
Umpqua Comm Coll (OR)
Vincennes U (IN)

PHYSICAL SCIENCES RELATED

Dakota Coll at Bottineau (ND)

PHYSICAL SCIENCE TECHNOLOGIES RELATED

Westmoreland County Comm Coll (PA)

PHYSICAL THERAPY

Amarillo Coll (TX)
Athens Tech Coll (GA)
Blackhawk Tech Coll (WI)
Central Oregon Comm Coll (OR)
Genesee Comm Coll (NY)
Gwinnett Tech Coll (GA)
Housatonic Comm Coll (CT)
Indian River State Coll (FL)
Kent State U at Ashtabula (OH)
Kent State U at East Liverpool (OH)
Kilgore Coll (TX)
Kingsborough Comm Coll of the City U of New York (NY)
Metropolitan Comm Coll–Penn Valley (MO)
Mid Michigan Comm Coll (MI)
Monroe County Comm Coll (MI)
Oklahoma City Comm Coll (OK)
Palm Beach State Coll (FL)
Seminole State Coll of Florida (FL)
Stark State Coll (OH)
State Coll of Florida Manatee-Sarasota (FL)
Tarrant County Coll District (TX)
Trident Tech Coll (SC)
Tunxis Comm Coll (CT)
Wytheville Comm Coll (VA)

PHYSICAL THERAPY TECHNOLOGY

Anne Arundel Comm Coll (MD)
Anoka-Ramsey Comm Coll (MN)
Austin Comm Coll (TX)
Berkshire Comm Coll (MA)
Carl Albert State Coll (OK)
Carroll Comm Coll (MD)
Chattanooga State Comm Coll (TN)
Chippewa Valley Tech Coll (WI)
Colby Comm Coll (KS)
Coll of Central Florida (FL)
Coll of DuPage (IL)
Coll of Southern Maryland (MD)
Comm Coll of Allegheny County (PA)
Comm Coll of Rhode Island (RI)
Delaware Tech & Comm Coll, Jack F. Owens Campus (DE)
Delaware Tech & Comm Coll, Stanton/Wilmington Campus (DE)
Dutchess Comm Coll (NY)
Edison Comm Coll (OH)
Elgin Comm Coll (IL)
El Paso Comm Coll (TX)
Fayetteville Tech Comm Coll (NC)
Fiorello H. LaGuardia Comm Coll of the City U of New York (NY)
Florida State Coll at Jacksonville (FL)
Fox Coll (IL)
GateWay Comm Coll (AZ)
Gateway Tech Coll (WI)
Guilford Tech Comm Coll (NC)
Gulf Coast State Coll (FL)
Gwinnett Tech Coll (GA)
Hawkeye Comm Coll (IA)
H. Councill Trenholm State Tech Coll (AL)
Hesser Coll, Concord (NH)
Hesser Coll, Manchester (NH)
Houston Comm Coll System (TX)
Hutchinson Comm Coll and Area Vocational School (KS)
Illinois Central Coll (IL)
Indian River State Coll (FL)
Ivy Tech Comm Coll–East Central (IN)
Jefferson State Comm Coll (AL)
Kankakee Comm Coll (IL)
Kaskaskia Coll (IL)
Kilgore Coll (TX)
Kingsborough Comm Coll of the City U of New York (NY)
Lake Area Tech Inst (SD)
Laramie County Comm Coll (WY)
Lehigh Carbon Comm Coll (PA)
Linn State Tech Coll (MO)
Macomb Comm Coll (MI)
Manchester Comm Coll (CT)

Massachusetts Bay Comm Coll (MA)
Miami Dade Coll (FL)
Mohave Comm Coll (AZ)
Montana State U–Great Falls Coll of Technology (MT)
Montgomery Coll (MD)
Mott Comm Coll (MI)
Mount Wachusett Comm Coll (MA)
Murray State Coll (OK)
Niagara County Comm Coll (NY)
Northeast Comm Coll (NE)
North Shore Comm Coll (MA)
Oakland Comm Coll (MI)
Olympic Coll (WA)
Onondaga Comm Coll (NY)
Owens Comm Coll, Toledo (OH)
Pasco-Hernando Comm Coll (FL)
Penn State DuBois (PA)
Penn State Hazleton (PA)
Penn State Mont Alto (PA)
Penn State Shenango (PA)
Pensacola State Coll (FL)
Polk State Coll (FL)
Randolph Comm Coll (NC)
St. Philip's Coll (TX)
Salt Lake Comm Coll (UT)
San Jacinto Coll District (TX)
San Juan Coll (NM)
Southwestern Illinois Coll (IL)
Southwestern Oklahoma State U at Sayre (OK)
Springfield Tech Comm Coll (MA)
State Coll of Florida Manatee-Sarasota (FL)
Union County Coll (NJ)
Vincennes U (IN)
Volunteer State Comm Coll (TN)
Waukesha County Tech Coll (WI)
Western Iowa Tech Comm Coll (IA)
West Kentucky Comm and Tech Coll (KY)

PHYSICIAN ASSISTANT

Foothill Coll (CA)
Moreno Valley Coll (CA)
San Joaquin Valley Coll, Visalia (CA)
State Coll of Florida Manatee-Sarasota (FL)

PHYSICS

Amarillo Coll (TX)
Austin Comm Coll (TX)
Bunker Hill Comm Coll (MA)
Burlington County Coll (NJ)
Casper Coll (WY)
Cecil Coll (MD)
Cochise Coll, Sierra Vista (AZ)
Comm Coll of Allegheny County (PA)
Eastern Arizona Coll (AZ)
Foothill Coll (CA)
Indian River State Coll (FL)
Kilgore Coll (TX)
Kingsborough Comm Coll of the City U of New York (NY)
Lake Michigan Coll (MI)
Los Angeles Harbor Coll (CA)
Miami Dade Coll (FL)
Monroe Comm Coll (NY)
Northampton Comm Coll (PA)
Northeast Comm Coll (NE)
Northwest Coll (WY)
Northwest Florida State Coll (FL)
Oklahoma City Comm Coll (OK)
Oklahoma State U, Oklahoma City (OK)
Orange Coast Coll (CA)
Pensacola State Coll (FL)
Salt Lake Comm Coll (UT)
San Jacinto Coll District (TX)
San Juan Coll (NM)
Santa Rosa Jr Coll (CA)
Snow Coll (UT)
Springfield Tech Comm Coll (MA)
State Coll of Florida Manatee-Sarasota (FL)
Terra State Comm Coll (OH)
Texarkana Coll (TX)
Truckee Meadows Comm Coll (NV)
Tyler Jr Coll (TX)

PHYSICS TEACHER EDUCATION

Anne Arundel Comm Coll (MD)

The Comm Coll of Baltimore County (MD)
Harford Comm Coll (MD)
Montgomery Coll (MD)
State Coll of Florida Manatee-Sarasota (FL)

PIPEFITTING AND SPRINKLER FITTING

GateWay Comm Coll (AZ)
Ivy Tech Comm Coll–Bloomington (IN)
Ivy Tech Comm Coll–Central Indiana (IN)
Ivy Tech Comm Coll–Columbus (IN)
Ivy Tech Comm Coll–East Central (IN)
Ivy Tech Comm Coll–Kokomo (IN)
Ivy Tech Comm Coll–Lafayette (IN)
Ivy Tech Comm Coll–North Central (IN)
Ivy Tech Comm Coll–Northeast (IN)
Ivy Tech Comm Coll–Northwest (IN)
Ivy Tech Comm Coll–Richmond (IN)
Ivy Tech Comm Coll–Southern Indiana (IN)
Ivy Tech Comm Coll–Southwest (IN)
Ivy Tech Comm Coll–Wabash Valley (IN)
Moraine Park Tech Coll (WI)
Oakland Comm Coll (MI)
Southwestern Illinois Coll (IL)

PLANT NURSERY MANAGEMENT

Comm Coll of Allegheny County (PA)
Miami Dade Coll (FL)

PLANT SCIENCES

Reedley Coll (CA)

PLASTICS AND POLYMER ENGINEERING TECHNOLOGY

Coll of DuPage (IL)
El Paso Comm Coll (TX)
Grand Rapids Comm Coll (MI)
Kent State U at Tuscarawas (OH)
Macomb Comm Coll (MI)
Mount Wachusett Comm Coll (MA)
Terra State Comm Coll (OH)
West Georgia Tech Coll (GA)

PLATEMAKING/IMAGING

Illinois Central Coll (IL)

PLAYWRITING AND SCREENWRITING

Minneapolis Comm and Tech Coll (MN)
Northwest Coll (WY)

PLUMBING TECHNOLOGY

GateWay Comm Coll (AZ)
Macomb Comm Coll (MI)
Moraine Park Tech Coll (WI)
North Dakota State Coll of Science (ND)
Northeast Iowa Comm Coll (IA)
Olympic Coll (WA)
St. Cloud Tech & Comm Coll (MN)
Southern Maine Comm Coll (ME)
State U of New York Coll of Technology at Alfred (NY)

POLITICAL SCIENCE AND GOVERNMENT

Austin Comm Coll (TX)
Bainbridge Coll (GA)
Casper Coll (WY)
Cochise Coll, Sierra Vista (AZ)
Eastern Arizona Coll (AZ)
Foothill Coll (CA)
Georgia Highlands Coll (GA)
Indian River State Coll (FL)
Iowa Lakes Comm Coll (IA)
Lake Michigan Coll (MI)
Lansing Comm Coll (MI)
Laramie County Comm Coll (WY)
Miami Dade Coll (FL)

Monroe Comm Coll (NY)
Northern Essex Comm Coll (MA)
Northwest Coll (WY)
Oklahoma City Comm Coll (OK)
Orange Coast Coll (CA)
Otero Jr Coll (CO)
Palm Beach State Coll (FL)
St. Philip's Coll (TX)
Salt Lake Comm Coll (UT)
San Diego City Coll (CA)
San Jacinto Coll District (TX)
Santa Rosa Jr Coll (CA)
Snow Coll (UT)
Texarkana Coll (TX)
Tyler Jr Coll (TX)
Umpqua Comm Coll (OR)
Vincennes U (IN)

POLYMER/PLASTICS ENGINEERING

Central Oregon Comm Coll (OR)

POLYSOMNOGRAPHY

Catawba Valley Comm Coll (NC)
Genesee Comm Coll (NY)
Minneapolis Comm and Tech Coll (MN)

PORTUGUESE

Miami Dade Coll (FL)

POULTRY SCIENCE

Crowder Coll (MO)
Delaware Tech & Comm Coll, Jack F. Owens Campus (DE)

PRECISION METAL WORKING RELATED

Oakland Comm Coll (MI)
Reedley Coll (CA)

PRECISION PRODUCTION RELATED

Lake Michigan Coll (MI)
Mineral Area Coll (MO)
Mott Comm Coll (MI)
Salem Comm Coll (NJ)

PRECISION PRODUCTION TRADES

Bucks County Comm Coll (PA)
Coll of DuPage (IL)
Mineral Area Coll (MO)
Owensboro Comm and Tech Coll (KY)

PRE-DENTISTRY STUDIES

Austin Comm Coll (TX)
Casper Coll (WY)
Howard Comm Coll (MD)
Iowa Lakes Comm Coll (IA)
Kilgore Coll (TX)
Lake Michigan Coll (MI)
Northeast Comm Coll (NE)
Pensacola State Coll (FL)
St. Philip's Coll (TX)
Vincennes U (IN)

PRE-ENGINEERING

Amarillo Coll (TX)
Anoka-Ramsey Comm Coll (MN)
Anoka-Ramsey Comm Coll, Cambridge Campus (MN)
Chipola Coll (FL)
Coll of the Canyons (CA)
Colorado Mountain Coll, Alpine Campus (CO)
Comm Coll of Philadelphia (PA)
Corning Comm Coll (NY)
Cowley County Comm Coll and Area Vocational–Tech School (KS)
Crowder Coll (MO)
Highline Comm Coll (WA)
Housatonic Comm Coll (CT)
Illinois Valley Comm Coll (IL)
Indian River State Coll (FL)
Iowa Lakes Comm Coll (IA)
Itasca Comm Coll (MN)
Lake Michigan Coll (MI)
Los Angeles Harbor Coll (CA)
Macomb Comm Coll (MI)
Metropolitan Comm Coll–Longview (MO)

Metropolitan Comm Coll–Maple Woods (MO)
Miami Dade Coll (FL)
Mid Michigan Comm Coll (MI)
Monroe County Comm Coll (MI)
Northeast Comm Coll (NE)
Northeastern Jr Coll (CO)
North Hennepin Comm Coll (MN)
North Shore Comm Coll (MA)
Northwestern Connecticut Comm Coll (CT)
Oklahoma City Comm Coll (OK)
Oklahoma State U, Oklahoma City (OK)
Otero Jr Coll (CO)
Palm Beach State Coll (FL)
Polk State Coll (FL)
Rainy River Comm Coll (MN)
Randolph Comm Coll (NC)
St. Philip's Coll (TX)
San Diego City Coll (CA)
Snow Coll (UT)
Southern Maine Comm Coll (ME)
Three Rivers Comm Coll (CT)
Umpqua Comm Coll (OR)
Valencia Coll (FL)
Virginia Western Comm Coll (VA)
Westmoreland County Comm Coll (PA)

PRE-LAW STUDIES
Anne Arundel Comm Coll (MD)
Carl Albert State Coll (OK)
Casper Coll (WY)
Central Oregon Comm Coll (OR)
Central Wyoming Coll (WY)
Foothill Coll (CA)
Iowa Lakes Comm Coll (IA)
Kilgore Coll (TX)
Lake Michigan Coll (MI)
Laramie County Comm Coll (WY)
Northeast Comm Coll (NE)
Pensacola State Coll (FL)
St. Philip's Coll (TX)

PREMEDICAL STUDIES
Austin Comm Coll (TX)
Casper Coll (WY)
Central Oregon Comm Coll (OR)
Dakota Coll at Bottineau (ND)
Eastern Arizona Coll (AZ)
Howard Comm Coll (MD)
Iowa Lakes Comm Coll (IA)
Kilgore Coll (TX)
Lake Michigan Coll (MI)
Lansing Comm Coll (MI)
Northeast Comm Coll (NE)
Pensacola State Coll (FL)
St. Philip's Coll (TX)
San Juan Coll (NM)
Springfield Tech Comm Coll (MA)
Vincennes U (IN)

PRENURSING STUDIES
Dakota Coll at Bottineau (ND)
Edison Comm Coll (OH)
Iowa Lakes Comm Coll (IA)
Northeast Comm Coll (NE)
Oklahoma State U, Oklahoma City (OK)
Pensacola State Coll (FL)
Randolph Comm Coll (NC)
St. Philip's Coll (TX)
Southwestern Michigan Coll (MI)
Texas State Tech Coll Harlingen (TX)

PRE-OCCUPATIONAL THERAPY
Casper Coll (WY)

PRE-OPTOMETRY
Casper Coll (WY)

PRE-PHARMACY STUDIES
Amarillo Coll (TX)
Austin Comm Coll (TX)
Casper Coll (WY)
Central Oregon Comm Coll (OR)
Eastern Arizona Coll (AZ)
Howard Comm Coll (MD)
Iowa Lakes Comm Coll (IA)
Kilgore Coll (TX)
Lake Michigan Coll (MI)
Laramie County Comm Coll (WY)
Monroe Comm Coll (NY)

Northeast Comm Coll (NE)
Northwest Coll (WY)
Pensacola State Coll (FL)
St. Philip's Coll (TX)
State Coll of Florida Manatee-Sarasota (FL)
Vincennes U (IN)

PRE-PHYSICAL THERAPY
Casper Coll (WY)

PRE-VETERINARY STUDIES
Austin Comm Coll (TX)
Casper Coll (WY)
Dakota Coll at Bottineau (ND)
Howard Comm Coll (MD)
Iowa Lakes Comm Coll (IA)
Kilgore Coll (TX)
Lake Michigan Coll (MI)
Northeast Comm Coll (NE)
Pensacola State Coll (FL)
Vincennes U (IN)

PRINTING MANAGEMENT
Moraine Park Tech Coll (WI)

PRINTING PRESS OPERATION
Iowa Lakes Comm Coll (IA)

PRINTMAKING
Florida State Coll at Jacksonville (FL)

PROFESSIONAL, TECHNICAL, BUSINESS, AND SCIENTIFIC WRITING
Austin Comm Coll (TX)
Coll of Lake County (IL)
Gateway Tech Coll (WI)
Oklahoma State U, Oklahoma City (OK)
Southwestern Michigan Coll (MI)
Three Rivers Comm Coll (CT)

PROJECT MANAGEMENT
ITT Tech Inst, Lake Mary (FL)

PSYCHIATRIC/MENTAL HEALTH SERVICES TECHNOLOGY
Anne Arundel Comm Coll (MD)
Comm Coll of Allegheny County (PA)
The Comm Coll of Baltimore County (MD)
Dutchess Comm Coll (NY)
El Paso Comm Coll (TX)
Fiorello H. LaGuardia Comm Coll of the City U of New York (NY)
Guilford Tech Comm Coll (NC)
Gulf Coast State Coll (FL)
Hagerstown Comm Coll (MD)
Harford Comm Coll (MD)
Hillsborough Comm Coll (FL)
Houston Comm Coll System (TX)
Illinois Central Coll (IL)
Ivy Tech Comm Coll–Bloomington (IN)
Ivy Tech Comm Coll–Central Indiana (IN)
Ivy Tech Comm Coll–Columbus (IN)
Ivy Tech Comm Coll–East Central (IN)
Ivy Tech Comm Coll–Kokomo (IN)
Ivy Tech Comm Coll–Lafayette (IN)
Ivy Tech Comm Coll–Northeast (IN)
Ivy Tech Comm Coll–Northwest (IN)
Ivy Tech Comm Coll–Richmond (IN)
Ivy Tech Comm Coll–Southeast (IN)
Ivy Tech Comm Coll–Southern Indiana (IN)
Ivy Tech Comm Coll–Southwest (IN)
Ivy Tech Comm Coll–Wabash Valley (IN)
Kingsborough Comm Coll of the City U of New York (NY)
Montgomery Coll (MD)
Montgomery County Comm Coll (PA)
Mount Wachusett Comm Coll (MA)
North Dakota State Coll of Science (ND)

PSYCHOLOGY
Amarillo Coll (TX)
Austin Comm Coll (TX)
Bainbridge Coll (GA)
Berkeley City Coll (CA)
Bucks County Comm Coll (PA)
Bunker Hill Comm Coll (MA)
Burlington County Coll (NJ)
Carroll Comm Coll (MD)
Casper Coll (WY)
Central Wyoming Coll (WY)
Chandler-Gilbert Comm Coll (AZ)
Cochise Coll, Sierra Vista (AZ)
Coll of the Canyons (CA)
Colorado Mountain Coll (CO)
Comm Coll of Allegheny County (PA)
Comm Coll of Philadelphia (PA)
Crowder Coll (MO)
Dakota Coll at Bottineau (ND)
Delaware County Comm Coll (PA)
Eastern Arizona Coll (AZ)
Foothill Coll (CA)
Genesee Comm Coll (NY)
Georgia Highlands Coll (GA)
Harper Coll (IL)
Hesser Coll, Concord (NH)
Hesser Coll, Manchester (NH)
Hesser Coll, Nashua (NH)
Hesser Coll, Portsmouth (NH)
Hesser Coll, Salem (NH)
Highline Comm Coll (WA)
Howard Comm Coll (MD)
Hutchinson Comm Coll and Area Vocational School (KS)
Indian River State Coll (FL)
Iowa Lakes Comm Coll (IA)
Itasca Comm Coll (MN)
Kankakee Comm Coll (IL)
Kilgore Coll (TX)
Kilian Comm Coll (SD)
Lake Michigan Coll (MI)
Lansing Comm Coll (MI)
Laramie County Comm Coll (WY)
Lehigh Carbon Comm Coll (PA)
Mendocino Coll (CA)
Miami Dade Coll (FL)
Mid Michigan Comm Coll (MI)
Mohave Comm Coll (AZ)
Monroe County Comm Coll (MI)
Montgomery County Comm Coll (PA)
Northeast Comm Coll (NE)
Northeastern Jr Coll (CO)
Northwest Coll (WY)
Oklahoma City Comm Coll (OK)
Oklahoma State U, Oklahoma City (OK)
Otero Jr Coll (CO)
Palm Beach State Coll (FL)
Pensacola State Coll (FL)
St. Philip's Coll (TX)
Salt Lake Comm Coll (UT)
San Diego City Coll (CA)
San Jacinto Coll District (TX)
San Juan Coll (NM)
Santa Rosa Jr Coll (CA)
State Coll of Florida Manatee-Sarasota (FL)
Terra State Comm Coll (OH)
Truckee Meadows Comm Coll (NV)
Tyler Jr Coll (TX)
Umpqua Comm Coll (OR)
Vincennes U (IN)

PSYCHOLOGY RELATED
Cayuga County Comm Coll (NY)
Murray State Coll (OK)

PUBLIC ADMINISTRATION
Fayetteville Tech Comm Coll (NC)
Housatonic Comm Coll (CT)
Houston Comm Coll System (TX)
Laramie County Comm Coll (WY)
Miami Dade Coll (FL)
Minneapolis Comm and Tech Coll (MN)
Mohawk Valley Comm Coll (NY)
Owens Comm Coll, Toledo (OH)
Scottsdale Comm Coll (AZ)
State Coll of Florida Manatee-Sarasota (FL)
Tallahassee Comm Coll (FL)
Three Rivers Comm Coll (CT)
Westchester Comm Coll (NY)

PUBLIC ADMINISTRATION AND SOCIAL SERVICE PROFESSIONS RELATED
Cleveland State Comm Coll (TN)
Erie Comm Coll (NY)
J. Sargeant Reynolds Comm Coll (VA)
Oklahoma State U, Oklahoma City (OK)
Onondaga Comm Coll (NY)

PUBLIC HEALTH
Anne Arundel Comm Coll (MD)

PUBLIC HEALTH EDUCATION AND PROMOTION
Berkeley City Coll (CA)

PUBLIC HEALTH RELATED
Berkeley City Coll (CA)
Salt Lake Comm Coll (UT)

PUBLIC RELATIONS, ADVERTISING, AND APPLIED COMMUNICATION RELATED
Harper Coll (IL)

PUBLIC RELATIONS/IMAGE MANAGEMENT
Amarillo Coll (TX)
Cecil Coll (MD)
Crowder Coll (MO)
Vincennes U (IN)

QUALITY CONTROL AND SAFETY TECHNOLOGIES RELATED
Blue Ridge Comm and Tech Coll (WV)
Ivy Tech Comm Coll–Lafayette (IN)
Ivy Tech Comm Coll–Wabash Valley (IN)
John Tyler Comm Coll (VA)
Macomb Comm Coll (MI)

QUALITY CONTROL TECHNOLOGY
Central Carolina Comm Coll (NC)
Central Comm Coll–Columbus Campus (NE)
Central Comm Coll–Hastings Campus (NE)
Comm Coll of Allegheny County (PA)
Gateway Tech Coll (WI)
Grand Rapids Comm Coll (MI)
Illinois Eastern Comm Colls, Frontier Community College (IL)
Illinois Eastern Comm Colls, Lincoln Trail College (IL)
Ivy Tech Comm Coll–Lafayette (IN)
Macomb Comm Coll (MI)
Metropolitan Comm Coll–Business & Technology Campus (MO)
Monroe Comm Coll (NY)
Northampton Comm Coll (PA)
Owens Comm Coll, Toledo (OH)
Salt Lake Comm Coll (UT)
Tarrant County Coll District (TX)

RADIATION PROTECTION/ HEALTH PHYSICS TECHNOLOGY
Aiken Tech Coll (SC)

RADIO AND TELEVISION
Alvin Comm Coll (TX)
Amarillo Coll (TX)
Austin Comm Coll (TX)
Bucks County Comm Coll (PA)
Central Carolina Comm Coll (NC)
Central Wyoming Coll (WY)
Colby Comm Coll (KS)
Coll of the Canyons (CA)
Gulf Coast State Coll (FL)
Illinois Eastern Comm Colls, Wabash Valley College (IL)
International Coll of Broadcasting (OH)
Iowa Lakes Comm Coll (IA)
Miami Dade Coll (FL)
Northwest Coll (WY)
Onondaga Comm Coll (NY)
San Diego City Coll (CA)

Santa Monica Coll (CA)
State Coll of Florida Manatee-Sarasota (FL)
Sullivan County Comm Coll (NY)
Virginia Western Comm Coll (VA)

RADIO AND TELEVISION BROADCASTING TECHNOLOGY
Central Comm Coll–Hastings Campus (NE)
Gateway Tech Coll (WI)
Houston Comm Coll System (TX)
Iowa Lakes Comm Coll (IA)
Lehigh Carbon Comm Coll (PA)
Miami Dade Coll (FL)
Mineral Area Coll (MO)
Mount Wachusett Comm Coll (MA)
Northampton Comm Coll (PA)
Northeast Comm Coll (NE)
Oakland Comm Coll (MI)
St. Clair County Comm Coll (MI)
Salt Lake Comm Coll (UT)
San Jacinto Coll District (TX)
Springfield Tech Comm Coll (MA)
State Coll of Florida Manatee-Sarasota (FL)
Tompkins Cortland Comm Coll (NY)
Vincennes U (IN)
Westmoreland County Comm Coll (PA)

RADIOLOGIC TECHNOLOGY/ SCIENCE
ACT Coll, Arlington (VA)
Amarillo Coll (TX)
Austin Comm Coll (TX)
Blackhawk Tech Coll (WI)
Brookhaven Coll (TX)
Career Tech Coll (LA)
Carl Albert State Coll (OK)
Carolinas Coll of Health Sciences (NC)
Casper Coll (WY)
Central Oregon Comm Coll (OR)
Century Coll (MN)
Clark Coll (WA)
Comm Coll of Rhode Island (RI)
Delaware Tech & Comm Coll, Jack F. Owens Campus (DE)
Delaware Tech & Comm Coll, Stanton/Wilmington Campus (DE)
El Centro Coll (TX)
Elgin Comm Coll (IL)
El Paso Comm Coll (TX)
Fayetteville Tech Comm Coll (NC)
Foothill Coll (CA)
Gadsden State Comm Coll (AL)
GateWay Comm Coll (AZ)
Georgia Highlands Coll (GA)
Harper Coll (IL)
H. Councill Trenholm State Tech Coll (AL)
Houston Comm Coll System (TX)
Illinois Central Coll (IL)
Jefferson State Comm Coll (AL)
John Wood Comm Coll (IL)
Kankakee Comm Coll (IL)
Kaplan Coll, Las Vegas Campus, Las Vegas (NV)
Kaskaskia Coll (IL)
Kilgore Coll (TX)
Lake Michigan Coll (MI)
Laramie County Comm Coll (WY)
Lincoln Land Comm Coll (IL)
Miami Dade Coll (FL)
Minnesota State Coll–Southeast Tech (MN)
Mitchell Tech Inst (SD)
Montana State U–Great Falls Coll of Technology (MT)
Montgomery County Comm Coll (PA)
Moraine Valley Comm Coll (IL)
Northampton Comm Coll (PA)
Northeast Iowa Comm Coll (IA)
Northern Essex Comm Coll (MA)
Oklahoma State U, Oklahoma City (OK)
Pasco-Hernando Comm Coll (FL)
Piedmont Virginia Comm Coll (VA)
Polk State Coll (FL)
Quinsigamond Comm Coll (MA)
Randolph Comm Coll (NC)
Red Rocks Comm Coll (CO)
San Jacinto Coll District (TX)

Santa Rosa Jr Coll (CA)
Southern Maine Comm Coll (ME)
South Suburban Coll (IL)
Southwestern Illinois Coll (IL)
Southwest Virginia Comm Coll (VA)
Spencerian Coll (KY)
Springfield Tech Comm Coll (MA)
State Coll of Florida Manatee-Sarasota (FL)
Truckee Meadows Comm Coll (NV)
Union County Coll (NJ)
Valencia Coll (FL)
Virginia Western Comm Coll (VA)
Westmoreland County Comm Coll (PA)

RADIO, TELEVISION, AND DIGITAL COMMUNICATION RELATED
Cayuga County Comm Coll (NY)
Mitchell Tech Inst (SD)
Montgomery County Comm Coll (PA)
Northwest Coll (WY)

RANGE SCIENCE AND MANAGEMENT
Casper Coll (WY)
Central Wyoming Coll (WY)
Northwest Coll (WY)
Snow Coll (UT)

REAL ESTATE
Amarillo Coll (TX)
Austin Comm Coll (TX)
Coll of DuPage (IL)
Coll of the Canyons (CA)
Comm Coll of Allegheny County (PA)
Edison Comm Coll (OH)
El Paso Comm Coll (TX)
Florida State Coll at Jacksonville (FL)
Foothill Coll (CA)
Gavilan Coll (CA)
Houston Comm Coll System (TX)
Iowa Lakes Comm Coll (IA)
Kent State U at Ashtabula (OH)
Lansing Comm Coll (MI)
Los Angeles Harbor Coll (CA)
Mendocino Coll (CA)
Montgomery County Comm Coll (PA)
Norco Coll (CA)
Northeast Comm Coll (NE)
Northern Essex Comm Coll (MA)
North Seattle Comm Coll (WA)
Northwest Florida State Coll (FL)
Rainy River Comm Coll (MN)
Red Rocks Comm Coll (CO)
Riverside City Coll (CA)
San Diego City Coll (CA)
San Jacinto Coll District (TX)
Santa Rosa Jr Coll (CA)
Scottsdale Comm Coll (AZ)
Southern State Comm Coll (OH)
Terra State Comm Coll (OH)
Texarkana Coll (TX)
Waukesha County Tech Coll (WI)
Westmoreland County Comm Coll (PA)

RECEPTIONIST
Dakota Coll at Bottineau (ND)
Iowa Lakes Comm Coll (IA)

RECORDING ARTS TECHNOLOGY
The Art Inst of Seattle (WA)
Comm Coll of Philadelphia (PA)
Fiorello H. LaGuardia Comm Coll of the City U of New York (NY)
Guilford Tech Comm Coll (NC)
The Inst of Production and Recording (MN)
International Coll of Broadcasting (OH)
Kansas City Kansas Comm Coll (KS)
Lehigh Carbon Comm Coll (PA)
Miami Dade Coll (FL)
Minneapolis Comm and Tech Coll (MN)
Montgomery County Comm Coll (PA)

Northeast Comm Coll (NE)
Springfield Tech Comm Coll (MA)
Union County Coll (NJ)
Vincennes U (IN)

REGISTERED NURSING, NURSING ADMINISTRATION, NURSING RESEARCH AND CLINICAL NURSING RELATED
John Wood Comm Coll (IL)
Red Rocks Comm Coll (CO)

REGISTERED NURSING/ REGISTERED NURSE
Aiken Tech Coll (SC)
Alvin Comm Coll (TX)
Amarillo Coll (TX)
Ancilla Coll (IN)
Anne Arundel Comm Coll (MD)
Anoka-Ramsey Comm Coll (MN)
Anoka-Ramsey Comm Coll, Cambridge Campus (MN)
Athens Tech Coll (GA)
Austin Comm Coll (TX)
Bainbridge Coll (GA)
Beaufort County Comm Coll (NC)
Berkshire Comm Coll (MA)
Bevill State Comm Coll (AL)
Big Bend Comm Coll (WA)
Blackhawk Tech Coll (WI)
Bluegrass Comm and Tech Coll (KY)
Brookhaven Coll (TX)
Bucks County Comm Coll (PA)
Bunker Hill Comm Coll (MA)
Burlington County Coll (NJ)
Cape Fear Comm Coll (NC)
Carl Albert State Coll (OK)
Carolinas Coll of Health Sciences (NC)
Carroll Comm Coll (MD)
Casper Coll (WY)
Catawba Valley Comm Coll (NC)
Cayuga County Comm Coll (NY)
Cecil Coll (MD)
Central Carolina Comm Coll (NC)
Central Carolina Tech Coll (SC)
Central Comm Coll–Grand Island Campus (NE)
Central Maine Comm Coll (ME)
Central Oregon Comm Coll (OR)
Central Wyoming Coll (WY)
Century Coll (MN)
Chandler-Gilbert Comm Coll (AZ)
Chattahoochee Valley Comm Coll (AL)
Chattanooga State Comm Coll (TN)
Chipola Coll (FL)
Chippewa Valley Tech Coll (WI)
The Christ Coll of Nursing and Health Sciences (OH)
City Colls of Chicago, Harry S. Truman College (IL)
Clark Coll (WA)
Cleveland State Comm Coll (TN)
Clinton Comm Coll (NY)
Cochise Coll, Sierra Vista (AZ)
Colby Comm Coll (KS)
Coll of Central Florida (FL)
Coll of DuPage (IL)
Coll of Lake County (IL)
Coll of Southern Maryland (MD)
Coll of the Canyons (CA)
Colorado Mountain Coll (CO)
Columbus Tech Coll (GA)
Comm Coll of Allegheny County (PA)
Comm Coll of Philadelphia (PA)
Comm Coll of Rhode Island (RI)
Copiah-Lincoln Comm Coll (MS)
Corning Comm Coll (NY)
Crowder Coll (MO)
Dakota Coll at Bottineau (ND)
Delaware County Comm Coll (PA)
Delaware Tech & Comm Coll, Jack F. Owens Campus (DE)
Delaware Tech & Comm Coll, Stanton/Wilmington Campus (DE)
Delaware Tech & Comm Coll, Terry Campus (DE)
Do&nna Ana Comm Coll (NM)
Dutchess Comm Coll (NY)
Dyersburg State Comm Coll (TN)
Eastern Arizona Coll (AZ)

Eastern Idaho Tech Coll (ID)
Edison Comm Coll (OH)
El Centro Coll (TX)
Elgin Comm Coll (IL)
Ellis School of Nursing (NY)
El Paso Comm Coll (TX)
Erie Comm Coll (NY)
Erie Comm Coll, North Campus (NY)
Fayetteville Tech Comm Coll (NC)
Fiorello H. LaGuardia Comm Coll of the City U of New York (NY)
Florida State Coll at Jacksonville (FL)
Fox Valley Tech Coll (WI)
Front Range Comm Coll (CO)
Gadsden State Comm Coll (AL)
GateWay Comm Coll (AZ)
Gateway Comm Coll (CT)
Gateway Tech Coll (WI)
Gavilan Coll (CA)
Genesee Comm Coll (NY)
Georgia Highlands Coll (GA)
Good Samaritan Coll of Nursing and Health Science (OH)
Goodwin Coll (CT)
Grand Rapids Comm Coll (MI)
Guilford Tech Comm Coll (NC)
Gulf Coast State Coll (FL)
Hagerstown Comm Coll (MD)
Harford Comm Coll (MD)
Harper Coll (IL)
Hawkeye Comm Coll (IA)
Highland Comm Coll (IL)
Highline Comm Coll (WA)
Hillsborough Comm Coll (FL)
Holyoke Comm Coll (MA)
Housatonic Comm Coll (CT)
Houston Comm Coll System (TX)
Howard Comm Coll (MD)
Hutchinson Comm Coll and Area Vocational School (KS)
Illinois Central Coll (IL)
Illinois Eastern Comm Colls, Frontier Community College (IL)
Illinois Eastern Comm Colls, Olney Central College (IL)
Illinois Valley Comm Coll (IL)
Indian River State Coll (FL)
Iowa Lakes Comm Coll (IA)
ITT Tech Inst, Bessemer (AL)
ITT Tech Inst, Madison (AL)
ITT Tech Inst, Mobile (AL)
ITT Tech Inst, Phoenix (AZ)
ITT Tech Inst, Rancho Cordova (CA)
ITT Tech Inst, Fort Lauderdale (FL)
ITT Tech Inst, Fort Myers (FL)
ITT Tech Inst, Jacksonville (FL)
ITT Tech Inst, Lake Mary (FL)
ITT Tech Inst, Miami (FL)
ITT Tech Inst, Pinellas Park (FL)
ITT Tech Inst, Tallahassee (FL)
ITT Tech Inst, Tampa (FL)
ITT Tech Inst (ID)
ITT Tech Inst, Orland Park (IL)
ITT Tech Inst, Fort Wayne (IN)
ITT Tech Inst, Merrillville (IN)
ITT Tech Inst, Newburgh (IN)
ITT Tech Inst, Louisville (KY)
ITT Tech Inst, Canton (MI)
ITT Tech Inst, Earth City (MO)
ITT Tech Inst, Henderson (NV)
ITT Tech Inst (NM)
ITT Tech Inst, High Point (NC)
ITT Tech Inst, Akron (OH)
ITT Tech Inst, Dayton (OH)
ITT Tech Inst, Hilliard (OH)
ITT Tech Inst, Norwood (OH)
ITT Tech Inst, Strongsville (OH)
ITT Tech Inst, Warrensville Heights (OH)
ITT Tech Inst, Youngstown (OH)
ITT Tech Inst, Tulsa (OK)
ITT Tech Inst, Portland (OR)
ITT Tech Inst, Nashville (TN)
ITT Tech Inst, Richardson (TX)
ITT Tech Inst, Norfolk (VA)
ITT Tech Inst, Salem (VA)
ITT Tech Inst (WV)
Ivy Tech Comm Coll–Bloomington (IN)
Ivy Tech Comm Coll–Central Indiana (IN)
Ivy Tech Comm Coll–East Central (IN)

Ivy Tech Comm Coll–Lafayette (IN)
Ivy Tech Comm Coll–North Central (IN)
Ivy Tech Comm Coll–Northwest (IN)
Ivy Tech Comm Coll–Richmond (IN)
Ivy Tech Comm Coll–Southeast (IN)
Ivy Tech Comm Coll–Southern Indiana (IN)
Ivy Tech Comm Coll–Southwest (IN)
Ivy Tech Comm Coll–Wabash Valley (IN)
Jackson Comm Coll (MI)
James Sprunt Comm Coll (NC)
Jamestown Comm Coll (NY)
Jefferson Comm Coll (NY)
Jefferson State Comm Coll (AL)
Johnston Comm Coll (NC)
John Tyler Comm Coll (VA)
J. Sargeant Reynolds Comm Coll (VA)
Kankakee Comm Coll (IL)
Kansas City Kansas Comm Coll (KS)
Kaplan Coll, Dayton Campus (OH)
Kaplan Coll, Las Vegas Campus, Las Vegas (NV)
Kaskaskia Coll (IL)
Kent State U at Ashtabula (OH)
Kent State U at East Liverpool (OH)
Kent State U at Tuscarawas (OH)
Kilgore Coll (TX)
Kingsborough Comm Coll of the City U of New York (NY)
Kirtland Comm Coll (MI)
Lake Michigan Coll (MI)
Laramie County Comm Coll (WY)
Lawson State Comm Coll (AL)
Lehigh Carbon Comm Coll (PA)
Lincoln Land Comm Coll (IL)
Los Angeles Harbor Coll (CA)
Lower Columbia Coll (WA)
Lurleen B. Wallace Comm Coll (AL)
Macomb Comm Coll (MI)
Massachusetts Bay Comm Coll (MA)
McHenry County Coll (IL)
Metropolitan Comm Coll–Penn Valley (MO)
Miami Dade Coll (FL)
Mid Michigan Comm Coll (MI)
Mid-Plains Comm Coll, North Platte (NE)
Mineral Area Coll (MO)
Minneapolis Comm and Tech Coll (MN)
Minnesota State Coll–Southeast Tech (MN)
Missouri State U–West Plains (MO)
Mohave Comm Coll (AZ)
Mohawk Valley Comm Coll (NY)
Monroe Comm Coll (NY)
Monroe County Comm Coll (MI)
Montcalm Comm Coll (MI)
Montgomery Coll (MD)
Montgomery County Comm Coll (PA)
Moraine Park Tech Coll (WI)
Moraine Valley Comm Coll (IL)
Motlow State Comm Coll (TN)
Mott Comm Coll (MI)
Mount Wachusett Comm Coll (MA)
Murray State Coll (OK)
Muskegon Comm Coll (MI)
New Mexico State U–Alamogordo (NM)
Niagara County Comm Coll (NY)
Normandale Comm Coll (MN)
Northampton Comm Coll (PA)
North Dakota State Coll of Science (ND)
Northeast Alabama Comm Coll (AL)
Northeast Comm Coll (NE)
Northeastern Jr Coll (CO)
Northeast Iowa Comm Coll (IA)
Northern Essex Comm Coll (MA)
North Hennepin Comm Coll (MN)
North Seattle Comm Coll (WA)
North Shore Comm Coll (MA)
Northwest Coll (WY)
Northwest Florida State Coll (FL)
Northwest-Shoals Comm Coll (AL)
Northwest Tech Coll (MN)

Oakland Comm Coll (MI)
Ocean County Coll (NJ)
Oklahoma City Comm Coll (OK)
Oklahoma State U, Oklahoma City (OK)
Olympic Coll (WA)
Onondaga Comm Coll (NY)
Otero Jr Coll (CO)
Owensboro Comm and Tech Coll (KY)
Owens Comm Coll, Toledo (OH)
Palau Comm Coll (Palau)
Palm Beach State Coll (FL)
Panola Coll (TX)
Pasco-Hernando Comm Coll (FL)
Peninsula Coll (WA)
Penn State Fayette, The Eberly Campus (PA)
Penn State Mont Alto (PA)
Penn State Worthington Scranton (PA)
Pensacola State Coll (FL)
Piedmont Virginia Comm Coll (VA)
Polk State Coll (FL)
Quinsigamond Comm Coll (MA)
Randolph Comm Coll (NC)
Raritan Valley Comm Coll (NJ)
Riverside City Coll (CA)
Rockingham Comm Coll (NC)
Rockland Comm Coll (NY)
Rogue Comm Coll (OR)
St. Cloud Tech & Comm Coll (MN)
St. Elizabeth Coll of Nursing (NY)
St. Joseph's Coll of Nursing (NY)
Salem Comm Coll (NJ)
Salt Lake Comm Coll (UT)
San Diego City Coll (CA)
San Jacinto Coll District (TX)
San Joaquin Valley Coll, Visalia (CA)
San Juan Coll (NM)
Santa Monica Coll (CA)
Santa Rosa Jr Coll (CA)
Scottsdale Comm Coll (AZ)
Seminole State Coll of Florida (FL)
Shawnee Comm Coll (IL)
Southeastern Comm Coll (IA)
Southeast Missouri Hospital Coll of Nursing and Health Sciences (MO)
Southeast Tech Inst (SD)
Southern Maine Comm Coll (ME)
Southern State Comm Coll (OH)
Southwestern Illinois Coll (IL)
Southwestern Michigan Coll (MI)
Southwestern Oklahoma State U at Sayre (OK)
Southwest Georgia Tech Coll (GA)
Southwest Mississippi Comm Coll (MS)
Southwest Virginia Comm Coll (VA)
Spencerian Coll (KY)
Springfield Tech Comm Coll (MA)
Stark State Coll (OH)
State Coll of Florida Manatee-Sarasota (FL)
State U of New York Coll of Technology at Alfred (NY)
Sullivan County Comm Coll (NY)
Tallahassee Comm Coll (FL)
Tarrant County Coll District (TX)
Terra State Comm Coll (OH)
Texarkana Coll (TX)
Three Rivers Comm Coll (CT)
Tompkins Cortland Comm Coll (NY)
Trident Tech Coll (SC)
Truckee Meadows Comm Coll (NV)
Tyler Jr Coll (TX)
Umpqua Comm Coll (OR)
Union County Coll (NJ)
U of Arkansas Comm Coll at Morrilton (AR)
Valencia Coll (FL)
Vincennes U (IN)
Virginia Western Comm Coll (VA)
Waukesha County Tech Coll (WI)
Westchester Comm Coll (NY)
Western Iowa Tech Comm Coll (IA)
West Kentucky Comm and Tech Coll (KY)
Westmoreland County Comm Coll (PA)
West Virginia Northern Comm Coll (WV)
White Mountains Comm Coll (NH)

Wilson Comm Coll (NC)
Wytheville Comm Coll (VA)

REHABILITATION AND THERAPEUTIC PROFESSIONS RELATED

Central Wyoming Coll (WY)
Iowa Lakes Comm Coll (IA)
Union County Coll (NJ)

RELIGIOUS STUDIES

Amarillo Coll (TX)
Cowley County Comm Coll and Area Vocational–Tech School (KS)
Kilgore Coll (TX)
Lansing Comm Coll (MI)
Laramie County Comm Coll (WY)
Orange Coast Coll (CA)
Palm Beach State Coll (FL)
Pensacola State Coll (FL)
Santa Rosa Jr Coll (CA)
State Coll of Florida Manatee-Sarasota (FL)

RESORT MANAGEMENT

Lehigh Carbon Comm Coll (PA)

RESPIRATORY CARE THERAPY

Alvin Comm Coll (TX)
Amarillo Coll (TX)
Arkansas State U–Mountain Home (AR)
Athens Tech Coll (GA)
Augusta Tech Coll (GA)
Berkshire Comm Coll (MA)
Bluegrass Comm and Tech Coll (KY)
Burlington County Coll (NJ)
Casper Coll (WY)
Catawba Valley Comm Coll (NC)
Chattanooga State Comm Coll (TN)
Chippewa Valley Tech Coll (WI)
Coll of DuPage (IL)
Comm Coll of Allegheny County (PA)
The Comm Coll of Baltimore County (MD)
Comm Coll of Philadelphia (PA)
Comm Coll of Rhode Island (RI)
Delaware County Comm Coll (PA)
Do&nna Ana Comm Coll (NM)
El Centro Coll (TX)
El Paso Comm Coll (TX)
Erie Comm Coll, North Campus (NY)
Fayetteville Tech Comm Coll (NC)
Florida State Coll at Jacksonville (FL)
Foothill Coll (CA)
GateWay Comm Coll (AZ)
Genesee Comm Coll (NY)
Goodwin Coll (CT)
Gulf Coast State Coll (FL)
Gwinnett Tech Coll (GA)
Hawkeye Comm Coll (IA)
Highline Comm Coll (WA)
Hillsborough Comm Coll (FL)
Houston Comm Coll System (TX)
Hutchinson Comm Coll and Area Vocational School (KS)
Illinois Central Coll (IL)
Indian River State Coll (FL)
Ivy Tech Comm Coll–Central Indiana (IN)
Ivy Tech Comm Coll–Lafayette (IN)
Ivy Tech Comm Coll–Northeast (IN)
Ivy Tech Comm Coll–Northwest (IN)
Ivy Tech Comm Coll–Southern Indiana (IN)
J. Sargeant Reynolds Comm Coll (VA)
Kankakee Comm Coll (IL)
Kansas City Kansas Comm Coll (KS)
Kaplan Career Inst, Franklin Mills Campus (PA)
Kaplan Coll, Phoenix Campus (AZ)
Kaskaskia Coll (IL)
Kent State U at Ashtabula (OH)
Macomb Comm Coll (MI)
Manchester Comm Coll (CT)
Massachusetts Bay Comm Coll (MA)
Metropolitan Comm Coll–Penn Valley (MO)
Miami Dade Coll (FL)

Mohawk Valley Comm Coll (NY)
Monroe County Comm Coll (MI)
Montana State U–Great Falls Coll of Technology (MT)
Moraine Park Tech Coll (WI)
Moraine Valley Comm Coll (IL)
Mott Comm Coll (MI)
Northeast Iowa Comm Coll (IA)
Northern Essex Comm Coll (MA)
North Shore Comm Coll (MA)
Oakland Comm Coll (MI)
Oklahoma City Comm Coll (OK)
Onondaga Comm Coll (NY)
Orange Coast Coll (CA)
Polk State Coll (FL)
Quinsigamond Comm Coll (MA)
Raritan Valley Comm Coll (NJ)
Rockingham Comm Coll (NC)
Rockland Comm Coll (NY)
St. Philip's Coll (TX)
San Jacinto Coll District (TX)
San Joaquin Valley Coll, Bakersfield (CA)
San Joaquin Valley Coll, Visalia (CA)
San Juan Coll (NM)
Santa Monica Coll (CA)
Seminole State Coll of Florida (FL)
Southeastern Comm Coll (IA)
Southern Maine Comm Coll (ME)
Southern State Comm Coll (OH)
Southwestern Illinois Coll (IL)
Southwest Georgia Tech Coll (GA)
Southwest Virginia Comm Coll (VA)
Spencerian Coll (KY)
Springfield Tech Comm Coll (MA)
Stark State Coll (OH)
State Coll of Florida Manatee-Sarasota (FL)
Tallahassee Comm Coll (FL)
Tarrant County Coll District (TX)
Trident Tech Coll (SC)
Tyler Jr Coll (TX)
Union County Coll (NJ)
Valencia Coll (FL)
Volunteer State Comm Coll (TN)
Westchester Comm Coll (NY)
West Kentucky Comm and Tech Coll (KY)
West Virginia Northern Comm Coll (WV)

RESPIRATORY THERAPY TECHNICIAN

Augusta Tech Coll (GA)
Bunker Hill Comm Coll (MA)
Career Tech Coll (LA)
Columbus Tech Coll (GA)
Delaware Tech & Comm Coll, Jack F. Owens Campus (DE)
Delaware Tech & Comm Coll, Stanton/Wilmington Campus (DE)
Georgia Northwestern Tech Coll (GA)
Kansas City Kansas Comm Coll (KS)
Kaplan Coll, Modesto Campus (CA)
Miami Dade Coll (FL)
Mineral Area Coll (MO)
Missouri State U–West Plains (MO)
Northern Essex Comm Coll (MA)
Okefenokee Tech Coll (GA)
San Joaquin Valley Coll, Rancho Cordova (CA)
Southeastern Tech Coll (GA)
Southern Crescent Tech Coll (GA)

RESTAURANT, CULINARY, AND CATERING MANAGEMENT

Central Comm Coll–Hastings Campus (NE)
Coll of Central Florida (FL)
Coll of DuPage (IL)
Coll of Lake County (IL)
Coll of the Canyons (CA)
Comm Coll of Allegheny County (PA)
Delaware Tech & Comm Coll, Stanton/Wilmington Campus (DE)
Elgin Comm Coll (IL)
Erie Comm Coll, North Campus (NY)
Fox Valley Tech Coll (WI)
Gateway Tech Coll (WI)

Gulf Coast State Coll (FL)
Hillsborough Comm Coll (FL)
Iowa Lakes Comm Coll (IA)
John Wood Comm Coll (IL)
Mohawk Valley Comm Coll (NY)
Moraine Park Tech Coll (WI)
Moraine Valley Comm Coll (IL)
Orange Coast Coll (CA)
Pensacola State Coll (FL)
Raritan Valley Comm Coll (NJ)
San Jacinto Coll District (TX)
Southwestern Illinois Coll (IL)
Vincennes U (IN)
Waukesha County Tech Coll (WI)
Westmoreland County Comm Coll (PA)

RESTAURANT/FOOD SERVICES MANAGEMENT

Burlington County Coll (NJ)
Fiorello H. LaGuardia Comm Coll of the City U of New York (NY)
Hillsborough Comm Coll (FL)
Iowa Lakes Comm Coll (IA)
Minneapolis Comm and Tech Coll (MN)
Northampton Comm Coll (PA)
Oakland Comm Coll (MI)
Owens Comm Coll, Toledo (OH)
Quinsigamond Comm Coll (MA)
The Restaurant School at Walnut Hill Coll (PA)
St. Philip's Coll (TX)
Santa Rosa Jr Coll (CA)

RETAILING

Bradford School (PA)
Bucks County Comm Coll (PA)
Burlington County Coll (NJ)
Casper Coll (WY)
Central Oregon Comm Coll (OR)
Clark Coll (WA)
Coll of DuPage (IL)
Comm Coll of Allegheny County (PA)
Delaware County Comm Coll (PA)
Elgin Comm Coll (IL)
Florida State Coll at Jacksonville (FL)
Fox Coll (IL)
Holyoke Comm Coll (MA)
Hutchinson Comm Coll and Area Vocational School (KS)
Illinois Central Coll (IL)
Iowa Lakes Comm Coll (IA)
Minnesota State Coll–Southeast Tech (MN)
Moraine Valley Comm Coll (IL)
Orange Coast Coll (CA)
Wood Tobe–Coburn School (NY)

RETAIL MANAGEMENT

Oakland Comm Coll (MI)

RHETORIC AND COMPOSITION

Amarillo Coll (TX)
Austin Comm Coll (TX)
Bainbridge Coll (GA)
Carl Albert State Coll (OK)
Gavilan Coll (CA)
Indian River State Coll (FL)
Iowa Lakes Comm Coll (IA)
Mendocino Coll (CA)
Monroe County Comm Coll (MI)
Northeast Comm Coll (NE)
St. Philip's Coll (TX)
San Diego City Coll (CA)
San Jacinto Coll District (TX)
Santa Monica Coll (CA)
State Coll of Florida Manatee-Sarasota (FL)

ROBOTICS TECHNOLOGY

Casper Coll (WY)
Coll of DuPage (IL)
Comm Coll of Allegheny County (PA)
Delaware County Comm Coll (PA)
Illinois Central Coll (IL)
Ivy Tech Comm Coll–Columbus (IN)
Ivy Tech Comm Coll–Lafayette (IN)
Ivy Tech Comm Coll–North Central (IN)
Ivy Tech Comm Coll–Northeast (IN)
Ivy Tech Comm Coll–Richmond (IN)

Ivy Tech Comm Coll–Southwest (IN)
Ivy Tech Comm Coll–Wabash Valley (IN)
Lake Area Tech Inst (SD)
Macomb Comm Coll (MI)
Oakland Comm Coll (MI)
St. Clair County Comm Coll (MI)
State U of New York Coll of Technology at Alfred (NY)
Sullivan Coll of Technology and Design (KY)
Terra State Comm Coll (OH)
Vincennes U (IN)

ROMANCE LANGUAGES

Highline Comm Coll (WA)

RUSSIAN

Austin Comm Coll (TX)

RUSSIAN, CENTRAL EUROPEAN, EAST EUROPEAN AND EURASIAN STUDIES

State Coll of Florida Manatee-Sarasota (FL)

RUSSIAN STUDIES

State Coll of Florida Manatee-Sarasota (FL)

SALES, DISTRIBUTION, AND MARKETING OPERATIONS

Aiken Tech Coll (SC)
Anoka-Ramsey Comm Coll (MN)
Anoka-Ramsey Comm Coll, Cambridge Campus (MN)
Burlington County Coll (NJ)
Central Carolina Tech Coll (SC)
Coll of DuPage (IL)
Coll of the Canyons (CA)
Edison Comm Coll (OH)
Gadsden State Comm Coll (AL)
Harper Coll (IL)
Hawkeye Comm Coll (IA)
Iowa Lakes Comm Coll (IA)
Lake Area Tech Inst (SD)
Lake Region State Coll (ND)
Lansing Comm Coll (MI)
Minnesota State Coll–Southeast Tech (MN)
Montgomery County Comm Coll (PA)
Northeast Iowa Comm Coll (IA)
Northwest Tech Coll (MN)
Owens Comm Coll, Toledo (OH)
St. Cloud Tech & Comm Coll (MN)
Santa Monica Coll (CA)
Western Iowa Tech Comm Coll (IA)
Westmoreland County Comm Coll (PA)

SALON/BEAUTY SALON MANAGEMENT

Mott Comm Coll (MI)
Oakland Comm Coll (MI)

SCIENCE TEACHER EDUCATION

Dutchess Comm Coll (NY)
Iowa Lakes Comm Coll (IA)
Moraine Valley Comm Coll (IL)
San Jacinto Coll District (TX)
Snow Coll (UT)
State Coll of Florida Manatee-Sarasota (FL)
Vincennes U (IN)

SCIENCE TECHNOLOGIES RELATED

Cascadia Comm Coll (WA)
Cayuga County Comm Coll (NY)
Cleveland State Comm Coll (TN)
Comm Coll of Allegheny County (PA)
The Comm Coll of Baltimore County (MD)
Dakota Coll at Bottineau (ND)
Delaware County Comm Coll (PA)
Delaware Tech & Comm Coll, Stanton/Wilmington Campus (DE)
Front Range Comm Coll (CO)
Harford Comm Coll (MD)

North Dakota State Coll of Science (ND)
Oakland Comm Coll (MI)
Red Rocks Comm Coll (CO)
West Virginia Northern Comm Coll (WV)

SCULPTURE

Salem Comm Coll (NJ)

SECONDARY EDUCATION

Ancilla Coll (IN)
Austin Comm Coll (TX)
Brookhaven Coll (TX)
Carl Albert State Coll (OK)
Central Wyoming Coll (WY)
Eastern Arizona Coll (AZ)
Georgia Highlands Coll (GA)
Howard Comm Coll (MD)
Kankakee Comm Coll (IL)
Lake Michigan Coll (MI)
Lansing Comm Coll (MI)
Mid Michigan Comm Coll (MI)
Mohawk Valley Comm Coll (NY)
Montgomery County Comm Coll (PA)
Northampton Comm Coll (PA)
Northeast Comm Coll (NE)
Northwest Coll (WY)
Panola Coll (TX)
San Jacinto Coll District (TX)
San Juan Coll (NM)
Springfield Tech Comm Coll (MA)
State U of New York Coll of Technology at Alfred (NY)
Vincennes U (IN)

SECURITIES SERVICES ADMINISTRATION

Vincennes U (IN)
Western Iowa Tech Comm Coll (IA)

SECURITY AND LOSS PREVENTION

Union County Coll (NJ)
Vincennes U (IN)

SELLING SKILLS AND SALES

Central Wyoming Coll (WY)
Clark Coll (WA)
Coll of DuPage (IL)
Coll of Lake County (IL)
Illinois Valley Comm Coll (IL)
Iowa Lakes Comm Coll (IA)
John Wood Comm Coll (IL)
Lansing Comm Coll (MI)
McHenry County Coll (IL)
Minnesota State Coll–Southeast Tech (MN)
Orange Coast Coll (CA)
Santa Monica Coll (CA)
Southwestern Illinois Coll (IL)

SHEET METAL TECHNOLOGY

Comm Coll of Allegheny County (PA)
GateWay Comm Coll (AZ)
Ivy Tech Comm Coll–Central Indiana (IN)
Ivy Tech Comm Coll–Lafayette (IN)
Ivy Tech Comm Coll–North Central (IN)
Ivy Tech Comm Coll–Northeast (IN)
Ivy Tech Comm Coll–Northwest (IN)
Ivy Tech Comm Coll–Southern Indiana (IN)
Ivy Tech Comm Coll–Southwest (IN)
Ivy Tech Comm Coll–Wabash Valley (IN)
Macomb Comm Coll (MI)
Southwestern Illinois Coll (IL)
Terra State Comm Coll (OH)
Vincennes U (IN)

SIGN LANGUAGE INTERPRETATION AND TRANSLATION

Austin Comm Coll (TX)
Berkeley City Coll (CA)
Burlington County Coll (NJ)
Coll of the Canyons (CA)
Comm Coll of Allegheny County (PA)
The Comm Coll of Baltimore County (MD)

Comm Coll of Philadelphia (PA)
El Paso Comm Coll (TX)
Florida State Coll at Jacksonville (FL)
Front Range Comm Coll (CO)
Gateway Tech Coll (WI)
Houston Comm Coll System (TX)
Illinois Central Coll (IL)
Lake Region State Coll (ND)
Lansing Comm Coll (MI)
Miami Dade Coll (FL)
Mohawk Valley Comm Coll (NY)
Mott Comm Coll (MI)
Northern Essex Comm Coll (MA)
Northwestern Connecticut Comm Coll (CT)
Oakland Comm Coll (MI)
Ocean County Coll (NJ)
Oklahoma State U, Oklahoma City (OK)
Riverside City Coll (CA)
Salt Lake Comm Coll (UT)
Southwestern Illinois Coll (IL)
Tarrant County Coll District (TX)
Tyler Jr Coll (TX)
Union County Coll (NJ)
Wilson Comm Coll (NC)

SMALL BUSINESS ADMINISTRATION
Coll of the Canyons (CA)
Dakota Coll at Bottineau (ND)
Harper Coll (IL)
Iowa Lakes Comm Coll (IA)
Lake Area Tech Inst (SD)
Lake Region State Coll (ND)
Moraine Valley Comm Coll (IL)
North Hennepin Comm Coll (MN)
Raritan Valley Comm Coll (NJ)
South Suburban Coll (IL)
Southwestern Illinois Coll (IL)
Springfield Tech Comm Coll (MA)

SMALL ENGINE MECHANICS AND REPAIR TECHNOLOGY
Iowa Lakes Comm Coll (IA)
Kirtland Comm Coll (MI)
Mitchell Tech Inst (SD)
North Dakota State Coll of Science (ND)

SOCIAL PSYCHOLOGY
Macomb Comm Coll (MI)
State Coll of Florida Manatee-Sarasota (FL)

SOCIAL SCIENCES
Amarillo Coll (TX)
Burlington County Coll (NJ)
Carl Albert State Coll (OK)
Central Oregon Comm Coll (OR)
Central Wyoming Comm Coll (WY)
Clinton Comm Coll (NY)
Coll of the Canyons (CA)
Colorado Mountain Coll (CO)
Colorado Mountain Coll, Alpine Campus (CO)
Comm Coll of Allegheny County (PA)
Comm Coll of Vermont (VT)
Corning Comm Coll (NY)
Dakota Coll at Bottineau (ND)
Dutchess Comm Coll (NY)
Foothill Coll (CA)
Gavilan Coll (CA)
Highline Comm Coll (WA)
Housatonic Comm Coll (CT)
Howard Comm Coll (MD)
Hutchinson Comm Coll and Area Vocational School (KS)
Indian River State Coll (FL)
Iowa Lakes Comm Coll (IA)
J. Sargeant Reynolds Comm Coll (VA)
Kilgore Coll (TX)
Lansing Comm Coll (MI)
Laramie County Comm Coll (WY)
Massachusetts Bay Comm Coll (MA)
Mendocino Coll (CA)
Miami Dade Coll (FL)
Monroe Comm Coll (NY)
Montgomery County Comm Coll (PA)
Niagara County Comm Coll (NY)

Northeast Comm Coll (NE)
Northeastern Jr Coll (CO)
Northwest Coll (WY)
Northwestern Connecticut Comm Coll (CT)
Northwest Florida State Coll (FL)
Orange Coast Coll (CA)
Otero Jr Coll (CO)
Palm Beach State Coll (FL)
Reedley Coll (CA)
San Diego City Coll (CA)
San Jacinto Coll District (TX)
Santa Rosa Jr Coll (CA)
Southwest Mississippi Comm Coll (MS)
State Coll of Florida Manatee-Sarasota (FL)
Terra State Comm Coll (OH)
Texarkana Coll (TX)
Tyler Jr Coll (TX)
Umpqua Comm Coll (OR)
Westchester Comm Coll (NY)

SOCIAL SCIENCES RELATED
Berkeley City Coll (CA)

SOCIAL STUDIES TEACHER EDUCATION
Casper Coll (WY)
State Coll of Florida Manatee-Sarasota (FL)

SOCIAL WORK
Amarillo Coll (TX)
Austin Comm Coll (TX)
Casper Coll (WY)
Central Carolina Comm Coll (NC)
Chandler-Gilbert Comm Coll (AZ)
Chipola Coll (FL)
Cochise Coll, Sierra Vista (AZ)
Coll of Lake County (IL)
Comm Coll of Allegheny County (PA)
Comm Coll of Rhode Island (RI)
Cowley County Comm Coll and Area Vocational–Tech School (KS)
Edison Comm Coll (OH)
Elgin Comm Coll (IL)
El Paso Comm Coll (TX)
Holyoke Comm Coll (MA)
Illinois Eastern Comm Colls, Wabash Valley College (IL)
Illinois Valley Comm Coll (IL)
Indian River State Coll (FL)
Iowa Lakes Comm Coll (IA)
Kilian Comm Coll (SD)
Lawson State Comm Coll (AL)
Manchester Comm Coll (CT)
Miami Dade Coll (FL)
Monroe County Comm Coll (MI)
Northampton Comm Coll (PA)
Northeastern Jr Coll (CO)
Northeast Iowa Comm Coll (IA)
Northwest Florida State Coll (FL)
Owensboro Comm and Tech Coll (KY)
Palm Beach State Coll (FL)
Rogue Comm Coll (OR)
St. Philip's Coll (TX)
Salt Lake Comm Coll (UT)
San Diego City Coll (CA)
San Juan Coll (NM)
Shawnee Comm Coll (IL)
South Suburban Coll (IL)
Southwestern Illinois Coll (IL)
Southwestern Michigan Coll (MI)
State Coll of Florida Manatee-Sarasota (FL)
Terra State Comm Coll (OH)
Umpqua Comm Coll (OR)
The U of Akron–Wayne Coll (OH)
Vincennes U (IN)
West Georgia Tech Coll (GA)
West Virginia Northern Comm Coll (WV)

SOCIAL WORK RELATED
Berkeley City Coll (CA)

SOCIOLOGY
Austin Comm Coll (TX)
Bainbridge Coll (GA)
Berkeley City Coll (CA)
Bunker Hill Comm Coll (MA)

Burlington County Coll (NJ)
Casper Coll (WY)
Cochise Coll, Sierra Vista (AZ)
Coll of the Canyons (CA)
Comm Coll of Allegheny County (PA)
Delaware County Comm Coll (PA)
Eastern Arizona Coll (AZ)
Foothill Coll (CA)
Georgia Highlands Coll (GA)
Indian River State Coll (FL)
Iowa Lakes Comm Coll (IA)
Kilian Comm Coll (SD)
Lake Michigan Coll (MI)
Lansing Comm Coll (MI)
Laramie County Comm Coll (WY)
Miami Dade Coll (FL)
Mid Michigan Comm Coll (MI)
Mohave Comm Coll (AZ)
Northwest Coll (WY)
Oklahoma City Comm Coll (OK)
Orange Coast Coll (CA)
Pensacola State Coll (FL)
St. Philip's Coll (TX)
Salt Lake Comm Coll (UT)
San Diego City Coll (CA)
San Jacinto Coll District (TX)
Santa Rosa Jr Coll (CA)
Snow Coll (UT)
Umpqua Comm Coll (OR)
Vincennes U (IN)

SOCIOLOGY AND ANTHROPOLOGY
Harper Coll (IL)

SOIL SCIENCE AND AGRONOMY
Iowa Lakes Comm Coll (IA)
Snow Coll (UT)

SOLAR ENERGY TECHNOLOGY
Comm Coll of Allegheny County (PA)
San Juan Coll (NM)

SPANISH
Austin Comm Coll (TX)
Berkeley City Coll (CA)
Coll of the Canyons (CA)
Fiorello H. LaGuardia Comm Coll of the City U of New York (NY)
Foothill Coll (CA)
Gavilan Coll (CA)
Indian River State Coll (FL)
Iowa Lakes Comm Coll (IA)
Laramie County Comm Coll (WY)
Mendocino Coll (CA)
Miami Dade Coll (FL)
Northwest Coll (WY)
Orange Coast Coll (CA)
St. Philip's Coll (TX)
Santa Rosa Jr Coll (CA)
Snow Coll (UT)
State Coll of Florida Manatee-Sarasota (FL)

SPANISH LANGUAGE TEACHER EDUCATION
Anne Arundel Comm Coll (MD)
The Comm Coll of Baltimore County (MD)
Harford Comm Coll (MD)
Montgomery Coll (MD)

SPECIAL EDUCATION
Comm Coll of Rhode Island (RI)
J. Sargeant Reynolds Comm Coll (VA)
Kankakee Comm Coll (IL)
Lehigh Carbon Comm Coll (PA)
Lincoln Land Comm Coll (IL)
Moraine Valley Comm Coll (IL)
Normandale Comm Coll (MN)
Pensacola State Coll (FL)
San Juan Coll (NM)
Truckee Meadows Comm Coll (NV)
Vincennes U (IN)

SPECIAL EDUCATION (ADMINISTRATION)
Foothill Coll (CA)

SPECIAL EDUCATION–EARLY CHILDHOOD
Itasca Comm Coll (MN)
Motlow State Comm Coll (TN)
Santa Monica Coll (CA)

SPECIAL EDUCATION–ELEMENTARY SCHOOL
Truckee Meadows Comm Coll (NV)
Westmoreland County Comm Coll (PA)

SPECIAL EDUCATION–INDIVIDUALS WITH HEARING IMPAIRMENTS
Hillsborough Comm Coll (FL)

SPECIAL PRODUCTS MARKETING
Copiah-Lincoln Comm Coll (MS)
Dutchess Comm Coll (NY)
El Centro Coll (TX)
Gateway Comm Coll (CT)
Indian River State Coll (FL)
Metropolitan Comm Coll–Penn Valley (MO)
Monroe Comm Coll (NY)
Muskegon Comm Coll (MI)
Orange Coast Coll (CA)
Palm Beach State Coll (FL)
San Diego City Coll (CA)
Scottsdale Comm Coll (AZ)
Three Rivers Comm Coll (CT)

SPEECH COMMUNICATION AND RHETORIC
Brookhaven Coll (TX)
Bucks County Comm Coll (PA)
Bunker Hill Comm Coll (MA)
Casper Coll (WY)
Central Oregon Comm Coll (OR)
Cochise Coll, Sierra Vista (AZ)
Delaware County Comm Coll (PA)
Dutchess Comm Coll (NY)
Edison Comm Coll (OH)
El Paso Comm Coll (TX)
Erie Comm Coll, South Campus (NY)
Fiorello H. LaGuardia Comm Coll of the City U of New York (NY)
Harper Coll (IL)
Hutchinson Comm Coll and Area Vocational School (KS)
Jamestown Comm Coll (NY)
Laramie County Comm Coll (WY)
Lehigh Carbon Comm Coll (PA)
Macomb Comm Coll (MI)
Manchester Comm Coll (CT)
Massachusetts Bay Comm Coll (MA)
Montgomery Coll (MD)
Montgomery County Comm Coll (PA)
Northampton Comm Coll (PA)
Northwest Coll (WY)
Onondaga Comm Coll (NY)
Pensacola State Coll (FL)
Salt Lake Comm Coll (UT)
San Jacinto Coll District (TX)
Tompkins Cortland Comm Coll (NY)
Tyler Jr Coll (TX)

SPEECH-LANGUAGE PATHOLOGY
Coll of DuPage (IL)

SPEECH-LANGUAGE PATHOLOGY ASSISTANT
Fayetteville Tech Comm Coll (NC)
Mitchell Tech Inst (SD)

SPORT AND FITNESS ADMINISTRATION/MANAGEMENT
Bucks County Comm Coll (PA)
Cayuga County Comm Coll (NY)
Central Oregon Comm Coll (OR)
Century Coll (MN)
Clark Coll (WA)
Garrett Coll (MD)
Holyoke Comm Coll (MA)
Howard Comm Coll (MD)

Iowa Lakes Comm Coll (IA)
Kingsborough Comm Coll of the City U of New York (NY)
Lehigh Carbon Comm Coll (PA)
Niagara County Comm Coll (NY)
Northampton Comm Coll (PA)
Salt Lake Comm Coll (UT)
Springfield Tech Comm Coll (MA)
State U of New York Coll of Technology at Alfred (NY)
Sullivan County Comm Coll (NY)
Tompkins Cortland Comm Coll (NY)
Union County Coll (NJ)
Vincennes U (IN)

STATISTICS
State Coll of Florida Manatee-Sarasota (FL)

STATISTICS RELATED
Casper Coll (WY)

STRUCTURAL ENGINEERING
Moraine Park Tech Coll (WI)

SUBSTANCE ABUSE/ADDICTION COUNSELING
Alvin Comm Coll (TX)
Amarillo Coll (TX)
Anne Arundel Comm Coll (MD)
Austin Comm Coll (TX)
Casper Coll (WY)
Central Oregon Comm Coll (OR)
Century Coll (MN)
Chippewa Valley Tech Coll (WI)
Clark Coll (WA)
Colby Comm Coll (KS)
Coll of DuPage (IL)
Coll of Lake County (IL)
Comm Coll of Allegheny County (PA)
The Comm Coll of Baltimore County (MD)
Comm Coll of Rhode Island (RI)
Corning Comm Coll (NY)
Dawson Comm Coll (MT)
Delaware Tech & Comm Coll, Stanton/Wilmington Campus (DE)
Delaware Tech & Comm Coll, Terry Campus (DE)
El Paso Comm Coll (TX)
Erie Comm Coll (NY)
Florida State Coll at Jacksonville (FL)
Fox Valley Tech Coll (WI)
Gadsden State Comm Coll (AL)
Gateway Comm Coll (CT)
Genesee Comm Coll (NY)
Guilford Tech Comm Coll (NC)
Harford Comm Coll (MD)
Housatonic Comm Coll (CT)
Howard Comm Coll (MD)
Illinois Central Coll (IL)
Kansas City Kansas Comm Coll (KS)
Kilian Comm Coll (SD)
Lower Columbia Coll (WA)
Mendocino Coll (CA)
Miami Dade Coll (FL)
Minneapolis Comm and Tech Coll (MN)
Mohave Comm Coll (AZ)
Mohawk Valley Comm Coll (NY)
Moraine Park Tech Coll (WI)
Moraine Valley Comm Coll (IL)
North Shore Comm Coll (MA)
Northwestern Connecticut Comm Coll (CT)
Oklahoma State U, Oklahoma City (OK)
Olympic Coll (WA)
Peninsula Coll (WA)
Southeastern Comm Coll (IA)
Southern State Comm Coll (OH)
Sullivan County Comm Coll (NY)
Texarkana Coll (TX)
Three Rivers Comm Coll (CT)
Tompkins Cortland Comm Coll (NY)
Truckee Meadows Comm Coll (NV)
Tunxis Comm Coll (CT)
Tyler Jr Coll (TX)
Westchester Comm Coll (NY)

SURGICAL TECHNOLOGY
Anne Arundel Comm Coll (MD)
Anthem Coll–Maryland Heights (MO)
Athens Tech Coll (GA)
Augusta Tech Coll (GA)
Austin Comm Coll (TX)
Bluegrass Comm and Tech Coll (KY)
Cape Fear Comm Coll (NC)
Career Tech Coll (LA)
Central Carolina Tech Coll (SC)
Coll of DuPage (IL)
Columbus Tech Coll (GA)
Comm Care Coll (OK)
Comm Coll of Allegheny County (PA)
Delaware County Comm Coll (PA)
Eastern Idaho Tech Coll (ID)
El Centro Coll (TX)
El Paso Comm Coll (TX)
Fayetteville Tech Comm Coll (NC)
GateWay Comm Coll (AZ)
Gateway Tech Coll (WI)
Georgia Northwestern Tech Coll (GA)
Georgia Piedmont Tech Coll (GA)
Guilford Tech Comm Coll (NC)
Illinois Central Coll (IL)
Iowa Lakes Comm Coll (IA)
Ivy Tech Comm Coll–Central Indiana (IN)
Ivy Tech Comm Coll–Columbus (IN)
Ivy Tech Comm Coll–East Central (IN)
Ivy Tech Comm Coll–Kokomo (IN)
Ivy Tech Comm Coll–Lafayette (IN)
Ivy Tech Comm Coll–Northwest (IN)
Ivy Tech Comm Coll–Southwest (IN)
Ivy Tech Comm Coll–Wabash Valley (IN)
Kilgore Coll (TX)
Kirtland Comm Coll (MI)
Lanier Tech Coll (GA)
Lansing Comm Coll (MI)
Laramie County Comm Coll (WY)
Lincoln Land Comm Coll (IL)
Macomb Comm Coll (MI)
Manchester Comm Coll (CT)
Mohave Comm Coll (AZ)
Montana State U–Great Falls Coll of Technology (MT)
Montgomery Coll (MD)
Montgomery County Comm Coll (PA)
Moraine Park Tech Coll (WI)
Niagara County Comm Coll (NY)
Northampton Comm Coll (PA)
Northeast Comm Coll (NE)
Oakland Comm Coll (MI)
Okefenokee Tech Coll (GA)
Oklahoma City Comm Coll (OK)
Owens Comm Coll, Toledo (OH)
Pittsburgh Tech Inst, Oakdale (PA)
Rasmussen Coll Brooklyn Park (MN)
Rasmussen Coll St. Cloud (MN)
St. Cloud Tech & Comm Coll (MN)
San Jacinto Coll District (TX)
San Joaquin Valley Coll, Bakersfield (CA)
San Joaquin Valley Coll, Fresno (CA)
San Juan Coll (NM)
Savannah Tech Coll (GA)
Southeast Tech Inst (SD)
Southern Crescent Tech Coll (GA)
Southern Maine Comm Coll (ME)
Southwest Georgia Tech Coll (GA)
Spencerian Coll (KY)
Springfield Tech Comm Coll (MA)
Tarrant County Coll District (TX)
Texas State Tech Coll Harlingen (TX)
Tyler Jr Coll (TX)
Vincennes U (IN)
Waukesha County Tech Coll (WI)
Western Iowa Tech Comm Coll (IA)
West Kentucky Comm and Tech Coll (KY)
West Virginia Northern Comm Coll (WV)
Wilson Comm Coll (NC)

SURVEYING ENGINEERING
Comm Coll of Rhode Island (RI)

SURVEYING TECHNOLOGY
Austin Comm Coll (TX)
Clark Coll (WA)
Coll of the Canyons (CA)
Delaware Tech & Comm Coll, Jack F. Owens Campus (DE)
Delaware Tech & Comm Coll, Stanton/Wilmington Campus (DE)
Fayetteville Tech Comm Coll (NC)
Gateway Tech Coll (WI)
Guilford Tech Comm Coll (NC)
Indian River State Coll (FL)
Lansing Comm Coll (MI)
Macomb Comm Coll (MI)
Mohawk Valley Comm Coll (NY)
Oklahoma State U, Oklahoma City (OK)
Palm Beach State Coll (FL)
Penn State Wilkes-Barre (PA)
Salt Lake Comm Coll (UT)
Santa Rosa Jr Coll (CA)
Southeast Tech Inst (SD)
Stark State Coll (OH)
State U of New York Coll of Environmental Science & Forestry, Ranger School (NY)
State U of New York Coll of Technology at Alfred (NY)
Sullivan County Comm Coll (NY)
Tyler Jr Coll (TX)
U of Arkansas Comm Coll at Morrilton (AR)
Valencia Coll (FL)
Vincennes U (IN)
White Mountains Comm Coll (NH)

SYSTEM, NETWORKING, AND LAN/WAN MANAGEMENT
Bradford School (OH)
Coll of Business and Technology (FL)
El Paso Comm Coll (TX)
Guilford Tech Comm Coll (NC)
Iowa Lakes Comm Coll (IA)
ITT Tech Inst, Orange (CA)
ITT Tech Inst, Sylmar (CA)
ITT Tech Inst, Atlanta (GA)
ITT Tech Inst, Duluth (GA)
ITT Tech Inst, Kennesaw (GA)
ITT Tech Inst, Mount Prospect (IL)
ITT Tech Inst, Oak Brook (IL)
ITT Tech Inst, Orland Park (IL)
ITT Tech Inst, Owings Mills (MD)
ITT Tech Inst, Norwood (MA)
ITT Tech Inst, Wilmington (MA)
ITT Tech Inst, Earth City (MO)
ITT Tech Inst (NJ)
ITT Tech Inst, Cary (NC)
ITT Tech Inst, Charlotte (NC)
ITT Tech Inst, High Point (NC)
ITT Tech Inst, Strongsville (OH)
ITT Tech Inst, Bensalem (PA)
ITT Tech Inst, Dunmore (PA)
ITT Tech Inst, Harrisburg (PA)
ITT Tech Inst, King of Prussia (PA)
ITT Tech Inst, Pittsburgh (PA)
ITT Tech Inst, Tarentum (PA)
ITT Tech Inst, Greenville (SC)
Metropolitan Comm Coll–Business & Technology Campus (MO)
Mineral Area Coll (MO)
Moraine Valley Comm Coll (IL)
MTI Coll, Sacramento (CA)
Oklahoma City Comm Coll (OK)
St. Philip's Coll (TX)
San Jacinto Coll District (TX)
Southwestern Indian Polytechnic Inst (NM)

SYSTEMS ENGINEERING
Kent State U at Trumbull (OH)

TEACHER ASSISTANT/AIDE
Bluegrass Comm and Tech Coll (KY)
Casper Coll (WY)
Central Maine Comm Coll (ME)
Central Wyoming Coll (WY)
Century Coll (MN)
Comm Coll of Vermont (VT)
Dakota Coll at Bottineau (ND)
El Centro Coll (TX)
Fiorello H. LaGuardia Comm Coll of the City U of New York (NY)
Gateway Tech Coll (WI)

Highland Comm Coll (IL)
Illinois Central Coll (IL)
Illinois Eastern Comm Colls, Lincoln Trail College (IL)
Illinois Valley Comm Coll (IL)
Indian River State Coll (FL)
Kankakee Comm Coll (IL)
Kaskaskia Coll (IL)
Kingsborough Comm Coll of the City U of New York (NY)
Kirtland Comm Coll (MI)
Lansing Comm Coll (MI)
Lehigh Carbon Comm Coll (PA)
Lincoln Land Comm Coll (IL)
Manchester Comm Coll (CT)
Miami Dade Coll (FL)
Montcalm Comm Coll (MI)
Montgomery County Comm Coll (PA)
Moraine Park Tech Coll (WI)
Moraine Valley Comm Coll (IL)
Northampton Comm Coll (PA)
Olympic Coll (WA)
St. Clair County Comm Coll (MI)
St. Cloud Tech & Comm Coll (MN)
St. Philip's Coll (TX)
Salt Lake Comm Coll (UT)
San Diego City Coll (CA)
Southern State Comm Coll (OH)
Southwestern Illinois Coll (IL)
Southwestern Michigan Coll (MI)
Texas State Tech Coll Harlingen (TX)
Vincennes U (IN)
Waukesha County Tech Coll (WI)

TEACHING ASSISTANTS/AIDES RELATED
Terra State Comm Coll (OH)

TECHNICAL TEACHER EDUCATION
Mineral Area Coll (MO)

TECHNOLOGY/INDUSTRIAL ARTS TEACHER EDUCATION
Casper Coll (WY)
Cowley County Comm Coll and Area Vocational–Tech School (KS)
Eastern Arizona Coll (AZ)
Iowa Lakes Comm Coll (IA)
State Coll of Florida Manatee-Sarasota (FL)

TELECOMMUNICATIONS TECHNOLOGY
Amarillo Coll (TX)
Carl Albert State Coll (OK)
Cayuga County Comm Coll (NY)
Central Carolina Comm Coll (NC)
Clark Coll (WA)
Delaware County Comm Coll (PA)
Dutchess Comm Coll (NY)
Georgia Piedmont Tech Coll (GA)
Guilford Tech Comm Coll (NC)
Howard Comm Coll (MD)
Illinois Eastern Comm Colls, Lincoln Trail College (IL)
Ivy Tech Comm Coll–North Central (IN)
Ivy Tech Comm Coll–Northwest (IN)
Miami Dade Coll (FL)
Mitchell Tech Inst (SD)
Monroe Comm Coll (NY)
Northern Essex Comm Coll (MA)
North Seattle Comm Coll (WA)
Penn State DuBois (PA)
Penn State Fayette, The Eberly Campus (PA)
Penn State Hazleton (PA)
Penn State New Kensington (PA)
Penn State Schuylkill (PA)
Penn State Shenango (PA)
Penn State Wilkes-Barre (PA)
Penn State York (PA)
Quinsigamond Comm Coll (MA)
Salt Lake Comm Coll (UT)
San Diego City Coll (CA)
Seminole State Coll of Florida (FL)
Springfield Tech Comm Coll (MA)
Texas State Tech Coll Harlingen (TX)
Trident Tech Coll (SC)
Union County Coll (NJ)

THEATER DESIGN AND TECHNOLOGY
Carroll Comm Coll (MD)
Casper Coll (WY)
Central Wyoming Coll (WY)
Florida State Coll at Jacksonville (FL)
Foothill Coll (CA)
Gavilan Coll (CA)
Harford Comm Coll (MD)
Howard Comm Coll (MD)
Normandale Comm Coll (MN)
Red Rocks Comm Coll (CO)
San Juan Coll (NM)
Southwestern Michigan Coll (MI)
Vincennes U (IN)

THEATER/THEATER ARTS MANAGEMENT
Harper Coll (IL)

THERAPEUTIC RECREATION
Austin Comm Coll (TX)
Colorado Mountain Coll (CO)
Comm Coll of Allegheny County (PA)
Northwestern Connecticut Comm Coll (CT)

TOOL AND DIE TECHNOLOGY
Bevill State Comm Coll (AL)
Gadsden State Comm Coll (AL)
Ivy Tech Comm Coll–Bloomington (IN)
Ivy Tech Comm Coll–Central Indiana (IN)
Ivy Tech Comm Coll–Columbus (IN)
Ivy Tech Comm Coll–East Central (IN)
Ivy Tech Comm Coll–Kokomo (IN)
Ivy Tech Comm Coll–Lafayette (IN)
Ivy Tech Comm Coll–North Central (IN)
Ivy Tech Comm Coll–Northeast (IN)
Ivy Tech Comm Coll–Northwest (IN)
Ivy Tech Comm Coll–Richmond (IN)
Ivy Tech Comm Coll–Southern Indiana (IN)
Ivy Tech Comm Coll–Southwest (IN)
Ivy Tech Comm Coll–Wabash Valley (IN)
Macomb Comm Coll (MI)
Moraine Park Tech Coll (WI)
Oakland Comm Coll (MI)
Owens Comm Coll, Toledo (OH)
Southwestern Michigan Coll (MI)
Texas State Tech Coll Harlingen (TX)
Vincennes U (IN)
Western Iowa Tech Comm Coll (IA)

TOURISM AND TRAVEL SERVICES MANAGEMENT
Albany Tech Coll (GA)
Amarillo Coll (TX)
Athens Tech Coll (GA)
Atlanta Tech Coll (GA)
Bradford School (OH)
Bucks County Comm Coll (PA)
Bunker Hill Comm Coll (MA)
Central Georgia Tech Coll (GA)
Coll of DuPage (IL)
Consolidated School of Business, York (PA)
Dutchess Comm Coll (NY)
El Paso Comm Coll (TX)
Fiorello H. LaGuardia Comm Coll of the City U of New York (NY)
Genesee Comm Coll (NY)
Gwinnett Tech Coll (GA)
Highline Comm Coll (WA)
Houston Comm Coll System (TX)
Kingsborough Comm Coll of the City U of New York (NY)
Miami Dade Coll (FL)
Monroe Comm Coll (NY)
Moraine Valley Comm Coll (IL)
Niagara County Comm Coll (NY)
Northern Essex Comm Coll (MA)
North Shore Comm Coll (MA)
Ogeechee Tech Coll (GA)
Rockland Comm Coll (NY)
San Diego City Coll (CA)
Savannah Tech Coll (GA)
Sullivan County Comm Coll (NY)

Three Rivers Comm Coll (CT)
Valencia Coll (FL)
Westmoreland County Comm Coll (PA)
Wood Tobe–Coburn School (NY)

TOURISM AND TRAVEL SERVICES MARKETING
Coll of DuPage (IL)
Florida State Coll at Jacksonville (FL)
Montgomery County Comm Coll (PA)

TOURISM PROMOTION
Coll of DuPage (IL)
Comm Coll of Allegheny County (PA)

TRADE AND INDUSTRIAL TEACHER EDUCATION
Copiah-Lincoln Comm Coll (MS)
Iowa Lakes Comm Coll (IA)
Northeastern Jr Coll (CO)
Snow Coll (UT)
Southeastern Comm Coll (IA)
State Coll of Florida Manatee-Sarasota (FL)

TRANSPORTATION AND HIGHWAY ENGINEERING
Gateway Tech Coll (WI)

TRANSPORTATION AND MATERIALS MOVING RELATED
Cecil Coll (MD)
Coll of DuPage (IL)
Highline Comm Coll (WA)
Mid-Plains Comm Coll, North Platte (NE)
Muskegon Comm Coll (MI)
St. Clair County Comm Coll (MI)
San Diego City Coll (CA)

TRANSPORTATION/MOBILITY MANAGEMENT
Cecil Coll (MD)
Hagerstown Comm Coll (MD)
Polk State Coll (FL)

TRUCK AND BUS DRIVER/COMMERCIAL VEHICLE OPERATION/INSTRUCTION
Central Comm Coll–Hastings Campus (NE)
Eastern Idaho Tech Coll (ID)
Mohave Comm Coll (AZ)

TURF AND TURFGRASS MANAGEMENT
Catawba Valley Comm Coll (NC)
Coll of Lake County (IL)
Comm Coll of Allegheny County (PA)
Delaware Tech & Comm Coll, Jack F. Owens Campus (DE)
Guilford Tech Comm Coll (NC)
Houston Comm Coll System (TX)
Iowa Lakes Comm Coll (IA)
Lake Michigan Coll (MI)
Linn State Tech Coll (MO)
North Georgia Tech Coll (GA)
Oklahoma State U, Oklahoma City (OK)
Southeast Tech Inst (SD)
Western Iowa Tech Comm Coll (IA)
Westmoreland County Comm Coll (PA)

URBAN FORESTRY
Dakota Coll at Bottineau (ND)
State U of New York Coll of Technology at Alfred (NY)

VEHICLE AND VEHICLE PARTS AND ACCESSORIES MARKETING
Central Comm Coll–Hastings Campus (NE)

VEHICLE MAINTENANCE AND REPAIR TECHNOLOGIES
Red Rocks Comm Coll (CO)

VEHICLE MAINTENANCE AND REPAIR TECHNOLOGIES RELATED

Central Maine Comm Coll (ME)
Guilford Tech Comm Coll (NC)
J. Sargeant Reynolds Comm Coll (VA)
North Dakota State Coll of Science (ND)
Pennco Tech (PA)
State U of New York Coll of Technology at Alfred (NY)

VETERINARY/ANIMAL HEALTH TECHNOLOGY

Athens Tech Coll (GA)
Bradford School (OH)
Central Carolina Comm Coll (NC)
Central Georgia Tech Coll (GA)
Chattanooga State Comm Coll (TN)
Colby Comm Coll (KS)
Coll of Central Florida (FL)
Colorado Mountain Coll (CO)
Comm Care Coll (OK)
The Comm Coll of Baltimore County (MD)
Delaware Tech & Comm Coll, Jack F. Owens Campus (DE)
Fiorello H. LaGuardia Comm Coll of the City U of New York (NY)
Foothill Coll (CA)
Fox Coll (IL)
Front Range Comm Coll (CO)
Genesee Comm Coll (NY)
Gwinnett Tech Coll (GA)
Hillsborough Comm Coll (FL)
Holyoke Comm Coll (MA)
International Business Coll, Indianapolis (IN)
Jefferson State Comm Coll (AL)
Kaplan Coll, Phoenix Campus (AZ)
Kaskaskia Coll (IL)
Kent State U at Tuscarawas (OH)
Lansing Comm Coll (MI)
Lehigh Carbon Comm Coll (PA)
Macomb Comm Coll (MI)
Metropolitan Comm Coll–Maple Woods (MO)
Minnesota School of Business–Plymouth (MN)
Minnesota School of Business–St. Cloud (MN)
Minnesota School of Business–Shakopee (MN)
Moraine Park Tech Coll (WI)
Murray State Coll (OK)
Northampton Comm Coll (PA)
Northeast Comm Coll (NE)
North Shore Comm Coll (MA)
Northwest Coll (WY)
Northwestern Connecticut Comm Coll (CT)
Oakland Comm Coll (MI)
Ogeechee Tech Coll (GA)
Oklahoma State U, Oklahoma City (OK)
San Joaquin Valley Coll, Fresno (CA)
San Juan Coll (NM)
State U of New York Coll of Technology at Alfred (NY)
Trident Tech Coll (SC)
Truckee Meadows Comm Coll (NV)
Vet Tech Inst (PA)
Vet Tech Inst at Bradford School (OH)
Vet Tech Inst at Fox Coll (IL)
Vet Tech Inst at Hickey Coll (MO)
Vet Tech Inst at International Business Coll, Fort Wayne (IN)
Vet Tech Inst at International Business Coll, Indianapolis (IN)
Vet Tech Inst of Houston (TX)
Volunteer State Comm Coll (TN)
Westchester Comm Coll (NY)

VISUAL AND PERFORMING ARTS

Amarillo Coll (TX)
Berkshire Comm Coll (MA)
Bucks County Comm Coll (PA)
Chandler-Gilbert Comm Coll (AZ)
The Comm Coll of Baltimore County (MD)
Fiorello H. LaGuardia Comm Coll of the City U of New York (NY)
Gavilan Coll (CA)
Harford Comm Coll (MD)
Hutchinson Comm Coll and Area Vocational School (KS)
Moraine Valley Comm Coll (IL)
Normandale Comm Coll (MN)
Piedmont Virginia Comm Coll (VA)
Rogue Comm Coll (OR)

VISUAL AND PERFORMING ARTS RELATED

Comm Coll of Allegheny County (PA)
Florida State Coll at Jacksonville (FL)
John Tyler Comm Coll (VA)
J. Sargeant Reynolds Comm Coll (VA)
Kankakee Comm Coll (IL)
Northwest Coll (WY)

VITICULTURE AND ENOLOGY

James Sprunt Comm Coll (NC)
Kent State U at Ashtabula (OH)
Lake Michigan Coll (MI)

VOCATIONAL REHABILITATION COUNSELING

State Coll of Florida Manatee-Sarasota (FL)

VOICE AND OPERA

Alvin Comm Coll (TX)
Iowa Lakes Comm Coll (IA)
Oakland Comm Coll (MI)
Reedley Coll (CA)
Snow Coll (UT)

WATCHMAKING AND JEWELRYMAKING

Austin Comm Coll (TX)
North Seattle Comm Coll (WA)

WATER QUALITY AND WASTEWATER TREATMENT MANAGEMENT AND RECYCLING TECHNOLOGY

Casper Coll (WY)
Coll of the Canyons (CA)
Delaware Tech & Comm Coll, Jack F. Owens Campus (DE)
Florida State Coll at Jacksonville (FL)
GateWay Comm Coll (AZ)
Moraine Park Tech Coll (WI)
Ogeechee Tech Coll (GA)
Red Rocks Comm Coll (CO)
St. Cloud Tech & Comm Coll (MN)

WATER, WETLANDS, AND MARINE RESOURCES MANAGEMENT

Iowa Lakes Comm Coll (IA)

WEB/MULTIMEDIA MANAGEMENT AND WEBMASTER

Blackhawk Tech Coll (WI)
Casper Coll (WY)
Clark Coll (WA)
Comm Coll of Rhode Island (RI)
Delaware County Comm Coll (PA)
Florida State Coll at Jacksonville (FL)
Fox Valley Tech Coll (WI)
Gateway Tech Coll (WI)
Illinois Central Coll (IL)
ITT Tech Inst, Norwood (MA)
ITT Tech Inst, Wilmington (MA)
ITT Tech Inst, Troy (MI)
ITT Tech Inst, Arnold (MO)
ITT Tech Inst, Albany (NY)
ITT Tech Inst, Norwood (OH)
ITT Tech Inst, Strongsville (OH)
ITT Tech Inst, Portland (OR)
ITT Tech Inst, Tarentum (PA)
ITT Tech Inst, Greenville (SC)
ITT Tech Inst, Norfolk (VA)
Kaskaskia Coll (IL)
Kilgore Coll (TX)

Kirtland Comm Coll (MI)
Metropolitan Comm Coll–Business & Technology Campus (MO)
Monroe County Comm Coll (MI)
Montgomery County Comm Coll (PA)
Moraine Valley Comm Coll (IL)
Northern Essex Comm Coll (MA)
Piedmont Virginia Comm Coll (VA)
Red Rocks Comm Coll (CO)
St. Clair County Comm Coll (MI)
San Jacinto Coll District (TX)
Seminole State Coll. of Florida (FL)
Southwestern Illinois Coll (IL)
Southwest Mississippi Comm Coll (MS)
Stark State Coll (OH)
Sullivan County Comm Coll (NY)
Tompkins Cortland Comm Coll (NY)
Trident Tech Coll (SC)
Truckee Meadows Comm Coll (NV)
Vincennes U (IN)
West Virginia Jr Coll–Bridgeport (WV)

WEB PAGE, DIGITAL/MULTIMEDIA AND INFORMATION RESOURCES DESIGN

The Art Inst of New York City (NY)
The Art Inst of Ohio–Cincinnati (OH)
The Art Inst of Seattle (WA)
Berkeley City Coll (CA)
Blackhawk Tech Coll (WI)
Bucks County Comm Coll (PA)
Bunker Hill Comm Coll (MA)
Casper Coll (WY)
Cecil Coll (MD)
Central Georgia Tech Coll (GA)
Chattahoochee Tech Coll (GA)
Chattanooga State Comm Coll (TN)
Columbus Tech Coll (GA)
Delaware County Comm Coll (PA)
Dyersburg State Comm Coll (TN)
Edison Comm Coll (OH)
El Centro Coll (TX)
Florida State Coll at Jacksonville (FL)
GateWay Comm Coll (AZ)
Georgia Northwestern Tech Coll (GA)
Hagerstown Comm Coll (MD)
Harper Coll (IL)
Hawkeye Comm Coll (IA)
Highline Comm Coll (WA)
ITT Tech Inst, Wilmington (MA)
ITT Tech Inst, Strongsville (OH)
Lanier Tech Coll (GA)
Lehigh Carbon Comm Coll (PA)
Metropolitan Comm Coll–Business & Technology Campus (MO)
Middle Georgia Tech Coll (GA)
Minneapolis Comm and Tech Coll (MN)
Minnesota State Coll–Southeast Tech (MN)
Monroe County Comm Coll (MI)
Montana State U–Great Falls Coll of Technology (MT)
Montgomery Coll (MD)
Moraine Park Tech Coll (WI)
Motlow State Comm Coll (TN)
Mott Comm Coll (MI)
Moultrie Tech Coll (GA)
Mount Wachusett Comm Coll (MA)
Niagara County Comm Coll (NY)
Northampton Comm Coll (PA)
North Dakota State Coll of Science (ND)
Northern Essex Comm Coll (MA)
North Georgia Tech Coll (GA)
North Shore Comm Coll (MA)
Oklahoma State U, Oklahoma City (OK)
Palm Beach State Coll (FL)
Pasco-Hernando Comm Coll (FL)
Peninsula Coll (WA)
Pittsburgh Tech Inst, Oakdale (PA)
Quinsigamond Comm Coll (MA)
Raritan Valley Comm Coll (NJ)
Rasmussen Coll Aurora (IL)
Rasmussen Coll Bismarck (ND)
Rasmussen Coll Bloomington (MN)

Rasmussen Coll Brooklyn Park (MN)
Rasmussen Coll Eagan (MN)
Rasmussen Coll Fargo (ND)
Rasmussen Coll Fort Myers (FL)
Rasmussen Coll Green Bay (WI)
Rasmussen Coll Lake Elmo/Woodbury (MN)
Rasmussen Coll Mankato (MN)
Rasmussen Coll Moorhead (MN)
Rasmussen Coll New Port Richey (FL)
Rasmussen Coll Ocala (FL)
Rasmussen Coll St. Cloud (MN)
Red Rocks Comm Coll (CO)
St. Cloud Tech & Comm Coll (MN)
Seminole State Coll of Florida (FL)
Southeastern Tech Coll (GA)
Southern Crescent Tech Coll (GA)
Springfield Tech Comm Coll (MA)
Stark State Coll (OH)
Sullivan Coll of Technology and Design (KY)
Terra State Comm Coll (OH)
Trident Tech Coll (SC)
Volunteer State Comm Coll (TN)
West Georgia Tech Coll (GA)
Westmoreland County Comm Coll (PA)
Wiregrass Georgia Tech Coll (GA)
Wisconsin Indianhead Tech Coll (WI)

WELDING ENGINEERING TECHNOLOGY

Mitchell Tech Inst (SD)

WELDING TECHNOLOGY

Arkansas State U–Mountain Home (AR)
Austin Comm Coll (TX)
Bainbridge Coll (GA)
Beaufort County Comm Coll (NC)
Big Bend Comm Coll (WA)
Bluegrass Comm and Tech Coll (KY)
Casper Coll (WY)
Central Comm Coll–Columbus Campus (NE)
Central Comm Coll–Grand Island Campus (NE)
Central Comm Coll–Hastings Campus (NE)
Central Wyoming Coll (WY)
Clark Coll (WA)
Cochise Coll, Sierra Vista (AZ)
Coll of DuPage (IL)
Coll of the Canyons (CA)
Comm Coll of Allegheny County (PA)
Cowley County Comm Coll and Area Vocational–Tech School (KS)
Dawson Comm Coll (MT)
Do&nna Ana Comm Coll (NM)
Eastern Arizona Coll (AZ)
Eastern Idaho Tech Coll (ID)
Fox Valley Tech Coll (WI)
Front Range Comm Coll (CO)
Grand Rapids Comm Coll (MI)
Hutchinson Comm Coll and Area Vocational School (KS)
Illinois Central Coll (IL)
Iowa Lakes Comm Coll (IA)
Jamestown Comm Coll (NY)
Kankakee Comm Coll (IL)
Kaskaskia Coll (IL)
Kilgore Coll (TX)
Kirtland Comm Coll (MI)
Lake Area Tech Inst (SD)
Lansing Comm Coll (MI)
Linn State Tech Coll (MO)
Lower Columbia Coll (WA)
Macomb Comm Coll (MI)
Mid-Plains Comm Coll, North Platte (NE)
Mohave Comm Coll (AZ)
Monroe County Comm Coll (MI)
Montana State U–Great Falls Coll of Technology (MT)
Montcalm Comm Coll (MI)
Moraine Park Tech Coll (WI)
Muskegon Comm Coll (MI)
North Dakota State Coll of Science (ND)
Northeast Comm Coll (NE)

Northwest Coll (WY)
Northwest Florida State Coll (FL)
Oakland Comm Coll (MI)
Oklahoma Tech Coll (OK)
Olympic Coll (WA)
Orange Coast Coll (CA)
Owens Comm Coll, Toledo (OH)
Red Rocks Comm Coll (CO)
Reedley Coll (CA)
Riverside City Coll (CA)
Rogue Comm Coll (OR)
St. Clair County Comm Coll (MI)
St. Cloud Tech & Comm Coll (MN)
St. Philip's Coll (TX)
Salt Lake Comm Coll (UT)
San Diego City Coll (CA)
San Jacinto Coll District (TX)
San Juan Coll (NM)
Shawnee Comm Coll (IL)
Southeastern Comm Coll (IA)
Southeast Tech Inst (SD)
Southwestern Illinois Coll (IL)
Southwestern Michigan Coll (MI)
Southwest Mississippi Comm Coll (MS)
State U of New York Coll of Technology at Alfred (NY)
Tarrant County Coll District (TX)
Terra State Comm Coll (OH)
Texarkana Coll (TX)
Texas State Tech Coll Harlingen (TX)
Truckee Meadows Comm Coll (NV)
Tyler Jr Coll (TX)
U of Alaska Anchorage, Kodiak Coll (AK)
The U of Montana–Helena Coll of Technology (MT)
Westmoreland County Comm Coll (PA)

WELL DRILLING

Southwest Mississippi Comm Coll (MS)

WILDLIFE BIOLOGY

Eastern Arizona Coll (AZ)
Iowa Lakes Comm Coll (IA)

WILDLIFE, FISH AND WILDLANDS SCIENCE AND MANAGEMENT

Casper Coll (WY)
Dakota Coll at Bottineau (ND)
Front Range Comm Coll (CO)
Garrett Coll (MD)
Iowa Lakes Comm Coll (IA)
Itasca Comm Coll (MN)
Laramie County Comm Coll (WY)
Ogeechee Tech Coll (GA)
Penn State DuBois (PA)
Shawnee Comm Coll (IL)

WINE STEWARD/SOMMELIER

Cayuga County Comm Coll (NY)

WOMEN'S STUDIES

Casper Coll (WY)
Foothill Coll (CA)
Northern Essex Comm Coll (MA)
Santa Monica Coll (CA)
Santa Rosa Jr Coll (CA)
State Coll of Florida Manatee-Sarasota (FL)

WOOD SCIENCE AND WOOD PRODUCTS/PULP AND PAPER TECHNOLOGY

Copiah-Lincoln Comm Coll (MS)
Ogeechee Tech Coll (GA)

WOODWIND INSTRUMENTS

Iowa Lakes Comm Coll (IA)

WOODWORKING

Red Rocks Comm Coll (CO)
Vincennes U (IN)

WORD PROCESSING

Corning Comm Coll (NY)
ETI Tech Coll of Niles (OH)
Florida State Coll at Jacksonville (FL)
Gateway Comm Coll (CT)

Iowa Lakes Comm Coll (IA)
Metropolitan Comm Coll–Business
  & Technology Campus (MO)
Monroe County Comm Coll (MI)
Northwest Florida State Coll (FL)
Orange Coast Coll (CA)

Owensboro Comm and Tech Coll
  (KY)
Palm Beach State Coll (FL)
Seminole State Coll of Florida (FL)
Stark State Coll (OH)

Tallahassee Comm Coll (FL)
Valencia Coll (FL)

WRITING
Austin Comm Coll (TX)

Berkeley City Coll (CA)
Cayuga County Comm Coll (NY)

ZOOLOGY/ANIMAL BIOLOGY
Dakota Coll at Bottineau (ND)

Northeastern Jr Coll (CO)
Palm Beach State Coll (FL)
Pensacola State Coll (FL)
Snow Coll (UT)

Associate Degree Programs at Four-Year Colleges

ACCOUNTING
AIB Coll of Business (IA)
Baker Coll of Allen Park (MI)
Baker Coll of Auburn Hills (MI)
Baker Coll of Clinton Township (MI)
Baker Coll of Owosso (MI)
Boston U (MA)
Broadview U–Boise (ID)
Broadview U–Layton (UT)
Broadview U–Orem (UT)
Broadview U–West Jordan (UT)
California U of Pennsylvania (PA)
Calumet Coll of Saint Joseph (IN)
Central Penn Coll (PA)
Clarke U (IA)
Cleary U (MI)
Coll of Mount St. Joseph (OH)
Coll of St. Joseph (VT)
Coll of Staten Island of the City U of New York (NY)
Davenport U, Grand Rapids (MI)
Elizabethtown Coll (PA)
Everest U, Lakeland (FL)
Florida Inst of Technology (FL)
Florida National Coll (FL)
Franciscan U of Steubenville (OH)
Franklin U (OH)
Globe U–Appleton (WI)
Globe U–Eau Claire (WI)
Globe U–Green Bay (WI)
Globe U–La Crosse (WI)
Globe U–Madison East (WI)
Globe U–Madison West (WI)
Globe U–Minneapolis (MN)
Globe U–Sioux Falls (SD)
Globe U–Wausau (WI)
Globe U–Woodbury (MN)
Goldey-Beacom Coll (DE)
Gwynedd-Mercy Coll (PA)
Hawai`i Pacific U (HI)
Husson U (ME)
Immaculata U (PA)
Indiana Tech (IN)
Indiana U of Pennsylvania (PA)
Indiana Wesleyan U (IN)
Inter American U of Puerto Rico, Bayamón Campus (PR)
Inter American U of Puerto Rico, Fajardo Campus (PR)
Inter American U of Puerto Rico, Ponce Campus (PR)
Inter American U of Puerto Rico, San Germán Campus (PR)
Johnson State Coll (VT)
Lake Superior State U (MI)
Lebanon Valley Coll (PA)
Liberty U (VA)
Maria Coll (NY)
Minnesota School of Business–Blaine (MN)
Minnesota School of Business–Elk River (MN)
Minnesota School of Business–Lakeville (MN)
Minnesota School of Business–Moorhead (MN)
Minnesota School of Business–Rochester (MN)
Missouri Southern State U (MO)
Morrisville State Coll (NY)
Mountain State U (WV)
Mount Aloysius Coll (PA)
Mount Marty Coll (SD)
Mount St. Mary's Coll (CA)
Muhlenberg Coll (PA)
Point Park U (PA)
Post U (CT)

Potomac Coll (DC)
Rasmussen Coll Appleton (WI)
Rasmussen Coll Blaine (MN)
Rasmussen Coll Land O' Lakes (FL)
Rasmussen Coll Mokena/Tinley Park (IL)
Rasmussen Coll Romeoville/Joliet (IL)
Rasmussen Coll Tampa/Brandon (FL)
Rasmussen Coll Wausau (WI)
Regent U (VA)
Rogers State U (OK)
Saint Francis U (PA)
Saint Mary-of-the-Woods Coll (IN)
Shawnee State U (OH)
Southern New Hampshire U (NH)
South U (GA)
South U (TX)
Southwest Minnesota State U (MN)
State U of New York Coll of Technology at Delhi (NY)
Sullivan U (KY)
Thiel Coll (PA)
Thomas More Coll (KY)
Tiffin U (OH)
Trine U (IN)
Union Coll (NE)
Universidad del Turabo (PR)
U of Alaska Anchorage (AK)
U of Cincinnati (OH)
The U of Findlay (OH)
U of Rio Grande (OH)
The U of Toledo (OH)
The U of West Alabama (AL)
Utah Valley U (UT)
Walsh U (OH)
Webber International U (FL)
Wilson Coll (PA)
Youngstown State U (OH)

ACCOUNTING AND BUSINESS/MANAGEMENT
AIB Coll of Business (IA)
Kansas State U (KS)

ACCOUNTING AND FINANCE
AIB Coll of Business (IA)

ACCOUNTING RELATED
AIB Coll of Business (IA)
Bayamón Central U (PR)
Caribbean U (PR)
Franklin U (OH)
Montana State U Billings (MT)

ACCOUNTING TECHNOLOGY AND BOOKKEEPING
American Public U System (WV)
Baker Coll of Flint (MI)
DeVry U, Pomona (CA)
DeVry U, Westminster (CO)
DeVry U, Miramar (FL)
DeVry U, Orlando (FL)
DeVry U, Decatur (GA)
DeVry U, Federal Way (WA)
DeVry U Online (IL)
Ferris State U (MI)
Florida National Coll (FL)
Gannon U (PA)
Hickey Coll (MO)
Hilbert Coll (NY)
Indiana U Southeast (IN)
International Business Coll, Fort Wayne (IN)

Kent State U at Geauga (OH)
Lewis-Clark State Coll (ID)
Mercy Coll (NY)
Miami U (OH)
Montana State U Billings (MT)
Montana Tech of The U of Montana (MT)
New York City Coll of Technology of the City U of New York (NY)
New York Inst of Technology (NY)
Pennsylvania Coll of Technology (PA)
Post U (CT)
State U of New York Coll of Technology at Canton (NY)
The U of Akron (OH)
U of Alaska Fairbanks (AK)
U of Cincinnati (OH)
U of Rio Grande (OH)

ACTING
Pacific Union Coll (CA)

ADMINISTRATIVE ASSISTANT AND SECRETARIAL SCIENCE
Arkansas Tech U (AR)
Baker Coll of Auburn Hills (MI)
Baker Coll of Cadillac (MI)
Baker Coll of Clinton Township (MI)
Baker Coll of Jackson (MI)
Baker Coll of Muskegon (MI)
Baker Coll of Owosso (MI)
Ball State U (IN)
Baptist Bible Coll of Pennsylvania (PA)
Bayamón Central U (PR)
Black Hills State U (SD)
Campbellsville U (KY)
Caribbean U (PR)
Clarion U of Pennsylvania (PA)
Clayton State U (GA)
Columbia Centro Universitario, Caguas (PR)
Columbia Centro Universitario, Yauco (PR)
Concordia Coll–New York (NY)
Dordt Coll (IA)
EDP Coll of Puerto Rico, Inc. (PR)
EDP Coll of Puerto Rico–San Sebastian (PR)
Faith Baptist Bible Coll and Theological Seminary (IA)
Florida National Coll (FL)
Fort Hays State U (KS)
Free Will Baptist Bible Coll (TN)
Hickey Coll (MO)
Idaho State U (ID)
Inter American U of Puerto Rico, Bayamón Campus (PR)
Inter American U of Puerto Rico, San Germán Campus (PR)
International Business Coll, Fort Wayne (IN)
Lamar U (TX)
Lewis-Clark State Coll (ID)
Miami U (OH)
Montana State U Billings (MT)
Montana Tech of The U of Montana (MT)
Mountain State U (WV)
New York Inst of Technology (NY)
Northern Michigan U (MI)
Oakland City U (IN)
Ohio U–Chillicothe (OH)
Rider U (NJ)

State U of New York Coll of Technology at Canton (NY)
Sul Ross State U (TX)
Tabor Coll (KS)
Trinity Baptist Coll (FL)
The U of Akron (OH)
U of Central Missouri (MO)
U of Puerto Rico at Ponce (PR)
U of Rio Grande (OH)
U of the District of Columbia (DC)
The U of Toledo (OH)
Washburn U (KS)
Weber State U (UT)
Williams Baptist Coll (AR)

ADULT AND CONTINUING EDUCATION ADMINISTRATION
Concordia Coll–New York (NY)

ADULT DEVELOPMENT AND AGING
The U of Toledo (OH)

ADVERTISING
Academy of Art U (CA)
The Art Inst of California, a college of Argosy U, San Diego (CA)
Fashion Inst of Technology (NY)
Inter American U of Puerto Rico, San Germán Campus (PR)
U of the District of Columbia (DC)
Xavier U (OH)

AERONAUTICAL/AEROSPACE ENGINEERING TECHNOLOGY
Purdue U (IN)
Vaughn Coll of Aeronautics and Technology (NY)

AERONAUTICS/AVIATION/AEROSPACE SCIENCE AND TECHNOLOGY
Embry-Riddle Aeronautical U–Worldwide (FL)
Florida Inst of Technology (FL)
Indiana State U (IN)
Montana State U (MT)
Ohio U (OH)
Pacific Union Coll (CA)
U of Cincinnati (OH)
Vaughn Coll of Aeronautics and Technology (NY)

AFRICAN AMERICAN/BLACK STUDIES
U of Cincinnati (OH)

AGRIBUSINESS
Morehead State U (KY)
Morrisville State Coll (NY)
Southern Arkansas U–Magnolia (AR)
Southwest Minnesota State U (MN)
Vermont Tech Coll (VT)

AGRICULTURAL BUSINESS AND MANAGEMENT
Coll of Coastal Georgia (GA)
North Carolina State U (NC)

AGRICULTURAL BUSINESS AND MANAGEMENT RELATED
Penn State Abington (PA)
Penn State Altoona (PA)
Penn State Berks (PA)
Penn State Erie, The Behrend Coll (PA)
Penn State U Park (PA)
U of Guelph (ON, Canada)

AGRICULTURAL ENGINEERING
Morrisville State Coll (NY)

AGRICULTURAL MECHANICS AND EQUIPMENT TECHNOLOGY
Montana State U–Northern (MT)

AGRICULTURAL PRODUCTION
Eastern New Mexico U (NM)
U of Arkansas at Monticello (AR)
Western Kentucky U (KY)

AGRICULTURE
Morrisville State Coll (NY)
North Carolina State U (NC)
South Dakota State U (SD)
U of Delaware (DE)
U of Guelph (ON, Canada)

AGRICULTURE AND AGRICULTURE OPERATIONS RELATED
Eastern Kentucky U (KY)

AIRCRAFT POWERPLANT TECHNOLOGY
Embry-Riddle Aeronautical U–Daytona (FL)
Embry-Riddle Aeronautical U–Worldwide (FL)
Idaho State U (ID)
Pennsylvania Coll of Technology (PA)
U of Alaska Fairbanks (AK)

AIRFRAME MECHANICS AND AIRCRAFT MAINTENANCE TECHNOLOGY
Kansas State U (KS)
Lewis U (IL)
Northern Michigan U (MI)
Piedmont International U (NC)
Thomas Edison State Coll (NJ)
U of Alaska Anchorage (AK)

AIRLINE FLIGHT ATTENDANT
Liberty U (VA)

AIRLINE PILOT AND FLIGHT CREW
Baker Coll of Flint (MI)
Baker Coll of Muskegon (MI)
Kansas State U (KS)
Lewis U (IL)
New England Inst of Technology (RI)
Southern Illinois U Carbondale (IL)
U of Alaska Anchorage (AK)
U of Alaska Fairbanks (AK)
Utah Valley U (UT)

AIR TRAFFIC CONTROL
LeTourneau U (TX)
Lewis U (IL)
Thomas Edison State Coll (NJ)
U of Alaska Anchorage (AK)

AIR TRANSPORTATION RELATED
Thomas Edison State Coll (NJ)

ALLIED HEALTH AND MEDICAL ASSISTING SERVICES RELATED
Clarion U of Pennsylvania (PA)
Florida National Coll (FL)
Jones Coll, Jacksonville (FL)
Thomas Edison State Coll (NJ)
Widener U (PA)

ALLIED HEALTH DIAGNOSTIC, INTERVENTION, AND TREATMENT PROFESSIONS RELATED
Ball State U (IN)
Cameron U (OK)
Gwynedd-Mercy Coll (PA)
Pennsylvania Coll of Technology (PA)
Thomas Edison State Coll (NJ)

AMERICAN NATIVE/NATIVE AMERICAN LANGUAGES
Idaho State U (ID)
U of Alaska Fairbanks (AK)

AMERICAN SIGN LANGUAGE (ASL)
Bethel Coll (IN)
Idaho State U (ID)
Madonna U (MI)

ANESTHESIOLOGIST ASSISTANT
Thompson Rivers U (BC, Canada)

ANIMAL/LIVESTOCK HUSBANDRY AND PRODUCTION
North Carolina State U (NC)
U of Connecticut (CT)

ANIMAL SCIENCES
Becker Coll (MA)
Sul Ross State U (TX)
U of Connecticut (CT)
U of New Hampshire (NH)

ANIMAL TRAINING
Becker Coll (MA)

ANIMATION, INTERACTIVE TECHNOLOGY, VIDEO GRAPHICS AND SPECIAL EFFECTS
Academy of Art U (CA)
Broadview U–Salt Lake City (UT)
Colorado Mesa U (CO)
National U (CA)
New England Inst of Technology (RI)

ANTHROPOLOGY
Midland Coll (TX)

APPAREL AND TEXTILE MANUFACTURING
Fashion Inst of Technology (NY)

APPAREL AND TEXTILE MARKETING MANAGEMENT
The Art Inst of Philadelphia (PA)
U of the Incarnate Word (TX)

APPLIED HORTICULTURE/ HORTICULTURAL BUSINESS SERVICES RELATED
Morrisville State Coll (NY)
U of Massachusetts Amherst (MA)

APPLIED HORTICULTURE/ HORTICULTURE OPERATIONS
Farmingdale State Coll (NY)
Kent State U at Geauga (OH)
Oakland City U (IN)
Pennsylvania Coll of Technology (PA)
Temple U (PA)
U of Connecticut (CT)
U of Massachusetts Amherst (MA)
U of New Hampshire (NH)

APPLIED MATHEMATICS
Central Methodist U (MO)
Clarion U of Pennsylvania (PA)

APPLIED PSYCHOLOGY
Florida Inst of Technology (FL)

AQUACULTURE
Morrisville State Coll (NY)

ARCHITECTURAL DRAFTING AND CAD/CADD
Baker Coll of Flint (MI)
Baker Coll of Muskegon (MI)
Broadview U–West Jordan (UT)
Globe U–Madison East (WI)
Globe U–Woodbury (MN)
Indiana U–Purdue U Indianapolis (IN)
Minnesota School of Business–Blaine (MN)
New York City Coll of Technology of the City U of New York (NY)
Purdue U North Central (IN)
Universidad del Turabo (PR)
The U of Toledo (OH)
Western Kentucky U (KY)

ARCHITECTURAL ENGINEERING TECHNOLOGY
Baker Coll of Clinton Township (MI)
Baker Coll of Owosso (MI)
Baker Coll of Port Huron (MI)
Bluefield State Coll (WV)
Ferris State U (MI)
Indiana U–Purdue U Fort Wayne (IN)
New England Inst of Technology (RI)
Norfolk State U (VA)
Northern Kentucky U (KY)
Purdue U North Central (IN)
State U of New York Coll of Technology at Delhi (NY)
U of Alaska Anchorage (AK)
U of the District of Columbia (DC)
Vermont Tech Coll (VT)

ARCHITECTURAL TECHNOLOGY
Pennsylvania Coll of Technology (PA)

ARCHITECTURE
Morrisville State Coll (NY)

ARCHITECTURE RELATED
Abilene Christian U (TX)
New York Inst of Technology (NY)

ART
Coll of Coastal Georgia (GA)
Coll of Mount St. Joseph (OH)
Eastern New Mexico U (NM)
Felician Coll (NJ)
Hannibal-LaGrange U (MO)
Indiana Wesleyan U (IN)
Kent State U at Stark (OH)
Keystone Coll (PA)
Lourdes U (OH)
Macon State Coll (GA)
Midland Coll (TX)
Northern Michigan U (MI)
Rivier Coll (NH)
State U of New York Empire State Coll (NY)
U of Cincinnati (OH)
U of Rio Grande (OH)
The U of Toledo (OH)

ART HISTORY, CRITICISM AND CONSERVATION
Clarke U (IA)

Thomas More Coll (KY)
U of Saint Francis (IN)

ARTIFICIAL INTELLIGENCE
Lamar U (TX)

AUDIOLOGY AND SPEECH-LANGUAGE PATHOLOGY
U of Cincinnati (OH)

AUDIOVISUAL COMMUNICATIONS TECHNOLOGIES RELATED
AIB Coll of Business (IA)

AUTOBODY/COLLISION AND REPAIR TECHNOLOGY
Idaho State U (ID)
Lewis-Clark State Coll (ID)
Montana State U Billings (MT)
New England Inst of Technology (RI)
Utah Valley U (UT)

AUTOMOBILE/AUTOMOTIVE MECHANICS TECHNOLOGY
Baker Coll of Auburn Hills (MI)
Baker Coll of Cadillac (MI)
Baker Coll of Clinton Township (MI)
Baker Coll of Flint (MI)
Baker Coll of Owosso (MI)
Baker Coll of Port Huron (MI)
Colorado Mesa U (CO)
Dixie State Coll of Utah (UT)
Ferris State U (MI)
Idaho State U (ID)
Lamar U (TX)
Lewis-Clark State Coll (ID)
Midland Coll (TX)
Montana State U Billings (MT)
Montana State U–Northern (MT)
Montana Tech of The U of Montana (MT)
Morrisville State Coll (NY)
New England Inst of Technology (RI)
Northern Michigan U (MI)
Oakland City U (IN)
Pennsylvania Coll of Technology (PA)
Pittsburg State U (KS)
State U of New York Coll of Technology at Canton (NY)
U of Alaska Anchorage (AK)
Utah Valley U (UT)
Weber State U (UT)

AUTOMOTIVE ENGINEERING TECHNOLOGY
Vermont Tech Coll (VT)
Weber State U (UT)

AVIATION/AIRWAY MANAGEMENT
Florida Inst of Technology (FL)
Mountain State U (WV)
U of Alaska Anchorage (AK)
U of the District of Columbia (DC)
Vaughn Coll of Aeronautics and Technology (NY)

AVIONICS MAINTENANCE TECHNOLOGY
Baker Coll of Flint (MI)
Excelsior Coll (NY)
U of Alaska Anchorage (AK)
U of the District of Columbia (DC)
Vaughn Coll of Aeronautics and Technology (NY)

BAKING AND PASTRY ARTS
The Art Inst of Austin (TX)
The Art Inst of California, a college of Argosy U, Inland Empire (CA)
The Art Inst of California, a college of Argosy U, Los Angeles (CA)
The Art Inst of California, a college of Argosy U, Orange County (CA)
The Art Inst of California, a college of Argosy U, Sacramento (CA)
The Art Inst of California, a college of Argosy U, San Diego (CA)
The Art Inst of California, a college of Argosy U, San Francisco (CA)
The Art Inst of Charleston (SC)

The Art Inst of Colorado (CO)
The Art Inst of Dallas (TX)
The Art Inst of Fort Lauderdale (FL)
The Art Inst of Houston (TX)
The Art Inst of Indianapolis (IN)
The Art Inst of Las Vegas (NV)
The Art Inst of Phoenix (AZ)
The Art Inst of Pittsburgh (PA)
The Art Inst of Salt Lake City (UT)
The Art Inst of San Antonio (TX)
The Art Inst of Tampa (FL)
The Art Inst of Tennessee–Nashville (TN)
The Art Inst of Tucson (AZ)
The Art Inst of Washington (VA)
The Art Insts International–Kansas City (KS)
The Art Insts International Minnesota (MN)
The Culinary Inst of America (NY)
Lincoln Culinary Inst (FL)
Pennsylvania Coll of Technology (PA)
Southern New Hampshire U (NH)
Sullivan U (KY)

BANKING AND FINANCIAL SUPPORT SERVICES
Brescia U (KY)
Caribbean U (PR)
Hilbert Coll (NY)
Touro Coll (NY)
Utah Valley U (UT)
Washburn U (KS)

BEHAVIORAL SCIENCES
Granite State Coll (NH)
Lewis-Clark State Coll (ID)
Midland Coll (TX)
Utah Valley U (UT)

BIBLICAL STUDIES
Alaska Bible Coll (AK)
Barclay Coll (KS)
Bethel Coll (IN)
Beulah Heights U (GA)
Boston Baptist Coll (MA)
Briercrest Coll (SK, Canada)
Calvary Bible Coll and Theological Seminary (MO)
Carolina Christian Coll (NC)
Carver Bible Coll (GA)
Cincinnati Christian U (OH)
Clear Creek Baptist Bible Coll (KY)
Corban U (OR)
Covenant Coll (GA)
The Criswell Coll (TX)
Dallas Baptist U (TX)
Eastern Mennonite U (VA)
Emmaus Bible Coll (IA)
Faith Baptist Bible Coll and Theological Seminary (IA)
Free Will Baptist Bible Coll (TN)
Grace Coll (IN)
Heritage Christian U (AL)
Hillsdale Free Will Baptist Coll (OK)
Houghton Coll (NY)
Howard Payne U (TX)
Kentucky Mountain Bible Coll (KY)
Lincoln Christian U (IL)
Maple Springs Baptist Bible Coll and Seminary (MD)
Mid-Atlantic Christian U (NC)
Piedmont International U (NC)
Point U (GA)
Simpson U (CA)
Southeastern Bible Coll (AL)
Southwestern Assemblies of God U (TX)
Trinity Coll of Florida (FL)
Tri-State Bible Coll (OH)

BIOCHEMISTRY
Saint Joseph's Coll (IN)

BIOLOGICAL AND BIOMEDICAL SCIENCES RELATED
Gwynedd-Mercy Coll (PA)
Roberts Wesleyan Coll (NY)

BIOLOGICAL AND PHYSICAL SCIENCES
Ferris State U (MI)
Free Will Baptist Bible Coll (TN)
Ohio U–Zanesville (OH)

Penn State Altoona (PA)
Purdue U North Central (IN)
State U of New York Empire State Coll (NY)
Trine U (IN)
Valparaiso U (IN)

BIOLOGY/BIOLOGICAL SCIENCES
Brewton-Parker Coll (GA)
Cleveland Chiropractic Coll–Kansas City Campus (KS)
Coll of Coastal Georgia (GA)
Dalton State Coll (GA)
Free Will Baptist Bible Coll (TN)
Immaculata U (PA)
Indiana U–Purdue U Fort Wayne (IN)
Indiana U South Bend (IN)
Indiana Wesleyan U (IN)
Lourdes U (OH)
Midland Coll (TX)
Mount St. Mary's Coll (CA)
Pine Manor Coll (MA)
Presentation Coll (SD)
Rogers State U (OK)
Shawnee State U (OH)
Thomas Edison State Coll (NJ)
Thomas More Coll (KY)
U of Cincinnati (OH)
U of New Hampshire at Manchester (NH)
U of Puerto Rico at Ponce (PR)
U of Rio Grande (OH)
The U of Tampa (FL)
The U of Toledo (OH)
Utah Valley U (UT)
Wright State U (OH)
York Coll of Pennsylvania (PA)

BIOLOGY/BIOTECHNOLOGY LABORATORY TECHNICIAN
U of the District of Columbia (DC)
Weber State U (UT)

BIOMEDICAL TECHNOLOGY
Baker Coll of Flint (MI)
Indiana U–Purdue U Indianapolis (IN)
Penn State Altoona (PA)
Penn State Berks (PA)
Penn State Erie, The Behrend Coll (PA)
Thomas Edison State Coll (NJ)

BIOTECHNOLOGY
Indiana U–Purdue U Indianapolis (IN)
Universidad del Turabo (PR)

BRASS INSTRUMENTS
McNally Smith Coll of Music (MN)

BROADCAST JOURNALISM
Evangel U (MO)
Ohio U–Zanesville (OH)

BUILDING/CONSTRUCTION FINISHING, MANAGEMENT, AND INSPECTION RELATED
Baker Coll of Flint (MI)
John Brown U (AR)
Pratt Inst (NY)
State U of New York Coll of Technology at Delhi (NY)
Weber State U (UT)
Wentworth Inst of Technology (MA)

BUILDING/CONSTRUCTION SITE MANAGEMENT
Utah Valley U (UT)
Wentworth Inst of Technology (MA)

BUILDING/HOME/ CONSTRUCTION INSPECTION
Utah Valley U (UT)

BUILDING/PROPERTY MAINTENANCE
State U of New York Coll of Technology at Canton (NY)
Utah Valley U (UT)

BUSINESS ADMINISTRATION AND MANAGEMENT

AIB Coll of Business (IA)
Alaska Pacific U (AK)
Albertus Magnus Coll (CT)
The American U of Rome (Italy)
Anderson U (IN)
Anna Maria Coll (MA)
Austin Peay State U (TN)
Baker Coll of Allen Park (MI)
Baker Coll of Auburn Hills (MI)
Baker Coll of Flint (MI)
Baker Coll of Owosso (MI)
Ball State U (IN)
Bauder Coll (GA)
Bay Path Coll (MA)
Benedictine Coll (KS)
Benedictine U (IL)
Bethel Coll (IN)
Brewton-Parker Coll (GA)
Broadview U–Boise (ID)
Broadview U–Layton (UT)
Broadview U–Orem (UT)
Broadview U–West Jordan (UT)
California Coast U (CA)
California U of Pennsylvania (PA)
Calumet Coll of Saint Joseph (IN)
Cameron U (OK)
Campbellsville U (KY)
Cardinal Stritch U (WI)
Carroll Coll (MT)
Central Penn Coll (PA)
Chaminade U of Honolulu (HI)
Clarion U of Pennsylvania (PA)
Cleary U (MI)
Coll of Coastal Georgia (GA)
Coll of Mount St. Joseph (OH)
Coll of St. Joseph (VT)
Coll of Saint Mary (NE)
Columbia Centro Universitario, Caguas (PR)
Columbia Centro Universitario, Yauco (PR)
Columbia Southern U (AL)
Concordia Coll–New York (NY)
Corban U (OR)
Dakota State U (SD)
Dallas Baptist U (TX)
Dallas Christian Coll (TX)
Dalton State Coll (GA)
Davenport U, Grand Rapids (MI)
Dixie State Coll of Utah (UT)
Edinboro U of Pennsylvania (PA)
EDP Coll of Puerto Rico, Inc. (PR)
EDP Coll of Puerto Rico–San Sebastian (PR)
Elizabethtown Coll (PA)
Everest U, Lakeland (FL)
Excelsior Coll (NY)
Faulkner U (AL)
Ferris State U (MI)
Five Towns Coll (NY)
Florida Inst of Technology (FL)
Florida National Coll (FL)
Franciscan U of Steubenville (OH)
Franklin U (OH)
Free Will Baptist Bible Coll (TN)
Friends U (KS)
Geneva Coll (PA)
Globe U–Appleton (WI)
Globe U–Eau Claire (WI)
Globe U–Green Bay (WI)
Globe U–La Crosse (WI)
Globe U–Madison East (WI)
Globe U–Madison West (WI)
Globe U–Minneapolis (MN)
Globe U–Sioux Falls (SD)
Globe U–Wausau (WI)
Globe U–Woodbury (MN)
Goldey-Beacom Coll (DE)
Gwynedd-Mercy Coll (PA)
Hawai'i Pacific U (HI)
Hilbert Coll (NY)
Husson U (ME)
Immaculata U (PA)
Indiana Tech (IN)
Indiana U of Pennsylvania (PA)
Indiana U–Purdue U Fort Wayne (IN)
Indiana Wesleyan U (IN)
Inter American U of Puerto Rico, Bayamón Campus (PR)
Inter American U of Puerto Rico, Fajardo Campus (PR)
Inter American U of Puerto Rico, Ponce Campus (PR)

Inter American U of Puerto Rico, San Germán Campus (PR)
ITT Tech Inst, Tempe (AZ)
ITT Tech Inst, Clovis (CA)
ITT Tech Inst, Concord (CA)
ITT Tech Inst, Corona (CA)
ITT Tech Inst, Indianapolis (IN)
ITT Tech Inst, South Bend (IN)
ITT Tech Inst, Wichita (KS)
ITT Tech Inst, Lexington (KY)
ITT Tech Inst (MS)
ITT Tech Inst, Springfield (MO)
ITT Tech Inst, Oklahoma City (OK)
Johnson State Coll (VT)
Jones Coll, Jacksonville (FL)
Jones International U (CO)
Kent State U (OH)
Kent State U at Geauga (OH)
Kent State U at Stark (OH)
Keystone Coll (PA)
King's Coll (PA)
Lake Superior State U (MI)
Lebanon Valley Coll (PA)
Lincoln Memorial U (TN)
Lock Haven U of Pennsylvania (PA)
Long Island U–Brooklyn Campus (NY)
Macon State Coll (GA)
Madonna U (MI)
Maria Coll (NY)
Marietta Coll (OH)
Medaille Coll (NY)
Medgar Evers Coll of the City U of New York (NY)
Mercy Coll (NY)
MidAmerica Nazarene U (KS)
Minnesota School of Business–Blaine (MN)
Minnesota School of Business–Elk River (MN)
Minnesota School of Business–Lakeville (MN)
Minnesota School of Business–Moorhead (MN)
Minnesota School of Business–Rochester (MN)
Missouri Baptist U (MO)
Montana State U Billings (MT)
Montreat Coll, Montreat (NC)
Morrisville State Coll (NY)
Mount Aloysius Coll (PA)
Mount Marty Coll (SD)
Muhlenberg Coll (PA)
Newbury Coll (MA)
New England Inst of Technology (RI)
Newman U (KS)
New Mexico Inst of Mining and Technology (NM)
Niagara U (NY)
Nichols Coll (MA)
Northwood U, Michigan Campus (MI)
Nyack Coll (NY)
Oakland City U (IN)
Ohio U–Chillicothe (OH)
Peirce Coll (PA)
Pennsylvania Coll of Technology (PA)
Point Park U (PA)
Post U (CT)
Potomac Coll (DC)
Providence Coll (RI)
Rasmussen Coll Appleton (WI)
Rasmussen Coll Blaine (MN)
Rasmussen Coll Land O' Lakes (FL)
Rasmussen Coll Mokena/Tinley Park (IL)
Rasmussen Coll Romeoville/Joliet (IL)
Rasmussen Coll Tampa/Brandon (FL)
Rasmussen Coll Wausau (WI)
Regent U (VA)
Rivier U (NH)
Robert Morris U Illinois (IL)
Rogers State U (OK)
Roger Williams U (RI)
Rust Coll (MS)
Saint Francis U (PA)
St. John's U (NY)
Saint Joseph's U (PA)
Saint Peter's Coll (NJ)
St. Thomas Aquinas Coll (NY)
Shawnee State U (OH)

Shaw U (NC)
Shorter U (GA)
Siena Heights U (MI)
Southern New Hampshire U (NH)
Southern Vermont Coll (VT)
South U (AL)
South U (GA)
South U (MI)
South U, Columbia (SC)
South U (TX)
South U, Glen Allen (VA)
Southwestern Assemblies of God U (TX)
Southwest Minnesota State U (MN)
State U of New York Coll of Technology at Canton (NY)
State U of New York Coll of Technology at Delhi (NY)
State U of New York Empire State Coll (NY)
Stevens Inst of Business & Arts (MO)
Taylor U (IN)
Thomas Edison State Coll (NJ)
Thomas More Coll (KY)
Tiffin U (OH)
Touro Coll (NY)
Trine U (IN)
Tulane U (LA)
Union Coll (NE)
Universidad del Turabo (PR)
The U of Akron (OH)
U of Alaska Anchorage (AK)
U of Alaska Fairbanks (AK)
U of Arkansas–Fort Smith (AR)
U of Central Arkansas (AR)
U of Cincinnati (OH)
The U of Findlay (OH)
U of Maine at Augusta (ME)
U of Maine at Fort Kent (ME)
The U of Montana Western (MT)
U of New Hampshire (NH)
U of New Hampshire at Manchester (NH)
U of New Haven (CT)
U of Pennsylvania (PA)
U of Pikeville (KY)
U of Rio Grande (OH)
U of Saint Francis (IN)
The U of Scranton (PA)
U of the Incarnate Word (TX)
The U of Toledo (OH)
Upper Iowa U (IA)
Utah Valley U (UT)
Vermont Tech Coll (VT)
Villa Maria Coll of Buffalo (NY)
Walsh U (OH)
Wayland Baptist U (TX)
Webber International U (FL)
Western International U (AZ)
Western Kentucky U (KY)
Williams Baptist Coll (AR)
Wilson Coll (PA)
Wright State U (OH)
Xavier U (OH)
York Coll of Pennsylvania (PA)
Youngstown State U (OH)

BUSINESS ADMINISTRATION, MANAGEMENT AND OPERATIONS RELATED

AIB Coll of Business (IA)
Dixie State Coll of Utah (UT)
Embry-Riddle Aeronautical U–Worldwide (FL)
Mountain State U (WV)
U of Cincinnati (OH)

BUSINESS AND PERSONAL/FINANCIAL SERVICES MARKETING

Dixie State Coll of Utah (UT)

BUSINESS AUTOMATION/TECHNOLOGY/DATA ENTRY

Baker Coll of Clinton Township (MI)
Colorado Mesa U (CO)
Mercy Coll (NY)
Midland Coll (TX)
Montana State U Billings (MT)
Montana State U–Northern (MT)
Northern Michigan U (MI)
U of Rio Grande (OH)
The U of Toledo (OH)
Utah Valley U (UT)

BUSINESS/COMMERCE

Adams State Coll (CO)
AIB Coll of Business (IA)
Alvernia U (PA)
American Public U System (WV)
Baker Coll of Flint (MI)
Bayamón Central U (PR)
Brescia U (KY)
Caribbean U (PR)
Castleton State Coll (VT)
Coll of Staten Island of the City U of New York (NY)
Columbia Coll (MO)
Crown Coll (MN)
Delaware Valley Coll (PA)
Ferris State U (MI)
Gannon U (PA)
Glenville State Coll (WV)
Granite State Coll (NH)
Hillsdale Free Will Baptist Coll (OK)
Idaho State U (ID)
Indiana U East (IN)
Indiana U Kokomo (IN)
Indiana U Northwest (IN)
Indiana U South Bend (IN)
Indiana U Southeast (IN)
Liberty U (VA)
Limestone Coll (SC)
Lourdes U (OH)
Mayville State U (ND)
Midland Coll (TX)
Missouri Southern State U (MO)
Montana State U Billings (MT)
Mount Vernon Nazarene U (OH)
New York U (NY)
Northern Kentucky U (KY)
Northern Michigan U (MI)
Northwestern State U of Louisiana (LA)
Pacific Union Coll (CA)
Penn State Abington (PA)
Penn State Altoona (PA)
Penn State Berks (PA)
Penn State Erie, The Behrend Coll (PA)
Penn State Harrisburg (PA)
Penn State U Park (PA)
Saint Leo U (FL)
Saint Mary-of-the-Woods Coll (IN)
Southern Arkansas U–Magnolia (AR)
Southwest Baptist U (MO)
Southwestern Assemblies of God U (TX)
Spalding U (KY)
Thomas More Coll (KY)
Thomas U (GA)
Troy U (AL)
Tulane U (LA)
U of Bridgeport (CT)
U of Cincinnati (OH)
U of New Hampshire (NH)
U of Puerto Rico at Ponce (PR)
The U of Toledo (OH)
Wright State U (OH)
Youngstown State U (OH)

BUSINESS MACHINE REPAIR

Lamar U (TX)
U of Alaska Anchorage (AK)

BUSINESS, MANAGEMENT, AND MARKETING RELATED

Ball State U (IN)
Caribbean U (PR)
Presentation Coll (SD)
Purdue U North Central (IN)
Sacred Heart U (CT)
Sullivan U (KY)

BUSINESS/MANAGERIAL ECONOMICS

Caribbean U (PR)
Saint Peter's Coll (NJ)

BUSINESS OPERATIONS SUPPORT AND SECRETARIAL SERVICES RELATED

Thomas Edison State Coll (NJ)

BUSINESS TEACHER EDUCATION

Wright State U (OH)

CABINETMAKING AND MILLWORK

Utah Valley U (UT)

CAD/CADD DRAFTING/DESIGN TECHNOLOGY

The Art Insts International Minnesota (MN)
Ferris State U (MI)
Idaho State U (ID)
ITT Tech Inst, Springfield (IL)
ITT Tech Inst, Charlotte (NC)
ITT Tech Inst, Durham (NC)
Montana Tech of The U of Montana (MT)
Northern Michigan U (MI)
Shawnee State U (OH)
U of Arkansas–Fort Smith (AR)

CARDIOVASCULAR TECHNOLOGY

Gwynedd-Mercy Coll (PA)
Mercy Coll of Ohio (OH)
Molloy Coll (NY)
New York U (NY)
Thompson Rivers U (BC, Canada)
The U of Toledo (OH)

CARPENTRY

Idaho State U (ID)
Montana State U Billings (MT)
Montana State U–Northern (MT)
Montana Tech of The U of Montana (MT)
New England Inst of Technology (RI)
Thompson Rivers U (BC, Canada)
U of Alaska Fairbanks (AK)

CHEMICAL ENGINEERING

U of the District of Columbia (DC)

CHEMICAL TECHNOLOGY

Ball State U (IN)
Excelsior Coll (NY)
Ferris State U (MI)
Indiana U–Purdue U Fort Wayne (IN)
Lawrence Technological U (MI)
Miami U (OH)
Millersville U of Pennsylvania (PA)
New York City Coll of Technology of the City U of New York (NY)
U of Cincinnati (OH)
U of Puerto Rico at Humacao (PR)
The U of Toledo (OH)
Weber State U (UT)

CHEMISTRY

Castleton State Coll (VT)
Central Methodist U (MO)
Clarke U (IA)
Coll of Coastal Georgia (GA)
Dalton State Coll (GA)
Immaculata U (PA)
Indiana U–Purdue U Indianapolis (IN)
Indiana U South Bend (IN)
Indiana Wesleyan U (IN)
Lake Superior State U (MI)
Lindsey Wilson Coll (KY)
Macon State Coll (GA)
Presentation Coll (SD)
Purdue U North Central (IN)
Southern Arkansas U–Magnolia (AR)
Thomas More Coll (KY)
U of Cincinnati (OH)
U of Rio Grande (OH)
The U of Tampa (FL)
U of the Incarnate Word (TX)
Utah Valley U (UT)
Wichita State U (KS)
Wright State U (OH)
York Coll of Pennsylvania (PA)

CHILD-CARE AND SUPPORT SERVICES MANAGEMENT

Bob Jones U (SC)
Eastern Kentucky U (KY)
Eastern New Mexico U (NM)
Ferris State U (MI)
Idaho State U (ID)
Mount Vernon Nazarene U (OH)

Nicholls State U (LA)
Pine Manor Coll (MA)
Post U (CT)
Southeast Missouri State U (MO)
Thompson Rivers U (BC, Canada)
Youngstown State U (OH)

CHILD-CARE PROVISION
American Public U System (WV)
Eastern Kentucky U (KY)
Mayville State U (ND)
Midland Coll (TX)
Pennsylvania Coll of Technology (PA)
Saint Mary-of-the-Woods Coll (IN)
Trevecca Nazarene U (TN)

CHILD DEVELOPMENT
Arkansas Tech U (AR)
Evangel U (MO)
Franciscan U of Steubenville (OH)
Grambling State U (LA)
Lamar U (TX)
Lewis-Clark State Coll (ID)
Madonna U (MI)
Northern Michigan U (MI)
Ohio U (OH)
Ohio U–Chillicothe (OH)
U of the District of Columbia (DC)
Youngstown State U (OH)

CHRISTIAN STUDIES
Crown Coll (MN)
Dallas Baptist U (TX)
Huntington U (IN)
Regent U (VA)
Wayland Baptist U (TX)

CINEMATOGRAPHY AND FILM/VIDEO PRODUCTION
Academy of Art U (CA)
The Art Inst of Atlanta (GA)
The Art Inst of California, a college of Argosy U, Los Angeles (CA)
The Art Inst of Charlotte (NC)
The Art Inst of Colorado (CO)
The Art Inst of Dallas (TX)
The Art Inst of Fort Lauderdale (FL)
The Art Inst of Philadelphia (PA)
The Art Inst of Pittsburgh (PA)
The Art Inst of Tennessee–Nashville (TN)
The Art Inst of Washington (VA)
New England Inst of Technology (RI)
Pacific Union Coll (CA)

CIVIL ENGINEERING TECHNOLOGY
Bluefield State Coll (WV)
Fairmont State U (WV)
Ferris State U (MI)
Idaho State U (ID)
Indiana U–Purdue U Fort Wayne (IN)
Indiana U–Purdue U Indianapolis (IN)
Michigan Technological U (MI)
Montana State U–Northern (MT)
Montana Tech of The U of Montana (MT)
New York City Coll of Technology of the City U of New York (NY)
Pennsylvania Coll of Technology (PA)
Point Park U (PA)
Purdue U North Central (IN)
State U of New York Coll of Technology at Canton (NY)
U of New Hampshire (NH)
U of Puerto Rico at Bayamón (PR)
U of Puerto Rico at Ponce (PR)
U of the District of Columbia (DC)
The U of Toledo (OH)
Vermont Tech Coll (VT)
Youngstown State U (OH)

CLINICAL LABORATORY SCIENCE/MEDICAL TECHNOLOGY
Arkansas State U (AR)
Dalton State Coll (GA)
Ferris State U (MI)
Lake Superior State U (MI)
Shawnee State U (OH)
Thomas Edison State Coll (NJ)

U of Cincinnati (OH)
The U of Toledo (OH)

CLINICAL/MEDICAL LABORATORY ASSISTANT
U of Maine at Augusta (ME)

CLINICAL/MEDICAL LABORATORY SCIENCE AND ALLIED PROFESSIONS RELATED
Mississippi State U (MS)
Youngstown State U (OH)

CLINICAL/MEDICAL LABORATORY TECHNOLOGY
Baker Coll of Owosso (MI)
Boston U (MA)
Coll of Coastal Georgia (GA)
Dalton State Coll (GA)
Eastern Kentucky U (KY)
Farmingdale State Coll (NY)
Ferris State U (MI)
The George Washington U (DC)
Indiana U Northwest (IN)
Indiana U South Bend (IN)
Marshall U (WV)
Mount Aloysius Coll (PA)
Our Lady of the Lake Coll (LA)
U of Alaska Anchorage (AK)
U of Maine at Presque Isle (ME)
U of Rio Grande (OH)
U of the District of Columbia (DC)
Weber State U (UT)
Youngstown State U (OH)

COMMERCIAL AND ADVERTISING ART
Academy of Art U (CA)
Baker Coll of Auburn Hills (MI)
Baker Coll of Clinton Township (MI)
Baker Coll of Muskegon (MI)
Baker Coll of Owosso (MI)
Baker Coll of Port Huron (MI)
Central Penn Coll (PA)
Fashion Inst of Technology (NY)
Mercy Coll (NY)
Midland Coll (TX)
Mitchell Coll (CT)
Montana State U–Northern (MT)
New York City Coll of Technology of the City U of New York (NY)
Northern State U (SD)
Pennsylvania Coll of Technology (PA)
Pratt Inst (NY)
Robert Morris U Illinois (IL)
Suffolk U (MA)
U of Cincinnati (OH)
U of the District of Columbia (DC)
Utah Valley U (UT)
Villa Maria Coll of Buffalo (NY)

COMMERCIAL PHOTOGRAPHY
Academy of Art U (CA)
The Art Inst of Atlanta (GA)
The Art Inst of Washington (VA)
Fashion Inst of Technology (NY)
Harrington Coll of Design (IL)

COMMUNICATION
Thomas More Coll (KY)
Xavier U (OH)

COMMUNICATION AND JOURNALISM RELATED
Clarke U (IA)
Immaculata U (PA)
Keystone Coll (PA)
Macon State Coll (GA)
Madonna U (MI)
Tulane U (LA)
Valparaiso U (IN)

COMMUNICATION AND MEDIA RELATED
Elizabethtown Coll (PA)
Keystone Coll (PA)
Lebanese American U (Lebanon)

COMMUNICATION SCIENCES AND DISORDERS
Ohio U–Chillicothe (OH)

COMMUNICATIONS SYSTEMS INSTALLATION AND REPAIR TECHNOLOGY
Idaho State U (ID)
Thompson Rivers U (BC, Canada)

COMMUNICATIONS TECHNOLOGY
AIB Coll of Business (IA)
Colorado Mesa U (CO)
East Stroudsburg U of Pennsylvania (PA)
ITT Tech Inst, Tempe (AZ)
ITT Tech Inst, Clovis (CA)
ITT Tech Inst, Concord (CA)
ITT Tech Inst, Corona (CA)
ITT Tech Inst, Indianapolis (IN)
ITT Tech Inst, South Bend (IN)
ITT Tech Inst, Wichita (KS)
ITT Tech Inst, Lexington (KY)
ITT Tech Inst, Hanover (MD)
ITT Tech Inst (MS)
ITT Tech Inst, Springfield (MO)
ITT Tech Inst, Oklahoma City (OK)
U of Puerto Rico at Humacao (PR)

COMMUNITY HEALTH AND PREVENTIVE MEDICINE
Utah Valley U (UT)

COMMUNITY ORGANIZATION AND ADVOCACY
Montana State U–Northern (MT)
State U of New York Empire State Coll (NY)
Touro Coll (NY)
U of Alaska Fairbanks (AK)
The U of Findlay (OH)
U of New Hampshire (NH)

COMPARATIVE LITERATURE
Midland Coll (TX)

COMPUTER AND INFORMATION SCIENCES
Baker Coll of Allen Park (MI)
Ball State U (IN)
Black Hills State U (SD)
Chaminade U of Honolulu (HI)
Clarke U (IA)
Coll of Mount St. Joseph (OH)
Columbia Coll (MO)
Delaware Valley Coll (PA)
Edinboro U of Pennsylvania (PA)
Franklin U (OH)
Herzing U, Madison (WI)
Indiana Wesleyan U (IN)
Inter American U of Puerto Rico, Fajardo Campus (PR)
Inter American U of Puerto Rico, Ponce Campus (PR)
Jones Coll, Jacksonville (FL)
King's Coll (PA)
Lewis-Clark State Coll (ID)
Lincoln U (MO)
Manchester Coll (IN)
Montana State U Billings (MT)
Montana State U–Northern (MT)
Morrisville State Coll (NY)
New England Inst of Technology (RI)
New York City Coll of Technology of the City U of New York (NY)
Rogers State U (OK)
St. John's U (NY)
Southern New Hampshire U (NH)
Troy U (AL)
Tulane U (LA)
U of Alaska Anchorage (AK)
U of Arkansas–Fort Smith (AR)
U of Cincinnati (OH)
U of Maine at Augusta (ME)
The U of Tampa (FL)
Utah Valley U (UT)
Washburn U (KS)
Webber International U (FL)

COMPUTER AND INFORMATION SCIENCES AND SUPPORT SERVICES RELATED
Cleary U (MI)
Florida National Coll (FL)
Husson U (ME)
Montana State U Billings (MT)

Potomac Coll (DC)
Utah Valley U (UT)

COMPUTER AND INFORMATION SCIENCES RELATED
Limestone Coll (SC)
Lindsey Wilson Coll (KY)
Madonna U (MI)

COMPUTER AND INFORMATION SYSTEMS SECURITY
Davenport U, Grand Rapids (MI)
Florida National Coll (FL)
Potomac Coll (DC)
St. John's U (NY)

COMPUTER ENGINEERING
New England Inst of Technology (RI)
The U of Scranton (PA)

COMPUTER ENGINEERING RELATED
Thompson Rivers U (BC, Canada)

COMPUTER ENGINEERING TECHNOLOGIES RELATED
Thomas Edison State Coll (NJ)
Universidad del Turabo (PR)

COMPUTER ENGINEERING TECHNOLOGY
Baker Coll of Owosso (MI)
California U of Pennsylvania (PA)
Dalton State Coll (GA)
Eastern Kentucky U (KY)
Indiana U–Purdue U Indianapolis (IN)
ITT Tech Inst, Springfield (IL)
ITT Tech Inst, Charlotte (NC)
ITT Tech Inst, Durham (NC)
Northern Michigan U (MI)
Oakland City U (IN)
Oregon Inst of Technology (OR)
U of Hartford (CT)
U of the District of Columbia (DC)
Vermont Tech Coll (VT)
Weber State U (UT)

COMPUTER GRAPHICS
Baker Coll of Cadillac (MI)
Florida National Coll (FL)
Indiana Tech (IN)
Mountain State U (WV)
Thompson Rivers U (BC, Canada)

COMPUTER/INFORMATION TECHNOLOGY SERVICES ADMINISTRATION RELATED
Keystone Coll (PA)
Limestone Coll (SC)
Maria Coll (NY)
Mercy Coll (NY)
Pennsylvania Coll of Technology (PA)

COMPUTER INSTALLATION AND REPAIR TECHNOLOGY
Dalton State Coll (GA)
Inter American U of Puerto Rico, Bayamón Campus (PR)
Inter American U of Puerto Rico, Fajardo Campus (PR)
Sullivan U (KY)
Thompson Rivers U (BC, Canada)
U of Alaska Fairbanks (AK)

COMPUTER PROGRAMMING
Baker Coll of Muskegon (MI)
Baker Coll of Owosso (MI)
Baker Coll of Port Huron (MI)
Bayamón Central U (PR)
Black Hills State U (SD)
Caribbean U (PR)
Castleton State Coll (VT)
Coll of Staten Island of the City U of New York (NY)
Dakota State U (SD)
Delaware Valley Coll (PA)
EDP Coll of Puerto Rico, Inc. (PR)
EDP Coll of Puerto Rico–San Sebastian (PR)

Everest U, Lakeland (FL)
Farmingdale State Coll (NY)
Florida National Coll (FL)
Gwynedd-Mercy Coll (PA)
Hickey Coll (MO)
International Business Coll, Fort Wayne (IN)
Limestone Coll (SC)
Medgar Evers Coll of the City U of New York (NY)
Missouri Southern State U (MO)
New England Inst of Technology (RI)
Oakland City U (IN)
Oregon Inst of Technology (OR)
Saint Francis U (PA)
U of Arkansas at Little Rock (AR)
The U of Toledo (OH)
Youngstown State U (OH)

COMPUTER PROGRAMMING RELATED
Florida National Coll (FL)
Herzing U, Madison (WI)

COMPUTER PROGRAMMING (SPECIFIC APPLICATIONS)
Florida National Coll (FL)
Idaho State U (ID)
Indiana U East (IN)
Indiana U South Bend (IN)
Indiana U Southeast (IN)
Midland Coll (TX)
The U of Toledo (OH)

COMPUTER SCIENCE
Baker Coll of Allen Park (MI)
Baker Coll of Owosso (MI)
Black Hills State U (SD)
Boston U (MA)
Calumet Coll of Saint Joseph (IN)
Carroll Coll (MT)
Central Methodist U (MO)
Central Penn Coll (PA)
Coll of Coastal Georgia (GA)
Creighton U (NE)
Dalton State Coll (GA)
Everest U, Lakeland (FL)
Farmingdale State Coll (NY)
Felician Coll (NJ)
Florida National Coll (FL)
Franklin U (OH)
Hawai`i Pacific U (HI)
Inter American U of Puerto Rico, Bayamón Campus (PR)
Inter American U of Puerto Rico, Ponce Campus (PR)
Inter American U of Puerto Rico, San Germán Campus (PR)
Lake Superior State U (MI)
Madonna U (MI)
Morrisville State Coll (NY)
Mountain State U (WV)
New England Inst of Technology (RI)
New York City Coll of Technology of the City U of New York (NY)
Oakland City U (IN)
Southwest Baptist U (MO)
Thomas Edison State Coll (NJ)
The U of Findlay (OH)
U of Maine at Fort Kent (ME)
U of New Haven (CT)
U of Rio Grande (OH)
Utah Valley U (UT)
Walsh U (OH)
Weber State U (UT)

COMPUTER SOFTWARE AND MEDIA APPLICATIONS RELATED
International Academy of Design & Technology (FL)
ITT Tech Inst, Indianapolis (IN)

COMPUTER SOFTWARE ENGINEERING
Rasmussen Coll Appleton (WI)
Rasmussen Coll Blaine (MN)
Rasmussen Coll Land O' Lakes (FL)
Rasmussen Coll Tampa/Brandon (FL)
Rasmussen Coll Wausau (WI)
Vermont Tech Coll (VT)

COMPUTER SOFTWARE TECHNOLOGY
Globe U–Woodbury (MN)
ITT Tech Inst, Clovis (CA)
ITT Tech Inst, Indianapolis (IN)
ITT Tech Inst, South Bend (IN)
ITT Tech Inst, Lexington (KY)
ITT Tech Inst, Charlotte (NC)
ITT Tech Inst, Durham (NC)
ITT Tech Inst, Oklahoma City (OK)

COMPUTER SYSTEMS ANALYSIS
Davenport U, Grand Rapids (MI)
New England Inst of Technology (RI)
The U of Akron (OH)
The U of Toledo (OH)

COMPUTER SYSTEMS NETWORKING AND TELECOMMUNICATIONS
Baker Coll of Allen Park (MI)
Baker Coll of Flint (MI)
Broadview U–Boise (ID)
Broadview U–Layton (UT)
Broadview U–Orem (UT)
Broadview U–West Jordan (UT)
Clayton State U (GA)
DeVry Coll of New York (NY)
DeVry U, Phoenix (AZ)
DeVry U, Pomona (CA)
DeVry U, Westminster (CO)
DeVry U, Miramar (FL)
DeVry U, Orlando (FL)
DeVry U, Decatur (GA)
DeVry U, Chicago (IL)
DeVry U, Kansas City (MO)
DeVry U, North Brunswick (NJ)
DeVry U, Columbus (OH)
DeVry U, Fort Washington (PA)
DeVry U, Houston (TX)
DeVry U, Irving (TX)
DeVry U, Arlington (VA)
DeVry U, Federal Way (WA)
DeVry U Online (IL)
Florida National Coll (FL)
Globe U–Eau Claire (WI)
Globe U–Green Bay (WI)
Globe U–La Crosse (WI)
Globe U–Madison East (WI)
Globe U–Madison West (WI)
Globe U–Minneapolis (MN)
Globe U–Wausau (WI)
Globe U–Woodbury (MN)
Herzing U, Madison (WI)
Hickey Coll (MO)
Idaho State U (ID)
Indiana Tech (IN)
International Business Coll, Fort Wayne (IN)
Minnesota School of Business–Blaine (MN)
Minnesota School of Business–Elk River (MN)
Minnesota School of Business–Lakeville (MN)
Minnesota School of Business–Moorhead (MN)
Minnesota School of Business–Rochester (MN)
Montana Tech of The U of Montana (MT)
Pace U (NY)
Robert Morris U Illinois (IL)
The U of Akron (OH)

COMPUTER TEACHER EDUCATION
Baker Coll of Flint (MI)

COMPUTER TECHNOLOGY/ COMPUTER SYSTEMS TECHNOLOGY
Dalton State Coll (GA)
Eastern Kentucky U (KY)
Morrisville State Coll (NY)
New England Inst of Technology (RI)
Southeast Missouri State U (MO)
Thompson Rivers U (BC, Canada)
U of Cincinnati (OH)

COMPUTER TYPOGRAPHY AND COMPOSITION EQUIPMENT OPERATION
Baker Coll of Auburn Hills (MI)
Baker Coll of Cadillac (MI)
Baker Coll of Clinton Township (MI)
Baker Coll of Flint (MI)
Baker Coll of Jackson (MI)
U of Cincinnati (OH)
The U of Toledo (OH)

CONSTRUCTION ENGINEERING TECHNOLOGY
Baker Coll of Owosso (MI)
Coll of Staten Island of the City U of New York (NY)
Ferris State U (MI)
Lawrence Technological U (MI)
New England Inst of Technology (RI)
New York City Coll of Technology of the City U of New York (NY)
Pennsylvania Coll of Technology (PA)
State U of New York Coll of Technology at Canton (NY)
State U of New York Coll of Technology at Delhi (NY)
The U of Akron (OH)
The U of Toledo (OH)
Vermont Tech Coll (VT)

CONSTRUCTION MANAGEMENT
U of Alaska Fairbanks (AK)
Vermont Tech Coll (VT)

CONSTRUCTION TRADES
Colorado Mesa U (CO)
Morrisville State Coll (NY)
Northern Michigan U (MI)
Utah Valley U (UT)

CONSTRUCTION TRADES RELATED
John Brown U (AR)
Utah Valley U (UT)

CONSUMER MERCHANDISING/ RETAILING MANAGEMENT
Baker Coll of Owosso (MI)
Madonna U (MI)
The U of Toledo (OH)

COOKING AND RELATED CULINARY ARTS
Colorado Mesa U (CO)
Hickey Coll (MO)

CORRECTIONS
Baker Coll of Muskegon (MI)
Lake Superior State U (MI)
Lamar U (TX)
Mount Aloysius Coll (PA)
U of the District of Columbia (DC)
The U of Toledo (OH)
Xavier U (OH)

CORRECTIONS ADMINISTRATION
John Jay Coll of Criminal Justice of the City U of New York (NY)

CORRECTIONS AND CRIMINAL JUSTICE RELATED
Cameron U (OK)
Florida Inst of Technology (FL)
Inter American U of Puerto Rico, Fajardo Campus (PR)
Rasmussen Coll Appleton (WI)
Rasmussen Coll Blaine (MN)
Rasmussen Coll Land O' Lakes (FL)
Rasmussen Coll Mokena/Tinley Park (IL)
Rasmussen Coll Romeoville/Joliet (IL)
Rasmussen Coll Tampa/Brandon (FL)
Rasmussen Coll Wausau (WI)

COSMETOLOGY
Lamar U (TX)

COUNSELING PSYCHOLOGY
Point U (GA)

COURT REPORTING
AIB Coll of Business (IA)

CREATIVE WRITING
U of Maine at Presque Isle (ME)

CRIMINAL JUSTICE/LAW ENFORCEMENT ADMINISTRATION
American Public U System (WV)
Anderson U (IN)
Arkansas State U (AR)
Bemidji State U (MN)
Boise State U (ID)
Broadview U–Boise (ID)
Broadview U–Layton (UT)
Broadview U–Orem (UT)
Broadview U–West Jordan (UT)
California Coast U (CA)
Calumet Coll of Saint Joseph (IN)
Campbellsville U (KY)
Castleton State Coll (VT)
Clarion U of Pennsylvania (PA)
Coll of Coastal Georgia (GA)
Coll of St. Joseph (VT)
Colorado Mesa U (CO)
Columbia Coll (MO)
Dalton State Coll (GA)
Farmingdale State Coll (NY)
Faulkner U (AL)
Florida National Coll (FL)
Glenville State Coll (WV)
Globe U–Appleton (WI)
Globe U–Eau Claire (WI)
Globe U–Green Bay (WI)
Globe U–La Crosse (WI)
Globe U–Madison East (WI)
Globe U–Madison West (WI)
Globe U–Minneapolis (MN)
Globe U–Sioux Falls (SD)
Globe U–Wausau (WI)
Globe U–Woodbury (MN)
Hannibal-LaGrange U (MO)
Hawai`i Pacific U (HI)
ITT Tech Inst, Charlotte (NC)
ITT Tech Inst, Durham (NC)
Lake Superior State U (MI)
Lincoln U (MO)
Lock Haven U of Pennsylvania (PA)
Macon State Coll (GA)
Mansfield U of Pennsylvania (PA)
Minnesota School of Business–Blaine (MN)
Minnesota School of Business–Elk River (MN)
Minnesota School of Business–Lakeville (MN)
Minnesota School of Business–Rochester (MN)
Morrisville State Coll (NY)
New England Inst of Technology (RI)
Northern Michigan U (MI)
Peirce Coll (PA)
Regent U (VA)
Reinhardt U (GA)
Roger Williams U (RI)
St. John's U (NY)
Southern Vermont Coll (VT)
South U (AL)
South U, Royal Palm Beach (FL)
South U, Tampa (FL)
South U (GA)
South U, Glen Allen (VA)
South U, Virginia Beach (VA)
Suffolk U (MA)
Thomas U (GA)
Tiffin U (OH)
Trine U (IN)
U of Arkansas at Monticello (AR)
U of Arkansas–Fort Smith (AR)
The U of Findlay (OH)
U of Maine at Fort Kent (ME)
U of Maine at Presque Isle (ME)
Utah Valley U (UT)
Washburn U (KS)
Wayland Baptist U (TX)
York Coll of Pennsylvania (PA)

CRIMINAL JUSTICE/POLICE SCIENCE
Arkansas State U (AR)
Armstrong Atlantic State U (GA)
Caribbean U (PR)
Columbia Southern U (AL)
Dalton State Coll (GA)
Ferris State U (MI)
Grambling State U (LA)
Hilbert Coll (NY)
Husson U (ME)
Idaho State U (ID)
John Jay Coll of Criminal Justice of the City U of New York (NY)
Lake Superior State U (MI)
Miami U (OH)
Midland Coll (TX)
Missouri Southern State U (MO)
Missouri Western State U (MO)
Northern Kentucky U (KY)
Northwestern State U of Louisiana (LA)
Ohio U–Chillicothe (OH)
Rasmussen Coll Blaine (MN)
Rogers State U (OK)
State U of New York Coll of Technology at Canton (NY)
The U of Akron (OH)
U of Arkansas at Little Rock (AR)
U of Louisiana at Monroe (LA)
U of New Haven (CT)
U of the District of Columbia (DC)
The U of Toledo (OH)

CRIMINAL JUSTICE/SAFETY
Arkansas Tech U (AR)
Ball State U (IN)
Bauder Coll (GA)
Bethel Coll (IN)
Central Penn Coll (PA)
Columbus State U (GA)
Dixie State Coll of Utah (UT)
Edinboro U of Pennsylvania (PA)
Everest U, Lakeland (FL)
Florida National Coll (FL)
Gannon U (PA)
Husson U (ME)
Idaho State U (ID)
Indiana Tech (IN)
Indiana U East (IN)
Indiana U Kokomo (IN)
Indiana U Northwest (IN)
Indiana U–Purdue U Indianapolis (IN)
Indiana U South Bend (IN)
Indiana Wesleyan U (IN)
Kent State U at Stark (OH)
Keystone Coll (PA)
King's Coll (PA)
Liberty U (VA)
Lourdes U (OH)
Madonna U (MI)
Manchester Coll (IN)
Mountain State U (WV)
New Mexico State U (NM)
Northern Michigan U (MI)
Penn State Altoona (PA)
Shaw U (NC)
Sullivan U (KY)
Thomas Edison State Coll (NJ)
Thomas More Coll (KY)
U of Cincinnati (OH)
U of Maine at Augusta (ME)
U of Pikeville (KY)
The U of Scranton (PA)
Weber State U (UT)
Xavier U (OH)
Youngstown State U (OH)

CRIMINOLOGY
Chaminade U of Honolulu (HI)
Elizabethtown Coll (PA)
Faulkner U (AL)
U of the District of Columbia (DC)

CRISIS/EMERGENCY/DISASTER MANAGEMENT
Arkansas State U (AR)

CROP PRODUCTION
North Carolina State U (NC)
U of Massachusetts Amherst (MA)

CULINARY ARTS
The Art Inst of Atlanta (GA)
The Art Inst of Austin (TX)
The Art Inst of California, a college of Argosy U, Hollywood (CA)
The Art Inst of California, a college of Argosy U, Inland Empire (CA)
The Art Inst of California, a college of Argosy U, Los Angeles (CA)
The Art Inst of California, a college of Argosy U, Orange County (CA)
The Art Inst of California, a college of Argosy U, Sacramento (CA)
The Art Inst of California, a college of Argosy U, San Diego (CA)
The Art Inst of California, a college of Argosy U, San Francisco (CA)
The Art Inst of California, a college of Argosy U, Sunnyvale (CA)
The Art Inst of Charleston (SC)
The Art Inst of Charlotte (NC)
The Art Inst of Colorado (CO)
The Art Inst of Dallas (TX)
The Art Inst of Fort Lauderdale (FL)
The Art Inst of Houston (TX)
The Art Inst of Indianapolis (IN)
The Art Inst of Jacksonville (FL)
The Art Inst of Las Vegas (NV)
The Art Inst of Michigan (MI)
The Art Inst of Philadelphia (PA)
The Art Inst of Phoenix (AZ)
The Art Inst of Pittsburgh (PA)
The Art Inst of Portland (OR)
The Art Inst of Raleigh-Durham (NC)
The Art Inst of Salt Lake City (UT)
The Art Inst of San Antonio (TX)
The Art Inst of Tampa (FL)
The Art Inst of Tennessee–Nashville (TN)
The Art Inst of Tucson (AZ)
The Art Inst of Virginia Beach (VA)
The Art Inst of Washington (VA)
The Art Insts International–Kansas City (KS)
The Art Insts International Minnesota (MN)
Baker Coll of Muskegon (MI)
Bob Jones U (SC)
The Culinary Inst of America (NY)
Idaho State U (ID)
The Illinois Inst of Art–Chicago (IL)
Keystone Coll (PA)
Lincoln Culinary Inst (FL)
Mountain State U (WV)
Newbury Coll (MA)
Nicholls State U (LA)
Oakland City U (IN)
Pennsylvania Coll of Technology (PA)
Robert Morris U Illinois (IL)
Southern New Hampshire U (NH)
State U of New York Coll of Technology at Delhi (NY)
Sullivan U (KY)
The U of Akron (OH)
U of Alaska Anchorage (AK)
U of Alaska Fairbanks (AK)
Utah Valley U (UT)

CULINARY ARTS RELATED
Delaware Valley Coll (PA)
Keystone Coll (PA)

DAIRY SCIENCE
Morrisville State Coll (NY)
Vermont Tech Coll (VT)

DANCE
Utah Valley U (UT)

DATA ENTRY/ MICROCOMPUTER APPLICATIONS
Baker Coll of Allen Park (MI)
Florida National Coll (FL)
The U of Akron (OH)

DATA ENTRY/ MICROCOMPUTER APPLICATIONS RELATED
Baker Coll of Allen Park (MI)
Florida National Coll (FL)

DATA MODELING/ WAREHOUSING AND DATABASE ADMINISTRATION

American Public U System (WV)
Midland Coll (TX)

DATA PROCESSING AND DATA PROCESSING TECHNOLOGY

American Public U System (WV)
Baker Coll of Auburn Hills (MI)
Baker Coll of Cadillac (MI)
Baker Coll of Clinton Township (MI)
Baker Coll of Flint (MI)
Baker Coll of Jackson (MI)
Baker Coll of Muskegon (MI)
Baker Coll of Owosso (MI)
Baker Coll of Port Huron (MI)
Campbellsville U (KY)
Dordt Coll (IA)
Everest U, Lakeland (FL)
Farmingdale State Coll (NY)
Florida National Coll (FL)
Lamar U (TX)
Miami U (OH)
Montana State U Billings (MT)
Mount Vernon Nazarene U (OH)
New York Inst of Technology (NY)
Northern State U (SD)
Pace U (NY)
Saint Peter's Coll (NJ)
U of Cincinnati (OH)
U of Puerto Rico at Ponce (PR)
The U of Toledo (OH)
Utah Valley U (UT)
Western Kentucky U (KY)
Youngstown State U (OH)

DENTAL ASSISTING

Boston U (MA)
U of Alaska Anchorage (AK)
U of Alaska Fairbanks (AK)
U of Southern Indiana (IN)

DENTAL HYGIENE

Baker Coll of Port Huron (MI)
Coll of Coastal Georgia (GA)
Dalton State Coll (GA)
Dixie State Coll of Utah (UT)
Farmingdale State Coll (NY)
Ferris State U (MI)
Florida National Coll (FL)
Indiana U Northwest (IN)
Indiana U–Purdue U Fort Wayne (IN)
Indiana U–Purdue U Indianapolis (IN)
Indiana U South Bend (IN)
Lamar U (TX)
Missouri Southern State U (MO)
Mount Ida Coll (MA)
New York City Coll of Technology of the City U of New York (NY)
New York U (NY)
Pennsylvania Coll of Technology (PA)
Shawnee State U (OH)
State U of New York Coll of Technology at Canton (NY)
Thomas Edison State Coll (NJ)
U of Alaska Anchorage (AK)
U of Alaska Fairbanks (AK)
U of Arkansas–Fort Smith (AR)
U of Bridgeport (CT)
U of Cincinnati (OH)
U of Maine at Augusta (ME)
U of Medicine and Dentistry of New Jersey (NJ)
U of New Haven (CT)
Utah Valley U (UT)
Vermont Tech Coll (VT)
Western Kentucky U (KY)
West Liberty U (WV)
Wichita State U (KS)
Youngstown State U (OH)

DENTAL LABORATORY TECHNOLOGY

Florida National Coll (FL)
Idaho State U (ID)
Indiana U–Purdue U Fort Wayne (IN)
New York City Coll of Technology of the City U of New York (NY)

DESIGN AND APPLIED ARTS RELATED

U of Maine at Presque Isle (ME)
U of Saint Francis (IN)
Washburn U (KS)

DESIGN AND VISUAL COMMUNICATIONS

Academy of Art U (CA)
ITT Tech Inst, Charlotte (NC)
ITT Tech Inst, Durham (NC)
U of Cincinnati (OH)
Utah Valley U (UT)

DESKTOP PUBLISHING AND DIGITAL IMAGING DESIGN

Academy of Art U (CA)
Ferris State U (MI)
New England Inst of Technology (RI)
Thompson Rivers U (BC, Canada)

DEVELOPMENTAL AND CHILD PSYCHOLOGY

Midland Coll (TX)

DIAGNOSTIC MEDICAL SONOGRAPHY AND ULTRASOUND TECHNOLOGY

Arkansas State U (AR)
Baker Coll of Auburn Hills (MI)
Baker Coll of Owosso (MI)
Baker Coll of Port Huron (MI)
Ferris State U (MI)
Florida National Coll (FL)
Keystone Coll (PA)
Mercy Coll of Health Sciences (IA)
Mountain State U (WV)
St. Catherine U (MN)

DIESEL MECHANICS TECHNOLOGY

Idaho State U (ID)
Lewis-Clark State Coll (ID)
Montana State U Billings (MT)
Montana State U–Northern (MT)
Morrisville State Coll (NY)
Pennsylvania Coll of Technology (PA)
U of Alaska Anchorage (AK)
Utah Valley U (UT)
Vermont Tech Coll (VT)
Weber State U (UT)

DIETETICS

Life U (GA)

DIETETIC TECHNOLOGY

Morrisville State Coll (NY)
Youngstown State U (OH)

DIETITIAN ASSISTANT

Eastern Kentucky U (KY)
Youngstown State U (OH)

DIGITAL COMMUNICATION AND MEDIA/MULTIMEDIA

Corcoran Coll of Art and Design (DC)
Indiana U–Purdue U Indianapolis (IN)
Vaughn Coll of Aeronautics and Technology (NY)

DIVINITY/MINISTRY

Carson-Newman Coll (TN)
Clear Creek Baptist Bible Coll (KY)
Great Lakes Christian Coll (MI)
Providence Coll (RI)
Southeastern Baptist Theological Seminary (NC)

DOG/PET/ANIMAL GROOMING

Becker Coll (MA)

DRAFTING AND DESIGN TECHNOLOGY

The Art Inst of Las Vegas (NV)
Baker Coll of Auburn Hills (MI)
Baker Coll of Clinton Township (MI)
Baker Coll of Owosso (MI)
Baker Coll of Port Huron (MI)
Black Hills State U (SD)
Caribbean U (PR)

Dalton State Coll (GA)
Eastern Kentucky U (KY)
Herzing U, Madison (WI)
ITT Tech Inst, Tempe (AZ)
ITT Tech Inst, Clovis (CA)
ITT Tech Inst, Concord (CA)
ITT Tech Inst, Corona (CA)
ITT Tech Inst, Deerfield Beach (FL)
ITT Tech Inst, West Palm Beach (FL)
ITT Tech Inst, Indianapolis (IN)
ITT Tech Inst, Indianapolis (IN)
ITT Tech Inst, South Bend (IN)
ITT Tech Inst, Overland Park (KS)
ITT Tech Inst, Wichita (KS)
ITT Tech Inst, Lexington (KY)
ITT Tech Inst, Grand Rapids (MI)
ITT Tech Inst, Southfield (MI)
ITT Tech Inst (MS)
ITT Tech Inst, Springfield (MO)
ITT Tech Inst, Oklahoma City (OK)
ITT Tech Inst, Salem (OR)
ITT Tech Inst, Germantown (WI)
Kentucky State U (KY)
Lamar U (TX)
LeTourneau U (TX)
Lewis-Clark State Coll (ID)
Lincoln U (MO)
Midland Coll (TX)
Montana State U (MT)
Montana State U Billings (MT)
Montana State U–Northern (MT)
Morrisville State Coll (NY)
New England Inst of Technology (RI)
Robert Morris U Illinois (IL)
Thompson Rivers U (BC, Canada)
The U of Akron (OH)
U of Alaska Anchorage (AK)
U of Alaska Fairbanks (AK)
U of Puerto Rico at Ponce (PR)
U of Rio Grande (OH)
The U of Toledo (OH)
Utah Valley U (UT)
Weber State U (UT)
Wright State U (OH)
Youngstown State U (OH)

DRAFTING/DESIGN ENGINEERING TECHNOLOGIES RELATED

Pennsylvania Coll of Technology (PA)
Thomas Edison State Coll (NJ)

DRAMATIC/THEATER ARTS

Adams State Coll (CO)
Clarke U (IA)
Macon State Coll (GA)
Pine Manor Coll (MA)
Thomas More Coll (KY)
Utah Valley U (UT)

DRAMATIC/THEATER ARTS AND STAGECRAFT RELATED

Utah Valley U (UT)

DRAWING

Academy of Art U (CA)
Midland Coll (TX)
Pratt Inst (NY)

EARLY CHILDHOOD EDUCATION

Adams State Coll (CO)
Baker Coll of Allen Park (MI)
Baker Coll of Jackson (MI)
Baptist Bible Coll of Pennsylvania (PA)
Bethel Coll (IN)
Coll of Saint Mary (NE)
Cornerstone U (MI)
Dixie State Coll of Utah (UT)
Gannon U (PA)
Granite State Coll (NH)
Great Lakes Christian Coll (MI)
Indiana U–Purdue U Indianapolis (IN)
Indiana U South Bend (IN)
Keystone Coll (PA)
Lake Superior State U (MI)
Lincoln Christian U (IL)
Lincoln U (MO)
Lindsey Wilson Coll (KY)
Manchester Coll (IN)
Maranatha Baptist Bible Coll (WI)

Mitchell Coll (CT)
Morrisville State Coll (NY)
Mount Aloysius Coll (PA)
Nova Southeastern U (FL)
Oakland City U (IN)
Pacific Union Coll (CA)
Point Park U (PA)
Rasmussen Coll Appleton (WI)
Rasmussen Coll Blaine (MN)
Rasmussen Coll Land O' Lakes (FL)
Rasmussen Coll Mokena/Tinley Park (IL)
Rasmussen Coll Romeoville/Joliet (IL)
Rasmussen Coll Tampa/Brandon (FL)
Rasmussen Coll Wausau (WI)
Rust Coll (MS)
Southwestern Assemblies of God U (TX)
State U of New York Coll of Technology at Canton (NY)
Sullivan U (KY)
Taylor U (IN)
Texas Coll (TX)
Thompson Rivers U (BC, Canada)
U of Alaska Fairbanks (AK)
U of Arkansas–Fort Smith (AR)
U of Great Falls (MT)
The U of Montana Western (MT)
U of Southern Indiana (IN)
Washburn U (KS)
Washington Adventist U (MD)
Western Kentucky U (KY)
Xavier U (OH)

ECONOMICS

Hawai'i Pacific U (HI)
Immaculata U (PA)
Midland Coll (TX)
State U of New York Empire State Coll (NY)
Thomas More Coll (KY)
The U of Tampa (FL)

EDUCATION

Baker Coll of Auburn Hills (MI)
Baker Coll of Cadillac (MI)
Cincinnati Christian U (OH)
Corban U (OR)
Dalton State Coll (GA)
Florida National Coll (FL)
Kent State U (OH)
Lamar U (TX)
Montana State U Billings (MT)
Montreat Coll, Montreat (NC)
Morrisville State Coll (NY)
National U (CA)
Saint Francis U (PA)
Southwestern Assemblies of God U (TX)
State U of New York Empire State Coll (NY)
U of Cincinnati (OH)
The U of Montana Western (MT)

EDUCATIONAL/ INSTRUCTIONAL TECHNOLOGY

Bayamón Central U (PR)
Cameron U (OK)

EDUCATION (MULTIPLE LEVELS)

Coll of Coastal Georgia (GA)

EDUCATION RELATED

The U of Akron (OH)

ELECTRICAL AND ELECTRONIC ENGINEERING TECHNOLOGIES RELATED

Inter American U of Puerto Rico, San Germán Campus (PR)
Lawrence Technological U (MI)
Northern Michigan U (MI)
Point Park U (PA)
Rochester Inst of Technology (NY)
Thomas Edison State Coll (NJ)
Vaughn Coll of Aeronautics and Technology (NY)
Youngstown State U (OH)

ELECTRICAL AND ELECTRONICS ENGINEERING

Fairfield U (CT)
Lake Superior State U (MI)
Merrimack Coll (MA)
Thompson Rivers U (BC, Canada)
The U of Scranton (PA)

ELECTRICAL AND POWER TRANSMISSION INSTALLATION

State U of New York Coll of Technology at Delhi (NY)

ELECTRICAL, ELECTRONIC AND COMMUNICATIONS ENGINEERING TECHNOLOGY

Baker Coll of Cadillac (MI)
Baker Coll of Owosso (MI)
Bluefield State Coll (WV)
California U of Pennsylvania (PA)
Cameron U (OK)
Columbia Centro Universitario, Caguas (PR)
Dalton State Coll (GA)
DeVry Coll of New York (NY)
DeVry U, Phoenix (AZ)
DeVry U, Pomona (CA)
DeVry U, Westminster (CO)
DeVry U, Miramar (FL)
DeVry U, Orlando (FL)
DeVry U, Decatur (GA)
DeVry U, Chicago (IL)
DeVry U, Kansas City (MO)
DeVry U, North Brunswick (NJ)
DeVry U, Columbus (OH)
DeVry U, Fort Washington (PA)
DeVry U, Houston (TX)
DeVry U, Irving (TX)
DeVry U, Federal Way (WA)
DeVry U Online (IL)
Eastern Kentucky U (KY)
Fairmont State U (WV)
Herzing U, Madison (WI)
Idaho State U (ID)
Indiana State U (IN)
Indiana U–Purdue U Fort Wayne (IN)
Indiana U–Purdue U Indianapolis (IN)
Inter American U of Puerto Rico, San Germán Campus (PR)
ITT Tech Inst, Tempe (AZ)
ITT Tech Inst, Clovis (CA)
ITT Tech Inst, Concord (CA)
ITT Tech Inst, Corona (CA)
ITT Tech Inst, Deerfield Beach (FL)
ITT Tech Inst, West Palm Beach (FL)
ITT Tech Inst, Indianapolis (IN)
ITT Tech Inst, Indianapolis (IN)
ITT Tech Inst, South Bend (IN)
ITT Tech Inst, Overland Park (KS)
ITT Tech Inst, Wichita (KS)
ITT Tech Inst, Hanover (MD)
ITT Tech Inst, Grand Rapids (MI)
ITT Tech Inst, Southfield (MI)
ITT Tech Inst (MS)
ITT Tech Inst, Springfield (MO)
ITT Tech Inst, Oklahoma City (OK)
ITT Tech Inst, Salem (OR)
ITT Tech Inst, Germantown (WI)
Kentucky State U (KY)
Lake Superior State U (MI)
Lamar U (TX)
Lawrence Technological U (MI)
Michigan Technological U (MI)
Midland Coll (TX)
New England Inst of Technology (RI)
New York City Coll of Technology of the City U of New York (NY)
Northern Michigan U (MI)
Northwestern State U of Louisiana (LA)
Oregon Inst of Technology (OR)
Penn State Altoona (PA)
Penn State Berks (PA)
Penn State Erie, The Behrend Coll (PA)
Pennsylvania Coll of Technology (PA)
Purdue U North Central (IN)
State U of New York Coll of Technology at Canton (NY)
Thomas Edison State Coll (NJ)

Universidad del Turabo (PR)
The U of Akron (OH)
U of Alaska Anchorage (AK)
U of Arkansas at Little Rock (AR)
U of Hartford (CT)
U of Massachusetts Lowell (MA)
U of Puerto Rico at Humacao (PR)
U of the District of Columbia (DC)
The U of Toledo (OH)
Utah Valley U (UT)
Vermont Tech Coll (VT)
Youngstown State U (OH)

ELECTRICAL/ELECTRONICS EQUIPMENT INSTALLATION AND REPAIR
Lewis-Clark State Coll (ID)
New England Inst of Technology (RI)
U of Arkansas–Fort Smith (AR)

ELECTRICAL/ELECTRONICS MAINTENANCE AND REPAIR TECHNOLOGY RELATED
Inter American U of Puerto Rico, San Germán Campus (PR)
Pittsburg State U (KS)

ELECTRICIAN
Pennsylvania Coll of Technology (PA)
Thompson Rivers U (BC, Canada)
Universidad del Turabo (PR)
Weber State U (UT)

ELECTROMECHANICAL TECHNOLOGY
Idaho State U (ID)
John Brown U (AR)
Michigan Technological U (MI)
New York City Coll of Technology of the City U of New York (NY)
Northern Michigan U (MI)
Shawnee State U (OH)
Utah Valley U (UT)

ELECTRONEURODIAGNOSTIC / ELECTROENCEPHALOGRAPHIC TECHNOLOGY
DeVry U, North Brunswick (NJ)

ELEMENTARY EDUCATION
Adams State Coll (CO)
Alaska Pacific U (AK)
Dalton State Coll (GA)
Edinboro U of Pennsylvania (PA)
Ferris State U (MI)
Hillsdale Free Will Baptist Coll (OK)
Mountain State U (WV)
Mount St. Mary's Coll (CA)
New Mexico Highlands U (NM)
Rogers State U (OK)
U of Cincinnati (OH)
Wilson Coll (PA)

EMERGENCY CARE ATTENDANT (EMT AMBULANCE)
Trinity Coll of Nursing and Health Sciences (IL)

EMERGENCY MEDICAL TECHNOLOGY (EMT PARAMEDIC)
Baker Coll of Cadillac (MI)
Baker Coll of Clinton Township (MI)
Baker Coll of Muskegon (MI)
Colorado Mesa U (CO)
Creighton U (NE)
Dixie State Coll of Utah (UT)
EDP Coll of Puerto Rico, Inc. (PR)
EDP Coll of Puerto Rico–San Sebastian (PR)
Idaho State U (ID)
Indiana U–Purdue U Indianapolis (IN)
Indiana U South Bend (IN)
Indiana U Southeast (IN)
Kent State U at Geauga (OH)
Mercy Coll of Health Sciences (IA)
Midland Coll (TX)
Montana State U Billings (MT)

Mountain State U (WV)
Pacific Union Coll (CA)
Pennsylvania Coll of Technology (PA)
Purdue U Calumet (IN)
Rogers State U (OK)
Saint Joseph's Coll (IN)
Shawnee State U (OH)
Southwest Baptist U (MO)
Spalding U (KY)
Trinity Coll of Nursing and Health Sciences (IL)
U of Alaska Anchorage (AK)
U of Cincinnati (OH)
U of Pittsburgh at Johnstown (PA)
The U of Toledo (OH)
Weber State U (UT)
Western Kentucky U (KY)
Youngstown State U (OH)

ENERGY MANAGEMENT AND SYSTEMS TECHNOLOGY
Baker Coll of Flint (MI)
Idaho State U (ID)
Montana State U Billings (MT)
U of Rio Grande (OH)

ENGINEERING
Brescia U (KY)
Coll of Staten Island of the City U of New York (NY)
Dixie State Coll of Utah (UT)
Ferris State U (MI)
Geneva Coll (PA)
Lake Superior State U (MI)
Lindsey Wilson Coll (KY)
Mountain State U (WV)
Palm Beach Atlantic U (FL)
Purdue U North Central (IN)
State U of New York Coll of Technology at Canton (NY)
Thompson Rivers U (BC, Canada)
Union Coll (NE)
Utah Valley U (UT)
Washington Adventist U (MD)

ENGINEERING RELATED
Eastern Kentucky U (KY)
McNally Smith Coll of Music (MN)

ENGINEERING SCIENCE
Rochester Inst of Technology (NY)
State U of New York Coll of Technology at Delhi (NY)
U of Pittsburgh at Bradford (PA)

ENGINEERING TECHNOLOGIES AND ENGINEERING RELATED
Arkansas State U (AR)
McNally Smith Coll of Music (MN)
Missouri Southern State U (MO)
Rogers State U (OK)
State U of New York Maritime Coll (NY)
Thomas Edison State Coll (NJ)
U of Puerto Rico at Bayamón (PR)
Utah Valley U (UT)

ENGINEERING TECHNOLOGY
Austin Peay State U (TN)
Brescia U (KY)
Excelsior Coll (NY)
Fairmont State U (WV)
Kansas State U (KS)
Lake Superior State U (MI)
Lincoln U (MO)
Macon State Coll (GA)
McNeese State U (LA)
Miami U (OH)
Michigan Technological U (MI)
Northern Kentucky U (KY)
State U of New York Coll of Technology at Delhi (NY)
U of Alaska Anchorage (AK)
Wright State U (OH)
Youngstown State U (OH)

ENGLISH
Calumet Coll of Saint Joseph (IN)
Carroll Coll (MT)
Central Methodist U (MO)
Coll of Coastal Georgia (GA)
Dalton State Coll (GA)

Felician Coll (NJ)
Hannibal-LaGrange U (MO)
Hillsdale Free Will Baptist Coll (OK)
Immaculata U (PA)
Indiana Wesleyan U (IN)
Lourdes U (OH)
Macon State Coll (GA)
Madonna U (MI)
Midland Coll (TX)
Pine Manor Coll (MA)
Southwestern Assemblies of God U (TX)
Thomas More Coll (KY)
U of Cincinnati (OH)
The U of Tampa (FL)
Utah Valley U (UT)
Xavier U (OH)

ENGLISH AS A SECOND/ FOREIGN LANGUAGE (TEACHING)
Briercrest Coll (SK, Canada)
Cornerstone U (MI)
Lincoln Christian U (IL)

ENGLISH LANGUAGE AND LITERATURE RELATED
Presentation Coll (SD)

ENTREPRENEURSHIP
Baker Coll of Flint (MI)
Central Penn Coll (PA)
Cogswell Polytechnical Coll (CA)
U of the District of Columbia (DC)

ENVIRONMENTAL CONTROL TECHNOLOGIES RELATED
Montana Tech of The U of Montana (MT)

ENVIRONMENTAL ENGINEERING TECHNOLOGY
Baker Coll of Flint (MI)
Baker Coll of Owosso (MI)
Baker Coll of Port Huron (MI)
New York City Coll of Technology of the City U of New York (NY)
Ohio U–Chillicothe (OH)
U of the District of Columbia (DC)
The U of Toledo (OH)

ENVIRONMENTAL SCIENCE
Thomas Edison State Coll (NJ)

ENVIRONMENTAL STUDIES
Columbia Coll (MO)
Mountain State U (WV)
The U of Findlay (OH)
The U of Toledo (OH)

EQUESTRIAN STUDIES
Centenary Coll (NJ)
Saint Mary-of-the-Woods Coll (IN)
The U of Findlay (OH)
U of Massachusetts Amherst (MA)
The U of Montana Western (MT)

EXECUTIVE ASSISTANT/ EXECUTIVE SECRETARY
Baker Coll of Allen Park (MI)
Baker Coll of Flint (MI)
Thompson Rivers U (BC, Canada)
U of Arkansas–Fort Smith (AR)
U of Cincinnati (OH)
Western Kentucky U (KY)

EXPLOSIVE ORDINANCE/ BOMB DISPOSAL
American Public U System (WV)

FAMILY AND COMMUNITY SERVICES
Baker Coll of Flint (MI)

FAMILY AND CONSUMER SCIENCES/HUMAN SCIENCES
Mount Vernon Nazarene U (OH)
U of Alaska Anchorage (AK)

FASHION/APPAREL DESIGN
Academy of Art U (CA)

The Art Inst of California, a college of Argosy U, Hollywood (CA)
The Art Inst of California, a college of Argosy U, San Francisco (CA)
The Art Inst of Dallas (TX)
The Art Inst of Fort Lauderdale (FL)
The Art Inst of Philadelphia (PA)
The Art Inst of Portland (OR)
Bauder Coll (GA)
EDP Coll of Puerto Rico, Inc. (PR)
Fashion Inst of Technology (NY)
Miami International U of Art & Design (FL)
Universidad del Turabo (PR)

FASHION MERCHANDISING
The Art Inst of California, a college of Argosy U, Hollywood (CA)
The Art Inst of California, a college of Argosy U, San Francisco (CA)
The Art Inst of Charlotte (NC)
The Art Inst of Michigan (MI)
The Art Inst of Raleigh-Durham (NC)
Bauder Coll (GA)
Fashion Inst of Technology (NY)
The Illinois Inst of Art–Chicago (IL)
The Illinois Inst of Art–Schaumburg (IL)
The Illinois Inst of Art–Tinley Park (IL)
Immaculata U (PA)
Miami International U of Art & Design (FL)
New York City Coll of Technology of the City U of New York (NY)
Southern New Hampshire U (NH)
Stevens Inst of Business & Arts (MO)
U of Bridgeport (CT)
U of the District of Columbia (DC)

FASHION MODELING
Fashion Inst of Technology (NY)

FIBER, TEXTILE AND WEAVING ARTS
Academy of Art U (CA)

FILM/CINEMA/VIDEO STUDIES
Burlington Coll (VT)

FINANCE
AIB Coll of Business (IA)
Davenport U, Grand Rapids (MI)
Franklin U (OH)
Hawai`i Pacific U (HI)
Indiana Wesleyan U (IN)
Saint Peter's Coll (NJ)
The U of Findlay (OH)
Youngstown State U (OH)

FINE ARTS RELATED
Academy of Art U (CA)
Madonna U (MI)
Pennsylvania Coll of Technology (PA)
Saint Francis U (PA)

FINE/STUDIO ARTS
Academy of Art U (CA)
Adams State Coll (CO)
Corcoran Coll of Art and Design (DC)
Fashion Inst of Technology (NY)
Keystone Coll (PA)
Lindsey Wilson Coll (KY)
Madonna U (MI)
Midland Coll (TX)
New Mexico State U (NM)
Pratt Inst (NY)
Thomas More Coll (KY)
U of Maine at Augusta (ME)
U of New Hampshire at Manchester (NH)
Villa Maria Coll of Buffalo (NY)
York Coll of Pennsylvania (PA)

FIRE PREVENTION AND SAFETY TECHNOLOGY
Montana State U Billings (MT)
Thomas Edison State Coll (NJ)
The U of Akron (OH)
U of Nebraska–Lincoln (NE)

U of New Haven (CT)
The U of Toledo (OH)

FIRE PROTECTION RELATED
The U of Akron (OH)

FIRE SCIENCE/FIREFIGHTING
Columbia Southern U (AL)
Idaho State U (ID)
Lake Superior State U (MI)
Lamar U (TX)
Lewis-Clark State Coll (ID)
Madonna U (MI)
Midland Coll (TX)
Mountain State U (WV)
Providence Coll (RI)
U of Alaska Anchorage (AK)
U of Alaska Fairbanks (AK)
U of Cincinnati (OH)
Utah Valley U (UT)
Vermont Tech Coll (VT)

FIRE SERVICES ADMINISTRATION
American Public U System (WV)
Midland Coll (TX)

FOOD PREPARATION
Washburn U (KS)

FOODS AND NUTRITION RELATED
U of Guelph (ON, Canada)

FOOD SCIENCE
Lamar U (TX)

FOOD SERVICE SYSTEMS ADMINISTRATION
Northern Michigan U (MI)
U of New Hampshire (NH)

FOODS, NUTRITION, AND WELLNESS
Madonna U (MI)
Morrisville State Coll (NY)

FOOD TECHNOLOGY AND PROCESSING
Arkansas State U (AR)
U of the District of Columbia (DC)
Washburn U (KS)

FOREIGN LANGUAGES AND LITERATURES
Coll of Coastal Georgia (GA)
Midland Coll (TX)
Southwestern Assemblies of God U (TX)

FOREIGN LANGUAGES RELATED
Macon State Coll (GA)
U of Alaska Fairbanks (AK)

FORENSIC SCIENCE AND TECHNOLOGY
Arkansas State U (AR)
ITT Tech Inst, Tempe (AZ)
ITT Tech Inst, Clovis (CA)
ITT Tech Inst, Concord (CA)
ITT Tech Inst, Corona (CA)
ITT Tech Inst, South Bend (IN)
ITT Tech Inst, Wichita (KS)
ITT Tech Inst, Lexington (KY)
ITT Tech Inst (MS)
ITT Tech Inst, Springfield (MO)
ITT Tech Inst, Oklahoma City (OK)
U of Arkansas at Monticello (AR)
U of Arkansas–Fort Smith (AR)
U of Saint Francis (IN)

FORESTRY
Coll of Coastal Georgia (GA)
U of Maine at Fort Kent (ME)

FOREST TECHNOLOGY
Glenville State Coll (WV)
Keystone Coll (PA)
Michigan Technological U (MI)
Pennsylvania Coll of Technology (PA)

State U of New York Coll of
Technology at Canton (NY)
U of Maine at Fort Kent (ME)
U of New Hampshire (NH)

FRENCH
Idaho State U (ID)
Midland Coll (TX)
Thomas More Coll (KY)
U of Cincinnati (OH)
The U of Tampa (FL)
Xavier U (OH)

FUNERAL SERVICE AND MORTUARY SCIENCE
Ferris State U (MI)
Mount Ida Coll (MA)
Point Park U (PA)
State U of New York Coll of
Technology at Canton (NY)
U of the District of Columbia (DC)

GAME AND INTERACTIVE MEDIA DESIGN
Academy of Art U (CA)

GENERAL STUDIES
AIB Coll of Business (IA)
Alverno Coll (WI)
American Public U System (WV)
Anderson U (IN)
Arkansas State U (AR)
Arkansas Tech U (AR)
Asbury U (KY)
Austin Peay State U (TN)
Averett U (VA)
Baptist Bible Coll of Pennsylvania
(PA)
Barclay Coll (KS)
Belhaven U (MS)
Black Hills State U (SD)
Bob Jones U (SC)
Brewton-Parker Coll (GA)
Burlington Coll (VT)
Butler U (IN)
California Coast U (CA)
Calumet Coll of Saint Joseph (IN)
Cameron U (OK)
Castleton State Coll (VT)
Chaminade U of Honolulu (HI)
City U of Seattle (WA)
Clearwater Christian Coll (FL)
Coll of Mount St. Joseph (OH)
Columbia Coll (MO)
Columbia Southern U (AL)
Concordia U Ann Arbor (MI)
Concordia U, St. Paul (MN)
Concordia U Texas (TX)
Dakota State U (SD)
Dalton State Coll (GA)
Dixie State Coll of Utah (UT)
Eastern Connecticut State U (CT)
Eastern Mennonite U (VA)
Ferris State U (MI)
Fort Hays State U (KS)
Franciscan U of Steubenville (OH)
Friends U (KS)
Great Lakes Christian Coll (MI)
Hillsdale Free Will Baptist Coll (OK)
Hope International U (CA)
Idaho State U (ID)
Indiana Tech (IN)
Indiana U East (IN)
Indiana U Kokomo (IN)
Indiana U Northwest (IN)
Indiana U of Pennsylvania (PA)
Indiana U–Purdue U Indianapolis
(IN)
Indiana U South Bend (IN)
Indiana U Southeast (IN)
Indiana Wesleyan U (IN)
John Brown U (AR)
Johnson State Coll (VT)
La Salle U (PA)
Lawrence Technological U (MI)
Lebanon Valley Coll (PA)
Lincoln Christian U (IL)
Macon State Coll (GA)
McNeese State U (LA)
Mercy Coll of Ohio (OH)
Miami U (OH)
Mid-Continent U (KY)
Monmouth U (NJ)
Montana State U Billings (MT)
Morehead State U (KY)
Mount Aloysius Coll (PA)
Mount Marty Coll (SD)

Mount Vernon Nazarene U (OH)
Newbury Coll (MA)
New Mexico Inst of Mining and
Technology (NM)
New Mexico State U (NM)
Nicholls State U (LA)
Northern Michigan U (MI)
Northwest Christian U (OR)
Northwestern State U of Louisiana
(LA)
Northwest U (WA)
The Ohio State U at Lima (OH)
Our Lady of the Lake Coll (LA)
Pace U (NY)
Pacific Union Coll (CA)
Peirce Coll (PA)
Point U (GA)
Presentation Coll (SD)
Regent U (VA)
Shawnee State U (OH)
Siena Heights U (MI)
Simpson U (CA)
South Dakota School of Mines and
Technology (SD)
South Dakota State U (SD)
Southeastern Louisiana U (LA)
Southern Arkansas U–Magnolia
(AR)
Southwest Baptist U (MO)
Southwestern Assemblies of God U
(TX)
Southwestern Christian U (OK)
State U of New York Coll of
Technology at Delhi (NY)
Temple U (PA)
Texas Coll (TX)
Thompson Rivers U (BC, Canada)
Tiffin U (OH)
Trevecca Nazarene U (TN)
Trinity Coll of Florida (FL)
Truett-McConnell Coll (GA)
U of Alaska Fairbanks (AK)
U of Arkansas at Little Rock (AR)
U of Arkansas at Monticello (AR)
U of Arkansas–Fort Smith (AR)
U of Bridgeport (CT)
U of Central Arkansas (AR)
U of Cincinnati (OH)
U of La Verne (CA)
U of Louisiana at Monroe (LA)
U of Maine at Fort Kent (ME)
U of Mobile (AL)
U of Rio Grande (OH)
The U of Toledo (OH)
U of Wisconsin–Superior (WI)
Utah State U (UT)
Utah Valley U (UT)
Valley Forge Christian Coll
Woodbridge Campus (VA)
Viterbo U (WI)
Weber State U (UT)
Western Kentucky U (KY)
Wichita State U (KS)
Widener U (PA)
Winona State U (MN)
York Coll of Pennsylvania (PA)

GEOGRAPHIC INFORMATION SCIENCE AND CARTOGRAPHY
The U of Akron (OH)

GEOGRAPHY
The U of Tampa (FL)
Wright State U (OH)

GEOGRAPHY RELATED
Adams State Coll (CO)

GEOLOGICAL AND EARTH SCIENCES/GEOSCIENCES RELATED
Utah Valley U (UT)

GEOLOGY/EARTH SCIENCE
Coll of Coastal Georgia (GA)
Midland Coll (TX)
U of Cincinnati (OH)
Wright State U (OH)

GERMAN
Midland Coll (TX)
U of Cincinnati (OH)
Xavier U (OH)

GERONTOLOGY
Holy Cross Coll (IN)

Madonna U (MI)
Manchester Coll (IN)
Siena Heights U (MI)
Thomas More Coll (KY)
The U of Toledo (OH)
Washburn U (KS)

GRAPHIC AND PRINTING EQUIPMENT OPERATION/ PRODUCTION
Dixie State Coll of Utah (UT)
Idaho State U (ID)
Lewis-Clark State Coll (ID)
New England Inst of Technology
(RI)

GRAPHIC COMMUNICATIONS
ITT Tech Inst, Tempe (AZ)
ITT Tech Inst, Clovis (CA)
ITT Tech Inst, Concord (CA)
ITT Tech Inst, Corona (CA)
ITT Tech Inst, Indianapolis (IN)
ITT Tech Inst, South Bend (IN)
ITT Tech Inst, Wichita (KS)
ITT Tech Inst, Lexington (KY)
ITT Tech Inst, Hanover (MD)
ITT Tech Inst (MS)
ITT Tech Inst, Springfield (MO)
ITT Tech Inst, Oklahoma City (OK)
New England Inst of Technology
(RI)
Pennsylvania Coll of Technology
(PA)

GRAPHIC DESIGN
Academy of Art U (CA)
The Art Inst of Atlanta (GA)
The Art Inst of Atlanta–Decatur
(GA)
The Art Inst of Austin (TX)
The Art Inst of California, a college
of Argosy U, Hollywood (CA)
The Art Inst of California, a college
of Argosy U, Inland Empire (CA)
The Art Inst of California, a college
of Argosy U, Los Angeles (CA)
The Art Inst of California, a college
of Argosy U, Orange County (CA)
The Art Inst of California, a college
of Argosy U, Sacramento (CA)
The Art Inst of California, a college
of Argosy U, San Diego (CA)
The Art Inst of California, a college
of Argosy U, San Francisco (CA)
The Art Inst of California, a college
of Argosy U, Sunnyvale (CA)
The Art Inst of Charleston (SC)
The Art Inst of Charlotte (NC)
The Art Inst of Colorado (CO)
The Art Inst of Dallas (TX)
The Art Inst of Fort Lauderdale (FL)
The Art Inst of Fort Worth (TX)
The Art Inst of Houston (TX)
The Art Inst of Houston - North (TX)
The Art Inst of Indianapolis (IN)
The Art Inst of Jacksonville (FL)
The Art Inst of Michigan (MI)
The Art Inst of Philadelphia (PA)
The Art Inst of Phoenix (AZ)
The Art Inst of Pittsburgh (PA)
The Art Inst of Portland (OR)
The Art Inst of Raleigh-Durham
(NC)
The Art Inst of Salt Lake City (UT)
The Art Inst of San Antonio (TX)
The Art Inst of Tampa (FL)
The Art Inst of Tennessee–
Nashville (TN)
The Art Inst of Tucson (AZ)
The Art Inst of Virginia Beach (VA)
The Art Inst of Washington (VA)
The Art Inst of Washington–Dulles
(VA)
The Art Inst of Wisconsin (WI)
The Art Insts International–Kansas
City (KS)
The Art Insts International
Minnesota (MN)
Bauder Coll (GA)
Coll of Mount St. Joseph (OH)
Corcoran Coll of Art and Design
(DC)
Ferris State U (MI)
Globe U–Woodbury (MN)
Hickey Coll (MO)
The Illinois Inst of Art–Chicago (IL)

The Illinois Inst of Art–Schaumburg
(IL)
The Illinois Inst of Art–Tinley Park
(IL)
International Academy of Design &
Technology (FL)
International Business Coll, Fort
Wayne (IN)
Madonna U (MI)
Montana State U–Northern (MT)
Mountain State U (WV)
Pacific Union Coll (CA)
Pratt Inst (NY)
South U, Columbia (SC)
Thompson Rivers U (BC, Canada)
Union Coll (NE)
Villa Maria Coll of Buffalo (NY)

HAZARDOUS MATERIALS MANAGEMENT AND WASTE TECHNOLOGY
Ohio U–Chillicothe (OH)

HEALTH AND PHYSICAL EDUCATION/FITNESS
Coll of Coastal Georgia (GA)
Robert Morris U Illinois (IL)
State U of New York Coll of
Technology at Delhi (NY)
Utah Valley U (UT)

HEALTH AND PHYSICAL EDUCATION RELATED
Mount Vernon Nazarene U (OH)
Pennsylvania Coll of Technology
(PA)

HEALTH AND WELLNESS
Howard Payne U (TX)
Presentation Coll (SD)

HEALTH/HEALTH-CARE ADMINISTRATION
Baker Coll of Auburn Hills (MI)
Baker Coll of Flint (MI)
California Coast U (CA)
Florida Inst of Technology (FL)
Madonna U (MI)
Park U (MO)
The U of Scranton (PA)
Washburn U (KS)

HEALTH INFORMATION/ MEDICAL RECORDS ADMINISTRATION
AIB Coll of Business (IA)
Baker Coll of Auburn Hills (MI)
Baker Coll of Cadillac (MI)
Baker Coll of Clinton Township (MI)
Baker Coll of Flint (MI)
Baker Coll of Jackson (MI)
Baker Coll of Port Huron (MI)
Boise State U (ID)
Dalton State Coll (GA)
Inter American U of Puerto Rico,
San Germán Campus (PR)
Montana State U Billings (MT)

HEALTH INFORMATION/ MEDICAL RECORDS TECHNOLOGY
Baker Coll of Flint (MI)
Baker Coll of Jackson (MI)
Dakota State U (SD)
Davenport U, Grand Rapids (MI)
DeVry U, Pomona (CA)
DeVry U, Decatur (GA)
DeVry U, Chicago (IL)
DeVry U, North Brunswick (NJ)
DeVry U, Columbus (OH)
DeVry U, Fort Washington (PA)
DeVry U, Houston (TX)
DeVry U, Irving (TX)
DeVry U Online (IL)
Ferris State U (MI)
Gwynedd-Mercy Coll (PA)
Hodges U (FL)
Idaho State U (ID)
Indiana U Northwest (IN)
Indiana U South Bend (IN)
Indiana U Southeast (IN)
ITT Tech Inst, Indianapolis (IN)
Macon State Coll (GA)
Mercy Coll of Ohio (OH)
Midland Coll (TX)

Molloy Coll (NY)
New England Inst of Technology
(RI)
Northern Michigan U (MI)
Peirce Coll (PA)
Pennsylvania Coll of Technology
(PA)
Rasmussen Coll Appleton (WI)
Rasmussen Coll Blaine (MN)
Rasmussen Coll Land O' Lakes
(FL)
Rasmussen Coll Mokena/Tinley
Park (IL)
Rasmussen Coll Romeoville/Joliet
(IL)
Rasmussen Coll Tampa/Brandon
(FL)
Rasmussen Coll Wausau (WI)
St. Catherine U (MN)
Washburn U (KS)
Weber State U (UT)
Western Kentucky U (KY)

HEALTH/MEDICAL PREPARATORY PROGRAMS RELATED
Immaculata U (PA)
Ohio Valley U (WV)
U of Cincinnati (OH)

HEALTH PROFESSIONS RELATED
Arkansas Tech U (AR)
Lock Haven U of Pennsylvania (PA)
Morrisville State Coll (NY)
National U (CA)
Newman U (KS)
New York U (NY)
Northwest U (WA)
Ohio U–Chillicothe (OH)
Point Park U (PA)
Saint Mary's Coll of California (CA)
Saint Peter's Coll (NJ)
Thompson Rivers U (BC, Canada)
U of Cincinnati (OH)
U of Hartford (CT)
U of Saint Francis (IN)
Villa Maria Coll of Buffalo (NY)

HEALTH SERVICES ADMINISTRATION
Florida National Coll (FL)

HEALTH SERVICES/ALLIED HEALTH/HEALTH SCIENCES
Florida National Coll (FL)
Howard Payne U (TX)
Lindsey Wilson Coll (KY)
Pennsylvania Coll of Technology
(PA)
Pine Manor Coll (MA)
U of Hartford (CT)
Weber State U (UT)

HEATING, AIR CONDITIONING, VENTILATION AND REFRIGERATION MAINTENANCE TECHNOLOGY
Lamar U (TX)
Lewis-Clark State Coll (ID)
Midland Coll (TX)
Montana State U Billings (MT)
New England Inst of Technology
(RI)
Oakland City U (IN)
State U of New York Coll of
Technology at Delhi (NY)
U of Alaska Anchorage (AK)

HEATING, VENTILATION, AIR CONDITIONING AND REFRIGERATION ENGINEERING TECHNOLOGY
Ferris State U (MI)
Northern Michigan U (MI)
Oakland City U (IN)
Pennsylvania Coll of Technology
(PA)
State U of New York Coll of
Technology at Canton (NY)
State U of New York Coll of
Technology at Delhi (NY)

HEAVY EQUIPMENT MAINTENANCE TECHNOLOGY
Ferris State U (MI)
Pennsylvania Coll of Technology (PA)
U of Alaska Anchorage (AK)

HEBREW
U of Cincinnati (OH)
Yeshiva U (NY)

HISTOLOGIC TECHNICIAN
Indiana U–Purdue U Indianapolis (IN)
Indiana U South Bend (IN)
Northern Michigan U (MI)
The U of Akron (OH)

HISTOLOGIC TECHNOLOGY/ HISTOTECHNOLOGIST
Tarleton State U (TX)

HISTORIC PRESERVATION AND CONSERVATION
Montana Tech of The U of Montana (MT)

HISTORY
American Public U System (WV)
Clarke U (IA)
Coll of Coastal Georgia (GA)
Dalton State Coll (GA)
Indiana U East (IN)
Indiana Wesleyan U (IN)
Lindsey Wilson Coll (KY)
Lourdes U (OH)
Macon State Coll (GA)
Midland Coll (TX)
Regent U (VA)
Rogers State U (OK)
State U of New York Empire State Coll (NY)
Thomas More Coll (KY)
U of Cincinnati (OH)
U of Rio Grande (OH)
The U of Tampa (FL)
Utah Valley U (UT)
Wright State U (OH)
Xavier U (OH)

HOME FURNISHINGS AND EQUIPMENT INSTALLATION
Eastern Kentucky U (KY)

HOMELAND SECURITY, LAW ENFORCEMENT, FIREFIGHTING AND PROTECTIVE SERVICES RELATED
Idaho State U (ID)
Universidad del Turabo (PR)

HORSE HUSBANDRY/EQUINE SCIENCE AND MANAGEMENT
Morrisville State Coll (NY)
U of Guelph (ON, Canada)

HORTICULTURAL SCIENCE
Andrews U (IN)
Morrisville State Coll (NY)
State U of New York Coll of Technology at Delhi (NY)
U of Connecticut (CT)
U of Guelph (ON, Canada)

HOSPITALITY ADMINISTRATION
AIB Coll of Business (IA)
Baker Coll of Flint (MI)
Baker Coll of Owosso (MI)
Colorado Mesa U (CO)
Florida National Coll (FL)
The Illinois Inst of Art–Chicago (IL)
The Illinois Inst of Art–Schaumburg (IL)
Lewis-Clark State Coll (ID)
Morrisville State Coll (NY)
New York City Coll of Technology of the City U of New York (NY)
Sullivan U (KY)
The U of Akron (OH)

U of Cincinnati (OH)
U of the District of Columbia (DC)
Utah Valley U (UT)
Webber International U (FL)
Western Kentucky U (KY)
Youngstown State U (OH)

HOSPITALITY ADMINISTRATION RELATED
Indiana U–Purdue U Indianapolis (IN)
Morrisville State Coll (NY)
Penn State Berks (PA)
Purdue U (IN)
U of the District of Columbia (DC)

HOSPITALITY AND RECREATION MARKETING
Ferris State U (MI)
State U of New York Coll of Technology at Delhi (NY)
Thompson Rivers U (BC, Canada)

HOTEL/MOTEL ADMINISTRATION
Baker Coll of Muskegon (MI)
Baker Coll of Owosso (MI)
Baker Coll of Port Huron (MI)
Inter American U of Puerto Rico, Fajardo Campus (PR)
International Business Coll, Fort Wayne (IN)
State U of New York Coll of Technology at Delhi (NY)
Thompson Rivers U (BC, Canada)
The U of Akron (OH)

HUMAN DEVELOPMENT AND FAMILY STUDIES
Mount Vernon Nazarene U (OH)
Penn State Abington (PA)
Penn State Altoona (PA)
Penn State Berks (PA)
Penn State Erie, The Behrend Coll (PA)
Penn State U Park (PA)
State U of New York Empire State Coll (NY)

HUMAN DEVELOPMENT AND FAMILY STUDIES RELATED
The U of Toledo (OH)
Utah State U (UT)

HUMANITIES
Briercrest Coll (SK, Canada)
Faulkner U (AL)
Harrison Middleton U (AZ)
Michigan Technological U (MI)
Ohio U (OH)
Ohio U–Chillicothe (OH)
Saint Peter's Coll (NJ)
State U of New York Coll of Technology at Delhi (NY)
State U of New York Empire State Coll (NY)
Thomas More Coll (KY)
The U of Findlay (OH)
Utah Valley U (UT)
Valparaiso U (IN)
Washburn U (KS)

HUMAN RESOURCES DEVELOPMENT
Park U (MO)

HUMAN RESOURCES MANAGEMENT
Baker Coll of Owosso (MI)
King's Coll (PA)
Montana State U Billings (MT)
Mountain State U (WV)
Rasmussen Coll Appleton (WI)
Rasmussen Coll Blaine (MN)
Rasmussen Coll Land O' Lakes (FL)
Rasmussen Coll Tampa/Brandon (FL)
Rasmussen Coll Wausau (WI)
Regent U (VA)
The U of Findlay (OH)
U of Saint Francis (IN)
The U of Scranton (PA)

HUMAN RESOURCES MANAGEMENT AND SERVICES RELATED
American Public U System (WV)

HUMAN SERVICES
Baker Coll of Clinton Township (MI)
Baker Coll of Flint (MI)
Baker Coll of Muskegon (MI)
Beacon Coll (FL)
Bethel Coll (IN)
Brescia U (KY)
Caribbean U (PR)
Coll of St. Joseph (VT)
Columbia Coll (MO)
Elizabethtown Coll (PA)
Hilbert Coll (NY)
Indiana U East (IN)
Mercy Coll (NY)
Morrisville State Coll (NY)
Mount Vernon Nazarene U (OH)
New York City Coll of Technology of the City U of New York (NY)
Rasmussen Coll Appleton (WI)
Rasmussen Coll Blaine (MN)
Rasmussen Coll Land O' Lakes (FL)
Rasmussen Coll Tampa/Brandon (FL)
Rasmussen Coll Wausau (WI)
State U of New York Empire State Coll (NY)
Thomas Edison State Coll (NJ)
U of Alaska Anchorage (AK)
U of Great Falls (MT)
U of Maine at Fort Kent (ME)
The U of Scranton (PA)
Walsh U (OH)
Wayland Baptist U (TX)

HYDROLOGY AND WATER RESOURCES SCIENCE
Lake Superior State U (MI)
U of the District of Columbia (DC)

ILLUSTRATION
Academy of Art U (CA)
Fashion Inst of Technology (NY)
Pratt Inst (NY)

INDUSTRIAL AND PRODUCT DESIGN
Academy of Art U (CA)
The Art Inst of Pittsburgh (PA)
Oakland City U (IN)

INDUSTRIAL ELECTRONICS TECHNOLOGY
Dalton State Coll (GA)
Ferris State U (MI)
Lewis-Clark State Coll (ID)
Pennsylvania Coll of Technology (PA)
Thompson Rivers U (BC, Canada)

INDUSTRIAL ENGINEERING
Indiana Tech (IN)
The U of Toledo (OH)

INDUSTRIAL MECHANICS AND MAINTENANCE TECHNOLOGY
Northern Michigan U (MI)
Pennsylvania Coll of Technology (PA)
U of Arkansas at Monticello (AR)

INDUSTRIAL PRODUCTION TECHNOLOGIES RELATED
Austin Peay State U (TN)
California U of Pennsylvania (PA)
Clarion U of Pennsylvania (PA)
Ferris State U (MI)
U of Alaska Fairbanks (AK)

INDUSTRIAL RADIOLOGIC TECHNOLOGY
Baker Coll of Owosso (MI)
The George Washington U (DC)
Lamar U (TX)
Our Lady of the Lake Coll (LA)
U of the District of Columbia (DC)
Widener U (PA)

INDUSTRIAL TECHNOLOGY
Arkansas Tech U (AR)
Baker Coll of Muskegon (MI)
Dalton State Coll (GA)
Edinboro U of Pennsylvania (PA)
Indiana U–Purdue U Fort Wayne (IN)
Kansas State U (KS)
Kent State U at Geauga (OH)
Millersville U of Pennsylvania (PA)
Montana State U–Northern (MT)
New England Inst of Technology (RI)
Purdue U North Central (IN)
Southeastern Louisiana U (LA)
Southern Arkansas U–Magnolia (AR)
U of Puerto Rico at Bayamón (PR)
U of Puerto Rico at Ponce (PR)
U of Rio Grande (OH)
The U of Toledo (OH)
Washburn U (KS)

INFORMATION RESOURCES MANAGEMENT
Rasmussen Coll Land O' Lakes (FL)
Rasmussen Coll Tampa/Brandon (FL)

INFORMATION SCIENCE/ STUDIES
Baker Coll of Clinton Township (MI)
Baker Coll of Owosso (MI)
Beacon Coll (FL)
Campbellsville U (KY)
Elizabethtown Coll (PA)
Farmingdale State Coll (NY)
Faulkner U (AL)
Florida Inst of Technology (FL)
Goldey-Beacom Coll (DE)
Husson U (ME)
Immaculata U (PA)
Indiana U–Purdue U Fort Wayne (IN)
Johnson State Coll (VT)
Mansfield U of Pennsylvania (PA)
Newman U (KS)
Oakland City U (IN)
Penn State Abington (PA)
Penn State Altoona (PA)
Penn State Berks (PA)
Penn State Erie, The Behrend Coll (PA)
Penn State U Park (PA)
Saint Peter's Coll (NJ)
State U of New York Coll of Technology at Canton (NY)
Touro Coll (NY)
Tulane U (LA)
U of Alaska Anchorage (AK)
U of Cincinnati (OH)
U of Massachusetts Lowell (MA)
U of Pittsburgh at Bradford (PA)
The U of Scranton (PA)
The U of Toledo (OH)
Wright State U (OH)

INFORMATION TECHNOLOGY
AIB Coll of Business (IA)
Arkansas Tech U (AR)
Cameron U (OK)
Ferris State U (MI)
Florida National Coll (FL)
Franklin U (OH)
Indiana U–Purdue U Fort Wayne (IN)
Kent State U at Geauga (OH)
Keystone Coll (PA)
McNeese State U (LA)
Mercy Coll (NY)
New England Inst of Technology (RI)
Peirce Coll (PA)
Point Park U (PA)
Regent U (VA)
South U (AL)
South U, Tampa (FL)
South U (GA)
South U (MI)
South U, Columbia (SC)
South U (TX)
South U, Glen Allen (VA)
South U, Virginia Beach (VA)
Thomas More Coll (KY)
Tiffin U (OH)

Trevecca Nazarene U (TN)
Vermont Tech Coll (VT)
Youngstown State U (OH)

INFORMATION TECHNOLOGY PROJECT MANAGEMENT
Pace U (NY)

INSTITUTIONAL FOOD WORKERS
Immaculata U (PA)

INSTRUMENTATION TECHNOLOGY
Idaho State U (ID)
U of Puerto Rico at Bayamón (PR)

INSURANCE
AIB Coll of Business (IA)
Caribbeán U (PR)

INTERCULTURAL/ MULTICULTURAL AND DIVERSITY STUDIES
Baptist U of the Americas (TX)

INTERDISCIPLINARY STUDIES
Cardinal Stritch U (WI)
Central Methodist U (MO)
John Brown U (AR)
Kansas State U (KS)
State U of New York Empire State Coll (NY)
Suffolk U (MA)
Trinity Baptist Coll (FL)

INTERIOR ARCHITECTURE
Villa Maria Coll of Buffalo (NY)

INTERIOR DESIGN
Academy of Art U (CA)
The Art Inst of Charlotte (NC)
The Art Inst of Colorado (CO)
The Art Inst of Dallas (TX)
The Art Inst of Fort Lauderdale (FL)
The Art Inst of Michigan (MI)
The Art Inst of Philadelphia (PA)
The Art Inst of Pittsburgh (PA)
The Art Insts International Minnesota (MN)
Baker Coll of Allen Park (MI)
Baker Coll of Auburn Hills (MI)
Baker Coll of Clinton Township (MI)
Baker Coll of Muskegon (MI)
Baker Coll of Owosso (MI)
Baker Coll of Port Huron (MI)
Bauder Coll (GA)
Bay Path Coll (MA)
Chaminade U of Honolulu (HI)
Coll of Mount St. Joseph (OH)
EDP Coll of Puerto Rico, Inc. (PR)
Fashion Inst of Technology (NY)
Indiana U–Purdue U Fort Wayne (IN)
Indiana U–Purdue U Indianapolis (IN)
International Academy of Design & Technology (FL)
Montana State U (MT)
New England Inst of Technology (RI)
New York School of Interior Design (NY)
Robert Morris U Illinois (IL)
Stevens Inst of Business & Arts (MO)
Weber State U (UT)

INTERMEDIA/MULTIMEDIA
Academy of Art U (CA)

INTERNATIONAL BUSINESS/ TRADE/COMMERCE
AIB Coll of Business (IA)
The American U of Rome (Italy)
Potomac Coll (DC)
Regent U (VA)
Saint Peter's Coll (NJ)
Utah Valley U (UT)

INTERNATIONAL/GLOBAL STUDIES
Briercrest Coll (SK, Canada)

Holy Cross Coll (IN)
Thomas More Coll (KY)

INTERNATIONAL RELATIONS AND AFFAIRS
U of Cincinnati (OH)

JAZZ/JAZZ STUDIES
Five Towns Coll (NY)
Villa Maria Coll of Buffalo (NY)

JOURNALISM
Indiana U Southeast (IN)
John Brown U (AR)
Madonna U (MI)
Manchester Coll (IN)
Midland Coll (TX)
Morrisville State Coll (NY)

JOURNALISM RELATED
Adams State Coll (CO)

KEYBOARD INSTRUMENTS
McNally Smith Coll of Music (MN)

KINDERGARTEN/PRESCHOOL EDUCATION
Baker Coll of Clinton Township (MI)
Baker Coll of Muskegon (MI)
Baker Coll of Owosso (MI)
California U of Pennsylvania (PA)
Keystone Coll (PA)
Maria Coll (NY)
Miami U (OH)
Mount St. Mary's Coll (CA)
Piedmont International U (NC)
Saint Mary-of-the-Woods Coll (IN)
Shawnee State U (OH)
U of Cincinnati (OH)
U of Great Falls (MT)
U of Rio Grande (OH)
Wilmington U (DE)

KINESIOLOGY AND EXERCISE SCIENCE
Southwestern Adventist U (TX)
Thomas More Coll (KY)

LABOR AND INDUSTRIAL RELATIONS
Indiana U–Purdue U Fort Wayne (IN)
Indiana U Southeast (IN)
Rider U (NJ)
State U of New York Empire State Coll (NY)
Youngstown State U (OH)

LABOR STUDIES
Indiana U Kokomo (IN)
Indiana U Northwest (IN)
Indiana U–Purdue U Indianapolis (IN)
Indiana U South Bend (IN)

LANDSCAPE ARCHITECTURE
Academy of Art U (CA)
Keystone Coll (PA)
Morrisville State Coll (NY)
State U of New York Coll of Technology at Delhi (NY)

LANDSCAPING AND GROUNDSKEEPING
Farmingdale State Coll (NY)
North Carolina State U (NC)
Pennsylvania Coll of Technology (PA)
State U of New York Coll of Technology at Delhi (NY)
U of Massachusetts Amherst (MA)
Vermont Tech Coll (VT)

LASER AND OPTICAL TECHNOLOGY
Idaho State U (ID)

LAY MINISTRY
Howard Payne U (TX)
Maranatha Baptist Bible Coll (WI)
Nyack Coll (NY)
Southeastern Bible Coll (AL)

LEGAL ADMINISTRATIVE ASSISTANT/SECRETARY
Baker Coll of Auburn Hills (MI)
Baker Coll of Clinton Township (MI)
Baker Coll of Flint (MI)
Baker Coll of Jackson (MI)
Baker Coll of Muskegon (MI)
Baker Coll of Owosso (MI)
Baker Coll of Port Huron (MI)
Clarion U of Pennsylvania (PA)
Dordt Coll (IA)
Florida National Coll (FL)
Hickey Coll (MO)
International Business Coll, Fort Wayne (IN)
Lamar U (TX)
Lewis-Clark State Coll (ID)
Shawnee State U (OH)
Sullivan U (KY)
U of Cincinnati (OH)
U of Rio Grande (OH)
U of the District of Columbia (DC)
The U of Toledo (OH)
Washburn U (KS)
Youngstown State U (OH)

LEGAL ASSISTANT/PARALEGAL
American Public U System (WV)
Anna Maria Coll (MA)
Bauder Coll (GA)
Broadview U–Boise (ID)
Broadview U–Layton (UT)
Broadview U–Orem (UT)
Broadview U–West Jordan (UT)
Central Penn Coll (PA)
Clayton State U (GA)
Coll of Mount St. Joseph (OH)
Coll of Saint Mary (NE)
Davenport U, Grand Rapids (MI)
Everest U, Lakeland (FL)
Faulkner U (AL)
Ferris State U (MI)
Florida National Coll (FL)
Gannon U (PA)
Globe U–Appleton (WI)
Globe U–Eau Claire (WI)
Globe U–Green Bay (WI)
Globe U–La Crosse (WI)
Globe U–Madison East (WI)
Globe U–Madison West (WI)
Globe U–Minneapolis (MN)
Globe U–Sioux Falls (SD)
Globe U–Wausau (WI)
Globe U–Woodbury (MN)
Grambling State U (LA)
Hickey Coll (MO)
Hilbert Coll (NY)
Hodges U (FL)
Husson U (ME)
Idaho State U (ID)
International Business Coll, Fort Wayne (IN)
ITT Tech Inst, Tempe (AZ)
ITT Tech Inst, Clovis (CA)
ITT Tech Inst, Concord (CA)
ITT Tech Inst, Corona (CA)
ITT Tech Inst, Springfield (IL)
ITT Tech Inst, Indianapolis (IN)
ITT Tech Inst, Indianapolis (IN)
ITT Tech Inst, South Bend (IN)
ITT Tech Inst, Wichita (KS)
ITT Tech Inst, Lexington (KY)
ITT Tech Inst (MS)
ITT Tech Inst, Springfield (MO)
ITT Tech Inst, Oklahoma City (OK)
Jones Coll, Jacksonville (FL)
Lewis-Clark State Coll (ID)
Madonna U (MI)
Maria Coll (NY)
McNeese State U (LA)
Midland Coll (TX)
Minnesota School of Business–Blaine (MN)
Minnesota School of Business–Elk River (MN)
Minnesota School of Business–Lakeville (MN)
Minnesota School of Business–Moorhead (MN)
Minnesota School of Business–Rochester (MN)
Missouri Western State U (MO)
Mountain State U (WV)
Mount Aloysius Coll (PA)
Newman U (KS)
New York City Coll of Technology of the City U of New York (NY)
Peirce Coll (PA)
Pennsylvania Coll of Technology (PA)
Post U (CT)
Rasmussen Coll Appleton (WI)
Rasmussen Coll Blaine (MN)
Rasmussen Coll Land O' Lakes (FL)
Rasmussen Coll Mokena/Tinley Park (IL)
Rasmussen Coll Romeoville/Joliet (IL)
Rasmussen Coll Tampa/Brandon (FL)
Rasmussen Coll Wausau (WI)
Robert Morris U Illinois (IL)
Saint Mary-of-the-Woods Coll (IN)
Shawnee State U (OH)
South U (AL)
South U, Royal Palm Beach (FL)
South U (GA)
South U, Columbia (SC)
South U, Glen Allen (VA)
South U, Virginia Beach (VA)
Stevens Inst of Business & Arts (MO)
Suffolk U (MA)
Sullivan U (KY)
Tulane U (LA)
The U of Akron (OH)
U of Alaska Anchorage (AK)
U of Alaska Fairbanks (AK)
U of Arkansas–Fort Smith (AR)
U of Cincinnati (OH)
U of Great Falls (MT)
U of Hartford (CT)
U of Louisville (KY)
The U of Toledo (OH)
Utah Valley U (UT)
Washburn U (KS)
Western Kentucky U (KY)
Widener U (PA)
William Woods U (MO)

LEGAL PROFESSIONS AND STUDIES RELATED
Florida National Coll (FL)

LEGAL STUDIES
Maria Coll (NY)
St. John's U (NY)
U of Hartford (CT)
U of New Haven (CT)

LIBERAL ARTS AND SCIENCES AND HUMANITIES RELATED
Adams State Coll (CO)
Ball State U (IN)
Colorado Mesa U (CO)
Ferris State U (MI)
Marymount Coll, Palos Verdes, California (CA)
Mount Aloysius Coll (PA)
New York U (NY)
Nyack Coll (NY)
Pennsylvania Coll of Technology (PA)
Sacred Heart U (CT)
Southern New Hampshire U (NH)
Taylor U (IN)
U of Hartford (CT)
U of Wisconsin–Green Bay (WI)
U of Wisconsin–La Crosse (WI)
Walsh U (OH)
Wayland Baptist U (TX)

LIBERAL ARTS AND SCIENCES/LIBERAL STUDIES
Adams State Coll (CO)
Adelphi U (NY)
Alvernia U (PA)
Alverno Coll (WI)
American U (DC)
The American U of Rome (Italy)
Amridge U (AL)
Aquinas Coll (MI)
Arkansas State U (AR)
Armstrong Atlantic State U (GA)
Ball State U (IN)
Bard Coll (NY)
Bard Coll at Simon's Rock (MA)
Bay Path Coll (MA)
Beacon Coll (FL)
Bemidji State U (MN)
Bethel Coll (IN)
Bethel U (MN)
Brenau U (GA)
Brescia U (KY)
Briar Cliff U (IA)
Bryn Athyn Coll of the New Church (PA)
California U of Pennsylvania (PA)
Calumet Coll of Saint Joseph (IN)
Cardinal Stritch U (WI)
Centenary Coll (NJ)
Charter Oak State Coll (CT)
Chestnut Hill Coll (PA)
Christendom Coll (VA)
Clarke U (IA)
Clayton State U (GA)
Coll of Coastal Georgia (GA)
Coll of St. Joseph (VT)
Coll of Staten Island of the City U of New York (NY)
Colorado Mesa U (CO)
Columbia Coll (MO)
Columbus State U (GA)
Concordia Coll–New York (NY)
Concordia U (CA)
Concordia U Texas (TX)
Dallas Baptist U (TX)
Dalton State Coll (GA)
Dominican Coll (NY)
Eastern New Mexico U (NM)
Eastern U (PA)
Emmanuel Coll (GA)
Emory U (GA)
Endicott Coll (MA)
Excelsior Coll (NY)
Fairfield U (CT)
Fairleigh Dickinson U, Metropolitan Campus (NJ)
Farmingdale State Coll (NY)
Faulkner U (AL)
Felician Coll (NJ)
Ferris State U (MI)
Five Towns Coll (NY)
Florida A&M U (FL)
Florida Atlantic U (FL)
Florida Coll (FL)
Florida Inst of Technology (FL)
Florida National Coll (FL)
Florida State U (FL)
Franklin Coll Switzerland (Switzerland)
Gannon U (PA)
Glenville State Coll (WV)
Granite State Coll (NH)
Gwynedd-Mercy Coll (PA)
Hilbert Coll (NY)
Holy Cross Coll (IN)
Houghton Coll (NY)
Indiana State U (IN)
Indiana U Kokomo (IN)
Indiana U Northwest (IN)
Indiana U–Purdue U Indianapolis (IN)
Indiana U South Bend (IN)
Indiana U Southeast (IN)
Johnson State Coll (VT)
Kent State U (OH)
Kent State U at Geauga (OH)
Kent State U at Stark (OH)
Kentucky State U (KY)
Keystone Coll (PA)
Lake Superior State U (MI)
Lewis-Clark State Coll (ID)
Limestone Coll (SC)
Long Island U–Brooklyn Campus (NY)
Lourdes U (OH)
Maria Coll (NY)
Marymount Coll, Palos Verdes, California (CA)
Medaille Coll (NY)
Medgar Evers Coll of the City U of New York (NY)
Mercy Coll (NY)
Merrimack Coll (MA)
MidAmerica Nazarene U (KS)
Midland Coll (TX)
Midwestern State U (TX)
Minnesota State U Mankato (MN)
Minnesota State U Moorhead (MN)
Missouri Southern State U (MO)
Mitchell Coll (CT)
Molloy Coll (NY)
Montana State U Billings (MT)
Montreat Coll, Montreat (NC)
Morrisville State Coll (NY)
Mountain State U (WV)
Mount Aloysius Coll (PA)
Mount Marty Coll (SD)
Mount St. Mary's Coll (CA)
Neumann U (PA)
New England Coll (NH)
Newman U (KS)
New Saint Andrews Coll (ID)
New York City Coll of Technology of the City U of New York (NY)
New York U (NY)
Niagara U (NY)
Northern Kentucky U (KY)
Northern State U (SD)
Northwestern Coll (MN)
Nyack Coll (NY)
Oakland City U (IN)
The Ohio State U at Marion (OH)
The Ohio State U–Mansfield Campus (OH)
The Ohio State U–Newark Campus (OH)
Ohio U (OH)
Ohio U–Chillicothe (OH)
Ohio Valley U (WV)
Okanagan Coll (BC, Canada)
Oregon Inst of Technology (OR)
Penn State Abington (PA)
Penn State Altoona (PA)
Penn State Berks (PA)
Penn State Erie, The Behrend Coll (PA)
Penn State Harrisburg (PA)
Penn State U Park (PA)
Post U (CT)
Providence Coll (RI)
Quincy U (IL)
Reinhardt U (GA)
Rider U (NJ)
Rivier Coll (NH)
Rocky Mountain Coll (MT)
Rogers State U (OK)
Roger Williams U (RI)
St. Catherine U (MN)
St. John's U (NY)
Saint Joseph's U (PA)
Saint Leo U (FL)
Saint Louis Christian Coll (MO)
Saint Mary-of-the-Woods Coll (IN)
St. Thomas Aquinas Coll (NY)
Salve Regina U (RI)
Schreiner U (TX)
Southeastern Baptist Theological Seminary (NC)
Southern Polytechnic State U (GA)
Southern Vermont Coll (VT)
Spring Arbor U (MI)
State U of New York Coll of Technology at Canton (NY)
Stephens Coll (MO)
Suffolk U (MA)
Thiel Coll (PA)
Thomas Edison State Coll (NJ)
Thomas More Coll (KY)
Thomas U (GA)
Thompson Rivers U (BC, Canada)
Touro Coll (NY)
Trine U (IN)
Troy U (AL)
Truett-McConnell Coll (GA)
The U of Akron (OH)
U of Alaska Fairbanks (AK)
U of Arkansas–Fort Smith (AR)
U of Cincinnati (OH)
U of Delaware (DE)
U of Hartford (CT)
U of La Verne (CA)
U of Maine at Augusta (ME)
U of Maine at Fort Kent (ME)
U of Maine at Presque Isle (ME)
U of New Hampshire at Manchester (NH)
U of North Florida (FL)
U of Pittsburgh at Bradford (PA)
U of Saint Francis (IN)
U of Saint Mary (KS)
The U of South Dakota (SD)
U of South Florida (FL)
U of the Incarnate Word (TX)
The U of Toledo (OH)
U of West Florida (FL)
U of Wisconsin–Eau Claire (WI)
U of Wisconsin–Platteville (WI)
U of Wisconsin–Stevens Point (WI)
U of Wisconsin–Superior (WI)
U of Wisconsin–Whitewater (WI)
Upper Iowa U (IA)
Valdosta State U (GA)
Villa Maria Coll of Buffalo (NY)
Waldorf Coll (IA)
Washburn U (KS)
Western Connecticut State U (CT)
Western New England U (MA)

Wichita State U (KS)
Williams Baptist Coll (AR)
William Woods U (MO)
Wilson Coll (PA)
Winona State U (MN)
Xavier U (OH)
Youngstown State U (OH)

LIBRARY AND ARCHIVES ASSISTING
U of Maine at Augusta (ME)

LICENSED PRACTICAL/VOCATIONAL NURSE TRAINING
Campbellsville U (KY)
Inter American U of Puerto Rico, Ponce Campus (PR)
Inter American U of Puerto Rico, San Germán Campus (PR)
Lamar U (TX)
Lewis-Clark State Coll (ID)
Maria Coll (NY)
Medgar Evers Coll of the City U of New York (NY)
Montana State U Billings (MT)
Ohio U–Chillicothe (OH)
Thompson Rivers U (BC, Canada)
U of the District of Columbia (DC)
Virginia State U (VA)

LINEWORKER
Pennsylvania Coll of Technology (PA)
Utah Valley U (UT)

LOGISTICS, MATERIALS, AND SUPPLY CHAIN MANAGEMENT
Park U (MO)
Sullivan U (KY)
The U of Akron (OH)
The U of Toledo (OH)

MACHINE SHOP TECHNOLOGY
Missouri Southern State U (MO)

MACHINE TOOL TECHNOLOGY
Colorado Mesa U (CO)
Idaho State U (ID)
Lamar U (TX)
Pennsylvania Coll of Technology (PA)

MANAGEMENT INFORMATION SYSTEMS
Arkansas State U (AR)
Bayamón Central U (PR)
Columbia Centro Universitario, Caguas (PR)
Columbia Centro Universitario, Yauco (PR)
Husson U (ME)
Inter American U of Puerto Rico, Bayamón Campus (PR)
Johnson State Coll (VT)
Lake Superior State U (MI)
Liberty U (VA)
Lindsey Wilson Coll (KY)
Lock Haven U of Pennsylvania (PA)
Morehead State U (KY)
Ohio U–Chillicothe (OH)
Shawnee State U (OH)
Thiel Coll (PA)
Universidad del Turabo (PR)
Weber State U (UT)
Wilson Coll (PA)
Wright State U (OH)

MANAGEMENT INFORMATION SYSTEMS AND SERVICES RELATED
Indiana U–Purdue U Indianapolis (IN)
Mount Aloysius Coll (PA)
Purdue U North Central (IN)
Rasmussen Coll Appleton (WI)
Rasmussen Coll Blaine (MN)
Rasmussen Coll Land O' Lakes (FL)

Rasmussen Coll Mokena/Tinley Park (IL)
Rasmussen Coll Romeoville/Joliet (IL)
Rasmussen Coll Tampa/Brandon (FL)
Rasmussen Coll Wausau (WI)

MANAGEMENT SCIENCE
Hawai`i Pacific U (HI)

MANUFACTURING ENGINEERING
New England Inst of Technology (RI)

MANUFACTURING ENGINEERING TECHNOLOGY
Colorado Mesa U (CO)
Edinboro U of Pennsylvania (PA)
Excelsior Coll (NY)
Lawrence Technological U (MI)
Lewis-Clark State Coll (ID)
Missouri Western State U (MO)
Morehead State U (KY)
New England Inst of Technology (RI)
Pennsylvania Coll of Technology (PA)
Thomas Edison State Coll (NJ)
Thompson Rivers U (BC, Canada)
The U of Akron (OH)
Weber State U (UT)
Western Kentucky U (KY)
Wright State U (OH)

MARINE MAINTENANCE AND SHIP REPAIR TECHNOLOGY
New England Inst of Technology (RI)

MARKETING/MARKETING MANAGEMENT
AIB Coll of Business (IA)
Baker Coll of Allen Park (MI)
Baker Coll of Auburn Hills (MI)
Baker Coll of Cadillac (MI)
Baker Coll of Clinton Township (MI)
Baker Coll of Owosso (MI)
Broadview U–Boise (ID)
Broadview U–Layton (UT)
Broadview U–Orem (UT)
Broadview U–West Jordan (UT)
California Coast U (CA)
Central Penn Coll (PA)
Cleary U (MI)
Dalton State Coll (GA)
Everest U, Lakeland (FL)
Florida Inst of Technology (FL)
Globe U–Eau Claire (WI)
Globe U–Green Bay (WI)
Globe U–La Crosse (WI)
Globe U–Madison West (WI)
Globe U–Minneapolis (MN)
Globe U–Sioux Falls (SD)
Globe U–Wausau (WI)
Globe U–Woodbury (MN)
Hawai`i Pacific U (HI)
Idaho State U (ID)
Miami U (OH)
Minnesota School of Business–Blaine (MN)
Minnesota School of Business–Elk River (MN)
Minnesota School of Business–Lakeville (MN)
Minnesota School of Business–Moorhead (MN)
Minnesota School of Business–Rochester (MN)
Mount St. Mary's Coll (CA)
New York City Coll of Technology of the City U of New York (NY)
Post U (CT)
Rasmussen Coll Appleton (WI)
Rasmussen Coll Blaine (MN)
Rasmussen Coll Land O' Lakes (FL)
Rasmussen Coll Tampa/Brandon (FL)
Rasmussen Coll Wausau (WI)
Regent U (VA)
Saint Peter's Coll (NJ)
Southern New Hampshire U (NH)
Southwest Minnesota State U (MN)

State U of New York Coll of Technology at Delhi (NY)
Tulane U (LA)
The U of Akron (OH)
U of Cincinnati (OH)
Walsh U (OH)
Webber International U (FL)
Wright State U (OH)
Youngstown State U (OH)

MARKETING RELATED
Sullivan U (KY)

MASONRY
Pennsylvania Coll of Technology (PA)

MASSAGE THERAPY
Broadview U–Boise (ID)
Broadview U–Layton (UT)
Broadview U–Orem (UT)
Broadview U–West Jordan (UT)
Globe U–Appleton (WI)
Globe U–Eau Claire (WI)
Globe U–Green Bay (WI)
Globe U–La Crosse (WI)
Globe U–Madison East (WI)
Globe U–Madison West (WI)
Globe U–Sioux Falls (SD)
Globe U–Wausau (WI)
Globe U–Woodbury (MN)
Idaho State U (ID)
Minnesota School of Business–Blaine (MN)
Minnesota School of Business–Elk River (MN)
Minnesota School of Business–Lakeville (MN)
Minnesota School of Business–Moorhead (MN)
Minnesota School of Business–Rochester (MN)
Morrisville State Coll (NY)

MASS COMMUNICATION/MEDIA
Adams State Coll (CO)
Black Hills State U (SD)
Inter American U of Puerto Rico, Bayamón Campus (PR)
Midland Coll (TX)
Pennsylvania Coll of Technology (PA)
Southwestern Assemblies of God U (TX)
U of Rio Grande (OH)
U of the Incarnate Word (TX)
York Coll of Pennsylvania (PA)

MATHEMATICS
Clarke U (IA)
Coll of Coastal Georgia (GA)
Creighton U (NE)
Dalton State Coll (GA)
Hawai`i Pacific U (HI)
Idaho State U (ID)
Indiana Wesleyan U (IN)
Midland Coll (TX)
Purdue U North Central (IN)
Shawnee State U (OH)
State U of New York Coll of Technology at Delhi (NY)
State U of New York Empire State Coll (NY)
Thomas Edison State Coll (NJ)
Thomas More Coll (KY)
Thomas U (GA)
Trine U (IN)
U of Cincinnati (OH)
U of Great Falls (MT)
U of Rio Grande (OH)
The U of Tampa (FL)
Utah Valley U (UT)

MATHEMATICS AND COMPUTER SCIENCE
Immaculata U (PA)

MECHANICAL DRAFTING AND CAD/CADD
Baker Coll of Flint (MI)
Broadview U–West Jordan (UT)
Cameron U (OK)
Globe U–Appleton (WI)

Globe U–Madison East (WI)
Globe U–Woodbury (MN)
Indiana U–Purdue U Indianapolis (IN)
Minnesota School of Business–Blaine (MN)
New York City Coll of Technology of the City U of New York (NY)

MECHANICAL ENGINEERING
Fairfield U (CT)
New England Inst of Technology (RI)

MECHANICAL ENGINEERING/MECHANICAL TECHNOLOGY
Baker Coll of Flint (MI)
Bluefield State Coll (WV)
Fairmont State U (WV)
Farmingdale State Coll (NY)
Ferris State U (MI)
Idaho State U (ID)
Indiana U–Purdue U Fort Wayne (IN)
Lake Superior State U (MI)
Lawrence Technological U (MI)
Miami U (OH)
Michigan Technological U (MI)
Morrisville State Coll (NY)
New York City Coll of Technology of the City U of New York (NY)
Penn State Altoona (PA)
Penn State Berks (PA)
Penn State Erie, The Behrend Coll (PA)
Point Park U (PA)
State U of New York Coll of Technology at Canton (NY)
Thomas Edison State Coll (NJ)
Universidad del Turabo (PR)
The U of Akron (OH)
U of Arkansas at Little Rock (AR)
U of Rio Grande (OH)
U of the District of Columbia (DC)
The U of Toledo (OH)
Vermont Tech Coll (VT)
Weber State U (UT)
Youngstown State U (OH)

MECHANICAL ENGINEERING TECHNOLOGIES RELATED
Indiana U–Purdue U Indianapolis (IN)
Purdue U North Central (IN)

MECHANIC AND REPAIR TECHNOLOGIES RELATED
Pennsylvania Coll of Technology (PA)
Thomas Edison State Coll (NJ)
Washburn U (KS)

MECHANICS AND REPAIR
Idaho State U (ID)
Lewis-Clark State Coll (ID)
Utah Valley U (UT)

MEDICAL ADMINISTRATIVE ASSISTANT AND MEDICAL SECRETARY
Baker Coll of Auburn Hills (MI)
Baker Coll of Cadillac (MI)
Baker Coll of Clinton Township (MI)
Baker Coll of Flint (MI)
Baker Coll of Jackson (MI)
Baker Coll of Muskegon (MI)
Baker Coll of Owosso (MI)
Baker Coll of Port Huron (MI)
Boise State U (ID)
Broadview U–Boise (ID)
Broadview U–Layton (UT)
Broadview U–Orem (UT)
Florida National Coll (FL)
Globe U–Appleton (WI)
Globe U–Eau Claire (WI)
Globe U–Green Bay (WI)
Globe U–La Crosse (WI)
Globe U–Madison East (WI)
Globe U–Madison West (WI)
Globe U–Sioux Falls (SD)
Globe U–Wausau (WI)
Globe U–Woodbury (MN)
Lamar U (TX)

Globe U–Madison East (WI)
Globe U–Woodbury (MN)
Indiana U–Purdue U Indianapolis (IN)
Minnesota School of Business–Blaine (MN)
New York City Coll of Technology of the City U of New York (NY)

MECHANICAL ENGINEERING
Fairfield U (CT)
New England Inst of Technology (RI)

Minnesota School of Business–Blaine (MN)
Minnesota School of Business–Elk River (MN)
Minnesota School of Business–Moorhead (MN)
Minnesota School of Business–Rochester (MN)
Montana State U Billings (MT)
Mountain State U (WV)
Rasmussen Coll Appleton (WI)
Rasmussen Coll Blaine (MN)
Rasmussen Coll Land O' Lakes (FL)
Rasmussen Coll Mokena/Tinley Park (IL)
Rasmussen Coll Romeoville/Joliet (IL)
Rasmussen Coll Tampa/Brandon (FL)
Rasmussen Coll Wausau (WI)
U of Cincinnati (OH)
U of Rio Grande (OH)

MEDICAL/CLINICAL ASSISTANT
Arkansas Tech U (AR)
Baker Coll of Allen Park (MI)
Baker Coll of Auburn Hills (MI)
Baker Coll of Cadillac (MI)
Baker Coll of Clinton Township (MI)
Baker Coll of Flint (MI)
Baker Coll of Jackson (MI)
Baker Coll of Muskegon (MI)
Baker Coll of Owosso (MI)
Baker Coll of Port Huron (MI)
Broadview U–Boise (ID)
Broadview U–Layton (UT)
Broadview U–Orem (UT)
Broadview U–West Jordan (UT)
Central Penn Coll (PA)
Davenport U, Grand Rapids (MI)
Eastern Kentucky U (KY)
Florida National Coll (FL)
Globe U–Appleton (WI)
Globe U–Eau Claire (WI)
Globe U–Green Bay (WI)
Globe U–La Crosse (WI)
Globe U–Madison East (WI)
Globe U–Madison West (WI)
Globe U–Sioux Falls (SD)
Globe U–Wausau (WI)
Globe U–Woodbury (MN)
Hodges U (FL)
Idaho State U (ID)
International Business Coll, Fort Wayne (IN)
Mercy Coll of Health Sciences (IA)
Minnesota School of Business–Blaine (MN)
Minnesota School of Business–Elk River (MN)
Minnesota School of Business–Lakeville (MN)
Minnesota School of Business–Moorhead (MN)
Minnesota School of Business–Rochester (MN)
Montana State U Billings (MT)
Montana Tech of The U of Montana (MT)
Mountain State U (WV)
Mount Aloysius Coll (PA)
New England Inst of Technology (RI)
Ohio U–Chillicothe (OH)
Presentation Coll (SD)
Rasmussen Coll Appleton (WI)
Rasmussen Coll Blaine (MN)
Rasmussen Coll Land O' Lakes (FL)
Rasmussen Coll Mokena/Tinley Park (IL)
Rasmussen Coll Romeoville/Joliet (IL)
Rasmussen Coll Tampa/Brandon (FL)
Rasmussen Coll Wausau (WI)
Robert Morris U Illinois (IL)
South U (AL)
South U (GA)
South U, Columbia (SC)
Sullivan U (KY)
The U of Akron (OH)
U of Alaska Anchorage (AK)
U of Alaska Fairbanks (AK)

U of Cincinnati (OH)
The U of Toledo (OH)
Youngstown State U (OH)

MEDICAL/HEALTH MANAGEMENT AND CLINICAL ASSISTANT
Florida National Coll (FL)
Lewis-Clark State Coll (ID)

MEDICAL INFORMATICS
Idaho State U (ID)
Montana Tech of The U of Montana (MT)

MEDICAL INSURANCE CODING
Baker Coll of Allen Park (MI)

MEDICAL INSURANCE/MEDICAL BILLING
Baker Coll of Allen Park (MI)

MEDICAL MICROBIOLOGY AND BACTERIOLOGY
Florida National Coll (FL)

MEDICAL OFFICE ASSISTANT
Hickey Coll (MO)
Lewis-Clark State Coll (ID)
Mercy Coll of Health Sciences (IA)

MEDICAL OFFICE COMPUTER SPECIALIST
Baker Coll of Allen Park (MI)

MEDICAL OFFICE MANAGEMENT
Dalton State Coll (GA)
Presentation Coll (SD)
Sullivan U (KY)
The U of Akron (OH)

MEDICAL RADIOLOGIC TECHNOLOGY
Arkansas State U (AR)
Ball State U (IN)
Bluefield State Coll (WV)
Boise State U (ID)
Coll of Coastal Georgia (GA)
Ferris State U (MI)
Gannon U (PA)
Idaho State U (ID)
Indiana U–Purdue U Fort Wayne (IN)
Inter American U of Puerto Rico, Ponce Campus (PR)
Inter American U of Puerto Rico, San Germán Campus (PR)
Keystone Coll (PA)
La Roche Coll (PA)
Mercy Coll of Health Sciences (IA)
Mercy Coll of Ohio (OH)
Midland Coll (TX)
Missouri Southern State U (MO)
Morehead State U (KY)
Mount Aloysius Coll (PA)
Newman U (KS)
New York City Coll of Technology of the City U of New York (NY)
Northern Kentucky U (KY)
Pennsylvania Coll of Technology (PA)
St. Catherine U (MN)
Shawnee State U (OH)
Thomas Edison State Coll (NJ)
Trinity Coll of Nursing and Health Sciences (IL)
The U of Akron (OH)
U of Cincinnati (OH)
U of New Mexico (NM)
U of Saint Francis (IN)

MEDICAL TRANSCRIPTION
Baker Coll of Flint (MI)
Baker Coll of Jackson (MI)
Mercyhurst Coll (PA)
U of Cincinnati (OH)

MEETING AND EVENT PLANNING
Cleary U (MI)

MENTAL AND SOCIAL HEALTH SERVICES AND ALLIED PROFESSIONS RELATED
Clarion U of Pennsylvania (PA)
U of Alaska Fairbanks (AK)
U of Maine at Augusta (ME)
Washburn U (KS)

MENTAL HEALTH COUNSELING
The U of Toledo (OH)

MERCHANDISING
The Art Inst of Philadelphia (PA)
The U of Akron (OH)

MERCHANDISING, SALES, AND MARKETING OPERATIONS RELATED (GENERAL)
Inter American U of Puerto Rico, San Germán Campus (PR)
Post U (CT)

METAL AND JEWELRY ARTS
Academy of Art U (CA)
Fashion Inst of Technology (NY)

METALLURGICAL TECHNOLOGY
Penn State Altoona (PA)
Penn State Berks (PA)
Penn State Erie, The Behrend Coll (PA)

METEOROLOGY
Florida Inst of Technology (FL)

MIDDLE SCHOOL EDUCATION
U of Cincinnati (OH)
Wright State U (OH)

MILITARY HISTORY
American Public U System (WV)

MILITARY STUDIES
Hawai`i Pacific U (HI)

MILITARY TECHNOLOGIES AND APPLIED SCIENCES RELATED
Thomas Edison State Coll (NJ)

MINING TECHNOLOGY
Mountain State U (WV)

MISSIONARY STUDIES AND MISSIOLOGY
Faith Baptist Bible Coll and Theological Seminary (IA)
Hillsdale Free Will Baptist Coll (OK)

MODERN LANGUAGES
Midland Coll (TX)

MULTI/INTERDISCIPLINARY STUDIES RELATED
Arkansas Tech U (AR)
Miami U (OH)
Montana Tech of The U of Montana (MT)
Ohio U–Chillicothe (OH)
Pennsylvania Coll of Technology (PA)
Providence Coll (RI)
Thomas Edison State Coll (NJ)
U of Alaska Fairbanks (AK)
U of Arkansas at Monticello (AR)
U of Arkansas–Fort Smith (AR)
U of Cincinnati (OH)
The U of Toledo (OH)
Utah Valley U (UT)

MUSIC
Alverno Coll (WI)
Clayton State U (GA)
Five Towns Coll (NY)
Hannibal-LaGrange U (MO)
Hillsdale Free Will Baptist Coll (OK)
Macon State Coll (GA)
Midland Coll (TX)
Mount Vernon Nazarene U (OH)

Musicians Inst (CA)
Nyack Coll (NY)
Pacific Union Coll (CA)
Southwestern Assemblies of God U (TX)
Thomas More Coll (KY)
U of Maine at Augusta (ME)
U of Rio Grande (OH)
Utah Valley U (UT)
Villa Maria Coll of Buffalo (NY)
Williams Baptist Coll (AR)
York Coll of Pennsylvania (PA)

MUSIC MANAGEMENT
Five Towns Coll (NY)
Globe U–Madison East (WI)
McNally Smith Coll of Music (MN)
Villa Maria Coll of Buffalo (NY)

MUSIC PERFORMANCE
Musicians Inst (CA)

MUSIC RELATED
Academy of Art U (CA)
Alverno Coll (WI)

MUSIC TEACHER EDUCATION
Midland Coll (TX)
Wright State U (OH)

MUSIC TECHNOLOGY
McNally Smith Coll of Music (MN)

NATURAL RESOURCES/CONSERVATION
Morrisville State Coll (NY)
State U of New York Coll of Environmental Science and Forestry (NY)
Suffolk U (MA)

NATURAL RESOURCES MANAGEMENT AND POLICY
Lake Superior State U (MI)
U of Alaska Fairbanks (AK)

NATURAL RESOURCES MANAGEMENT AND POLICY RELATED
U of Guelph (ON, Canada)

NATURAL SCIENCES
Indiana U East (IN)
Lourdes U (OH)
Madonna U (MI)
Roberts Wesleyan Coll (NY)
U of Alaska Fairbanks (AK)
The U of Toledo (OH)
Washburn U (KS)

NETWORK AND SYSTEM ADMINISTRATION
Florida National Coll (FL)
ITT Tech Inst, Tempe (AZ)
ITT Tech Inst, Clovis (CA)
ITT Tech Inst, Concord (CA)
ITT Tech Inst, Corona (CA)
ITT Tech Inst, Deerfield Beach (FL)
ITT Tech Inst, West Palm Beach (FL)
ITT Tech Inst, Indianapolis (IN)
ITT Tech Inst, Indianapolis (IN)
ITT Tech Inst, South Bend (IN)
ITT Tech Inst, Overland Park (KS)
ITT Tech Inst, Wichita (KS)
ITT Tech Inst, Lexington (KY)
ITT Tech Inst, Grand Rapids (MI)
ITT Tech Inst, Southfield (MI)
ITT Tech Inst (MS)
ITT Tech Inst, Springfield (MO)
ITT Tech Inst, Oklahoma City (OK)
ITT Tech Inst, Salem (OR)
ITT Tech Inst, Germantown (WI)
Midland Coll (TX)
Thompson Rivers U (BC, Canada)

NUCLEAR ENGINEERING TECHNOLOGY
Arkansas Tech U (AR)
Thomas Edison State Coll (NJ)

NUCLEAR MEDICAL TECHNOLOGY
Ball State U (IN)

The George Washington U (DC)
Molloy Coll (NY)
Thomas Edison State Coll (NJ)
U of Cincinnati (OH)
The U of Findlay (OH)

NUCLEAR/NUCLEAR POWER TECHNOLOGY
Excelsior Coll (NY)

NURSING EDUCATION
Macon State Coll (GA)

NURSING SCIENCE
EDP Coll of Puerto Rico, Inc. (PR)
EDP Coll of Puerto Rico–San Sebastian (PR)
Emmaus Bible Coll (IA)
National U (CA)
Trinity Coll of Nursing and Health Sciences (IL)

NUTRITION SCIENCES
U of Cincinnati (OH)

OCCUPATIONAL SAFETY AND HEALTH TECHNOLOGY
Columbia Southern U (AL)
Fairmont State U (WV)
Indiana U Southeast (IN)
Lamar U (TX)

OCCUPATIONAL THERAPIST ASSISTANT
Arkansas Tech U (AR)
Baker Coll of Muskegon (MI)
Inter American U of Puerto Rico, Ponce Campus (PR)
Maria Coll (NY)
Mercy Coll (NY)
Mountain State U (WV)
New England Inst of Technology (RI)
Newman U (KS)
Penn State Berks (PA)
Pennsylvania Coll of Technology (PA)
St. Catherine U (MN)
U of Louisiana at Monroe (LA)
U of Puerto Rico at Humacao (PR)
U of Southern Indiana (IN)
Washburn U (KS)

OCCUPATIONAL THERAPY
Coll of Coastal Georgia (GA)
Keystone Coll (PA)
Shawnee State U (OH)
Touro Coll (NY)

OFFICE MANAGEMENT
Baker Coll of Jackson (MI)
Dalton State Coll (GA)
Emmanuel Coll (GA)
Inter American U of Puerto Rico, Fajardo Campus (PR)
Inter American U of Puerto Rico, Ponce Campus (PR)
Inter American U of Puerto Rico, San Germán Campus (PR)
Maranatha Baptist Bible Coll (WI)
Mercyhurst Coll (PA)
Miami U (OH)
Mount Vernon Nazarene U (OH)
Shawnee State U (OH)
Sullivan U (KY)
Thompson Rivers U (BC, Canada)
Universidad del Turabo (PR)
Washburn U (KS)

OFFICE OCCUPATIONS AND CLERICAL SERVICES
Bob Jones U (SC)
Morrisville State Coll (NY)

OPERATIONS MANAGEMENT
Indiana U–Purdue U Fort Wayne (IN)
Indiana U–Purdue U Indianapolis (IN)
Purdue U North Central (IN)

OPHTHALMIC LABORATORY TECHNOLOGY
Rochester Inst of Technology (NY)

OPTICAL SCIENCES
Indiana U of Pennsylvania (PA)

OPTICIANRY
New York City Coll of Technology of the City U of New York (NY)

OPTOMETRIC TECHNICIAN
Inter American U of Puerto Rico, Ponce Campus (PR)

ORGANIZATIONAL BEHAVIOR
Hawai`i Pacific U (HI)
Regent U (VA)

ORGANIZATIONAL COMMUNICATION
Creighton U (NE)
Xavier U (OH)

ORGANIZATIONAL LEADERSHIP
AIB Coll of Business (IA)
Beulah Heights U (GA)
Grace Coll (IN)
Huntington U (IN)
Point U (GA)

ORNAMENTAL HORTICULTURE
Farmingdale State Coll (NY)
Ferris State U (MI)
Vermont Tech Coll (VT)

ORTHOTICS/PROSTHETICS
Baker Coll of Flint (MI)

PAINTING
Academy of Art U (CA)
Pratt Inst (NY)

PALLIATIVE CARE NURSING
Madonna U (MI)

PARKS, RECREATION AND LEISURE
Indiana U Southeast (IN)
State U of New York Coll of Technology at Delhi (NY)

PARKS, RECREATION AND LEISURE FACILITIES MANAGEMENT
Coll of Coastal Georgia (GA)
Indiana Tech (IN)
Indiana U Southeast (IN)
State U of New York Coll of Technology at Delhi (NY)
Webber International U (FL)

PARKS, RECREATION, LEISURE, AND FITNESS STUDIES RELATED
Indiana U Southeast (IN)

PASTORAL COUNSELING AND SPECIALIZED MINISTRIES RELATED
Brescia U (KY)

PASTORAL STUDIES/COUNSELING
Indiana Wesleyan U (IN)
William Jessup U (CA)

PERCUSSION INSTRUMENTS
Five Towns Coll (NY)
McNally Smith Coll of Music (MN)

PERFUSION TECHNOLOGY
Thompson Rivers U (BC, Canada)

PERSONAL AND CULINARY SERVICES RELATED
U of Cincinnati (OH)

PETROLEUM TECHNOLOGY
Montana State U Billings (MT)
Nicholls State U (LA)
U of Alaska Anchorage (AK)

PHARMACOLOGY
Universidad del Turabo (PR)

PHARMACY, PHARMACEUTICAL SCIENCES, AND ADMINISTRATION RELATED
EDP Coll of Puerto Rico–San Sebastian (PR)
Universidad del Turabo (PR)

PHARMACY TECHNICIAN
Baker Coll of Flint (MI)
Baker Coll of Jackson (MI)
Baker Coll of Muskegon (MI)
Rasmussen Coll Appleton (WI)
Rasmussen Coll Blaine (MN)
Rasmussen Coll Land O' Lakes (FL)
Rasmussen Coll Mokena/Tinley Park (IL)
Rasmussen Coll Romeoville/Joliet (IL)
Rasmussen Coll Tampa/Brandon (FL)
Rasmussen Coll Wausau (WI)
Robert Morris U Illinois (IL)

PHILOSOPHY
Carroll Coll (MT)
Coll of Coastal Georgia (GA)
Thomas More Coll (KY)
U of Cincinnati (OH)
The U of Tampa (FL)
Utah Valley U (UT)

PHOTOGRAPHIC AND FILM/ VIDEO TECHNOLOGY
St. John's U (NY)
U of Cincinnati (OH)
Villa Maria Coll of Buffalo (NY)

PHOTOGRAPHY
Academy of Art U (CA)
The Art Inst of California, a college of Argosy U, Hollywood (CA)
The Art Inst of California, a college of Argosy U, Orange County (CA)
The Art Inst of Charlotte (NC)
The Art Inst of Colorado (CO)
The Art Inst of Dallas (TX)
The Art Inst of Fort Lauderdale (FL)
The Art Inst of Fort Worth (TX)
The Art Inst of Indianapolis (IN)
The Art Inst of Philadelphia (PA)
The Art Inst of Pittsburgh (PA)
Corcoran Coll of Art and Design (DC)
International Academy of Design & Technology (FL)
The New England Inst of Art (MA)
Pacific Union Coll (CA)
Paier Coll of Art, Inc. (CT)
Thomas Edison State Coll (NJ)

PHYSICAL EDUCATION TEACHING AND COACHING
Hillsdale Free Will Baptist Coll (OK)
Midland Coll (TX)
U of Rio Grande (OH)

PHYSICAL FITNESS TECHNICIAN
Broadview U–West Jordan (UT)
Globe U–Madison West (WI)
Globe U–Woodbury (MN)

PHYSICAL SCIENCES
Hillsdale Free Will Baptist Coll (OK)
Kent State U at Geauga (OH)
New York City Coll of Technology of the City U of New York (NY)
Roberts Wesleyan Coll (NY)
U of Cincinnati (OH)
U of the District of Columbia (DC)
Utah Valley U (UT)

PHYSICAL THERAPY
Clarkson Coll (NE)
Coll of Coastal Georgia (GA)

EDP Coll of Puerto Rico–San Sebastian (PR)
Touro Coll (NY)

PHYSICAL THERAPY TECHNOLOGY
Arkansas State U (AR)
Arkansas Tech U (AR)
Baker Coll of Flint (MI)
Baker Coll of Muskegon (MI)
California U of Pennsylvania (PA)
Central Penn Coll (PA)
Dixie State Coll of Utah (UT)
EDP Coll of Puerto Rico, Inc. (PR)
EDP Coll of Puerto Rico–San Sebastian (PR)
Idaho State U (ID)
Inter American U of Puerto Rico, Ponce Campus (PR)
Louisiana Coll (LA)
Maria Coll (NY)
Mercy Coll of Health Sciences (IA)
Mercyhurst Coll (PA)
Missouri Western State U (MO)
Mountain State U (WV)
Mount Aloysius Coll (PA)
New England Inst of Technology (RI)
Our Lady of the Lake Coll (LA)
St. Catherine U (MN)
Shawnee State U (OH)
Southern Illinois U Carbondale (IL)
South U (AL)
South U, Royal Palm Beach (FL)
South U, Tampa (FL)
South U (GA)
State U of New York Coll of Technology at Canton (NY)
U of Cincinnati (OH)
U of Evansville (IN)
U of Indianapolis (IN)
U of Maine at Presque Isle (ME)
U of Puerto Rico at Humacao (PR)
U of Puerto Rico at Ponce (PR)
U of Saint Francis (IN)
Villa Maria Coll of Buffalo (NY)
Washburn U (KS)

PHYSICIAN ASSISTANT
Coll of Coastal Georgia (GA)

PHYSICS
Coll of Coastal Georgia (GA)
Dalton State Coll (GA)
Idaho State U (ID)
Macon State Coll (GA)
Midland Coll (TX)
Purdue U North Central (IN)
Rogers State U (OK)
Thomas More Coll (KY)
Utah Valley U (UT)
York Coll of Pennsylvania (PA)

PIPEFITTING AND SPRINKLER FITTING
New England Inst of Technology (RI)
State U of New York Coll of Technology at Delhi (NY)
Thompson Rivers U (BC, Canada)

PLANT PROTECTION AND INTEGRATED PEST MANAGEMENT
North Carolina State U (NC)

PLASTICS AND POLYMER ENGINEERING TECHNOLOGY
Ferris State U (MI)
Penn State Erie, The Behrend Coll (PA)
Pennsylvania Coll of Technology (PA)
Shawnee State U (OH)

PLAYWRITING AND SCREENWRITING
Pacific Union Coll (CA)

PLUMBING TECHNOLOGY
Montana State U–Northern (MT)
Thompson Rivers U (BC, Canada)

POLITICAL SCIENCE AND GOVERNMENT
Adams State Coll (CO)
Coll of Coastal Georgia (GA)
Dalton State Coll (GA)
Holy Cross Coll (IN)
Immaculata U (PA)
Macon State Coll (GA)
Midland Coll (TX)
Mount St. Mary's Coll (CA)
Thomas More Coll (KY)
U of Cincinnati (OH)
The U of Tampa (FL)
The U of Toledo (OH)
Xavier U (OH)
York Coll of Pennsylvania (PA)

POLYSOMNOGRAPHY
Mercy Coll of Health Sciences (IA)

PRECISION METAL WORKING RELATED
Montana Tech of The U of Montana (MT)

PRE-DENTISTRY STUDIES
Coll of Coastal Georgia (GA)
Macon State Coll (GA)
U of Cincinnati (OH)

PRE-ENGINEERING
Coll of Coastal Georgia (GA)
Dixie State Coll of Utah (UT)
Eastern Kentucky U (KY)
Macon State Coll (GA)
Midland Coll (TX)
Newman U (KS)
Niagara U (NY)
Northern State U (SD)
Siena Heights U (MI)

PRE-LAW STUDIES
Calumet Coll of Saint Joseph (IN)
Ferris State U (MI)
Immaculata U (PA)
Northern Kentucky U (KY)
Thomas More Coll (KY)
U of Cincinnati (OH)
Wayland Baptist U (TX)

PREMEDICAL STUDIES
Coll of Coastal Georgia (GA)
U of Cincinnati (OH)

PRENURSING STUDIES
Anna Maria Coll (MA)
Keystone Coll (PA)
Lincoln Christian U (IL)
Reinhardt U (GA)

PRE-PHARMACY STUDIES
Coll of Coastal Georgia (GA)
Dalton State Coll (GA)
Emmanuel Coll (GA)
Ferris State U (MI)
Keystone Coll (PA)
Macon State Coll (GA)
Madonna U (MI)
Thompson Rivers U (BC, Canada)
U of Cincinnati (OH)

PRE-THEOLOGY/PRE- MINISTERIAL STUDIES
Eastern Mennonite U (VA)

PRE-VETERINARY STUDIES
Coll of Coastal Georgia (GA)
Macon State Coll (GA)
U of Cincinnati (OH)

PRINTMAKING
Academy of Art U (CA)

PROFESSIONAL, TECHNICAL, BUSINESS, AND SCIENTIFIC WRITING
Ferris State U (MI)
Florida National Coll (FL)

PSYCHIATRIC/MENTAL HEALTH SERVICES TECHNOLOGY
Lake Superior State U (MI)
Pennsylvania Coll of Technology (PA)
The U of Toledo (OH)

PSYCHOLOGY
California Coast U (CA)
Central Methodist U (MO)
Coll of Coastal Georgia (GA)
Dalton State Coll (GA)
Eastern New Mexico U (NM)
Ferris State U (MI)
Hillsdale Free Will Baptist Coll (OK)
Indiana U–Purdue U Fort Wayne (IN)
Liberty U (VA)
Macon State Coll (GA)
Midland Coll (TX)
Montana State U Billings (MT)
Muhlenberg Coll (PA)
Regent U (VA)
Siena Heights U (MI)
Southwestern Assemblies of God U (TX)
Thomas More Coll (KY)
U of Cincinnati (OH)
U of Rio Grande (OH)
The U of Tampa (FL)
Utah Valley U (UT)
Wright State U (OH)
Xavier U (OH)

PSYCHOLOGY RELATED
Mountain State U (WV)

PUBLIC ADMINISTRATION
Central Methodist U (MO)
Ferris State U (MI)
Florida National Coll (FL)
Indiana U Northwest (IN)
Indiana U–Purdue U Indianapolis (IN)
Indiana U South Bend (IN)
Point Park U (PA)
Universidad del Turabo (PR)
U of Maine at Augusta (ME)

PUBLIC ADMINISTRATION AND SOCIAL SERVICE PROFESSIONS RELATED
Point Park U (PA)
State U of New York Empire State Coll (NY)
The U of Akron (OH)

PUBLIC HEALTH
American Public U System (WV)
U of Alaska Fairbanks (AK)

PUBLIC HEALTH EDUCATION AND PROMOTION
U of Cincinnati (OH)

PUBLIC POLICY ANALYSIS
Saint Peter's Coll (NJ)

PUBLIC RELATIONS, ADVERTISING, AND APPLIED COMMUNICATION RELATED
John Brown U (AR)
U of Maine at Presque Isle (ME)

PUBLIC RELATIONS/IMAGE MANAGEMENT
John Brown U (AR)
Xavier U (OH)

PURCHASING, PROCUREMENT/ ACQUISITIONS AND CONTRACTS MANAGEMENT
Mercyhurst Coll (PA)

QUALITY CONTROL AND SAFETY TECHNOLOGIES RELATED
Lamar U (TX)
Madonna U (MI)
Rochester Inst of Technology (NY)

QUALITY CONTROL TECHNOLOGY
Baker Coll of Cadillac (MI)
Baker Coll of Flint (MI)
Baker Coll of Muskegon (MI)
Eastern Kentucky U (KY)
Universidad del Turabo (PR)

RADIATION PROTECTION/ HEALTH PHYSICS TECHNOLOGY
Indiana U South Bend (IN)
Indiana U Southeast (IN)
Thomas Edison State Coll (NJ)

RADIO AND TELEVISION
Lawrence Technological U (MI)
Northwestern Coll (MN)
Ohio U–Zanesville (OH)
Xavier U (OH)

RADIO AND TELEVISION BROADCASTING TECHNOLOGY
The New England Inst of Art (MA)
New England Inst of Technology (RI)
New York Inst of Technology (NY)

RADIOLOGIC TECHNOLOGY/ SCIENCE
Allen Coll (IA)
Baker Coll of Clinton Township (MI)
Baker Coll of Muskegon (MI)
Clarkson Coll (NE)
Coll of St. Joseph (VT)
Colorado Mesa U (CO)
Dalton State Coll (GA)
Dixie State Coll of Utah (UT)
Fairleigh Dickinson U, Metropolitan Campus (NJ)
Florida National Coll (FL)
Fort Hays State U (KS)
Holy Family U (PA)
Indiana U Kokomo (IN)
Indiana U Northwest (IN)
Indiana U–Purdue U Indianapolis (IN)
Indiana U South Bend (IN)
Keystone Coll (PA)
Lewis-Clark State Coll (ID)
Mansfield U of Pennsylvania (PA)
Midland Coll (TX)
Montana Tech of The U of Montana (MT)
Mountain State U (WV)
Newman U (KS)
Northern Michigan U (MI)
Presentation Coll (SD)
Regis Coll (MA)
Trinity Coll of Nursing and Health Sciences (IL)
U of Arkansas–Fort Smith (AR)
U of Rio Grande (OH)
Washburn U (KS)
Widener U (PA)
Xavier U (OH)

RADIO, TELEVISION, AND DIGITAL COMMUNICATION RELATED
Keystone Coll (PA)
Lawrence Technological U (MI)
Madonna U (MI)

REAL ESTATE
American Public U System (WV)
Caribbean U (PR)
Lamar U (TX)
Miami U (OH)
Saint Francis U (PA)

RECEPTIONIST
Baker Coll of Allen Park (MI)

RECORDING ARTS TECHNOLOGY
Broadview U–Salt Lake City (UT)
Five Towns Coll (NY)
New England Inst of Technology (RI)

REGISTERED NURSING, NURSING ADMINISTRATION, NURSING RESEARCH AND CLINICAL NURSING RELATED
Anna Maria Coll (MA)

REGISTERED NURSING/ REGISTERED NURSE
Alcorn State U (MS)
Angelo State U (TX)
Anna Maria Coll (MA)
Arkansas State U (AR)
Baker Coll of Allen Park (MI)
Baker Coll of Auburn Hills (MI)
Baker Coll of Cadillac (MI)
Baker Coll of Clinton Township (MI)
Baker Coll of Flint (MI)
Baker Coll of Muskegon (MI)
Baker Coll of Owosso (MI)
Bayamón Central U (PR)
Becker Coll (MA)
Bethel Coll (IN)
Bluefield State Coll (WV)
Broadview U–West Jordan (UT)
California U of Pennsylvania (PA)
Campbellsville U (KY)
Cardinal Stritch U (WI)
Castleton State Coll (VT)
Clarion U of Pennsylvania (PA)
Coll of Coastal Georgia (GA)
Coll of Saint Mary (NE)
Coll of Staten Island of the City U of New York (NY)
Colorado Mesa U (CO)
Columbia Centro Universitario, Caguas (PR)
Columbia Centro Universitario, Yauco (PR)
Columbia Coll (MO)
Dalton State Coll (GA)
Dixie State Coll of Utah (UT)
Excelsior Coll (NY)
Fairmont State U (WV)
Farmingdale State Coll (NY)
Ferris State U (MI)
Florida National Coll (FL)
Gardner-Webb U (NC)
Gwynedd-Mercy Coll (PA)
Hannibal-LaGrange U (MO)
Idaho State U (ID)
Indiana U East (IN)
Indiana U Kokomo (IN)
Indiana U Northwest (IN)
Indiana U–Purdue U Indianapolis (IN)
Inter American U of Puerto Rico, Ponce Campus (PR)
ITT Tech Inst, Deerfield Beach (FL)
ITT Tech Inst, West Palm Beach (FL)
ITT Tech Inst, Indianapolis (IN)
ITT Tech Inst, South Bend (IN)
ITT Tech Inst, Wichita (KS)
ITT Tech Inst, Oklahoma City (OK)
Judson Coll (AL)
Kent State U (OH)
Kentucky State U (KY)
Lamar U (TX)
La Roche Coll (PA)
Lincoln Memorial U (TN)
Lincoln U (MO)
Lock Haven U of Pennsylvania (PA)
Maria Coll (NY)
Marshall U (WV)
McNeese State U (LA)
Mercy Coll of Health Sciences (IA)
Mercy Coll of Ohio (OH)
Miami U (OH)
Midland Coll (TX)
Mississippi U for Women (MS)
Montana State U Billings (MT)
Montana State U–Northern (MT)
Montana Tech of The U of Montana (MT)
Morehead State U (KY)
Morrisville State Coll (NY)
Mount Aloysius Coll (PA)
Mount St. Mary's Coll (CA)
New England Inst of Technology (RI)
New York City Coll of Technology of the City U of New York (NY)
Norfolk State U (VA)
Northern Kentucky U (KY)
North Georgia Coll & State U (GA)
Northwestern State U of Louisiana (LA)

Our Lady of the Lake Coll (LA)
Pacific Union Coll (CA)
Park U (MO)
Penn State Altoona (PA)
Penn State Berks (PA)
Penn State Erie, The Behrend Coll (PA)
Penn State U Park (PA)
Pennsylvania Coll of Technology (PA)
Presentation Coll (SD)
Purdue U North Central (IN)
Queens U of Charlotte (NC)
Regis Coll (MA)
Reinhardt U (GA)
Rivier Coll (NH)
Robert Morris U Illinois (IL)
Rogers State U (OK)
Shawnee State U (OH)
Southern Arkansas U–Magnolia (AR)
Southern Vermont Coll (VT)
Southwest Baptist U (MO)
State U of New York Coll of Technology at Canton (NY)
State U of New York Coll of Technology at Delhi (NY)
Sul Ross State U (TX)
Thomas U (GA)
Trinity Coll of Nursing and Health Sciences (IL)
Troy U (AL)
U of Alaska Anchorage (AK)
U of Arkansas at Little Rock (AR)
U of Arkansas at Monticello (AR)
U of Arkansas–Fort Smith (AR)
U of Charleston (WV)
U of Cincinnati (OH)
U of Guam (GU)
U of Maine at Augusta (ME)
U of Mobile (AL)
U of Pikeville (KY)
U of Pittsburgh at Bradford (PA)
U of Rio Grande (OH)
U of Saint Francis (IN)
The U of South Dakota (SD)
The U of Toledo (OH)
The U of West Alabama (AL)
Utah Valley U (UT)
Vermont Tech Coll (VT)
Western Kentucky U (KY)

REHABILITATION AND THERAPEUTIC PROFESSIONS RELATED
U of Cincinnati (OH)
U of Medicine and Dentistry of New Jersey (NJ)

RELIGIOUS EDUCATION
Apex School of Theology (NC)
Cincinnati Christian U (OH)
Hillsdale Free Will Baptist Coll (OK)
Lincoln Christian U (IL)
Oakland City U (IN)
Piedmont International U (NC)

RELIGIOUS/SACRED MUSIC
Briercrest Coll (SK, Canada)
Cincinnati Christian U (OH)
Dallas Baptist U (TX)
Hillsdale Free Will Baptist Coll (OK)
Immaculata U (PA)
Indiana Wesleyan U (IN)
Mount Vernon Nazarene U (OH)

RELIGIOUS STUDIES
Brewton-Parker Coll (GA)
Calumet Coll of Saint Joseph (IN)
Concordia Coll–New York (NY)
Corban U (OR)
The Criswell Coll (TX)
Huntington U (IN)
Liberty U (VA)
Lourdes U (OH)
Madonna U (MI)
Mount Marty Coll (SD)
Mount Vernon Nazarene U (OH)
Northwest U (WA)
Presentation Coll (SD)
Shaw U (NC)
Thomas More Coll (KY)
The U of Findlay (OH)
Xavier U (OH)

RESORT MANAGEMENT
Thompson Rivers U (BC, Canada)

RESPIRATORY CARE THERAPY
Boise State U (ID)
Coll of Coastal Georgia (GA)
Dakota State U (SD)
Dixie State Coll of Utah (UT)
Ferris State U (MI)
Gannon U (PA)
Gwynedd-Mercy Coll (PA)
Hannibal-LaGrange U (MO)
Idaho State U (ID)
Indiana U Northwest (IN)
Indiana U South Bend (IN)
Lamar U (TX)
Macon State Coll (GA)
Mansfield U of Pennsylvania (PA)
Midland Coll (TX)
Molloy Coll (NY)
Morehead State U (KY)
Newman U (KS)
Northern Kentucky U (KY)
Shawnee State U (OH)
Thomas Edison State Coll (NJ)
Trinity Coll of Nursing and Health Sciences (IL)
The U of Akron (OH)
U of Cincinnati (OH)
U of Medicine and Dentistry of New Jersey (NJ)
U of Pittsburgh at Johnstown (PA)
U of Southern Indiana (IN)
U of the District of Columbia (DC)
The U of Toledo (OH)
Vermont Tech Coll (VT)
Washburn U (KS)
York Coll of Pennsylvania (PA)

RESPIRATORY THERAPY TECHNICIAN
Clarion U of Pennsylvania (PA)
Dalton State Coll (GA)
Florida National Coll (FL)
Northern Michigan U (MI)
Thompson Rivers U (BC, Canada)

RESTAURANT, CULINARY, AND CATERING MANAGEMENT
Arkansas Tech U (AR)
The Art Inst of Atlanta (GA)
The Art Inst of Austin (TX)
The Art Inst of Charleston (SC)
The Art Inst of Dallas (TX)
The Art Inst of Houston (TX)
The Art Inst of San Antonio (TX)
The Art Inst of Washington (VA)
Bob Jones U (SC)
Ferris State U (MI)
Lincoln Culinary Inst (FL)
State U of New York Coll of Technology at Delhi (NY)
Sullivan U (KY)

RESTAURANT/FOOD SERVICES MANAGEMENT
American Public U System (WV)
Morrisville State Coll (NY)
Pennsylvania Coll of Technology (PA)
The U of Akron (OH)

RETAILING
American Public U System (WV)
International Business Coll, Fort Wayne (IN)
Stevens Inst of Business & Arts (MO)
Weber State U (UT)

RHETORIC AND COMPOSITION
Ferris State U (MI)
Midland Coll (TX)

ROBOTICS TECHNOLOGY
Indiana U–Purdue U Indianapolis (IN)
Pennsylvania Coll of Technology (PA)
Purdue U (IN)
U of Rio Grande (OH)

RUSSIAN
Idaho State U (ID)

SALES AND MARKETING/ MARKETING AND DISTRIBUTION TEACHER EDUCATION
Wright State U (OH)

SALES, DISTRIBUTION, AND MARKETING OPERATIONS
AIB Coll of Business (IA)
Baker Coll of Flint (MI)
Baker Coll of Jackson (MI)
Dalton State Coll (GA)
Thompson Rivers U (BC, Canada)
The U of Findlay (OH)

SCIENCE TEACHER EDUCATION
Wright State U (OH)

SCIENCE TECHNOLOGIES
Washburn U (KS)

SCIENCE TECHNOLOGIES RELATED
Madonna U (MI)
Maria Coll (NY)
Ohio Valley U (WV)
U of Alaska Fairbanks (AK)
U of Cincinnati (OH)

SCULPTURE
Academy of Art U (CA)

SECONDARY EDUCATION
Ferris State U (MI)
Mountain State U (WV)
Ohio U–Chillicothe (OH)
Rogers State U (OK)
U of Cincinnati (OH)
Utah Valley U (UT)

SECURITIES SERVICES ADMINISTRATION
Davenport U, Grand Rapids (MI)

SECURITY AND LOSS PREVENTION
John Jay Coll of Criminal Justice of the City U of New York (NY)

SELLING SKILLS AND SALES
Inter American U of Puerto Rico, San Germán Campus (PR)
The U of Akron (OH)

SHEET METAL TECHNOLOGY
Montana State U Billings (MT)

SIGN LANGUAGE INTERPRETATION AND TRANSLATION
Bethel Coll (IN)
Cincinnati Christian U (OH)
Mount Aloysius Coll (PA)
St. Catherine U (MN)
U of Arkansas at Little Rock (AR)
U of Louisville (KY)

SMALL BUSINESS ADMINISTRATION
Lewis-Clark State Coll (ID)
The U of Akron (OH)

SOCIAL SCIENCES
Briercrest Coll (SK, Canada)
Campbellsville U (KY)
Faulkner U (AL)
Hillsdale Free Will Baptist Coll (OK)
Long Island U–Brooklyn Campus (NY)
Ohio U–Zanesville (OH)
Saint Peter's Coll (NJ)
Shawnee State U (OH)
Southwestern Assemblies of God U (TX)
State U of New York Coll of Technology at Delhi (NY)
State U of New York Empire State Coll (NY)
Trine U (IN)
U of Cincinnati (OH)
The U of Findlay (OH)
U of Puerto Rico at Ponce (PR)

U of Southern Indiana (IN)
The U of Toledo (OH)
Valparaiso U (IN)
Wayland Baptist U (TX)

SOCIAL SCIENCES RELATED
Concordia U Texas (TX)

SOCIAL WORK
Elizabethtown Coll (PA)
Ferris State U (MI)
Northern State U (SD)
Suffolk U (MA)
U of Cincinnati (OH)
U of Rio Grande (OH)
The U of Toledo (OH)
Wright State U (OH)
Youngstown State U (OH)

SOCIAL WORK RELATED
Macon State Coll (GA)
The U of Akron (OH)

SOCIOLOGY
Coll of Coastal Georgia (GA)
Holy Cross Coll (IN)
Lourdes U (OH)
Macon State Coll (GA)
Marymount Manhattan Coll (NY)
Midland Coll (TX)
Montana State U Billings (MT)
Thomas More Coll (KY)
U of Cincinnati (OH)
U of Rio Grande (OH)
The U of Scranton (PA)
The U of Tampa (FL)
Wright State U (OH)
Xavier U (OH)

SOLAR ENERGY TECHNOLOGY
Pennsylvania Coll of Technology (PA)

SPANISH
Holy Cross Coll (IN)
Immaculata U (PA)
Midland Coll (TX)
Thomas More Coll (KY)
U of Cincinnati (OH)
The U of Tampa (FL)
Xavier U (OH)

SPECIAL EDUCATION
Edinboro U of Pennsylvania (PA)
Montana State U Billings (MT)
U of Cincinnati (OH)

SPECIAL EDUCATION RELATED
Minot State U (ND)

SPECIAL PRODUCTS MARKETING
Lamar U (TX)

SPEECH COMMUNICATION AND RHETORIC
American Public U System (WV)
Baker Coll of Jackson (MI)
Carroll Coll (MT)
Central Penn Coll (PA)
Coll of Mount St. Joseph (OH)
Indiana Wesleyan U (IN)
Presentation Coll (SD)
Thomas Edison State Coll (NJ)
Trine U (IN)
Tulane U (LA)
U of Rio Grande (OH)
Utah Valley U (UT)
Wright State U (OH)

SPEECH-LANGUAGE PATHOLOGY
Baker Coll of Muskegon (MI)

SPORT AND FITNESS ADMINISTRATION/ MANAGEMENT
AIB Coll of Business (IA)
Lake Superior State U (MI)
Mount Vernon Nazarene U (OH)
Thompson Rivers U (BC, Canada)
U of Cincinnati (OH)

STRINGED INSTRUMENTS
Five Towns Coll (NY)
McNally Smith Coll of Music (MN)

SUBSTANCE ABUSE/ ADDICTION COUNSELING
Indiana Wesleyan U (IN)
Midland Coll (TX)
Newman U (KS)
The U of Akron (OH)
U of Great Falls (MT)
The U of Toledo (OH)
Washburn U (KS)

SURGICAL TECHNOLOGY
Baker Coll of Clinton Township (MI)
Baker Coll of Flint (MI)
Baker Coll of Jackson (MI)
Baker Coll of Muskegon (MI)
Lincoln U (MO)
Mercy Coll of Health Sciences (IA)
Montana State U Billings (MT)
Mount Aloysius Coll (PA)
New England Inst of Technology (RI)
Northern Michigan U (MI)
Our Lady of the Lake Coll (LA)
Pennsylvania Coll of Technology (PA)
Presentation Coll (SD)
Robert Morris U Illinois (IL)
Trinity Coll of Nursing and Health Sciences (IL)
The U of Akron (OH)
U of Arkansas–Fort Smith (AR)
U of Cincinnati (OH)
U of Pittsburgh at Johnstown (PA)
U of Saint Francis (IN)
Washburn U (KS)

SURVEYING TECHNOLOGY
Ferris State U (MI)
Glenville State Coll (WV)
Pennsylvania Coll of Technology (PA)
The U of Akron (OH)
U of Alaska Anchorage (AK)
U of Arkansas at Monticello (AR)

SYSTEM, NETWORKING, AND LAN/WAN MANAGEMENT
Baker Coll of Auburn Hills (MI)
Dakota State U (SD)
ITT Tech Inst, Springfield (IL)
ITT Tech Inst, Hanover (MD)
ITT Tech Inst, Charlotte (NC)
ITT Tech Inst, Durham (NC)
Midland Coll (TX)
Sullivan U (KY)
Thompson Rivers U (BC, Canada)

TEACHER ASSISTANT/AIDE
Alverno Coll (WI)
Dordt Coll (IA)
Eastern Mennonite U (VA)
Lamar U (TX)
U of Alaska Fairbanks (AK)
Valparaiso U (IN)

TECHNICAL TEACHER EDUCATION
Northern Kentucky U (KY)
Western Kentucky U (KY)

TELECOMMUNICATIONS TECHNOLOGY
Inter American U of Puerto Rico, Bayamón Campus (PR)

New York City Coll of Technology of the City U of New York (NY)
Pace U (NY)
St. John's U (NY)

TERRORISM AND COUNTERTERRORISM OPERATIONS
American Public U System (WV)

THEATER DESIGN AND TECHNOLOGY
Johnson State Coll (VT)
U of Rio Grande (OH)

THEOLOGICAL AND MINISTERIAL STUDIES RELATED
California Christian Coll (CA)
Lincoln Christian U (IL)

THEOLOGY
Briar Cliff U (IA)
Creighton U (NE)
Franciscan U of Steubenville (OH)
Immaculata U (PA)
Missouri Baptist U (MO)
Piedmont International U (NC)
Sacred Heart Major Seminary (MI)
William Jessup U (CA)
Williams Baptist Coll (AR)

THEOLOGY AND RELIGIOUS VOCATIONS RELATED
Anderson U (IN)

TOOL AND DIE TECHNOLOGY
Ferris State U (MI)

TOURISM AND TRAVEL SERVICES MANAGEMENT
AIB Coll of Business (IA)
Baker Coll of Flint (MI)
Baker Coll of Muskegon (MI)
Black Hills State U (SD)
Morrisville State Coll (NY)
State U of New York Coll of Technology at Delhi (NY)
Stevens Inst of Business & Arts (MO)
Sullivan U (KY)
The U of Akron (OH)

TOURISM PROMOTION
Thompson Rivers U (BC, Canada)

TRADE AND INDUSTRIAL TEACHER EDUCATION
Cincinnati Christian U (OH)

TRANSPORTATION AND MATERIALS MOVING RELATED
Baker Coll of Flint (MI)
The U of Toledo (OH)

TURF AND TURFGRASS MANAGEMENT
North Carolina State U (NC)
Penn State U Park (PA)
U of Guelph (ON, Canada)
U of Massachusetts Amherst (MA)

URBAN STUDIES/AFFAIRS
Saint Peter's Coll (NJ)
U of Cincinnati (OH)

VEHICLE AND VEHICLE PARTS AND ACCESSORIES MARKETING
Pennsylvania Coll of Technology (PA)

VETERINARY/ANIMAL HEALTH TECHNOLOGY
Baker Coll of Cadillac (MI)
Baker Coll of Jackson (MI)
Baker Coll of Muskegon (MI)
Baker Coll of Port Huron (MI)
Becker Coll (MA)
Broadview U–Boise (ID)
Broadview U–Layton (UT)
Broadview U–Orem (UT)
Broadview U–West Jordan (UT)
Globe U–Appleton (WI)
Globe U–Eau Claire (WI)
Globe U–Green Bay (WI)
Globe U–La Crosse (WI)
Globe U–Madison East (WI)
Globe U–Madison West (WI)
Globe U–Sioux Falls (SD)
Globe U–Wausau (WI)
Globe U–Woodbury (MN)
Hickey Coll (MO)
International Business Coll, Fort Wayne (IN)
Lincoln Memorial U (TN)
Medaille Coll (NY)
Minnesota School of Business–Blaine (MN)
Minnesota School of Business–Elk River (MN)
Minnesota School of Business–Lakeville (MN)
Minnesota School of Business–Moorhead (MN)
Minnesota School of Business–Rochester (MN)
Morehead State U (KY)
Mount Ida Coll (MA)
New England Inst of Technology (RI)
Northwestern State U of Louisiana (LA)
Purdue U (IN)
State U of New York Coll of Technology at Canton (NY)
State U of New York Coll of Technology at Delhi (NY)
Sul Ross State U (TX)
Thomas Edison State Coll (NJ)
Thompson Rivers U (BC, Canada)
Universidad del Turabo (PR)
U of Cincinnati (OH)
U of Guelph (ON, Canada)
U of Maine at Augusta (ME)
Vermont Tech Coll (VT)

VISUAL AND PERFORMING ARTS
Pine Manor Coll (MA)

VOICE AND OPERA
Five Towns Coll (NY)
McNally Smith Coll of Music (MN)

WATER QUALITY AND WASTEWATER TREATMENT MANAGEMENT AND RECYCLING TECHNOLOGY
Colorado Mesa U (CO)
Lake Superior State U (MI)
U of the District of Columbia (DC)
Western Kentucky U (KY)

WEAPONS OF MASS DESTRUCTION
American Public U System (WV)

WEB/MULTIMEDIA MANAGEMENT AND WEBMASTER
American Public U System (WV)
Indiana Tech (IN)
Lewis-Clark State Coll (ID)
Montana Tech of The U of Montana (MT)
Mountain State U (WV)

WEB PAGE, DIGITAL/ MULTIMEDIA AND INFORMATION RESOURCES DESIGN
Academy of Art U (CA)
The Art Inst of Atlanta (GA)
The Art Inst of Atlanta–Decatur (GA)
The Art Inst of Austin (TX)
The Art Inst of California, a college of Argosy U, Hollywood (CA)
The Art Inst of California, a college of Argosy U, Los Angeles (CA)
The Art Inst of California, a college of Argosy U, Orange County (CA)
The Art Inst of California, a college of Argosy U, Sacramento (CA)
The Art Inst of California, a college of Argosy U, San Francisco (CA)
The Art Inst of California, a college of Argosy U, Sunnyvale (CA)
The Art Inst of Charleston (SC)
The Art Inst of Charlotte (NC)
The Art Inst of Colorado (CO)
The Art Inst of Fort Lauderdale (FL)
The Art Inst of Fort Worth (TX)
The Art Inst of Houston (TX)
The Art Inst of Houston - North (TX)
The Art Inst of Jacksonville (FL)
The Art Inst of Michigan (MI)
The Art Inst of Philadelphia (PA)
The Art Inst of Pittsburgh (PA)
The Art Inst of Raleigh-Durham (NC)
The Art Inst of San Antonio (TX)
The Art Inst of Tennessee–Nashville (TN)
The Art Inst of Virginia Beach (VA)
The Art Inst of Washington (VA)
The Art Inst of Washington–Dulles (VA)
The Art Insts International Minnesota (MN)
Baker Coll of Allen Park (MI)
DeVry U, Phoenix (AZ)
DeVry U, Pomona (CA)
DeVry U, Westminster (CO)
DeVry U, Miramar (FL)
DeVry U, Orlando (FL)
DeVry U, Decatur (GA)
DeVry U, Chicago (IL)
DeVry U, Kansas City (MO)
DeVry U, North Brunswick (NJ)
DeVry U, Columbus (OH)
DeVry U, Fort Washington (PA)
DeVry U, Houston (TX)
DeVry U, Irving (TX)
DeVry U, Arlington (VA)
DeVry U, Federal Way (WA)
DeVry U Online (IL)
Florida National Coll (FL)
Idaho State U (ID)

The Illinois Inst of Art–Schaumburg (IL)
International Academy of Design & Technology (FL)
New England Inst of Technology (RI)
Rasmussen Coll Appleton (WI)
Rasmussen Coll Blaine (MN)
Rasmussen Coll Land O' Lakes (FL)
Rasmussen Coll Mokena/Tinley Park (IL)
Rasmussen Coll Romeoville/Joliet (IL)
Rasmussen Coll Tampa/Brandon (FL)
Rasmussen Coll Wausau (WI)
Thomas More Coll (KY)
Thompson Rivers U (BC, Canada)
Universidad del Turabo (PR)
Utah Valley U (UT)

WELDING TECHNOLOGY
Excelsior Coll (NY)
Ferris State U (MI)
Idaho State U (ID)
Lamar U (TX)
Lewis-Clark State Coll (ID)
Midland Coll (TX)
Oakland City U (IN)
Pennsylvania Coll of Technology (PA)
State U of New York Coll of Technology at Delhi (NY)
U of Alaska Anchorage (AK)
The U of Toledo (OH)
Weber State U (UT)

WILDLIFE, FISH AND WILDLANDS SCIENCE AND MANAGEMENT
Mountain State U (WV)

WOMEN'S STUDIES
Indiana U–Purdue U Fort Wayne (IN)

WOOD SCIENCE AND WOOD PRODUCTS/PULP AND PAPER TECHNOLOGY
Morrisville State Coll (NY)

WOODWIND INSTRUMENTS
Five Towns Coll (NY)

WOODWORKING
Burlington Coll (VT)
State U of New York Coll of Technology at Delhi (NY)

WORD PROCESSING
Baker Coll of Allen Park (MI)

WRITING
Carroll Coll (MT)
Indiana U South Bend (IN)
The U of Tampa (FL)

YOUTH MINISTRY
Calvary Bible Coll and Theological Seminary (MO)

Alphabetical Listing of Two-Year Colleges

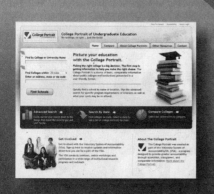

NOTES

NOTES

NOTES

NOTES

NOTES

NOTES

NOTES

08 12